CANADA
MAINE
Augusta
Portland
N.H.
VT.
Burlington
Montpelier
Concord
Manchester
Boston
MASS.
Providence
R.I.
Hartford
CONN.
Albany
NEW YORK
Buffalo
L. Ontario
St. Lawrence R.
L. Superior
L. Huron
L. Michigan
L. Erie
MICHIGAN
Lansing
Detroit
Duluth
MINNESOTA
St. Paul
Minneapolis
WISCONSIN
Milwaukee
Madison
Sioux Falls
IOWA
Des Moines
Omaha
Lincoln
Chicago
Gary
ILLINOIS
Springfield
INDIANA
Indianapolis
OHIO
Columbus
Cleveland
Wheeling
Cincinnati
PENNSYLVANIA
Pittsburgh
Harrisburg
Philadelphia
Newark
New York
Trenton
NEW JERSEY
Baltimore
MD.
Dover
DELAWARE
Annapolis
WASHINGTON D.C.
WEST VIRGINIA
Charleston
Richmond
VIRGINIA
Norfolk
APPALACHIAN MOUNTAINS
Kansas City
Jefferson City
St. Louis
MISSOURI
Topeka
Frankfort
Louisville
KENTUCKY
Nashville
Knoxville
TENNESSEE
NORTH CAROLINA
Raleigh
Charlotte
SOUTH CAROLINA
Columbia
Charleston
Atlantic Ocean
Oklahoma City
ARKANSAS
Little Rock
Memphis
Birmingham
ALABAMA
Montgomery
Atlanta
GEORGIA
MISSISSIPPI
Jackson
LOUISIANA
Baton Rouge
New Orleans
Dallas
Houston
Tallahassee
Jacksonville
FLORIDA
Miami
Gulf of Mexico
BAHAMAS
CUBA
Wisconsin R.
Mississippi R.
Illinois R.
Wabash R.
Missouri R.
Ohio R.
Cumberland R.
Allegheny R.
Potomac R.
Roanoke R.
Hudson R.
Cape Fear R.
Santee R.
Tennessee R.
Chattahoochee R.
Altamaha R.
Alabama R.
Arkansas R.
Canadian R.
Red R.
Sabine R.
Trinity R.
67°
66°
Atlantic Ocean
San Juan
PUERTO RICO
Ponce
18°
Caribbean Sea
0
50
Miles
Elevation
Feet
Meters
9,843
3,000
6,562
2,000
3,281
1,000
1,640
500
656
200
0
0
Below sea level
Below sea level
0
200
400
Miles
95°
90°
85°
80°
75°

Yu-Ting Ma
Ms. Duenzen

America's History

John White Allen Scott *Boston Harbor, 1853,* Oil on panel
The Bostonian Society/Old State House

John White Allen Scott (1815–1907), a portrait, landscape, and marine painter, also dabbled in lithography. He intended this painting of Boston Harbor to be engraved to make decorative prints for the burgeoning middle class, a practice pioneered by his New York contemporaries Currier and Ives.

The painting conveys the bustle and activity of Broad Street, a major commercial thoroughfare since 1805, when Uriah Cotting's Broad Street Association transformed the waterfront by building new wharves.

SECOND EDITION

America's History

James A. Henretta
University of Maryland

W. Elliot Brownlee
University of California, Santa Barbara

David Brody
University of California, Davis

Susan Ware
New York University

Worth Publishers

America's History, *Second Edition*

Manufactured in the United States of America

Library of Congress Catalog Card Number: 92-61800

ISBN: 0–87901–552–7

Printing: 4 5—97 96 95

Development editor: Jennifer Sutherland

Design: Malcolm Grear Designers

Art director: George Touloumes

Production editor: Toni Ann Scaramuzzo

Production supervisor: Stacey B. Alexander

Layout: Patricia Lawson

Picture editor: Deborah Bull/Photosearch

Picture researcher: Joanne Polster/Photosearch

Line art: Demetrios Zangos

Advisory editor for cartography: Michael P. Conzen

Cartography: Mapping Specialists, Ltd.

Composition and separations: TSI Graphics

Printing and binding: R. R. Donnelley & Sons Company

Cover and frontispiece: John White Allen Scott, *Boston Harbor, 1853* (detail), 1853. Courtesy of the Bostonian Society/Old State House.

Illustration credits and copyright notices begin on page IC-1, and constitute an extension of the copyright page.

Worth Publishers
33 Irving Place
New York, New York 10003

For our families

Contents in Brief

Preface xxvii

PART 1

The Creation of American Society, 1450–1775 1

1 *Europe and America, 1450–1630* 3

2 *Invasion and Settlement, 1600–1675* 35

3 *The British Empire in America, 1660–1750* 67

4 *Growth and Crisis in American Society, 1720–1765* 99

5 *Toward Independence: Years of Decision, 1763–1775* 133

PART 2

The New Republic, 1775–1820 162

6 *War and Revolution, 1775–1783* 165

7 *The New Political Order, 1776–1800* 193

8 *Toward a Continental Nation, 1790–1820* 223

9 *The Capitalist Protestant Republic, 1790–1820* 257

PART 3

Early Industrialization and the Sectional Crisis, 1820–1877 284

10 *The Industrial Revolution, 1820–1840* 287

11 *A Democratic Revolution, 1820–1844* 319

12 *Freedom's Crusaders, 1820–1860* 349

13 *Sections and Sectionalism, 1840–1860* 375

14 *Disrupting the Union, 1844–1860* 413

15 *Two Societies at War, 1861–1865* 443

16 *The Union Reconstructed, 1865–1877* 481

PART 4

A Maturing Industrial Society, 1877–1914 513

17 *The American West, 1865–1890* 515

18 *Capital and Labor in the Age of Enterprise, 1877–1900* 547

19 *The Politics of Late Nineteenth-Century America* 579

20 *The Rise of the City* 607

21 *The Progressive Era, 1900–1914* 639

22 *An Emerging World Power, 1877–1914* 669

PART 5

The Modern State and Society, 1914–1945 695

23 *War and the American State, 1914–1920* 697

24 *Modern Times: The 1920s* 727

25 *The Great Depression* 757

26 *The New Deal, 1933–1939* 787

27 *The World at War, 1939–1945* 817

PART 6

America and the World, 1945 to the Present 851

28 *Cold War America, 1945–1960* 853

29 *Affluence and Its Contradictions, 1945–1965* 885

30 *Kennedy, Johnson, and the Liberal Consensus, 1960–1968* 917

31 *The Struggles for Equality and Diversity, 1954–1975* 945

32 *A More Conservative Era, 1968–1980* 977

33 *Toward a New World Order, 1980 to the Present* 1007

Appendix A-1

Illustration Credits IC-1

Index I-1

Contents

Preface xxvii

PART 1

The Creation of American Society, 1450–1775 1

1 ***Europe and America, 1450–1630*** 3

Native American Worlds 3

The First Americans 3
The Maya and the Aztecs 4
The Indians of Eastern North America 6

NEW TECHNOLOGY
Native American Agriculture 7

AMERICAN VOICES
A Creek Migration Legend 9
Recounted by Chief Tchikilli

Traditional European Society 10

The Peasantry 10
Hierarchy and Authority 12
The Power of Religion 13

The Expansion and Transformation of Europe, 1450–1630 15

The Renaissance 16
Portuguese Innovation 18
Spain Dispatches Columbus 19
The Spanish Conquest 20

AMERICAN VOICES
The Spanish Conquest Condemned 22
Bartholomé de Las Casas

The Protestant Reformation 23
Spain's Rise and Decline 25

The Background of English Colonization, 1550–1630 26

Prices and Society in England 26
Mercantilist Expansion 28
The English Reformation 29

2 ***Invasion and Settlement, 1600–1675*** 35

Spanish, French, and Dutch Goals 35

New Spain: Territory and Missions 35
New France: Fur Trade and Conversion 36
New Netherland: Commercial Expansion 37

AMERICAN VOICES
Mohawk Customs, 1644 39
A Dutch Clergyman in New Netherland

Social Conflict in the Chesapeake 39

The Invasion of the Chesapeake 39
Tobacco and Disease 42
Indentured Servitude 43

AMERICAN LIVES
Margaret Brent: A Woman of Property 44

The Seeds of Revolt 46
Bacon's Rebellion 47

Puritan New England 48
The Puritan Migration 49

AMERICAN VOICES
A Letter from New England 51
Edward Trelawney

The Religious Covenant 52
The Puritans and the Pequot 53
The Suppression of Dissent 54
The Halfway Covenant 55
The Puritan Imagination 57
A Freeholding Society 57

The Indians' New World 60
Metacom's War 60

AMERICAN VOICES
Captivity Narrative 61
Mary Rowlandson

The Fate of the Seaboard Tribes 62

3 *The British Empire in America, 1660–1750* 67

The Politics of Empire, 1660–1713 67

The Restoration Colonies 67
The New Mercantilism 69
The Dominion of New England 71
The Glorious Revolution of 1688 71
Ethnic Rebellion in New York 73
The Empire in 1713 74

The Imperial Slave Economy 76

The South Atlantic System 76
The Impact on Africa 77
Virginia's Decision for Slavery 78

AMERICAN VOICES
The Brutal "Middle Passage" 79
Olaudah Equiano

The Economics of Slavery 80
The Creation of an African-American Community 81

NEW TECHNOLOGY
Rice: Riches and Wretchedness 82

Oppression and Resistance 84

America in the Empire, 1690–1750 85

The Southern Social Order 85
The Northern Urban Economy 87
Seaport Society 88
The Rise of the Assembly 90

AMERICAN VOICES
The Waning of British Authority 92
Governor George Clinton

Salutary Neglect 93
Imperial Expansion 94
The Politics of Mercantilism 95

4 *Growth and Crisis in American Society, 1720–1765* 99

Freehold Society in New England 99

The Farm Family 99
Women's Place 100
The Crisis of Freehold Society 103

The Mid-Atlantic: Toward a New Society, 1720–1765 105

The Quaker Experiment 105
Ethnic Diversity 106

AMERICAN VOICES
The Perils of Migration 107
Gottlieb Mittelberger

Opportunity and Equality 108
A Pluralistic Society 111

The Enlightenment and the Great Awakening, 1740–1765 112

The Enlightenment in America 113
Pietism in America 114
George Whitefield and the Great Awakening 115
Religious Upheaval 115

AMERICAN LIVES
Jonathan Edwards: Preacher, Philosopher, Pastor 116

AMERICAN VOICES
The Religious Tribulations of a New Light 118
Nathan Cole

Social and Religious Conflict in the South 119

The Mid-Century Challenge: War, Trade, and Land 121

The French and Indian War 121
The Great War for Empire 124
British Economic Growth 125
Land Conflicts 127
Uprisings in the West 128

5 *Toward Independence: Years of Decision, 1763–1775* 133

The Reform Movement, 1763–1765 133

The Imperial System in 1763 133
The Financial Legacy of the War 135
British Reform Strategy 136
The Stamp Act 138

The Dynamics of Rebellion, 1765–1766 139

The Crowd Rebels 139

AMERICAN VOICES
A Stamp Act Riot, 1765 141
A Rhode Island Loyalist

Ideological Roots of Resistance 142
The Informal Compromise of 1766 143

The Growing Confrontation, 1767–1770 145

The Townshend Initiatives 145
America Again Resists 146
The Second Compromise 148

The Road to War, 1771–1775 150

The Tea Act 150

AMERICAN VOICES
***Letter to Captain Ayres, of the Ship* Polly** 151
Committee on Tar and Feathering

The Continental Congress Responds 153

AMERICAN LIVES
George R. T. Hewes and the Meaning of the Revolution 154

The Rising of the Countryside 156
The Failure of Compromise 158

PART 2

The New Republic, 1775–1820 162

6 *War and Revolution, 1775–1783* 165

Toward Independence, 1775–1776 165

Civil War 165
Common Sense 166
Independence Declared 168

The Perils of War and Finance, 1776–1778 169

War in the North 169
Armies and Strategies 170
Victory at Saratoga 172
Wartime Trials 173

AMERICAN VOICES
The Hardships of Life at Valley Forge 174
The Diary of a Surgeon

The Path to Victory, 1778–1783 175

The French Alliance 175
War in the South 179
The Patriot Advantage 179

AMERICAN LIVES
The Enigma of Benedict Arnold 180

Diplomatic Triumph 182

Republicanism in Action 183

Republicanism Defined and Tested 183

AMERICAN VOICES
The Tories Condemned, 1779 185
Letter from "A Whig"

The Loyalist Exodus 186
The Problem of Slavery 187
A Republican Religious Order 188

7 *The New Political Order, 1776–1800* 193

Creating New Institutions, 1776–1787 193

The State Constitutions: How Much Democracy? 193
Women and Republicanism 196
The Articles of Confederation 197
The Postwar Crisis 199

The Constitution of 1787 201

The Rise of a Nationalist Faction 201
The Philadelphia Convention 201
The Debate over Ratification 204

AMERICAN VOICES
A Farmer Praises the Constitution 206
Jonathan Smith

The Constitution Implemented 207

The Political Crisis of the 1790s 208

The Hamiltonian Program 208

AMERICAN VOICES
Hamilton's Funding Scheme Attacked, 1790 210
A Pennsylvania Farmer

NEW TECHNOLOGY
Technology and Republican Values 212

Jefferson's Vision 213
War and Politics 214
The Rise of Parties 217
The Crisis of 1798–1800 218

8 ***Toward a Continental Nation, 1790–1820*** 223

Westward Expansion 223
Native American Resistance 223
Farmers Move West 225
The Transportation Bottleneck 227
Speculators and Settlers 228

Republican Policy and Diplomacy 230
The Jeffersonian Presidency 230
Jefferson and the West 231
Crisis at Sea 234
The Embargo of 1807 235
Madison as President 235

AMERICAN VOICES
The Battle of Tippecanoe 237
Chief Shabonee

The War of 1812 237

Regional Diversity and National Identity 240
The Seaboard Societies 240
The Old Northwest 241
The Old Southwest 243
African-American Society and Culture 245

AMERICAN LIVES
Richard Allen and African-American Identity 248

The Fate of Native Americans 250

AMERICAN VOICES
A Seneca Chief's Understanding of Religion 251
Red Jacket

Diplomacy and the West 252

9 ***The Capitalist Protestant Republic, 1790–1820*** 257

Political Economy: The Capitalist Commonwealth 257
A Capitalist Society 257
State Mercantilism 261
The Law of the "Commonwealth" 261
The Federalist Law of John Marshall 262

A Republican Society 264
Democracy Extended 265
An Educated Republic 266

AMERICAN VOICES
Manners in the New Republic 268
An English Traveler

Republican Marriages 269

AMERICAN VOICES
The Dilemmas of Womanhood 270
Eliza Southgate

Raising Republican Children 271
Women's Sphere 273
Women, Religion, and the State 273

AMERICAN LIVES
Jemima Wilkinson, The Universal Friend 274

The National Character 276
The Second Great Awakening 276
Religion and Reform 278
Tocqueville's America 279

PART 3

Early Industrialization and the Sectional Crisis, 1820–1877 284

10 ***The Industrial Revolution, 1820–1840*** 287

The Rise of Northeastern Manufacturing 287
New Organization and New Technology 287
The Textile Industry 289

NEW TECHNOLOGY
Cotton-Spinning Machines 290

The Boston Manufacturing Company 291

AMERICAN VOICES
Early Days at Lowell 293
Lucy Larcom

American Mechanical Genius 294

The Expansion of Markets 296
Regional Trade Patterns 296
The Growth of Cities and Towns 297
The West: Farming New Land 299
The Transportation Revolution 300
Government and the Business Corporation 305

Social Structure in an Industrializing Society 305
The Concentration of Wealth 305
The New Urban Poor 306

AMERICAN VOICES
A Food Riot in New York 308
Philip Hone

The Rise of the Business Class 309
The Benevolent Empire 311
Business-Class Revivalism and Reform 311

11 ***A Democratic Revolution, 1820–1844*** 319

Democratizing Politics, 1820–1829 319
Democratic Institutions 319
The Election of 1824 320

AMERICAN VOICES
Politics on the Tennessee Frontier 321
Davy Crockett

The Presidency of John Quincy Adams, 1825–1829 322
The Election of 1828: The Birth of the Democratic Party 323

The Jacksonian Presidency, 1829–1837 325
Party Government 325
Jackson and the Native Americans 325

AMERICAN VOICES
Prelude to the Black Hawk War 326
Black Hawk

Jackson Versus the Bank 328
The Tariff and the Nullification Crisis 330
Andrew Jackson's Legacy 332
The Texas Rebellion 333

The Early Labor Movement, 1794–1836 334
Artisan Self-Consciousness 334
Workers in the Building Trades 334
The Threatened Mechanics 335

AMERICAN LIVES
Frances Wright: Radical Reformer 336

Factory Workers 338
Employers on the Counterattack 339

Democrats and Whigs: The Second Party System, 1836–1844 339
The Emergence of the Whigs 340
The Whig Coalition 341
The Depression of 1837–1843 342
The Election of 1840 344
The Resurgence of the Democratic Party 345

12 ***Freedom's Crusaders, 1820–1860*** 349

Transcendentalists and Utopians 350
Ralph Waldo Emerson 350
Emerson's Disciples 351
Brook Farm 353
The Phalanxes 355
The Shakers 355

AMERICAN VOICES
The Shakers 356
Rebecca Cox Jackson

The Oneida Community 356

Women and Reform 357
Origins of the Women's Movement 357
Abolitionism and Women 359
The Program of Seneca Falls 360

AMERICAN VOICES
The Question of Women's Rights 362
Lucy Stone

The Antislavery Movement 363
African Colonization 363
A Radical Solution 364
Evangelical Abolitionism, to 1840 364
Hostility to Abolition 367
Antislavery After 1840: The Rise of the Free-Soil Movement 368

AMERICAN LIVES
Frederick Douglass: Development of an Abolitionist 370

13 ***Sections and Sectionalism, 1840–1860*** 375

The Slave South: A Distinctive Society 375
The Slave Economy 378
Realities and Ideals of the Planter Class 378
Slave Life 379

AMERICAN VOICES
A Slaveholder's Diary 380
Mary Boykin Chesnut

AMERICAN VOICES
Slave Songs 383
Frederick Douglass

Resistance and Rebellion 383
Southern Imperialism 385

The Northeast: The Industrial Revolution Accelerates 385
Factories Triumphant 385
Immigration 387

AMERICAN VOICES
A German Immigrant in Chicago 388
Nikolaus Schwenck

Irish Identity and Anti-Catholicism 389
Business-Class Consumption 391
Middle-Class Literature 394
Education 395
Family Planning and Population Growth 395

AMERICAN LIVES
The Beecher Family 396

The Dynamic West 398

The Old Northwest 398
Manifest Destiny 402
The "Great American Desert" and "Oregon Fever" 403
The Mormons and the Great Basin Frontier 404
Expansion into California 406

14 ***Disrupting the Union, 1844–1860*** 413

Sectional Conflict and Compromise, 1844–1850 413

The Election of 1844 413
The Agenda of the Polk Administration 415
The Mexican War, 1846–1848 416

AMERICAN VOICES
A Mexican War Diary 419
Henry S. Lane

The Election of 1848 420
Alternatives to the Wilmot Proviso 421
The Compromise of 1850 422

Sectional Strife and Third Party System, 1850–1858 423

The Fugitive Slave Act 424
The Election of 1852: A Shift in the Party Balance 425
Latin American Schemes 426
Kansas-Nebraska and the Republicans 427
Republican Ideology Versus the Defense of Slavery 428
"Bleeding Kansas" 429

AMERICAN VOICES
Six Months in "Bleeding Kansas" 430
Hannah Anderson Ropes

The Election of 1856 431
The Democratic Blunders of 1857–1858 432

Abraham Lincoln and the Breaking of Union, 1858–1860 433

Lincoln's Early Career 433
Lincoln Versus Douglas 436
The Election of 1860 437

15 ***Two Societies at War, 1861–1865*** 443

Choosing Sides, 1861 443

The Secession Crisis 443
The Contest for the Upper South 445
War Aims and Resources, North and South 446

NEW TECHNOLOGY
The Rifle-Musket 449

War Machines, North and South 450

Mobilizing Armies 450
Mobilizing Money 452
The Union and Confederate Economic Programs 453
The Home Front: Civilian Support for the War 454

Military Deadlock, 1861–1863 455

Early Stalemate, 1861–1862 455

AMERICAN VOICES
The Union Home Front, 1865 456
Sarah Beaulieu

Emancipation 461
Union Gains in 1863 464

AMERICAN VOICES
The Diary of a Union Soldier 466
Elisha Hunt Rhodes

Wartime Diplomacy 467

The Union Victorious, 1864–1865 467

African-American Soldiers 468
The New Military Strategy 469

AMERICAN VOICES
The Confederate Home Front 472
Cornelia Peake McDonald

Sherman, Atlanta, and the Election of 1864 473
Sherman's "March to the Sea" 474
The End of the War 475

16 ***The Union Reconstructed, 1865–1877*** 481

Presidential Restoration 481

Restoration Under Lincoln 482
The Assassination of Lincoln 483
Restoration Under Johnson 483
Acting on Freedom 485

AMERICAN VOICES
Report on the Freedmen's Bureau 486
Eliphalet Whittlesey

Congressional Initiatives 488

Radical Reconstruction 490

The Congressional Program 490
The Issue of Suffrage for Women 491
The South During Radical Reconstruction 493
The Counterrevolution of the Planters 497

AMERICAN VOICES
The Intimidation of Black Voters 498
Harriet Hernandes

The Economic Fate of the Former Slaves 499

AMERICAN LIVES
Nathan Bedford Forrest 500

The North During Reconstruction 503

A Dyamic Economy 504
Republican Foreign Policy 504
The Politics of Corruption and the Grant Administration 505
The Political Crisis of 1877 507

PART 4

A Maturing Industrial Society, 1877–1914 513

17 ***The American West, 1865–1890*** 515

The Great West 515

Indians of the Great Plains 516
Intruders 518

AMERICAN LIVES
Buffalo Bill and the Wild West 522

The Impact on the Indians 524

AMERICAN VOICES
Wounded Knee: "Something Terrible Happened. . . ." 528
Black Elk

California and the Far West 529

Hispanics, Chinese, Anglos 530
The Golden West 533

The Agricultural Interest 536

The Farmers' Last Frontier 536

AMERICAN VOICES
Swedish Emigrant in Frontier Kansas 537
Ida Lindgren

The Farming Business 539
Agrarian Distress 540

18 ***Capital and Labor in the Age of Enterprise, 1877–1900*** 547

Industrial Capitalism Triumphant 547

Basic Industry 548

NEW TECHNOLOGY
Iron and Steel 550

The Railroads 550
Mass Markets and Large-Scale Enterprise 553
The Managerial Revolution 556
The New South 558

The World of Work 561

Autonomous Labor 561
Labor Recruits 561
Working Women 564
Systems of Control 566

AMERICAN VOICES
The Impact of Mechanization 567
John Morison

The Labor Movement 569

Reformers and Unionists 569
The American Federation of Labor 570

AMERICAN VOICES
On Strike 571
H. J. Thomas

Industrial War 572
American Radicalism in the Making 574

19 ***The Politics of Late Nineteenth-Century America*** 579

The Politics of the Status Quo, 1877–1893 579

The National Scene 579
The Ideology of Individualism 582
Cultural Politics 584
Organizational Politics 586
Women's Political Culture 588

AMERICAN VOICES
The Case for Women's Political Rights 589
Helen Potter

The Crisis of American Politics: The 1890s 590

The Populist Revolt 590
Money and Politics 592

AMERICAN VOICES
The Nomination of William Jennings Bryan 594
Edgar Howard

Race and Politics in the South 597
The Failure of Biracial Politics 597
The Black Response 599

AMERICAN LIVES
Robert Charles: Black Militant 600

20 ***The Rise of the City*** 607

Urbanization 607
The Sources of City Growth 607
City Building 609
The Private City 612

City People 615
Immigrants 615
Ward Politics 618
Religion and Ethnic Identity 619

AMERICAN LIVES
Big Tim Sullivan: Tammany Politician 620

AMERICAN VOICES
The Salvation Army at Work 623
Maud Ballington Booth

Leisure in the City 624

Upper Class/Middle Class 626
The Urban Elite 627
The Middle Class 628

AMERICAN VOICES
Throwing a Great Party During Hard Times 629
Frederick Townshend Martin

Families 631
The Higher Culture 633

21 ***The Progressive Era, 1900–1914*** 639

The Course of Reform 639
The Intellectual Roots of Progressivism 640
Political Reformers 642

AMERICAN VOICES
The Shame of the Cities 643
Lincoln Steffens

The Woman Progressive 645

AMERICAN LIVES
Frances Kellor: Woman Progressive 646

Urban Liberalism 650

AMERICAN VOICES
Working for the Triangle Shirtwaist Company 653
Pauline Newman

Racism in an Age of Reform 654

Progressivism and National Politics 656
The Making of a Progressive President 656
The Fracturing of Republican Progressivism 660
Woodrow Wilson and the New Freedom 662

22 ***An Emerging World Power, 1877–1914*** 669

The Roots of Expansionism 669
Diplomacy in the Gilded Age 669
Economic Sources of Expansionism 671
The Making of an Expansionist Foreign Policy 674

An American Empire 676
The Cuban Crisis 676
The Spoils of War 678

AMERICAN VOICES
Black Soldiers in a White Man's War 680
George W. Prioleau

The Imperial Experiment 681

AMERICAN VOICES
Subduing the Filipinos—the Ideal 682
Major General Arthur MacArthur

AMERICAN VOICES
Subduing the Filipinos—the Realities 682
F. A. Blake and Richard T. O'Brien

Onto the World Stage 684
A Power Among Powers 684
The Caribbean—An American Lake 685
The Open Door 687
Woodrow Wilson and Mexico 689
The Gathering Storm in Europe 690

PART 5
The Modern State and Society, 1914–1945 695

23 ***War and the American State, 1914–1920*** 697

The Great War, 1914–1918 697
War in Europe 697
The Perils of Neutrality 699
Over There 702

AMERICAN VOICES
Mustard Gas 705
Frederick Pottle

The American Fighting Force 705

AMERICAN LIVES
Edward Vernon Rickenbacker, Fighter Pilot 706

Mobilizing the Home Front 709

Financial and Economic Mobilization 710
Mobilizing American Workers 711
Women and the War Effort 712
Promoting National Unity 714

AMERICAN VOICES
An Imprisoned Suffrage Militant 716
Rose Winslow

An Unsettled Peace, 1919–1920 717

The Treaty of Versailles 717
The Fate of the Treaty 718
Racial Strife 719
Labor Unrest 720
The Eighteenth Amendment 721
The Red Scare 722

24 ***Modern Times: The 1920s*** 727

The Business-Government Partnership of the 1920s 727

The Economy 728
The Republican Ascendancy 729
Corporate Capitalism 731
Labor and Welfare Capitalism 732
Economic Expansion Abroad 732
Foreign Policy in the 1920s 733

A New National Culture 734

Consumption and Advertising 734
The Automobile Culture 736

AMERICAN VOICES
The Automobile Culture 737
The Residents of "Middletown"

The Movies and Mass Culture 738

AMERICAN LIVES
Clara Bow: The "It" Girl 740

New Patterns of Leisure 743

Dissenting Values and Cultural Conflict 744

Urban Majority, Rural Minority 744
The Rise of Nativism 744

AMERICAN VOICES
The Klan Comes to Kokomo 747
Robert Coughlan

Religious Fundamentalism 748
Intellectual Currents and Crosscurrents 748
Prohibition 750
The 1928 Election 752

25 ***The Great Depression*** 757

The Coming of the Great Depression 757

The Causes of the Depression 757
The Deepening Economic Crisis 759

Hard Times 761

The Invisible Scar 761
The Family Faces the Great Depression 764
Demographic Trends 764
Women on the Job 765
Hard Times for Youth 766
Popular Culture 766

The Social Fabric of Depression America 770

Blacks and the Depression 770
Dust Bowl Migrations 772

AMERICAN VOICES
A Dust Bowl Diary 773
Ann Marie Low

NEW TECHNOLOGY
Rural Electrification 774

Mexican-American Communities 777

Herbert Hoover and the Great Depression 778

The Republican Response 778
Rising Discontent 779

AMERICAN VOICES
The Despair of the Unemployed 781

The 1932 Election 782

26 ***The New Deal, 1933–1939*** 787

The New Deal Takes Over, 1933–1935 787

The Roosevelt Style of Leadership 787
The Hundred Days 788
Consolidating the Hundred Days 791
Challenges from the Left 791

The Second New Deal, 1935–1939 792

Legislative Accomplishments 792
The 1936 Election 794
Stalemate 794

The New Deal's Impact on Society 796

Bureaucratic Growth 796
Women and the New Deal 797

AMERICAN LIVES
Frances Perkins, New Deal Reformer 798

AMERICAN VOICES
The Great Depression in Harlem 800
Nora Mair

Blacks and the New Deal 800
The Rise of Organized Labor 801

AMERICAN VOICES
Labor Militancy 803
Genora Johnson Dollinger

Other New Deal Constituencies 804
The New Deal and the Land 805
The Legacies of the New Deal 807

Culture and Commitment 808
New Deal Culture 808

AMERICAN VOICES
Artists on Relief 809
Anzia Yezierska

The Documentary Impulse 810
Intellectuals and the Popular Front 812

27 ***The World at War, 1939–1945*** 817

The Road to War 817
Depression Diplomacy 817
Aggression and Appeasement 818
American Neutrality, 1939–1941 820
The Attack on Pearl Harbor 822

Mobilizing for Victory 823
Defense Mobilization 823
Mobilizing the American Fighting Force 824
Women and the War Effort 825
Organized Labor 826

AMERICAN VOICES
"Rosie the Riveter" 827
Helen Studer

Politics in Wartime 828

Life on the Home Front 829
"For the Duration" 829
Rising Winds of Change for African-Americans 832
Japanese Relocation 833

AMERICAN VOICES
The Insult and Injury of Internment 834
Peter Ota

Fighting and Winning the War 835
Wartime Goals and Strategies 835

AMERICAN LIVES
The Quiet Diplomacy of Harry Hopkins 836

The War in Europe 838
The War in the Pacific 841

AMERICAN VOICES
The War in the Pacific 842
Anton Bilek

The American GIs 844
Wartime Diplomacy 845
The Onset of the Atomic Age 846

PART 6

America and the World, 1945 to the Present 851

28 ***Cold War America, 1945–1960*** 853

The Origins of the Cold War 853
Descent into Cold War, 1945–1946 853
From the Truman Doctrine to NATO, 1947–1949 855

AMERICAN LIVES
The Wise Men: Acheson, Bohlen, Harriman, Kennan, Lovett, and McCloy 856

The "Fall" of China 860
Containment Militarized: NSC-68 861
The Korean War 862

Harry Truman and the Fair Deal 865
The Challenge of Reconversion 865
The 1948 Election 866
Fair Deal Liberalism 868
The Great Fear 869

AMERICAN VOICES
Testifying Before the House Committee on Un-American Activities 870
Pete Seeger

Modern Republicanism 872
The Soldier Becomes President 872
The Hidden-Hand Presidency 874
Alliances and Arms 875

AMERICAN VOICES
An Atomic Bomb Veteran Remembers 878
George Mace

The Emerging Third World 879
Eisenhower's Farewell Address 880

29 *Affluence and Its Contradictions, 1945–1965* 885

Technology and Economic Change 885

The Economic Record 886
The Military-Industrial Complex 887

NEW TECHNOLOGY
The Computer Revolution 889

Corporate Strategies 890
The Changing World of Work 891
Challenges for the Labor Movement 892
The Agricultural Revolution 894

Cities and Suburbs 895

Metropolitan Life 895
The Growth of Suburbia 896
State and Local Government 898
City Dwellers and New Arrivals 899
Urban Neighborhoods, Urban Poverty 901

AMERICAN VOICES
Harlem: Dream and Reality 902
Claude Brown

American Society During the Baby Boom 903

Consumer Culture 903
Television 904
The Baby Boom 906
Youth Culture 908
Contraditions in Women's Lives 909

AMERICAN VOICES
The Feminine Mystique 910
Betty Friedan

The Fifties: The Way We Were? 912

30 *Kennedy, Johnson, and the Liberal Consensus, 1960–1968* 917

John Kennedy and the Politics of Expectation 917

The New Politics and the 1960 Campaign 918
The Kennedy Style 920
Activism Abroad 920

AMERICAN VOICES
A Peace Corps Veteran Remembers 921
Thaine Allison

Kennedy's Thousand Days 924
The Kennedy Assassination 925

Lyndon Johnson and the Great Society 926

The Great Coalition Builder 926
Enacting the Liberal Agenda 927
The War on Poverty 928
Cracks in the New Deal Coalition 929

America and the Vietnam Experience 930

The Roots of American Involvement 930
Escalation 932
Vietnam, From the Perspective of Americans Who Fought the War 935

AMERICAN LIVES
John Paul Vann 936

AMERICAN VOICES
A Vietnam Veteran Remembers 938
Ron Kovic

The Consensus Begins to Unravel 939
The Tet Offensive 941

31 *The Struggles for Equality and Diversity, 1954–1975* 945

The Civil Rights Movement 945

The Challenge to Segregation 945
Nonviolent Protest 947
JFK and Civil Rights 948

AMERICAN LIVES
Ella Baker 950

The March on Washington 952
Landmark Legislation 952

AMERICAN VOICES
Registering to Vote in Mississippi 953
Fannie Lou Hamer

Rising Militance 955
Summer in the City 957
The Spreading Demand for Equal Rights 959

The Challenge of Youth 962

Student Activism 962
The Rise of the Counterculture 965

The Revival of Feminism 967

Women's Changing Lives 967
Paths to Feminism 967
The High Tide of Feminism 969

AMERICAN VOICES
The Politics of Housework 970
Pat Mainardi

Stalemate 972

32 *A More Conservative Era, 1968–1980* 977

The Watershed Year: 1968 977

A Year of Shocks 977
Turmoil and Political Backlash 979

AMERICAN VOICES
The Siege of Chicago 980
Steve Lerner

The Nixon Years 982

Domestic Agendas 982
Foreign Policy 983
Nixon's War 984
The 1972 Election 985
American Withdrawal from Vietnam 986
Watergate 986

AMERICAN LIVES
Woodward and Bernstein, Investigative Reporters 988

Lowered Expectations and New Challenges 991

The Hydrocarbon Age 991
The Environmental Movement 992
Economic Trends 995
Lifestyles and Social Trends 996

AMERICAN VOICES
Busing in Boston 998
Phyllis Ellison

Post-Watergate Politics: Failed Leadership 998

Ford's Caretaker Presidency 998
The Outsider as President 1000
The Iranian Hostage Crisis 1002

33 *Toward a New World Order, 1980 to the Present* 1007

The Reagan Presidency 1007

Ronald Reagan and the Conservative Agenda 1007
The Reagan Style 1009
Reaganomics 1009
Foreign Relations 1010
Reagan's Second Term 1011
Reagan Legacies 1012

The Best of Times, The Worst of Times 1014

The Second Gilded Age 1014
The Struggling Middle Class 1015
Poverty in the 1980s 1016
The Two Worlds of Black America 1016
Toward a Pluralistic Society 1018

AMERICAN VOICES
L. A. Journal 1019
Rubén Martínez

Health Care Costs and the Challenge of AIDS 1020
Popular Culture and Popular Technology 1022
The End of the Eighties 1022

NEW TECHNOLOGY
The Electronic Office 1023

Beyond the Cold War 1024

The Bush Administration 1024
The Collapse of Communism 1026

AMERICAN VOICES
A Third-Wave Feminist 1027
Laurie Ouellette

War in the Persian Gulf 1030
The Spread of Environmentalism 1031
The 1992 Election 1033
The New World Order 1034

Appendix A-1

The Declaration of Independence A-1

The Constitution of the United States of America A-3

Amendments to the Constitution A-8

The American Nation A-13

Admission of States into the Union A-13
Territorial Expansion A-13
Presidential Elections A-14
Supreme Court Justices A-17

The American People: A Demographic Survey A-18

A Demographic Profile of the American People A-18
American Population A-19
The Ten Largest Cities by Population A-20
Foreign Origins of the American People A-21
Immigration by Decade A-21
Regional Origins of Immigrants A-21
The Labor Force A-22
Changing Labor Patterns A-22
The Aging of the U.S. Population A-23

The American Government and Economy A-24

The Growth of the Federal Government A-24
The Federal Government, 1900–1990 A-24
Total Federal Debt, 1900–1990 A-24
Gross National Product and GNP per Capita A-25
Consumer Price Index and Conversion Table A-25

Illustration Credits IC-1

Index I-1

Chapter Features

MAPS

Native American Peoples, 1492 **6**
Europeans Seek Control of World Trade **16**
The Spanish Conquest **20**
Religious Diversity in Europe **24**
North American Colonies in 1650 **38**
River Plantations in Virginia **40**
The Puritan Migration to America **50**
Settlement Patterns in New England **58**
The Dominion of New England **71**
Britain's American Empire, 1713 **75**
Africa and the Atlantic Slave Trade **78**
The Rise of the American Merchant **87**
Trade and Urban Growth in Pennsylvania, 1700–1750 **89**
Preserving a Farmstead: Billerica, Massachusetts **101**
Ethnic and Racial Diversity, 1775 **108**
The Hudson River Manors **111**
Religious Diversity in 1750 **112**
European Spheres of Influence, 1754 **122**
The Anglo-American Conquest of New France **125**
Westward Expansion and Armed Conflict **127**
Britain's American Empire in 1763 **134**
British Troop Deployments, 1763–1775 **147**
British Western Policy, 1763–1774 **152**
The War in the North **172**
The Campaign in the South **177**
The Confederation and Western Land Claims **198**
Ratifying the Constitution **205**
Expansion: Military and Diplomatic **224**
Land Divisions in the Northwest Territory **229**
The Louisiana Purchase, 1803 **233**
Regional Cultures Move West, 1720–1820 **242**
The Missouri Compromise, 1820 **245**
Defining the National Boundaries **252**
The Expansion of Voting Rights for White Men **267**
Ethnicity and Religious Institutions **277**
Early Industrial Enterprise in New England **292**
The Nation's Major Cities in 1840 **298**
Western Land Sales, 1820–1839 **299**
The Transportation Revolution: Roads and Canals, 1820–1860 **302**
The Speed of Business News **303**
The Removal of Native Americans **328**
The American Settlement of Texas **333**
Anatomy of a Panic: Bank Suspensions in May 1837 **343**
Communal Experiments Before 1860 **354**
The Distribution of Slave Population, 1790–1860 **376**
Western Land Sales, 1840–1862 **399**
Railroads of the North and South, 1850–1860 **400**
The New Mobility of Goods and People, 1800–1857 **401**
Territorial Conflict in Oregon **403**
Settlement of the Trans-Missouri West, 1840s **404**
The California Gold Rush **407**
The Mexican War, 1846–1848 **416**
The Compromise of 1850 and the Kansas-Nebraska Act, 1854 **427**
The Election of 1860 **439**
The Process of Secession **444**
The Western Campaigns, 1861–1862 **458**
The Eastern Campaign, 1861–1862 **459**
The Battle of Gettysburg **465**
The Closing Virginia Campaigns **471**
Sherman's March Through the Confederacy **475**
The Conquest of the South, 1861–1865 **477**
Reconstruction **494**
The Barrow Plantation **502**
The Election of 1876 **509**
The Natural Environment and Peoples of the West **516**
The Development of the West, 1860–1890 **519**

The Indian Frontier **524**
The Sioux Reservations in South Dakota, 1868–1890 **525**
The Settlement of the Pacific Slope **529**
The Rural Ethnic Mosaic: Blue Earth County, Minnesota, 1880 **538**
Agricultural Regions, 1900 **539**
The Westward Movement of Iron and Steel Production **548**
The Expansion of the Railroad System, 1870–1890 **552**
The Dressed Meat Industry **554**
The New South, 1900 **559**
The Heyday of Western Populism, 1892 **591**
The Election of 1896 **595**
Disfranchisement in the South **598**
The Growth of America's Cities, 1880–1900 **608**
The Expansion of Chicago **610**
The Lower East Side, New York City **616**
The Urban Ethnic Mosaic: Milwaukee, 1850–1890 **617**
Woman Suffrage, 1869–1918 **649**
The Election of 1912 **663**
The Spanish-American War **679**
The American Empire **686**
Policeman of the Caribbean, 1898–1917 **689**
Europe at the Start of World War I **698**
U.S. Participation on the Western Front, 1918 **704**
Prohibition on the Eve of the Eighteenth Amendment **721**
The Shift from Rural to Urban Population, 1920–1930 **745**
The Election of 1928 **753**
The Spread of Radio **769**
The Dust Bowl **776**
The Election of 1932 **782**
The Tennessee Valley Authority **806**
WRA Relocation Camps **835**
War in Europe, 1941–1945 **839**
War in the Pacific, 1941–1945 **843**
Cold War Europe, 1955 **860**
The Korean War, 1950–1953 **862**
The Election of 1948 **868**
Metropolitan Growth, 1950–1980 **895**
The Election of 1960 **919**
The United States and Cuba, 1961–1962 **922**
The Vietnam War, 1954–1975 **931**
Black Voter Registration in the South **955**
Racial Unrest in America's Cities, 1965–1968 **957**
American Indian Reservations **960**
States Ratifying the Equal Rights Amendment **972**
The Election of 1968 **982**
U.S. Troops Around the World, 1975 **994**
The Growth of the Sunbelt, 1970–1990 **1008**
American Hispanic Population, 1990 **1018**
The Collapse of Communism in Eastern Europe and the Soviet Union **1029**
U.S. Involvement in the Middle East, 1980–1992 **1031**
The Election of 1992 **1034**

FIGURES

The Yearly Rhythm of Rural Life **11**
Inflation and Living Standards **27**
The Structure of English Society: 1688 **28**
Average Life Expectancy at Age Twenty in New England and the Chesapeake, 1640–1700 **49**
The Growth of Slavery in South Carolina **81**
Wealth Inequality in Northern Cities **90**
Family Connections and Political Power **91**
Population Growth, Wheat Prices, and English Imports in the Middle Colonies **109**
Increasing Social Inequality in Chester County, Pennsylvania **110**
Church Growth by Denomination, 1700–1780 **119**
Population, British Imports, and the American Trade Deficit **126**
The Growing Power of the British State **136**
Coincidence of Trade and Politics, 1763–1776 **148**
Change in the Wealth of Elected Officials, 1765–1790 **195**
Hamilton's Fiscal Structure, 1792 **209**
Inland Freight Rates, 1784–1900 **303**
Church Growth by Denomination, 1780–1860 **314**
Changes in Voting Patterns, 1824–1840 **324**
Proportion of Black and White Population in the South, 1860 **378**
Immigration to the United States, 1820–1860 **386**
Birthrate by Race, 1800–1880 **398**
Population by Region, 1820–1860 **399**
Economies, North and South, 1860 **447**
Business Activity and Wholesale Prices, 1865–1900 **553**
The Organization of Armour & Company in 1907 **557**
Changes in the Labor Force, 1870–1910 **562**
American Immigration, 1870–1914 **563**
Ethnocultural Voting Patterns in the Midwest, 1870–1892 **585**
Wage Distributions of Black and White Workers in Virginia, 1907 **603**
Floor Plan of a Dumbbell Tenement **613**
Balance of U.S. Imports and Exports, 1870–1914 **672**
American Immigration Since World War I **746**
Statistics of the Depression **760**
Unemployment, 1915–1945 **761**
Gross National Product (GNP), 1929–1972 **886**
National Defense Spending, 1940–1965 **888**
Labor Union Strength, 1900–1990 **893**
Federal, State, and Local Government Employees, 1946–1970 **899**
The Declining American Birthrate, 1860–1980 **906**
Women in the Labor Force, 1800–1990 **967**
The Consumer Price Index, 1960–1990 **1000**
The Escalating Federal Debt, 1939–1992 **1013**

TABLES

European Colonies in North America Before 1660 **56**
English Colonies in North America, 1660–1750 **69**
Navigation Acts, 1651–1751 **70**
English Wars, 1650–1750 **74**
English Monarchs, 1660–1760 **93**
Diminishing Property in the Fuller Family, Kent, Connecticut **104**
Colonial Colleges **120**
Ministerial Instability in Britain **144**
Patriot Resistance, 1760–1775 **157**
African-American Naming Patterns **247**
Number of Lawyers in Three Selected States, to 1820 **266**
American Presidents and the Sectional Crisis, 1841–1861 **414**
Freight Rates for Transporting Crops **543**
Increasing Output of Heavy Industry, 1870–1910 **549**
Comparison of South and Non-South Value-Added per Worker, 1910 **560**
Ten Largest Cities by Population, 1870 and 1910 **609**
Foreign-Born Population of Philadelphia, 1870 and 1910 **615**
Exports to Canada and Europe Compared with Exports to Asia and Latin America **673**
American Banks and Bank Failures, 1920–1940 **789**
Major New Deal Legislation **796**
Trends in American Farming, 1935–1990 **894**

AMERICAN LIVES

Margaret Brent: A Woman of Property **44**
Jonathan Edwards: Preacher, Philosopher, Pastor **116**
George R. T. Hewes and the Meaning of the Revolution **154**
The Enigma of Benedict Arnold **180**
Richard Allen and African-American Identity **248**
Jemima Wilkinson, the Universal Friend **274**
Frances Wright: Radical Reformer **336**
Frederick Douglass: Development of an Abolitionist **370**
The Beecher Family **396**
Nathan Bedford Forrest **500**
Buffalo Bill and the Wild West **522**
Robert Charles: Black Militant **600**
Big Tim Sullivan: Tammany Politician **620**
Frances Kellor: Woman Progressive **646**
Edward Vernon Rickenbacker, Fighter Pilot **706**
Clara Bow: The "It" Girl **740**
Frances Perkins, New Deal Reformer **798**
The Quiet Diplomacy of Harry Hopkins **836**
The Wise Men: Acheson, Bohlen, Harriman, Kennan, Lovett, and McCloy **856**
John Paul Vann **936**
Ella Baker **950**
Woodward and Bernstein, Investigative Reporters **988**

Preface

At the core of *America's History* stands a vision of a "democratic" history, one not confined to the deeds of the great and powerful but concerned also with the experiences of ordinary women and men. We present political and social history in an integrated way, using each perspective to make better sense of the other. We believe that there is a continual interaction between the lives of ordinary people and the practice of politics—and that both are shaped by the political institutions, economic conditions, and moral values of the times. *America's History* thus offers a balanced and comprehensive narrative of our nation's past, from government and politics, diplomacy and war, to society, the economy, popular culture, and intellectual life. Just as important, it consistently places American history in a global context—for example, tracing aspects of American society to their origins in European and African cultures, and exploring the impact of American ideals, popular culture, and military power on the wider world today.

Organization

As history casts its net to draw in ever more diverse aspects of human experience, the need to organize and make sense of this abundance of disparate material for the student becomes more and more imperative. We have reorganized *America's History* to provide a clear chronology and a strong conceptual framework. The book is now divided into six Parts, corresponding to six distinct phases of the country's development. The Part breaks reflect not only the obvious turning points of revolution and war but also more gradual changes in the economy and society and the dynamic forces that produced them. Each Part begins with a two-page overview: first, a **Thematic Timeline** highlights the key developments in government, the economy, society, culture, and foreign affairs; then these themes are summarized in a brief Part essay. The Part essays focus on the crucial engines of historical change—in some eras primarily economic, in others political—that created new conditions of life and transformed social relations. The essays and the Part organization will help students to understand the major themes and periods of American history, to see that bits and pieces of historical data acquire significance as part of the larger, interconnected pattern of development.

Part 1, "The Creation of American Society, 1450–1775," tells the story of the emergence of a new American world, explaining the role and contributions of native Americans, Europeans, and Africans. Part 2, "The New Republic, 1775–1820," shows how the republican revolution of 1776 transformed not just government, but also economic institutions, religious values, and family life. Part 3, "Early Industrialization and the Sectional Crisis, 1820–1877," describes how the Industrial Revolution irrevocably changed American life, increasing prosperity but widening class divisions and sharpening sectional differences.

Part 4, "A Maturing Industrial Society, 1877–1914," explores the emergence of heavy industry and large-scale enterprise and describes their impact on how people lived and how they made a living. Part 5, "The Modern State and Society, 1914–1945," focuses on the formation of modern government and the emergence of a national culture—strong centralizing forces that gradually undermined earlier patterns of regionalism and local autonomy. Part 6, "America and the World, 1945 to the Present," describes how the Cold War drove government decision making, resulting in a massive military-industrial complex, and, by highlighting Americans' image of themselves as the defenders of democracy abroad, advanced the struggle for equality at home fought by African-Americans, Hispanics and other minorities, and women.

In telling this complex story, we have given equal attention to historical actors and to historical institutions, customs, and forces—writing what the historian Lawrence Stone has called the "new narrative history." At the center of our narrative are the actions of individual Americans: we show how the people of all classes and groups make their own history. But we also make clear how people's choices are influenced and constrained by the circumstances of their lives and times. Such a narrative not only conveys the rich diversity of life in the past but also will help students understand their own potential for purposeful action.

Changes in the Second Edition

Those familiar with the first edition will notice changes on virtually every page. In particular, we have greatly expanded our discussions of the War of Independence and the framing of the federal and state constitutions. We now devote full chapters to the Civil War (15) and the settling of the West (17), including a new section on California and its important Hispanic and Asian communities. American diplomacy in the late nineteenth and early twentieth centuries is the subject of a new foreign policy chapter, "An Emerging World Power, 1877–1914" (22). We retain two full chapters (25 and 26) on the Great Depression and the New Deal, but they have been extensively reorganized and rewritten. And the entire post-1945 section has been reorganized and refocused to place more emphasis on the dominant influence of the Cold War on foreign relations, domestic politics, the economy, and society. Finally, the last chapter, on the Reagan and Bush years through the 1992 election, is almost entirely new.

To enhance clarity and interest, we have strengthened the narrative line, added subheads on important topics, and enlivened the story with telling illustrations and examples. And, reflecting current scholarly interest, we have expanded the treatment of a variety of social groups, from Eastern Woodland Indians and Continental Army officers in the pre-1800 period to building trades workers, newly emancipated slaves, and steel and railroad magnates in the nineteenth century, to women bureaucrats in the New Deal and religious fundamentalists today. We think our text captures the quite remarkable social and cultural diversity of the United States even as it describes the evolution of America's political institutions and national identity.

Features

America's History contains a wealth of special features, all closely tied to the main text. In keeping with our emphasis on the experiences of individual Americans we include two new features, **American Voices** and **American Lives**. Each chapter contains two or three American Voices, contemporary first-person accounts from letters, diaries, autobiographies, and public testimony that paint a vivid portrait of the social or political life of the time. And most chapters include an American Lives essay, a short biography of a representative individual or group—from controversial generals and ardent social reformers to religious leaders and icons of popular culture. Nine major essays on **New Technology** focus on the technical aspects of innovations and how discoveries affected everyday life: what people ate, how they made a living, how they fought in battle. Together, these documents and essays will help students enter into the life of the past and see it from within.

At the end of each chapter a **Summary** and an expanded **Timeline** provide a convenient review. In addition, for courses that require a research paper, each chapter includes a **Topic for Research** (a broad topic that can be explored in a variety of short papers), and a **Bibliography**.

We have significantly expanded our illustration program. The text now has over 500 photographs, many from unusual sources. There are now 117 maps, 30 entirely new and 87 redrawn to improve readability or provide additional information. We have added 7 new figures and redrawn the remaining 35. We have doubled the number of tables, adding useful lists to help students disentangle complicated sequences of events, such as British colonial regulations and New Deal legislation. At the end of the text, in addition to lists of presidential elections, Supreme Court justices, population data, and economic statistics, we include two special charts: (1) lists of the ten largest American cities at selected dates from 1700 to 1990, and (2) a currency conversion chart that enables readers to convert any historic pound Sterling or U.S. dollar amount into a roughly equivalent amount in 1990 U.S. dollars.

Supplements

Student Guide

by Stephen J. Kneeshaw (College of the Ozarks), Timothy R. Mahoney (University of Nebraska, Lincoln), Barbara M. Posadas (Northern Illinois University), Gerald J. Goodwin (University of Houston), Linda Moore (Eastern New Mexico University), and Thomas R. Frazier (Baruch College)

Entirely new, the *Student Guide* is designed to help students improve their performance in the course. Not only will their comprehension of the textbook and their confidence in their abilities be advanced through its conscientious use, but they will develop better learning skills and study habits. The guide begins with an introduction by Gerald J. Goodwin on how to study history. Each chapter includes a summary of the essential facts and ideas of the text chapter, with fill-in questions; the timeline from the textbook with short explanations of the significance of each event; a glossary; skill-building exercises based on a map, table, or figure from the textbook; exercises for the American Voices documents and the American Lives and New Technology essays; and a self-test.

Instructor's Resource Manual

by Timothy R. Mahoney (University of Nebraska, Lincoln), Robert Weir (University of South Carolina), Linda Moore (Eastern New Mexico University), Clifford Egan (University of Houston), Kendall Staggs (Oklahoma Panhandle State University), and Thomas R. Frazier (Baruch College)

The *Instructor's Resource Manual* contains an abundance of material to aid instructors in planning the course and enhancing student involvement. For each chapter of the textbook the resources include chapter themes, a brief summary, the timeline from the textbook with additional details, lecture suggestions, class discussion starters, and topics for writing assignments. In addition, the manual includes sixteen historiographic essays on a variety of topics by outstanding scholars in these fields. For courses with a topical focus, special documents sets (modules) are provided for constitutional, southern, and diplomatic history, as well as the history of African-Americans, Latinos, native Americans, and women. The *Instructor's Resource Manual* also includes a guide to writing about history by Gerald J. Goodwin, a guide to the uses of computers in teaching history by James B. M. Schick (Pittsburg State University), and a film and video guide by Stephen J. Kneeshaw.

Test Bank

by Thomas L. Altherr and Adolph Grundman (Metropolitan State College of Denver)

There are 70 to 80 questions in various formats for each chapter, including multiple-choice factual and analytical questions, fill-ins, map questions, and short and long essay questions. Computerized test-generation systems are also available.

Documents Collection

by Harry Fritz (University of Montana), John K. Alexander (University of Cincinnati), Louis S. Gerteis (University of Missouri, St. Louis), Charles Stephenson (Central Connecticut State University), Melvin I. Urofsky (Virginia Commonwealth University), O. Vernon Burton (University of Illinois, Urbana-Champaign), Thomas E. Terrill (University of South Carolina), Douglas Bukowski (University of Illinois, Chicago), Maurice Isserman (Hamilton College), David Hammack (Case Western Reserve University), Barry D. Karl (University of Chicago), David Steigerwald (Ohio State University, Marion), and Katherine G. Aiken (University of Idaho)

The *Documents Collection*, containing 300 key documents, is packaged with the textbook (if required) or available separately. Each document is preceded by a brief introduction and followed by questions to help students understand its context and significance.

Transparencies

A set of 110 full-color acetate transparencies includes maps, charts, tables, and fine art from the textbook, along with teaching suggestions.

Acknowledgments

We wish to thank R. Jackson Wilson, who helped us conceive this project and whose vision we believe we have fulfilled in this edition. We are also extremely grateful to the many scholars and teachers who reviewed manuscript chapters of the second edition at various stages. Their comments and suggestions often challenged us to rethink or justify our interpretations and always provided a useful check on accuracy down to the smallest detail.

Richard Abbott, *Eastern Michigan University*
Katherine G. Aiken, *University of Idaho*

Sara Alpern, *Texas A&M University*
Thomas L. Altherr, *Metropolitan State College of Denver*
Virginia DeJohn Anderson, *University of Colorado, Boulder*
Anne Bailey, *Georgia Southern University*
Paula Baker, *University of Pittsburgh*
Ronald Bayor, *Georgia Institute of Technology*
Eugene H. Berwanger, *Colorado State University*
W. Roger Biles, *Oklahoma State University*
Thomas Blantz, *University of Notre Dame*
Frederick Blue, *Youngstown State University*
John B. Boles, *Rice University*
James Bradford, *Texas A&M University*
Elaine Breslaw, *Morgan State University*
Howard Brick, *University of Oregon*
William Brinker, *Tennessee Technological University*
Jane Turner Censer, *George Mason University*
James S. Chase, *University of Arkansas, Fayetteville*
Martin B. Cohen, *George Mason University*
John Cooper, *University of Wisconsin, Madison*
Richard Cramer, *San Jose State University*
George H. Daniels, *University of South Alabama*
Thomas Dublin, *Binghamton University*
Wayne K. Durrill, *University of Cincinnati*
Paul G. Faler, *University of Massachusetts, Boston*
Henry Ferrell, *East Carolina University*
Robert Fishman, *Rutgers University, Camden*
Dan Flores, *Texas Technological University*
Dee Garrison, *Rutgers University, New Brunswick*
Louis S. Gerteis, *University of Missouri, St. Louis*
Paul Gilje, *University of Oklahoma*
Joanne Abel Goldman, *University of Northern Iowa*
Lawrence B. Goodheart, *University of Connecticut, Hartford*
Barbara Graymont, Emeritus, *Nyack College*
Adolph Grundman, *Metropolitan State College of Denver*
Benjamin Harrison, *University of Louisville*
Herman M. Hattaway, *University of Missouri, Kansas City*
Margot A. Henriksen, *University of Hawaii at Manoa*
Joan Hoff, *Indiana University*
Herbert T. Hoover, *University of South Dakota*
Frederic Jaher, *University of Illinois, Urbana-Champaign*
Elizabeth Jameson, *University of New Mexico*
John Jameson, *Kent State University*
David A. Johnson, *Portland State University*
Maxine Jones, *Florida State University*
Lawrence Kelly, *University of North Texas*
Jeffrey P. Kimball, *Miami University (Ohio)*
Eve Kornfeld, *San Diego State University*
Barbara Loomis, *San Francisco State University*
Timothy R. Mahoney, *University of Nebraska, Lincoln*
Louis P. Masur, *City College of New York*
Cathy Matson, *University of Delaware*
Nancy McLean, *Northwestern University*
Samuel T. McSeveney, *Vanderbilt University*
Wilbur Miller, *State University of New York, Stony Brook*
John Muldowny, *University of Tennessee, Knoxville*
Edward Muller, *University of Pittsburgh*
Benjamin H. Newcomb, *Texas Technological University*
Patricia Ourada, *Boise State University*
Carla Pestana, *Ohio State University*
Barbara Posadas, *Northern Illinois University*
Howard N. Rabinowitz, *University of New Mexico*
Leo Ribuffo, *George Washington University*
Leonard R. Riforgiato, *Pennsylvania State University, Shenango Valley*
Jere Roberson, *Central State University (Oklahoma)*
Jerome L. Rodnitzky, *University of Texas, Arlington*
Naomi Rogers, *University of Alabama, Tuscaloosa*
Joy Scime, *Ohio State University*
Sharon Seager, *Ball State University*
Judith Sealander, *Wright State University*
Kathryn Kish Sklar, *Binghamton University*

Judith Stanley, *California State University, Hayward*

Mark Summers, *University of Kentucky*

Thomas E. Terrill, *University of South Carolina, Columbia*

Richard Turk, *Allegheny College*

David Walker, *University of Northern Iowa*

Robert M. Weir, *University of South Carolina, Columbia*

William Bruce Wheeler, *University of Tennessee, Knoxville*

John Wilson, *University of South Carolina, Columbia*

Randall B. Woods, *University of Arkansas, Fayetteville*

We would also like to thank Jennifer Sutherland, our main editor at Worth Publishers, for holding us to her high and exacting standards, Toni Ann Scaramuzzo, George Touloumes, and Stacey Alexander for guiding *America's History* through production, and Paul Shensa, Anne Vinnicombe, and Bob Worth for their valuable suggestions and unflagging encouragement and support. Their contributions, and those of Carol Bullock, Rory Dicker, Jeannie Jhun, Patricia Lawson, Demetrios Zangos, and many other members of the fine staff at Worth Publishers, have helped make this a more accessible and intellectually stimulating book.

Finally, we wish to state clearly that this is a collaborative work. For the past three years, the four of us have read and commented on each other's draft chapters, meeting periodically to thrash out differences on matters large and small—from organizational issues, to what topics should be covered, to how to turn a phrase. We believe this collaboration has strengthened each part of the book and afforded a greater cohesiveness to the whole. We hope that the students we introduce to America's history will develop an interest in some aspect of our nation's past and the skills to think critically about historical issues that will last long after the course is over.

James A. Henretta
W. Elliot Brownlee
David Brody
Susan Ware

January 1993

About the Authors

James A. Henretta is Priscilla Alden Burke Professor of American History at the University of Maryland, College Park. He received his undergraduate education at Swarthmore College and his Ph.D. from Harvard University. Professor Henretta has taught at the University of Sussex, England; Princeton University; UCLA; Boston University; as a Fulbright lecturer in Australia at the University of New England; and in 1991–92 at Oxford University as the Harmsworth Professor of American History. His publications include *The Evolution of American Society, 1700–1815: An Interdisciplinary Analysis; "Salutary Neglect": Colonial Administration Under the Duke of Newcastle; Evolution and Revolution: American Society, 1600–1820; The Origins of American Capitalism;* and important articles in early American and social history. He is presently working on a study of *The Rise and Decline of the Liberal State in America, 1800–1930.*

W. Elliot Brownlee is Professor of History at the University of California, Santa Barbara, and Chair of the Academic Senate of the University of California. He is a graduate of Harvard University, received his Ph.D. from the University of Wisconsin, Madison, and specializes in U.S. economic history. He has been awarded fellowships by the Charles Warren Center, Harvard University, and the Woodrow Wilson International Center for Scholars. He has been a visiting professor at Princeton, and was Bicentennial Lecturer at the U.S. Department of the Treasury. His published works include *Dynamics of Ascent: A History of the American Economy; Progressivism and Economic Growth: The Wisconsin Income Tax, 1911–1929; Women in the American Economy: A Documentary History, 1675–1929* (with Mary M. Brownlee); and *The Essentials of American History* (with Richard N. Current, T. Harry Williams, and Frank Freidel). His current projects include a history of the financing of World War I.

David Brody is Professor of History at the University of California, Davis. He received his B.A., M.A., and Ph. D. from Harvard University. He has taught at the University of Warwick in England, at Moscow State University in the former Soviet Union, and at Sydney University in Australia. He is the author of *Steelworkers in America; Workers in Industrial America: Essays on the 20th Century Struggle;* and, forthcoming, *Main Chapters in American Labor History: From Origins to the Present.* He has been awarded fellowships from the Social Science Research Council, the Guggenheim Foundation, and the National Endowment for the Humanities. He is past president (1991–92) of the Pacific Coast Branch of the American Historical Association. His current research is on industrial labor during the Great Depression.

Susan Ware is Associate Professor of History at New York University, where she specializes in twentieth-century U.S. history and the history of American women. She received her undergraduate degree from Wellesley College and her Ph.D. from Harvard University. Ware is the author of *Beyond Suffrage: Women in the New Deal; Holding Their Own: American Women in the 1930s; Partner and I: Molly Dewson, Feminism, and New Deal Politics; Modern American Women: A Documentary History;* and the forthcoming *Still Missing: Amelia Earhart and the Search for Modern Feminism.* She serves on the national advisory boards of the Franklin and Eleanor Roosevelt Institute and the Schlesinger Library of Radcliffe College and has been a historical consultant to numerous documentary film projects.

America's History

P A R T 1

The Creation of American Society, 1450–1775

THEMATIC TIMELINE

	Economy	Society	Government	Religion	Culture
	From Staple Crops to Internal Growth	**Ethnic, Racial, and Class Divisions**	**From Monarchy to Republic**	**From Hierarchy to Pluralism**	**The Creation of American Identity**
1450	Native American subsistence economy Europeans fish off North American coast	Sporadic warfare among Indian peoples Spanish conquest of Mexico, 1519–21	Rise of monarchical nation-states in Europe	Protestant Reformation, 1517	
1600	First staple crops: furs and tobacco	English-Indian warfare African servitude begins in Virginia, 1619	James I rules by "divine right" Virginia House of Burgesses, 1619	Persecuted English Puritans and Catholics migrate to America	Puritans implant Calvinism, education, and freehold ideal
1640	New England trade with sugar islands Mercantilist regulations: first Navigation Act, 1651	White indentured servitude in Chesapeake Indians retreat inland	Puritan Revolution Stuart restoration, 1660 Bacon's rebellion, 1675	Religious liberty in Rhode Island	Aristocratic aspirations in Chesapeake
1680	Tobacco trade stagnates Rice cultivation expands	Indian slavery in Carolinas Ethnic rebellion in New York, 1689	Dominion of New England, 1686–89 Glorious Revolution	Rise of toleration	Emergence of African-American language and culture
1720	Mature subsistence economy in North Imports from Britain increase	Scots-Irish and German migration Growing rural inequality	Rise of the assembly Challenge to "deferential" policies	German and Scots-Irish pietists in mid-Atlantic region Great Awakening	Expansion of colleges, newspapers, and magazines Franklin and the American Enlightenment
1760	Trade boycotts encourage domestic manufacturing	Uprisings by tenants and backcountry farmers Artisan protests	Ideas of popular sovereignty Battles of Lexington and Concord, 1775	Evangelical Baptists Quebec Act allows Catholicism, 1774	Sense of "American" identity Innovations in political theory

Societies are made, not born. They are the creation of decades, even centuries, of human endeavor and experience. America is no exception to this rule. The first Americans were tribal peoples who migrated to the Western Hemisphere from Asia many centuries ago. In much of North America, the native Americans developed stable societies based on subsistence farming and kinship ties. In the lower Mississippi region a hierarchical society emerged, influenced by the great civilizations of Mexico. The coming of Europeans tore the fabric of native American life into shreds. From now on native Americans would participate in the creation of a *new* American society, one dominated by men and women of European origin.

The Europeans who settled America sought to transplant their traditional society to the new world—their farming practices, their social hierarchies, their culture, and their religious ideas. But in learning to live in the new land, the Europeans in the English colonies of North America created a distinctly new society.

First of all, these settlers compiled an impressive record of economic achievement: the American colonies became the "best poor man's country" for migrants from the British Isles and Germany. Traditional Europe was made up of poor and unequal societies racked by periodic famines. But in the bountiful natural environment of North America, plenty replaced poverty, and the settlers created prosperous communities of independent farm families. By 1750 the American colonists had developed a thriving export trade and a bustling domestic economy.

Second, the new society became a place of oppressive captivity for Africans. Tens of thousands of Africans, from many tribes, were transported to America in chains to labor as slaves. Slowly, and with great effort, they and their descendants created an African-American culture, but most blacks remained subordinate members of a social order dominated by whites.

Third, whites in the new American society created an increasingly free and competitive political system. The first English settlers brought traditional authoritarian institutions to the colonies. But after 1689 these gradually gave way to governments based in part on representative assemblies. Eventually, the growth of self-government led to demands for political independence and a government based on the sovereignty of the people.

Fourth, the American experience profoundly changed religious institutions and values. Many migrants came to America in search of the right to practice their religion, and the society they created became increasingly religious, especially after 1740. But theological dogmas and church institutions became less rigid and authoritarian. Many Americans rejected the harshest Calvinist beliefs, while others embraced the rationalist views of the European Enlightenment. As a result, American Protestant Christianity became increasingly tolerant, democratic, and optimistic.

Fifth, the new American society was marked by change in the family and local community. The first English settlers lived in patriarchal families, in which the father exercised supreme authority. Their close-knit communities were strictly ruled by religious leaders or men of high status. By 1750, however, many American parents no longer tightly controlled their children's lives and lived themselves in more diverse and open communities. Personal independence had become a prominent trait of American life.

Sixth, the new American society was pluralistic, composed of men and women from varied backgrounds: English, Scots, Scots-Irish, Dutch, Germans, West Africans, and many native American peoples. Regional cultures developed in New England, the mid-Atlantic colonies, and the Chesapeake and Carolina areas. An American identity—based on the English language, British legal and political institutions, and shared experiences—emerged only slowly.

The story of the colonial experience is thus both exciting and tragic. The settlers created a new American world, one excluding native Americans and condemning most African-Americans to bondage, while offering whites rich opportunities for economic security, political freedom, and spiritual fulfillment.

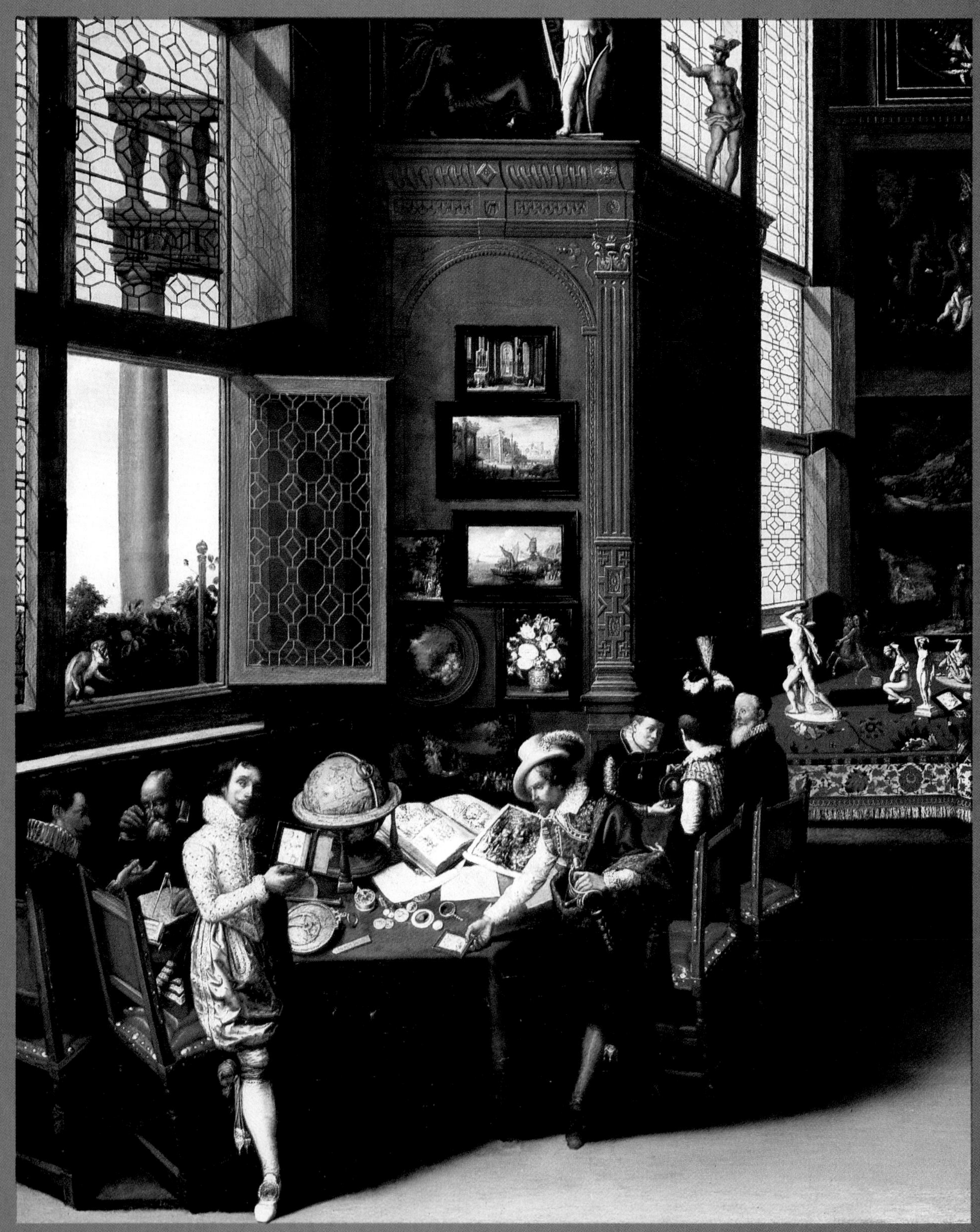

Europeans Seek to Understand the World

This detail from *The Cognoscenti*, a seventeenth-century Flemish painting, depicts a group of English scholars and navigators examining the discoveries of the age of exploration.

CHAPTER 1 *Europe and America,* 1450–1630

The United States had its origins in two separate historical dramas—first, the transformation of Europe from a static agricultural society to a dynamic commercial one and, second, the confrontation between adventurers from Europe and the peoples living in the Western Hemisphere. For a thousand years before 1450, most people in Europe had lived in poor agricultural communities. A small class of armed aristocrats, the feudal nobility, ruled over a mass of illiterate peasants. Except for the city-states of Italy, which had established themselves as vibrant centers of trade, this predominantly agricultural society had little potential for sustained economic growth or geographic expansion. During this period it was the Muslim peoples of the Mediterranean region who controlled the trade among Europe, Asia, and Africa, and who led the world in commerce and learning.

By 1630, the center of economic dynamism had shifted from the Mediterranean basin to the emergent nation-states of the North Atlantic. Portuguese and Dutch traders had replaced Arabs as the dominant force in world commerce, and Spain controlled huge amounts of land in the Western Hemisphere, with England and France claiming the rest. The Age of Exploration fueled economic activity in Europe and created an era of prosperity for the upper and middling classes.

For the native Americans, the European discovery was an unrelieved tragedy. At first the Europeans came to plunder their wealth and exploit their natural resources. Later, as the pace of economic development quickened, as peasants were forced off their land and religious dissenters were persecuted, thousands of Europeans came as settlers. They invaded the lands inhabited by native Americans for many centuries, threatening their institutions, their way of life, their very existence.

How did Europeans come to replace Arabs as the leaders in world trade and extend their influence across the Atlantic? What made native Americans vulnerable to conquest? And how did England, a small and insignificant European nation in 1492, rise to a position of considerable prominence in the Western Hemisphere during the two succeeding centuries? In the answers to these questions lie the origins of the United States.

Native American Worlds

When the Europeans arrived, millions of people were living in the Western Hemisphere, in environments as harsh as the Arctic and as lush as the tropics. In Mesoamerica (present-day Mexico and Central America) and Peru, native Americans had created civilizations that rivaled those of Europe and the Mediterranean in the complexity of their art, religion, social structure, and economic practices.

The First Americans

The first people to live in the Western Hemisphere were family bands of hunters and gatherers who migrated from northeastern Asia during the last great Ice Age, which ended about 12,000 years ago. They probably traveled from Siberia to Alaska across a land bridge formed when glaciation lowered the sea level and exposed dry land at the Bering Strait. In all likelihood, these first "migrants" were not consciously migrating at all, but were merely following the herds of wild game animals that moved ahead of them. Archeological evidence suggests that this haphazard peopling of the American continents continued in successive waves for thousands of years until the glaciers melted and the rising ocean waters submerged the land bridge. The people of the Western Hemisphere were then cut off from the rest of the world and would remain so for five hundred generations.

Following wild herds and looking for edible plants and fresh water, some of the earliest Americans gradually moved eastward from the Bering Strait. Crossing the northern Rocky Mountains, they found an ice-free corridor that stretched along the eastern side of the mountains from present-day Alaska to Montana, a land teeming with game animals, nuts, berries, and nutritious grasses. Over the generations they settled along the way or moved south through the corridor and spread out in all directions. By 10,000 years ago, groups of hunter-gatherers were established throughout the hemisphere, from the tip of South America to the Atlantic coast of North America. For another 3,000 years, these first Americans were content to live as foragers, living off the abundant wildlife and vegetation they found. Over the millennia their numbers grew into the millions.

Gold Piece From Peru

Skilled Inca artisans created gold jewelry of striking beauty. Note the intricate detail on the headdress and the stylized treatment of the face.

About 7,000 years ago, some native American peoples began to develop from foraging into horticultural societies—most notably in present-day Mexico and Peru. They discovered how to cultivate wild grasses, especially teocentli, which produced an ear of grain about the size of an acorn. Over the next 3,000 years, they bred teocentli into maize or Indian corn, a much larger, extremely nutritious plant that was a good deal hardier than wheat or rice, the staple cereals of Europe and Asia, and had more varieties and a higher yield per acre. They also learned to cultivate beans and squash and to plant them together with corn. Since the beans preserved the fertility of the soil by restoring its nitrogen, this trio of vegetables not only provided a balanced diet rich in calories and essential amino acids but also allowed intensive farming. Cultivation of these crops thus provided an agricultural surplus, laying the economic foundation for a settled society and a complex civilization.

The Maya and the Aztecs

By 700 B.C. native Americans in two regions of present-day Mexico—the people of Teotihuacán in the highlands and the Maya in the Yucatan Peninsula— had developed sophisticated cultures that remained vital for more than a thousand years. Both these civilizations were derived from the culture of the Olmec peoples, who created small ceremonial centers in the forested lowlands along the Gulf of Mexico beginning about 1000 B.C. Olmec sculptors created huge stone heads and intricate jade carvings to honor their jaguar god.

The Mayan peoples of southeastern Mexico adopted many Olmec symbols and beliefs, and built large religious centers in the rain forests where the flat Yucatan Peninsula rises gradually to the highlands of present-day Guatemala. These urban centers had elaborate systems of water storage and irrigation. Tikal, one of the largest, had at least 10,000 inhabitants, mostly farmers who worked nearby fields. An elite class of priests ruled Mayan society, living in splendor on the goods and taxes extracted from peasant families. Skilled artists decorated stone temples with magnificent friezes and paintings, which often depicted warrior gods. Mayan priests perfected a complex and mathematically precise calendar that told farmers when to plant their crops and predicted eclipses of the sun and the moon with remarkable accuracy, centuries in advance of their occurrence. Most fascinating of all, perhaps, was the Mayan hieroglyphic writing system, which recorded local rulers and major events of their reigns.

Around A.D. 900, Mayan civilization fell into decline, for reasons that are still not known for certain. Perhaps the farmers, dissatisfied with the taxes and duties imposed on them by the priestly elite, deserted

The Temples of Tikal
Tikal was one of the great Mayan cities, its ceremonial precinct covering a square mile and filled with dozens of stone temples. Set in the low hills that rise up from the flat Yucatan Peninsula, the city was served by an intricate irrigation system.

the temple cities, leaving them without workers to cultivate crops and vulnerable to conquest. Perhaps urban disease epidemics took their toll. Some Maya may have fled across the Gulf of Mexico and established new settlements in the lower Mississippi Valley.

Teotihuacán and Tula. A second major civilization developed in the highland region of Mexico. About 2,000 years ago people living at the northern end of the Valley of Mexico seized control of the trade between the highland and lowland regions. Their city, Teotihuacán, spread over 8 square miles and, at its zenith around A.D. 500, had more than 100 religious structures, at least 4,000 apartment buildings, and a population of between 50,000 and 75,000. It also boasted the Pyramid of the Sun, a huge religious monument that was as large at its base as the great pyramid of Cheops in Egypt.

The Teotihuacán people were agricultural innovators, developing a cultivation system known as *chinampas*—small, intensively cultivated artificial islands that were constructed on a network of natural and man-made lakes. At the top of the social order were religious leaders, priestly bureaucrats, and military officials, who ruled over a vast assemblage of farmers and a variety of artisans who worked in stone, pottery, cloth, leather, and obsidian (black volcanic glass used for weapons and tools). The religion incorporated the jaguar god of the earlier Olmec culture and added Quetzalcoatl, a feathered serpent god, Tlaloc, a rain god, and other deities.

Teotihuacán began to decline around A.D. 700, probably because of a long-term drop in rainfall and persistant invasions by various seminomadic peoples. Eventually the militant Toltecs from northern Mexico got control of the region and gradually absorbed its culture. The Toltecs built their capital at the ancient religious site of Tula and adopted Quetzalcoatl, the feathered serpent, as their major deity. Tula in its turn was captured in A.D. 1168 by other warrior tribes.

The Aztecs. The last great civilization of Mesoamerica was the Aztec empire. The Aztecs entered the Valley of Mexico from the north toward the end of the twelfth century. They attempted to settle among the Toltec survivors and others. Rebuffed, they finally found an unoccupied island in the middle of Lake Texcoco. Here, about A.D. 1325, they built a new capital, Tenochtitlán (present-day Mexico City), just 30 miles south of Teotihuacán. Like the Toltecs before them, they learned the settled ways of the resident peoples and mastered their complex irrigation systems. However, they remained an aggressive tribe. Led by the sun god, Huitzilopochtli, who was also their god of war, they eventually subjugated the entire central Valley of Mexico.

The Aztecs established themselves as a priestly and warrior caste who married exclusively among themselves and forced subordinate peoples to serve them as artisans, farmers, and common soldiers. Aztec merchants created trading routes throughout the highland regions and imported furs, gold, textiles, and food, while Aztec warriors used brute military force to extend the bounds of their empire. Aztec priests demanded both economic and human tribute from scores of subject tribes, gruesomely sacrificing untold thousands of men and women to Huitzilopochtli and other deities. By A.D. 1500 Tenochtitlán had grown into a great metropolis with splendid palaces and temples and over 200,000 inhabitants, a monument to centuries of agricultural ingenuity and the skills of its Aztec rulers.

The Indians of Eastern North America

At the height of Aztec power, perhaps three million native Americans were living in the heavily forested lands east of the Mississippi River. Like the residents of Mexico, the inhabitants of eastern North America were descendants of the hunter-gatherers who had crossed the land bridge from Asia—an epic journey that was kept alive from one generation to the next in stories and legends. A tale of the Tuscarora Indians, who occupied the area of present-day North Carolina, tells of a famine in the old world and a journey over ice toward "where the sun rises," a long trek that finally brought their ancestors to a lush forest with abundant food and game, where they settled.

The Woodland Indians. Unlike the peoples of Mexico, the Indians of the eastern woodlands of North America lived in small self-governing tribes composed of clans. A *clan* was a group of related families that shared a common identity and often a real or legendary common ancestor. Councils of clan elders regulated personal and ceremonial life in the interests of the tribe as a whole.

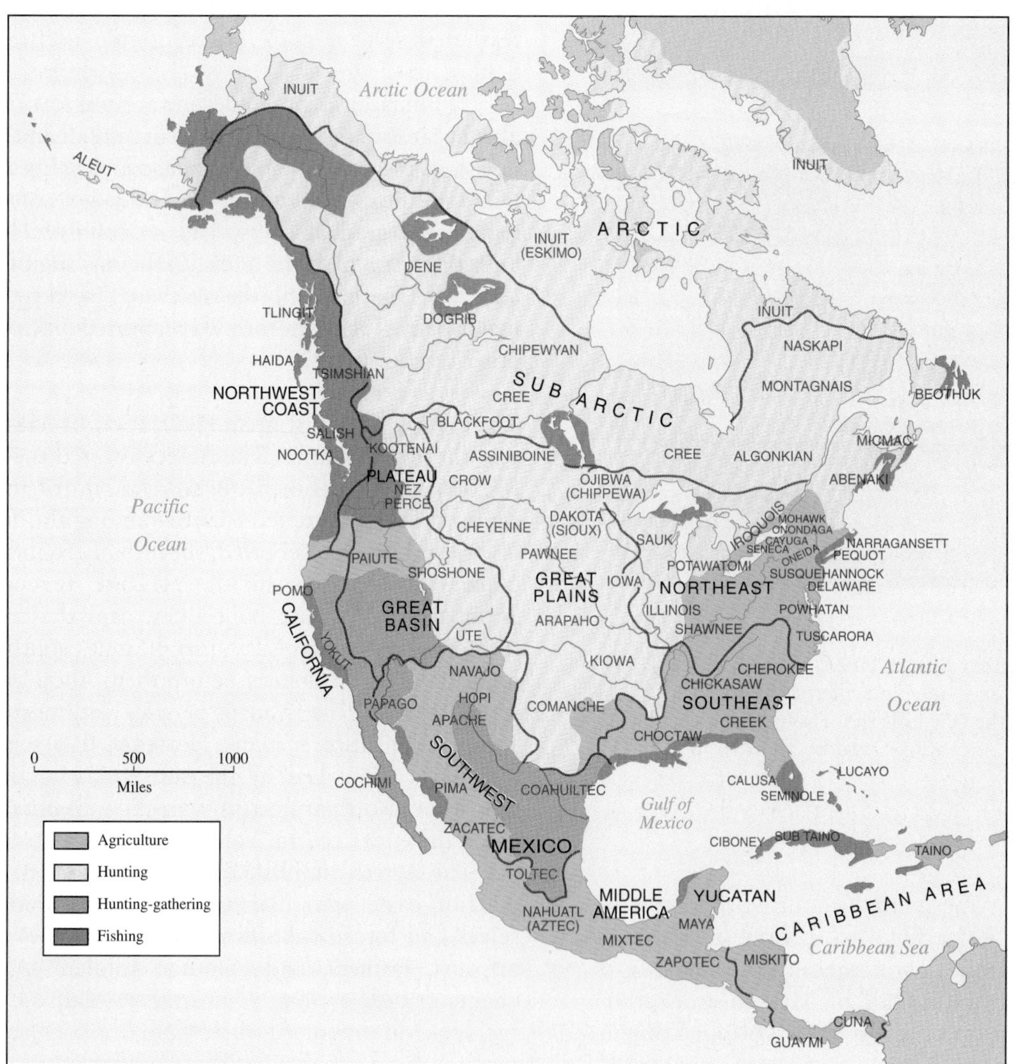

MAP 1.1

Native American Peoples, 1492

Native Americans populated the entire Western Hemisphere at the time of Columbus's arrival—having learned how to live in many environments. They created diverse cultures that ranged from the centralized agricultural-based empires of the Mayas and the Aztecs to seminomadic tribes of hunter-gatherers. The sheer diversity among Indians—of culture, language, tribal identity—inhibited united resistance to the European invaders.

New Technology *Native American Agriculture*

Corn was the dietary staple of most native Americans and its cultivation shaped their visions of the natural world. The Agawam Indians of Massachusetts began their year with the month of Squannikesas, a word that meant "when they set Indian corn," and subsequent months had names that prescribed the weeding, hilling, and ripening of corn. To appease the spirit forces in nature and ensure a bountiful harvest, the Seneca Indians of New York held a corn-planting ceremony. They asked the Thunderers, "our grandfathers," to water our crops, and beseeched the sun, "our older brother," not to burn them.

Among the eastern woodland tribes, growing corn was women's work. Indian women prepared the ground with wooden hoes tipped with bone, flint, or clamshells. According to a Dutch traveler, they made "heaps like molehills, each about two and a half feet from the others" and they planted "in each heap five or six grains." As the tall slender plants appeared, the women piled on more dirt to support the roots. They also "put in each hill three or four Brazilian [kidney] beans. When they grow up, they interlace with the corn, which reaches to a height of from five to six feet; and they keep the ground free of weeds."

Planting of corn and beans together represented a major technological advance, for it dramatically increased total yields. The beans fixed nitrogen in the soil, preserving fertility, and conserved moisture, preventing erosion. Beans and corn provided a diet rich in vegetable proteins. By cultivating two acres, an Indian woman typically harvested 60 bushels of shelled corn—half the calories required by five persons for a year.

This economic contribution gave the women of some tribes considerable political power. For example, among the Seneca and the other Iroquois nations, women chose the clan leaders. To preserve their status, women jealously guarded their productive role. A Quaker missionary reported as late as 1809 that "if a man took hold of a hoe to use it, the Women would get down his gun by way of derision & laugh and say such a Warrior is a timid woman."

In seventeenth-century America, English farmers appropriated Indian corn technology and made it part of their own culture. Now Protestant ministers as well as Indian spiritual leaders prayed for a bountiful harvest of corn. But among European settlers men and not women planted, tended, and harvested the crop—and they worked with horses and plows, not hoes. After clearing their fields of tree stumps, English farmers plowed furrows at three-foot intervals from north to south. Then they cut east-west furrows, heaping up the soil into Indian-style cornhills at the intersecting points. English planting methods were less labor-intensive than Indian techniques, and far less productive. Yields averaged from ten to fifteen bushels per acre, not thirty, and the fertility of the soil diminished much more quickly.

Nevertheless, corn became the premier American food crop, and with good reason. As a Welsh migrant to Pennsylvania noted, corn "produced more increase than any other Graine whatsoever." Pigs and chickens ate its kernels and cows munched its stalks and leaves. Ground into flour and made into bread, cakes, or porridge, corn became the dietary staple of poor people in the northern English colonies and of white tenant farmers and black slaves in the South and the West Indies.

The horticultural achievements of native Americans provided the English settlers not only with food for consumption but a valuable export crop, tobacco, which accounted for 27 percent of commodity exports from the mainland colonies in 1770. Thus, the standard of living enjoyed by white Americans was in no small measure the result of Indian technology.

Indian women hoeing and planting corn in hillocks.

For example, marriage between members of the same clan was prohibited (a rule that prevented genetic inbreeding), and families were granted use rights over certain planting grounds or hunting areas (the concept of private property being unknown in Indian culture). Tribal or clan leaders also resolved personal feuds, disciplined individuals who violated the customs of the tribe, and decided whether and when to go to war against a neighboring tribe. Their power was far less than that of Mayan or Aztec rulers, however, because their kinship-based system of government worked by consensus, not by coercion.

The peoples of eastern North America spoke many kindred but distinct languages belonging to a few language groups. Most of the Indians who lived between the St. Lawrence River and Chesapeake Bay, such as the Pequot and the Delaware, spoke Algonquian languages. The Five Nations of the Iroquois, who dominated the region between the Hudson River and the Great Lakes—the Mohawk, Oneida, Onondaga, Cayuga, and Seneca—spoke Iroquoian languages. The tribes in the territory between the southern Atlantic coast and the Mississippi River, such as the Creek and Choctaw, were primarily speakers of Muskhogean languages.

Each tribe claimed its own territory, but most Indians did not live in a permanent settlement. Rather, bands of people moved about, using different parts of the tribal domain on a seasonal basis. Throughout much of eastern North America, women and children gathered berries and seeds year-round, while men hunted and fished. In the summer, villages were established near arable lands, where women, using hoes, planted corn, squash, and beans. Among the Iroquois, women's central role in food production enhanced their authority considerably. It was the senior women of each clan who chose the (male) clan chief, and inheritance was *matrilineal,* with use rights to land and other property passing from mother to daughter.

After the harvest, tribes often broke again into bands so that the men of a family or clan could hunt together for large game in their territories. With this subsistence economy—a combination of hunting, gathering, and simple hoe agriculture—the woodland peoples did not make an intensive use of the environment, and their populations did not grow rapidly. Consequently, these tribes, unlike the native Americans in Mexico, did not live in densely populated communities with elaborate religious sites.

Each tribe's economic life depended on the climate and natural resources of its territory. For example, the short growing season along the St. Lawrence River diminished the importance of horticulture for northern Algonquians—such as the Abenaki and Penobscot of present-day Maine, who lived by hunting wild animals, fishing, and gathering wild grasses, nuts, and berries. In contrast, the more southerly Algonquians, such as the Nanticoke, Delaware, and Powhatan, depended on farming by women for most of their food. In many cases, the foraging tribes traded furs for the foodstuffs grown by the farming peoples. Thus a long-distance trade in corn, *wampum* (shell-money), and furs linked the distant communities of Long Island and Maine.

Mississippian Culture. Over the centuries, contact through trade or migration had brought the farming practices of the Indian civilizations of Mexico to the Mississippi Valley, and from there to the rest of eastern North America. In the lower Mississippi region the social institutions and religious beliefs of the high Mexican civilizations also had a significant impact. The resident peoples built earthen mounds for their religious ceremonies similar to the magnificent stone temple platforms in Mexico. One mound, near Emerald, Mississippi, stands 35 feet high and covers 7 acres; it must have taken decades to build. These mounds were the centers of urban areas, governed, as in Mexico, by a privileged class of nobles and priests, supported in comfort by the handiwork of skilled artisans and the agricultural surplus taken from the peasant class.

Snake Sculpture
Snake designs were characteristic of the Mississippian culture, which flourished in southeastern North America between 1000 and 1300 A.D. This sculpture was carved from a thin sheet of mica. (Peabody Museum, Harvard University)

AMERICAN VOICES

A Creek Migration Legend *Recounted by Chief Tchikilli*

Every culture has a story—part factual, part mythical—that expresses the meaning of its past and justifies its present values. This legend, recounted by a chief of the Upper and Lower Creek peoples in the 1830s, tells of the various migrations of this Creek tribe and of its decision to give up warfare as part of its way of life.

At a certain time, the Earth opened in the West, where its mouth is. The earth opened and the Cussitaws came out of its mouth, and settled near by. But the earth became angry and ate up their children; so that, full of dissatisfaction, they journeyed toward the sunrise. They came to a red, bloody river and heard a noise as of thunder. At first they perceived a red smoke, and then a mountain which thundered. This mountain they named the King of Mountains. It thunders to this day; and men are very much afraid of it.

On the mountain was a pole which was very restless and made a noise, nor could any one say how it could be quieted. At length, they took a motherless child, and struck it against the pole; and thus killed the child. They then took the pole, and carry it with them when they go to war. It was like a wooden tomahawk, such as they now use.

At this place, they also obtained a knowledge of herbs and of many other things. These herbs, they use as the best medicine to purify themselves at their Busk. Since they learned the virtues of these herbs, their women, at certain times, have a separate fire, and remain apart from the men five, six, and seven days, for the sake of purification. . . .

After this, they left that place, and came to a white foot-path. The grass and everything around were white; and they plainly perceived that people had been there and came to the belief that it might be better for them to follow that path. [After staying many years in various places], they came to a River which they called the Aphoosapheeskaw . . . . This is the place where now the tribe of Palachucolas live. The Palachucolas gave them black drink, as a sign of friendship, and said to them: Our hearts are white and yours must be white, and you must lay down the bloody tomahawk. . . . Since then they have always lived together.

Some settled on one side of the River, some on the other. Those on one side are called Cussetaws, those on the other, Cowetas; yet they are one people, and the principal towns of the Upper and Lower Creeks. Nevertheless, as the Cussetaws first saw the red smoke and the red fire, and make bloody towns, they cannot yet leave their red hearts, which are, however, white on one side and red on the other. They now know that the white path was the best for them.

Source: Albert S. Gatschet, *A Migration Legend of the Creek Indians* (Philadelphia: D. G. Brinton, 1884), I, 244–251.

By A.D. 1350, the largest centers of Mississippian civilization were in rapid decline, most likely because of the impact of diseases or military conquest. Still, the influence of this civilization lingered for centuries. Native Americans of the region venerated the abandoned temple mounds as sacred places. Indeed, the Choctaw regarded a mound in present-day Winston County, Mississippi, as *ishki chito,* the "great mother." There, according to a Choctaw legend, "the Great Spirit created the first Choctaws, and through a hole or cave, they crawled forth into the light of day."

The Natchez people of Mississippi maintained elements of the old temple mound culture even into modern times. French traders who encountered the Natchez around 1700 found a stratified society ruled by a monarch. There was an upper class of Suns, Nobles, and Honored People, while the mass of peasants, called Stinkards, cultivated the land. Less rigid class divisions persisted among some speakers of the Muskhogean languages—the Creek, Chickasaw, Choctaw, Seminole—and the Iroquoian-speaking Cherokee. Because of their hierarchical social order and cultural achievements, eighteenth-century British settlers called them the "Five Civilized Tribes."

For the rest of North America, the most important legacy of the Mississippian civilization was its agricultural practices, including the use of flint hoes and superior strains of corn, beans, and squash. This new horticultural technology permitted the tribes of the eastern region to enjoy a more fixed and stable way of life, with corn and beans now replacing wild game and fruits as the main foods. As better nutrition improved health and lengthened the life span, communities grew in size and developed more complex cultures. Prospering tribes built semipermanent villages of domed wigwams (or, among the Iroquois, longhouses) near their cornfields and lived there from April to October. They celebrated the yearly agricultural cycle with religious ceremonies, such as the Iroquois green corn and strawberry festivals. The men continued to hunt during the winter, but the tribes were no longer nomadic. By the time the Europeans invaded eastern North America, most of the Indian peoples had been living a relatively settled existence on their lands for generations.

Traditional European Society

Europeans came to America from a predominantly agricultural society. Before 1450—indeed, until the Industrial Revolution, which began about 1750—most Europeans lived in the countryside. The vast majority were peasants who farmed the soil and were at the mercy of forces beyond their control—from kings and aristocrats who imposed high taxes and rents to bandits, predatory armies, droughts, and plagues that threatened their safety and their livelihoods. The only comfort amid these dangers was the Christian church, which offered the hope of eternal salvation.

The Peasantry

There were only a few large cities in northwestern Europe before 1600—Paris, Amsterdam, London—home to merchants and artisans. More than 90 percent of the population lived in small, relatively isolated rural communities separated from each other by rolling hills or dense forests. Many of these settlements consisted of a compact village center in the midst of extensive fields. Each peasant family owned or leased a small dwelling in the center and had the right to farm several strips of land in the fields. These fields were "open"—that is, not divided by fences or hedges—making cooperative farming a necessity. Each year the male householders of the village decided which crops to plant and how many cows and sheep each family could graze on the commonly owned meadows.

This open-field system of land tenure produced a strong sense of community, reinforced by the confiningly primitive state of transport. Peasant villages were linked only by rough dirt roads and ox-drawn carts. Travel, at best, was slow and cumbersome, and in heavy rain or deep snow virtually impossible. Since there were few merchants, most peasant families exchanged surplus grain or meat with their relatives and neighbors, and bartered their produce for the services of local artisans—millers, weavers, blacksmiths, roof thatchers.

The character of village life was tightly restricted. Although peasants in Western Europe after 1450 were no longer serfs legally bound to the land, their mobility was still hampered by geographical isolation and the lack of work outside agriculture. A man might seek a job (or a wife) in a nearby village, or be forced to fight as a foot soldier in a distant war. A woman might leave her village to marry or to work as a domestic servant or to sell homespun textiles at a regional fair. If she was really lucky, she would make a pilgrimage to a famous shrine or cathedral, like Canterbury or Chartres. But these events were extraordinary. Most men and women lived hard, repetitious lives in the towns or regions of their birth.

The Seasonal Cycle. Nearly all aspects of peasant life followed a seasonal pattern. The agricultural year began in March, after the early spring thaw. As the soil dried, villagers plowed the land and prepared to plant.

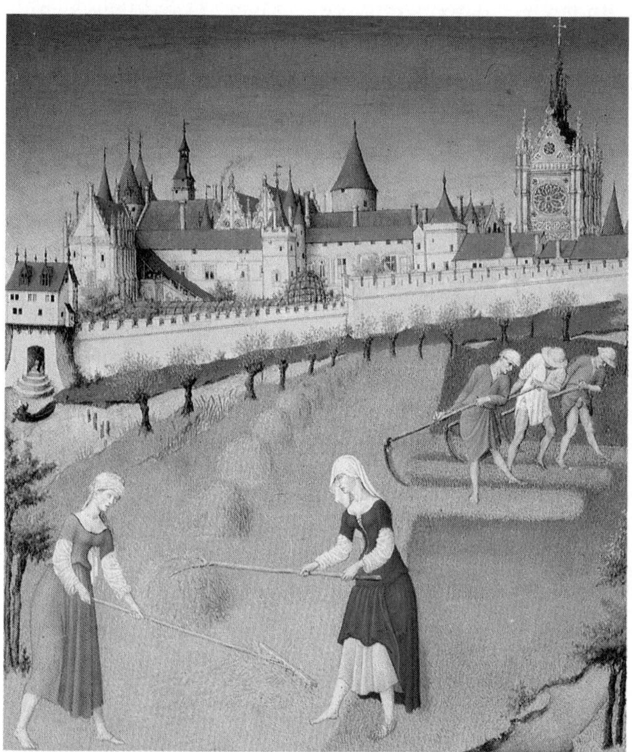

An Idealized Medieval World

In this illustration from a medieval manuscript, well-dressed peasants labor effortlessly in front of a beautiful palace. Only the fortifications and the moat hint at the exploitation and violence of the era.

In England, the farming year began on Lady Day, March 25, the day the Christian calendar celebrated the Annunciation to the Virgin Mary of the impending birth of Jesus Christ. Accordingly, in ceremonies reminiscent of pagan fertility rites, pious peasants prayed to the Virgin for a bountiful crop. With less enthusiasm, they paid the first quarterly installment of rent to their landlords.

Once the agricultural year was underway, the pace of life quickened. Peasants sowed their fields in April and May and cut the first crop of hay in June, storing it as winter fodder for their livestock. During these busy spring months, men sheared the thick winter coats of sheep, while women washed the wool and spun it into yarn. Following the law of supply and demand, cash and barter prices were always highest in the late spring after the depletion of winter supplies, and then dropped off sharply following the fall harvest.

After the exhausting work of spring planting and haymaking, which pushed peasant families to the limits of their endurance, life became more relaxed. Families took to mending their fences or repairing their barns and houses. Following the strenuous fall harvest, they celebrated with riotous bouts of merrymaking. As winter approached, peasants slaughtered excess livestock and salted or smoked the meat. During the cold months, they gradually completed the time-consuming tasks of threshing grain and weaving textiles and had more leisure time to visit friends or relatives in nearby villages. Just before the cycle began again in the spring, rural folk held carnivals to celebrate the end of the long winter night with drink and dance.

Death also followed a seasonal pattern. Many rural folk died in January and February, victims of the cold and of viral diseases. August and September were bad months too, when infants and old people succumbed to epidemics of fly-borne dysentery. More mysteriously, births too followed a seasonal rhythm. In European villages (and later in rural British America), the greatest number of babies were born in February and March, with a smaller peak in September and October. The precise causes of this pattern are unknown. Religious practices—for example the abstention from sexual intercourse by devout Christians during Lent—may have affected the number of conceptions at specific times of the year. Fluctuations in the food supply or in female work patterns from month to month may have altered the woman's ability to carry a child. Only one thing is certain. This seasonal pattern of births does not exist in modern urban societies, so it must have been a reflection of traditional rural life.

Over the generations, this pattern of exhausting effort during the spring and summer alternating with exuberant play during the fall and winter became a custom, and one that European migrants would bring with them to America. A German who settled in Pennsylvania refused to move farther south, because, a traveler reported, he loved his winter leisure. Without cold and snow, "people must work year in, year out, and that was not his fancy; winter, with a warm stove and sluggish days being indispensable to his happiness."

The Peasant's Lot. For most peasants, a difficult, unpredictable life and early, arbitrary death were the natural conditions of existence. Mere survival required heavy labor. Other than water- or wind-powered mills for grinding grain, raw muscle power was the major source of energy. While horses and oxen strained to break the soil with primitive wooden plows, men staggered as they guided them from behind. At harvest time, men cut hay, wheat, rye, and barley with hand sickles, and despite the help of women and children, who gathered up the grain, a man could reap only half an acre a day. Even when fine weather brought a good harvest, output was at most ten bushels of grain per acre—one-tenth of a modern yield.

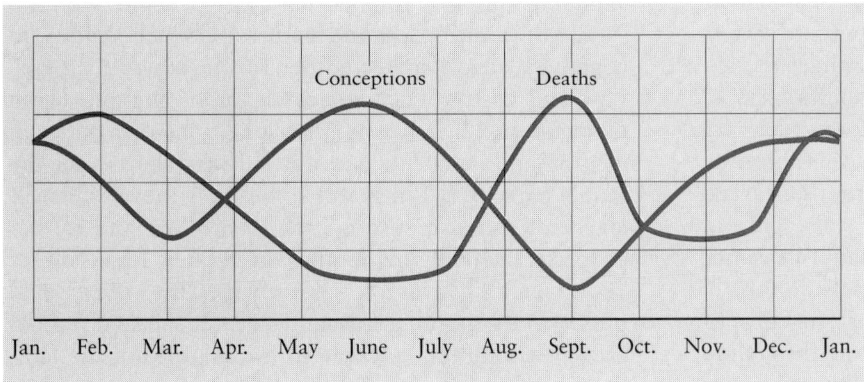

FIGURE 1.1

The Yearly Rhythm of Rural Life

The annual cycle of nature profoundly affected life in the traditional agricultural world. Summer was the healthiest season with the fewest deaths and the greatest number of successful conceptions (as measured by births nine months later).

Peasant Agriculture

Farming was hard work in the preindustrial era, for peasants plowed and harrowed their fields with primitive tools and carried sheaves of wheat to the barn on their backs.

The margin of existence was thin and corroded family relations. Before 1650 about half of those born in Europe died before the age of twenty-one. Malnourished mothers fed their babies sparingly, calling them "greedy and gluttonous" little beasts, and many newborn girls were "helped to die" so that older brothers would have enough to eat. Parents commonly sent eight-year-old children to live as servants in other households, to instill discipline and to relieve overcrowding at home. Those who survived the rigors of infancy and childhood found hunger, disease, and violence to be constant companions. "I have seen the latest epoch of misery," a French doctor reported as famine and plague struck. "The inhabitants . . . lie down in a meadow to eat grass, and share the food of wild beasts."

These circumstances gave rise to a fearful and pessimistic outlook. Scores of "sturdy beggars" and "swarmes of idle persons" roamed the English countryside, searching for food or something to steal, noted the philosopher Thomas Hobbes. In these circumstances, Hobbes argued in a famous passage that has echoed down the centuries, "every man is enemy to every man," there was "continual fear and the danger of violent death; and the life of every man, solitary, poor, nasty, brutish, and short." Seeking to restore order and stability, Hobbes wrote *Leviathan* (1651), an important political treatise that advocated a strong authoritarian government.

Destitute, exploited, dominated, many peasants simply accepted their condition. Others did not. It would be the deprived rural classes of Western Europe, hoping for a better life for themselves and their children, who would supply the majority of white migrants to British North America.

Hierarchy and Authority

Hobbes's *Leviathan* sought to reinforce the traditional European social order, in which authority came from above. Aristocrats, priests, and government officials intruded into the affairs of peasants, and the peasants organized their families and communities in a hierarchical manner. Nearly everywhere, the individual had to submit to the exigencies of scarcity, the discipline of superiors, or the consensus of the village community. There was little personal freedom and only a weak sense of individual identity. In myriad ways, a person's values and behavior were shaped by powerful social institutions—family, community, and nobility.

The Family. Social discipline began at home. The man was the head of the house, the patriarch who made all the important decisions. His power was justified by the teachings of St. Paul and the fathers of the Christian church. As one English pastor put it, "The woman is a weak creature not embued with like strength and constancy of mind." God and nature, a French gentleman concluded, had "subjected her to the power of man." Law and custom ensured female subordination. Upon marriage an English woman virtually lost her personal identity and independence; not only did she assume the family name of her husband and usually move to his village, but she also surrendered to her husband all her property, including her clothes. In her new legal state of "coverture," she was allowed only the "use" of personal possessions; upon her husband's death, she received her dower—usually the income from one-third of the family's land and goods. As a wife she was a dependent being, required under the threat of legally-sanctioned physical "correction" to submit to her husband's orders—be they for service or sexual favors.

Fathers controlled the lives of children in an equally encompassing and authoritarian way. Land-owning peasants in Western Europe normally retained legal control of farms until their physical strength ebbed. Only then, at age fifty to sixty, did they provide land to sons and doweries to daughters, permitting their children to marry. Most marriages were arranged, with fathers choosing partners of comparable wealth and status in order to protect the family's economic position. As a result of these customs, most young men and women worked for their fathers until they married, in their mid- or late twenties, enduring years of emotional domination and sexual deprivation. And when they finally did marry, it was often to someone not of their liking.

Within the family, children were not born equal: their social position depended on their sex and birth order. It was common practice for a father to bestow most of his property on his eldest son. That son became the new patriarch, responsible for the welfare of his siblings. Custom called for landless brothers and sisters to work on his farm in return for food and shelter, but the small size of most peasant holdings forced many younger children to join the ranks of the Hobbes's roaming poor, condemned to desperate lives on the edge of respectable society.

The Community. The price of survival in a world of scarcity was unremitting social discipline. On the level of the community, individual behavior was strictly regulated for the common good. For instance, German magistrates denied marriage licenses to couples without sufficient means in order to avoid the emergence of a dependent landless class. Communal controls were even more explicit in the manufacturing towns and commercial centers than in the countryside. Town councils limited the privileges of citizenship to specified "freemen"—usually artisans with substantial skill or property—and often expelled anyone who lacked this status. Similarly, craft guilds controlled admittance to various occupations, such as weaving, glassmaking, or goldsmithing, and regulated not only the scale of wages but also the quality and quantity of production—acting as a brake on individual initiative and competition in order to maintain a stable market and a rough equality among members. Town officials imposed similar limits on what could be charged for the staffs of life: a loaf of bread, a sack of flour or grain. Fearful of change, village elders and town officials alike discouraged economic innovation or social ambition. Tradition became the measure of all existence. "After a thing had been practiced for so long that it becomes a Custom," an English clergyman proclaimed, "that Custom is Law."

Manorial Lords. The monarchs of Western Europe owned vast tracts of land and lived in splendor off the labor of the masses of peasants. Gradually, the rulers extended their power, levying royal taxes, creating law courts, and conscripting men for military service. Yet they were far from supreme, given the power of the nobility, the descendants of the feudal lords, who still played a major role in the affairs of the villages and kingdoms of Western Europe.

Collectively, noblemen often challenged the authority of princes and kings. They had their own legislative institutions, such as the French *parlements* and the English House of Lords, and enjoyed special legal privileges. If accused of a crime, an aristocrat could demand a trial before a jury composed of his own (noble) peers. Monarchs had little choice but to appoint noblemen as their local political agents. Their authority as judges, magistrates, and militia officers further enhanced their power.

Such legacies of the medieval feudal order, when most kings were dependent on the nobility, worked against the formation of strong centralized states. Monarchs had little direct control over the peasantry, which had to submit to the demands of the local nobleman for goods, services, and loyalty. Other privileged groups whose wealth and status limited the rulers' power were the clergy and merchants. In the Beauvais region of France around 1650, the Catholic Church and absentee merchants, along with the aristocracy, controlled 60 percent of the land; individual peasants and village communities, who made up more than 95 percent of the population, owned only 40 percent.

The peasant community opposed domination by elite groups and ambition within its own ranks. Its members condemned the creation of large farms, whether by merchants, or enterprising peasant families. Most peasants wanted an egalitarian society composed of small-scale farmers who controlled enough land to support a family, but only a few were fortunate enough to live in such a community. Hierarchy and authority reigned supreme in the traditional European social order, and these values, which migrants carried with them to America, would shape the character of family life and the social order there for more than a century.

The Power of Religion

The Catholic Church served as one of the great unifying forces in European society. By A.D. 1000 the Christian church had completed its conversion of pagan Europe and its spiritual jurisdiction embraced Latins, Germans, Celts, Anglo-Saxons, and Slavs. The pope, as head of the Catholic Church, directed a vast institutional hierarchy of cardinals, bishops, and priests. Latin, the lan-

Christ's Crucifixion
This graphic protrayal of Christ's death on the cross, by the German painter Grünewald, sought to remind believers of the reality of death and the need for repentance. (Central panel of closed Isenheim Altarpiece, Colmar, Musée Unterlinden, Giraudon/Art Resource)

guage of scholarship, was preserved by Catholic priests and monks, and Catholic dogma provided a common understanding of God, the world, and human history. Equally important, the church provided another chain of authority and discipline in society.

Religion in Daily Life. Christian doctrine penetrated deeply into the everyday lives of peasants. Over the centuries, the church adopted a calendar that reflected the agricultural cycle and incorporated various pagan festivals. Pagans had long marked the winter solstice, celebrating the return of the sun and victory of light over darkness. The Christian celebration of the birth of Jesus Christ on December 25, a few days later, grafted a new religious meaning onto the solstice, encouraging pagan conversions.

In the spring, when the warmth of the sun revived the earth, the church celebrated Christ's resurrection from the dead on Easter Sunday. This holy day also reflected older pagan beliefs: in England, Anglo-Saxons had honored Eostre, the goddess of dawn, just after the vernal equinox (about March 21) and other European peoples held similar spring fertility festivals. Christian and pagan traditions blended again in the autumn months as ancient harvest festivals gradually evolved into holy days of thanksgiving.

This merging of the sacred and the agricultural cycles endowed all worldly events with a supernatural meaning. Few Christians believed that anything occurred by chance or as a result of natural causes. Rather, they thought that everything that happened was God's will. If crops rotted in the ground or withered under a hot sun, the Lord must be displeased with his people. According to the Bible, "The earth is defiled under its inhabitants' feet, for they have transgressed the law" (Isaiah 24:5). To avert calamities, peasants turned to their priests for spiritual guidance and to confess their transgressions of God's commands and the Church's laws. Every village had a church, and holy shrines dotted the map of Europe, tangible points of contact between the material and spiritual worlds. By offering prayers to Christ and the saints, whose statues stood in the shrines and churches, Christians hoped to stave off worldly disaster.

God's presence in the world was continually renewed through the ceremony of the Mass and the sacrament of Holy Communion. According to Roman Catholic doctrine, priests had the power to change sacramental bread and wine into the body and blood of Christ. After performing this miracle, called transubstantiation, priests placed the transformed (but still ordinary-looking) bread on the tongues of the faithful, thereby allowing the body and blood of Christ to mingle with that of human beings. In this way ordinary peasants—along with priests and aristocrats—partook of the divine.

There was another supernatural force at large in the world: Satan. Satan challenged the majesty of God by tempting people into evil. The heavenly millennium, the thousand-year period of Christ's peaceful rule on earth predicted in the book of Revelation, depended on God's triumph over Satan. Humans played a pivotal role in this titanic battle. If prophets spread unusual doctrines, they were surely the tools of Satan. If a devout Christian fell mysteriously ill, the sickness might be the result of an evil spell cast by a witch in league with Satan. Fear of Satan's wiles justified periodic purges of heretics, those men and women who questioned the Church's doctrine and practices.

The Crusades. As the Christian church consolidated its hold in Europe, popes and priests urged their followers to crush all those who held other religious beliefs. Muslims became a prime target. After the death of the prophet Muhammad in A.D. 632, the newly united tribes of Arabia set out to convert and conquer the world. They spread the Muslim faith and Arab civilization far beyond its homeland—into Africa, India, Indonesia, and deep into southern Europe. Between A.D. 1095 and 1272, successive armies of Christians, led by the flower of the nobility, embarked on a series of great Crusades against Muslim "infidels." They repelled Mus-

The Spice Trade
This French manuscript illustration (circa 1380) shows workers in Malabar (on the western coast of India) harvesting pepper for the spice trade. The white skinned man is meant to be Marco Polo, one of the few Europeans to visit India or China before the Portuguese voyages.

lim advances into southern Europe and invaded Palestine, seeking to expel Muslim Arabs from the Holy Land where Christ had lived.

As a spiritual movement, the Crusades strengthened the Christian identity of the majority of Western Europeans. The religious fervor created by the Crusades also contributed to the renewed persecution of Jews in many European countries. England expelled most of its Jewish population in 1290, and France did the same in 1306. Jewish refugees went mostly to Germany, the great center of European Jewry, only to be driven farther east, to Poland, over the next century.

At the same time, the Crusades broadened the intellectual and economic horizons of many Europeans. These expeditions opened a window onto another world, bringing the privileged classes of Western Europe into contact with the advanced learning of the Arab world and the luxury goods and spices carried out of Asia by Arab traders. A fresh wind blew through Europe, resulting in marked changes in that continent's commercial interests and military power—changes that in turn caused slower, but equally significant alterations in its traditional agricultural society.

The Expansion and Transformation of Europe, 1450–1630

Europe changed dramatically after 1450. First, Portugal found new trade routes to the Orient, and Spain discovered the riches to be had in the New World. Second, in 1517, a major schism over doctrine divided the Christian church and then plunged Europe into wars which lasted for decades. Spain tried to use its great wealth and military power to maintain the primacy of Roman Catholicism, but the newly formed Protestant states of Europe resisted fiercely. Finally, gold and silver from America set off a great inflation, which disrupted traditional European society and prompted the Protestant countries of England and Holland to start their own empires in America.

The Renaissance

Beginning about A.D. 1300 first Italy and then the countries of northern Europe experienced a rebirth of learning and of cultural life. The main stimulus came from the Crusaders' exposure to the highly developed civilization of the Arab world, a civilization fueled by Arab control of the wealthy trade routes between Europe and Asia. Arab traders had access to the fabulous treasures of the East—luxurious Chinese silks, brilliant Indian cottons, precious stones such as rubies and sapphires, and exotic spices including pepper, nutmeg, ginger, and cloves. Arab inventors had developed magnetic compasses, water-powered mills, and mechanical clocks, and from their trading contacts in China, they had discovered the properties and uses of gunpowder. In great

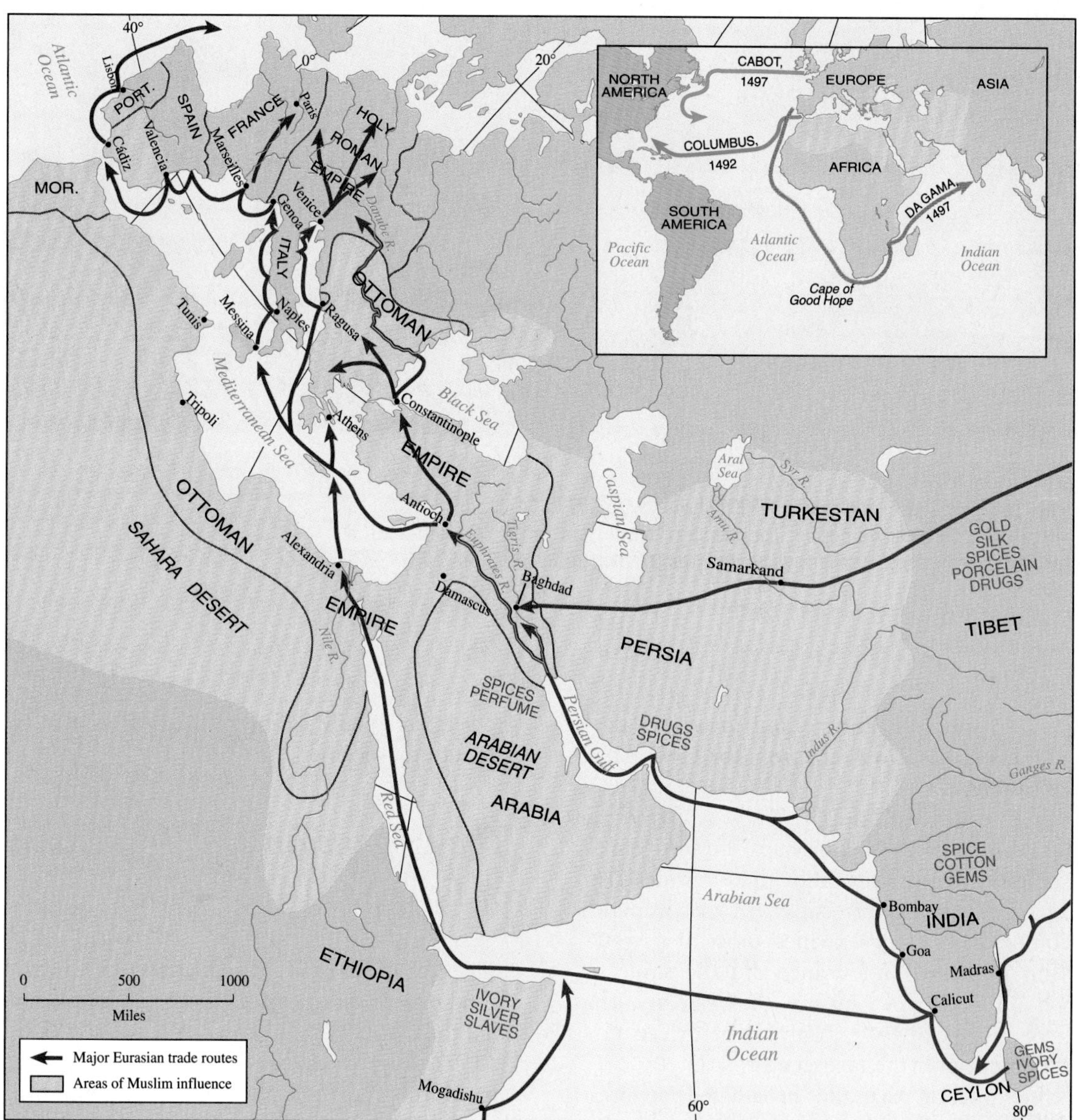

MAP 1.2

Europeans Seek Control of World Trade

For centuries the Mediterranean Sea had been the meeting point for the commerce of Europe, northern Africa, and southern Asia. Beginning in the 1490s, Portuguese, Spanish, and Dutch adventurers and merchants opened up new trade routes, challenging the primacy of the Muslim-dominated Mediterranean.

Astronomers at Istanbul, 1581

Arab scholars transmitted ancient texts and learning to Europeans in the Middle Ages and, during the age of discovery, contributed to the expansion of geographical and astronomical knowledge.

cultural centers, such as Alexandria and Cairo in Egypt, Arab scholars carried on the legacy of Christian Byzantine civilization which had preserved the great intellectual achievements of the pagan Greeks and Romans in religion, medicine, philosophy, mathematics, astronomy, and geography.

At the same time, from Toledo and other cities in Moorish Spain, Arab learning gradually filtered into Europe. The Moors were Arabs who had invaded the Iberian peninsula centuries before and still controlled its southern region. Moorish scholars had translated Aristotle, Ptolemy, and other ancient writers into Latin, reacquainting the peoples of Europe with their classical heritage.

The Italian Renaissance. Following the crusades, merchants from the Italian city-states of Venice, Genoa, and Pisa sought a share of the Arab trade with the east. Dispatching ships to Alexandria, Beirut, and other eastern Mediterranean ports, these merchants purchased goods that originally had come from China, India, Persia, and Arabia and, returning to their home ports, sold them throughout Europe. This wealth, in turn, gave rise to a new class of merchants, bankers, and textile manufacturers who conducted trade, loaned vast sums of money, and spurred technological innovation in silk and woolen production throughout Europe. This monied elite ruled the republican city-states of Italy, and, in *The Discourses,* Niccolò Machiavelli articulated its political culture of "civic humanism"—an ideology that would profoundly influence European and American conceptions of the state.

In what was to become the fashion of the age, wealthy Italian families became patrons of the arts and sciences, subsidizing a remarkable array of artistic and intellectual projects. Perhaps no other age in history has produced such a flowering of artistic genius. Michelangelo, Andrea Palladio, and Filippo Brunelleschi designed and built great architectural masterpieces, while Leonardo da Vinci and Raphael produced magnificent religious paintings—creating styles and setting standards that endured until the modern era.

Humanism. The Renaissance did not directly affect the average European peasant, but it had a profound impact on the upper classes. The artists and intellectuals of the Renaissance were optimistic in their view of human nature—they were humanists. Whereas traditional paintings had depicted, often grimly, religious themes and symbols, Renaissance works celebrated human potential, showing real individuals, with complex personalities and creative talents. Renaissance men and women saw themselves not as prisoners of blind fate or as victims of the forces of nature but rather they saw themselves as many-sided individuals with the capacity to change the world.

Renaissance Princes. The idea that the world could be shaped by man was particularly appealing to Renaissance rulers, who were eager to shape it to their own benefit. In *The Prince* (1513), Machiavelli provided unsentimental advice on how monarchs could increase their political power. Machiavelli's hero in this treatise was the Italian ruler Cesare Borgia, but his inspiration had been drawn from the state-building activities of the ambitious monarchs of northwestern Europe. These "new monarchs"—among them France's Louis XI (1461–1483), England's Henry VII (1485–1509), and Spain's Ferdinand of Aragon (1474–1516)—wanted to reduce the power of the landed classes and build strong

Renaissance Architecture

The columned buildings of the Renaissance recalled the classical world of Greece and Rome, while the symmetrical design reflected the impulse to create a world of ordered beauty. (Piero della Francesca, *The Ideal City*)

and prosperous national states. In England, the kings enhanced the authority of royal legal institutions and judges, thereby undermining the power of local lords. The French monarchs dispatched royal bureaucrats to every province, in an effort to establish direct control over peasant communities. Throughout Western Europe, kings and princes formed alliances with commercial interests, granting political privileges to artisan guilds, extending merchants the right to trade throughout their realms, and encouraging the expansion of both foreign trade and domestic manufacturing. In return, they extracted taxes from urban centers and loans from merchants to support their armies and bureaucracies. This alliance of monarchs, merchants, and royal bureaucrats challenged the primacy of the agrarian nobility and increased the wealth of the emergent nation-states. The rise of the monarchical nation-state laid the economic and administrative foundations for Europe's rise to world power, a rise that was ushered in by the European age of expansion.

Portuguese Innovation

In 1450 Western Europe was a relatively unimportant part of the world, a collection of poor agricultural societies lying isolated at the far edge of the Eurasian land mass. Strangely, it was Portugal, one of the smallest and most remote of the European countries, that led the way in the great surge of European exploration. A small Atlantic country, Portugal boasted a long tradition of seafaring and had a substantial merchant fleet. In the early part of the fifteenth century, it also had a prince, Henry the Navigator, who was determined to contest the dominant position of Muslim and Italian merchants by finding a new ocean route to the wealth of Asia.

Henry the Navigator. Prince Henry (1394–1460) was the younger brother of King Edward I of Portugal. Henry was a complex, many-sided individual, at once a Christian warrior and a Renaissance humanist. As a knight of the Order of Christ, Henry had fought against the Arabs in the important battle of Ceuta in North Africa (1415), an experience that reinforced his desire to extend Portuguese power and the bounds of Christendom. As a humanist, Henry patronized Renaissance thinkers who drew inspiration from classical Greek and Roman (rather than Christian) sources, and he relied on Arab and Italian geographers for the latest knowledge of the shape and size of the continents. In the activist spirit of the Renaissance, Henry sought to fulfill the predictions of his horoscope: "to engage in great and noble conquests and to attempt the discovery of things hidden from other men."

In the 1420s, Prince Henry established a center for exploration and ocean mapping on the coast of Portugal and from there sent out ships to sail the African coast and probe the Atlantic. His seamen soon discovered and settled the Madeira and Azores islands. By 1435, Portuguese sea captains were regularly roaming along the coast of West Africa, seeking ivory and gold in exchange for salt, wine, and fish. By the 1440s they were trading in humans as well. For centuries Arab merchants had conducted a brisk overland trade in slaves, buying sub-Saharan Africans captured during tribal conflicts and selling them throughout the Mediterranean region. The Portuguese extended this commerce, at first transporting West African blacks to Mediterranean sugar estates and eventually carrying hundreds of thousands of slaves across the Atlantic, where they would lead short, brutalized lives on sugar plantations in Brazil and the West Indies.

The Portuguese Maritime Empire. After Henry's death in 1460, Portuguese kings and navigators continued their explorations, looking for a direct ocean route to Asia. In 1488, Bartholomew Diaz rounded the Cape of Good Hope, the southern tip of Africa. Ten years later,

Vasco Da Gama sailed all the way to India. The Arab, Indian, and Jewish traders on India's Malabar Coast shunned Da Gama as a dangerous commercial rival, but he managed to return to Portugal with a valuable cargo of cinnamon and pepper, the latter in such great demand for flavoring and preserving meat that the voyage realized a profit of 6,000 percent. Da Gama returned to India in 1502, with twenty-one fighting vessels, and immediately attacked his rivals in a naked challenge for commercial dominance. Square-rigged Portuguese caravels outmaneuvered and outgunned Arab fleets, while on land Portuguese adventurers burned cities and seized the property of rival traders.

The Portuguese government set up fortified trading posts for its merchants at key points around the Indian Ocean, at Goa in India, Hormuz in Arabia, and Malacca in Malaysia; and soon had opened trade routes from Africa to Indonesia and up the coast of Asia to China and Japan. Portuguese merchants easily undersold Arab traders, for their ships held more and traveled faster than overland caravans. In a momentous transition, Portuguese Christians replaced Arab Muslims as the leaders in world commerce.

Spain Dispatches Columbus

Spain quickly followed Portugal's example. As Renaissance rulers, King Ferdinand of Aragon (1474–1516) and Queen Isabella of Castile (1474–1504) saw national unity and commerce as the keys to prosperity and power. Married in their teens in an arranged match, the young rulers had combined their kingdoms. In 1492, after their armies had expelled the Moors from Granada, the last outpost of Islam in Western Europe, they set about building a sense of "Spanishness" through religion, launching a brutal Inquisition against suspected heretics and expelling both Moors and Jews. Then they turned their attention to expansion, invading Moorish states in North Africa and looking across the seas for trading opportunities.

Because Portugal controlled the southern, or African, approach to Asia, Isabella and Ferdinand sought a western route, and soon were giving a hearing to the notions of a Genoese sea captain, Christopher Columbus. Columbus was familiar with the findings of Italian geographers who had rediscovered the maps of the ancient Greeks and recalculated the size of the continents. They reached the mistaken conclusion that Europe, Africa, and Asia covered more than half the earth's surface. Accepting these miscalculations, Columbus believed that the Atlantic Ocean, long feared by Arab sailors as an endless "green sea of darkness," was little more than a narrow channel of water separating Europe from Asia.

The Spanish monarchs were skeptical of Columbus's theories, but they were determined to match the success of the Portuguese. With the support of Spanish merchants, Ferdinand and Isabella mounted an expedition, commissioning Columbus "to discover and acquire islands and mainland in the Ocean Sea."

Columbus set sail with three small ships on August 3, 1492. Wanting not only to discover a new route to China but to find and rule new lands, he demanded, and received, from his monarch-patrons the titles of admiral, viceroy, and governor. To avoid the strong westerly winds of the North Atlantic, Columbus first sailed south, to the Canary Islands. From there he set a course due west, never losing faith in his mission and driving his crew hard while trying to calm their fears. On October 12, 1492, after a voyage of 3,000 miles, he landed at one of the islands of the present-day Bahamas. Whatever his original intentions, the Italian adventurer had "discovered" the lands of the Western Hemisphere for Europeans.

Columbus then set about exploring the Caribbean islands, claiming each for Spain and searching for signs of gold. The only gold he found, however, were trinkets given to him by the local Carib and Arawak peoples. Because he believed that he had reached Asia, or "the Indies" in fifteenth-century parlance, he called these native inhabitants "Indians," and the Caribbean islands thus became known as the "West Indies." Buoyed by the natives' stories of rivers of gold lying "to the west," Columbus left forty men on the island of Santo Domingo and returned triumphantly with several Caribs to display to Queen Isabella and King Ferdinand.

The monarchs were sufficiently impressed by Columbus's discovery that, over the next twelve years, they supported three more voyages, during which he found additional islands and the coast of South America. During these expeditions Columbus began the transatlantic trade in slaves, carrying a few hundred Indians to slavery in Europe and importing black slaves from Africa, but he failed to find great kingdoms or valuable goods. Indeed, his voyages produced so little of immediate value that Columbus fell into deep disfavor with his royal sponsors, and his death in 1506 was virtually unrecognized. In one of the more curious ironies of history, the two continents that Columbus revealed to Europe were named, by a German geographer, after the Florentine merchant Amerigo Vespucci, who had traveled in South America around 1500 and called it a *nuevo mundo,* a New World.

Spain's discovery of America was the climax of a century of nation building and commercial expansion by the Christian monarchs of Portugal and Spain. Renaissance learning and religious zeal had extended the horizons of these rulers and their merchant allies. They had sought power and wealth first in the Mediterranean, then in the Indian Ocean, and finally in the Western Hemisphere—spreading their influence to the far corners of the world.

The Spanish Conquest

The Spaniards who followed Columbus, settling on Cuba, Santo Domingo, and other Caribbean islands, were hardened men, many of whom had fought in the Moorish wars. They were eager to spread the Christian faith and determined, at all costs, to get rich. After subduing the native Arawak and Caribs, they quickly penetrated the North American continent in search of gold and other booty. Especially noteworthy were Juan Ponce de León, who explored the coast of Florida and gave the peninsula its name, and Vasco Núñez de Balboa, who crossed the Isthmus of Darien (Panama) in 1513, becoming the first European to see the Pacific Ocean.

The Spaniards were even more successful as conquerors. Between 1519 and 1535 small forces of Spanish adventurers seized control of the powerful Aztec empire in the Mexican highlands, the divided Mayan peoples of the Yucatan peninsula, and the rich Inca civilization in the mountains of Peru. Within a generation, the Spaniards had become masters of the wealthiest and most populous regions of the Western Hemisphere.

The Fall of the Aztecs. The onslaught against the Aztecs began in 1519, when Hernando Cortés, the first of the great Spanish *conquistadors* (conquerors) landed on the Mexican coast near Vera Cruz. Leading a Spanish force of 600 men, he marched inland, drawn by rumors of the golden splendor of the Aztec empire. Within two years Cortés and his men had conquered the Aztecs. This impressive feat was partly the result of a startling coincidence. Cortés arrived in the very year that Aztec mythology had predicted the return of the God Quetzalcoatl to his earthly kingdom. Believing that Cortés was indeed that god, Moctezuma, the Aztec

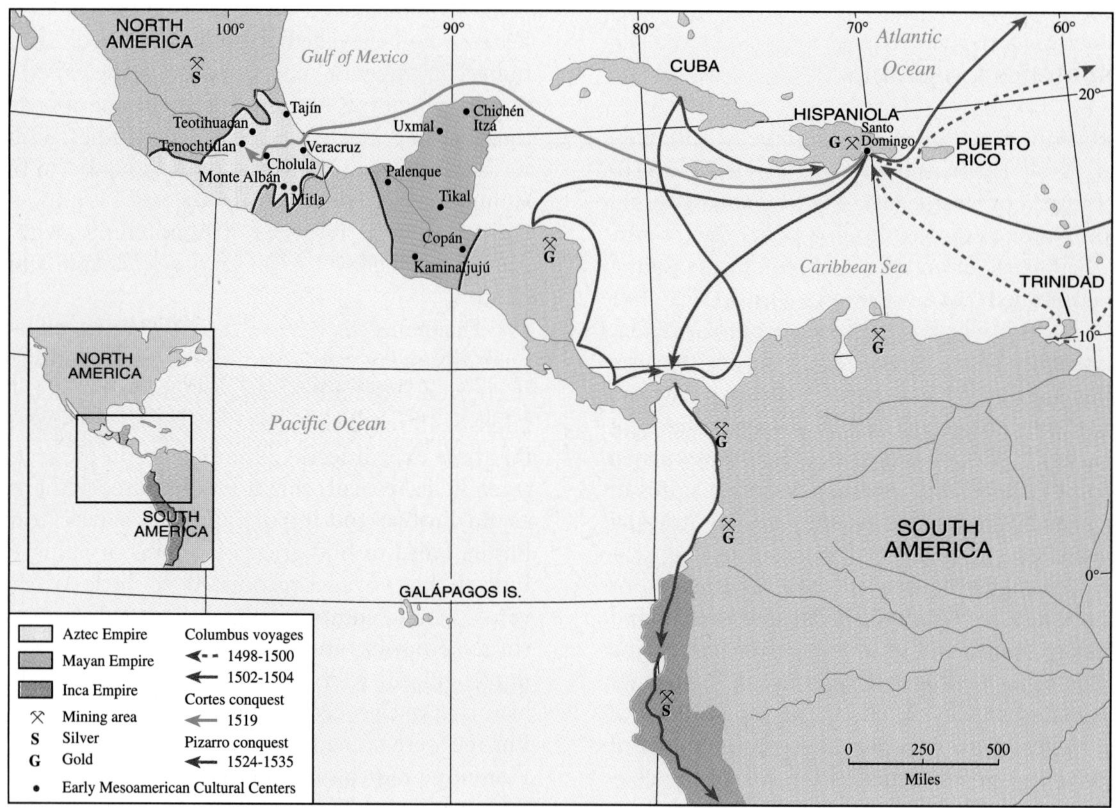

MAP 1.3

The Spanish Conquest

The Spanish first settled on the islands of the Caribbean. Rumors of a magnificent golden civilization led to Cortés's invasion of the Aztec empire in 1519. By 1535, other Spanish *conquistadors* had conquered the Mayan temple cities and the Inca empire in Peru—completing one of the great conquests in world history.

ruler, received him with great ceremony and initially allowed him free rein.

European technology was also an important factor in Cortés's triumph, both as a symbol of Cortés's divinity and as an instrument of warfare. The sight of the Spaniards in full armor, with guns that shook the heavens, made a deep impression on the Aztecs. The Aztecs had learned how to purify gold and fashion it into ornate religious objects, but they did not produce iron for tools or weapons. Moreover, they had no wheeled carts or cavalry, for horses, once abundant in the Western Hemisphere, had died out thousands of years before. Consequently, Aztec warriors, fighting on foot with flint- or obsidian-tipped spears and arrows, were no match for the Spanish conquistadors, seated high on their horses, protected by heavy armor, and wielding steel swords.

Still, the peoples of the Aztec empire, who numbered in the millions, could have crushed the European invaders if they had presented a united front. But Cortés brilliantly employed the age-old strategy of divide-and-conquer. The various tribes and nations dominated by the Aztecs had long resented their cruel and oppressive rulers, who had seized their finest goods and sacrificed vast numbers of their people to the Aztec gods. At the urging of Cortés, many of these subject peoples rebelled, providing the Spaniards with supplies, information, and thousands of soldiers. After a three-month siege, the main city of Tenochtitlán fell and the Aztec empire collapsed, the victim not only of superior Spanish military technology but of the rebellion by its subject Indian peoples.

The conquistadors took over the centralized political system of Moctezuma, who had been killed early in the struggle with Cortés, and soon extended their rule over the entire valley of Mexico. Cortés's lieutenants subdued the rest of the highland tribes and then moved against the Maya in the Yucatan, quickly conquering them as well.

The Spanish were able quickly to extend their control throughout the valley of Mexico and beyond because of the devastating impact of common European diseases. The Western Hemisphere had been isolated from the viral illnesses of Europe and Asia for thousands of years, so native Americans lacked immunity or resistance to smallpox, influenza, and measles. A savage smallpox epidemic devastated the Aztec capital of Tenochtitlán even as the Spanish attacked, and within a generation diseases took the lives of tens of thousands of native Americans.

These epidemics were swiftly spread throughout the region by Indian traders and Spanish explorers, facilitating the expansion of Spanish control. In the 1520s Francisco Pizarro embarked upon a long expedition to the mountains of Peru, home of the rich and powerful Inca empire. By the time he reached Peru, one-half of the Inca population had died from European diseases. Weakened militarily and emotionally by this abrupt loss of population, the Incas were easy prey for Pizarro and his conquistadors.

Indian Views of the Spanish Conquest

The Aztecs had a rich visual culture and wrote in pictograms. These illustrations, from the 1540s, depict the assault against Teochtitlán by Cortés and his Indian allies. (Conquest of Aztecs (top) and Attack on Great Temple (bottom), Codex Florentino, American Museum of Natural History)

The Legacy of the Conquest. The Spanish invasion forever changed the Western Hemisphere—first and foremost through its devastation of the native population. Although estimates vary, it seems likely that probably 20 million Indians were living in present-day Mexico and Guatemala at the time of the Spanish invasion of 1519. Disastrous epidemics in 1521, 1545, and 1575 took millions of lives. By 1650, only 3 million native Americans were left in this region.

AMERICAN VOICES

The Spanish Conquest Condemned *Bartholomé de Las Casas*

In 1542 Bartolomé de Las Casas, Dominican friar and Bishop of Chiapas (in present-day Mexico), wrote to the Spanish King to condemn the brutal treatment of native Americans by the conquistadors. Las Casas's books were widely read throughout Europe, creating the "Black Legend" of the Spanish conquest.

Now to come to the continent, we dare affirm of our own knowledge that there were ten kingdoms as large as the kingdom of Spain . . . . Of all this the inhumane and abominable villainies of the Spanish have made a wilderness, for though it was formerly occupied by vast and infinite numbers of men, it has been stripped of all people . . . over twelve million souls innocently perished, women and children being included in the sad and fatal list. . . .

As for those that came out of Spain, boasting themselves to be Christians, they had two ways of extirpating the Indian nation from the face of the earth: the first was by making bloody, unjust, and cruel wars against them; the second was by killing all those that so much as sought to recover their liberty, as some of the braver sort did. And as for the women and children that were left alive, the Spaniards let so heavy and grievous a yoke of servitude upon them that the condition of beasts was much more tolerable. . . .

What led the Spanish to these unsanctified impieties was the desire for gold to make themselves suddenly rich, in order to obtain dignities and honors that were in no way fit for them. . . . The Spanish so despised the Indians (I now speak what I have seen without the least untruth) that they used them not like beasts, for that would have been tolerable, but looked upon them as if they had been the dung and filth of the earth, and so little did they regard the health of their souls that they permitted the great multitude to die without the least light of religion. . . .

From which time forward the Indians began to think of ways that they might take to expel the Spaniards from their country. And when the Spanish saw this they came with their horsemen well armed with swords and lances, making a cruel havoc and slaughter among them, overrunning cities and towns and sparing neither sex nor age. Nor did their cruelty take pity on women with children, whose bellies they ripped up, taking out the infants to hew them to pieces. They would often lay wagers as to who could cleave or cut a man through the middle with the most dexterity, or who could cut off his head at one blow. The children they would take by the feet and dash their innocent heads against the rocks. . . .

Bartholomé de Las Casas

They erected a kind of gallows broad and low enough so that the tormented creatures might touch the ground with their feet, and upon each one of these they strung thirteen persons, blasphemously affirming that they did it in honor of our Redeemer and his apostles.

Source: Bartolomé de Las Casas, *The Tears of the Indians, Being an Historical and True Account of the Cruel Massacres and Slaughters of above Twenty Millions of Innocent People,* trans. John Phillips (London, 1656), pp. 4–9.

Warfare and brutal economic exploitation hastened the decline of the population. Following their victory over the Aztecs, the conquistadors betrayed their tribal allies, taking over the Aztec tribute system and forcing Indians to labor on vast new plantations. Building on Indian institutions, the Spanish created a hierarchical colonial system, much more rigid and exploitative than the later French and English empires in North America would be. The Spanish overlords expelled native Americans from their agricultural lands, which had provided corn, squash, and beans for human consumption, and used them to raise livestock for export to Europe. This new agricultural system altered the character of the environment as well as the lives of the native peoples, as imported European grains and grasses supplanted native flora. Horses, which were first brought over by Cortés, would run wild through the Americas within a century and change the way of life of hundreds of Indian communities.

The gold and silver that had honored Aztec gods now flowed into the counting houses of Spanish mine-owners and merchants and the treasury of the Spanish kings, but the Indian peoples received little in return. The Spanish monarchs dispatched royal governors, bureaucrats, and Catholic priests to manage the empire and to convert the Indian peoples, but they did little more than preside over a demographic, cultural, and ecological disaster. Within a century and a half, the once magnificent civilizations of Mexico and Peru lay in ruins, and the surviving native Americans lost much of their identity as a people. Some of the European invaders married Indian women, and their descendants eventually constituted a large *mestizo* population with a predominantly Spanish cultural outlook. Small groups of Maya and other peoples retreated into the mountains and preserved their traditional agricultural practices and values. In the centuries to come, their descendants would never gain the numbers or the military power to oust the Europeans. Unlike the inhabitants of Africa and India, native Americans were unable to preserve their culture following conquest by Europeans. For the original Americans, the consequences of being discovered by Columbus in 1492 were tragic and irreversible.

The Protestant Reformation

While Europeans were conquering the indigenous societies of the New World, traditional European society was under siege from within. For more than a millennium the peoples of Western and Central Europe had been united in a common faith and in their allegiance to the pope in Rome. The Protestant Reformation, which began in 1517, forever shattered that unity. It ushered in an era of wars and social turmoil that lasted more than a century, forcing every Christian, prince and peasant alike, to reexamine age-old beliefs, sometimes at the point of a sword.

At first, reformers wanted only to cleanse the church of corruption and abuses. Over the centuries, the Catholic church, through gifts, fees, and taxes, had become a large and wealthy institution, owning vast estates throughout Europe. Bishops and cardinals, the princes of the church, used the income from church lands to live well, often luxuriously. Abuse and corruption became a way of life within the church. Pope Leo X (1513–1521), a member of the powerful Italian Medici family, received half a million ducats a year from the sale of religious offices, a practice known as simony. In England, Cardinal Thomas Wolsey engaged in nepotism, giving jobs to his relatives; his illegitimate son held church positions with an income equal to that of 250 country priests. Ordinary priests and monks extracted their share of the spoils, using their authority to obtain economic or sexual favors. These abuses ignited a smoldering anticlericalism. One reformer proclaimed that the clergy were a "gang of scoundrels" who should be "rid of their vices or stripped of their authority." But until 1517 those raising their voices in protest had been ignored or condemned as heretics and executed.

Martin Luther. In 1517, Martin Luther, a German monk and a professor at the university in Wittenberg, publicly challenged church leaders by nailing his famous Ninety-five Theses to the door of the town cathedral. This document, which was soon reprinted in a number of major cities, condemned the church's pervasive and highly lucrative practice of selling indulgences—official dispensations that promised the purchasing sinner release from punishments in the afterlife. Luther charged not only that this practice was corrupt but also that indulgences were spiritually worthless; redemption could come only from God, through grace, not from the church, through a fee. When Luther refused to recant his position, he was excommunicated by Pope Leo X and threatened with punishment by Charles V, emperor of the Holy Roman Empire. The sentiment for reform was particularly strong in the German states, and northern German princes, eager to free the churches in their realms from papal control, embraced Luther's doctrines and protected him from arrest. Soon Europe was at war, as Charles V dispatched armies to restore his authority, and Catholicism, throughout the Holy Roman Empire.

Luther broadened his attack, lashing out at church dogma, ritual, and practices not explicitly based on Scripture. Essentially, his beliefs differed from Roman Catholic doctrine in four major respects. First, Luther rejected the doctrine of St. Thomas Aquinas, the great medieval philosopher, that Christians could win salvation either by their faith or by their good deeds (what Luther called "justification by works"). Stressing God's power and human weakness, Luther argued that people could be saved only by faith ("justification by faith"), and that faith—and salvation—came as a gift of grace from God, not as a result of human action.

Second, Lutherans—and all Protestants—rejected the spiritual authority of the pope, in part because of political developments. As the Reformation gathered force, the rulers in many Protestant states took over as the official head of the church, gaining the power to appoint bishops and to control the church's property. Third, Luther downplayed the role of priests as mediators between God and the people, denying, for example, that priests had the power to change bread and wine into Christ's body and blood or to grant absolution for sins. Instead he proclaimed the priesthood of all believers: "Our baptism consecrates us all without exception and makes us all priests." Fourth, Protestants considered the Bible the sole authority in matters of faith, raising the prospect of a multitude of individual interpretations. So that everyone could read the Bible, it was translated from Latin into the languages of the common people—German, French, and English. Luther himself did the German translation.

It was not Luther's intention to inspire social revolution, but his attacks on existing authority encouraged the proliferation of radical religious doctrines and, for a brief period, popular revolt. In 1524 the oppressed peasantry in Germany repudiated the legitimacy of manorial landlords, claiming economic as well as religious rights for themselves. The revolt was ruthlessly suppressed (a response that was applauded by Luther), but dissenting ideas continued to simmer below the surface. Ten years later a group of Anabaptists, religious radicals who rejected the doctrine of infant baptism, seized control of the city of Munster. They placed political power in the hands of "Saints"—those who felt God had saved them through grace—and this new government promptly abolished most rights to private property and instituted polygamy, as authorized by the Old Testament.

To forestall such social revolutions in southern Europe, most rulers there reaffirmed support for Catholicism, accepting the need to share power with the church in order to preserve religious and social order. Luther also affirmed the need for social discipline and supported the Protestant princes of northern Germany in their assertion of state power over religion. He argued that whereas spiritual liberty was a private matter, Christians owed complete obedience to established political authorities. In fact, when Charles V gave up his bid to control the Empire in 1555 and concluded the Peace of Augsburg, which gave every prince the right to decide whether his subjects were to be Catholic or Protestant, the northern German princes made Lutheranism the official state religion, to which all members of the realm had to conform. The ultimate control of these Lutheran state churches resided in the princes, whose dictates were channeled through the traditional hierarchy of bishops and clergy to the people. Thus the success of the Reformation in northern Germany was assured, setting the stage for its spread to France and England.

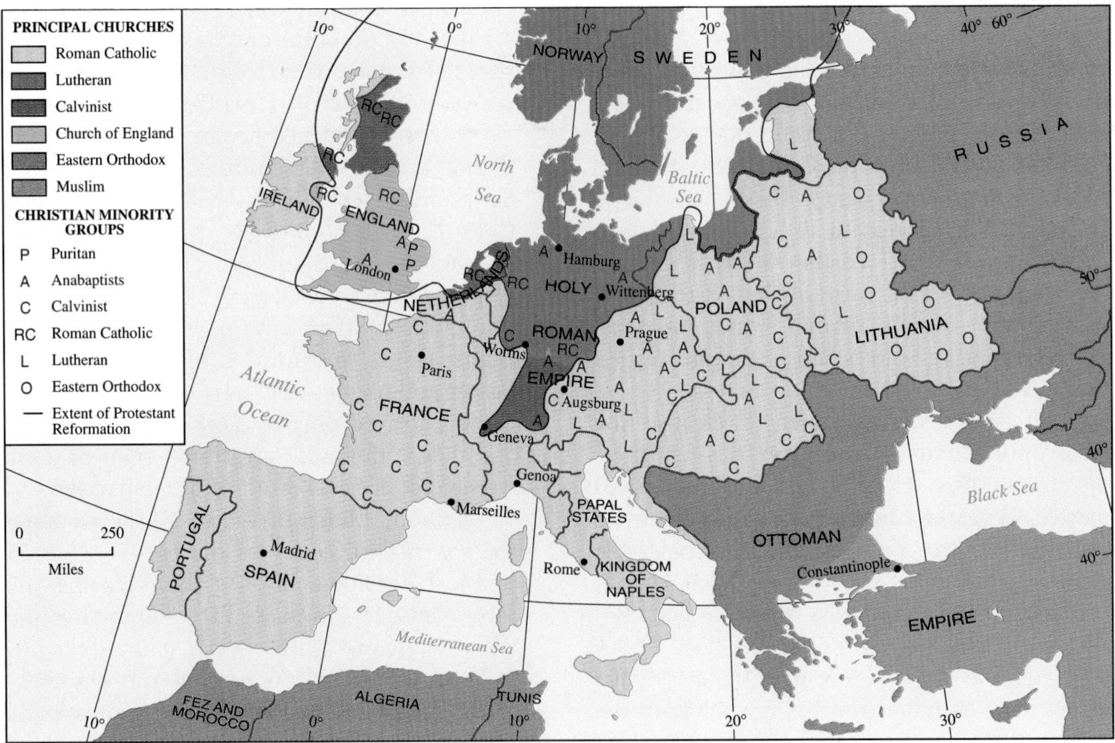

MAP 1.4

Religious Diversity in Europe

By 1600, Europe was permanently divided. Catholicism remained dominant in the south but Lutheran princes and monarchs ruled northern Europe and Calvinism had strongholds in Switzerland, Holland, and Scotland. Radical sects were persecuted by legally established Protestant churches as well as by Catholic clergy and monarchs. These religious conflicts encouraged the migration of minority sects to America.

The Teachings of John Calvin. A more rigorous version of Protestantism appeared in Geneva, Switzerland, under the leadership of a great French theologian, John Calvin. Even more than Luther, Calvin stressed the omnipotence of God and the corruption of human nature caused by Adam's sin. His masterly *Institutes of the Christian Religion* (1536) depicted God as an awesome and absolute sovereign governing the "wills of men so as to move precisely to that end directed by him." Relentlessly pursuing this train of thought to its ultimate conclusion, Calvin enunciated the doctrine of predestination—the idea that God had "predestined" certain women and men for salvation even before they were born and had condemned the rest to the eternal miseries of hell.

In Geneva, Calvin set up a model Christian community. He eliminated bishops altogether and placed spiritual power in the hands of ministers; the choice of a minister was up to the members of each congregation. In the eyes of Calvinists, the state was an instrument of the church; its duty was to remake society into a disciplined religious community. Accordingly, ministers and pious laymen ruled the city, prohibiting all frivolity and luxury and banishing those who resisted.

Calvinist precepts—of predestination and religious perfectionism—won converts all over Europe. Small communities of Calvinists appeared in Hungary, Poland, and Germany. Calvinism was the creed of the French Huguenots, of Protestants in Belgium and Holland, of Presbyterians in Scotland, and of Puritans in England and, eventually, America.

The Reformation produced a century and a half of social upheaval and bloody warfare. In the name of true faith, princes fought with each other, sometimes for religious principle, sometimes for dynastic gain. And they fought with their subjects, suppressing religious minorities in the name of national unity. Many Christians were forced by the state to conform to the religion of their ruler—or to leave their homeland. For many others there was the constant threat of more violent persecution. Both the Protestant and Catholic hierarchies accused thousands of women and men of heresy or witchcraft and sentenced them to death for their beliefs. Eventually, religious confusion and violence prompted thousands of Europeans, now belonging to many different churches, to escape from the bitter sectarian and national rivalries of Europe and seek freedom and safety in North America.

Spain's Rise and Decline

Luther's challenge to Catholicism in 1517 came just two years before Cortés conquered the Aztec empire, and the two sets of events remained linked. For more than a century, precious metals from America made Catholic Spain the wealthiest nation in Europe. Gold and silver from rich mines in Mexico and Peru poured into it at the rate of 3 million ducats per year between 1550 and 1575, and averaged about 9 million for the rest of the century. Twenty percent of this immense treasure—the "Royal Fifth"— went directly to the Spanish monarch, helping Philip II (1556–1598), the great-grandson of Ferdinand and Isabella, to become the most powerful ruler in Europe. From the Escorial, a massive administrative palace which he built outside Madrid, Philip presided over a vast empire that included the wealthiest states of Italy, the commercial and manufacturing provinces of the Spanish Netherlands (Holland and Belgium) and, after 1580, Portugal and all of its possessions in America, Africa, and the East Indies.

Philip sought to impose Spanish power and Catholicism on all of Europe. After defeating the Ottoman Turks in the famous battle of Lepanto in 1571, thereby securing Christian control of the western Mediterranean, he spent the last decades of his life trying to snuff out Protestantism in the Netherlands. Calvinism had taken strong root in these Dutch-and Flemish-speaking provinces, which had become wealthy from deep-sea fishing, commercial ties with the Portuguese empire, and the manufacture of woolen and linen fabrics. Their inhabitants feared that Philip would extend the Spanish Inquisition to wipe out their faith and take away their traditional political liberties. A popular anti-Catholic and anti-Spanish revolt in 1566 brought fierce repression by Philip's armies, but the revolt continued nonetheless.

Led by William of Orange in the province of Holland, the seven northern provinces declared their independence from Spain in 1581, becoming the Dutch Republic (or the Netherlands). To support this new Protestant state, Queen Elizabeth of England dispatched six thousand troops to the continent in 1585. In response, Philip assembled the Spanish Armada, the most powerful naval force the world had ever seen, and in 1588, he sent this fleet of 130 ships (with 30,000 men and 2,400 pieces of artillery) to attack England. To Philip, this assault represented the start of a holy crusade, for he intended to conquer England, reimpose Catholicism there, and then wipe out Calvinism in Holland.

The Armada failed utterly, as English ships and a fierce storm destroyed the Spanish fleet and Philip's dream of a Catholic Europe along with it. In 1609, Philip's successor tacitly accepted Dutch independence, and Amsterdam quickly emerged as the financial and commercial capital of northern Europe. Following the formation of the Dutch East India Company, which quickly gained a monopoly hold on trade with the In-

A Dutch Merchant Family

This painting captures the serious Calvinist ethos—and the prosperity—of Holland in the sixteenth century, and also the character of the patriarchal family, with its rigid hierarchy of gender and age. (Cornelius de Zeeuw, *Pierre de Moucheron and his Family*, Rijksmuseum, Amsterdam)

dies, the Netherlands replaced Portugal as the dominant European power in Asia and coastal Africa. The Dutch also looked across the Atlantic, investing in sugar plantations in Brazil and the Caribbean and establishing fur-trading posts in North America.

As the Netherlands prospered, Spain faltered. Philip had spent much of his American bullion outside Spain, drawing resources away from domestic development. Philip's massive expenditure of bullion also doubled the money supply of Europe, contributing to a runaway inflation, which historians now refer to as the "price revolution" of the sixteenth century. The price of a bushel of wheat, for example, rose by 300 percent between 1530 and 1600, both because more money was "chasing" the limited supply of food and handmade goods and because a sharp rise in Europe's population was increasing the demand for them. The chief beneficiaries of the price revolution were the northern European states of the Netherlands, France, and England. Stimulated by the influx of Spanish gold and silver, their economies boomed, enabling them to seize the initiative in commerce, manufacturing, and diplomacy. At Philip's death in 1598, Spain was in serious decline, exhausted financially and psychologically by war and inflation. In the century to come, it was not Spain but England, France, and the Netherlands that would exploit the riches of North America.

The Background of English Colonization, 1550–1630

England, too, was reshaped by the forces that swept the rest of Europe: monarchical nation building, the Protestant Reformation, and the price revolution. Indeed, it was the convergence of these three great historical changes that resulted in the English settlement of North America. Inflation, along with the enclosure of open fields, disrupted the lives of the peasantry, laying the foundation for a vast transatlantic migration. At the same time, English monarchs, seeking greater wealth, assisted the expansion of shipping and trade, thereby creating the maritime resources required to establish overseas colonies. Finally, the kings, trying to impose a single national Protestant church, persecuted Calvinist Protestants and Roman Catholics, prompting thousands to seek refuge in America.

Prices and Society in England

As on the continent, the price revolution in England was driven in part by rapid population growth. Due largely to a decline in the death rate (because of fewer plagues and epidemics) the population of England rose

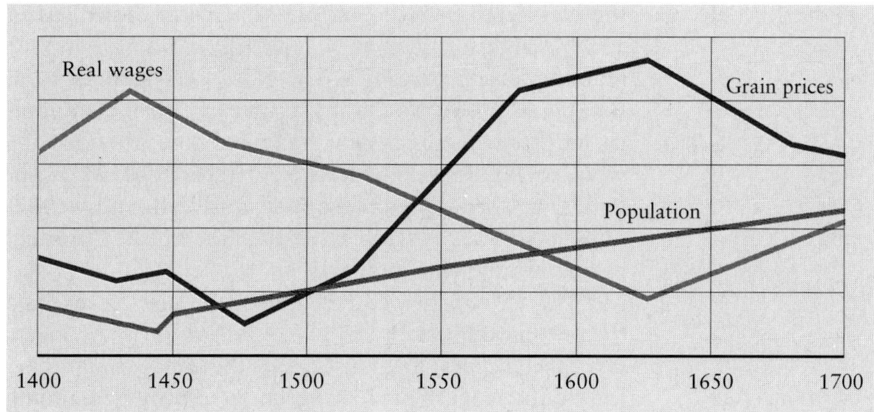

FIGURE 1.2

Inflation and Living Standards

The influx of Spanish bullion was the main cause of the great inflation in grain prices, but increased demand (from a constantly growing population) also caused the rise in prices. Higher costs cut real wages, resulting in lower living standards.

from 3 to 5 million between 1500 and 1630. A larger population created shortages of food, clothes, housing, and other goods, leading to a spiral of higher prices—an economic change that profoundly altered the traditional class structure.

Aristocracy, Gentry, Yeomanry. Most profoundly affected by the price revolution were the nobility, who had customarily rented out their estates on long leases for fixed rents. In the past, such arrangements had provided them with a secure income and plenty of leisure. As one English nobleman put it, "We eat and drink and rise up to play and this is to live like a gentleman." Then inflation struck. In the space of two generations, prices tripled on virtually everything, but the nobility's income from the rents on their farmlands remained the same. Consequently, the wealth and status of the aristocracy declined both in their local communities and in the nation as a whole.

However, there were two other social groups who benefited from the price revolution: the yeomen and the gentry. The gentry were substantial landholders who lacked the titles and legal privileges of the aristocracy. They usually owned smaller estates but managed them more efficiently. For instance, the gentry rented their lands on short leases, so they could raise rents to keep pace with inflation. Yeomen also benefited from rising prices. Described as "middle people of a condition between gentlemen and peasants," the yeomen owned land and worked it with family labor. Since their labor costs remained constant, the yeomen's sale of grain brought increasing profits, which they used to build substantial houses and to provide land for their children. Similarly, some tenants on noble estates were able to take advantage of rising prices to join the ranks of the yeomanry: they paid the customary fixed rent to the lord and, by selling surplus grain at increasingly higher prices, were able to buy small plots of land.

As aristocrats lost wealth, their branch of Parliament, the House of Lords, declined in influence. At the same time, members of the rising gentry, supported by the votes of other rural property owners, entered the House of Commons, the political voice of the freeholding classes. The gentry demanded new rights and powers for the Commons, such as the control of taxation. Thus the price revolution encouraged the rise of representative government in England, a development with profound consequences for American political history.

Peasants and Enclosures. Peasants and farm laborers made up three-fourths of the population of England, and their lives, too, were transformed by the great inflation. As in the rest of Europe, many of these rural folk lived in open-field settlements, owning or leasing a house plot in the village center and holding the right to farm strips of the large surrounding fields. After 1500, rising prices and a growing demand for wool disrupted this communal agricultural system. Profit-minded landlords and wool merchants used their influence in Parliament to pass *Enclosure* acts, which allowed owners to enclose the open fields with fences and put sheep to graze on them, pushing villagers off their lands.

Thus dispossessed, families moved to small cottages in the countryside, creating a new class of landless laborers known as *cotters.* Constantly on the brink of poverty, the cotters spun and wove the wool of the sheep that had taken their place on the land, or they worked as wage laborers on large estates owned by merchants or gentry. Wealthy men had "taken farms into their hands," a critical observer noted in 1600, "and rent them to those that will give most, whereby the peasantry of England is decayed and become servants to gentlemen." English agriculture thus became increasingly capitalistic, with a few families owning the land and many other families working for them.

These changes in English rural life precipitated a

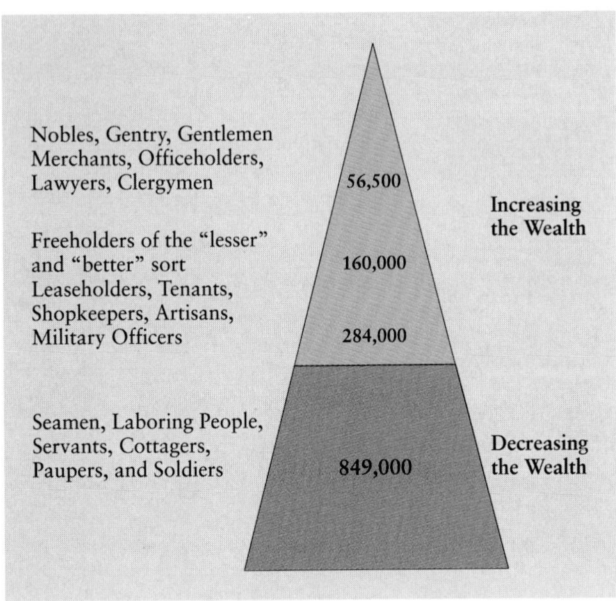

FIGURE 1.3

The Structure of English Society: 1688

During the 1680s Gregory King devised a famous table of the structure of English society. King argued that less than half the families of England (some 500,500) were independent and "Increasing the Wealth of the Kingdom," while the majority (849,000) were dependent and decreasing its wealth.

substantial migration to North America after 1600, as thousands of yeomen farm families migrated to the English colonies to maintain their status as landowners. Even greater numbers of dispossessed and impoverished peasants crossed the Atlantic as humble indentured servants, in hopes of a better life in the New World.

Mercantilist Expansion

The migration of so many English men and women would not have been possible without a vigorous and expanding merchant community. About 1550, English monarchs began giving assistance, such as subsidies and trade monopolies, to merchants to encourage foreign trade and increase national wealth. These incentives enabled merchants to expand domestic manufacturing and foreign commerce, providing England with the resources and expertise to establish colonies overseas.

The Wool Trade. England had engaged in little foreign trade before 1350. Then merchants began to sell high-quality English wool to manufacturers in France and the Netherlands, receiving fine textiles in return. After 1500, English merchants themselves became textile manufacturers, creating a new *outwork* system of rural household production that was an early form of capitalist industry. In this system the merchants provided the wool to landless cotters who, in return for wages or goods, washed the wool, spun it into yarn, and wove it into cloth. The merchants then sold the finished product in English and foreign markets.

The Crown helped merchant capitalists to expand the putting-out system. In 1563, the Statute of Artificers (artisan workers) gave justices of the peace the authority to fix wages, preventing cotters from demanding higher pay for their work. A new Poor Law in 1601 further ensured manufacturers a pool of cheap labor by making it more difficult for poor people to receive public assistance or private charity. Under the Tudor monarchs, especially Elizabeth I, special monetary bonuses were awarded to manufacturers who exported goods. Moreover, the government negotiated commercial treaties with foreign states and gave special privileges to merchant groups. In 1555, the Crown gave a royal charter to the Muscovy Company, providing it with a monopoly on the export of English cloth to Russia. Similar charters were granted to the Levant Company (Turkey) in 1581, the Guinea Company (Africa) in 1588, and the East India Company in 1600.

Mercantilism. This system of state-supported manufacturing and trade became known as *mercantilism.* English monarchs, like the rulers of many European states, used this system to increase national power and wealth. By encouraging merchants to invest in domestic manufacturing, the Crown reduced the import of foreign-made goods and boosted English exports, a strategy that gave England a favorable balance of trade. Gold and silver flowed into the country in payment for English manufactures, stimulating further economic expansion and enriching the merchant community. Increased trade meant higher revenues from import duties, which swelled the royal treasury and enhanced the power of the national government.

American Ventures. Before this mercantilist expansion, England was unable to challenge Spanish dominance in the Western Hemisphere. As early as 1497, John Cabot had explored the coasts of Newfoundland and Nova Scotia, but England had lacked the wealth, the shipping, and the sense of national purpose to colonize North America. For the next half-century it did little more than send fishing fleets across the Atlantic.

Then Spanish gold began to lure English adventurers to the Western Hemisphere. Sir John Hawkins and

Sir Walter Raleigh and His Son

Raleigh was one of the great figures of his age. A distinguished courtier (as this portrait suggests), he was also a man of action—as a conquering soldier in Ireland, an explorer in South America, and the organizer of England's first colonial ventures. (*Raleigh and Son,* 1602, National Portrait Gallery, London)

other "sea dogs" plundered Spanish possessions in the Caribbean in the 1560s. In 1577, Sir Francis Drake sailed around the tip of South America and attacked a Spanish bullion fleet in the Pacific. After landing in California, which he claimed for England, Drake sailed west to Asia. Circumnavigating the globe, he returned home with £600,000 in bullion, (equal to about $30 million in 1990) twenty times the annual income of the wealthiest aristocrat.

Adventures such as Drake's yielded private fortunes but not colonial settlements. The first attempts to establish a permanent English presence in America were small-scale attempts backed by individual aristocrats. All failed. In the 1580s, Sir Humphrey Gilbert's settlement in Newfoundland collapsed for lack of sufficient financial backing. Sir Ferdinando Gorges colony along the coast of Maine likewise failed because of inadequate supplies and the harsh climate. Sir Walter Raleigh's three expeditions to North Carolina also ended in failure, with one, the famous "lost" colony of Roanoke, completely vanishing, its one hundred men, women, and children gone without a trace or any apparent cause.

What finally made American colonization possible was the banding together of successful merchants in *joint-stock companies,* which sold shares of stock to many investors, thus raising substantial amounts of money for commercial enterprises. It was a joint-stock venture, the Virginia Company of London, that founded the first permanent English settlement in America at Jamestown (Virginia) in 1607. The investors hoped to grow rich by finding gold like the Spanish and by trading with the natives or exploiting their labor.

The English Reformation

While English merchants sought wealth in Virginia, thousands of other English men and women migrated to Massachusetts and Maryland to escape religious conflict and persecution. King Henry VIII (1509–1547) had initially opposed the spread of Protestantism in his kingdom. Then he petitioned the Spanish-controlled papacy for a divorce from Catherine of Aragon, an aunt of Charles V. When his request was denied, he broke with Rome, established a national Church of England (which granted his divorce) and declared himself supreme head of the Church of England with complete control over ecclesiastical appointments. This break from Rome set in motion a series of religious conflicts that ended in a massive migration to America and civil war in England.

The Church of England. As head of the Church of England, Henry VIII made few changes in traditional dogma, organization, or ritual. Priests, sacraments, and elaborate ceremonies remained important and spiritual authority still flowed downward in a hierarchical and authoritarian fashion—from king to bishops to priests and, finally, to the laity. Indeed, except for its emphasis on the authority of the Bible and its recognition of justification by faith, the Church of England under Henry was barely Protestant at all. But Henry's severance of the link with Rome was crucial. When his daughter Mary briefly restored Catholicism, her action was deeply resented, and her execution of three hundred Protestant clergymen further inflamed anti-Catholic sentiment.

By the time Henry's younger daughter, Elizabeth I (1558–1603), ascended the throne, pressure for Protestant reform was irresistible, and the new queen was

Elizabeth I (1558–1603)
This rather unflattering portrait of the "Virgin Queen" conveys nonetheless her commanding presence and her shrewd character, two keys to her success as a monarch. (*Elizabeth I*, c.1592, Marcus Gheeraerts, the Younger, National Portrait Gallery, London)

quick to respond to it. She repealed the pro-Rome legislation passed during Mary's reign and approved the Thirty-nine Articles as official dogma. The Articles were a carefully crafted compromise intended to appeal to as many English Christians as possible. They incorporated both the Lutheran doctrine of justification by faith and the Calvinist belief in predestination, but at the same time retained the clerical hierarchy of bishops and archbishops as well as traditional religious services—now conducted in English rather than Latin.

The Presbyterian Church. In an age of passionate religious controversy, Elizabeth's compromise was bound to be challenged. Many English Protestants condemned the power of bishops as "anti-Christian and devilish and contrary to the Scriptures" and called for a more radical change in church organization. Some reformers took inspiration from Calvin's Geneva, where the laity of each church controlled all of its affairs. Others preferred the presbyterian system devised by John Knox for the Calvinist Church of Scotland; there, local congregations elected lay elders ("presbyters"), who assisted ministers in running the church. Presbyters also represented the laity in church synods that formulated dogma, ordained new ministers, and enforced church discipline. By 1600, five hundred ministers within the Church of England wanted to eliminate bishops and install a presbyterian form of church government.

The Puritans. Many of these ministers called themselves Puritans. As their name implied, they wished to purify the church of "false" teachings and practices. These reformers appeared as early as 1559 and nearly gained control of a church convocation in 1562. Four years later, a community of Puritans, or "unspotted lambs of the Lord," formed in London. Although Puritans differed among themselves on many issues of doctrine and ritual, they were generally united on three basic principles. First, they wanted the authority over spiritual and financial matters to rest with the lay men and women who composed the local congregation. (Some accepted the presbyterian form of church organization; others were strict congregationalists, demanding local autonomy and complete lay control.) Second, Puritans asserted the priesthood of each individual, maintaining that all Christians, and not merely ministers, could understand and interpret the Bible. Third, they condemned most traditional religious rites as magical or idolatrous. Praying to saints could not change worldly events; sacraments such as Communion had no miraculous spiritual powers.

Puritans likewise rejected the view that God spoke to people through their *senses;* they were offended by elaborately robed priests and by gaudy churches filled with statues and fragrant with incense. According to the great Puritan poet John Milton, Catholics and traditionalists within the Church of England had made God "earthy and fleshy because they could not make themselves heavenly and spiritual." True spirituality and genuine religious knowledge, the Puritans argued, came through the *mind.* Consequently, they taught their children the importance of reading the Bible. The centerpiece of their religious service was the sermon—a finely wrought argument on dogma and ethics.

Religious Persecution. As head of the Church of England, King James I (1603–1625), a Scotsman and the first of the Stuart kings, continued Elizabeth's policy of resistance against radical religious reform. He remarked bitterly that Presbyterians favoring representative institutions of church government, "agreeth as well with a monarchy as God with the Devil." James endorsed absolutism, not democracy. In *The True Laws of Free Monarchy,* he maintained that kings drew their authority directly from God and thus had a "divine right" to rule. As for the congregationalist-minded Puritans, James threatened to "harry them out of the land, or else do worse."

Radical Protestants took the king at his word and fled England to avoid persecution. To preserve their "pure" Christian faith, some sects separated completely from the Church of England (and hence were called "Separatists"). One such group was the Pilgrims—who left England and settled among like-minded Dutch Calvinists, at Leiden in Holland. In time, however, some of these Separatist Pilgrims began to fear the loss of their English way of life. Migration to America seemed the only way to preserve both their religious freedom and their sense of national identity. Led by William Bradford, 35 Pilgrims, joined by 60 migrants from England, founded Plymouth colony in 1620.

During the next two decades, the repressive policies of James I and Charles I (1625–1649) drove thousands of other Puritans across the Atlantic to establish a settlement at Massachusetts Bay. Like the Pilgrims, the Puritans envisioned a reformed Christian society, a genuinely "new" England. However, rather than break with the Church of England, they hoped to reform it; hence they were "non-Separatist" congregationalists. They were strict Calvinists nonetheless and the colonies they founded embodied some of the most radical thought of the Protestant Reformation.

Religious intolerance drove English Catholics to America as well. Persecuted by the dominant Church of England both for their religious beliefs and for their allegiance to the pope, they began settling in America in 1632, establishing the colony of Maryland.

The English Legacy to America. The economic and religious transformation of England during the sixteenth century greatly influenced the character of its North American settlements. The aristocracy was on the decline between 1550 and 1630, and therefore played a small role in colonization, so the American settlements were never dominated by a legally privileged nobility. Conversely, the rise of English merchants enhanced their role in overseas expansion, and resulted in the rapid creation of a transatlantic trading economy. Moreover, the social upheaval produced by enclosures and agricultural capitalism in England prompted the transatlantic migration of thousands of yeomen and peasant families. Many more migrants to the Western Hemisphere came from England than from Spain, and they came seeking land to farm rather than native Americans to exploit. Finally, as a result of the influence of Calvinism on English Protestantism, many of these migrants carried strict forms of Christianity to North America.

The legacy was rich and complex. As products of traditional Europe, the settlers brought with them age-old principles of authority and a hierarchical social organization. Yet the old European order had already been partially overturned: the English colonies in America were founded by a nation in the midst of violent economic, political, and religious transformation. Their character—and their fate—were unpredictable.

Summary

The first inhabitants of the Western Hemisphere were hunter-gatherers from Asia, who migrated across a land bridge during the last Ice Age. Their descendants settled throughout North and South America, establishing a great variety of societies. In Mesoamerica the Mayan and Aztec peoples developed highly sophisticated systems of agriculture, religion, and politics. In North America, the peoples of the Mississippian culture also created elaborate ceremonial and urban sites. Most native Americans, however, lived in self-governing communities of foragers, hunters, and horticulturalists.

The Europeans who invaded America came from a traditional agricultural society in which a privileged elite ruled a mass of peasants. The Christian church gave emotional richness and meaning to life. Church and state alike endorsed the values of hierarchy and authority, demanding that people submit to strict discipline as the price of survival.

The Crusades opened Europeans' eyes to the wealth and learning of Asia, but trade with the East flowed through the Mediterranean, which was controlled by Arab Muslims. By A.D. 1450, the Italian Renaissance and the emergence of strong monarchical nation-states had begun the transformation of Western Europe from a static to a dynamic and expanding society. First to break the Arab monopoly of trade was Portugal, whose explorers found the southerly route to Asia around the African continent. Then Spain sent the Italian sea captain Christopher Columbus to find a westerly route, across the Atlantic. Instead of Asia, Columbus found a "new world." Within a generation Spanish *conquistadors* had pillaged the wealthy civilizations of Mexico and Peru. The coming of Europeans—and their diseases, horses, government, and religion—changed native American life forever. At the same time, American gold and silver helped trigger a price revolution that severely undermined traditional European society, already reeling from the religious wars unleashed by the Protestant Reformation.

In England inflation reduced the wealth and power of the nobility and enhanced the position of the gentry and the merchants. The Tudor monarchs used mercantilist policies to promote domestic manufacturing, foreign trade, and colonization. The enclosure movement and religious conflicts laid the social basis for a mass migration to America. Coming from a society in flux, the migrants carried both traditional and modern ideas and institutions across the Atlantic.

TOPIC FOR RESEARCH

The Environmental Consequences of 1492

Columbus's voyage to America changed the course of human history—and the natural environment of every continent. The Spanish carried European diseases to the Western Hemisphere and transmitted American viruses back to Europe. Likewise, the Spanish introduced horses and cattle to the New World, while the native Americans contributed corn and other plants to the world ecology. What was the precise impact of this transcontinental exchange of diseases, animals, and plants? How did it change the way that men and women lived—or died? What was its impact on the food supply? On the natural environment? Two books by Alfred W. Crosby, Jr., provide an overview: *The Columbian Exchange: Biological and Cultural Consequences of 1492* (1972) and *Ecological Imperialism: The Biological Expansion of Europe, 900–1900* (1986). Other works include E. L. Jones, *The European Miracle: Environments, Economics, and Geopolitics in the History of Europe and Asia* (1981), and William H. McNeill, *Plagues and Peoples* (1976). Studies that focus on North America are Henry F. Dobyns, *Their Numbers Became Thinned: Native American Population Dynamics in Eastern North America* (1983), and William Cronon, *Changes in the Land: Indians, Colonists, and the Ecology of New England* (1983).

BIBLIOGRAPHY

Native American Worlds

Brian M. Fagan, *The Great Journey; The People of Ancient America* (1987), is a good recent summary, while an earlier popular treatment is Peter Farb, *Man's Rise to Civilization, as Shown by the Indians of North America* . . . . For the civilizations of Mesoamerica, see Nigel Davies, *The Aztecs* (1973); John S. Henderson, *The World of the Maya* (1981); David Carrasco, *Quetzalcoatl and the Irony of Empire* (1982); and R. C. Padden, *The Hummingbird and the Hawk* (1962). Wilcomb B. Washburn, *The Indian in America* (1975), offers an overview of the development of the tribes of North America, as do Carl Waldman and Molly Braun, *Atlas of the North American Indian* (1985). See also Robert Silverberg, *Mound Builders of Ancient America: The Archaeology of a Myth* (1968).

Traditional European Society

Barbara W. Tuchman, *A Distant Mirror: The Calamitous Fourteenth Century* (1978), and Johan Huizinga, *The Waning of the Middle Ages,* present vivid portraits of the late medieval world. See also Pierre Goubert, *Louis XIV and Twenty Million Frenchmen* (1970). Other pathbreaking studies in the social and political history of early modern Europe include Marc Bloch, *Feudal Society* (1940); Philippe Ariès, *Centuries of Childhood* (1962); Norman Cohn, *The Pursuit of the Millennium* (1957); B. H. Slicher Van Bath, *The Agrarian History of Western Europe, A.D. 500–1850* (1963); and Emanuel Le Roy Ladurie, *The Peasants of Languedoc* (1974).

The Expansion and Transformation of Europe

W. H. McNeill, *The Rise of the West* (1963), offers an incisive description of European political and cultural development, while economic expansion is treated in Robert R. Reynolds, *Europe Emerges: Transition Toward an Industrial World-Wide Society, 600–1750* (1961). For southern Europe, read selectively in Fernand Braudel's massive and stimulating *The Mediterranean and the Mediterranean World in the Age of Philip II* (1949).

Paul H. Chapman, *The Norse Discovery of America* (1981), and Boies Penrose, *Travel and Discovery in the Renaissance, 1420–1620* (1952), illuminate the growth of geographical knowledge. Caro M. Cipolla, *Guns, Sails, and Empires* (1966), and J. H. Parry, *The Age of Reconnaissance* (1963), survey European expansion around the world. Samuel Eliot Morrison offers an exciting biography of Columbus in *Admiral of the Ocean Sea* (1942).

For the Spanish and Portuguese empires, see Leon Portilla, *Broken Spears: The Aztec Account of the Conquest of Mexico* (1962); Charles R. Boxer, *The Portuguese Seaborne Empire* (1969); James Lockhard and Stuart B. Schwartz, *Early Latin America: Colonial Spanish America and Brazil* (1984); J. H. Parry, *The Spanish Seaborne Empire* (1966); and G. V. Scammell, *The World Encompassed: The First European Maritime Empires* (1981). Classic accounts of the Spanish conquest include the memorable firsthand report by Bernal Diaz del Castillo, *The Discovery and Conquest of Mexico* (edited by I. A. Leonard, 1956), and William H. Prescott, *History of the Conquest of Mexico* (3 vols., 1843).

On the Reformation, consult Roland H. Bainton, *The Reformation of the Sixteenth Century* (1963); William J. Bouwsma, *John Calvin* (1987); and De Lamar Jensen, *Reformation Europe: Age of Reform and Revolution* (1981).

The Background of English Colonization

A brilliant and forceful portrait of English preindustrial society is offered by Peter Laslett, *The World We Have Lost* (3rd ed., 1984). Other important works are Keith Wrightson, *English Society, 1580–1680* (1982), and Carl Bridenbaugh, *Vexed and Troubled Englishmen, 1500–1642* (1968). Patrick Collinson, *The Elizabethan Puritan Movement* (1967), provides a good account of early Puritanism; Michael Walzer, *The Revolution of the Saints* (1965), and C. H. George and Katherine George, *The Protestant Mind of the English Reformation* (1961), continue the story. For various social groups, see Lawrence Stone, *The Crisis of the Aristocracy* (1965); Mildred Campbell, *The English Yeoman* (1942); and W. G. Hoskins, *The Midland Peasant* (1957).

Early English expansion is treated in Kenneth Andrews, *Trade, Plunder, and Settlement: Maritime Enterprise and the Genesis of the British Empire, 1480–1630* (1984), and Nicholas Canny, *Kingdom and Colony: Ireland in the Atlantic World, 1560–1800* (1988). See also A. L. Rowse, *Sir Walter Raleigh* (1962); David B. Quinn, *England and the Discovery of America, 1481–1620* (1974); and Karen O. Kupperman, *Roanoke* (1984).

TIMELINE

30,000–12,000 B.P.*	Settlement of eastern North America
5000–4000 B.P.	Cultivation of crops begins in Mesoamerica
300 B.C.–A.D. 700	Mayan civilization Teotihuacán civilization
700–1100	Spread of Arab Muslim civilization
1000–1300	Mississippian culture
1095–1272	Crusades bring Europeans into contact with Islamic civilization
1300–1450	Italian Renaissance
1325	Aztecs establish their capital at Tenochtitlán
1400–1500	Portuguese exploration
1492	Christopher Columbus's first voyage to America
1517	Martin Luther starts Protestant Reformation
1521	Hernando Cortés leads Spanish conquest of Mexico
1536	John Calvin's *Institutes of Christian Religion*
1550–1630	Price revolution English mercantilism Enclosure movement
1556	Philip II becomes king of Spain
1558–1603	Elizabeth I, queen of England
1560s	English Puritan movement begins
1570–1607	Unsuccessful English colonies in North America
1603–1625	James I, first Stuart king of England

**Before present*

Cloak Worn by Powhatan

This deerskin, decorated with shells, is believed to be one of the ceremonial cloaks worn by Powhatan, the leading chief of the Indians of eastern Virginia. It was taken from Jamestown to England in 1614, a few years after the colony was founded. (Ashmolean Museum)

CHAPTER 2

Invasion and Settlement, 1600–1675

By 1600, England stood poised to join Spain and France in claiming a share of the New World. English monarchs, having asserted control over church and state, dreamed of national power and glory. English merchants, many now experienced in international trade, had visions of greater wealth. The English common people, their ranks swelled by rapid population growth and divided by religious controversy, also looked to America—for new lands to farm and for a refuge from religious persecution.

English expansion began more modestly than did the colonial enterprises of its European rivals. In the fifteenth century Portugal had established a great commercial empire with outposts in Africa, Asia, and Brazil. Spain had conquered the peoples of Mexico and Peru in the sixteenth century, using Aztec and Inca silver and gold to become the most powerful nation in Europe. By the early seventeenth century England had founded only two small colonies: Jamestown and Plymouth, both in eastern North America. Yet these outposts were the beginnings of a new and different kind of empire, for, unlike Spain and Portugal, England sent substantial numbers of families to the New World and established vigorous settler colonies.

Between 1607 and 1675, tens of thousands of English men and women migrated to America, seizing land from the Indian peoples in New England and the Chesapeake Bay region. The new North Americans brought many traditions with them, but life in America pushed them in fresh directions. For example, with land easily available, many peasants became freeholders, fulfilling the dreams of generations of poor Europeans. Their success, however, came at the expense of the native Americans, who gradually—through European diseases, sporadic wars, and religious conversions—lost their lives, lands, and cultural values.

Spanish, French, and Dutch Goals

While English migrants were putting the stamp of their character on settlements along the eastern seaboard, other Europeans were exploring deep into the continent and claiming it as their own. Along with the explorers came missionaries—the Spanish in California and the French in Canada—who encouraged native Americans to renounce their ancestral religions and become Christians. French and Dutch fur merchants also went among the Indians, setting one tribe against another and igniting episodes of bloody warfare. To the Indians, all of these strangers were dangerous, but wherever Europeans went as missionaries or fur traders—in Spanish California, French Canada, or Dutch New Netherland—the white population remained small, and the Indians largely retained their traditional lands and tribal identities.

New Spain: Territory and Missions

As early as the 1540s, Spanish explorers penetrated to the heart of North America when Francisco de Coronado led an expedition northward from Mexico in search of the fabled seven cities of Cibola, said to be capped with golden towers. Coronado crossed the plains of what is now Texas and got all the way to central Kansas before abandoning his quest. Between 1538 and 1542, Hernando de Soto, likewise driven by visions of gold and glory, explored Florida and parts of Georgia, North Carolina, Tennessee, Arkansas, and Oklahoma—again without substantial result. Other adventurers established bases to protect Spanish interests. In 1565, for example, a contingent of Spaniards built a fort in Florida—St. Augustine. It was the first permanent European settlement in the future United States, one that secured Spanish control of the Florida peninsula for the next two hundred years. Apart from Florida, Spain had no settlements east of the Mississippi River; its North American empire lay primarily in the semiarid west—the present-day states of Texas, New Mexico, Arizona, and California—which attracted few Spanish migrants and generated little wealth.

The Catholic Church was the primary force in colonizing New Spain north of the Rio Grande. Throughout the seventeenth century, Spanish priests spread the gospel among the Navaho and Pueblo people of Arizona and New Mexico. The Pueblo Indians, a large group of culturally related communities including the Zuni and Hopi, lived in impressive multistory buildings (*pueblos*), usually on cliffs not far from rivers. Well organized and with a rich cultural heritage, the Pueblos resisted conversion to Christianity. They mounted several major revolts before being brought under Spanish control.

In 1769 the Spanish began to consolidate their authority in western North America by building the first of several *presidios* (military garrisons) at San Diego, on the coast of California. Simultaneously, Junipero Serra and other Franciscan monks established a string of missions, which eventually became such cities as Santa Barbara and San Francisco.

For the Franciscans, religious conversion and cultural assimilation went hand in hand. By persuading members of such California peoples as the Serrano and Chumash to live and work at the missions and by using Spanish military units to force other Indians to join their ranks, the monks tried to create permanent agricultural settlements. The missionaries required the new residents to adopt European agricultural practices, with men instead of women growing most of the crops, and they preached the basic doctrines of Christianity, including the concepts of sin and Heaven and Hell—all new ideas for the Indians. From the native Americans' perspective, the missions were coercive institutions that challenged their traditional values and way of life.

New France: Fur Trade and Conversion

Like Spain, France sent its clergy to convert the Indians and its explorers to claim vast tracts of North America. During the 1530s Jacques Cartier sailed into the Gulf of St. Lawrence in search of a northwest passage to Asia and laid France's claim to all the adjacent lands. It was another seventy years, however, before France established a permanent settlement. In 1608 Samuel de Champlain founded the royal colony of Quebec, and in 1627 the king chartered the Company of New France to encourage migration to the settlement.

New France offered few enticements to potential migrants, however, and by 1666 it had a mere 3,200 settlers. The pressures of a growing population in need of food and land were not as severe in France as they were in England. French peasants enjoyed more legal rights to their village lands than did the English rural population, and fewer had been displaced by the enclosure of common fields. Even landless French peasants refused to move to Quebec, having heard about the long cold Canadian winters. In addition, the French government actively discouraged migration to ensure an ample supply of farm laborers and military recruits—and thereby preserve French hegemony in Western Europe. Finally, the Catholic monarchy of France barred Huguenots (French Protestants) from seeking refuge in the colony, where the crown feared they might undermine state interests. Consequently, New France proved a failure as a settler colony: in 1698 its European population was only 15,200, much less than the 100,000 settlers then residing in the English colonies.

Instead, French Canada became a vast fur-trading enterprise. The *coureurs de bois* (runners of the woods) went deep into the interior to exchange European manufactures, such as blankets and knives, for deerskins and beaver pelts from the Indians. They took these furs, which the Indians had partially tanned, by canoe and packhorse to Montreal, where merchant firms shipped them to Europe to be made into felt hats, fur coats, and luxurious rugs.

French explorers traveled deep into the continent seeking new supplies of furs and claiming new lands for the French crown. In 1673, Jacques Marquette, a priest of the Society of Jesus (Jesuits), journeyed west from Quebec with the fur trader Louis Joliet, eventually reaching the Mississippi River and traveling down it from present-day Wisconsin to Arkansas. René Robert Cavelier, Sieur de La Salle, completed exploration of the majestic river in 1681, claiming French sovereignty over the entire region drained by the Great Lakes and the Mississippi River system and naming the area Louisiana, in honor of Louis XIV, the Sun King. By the early eighteenth century, New France included a thriving port at New Orleans, on the Gulf of Mexico.

The French presence in North America had a strong Jesuit flavor. Between 1625 and 1763, hundreds of priests attempted to spread the Catholic faith among the Micmac, the Abenaki, and especially the Huron, an Iroquoian-speaking people in Canada and the prime suppliers of furs to the French. Unlike the Spanish friars, French priests tried to understand the Indians' values and their ways of looking at the world. For example, one Jesuit reported a belief among the Huron that "our souls have desires which are inborn and concealed, yet are made known by means of dreams." He used this Indian concept of a soul to explain the Christian doctrines of immortality and salvation. Another instance of the missionaries' adaptation of the Christian message is the Huron Carol. Written by Jesuits in the seventeenth century, it tells of Jesus being born in "a lodge of broken bark," wrapped in "a ragged robe of rabbit skin." Also unlike the Spanish, the French missionaries usually lived in the Indians' villages and did not remove them for forced labor. In New France religious and cultural contact was much less coercive than in New Spain.

Neither the Spanish Franciscans nor the French Jesuits converted many Indians to Christianity. Most native Americans held on to their traditional religion and culture as long as they could. It was only much later, when native Americans had been subdued by force and confined to reservations, that European religions won a significant number of adherents, dividing many tribes into bitterly opposed factions of Christians and traditionalists.

New Netherland: Commercial Expansion

Unlike the French and Spanish, the first Dutch settlers in North America had little interest in religious conversion or territorial empire. Commerce was their overriding concern. The Dutch settlements, sponsored by private companies, were part of an expanding mercantile network that made the Dutch Republic the commercial hub of Europe during the seventeenth century. Henry Hudson, an Englishman in the service of the Dutch East India Company, found and named the Hudson River in 1609, and a few years later the Dutch established fur-trading posts on Manhattan Island and at Fort Nassau (present-day Albany). In 1621, the Dutch government chartered the West India Company, giving it a trade monopoly in West Africa and the exclusive authority to establish settlements in America. The new company took over the settlement at Fort Nassau (which it renamed Fort Orange) and set up trading posts in Connecticut, New Jersey, Delaware, and Pennsylvania. In 1624 the director of the company, Peter Minuit, "purchased" all of Manhattan Island from the Indians and founded the settlement of New Amsterdam as the capital of the New Netherland colony.

These wilderness outposts attracted few settlers because the Netherlands did not have a surplus agricultural population and its prosperous commercial economy provided ample work for seamen and artisans. The small size of its settlements alarmed the Dutch West India Company, which feared their being invaded by New England or New France. To encourage migration, the company granted huge estates along the Hudson River to wealthy Dutchmen, stipulating that each pro-

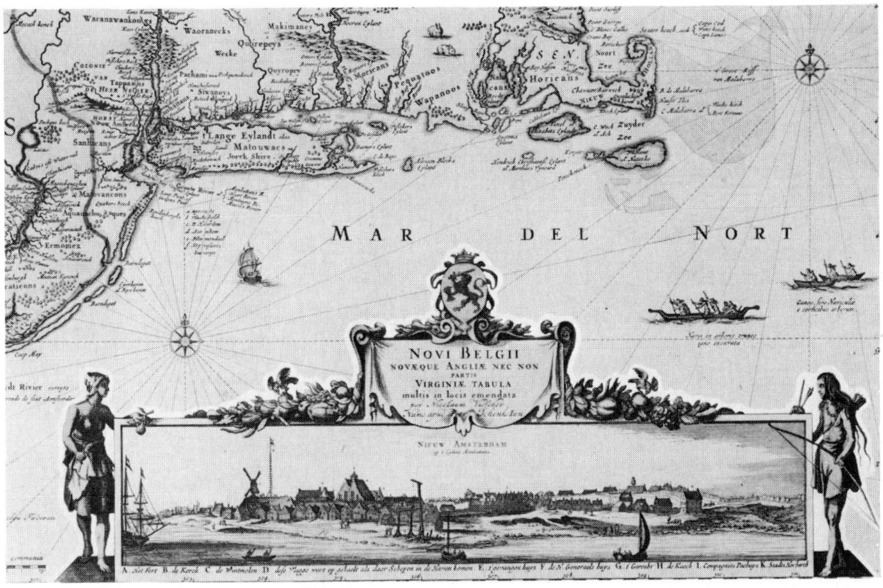

View of New Amsterdam, 1655

This Dutch map deserves close attention. Its title is in Latin, still the language of educated Europeans, but most place names and the description of New Amsterdam are in Dutch, while Indian tribes (such as the Pequatoos—the Pequot) are accurately located.

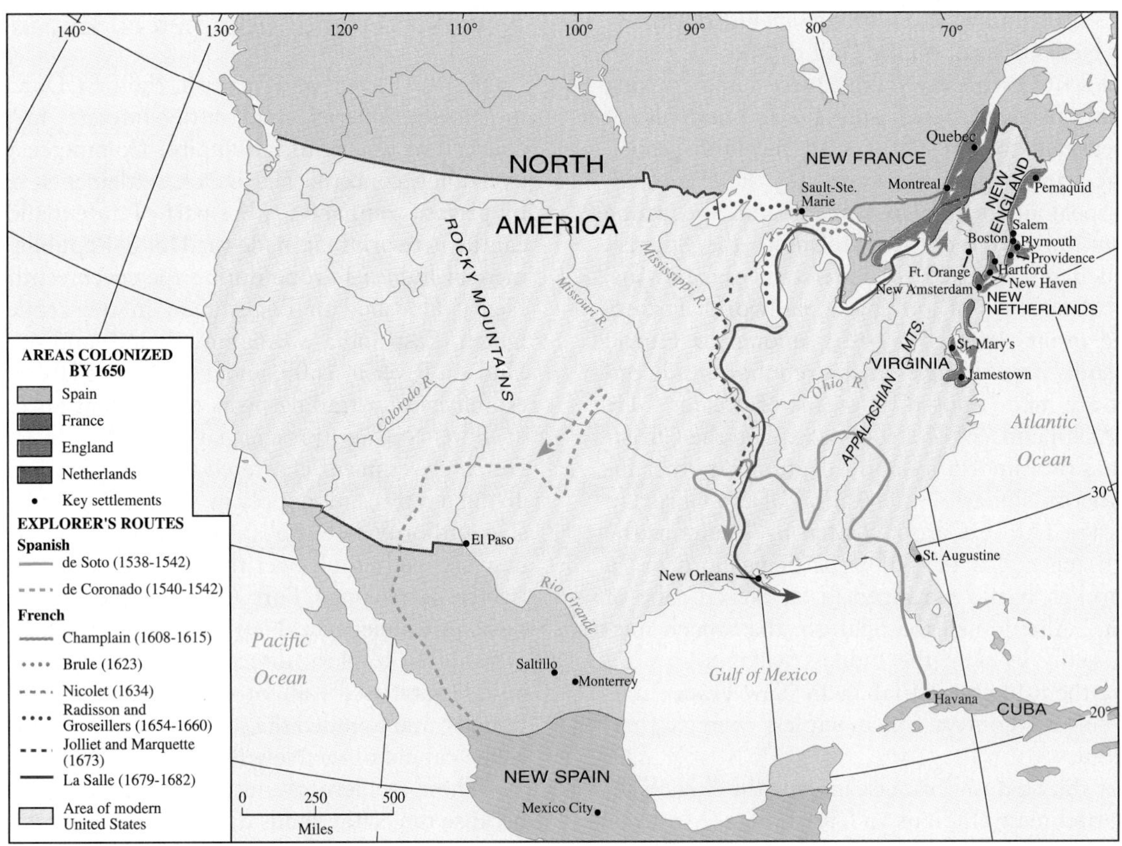

MAP 2.1

North American Colonies in 1650

Europeans had explored only a small part of North America by 1650 and had established colonies only on the very fringes of the continent. It would take another century before English settlers reached the Appalachian Mountains.

prietor, or *patroon,* settle fifty tenants on his land within four years or the estate would revert to the company. Of all the patroons, only Kiliaen Van Rensselaer, a diamond merchant, brought over enough peasant-tenants to retain his vast American holding, the manor of Rensselaerswyck. By 1646 the number of Dutch men and women in North America was still only 1,500.

Although New Netherland failed as a settler colony, it flourished briefly as a fur-trading enterprise, albeit a bloodythirsty one. In the 1640s, Governor William Kieft tried to rid the countryside of potential enemies by dispatching armed Dutch bands to slaughter Indians. The Dutch then seized prime farming land and sought control of the trading system run by Algonquian "River Indians," who had long exchanged corn and wampum from Long Island for furs from Maine. Threatened by the Dutch guns supplied to their traditional Iroquois enemies, the Algonquian tribes responded with force. By the end of "Kieft's War" (1643–1646), more than two hundred Dutch residents and a thousand Indians had been killed, many in brutal massacres of women, children, and elderly men.

The Dutch West India Company largely ignored its crippled North American settlement, concentrating instead on the profitable trade in African slaves to the sugar colonies in America, including its own plantations in Brazil. This left the company-appointed governors in New Amsterdam with virtually unchecked power. In 1655, for example, Kieft's successor Peter Stuyvesant ordered the conquest of New Sweden, a small fur-trading rival established in 1638 on the Delaware River. Stuyvesant also rejected the demands of English settlers on Long Island for a representative system of government, demonstrating a harsh and arbitrary attitude that alienated the colony's increasingly diverse population of Dutch, English, and Swedes. Consequently in 1664, during one of a series of Anglo-Dutch wars, the population of New Amsterdam offered little resistance to En-

AMERICAN VOICES

Mohawk Customs, 1644

A letter from a Dutch clergyman in New Netherland

The tribal societies of North America had rules and institutions that were very different from those of Europe. Here a Dutch clergyman describes Indian life, the adoption practices used to maintain kin networks, and the sense of social responsibility among members of a tribe.

The principal nation of all the savages and Indians hereabouts with which we have the most intercourse is the Mohawks. They are like us Dutchmen in body and stature; some of them have well formed features, bodies and limbs; they all have black hair and eyes, but their skin is yellow. In summer they go naked, having only their private parts covered with a patch. The children and young folks to ten, twelve and fourteen years of age go stark naked. In winter, they hang about them simply an undressed deer or bear or panther skin; or they take some beaver and otter skins, wild cat, racoon, martin, otter, mink, squirrel or such like skins, which are plenty in this country, and sew some of them to others . . . .

Our Mohawks carry on great wars against the Indians of Canada, on the River Saint Lawrence, and take many captives . . . . They spare all the children from ten to twelve years old, and all the women whom they take in war, unless the women are very old, and then they kill them too. Though they are so very cruel to their enemies, they are very friendly to us, and we have no dread of them . . . .

The chiefs are generally the poorest among them, for instead of their receiving from the common people as among Christians, they are obliged to give to the mob; especially when any one is killed in war, they give great presents to the next of kin of the deceased; and if they take any prisoners they present them to that family of which one has been killed, and the prisoner is then adopted by the family into the place of the deceased person.

Source: Peter Force, ed., Tracts . . . , *Relating to the Origin, Settlement and Progress of the Colonies. . .* , 4 vols (Washington; Peter Force, 1836–1847).

glish forces; most residents of the renamed colony of New York peacefully accepted English rule. For the rest of the century, New York City and Albany remained small fur-trading centers, Dutch-English outposts in a region still dominated by native Americans.

Social Conflict in the Chesapeake

The English came to the Chesapeake region, the low-lying Tidewater lands adjacent to the Chesapeake Bay, seeking gold, furs, and trading opportunities. They might easily have created colonies like those in New France and New Netherland, but quite unexpectedly, they developed a settler-society with a booming tobacco economy, based on the exploitation of native American lands and the labor of white indentured servants. The Chesapeake settlements were an economic success but a social and moral failure. Settlers fought with Indians to acquire the land, and prominent families used wealth, deceit, and force of arms to rule the society.

The Invasion of the Chesapeake

Like New Netherland, the first English settlement in North America was a *corporate colony*, an enterprise of ambitious merchants. In 1606 the merchant stockholders of the Virginia Company of London received a charter from James I granting them the right to exploit the riches of North America from present-day North Carolina to southern New York. The company's directors had chosen the name Virginia both to honor Elizabeth I, the "Virgin Queen" who had died in 1603 and to enhance their chances of obtaining a charter. As an additional inducement, they promised to "propagate the *Christian* religion" among "infidels and Savages." Charter in hand, the company directors were able to raise funds from no fewer than 56 London commercial firms and 659 individual investors.

In 1607 the company dispatched an expedition to Virginia to found a trading outpost, not a settler colony. Thus only men and boys were aboard the three small ships—*Sarah Constant, Goodspeed,* and *Discovery*—

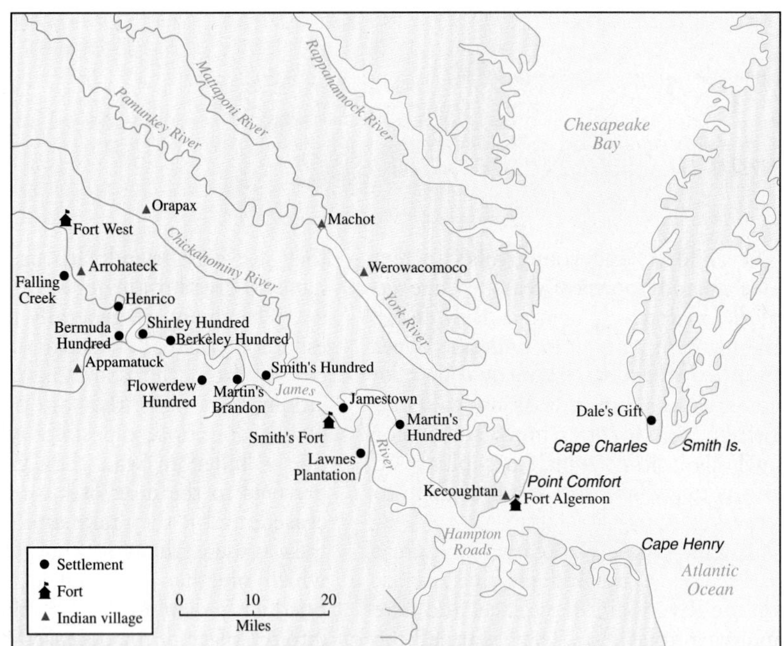

MAP 2.2

River Plantations in Virginia

The first migrants settled in widely dispersed plantations along the James River. The growth of the tobacco economy continued this pattern, as wealthy planter-merchants traded with English ship captains from their river-front plantations. Consequently, few towns or trading centers developed in the Chesapeake region.

that set sail from London. The company retained ownership of all the land and appointed a governor and a small council to direct the migrants, who were its employees or "servants." The company expected its employees to raise or procure their own food and to ship anything of value—gold, exotic crops, or Indian merchandise—back to England.

These migrants were unprepared for the challenges they faced. Some were young gentlemen with financial or personal ties to the shareholders of the Virginia Company but no experience in living off the land—a bunch of "unruly Sparks, packed off by their Friends to escape worse Destinies at home," as one observer put it. The rest were cynical adventurers, men bent on conquering natives or turning quick profits. Like the company's directors, they expected to find established towns with ample supplies of food and labor and Indians with hoards of gold and other valuable treasures, eager to trade them for English goods such as cloth and tinware.

The "Starving Time." They were soon disappointed. The expedition arrived in April, after a hazardous voyage of four months. By May, the newcomers had begun to lay out the settlement of Jamestown on a swampy peninsula on the James River (both named after the new king) and to explore the region. They found forty small Indian tribes, among them the Monacan and the Chickahominy, who willingly traded corn for English goods but had little else to offer and no interest in working for the traders. And the traders were not much interested in working for themselves, at least not in planting crops and raising food. All they wanted, one of them noted, was to "dig gold, refine gold, load gold"—though, in fact, there wasn't any gold.

Of the 120 Englishmen who embarked on the expedition, only 38 were still alive after nine months in America, the rest having fallen victim to malnutrition and disease. Only the determination of Governor John Smith, a soldier of fortune who ran the infant colony like a dictator, saved the infant colony from total collapse. The settlement survived only to be threatened by a new "starving time" and hostility from Indians. As of 1610, the Virginia Company had sent 1,200 servants to Jamestown; by the following year, less than half remained. "Our men were destroyed with cruell diseases, as Swellings, Fluxes, Burning Fevers, and by warres," one of the leaders reported, "but for the most part they died of meere famine." Desperate for food, survivors raided Indian villages, provoking their hostility. The new governor, Thomas West, imposed military discipline on the migrants and demanded that the native Americans acknowledge the sovereignty of James I.

Powhatan, the leading chief of a loose confederation of some two dozen tribes, accused the English of coming "not to trade but to invade my people and possess my country." Nevertheless, he agreed to extend privileges to the English traders if they would support him against his Indian rivals. To cement this agreement, Powhatan, whom Smith described as a "grave majestical man," gave his daughter Pocahontas in marriage to the adventurer John Rolfe in 1614.

Rolfe had come to Virginia in 1610, and he played a leading role in the colony until his death in 1622. Within two years of his arrival, Rolfe had imported tobacco seeds from the West Indies and begun to cultivate the crop. Tobacco was already popular in England as a result of imports from Spanish America. Within a few years Virginia was exporting tobacco to London; and the colony's leading men sought workers to grow it. In 1619, Rolfe noted that "a Dutch man of warre . . . sold us twenty Negars." These black laborers, who probably worked as servants rather than slaves, are thought to be the first Africans to set foot on the North American continent—and, in a sense, the first African-Americans.

To attract English settlers, the company had already instituted a new and far-reaching set of policies. In 1617 it began to allow individual settlers to own land. The company started by granting 100 acres of land to every freeman in Virginia. To attract new migrants it established a *headright* system, whereby every head of household had a right to 50 acres of land for himself and 50 additional acres for every adult family member or servant he brought to Virginia. The company also approved a new "charter of privileges, orders, and Lawes" that provided for a system of representative government. The House of Burgesses (so-called because its electoral procedures followed those of the English boroughs or "burgs") was first convened by Governor George Yeardley in Jamestown in 1619. This body had the authority to make laws and levy taxes, although its legislative acts could be vetoed by the governor or nullified by the company. Together, these two incentives—land ownership and local self-government—achieved the desired result: between 1617 and 1622, about 4,500 new recruits set sail from England. Virginia was about to become a settler colony.

The Indian Uprising of 1622. The sudden influx of settlers brought about a major conflict with the resident Indians. The new migrants were yeoman farmers who wanted land that the Indians had long since cleared and were using for their own crops. The Englishmen's demands alarmed Opechancanough, Powhatan's brother and his successor as the leading chief of the region. Opechancanough realized that the invaders were too numerous and too intent on settlement to be stopped by negotiation or small-scale raids. He therefore formed an alliance with other Chesapeake tribes and in 1622 they launched a surprise attack. The Indians killed 347 settlers, nearly a third of the white population, and vowed to drive the rest back across the ocean. The English retaliated by burning the Indians' cornfields, depriving them of food, a strategy that gradually secured the safety of the colony. Opechancanough attacked again in 1644, but was again defeated.

The cost of the war was high for both sides. The Indians killed many settlers and burned a lot of property, but their own losses were even worse. Moreover, they

James Forte

Aware that the Indians saw them as dangerous intruders, the Virginia adventurers barricaded themselves inside this fort at Jamestown. To symbolize the danger, the artist shows the militia training in front of the stockade and Powhatan raising an arrow.

were now depicted as the aggressors, and, as one militiaman put it, the English invaders now felt that

> [we could] by right of Warre, and law of Nations, invade the Country, and destroy them who sought to destroy us; whereby wee shall enjoy their cultivated places, turning the labourious Mattock [hoe] into the victorious Sword (wherein there is more ease, benefit, and glory) and possessing the fruits of others' labour.

Royal Government. Two years after the Indian uprising of 1622, James I dissolved the Virginia Company. He accused its directors of mismanagement, saying they had come dangerously close to losing the increasingly valuable tobacco colony. Thereafter, Virginia became a *royal colony,* the first in English history. A governor and members of a small advisory council were appointed by the king; the settlers were allowed to retain their representative assembly, the House of Burgesses, but any legislation it enacted now required ratification by the king's own Privy Council. James I also legally established the Church of England in Virginia, which meant that all property owners would now have to pay taxes to support the clergy. These institutions—a royal governor, an elected assembly, and an established Anglican church—became the model for royal colonies throughout America.

The Founding of Maryland. The neighboring settlement of Maryland was founded on a completely different political and religious basis. Maryland was a *proprietary colony,* meaning that it was owned by a "proprietor." In 1632 Charles I (1625–1649), James's successor, gave Cecilius Calvert, Lord Baltimore, a charter that made him the proprietor of the territory between the Potomac River and the Delaware Bay. Lord Baltimore owned all the land in his colony; he could sell it, lease it, or give it away as he wished. He also had the authority to appoint the governor and all public officials, and he could found churches and appoint ministers.

A Catholic himself, Baltimore wanted Maryland to become a refuge for his co-religionists, who were being persecuted in England. He therefore devised a policy of religious toleration that would minimize confrontations between Catholics and Protestants. He instructed the governor (his brother, Leonard Calvert) to allow "no scandall nor offence to be given to any of the Protestants" and to "cause All Acts of Romane Catholicque Religion to be done as privately as may be."

The settlement of Maryland began in 1634. Twenty gentlemen, mostly Catholics, and 200 artisans and laborers, mostly Protestants, established St. Mary's City, high on a bluff overlooking the mouth of the Potomac River. The population grew quickly, for the Potomac Indians were friendly and willing to sell their coastal lands. The Calvert family carefully planned and supervised the colony's development. They provided settlers with lists of things to take with them to America, including foodstuffs and tools. They hired skilled artisans and offered ample grants of land to wealthy migrants. Since Maryland's soil proved almost as suitable for the cultivation of tobacco as Virginia's, the booming European market for the new crop helped to ensure the success of the colony.

The main problems were political. Baltimore's charter specified that the proprietor had to govern with the "Advice, Assent, and Approbation" of the freemen of the colony. However, Governor Leonard Calvert tried to ignore that stipulation. Beginning in 1638, a representative assembly elected by the freemen insisted on the right to initiate legislation, which Baltimore grudgingly granted. In 1649, the assembly enacted a Toleration Act, granting religious freedom to all Christians, thus protecting the Catholic settlers, who remained a minority of the population of Maryland. By 1650, Baltimore had accepted the separation of the legislature into an upper house, composed of an appointed council, and a lower house, representing the interests of the people. As in Virginia, local self-government was balanced by limits on the settlers' autonomy; all laws passed by the assembly and the council and approved by the proprietor had to be consistent with those in England. But the fluid conditions of life in America—notably the absence of traditional authoritarian institutions—enhanced the political power of ordinary people and their ambitious leaders.

Tobacco and Disease

Tobacco and disease shaped the early history of the Chesapeake colonies. Indians in North America and the West Indies had long cultivated the tobacco plant, using its leaves as a medicine and stimulant. By 1600 tobacco was popular in England as well, especially among the upper classes. Soon English men and women of the middling and lower classes as well developed a craving for tobacco and the nicotine it contained. They found many ways to use tobacco: smoking, chewing, or snorting it in powdered form, snuff. Initially, King James I had been unimpressed. He condemned the use of this "vile Weed" and warned that its "black stinking fumes" were "baleful to the nose, harmful to the brain, and dangerous to the lungs." But his attitude changed as "the vile weed" proved to be a valuable crop. In 1619, he imposed a duty on imported tobacco and the revenues filled the royal coffers.

The Tobacco Economy

Poor farmers as well as slave-owning planters raised tobacco, for it grew well in small fields and was easy to process. The tobacco stalk was hung to cure for several months in a well-ventilated shed, then the leaves were stripped and packed tightly into large barrels, or "hogsheads," for shipment to Europe.

European demand for tobacco set off a forty-year economic boom. The exotic crop commanded such high prices that thousands of profit-hungry migrants flocked to the Chesapeake region, where tobacco thrived in the warm, humid climate. "All our riches for the present do consist in tobacco," a happy planter remarked in 1630. The Chesapeake colonies exported about 3 million pounds of the substance in 1640 and 10 million pounds in 1660. Tobacco became the symbol of the new colonies of Virginia and Maryland, and the tobacco plantation became a characteristic form of settlement. Planters moved up the river valleys, establishing large farms at a considerable distance from one another but within easy access by water. Few towns grew in the Chesapeake colonies, and there was a much weaker sense of community there than in the open-field villages of rural England.

Unfortunately, tobacco was not the only thing that flourished in the mild Chesapeake climate. Mosquitoes bred quickly, and spread malaria through their bite. Malaria made people weak to the point where they were unable to resist other diseases. It struck pregnant women especially hard; many died after bearing their first or second child, and so settler families were small. Malaria and other sicknesses—smallpox, fevers, dysentery—took such a toll that although more than 15,000 settlers arrived in Virginia between 1622 and 1640, the population rose only from 2,000 to 8,000.

For most of the seventeenth century, harsh conditions made life in the Chesapeake colonies truly, in the words of Thomas Hobbes, "solitary, poor, nasty, brutish, and short." Most men never married because there were few women settlers. The marriages that did take place ended abruptly with early deaths, destroying the normal bonds of family, friendship, and community. Rarely did both parents survive to see their children grow to adulthood. Unmarried young men and orphaned children accounted for a substantial portion of the population.

The precarious state of family life altered the traditional male system of authority in the household. Because men could expect their male relatives to die young, many Chesapeake husbands deviated from custom and named their wives as executors of their wills. These wills enhanced the position of widows (in relation to child-heirs) by giving them the use of more of the family property than was strictly required by law. Frequently a man's will permitted his widow to retain ample legacies even if she remarried, as most women did. In fact, those women who survived the rigors of life in the Chesapeake often improved their social position and legal privileges through marriage and inheritance.

Indentured Servitude

Despite the dangers, the lure of owning land in America and becoming well-to-do by growing tobacco was so strong that between 1640 and 1700 over 80,000 English settlers moved to Virginia and thousands more sought their fortunes in Maryland. Many were so destitute, lacking land or work in their own villages, that they paid for their passage to America by signing labor contracts called *indentures*. Indentures bound the migrants to labor for a period of four or five years (or, in the case of younger servants, until the age of twenty-one). Shipping registers from the port of Bristol provide a glimpse at the lives of 5,000 people who left England as indentured servants during the seventeenth century.

AMERICAN LIVES

Margaret Brent: A Woman of Property

In 1647 the new Maryland colony was in crisis. Protestants had revolted against the Catholic government and seized control of the colony. To preserve Maryland as a refuge for Catholics and safeguard his family's interests, Governor Leonard Calvert hired mercenary soldiers from Virginia. Lacking hard currency to pay them, he pledged his estate and that of his brother, Cecilius Calvert (Lord Baltimore, the proprietor of Maryland), as security for their wages. But Governor Calvert died just as his soldiers put down the revolt, plunging the government into disarray, without authority or funds to pay off the restless mercenaries. On his deathbed Leonard Calvert named Thomas Green to succeed him as governor, but he entrusted his personal estate to a prominent landowner, Margaret Brent. Telling her to "Take all, pay all," he left the resolution of the crisis in her hands.

Margaret Brent was born around 1601 in Gloucestershire, England, into a substantial gentry family. But as Catholics, the Brents' faith and fortune were increasingly precarious. Since the death of Queen Mary in 1557, English Catholics had endured almost continuous

A nineteenth-century painting depicts Margaret Brent asking for voting rights in the Maryland assembly.

religious persecution; the growing power of militant Puritans during the 1630s promised new hardships for the Brents and other Catholics. The family faced a troubled financial future as well. With thirteen children, Margaret Brent's parents had done their utmost to propagate their Catholic faith, but their fruitfulness threatened the next generation with economic decline. In migrating to Maryland, the Brent children hoped to use the modest funds provided by their parents and their ties with the Calverts to maintain their gentry status.

Margaret Brent, her sister Mary, and their brothers Giles and Fulke arrived in Maryland in 1638. They carried a letter from their co-religionist Lord Baltimore recommending that they be granted land on favorable terms, and it was. Margaret and Mary took up the "Sisters Freehold" of 70 acres in St. Mary's City, the capital of the colony. Four years later Margaret acquired another 1,000 acres on Kent Island from her brother Giles. Margaret soon won the trust and favor of Governor Calvert, sharing with him the guardianship of Mary Kitomaquund, the daughter of a Piscataway chief, who was being educated among the English.

The governor's death during the 1647 crisis threatened all the Brents' ambitions, which depended on Catholic rule and access to the governing family and its allies in the assembly. To preserve her family's religious freedom—and its influence—Margaret Brent would have to save the colony from the mutinous soldiers. Now a mature woman of forty-six, Brent was unusually qualified for this task. Like many women of gentle birth, she had some preparation for public affairs; she had received a basic education in England and had watched her father conduct the business of his estate. But, almost unheard of for a woman, she also had considerable experience in the public arena. As a single woman of property in Maryland, she had appeared frequently before the Provincial Court to file suits against her debtors. In addition, she had occasionally acted as an attorney, pleading the cases of other litigants before the court.

Brent did not hesitate to use the power and authority Calvert had assigned to her. First, since food was in short supply and the soldiers camped in St. Mary's City were demanding bread, she arranged for corn to be imported from Virginia. Then, to pay the soldiers off, she spent all of Leonard Calvert's personal estate. When that proved inadequate, she adroitly exploited her position as the governor's legal executor to draw on the resources of the Lord Proprietor. Using the power of attorney Governor Calvert had held as Baltimore's representative, Brent sold off the proprietor's cattle to pay the troops. Once paid, the soldiers promptly dispersed—some becoming settlers—allowing Governor Green to restore order to the colony. To stave off a new revolt, Lord Baltimore had the assembly pass a Toleration Act (1649), which allowed the free exercise of religion by all Christians.

Margaret Brent's vigorous advocacy of the interests of her family and the Calverts did not go unchallenged. In January 1648 she demanded two votes in the assembly, one for herself as a freeholder and one in her role as the proprietor's attorney. For reasons that do not appear on the record Governor Green opposed her claim: he "denyed that the s[ai]d Mrs. Brent should have any vote in the house." From England, Lord Baltimore protested against the sale of his cattle, accusing Brent of wasting his estate. His attack was partly designed to convince the Puritan Parliament, which had just defeated the king in the English Civil War, that he did not favor Catholics. Baltimore also hoped to recover some of his property, which he suspected had fallen into the hands of the Brent family. Although the Maryland assembly declined to grant Margaret Brent a vote, it did defend her stewardship of Baltimore's estate, advising him that it "was better for the Collonys safety at that time in her hands than in any mans . . . for the Soldiers would never have treated any others with that Civility and respect. . . ."

No longer assured of the proprietor's favor, the Brents turned to new strategies to advance their interests. Giles Brent married Mary Kitomaquund, the Piscataway Indian, perhaps hoping to gain land or power from her influential father. He moved with her to Virginia in 1650. The following year Margaret and Mary Brent also took up lands in Virginia, on the Northern Neck, gradually settling their estate with migrants from England. Margaret Brent died on her Virginia plantation, named "Peace," around 1671, bequeathing extensive property in Virginia and Maryland to her heirs.

Margaret Brent is often hailed as an early feminist and woman lawyer, but, viewed in the context of the time, her actions and achievements were essentially those of a "soldier of fortune" and a woman of property. Born into privileged circumstances, to maintain that status she had struck out on her own—settling in the wilderness of Maryland, defending her interests before the Provincial Court, asserting her rights as a property owner in the assembly, and helping to save the colony—and her family's fragile stake in America—in a time of crisis.

Three-quarters of them were men, and most of them were under twenty-five years old; many had traveled hundreds of miles to Bristol, some intent on embarking for Virginia, others simply looking for work. Taking full advantage of the situation, merchants or sea captains concluded indentures with migrants on the docks of Bristol or London. Then, upon reaching Virginia or Maryland, the entrepreneurs assigned the contracts to local planters in return for cash or tobacco.

Indentured servitude was very profitable for those who owned the contracts. For merchants, servants were valuable cargo, because they fetched high prices in the labor-starved Chesapeake. For plantation owners, they were an incredible bargain. Planters had to provide food, clothing, and shelter for their indentured workers, but in return they received all the profits of their servants' labor for four or five years. With the price of tobacco at six pence a pound, a male indentured servant could produce five times his purchase price in a single year. Furthermore, indentured servants fell under the headright policy, so that planters received another 50 acres of land for every servant they brought over.

Masters had the legal right to regulate nearly every aspect of their servants' lives. They could beat them for disobeying or slacking off, they could withhold permission to marry. If a servant ran away or became pregnant, a master could go to court to increase the servant's term of service. Planters often abused their female servants. As a Virginia law of 1692 put it, "dissolute masters have gotten their maids with child; and yet claim the benefit of their service." Planters got rid of uncooperative servants by selling their contracts to new masters. One Englishman in Virginia remarked in disgust that "servants were sold up and down like horses."

And so, for the servants themselves indentured servitude was a disaster. Half of the men died before they received their freedom, and half of the servants who survived remained poor. The remaining quarter got some benefit for their ordeal but it was short-lived, because the tobacco market crashed after 1660. Only a few male servants rose significantly in the world, acquiring property and respectability. Many women servants did better, prospering because men in the Chesapeake had grown "very sensible of the Misfortune of Wanting Wives." Some married their masters, while others married older men with substantial incomes. By migrating to America, these few—and very fortunate—men and women escaped a life of landless poverty in England.

The Seeds of Revolt

During the boom years of the 1620s tobacco sold for two shillings or more a pound; forty years later, it fetched only a few pence per pound—barely one-tenth as much. Overproduction in the Chesapeake was the prime cause of the bust in the tobacco market, but political decisions made in England also played a role.

The Navigation Acts. In 1651 Parliament, wanting to exclude Dutch ships and merchants from its overseas possessions, passed an *Act of Trade and Navigation.* As revised and extended in 1660 and 1663, the Navigation Acts permitted only English or colonial-owned ships to enter American ports. They also required the colonists to ship certain "enumerated articles," including tobacco, only to England. Chesapeake planters could thus no longer legally trade with Dutch merchants, who traditionally paid the highest prices for tobacco and offered European goods at the best rates.

Moreover, the English monarchs continually raised the customs duty on tobacco in order to increase royal revenues. These duties, by keeping the price of imported tobacco high, ultimately reduced the demand, and the market price of the Chesapeake's staple crop fell to one penny a pound by the 1670s. Yet as living conditions improved and more children were born and survived to adulthood, the number of planters in Virginia and Maryland grew each year, as did tobacco exports—from about 20 million pounds of tobacco annually in the 1670s to 41 million pounds between 1690 and 1720, much more than the market could absorb. Profit margins were very thin and few planters prospered.

Poor Tenants, Rich Planters. Economic stagnation after 1660 meant that the Chesapeake ceased to be a land of upward social mobility. With tobacco at one penny a pound, yeomen families earned just enough to scrape by. Each year they grew about 1,800 pounds of marketable tobacco. Taxes took 200 pounds from the earnings; clothes accounted for another 800, leaving the income from only about 800 pounds for the purchase of supplies, equipment, or additional land. Many freeholders fell into debt and had to sell their land.

Even harder hit were newly freed indentured servants, who now found it nearly impossible to save the money required to become property owners. Under the headright system, freed servants could *patent* (be granted) 50 acres of uncleared land. However, they first had to pay the fees for surveying the land and recording the deed. Then, to become planters they had to buy tools, seed, and livestock. Few succeeded, and most had to sell their labor once again—as wage laborers, tenant farmers, or even servants.

Established planters weathered the decline in tobacco prices with greater success. Many had accumulated large landholdings; now they leased small plots to the growing army of tenant farmers. They also lent money at high rates of interest to hard-pressed yeomen families who, because of the fall in tobacco prices, could not pay for farm implements and other basic necessities. Some well-to-do planters became commercial middlemen, setting up small retail stores or charging a commission for storing the tobacco of their poorer neighbors or for selling it to English merchants.

Gradually the economic life of the Chesapeake colonies came to be dominated by this elite of planter-merchants. In Virginia, these men accumulated nearly half the patented land by claiming headright shares for fictitious migrants and by using their political power to extract huge land grants from the royal governor. In Maryland wealthy planters controlled labor with equal success; in Charles County, they owned about 40 percent of the work force through the indenture system. As aggressive entrepreneurs confronted a growing number of young, landless laborers, social divisions intensified.

Governor William Berkeley. The political corruption of the royal governor, William Berkeley, and his associates raised tensions in Chesapeake society to a dangerous level. Berkeley, who served as governor of Virginia between 1642 and 1652, had won fame fighting Indians during the uprising of 1644. When he again became governor in 1660, he made large land grants to himself and members of his council. Berkeley's "Green Spring" faction, named after his country estate, soon became a corrupt oligarchy. Council members exempted their own lands from taxation and appointed friends as county judges and local magistrates. Berkeley suppressed dissent in the House of Burgesses by a lavish use of patronage, assigning land grants to friendly legislators and appointing their relatives to the profitable posts of sheriff, tax collector and justice of the peace.

Berkeley staved off every challenge to his rule for fifteen years. Once his favorites were in office, he refused to call new elections. When the demand for legislative elections could no longer be ignored, the corrupt Burgesses changed the voting system to exclude landless freemen, who constituted half the adult white men. Property-holding yeomen retained the vote, but they were unhappy about falling tobacco prices, rising taxes, and political corruption. The Virginia elite—unlike the English aristocracy and gentry—was too newly formed and too crudely ambitious to command the respect of the lower orders. Social and political unrest began to reach the boiling point.

Bacon's Rebellion

Conflict with the Indians. Racial warfare sparked the explosion. In 1675 there were 40,000 whites in Virginia, and their views of frontier issues were divided along the lines of class and geography. Most of the wealthy planters lived in the coastal districts and opposed a policy of armed expansion into Indian territory, as did planter-merchants who traded with the Indians for furs. Poor freeholders and aspiring tenant farmers had settled farther inland. Having moved to the frontier for cheap land, they insisted that the Indians be expelled or exterminated.

The Indians meanwhile were few and weak, their numbers having dwindled from about 30,000 in 1607 to only 2,000 in 1675. Most lived north of the York River, on lands guaranteed by treaty—lands now coveted by the frontier settlers. Then the Susquehannock migrated from the north, settled on the upper reaches of the Potomac River, and actively encouraged the other Indians to resist white expansion.

War broke out in the summer of 1675, when Virginia militiamen crossed the Potomac River into Maryland and murdered thirty Indians indiscriminately. Defying orders from Governor Berkeley, a larger force of 1,000 militiamen then surrounded a fortified Susquehannock village. Under a flag of truce, they lured four chiefs out of the stockade and killed them on the spot. The outraged Susquehannock retaliated by killing eighty whites in raids on outlying plantations.

Attempting to restore peace, Berkeley proposed a defensive military policy that served the interests of coastal planters and fur traders. In March 1676, the governor asked the House of Burgesses to raise the money to build and arm a series of forts to protect the frontier plantations. Western settlers dismissed this

Green Spring

Governor Berkeley ran Virginia from his country estate at Green Spring, with its large but architecturally undistinguished residence. The wooden outbuildings housed equipment and the indentured servants who worked as farm laborers.

strategy as useless against roving Indian bands and a blatant excuse to levy high taxes. Berkeley's plan, one freeholder argued, was a plot by the political elite—the "grandees," as he called them—to break the freeholders financially and to take "all our tobacco into their own hands."

Nathaniel Bacon. Nathaniel Bacon emerged as the leader of the western settlers. Bacon, a wealthy young man and a member of the governor's council, had recently arrived from England and settled on a frontier estate. Although he was only twenty-eight, he commanded the respect of his neighbors partly because of his social position but more so because of his personality. Bacon was forceful and bold—confident of his goals and purposeful in pursuing them. After the Susquehannock raids, the frontiersmen wanted Bacon to lead them in battle, but Berkeley refused to grant him a military commission. Bacon and his men marched against the Indians anyway, slaughtering members of the peaceful Doeg tribe.

This massacre triggered a political upheaval that completely overshadowed the Indian question. Condemning Bacon's men as "rebels and mutineers," Berkeley expelled Bacon from the council and placed him under arrest. Then, realizing that the rebel leader commanded a larger military force than he himself could muster, Berkeley reversed his decision and reinstated Bacon. Now on the defensive, the governor finally gave in to the demand for legislative elections and accepted far-reaching political reforms enacted by the new House. The Burgesses, who now included influential supporters of Bacon, curbed the powers of the governor and the council to grant lands or allow tax exemptions. And, to cut the patronage powers of the Green Spring faction, the Burgesses made many local offices into elected posts, thus giving yeoman freeholders more control over government. The legislature also restored voting rights to landless freemen.

These much-needed reforms did not end the rebellion, however. Bacon, who was well-educated and highly connected in England, was bitter at having been treated by the governor as a young upstart; the men in his army, resentful of exploitation by the "grandees," were eager to flaunt their newly won power. Backed by four hundred armed men, Bacon forced the Burgesses to commission him "General of Virginia." Then he toppled Berkeley and seized control of the colony.

Popular Rebellion. In August 1676, Bacon announced his goals in an uncompromising "Manifesto and Declaration of the People." It demanded the death or removal of all native Americans and an end to the rule of wealthy "parasites." "The poverty of the country," Bacon proclaimed, "is such that all the power and sway is got into the hands of the rich, who by extorious advantages, having the common people in their debt, have always curbed and oppressed them in all manner of ways."

Bacon's coup brought civil war to Virginia. Berkeley led five hundred armed supporters in a successful attack on Jamestown, whereupon Bacon's army promptly recaptured the capital, burned it to the ground, and plundered the plantations of Berkeley's allies. Only Bacon's sudden death from dysentery in October gave Berkeley the upper hand. The governor dispersed Bacon's army of frontiersmen and servants, and then took his revenge, seizing the estates of well-to-do rebels and hanging twenty-three men.

Bacon's rebellion was a pivotal event in the history of the Chesapeake region. Planter-merchants continued to dominate the colony, but they realized it was dangerous to let a governor and a corrupt oligarchy rule unchecked. In the future, they limited the governor's authority and found public positions for substantial property owners who, like Bacon, had political ambitions. These budding aristocrats also learned how to contain the fury of the lower social orders. They now supported an expansionist military policy, buying the votes of tenants and poor yeomen with Indian lands.

This uprising had another far-reaching effect on the colony. It contributed to the emergence of a new labor system: African slavery. This system arose partly from economic factors, such as the declining availability of English indentured servants and a major surge in the transatlantic African slave trade. But it was also motivated by the Chesapeake elite's desire to forstall another white rebellion by using more and more African slaves on their plantations. In All Hallows Parish in Maryland, Africans made up 10 percent of the population in 1675; by 1700 they accounted for 35 percent. Thus, to maintain their privileged class position, the leaders of Virginia and Maryland committed themselves, and their descendants, to a social system based on the exploitation of black slaves.

Puritan New England

Adopting the Puritans' own view of themselves, many historians depict the Puritan exodus to America as a heroic effort to preserve the "pure" Christian faith. Yet many Puritans migrated for economic reasons, and their lust for land, to provide food and farmsteads for their growing families, was only slightly less intense than that of their openly profit-minded counterparts in Virginia. Puritan magistrates found biblical justifications for seizing lands from the native Americans, and they imposed strict religious orthodoxy on their own followers. Yet the Puritan story does have impressive qualities. These religious migrants created a stable society of independent farm families in New England and gave a moral definition to American history.

The Puritan Migration

The Pilgrims at Plymouth. The histories of New England and Virginia differed from the very beginning. Jamestown was settled by unruly male adventurers; Plymouth, the first permanent community in New England, was filled with pious Protestant families—Pilgrims who had settled in Holland and other religious dissenters who wished, as they put it, to advance the true "gospell of the Kingdome of Christ in those remote parts of the world."

Before sailing to America aboard the *Mayflower* in September 1620, the Pilgrims had organized themselves into a joint-stock corporation so as to secure financial backing from sympathetic Puritan merchants. Their stated intention was to settle in the territory granted to the Virginia Company; but, either by accident or, more likely, by design, they landed far to the north, on the rocky coast of New England. There, outside the jurisdiction of Virginia, they were free to devise their own institutions. Lacking a charter from King James I, they created their own frame of government, the Mayflower Compact, to "combine ourselves together into a civill body politick." This document, signed by forty-one adult men, was the first "constitution" adopted in North America. It translated into political terms the Pilgrims' long-standing demands for self-rule and produced a system of congregational autonomy and popular self-government based on the rule of law.

That first winter in America tested the Pilgrims' spiritual mettle. In Plymouth, as in Jamestown, hunger and disease took a heavy toll at first: of the 100 migrants who arrived in November, only half survived till spring. Thereafter, Plymouth—unlike Virginia—became a healthy and thriving community, thanks to the cold climate, which inhibited the spread of disease, and to the religious discipline of the determined settlers. Unlike the gold-hungry adventurers in Virginia, the Pilgrims immediately set about building small, solid houses and planting ample crops of grain and vegetables. The settlement grew quickly, through natural increase and migration, and had a population of 3,000 inhabitants by 1640. Aided by epidemics that killed off the Indians, the settlers spread across the landscape and established ten new towns with extensive powers of self-government. In 1636, they adopted a legal code that provided for a colony-wide system of representative government and contained a rudimentary bill of rights.

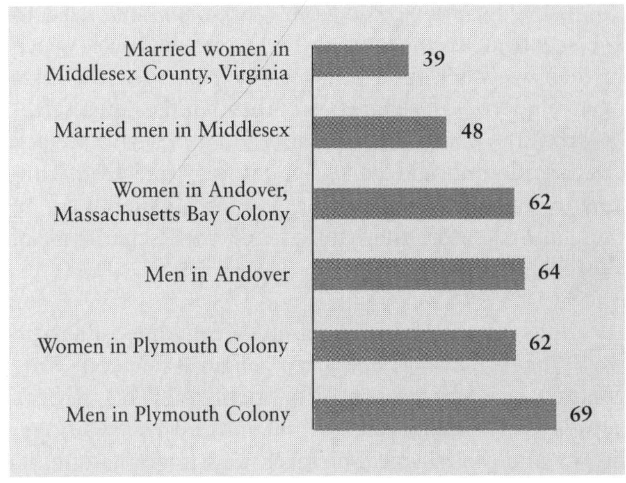

FIGURE 2.1
Average Life Expectancy at Age Twenty in New England and the Chesapeake, 1640–1700

A Seventeenth-Century House
Migrants to New England built small houses, with low ceilings, dark interiors, and only a few pieces of furniture. Depending on the time of day, rooms were used for different purposes—eating, working, or sleeping.

The Pilgrims were devout Christians and tried to live according to the laws and ethics of the Bible, which in their view required limiting the power of the state over religion. As "Separatists," they had cut themselves off from the Church of England and believed that each congregation should be self-governing, free from control by either a religious or a political hierarchy. In that limited sense, they anticipated the "separation of church and state."

Religious Conflict in England. Meanwhile, England was plunging ever deeper into religious turmoil. King Charles I, James I's successor, reaffirmed his father's support for the Church of England and its traditional liturgy and ecclesiastical hierarchy. As James had put it, "No bishop, no king." Charles personally repudiated some of the long-established Calvinist doctrines of the Anglican creed, such as justification by faith. The Puritans, who had gained many seats in Parliament, directly challenged the king, accusing him of "popery."

Charles's response was to dissolve Parliament in 1629. For the next decade he ruled on his own authority, invoking his "divine right" to raise money through royal edicts, higher customs duties, and the sale of monopolies. The king's arbitrary rule struck at the dignity of the landed gentry, who expected to exercise authority through the House of Commons. The merchant community, another stronghold of Puritanism, was also displeased, as higher taxes ate away at their profits.

Religious and political strife intensified when the

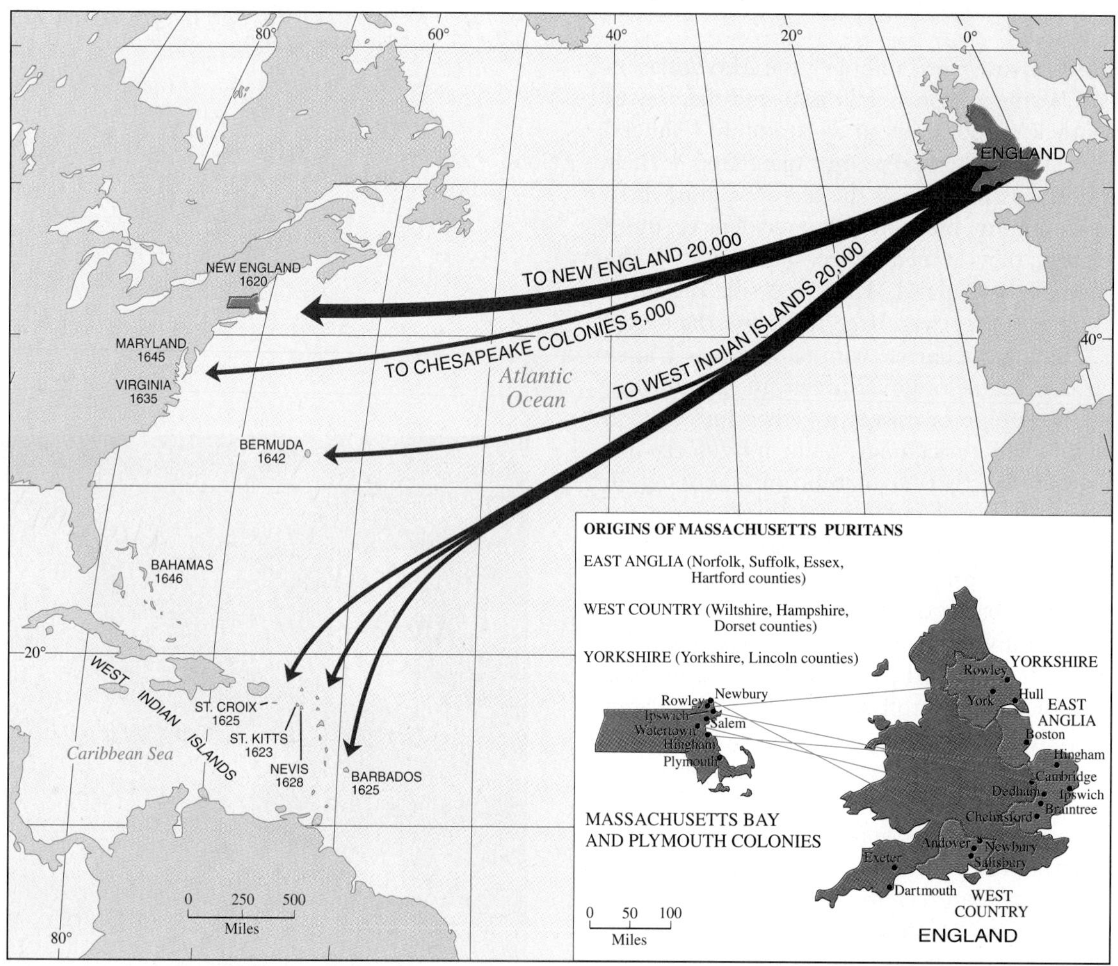

MAP 2.3

The Puritan Migration to America

Nearly 50,000 Puritans left England between 1620 and 1640. In New England, migrants from the three major areas of English Puritanism—Yorkshire, East Anglia, and the West Country—commonly settled among those from their own region. They named American communities after their English towns of origin and transplanted regional customs, such as the open-field agriculture practiced in Rowley in Yorkshire and Rowley in Massachusetts Bay.

AMERICAN VOICES

A Letter from New England, 1635

Edward Trelawney to Robert Trelawney

This letter—from a young man sent out as an agent by his brother, a merchant in Plymouth, England—testifies to the appeal of the Puritan communities of New England. Such letters prompted thousands of Puritans to migrate to New England during the 1630s.

For my part I have just cause even to bless the Lord for so high a favor in bringing me hither. Oh dear brother, I now find what it is to be a Christian. After many a temptation, many a hard conflict and buffetting with Satan, many a heavy sign, deep groan, salt and sorrowful tear, I thank God through Jesus Christ our Lord, who hath brought me out of darkness into His glorious light. Oh Newe England, Newe England, how much am I bound to the Lord for granting me so great mercy as to tread on thy grounds. Oh that Old England could but speak in thy language; then would not the holy and heavenly and sacred name of the great and glorious God be so irreverently tossed and tumbled, so profanely torn in pieces in men's mouths; then would not there be so many abominations and wickedness committed in the hearth and houses of thy people, but thou shouldst then be blest and beloved of the Lord as New England is.

And what is the reason of all this? Surely one is (as I conceive) that as God's people are come into a new country, where they may freely enjoy the liberty of his holy ordinance without any trouble or molestation at all, either of bishop, archbishop, or any other inferior carping minister or gaping officer, so they come unto the land and to the Lord with new hearts and new lives, and enter into a new covenant.

Source: Everett Emerson, ed., *Letters from New England: The Massachusetts Bay Colony, 1629–1638* (Amherst: University of Massachusetts Press, 1976).

king chose William Laud to be archbishop of Canterbury. Laud loathed Puritans and was determined to preserve the traditions and doctrines of the Anglican Church. He banished hundreds of Puritan ministers from their pulpits and forced Anglican rituals on their congregations. Tens of thousands of ordinary men and women now felt the impact of arbitrary rule in their religious lives. However, their faith in the Puritan creed remained unshaken: they conducted services in secret, and some of them went further, plotting to escape Laud's harassment by seeking refuge in America.

The Massachusetts Bay Colony. In 1630, 900 Puritans boarded eleven ships and sailed across the Atlantic under the leadership of John Winthrop, a well-educated, highly regarded country squire. Having obtained a charter from Charles I, the Puritans established a new settlement, the Massachusetts Bay colony, in the area around Boston. Even more than the Pilgrims, the Puritans saw themselves as central actors in a great historical drama. They were a "saving remnant" chosen by God to preserve the true faith in America. The Lord "has sifted a whole nation," a Puritan minister declared, "that he might send choice grain over into this Wilderness."

Governor John Winthrop

This portrait captures the determination and intensity of Winthrop, whose policies of religious orthodoxy and elite rule shaped the early history of the Massachusetts Bay colony.

Winthrop decided to go to America for economic as well as religious reasons. Believing England to be corrupt in morals and "overburdened with people," he sought land and opportunity for his children in the New World. But he also saw a chance to preserve the true Christian church and to set an example for all of Europe to follow. "We must consider that we shall be as a City upon a Hill," Winthrop told his fellow passengers aboard the ship *Arbella* in 1630. "The eyes of all people are upon us." Though the Puritan experiment has long since vanished, Winthrop's words still evoke in Americans a vision of their destiny as a people and a nation.

Once they arrived in America, Winthrop and his associates transformed their joint-stock corporation, the General Court of shareholders, from an economic into a political institution. The Puritan leaders persuaded the English stockholders to give up their claim to a monetary dividend and they made the General Court into a legislature, which was empowered to enact laws for the new colony.

Over the next decade, about 10,000 Puritans migrated to the Massachusetts Bay colony, along with 10,000 others—peasants, indentured servants, and artisans—fleeing from poverty. To ensure their continued dominance, the Puritans enacted a law limiting the right to vote and hold office to men who were members of an approved Puritan church. By the mid-1630s, the General Court had become a representative assembly, elected by the members of Puritan congregations in the various towns. With John Winthrop as governor (he served for fifteen years), the court sought to create a religious commonwealth, establishing Puritanism as the official state-supported religion and barring members of other faiths from conducting services. The Bible was the basis for some laws enacted by the Massachusetts Bay government. For example, the Puritans followed a Biblical rule by dividing inheritances among all heirs, with a double portion to the eldest son, thereby rejecting the custom of many English families to give all the land to the eldest son. "Where there is no Law," the court advised local magistrates, they should rule "as near the law of God as they can."

The Religious Covenant

Unlike the Pilgrims, the Puritans did not separate from the Church of England; both in England and America, their goal was to reform it from within. Consequently, the Puritans created a religious system without ostentatious "Catholic" features. Disposing of bishops and elaborate rituals, they followed what they believed to be the practice of the first Christians, devising a simple church structure controlled by the laity, or ordinary members of the congregation. Hence their name, *Congregationalists.*

According to Puritan theology, which derived mainly from the teachings of John Calvin (see Chapter 1, page 25), God had chosen a few "elect" men and women for salvation—they were predestined for heaven, even before they were born. The doctrine of predestination was a harsh one, because although members of New England churches were among the elect, a majority of the adult population lived and died without ever being admitted to a congregation. Church members, or Saints, as they were called, set extraordinarily high standards for membership. Many people didn't even bother to apply and those who did were subjected to rigorous oral examinations on their morals and beliefs. Even the Saints lived in great anxiety, for they owed their status to mere mortals and could never be sure that they were *really* among the elect. Consequently, Puritan deathbeds were scenes of agony and doubt. "I have seen Persons Quaking on their Death

A Puritan Meetinghouse

Puritan churches were plain but handsome buildings. Inside, the most prominent feature was the pulpit, symbolizing the importance of the sermon and the Word of God. Outside, most meetinghouses were painted in bright colors (not white, as they are today).

Changing Images of Death
Death—sudden and arbitrary—was a constant presence in the preindustrial world. Pre-1700 New England gravestones often depicted death as a frightening skull, crowned with a laurel to signify its inevitable victory. After 1700 a smiling cherub adorned many gravestones, suggesting a more optimistic view of eternal life.

Beds, and their very beds therewith Shaking under them," the minister Cotton Mather reported. The deathbed utterances of the Saints likewise testified to their terror: "O! The wrath of a Dreadful God, Makes me Tremble; I Tremble, I Tremble, at that wrath."

Puritans dealt with the uncertainties of divine election in three ways. Some congregations pointed to the transforming effect of grace—the overwhelming feeling of God's presence within that often accompanied the conversion experience: as God infused the sinner's soul with grace, he or she was "born again," and *knew* that salvation was at hand. Other Puritans stressed "preparation," the confidence that came from years of spiritual guidance and church discipline. Many of these "preparationists" followed the Dutch Protestant theologian Jacob Arminius in conceiving of God as a more reasonable and merciful deity than the one portrayed by Calvin. If a person expressed "the merest desire to be saved," declared one Arminian-influenced Puritan, God would bestow His saving grace. Still other New England Puritans reassured themselves by embracing a collective interpretation of their destiny. They believed that God had entered into a *covenant,* or contract, with them: He promised to treat them as a divinely "chosen people" as long as they cleaved to the faith and ordered their lives in accordance with God's laws. To do otherwise was to risk divine wrath and the loss of their elect status.

The Puritans and the Pequot

The Puritans' conception of themselves as a chosen people shaped their relations with native Americans. Initially, they felt obliged to justify their intrusion into the Indians' domain. "By what right or warrant can we enter into the land of the Savages," they asked themselves while still in England, "and take away their rightfull inheritance from them and plant ourselves in their places?" One answer to this question was provided by a smallpox epidemic that broke out in 1633 and killed hundreds of Indians. John Winthrop interpreted this disaster as a mark of divine favor. "If God were not pleased with our inheriting these parts," he asked, "Why doth he still make roome for us by diminishing them as we increase?"

For a second justification, the Puritans turned to the book of Genesis, which instructed them to "be fruitful, and multiply, and replenish the earth, and subdue it." From this, the magistrates of Massachusetts Bay argued that because the Indians had not "subdued" most of the earth by plowing or fencing the land, they had no "just right" to it. "If we leave them sufficient for their own use," Winthrop maintained, "we may lawfully take the rest, there being more than enough for them and us." One of the most brutal instances of this occurred in 1637, when Puritans settled on the fertile lands of the Pequot tribe in the Connecticut River Valley. Finding themselves at war, Puritan militiamen and their Indian allies led a surprise attack on a Pequot village and massacred about five hundred men, women, and children. "God laughed at the Enemies of his People," one soldier boasted, "filling the Place with Dead Bodies." Puritan forces ruthlessly tracked down the survivors, selling many into slavery in the sugar islands of the Caribbean. In the end, the Pequot tribe was virtually exterminated.

Like most Europeans, the English invaders viewed the Indians as culturally inferior people who did not deserve civilized treatment. Indeed, to some Puritans, the Indians were latter-day "Philistines"—a biblical tribe that had been justly slain by the Jews, God's original chosen people. Yet the Puritans were not racist as we understand the term today. To them, native Americans were not genetically inferior—they were white people with sun-darkened skins. Not race but sin accounted for the Indians' "degenerate" condition. "Probably the devil" delivered these "miserable savages" to America, wrote the Puritan divine Cotton Mather, "in hopes that the gospel of the Lord Jesus Christ would never come here to destroy or disturb his absolute empire over them."

This interpretation of Indian history inspired attempts at conversion. John Eliot, a Puritan minister, translated the Bible into Algonquian and undertook missions to Indians outside Boston and on Cape Cod. His efforts were even less successful than those of the Jesuits in New France. Puritans demanded that the Indians conform to English customs and master Puritan theology, but only a few native Americans became full members of Puritan congregations. Still, within a generation, there were more than a thousand "praying Indians" who lived under Puritan supervision in fourteen special mission towns. This pacification of those Indians who had not been killed by European diseases or English arms completed the Puritan invasion of New England and guaranteed, at least temporarily, the safety of its new white inhabitants.

The Suppression of Dissent

Like nearly all Europeans of the seventeenth century, John Winthrop and his fellow magistrates believed that social stability required religious uniformity. While they sought God's help against the Pequots in the mid-1630s, they purged their own society of religious dissidents.

Roger Williams and Rhode Island. In Massachusetts Bay, religious liberty meant the freedom to worship "correctly." The first challenge to this policy came from Roger Williams, who became minister of the Puritan church in Salem in 1634. Williams urged his congregation—and all Puritans in the colony—to follow the example of the Separatist Pilgrims and break completely from the Church of England. He condemned the legal establishment of Congregationalism in Massachusetts Bay and applauded the Pilgrims' separation of church and state. The Salem minister taught that political magistrates should have authority only over the "bodies, goods, and outward estates of men," not over their spiritual lives. Moreover, the outspoken preacher questioned the moral and legal justification for the seizure of Indian lands. When Williams refused to stop his criticism, the Puritan magistrates banished him from Massachusetts Bay in 1635.

Williams and his followers resettled in Rhode Island, founding the town of Providence in 1636 on land bought from the Narragansett Indians. Other religious dissidents joined him in nearby Portsmouth and Newport. In 1644, these towns obtained a corporate patent from the English Parliament, then controlled by Puritans, granting them full power and authority "to rule themselves." Rhode Islanders used their new political freedom to ensure their religious freedom. In Rhode Island, there was no legally established church—every congregation was autonomous and individual men and women could worship God as they pleased.

The Heresy of Anne Hutchinson. Following Williams's banishment, Puritan magistrates detected another threat to their holy commonwealth in the person of Anne Hutchinson, a middle-aged woman, the wife of a merchant and the mother of seven, who worked as a midwife and acted as a spiritual adviser. Hutchinson held weekly prayer meetings in her house—often attended by as many as sixty women—in which she attacked the teachings of certain Boston clergymen, saying they placed undue stress on church laws and good behavior. In words that recalled Martin Luther's rejection of indulgences, Hutchinson argued that salvation was not something that people could earn; there was no "covenant of works." Rather, salvation was bestowed by God through the "covenant of grace." Hutchinson stressed the importance of revelation: the direct communication of truth by God to the individual believer. Since this doctrine diminished the role of ministers, Puritan magistrates found it threatening.

The magistrates also resented Hutchinson because of her sex. Like other Christians, Puritans believed in the equality of souls—both men and women could be saved—but when it came to practical matters regarding governance of church and state, women were deemed inferior to men. On this point, the Puritans agreed with the Pilgrim minister John Robinson, who asserted that women "are debarred by their sex from ordinary prophesying, and from any other dealing in the church wherein they take authority over the man." Puritan women could never be ministers, or lay preachers, or even voting members of the church.

This patriarchal attitude came to the fore when the magistrates put Hutchinson on trial for heresy as an *antinomian,* that is, a person who looks inward for grace or truth and asserts freedom from the rules of the church. Hutchinson defended her beliefs with great skill and tenacity, and even Winthrop admitted that she was "a woman of fierce and haughty courage." But the odds were against her. The judges not only found Hutchinson guilty of heresy for claiming a direct relationship with God, but also condemned her for exceeding her proper station in life. In Winthrop's words, she should have "attended her household affairs, and such things as belong to women."

The General Court banished Hutchinson from the Massachusetts Bay colony in 1637. Her allies in the merchant community, affluent men who also resented the power of the clergy, were unable to protect her. Defeated, she followed Roger Williams into exile in Rhode Island, where she and a small group of supporters founded Portsmouth. Later Hutchinson moved to Westchester County, New York, where she was killed in an Indian raid. Puritan magistrates noted Hutchinson's death with grim satisfaction, interpreting it as a sign of God's approval for their efforts to enforce religious orthodoxy.

The Connecticut Colony. The banishment of dissidents bothered some devout Puritans, among them the Reverend Thomas Hooker of Newtown (Cambridge), who questioned the authority of the Massachusetts Bay magistrates. In 1636 Hooker led a hundred settlers to the Connecticut River valley, where they established the town of Hartford. Other Bay colony residents followed, creating separate settlements along the river at Wethersfield and Windsor. In 1639 the Connecticut Puritans adopted the Fundamental Orders, a plan of government that included a representative assembly and a popularly elected governor. A royal charter from King Charles II in 1662 bestowed self-government on these Connecticut towns, whose population had grown to almost 5,000, and joined them to another Puritan settlement at New Haven. Connecticut was patterned after Massachusetts Bay, with a firm union of church and state and a congregational system of church government, but voting rights were extended to most property-owning men—not just church members. Thus it had a more democratic franchise.

The Halfway Covenant

The trend toward greater democracy was felt within the Puritan churches of New England as well. Gradually, magistrates and ministers, such as John Winthrop and John Cotton, gave up their efforts to impose a single definition of Puritan orthodoxy. In the Cambridge Platform of 1648, the laity won a written guarantee that each church was independent and equal. Puritan congregations with diverse theological persuasions now went their separate ways, deciding matters of doctrine, choosing and dismissing their ministers, and admitting new members. The Cambridge Platform also specified that "consociations" of clergy and leading laymen might meet to discuss church dogma and discipline. This provision appeased ministers and magistrates, who had resisted lay control as well as autonomy, but the lay congregation increasingly became the dominant institutional force.

The Puritan Revolution. Many migrants had expected that the settlement of New England would be the beginning of the *millennium,* the thousand-year rule of Christ on earth predicted in the book of Revelation. At first, events in England appeared to bear them out. In 1637 Archbishop Laud imposed a new prayer book on Presbyterian Scotland and threatened to send bishops to impose religious discipline. Popular riots against Laud's edicts led to armed resistance. In 1639, a Scottish Presbyterian army marched on England, forcing Charles to call Parliament into session to vote funds for the war.

Richard Mather (1596-1669)
Mather migrated to New England in 1635 when Archbishop Laud stripped him of his pulpit. His son Increase Mather was a leading Boston clergyman as was his grandson, Cotton Mather, the author of *Magnalia Christi Americana*, an epic of the Puritan adventure in New England.

TABLE 2.1

European Colonies in North America before 1660

	Date	First Settlement	Type	Religion	Chief Export or Economic Activity
New France	1608	Quebec	Royal	Catholic	Furs
New Netherland	1613	New Amsterdam	Corporate	Dutch Reformed	Furs
New Sweden	1628	Fort Christina	Corporate	Lutheran	Furs; farming
English Colonies					
Virginia	1607	Jamestown	Corporate (Merchant)	Anglican	Tobacco
Plymouth	1620	Plymouth	Corporate (Religious)	Separatist Puritan	Mixed farming; livestock
Massachusetts Bay	1629	Boston	Corporate (Religious)	Puritan	Mixed farming; livestock
Connecticut	1635	Hartford	Corporate (Religious)	Puritan	Mixed farming; livestock
Maryland	1634	St. Mary's	Proprietary	Catholic	Tobacco; grain
Rhode Island	1636	Providence	Corporate (Religious)	Separatist Puritan	Mixed farming; livestock

The Puritan-dominated House of Commons seized the chance to demand an end to arbitrary measures. When Charles resisted, the nation divided into Royalist and Parliamentary factions. In 1642 thousands of English Puritans—and scores of Puritans who had returned from America—took up arms against the king. After four years of civil war, the Parliamentary forces led by Oliver Cromwell were victorious. In 1649 Parliament executed Charles, proclaimed a republican Commonwealth, and imposed Presbyterianism on the Church of England. God's rule on earth seemed imminent.

But the Puritan experiment lasted just a decade. Popular support for saintly rule quickly declined, especially when Cromwell took dictatorial control of the English government in 1653. After Cromwell's death a repentant Parliament summoned Charles I's son, Charles II, back to the throne. In 1660 the monarchy was restored and bishops reclaimed their authority in the Church of England. For many steadfast Puritans, the Restoration was the victory of the Antichrist.

The outlook in New England seemed equally grim. Puritans in America were experiencing grave doubts about the meaning of their religious "errand into the wilderness." In many congregations, the second generation had not sustained the intense religious spirit of the original migrants. The new generation had been baptized as infants but had not experienced conversion and become full church members. Their "deadness of soul" threatened to end the Puritan experiment, since the unconverted could not present their children for baptism. Saints had never numbered more than a bare majority of the population; they had imposed their religious vision out of determination, not numbers. Now it appeared that they might be reduced to a small minority and lose control of the colony.

To keep the churches vigorous and remain in power, Puritan ministers devised the Halfway Covenant in 1662. This covenant proposed new, and more lenient, criteria for church membership. Under its terms, the children of all baptized Puritans could be presented for baptism and thus become "halfway" members. While growing up and awaiting conversion to sainthood, they could participate in church affairs.

The Halfway Covenant altered Calvinist theology by making salvation more predictable. As Increase Mather, a leading Puritan minister, explained, "God has cast the line of election so that generally elect Children are cast upon elect Parents." By stressing the hereditary nature of election, the covenant strengthened the Puritans' sense of "tribalism." In future generations, those born into the elect would dominate the Congregational churches of New England. For example, the First Church of Milford, Connecticut, had 962 members in the period 1639–1770. No fewer than 693 of these

Puritan Saints (72 percent) were descendants of the thirty-six families who had established the original congregation.

The Halfway Covenant began a new phase of the Puritan experiment. Puritans had come to America to preserve the "pure" Christian church; many of them half-expected to return in triumph to a Europe ready to receive the true Gospel. In the course of events, that sacred mission had been dashed, so that Puritan ministers laid out a new goal. They exhorted their congregations to maintain their identity as a chosen people and to create in the American wilderness a new society based on high moral and intellectual principles.

The Puritan Imagination

The Puritans (and other seventeenth-century English men and women) believed that the physical world was full of supernatural forces and terrifying demons. Ordinary people still held many pagan beliefs and even highly educated individuals were subject to superstitions. The diary of Samuel Sewall provides a glimpse into the Puritan imagination.

Sewall was born in England in 1652 and educated at Harvard College, founded by Massachusetts Bay Puritans in 1635. He enjoyed a long and distinguished life as a Boston merchant, politician, and judge. Sewall was a devout Puritan: the Bible shaped his view of the world and he interpreted ordinary bits of news from Europe in biblical terms. Reading in a Boston newspaper of a proposal to establish a new Protestant colony in America, Sewall quickly concluded that "God will [use it] for pulling down the throne of Antichrist, as is so designed in the Revelation."

Sewall and other Puritans constantly sought a supernatural design in natural events. For example, Sewall spent an evening with Cotton Mather, an influential minister, discussing why "more Ministers' Houses than others proportionably had been smitten with Lightning; inquiring what the meaning of God should be in it." At times, this belief in supernatural forces led Sewall into pagan practices. Before occupying a new addition to his house, he drove a metal pin into the floor, to fend off evil spirits. Years later, he placed two wooden carvings of "cherubims heads" on his gateposts to signify protective spiritual forces.

Devout Protestants like Sewall received many celestial signs or warnings from God, in the form of blazing stars, monstrous births, and rainstorms of blood. They also followed pagan astrological charts printed in farmers' almanacs. These charts, along with diagrams and pictures, correlated the movements of the planets and stars with the signs of the zodiac. By deciphering the charts, farmers determined the best times to plant crops, to marry off their children, to make important decisions.

Christian ministers condemned anyone who claimed to have special powers as a healer or prophet. Fearful of challenges to their spiritual authority, they attacked such people as "cunning." Ordinary Christians often looked on them as "wizards" or "witches," acting at the command of Satan. Between 1647 and 1662, civil authorities in Massachusetts and Connecticut hanged fourteen people, mostly women, for witchcraft. Witchcraft trials continued for another generation.

The most dramatic episode of witch hunting took place in Salem, Massachusetts, in 1692. A group of poor Puritan farmers in Salem village sought to avenge themselves against certain wealthier church members, who lived near Salem town, a rising seaport, and whom they resented on personal and economic grounds, by bringing charges of witchcraft against their families and friends. This community conflict quickly got out of hand and, before it ended, Massachusetts authorities had arrested 175 men and women and executed 22 of them. Fear and suspicion spread into the neighboring village of Andover. Its people "were much addicted to sorcery," claimed one observer, and "there were forty men in it that could raise the Devil as well as any astrologer."

Ultimately, the hysteria—and the mass executions—of the Salem episode brought an end to legal prosecutions for witchcraft. After 1700, judges refused to accept spectral evidence—unsubstantiated claims by witnesses that they had seen the accused individuals assume the shapes of strange animals or mysterious creatures. The European Enlightenment gave educated men and women a more critical, more rational view of the natural world (see Chapter 4). Unlike Sewall and Cotton Mather, well-read men of the next generation, like Benjamin Franklin, would conceive of lightning not as a supernatural sign but as a natural phenomenon. Superstition began to lose its grip on people.

A Freeholding Society

Essential to the Puritans' God-fearing "just society" was the freeholder ideal. In creating New England communities, they consciously avoided the worst features of the traditional agricultural regime of Europe. They did not wish to live in a society dominated by a harsh class of gentlemen landlords, with a strong central government that levied oppressive taxes and a large population of poor landless laborers. The Puritans wanted a society of independent communities and churches made up of landowning, socially responsible families.

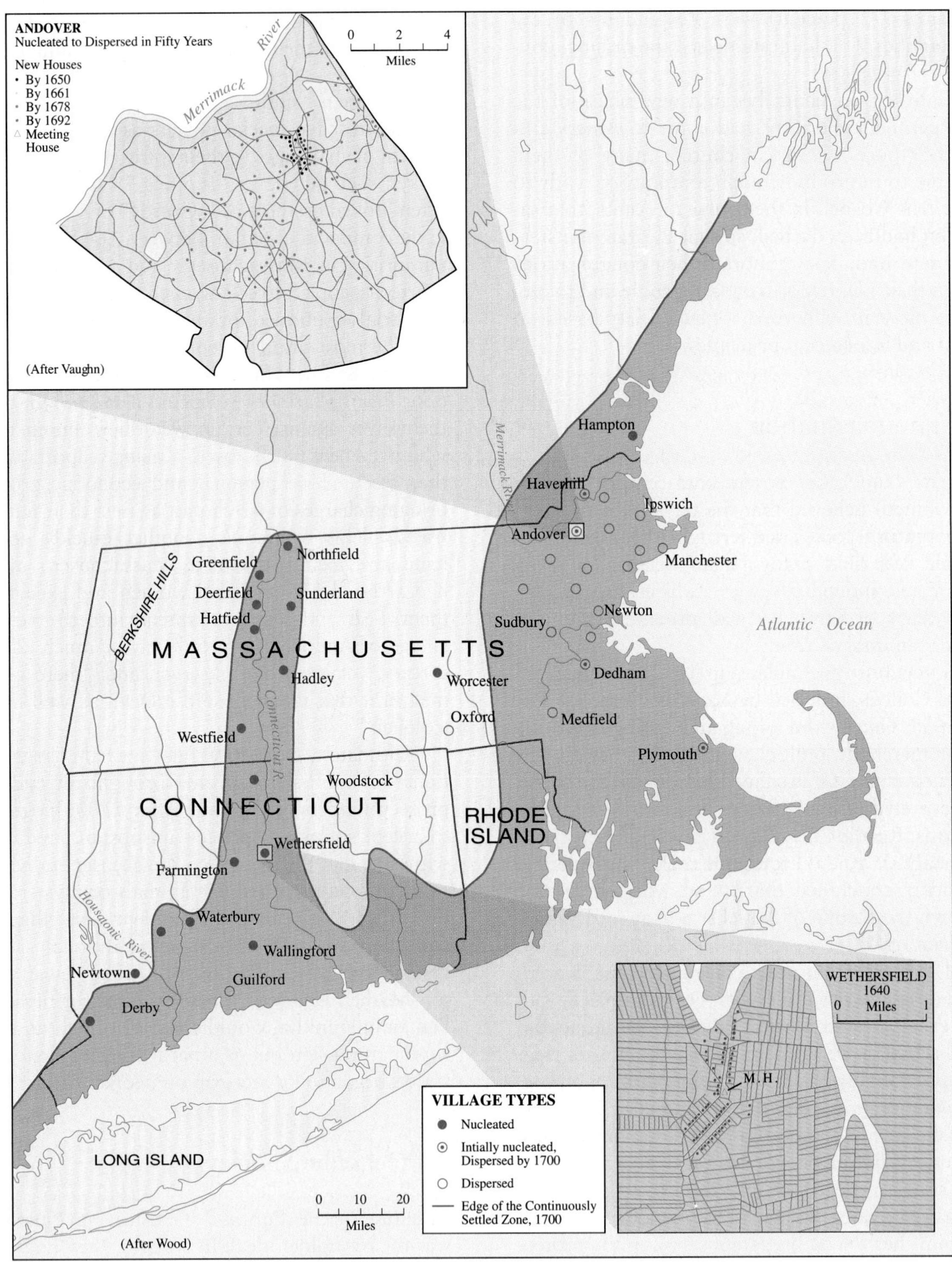

MAP 2.4

Settlement Patterns in New England

Initially, most Puritan towns were compact; families lived close to one another in the "nucleated" village center and traveled daily to the surrounding fields. In 1640, this pattern was apparent in Wethersfield, which was situated on the broad plains of the Connecticut River Valley. The rugged geography of eastern Massachusetts encouraged a more dispersed form of settlement. By 1692 many residents of Andover, Massachusetts, lived outside the village center—on their own farms.

New England governments fashioned a new social order through their land-grant policies. The General Courts of Massachusetts Bay and Connecticut did not adopt the Chesapeake headright system, which enabled wealthy planters to accumulate land patents. Nor did they normally give thousands of acres of land to favored individuals. Instead, they bestowed the title to a township—usually measuring about 6 miles by 10 miles—on a group of settlers. These settlers, or *proprietors,* then distributed the land among themselves, often giving the largest amounts to men of high social status. Subsequently, the male heads of families ran the community through the *town meeting,* the main institution of local government. Each year the town meeting chose *selectmen* to manage town affairs. It also levied taxes; enacted ordinances regarding fencing, lot sizes, and road building; and regulated the common fields used for grazing livestock and cutting firewood.

New England town meetings were not completely democratic institutions. Voting was limited to male householders, and the town's leaders were usually men of means. However, political participation was widespread and towns ran their own affairs. Communities in New England had much more freedom than most peasant villages in Europe.

The political power of the towns determined the structure of colony-wide government. Beginning in 1634, each town in the Massachusetts Bay colony elected its own representatives to the General Court. As the number of towns increased, they assumed more and more control over their own affairs, shifting power away from the governor and the magistrates in Boston. Thus, when Governor John Winthrop intervened in a local dispute over militia officers in the town of Hingham, he met stout resistance. As one Hingham militiaman put it, he would "die at the sword's point, if he might not have the choice of his own officers."

The political autonomy of the towns encouraged a certain amount of diversity. For instance, most of the settlers of Rowley, Massachusetts, came from the East Riding of Yorkshire in northern England and brought with them many Yorkshire manorial customs, such as communally regulated open-field agriculture. In contrast, the proprietors of Watertown, who came primarily from the East Anglia region northeast of London, quickly duplicated that area's system of enclosed fields and separate family farmsteads.

Whatever their county of origin, Puritans were careful not to transplant feudal land customs. New England governments granted land to the town proprietors or to individuals in *fee simple.* This form of title meant that the holders owned the land outright, free from manorial obligations or feudal dues; they could sell, lease, or rent it as they pleased. Moreover, fee simple owners did not have to pay the government (or an aristocrat) even an annual *quitrent,* a token sum of money that symbolized the authority of the state or the lord. Puritan leaders wanted a society of independent freeholders.

Widespread ownership of land did not imply equality of wealth or status. Puritans accepted—indeed, they embraced—a social and economic hierarchy and invoked God's will to justify it. "God had Ordained different degrees and orders of men," proclaimed the wealthy Boston import merchant John Saffin, "some to be Masters and Commanders, others to be Subjects, and to be commanded." Otherwise, Saffin noted with disdain, "there would be a meer parity among men."

Migrants from privileged English backgrounds brought their social status with them to America, and their prestige yielded immediate material benefits. In most New England towns, the most influential proprietors were able to bestow the lion's share of land upon themselves. Edward Johnson came to New England from Kent, where he had been a substantial landowner

An Affluent Puritan Woman

This well-known painting of Elizabeth Freake and her daughter, Mary, is perhaps the finest portrait of a seventeenth-century American, and suggests the growing prosperity of New England. (*Mrs. Elizabeth Freake and Baby,* c. 1671–1674, Worcester Art Museum)

and a man of "rank and quality." Johnson became well known on both sides of the Atlantic as the author of the *Wonder-Working Providence of Zion's Saviour,* a prophetic tract published in 1650, but he prospered in Massachusetts Bay primarily because his social status enabled him to claim a large land grant as one of the proprietors of the town of Woburn. In Windsor, Connecticut, when the proprietors divided up the land in 1640, the upper tenth of them received 40 percent of it, while the lowest fifth got only 4 percent.

Occasionally the General Court made large grants to individuals. John Pynchon owned thousands of acres along the Connecticut River at Springfield, Massachusetts, a reward from the Court for his exploits as an Indian fighter. More than most important migrants, Pynchon was able to live like a landed English gentleman, presiding over dozens of tenants. In 1685, Pynchon rented land or housing to 49 of the 120 male adults in Springfield. Because of his economic power, he dominated the political life of the town.

In settlements composed primarily of yeomen farm families, economic inequality increased over the years. Initially, the larger proprietors owned sizable farms, ranging in area from 200 to 600 acres—enough land to establish all of their sons, who before 1700, usually numbered three or four, within the community. Smallholders were less fortunate and could usually provide land for only some of their sons. Nonproprietors were the least well off, for they had to buy land or work as tenants or laborers. By 1702, in Windsor, Connecticut, about 30 percent of the adult male taxpayers were landless. It would take years of saving, or migration to a new town, for these men and their families to become freeholders.

Despite these inequalities, nearly all New England settlers had a real opportunity to acquire property, and even those at the bottom of the social scale enjoyed some economic security. Nathaniel Fish was one of the poorest men in Barnstable, Massachusetts, when he died in the 1690s, yet he owned a two-room cottage, 8 acres of land, an ox, and a cow. For him, and thousands of other settlers, New England had proved to be the promised land, a new world of opportunity.

The Indians' New World

Native Americans, whose ancestors had lived on the American continents for millennia, found that they too were living in a new world, but for them it was a bleak, dangerous, and conflict-ridden place, rendered deadly by European diseases and by the hardly less benign presence of thousands of armed settlers.

Metacom's War

By the 1670s, the white population of New England had reached 55,000, and Puritan communities stretched for 50 miles along the Massachusetts coast and throughout the Connecticut River valley. Displaced from their lands and beset by European diseases, the Indian population in southern New England dropped from 120,000 in 1570, to 70,000 in 1620, to barely 12,000 in 1670.

Like Opechancanough in Virginia a generation earlier, Metacom, leader of the Wampanoag tribe, concluded that only united resistance could stop the relentless advance of the English. He hesitated to act until he was hauled into an English court to answer an unfounded charge of murder. Released for lack of evidence, Metacom now forged a military alliance with the Narragansett and Nipmuck peoples. Many frightened

Metacom (King Philip), Chief of the Wampanoag
The Indian uprising of 1675 left an indelible mark on the historical memory of New England. This painting of 1850 was used by travelling performers to tell the story of King Philip's War, and was done on a window shade, so that it could be lit from behind for dramatic effect.(Shelburne Museum)

AMERICAN VOICES

Captivity Narrative *Mary Rowlandson*

Mary Rowlandson, a minister's wife in Lancaster, Massachusetts, was one of many settlers taken captive by the Indians during Metacom's War. She spent eleven weeks and five days with them, traveling constantly, until her family ransomed her for £20. Her account of her captivity, published in 1682, became one of the most popular prose works of its time.

On the tenth of February 1675, came the Indians with great numbers upon Lancaster: their first coming was about sunrising; hearing the noise of some guns, we looked out; several houses were burning, and the smoke ascending to heaven. . . . [T]he Indians laid hold of us, pulling me one way, and the children another, and said, "Come go along with us"; I told them they would kill me: they answered, if I were willing to go along with them, they would not hurt me. . . .

The first week of my being among them I hardly ate any thing; the second week I found my stomach grow very faint for want of something; and yet it was very hard to get down their filthy trash; but the third week . . . they were sweet and savory to my taste. I was at this time knitting a pair of white cotton stockings for my mistress; and had not yet wrought upon a sabbath day. When the sabbath came they bade me go to work. I told them it was the sabbath-day, and desired them to let me rest, and told them I would do as much more tomorrow; to which they answered me they would break my face. . . .

Then I went to see King Philip. He bade me come in and sit down, and asked me whether I would smoke . . . but this no way suited me. For though I had formerly used tobacco, yet I had left it ever since I was first taken. It seems to be a bait the devil lays to make men lose their precious time. . . .

. . . During my abode in this place, Philip spake to me to make a shirt for his boy, which I did, for which he gave me a shilling. I offered the money to my master, but he bade me keep it; and with it I bought a piece of horse flesh. Afterwards he asked me to make a cap for his boy, for which he invited me to dinner. I went, and he gave me a pancake, about as big as two fingers. It was made of parched wheat, beaten, and fried in bear's grease, but I thought I never tasted pleasanter meat in my life. . . .

Hearing that my son was come to this place, I went to see him. . . . He told me also, that awhile before, his master (together with other Indians) were going to the French for powder; but by the way the Mohawks met with them, and killed four of their company, which made the rest turn back again, for which I desire that myself and he may bless the Lord; for it might have been worse with him, had he been sold to the French, than it proved to be in his remaining with the Indians. . . .

My master had three squaws, living sometimes with one, and sometimes with another one. . . . [It] was Weetamoo with whom I had lived and served all this while. A severe and proud dame she was, bestowing every day in dressing herself near as much time as any of the gentry of the land: powdering her hair, and painting her face, going with necklaces, with jewels in her ears, and bracelets upon her hands. When she had dressed herself, her work was to make girdles of wampom and beads. . . .

About that time there came an Indian to me and bid me come to his wigwam at night, and he would give me some pork and ground-nuts. Which I did, and as I was eating, another Indian said to me, he seems to be your friend, but he killed two Englishmen at Sudbury, and there lie their cloaths behind you. I looked behind me, and there I saw bloody cloaths, with bullet-holes in them. Yet the lord suffered not this wretch to do me any hurt. . . .

On Tuesday morning they called their general court (as they call it) to consult and determine, whether I should go home or no. And they all as one man did seemingly consent to it, that I should go home. . . .

Source: C. H. Lincoln, ed., *Original Narratives of Early American History, Narratives of Indian Wars, 1675–1699*, vol. 14 (New York: Barnes and Noble, 1952).

colonists abandoned their farms for the safety of Plymouth. When a settler in the outlying village of Swansea shot and killed one of the Indians scavenging in the deserted town, full-scale war broke out. Metacom, whom the Puritans called King Philip, and his allies attacked white settlements throughout New England. Bitter fighting continued into 1676, ending only when Metacom was killed. By the end of King Philip's

Indians Hunting Deer
This stylized engraving by a French artist implicitly contrasted European and native American hunting methods. Such artists were essentially anthropologists and their work provides vital clues to the values and outlook of both the resident Indians and the European intruders.

War, the Indians had burned 20 percent of the English towns in Massachusetts and Rhode Island and killed 5 percent of the adult white population. But the Indians' losses—from war, famine, and disease—were even higher: 4,000 native Americans or 25 percent of an already severely diminished population. And many of the survivors were sold into slavery, including Metacom's wife and nine-year-old son.

All-out warfare lowered the moral standards of both peoples. Indian warriors had traditionally demonstrated their fighting skills in small-scale raids against neighboring tribes. Now they became increasingly violent, torturing male captives seized from their tribal enemies. As for whites, the Indians wished to annihilate them totally. The Puritans also sank to a new low. A fisherman reported that once when his ship had brought two captured Indians into Marblehead, Massachusetts, "the women surrounded them, drove us by force from them, and then with stones, billets of wood, and what else they might, they made an end of these Indians." Once aroused, racial hatred did not easily die.

The Fate of the Seaboard Tribes

The fate of Metacom's revolt was all too typical. By 1700, the English invaders in New England and the Chesapeake had conquered many of the tribes of the Atlantic seaboard. Small remnants of these tribes, stripped of their lands and traditions, lived on the margins of white society. They had suffered a double tragedy, failing both to repel the English and to maintain their cultural identity.

The Impact of the Fur Trade. For the time being, the Indian tribes in the interior of North America were able to maintain their identity and independence, even though they could not preserve their traditional way of life. White traders had introduced rum and European diseases, and drunkenness and epidemics soon sapped the vitality of many tribes. Even European manufactures were a mixed blessing. As native Americans acquired iron hoes and pots, they lost their motivation to work with flint and clay. In two generations they could no longer produce what they needed, and they became dependent on the fur trade—and on Europeans—for basic necessities.

The competition for beaver furs and deer pelts increased conflict among native Americans. Families or villages within a tribe would claim exclusive hunting and trapping rights over an area, undermining clan and tribal unity. Conflict between tribes also increased as the population of the fur-bearing animals dwindled, and rival bands of hunter-warriors competed for new trapping areas. The Iroquois, aggressive and well organized, stole pelts bound for Montreal and ultimately subdued the Huron and Erie peoples after decades of warfare. The Iroquois then extended their dominion to include the Delaware and the Susquehannock tribes. As in all societies, a commitment to warfare increased the influence of those who made war, so the balance of power shifted within the tribes as elders lost sway over headstrong young warriors.

The fur trade also transformed the Indians' relationship with the natural world. Native Americans were animists in religion: they believed that everything in nature—animals, trees, rocks—had a living spirit that demanded respect. Each clan within a tribe venerated an animal as its *totem,* or symbol. Tribesmen could hunt these totem animals—fox, deer, beavers—but only if they followed certain customs. As they skinned beavers or butchered deer, they thanked the spirits of the animals for giving them clothing and food. Later they respectfully buried the carcasses and the entrails. To throw the bones into a fire or a river was taboo—that might bring misfortune on the tribe.

The European fur trade brought spiritual upheaval to the Indians at the same time as it cut into the abundant wildlife of the continent. Warriors now hunted ceaselessly, to feed and clothe their clan, to trade with the French in Quebec and the Dutch and English in New York. As they killed more and more deer and beaver, the Indians sensed the displeasure of the spirits in nature. The epidemics that swept their communities were taken as a confirmation of their fears: the spirits of the animals were taking their revenge. The warriors of the Micmac of Nova Scotia confessed that they no longer knew "whether the beavers are among our friends or our enemies." No less than military conquest and religious conversion, the fur trade drastically altered the character of Indian society, bringing disease, drunkenness, and a warrior mentality to many tribes.

America had become a new world for Indians as well as for Europeans. All of the invaders—Dutch and French fur traders no less than Spanish conquistadors and English settlers—destroyed traditional native American societies, forcing their members to fashion new ways of life.

Summary

For seventy-five years after the conquest of Mexico, Spain enjoyed a monopoly in colonizing North America. Spain added Florida, New Mexico, and California to its empire by establishing military garrisons and, in the Southwest, by sending Franciscan monks to convert the Indians.

Beginning in 1607 England, France, Holland, and Sweden joined Spain in establishing colonies in North America. The French, Dutch, and Swedes all settled far north of New Spain, setting up trading posts and small agricultural settlements. The fur trade was the lifeblood of New France, New Netherland, and New Sweden. French fur traders and Jesuit priests probed deep into the heart of the North American continent, extending France's influence into the Mississippi Valley.

The English came primarily as settlers, and their relentless quest for land brought war with the Indian peoples. Chesapeake Indians nearly wiped out the Virginia colony in 1622, the Pequot contested Puritan claims in 1635, and Metacom's forces dealt New England a devastating blow in 1675–1676. By 1700, however, the native Americans of the Atlantic seaboard had been nearly annihilated by the force of English arms and diseases.

The English created two very different types of colonies in North America. Settlers in the Chesapeake region concentrated on raising tobacco for export to Europe. Wealthy planters and corrupt officials controlled Chesapeake society, dominating a population of yeomen farmers, propertyless freemen, and white indentured servants. The pursuit of self-interest by Governor Berkeley and his faction in Virginia and economic hardship following the end of the tobacco boom, prompted Nathaniel Bacon's unsuccessful rebellion of 1675–1676; subsequently, planters turned increasingly to slave labor.

The English colonies planted in the rocky soil and harsh climate of New England raised crops mostly for their own consumption rather than for export. They created strong communities of independent, God-fearing freeholders. Puritan magistrates enforced religious orthodoxy, banishing Roger Williams, Anne Hutchinson, and other religious dissidents, but gave extensive power to the lay members of Congregational churches, thereby ensuring political stability.

TOPIC FOR RESEARCH

The Puritans' Decision to Migrate to America

Between 1630 and 1640 thousands of English Puritans left their homeland to seek a new life in America. What prompted these men and women to make such a momentous decision? Did they act solely from religious motives, or were other factors also important? One way to address these questions is by examining the migrants' lives in England; a second way is by reading their letters and correspondence; yet a third approach is by studying the kinds of communities they established in America.

Important books dealing with one or more of these approaches include Bernard Bailyn, *The New England Merchants in the Seventeenth Century* (1955); Edmund S. Morgan, *The Puritan Dilemma: The Story of John Winthrop;* Sumner Chilton Powell, *Puritan Village: The Formation of a New England Town* (1963); Francis J. Bremer, *The Puritan Experiment* (1976); Everett Emerson, ed., *Letters from New England: The Massachusetts Bay Colony, 1629–1638* (1976); David Grayson Allen, *In English Ways: The Movement of Societies and the Transferral of English Local Law and Custom to Massachusetts Bay in the Seventeenth Century* (1981); and David Cressy, *Coming Over: Migration and Communication between England and New England in the Seventeenth Century* (1987). This topic may also be studied through the intensive examination of John Winthrop's "*A Model of Christian Charity*," which is reproduced in the *student's guide.* Two works that explicate this document are Darrett B. Rutman, *John Winthrop's Decision for America: 1629* (1975), and Stephen Nissenbaum's commentary in David Nasaw, ed., *The Course of United States History: To 1877* (1987), pp. 31–51.

BIBLIOGRAPHY

The Europeans Come to North America

Gary B. Nash, *Red, White, and Black: The Peoples of Early America* (l982), provides a good introduction to the cultural interaction among various European and Indian peoples, as do two works by James Axtell, *The European and the Indian* (1981), and *The Invasion Within: The Contest of Cultures in Colonial North America* (1985). Francis Jennings, *The Invasion of America* (1975), views the impact of European settlement from a critical perspective, as does W. R. Jacobs, *Dispossessing the American Indian: Indians and Whites on the Colonial Frontier* (1972).

Important specific studies include Bruce G. Trigger, *The Children of Aataentsic: A History of the Huron People to 1660* (1976); Karen Ordahl Kupperman, *Settling with the Indians: The Meeting of English and Indian Cultures in America, 1580–1640* (1981); James Bradley, *Evolution of the Onondaga Iroquois* (1987); and Kenneth Morrison, *The Embattled Northeast: The Elusive Ideal of Alliance in Abeneki-European Relations* (1984). An illuminating study of the fur trade is Calvin Martin, *Keepers of the Game: Indian-Animal Relations and the Fur Trade* (1978).

For the story of early settlement from the English point of view, see Alden Vaughan, *American Genesis: Captain John Smith and the Founding of Virginia* (1975), and *New England Frontier: Puritans and Indians, 1620–1675* (1965). See also A. W. Trelease, *Indian Affairs in Colonial New York: The Seventeenth Century* (1960).

Social Conflict in the Chesapeake

Edmund S. Morgan, *American Slavery, American Freedom: The Ordeal of Colonial Virginia* (1975), provides a brilliant analysis of life in the new colony. Important supplemental essays appear in Thad W. Tate and David L. Ammerman, eds., *The Chesapeake in the Seventeenth Century* (1979), and Lois Green Carr, Philip D. Morgan, and Jean B. Russo, *Colonial Chesapeake Society* (1989). Significant community studies include Carville Earle, *The Evolution of a Tidewater Settlement Pattern: All Hallows Parish, Maryland, 1650–1783* (1975), and Darrett Rutman and Anita Rutman, *A Place in Time: Middlesex County, Virginia, 1650–1750* (1984). See also Gloria L. Main, *Tobacco Colony: Life in Early Maryland, 1650–1720* (1982).

For a discussion of political institutions, see W. F. Craven, *The Southern Colonies in the Seventeenth Century, 1607–1689* (1949), and David W. Jordan, *Foundations of Representative Government in Maryland, 1632–1715* (1988). Contrasting accounts of Bacon's Rebellion are T. J. Wertenbaker, *Torchbearer of the Revolution* (1940), and Wilcomb B. Washburn, *The Governor and the Rebel* (1958).

Puritan New England

The Puritan migration is explored in the works listed in the Topic for Research. Puritanism as an intellectual movement is best explored in the many works of Perry Miller. See *The*

New England Mind: The Seventeenth Century (1939) and *Orthodoxy in Massachusetts, 1630–1650* (1933). Charles Hambrick-Stowe, *The Practice of Piety: Puritan Devotional Disciplines* (1982), discusses the emotional dimension of Puritanism, while David D. Hall, *World of Wonder, Days of Judgment: Popular Religious Belief in Early New England* (1989), explores its nonrational aspects. Two fine biographies that convey the shifting currents of orthodoxy are Edmund S. Morgan, *The Puritan Dilemma: The Story of John Winthrop* (1958), and Robert Middlekauff, *The Mathers: Three Generations of Puritan Intellectuals, 1596–1728* (1971). See also the powerful study by Andrew Delbanco, *The Puritan Ordeal* (1989).

For a discussion of dissent in early New England, consult Philip Gura, *A Glimpse of Sion's Glory: Puritan Radicalism in New England, 1620–1660* (1984). See also Ola Winslow, *Master Roger Williams* (1957); Emery Battis, *Saints and Sectaries: Anne Hutchinson and the Antinomian Controversy* (1962); Amy Schrager Lang, *Prophetic Woman: Anne Hutchinson and the Problem of Dissent in the Literature of New England* (1987); and the controversial analysis by Lyle Kohler, *A Search for Power: The Weaker Sex in Seventeenth-Century New England* (1980).

Community studies that reveal the lives of ordinary New England men and women are John Demos, *The Little Commonwealth: Family Life in Plymouth Colony* (1971); Kenneth A. Lockridge, *A New England Town . . . Dedham, Massachusetts, 1636–1736* (1970); Philip J. Greven, Jr., *Four Generations: Population, Land, and Family in Colonial Andover, Massachusetts* (1970); Paul Boyer and Steven Nissenbaum, *Salem Possessed: The Social Origins of Witchcraft* (1974); and Carol F. Karlsen, *The Devil in the Shape of a Woman: Witchcraft in New England* (1987).

The Indians' New World

James H. Merrell, *The Indians' New World: Catawbas and Their Neighbors from European Contact through the Era of Removal* (1989), is a path-breaking study. Douglas Leach, *Flinthawk and Tomahawk: New England in King Philip's War* (1958), is the standard treatment of the conflict. See also Bernard Sheehan, *Savagism and Civility: Indians and Englishmen in Colonial Virginia* (1980), and Daniel K. Richter and James H. Merrell, eds., *Beyond the Covenant Chain: The Iroquois and Their Neighbors in Indian North America* (1987).

TIMELINE

1565	Spain establishes St. Augustine, Florida
1603–1625	King James I of England
1607	English adventurers settle Jamestown, Virginia
1608	Samuel de Champlain founds Quebec
1613	Dutch set up fur-trading post on Manhattan Island
1619	First Africans arrive in Chesapeake Virginia House of Burgesses convened
1620	Pilgrims found Plymouth colony
1620–1660	Tobacco boom in Chesapeake colonies
1622	Opechancanough's uprising
1624	Virginia becomes a royal colony
1625–1649	King Charles I
1629	Puritans found Massachusetts Bay colony
1632/1634	Maryland chartered/settled
1636	Roger Williams and his followers settle Rhode Island
1637	Pequot War
1649–1660	Puritan Commonwealth in England
1651	First Navigation Act passed
1660	William Berkeley Governor of Virginia until 1678
1660–1720	Poor tobacco market; prices level
1662	Connecticut receives royal charter Halfway Covenant
1664	English conquer New Netherland
1670s	Indentured servitude declines
1675–1676	Bacon's rebellion Metacom's uprising
1692	Salem witchcraft trials

Bristol Docks and Quay (detail)

The bustle and prosperity of the English port of Bristol is well conveyed in this eighteenth-century painting. Bristol, a hub of the triangular trade with Africa, the West Indies, and the American colonies, was the departure point for many American settlers. (City of Bristol Museum and Art Gallery)

CHAPTER 3 *The British Empire in America,* 1660–1750

By 1660, English traders and settlers had founded two clusters of colonies along the eastern coast of North America. The English government now sought to profit from their products and commerce, and to protect them from European rivals, particularly the Dutch in New Netherland and the French in Quebec. To do so, officials expanded the English navy and tried to bring the Chesapeake and New England colonies under the yoke of a single imperial system that would also include England's valuable holdings in the West Indies.

The sugar islands of the West Indies were England's most prized overseas possessions. Sugar produced with slave labor on large plantations brought wealth to English planters and merchants and made England a world power. The settler colonies on the mainland of North America bolstered this economic empire by providing crucial supplies to the sugar islands and by shipping valuable crops of tobacco and rice to European markets. By the mid-eighteenth century the mainland colonies were also buying large quantities of English manufactures and were becoming an important part of the empire.

Britain's dominion in America rested on a strange combination of force and consent. English planters used brute force to control the tens of thousands of African slaves who labored on the plantations, while English governors and bureaucrats won the voluntary support of the white settlers by consenting to a measure of self-government. The result, as defined by a proud British imperialist in 1745, "was a magnificent superstructure of American commerce and British naval power on an African foundation."

The Politics of Empire, 1660–1713

In 1660, England had thriving colonies in America but no firm and uniform policy for governing them. For the most part the colonies had simply been left to develop as they might. Over the next twenty-five years, as their financial importance grew, England tried to tighten its control, first by imposing strict trade regulations and then by centralizing colonial government. Accustomed to running their own affairs, the colonists resisted these efforts, sometimes through open rebellion. Finally, upheaval in England brought to power new political leaders who allowed for American self-government within an empire based on trade.

The Restoration Colonies

In 1660 the Stuart monarchy was restored to England and Charles II (1660–1685) returned from exile. Like previous Stuarts, Charles II supported the Anglican Church and believed in the divine right of kings. A robust and vigorous man, he offended many of his subjects by marrying a Portuguese Catholic princess and presiding over a sexually carefree royal entourage. His generosity and extravagance kept him constantly in debt—a fact of considerable importance for American affairs.

On ascending the throne, Charles rewarded the aristocrats who supported the Restoration by giving them millions of acres of land in America. In 1663 he gave the Carolinas to eight aristocrats, including the duke of Albemarle, Sir George Carteret, Lord John Berkeley, and his brother Sir William Berkeley, the governor of Virginia. In 1664 the king granted all the territory between the Delaware and Connecticut rivers to his brother James, the duke of York. Later that year, James also took possession of the newly captured Dutch colony of New Netherland, renaming it New York after his title. Because he wished to concentrate his energies on governing New York personally, James gave ownership of New Jersey to two of the Carolina proprietors, Sir George Carteret and Lord John Berkeley. And so, in just two years, vast tracts of land had fallen into the hands of a few English noblemen.

The new colonies were proprietorships, like Maryland, not commercial ventures like the settlements in Virginia and New England. Their charters required only that their laws conform broadly to those of England, generous provisions that allowed the proprietors to shape their social and institutional character. Moreover, the proprietors of New York, New Jersey, and the Carolinas owned all of the land in their domains, to do with as they pleased.

The Carolinas. The Carolina proprietors had no wish to create communities of independent yeoman farm families, as in New England. Instead they tried to recreate a traditional European rural society. They instructed John Locke, the future political theorist of individualism and popular government, to devise a scheme of government for the new colony. The result, the Fundamental Constitutions of Carolina (1669), prescribed an archaic feudal society: noble "landgraves" were to preside over baronies populated both by free families and by "leet men"—serfs bound to the land.

This aristocratic fantasy could not have been further removed from reality. The first settlers in North Carolina, poor families from Virginia, refused to work on large manors and lived on modest farms, raising crops of grain and tobacco. The proprietors, despite the failure of their manorial plans, continued to grant deeds that required the payment of an annual quitrent. Farmers in Albemarle County, angered by the cost of this claim of lordship and by taxes on tobacco exports, rose in rebellion in 1677. Led by John Culpepper, they deposed the governor and took control of North Carolina.

The settlement of South Carolina was equally unsuccessful for the proprietors. The colonists, many of whom came from Barbados, by now an overcrowded sugar island, refused to accept the Fundamental Consti-

A King in Waiting, c. 1655

While Oliver Cromwell imposed stern Puritan rule on England, the future Charles II (1660–1685) danced his way across Europe. As king, Charles presided over a court known for its extravagance and debauchery.

TABLE 3.1

English Colonies in North America, 1660–1750

	Date	Type	Religion	Status in 1775	Chief Export or Economic Activity
Carolina	1663	Proprietary	Church of England	Royal	
North	1691				Mixed farming; naval stores
South	1691				Rice; indigo
New Jersey	1664	Proprietary	Church of England	Royal	Wheat
New York	1664	Proprietary	Church of England	Royal	Wheat
Pennsylvania	1681	Proprietary	Quaker	Proprietary	Wheat
Georgia	1732	Trustees	Church of England	Royal	Rice
New Hampshire (Separated from Massachusetts)	1739	Royal	Congregationalist	Royal	Mixed farming; lumber; naval stores
Nova Scotia	1749	Royal	Church of England	Royal	Fishing; mixed farming; naval stores

tutions or the proprietors' demands for quitrents. The Barbadians introduced slavery, though the number of blacks remained small until 1700, and opened up a lucrative commerce with native Americans, exchanging English manufactures for furs and for Indian slaves captured in intertribal warfare. This commerce brought war with the Yamassee and other tribes, making South Carolina a turbulent and dangerous society for half a century.

William Penn and Pennsylvania. In stark contrast, the proprietary colony of Pennsylvania developed into a peaceful and prosperous settlement. In 1681, Charles II bestowed this land on William Penn, primarily in payment of a large debt the king owed to Penn's father, the admiral Sir William Penn.

The younger Penn was an enigmatic man. Born to wealth and influence, he had seemed destined for renown as a friend and servant of kings but, in his early twenties, he converted to the Society of Friends (Quakers), a radical Protestant sect, and became one of its more ardent supporters. His pamphlet *No Cross, No Crown* offered an articulate defense of the Quakers' beliefs in religious liberty, and he used his wealth and prestige to spread their influence. Pennsylvania, his greatest achievement, was designed as a refuge for Quakers, who were persecuted in England because they refused to serve in the army or pay taxes to support the Church of England.

Penn's Frame of Government, which he drew up for his colony in 1681, guaranteed political liberty and religious freedom: it called for no established church and no religious taxes and allowed Christians of all faiths to vote and hold office. During the 1680s, thousands of Quakers, primarily from the middling classes of northwestern England, came to Pennsylvania. Most settled along the Delaware River, in or near the city of Philadelphia, which Penn himself planned. To attract additional settlers, the proprietor sold land at low prices—and in *fee simple*, without quitrents or other feudal restraints—and had his *Brief Account of the Province of Pennsylvania* translated into Dutch and German. In 1683 migrants from Krefeld in Saxony founded Germantown—just outside Philadelphia—and thousands of other Germans soon joined them.

Penn was given another colony, Delaware, which he governed in an equally enlightened fashion. Originally a Swedish settlement, Delaware had been conquered first by the Dutch and then, in 1664, by the English. James, duke of York, ruled the small colony until 1682, when he gave it to Penn. The Quaker leader incorporated the Delaware settlements into Pennsylvania as the Lower Counties, but he allowed the inhabitants to select their own representative assembly (1703). The constitution and social order of Pennsylvania and the Lower Counties were by far the most open and democratic of all the Restoration colonies.

The New Mercantilism

To pay his political and financial debts, Charles II had relinquished royal control over vast areas of his colonial domain. Although the king was generous with land, he kept a tight grip on colonial trade, to increase the value of the empire and to raise royal revenues from custom duties. His trade policies accelerated a new phase of English mercantilism that had been initiated during the Commonwealth.

Before 1650, the English government had sought to enhance national wealth chiefly by accumulating specie. Its policies encouraged exports while restricting imports, giving England a favorable balance of trade with European countries and forcing them to pay the difference in gold or silver. After 1650, as the economic potential of the colonies became apparent, the government expanded mercantilism by regulating the trade of the American settlements. The initial phase of this policy, expressed in the Navigation Act of 1651, was aimed expressly at Dutch merchants who supplied the English colonies with European manufactures and carried their sugar and tobacco directly to European markets. To curb these traders (and secure shipping fees for English merchants), the act required that all goods imported into England or the colonies be carried on ships registered in England, Ireland, or the colonies themselves.

Upon coming to the throne in 1660, Charles II endorsed the Navigation Act. He felt that England could reap the full benefit of its overseas empire only by monopolizing colonial commerce. To this end, the king created a new committee of the Privy Council, the Lords of Trade and Plantations, to formulate colonial policy, and had Parliament pass a new Navigation Act (1660) that strengthened the ban on foreign shipping and stipulated that sugar, tobacco, and indigo, a deep violet-blue dye extracted from a subtropical plant, could be shipped only to other English possessions. In 1663, the Staple Act required that these crops be sent directly to England, from where they could be reexported to other countries at great profit. The Staple Act also required that European exports to America be shipped through England, inflating the price of those goods and increasing the sale of lower-priced English manufactures. To enforce these laws and to raise money, Parliament passed the Revenue Act of 1673 which imposed a special "plantation duty" on certain American exports and created, for the first time, a staff of customs officials to collect the levy in American ports. In 1696 a final Navigation Act increased the legal powers of the customs agents and replaced the Lords of Trade with a new administrative body, the Board of Trade, composed of politicians and officials with knowledge of colonial affairs. The act also required all American governors to enforce trade regulations under penalty of dismissal.

The English government backed up its policy with force. "What we want," declared the duke of Albemarle, "is more of the trade the Dutch now have." In three commercial wars between 1652 and 1674, the English navy broke Dutch supremacy in world trade, driving the Dutch from New Netherland, their only base in North America, and ending their monopoly of the West African slave trade. While the English navy was winning control of the seas, English merchants were building their fleets and establishing a dominant position in world commerce.

TABLE 3.2

Navigation Acts, 1651–1751

	Date	Purpose	Result
Act of 1651	1651	Cut Dutch trade	Mostly ignored
Act of 1660	1660	Ban foreign shipping; Enumerated goods only to England	Partially obeyed
Act of 1663	1663	European imports only through England	Partially obeyed
Staple Act	1673	Ensure enumerated goods go only to England	Mostly obeyed
Act of 1696	1696	Prevent frauds; Create Vice-Admiralty Courts	Mostly obeyed
Woolen Act	1699	Prevent export or intercolonial sale of textiles	Partially obeyed
Hat Act	1732	Prevent export or intercolonial sale of hats	Partially obeyed
Molasses Act	1733	Cut American imports of molasses from French West Indies	Extensively violated
Iron Act	1750	Prevent manufacture of finished iron products	Extensively violated
Currency Act	1751	End use of paper currency as legal tender in New England	Mostly obeyed

The Dominion of New England

For England, the new mercantilism was a spectacular success. In the colonies, however, Charles II's policies were deeply resented. Not only were the laws an economic burden, but they allowed royal bureaucrats unprecedented intervention into the colonies' internal affairs. Most of the colonies resisted the new measures. In Massachusetts, a customs official named Edward Randolph reported that the Puritan government took "no notice of the laws of trade," welcoming Dutch merchants as usual and importing goods from the French sugar islands. Indeed, Puritan leaders claimed that their original royal charter exempted them from most of the regulations. Outraged, Randolph called on his superiors to use English troops to "reduce Massachusetts to obedience."

At the urging of officials like Randolph, the Lords of Trade and Plantations decided to assert their authority over the Puritan colonies. In 1679, they denied the claim the Massachusetts Bay colony had laid to the adjoining frontier province of New Hampshire and created instead a separate colony there with a royal governor. In 1684, the Lords of Trade won a major legal victory when the English Court of Chancery annulled the charter of Massachusetts Bay on the grounds that the Puritan government discriminated against members of the Church of England and had violated the Navigation Acts.

The accession of James, duke of York, to the throne as James II (1685–1688) gave the Lords of Trade a perfect opportunity to increase royal authority. James was an avid admirer of Louis XIV, the despotic king of France, and he was bent on curbing the power of Parliament at home and of representative institutions in America. With James's support, in 1686 the Lords revoked the corporate charters of Connecticut and Rhode Island and merged them with the Massachusetts Bay and Plymouth colonies to form a new royal province, the Dominion of New England. Two years later, the Lords added New York and New Jersey to the dominion, thereby creating one huge colony stretching from the Delaware River to Maine.

The Dominion of New England represented a new authoritarian model of colonial administration. As the name implied, New England was to be the king's own "dominion." James named Sir Edmund Andros, a military officer and former governor of New York, to rule the new colony. Dispatched to Boston with orders to abolish the existing legislative assemblies, Andros ruled Massachusetts Bay by administrative fiat. He proceeded to attack all the major institutions of Puritan society. He advocated public worship in the Church of England, which offended Puritan Congregationalists. He banned town meetings, which aroused the ire of colonists in scores of rural villages, who treasured local autonomy.

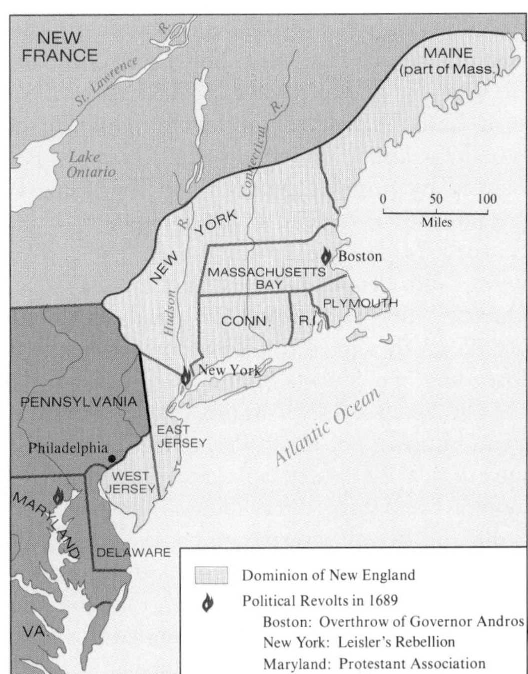

MAP 3.1

The Dominion of New England

The Dominion created a vast new royal colony—stretching nearly 500 miles along the Atlantic coast. Following the Glorious Revolution in England, revolts in Boston and New York City ousted royal officials—effectively ending the Dominion. In Maryland, a Protestant Association mounted a third revolt, deposing the Catholic proprietary governor.

And he levied arbitrary taxes and challenged the validity of all land titles granted under the original Massachusetts charter. While he offered to provide new deeds, they would not be in fee simple; owners would have to pay an annual quitrent.

The Puritans protested vigorously against the new regime, sending the eminent minister Increase Mather to London to plead with James II to restore the old charter, but the king refused.

The Glorious Revolution of 1688

Fortunately for the colonists, James had made as many enemies at home as Andros had in the colonies. The new monarch had angered political leaders by revoking the charters of many English towns, charities, and corporations—to make them more dependent on the crown—and by rejecting the advice of Parliament. He had offended the majority of the English people by openly practicing Roman Catholicism and prosecuting Anglican bishops when they defied his attempt to control Church of England appointments. The turning point came in 1688, when James's second wife, a Spanish Catholic princess, gave birth to a son. The prospect of a Catholic heir to the throne ignited a quick and bloodless coup, known as the Glorious Revolution. Backed by popular protests and the army, Protestant parliamentary leaders forced James into exile and enthroned Mary, his Protestant daughter (by his first wife), and her Dutch husband, William of Orange. Queen Mary II (1689–1694) and King William III (1689–1701) agreed to rule as constitutional monarchs, foregoing the Stuarts' claim to a "divine right," and they accepted a Bill of Rights that guaranteed many of the traditional powers of Parliament. The new system of government promoted economic growth throughout the empire by curbing royal monopolies (such as the East India and Royal African companies) and by giving free rein to enterprising merchants and financiers. (The Bank of England, the nation's central bank and guarantor of financial stability, was founded in 1694.) In *Two Treatises on Government*, published in 1690, John Locke justified the Glorious Revolution. He argued that individuals are endowed with inalienable natural rights to life, liberty, and property and that the legitimacy of government rests on the consent of the governed. Locke's views on liberty and popular sovereignty—and the growing power of Parliament—had a lasting influence on many Americans, especially those who sat in the colonial assemblies and wanted to increase their powers. More immediately, the Glorious Revolution sparked popular rebellions in Massachusetts, Maryland, and New York.

The Target of the Glorious Revolution
James II (1685–1688) was a forceful but arrogant ruler, whose arbitrary measures and Catholic sympathies prompted rebellions in England and America, and cost him the throne. (Godfrey Kneller, *James II*, National Portrait Gallery, London)

The Fall of the Dominion. News of the accession of William and Mary in November 1688 finally reached Boston the following April. The city's residents immediately circulated a printed Manifesto—probably the work of Congregational ministers or their followers—calling on the townspeople to "seize the vile persons who oppressed us." The town militia took Andros prisoner and a hastily formed Committee of Safety forced him to return to England. In London, Increase Mather petitioned the new monarchs for the restoration of the old charter of 1629.

William and Mary agreed to break up the Dominion of New England, which many English Parliamentary leaders viewed as a symbol of Stuart despotism. However, they insisted on retaining close supervision of the northern colonies, especially with regard to trade. In 1691 a new charter combined Massachusetts Bay, Plymouth, and Maine into the new royal colony of Massachusetts. Henceforth, the Crown would appoint the governor (and naval officers to supervise the ports), while the townspeople would elect delegates to the assembly, the House of Representatives. The charter broadened the franchise, extending the vote to property owners who were not members of Puritan congregations, and guaranteed religious freedom to members of the Church of England. This new charter, which gave Massachusetts considerable political autonomy while increasing royal control over trade and military defense, worked well for the next seventy years.

Uprising in Maryland. In Maryland the response to the news of James II's overthrow was similar. A Protestant Association led by John Coode quickly removed the officials appointed by the Catholic proprietor, Lord Baltimore, accusing them of "Popish Idolatry and Superstition." The rebellion was a result of longstanding conflict between Protestants and Catholics in Maryland, aggravated by economic problems. The stagnant tobacco market had struck hard at the finances of smallholders, tenant farmers, and former indentured servants. Like Nathaniel Bacon's followers in Virginia, they were suffering not only from falling prices but also from rising taxes and the high fees imposed by government officials.

Coode's Protestant Association ruled Maryland for two years, until the Lords of Trade suspended the proprietorship, imposed royal government, and established the Church of England as the colony's official church. Maryland continued to be ruled by governors appointed by the monarch until Lord Baltimore's death in 1715. Since his son, Benedict Calvert, the fourth Lord Baltimore, had earlier converted to the Anglican faith, the Crown decided to restore the family's power to govern the colony, which then continued as a proprietorship until the American Revolution.

Like Virginia, Maryland remained a divided society, with a planter elite controlling a population of servants, slaves, and tenants and dominating the representative institutions. However, the proprietor's commitment to Protestantism, with religious freedom for Catholics, diminished political conflicts, and a united governing class emerged. In Maryland, as in Massachusetts, the uprisings of 1689 resulted in the creation of stable political institutions.

Ethnic Rebellion in New York

In New York, however, the Glorious Revolution produced many years of ethnic strife, class tension, and political instability. After England conquered New Netherland in 1664, James II (as Duke of York) had imposed strict authoritarian rule on the colony, prohibiting representative institutions. However, he allowed the Rensselaers and other Dutch manorial lords to retain their large holdings, and most of the other Dutch inhabitants—fur traders, farmers, urban artisans—remained in the colony as well. Thirty years later, nearly 60 percent of the taxpayers in New York City were Dutch artisans and shopkeepers. As proud Protestants from Holland, they welcomed the accession of Mary and her Dutch husband to the English throne.

A month after the uprising in Boston, the New York militia ousted Colonel Francis Nicholson, who, under Sir Edmund Andros, was lieutenant governor of New York and New Jersey. Dutch artisans in New York City joined with Puritan farmers on Long Island in this attack on Nicholson, an alleged Catholic sympathizer, and other "Popish Doggs & Divells" appointed by James II. They replaced Nicholson with Jacob Leisler, a migrant German soldier who had married into a prominent Dutch merchant family. At first Leisler had the support of upper and lower classes and of all ethnic groups, but when his sympathy for the common people led him to free debtors from prison and to urge the creation of a more democratic, town-meeting form of government, this solidarity disintegrated.

Dutch artisans in New York City sided with Leisler, taking control of the ten-member Board of Aldermen, while wealthy merchants, who had traditionally controlled the city government, attacked the legitimacy of Leisler's seizure of power. The class animosity underlying this split was reflected in a pamphlet written by a merchant, Nicholas Bayard, who accused Leisler of being like a "Masaniello," the peasant fishmonger who in 1647 had led a popular revolt in Naples, Italy. Leisler held on to power until 1691, when he was forced to surrender to Henry Sloughter, the new royal governor. Influenced by Bayard and his wealthy merchant friends, Sloughter had Leisler and seven of his associates indicted for treason. An English jury convicted Leisler and Jacob Milburne, his brother-in-law, and the two men were hanged and then decapitated—a form of execution reserved for those found guilty of the most heinous crimes. At the same time, a new Board of Aldermen, dominated once again by merchants, passed ordinances reducing artisan wages. These measures broke the power of the Dutch artisans, but political conflict between the Leislerian and anti-Leislerian factions continued until the 1710s.

The events of 1689 marked a turning point in the political history of the American colonies. The uprisings in Boston and New York toppled the authoritarian

A Prosperous Dutch Farmstead

Most Dutch farmers in the Hudson River Valley lived well, because of easy access to market and their exploitation of black slaves. To record his success, Martin Van Bergen of Leeds, New York, had this mural painted over his mantelpiece.

institutions of the Dominion of New England and restored internal self-government. Subsequently, the imperial presence would be felt primarily through a close supervision of colonial trade.

The Empire in 1713

At the end of the seventeenth century, England fought two more great wars, the first against France—the War of the League of Augsburg (1689–1697)—and the second against France and Spain—the War of the Spanish Succession (1702–1714). England's goal was to prevent Louis XIV (the "Sun King") from extending France's boundaries to the Rhine River and thus gaining dominance on the Continent. Although most of the battles took place in Europe, conflict spilled over to the English and French empires in North America.

War in America. During the War of the League of Augsburg (known in America as King William's War) New England troops and their Iroquois allies fought against French troops and their Algonquian allies in the wide belt of Indian territory between New England and New France. French and Indian forces destroyed Schenectady, New York, in 1690, while Massachusetts troops captured Port Royal, the capital of Acadia. The Treaty of Ryswick, which ended the war in 1697, provided for the return of all captured territory.

During the War of the Spanish Succession (or Queen Anne's War), Abenaki warriors joined with the French to destroy English settlements in Maine, and in 1704, they massacred many of the residents of the western Massachusetts town of Deerfield. The New York frontier remained quiet, chiefly because the English and French governments decided not to embark on any military expeditions that would disrupt the lucrative fur trade with the Indians. In 1710 British troops, augmented with New England volunteers, again seized Port Royal, but a major expedition against the French stronghold at Quebec in 1711 failed miserably, despite the presence of twelve British men-of-war, forty transports, and more than 5,000 troops.

For the British, the stakes in these American confrontations were not high, and, with the exception of the Quebec assault, the imperial government committed few military resources to them. New England governments strongly supported the expeditions to conquer Acadia and New France, for they feared the Catholicism of the French as well as their privateers and Indian allies.

Native Americans, caught in the middle of these European-bred conflicts, maneuvered to protect their interests. The Iroquois tribes of New York—the Mohawk, Oneida, Onondaga, Cayuga, and Seneca—had long lived in a political confederation that stretched from the Hudson River to the Great Lakes. Having suffered losses by supporting the British in King William's War, they moved toward neutrality. By means of astute diplomacy, the Iroquois created a "covenant chain" of treaties with tribes in Pennsylvania and the Ohio River Valley. Beginning with Queen Anne's War and continuing to the 1750s, the Iroquois and their allies adopted a policy of "aggressive neutrality," exploiting their central geographic location by trading with both nations, English and French, but refusing to fight for either. The Delaware leader Teedyuscung explained this strategy to his tribe as he showed them a pictorial message from the Iroquois: "You see a Square in the Middle, meaning the Lands of the Indians; and at one End, the Figure of a Man, indicating the English; and at the other End, another, meaning the French. Let us join together to defend our land against both."

The Treaty of Utrecht ended this series of wars in 1713 and provided Britain with major territorial and

TABLE 3.3

English Wars, 1650–1750

	Date	Purpose	Result
Anglo-Dutch	1652–1654	Commercial markets	Stalemate
Anglo-Dutch	1664	Markets-Conquest	England takes New Amsterdam
Anglo-Dutch	1673	Commercial markets	England makes maritime gains
King William's	1689–1697	Maintain European balance of power	Stalemate in North America
Queen Anne's	1702–1713	Maintain European balance of power	British get Hudson Bay and Nova Scotia
Jenkins' Ear	1739	Expand markets in Spanish America	Stalemate
King George's	1740–1748	Maintain European balance of power	Capture and return of Louisbourg

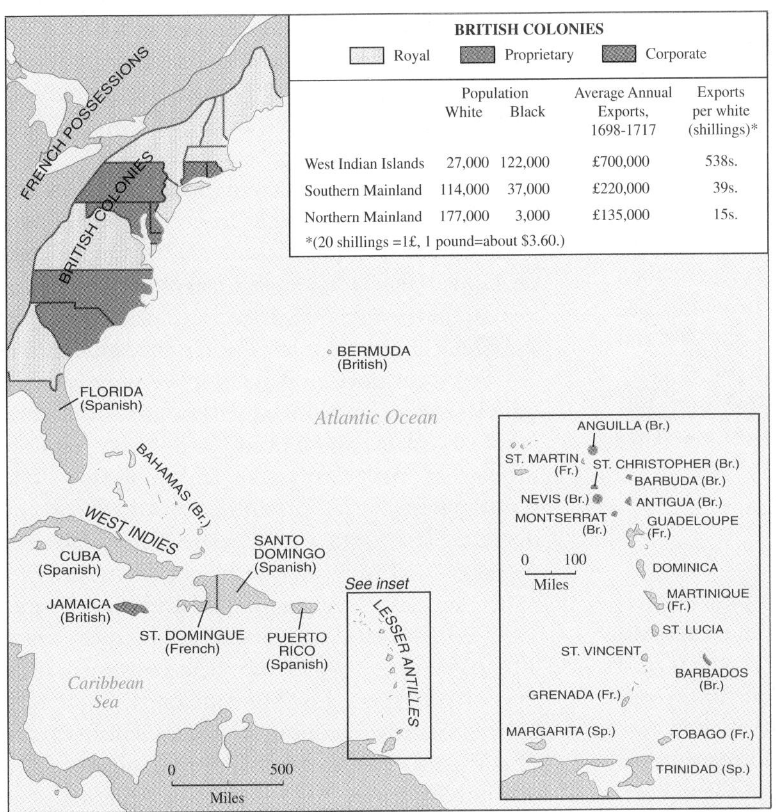

BRITISH COLONIES

Royal | Proprietary | Corporate

	Population White	Population Black	Average Annual Exports, 1698-1717	Exports per white (shillings)*
West Indian Islands	27,000	122,000	£700,000	538s.
Southern Mainland	114,000	37,000	£220,000	39s.
Northern Mainland	177,000	3,000	£135,000	15s.

*(20 shillings =1£, 1 pound=about $3.60.)

MAP 3.2

Britain's American Empire, 1713

Britain's West Indian possessions were small—mere dots on the Caribbean Sea—but in 1713 they were by far the most valuable parts of the Empire, their sugar crops bringing wealth to English merchants, trade to the northern colonies, and a brutal life (and early death) to the African workers.

commercial gains. From France, Britain obtained Newfoundland, Acadia (Nova Scotia), and the Hudson Bay region of northern Canada; from France's ally, Spain, Britain acquired commercial privileges in Spanish America and the strategic fortress of Gibraltar at the entrance to the Mediterranean. This British military and diplomatic triumph solidified its commercial supremacy and made the island nation a major European power. It also brought peace to North America for the next generation, leaving the colonies free to develop their social and political institutions.

Limited Administrative Reform. During the seventeenth century, the English empire in America had developed in a haphazard fashion. Some colonies produced crops for export and were closely tied to England by commerce; others were settlements of religious dissidents who wanted to be left alone. Some colonies had corporate charters; others were proprietary ventures; still others had royal governors.

In 1696, Parliament had created a new Board of Trade, consisting of rising politicians and experienced bureaucrats. This new Board of Trade's policies were designed to increase trade, and reflected the thinking of leading political philosophers and economists—such as John Locke. The Board sought to install royal governors and a uniform set of administrative institutions in all the American settlements, however they lacked the political influence to do so. Colonists and proprietors resisted such reforms, and so did English political leaders: Parliament had just overthrown a power-hungry monarch at home and was unwilling to increase royal power in America.

Consequently, the empire retained the complex institutional structure of the seventeenth century. New York continued as a royal province, with New Jersey coming under royal control in 1702. As in the first royal colony of Virginia and in Massachusetts after 1691, a governor was appointed by the crown and an assembly was elected by the people. Connecticut and Rhode Island, as corporate colonies, had greater political autonomy. They were bound by the Navigation Acts and their laws were subject to review by the Privy Council in London, but they elected their governors and all other officials. The proprietors retained uneasy control of Carolina, which was formally divided into two colonies in 1713, when different governors were appointed for North and South Carolina. Likewise in Maryland and Pennsylvania, the Calvert and Penn families retained their land rights and political authority. In 1713, as in 1660, the English settlements in North America resembled a patchwork quilt, its diverse colors and textures representing corporate, proprietary, and royal colonies. However, these colonies were no longer religious outposts or baronial fantasies but parts of a thriving commercial empire.

The Imperial Slave Economy

During the seventeenth century, Europeans created a revolutionary agricultural system in the Western Hemisphere. Using land seized from native Americans and the labor of millions of enslaved people from Africa, they raised sugar, tobacco, and other valuable crops, which merchants then brought to markets in Europe. This transoceanic commerce, known as the South Atlantic system, changed the history of four continents. It sapped the human resources of Africa, set off a commercial revolution in Europe, and populated the Western Hemisphere with a score of racially mixed societies.

The South Atlantic System

Sugar from Brazil and the West Indies was the cornerstone of the South Atlantic system, an edifice of agricultural plantations and oceanic trade whose products also included tobacco, rice, and indigo from the North American mainland. Before 1500 Europeans had few sources of sweetness—primarily honey and fruit juices. The cultivation of sugar cane, and later the sugar beet, changed the diet of Europe and the world. Once people had tasted sweetness, they craved it. They added sugar to tea and coffee, pies and cakes, and ate it straight in the form of candy. (By 1900 sugar accounted for 20 percent of the calories consumed by humans throughout the world.)

Like other European nations, England sought to meet the demand for sugar by continually expanding its plantations. Beginning about 1650, English merchants developed Barbados as a sugar colony. They invested heavily in the Leeward Islands around 1700, and made Jamaica a major supplier during the eighteenth century.

Sugar production was complex and expensive. It required fertile land on which to grow the cane, slave labor to plant and cut it, and heavy equipment to process it into raw sugar and molasses. Since only wealthy merchants or landowners had the capital to outfit a plantation, a planter-merchant elite grew up in the sugar industry. At the height of its prosperity, Jamaica had 700 sugar plantations, worked by more than 105,000 African slaves. Successful planters earned from 8 to 10 percent annually on their investment, double the rate of return on government bonds. Such enrichment led the Scottish economist Adam Smith to declare in *The Wealth of Nations* (1776) that sugar was the most profitable crop in either Europe or America.

The South Atlantic system made England a wealthy

Sea Captains in Surinam

Flouting the Navigation Acts, New England merchants developed a flourishing trade with the Dutch colony of Surinam. This tavern scene, painted by Boston artist John Greenwood in the 1750s, pokes fun at the hard-drinking sea captains. (The Saint Louis Art Museum) nation, stimulating its economy in four ways. First, the direct profits of sugar production returned to England because most West Indian planters lived in England as "absentees." Second, the Navigation Acts, requiring that all staple crops from America be exported by way of England, artificially raised English exports; indeed, by 1750 the reexport of American and West Indian products accounted for half of all British exports. Third, the South Atlantic system made Britain the leading commercial and naval power in Europe. English and American shipyards built hundreds of vessels to transport slaves, machinery, food, and settlers to the Western Hemisphere. Commercial expansion also enhanced Britain's maritime expertise and provided a supply of experienced sailors, helping to make the Royal Navy the most powerful fleet in Europe. Finally, transatlantic commerce expanded Britain's domestic economy, creating thousands of jobs as men built the port facilities, warehouses, and dwellings of Liverpool, London, and Glasgow—the cities that became the centers of the trade in slaves, sugar, and tobacco. Other men and women worked as sugar or tobacco refiners, rum distillers, or manufacturers of textiles and iron products for the growing markets in America.

England no longer depended for its prosperity on the wool trade, which, by 1700, accounted for less than half of its exports. The South Atlantic system and the mercantilist policies of the Navigation Acts had made England a wealthy nation.

An African King
This striking bronze plaque from Benin, an important kingdom in West Central Africa, depicts a mounted king, his attendants, and (probably) his children. (c.1550–1680, The Metropolitan Museum of Art)

The Impact on Africa

Whatever the benefits for Europeans, the South Atlantic system was a tragedy for West Africa, and for certain parts of East Africa, such as Madagascar. Between 1450 and 1870, the transatlantic slave trade uprooted between 10 and 12 million Africans, draining the human resources of the continent and lowering the living standards of its people.

When the Portuguese began trading with West Africa in the 1430s, they encountered a world of cultural diversity. Africans spoke many different languages and practiced many different faiths, including Islam. Some Africans lived in strong, relatively centralized states, such as Benin and Mali. Others were members of tribal communities based primarily on kinship connections, like native American tribes. Clan elders enforced customary rules, allocated economic privileges, and decided questions of war and peace.

Slavery had existed on a small scale in West Africa from an early date, primarily as a domestic system of labor. Slaves were usually prisoners of war, debtors, or people sold into servitude by their rulers or priests. Although owned as property, these slaves often retained certain rights, including the right to marry, and their children were usually free. Only a small proportion were sold from one kingdom to another or carried overland to the Mediterranean region, mostly by Arab Muslim traders.

The demand for labor in Europe's New World plantations gradually transformed the scale and nature of African slavery. Between 1440 and 1550, Portuguese traders carried thousands of Africans to enslavement on sugar plantations in the Madeira and Canary islands. Then, between 1550 and 1700, Dutch and Spanish traders transported tens of thousands more across the Atlantic to plantations in Brazil and the Caribbean. Following England's triumph in the Anglo-Dutch wars, English and French merchants took over the trade in humans, developing African-run slave-catching systems that extended far into the interior. Between 1700 and 1810, they carried over 6 million Africans to toil and die in the Americas, primarily on sugar plantations in the West Indies.

This vast commerce in human lives brought great profits to Europeans and mostly suffering, economic

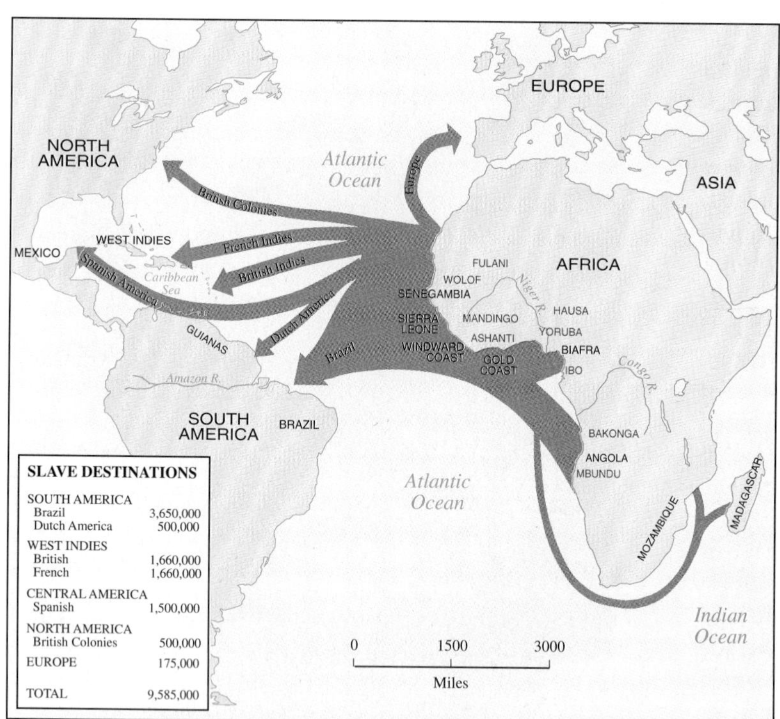

MAP 3.3

Africa and the Atlantic Slave Trade

Between 1520 and 1810 twelve million Africans were forcibly carried to the Western Hemisphere, and two million of them died en route. Most slaves labored in the sugar industry of Brazil and the Caribbean islands, where they perished quickly from overwork and disease. North America, which received the fewest Africans, had the only self-reproducing slave society.

and spiritual, to Africa. In the 1680s, the English Royal African Company sold male slaves in the West Indies for five or six times as much as it had paid for them. European planters reaped equally great profits. Before dying of disease or overwork, slaves produced sugar that sold for two to three times their purchase price. At the same time, the rum, tinware, or cloth that entered the African economy in exchange for slaves was worth only one-tenth as much as the goods those slaves produced. Thus, the growing wealth of Europe was directly related to the impoverishment of Africa.

The spiritual cost to Africa produced by the slave trade cannot be calculated. European demand for slaves made kidnapping common throughout much of West Africa, disrupting the lives of millions of families. It encouraged violence among the tribes for control of the slave trade, which in turn transformed the traditional political structure; loose tribal federations became powerful centralized slave-trading states. Class divisions also hardened, as people of noble birth sold those of lesser status into slavery. Slavery eroded the dignity of human life in Africa as well as on the plantations of the Western Hemisphere.

Virginia's Decision for Slavery

Africans had first arrived in Virginia in 1619, but they were not legally enslaved and their numbers remained small. English common law acknowledged various degrees of bondage, such as indentured servitude, but not the concept of *chattel slavery*—the ownership of one human being by another. If legalized slavery were to exist in the English colonies, the colonists themselves would have to create it.

The decision in favor of slavery was easy for some migrants. The English sugar planters in the West Indies—and those who migrated from there to South Carolina—simply imitated the labor system used by the Spanish, Portuguese, and Dutch and soon gave it legal form. In the tobacco colonies of Maryland and Virginia slavery developed more slowly. Three or four hundred Africans lived in the Chesapeake colonies in 1649, making up about 2 percent of the population; by 1670, the proportion of blacks had risen to 5 percent. Many of these Africans were treated more strictly than English indentured servants, particularly in the case of runaways. However, some of the first black workers eventually received their freedom, apparently as a result of having converted to Christianity. A few African Christian freemen even purchased slaves themselves or bought the labor contracts of white servants.

The success of these Africans suggests that initially religion may have been as important as race in determining social status. The English in the Chesapeake had always seen Africans as "different." In personal letters and official documents, whites sometimes described the difference in terms of skin color, bone structure, and language, but in a world dominated by passionate theological conflict, religion was the primary point of con-

AMERICAN VOICES

The Brutal "Middle Passage" *Olaudah Equiano*

Olaudah Equiano, also known as Gustavus Vasa, was sold into slavery in Africa by a conquering tribe. Shipped first to Barbados, then to Virginia, he eventually bought his freedom from his owner in 1766. Twenty years later he published a famous memoir of his experiences; in this excerpt he describes the horrors of his transatlantic passage.

The first object which saluted my eyes when I arrived on the coast was the sea, and a slave ship which was then riding at anchor, and waiting for its cargo. I now saw myself deprived of all chance of returning to my native country.

I was not long suffered to indulge my grief; I was soon put down under the decks, and there I received such a salutation in my nostrils as I had never experienced in my life: so that with the loathsomeness of the stench, and crying together, I became so sick and low that I was not able to eat, nor had I the least desire to taste any thing. I now wished for the last friend, death, to relieve me; but soon, to my grief, two of the white men offered me eatables; and, on my refusing to eat, one of them held me fast by the hands, and laid me across, I think the windlass, and tied my feet, while the other flogged me severely. I had never experienced any thing of this kind before: and, although not being used to the water, I naturally feared that element the first time I saw it, yet, nevertheless, if could I have got over the nettings, I would have jumped over the side, but I could not; and, besides, the crew used to watch us very closely who were not chained down to the decks, lest we should leap into the water: and I have seen some of these poor African prisoners most severely cut for attempting to do so, and hourly whipped for not eating.

Olaudah Equiano
(The Library Company of Philadelphia)

Source: The Interesting Narrative of the Life of Olaudah Equiano, or Gustavus Vasa, the African, Written By Himself (London, 1789).

trast. To the colonists, Africans were first and foremost pagans or Muslims. Thus by becoming a Christian and a planter, an enterprising African might aspire to near-equality with the English settlers.

Beginning in the 1660s, however, new laws gradually lowered the status of all Africans, regardless of religion. The reason for this is not clear. Perhaps the English elite grew more conscious of race as the number of Africans increased, or perhaps they were responding to the end of the tobacco boom by bringing blacks under firmer control along with white servants and poor farmers. In any event, new legislation in Virginia forbade Africans to own guns or to join the militia. In 1670 the House of Burgesses abridged the property rights of Africans, barring them—"tho baptized and enjoying their own Freedom"—from buying the labor contracts of white servants.

Being black was now becoming a permanent mark of inferiority. Legislation enacted between 1667 and 1671 specified that conversion to Christianity did not qualify Africans for eventual freedom; black workers were bound for life. In the two decades following Bacon's Rebellion of 1675–1676, planters imported thousands of Africans, primarily because it was now cheaper to buy blacks than to import white servants and also because slaves had few legal rights and might be more strictly disciplined. A law of 1692 prohibiting sexual intercourse between English and Africans sharply divided the two laboring groups. As a result of legal restrictions, black laborers found that their servitude was permanent and hereditary, binding their children as well as themselves. Finally, in 1705, a Virginia statute explicitly and formally defined virtually all resident Africans as slaves: "All servants imported or brought into this country by sea or land who were not Christians in their native country shall be accounted and be slaves." The English in the Chesapeake colonies had chosen to create a society based on slave labor.

The Economics of Slavery

At every step, in every respect, eighteenth-century slavery was a brutal experience for Africans. After being torn from their villages, they were marched in chains to coastal ports. From there they made the infamous "middle passage"—the perilous voyage to the New World on disease-ridden ships so overcrowded there was barely room to move. Some Africans jumped overboard, preferring to lose their lives rather than lose their liberty or endure more suffering. Others—no fewer than 750,000 during the eighteenth century alone—died from disease aboard ship. The survivors, headed mostly for Brazil or the West Indies, were in for a degrading life of backbreaking labor.

The Sugar Islands. Sugar was a killer crop. To plant and harvest the cane required intense labor under a subtropical sun, its tempo often set by the overseer's whip. Many planters were themselves little more than killers. With sugar prices high and the cost of slaves low, many European planters simply worked their slaves to death, and then imported more.

The waste of human life was staggering. Thousands of Africans died in epidemics of yellow fever, smallpox, and measles. Thousands more were literally killed by inadequate food, oppressive labor, and inhuman living conditions. The mortality rate was so high that although British sugar planters on Barbados imported about 85,000 Africans between 1708 and 1735, the black population of the island increased by only 4,000 (from 42,000 to 46,000).

Contributing to these devastating demographics was the fact that because West Indian planters purchased six men for every woman, most slaves could not marry. Those who did form unions had few children, since planters forced pregnant women to work in the fields right up to the birth and miscarriages were frequent. In the sugar colonies, the African population did not increase through natural reproduction until after slavery was abolished.

Two Views of the Middle Passage
As the slave trade boomed, ship designers packed in more and more cargo, treating enslaved Africans with no more respect than hogsheads of sugar or tobacco. By contrast, the watercolor, painted by a naval officer, captures their humanity and dignity. (left: National Maritime Museum, London)

The Chesapeake. In the mainland colonies, living conditions for slaves were less severe. Producing tobacco was less physically demanding than growing sugar and, because plantations in Maryland and Virginia were small and dispersed, epidemic diseases did not spread as easily. Moreover, since tobacco planting was only modestly profitable, planters could not constantly buy new slaves and therefore treated the ones they had less harshly. As a result, many slaves in the Chesapeake region lived relatively long lives.

Unlike the sugar planters in the islands, tobacco planters sought to increase their work force through reproduction, purchasing larger numbers of female slaves and giving Africans the opportunity to create families. Women made up about a third of the African population of Maryland before 1720, by which time the Chesapeake black population had begun to increase through reproduction. Female slaves born in America had children at an earlier age and at more frequent intervals than did slaves who had been born in Africa, a fact that prompted masters to encourage large families among their slaves. Thus an absentee owner instructed his plantation agent "to be kind and indulgent to the breeding wenches, and not to force them when with child upon any service or hardship that will be injurious to them." And, he added, "the children are to be well looked after."

Planters imported Africans again when tobacco prices rose after 1720, but by mid-century American-born slaves formed a majority of Chesapeake blacks. The character of the tobacco economy, with its relatively healthful plantations and its modest profit margins, permitted the emergence of a large African-American population.

South Carolina. In South Carolina, which was settled by land-hungry whites from Barbados in the 1680s, slaves lived under a more demanding regime. South Carolina grew slowly at first because it lacked a profitable export. English planters had cultivated rice as early as 1685, but it was African slaves who turned it into a major crop. Some Africans came from rice-growing cultures and knew how to plant, harvest, and process this nutritious grain. Equally important, as slaves they could be forced to work in the malaria-ridden swamps where the crop was grown. By 1730 Charleston merchants were shipping about 17 million pounds of rice a year to southern Europe, where it was in high demand; by 1775, rice exports reached 75 million pounds.

In South Carolina, as in the West Indies, epidemic diseases spread quickly on densely settled plantations, so the death rate was high and the rate of natural reproduction was low. In order to sustain production of their lucrative crop, white planters and merchants imported tens of thousands of African slaves. As early as the 1710s, blacks made up a majority of the population of South Carolina and about 80 percent of those living in the rice-growing lowlands, but most of them met an early death.

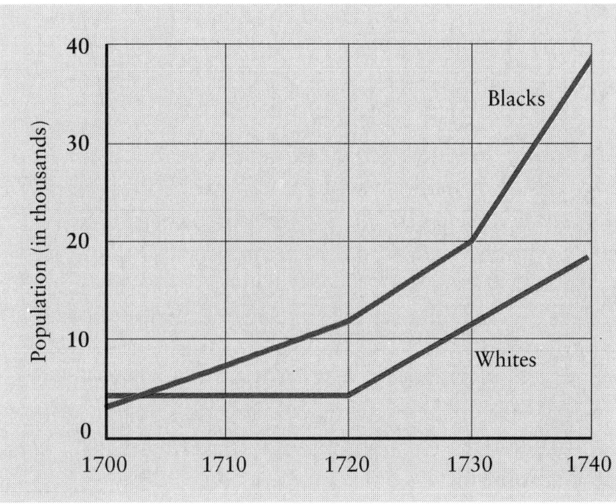

FIGURE 3.1

The Growth of Slavery in South Carolina

To grow more rice, white planters imported thousands of African slaves. By 1740 South Carolina had a black majority, prompting plantation owners to impose a rigorous system of discipline.

Throughout the southern colonies, as in South Carolina, the importance of staple crop exports caused slavery to become deeply embedded in the economic and social order. By 1770 slaves numbered about 500,000 and made up about a third of the southern population. Yet black slavery became an institution not because it was "necessary"—whites grew most of the tobacco and could have cultivated rice and sugar—but because it meant less work and greater profits for those who owned slaves. African labor not only supported a wealthy elite of planter-merchants—such as the Carters, Lees, Burwells, and Randolphs in the Chesapeake and the Bulls, Pinckneys, and Gadsdens in South Carolina—but it also raised the living standards of white southerners as well: 60 percent of farm families owned at least one slave by the 1770s. The economic opportunities afforded by the South Atlantic system prompted whites to adopt an exploitative slave-based society.

The Creation of an African-American Community

Slaves came from many regions of West Africa. Chesapeake planters imported tribal peoples from Senegambia, the Gold Coast, Nigeria, and Angola. South

NEW TECHNOLOGY *Rice: Riches and Wretchedness*

Technology always has cultural significance—for its use reveals the systems of value and power in a society. Occasionally, as in the case of the introduction of rice to America, the relation between culture and technology is particularly dramatic. Rice was not grown in England, and the first white settlers in South Carolina failed during the 1670s and 1680s to plant it successfully. As a planter later recalled, "The people being unacquainted with the manner of cultivating rice, many difficulties attended to the first planting and preparing it, as a vendable commodity."

Unlike Europeans, many West Africans had a thorough knowledge of rice. Along the Windward Coast of Africa, an English traveler noted, rice "forms the chief part of the African's sustenance." As he explained, "The rice fields or *lugars* are prepared during the dry season, and the seed sown in the tornado season, requiring about four or five months to bring it to perfection." Enslaved blacks brought these skills to South Carolina. As early as 1690 an Englishman named John Steward was actively promoting rice production, both as a potential export and as a cheap food for his slaves. For their part, Africans welcomed the cultivation of a familiar food and their knowledge was crucial to its success.

English settlers had been unable to master not only the planting and harvesting of rice but its hulling. At first they tried to come up with a machine—a "rice mill" to separate the tough husk of the rice seed from the nutritious grain inside. Thus, in 1691 the government awarded Peter Jacob Guerard a two-year patent on a "Pendulum Engine, which doeth much better, and in lesser time and labour, huske rice." Machines did not prove equal to the task, and English planters turned to African technology. In 1700, a royal official informed the English Board of Trade that the settlers had "found out the true way of raising and husking rice," by having slave women use traditional mortar and pestle methods to process it. The women placed the grain in large wooden mortars hollowed from the trunks of pine or cypress trees, and then pounded it with long wooden pestles, quickly removing the husks and whitening the grains. Their labor was prodigious. By the 1770s slaves were processing 75 million tons of rice for export and millions more for their own consumption.

Enslaved women use African technology to hull rice in South Carolina

African labor and technology brought both wealth and wretchedness to South Carolina. The planter-merchant aristocracy who controlled the rice industry became immensely wealthy; for example, nine of the ten richest Americans who died in 1770 came from South Carolina and had grown rich on rice. The tens of thousands of enslaved Africans who labored in the rice swamps and plantations lived hard and difficult lives; many died of disease and, until the late eighteenth century, those slaves who survived had little to show—in material comforts or family life—for their years of labor. Although the technology of rice production was not inherently elitist, its use in America helped to create a slave-based plantation society with immense racial and economic divisions.

Carolina slaveowners preferred Angolan laborers, getting more than 30 percent of their work force from that region. In no colony, however, did any African tribe or language group become dominant, primarily because white planters consciously aimed for cultural diversity. "The safety of the Plantations," declared a widely read English pamphlet, "depends upon having Negroes from all parts of *Guiny*, who do not understand each other's languages and Customs and cannot agree to Rebel."

Slaves themselves regarded each other not as "Africans" but as members of specific tribes and language groups. Gradually, however, slaves found it in their interests to transcend their tribal identities. In the lowlands of South Carolina, populated largely by African-born blacks, slaves created a new language, the Gullah dialect, which incorporated English and African words within an African grammatical structure and consequently was understood by people from a wide variety of tribes. In the Chesapeake, where there were more American-born blacks and the slave population was less concentrated, many Africans gave up their native tongues for English. "All the blacks spoke very good English," a European visitor to Virginia in the mid-eighteenth century noted with surprise.

The acquisition of a common language, whether Gullah or English, was a prerequisite for the creation of an African-American community. The growth of stable families was another. In South Carolina a high death rate prevented this, but between 1725 and 1750 the more favorable conditions of their existence allowed Chesapeake blacks to create strong nuclear-family bonds and extended kin relationships. This first African-American generation gradually developed a culture of its own—passing on family names, traditions, and knowledge to the next generation.

These African-Americans were the founders of a new society. Aspects of their African heritage could be seen in wood carvings, in the giant wooden mortars and pestles they used for hulling rice, and in the design of their shacks, which often had rooms arranged from front-to-back in a distinctive "I" pattern (and not side-by-side, as was common in English houses). Many continued to hold traditional religious beliefs, observing Muslim religious practices or relying on the spiritual powers of conjurers. Others adopted the Protestant Christian faith, reshaping doctrines, ethics, and rituals to fit their own needs. African musical rhythms persisted and were taken up by white society. Virginians

African Culture in South Carolina

The dance and the musical instruments are of Yoruba origin, the contribution of Africans from the Niger River-Gold Coast region (the homeland of the Yoruba), an area that accounted for one-sixth of the slaves imported into South Carolina. (*The Old Plantation,* late-eighteenth century, Abby Aldrich Rockefeller Folk Art Center)

African-American Identity
Like other peoples who came to the New World, Africans preserved traditional forms in their art and architecture. This earthenware face vessel, made in South Carolina about 1860, shows the persistence of African motifs. (Augusta-Richmond Art Museum)

have "what I call everlasting jigs," reported Nicholas Creswell, an Englishman. "A Couple gets up and begins to dance a jig (to some Negro tune)."

Yet slavery limited African-American creativity by limiting their opportunities for education and self-expression. Most blacks worked as farm laborers and accumulated few material goods. "We entered the huts of the Blacks," commented a well-traveled European who visited Virginia in the late eighteenth-century:

> They are more miserable than the most miserable of the cottages of our peasants. The husband and wife sleep on a mean pallet, the children on the ground; a very bad fireplace, some utensils for cooking, but in the middle of this poverty some cups and a teapot. . . . They work all week, not having a single day for themselves except for holidays.

He concluded that, without question, "the condition of our peasants is infinitely happier."

The comparison between slaves and peasants was apt. Both American slaves and European peasants were peoples who, because of their poverty and dependent position, could express their identity only within a limited sphere. They bequeathed to posterity not great works of art or literature but distinctive cultures based on language, family, community, and religion. Moreover, African-American society was new, still in the process of formation. The parents or grandparents of the first African-Americans had come to the English colonies in chains and as strangers to one another. Yet, unlike their fellow Africans in the West Indies, the slaves on the mainland not only survived but developed family networks, a common language, and a culture of their own.

The power of that culture is conveyed by a story told by a traveler in the southern backcountry. He came upon an African-American who had been taken prisoner by Indians. The Indians had adopted him into their tribe and given him "a wife, a mother, and plenty of land to cultivate if he chose it, and the liberty of doing everything but making his escape." But the black man rejected this offer preferring "to render himself up a voluntary slave to his former master, that he might there once more embrace those friends and relatives from whom he had been so long separated." To this African-American, his family and cultural identity were worth more to him than greater freedom in an alien Indian society.

Oppression and Resistance

To return to slavery was an act of great courage: slaveowners were not a forgiving group. They came from a culture in which the poor were systematically oppressed, religious rebellions ended in bloodshed, and minor crimes were punishable by death. Masters did not scruple to impose harsh discipline even on white indentured servants, whipping them without mercy or doubling their time of service for running away, and when race entered into it, moral restraints vanished. In the West Indies English planters routinely branded troublesome slaves with hot irons. Chesapeake planters resorted to castration, nose slitting, and the amputation of fingers, toes, and ears to keep their slaves in submission. The worst aspects of human nature found ample expression in a slave-based society.

White violence was related to the size and density of the slave population. On the lowland plantations of South Carolina a few whites generally had charge of between twenty-five and one hundred slaves, and they maintained their authority by exerting strict control. Black workers were forbidden to leave the plantation without special passes and night watches and rural patrols enforced these regulations. Slaves who disobeyed, refused to work, or ran away were brutally punished. Even in the Chesapeake, where slaves were a minority of the population, planters often resorted to the whip.

Whites who grew up in this society were conditioned to use terror to maintain their superiority. No one knew this better than Thomas Jefferson, who witnessed it personally on his father's plantation. Each generation of whites, he noted, was "nursed, educated, and daily exercised in tyranny," for the relationship "between master and slave is a perpetual exercise of the most unremitting despotism on the one part, and degrading submission on the other. Our children see this and learn to imitate it."

Slaves dealt with their plight in a variety of ways. Some cooperated with their masters, agreeing to extra work in return for better food or clothes. Others resisted by working slowly or carelessly, or by stealing from their masters. Still others attacked their owners or overseers, taking a small measure of revenge though it was punishable by mutilation or death.

A successful rebellion was nearly impossible on the mainland, because whites were both numerous and armed. Full-fledged slave revolts occurred mostly on densely settled sugar plantations—and then only in places, such as Jamaica, where nearby mountains offered a secure refuge. But some mainland slaves, especially newly arrived Africans, did try to escape to the frontier, where they often married into Indian tribes. Others, especially those who were fluent in English, fled to towns, where they tried to pass as free blacks.

The Stono Rebellion. The first major slave revolt in American history took place in the late 1730s when the governor of Spanish Florida promised freedom and land to any black in South Carolina who fled to Florida. In November 1738 it was reported that sixty-nine slaves had escaped to St. Augustine. The following February, rumors circulated "that a Conspiracy was formed by Negroes in Carolina to rise and make their way out of the province." When war between England and Spain broke out later that year, the conspirators acted. Banding together near the Stono River, seventy-five slaves killed a number of whites, stole guns and ammunition, and marched south toward Florida "with Colours displayed and two Drums beating." Unrest swept the countryside, but the white militia killed many of the Stono rebels and dispersed the rest before they reached Florida, preventing a general uprising.

The Stono rebellion frightened whites throughout the mainland. For a decade afterward South Carolina planters bought fewer new Africans so as to keep the slave population at a manageable level, and slaveholders everywhere acted vigorously to quell discontent. Following several unexplained fires and burglaries in New York City in 1741, authorities alleged a plot among slaves, who formed almost 20 percent of the population. After a judicial inquisition, they hanged or burned to death twenty blacks and four whites—alleged accomplices in the conspiracy—and transported eighty slaves to the West Indies. Such repressive measures served as a warning to the slaves, a reminder of the price of active resistance.

America in the Empire, 1690–1750

For most white Americans, the South Atlantic system offered no cause for complaint. It made possible the genteel life of the planter aristocracy in the South, provided markets for farmers in the North, and stimulated the growth of northern seaports and merchant communities. The British government, pleased with its prosperous trade in staple crops, ruled its colonies with a gentle hand. This policy of "salutary neglect" gave the colonists a significant degree of self-government.

The Southern Social Order

Chesapeake society changed significantly after 1700. As settlement moved inland, away from swampy lowlands, diseases took fewer lives, so people lived long enough to form stable families and communities. Men reassumed their traditional role within the family. By 1750, most Chesapeake husbands who wrote wills had reverted to naming their male kin rather than their wives as executors of their estates and as the legal guardians of their children. Widows' estates were once again restricted to the customary one-third share.

The Chesapeake Aristocracy. The reappearance of patriarchy within the family mirrored larger social developments. After Bacon's rebellion, the planter elite gradually consolidated its authority and created a traditional rural social order, with a few gentry families on the top, a small yeoman class, and an army of dependent laborers. Wealthy planters bought thousands of slaves and put them to work on a variety of tasks. Blacks grew their masters' food as well as their export tobacco; they built houses, wagons, and tobacco casks; and they made shoes, clothes, and other necessities. This increased self-sufficiency helped wealthy planters to weather the depressed tobacco market. Small-scale planters fared less well between 1680 and 1720. Their income declined and they fell deeper into debt to their creditors among the elite.

The Virginia gentry wanted to keep middling and poor whites on their side in case of a black revolt and went after their political support by reducing their taxes. Before Bacon's rebellion, the annual poll tax paid by every free man amounted to 45 pounds of tobacco.

By 1700, the House of Burgesses had reduced the tax to 11 pounds a year, and between 1701 and 1750, to only 5 pounds a year. As one royal governor, Alexander Spotswood, observed, the Burgesses have "declared their resolution to raise no Tax upon the people, let the occasion be what it may."

By such means, the eighteenth-century Chesapeake gentry created a political culture that united, rather than divided, the white population. When Alexander Spotswood tried to increase the amount of land a man had to own in order to vote, leading property owners strongly opposed him. The gentry curried the favor of voters at election time, bribing them with rum, food, and money and, once in office, they enacted legislation that favored the small-scale farmers. In return, yeomen planters regularly returned their wealthy neighbors to political office and deferred to their authority. By creating solidarity among whites, this political compromise prevented a black uprising; by enhancing the power of the planter elite, it also inhibited the expansion of imperial control.

One important factor facilitating the compromise was the common culture shared by most Chesapeake whites. The gentry was still a boisterous, aggressive class, and poor and wealthy planters enjoyed many of the same amusements, from drinking and gambling on horse races and cockfights to sharing tales of their manly prowess. As time passed, however, Chesapeake planters took on the trappings of wealth, modeling themselves after the English aristocracy. Between 1720 and 1750, they replaced their modest wooden houses with mansions of brick and mortar. Increasingly planters—and their wives—sought elegance and refinement, avidly reading English newspapers and pamphlets, importing English clothes, and dining in the English fashion, taking an elaborate afternoon tea. They hired English tutors to teach etiquette to their daughters and sent their sons to London to be educated as gentlemen. Hundreds of young men from the Chesapeake and the Carolinas passed a few years at the Inns of Court, the training ground for English lawyers. Most of them returned to America and married a young lady (preferably a charming and rich one), and took up the life of a slaveowning planter, managing a plantation and participating in politics.

Unlike the absentee sugar producers of the West Indies, the planter-merchants of the southern mainland were committed to life in America. They used the profits from the South Atlantic system to form a stable ruling class, increasingly well-educated and refined.

Fox Hunting in Virginia

Virginians had always been hunters but after 1750 they emulated the English landed classes by "riding to the hounds" in elaborate dress. Only the spectators were different, with enslaved African-Americans rather than landless English cotters watching their masters at play. (*The End of the Hunt*, c.1800, National Gallery of Art)

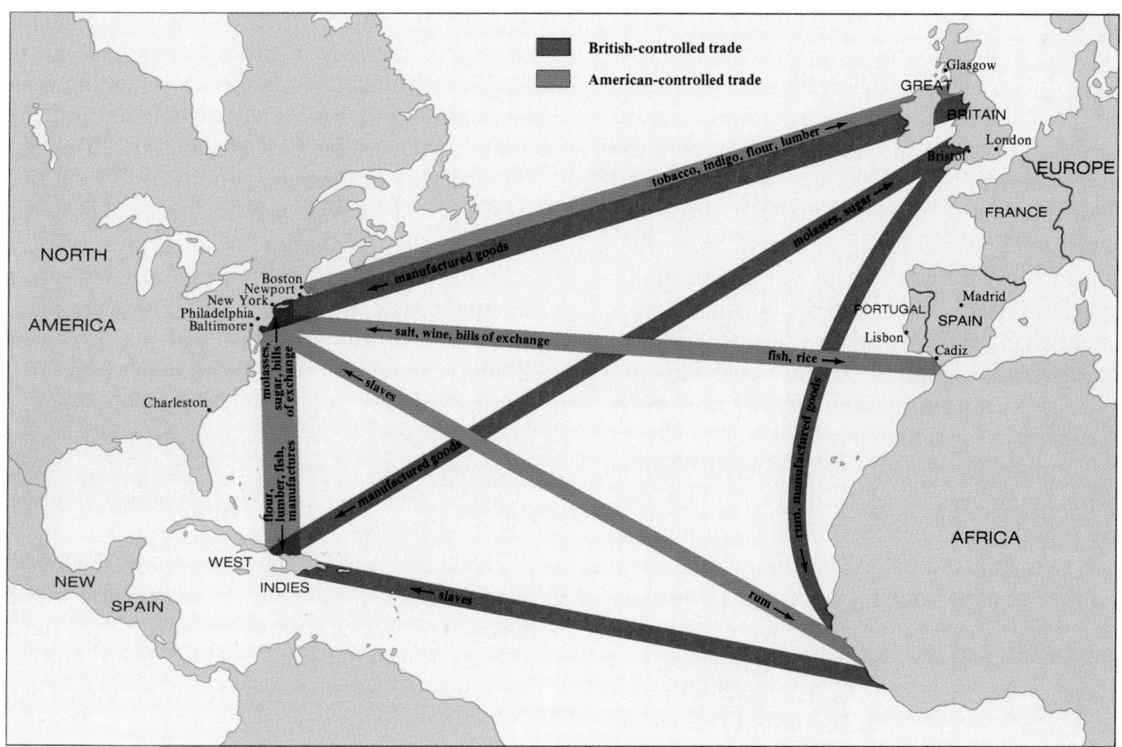

MAP 3.4

The Rise of the American Merchant

In accord with mercantilist doctrine, British merchants controlled most of the transatlantic trade in manufactures, sugar, tobacco, and slaves. However, merchants in Boston, New York, and Philadelphia seized control of the West Indian trade, while Newport traders imported slaves from Africa and Charleston merchants carried rice to southern Europe.

The Northern Urban Economy

The West Indies Trade. The South Atlantic system also stimulated the northern rural economy. The plantations of the sugar islands provided a ready market for American bread, lumber, fish, and meat. As a West Indian explained as early as 1647, planters in the islands "had rather buy food at very dear rates than produce it by labour, so infinite is the profit of sugar works." By 1700, the economic systems of the West Indies and New England were tightly interwoven. In "An Essay on the Trade of New England" (1714), Thomas Bannister noted that although the region exported no staple crops to Europe, its farmers had a decent standard of living because they sent "Pork, Beef, [barrel] Staves, bread, butter and Flour" to the sugar islands. After 1720, farmers and merchants in New York, New Jersey, and Pennsylvania entered this trade, shipping wheat, corn, and bread to the West Indies.

This commerce tied the empire together economically. In return for sugar exports, West Indian planters received bills of exchange—basically credit slips—from London merchant houses. The planters then used these bills to pay mainland merchants for the agricultural goods produced by northern farmers, and the merchants, in turn, exchanged them for British manufactures, thus completing the cycle.

The West Indian trade created the first American merchant fortunes and the first major urban industries. New England merchants built factories in Boston, Newport, and Providence to process raw sugar, imported from the islands, into refined sugar, which previously had been imported from England. They also invested in distilleries to turn West Indian molasses into rum for domestic and foreign consumption. By the 1740s, Boston distillers exported more than half a million gallons of rum annually.

Seaboard Cities. As a result of this mercantile activity, the American port cities grew rapidly. By the middle of the eighteenth century, Newport, Rhode Island, and Charles Town, South Carolina, had nearly 10,000 residents apiece, Boston had 15,000 and New York had almost 18,000. The largest colonial city, Philadelphia, whose population would reach 30,000 by 1776, had as many inhabitants as most European provincial centers.

Trade was the lifeblood of these cities. Merchants in Boston and Philadelphia handled most of the mainland's imports from Britain and managed exports to the West Indies; along with New York, they also dominated the short-haul commerce among American cities and the trade with small coastal towns and river ports. Baltimore was transformed from a sleepy village to a major port within a few decades thanks to the bustling export trade in wheat that developed after 1740. Charleston, the only major southern seaport, shipped deerskins, indigo, and rice to European markets. In addition, New England merchants, operating out of Boston, Salem, Marblehead, and smaller ports, built up a major fishing industry, providing mackerel and cod to feed the slaves of the sugar islands and to export to southern Europe. By 1750, the New England fishing fleet numbered more than 600 ships and provided employment for over 4,000 men.

Coastal towns were centers of the shipbuilding and lumber industries. By the 1740s, seventy sawmills dotted the Piscataqua River in New Hampshire, providing low-cost wood for homes, warehouses, and especially for shipbuilding. Artisans in small coastal villages built the boats of the New England fishing fleet, while scores of shipwrights turned out ocean-going vessels in yards near the major port cities. Hundreds of other artisans made the ropes, sails, and metal fittings for the new fleet. Shipyards in Boston and Philadelphia launched about 15,000 tons of freighters annually, competing so successfully with English builders that colonial-built ships eventually made up about a third of the British merchant fleet.

Interior Towns. The impact of the South Atlantic system extended far into the interior of North America, facilitated by an intricate transportation network that connected the seaport cities to the agricultural hinterland. For instance, a small fleet of trading vessels sailed back and forth between Philadelphia and the villages along the Delaware Bay and its tributaries, exchanging their cargoes of European goods for barrels of flour and wheat. Land-based transport in this region, meanwhile, was handled by hundreds of professional teamsters, who moved the cargo from inland farms to river ports or the coast. By the 1750s, for example, 370,000 bushels of wheat and corn and the 16,000 barrels of flour, representing ten thousand wagon trips, were being exported yearly from the eastern shore of Maryland. To accommodate this traffic, entrepreneurs and artisans set up taverns, livery stables, and wheel repair shops in small towns along the wagon roads, providing additional jobs.

The towns in the interior became the locus of small-scale artisan production, which often depended on trade. Coopers in scores of towns turned out hundreds of barrels to hold flour, pickled meat, and other local food products. Prosperous towns attracted a wide variety of artisans so that, for example, Lancaster, Pennsylvania, had more than two hundred German and English artisans, who practiced many crafts and played a central role in the town's economic and political life. The South Atlantic system, then, provided not only markets for farmers, by far the largest group of northern residents, but also opportunities for merchants, artisans, and workers in country towns and seaport cities.

Seaport Society

American Merchants. A small group of wealthy merchants stood at the top of society in the seaport cities. The Apthorp, Bowdoin, Faneuil, and Oliver families in

A View of Philadelphia

By 1750 Penn's city on the Delaware River was the largest and wealthiest seaport in North America, the home of prosperous Anglican and Quaker merchants, English, German, and Scots-Irish artisans, and thousands of African-American laborers. (*Southeast Prospect of the City of Philadelphia,* 1720, Peter Cooper, The Library Company of Philadelphia)

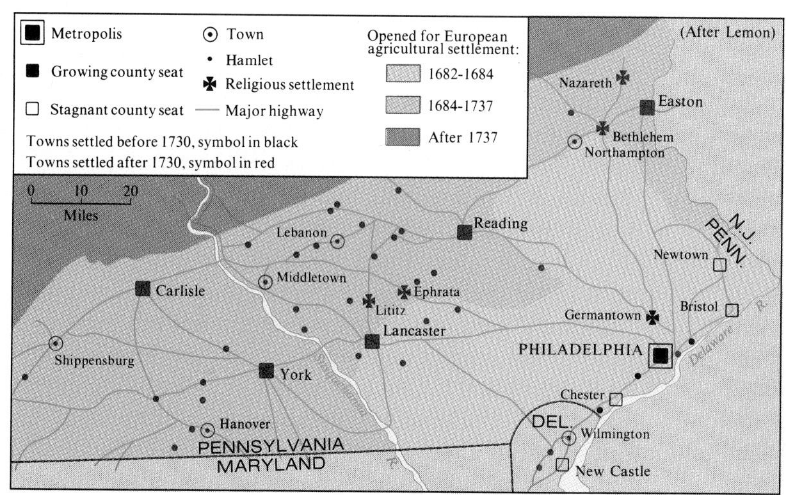

MAP 3.5

Trade and Urban Growth in Pennsylvania, 1700–1750

As settlers moved west, villages of artisans and shopkeepers appeared. Some villages grew into county seats and trading centers, crucial parts of a far-flung system of commerce that sent agricultural goods to the West Indies and Europe in return for sugar products and manufactures.

Boston; the Beekmans, Crugers, Waltons, and Roosevelts in New York; the Norris and Pemberton clans in Philadelphia were among the first great American entrepreneurs, whose ventures in the West Indian and European trades reaped handsome profits. By the mid-eighteenth century, about 150 merchants controlled 70 percent of Philadelphia's trade. Their taxable assets averaged £3,000, a huge sum at the time.

Like the Chesapeake gentry, wealthy northern merchants imitated the British upper classes in their cultural tastes and increasingly in the design of their housing. Guided by imported design books from England, merchants built mansions in the new Georgian architectural style—grand houses that, with their large windows symmetrically flanking elaborate columned porticos, conveyed the ordered lives and conservative social values of the merchant class and offered material evidence of their wealth and status.

Artisans. Artisans and their families constituted nearly half the population of the seaport cities and provided the residents with food, housing, and clothing. Their ranks included butchers, seamstresses, shoemakers, weavers, bakers, carpenters, masons, and dozens of other specialists. Well-to-do artisans owned their own tools, shops, and houses, and had taxable assets averaging about £300, a tenth that of the merchants. Most craft workers were not well-to-do, however. A tailor was lucky to accumulate £30 worth of property in his lifetime, a mere 1 percent of the wealth of the average merchant.

Artisans had their own culture, usually centered on their particular craft and its traditions. They tended to socialize among themselves and sometimes formed mutual-help societies that assisted members in times of need. Wives and husbands often worked as a team, and over time taught the "mysteries of the craft" to their children. The goal of most artisans was a "competency"—sufficient income to maintain the family in modest comfort and dignity.

Laborers and Slaves. Laboring men and women formed the lower ranks of the urban social order. There were no motor-driven cranes to transfer goods from ocean-going ships to warehouses and coastal freighters, so hundreds of men worked as stevedores on the docks of Boston, Philadelphia, and New York, unloading tons of manufactured goods or molasses from inbound ships and then loading them up with barrels of wheat, fish, or rice for export. Hundreds of other men and women worked for wages in a variety of semiskilled jobs: helping artisans, building roads, caring for horses, washing clothes, and cleaning houses.

Black slaves and white indentured servants performed many of these menial yet demanding jobs. In Philadelphia, slaves and indentured German migrants made up about 20 percent of the city's residents and held nearly half the laboring jobs. The situation was much the same around 1750 in Boston, where African-Americans made up about 10 percent of the population and in New York City, where they numbered 20 percent of the residents. Whether enslaved, indentured, or merely poor, these laborers and their families were indispensable to the economy of every port city.

Altogether day laborers, merchant seamen, and other wage-earners made up 30 percent of the workforce in the seaport cities but owned little property. Most lived in small rented houses or tenements in the back alleys of the crowded waterfront districts. Many scraped by on household budgets that left no margin for

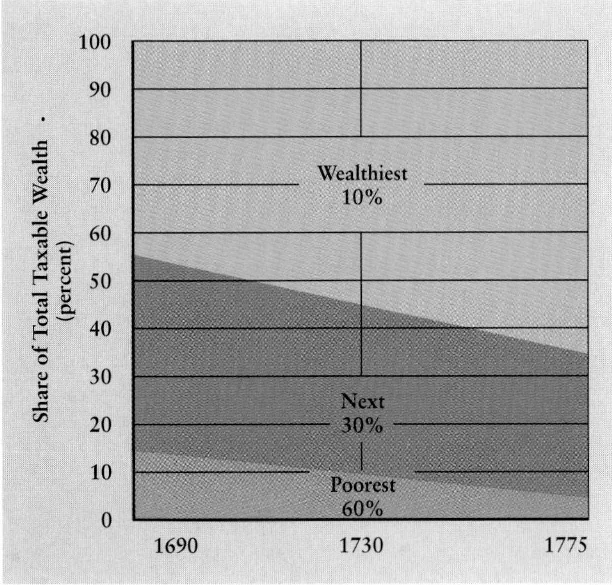

FIGURE 3.2

Wealth Inequality in the Northern Cities

As commerce expanded, the wealth of merchants grew much faster than that of artisans and laborers. By the 1770s the poorest 60 percent of the taxable inhabitants of Boston, New York, and Philadelphia owned less than 5 percent of the taxable wealth, while the top 10 percent—the merchant elite and their allies—controlled 65 percent.

sickness, accidents, or unemployment. To make ends meet, women took in washing and sewing, and children were sent out to work as soon as they were able. In good economic times, such personal sacrifices brought economic security or, for many sailors and laborers, enough money to drink cheap New England rum in waterfront taverns, often in the company of adventurous or poor women, who worked as prostitutes. But periods of depressed trade meant irregular work, hunger, dependence on the charity handed out by the town-appointed overseers of the poor, and—for the most desperate—a turn to a life of petty thievery.

Periods of stagnant commerce affected all townspeople, the rich as well as the poor. Even the most astute merchants faced financial hardship and possible bankruptcy when prices plunged in the transatlantic marketplace. Commerce brought wealth to residents of the seacoast cities, but also uncertainty. American cities and towns had become part of a complex and unpredictable system of worldwide trade.

The Rise of the Assembly

Before 1689, political affairs in most colonies were dominated by authoritarian elites. The duke of York ran New York by fiat; Puritan magistrates suppressed dissent in New England; and Governor Berkeley and his Green Spring faction ruled Virginia with an iron hand. The oligarchs denounced critics of their policies as traitors and condemned opposition groups as illegitimate "factions." Such arrogance reflected a widespread belief that power came from above, not below. In the words of Robert Filmer, a royalist political philosopher in England, "Authority should Descend from *Kings* and *Fathers* to *Sons* and *Servants*."

As the American settlements became mature provinces, they began to develop a more representative system of politics. The seeds of this change were planted by the Glorious Revolution in England, when the political faction known as the *Whigs* led the fight for a constitutionally limited monarchy rather than an absolute one. Whigs did not believe in democracy, but they did believe ordinary property owners (the "commons") should have political power, especially with regard to the levying of taxes. Their ideal was a "mixed government," one that divided power among the three social orders: the monarchy, the aristocracy, and the commons. In 1689, Whig politicians forced William and Mary to accept a Bill of Rights; subsequently, they strengthened the powers of Parliament—especially of the House of Commons—at the expense of the Crown.

Following the example of the English Whigs, the leaders of the American representative assemblies increased the power of their assemblies by instituting procedures similar to those of the House of Commons. They established the same committees as the Commons, such as those on Rights and Privileges, safeguarded the assemblies' authority to levy taxes, and demanded a position of constitutional equality with the royal or proprietary governor. Gradually, colonial leaders won control of patronage and of the budget, angering imperial bureaucrats and absentee proprietors. "The people in power in America," complained proprietor William Penn during a struggle with the Pennsylvania Assembly, "think nothing taller than themselves but the Trees."

The changing character of American politics and society helped the assemblies to increase their power. After 1700, most property-owning white adult men had the right to vote in regular elections. In some colonies—Virginia and South Carolina, for example—only men of considerable wealth and status stood for election, but the political competition in most of the northern colonies was much more open. Increasingly ordinary men—and ethnic and religious groups—elected repre-

The Rise of an American Gentry

George Wyllys (1710-1796) came from a family of political leaders in Connecticut, and served as Secretary of the colony from 1730 to 1796. The emergence of such well-established, educated, and capable men greatly enhanced the power of the American representative assemblies. (Joseph Steward, c.1770, The Connecticut Historical Society)

sentatives to office who were conscious of their views and interests.

Yet the political system was far from democratic. In the Chesapeake colonies, for example, with the decline in the white death rates after 1700, influential families were able to transmit wealth and political influence along to succeeding generations and thus create colony-wide political networks. By the 1750s seven members of the Lee family, representing five counties, sat in the Virginia House of Burgesses and—along with members of other powerful Virginia families such as the Byrds, Randolphs, and Carters—dominated its major committees.

Similar family dynasties and alliances appeared in the northern colonies. In New England, the children and grandchildren of the original Puritans had intermarried and formed a core of political leaders. "Go into every village in New England," John Adams said in 1765, "and you will find that the office of justice of the peace, and even the place of representative, have generally descended from generation to generation, in three or four families at most." Marriage ties created powerful political networks. A European traveler noted that the political leaders in New Brunswick, New Jersey, were "General White, Colonel Bayard, and Judge Patterson—all these families are related and live in close contact."

Political authority came increasingly to reside in these local leaders, and in the assemblies in which they sat. Most assemblymen had first been elected to office as town selectmen, county justices of the peace, or officers in the militia. They had deep roots in the community and could count on local support in the face of opposition from governors or royal bureaucrats. These self-confident American politicians used the "power of the purse"—their control of taxation and revenue—to keep governors from implementing unpopular imperial policies. In Massachusetts during the 1720s, for example, the assembly refused repeatedly to obey the king's instructions to provide a permanent salary for the royal governor and—adding insult to injury—refused to pay even a yearly stipend to Governor Shute as long as he continued to press the issue.

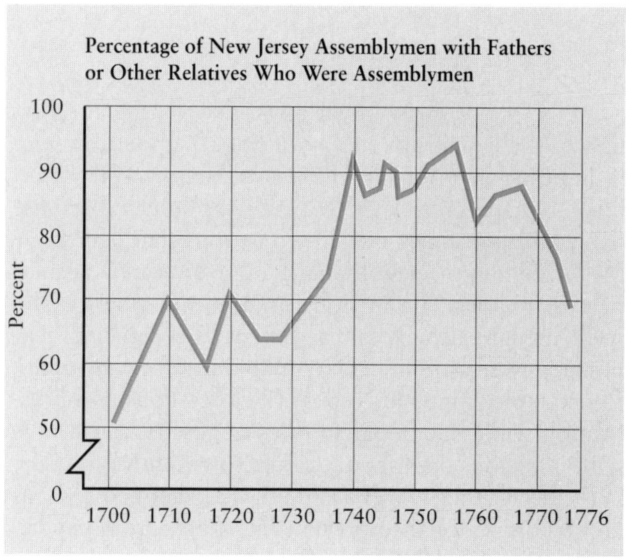

FIGURE 3.3

Family Connections and Political Power

By the 1750s nearly every member of the New Jersey assembly came from a family with a history of political leadership, clear testimony to the emergence of an experienced governing elite in the colonies.

AMERICAN VOICES

The Waning of British Authority *Governor George Clinton*

Authority has to be exercised firmly to command respect. Lax administration in London and weak officials in America opened the way for colonial assemblies to defy imperial policy. In a letter to the Lords of Trade written in 1742, Governor Clinton confesses his inability to control the provincial New York Assembly.

My Lords,

I have in my former letters inform'd Your Lordships what Incroachments the Assemblys of this province have from time to time made on His Majesty's Prerogative & Authority in this Province in drawing an absolute dependence of all the Officers upon them for their Saleries & Reward of their services, & by their taking in effect the Nomination to all Officers . . . .

1stly, That the Assembly refuse to admit of any amendment to any money bill, in any part of the Bill; so that the Bill must pass as it comes from the Assembly, or all the Supplies granted for the support of Government, & the most urgent services must be lost.

2ndly, It appears that they take the Payment of the [military] Forces, passing of Muster Rolls into their own hands by naming the Commissaries for those purposes in the Act.

3rdly, They by granting the Saleries to the Officers personally by name & not to the Officer for the time being, intimate that if any person be appointed to any Office his Salery must depend upon their approbation of the Appointment . . . .

I must now refer it to Your Lordships' consideration whether it be not high time to put a stop to these usurpations of the Assembly on His Majesty's Authority in this Province and for that purpose may it not be proper that His Majesty signify his Disallowance of the Act at least for the payment of Saleries.

Source: E.B. O'Callaghan, ed., *Documents Relative to the Colonial History of the State of New York,* (Albany, 1860–).

Like Shute, most royal governors during the first half of the eighteenth century lacked the political clout to impose controversial policies on the powerful assemblies. Nor did they have the military force to impose them on the people. The crowd actions that overthrew the Dominion of New England in 1689 were a regular part of political life in both Britain and America and were used to achieve aims that were social and economic as well as political. To uphold community values, for example, a mob in New York closed houses of prostitution while one in Salem, Massachusetts, ran people with infectious diseases out of the town. In Boston during Queen Anne's War (1702–1713), hungry artisans and laborers rioted to prevent merchants from exporting much-needed grain. A generation later in New Jersey, farmers closed down the law courts to prevent proprietary claimants from seizing disputed lands. In New England, lumbermen attacked Surveyors of the Woods when those royal officials tried to prevent them from cutting certain tall pine trees reserved as masts for the British navy.

Crowds were often outmaneuvered by astute officials, who waited for their passion to subside, or they were outlasted by entrepreneurs or land speculators, who had money and often law on their side. But mobs were forces to be reckoned with, both because of their power and their claim to moral and political legitimacy. The "violence" of New Jersey land rioters had been justified, one participant explained, since the people had been "wronged and oppressed." When officials in Boston, seeking to favor established retailers over country hawkers, attempted to force residents to buy farm produce only at a designated public market, a crowd destroyed the building and defied the authorities to arrest them. "If you touch One you shall touch All," an anonymous letter warned Sheriff Edward Winslow, "and we will show you a Hundred Men where you can show one."

The letter put it in a nutshell. The expression of popular opinion—in the give-and-take of New England town meetings, in the rum-warmed conviviality of Virginia electioneering, in the political contests between ambitious men in the Middle Colonies, and, ultimately, in the actions of rebellious mobs—gradually undermined the old authoritarian system. In its place stood political institutions—local governments and provincial assemblies—that were broadly responsive to popular pressure and increasingly immune from British control.

Salutary Neglect

Contributing significantly, though unwittingly, to the rise of American self-government were the policies pursued by British politicians and bureaucrats. During the reigns of George I (1714–1727) and George II (1727–1760), royal bureaucrats relaxed their supervision of internal colonial affairs, focusing instead on the military defense of the colonies and the expansion of their trade. Two generations later, the eminent British political philosopher Edmund Burke would praise this strategy of mild rule as one of "salutary neglect," a mercantilist strategy Burke believed had contributed to the colonies' wealth and population growth.

Sir Robert Walpole. "Salutary neglect" was in part a by-product of the political system developed by Sir Robert Walpole. Walpole was the leader of the Whig party and served as the king's chief adviser and leader of the House of Commons between 1720 and 1742. By strategically dispensing appointments, pensions, and gifts, Walpole won parliamentary support for the policies of the king's ministers, thereby transforming the once-antagonistic relationship between king and Parliament into one of harmonious cooperation. In effect, he governed in the monarch's name but with Parliament's consent.

Walpole's political tactics offended some members of Parliament, who condemned him for using patronage and bribery to create a *Court party*, a group of politicians closely tied to the royal government. Articulating arguments that would be picked up by many Americans, Walpole's critics argued that such corruption undermined the independence of the legislative body. They also pointed to his creation of a large national debt as the cause of high taxes and warned that a bloated royal bureaucracy and a standing army threatened the liberties of the people.

Walpole's chief opponents, who called themselves the Real Whigs, maintained that by increasing the power of the Crown, the prime minister had betrayed the constitutional monarchy established by the Whigs' Glorious Revolution of 1688. Other critics, landed gentlemen with *Tory* (royalist) principles, likewise opposed Walpole's use of patronage and his close ties with merchants and financial institutions such as the Bank of England. They constituted a *Country party*—one that celebrated the independence of the individual members of Parliament. As country gentlemen, they feared the power wielded by the Court party in London and the expanding royal bureaucracy. Indeed, Walpole's support for mercantilist trade policies, and the wealthy community of merchants and financiers that they benefited, directly threatened the political power of the landed classes.

TABLE 3.4

English Monarchs, 1660–1760

	Dates of Reign	Family/Dynasty of Origin
Charles II	1660–1685	Stuart
James II	1685–1688	Stuart
Mary II and	1689–1694	Stuart
William III	1689–1702	House of Orange
Anne	1702–1714	Stuart
George I	1714–1727	House of Hanover
George II	1727–1760	House of Hanover

American Real Whigs. Many Americans who wanted to preserve the hard-won powers of the provincial assemblies adopted the outlook of the Real Whigs and the Country party. In their eyes, the royal governors in America still had too much arbitrary power: they could call and dissolve the provincial assemblies at their pleasure; they could veto legislation; and they could use land grants and political appointments to influence the votes of legislators. "By increasing the number of officers dependent on the Crown," a writer in the Boston *Weekly Newsletter* charged, the royal governor sought to destroy "the liberties of the people." Such rhetoric was excessive, for few governors could actually wield such powers, but it was believed nevertheless, and stirred public anxiety.

In fact, however, even as Walpole's political tactics were alarming Americans, his patronage policies were actually undermining the royal bureaucracy in America. His ministers were filling colonial posts with mediocre officials who happened to have good political connections, and whose main goal was not to advance imperial policies but to enrich themselves. In New York, for example, Walpole's patronage system had dire administrative consequences. During the 1730s, William Cosby became governor of the colony primarily because his wife was related to Lord Halifax, an influential aristocrat. Hungry for money, Cosby's salary demands and his selling of offices threw the province into political chaos for a decade. His successor, George Clinton, appointed through a family connection with the duke of Newcastle, Walpole's chief political manager, lacked the will or political acumen to uphold imperial interests. In 1744, he responded to a rumor of an impending stamp tax by cautioning his superiors against it. "The people in North America are quite strangers to any Duty but such as they raise themselves," he warned. Rather than challenging the authority of the provincial assembly, Clinton simply accepted it as a fact of political life.

Patronage also weakened the Board of Trade as Walpole and Newcastle packed it with their supporters in Parliament. The presence of these mediocre *placemen* (so-called because they did little work but merely occupied a "place") weakened the morale of capable imperial officials. Governor Gabriel Johnson went to North Carolina in the 1730s determined to "make a mighty change in the face of affairs" by taking control of patronage and curbing the power of the assembly, but he soon became discouraged by the lack of support at home. Though he started out as a potential reformer, Johnson became a cautious, do-nothing governor. Like many other imperial officials during the era of salutary neglect, he resolved "to do nothing which can be reasonably blamed, and leave the rest to time, and a new set of inhabitants."

Thus Walpole's political strategy weakened imperial rule in America in three different ways. First, his support for the merchant community and the expansion of trade inhibited forceful imperial rule, allowing the "rise of the assembly" in America. Second, the ideological attacks mounted by Walpole's Real Whig opponents persuaded some colonists that British rule posed a threat to their liberties, weakening respect for royal governors and imperial policies. Third—and most directly—his patronage system weakened the royal bureaucracy and the authority of the imperial government in America. Salutary neglect did not "cause" Americans to seek independence—in fact, mild rule actually strengthened the colonists' allegiance to Britain (as did the increasing popularity of British goods and culture). But it did encourage Americans to expect a position of political equality within the empire, and eventually to claim it.

Imperial Expansion

Walpole's ministry did act decisively in protecting British interests in America from foreign threats, both military and commercial. One of its first gestures in this direction was the provision of a subsidy for the founding of the colony of Georgia.

The Founding of Georgia. In the early 1730s, General James Oglethorpe and a group of social reformers influenced by the Enlightenment (see Chapter 4) successfully petitioned King George II for land south of the Carolinas to establish a new American colony. They named the settlement Georgia (in honor of the king) and planned it as a refuge for England's poor. Envisioning a colony of small farms worked by independent landowners and white indentured servants, the trustees of Georgia limited most land grants to 500 acres and outlawed slavery.

Walpole provided Georgia with a subsidy from Parliament not because he shared the founders' vision but because he wished to protect the increasingly valuable rice colony of South Carolina by establishing a buffer between it and Spanish Florida. Spain had long resented the British presence in Carolina and was outraged by the expansion into Georgia, whose territory it claimed. Concerned with the threat from Spanish troops in Florida and Spanish naval vessels in the Caribbean, Walpole dispatched a regiment of troops to Georgia in 1737 and appointed Oglethorpe as commander-in-chief of all military forces in Georgia and South Carolina. Simultaneously, merchant interests in Parliament formed an alliance with the Georgia trustees to push for an aggressive anti-Spanish policy. Following the Treaty of Utrecht in 1713, British merchants had steadily increased their control of the trade in slaves and manufactured goods in the Spanish empire. Spanish officials had now begun to resist this commercial imperialism, so the merchants wanted their government to go to war.

War with Spain. In 1739, Spanish naval forces sparked the so-called War of Jenkins' Ear by physically mutilating Robert Jenkins, an English sea captain who was trading illegally with the Spanish West Indies. Britain immediately struck back, and started the first significant military conflict in America in a generation. In 1740 British regulars commanded by Oglethorpe, together with provincial troops from South Carolina and Georgia and some Indian allies, launched an unsuccessful expedition against St. Augustine in Spanish Florida. Later that year, the governors of the eleven colonies stretching from New England to North Carolina raised 2,500 volunteers for service in the West Indies. These troops joined a British naval force in an assault on the Spanish seaport of Cartagena in Panama. The attack failed and instead of enriching themselves with Spanish booty, as they had hoped, hundreds of colonial volunteers died of tropical diseases.

The War of Jenkins' Ear became part of a general European conflict, the War of the Austrian Succession, in 1740. This struggle pitted Britain and its traditional ally Austria against Spain, France, and Prussia. Although the British and French navies clashed in the West Indies, the long frontier between the mainland colonies and French Canada remained calm. Then, in 1745, more than 3,000 New England militiamen, supported by a British naval squadron, captured the powerful French naval fortress of Louisbourg, on Cape Breton Island near the mouth of the St. Lawrence River, which surrendered without a fight.

The Treaty of Aix-la-Chapelle, which ended the war in 1748, mandated the return of all captured territory in North America, which bitterly disappointed the New England provinces. Yet the war secured the territorial integrity of Georgia by reaffirming British military superiority in the region, and British commercial power within the Spanish empire continued to expand.

The Politics of Mercantilism

The expansion of British mercantilism that had opened the way to the era of salutary neglect ultimately brought it to a close. As the economic growth of the colonies began to threaten certain British financial interests, pressure mounted in England to assert control over the internal administration of the American colonies. In general, mercantilist policy called for colonies to produce only agricultural goods and raw materials, reserving the more profitable provision of manufactured goods and commercial services for the artisans and merchants of the home country. British mercantilists sought to implement this policy in the colonies by securing such legislation as the Woolens Act of 1699 and the Hat Act of 1732, which prohibited the intercolonial sale of American-produced textiles and hats, and the Iron Act of 1750, which banned the construction of new mills, forges, and furnaces in the colonies.

The Navigation Acts, however, had an inherent flaw. Because they encouraged Americans to own ships and transport goods, they enabled colonial merchants to gain control of the commerce between the mainland and the West Indies—about 95 percent control by the 1740s. American firms also carried three-quarters of the manufactured goods imported into the colonies from London and Bristol. Quite unexpectedly, British mercantilism had created a dynamic and wealthy community of colonial merchants.

The Molasses Act. American enterprise eventually clashed with powerful British economic interests. Since the rapidly growing mainland settlements were producing more goods than the British sugar islands had use for, in the 1720s colonial merchants began to trade with the French West Indies. Inexpensive imports of corn, fish, and supplies from British North America enabled French planters to produce an abundance of correspondingly low-cost sugar, and thus to capture control of the competitive European market. American rum distillers imported cheap French molasses, cutting off another market for British sugar products. By the 1730s, the British sugar industry was on the verge of collapse.

British sugar producers petitioned Parliament for help and won passage of the Molasses Act of 1733. The act permitted the mainland colonies to continue the export of fish and farm products to the French islands, but it placed a high duty (6 pennies per gallon) on molasses imported from non-British colonies. The imperial government expected the act to benefit British planters by making their prices competitive.

American merchants and public officials strongly protested the Molasses Act, arguing not only that the act would diminish their trade with the French islands and cripple their distilling industry but also that the resulting loss of revenues would make it more difficult for colonists to purchase British manufactures. When Parliament ignored their protests, American merchants simply refused to obey the new act. They continued to import shiploads of French molasses, and bribed customs officials to circumvent the tax. Fortunately for the Americans, sugar prices rose in the mid-1730s, quieting the concerns of the British planters. As a result, the imperial government never enforced the act, and the Royal Customs Service collected only a pittance. But the act itself foreshadowed increased imperial control that was soon to come.

Currency Problems. The impulse to greater imperial control was also excited by the internal economic policies of the provincial assemblies. Because American merchants used most of the gold, silver, and bills of exchange from the West Indian trade to pay for British manufactures, the colonists lacked an adequate amount of currency. To create a domestic money supply, the assemblies of ten colonies established land banks which lent money. Farmers gave the banks a mortgage on their land (hence the term *land bank*) and received loans in the form of paper currency. This imaginative system of finance provided landowners with money to invest in equipment, and also increased trade by creating a paper currency that could be exchanged for goods.

In some colonies, however, paper currency created conflicts with merchants, both British and American. The Rhode Island assembly paid its expenses by printing as much paper money as it needed, thereby producing a severely depreciated currency. A Rhode Island bill with a face value of £10 would buy only £5 worth of goods, and creditors rightly complained that they were being financially harmed because Rhode Islanders could pay off old debts with new, depreciated currency.

Because Rhode Island was a small colony and did not have a royal governor, British officials tolerated this fiscal abuse. But when Massachusetts tried to create a land bank in 1740, the British government intervened, strongly supporting Governor Belcher's veto of the land bank. Then, in 1751, Parliament passed a broad Currency Act that prevented all the New England colonies from establishing new land banks and, with Rhode Island in mind, prohibited public bills of credit from being used to pay private debts. Many British merchants thought such decisive action was long overdue.

Imperial officials were equally distressed by the growing power of the provincial assemblies and seized upon the currency issue as a case in point. Charles Townshend of the Board of Trade charged that the American assemblies had assumed many of the "ancient and established prerogatives wisely preserved in the Crown." By 1750, many British political and financial leaders were determined to replace "salutary neglect" with a more rigorous system of imperial control.

Summary

When Charles II was restored to the English throne in 1660, he took an active part in shaping colonial policy. To pay his political and personal debts he bestowed land in America as proprietary colonies. The Carolina colony was given to a group of aristocrats headed by the duke of Albemarle. New York and New Jersey, conquered from the Dutch in 1664, fell to Charles's brother James, duke of York. And Pennsylvania was awarded to William Penn. The crown continued to control all the colonies' external economic affairs, however, and Charles secured the enactment of new Navigation Acts to tighten the regulation of colonial exports and imports. In 1685, the new king, James II, tried to impose tighter political controls as well, abolishing the existing charters of the northern mainland colonies and creating the Dominion of New England. The Glorious Revolution of 1688 cost James his throne, and revolts in Boston, New York, and Maryland helped secure the restoration of the colonists' traditional rights and institutions.

The South Atlantic system, based on the West Indian sugar trade, laid the foundation for England's wealth and power. To work the sugar plantations of the West Indies and Brazil, millions of Africans were forced into slavery and premature death. In Virginia, where Africans mainly raised tobacco and the conditions of servitude were less severe, the number of black laborers grew dramatically, by importation and by natural increase. In America, the South Atlantic system brought great profits to white planters, the creation of African-American communities, and prosperity for northern seaports, merchants, and farmers.

The 1713 Treaty of Utrecht ushered in a generation of peace, leaving the colonies free to develop their social and political institutions. Aided by the unofficial British policy of salutary neglect, American political leaders strengthened the power of the provincial assemblies. Colonial politics became more responsive to the views of ordinary people, in part because of a broad property-based suffrage and frequent elections and in part because of a tradition of crowd actions.

In 1733, alarmed at the increasingly large share of West Indian commerce controlled by colonial merchants—and their eagerness to trade with the French sugar islands—the British passed the Molasses Act, once again tightening mercantilist controls on colonial trade. Additional legislation restricting manufacturing in the colonies and regulating their financial policies signaled that, by 1750, the era of salutary neglect was rapidly coming to an end.

TOPIC FOR RESEARCH

The English Empire in America

What was the nature of the English empire in America and how did its character change over time? What goals were English policy makers attempting to achieve when they enacted legislation relating to the colonies? You can begin to formulate an answer to these questions by reading parliamentary laws, especially the provisions of the various Acts of Trade and Navigation. These documents provide insight into the original conception of the empire held by English political leaders and how it evolved over three decades. Various secondary works address these questions and other aspects of English imperial policy between 1650 and 1750: Lawrence A. Harper, *The English Navigation Laws* (1939); Charles M. Andrews, *The Colonial Period of American History* (vol. 4, 1938); Viola Barnes, *The Dominion of New England* (1923); Thomas C. Barrow, *Trade and Empire:The British Customs Service in Colonial America, 1660–1775* (1967); Michael G. Hall, *Edward Randolph and the American Colonies, 1676–1703* (1960); James A. Henretta, *"Salutary Neglect": Colonial Administration under the Duke of Newcastle* (1972); I. K. Steele, *Politics of Colonial Policy: The Board of Trade in Colonial Administration, 1696–1720* (1968); and Stephen S. Webb, *1676: The End of American Independence* (1984).

BIBLIOGRAPHY

The Politics of Empire

The best short overview is Michael Kammen, *Empire and Interest: The American Colonies and the Politics of Mercantilism* (1970). More detailed studies are Alison G. Olson, *Anglo-American Politics, 1660–1775* (1973); Jack M. Sosin, *English America and the Restoration Monarchy of Charles II: Transatlantic Politics, Commerce, and Kinship* (1980); and W. F. Craven, *New Jersey and the English Colonization of North America* (1964).

For the events of 1688–1689 see David S. Lovejoy, *The Glorious Revolution in America* (1972). More specific studies include Jack M. Sosin, *English America and the Revolution of 1688: Royal Administration and the Structure of Provincial Government* (1982); and Lois Green Carr and David W. Jordan, *Maryland's Revolution of Government, 1689–1692* (1974). Ethnic tension in New York can be traced in Robert C. Ritchie, *The Duke's Province: Politics and Society in New York, 1660–1691* (1977); Thomas J. Archdeacon, *New York City, 1664–1710: Conquest and Change* (1976); and Jerome R. Reich, *Leisler's Rebellion: A Study of Democracy in New York, 1664–1720*. Jack M. Sosin, *English America and Imperial Inconstancy: The Rise of Provincial Autonomy, 1696–1715* (1985), outlines the new imperial system.

The Imperial Slave Economy

Richard S. Dunn, *Sugar and Slaves: The Rise of the Planter Class in the English West Indies, 1624–1713* (1972), provides a graphic portrait of the brutal slave-based economy, while Sidney W. Mintz, *Sweetness and Power: The Place of Sugar in Modern History* (1985), explores the impact of its crop. Studies of forced African migration include Philip Curtin, *The Atlantic Slave Trade: A Census* (1969); Paul Lovejoy, ed., *Africans in Bondage: Studies in Slavery and the Slave Trade* (1986); and James A. Rawley, *The Transatlantic Slave Trade* (1981). For the effect on African society, see Basil Davidson, *The African Genius* (1970); Richard Olaniyan, *African History and Culture* (1982); and Walter Rodney, *West Africa and the Atlantic Slave Trade* (1969).

Winthrop D. Jordan, *White over Black, 1550–1812* (1968), remains the best account of Virginia's decision for slavery. T. H. Breen and Stephen Innes, *"Myne Owne Ground": Race and Freedom on Virginia's Eastern Shore, 1640–1676* (1980), closely examines the lives of the first slaves and free blacks. For the creation of African-American society see Allan Kulikoff, *Tobacco and Slaves: Southern Cultures in the Chesapeake, 1680–1800* (1986); Daniel C. Littlefield, *Rice and Slaves: Ethnicity and the Slave Trade in Colonial South Carolina* (1981); and Peter H. Wood, *Black Majority: Negroes in Colonial South Carolina Through the Stono Rebellion* (1974).

Excellent comparative studies of slave societies include Orlando Patterson, *Slavery and Social Death: A Comparative Study* (1982), and Carl Degler, *Neither Black nor White: Slavery and Race Relations in Brazil and the United States* (1971). On the possibilities for resistance, see Richard Price, ed., *Maroon Societies: Rebel Slave Communities in the Americas* (1973), and Gerald W. Mullin, *Flight and Rebellion: Slave Resistance in Eighteenth-Century Virginia* (1972).

America in the Empire

On white society in the South, see Daniel Blake Smith, *Inside the Great House: Planter Family Life in Eighteenth-Century Chesapeake Society* (1980); Rhys Isaac, *The Transformation of Virginia, 1740–1790* (1982); and Timothy H. Breen, *Tobacco Culture* (1985). Urban society and trade are explored in Gary B. Nash, *The Urban Crucible* (1979); Gary M. Walton and James F. Shephard, *The Economic Rise of Early America* (1979); and Christine L. Heyrman, *Commerce and Culture: The Maritime Communities of Colonial Massachusetts, 1690–1750* (1984). See also Marcus Rediker, *Between the Devil and the Deep Blue Sea: Merchant Seamen, Pirates, and the Anglo-American Maritime World, 1700–1750* (1987).

The appearance of a distinctive American polity is traced in Jack P. Greene, *The Quest for Power: The Lower Houses of Assembly in the Southern Royal Colonies, 1689–1776* (1963); Bernard Bailyn, *The Origins of American Politics* (1968); Patricia U. Bonomi, *A Factious People: Politics and Society in Colonial New York* (1971); A. Roger Ekirch, *"Poor Carolina": Politics and Society in Colonial North Carolina, 1729–1776* (1981); and Richard Bushman, *King and People in Provincial Massachusetts* (1985). John Schutz, *William Shirley* (1961), shows how a competent colonial governor wielded power.

Douglas E. Leach, *Roots of Conflict: British Armed Forces and Colonial Americans, 1677–1763*, and Howard H. Peckham, *The Colonial Wars, 1689–1762*, cover the diplomatic and military conflicts of the period.

TIMELINE

1651	First Navigation Act
1660	Restoration of Charles II as king of England
1660s	Trend toward legalization of slavery in Virginia
1663	Carolina colony founded
1681	William Penn founds Pennsylvania colony
1685	James II king of England
1685–1689	Dominion of New England
1688	Glorious Revolution
1689–1702	Mary II and William III
1689–1692	Jacob Leisler's rebellion in New York
1696	Board of Trade created
1699	Woolens Act
1714–1750	"Salutary neglect"
1720–	Black natural increase African-American society created
1720–1742	Sir Robert Walpole serves as chief minister
1732	Georgia colony chartered
1732/1733	Hat Act/Molasses Act
1739	Stono rebellion War of Jenkins' Ear
1740–1748	War of the Austrian Succession
1751	Currency Act

Chandler Wedding Tapestry, 1756

It was fashionable at this time for upper-class couples to commemorate their wedding by having a tapestry made. This detail shows the wedding party arriving at the church.

CHAPTER 4 *Growth and Crisis in American Society,* 1720–1765

The British settlements on the mainland grew spectacularly during the eighteenth century. A population explosion in Europe prompted another migration of whites to America, and the continuing importation of Africans greatly increased the number of blacks. The mainland colonies had about 400,000 residents in 1720, and nearly 2 million by 1765. They sent huge quantities of tobacco, rice, and wheat to European markets and, after 1750, consumed about 15 percent of all British exports. No longer primitive colonies, the British possessions were mature provinces within a transatlantic imperial system.

The first generations of Americans lived much simpler lives than Europeans, because they were unable to recreate the cultural sophistication of their homelands. But after 1720, Americans began participating in the intellectual and religious movements of the larger European world. Many educated Americans embraced the ideas of the European Enlightenment or Age of Reason. Far more Americans were swept up in a new wave of religious enthusiasm that derived from European pietism.

Yet the provinces remained distinctly "American" in character. The widespread ownership of land made the farming communities of New England very different from the peasant villages of Europe. The middle colonies had more ethnic and religious diversity than any society in Western Europe. In a variety of ways, the American provinces were coming of age.

Freehold Society in New England

However much their religious vision had faltered after a century in America, the Puritans did achieve many of their social goals. By 1720 rural New England boasted a freeholding yeomen society dominated by families of Puritan descent. Most of the farmers owned their own land, which they worked with the help of their families. Few New Englanders were tenants; fewer still were wage-laborers. But the system was stable only so long as there was enough arable or pasture land for every household. By 1750 the population threatened to outstrip the supply of land and posed a severe challenge to the freehold ideal.

The Farm Family

Whereas in England the nobility and the gentry owned 75 percent of the arable land, and leased it to tenants, 70 percent of the settled land in the northern mainland colonies was owned and worked by freeholding families. "The hope of having land of their own & becoming independent of Landlords is what chiefly induces people into America," an official reported in the 1730s.

Not that it was easy to get hold of even a small farm in the colonies. Children who came from poor families often began their working lives as indentured servants. Their parents, unable to provide them with work or food, bound them out to farmers who could. Young men ended their indentures, at age eighteen or twenty-one, with many farming skills but without land. For ten or twenty years they struggled as wage-earning farm laborers or tenants to save enough to buy a few acres of their own. Then they needed to acquire enough property to leave a landed estate to their children, or the children would have to repeat the slow climb up the agricultural ladder: from servant, to laborer, to tenant, to freeholder.

Having learned through bitter experience in Europe the importance of a landed inheritance, most yeomen farmers assumed responsibility for the economic fate of their children. As their sons and daughters reached marriageable age—usually twenty-three to twenty-five—their parents provided them with a *marriage portion*, consisting of land, livestock, and sometimes farm equipment. The marriage portion repaid children for their labor on the parents' farm and ensured their future loyalty. Parents knew they would need help in their old age (there were no pension or social security systems). To guarantee that they would not be left helpless, some farmers kept legal title to the land until they died.

Since parents began to transfer their hard-earned land and goods to the children upon marriage, the family's future prosperity depended on the wise choice of marriage partners. Yeomen parents usually decided whom their children would marry. Normally, children had the right to refuse an unacceptable match, but they did not have the luxury of "falling in love" with whomever they pleased.

Keeping the Farm Intact. To preserve the ideal of a freehold society, American farmers followed a number of strategies. Some fathers used the traditional English legal device of *entail* to keep the farmstead intact. They willed the farm to a male child and specified that it remain in his family forever. For example, Ebenezer Perry of Barnstable, Massachusetts, willed his land to his son Ebenezer, Jr., stipulating that it devolve in turn on Ebenezer, Jr.'s "eldest son surviving and so on to the male heirs of his body lawfully begotten forever."

Other farm parents in New England used a *stem family* system to preserve a freehold estate. They chose a married son or son-in-law to work the farm with them and he became the "stem" or center of the entire family, inheriting the farm upon the father's death. These parents, like those using entails, often provided their other children with money, apprenticeship contracts, or frontier land tracts to enable them to become freeholders in other communities. Still other parents wrote wills that gave the family farm to the eldest son but required that he pay money or goods to the younger children. All these devices—entail, the stem system, legally binding wills—favored one son in order to keep the family's farm intact across the generations.

Dividing Up the Farm. Many farmers in New England wished to give land to all their male children. Thus about 90 percent of the fathers in Chebacco, Massachusetts, rather than bequeath their farms to a single heir, divided them up. This could be a risky strategy, however. The sons had some land—but not enough to provide a comfortable living. A better solution, chosen by other equality-minded farmers, was to move their young families to frontier regions, where land was cheap and abundant. "The Squire's House stands on the Bank of the Susquehannah," a traveler named Philip Fithian reported from the Pennsylvania backcountry in the late colonial period. "He tells me that he will be able to settle all his sons and his fair Daughter Betsy on the Fat of the Earth."

The great historic accomplishment of New England farmers was the creation of communities composed of independent property owners. A French visitor remarked that the sense of personal worth and dignity in this rural world contrasted sharply with European peasant life. In America, he found "men and women whose features are not marked by poverty, by lifelong deprivation of the necessities of life, or by a feeling that they are insignificant subjects and subservient members of society."

Women's Place

In America, as in Europe, law and custom gave men greater power and importance than women. Men claimed not only political power in the state but also domestic authority within the family. As the Reverend Benjamin Wadsworth of Boston advised women in his pamphlet *The Well-Ordered Family* (1712), it made no difference if they were richer, more intelligent, or of higher social status than their husbands: "Since he is thy Husband, God has made him the head and set him above thee." Therefore, Wadsworth concluded, it is "thy duty to love and reverence him."

Women's Property Rights. All through their lives, women had it impressed on them that theirs was a subordinate role. Small girls watched their mothers defer to their fathers. As they grew to adulthood, they learned that their marriage portions would be different and smaller than those of their brothers. They would receive not land but money, livestock, or household goods. In a typical will, Ebenezer Chittendon of Guilford, Connecticut, left all his land to his sons, decreeing that "Each Daughter have half so much as Each Son, one half in money and the other half in Cattle."

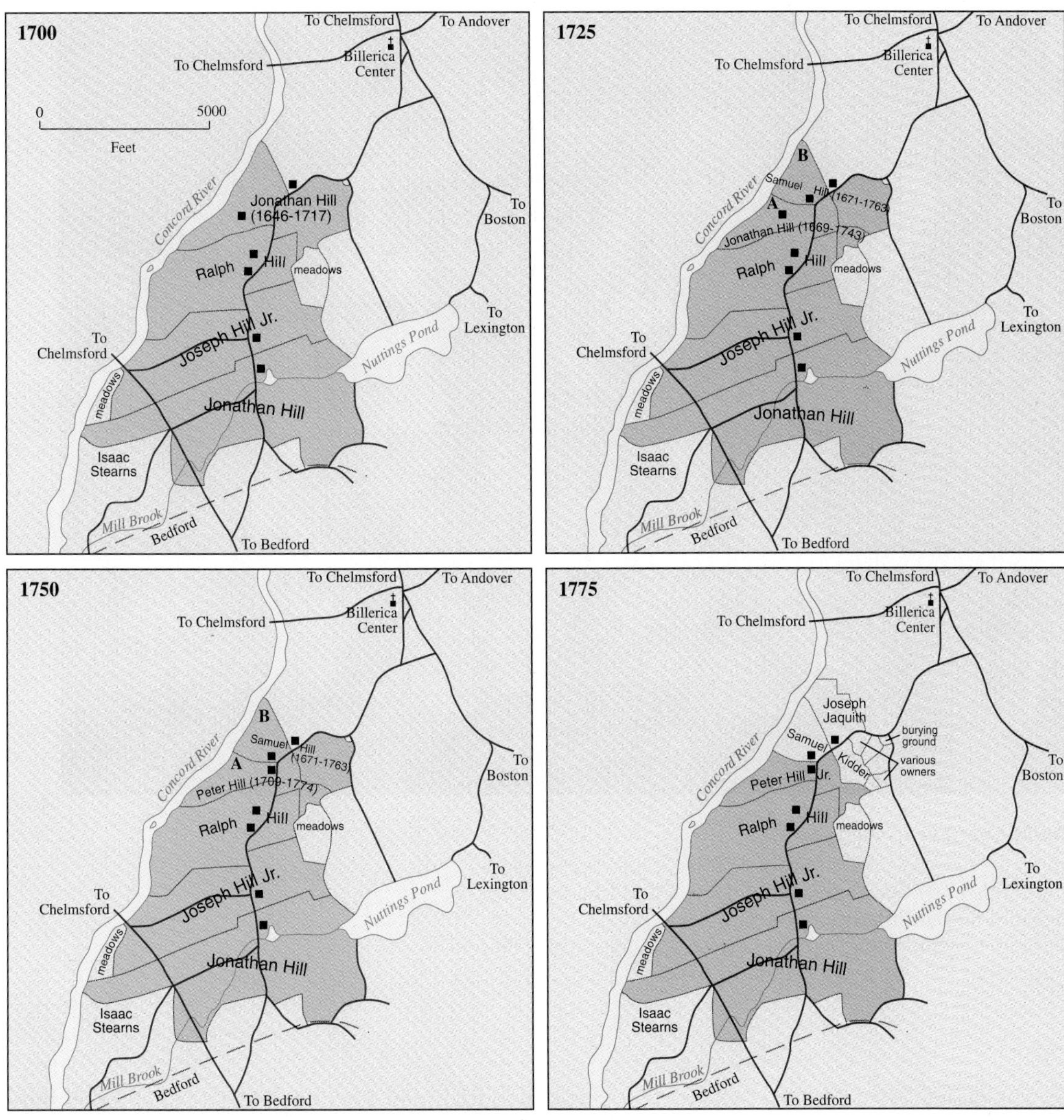

MAP 4.1

Preserving a Farmstead: Billerica, Massachusetts

In 1700 Jonathan Hill (1646–1717) owned a farm of about 170 acres, part of a larger tract that his father Ralph (d. 1663), one of the original proprietors of the town, had divided among his three sons.

Jonathan divided his 170 acres between two sons, Jonathan Jr. (1669–1743) and Samuel (1671– 1763); another son died young and needed no land while his two daughters, Mary and Sarah, received none.

PLOT A: Jonathan Jr. had five children (two sons and three daughters) who survived to adulthood but, to preserve an economically viable farmstead of 80+ acres only one son (Peter, 1709–1774) received this Billerica property, which he passed on to his son, Peter Jr. (1747–1823), one of the fifth generation of Hills to live in the town. Peter Jr. bequeathed it to his daughter Elizabeth Hill who, in 1827, married Benjamin Judkins, whereupon—after five generations and 180 years—the farm no longer carried the name of the Hill family. (However, descendants of the Hills retained ownership under different surnames until 1969).

PLOT B: Samuel had one son, Samuel Jr. (1699–1749), who predeceased him, and five daughters; at his death in 1763 he willed 65 acres to the widow of his dead son and 17 acres to his five daughters and their husbands jointly—who sold it in small parcels. Samuel Jr.'s widow died in 1768, bequeathing her 65 acres to her daughter Abigail, who had married Samuel Kidder in 1749. So this half of the property passed out of the ownership of those named Hill after a mere three generations and 110 years.

These complicated transactions (revealed by the research of Samuel Brainerd) show some basic principles: a great reluctance to divide farms below 60-80 acres; the consequent migration of many children; the superior inheritance rights of sons; and, perhaps most important of all, the centuries-long link between some families and their land.

The Character of Family Life: The Cheneys
Life in a large colonial family was very different from that in a small modern one as depicted in this painting entitled *The Cheney Family*, c. 1795. Mrs. Cheney's face shows the rigors of having borne ten children, a task that would occupy her entire adult life. Her children grew up with much older (or younger) siblings, which blurred differences between the generations. (National Gallery of Art)

Once married, a woman had fewer property rights than her husband or her children. A new bride gave legal ownership of all her personal property to her husband. Any land a woman might possess fell under the control of her husband during his lifetime and upon his death would normally bypass her and go straight to the children.

English and colonial law compensated married women for this loss of property by giving them *dower rights*. When a woman's husband died, she had the right to use a third of the family's estate during her lifetime. However, if she remarried, she forfeited this right. And she could not sell her one-third interest, for it legally belonged to her children; her rights were restricted to use. The wife's property rights were subordinated to those of the family "line" which stretched, through the children, across the generations.

Women's Duties. In New England—indeed, throughout the colonies—a woman's place was as a dutiful daughter to her father and a helpmeet (help-mate) to her husband. Some women fulfilled these roles in exemplary fashion by working full-time as farm wives. They spun thread from flax or wool and wove it into shirts and gowns; knitted sweaters and stockings; churned butter, preserved food, made candles and soap, and mastered dozens of other productive household tasks.

The community lavished praise on these "notable" women, setting them up as models. "I have a great longing desire to be very notable," one woman wrote upon her marriage. Women who lacked skills felt their shortcomings keenly, although their labor was no less crucial to the rural household economy. As Abigail Hyde, a New England farm wife, confessed in a letter, "The conviction of my deficiencies as a mother is overwhelming."

Bearing and raising children was no easy task. Most women in the northern colonies married in their early twenties and bore five to seven children before the onset of menopause, in their early forties. There were no drugs to ease the pain of women in labor, no antibacterial medications to prevent infections. Yet most women survived numerous childbirths, helped by midwives—women who prepared them emotionally for the experience of giving birth, stayed with them during labor, and attended to the needs of newborn and mother. A large family sapped a woman's emotional strength and kept her energies focused on domestic activities. For about twenty of her most active years, a woman was either pregnant or breastfeeding. Sarah Ripley Stearns, a Massachusetts farmwife, explained that she had no time for religious activities because "the care of my Babes takes up so large a portion of my time and attention."

Over time, many couples with small farms chose to have fewer children. After 1750, families in such long-settled communities as Andover, Massachusetts, had an average of only four children. Smaller families meant women had fewer mouths to feed, fewer clothes to wash and mend, and more time to pursue other tasks. Susan Huntington of Boston, who had the good fortune to be rich, spent more time in "the care & culture of children, and the perusal of necessary books, including the scriptures." With fewer children, ordinary farm women could make extra yarn, cloth, or cheese to exchange with their neighbors or sell to shopkeepers, thus enhancing the family's standard of living. After 1770 some became wage workers in a new merchant-run putting-out system, stitching the soft upper parts of women's shoes.

But women's participation in the daily affairs of life was limited, especially in Puritan communities, by cultural rules. Puritan men were reluctant to have their wives work in the fields. "Women in New England," Timothy Dwight reported approvingly, "are employed only in and about the house and in the proper business of the sex." Many strong-minded wives found ways to let their preferences be known and to assume authority within the household or on the farm. The stress on domestic concerns gave many Puritan women the chance to learn to read and write, as did their church's emphasis on reading the Bible. Yet whatever their literary or religious accomplishments, women were not full participants in church affairs. Ezra Stiles, the president of Yale College, noted that he "never knew or read of the Sisters [women] voting" in Congregational churches. "They often stay with the brethren & see & hear what is transacted," he continued, "but don't even speak in Church." Only a few radical Protestant churches gave women an active role in religious matters. For example, Quakers believed "that women can be called to the ministry as well as men," as a French visitor noted, and Baptists in Rhode Island permitted women to vote on church affairs.

However, these differences among churches were only variations on the general theme of female subordination. Despite their increasing freedom from child raising, most American women remained in an inferior position, their lives tightly bound by a web of laws, cultural expectations, and religious restrictions.

Tavern Culture

Although women's participation in daily affairs was restricted to the home, after 1770 some became wage earners. By 1790, taverns were often run by women, such as this "Charming Patroness." It was in taverns, declared puritanical John Adams, that "diseases, vicious habits, bastards, and legislators are frequently begotten."

The Crisis of Freehold Society

Men's lives in New England were also getting more restricted, not because of cultural rules but because of overpopulation. From the beginning of white settlement, the number of residents had doubled with each generation, mostly from natural increase. The Puritan colonies had about 100,000 people in 1700, 200,000 in 1725, and almost 400,000 by 1750.

Rapid population growth threatened to overcrowd long-settled areas. Lands that had been ample for the original migrant families had been divided and then subdivided until by 1750 many parents could no longer provide land for their children. The Reverend Samuel Chandler of Andover, Massachusetts, noted in the 1740s that he had "been much distressed for land for his children," seven of whom were boys. Dispersing the land among so many heirs usually meant a decline in living standards. In Concord, Massachusetts, by the 1750s, about 60 percent of farmers owned less land than their fathers had.

TABLE 4.1

Diminishing Property in the Fuller Family, Kent, Connecticut

	Date of Birth	Highest Assessment on Tax List
First Generation		
Joseph Fuller	1699	203 pounds
Second Generation		
Joseph Jr.	1723	42
Zachariah	1725	103
Jeremiah	1728	147
Nathaniel	?	67
Adijah	?	46
Simeon	?	49
Abraham	1737	136
Jacob	1738	59
Isaac	1741	7
	Average:	72 pounds
Third Generation		
Abel	?	40
Abraham, Jr.	?	50
Oliver	1747	50
Daniel	1749	65
Howard	1750	28
Benejah	1757	32
Ephraim	1760	100
John	1760	?
Asahel	1770	48
James	1770	40
Revilo	1770	35
Samuel	?	14
	Average:	42 pounds

Because parents had less to give their children, they had less control over their children's lives. The system of arranged marriages broke down. Young people moved to newly settled regions, or they had premarital sex and used pregnancy to win permission to marry. The number of firstborn children conceived before marriage rose spectacularly throughout New England, from about 10 percent in the 1710s to 30 percent in the 1740s and, in some communities, to 40 percent by the 1760s. If these young people had it to do over, they "would do the same again," an Anglican minister observed, "because otherwise they could not obtain their parents' consent to marry."

On the eve of the American Revolution, farm communities in New England responded to the threat to their freehold ideal in three basic ways. First, many towns petitioned the provincial government for new land grants along the frontier. Settlers continually moved inland from the Massachusetts coast and up the Connecticut River Valley, hacking new farms out of the virgin forest and creating new communities of freehold farmers.

Second, settlers who remained on the original farmsteads planted different crops. Even before 1750, they had replaced the traditional English crops of wheat and barley (for bread and beer) with a grazing economy based on corn, cattle, and hogs. Corn provided a hardy food for humans and its abundant leaves furnished feed for cattle or pigs. Farmers then butchered the livestock and preserved the meat. The physician William Douglass observed in the 1720s that poor people in New England subsisted on "salt pork and Indian beans, with bread of Indian corn meal, and pottage of this meal with milk for breakfast and supper." After 1750, New England farmers raised the output of this mixed-crop grazing economy by planting potatoes, whose high yields offset the disadvantage of smaller farms. Farmers also introduced nutritious English grasses, such as red clover and timothy, to provide forage for their livestock and nitrogen for the depleted soil (though they didn't know the chemistry). These innovative measures not only averted a food shortage but generated a surplus for export. New England became the major supplier of salted and pickled meat to the West Indies; in 1770 preserved meat accounted for about 5 percent of the value of all exports from the mainland colonies.

Third, to compensate for the reduced size and limited resources of their properties, farmers increased productivity by constantly helping one another. Men loaned each other tools, draft animals, and grazing land. Women and children joined other families in spinning yarn, sewing quilts, or shucking corn. Farmers plowed the fields of artisans, who in turn fixed pots, plows, and furniture brought to them for repair. By sharing labor and goods, every farm—and the entire

Lady Undressing for a Bath, c. 1730–40

This delightful painting attributed to Gerardus Duyckinck captures a moment of intimacy between an unknown American couple. Many marriages were "arranged" and grew into love matches. Others began with strong emotional bonds. An affluent Philadelphia woman expressed this rapport, writing to her husband: "Our Hearts have been united from the first, in so firm, so strong, so sweet an affection, that words are incapable of setting it forth." (National Gallery of Art)

economy—was able to achieve maximum output at the minimum cost.

This exchange system—the "household mode of production," as one historian has called it—worked well because New England was a homogeneous, close-knit society. Typically, no money changed hands between relatives or neighbors. Instead, farmers, artisans, and shopkeepers recorded debts and credits in personal account books, and every few years the accounts were "balanced" with the transfer of small amounts of cash. Thus, New England farmers averted a social crisis and preserved their freehold society well into the nineteenth century.

The Mid-Atlantic: Toward a New Society, 1720–1765

The middle colonies—New York, New Jersey, and Pennsylvania—lacked the cultural and religious uniformity of New England, containing instead a mixture of settlers from many European countries, with diverse religious backgrounds. Yet these settlements had more order and purpose than would at first appear. Strong ethnic ties bound German settlers to one another, as did deep religious loyalties among the members of various churches: Scots-Irish Presbyterians, English and Welsh Quakers, German Lutherans, and Dutch Reformed Protestants.

The Quaker Experiment

When the Swedish traveler Peter Kalm visited Philadelphia in 1748, he found no fewer than twelve religious denominations, including Anglicans, Quakers, Swedish and German Lutherans, Scots-Irish Presbyterians, and even Roman Catholics. Large communities of German sectarians, such as the Moravians in the Pennsylvania towns of Bethlehem and Nazareth, added to this religious diversity.

Quakers were the dominant social group in Pennsylvania—at first because they outnumbered the others and later because, despite a huge influx of new migrants after 1720, they retained wealth and influence. Quakers controlled Pennsylvania's representative assembly (established by proprietor William Penn's Frame of Government) until the 1750s, and they exercised considerable control over New Jersey, too. Like the Puritan migrants to New England, Quakers wanted to restore to religion the simplicity and spirituality of early Christianity. But Quakers were not Calvinists; they did not believe that just a small elect could achieve salvation. They followed the teachings of their founder, the English visionary George Fox, who argued that all women and men could be saved. Fox maintained that God had imbued each person with an inner "light" of grace or understanding. The principal Quaker religious institution—the weekly meeting for worship—was designed to assist members to discover this inner light. The meetings were not led by a minister or centered around

A Quaker Meeting for Worship
Quakers dressed plainly and met in plain buildings. They sat in silence, speaking only when inspired by the "inner light." Women spoke frequently and with near-equality to men, an experience that prepared Quaker women to take a leading part in the nineteenth-century women's rights movement. This British work was done in the late eighteenth or early nineteenth century and is entitled *Quaker Meeting.* (Museum of Fine Arts, Boston)

a sermon or a passage from the Bible. Rather, Quakers encouraged anyone, man or woman, who felt the promptings of the inner light to speak. "Nearest the front by the wall are two benches," Peter Kalm reported following a visit to a Philadelphia meetinghouse in 1749. "In these pews sit those of both sexes who either are already accustomed to preach or expect to be inspired by the Holy Ghost."

This emphasis on religious equality shaped the Quaker social ethic. Quakers wore plain clothes without elaborate decorations and refused to defer to their "superiors" by removing their hats. In talking among themselves and with strangers, they used the familiar "thee" and "thou" rather than the more formal "you." The Society of Friends refused to use law courts to settle disputes among themselves, relying instead on arbitrators to judge what was "right"—and not simply what was "legal." Around 1750 some Quakers extended these egalitarian values to their relations with blacks, freeing their own slaves. Indeed, some Quaker meetings condemned the institution of slavery and expelled from their meetings any members who continued to keep slaves—making Quakers the first religious group to advocate the abolition of slavery.

Quakers were pacifists, and so they avoided war with Native Americans. Penn himself negotiated the first treaty with the Indians in 1682, and the Pennsylvania government purchased Indian land rather than seize it by force. These conciliatory policies irritated non-Quaker settlers on the frontier and did not completely eliminate conflict with the Indians. However, Pennsylvania did avoid a major Indian war until the 1750s, a record unmatched elsewhere in the British colonies. In diplomacy, as in religious matters, the Quakers' radical social experiment was largely successful.

Ethnic Diversity

To thousands of eighteenth-century Europeans who fled their homelands because of war, religious persecution, and poverty, the mid-Atlantic region seemed like the Promised Land. Most of them managed to improve their lives. As the German minister Gottlieb Mittelberger reported from Pennsylvania in the 1750s, "Even in the humblest or poorest houses, no one eats bread without butter or cheese."

The Pennsylvania Germans. Germans came to the middle colonies in a series of waves. First to arrive, in 1683, were a group of Mennonites attracted by Penn's pamphlet promising religious freedom. Beginning in 1709, boatloads of impoverished peasants from the Palatine region of western Germany, an area devastated by religious warfare, settled as tenants on Hudson River manors. Then, in the 1720s, continuing religious

AMERICAN VOICES

The Perils of Migration *Gottlieb Mittelberger*

The lure of ample land and a better life prompted thousands of Germans to endure the hardships of migration, described here in a book published by Gottlieb Mittelberger in 1750. A Lutheran minister who returned to Germany, Mittelberger viewed America with a critical eye—warning his readers of the difficulties of life in a competitive, pluralistic society.

[The journey from Germany to Pennsylvania, via Holland and England] lasts from the beginning of May to the end of October, fully half a year, amid such hardships as no one is able to describe adequately with their misery. Both in Rotterdam and in Amsterdam the people are packed densely, like herrings so to say, in the large sea-vessels. One person receives a place of scarcely 2 feet width and 6 feet length in the bedstead, while many a ship carries four to six hundred souls; not to mention the innumerable implements, tools, provisions, water-barrels and other things which likewise occupy much space. . . .

When the ships have for the last time weighed their anchors near the city of Cowes in England, the real misery begins with the long voyage. For from there the ships, unless they have good wind, must often sail 8, 9, 10 to 12 weeks before they reach Philadelphia. But even with the best wind the voyage lasts 7 weeks. But during the voyage there is on board these ships terrible misery, stench, fumes, horror, vomitting, many kinds of seasickness, fever, dysentery, headache, heat, constipation, boils, scurvy, cancer, mouthrot, and the like, all of which come from old and sharply salted food and meat, also from very bad and foul water, so that many die miserably.

Children from 1 to 7 years rarely survive the voyage; and many a time parents are compelled to see their children miserably suffer and die from hunger, thirst and sickness, and then to see them cast into the water. I witnessed such misery in no less than 32 children in our ship, all of whom were thrown into the sea. The parents grieve all the more since their children find no resting-place in the earth, but are devoured by the monsters of the sea.

Source: Gottlieb Mittelberger, *Journey to Pennsylvania* (1756), ed. and trans., Oscar Handlin and John Clive (Cambridge, Mass.: Harvard University Press, 1960).

upheaval and population growth in southwestern Germany and Switzerland stimulated another wave of migrants. "Wages were far better than here," Heinrich Schneebeli reported to his friends in Zurich after an exploratory trip to Pennsylvania, and "one also enjoyed there a free unhindered exercise of religion." Thirty citizens of Zurich immediately asked the authorities for permission to emigrate. Many Germans and Swiss had sufficient resources to pay their own way; they migrated to provide better opportunities for their children. Others signed on as *redemptioners*, a kind of indentured servant, to get to Pennsylvania.

Seventeen shiploads of German settlers arrived in Pennsylvania in 1732. This was the beginning of a major influx, which reached a peak in 1749, when twenty-four ships deposited over 6,000 Germans in Philadelphia. In less than two decades, more than 125,000 Germans and Swiss had poured into the middle colonies. Their settlements dominated certain areas of the rich Lancaster plain in Pennsylvania. Other groups of Germans and Swiss moved down the Shenandoah Valley into the western districts of Maryland, Virginia, and the Carolinas.

German Artisanry
German artisans in Pennsylvania, like those in Germany, frequently decorated their furniture with abstract designs and simple folk motifs, such as the angels on this chest of drawers. (Philadelphia Museum of Art)

Once in the colonies, Germans formed their own communities, guarding their linguistic and cultural heritage. One German minister in North Carolina explained to his congregation, "We owe it to our native country to do our part that German blood and the German language be preserved in America." He admonished them "not to contract any marriages with the English or Irish." In fact, most American-born Germans took marriage partners of their own ancestry, spoke to each other and read newspapers in German, and attended church services conducted in German. They also continued German agricultural practices: English visitors to the middle colonies remarked that German women were "always in the fields, meadows, stables, etc. and do not dislike any work whatsoever."

The Scots-Irish. The Scots-Irish made up the largest group of new migrants to British North America, some 150,000 arriving between 1720 and 1776. They settled throughout the mainland but primarily in the middle colonies and in the southern backcountry. These migrants were Presbyterians, the descendants of Scots sent to northern Ireland to bolster English control there in the mid-seventeenth century. In Ireland, the Scots had faced discrimination. For example, the Test Act of 1704 excluded both Scottish Presbyterians and Irish Catholics from holding public office in Ireland, reserving this privilege for members of the Church of England. English mercantilist regulations placed heavy import duties on the woolen goods produced by Scots-Irish farmers and weavers.

Rising taxes and poor harvests set off a major Scots-Irish migration to America during the 1720s. "Read this letter, Rev. Baptist Boyd," one New York settler wrote back to his minister, "and tell all the poor folk of ye place that God has opened a door for their deliverance. . . . all that a man works for is his own; there are no revenue hounds [tax collectors] to take it from us here." Lured by such reports, thousands of Scots-Irish sailed for Philadelphia and spread out across the mid-Atlantic region and southward down the Shenandoah Valley. Like the Germans, the Scots-Irish were determined to keep the culture of their homelands alive from generation to generation. They held to their Presbyterian faith and encouraged marriages within the church.

The middle colonies were not a "melting pot"; the diverse European cultures did not blend together to produce a homogeneous "American" outlook but kept their separate identities. The only exception were the Huguenots, French Calvinists who were expelled from France and settled in New York and various seacoast cities; they intermarried with other Protestants during the eighteenth century. More typical was the experience of Welsh Quakers; 70 percent of the children of the original migrants to Chester County, Pennsylvania, married other Welsh Quakers, as did 60 percent of the third generation. By marrying among themselves, European settlers created a pluralistic society of diverse nationalities, cultures, and religions in the middle colonies.

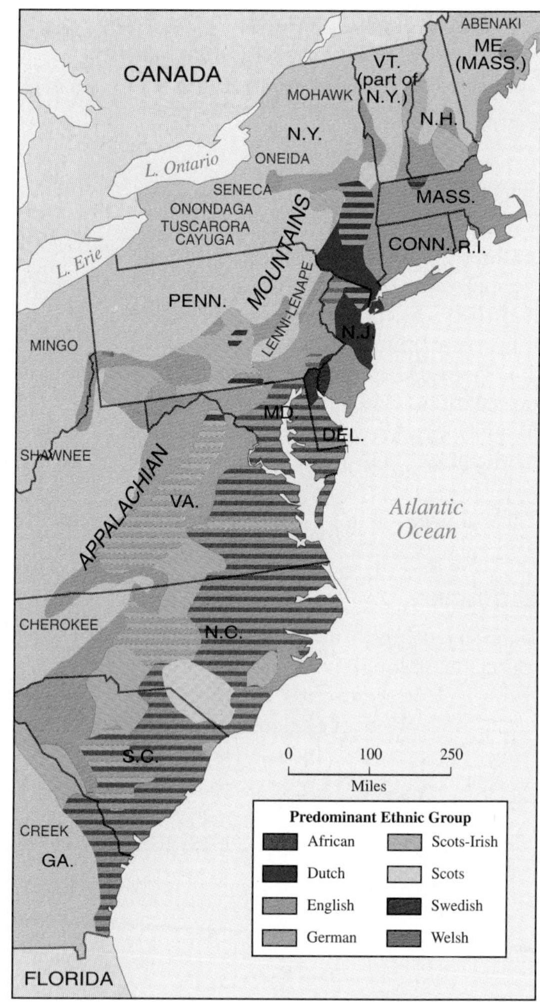

MAP 4.2

Ethnic and Racial Diversity, 1775

In 1700 most colonists were English but by 1775 women and men of English descent were a minority. African-Americans accounted for one-third of the population of the South, while Germans and Scots-Irish made the middle colonies and the southern backcountry one of the most ethnically and religiously diverse regions in the western world.

Opportunity and Equality

Pennsylvania, New York, and New Jersey attracted huge numbers of migrants in the eighteenth century, the combined population rising from 50,000 in 1700, to

120,000 in 1720, to 350,000 by 1765. An ample supply of fertile land and a long frost-free growing season of about 180 days attracted migrants to the region, but the main reason the middle colonies prospered was that the population explosion in Western Europe created a huge demand for wheat, which they were able to supply. Wheat prices doubled in the Atlantic world between 1720 and 1770, and profits from wheat financed the settlement of the region. By 1770, the value of wheat, corn, flour, and bread shipped from the middle colonies amounted to over 15 percent of all colonial exports.

Many yeomen farm families prospered from growing grain, but few became large-scale producers, because preindustrial technology greatly limited output. A worker with a hand sickle could reap only half an acre a day and if ripe grain was not cut promptly it sprouted, rendering it useless. The *cradle*, a long-handled scythe with wooden fingers that arranged the wheat for easy collection and binding, was introduced during the 1750s, and this innovation doubled or tripled the amount a worker could cut. Even so, a family with two adult workers could not usually harvest more than about 15 acres of wheat in a growing season, from which it could thresh perhaps 150–180 bushels of grain. After meeting its own needs, the family might sell the surplus for £15. This cash income paid for store goods such as salt and sugar, tools, cloth, and perhaps the purchase of a few acres of new land, but nobody got rich on it.

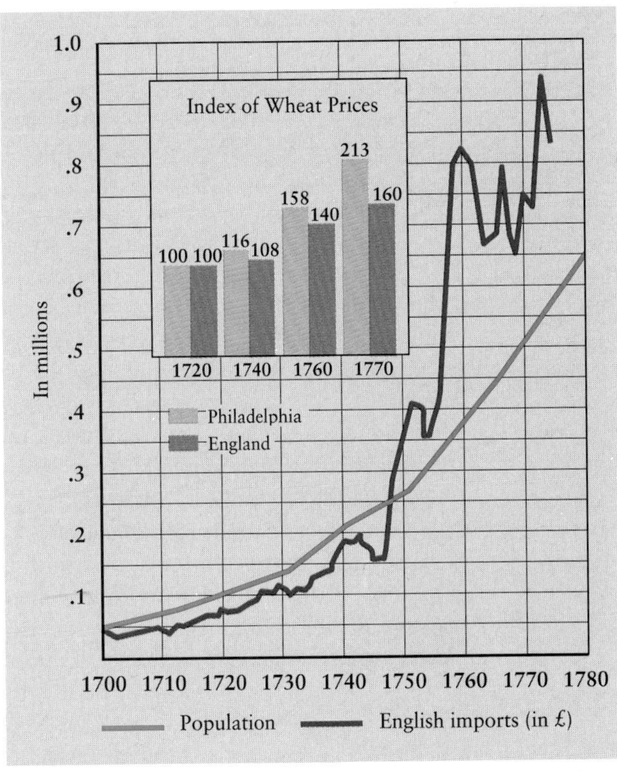

FIGURE 4.1

Population Growth, Wheat Prices, and English Imports in the Middle Colonies

The Emergence of Inequality. Initially, there was economic equality in rural Pennsylvania. In Chester County, for example, the original migrants came with approximately the same resources. In 1693, the poorest 30 percent of the taxpayers owned a substantial 17 percent of the assessed wealth and the top 10 percent controlled 23 percent. Most families lived in small houses, with one or two rooms. Their furniture consisted of a few benches or stools plus a bed in a loft. Only the wealthiest families ate off pewter or ceramic plates imported from England or Holland. The great majority consumed their simple fare from wooden *trenchers* (platters) and drank from wooden *noggins* (cups).

The rise of the wheat trade—and the influx of poor settlers—introduced social divisions among the farmers. By the 1760s, some farmers had grown wealthy by hiring the poor and using their labor to raise large quantities of wheat for market sale. Others had become successful entrepreneurs, providing newly arrived settlers with land, equipment, goods, and services. These large-scale farmers, rural landlords, speculators, storekeepers, and gristmill operators gradually formed a new class of wealthy agricultural *capitalists*—the owners of productive property. The estate inventories of this economic elite include mahogany tables, four-poster beds,

Harvesting Wheat in Western Maryland, 1738

Beginning in the 1730s, wheat became a major export crop in Maryland and Virginia. This engraving probably depicts a German farm, for the harvesters are using oxen, not horses, and women are working in the field alongside men.

couches, table linen, imported Dutch dinnerware—all of which testify to the growth of economic inequality. In the 1760s the richest 10 percent of the Chester County's property-owning families controlled 30 percent of their communities' assets, while the poorest 30 percent held a mere 6 percent of the wealth.

Moreover, a new landless class, one with no taxable property, had appeared at the bottom of the social order. In five agricultural towns in New Jersey by the 1760s, half of the white men aged eighteen to twenty-five were without land, while in Chester County, Pennsylvania, nearly half of *all* white men were propertyless. Some landless men were the sons of property owners and would eventually inherit at least a part of the family's estate. But in Pennsylvania, there were many Scots-Irish *inmates*, single men or families "such as live in small cottages and have no taxable property, except a cow," as the tax assessor in the Scots-Irish township of Londonderry explained. There was also an "abundance of Poor people" in the predominantly German settlement of Lancaster, Pennsylvania. A merchant noted that they "maintain their Families with great difficulty by day Labour."

These landless Scots-Irish and German migrants hoped to improve their lot by becoming tenants and then landowners, but such goals were either unrealistic or very hard to achieve. Land prices had risen sharply in settled areas convenient to transportation, and the acquisition of a farmstead was the work of a lifetime. Merchants and artisans took advantage of the ample supply of labor by organizing a small putting-out system: they bought wool or flax from some farm families and paid others to spin it into yarn or weave it into cloth. An English traveler reported in the 1760s that hundreds of Pennsylvanians had turned "to manufacture, and live upon a small farm, as in many parts of England." By this time, eastern areas of the middle colonies, as well as of New England, had become as crowded and socially divided as many regions of rural England.

Tenancy on the Hudson Manors. German and Scots-Irish migrants in New York faced an even more arduous road to land ownership. Long-established Dutch families—the Rensselaers, the Van Cortlandts, and the Philipses—still presided over the patroonships created by the Dutch West India Company in the fertile Hudson River Valley. The first English governors of New York augmented the ranks of this landowning class by bestowing huge tracts of land on the Livingston, Morris, and Heathcote families. These clans had a stranglehold on the best land and refused to sell an acre of it. They wanted to live like European aristocrats, masters of scores of tenant families.

For that reason, many migrants refused to settle in the Hudson River Valley. In 1714, the manor of Rensselaerswyck had only 82 tenants on hundreds of thousands of acres. But gradually population growth caused a scarcity of freehold land in New York, and more families were forced to accept tenancy leases. To attract tenants, the lords of the manors had begun to offer better terms. They gave tenants long leases and the right to sell (to the next tenant) any improvements made to the property. Thus, Rensselaerswyck had 345 tenants in 1752 and nearly 700 by 1765. With determination, luck, and wheat profits, some tenants saved enough to buy freehold property, but the Hudson River Valley remained primarily a region of tenant farmers, distinct from the predominantly freehold communities in Pennsylvania, New Jersey, and New England.

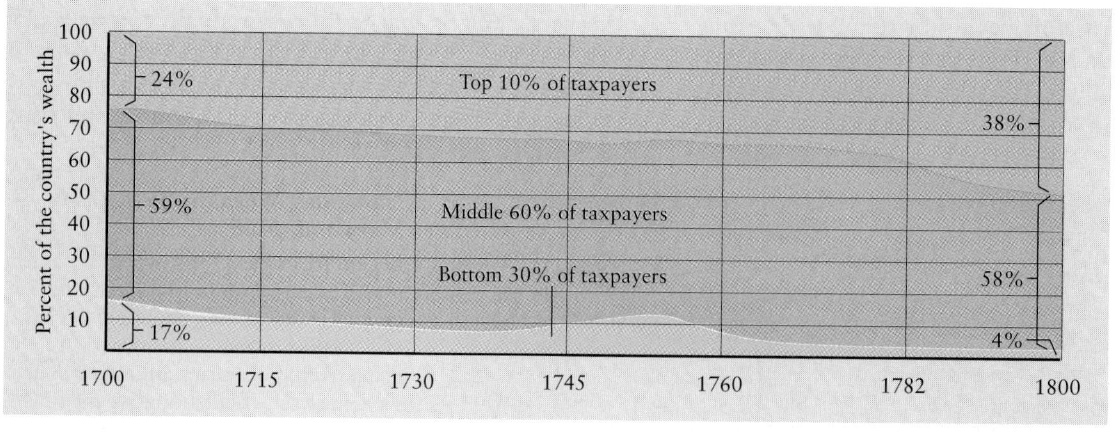

FIGURE 4.2

Increasing Socal Inequality in Chester County, Pennsylvania

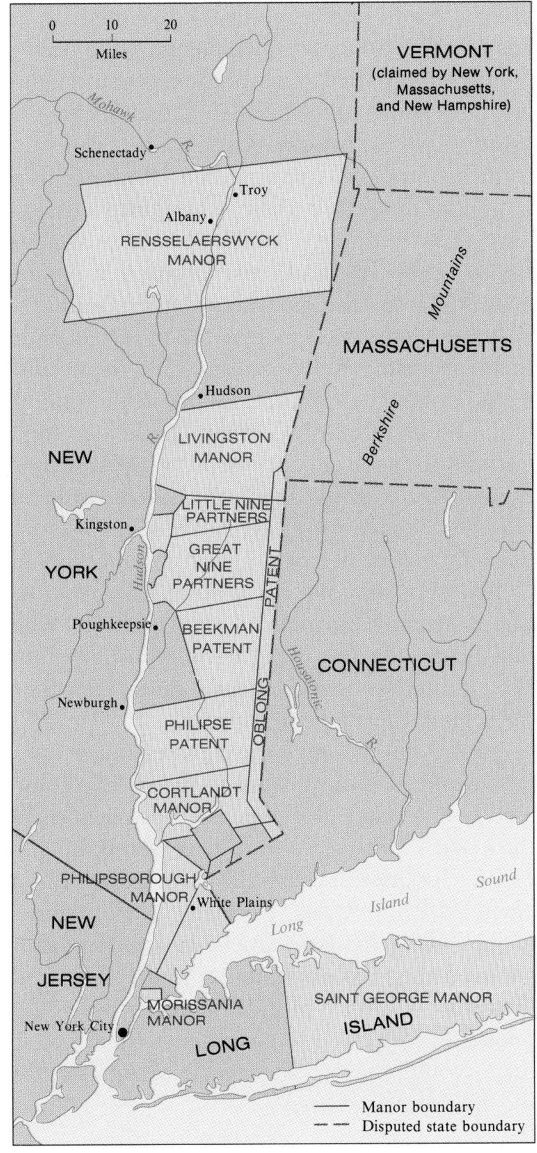

MAP 4.3

The Hudson River Manors

Dutch and English manorial lords dominated the fertile eastern shores of the Hudson River Valley—leasing their farms to German tenant families and refusing to sell farms to migrants from overcrowded New England. The landed elite used its political power to suppress tenant uprisings and rebuff the schemes of New England speculators and settlers.

By the middle of the eighteenth century, even communities of yeomen farm families stood divided by economic interests and class position. In Pennsylvania, gentlemen farmers and commercial middlemen had grown rich while German and Scots-Irish inmates still struggled for subsistence. In New England, which lacked a major export crop, many small-scale freeholders had fallen into debt—even the most creative farmers could generate only a limited surplus. The demands of yeomen farmers for land banks to provide loans and for paper currency to stimulate trade led to sharp political confrontations in Rhode Island in the 1730s and in Massachusetts in 1740. American creditors as well as British merchants feared a depreciated currency and insisted on "hard money" policies.

The boom in agricultural exports, both to the West Indies and to Western Europe, had subjected American farmers to the uncertainties of the international marketplace. In aspects of its economy, life in the colonies, especially in the long-settled regions, was beginning to resemble life in Europe. Yeomen farm families worried about finding sufficient land to give their children and feared—with good reason—a return to the exploited status of the European peasantry.

A Pluralistic Society

In their religious and ethnic diversity, if not in their economic divisions, the colonies remained distinct from Europe. In Western Europe, pluralism in religion was an untried experiment. Most European-trained ministers remained committed to religious uniformity enforced by an established church, backed by the government. "Throughout Pennsylvania the preachers do not have the power to punish anyone, or to force anyone to go to church," Gottlieb Mittelburger complained. As a result, "Sunday is very badly kept. Many people plough, reap, thresh, hew or split wood and the like." He concluded that "Liberty in Pennsylvania does more harm than good to many people, both in soul and body."

Mittelburger failed to appreciate the power of communal self-discipline. The various religious sects in Pennsylvania enforced moral behavior among their members. Each Quaker family, for example, regularly attended a weekly meeting for worship and was part of a monthly meeting that handled discipline. A committee met with each family four times a year and made certain that its children received proper religious instruction. The committee also reported on the moral behavior of adults. In Chester County, the men acted on such a report by disciplining one of their members "to reclaim him from drinking to excess and keeping vain company."

In the Quaker community, permission to marry was granted only to couples with sufficient land, livestock, and equipment to support themselves and their future children. Marriage with non-Quakers was usually prohibited and those who disobeyed were treated as outcasts. In Chester County, about two-thirds of the young men and women who married outside the faith were barred from Quaker meetings.

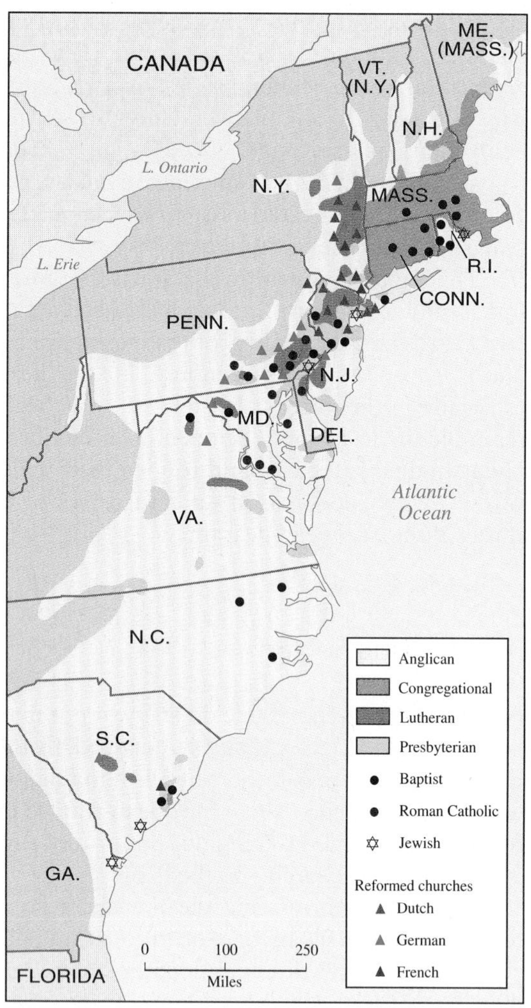

MAP 4.4

Religious Diversity in 1750

By 1750 religious diversity was the norm in many colonies. Baptists had become an important force in New England, long the stronghold of Congregationalism, while Presbyterians and Lutherans populated the backcountry of the southern colonies, where Anglicanism was the established religion.

Over the generations, this strict system shaped the character of the Quaker community. The children of well-to-do Friends had ample marriage portions and usually married within the sect. Those who lacked the resources remained unmarried or left the Society. Thus the Quakers created a prosperous religious community of urban merchants and freeholding families. Clearly it was not necessary to have an established church to avoid social chaos.

However, Pennsylvania did not escape the tensions inherent in a society composed of distinct ethnic groups. By the 1750s, Pennsylvania politics was sharply divided along cultural and religious lines. Scots-Irish Presbyterians on the frontier were challenging the pacifism of the Quaker-dominated assembly and demanding a more aggressive policy toward the Indians. Germans in frontier areas, many of whom belonged to Lutheran and Reformed churches, opposed the Quakers; they wanted laws that respected their inheritance customs (which gave the community some say in the disposition of a family's property) and representation in the assembly in proportion to their numbers. Other Germans, particularly the Mennonites, supported the Quakers because of their pacifism. Religious outlook increasingly determined political allegiance. As one observer noted, Scots-Irish Presbyterians, German Baptists, and German Lutherans had begun to form "a general confederacy" against the "ruling party" of Quakers in Pennsylvania, but this alliance was fragile. These diverse peoples still lived in peace, a foreign visitor remarked during the 1750s, yet "they have a mutual jealousy, for religious zeal is secretly burning." Latent passions would break out during the following decade and again during the War for Independence, nearly destroying the fabric of the social order in Pennsylvania.

But during most of the eighteenth century, the many ethnic and religious groups in the middle colonies tolerated one another, developed self-governing churches of their own, and created an increasingly open and competitive political system. Ethnic tensions continued—particularly between German- and English-speaking groups—but this experiment in freedom and diversity survived the revolutionary era and offered a glimpse of the future. Cultural pluralism and an open religious and political order given to passionate ethnic and social conflicts would characterize much of American society in the nineteenth century.

The Enlightenment and the Great Awakening, 1740–1765

Two great European cultural movements swept across the Atlantic to America between the 1730s and the 1760s: the Enlightenment and Pietism. The *Enlightenment* emphasized the power of human reason to shape the world; it appealed especially to better-educated men and women, mostly those from merchant or planter families, and to urban artisans. *Pietism* was an emotional evangelical religious movement that stressed human beings' dependence on God. Although Pietism attracted all social groups, it was most successful among farmers, urban laborers, and slaves. Both the Enlightenment and Pietism promoted independent thinking, but in different ways; together, they transformed American intellectual and cultural life.

The Enlightenment in America

From the time of the earliest colonial settlements, most Americans saw the world in religious terms. However, theological doctrines were often less persuasive to ordinary Christians than superstitions and folk wisdom. Even trained ministers believed in magic. When a measles epidemic struck Boston in the 1710s, the Puritan minister Cotton Mather recommended "getting the Blood of the Great Passover sprinkled on our Houses." Like most Christians of the time, Mather believed that God intervened directly in human affairs. Indeed, some Europeans who settled in British America saw the world in animistic terms: spirits and powers were everywhere and could be used for good or evil. Swedish settlers in Pennsylvania ascribed magical powers to the great white mullein, a common wild plant. When they had a fever, a traveler reported, they "tie the leaves around their feet and arms."

The New Learning. The Scientific Revolution of the seventeenth century challenged these traditional world views. The observation of the sixteenth-century astronomer Copernicus that the earth traveled around the sun, and not vice versa, had offered a new and more modest view of humanity's place in the universe. Other scholars conducted experiments using empirical methods—actual observed experience—to discover the facts about natural phenomena, such as earthquakes and lightning. These intellectual innovations convinced many educated Europeans that human beings could analyze—and ultimately understand and improve—the world in which they lived.

The European Enlightenment began around 1675, when laws that governed the natural world were discovered and critical, rational modes of thought were applied to the understanding of human society. The Enlightenment was a complex intellectual movement, but it was based on four fundamental principles: a belief in the power of human reason, the existence of natural laws, the rejection of "divine right" government, and the possibility of the progressive improvement of society.

The English scientist Isaac Newton did more than anyone to advance this "new learning." His *Principia Mathematica* (1687) used mathematics to explain the movement of the planets around the sun. Newton's laws of motion and his concept of gravity described how the universe could operate without the constant intervention of a god, thus challenging traditional Christian explanations of the cosmos. Similarly, John Locke in his *Essay Concerning Human Understanding* (1690) rejected the belief that human beings were born with God-given "innate" ideas. On the contrary, Locke argued that the infant's mind was a *tabula rasa*, a "blank slate" that was gradually filled with information conveyed by the senses and arranged by reason. By emphasizing the impact of experience and environment on human thought and behavior, Locke proposed that the character of people and societies could be changed through education and purposeful action. Indeed, in his *Two Treatises on Government* (1690), justifying the Glorious Revolution of 1688, Locke advanced a revolutionary theory of government: political authority was not divinely ordained but sprang from "*social compacts*" among people. Legitimacy came from the agreement among individuals to form a political society and, subsequently, to change their form of government by the decision of a majority.

Impact in America. Enlightenment ideas were brought to America in books and by travelers during the first decades of the eighteenth century. When a smallpox epidemic threatened Boston in the 1720s—ten years after the measles epidemic—Cotton Mather sought a scientific remedy, joining with Zabdiel Boylston, a prominent Boston physician, in supporting the new technique of inoculation against the disease. Also in the 1720s, the Reverend John Wise of Ipswich, Massachusetts, combined Locke's political principles and Calvinist theology to defend the decision of Congregational churches to vest power in the laity (rather than in bishops, as in the Church of England). Wise argued that just as the "social compact" formed the basis of political society, the religious covenant made the congregation—and not bishops or kings—the source of spiritual authority.

By mid-century, Enlightenment ideas had become second nature to many educated Americans. Elizabeth Smith, an upper-class mother, invoked Lockean principles when, in a letter to a friend, she wrote about her newborn child: "The Infant Mind is a blank that easily receives my impression." Some upper-class colonists—Virginia planters, New York merchants, urban artisans—became *deists*. Influenced by Enlightenment science, deists believed that God had created the world and then allowed it to operate according to the laws of nature. Their God was a rational being, a divine "watchmaker" who did not intervene in the historical process.

Franklin and the Enlightenment. Benjamin Franklin was the epitome of an Enlightenment thinker in America. Born into the family of a candlemaker in Boston in 1706, Franklin had little formal schooling. He was self-taught, having acquired a taste for knowledge as a printer's apprentice, and he mastered a wide variety of political and scientific works. Franklin's imagination was shaped by Enlightenment literature, not by the Christian Bible. In fact, as he explained in his *Autobiography*, "from the different books I read, I began to doubt of Revelation itself." Franklin became a deist.

Enlightenment Philanthropy: The Pennsylvania Hospital
This imposing structure, built in 1753 with public funds and private donations, embodied two principles of the Enlightenment—the belief that purposeful action could improve society and the importance of reason and order, expressed here in the symmetrical facade. It is illustrated beautifully in this painting, *A Southeast Prospect of the Pennsylvania Hospital*, c. 1761 by John Steeper and Henry Dawkins. (The Library Company of Philadelphia)

As a tradesman, printer, and journalist in Philadelphia, Franklin formed "a club of mutual improvement," which met every Friday evening to discuss "Morals, Politics, or Natural Philosophy." He propagated the outlook of the Enlightenment—optimistic, secular, and materialistic—in *Poor Richard's Almanac*, which was read by thousands of farmers. In 1743 he helped found the American Philosophical Society, an institution devoted to "the promotion of useful knowledge." He came up with an improved stove (the Franklin stove) and invented bifocal lenses for spectacles, and the lightning rod. His research in the infant science of electricity won international acclaim. In fact, the English scientist Joseph Priestly praised Franklin's book on electricity, first published in England in 1751, as the greatest contribution to science since the work of Isaac Newton.

The Legacy of the Enlightenment. Franklin's Philadelphia became the showplace of the American Enlightenment. It boasted a circulating library filled with the latest scientific treatises from Europe. The first American medical school was founded there in 1765. Quaker and Anglican merchants built a Hospital for the Sick Poor in 1751 and then, in 1767, added a Bettering House to shelter the aged and disabled and to offer employment to the poor. These philanthropists were acting as much from economic self-interest as from moral conviction, for they hoped these institutions would reduce the taxes they paid for relief of the poor. Nonetheless, the hospital and the bettering house were expressions of the Enlightenment belief that purposeful human action could improve society.

By the mid-eighteenth century, educated Americans were showing increased self-confidence and a growing sense of social identity. A host of clubs, schools, and publications appeared. The first American newspapers had appeared in Boston in 1704 and Philadelphia in 1719, but their numbers increased dramatically after 1740; by 1765, nearly every colony had a regularly published newspaper. Ambitious printers began magazines aimed at wealthy gentlemen, including the *New York*, the *Massachusetts*, and Franklin's *General*. Although most of them were failures—local newspapers and books from Europe filled the needs of the reading public—they were the first significant non-religious publications (apart from newspapers) to appear in the colonies. The European Enlightenment had added a secular dimension to colonial intellectual life, preparing the way for the great American contributions to republican political theory during the Revolutionary Era.

Pietism in America

While some Americans were abandoning an old religious world view, others were embracing a new one: the European religious movement known as *pietism*. Pietism paid little attention to theological dogmas, emphasizing instead moral behavior, emotional church services, and a mystical union with God. Pietist preachers appealed to the hearts, not the minds, of their followers. They exhorted people to be devout—that is, "pious"—Christians; hence the name. Their teachings were particularly popular among the lower orders of European society. Peasants, artisans, and laborers joined pietistic churches by the thousands.

Pietism came to America with German migrants beginning in the 1720s and led to a religious revival in the middle colonies. The Dutch minister Theodore Jacob Frelinghuysen moved from church to church, preaching to German settlers in Pennsylvania and members of the Dutch Reformed Church in New Jersey. He sought first to arouse them by delivering vigorous, emotional sermons. Then he harnessed their enthusiasm, organizing private prayer meetings and encouraging lay members of the congregation to preach. William Tennent and his son Gilbert were Presbyterian clergymen who copied Frelinghuysen's approach. During the 1730s the Tennents led a series of revivals among Scots-Irish migrants in New Jersey and Pennsylvania.

Simultaneously, an American pietistic movement was born in the Puritan colonies. Puritanism itself had been part of a pietistic upsurge in sixteenth-century England, but over the years many Puritan congregations had lost their religious zeal. During the 1730s Jonathan Edwards sought to restore spiritual commitment to the Congregational churches of the Connecticut River Valley, urging people—especially young men and women—to commit themselves to a life of piety and prayer.

Edwards was a philosopher as well as a defender of revivalism. He was well-versed in the literature of the Enlightenment and tried to reconcile the new learning with traditional religious thought. For example, Edwards used Locke's theory of knowledge to explain and justify emotional preaching. He argued that by stimulating the passions, a minister could make people more receptive to God's grace.

Edwards himself was not an emotional preacher but he was an extremely effective one, holding his audience through the sheer force of his ideas and his vivid imagery. He told congregations that they were "helpless and hopeless creatures"; to be saved, they had to renounce their pride and humble themselves before God. In his most famous sermon, *Sinners in the Hands of an Angry God* (1742), Edwards warned the congregation that the Creator held them "by a thin thread over the abyss of *hell*." Edwards's vigorous defense of revivalism and his insistence on strict standards for church admission and communion angered his congregation in Northampton, Massachusetts: it dismissed him as their minister in 1750.

George Whitefield and the Great Awakening

Revivalism was carried to new heights in the 1740s by George Whitefield, a young English evangelist. Whitefield had experienced conversion in England after reading German pietistic tracts. He became a disciple of John Wesley, the founder of Methodism, who himself had been inspired by German Moravian Pietists during a stay in Georgia. Wesley combined enthusiastic preaching with disciplined "methods" of worship. Soon he had persuaded thousands of Anglicans and scores of ministers to become pietistic Methodists within the Church of England.

Whitefield preached with equal success in America, where, especially in the South, he found a society with few ministers and a weak church-going tradition. He established an orphanage in Georgia in 1738 and then returned to preach throughout the colonies from 1739 to 1741. Huge crowds of "enthusiasts" greeted the young preacher wherever he went, from Georgia to Massachusetts. "Religion is become the Subject of most Conversations," the Pennsylvania *Gazette* reported. "No books are in Request but those of Piety and Devotion." The usually skeptical and restrained Benjamin Franklin was so moved by Whitefield's oratory that he emptied his pockets "wholly into the collector's dish, gold and all." By the time the evangelist reached Boston, the Reverend Benjamin Colman reported that the people were "ready to receive him as an angel of God."

Whitefield owed his appeal partly to his compelling personal presence. "He looked almost Angelical—a young, slim, slender youth," according to one Connecticut farmer. And he spoke magnificently and with great force, impressing on his audience that they had sinned and must seek salvation. Like most evangelical preachers, Whitefield did not read his sermons but spoke from memory, as if inspired, raising his voice for dramatic effect, gesturing eloquently, and making striking use of biblical metaphors. The young preacher evoked a deep emotional response. Hundreds of men and women suddenly felt the "new light" of God's grace within them; strengthened and self-confident, these New Lights were prepared to follow in Whitefield's footsteps. The evangelist's eloquence transformed local revivals into a genuine Great Awakening.

Religious Upheaval

Old Lights versus New Lights. Like all cultural explosions, the revival was controversial. Conservative ministers, such as Charles Chauncy of Boston, condemned the "cryings out, faintings and convulsions" produced by emotional preaching. These "Old Lights," as they were called by the awakeners, feared—with good reason—that revivalism might destroy the established churches. Inspired by Whitefield's example, dozens of farmers, women, and artisans were now roaming the countryside, preaching to all who would listen, condemning the Old Lights as "unconverted" sinners.

AMERICAN LIVES

Jonathan Edwards: Preacher, Philosopher, Pastor

Jonathan Edwards did not mince words. Echoing the harsh theology of John Calvin, Edwards preached that men and women were helpless creatures completely dependent on God: "There is Hell's wide gaping mouth open; and you have nothing to stand upon, nor any thing to take hold of: there is nothing between you and Hell but the air; 'tis only the power and mere pleasure of God that holds you up."

Edwards was very certain of the torments that awaited those who fell into the eternal flames:

> How dismal will it be . . . to know assuredly that you never, never shall be delivered from them; . . . after you shall have endured these torments millions of ages . . . your bodies, which shall have been burning and roasting all this while in these glowing flames, yet shall not have been consumed, but will remain to roast through an eternity yet. . . .

Such was the terrible fate Edwards promised to the complacent members of his congregation who had not repented and undergone a conversion experience:

> Thus are all you that never passed under a great change of heart, by the mighty power of the spirit of God upon your souls; all that were never born again, and made new creatures, and raised from being dead in sin, to a state of new, and before altogether unexperienced light and life. . . .

With such impassioned words, Edwards inspired a religious revival in the Connecticut River Valley in the mid-1730s and helped George Whitefield stir up an even greater one in the 1740s. But this hellfire-and-brimstone preacher, one of the leading revivalists of his age, was also a profound and original philosopher, perhaps the most intellectually brilliant of all colonial Americans.

Jonathan Edwards was born in East Windsor, Connecticut, in 1703. His father was a rural minister, and his mother was the daughter of Solomon Stoddard, a great revivalist and the most famous churchman in Connecticut. Edwards displayed a quick and enquiring mind even as a child, and he enrolled at Yale College before he turned thirteen. While preparing for the ministry at Yale, Edwards read the works of Isaac Newton, John Locke, and other Enlightenment thinkers, starting a lifetime of philosophical inquiry into the meaning of words and things. He accepted Locke's argument, in the *Essay Concerning Human Understanding* (1690), that words are only noises—having meaning merely as the result of social convention. But if words do not embody things or concepts, how can we come to know the world? Or, as Edwards posed the question, how could we escape from "the ambiguity of words, so that the ideas shall be left naked."

Locke had argued that ideas were the product of our senses—our ability to see, hear, feel, and taste. A person who has never *tasted* a pineapple, said Locke, will never have "the true idea of the relish of that celebrated and delicious fruit." But Locke's theory was less successful in explaining *abstract* ideas—God, man, angel, love, salvation—and it was here that Edwards made his contribution. Locke had suggested that such ideas were the result of the mind mixing together various sense experiences; but Edwards argued that they involved emotional apprehension as well—since, for example, "love" (whether of God or a fellow human) was "felt" and not merely understood. It followed that abstract ideas were emotional as well as rational entities, the product of the passions as well as the senses.

Edwards used his theory of knowledge to justify his enthusiastic style of preaching, arguing that vivid words promoted conversions by conveying abstract ideas in their full emotional intensity. As he put it in *A Treatise Concerning Religious Affections* (1746), "true religion, in great part, consists in holy affection"—an emotional state created by words that evoked the terrors of eternal damnation and the necessity of repentance. It was reasonable, Edwards declared, "to endeavor to fright persons away from Hell." In the end the philosopher was at one with the preacher.

This portrait by Joseph Badger shows the Rev. Jonathan Edwards as a young man in 1720. (Yale University Art Gallery)

Edwards put these ideas into practice as pastor of the Congregational Church in Northampton, Massachusetts, taking over that position from his grandfather, Solomon Stoddard, in 1727. He more than matched his grandfather's success as a revivalist. Beginning in 1734, Edwards reported, "the number of true saints multiplied . . . the town seemed to be full of the presence of God: it never was so full of love, nor so full of joy; and yet so full of distress as it was then." News of the Northampton revival stimulated religious fervor up and down the Connecticut River Valley "till there was a general awakening."

Edwards interpreted his success as "a remarkable Testimony of God's Approbation of the Doctrine . . . that we are justified only by faith in Christ, and not by any manner of virtue or goodness of our own." He maintained that uncompromising Calvinist position during the widespread revivals of the 1740s. Seeking to restore an older communal order, he took issue with the New Lights who asserted "the absolute Necessity for every Person to act singly . . . as if there was not another human Creature upon earth." Repudiating this spirit of individualism, Edwards insisted that aspiring Saints should heed their pastors, who were "skilful guides," and then make "a credible Relation of their inward Experience" to the congregation, thus strengthening the covenant bonds that knit members together in a visible church. Edwards extended his critique of individualism to economic affairs, speaking out against "a narrow, private spirit" among merchants and landlords, those men who "are not ashamed to hit and bite others [and] grind the faces of the poor. . . . "

Edwards's rigorous standards and his assault on religious and economic individualism deeply offended the wealthiest and most influential members of his congregation. The final break came in 1750, after Edwards repudiated Stoddard's practice of admitting almost all applicants for church membership—adhering instead to the Calvinist doctrine that God bestowed grace only upon chosen Saints. Dismissed from his Northampton pulpit, Edwards moved to Stockbridge, Massachusetts, a small frontier outpost. There he ministered to the Housatonic Indians and wrote his great philosophical works, *Freedom of the Will* and *Original Sin*. Just as he was about to take up the presidency of the College of New Jersey (Princeton) in 1757, Edwards was inoculated against smallpox, took the inoculation badly, and died.

As he lay dying, this turn of fate puzzled America's first great philosopher. Why had God called him to Princeton only to give him no time to undertake his duties? As a preacher and pastor Edwards had always responded to such questions by stressing God's arbitrary power and the "insufficiency of reason" to understand God's purpose. Now he himself had to accept that grim and emotionally unsatisfying answer, showing through his personal experience why Calvinism was such a hard faith by which to live . . . or die.

AMERICAN VOICES

The Religious Tribulations of a New Light *Nathan Cole*

George Whitefield transformed the lives of thousands of Americans, such as the Connecticut farmer Nathan Cole, by convincing them of their sinfulness. Here Cole describes his subsequent months of agony as he waited and prayed for a sign that he was worthy enough to merit God's grace and eternal salvation.

When I saw Mr. Whitefield come upon the Scaffold he lookt almost Angelical; a young, Slim, slender Youth before some thousands of people with a bold undaunted Countenance, and my hearing how God was with him every where as he came along it Solemnized my mind; and put me into a trembling fear before he began to preach; for he looked as if he was Cloathed with Authority from the Great God. . . . And a sweet solleme solemnity sat upon his brow and my hearing him preach, gave me a heart wound; By Gods blessing: my old Foundation was broken up, and I saw that my righteousness would not save me; then I was convinced of the doctrine of Election: and went right to quarrelling with God about it; because that all I could do would not save me; and he had decreed from Eternity who should be saved and who not: I began to think I was not Elected, and that God made some for heaven and me for hell. And I thought God was not Just in sodoing, I thought I did not stand on even Ground with others, if as I thought; I was made to be damned; My heart then rose against God exceedingly, for his making me for hell; Now this distress lasted Almost two years—Poor—Me—Miserable me. . . .

Hell fire was most always in my mind; and I have hundreds of times put my fingers into my pipe when I have been smoaking to feel how fire felt: And to see how my Body could bear to lye in Hell fire for ever and ever. . . . And while these thoughts were in my mind God appeared unto me and made me Skringe: before whose face the heavens and the earth fled away; and I was Shrinked into nothing; I knew not whether I was in the body or out, I seemed to hang in open Air before God, and he seemed to Speak to me in an angry and Sovereign way what won't you trust your Soul with God; My heart answered Oh yes, yes, yes.

I was set free, my distress was gone, and I was filled with a pineing desire to see Christs own words in the bible. I saw was the 15th Chap: John—on Christs own words and they spake to my very heart and every doubt and scriple that rose in my heart about the truth of Gods word was took right off. I got the bible up under my Chin and hugged it; it was sweet and lovely; the word was nigh me in my hand, then I began to pray and to praise God; . . .

George Whitefield, c. 1742

This is John Wollaston's painting of the evangelist. Perhaps no painting captured Whitefield's magic. When he spoke to a crowd near Philadelphia, his sermon "was sharper than a two-edged sword . . . . Some of the people were pale as death; others were wringing their hands . . . and most lifting their eyes to heaven and crying to God for mercy." (The National Portrait Gallery, London)

Source: Richard Bushman, *The Great Awakening: Documents on the Revival of Religion, 1740–1745,* (University of North Carolina Press, 1989).

To silence the revivalists, the Old Lights in Connecticut persuaded the legislative assembly to prohibit traveling preachers from speaking to established congregations without the ministers' permission. Thus when Whitefield returned to Connecticut in 1744, he found many pulpits closed to him. But the New Lights stoutly resisted attempts by civil authorities to silence them. "I shall bring glory to God in my bonds," a dissident preacher wrote from a Massachusetts jail. The New Lights won repeal of the Connecticut law in 1750. But the battle was far from over.

The Awakening's Significance. Because of this and similar struggles throughout the northern colonies, the Great Awakening escalated into a social and intellectual upheaval. Before it had run its course, Americans had questioned religious taxes, the idea of an established church, the authority of ministers—even the morality of economic competition.

Many New Lights and Baptists questioned government involvement in religion and favored a greater separation between church and state. According to the Baptist preacher Isaac Backus, "God never allowed any civil state upon earth to impose religious taxes." In New England many New Lights simply left the established Congregational Church; by 1754 they had founded 125 "separatist" churches. Other dissidents joined Baptist congregations, which grew tremendously. In New York and New Jersey, the Dutch Reformed Church split into two factions, as New Lights resisted the conservative church authorities in the Netherlands. Following the Great Awakening, church membership throughout the colonies became a voluntary act, not a civic duty.

The Awakening challenged the authority of the ministry. Traditionally, preachers had commanded respect because of their education in theology and knowledge of the Bible. But Gilbert Tennent questioned these criteria in his influential pamphlet, *The Dangers of an Unconverted Ministry* (1740). Tennent maintained that what qualified ministers to hold office was not theological training but the conversion experience. Thus, anyone who was saved could speak with ministerial authority. Traditional churches—formal, hierarchical, doctrine-bound—were starting to give way to denominations, such as the Baptists, that emphasized piety rather than theology, emotions rather than dogma, lay preaching rather than clerical wisdom.

The Pietist revivals also reinforced the strong community values held by rural people. Many Pietist leaders were suspicious of merchants and land speculators. They feared that the mercenary values of the marketplace had eroded traditional moral principles. Jonathan Edwards spoke for many rural Americans when he said that a "private niggardly spirit" was more suitable "for wolves and other beasts of prey, than for human beings." By joining religious revivals, many farm families reaffirmed their commitment to the cooperative ethic of rural life. "In any truly Christian society," Gilbert Tennent explained, "mutual *Love* is the *Band* and *Cement*."

At the same time, the Awakening injected new vigor into education and intellectual pursuits, for the various churches founded new colleges to educate youth and to train ministers. New Light Presbyterians established the College of New Jersey (Princeton) in 1747, and New York Anglicans founded King's College (Columbia) in 1754. Baptists set up the College of Rhode Island (Brown); the Dutch Reformed Church subsidized Queen's College (Rutgers) in New Jersey. However, the true intellectual legacy of the revival was not education for the few but a new sense of spiritual power and independence among the many. The Baptist preacher Isaac Backus captured the democratic thrust of the Awakening when he noted that "the common people now claim as good a right to judge and act in matters of religion as civil rulers or the learned clergy."

Social and Religious Conflict in the South

In the southern colonies religious conflict took an intensely social form, especially in Virginia. The Church of England, the established church, was supported by public taxes, yet it had never ministered to most Virginians. About 40 percent of the population was made up of blacks, who were generally excluded from church membership. Whites were required by law to attend Sunday services, but many landless families—another 20 percent of the population—came irregularly. Middling white freeholders, who made up 35 percent of the

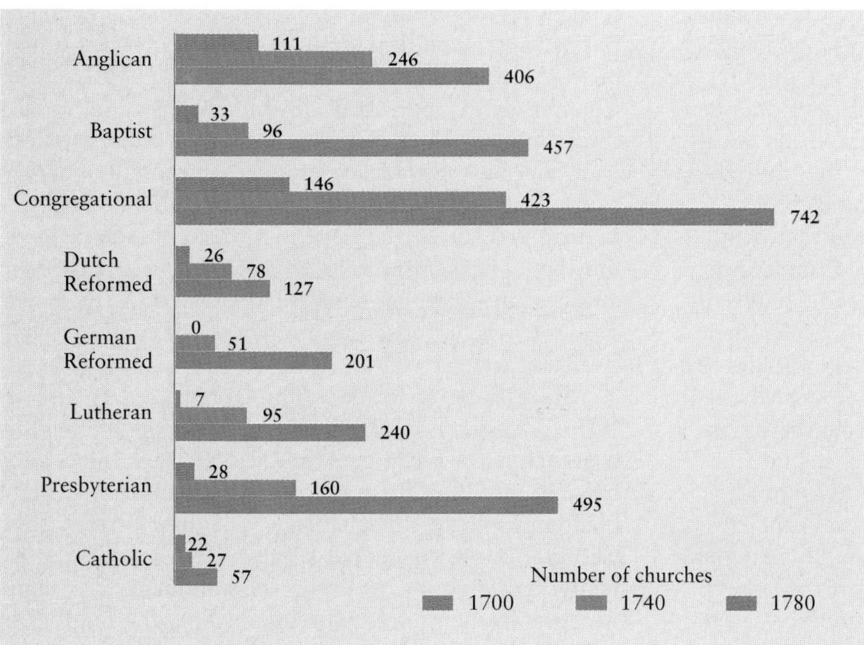

FIGURE 4.3

Church Growth by Denomination, 1700–1780

TABLE 4.2

Colonial Colleges

	Date of Founding	Colony	Religious Affiliation
Harvard	1636	Massachusetts	Puritan
William and Mary	1693	Virginia	Church of England
Yale	1701	Connecticut	Puritan
College of New Jersey (Princeton)	1746	New Jersey	Presbyterian
King's (Columbia)	1754	New York	Church of England
College of Philadelphia (University of Pennsylvania)	1755	Pennsylvania	None
Brown	1764	Rhode Island	Baptist
Queen's (Rutgers)	1766	New Jersey	Dutch Reformed
Dartmouth	1769	New Hampshire	Congregationalist

population, formed the core of most Anglican congregations, but it was the remaining 5 percent, the prominent planters, who held power in the church. They controlled the parish vestries, the lay organizations that helped ministers manage church affairs. Indeed, these wealthy vestrymen used their control of parish finances to keep Anglican ministers under control. One clergyman complained that vestrymen dismissed any minister who "had the courage to preach against any Vices taken into favor by the leading Men of his Parish."

But the vestry's power could not dam up the new religious fervor. In 1743 a bricklayer named Samuel Morris, who had been inspired by reading George Whitefield's sermons, led a group of Virginia Anglicans out of the established church to seek a more vital experience. Morris and his followers invited New Light Presbyterian ministers from Scots-Irish settlements along the Virginia frontier to lead prayer meetings. Soon local revivals spread across the backcountry and into the so-called Tidewater region along the Atlantic coast.

The political leaders of Virginia feared that a full-scale Presbyterian pietistic revival would undermine their authority. It was their custom to attend Church of England services with their families and to display their fine clothes, well-bred horses, and elaborate carriages to the assembled community. Vestrymen often waited outside the church until the minister had started the service before marching in a body to their seats in the front row. These opportunities for a show of their authority would vanish if freeholders joined the New Light Presbyterians, and religious pluralism would threaten the gentry's ability to tax the masses to support the Church of England. The fate of the established church seemed to hang in the balance.

To restrain the New Light Presbyterians, Governor William Gooch denounced their "false teachings." Anglican justices of the peace closed down Presbyterian meetinghouses and harassed Samuel Davies, a popular New Light preacher. These actions kept most white yeomen within the Church of England, as did the elitist outlook of the Presbyterians themselves. Presbyterian ministers—even the New Lights—were highly educated, and they sought converts among skilled workers and propertied farmers, seldom preaching to poor whites and never to black slaves.

Baptist Revivals and Black Protestantism. Baptists succeeded where Presbyterians failed. Like the Quakers, Baptists were a radical offshoot of the Protestant Reformation, direct descendants of the Anabaptists (see Chapter 1). Condemned or outlawed by authorities throughout Europe, Baptists drew their congregations from among the poor, developing emotionally charged rituals—such as baptizing adults by full immersion—that offered solace and hope in a world of trouble. During the 1760s, thousands of yeomen and tenant farm families in Virginia flocked to revivalist meetings, drawn by the enthusiasm and democratic ways of Baptist preachers.

Slaves were welcome at Baptist revivals. As early as 1740, George Whitefield had openly condemned the brutality of slaveholders and urged that blacks be brought into the Christian fold. A handful of New Light planters took up this challenge in South Carolina and Georgia, but with limited success. The hostility of the white population and the commitment of many Africans to their ancestral religions kept the number of converts low. The first large-scale conversion of slaves took place two decades later, among African-Americans in Virginia. Hundreds of slaves joined Baptist churches, run by ministers who taught that all men and women were equal in God's eyes.

The ruling gentry reacted violently to this courting of blacks and poor whites. Anglican sheriffs and justices of the peace organized armed bands of planters, who broke up Baptist services by force. In Caroline County, Virginia, according to the report of a Baptist, an Anglican posse attacked one Brother Waller. Waller was attempting to pray when "he was violently jerked off the stage; they caught him by the back part of his neck, beat his head against the ground, and a gentleman gave him twenty lashes with his horsewhip."

The intensity of the gentry's response reflected class antagonism, loyalty to the Anglican church, and fear: the Baptists posed a threat to their traditional culture. Baptist ministers condemned as vices such customary pleasures of Chesapeake men as horse racing, gambling, drinking, whoring, and cockfighting. They proposed to replace these boisterous habits with puritanical, cooperative Christian living. Baptist preachers urged their followers to work hard and lead virtuous lives. They emphasized equality by calling one another "brother" and "sister."

The central ritual, of course, was baptism. In contrast to most other Christian churches, which baptized infants, Baptists received this sacrament as adults, often by complete immersion in water. Once men and women had experienced the infusion of grace—had been "born again"—they were baptized in an emotional public ceremony that was a celebration of shared fellowship. One Sunday "about 2,000 people came together," a Baptist minister noted,

> We went to a field and making a circle in the center, there laid hands on the persons baptized. The multitude stood around weeping, but when we sang *Come we that love the lord* they lifted up their hands and faces toward heaven and discovered such cheerful countenances in the midst of flowing tears as I have never seen before.

The appeal of Baptist preaching and ritual was overwhelming. Despite fierce resistance from the gentry, by 1775 about 20 percent of Virginia's whites and thousands of enslaved blacks belonged to Baptist churches.

Anglican slaveholders retained their economic and political power, but the revival threatened their privileged position. For one thing, it spread democratic principles of church organization among white yeomen and tenant farmers. Then, belief in a living God gave meaning to the lives of poor families and better prepared them to assert their economic interests. Finally, when Baptist—and, later, Methodist—ministers began to spread Christianity among the slaves, the cultural gulf between blacks and whites grew smaller, undermining one justification for slavery and giving blacks a new sense of spiritual identity. Within a generation, African-Americans would develop their own version of Protestant Christianity.

The Mid-Century Challenge: War, Trade, and Land

Besides the intellectual and religious crisis of the eighteenth century, three other sets of events transformed colonial life between 1740 and 1765 and redefined the British empire in North America. First, Britain embarked on a major war in America, the so-called French and Indian War, which became a worldwide conflict. Second, the expansion of transatlantic trade increased colonial prosperity but put Americans into debt to British creditors. Third, Britain's ouster of the French from North America following the French and Indian War prompted a great westward movement that led to new battles with the Indians, armed conflicts between migrants and landowners, and frontier rebellions against eastern governments.

The French and Indian War

In the aftermath of the War of Jenkins' Ear and New England's capture of Louisbourg, British officials began to appreciate the potential of the colonial empire. Governor William Shirley of Massachusetts predicted that within a century the population of the mainland colonies would equal that of France and "lay a foundation for a Superiority of British power upon the continent of Europe."

Population and Diplomacy. Before the middle of the eighteenth century few Europeans had penetrated the region west of the Appalachians. The main French settlements, including the fur-trading centers of Montreal and Quebec, were along the St. Lawrence River, with only forts and fur-trading posts dotting the interior of the North American continent. British settlers had not moved across the Appalachians because there were few natural transportation routes. Moreover, the territory was a stronghold of the Iroquois and other tribes, still allied in a covenant chain. For a generation the Iroquois had traded with both the English and the French for guns and supplies, holding off white settlements with threats of war. In the late 1740s this "play-off" system began to break down because of the land crisis in neighboring New England and the influx of European migrants into the middle colonies. William Johnson, the Indian agent for the British government, wanted to settle Scottish migrants in the Mohawk valley, west of

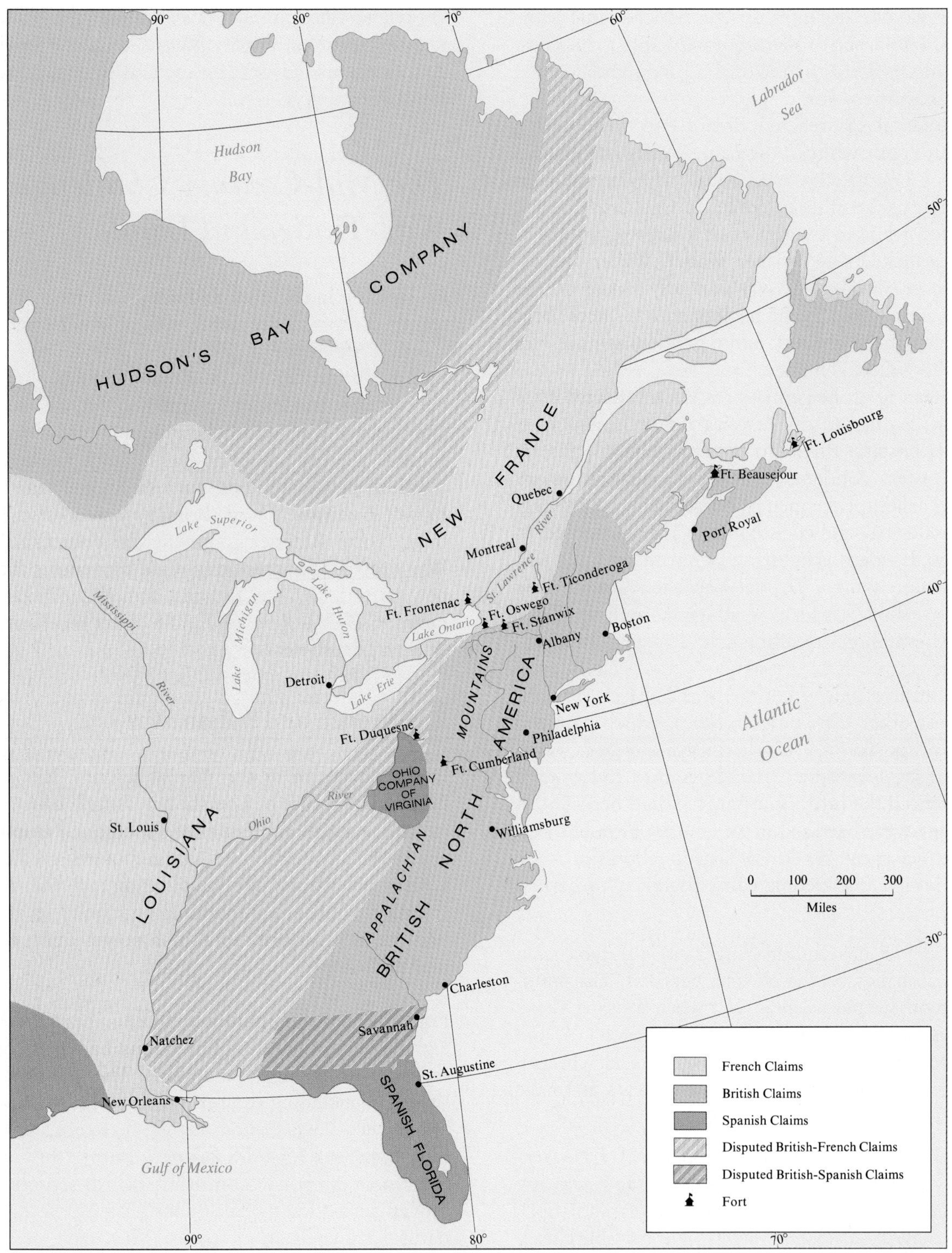

MAP 4.5

European Spheres of Influence, 1754

Britain, France, and Spain laid claim to vast areas of North America, seeking Indian allies but often disregarding their land rights. For their part, native Americans played off one European power against another. As a British official commented: "To preserve the Ballance between us and French is the great ruling Principle of Modern Indian Politics." The Great War for Empire disrupted this system, unleashing new white settlements and new Indian wars.

Albany, New York. To win over the Mohawk tribe, Johnson bestowed a huge amount of manufactured goods on them.

In the South also the movement of European migrants into the backcountry prompted land speculators to encroach on Indian territory. In 1749, Governor Robert Dinwiddie of Virginia and a group of prominent planters organized the Ohio Company, which enlisted the support of John Hanbury and other London merchants with political connections and obtained a royal land grant of 200,000 acres along the upper Ohio River and the promise of 300,000 acres more.

The Road to War. To secure British claims to the Ohio region, Governor Dinwiddie sent Colonel George Washington—a young planter, eager to speculate in western lands—with a force of the Virginia militia to ward off the French. This Virginia initiative raised the prospect of war. French merchants controlled the fur trade in this region and could only view Washington's expedition as a threat to their interests. Moreover, the French government sensed a larger danger to its claims of sovereignty over the interior of the North American continent. French officials in Canada responded to Dinwiddie's actions by constructing Fort Duquesne at the point where the Monongahela and Allegheny rivers join to form the Ohio (present-day Pittsburgh). French troops repulsed the Virginia force and captured Washington and the garrison at Fort Necessity (a hastily built military redoubt 60 miles south of Fort Duquesne) in July 1754. Virginia was at war with France in the American backcountry.

The British government had no desire to see this fighting continue. Its coffers were still empty from a long and expensive war against France that ended in 1748. Wars meant new taxes which were strongly opposed in Parliament. Prime Minister Henry Pelham knew this all too well: "There is such a load of debt, and such heavy taxes already laid upon the people, that nothing but an absolute necessity can justifie our engaging in a new War."

But Pelham could not control the march of events. William Pitt, a rising statesman, demanded a policy of expansionism in the colonies, as did Lord Halifax, the energetic new head of the Board of Trade. To coordinate the efforts of the American settlements, the board proposed a "union between ye Royal, Proprietary, & Charter Governments." American political leaders were thinking along similar lines. Delegates from most of the northern governments and the Six Iroquois Nations had met at Albany in June 1754 and adopted a "Plan of Union," primarily the work of Benjamin Franklin. Under the Albany plan, each colony would send delegates to an American continental assembly, which would be presided over by a royal governor-general. This assembly would assume responsibility for all western affairs—trade, Indian policy, and defense. The proposed union never happened because the provincial assemblies wanted to preserve their autonomy and the imperial government feared the consequences of convening a great American assembly.

To counter the French presence in the Ohio region, Britain dispatched Sir Edward Braddock and two regiments of troops to America. In May 1755 Braddock started marching through the wilderness with this force of 1,400 regulars and 450 Virginia militiamen. He never reached Fort Duquesne. In July, a small force of French and native Americans launched a surprise attack, fighting Indian style in the forest, and killed Braddock and half his men. With this battle, the skirmish between France and Virginia escalated into a European war.

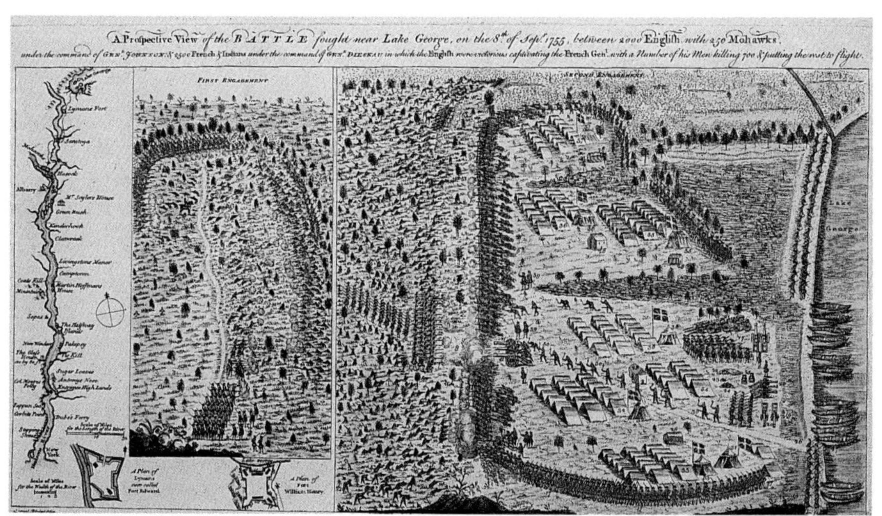

Battle of Lake George, 1755

Following European practice, French and British troops did battle in America in disciplined ranks or behind well-constructed earthworks. Only their native American allies (and a few colonial militiamen) fought "Indian-style" in small, irregular formations.

Not much fighting took place in the first years of the war. Hundreds of miles of forest separated the opposing forces, and military action was limited primarily to water-borne expeditions. In June 1755 British and New England naval and military forces captured Fort Beauséjour in Nova Scotia (Acadia). To eliminate the French from this region, the British deported 6,000 Acadians to Louisiana and South Carolina. Just before war was formally declared in 1756, the French sent the Marquis de Montcalm to command their forces in North America. Montcalm promptly captured and destroyed Fort Oswego on Lake Ontario.

The Great War for Empire

The two years of fighting in America precipitated the Seven Years' War in Europe and minor campaigns in South Asia and West Africa. In 1756, France made a pact with Austria, Britain's longtime continental ally, giving France the upper hand in Europe. French and Austrian armies threatened Hanover, the homeland of King George II of England, as well as Prussia, the territory of Britain's new ally, Frederick the Great.

Pitt's Imperial Strategy. In 1757, William Pitt replaced the irresolute Henry Pelham as first minister. With Pitt at the helm, the Seven Years' War would not be just another in a long string of European dynastic struggles with colonial episodes. Instead, it became the Great War for Empire. For Pitt was determined not merely to repel France in America and India, but to crush it completely.

Pitt honored Britain's commitment to its Prussian ally by sending large subsidies and a small expeditionary force. But his main interest lay overseas. Britain had reaped unprecedented wealth from its trading empire in the Caribbean, America, and India, and the French navy was the main obstacle to further expansion. Pitt ordered the British fleet to keep the French bottled up in their home ports so they could not respond to the various offensives he planned against their possessions.

Pitt planned the critical campaign against New France with special care. He sought out vigorous military leaders, giving top commands to three impressive young officers: James Wolfe, Jeffrey Amherst, and William Howe. And he took advantage of the fact that Britain's 2 million American colonists outnumbered the French settlers by fourteen to one. Pitt provided the colonies with generous subsidies, agreeing to pay half the cost of the troops raised there and to supply them with arms and equipment. Finally, he committed main units of the British navy and thousands of British regulars to the American conflict.

The Capture of Quebec. In 1758 the British launched attacks on the perimeter of New France's defenses, forcing the French to abandon Fort Duquesne and capturing Louisbourg. The following year, they moved on Quebec itself, from three directions. Colonel John Stanwix moved northward from Fort Duquesne—now Fort Pitt—and General Amherst led an Anglo-American army northward from New York. These expeditions were designed to distract French forces and their Indian allies from the major British force—50 warships, 200 transports, and 8,500 troops—which sailed up the St. Lawrence River under the command of General Wolfe in June 1759.

The attack on Quebec was the turning point of the war in North America. General Wolfe probed the city's strong defenses for three months. Then one day, in the hours before dawn, four thousand British troops scaled the 200-foot cliffs behind the city and took up positions on the high plains. French troops led by Montcalm advanced against Wolfe's army but were overwhelmed by British discipline and firepower, and Quebec fell. The Royal Navy prevented French reinforcements from crossing the Atlantic, and when British forces captured Montreal in 1760, the conquest of Canada was complete.

Still, the war in America did have one more scene to play, a quite unexpected one. Early in 1763 the Ottawa chief Pontiac organized a general uprising of the tribes of the Ohio River Valley. The Indians had generally coexisted well with French fur-traders and assimilated their culture; Pontiac himself said "I am French, and I want to die French." During the war, the tribes had been mistreated by British traders and soldiers and they feared an influx of Anglo-American settlers. Pontiac besieged the British fort at Detroit, while his allies captured nearly every British garrison west of Fort Niagara. Pontiac's forces defeated two British relief expeditions but when help from the French failed to arrive, the Indians signed peace treaties that protected their lands.

The Treaty of Paris. On the other battlefronts around the world, the British went from success to success. The East India Company captured French commercial outposts and took control of trade in large parts of India. British forces seized French Senegal in West Africa, the French sugar island of Martinique, as well as the Spanish colonies of Cuba and the Philippine Islands. When the war ended, Pitt was no longer in office, but his maritime strategy had extended British power all over the world. The first British Empire was at the height of its power.

The Treaty of Paris of 1763 confirmed the triumph of British arms. Britain gained sovereignty over half the continent of North America, including French Canada, all French territory east of the Mississippi River, and Spanish Florida. In recompense, Spain received French

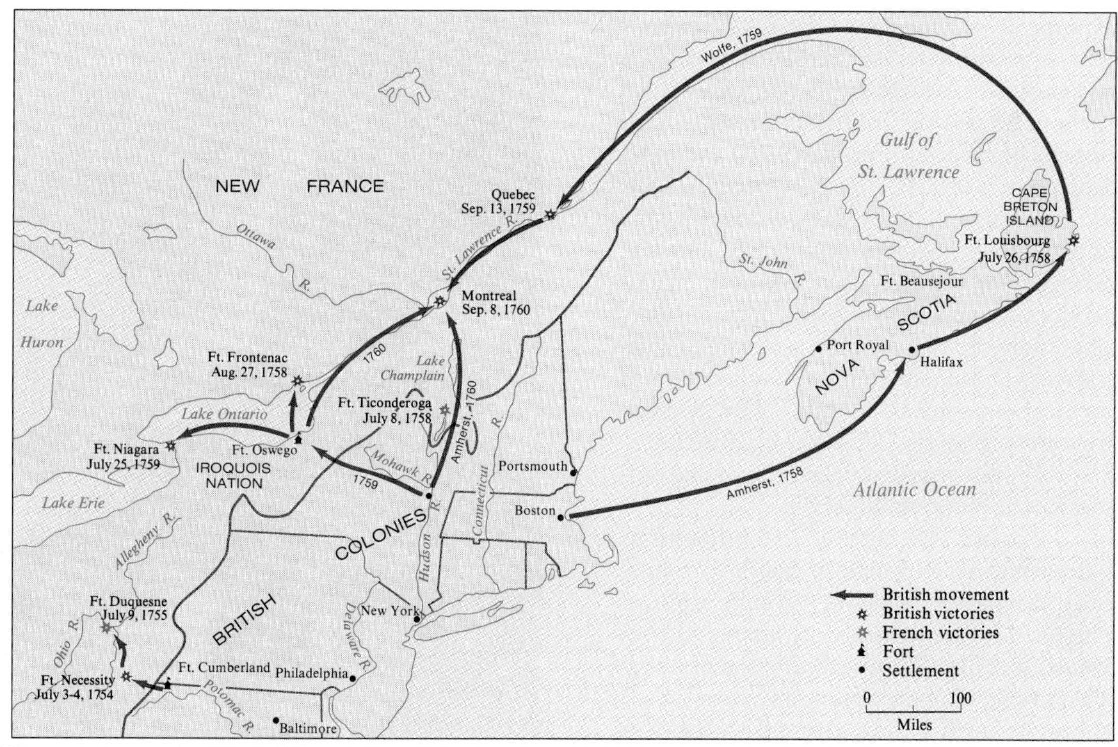

MAP 4.6

The Anglo-American Conquest of New France

After years of preparation, British and American forces attacked the heartland of New France, capturing Quebec in 1759. The conquest both united and divided the allies. Colonists celebrated the great victory—"The Illuminations and Fireworks exceeded any that had been exhibited before," reported the South Carolina *Gazette*—but British military leaders viewed provincial soldiers with contempt: "the dirtiest, most contemptible, cowardly dogs you can conceive."

Louisiana and the restoration of Cuba and the Philippines. The French empire in North America was reduced to a handful of valuable sugar islands in the West Indies and two rocky islands off the coast of Newfoundland.

British Economic Growth

Britain owed its triumph in large part to its unprecedented economic resources. Ever since it wrested control of many oceanic trade routes from the Dutch at the end of the seventeenth century, Britain had been the dominant commercial power. Now, at mid-eighteenth-century, Britain became the first country to undergo the Industrial Revolution. Its new system of technology and work-discipline made Britain the first—and for over a century the greatest—industrial nation in the world.

The Industrial Revolution. By 1750, British craftsmen had designed and built water- and steam-driven machines that powered lathes for shaping wood, jennies and looms for making textiles, and hammers for forging iron. The new machines produced goods far faster than human labor could. Furthermore, the entrepreneurs who ran the new factories drove their employees hard, forcing them to labor long hours and keep pace with the machines. This new work-discipline made it possible for the British to produce more wool and linen textiles, iron tools, paper, chinaware, and glass than ever before—and sell them at lower prices.

English and Scottish merchants launched aggressive campaigns to market these products in the rapidly growing mainland colonies. They extended a full year's credit to American traders, instead of the traditional six months. Colonial shopkeepers and merchants took advantage of these liberal terms to expand their inventories and increase their sales to distant backcountry farmers. Americans increased their consumption, and soon accounted for 20 percent of all British exports. The settlers bought equipment for their farms and all kinds of household goods—cloth, blankets, china, and cooking utensils. This "consumer revolution," as some historians have called it, raised the living standard of many Americans.

American Exports. To pay for these imports, Americans increased their agricultural exports. Tobacco from the Chesapeake remained the most important export, accounting for about 25 percent of the total. Planters sent 52 million pounds of tobacco abroad in 1740 and more than 75 million pounds in 1765. Entrepreneurs in Scotland financed this expansion by subsidizing Virginia planters and Scots-Irish migrants who moved into the Piedmont, a region of rolling plains and hills inland from the Tidewater counties. Scottish-run stores granted ample credit to these white settlers—to purchase land, slaves, and equipment—and took part of their tobacco crop in payment. By the 1760s, Scottish merchants were buying nearly half of the annual Chesapeake tobacco crop, re-exporting most of it to expanding markets in France and central Europe.

Agricultural exports also supported the luxurious life style of the white slaveowners of South Carolina. The British government subsidized the cultivation of indigo and, by the 1760s, planters were annually sending indigo valued at £117,000 to English textile factories as well as carrying on their traditional export trade to southern Europe—which now averaged about 65 million pounds of rice a year.

A booming export trade in wheat and flour permitted residents of the mid-Atlantic region to participate in the consumer revolution. With Europe in the throes of a population explosion, continental merchants were buying wheat from America—at first only in poor harvest years, then regularly. Wheat prices in Philadelphia jumped almost 50 percent between 1740 and 1765, bringing high profits to farmers and merchants. New

A Philadelphia Merchant

James Tulley stands well-dressed and proud, his arm resting on the ledger of his counting house, his ships in the background, preparing for the next voyage. Merchants like Tulley were the first great American entrepreneurs, organizing trade between the mainland, the West Indies, and Britain.

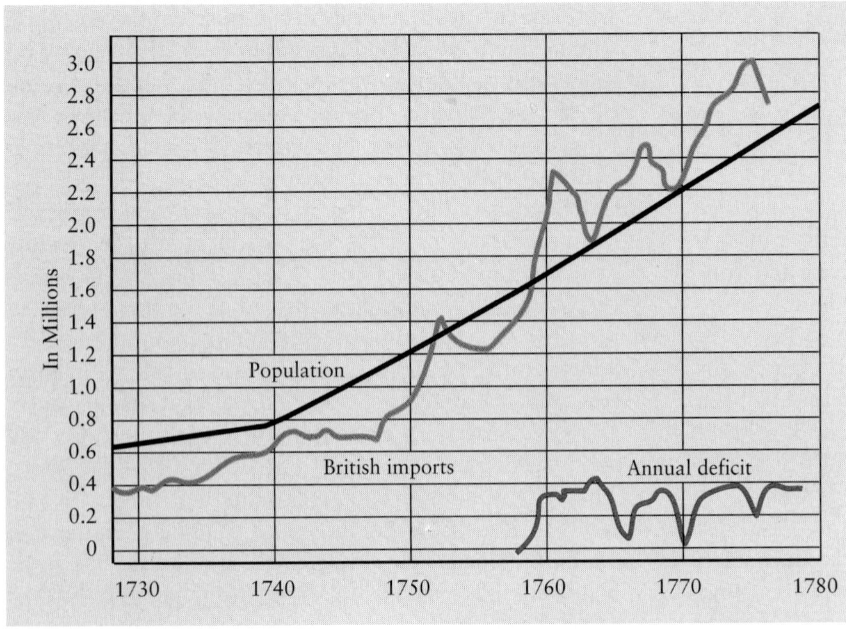

FIGURE 4.4

Population, British Imports, and the American Trade Deficit

York, Pennsylvania, Maryland, and Virginia became the breadbasket of the Atlantic world.

But even this boom in exports was not enough to defray the cost of the consumer frenzy. During the 1750s and 1760s exports paid for only 80 percent of the imported British goods. The remaining 20 percent—millions of pounds—was financed by British merchants who extended credit. The first American spending binge, like most subsequent splurges, landed many consumers in debt.

The return of peace after the Great War for Empire brought an end to boom times. Britain slashed its troop levels and military expenditures in America, and the loss of military markets, contracts, and cash subsidies made it more difficult for Americans to purchase British goods. Merchants looked anxiously at their overstocked warehouses and feared bankruptcy. "I think we have a gloomy prospect before us," a Philadelphian noted in 1765, "as there are of late some Persons failed, who were in no way suspected." The increase in transatlantic trade had raised living standards but had also made Americans more dependent on overseas creditors and the world economy.

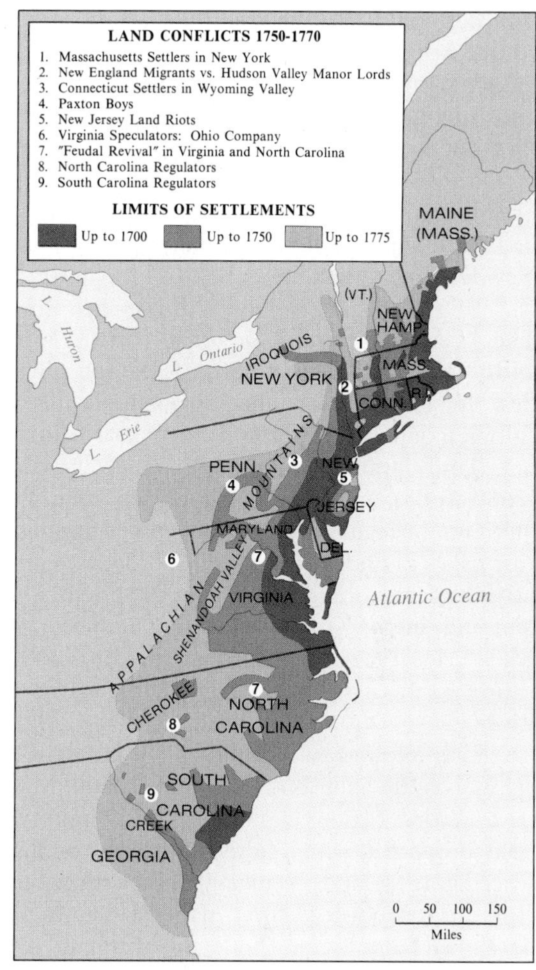

MAP 4.7

Westward Expansion and Armed Conflict

Between 1750 and 1775 the American population more than doubled—from 1.2 million to 2.5 million—sparking legal battles over land rights. Violence was particularly widespread in newly settled lands as backcountry farmers fought with Indians, rival claimants, and eastern-dominated governments.

Land Conflicts

In times of prosperity and in times of stagnating trade, the colonial population continued to grow. By 1750, the shortage of arable land in long-settled areas had become so acute that political conflicts broke out over land rights. With each new generation the problem got worse. In 1738, for example, men and women who traced their American ancestry back four generations founded the new town of Kent in western Connecticut. Their families had been moving slowly north and west for a century, and Kent was at the generally accepted western boundary of the colony. The next generation would have to find someplace else to go.

Migration Out of New England. In the 1750s, Connecticut farmers formed the Susquehannah Company and petitioned the Connecticut legislature to help them claim lands in the West. According to the colony's seventeenth-century charter, its boundaries stretched all the way to the Pacific Ocean; however, these claims crossed land also granted to William Penn. The Susquehannah Company persuaded the legislature to assert jurisdiction over disputed territory in the Wyoming Valley in northeastern Pennsylvania, and then sold land titles to Connecticut migrants who settled there.

The Penn family resisted this intrusion into its domain. With the support of the Pennsylvania assembly, the Penns reaffirmed their proprietary rights over the Wyoming Valley and issued land patents to its own settlers. Rival groups of land claimants proceeded to burn down each other's houses. To avert further violence, the Pennsylvania and Connecticut governments referred the dispute to British authorities in London, where it remained, undecided, at the time of independence.

Land disputes also broke out on New York's border with Massachusetts and New Hampshire. The boundaries were not precise and hundreds of families from New England moved into disputed territory in the Hudson River Valley. New England yeomen farmers refused to accept the tenancy leaseholds that were customary on the great New York manorial estates. Instead, they purchased freehold titles from Massachusetts land speculators and roused the long-settled Dutch and German tenants to repudiate their manorial leases.

Manorial lords enforced their claims in New York courts, setting off a rebellion. In 1766, New England migrants and tenant farmers in Westchester, Dutchess, and Albany counties refused to pay rent and used the threat of mob violence to close the courts. At the behest of the royal governor, General Thomas Gage led two British regiments to assist local sheriffs and manorial bailiffs in suppressing the tenant uprising and evicting New England squatters.

The "Feudal Revival." In other colonies proprietors with "feudal" claims also won legal and political battles. In New Jersey and throughout the southern colonies, landowners and English aristocrats revived old land grants from the time of Charles II (1660–1685), and judges supported their claims to quitrents in regions settled by yeomen farmers and to vast tracts of undeveloped land. Lord Granville, an heir of one of the original Carolina proprietors, collected quitrents in the Granville district of North Carolina, while a legal suit gave Lord Fairfax ownership of the entire northern neck of Virginia, along the Potomac River.

Long-established proprietary families profited anew from the increased demand for land. Many farmers in settled regions could not afford "improved" freehold properties with cultivated fields, orchards, and fenced grazing land. Reluctantly, they turned to proprietors for tenancy leases on manorial estates or for undeveloped land. By the 1760s, the Maryland proprietor, Lord Baltimore, was one of the richest men in England, thanks to his American real estate. The Penn family likewise reaped great profits from land sales and rents in Pennsylvania.

This "feudal revival" underscored the growing resemblance between rural society in Europe and America. High-quality land east of the Appalachians was getting more expensive, and much of it was controlled by English aristocrats, manorial landlords, or wealthy speculators. Unless something changed, tenants and even yeomen farmers might soon be reduced to the status of European peasants.

Uprisings in the West

As farmers moved west in search of land, they found themselves in the midst of new political and economic conflicts. Indian policy, political representation, and bankruptcy erupted in violence on the frontiers of Pennsylvania and North and South Carolina.

The Paxton Boys. In Pennsylvania, the white community came to blows over Indian policy. As long as Quakers dominated Pennsylvania politics, relations with native American tribes had remained peaceful, but when large numbers of Scots-Irish migrants settled along the frontier after 1740, they wanted to push the Indians off the land. When the Quakers refused to help them, the frontiersmen reacted with violence. In 1763 the Paxton Boys, a band of Scots-Irish farmers, massacred twenty members of the Conestoga tribe, which included the last remnants of the once numerous Susquehannock people. Governor John Penn attempted to protect the tribe and bring the murderers to justice, in response to which about 250 armed Scots-Irish advanced on Philadelphia, forcing the governor to mobilize the militia to defend the city. Benjamin Franklin intercepted the angry mob at Lancaster to seek a compromise, and a battle outside Philadelphia was narrowly averted. Ultimately, the prosecution of the accused men failed for lack of witnesses. The Scots-Irish dropped their demands for the expulsion of the Indians but the episode left a legacy of racial hatred and political resentment. During the independence crisis, the Scots-Irish would take their revenge against Quaker and Anglican leaders.

Philadelphia Mobilizes
The march of the Paxton Boys toward Philadelphia threw the city into alarm, bringing a hasty call-up of the militia. This cartoon of 1764, entitled "Paxton Boys vs. Philadelphia Quakers," satirizes the Quakers, who were pacifists, for their support of military action. (The Library Company of Philadelphia)

The South Carolina Regulators. During the French and Indian War, there had been brutal warfare between land-hungry whites and Cherokee Indians in the backcountry of South Carolina. Following the war, outlaw bands of whites continued to roam the countryside, unchallenged by government authority.

To subdue the outlaw bands and restore order, slaveowning planters and yeomen farmers banded together in an armed vigilante group called the Regulators. They took it upon themselves to impose moral discipline on the "low people"—the hunters, squatters, and landless laborers who lived on the fringes of society. They whipped people suspected of poaching or stealing goods. The Regulators also struggled for western rights, presenting a list of demands to the eastern authorities: they wanted more local courts, fairer taxes, and greater representation in the provincial assembly.

The South Carolina government accepted Regulator rule in the west despite its illegal character. Both the royal governor and the members of the provincial assembly were afraid to send the militia to the backcountry because it was needed to forestall slave revolts on the lowland rice plantations. They therefore compromised with backcountry insurgents, creating locally controlled courts in the west in 1767 and reducing the fees for legal documents. However, lowland planters and merchants kept a firm grip on political power, refusing to reapportion the legislature to provide western settlers with representation equal to their growing numbers. The assembly likewise continued to tax the thin soil of the upland region at the same rate as the fertile lands of the low country.

The Regulators could not continue the struggle because many western residents resisted their arbitrary assumption of power. Vowing to end Regulator rule, men who had previously served as justices of the peace in the backcountry organized a Moderator movement. In March 1769, six hundred armed supporters of each faction met near the Saluda River and exchanged angry words, then gunshots. Only an agreement to restore authority to the provincial government averted wholesale violence. Like the Paxton Boys in Pennsylvania, the Regulators attracted attention to western interests but failed to alter the balance of power. Eastern interests remained dominant.

The North Carolina Regulators. In North Carolina, the key issue dividing east and west was commercial credit. By the 1760s, the transatlantic market system extended far into the backcountry. At small stores owned by Scottish merchants, farmers and planters exchanged their tobacco, wheat, and hides for manufactured goods and bought land and slaves on credit. The more ambitious among them created small-scale slave plantations, so that the number of blacks rose. In Orange County, North Carolina, the number of African-Americans jumped from 45 in 1754 to 729 by 1767.

But the commercial slump following the Great War for Empire made tobacco prices plummet and many farmers were soon deeply in debt. In one three-year period, merchants in Granville County brought 350 debt suits to local courts. Judges directed sheriffs to seize the property of bankrupt farmers and sell it at auction to pay creditors and court costs. Backcountry farmers resented this recourse to the courts, both because it generated high fees for corrupt lawyers and court officials and because it violated local custom. As in rural communities in New England, loans among neighbors were based on trust and often ran for years.

To save their farms, North Carolina debtors created their own Regulator movement. At first, the Regulators intimidated judges, closed courts by force, and broke into jails to free their leaders. Then they sought to elect planters and farmers to the legislature. Their leader, a migrant from Maryland named Herman Husband, told his followers not to vote for "any Clerk, Lawyer, or Scotch merchant. We must make these men subject to the laws or they will enslave the whole community." The Regulators demanded a law allowing them to pay their taxes in the "produce of the country," rather than in cash; they also wanted legal fees reduced, and—like the South Carolina Regulators—they asked for fairer taxes and greater legislative representation.

The North Carolina Regulators developed the most broad-based and democratic program of all the backcountry movements. In Anson County, the Regulators argued that each person should pay taxes "in proportion to the profits arising from his estate." But the North Carolina insurgents were no more successful than other western protesters. In 1771, Governor William Tryon mobilized the militia and defeated a large Regulator force at the Alamance River. Then Tryon hunted down and hanged seven insurgent leaders. Not since Leisler's 1689 revolt in New York had political conflict in America resulted in so much bloodshed.

In 1771 as in 1689, colonial conflicts became intertwined with imperial politics. In far-off Connecticut, the Reverend Ezra Stiles defended the Regulators. "What shall an injured & oppressed people do," he asked, when they are faced with "Oppression and tyranny (under the name of Government)?" Stiles was an American Patriot and his condemnation of Governor Tryon in 1771 reflected American resistance to new British imperial controls. Reverend Stiles's remarks also served as a commentary on developments in the colonies between 1720 and 1765. These were years of crisis—agricultural, religious, ethnic, and military—and also of transformation. By 1765 America was still a dependent society, closely tied to Britain by trade, culture, and politics, but an increasingly complex, mature, and self-confident one. The colonies' potential for an independent existence was becoming apparent.

Summary

By 1720 a freeholding yeomen society had developed in New England. When rapid population growth began to threaten the freehold ideal, New England farmers averted a crisis by planting new, higher-yielding crops, and sharing their labor and goods with each other, and moving to land farther west.

In the middle colonies, the rising European demand for wheat, their principal crop, brought prosperity to many farmers. A great influx of German and Scots-Irish migrants created an ethnically diverse society, where religious groups held to their own beliefs but tolerated the traditions of others. Ethnic conflict did break out, especially over the Quakers' Indian policy, but the greater problem was the emergence of stark economic inequality. While some gentlemen farmers and entrepreneurs grew wealthy, a new landless class began to appear at the bottom of the social order.

As the American colonies became more integrated into the world economy, they also participated more fully in the intellectual life of the larger European world. Enlightenment rationalism and pietistic religion both reached America by 1730. The Great Awakening brought spiritual renewal to thousands of Americans, but not without sparking conflict. In the northern colonies New Lights condemned Old Lights, and in Virginia Baptists challenged the Anglican elite.

Beginning in the 1740s, the mainland colonies experienced a series of upheavals. Manorial lords in New York suppressed tenant uprisings, and proprietors in many colonies successfully asserted their economic, legal, and "feudal" rights. Yeomen families who had migrated into the backcountry fought with native Americans and with other settlers over land, and challenged the authority of eastern political leaders. And British and American soldiers fought a major war against the French, conquering Quebec and driving the French out of North America.

These conflicts testified to the growing involvement of the colonies in the diplomacy, commerce, and intellectual life of Europe. Britain's North American provinces were growing—in economic complexity, political vitality, and military potential.

TOPIC FOR RESEARCH

The Great Awakening

The Great Awakening was a pivotal event in American history, for it began a century-long process which made evangelical Protestantism a dominant cultural force in the United States. What was the message preached by the revivalists and why did thousands of Americans embrace it? Examine one of the sermons of the great evangelist George Whitefield, "The Marriage of Cana." What religious *doctrine*, if any, does Whitefield espouse, and how must he have delivered this sermon to elicit such a passionate response? (To understand this, you should deliver it out loud—with gusto!) The following secondary works analyze revivalists and the social conditions that accounted, in part, for their success: William G. McLouglin, *Revivals, Awakenings, and Reform: An Essay on Religion and Social Change in America, 1607–1977* (1978); David S. Lovejoy, *Religious Enthusiasm in the New World: Heresy to Revolution* (1985); Patricia U. Bonomi, *Under the Cope of Heaven: Religion, Society, and Politics in Colonial America* (1986); Jon Butler, *Awash in a Sea of Faith: Christianizing the American People* (1990); Richard Hofstadter, *America in 1750* (1971); Harry S. Stout, *The New England Soul: Preaching and Religious Culture in Colonial New England* (1986); Marilyn J. Westerkamp, *Triumph of the Laity: Scots-Irish Piety and the Great Awakening, 1625–1760* (1988); C. C. Goen, *Revivalism and Separatism in New England, 1740–1800* (1962); Alan Heimart, *Religion and the American Mind* (1966); and W. G. McLoughlin, *Isaac Backus and American Pietistic Tradition* (1957). Two good biographies of revivalists are Patricia Tracy, *Jonathan Edwards, Pastor* (1979) and Christopher Jedrey, *The World of John Cleaveland* (1979). Richard Bushman, ed., *The Great Awakening* (1989), and Rhys Isaac, *The Transformation of Virginia, 1740–1790* (1982), capture the emotions of ordinary participants.

BIBLIOGRAPHY

Freehold Society in New England

Two fine local studies are Christopher Jedrey, *The World of John Cleaveland: Family and Community in New England* (1979), and Robert Gross, *The Minutemen and Their World* (1976). For a broader approach, see Richard Bushman, *From Puritan to Yankee: Character and the Social Order in Connecticut, 1690–1765* (1967), and Michael Zuckerman, *Peaceable Kingdoms: New England Towns in the Eighteenth Century* (1970). On women's lives, see Laurel Thatcher Ulrich, *Good Wives: Image and Reality in the Lives of Women of Northern New England, 1650–1750* (1982), and Marylynn Salmon, *Women and the Law of Property in Early America* (1986). Studies of the material culture that reveal the character of society include James B. Deetz, *In Small Things Forgotten* (1977), and Robert B. St. George, ed., *Material Life In America, 1600–1860* (1988).

The Mid-Atlantic: Toward a New Society

On Pennyslvania, consult Gary B. Nash, *Quakers and Politics: Pennsylvania, 1681–1726* (1968); Allan Tully, *William Penn's Legacy: Pennsylvania, 1726–1755* (1978); and Barry J. Levy, *Quakers and the American Family* (1988). James T. Lemon, *The Best Poor Man's Country* (1972), explores Pennsylvania rural society with some attention to ethnicity. On white indentured servants and immigration, see the classic study by Abbot E. Smith, *Colonists in Bondage* (1947), and also R. J. Dickson, *Ulster Immigration to Colonial America, 1718–1775* (1966); James H. Kettner, *The Development of American Citizenship, 1608–1870* (1978); Jon Butler, *The Huguenots in America* (1983); Ned Landsman, *Scotland and Its First American Colony, 1683–1775* (1985); and A. Roger Ekirch, *Bound for America: The Transportation of British Convicts to the Colonies, 1718–1775* (1987). Other important studies include Sung Bok Kim, *Landlord and Tenant in Colonial New York: Manorial Society, 1664–1775* (1978), and Thomas L. Purvis, *Proprietors, Patronage, and Money: New Jersey, 1703–1776* (1986).

The Enlightenment and the Great Awakening

Henry F. May, *The Enlightenment in America* (1976), is the standard treatment, but see also Paul Merrill Spurlin, *The French Enlightenment in America* (1984). The growth of medical knowledge is covered in Richard Shryock, *Medicine and Society in America, 1660–1860* (1960), while the rise of scientific thinking is explored in Brooke Hindle, *The Pursuit of Science in Revolutionary America, 1735–1789* (1956); Raymond P. Stearns, *Science in the British Colonies of America* (1970); and James H. Cassedy, *Demography in Early America: Beginnings of the Statistical Mind, 1600–1800* (1976).

Bernard Bailyn, *Education in the Forming of American Society* (1960), is a stimulating introduction, while Lawrence A. Cremin, *American Education: The Colonial Experience* (1970), is a comprehensive study. Richard Warch captures the spiritual tenor of higher education in *School of the Prophets: Yale College, 1701–1740* (1973). See also James Axtell, *The School upon a Hill* (1974). Russell B. Nye provides a useful survey of *American Literary History, 1607–1830* (1970), while William L. Joyce et al., eds., *Printing and Society in Early America* (1983), assesses the impact of books, pamphlets, and newspapers on the American mind. Studies of religion and the Awakening are listed in the Topic for Research.

The Mid-Century Challenge: War, Trade, and Land

Douglas E. Leach, *Roots of Conflict: British Armed Forces and Colonial Americans, 1677–1763* (1989), sets the Great War for Empire in a larger context. See also Edward P. Hamilton, *The French and Indian Wars* (1962); Guy Fregault, *Canada: The War of the Conquest* (1969); George F. G. Stanley, *New France: The Last Phase, 1744–1760* (1968); and Fred Anderson, *A People's Army: Massachusetts Soldiers and Society in the Seven Years' War* (1984). Francis Jennings, *Empire of Fortune: Crown, Colonies, and Tribes in the Seven Years' War* (1988), shows the crucial part played by Indians in the conflict. See also Richard Aquila, *The Iroquois Restoration: Iroquois Diplomacy on the Colonial Frontier, 1701–1754* (1983); David H. Corkran, *The Cherokee Frontier: Conflict and Survival, 1740–1762* (1966); and W. R. Jacobs, *Wilderness Politics and Indian Gifts: The Northern Colonial Frontier, 1748–1763* (1950).

Gary M. Walton and James F. Shepherd, *The Economic Rise of Early America* (1979), traces the growing importance of commerce. See also Paul G. E. Clemens, *The Atlantic Economy and Colonial Maryland's Eastern Shore: From Tobacco to Grain* (1980); Jacob M. Price, *Capital and Credit in British Overseas Trade: The View from the Chesapeake, 1700–1776* (1980); and John J. McCusker and Russell R. Menard, *The Economy of British America, 1607–1783* (1985).

Backcountry political agitation forms the focus of Richard D. Brown, *The South Carolina Regulators* (1963), and some of the essays in Alfred Young, ed., *The American Revolution: Essays in the History of American Radicalism* (1976). See also W. Stitt Robinson, *The Southern Colonial Frontier, 1607–1763* (1979); Charles E. Clark, *The Eastern Frontier: The Settlement of Northern New England, 1610–1763* (1970); and Richard Beeman, *The Evolution of the Southern Backcountry* (1984).

TIMELINE

1700–	Female literacy in New England expands
1700–1714	New Hudson River manors created
1714–	German migrants settle in middle colonies
1720s	Enlightenment ideas spread to America Frelinghuysen revivals
1730–	Scots-Irish migration grows
1730s	Tennents lead revivals among Presbyterians
1734–1736	Jonathan Edwards leads New England revivals
1739–	George Whitefield and the Great Awakening
1739	War of Jenkins' Ear
1740–	Population pressure in New England Increase in premarital pregnancies
1740s	Churches divide between Old Lights and New Lights
1740–	Rising grain and tobacco prices
1749	Ohio company formed
1750s	"Feudal Revival" American imports from England increase
1754	French and Indian War begins
1759	Fall of Quebec
1763	Treaty of Paris ends Great War for Empire Postwar recession begins Paxton Boys in Pennsylvania
1760s	Land conflicts along New York/New England border Regulator movements in the Carolinas Evangelical Baptists in Virginia

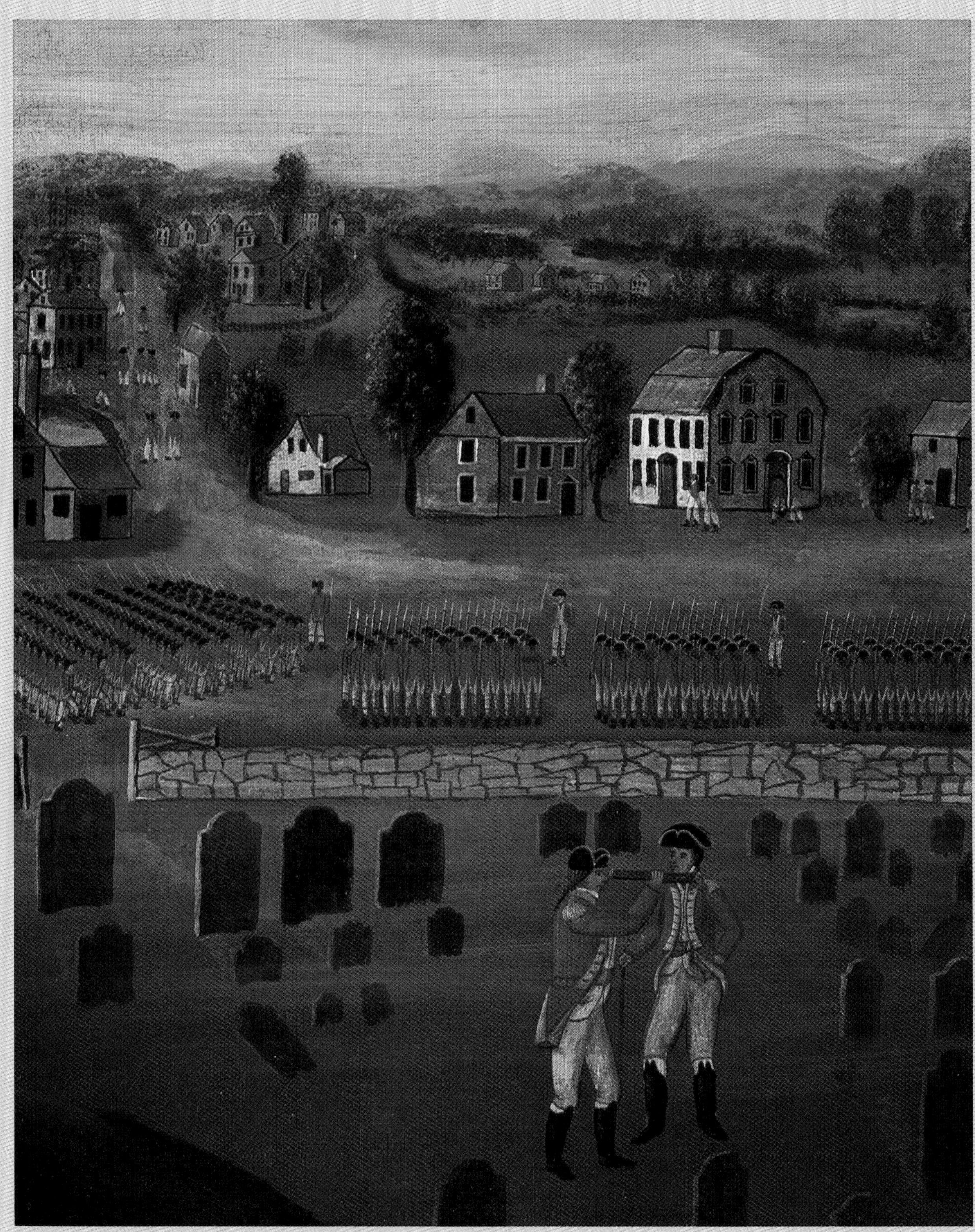

Occupation of Concord by the British (detail)

The New England portraitist Ralph Earl produced some of the earliest historical paintings in America. After hearing of the skirmishes at Lexington and Concord in 1775, he visited the sites, creating this and other paintings of the campaign. (Concord Antiquarian Museum)

CHAPTER 5 *Toward Independence: Years of Decision, 1763–1775*

At the end of the Great War for Empire, the American colonists were loyal subjects of Great Britain. Twelve years later, they stood on the brink of civil war—angry, armed, and resistant to British authority. How had it happened, asked the president of King's College in New York, that such a "happily situated" people should decide to "hazard their Fortunes, their Lives, and their Souls, in such a Rebellion"?

This rapid and unexpected change had two broad sets of causes. First, the character of the American political and social system fostered dreams of independence. Unlike many colonial peoples, Americans lived in a prosperous, stable society with a strong tradition of representative government. This unique historical experience created a group of vigorous, experienced leaders and a self-confident populace capable of supporting an independence movement. Still, most Americans had been content for generations under British rule. What sparked them to rebel—the second, and immediate, cause—was Britain's attempt to reform the imperial system.

The Great War for Empire had emptied the British treasury and prompted a campaign to enhance the power of royal officials in America and use them to raise revenue from the colonies. This British initiative began during the war and culminated in the Stamp Act of 1765, which escalated the confrontation into a major conflict over economic burdens and constitutional principles. Ultimately the passions stirred up by the reform movement would produce a civil war within the British empire.

The Reform Movement, 1763–1765

Military power made Britain the dominant nation in Europe following the Great War for Empire. France had finally been checked on the continent and Britannia ruled the waves for the next century and a half. By driving the French out of Canada, Britain had also achieved dominance over North America. The way was now clear for Britain to impose central control on its American colonies.

The Imperial System in 1763

The Great War for Empire strained the imperial political system and brought to light deep-seated differences between Britain and its colonies. Before 1754, only royal governors and a few British merchants and naval officers had personally experienced the American provinces. During the conflict, however, hundreds of British army officers and middle-level bureaucrats came to the mainland colonies, and they did not like what they saw. Provincial soldiers were "the dirtiest, most contemptible, cowardly dogs that you can conceive," General James Wolfe told a friend. "There is no depending on them in action." For their part, Americans were shocked by the arrogance of upper-crust British officers and by the rigors of military discipline. British regulars, a Massachusetts militiaman wrote in his diary, "are but little better than slaves to their officers."

The war also exposed the weakness of British administrative control, especially as wielded by the royal governors. In theory, governors had extensive political powers, including command of the provincial militia. In reality, they were completely dependent on the colonial assemblies to appropriate funds for troops and supplies. Many assemblies refused to support the war effort unless the governor relinquished control over military appointments and operations. Britain's Board of Trade complained that in Massachusetts, "almost every act of executive and legislative power is ordered and directed by votes and resolves of the General Court."

In Virginia, the assembly refused to levy additional taxes to pay for the war. The Burgesses resorted instead to deficit financing, printing paper currency in amounts sufficient to pay the province's bills. As the Virginia government bought military supplies and paid troops, the value of the currency fell by nearly 20 percent. Yet Virginia law required merchants and other creditors to accept the currency as legal tender, at face value. British merchants in the colony refused to accept payment in depreciated currency and applied to Parliament for relief. Parliament had helped before, passing a Currency Act in 1751 that placed strict regulations on the is-

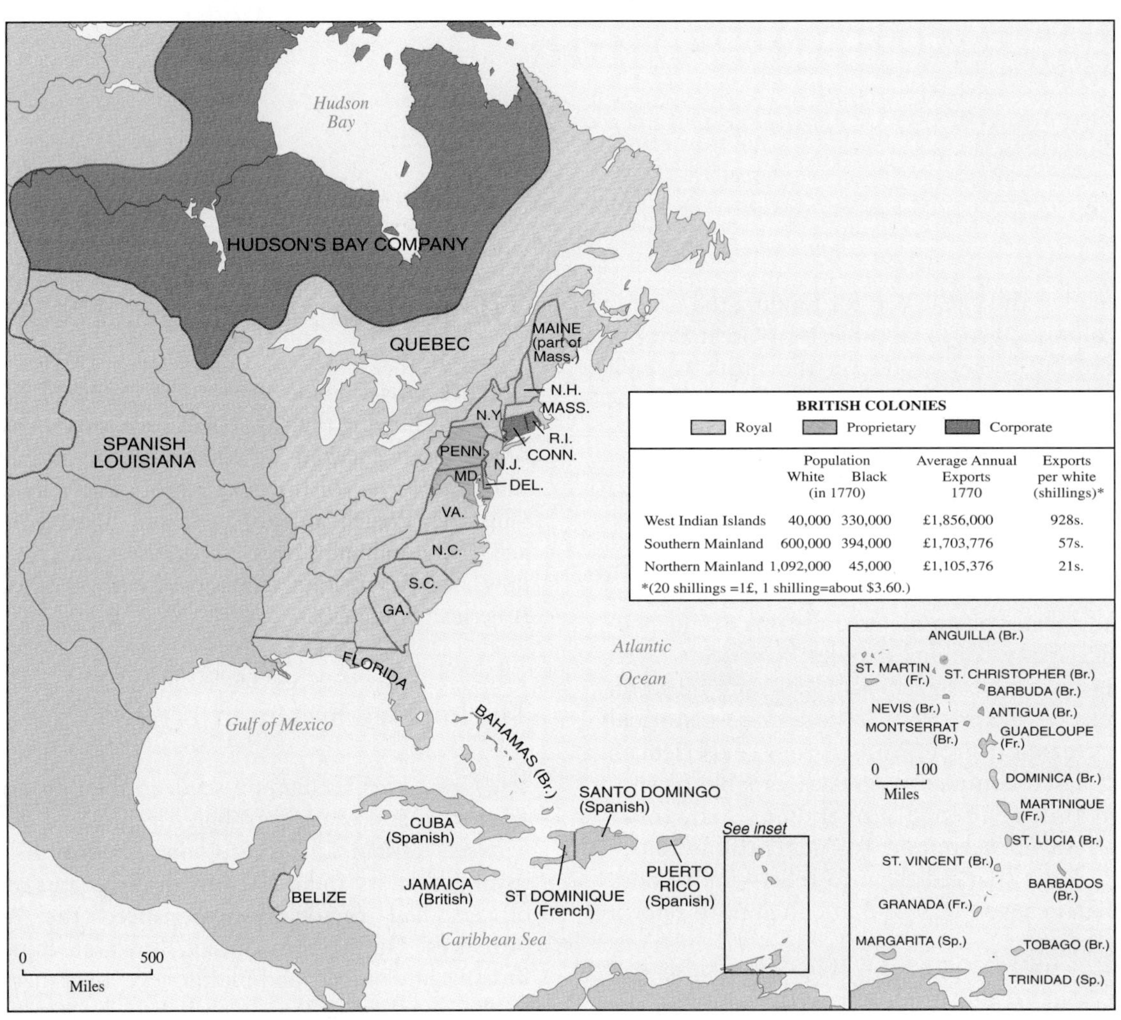

	Population White (in 1770)	Population Black (in 1770)	Average Annual Exports 1770	Exports per white (shillings)*
West Indian Islands	40,000	330,000	£1,856,000	928s.
Southern Mainland	600,000	394,000	£1,703,776	57s.
Northern Mainland	1,092,000	45,000	£1,105,376	21s.

*(20 shillings =1£, 1 shilling=about $3.60.)

MAP 5.1

Britain's American Empire in 1763

In 1763 Britain was dominant in the West Indies and North America. British ministers created the new colony of Quebec and, by the Proclamation Line of 1763, sought to prevent Anglo-American settlement west of the Appalachian Mountains. Later, the Quebec Act of 1774 vastly expanded the new colony's boundaries, greatly angering American settlers, speculators, and political officials.

suance of government bills of credit by the New England colonies and prohibited their use as legal tender in payment of private debts. Now the British legislature passed the Currency Act of 1764, banning the use of paper money as legal tender in Virginia and all the colonies. Subsequently, Americans had to pay their debts to merchants with British currency, foreign coins, or bills of exchange.

Imperial authorities also began more strictly to enforce the Navigation Acts regulating colonial trade. Before the war, American merchants had bribed colonial customs officials to circumvent the Molasses Act of 1733. To curb such corruption, Parliament in 1762 passed a Revenue Act, which required officeholders in the customs department to serve in person and prohibited them from leasing offices to deputies—who had often accepted bribes to support themselves while paying the officeholder. Moreover, the Royal Navy was instructed to block all trade with the French islands. Royal officials had been shocked to find that during the war with France colonial merchants continued to ship food and supplies to the French islands. It was absurd, declared an outraged British politician, that French armies attempting "to Destroy one English province, are actually supported by Bread raised in another." Such commerce, the British ministry charged, allowed the French "to sustain and protract this long and expensive war."

British Troops in America. The most striking evidence of British determination to control its colonies was the decision in 1763 to station a large peacetime army—fifteen regiments of infantry, about 10,000 men—in North America. There were three reasons for this move. First, because thousands of French settlers still lived in Canada, Britain needed the troops to discourage rebellion in the newly captured province. British troops likewise occupied Florida, in case the Spanish colonial authorities in Mexico might promote unrest.

Second, officials in London feared another Indian war. The rising led by the Ottawa chief Pontiac in May 1763 had been put down only with great difficulty (see Chapter 4). To meet further threats, the British wanted to maintain substantial garrisons in the forts they had taken over from the French. Pontiac's rebellion had also taught the British that what the Indians most feared was white settlement. So in October, as an additional step to prevent trouble in the Ohio River Valley, King George III issued the Proclamation of 1763, which prohibited white settlement west of the crest of the Appalachians and regulated the fur trade with the Indian peoples. The Proclamation angered American land speculators, whose drive for expansion into the Ohio River Valley had started the war in the first place.

The third reason for deploying the troops was the apprehension on the part of British politicians of a possible American independence movement, a fear that had been growing since the late 1740s. "I have been publickly told," the Swedish traveler Peter Kalm reported from America in 1748, "that within thirty or fifty years, the English colonies may constitute a separate state, wholly independent of England." Only the danger of a French invasion from Canada, Kalm thought, deterred colonists from demanding greater autonomy. For that reason, some British officials argued, during the peace negotiations of 1763, that it would be prudent to return Canada to France in exchange for the West Indian sugar island of Martinique. Given the decision to keep Canada, officials such as Henry Knox, a former treasury official in Georgia, recommended a strong British military presence in the mainland colonies. Indeed, Knox wrote in a memorandum to policy makers, "The main purpose of Stationing a large Body of Troops in America is to secure the Dependence of the Colonys on Great Britain."

Of course, the mere presence of British troops would not necessarily stop Americans from demanding political autonomy. In the 1740s, when land riots nearly resulted in the dispatch of military forces to New Jersey, Governor Jonathan Belcher advised royal authorities that simply stationing troops in the colony would not "drive Assemblies or people from their Obstinate ways of Thinking, into reasonable measures." To be effective, military power could not just be displayed but had to be used—to impose royal edicts or to curb the power of local officeholders. In establishing a serious military presence in America, the British ministry showed that it might be prepared to use force to preserve and extend imperial rule.

The Financial Legacy of the War

Britain paid a substantial price at home for its military successes abroad. During the Great War for Empire, the British East India Company had routed the French in India, opening up the rich subcontinent to British commerce and eventual conquest, but the conflict had drained the company. Its well-connected officials looked to the British government for new subsidies and privileges, but the treasury was empty. The government had borrowed heavily from British and Dutch bankers to finance the war and by 1763 the national debt had almost doubled, from £75 million in 1754 to £133 million in 1763.

This huge war debt placed a new financial burden on the British prime minister Lord Bute, the lackluster favorite of George III who had replaced William Pitt in 1761. As the war came to a close, Bute's ministry had to find funds to pay the interest on its debts as well as its

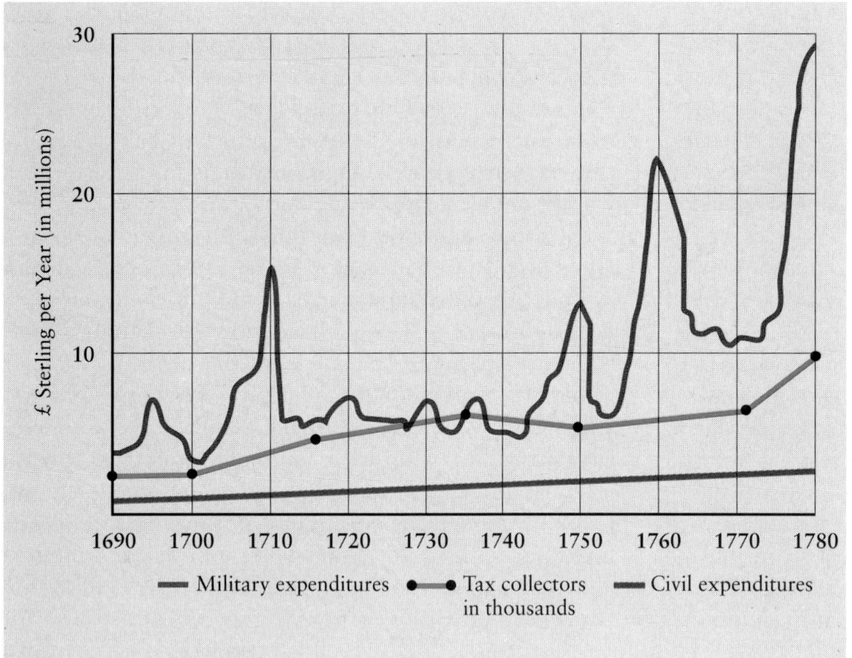

FIGURE 5.1

The Growing Power of the British State

normal expenses. Treasury officials advised against raising the British land tax, which was already at an all-time high and which bore directly on the propertied classes, whose support the government needed. The ministry therefore imposed higher import duties on tobacco and sugar, which manufacturers passed on to consumers in the form of higher prices. The government also increased excise levies—sales taxes—on other goods, such as salt and beer and distilled spirits, once again passing along the costs of the war to ordinary people.

In order to collect these taxes and duties, the British government had to expand its bureaucracy. Between 1750 and 1775, the total number of royal officials in Britain jumped from about 5,000 to more than 11,000. Parliament gave the new bureaucrats increased administrative and legal powers. Customs agents and informers patrolled the coasts of southern England, arresting smugglers and seizing tons of goods—such as French wines and Flemish textiles—on which import duties had not been paid. Convicted smugglers faced heavy penalties, including death or "transportation" to America as indentured servants.

The legacy of the war was a paradoxical mix. Along with immense military power and increased national pride came huge debts, tighter governmental controls, and rising domestic dissent. Beginning with the ascendancy of Sir Robert Walpole in the 1730s, radical Real Whigs and conservative Country Party landlords had emphasized the dangers of unlimited government, and now their worst fears had come to pass. The treasury was at the mercy of the "monied interest"—the banks and financiers who had paid for the war and now reaped millions of pounds in interest from government bonds. And with the number of royal officers skyrocketing, the evils of patronage and administrative abuse became ever more apparent. Reformers warned that a corrupt Parliament filled with "worthless *pensioners* and *placemen*" had embarked on a systematic plan to extinguish British liberty. In 1763, the radical Whig John Wilkes launched a campaign to reform Parliament, demanding an end to *rotten boroughs*—tiny districts whose voters were controlled by wealthy aristocrats and merchants.

British Reform Strategy

The Great War for Empire brought a decisive end to the era of salutary neglect. During the war, a new generation of British political leaders had come to power, determined not only to defeat France but also to reform the imperial system. Charles Townshend of the Board of Trade and Prime Minister William Pitt had a broad vision. They agreed with Thomas Pownall, the former governor of Massachusetts, that "the spirit of *commerce* will become the predominant power, which will rule the powers of Europe," and that the American colonies were the key to commercial success. In their eyes, the reform of imperial administration and taxation was crucial to the continued growth of British trade and national power.

At first, political instability in Britain hampered the quest for imperial reform. When George III came to the throne in 1760, he reasserted the power of the monarchy, disrupting Walpole's system of cooperation between the king and Parliament. In particular, King George insisted on installing Lord Bute, his favorite, as prime minister in 1761 even though Bute did not control a majority in the House of Commons. Bute successfully negotiated the Treaty of Paris, ending the war, but resigned in 1763, unable to resolve the growing financial crisis. The king then turned reluctantly to a commoner, George Grenville, who enjoyed strong support in Parliament.

The Sugar Act. Grenville was an astute politician and embraced the cause of imperial reform. As prime minister, he introduced the Sugar Act of 1764. This new Navigation Act, a revision of the Molasses Act of 1733, resulted from a wide-ranging review of the West Indian trade system by Treasury officials Thomas Whatley and Charles Jenkinson. Whatley and Jenkinson understood how transatlantic commerce worked, from their long experience in the government and from their contacts with colonial agents—resident Americans or English merchants who represented the interests of the provincial assemblies in London. They understood that the mainland settlers had to sell their wheat, fish, and lumber in the French islands. Without the molasses, sugar, and bills of exchange earned through these sales, the colonists would lack the funds to buy British manufactured goods. The Treasury officials therefore resisted demands from British sugar planters to cut off this trade by enforcing Molasses Act's high duty of 6 pence per gallon on the molasses imported from the French West Indies, instituting instead a smaller duty of 3 pence per gallon. They argued that this levy would allow British molasses to compete with the cheaper French product without destroying the mainland's export trade or its distilling industry.

But American merchants and manufacturers refused to accept this compromise. Many New England traders, such as John Hancock of Boston, had made their fortunes by importing huge quantities of French molasses without paying any duty. Their businesses would be threatened—perhaps destroyed—by the new regulations. The merchants, joined by New England distillers, who feared higher costs, protested publicly that the 3 pence tax called for in the Sugar Act would wipe out trade with the French islands. Privately, they vowed to evade the duty, by smuggling or by bribing officials.

Imperial reform had legal and political as well as economic implications. Colonial political leaders raised constitutional objections to the Sugar Act. Thomas Cushing, Speaker of the Massachusetts House of Representatives, argued that the duties constituted a "tax," and as such, the Sugar Act was "contrary to a fundamental Principall of our Constitution: That all Taxes ought to originate with the people." A House committee went further, declaring that such parliamentary acts "have a tendency to deprive the colonies of some of their most essential Rights as British subjects." Whatley and Jenkinson's attempt to balance the interests of British sugar planters and mainland settlers had become a bitterly contested constitutional issue. The terms of debate had shifted, and fatefully so.

Vice-Admiralty Courts and the "Rights of Englishmen." In addition to levying duties, the Sugar Act of 1764 extended the jurisdiction of *vice-admiralty courts*—mar-

Britain Triumphant

This painting celebrates the Great War of Empire by praising two of its heroes, Prime Minister William Pitt and General James Wolfe. It also conveys a political message with Real Whig overtones—warning the King against "Evil and Corrupt Ministers."

itime tribunals that operated without the procedures and protections of English common law. There was no trial by jury in these courts. Rather, a judge heard arguments and decided cases solely on the basis of parliamentary legislation. For half a century, colonial legislatures had vigorously opposed vice-admiralty tribunals, primarily by extending the jurisdiction of their own courts over all customs offenses occurring in American seaports or coastal waters. Thus merchants charged with violating the Navigation Acts were often acquitted by well-disposed common-law juries or American-born judges. By extending the jurisdiction of vice-admiralty courts to all customs offenses wherever they occurred, the Sugar Act closed up this loophole.

The powers given to the vice-admiralty courts revived old American fears and raised new constitutional objections. Richard Bland, an influential Virginia planter, charged that the courts discriminated against British subjects living in America. The colonists were "born equally free, and entitled to the same civil rights," Bland argued. "*Rights* imply *Equality*," he declared; the colonists "were not sent out to be the Slaves but to be the Equals of those that remained behind."

John Adams, a young Massachusetts lawyer who defended John Hancock on a charge of smuggling, took a similar position.

> Here is the contrast that stares us in the face. The Parliament in one Clause guarding the People of the Realm, and securing to them the benefit of a Tryal by the Law of the Land, and by the next Clause, depriving all Americans of that Privilege. What shall we say to this Distinction? Is there not in this Clause a Brand of Infamy, or Degradation, and Disgrace, fixed upon every American? Is he not degraded below the rank of an Englishman?

The logic of Adams and Bland was compelling, though they had some of their facts wrong. Vice-admiralty courts had long played a major role in British commercial life. Adams and Bland were either unaware of this, or, caught up in the debate over imperial reform and American rights, they were deliberately misleading their fellow colonists. In any case, the new vice-admiralty legislation did not discriminate against Americans; rather it extended British practices—albeit unpopular ones—to America.

The real issue was not the suppression of American liberties but the growing authority of the British state, both at home and abroad. The expanded royal bureaucracy was determined to root out smuggling and to raise revenues both in Britain and in North America. The colonists' righteous anger reflected their naivete; raised under a policy of salutary neglect, they instinctively resisted the new rules and procedures.

Yet in a larger sense, knowledgeable Americans like Bland and Adams were right when they claimed that British policy was discriminatory, for legislation such as the Sugar Act challenged the legitimacy of American constitutional claims. Following the war, many British officials denied that the colonists could claim the traditional "rights of Englishmen." For example, when Royal Governor Francis Bernard of Massachusetts heard that the Massachusetts assembly had objected to the Sugar Act on the grounds of no taxation without representation, he said that the people in America did not have that constitutional right. "The rule that a *British* subject shall not be bound by laws or liable to taxes, but what he has consented to by his representatives," Bernard argued, "must be confined to the inhabitants of Great Britain only." In Bernard's eyes, and those of many British political leaders, Americans were second-class subjects of the king, their rights limited by the Navigation Acts and the national interests of the British state.

The Stamp Act

The issue of taxation brought about the first great imperial crisis. When Grenville introduced the Sugar Act in Parliament in 1764, he also announced his intention to seek a colonial stamp tax the following year. He hoped that part of the £200,000 per year needed to clothe, house, feed, and pay the 10,000 soldiers the ministry planned to station in America would be covered by this new measure, which would require tax stamps on court documents, land titles, contracts, playing cards, newspapers, and other printed items. A similar English tax, levied since 1694, had yielded an annual revenue of £290,000 and Grenville hoped the American levy would raise at least £60,000 (about $5 million, today). The prime minister knew that some Americans would object to this tax on constitutional grounds, so he asked explicitly if any member of the House of Commons doubted "the power and sovereignty of Parliament over every part of the British dominions, for the purpose of raising or collecting any tax." No one rose.

Grenville informed the American assemblies that unless they could themselves "raise a sum adequate to their defence" a stamp tax would be voted in 1765. This challenge threw the London agents of the colonial legislatures into confusion. They all agreed that the assemblies could not apportion the defense budget among themselves—for there was no intercolonial political institution to assume such a task. Agent Richard Jackson, an English merchant, advised the assemblies to accept the stamp tax because he believed that their long-standing claim of the sole right of taxation lacked a firm legal or constitutional basis and that the tax would be imposed upon them whether they liked it or not.

George Grenville, Architect of the Stamp Act
As prime minister from 1764 to 1766, Grenville assumed leadership of the movement for imperial reform and taxation. But most British politicians believed that the colonies should be better regulated and share the cost of the empire.

Benjamin Franklin, representing the Pennsylvania assembly, countered with a proposal for American representation in Parliament. "If you chuse to tax us," he suggested to a British friend, "give us Members in your Legislature, and let us be one People." But with the exception of William Pitt, who prepared a draft proposal for American representation in Parliament, British politicians rejected this radical idea. They argued that the colonists were "virtually" represented by the merchants who sat in Parliament and by other members with interests in America. Even colonial leaders were skeptical of Franklin's plan; they were "situate at a great Distance from their Mother Country," the Connecticut Assembly declared in a printed pamphlet dispatched to London, and therefore "cannot participate in the general Legislature of the Nation." Influential Philadelphia merchants, worried that a handful of colonial delegates would be powerless in Parliament, warned Franklin "to beware of any measure that might extend to us seats in the Commons."

American leaders had no alternative to the plan proposed by Grenville, who was determined to assert the constitutional supremacy of Parliament. The Stamp Act was "the great measure of the Sessions," Grenville's chief assistant observed, "on account of the important point it establishes, the Right of Parliament to lay an internal Tax upon the Colonies." The ministry's plan worked smoothly. The House of Commons refused to accept American petitions opposing the new legislation, which it passed by the overwhelming vote of 205 to 49. Parliament also approved George Grenville's proposal that violations of the Stamp Act would be tried in vice-admiralty tribunals, so the colonists had no hope of acquittal by friendly juries in local common law courts.

Finally, at the request of General Thomas Gage, commander of British military forces in America, the home legislature passed a Quartering Act, directing colonial governments to provide barracks and food for British troops stationed in the seaboard colonies. During the French and Indian War the assemblies of Massachusetts and New York had refused to accept the financial burden of accommodating British troops, and the ministry was determined that this should not happen again.

Grenville's design was complete. He had provoked a constitutional confrontation with the American assemblies, not only on the crucial issue of taxes but also on the right to a trial by jury and on compulsory support of a standing army. Imperial reform had begun in earnest.

The Dynamics of Rebellion, 1765–1766

With the Sugar and Stamp acts Grenville had thrown down the gauntlet to the American colonists. Would they resist this curtailment of the political autonomy achieved during the decades of salutary neglect? And what were their chances of success? Settlers in various colonies had opposed unpopular laws or arbitrary governors, but they had never before faced a reform-minded ministry and Parliament. Some Patriots—as the defenders of American rights came to be called—resisted the new British measures forcefully, participating in large-scale riots or delivering speeches that bordered on treason. Many other Americans, moved by anti-imperialist sentiments, economic self-interest, religious and constitutional principles, rallied to the Patriot side.

The Crowd Rebels

The American response to the Stamp Act was more drastic than Grenville had predicted. Disciplined mobs,

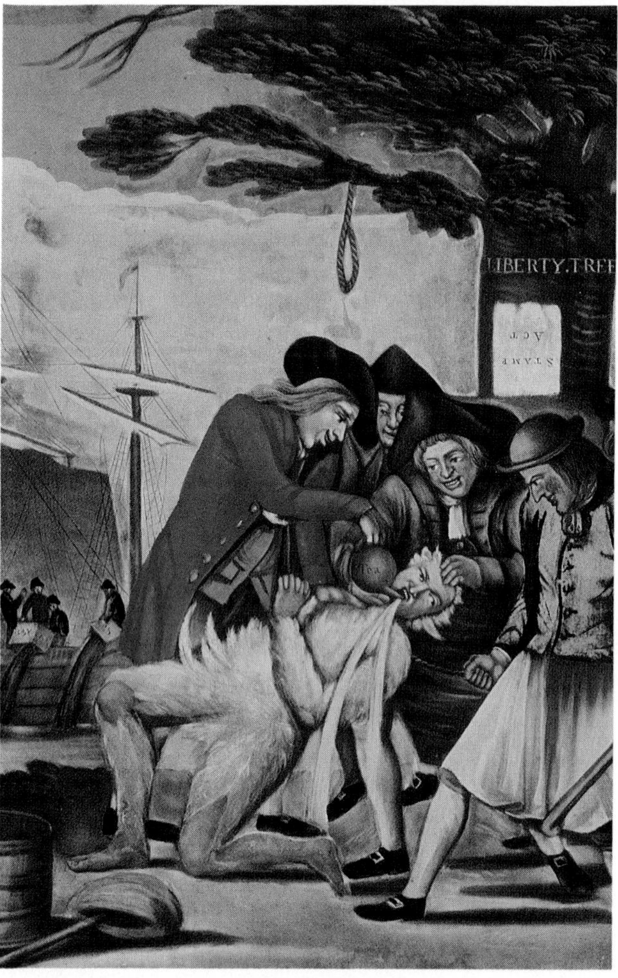

A British View of American Mobs
The artist depicts the Sons of Liberty as sadists, subjecting a British excise officer to physical abuse, and as wanton destroyers of property, dumping tea into the harbor. The Liberty Tree in the background raises the question: Does Liberty mean Anarchy?

led by men who called themselves the Sons of Liberty, demanded the resignation of newly appointed stamp-tax collectors, most of whom were native-born colonists. One of the first incidents took place in Boston in August 1765, when the Boston Sons of Liberty made an effigy of collector Andrew Oliver, which they then beheaded and burned before destroying a new brick building that he owned. Boston merchants who opposed the Stamp Act advised Oliver to resign; otherwise "his House would be immediately destroyed and his Life in Continual Danger." Two weeks later, Bostonians attacked the house of Lieutenant Governor Thomas Hutchinson. As a defender of social privilege and imperial authority, Hutchinson had many enemies. Now, in the heat of crisis, the common people took their revenge by plundering his wine cellar and burning his library.

In nearly every colony, similar crowds of angry but purposeful people—the "rabble," as their American and British detractors called them—intimidated royal officials. In Connecticut, 500 farmers and artisans confronted tax collector Jared Ingersoll near Wethersfield. Ingersoll had been born into a prominent Connecticut family and had served as the assembly's agent in London. He worked actively against the Stamp Act, but once it had passed he sought to profit from it by collecting the tax. Ingersoll paid dearly for that decision. He debated with the leaders of the crowd for hours but they refused to be swayed by his previous service to the colony or his high social status. He "lookt upon this as the Cause of the People," an observer heard one rioter shout, and would not "take Directions about it from any Body." Ingersoll finally capitulated. At the behest of the mob, he gave three cheers for "Liberty and Property," tossed his hat into the air, and resigned his office.

The Motives of the Crowd. The strength of the Liberty mobs was surprising, but the existence of such crowd actions was a fact of political life in both Britain and America. For example, Protestant mobs burned the Pope in effigy every November 5 to celebrate the failure of Guy Fawkes, a Catholic, to overturn the English government in 1605. Colonial mobs had often expressed anti-imperial sentiments. In 1747, Boston crowds rioted for three days to protest the impressment of merchant seamen for forced service in the Royal Navy. The Stamp Act mobs were simply acting according to tradition—beheading an effigy of Oliver re-enacted the ritual killing of the Pope on Guy Fawkes Day—and gave the Sons of Liberty a sense of identity and of moral purpose.

Some urban artisans joined the Liberty mobs out of economic self-interest. Imports of low-priced British shoes and other products were threatening their livelihood, and they feared that the Stamp Tax would lower their standard of living still further—for the benefit of a rich governing class in England and America. Unlike "the Common people of England," a well-traveled colonist observed, "the people of America . . . never would submitt to be taxed that a few may be loaded with palaces and Pensions and riot in Luxury and Excess, while they themselves cannot support themselves and their needy offspring with Bread."

The religious passions aroused by the Great Awakening were yet another source of popular resistance. Some skilled workers were evangelical Protestants who led disciplined, hard-working lives, and they resented the arrogance and immorality of many British officers and the corrupt behavior of many royal bureaucrats. The image of the greedy British official seeking only the "gratification of his private Passions" loomed large in the pages of the *Independent Reflector*, a Real Whig newspaper published in New York during the 1750s.

AMERICAN VOICES

A Stamp Act Riot, 1765 *A Rhode Island Loyalist*

The Sons of Liberty attacked Stamp Collectors in many cities, including Newport, Rhode Island. This letter, probably written by the wife of a pro-British merchant to her daughter, suggests the high emotional and material price paid by those who remained loyal to the Crown.

In the morning of the 27th Inst. between five and six a Mob Assembled and Erected a Gallows near the Town House and then Dispers'd, and about Ten A Clock Reassembled and took The Effigys of the Above Men and the Stamp Master and Carted them up Thames Street, then up King Street to the said Gallows where they was hung up by the Neck and Suspended near 15 feet in the Air, And on the Breast of the Stamp Master, was this Inscription THE STAMP MAN...and upon the Breast of the Doct'r was write, THAT INFAMOUS, MISCREATED, LEERING JACOBITE DOCT'R MURFY.... And about five A Clock in the Afternoon they made a Fire under the Gallows which Consum'd the Effigy's, Gallows and all, to Ashes. I forgot to tell you that a Boot hung over the Doctor's Shoulder with the Devil Peeping out of it . . . we thought it was all over. But last Night about Dusk they all Muster'd Again, and first they went to Martin Howard's, and Broke Every Window in his house Frames and all, likewise Chairs Tables, Pictures and every thing they cou'd come across . . . this Moment I'v Rec'd a Peace of News which Effects me so Much that I Cant write any More, which is the Demolition of your worthy Daddy's house and Furniture etc. But I must just let you know that the Stamp Master has Resign'd. . . .

Source: Alden Vaughan, ed., *Eyewitness Accounts of the American Revolution* (New York: Harper Torch Books).

Still other artisans had carried over from England the anti-monarchical sentiments of the seventeenth-century Puritan Revolution. A letter sent to a Boston newspaper promising to save "all the Freeborn Sons of America" from "tyrannical ministers" was signed "Oliver Cromwell." In other letters and handbills signed "O.C." British officials and sympathizers were threatened with violence. The cry of "Liberty and Property" forced on Jared Ingersoll echoed ideological resistance to the taxes imposed by the Stuart kings.

The social composition of the crowds made them a potent political force. Most mobs were formed by men and women who knew one another—in jobs, churches, or neighborhoods. For example, of the thirty-six young men who formed the Sons of Liberty of Albany, New York, in 1765, twenty belonged to the same firefighter's club, and twelve sat together in the balcony of the Dutch Reformed Church. These personal ties made the Sons of Liberty into a political force that sustained its purpose from month to month and from crisis to crisis.

When the Stamp Act went into effect on November 1, 1765, most influential Americans advocated nonviolent resistance. In New York City, two hundred merchants announced a boycott, vowing not to import British goods. Traders in Boston and Philadelphia quickly followed their example. But popular resentment against British policy was not easily contained. In New York less prosperous merchants such as Isaac Sears mobilized shopkeepers, tradesmen, artisans, laborers, and seamen in a mass protest meeting. They marched through the streets, breaking streetlamps and windows and crying "Liberty!" On November 2, 3,000 New Yorkers plundered the house of an unpopular British officer and surrounded Fort George where the tax stamps were stored, threatening to seize and destroy them.

As Guy Fawkes Day on November 5 approached, Lieutenant Governor Cadwallader Colden feared an open assault on the fort. He called upon General Gage to use his small military force against the crowd, but the British commander refused. "Fire from the Fort might disperse the Mob, but it would not quell them;" he told Colden, "and the consequence would in all appearances be an Insurrection, the Commencement of Civil War." Colden had to surrender the tax stamps.

Popular resistance nullified the Stamp Act throughout the colonies. Frightened collectors distributed few stamps to angry Americans. Royal officials and judges were at a loss; the state of communications across the Atlantic was such that the ministry's response to the riots would not be known until the following spring and so in the meantime they had no choice but to accept legal documents without the stamps.

The popular revolt of 1765 not only repudiated British authority but gave a democratic cast to the emerging sense of American political identity. "Nothing is wanting but your own Resolution," a New York Son of Liberty declared during the upheaval, "for great is the Authority and Power of the People." Royal officials could no longer count on the deferential behavior that had ensured political stability for three generations. "What can a Governor do without the assistance of the Governed?" the Philadelphia customs collector lamented. The Stamp Act crisis of 1765 eroded the emotional foundations of power, and left the British government on the defensive in America.

Ideological Roots of Resistance

The American resistance movement began in the seaport cities, and for good reason. Urban residents—artisans, merchants, and lawyers—were directly affected by British policies. The Stamp Act taxed city-based products and services, such as newspapers and legal documents. The Sugar Act and accompanying customs reform raised the cost of molasses to American merchants and distillers, while the Currency Act complicated trade and financial transactions. To make matters worse, beginning in the early 1750s British firms had begun to sell goods directly to colonial shopkeepers at special auction sales, bypassing American mercantile houses and cutting their profits. The combination of British governmental regulation and business competition undermined the merchants' loyalty to the empire. As an official in Rhode Island reported in 1765, the interests of Britain and the colonies were increasingly "deemed by the People almost altogether incompatible in a Commercial View."

American lawyers were prominent in mobilizing public opinion against the British. In part, lawyers reflected the views of the merchants who hired them to prevent seizure of their ships by zealous customs officials or vice-admiralty judges. But their own professional values also prompted lawyers to contest the legality of various imperial measures. When the Board of Trade changed the terms of appointment for colonial judges from "during good behavior" to "at the pleasure" of the royal governor, lawyers protested that the new procedure compromised the independence of the judiciary. The American bar also opposed the extension of vice-admiralty courts; as men trained in the English common law, they favored trials by jury. A deep respect for established institutions ultimately led many older lawyers to remain loyal to the Crown, but young lawyers embraced the revolutionary cause; of the 56 men who signed the Declaration of Independence in 1776, 25 were lawyers.

Merchants and lawyers debated political and constitutional issues in taverns and coffeehouses, on street corners, and in public meetings. They drew upon the works of seventeenth-century English philosophers such as Thomas Hobbes, James Harrington, and John Locke; on the French theorists Montesquieu and Voltaire; and on the Scottish Enlightenment thinkers David Hume and Frances Hutcheson. Pamphlets of remarkable political sophistication circulated throughout the colonies, providing the resistance movement with an intellectual rationale and a political agenda. This urban-based political agitation stimulated representatives of rural communities, who dominated the American assemblies numerically, and encouraged them to make a principled defense of American rights.

Intellectual Traditions. Lawyers and other educated colonists drew on three intellectual traditions to build their arguments. The first was the common law, the great body of legal rules and procedures that had been used for centuries in the courts of England and transferred, in large measure, to the colonies. Common law protected the king's subjects against arbitrary acts, by other subjects or by the government itself. As early as 1761, James Otis of Boston had cited English legal precedents in the famous Writs of Assistance case, disputing the constitutionality of a general search warrant that permitted customs officials to inspect the property and possessions of any person they wished. Similarly, when John Adams defended John Hancock's right to a trial by jury when the influential Boston merchant was accused of smuggling, he relied on the common-law principles outlined in his *Dissertation on the Canon and Feudal Law* (1765). "This 29th Chap. of Magna Charta" respecting jury trials, Adams argued, "has for many Centuries been esteemed by Englishmen, as one of the noblest Monuments, one of the firmest Bulwarks of their Liberties." An essential argument of Otis, Adams, and other New England lawyers was that customary or common-law rights could not be abridged by parliamentary statutes; because the colonists' "essential rights as British subjects" were being violated, resistance was justified.

A second major intellectual resource for educated Americans was the rationalism cultivated during Enlightenment. Unlike common-law attorneys, who valued precedent and venerated the ways of the past, Enlightenment philosophers questioned the past and used reason to discover and correct the ills of society. Most Enlightenment thinkers followed John Locke in believing that all individuals possessed certain "natural rights"—such as life, liberty, and property—and that it was the responsibility of government to protect those rights. For many educated colonists, this belief provided an intellectual justification for resistance to British au-

Sam Adams, Boston Agitator

John Singleton Copley, the important Boston painter, shows Adams pointing to the Massachusetts Charter of 1692, suggesting that "charter rights" accounted for Adams's opposition to Britain. Adams was also influenced by the natural rights tradition. This work, *Samuel Adams,* was painted c. 1772. (Museum of Fine Arts, Boston)

thority. Samuel Adams, John's cousin and a radical Patriot, asked—rhetorically—if it was "lawful to resist the Supreme Magistrate, if the Commonwealth cannot be otherwise preserved," and used arguments based on the individual's natural rights to justify the Stamp Act uprising.

English political tradition provided a third ideological basis for the American Patriot movement. The provincial assemblies had long applauded the Glorious Revolution of 1688 and the various constitutional restrictions placed on the monarchy by the English Whigs, such as the ban on royally imposed taxes. Subsequently, many educated Americans absorbed the arguments of Real Whig spokesmen such as John Trenchard and Thomas Gordon (the authors of *Cato's Letters*), who attacked the power of government financiers and condemned the idea of standing armies. Well-informed colonists also joined in the criticism of Walpole and his successors as leaders of political corruption. "Bribery is so common," John Dickinson of Pennsylvania noted during a visit to London in the 1750s, "that there is not a borough in England where it is not practiced." This critical Real Whig view of British politics predisposed many Americans to distrust any attempt at imperial reform. Joseph Warren, a Boston physician and Patriot, reported that many townspeople thought the Stamp Act was intended "to force the colonies into rebellion," whereupon the ministry would use "military power to reduce them to servitude."

The rhetoric was exaggerated, but the charges had a basis in fact. British administrative reform threatened the interests of many Americans. The Proclamation Line of 1763 curbed the activities of land speculators, fur traders, and westward migrants. The Sugar Act of 1764 extended the jurisdiction of the vice-admiralty courts, which tried defendants without a jury. The Stamp Act of 1765 imposed British taxes directly on Americans for the first time. Finally, Britain's growing economic presence threatened the colonists' sense of control over their financial lives. It seemed to one pamphleteer that Americans were being compelled to give the British "our money, as oft and in what quantity they please to demand it."

Many Americans responded to these events narrow-mindedly, as threats to their own self-interest, but common-law attorneys, natural-rights theorists, and Real Whig critics of ministerial policy stated their objections in philosophical terms. Their ideological statements endowed colonial opposition to British control with moral significance. Increasingly, Americans saw themselves as defenders of venerable political rights. The moral passion and ideological energy thus produced turned a series of tax-protests into a broad resistance movement.

The Informal Compromise of 1766

While mobs protested in the streets, politicians sharpened their arguments in the assemblies. In May 1765 the eloquent young Virginian Patrick Henry urged the House of Burgesses to condemn the Stamp Act. The Burgesses were alarmed when Henry, comparing George III to Charles I, seemed to call for a new Oliver Cromwell to seize power in England, but they endorsed most of his resolutions, declaring that any attempt to tax the colonists without their consent "has a manifest Tendency to Destroy AMERICAN FREEDOM." More significantly, the Stamp Act led to the first effort by the colonial assemblies to speak with one voice. Even before the Burgesses' resolutions reached Boston, the Massachusetts House of Representatives had called for a meeting of the colonies in New York in October to consider a "loyal and humble representation" to the king and Parliament "to implore Relief."

Patrick Henry, A Great Orator
Henry drew on the evangelical tradition to create a new mode of political oratory. "His figures of speech . . . were often borrowed from the Scriptures," a contemporary noted, while his style and speech conveyed "the earnestness depicted in his own features." (Shelburne Museum, Shelburne, Vt. Photograph by Ken Burris)

Nine of the colonial assemblies sent delegates to the Stamp Act Congress. As politicians trained in the art of compromise, the twenty-eight delegates did not threaten to rebel, but devised a set of Stamp Act Resolves, in which they contested the constitutionality of the Stamp and Sugar acts, arguing that only the colonists' elected representatives could impose taxes on them. They protested strongly against the loss of American "rights and liberties," especially trial by jury. Then, assuring Parliament that Americans "glory in being subjects of the best of Kings having been born under the most perfect form of government," the delegates humbly petitioned for repeal of the Stamp Act.

The Stamp Act Resolves were received by a Parliament in turmoil. George III had lost confidence in Grenville (because of issues unrelated to the Stamp Act) and replaced him as prime minister with Lord Rockingham. From the American point of view, Rockingham was an ideal prime minister. Young, inexperienced, and open to persuasion, he led a party of Old Whigs who were hostile to Grenville's American policies. Indeed, the Rockingham Whigs stood for the old imperial policy of salutary neglect, believing that America was important as a source of "flourishing and increasing trade," which added to the national wealth, and not as a source of tax revenue. Many Old Whigs even agreed with the colonists that it was unconstitutional to tax them. Lord Camden, Chief Justice of the Court of Common Pleas, spoke for many Old Whigs when he told his parliamentary colleagues, "Taxation and representation are inseparably united," and concluded, "I can never give my assent to any bill for taxing the American colonies while they remain unrepresented."

British merchants likewise favored the colonists' cause. The decision by most American traders not to import British goods had caused a drastic fall in sales and Britain had large inventories of goods on hand. "The Avenues of Trade are all shut up," a Bristol merchant complained. "We have no Remittances and are at our Witts End for want of Money to fulfill our Engagements with our Tradesmen." In January 1766, the leading commercial centers of London, Liverpool, Bristol, and Glasgow deluged Parliament with petitions. They pointed out that as a result of the colonial boycott the Stamp Act threatened British prosperity.

Though colonial politicians tried to be conciliatory, the popular rebellion in America had generated intense anger in Britain. Outraged members of Parliament demanded that substantial numbers of British regulars be sent to the seaport cities to suppress the riots. They formulated a statement of British constitutional supremacy and demanded that the Americans submit to Parliament. "The British legislature," declared Chief Justice Sir James Mansfield, "has authority to bind every part and every subject, whether such subjects have a right to vote or not." And he insisted that the ministry discipline the upstart colonists, warning that "when the supreme power abdicates, the government is dissolved."

TABLE 5.1

Ministerial Instability in Britain

Leading Minister	Dates of Ministry	American Policy
Lord Bute	1760–1763	Mildly reformist
George Grenville	1763–1765	Ardently reformist
Lord Rockingham	1765–1766	Accommodationist
William Pitt/ Charles Townshend	1766–1770	Ardently reformist

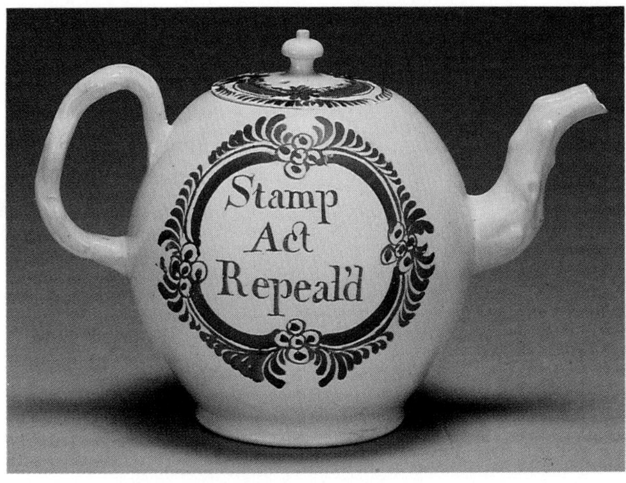

***Mixing Business and Politics.* 1766**
Hurt by the colonists' trade boycott, British manufacturers campaigned for repeal of the Stamp Act. To celebrate repeal—and to expand the market for its teapots in America—the Cockpit Hill factory in Derby quickly produced a commemorative design.

William Pitt, pro-American in sentiment yet firmly committed to British national power, devised yet a third, more ambiguous, response to the American resistance movement. Stating that Parliament had no right to tax the colonies, Pitt demanded that "the Stamp Act be repealed absolutely, totally, and immediately," but at the same time he acknowledged that British authority over America was "sovereign and supreme, in every circumstance of government and legislation whatsoever."

Rockingham tried to reconcile these conflicting opinions and factions. First, to mollify colonial opinion and assist British merchants, he repealed the Stamp Act. He also instructed army commanders in the colonies not to use their troops against the crowds, and he refused to send additional troops to the seaport cities. Next, Rockingham fashioned a compromise on the Sugar Act: He reduced the duty on French molasses from 3 pence to 1 penny a gallon, but he risked another constitutional confrontation by applying the duty to imports of British molasses as well. Thus, the revised Sugar Act not only regulated foreign trade, which most American politicians accepted, but also raised revenue through a tax on a British product, which some colonists challenged as unconstitutional. Rockingham sharpened the constitutional debate—and pacified the imperial reformers—with the Declaratory Act of 1766, which explicitly reaffirmed the "full power and authority" of the British Parliament to "bind the colonies and people of America in all cases whatsoever."

Despite these strong words, the Stamp Act crisis ended in an informal compromise. The Americans had won an important victory. Their riots, their boycott, and their humble petitions had secured repeal of the hated tax. Yet Grenville and other advocates of imperial reform also triumphed: They had provoked a showdown with the provincial assemblies and obtained a statement of parliamentary supremacy. Rockingham's compromise gave each side just enough to claim victory. Because the confrontation had ended quickly, it seemed possible that it might be forgotten even more quickly. The constitutional status of the American provinces remained uncertain, but political positions had not yet hardened. Leaders of good will could still hope to work out an imperial relationship acceptable to both sides.

The Growing Confrontation, 1767–1770

The compromise of 1766 was short-lived. Within a year, political rivalries in Britain sparked a new and more prolonged struggle over taxes. Economic self-interest and ideological rigidity on both sides of the Atlantic aggravated the conflict. Only after a lengthy commercial boycott and the threat of military action was a second compromise finally achieved.

The Townshend Initiatives

Often the course of history is changed by a small event—a leader's illness, a personal grudge, a chance remark. So it was in 1767, when Rockingham's Old Whig ministry collapsed and George III named William Pitt to head a new ministry. Pitt, the master strategist of the Great War for Empire, now sat in the House of Lords as the Earl of Chatham, but he was chronically ill with spells of gout. Because of Chatham's frequent absences from cabinet meetings and parliamentary debates, Chancellor of the Exchequer Charles Townshend assumed command. Chatham was sympathetic toward America; Townshend was not. Since his service on the Board of Trade in the 1750s, the Chancellor of the Exchequer had favored imperial reform; now he had the power to push it through.

What prompted Townshend to act was a chance confrontation with his political rival, George Grenville. As the Chancellor presented the military budget to Parliament in 1767, Grenville rose from his seat to demand that the colonists pay for the British troops in America. Grenville's challenge put Townshend on the defensive and he made an unplanned, fateful policy decision. Convinced of the necessity of imperial reform and anxious to reduce the English land tax, Townshend promised that he would find a new source of revenue in America.

The new tax legislation, known as the Townshend Act of 1767, imposed duties on paper, paint, glass, and tea imported into the colonies. The tax was expected to raise between £35,000 and £40,000 a year—a small sum, but one that Townshend was determined to use shrewdly. To mollify Grenville, he allocated part of the revenue for military expenses, but reserved the major part "to defray the costs of Civil Government"—that is, to pay the salaries of governors, judges, and other imperial officials.

This initiative had the potential to change the political balance of power in the colonies by freeing royal officials from financial dependence on the American legislatures. Thus, they could more strictly enforce parliamentary laws and royal directives, and the colonial assemblies would be deprived of much of their political leverage. To enhance the power of the royal bureaucracy still more, Townshend devised the Revenue Act of 1767, reorganizing the Customs Service. The new Act created a Board of American Customs Commissioners in Boston and four vice-admiralty courts, in Halifax, Boston, Philadelphia, and Charleston. These administrative innovations were far-reaching and posed a greater threat to American autonomy than the small sums raised by the import duties themselves.

In fact, Townshend's overriding concern was to diminish the powers of the American representative assemblies, and events in New York gave him a chance. The New York assembly had refused to comply with the Quartering Act of 1765 by lodging British troops. Fearing an unlimited drain on its treasury, the New York legislature initially denied General Gage's requests for barracks and supplies, and later limited its assistance to the housing of two infantry battalions and one artillery company. The struggle intensified when the ministry instructed the New Yorkers to assume financial responsibility for defense against Indian attacks. Members of Parliament proposed an extra port duty to raise the needed funds.

The secretary of state, William Petty, earl of Shelburne, came up with a stronger, more coercive, set of policies. He suggested a military governor for New York, with authority to seize funds from the colony's treasury to quarter the troops and "to act with Force or Gentleness as circumstances might make necessary."

In June 1767 Townshend decided on a less coercive measure, pushing through Parliament the so-called Restraining Act, which suspended the New York assembly until it submitted to the Quartering Act. Faced with the loss of self-government, the stubborn New Yorkers finally gave in. They appropriated funds to support the resident military garrison and to defend themselves against Indian attacks.

The Restraining Act was an important innovation. The British Privy Council had always supervised the colonial assemblies, over the decades invalidating about 5 percent of all colonial laws—such as those establishing land banks or vesting new powers in the assemblies—as contrary to British practice or policy. The Restraining Act was a much more powerful administrative weapon because it threatened not just particular laws but the existence of the law-making body. Townshend, like his critic Grenville, was determined to tax the colonists and to undermine their representative political institutions.

America Again Resists

The debate on the Townshend duties, which most American public officials condemned as unconstitutional, hinged on the distinction between "internal" and "external" taxes. In response to the Stamp Act, Daniel Dulany, a conservative Maryland lawyer, had suggested that Americans accepted external duties on trade but opposed internal taxes. Benjamin Franklin had reinforced this distinction when he went before the House of Commons to ask for repeal of the Stamp Act. Townshend personally thought this distinction between the two forms of taxation "perfect nonsense," but he told Parliament that "since Americans were pleased to make that distinction, he was willing to indulge them [and] . . . to confine himself to regulations of Trade."

In reality, only a few colonial leaders made the distinction between internal taxes and external duties, the majority agreeing with John Dickinson, author of *Letters from a Farmer in Pennsylvania* (1768), that the issue was not the *form* of the legislation but the *intention*. The Townshend duties were not designed to regulate trade but to bring revenue to the imperial government and thus they were taxes imposed without consent.

The Massachusetts House of Representatives took the lead in opposing the new duties. In February 1768, it sent a letter to other assemblies condemning the Townshend Act as infringing on the colonists' "natural & constitutional Rights." This initiative received a lukewarm response, primarily because the merchant community was divided. Boston merchants began a new boycott of British imports in April 1768, to pressure Parliament to repeal the legislation; New York traders followed suit in August. However, Philadelphia merchants refused to join the boycott, because they were more heavily involved in direct trade with Britain than traders in Boston and New York and felt they had too much to lose. Not only the merchants of Philadelphia but also the sailors and dockworkers of the city feared that a lengthy boycott would ruin them financially. In Philadelphia, therefore, protests were confined to words: residents encouraged the Pennsylvania assembly to petition the king for repeal of the Townshend duties.

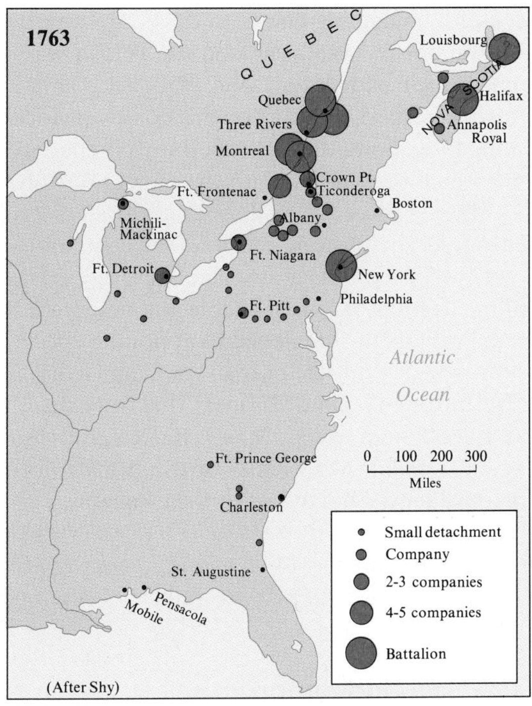

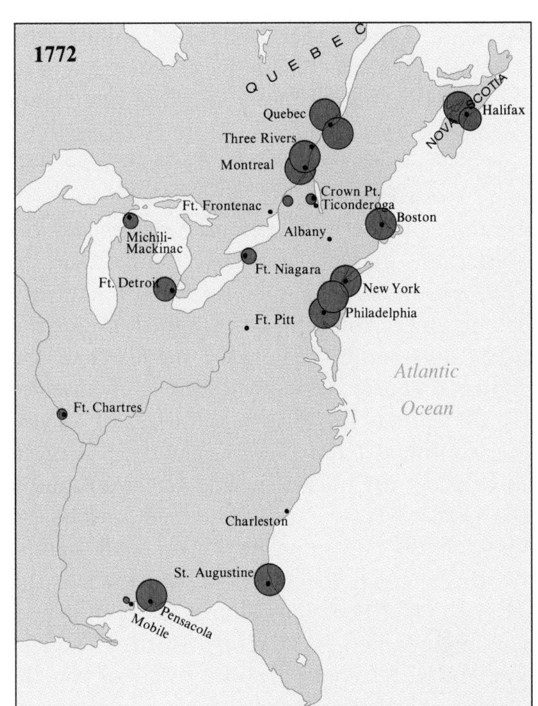

Nonimportation. In 1768, unlike 1765, not all Americans accepted the wisdom of a nonimportation strategy. Nonetheless, public support for the boycott gradually spread from Boston and New York to smaller port cities, like Salem, Newport, and Baltimore, and into the countryside. In Puritan New England, ministers and public officials condemned "luxury and dissipation" and decried the use of "foreign superfluities." They discouraged reliance on imported goods and promoted the domestic manufacture of such necessities as cloth and paper.

American women, ordinarily excluded from involvement in politics, rose to the challenge, using their traditional skills to enter the public arena. Cheered on by their neighbors, "Daughters of Liberty" spun wool into yarn and then wove it into rough fabric—"homespun." Newspapers celebrated these patriotic heroines, whose production of cloth made America less dependent on British textile imports, which totaled about 10 million yards a year. It was a newsworthy event when the women of the Freeman, Smith, and Heard families of Woodbridge, New Jersey, announced they had attained an annual household output of 500 yards. Town-wide production was also a source of pride. One Massachusetts town claimed an annual output of 30,000 yards of cloth; East Hartford, Connecticut, reported 17,000 yards.

In Boston and New York the Sons of Liberty had other methods of promoting nonimportation. They published the names of merchants who refused to comply with the boycott, broke their store windows, and harassed their employees. In Charleston, South Car-

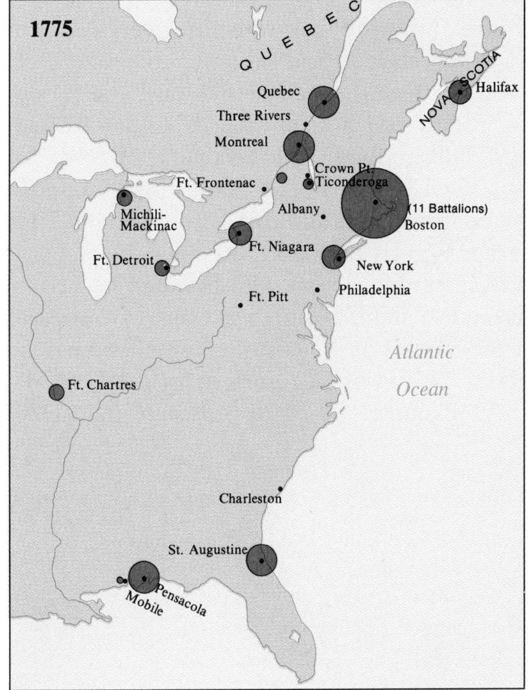

MAP 5.2

British Troop Deployments, 1763–1775

As the imperial crisis deepened, British military priorities changed. In 1763 most British battalions (the large circles representing 350 men) were stationed in Canada to deter Indian attacks and French-Canadian revolts. Following the Stamp Act riots of 1765, the British established larger garrisons in New York and Philadelphia. By 1775, eleven battalions of British regulars occupied Boston, the center of the American Patriot movement.

olina, merchant Christopher Gadsden joined the Liberty Boys and helped persuade his fellow traders to support the boycott. But in many seaports merchants deeply resented the crowd's attacks on their reputations and property. They condemned nonimportation and stood by the royal governors, fearing mob rule.

Despite this split between radical Patriots and future Loyalists, the boycott gathered momentum. In March 1769, responding to public pressure, a majority of Philadelphia merchants finally stopped importing British goods. Two months later, the members of the Virginia House of Burgesses agreed among themselves not to buy dutied articles, British luxuries, or slaves. "The whole continent from New England to Georgia seems firmly fixed," the Massachusetts *Gazette* proudly announced, "like a strong, well-constructed arch, the more weight there is laid upon it, the firmer it stands; and thus with America, the more we are loaded, the more we are united." Reflecting colonial self-confidence, Benjamin Franklin called for a return to the pre-1763 imperial system. "It is easy to propose a plan of conciliation," Franklin declared: "*repeal* the laws, *renounce* the right, *recall* the troops, *refund* the money, and *return* to the old method of requisition."

The home authorities had something very different in mind. The new boycott had exhausted their patience. When a copy of the Massachusetts House's letter opposing the Townshend duties reached London in mid-1768, Lord Hillsborough, the Secretary of State for American affairs, branded it as "unjustifiable opposition to the constitutional authority of Parliament." He told Governor Francis Bernard to dissolve the House if it refused to rescind its action. Hillsborough backed up his words by dispatching four regiments of troops to Boston at the request of the customs commissioners, to strengthen the "Hand of Government." (In June 1768, customs commissioners trying to prosecute John Hancock for smuggling had been forced by a mob of furious Bostonians to take refuge on the British warship *Romney*, which had seized John Hancock's ship *Liberty* in Boston harbor.) Hillsborough's goal was not to prevent smuggling along the seacoast but to prepare for a possible armed showdown with the radical Boston Patriots.

By the end of 1768 a thousand British regulars were encamped in Boston, and military coercion was a very real prospect. General Gage accused Massachusetts public leaders of "Treasonable and desperate Resolves," and Parliament threatened to appoint a special commission to hear evidence of treason. King George supported Hillsborough's plan to repeal the Townshend duties in all the colonies except Massachusetts, thus isolating the agitators, and then use the British army to bring the rebellious New Englanders to their knees.

The stakes had risen. In 1765, American resistance to taxation had provoked an argument in Parliament; in 1768, it produced a plan for military coercion.

The Second Compromise

At this critical moment, the British ministry's resolve faltered. England was having domestic problems. Poor harvests caused a food shortage in 1768, and riots swept the countryside. Mobs protested against high prices and raided supplies of grain and bread. In the highly publicized "Massacre of Saint George Fields," troops killed seven demonstrators. Opposition politicians exploited the situation and called for a new ministry. Radical Whig John Wilkes stepped up his attacks on government corruption and won election to Parliament. American Patriots identified with Wilkes and drank toasts in his honor. They followed events apprehensively as on four occasions the ministry denied Wilkes his seat when the popular leader was elected,

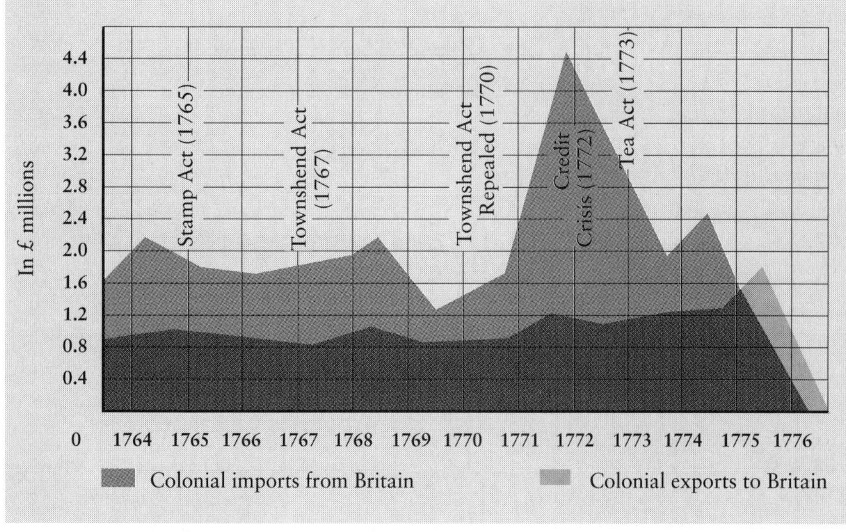

FIGURE 5.2

Coincidence of Trade and Politics, 1763–1776

and reelected, to Parliament in 1768 and 1769. Riots in Ireland over the growing military budget there added to the ministry's difficulties.

The American trade boycott likewise began to hurt. Normally, the mainland colonies had an annual deficit of £500,000 in their trade with Great Britain, but in 1768 they imported far fewer goods, cutting the deficit to £230,000. In 1769, the boycott had a major impact on the British economy. By continuing to export tobacco, rice, fish, and other goods to Britain while refusing to buy its manufactured goods, Americans accumulated a huge trade surplus of £816,000. British merchants and industrialists petitioned Parliament for repeal of the Townshend duties, in order to revive their flagging fortunes.

By late 1769, merchant petitions had persuaded some ministers that the Townshend duties were a mistake. The king no longer supported Hillsborough's scheme to punish the Massachusetts Patriots, and the danger of military coercion seemed to have passed. Early in 1770, Lord North became chief minister, and he pointed out that it was "contrary to the true principles of commerce" for Britain to tax its own exports to America, because the goal of mercantilism was to encourage consumption of British products in the colonies. North arranged a compromise whereby Parliament repealed the Townshend Act's duties on glass, paper, paint, and other manufactured items, but retained the tax on tea as a symbol of Parliament's supremacy. This stratagem worked. In a spirit of good will (and to restore their own flagging fortunes), merchants in New York and Philadelphia rejected pleas from Patriots in Boston to continue the boycott. Most Americans did not insist on strict adherence to their constitutional principles, contesting neither the duty on British molasses required by the Sugar Act of 1766 nor the symbolic tax on tea. They simply avoided paying these taxes by smuggling and bribing customs agents.

Not even a new outbreak of violence in New York City and Boston in 1770 could disrupt the spirit of compromise. During the boycott, New York artisans and workers had taunted British regulars in the resident garrison—mostly with words, but occasionally with stones and fists. In January 1770 the troops responded by tearing down a Liberty Pole in front of a tavern, setting off a week of sporadic street-fighting—the Golden Hill riots—in which both sides suffered only minor injuries. In Boston, where British soldiers competed with townsmen for the favor of local women and for part-time jobs, tensions came to a head in the "Boston Massacre" of March 1770. A mob of laborers and seamen attacked a group of soldiers, who fired into the crowd, killing five men, including one of the leaders—Crispus Attucks, a mulatto who had escaped from slavery in Massachusetts in 1750 and worked as a seaman. The British soldiers were defended in a Boston court by no less a Patriot than John Adams, who blamed the incident on "a motley rabble of saucy boys, negroes and mulattoes, Irish teagues and outlandish jack tarrs," and won their acquittal. However, another Patriot, James Bowdoin, wrote *A Short Narrative of the Horrid Massacre in Boston*, accusing the British of deliberately planning the killing. This pamphlet circulated widely in the colonies and further inflamed public opinion against the imperial authorities.

John Wilkes, British Radical

Wilkes won fame as the author of "North Briton, Number 45", a pamphlet that called for political reform in Britain. At a dinner in Boston, Radical Whigs raised their glasses to Wilkes—toasting him 45 times!

Sovereignty Debated. Most Americans still remained loyal to the empire, but five years of conflict over taxes and constitutional principles built ill will on both sides of the Atlantic. Even Lord Chatham thought the American merchants and assemblies had carried "their notions of freedom too far" and were unwilling, on a number of crucial issues, to "be subject to the laws of this country." Benjamin Franklin recognized that the colonies had repudiated the power of Parliament to impose taxes and had questioned other aspects of its authority as well. He wanted to redefine the imperial relationship, giving America political equality within the empire. Franklin suggested that the colonies were now "distinct and separate states" but "having the same Head, or Sovereign, the King."

Thomas Hutchinson, the American-born royal governor of Massachusetts, was horrified at Franklin's proposal. He rejected the idea of "two independent legislatures in one and the same state." For Hutchinson, sovereignty was indivisible—it was all or nothing. "I know of no line," he told the Massachusetts House of Representatives, "that can be drawn between the supreme authority of Parliament and the total independence of the colonies." But a House committee disagreed, adopting Franklin's position: If Britain and its American colonies were united by the king as their "one head and common sovereign," they could "live happily in that connection." (More than a century and a half later this idea would come to fruition in the British Commonwealth of Nations.)

The second crisis—and compromise—had significantly altered the terms of the debate. In 1765, American public leaders had accepted Parliament's authority. The Stamp Act Resolves had opposed only certain "unconstitutional" legislation. By 1770 the most outspoken Patriots—including Franklin, Patrick Henry of Virginia, and Samuel Adams and his followers in the Massachusetts House—had repudiated Parliament and claimed equality for their own assemblies under the king. Nor did they flinch when reminded that George III condemned their agitation. As the Massachusetts House told Hutchinson, "There is more reason to dread the consequences of absolute uncontrolled supreme power, whether of a nation or a monarch, than those of total independence."

There the matter rested. The British had twice tried to impose taxes on the colonies and American Patriots had twice forced them to retreat. It was now clear that if Parliament insisted on exercising its claim to sovereignty, at least some Americans would have to be subdued by force. Fearful of civil war, the ministry hesitated to take the final fateful step.

The Road to War, 1771–1775

The repeal of most of the Townshend duties in 1770 restored harmony to the British empire and for the next three years most disputes were resolved peacefully or confined to individual colonies. The continued existence of the empire seemed assured. However, history moves in unseen and unpredictable ways, and below the surface lay strong fears and passions—and mutual distrust. Suddenly in 1773 these undercurrents erupted, overwhelming hope for compromise. In less than two years the Americans and the British stood on the brink of war.

The Tea Act

Lord North's repeal of the Townshend duties did not satisfy radical Patriots, who now wanted American independence. They kept the Boston Massacre vivid in public memory and exploited events, such as a British credit crisis in 1772 that caused economic distress in the colonies, to warn Americans of the dangers of imperial domination. In November 1772, Samuel Adams persuaded the Boston town meeting to establish a Committee of Correspondence "to state the Rights of the Colonists of this Province." Within a few months, eighty Massachusetts towns had set up similar committees. This movement spread to other colonies when, in January 1773, the British government set up a royal commission to investigate an incident involving the *Gaspée*, a British customs vessel which Rhode Island Patriots had burned in June 1772, to protest the diligence of its captain in enforcing the Navigation Acts. The royal commission's powers, particularly its authority to send Americans to England for trial, aroused Patriot sentiment. In Virginia, the House of Burgesses created a Committee of Correspondence "to communicate with the other colonies" respecting the situation in Rhode Island. By July 1773, similar committees had sprung up in Connecticut, New Hampshire, and South Carolina.

However, the first link in the chain of events that led directly to revolution was Parliament's passage of a Tea Act in May 1773. The purpose of the Act was to provide financial relief to the British East India Company, a royally chartered firm that was deeply in debt, both because of mismanagement and because of the cost of military expeditions that extended British trade in India. The Tea Act provided a government loan to the company and, more important, eliminated the customs duties on the tea that the company brought to England and then reexported to America. This provision cut costs for the East India Company, allowing it to undersell other British merchants, who had to pay the customs levies, and giving it a virtual monopoly of the provincial market.

Lord North knew that the Tea Act would be unpopular in America, but he failed to gauge just how unpopular it would be. Since 1768, when the Townshend Act placed a duty of 3 pence a pound on tea, Americans had boycotted the British product, buying illegally imported tea from the Dutch instead. By the 1770s, about 90 percent of the tea consumed in America was contraband. But the Tea Act would make the East India Company tea competitive with the smuggled Dutch tea, and many Americans, in these circumstances, might choose to buy the British tea—and pay the 3 pence Townshend duty. Colonial opponents of the act charged that the ministry was bribing Americans to give up their principles, "to

AMERICAN VOICES

Letter to Captain Ayres, of the Ship *Polly*

COMMITTEE ON TAR AND FEATHERING

In 1773 Patriots throughout the colonies prevented the landing of taxed tea by the agents of the East India Company. This letter from a self-appointed "Committee on Tar and Feathering" in Philadelphia, although undoubtedly written by a highly educated American, suggests the fears—and the determination—of ordinary members of the Sons of Liberty.

Sir:

We are informed that you have imprudently taken charge of a quantity of tea which has been sent out by the India Company, under the auspices of the Ministry, as a trial of American virtue and resolution.

Now, as your cargo, on your arrival here, will most assuredly bring you into hot water, and as you are perhaps a stranger to these parts, we have concluded to advise you of the present situation in Philadelphia, that, taking time by the forelock, you may step short in your dangerous errand, secure your ship against the rafts of combustible matter which may be sent on fire and turned loose against her; and more than all this, that you may preserve your own person from the pitch and feathers that are prepared for you.

In the first place, we must tell you that the Pennsylvanians are, to a man, passionately fond of freedom, the birthright of Americans, and at all events are determined to enjoy it.

That they sincerely believe no power on the face of the earth has a right to tax them without their consent. . . .

You are sent out on a diabolical service; and if you are so foolish and obstinate as to complete your voyage by bringing your ship to anchor in this port, you may run such a gauntlet as will induce you in your last moments most heartily to curse those who have made you the dupe of their avarice and ambition.

What think you, Captain, of a halter around your neck—ten gallons of liquid tar decanted on your pate—with feathers of a dozen wild geese laid over that to enliven your appearance?

Only think seriously of this—and fly to the place from whence you came—fly without hesitation—without the formality of a protest—and above all, Captain Ayres, let us advise you to fly without the wild geese feathers.

The Committee on Tar
and Feathering

Source: Pennsylvania Magazine of History and Biography XV (1891), 391.

barter liberty for luxury," as they put it. This was exactly what North wanted. Like Grenville and Townshend before him, he was not content to declare Parliament's authority to tax the colonies—he wanted to demonstrate it.

North's insensitivity to the fragile state of the colonial relationship cost the empire dearly, for it revived American resistance. The East India Company decided to bypass American traders in London and to distribute the tea directly to shopkeepers in the major port cities, a tactic that shocked colonial merchants. The Tea Act would not only eliminate the illegal Dutch trade but also cut colonial merchants out of the British tea business. "The fear of an Introduction of a Monopoly in this Country," General Haldimand reported from New York, "has induced the mercantile part of the Inhabitants to be very industrious in opposing this Step and added Strength to a Spirit of Independence already too prevalent."

The Committees of Correspondence took the lead in organizing resistance to the Tea Act. All along the seaboard, the Sons of Liberty prevented East India Company ships from landing tea and forced the captains to return it to England or store it in public warehouses. By firm but peaceful means, Patriots effectively nullified the Tea Act.

The Boston Tea Party. In Boston events took a more ominous turn. For decades, Massachusetts had steadfastly resisted British authority and, in the 1760s, had assumed leadership of the anti-imperial movement. Boston lawyers James Otis and John Adams had raised the first constitutional objections to legislation enforcing imperial reform; Boston mobs were the first to oppose the Stamp Act; Boston merchants such as John Hancock had led the joint colonial opposition to the Townshend duties. As early as 1768 Bostonians had condemned the tax on tea as a devious plot by "the politicians who planned our ruin," and it was they who provoked the Boston Massacre two years later. Boston was destined to spark the final conflagration with Great Britain.

Chance also figured in this outcome. The governor of Massachusetts, Thomas Hutchinson, bitterly opposed the Patriots, and with good reason. Stamp Act rioters had looted his house; Benjamin Franklin and Boston Patriots had smeared his reputation by publishing his private correspondence; and the Massachusetts House had condemned his defense of parliamentary power. A combination of personal grudges and constitutional principles made Hutchinson determined to uphold the Tea Act.

The governor had a scheme to collect the tax and land the tea. As it happened, several of the agents chosen by the East India Company to handle the tea in Boston were Hutchinson's sons. When the tea arrived on the *Dartmouth*, the governor had his sons pass the ship through customs. Once this legal entry had been achieved, the *Dartmouth* could not depart without paying the duties on its cargo. Hutchinson had time on his side. If the tea duty was not paid within twenty days, customs officials could seize the cargo, land it with the help of the British army, and sell the tea at auction.

The Massachusetts Patriots met the governor's challenge. The Boston Committee of Correspondence sent Paul Revere, William Molineaux, and Thomas Young to lead a group of Patriots, most of whom were artisans, aboard the *Dartmouth*. On a cold night in December 1773 they boarded the ship, disguised as Indians, broke open the 342 chests of tea, and threw them into the harbor. "This destruction of the Tea is so bold and it must have so important Consequences," John Adams wrote in his diary, "that I cannot but consider it as an Epoch in History."

The Coercive Acts. Adams was not exaggerating. The British Privy Council was outraged, as was the king. There would be no more compromises: "Concessions have made matters worse," George III declared. "The time has come for compulsion." Parliament decisively rejected a proposal to repeal the duty on American tea. Instead, in the spring of 1774, it enacted four Coercive Acts to force Massachusetts into submission. A Port Bill closed Boston Harbor until the East India Company re-

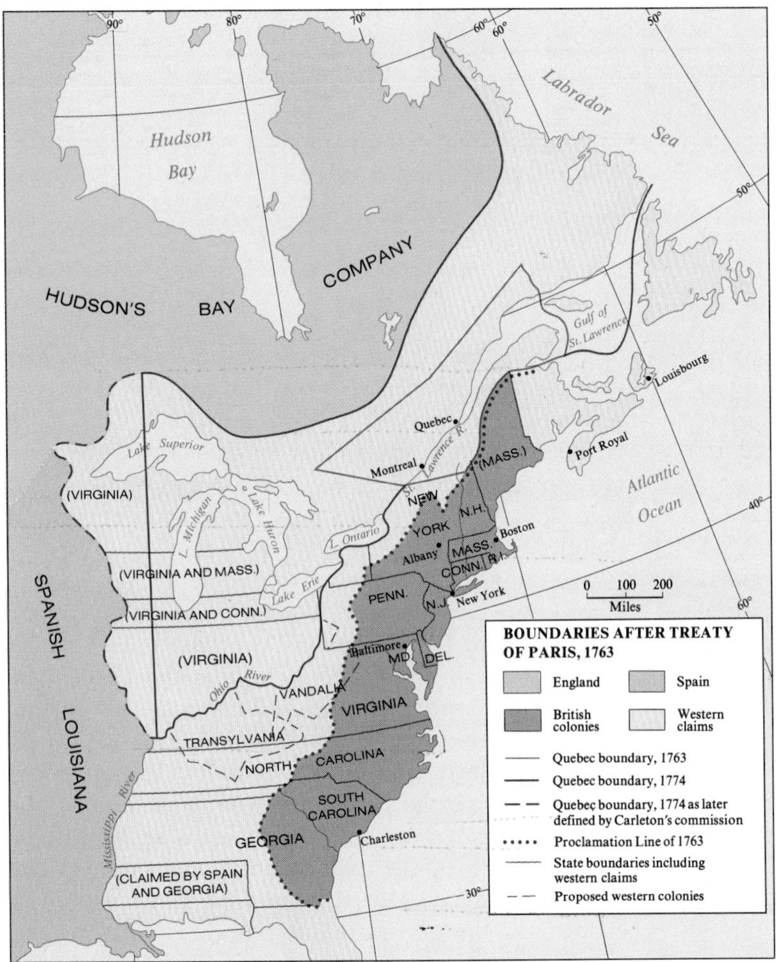

MAP 5.3

British Western Policy, 1763–1774

To prevent Indian wars, the Proclamation Line of 1763 restricted white settlement west of the Appalachian Mountains. Nevertheless, colonial land speculators planned the new colonies of Vandalia and Transylvania. The Quebec Act of 1774 designated these colonies as Indian Reserves and, by vastly increasing the boundaries of Quebec, eliminated the sea-to-sea land claims of many eastern colonies. The act angered American settlers and speculators and frightened colonial political leaders because it made no provision for a representative assembly in Quebec.

Religion and Rebellion

Many American Protestants hated bishops and the ecclesiastical power they represented. This cartoon warns that the Quebec Bill of 1774, which allowed the practice of Catholicism in Canada, was part of a plot by the hierarchy of the Church of England to impose bishops on the American colonies.

ceived payment for the destroyed tea. The Massachusetts House and local town meetings were deprived of the authority to enact many types of laws and regulations. Massachusetts was to pay for the quartering of troops. And royal officials accused of capital crimes in Massachusetts were allowed to be tried in other colonies or in Britain.

Hillsborough had proposed a similar "divide-and-rule" strategy in 1769, when he suggested isolating Massachusetts from the other mainland colonies. By 1774, however, the success of the boycott against the Townshend duties and the activities of the Committees of Correspondence had created a firm sense of unity among the colonies. "The cause of Boston, the despotick measures in respect to it, I mean," George Washington declared from Virginia, "now is and ever will be considered as the cause of America."

In 1774 Parliament passed the Quebec Act, heightening the Americans' sense of common danger. This law extended the boundaries of Quebec into the Ohio River Valley, thus threatening to restrict the western land boundaries of Virginia and other seaboard colonies. The Quebec Act also gave legal recognition to Roman Catholicism, a concession to the French residents of Canada that aroused old religious hatreds, especially in New England. The ministry had not intended the Quebec Act as a coercive measure, but many colonial leaders saw it as yet another demonstration of Parliament's power to intervene in American domestic affairs.

The Continental Congress Responds

To respond to the new British measures, American leaders called for a new all-colony assembly, the Continental Congress. The newer colonies—Florida, Quebec, Nova Scotia, and Newfoundland—did not attend, but delegates from all of the other mainland provinces except Georgia, whose assembly was effectively controlled by a royal governor, met in Philadelphia in September 1774.

New England delegates to the First Continental Congress advocated political union and immediate military preparations. Southern leaders, convinced that there was a British plot "to overturn the constitution and introduce a system of arbitrary government," also favored resistance. Many delegates from the middle colonies held out for a political compromise. Led by Joseph Galloway of Pennsylvania, these men of "loyal principles" outlined a scheme for a new imperial system, resembling the Albany Plan of Union of 1754. Under Galloway's system, America would have a legislative council selected by the colonial assemblies and a president-general appointed by the king, with the new government having a veto over parliamentary legislation affecting America. The delegates refused to endorse Galloway's plan as the basis for a negotiated settlement, because, with British troops "occupying" Boston, it was thought to be too conciliatory.

Instead, the First Continental Congress passed a Declaration of Rights and Grievances that condemned the Coercive Acts and demanded their repeal. The Congress likewise repudiated the Declaratory Act of 1766, which had proclaimed Parliament's supremacy over the colonies, and demanded that Britain restrict its supervision of American affairs to matters of external trade. Finally, the Congress began a program of economic retaliation. New nonimportation and nonconsumption agreements would come into effect in December 1774, and if Parliament did not repeal the "Intolerable Acts," as the Patriots called them, by September 1775, all colonial exports to Britain, Ireland, and the West Indies would be cut off. Ten years of constitutional conflict had ended in all-out commercial warfare.

AMERICAN LIVES

George R.T. Hewes and the Meaning of the Revolution

★

George Robert Twelve Hewes was born in Boston in 1742. He was named George after his father, Robert after a paternal uncle, and Twelve after his maternal grandmother, whose maiden name was Twelves. Apart from his long name, Hewes received little from his parents—not size, for he was unusually short, five feet, one inch; not wealth, for his father, a failed tanner, died a poor soap boiler when Hewes was seven; not even love, for Hewes spoke of his mother only as someone who whipped him for disobedience. At the age of fourteen Hewes was apprenticed to a shoemaker, one of the lower trades.

George Hewes, 1835
This portrait of George Hewes was painted by Joseph Cole.

This harsh upbringing shaped Hewes's personality. As an adult he spoke out against all brutality—even the tar-and-feathering of a Tory who had almost killed him. And throughout his life he was extremely sensitive about his class status. He was "neither a rascal nor a vagabond," Hewes retorted to a Boston gentleman who pulled rank on him, "and though a poor man was in as good credit in town as he was."

The occupation of Boston by 4,000 British soldiers in 1768 drew the twenty-six-year-old Hewes into the resistance movement. At first his concerns were personal: he took offense when British sentries challenged him and when a soldier refused to pay for a pair of shoes. Then they became political: Hewes grew angry when some of the poorly paid British soldiers moonlighted, taking jobs away from Bostonians, and angrier still when a Tory merchant fired into a crowd of apprentices who were picketing his shop, killing one of them. And so on March 5, 1770, when British soldiers came out in force to clear the streets of rowdy civilians, Hewes joined his fellow townspeople: "They were in the king's highway, and had as good a right to be there" as the British troops, he said.

Fate—and his growing political consciousness—had placed Hewes in the midst of the Boston Massacre. Not only did he know four of the five workingmen shot down that night by British troops, but one of them, James Caldwell, was standing by his side and Hewes caught him as he fell. Outraged, Hewes armed himself with a cane, only to be confronted by Sergeant Chambers of the 29th British Regiment and eight or nine soldiers, "all with very large clubs or cutlasses." Chambers seized his cane, but, as Hewes stated in a legal deposition, "I told him I had as good a right to carry a cane as they had to carry clubs." This deposition, which went on to tell of the soldiers' threats to kill more civilians, was included in *A Short Narrative of the Horrid Massacre in Boston,* published by a group of Boston Patriots.

Hewes had chosen sides, and his political radicalism did not go unpunished. His outspokenness roused the ire of one of his creditors, a Tory merchant tailor. Hewes had never really made a go of it as a shoemaker and constantly struggled on the brink of poverty. Unable to make good on a two-year-old debt of £6. 8s. 3p. (about $300 today) for "a sappled coat & breeches of fine cloth," he landed in debtor's prison in September 1770. Such extravagance of dress on Hewes's part was rare, the desperate ploy of a propertyless artisan to win the hand of Sally Summer, the daughter of the sexton of the First Baptist Church, whom he had married in 1768. Prison did not blunt Hewes's enthusiasm for the Patriot cause. On the night of December 16, 1773, he turned up as a volunteer at the Tea Party organized by the radical Patriot leaders of Boston. He "daubed his face and hands with coal dust in the shop of a blacksmith" and then found, somewhat to his surprise, that "the commander of the division to which I belonged, as soon as we were on board the ship, appointed me boatswain, and ordered me to go to the captain and demand of him the keys to the hatches." Hewes had been singled out and made a minor leader, and he must have played the part well. Thompson Maxwell, a volunteer sent to the Tea Party by John Hancock, recalled that "I went accordingly, joined the band under one Captain Hewes; we mounted the ships and made tea in a trice." In the heat of conflict the small man with the large name had been elevated from a poor shoemaker to "Captain Hewes."

A man of greater ability or ambition might have seized the moment, using his prominence as a Patriot to win fame or fortune, but that was not Hewes's destiny. During the War of Independence, he fought as an ordinary sailor and soldier—shipping out twice on privateering voyages and enlisting at least four times in the militia, about twenty months of military service in all. He did not win riches as a privateer (although, with four children to support, that was his hope), or find glory in battle, or even adequate pay: "we received nothing of the government but paper money, of very little value, and continually depreciating." Indeed, the war cost Hewes the little stake he had in society: "The shop which I had built in Boston, I lost"; it was pulled down and burned by British troops.

In material terms, the American Revolution did about as much for Hewes as his parents had. When a journalist found the shoemaker in New York State in the 1830s, he was still "pressed down by the iron hand of poverty." The spiritual reward was greater. As his biographer Alfred Young put it: "He was a nobody who briefly became a somebody in the Revolution and, for a moment near the end of his life, a hero." Because Americans had begun to celebrate the memory of the Revolution Hewes was brought back to Boston in 1835 in triumph, as one of the last surviving participants in the Tea Party—the guest of honor on Independence Day.

But a more fundamental spiritual reward had come to Hewes when he became a revolutionary, casting off the deferential status of "subject" in a monarchy and becoming a proud and equal "citizen" in a republic. What this meant to Hewes, and to thousands of other poor and obscure Patriots, appeared in his relationship—both real and fictitious—with John Hancock. As a young man Hewes had sat tongue-tied and deferential in the rich merchant's presence. But in his story of the Tea Party, Hewes made Hancock his equal, placing him at the scene (which was almost certainly not the case) and claiming that he "was himself at one time engaged with him in the demolition of the same chest of tea." In this lessening of social distance—this declaration of *equality*—lay the meaning of the American Revolution.

The Boston "Tea Party"

Led by radical Patriots disguised as Mohawk Indians, Bostonians dump taxed British tea into the harbor. The rioters underlined their political motives by punishing those who sought personal gain; one man who stole some of the tea was "stripped of his booty and his clothes together, and sent home naked."

The British ministry was unyielding. The government branded the Continental Congress an illegal assembly and reaffirmed its coercive policy. A few British leaders continued to hope for a compromise. In January 1775 the Earl of Chatham (William Pitt) proposed the removal of British troops from Boston and asked Parliament to give up its claim to tax the colonies and to recognize the Continental Congress as a lawful body. In return for these and other concessions, he asked that the Congress acknowledge parliamentary supremacy and grant a continuing revenue to cover part of the British national debt. But Chatham's dramatic intervention, like Galloway's in the colonies, was doomed to failure. The British ministry had twice backed down; a third retreat was impossible. The honor of the nation was at stake. The ministry rejected Chatham's plan and also a proposal by Lord Dartmouth, the colonial secretary, to send commissioners to America to negotiate a settlement.

Instead, Lord North set stringent terms. Americans must pay for their own defense and administration; and they must acknowledge Parliament's authority to tax them. To give teeth to these demands, North imposed a naval blockade on American trade with foreign nations and ordered General Gage to suppress dissent in Massachusetts. Former Governor Thomas Hutchinson, now living in exile in London, reported that the British prime minister had told him, "Now the case seemed desperate. Parliament would not—could not—concede. For aught he could see it must come to violence."

The Rising of the Countryside

Although the Patriot movement began in the seaport cities, its success depended on the support of the predominantly rural population. Most farmers initially had little interest in imperial issues. Their lives were deeply rooted in the soil, and their prime allegiance was to their families and communities. Then the French and Indian War took their sons away from home and nibbled at their income. In the community of Newtown on Long Island, farmers had paid an average of 10 shillings (about $20 today) in taxes before 1754; by 1756 taxes had jumped to 30 shillings to cover New York's military expenses. Peace brought only slight relief; the Quartering Act cost Newtown residents 20 shillings in taxes in 1771. Many Americans found these exactions onerous, although in fact they paid much less in taxes than most Britons.

Political as well as economic issues infiltrated from the cities into the countryside. Rural Patriots rallied to support the nonimportation movements of 1765 and 1769, and the Daughters of Liberty in hundreds of small towns and villages spun and wove wool into homemade cloth to support American resistance. It was this outburst of rural patriotism that encouraged the Continental Congress to declare a new economic boycott of British goods in 1774 and to create a network of local associations to enforce it. The Congress condemned Americans who wore expensive imported clothes at funerals, approving only "a black crape or ribbon on the arm or hat for gentlemen, and a black ribbon and necklace for ladies."

These symbolic affirmations of traditional rural thriftiness reflected harsh economic realities. The yeoman tradition of agricultural independence was everywhere under attack. Arable land was scarce and expensive in long-settled regions. Aristocratic landlords were demanding high rents, and entrepreneurial speculators controlled large frontier tracts. Merchants were seizing farmsteads for delinquent debts. The new demands of the British government would further drain

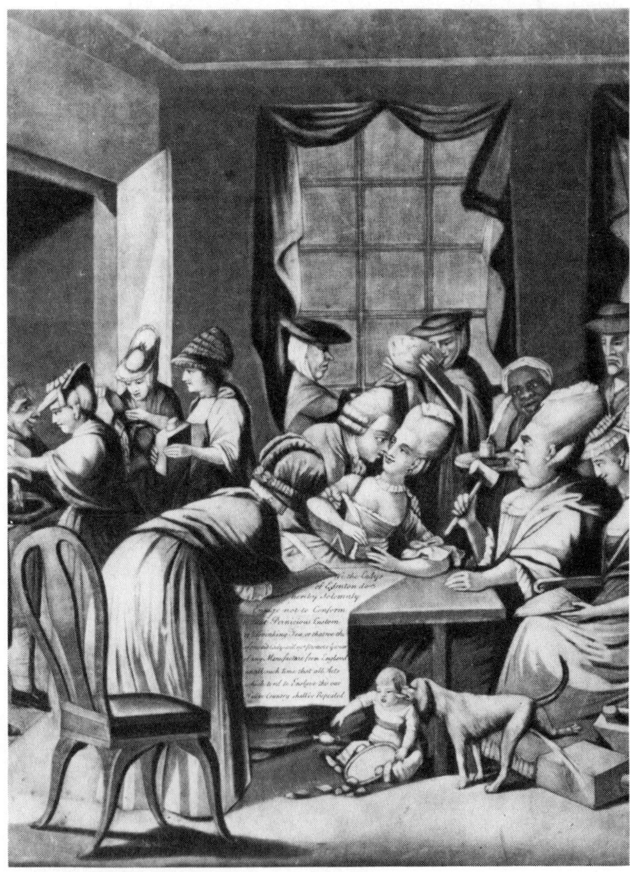

Political Propaganda: The Empire Strikes Back

A British print attacks the women of Edenton, North Carolina, for supporting the boycott of British trade, hinting at their sexual lasciviousness and—by showing an enslaved black woman among these advocates of American liberty—their moral hypocrisy.

TABLE 5.2

Patriot Resistance, 1760–1775

British Action	Date	Patriot Response
Revenue Act	1762	Merchants complain privately
Proclamation Line	1763	Land speculators voice discontent
Sugar Act	1764	Massachusetts Assembly protests
Stamp Act	1765	Riots by Sons of Liberty Stamp Act Congress First nonimportation movement
Quartering Act	1765	New York Assembly refuses to implement until 1767
Townshend Duties	1767	Second nonimportation movement Harassment of pro-British merchants
Troops occupy Boston	1768	Harassment; Boston Massacre of 1770
Gaspée affair	1772	Committees of correspondence created
Tea Act	1773	Widespread resistance Boston Tea Party
Coercive Acts and Quebec Act	1774	First Continental Congress Third nonimportation movement
British raids on Lexington and Concord	1775	Armed resistance by Minutemen Second Continental Congress

"this People of the Fruits of their Toil," complained the town meeting of rural Petersham, Massachusetts. "The duty on tea," added a Patriot pamphlet, "was only a prelude to a window tax, hearth-tax, land-tax, and poll-tax, and these were only paving the way for reducing the country to lordships." By the 1770s many northern yeomen felt personally threatened by British policies.

Chesapeake slaveowners had similar fears, despite their much higher standard of living. Beginning in the 1750s, many planters had sunk deep into debt. A Virginia planter observed in 1766 that a debt of £1,000 was once considered excessive, but "ten times that sum is now spoke of with indifference and thought no great burthen on Some Estates." High living had led to economic anxiety. Slaveowners, accustomed to being masters on their own plantations, resented their financial dependence on British merchants.

The southern countryside, like that of the North, became increasingly committed to the Patriot movement. The Coercive Acts raised the threat of political dependence in the minds of many planters. They worried that once Parliament had subdued Massachusetts, it might seize control of Virginia's county courts and the House of Burgesses. This prospect moved many planters to action. "The spark of liberty is not yet extinct among our people," one planter declared, "and if properly fanned by the Gentlemen of influence will, I make no doubt, burst out again into a flame."

The Loyalists. Support for the Patriot cause was not unanimous, however. As early as 1765, various groups of Americans had feared that resistance to Britain would destroy respect for all political institutions and end in mob rule. This fear was particularly strong among propertied families—large landowners, substantial slaveowners, and wealthy merchants—but it was shared by thousands of ordinary colonists. Their fears increased as the Sons of Liberty used violence to enforce nonimportation. One well-to-do New Yorker complained, "No man can be in a more abject state of bondage than he whose Reputation, Property and Life are exposed to the discretionary violence . . . of the community."

Beginning in 1774, conservative Americans of "loyal principles" began joining together to denounce Patriot schemes of independence. Royal governors—such as Thomas Hutchinson of Massachusetts, Benning Wentworth of New Hampshire, and Lord Dunmore of Virginia—stood at the head of the Loyalists. They mobilized royal officials, merchants with military contracts, clergy of the Church of England, and well-established lawyers into a small but wealthy and articulate pro-British party. Clergymen such as Jonathan Boucher of Virginia denounced Patriot agitators from their pulpits, while landlords and merchants used the threat of economic retaliation to persuade indebted tenants and workers to oppose radical demands. But there were too few Loyalists, and they were too poorly organized, to affect events in 1774 and 1775. A Tory Association started by Governor Wentworth in New Hampshire had only fifty-nine members—fourteen of whom were Wentworth's relatives. At this crucial point, Americans who favored resistance to British rule commanded the allegiance—or at least the acquiescence—of the majority of white Americans.

The Failure of Compromise

When the Continental Congress met in September 1774, New England already stood in open defiance of British authority. In August, 150 delegates from neighboring towns had gathered in Concord, Massachusetts, for a Middlesex County Congress, an illegal county convention at which the people were advised to close the royal courts of justice and transfer their political allegiance to the popularly elected House of Representatives. Crowds of armed men prevented the Court of General Sessions from meeting, and rural Patriots harassed supporters of the royal regime.

Governor Gage tried desperately to maintain imperial power. In September 1774, British troops marched out of Boston and seized Patriot armories and storehouses at Charlestown and Cambridge. Far from subduing the Patriots, this action only created more support for their cause. Twenty thousand colonial militiamen mobilized to safeguard depots of military supplies at Concord and Worcester. The Concord town meeting voted to raise two companies of troops to "Stand at a minutes warning in Case of alarm"—the famous "minutemen." Eighty percent of the male heads of families and a number of single women in Concord signed a Solemn League and Covenant vowing support for non-

The Battle of Lexington

At dawn, 70 militiamen (half the town's men) confronted 700 British soldiers. "Ye vilans, ye Rebels, disperse," shouted a British officer. "Damn you, disperse." Someone fired a shot. Panicked, the soldiers fired at will, killing eight Minutemen and wounding nine. This was painted in the late eighteenth century by Amos Doolittle. (The Carnegie Museum of Art) importation, and other rural towns likewise expressed allegiance to the rebellious Patriot government. Gage's authority was increasingly limited to Boston, where it rested primarily on the bayonets of his 3,500 troops.

This stalemate lasted for six months. Gage, unwilling to undertake new raids that might precipitate an armed conflict, waited for orders from Britain. In the meantime, the Massachusetts House met on its own authority. It issued regulations for the collection of taxes, assumed the responsibilities of government, and strengthened the militia. Even before the news of Massachusetts' defiance reached London, Colonial Secretary Lord Dartmouth declared Massachusetts to be in a state of "open rebellion." He told Gage that "force should be repelled by force" and sent orders to the governor to march quickly against the "rude rabble." On the night of April 18, Gage dispatched troops to capture colonial leaders and supplies at Concord. However, Paul Revere and two other Bostonians warned the Patriots, and at dawn on April 19 local militiamen met the British at Lexington. Shots rang out, and a British volley killed 8 Americans and wounded several others. Pressing on to Concord, the 700 British soldiers confronted 400 Patriots. This time the British took the heavier losses, 3 dead and 12 wounded. The worst was yet to come. As the British retreated along the narrow, winding roads to Boston, they were repeatedly ambushed by 1,000 militiamen from neighboring towns. By the end of the day, 73 British soldiers lay dead, 174 were wounded, and 26 were missing. British fire had killed 49 American militiamen and wounded 39.

Now too much blood had been spilled to allow a peaceful compromise. Twelve years of economic conflict and constitutional debate had ended in civil war.

Summary

The Great War for Empire brought a decisive end to the era of salutary neglect. The war had exposed the weakness of imperial control over the American colonies and had left Britain with a crushing load of debt. When George Grenville became prime minister in 1763 he embraced the cause of imperial reform. To raise money—and reassert British authority—he enacted the Sugar Act, which extended the jurisdiction of vice-admiralty courts, and the Stamp Act, which imposed a direct tax for the first time. The colonists protested against the stamp duty through mob violence, a trade boycott, and an extralegal Stamp Act Congress. Parliament was forced to repeal the Stamp Act in 1766, but it explicitly reaffirmed its complete authority over the colonies.

Between 1765 and 1770, American and British politicians vigorously debated constitutional issues. Educated colonists based their arguments for American rights on English common law, Enlightenment thought, and the writings of Real Whigs, while the Sons and Daughters of Liberty drew inspiration from evangelical Protestantism and the English republican tradition.

In 1767 Charles Townshend undermined the first informal compromise by imposing a new tax on trade. Americans responded with a second nonimportation movement. While the British ministry nearly adopted a plan to crush American resistance by force, domestic problems prompted it to repeal most of the Townshend duties by 1770.

Lord North disrupted this second compromise by passing the Tea Act in 1773. When Bostonians resisted the new law, the British used coercion in Massachusetts to try to destroy the Patriot resistance movement. In 1774, American political leaders met in the First Continental Congress, which challenged British authority and devised a new program of economic warfare. The Congress had the support of a majority of American farmers and planters, who were now prepared to resist arbitrary British rule. The failure to find a new compromise resulted in bloodshed at Lexington and Concord in April 1775, and civil war.

TOPIC FOR RESEARCH

Why Did the Patriots Revolt? The Search for Motives

For decades historians have sought the causes of the American Revolution. At times they have stressed economic causes—the impact of the Navigation Acts or the fear of taxes. More recently they have looked to political ideology and cultural values to explain the motivations of Patriot leaders and the Sons and Daughters of Liberty. In November 1772, a committee of the Boston town meeting headed by Samuel Adams, James Otis, and Joseph Warren composed "The State of the Rights of the Colonists" and a "List of Infringements." Read these documents carefully. How would you characterize the motives of these Patriots? Secondary works that address this issue include Pauline Maier, *The Old Revolutionaries: Political Lives in the Age of Samuel Adams* (1980); Library of Congress Symposium, *The Development of a Revolutionary Mentality* (1972); John C. Miller, *Samuel Adams: Pioneer in Propaganda* (1936); Milton E. Flower, *John Dickinson, Conservative Revolutionary* (1983); Richard R. Beeman, *Patrick Henry: A Biography* (1974); John R. Alden, *George Washington: A Biography* (1984); Helen Hill Miller, *George Mason: Gentleman Revolutionary* (1975); John J. Waters, Jr., *The Otis Family in Provincial and Revolutionary Massachusetts* (1968); Page Smith, *John Adams* (1962); Richard Walsh, *Charleston's Sons of Liberty* (1959); and Eric Foner, *Tom Paine and Revolutionary America* (1976).

BIBLIOGRAPHY

The Reform Movement

For the impact of the war and the state of the empire in 1763, see the classic study by Lawrence H. Gipson, *The Coming of the Revolution, 1763–1775* (1954), and the following works: Richard Middleton, *The Bells of Victory: The Pitt-Newcastle Ministry and the Conduct of the Seven Years' War, 1757–1762* (1985); Alan Rogers, *Empire and Liberty: American Resistance to British Authority, 1755–1763* (1974); Howard H. Peckham, *Pontiac and the Indian Uprising* (1947); and Joseph A. Ernst, *Money and Politics in America, 1755–1775* (1973). Marc Egnal, *A Mighty Empire: The Origins of the Revolution* (1988), attempts an interpretive synthesis.

British politics and imperial reform can be traced in John Brewer, *Party Ideology and Popular Politics at the Accession of George III* (1976); P. D. G. Thomas, *British Politics and the Stamp Act Crisis: The First Phase of the American Revolution, 1763–1767* (1975); Thomas C. Barrow, *Trade and Empire: The British Customs Service in Colonial America, 1660–1775* (1967); John L. Bullion, *A Great and Necessary Measure: George Grenville and the Genesis of the Stamp Act, 1763–1765* (1982); Michael Kammen, *A Rope of Sand: The Colonial Agents, British Politics, and the American Revolution* (1968); Carl Ubbelohde, *The Vice-Admiralty Courts and the American Revolution* (1960); and Philip Lawson, *George Grenville: A Political Life* (1984).

The Dynamics of Rebellion

For the American response to the British reform laws, see Edmund S. Morgan and Helen M. Morgan, *The Stamp Act Crisis: Prologue to Revolution* (1963); Dirk Hoerder, *Crowd Action in Revolutionary Massachusetts, 1765–1780* (1977); Pauline Maier, *From Resistance to Revolution: Colonial Radicals and the Development of American Opposition to Britain, 1765–1776* (1972); and Gary B. Nash, *The Urban Crucible: Social Change, Political Consciousness, and the Origins of the American Revolution* (1979). Merrill Jensen, *The Founding of a Nation: A History of the American Revolution, 1763–1776* (1968), and Robert Middlekauff, *The Glorious Cause: The American Revolution, 1763–1789* (1982), provide detailed narratives of the struggle.

Studies of individual colonies capture the spirit of the resistance movement. See David Lovejoy, *Rhode Island Politics and the American Revolution* (1958); Ronald Hoffman, *A Spirit of Dissension: Economics, Politics, and the Revolution in Maryland* (1973); and David C. Skaggs, *Roots of Maryland Democracy* (1973). For biographical studies of Patriot leaders, consult the Topic for Research.

The most important recent study of Patriot ideology is Bernard Bailyn, *The Ideological Origins of the American Revolution* (1967); but see also Caroline Robbins, *The Eighteenth-Century Commonwealthman* (1959); Morton White, *The Philosophy of the American Revolution* (1978); Garry Wills, *Inventing America: Jefferson's Declaration of Independence* (1978); and H. T. Dickinson, *Liberty and Property: Political Ideology in Eighteenth-Century Britain* (1978). For a discussion of the legal tradition, see Charles H. McIlwain, *The American Revolution: A Constitutional Interpretation* (1923), and John Phillip Reid, *Constitutional History of the American Revolution: The Authority of Rights* (1986).

The Growing Confrontation

Peter D. G. Thomas, *The Townshend Duties Crisis: The Second Phase of the American Revolution, 1767–1773* (1987), is the most comprehensive treatment; but see Colin Bonwick, *English Radicals and the American Revolution* (1977), and Ian R. Christie and Benjamin W. Labaree, *Empire or Independence, 1760–1776* (1976). On American resistance, consult Richard Alan Ryerson, *The Revolution Is Now Begun: The Radical Committees of Philadelphia, 1765–1776* (1978); Peter Shaw, *American Patriots and the Rituals of Revolution* (1981); and Stanley Godbold, Jr. and Robert W. Woody, *Christopher Gadsden* (1982). The confrontation between Patriots and British authority is covered in John Shy, *Toward Lexington: The Role of the British Army in the Coming of the American Revolution* (1965), and Hiller B. Zobel, *The Boston Massacre* (1970).

The Road to War

Benjamin Labaree, *The Boston Tea Party* (1964), is comprehensive and stimulating. It should be read in conjunction with Bernard Donoughue, *British Politics and the American Revolution: The Path to War, 1773–75* (1972); David Ammerman, *In the Common Cause: American Response to the Coercive Acts of 1774*; Richard D. Brown, *Revolutionary Politics in Massachusetts: The Boston Committee of Correspondence and the Towns, 1772–1774* (1970). A fine study of the course of resistance is Edward F. Countryman, *A People in Revolution: The American Revolution and Political Society in New York* (1983). On prewar Loyalism, see Bernard Bailyn, *The Ordeal of Thomas Hutchinson* (1974), and Janice Potter, *The Liberty We Seek: Loyalist Ideology in Colonial New York and Massachusetts* (1983). For the rising of the countryside, see Gregory H. Nobles, *Divisions Throughout the Whole: Politics and Society in Hampshire County, Massachusetts, 1740–1775* (1983); Jere R. Daniell, *Experiment in Republicanism: New Hampshire Politics and the Revolution, 1741–1790* (1970); and Richard Bushman, *King and People in Provincial Massachusetts* (1985). The transfer of authority is described in Jerrilyn Greene Marston, *King and Congress: The Transfer of Political Legitimacy, 1774–1776* (1987).

TIMELINE

1754	"Salutary Neglect" ends
1760	George III becomes king
1762	Revenue Act
1763	Treaty of Paris ends Great War for Empire Proclamation Line restricts settlement Peacetime army in America Grenville becomes prime minister
1764	Currency Act Sugar Act Colonists claim "rights of Englishmen"
1765	Stamp Act Stamp Act Congress; riots by Sons of Liberty
1765	Constitutional debate in Britain and America
1765–1766	First nonimportation movement
1766	Rockingham repeals Stamp Act Declaratory Act
1767	Townshend Duties "Restraining Act" in New York Second nonimportation movement begins Daughters of Liberty make homespun cloth
1768	British army occupies Boston
1770	North repeals most Townshend Duties Golden Hill riots; Boston Massacre
1772	Colonial Committees of Correspondence
1773	Tea Act Boston Tea Party
1774	Coercive Acts Quebec Act First Continental Congress meets in Philadelphia Third nonimportation movement
1775	Battles of Lexington and Concord

PART 2

The New Republic, 1775–1820

THEMATIC TIMELINE

	Government	Diplomacy	Economy	Society	Culture
	Creating republican institutions	**European entanglements**	**Expansion of commerce and manufacturing**	**Defining liberty and equality**	**Pluralism and national identity**
1775	State constitutions written	Independence declared (1776) French Alliance (1778)	Wartime expansion of manufacturing	Slavery abolished in the North Murray, "On the Equality of the Sexes" (1779)	Paine's *Common Sense* calls for a republic
1780	Articles of Confederation ratified (1781) Legislative supremacy in states Philadelphia Convention drafts U.S. Constitution (1787)	Treaty of Paris (1783) British trade restrictions	Bank of North America (1781) Commercial recession (1783–1789) Western land speculation	Virginia Statute of Religious Freedom (1786) Idea of republican motherhood	Land ordinances create a national domain in the West German settlers preserve own language Webster defines American English
1790	Bill of Rights (1791) First national parties: Federalists and Republicans	Wars of the French Revolution Jay's and Pinckney's treaties (1795) Undeclared war with France (1798)	First Bank of the United States (1792–1812) States charter business corporations Outwork system expands	Sedition Act limits freedom of the press (1798)	Indians form Western Confederation Sectional divisions emerge between South and North
1800	Revolution of 1800 Activist state legislatures Chief Justice Marshall asserts judicial power	Napoleonic wars (1802–1815) Louisiana Purchase (1803) Embargo of 1807	Cotton expands into Old Southwest Farm productivity improves Embargo encourages domestic manufacturing	Youth-run marriage system New Jersey ends woman suffrage (1807) Atlantic slave trade legally ended (1808)	African-Americans absorb Protestant Christianity Tecumseh develops Indian identity
1810	Triumph of Republican party State constitutions democratized	War of 1812 Treaty of Ghent (1816) Monroe Doctrine (1823)	Second Bank of the United States (1816–1836) Supreme Court protects contracts and corporations Emergence of a national economy	Expansion of suffrage for white men New England abolishes established church	War of 1812 tests national unity Second Great Awakening shapes American identity Tocqueville defines American character (1835)

The American war is over, the Philadelphia Patriot Benjamin Rush declared in 1787, "but this is far from being the case with the *American revolution.* On the contrary, nothing but the first act of the great drama is closed. It remains yet to establish and perfect our new forms of government." The job was even greater than Rush imagined, for the republican revolution of 1776 challenged the values and institutions of the colonial social order, forcing changes in many spheres of life—economic, religious, cultural.

The first and most fundamental task was to devise a republican system of government. In 1775 no one in America knew what powers the central and state governments should have or how they should be organized. It took time and experience to find out. The states wrote constitutions by 1780, but the prodebtor policies pursued by their legislatures were controversial. It took another decade to reach agreement on a national government, and even longer to assimilate a new institution, the political party, into the workings of government. These years of experiment and party strife witnessed the success not only of popular sovereignty—government of the people—but also the rise of activist state legislatures—government for the people—and a slow but steady movement toward political democracy—government by the people.

Second, to create and preserve their new republic, Americans had to fight two wars against Great Britain, an undeclared war against France, and many battles with Indian tribes and confederations. The wars against Britain divided the country into bitter factions—Patriots versus Loyalists in 1776, and prowar Republicans against antiwar Federalists in 1812—and expended much blood and treasure. Tragically, the extension of American sovereignty over the trans-Appalachian West brought about the demise of many Indian peoples—their lives taken by European diseases, their lands by white settlers. Yet by 1820 the United States was a strong independent state, free at last from a half-century of entanglement in the wars and diplomacy of Europe.

Third, by this time the expansion of the market system had laid the foundations for a strong national economy. Merchants financed a banking system and devised an extensive outwork industry. State governments used charters and legal incentives to spur improvements in transportation, finance, and manufacturing. Southern planters carried slavery west to Alabama and Mississippi and grew rich by exporting a new crop—cotton—to markets in Europe and the North. Vast numbers of farm families settled new lands in the West or undertook additional labor as handicraft workers in the Northeast. By 1820 the new American republic had achieved economic as well as political independence.

Fourth, Americans tried to define the nature of their republican society, but found themselves divided along lines of gender, race, religion, and class. Then, as now, Americans disagreed on fundamental issues—legal equality for women, the future status of slavery, the meaning of free speech and religious liberty, and the extent of public responsibility for social inequality. These years saw the triumph of liberty of conscience and, except in New England, the end of established churches. The northern states abolished slavery, but social equality—not only for blacks, but for women and many white men—remained elusive. In 1820, as in 1775, authority in the family and society remained firmly in the hands of men of property.

The fifth and final task Americans set themselves—creating a distinct culture and identity—was very hard to achieve. The United States remained a land of diverse peoples and distinct regions. Native Americans still lived in their own tribes and nations, while black Americans, one-fifth of the enumerated population, were developing a new, African-American culture. The white inhabitants, divided among those of English, Scots-Irish, German, and Dutch ancestry, also preserved many aspects of their traditional cultures. Nevertheless, political institutions united Americans, as did their engagement in the market economy, and their increasing participation in evangelical Protestant churches. By 1820, to be an American meant, for the dominant white population, being a republican, a Protestant, and an enterprising individual in a capitalist-run market system.

The Attack on Bunker Hill with the Burning of Charles Town (detail)

The British attacked Patriot militiamen on Bunker Hill on June 17, 1775, suffering heavy losses before dislodging the Patriots. (c. 1783, National Gallery of Art)

CHAPTER 6 *War and Revolution,* 1775–1783

With the battles at Lexington and Concord in April 1775, the American Patriots became rebels, prepared to use military force to achieve their political ends. Independence was the goal of only a minority of Patriots at this point, but the outbreak of fighting gave the advantage to the most intrepid, perhaps even the most foolhardy. During the last months of 1775 radical Patriots took over local meetings, provincial assemblies, and the Continental Congress, urging a complete break from British rule.

On July 4, 1776, rebels became revolutionaries when they signed a Declaration of Independence, severing their ties to Great Britain. In a decision that changed the course of world history, Americans repudiated aristocratic and monarchical rule and created a republic, vesting authority in the hands of the people. Thus began the age of the democratic revolutions. To defend their new republican state governments, Patriot men and women became warriors, committing their property and their lives to the struggle against Great Britain. The War of Independence took six years and brought destruction and economic deprivation to the American people, sharpening the social divisions among them, nearly destroying their new financial institutions, and testing their commitment to republican ideals.

Toward Independence, 1775–1776

The battle of Concord was fought on April 19, 1775, but it would be another fourteen months before the Americans made a final break with Britain. In the intervening time, the most vocal Patriots decided that preserving the "rights of Englishmen" wasn't enough: they wanted independence. In one state after another, Patriot legislators threw out their royal governors and created the two essentials for independence: a government and an army. Loyalists protested in vain against the patriotic fervor sweeping the colonies.

Civil War

The Second Continental Congress. The outbreak of fighting in Massachusetts lent great urgency to the Second Continental Congress, which met in Philadelphia in May 1775. With John Adams exhorting them to rise to "the defense of American liberty," Patriot leaders pressed for the creation of a Continental army. They wanted George Washington of Virginia to take command of the New England forces that had surrounded the British in Boston, and they wanted to put out a call for new volunteers. More cautious delegates and those with Loyalist sympathies opposed these measures, warning that they would lead to more violence and commit the colonists irretrievably to rebellion. After bitter debate, Congress approved the proposals—but, as Adams lamented, only "by bare majorities."

While Congress deliberated in Philadelphia, hostilities continued to rage in Massachusetts. On June 17, more than 3,000 British troops attacked new American fortifications on Breed's Hill and Bunker Hill. It took three assaults, during which the British suffered heavy casualties, to dislodge the Patriot militiamen. Even when the delegates learned of the new bloodshed, a majority still hoped for reconciliation with Britain. Led by John Dickinson of Pennsylvania, a moderate Patriot, they passed an Olive Branch petition, expressing loyalty to George III and asking him to repeal oppressive parliamentary legislation. Zealous Patriots in the Congress countered by winning passage of a virtually contradictory Declaration of the Causes and Necessities of Taking Up Arms, asserting that Americans dreaded the "calamities of civil war" but were "resolved to die Freemen rather than to live [as] slaves."

King George did not exploit these internal conflicts. He refused even to receive the Olive Branch petition, which the Loyalist Richard Penn brought to London in August. Instead, he issued a Proclamation for Suppressing Rebellion and Sedition, expressing his determination to crush the American revolt. By that time his intemperate words were perhaps justified, for Congress had decided at the end of June to invade Canada, hoping to unleash a popular uprising there and add a fourteenth colony to the rebellion. Patriot forces easily took Montreal, but in December 1775 they failed to capture Quebec.

Meanwhile, Patriot merchants resorted to economic warfare, implementing Congress's resolution to cut off all exports to Britain and its West Indian possessions. By disrupting the tobacco trade and sugar production, they hoped to undermine British commerce. Parliament retaliated in December 1775 with a Prohibitory Act outlawing all trade with its rebellious colonies.

Rebellion in the South. In the meantime, the fighting in Massachusetts had sparked skirmishes between Patriots and Loyalists in the southern colonies. When the House of Burgesses seized authority in Virginia in June 1775, the royal governor, Lord Dunmore, took refuge on a British warship in Chesapeake Bay. From there he organized two military forces, one of whites, the Queen's Own Loyal Virginians, and one of blacks, the Ethiopian Regiment. In accordance with the king's proclamation of rebellion, Dunmore branded the Patriots "traitors" and declared martial law. Then, in November, the governor issued a controversial proclamation of his own, offering freedom to slaves and indentured servants who belonged to rebels but who joined the Loyalist cause. The leaders of Chesapeake society now faced the possibility of black uprisings as well as military attack. Alarmed by Dunmore's proclamation, many planters threatened runaway slaves with death and called for a final break with Great Britain.

In the Carolinas too, demands for independence grew more insistent in response to British military threats. Early in 1776, North Carolina's royal governor, Josiah Martin, tried to reestablish authority over the rebellious colony with a force of 1,500 Scottish Highlanders from the Carolina backcountry. The Patriot militia quickly mobilized, and in February they defeated Martin's army in the Battle of Moore's Creek Bridge, capturing more than 800 of his troops. In Charleston, South Carolina, in June 1776, a group of artisans took up arms alongside three Continental regiments and successfully repelled a British naval assault.

As the violence escalated, it pushed the rebels in the South toward independence. Early in 1776, Patriots transformed the North Carolina assembly into an independent Provincial Congress; in April that body instructed its representatives "to concur with the Delegates of other Colonies in declaring Independency, and forming foreign alliances." Virginia followed suit. Led by George Mason, James Madison, Edmund Pendleton, and Patrick Henry, Patriots called a special convention in May at which they resolved unanimously "to declare the United Colonies free and independent states."

Common Sense

For the colonists to become completely independent, they had to repudiate not only Parliament—the author of the hated tax laws—but also King George III, whose health they had toasted following the repeal of the Stamp Act. Most Americans retained a deep loyalty to the Crown. In virtually every anti-imperial demonstration, most Americans condemned the legislation enacted by Parliament, not the king or the institution of monarchy.

A Liberty Pole: Symbol of Revolution

Patriots had rallied around Liberty Poles since the Stamp Act riots, using these festivities to mobilize public support for their cause.

The roots of American loyalty ran deep into the structure of society. Like most men and women in the early modern world, Americans used metaphors of age and family to describe the system of social authority and imperial rule. Colonists often pictured their society as the dependent offspring—the child—of England, the "mother country." They respected "elders" in town meetings and church congregations. In their minds, the family itself was a "little commonwealth" ruled by its male head, and the king was the "father" of his people. Denial of the legitimacy of the monarchy threatened paternal authority and the hierarchical order of society.

Yet events had prepared Americans to reject their political father. By 1775 zealous Patriots were accusing George III of supporting ministers who passed oppressive legislation and of ordering the use of military force against them. Agitation against the king became especially intense in Philadelphia, the largest American city, but not previously a bastion of Patriot sentiment. About half of the city's population were artisans, and they owned nearly 40 percent of its wealth. Many artisans now felt that British imports threatened their small-scale manufacturing enterprises and that Parliament was bent on eliminating their "just Rights and Privileges." When the outbreak of fighting in Massachusetts discredited pro-British merchants, the artisans of Philadelphia, now organized into a Mechanics Association, became a powerful force in the Patriot movement. In February 1776, forty artisans were sitting alongside forty-seven merchants on the Philadelphia Committee of Resistance, the extralegal body that enforced the latest trade boycott.

Philadelphia artisans were deeply hostile to Britain and had strong republican sentiments. Many of them were Scots-Irish Presbyterians who had migrated to Pennsylvania to escape oppressive British rule in northern Ireland, and many adhered to the doctrine of religious equality propounded by Gilbert Tennent and other New Light ministers. As pastor of Philadelphia's Second Presbyterian Church, Tennent had told his congregation that all men and women were equal before God. Translating religious equality into political terms, New Light Presbyterians shouted in street demonstrations that they had "no king but King Jesus." In addition, republican ideas derived from the European Enlightenment circulated freely in Pennsylvania. Well-educated scientists and statesmen—such as Benjamin Franklin, David Rittenhouse, Charles Thomson, and Benjamin Rush—joined artisans in questioning not only the wisdom of George III but the legitimacy of the monarchy itself.

At this pivotal moment, with popular sentiment in a state of flux, a single pamphlet tipped the balance. In January 1776, Thomas Paine published *Common Sense*, a call for independence and republicanism. Paine, a corset maker and minor bureaucrat in Britain, had been fired from the English Customs Service for agitating for higher wages. He migrated to Philadephia in 1774, armed with a letter of introduction from Benjamin Franklin. There he met Benjamin Rush and others who shared his republican sentiments. "Monarchy and hereditary succession have laid the world in blood and ashes," Paine proclaimed in *Common Sense*. Mixing insults with biblical quotations, Paine leveled a blast at

The Royal Family

George III strikes a regal pose, surrounded by his queen and numerous offspring, all brilliantly attired. Patriots repudiated not only monarchy but also the fancy dress and aristocratic manners of the *ancien régime*, championing a society of republican simplicity.

the British system of "mixed government" which yielded only tyranny—"monarchical tyranny in the person of the King and aristocratical tyranny in the persons of the peers."

Paine presented the case for independence in a way that the general public could understand and respond to. *Common Sense* went through twenty-five editions and reached into hundreds of thousands of homes. Its message was clear: reject the arbitrary powers of king and Parliament and create independent republican states. "A government of our own is our natural right," Paine concluded. "'TIS TIME TO PART."

Independence Declared

Fired by Paine's arguments and the escalating military conflict with Loyalists, the American call for a break with Britain sounded with increasing urgency in Patriot conventions throughout the colonies. In June 1776 these disparate demands were given a single voice in the Continental Congress, when Richard Henry Lee presented the Virginia Convention's resolution: "That these United Colonies are, and of right ought to be, free and independent states . . . absolved from all allegiance to the British Crown." Faced with certain defeat, staunch Loyalists and anti-independence moderates withdrew from the Congress, leaving committed Patriots to take the fateful step. On July 4, 1776, the Congress approved the Declaration of Independence.

The main author of the Declaration was Thomas Jefferson, a young Virginia planter and legislative leader whose pamphlet *A Summary View of the Rights of British America* had mobilized resistance to the Coercive Acts. In composing the Declaration, Jefferson's primary purpose was to justify Congress's action, both to domestic critics and foreign observers, by putting the blame for the rupture on the king. To this end, he enumerated the acts of the imperial government that had oppressed Americans, thereby giving a prominent and enduring place to the view that powerful centralized governments are inherently dangerous to liberty. Simultaneously, he provided a detailed indictment of the king's conduct, discrediting monarchical rule. By the sheer power of his prose, Jefferson sought to convince his fellow Americans of the perfidy of George III: "He has plundered our seas, ravaged our coasts, burned our towns, and destroyed the lives of our people. . . . A prince, whose character is thus marked by every act which may define a tyrant, is unfit to be the ruler of a free people."

In ringing phrases Jefferson proclaimed a series of self-evident truths: "That all men are created equal"; that they possess the "unalienable rights" of "life, liberty, and the pursuit of happiness"; that government derives its "just powers from the consent of the governed" and can rightly be overthrown if it "becomes destructive of these ends." His prose, steeped in the ideas and rhetoric of the European Enlightenment and the Glorious Revolution of 1688, celebrated the doctrines of individual liberty and popular sovereignty. All Americans are heirs of this revolutionary republican tradition.

For Jefferson, as for Paine, the pen was mightier than the sword. Almost overnight, many half-hearted Americans were radicalized into republican revolution-

Signing the Declaration of Independence

The mood in the room is solemn as Congress declares independence from Great Britain. The delegates were now traitors to their country and king, their fortunes and even their lives hinging on the success of Patriot arms.

aries. In rural hamlets and seaport cities, crowds celebrated the Declaration by burning George III in effigy; in New York City, they toppled a statue of the king. With these acts of destruction, Patriots broke their psychological ties to the mother country and the father monarch. Americans were now ready to create a republic, a government that derived its authority from the people.

The Perils of War and Finance, 1776–1778

The Declaration of Independence brought an end to the minor skirmishing of civil war. For the next two years Britain mounted large-scale offensives against the Continental army commanded by George Washington, defeating the rebel forces in nearly every battle. A few spectacular American victories kept the rebellion alive, but in late 1776 and again during the winter of 1777-1778, at Valley Forge, the fate of the Patriot cause hung in the balance.

War in the North

Early in 1776, the British ministry made a decision to use overwhelming military force to crush the American rebellion. It looked easy. Great Britain had a population of 11 million, compared to about 2.5 million in the thirteen rebel colonies, nearly 20 percent of whom were African-American slaves. The British enjoyed an equally great economic advantage, both because of the immense profits of the South Atlantic system and the coming of the Industrial Revolution. Militarily, Britain enjoyed a clear superiority: it had a standing army of 48,000 men (and the financial resources to hire or raise thousands more) and the largest, most powerful navy in the world. The imperial government also expected support from the tens of thousands of Loyalists in America and from various Indian tribes hostile to white expansion. In contrast, the rebellious Americans had no navy and its small Continental army consisted mostly of militiamen whose enlistments would expire at the end of 1776. True, the Patriots could field thousands of militiamen, but only for short periods of time and only in the vicinity of their own farms or towns. Assessing the two antagonists in 1776, few observers would have given the rebels a chance of victory.

Alarmed by the American invasion of Canada in 1775, Lord North, who was still the prime minister, ordered an ambitious military mobilization. The ineffective General Gage was replaced as overall commander by General William Howe. Howe had served in the colonies during the French and Indian War and had distinguished himself in Wolfe's siege of Quebec. He had orders to capture New York City and seize control of the Hudson River, thus isolating the radical Patriots in New England from the rest of the colonies.

In March 1776 Howe withdrew his forces from Boston and established military headquarters in Halifax, Nova Scotia. While the Continental Congress was declaring independence in Philadelphia, Howe was landing 10,000 troops—British regulars and German mercenaries—outside New York City. By August, the invading force had swollen to 32,000 soldiers, supported by a fleet of thirty warships and 10,000 sailors. On the American side was General Washington's newly formed, poorly trained army of about 19,000 troops, nearly half of whom were short-term militiamen hastily recruited by the state governments of Virginia and New England. Many American officers were capable men who had served in the Seven Years' War, but even the most experienced of them had never commanded a large force or faced a disciplined army capable of executing the intricate maneuvers of European warfare. The advantage of the British forces was overwhelming; their officers had been tested in combat and their soldiers were disciplined and well armed.

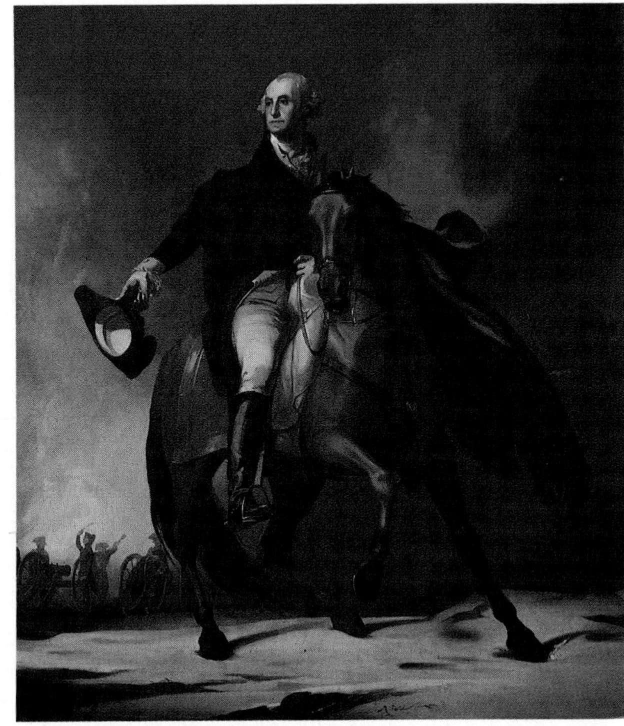

Washington at the Battle of Trenton

Washington told Congress that "on our side the War should be defensive," but his bold attack across the Delaware on Christmas night, 1776, gave Americans their first military victory.

The Battle of Princeton
Pursued by Cornwallis after his victory at Trenton, Washington confronted three regiments of redcoats at Princeton and, having an advantage in numbers, put them to flight—but only after withstanding a bayonet charge that nearly crushed the American vanguard.

British superiority was immediately apparent. On August 27, 1776, Howe attacked the Americans in the Battle of Long Island and forced them to retreat to Manhattan Island. There Howe outflanked Washington's troops, nearly trapping them on several occasions. Outgunned and outmaneuvered, the Continental army again retreated, first to Harlem Heights, then to White Plains, and finally across the Hudson River to New Jersey. The British pursued the Americans cautiously, seeking to envelop Washington's main force in a pincer movement. By December, the British army had pushed the Continental troops across the Delaware River into Pennsylvania, and Congress was forced to flee to Baltimore.

It was customary in the eighteenth century to halt military campaigns during the winter. As the weather grew cold and snowy, the British let down their guard and the Patriots managed to score a few triumphs. On Christmas night 1776, Washington crossed the Delaware River and staged a surprise attack on Trenton, New Jersey. About a thousand Hessians, the German mercenaries who had long fought for the British army, were forced to surrender. Then, on January 3, 1777, the Continental army won a small engagement at nearby Princeton. These victories raised sagging Patriot morale and prompted the British to evacuate New Jersey, a withdrawal that allowed the Patriot Congress to return to Philadelphia and worried potential Loyalists throughout America. Bright stars in a dark night, the American triumphs could not mask British military superiority. These were the times, wrote Tom Paine, that "tryed men's souls."

Armies and Strategies

British superiority did not break the will of the Continental army, and the rebellion continued. Howe himself was partly responsible for prolonging the conflict. While in England, he had opposed the Coercive Acts and as the British military commander he still hoped for a compromise—indeed he even had authority to negotiate with the rebels. Consequently, instead of following up his early victories with a ruthless pursuit of the retreating American army, Howe was content to show his superior power and tactics, hoping to convince the Continental Congress that resistance was futile.

Howe's cautiousness reflected the conventions of eighteenth-century warfare, in which generals sought to outmaneuver the opposing forces and win their surrender rather than destroy them. Of course, he was aware that his troops were 3,000 miles from supplies and reinforcements; in case of a major defeat, it would take six months to replenish his forces. Neither the ministry nor the royal governors had encouraged Loyalists to join or supply the army. Howe's tactics were understandable but they cost the British the opportunity to nip the rebellion in the bud. Instead, he allowed the American army to claim victories at Trenton and Princeton and survive to fight another day.

Howe's failure contrasted sharply with Washington's military successes. The American general told Congress that "on our Side the War should be defensive." He, too, was cautious, challenging Howe's army on selected occasions but retreating when he met superior strength. Washington's strategy was to draw the British away from the seacoast, extending their lines of supply and sapping their morale. His primary goal was to keep the Continental army intact as a symbol and instrument of American resistance.

In achieving this goal, Washington had more to contend with than Howe. Congress tried to field a regular force of 75,000 men, but the Continental army never reached half that number; at its peak Washington's main force had only 18,000 men, few of whom were experienced soldiers. Yeomen farmers and trained militiamen preferred to serve in local units near their fields and families and refrained from joining the Continental forces. The American army drew its recruits from the lower ranks of society. For example, the soldiers in the Continental units commanded by General William Smallwood of Maryland were either poor American-born youths or older foreign-born men—British ex-convicts or former indentured servants. They enlisted not to express their patriotic fervor but to make their way in the world. Congress could compete with the various state governments for recruits only by offering short (one-year) terms of service or by promising a bounty of 100 acres of land and $20 in cash (about $200 today) for three-year enlistments. Even so, the declining value of Continental currency hurt the soldiers and their families financially and undermined their morale. Moreover, it took time to mold these men into a fighting force. In the face of a British artillery bombardment or a flank attack, many recruits panicked; hundreds of others deserted, unwilling to submit to the discipline and danger of military life. They also resented the contemptuous way Washington and other American officers treated the camp followers—the women who lived with and cared for the soldiers.

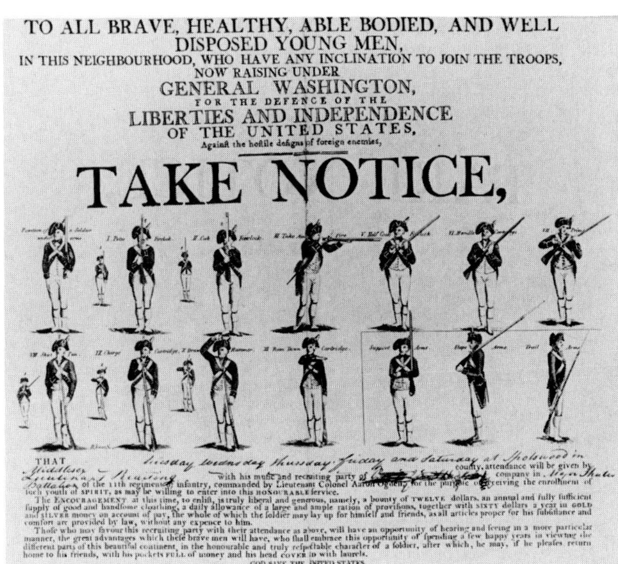

Patriots Recruit an Army

Some Americans became soldiers because of the glamor of bearing arms, but the citizens of Peacham, New Hampshire marched to a different drummer: "Although we . . . had but six or eight men in the town, we sent two of them . . . for we feared if the British were not going to be stopped, we shall all be ruined."

The Continental army did not receive much public support. Many Patriots had long viewed the British standing army as a threat to liberty and had no desire to create one of their own. They placed their hopes in the local militia, men organized in community units, supplied and aided by their wives and families. The Continental army went begging, without adequate goods from the populace or money from the Congress. General Philip Schuyler of New York complained that his troops were "weak in numbers, dispirited, naked, destitute of provisions, without camp equipage, with little ammunition, and not a single piece of cannon." Given this situation, Washington was fortunate, in the first year of the war, not to have suffered an overwhelming defeat.

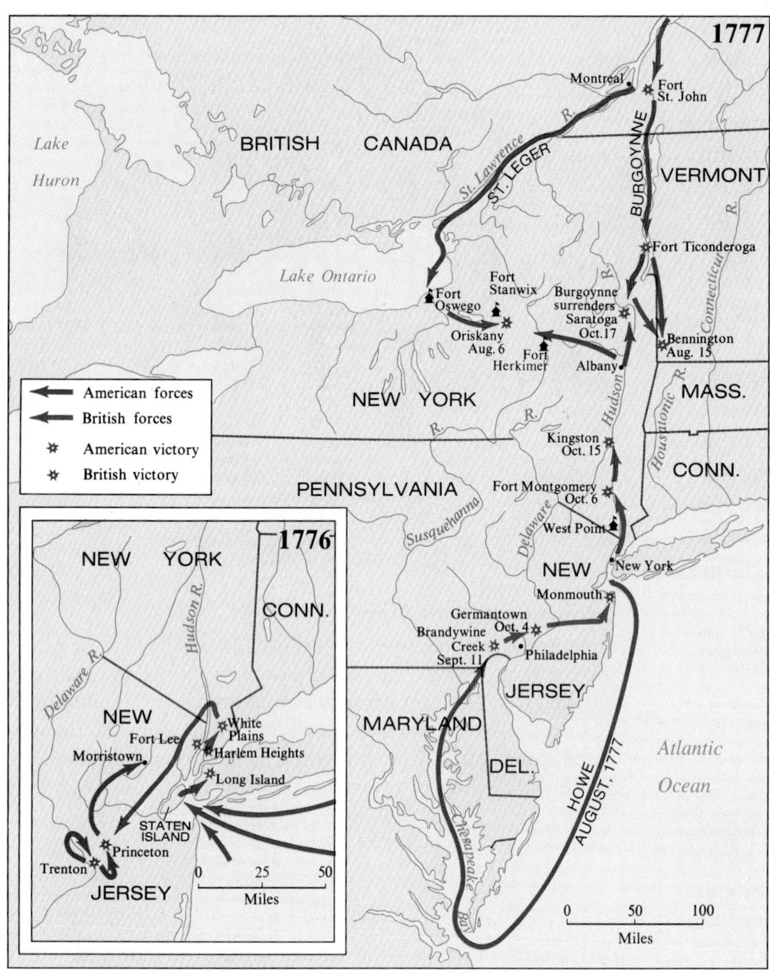

MAP 6.1

The War in the North

In 1776 the British army drove Washington's forces across New Jersey into Pennsylvania. The Americans counterattacked at Trenton and Princeton, setting up winter headquarters at Morristown. In 1777 General Howe captured Philadelphia from the south, while General Burgoyne and Colonel St. Leger launched invasions from Canada. Aided by thousands of New England militia, General Horatio Gates defeated Burgoyne at Bennington and then at Saratoga, the military turning point of the war.

Victory at Saratoga

Howe's failure to achieve a decisive victory surprised Lord North and his ministers, who now realized that restoration of the empire would require a long-term military commitment similar to that in the French and Indian War. Accepting the challenge, the government increased the British land tax to finance the war, and prepared to mount a major campaign in 1777.

The isolation of New England remained the primary British goal. To accomplish this the colonial secretary Lord George Germain devised a three-pronged attack converging on Albany, New York. General John Burgoyne was to lead the main force, a large contingent of British regulars, from Quebec via Lake Champlain and the Hudson River. A second, smaller force under Lieutenant Colonel Barry St. Leger would attack Albany from the west, moving through the Mohawk River Valley. Leger's troops were mostly Iroquois warriors from central New York. The Iroquois had allied themselves with the British in the hope of protecting their land from American settlers, and Germain was confident they would cut down the rebels all along the New York frontier. Finally, to reinforce Burgoyne from the south, Germain ordered Howe to dispatch a contingent from the troops commanded by Sir Henry Clinton in New York City.

Howe had a plan of his own. He proposed to attack Philadelphia, the home of the Continental Congress, hoping to force Washington into a fixed battle and end the rebellion with a single major victory. With Germain's apparent approval, Howe set his forces in motion—but very slowly. Rather than march overland through New Jersey, the troops sailed south from New York and then up Chesapeake Bay, to approach Philadelphia from the southwest. Once again, British numbers and tactics paid off. Howe's troops easily outflanked the American positions along Brandywine Creek, forcing Washington to withdraw. The British marched triumphantly into Philadelphia on September 26, half-assuming that the capture of the rebels' capital would end the uprising. However, the Continental Congress fled into the interior, first to Lancaster and then to York, and would hear no words of surrender.

Joseph Brant
The Mohawk chief Thayendanegea, known to the whites as Joseph Brant, secured the support of four of the Six Iroquois Nations for the British. In 1778 and 1779 he led Iroquois warriors and Tory Rangers in attacks on American settlements throughout western New York. This portrait by Charles Willson Peale was painted in 1797.

The British paid a high price for this victory. Howe's leisurely advance against Philadelphia exposed Burgoyne to defeat in the north. Initially, Burgoyne's Canadian expedition had sped across Lake Champlain, overwhelming the American defenses at Fort Ticonderoga and driving onward toward the upper reaches of the Hudson River. Then they stalled, for Burgoyne—"Gentleman Johnny," as he was called—fought with style, not speed. His heavy baggage train, weighed down with comfortable tents and ample stocks of food and wine, moved slowly. Its progress was further impeded by the Continental forces of General Horatio Gates, who felled trees across the crude wagon trail and raided the long, thinly stretched supply lines to Canada. By the end of the summer, Burgoyne's army—6,000 regulars (half of them German mercenaries) and 600 Loyalists and Indians—was in serious trouble, bogged down in the American wilderness.

It was left to the Patriot militia to deliver the final blow. Two thousand militiamen left their farms to fight a bitter pitched battle on August 16 at Bennington, Vermont, to protect American military supplies from British raiders, depriving them of much-needed supplies of food, horses, and oxen. Burgoyne received more bad news: Patriot militia in the Mohawk Valley had forced St. Leger's troops to retreat. And in New York City General Clinton had to recall the relief force he had sent toward Albany in order to meet Howe's request for additional troops to occupy Philadelphia. While Burgoyne waited in vain for help, thousands of Patriot militiamen from Massachusetts, New Hampshire, and New York joined Gates's forces. Surrounding the British troops at Saratoga, New York, they "swarmed around the army like birds of prey," an English sergeant wrote in his journal, and forced Burgoyne to surrender on October 17, 1777.

The battle of Saratoga proved to be the turning point of the war. The Americans captured 5,000 British troops and their equipment—a price in men and matériel that far outweighed Howe's capture of Philadelphia. More important still, it virtually assured the success of American diplomats in Paris, who were seeking a military alliance with France. Patriots on the home front were equally delighted, though their joy was muted by an acute awareness of the difficulties that lay ahead.

Wartime Trials

Financial Crisis. Wars are not won by guns alone. Armies have to be fed, clothed, and paid. Victory often goes to the side with the most money or the one prepared to make the most financial sacrifices. When the War of Independence began, the new American governments were neither wealthy nor politically secure. Since opposition to taxes had fueled the independence movement in the first place, Patriot officials were reluctant to increase taxes for fear of undermining their fragile authority. To finance the war, the state governments first borrowed money, in gold or silver or British currency, from wealthy individuals. These funds quickly ran out, so the states created a new paper currency—the dollar—and issued notes with a face value of $260 million, using it to pay soldiers and purchase supplies. Since the new notes were not backed by gold or silver or by tax revenues, they quickly depreciated. Indeed, North Carolina's paper money was worth so little that the state government itself refused to accept it. Many state governments teetered on the brink of bankruptcy.

The monetary system created by the Continental Congress collapsed as well, despite the best efforts of Philadelphia merchant Robert Morris, the "financier of the Revolution." Until 1781 the Congress was essentially a coalition of independent state governments, without legal authority and completely dependent on funds requisitioned from the member states, which frequently paid late or not at all. To obtain funds, Congress borrowed $6 million from France and pledged it as security; wealthy Americans promptly purchased $27

AMERICAN VOICES

The Hardships of Life at Valley Forge *The Diary of a Surgeon*

The Continental army nearly disintegrated during the winter of 1777–1778 because of desperate living conditions. This diary entry conveys both the hardships of camp life and the allure of civilian existence.

December 14. Prisoners and deserters are continually coming in. The army, which has been surprisingly healthy hitherto, now begins to grow sickly from the continued fatigues they have suffered this campaign. Yet they still show a spirit of alacrity and contentment not to be expected from so young troops. I am sick—discontented—and out of humour. Poor food—hard lodging—cold weather—fatigue—nasty cloathes—nasty cookery—vomit half my time—smoked out of my senses—the Devil's in't—I can't endure it—Why are we sent here to starve and freeze?—What sweet felicities have I left at home: A charming wife—pretty children—good bed—good food—good cooking—all agreeable—all harmonious! Here all confusion—smoke and cold—hunger and filthyness—a pox on my bad luck! People who live at home in luxury and ease, quietly possessing their habitations, enjoying their wives and families in peace, have but a very faint idea of the unpleasing sensations and continual anxiety the man endures who is in a camp, and is the husband and parent of an agreeable family. These same people are willing we should suffer every thing for their benefit and advantage and yet are the first to condemn us for not doing more!!

Source: "Valley Forge, 1777–1778: Diary of Surgeon Albigence Waldo of the Connecticut Line," *Pennsylvania Magazine of History and Biography* 21 (1897), 304–309.

A Flood of Paper Currency

The Continental Congress issued this bill in 1776, declaring it to be worth "SIX Spanish Milled DOLLARS" or the equivalent in gold or silver, but by 1780 its value had collapsed—giving rise to the phrase, "not worth a continental."

million in Continental loan certificates. When these and other loans from the French and Dutch were exhausted, Congress followed the lead of the states and financed the war simply by printing money. Between 1775 and 1779, it issued currency with a face value of $191 million. By 1780, tax revenues from the states had retired only $3 million of these bills from circulation, so the value of the remaining bills continued to fall.

Indeed, the enormous increase in the volume of paper currency created the worst inflation in American history. The amount of goods—grain, clothes, tools—available for purchase had decreased significantly because of the British naval blockade and the onset of fighting, yet the amount of currency had vastly increased. Inevitably, consumers "bid up" the price of goods. In Maryland a bag of salt that had cost $1 in 1776 was valued at $3,900 a few years later. Many farmers refused to accept currency for their goods and resorted to barter—trading wheat for tools or clothes—or demanded payment in gold or silver. This soaring inflation forced nearly every family to look out for its own interests and undermined support for the rebel cause, especially among hard-hit ordinary Americans. Even some Patriot leaders began to doubt that the rebellion could succeed.

Valley Forge. Fears reached their peak during the winter of 1777–1778. Following the capture of Philadelphia, Howe established winter quarters there, and he and his officers partook of the finest wines, foods, and entertainment it could offer. Washington's army retreated to the countryside, establishing its base for the winter some 20 miles west of Philadelphia, in Valley Forge. About 12,000 soldiers, accompanied by hundreds of camp followers, arrived at the camp in December. Everyone suffered horribly. "The army . . . now begins to grow sickly," a surgeon confided to his diary. Poor food—hard lodging—cold weather—fatigue—nasty clothes—nasty cookery. . . . Why are we sent here to starve and freeze?" Many soldiers deserted, unable to endure the harsh conditions; by spring, over a thousand men had vanished into the countryside. Nearly 3,000 soldiers and scores of camp followers died from malnutrition and disease. One winter at Valley Forge took as many American lives as had two years of fighting against General Howe.

Public support for the rebellion was in as precarious a state as the Continental army itself. The population of the region near Valley Forge was split along lines of ethnicity, religion, and class, and these divisions had a direct impact on military operations. For example, most New Light members of the Dutch Reformed Church in New Jersey actively supported the American cause, joining the militia and raiding British encampments; but many Old Lights were Loyalists and fed information and supplies to the British. A number of Quakers and German sectarians in Pennsylvania were pacifists, unwilling to support either side.

Pure self-interest also contributed to the deprivation of Washington's army at Valley Forge. Many farmers hoarded their grain over the winter, hoping to profit from high prices in the spring. Others fought their way through Patriot roadblocks to Philadelphia, where British quartermasters paid in gold and silver. Even farmers who supported the rebellion could not afford to supply the American army when their labors were rewarded with rapidly depreciating Continental Congress dollars. "Such a dearth of public spirit, and want of public virtue," Washington complained—but to no effect. The suffering at Valley Forge continued, graphic testimony to the American Congress's inability to raise sufficient revenue.

In this dark hour, Baron von Steuben, a former Prussian military officer, raised the morale and self-respect of both officers and enlisted men by instituting a standardized system of drill and maneuver at Valley Forge. Von Steuben was one of a handful of foreigners who had volunteered their services to the American cause. His efforts encouraged officers to become more professional in their demeanor and behavior, and instilled greater order and discipline in the ranks. Thanks to von Steuben, the smaller Continental army that emerged from Valley Forge in the spring was tougher, with a renewed sense of purpose.

The Path to Victory, 1778–1783

Patriot prospects improved dramatically in 1778, when the United States formed a military alliance with France, the most powerful nation on the European continent. The alliance not only brought the Americans money, troops, and supplies but also changed the conflict from a colonial rebellion into an international war.

The French Alliance

Negotiating the Treaty. In 1777, Benjamin Franklin and two other diplomats, Arthur Lee and Silas Deane, had begun negotiations for a commercial and military treaty with France. Since 1763, France had been seeking revenge for its defeat in the Seven Years' War and its loss of Canada. The French Foreign Minister, the Comte de Vergennes, was a determined opponent of Britain and an early supporter of American independence. In 1776, he persuaded King Louis XVI to extend a secret loan to the rebellious colonies and supply them with gunpowder. When news of Saratoga reached Paris in December 1777, Vergennes urged the king to approve a formal alliance with the Continental Congress.

Franklin and his associates craftily exploited the rivalry between France and Britain. They used the threat of a negotiated settlement with Britain to win an explicit French commitment to American independence. The Treaty of Alliance of February 6, 1778, specified that after France entered the war against Great Britain, neither partner would sign a separate peace before the "liberty, sovereignty, and independence" of the United States was assured. In return, the American diplomats pledged that their government would recognize any French conquests in the West Indies.

France and America were unlikely partners. France was Catholic and a monarchy; the United States was Protestant and a republic. The two peoples had been on opposite sides in wars from 1689 to 1763. But now they were united against a common enemy: Great Britain. After two years of armed resistance, the fledgling American republic had earned the respect of the nations of Europe; it figured in the international balance of power. Britain was now isolated diplomatically and its forces were spread thin—it was not only confronting the Patriots in North America but defending Gibraltar against Spain, and the West Indies, India, and England itself against France. 

The British Response. The war had never been popular in Britain. Radical agitators and artisans supported American demands for greater rights and campaigned for political reforms at home—broadening the right to vote and eliminating electoral corruption. The landed gentry and urban merchants protested against rising taxes. To meet the military budget, the government had already increased the land tax and the stamp duty and imposed new levies on carriages, wine, and imported goods. "It seemed we were to be taxed and stamped ourselves instead of inflicting taxes and stamps on others," one British politician complained. Yet George III continued to demand that the rebellion be crushed, whatever the financial cost. If America won independence, he warned Lord North, "the West Indies must follow them. Ireland would soon follow the same plan and be a separate state, then this island would be reduced to itself, and soon would be a poor island indeed."

Fearful of an imminent Franco-American alliance—which, in fact, had already been sealed—on February 17, 1778, North announced his intention to seek a negotiated constitutional settlement. At his bidding, Parliament repealed the Tea and Prohibitory acts and, in an amazing concession, renounced its right to tax the American colonies. North appointed a commission, headed by Lord Carlisle, to negotiate with the Continental Congress and offer a return to the constitutional relationship that existed in 1763, before the Sugar and Stamp acts. But it was too late. By 1778, many Americans had already embraced independence.

The Impact of the Alliance. The alliance with France infused new life into the Patriot cause. With access to military supplies and European loans, the condition of the American army improved immediately. "There has been a great change in this state since the news from France," a Patriot soldier reported from Pennsylvania; farmers—"mercenary wretches," he called them—were "as eager for Continental Money now as they were a few weeks ago for British gold."

Many financial problems remained, but Congress was finally able to meet the officer corps' demand for pensions. Most officers came from the upper ranks of society and used their own funds not only to keep up appearances but to equip themselves, and sometimes their men; in return they demanded pensions for life at half-pay. Congress now agreed to give them half-pay after the end of the war, though only for seven years. Washington himself had urged Congress to make this concession, warning the lawmakers that, "the salvation of the cause depends upon it."

War in the South

The French alliance expanded the war but did not bring it to a rapid conclusion. When France entered the conflict in June 1778, it had other goals in mind besides a quick victory over the British forces in North America. Hoping to capture a rich sugar island, France concentrated its naval forces in the West Indies. Spain, which entered the war in 1779, also had its own agenda: in return for providing naval assistance to France, it hoped to win back Florida and Gibraltar in the peace settlement. The destiny of the new American republic was now enmeshed in a web of European alliances and territorial quarrels.

These maneuvers gave Britain one more opportunity to crush the rebellion—or, at least, to limit it. Saratoga had spelled an end to British hopes of recapturing New England and holding all thirteen colonies. But in many ways New England was the least valuable part of the empire. Far more important to the South Atlantic system were the southern colonies, with their rich crops of rice and tobacco. So the British ministry, beset by a war on many fronts, settled on a more modest strategy in America. It would recapture Virginia, the Carolinas, and Georgia, relying on Loyalists to hold and administer the reconquered territory.

Up to now the British had made little use of the Americans who remained loyal to the king. But they knew that recent migrants with little sympathy for the rebel cause made up a sizeable portion of the population of the southern backcountry. Some, such as the Scottish Highlanders in North Carolina, retained an especially strong allegiance to the Crown. The British hoped to recruit other Loyalists from the ranks of the Regulators, who had opposed the political dominance of low-country planters. They also hoped to take advantage of racial divisions in the South. Over 1,000 Virginia slaves had fought for Lord Dunmore in 1776 under the banner "Liberty to Slaves!" and thousands more might support a new British offensive. At the least, racial divisions would undermine the Patriots' military efforts. Blacks formed from 30 to 50 percent of the population, yet whites were afraid to arm them. Many planters refused to allow their sons or white overseers to join the Continental forces, keeping them home to prevent slave revolts.

Charged with implementing its southern strategy was Sir Henry Clinton, who had replaced the discredited Howe early in 1778. In June 1778 Clinton ordered the main British army to evacuate Philadelphia and move to safer quarters in New York. In December he finally launched his southern campaign, landing a force

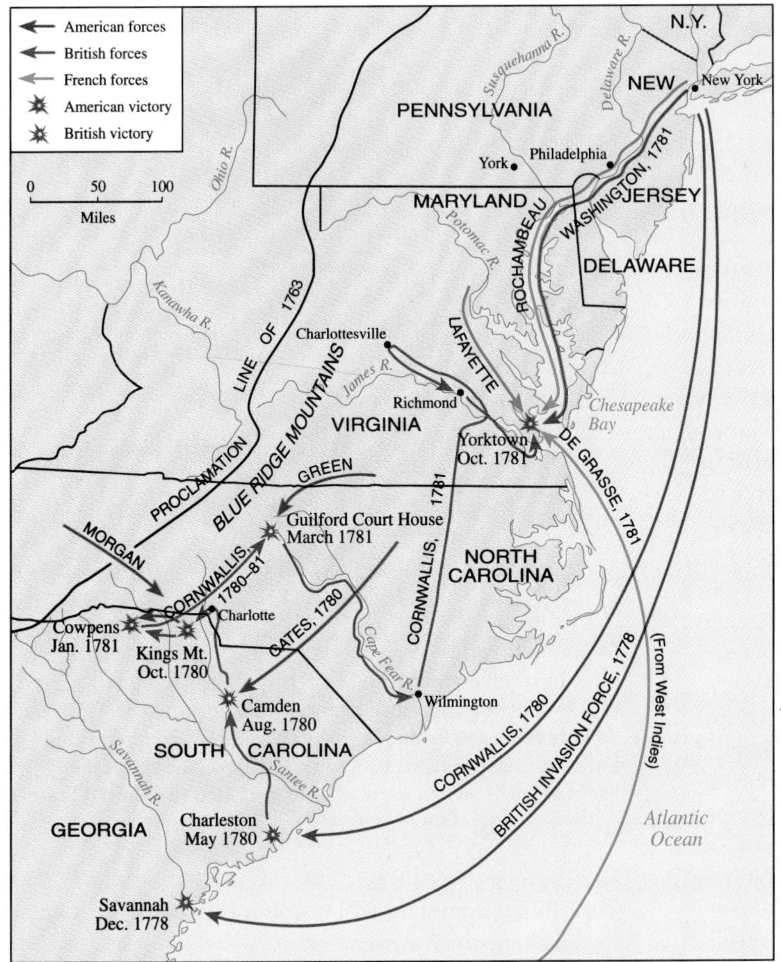

MAP 6.2

The Campaign in the South

The British ministry's southern strategy started well. British forces captured Savannah in December 1778 and Charleston in May 1780. Brutal warfare raged in the interior over the next eighteen months, fought more by small bands of irregulars than by disciplined armies. When Cornwallis carried the battle into Virginia in late 1781, Washington and Lafayette surrounded his forces at Yorktown, aided by the French fleet under Admiral de Grasse.

of 3,500 men near Savannah, Georgia. The British army took the city, mobilized hundreds of blacks to build barricades and unload military supplies, and then moved inland, capturing Augusta early in 1779. By the end of the year the British had reconquered Georgia and had 10,000 troops poised for an assault on South Carolina. To counter this, the Continental Congress suggested that South Carolina raise 3,000 black troops, but this proposal was overwhelmingly rejected by the South Carolina assembly.

During most of 1780, British forces moved from one victory to another. In April, Clinton laid siege to Charleston, South Carolina, which surrendered six weeks later. He captured General Benjamin Lincoln and his 5,000 troops, in the single largest American surrender of the war. Following this success, Lord Cornwallis assumed control of the British forces and sent out expeditions to secure the countryside. In August he routed an American force commanded by General Horatio Gates, the hero of Saratoga, at Camden in the heart of the Carolina pine barrens, giving the British control of South Carolina.

This victory seemed to confirm the wisdom of the southern strategy. Following the British invasion, hundreds of blacks fled to Florida and hundreds more sought protection behind British lines, providing labor for the invading army. Finally, the ministry was making good use of the Loyalists. Southern Tories formed military units and assisted British forces as they moved through Georgia and South Carolina, providing them with supplies and auxiliary troops. In contrast, the local Patriots were of little use to General Gates's army. Only about 1,200 militiamen joined Gates at Camden—a fifth of the number of local Patriots at Saratoga—and many of them panicked and fled without firing a shot.

Then the tide of battle turned. Far off in Europe, the Dutch declared war against Britain, making its diplomatic isolation complete, and, for the first time, the French dispatched troops to America. In July 1780, a French army of 5,500 men, commanded by General Comte de Rochambeau, arrived in Newport, Rhode Island, where it posed a threat to the British forces in New York. In the South, a militia force of Patriot farmers defeated a regiment of Loyalists at King's Mountain, North Carolina, in October 1780, taking about a thousand prisoners. Washington replaced Gates with Nathanael Greene as the American commander in the South, and Greene immediately devised new military tactics. To make the best use of the Patriot militia, many of whom were "without discipline and addicted to plundering," Greene divided them into small groups under strong leaders, and used them to harass the larger but less mobile British forces. American guerrillas led by the "Swamp Fox," General Francis Marion, won a series of small but fierce battles in South Carolina, while General Daniel Morgan led another American force to a bloody victory over a British regiment at Cowpens, North Carolina, in January 1781. On March 15, General Greene himself fought Cornwallis's seasoned army to a draw at North Carolina's Guilford Court House.

Patriot forces had broken the back of the British offensive, but Loyalist garrisons and militia remained powerful. The well-organized Cherokee posed an additional threat to Patriot forces. Determined to protect their lands, the Cherokee attacked American settlers in the backcountry, preventing them from joining the battle against the British. Nonetheless, Greene's army slowly began to reconquer the Carolinas and Georgia. "We fight, get beaten, and fight again," lamented General Greene.

In the spring of 1781, Lord Cornwallis made a crucial decision: to concede the southernmost states to Greene and seek a decisive victory in Virginia. Aided by reinforcements from Clinton in New York, Cornwallis moved through eastern North Carolina and into the Tidewater region of Virginia. His forces, led by Benedict Arnold, the infamous traitor to the Patriot cause, ranged up and down the James River, meeting only slight resistance from a small American force commanded by the Marquis de Lafayette. Lafayette was a republican-minded French aristocrat who had offered his services to the American cause long before the alliance of 1778. Early in 1780, he had returned temporarily to France to persuade Louis XVI to change French military priorities. Partly as a result of Lafayette's intercession, the French government decided to prosecute the war more vigorously and dispatched the army commanded by General Comte de Rochambeau to Rhode Island. Now, in May 1781, as Lafayette dueled with Cornwallis near the York Peninsula in Virginia, the French monarch ordered the large fleet in the

James Lafayette

Born into slavery in Virginia, in 1781 James Lafayette served as a spy for the American army commanded by the Marquis de Lafayette, receiving his freedom as a reward and taking Lafayette's surname as his own. The two Lafayettes met again in 1824, when the Frenchman visited the United States.

West Indies commanded by Admiral François de Grasse to sail to North America.

Emboldened by the ample forces at his disposal, Washington launched a well-coordinated attack. He feinted an assault on New York City to keep Clinton's troops in the north and secretly had General Rochambeau's army march from Rhode Island to Virginia, where it joined Washington's own troops. Simultaneously Admiral de Grasse positioned his fleet off the coast of Virginia, where, in combination with a smaller French naval force from Rhode Island, it established control of Chesapeake Bay. Cornwallis suddenly found himself surrounded, his army of 9,500 men outnumbered two to one on land and cut off from reinforcement or retreat by sea. Abandoned by the British navy, he surrendered at Yorktown on October 19, 1781.

The Franco-American victory at Yorktown broke the resolve of the British government. "Oh God! It is all over!" exclaimed Lord North when he heard the news. His ministry lacked the will or the resources to raise a new army to fight a long war of attrition in America. Britain's position vis-à-vis its European rivals was even more troubling. The combined fleets of France and Spain were menacing the British sugar islands, Dutch merchants were recapturing American and European

American Soldiers at Yorktown, 1781
A French observer captured the diversity of the American army: a black infantryman from Rhode Island, a Canadian volunteer, a buckskin-clad rifleman from Virginia, and (holding the gunnery torch) an artilleryman from the Continental Army.

markets from English and Scottish traders, and a newly formed group of European states—the League of Armed Neutrality—was threatening to use force to break Britain's commercial blockade of France. Isolated diplomatically in Europe, stymied militarily in America, and—perhaps most important—lacking public support at home, the British ministry gave up the active prosecution of the war. Only isolated attacks by Loyalists and Indians reminded Americans that their country was still at war.

The Patriot Advantage

The military outcome of the American War of Independence left angry members of Parliament calling for an explanation. In 1763, Britain had been a major power in Europe with formidable financial and military resources. How could it be defeated by a motley group of upstart colonists? The ministry blamed the military leadership, pointing—with some justification—to a series of blunders made by British generals. Why had Howe not been more ruthless in his pursuit of Washington's army in 1776? How could Germain have failed to coordinate the movements of Howe's and Burgoyne's armies in 1777? Why was Cornwallis allowed to march deep into the powerful rebel state of Virginia in 1781?

Historians have been equally critical of the military command, but they have also pointed out the high odds against British success, despite Britain's apparent superiority. While only a third of the white population was deeply committed to the rebellion, another third willingly accepted the laws and paid the taxes imposed by the state governments. Unlike most revolutionaries, the Patriots had assumed control of well-established institutions and their leaders were experienced politicians. And while the Continental army had to be built from scratch and was never very large, it was fighting on its own territory, with the assistance of thousands of militia. Even the substantial number of Loyalists and Indian allies—more than 30,000 Tories fought as regular soldiers during the war, and thousands of native Americans served as auxiliary troops—could not offset these advantages. Once the rebels had the military, diplomatic, and financial support of France, they could reasonably hope for victory. A charismatic leader in Britain, such as William Pitt, or a great general might have rallied British political opinion to the cause, suppressed the American rebellion, and restored imperial authority. But ordinary politicians and mediocre generals were destined to fail.

Americans, by contrast, were extremely lucky in Congress's appointment of George Washington as commander of the Continental army. He was a brilliant choice, for his leadership was long-lasting and inspired. The American general deferred to the civil authorities, winning respect—and political and financial support—from the Congress and the state governments alike. He exercised firm control over his subordinates yet supported their just complaints. Confident of his own abilities, he recruited outstanding men, such as Baron von Steuben, to instill discipline into the ranks of the fledgling Continental army and turn it into a respectable fighting force. Washington also understood the character of warfare in an agricultural society and made deft use of the rural militia units.

AMERICAN LIVES

The Enigma of Benedict Arnold

Benedict Arnold is one of the few men to have been a military hero for both sides in the same war. He began his career as an American Patriot in May 1775, when he and Ethan Allen led the capture of Fort Ticonderoga on Lake Champlain. His heroics continued in September 1775, when he led an expedition of 1,150 Virginia and Pennsylvania riflemen against Quebec, the capital of British Canada. He drove his men hard through the Maine wilderness, overcoming leaky boats, spoiled provisions, treacherous rivers, and near-starvation to arrive before Quebec in November, his force reduced to 650 men. These losses did not deter Arnold. Joined by General Richard Montgomery, who had arrived with 300 troops after capturing Montreal, he attacked the strongly fortified city, only to have the assault end in disaster. A hundred Americans were killed, including Montgomery, 400 were captured, and many wounded, including Arnold, who fell as he stormed through a barricade, a ball through his leg.

Benedict Arnold

For five years Arnold served the Patriot side with distinction in many battles, including a dangerous assault against the center of the British line at Saratoga, when he was again wounded in the leg. No general was more imaginative than Arnold, no field officer more daring, no soldier more courageous.

Yet Arnold has gone down in history not as a hero but as a villain, a military traitor who, as commander of the American fort at West Point, New York, in 1780, schemed to hand it over to the British. Of his role in this plan there is no doubt. His British contact, Major John André, was caught with incriminating documents in Arnold's handwriting—including routes of access to the fort. Arnold himself, fleeing down the Hudson River on a British ship, defended his actions in a letter to Washington: "love to my country actuates my present conduct, however it may appear inconsistent to the world, who very seldom judge right of any man's actions."

But judge we must. Why did Arnold desert the cause for which he had fought so gallantly and twice been wounded? And was there any justification for his conduct?

When the fighting began at Lexington and Concord in April 1775, Arnold was thirty-four, an apothecary and minor merchant in New Haven, Connecticut—and also a militia captain and ardent Patriot. Eager to support the rebellion, he threatened the town's selectmen, who preferred a more cautious course, forcing them to supply powder and ball to his men. He promptly marched his troops off to Boston, then under siege by the New England militia. On the way Arnold thought up the attack on Fort Ticonderoga (realizing that the fort's cannon could be used to force the British out of Boston), and persuaded the Massachusetts Committee of Safety to approve his plan and make him a colonel.

Major John André, Executed as a British Spy
Unable to catch the traitor Benedict Arnold, the American army executed his British accomplice, whose elegance, intelligence, and dignity won the hearts of his captors: "He died universally esteemed and universally regretted," noted Alexander Hamilton.

This done, he raced to New York to take command, so that the glory would be his and not go to Ethan Allen and the Green Mountain Boys. The victory achieved, Arnold submitted a rather large claim for expenses (£1,060 in Massachusetts currency, about $60,000 today) and protested vehemently when the suspicious legislators closely examined each item.

These events at the outset of the war illuminate Arnold's great strengths and fatal flaws, and were prophetic of his ultimate fate. He was bold and creative, a man who sized up a situation and acted quickly. He was ambitious and extravagant, a man who craved power and the financial rewards that came with it. He was intrepid and ruthless, willing to risk his life—and those of others—to get what he wanted.

Such men are often resented as much as they are admired, and so it was with Arnold. At Quebec some New England officers accused him of arrogance and tried to withdraw from his command, but his advocates in Congress rewarded the intrepid colonel by making him a general. When Arnold again distinguished himself in battle in early 1777—having his horse shot out from under him—Congress promoted him to major general and gave him a new horse, "as a token of their admiration of his gallant conduct." But then, in the midst of the struggle at Saratoga, General Horatio Gates, the American commander, relieved Arnold of his command, partly for insubordination and partly because Gates considered him a "pompous little fellow." Washington rewarded Arnold nonetheless, appointing him commandant at Philadelphia in July 1778, following the British evacuation of the city.

By then Arnold was an embittered man, disdainful of his fellow officers and resentful of Congress for not promoting him more quickly and to even higher rank. A widower, he threw himself into the social life of the city, holding grand parties, courting and marrying Margaret Shippen—a talented young woman of good family, who, at nineteen, was half his age—and falling deeply into debt. Arnold's extravagance drew him into shady financial schemes and into disrepute with Congress, which investigated his accounts and recommended a court martial.

Faced with financial ruin, uncertain of future promotion, and disgusted with congressional politics, Arnold made a fateful decision: he would seek fortune and fame in the service of Great Britain. With cool calculation, he initiated correspondence with Sir Henry Clinton, the British commander, promising to deliver West Point and its 3,000 defenders for £20,000 sterling (about $1 million), meanwhile persuading Washington to place the fort under his command. By September 1780, Arnold's plan was in place, only to fail when André was captured—and executed as a spy. Arnold still received £6,000, as well as a British generalship.

Arnold served the king with the same skill and daring he had shown in the Patriot cause. In 1781, as a British brigadier general, he led devastating strikes on Patriot supply depots. In Virginia he looted Richmond and destroyed munitions and grain intended for the American army opposing Lord Cornwallis; in Connecticut, he burned ships, warehouses, and much of the town of New London, a major port for Patriot privateers.

In the end, Benedict Arnold's moral failure lay not in his disenchantment with the American cause—for other officers had become disgusted and returned to civilian life; nor even in his decision to switch his allegiance to the British side—for other Patriots chose to become Loyalists, sometimes out of principle but just as often for personal gain. Arnold's perfidy lay in the abuse of his position of authority and trust: he would betray West Point and its garrison—and if necessary the entire American war effort—to secure his own success. His treason was not that of a principled man but a selfish one, and he never lived that down. Hated in America, Arnold was treated with coldness and even contempt in Britain, and he died as he lived—a man without a country.

Making Peace
Benjamin West's painting, *American Commission of the Preliminary Peace Negotiation with Great Britain* (detail), portrays the American negotiators, including Benjamin Franklin, John Jay, and John Adams in 1783. The Americans bargained hard with British during the fall of 1782, and signed the preliminary treaty on November 30. A Patriot diplomatic triumph, the treaty acknowledged the independence of the United States and extended its boundaries to the Mississippi River. (Winterthur Museum)

Washington also had a greater margin for error than did the British generals who opposed him. For every active Loyalist, there were two avid Patriots—and the Patriots usually controlled the local governments. Though they often wavered in their support of the Patriot cause, these ordinary citizens mobilized the economic resources required to fight a long war, and they came through at crucial moments in the military campaigns. Thousands of militiamen besieged General Gage in Boston in 1775, surrounded Burgoyne at Saratoga in 1778, and forced Cornwallis to relinquish the Carolinas in 1781.

In the end, the allegiance of the American people decided the outcome of the conflict. Patriot partisans and guerrillas deprived the British troops of safe camps and local supplies. Preferring Patriot rule, the majority of farmers and artisans refused to support Loyalist forces or accept imperial control in areas occupied by the British army. Consequently, though the British won many military victories, they achieved little, whereas their two major defeats—at Saratoga and Yorktown—proved catastrophic.

Diplomatic Triumph

It was two years after the battle of Yorktown before diplomats achieved a formal end to the war. Peace talks began in Paris in April 1782, but the French and Spanish stalled for time, hoping for a major naval victory or territorial conquest. Their delaying tactics infuriated the American diplomats—Benjamin Franklin, John Adams, and John Jay—for they feared that drawn-out negotiations would tempt France to sacrifice American interests. Consequently, the Americans negotiated secretly with the British; they were prepared, if necessary, to cut their ties with France and sign a separate peace. The British ministry was also anxious to obtain a quick settlement, because many members of Parliament no longer supported the war and ministers feared the loss of a rich sugar island in the West Indies or the creation of a new French empire in North America.

Astutely exploiting the rivalry between Britain and France, Franklin and his colleagues won a major victory at the bargaining table. The Treaty of Paris, signed in the French capital on September 3, 1783, formally recognized the independence of the United States. Britain retained Canada, but only the territory north of the Great Lakes. All the land between the Appalachian Mountains and the Mississippi River that Britain had wrested from France twenty years before was ceded to the new American republic. This was still the domain of native Americans, but Britain made no attempt to secure the land rights of its Indian allies. Instead it promised to withdraw its garrisons, scattered across the trans-Appalachian West, "with all convenient speed."

Other provisions of the treaties granted Americans fishing rights off Newfoundland and Nova Scotia and guaranteed freedom of navigation on the Mississippi to British and American citizens "forever." In its only concession, the United States government promised to recommend to the state governments that they return Loyalist property seized in the war.

In the Treaty of Versailles, signed at the same time as the Treaty of Paris, Britain also made peace with France and Spain. France had the satisfaction of seeing the British defeated, but its only territorial gain was the Caribbean island of Tobago. More important, its support for liberty in America had quadrupled the national debt, and in six years cries for tax relief and for political liberty would lead to the French Revolution. Spain failed in its main objective of retaking Gibraltar, but it did reacquire Florida from Britain. Americans welcomed the return of Spanish rule to Florida, for Spain was a far weaker power than Britain or France.

The two treaties were vague in defining the boundaries between the United States and its British and Spanish neighbors, and territorial disputes would mar relations for another thirty years. But the peace settlement opened the interior of the continent to American expansion and made possible the development of a large and powerful nation.

Republicanism in Action

Americans began to define the character of their new republic at the moment of its creation. In the Declaration of Independence Thomas Jefferson proclaimed that all individuals have the right to "life, liberty, and the pursuit of happiness." Jefferson drew his list from the writings of John Locke, but he substituted the word *happiness* for Locke's *property*. Jefferson's choice reflected the idealism of many Americans and their commitment to *republican virtue*, an enlightened quest for the public interest. But it also suggested that many Americans considered the private ownership of property as a prerequisite for happiness. The tension between self-interest and the public interest—between individual property rights and the rights of the community—would shape the political and social debates of the new nation.

Republicanism Defined and Tested

The Republican Ideal. In its simplest terms, a republic is a state without a monarch. But for Americans, republicanism was much more. It was not only a political ideology but also a social philosophy. "The word *republic*," wrote Thomas Paine, "means the *public good*, or the good of the whole" (from the Latin *republica*: thing, *res*, of the people, *publica*). It followed that members of a republic assumed important responsibilities. "Every man in a republic is public property," asserted Philadelphia Patriot Benjamin Rush (eventually he extended this notion to include women as well). "His time and talents—his youth—his manhood—his old age—nay more, life, all belong to his country."

During the war this collectivist vision shaped American policy. When a local Committee of Safety suppressed dissent or controlled prices, its members saw themselves as acting in the public interest, according to the maxim of ancient Rome: "Take care that the commonwealth should receive no damage." Similarly, when General Howe occupied Philadelphia in 1777, the Pennsylvania assembly invoked republican principles to justify its extreme steps to safeguard the state. It required loyalty oaths of all people in areas still under its control, expelled suspected Tories, and executed two Quakers on charges of treason. The assembly, dominated by Scots-Irish Presbyterians, even outlawed gambling, horse-racing, theatrical shows, and all "evil practices which tend to debauch the minds and corrupt the morals of the subjects of the Commonwealth."

The Ideal Tested: The Military. Patriot leaders lauded the self-sacrifice of the militiamen who fought and fell at Lexington and Concord, Saratoga, and Camden. In contrast, they saw in the Continental officer corps's demand for lifetime pensions no less than a "total loss of virtue," as Henry Laurens of South Carolina put it. Gentlemen were supposed to be the prime exemplars of the republican ideal—far from demanding recompense, they should give freely to the republic. As the war continued, the zeal for self-sacrifice diminished throughout the military. Continental troops stationed at Morristown, New Jersey, mutinied during the winters of 1779 and 1780, unable or unwilling to endure the harsh conditions. To restore authority, Washington ordered the execution of several ringleaders, and Congress resorted to monetary incentives—back pay and new clothing—to pacify the rest. At Newburgh, New York, in 1783, Washington had to use his personal authority to thwart a potentially dangerous military challenge to Congress's policies by a group of disgruntled officers.

Virtue versus Self-Interest. Civilians likewise found it difficult to sustain their virtue as economic struggles brought the war closer to home. The British naval blockade nearly eliminated the New England fishing industry along the Atlantic coast and cut off the supply of European manufactured goods to American consumers. Domestic trade and production declined as well. The British occupation of Boston, New York, and Philadelphia put thousands of people out of work. Unemployed shipwrights, dock laborers, masons, coopers, and bakers left the cities and drifted into the countryside; the population of New York City declined from 21,000 in 1774 to less than half that at war's end. In the Chesapeake, the British blockade deprived tobacco planters of markets in Europe, forcing them to turn to the cultivation of wheat, corn, and other foodstuffs. All across the land, the pace of commercial activity slackened as farmers and artisans adapted to a war economy.

The scarcity of imported goods brought a sharp rise in prices and widespread appeals for government regulation. Consumers decried merchants and traders as "enemies, extortioners, and monopolizers." In 1777 a convention of New England states restricted increases in the price of domestic commodities and imported goods to 75 percent above their prewar level; to enforce this directive, the Massachusetts legislature passed an "Act to prevent Monopoly and Oppression." However, many farmers and artisans simply refused to sell goods at the established prices. Some were passing along their own costs, but others were just plain greedy, determined to profit from wartime shortages. In the end, consumers had to pay the market price, a government official admitted, "or submit to starving."

Personal distress prompted many Americans to reexamine the meaning of republican virtue. Philadelphia, where severe food shortages and soaring prices followed the British withdrawal in 1778, saw the most spirited debate. In May 1779 a crowd of artisans and laborers, having caught a merchant illegally exporting flour, called a town meeting and created a Committee on Prices that set wholesale and retail rates for thirty-two commodities. The committee, composed primarily of artisans, justified these restraints by invoking the traditional concept of the "just price," reflecting their fear of exploitation by well-to-do merchants or calculating storekeepers.

Led by the influential Patriot financier Robert Morris, Philadelphia merchants argued against price controls: regulation would only cause hoarding, while allowing prices to rise would bring goods to market and relieve scarcity. When the Continental Congress returned to the city, many members supported the merchants' position, including Benjamin Franklin, who condemned price controls as "contrary to the nature of commerce."

But most Philadelphians were skeptical. At a town meeting in August 1779, 2,115 voters endorsed government regulation of the market and only 281 opposed it. This vote showed the strength of republican feeling among craft-workers and laborers—at least in *principle*. In practice, many artisan-republicans—shoemakers, tanners, and bakers—refused to abide by the fixed prices, saying that these denied them a living wage. In civilian life, as in the military, self-interest tended to triumph over republican virtue.

Women and the War. Faced with constantly rising prices, government officials found it nearly impossible to purchase supplies for the troops. They met this challenge by requisitioning goods directly from the people. For example, in 1776, Connecticut officials called upon the citizens of Hartford to provide 1,000 coats and 1,600 shirts. They assessed smaller towns on a proportionate basis. In 1777, officials again asked the people to provide shirts, stockings, and shoes for the men of their community serving in the Continental army.

Soldiers added their own pleas to these exhortations. During the Battle of Long Island Captain Edward Rogers lost "all the shirts except the one on my back," he wrote to his wife. "The making of cloath . . . must go on. . . . I must have shirts and stocking & a jacket sent me as soon as possible & a blankit."

Patriot women seized this opportunity to contribute to the war effort, increasing their production of homespun cloth. One Massachusetts town claimed an annual output of 30,000 yards of cloth, while women in Elizabeth, New Jersey, promised "upwards of 100,000 yards of linnen and woolen cloth."

With their husbands and sons away, many women assumed the burden of farm production. Some went into the fields themselves, plowing fields or cutting and loading grain. Others supervised hired laborers or slaves, acquiring a taste for decision making in the process. "We have sow'd our oats as you desired," Sarah Cobb Paine wrote to her absent husband, "had I been master I should have planted it to Corn." Taught from childhood to act selflessly—to promote the welfare of their fathers, brothers, and husbands above their own—most Patriot women did not experience the conflict between virtue and self-interest that plagued the men. The production of cloth, meat, and grain boosted their self-esteem as it contributed to the war effort.

Fiscal Crisis. Nearly all Americans—women as well as men—found they had to calculate more closely to main-

AMERICAN VOICES

The Tories Condemned, 1779 *Letter from "A Whig"*

The pressures of war always inflame passions. As the war entered its fourth year and Continental currency lost value, Patriots took out their frustration on resident Tories, as in the letter to the *Pennsylvania Packet*. Fueled by this rhetoric, Patriots attacked many Loyalists (and neutrals), sharpening social tensions in hundreds of American communities.

Among the many errors America has been guilty of during her contest with Great Britain, few have been greater, or attended with more fatal consequences to these States, than her lenity to the Tories. . . . We are all crying out against the depreciation of our money, and entering into measures to restore it to its value; while the Tories, who are one principal cause of the depreciation, are taken no notice of, but suffered to live quietly among us.

Who do all in their power to depreciate it? The Tories! Who propagate lies among us to discourage the Whigs? The Tories! Who hold a traitorous correspondence with the enemy? The Tories! Who daily send them intelligence? The Tories! Who take the oaths of allegiance to the States one day and break them the next? The Tories! Who prevent your battalions being filled? The Tories! Who persuade those who have enlisted to desert? The Tories! Who harbor those who do desert? The Tories! In short, who wish to see us conquered, to see us slaves, to see us hewers of wood and drawers of water? The Tories!

Awake, Americans, to a sense of your danger. No time to be lost. Instantly banish every Tory from among you. Let America be sacred alone to freemen.

Source: Pennsylvania Packet, August 5, 1779; reprinted in Thomas A. Bailey, ed., *The American Spirit: United States History as Seen by Contemporaries* (Boston: Heath, 1963), pp. 117–18.

tain their standard of living during the war, mostly because of the fiscal crisis. Those who accepted the currency issued by the Continental Congress at face value courted financial disaster. By 1778 so much currency had been printed that it took $7 in Continental bills to buy goods worth $1 in gold or silver. And the ratio continued to increase—it was 42 to 1 in 1779, and 100 to 1 in 1780. When the rate of exchange between Continental currency and specie reached 146 to 1 in 1781, not even the most virtuous Patriots would accept paper money.

Congress sought to halt the spiraling inflation by redeeming its currency and removing it from circulation. In 1780 it asked the states to assess taxes that could be paid in Continental currency at the rate of 40 paper dollars for every silver dollar owed by the taxpayer. This scheme resulted in the redemption of $120 million in Continental bills, and yielded a substantial profit to astute speculators, who had seen a future value in the currency. They had accumulated Continental bills from thousands of ordinary citizens at rates of 80, 100, or 120 to 1, and they now used these bills to pay their taxes, receiving credits worth double or triple their investment. At the end of the war speculators still held $71 million in Continental notes, hoping that the currency would eventually be redeemed at its face value, giving them an even greater profit.

The big losers in this game were farmers and artisans who had received the bills for supplies and soldiers who received them as military pay. The currency depreciated in their pockets week by week, constantly losing purchasing power. Individually, these losses were small, amounting to a tiny "tax" every time an ordinary citizen spent a dollar. But collectively these "currency taxes" paid the huge cost of the war.

It was the personal sacrifices, willing or not, of hundreds of thousands of American citizens that won the struggle for independence. The experience was a sobering one. "Private Interest seemed to predominate over the public weal," a leading Patriot complained as the war came to an end, and "avaricious and ambitious men" seemed to be everywhere. Was this the society for which Americans had fought and died? "Let us have patience," Benjamin Rush replied to such questions. Self-interest might now be in the ascendancy, "but our republican forms of government will in time beget republican opinions and manners. All will end well." Events would not completely bear this out, but for Rush and many other Patriots, public virtue remained the guiding principle of the new American republic.

The Loyalist Exodus

The world wars of the twentieth century disrupted the lives of millions of ordinary women and men—mobilizing them to produce weapons, destroying their property, turning them into refugees, taking their lives. On a much smaller scale, the American War of Independence exposed tens of thousands of civilians to deprivation, displacement, and death. "An army, even a friendly one, are a dreadful scourge to any people," a Connecticut soldier wrote home from Pennsylvania. "You cannot imagine what devastation and distress mark their steps." New Jersey was particularly hard hit by the fighting, as British and American armies marched back and forth across the state. Well-known Patriots and Loyalists fled from their homes to escape arrest. Soldiers and partisans looted farms, seeking food or political revenge. Drunk and disorderly troops harassed or raped women and girls. Wherever the armies went, people lived in fear.

People learned to fear their neighbors as well, for the War of Independence was in many respects a civil war. Mobs of Patriot farmers in New England beat suspected Tories or destroyed their property. "Every Body submitted to our Sovereign Lord the Mob," a Loyalist preacher lamented. "Now we are reduced to a State of Anarchy." Patriots in most communities quickly organized a new institution of local government called a Committee of Safety. These committees collected taxes, sent food and clothing to the Continental army, and imposed fines or jail sentences on those who failed to support the Patriot cause. Declared the Committee of Safety of Farmington, Connecticut: "There is no such thing as remaining neutral."

Thomas Hutchinson, Loyalist

The secure world of his American ancestors crumbling around him, Hutchinson left Boston in 1774, never to return. The leader of the Loyalist community in London, he died there in 1780, never quite reconciled to his fate as an exile.

Because of the war, the Loyalists faced disaster. More than 100,000 Tories emigrated to Canada, the West Indies, or Britain, during and after the war. This exodus disrupted the established social order, for many of the Loyalists were wealthy and politically powerful merchants, lawyers, and landowners. Some of those who migrated to Canada—where they became known as the United Empire Loyalists—assumed the leadership of the English-speaking colonies of Nova Scotia, New Brunswick, and Ontario. Hundreds of black Loyalists—former slaves in the South—found their way to Nova Scotia, and to Sierra Leone in Africa.

The land, buildings, and goods left behind by the Loyalists raised the touchy issue of the sanctity of property rights. Some Patriots wanted to confiscate the property of these "traitors," and the passions of war lent urgency to their arguments. Initially, the government of North Carolina rented out Loyalists' estates, but when the British army invaded the South, the Patriots confiscated the estates outright. Officials in New York also seized Loyalists' lands and goods, claiming the "sovereignty of the people of this state in respect to all property."

However, many public officials opposed the seizure of Loyalist property. The Massachusetts Constitution of 1780 declared that every citizen should be protected "in the enjoyment of his life, liberty, and property, according to the standing laws," and state officials extended these rights to Loyalists. Most Tory property in Massachusetts was handled by the court system under the Act to Provide for the Payment of Debts. The courts mandated the seizure of land and goods needed to reimburse creditors, but the remaining property reverted to the agents of departed Loyalists or to their resident wives or widows.

This respect for property rights prevented an extensive redistribution of Tory lands and goods, as did the states' need to raise revenue. Most states seized the property only of leading Loyalists, selling it to the highest bidder. Consequently, there were few attempts to break up large Tory estates to provide land for yeomen farmers. For example, Georgia seized 128,000 acres of land from 166 Tories and sold it to only 188 Patriots. There were a few exceptions where the sale of Loyalist property produced a somewhat more democratic result. In North Carolina about half the new owners of Loyalist lands were small-scale farmers. And on the Philipsburg manor in New York, tenants successfully converted their leases into fee-simple ownership. But unlike France after 1789 or Russia after 1917, the revolutionary upheaval did not drastically alter the structure of rural society.

Social turmoil was greater in the cities, as upwardly mobile Patriot merchants replaced Tories at the top of the economic ladder. The Lowell, Higginson, Jackson, and Cabot families moved their trading enterprises to Boston to fill the vacuum created by the departure of the Hutchinsons and Apthorps and their friends. Small-scale traders in Philadelphia and its environs likewise stepped into the vacancies created by the collapse of Anglican and Quaker mercantile firms during the war. In the counting houses, as on the battlefield, Patriots emerged triumphant. The War of Independence had driven thousands of Loyalists from their homes and replaced a conservative economic elite—one that invested primarily in foreign trade and urban real estate—with a group of entrepreneurial-minded republican merchants.

The Problem of Slavery

The American Revolution generated intense debate over the institution of slavery, in part because of the active role played by African-Americans on both sides of the struggle. Thousands of slaves had fought or worked for the British, while free blacks from New England had enrolled in Patriot units such as the First Rhode Island Company and the Massachusetts "Bucks." In Maryland Patriots had recruited a large number of slaves for military duty and freed them in return for their service, a policy rejected by other southern states.

Thousands of enslaved blacks in the South therefore sought freedom on their own, usually by seeking refuge behind British lines. Two neighbors of Richard Henry Lee, the Virginia Patriot, lost "every slave they had in the world" during the war. Fifty-three blacks, including eight mothers and their children, fled from another Virginia plantation. When the British army evacuated Charleston, more than 6,000 former slaves went with them; another 4,000 left Savannah with the British. Other slaves struck informal bargains with their Patriot masters, trading loyalty in wartime for a promise of liberty. Virginia passed a Manumission Act in 1782, and planters freed 10,000 slaves within a decade.

These wartime events revealed a contradiction in republican ideology. Many white Patriots, demanding liberty for themselves, realized it was inconsistent to hold blacks in perpetual bondage. "I wish most sincerely there was not a Slave in the province," Abigail Adams wrote her husband John as Massachusetts went to war. "It always appeared a most iniquitous Scheme to me—to fight ourselves for what we are daily robbing and plundering from those who have as good a right to freedom as we have."

Abolition in the North. This intense questioning of slavery was fairly new. The first to condemn slavery as immoral were the Quakers. As early as the 1750s, evangelist John Woolman and a few other Quakers had urged their coreligionists to free their slaves. The outbreak of the war led many North Carolina Quakers to "clear their hands" of the institution by *manumitting* (literally, letting go from the hand) their slaves. Other pietistic groups, notably the Methodists and the Baptists, advocated emancipation and admitted both enslaved and free blacks into their congregations. In 1784 a conference of Virginia Methodists declared that slavery was "contrary to the Golden Law of God on which hang all the Law and Prophets."

Enlightenment principles also played a role in the debate over slavery. John Locke had argued that ideas were not innate but stemmed from impressions and experience. Accordingly, Enlightenment thinkers argued that the oppressive conditions of slavery accounted for the debased situation of the black race; they were not an inherently inferior people. "A state of slavery has a mighty tendency to shrink and contract the minds of men," one American observer noted. Anthony Benezet, a Quaker philanthropist who funded a school for blacks in Philadelphia, contradicted popular belief by declaring that African-Americans were "as capable of improvement as White People."

These religious and secular arguments temporarily prevailed over the defenses of slavery, at least in the North. By 1784, four states—Massachusetts, Pennsyl-

Symbols of Slavery—and Freedom

The scar on the forehead of this black woman, widely known as "Mumbet," underlined the cruelty of slavery. Winning emancipation through a legal suit, she chose a name befitting her new status: Elizabeth Freeman.

vania, Connecticut, and Rhode Island—had either abolished slavery or provided for its gradual end. Within two decades, every state north of Delaware adopted similar legislation. But liberty came slowly to African-Americans. The New York Emancipation Edict of 1799, for example, granted freedom only to the *children* of presently enslaved blacks, and only when they reached the age of twenty-five. As late as 1810, 30,000 slaves in the northern states—nearly a fourth of their African-American populations—still served masters.

One reason that emancipation was so slow was the whites' fear that a large community of free blacks would create conflict with whites over jobs, housing, and cultural values. Moreover, gradual emancipation provided compensation to slaveowners, in the form of a few more years of slave labor. Even in the North, the whites' right to property had priority over the blacks' rights to liberty. And liberty did not mean equality, for racial prejudice remained strong. A Massachusetts law of 1786 prohibited whites from marrying blacks, Indians, or mulattoes.

Emancipation in the Chesapeake Region. The tension between the republican values of liberty and property was greatest in the South. Slaves made up from 30 to 60 percent of the population and represented a huge financial investment. Most of the political leaders were slaveholders, and they used state power to preserve slavery. In 1776 the North Carolina legislature condemned Quaker manumissions as "highly criminal and reprehensible," ordering the seizure of freed blacks and their sale at public auction. However, many Chesapeake slaveholders, moved by religious principles or oversupplied with workers on their plantations, allowed blacks to buy their freedom through paid work as artisans or laborers. By 1810, manumission and self-purchase had raised the number of freed blacks in Maryland to about a third of its African-American population. In Delaware, freed blacks outnumbered slaves three to one.

But none of this was strong enough to overthrow slavery in the Chesapeake. Most whites did not want a society filled with freed blacks. In 1792 the Virginia legislature imposed various financial conditions that made it more difficult for whites to free their slaves. Following the lead of Thomas Jefferson, who owned more than a hundred slaves, many Chesapeake planters now argued that slavery was a "necessary evil" required to maintain white supremacy and their elaborate lifestyles.

And so, within a decade of the end of the Revolution, the tide had turned against emancipation in the Chesapeake. (It was never seriously considered in South Carolina and Georgia.) Its fate was sealed in 1800 when Virginia authorities discovered and prevented a slave uprising planned by Gabriel Prosser and hanged him, along with about thirty of his followers. "Liberty and equality have brought the evil upon us," a letter to the Virginia *Herald* proclaimed in the aftermath of the abortive rebellion, for such doctrines are "dangerous and extremely wicked in this country, where every white man is a master, and every black man is a slave." Throughout the South, most whites reaffirmed their commitment to slavery and white property rights, whatever the cost to republican principles.

A Republican Religious Order

Shifts in American religious institutions paralleled the political changes of the revolutionary years. To win popular support for the war, Patriot leaders in Virginia stopped harassing New Light Presbyterians and Baptists. In 1776, James Madison persuaded the Virginia Convention to issue a Declaration of Rights that guaranteed the "free exercise of religion." Later that year, the Virginia legislature passed an act exempting dissenters from paying taxes to support the Anglican Church. Throughout the South the Church of England lost its status as the established church. Anglicans renounced allegiance to the king, the head of the Church of England, and reorganized themselves as the Protestant Episcopal Church of America.

The Separation of Church and State. After the war Patriots began to devise a new relationship between churches and state governments. The two major issues they confronted were compulsory religious taxes and freedom of worship. In general, Baptists opposed all taxes to support religion. Their influence in Virginia prompted lawmakers to reject a bill supported by George Washington and Patrick Henry that would have imposed a general assessment tax to provide funds for all Christian churches. Instead, in 1786 the legislature enacted Thomas Jefferson's Bill for Establishing Religious Freedom, which made all churches equal before the law and granted direct financial support to none. The bill also endorsed the principle of liberty of conscience and outlawed religious requirements for political and civil posts.

Yet many Americans still clung to traditional European principles, arguing that a firm union of church and state promoted morality and respect for authority. "Pure religion and civil liberty are inseparable companions," one group of North Carolinians advised their minister. "It is your particular duty to enlighten mankind with the unerring principles of truth and justice, the main props of all civil government."

So change came slowly, especially in New England, where Congregationalist ministers had strongly supported the independence movement and used their prestige to maintain a legally established church until the 1830s. However, Congregationalists no longer attempted to suppress Baptist and Methodist churches and allowed them to use religious taxes to support their own ministers. In the Middle Atlantic states, the sheer number of churches—Episcopalian, Presbyterian, Dutch Reformed, Lutheran, and Quaker, among others—prevented legislative agreement on an established church or compulsory religious taxes, and religious freedom blossomed.

Before 1776, only Quakers in Pennsylvania and Baptists in Rhode Island had severed the traditional link between church and state. The Revolution ushered in a new era in American religion. Virginia and the other southern states repudiated an established church as well as taxation for religious purposes, and legislative bodies in many states affirmed the principle of religious liberty.

Freedom of Religion. Nonetheless, some states continued to offer tax exemptions on church property, enforce religious criteria for voting and office holding, and penalize individuals who questioned the doctrines of Protestant Christianity. For example, the North Carolina Constitution of 1776 disqualified from public office any citizen "who shall deny the being of God, or the Truth of the Protestant Religion, or the Divine Authority of the Old or New Testament." New Hampshire had a similar provision in its constitution until 1868.

In one celebrated case Chancellor James Kent of the New York Supreme Court flouted the principle of religious liberty by upholding the conviction of Timothy Ruggles for blasphemy (publicly and disrespectfully shouting the name of Christ). Kent overruled Ruggles's contention that the charge infringed his liberty of conscience under the New York Constitution of 1777, which guaranteed "the free, equal and undisturbed enjoyment of religious opinion." Kent declared that "the people of this State profess the general doctrines of Christianity," and for Ruggles to slander Christ was "to strike at the root of moral obligation and weaken the security of social ties." For Kent, the good of the republic had a higher priority than the individual's right of free speech.

Americans influenced by the Enlightenment condemned interference in religious affairs, by courts or by the churches themselves. Thomas Paine attacked churches as "no other than human inventions set up to terrify and enslave mankind, and monopolize power and profit." Rationalist thinkers extended republican principles to religion, teaching that God had given human beings the power of reason so they could determine moral truths for themselves. Ethan Allen of Vermont, the leader of the Green Mountain Boys during the war, wrote a widely circulated pamphlet called *Reason, The Only Oracle of Man* (1784).

Many of the founders of the new American republics, like Thomas Jefferson and Benjamin Franklin, were *deists*. They thought God had created the world the way a watchmaker builds a clock; once set in motion, it ran according to its own laws. "God Almighty is himself a Mechanic," proclaimed Thomas Cooper, president of the College of South Carolina. Philip Freneau, an ardent Patriot poet and deist, wrote that in "Nature" one could

> see, with most exact design,
> The world revolve, the planets shine.
> The nicest order, all things meet,
> A structure in itself complete.

To protect society from what they called "ecclesiastical tyranny," rationalists demanded complete freedom of expression. Many American Protestants also favored freedom of conscience, but their goal was to protect themselves and their churches from state control. Isaac Backus warned New England Baptists not to incorporate their churches or to accept tax funds under the general assessment laws of Massachusetts. Instead, Backus favored voluntary church support. In Connecticut a devout Congregationalist layman likewise approved of voluntarism, because it undermined the clerical hierarchy and thus furthered "the spirit of toleration" and "the principles of republicanism." In the aftermath of the Revolution, American Protestant Christianity thus became increasingly republican in structure and spirit.

Summary

Civil war disrupted the British empire beginning in April 1775. Bloodshed between British and Patriot forces made compromise difficult, as did George III's determination to crush the rebellion. Thomas Paine's *Common Sense* attacked the monarchical system and persuaded many Americans to support independence, which was declared by the Continental Congress on July 4, 1776.

British troops under General Howe defeated Washington's Continental army in a series of battles during 1776, but Patriot triumphs at Trenton and Princeton revived American morale. As a result of poor British planning, the rebels won a major victory at Saratoga in October 1777, then nearly lost their main army to cold and hunger at Valley Forge during the winter of 1777–1778.

An alliance with France in 1778 aided the Patriot cause financially, militarily, and diplomatically. British troops won major victories in Georgia and the Carolinas during 1779 and 1780, but Patriot troops and guerrillas finally forced General Cornwallis into Virginia, where he suffered a major defeat at Yorktown, the last major battle of the war. The Treaty of Paris of 1783 acknowledged American independence and opened the west for settlement.

Idealist-minded Americans sought to create a republican society based on the individual's commitment to the common good. However, soldiers and civilians responded to wartime hardships by pursuing their economic self-interest. Most Americans suffered financially because of inflation—a hidden tax that paid for the war. Independence and republicanism significantly changed American society—bringing the departure of the Loyalists, the abolition of slavery in the North, the gradual separation of church and state, and freedom of worship.

TOPIC FOR RESEARCH

The Outcome of the War for Independence

Why and how did the United States emerge victorious in the armed struggle against Great Britain? Historians have treated this question from a variety of perspectives—military, diplomatic, and geographic, among others. In addressing this issue, you may wish to focus on a particular development, such as the Franco–American alliance, or adopt a broader approach, discussing the combination of American strengths and British weaknesses that resulted in a Patriot victory.

Four good general accounts are John Richard Alden, *The American Revolution, 1775–1783* (1964); Piers Mackesy, *The War for America, 1775–1783* (1964); Don Higginbotham, *The War of American Independence: Military Attitudes, Policies, and Practice, 1763–1789* (1971); and James L. Stokesbury, *A Short History of the American Revolution* (1991). Eric Robson, *The American Revolution in Its Political and Military Aspects* (1954), and Ronald Hoffman and Peter Albert, eds., *Arms and Independence: The Military Character of the American Revolution* (1984), offer a more analytical perspective. The role of ordinary Patriots is assessed in John Shy, *A People Numerous and Armed: Reflections on the Military Struggle for Independence* (1976), and Charles Royster, *A Revolutionary People at War: The Continental Army and American Character, 1775–1783* (1979).

Studies of the soldiers who fought the war include Rodney Attwood, *The Hessians* (1980); Sylvia R. Frey, *The British Soldier in America* (1981); Robert K. Wright, Jr., *The Continental Army* (1983); and John C. Dann, ed., *The Revolution Remembered: Eyewitness Accounts of the War for Independence* (1980). The crucial role played by the military bureaucracy is assessed in R. Arthur Bowler, *Logistics and the Failure of the British Army in America, 1775–1783* (1975), and E. Wayne Carp, *To Starve the Army at Pleasure: Continental Army Administration and American Political Culture, 1775–1783* (1984).

BIBLIOGRAPHY

Toward Independence

Jerrilyn Green Marston, *King and Congress: The Transfer of Political Legitimacy, 1774–1776* (1987), and Jack N. Rakove, *The Beginnings of National Politics: An Interpretative History of the Continental Congress* (1979), discuss the deliberations that preceded the Declaration of Independence, while Robert Middlekauff, *The Glorious Cause: The American Revolution, 1763–1789* (1982), sets these events in a broader context. The identity and activities of Loyalists both before and after 1776 are discussed by William N. Nelson, *The American Tory* (1961); Wallace Brown, *The King's Friends* (1966); Robert M. Calhoon, *The Loyalists in Revolutionary America, 1760–1781* (1973); Bernard Bailyn, *The Ordeal of Thomas Hutchinson* (1974); Adele Hast, *Loyalism in Revolutionary Virginia* (1982); and Robert S. Allen, ed., *The Loyal Americans: The Military Role of the Loyalist Provincial Corps and Their Settlement in British North America 1775–1784* (1983).

The Perils of War and Finance, 1776–1778

In addition to the studies cited in the Topic for Research, the military history of the war in the North can be followed in Ira D. Gruber, *The Howe Brothers and the American Revolution* (1972); Richard J. Hargrove, Jr., *General John Burgoyne* (1983); Paul David Nelson, *General Horatio Gates* (1976); and Don Higginbotham, *George Washington and the American Military Tradition* (1985). Local studies that examine the impact of the war include Robert A. Gross, *The Minutemen and Their World* (1976); Richard Buel, Jr., *Dear Liberty: Connecticut's Mobilization for the Revolutionary War* (1980); Hugh Rankin, *The North Carolina Continentals* (1971); and Donald Wallace White, *A Village at War: Chatham, New Jersey, and the American Revolution* (1979).

African-American participation in the war is discussed by Gary A. Puckrein, *The Black Regiment in the American Revolution* (1978), and Sidney Kaplan, *The Black Presence in the Era of the American Revolution* (rev. ed., 1989). The role of native Americans is described in Barbara Graymont, *The Iroquois in the American Revolution* (1972); Isabel T. Kelsey, *Joseph Brant, 1743–1807* (1984); James H. O'Donnell III, *Southern Indians in the American Revolution* (1973); and Anthony F. C. Wallace, *The Death and Rebirth of the Seneca* (1969).

For good older discussions of the fiscal problems created by the war, see E. James Ferguson, *The Power of the Purse: A History of American Public Finance: 1776–1790* (1961), and Clarence L. Ver Steeg, *Robert Morris, Revolutionary Financier* (1954). A more recent study is William G. Anderson, *The Price of Liberty: The Public Debt of the American Revolution* (1983).

The Path to Victory, 1778–1781

Jonathan R. Dull, *A Diplomatic History of the American Revolution* (1985), and Reginald Horsman, *The Diplomacy of the New Republic, 1776–1815* (1985), provide good overviews of this topic. More specialized studies include James H. Hutson, *John Adams and the Diplomacy of the American Revolution* (1980); William C. Stinchcombe, *The American Revolution and the French Alliance* (1969); Richard B. Morris, *The Peacemakers: The Great Powers and American Independence* (1965); and Ronald Hoffman and Peter Albert, eds., *Peace and the Peacemakers: The Treaty of 1783* (1986).

For the war in the South, consult W. Robert Higgins, ed., *The Revolutionary War in the South* (1979); Ronald Hoffman, Thad W. Tate, and Peter J. Albert, eds., *An Uncivil War: The Southern Backcountry During the American Revolution* (1985); and Jeffrey J. Crow and Larry E. Tise, eds., *The Southern Experience in the American Revolution* (1978). Studies of military action include Hugh F. Rankin, *Francis Marion: The Swamp Fox* (1973); Don Higginbotham, *Daniel Morgan* (1961); and John S. Pancake, *The Destructive War, 1780–1782* (1985).

Republicanism in Action

Eric Foner, *Tom Paine and Revolutionary America* (1976), provides a good discussion of conflicting views among republican Patriots in Philadelphia, while Ronald Hoffman, *A Spirit of Dissension: Economics, Politics, and the Revolution in Maryland* (1973), examines similar conflicts in that state. Women's lives are analyzed in Mary Beth Norton, *Liberty's Daughters: The Revolutionary Experience of American Women, 1750–1800* (1980); Lynn Withey, *Dearest Friend: A Life of Abigail Adams* (1980); and Joy Day Buel and Richard Buel, Jr., *The Way of Duty: A Woman and Her Family in Revolutionary America* (1984).

On the black experience, see Ira Berlin and Ronald Hoffman, eds., *Slavery and Freedom in the Age of the American Revolution* (1983); Duncan J. Macleod, *Slavery, Race, and the American Revolution* (1974); Gary Nash, *Forging Freedom: The Formation of Philadelphia's Black Community, 1720–1840* (1988); and David Brion Davis, *The Problem of Slavery in the Age of Revolution, 1770–1823*. See also James W. St. G. Walker, *The Black Loyalists: The Search for a Promised Land in Nova Scotia and Sierra Leone, 1783–1870* (1976), and Arthur Zilversmit, *The First Emancipation: The Abolition of Slavery in the North* (1967).

On changes in American religion, see Rhys Isaac, *The Transformation of Virginia, 1740–1790* (1982), and Fred Hood, *Reformed America 1783–1837* (1980). The spiritual roots of a new secular religion are traced by Catharine Albanese, *Sons of the Fathers: The Civil Religion of the American Revolution* (1976), and Ruth Bloch, *Visionary Republic: Millennial Themes in American Thought* (1985).

TIMELINE

1775	Second Continental Congress meets in Philadelphia Battle of Bunker Hill American invasion of Canada
1776	Thomas Paine's *Common Sense* Declaration of Independence (July 4) William Howe defeats George Washington in New York and New Jersey Virginia Declaration of Rights American victories at Trenton (December 26) and Princeton (January 3, 1777)
1777	Howe occupies Philadelphia Horatio Gates accepts surrender of John Burgoyne's army at Saratoga (October 17) Patriot governments issue paper currency to pay for war; inflation increases Continental army suffers at Valley Forge
1778	Franco-American alliance (February 6) British begin "southern" strategy by capturing Savannah
1780	Nathanael Greene's forces harass Lord Cornwallis and begin reconquest of Carolinas Continental currency depreciates
1781	Cornwallis invades Virginia; surrenders at Yorktown (October 19) Loyalists begin to emigrate to Canada and Britain
1782	Slave manumission act in Virginia; reversed in 1792
1783	Treaty of Paris (September 3)
1786	Virginia Bill for Establishing Religious Freedom
1800	Gabriel Prosser's rebellion in Virginia

The American Star

This idealized portrait of Washington by Frederick Kemmelmeyer celebrates Washington and the creation of a nation. (The Metropolitan Museum of Art)

CHAPTER 7 *The New Political Order,* 1776–1800

Many wars for national independence have resulted in military rule or political chaos. The United States escaped those unhappy fates. The departure of the Loyalists eliminated a potential threat to the new republic from a group of monarchists. General Washington refused to consider any suggestion that he become king, and returned to his plantation in Virginia. Authority remained firmly in the hands of the leaders of the resistance movement, who wished to establish governments based on popular sovereignty and republican principles.

Patriot leaders had to act swiftly and decisively to establish the legitimacy of their rule. Beginning in 1776, state officials faced the daunting task of devising new constitutions acceptable to the people. The Continental Congress likewise needed a constitutional mandate for its rule, especially given the need to address the vexing issues of war finance, the disposition of western lands, and social unrest. Following the war, the new Confederation Congress faced the ever-present prospect of the British stirring up trouble and trying to restore imperial rule.

Despite the problems—inflation, public debt, depressed trade, political conflict—the period between 1776 and 1800 was the most creative era in American political and constitutional development. The postrevolutionary years produced two national charters—the Articles of Confederation of 1781 and the Constitution of 1787—as well as a successful, if controversial, system of public finance and the rise of organized political parties. Everywhere, people with enlightened and democratic views saw the United States as the exemplar of political liberty—and, as Tom Paine had put it, "the last best hope of mankind."

Creating New Institutions, 1776–1787

The Revolution of 1776 was both a struggle for home rule (independence) and, in the words of the historian Carl Becker, a conflict over "who should rule at home." The first conflict had been successfully resolved with a military victory over Britain. The second, a struggle over the form and nature of the state constitutions, was both an intellectual effort—a debate over centuries-old issues of political theory—and a matter of practical politics. Who would control the new republican institutions, traditional elites or ordinary citizens?

The State Constitutions: How Much Democracy?

On May 10, 1776, Congress urged Patriots in all the states to suppress royal authority and establish institutions based on popular rule. Most states readily complied. By the end of 1776, Virginia, Maryland, North Carolina, New Jersey, Delaware, and Pennsylvania had written new constitutions; Connecticut and Rhode Island transformed their colonial charters, which provided for extensive self-government, into republican charters by deleting all references to the king.

The Declaration of Independence stated the principle of popular sovereignty, that governments derive "their just powers from the consent of the governed," but it left unclear exactly what this meant in practice. The Delaware Constitution of 1776 directly linked popular sovereignty with the exercise of political power: "the Right of the People to participate in the Legislature, is the Foundation of Liberty and of all free government."

But which people? During the colonial period most political offices were occupied by the rich and wellborn, and ordinary Americans willingly deferred to their "social betters." Even after the Revolution, most Patriots held a narrow definition of the political nation: voting and office holding were the province of propertied white men; women, blacks, native Americans, and propertyless whites were excluded. Conservative Patriots went much further, denying that popular sovereignty meant popular rule. Thus Jeremy Belknap of New Hampshire allowed that "Government originates from the people" but insisted that "the people be taught . . . that they are not able to govern themselves."

Radical Patriots refused to be excluded from power. In the heat of revolution, they frankly embraced a democratic outlook: every citizen who supported the rebellion had "an equal claim to all privileges, liberties and immunities," declared an article in the Maryland *Gazette*. The backcountry farmers of Mecklenburg County, North Carolina, instructed their representatives to the state's constitutional convention of 1776 to "oppose everything that leans to aristocracy or power in the hands of the rich and chief men exercised to the oppression of the poor." Voters in Virginia felt the same way, electing a new assembly that, an observer remarked, "was composed of men not quite so well dressed, nor so politely educated, nor so highly born . . . . They are the People's men," he concluded, "and the people in general are right."

Democratic-republicanism received fullest expression in Pennsylvania, where a coalition of Scots-Irish farmers, Philadelphia artisans, and Enlightenment-influenced intellectuals took control of state politics and formulated a constitution that created the most democratic institutions of government in America or Europe. The Pennsylvania constitution of 1776 abolished property-owning as a qualification for political participation, giving all men who paid taxes the right to vote and hold office. The constitution also rejected the system of mixed government and created a *unicameral* (one-house) assembly that had complete legislative power. There was no council or upper house reserved for the wealthy, and no governor. Other constitutional clauses mandated an extensive system of elementary education, protected citizens from imprisonment for debt, and called for a society composed of economically independent freemen.

Pennsylvania's democratic—even radical—constitution alarmed leading Patriots in other states, for most of them did not believe in democratic government. Conservatives feared that popular rule would lead to the tyranny of legislative majorities, with ordinary citizens using their numerical advantage to tax the rich. In Philadelphia, prosperous Anglican merchants founded a Republican Society to lobby for repeal of the constitution. In Boston, John Adams denounced Pennsylvania's unicameral legislature as "so democratical that it must produce confusion and every evil work."

To prevent the spread of democratic institutions, Adams dispatched copies of his own *Thoughts on Government* to friends at constitutional conventions in other states. In this political treatise, Adams adapted the theory of mixed government devised by English Whigs (monarch, house of lords, house of commons) to a republican society. Instead of dividing state power along social lines, he assigned each function—lawmaking, administering, and judging—to a distinct branch of government. Adams argued that his scheme was republican, because the people would elect the chief executive and the members of a two-house (*bicameral*) legislature. It would also preserve liberty, because the various branches would check and balance each other: men of property and status in the upper house could check any excesses of popular majorities in the lower house, and an appointed—not elected—judiciary would review legislation. As a further curb on democracy, an elected governor would have the power to veto laws.

Patriots in most states preferred Adams's mixed and balanced government, in part because it was less democratic than Pennsylvania's system and in part because Adams's system was more familiar. Most colonies had an elected assembly, an appointed council (upper house), and a royal governor; it seemed easier to adapt existing institutions than to begin anew. Consequently, the framers of most state constitutions retained the existing bicameral legislature, but made both houses elective. Reacting against royal governors, they reduced the powers of the executive; only three constitutions gave veto power to the governor. One of these was New York, where the elite who led the independence movement sought to prevent popular rule. The New York Constitution of 1777, written chiefly by John Jay (with a copy of Adams's *Thoughts on Government* by his side), provided for a bicameral legislature, with the lower house fairly apportioned by population; a governor with veto powers; an appointed judiciary; and a suffrage limited by property qualifications, so that, in practice, the governor and members of the upper house were elected by only 40 percent of white men.

The most flagrant use of property qualifications to maintain elite power was in the South Carolina constitution of 1778. It required candidates for governor to have a debt-free estate of £10,000 (about $450,000),

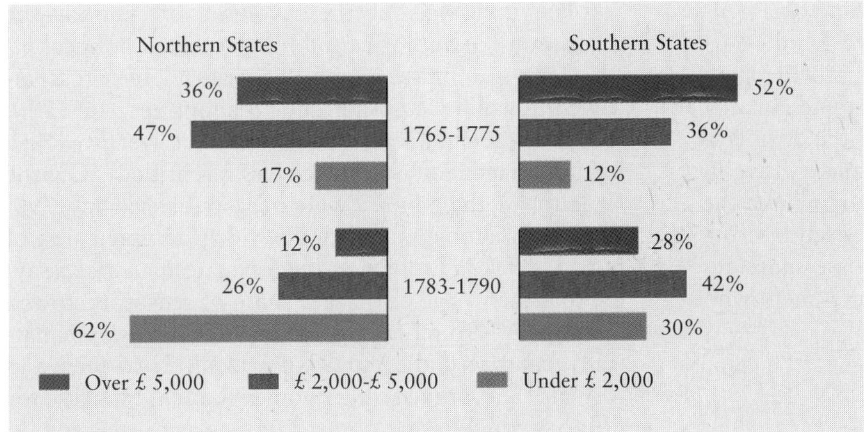

FIGURE 7.1

Change in the Wealth of Elected Officials, 1765–1790

Before the Revolution the membership of colonial assemblies was dominated by men of wealth and property. In the new republic the proportion of less prosperous men in state legislatures increased dramatically, especially in the North.

Source: Adapted from Jackson T. Main, "Government by the People: The American Revolution and the Democratization of the Legislatures," *William and Mary Quarterly,* 3rd ser., vol. 23 (1966).

senators to be worth £2,000, and assemblymen to have property valued at £1,000. This ruled out about 90 percent of the white adult population. High property qualifications likewise restricted the voting franchise to a minority of South Carolina's white men. Pennsylvania—and Vermont, which copied Pennsylvania's constitution—were exceptions in 1776. They were the only states in which radical Patriots were able to seize power and create new democratic-republican institutions.

Toward a Democratic Polity. Nonetheless, the character of American politics became more open and competitive—more democratic—mostly as a result of the broader franchise in many states and a fairer apportionment of seats in the legislatures. Yeomen farmers in western areas at last got the representation they desired. The new democratic institutions also reflected a raised consciousness. During the war, Patriot militiamen had claimed the right to elect their own officers, "for annual election is so essentially necessary to the Liberty of Freemen." Subsequently, many veterans, whether or not they had property, demanded the right to vote. Those who had the vote no longer automatically elected their social betters; rather, one observer noted, they chose men of "middling circumstances" who knew "the wants of the poor."

These democratic tendencies changed the composition of American legislatures. Before the war, 85 percent of the assemblymen in the six colonies of New York, New Hampshire, New Jersey, Maryland, Virginia, and South Carolina were wealthy men, with estates averaging in excess of £2,000. By 1784 middling farmers and artisans formed a majority in the lower houses of the three northern states and a sizable minority in those of the three southern states. Flexing their new political muscles, these ordinary citizens successfully opposed the collection of back taxes and other measures that tended "toward the oppression of the people." In most states, backcountry residents won the transfer of the state capital from merchant-dominated seaports (such

John and Abigail Adams

Both Adamses had strong personalities. In 1794 John fondly accused his wife of being a "Disciple of Wollstonecraft," but Abigail's commitment to legal equality for women long predated Wollstonecraft's treatise, *A Vindication of the Rights of Woman* (1792).

as New York City and Philadelphia) to inland cities (Albany and Harrisburg); even conservative South Carolina moved its seat of government inland from Charleston to Columbia. Adams and like-minded Patriots had succeeded in blunting the edge of the democratic movement, in that most states were conservative in the *structure* of their political institutions. However, the political system itself—the day-to-day electioneering and interest-group bargaining—had become more responsive to a broader segment of white men who owned property.

Women and Republicanism

War and constitution making affected everyone, but only men were expected to engage in political discourse and affect events. The extraordinary excitement of the Revolutionary Era tested this tradition, as some upper-class women bridled under the restrictions. They filled their letters and diaries with their opinions on political issues. "The men say we have no business [with politics]," Eliza Wilkinson of South Carolina complained in 1783, "but I won't have it thought that because we are the weaker sex as to bodily strength we are capable of nothing more than domestic concerns. They won't even allow us liberty of thought, and that is all I want."

Indeed, Wilkinson was not asking for much. Most American women—even those who were wealthy or well educated—did not demand complete political equality with men, or even voting rights. Rather, like Abigail Adams, they asked men to create a republican legal order that would enhance the position of married women, who were completely subordinate to their husbands under the common law. "All men would be tyrants if they could," Abigail Adams chided her husband John in a famous exchange of letters. "If particular care is not paid to the ladies," she continued in a tone that was only half-joking, "we will not hold ourselves bound by any laws in which we have no voice or representation." Even as her husband and other Patriots were busy "emancipating all nations," she pointed out, "you insist upon retaining absolute power over Wives."

Male leaders ignored women's requests for legal equality and a political voice. The state constitutions either explicitly restricted suffrage to men or imposed property qualifications for voting that effectively excluded married women, who had few ownership rights. An exception—accidentally—was New Jersey. Its constitution of 1776 granted suffrage to *all inhabitants* worth £50, an ambiguous phrasing that permitted widows and unmarried women with property to vote. Few women exercised the franchise until the 1790s, when a series of fierce electoral battles drew them to the polls. To preserve men's prerogatives, in 1807 the New Jersey legislature revoked the voting rights of property-owning women while extending the franchise to all white men.

The upheavals of the revolutionary period—the questioning of authority and long-accepted political institutions—prompted a few American women to challenge prevailing customs and assumptions. In 1779, Judith Sargent Murray, daughter of a wealthy New England merchant, wrote an essay entitled "On the Equality of the Sexes," which she published in 1790. This treatise took issue with the widely accepted view of Lord Halifax, a prominent English statesman and essayist, that men "had the larger share of reason bestowed upon them." To refute this statement, Murray systematically compared the intellectual faculties of men and women. She argued that women had a capacity for memory equal to that of men, and more imagination. In judgment and reasoning, she conceded that most women were inferior to men, but argued that this was due to lack of training. "We can only reason from what we know," she wrote, and most women had been denied "the opportunity of acquiring knowledge." Educa-

The Cultivation of Young Minds

Between 1780 and 1830 young American women stitched thousands of samplers similar to this one, from Mary Balch's famous school for girls in Providence, Rhode Island. Samplers often carried republican messages, such as faith in the value of education. (Museum of Art, Rhode Island School of Design) tion would in time permit women to assume a more equal position in society, Murray concluded.

The most famous call for equality of the sexes—in politics as well as education—came not from America but from England. In 1792 Mary Wollstonecraft, an English republican influenced by the French Revolution, published the path-breaking feminist manifesto *A Vindication of the Rights of Woman*. Reasoning from republican principles of civic equality, she demanded equal status for women in all public and political activities. Her demands received mixed reviews in elite social circles in America. Women generally condemned Wollstonecraft's sexually adventurous personal life, but they could respect her political arguments. American men read the *Rights of Woman* with a disdain born of a lack of understanding. Despite their commitment to republican principles, they were unable to envision a political role for their wives and daughters. Women remained second-class citizens, unable to participate directly in American political life.

The Articles of Confederation

In the days before the Declaration of Independence, the Continental Congress directed a committee to devise a more permanent governing body. Most Patriot leaders envisioned a central government with limited powers. For example, Carter Braxton of Virginia thought Congress should have the power "to adjust disputes between Colonies, regulate the affairs of trade, war, peace, alliances, &c." but "should by no means have authority to interfere with the internal police or domestic concerns of any Colony."

The Articles of Confederation, based on a draft by John Dickinson of Pennsylvania and finally passed by Congress on November 15, 1777, was the first national constitution. It provided for a loose confederation in which "each state retains its sovereignty, freedom, and independence" and all powers and rights not "expressedly delegated" to the United States. Most delegated powers pertained to diplomacy and defense. The Confederation government had the authority to declare war and peace, to make treaties with foreign nations, to adjudicate disputes between the states, to borrow and print money, and to requisition funds from the states "for the common defense or general welfare." The body charged with exercising these powers was a central legislature, or Congress, in which each state had one vote, regardless of its population. There was no separate executive branch. Important laws and decisions had to be approved by at least nine of the thirteen states. The Articles were not innovative; they simply described the way the Continental Congress had been operating since 1775.

Nonetheless, the Articles of Confederation were not ratified by all the states until 1781. The Articles gave Congress authority over land disputes between states, but did not provide for a national domain under Congressional control. Consequently, states having no western land claims, such as Maryland and Pennsylvania, would not ratify the Articles until states that did have claims to western lands—charter rights granted by the king that extended in principle to the Pacific Ocean—relinquished them to Congress. Virginia, for instance, bitterly resisted proposals to confine its territory. The pressure of war finally broke the deadlock. Threatened by Cornwallis's army, Virginia ceded its land claims to Congress in 1781, and Maryland, the final holdout, ratified the Articles.

Formal ratification was anticlimactic, since the Confederation Congress had been exercising de facto constitutional authority for four years. It was the Confederation Congress that raised the Continental army, negotiated the Franco-American treaty of 1778, and financed the war effort. The failures of the Congress stemmed primarily from its limited fiscal powers. Without the authority to impose taxes, all it could do was requisition funds from the state legislatures and hope they paid; it had no means of disciplining states that did not pay. Consequently, the prospect of bankruptcy loomed ever larger, threatening the war effort. In 1780, Washington called urgently for a national system of taxation, warning Patriot leaders that "unless the Congress are vested with powers competent to the great purposes of the war, our cause is lost."

In response, nationalist-minded members of Congress tried to amend the Articles to give more powers to the Confederation. Upon becoming superintendent of finance in 1781, Robert Morris developed a comprehensive financial plan. He succeeded in winning a Confederation charter for the Bank of North America, a private Philadelphia institution, hoping to use its notes to stabilize the currency throughout the country. He also undertook to apportion some war expenses among the states according to the value of their respective landed wealth, while keeping control of Continental army expenditures and foreign debts in the hands of Congress. Morris hoped that the existence of a national debt would demonstrate the continuing importance of the Confederation and its need to impose taxes.

But when Morris tried to complete his plan by raising revenue, he suffered defeat. Unanimous consent was required to amend the Articles and in 1781 Rhode Island rejected Morris's proposal for a national *tariff*, an import duty of 5 percent on foreign goods. Two years later New York exercised a similar veto, blocking another proposed national tariff. State leaders had not resisted import duties imposed by the British in order to allow similar levies by another central government, even their own. In another setback to Morris's plans, the states began to pay interest on their share of the national debt directly to those of their own citizens who held part of the debt, rather than send funds to Congress, which might use them to pay citizens of other states. By 1786 Pennsylvania, Maryland, New York, and New Jersey had assumed nearly one-third of the national debt.

Western Lands and the Northwest Ordinance. The most enduring accomplishment of the Confederation Congress was its plan for settling the trans-Appalachian West, which it had acquired as a result of the Treaty of Paris and the cessions of the states. The Congress had two goals. First, it needed to assert its title to this great treasure so that it could sell most of it to help pay the government's expenses. Standing in the way of this scheme were the native Americans who occupied most of these lands, as well as thousands of white squatters, who asserted ownership rights. In 1783 Congress began negotiating with Indian tribes to persuade them that the Treaty of Paris had extinguished their land rights. It also rejected the claims of white squatters, allowing them to stay only if they paid the Confederation government for their lands.

Second, Congress was determined to bind western settlements to the United States by providing for their orderly settlement and eventual admission to the Union. Given the geographic barriers between the seaboard and the interior, Congress feared that westerners might seek to create states on their own, or establish separate republics, or even link up with Spanish Louisiana. The danger was real: in 1784 thousands of settlers in what is now east Tennessee had set up a new state, Franklin, and applied for admission to the Confederation; their petition was rejected by Congress.

To thwart similar movements, Congress directed that the western lands south of the Ohio River remain temporarily under the administrative control of Virginia, North Carolina, and Georgia. The territory north of the Ohio, however, became a national domain. In three ordinances between 1784 and 1787, Congress set forth its policy for the settlement and administration of this Northwest Territory. The Ordinance of 1784, written by Thomas Jefferson, called for the admission of the states carved out of the Territory as soon as their populations equaled that of the smallest state. The Land Ordinance of 1785 set out a rectangular grid system for surveying land (see Map 8.2, p. 229). It required that western lands be surveyed prior to settlement—to deter

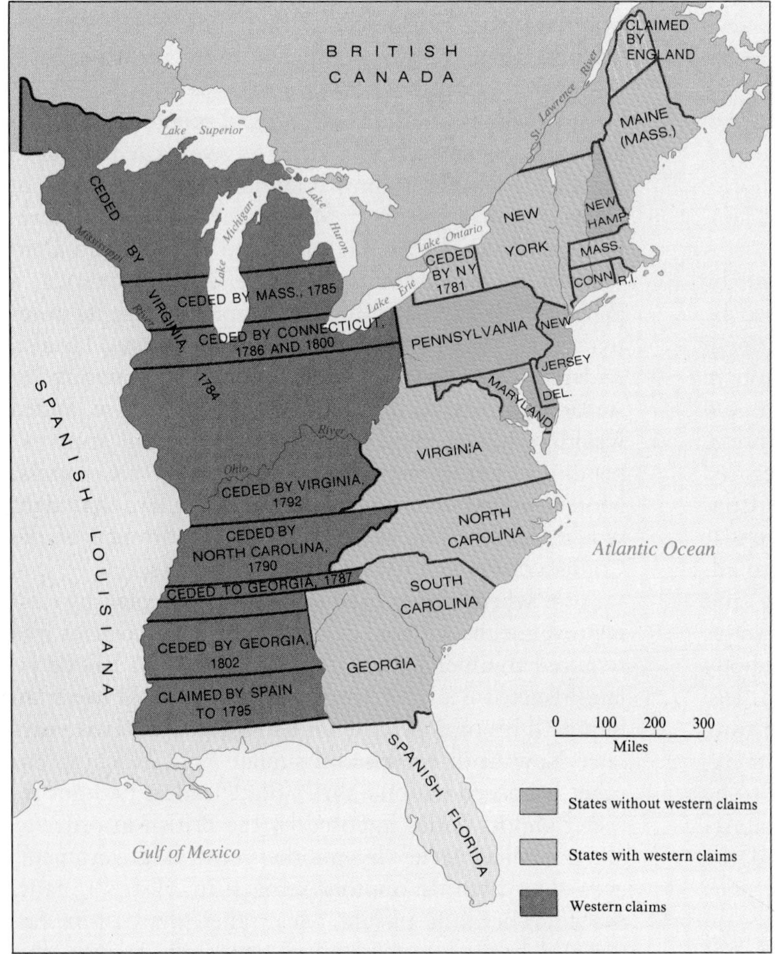

MAP 7.1

The Confederation and Western Land Claims

The Confederation Congress resolved the conflicting land claims of the states by creating a "national domain," the Northwest Territory, north of the Ohio River. From 1781 to 1802 all the seaboard states with western land claims ceded them to the national government. The Confederation Congress declared the Northwest Territory open to settlement by citizens from every state and provided for the establishment of democratic political institutions there.

Gouverneur Morris, Federalist Statesman
Morris almost became a Loyalist because he was a snob who liked privilege and feared the people ("The mob begins to think and reason," he once noted with disdain), and for similar reasons he became a Federalist, helping to write Philadelphia Constitution and strongly supporting the Federalist party. (City of Bristol Museum and Art Gallery)

squatters—and sold mostly in large blocs—which favored large-scale investors and land speculators. In specifying that lands be sold in fee simple, without quit rents or other feudal dues, the Land Ordinance encouraged the transition to a full-fledged capitalist economy in the United States.

The Northwest Ordinance of 1787 applied these general principles by providing for the creation of three to five territories in the Old Northwest—the national domain north of the Ohio River, eventually comprising the states of Ohio, Indiana, Illinois, Michigan, and Wisconsin. Reflecting the antislavery sentiments of Jefferson and many other Patriots, the ordinance prohibited slavery in these territories. It encouraged education, directing funds from the sale of certain lands toward the support of schools. It specified that initially each new territory would be ruled by a governor and judges appointed by Congress. Once the number of free adult men reached 5,000, the settlers could elect their own legislature. When the population grew to 60,000, the residents could write a republican constitution and apply to join the Union. Once admitted, the new state would enjoy all the rights and privileges of existing states.

The ordinances of the 1780s were a great achievement. They encouraged settlement of the west while reducing the prospect of secessionist movements and preventing the emergence of dependent "colonies." Moreover, by asserting national control over land sales, the Confederation government turned the Northwest Territory into a source of revenue. Lastly, in providing for geographic expansion, the ordinances added a new dimension to the national identity. Whatever the continuing problems in the west—besides native American land claims there were still illegal British forts and threats from Spanish officials—the United States was no longer confined to thirteen governments on the eastern seaboard. It was a dynamic, expanding society.

The Postwar Crisis

The 1780s was a critical decade for the new nation. Peace did not bring a return of prewar prosperity. The war had destroyed many American merchant ships and disrupted trade; exports—especially Chesapeake tobacco—declined because of the loss of long-established ties with British merchant houses. Deprived of a subsidy from the British government, South Carolina's lucrative indigo industry nearly vanished. The British Navigation Acts, which had contributed to the expansion of colonial commerce, now worked against the United States: American-owned ships were barred from trading with the sugar islands in the British West Indies.

The postwar recession lowered the American standard of living. The population of the United States continued to grow—from 2.4 to 3.6 million between 1775 and 1787—but exports increased only slightly, from \$10.7 to \$11.6 million. As a result, individual Americans had less income to buy imported manufactures. Nevertheless, low-priced British goods flooded urban markets, driving many artisans and war-created textile firms out of business. Responding to artisan protests, New York, Rhode Island, Pennsylvania, and Massachusetts imposed tariffs on imported manufactures.

The financial legacy of the war compounded the problems. Most state governments emerged from the conflict with worthless currencies and big debts. North Carolina owed its creditors \$1.7 million, while Virginia was liable for \$2.7 million in war bonds. Speculators—wealthy merchants and landowners—had purchased many state debt certificates for far less than their face value. Now these shrewd and influential men advocated high taxes so the states could redeem the bonds quickly and at full value.

Major political battles broke out in many states. To avert a radical Regulator movement, such as the one that had swept North Carolina in the late 1760s, and to preserve elite rule, Charles Carroll of Carrollton persuaded other wealthy Maryland landowners to adopt conciliatory economic policies toward yeomen and tenant farmers. Accordingly, the Maryland legislature replaced the customary poll tax, which bore hard on the poor, with a graduated property tax. In South Carolina, hard-pressed farmers won passage of a law that prevented sheriffs from selling seized farm lands to repay debts; instead, creditors had to accept installment payments over a three-year period. South Carolina legislators also assisted debtors by increasing the supply of paper currency. But these prodebtor measures were controversial. David Ramsay, a physician and the future author of the well-known *History of the American Revolution* (1789), assailed the South Carolina legislature for undermining "the just rights of creditors." When the Maryland House of Delegates enacted a profarmer and prodebtor program in 1785 and 1786, it was rejected by a procreditor majority in the more conservative state senate.

As James Madison of Virginia pointed out, these political struggles were not primarily between "the Class with, and Class without, property." The real battle was between wealthy merchants and landowners on the one hand and a larger coalition of middling farm owners, small-scale traders, artisans, and tenant farmers on the other. Economic recession and high taxes pressed hard on debtors, who sought political solutions to their financial problems. Creditors might grow angry over legislation favoring farmers and artisans, but prodebtor laws eased the financial strain and probably prevented a major social upheaval.

Shays's Rebellion. The first armed uprising of the new nation was provoked by the absence of debtor-relief legislation in Massachusetts. When the war ended, eastern Massachusetts merchants and creditors lobbied successfully for high taxes and against paper money. These procreditor policies facilitated rapid repayment of the state's war debt but undermined the fragile finances of farmers in newly settled areas. Creditors and sheriffs hauled delinquent farmers into court, saddled them with high legal fees, and threatened to imprison them for debt or repossess their property. In 1786, residents of western counties called meetings similar to those at which they had repudiated British authority in 1774 and 1775. At these extralegal meetings, they protested against high taxes and aggressive eastern creditors. Meanwhile, bands of angry farmers closed the law courts by force and freed debtors and fellow protesters from jail. Resistance gradually grew into a full-scale revolt. When the legislature continued to ignore their demands, hundreds of farmers in western and central Massachusetts organized an army, under the leadership of Daniel Shays, a former Continental army captain, and prepared to use force to resist state authority.

Daniel Shays and Job Shattuck

"Liberty is still the object I have in view," a Shaysite declared, but the former radical Sam Adams would have none of it: "The man who dares to rebel against the laws of a republic ought to suffer death." Shattuck was sentenced to death for treason but then pardoned; Shays fled to New York State where he died in 1821, still a poor farmer. (National Portrait Gallery)

Shays's Rebellion, as a struggle against high taxes and nonlocal political control, resembled the American resistance movements between 1763 and 1775. "The people have turned against their teachers the doctrines which were inculcated to effect the late revolution," complained the conservative Massachusetts political leader Fisher Ames. Radical Patriots were no less troubled. As Samuel Adams put it, "those Men, who . . . would lessen the Weight of Government lawfully exercised must be Enemies to our happy Revolution and Common Liberty."

To preserve its authority, the Massachusetts legislature passed a Riot Act outlawing illegal assemblies. With the financial support of nervous eastern merchants, Governor James Bowdoin was able to equip a strong fighting force to put down the rebellion. At Bowdoin's request, the Confederation Congress prepared to dispatch an additional 1,300 soldiers, but a national army was not needed. Shays's army dwindled away during the winter of 1786–1787, falling victim to freezing weather and inadequate supplies. Bowdoin's military force easily dispersed the rebels and state authority was restored.

Though the rebellion collapsed, the discontent that caused it was not so easily suppressed. Massachusetts voters turned Governor Bowdoin and other established leaders out of office, and farmers in New York, northern Pennsylvania, New Hampshire, and Vermont (still a separate republic) grew increasingly restless. British officials in Canada predicted the imminent demise of the United States. Many Americans saw in the economic crisis and mounting social unrest a threat to the very existence of the new republic.

The Constitution of 1787

In a great burst of intellectual and political energy, the states implemented new constitutions between 1776 and 1780. This great task completed, Americans turned their creative talents to a second pressing issue: how to distribute power between the states and the central government. After a decade of efforts to revise the Articles of Confederation and two years of intense debate over a new charter, American politicians produced a constitution that dramatically strengthened the authority of the national government.

The Rise of a Nationalist Faction

Shays's Rebellion was more important for its political impact than for anything the uprising actually accomplished. It prompted leaders with a national perspective to redouble their efforts to create a stronger central government. Prominent among the nationalists were military officers, diplomats, and officials who had served in the Continental Congress, experiences that made their political outlook more national, rather than state or local. General Washington, financier Robert Morris, diplomats Benjamin Franklin, John Jay, and John Adams were all advocates of strong national policies on issues presently controlled by the states, such as tariffs and tax revenues.

Nationalists had been trying to enhance the powers of the Confederation government since 1781, with little success. Key commercial states in the North—New York, Massachusetts, Pennsylvania—had devised their own trade policies, imposing protective tariffs. Proposals to place trade in the hands of Congress ran afoul of regional interests: southern planters wanted free trade with Europe, whereas northern merchants, artisans, and manufacturers called for protective tariffs and preferential treatment for American ships.

Nationalist leaders were particularly troubled by the poverty of the Confederation government. The refusal by Rhode Island and New York to levy a national import duty and the decision by other states to assume much of the national debt had completely undermined Robert Morris's scheme to prop up the Confederation. Without tax revenue or state contributions, Congress was unable to pay the interest on the foreign debt. To many nationalists, the American republic seemed on the verge of collapse. "I am really more distressed by the posture of our public affairs, than I ever was by the most gloomy appearances during the war," confessed William Livingston of New Jersey. Livingston's remarks summed up a decade of frustration for the nationalists. The "stubborn Dignity" of the states, another nationalist complained, "will never permit a federal Government to exist."

By 1786 nationalists had yet another reason for concern—the financial weakness and prodebtor policies of the states. Legislatures in Virginia and other southern states were granting tax relief to various groups of citizens, thus diminishing public revenue and delaying redemption of the state debt. Public creditors feared their bonds would become worthless because, as Charles Lee of Virginia lamented, taxpayers had been led to believe "they will never be compelled to pay." The sanctity of private debts was also in jeopardy, since many state governments approved some form of relief for debtors—staying the collection of private debts or exempting personal property from seizure. Four states had gone much further, forcing merchants and creditors to accept depreciated paper currency in payment for debts. "The debtor interest . . . operates in all the forms of injustice & oppression," a South Carolina creditor complained. "While men are madly accumulating enormous debts, their legislators are making provisions for their nonpayment." The nationalists added these concerns to their agenda. Now they wanted not only to shore up the fiscal strength of the central government but also to give it the power to correct what James Madison of Virginia, in an important memorandum of 1787, would call the "Vices of the Political System of the United States."

The nationalists took the initiative in 1786, when Madison persuaded the Virginia legislature to call a commercial convention in Annapolis, Maryland, to discuss tariff and taxation policies. When only twelve delegates from five states showed up, a new meeting was proposed in Philadelphia, to undertake a broad review of the responsibilities and powers of the Confederation. News of Shays's Rebellion underscored the need for action; nationalists in Congress were afraid that western farmers in other states and along the frontier would foment a social revolution. In January 1787, nationalists won passage of a Congressional resolution supporting the revision of the Articles of Confederation to make them "adequate to the exigencies of government and the preservation of the Union." To many nationalists, the Philadelphia meeting seemed the last opportunity to save the republic. "Nothing but the adoption of some efficient plan from the Convention," a fellow Virginian wrote to James Madison, "can prevent anarchy first & civil convulsions afterwards."

The Philadelphia Convention

The Philadelphia convention began in May 1787. Fifty-five delegates attended, representing every state except Rhode Island, whose legislature opposed any increase in central authority. Some members, such as Benjamin Franklin of Pennsylvania, had been leaders of the independence movement. Others, including George Washington and Robert Morris, had come to prominence during the war. Most were merchants, slaveholding planters or "monied men"; there were no artisans, no westerners, no tenants, and only a solitary yeoman farmer.

Several of the most famous Patriots missed the convention. John Adams and Thomas Jefferson were in Europe, serving as the American ministers to Britain and France. Thomas Paine was also in Europe, and his fellow radical Samuel Adams was not chosen as a delegate by the Massachusetts legislature. The Virginia firebrand Patrick Henry was selected but refused to attend because he favored a limited national government. Their places were taken by capable younger men, such as James Madison and Alexander Hamilton. Both were nationalists, committed to the creation of a central government that, as Hamilton put it, would protect the republic from "the imprudence of democracy" in the state legislatures.

Many of the delegates had nationalist sympathies, stemming from their opposition to the prodebtor financial policies of the state governments. As the historian Charles A. Beard pointed out in *An Economic Interpretation of the Constitution of the United States* (1913), the Philadelphia convention was filled with men who supported procreditor factions in their own states. The delegates therefore shared the goal of a stronger central government—one that would curb what Madison called the "vicious" character of state legislation, "base and selfish measures, masked by pretexts of public good and apparent expediency." They differed only in the means by which to accomplish this goal.

Portrait of James Madison, 1805–1807, by Gilbert Stuart
An intellectual, Madison was also a successful politician, especially in the decade after 1785—when he helped to enact the Virginia Statute of Religious Liberty, to write and ratify the Constitution of 1787, to win passage of the Bill of Rights, and to found the Democratic-Republican party. (Bowdoin College Museum of Art)

The Virginia Plan. The delegates began the convention by electing Washington as the presiding officer and deciding to deliberate behind closed doors in order to forestall popular opposition. (In fact, Americans knew little about the proceedings of the convention until the 1840s, when Madison's notebooks were discovered and published.) They agreed that each state would have one vote at the convention, as in the Confederation, and that a majority would decide an issue. Then the delegates exceeded their mandate to revise the Articles of Confederation and began to create a completely different constitutional framework. They took this extra legal step when they agreed to consider the Virginia Plan, a scheme devised by James Madison that called for a truly national government.

Madison arrived in Philadelphia determined to fashion a new political order. He had graduated from Princeton, where he read classical and modern political theory, and had served in both the Confederation Congress and the Virginia assembly. His experience in Virginia convinced him of the "narrow ambition" of many state political leaders and their lack of public virtue. He wanted to design a national government that would curb the spirit of faction and ensure the rule of men of high character.

The Virginia Plan differed from the Articles of Confederation in two crucial respects. First, it rejected state sovereignty in favor of the "supremacy of national authority." In Madison's scheme, the central government had the power "to legislate in all cases to which the separate States are incompetent" and to overturn state laws. Second, it called for a *national* republic that drew its authority directly from all the people of the United States. They would vote directly for some of its officials, who would, in turn, have direct power over them. As Madison explained, the new central government would bypass the states and operate directly "on the individuals composing them."

The Virginia Plan also applied to the national government the lessons in republican political theory learned from constitution making in the states. It implemented the doctrine of the separation of powers by calling for a government of three parts: a lower house elected by the voters, an upper house elected by the lower house, and an executive and judiciary chosen by the entire legislature.

This constitutional innovation would increase the power of the national government, since, with the people directly represented in the lower house, it would have a stronger case for imposing taxes. It would increase the leverage of the larger states as well, since representation in the lower house was based on population. Delegates from the less populous states rejected this scheme out of hand, arguing that it would give a few large states control of the entire central government. The populous states would "crush the small ones whenever they stand in the way of their ambitious or interested views," proclaimed a delegate from Delaware.

To protect their interests, small-state delegates rallied behind a plan devised by William Paterson, the former attorney general of New Jersey. The New Jersey Plan had many nationalist aspects: it would transform the Confederation by giving the central government the power to raise revenue, control commerce, and make binding requisitions upon the states. However, it would protect state power by allowing each state one vote in a unicameral legislature, as in the Articles of Confederation. Of course, this provision made the New Jersey Plan unacceptable to delegates from the larger states. After a month of debate, a bare majority of the states voted to accept the Virginia Plan as the basis for negotiations.

The decision to commit the convention to a new constitutional structure changed the course of American history. Although two New York delegates walked out in protest, the rest redoubled their efforts. They met six days a week during the hot, humid summer of 1787, debating high principles and working through a multitude of technical details. As experienced and realistic politicians, the delegates knew their plan had to be acceptable to existing political factions and powerful social groups. Pierce Butler of South Carolina expressed it by drawing on a classical Greek precedent: "We must follow the example of Solon, who gave the Athenians not the best government he could devise but the best they would receive."

The Great Compromise. Representation remained the central problem. To satisfy all the states, large and small, the Connecticut delegates suggested changing the Virginia Plan so that the upper house, or Senate, would have two members from each state, regardless of its size. In the lower chamber, the House of Representatives, seats would be apportioned on the basis of population, determined every ten years by a national census. Delegates from the large states accepted this Great Compromise, but only after bitter debate; it seemed to them less a compromise than a victory for the smaller states.

Having resolved the major issue that divided them, the delegates quickly settled a series of other matters, many involving the interests of the existing state governments. One delegate objected to a proposal to extend the national judiciary into the states, declaring that "the states will revolt at such encroachments." The convention therefore defined the judicial power of the United States in broad terms and vested it "in one supreme Court"; but it stopped short of establishing lower national courts within the states, leaving that thorny issue to the new national legislature. The convention also decided against imposing a nationwide freehold property qualification for voting in national elections. "Eight or nine states have extended the right of suffrage beyond the freeholders," George Mason of Virginia pointed out. "What will people there say if they should be disfranchised?"

Ultimately, the delegates devised ingenious ways to give the states a prominent role in the new constitutional structure. For example, they placed the selection of the president, the chief executive official, in the hands of an *electoral college* to be chosen on a state-by-state basis. The delegates also specified that state legislatures, not the voters at large, would elect the members of the Senate. By giving the state governments an important role in the new system, the delegates hoped those governments would accept the reduction of their sovereign power.

Compromise Over Slavery. Although the differences between the large and small states dominated the convention's debates, another kind of division, a regional or *sectional* division between the North and South on the slavery issue, also began to emerge. Although no one proposed the abolition of slavery, Gouverneur Morris of New York did take the floor to condemn it as "a nefarious institution." Debate was silenced when John Rutledge of South Carolina reminded his colleagues that "the true question at present is whether the Southern states shall or shall not be parties to the Union."

To maintain national unity, the delegates treated slavery as a political question, not as a moral issue. They won the support of white planters in Georgia and the Carolinas by providing a legal mechanism whereby owners could reclaim slaves who had taken refuge in "free" states. They also denied Congress the power to regulate the importation of slaves for twenty years following ratification. To mollify antislavery sentiment in the northern states, the delegates agreed that the slave trade could thereafter be abolished by legislative action.

A second sectional compromise resolved the slavery-related issues of taxation and representation. Southern delegates wanted to include slaves in a state's population for the purpose of determining representation in the House of Representatives. Northerners objected, arguing that propertyless slaves, lacking the vote, were not full members of the republic. The convention finally agreed that for the purposes of representation slaves (carefully referred to in the Constitution as "all other Persons") would be counted as three-fifths of a free person.

National Power. Having allayed the concerns of the small states and the slave states, the delegates proceeded to fulfill their goal of creating a powerful, procreditor national government. The finished document declared that the Constitution and all national legislation and treaties made under its authority were to be the supreme law of the land. It gave the national government broad powers over taxation, military defense, and external commerce, as well as the authority to make all laws that were "necessary and proper" to implement these and other provisions. It also created a strong president—with veto power, military authority as commander-in-chief, and a considerable number of patronage appointments. To establish the fiscal authority of the central government, the Constitution mandated that the United States would honor the existing national debt. Under the new charter, the states lost the power to issue money, which protected creditors from the fluctuations of paper currency. And state legislatures were forbidden to enact any "Law impairing the Obligation of Contracts," thus prohibiting debtor relief legislation and encouraging the expansion of capitalist enterprise.

The proposed Constitution was not a "perfect production," Benjamin Franklin admitted on September 17, 1787, as he urged the forty-one delegates still present to sign it. Yet the great diplomat confessed his astonishment "to find this system approaching so near to perfection as it does." His colleagues apparently agreed; all but three signed the document. Their handiwork would now be judged by their fellow Americans.

The Debate over Ratification

The procedures for ratifying the new Constitution were controversial. The convention hesitated to submit its nationalist scheme of government for the unanimous consent of the state legislatures, as required by the Articles of Confederation, since it would undoubtedly be rejected by Rhode Island and possibly by a few other states. The delegates therefore specified a quite different procedure. The Constitution would go into effect upon ratification by special conventions in at least nine of the thirteen states. Because of its nationalist sympathies, the Confederation Congress winked at this extralegal procedure and sent the new Constitution to the states. More surprisingly, the state legislatures complied, calling for the election of delegates to state ratification conventions.

A great national debate began almost immediately. The nationalists seized the initiative with two bold moves. They called themselves "Federalists," a term that suggested a loose, decentralized system of government and thus partially obscured their nationalist goals. And they undertook a coordinated political campaign, publishing dozens of pamphlets and newspaper articles. In this literature they argued that the proposed Constitution would remedy acknowledged defects of the Articles of Confederation and create a strong and prosperous union.

The Antifederalists. The opponents of the Constitution became known as the Antifederalists. They came from diverse backgrounds and were less well organized. Some, like Governor George Clinton of New York, enjoyed great power and patronage in their states and feared losing it. Others came from the ranks of agrarian democrats who had long opposed merchants and creditors. "These lawyers and men of learning and monied men," argued a Massachusetts farmer, "expect to be managers of this Constitution and get all the power and all the money into their own hands and then they will swallow up all of us little folks . . . just as the whale swallowed up Jonah."

Many highly educated Americans became Antifederalists for ideological reasons. They feared that a strong national administration would restore the worst features of British rule—high taxes, an oppressive bureaucracy, and a standing army controlled by a tyrant—thus ending the republican experiment in popular government. George Mason of Virginia, one of the three delegates who refused to sign the Constitution, argued that it was "totally subversive of every principle which has hitherto governed us. This power is calculated to annihilate totally the state governments." Antifederalists had no alternative program to offer, but they maintained that keeping the old Articles was preferable to adopting a new document with such obvious defects.

Antifederalist arguments were based on the fear of tyranny and elite rule. Melancton Smith of New York warned that the Constitution's provision for large electoral districts would inevitably lead to the concentration of power in the hands of a few wealthy upper-class men, since only such men would be prominent enough to be elected. Yet it was well known, Smith maintained, that "a representative body, composed principally of respectable yeomanry, is the best possible security to liberty." Patrick Henry of Virginia called attention to the immense taxing power of the central government. "A great and mighty President" would "be supported in extravagant munificence," he predicted; "the whole of our property may be taken by this American government, by laying what taxes they please, and suspending our laws at their pleasure."

The Antifederalists' fears stemmed from their belief, following the argument of the French political philosopher Montesquieu, that republican institutions were suitable only for cities or small states. "No extensive empire can be governed on republican principles," James Winthrop of Massachusetts declared. Like most Antifederalists, Winthrop wanted the new nation to be a collection of small sovereign republics, tied together only for purposes of trade and defense—not the "United States" but the "States United."

The Federalist. In New York, where ratification was hotly contested, James Madison, John Jay, and Alexander Hamilton countered these arguments in a series of newspaper articles called *The Federalist.* These ardent nationalists stressed the need for a strong government to conduct foreign affairs and insisted that it would not foster domestic tyranny. Power within the national government was divided among a president, a bicameral legislature, and a judiciary, they pointed out, and each branch of government would "check and balance" the others, thus preserving liberty. In his *Thoughts on Government*, John Adams had adapted this argument from Montesquieu's well-known analysis of British institutions, *The Spirit of the Laws* (1748).

Internal checks were one guarantee of liberty, James

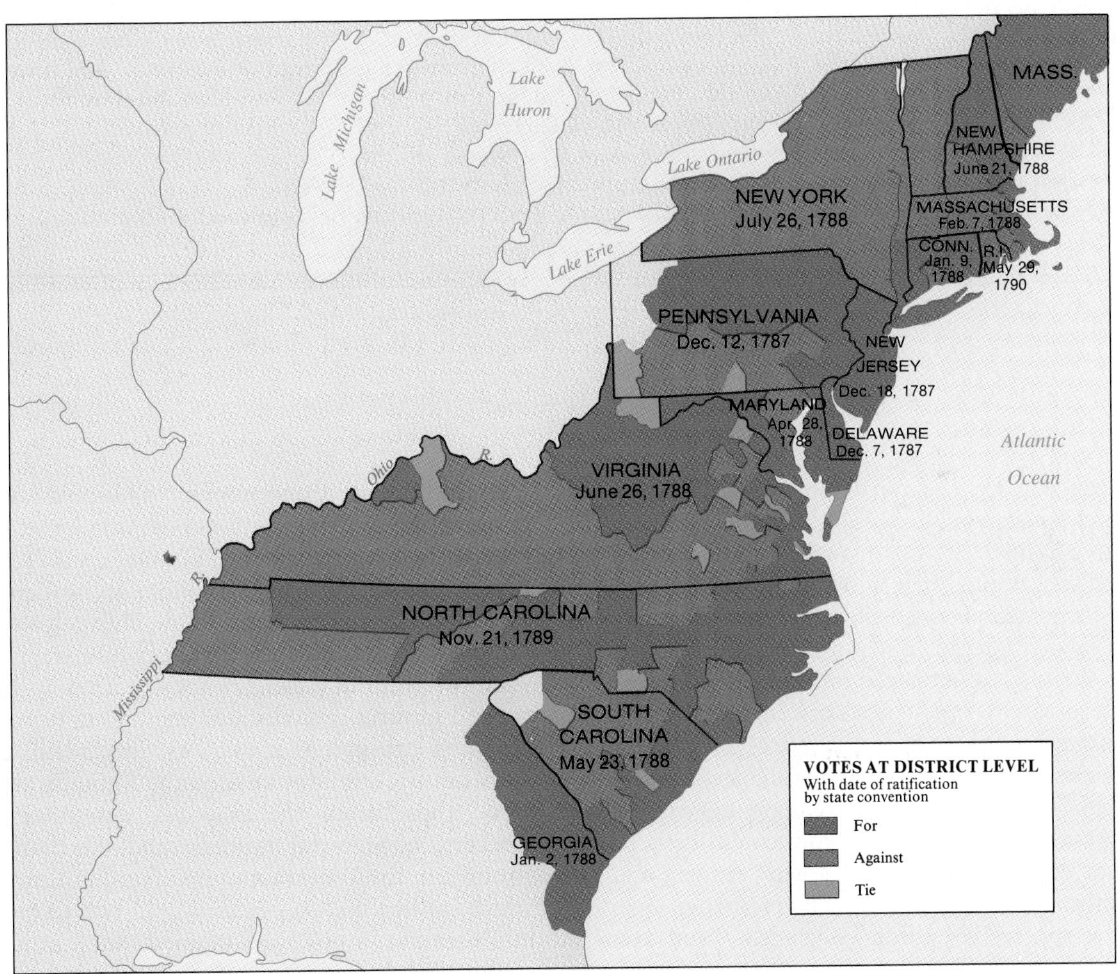

MAP 7.2

Ratifying the Constitution

In 1907 the geographer Owen Libby plotted the votes of the state ratification conventions on a map. He noted that most delegates from seaboard or commercial farming districts favored the Constitution, while those from backcountry areas opposed it. Subsequent research has confirmed Libby's socioeconomic interpretation in North and South Carolina and Massachusetts; however, other factors influenced delegates in some states, such as Georgia, where the Constitution was ratified unanimously.

AMERICAN VOICES

A Farmer Praises the Constitution *Jonathan Smith*

Scores of ordinary men—middling farmers, shopkeepers, artisans—sat alongside their social betters in the state ratifying conventions; their opinions and votes were often crucial to the outcome. Here a farmer explains his support of the Constitution to the Massachusetts convention.

Mr. President, I am a plain man, and get my living by the plough. I am not used to speak in public . . . . I have lived in a part of the country where I have known the worth of good government by the want of it. There was a black cloud [Shays's Rebellion] that rose in the east last winter, and spread over the west. It brought on a state of anarchy that let to tyranny. . . . People, I say, took up arms, and then, if you went to speak to them, you had the musket of death presented to your breast. They would rob you of your property, threaten to burn your houses . . . .

When I saw this Constitution, I found that it was a cure for these disorders. I got a copy of it and read it over and over. I had been a member of the convention to form our own state constitution, and had learnt something of the checks and balances of power; and I found them all here . . . .

I don't think the worse of the Constitution because lawyers, and men of learning, and moneyed men are fond of it. [They] are all embarked in the same cause with us, and we must all swim or sink together. Suppose two or three of you had been at the pains to break up a piece of rough land, and sow it with wheat—would you let it lie waste because you could not agree what sort of fence to make? There is a time to sow and a time to reap. We sowed our seed when we sent men to the federal convention. Now is the harvest; now is the time to reap the fruit of our labor. And if we won't do it now, I am afraid we never shall have another opportunity.

Source: Jonathan Elliot, *The Debates on the Federal Constitution*(1836), II, 101–2.

Madison argued in *The Federalist*, No. 10, but the sheer size of the national republic would be an even greater deterrent to tyranny. It was "sown in the nature of man," Madison wrote, that individuals would seek power and form factions to advance their own interests. Indeed, "a landed interest, a manufacturing interest, a mercantile interest, a moneyed interest, with many lesser interests, grow up of necessity in civilized nations." The task of government in a free society, the young Virginian continued with true brilliance, was not to suppress these groups but to prevent any one faction from becoming dominant. This end could best be achieved not in a small republic, as Montesquieu and James Winthrop had maintained, but in a large one. "Extend the sphere," Madison concluded, "and you take in a greater variety of parties and interests; you make it less probable that a majority of the whole will have a common motive to invade the rights of other citizens."

Madison's hard-headed realism—his emphasis on self-interest as the spring of human conduct—was tempered by a traditional republican belief in public virtue. "I go by this great republican principle," Madison told the Virginia ratifying convention, "that the people have virtue and intelligence to select men of virtue and wisdom"—and, he undoubtedly hoped, to ratify the new Constitution.

The Ratification Conventions. Madison's hopes were tested in the ratifying conventions, which met in twelve states between December 1787 and June 1788. (Rhode Island, again, was the exception; it ratified only in 1790.) Unlike the delegates to the Philadelphia convention, the delegates to the state caucuses represented a wide spectrum of American society. They included untutored farmers and educated gentlemen, middling artisans and prosperous merchants. In general, delegates from the backcountry favored the Antifederalist cause, while those from the seacoast, representing urban workers, commercial farmers, and merchants, stood strongly in the Federalist camp. Thus, in Pennsylvania, which ratified the Constitution by a two to one margin in December, a coalition of merchants, artisans, and commercial farmers from Philadelphia and the vicinity spearheaded the Federalist victory. Other early Federalist successes came in the smaller or less populous states. Delaware and New Jersey ratified the Constitution in December 1787, and Georgia and Connecticut quickly followed. In each case, the delegates hoped that a stronger national government would offset the power of large neighboring states.

The first real test came in January 1788 in Massachusetts, one of the most populous states and a hotbed of Antifederalist sentiment. Influential Patriots—including Sam Adams and John Hancock—publicly opposed

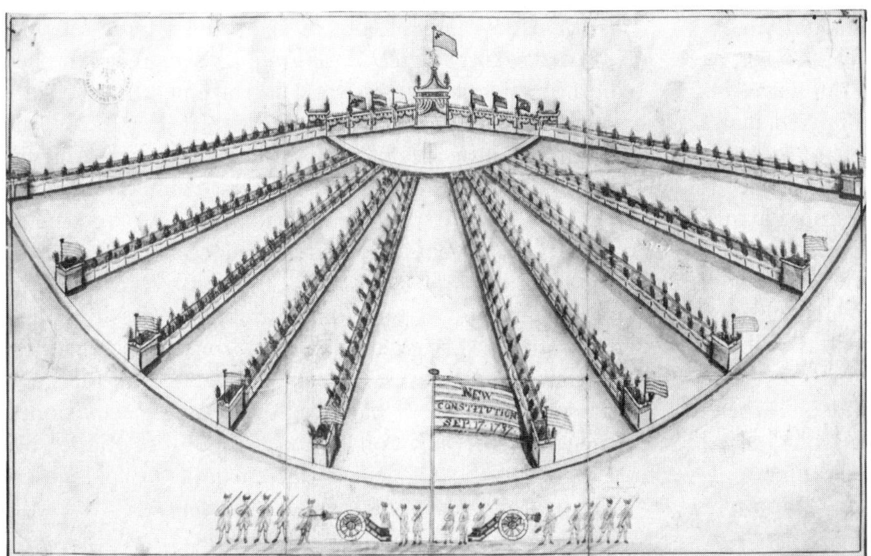

Federalists Celebrate New York's Ratification

Let the banquet begin! Ten long tables radiate outward from the speaker's platform, representing the ten states who, by July 1788, had ratified the new national Constitution. Only Virginia, North Carolina, and Rhode Island had not yet acted.

the new Constitution. When the convention opened, Antifederalists were in the majority, their ranks swelled by Shaysite sympathizers from the west. Astute Federalist politicians persuaded—even coerced—several wavering delegates to change their minds by warning of political chaos, and they won over some of Governor John Hancock's followers by hinting they would support Hancock for the presidency of the United States. Boston artisans, who hoped for tariff protection from British imports, worked on Sam Adams, ultimately persuading him to support ratification. By a close vote of 187 to 168, the Federalists carried the day.

Spring brought Federalist victories in Maryland and South Carolina. When New Hampshire ratified in June (by 57 votes to 47), the required nine states had approved the Constitution. But the outcome was still in doubt, for the powerful states of Virginia and New York had not yet acted. Now Madison, Jay, and Hamilton, writing in *The Federalist*, used their superb rhetorical skills to win over delegates in those key states. In addition, leading Federalists now promised that the Constitution would be amended to include a Bill of Rights. This addressed the most powerful argument of the Antifederalists, that the new national Constitution, unlike most state constitutions, failed to protect basic individual rights, such as the liberty of conscience in religious matters and the right to a jury trial. The expectation that George Washington would be the first president finally inclined many Virginians to support ratification. In the end, the Federalists won a narrow victory in Virginia, 89 votes to 79, and this momentum—as well as New York City's threat to secede from the state and join the union—carried them to victory in New York, by the even smaller margin of 30 votes to 27.

Few Federalists had expected a more resounding victory, given the prejudice against a strong central government during the 1780s. Working against great odds, they had brought about a fundamental change in the American system of government. Their triumph had ideological and social implications as well: the United States Constitution of 1787 represented the resurgence of the traditional political elite and the decline of the yeomanry. At least temporarily, creditors and merchants were in the ascendancy. The Revolutionary Era had come to an end.

The Constitution Implemented

The Constitution gave American political life a new, national dimension. Previously voters had chosen local and state officials; now they elected national officeholders as well. A single political system was beginning to tie together the interests and concerns of Georgia planters, Pennsylvania artisans, Massachusetts merchants, and scores of other social groups.

The men who had devised the Constitution dominated the new national government: Federalists swept the election of 1788. No fewer than 44 of the 91 members of the first United States Congress, which met in 1789, had helped write or ratify the Constitution. Only eight Antifederalists were elected to the House of Representatives; they soon vanished as a coherent political force, leaving behind their suspicion of a national government dominated by an elite. The Constitution specified that "electors" chosen by voters in the various states would select the president and vice-president. As expected, the electors chose George Washington of Virginia as president; John Adams of Massachusetts received the second-highest number of electoral votes and became vice-president. The newly elected officials took up their posts in New York City, the temporary home of the national government.

Washington, the military savior of his country, now became its political father. At fifty-seven years of age, he was a man of great personal dignity and influence. Instinctively cautious, the new president followed many administrative practices of the Confederation government. He asked Congress to reestablish existing executive departments—Foreign Affairs (or State), Finance (or Treasury), and War—but put the administrative bureaucracy under the president's control. The chief executive had the power to appoint major officials, with the consent of the Senate, and to remove them at will. To head the Department of State, Washington chose Thomas Jefferson, a fellow Virginian and an experienced diplomat. For secretary of the treasury, he turned to Alexander Hamilton, a lawyer and a wartime military aide. Washington designated Jefferson, Hamilton, and Secretary of War Henry Knox as his *cabinet*, or body of advisers.

Congress also set about implementing the Constitution. The new national charter created a Supreme Court but left it to Congress to establish lower courts. The Judiciary Act of 1789 created 13 district courts, one for each state, and three circuit courts to hear appeals from the district tribunals, with the final decision remaining in the hands of the Supreme Court. Nationalists insisted on this comprehensive hierarchical system, defeating proposals that would have given state courts jurisdiction over federal issues. In law as in politics, the Federalists wanted national institutions to supersede state institutions and act directly on individual citizens. Moreover, the Judiciary Act permitted appeals from state courts to the Supreme Court on federal issues, thus ensuring that national judges could overturn state tribunals on the interpretation of the Constitution.

The Bill of Rights. The Federalists kept their promise to add a Bill of Rights to the Constitution. Drawing on similar bills in state constitutions, James Madison, now a member of the House of Representatives, submitted nineteen amendments to the first Congress—after carefully weeding out any that would have weakened the national government. Ten amendements received legislative approval and were ratified by the states. Of these first ten amendments to the Constitution, many guaranteed legal procedures, such as the right to a jury trial and freedom from arbitrary arrest; others safeguarded sacred political rights, such as freedom of speech and freedom of assembly. The Tenth Amendment limited the potential authority of the national government by reserving nondelegated powers to the states or the people.

As a political maneuver, the Bill of Rights yielded immediate results, quieting the fears of many Antifederalists and enhancing the legitimacy of the Constitution of 1787. As a constitutional safeguard, the amendments have had a complex history. They always protected rights to life, liberty, and property against actions of the national government, but in 1833 the Supreme Court (in the case of *Barron v. Baltimore*) declared that they did not safeguard rights from infringement by the state governments. Nearly a century later, in the 1920s, the national courts began to use the Fourteenth Amendment (1868) to protect these rights enumerated in the first Ten Amendments against violation by governments at every level—national, state, and local.

The ratification of the Bill of Rights completed the implementation of the Constitution. The president and the Congress had given definite form to the executive, legislative, and judicial departments, creating the intricate mechanism of "balanced" government envisioned by the Philadelphia convention. The Bill of Rights, demanded by the Antifederalists, ensured broad political support for the new national government.

The Political Crisis of the 1790s

Although the new Constitution was in place by 1790, the final decade of the century brought fresh political crises. The Federalists split into two irreconcilable factions over financial policy, and the French Revolution caused rifts over political ideology. The wars of the French Revolution (1792–1801) expanded American trade, bringing substantial profits to farmers and spectacular fortunes to merchants, but they also divided American public opinion between pro-British Federalists and pro-French Republicans. Political conflict culminated in an undeclared naval war against France in the Atlantic and the repression of free speech at home.

The Hamiltonian Program

One of George Washington's most important decisions was his choice of Alexander Hamilton to be secretary of the treasury. Hamilton was an ambitious, self-made man. The son of a Scottish merchant in the West Indies, Hamilton was raised by his mother, Rachel Faucett, after his father abandoned the family. The precocious child learned the ways of trade from his mother, who ran a small store; he was soon apprenticed to a prominent import-export firm. Hamilton moved to the mainland in 1772, after his mother died, and enrolled in King's College in New York. His military abilities and personal charm impressed Washington, who chose him as a personal aide during the war. During the 1780s Hamilton married Elizabeth Schuyler, the daughter of a wealthy Hudson River landowner, and established close connections with the mercantile community, becoming one of the leading lawyers in New York City. At the Philadelphia convention, he had condemned the "amazing violence and turbulence of the democratic spirit" and called for an authoritarian government headed by a

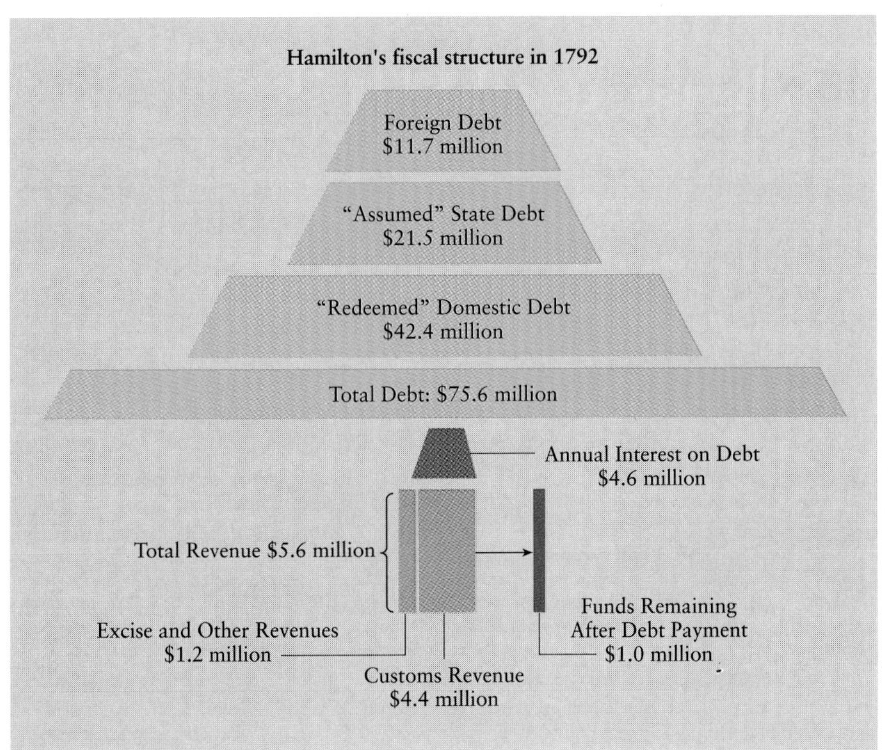

FIGURE 7.2

Hamilton's Fiscal Structure, 1792

Hamilton used excise taxes and customs revenues to defray the annual interest on the debt. He did not pay off the debt, for he wanted to tie wealthy American bondholders to the new national government.

president with nearly monarchical powers. Though he left the convention early, Hamilton championed the work of his fellow delegates in *The Federalist*.

As treasury secretary, Hamilton devised innovative financial policies to overcome the fiscal problems that had bedeviled the Confederation. Not surprisingly, the ambitious program Hamilton presented to Congress favored men of his immediate acquaintance—seaport merchants and financiers. His recommendations took the form of three major reports: on public credit (January 1790), on a national bank (December 1790), and on manufactures (December 1791).

Public Credit. The financial and social implications of Hamilton's "Report on the Public Credit" made it instantly controversial. The report was welcomed by foreign and domestic creditors, because it proposed to redeem at face value the millions of dollars of securities issued by the Confederation government. Redeeming the debt would bolster the faith of monied men in the national government's credit and increase its prestige. It would also give an enormous windfall profit to the speculators among them. For example, in one transaction the Burrell & Burrell merchant house of Boston had paid about $600 for Confederation notes with a face value of $2,500. If these notes were paid off at face value, the Burrells would reap an enormous profit. Hamilton's plan was to have these and other financiers continue in their role as public creditors. He proposed to redeem the old notes with new government securities, which would pay interest at about 4 percent. The creation of this permanent debt would tie the interests of wealthy Americans to the new national government.

Hamilton's scheme reawakened fears of British monopolies and government corruption. Republican ideology warned that wealth—and the luxury that inevitably went with it—undermined public virtue, a danger that seemed particularly clear to leaders from the southern agricultural states. "Money in a state of civilization is power," argued John Taylor of Virginia, who was wary of the rising wealth and power of the northern commercial elite. His thought might have been finished by Patrick Henry, who proclaimed on behalf of the Virginia assembly, that "to erect, and concentrate, and perpetuate a large monied interest, must prove fatal to the existence of American liberty."

But Hamilton ignored these objections and went on to advance a second proposal that favored wealthy creditors over southern planters. He devised an *assumption* plan: the national government would assume all the outstanding war debts of the states. This proposal unleashed a flurry of financial speculation, even an instance of governmental corruption. Before Hamilton announced his assumption plan, Assistant Secretary of the Treasury William Duer used his insider knowledge and bought up the depreciated bonds of the southern states. By the end of 1790, Duer and other northern speculators owned more than half the war bonds of Virginia and the Carolinas, selling them as their value rose.

Secretary of State Jefferson and other southern leaders condemned such shady dealings and the "corrupt squadron of paper dealers" who arranged them.

AMERICAN VOICES

Hamilton's Funding Scheme Attacked, 1790

A Pennsylvania Farmer

Hamilton's plan to redeem at full value the remaining war debt of the Continental Congress roused widespread anger, for most of the money—which would be raised by import duties on goods like tea and sugar—would go to speculators, not to the soldiers and farmers who originally held the certificates.

In a former letter I took notice of the injuries which the proposed funding system will do the soldiers and other original holders of certificates, by compelling them to pay taxes in order to increase the value of certificates in the hands of quartermasters, speculators, and foreigners. The Secretary of the Treasury has declared that these people sold their certificates from choice. This I believe is true only in a few instances. A hungry creditor, a distressed family, or perhaps, in some instances, the want of a meals victuals, drove most of them to the brokers' offices, or compelled them to surrender up their certificates . . . .

This case I shall mention is of a sick soldier, who sold his certificates of £69.7.0 for £3.0.11 to a rich speculator. He went to this speculator after he recovered, and offered to redeem his certificate—but he refused to give it up. Now, can it be right that this poor soldier, every time he sips his bohea tea, or tastes a particle of sugar, should pay a tax to raise £3.0.11 to £67.7.0 in the hands of this speculator?

Thus we see public credit (that much hackneyed and prostituted phrase) must be established at the expense of national justice, gratitude, and humanity . . . .

Would it not be proper for the farmers to unite immediately, and remonstrate against all these evils? They never were in half the danger of being ruined by the British government that they now are by their own.

Had any person told them in the beginning of the war that, after paying the yearly rent of their farms for seven years to carry on this war, at the close of it their farms would only be worth one-fourth of their original cost and value, in consequence of a funding system—is there a farmer that would have embarked in the war? No, there is not. Why then should we be deceived, duped, defrauded, and ruined by our new rulers?

Source: Pennsylvania Gazette, February 3, 1790.

Concerned members of Congress pointed out that some states, such as Virginia and Maryland, had already levied high taxes in order to pay their war debts; now they would be taxed to pay the debts of other states as well—mostly for the benefit of rich northern speculators. To win support for assumption, Hamilton struck a deal. He agreed to support a plan proposed by members of Congress from Maryland and Virginia to lay out a special "district" as the nation's capital, as provided for in the Constitution, along the banks of the Potomac River. In return, they gave him the votes he needed to secure passage of his assumption plan in the House of Representatives.

This bargain only sharpened fears of what Hamilton was up to. James Madison had already questioned the morality of Hamilton's redemption and assumption proposals, since the financial rewards would go to the present holders of Confederation securities and not the original owners—the thousands of shopkeepers, farmers, and soldiers who had accepted government certificates during the dark days of the war. Madison therefore presented Congress with legislation that would give present holders only "the highest price which has prevailed in the market," with the remaining funds going to the original owner. His scheme, Madison argued, "will do more real justice . . . than any other expedient."

Madison's intervention was unavailing. Nearly half the members of the House of Representatives owned Continental or Confederation securities; they were not about to share their profits. The House defeated Madison's proposal by a solid margin of 36 to 13. Madison now became an avowed opponent of Hamilton's economic program—and he was not alone. By way of protest, an angry citizen composed an ode, "On the Rejection of Mr. Madison's Motion":

> A soldier's pay are rags and fame,
> A wooden leg—a deathless name.
> To specs, both *in* and *out* of Cong.
> The four and six per cents belong.

The Bank of the United States. Hamilton outraged Madison again by asking Congress to charter a national financial institution, the Bank of the United States. The

Bank's stock would be owned by both private investors and the national government. The Bank would make loans to merchants, handle government funds, and issue financial notes, thus providing a respected medium of exchange for the specie-starved American economy. These considerable benefits persuaded a majority of both houses to enact the bank bill and send it to President Washington for his approval.

At this critical juncture, Secretary of State Thomas Jefferson joined ranks with Madison against Hamilton. Jefferson believed that Hamilton's scheme for a national bank was unconstitutional. "The incorporation of a Bank," Jefferson argued in private conversation with President Washington, was not "delegated to the United States by the Constitution." Adopting a *strict* interpretation of the national charter, Jefferson maintained that the central government had only the limited powers explicitly assigned to it in the document.

In response, Hamilton articulated a *loose* interpretation of the Constitution. Article I, Section 8, empowered Congress to make "all Laws which shall be necessary and proper" to carry out the Constitution. So, in Hamilton's view, "if the *end* be clearly comprehended within any of the specified powers, and if the measure is not forbidden by any particular provision of the Constitution, it may safely be deemed to come within the compass of national authority." Washington agreed with Hamilton and signed the legislation creating the bank, which was to have its headquarters in Philadelphia.

The Report on Manufactures. As an advocate of an economically powerful nation, Hamilton had a vision of America as self-sufficient in manufactures. In 1790 he appointed Tench Coxe, the secretary of the Pennsylvania Manufacturing Society, as an assistant secretary of the treasury. With Coxe's aid, Hamilton prepared a "Report on Manufactures," which provided the first comprehensive survey of American manufacturing and, more important, presented a coherent rationale for an American mercantilist system. In the report, Hamilton took issue with the view put forth by the Scottish economist Adam Smith in his influential treatise *The Wealth of Nations*, published the same year as the Declaration of Independence. Smith had condemned traditional state-directed mercantilist regulations, arguing that they subsidized inefficient producers and inhibited personal enterprise. Instead he had advocated a *laissez faire* (leave alone) system of political economy, in which the demand for goods would determine their production and price. Following this logic, Smith suggested that the United States raise farm products—which it could do more cheaply than European countries—and exchange them for foreign manufactures, which were less expensive than American products.

Hamilton disputed Smith's reasoning, pointing out that American production costs could be altered in two ways: by technological innovation or by public policy. If American manufacturers were given tariff protection or direct subsidies—what Hamilton called "the patronage of government"—they could compete with European producers. Hamilton did impose a modest tariff as a way to raise government revenue, but effective national support for manufacturing came only in the 1820s, when a new generation of politicians took up his ideas. Hamilton also joined with Coxe to create a private Society for Establishing Useful Manufactures to encourage merchants to invest in technologically innovative factories, but that too had little success.

Factions and Taxes. As Washington began his second four-year term as president in 1793, Hamilton's financial measures split the national legislature into irreconcilable factions. Hamilton had formed political alliances in Congress to support his program, and now Madison organized the opposition. Jefferson, who resigned as secretary of state at the end of 1793, sided with Madison. "Mr. Madison, co-operating with Mr. Jefferson," Hamilton complained, "is at the head of a faction decidedly hostile to me . . . and subversive of good government." At first these factions divided along North-South lines. For example, northern congressmen had supported the Bank of the United States by a margin of 33 to 1, while southern representatives had opposed it by 19 to 6. By the elections of 1794, the factions had a more diverse makeup and had acquired names—Federalists supported Hamilton, Democratic-Republicans followed Madison and Jefferson.

Two Visions of America

Thomas Jefferson and Alexander Hamilton confront each other here—as they did during the 1790s. Jefferson was pro-French; Hamilton, pro-British. Jefferson favored farmers and artisans; Hamilton supported merchants and financiers. Jefferson believed in democracy and rule by legislative majorities; Hamilton argued for a strong executive and for judicial review.

NEW TECHNOLOGY *Technology and Republican Values*

In 1805 the young American scientist Benjamin Silliman visited the industrial city of Manchester, England. Silliman was impressed by the great factories, "the wonder of the world and the pride of England," but disturbed by the condition of the workers—"at best an imbecile people," degraded by the conditions in which they lived and worked. "Heaps of dung, rubble from buildings, putrid, stagnant pools are found here and there among the houses, and a sort of black smoke covers the city," another visitor reported. "Under this half daylight 300,000 human beings are ceaselessly at work . . . the crunching wheels of machinery, the shriek of steam from boilers, the regular beat of the looms, the heavy rumble of the carts, these are the noises from which you can never escape."

Silliman contrasted this dismal scene with a peaceful image of rural America: "fields and forests, in which pure air . . . and simple manners, give vigour to the limbs, and a healthful aspect to the face." Were the wonders of English technology, he asked, worth "the physical and . . . moral evils which they produce?"

No American struggled harder with this question than Thomas Jefferson. "Those who labour in the earth are the chosen people of God," Jefferson wrote in his *Notes on Virginia* (1785), and he remained committed to the moral superiority of a society of yeoman farm families. Yet Jefferson also knew that "a people who are *entirely* dependent upon foreigners for food or clothes, must always be subject to them." Even before the Embargo of 1807 and the War of 1812 convinced him of the necessity of American manufacturing, Jefferson advocated the use of advanced farm technology. He introduced cast-iron plows and improved threshing machines on his Monticello, Virginia, plantation, and rotated crops according to the latest scientific theory.

The Household as Factory

Jefferson championed manufacturing on the plantation as well. As early as 1796 he bought an iron-cutting machine to make nails and, by employing a dozen slave men, made ten thousand nails a day. By 1812 Jefferson had built two water-powered mills at another plantation and equipped his Monticello slaves to manufacture textiles. He and other Americans, the former president boasted to a European friend, "have reduced the large and expensive machinery for most things to the compass of a private family . . . . I need 2,000 yards of linen,

Meanwhile, Hamilton pushed for the enactment of the final element of his financial system: national taxes. Taxes on domestic and foreign commodities were needed to pay interest charges on the permanent debt. At Hamilton's insistence, Congress imposed a variety of domestic excise taxes, including a duty on spirits, such as whiskey, distilled within the United States. It also revised the schedule of tariffs. In 1789, Congress had imposed a tax of 50 cents a ton on foreign ships entering American ports and a duty of 5 to 15 percent on the value of imported goods. Hamilton did not propose drastic increases—high "protective" tariffs that would exclude foreign goods—because that would have hurt his merchant allies and cut revenues. But he won Congressional approval for a modest increase in customs duties. As a result, customs revenue rose steadily, providing about 90 percent of the national government's income from 1790 to 1820 and ensuring the financial success of Hamilton's redemption and assumption programs.

The "dark Satanic mills" of industrial England

cotton and woolen yearly, to cloth my family [of slaves], which this machinery, costing $150 only, and worked by two women and two girls, will more than furnish."

Here, then, was Jefferson's way of avoiding the "dark satanic mills" of Manchester. Each American household would become a small factory, using the labor of "women, children, and invalids" to enhance the independence of American freehold farmers. For Jefferson, the key was democratic ownership of the means of industrial production.

Jefferson's vision was noble and not unrealistic. America did become a nation of household producers between 1790 and 1820 (see Chapter 9). Hundreds of rural families made nails; thousands manufactured shoes and textiles for their own use and for market sale.

Yet Jefferson's vision was limited in scope and flawed by internal contradictions. Was the slave labor that made his nails more moral or republican than wage labor in Manchester factories? And, over the long run, could household producers compete successfully with the water- and steam-driven factories owned by wealthy capitalists?

A candid observer must answer "no" to both questions. Jefferson had addressed the crucial issues of the social organization of production and who should benefit financially from it, but he was unable to show how technological advance could be made compatible with the republican value of liberty and the democratic ideal of equality. That question remains unresolved to this day.

Hamilton's design was now complete. His bold, if controversial, policies had given the national government new financial powers and protected the investments and commercial interests of the merchant class.

Jefferson's Vision

Few southern planters or western farmers shared Hamilton's enthusiasm for his version of the American future, and James Madison and Thomas Jefferson spoke for them. Jefferson deplored the idea of an urban industrial society, and his views were grounded in personal observation. He had visited the manufacturing regions of England and seen the masses of propertyless laborers there. These workers, poor and dependent on their employers, lacked the independence required to sustain a republican polity.

Jefferson's vision of the American future was more agrarian and more democratic. Although he had grown up as a privileged and well-educated slaveowner among the Virginia elite, he understood the values and needs of yeomen farmers and other ordinary white Americans. Jefferson was well read in architecture, natural history, scientific farming, and political theory, and he embraced the optimistic spirit of the Enlightenment, declaring his firm conviction in the "improvability of the human race."

Jefferson devoted his political career to the creation of a democratic republic. In the Declaration of Independence, he had proclaimed the primacy of "life, liberty, and the pursuit of happiness," and he gave form and substance to this vision in his *Notes on Virginia* (1785). "Those who labor in the earth are the chosen people of God," Jefferson declared; independent yeomen farmers formed the very soul of the republic. When Jefferson drafted the Ordinance of 1784, he pictured the west settled with families who would produce bountiful harvests. Their grain and meat would feed European nations, who "would manufacture and send us in exchange our clothes and other comforts." Jefferson hoped that westward expansion and foreign commerce would remedy two of the worst features of eighteenth-century agriculture—widespread tenancy in the South and subdivided farms in New England—while preserving its best features. He wanted to ban slavery from the territories (though he did not advocate abolishing it in the South), so that the American west would become a vigorous, incorruptible society of independent white yeoman farm families.

War and Politics

Events in Europe pulled the United States out of the economic doldrums of the 1780s, creating opportunities for both Hamiltonian merchants and Jeffersonian farmers. The French Revolution began in 1789; four years later, the French republican government went to war against a British-led coalition of monarchical states. With the war disrupting European farming, wheat prices in Europe leapt from five to eight shillings a bushel and remained at that level for twenty years. Farmers in the Chesapeake and in the Middle Atlantic states capitalized on the situation, increasing their grain exports to Europe and reaping substantial profits.

Simultaneously, a boom in cotton exports revived the southern economy. Americans had expanded cotton production during the War of Independence in order to make their own textiles. Subsequently, the mechanization of cloth production in England created a huge market for raw cotton. During the 1790s the invention of gins—machines that combed seeds from cotton fibers—cut the cost of production dramatically (see Chapter 8). Soon the annual value of American cotton exports outstripped that of tobacco, the traditional southern export crop. As Jefferson had hoped, European markets brought high prices and prosperity to many American planters and farmers.

American merchants profited even more handsomely from the war. President Washington issued a Proclamation of Neutrality, enabling United States citizens to trade legally with the belligerents on both sides. As neutral carriers able to pass through the British naval blockade of the French coastline, American merchant ships took over the lucrative trade between France and its West Indian sugar islands. The American merchant fleet became one of the largest in the world, increasing from 355,000 tons in 1790 to more than 1.1 million tons in 1808. Commercial earnings rose spectacularly, averaging $20 million annually in the 1790s—twice the value of cotton and tobacco exports.

After two decades of stagnation, American ports came alive. Shipowners invested part of their rising profits in new vessels, providing work for thousands of shipwrights, sailmakers, laborers, and seamen. Hundreds of carpenters, masons, and cabinetmakers found work building warehouses and elegant Federal-style town houses for newly affluent merchants. New buildings went up in Philadelphia, a European visitor reported: "chiefly of red brick, and in general three stories high. A great number of private houses have marble steps to the street door, and in other respects are finished in a style of elegance." Real estate values jumped,

Urban Affluence
New York merchants built large town houses and furnished them with fine pieces of furniture. John Rubens Smith's painting *The Shop and Warehouse of Duncan Phyfe,* illustrates the success of America's most skilled artisan entreprenuer. (The Metropolitan Museum of Art)

Federalist Gentry

The artist Ralph Earl captured the importance of the Ellsworths in 1792 by giving them an aristocratic demeanor and by prominently displaying their mansion (in the window). Oliver Ellsworth served as Chief Justice of the United States (1796-1800), while Abigail Wolcott Ellsworth was the daughter of a Governor of Connecticut. (Wadsworth Atheneum)

reflecting the growth in population and wealth. During the 1790s the assessed value of property in New York City soared from $5.8 to $20.7 million.

Economic prosperity had its price. Americans got caught up in the differing political ideologies and naval policies of the European belligerents. Many had welcomed the French Revolution of 1789 because it abolished the last vestiges of feudalism and set up a constitutional monarchy. However, the creation of the more democratic French Republic in 1792 and the execution of King Louis XVI the next year divided public opinion in the United States.

On one side many American artisans praised the egalitarianism of the French republicans. They founded Democratic-Republican clubs modeled on the radical Jacobin clubs in Paris. In Philadelphia, Democratic-Republicans had a dinner to celebrate the beheading of Louis XVI; there, an observer reported, "the head of a roasted pig was severed from its body, and being recognized as an emblem of the murdered King of France, was carried round to the guests. Each one placing the cap of liberty on its head, pronounced the word "tyrant." Adopting French republican practice, many Americans began addressing each other as "citizen," as a symbol of equality. Their objection to Hamilton's economic policies was that they were "aristocratic."

On the other side of this ideological controversy were men and women of wealth, conservative religious convictions, or Hamiltonian sympathies. They denounced the Reign of Terror—the executions of Louis XVI and his aristocratic supporters—and condemned the new French regime for abandoning Christianity in favor of a new religion of Reason.

American politics were soon dominated by the passions of the French Revolution. When the Frenchman Edmond Genêt arrived in the United States on a diplomatic mission, many admirers of the French Republic held parades in his honor. They supported Genêt's efforts to persuade individual Americans—and the United States government—to join their old ally France in a new war against Great Britain. "The cause of France is the cause of man, and neutrality is desertion," proclaimed the novelist Hugh Henry Brackenridge, an influential Democratic-Republican politician from Pennsylvania. However, leading Federalists accused Genêt of violating Washington's Proclamation of Neutrality and persuaded the president to demand his recall. In 1794 the Federalist-dominated Congress passed a Neutrality Act, prohibiting American citizens from fighting in the war and barring both French and British naval vessels from American ports.

Meanwhile, violence broke out in the United States

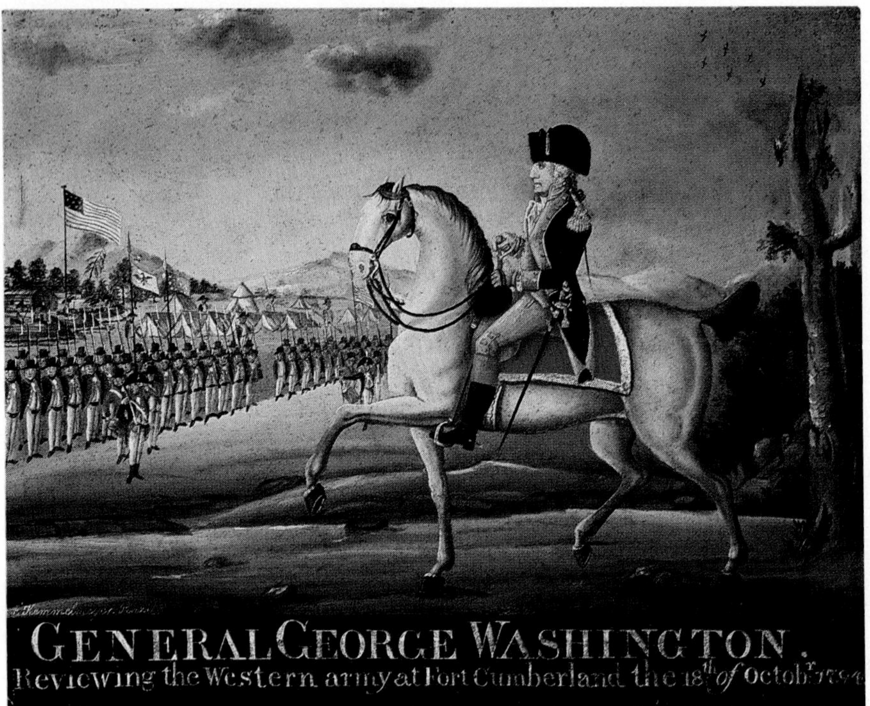

GENERAL GEORGE WASHINGTON.
Reviewing the Western army at Fort Cumberland the 18th of Octobr 1794

Washington Puts Down the Whiskey Rebels

Because of his speculations in western lands, President Washington took a personal interest in the suppression of the Whiskey Rebellion. He raised a sizeable army and traveled to Fort Cumberland to review it. (Winterthur Museum)

over a domestic issue. In 1792, farmers in western Pennsylvania began protesting against Hamilton's excise tax on spirits. The tax had raised the price—and thus cut the demand—for the corn whiskey that the farmers sold locally and bartered with the East for manufactures. In the Whiskey Rebellion, an extralegal assembly in Pittsburgh challenged the constitutionality of the tax, and rebels armed with guns, swords, and pitchforks attacked tax collectors and waved banners proclaiming the French revolutionary slogan "Liberty, Equality, and Fraternity!" The ideology of the French Revolution had sharpened the debate over Hamilton's economic policies and helped justify domestic rebellion. To uphold national authority (and deter secessionist movements along the frontier, where he owned extensive property), President Washington raised an army of 15,000 troops and suppressed the Whiskey Rebellion.

Britain's maritime strategy widened the growing political divisions in the United States. In November 1793, the Royal Navy began seizing American ships bound for France from the West Indies. In six months the British took more than 250 vessels and confiscated their cargoes of sugar as contraband, invoking the so-called Rule of 1756. (This British legal doctrine restricted the volume of commerce neutral states could conduct with belligerents during wartime to the amount conducted during peace.) Federalist merchants argued that the rule was not an accepted principle of international law, but their claims were usually rejected by judges in British admiralty courts. American merchants refrained from demanding that their country retaliate against the Royal Navy, fearing that a war against Great Britain would throw the United States into the arms of radical French republicans, destroy the American merchant fleet, and undermine Hamilton's system of public finance.

To avert war, President Washington sent John Jay to negotiate with Britain. Jay returned with a comprehensive agreement that addressed the maritime issues as well as territorial and financial disputes dating back to the War of Independence. The treaty required the United States to make "full and complete compensation" to British merchants for all prewar debts owed by American citizens. It also acknowledged Britain's right to remove French property from neutral ships, thus relinquishing the American merchants' claim that "free ships make free goods." In return, Jay's Treaty required the British to abide by the terms of the peace treaty of 1783, which mandated the withdrawal of British military garrisons from six forts in the American Northwest; to end British aid to western Indian tribes; and to allow American merchants to submit claims of illegal seizures to an arbitration tribunal.

Jefferson and his Democratic-Republican followers denounced Jay's Treaty as too conciliatory to America's former enemy, and tried to prevent its ratification. The Senate did ratify the treaty in June 1795, but only by a vote of 20 to 10, barely meeting the two-thirds majority required by the Constitution. This outcome reaffirmed the government's diplomatic position. As long as Hamilton and his Federalist allies were in power, the United States would have a pro-British foreign policy.

The Rise of Parties

The Election of 1796. The presidential election of 1796 marked a new stage in the organization of political parties in the United States. Politicians now sought office not as individuals but as representatives of a *party* that stood for certain political principles. To prepare for the election, the Federalists and Democratic-Republicans (now known simply as Republicans) called legislative caucuses in Congress and in the various states. Members of these informal conventions nominated candidates and mobilized support among the voters.

Parties were a new phenomenon. Colonial legislatures had often divided into factions, based on family alliances, ethnic groups, or regional concerns, but these groups were poorly organized and usually temporary. The state and national constitutions of the Revolutionary Era likewise made no provision for parties, because their authors assumed that representative institutions adequately expressed the will of the people. Other political groups—Shaysite mobs, factions in state legislatures, ideological parties—were unnecessary and dangerous. They violated the basic republican premise that citizens should be independent and virtuous, using their vote not for partisan advantage but for the public interest. "If I could not go to heaven but with a party, I would not go there at all," Jefferson declared. As president, Washington had tried to stand above parties, but his continuing support for Hamilton's policies exposed him to partisan attack. In fact, Washington's refusal to seek a third presidential term in 1796 stemmed in part from his disillusionment with party strife. Only Madison accepted the inevitability of political parties in a free society, and he assumed they would be temporary coalitions that would form around a specific issue and then disappear.

By encouraging a politically active citizenry, the revolutionary ideology of popular sovereignty laid the basis for a competitive party system. At first, most social groups entered politics only on a sporadic basis. In Virginia, for example, the Antifederalists who opposed ratification of the Constitution did not become active again until the formation of the Republican party. Once political parties appeared, however, they attracted the long-term allegiance of certain regional or occupational groups. Merchants and creditors in the northeastern states supported the Federalist party, as did wheat-exporting slaveholders in the Tidewater districts of the Chesapeake states. The Republican coalition was more diverse. By the mid-1790s it included mechanics and artisans in seaport cities, southern tobacco planters, German and Scots-Irish settlers, and subsistence farmers throughout the country. Republican policies appealed to a wider range of social groups, but the Federalists' prestige, wealth, and experience made them a potent political force.

In 1796, in an election dominated by conflict over ideology and foreign policy, Federalist candidates triumphed, winning a majority of seats in Congress and in the electoral college. The electors chose John Adams as president; when some Federalist electors refused to vote for Adams's official running mate, Thomas Pinckney of South Carolina (they were offended by a treaty he had negotiated with Spain), Thomas Jefferson, the Republican candidate for president, became vice-president. Thus the nation had a divided administration.

As chief executive, John Adams upheld the Federalists' pro-British foreign policy. He condemned French seizures of American merchant ships and accused France of meddling in the United States' domestic affairs. When three agents of Prince Talleyrand, the French foreign minister, solicited a loan and a bribe from American diplomats, Adams urged Congress to prepare for war. To overcome Republican objections, he charged that Talleyrand's agents, whom he dubbed X, Y, and Z, had insulted American honor. The Federalist-controlled Congress cut off trade with France and authorized American privateers to seize French ships. Between 1798 and 1800 the United States became an unofficial ally of Great Britain—a monarchy and its recent enemy—and fought an undeclared war against

An Anti-French Cartoon

A five-headed monster, representing France, demands a bribe ("Money, Money, Money") from American diplomats. Federalists used the incident, named the XYZ affair for the three anonymous French agents, to whip up anti-French sentiment in the United States and to launch an undeclared naval war.

France, a republic and its major supporter during the War of Independence.

The Crisis of 1798–1800

The Alien and Sedition Acts. For the first—but not the last—time in American history, a controversial foreign war prompted domestic protest and governmental repression. Pro-French immigrants from Ireland viciously attacked Adams's foreign policy in newspapers and pamphlets. To silence them, the administration enacted an Alien Act in 1798 that authorized the deportation of foreigners. A few Federalist supporters favored even harsher treatment. "Were I president, I would hang them for otherwise they would murder me," declared a Philadelphia pamphleteer. To allay such exaggerated concerns, the administration passed a Naturalization Act, which increased the residence requirement for citizenship from five to fourteen years. Also in 1798, the Federalist Congress enacted a harsh Sedition Act, prohibiting the publication of ungrounded or malicious attacks against the president or Congress. "He that is not for us is against us," thundered the Federalist *Gazette of the United States*. Using the legal powers of the new act, Federalist prosecutors arrested more than twenty Republican newspaper editors, charged them with sedition, and sent some of them to prison.

Republicans assailed the Sedition Act as contrary to the Bill of Rights. The First Amendment to the Constitution prohibits the national government from "abridging the freedom of speech, or of the press." The Sedition Act was probably unconstitutional, but Republican leaders did not turn to the Supreme Court for redress. The Court's powers were still vague, particularly with regard to the "judicial review" of Congressional legislation. Besides, the Court was an appointed body presently packed with Federalists, who would probably uphold the Sedition Act.

So Madison and Jefferson took the fight to elected bodies, the state legislatures that were not dominated by Federalists. In November 1798 the legislature of Kentucky—the first western territory to become a state, in 1792—passed a resolution drafted by Jefferson. It declared the Alien and Sedition Acts to be "unauthoritative, void, and of no force." More important, the resolution asserted that the national government owed its existence to a compact among the states. "As in all other cases of compact among parties having no common Judge," the resolution declared, "each party has an equal right to judge by itself." A resolution Madison drafted for the Virginia legislature similarly claimed that the states had the right to refuse to enforce laws passed by Congress that exceeded the powers granted that body by the Constitution. The Kentucky and Virginia resolutions thus laid the theoretical basis for subsequent "states's rights" interpretations of the Constitution.

In 1798, as at the ratification conventions in 1788, Federalist assertions of national authority provoked a debate over the nature of the Union. Even Madison—the architect of the Constitution—had second thoughts. At the Philadelphia convention, he had advocated a strong central government created by and responsible to the people; now he was swayed by the dubious argument that the Constitution had resulted from a compact among the states. Similarly, in the heat of partisan conflict, Jefferson modified his ideological opposition to political parties. He now believed that parties were valuable "to watch and relate to the people" the activities of the government.

The Election of 1800. The debate over the Sedition Act set the stage for the election of 1800. Republicans supported Jefferson's bid for the presidency by pointing to the wrongful imprisonment of newspaper editors and championing the rights of the states. President Adams responded to these attacks by reevaluating his foreign policy. Adams was a complicated man, often vain, easily offended, and dogmatic, but possessed of great personal strength and determination. He showed his quality as a statesman by rejecting the advice of Hamilton and other Federalist leaders to intensify the undeclared war with France and benefit politically from nationalist fervor. Instead, Adams entered into diplomatic negotiations that brought the war to an end.

Federalists attempted to win the election by depicting Jefferson as an irresponsible pro-French radical—"the archapostle of irreligion and free thought"—but they were unsuccessful. The Republicans won a resounding victory. Voters registered their protest against a foreign war—and a special national tax on land and houses levied in 1798 to pay for it—by giving Republicans a majority in both houses of Congress as well as a narrow edge in the electoral college. However, the electors gave Jefferson and Aaron Burr of New York (his vice-presidential running mate on the Republican ticket) the same number of votes for the office of president. In the event of such a tie, the Constitution specified that the House of Representatives would select the president, with each state having one vote. (The Twelfth Amendment, ratified in 1804, remedied this constitutional defect by requiring the electors to cast separate ballots for president and vice-president.)

Alexander Hamilton played a crucial role in the drama that followed. For thirty-five ballots, Federalists in the House of Representatives blocked Jefferson's election. Then the former treasury secretary intervened. Calling Burr an "embryo Caesar" and the "most unfit man in the United States for the office of president," Hamilton persuaded key Federalists to permit the selection of Jefferson, his longtime rival. The Federalists' concern for political stability also played a role. As Senator James Bayard of Delaware explained, "It was admitted on all hands that we must risk the Constitution and a Civil War or take Mr. Jefferson."

Jefferson called the election the "revolution of 1800," and so it was. It signaled the twilight of Federalism and its aristocratic outlook and the dawn of a more democratic era. The election also testified to the strength of the American experiment in self-government. The Federalists had attacked the Republicans as social radicals, traitors, and atheists for nearly a decade, with all sincerity, yet they peacefully relinquished power to their enemies. This bloodless transfer of power was genuinely revolutionary. It demonstrated that governments elected by the people could be changed by the people in an orderly, civilized way, even in times of bitter partisan conflict.

In his inaugural address in 1801, Jefferson referred to this achievement, declaring: "We are all Republicans, we are all Federalists." The new president reminded Americans of their common political heritage of popular sovereignty and representative government, and expanded it to include peaceful dissent and equal rights. He asked his audience to

> bear in mind this sacred principle, that though the will of the majority is in all cases to prevail, that will to be rightful must be reasonable; that the minority possess their equal rights, which equal laws must protect, and to violate would be oppression.

Over the course of a quarter-century, Jefferson had remained true to his principles. In 1801, as in the Declaration of Independence of 1776, he defined the American republic as a government based on the twin principles of liberty and equality.

Summary

The state constitutions of 1776–1780 created new institutions of republican government. Most had property qualifications for voting and a separation of powers that inhibited popular rule. The Pennsylvania and Vermont constitutions were more democratic, with broad voting rights for men and a powerful one-house legislature. Women continued to be excluded from the political sphere but sought greater legal rights.

The national government created by the Articles of Confederation began the orderly settlement of the trans-Appalachian West, but it lacked the authority to regulate foreign trade or to raise enough revenue to pay off wartime debts. Power remained with the states, where clashes over financial policy culminated in Shays's Rebellion, an uprising of indebted farmers in western Massachusetts.

The weaknesses of the Confederation led to a constitutional convention in Philadelphia in 1787 that was dominated by nationalists and creditors. The delegates devised a new constitution that derived its authority directly from the people, who were represented in the lower house of the legislature, bypassing the states. They also created a strong national government, with the power to levy taxes, issue money, and control trade. Its laws were to be the supreme law of the land. In several important states the Constitution was ratified by only narrow margins, because it diminished the sovereignty of the states and seemed to provide for a powerful central government immune from popular control.

George Washington served as the first president of the United States and, along with the first Congress, established the executive and judicial departments. The economic policies of Washington's secretary of the treasury, Alexander Hamilton, favored northern merchants and financiers. To oppose them, Thomas Jefferson and James Madison organized farmers, planters, and artisans into the Democratic-Republican party. The French Revolution and naval warfare led to bitter ideological struggles and, during an undeclared war with France, to political repression in the Alien and Sedition acts of 1798. The peaceful transfer of power to Jefferson in 1800 ended a decade of political strife.

TOPIC FOR RESEARCH

American Constitutionalism

Between 1776 and 1789 American political leaders wrote constitutions establishing state and national institutions of government. What principles are embodied in these charters? What type of political institutions did they create? How do the various state constitutions differ from one another and from the national constitutions? And how do the national charters differ from one another? Carefully read the Articles of Confederation and the Constitution of 1787, as well as the Constitutions of Pennsylvania (1776) and New York (1777). In addressing these questions, you can either deal with a specific topic—for example, the extent of legislative or executive power—or attempt a broader comparison.

Important studies of state constitutions include Willi Paul Adams, *The First American Constitutions: Republican Ideology and the Making of the State Constitutions in the Revolutionary Era* (1980); Edward Countryman, *A People in Revolution: The American Revolution and Political Society in New York, 1760–1790* (1981); Donald Lutz, *Popular Consent and Popular Control: Whig Political Theory in the Early State Constitutions* (1980); and J. R. Pole, *Political Representation in England and the Origins of the American Republic* (1966).

Gordon Wood, *The Creation of the American Republic, 1776–1790* (1965), is a magisterial analysis that links the state and national documents. It can be supplemented by Merrill Jensen, *The Articles of Confederation, 1774–1781* (1940); Richard R. Beeman, Stephen Botein, and Edward C. Carter II, eds., *Beyond Confederation: Origins of the Constitution and American National Identity* (1987); and Christopher Collier and James L. Collier, *Decision in Philadelphia* (1987).

BIBLIOGRAPHY

Creating New Institutions

Elisha P. Douglass, *Rebels and Democrats* (1965), and Jackson Turner Main, *Political Parties Before the Constitution* (1973), document the struggle for equal political rights during the war. See also Stephen E. Patterson, *Political Parties in Revolutionary Massachusetts* (1973); Jackson T. Main, *The Sovereign States, 1775–1783* (1973); and Ronald L. Hoffman and Peter Albert, eds., *Sovereign States in an Age of Uncertainty* (1981). Linda K. Kerber, *Women of the Republic: Intellect and Ideology in Revolutionary America* (1980), discusses the idea of republican motherhood.

Readings on the Articles of Confederation are listed in the Topic for Research. See also H. James Henderson, *Party Politics in the Continental Congress* (1974); Joseph L. Davis, *Sectionalism in American Politics, 1774–1787* (1977); and Peter S. Onuf, *The Origins of the Federal Republic: Jurisdictional Controversies in the United States, 1775–1787* (1983).

In 1883 John Fiske called the decade of the 1780s *The Critical Period of American History*; for a more positive view see Merrill Jensen, *The New Nation*, 1781–1789 (1950). More recent studies include Dale W. Forsythe, *Taxation and Political Change in the Young Nation, 1781–1833* (1977); Richard B. Morris, *The Forging of the Union, 1781–1789* (1987); and David Szatmary, *Shays' Rebellion: The Making of an Agrarian Insurrection* (1980).

The Constitution of 1787

The modern study of the Constitution began in 1913 with the publication of works by Charles A. Beard, *An Economic Interpretation of the Constitution of the United States*, and Max Farrand, *The Framing of the Constitution*. For critiques of Beard's work, see Leonard Levy, ed., *Essays on the Making of the Constitution* (rev. ed., 1987); for recent studies similar to Farrand's, see Clinton Rossiter, *1787: The Grand Convention* (1973), and Richard B. Bernstein and Kym S. Rice, *Are We to Be a Nation? The Making of the Constitution* (1987).

Other important works (in addition to those cited in the Topic for Research) include Forrest McDonald, *Novus Ordo Seculorum: The Intellectual Origins of the Constitution* (1985); Edmund S. Morgan, *Inventing the People: The Rise of Popular Sovereignty in England and America* (1988); and Michael Kammen, *A Machine That Would Go by Itself: The Constitution in American Culture* (1986).

On the Antifederalists and the ratification struggle, see Stephen R. Boyd, *The Politics of Opposition: Antifederalists and the Acceptance of the Constitution* (1979); Stephen L. Schechter, *The Reluctant Pillar: New York and the Adoption of the Federal Constitution* (1985); Jackson Turner Main, *The Antifederalists: Critics of the Constitution, 1781–1788* (1961); Robert A. Rutland, *The Ordeal of the Constitution: The Anti-Federalists and the Ratification Struggle of 1787–88* (1966); and Herbert Storing, *The Antifederalists* (1985). Two recent studies of the Federalist papers are David F. Epstein, *The Political Theory of "The Federalist"* (1984), and Charles R. Kesler, ed., *Saving the Revolution: "The Federalist Papers" and the American Founding* (1987). See also R. A. Rutland, *The Birth of the Bill of Rights, 1776–1791* (rev. ed., 1983), and Bernard Schwartz, *The Great Rights of Mankind: A History of the American Bill of Rights* (1977).

The Political Crisis of the 1790s

John C. Miller, *The Federalist Era, 1789–1800* (1960), remains the standard political history of the decade. Studies of important statesmen are Forrest McDonald, *Alexander Hamilton: A Biography* (1979); Gerald Stourzh, *Alexander Hamilton and the Idea of Republican Government* (1970); James T. Flexner, *George Washington and the New Nation, 1783–1793* (1970), and *George Washington: Anguish and Farewell, 1793–1799* (1972). Recent analyses of Jeffersonian ideology include Joyce Appleby, *Capitalism and a New Social Order: The Republican Vision of the 1790s* (1984); Drew McCoy, *The Elusive Republic: Political Economy in Jeffersonian America* (1982); Lance Banning, *The Jeffersonian Persuasion: The Evolution of a Party Ideology* (1978); and John R. Nelson, Jr., *Liberty and Property: Political Economy and Policymaking in the New Nation, 1789–1812* (1987).

Richard Hofstadter, *The Idea of a Party System: The Rise of Legitimate Opposition in the United States, 1790–1840* (1969), offers an overview of the subject; more detailed studies of the 1790s are Joseph Charles, *The Origins of the American Party System* (1956); Noble Cunningham, *The Jeffersonian Republicans: The Formation of Party Organization, 1789–1801* (1957), William Nisbet Chambers, *Political Parties in the New Nation: The American Experience* (1963); and John F. Hoadley, *Origins of American Political Parties, 1789–1803* (1986). The impact of social and economic conflict on politics forms a main theme in Thomas P. Slaughter, *The Whiskey Rebellion: Frontier Epilogue to the American Revolution* (1986), and Alfred Young, *The Democratic-Republicans of New York: The Origins, 1763–1797* (1967). On diplomatic and military history, consult Henry Ammon, *The Genêt Mission* (1973); Jerald A. Combs, *The Jay Treaty* (1970); Alexander DeConde, *Entangling Alliance: Politics and Diplomacy Under George Washington* (1958); Richard H. Kohn, *Eagle and Sword: The Federalists and the Creation of the Military Establishment in America, 1783–1802* (1975); and Lawrence D. Cress, *Citizens in Arms: The Army and the Military to the War of 1812* (1982).

On Adams's administration, see Ralph Brown Adams, *The Presidency of John Adams* (1975), and Stephen G. Kurtz, *The Presidency of John Adams: The Collapse of Federalism, 1795–1800* (1957). More specialized studies are William Sinchcombe, *The XYZ Affair* (1980); Leonard Levy, *The Emergence of a Free Press* (1985); and James M. Smith, *Freedom's Fetters: The Alien and Sedition Laws and American Civil Liberties* (rev. ed., 1966).

Good studies of state history include Patricia Watlington, *The Partisan Spirit: Kentucky Politics, 1779–1792* (1972); Richard R. Beeman, *The Old Dominion and the New Nation, 1788–1801* (1972); Paul Goodman, *The Democratic Republicans of Massachusetts* (1964); and Mary K. Bonsteel Tachau, *Federal Courts in the Early Republic: Kentucky, 1789–1816* (1978).

TIMELINE

1776	First state constitutions John Adams, *Thoughts on Government*
1777	Articles of Confederation (ratified 1781)
1779	Judith Sargent Murray, "On the Equality of the Sexes"
1780s	Postwar commercial recession Burdensome state debts Creditor-debtor conflicts in states
1786	Annapolis commercial convention Shays's Rebellion
1787	Northwest Ordinance Philadelphia convention
1788–1789	Ratification conventions *The Federalist*
1789	George Washington becomes first president Outbreak of French Revolution Judiciary Act establishes federal court system
1790	Alexander Hamilton's program: public credit and a national bank
1791	Bill of Rights ratified
1792	Mary Wollstonecraft, *A Vindication of the Rights of Woman*
1793	Democratic-Republican party emerges under leadership of Madison and Jefferson War between Britain and France Britain begins seizing American merchant ships
1794	Whiskey Rebellion
1795	Jay's Treaty
1797	John Adams becomes president
1798	Undeclared war against France Alien, Sedition, and Naturalization acts Kentucky and Virginia resolutions
1800	"Revolution of 1800"
1801–1809	Presidency of Thomas Jefferson

Settlers Move West Through Pennsylvania

Thomas Birch captured the spirit of westward expansion in his painting, *Conestoga Wagon on the Pennsylvania Turnpike*, 1816. (Shelburne Museum)

CHAPTER 8 *Toward a Continental Nation*, 1790–1820

For the first century and a half of their history, the thirteen colonies were confined to a narrow strip of land along the Atlantic seaboard. But in 1783, Britain surrendered its claim not only to the settled territory of the colonies but also to vast stretches of the North American interior, more than tripling the size of the new United States. The land beyond the Appalachians was mostly forested, dotted with French and British forts and fur-trading posts, and peopled by tens of thousands of native Americans. Yet within fifty years, white Americans had driven the Indians from their lands, hacking out millions of acres of farms in the Old Northwest and creating a new plantation economy based on slave-produced cotton in the Old Southwest.

Even before this process was well begun, Jefferson doubled the size of the nation again. The Louisiana Purchase added most of the lands between the Mississippi River and the Rocky Mountains to the United States. It would take nearly a century to populate this huge "inland empire," but the acquisition of western lands had an immediate and continuing impact on all aspects of American life, drawing migrants from the eastern states and from Europe, stirring controversy over land policy, sharpening the division between free and slave states, and changing the goals of American diplomacy. A new phase of American history had begun.

Westward Expansion

In 1776 the United States had 2.5 million people, most of whom lived within 50 miles of the Atlantic Ocean. By 1790, the white and black population had grown to 3.9 million, but of these only 200,000 resided west of the Appalachian Mountains. During the next thirty years the geographic dimensions of American life multiplied along with the population. By 1820, there were 9.6 million white and black Americans, and 2 million of them—a number almost as large as the total population in 1776—now inhabited nine new states and three territories west of the Appalachians.

Native American Resistance

Although many native American tribes had fought on the British side during the War of Independence, British negotiators failed to protect Indian lands or independence at the Paris peace conference. As one British statesman put it, the Indian nations were "remitted to the care of neighbours." That care was far from benevolent. The new American republic asserted its ownership to all Indian lands west of the Appalachians, both by right of conquest and by the terms of the Paris treaty of 1783. Native Americans refused to honor this claim, pointing out that they had not signed the treaty and had never been conquered by Europeans.

In 1784, the Confederation Congress sent commissioners, accompanied by a military guard, to meet with representatives of the four pro-British Iroquois tribes—the Mohawk, Onondaga, Cayuga, and Seneca. The commissioners imposed peace by threatening to use military force. In the Treaty of Fort Stanwix, signed in October 1784, the Iroquois lost most Seneca land in Pennsylvania and western New York and all Iroquois land in Ohio. And that was just a taste of what was to follow. Pennsylvania officials coerced the Iroquois into relinquishing more territory, as did Governor George Clinton of New York. Freely dispensing liquor, manufactured goods, and bribes, New York officials and land speculators secured new treaties that gave them title to millions of acres of Indian land in central and western New York. By 1800 the once-powerful Iroquois peoples were confined to relatively small reservations. Even the Oneida and Tuscarora, who had supported the Patriot cause, lost most of their lands.

The American commissioners used similar tactics to extract agreements from tribes farther west. In 1785 the Chipewyan, Delaware, Ottawa, and Wyandot signed away most of the future state of Ohio, but later repudiated the agreements, claiming—justifiably—that the treaties had been signed under duress. In the Northwest Territory, the Miami, Shawnee, Potawatomi, and Chipewyan formed a Western Confederacy to defend their lands. Led by Little Turtle, they crushed American expeditionary forces commanded by General Josiah Harmar and General Arthur St. Clair in Ohio in 1790 and 1791.

The United States government's aggressive stance toward the Indians divided political opinion in the new republic. Some critics charged that it was immoral to use force against native Americans. Others worried that if the national government were permitted to raise a permanent army to fight Indians, it might then use that army to suppress political dissent among whites. Yet a majority in Congress found the strength of the Western Confederacy menacing enough that they supported President Washington's decision to double the army to five thousand men. Washington chose General "Mad Anthony" Wayne to lead the western army. The cautious Wayne spent two years equipping and training his forces for a confrontation with the Western Confederacy. In August 1794 he defeated the Indian allies in the Battle of Fallen Timbers (near present-day Toledo, Ohio).

The negotiations following the battle produced the Treaty of Greenville (Ohio) in 1795, in which the United States renounced its general claim to ownership of Indian land by right of conquest. In return for annuities of about $10,000, the native American chiefs ceded the southeastern corner of the Northwest Territory as

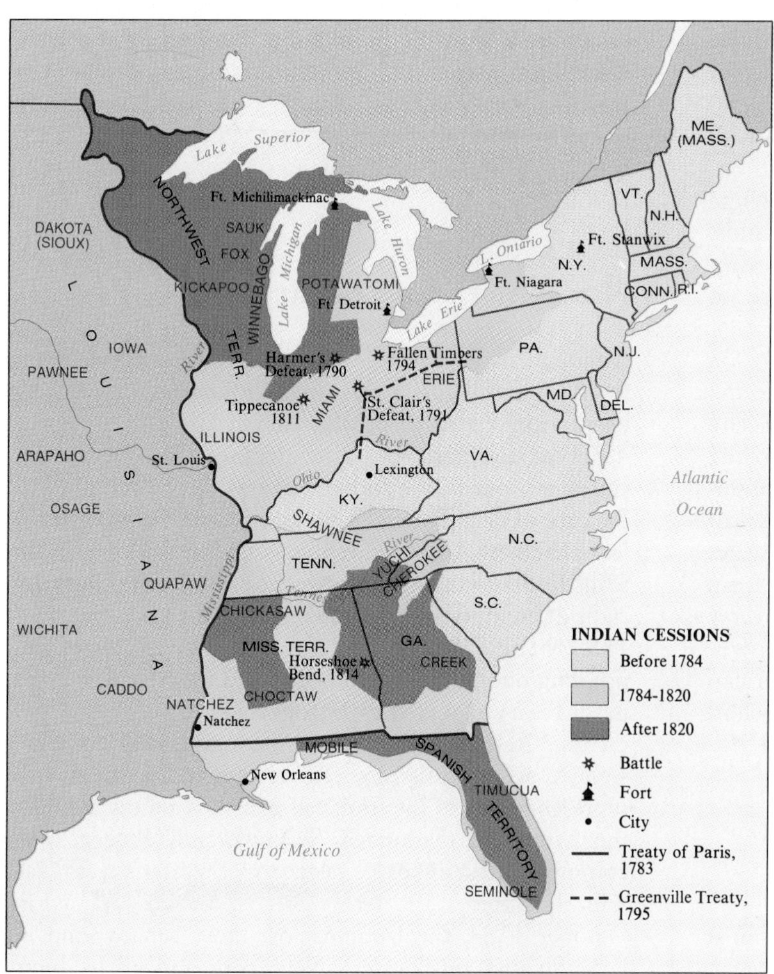

MAP 8.1

Expansion: Military and Diplomatic

The United States claimed sovereignty over the entire trans-Appalachian West by right of conquest over Great Britain. When the tribes of the Western Confederacy contested this claim, the American government upheld it by force, sending armies into the West in the 1790s and during the War of 1812. This armed diplomacy forced the cession by treaty of most native American lands east of the Mississippi River.

Treaty Negotiations at Greenville
In 1785 the Shawnee, Chippewyan, Ottawa, Miami, and other tribes formed the Western Confederacy to stop white settlement at the Ohio River. The American victory at the Battle of Fallen Timbers (1794) opened up the region, but the Treaty of Greenville (1795) recognized many Indian rights.

well as certain strategic areas on the Great Lakes, including Detroit and the future site of Chicago, and acknowledged American sovereignty over the entire region. Indeed, the Indians agreed to place themselves "under the protection of the United States, and no other Power whatever." This agreement increased the likelihood that Great Britain would comply with its obligation (reaffirmed in Jay's Treaty of 1795) to withdraw its military garrisons from American territory between the Appalachians and the Mississippi River.

White families were moving westward now, establishing their presence in the region. Ohio entered the Union in 1803 and two years later had more than 100,000 residents, many of them clamoring for fertile Indian lands. Thousands more migrants moved into Indiana and Illinois. To meet their demands for land, William Henry Harrison, governor of the Indiana Territory, used threats, bribes, and deceit to purchase millions of acres from native American tribes. State officials and land speculators in Georgia, Tennessee, and the Mississippi Territory made similar deals. All along the western frontier, native Americans were threatened with imminent eviction from their ancestral lands by the remorseless advance of white civilization.

Farmers Move West

From North and South, migrants poured across the Appalachians into the fertile, well-watered lands of western New York, Kentucky and Tennessee, and the Northwest Territory. Those settlers taking the southern route came from the states of the Chesapeake region and consisted primarily of white tenant farmers, poor yeomen, and young couples. Fleeing the depleted soils and planter elite of the Tidewater region, these migrants sought social freedom and land of their own. Landlords tried to stop this massive exodus of farm labor, but without success. As early as 1785 a worried planter warned readers of the Maryland *Gazette* that "boundless settlements open a door for our citizens to run off and leave us, depreciating all our landed property and disabling us from paying taxes."

A Roadside Inn
Dozens of inns dotted the roads of the new republic, providing food and accommodation for settlers moving west and for cattle drovers and teamsters taking western goods to the east.

By 1790 more than 100,000 southerners had defied their planter landlords. Along with migrants from Pennsylvania, they moved through the Cumberland Gap into Kentucky or along the Knoxville Road into Tennessee. Kentucky and Tennessee soon had enough residents to apply for statehood, joining the Union in 1792 and 1796, respectively. Thousands of new settlers flocked across the mountains after 1800, confident that they would prosper by growing cotton and hemp—which were in great demand. By 1820, Kentucky and Tennessee had a combined population of nearly a million.

The northern wave of migrants flowed out of New England into New York State and beyond, seeking arable land. The need for land had already taken New England farmers north into New Hampshire and Vermont, east along the coast of Maine, and west as far as the Appalachians. Now, after two centuries of population growth, many New England communities were overcrowded, their rocky soils on the verge of exhaustion and their families unable to provide farmsteads for the four or five children who survived to adulthood. In 1796 there were 103 farmsteads in Kent, Connecticut (founded only in 1738), and they were inhabited by 100 fathers and 109 adult sons. All the other sons, and the daughters who had not married local men, had moved away. Previous generations of Kent parents had been able to subdivide their farms to provide land for most of their sons, but now the farms were too small to support more than one heir.

In 1796 ten Kent families moved to Amenia, New York. By selling their small but well-established farms in Kent for $20 to $30 per acre, they were able to buy enough western land—at $2 to $3 per acre—to support themselves and to provide farmsteads for all their children. Hundreds—then thousands—of farm families followed their example. They hitched their oxen and horses to wagons, and carried tools, plows, and household goods across the Appalachians into the plains and rolling hills of upstate New York. By 1820, 800,000 migrants were living in a string of settlements stretching from Albany to Buffalo. Thousands more New Englanders traveled on to Ohio.

This vast folk migration was carefully organized, not by joint-stock companies or governments, but by the people themselves, using their own social ties. To lighten the economic and emotional burdens of migration, many settlers moved in large family groups. As an astonished traveler reported from central New York: "The town of Herkimer is entirely populated by families come from Connecticut. We stayed at Mr. Snow's who came from New London with about ten male and female cousins." Members of Congregational churches likewise migrated together, transplanting the strong religious and cultural traditions of New England directly into western communities.

Agricultural Change. The massive exodus to the west left eastern towns drained of labor and capital. Many eastern farmers compensated by planting different crops and improving methods of cultivation. In New England, more farmers turned to potatoes, a high-yielding, nutritious crop. In the wheat-growing Middle Atlantic states, enterprising farmers replaced their metal-tipped wooden plows with cast-iron models, which dug a deeper furrow and required a single yoke of oxen, instead of two or three. By saving on livestock and labor, cast-iron plows enabled small-scale farmers to keep up production, even though their sons and daughters had gone west.

The "Onion Maidens" of Wethersfield, Connecticut

Nearly 200 years old by the early nineteenth century, Wethersfield remained prosperous through agricultural innovation—turning to market gardening and becoming, for a few decades, the "onion capital" of the United States.

Wealthier eastern farmers prospered by adopting the progressive farming methods advocated by British agricultural reformers. They began rotating their crops to maintain the fertility of the soil, ordering their workers or tenants to plant nitrogen-rich clover and follow it with wheat, corn, wheat, and then clover again. In Pennsylvania and the Chesapeake region, rotation raised the average wheat yield from 12 to 25 bushels per acre.

Yeomen also adopted crop rotation in order to increase the variety and quantity of what they produced. In the fall they planted winter wheat to sell as a market crop and to provide bread for their families. In the spring they planted corn to feed milk cows during the winter. Women and girls milked the cows and made butter and cheese for market sale.

Rural families now worked harder, laboring all twelve months of the year, but whether they were hacking fields out of western forests or carting manure to replenish eastern soils, their labor was rewarded by higher output and income. Westward migration thus boosted the entire American economy and improved the quality of rural life.

The Transportation Bottleneck

For centuries the pattern of trade and settlement had been determined by water routes. Chesapeake planters and Hudson River manor lords relied on river transportation—convenient and cheap, at a cost of 5 or 6 cents a ton-mile—to get their crops to market. Farmers without access to rivers had to haul their crops by ox cart over narrow dirt trails that turned into mudholes at the spring thaw or during a heavy rain. Even in dry weather, ox-drawn carts moved slowly and carried only small loads. They were expensive too, costing farmers 30 cents a ton-mile to ship wheat or corn to market. Pennsylvania farmers spent as much to send their grain 30 miles overland to Philadelphia as they did to ship it from Philadelphia to London by sea. Settlers in most western regions could not afford to send goods by cart to eastern markets.

The improvement of inland travel and trade was one of the priorities of the new state governments, and they actively encouraged transportation ventures. The Pennsylvania legislature granted corporate charters to fifty-five private turnpike companies between 1793 and 1812; Massachusetts chartered over a hundred similar enterprises. The turnpike companies charged tolls for the use of the level, graveled roads they built, but the roads cut travel time significantly. Even the best roads remained less efficient than water transportation, however, so state governments and private entrepreneurs also undertook the construction of inland waterways.

The River Town of Cincinnati
Cincinnati was still a small settlement in 1800 but, thanks to its location on the Ohio River, it would soon become one of the great market cities of the trans-Appalachian west and, for a time, a major outpost of New England culture.

They dredged rivers to make them navigable and constructed canals to bypass waterfalls or rapids. In 1816, the entire United States had about 100 miles of canals, but only three of them were more than 2 miles long.

Rivers remained the best means of transportation, and they determined the location of settlements in the West. People paid premium prices for land along navigable streams, and speculators bought up likely sites for towns along the Ohio, Tennessee, and Mississippi rivers. To take cotton and surplus grain and meat to market, western farmers and merchants built shallow barges and floated them down this great interconnected river system to the Spanish port of New Orleans. By 1815 the southern port was processing about $5 million in agricultural products yearly.

Migrants in the interior of New York faced an even bigger transportation problem, for they had no river at all by which to get their goods to the markets of the East. As one pioneer recalled:

> In the early years, there was none but a home market and that was mostly barter—it was so many bushels of wheat for a cow; so many bushels for a yoke of oxen. The price of a common pair of cowhide boots would be $7, payable in wheat at 62 cents per bushel.

It was only in 1819, when the first section of the Erie Canal connected the central counties of New York with the Hudson River, that farmers could ship their crops to eastern markets (see Chapter 10).

Speculators and Settlers

The settlement of the Old Northwest had been carefully planned by the Confederation Congress. The ordinances of 1785 and 1787, which created the Northwest Territory, also divided it into uniform sections or *townships.* Townships were about the same size as New England communities, 6 miles square, and were divided into thirty-six sections of 1 square mile, or 640 acres. However, unlike New England, where property lines followed the contours of the land, the Northwest Territory was surveyed in a grid pattern, without regard to topography. The ordinance of 1785 favored speculators by specifying a minimum price of $1 per acre and requiring that half of the townships be sold entire, in single blocks of 23,040 acres each. The other half of the townships were divided into parcels of 640 acres. But even this was too expensive for many migrants; only well-to-do farmers could afford the $640 cash price for an ordinary farmstead, not to mention the considerably higher amount needed to buy high-quality or well-placed land.

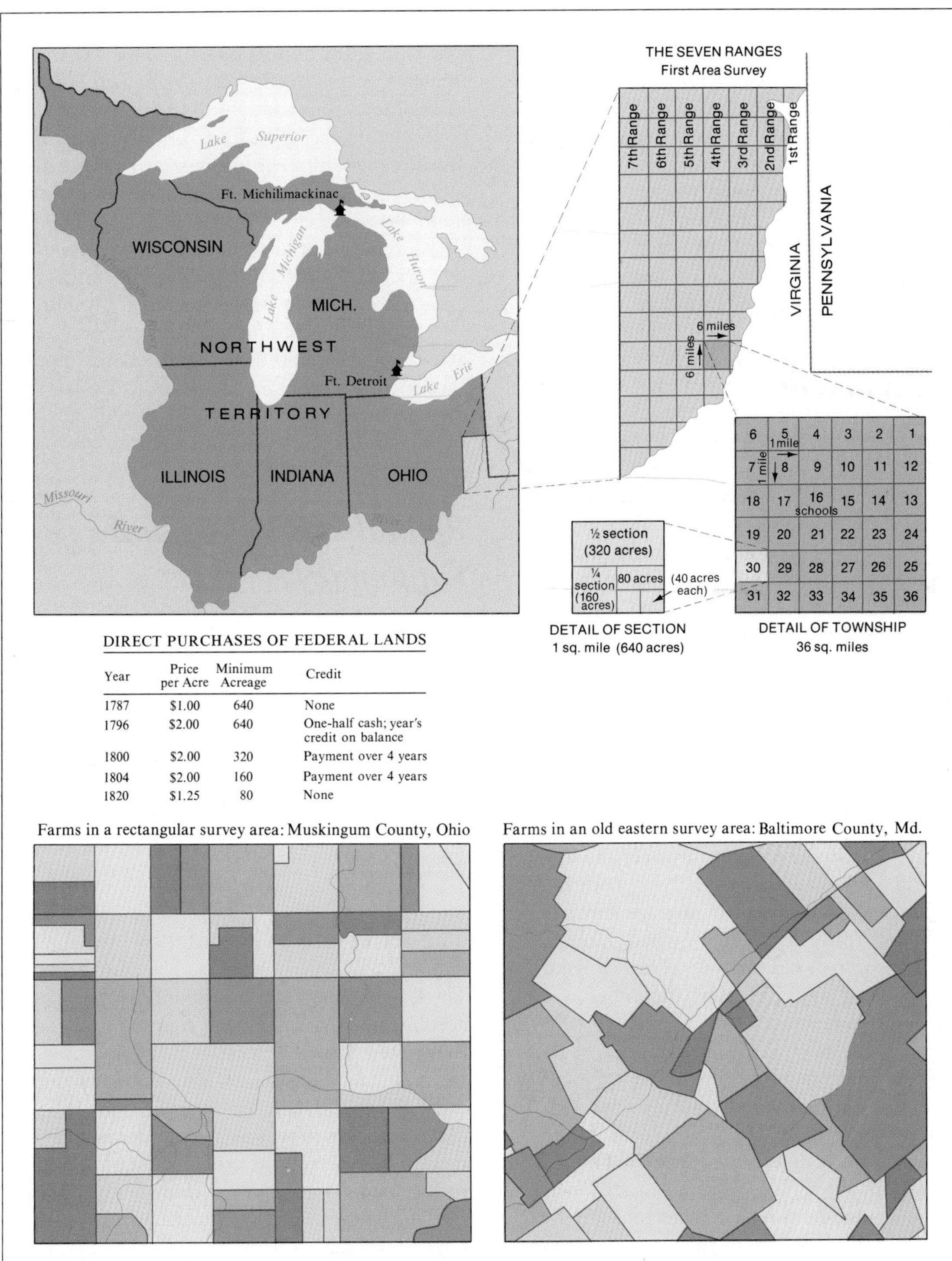

DIRECT PURCHASES OF FEDERAL LANDS

Year	Price per Acre	Minimum Acreage	Credit
1787	$1.00	640	None
1796	$2.00	640	One-half cash; year's credit on balance
1800	$2.00	320	Payment over 4 years
1804	$2.00	160	Payment over 4 years
1820	$1.25	80	None

MAP 8.2

Land Divisions in the Northwest Territory

Throughout the Northwest Territory, surveyors imposed a rectangular grid on the landscape in advance of settlement, so that farmers bought neatly defined properties. Thus the right-angled property lines in Muskingum County, Ohio (lower left), contrasted sharply with those in Baltimore County, Maryland (lower right), where—as in most eastern states—boundaries followed the contours of the land.

The poorer migrants demanded better terms, but the Federalist-dominated Congresses of the 1790s turned a deaf ear. Many Federalist politicians were eastern landlords, and they had no desire to lose their tenants to cheap land in the West. In fact, the Federalist Land Act of 1796 *doubled* the minimum price to $2 per acre. But Thomas Jefferson wanted to see the West populated with yeomen farm families, so under his leadership the Democratic-Republican party pressured Congress to pass legislation that assisted cash-poor migrants. New laws in 1800 and 1804 reduced the minimum allotment to 320 acres and then to 160 acres, and allowed payment in installments over four years. Eventually, the Land Act of 1820 reduced the minimum purchase to 80 acres and the price to $1.25 per acre, enabling a farmer with only $100 in cash to buy a farm in the West.

Few individual settlers bought farms directly from the government, however, because much of the best land fell into the hands of speculators—as the authors of the ordinances had intended. To raise money to pay the public debt, the national government had sold millions of acres in the Northwest Territory to the Ohio and Scioto land companies, for as little as a few cents an acre. Terrible abuses occurred in the western land sales of the eastern states. In the 1780s, the financier Robert Morris acquired 1.3 million acres of land in the Genesee region of central New York for a mere $75,000—about 6 cents an acre. Morris took a quick profit, selling the land to a group of English investors headed by Sir William Pulteney, who made their profits over the long run. By 1829, Pulteney's land agents in New York had received $1.2 million from sales to migrant farmers. Elsewhere in New York, the Dutch-owned Holland Land Company acquired millions of acres of land, while the Transylvania and Vandalia companies won control of vast tracts in Kentucky.

Because land speculators drove up the price of the best western farms, many aspiring yeomen found it difficult to realize their dream of landed independence. In New York's Genesee region, the Wadsworth family bought thousands of acres and created leasehold estates similar to the manors of the Hudson River Valley. To attract tenants, the Wadsworths leased farms rent-free for the first seven years. But because of their cultural ideal of freehold ownership, many New England yeomen shunned these terms. They preferred to sign lease-purchase agreements with the Holland Land Company, so they could work the land while saving the money to buy it—or so they thought. In fact, high interest rates and the difficulty of transporting goods to market put many farmers in debt and forced them to remain tenants indefinitely. Soon the combined debt of farmers in the counties west of the Genesee River amounted to $5 million, and tenant farmers far outnumbered freeholders.

It looked as if American farmers had fled declining prospects in the East only to find themselves at the bottom of a new economic hierarchy in the West. Indeed, many migrant families—especially in areas without low-cost access to markets—remained in debt to landlords or land companies for decades. Yet white Americans continued to move westward, in the belief that present sacrifices would yield future security. In any new settlement it took the labor of a generation to clear land, build houses, barns, and roads, and plant orchards. Whatever the labor and crude living conditions—and the financial burdens—a western farmstead would eventually provide an independent livelihood for the settlers and their children. Taken together, the humble achievements of thousands of farm families transformed the landscape of the trans-Appalachian West, turning forests into farms and beginning the conquest of the interior of the North American continent.

Republican Policy and Diplomacy

Between 1801 and 1825, three Republicans from Virginia—Thomas Jefferson, James Madison, and James Monroe—each served two terms as president. Supported by strong majorities in Congress, they reversed many Federalist policies, completing what Jefferson called the Revolution of 1800. Although the attention of much of the nation was focused on the settlement of the West, maritime disputes with Great Britain precipitated the War of 1812.

The Jeffersonian Presidency

Thomas Jefferson was a brilliant man, perhaps the most accomplished and versatile statesman in the history of the United States. A seasoned diplomat and an insightful political philosopher, he was also a superb politician. When he became president in 1801, Jefferson moved quickly to win over his Federalist opponents. Although he reserved the crucial post of Secretary of State for his Virginia ally, James Madison, he appointed three men from New England to major government posts: Levi Lincoln as attorney general, Henry Dearborn as secretary of war, and Gideon Granger as postmaster general. At the same time, Jefferson prepared for new electoral battles, using patronage appointments to bolster the Republican party in New England.

Politics and the Court System. Jefferson was the first chief executive to be inaugurated in the District of Columbia, the new national capital. But Jefferson did not begin with a clean slate, for after a dozen years of Federalist presidents, he inherited a government filled with his political opponents. In addition to the bureaucrats who managed the day-to-day operations of the small national government, the judiciary was packed with Federalists. Of these the most important was John Marshall of Virginia, who had been appointed chief justice of the United States by John Adams in January 1801 (he would serve until 1835). In addition, the outgoing Federalist-controlled Congress had passed a Judiciary Act in 1801 creating sixteen new judgeships, six additional circuit courts, and a variety of posts for marshals and court clerks. Adams filled these positions in a series of "midnight appointments" just before he left office. The Federalists "have retired into the judiciary as a stronghold," Jefferson complained, ". . . and from that battery all the works of Republicanism are to be beaten down and destroyed."

The Republicans fought back. The new Congress repealed the controversial Judiciary Act, dismissing the midnight judges as superfluous. They used provisions in the Constitution to punish Federalist judges for their political partisanship on the bench. The Constitution empowered the House of Representatives to bring impeachment charges against officials for "high crimes and misdemeanors"; the accused was then brought to trial before the Senate. First, the House impeached a mentally unstable judge, John Pickering of New Hampshire, and won his removal from office. Then House Republicans brought impeachment charges against Supreme Court Justice Samuel Chase, in retaliation for his overzealous enforcement of the Sedition Act. But enough senators quailed at the obviousness of this political move that Chase escaped removal by a narrow vote.

The "Revolution of 1800." President Jefferson pursued a more conciliatory policy. He supported repeal of the recent Judiciary Act, but he judged Federalist bureaucrats on the basis of ability, not party loyalty. During his eight years as chief executive, he removed only 109 of 433 Federalist officeholders, 40 of them the controversial midnight appointees of Adams.

Yet Jefferson was determined to change the character of the national government. The Federalists, he charged, had swollen its size and power; Republicans would shrink it back to the right constitutional size and shape. When the Alien and Sedition acts expired in 1801, Congress did not reenact them, charging that they were politically motivated and unconstitutional. The Naturalization Act was amended to permit resident aliens to become citizens after five years.

For his part, Jefferson modified many Federalist policies. During the 1790s, Federalist administrations had paid tribute to the Barbary States of North Africa—that is, bribed them to spare American merchant ships from attack in the Mediterranean Sea. Jefferson stopped these payments in 1801, and when the city-states of Tunis, Morocco, Tripoli, and Algiers renewed their assaults on the ships, he ordered U.S. naval and marine units to retaliate. But Jefferson knew that an extended campaign would require a buildup of the army and navy, which would increase taxes and the national debt. He therefore accepted a diplomatic solution, reviving the old Federalist tribute system but, by threatening new military action, at a much better rate.

In domestic affairs, too, Jefferson set his own course—moderate but clearly Republican. He abolished all internal taxes, including the excise tax that had sparked the Whiskey Rebellion of 1794. Addressing his party's fears of a military takeover of the government, Jefferson reduced the size of the permanent army. He came to accept the Bank of the United States, which he had condemned as unconstitutional in 1791, because of its importance to the nation's economy, but he was still opposed to a large public debt. One of his most important appointments was that of Albert Gallatin, a brilliant Swiss-born Republican, as secretary of the treasury. Gallatin was a fiscal conservative who believed that the national debt was "an evil of the first magnitude." By carefully controlling government expenditures and using customs revenues to redeem government bonds, he reduced the debt from $83 million in 1801 to $45 million in 1808. Jefferson and Gallatin saw to it, following the "revolution of 1800," that the nation was no longer run in the interests of northeastern creditors and merchants.

Jefferson and the West

The main objective of the Jefferson administration was to help the ordinary farm families who were settling the West. Long before his presidency, Jefferson had envisioned a prosperous yeoman society in the West. He had celebrated the pioneer farmer in *Notes on Virginia* (1785) and strongly supported Pinckney's Treaty of 1795, which allowed westerners to ship crops down the Mississippi for export through Spanish-held New Orleans.

The Louisiana Purchase. Jefferson's dream was jeopardized by the sudden rise of Napoleon Bonaparte, a daring thirty-year-old general who had seized power in revolution-torn France in 1799. Almost immediately, the young dictator began an ambitious campaign for a French empire. Napoleon sought not only to dominate Europe but also to establish a new French colonial empire in America. In 1800 he forced Spain to sign a secret treaty that returned Louisiana to France; two years later Spanish officials began restricting American access to New Orleans. Meanwhile, Napoleon mobilized an expeditionary force to restore French rule in Haiti, the rich sugar island then called Saint-Domingue, which was now under the control of rebellious blacks led by Toussaint L'Ouverture.

Napoleon's actions prompted Jefferson to question the traditional pro-French foreign policy of the Repub-

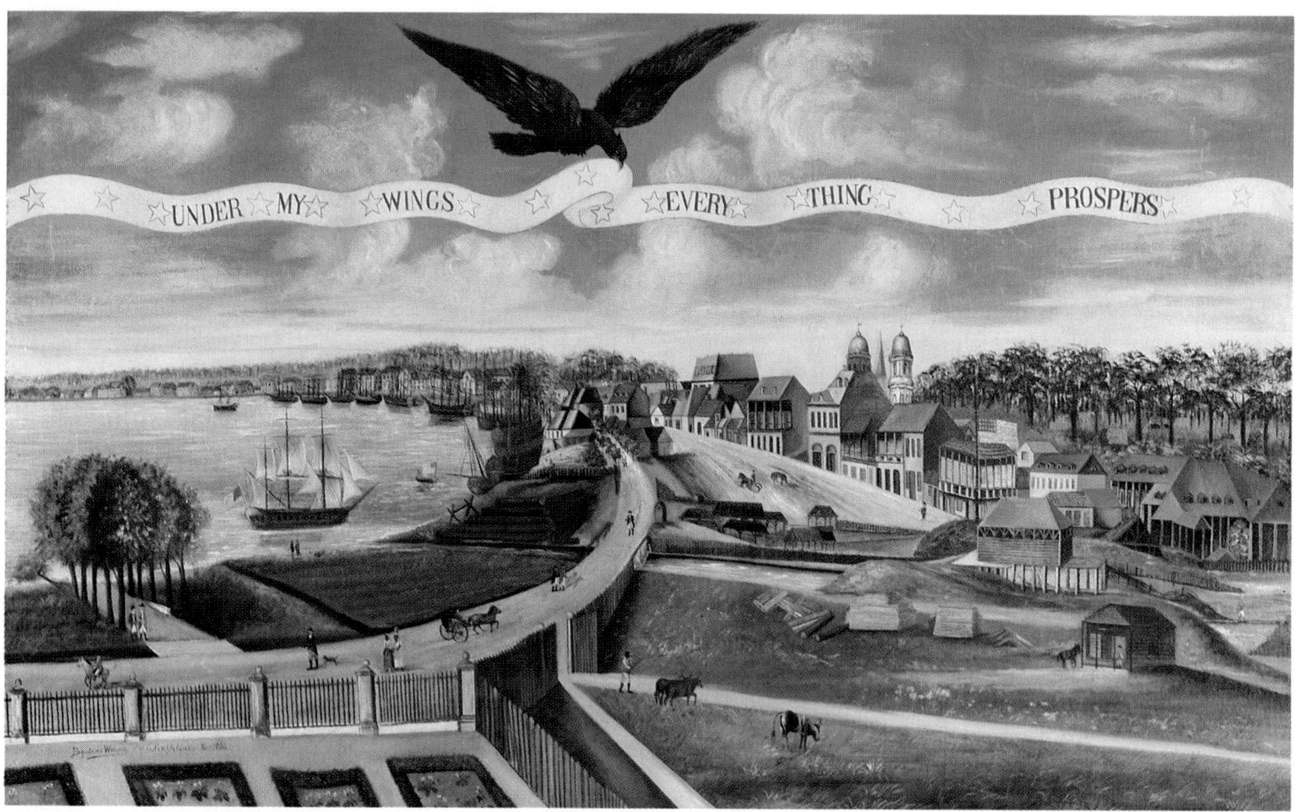
UNDER MY WINGS EVERY THING PROSPERS

The American Eagle Over New Orleans
Jefferson's purchase of Louisiana made New Orleans an American city, but the culture of the French settlers (or Creoles) remained strong for decades. A traveller noted that "the great enmity existing between the Creoles . . . & the Americans results in fights and Challenges—there are some of both sides in jail."

lican party. The trade guaranteed by Pinckney's Treaty was crucial to the West; any nation that denied Americans access to New Orleans, Jefferson declared, must be "our natural and habitual enemy." To avoid crossing swords with Napoleon, he instructed Robert R. Livingston, the United States minister in Paris, to purchase New Orleans. Simultaneously Jefferson sent James Monroe, a former congressman and governor of Virginia, to Britain to seek its assistance in case of war. "The day that France takes possession of New Orleans," the president warned, "we must marry ourselves to the British fleet and nation." Secretary of State James Madison took the first step toward war by encouraging American merchants to cooperate with the black government of Haiti in its resistance against the French.

Jefferson's determined diplomacy yielded a magnificent prize—the entire territory of Louisiana. By 1802 the French invasion of Haiti had faltered, the victim of yellow fever and spirited black resistance. Napoleon hesitated to send reinforcements because a new war with Britain was threatening to break out in Europe. In fact, the French dictator now feared that American troops would invade Louisiana. Acting with characteristic decisiveness, Napoleon gave up his dream of an empire in America, and in April 1803 he offered to sell not only New Orleans but the entire territory of Louisiana as well. For about $15 million ($180 million today), Livingston and Monroe, who had joined him in Paris, concluded what became known as the Louisiana Purchase. "We have lived long," Livingston remarked to Monroe, "but this is the noblest work of our lives." The Republican statesmen had acquired the vast region between the Mississippi River and the Rocky Mountains, doubling the size of the nation.

The sheer magnitude of the Louisiana Purchase overwhelmed the president's reservations. Jefferson had always given a strict construction to the Constitution; for example, he had argued that the Constitution limited the national government to "expressly" delegated powers. The Constitution contained no provision for adding new territory to the Union. Yet given an opportunity to fulfill his vision of a freeholding yeoman society in the West, Jefferson was pragmatic. He used the treaty-making powers in the Constitution to complete the deal with France. Federalists roundly criticized Jefferson's inconsistency, but they largely approved his diplomatic triumph, with the Senate ratifying the treaty by a vote of 26 to 6.

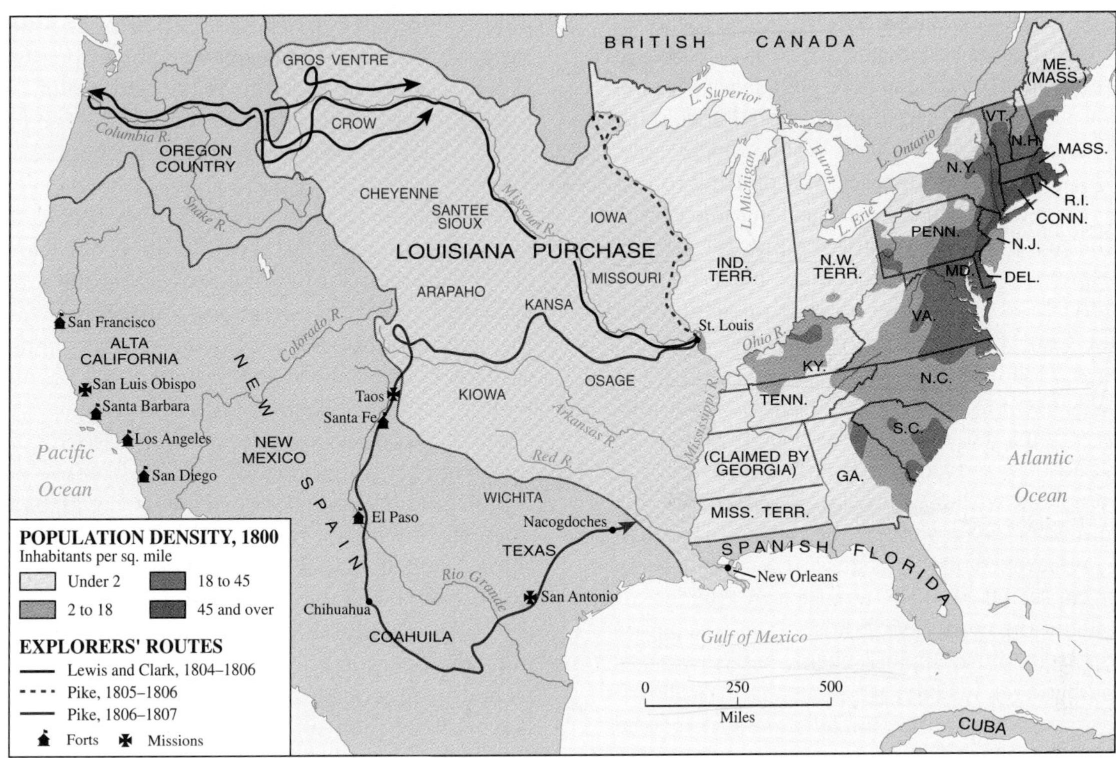

MAP 8.3

The Louisiana Purchase, 1803

The Louisiana Purchase ended forever France's claims to North America. It virtually doubled the size of the United States, prompting Jefferson to predict that the vast Mississippi Valley "from its fertility . . . will ere long yield half of our whole produce, and contain half of our whole population." Now only Spain stood in the way of an American continental empire.

The Continent Described

Meriweather Lewis and William Clark fulfilled Jefferson's injunction to explore the west, filling their journals with drawings and descriptions of its topography, plants, and animals, such as this detailed report on the white salmon trout.

A scientist as well as a statesman, Jefferson wanted detailed information about the physical features of the Louisiana Territory and its plant and animal life. He sent out his personal secretary, Meriwether Lewis, to explore the region. Lewis and William Clark, an army officer, traveled up the Missouri River, across the Rocky Mountains, and down the Columbia River to the Pacific Ocean. After two years, the explorers returned with the first maps of this immense wilderness and vivid accounts of its natural resources and native American inhabitants.

Threats to Union. The Louisiana Purchase had been a magnificent acquisition, but it brought in its wake a threat to the American Union. New England Federalists had long feared that western expansion would diminish their region's political power. Now, despite the fact that few Americans would settle west of the Mississippi for another half-century, some Federalists, including the Massachusetts congressman Timothy Pickering and the geographer Jedidiah Morse, talked openly of the secession of the northeastern states. They approached Alexander Hamilton, but the great New York Federalist refused to support their plan for a separate Northern

Confederacy—a scheme that they continued to advocate until 1815. The secessionists then turned to Aaron Burr, the ambitious Republican vice-president, who expressed some interest. When Burr accepted Federalist support in his campaign for the governorship of New York in 1804, Hamilton accused him of plotting to dismember the Union. Burr challenged his longtime enemy to a duel, the preferred aristocratic method for settling personal disputes. The illegal duel took place in New Jersey in July 1804. Hamilton died from a gunshot wound, and Burr was indicted for murder by state courts in New York and New Jersey.

This tragic event led Burr to yet another secessionist scheme. He completed his term as vice-president in early 1805 and then moved west to avoid prosecution. There he conspired with General James Wilkinson, the American military governor of the Louisiana Territory—to do what, remains a mystery. It had something to do with capturing Spanish territory in Mexico or leading a rebellion to establish Louisiana as a separate nation, headed by Burr. In any event, Wilkinson got cold feet and betrayed his ally, arresting him on a charge of treason as the former vice-president led an armed force down the Ohio River. Chief Justice Marshall presided over Burr's trial, which was both a political and a legal contest. Jefferson tried to get Burr convicted by giving a loose construction to the definition of treason in the Constitution. But Marshall repeatedly intervened from the bench, insisting, for a change, on a strict reading of the Constitution, with the result that Burr was acquitted.

The decision in Burr's trial was less important than the events leading up to it, beginning with the Louisiana Purchase. The Republicans' expansionist policies had increased sectional tension and party conflict within the nation.

Crisis at Sea

The outbreak of the Napoleonic Wars (1802–1815) distracted attention from the growing significance of the American West. The United States had no desire to become enmeshed in European political conflicts but was drawn in nonetheless. Great Britain and France, the major belligerent powers, refused to respect American neutrality, claiming the right to board merchant ships and confiscate their cargoes, just as they had done in the wars of the 1790s. This economic warfare intensified in 1805, when Admiral Horatio Nelson resoundingly defeated the French navy in the Battle of Trafalgar, enabling Britain to tighten its naval blockade of the Continent. The British navy promptly seized the American freighter *Essex* for carrying sugar and molasses from the West Indies to France. A British vice-admiralty judge refused to classify these products as American re-exports, although the *Essex* had intentionally stopped at a U.S. port in order to make that claim. This new British restriction on neutral trade threatened the profits of American merchants and revived anti-British sentiment.

Napoleon replied to the British blockade with a blockade of his own. The Berlin (1806) and Milan (1807) decrees, known collectively as the Continental System, banned British ships—and neutral vessels that stopped in Britain—from European ports under French control. If the Continental System could be enforced, it would virtually destroy Britain's export trade. To counter Napoleon's strategy, the British required neutral shippers to obtain a special license—and carry British goods—to pass through its naval blockade of Europe. American merchants were trapped. If their ships stopped at a British port to pick up a license or cargo, they faced seizure by France and its allies at their next port of call; but if they refused to carry British permits, their cargoes might be seized by the British as contraband. American traders were more afraid of the Royal Navy than of French customs officials, so they took out thousands of permits and carried British goods to Europe, thus undermining Napoleon's Continental System.

Impressment. Both Federalists and Republicans resented British high-handedness, but there was little they could do about it. Even when the British stopped American ships on the high seas to search for deserters from the Royal Navy and *impress* them (force them back into service), American merchants did not resist. The phenomenal expansion of American commerce was partly responsible for impressment, as American merchantmen provided about 4,000 new jobs for sailors each year and hundreds of British sailors had fled the Royal Navy to fill these positions. Some of the men seized by the British were Englishmen carrying forged identity papers; others were Americans impressed by accident—or, more and more frequently, by design. During the wars of the 1790s, British warships had seized about 2,400 sailors from American ships; between 1802 and 1811, they impressed nearly 8,000.

Long-simmering American resentment erupted in 1807. When the U.S. frigate *Chesapeake* refused to be boarded, the British warship *Leopard* attacked it, killing or wounding twenty-one men and seizing four alleged deserters. "Never since the battle of Lexington have I seen this country in such a state of exasperation as at present," Jefferson declared. But instead of retaliating, Jefferson demanded monetary reparations and an end to impressment. To demonstrate his resolve, he barred British warships from entering American ports for resupply. The astute British government apologized for the attack. It promised eventual compensation for the loss of lives and property, but defended its blockade and impressment policies.

The Embargo of 1807

To protect American interests while avoiding war, Jefferson adopted a policy of *peaceful coercion*. Working closely with Secretary of State Madison, the president devised the Embargo Act of 1807. As passed by Congress, this legislation prohibited American ships from leaving their home ports to carry goods to any nation until Britain and France repealed their restrictions on United States trade. The embargo was imaginative—an economic weapon similar to the nonimportation movements between 1765 and 1775—but naive. Jefferson and Madison overestimated the commercial importance of the United States. Neither Britain nor France was dependent on American shipping—and, in any event, both countries were determined to continue the war regardless of the cost to commerce. The Republican leaders also underestimated the cunning of Federalist merchants, who subverted the Embargo Act by ordering their captains to steer clear of American harbors and sail between foreign ports until the embargo was lifted. Trade was the merchants' lifeblood—they were prepared to take their chances with the British navy and Napoleon's officials rather than pass up wartime profits.

The embargo crippled the American export trade. Exports plunged from $108 million in 1806 to $22 million in 1808. The Federalists who represented the interests of New England merchants in Congress attacked Jefferson and Madison for jeopardizing the nation's economy. Federalists grew more alarmed when the Republican Congress passed a Force Act to prevent smuggling across the border between New England and Canada. The act gave customs officials extraordinary legal powers, reviving fears of government tyranny. "Would to God," exclaimed one Federalist, "that the Embargo had done as little evil to ourselves as it has done to foreign nations."

I Josiah the first do by this my Royal Proclamation announce myself King of New England, Nova Scotia and Passamaquoddy, Grand Master of the noble order of the Two Cod fishes.

Poking Fun at the Federalists

A Republican cartoon of 1812 shows Federalist Josiah Quincy—whose wealth came from the fish trade—as Grand Master of the Cod Fishes and gives him the face of a fish, effectively undercutting the Federalists' claims to social superiority.

Madison as President

Despite public discontent with the embargo, the voters elected one of its authors, James Madison, to the presidency in 1808, giving him 122 electoral votes to 47 for Federalist Charles C. Pinckney. As the main architect of the Constitution, an advocate of the Bill of Rights, a congressman and party leader, Madison had served the nation well; but he was not a diplomat—he had performed poorly as secretary of state—and he lacked administrative skills. As John Beckley, a loyal Republican activist, observed in 1806, "Madison is deemed by many too timid and indecisive as a statesman." Beckley had urged James Monroe to fight for the Republican nomination, praising him for "the known energy and decision of your character" in contrast with Madison's timidity. But Beckley's call went unheeded, and at a crucial juncture in foreign affairs, a man with little understanding of the devious, cutthroat world of international politics became president.

Madison did try to find an effective diplomatic policy. In 1809 he acknowledged the failure of the embargo, secured its repeal, and replaced it with the Nonintercourse Act. This legislation benefited merchants by permitting trade with all nations except France and Britain, and it offered the two belligerents the promise of normal commerce if they respected America's neutral rights. When Britain and France ignored this overture, Madison bowed to pressure from Congress and accepted a legislative act, called Macon's Bill No. 2, after Congressman Nathaniel Macon. The act reopened legal trade with Britain and France in 1810 but authorized new sanctions if either nation interfered with American commerce. The British ministry refused to alter its policies, daring the United States to cut off trade. Napoleon exploited this ill-conceived legislation more astutely. Publicly he exempted American commerce from the Berlin and Milan decrees, but privately he instructed customs officials to enforce them. "The Devil himself could not tell which government, England or France, is the most wicked," the exasperated Macon declared.

Tecumseh's Challenge. Other Republicans were pretty sure it was England. Eastern party leaders, such as George Clinton of New York, Madison's vice-president, began to take a stand against British maritime policies in 1809. The following year, Republican congressmen from the West—the future War Hawks of 1812—accused Britain of arming the Indian tribes in the trans-Appalachian region. Governor General James Craig of Canada had, in fact, quietly renewed military assistance to native Americans in the Ohio River valley, hoping that the Indians could defend their territory and continue to trade with the British. The Shawnee chief Tecumseh, assisted by his brother, the Prophet Tenskwatawa, revived the Western Confederacy of the 1790s and extended it to the southern tribes. They vowed to push white settlers back across the Ohio River.

Tenskwatawa, "The Prophet," 1836

Tenskwatawa added a spiritual dimension to Indian resistance, urging a holy war against the invading whites. His religious message transcended tribal differences and helped to create a formidable fighting force. (Library Company of Philadelphia)

Tecumseh and Tenskwatawa appealed to ancestral religious values. Christian missionaries had won native American converts in many tribes, creating rival factions and prompting revivals of traditional spiritual beliefs. The Shawnee leaders exploited pride in Indian ways to encourage military alliances among the western tribes. Moreover, Tenskwatawa prophesied that warriors would emerge from battle unscathed. Tecumseh centered his confederacy at a sacred town at the junction of the Tippecanoe and Wabash rivers, as a symbol of the religious roots of Indian resistance. He traveled widely among southern tribes to win their allegiance, sowing the prospect of war along the entire frontier.

A generation of westward expansion now began to affect American foreign policy. British support for the Western Confederacy played into the hands of southern expansionists in Congress, giving them an excuse to retaliate by seizing Florida from Spain, Britain's ally. Some Americans invaded western Florida and sought to annex it to the United States. Southern planters campaigned for the conquest of eastern Florida to prevent slaves from taking refuge there among the Seminole Indians. "I wish you would authorize the President to take possession of East Florida immediately," Thomas Jefferson wrote to his son-in-law, a member of the House of Representatives. "The militia of Georgia will do it in a fortnight."

Meanwhile, Republican politicians in the West claimed that it would be just as easy to conquer British Canada. Henry Clay, an avowed War Hawk from Kentucky and the new Speaker of the House of Representatives, pushed Madison toward war with Great Britain, as did John C. Calhoun, a rising young congressman from South Carolina. The outbreak of fighting with the Shawnee in the Indiana Territory may have decided the issue. In 1811, Governor William Henry Harrison defeated the Shawnee in the Battle of Tippecanoe and burned their sacred town.

With influential Republicans in Congress pressing for war—and national elections quickly approaching—Madison abandoned the strategy of economic coercion. He demanded that the British respect American territorial sovereignty in the West and neutral rights in the Atlantic. When the British failed to respond quickly, Madison asked Congress to declare war. In June 1812, a sharply divided Senate voted 19 to 13 for war; the House of Representatives concurred, 79 to 49.

The causes of the War of 1812 have been much debated. Officially, the United States went to war because of violations of its neutral rights—the seizure of its

AMERICAN VOICES

The Battle of Tippecanoe *Chief Shabonee*

His mind sharpened by defeat, the Potawatomi chief Shabonee offers a penetrating view of reality: the unfaithfulness of allies, the determination of some men and women, and the false hopes of war leaders.

It was fully believed among the Indians that we should defeat General Harrison, and that we should hold the line of the Wabash and dictate terms to the whites. The great cause of our failure, was the Miamies, whose principal country was south of the river, and they wanted to treat with the whites so as to retain their land, and they played false to their red brethern and yet lost all. They are now surrounded and will be crushed. The whites will shortly have all their lands and they will be driven away. . . .

Our young men said: We are ten to their one. If they stay upon the other side, we will let them alone. If they cross the Wabash, we will take their scalps or drive them into the river. They cannot swim. Their powder will be wet. The fish will eat their bodies. The bones of the white men will lie upon every sand bar. Their flesh will fatten buzzards. These white soldiers are not warriors. Their hands are soft. Their faces are white. One half of them are calico peddlers. The other half can only shoot squirrels. They cannot stand before men. They will all run when we make a noise in the night like wild cats fighting for their young. . . .

Such were the opinions and arguments of our warriors. They did not appreciate the great strength of the white men. I knew their great war chief, and some of his young men. He was a good man, very soft in his words to his red children, as he called us; and that made some of our men with hot heads mad. I listened to his soft words, but I looked into his eyes. They were full of fire. I knew that they would be among his men like coals of fire in the dry grass. The first wind would raise a great flame. I feared for the red men that might be sleeping in its way. . . .

Our women and children were in the town only a mile from the battle-field waiting for victory and its spoils. They wanted white prisoners. The Prophet had promised that every squaw of any note should have one of the white warriors to use as her slave, or to treat as she pleased. Oh how these women were disappointed! Instead of slaves and spoils of the white men coming into town with the rising sun, their town was in flames and women and children were hunted like wolves and killed by hundreds or driven into the river and swamps to hide. With the smoke of that town and the loss of that battle I lost all hope of the red men being able to stop the whites.

Source: David J. Rothman and Sheila Rothman, eds., *Sources of the American Social Tradition*, (New York: Basic Books, 1975).

ships and impressment of its sailors. But the results of the election of 1812 suggest otherwise. The war was opposed by Federalist merchants and seamen as well as by a majority of voters in the maritime states. The Federalist candidate for president, De Witt Clinton of New York, received 89 electoral votes, primarily from New England and the Middle Atlantic states.

In contrast, Madison amassed 128 electoral votes, mostly from the South and West—regions that tended to favor a resort to arms, for a variety of reasons. Western farmers were angry because the British blockade had cut the price of their crops. War Hawks representing frontier districts in Congress wanted to see the Indians defeated in the West. Some had their eye on expansion into Florida; others dreamed of annexing British Canada. Moreover, many Republicans saw political advantage in a war against Great Britain. It might discredit the Federalists and drive home once and for all America's independence from Britain.

With the election result so divided along regional lines, some historians have argued that the War of 1812 was "a western war with eastern labels"—that is, a war fought for land rather than maritime rights. Whatever their motives, the Republicans translated them into elevated moral principles, claiming that the pride of the nation was at stake. As President Madison declared in his second inaugural address of March 1813, when the fighting was already well under way, "National honor is national property of the highest value."

The War of 1812

The War of 1812 was a near disaster for the United States, both militarily and politically. Republican congressmen had predicted an easy military victory in Canada, but when General William Hull, governor of the Michigan Territory, invaded western Canada in the summer of 1812, he had to retreat almost immediately because of attacks from Indians under Tecumseh and lack of reinforcements. But U.S. forces enjoyed naval superiority on the Great Lakes and remained on the offensive in the West. Commodore Oliver Perry defeated a small British flotilla on Lake Erie. General William Henry Harrison launched a land attack on British and Indian forces near Detroit, forcing the British to withdraw and killing Tecumseh at the Battle of the Thames in October 1813. Another United States force captured and burned the Upper Canada capital of York (now Toronto) but, short of men and supplies, immediately withdrew.

Political divisions within the United States made a major invasion of Canada impossible. New England governors opposed the war effort and prohibited state militiamen from fighting outside the United States. Boston merchants and banks declined to lend money to the national government, making it difficult to finance the war—in fact they invested in British funds instead. In Congress, Daniel Webster, a dynamic young representative from New Hampshire, led Federalist opposition to higher taxes and tariffs. He also discouraged army enlistments and prevented the conscription of state militiamen into the American army, in order to force a negotiated peace. Having led a divided nation into war, Madison and the Republicans were unable to strike the British in Canada—their weakest point.

The American navy was no more successful in the Atlantic Ocean, because Britain had the strongest navy in the world. The British lost scores of merchant vessels to American privateers in the first months of the war, but thereafter the Royal Navy redeployed its fleet and British commerce moved in relative safety. By 1813, Britain had retaken the initiative at sea. A flotilla of British warships moved up and down the American coastline, interfering with shipping and threatening seaport cities. In 1814, the fleet sailed up Chesapeake Bay and British army units stormed ashore. They attacked the District of Columbia and set government buildings on fire, in retaliation for the burning of York. The British then advanced on Baltimore but were repulsed by courageous American resistance at Fort McHenry, in the battle that inspired Francis Scott Key to write "The Star-Spangled Banner." After two years of sporadic warfare, the United States was stalemated in Canada and on the defensive along the Atlantic coast, its new capital city in ruins.

Sectional opposition to the war entered a new phase in 1814. The Massachusetts legislature called for a convention "to lay the foundation for a radical reform in the National Compact." In response, Federalists from all the New England states gathered in Hartford, Connecticut, in December. Some delegates to the Hartford convention proposed secession from the Union, but the majority moderately called for a revision of the Constitution. Their object was to reverse the declining role of the Federalist party—and of New England—in the expanding nation. To end the Virginia Dynasty, delegates proposed a constitutional amendment limiting the presidency to one four-year term and rotating the office among citizens from different states. Other Federalists suggested amendments restricting commercial embargoes to sixty days and requiring a two-thirds majority in Congress to declare war, prohibit trade, or admit a new state into the Union. A minority in the nation and divided among themselves, the Federalists could not hope to prevail unless the war continued to go badly.

That was a very real prospect. An American naval victory at the Battle of Lake Champlain in the late summer of 1814 had narrowly averted a major British invasion of the Hudson River Valley. In December, British transports landed thousands of seasoned veterans at New Orleans, threatening to cut off the West's access to the sea. The United States was now under siege from both north and south. The only hopeful sign was that Britain had finally defeated Napoleon in Europe and was interested in securing peace with the United States as well, to lower taxes at home and reestablish trade with America.

The British entered into negotiations with an American delegation at Ghent in Belgium late in 1814. The American commissioners—John Quincy Adams, Albert Gallatin, and Henry Clay—initially demanded territorial gains in Canada and Florida. British diplomats insisted on a buffer state between the United States and Canada, to serve as a refuge for their native American allies. In the end, both sides realized that the small concessions that might be won at the bargaining table were not worth the cost of protracting the war. The Treaty of Ghent, signed on Christmas Eve, 1814, restored the prewar borders and referred the unresolved disputes to future negotiations.

Andrew Jackson and the Battle of New Orleans. These results hardly justified three years of fighting and a sharply divided nation. Indeed, the outcome confirmed the view of contemporary critics (and later historians) that the War of 1812 was unnecessary and undertaken primarily for partisan reasons. But a final victory in combat lifted American morale and, for many citizens, justified the fighting. Before news of the Treaty of Ghent reached the United States, newspaper headlines proclaimed, "ALMOST INCREDIBLE VICTORY!! GLORIOUS NEWS." On January 8, 1815, troops commanded by General Andrew Jackson crushed the British forces attacking New Orleans.

The victory at New Orleans ushered a very different kind of leader onto the American national scene. A son of the West, Jackson was a rugged slaveowning planter from Tennessee. He first came to public attention as an Indian-fighter, having led a troop of militia in a series of battles against the Creek in 1813 and 1814. After winning the Battle of Horseshoe Bend, he forced

The Battle of New Orleans
As shown in Jean Hyacinthe de Laclotte's painting, British troops advanced along the riverbank, seeking to outflank the Americans. Secure behind their battlements, Jackson's troops repelled the assault and inflicted hundreds of casualties. (New Orleans Museum of Art)

the Indian chiefs to sign a treaty ceding 23 million acres of land. These actions earned Jackson a reputation as a ruthless man, determined to remove the Indians in one way or another from the path of white settlement.

Jackson's victory at New Orleans made him a national hero and a symbol of the emerging West, the land of frontier fighters. Yet he won the contest at New Orleans not with Kentucky sharpshooters in coonskin caps but with a traditional deployment of regular troops, including a contingent of French-speaking black Americans, the Corps d'Afrique. The Americans fought from carefully constructed breastworks and were amply supplied with cannon, which pounded the massed British formations. "Our artillery fired upon their whole columns . . . with grapeshot and cannister bombs," reported one American witness. "The slaughter must have been great." Indeed it was. The British lost thousands of their finest troops, with 700 dead and 10,000 wounded or taken prisoner. American casualties totaled only 13 dead and 58 wounded.

For Americans, the Battle of New Orleans was the most significant event of the war, testifying, as one headline put it, to the "RISING GLORY OF THE AMERICAN REPUBLIC!" It redeemed the nation's battered pride and, along with the coming of peace, undercut Federalist demands for a revision of the Constitution. The political institutions of the new nation had survived a war and a generation of sectional strife.

Regional Diversity and National Identity

The political divisions that emerged during the War of 1812 showed that regional differences were still strong. There were four American cultures—New England, Middle Atlantic, Chesapeake, and Carolinian—each with distinctive values and political interests. As migrants transplanted these cultures to the Old Northwest and the Old Southwest after the war, American life became even more diverse, divided between complex seaboard societies and frontier farming regions. To unify this increasingly fragmented society, politicians and statesmen defined a new national identity: a continental American empire.

The Seaboard Societies

Generations of observers had contrasted the racially and class-divided society of the Chesapeake with the freehold farming regions of the North—particularly New England. Popular speech reflected some of these differences: "Yankee," a foreign traveler learned, was "a name given derisively, or merely jestingly," to the residents of New England because of their shrewd bargaining habits. "The name of 'Buckskin'," he went on to observe, "is given to the inhabitants of Virginia, because their ancestors were hunters and sold buck, or rather deer skins."

European visitors saw genuine cultural differences in the popular stereotypes. In 1800, an Englishman detected religious "fanaticism" in New England as well as "a great strain of industry among all ranks of people." He thought that "the lower orders of citizens have a better education, are more intelligent, and better informed" than those he met in the southern states. Visitors to the Chesapeake commented on the rude manners and heavy drinking habits of white tenant farmers and small freeholders. They had a "passion for gaming at the billiard table, a cock-fight or cards."

New Englanders did indeed set a higher store by education than did residents of the Chesapeake. The Puritan legacy included strong traditions of primary schooling and Bible reading. As a result, most men and more than half the women in New England in 1790 could read and write. In Virginia, most white women and a third of the adult white men could not even write their names; they signed legal documents, such as wills and marriage licenses, with an "X" or some other mark. This disparity in the literacy rate reflected different social and fiscal priorities. The slaveholding elite that ruled southern society refused to provide services or schooling for ordinary white families. In 1800, the

Puritan Culture Persists
Like good Puritans, this prosperous New England couple wear plainly cut clothes and hold the symbols of literacy —a book and a pen. The artist shows the woman, his stepmother, looking directly at him (and us), suggesting that he enjoyed a better relationship with her than with his stern-faced father, a traditional New England patriarch.

4,000 free inhabitants of Essex County in Virginia spent about $1,000 for local government, including schooling. That same year, the 900 residents of Acton, Massachusetts, spent $950 for public purposes—four times as much per capita as in Essex County—$550 on education alone.

Regional differences were also apparent in the observance of holidays. In Virginia, South Carolina, and other states with an Anglican heritage, Christmas was an occasion for feasting and celebration. Not so in New England, where Puritans condemned such celebrations as profane. Most New England churches did not celebrate Christmas until the 1850s; for them, Thanksgiving Day, commemorating the trials and triumphs of the first Pilgrim and Puritan settlers, was the focus of festivities. During the War of Independence, New England customs had become political symbols, as Congress frequently declared days of fasting and thanksgiving.

Regional identity was especially intense in New England because of ethnic and religious uniformity. By

1820 most men and women in New England could trace their American roots back six or seven generations. No fewer than 281 members of the Newhall family resided in Lynn, Massachusetts, in 1830, along with 259 Breeds, 195 Alleys, and 162 Johnsons. A list of only twelve family names encompassed 1,660 persons, 27 percent of the town's population. In a very real sense, New England was a "big family" composed of large, interrelated groups.

The cultures of the Middle Atlantic and the two southern regions were more diverse, because the people came from different ethnic and racial backgrounds. In Pennsylvania and New Jersey, Quakers, Germans, and Scots-Irish married largely within their own ethnic groups, and to a lesser extent so did the Dutch. Germans held on to their language as well as their customs, especially in the small agricultural villages of Pennsylvania and the backcountry districts of Maryland, Virginia, and North Carolina. A visitor to Hanover, Maryland, noted around 1820, "The inhabitants are all German. Habits, speech, newspapers, cooking—all German." In nearby Frederick Town, the Lutheran church not only held services and Sunday-school classes in German but kept all records in German as well. In the Tidewater districts of the South, whites and blacks lived in different worlds, sharing certain experiences, mainly in religion and music, but otherwise developing distinct cultures of their own.

German Dress and Manners in America

A gentlemen in traditional dress strolls among giant tulips, a familiar motif in Pennsylvania German folk art. The lace cuffs, white stockings, and walking stick suggest his high social status, as does the genteel way he holds his pipe. (Rare Book Dept., Free Library of Philadelphia)

This diversity among and within the various regions inhibited the growth of an American national identity. In day-to-day life, the people of New England, the Middle Atlantic states, and the South upheld the traditions of their ancestors. Only certain political events—especially national elections or wars—reminded people that they were citizens of the United States. For example, the term "Uncle Sam" came into use during the War of 1812. "This cant name for our government has got almost as common as John Bull [for the British]," a newspaper in Troy, New York, reported. "The letters U.S. on government waggons &c are supposed to have given rise to it."

Newspapers played an increasingly important role in fostering national identity and common cultural values. By 1820 the cities of the United States boasted thirty daily newspapers. Another thousand newspapers, mostly four-page weeklies, provided national news, market information, and advertisements to people in small towns and rural areas. Political parties subsidized some of these newspapers, thereby creating a national debate on various legislative issues. The influential *Niles Weekly Register*, established in Baltimore in 1811, and the *North American Review*, founded in Boston in 1815, carried news from Europe and the East to every region. But only members of certain elites—merchants, politicians, lawyers—participated fully in this national culture. Most Americans lived out their lives within the regional culture into which they had been born.

The Old Northwest

When Jedidiah Morse published his *American Geography* in 1793, he listed three "grand divisions of the United States": northern, middle, and southern. In the edition of 1819, he added a new section: "Western States and Territories." But was there a distinct culture of the West? Some seventy years later, in an essay called "The Significance of the Frontier in American History" (1893), the historian Frederick Jackson Turner placed the West at the center of the American experience. Turner argued that an identifiable national character first came into being in the West because its develop-

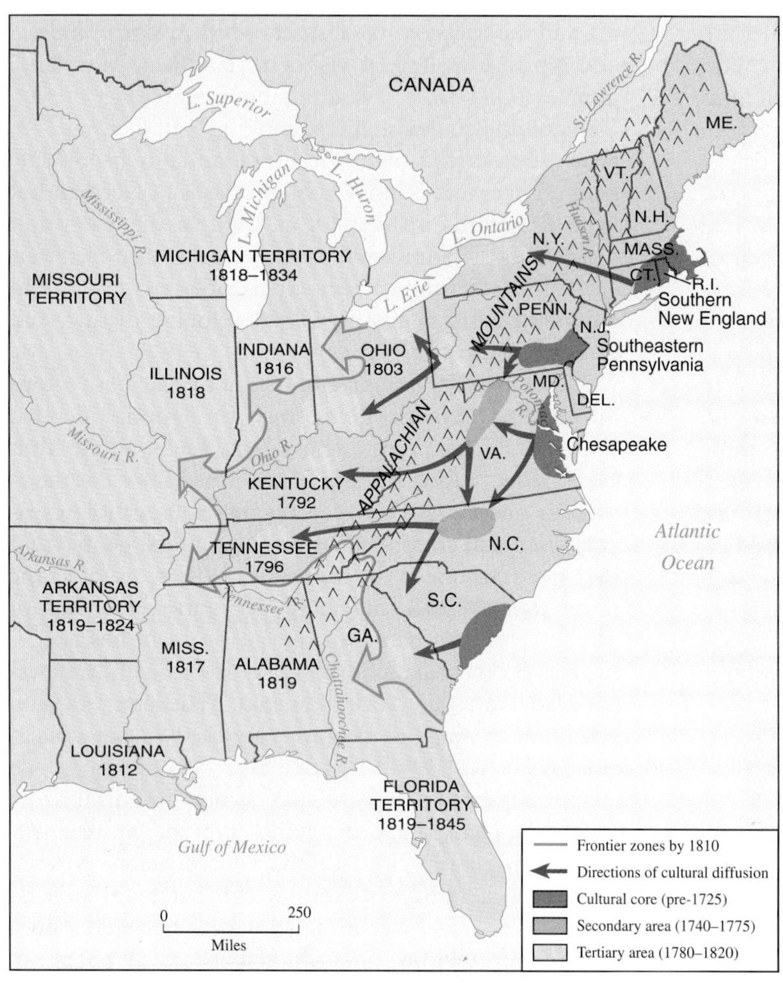

MAP 8.4

Regional Cultures Move West, 1720–1820

By 1720 four distinct "core" cultures had developed along the Atlantic coast and, by 1775, those of the Middle Atlantic and Chesapeake regions had been carried into the southern backcountry. Then, between 1780 and 1820, settlers transplanted all four regional cultures into different parts of the trans-Appalachian West. Extensive cultural intermixture—and conflict—occurred only in certain regions, such as southern Ohio, Kentucky, and Tennessee.

ment was controlled by the national government. He also maintained that the western frontier experience itself—the life-or-death struggle with nature—created a character and system of values that was distinctly American: individualistic, optimistic, pragmatic, and democratic.

Turner's theories provoked a generation of scholarly research and debate, but historians no longer accept many of his views. For instance, Turner underestimated the force of cultural tradition. Most migrants to the West, like most Europeans who came to America, sought to preserve their old values and customs. Thus, when 176 residents of Granville, Massachusetts, decided to move to Ohio, they carefully chose a site whose "peculiar blending of hill and valley" resembled the landscape of their New England community. They transplanted their Congregational Church to Ohio whole, complete with ministers and elders, along with their system of freehold agriculture. So it was throughout the West: in many respects, "new" communities were not new—they were old communities that had moved inland.

Yet Turner was right about the primitive conditions of frontier living. Cut off from outside markets, settlers made their own clothes, repaired old tools, and lived in a barter economy, exchanging goods or labor with their neighbors. "A noble field of Indian corn stretched away into the forest on one side," an English visitor to an Ohio farm in the 1820s noted, waxing romantic,

> and immediately before the house was a small potato garden, with a few peach and apple trees. The woman told me that they spun and wove all the cotton and woollen garments of the family, and knit all the stockings; her husband, though not a shoemaker by trade, made all the shoes. She manufactured all the soap and candles they use. All she wanted with money, she said, was to buy coffee, tea, and whiskey, and she could "get enough any day by sending a batch of butter and chickens to market."

A low standard of living prevailed for this and other farm families for more than a generation. As late as 1840, per capita income in the Old Northwest was only 70 percent of the national average.

Apart from its relative poverty, the distinctiveness of the region lay in the conflict among competing cultural traditions. In Indiana, education-conscious migrants from New England set up a system of public primary schools, but only after a twenty-year battle with tax-shy yeomen from the southern states. Societies in the Old Northwest developed largely along the model of the Middle Atlantic states—Pennsylvania, New Jersey, and New York—with their diverse cultural traditions and ethnic political factions.

The Old Southwest

Slavery Moves Southwest. As poor white farmers and tenants fled from the plantation economy of the Chesapeake states to Kentucky and Tennessee, wealthy planters and up-and-coming young men from the Chesapeake and the Carolinas set up new slave plantations in the Old Southwest—the future states of Alabama, Mississippi, and Louisiana. Consequently, the southwestern frontier became a stronghold, not of Turner's individualism and democracy, but of slavery.

Indeed, slavery increased dramatically in extent and importance in the United States following independence. Rice planters in Georgia and South Carolina had used their influence at the Philadelphia convention of 1787 to exempt the importation of slaves from national regulation for twenty years. When the time limit expired in 1808, Congress banned American participation in the transatlantic trade in slaves in response to antislavery sentiment in the North. By then planters had purchased 250,000 new Africans, a number equal to the total of all slaves imported during the colonial period. The black population had also grown through reproduction. Unlike the West Indies, in the United States more blacks were born than died each year. Between 1775 and 1820, the slave population grew from 0.5 million to 1.8 million.

Many of these Africans and African-Americans still toiled on tobacco and rice plantations. When tobacco production stagnated in the Chesapeake region because of soil exhaustion, white planters took the crop into North Carolina, Kentucky, and Tennessee. The rice industry of South Carolina and Georgia grew until the 1820s, when many of its overseas markets were lost to cheaper rice from Asia. By that time, white planters in Louisiana—some of them refugees from black-controlled Haiti—had established a booming economy based on sugar. Slaves in Louisiana, like those on the sugar plantations of the West Indies, died quickly from disease and overwork.

The Coming of Cotton. However, it was a new crop—cotton—that provided the main economic base for the slave regime in the South after 1790. For centuries, most Europeans had worn clothing made from wool or flax; cotton imported from India was only for the rich. Cotton spinning and weaving had been taken up in England in the mid-seventeenth century but had remained a minor industry. Then, after 1750 the European population explosion increased the demand for woolen and cotton cloth, just as the technological breakthroughs of the Industrial Revolution boosted production and lowered prices. Soon there was an insatiable demand for raw cotton to feed the newly invented water-powered spinning jennies and weaving mules.

Beginning in the 1780s American planters responded to this demand by importing a rot-resistant, smooth-seed, long-fiber variety of cotton from the West Indies and planting it on sea islands along the southern Atlantic coast. Then, in the 1790s, a number of inventors—including Connecticut-born Eli Whitney—developed machines to separate the seeds from the fiber of short-staple cotton, which grew well in many regions of the South.

The combination of English demand and American invention created a new industry—and a massive demand for land and labor. Thousands of white planters moved into the interior of South Carolina and Georgia to grow cotton. Following the War of 1812, production spread into Mississippi and Alabama, which entered the Union in 1817 and 1819, respectively. In a single year, a government land office in Huntsville, Alabama, took in $7 million. The expression "doing a land-office business"—a metaphor for rapid commercial expansion—dates from this time.

For blacks the coming of cotton meant being uprooted from the Chesapeake or Carolina regions and forced to move west with their owners or sold to other migrating planters through a new internal slave trade. Within two generations, whites had displaced more than 835,000 slaves from their birthplaces to the booming cotton states.

The history of the Tayloe family's Mount Airy plantation in Virginia illustrates the impact of cotton on the lives of blacks. In 1747, John Tayloe owned 167 slaves at Mount Airy. Over the next sixty years, twice as many slaves were born as died on this plantation, creating a large, interrelated African-American community—and, from the Tayloes' point of view, a "surplus" of workers. Hence, in 1792 John Tayloe III advertised a sale of 200 slaves, at least 50 of whom came from Mount Airy. Between 1828 and 1860 Tayloe and his sons moved 180 Mount Airy slaves to their new cotton plantations in Alabama.

These sales and migrations brought great wealth to white families like the Tayloes and untold misery to blacks. Torn from their loved ones, African-Americans had to rebuild their lives, laboring "from day clean to first dark" on frontier plantations in Alabama and Mississippi. "I am Sold to a man by the name of Peterson a

Arise! Arise! and weep no more
dry up your tears, we Shall part
no more. Come rose we go to
Tennessee,
that happy Shore. to old virginia
never — never — return. —

The Internal Slave Trade

Mounted whites escort a convoy of slaves from Virginia to Tennessee in Louis Miller's *Slave Trader, Sold to Tennessee*. The trade was a lucrative one for whites, pumping money into the declining Chesapeake economy and valuable workers into the labor-starved plantations of the cotton belt. For blacks it was traumatic, breaking up families and communities. (Abby Aldrich Rockefeller Folk Art Center)

trader," lamented one Georgia slave. "My Dear wife for you and my Children my pen cannot Express the griffe I feel to be parted from you all."

Antislavery Movements. The expansion of slavery into the Old Southwest destroyed the hopes of those who thought slavery would "die a natural death" along with the decline of the tobacco economy. Antislavery advocates in the North reluctantly accepted the existence of slavery; all they could do was try to control its spread. Some reformers worked to prevent the illegal importation of slaves from Africa. Others persuaded the legislatures of northern states to pass *personal liberty laws*, protecting free blacks from kidnapping or seizure under the terms of the Fugitive Slave Act of 1793.

More important, reformers opposed the expansion of slavery into the western territories. During the 1810s, Louisiana, Mississippi, and Alabama joined the Union with state constitutions permitting slavery. When Missouri applied for admission on a similar basis in 1819, antislavery forces rallied. Congressman James Tallmadge of New York proposed a ban on the importation of slaves into Missouri and the gradual emancipation of its black inhabitants. When Missouri whites rejected these conditions, the northern majority in the House of Representatives blocked the territory's admission to the Union. In response, southerners used their power in the Senate, which was equally divided between eleven free and eleven slave states, to withhold statehood from Maine, which was seeking to separate itself from Massachusetts. Tempers flared in the heat of debate. "You have kindled a fire which all the waters of the ocean cannot put out," Senator Thomas W. Cobb of Georgia warned Tallmadge, and "which seas of blood can only extinguish."

Controversy raged for two years before Congress resolved the stalemate. Representative Henry Clay of Kentucky and other skilled politicians put together a series of agreements known collectively as the Missouri Compromise, by which Maine entered the Union as a

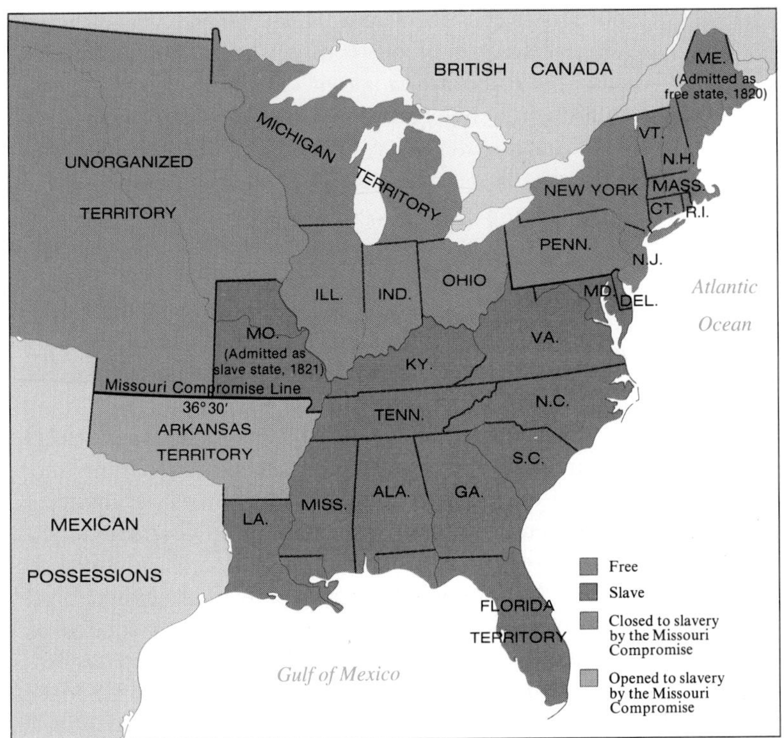

MAP 8.5

The Missouri Compromise, 1820

The Missouri Compromise resolved for a generation the issue of slavery in the lands of the Louisiana Purchase. Slavery was forbidden north of the Missouri Compromise line (36° 30' north latitude), with the exception of the state of Missouri. To maintain an equal number of free and slave states in the U.S. Senate, the Compromise provided for the nearly simultaneous admission of Maine and Missouri.

free state in 1820, and Missouri was admitted as a slave state the following year. This bargain preserved the existing sectional balance in the Senate and set a precedent for the future admission of states—in pairs, one free, one slave. To mollify antislavery sentiment in the House of Representatives, southern congressmen accepted the restriction of slavery in the rest of the Louisiana Territory north of latitude 36° 30', the southern boundary of Missouri.

The tradition of compromise on the issue of slavery was thus continued. In 1821, as in 1787, northern and southern political leaders gave priority to the Union, finding complex but workable ways to reconcile the interests of their regions. But the task had become more difficult. The Philadelphia delegates had resolved their sectional differences in two months; Congress took two years to work out the Missouri Compromise, and there was no guarantee that it would work. The fate of the West, the Union, and the black race were inextricably intertwined. American politicians feared that the North and the South, with their conflicting systems of free and slave labor, would compete for dominance in the new territories and that whoever succeeded would take control of the national government, pushing the losing side toward civil war. "This momentous question, like a firebell in the night, awakened and filled me with terror," Thomas Jefferson wrote, at the time of the Missouri controversy.

African-American Society and Culture

In the early decades of the nineteenth century, a more unified African-American culture began to develop in the United States, for two main reasons. First, the end of the legal transatlantic slave trade in 1808 reduced the flow of new Africans to a trickle, cutting blacks off from cultural contact with their home continent and eliminating the need to assimilate newly arrived Africans into African-American society. Second, the westward movement reduced differences among slaves; as African-Americans from the Chesapeake region and the Carolinas mingled in the states of the Old Southwest, they created a more unified culture. For example, the black Gullah dialect of the Carolinas disappeared on the cotton plantations of Alabama and Mississippi because slaves from the Chesapeake had adopted English.

Many African elements persisted in the new African-American culture. As the traveler Isaac Holmes reported in 1821:

> In Louisiana, and the state of Mississippi, the slaves . . . dance for several hours during Sunday afternoon. The general movement is in what they call the Congo dance; their music often consists of nothing more than an excavated piece of wood . . . one end of which is a piece of parchment.

African-American Banjos

In 1794 an Englishman in Virginia watched African-Americans dancing to the music of a banjo, "made of a gourd something in the imitation of a Guitar, with only four strings and played with the fingers in the same manner."

Similar descriptions of blacks who "danced the Congo and sang a purely African song to the accompaniment of . . . a drum made by stretching a skin over a flour barrell" appeared as late as 1890.

Marriage and Family Life. The white elite of South Carolina routinely married their cousins in order to keep property in the family and maintain an intermarried ruling group. African-Americans had different incest rules, in part because of African customs. Blacks shunned marriages between cousins, even on relatively self-contained plantations. On the Good Hope plantation in South Carolina about 175 slave children were born between 1800 and 1857, 40 percent of whom were related by blood to three slaves from Africa. Despite the elaborate tangle of kinship in this black community, only one marriage between cousins took place.

Masters and slaves also had different ideas about the sanctity of marriage. Whereas whites insisted on legally binding marriage contracts among themselves, both to regulate morals and to establish the ownership of property, they forbade legal marriage between blacks. Owners wanted to be able to sell their slaves without breaking a marriage bond. As so often in the history of slavery, a concern for property rights overrode moral principles.

Slaves therefore devised their own marriage rituals. Young men and women first asked their parents' consent to marry, then sought their owner's permission to live together in their own cabin. Following African custom, many couples signified their union in a public ceremony by jumping over a broomstick together. Blacks who were Christians often had a religious service performed by a white or a black preacher. These rites never ended with the customary phrase "Until death do you part." Everyone knew that black marriages could end with the sale of one or both parties.

Most married slaves who were not separated by sale lived in stable unions. Among the slaves on the Good Hope Plantation in South Carolina, about 70 percent of the women had all their children by the same man. Most other women had their first child before marriage, in what the community called an "outside" birth, and bore the rest of their children within a stable union. On plantations in Louisiana black family ties were much more fragile, in part because labor in the sugar fields killed many men. Thirty percent of the slave women on one Louisiana plantation lived alone with their children, who were fathered by a succession of men.

The oppressive conditions of slavery thus partially undermined blacks' efforts to create solid family bonds. To maintain their identity, some slaves bestowed African names on their children; males born on Friday were often called Cuffee—the name of that day in various West African languages. The majority of slaves chose names of British origin and bound one generation to another by naming sons after fathers, uncles, or grandfathers; daughters were often named after grandmothers. Names had symbolic importance, for they gave cultural significance to the biological ties of kinship. Like incest rules and marriage rituals, naming patterns created order in a harsh and arbitrary world.

As an African-American cultural community developed, the quality of slave life gradually improved. During the eighteenth century, a lack of social organization among African-born slaves (because of their diverse

TABLE 8.1

African-American Naming Patterns

Good Hope Plantation Slaves, Orangebury, South Carolina

Date of Birth	Baby's Name	Parents' Names	Source of Baby's Name
1793	Hector	Bess, Hector	Father
1806	Clarinda	Patty, Primus	Mother's mother
1811	Sambo	Affy, Jacob	Mother's father
1813	Primus	Patty, Primus	Father
1824	Sarah	Phoebe, Jack	Mother's mother
1828	Major	Clarinda, Abram	Father's father

tribal origins) had made it easy for white men to take advantage of blacks. They had raped women and punished defiant men in horrible ways, branding them or cutting off their fingers or ears or even castrating them. Such abuses did not stop after 1800, but they were questioned more often. White politicians condemned rape as an aristocratic vice, ill suited to life in a republican society. The spread of evangelical Christianity encouraged many masters to treat their slaves more humanely. African-Americans also put themselves in a better position to resist the worst forms of oppression by forming stable families and strong communities. A brutal master faced the prospect that a slave's relative might retaliate for violence, by arson, poison, or destruction of crops or equipment.

Blacks in the lowlands of South Carolina were particularly successful in gaining control over their work lives. By the Revolutionary Era, these slaves had won the right to labor by the *task*. Each day, a worker had to complete a precisely defined task—turn up a quarter-acre of rice land, hoe a half-acre, or pound seven mortars of rice. Many slaves finished their task "by one or two o'clock in the afternoon," a Methodist preacher reported. They had "the rest of the day for themselves, which they spend in working their own private fields, consisting of 5 or 6 acres of ground . . . planting rice, corn, potatoes, tobacco &c. for their own use and profit." African-Americans jealously guarded these hard-won rights. "Should any owner increase the work beyond what is customary," a South Carolina planter said, "he subjects himself . . . to such discontent amongst his slaves as to make them of little use to him."

White masters still had virtually unlimited legal power over their slaves. They could sell those who were recalcitrant or punish those they viewed as lazy—and many did not hesitate to do so. But among some planters a new conception of blacks evolved. No longer called "pagans" or "savages," African-Americans over several generations came to be referred to as the "children" of the plantation, and the slave community as part of the plantation "family." St. George Tucker's novel *The Valley of the Shenandoah* (1824) offered the first literary depiction of slaveowners as the paternalistic guardians of their black laborers.

Though somewhat more benevolent, the new paternalism was still based on feelings of ownership, and slaves resisted it just as they had resisted the old tyranny. Some, such as Gabriel Prosser of Virginia, went so far as to plot mass uprisings and murders. Denmark Vesey, a free black married to a slave woman, planned a rebellion in Charleston, South Carolina, in 1822, but, like Prosser's, it was discovered and crushed at the last moment. Most blacks knew that a successful revolt was impossible, in the face of white strength in numbers and military superiority. Flight was also out of the question. An ocean separated blacks from their African homeland, and the northern and western states were hotbeds of racial prejudice, where their masters could track them down and use the Fugitive Slave Law (1793) to carry them back to bondage. The one available avenue of escape—to Spanish Florida—was cut off in 1818 when the United States annexed Florida. Slaves had no option but to build the best possible lives for themselves where they were. As the black abolitionist Frederick Douglass would later observe, slave communities were "pegged down to a single spot" and "must take root there or nowhere."

And so enslaved African-Americans developed a culture similar to that of European peasants. They worked as dependent agricultural laborers and lived in close-knit communities based on family, kinship, and religion.

AMERICAN LIVES

Richard Allen and African-American Identity

Richard Allen was a success. Born into slavery in Philadelphia in 1760, he died in 1831 not only a free man but an influential one, a founder of the African Methodist Episcopal Church and its first bishop. Allen's rise from poverty and obscurity to affluence and fame has much of the classic American success story about it. But there is a larger significance, since Allen, as one of the first blacks to be emancipated, had to forge an identity for his people as well as for himself.

Sold as a child along with his family to a farmer in Delaware, Allen's ascent began in 1777, when he was converted to Methodism by Freeborn Garretson, an itinerant preacher. Garretson also converted Allen's master and convinced him that, on Judgment Day, slaveholders would be "weighted in the balance, and . . . found wanting." Allowed by his repentant owner to buy his freedom, Allen earned a living sawing cordwood and driving a wagon during the Revolutionary War. After the war he furthered the Methodist cause by becoming a "licensed exhorter," preaching to blacks and whites from New York to South Carolina. He attracted the attention of Francis Asbury, the first American bishop of the Methodist church, and other Methodist leaders, and in 1786 the Methodist elder in charge in Philadelphia sent for Allen. Allen took up residence in Phildelphia, ministering to the racially mixed congregation of St. George's Methodist Church. The following year he and Absalom Jones joined other ex-slaves and Quaker philanthropists to form the Free African Society, a quasi-religious benevolent organization that offered fellowship and mutual aid to "free Africans and their descendants."

Allen remained a staunch Methodist throughout his life. In 1789, when the Free African Society adopted various Quaker practices, such as having fifteen minutes of silence at its meetings, Allen led a withdrawal of those who preferred the more enthusiastic Methodist practices. In 1794 he rejected an offer to become the pastor of the church the Free African Society had built, St. Thomas's African Episcopal Church. A large majority of the society had chosen to unite with the Episcopal (formerly Anglican) Church, since much of the city's black community had been Anglican since the 1740s. "I informed them that I could not be anything else but a Methodist, as I was born and awakened under them," Allen recalled. (The pastorate of St. Thomas's was finally accepted by Absalom Jones.)

To reconcile his faith and his African-American identity, Allen decided he had to form his own congregation. He gathered a group of ten black Methodists and converted a blacksmith's shop into a church, Bethel African Methodist Episcopal Church. Although the church was opened by Bishop Francis Asbury in July 1794, its tiny congregation worshiped "separate from our white brethren."

Allen's decision to found a black congregation was partly a response to white racism. Although most white Methodists favored emancipation in the 1790s, they did not treat free blacks as equals. They refused to support a fund-raising drive for an African-American church, and, in a famous incident in 1792, segregated blacks into a newly built gallery of St. George's Methodist Church. But Allen's action also reflected a desire among African-Americans to control their religious lives, to have the power, for example,"to call any brother that appears to us adequate to the task to preach or exhort as a local preacher, without the interference of the Conference." By 1795 the congregation of Allen's Bethel Church numbered 121; a decade later it had grown to 457, and by 1813, to 1,272.

Bethel's rapid growth showed the appeal of Methodist practices. Newly freed blacks welcomed "love feasts," which allowed the full expression of emotions repressed under slavery. They were attracted as

The Mount Bethel African Methodist Episcopal Church, Philadelphia

well by the church's strict system of discipline, which assisted them in bringing order to their lives. Allen's preaching also played a role; the excellence of his sermons was recognized in 1799, when Bishop Asbury ordained him the first black deacon of the Methodist Church.

But over the years Allen and other blacks grew dissatisfied with Methodism, as white churchmen retreated from their antislavery principles and attempted to curb the autonomy of African-American congregations. In 1807 the Bethel Church added an "African Supplement" to its articles of incorporation; in 1816 it won legal recognition as an independent church. In the same year Allen and representatives from four other black Methodist congregations (in Baltimore; Wilmington, Delaware; Salem, New Jersey; and Attleboro, Pennsylvania) met at Bethel Church to organize a new denomination, the African Methodist Episcopal Church. Allen was chosen as the first bishop of the church, the first fully independent black denomination in America. Allen had succeeded in charting a separate religious identity for African-Americans.

Allen also recognized the importance of education to the future of the African-American community and identity. In 1795 he opened a day school for sixty children, and in 1804 he founded the "Society of Free People of Colour for Promoting the Instruction and School Education of Children of African Descent."

But where did Allen think "free people of colour" should look for their future? This question had arisen in Philadelphia in 1787, when William Thornton promoted a plan devised by antislavery groups in London to colonize free American blacks (and emancipted slaves from the West Indies) in Sierra Leone, an independent state they had founded on the west coast of Africa. Many blacks in Boston and Newport had endorsed this scheme, but Philadelphia's Free African Society had preferred to seek advancement in America. In 1815 the city's black population, now numbering about 12,000, again rejected colonization: only four people signed up for emigration to Sierra Leone.

Instead, Philadelphia's black community petitioned the state and national governments to end slavery and the slave trade and asked for repeal of the Fugitive Slave Act of 1793, which allowed slaveowners to seize blacks without a warrant. As if to underline the importance of these political initiatives, in 1806 Allen himself was temporarily seized as a fugitive slave, showing that even the most prominent northern blacks could not be sure of their freedom. This experience may account for Allen's initial support for the American Colonization Society, an organization founded in 1817 to promote the settlement of free blacks in Africa. This scheme was immediately condemned by a mass meeting of nearly 3,000 Philadelphia blacks, who set forth a different vision of the African-American future: "Whereas our ancestors (not of choice) were the first successful cultivators of the wilds of America, we their descendants feel ourselves entitled to participate in the blessings of her luxuriant soil."

Philadelphia's black community, including Allen, was more favorably inclined toward the Haitian Emigration Society, founded in 1824 to help African-Americans settle on that island republic. But when that venture failed, Allen forcefully urged blacks to remain in the United States. In November 1827, he made a compelling argument in *Freedom's Journal*, the nation's first black newspaper: "This land which we have watered with our *tears* and *our blood* is now our *mother country*."

Born a slave of African ancestry, Allen had come to terms with freedom and with white America. He had risen to a position of eminence and he had created separate African-American institutions. But he had ultimately decided to cast his lot, and that of his descendants, with a society pervaded by racism. It was a brave decision, characteristic of the man who made it, and one whose wisdom has yet to be determined.

Black Religion. After the family, the religious community played the most important role in African-American life. Some blacks kept up African practices, invoking traditional spirits in time of need. Some slaves who had been moved from Haiti to Louisiana practiced the folk religion of voodoo, a blend of African and Catholic customs. Most African-Americans became Christians, absorbing the religious views of white Baptists and Methodists but putting their own interpretation on them, reflecting their own experiences and values. Black theology generally ignored the doctrines of original sin and predestination. It also downplayed those biblical passages in which the church is viewed as lawgiver and symbol of authority. Black Christians preferred to envision God as a warrior who had liberated his chosen people. "Their cause was similar to the 'Israelites'," Martin Prosser, Gabriel's brother, told his fellow slave conspirators during the thwarted rebellion in Virginia in 1800. "I have read in my Bible where God says, if we worship him, we should have peace in all our land and five of you shall conquer a hundred and a hundred of you a hundred thousand of our enemies."

The Christian message promoted spiritual endurance as well as physical resistance. Some slaves identified with the persecuted Christ, who had suffered and died so his followers might find peace and justice in the next world. Amid the manifest injustice of their own lives, these African-Americans used Christian principles to affirm their equality with whites in the eyes of God. Slaves had taken the language and religion of their masters, but then adapted them for their own ends. Trapped in a bicultural world, they learned from whites but lived as blacks.

The Fate of Native Americans

"Next to the case of the black race within our bosom," James Madison remarked as he left the presidency in 1817, "that of the red race on our borders is the problem most baffling to the policy of our country." Most American political leaders did not suffer misgivings on this score. They wanted to open lands in the trans-Appalachian West, and they were determined to assimilate or expel the native American inhabitants. "The savage must ever recede before the march of civilization," proclaimed one southerner. For many educated whites, the conquest of the interior and its aboriginal inhabitants represented the historical progress of mankind: primitive life was replaced by higher cultural forms. As a congressional committee put it in 1818, "Those sons of the forest should be moralized or exterminated."

In the name of "civilization," government officials sought to destroy the traditional economic, political, and religious practices of the native Americans. Henry Knox, Washington's first secretary of war, had advocated breaking up commonly owned tribal lands and distributing farming plots to individual Indian families as their private property, a concept that was alien to the Indians. Other white leaders demanded that Indians abandon allegiance to their tribal governments and submit to the authority of the state and the nation. Public officials also encouraged the efforts of missionaries to change the Indians' religious beliefs. The object, as one Kentucky minister put it, was to make the Indian "a farmer, a citizen of the United States, and a Christian."

Few native Americans willingly accepted this definition of their identity. Many tribes drove out white missionaries and forced converts among their own people to participate in traditional rites. To justify their ancestral values, Indian leaders devised theories of cultural and religious dualism. They argued that the Great Spirit had made the two races different and intended them to have different ways of life. Nevertheless, under pressure from missionaries and the military, many tribes broke into hostile religious factions. Among the Seneca of New York, for example, the prophet Handsome Lake adopted some Christian precepts, such as belief in heaven and hell, and used them to discourage his followers from drinking alcohol, gambling, or practicing witchcraft. But Handsome Lake also promoted traditional agricultural ceremonies—the green corn dance, the strawberry festival, and the false-face pageant—that gave ritual thanks to the earth, plants, animals, water, and sun. More conservative people among the Seneca clung to the old ways, believed in witchcraft, and resisted the influence of white missionaries. Handsome Lake's political enemy Red Jacket led the Seneca in opposing such innovations as men working in the fields, a practice that turned their values upside down.

Even Indian Christians would not give up their tribal identity. They viewed themselves not as individuals but as members of a clan, all descendants of the same person. Most clans adopted an animal—a deer, turtle, fox, or bear—as their *totem*, or designation, often because of some vision of their original ancestor. Indians also superimposed new Christian identities onto familiar clan spirits.

Strong ancestral values likewise prompted Indians to reject European agricultural methods. White farm women lived in a male-dominated cultural world and accepted an inferior position with respect to sex roles, property rights, and marriage. By comparison, the women in most Eastern Woodland tribes had greater economic importance, growing corn, squash, beans, and other basic foods, and often controlling (in *matrilineal* fashion) the inheritance of cultivation rights on certain lands. Indian women resisted being taken out of the fields, and few Indian men wished to replace them there, preferring the manly roles of hunter and warrior.

AMERICAN VOICES

A Seneca Chief's Understanding of Religion *Red Jacket*

The Seneca chief Red Jacket (c. 1758–1830) acquired his unusual name during the Revolutionary War, when he fought for the British "redcoats." He reconciled himself to American rule and joined an Indian delegation that met George Washington. He rejected Christianity, however, and in 1805 he explained why to a group of missionaries.

Brother: Continue to listen. You say that you are sent to instruct us how to worship the Great Spirit agreeably to his mind; and, if we do not take hold of the religion which you white people teach, we shall be unhappy hereafter. You say that you are right, and we are lost. How do we know this to be true? We understand that your religion is written in a book. If it was intended for us as well as you, why has not the Great Spirit given to us, and not only to us, but why did He not give to our forefathers, the knowledge of the book, with the means of understanding it rightly?

Brother: The Great Spirit has made us all, but he has made a great difference between his white and red children. He has given us different complexions and different customs. To you He has given the arts. To these He has not opened our eyes. We know these things to be true. Since He has made a great difference between us in other things, why may we not conclude that He has given us different religion according to our understanding? The Great Spirit does right. He knows what is best for his children; we are satisfied.

Source: David J. Rothman and Sheila Rothman, eds., *Sources of the American Social Tradition* (New York: Basic Books, 1975).

To accept European values would be to repudiate clan identity and the essence of Indian life.

The Cherokee. Native Americans assimilated European ways only under special circumstances and for specific purposes. Beginning in the late eighteenth century, the Cherokee of Georgia and the Carolinas organized an unusually centralized political system in order to resist more effectively the advancing white settlers who wanted their lands for growing cotton. A Cherokee national council, headed by two respected chiefs, oversaw all thirteen thousand members of the tribe with respect to certain activities—maintaining a mounted police force, abolishing clan revenge for murder, and establishing a limited *patrilineal* inheritance system.

These innovations were implemented by a small faction of Christian Cherokee mixed-bloods. Most mixed-bloods were the offspring of white fur traders and Indian women. Growing up in a bicultural world, they learned the language and political ways of white people. To resist attempts to oust them from their ancestral lands in 1806 and again in 1817, Christian Cherokee mixed-bloods found ways to forge a strong tribal identity among their people. Sequoyah, a mixed-blood, developed a system of writing for the Cherokee language, and the tribe published a newspaper. In 1827, the Cherokee introduced a new charter of government modeled directly on the U.S. Constitution. By this time,

Divisions Among the Cherokee
In 1821 Sequoyah, a mixed-blood, devised a written script for the Cherokee language and the tribe published a newspaper, printed both in English and Cherokee. Few full-blooded Cherokee could read either language and continued their traditional oral culture. (Philadelphia Museum of Art)

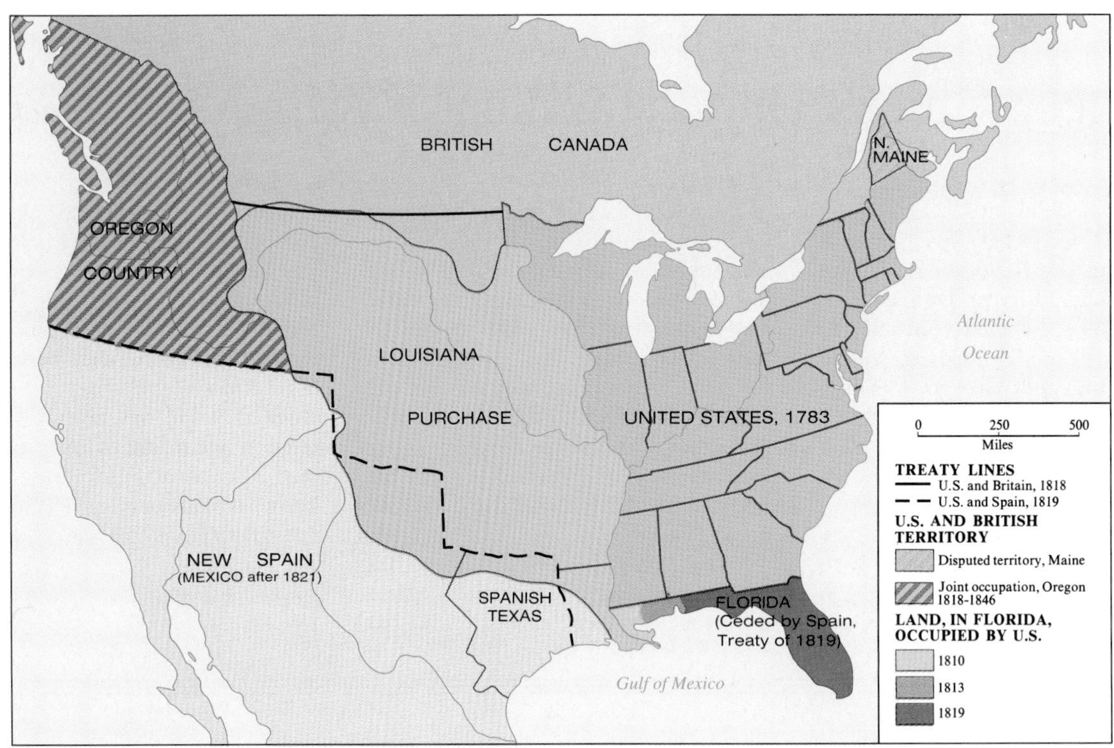

MAP 8.6

Defining the National Boundaries

Following the War of 1812, American statesmen negotiated treaties with Great Britain and Spain that defined the boundary with Canada in the north and with New Spain (which in 1821 became the independent nation of Mexico) in the west. These treaties eliminated the threat of war until the 1840s, providing the young American nation with a much-needed period of peace and security.

many mixed-bloods had abandoned traditional ways, and dressed and behaved much like white planters. A few were quite prosperous. James Vann, a Georgia Cherokee, owned more than twenty black slaves, two trading posts, and a grist mill. Forty other Cherokee mixed-blood families owned a total of more than 1,000 slaves.

Mixed-blood Christians were caught between two cultures, never fully accepted by either. Whites treated them as Indians, to be pushed ever westward, and full-blooded Cherokee condemned their white values. Full-bloods seized power in the Great Smoky Mountains and, because of their numbers, gradually took control of the national council, which then resisted both cultural assimilation and forced removal. Like most native Americans, the Indians of the Southeast wanted to practice their traditional culture on ancestral lands. "We would not receive money for land in which our fathers and friends are buried," a Creek chief declared. "We love our land; it is our mother." Unfortunately for the Indians, historical events turned the attention of white Americans increasingly to the West.

Diplomacy and the West

The tumultuous era of the early republic came to an end around 1820. Peace in Europe ended two decades of conflict in America over foreign policy, and the continuing success of the Republicans brought about the demise of the Federalists, whose eastern-oriented policies and elitist outlook received little support in an expanding, increasingly democratic nation. "No Federal character can run with success," Gouverneur Morris of New York lamented, and the election results of 1818 bore out his pessimism. Following the voting, Republicans outnumbered Federalists in the Senate by 37 to 7 and in the House of Representatives by 156 to 27.

The decline of the Federalists prompted contemporary observers to call the two terms of President James Monroe, from 1817 to 1825, the Era of Good Feeling. Actually, national political harmony was more apparent than real, for the dominant Republican party—now home to many former Federalists—split into factions that struggled among themselves over power and patronage.

Among the Federalists who joined the Republican party was John Quincy Adams, the son of John Adams. A dour and suspicious man, John Quincy greatly resembled his Federalist father. But the younger Adams feared British power more than French ideology, so even before the War of 1812, he had joined the Republicans. As secretary of state under Monroe, the younger Adams pursued an expansionist western policy that would have astounded his father. In 1817, when General Andrew Jackson led an expedition into East Florida, seized two Spanish forts, and executed two British subjects, accusing them of promoting Seminole raids into the United States, Adams defended the general, despite strong reservations about his character and conduct.

Indeed, Adams used the diplomatic crisis created by Jackson's attack to put Spain on the defensive. Threatening to invade Florida, Adams secured a treaty in 1819 by which East Florida was annexed to the United States. In return, the American government accepted responsibility for the financial claims of American citizens against Spain, renounced its dubious claim to Spanish Texas, and agreed on a boundary between New Spain and the Louisiana Territory.

Adams also negotiated important agreements with Great Britain. The Rush-Bagot treaty of 1817 eliminated a longstanding source of conflict by limiting British and U.S. naval forces on the Great Lakes. More important, in 1818 the two countries agreed to establish the border between the Louisiana Territory and British Canada at the 49th parallel. As a result of Adams's efforts, the United States gained undisputed possession of nearly all the land south of the 49th parallel and between the Great Lakes and the Rocky Mountains.

Secretary Adams and President Monroe had this continental empire in mind when they outlined a new foreign policy which, thirty years later, became known as the Monroe Doctrine. In an address to Congress in 1823, Monroe, at Adams's behest, gave a warning to Spain and other European powers to stay out of the Western Hemisphere. During and after the Napoleonic Wars, patriots in Mexico and other Latin American countries had revolted against Spanish rule and established independent republics. The United States had extended diplomatic recognition to the new republics, and now Monroe warned Spain not to try to subdue them. The president, hoping as well to prevent the Russians from extending their fishing camps and fur-trading posts south of Alaska, also declared that the American continents were not "subject for further colonization" by the nations of Europe. In return, Monroe reiterated that it was the policy of the United States "not to interfere in the internal concerns" of European nations. Monroe and Adams had turned their backs on Europe. They now looked purposefully westward, envisioning an American empire that stretched from the Atlantic to the Pacific.

Summary

With the acquisition of Louisiana and white settlement of the trans-Appalachian West, the United States became a continental nation. The pace of white advance was slowed by native Americans fighting to defend their lands, by the difficulties of transport and trade across the mountains, and by the high price of land sold by the U.S. government and by speculators. Nonetheless, by 1820 two million white and black Americans were living west of the Appalachians.

Led by Thomas Jefferson, the Republicans wrested political power from the Federalists by gaining western support. While retaining the Bank of the United States and many Federalist bureaucrats, Jefferson eliminated excise taxes, reduced the national debt, and cut the size of the army. Faced with British and French seizures of American ships and sailors, he devised the Embargo of 1807, but it failed to change the belligerents' policies. Eventually, Indian uprisings and expansionist demands by western Republicans led President Madison into the War of 1812. The war split the nation, prompting a secessionist movement in New England, but ultimately confirming American sovereignty over the southern half of North America.

The war strengthened American national identity, but regional customs remained strong. Migrants from New England carried their way of life to the Old Northwest, while southerners created a slave-based cotton economy in the Old Southwest. Blacks adopted some white religious practices but devised a distinct African-American culture. James Monroe and John Quincy Adams envisioned a continental nation, but American society was increasingly divided by region and race, creating a sectional confrontation over slavery that the Missouri Compromise of 1820 did not fully resolve.

TOPIC FOR RESEARCH

The Subject Races

Native Americans and African-Americans came from cultures that were very different from those of the European settlers who controlled the United States. And so, when Americans of European descent sought to impose their values, blacks and Indians resisted, seeking to preserve their own cultural identities. To what extent did they succeed? In what ways did native Americans and African-Americans retain their original cultural identities? In what ways did they assimilate European-American customs or beliefs? Did they create any new cultural forms?

Works dealing with native Americans include Robert F. Berkhofer, Jr., *Salvation and Savage: An Analysis of Protestant Missions and American Indian Response, 1787–1862* (1965); Henry Warner Bowden, *American Indians and Christian Missions: Studies in Cultural Conflict* (1981); William W. Fitzhugh, ed., *Cultures in Contact* (1985); William G. McLoughlin, *Cherokees and Missionaries, 1789–1839* (1984) and *Cherokee Renascence in the New Republic* (1986); and J. Leitch Wright, Jr., *Creeks and Seminoles: The Destruction and Regeneration of the Muscogulge People* (1986).

Studies dealing with African-Americans are Ira Berlin, *Slaves Without Masters: The Free Negro in the Antebellum South* (1974); Dena J. Epstein, *Sinful Tunes and Spirituals: Black Folk Music to the Civil War* (1977); Mechal Sobel, *The World They Made Together: Black and White Values in Eighteenth-Century Virginia* (1987); and Herbert Gutman, *The Black Family in Slavery and Freedom, 1750–1925* (1976).

BIBLIOGRAPHY

Westward Expansion

The interaction of whites and native Americans can be traced in Francis Paul Prucha, *American Indian Policy in the Formative Years: The Indian Trade and Intercourse Acts, 1790–1834* (1962); Bernard Sheehan, *Seeds of Extinction: Jeffersonian Philanthropy and the American Indian* (1973); Reginald Horsman, *Expansion and American Indian Policy, 1783–1812* (1967) and *The Frontier in the Formative Years, 1783–1815* (1970); and Dorothy Jones, *License for Empire: Colonialism by Treaty in Early America* (1982). See also Richard Slotkin, *Regeneration Through Violence: The Mythology of the American Frontier* (1973).

Malcolm J. Rohrbough, *The Land Office Business* (1968), discusses the disposal of public lands, while his *The Transappalachian Frontier: Peoples, Societies, and Institutions, 1775–1850* (1978) offers a broader account. Developments in farming are discussed in Clarence Danhof, *Change in Agriculture: The Northern United States, 1820–1870* (1969), and Richard Ellis, *Farmers and Landlords* (1958). See also John Mack Faragher, *Sugar Creek: Life on the Illinois Prairie* (1986).

Republican Policy and Diplomacy

Two good general accounts are Marshall Smelser, *The Democratic Republic, 1801–1815* (1968), and Ralph Ketcham, *Presidents Above Party: The First American Presidency, 1789–1829* (1984). Detailed studies of Jefferson's presidency include Daniel Sisson, *The Revolution of 1800* (1974); Dumas Malone, *Jefferson the President* (2 vols., 1970 and 1974); Richard E. Ellis, *The Jeffersonian Crisis: Courts and Politics in the New Republic* (1971); Raymond Waters, Jr., *Albert Gallatin: Jeffersonian Financier and Diplomat* (1957); Noble Cunningham, Jr., *The Process of Government Under Jefferson* (1978); and Merrill Peterson, *Thomas Jefferson and the New Nation* (1970). For the Louisiana Purchase, see Alexander DeConde, *This Affair of Louisiana* (1976), and A. P. Whitaker, *The Mississippi Question* (1934). Donald Jackson, *The Letters of the Lewis and Clark Expedition* (1963), and James P. Ronda, *Lewis and Clark Among the Indians* (1984), describe the excitement of their expedition.

The activities of Aaron Burr are covered in Thomas P. Abernethy, *The Burr Conspiracy* (1954), and Milton Lomask, *Aaron Burr* (1979), while the Federalists are discussed in David Hackett Fischer, *The Revolution of American Conservatism: The Federalist Party in the Age of Jeffersonian Democracy* (1965); Linda K. Kerber, *Federalists in Dissent: Imagery and Ideology in Jeffersonian America* (1970); and James Banner, *To the Hartford Convention: The Federalists and the Origins of Party Politics in the Early Republic, 1789–1815* (1970).

American attempts to avoid involvement in the Napoleonic Wars are traced in Lawrence Kaplan, *"Entangling Alliances with None": American Foreign Policy in the Age of Jefferson* (1987), and Bradford Perkins, *The First Rapprochement: England and the United States, 1795–1805* (1967) and *Prologue to War: England and the United States, 1805–1812* (1961). See also Clifford L. Egan, *Neither Peace nor War: Franco-American Relations, 1803–1812* (1983), and Burton Spivak, *Jefferson's English Crisis: Commerce, the Embargo, and the Republican Revolution* (1979). On Madison, see Robert A. Rutland, *James Madison: The Founding Father* (1987); J. C. A. Stagg, *Mr. Madison's War: Politics, Diplomacy, and Warfare in the Early Republic, 1783–1830* (1983); and Robert A. Rutland, *Madison's Alternatives: Jeffersonian Republicans and the Coming of War, 1805–1812* (1975). See also Reginald Horsman, *The Causes of the War of 1812* (1962), and R. H. Brown, *The Republic in Peril: 1812* (1964).

Native American resistance is discussed in R. David Edmunds, *The Shawnee Prophet* (1983) and *Tecumseh and the Quest for Indian Leadership* (1984), as well as H. S. Halbert and T. H. Ball, *The Creek War of 1813 and 1814* (1970). The war is treated in detail in Harry L. Coles, *The War of 1812* (1965), while its conclusion is the subject of Fred L. Engleman, *The Peace of Christmas Eve* (1962), and John William Ward, *Andrew Jackson: Symbol for an Age* (1963).

Regional Diversity and National Identity

For life in the northern seaboard states, see Benjamin W. Labaree, *The Merchants of Newburyport, 1764–1815* (1962); Howard Rock, *Artisans of the New Republic: Tradesmen of New York City in the Age of Jefferson* (1979); Charles G. Steffan, *The Mechanics of Baltimore: Workers and Politics in the Age of Revolution, 1763–1812* (1984); and Sean Wilentz, *Chants Democratic: New York City and the Rise of the American Working Class, 1788–1850* (1984). The evolution of the South can be traced in James Sterling Young, *The Washington Community, 1800–1828* (1966); John Boles, *The Great Revival in the South, 1787–1805* (1972); Clement Eaton, *The Growth of Southern Civilization* (1961); and William R. Taylor, *Cavalier and Yankee: The Old South and American National Character* (1961).

F. S. Philbrick, *The Rise of the West, 1754–1830* (1964), provides an overview of life in the Old Northwest. More detailed studies include Richard C. Wade, *The Urban Frontier: The Rise of Western Cities, 1790–1840* (1973), and Andrew Cayton, *The Frontier Republic: Ideology and Politics in the Ohio Country, 1789–1812* (1986). The expansion of slavery is analyzed in Ira Berlin and Ronald Hoffman, eds., *Slavery and Freedom in the Age of the American Revolution* (1983); Donald L. Robinson, *Slavery in the Structure of American Politics, 1765–1820* (1971); and Albert Raboteau, *Slave Religion* (1968). For blacks in the northern states, see Leon Litwack, *North of Slavery: The Negro in the Free States, 1790–1860* (1961), and Gary B. Nash, *Forging Freedom: Philadelphia's Black Community, 1720–1840* (1988). Glover Moore, *The Missouri Compromise* (1953), provides a detailed analysis of that crisis. See also William M. Wiecek, *The Sources of Antislavery Constitutionalism in America, 1760–1848* (1977).

Diplomatic history following the War of 1812 is presented in Samuel F. Bemis, *John Quincy Adams and the Foundations of American Foreign Policy* (1949); Walter LaFeber, ed., *John Quincy Adams and American Continental Empire* (1965); and Ernest May, *The Making of the Monroe Doctrine* (1976). See also Henry Ammon, *James Monroe: The Quest for National Identity* (1971), and George Dangerfield, *The Era of Good Feeling* (1952).

TIMELINE

1784	Treaty of Fort Stanwix
1787	Northwest Ordinance
1790s	Western (Indian) Confederacy White settlement of Northwest Territory Slave imports increase Cotton production expands
1794	Battle of Fallen Timbers
1795	Treaty of Greenville Jay's Treaty Pinckney's Treaty
1800s	African-American culture develops Rise of black Protestantism Missionaries seek Indian converts
1800	Gabriel Prosser's rebellion in Virginia
1801–1835	John Marshall, chief justice
1801–1809	Presidency of Thomas Jefferson National debt declines
1803	*Marbury v. Madison* Louisiana Purchase
1804–1805	Lewis and Clark expedition Aaron Burr and western secession
1807	*Chesapeake* attacked Embargo of 1807
1808	Tecumseh mobilizes western tribes Slave imports outlawed
1811	Battle of Tippecanoe
1812–1815	War of 1812
1815	Battle of New Orleans Treaty of Ghent signed
1816	Expansion of slavery into Old Southwest Cherokee resist white advance Decline of Federalist party
1817	Rush-Bagot Treaty
1817–1825	Era of Good Feeling
1819	Annexation of East Florida
1820	Missouri Compromise
1823	Monroe Doctrine

The Bustling Port of New York

Following independence, New York City quickly became the largest American seaport. This burgeoning waterfront was captured in Francis Guy's *Tontine Coffee House* (detail), c. 1747. (The New-York Historical Society)

CHAPTER 9 *The Capitalist Protestant Republic,* 1790–1820

On the fiftieth anniversary of the founding of the United States, white Americans had cause for celebration. They lived free of an arbitrary government that imposed high taxes and of an established church that inflicted rigid dogmas. They also had cause for mourning. On July 4, 1826, within a few hours of each other, John Adams and Thomas Jefferson died. The death of the two former presidents on Independence Day seemed to many Americans, perhaps paradoxically, to be a sign that God looked with favor on their experiment in self-government. Two of the greatest Founders had died, but the republic lived on.

Although few people noted it at the time, the 1820s marked a more significant milestone in the nation's history: the passing of the "old America." For two centuries, colonists and then citizens had lived in tightly knit communities, on farms or plantations. They had measured their lives by natural rhythms—the rising and setting of the sun, the passage of the seasons, the cycle of the agricultural year. They had lived in a relatively stable world and were apprehensive of change. Now society had become dynamic, embracing change. Nearly 10 percent of the population resided in cities or small towns, and more people were contributing crops and manufactured products to the market economy, thus creating a mature commercial capitalist society.

A prominent feature of this "new America" was an increasingly republican and Protestant culture. Beginning in 1776 white Americans applied the republican principle of liberty not only to the political system but also to social institutions—families, churches, and schools. Individuals—women as well as men—now had more freedom to choose their marriage partners, social values, and religious faiths. Yet they made these decisions within an increasingly well organized and well governed Christian society—the product of a continuous wave of religious revivals. The resulting society neatly balanced private freedom with public responsibility. "The temperate zone of North America," a Kentucky judge declared in a speech on the Fourth of July, "already exhibits many signs that it is the promised land of civil liberty, and of institutions designed to liberate and exalt the human race."

Political Economy: The Capitalist Commonwealth

The nation that declared its independence in 1776 was overwhelmingly agrarian, dependent on Great Britain for markets, credit, and manufactured goods. Over the next fifty years the United States achieved a measure of economic independence, as rural Americans became manufacturers, bankers supplied credit to expand industry and trade, merchants developed regional market economies, and state governments took an active role in encouraging economic development.

A Capitalist Society

American Merchants. Merchants had dominated the economic life of port cities in colonial times, and with the departure of the British they began to set the social and cultural tone as well. "It is a Nation of Merchants," an English visitor reported from Philadelphia in 1798, "always alive to their interests; and keen in the pursuit of wealth in all the various modes of acquiring it."

After the economic contraction that followed independence, the European wars from 1792 to 1815 brought rising profits to established merchant houses and fortunes to daring entrepreneurs. Among the many success stories were two immigrants, Robert Oliver and John Jacob Astor, who succeeded phenomenally. Oliver arrived in Baltimore in 1783 as the American agent for Irish merchants who sold linens in the United States and foodstuffs in the West Indies. Two years later, he began his own business—a mercantile partnership—and watched his investment of £2,000 grow slowly to £3,300 during the recession of the 1780s. Then, during the wartime shipping boom, his firm's assets soared to £110,000 by 1800. Caught up in a restless pursuit of wealth, Oliver began to trade on his own, reaping enormous profits from the West Indian coffee trade and speculating in Mexican gold and silver. By 1807 he was a millionaire.

John Jacob Astor migrated from Germany to New York City in 1784 and became a wealthy man by exploiting the trade in furs from the Pacific Northwest. Soon Astor emerged as the leading New York merchant trading with China. Investing his profits in real estate, he became the largest landowner in the rapidly growing port of New York. Astor's success was unusual only in its extent; the wartime commercial boom brought prosperity to the mercantile elite in all the seacoast cities.

Banking and Credit. To finance the expansion of mercantile enterprise, Americans had to devise an entirely new banking system. Before 1776 the colonists had few places to turn to for credit. Farmers had relied on government-sponsored land banks, pledging their land as security, while merchants like Oliver arranged partnerships, took out personal loans, or relied on British suppliers to extend credit. Then, in 1781, several Philadelphia merchants, Robert Morris among them, persuaded the Confederation Congress to charter the Bank of North America to provide short-term commercial loans, and traders in Boston and New York founded similar banks in 1784. These institutions provided merchants with the credit they needed to finance their transactions.

Alexander Hamilton expanded the American financial system and tried to centralize it by having Congress charter the Bank of the United States in 1791. The Bank had the power to issue notes and make commercial loans—powers the Bank's managers used cautiously, limiting loans to three times the value of the Bank's holdings in gold and silver. Profits still averaged a handsome 8 percent annually, and by 1805 the managers had set up branches in eight major cities, in response to the continuing demand for commercial credit. When the Bank's twenty-year charter expired in 1811, President Madison did not seek its renewal, primarily because the Bank had been dominated by Federalists. Merchants persuaded state legislatures to support banking, and by the time Madison rechartered the Bank of the United States in 1816, for another twenty years, there were already 246 state-chartered banks. Unfortunately, many of the state banks issued notes without adequate reserves of specie, causing the notes to fall in value and inhibiting commercial growth.

Nonetheless, the rapid emergence of this banking system signaled a new stage in the American economy. Many merchants had become bankers, providing not only goods to shopkeepers and farmers but credit and cash to other traders and entrepreneurs. The United States was no longer completely dependent on British credit but had its own financial institutions to promote foreign trade and domestic development.

Rural Manufacturing. Since colonial times American artisans had handcrafted furniture, tools, wagons, shoes, saddles, clothes, and dozens of other items. Especially in New England and the Middle Atlantic states, many artisans enjoyed a modest but comfortable life from their labors, selling or exchanging their goods mostly within the local community. For example, during the 1780s, John Hoff of Lancaster, Pennsylvania, sold his fine wooden-cased clocks locally or bartered them with his neighbors for a dining table, a bedstead, shoes, pine boards, and even labor on his small farm.

Some artisans—especially those who worked in large, specialized groups—did have their eyes on more distant markets. Shipbuilders in seacoast towns, iron smelters in Pennsylvania and Maryland, shoemakers in Lynn, Massachusetts—all sold their products to customers outside their regions. During the Revolutionary War, merchants financed the expansion of various enterprises, encouraging rural men and women to make cheese, textiles, paper, and gunpowder. After the war nationalist pride prompted calls for the expansion of *all* domestic handicrafts. "Until we manufacture more," the Boston *Gazette* declared in 1788, "it is absurd to celebrate the Fourth of July as the birthday of our independence."

With peace restored, many merchants ignored the plea to invest in domestic manufacturing, since it was more profitable for them to sell low-priced British goods. Still, some entrepreneurs continued to develop wider markets for rural manufactures. For instance, merchants sold cheese made on Massachusetts farms not only in Boston but in all the seaport towns of New England. As a Polish traveler in central Massachusetts reported in 1798, "Along the whole road from Boston, we saw women engaged in making cheese."

Some inland merchants were not content with

A Cloth Merchant

Elijah Boardman and other American merchants annually imported millions of yards of cloth from Britain. When war cut off trade, some merchants encouraged domestic production, first in rural households and then in factories. (Ralph Earl, *Elijah Boardman*, 1782, The Metropolitan Museum of Art)

merely marketing farm products and handicrafts. They actively recruited and organized rural households to manufacture specific goods, developing their own version of the European *outwork* or *putting-out system* (see Chapter 1, p. 28). The experience of Berlin, New Hampshire, was typical. For many years Berlin artisans had made tinware—baking pans, cups, eating utensils, lanterns—and carried it to local farmers with "a horse and two baskets." After the Revolutionary War, merchants in Berlin paid artisans to increase their output and hired young men, whom they furnished "with a horse and a cart covered with a box or with a wagon," to market the tinware in the South.

The greatest success of the putting-out system was in the shoe and boot trade. In the 1780s merchants and master craftsmen in Lynn, Massachusetts, began buying large quantities of leather, thread, and awls, and put thousands of families in the New England countryside to work. Farm women and children stitched together the thin leather and canvas uppers of the shoes, and the half-finished shoes were taken by wagon to Lynn for assembly by journeymen shoemakers. When the Embargo of 1807 cut off the competition from British-made shoes, merchants in Lynn and over thirty other Massachusetts towns expanded production. By the 1820s these entrepreneurs had mobilized an enormous work force in the New England countryside and were selling millions of shoes throughout the nation. They had established the beginnings of a *national* market linking the northern and southern states.

The putting-out system owed its success to innovations in organization, not innovations in technology. Tinworkers, shoemakers, and other artisans continued to use their traditional *preindustrial* hand-craft technology. The use of power-driven machines—the product of the Industrial Revolution in Britain—came slowly to America, beginning with the textile industry.

In the 1780s merchants built hundreds of small mills along the creeks and rivers of New England and the Middle Atlantic states. They installed water-powered machines and hired workers to card and comb wool—and later cotton—into long strands. For several decades, the next steps were accomplished under the outwork system. Farm women and children spun the strands into yarn, receiving wages for their work, while men, usually in other households, wove the yarn into cloth. Finally, the woolen cloth was pounded flat and finished in water-powered fulling mills. Though the full industrialization of the textile industry was still to come, by 1820 the nation already boasted a dynamic group of merchant entrepreneurs, a nascent banking system, and a well-developed system of rural manufacturing.

The Market Economy. With the advances in rural manufacturing, the United States took yet another step toward a capitalist society. In his *Letter on Manufactures* (1810), Secretary of the Treasury Albert Gallatin reported that there were about 2,500 outwork weavers in New England. A decade later, more than 12,000 household workers in the region were weaving cloth, and hundreds of thousands more were making cheese, yarn, shoes, nails, and dozens of other products. Many families now combined farming with manufacturing. When a French traveler visited central Massachusetts in 1795, he found "almost all these houses . . . inhabited by men who are both cultivators and artisans; one is a tanner, another a shoemaker, another sells goods, but all are farmers."

The rise of rural manufacturing changed the character of agriculture. To supply merchants and artisans with raw materials, many farmers switched from mixed-crop agriculture to raising livestock. The shoe

Ebenezer Breed, Quaker Entrepreneur
Breed was one of the great shoe merchant-manufacturers of Lynn, Massachusetts, organizing the production and sale of millions of shoes. But he died in poverty, his business and health destroyed by the competitive pressures of the capitalist market economy.

business consumed thousands of hides each year, and it took large herds of dairy cows to supply the new cheese industry. Textile producers purchased the wool off the backs of tens of thousands of sheep. The demand for materials brought prosperity to many farming towns. In 1792 there was one slaughterhouse and five small tanneries in Concord, Massachusetts. A decade later there were eleven slaughterhouses and six large tanneries in the town. Foul odors from the stockyards and tanning pits drifted over Concord, but its people lived better.

The "old America" of quiet rural towns began to disappear. Rural producers and merchant capitalists together were giving more importance to the market economy. As farm families joined the outwork system, they stopped producing all their own food and making their own clothing and bedding. Instead of bartering their surplus crops for household necessities, they supplied merchants with specialized goods in return for cash or store credit. "Straw hats and Bonnets are manufactured by many families," noted a Maine official in the Census of Manufacturing of 1820, while another observer noted that "probably 8,000 females" in the vicinity of Foxborough, Massachusetts, braided rye straw into hats for market sale. These women used the income from the sale of their labor to shop in local stores.

The new system had its drawbacks. Rural parents—and their children—worked longer and harder than ever. Perhaps more important, they lost some of their economic independence. Instead of working for themselves as yeomen farm families, they now toiled as wage laborers for merchants and manufacturers. The new market economy made whole communities less self-sufficient.

As the income of farm families rose, so did the wealth of the United States. Beginning around 1800, the per capita income of Americans increased at a rate of more than 1 percent per year—more than 30 percent each generation. By the 1820s this extraordinary increase in output, artisan skills, and merchant capital had laid the foundation for the American Industrial Revolution (see Chapter 10). After a half-century of political independence, the nation was beginning to achieve economic independence from British credit and manufactures.

State Mercantilism

Throughout the nineteenth century, state governments were the most important political institutions in the United States. Responding to changing needs, state constitutional conventions regularly proposed new government charters. State legislatures took the lead in regulating social life—abolishing slavery in the North and retaining it in the South. State governments enacted the laws governing criminal and civil affairs, set voting requirements, established the taxation system, and oversaw county, city, and town officials. Consequently, state governments—and particularly state legislatures—had a much greater impact on the day-to-day lives of Americans than did the national government.

Beginning in the 1790s, many state legislatures sought to promote commerce by devising a new, American system of mercantilism. Just as the British Parliament had promoted the imperial economy by passing Acts of Trade, the state legislatures enacted measures to stimulate commerce and economic development in America. In particular, state governments granted hundreds of *corporate charters* to private businesses. Chartered companies were not new, of course—English investors had used them to establish the first American colonies. However, under English law, colonial governments were prevented from creating corporations, so merchants had financed mills, shipyards, and trading ventures through private partnerships, which lacked the legal and economic advantages of government-chartered corporations.

American state governments gave a high priority to resolving the transportation problems that were hampering trade. They issued numerous charters of incorporation to promote investment in roads, bridges, and canals. For example, the Lancaster Turnpike Company opened a graded gravel road between Lancaster and Philadelphia in 1794. Its success set off a boom in turnpike construction, and soon dozens of inland market centers were connected to one another and to seaport cities. By 1800 state governments had granted more than three hundred corporate charters, mostly for transportation projects.

Legal incorporation transformed the status of private companies in two ways. First, some charters included the new protection of *limited liability:* in the event of business failure, the shareholders' personal assets could not be used to pay the debts of the corporation. Second, most transportation charters included the power of *eminent domain*, a legal device that allowed turnpike, bridge, and canal corporations to force the sale of land along their rights-of-way. This power—previously available only to the government itself—allowed private corporations to take lands from property owners for a reasonable price, even if the owners did not want to sell.

State courts consistently upheld such grants of eminent domain, even though they infringed on private property rights, because they were in the interest of economic development and the public welfare. A New Jersey court declared that "the opening of good and easy internal communications is one of the highest duties of government" and judged it lawful to delegate this task to a private corporation.

State mercantilism soon encompassed much more than transportation. Following the Embargo of 1807, which cut off goods and credit from Europe, the New England state governments awarded charters to two hundred iron-mining, textile-manufacturing, and banking firms. Subsequently, many states invested government funds directly in public and private ventures.

During the 1790s Alexander Hamilton had used the powers of the United States government to encourage economic development through tariff and banking policies, and most Federalists supported his program of *national* mercantilism. After the War of 1812 some Republicans, led by Henry Clay of Kentucky, began counting themselves among the economic nationalists. As Speaker of the House of Representatives, Clay supported the creation of the Second Bank of the United States in 1816. The following year he won passage of the Bonus Bill, sponsored by Representative John C. Calhoun of South Carolina, which would have established a national fund for roads and other internal improvements. But many American political leaders still opposed national mercantilist policies. They agreed with President Madison, who vetoed the Bonus Bill, arguing that it exceeded the powers delegated to the national government by the Constitution. This fundamental disagreement over the proper role of the national government would be a major issue of political debate for the next thirty years (see Chapter 11).

The Law of the "Commonwealth"

By the early nineteenth century the innovative policies of the state governments had created a new political economy known as the *commonwealth* system. This system had two distinct features. First, it elevated the good of the public—the common-wealth—above that of private individuals, reflecting the republican doctrine of popular sovereignty. Second, it assumed the existence of state governments that actively sought to improve the general welfare through legislation. Missouri lawmakers incorporated this outlook into their first constitution (1820), specifying that "internal improvements shall forever be encouraged by the government of this state."

Both Federalists and Republicans endorsed commonwealth ideology, but they interpreted it in different ways. Federalists looked to the national government for economic leadership, while Republicans relied on the state legislatures. Some Federalists clung to a *static* conception of property rights, as something that did not change; many Republicans leaned toward a more *dynamic* view, arguing that property rights should evolve along with the economic system.

Common Law and Statute Law. The differing ideas of property rights stemmed in part from different perspectives on the law. English common law had shaped American jurisprudence from the earliest colonial times. When deciding cases, judges relied on *precedents*—that is, decisions in similar earlier cases—and they assumed, as a Maryland lawyer put it, that "the Common Law takes in the Law of Nature, the Law of Reason and the Revealed Law of God." In this view, law—including property rights—was a venerable and unchanging entity.

The doctrine of popular sovereignty undermined the intellectual foundations of this old legal order. As Americans debated constitutional principles, many of them recognized that law was a human invention—the product of politics—and not a sacred body of timeless truths. Indeed, Thomas Jefferson and other leaders of the Republican party directly attacked the common-law system during the 1790s. They maintained that law made by judges following common-law precedents was inferior to the statute (or "positive") law enacted by the representatives of the people. As one Republican jurist put it, a magistrate "should be governed himself by *positive* law, and executes and enforces the will of the supreme power, which is the will of THE PEOPLE."

Federalist judges and politicians warned that popular sovereignty and representative government might result in the "tyranny of the majority." They favored only those statutes that did not infringe on the existing property rights of individuals. To keep these rights from being overridden by state legislatures, Federalist lawyers invoked the principles of common law and natural law (see Chapter 4). They also asserted that judges had the power to interpret laws and to void them if they were unconstitutional.

Common Law versus Development. As state legislatures implemented the commonwealth system, they provoked an inevitable confrontation between common law precedents, which tended to discourage economic development, and the principles of state mercantilism, which promoted it. Capitalist entrepreneurs who needed to erect dams to operate flour or textile mills often flooded adjacent farmlands; outraged farmers sued, arguing that the dams not only infringed their property rights but were a "nuisance" to the public and should be pulled down. At first the farmers won most such cases. In 1795, for example, a New Jersey court used common-law precedents in ruling that it was illegal to interfere with the natural flow of a river for nonfarming purposes "without the consent of all who have an interest in it."

Such decisions threatened to stifle economic development. Consequently state legislatures enacted statutes that overrode the common law by limiting the legal recourse available to landowners. In Massachusetts, the Mill Dam Act of 1795 allowed mill proprietors to flood adjacent farmlands and prevented farmers from blocking the construction of dams or seeking damages, forcing them to accept "fair compensation" for their lost acreage. This prodevelopment legislation justified the taking of private property by asserting the superior rights of individuals who made a dynamic, rather than a static, use of their property.

State judges accepted the doctrines of popular sovereignty and legislative power and therefore usually upheld the mill acts, just as they supported legislative statutes that granted eminent domain to private turnpike and canal corporations. To these judges, *social utility*—the greatest good for the greatest number—justified the government's intrusion on the property rights of individual citizens.

Such rulings shocked Daniel Webster, the great Federalist lawyer and politician, who considered them no less than a "revolution against the foundations on which property rests." In point of fact, the judges—like the state legislatures—were redefining property rights to benefit the commonwealth. Thus the New York Court of Appeals ruled, in the case of *Palmer v. Mulligan* (1805), that a dam owner could not prevent the construction of a new milldam elsewhere on the river. As the court declared: "The public, whose advantage is always to be regarded, would be deprived of the benefits which always attend competition and rivalry."

The Federalist Law of John Marshall

The legal career of John Marshall was closely interwoven with the debates over property rights and the respective powers of legislatures and judges. The great Virginia Federalist served as chief justice of the United States from 1801 to 1835. Marshall's gift lay not in the mastery of legal principles and doctrines—indeed, his opinions usually cited very few precedents—but in the power of his logic and the force of his personality. Until 1821, Marshall dominated his colleagues on the Supreme Court; they accepted both his definition of its powers and his interpretation of the law.

Three principles shaped Marshall's jurisprudence: a commitment to judicial power, the supremacy of national over state legislation, and a traditional view of property rights.

Chief Justice John Marshall
Marshall had a commanding personal presence and made over the United States Supreme Court in his image—elevating it from a minor department into a major institution in American legal and political life. (Boston Atheneum)

Judicial Power: *Marbury v. Madison.* The celebrated case of *Marbury v. Madison* (1803) demonstrated Marshall's commitment to the preeminent authority of the judiciary. The case arose out of the controversial "midnight" appointments of President John Adams in 1801. As Jefferson's secretary of state, James Madison had refused to deliver a commission as justice of the peace to William Marbury. When Marbury took his case to the Supreme Court, Marshall ruled that while Marbury had a right to his commission, that right was unenforceable. Marshall declared that the section of the Judiciary Act of 1789 that gave the Supreme Court the power to issue a writ ordering the secretary of state to deliver the commission was unconstitutional. Marshall's decision was politically astute, condemning Madison's actions while avoiding a direct confrontation with the Republican administration.

More important, this decision marked the first time the Supreme Court had overturned a national law. Five years earlier the Kentucky and Virginia legislatures had asserted the authority of state legislatures to determine the constitutionality of national laws. But the Constitution implied that the Supreme Court had this power of *judicial review*, and now Marshall claimed it explicitly: "It is emphatically the province and duty of the judicial department to say what the law is." The doctrine of judicial review evolved slowly. During the first half of the nineteenth century, the Supreme Court and the state courts used the principle of judicial review to overturn state laws that conflicted with constitutional principles, but not until the *Dred Scott* decision of 1857 did the Supreme Court void another national law. After the Civil War, however, the Court frequently invoked judicial review to overturn Congressional as well as state legislation.

Nationalism: *McCulloch v. Maryland.* Marshall's nationalism was most eloquently expressed in the controversial case of *McCulloch v. Maryland* (1819). When Congress created the Second Bank of the United States in 1816, the Bank was given the authority to handle the notes of the state banks, a power it used to monitor their financial reserves and to create a national system of credit.

Many state governments resented the dominant position of the new national Bank. The Maryland legislature imposed an annual tax of $15,000 on the notes issued by the Baltimore branch of the Second Bank and limited its powers, in order to preserve the independence and competitive position of its own state-chartered banks. The Second Bank contested the constitutionality of the state's action, claiming that it infringed on the powers of the national government. In response, lawyers for the state of Maryland adopted Jefferson's argument against the First Bank of the United States. They maintained that Congress lacked the constitutional authority to charter a national bank. And even if the Bank could be created, the lawyers argued, Maryland had a right to tax its activities within the state.

Marshall firmly rejected both arguments. He declared that the Second Bank was constitutional because its existence was "necessary and proper," given the national responsibility to control currency and credit. Like Alexander Hamilton and other Federalists, Marshall gave a loose construction to the Constitution: "Let the end be legitimate, let it be within the scope of the Constitution and all means which are appropriate, which [are consistent] . . . with the letter and the spirit of the constitution, are constitutional."

As for Maryland's right to tax all institutions within its borders, the chief justice embraced the nationalist position advanced by Daniel Webster, a fellow Federalist and legal counsel to the Second Bank. "The power to tax involves the power to destroy," Marshall observed. Following his own logic, the chief justice declared that Maryland's tax would render the national government "dependent on the states"—a situation that "was not intended by the American people" when their representatives ratified the Constitution. With this decision, Marshall asserted the dominance of national statutes over state legislation and, by outlining a broad interpretation of the Constitution, laid the legal foundation for the subsequent expansion of national authority.

Two years later, Marshall declared the supremacy of national courts of law over state tribunals. In the case of *Cohens v. Virginia* (1821), he proclaimed that the Constitution had diminished the sovereignty of the states. State courts did not have the last say on issues that fell within the purview of the national Constitution, and their decisions could be appealed to the federal judiciary.

Property Rights: *Fletcher v. Peck.* Marshall found in the national Constitution the basis for legal guarantees supporting a traditional conception of property rights. The *contract clause* of the Constitution prohibits the states from passing any law "impairing the obligation of contracts." The delegates had included this clause primarily to assist merchants and other creditors by voiding state laws that protected debtors. Marshall, however, used the contract clause to defend other property rights against legislative challenge. For example, the case of *Fletcher v. Peck* (1810) involved a large grant of land made by the Georgia legislature to the Yazoo Land Company. A newly elected state legislature canceled the grant, alleging that it had been obtained through fraud and bribery, but speculators in other states who had purchased Yazoo lands appealed to the Supreme Court. Speaking for the Court, Marshall ruled that the original legislative grant constituted a contract and could not be broken. This decision gave security to those who purchased state-owned lands, protecting their rights against subsequent state legislation.

The case of *Dartmouth College v. Woodward* (1819) gave property owners even greater protection against state interference. Dartmouth was a private institution, established by a charter granted by King George III in 1769. In 1816 the Republican-dominated legislature of New Hampshire tried to convert the college into a public university, invoking the ideology of the commonwealth system. The Dartmouth trustees resisted the plan and engaged Daniel Webster to plead their case before the Supreme Court. Webster based his argument squarely on the court's decision in *Fletcher v. Peck.* The royal charter had bestowed "corporate rights and privileges" on the college, Webster maintained; therefore the charter constituted a contract and could not be tampered with by the New Hampshire legislature.

Marshall had difficulty persuading his colleagues to accept Webster's argument. Although he was still the dominant member of the Court, by 1819 five Supreme Court justices had been appointed by the Republican presidents Jefferson, Madison, and Monroe. Some of these justices favored the commonwealth system; others hesitated to restrict the powers of the state legislatures or to endorse the broad legal protections for property rights set forth in *Fletcher v. Peck.* It was only after months of deliberation—and the preparation of a precedent-filled decision by Associate Justice Joseph Story, a New England jurist with strong Federalist leanings—that the justices followed Marshall and ruled in favor of the college. *Dartmouth v. Woodward* not only endorsed a static conception of property rights (repudiating the dynamic, commonwealth-oriented view of the New Hampshire legislature) but extended those rights from individuals to business corporations. Thereafter, corporations would claim that their state-granted charters were "contracts" that protected them—forever—from regulation or control by the governments that created them.

Marshall's triumph seemed complete. In the decisions handed down between 1819 and 1821—*Dartmouth, McCulloch, Cohens*—he had incorporated Federalist principles into the law of the land, championing judicial review, nationalism, and a static conception of property rights. But his victory was short-lived. After 1821 Marshall had to fight a rearguard action to defend his jurisprudence from the attacks of Republican jurists who believed in legislative supremacy (as opposed to judicial review), in the exercise of broad authority by state governments, and in a dynamic conception of property rights. By the time Marshall died in 1835, the Republican definition of commonwealth ideology had superseded Marshall's Federalist vision. Two generations of the purposeful use of statute law by state legislators and judges had paved the way for aggressive economic development in America.

A Republican Society

During the generation following independence, Americans tried to become "republicans" in social behavior and cultural values. To accomplish this, people strove for greater equality in their social relations. They condemned the aristocratic pretensions of old-style politicians and lawyers and the cold formality of conservative clergymen. Some young people sought more egalitarian marriages and a more affectionate family life. In addition, thousands of women tried to gain a more respected public identity for themselves, channeling their energy into religious and educational projects. Gradually, the pursuit of republican ideals by hundreds of thousands of people changed the character of American society.

Democracy Extended

Many Americans agreed that in a republic men and women should be valued not for their "wealth, titles, or connections"—as one letter to a newspaper put it—but rather for their "talents, integrity, and virtue." Politicians who flaunted their high social status fell into disfavor. An observer noted with disdain that many Federalists remained aristocratic in their dress as well as their behavior, with their hair in "powder and queues" and their "top boots, breeches, and shoe buckles." In contrast, many Republican politicians resembled the common people in their style of dress.

Republicans embraced a political philosophy that appealed to the middle and lower ranks of society. In 1807 a Republican-dominated legislature in New Jersey abolished the property-holding requirements for voting; Maryland did the same in 1810. Constitutions for the new states of Indiana (1816), Illinois (1818), and Alabama (1819) likewise prescribed a broad franchise. Between 1818 and 1821, reform-minded politicians in Connecticut, Massachusetts, and New York pushed through important revisions in their state constitutions, reapportioning their legislatures on the basis of population and instituting more democratic forms of local government—such as the election rather than the appointment of judges and justices of the peace.

Most Federalist leaders opposed these innovations. They wanted to restrict politics to the upper levels of society and, in the words of Thurlow Weed, a Federalist politician in New York, they "dreaded the effect of extending and cheapening suffrage." But they could not turn back the tide of democracy. With only three exceptions—Rhode Island, Virginia, and Louisiana—all the states had instituted universal white male suffrage by the end of the 1820s and eliminated property qualifications for officeholding. If such "democratic doctrines" had been advanced ten years earlier, Chancellor James Kent of New York protested, they "should have struck the public mind with astonishment and terror."

Creating a National Identity

As British subjects, Americans celebrated the birthday of the King. As citizens, they marked the birthday of the nation, the Fourth of July, recalling the exploits of military heroes who secured and preserved American independence, such as John Paul Jones, whose picture tops the tent at the left, and the soldiers at the Battle of New Orleans (right tent).

The Legal Profession. A similar revolution took place in the legal profession. During the Revolutionary Era, American attorneys had raised the standards of their profession by establishing bar associations and winning legislation that prevented untrained lawyers—whom they called "pettifoggers"—from practicing law. By 1800, most of the sixteen states required lawyers to have three to seven years of formal schooling or apprenticeship training. Harvard, Columbia, and William and Mary colleges all offered lectures on legal issues, and in 1784 Judge Tapping Reeve founded the famous Litchfield, Connecticut, law school. By the 1820s Litchfield had graduated more than a thousand lawyers, including three future Supreme Court justices and two vice-presidents (Aaron Burr of New York and John C. Calhoun of South Carolina).

As state legislatures became activist institutions, enacting hundreds of laws affecting many aspects of life, the legal profession grew in importance. In many states (as Table 9.1 suggests), the number of lawyers grew faster than the population. As lawyers gained in prestige, impressing the voters through their eloquence in local courtrooms, they increasingly won election to public office. As early as 1820, 15 percent of the Massachusetts Assembly and 35 percent of its Senate were lawyers, though men of the law constituted only 1 percent of the state's male population.

TABLE 9.1

Number of Lawyers in Three Selected States, to 1820

	Number of Lawyers	Lawyers per 10,000 Population
Massachusetts (including Maine)		
1740	15	10
1775	71	24
1780	34	11
1785	92	24
1790	112	24
1800	200	35
1810	492	70
1820	710	87
Connecticut		
1790	129	54
1800	169	67
1820	248	90
South Carolina		
1771	24	19
1820	200	40

Source: George Dargo, *Law in the New Republic: Private Law and the Public Estate* (New York: Knopf, 1983), 49. Reprinted by permission of McGraw-Hill, Inc.

The apparent power of the legal profession inspired calls for its reform. Critics attacked what they called the "professional aristocracy" of lawyers, demanding the regulation of attorney's fees and the creation of small-claims courts in which ordinary citizens could represent themselves. They also succeeded in obtaining more relaxed standards for admission to the bar. By the 1820s, only eleven of the twenty-six states required a fixed period of legal instruction. These reforms lowered the intellectual quality of the legal profession but made it more democratic in composition and spirit.

An Educated Republic

Education Debated. Before 1800, formal education played a minor role in the lives of most Americans. In New England locally funded public schools provided most children with basic instruction in reading and writing. In other regions fewer children were given an education: about a quarter of the boys and perhaps 10 percent of the girls attended privately funded schools or had personal tutors. Even in New England, only a small fraction of the men—and almost .no women—went on to grammar (or high) school, and only 1 percent of the men graduated from college.

Following independence Caleb Bingham, an influential textbook author from Boston, called for "an equal distribution of knowledge to make us emphatically a 'republic of letters'." Thomas Jefferson and Benjamin Rush, the Philadelphia physician, separately proposed ambitious schemes for educational reform. Both mapped out plans for a comprehensive system of primary and secondary schooling, followed by colleges to educate young men (but not women) in the liberal arts—classical literature, history, and philosophy. They also proposed the establishment of a university, where distinguished scholars would lecture on law, medicine, theology, and political economy.

These ideas fell on deaf ears. To ordinary citizens, such schemes smacked of elitism. "Let anybody show what advantage the poor man receives from colleges," an anonymous "Old Soldier" wrote to the Maryland *Gazette.* "Why should they support them, unless it is to serve those who are in affluent circumstances, whose children can be spared from labor, and receive the benefits." The argument had merit; even Jefferson assumed that the majority of Americans would receive only a minimal education. "The mass of our citizens may be divided into two groups, the laboring and the learned," Jefferson wrote.

Educational schemes made little headway before 1820, when a new generation of reformers campaigned successfully for the improvement of public elementary schools. Led by merchants and manufacturers, they raised standards by certifying qualified teachers and

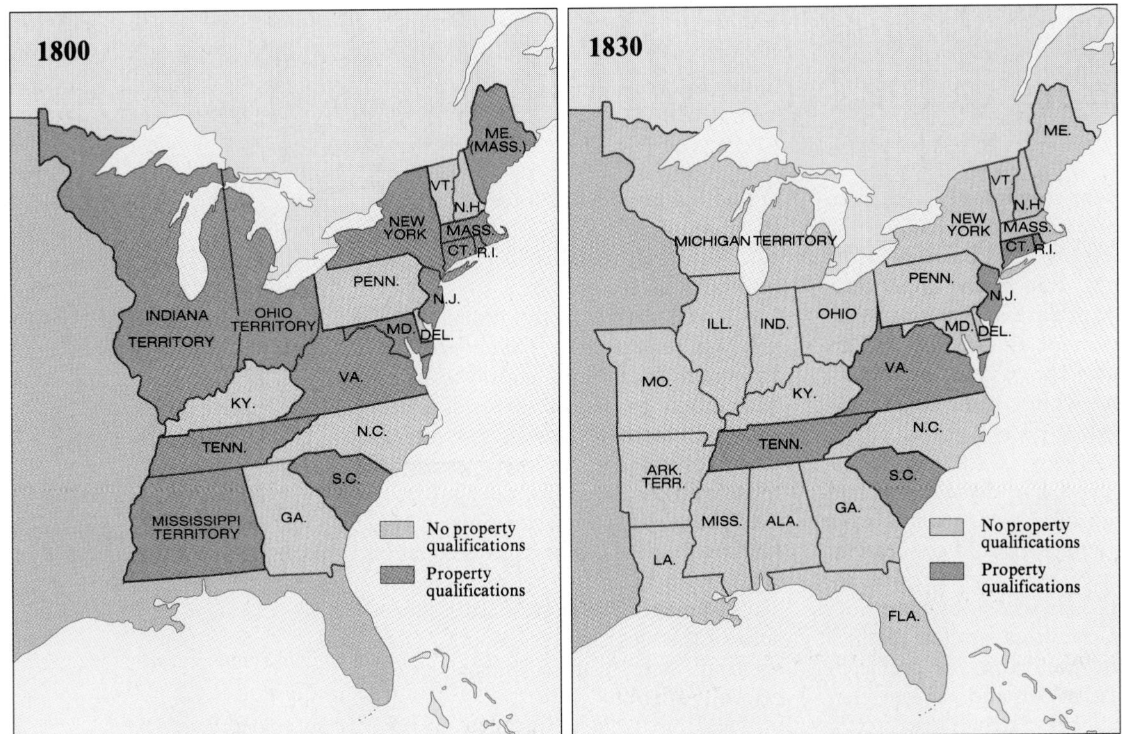

MAP 9.1

The Expansion of Voting Rights for White Men

Between 1800 and 1830 the United States moved steadily toward political democracy. Many existing states revised their constitutions, removing property qualifications for voting and enfranchising white men (and, in some states, free black men) who paid taxes; most new states in the West extended the suffrage to all adult white men. As parties sought votes from a broader electorate, the tone of politics became more open and competitive—swayed by the interests and values of ordinary people.

appointing state superintendents of education. Self-interest as well as public virtue motivated these gentlemen reformers, many of whom were old Federalists suspicious of the popular will. They wanted schools to instill the virtues of self-discipline and individual enterprise. Consequently, textbooks praised honesty and hard work while condemning gambling, drinking, and laziness.

The goals and the curriculum of the schools remained controversial, for Americans did not agree on what should be taught. Wealthy citizens preferred an elitist system that focused on higher education and the upper-class European customs of reading and appreciation of the arts. Farmers, artisans, and laborers looked to schools for basic instruction in the "three R's": reading, 'riting, and 'rithmetic. They supported public funding for primary schools, but not for secondary schools or colleges. By the time their children were twelve, they

The Battle Over Education

The artist pokes fun at a tyrannical schoolmaster and, indirectly, at the evangelicals' strict approach to childrearing. The children's faces reflect the rationalist outlook of the artist; we see in their eyes "the first dawn of reason, beaming forth its immortal rays."

AMERICAN VOICES

Manners in the New Republic *An English Traveler*

Most European immigrants were from the poorer classes and welcomed the absence of strong class barriers in the United States, but many upper-class visitors took offense at American presumptions of social equality. This document also shows that the dignity felt by some whites came at the expense of blacks.

Let me suppose, like myself, you had fallen in with an American innkeeper who at the moment would condescend to take the trouble to procure you refreshment. . . . He will sit by your side, and enter in the most familiar manner into conversation; which is prefaced, of course, with a demand of your business, and so forth. He will then start a political question (for here every individual is a politician), force you to answer, contradict, deny, and, finally, be ripe for a quarrel, should you not acquiesce in all his opinions. . . .

If you arrive at the dinner hour, you are seated with "mine hostess" and her dirty children, with whom you have often to scramble for a plate. This is esteemed wit, and consequently provokes a laugh, at the expense of those who are paying for the board. . . .

The arrogance of servants in this land of republican liberty and equality is particularly calculated to excite the astonishment of strangers. To call persons of this description servants, or to speak of their master or mistress, is a grievous affront.

Having called one day at the house of a gentleman of my acquaintance, on knocking at the door, it was opened by a servant-maid, whom I had never before seen, as she had not been long in his family. The following is the dialogue, word for word, which took place on this occasion:

"Is your master at home?"

"I have no master."

"Don't you live here?"

"I stay here."

"And who are you then?"

"Why, I am Mr. ______ 's help. I'd have you to know, man, that I am no sarvant. None but negers are sarvants."

Source: C. W. Janson, *The Stranger in America, 1793–1806* (1807), 85–88.

were working as apprentices, domestic servants, or farm laborers. New (or revised) state constitutions responded to the wishes of the majority by calling for the legislatures to fund a broad system of primary education.

Gentlemen reformers demanded that students be required to study American history, for they thought patriotic instruction would foster shared cultural ideals. The experience of Thomas Low, a New Hampshire schoolboy of the 1820s, would have satisfied their fondest hopes:

> We were taught every day and in every way that ours was the freest, the happiest, and soon to be the greatest and most powerful country of the world. This is the religious faith of every American. He learns it in his infancy and can never forget it.

The task of educators had been to transmit widely accepted knowledge and values from one generation to the next. In the new republican society, they were also entrusted with the mission of instilling patriotism.

The Literary World. Before independence most American writers were ministers who published sermons, moral tracts, or commentaries on religious experience. Likewise, many books imported from Europe were religious in character—the Bible, commentaries on Scripture, moral advice, and the like. Most of the political treatises and literary works read in America were also by European writers. Consequently, as far as a literary tradition went, the United States remained a dependent society.

Despite the absence of an intellectual milieu, individual Americans did attempt to contribute to the world of literature. Joel Barlow, a Yale graduate and ardent Jeffersonian Republican, called for an epic literature that would celebrate America. To that end he offered his own epic poem *The Columbiad* (1807), which was ambitious but undistinguished. Charles Brockden Brown of Philadelphia, the first American novelist, wrote six psychological novels between 1798 and 1801, but they attracted few readers. Mercy Otis Warren's *History of the Revolution* (1805) contained stirring portraits of leading American patriots, as did the best-selling *Life of Washington,* written around 1800 by "Parson" Mason Weems, an Episcopal minister. Neither work had much literary or historical merit; still, they won acclaim as contributions to popular culture and patriotism.

The most accomplished and successful writer in the new republic was Washington Irving, a Federalist in politics and in outlook. His essays and histories, including *Salmagundi* (1807), *Diedrich Knickerbocker's History of New York* (1809), and *The Sketch Book* (1819), had substantial American sales and won him fame abroad, because Europeans were fascinated with his tales of Dutch-American life. Irving himself lived in Europe for seventeen years, drawn by its aristocratic manners and intense intellectual life.

Apart from Irving and James Fenimore Cooper (who published *The Spy* in 1821 and *The Leatherstocking Tales* between 1823 and 1841), no American author was well known in Europe, partly because most writers had other careers as planters, merchants, or lawyers. "Literature is not yet a distinct profession with us," Thomas Jefferson told an English friend, explaining the dearth of intellectual life in the United States. "Now and then a strong mind arises, and at its intervals from business emits a flash of light. But the first object of young societies is bread and covering."

Cultural autonomy came harder to Americans than political or economic independence. A bleak cultural environment challenged the ingenuity of writers and educators. "America must be as independent in *literature* as she is in politics," proclaimed Noah Webster. Webster's contribution, in his *Dissertation on the English Language* (1789), was to standardize the American spelling of various words (such as *labor* for the British *labour*). His "blue-backed speller," published in 1783, sold 60 million copies over the next half-century and helped give Americans a common vocabulary and grammar. Webster blended instruction in grammar and pronunciation with moral principles: "Vir-tue ex-alt-eth a na-tion, but sin is a re-proach to a-ny peo-ple" was a typical example. In other works, Webster called on his fellow republican citizens to detach themselves "from the dependence on foreign opinions and manners, which is fatal to the efforts of genius in this country." His plea was premature. Not until the so-called American Renaissance of the 1840s and 1850s would native-born authors make any real contribution to the elite literature of the Western world (see Chapter 12).

Republican Marriages

Republicanism challenged the traditional concept of family life, which was patriarchal and constricting. In the "Old America," husbands had dominated wives and maintained legal control over the family's property. Parents had arranged the marriages of their children to protect themselves during their old age and to safeguard the young people as well. Wealthy fathers often placed funds in legal trusts for their daughters at the time of marriage so they would not be completely dependent on their husbands. As one Virginia planter wrote to his lawyer, "I rely on you to see the property settlement properly drawn *before the marriage,* for I by no means

The Genius of Washington Irving
Ichabod Crane (shown here with the "Headless Horseman") was one of Irving's most popular characters, many of whom were drawn from the folk tradition of the early Dutch settlers in New York. (National Gallery of Art)

AMERICAN VOICES

The Dilemmas of Womanhood *Eliza Southgate*

Eliza Southgate was born into a wealthy Maine family in 1783. At school in Boston, she discovered both radical doctrines of sexual equality and the reality of female subordination. In this letter to a male cousin, written in 1801, she tries to resolve these contradictory messages and to define her own stance toward the world of men.

But every being who has contemplated human nature on a large scale will certainly justify me when I declare that the inequality of privilege between the sexes is sensibly felt by us females, and in no instance it is greater than in the liberty of choosing a partner in marriage; true, we have the liberty of refusing those we don't like, but not of selecting those we do. This is undoubtedly as it should be....

I never was of opinion that the pursuits of the sexes ought to be the same; on the contrary, I believe it would be destructive to happiness, there would be a degree of rivalry incompatible with the harmony we wish to establish. I have ever thought it necessary that each should have a separate sphere of action—in such a case there could be no clashing unless one or the other should leap their respective bounds. Yet to cultivate the qualities with which we are endowed can never be called infringing the prerogatives of man....

The cultivation of the power we possess, I have ever thought a privilege (or I may say duty) that belonged to the human species, and not man's exclusive prerogative. Far from destroying the harmony that ought to subsist, it would fix it on a foundation that would not totter at every jar. Women would be under the same degree of subordination that they now are; enlighten and expand their minds, and they would perceive the necessity of such a regulation to preserve the order and happiness of society....

It does not follow (O what pen!) that every female who vindicates the capacity of the sex is a disciple of Mary Wolstoncraft. Though I allow her to have said many things which I cannot approve, I confess I admire many of her sentiments.

Source: David J. Rothman and Sheila Rothman, eds., *Sources of the American Social Tradition.,* (New York: Basic Books, 1975).

consent that Polly shall be left to the Vicissitudes of Life."

Two developments undermined this system of parent-controlled marriage. First, as land holdings shrank in long-settled rural communities, parents could no longer bequeath substantial farms to their children and so lost control of their children's lives. Increasingly, sons and daughters chose their own partners.

Second, the cultural attitude of ***sentimentalism***—a new, more romantic way of perceiving the world—swept the country. Originating in Europe, during the so-called Romantic movement of the late eighteenth century, sentimentalism celebrated the importance of "feeling"—that is, an emotional understanding of life's experiences. Those influenced by sentimentalism sought a physical, sensuous appreciation of God, nature, and other human beings. By 1800 sentimentalism had touched all classes of American society. It dripped from the pages of German and English literary works read in educated circles. It fell from the lips of actors in melodramas, which soon became the most popular type of theatrical entertainments in the United States. Religious revivals likewise relied on an emotional rather than an intellectual commitment, appealing to the passions of the heart over the cool logic of the brain.

Sentimentalism encouraged couples to marry for love. Parents had always taken physical attraction and emotional compatibility into account when arranging marriages for their children, but romance did not have a high cultural value. Parents were more influenced by the character and financial resources of a prospective son- or daughter-in-law. One skeptical Virginia mother argued that young women should remain single "till they were old enough to form a proper *judgement* of mankind" and not be deceived by their emotions.

The tide of sentimentalism could not be stopped. Before 1800 the few people who petitioned for divorce had charged their spouses with neglect, abandonment, or adultery—serious offenses against the moral order of society. Subsequently, the grounds for divorce were expanded in some states to include personal cruelty and drunkenness, and divorces were made available through judicial decree, rather than, as in the past, only through a special act of the legislature. Emotional complaints now dominated divorce petitions. One woman complained that her husband had "ceased to cherish her," while a male petitioner lamented that his wife had "almost broke his heart."

The new child-run marriage system gave young adults greater freedom. They now had the opportunity to seek a spouse who was, as Eliza Southgate of Maine put it, "calculated to promote my happiness." Yet many young adults lacked the maturity and experience to choose wisely. They married for love, only to be disappointed when their spouses failed them as financial providers or faithful companions.

Many urban Americans of middling status embraced the republican idea of a companionate marriage, in which husbands and wives were equal, sharing responsibility for decisions and treating each other with respect. This noble ideal foundered in the face of cultural rules that favored men and placed all property in their hands. Moreover, since the new marriage system discouraged parents from playing an active role in their children's lives, young wives could no longer rely on their parents for emotional or financial support and became more dependent on their husbands.

Republican marriages diminished the control of parents over children but not the power of husbands over wives. The marriage contract "is so much more important in its consequences to females than to males," a young man at the Litchfield Law School noted astutely in 1820, "for besides leaving everything else to unite themselves to one man, they subject themselves to his authority. He is their all—their only relative—their only hope."

Raising Republican Children

Smaller Families. The creation of a republican society coincided with a dramatic fall in the birth rate. In the farm village of Sturbridge, Massachusetts, for example, women who had married around 1750 bore an average of 8.8 children, while women who married around 1810 bore an average of 6 children. The decline was even greater in the urban areas of Massachusetts, where by the 1820s native-born white women bore an average of 4 children. This urban birth rate barely sufficed to maintain the population, for one-third of all children in the cities died from measles, diphtheria, or smallpox.

The United States was one of the first countries in the world to experience this sharp decline in the birth rate, known as the *demographic transition.* The causes were several. The migration of thousands of young men to the trans-Appalachian West left many women without marriage partners and delayed the marriages of many more. Women who married later—say, at age 26 rather than at age 20—had fewer children because they were married for fewer of their most fertile years. More important, thousands of white American couples deliberately limited the size of their families. After having four or five children, they used various methods of birth control or abstained from sexual intercourse to avoid conception. Farms were shrinking in size, and parents wanted to provide each of their children with an adequate inheritance.

The New Conjugal Family

Grace and Philip Schuyler pose informally with their daughters and encourage their musical and literary talents. The affectionate mood of this scene stands in sharp contrast to the hierarchy and discipline of the family portraits shown in earlier chapters (see pp. 26 and 102).

Separate Spheres

Art often reveals cultural values—here the new emphasis on childrearing and women's domestic authority. The mother sits in the center of the room, controlling the household domain. The father enters from the outside, his prime concerns now lying elsewhere, in the world of business. (*The Sargent Family*, 1800, National Galley of Art)

Republican Children. American parents now had fewer children, and they raised them in new ways. Child-rearing practices are difficult to document, not being matters of public record, but we know that most foreign visitors thought American parents indulged their children and failed to discipline them. "Mr. Schuyler's second son is a spoiled little child, as are all American children, very willful, mischievous, and likeable," the Marquis de Chastelleux observed in 1780.

Visitors attributed this behavior, at least in part, to republican ideology. Because of the "general ideas of Liberty and Equality engraved on their hearts," a Polish aristocrat argued, American children had "scant respect" for their parents. A British traveler was dumbfounded when an American father excused his son's "resolute disobedience" with a smile and the remark "A sturdy republican, sir." Foreigners guessed that parents encouraged such independence to enable young people to "go their own way" in the world.

The child-rearing literature of the period supports this interpretation to a degree. Most of the pamphlets and books giving advice on children were written by ministers. Religious writers influenced by John Locke and the Enlightenment argued that children were "rational creatures" who should be encouraged to act correctly by praise, advice, and reasoned restraint. At the opposite end of the spectrum, however, Calvinist preachers still taught that infants were "full of the stains and pollution of sin" and needed strict discipline.

These two approaches—the authoritarian Calvinist and the affectionate rationalist—appealed to different social and religious groups in the United States. Educated or wealthy Americans usually treated their children kindly. Since foreign travelers usually mixed with well-to-do Americans, often members of Anglican or Presbyterian churches, their customs were viewed as the norm. Actually, most yeomen and tenant farmers were much stricter and more authoritarian in their dealings with children, especially in families that belonged to Baptist or Calvinist-oriented Congregational churches.

Republican ideals affected both of these outlooks. Evangelical Baptists and Methodists in the early nineteenth century still insisted on the need to instill humility in children and teach them to subordinate their will to God's. Fear was a "useful and necessary principle in family government," minister John Abbott advised parents in an essay of 1833; a child "should submit to your authority, not to your arguments or persuasions." Yet even Abbott cautioned that it was wrong "exclusively to control him by this motive."

Rationalist writers placed more and more emphasis on children's capacity for education. They suggested that the goal of training should be to develop children's consciences, which would permit young people to police their own behavior. To this end, affectionate parents would read their children stories that stressed self-discipline and neatness. They encouraged their children to accept the burdens of independence: they must think and act for themselves. Foreigners observed that these American children had greater freedom than their counterparts in Europe. What passed unnoticed was the responsibility young Americans had to assume for their own lives. In private life as in public, republicanism balanced rights with duties.

Women's Sphere

Republican ideology raised the question of women's rights, challenging traditional assumptions of inferiority, but the issue was decided by men with patriarchal values. Deeply ingrained cultural patterns of male dominance were not easily overcome. Few American men could envision a political role for women. To justify the exclusion of women, legislators invoked traditional biological and social arguments. As one letter to a newspaper put it,

> Women, generally, are neither by nature, nor habit, nor education, nor by their necessary condition in society fitted to perform this duty with credit to themselves or advantage to the public.

A few American leaders responded more positively to white women's demands for greater equality, but they did so with men's needs in mind. In his *Thoughts on Female Education* (1787), Benjamin Rush argued that a young woman should be given intellectual training so that she would "be an agreeable companion for a sensible man." Rush and other men of affairs likewise welcomed the emergence of loyal "republican mothers" who would instruct "their sons in the principles of liberty and government." As a list of "Maxims for Republics" put it, "Some of the first patriots of ancient times were formed by their mothers."

Ministers embraced the idea of republican motherhood and devised new roles for women in moral and religious education. "Preserving virtue and instructing the young are not the fancied, but the real 'Rights of Women'," the Reverend Thomas Bernard told the Female Charitable Society of Salem, Massachusetts, in 1803. He urged his audience to forget about the public roles advocated by Mary Wollstonecraft and other feminists. Instead, women should remain content to care for their children, because this gave them "an extensive power over the fortunes of man in every generation." Bernard also wanted women to remain in their traditional sphere, while insisting that its value should be enhanced.

Many American women from the middling classes accepted this limited revision of their identity. As a young New England woman wrote in 1803, "She is still *woman,* with duties prescribed her by the God of Nature essentially different from those of *man.*" However, some educated upper-class women insisted on the equality of the separate male and female worlds. "I will never consent to have our sex considered in an inferior point of light," Abigail Adams, the wife of President John Adams, proclaimed in 1799. "Let each planet shine in their own orbit. God and nature designed it so—if man is *Lord,* woman is *Lordess.*" Such strong private arguments notwithstanding, women's status remained greatly inferior to that of men.

Women, Religion, and the State

The Christian Church had traditionally assigned women a subordinate role. In fact, many religious writers viewed women as morally inferior to men—they were sexual temptresses or witches. By 1800 the clergy had reversed this image; they now put the blame for sexual misconduct on men with bad habits associated with aristocratic privileges rather than on women's voluptuousness. Moralists now claimed that modesty and purity were inherent in the nature of women, giving them a unique ability to educate the spirit. As Thomas Grimké, a South Carolina reformer, said, "Give me a host of educated pious mothers and sisters and I will revolutionize a country, in moral and religious taste."

Women in England and America took new religious initiatives in the late eighteenth century. Mother Ann Lee founded the Shaker sect in England and migrated in 1774 to America, where she and a handful of followers attracted numerous recruits. The Shakers were a controversial sect; their enthusiasm, clannishness, celibacy, and commitment to female equality set them apart. But by the 1820s, Shaker communities dotted the countryside from New Hampshire to Kentucky and Indiana (see Chapter 12). In Rhode Island, Jemima Wilkinson, a female revivalist, won dozens of converts to her own sect. Women in traditional churches also became more active. In Boston, they created the Female Society for Missionary Purposes, while in New Hampshire, women managed more than fifty local "cent" societies which raised funds for the Society for Promoting Christian Knowledge.

Women became active in religion partly because they were excluded from other spheres of public life and partly because of their numerical predominance in many denominations. After 1800 about 70 percent of the members of New England Congregational churches were women; their substantial presence encouraged changes in religious practice. In many Protestant faiths men and women traditionally sat on opposite sides of the church during regular Sunday services, and ministers often conducted separate prayer meetings for each sex. Now evangelical Methodist and Baptist preachers encouraged mixed praying, which critics condemned as "promiscuous." Presbyterian and Congregational churches in frontier areas adopted this innovation, with impressive results. "Our prayer meetings have been one of the greatest means of the conversion of souls," a minister in central New York reported in the 1820s, "especially those in which brothers and sisters have prayed together."

AMERICAN LIVES

Jemima Wilkinson, the Universal Friend

★

1776 was a year of new beginnings: In July, the thirteen colonies repudiated 150 years of monarchical rule and declared themselves independent republics—as the United States of America. In October, Jemima Wilkinson of Cumberland, Rhode Island, became ill with a fever and had a vision that she had died and that her body was now inhabited by the "Spirit of Light"; repudiating her birthname, she declared herself the founder of a new religion—as the Publick Universal Friend.

George Whitefield had a hand in both new beginnings. Since 1739 the great English evangelist had inspired Americans to turn to God and to question established authority. By the 1760s, New Light Presbyterians in Philadelphia and elsewhere declared they had "no king but King Jesus" and joined the Patriot movement. At about the same time—around 1768, when she was sixteen—Jemima Wilkinson discovered Whitefield, reading his sermons and joining in the religious revival that followed his final visit to New England in 1770. By 1776 she had forsaken Quakerism, the faith of four generations of Rhode Island Wilkinsons, and joined the New Light Baptists. Whitefield had a way of "turning the world up-side down."

And so did Wilkinson. A tall and graceful woman, with dark hair and dark eyes, she had a magnetic personality and a powerful preaching style that won fervent disciples. Judge William Potter of Rhode Island was so moved by the Universal Friend that he gave up a promising political career, freed his slaves, and built a fourteen-room addition to his mansion for Wilkinson to use. Another wealthy farmer provided her with a home in Pennsylvania, and supporters built churches in three New England towns.

Wilkinson's religious teachings were not particularly new, mostly an amalgam of Calvinist and Quaker principles. From New England's Great Awakening she took the theme of sin and repentance, warning "a lost and guilty, gossiping, dying World to flee from the wrath . . . to come." From the Quakers she derived a progressive social gospel, advocating plain dress, pacifism, and slave emancipation. Wilkinson added a few new elements that reflected the revolutionary spirit of the age. Like Mother Ann Lee, the founder of the Shakers, she preached celibacy and never married. More controversial, she dressed like a man, wearing a black robe similar to a clergyman's gown, and—emphasizing the ambiguity of her gender—told her followers to address her not as "she" or "her" but as "the Friend."

Jemima Wilkinson, the "Universal Friend"

This radicalism—of social doctrine and personal identity—alienated more people than it attracted. Some of her disciples claimed that Wilkinson was a messiah, although she denied having any divine powers. Still, her attempts at faith healing and prophesizing scandalized most orthodox Christians and even the tolerant Quakers and Baptists of Rhode Island. An outcast in her native colony, the Universal Friend moved to Philadelphia in 1783. There she encountered even fiercer opposition—at one gathering being attacked by a stone-throwing mob—forcing her to return to Rhode Island after two years.

Wilkinson now made a fateful decision. Forsaking evangelism, she gave up her ministry of preaching to the "wicked world" and turned to utopianism. She decided to create a colony for her sect "where no intruding foot could enter." Around 1790, Wilkinson and her followers moved to the frontier, near Seneca Lake in western New York, where they established the community of Jerusalem. The fertile land yielded bountiful harvests, and, once some conflicts among members over property rights had been resolved, the colony prospered. By 1800 the settlement had some 260 inhabitants.

But Jerusalem suffered the fate of many utopian experiments, declining as its purpose and energy gradually drained away. Few new recruits joined the colony, and critics continued to heap abuse on Wilkinson, charging her with sexual misconduct and dictatorial rule. More important, the Universal Friend lost her messianic vision: she no longer claimed to have a message for, or a mission in, the wider society, and she did not seek new converts to her religion. Instead, she turned inward, seeking a spiritually fulfilling life in Jerusalem, opening her house to travelers and becoming a leading citizen in the region. The local Indians called her Squaw Shinnewanagistawge (Great Woman Preacher), and she mediated disputes between them and white settlers. The result was predictable. Within two decades of Wilkinson's death in 1819, her sect had disappeared. Its only legacy is a short doctrinal pamphlet, *The Universal Friend's Advice to Those of the Same Religious Society* (1794).

In the broad sweep of history, Jemima Wilkinson was of minor significance. Her religious vision and personal presence were unequal to the task of redeeming Americans and their society. But the life of the Universal Friend is important for what it reveals about the age in which she lived. Wilkinson attacked slavery, and so did many others in the North, bringing its gradual demise. She called for a more enthusiastic religion, and, along with other inspired preachers, sparked the Second Great Awakening. She showed that women could take an active part in religious affairs, and thousands of American women did likewise, gradually changing the composition, practice, and outlook of many Protestant churches.

But Jemima Wilkinson was more than just a reformer, and that, in a sense, proved her undoing. She had the personality and the drive of a social revolutionary, challenging slavery, war, and customary gender roles. And she had the unbending will of a messianic preacher, declaring "Ye cannot be my friends except ye do whatsoever I command you." Her uncompromising radicalism placed Wilkinson outside the bounds of accepted discourse even in an age of political revolution, kept her from attracting a large number of followers, and ultimately forced her into exile in the wilderness.

First Residence of the Friend in Jerusalem

Many laymen resented the emphasis on women's moral superiority and the religious and social activism that sprang from it. "Women have a different *calling,*" one man argued. "They are neither required nor permitted to be exhorters or leaders in public assemblies. . . . That they *be chaste, keepers at home* is the Apostle's direction."

Ministers nevertheless encouraged the creation of women's organizations, and women became increasingly conscious of their new social power. By the 1820s mothers throughout the United States had founded local maternal associations to encourage Christian child raising. Newsletters like *Mother's Magazine* were widely read in hundreds of small towns and villages. A sense of shared purpose and identity arose among many women.

In their capacity as moral paragons, women were able to have an effect on American society. Many young women and the men who courted them upheld female virtue by postponing sexual intercourse until after marriage—a form of self-restraint that had not been common in the eighteenth century. In Hingham, Massachusetts, about 30 percent of the women who married between 1750 and 1800 had borne a child within eight months of their wedding day; by the 1820s the proportion had dropped to 15 percent.

Moreover, women's activism in the churches helped to bring about a new era in the history of women, because churches responded by supporting scores of seminaries where girls were given a sound education. Emma Willard, the first American who publicly advocated higher education for women, opened the Middlebury Female Seminary in Vermont in 1814 and later founded schools for girls in Waterford and Troy, New York. Women educated in female seminaries and academies began to displace men from their traditional roles as teachers in locally supported public schools. By the 1820s women were teaching summer sessions in many schools; in the following decade they worked the more demanding winter sessions as well. One reason that women were able to take over the teaching in primary schools was that school authorities could pay them less than they paid men, because women had few other job opportunities. Women earned $12 to $14 per month as schoolteachers, with room and board—less than a farm laborer. But they had moral and intellectual responsibilities and an acknowledged place in public life, both of which had been beyond their reach in the colonial and Revolutionary periods.

The National Character

Beginning in the 1820s, a distinct national character began to emerge in the United States, reflecting three long-term historical developments that shaped the lives of most free Americans. First, as a result of their involvement in an ever-shifting capitalist market economy, Americans became a "calculating" people. Second, republican precepts of liberty and equality made for a citizenry that was suspicious of—if not hostile toward—anyone with aristocratic pretensions. Finally, in the wake of the Second Great Awakening, many Americans became fervent Protestants. This new religious identity gave otherwise diverse social groups a common vocabulary and set of goals.

The Second Great Awakening

American Churches. Following independence, Americans scrutinized their churches to find those best suited to a republican society. The hierarchical structure of the Roman Catholic Church had always troubled Protestants who embraced Luther's doctrine of the priesthood of all believers. In the Episcopal Church power likewise flowed downward—from bishops to ministers and then to the congregations. In contrast, the Presbyterian Church was more "republican," because ordinary members elected laymen to the synods (or congresses) where doctrine and practice were formulated.

The most democratic forms of church government belonged to Quakers, Baptists, and Congregationalists. No bishops or governing bodies stood above the local congregations; most church decisions—on matters of theology as well as administration—rested in the hands of church members. Methodism retained a religious hierarchy but added democratic features as well. Bishops took the lead on theological issues and enforced order in the church; yet the evangelical fervor of early Methodism fostered lay preaching, emotional worship, and communal singing, creating an egalitarian religious culture. Partly because of their democratic features, Methodist and Baptist churches grew spectacularly, and by the early nineteenth century they had become the largest religious denominations in America.

Revivalism. Between 1790 and 1830, every decade brought another upsurge of Protestantism somewhere in the new nation. Baptists and Shakers evangelized the backcountry of New England. A new sect of Universalists, who repudiated the Calvinist doctrines of predestination and eternal damnation and taught that salvation was universal, attracted thousands of converts in northern New England.

After 1800 camp meeting revivals swept across the frontier regions of South Carolina, Kentucky, Tennessee, and Ohio. James McGready, a Scots-Irish Presbyterian preacher, "could so array hell before the wicked," an eyewitness reported, "that they would tremble and Quake, imagining a lake of fire and brim-

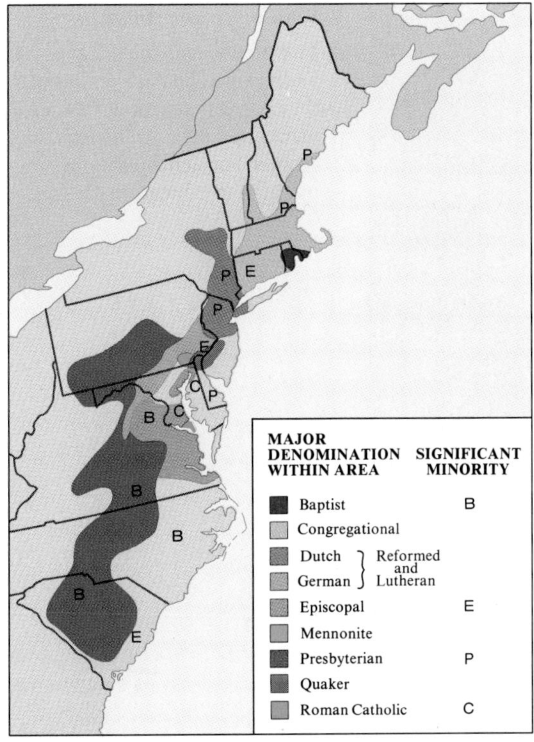

MAP 9.2

Ethnicity and Religious Institutions

The diversity of ethnic groups in the Middle Atlantic region had undermined support for the idea of a legally established church long before the Revolution. In the South, responding to the demands of Scots-Irish Presbyterians and German Lutherans in the backcountry, legislatures ended religious taxation during the 1780s and made all churches equal before the law. In New England, however, the established Congregational Church persisted until the 1830s because of the numerical dominance of English settlers and the strength of the Puritan tradition.

stone yawning to overwhelm them." When frontier preachers got together at a revival meeting, they were electrifying. As a lad of twenty, James Finley attended the Cane Ridge, Kentucky, revival of 1802 and was so moved that he became a Methodist minister:

> The noise was like the roar of Niagara. The vast sea of human beings seemed to be agitated as if by a storm. I counted seven ministers, all preaching at one time, some on stumps, others on wagons. . . . Some of the people were singing, others praying, some crying for mercy. A peculiarly strange sensation came over me. My heart beat tumultuously, my knees trembled, my lips quivered, and I felt as though I must fall to the ground.

Through such revivals, Baptist and Methodist preachers reshaped the spiritual landscape of the South and the Old Southwest. They won over most of the white population and, with the assistance of black ministers, implanted evangelical Protestant Christianity firmly among African-Americans as well.

The First Great Awakening of the 1740s had split many congregations and churches into hostile New and Old Light factions. The Second Great Awakening had a different effect, as Protestant churches began to engage in friendly competition, each seeking new members among the unconverted. New methods of spreading the faith arose. In New England and the Middle Atlantic states, women supplemented the work of preachers and lay elders, doubling the amount of organized spiritual energy. In the South and West, Baptist and Methodist preachers traveled constantly. Instead of settling among a congregation, a Methodist cleric followed a circuit, "riding a hardy pony or horse . . . with his Bible, hymnbook, and Discipline." Wherever he went, he established new churches by searching out devout families, bringing them together for worship, and then appointing lay elders to lead the congregation and enforce moral discipline until he returned.

It was these missionary innovations that caused the denominational base of American religion to shift toward the Baptists, Methodists, Presbyterians, and other evangelical churches, which grew rapidly because they actively sought converts. The leading churches of the Revolutionary Era—the Congregationalists, Episcopalians, and Quakers—declined in relative importance. Their leaders and members were content, for the most part, to maintain existing congregations or to grow slowly through natural increase.

Evangelical ministers copied the techniques of George Whitefield and other eighteenth-century revivalists. In fact, they codified the intuitive genius of the early New Light preachers, preparing manuals on "practical preaching." Preachers were advised to emphasize piety as opposed to theology and learning. Extemporaneous speech was more powerful than a written sermon. "Preach without papers," advised one minister, "seem earnest & serious; & you will be listened to with Patience, & Wonder; both of your hands will be seized, & almost shook off as soon as you are out of the Church." Vigorous preaching imparted enthusiasm and a sense of purpose to hundreds of local revivals.

The Second Great Awakening was solidified and its cultural impact extended by the founding of new theological seminaries, such as the Congregationalist institutions of Andover in Massachusetts and Lane in Ohio. Even more than the older divinity schools at Harvard, Yale, Princeton, and other colleges, these institutions fostered cooperation among clergymen, creating loyalty to nationwide denominations. The ties among clergy-

Women in the Awakening
The preacher is male but women fill the audience. The Awakening was one of the most far-reaching women's movements in American history, mobilizing women for action not only in religion but also in education and social reform.

men—and an expanded religious publication program—united local congregations with one another; for the first time in America, men and women in small villages scattered across the landscape saw themselves as part of a large religious organization.

As individual clergymen cooperated with one another, American Protestant churches became less dogmatic in their teachings. Many congregations abandoned books and pamphlets that contained controversial theological doctrines, such as the orthodox *Watts Hymnal,* replacing them, as a layman explained, with publications that would not give "offense to the serious Christians of any denomination."

Five interdenominational societies were founded between 1815 and 1826—the American Education Society (1815), the American Bible Society (1816), the American Sunday School Union (1824), the American Tract Society (1824), and the American Home Missionary Society (1826). These new organizations were based in New York, Boston, and Philadelphia, but they ministered to a national—and eventually to an international—audience. Each year they dispatched hundreds of missionaries to frontier regions and foreign lands—Africa, India, China—and distributed tens of thousands of religious pamphlets.

Organization on this scale gave momentum and a sense of power to the Second Great Awakening. National institutions united the individual energies of thousands of church members in a great collective undertaking, unleashing their ambitions and freeing their imaginations. "I want to see our state evangelized," declared one pious New York layman:

> Suppose the great State of New York in all its physical, political, moral, commercial, and pecuniary resources should come over to the Lord's side. Why it would turn the scale and could convert the world. I shall have no rest until it is done.

Religion and Reform

Before the Second Great Awakening, Calvinist theology, with its emphasis on human depravity and weakness, had shaped the thinking of many writers, teachers, and statesmen. Then, in the early nineteenth century, ministers—whether or not they were revivalists—began placing greater stress on human ability and individual free will. This view imparted a new optimism to the intellectual culture of the United States.

In New England, the primary source of the new theology, many educated and economically well-off Congregationalists became Unitarians. Rejecting the concept of the Trinity—God the Father, Son, and Holy Spirit—Unitarians believed in an indivisible and "united" God (hence the name Unitarians). In reaction against the emotionalism of Methodist and Baptist services, Unitarians stressed the power of human reason. "The ultimate reliance of a human being is, and must be, on his own mind," argued the famous Unitarian minister William Ellery Channing, "for the idea of God is the idea of our own spiritual nature, purified and enlarged to infinity." This emphasis on a believer's reason gave Unitarianism a humanistic and individualistic thrust.

Similar ideas affected mainstream Congregationalist churches as well. Lyman Beecher, the leading New England clergyman of the early nineteenth century, accepted the anti-Calvinist idea of universal salvation. Although Beecher insisted, as had his Calvinist predecessors, that humans had a natural tendency to sin, he repudiated the doctrine of predestination, declaring that all men and women had the capacity to choose God. In Beecher's sermons, redemption referred to a self-induced spiritual awakening, not an arbitrary summons from a stern God. By emphasizing choice—the free will of the believer—he testified to the growing confidence in the power of human action.

Samuel Hopkins—a disciple of the great philosopher of the First Awakening, Jonathan Edwards—linked individual salvation with social reform through the concept of religious *benevolence*. Hopkins argued that individuals who received God's sanctifying grace had an obligation to help others find salvation. Benevolence resembled republican "virtue" and soon led to the creation of benevolent organizations whose members sought to reform the social order. Indeed, by the 1820s, some conservative church leaders complained that through their benevolence lay men and women were devoting themselves to secular reforms—such as temperance—and neglecting spiritual goals.

Yet as a result of the Second Awakening, religion had become too important a force in American society to be kept separate from secular affairs. On July 4, 1827, the Reverend Ezra Stiles Ely called on the members of the Seventh Presbyterian Church in Philadelphia to begin a "Christian party in politics." In his sermon, entitled "The Duty of Christian Freemen to Elect Christian Rulers," Ely set out a new goal for the American republic—a religious goal that Thomas Jefferson and John Adams would have found strange, if not troubling. The two presidents, who had died only the year before, believed America's mission was to spread political republicanism. Ely urged the United States to become an evangelical Christian nation, dedicated to religious conversion at home and abroad. As Ely put it, "All our rulers ought in their official capacity to serve the Lord Jesus Christ." The Second Great Awakening had added a religious dimension to the emerging American national identity.

Tocqueville's America

In the half-century following independence, hundreds of well-educated Europeans visited the United States to acquire first-hand knowledge of life in a republican society. These visitors came from countries characterized by political hierarchy, limited economic opportunity, religious orthodoxy, patriarchal families, and profound social inequality. They wondered—as successive generations of historians have wondered—whether America represented a more just social order. The French-born essayist St. Jean de Crèvecoeur had no doubts. Comparing the Old World and the New in his famous *Letters from an American Farmer* (1782), Crèvecoeur wrote that European society was composed "of great lords who possess everything, and of a herd of people who have nothing." In America, by contrast, there "are no aristocratical families, no courts, no kings, no bishops."

To many Europeans, American distinctiveness stemmed from the availability of economic opportunity—it was the "best poor man's country," at least for whites. As an Englishman explained, "A consciousness of independence forms the character of the American because the means of subsistence being so easy in this country, and their dependence on each other consequently so trifling, the spirit of servility to those above them so prevalent in European manners is wholly unknown to them."

Republican ideology further undermined traditional hierarchical authority through its emphasis on legal equality. "The law is the same for everyone both as it protects and as it punishes," one European noted. "In the course of daily life everyone is on the most perfect footing of equality." Foreign visitors were well aware that class divisions existed in the United States but saw them as different from those in Europe. The American colonies had never had—and the republican state and national constitutions prohibited—a legally defined and privileged class of nobility.

The absence of an aristocracy of birth (and the ready availability of freehold land) encouraged enterprising Americans to seek upward social mobility and to justify class divisions based on achievement. "In Europe to say of someone that he rose from nothing is a disgrace and a reproach," an aristocratic Polish visitor explained. "It is the opposite here. To be the architect of your own fortune is honorable. It is the highest recommendation."

Alexis de Tocqueville gave classic expression—and a new description, *individualism*—to the character of the American people. Tocqueville was a French aristocrat who visited the United States in 1831 to inspect its novel prison system; after returning to France he composed a famous treatise, *Democracy in America* (1835), which explored the character of republican society. In Europe, he pointed out, "aristocracy had made a chain of all the members of the community from the peasant to the king." In America, however, "democracy breaks that chain and severs every link of it." Consequently, Americans could not rely on the security and predictability of life in an established hierarchical society. Rather, the individual was thrown "back forever upon himself alone."

A Country Tavern

The stylishly dressed dancers command the attention of the onlookers, but the scene reveals the relative social equality of rural communities and the spontaneous character of leisure-time activities.

Tocqueville's verdict on the new republican society was mixed. In America, he declared, "I saw the freest and most enlightened men placed in the happiest condition that there is in the world." Yet he detected a peculiar unhappiness, "as if a kind of cloud habitually covered every visage." He traced this discontent to the American "taste for material enjoyments" and the "universal competition" in an open society. "When men are almost alike and all follow the same route," he concluded on a pessimistic note, they must always strive for superiority and can never achieve "an easy and tranquil existence."

Tocqueville delivered his judgments from a perspective that was far from neutral. Like most aristocrats, he feared a competitive society composed of equal men. (And in common with most other men of the age, he could not conceive of equality between men and women.) Americans who owed their position to inherited wealth and social status also questioned the moral legitimacy of a social order determined by personal financial achievement. "The aristocracy of Kingston [New York] is more one of money than any village I have ever seen," complained Nathaniel Booth in 1825. Booth's ancestors had once ruled Kingston but had now lost predominance in the rapidly growing Hudson River town. "Man is estimated by dollars," he lamented, "what he is worth determines his character and his position at once." Booth and Tocqueville knew only too well that competitive capitalist individualism, like republicanism and evangelical Protestantism, was a revolutionary doctrine in a world of aristocrats, inherited status, and established churches.

However, individualism by itself did not adequately encompass the American character in the 1820s. In the first place, the self-reliant, independent behavior it suggested did not reflect the life-experiences of African-Americans, native Americans, most white women, and even many white men. Legal rules or social customs severely limited the freedom of action of all these groups, who together constituted a majority of the population. Second, as Tocqueville himself pointed out, the continuing importance of republican virtue balanced the pursuit of private advantage. "The principle of self-interest rightly understood," he concluded, prompted Americans "to assist one another and inclines them willingly to sacrifice a portion of their time and property to the welfare of the state." And the republican governments of the states, Tocqueville might have pointed out, sought to increase not only the liberty of individuals but also the "commonwealth" of society.

Thus republicanism as well as competitive individualism (and fervent Protestantism) formed the core of the emerging national identity. This complex set of values and practices was the product of the shared historical experiences of hundreds of thousands of white Americans between the 1770s and the 1820s. During this half-century, the citizens of the United States won a war for political independence and created republican political and social institutions. Many became artisan manufacturers in the East; many more migrated to the West; still more—blacks and Indians as well as whites, women as well as men—participated in intense religious revivals. This process of change challenged old values. Many Americans no longer accepted aristocratic poli-

tics, established religions, or the authority of the family patriarch. Slowly but surely, they created a new American culture based on the principles of republicanism, commercial capitalism, and free-will Protestant Christianity. Within this new framework of life and thought, they struggled to work out their individual destinies.

Summary

Between 1780 and 1820 the United States became a mature commercial society. Merchant capitalists created a flourishing outwork system of rural manufacturing, while state governments devised a commonwealth system of political economy—awarding corporate charters and subsidies to assist transportation companies, manufacturers, and banks. The Supreme Court initially upheld traditional concepts of ownership, but economic competition and the activist policies of state governments and jurists gradually produced a more dynamic legal definition of property rights.

The private lives of many Americans changed as well. Sentimentalism encouraged marriage for love as well as for economic security, and parents often used reason rather than authority in raising children. Women assumed greater moral authority and a more significant role in religious affairs. The Second Great Awakening made religion a more significant part of American life, dramatically increasing the influence of the evangelical Protestant churches of Baptists and Methodists. The United States became, for the first time in its history, a fervent Protestant nation.

By the 1820s a national character had taken shape, even as regional customs and identities remained strong. The emergent image of the American character was complex and did not encompass the lives of women and men from disadvantaged social groups. Nonetheless, most European observers regarded the United States as an increasingly democratic society, filled with men committed to individual ambition and self-achievement.

TOPIC FOR RESEARCH

The Character of American Law

At the time of independence John Adams declared that the United States would be a "government of laws and not of men." By this Adams meant that legal rules would be enforced uniformly—and not arbitrarily according to the whim of an aristocrat or a government official. But who was to determine what the law was? In any event, this task did indeed fall to men (and later women as well)—the judges who interpreted the meaning of legislative statutes, sometimes through textual analysis and other times by reference to common law doctrines and precedents.

The legal decisions of the period present conflicting interpretations of property rights. What arguments or legal doctrines are used by the various judges? Which decisions and doctrines would promote economic development? Which ones would inhibit the creation of new forms of enterprise? On the basis of your reading of these cases, what role does law play in the economic system?

Two good introductions to the legal and economic history of this period are George Dargo, *Law in the Early Republic* (1982), and Jamil S. Zainaldin, *Law in Antebellum Society* (1983). Other important studies are J. Williard Hurst, *Law and the Conditions of Freedom* (1956); Morton Horwitz, *The Transformation of American Law, 1790–1860* (1976); and William Nelson, *Americanization of the Common Law: The Impact of Legal Change on Massachusetts Society, 1780–1830* (1975).

BIBLIOGRAPHY

Political Economy: The Capitalist Commonwealth

Thomas Doerflinger, *A Vigorous Spirit of Enterprise: Merchants and Economic Development in Revolutionary Philadelphia* (1986), and Stuart Bruchey, *Robert Oliver: Merchant of Baltimore* (1956), are fine studies of merchant enterprise. Complementary broader studies include Douglass C. North, *The Economic Growth of the United States, 1790–1860* (1961), and Stuart Bruchey, *The Roots of American Economic Growth, 1607–1861* (1965), while the standard treatment of the period remains Curtis R. Nettels, *The*

Emergence of a National Economy, 1775–1815 (1965). See also Diane Lindstrom, *Economic Development in the Philadelphia Region, 1810–1860* (1983), and Ronald Hoffman, John J. McCusker, and Peter Albert, eds., *The Economy of Revolutionary America* (1987).

The best analysis of early banking remains Bray Hammond, *Banks and Politics in America* (1957). Studies of early manufacturing are Thomas C. Cochran, *Frontiers of Change: Early Industrialism in America* (1981); Rolla S. Tryon, *Household Manufactures in the United States* (1916); David Jeremy, *Transatlantic Industrial Revolution: The Diffusion of Textile Technology Between Britain and America, 1790–1830* (1981); and Caroline F. Ware, *The Early New England Cotton Manufacture* (1931).

The classic study of state assistance to economic development is Oscar and Mary Handlin, *Commonwealth: A Study of the Role of Government in the American Economy: Massachusetts, 1774–1861* (1947). Other important studies include Louis Hartz, *Economic Policy and Democratic Thought: Pennsylvania, 1776–1860* (1948), and E. M. Dodd, *American Business Corporations Until 1860* (1954). State support for transportation can be traced in Carter Goodrich, *Government Promotion of American Canals and Railroads* (1960); Erik F. Hiates et al., *Western River Transportation: The Era of Early Internal Development, 1810–1860* (1975); Philip Jordan, *The National Road* (1948); and Harry N. Scheiber, *Ohio Canal Era: A Case Study of Government and the Economy* (1969).

The conflict in legal doctrine in the state courts is discussed in the Topic for Research. In addition, see the fine study by Leonard Levy, *The Law of the Commonwealth and Chief Justice Shaw* (1955), and Lawrence M. Friedman, *A History of American Law* (2nd ed., 1985). On Marshall, Albert J. Beveridge, *The Life of John Marshall* (4 vols., 1916–1919), is a classic biography. See also Robert K. Faulkner, *The Jurisprudence of John Marshall* (1968); Leonard Baker, *John Marshall: A Life in the Law* (1974); R. Kent Newmyer, *The Supreme Court Under Marshall and Taney* (1968); and Francis N. Stites, *John Marshall: Defender of the Constitution* (1981). A fine study of a single case is C. Peter McGrath, *Yazoo: Law and Politics in the New Republic: The Case of Fletcher v. Peck* (1966).

A Republican Society

Clement Eaton, *Henry Clay and the Art of American Politics* (1957), perceptively describes the emergence of a more open political system, a theme that is enlarged upon by Ronald Formisano, *The Transformation of Political Culture: Massachusetts Parties, 1790s–1840s* (1983). Chilton Williamson, *American Suffrage from Property to Democracy* (1960), discusses the extension of the vote; other constitutional reforms are outlined in Fletcher C. Green, *Constitutional Development in the South Atlantic States, 1776–1860* (1930), and Merrill D. Peterson, ed., *Democracy, Liberty, and Property: The State Constitutional Conventions of the 1820s* (1966).

Lawrence Cremin, *American Education: The National Experience, 1783–1861* (1981), and Carl F. Kaestle, *Pillars of the Republic: Common Schools and American Society, 1780–1860* (1983), are the standard studies. More specialized analyses include Michael Katz, *The Irony of Early School Reform* (1968); Stanley K. Schultz, *The Culture Factory: Boston Public Schools, 1789–1860* (1973); and Carl F. Kaestle, *The Evolution of an Urban School System: New York City, 1750–1850* (1973).

Russell B. Nye, *The Cultural Life of the New Nation, 1776–1830* (1960), and Kenneth Silverman, *A Cultural History of the American Revolution* (1976), offer comprehensive coverage of cultural life. Two fine specialized studies are Neil Harris, *The Artist in American Society, 1790–1860* (1966), and Joseph Ellis, *After the Revolution: Profiles of Early American Culture* (1975). Important interpretative works of literary history include Cathy N. Davidson, *Revolution and the Word: The Rise of the Novel in America* (1986); Emory Elliot, *Revolutionary Writers: Literature and Authority in the New Republic, 1725–1810* (1982); Robert A. Ferguson, *Law and Letters in American Culture* (1984); and Jay Fliegelman, *Prodigals and Pilgrims: The American Revolution Against Patriarchal Authority, 1750–1800* (1982). See also William L. Hedges, *Washington Irving: An American Study, 1802–1832* (1965); Myra Jehlen, *American Incarnation: The Individual, the Nation, and the Continent* (1986); and Cecelia Tichi, *New World, New Earth: Environmental Reform in American Literature from the Puritans Through Whitman* (1980).

Lawrence Stone, *Family, Sex, and Marriage in England* (1979) provides a broad overview of the history of the family, while Michael Grossberg, *Governing the Hearth* (1985), discusses changes in legal doctrines and ideology pertaining to marriage and child custody in America. Catherine M. Scholten, *Childrearing in American Society, 1650–1850* (1985) should be supplemented by Linda Gordon, *Woman's Body, Woman's Right: A History of Birth Control in America* (1976). Philip Greven, *The Protestant Temperament: Patterns of Childrearing, Religious Experience, and the Self in Early America* (1977), is a path-breaking analysis. Other important studies include Daniel Blake Smith, *Inside the Great House: Planter Family Life in Eighteenth-Century Chesapeake Society* (1980); Bernard Wishy, *The Child and the Republic* (1970); Jan Lewis, *The Pursuit of Happiness: Family and Values in Jefferson's Virginia* (1983); and John Demos, *Past, Present, and Personal: The Family and the Life Course in American History* (1986).

The changing situation of white women following independence is assessed in Linda Kerber, *Women of the Republic: Intellect and Ideology in Revolutionary America* (1980); Janet Wilson James, *Changing Ideas About Women in the United States, 1776–1825* (1981); Joan M. Jensen, *Loosening the Bonds: Mid-Atlantic Farm Women, 1750–1850* (1986); and Nancy F. Cott, *The Bonds of Womanhood: "Women's Sphere" in New England, 1780–1835* (1977). Three works that use legal records to discuss women's rights and circumstances are Marylynn Salmon, *Women and the Law of Property in Early America* (1986); Susanne Lebsock, *The Free Women of Petersburg: Status and Culture in a Southern Town, 1784–1860* (1984); and Toby L. Ditz, *Property and Kinship: Inheritance in Early Connecticut, 1750–1820* (1986). See also Christine Stansell, *City of Women: Sex and Class in New York, 1789–1860* (1986).

For women's religious initiatives, consult Mary P. Ryan, *Cradle of the Middle Class* (1981); Barbara Epstein, *The Poli-*

tics of Domesticity: Women, Evangelism, and Temperance (1978); and Keith Melder, *Beginnings of Sisterhood: The American Women's Rights Movement, 1800–1850* (1977), which also traces the growing importance of female academies.

The National Character

Perry Miller, *The Life of the Mind in America: From the Revolution to the Civil War* (1966) explores the impact of religion and revivalism on American thought, while William G. McLoughlin, *Revivals, Awakenings, and Reform: An Essay on Religion and Social Change in America, 1607–1977,* discusses their impact on society. For revivalism see Stephen A. Marini, *Radical Sects of Revolutionary New England* (1982); John B. Boles, *Religion in Antebellum Kentucky* (1976); and Jon Butler, *Awash in a Sea of Faith* (1989). Three older works remain valuable: C. A. Johnson, *The Frontier Camp Meeting* (1955); Bernard A. Weisberger, *They Gathered at the River* (1958); and Wilbur D. Cross, *The Burned Over District* (1950). For the decline of New England Calvinism, see Conrad Wright, *The Beginnings of Unitarianism* (1955); D. P. Edgell, *William Ellery Channing* (1955); and Daniel Walker Howe, *The Unitarian Conscience* (1970).

A growing sense of American identity can be traced in Loren Baritz, *City on a Hill: A History of Ideas and Myths in America* (1964); Stephen Watts, *The Republic Reborn: War and the Making of Liberal America, 1790–1820* (1987); and Paul C. Nagel, *One Nation Indivisible* (1964). Warren S. Tryon, *A Mirror for Americans: Life and Manners in the United States, 1790–1870, as Recorded by American Travelers* (3 vols., 1952) is a useful collection. Perceptive accounts by foreigners include Michael Chevalier, *Society, Manners, and Politics in the United States* (1839); Frances Trollope, *Domestic Manners of the Americans* (1832); and, of course, Alexis de Tocqueville, *Democracy in America* (1835).

TIMELINE

1780s	Rural outwork system, especially shoes and textiles
1781	Philadelphia merchants found Bank of North America
1782	St. Jean de Crèvecoeur, *Letters from an American Farmer*
1783	Noah Webster's ("the Blue-backed Speller") *American Spelling Book*
1790s	State mercantilism encourages economic development Parents limit family size Second Great Awakening
1791	(First) Bank of the United States founded; dissolved in 1811
1794	Lancaster Turnpike Company
1795	Massachusetts Mill Dam Act
1800s	State-chartered banks proliferate Legal profession democratized Rise of sentimentalism and republican marriage system Female religious activism Spread of evangelical Baptists and Methodists
1801	John Marshall becomes chief justice of the United States
1803	*Marbury v. Madison* states theory of judicial review
1805	*Palmer v. Mulligan* (New York) supports economic competition
1810	Albert Gallatin *Report on Manufactures* *Fletcher v. Peck* expands contract clause
1816	Second Bank of the United States chartered
1819	*McCulloch v. Maryland* enhances power of national government *Dartmouth College v. Woodward* protects corporate property rights
1818–1821	Democratic revision of state constitutions
1820s	Expansion of public primary school system
1821	*Cohens v. Virginia* declares supremacy of national courts
1835	Alexis de Tocqueville, *Democracy in America*

PART 3

Early Industrialization and the Sectional Crisis, 1820–1877

THEMATIC TIMELINE

	Economy	Society	Culture	Politics and Government	Sectionalism
	The Industrial Revolution begins	**The emergence of a new class structure**	**Reform and reaction to reform**	**Democratization and western expansion**	**From compromise to Civil War and Reconstruction**
1820	Waltham textile factory (1814) Erie Canal (1825)	Business class emerges Rural women and girls recruited as factory workers	The Benevolent Empire dominates reform Charles Finney leads revivals	Most adult white men gain the vote The rise of Andrew Jackson and the Democratic party	Missouri Compromise (1820) South becomes world's largest cotton producer
1830	American textile manufacturers achieve competitive superiority over British Panic of 1837	Mechanics form craft unions Depression shatters labor movement	Joseph Smith founds Mormon church (1830) Garrisonian abolitionism (1831)	Indian Removal Act (1830) Whig party formed (1834); Second Party System emerges	Nullification crisis (1832) Compromise Tariff (1833) Texas Republic
1840	Stationery steam engines used to power factories Modern factories built in East-coast cities	Working-class districts emerge in cities Irish immigration accelerates	Brook Farm (1841) Seneca Falls convention (1848)	Manifest Destiny (1845) Mexican War (1846–47) Free Soil party (1848)	South attempts to win guarantees for slavery
1850	Railroad trunk lines Panic of 1857	Settlement of Oregon and California	*Uncle Tom's Cabin* (1852)	Whig party disintegrates; Third Party System emerges *Dred Scott* (1857)	Compromise of 1850 Kansas-Nebraska Act (1854) John Brown's raid
1860	War industries thrive in the North Republicans enact economic program	Emancipation Proclamation (1863) Free blacks struggle for control of land	Thirteenth Amendment abolishes slavery (1866) Fifteenth Amendment	Lincoln elected (1860) Civil War (1861–65) Reconstruction	South Carolina secedes (1860) Confederate States of America (1861–65)
1870	Panic of 1873	Rise of debt peonage in the South	African-Americans build new communities	Compromise of 1877	Southern states readmitted to Union

In 1820 America was still a predominantly agricultural society. By 1877 it had become one of the world's most powerful industrial economies. This profound transformation began slowly in the Northeast and then, during the 1840s and 1850s, accelerated and spread throughout the northern states. The Industrial Revolution had an impact on virtually every aspect of American life over the period.

First, the technological and organizational innovations transformed the American economy. High-speed machines and a new system of factory labor boosted production, while canals and railroads created a vast national market. The industrial sector produced an ever-increasing share of the country's wealth—from a negligible amount in 1820 to a third in 1877.

Second, industrialization spurred the creation of a society divided by class. Many Americans—middle-class people as well as the very wealthy—benefited from the new economic opportunities. An ambitious and powerful business class emerged, which sought to assert its leadership, often enlisting religion to justify the new economic order and promote its reform agenda. Many other Americans, however, lost wealth or status. Especially threatened were the artisans whose skills were made redundant by technological advances. By 1840, as many as half the nation's free workers labored for wages, and income and wealth had become more concentrated in the hands of relatively fewer families.

Third, industrialization increased pressures to democratize political life. Most important, rival social groups organized to advance their interests and, at times, even to challenge the power of the business class. Farmers turned to political action to address problems of land, credit, and monopoly power. Some workers proposed the reform of industrial society, through the workingmen's parties of the 1820s and 1830s. And immigrant groups—arriving from Ireland, Germany, and Canada during the 1840s and 1850s—espoused social and religious values that often differed from those of the business class. Under the leadership of Andrew Jackson, the Democratic party became the major vehicle for advancing the interests of these groups. To compete with the Democratic party, the parties of the business-class, first the Whigs, then the Republicans, embraced democratic tactics.

Fourth, many Americans became profoundly troubled by the changes sweeping the country. Some sought radical reform—equal rights for women and the abolition of slavery. Abolitionists first condemned slavery as a sinful expression of arbitrary personal power, but during the 1840s many shifted their ground, attacking a "Slave Power" that seemed to threaten free labor and the economic foundations of the republic.

Fifth, and finally, industrialization sharpened sectional divisions. The North was developing an urban industrial economy, while the South remained a predominantly rural slave-holding society. During the 1840s and 1850s, each section tried to impose its distinctive labor system on the West. It was the defeat of the South in this competition, and the fear that it could no longer protect its vital interests, that led to the secession movement. Secession of a large number of southern states, met by the resolve of Abraham Lincoln's Republican government to preserve the Union, produced the Civil War.

Each side believed that it was fighting to preserve its fundamental institutions and values. Each side fought to preserve a democratic republic and a labor system regarded as essential to democracy. Eventually, the North declared its intention to smash slavery. The war became a total war—a war between two societies as well as two armies—and with industrial technology at their disposal, the two sides endured unprecedented casualties and costs.

The war dragged on long enough for the North to build the most potent military machine in the world. The fruits of victory were substantial. During Reconstruction, the North imposed its interpretation of the Constitution on the nation, built an enduring base of power for the Republican party, eradicated slavery, and began to extend the benefits of democracy to African-Americans. But the North lacked the will to complete its work—to undertake the economic restructuring that was required to enable the freed slaves to participate with full equality in American society.

Lockport on the Erie Canal, (detail)

This 1852 watercolor by artist Mary Keys portrays Lockport, New York, a town that grew up around the locks of the Erie Canal near Buffalo. (Munson-Williams-Proctor Institute Museum of Art)

CHAPTER 10 *The Industrial Revolution,* 1820–1840

In 1831–1832 Alexis de Tocqueville observed Americans at work and remarked, "What most astonishes me . . . is not so much the marvelous grandeur of some undertakings, as the innumerable magnitude of small ones." Tocqueville astutely identified a key feature of the Industrial Revolution in America: it was the product of thousands of small innovations—and thousands of small innovators.

In the late eighteenth century these innovators began the transformation of America from a predominantly agricultural society to what would become, a century later, the world's most powerful industrial economy. The 1820s and 1830s were crucial decades in this process, for they saw the most dramatic acceleration of the innovations in manufacturing that had begun so tentatively and piecemeal in the 1790s. And even though most Americans remained farmers and most manufacturing was done by craftsmen in traditional shops until after the Civil War, the era of early industrialization was quite distinct from the preindustrial period.

For one thing, by the 1820s the very meaning of the word *manufacturing* had changed. From its original sense of making things by hand it had come to mean production carried on in factories by workers tending power-driven machinery. More important, industrialization enabled Americans to produce far more goods and services per person than ever before. And innovations in the pioneering industries triggered additional advances—in agriculture, transportation, and other industries—which increased productivity further. Thus the new, more productive era that began in the 1820s provided the basis for a great increase in the living standards of the vast majority of Americans.

Americans sensed they were in a new era. Some welcomed it but many feared the changes in traditional social relationships. For many, religion provided the glue to keep society—and the new social classes—together.

The Rise of Northeastern Manufacturing

The Industrial Revolution had originated in Great Britain in the middle of the eighteenth century (see Chapter 4). Britain's head start gave it an early advantage that endured for many years. The first factories of the American Industrial Revolution, concentrated in the Northeast, copied British machines and were often supervised by British technicians. But by 1840, Americans had reduced their reliance on British technology and British innovators and were developing their own machinery and factory organization in order to exploit America's main advantage—an abundance of natural resources.

New Organization and New Technology

The first increases in productivity had come from the outwork system of rural manufacturing organized by merchants after the Revolutionary War (see Chapter 9).

Upper Falls of the Genessee River, 1835

Like many early industrial sites, these prosperous flour mills at Rochester, New York, were located to take advantage of natural resources. The Genessee River provided water to irrigate the wheat farms of the Genessee Valley, it offered transportation of grain to the mills, and its falls powered the mill machinery.

The new ways of organizing workers made manufacturing more efficient, even without any technological improvements. As late as 1850, shoe manufacturers running complex outwork systems were the largest employers in Massachusetts but still used no modern machinery.

For tasks that did not lend themselves to the outwork system, manufacturers developed a different approach to organizing workers: they brought them all together under one roof. They created the modern *factory,* which concentrated as many of the elements of production as possible in one place and divided up the work into specialized tasks. For example, Cincinnati merchants in the 1830s built slaughterhouses that included "disassembly" lines for butchering hogs. A simple system of overhead rails moved the carcasses past workers who were assigned specific tasks: splitting the animals, removing various organs, trimming, weighing, and, finally, hosing down the cleaned carcasses before packers pickled them and stuffed them in barrels. All of these tasks could have been done on any Ohio farm, and the workers were no more skilled than the typical Ohio farmer. But in the factory the entire butchering and packing process required less than one minute. By the 1840s, Cincinnati was disassembling so many hogs that the city had become known as "Porkopolis."

Technological improvements alone could also increase productivity. As early as 1782, the prolific Delaware inventor Oliver Evans built a highly automated labor-saving flour mill driven by water power.

His machinery lifted the grain to the top of the mill, cleaned the grain as it fell into hoppers, ground it into flour, conveyed the flour back to the top of the mill, and then cooled the flour during its descent into barrels. Evans needed only six men to mill a hundred thousand bushels of grain a year, and his labor-saving techniques spread quickly as permanent elements in flour-milling.

What made industrial development distinctive during the 1820s and 1830s was that for the first time manufacturers *combined* organizational and technological innovations. By applying technological advances to a factory setting, Americans finally achieved the dramatic productivity gains of the Industrial Revolution. In the United States the first technologically advanced factories were the New England mills that made woolen and cotton cloth.

The Textile Industry

The Industrial Revolution had begun in the textile mills of northern England in the middle of the eighteenth century. After the Revolutionary War, their cheap, factory-made cloth flooded the American market, threatening the livelihood of American hand spinners and weavers. Desperate to recapture the domestic market, American merchants resolved to copy—or steal if necessary—the new British technology.

The earliest practitioners of industrial espionage in America were a group of British *mechanics*, as skilled workers were called during the early Industrial Revolution. Lured by high wages or offers of partnerships, thousands of British mechanics—who often were machine builders—pirated the detailed and up-to-date information that American manufacturers coveted and set sail for the United States. Since British law prohibited the emigration of mechanics as well as the export of textile machinery, many artisans disguised themselves as ordinary laborers—or crossed the Atlantic hidden in barrels. In 1812 there were more than three hundred British mechanics at work in the Philadelphia area alone.

Samuel Slater. The most important of the British mechanics was Samuel Slater, who emigrated from the industrial district of Derbyshire, England, in 1789. He had served as an apprentice to Jedediah Strutt, a partner of Richard Arkwright, the inventor and current operator of the most advanced machinery for spinning cotton. Having memorized the design of Arkwright's machinery, the young Slater, disguised by a beard, set sail for New York. There he contacted Moses Brown, a wealthy merchant who had been trying unsuccessfully to duplicate English spinning machinery in his cotton mill in Providence, Rhode Island. Slater took over the management of Brown's mill and replicated the entire set of Arkwright's machines. This was now by far the most advanced mill in America, and for that reason the year of its opening—1790—is often considered to mark

the beginning of the Industrial Revolution in the United States.

Problems of Competition. Even a mill as advanced as Slater's, however, had difficulty competing with British mills. Americans had one major advantage—an abundance of natural resources. Not only did America's rich agriculture produce a wealth of cotton and wool, but its rivers provided a cheap source of energy. All along the *fall line*, from Maine to Delaware, where the Appalachian foothills drop to the Atlantic coastal plain, the rivers cascade downhill in falls and rapids that can easily be harnessed to run power machinery.

Pork Packing in Cincinnati
This pork-packing plant in Cincinnati used little modern technology except an overhead moving pulley system that carried hog carcasses past the workers. The plant's efficiency was primarily organizational; each worker was assigned a specific task. Such plants pioneered the design of the moving assembly lines that reached their sophisticated development in the twentieth-century automobile factories of Henry Ford.

NEW TECHNOLOGY *Cotton-Spinning Machines*

The Industrial Revolution in America began in the textile factories of New England. By 1800, a wide array of machines were in use to clean and fluff raw cotton fibers and to prepare the fibers for weaving. Carding machines, which consisted of two cylinders full of wire pins, combed the fibers into parallel strands. Roving machines rolled the carded cotton into a loose roll called a roving.

The real revolution in textile manufacturing came with changes in spinning technology. Rates of production had been severely limited by the slow process of spinning cotton fibers into yarn. As late as the 1760s, all yarn was spun by individuals at hand-turned spinning machines. In 1765, the British inventor James Hargreaves invented the *spinning jenny,* also called the hand jenny. The key tool in spinning had always been the spindle, which first elongated and then twisted together strands of fiber to make yarn. Hargreaves's spinning jenny imitated the function of spinning wheels. The operator manually turned a wheel that spun a series of spindles, each of which simultaneously drew out the roving and twisted it into thread.

Jennies saved labor by spinning from twenty-four to more than a hundred spindles at once. However, a jenny required a skilled operator. The spinner placed bobbins (spools) with roving on the machine's frame and tied a bit of roving from each bobbin to a spindle, first passing the fibers through a carriage that moved back and forth on the frame. After elongating the roving by moving the carriage, the spinner clamped the rovings to the carriage and then turned the wheel to spin the spindles. When the thread had been given enough twist, the operator moved the carriage forward again while turning the spindles more slowly to wind the thread onto the bobbins. The jenny had to be stopped between the drawing and the twisting, and slowed before winding, so it had to be driven by hand. Because of the labor costs involved, relatively few manufacturers adopted jennies for cotton spinning in America.

Americans preferred the *spinning frame, or water frame,* a machine patented in England in 1769 by Richard Arkwright and brought to the United States by Samuel Slater. Its chief innovation was to separate the functions of drawing and twisting. After two pairs of rollers had elongated the thread, it was passed down the arm of a flier, a device attached to a spindle. The flier

A Photograph of Samuel Slater's Water Frame
Samuel Slater's water frame had two rows of bobbins, twenty-four in each row, on the front and back of the lower portion of the machine.

twisted the thread and wound it onto a bobbin attached to the spindle.

The only skill needed to operate a water frame was the ability to knot a broken thread. The machine ran continuously on inexpensive water power. In addition to saving expensive labor, the frame worked much faster than the jenny. A single water frame produced as much yarn as several hundred spinning wheels working together. Moreover, the water frame produced a yarn that was coarse enough for the rugged cloth used for most clothing in America. Even more significantly, its yarn was strong enough to be used on power looms for the warp, the vertical rows of yarn strung in tension, through which the weft yarn was woven to form the finished cloth.

American inventors quickly made significant improvements in the water frame. By 1830 virtually all the processes involved in the manufacture of cotton cloth had been mechanized in the United States, and most new mills had separate departments for carding, dressing, spinning, and power-loom weaving. The enormous gains in textile productivity and profitability inspired a host of inventors and entrepreneurs to mechanize other kinds of industry. The Industrial Revolution had seized the American imagination.

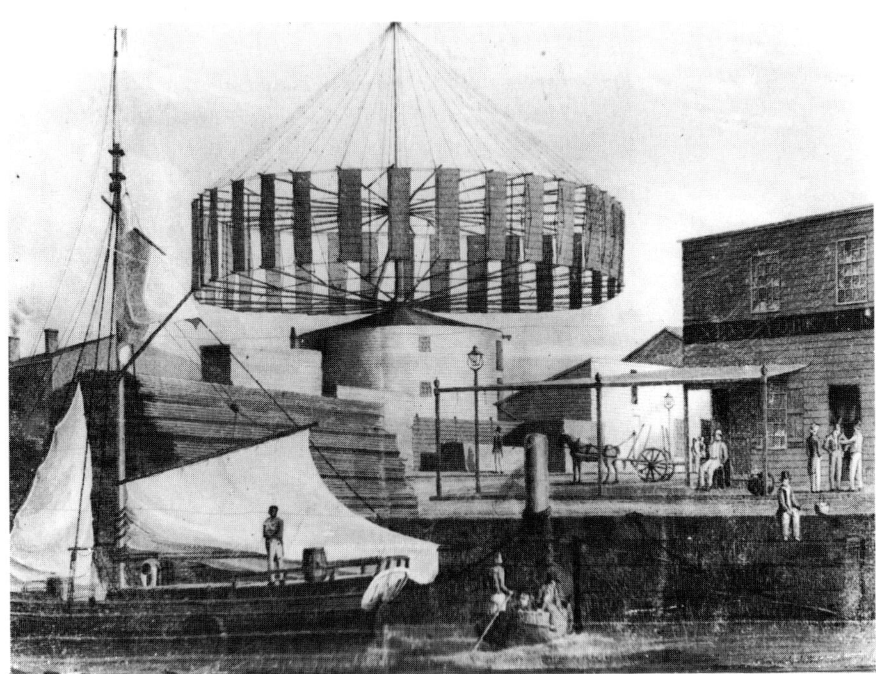

A Rotary Windmill, 1833
In towns and cities that were not located along the fall line, manufacturers had difficulty finding a source of cheap power. All such experiments—including this circular windmill, built in New York City—proved impractical until the development of stationary steam engines in the 1840s. (J.W. Hill, *The Rotary or Circular Windmills,* The Metropolitan Museum of Art)

Against this the British had numerous advantages. For one thing, falling shipping rates made it cheaper to ship goods across the Atlantic than to transport them within the United States, given its primitive transportation network. British interest rates were lower too, so British firms could build factories and market their goods less expensively. And because British companies were better established, they could afford to engage in occasional cutthroat competition, cutting prices briefly but sharply in order to drive the newer American firms out of business.

But the most important British advantage was cheap labor. Britain had a larger population—about 12.6 million in 1810, compared with 7.3 million Americans—and its workers were paid less. Landless agricultural workers and underemployed urban laborers were more than willing to perform simple, repetitive factory jobs, even for low wages. Since unskilled American workers could obtain good pay for farm or construction work, American manufacturers had to offer relatively high wages to attract them to factory jobs.

To make matters worse, the federal government did little to protect the nation's high-wage workers and high-cost industries as they learned how to meet the British competition. Congress did not pass its first protective *tariff*—a tax on imported goods—until 1824. The measure levied a fairly modest 35 percent tax on imported iron, woolens, cotton, and hemp. But in 1833, under pressure from southern planters and western farmers who wanted to keep down the price of manufactured goods, Congress began to reduce even those tariffs (see Chapter 11).

The sad consequence of all these factors was that American textile manufacturers often failed. Even those who survived made good profits only when the Embargo of 1807 and the War of 1812 cut off British competition. To overcome their British rivals, American textile manufacturers would have to address the central problem of low-cost British labor.

The Boston Manufacturing Company

In 1811, Francis Cabot Lowell, a wealthy Boston merchant, spent an apparently casual holiday touring English textile mills. A well-educated and charming young man, he flattered his hosts by asking thousands of questions. But his easy manner hid a serious purpose. He paid close attention to the answers he received, and later, in his hotel rooms, secretly made detailed drawings of the mills and power machinery he had seen. On returning to the United States, Lowell turned over his drawings to an experienced American mechanic, Paul Moody, who made additional improvements. Lowell then joined with two other merchants, Nathan Appleton and Patrick Tracy Jackson, to raise the staggering sum of $400,000 to form the Boston Manufacturing Company. In 1814, they opened a textile plant in Waltham, Massachusetts, on the Charles River. Waltham was the first plant in America to perform all the operations of cloth making under one roof. More important, thanks to Moody's improvements, Waltham's innovative power looms operated at even higher speeds than those Lowell had seen in England, making it pos-

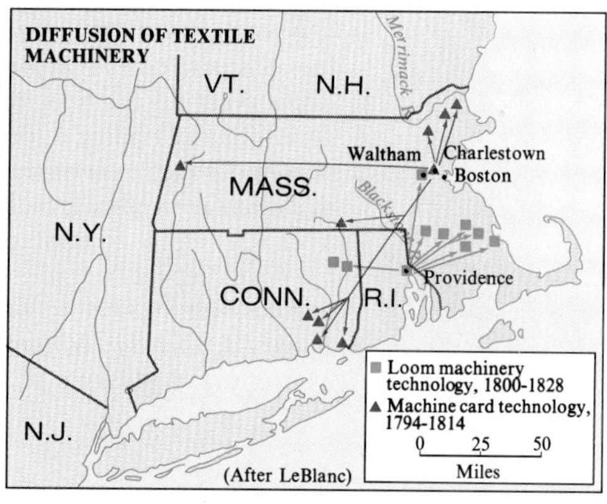

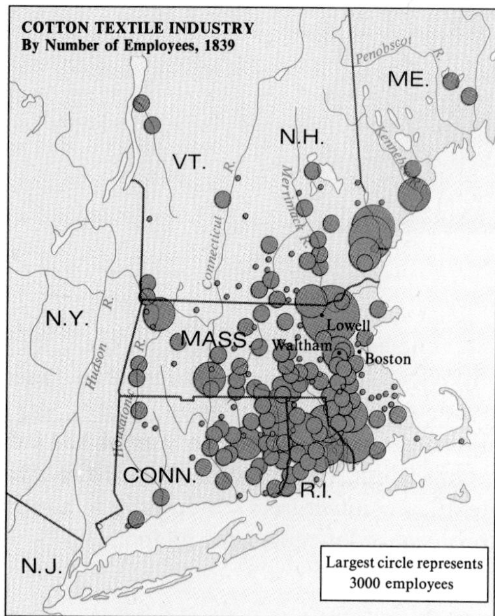

MAP 10.1

Early Industrial Enterprise in New England

As new and improved textile machinery spread across New England, modern textile factories sprang up and became concentrated at locations such as Waltham and Lowell in eastern Massachusetts. On the lower map, each circle is focused on a town with one or more textile factories. The size of each circle indicates the relative number of spindles or employees in that town; the data are sufficiently similar for historians to be able to trace and compare the development of the industry over this period.

sible to produce cloth with fewer workers. Improved technology was one part of the answer to Britain's cheaper labor; finding a less expensive group of American workers was the other.

The Waltham Plan. The Boston Manufacturing Company solved the other part of its problem by pioneering a manufacturing system that became known as the Waltham plan. It recruited thousands of farm girls and women as operators of its textile machinery, offering them higher wages than they could earn in the outwork system of shoe and broom production or in service as maids or cooks. In addition, manufacturers provided company-run boarding houses and cultural activities, such as evening lectures. The mill owners reassured anxious parents by enforcing strict curfews, prohibiting alcoholic beverages, and requiring regular church attendance. At Lowell (1822), Chicopee (1823), and other sites in Massachusetts and New Hampshire, the Boston company built new cotton factories on the Waltham plan. During the 1820s and 1830s, other Boston-owned firms, such as the Hamilton, Suffolk, and Tremont corporations, also adopted the Waltham plan.

Women Workers in a Textile Mill

This lithograph shows women working in an English cotton factory that closely resembled those in America. They tended spinning machines and looms driven by water power transmitted by a system of belts and wheels. The women here are probably knotting broken threads, while the man is most likely adjusting the machinery. (Barfoot for Darton, *Progress of Cotton: No. 6, Spinning,* Yale University Art Gallery)

AMERICAN VOICES

Early Days at Lowell *Lucy Larcom*

Lucy Larcom (1824–1893) went to work in a textile mill in Lowell, Massachusetts, when she was eleven years old. She remained there until 1846, when she moved west to Illinois with her sisters and a great tide of other New Englanders. In later life she became a teacher and a writer; this selection is from her autobiography, *A New England Girlhood.*

I never cared much for machinery. The buzzing and hissing and whizzing of pulleys and rollers and spindles and flyers around me often grew tiresome. I could not see into their complications, or feel interested in them. But in a room below us we were sometimes allowed to peer in through a sort of blind door at the great waterwheel that carried the works of the whole mill. It was so huge we could only watch a few of its spokes at a time, and part of its dripping rim, moving with a slow, measured strength through the darkness that shut it in. It impressed me with something of the awe which comes to us in thinking of the great Power which keeps the mechanism of the universe in motion.

. . . We did not call ourselves ladies. We did not forget that we were working girls, wearing coarse aprons suitable to our work, and that there was some danger of our becoming drudges. I know that sometimes the confinement of the mill became very wearisome to me. In the sweet June weather I would lean far out of the window, and try not to hear the unceasing clash of sound inside. Looking away to the hills, my whole stifled being would cry out

> Oh, that I had wings!

Still I was there from choice, and

> The prison unto which we doom
> ourselves,
> No prison is.

I regard it as one of the privileges of my youth that I was permitted to grow up among these active, interesting girls, whose lives were not mere echoes of other lives, but had principle and purpose distinctly their own. Their vigor of character was a natural development. The New Hampshire girls who came to Lowell were descendants of the sturdy backwoodsmen who settled that State scarcely a hundred years before. Their grandmothers had suffered the hardships of frontier life. . . . Those young women did justice to their inheritance. They were earnest and capable; ready to undertake anything that was worth doing. My dreamy, indolent nature was shamed into activity among them. They gave me a larger, firmer ideal of womanhood. . . .

Country girls were naturally independent, and the feeling that at this new work the few hours they had of every-day leisure were entirely their own was a satisfaction to them. They preferred it to going out as "hired help." It was like a young man's pleasure in entering upon business for himself. Girls had never tried that experiment before, and they liked it. It brought out in them a dormant strength of character which the world did not previously see.

Source: Lucy Larcom, *A New England Girlhood* (Boston: Houghton Mifflin, 1889), 153–55, 181–83, 196–200.

Some of the young women working under the Waltham plan banked their wages for later use. One such worker wrote to a cousin in the 1830s that she wanted to attend Oberlin College (the first coeducational U.S. college, founded in 1833) "because I think it the best way of spending the money I have worked so hard to earn." Others used their wages to help support their families and parents. A girl might help her father to pay off a farm mortgage, a brother to acquire more schooling, or her family to accumulate a dowry for her own marriage. In 1835, eleven-year-old Lucy Larcom of Lowell, Massachusetts, went to work in a textile mill. In 1889 she recalled that she started work "with a light heart" because the work meant that she "was not a trouble or burden or expense" to her widowed mother. Regardless of what the young women did with their wages, they enjoyed the greater degree of personal independence that their incomes provided. "Don't I feel independent!" another mill worker wrote to her sister in the 1840s. "The thought that I am living on no one is a happy one indeed to me."

Throughout the 1820s and 1830s, young women made up a majority of all workers in the cotton-textile industry and nearly half of the workers in woolen-textile manufacturing. In the early 1830s, more than 40,000 women were working in textile mills. Most of the remaining 20,000 textile workers were children under the age of fourteen, and most of these were girls. Men comprised only a small fraction of the textile operatives. The few men in the industry worked primarily in

Rhode Island, under the Fall River plan, which offered unskilled factory work to entire families. The success of the Waltham and Fall River plans was largely due to the meager profitability of New England agriculture and the high birth rate among New England farm families. The region's poorer farms could not hold young people, who quickly turned to factory work, even though it meant operating fast-moving machines, doing highly repetitive tasks, and disrupting traditional family life.

It was hard to argue with success. Less than forty years after the founding of Slater's mill, New England companies finally established their competitive superiority over the British in American markets. In 1825, Thomas Jefferson—who had earlier warned against the dehumanizing perils of industrialization—was moved to express his pride in the American achievement. "Our manufacturers are now very nearly on a footing with those of England. [England] has not a single improvement which we do not possess, and many of them adopted by ourselves to our ordinary use."

The Waltham and Fall River plans also gave New England manufacturers a competitive edge over other American textile manufacturers. In New York and Pennsylvania, where agricultural employment was far better paid than in New England, textile producers were slower to adopt the technology of the Industrial Revolution. They concentrated their innovative efforts in modifying traditional technology to produce higher-quality cloth than the British and New England mills manufactured. In the South, textile entrepreneurs almost always failed because they lacked a cheap supply of labor. Poor whites disdained factory work, and the cost of buying or renting slaves was prohibitive because of the huge profits the slaveowners could earn by producing cotton. The southern textile industry languished until after the Civil War.

American Mechanical Genius

Until the 1840s, individuals of modest wealth provided most of the capital required to start new manufacturing firms. Only in Massachusetts did wealthy merchant capitalists—such as Francis Cabot Lowell—invest in modern industry. More typically, it was mechanics and small merchants who took the risks, pooling their capital and often borrowing from family and friends to start factories. Some storekeepers invested in small mills, hoping to expand their business. A mill could increase a storekeeper's ability to purchase supplies for his store and, by generating jobs and income, increase the local market for his goods. Storekeeper-manufacturers commonly tried to pay workers with credit at their stores, thus making certain they spent their wages on store goods.

Rockdale. The early history of industry in Rockdale, Pennsylvania, a small mill village in the Delaware Valley near Philadelphia, illustrates the entrepreneurial role of small manufacturers. In 1825 there were four cloth manufacturers in Rockdale. One was William Martin, a young, modestly wealthy Philadelphia merchant who had purchased his mills in a sheriff's sale (a sale of bankrupted property) using his own savings and those of his brother-in-law. He expanded the mills with money borrowed from an uncle and a mortgage on the property. In 1829, however, cloth prices tumbled and he was forced into bankruptcy. The second manufacturer was John Phillips, the son of a once prominent Philadelphia merchant who had fallen on hard times. John had married well, and he borrowed from his new brother-in-law to buy mills. Strong family support and prudent management enabled him to survive and, in 1835, to relocate his machinery to a new mill in Philadelphia. The

The Lenni Mill

Owned first by William Martin, this was one of the most important early mills in Rockdale. It was named after the site's original inhabitants, the Lenni Lenape, or Delaware Indians. The millrace in the foreground is the beginning of a water system—dam, gates, wheel, and pit—that required extensive labor by local millwrights, masons, and day-laborers to maintain.

third entrepreneur was John Crozer, a farmer and the owner of a failing sawmill. He bought a textile mill at a sheriff's sale by mortgaging his farm and borrowing from a brother-in-law. With enormous personal energy and sustained family assistance, he built the mill into a thriving business and became one of the wealthiest men in Rockdale. The fourth manufacturer, John Carter, was an immigrant and the only one of the four with experience in textiles, from his years as a mill manager in England. Because of his expertise, he was able to borrow extensively from local banks. Nonetheless, largely because he lacked relatives with capital, he suffered a devastating bankruptcy in 1826. The lesson was clear: success was impossible without determination, skill, and family finances.

Mechanics often crossed into the ranks of small manufacturing entrepreneurs, either by starting their own manufacturing firms or by joining them as partners. Literally thousands of modest mechanics developed the simple inventions that, cumulatively, revolutionized American manufacturing. Few of these craftsmen had formal education, but they had learned about machinery in small, traditional craft shops and, increasingly, in modern factories.

One such inventor, Richard Garsed, started working in a textile mill in New Hope, Pennsylvania, when he was only eight years old. Ten years later, in 1837, after his father had purchased a small mill in Rockdale, Garsed began making experimental improvements on his father's power looms. In three years, he nearly doubled their speed. By 1842, he had invented a cam and harness device (patented in 1846) that allowed elaborately figured fabrics, such as damask, to be woven by machine.

The Sellars Family and the Franklin Institute. Garsed was only one of the many American mechanics who, by the 1820s, had replaced British immigrants at the cutting edge of technological innovation usually basing their success on elaborate ties of family and friendship. In the Delaware Valley, the remarkable Sellars family dominated an interrelated group of inventors who transmitted their mechanical knowledge from one generation to the next. Samuel Sellars, Jr., invented a machine for twisting worsted woolen yarn. His son John harnessed water power for the efficient operation of the family's saw and grist mills, and devised a machine to weave wire sieves. John's sons and grandsons, in turn, built machine shops that turned out a variety of new products—riveted leather fire hoses, paper-making equipment, and eventually locomotives.

In 1824, members of the Sellars family and other mechanics and small manufacturers founded the Franklin Institute in Philadelphia. Named after Benjamin Franklin, whom the mechanics admired for his scientific accomplishments and his idealization of hard work, the institute fostered the mechanics' sense of professional identity. It published a journal, provided high school instruction in mechanics, chemistry, mathematics, and mechanical drawing, and organized annual fairs for exhibiting the most advanced products and rewarding their designers. At the 1842 fair the institute judges awarded a silver medal to Richard Garsed for cotton and worsted damask tablecloths that promised "successful competition with the imported." Craftsmen in Ohio and other states soon established their own mechanics institutes, offering the same kinds of programs that the Franklin Institute had pioneered.

Machine Tools. The most outstanding contribution of American mechanics to the Industrial Revolution was the development of machines capable of making other machines—that is, *machine tools*. In the textile industry, mechanics invented devices—lathes, planers, and boring machines—that could make interchangeable textile-machine parts. These machine-tooled parts, which required only a minimum of filing or fitting, made it possible to manufacture textile machinery that was low in price and precise enough in design and construction to operate at higher speeds than British equipment.

Once American craftsmen had perfected machine tools for the textile industry, the Industrial Revolution swept through the rest of American manufacturing. If anything, the impact of machine tools was even greater in the industries producing goods made of iron or steel—such as plows, scythes, and axes. In 1832 the mechanics David Hinman and Elisha K. Root, employed by Samuel W. Collins in his Connecticut ax-making company, built a vastly improved die-forging machine—a device that pressed and hammered hot metal into *dies,* or cutting forms. Using the improved machine, a skilled worker could increase his production of ax heads from twelve to three hundred a day.

Eli Whitney: Machine Builder. Some of the most significant machine-building innovators worked in the firearms industry, and none was more influential than Eli Whitney. Whitney's mechanical bent manifested itself early. When he was only fourteen, he persuaded his father to install a forge on their Massachusetts farm so that he could produce nails and knife blades for local markets.

In 1792, after graduating from Yale College, Whitney was employed as a tutor on the Georgia plantation of Catherine Greene, the young widow of Revolutionary War general Nathanael Greene. It was there that he built the first prototype cotton gin, the machine that would revolutionize cotton production (see Chapter 8). In 1793, Whitney returned to New Haven, where he tried to manufacture the gins in quantity using special machine tools he had also developed. Whitney hoped he could maintain a monopoly for his gin, which he had

Eli Whitney's Factory and Village Whitney's Mill Rock armory, which he began building in 1798 near New Haven, Connecticut, produced inexpensive, high-quality guns until his death in 1825. Whitney tried to supervise every detail of his workers' lives in the mill village, called Whitneyville. (William Giles Munson, *The Eli Whitney Gun Factory,* 1826–28, Yale University Art Gallery)

patented in 1794. But the patent did not protect him from the numerous planters who made their own gins or from manufacturers who made slight improvements on his design.

Disgusted and in debt, Whitney turned his attention to a product with a larger, guaranteed market—firearms. In 1798 he obtained a federal contract to manufacture ten thousand muskets. He believed he could design machine tools that would enable him to produce interchangeable musket parts. Consequently, he promised to produce the muskets in only twenty-eight months. He would, he said, "form the tools so that the tools themselves shall fashion the work and give to every part its just proportion—which when once accomplished will give expeditious uniformity, and exactness to the whole." He devised improved forms and jigs to guide the hands of mechanics; he crafted the first milling machine, which used sharp teeth on a gearlike wheel to cut metal; and he achieved a greater degree of interchangeability of parts than anyone before him.

But it took Whitney ten years to fulfill his original contract, and he had to resort to much traditional hand-crafted production. The federal government, largely because of Thomas Jefferson's interest, continued to issue Whitney contracts so that he could perfect his technique. But he died in 1825 without achieving his goal of complete mass production.

After Whitney's death, his work was completed by his partner John H. Hall, an engineer at the federal armory at Harpers Ferry, Virginia. Hall developed all the basic machine tools required to produce modern arms—turret lathes, milling machines, and precision grinders. By 1840, Hall and other American mechanics had created the first modern machine-tool industry in the world. Thereafter, manufacturers could use the machine tools to produce complicated machinery at high speeds and in great quantity. Such machinery enabled the Industrial Revolution to spread relentlessly throughout American manufacturing during the next fifty years.

The Expansion of Markets

During the 1820s and the 1830s, the Industrial Revolution stimulated the rapid expansion of the American marketplace. Manufacturers and merchants in the industrializing Northeast developed a national system of markets, stimulated the growth of cities and towns, and promoted the construction of a massive transportation system to link the Northeast and the Old Northwest.

Regional Trade Patterns

In the first forty years after independence, Americans continued to rely on the export of farm products to Europe. Between 1790 and 1810, as much as 15 percent of the national product was exported—roughly the same level as had prevailed in the mid-eighteenth century. However, this changed dramatically during the 1820s. Americans sharply reduced their reliance on European markets and by 1830 were exporting only 6 percent of the national product, a level that remained constant until the mid-twentieth century.

As exports declined in significance, the domestic trade in agricultural and manufacturing goods flourished. Americans traded with one another in two ways. First, they exchanged goods *within* regions. Philadelphians, for example, traded locally manufactured textiles for farm products grown nearby: flour and corn, dairy products, fruits and vegetables, hay for the horses that pulled carriages, coaches, and omnibuses, and wood for heating and cooking. Second, Americans exchanged products *among* regions. Most important, merchants in the industrializing Northeast traded textiles, clothing, boots and shoes, muskets, and farm equipment for wheat, corn, whiskey, and hogs from the farms of the Great Lakes basin and the Ohio Valley. Manufacturers and farmers in the Northeast and the Old Northwest specialized in production for shipment to other regions. Because this interregional trade grew rapidly, they increased their scale of production, became more efficient, and enlarged their profits.

The exception to the trend of increased domestic trade was the South, which continued to produce primarily for international markets. As the Cotton Kingdom expanded across the Old Southwest, the United States became the world's largest cotton producer. Although southern farmers supplied the textile mills of the Northeast, they exported most of their cotton to Britain and imported the majority of their manufactured goods from British suppliers. Southerners also obtained most of their finance and marketing services from British import houses. Food did not figure in this trade. Southerners fed themselves almost entirely from nearly self-sufficient plantations or small farms on the fringe of the cotton economy.

Thus the South's economy remained tied not to other parts of the United States but to Britain. Its plantation economy more closely resembled those of such colonies as Brazil or Cuba. As in those areas, the earnings from exports went largely to Europeans and to the local planters. Like the landed classes of other plantation societies, southern planters reinvested their profits by expanding their slave labor force and increasing the size of their estates.

The Growth of Cities and Towns

Northern cities and towns flourished in the 1820s, stimulated by industrialization and the expansion of interregional trade. For the first time urban places—defined as localities with more than 2,500 inhabitants—began to grow more rapidly than the population as a whole. There were now also more such places: the number of towns and cities with between 2,500 and 50,000 people more than doubled in twenty years, from 58 towns in 1820 to 126 in 1840. The total urban population grew fourfold, from 443,000 in 1820 to 1,844,000 in 1840.

Fall-Line Towns. The most rapidly growing cities were the new industrial towns. Since the early mills relied on water power to run their machinery, factory towns sprang up all along the fall line. In 1822, for example, the Boston Manufacturing Company decided to build a new complex of mills in East Chelmsford, Massachusetts, on the Merrimack River. Within a few years the sleepy village had been transformed into a bustling town, now named Lowell in honor of the company's founder. Hartford, Connecticut, Trenton, New Jersey, and Wilmington, Delaware, also surged, as mill owners recruited workers from the surrounding countryside.

Western Cities. Western cities grew almost as rapidly. In 1830, New Orleans, Pittsburgh, Cincinnati, and Louisville accounted for almost three-quarters of the urban population in the West. St. Louis joined the West's largest cities by 1840, its growth stimulated by increased traffic to and from the territory west of the Mississippi. Rochester, Buffalo, Cleveland, Detroit, and Chicago also grew rapidly during the 1830s. The initial expansion of all of these cities resulted from their loca-

The Yankee Peddler

Even as late as 1830, the approximate date of this painting, most Americans lived too far from town markets to shop there regularly. Farm families, like this affluent one represented by an unknown artist, purchased most of their tinware, silverware, clocks, yardgoods, pins and needles, and notions from peddlers, often New Englanders, who traveled far and wide with their vans.

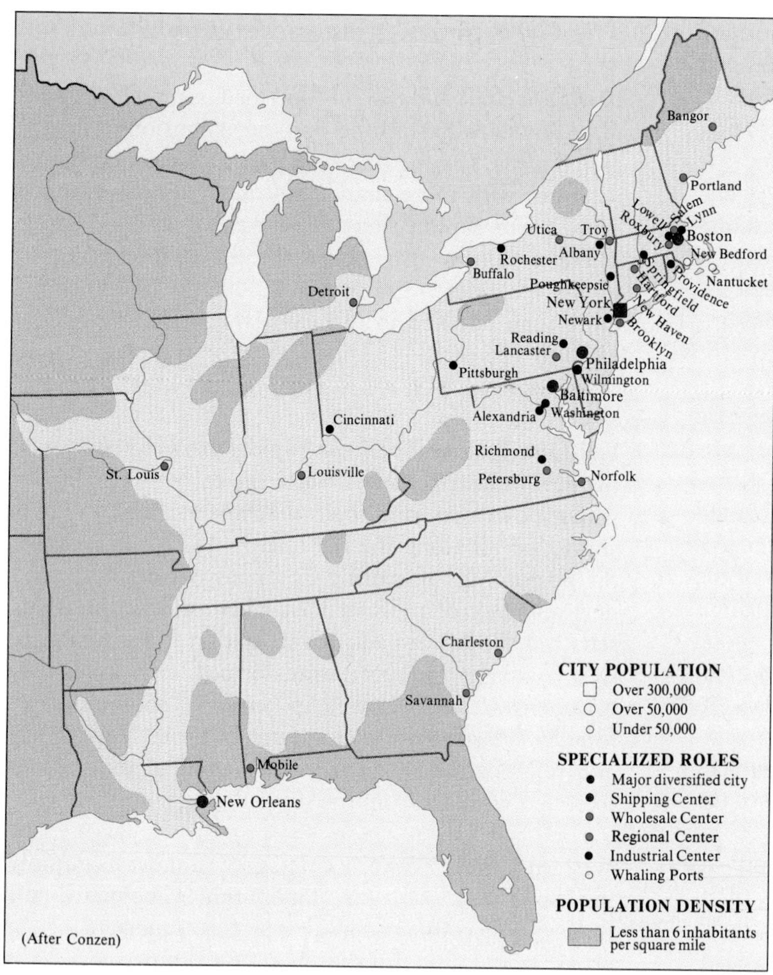

MAP 10.2

The Nation's Major Cities in 1840

By 1840, American cities developed specialized roles—Cincinnati and Pittsburgh became industrial centers, Hartford and Lancaster grew as regional centers for farm communities, and Brooklyn and Buffalo developed as wholesaling centers. The oldest ports on the Atlantic seaboard remained the most diversified and played a critical role in managing and organizing the national economy.

tion at points where goods had to be transferred from one mode of transport, such as canal boats or farmers' wagons, to another, such as steamboats or sailing vessels. Merchants and bankers took advantage of the special location of these cities to develop the marketing, provisioning, and financial services that were essential to farmers and to small-town merchants in the hinterland. Despite their commercial dynamism, however, the manufacturing in these communities remained mostly traditional in technology and organization. No western city challenged the industrial preeminence of the eastern seaport cities.

The Rise of New York. The old Atlantic seaports—Boston, New York, Philadelphia, and Baltimore—remained the largest American cities, but of the four only New York grew more rapidly than the population as a whole. New York's growth rate was phenomenal, twice that of the nation as a whole during the 1820s and 1830s. New York overtook Philadelphia as the nation's largest city in 1810 and became the economic center of the nation over the next two decades.

New York boasted the best harbor in the United States. Ocean vessels could sail or steam 150 miles up the Hudson River to Albany; no other Atlantic port provided such deep penetration of the interior. Moreover, ships had unobstructed, yet protected, access to the docks on Manhattan Island. And New York merchants were unusually enterprising. They had made their city the smuggling center of British North America during the eighteenth century and had used their wits to survive British occupation during the Revolution. New York merchants, more so than the merchants in Boston or Philadelphia, welcomed outsiders and their money. In 1817 New York merchants founded the New York Stock Exchange, which soon became the nation's chief market for securities.

In their most aggressive stroke, New York merchants convinced their state government to enact a law that earmarked tax revenues to construct a project that private investors regarded as too risky—the Erie Canal from Albany to Buffalo and Lake Erie. Opened in 1825, the Erie Canal connected New York City and Albany with the vast interior—the burgeoning farming communities of upstate New York and the entire Great Lakes region (see pages 301–302).

New York merchants sought to control foreign commerce as well. In 1818 four Quaker merchants founded the Black Ball Line to carry goods between New York and European ports such as Liverpool, London, and Le Havre. This was the first transatlantic *packet service*, carrying cargo, people, and mail on a regular schedule, and this dependability made the service extremely attractive to international traders. New York merchants also gained an unassailable lead in commerce with the newly independent Latin American nations of Brazil, Peru, and Venezuela. Finally, they controlled a small but growing portion of the cotton trade. Their agents in southern ports offered finance, insurance, and shipping to cotton exporters and won for New York a dominant share of the cotton that passed through northern harbors. By 1840, New York's mercantile community controlled almost two-thirds of the nation's foreign imports and almost half of all foreign trade, both imports and exports.

The West: Farming New Land

The Industrial Revolution affected farming people in the United States in a far different way than in Europe. In Europe, it forced a massive reduction and relocation of rural populations. In the United States it promoted the rapid occupation of new lands by farmers and a huge increase in the rural population. (Map 10.3 shows how the patterns of land sales and settlement changed during this period.) At the same time that the nation's industrial towns and seaport cities were gaining in size and importance, millions of farming families were still moving west.

Routes of Migration. These pioneers migrated in three great streams. In the South, cotton producers continued the migration that had begun after the War of 1812. They moved their slaves and the Cotton Kingdom into the new states of Mississippi (admitted to the Union in 1817) and Alabama (1819), and on into Louisiana (1812), Missouri (1821), Arkansas (1836), and Texas (1845). Southerners also pioneered the early settlement of the Old Northwest. Small farmers from the upper South, especially Virginia and Kentucky, created a second stream as they followed westward routes they had established as early as the 1790s. They ferried their wagons across the Ohio River and introduced corn and hog farming to the southern parts of Ohio (1803), Indiana (1816), and Illinois (1818).

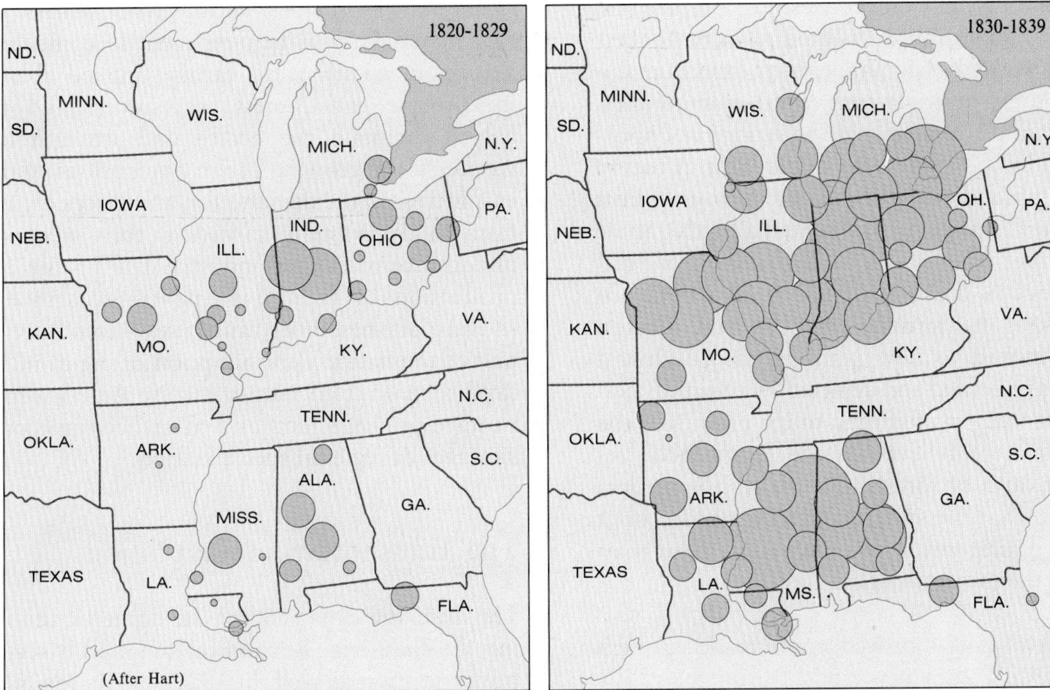

MAP 10.3

Western Land Sales, 1820–1839

Land offices opened up on the frontier to sell government land. Each of the circles centers on a land office, and the area of each circle represents the relative amount of land sold at that office. The maps show how settlement spread and intensified in the farm lands of the Ohio Valley and the cotton plantations of the old Southwest during the 1820s and the 1830s.

The third stream of migrants came from the Northeast. This flow had begun during the 1790s when settlers had poured into upstate New York; the stream reached the trans-Appalachian West during the 1820s. During that decade and the next, settlers from New England and the Middle Atlantic states, particularly New York, traveled along the Erie Canal to establish wheat farms in the Great Lakes basin—northern Ohio, northern Illinois, Michigan (1837), and Wisconsin (1848).

Westward migration significantly shifted the population center of American society. In 1830 about 3 million people—more than a fourth of the nation's population—were living west of the Appalachians. By 1840 the figure was over 5 million, more than a third of all Americans. Western growth often meant the stagnation or decline of eastern communities. Vast numbers of men and women left the seaboard states where they were born, taking with them their savings, personal property, and skills. During the 1820s and 1830s, the Carolinas, Vermont, and New Hampshire lost nearly as many people through migration as they gained through the excess of births over deaths. In New England, abandoned farms and homes dotted the countryside, their owners gone in search of better lands farther west.

The Motivation. Farmers moved west for complex and varying reasons. Some simply wanted to increase their profits. Others wanted to acquire enough land to maintain their children in traditional rural communities. However, all farmers appreciated the economic opportunities offered by the virgin soils of the West. A cotton planter from upland Georgia, a prosperous wheat farmer from the Connecticut Valley, and a hardscrabble subsistence farmer from Vermont might have very different values, but all could recognize the economic advantage of taking up farming on new land. Cotton planters who moved to new lands in the Southwest were glad to leave behind soil depleted by relentless cultivation. Wheat farmers migrating to the prairies of the Old Northwest were relieved of the heavy labor required to clear land of forests and rocks. The settlers soon discovered that the sweat and toil expended on a patch of fresh prairie yielded a much larger crop than could a plot of the same size in the East.

The Tools. New and improved tools made farmers even more eager to occupy new lands. During the 1830s farmers throughout the North bought the new cast-iron plow invented in 1819 by Jethro Wood, a farmer in upstate New York. With this single device, farmers could cut their plowing time in half and could till much larger fields. Wood's plow, which could be repaired with replaceable cast-iron parts, spelled doom for village blacksmiths. Their handmade product could not compete with this low-cost, high-quality product of northeastern foundries. Western farmers purchased many other sturdy, inexpensive, mass-produced necessities: shovels and spades, which Alan Wood, at his Delaware Iron Works, began fabricating from rolled iron in 1826; axes, which the Collins Company of Connecticut began forging in the same year; and horseshoes, which Henry Burden of Troy, New York, began to make in 1835.

The Land. Cheap land prices made western settlement an even more practical choice. In 1820 Congress reduced the price of federal land from $2.00 an acre to $1.25—just enough to cover the cost of surveying and sale. For $100, a farmer could buy 80 acres, the minimum required under federal law. With the federal government offering huge quantities of public land at this price, the basic market price for all undeveloped land remained low. Purchasing land was well within the reach of most migrating people. During the 1820s and 1830s, the average American family could save enough in two years to make the minimum purchase, even without raising any money from the sale of an old farm.

Effects on Industrialization. Although farms, not factories, dominated the economic life of the West, western settlement did promote industrial development indirectly. Efficient western farms provided eastern manufacturers with low-cost cotton, wool, leather, and other raw materials, thus helping them to compete with the British. In addition, the farms supplied abundant and inexpensive grain, meat, vegetables, and fruit that helped maintain the health and strength of factory workers. The growing urban populations of the Northeast increased the demand for, and prices of, all types of farm goods. Western markets, in turn, were of growing importance to eastern industry. During the 1830s, the production of farm implements—horseshoes, plows, shovels, scythes, hoes, and axes—accounted for fully half of the nation's consumption of pig iron. Westward expansion enabled industrializing America to take advantage of cheap land and to realize the economic advantages of regional specialization.

The Transportation Revolution

The dramatic expansion of the domestic economy during the Industrial Revolution required a revolution in transportation as well. In 1820, the nation had no true road system, particularly in the West. Spring thaws, rainstorms, and snow made dirt roads impassable. Western settlers complained to the federal government that they lacked even roads to get their goods to market. To correct these inadequacies and to integrate great chunks of territory into their buoyant economy, Americans rapidly built a transportation system of unprecedented size, complexity, and cost.

Road Transportation, 1838

This coach has just passed over one of the best western thoroughfares, a "corduroy road" made of tree trunks laid across a swamp. In 1842 the English author Charles Dickens traveled on such a road and wrote: "The very slightest of the jolts with which the ponderous carriage fell from log to log was enough . . . to have dislocated all the bones in the human body." (George Tattersall, *Highways and Byeways of the Forest,* Museum of Fine Arts, Boston)

Roads. Through the 1830s, in cooperation with state governments, the federal government built interregional roads for pedestrians, horses, herds of livestock, and heavily loaded wagons. The federal government regarded creating this vital infrastructure as a legitimate part of its responsibilities. The most significant feat was the National Road, which started in Cumberland, Maryland, passed Wheeling (then in Virginia) in 1818, crossed the Ohio River in 1833, and reached Vandalia, Illinois, in 1850. By that time construction of major interregional roads had ceased, their role taken over by canals and railroads. Although local road building continued, the quality of roads did not improve until the introduction of automobiles in the early twentieth century.

Canals. A canal frenzy swept the nation, and canals became the most important part of the transportation revolution. After the War of 1812, Americans had begun to build canals to connect the inland areas along rivers and lakes with the nation's coastal cities and towns. But progress had come slowly. When the New York legislature initiated the Erie Canal in 1817, no canal in the United States was longer than 28 miles—a reflection of the huge capital investment required for canals as well as of the lack of engineering expertise.

New Yorkers drove hard to complete the Erie Canal. Three key advantages made this project possible: the vigorous support of New York City merchants; the backing of De Witt Clinton, New York's powerful governor; and the relative gentleness of the terrain. Even amateur surveyors—such as James Geddes and Benjamin Wright, who had been trained as lawyers—were able to design and construct much of the canal.

Construction of the Erie Canal

Gangs of construction workers on the Erie Canal had to excavate deep cuts through rough land. The artist who sketched this scene, like the canal planners, was more interested in the scale of the project than the personalities of the faceless workers. Working conditions were even worse in the marshes near Syracuse where, in 1819, a thousand workers fell ill with fever and many died.

The Erie Canal was an instant success. The first section, a stretch of 75 miles opened in 1819, immediately generated large revenues for New York State. When the entire canal was completed in 1825, the 40-foot-wide ribbon of water, complete with locks to raise and lower

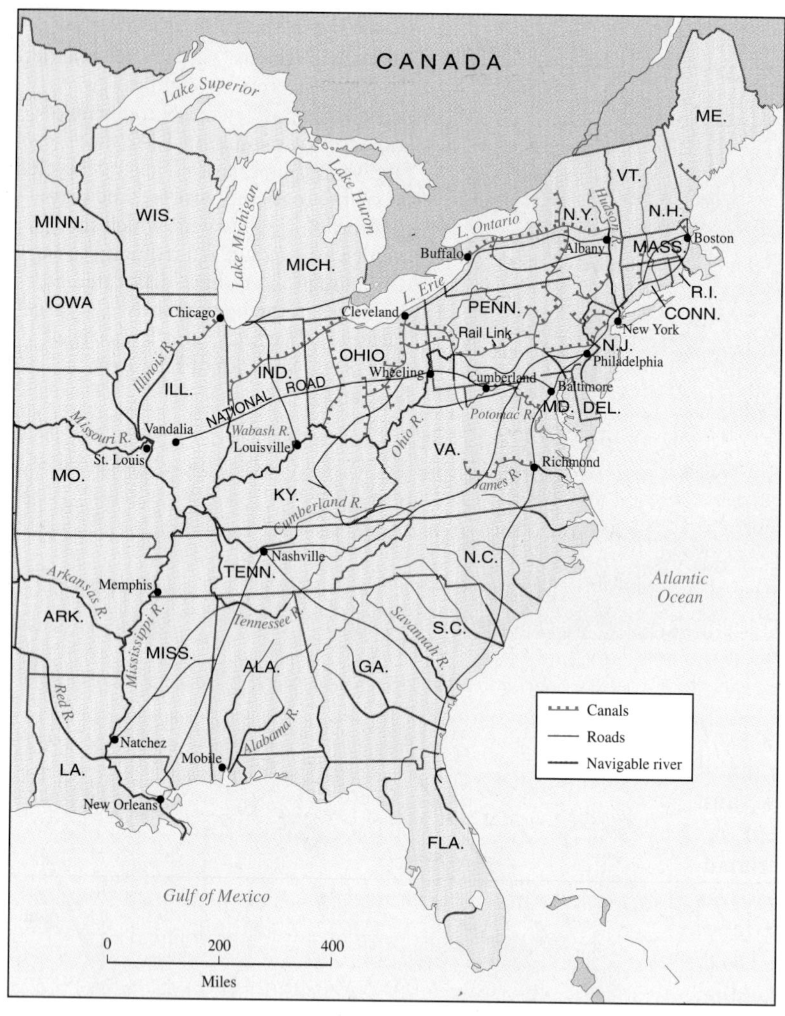

MAP 10.4

The Transportation Revolution: Roads and Canals, 1820–1860.

By 1840 the United States had completed a transportation system based on roads, natural waterways, and canals. Even though this system lacked railroads until the 1840s, it was adequate for launching the Industrial Revolution.

boats, reached 364 miles from Albany to Buffalo and reduced the journey for passengers traveling from New York City to Buffalo from twenty days to six. The canal also greatly accelerated the flow of goods. On a road in upstate New York, four horses would take an entire day to pull a 1-ton load 12 miles. On the canal, only two horses could pull a 100-ton load 24 miles in a day.

The Erie Canal fulfilled every promise of its promoters. It moved settlers from New England and New York to the Old Northwest. It gave the new western farmers of the Great Lakes basin, as well as those of upstate New York, cheap access to the port of New York. And it placed western communities within easy reach of eastern manufacturers and the merchants of New York City.

After a trip on the Erie Canal in 1830, the novelist Nathaniel Hawthorne wrote:

> Surely the water of this canal must be the most fertilizing of all fluids, for it causes towns with their masses of brick and stone, their churches and theaters, their business and hubbub, their luxury and refinement, their gay dames and polished citizens, to spring up, till in time the wondrous stream may flow between two continuous lines of buildings, through one thronged street, from Buffalo to Albany.

The spectacular benefits and profits brought about by the Erie Canal prompted a national canal boom. Civic and business leaders in major cities and towns competed to build their own canals to capture trade with the West. Some canal promoters took advantage of New York's experience by hiring the young men who had learned canal engineering while building the Erie. Many promoters also copied New York's fiscal innovations. They persuaded their state governments to charter companies, to guarantee the companies' credit, and to invest directly in them or force mutual savings banks to do so—sometimes even to take over the ownership of such companies. Altogether, state governments provided—often by borrowing from English and Dutch investors—almost three-quarters of the $200 million invested in canals by 1840. By then, new canals had provided three critical transportation links: (1) from the coastal plain to the upcountry of the Atlantic seaboard states; (2) from the seaboard states to the Great Lakes basin and the Ohio Valley; and (3) from the Great Lakes to the Ohio and Mississippi rivers.

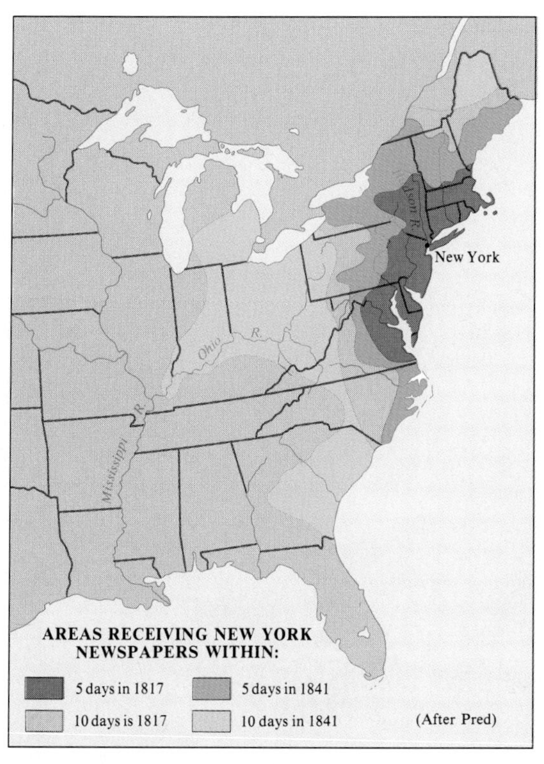

MAP 10.5

The Speed of Business News

The transportation revolution and aggressive entrepreneurs increased the speed of trade and communication between the Atlantic seaboard and the interior. The national circulation of newspapers grew along with trade, and New York's dailies became the most important sources of economic news. This map shows the dramatic improvements in communication between 1817 and 1841.

Steamboats. The steamboat, another product of the industrial age, ensured the success of America's vast water transportation system. On canals, rivers, and lakes, steamboats traveled faster, met tighter schedules, and carried more cargo than did sailing ships.

The engineer-inventor Robert Fulton built the first American steamboat, the *Clermont,* which he navigated up the Hudson in 1807. But steamboats' large consumption of wood or coal fuel made them very expensive to run, and they could not navigate shallow western rivers. During the 1820s, engineers broadened the hulls of the boats—to increase their cargo capacity and, most important, to give them a shallower draft—

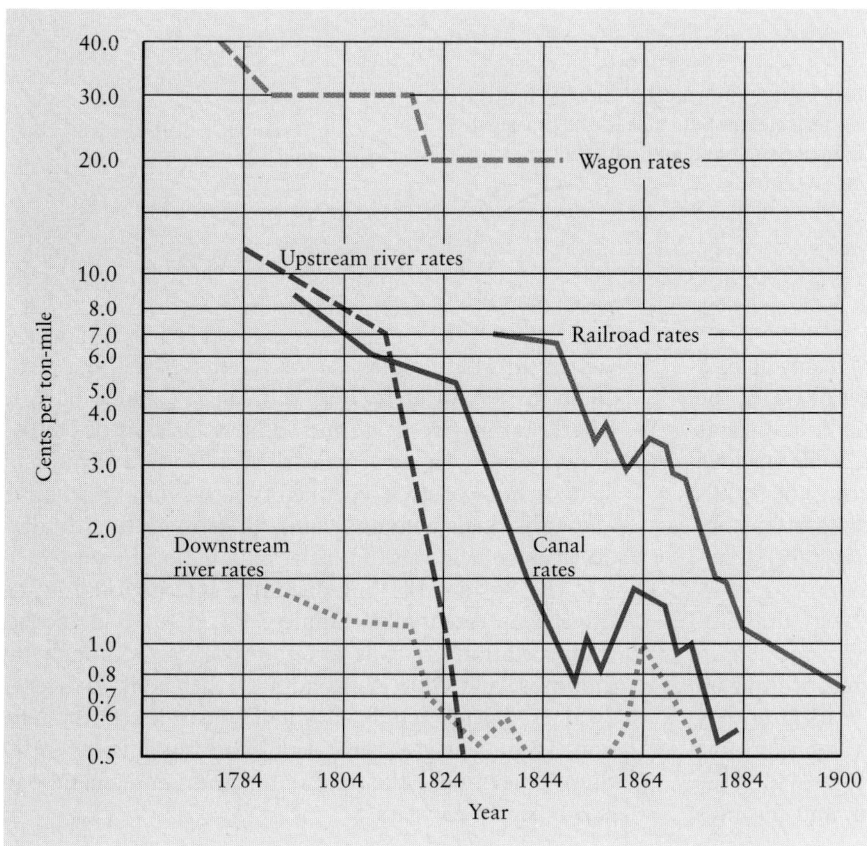

FIGURE 10.1

Inland Freight Rates, 1784–1900

The costs of shipping goods inland on rivers, canals, and railroads fell as new technologies developed between 1784 and 1900. If a logarithmic scale had not been used for cents per ton-mile, a much larger chart would have been necessary to show the enormous gap between wagon rates and the other rates.

An Eastern Steamboat

This watercolor by Russian artist Pavel Petrovich Svinin (1787–1839) portrays deck life on the *Paragon*, which was owned by Robert Fulton and traveled on the Hudson River. Designed primarily for passengers, the eastern steamboats lacked the great paddle wheels and superstructures that became characteristic of steamboats on western rivers during the 1840s. (The Metropolitan Museum of Art)

and reduced the weight of the boats by using lighter wood. Able to navigate in as little as 3 feet of water, the new steamboats could maneuver around tricky snags and sandbars. Moreover, the wider, flat decks speeded the loading and unloading of cargo. During the 1820s alone, the new steamboats cut in half the costs of upstream river transport. By 1830, steamboat travel dominated the major rivers and lakes of the country.

The canals and the new boat technology dramatically increased the flow of goods. In 1835, farmers in the Old Northwest shipped 268,000 barrels of flour on canal boats to eastern markets; just five years later they shipped more than a million barrels. Water transport also enabled people to travel more cheaply and sped the exchange of news, technical information, and business advice. In 1830, a traveler or a letter from New York could go by water to Boston in a day and a half, to Charleston in five days, and to New Orleans or Detroit in two weeks. Thirty years earlier, the same journeys, by road or sail, would have taken twice as long. Businesses and individuals communicated far more efficiently than ever before, and this in turn stimulated business.

The system of long-distance, interregional water travel was essentially complete by 1840. But another transportation era was about to dawn. Although the Baltimore and Ohio Railroad had received its charter in 1828, railroads remained small, unconnected systems until 1840. The great era of railroad building lay in the future; meanwhile the heyday of canals and steamboats lasted nearly 25 years.

Government and the Business Corporation

State governments had been granting charters to corporations since the 1790s (see Chapter 9). By extending such privileges to transportation companies in the 1820s, states accelerated the accumulation of the huge amounts of capital needed to build transportation systems and reduced the need to tax the public for that purpose. Banks also incorporated, but few mercantile firms and almost no manufacturers did. Until after the Civil War, manufacturers did not need large accumulations of capital. They preferred to continue as partnerships or sole proprietorships so as to remain free from state regulation.

States gradually made the ability to incorporate a right rather than a privilege. During the 1820s the states reduced the conditions necessary for incorporation, and in the 1830s legislatures ceased granting corporate charters one by one through the passing of special acts. Instead, they established general incorporation acts that turned over the chartering process to administrators. As more businesses received charters, however, it became difficult to protect the monopoly privileges that corporate charters often guaranteed. Younger entrepreneurs often challenged the monopoly privileges of established businesses as inconsistent with the ideals of a republic. The state courts responded to these challenges by weakening the legal definition of corporate privilege and thus promoting more entrepreneurial uses of property.

The Supreme Court under John Marshall contributed to this trend of encouraging business enterprise. In the crucial case of *Gibbons v. Ogden* (1824), the Court struck down a monopoly that the New York legislature had granted to Aaron Ogden for steamboat passenger service across the Hudson River between Manhattan and Elizabethport, New Jersey. The Court's ruling, however, did not clearly favor an instrumental view of property—that is, a view hostile to the granting of monopolies. The Court overturned the Ogden monopoly because the competitor, Thomas Gibbons, had a federal coasting license, and the Court believed that the federal government had paramount authority over the regulation of interstate commerce.

An entrepreneurial (instrumental) view of property triumphed fully only after John Marshall died in 1835. In the landmark case of *Charles River Bridge v. Warren Bridge* (1837), the new chief justice, Roger B. Taney, ruled in favor of the Warren Bridge Company, which in 1828 had received a charter from the Massachusetts legislature to collect tolls across the Charles River. He ruled against the Charles River Bridge Company, which had received an earlier charter that, the company claimed, granted an *exclusive* right to collect bridge tolls on the river. Taney did adhere to Marshall's doctrine that state governments had to respect charters, but he also argued that a legislature could not be *presumed* to have granted an exclusive, monopolistic right. His language affirmed wide access to the benefits of government: "While the rights of private property are sacredly guarded, we must not forget that the community also has rights, and the happiness and well-being of every citizen depends on their faithful preservation." In effect, he claimed that the destruction of monopoly and the consequent stimulation of competition were in the best interests of the community.

The courts thus reconciled government-granted privileges with the ideals of a republican society. State governments could follow both Marshall and Taney. Following Marshall, they could protect the privileges granted in corporate charters. Following Taney, they could diffuse those privileges as widely as possible through society. State governments could maintain privilege but reduce its significance. Widening access to privilege increased the flow of capital to corporations and promoted the construction of the national transportation system.

Social Structure in an Industrializing Society

The Industrial Revolution transformed the material life of people in the United States. For most Americans the bonanza of factory-produced goods meant an improved standard of living. But industrialization was a socially disruptive process; the new affluence had its costs. The economic system sharpened and widened class distinctions based on the ownership and use of property, and stirred up animosities between classes. For a small elite—mostly merchants, factory owners, and financiers concentrated in northeastern cities and towns—industrialization meant great wealth. But for wage earners who did not own property, industrialization sometimes meant a loss of status and an uncertain future. Industrialization thus posed an unprecedented challenge to American republican ideals.

The Concentration of Wealth

By 1800, 10 percent of the nation's families owned between one-third and one-half of the nation's wealth. By 1860, 10 percent owned more than two-thirds of the nation's wealth.

Especially in the major Atlantic seaports, wealthy people owned most of the property. In 1840 the richest 1 percent in these cities owned as much as 10 percent of the population had owned fifty years before. This top 1 percent owned more than 40 percent of all *tangible* property—land, ships, buildings, and household furnishings. In New York City, the richest 4 percent of the population owned more than three-quarters of the tangible property. Their share of *intangible* property—stocks, bonds, and mortgages—was even greater.

The growing concentration of wealth in the cities had come about primarily as a result of the opportunities created by industrial and commercial expansion. Hence great concentrations of wealth were less common in smaller towns or agricultural areas. Yet similar trends existed there as well. Even in modest-sized, nonindustrial Massachusetts towns the richest 10 percent of families increased their holdings, so that by 1840 they typically owned 50 percent or more of the tangible property.

The new manufacturers, like Francis Cabot Lowell, increased their fortunes most rapidly. More generally, the Americans whose incomes rose most were those who exploited the innovations of the Industrial Revolution. Since technical advances were concentrated primarily in the textile, machine-tool, and firearm industries, owners and skilled workers in those industries benefited the most. Individuals who designed or adapted the most modern machinery and mobilized and disciplined the labor needed to operate that machinery enjoyed the most rapidly growing profits, salaries, or wages.

The concentration of wealth increased more rapidly than the pace of technological and organizational change. This was so partly because the wealthy, often linked by business and family ties, could more easily acquire the best information about new investment opportunities. Moreover, nineteenth-century governments almost never taxed inheritances or intangible property, and they usually taxed real estate and personal property (furniture, tools, and machinery, for example) at extremely low rates. Although wealthy Americans paid the largest share of state and local taxes, government was small and taxes were modest. Therefore, wealthy manufacturing and mercantile families could retain their fortunes, and their economic power, into the second or third generation.

But wealthy families often failed to keep their hard-earned assets—through foolish investments, poor business sense, imprudent living, or simple bad luck. In fact, the Industrial Revolution increased the rate at which fortunes, large and small, were lost. Financial panics drove growing numbers of even the most cautious and calculating investors into bankruptcy. Jeremiah Thompson, New York's largest cotton trader and one of the organizers of the Black Ball Line, went bankrupt in 1827. Philip Hone, wealthy merchant and mayor of New York in the 1820s, never recovered from his losses and the bankruptcy of his son during the Panic of 1837, the worst financial crisis before the Civil War.

Middle Class Property Owners. Far more people, however, improved their economic and social standing than lost ground. The middle class grew rapidly in size and importance. Most mechanics found their skills in high demand and their wages rising. Likewise, building contractors, grocers, shopkeepers, and butchers in booming urban areas profited from an abundance of prosperous customers. The growing urban demand for meat, dairy products, and perishables, as well as for the staples of wheat, corn, and cotton, increased farmers' incomes. Most Americans saved about 15 percent of their income, often placing their surplus funds in local banks and new savings institutions. Many eventually bought property with their savings. By 1840 about half of all free American men over the age of thirty had acquired at least moderate wealth—a house, furniture, a little land, and some savings. In agricultural communities an even higher percentage owned some land. The new members of the middle class hoped to pass on to their children advantages of skills, education, and property ownership.

The New Urban Poor

For many Americans, however, the Industrial Revolution meant a loss of opportunity and a betrayal of republican ideals. By 1840, as many as half the nation's free workers were laboring for wages, rather than for their own profits. Of these, the laborers who lacked skills, education, or property found that even though their real wages might be rising, the gap between themselves and other Americans was widening. For ordinary laborers, social mobility was extremely limited and difficult. They could look forward only to a life of work for others—in factories, machine shops, and stores, on construction projects and sanitation crews. No matter how hard they worked or how thrifty they were, most could accumulate only modest savings. And even so, an economic recession or sickness could quickly dash their hopes of rising in the world. They faced a high probability of a lifetime with little chance to buy a home or land, let alone start a business. For wage laborers who acquired no property, hope for upward social mobility rested with their children. But these workers had few resources to pass on. In fact, most could not afford to educate their offspring, to apprentice them, or to accumulate small dowries so that their daughters could marry men with better prospects. Instead, their children had to work to help support their families.

In Massachusetts in 1825, the daily wage of a common (unskilled) laborer—about 75 cents—was about two-thirds that of a mechanic. By the 1840s, the laborer's wage had increased to about $1 but was now less than half the typical mechanic's. Moreover, the poorest workers in the cities in the 1830s had to spend $2 out of every $3 they earned just to feed their families, so they had relatively less money left to take advantage of the rapidly falling prices of manufactured goods. Middle-class families, in contrast, could feed themselves on less than a third of their earnings. Thus during the early years of the Industrial Revolution people who lacked skills or property were even worse off, in relative terms, than their low wages indicated.

And unskilled work offered little satisfaction. Raised in rural areas, most wage laborers were accustomed to the seasonal and task-oriented work regime of agricultural society. They resented the strict, year-round labor schedule typical of most urban jobs. These workers often did not report to their jobs on time, and they skipped whole days of work when not in dire need of money.

The wage laborers who faced the worst conditions were casual workers—those hired on a short-term basis, often by the day, for the most arduous jobs. Altogether, casual workers accounted for about 10 percent of the labor force. The day laborers who dug out dirt and stones to build canals, who carried lumber and bricks for construction projects, who loaded and unloaded ships and wagons, were the most numerous. In 1840 nearly twenty-five thousand day laborers worked on the Erie Canal. Of the casual workers the poorest were free African-Americans and Irish immigrants, who began arriving in the cities of the Northeast during the 1830s (see Chapter 14).

Day laborers owned no property except the clothes they wore, and their work provided no economic security. In depressions they bore the brunt of unemployment, and even in the best of times their jobs were unpredictable, seasonal, and dangerous. Serious injury, which was common, often meant that a worker could no longer support his family. Disease could be rampant. Laborers building canals through swamps often contracted malaria and yellow fever. In 1831 the economist Mathew Carey reported that 5 percent of the workers on the Erie Canal returned to their families in the winter with their health broken "by fevers and agues."

Since nothing tied them down, casual laborers were the most geographically mobile of all workers, and many looked eagerly to the West. Joining casual laborers on the way west were people who had once been more prosperous but had suffered economic reversals. Many household weavers, blacksmiths, and harness makers, for example, left eastern towns as their customers turned to cheap goods produced in factories. Some craftsmen were able to reestablish their trade farther west, where high transportation costs made goods

A Chimney Sweep
The low-paid and exceedingly dirty and unhealthy work of cleaning chimneys, which were a major fire hazard in the cities of the Northeast, became largely the work of Irish immigrants and African-Americans. An Italian artist, Nicolino Calyo, painted this portrait in New York City in the early 1840s. (George Cousin, *The Patent Chimney Sweep Cleaner,* Museum of the City of New York)

The Hot Corn Seller
Free African-Americans, such as this woman painted (1840–44) by Nicolino Calyo, persisted in the face of both discrimination and harsh economic conditions. She may have been lucky enough to have a garden plot that grew more food than her family needed to survive. The extra produce offered an opportunity to supplement her meager income. (Museum of the City of New York)

AMERICAN VOICES

A Food Riot in New York *Philip Hone*

Philip Hone (1780–1851) was a carpenter's son who made a fortune in the New York auction business. He entered civic affairs and, in 1825, was elected to a one-year term as mayor. He presided over New York's reception of Lafayette and the opening of the Erie Canal. From 1828 until five days before his death, he kept a secret diary, which presents a detailed picture of New York life.

Monday, Feb. 13 [1837]—*Riots.* This city was disgraced this morning by a mob regularly convened by public notice in the park for the notable purpose of making bread cheaper by destroying the flour in the merchants' warehouses. The following notice was extensively published on Saturday by placards at the corners of the streets:

> Bread, Meat, Rent, Fuel—Their Prices Must Come Down.
>
> The Voice of the People Shall be Heard and Will Prevail.
>
> The People will meet in the Park, rain or shine, at four o'clock on Monday afternoon to inquire into the cause of the present unexampled distress, and devise a suitable remedy. All friends of humanity, determined to resist Monopolists and Extortioners, are invited to attend.

Many thousands assembled on this call. The day was bitter cold and the wind blew a hurricane, but there was fire enough in the speeches of Messrs. Windt and Ming to inflame the passions of the populace. These two men . . . did not tell them in so many words to attack the stores of the flour merchants, but stigmatized them as monopolists and extortioners, who enriched themselves at the expense of the laboring poor. They said that Eli Hart & Co. had 50,000 barrels of flour in their store, which they held at an exorbitant price whilst the poor of the city were starving. This was a firebrand suddenly thrown into the combustible mass which surrounded the speaker, and away went the mob to Hart's store in Washington near Cortland Street, which they forced open, threw 400 or 500 barrels of flour and large quantities of wheat into the street, and committed all the extravagant acts which usually flow from the unlicensed fury of a mob. The mayor and other magistrates, with the police officers, repaired to the spot, and with the assistance of many well-disposed citizens, succeeded after a time in clearing and getting possession of the store. From thence the mob went to Herrick & Co. in Water Street, and destroyed about fifty barrels of flour. The mayor ordered out a military force, which with the other measures adopted, kept the rioters in check.

Source: Allan Nevins, ed., *The Diary of Philip Hone* (New York: Dodd, Mead, 1936), 241–242.

from eastern factories more expensive. But others with traditional skills had to work for wages in the West, even as casual laborers, easing their hardship by maintaining a garden or keeping a few animals to supplement the family diet. This recourse, however, was of only slight assistance during the winter, when food was scarce and when storms and frozen rivers and canals could shut down trade. Winter was often a season of appealing for charity and searching continuously, sometimes fruitlessly, for a little work chopping wood or cutting ice.

In cities, most wage laborers and their families lived under conditions that discouraged any sense of hope for the future. By the 1830s, factory workers, journeymen, and unskilled casual laborers in northeastern towns and cities lived in well-defined neighborhoods. Certain blocks became dominated by large, congested boarding houses, where many single men and women lived crowded together under unhealthy conditions. Landlords converted houses, including basements and attics, into apartments and then used the profits from rentals to build more tenements. Often they squeezed onto a single lot a number of buildings, interspersed with outhouses and connected by foul-smelling courtyards and dark alleys.

Under such conditions, the lives of many wage earners deteriorated. Emotional tension and insecurity took hold; they became anxious over the breakdown of the traditional order, over their loss of social status, and over their worsening working and living conditions. To alleviate their distress, many workers turned to the dubious solace of alcohol.

In the eighteenth century, liquor had been an integral and accepted fact of American life; it had lubricated ceremonies, celebrations, work breaks, barn raisings, and games. But during the 1820s, urban wage earners led Americans to new heights of alcohol consumption. Aiding in this consumption were the nation's farmers, who increasingly chose to distill gin and whiskey as a low-cost way to get their grain to market. Falling prices led drinkers to switch from rum to these "spirits." By 1830, per capita consumption of gin and whiskey had risen to more than 5 gallons a year, more than twice the present-day levels of liquor consumption.

Drinking habits changed as well. At work, those who were not members of craft unions committed to abstinence began to drink on the job—and not just during the traditional 11 A.M. and 4 P.M. "refreshers." The journeymen used apprentices to smuggle whiskey into shops, and then, as one baker recalled, "One man was stationed at the window to watch, while the rest drank." Grog shops and tippling houses appeared on almost every block in working-class districts, and many workers who frequented these saloons became less interested in casual camaraderie than in solitary and heavy drinking. The saloons became focal points for urban disorder and crime, including assaults, burglary, and vandalism. Fueled by unrestrained drinking, a fist fight among young men one night could turn into a brawl the second night and a full-scale riot the third. The urban police forces, consisting of low-paid watchmen and amateur constables, were not able to contain the lawlessness.

The Rise of the Business Class

In 1800, most whites in rural America shared a common culture. Gentlemen farmers talked easily to yeomen about crop yields, livestock breeds, and the unpredictability of the weather. Poor southern whites and aristocratic slaveowners shared the same forms of amusement—gambling, cockfighting, and horse racing. In the North, poor and rich Quakers attended the same meeting house, as did Presbyterians, Episcopalians, and Congregationalists of different economic groups. "Almost everyone eats, drinks, and dresses in the same way," a European visitor to Hartford, Connecticut, reported in 1798, "and one can see the most obvious inequality only in the dwellings." Social hierarchies existed in these farming towns and villages, but the various levels of society shared many cultural and religious values.

Origins of the Business Class. The Industrial Revolution shattered this unified social order. The wealthiest merchants and manufacturers—the new business elite—had begun the process of fragmentation by setting themselves apart as a social group. They did this first by reorganizing work in ways that separated them from their wage earners. With the outwork and factory modes of organization, a new, more impersonal system of wage labor and large-scale production replaced the small, intimate shops where masters, journeymen, and apprentices had worked side by side. This separation of employers and wage earners in turn affected residential patterns. Before the Industrial Revolution, most wage earners had lived close to their employers, often in the same homes. By the 1830s, though, most employers in the largest northeastern cities had stopped providing their employees with housing, and many had fled to residential communities on the urban fringe, thus destroying the continuity between the household and the workplace.

During the 1820s and 1830s, another social group emerged of affluent property owners who were, in economic terms, literally a "middle class"—standing between the extremely wealthy factory owners, merchants, financiers, and landowners at one extreme and the nonpropertied wage earners at the other. Middle-class men and women felt growing differences between themselves and the rapidly increasing number of people who owned nothing and had to struggle just to survive. Their education, material well-being, and aspirations led growing numbers of middle-class Americans, especially in the North, to identify with the wealthy families of the business elite. Together these two groups, the middle class and the business elite, formed a truly new social stratum—the *business class*. There might be an enormous economic gulf between a wealthy factory owner and his clerks, foremen, and mechanics. But they were beginning to share the same moral and religious ideas and, therefore, membership in the business class.

Most members of the business class were the families of the men who had accumulated enough money to live comfortably. They were the contractors, foremen, and mechanics valued by the manufacturers; they were prosperous farmers; they were professional men of modest means; they were shopkeepers or manufacturers' clerks and agents; they owned small enterprises or worked in large banks, firms, or stores that they did not own. Typically, they had been able to buy a house and perhaps a little land.

Such people dressed well. They could afford a small carriage and a good horse or two. Their wives and daughters were literate and could play the pianos that graced the carefully decorated front parlors of their well-built houses. There were books on their shelves and usually a servant or two in the kitchen and stables. They attended church and sent their sons and daughters to good schools. They were most numerous in New England, but there were business-class families in every American town, even in the agrarian South.

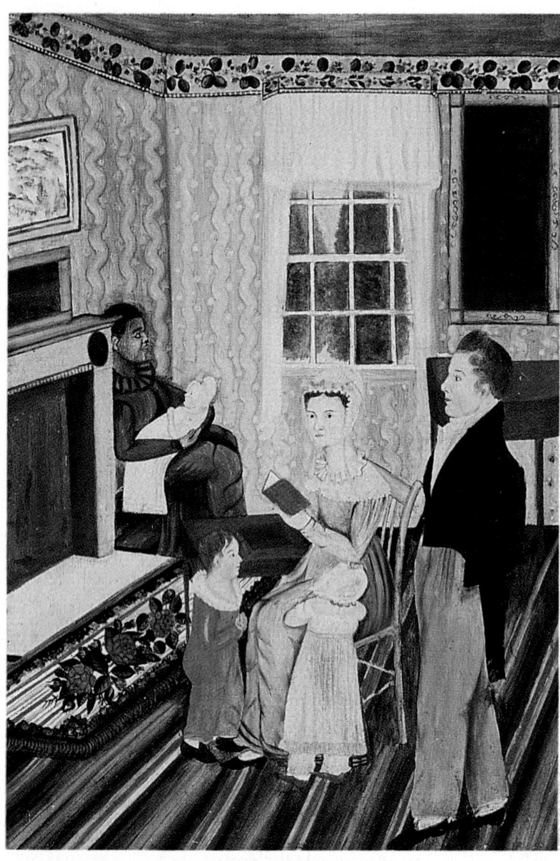

Pennsylvania Family with Servant
Women as well as men worked as day laborers, usually in domestic service. Discrimination that limited employment opportunities for free African-Americans meant that they were forced to work in disproportionate numbers as domestic servants, like the woman in this middle-class family painted by an unknown artist in York, Pennsylvania. (*York Pennsylvania Family with Negro Servant,* c. 1828, The Saint Louis Art Museum)

Ideology of the Business Class. The members of the business class defined themselves by how they thought about themselves and their relationship to society. They developed their own ideology of work, redefining the traditional Christian moral injunctions. The founders of seventeenth-century New England had believed that hard work in an earthly "calling" was a duty that people owed to God. The Puritans had stopped short of believing that God would reward good Christians with worldly riches. In contrast, the business class embraced a secular ideal of work. In the late eighteenth century Benjamin Franklin had expressed this secular ideal in his *Autobiography,* in which he implied that an industrious man would become a rich one. When Franklin's *Autobiography* was finally published in full in 1818, it found a huge audience, mostly young men ready and willing to believe that if they followed Franklin's example—worked hard, saved their money, and were temperate in their habits and honest in their dealings—success would be theirs. The same lessons were taught in countless magazines, children's books, manuals for young men, and novels. The business class made the ideal of the "self-made man" a central part of American popular culture.

Perceptive members of the business class sensed a contradiction between their wealth and their ideology. They urged all Americans to adopt the virtues of industry and to rise in the world. At the same time, they recognized that industrialization had widened economic divisions, and that many Americans would never improve their status. A yeoman society made up of independent families of farmers and artisans no longer seemed possible. "Entire independence ought not to be wished for," Ithamar A. Beard, the paymaster of the Hamilton Manufacturing Company, told a mechanics association in 1827. "In large manufacturing towns, many more must fill subordinate stations and must be under the immediate direction and control of a master or superintendent, than in the farming towns."

The message was clear. Business-class values were democratic, but the economic system that supported them was not. The clash between the democratic values of the business class and its privileged financial position became a persistent preoccupation for many Americans.

Every day, the contradiction was visible in the streets of cities and towns when employers and middle-class property owners brushed up against the new urban poor. Even though neighborhoods were growing more distinct, no class dominated any single section of the city. People across the social spectrum retained a high degree of day-to-day physical proximity, even in the largest cities. These were cities where most people lived within walking distance of work, school, church, shops, and saloons. Most middle-class housing remained within walking distance of cheap rooming houses and factories. As the horse-drawn bus—too costly for most workers—moved slowly through the late afternoon crowds, the wealthy could not avoid the sight of disorderly, sometimes drunken crowds in the muddy cobblestone streets.

When the wealthy began to ponder this disturbing reality and attempted to resolve conflicts of conscience, they did not seek to halt or reverse the Industrial Revolution. Instead, they worked to eradicate its negative aspects and to control the social disorder it had created. They attempted to introduce new forms of discipline, first into their own lives and then into the lives of ordinary working people.

The Benevolent Empire

The leaders of the business class attempted to create a society marked by moral discipline. During the 1820s, ministers in Congregational and Presbyterian churches, together with well-established merchants—and their wives—launched programs of social regulation. One of the ministers' leading spokesmen, Presbyterian Lyman Beecher of Boston, proclaimed their purpose: to restore "the moral government of God." Because of their aggressive quest for moral purity and their firm belief in charity, historians have labeled this movement the "Benevolent Empire." It was never a formal organization, however, just a collection of reform organizations linked by overlapping membership and shared ideals.

The Benevolent Empire targeted age-old evils like drunkenness, prostitution, and crime, but its methods were new. Instead of relying on charity, church sermons, or other traditional local initiatives, the reformers set out to institutionalize charity and combat evil systematically. They established large-scale regional and even national organizations—for example, the Prison Discipline Society and the American Society for the Promotion of Temperance. Each of these organizations had a managing staff, a network of volunteers and chapters, and a newspaper. Together the groups set out to "rescue" prostitutes and save the abandoned children of the poor. Some reformers worked to have the insane taken from attics and cellars and put into well-ordered and disciplined asylums. Other reformers labored to change the mission of the criminal justice system from the punishment and humiliation of criminals to their rehabilitation in penitentiaries where moral self-discipline would be emphasized. By removing from their midst those individuals whom they viewed as both incompetent and evil, the reformers claimed they would ensure the vitality and independence of the citizenry and consequently strengthen the republic.

Women played an increasingly active role in reforms inspired by the Benevolent Empire. Since the 1790s upper-class women had sponsored a number of charitable organizations, such as the Society for the Relief of Poor Widows with Small Children, founded in New York in 1797 by Isabella Graham, a devout Presbyterian and a widow herself. By the 1820s, Graham's society was assisting hundreds of widows and their children in New York City. Her daughter, Joanna Bethune, set up other charitable institutions, including the Orphan Asylum Society and the Society for the Promotion of Industry, which gave subsidized employment to hundreds of poor women.

Keeping the Sabbath. The most deeply held conviction of the men and women who ran the Benevolent Empire was that religion provided the answers to social problems. One of the greatest threats they saw to the "moral government of God" was the decline of the traditional Sabbath. The conduct of business on Sunday became increasingly common during the 1820s, especially among merchants and shippers who did not want their goods and equipment to lie idle one day of every seven. Congress had even passed a law in 1810 that allowed mail to be transported—though not delivered—on Sunday. In 1828, Lyman Beecher and other Congregationalist and Presbyterian ministers formed the General Union for Promoting the Observance of the Christian Sabbath. To the General Union reformers, the question of the Sunday mail law was not important in itself. It was a symbolic issue, chosen to rally Christians to the task of social purification. The Union spread its chapters—usually with women's auxiliaries—from Maine to the Ohio valley. It lobbied for local Sabbath regulations, collected funds, published tracts, organized rallies, and circulated petitions. The Union behaved, in short, much like a political party.

Although the Benevolent Empire found support in every community, it did meet resistance, especially with respect to keeping the Sabbath. Owners of barges on the Erie Canal, and of taverns and hotels, refused to close on Sundays. Working men, who labored twelve or fourteen hours a day, six days a week, scorned the notion that they ought to spend their one day of recreation in meditation and prayer. Baptist and Methodist clergymen, whose congregations tended to be poorer than those of the Congregationalists or Presbyterians, objected to the patronizing tone of the General Union. And when the Benevolent Empire proposed to teach Christianity to the slaves, or to send missionaries among the Indians, white southerners were outraged.

Such popular resistance or indifference limited the success of the Benevolent Empire, whose purpose was all too obviously to regulate the behavior of others—by persuasion if possible, but by law if necessary. A different kind of message was required if religious reformers were to do more than preach to the already converted and discipline the already disciplined.

Business-Class Revivalism and Reform

Charles Grandison Finney. Beginning in 1825, the Presbyterian minister Charles Grandison Finney began bringing a new message to the people living along the Erie Canal—evil was avoidable and *all* sinners could be saved. His ministry accelerated the pace of the Second Great Awakening—the wave of Protestant revivalism that had begun after the Revolution (see Chapter 9). Finney was not part of a traditional religious elite. Born to poor farmers in Connecticut in 1792, Finney determined to make himself part of the new middle class as a lawyer. But in 1821 he underwent a highly emotional conversion experience and was ordained as a minister after two years of informal religious study.

In strikingly emotional revival meetings, Finney preached that God waited to welcome any sinner who truly wanted salvation and that only God's grace, poured into the heart of the believer, made a moral life possible. He rejected an emphasis on original sin and stressed that the exercise of free will—submission to the Holy Spirit—could lead to a Christian conversion. He believed that religious instruction in official church doctrine by a trained minister did not bring—and might even hinder—salvation. What counted, Finney proclaimed, was not a person's belief in the technical doctrines of a church but the will to be saved. His was an emotional faith that rejected the intellectually based faith of many established Protestant churches.

Wherever he preached Finney won converts among churchgoing Protestants and among those who had drifted away from their churches. The conversions were dramatic, and often tearful. Although most of Finney's converts were members of the middle class, he became famous for converting wealthy individuals and the poor, who seemed lost to drink, sloth, and misbehavior. Finney used religious conversion to bring everyone, rich and poor, into the same moral community. The pride of the rich (if not their wealth) and the shame of the poor (if not their poverty) would give way to an exultant celebration of a new brotherhood in Christ. Conversion changed not only people's eternal fate but also their moral standing—identifying them spiritually with earnest, pious, middle-class respectability.

Charles Finney, Evangelist
Finney (1792–1875) had a long and influential career after his New York revivals. In 1835, he established a theology department at the newly founded Oberlin College, where he helped train a generation of ministers. Finney served as president of the college from 1851 to 1866. This daguerreotype was taken in 1850, while Finney and his second wife, Elizabeth Atkinson, were on an evangelistic tour of Great Britain.

The Rochester Revival. Finney's most spectacular triumph came in 1830 when he moved his revivals from small towns to Rochester, New York, a major Erie Canal city, at the invitation of local business and political leaders. For six months he preached every day. He employed a new tactic—group prayer meetings in family homes, in which women played an active role. Finney's wife, Lydia, took a visible part in his ministry. She and other pious, middle-class wives visited the homes of the unconverted, often while disapproving husbands were at work. Week after week, Rochester was saturated with the evangelical message. Schools and businesses stopped for prayer. Spontaneous religious meetings were held in houses and even in the streets.

Finney won over members of the business elite and their wives, and soon claimed he had converted the "great mass of the most influential people" of Rochester—especially the manufacturers and merchants who shipped grain on the Erie Canal. As part of their conversion, these "influential people" often confessed that their lives had been overly governed by money and too little devoted to the moral well-being of their own souls and those of their employees. With this confession came a pledge to reform their own lives and to try to reform the lives of their workers. They would attend church, drink only water, work steady hours, and encourage their employees to follow suit. In 1831 one of Rochester's Presbyterian churches rewrote its covenant in a way that gave a new meaning to the concept of "business." Every member pledged to "renounce all the ways of sin, and to make it the business of our life to do good and promote the glory of God."

And so the business leaders of Rochester set out to reform their city. Their favorite target was alcohol, which seemed to be the most wasteful and damaging social habit of their workers and also the most obvious sign of a collapsing social order. But they also tried to meet what they thought were the workers' spiritual needs. In 1832 wealthy businessmen founded a new Free Presbyterian Church—called "free" because members did not have to pay for pew space. This church was specifically designed to serve canal workers, transients,

The Ecstasy of a Camp Meeting
In isolated rural areas, especially those with many Baptists and Methodists, the camp meeting was a more common forum for evangelical revivals than were church and prayer meetings. Such meetings, organized while farm work was slack, attracted families who camped in wagons and tents for as long as a week to join in the intense religious excitement and social life. (J. Maze Burbank, *Religious Camp Meeting* (detail), 1839, New Bedford Whaling Museum)

and the settled poor. Soon two similar evangelical churches were founded in the city. To reinforce the work of these churches, Rochester's business elite founded other institutions—a savings bank to encourage thrift, Sunday schools for poor children, and the Female Charitable Society to provide relief for the families of the unemployed.

Within limits, the attempt to create a harmonious community of morally disciplined Christians was effective. During the 1830s, many workers—often led by their wives—followed their employer's example and became converts and church members. And employers who had been "saved" often confirmed the respectability of the newly converted with raises, promotions, or bonuses. However, Finney's revival seldom moved poor people. Least responsive to the Protestant evangelists were the Irish Catholic immigrants who had recently begun arriving in American cities, including Rochester.

A Family's Morning Devotional
This 1842 illustration from *Godey's Lady's Book*, a leading influence on the tastes of the emerging business class, portrays the kind of family Bible reading and prayer that the Finney revivals encouraged. Here, *Godey's* idealizes an affluent young mother and father who are attempting to set a good example for their child and two servants.

Skilled workers who belonged to strong craft organizations—bootmakers, carpenters, stonemasons, and boat builders—also resisted the message. Some of them even supported newspapers opposing the revival, arguing that workers needed organization, higher wages, and schools more than sermons and prayers. But these critics only heightened the converts' zeal for rebuilding society into an evangelically defined Christian order.

The Spread of Business-Class Revivalism. During the 1830s revivals swept through cities and towns from New England to the Ohio Valley. Dozens of younger ministers—Baptist and Methodist as well as Congregationalist and Presbyterian—energetically adopted the evangelical message and its techniques. They succeeded wherever the middle class was large and considerable numbers of workers had reaped benefits from the Industrial Revolution. In New York City, where Finney successfully established himself soon after leaving Rochester, the wealthy silk merchants Arthur and Lewis Tappan founded a magazine, *The Christian Evangelist*, to promote his ideas. With the assistance of manufacturers and merchants, evangelists soon reached sinners the way the most aggressive businessmen reached customers. They standardized and simplified their religious message, aimed it at masses of people, and measured their success in quantitative terms—by the number of converts.

Temperance. The temperance movement proved to be the most effective arena for evangelical reform on a national scale. Evangelicals gained control over the American Temperance Society, which had been organized in 1828. By the mid-1830s it had grown to 2,000 chapters with more than 200,000 members. The society adapted the methods that had worked so well in the revivals—group confession and prayer, a focus on the family and the spiritual role of women, and sudden, emotional conversion—and took them into virtually every town and city in the North. These techniques worked best among the families of the business class, for whom drink was becoming a fearful mark of social disrepute. Some business-class wives may well have embraced temperance reform as a way to curb alcoholic husbands. On one day in New York City in 1841, 4,000 people took the temperance "pledge." The average annual consumption of spirits fell from about 5 gallons per person in 1830 to about 2 gallons in 1845.

The Work Ethic. Evangelical reformers also turned their efforts to revising and invigorating the work ethic that had been so important to the American tradition. They put a religious twist on Benjamin Franklin's formula for success. Laziness, drinking, and other wasteful

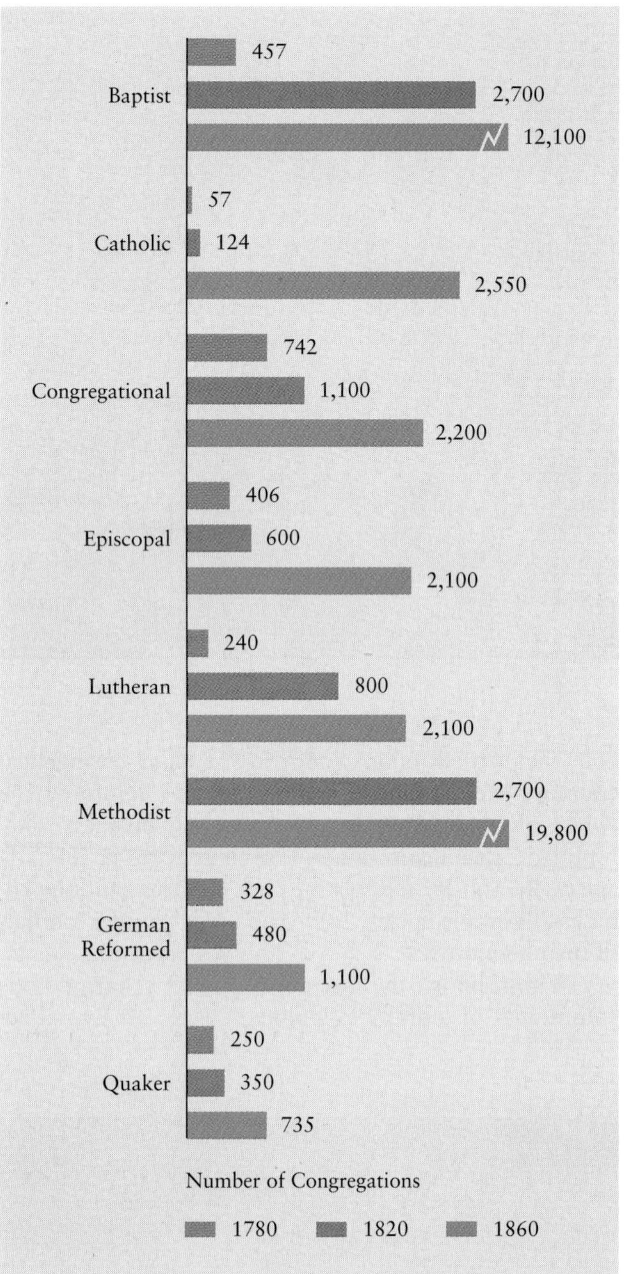

FIGURE 10.2

Church Growth by Denomination, 1780–1860

Christian congregations increased phenomenally between 1780 and 1860—nearly three times more rapidly than population. With the state now removed from religion, all denominations grew but revivalism played an especially important role in Protestant expansion.

habits could not, they preached, be cured simply by Franklin's patient methods of self-discipline. People had to undergo a profound change of heart, possible only through religious conversion. With God's grace would come the determination to put away drink, sloth, and sin. Then even the poorest family could look forward to a prosperous new life.

Only a minority of the large and diverse communities of laboring men and women actually joined the evangelical movement. Most of the religious converts were at least moderately prosperous and enjoyed a respectable standing in their communities. Evangelical religion reinforced the sense of common identity within the business class and this group's commitment to the concepts of individual enterprise, success, and moral discipline that comprised the ethic of the Industrial Revolution. Those middle-class Americans who joined the business class saw religion as a powerful cement for holding society together in the face of industrialization, which threatened to overwhelm the nation with social disorder and class animosities and conflict. But evangelical reform could not be contained within the Benevolent Empire, and it soon spilled over into radical and utopian movements, discussed in Chapter 12.

Summary

During the 1820s the nation's merchants, mechanics, and small manufacturers brought the Industrial Revolution to America. Through innovations in manufacturing organization and technology, Americans become more efficient producers. In the Northeast and Northwest they became economically independent of the British and developed a vigorous domestic trade in agricultural and manufactured goods. Southerners, however, remained dependent on the export of cotton, the import of British manufactured goods, and British commercial services. Based on industrial success, urbanization accelerated in the Northeast, led by New York City, which became the nation's leading trading center. Industrialization also stimulated the settlement of the West, resulting in increasing agricultural production that helped to sustain the nation's economic growth. To integrate the national market, Americans built a transportation system, based heavily on waterways, that was unprecedented in size and complexity.

Economic growth meant that most Americans, especially those who were able to take advantage of the modern technological change, improved their standard of living. But industrialization widened distinctions among classes, disrupted working relations and residential patterns, and offered little opportunity for the large number of Americans who did not acquire skills, education, or property.

Economic growth fostered the development of a new social class: the business class, consisting of middle-class property owners led by a business elite. Its members publicly acknowledged the disorder that accompanied industrialization and tried to harmonize class interests. They joined revivals led by evangelical clergymen such as Charles Finney, who believed that Christian conversions could mobilize the free will of individuals on behalf of worldly perfection. In Finney's revivals, business leaders and middle-class citizens pledged to attend church regularly, respect their families, abstain from alcohol, and urge others to embrace religion. A temperance pledge became an important badge of respectability. Revivalism and reform made the members of the business class even more certain that they were special—united, they believed, not only by material success but also by a moral and spiritual superiority.

TOPIC FOR RESEARCH

A Case Study of the Industrial Revolution

This text has surveyed the Industrial Revolution and reached some generalizations about its timing, sources, and effects in the United States. However, the Industrial Revolution was experienced differently in each of the hundreds of communities transformed by it during the first half of the nineteenth century. Choose one northeastern community—for example Hartford (Connecticut), Rochester (New York), Trenton (New Jersey), and Wilmington (Delaware)—that underwent industrialization during the 1820s and 1830s, and find out how the Industrial Revolution changed it. You might focus on the key industry and outline the major transformations in technology and organization of work that occurred. Alternatively, you could try to trace the rise of the business class, or consider the effects of these changes on the quality of everyday life—particularly on the working and living conditions of average citizens.

To identify communities from which you might choose, see the suggested readings at the end of this chapter. For the city of Lynn, Massachusetts, to take one example, you might begin by consulting the following books: Mary H. Blewett, *Men, Women, and Work: Class, Gender, and Protest in the New England Shoe Industry, 1780–1910* (1988); Alan Dawley, *Class and Community, The Industrial Revolution in Lynn, Massachusetts, 1780–1860* (1981); and Paul G. Faler, *Mechanics and Manufacturers in the Early Industrial Revolution: Lynn, Massachusetts* (1981). These books would, in turn, suggest sources from the time, such as diaries and other eyewitness accounts. For Lynn, for example, you would find that some historians have relied heavily on the reminiscences of David N. Johnson, a Lynn resident between 1830 and 1880. See Johnson, *Sketches of Lynn, or the Changes of Fifty Years* (1880).

You might also consider how well the Industrial Revolution in your chosen community compares with the general descriptions in the text. What were the important points of similarity? of difference?

BIBLIOGRAPHY

The Rise of Northeastern Manufacturing

Books on the role of technological change in the Industrial Revolution include H. J. Habakkuk, *American and British Technology in the Nineteenth Century: The Search for Labour-Saving Inventions* (1962); David A. Hounshell, *From the American System to Mass Production, 1800–1932: The Development of Manufacturing Technology in the United States* (1984); Melvin Kranzberg and Carroll W. Pursell, Jr., *Technology in Western Civilization* (1967); and Nathan Rosenberg, *Perspectives on Technology* (1976). The relationship between technological change and the development of the textile industry is worked out in Paul F. McGouldrick, *New England Textiles in the Nineteenth Century* (1968).

Stanley Lebergott, *Manpower in Economic Growth: The United States Record since 1800* (1964), provides a useful survey of the contribution of labor to the Industrial Revolution. An in-depth analysis of a critical group of women workers is Thomas Dublin, *Women at Work: The Transformation of Work and Community in Lowell, Massachusetts, 1826–1860* (1979). Tracing the history of early industrialization in another representative community, but from an anthropological perspective, is Anthony F. C. Wallace, *Rockdale: The Growth of an American Village in the Early Industrial Revolution* (1978). Regional studies of the early Industrial Revolution include Peter J. Coleman, *The Transformation of Rhode Island* (1963), and Dianne Lindstrom, *Economic Development in the Philadelphia Region, 1810–1850* (1978). Surveys of the broader economic impact of the Industrial Revolution include W. Elliot Brownlee, *Dynamics of Ascent: A History of the American Economy (1979);* Stuart Bruchey, *Enterprise: The Dynamic Economy of a Free People* (1990); Thomas C. Cochran, *Frontiers of Change: Early Industrialism in America* (1981); and Douglass C. North, *The Economic Growth of the United States, 1790-1860* (1961).

The Expansion of Markets

Urban development in this period is best explored through R. G. Albion, *The Rise of New York Port, 1815–1860* (1939); Eric E. Lampard, "The Evolving System of Cities in the United States: Urbanization and Economic Development," in *Issues in Urban Economics* (ed. Harvey S. Perloff and Lowdon Wingo, Jr., 1968); Richard C. Wade, *The Urban Frontier: Pioneer Life in Early Pittsburgh, Cincinnati, Lexington, Louisville, and St. Louis* (1964); and Alan R. Pred, *Urban Growth and the Circulation of Information: The United States System of Cities, 1790–1840* (1973). The best introductions to the agricultural expansion in this period are Paul W. Gates, *The Farmer's Age: Agriculture, 1815–1860* (1960), and Lewis C. Gray, *History of Agriculture in the Southern United States to 1860* (1933). The classic history of the role of transportation is George R. Taylor, *The Transportation Revolution, 1815–1860* (1951). On the role of canals, consult Carter Goodrich et al., *Canals and American Economic Development* (1961), and Ronald E. Shaw, *Canals for a Nation: The Canal Era in the United States, 1790–1860* (1990). On the contribution of the law to early industrialization, see Oscar Handlin and Mary Flug Handlin, *Commonwealth: A Study in the Role of Government in the American Economy, Massachusetts, 1774–1861* (1947); Morton J. Horwitz, *The Transformation of American Law, 1780–1860* (1977); and James Willard Hurst, *Law and the Conditions of Freedom in the Nineteenth-Century United States* (1964).

Social Structure in an Industrializing Society

The following provide a good introduction to the study of the distribution of wealth and income in the early nineteenth century: Frederick C. Jaher, *The Urban Establishment: Upper Strata in Boston, New York, Charleston, Chicago, and Los Angeles* (1982); Edward Pessen, *Riches, Class, and Power Before the Civil War* (1973); Lee Soltow, ed., *Six Papers on the Size Distribution of Wealth and Income* (1969); and Jeffrey G. Williamson and Peter H. Lindert, *American Inequality: A Macroeconomic History* (1980). These studies should be supplemented with analyses of social mobility such as Robert Doherty, *Society and Power: Five New England Towns, 1800–1860* (1977); Don H. Doyle, *The Social Order of a Frontier Community: Jacksonville, Illinois, 1825–1870* (1978); Michael B. Katz et al., *The Social Organization of Early Industrial Capitalism* (1982); Peter R. Knights, *The Plain People of Boston, 1830–1860* (1971); and Stanley Lebergott, *The American Economy: Income, Wealth, and Want* (1976). Some of the disruptive effects of mobility on urban life are addressed in Alan Dawley, *Class and Community: The Industrial Revolution in Lynn* (1976); Karen Haltunen, *Confidence Men and Painted Women: A Study of Middle-Class Culture in America, 1830–1870* (1982); Roger Lane, *Policing the City: Boston, 1822–1885* (1967); Bruce Laurie, *Working People of Philadelphia, The Coming of Industrial Order: Town and Factory Life in Rural Massachusetts* (1983); W. J. Rorabaugh, *The Alcoholic Republic: An American Tradition* (1979); Ian R. Tyrell, *Sobering Up: From Temperance to Prohibition in Antebellum America, 1800–1860* (1979); and Sam Bass Warner, Jr., *The Private City* (1968).

The Rise of the Business Class

The concept of the business class is developed in Michael Katz et al., *The Social Organization of Early Industrial Capitalism* (1982). Surveys of reform movements closely linked to the Second Great Awakening include C. S. Griffen, *The Ferment of Reform, 1830–1860* (1967); Alice F. Tyler, *Freedom's Ferment: Phases of Social History from the Colonial Period to the Outbreak of the Civil War* (1944); and Ronald G. Walters, *American Reformers, 1815–1860* (1978). Studies of the relationship between religious evangelism and reform are particularly abundant for communities in New York State. See Whitney R. Cross, *The Burned-Over District: The Social and Intellectual History of Enthusiastic Religion in Western New York, 1800–1850* (1950); Paul E. Johnson, *A Shopkeeper's Millennium: Society and Revivals in Rochester, New York, 1815–1837* (1978); and Mary Ryan, *Cradle of the Middle Class: The Family in Oneida County, New York, 1790–1865* (1981).

TIMELINE

1790	Samuel Slater's cotton mill opened in Providence, R.I.
1793	Eli Whitney manufactures cotton gins
1807	Robert Fulton launches the *Clermont*
1814	Boston Manufacturing Company builds Waltham cotton mill
1817	New York Stock Exchange founded Erie Canal begun
1819	Cast-iron plow invented
1820	Price of federal land reduced to $1.25 per acre
1824	Franklin Institute founded
1825	Erie Canal completed Jefferson proclaims U.S. technological independence
1828	Baltimore and Ohio Railroad chartered American Temperance Society founded
1831	Charles Grandison Finney begins Rochester revival
1832	First die-forging machine built
1833	National Road crosses Ohio River
1837	Supreme Court decides *Charles River Bridge v. Warren Bridge*

President's Levee

Andrew Jackson's chaotic 1829 inauguration, represented in this painting by Robert Cruikshank as "all Creation going to the White House," was the first "people's inaugural." (White House Historical Association)

CHAPTER 11 *A Democratic Revolution,* 1820–1844

The Industrial Revolution transformed the lives of millions of American men and women. In traditional society, where people lived and worked together in self-sufficient, close-knit communities, their institutions—the family, the village or urban neighborhood, the artisan's shop, the religious congregation, and the town meeting—all had functioned well. But the new economy drew people out of those intimate settings and into larger spheres, even into national and international affairs. The new world was less predictable, less personal, and far more complicated.

The dislocations and disorders caused by the Industrial Revolution had a profound effect on American politics. The turmoil fueled a process of political democratization, and it paved the way for the emergence of Andrew Jackson and his new political party, the Democratic party. In the early years of the republic the byword had been republicanism. Now the clarion cry was for democracy.

Jackson defined himself as the protector of farmers and workers, and he committed himself to advancing liberty by removing the "special privileges" of the rich and the business class. Jackson was a product of the democratization movement, and as president, he transformed his office and the federal government into potent instruments of democracy.

Jackson's opponents—the Whigs—gradually defined themselves as the party of economic improvement and prosperity; they would create opportunity by using the federal government to promote business, transportation, and industry. The Whig challenge to Jackson's Democratic party initiated what historians have called the Second Party System—a system that endured until the rise of the Republican party in the 1850s. This fiercely competitive system of two parties each striving to speak for "the people" completed a democratic revolution that, in its scope and significance, matched the Industrial Revolution.

Democratizing Politics, 1820–1829

The quest for political democracy, under way since the 1780s, accelerated because of the Industrial Revolution. With the exception of the most traditional elites in seaboard cities and in the plantation South, virtually all Americans supported democratization of the republic—especially through the expansion of male voting—as a way of fulfilling the ideals of the American Revolution. But the Industrial Revolution raised the tempo of democratization and took it beyond extension of the franchise—into the development of modern political parties.

Democratic Institutions

Industrialization created a public that was much more complex in its composition, better informed, and more emotionally involved in politics. Rapid economic change created new economic interests and intensified the conflict among social and economic groups, thus raising the stakes of politics. Many people saw the possibilities of using government to promote their own interests—or to oppose the interests of others. They could either promote or resist, through government, the forces of industrialization. At the same time, the growing ease of communication made state and national issues more important at the local level. In addition, the accelerating growth of western communities, where enthusiasm for broad participation in political life had always been greatest, increased the pressures for democratization.

The Right to Vote. Expansion of the franchise was the most dramatic expression of the democratic revolution (see Chapter 9). The removal of property requirements meant that even the poorest wage laborer could vote. By 1840 the electorate included more than 90 percent of the adult white male population. Most states also established the direct popular election of governors, presidential electors, and some judges.

And so, more than half a century after the American Revolution, the idea that all white men had the right to participate fully in the political life of the nation had finally triumphed. Democracy, however, still excluded more than half the population. Native Americans remained nations to themselves, with no voice in the halls of government where their fate was effectively determined. Every state denied women the franchise and the right to hold office. Almost every state denied the vote to free blacks. And in 1840 nearly 3 million African-Americans—about 17 percent of all Americans—lived in slavery, with no rights at all. But the essence of democracy's appeal was its universality, and when women and blacks launched their drives for equal rights in the 1840s and 1850s they drew heavily on the language of democracy first enunciated in the Declaration of Independence.

Political Parties. In response to the challenge of economic and social change, new parties emerged in every state during the 1820s and 1830s. They were more democratic than their predecessors, but they were as concerned with organization and discipline as they were with increasing participation. Party organization was the crucial ingredient required to shape a wide diversity of interests into workable coalitions—coalitions that could give the electorate clear choices and produce coherent legislation. In large and diverse states like New York, party loyalty and discipline were crucial. Party members had to be persuaded to support the party's candidate even if they disagreed with some of his ideas. In return, party members got a chance to participate, influence government, and benefit from patronage. Although unrecognized by the Constitution, political parties became central elements in American government.

During the 1820s, the New York politician Martin Van Buren pioneered in making party discipline an effective tool in governing. Using skills that earned him the nickname of the "Little Magician," Van Buren and his associates took over and transformed New York's Republican party. They introduced collective leadership, strong party loyalty and discipline, and an elaborate apparatus of party organization. Widely circulated party newspapers such as the Albany *Argus* promoted the party line and helped maintain party discipline. The focus of party activity was on legislative outcomes. Party members learned that they could advance their own interests in the New York legislature by accepting the majority decisions of the party caucus. On one crucial occasion, after seventeen Republicans in the state legislature had threatened to vote against the party line, Van Buren pleaded that they "magnanimously sacrifice individual preferences for the general good." They agreed and were rewarded with a banquet where, as one observer wrote, "something approaching divine honors were lavished on the Seventeen."

In a nation as diverse as the United States, parties had to embrace platforms that would appeal to a broad coalition of voters. The party leader most successful in reaching across sectional and class lines to establish a national constituency was Andrew Jackson.

The Election of 1824

While state parties became more vigorous and organized during the early 1820s, the national political parties were in disarray. The Federalist party had virtually disappeared and the Republican party was badly fragmented. In the election of 1824 to succeed Monroe, no fewer than five presidential candidates, all calling themselves Republicans, crowded the field. Three were veterans of Monroe's cabinet: Secretary of State John Quincy Adams, the son of John Adams; Secretary of War John C. Calhoun; and Secretary of the Treasury William H. Crawford. The fourth was Speaker of the House Henry Clay from Kentucky. The fifth was General Andrew Jackson, now a senator from Tennessee.

As a native of Nashville, where he was linked to the most influential families through marriage and his career as an attorney, cotton planter, and slaveowner, Jackson spoke most clearly for the voters of the Old Southwest. But virtually all Americans revered Jackson as the hero of the Battle of New Orleans. Tall and rough-hewn—nicknamed "Old Hickory" by the press—he embodied the nationalistic pride that had swelled in the wake of the War of 1812. And his rise to prominence from common origins demonstrated republican virtue, even suggested divine favor.

AMERICAN VOICES

Politics on the Tennessee Frontier *Davy Crockett*

The democratic revolution helped establish David Crockett (1786–1836) in American folklore. His autobiography described—with considerable exaggeration—his exploits as frontiersman, Indian fighter, humorist, and politician. This account of his election to the Tennessee legislature in 1821 suggests the importance in the new democratic political culture of the common touch—"natural" wisdom, antiestablishment humor, and forthright cunning.

Davy Crockett addresses a group of citizens on the Tennessee frontier while "electioneering" for the House of Representatives.

I . . . set out electioneering, which was a bran-fire new business to me. It now became necessary that I should tell the people something about the government, and an eternal sight of other things that I knowed nothing more about than I did about Latin, and law, and such things as that. . . .

I went first into Heckman county to see what I could do among the people as a candidate. Here they told me that they wanted to move their town nearer to the centre of the county, and I must come out in favour of it. There's no devil if I knowed what this meant, or how the town was to be moved; and so I kept dark, going on the identical same plan that I now find is called "non-committal." About this time there was a great squirrel hunt on Duck river, which was among my people. They were to hunt two days: then to meet and count the scalps, and have a big barbecue, and what might be called a tip-top country frolic. The dinner, and a general treat, was all to be paid for by the party having taken the fewest scalps. I joined one side, taking the place of one of the hunters, and got a gun ready for the hunt. I killed a great many squirrels, and when we counted scalps, my party was victorious.

The company had every thing to eat and drink that could be furnished in so new a country, and much fun and good humor prevailed. But before the regular frolic commenced, I mean the dancing, I was called on to make a speech as a candidate . . . .

How to begin I couldn't tell. I made many apologies, and tried to get off, for I know'd I had a man to run against who could speak prime, and I know'd too, that I wa'n't able to shuffle and cut with him. He was there, and knowing my ignorance as well as I did myself, he also urged me to make a speech. The truth is, he thought my being a candidate was a mere matter of sport; and didn't think, for a moment, that he was in any danger from an ignorant back-woods bear hunter. . . .

. . .They all roared out in a mighty laugh, and I told some other anecdotes, equally amusing to them, and believing I had them in a first-rate way, I quit and got down, thanking the people for their attention. But I took care to remark that I was as dry as a powder horn, and I thought it was time for us all to wet our whistles a little; and so I put off to the liquor stand, and was followed by the greater part of the crowd.

I felt certain this was necessary, for I knowed my competitor could open government matters to them as easy as he pleased. He had, however, mighty few left to hear him, as I continued with the crowd, now and then taking a horn, and telling good humored stories, till he was done speaking. . . .

The thought of having to make a speech made my knees feel mighty weak, and set my heart to fluttering almost as bad as my first love scrape with the Quaker's niece. But as good luck would have it, these big candidates spoke nearly all day, and when they quit, the people were worn out with fatigue, which afforded me a good apology for not discussing the government. But I listened mighty close to them, and was learning pretty fast about political matters. When they were all done, I got up and told some laughable story, and quit. I found I was safe in those parts, and so I went home, and didn't go back again till after the election was over. But to cut this matter short, I was elected, doubling my competitor, and nine votes over.

Source: David Crockett, *A Narrative of the Life of David Crockett of the State of Tennessee*, (Knoxville: University of Tennessee Press, 1973), 139–143.

Nominated for the presidency by the Tennessee legislature, Jackson followed tradition and did not actively campaign himself. But his supporters vigorously promoted him as a man of integrity who would root out corruption and preserve American freedom. They did not dwell on specific issues except to condemn the practice, customary under the First Party System, of having a *congressional caucus*—an informal meeting of each party's congressional leaders—nominate presidential candidates. They had especially harsh words for the congressional caucus of 1824, in which less than a third of the Republicans had chosen the "official" presidential candidate, William H. Crawford.

Significantly for Jackson, the 1824 election was the first in which most of the presidential electors were selected by the voters. Only six of the twenty-four states retained the practice of having the state legislature choose the electors.

The result was a complete surprise to political leaders: Jackson won 99 electoral votes, Adams 84, Crawford 41, and Clay only 37. Crawford, paralyzed by a stroke, won only Georgia, his home state, and Virginia, where he was born. Adams had broader national support, largely because of his prominence as secretary of state, but the public identified him as the candidate of New England. Clay's support was limited largely to the Ohio valley. (John C. Calhoun had bowed to political realities and switched over to the vice-presidential race, which he won easily with the support of the Jackson forces.)

Since no candidate had received an absolute majority, it fell to the House of Representatives to choose the president from among the three leading contenders. Many established politicians were horrified at the thought of the uncouth Tennesseean in the White House. Clay had been particularly derisive during the campaign, scorning Jackson as a mere "military chieftain." Out of the race himself, Clay resolved to block Jackson's election in the House, where Clay still served as Speaker. By the time the House met on February 9, 1825, Clay had put together a New England–Ohio valley coalition that threw the election to Adams. Adams showed his gratitude by appointing Clay secretary of state. This was a most significant appointment, since it had served the last three presidents as the final stepping stone to the highest office; but it was a fatal mistake for both men. Jackson's supporters immediately decried the arrangement as a "corrupt bargain" and began almost at once to prepare for the next election.

John Quincy Adams

A famous photograph of John Quincy Adams (1767–1848), taken about 1843 by Philip Haas, suggests the tenacity and moral commitment that contributed to his seventeen-year career as congressman from Massachusetts. Far more effective in Congress than he had been as president, Adams became a vigorous opponent of slavery. (The Metropolitan Museum of Art)

The Presidency of John Quincy Adams, 1825–1829

As president, Adams presented a bold and sweeping program to promote the nation's economic and social development. He fully embraced the basic features of Clay's American System: (1) a protective tariff to stimulate manufacturing; (2) internal improvements (e.g., roads and canals) to stimulate commerce; and (3) a national bank to promote a uniform currency and expand credit. But Adams had an even more expansive view of the federal government's responsibilities than Clay. In his first message to Congress in December 1825, he advocated legislation to promote "the cultivation of the mechanic and of the elegant arts, the advancement of literature and the progress of the sciences, ornamental and profound." And he called for the establishment of a national university in Washington, extensive scientific explorations of the Far West, the adoption of a uniform standard of weights and measures, and the building of a national observatory.

Many politicians attacked Adams's proposals as favoritism to his most loyal supporters, the business class of the Northeast. Thomas Jefferson, on his deathbed, argued that Adams was seeking to establish "a single and splendid government of an aristocracy . . . riding and ruling over the plundered ploughman and beggared yeomanry." There were constitutional objections as well. Madison had vetoed Calhoun and Clay's Bonus Bill in 1817 because he felt it would have exceeded the government's constitutional powers, and Adams's program was even more ambitious. Adams made matters worse by openly questioning the wisdom of democracy. He warned that America seemed to "proclaim to the world that we are palsied by the will of our constituents."

In the end, all that Adams was able to get out of a hostile Congress was a modest improvement in navigation and a start on extending the National Road from Wheeling, Virginia, into Ohio. He had no success in raising tariffs until the end of his term, and the tariff that was passed then was not of his devising.

In December 1827 the Jacksonians won control of Congress, and they decided to push through their own tariff measure to bolster their leader's prospects for the next election. The Tariff of 1824 had imposed a protective tax of 35 percent on imported iron, woolens, cotton, and hemp. The new tariff raised the rate on manufactured goods to about 50 percent of their value, providing significantly greater protection to New England cloth manufacturers. To appeal to voters in New York, Pennsylvania, Ohio, and Kentucky, where Jackson was also weak, the act also increased tariffs on imported raw materials—including flax, hemp, iron, lead, molasses, and raw wool. Despite his reservations, Adams signed the legislation. The tariff favored interests in the West and the North, but it was bitterly attacked in the South, which relied heavily on trade with Britain. The new tariffs raised the cost of British imports and, by restricting the flow of British goods, made it more difficult for the British to pay for the cotton they imported from the South. Southern politicians, especially in South Carolina, denounced it as the "Tariff of Abominations" and vowed to overturn it in the future, one way or another.

Adams's problems in the South were aggravated by his apparent support for the rights of native Americans. In 1825 the Creek nation had signed a treaty with Georgia ceding its remaining land in that state. Adams claimed Georgia had obtained the treaty through fraud, and he ordered that another be negotiated. When Georgia's governor, a backwoodsman named George M. Troup, defied Adams and threatened to take control of the Creek lands, Adams declared that it was the president's duty to uphold federal jurisdiction "by all the force committed for that purpose to his charge." Though the new treaty confirmed the cession of Creek land, Adams's concern for the legal niceties made it clear that he would not support the total removal of the Indians that many southerners were seeking.

Adams the patrician viewed the presidency as above politics. He ignored his waning popularity and disregarded the need to build support within his party. He failed to use presidential patronage to reward his supporters; he retained even hostile politicians as his appointees so long as they were competent. When he decided to run for reelection in 1828, he refused to pay any attention to his campaign. He reinforced this aloof, paternalistic image by telling supporters that he would not ask the American people to reelect him. "If my country wants my services," he said, "she must ask for them."

The Election of 1828: The Birth of the Democratic Party

As Adams's problems mounted, Jackson's campaign gathered momentum. He did not campaign personally, but his organization was brilliant. He assembled a broad, seemingly incongruous coalition of political leaders: his close friends in the Old Southwest; the South Carolina supporters of John C. Calhoun, who was again his semiofficial running mate; the Crawford supporters and the Virginians who had inherited power from Jefferson, Madison, and Monroe; the former Pennsylvania Federalists, who were drifting without a political home; and the skilled, disciplined leaders of Martin Van Buren's New York organization. The state leaders organized local groups that planned newspaper campaigns, mass meetings, torchlight parades, and barbecues to excite public interest.

An Anti-Jackson Political Cartoon
This 1828 lithograph predicted that the extreme emotionalism of Andrew Jackson's presidential campaign would lead American voters to reject him in favor of John Quincy Adams. (The comparison between the campaigns was suggested by the contemporary debate over high-pressure vs. low-pressure engines for steamboats.)

The Democrats' Message. Jackson's supporters conveyed the same message as in 1824, but they did so more thoroughly and with greater emotion. The republic, the Jacksonians charged, had been corrupted by "special privilege," which Jackson would ruthlessly root out. Though they championed Jefferson as their hero, they emphasized, more than he or the Republicans ever had, that forceful democratic measures, especially majority rule, were necessary to purify the republic. Their evolving party label reflected this new emphasis on democracy. Initially, the Jacksonians had called themselves "Democratic-Republicans," in contrast to other Republicans. But as the campaign wore on, the Jackson forces simplified their name to "Democrats."

Jackson's supporters attacked Adams as the very personification of the corrupt consequences of special privilege. Had he not stolen the presidency itself through a "corrupt bargain" with Clay? They even made the sensational (but untrue) charge that as minister to Russia, Adams had tried to procure an American girl for the tsar. In contrast, they exalted Jackson's virtue, making much of his frontier origins and stressing his rise to wealth and fame without benefit of formal education or association with a political faction. Jackson was described as a "natural" aristocrat, a man who had achieved success by his own efforts in an environment of liberty. The Jacksonians made their leader personify the potential of the republic and gave Americans an opportunity to express their nationalism by casting their votes for him.

Jacksonian hostility to special privilege—in particular Jackson's hatred of corrupt bankers—appealed especially to the urban workers and artisans of the Northeast who felt threatened by industrialization. But it also appealed to farmers and small property-owners who believed that the American System was unconstitutional favoritism and had narrowed economic opportunity.

In the South, the Jacksonians courted the planters and small farmers opposed to the American System. On the crucial question of the Tariff of Abominations, as on other issues, he avoided making concrete pledges that might alienate large numbers of voters. Instead he allowed his supporters to publish a letter in which he declared his preference for an unspecified "judicious" tariff. More important, most white southerners calculated that the famed Indian fighter shared their desire to remove the remaining native Americans from the Southeast.

In the West, although Jackson remained vague on how much support government should give to western expansion, his military record was crucial. It suggested that he would vigorously support the ambitions of westerners and of all those, throughout the country, for whom the West symbolized opportunity.

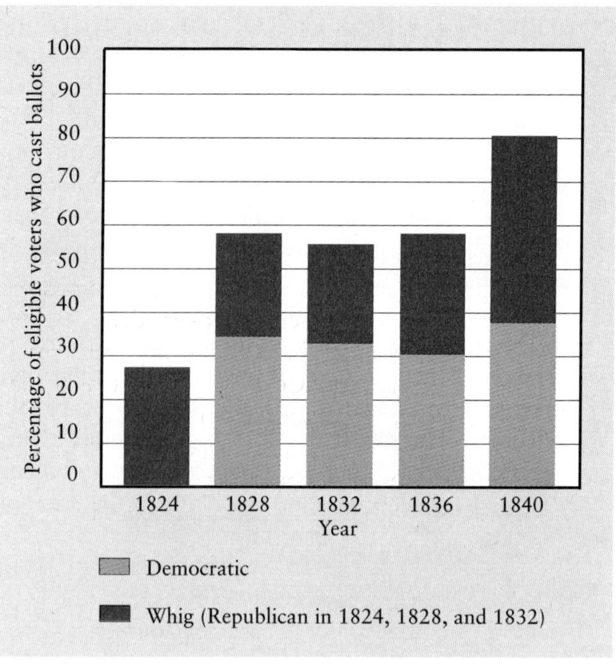

FIGURE 11.1

Changes In Voting Patterns, 1824–1840

With the return of two-party competition, voter participation soared in the critical presidential elections of 1828 and 1840.

The Democrats Triumph. The Jacksonian strategy worked. Whereas only about a fourth of the eligible electorate had voted in 1824, more than half voted in 1828, overwhelmingly for Jackson. There were now only two states, South Carolina and Delaware, where the legislature chose the presidential electors. Jackson and Calhoun received 178 of 261 electoral votes. Jackson and his supporters had fashioned a unified, national coalition that included urban workers, western settlers, and southern farmers—planters and yeomen alike. He was the first president to be elected from the West, and not from Virginia or Massachusetts.

Jackson's only area of weakness was New England, which Adams swept. To the northern business elite, Jackson's election was unsettling. After the election, Daniel Webster, an old Federalist, predicted to his business friends in Boston that when Jackson came to Washington, he would "bring a breeze with him. Which way it will blow, I cannot tell. . . . My *fear* is stronger than my *hope*." On inauguration day, after watching an unruly crowd clamber over the elegant furniture in the White House to shake the new president's hand, Supreme Court Justice Joseph Story declared, "The reign of King 'Mob' seemed triumphant."

The Jacksonian Presidency, 1829–1837

The democratizing of politics—the expansion of the franchise and the emergence of the first modern political party—had carried Andrew Jackson to the presidency. Now he turned his efforts to holding and enlarging his popular support. To accomplish this he transformed the basic institutions of government. He expanded the powers of the presidency as an instrument of popular will. In the process, he stripped Congress of control of national politics and gave that control, instead, to the Democratic party. Then, with powers greater than any president before him, he set out to smash any obstacles that impeded an independent citizenry intent on opportunity and expansion.

Party Government

To implement the people's will—the will of the majority—through party government, President Jackson reformed federal officeholding. He declared that long tenure in federal jobs encouraged officeholders to view their positions as personal fiefdoms. During the election he had promised to introduce rotation in office, so that every four years officials would have to return "to making a living as other people do." He dismissed the argument that rotation would deny the government the service of experienced officials. The duties of public service, Jackson said, were "so plain and simple that men of intelligence may readily qualify themselves for their performance." Other Democrats put it more bluntly. In the words of William L. Marcy, a Jackson supporter from New York, "To the victors belong the spoils." The policy of rotation—the *spoils system*—was a distinctly democratic principle. And, by giving the president greater flexibility to reward loyal Democrats with public office, it contributed to the building of a modern political party. Moreover, Jackson acted carefully in his dismissals, correcting some serious abuses of power and protecting talented bureaucrats.

President Jackson also used his highest-level political appointments to consolidate the power of his party. He selected cabinet officers purely for their ability to represent the various Democratic constituencies harmoniously. But Jackson never called cabinet meetings, relying instead on an informal group of advisers whose opinions he valued. Participating in this Kitchen Cabinet were several newspaper editors, among them Francis Preston Blair of Kentucky, who edited the *Washington Globe;* Roger B. Taney of Maryland, who was to become attorney general and chief justice of the United States; several Treasury Department officials, including Amos Kendall, also from Kentucky, who collaborated with Jackson on many of his state papers; and, most influential of all, Secretary of State Martin Van Buren.

Andrew Jackson
This painting by Ralph E.W. Earl, completed about 1830 and entitled *Tennessee Gentleman,* displays the striking blend of romance and force of character that reinforced Jackson's image as a "natural aristocrat." (Courtesy The Hermitage—The Home of Andrew Jackson)

Jackson and the Native Americans

Jackson quickly and effectively enlarged the western base of the Democratic party through his Indian policy. White westerners of all classes and occupations applauded when he sent regular army troops to frontier areas of Illinois in 1832 to remove Chief Black Hawk, a leader of the Sauk and Fox tribes, from rich farmland along the Mississippi in western Illinois. The troops refused Black Hawk's offer to surrender and pursued him into the Wisconsin Territory. On August 3, the army ended its pursuit with the eight-hour-long Bad Axe Massacre, leaving alive only 150 of the 1,000 warriors who had followed Black Hawk.

AMERICAN VOICES

Prelude to the Black Hawk War *Black Hawk*

Black Hawk (1767–1838), or Makataimeshekiakiak in the language of his people, was a chief of the Sauk and Fox Indians. He was born in the same year as Andrew Jackson in a Sauk village where present-day Rock Island, Illinois, is located. Also like Jackson, he was a warrior, leading armies of more than 500 by the time he was in his thirties. In 1833 he dictated his life story to the government interpreter, who in turn worked with a young Illinois newspaper editor to publish the narrative. In this passage, Black Hawk describes some of the events leading up to the Black Hawk War.

We had about eight hundred acres in cultivation. . . .The land around our village . . .was covered with bluegrass, which made excellent pasture for our horses. . . .The rapids of Rock river furnished us with an abundance of excellent fish, and the land, being good, never failed to produce good crops of corn, beans, pumpkins, and squashes. We always had plenty—our children never cried with hunger, nor our people were never in want. Here our village had stood for more than a hundred years. . . .

Nothing was now [1828] talked of but leaving our village. Ke-o-kuck [the principal chief] had been persuaded to consent to. . . remove to the west side of the Mississippi. . . . I . . . .raised the standard of opposition to Ke-o-kuck, with full determination not to leave my village. . . . I was of the opinion that the white people had plenty of land, and would never take our village from us. . . . During the winter [1828–29], I received information that three families of whites had arrived at our village, and destroyed some of our lodges, and were making fences and dividing our corn-fields for their own use. . . . I went to my lodge, and saw a family occupying it. . . . The interpreter wrote me a paper, and I went back to the village, and showed it to the intruders, but could not understand their reply. I expected, however, that they would remove, as I requested them.

. . . we came up to our village, and found that the whites had not left it—but that others had come, and that the greater part of our corn-fields had been enclosed. . . . the whites appeared displeased because we had come back. We repaired the lodges that had been left standing, and built others. . . .

In consequence of the improvements of the intruders on our fields, we found considerable difficulty to get ground to plant a little corn. Some of the whites permitted us to plant small patches in the fields they had fenced, keeping all the best ground for themselves. . . .

The white people brought whisky into our village, made people drunk, and cheated them out of their homes, guns, and traps!

That fall [1829] I paid a visit to the agent, before we started to our hunting grounds. . . . He said that the land on which our village stood was now ordered to be sold to individuals; and that, when sold, *our right* to remain, by treaty, would be at an end, and that if we returned next spring, we would be *forced* to remove!

I refused . . . to quit my village. It was here, that I was born—and here lie the bones of many friends and relatives. For this spot I felt a sacred reverence, and never could consent to leave it, without being forced therefrom. [1830]

I directed my village crier to proclaim, that my orders were, in the event of the war chief coming to our village to remove us, that not a gun should be fired, not any resistance offered. That if he determined to fight, for them to remain quietly in their lodges, and let them *kill them if he chose*! [Spring, 1831]

Source: David Jackson, ed., *Black Hawk, An Autobiography* (Urbana: University of Illinois Press, 1964), 88–113.

But Jackson's goal was not limited to breaking the resistance of western Indians to white settlement. As he made clear in his first message to Congress, he meant to remove all native Americans east of the Mississippi, even those in seaboard states who had adapted to white society and posed no threat to their white neighbors. As he had put it in a letter to President Monroe in 1817: "I have long viewed treaties with the Indians an absurdity not to be reconciled to the principles of our government." In Jackson's view, Indians were blocking the advance of citizen farmers and republican virtue; they were barbaric and could never become part of American society. Publicly, he also argued that removal of Indians was humane in that it sheltered an inferior people.

The "Five Civilized Tribes." The Cherokee and Creek in Georgia and Alabama; the Chickasaw and Choctaw in Mississippi, Alabama, and Tennessee; and the Seminole in Florida—the so-called five civilized tribes—remained in the South. They retained control of large enclaves, often with federal protection guaranteed by earlier treaties. The Cherokee were particularly success-

Black Hawk
This portrait was painted by George Catlin (1796–1872), who visited more tribes of western Indians than any other artist during the 1830s. He assembled nearly six hundred paintings in an "Indian Gallery" and traveled with it through America between 1837 and 1851, appealing to intrigued but unsympathetic audiences. (*Muk-a-tah-mish-o-kah-kaik, the Black Hawk*, Courtesy of the Gilcrease Institute)

ful because they had a centralized political system, a thriving agricultural economy, and leaders who worked to gain white sympathy by adopting the trappings of a plantation society. Tragically, the five tribes occupied high-quality cotton land that was directly in the path of white settlement.

Jackson's first move was to withdraw the federal troops protecting the tribal enclaves that had been created in the southeastern states after the War of 1812. He realized this action would leave the native Americans subject to state law, which he knew had a sharp anti-Indian edge. One state, Georgia, in 1825 and again in 1827, had forced the Creek to cede most of their territory to the state. In 1828, Georgia went further, declaring that the Cherokee were not an Indian nation but a collection of individuals who were tenants on state-owned land. Other states followed Georgia's example; they restricted the tribal rights of native Americans, thus opening the way for whites to acquire Indian property.

Next, Jackson pushed through the Indian Removal Act of 1830. It offered the southern Indians land west of the Mississippi in exchange for their eastern holdings. When Jackson sent agents to negotiate with the five tribes, he instructed them to tell the Indians "as friends and brothers to listen to their father." In the West, the agents should promise the tribes, "their white brothers will not trouble them, . . . will have no claim to the land," and the Indians "can live upon it, they and all their children, as long as grass grows and water runs." Realizing that Jackson was prepared to send federal troops to remove them, the tribes negotiated almost a hundred treaties for such exchanges.

Jackson carried out his Indian policy despite two rulings by the Supreme Court upholding Indian rights. In 1827, the Cherokee had adopted a constitution and proclaimed themselves a separate nation within the United States. After Georgia's 1828 declaration denied their claim to nationhood, the Cherokee appealed to the Supreme Court. The Cherokee argued that Georgia's denial of their independence violated the U.S. Constitution. Chief Justice John Marshall upheld their view. In *Cherokee Nation v. Georgia* (1831), speaking for a majority of the justices, he argued that the Indians were "domestic dependent nations" with a right to their land. In another case, *Worcester v. Georgia* (1832), Marshall held that the Indian nations were "distinct political communities, having territorial boundaries, within which their authority is exclusive . . . which is not only acknowledged, but guaranteed by the United States." Jackson reputedly responded, "John Marshall has made his decision; now let him enforce it." Because of the wide popularity of Jackson's Indian policy, no significant support emerged for the Court, and Marshall took no steps to implement his ruling.

The Trail of Tears. Still, the Cherokee refused to budge. They repudiated a treaty, forced on them by Georgia in 1835, which required them to leave by May 23, 1838. By the deadline, only 2,000 of the 17,000 Cherokee had left. During the summer, Martin Van Buren, who had assumed the presidency a year earlier, sent General Winfield Scott with an army of 7,000 men to enforce the treaty. Scott rounded up 15,000 Cherokee and concentrated them in government camps, where many died. A few escaped to isolated Cherokee villages in the mountains of North Carolina. In the fall and winter, the rest were forced to undertake a 1,200-mile march to the new Indian Territory in present-day Oklahoma—a route they remembered as the Trail of Tears. Only 11,000 reached Oklahoma; on the journey as many as 4,000 died of starvation and exposure, victims of racial prejudice and the ruthless hunger of whites for land. Now only the Seminole remained in the Southeast. Aided by runaway slaves, many of whom had married into the tribe, the Seminole fought a guerrilla war into the 1840s against federal troops and the state militia.

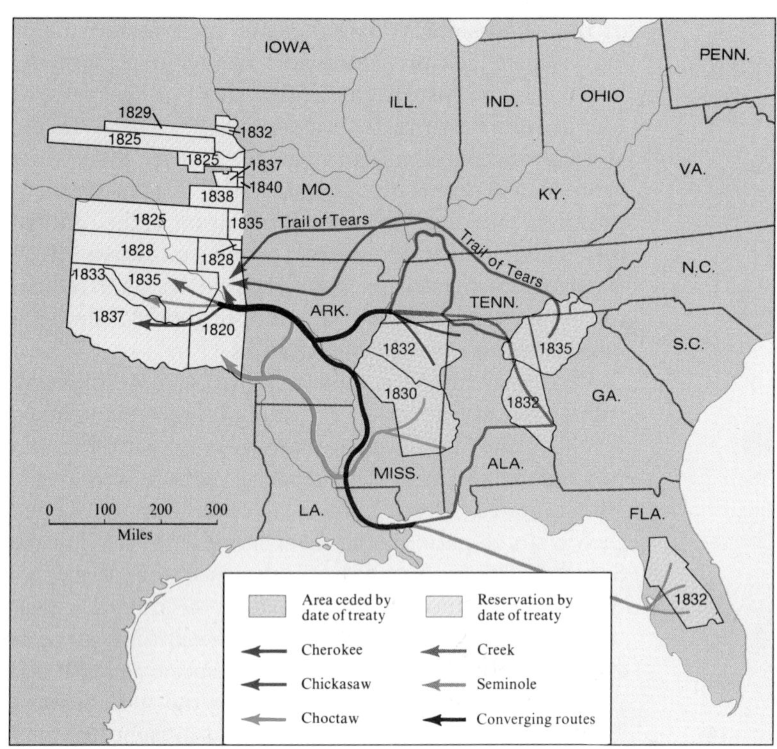

MAP 11.1

The Removal of Native Americans

This map shows the lands of the southeastern tribes before and after their removal during the 1820s and 1830s, and the routes of their forced migrations. A comparison of this map with the land sales on page 299 shows that the tribal lands ceded in Alabama and Mississippi became those most sought after by white settlers during the 1830s. No white settlers occupied land on the new reservations before the Civil War.

Jackson versus the Bank

Jackson's most vigorous political offensive was his attack on the Second Bank of the United States, one of the key elements of the American System. Jackson began to dismantle the American System in May 1830, when he vetoed a bill providing for the extension of the National Road from Maysville, Ohio, to Lexington, Kentucky. Jackson worried about the potential for corruption because the bill provided for federal purchase of stock in a Kentucky turnpike company. This issue was even more salient in Jackson's attack on the Bank.

The Second Bank of the United States. The Second Bank was a large commercial bank that the federal government had chartered in 1816 and partially owned (to the extent of 20 percent of the Bank's stock). Its federal charter would expire in 1836. The Bank's most important role was the stabilization of the nation's money supply. Most American money consisted of notes—in effect, paper money—that state-chartered commercial banks issued with the promise to redeem the notes with "hard" money—gold or silver coins, also known as *specie*—on demand. The Bank played its stabilizing role by regularly collecting these state bank notes at its various branch offices, returning them to the banks that had issued them, and demanding that the banks convert them into gold and silver coin. The intention was that, with the threat of collection hanging over them, the state banks would be conservative about extending credit. The state banks continued to issue more notes than they could redeem at any given time, thereby expanding the money supply; but under the discipline imposed by the Second Bank, they had to do so cautiously. During the prosperous 1820s, under the leadership of its president, Nicholas Biddle, the Second Bank performed especially well, maintaining steady, predictable increases in the money supply. By enhancing investors' confidence in the monetary stability of the developing West, Biddle and the bank promoted increases in the supply of capital for economic development, a role especially appreciated by bankers and entrepreneurs in Boston, New York, and Philadelphia.

Most Americans did not understand commercial banking, particularly the banks' capacity to enlarge the money supply through the lending of bank notes. Nor did they appreciate the role of the Second Bank in regulating credit. It was easy to believe that banking was a nonproductive, parasitic activity and that bankers earned their profits illegitimately through the exercise of special privileges. Many Americans had specific grievances against bankers. Jackson himself blamed them for financial instability in general and for large sums of money he had lost in speculative investments during the 1790s. Wage earners were especially distrustful and hostile. They sometimes received payment in highly depreciated notes issued by unstable state banks. In response, they often advocated the end to all banking so as to eliminate all money except specie. Various other groups played on popular prejudices for the purpose of killing the Second Bank. Wealthy New York bankers, including supporters of Martin Van Buren, wanted to see federal monies deposited in their banks instead; some bankers in the smaller cities, including the Nashville supporters of Jackson, wanted to be free of the inhibiting supervision of the Second Bank.

The Bank Veto. In 1832, Jackson's opponents in Congress, led by Henry Clay and Daniel Webster, united to embarrass Jackson. They knew that the president opposed the Second Bank. Anticipating that many Democrats in Congress favored the Bank, Clay and Webster hoped to lure Jackson into the trap of a divisive and unpopular veto just before the 1832 elections. So they persuaded Biddle, who would have preferred to remain neutral, to request an early recharter of the Bank, and they engineered passage of a bill to accomplish that.

Seeming to fall into the trap, Jackson vetoed the bill. The veto itself was highly unusual. Before Jackson, presidents had vetoed legislation only nine times, on constitutional grounds. But Jackson accompanied his veto with a powerful message that ranged far beyond constitutional issues to focus on the ways in which the bill was "dangerous to the liberties of the people." Using the vocabulary of the Revolution, he made the Bank the focus of resentment against the era's unsettling social and economic changes. He denounced the Bank as a nest of special privilege and monopoly power that promoted "the advancement of the few at the expense of the many." It damaged the "humbler members of society—the farmers, the mechanics, and laborers—who have neither the time nor the means of securing like favors to themselves." The president singled out the monopolists who had profited from special privilege and inside dealing. By inference, he attacked Webster, a director of the Boston branch of the Second Bank, for having drawn on the Bank for loans and received fees from it for legal services. Finally, Jackson made a connection that was especially damning in the eyes of republican patriots. He emphasized the heavy investment by British aristocrats in the Second Bank.

The Election of 1832. Riding on the popular appeal of his veto message, Jackson and his new running mate, Martin Van Buren, faced Henry Clay, who headed the National Republican ticket, in the presidential election of 1832. Clay attacked Jackson for his abuses of patronage and the veto power, reproclaimed the American System, and called for rechartering the Second Bank. Clay was a popular campaigner, but Jackson and Van Buren carried a majority of the popular vote and overwhelmed Clay in the electoral vote, 219 to 49.

Jackson's Bank veto and his parading of the veto in the campaign showed that he had a better sense of the public's anticorporate mood than did the champions of the Bank. His most fervent support came from a broad spectrum of people who resisted industrialization. But Jackson's position also won favor with some promoters of economic growth. Among them were state bankers who had originally supported the Second Bank but now believed its demise would open the way for more speculative investments by their banks. Also supporting Jackson were middle-class people who were not opposed to industrialization but wanted their rightful share of its benefits. Thus Jackson managed to include additional groups in his coalition, even though some held diametrically opposite positions on the value of banking and even of industrialization.

The Bank War. Immediately after his reelection, Jackson launched a new attack on the Second Bank, which still had four years left on its original charter. Jackson decided to destroy the Bank immediately by withdrawing the federal government's deposits. After removing two recalcitrant secretaries of the treasury, he appointed Roger B. Taney, an enemy of the Bank who had helped

The Bank War

This political cartoon shows Jackson ordering the withdrawal of federal funds from the Second Bank of the United States. Crushed by the collapse of the Bank are Nicholas Biddle, whom the cartoonist represented as the devil, Biddle's cronies, and the newspapers Biddle supported in the war with Jackson. The man behind Jackson is "Major Jack Downing," the pseudonym for Seba Smith, a pro-Jackson humorist.

Jackson with the veto message. He ordered Taney to move the government's cash to state banks—called "pet banks" by Jackson's opponents. This action may well have been a violation of the Bank's charter, but Jackson claimed that he had the authority to act because the recent election had given him a mandate to destroy the Bank. It was the first time a president claimed that his electoral victory gave him the power to act independently of Congress.

Congress and the Bank retaliated, turning the dispute into the "Bank war." While the House of Representatives defended Jackson, in March 1834 the Senate passed a resolution that censured him. Henry Clay had drafted it, and he declared: "We are in the midst of a revolution, hitherto bloodless, but rapidly descending towards a total change of the pure republican character of the Government, and the concentration of all power in the hands of one man." For his part Nicholas Biddle contracted the Bank's loans sharply, increasing the pressure on other banks to restrict their loans and creating a brief recession in 1834. But Jackson and Taney held firm, and in 1836 the Second Bank became a state bank chartered under the laws of Pennsylvania. Jackson rewarded Taney by appointing him chief justice of the United States in 1836, after the death of John Marshall. Until his death in 1864, Taney led the Court in giving constitutional legitimacy to Jackson's antimonopoly policy and implementing Jackson's belief that a government under control of the majority could be trusted to promote the common good.

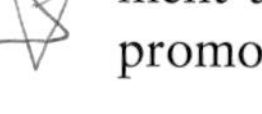

The Tariff and the Nullification Crisis

After the 1832 election, Jackson's eagerness to defend the destiny of the republic led him to attack a state

Charleston, South Carolina

The painting, by S. Bernard, a South Carolina artist, shows Charleston's Battery, the fashionable harborfront district. In this idealized scene, gentlemen and ladies stroll along the promenade, looking toward England which they tried to emulate. Beneath the confident exteriors of Charleston's elite lurked worries about their future in the only state with a slave majority. (*View Along the East Battery, Charleston,* c . 1831, Yale University Art Gallery) government. The occasion was the South Carolina nullification controversy, which stemmed from the chronic insecurity of South Carolina's slaveholding elite. The only state with a slave majority—56 percent of the population in 1830—South Carolina was more like Haiti, Jamaica, or Barbados than the rest of the South. In the rice-growing districts along the coast, the ratio of African-Americans to whites was more than ten to one. Like their West Indian counterparts, South Carolina planters lived in constant fear of slave rebellions—and the power of outside authorities to abolish slavery.

During the 1820s, South Carolina planters watched in apprehension as the British Parliament moved toward abolition of slavery in the West Indies. (Parliament took this action, with compensation for slave-owners, in August 1833.) Might the United States move in the same direction? South Carolina's leaders decided to contest the limits of federal power, choosing the tariff as their target.

They had reason to focus on tariffs. The planters had lost repeatedly on tariff questions, most recently in July 1832, when Congress had passed legislation that retained the high rates of the Tariff of Abominations on manufactured cloth and iron. In effect, northern majorities in Congress had used their votes to redistribute wealth from the South to northern manufacturers, who received an artificially high price for their goods. The economic damage to southern states raised an issue endemic to American federalism: What recourse do states have when the federal government takes actions which harm interests that those states regard as vital? Some southern delegates to the Philadelphia convention in 1787, anticipating the threat tariffs might pose to their states, had proposed that a two-thirds majority of Congress be required to enact tariff legislation.

Southern opposition to the tariff surged in the months after Jackson signed the bill. Antitariff forces under planter leadership won impressively in South Carolina's election that fall, and on November 24, 1832, a South Carolina state convention took a bold step. It adopted an Ordinance of Nullification, declaring the tariffs of 1828 and 1832 null and void and forbidding the collection of tariff duties within the state after February 1, 1833. Furthermore, should the federal government try to use force, South Carolina would secede.

John C. Calhoun (1782–1850)
This daguerreotype, made close to the time of Calhoun's death, suggests the emotional intensity he brought to bear on issues of states' rights and slavery. (The Gibbes Museum of Art)

Calhoun's *Exposition.* The state's act of nullification rested on the constitutional arguments of Jackson's first vice-president, John C. Calhoun, presented in his anonymous tract *The South Carolina Exposition and Protest* (1828). Calhoun had directly assaulted the Jacksonian position that majority rule should be at the heart of republican government. "Constitutional government and the government of a majority are utterly incompatible," Calhoun wrote. "An unchecked majority is a despotism," while "government is free, and will be permanent in proportion to the number, complexity, and efficiency of the checks, by which its powers are controlled."

Calhoun drew on the arguments of Jefferson and Madison in the Kentucky and Virginia resolutions of 1798. He returned to the Antifederalist argument that sovereignty lay not with the American people as a whole but with collections of people acting through their state governments. Only conventions like those that had ratified the Constitution could determine whether acts of Congress were constitutional. If any state decided that a federal law was unconstitutional, it could "interpose" by declaring the law null and void within its borders. The challenged law would remain nullified unless three-fourths of the other states ratified an amendment assigning Congress the power in question. And if such an amendment were adopted, the dissident state then had the option of seceding from the republic. Calhoun's ideas would form the basis of *states' rights* (or *state rights*) arguments well into the twentieth century.

Calhoun did not immediately admit authorship of the *Exposition,* but he took a public position on the issue of states' rights in 1830 following a long Senate debate between Robert Y. Hayne of South Carolina and Daniel Webster of Massachusetts over the nature of the Union. The debate began in January 1830 when Senator Hayne, protesting a resolution of Samuel A. Foot of Connecticut to restrict western land sales, suggested that the West should join forces with the South to oppose the land and tariff policies of the Northeast. Webster defended his section, turning from economic issues and challenging Hayne to debate the issue of states' rights. Hayne responded with the arguments of Calhoun's *Exposition,* while Calhoun looked on approvingly. Webster, often speaking directly to Calhoun, replied with a stirring defense of national power in which he concluded: "Liberty *and* Union, now and forever, one and inseparable!" What became known as Webster's "Second Reply to Hayne" circulated more widely than any previous congressional speech.

Jackson kept Republicans in suspense as to where he stood on the issue until April 1830 at a banquet to celebrate Jefferson's birthday. Opening the formal toasts, Jackson looked squarely at Calhoun and unequivocally declared: "Our Federal Union—it must be preserved." As vice-president, it was Calhoun's turn to rise next. His glass trembling in his hand, he delivered his toast: "The Union—next to our liberty the most dear! May we all remember that it can only be preserved by respecting the rights of the states and distributing equally the benefits and burdens of the Union."

In 1831, Calhoun finally admitted his authorship of the Exposition and elaborated his views further. Jackson—spurred on by Secretary of State Van Buren, who wanted the vice-presidency himself—dropped Calhoun from the ticket in May 1832.

Jackson Defends the Constitution. Jackson's response to the Ordinance of Nullification was swift and firm. On December 10 he issued a proclamation declaring that "disunion by armed force is *treason.*" Appealing to American patriotism, he declared that nullification violated the Constitution, was "unauthorized by its spirit, inconsistent with every principle on which it is founded, and destructive of the great object for which it was formed." Privately, he threatened to hang Calhoun. This was the final straw for Calhoun, who resigned as vice-president in December, with three months left of his term. From now on he would defend nullification from the floor of the Senate, to which he was immediately appointed by the South Carolina legislature.

South Carolina refused to relent, even when Jackson brandished federal power by reinforcing the federal forts in South Carolina and sending a warship and several armed boats to the port of Charleston. Finally, in January 1833, Jackson asked Congress to pass a "force bill" authorizing him to use the army and navy if necessary to compel obedience.

Jackson had firmly established national supremacy, but he wanted Congress to remove a principal source of the conflict, high tariffs. Henry Clay, determined to preserve protection for America's fledgling industries for at least a few more years, worked out a compromise. He proposed a new measure that provided for a gradual, annual reduction of the tariff so that by 1842 rates would return to the modest levels set in 1816. On March 1, 1833, Congress passed both the Compromise Tariff and the force bill. Jackson was satisfied. He believed he had established that no state could nullify a law of the United States.

Having saved face on the tariff issue, South Carolina's leaders promptly repealed the nullification ordinance. Significantly, no other state had joined South Carolina in its confrontation with federal power. Like Jackson, most southerners perceived no imminent threat to slavery. They held the Union in high regard and did not believe that restoring low tariffs warranted a challenge either to federal authority or to President Jackson, who was popular in the South. Still, South Carolinians resented their defeat over nullification, and support for Calhoun's theories remained widespread throughout the South. The compromise of 1833 was only a truce, not a definitive solution to the conflict over the meaning of the Union.

Andrew Jackson's Legacy

Jackson's aggressive defense of the national interest against the nullifiers won support throughout the North and the South. Americans of virtually all regions and classes saw the need for a strong central government to promote territorial expansion and preserve American democracy.

Jackson left the federal government—in particular the presidency—far stronger than he had found it. While he defended the republican values of Jefferson, he built a far more powerful, dynamic federal government than Jefferson had favored. And the constitutional argument Jackson set forth in his proclamation against nullification would provide the basis for Abraham Lincoln's response to the secession crisis of 1861.

Jackson opposed increased power for governments only when they fostered special privilege and corruption—as he believed they tended to do when legislatures were too powerful. "The President," Jackson declared in 1834, "is the direct representative of the American people." Acting on this belief, Jackson had freely used the veto power, fired federal office holders and replaced them with his political supporters, defied the Supreme Court and Congress, and mobilized force against a disobedient state. Jackson was convinced that when the people controlled the federal government, through their party and their president, the republic had nothing to fear.

The Texas Rebellion

Strong-willed and decisive, Jackson also recognized when the best policy was to do nothing. This proved to be the case with the Texas crisis, which bedeviled not only Jackson but the next three presidents as well.

After winning independence from Spain in 1821, Mexico began to encourage immigration to its Texas region north of the Rio Grande. During the 1820s, Stephen F. Austin and some other Americans from the lower Mississippi valley received grants for some of the best land in Texas. By 1830, about 30,000 Americans were living in Texas, far outnumbering the 4,000 Mexicans there. Looking forward to planting cotton, the American Texans had imported slaves by finding loopholes in Mexico's restrictions against slavery.

The Mexican government, worried about the strength of the American community in Texas, passed laws in 1830 that restricted American immigration and prohibited the importation of slaves. These actions, and the news that American abolitionists planned to establish a refuge for free African-Americans in Texas, led the American immigrants to begin violent protests. Protest turned to revolt after General Antonio López de Santa Anna became President of Mexico, appointed a military commandant for Texas, and centralized power in Mexico City. On March 2, 1836, Texas proclaimed its independence and adopted a constitution legalizing slavery.

At first the tide of battle went against the Texans. Only four days after the declaration of independence, Santa Anna wiped out the garrison, including Davy Crockett and Jim Bowie, that was defending the Alamo in San Antonio. But the defeat captured the attention of New Orleans and New York newspapers, whose correspondents romanticized the heroism of the Texans. Using some of the strongest anti-Catholic rhetoric of the day, the newspapers described the Mexicans as tyrannical butchers in the service of the pope. Thousands of adventurers, learning of Texan offers of land bounties, set sail from New York, the Gulf states, and the Mississippi valley. Reinforced by the new arrivals and led by General Sam Houston, the Texas rebels routed the Mexicans in the Battle of San Jacinto on April 21, 1836. Although Mexico refused to recognize the new republic, efforts to reconquer it were abandoned.

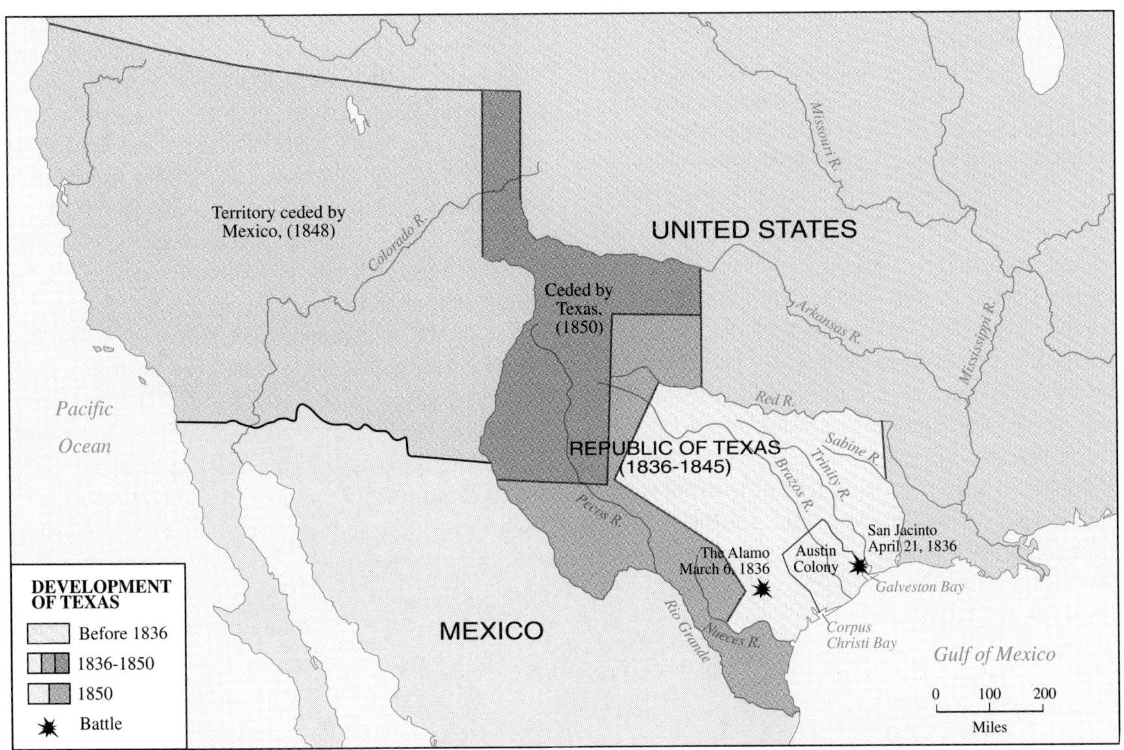

MAP 11.2

The American Settlement of Texas
The modern boundaries of Texas result from the organized settlement of the Texas region by Americans in the 1820s, the revolution for Texas independence (1836), annexation by the United States (1845), the Mexican War (1846–1848), and the organization of the territory of New Mexico (1850).

Davy Crockett at the Alamo
Cartoons like this from *Crockett's Almanac,* which appeared after his death, continued the myth-making that Crockett's *Narrative* had begun. They also helped establish the Alamo as a code for Texas heroism and Mexican brutality.

The Texans immediately voted by plebiscite for annexation by the United States. But Jackson and Martin Van Buren, who succeeded Jackson as president the following year, took no position on the issue. Jackson recognized that adding Texas as a state would disrupt the even balance of free and slave states established by the Missouri Compromise. In addition, he feared that such a step might lead to war with Mexico and division of the Democratic party into northern and southern factions. Privately, however, Jackson supported annexation and even encouraged the Texans to seize Mexican territory all the way to the Pacific Ocean.

The Early Labor Movement, 1794–1836

The movement for democratization extended beyond politics to the workshops—especially those directly affected by the Industrial Revolution. Some mechanics believed that they had gained independence and even prosperity from the Industrial Revolution, and saw little reason to challenge the inherently undemocratic nature of the new working conditions. They organized societies, associations, and unions, but only as a way to increase their share of the growing economic pie. Other mechanics organized with a more radical purpose—to resist the business class. Many mechanics with traditional skills had been hurt by industrialization, and they looked with suspicion on business-class efforts to reform society. To them the political task was not to create harmony between owners and workers but to recognize the inevitable conflict of interests between the people who sold their labor and the people who bought it.

Artisan Self-Consciousness

The earliest labor unions drew sustenance from the craft identity and social solidarity that had existed for generations among artisans—carpenters, shoemakers, shipbuilders, and other skilled workers. The skilled shoemakers in Philadelphia were representative. They had formed the Federated Society of Journeymen Cordwainers in 1794 to press for a uniform wage for their members. (Shoemakers took the name *cordwainers* from the high-quality Cordovan leather they worked.) Their repeated strikes against wage cuts had some limited success until 1806, when their leaders were convicted of criminal conspiracy under the common law in *Commonwealth v. Pullis.* The idea that a workers' combination was illegal—"a government unto themselves," in the words of the Philadelphia court—hampered the union movement for many years but did not stop it.

As the Industrial Revolution gathered momentum during the 1820s and 1830s, the mechanics developed a broader sense of social identity. Their group consciousness did not yet include black or women workers—not even the spouses who toiled alongside as "help-mates." And it did not include the growing numbers of unskilled workers, including the vast majority of factory workers. But the vision of the mechanics was expanding. They began to see themselves as linked not only with others skilled in their particular craft but as members of a larger class.

Workers in the Building Trades

During the 1820s and 1830s, the union movement was primarily carried forward not by factory workers but by workers with traditional skills still needed in the industrial era. Prominent among these were workers in the building trades—carpenters, house painters, stonecutters, masons, nailers, cabinetmakers. They were able to challenge employers in a sustained way because the Industrial Revolution, far from undermining their skills, actually increased the demand for them. They organized largely with the aim of increasing their remuneration—which they regarded as including leisure time as well as money—and their prospects for independence and security in the new industrial society.

Rapid urbanization during the 1820s and the construction of homes, stores, and factories triggered a strong demand for members of the building trades. The traditional hours of work for virtually all laborers were "sun to sun." But the quickening pace of economic activity was leading many employers to demand greater intensity of effort during working hours. For the building trades, the pressure became most intense during the spring and summer. Not only was construction then at fever pitch, but the regular working day exceeded twelve hours.

As demand for their skills increased, so did the bargaining position of the construction workers. They attempted to take advantage of this by forming labor unions and demanding a shorter work day. In 1825, about six hundred carpenters in Boston struck against their contractor-employers, demanding a ten-hour day, 6 A.M. to 6 P.M., with an hour each for breakfast and dinner. Their effort failed, but this had been the first great strike for the ten-hour day. Two years later a group of journeymen carpenters in Philadelphia had greater success. After a brief strike, several hundred of these workers won the ten-hour day and initiated coordinated action by groups of unions in the city. Their success led the building-trade workers to found the Mechanics' Union of Trade Associations. They reached out to other trades and formed the first effective citywide organization of wage earners in Philadelphia. "The real object . . . of this association," stated the constitution of the Mechanics' Union, is "to assist in establishing a just balance of power . . . between all the various classes and individuals which constitute society at large."

The building-trade workers went even further: they founded a political party, the Working Men's party, in 1828. The party's platform for increasing the power of labor included equal taxation, the abolition of banks, and universal education. For a time the Working Men held enough seats on the Philadelphia City Council to control it.

A large majority of workers considered the advance of public education their most important goal. They were convinced that public schools would enable their children to acquire skills that would not become obsolete and would allow them to advance more rapidly into the ranks of the propertied. So the Working Men's party demanded that the city and state provide all citizens with public education that would combine "one or more mechanical arts" with "literary and scientific instruction." Such training would "place the citizens of this extensive republic on an equality [and] bring the children of the poor and rich to mix together as a band of republican brethren," so that "united in youth in the acquisition of knowledge, they will grow up together, jealous of naught but the republican character of their country." The Working Men's party helped persuade Philadelphia to expand public schooling, and in 1834 the Pennsylvania legislature to authorize universal, free, tax-supported schools.

The members of the building-trade unions maintained their traditional values. They continued to take pride in their occupations and make a comfortable living from their work, and they stressed the importance of the communal solidarity of their respective crafts. In the growing urban economy of the 1820s and 1830s, their relative economic position improved, and they expanded their holdings of property significantly. Consequently, they had little reason to criticize the new industrial order in any fundamental way and considerable reason to promote their own version of social harmony.

The Threatened Mechanics

The position of mechanics directly threatened by industrialization was less happy. They faced declining incomes, unemployment, and loss of status. Hatters, printers, and weavers were among the most threatened workers, and during the 1820s and 1830s they banded together to form craft unions. Their leaders formulated a "producer's" ideology that defined their position in relation to both the business class and unskilled wage earners. They advanced a *labor theory of value,* arguing that the price of a product should reflect the labor required to make it, and that most of the income from its sale should be paid to the person who made it. The mechanics condemned the accumulation of wealth by capitalist employers and proclaimed their fear of becoming, as they put it, "slaves to a monied aristocracy."

A key group of threatened workers were journeymen shoemakers. In the 1820s and 1830s shoe manufacturers had begun to change the way shoes were made. They hired more journeymen but moved them to large, back-room shops where the workers cut leather into soles and "uppers." Then the masters sent out the uppers to shoebinders, usually women who worked at home binding the uppers and sewing in fabric linings. The employers then passed on the uppers and soles to journeymen who assembled entire shoes in small shops ("ten footers") commonly located in their backyards.

AMERICAN LIVES

Frances Wright: Radical Reformer

Frances Wright (1795–1852) arrived in New York City on New Year's Day, 1829, with a radical plan: to convince the city's workers to assault business-class power. She hoped that from New York her message would "spread far and wide, and invigorate the exertions of good and bold men throughout the land."

Born in Glasgow, Scotland, into the family of a wealthy merchant devoted to the republicanism of Thomas Paine, she discovered America at age sixteen. "From that moment on," she wrote, "my attention became rivetted on this country as upon the theatre where man might first awake to the full knowledge and exercise of his powers." She was among those Europeans drawn to American shores by the magnet of the Declaration of Independence.

In 1818 Wright made her first Atlantic crossing. When she returned to Britain in 1821, she published an enthusiastic account of life in America, *Views of Society and Manners in America*. Translated into three languages, the book reached a large international readership. Among the readers of her book was the French hero of the American Revolution, Marquis de Lafayette, who became her friend and patron. In 1824, Wright accompanied him on his triumphal return, which included a six-week stay with Thomas Jefferson at Monticello. There she revealed a bold plan to set up a utopian community of whites and freed slaves, who would live together in full equality.

Encouraged by Jefferson, Wright founded the community, called Nashoba, in 1825, on 320 acres of western Tennessee wilderness. She gathered support among other young idealists, enlarged Nashoba to nearly 2,000 acres, and purchased about thirty slaves. Her scheme was to allow them to earn emancipation by working on the land. During that time Nashoba would provide their children with an education.

Wright worked alongside the slaves in the arduous clearing and ditching of the marshy land. However, the slaves saw little improvement in their lives, and the summer heat and waves of malarial fevers wore down the enthusiasm of everyone—except Wright. Her dreams soared to embrace the ideals of Robert Owen, a Scottish industrialist and philanthropist who had formed his own utopian community in New Harmony, Indiana, in 1824. Following Owen's search for alternatives to private property, organized religion, and marriage, Wright declared that Nashoba would become a society "where affection shall form the only marriage, kind feelings and kind action the only religion, respect for the feelings and liberties of others the only restraint, and reunion of interest the bond of peace and security." But potential recruits were repelled by what the English author Frances Trollope described as the "savage aspect of the scene."

By 1828, Wright concluded that America had become too conservative for an "individual experiment" like Nashoba to succeed. What was required was to reform the "collective body politic." She left Nashoba and joined forces with Owen's son, Robert Dale Owen, who had become infatuated with her, and launched a lecture campaign, which took her to New York.

As a lecturer, Wright was a sensation. Rumors of free love and racial mixing at Nashoba did their part. And she challenged gender stereotypes: she was the first woman to address large mixed audiences in America. She would sweep onto a stage with a group of women apostles and throw off her cloak to reveal her revolutionary garb—a tunic of white muslin. Producing a copy of the Declaration of Independence, she would lecture in a resonant, musical voice. The poet Walt Whitman, who heard Wright as a young boy, remembered that "we all loved her; fell down before her: her very appearance seemed to enthrall us."

Wright announced to her packed audiences that the "laboring class of the community" faced oppression by a "monied aristocracy" and a "professional aristocracy of priests, lawyers, and politicians." She lashed out at evangelical ministers, calling them hypocritical and un-

Frances Wright
This 1826 painting is one of the thirty-two-year-old Frances Wright at Neshoba. She is wearing the simple, practical costume which the New Harmony community adopted for women—a coat reaching to the knees over pantaloons.

republican, challenging their claims of divine revelations, and describing the Benevolent Empire as the "would-be Christian Party in politics." She argued that the only way between the extremes of enslavement of all labor and violent revolution was reform focused on education. She called on Americans to educate all children between the ages of two and sixteen in compulsory boarding schools; these would enforce social equality and insulate children from organized religion. Among the beneficiaries would be women, who would learn to break their "mental chains" and attain equality under the law.

To nurture a radical culture among New York's workers, Wright and Owen took over an abandoned church near the Bowery, in the heart of the workers' neighborhood, and transformed it into a "Hall of Science." They established a newspaper office and a printing-press, a lecture auditorium, a day school, a deist Sunday school, a reading room, and a free medical dispensary.

Wright won a large following among mechanics and journeymen, some of whom turned to politics and energized the Working Men's party. In 1829, twenty men even wrote in her name on their ballots for the New York Assembly. Nonetheless, she failed to convert most of New York's radical workers; they believed that a maldistribution of wealth and opportunities—not religion—was at the heart of their powerlessness.

Disheartened, in 1831 Wright and Owen sold the Hall of Science to a new Methodist congregation. While Owen returned to New Harmony as a Democratic reform politician, Wright transported her freed-slaves to Haiti, and then sailed for Paris, where she married a French educational reformer and gave birth to a daughter.

Wright never abandoned her dreams, however. Inspired by stories of Jackson's Bank War, she returned to America in 1835. But her lectures, including speeches for Martin Van Buren, met with indifference or hostility. Newspaper editors called her the "Red Harlot of Infidelity," and pious parents used her name to frighten their children.

Wright settled in Cincinnati, where she lived out her life in oblivion, writing her memoirs, occasionally promoting her old causes, and winning a pioneering suit for divorce. In 1852, she died of complications from a broken hip. In her later years she became pessimistic about America. She felt as if she had "fallen from a strange planet among a race whose sense and perceptions are all different from my own."

Finally, the journeymen returned finished shoes to the central shops for inspection and packing. The new system of production made the master into a mere employer, the "shoe boss," and it eroded the workers' control over the pace and conditions of labor.

In 1830 the journeymen shoemakers of Lynn, Massachusetts, united to form the Mutual Benefit Society of Journeymen Cordwainers. Their goals were to defend their interests as employees and, insofar as possible, establish their independence from the shoe bosses. "The division of society into the producing and nonproducing classes," they explained, "and the fact of the unequal distribution of value between the two, introduced us at once to another distinction—that of capital and labor. . . . "Labor now becomes a commodity, wealth capital, and the natural order of things is entirely reversed." Therefore, "antagonism and opposition is introduced in the community; capital and labor stand opposed." In 1836 the cordwainers and journeymen printers each set up national craft unions to coordinate the activities of local unions.

The new unions of cordwainers and printers, and mechanics in similar situations, quickly turned to politics. Union members supported the Jacksonian movement, which in turn energized their own political efforts. Union members formed a small but vocal portion of the Democratic leadership. They became the most radical Democrats, agitating for antimonopoly legislation and antibanking regulations by the states, the adoption of universal suffrage for white men, and the abolition of imprisonment for debt. They also supported new taxes—general property taxes—that would apply to personal property such as stocks, bonds, machinery, and furniture as well as to real estate. In their political campaigns, the mechanics appealed to the spirit of the American Revolution. The revolution had destroyed the monopolies and special privileges created by the king, they said. Now a new revolution was needed to destroy the monopolies created by capital. Only then could individuals regain the dignity and independence befitting citizens of a republic.

During the 1830s, however, the threatened mechanics shifted away from politics to concentrate on the same economic issues being pressed by members of the building trades. Following the model of the Philadelphia building trades, unions formed citywide coalitions across craft lines. In 1834 federations from Boston to Philadelphia joined to form the National Trades' Union—the first national union of different trades. By 1836 federations from as far south as Washington, D.C., and as far west as Pittsburgh and Cincinnati had joined.

In a series of strikes and boycotts during the 1830s, workers across a broad spectrum of crafts successfully exploited their bargaining power; they forced employers to accept ten hours as the standard workday for most skilled workers in the large cities and for virtually all skilled workers in the building trades. Philadelphia was the scene of the most dramatic victories. In 1835 the Philadelphia city council set a ten-hour day on local public works, and the following year President Jackson, recognizing the importance of the support of the Philadelphia mechanics to his party, established a ten-hour day at the Philadelphia navy yard. The ten-hour day victories were significant: American skilled workers were the first in the industrializing world to wrest this concession from their employers.

Buoyed by their victories, the unions next turned their energies to winning increases in wages. They organized more than fifty strikes during 1836 and 1837. In most instances the strikers were victorious, often because of the cooperation of trade unions. For example, when the journeymen bookbinders in Philadelphia struck for higher wages in 1836, thirty-seven trade unions from New York to Washington provided the financial support that enabled the bookbinders to hold out for over two months. The grateful journeymen declared that their cause had become "the sacred cause of every skilled laborer in the civilized world."

Factory Workers

The success of the mechanics' organizations inspired another group of workers—factory laborers. They were a new group, without a history of organization or traditional craft identity, and they were poorer than the mechanics. Nonetheless, they marshalled the strength to resist the growing demands of their employers that they do more work for less pay.

There were about 20,000 cotton-mill operatives by the 1830s, mostly unskilled women and girls. To protest pay cuts or more stringent work rules, many of them engaged in sporadic strikes. In 1828, women mill workers in Dover, New Hampshire, had struck against two new rules. The first levied fines for lateness; the second initiated a system whereby employees leaving the mill would receive certificates of regular discharge only if they had been "faithful" employees. The strikers worried that rebellious workers would be fired and then be unable to find jobs because they lacked these certificates. The employers prevailed but in 1834 more than eight hundred Dover women struck again, protesting wage cuts. In Lowell, Massachusetts, 2,000 women backed up a strike in 1834 by withdrawing their savings from a Lowell bank owned by their employers. The *Boston Transcript* reported that "one of the leaders mounted a pump, and made a flaming . . . speech on the rights of women and the iniquities of the 'monied aristocracy.'" Nevertheless, the 1834 strikes failed. The employers fired the leaders, and the rest of the workers returned to the mills. The Lowell women remained restless and militant, however. Two years later, when the mill owners raised boardinghouse rents, Lowell workers organized again. This time their rallies, marches, and slowdown of production persuaded the owners to reduce or eliminate the rent increases.

Victories were rare, however. Strikes of unskilled operatives almost always failed. Overpowered by the employers and viewing factory employment as temporary and rather peripheral to their lives, women mill workers did not react to defeat by forming strong and permanent unions.

Employers on the Counterattack

Employers had resisted workers' demands since the end of the eighteenth century. But they had only rarely acted together to combat labor. Employers' cooperation had been limited to the regulation of production or the fixing of prices. In response to the waves of strikes in 1836 and 1837, however, employers from Massachusetts to St. Louis dramatically increased their mobilization against the unions. Among the antiunion tactics they developed was the *blacklist*. In 1836 employers in New York City agreed not to hire workers belonging to the Union Trade Society of Journeymen Tailors and circulated a list—a blacklist—of its members. The employers also used the courts. Their lawsuits targeted the *closed shop*—the requirement that employers hire only union members. Most unions secured closed shop agreements when they won wage increases. During the 1830s, employers sued the carpet weavers' union in Thompsonville, Connecticut; the shoemakers' unions in Geneva and Hudson, New York; the tailors' union in New York City; the plasterers' union in Philadelphia; and the union of journeymen cordwainers in Boston. Employers charged that closed shop agreements violated the common law or, in New York State, statutes that prohibited such "conspiracies."

The New York Supreme Court ruled against the Geneva shoemakers. The closed shop, the court held, had caused "an industrious man" to be "driven out of employment" and trade to be restricted. "It is important to the best interests of society," the court held, "that the price of labor be left to regulate itself." In other words, individual workers were denied the opportunity to organize. Following this precedent, a lower court found the New York tailors guilty of conspiracy.

Unions protested the decision. Twenty-seven thousand workers and their supporters demonstrated outside New York City Hall, and workers intimidated juries hearing similar cases. Later in 1836, juries acquitted the Hudson shoemakers, the Philadelphia plasterers, and the Thompsonville carpet makers.

The rising power of organized labor was particularly threatening to the business class. Unionization—the increasingly successful effort to democratize the workplace—was only part of the threat. At least as serious was the simultaneous democratization of national politics. It now appeared that workers, cooperating with other groups dissatisfied with the effects of the Industrial Revolution, might take control of government and try to check the power of the business class. In the mid-1830s, leaders of the business class themselves attempted to use the new, more democratic political system to win support, even among American workers, for their vision of American society.

Workers Protest, 1836

This poster appealed to workers to protest the conviction of the Geneva shoemakers for conspiracy. At the meeting held in the park fronting New York's City Hall, the crowd burned judges in effigy and passed resolutions calling for the creation of a new labor party.

Democrats and Whigs: The Second Party System, 1836–1844

Jackson's party and politics presented the northern business class with the first concerted threat to its power. To check the growing power of democracy, the leaders of the business class led in organizing a new national political grouping—the Whig party. The two parties that resulted, Democratic and Whig, constituted the Second Party System, which survived until the rise of the Republican party in the mid-1850s. Both political parties competed for support among farmers and urban workers, and in every electoral contest victory went to the party that appealed most successfully to Americans of modest wealth and social status.

The Emergence of the Whigs

As early as Jackson's first term, his opponents in Congress began to form an alliance. They called themselves "Whigs" and referred to Jackson as "King Andrew I." These names conjured up associations with the American and English parties—also called Whigs—that had opposed the power of King George III. Whigs charged that Jackson had violated the Constitution through tyrannical abuses of executive power and that Whigs were better defenders of the republic than Democrats. In effect, the Whigs were attempting to turn Jackson's republican rhetoric against him.

Initially, the congressional Whigs were united only by their common opposition to President Jackson. They included Senators Webster of Massachusetts, Clay of Kentucky, and Calhoun of South Carolina. Webster and Clay had a bond of common economic interests; Webster spoke on behalf of New England's business elite, and Clay represented the commercial interests of the Ohio and Mississippi valleys. Calhoun, having broken with Jackson over nullification, had little choice but to join the Whigs. However, as a representative of the planter class of the lower South, he had reservations about the economic ideas of his congressional allies.

Jackson's victory over Henry Clay in the 1832 presidential election deeply troubled Jackson's congressional opponents. They regarded Jackson's election as a popular mandate for his position on the Second Bank. Clay and Webster feared that Jackson had opened the door for the destruction of all privilege and the undermining of legislative government. In Webster's home state of Massachusetts, Whigs listened apprehensively as the Jacksonian George Bancroft told the workingmen of Northampton:

> The feud between the capitalist and the laborer, the house of Have and the house of Want, is as old as social union. . . . It is now for the yeomanry and the mechanics to march at the head of civilization. The merchants and the lawyers, that is, the moneyed interest, broke up feudalism. The day for the multitude has now dawned.

To check such democratization, the congressional Whigs began elaborating their own plan for the nation's future. By the 1836 election, they had formulated a well-defined alternative to the Democratic vision and had begun to popularize it among the northern middle class.

A Whig Cartoon

This political cartoon lampooned Andrew Jackson as a monarch decked out with the trappings of royalty and trampling on the Constitution. The cartoon emphasized Jackson's contempt for judges and criticized many of his political appointments. It concluded by asking, "Shall he reign over us, or shall the PEOPLE RULE?"

Whig Ideology. Whigs believed it was "natural" for a relatively few individuals to acquire a large share of the nation's wealth, to represent the people in a republican government, and to use government power as they thought necessary for the welfare of all. They attempted to reconcile their elitism with republican ideals in several ways. First, they asserted that American society was really classless because it did not ascribe permanent status to groups and individuals, and because its institutions fostered upward mobility. Second, they argued that in a republic it was "natural" for wealthy individuals to represent other citizens. Constrained by a republican Constitution and the moral influence of religion, elites would govern in the best interests of all. Third, pointing to the dramatic advances in banking, manufacturing, and transportation, the Whigs claimed that a strong ruling elite promoted economic growth, which strengthened the republic by creating a more prosperous citizenry and unifying labor and capital.

To the Whigs, even the most modern factories were sources of potential social harmony. In 1830, Edward Everett, a congressman from Massachusetts and a leading Whig publicist, told a Fourth of July crowd in Lowell that "the alliance which you have . . . established between labor and capital . . . may truly be called a holy alliance." He proclaimed that factories like those at Lowell "form a mutually beneficial connection between those who have nothing but their muscular power and those who are able to bring into the partnership . . . property which was itself, originally, the work of men's hands, but has been converted, by accumulation and thrift, from labor into capital." He concluded, "Woe to the land where labor and intelligence are at war! Happy the land whose various interests are united together by the bonds of mutual benefit and kind feeling!"

The Whigs criticized Jackson and the Democrats for underestimating the possibilities for upward mobility, for pitting the poor against the rich, and for disrupting social harmony. They attacked Jackson's strong presidency, warning against powerful, highly individualistic executives who pandered to the growing masses of voters. And the Whigs claimed that Democratic economic programs would turn back the clock, impoverishing and weakening the republic.

As an alternative, the Whigs offered legislative rule and a program of governmental intervention in the economy. They wanted to see a more vigorous national government, with Congress rather than the president exercising leadership. And the Whigs advocated the economic programs of the American System of Henry Clay and John Quincy Adams.

Calhoun's Appeal to Capitalists. The only congressional opponents of Andrew Jackson who had reservations about the full-blown Whig ideology and program were Calhoun and his southern followers. Calhoun's greatest concern was over the Whig objection to fixed classes, but he also disliked Whig nationalism and Clay's tariff policies. Calhoun argued that the Whig ideal of equal opportunity contradicted the realities of slavery and of an industrial society. In 1837 he wrote, "There is and always has been in an advanced stage of wealth and civilization a conflict between labor and capital." He argued that southern slaveowners and northern factory owners belonged to the same privileged class and faced the same threat from below. Calhoun therefore urged northern capitalists to join a defensive alliance with the planters. In his view, social harmony was possible only through the recognition, acceptance, and reinforcement of existing sharp distinctions of class. Whigs, he argued, ought to unite around a common defense of privilege and social order.

The other Whig leaders refused to accept Calhoun's antidemocratic analysis. Calhoun's description of "a clear and well-defined line between capital and labor," Daniel Webster agreed, might fit the South or Europe. But in the North, "this distinction grows less and less definite as commerce advances." Pointing to Massachusetts, Webster declared, "I do not believe there is on earth, in a highly civilized society, a greater equality in the condition of men than exists there." Webster maintained that Calhoun had neglected the growing importance of the northern middle class. As it turned out, it was the middle class, attracted by the promise of upward mobility, that became the backbone of the Whig, and later the Republican, party.

The Whig Coalition

Led by the congressional Whigs, a coalition of groups emerged to run candidates at the state and local levels in 1834 in opposition to the Jacksonian Democrats. These groups proved powerful enough to gain control of the House of Representatives in 1834. The coalition was strongest in New England, New York, and the new communities along the shores of the Great Lakes. The American System had the greatest appeal in those areas because they had the highest concentrations of prosperous farmers, small-town merchants, and the machinists and other skilled industrial workers who identified with their employers. Whig politicians realized that they had interests in common with business-class enthusiasts for moral reform. Government intervention along Whig lines could be seen as part of a comprehensive program designed to restore social harmony and invigorate the Industrial Revolution. And, on a practical level, Whig leaders found that those workers and farmers who had been drawn to the perfectionist message of evangelical Protestantism tended also to embrace Whig politics, with its emphasis on individual upward mobility and social improvement.

The Whig message, as publicized by Henry Clay, also won support from people of southern origin in the Ohio and Mississippi valleys. The farmers, bankers, and shopkeepers in the southern tier of the northwestern states differed from northern Whigs in their religious affiliations and culture. But they agreed that positive government action—conscious planning and collective effort—was needed for economic development. They found public investment in internal improvements particularly attractive, and they supported the ideal of a classless society led by "natural" elites. Consequently they gradually formed alliances with the business class to the north.

In the South, support for the Whig party was less cohesive, resting more on the appeal of specific elements in the Whig program than on the force of the Whigs' social vision. For example, many of the nonslaveholding whites in the backcountry, especially in western Virginia and the deepest hill country of the other seaboard states, were Whigs because they favored a federal program of banking and internal improvement to break the grip of planter elites. A significant Whig minority also existed among wealthy planters who had invested heavily in railroads, banks, and factories and maintained close ties to northern markets and New York capitalists. Finally, some states' rights Democrats in Virginia and South Carolina, upset with Andrew Jackson's threat of force to suppress nullification, joined the Whigs, at least temporarily.

The Election of 1836. In the 1836 presidential election, the voters faced Martin Van Buren—the Democratic candidate handpicked by Jackson as his successor. He ran on Jackson's record, which now included not only the Bank veto but also the Bank war. The Democrats claimed that they offered Americans "liberty"—in contrast with the coercion threatened by the Whigs and the social elites the Democrats said the Whigs represented. The Whigs ran three presidential candidates, hoping to maximize the opposition votes from the various sections and to force the election into the House of Representatives, which the Whigs now controlled. The plan failed. The total electoral votes collected by the Whigs—73 by William Henry Harrison of Ohio, 26 by Hugh L. White of Tennessee, and 14 by Daniel Webster—fell short of Van Buren's 170 votes. Van Buren's Democratic base of electoral support in the populous states of New York, Pennsylvania, and Virginia had proved decisive. Still, the size of the Whig vote showed that their message of social development—economic improvement and moral uplift—had strong appeal, not only to middle-class Americans but also to farmers and workers with little or no property. Van Buren had prevailed, but his political problems were just beginning.

The Depression of 1837–1843

The prolonged and steady expansion of the economy from 1820 to 1837 had led many citizens to believe that prosperity was a permanent feature of life. Few realized that their prosperity still depended heavily on events in Europe. True, American production for export was declining relative to production for domestic consumption and cotton exports were important primarily to the South. But any disruption of foreign credit flowing to the South had severe ripple effects on the entire economy. Furthermore, American industrialization and territorial expansion depended on large amounts of long-term investment from Europe, primarily from Great Britain, to finance the construction of canals and railroads. Whenever the flow of investment came to a halt, depression was apt to radiate throughout the American economy. Amplifying these problems was the fact that industrialization had made the economy more complex; its parts were more interdependent. Disruptions in any sector had more serious effects on the entire economy than they had previously.

The Panic of 1837. The Panic of 1837 began in Britain. In late 1836 the Bank of England, convinced that it was sending too much specie to the United States, curtailed the flow of investment. Partly as a result, British demand for cotton declined sharply, causing the bankruptcy of British and American mercantile firms whose lending was based on cotton as security. These events set off a wave of bankruptcies and restrictions of credit that affected merchants and bankers throughout the United States. Lacking adequate credit, American trade, manufacturing, and farming slid into a depression.

Years of Depression. The depression dragged on until 1843, becoming the most severe depression endured by the nation prior to the 1870s. The Bank of England continued to keep credit tight until the early 1840s. At the same time bumper cotton crops in the late 1830s drove down cotton prices, making matters even worse for merchants in international trade. Many states, unable to raise taxes or to borrow in depressed conditions, defaulted on the bonds they had issued to finance canal building and thereby undermined British confidence in American investments. To protect themselves, American

The Aftermath of the Panic of 1837

The cartoon pictures the Independence Day celebration in New York in 1837 as marred by the symptoms of economic depression—unemployed workers, mothers begging and pawning their possessions, goods that cannot be sold, Sheriff's sales of property, runs on banks, and alcoholism. A prison and almshouse are in the background.

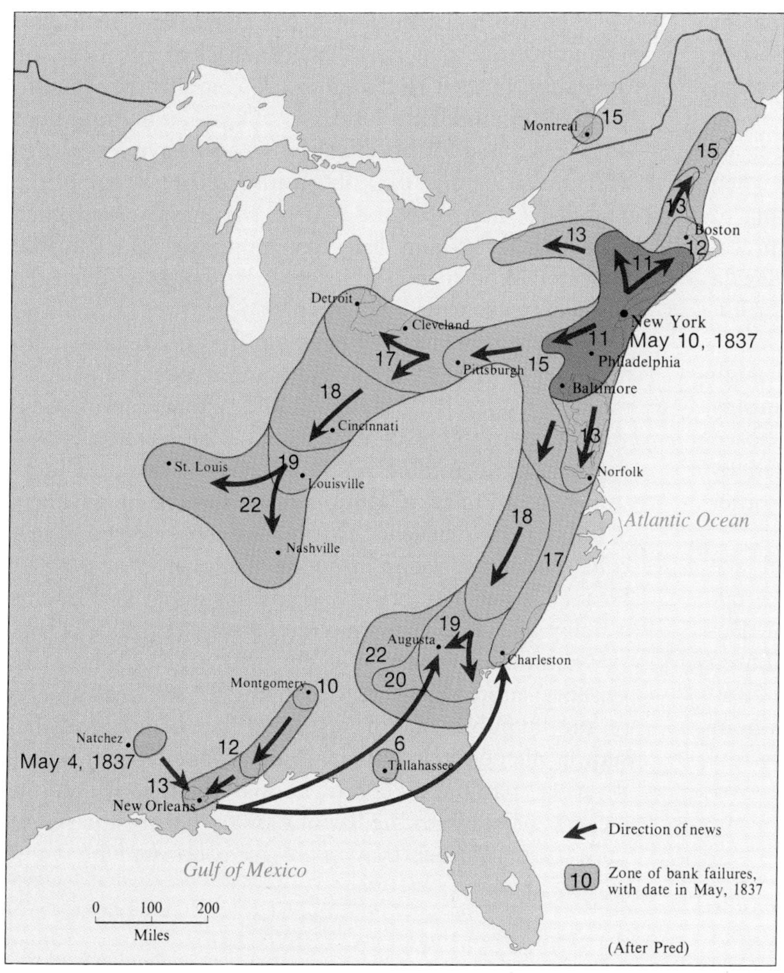

MAP 11.3

Anatomy of a Panic: Bank Suspensions in May 1837

Although the first bank failures occurred in Natchez and Tallahassee, it was the collapse of New York City banks several days later that precipitated a chain reaction of national panic. Rivers, canals, and post roads carried news of the panic from New York to St. Louis in just twelve days. The resulting pattern of bank failures provides a dramatic picture of the economic nerve system of the nation—a nerve system dominated by New York.

banks insisted on holding larger amounts of specie. But this cautious policy reduced the amount of money available to the general public. As a result, overall spending, capital investment, and prices declined even further, deepening the depression.

By 1843, as compared to 1837, prices on the average had fallen by almost half and overall investment in the American economy had declined by almost 25 percent—led by a 90 percent drop in canal construction. Investment in railroads and manufacturing also fell dramatically. Slumping investment and production forced workers out of jobs, and in 1838 unemployment rose to an unprecedented level of almost 10 percent; in seaports and industrial centers it approached 20 percent. Taken together with the bankruptcies of farms and businesses, a vast spectrum of Americans were stricken. In the words of Reverend Henry Ward Beecher:

> The world looked upon a continent of inexhaustible fertility (whose harvest had glutted the markets, and rotted in disuse), filled with lamentation, and its inhabitants wandering like bereaved citizens among the ruins of an earthquake, mourning for children, for houses crushed, and property buried forever.

Economic instability was now a significant part of American life. It heightened all the other disruptive forces of the Industrial Revolution. And its effects were particularly harsh on people who lacked property or skills.

The Destruction of the Labor Movement. As might be expected, the depression shattered the labor movement. Union successes in the early 1830s had been based on labor shortages. But now, for the first time in fifty years, there was a surplus of skilled workers. For example, in 1837 six thousand masons, carpenters, and other building-trade workers were discharged in New York City alone. The dramatic rise in unemployment among skilled workers decimated union membership.

The mechanics faced additional dilemmas. Factory competition had already forced large numbers of them to abandon their crafts and consequently their union movement. During the depression increasing numbers of mechanics, despairing of the possibility of organizing to oppose the forces of industrialization, simply dropped out of the labor movement. Consequently, most local unions and workers' assemblies and all the national labor organizations disappeared, along with their newspapers and other publications.

One of the few bright spots for the labor movement during the depression came in 1842, when Chief Justice Lemuel Shaw of Massachusetts handed down his ruling in *Commonwealth v. Hunt.* The case had begun in 1840, when the Whig district attorney for the city of Boston brought members of the Boston Journeymen Bootmakers' Society into municipal court for trying to enforce a closed shop. Shaw overturned earlier precedent by making two critical rulings: (1) a union was a criminal organization only if its *objectives* were criminal; and (2) union members were within their rights in attempting to enforce closed shops, even through strikes. This decision discouraged courts from finding that unions were inherently criminal or that the closed shop was socially harmful. But courts, dominated by unsympathetic Whig judges, still usually found other grounds to restrict strikes and boycotts.

Workers, with their unions destroyed and the movement for greater democracy in the workplace faltering, increasingly turned to politics, where the Democrats offered a warm welcome. President Van Buren continued Jackson's effort to court workers and in 1840 he signed an executive order establishing the ten-hour day for federal employees. Ironically, this victory, the most dramatic achievement of the early labor movement, came after the unions had lost their power in the marketplace.

The Election of 1840

The election of 1840, held in the midst of the depression, created a political crisis for the Democrats. Ironically, Andrew Jackson's success now proved to be a liability. In turning the presidency into an agent of the people, Jackson had convinced many Americans that the president could make a difference in maintaining prosperity. Most people did not understand the overwhelming influence of international forces on the business cycle, and they readily blamed Jackson and Van Buren for their economic troubles. In particular, they decided that Jackson had been wrong to attack the Second Bank and was responsible for the Panic of 1837.

President Van Buren seemed helpless in the face of the political crisis. The only substantial measures successfully sponsored by his administration were the ten-hour day for federal employees and the Independent Treasury Act. The latter confirmed the public's identification of the Democrats as the antibanking party by requiring the federal government to keep its cash in government vaults rather than in banks. Its chief objective was to prevent the government from playing favorites among bankers, and from using federal deposits to promote banking and expand the money supply.

William Henry Harrison. The Whigs made the most of their opponents' discomfiture. The depression was helping them—it was discrediting the Democrats, making it less important that the Whigs take clear positions on the issues. In their first national convention they renominated William Henry Harrison of Ohio, a military hero who was noted for his victories—over native Americans at Tippecanoe and over the British in the Battle of the Thames (Ontario) in the War of 1812. Harrison lacked executive ability and was sixty-eight years old. But that mattered little to the Whig leaders, Clay and Webster. They did not want a strong president; they planned to use Harrison as the rubber stamp for congressional enactment of the Whig program. Moreover, Harrison's military record, Virginia roots, and strong identification with western interests made him a Whig version of Andrew Jackson. And Harrison believed he matched Jackson's commitment to democracy, although he gave it a Whig twist. He believed that democracy coupled with a robust banking system provided "the only means, under Heaven, by which a poor industrious man may become a rich man without bowing to colossal wealth."

Economic events stacked the cards against Van Buren. A more charismatic man might have been able to retain the public's favor in spite of the economic ills besetting the country. But Van Buren was known primarily as a manipulative professional politician. And he lacked the ties with the Revolutionary generation or the military experience that might have boosted his vote-getting appeal.

The Log-Cabin Campaign. In the 1840 campaign, the Whigs concentrated on organizing the electorate and demonstrating their commitment to upward social mobility rather than taking a stand on issues. As a result, the Harrison campaign was the first in American history to be conducted as an exuberant carnival. The Whigs turned pamphleteering, songfests, parades, and well-orchestrated mass meetings into a new political style that would become the norm for American elections. The colorful Whig spectacles helped persuade participants and observers alike that they were all engaged in a fundamentally democratic cause. The Whigs also made the most of the democratic message in their nomination of a popular war hero who had worked himself up from the ranks. When a Democratic newspaper unwisely described Harrison as a man who would be happy to retire to a log cabin if he had a pension and an ample supply of hard cider, the Whigs quickly seized on the description to promote their candidate as a simple man who loved log cabins and cider. Although Harrison was actually a man of some wealth, the 1840 election became the "log-cabin" campaign, and the candidate demonstrated his common touch by breaking precedent and joining the campaign celebrations.

The Whigs succeeded in their strategy of portraying their candidate as a man of the people and blaming the

The Log-Cabin Campaign, 1840
Campaign banners such as this one portrayed Harrison as a simple, generous, and patriotic man of the people.

Democrats for the depression. Although their popular victory was a narrow one, the Whigs won an overwhelming electoral victory (including the votes of New York and Pennsylvania); and they won control of Congress. Popular interest in a presidential election had never been greater. Whereas less than 60 percent of the eligible voters had taken part in 1832 and 1836, more than 80 percent voted in 1840.

The Resurgence of the Democratic Party

The election of Harrison seemed to clear the way for the enactment of Henry Clay's economic program. The Whigs had the misfortune, however, of immediately losing the leader on whom they had pinned their hopes, when Harrison died of pneumonia one month after his inauguration. Succeeding him was Vice-President John Tyler, a Virginian who was far from being the typical southern Whig. Tyler actually opposed the urban commercial interests in his own state and had shared Andrew Jackson's hostility to the Second Bank. He had joined the Whig party because of his enthusiasm for states' rights and his disgust with Jackson's nationalism.

John Tyler. As president, Tyler betrayed the Whig party. He took it on himself to block, singlehandedly, the Whig program of economic nationalism. He vetoed two bills sponsored by Senator Henry Clay to reestablish the national bank. He also blocked major protective tariffs. Clay broke with Tyler in disgust. Then Tyler's cabinet, all of them Whigs, resigned, with the exception of Secretary of State Daniel Webster.

Whig successes during the Tyler administration were few and limited: repeal of the independent Treasury in 1841 and a modest increase in tariffs in 1842. The most important legislation of Tyler's administration—the Preemption Act—passed because strong western support for it had forced the Whigs to work with the Democrats.

The Preemption Act of 1841 gave most American citizens and also immigrants the right to stake a claim to 160 acres of land and then to purchase it later at the standard price of $1.25 an acre, provided they built a house on the land and made other "improvements"—such as clearing the land. The preemption process recognized that people commonly settled on public land before purchasing it from the government. Its intent was to give an advantage to actual settlers over land speculators; its effect was to accelerate the pace of westward expansion.

The New Democratic Coalition. Tyler's rejection of Clay's American System gave the Democrats some precious time—time they needed to consolidate their opposition to the Whigs. During the 1840s the Democratic party vigorously recruited support among the farming community: poor farmers in the North, planters and small farmers in the South. At the same time, the party went after the votes of the urban working class, in part by strongly opposing any economic program that seemed to offer benefits to wealthy members of the business class. Immigrant workers provided a new source of support—in particular, the Catholic immigrants, who were repelled by the insistent Protestantism of the Whigs and appreciated the Democrats' greater acceptance of religious and economic diversity. In New York City during the 1840s, about 95 percent of Irish Catholic voters supported Democratic candidates.

Thus for the first time two national parties were competing vigorously for the loyalties of a mass electorate. Each of the parties relied on a network of newspapers to convey its message; virtually every crossroads town had both a Jacksonian and Whig newspaper. In Washington, D.C., the *Washington Globe* represented the Democrats, while the *National Intelligencer* spoke for the Whigs. Each of the parties offered distinct visions of industrialization and of the social and political order, and they competed on terms that were reasonably equal. The Democrats held an edge in party discipline and mass loyalty. But in organizing popular appeals the Whigs had a major advantage in their wealth and the cohesiveness of their leadership and support. That support was based on the interests of the business class, yet the Whigs also managed to make powerful inroads among workers and farmers.

The Second Party System was in place. The new two-party competition invigorated American democracy. Both Democrats and Whigs built coalitions of diverse groups and interests. Each party tried to persuade Americans to use its ideas and rhetoric in approaching every public issue. Each party established a national identity and helped to dilute and diffuse sectional disagreements. The parties were managed by professional politicians who worked to create a political "product" that would satisfy as many different kinds of voters as possible. Together, the two parties molded a new political culture.

Summary

The rise of the business class stimulated group consciousness throughout American society. All groups saw politics as the best way to advance their interests (sometimes by blocking the interests of others), and their collective pressure forced a democratization of politics—a democratic revolution—during the 1820s and 1830s. That revolution swept Andrew Jackson into the presidency, and he mobilized the support of large numbers of laborers, farmers, and southern planters behind the Democratic party. He was the first president to regard himself as an instrument of democracy—of the will of the majority—and not simply as the enforcer of the nation's laws. In the process of implementing his vision he transformed his party and the presidency into powerful instruments for majority rule.

Some workers, especially those who practiced traditional skills, sought democracy in their places of work. They challenged the new industrial order and the power of the business class—not only through politics but also through a union movement. They sought to reform working conditions by forming labor unions to demand a ten-hour day and by establishing political parties to promote a more equitable society. Strikes increased during the 1830s, and the unions made some limited gains.

The democratic revolution, dramatized by Jackson's veto of the rechartering of the Second Bank of the United States, disturbed the emerging business class and stimulated the formation of the Whig party. Its initial goal was to check the power of the mass-based Democratic party. But the new political realities forced the Whigs to design a message that would have broad appeal to common people. Led by Henry Clay and Daniel Webster, the Whigs invited middle-class Americans to join the business class, and designed an ideology and a program to reconcile elitism with republican ideals. While Democrats emphasized liberty, the Whigs stressed material improvement and opportunity. This marked the beginning of the Second Party System. The democratic revolution was now carried forward by the intense competition between the Whig and Democratic parties, both of which established coalitions of support that were national in scope.

The depression following the Panic of 1837 halted both the labor movement and Jacksonianism and contributed to the election of a Whig president, William Henry Harrison. But the betrayal of the Whigs by Harrison's successor, John Tyler, blocked the enactment of the Whig economic program.

TOPIC FOR RESEARCH

Andrew Jackson and the Cherokee Nation

Andrew Jackson worked out his political and social philosophies in writing his various messages to Congress. In his second annual message to Congress, delivered on December 6, 1830, he outlined at some length the justification for removing the southern Indians. In 1835 representatives of the Cherokee nation sent Congress an eloquent statement of their own.

First read the two statements carefully and summarize the main arguments of each. Then go beyond the documents. Jackson and the Cherokee were each trying to persuade audiences. What audiences, do you think, each was trying to reach? How did the two sides differ in their understanding of American society? Was there any common ground between Jackson and the Cherokee? On the basis of the ideas expressed by Jackson and the Cherokee and what you know about the Jacksonian era, do you think there was any way whites and native Americans could have lived in harmony?

BIBLIOGRAPHY

Democratizing Politics and Andrew Jackson

Many books explore the Jacksonian era, but the most useful surveys are Edward Pessen, *Jacksonian America* (1970); Glydon Van Duesen, *The Jacksonian Era* (1959); and Harry L. Watson, *Liberty and Power: The Politics of Jacksonian America* (1990). Arthur M. Schlesinger, Jr., *The Age of Jackson* (1945), initiated modern reexamination of Andrew Jackson. Among the most provocative are other older studies: Lee Benson, *The Concept of Jacksonian Democracy: New York as a Test Case* (1961); Marvin Meyers, *The Jacksonian Persuasion: Politics and Belief* (1957); and John William Ward, *Andrew Jackson; Symbol for an Age* (1962). More recently scholars have studied Jacksonian democracy in the context of democratic political culture and the rise of the Second Party System (see below). Books treating Jackson's Indian policy and the Indians themselves include Ralph S. Cotterill, *The Southern Indians* (1954); Grant Forman, *Indian Removal* (1953); Michael D. Green, *The Politics of Indian Removal* (1982); William G. McLoughlin, *Cherokee Renascence in the New Republic* (1986); and Ronald N. Satz, *American Indian Policy in the Jacksonian Era* (1975). On the nullification crises, see William W. Freehling, *Prelude to Civil War* (1966), and Richard E. Ellis, *The Union at Risk* (1987). On the spoils system, see Leonard D. White, *The Jacksonians: A Study in Administrative History, 1828–1861* (1954). For biographies of leading figures, see Robert V. Remini, *Andrew Jackson and the Course of American Freedom, 1822–1833* (1977), *Andrew Jackson and the Course of American Democracy, 1833–1845* (1984), and *The Life of Andrew Jackson* (1988). On John Quincy Adams, see Samuel Flagg Bemis, *John Quincy Adams and the Union* (1956), and Leonard L. Richards, *The Life and Times of Congressman John Quincy Adams* (1986). On Martin Van Buren, see John Niven, *Martin Van Buren: The Romantic Age of American Politics* (1983); Robert V. Remini, *Martin Van Buren and the Making of the Democratic Party* (1959); and James C. Curtis, *The Fox at Bay* (1970). The Great Triumverate has attracted numerous biographers. On *John C. Calhoun,* see Richard N. Current, *John C. Calhoun* (1963), and Charles M. Wiltse, *John C. Calhoun* (3 vols., 1944–1951); on Daniel Webster, see Irving H. Bartlett, *Daniel Webster* (1978); and on Henry Clay, see Robert V. Remini, *Henry Clay: Statesman for the Union* (1991). For the presidency of John Tyler, see Robert J. Morgan, *A Whig Embattled* (1954).

The Early Labor Movement

An earlier generation of historians of labor emphasized the organization of unions during early industrialization. See Norman Ware, *The Industrial Worker, 1840–1860* (1924), and John R. Commons, *History of Labour in the United States,* Vol. 1 (1918). More recently, historians have carefully explored the political context of the labor movement. See Mary H. Blewett, *Men, Women, and Work: Class, Gender, and Protest in the New England Shoe Industry, 1780–1910* (1988); Alan Dawley, *Class and Community: The Industrial Revolution in Lynn Massachusetts, 1780–1860* (1981); Paul G. Faler, *Mechanics and Manufacturers in the Early Industrial Revolution: Lynn, Massachusetts* (1981); Susan E. Hirsch, *Roots of the American Working Class: The Industrialization of Crafts in Newark, 1800–1860* (1978); Bruce Laurie, *Working People of Philadelphia, 1800–1860* (1980); Jonathan Prude, *The Coming of the Industrial Order: Town and Factory Life in Rural Massachusetts, 1810–1860* (1983); and Sean Wilentz, *Chants Democratic, New York City and the Rise of the American Working Class, 1788–1850* (1984).

TIMELINE

1825	John Quincy Adams elected president by House of Representatives
1827	Philadelphia Working Men's Party organized
1828	The Tariff of Abominations Andrew Jackson elected *The South Carolina Exposition and Protest*
1830	Journeymen cordwainers organize Indian Removal Act
1831	*Cherokee Nation v. Georgia*
1832	Jackson vetoes renewal of charter of Second Bank of the United States South Carolina nullifies the Tariff of Abominations
1833	Force bill and Compromise Tariff
1835	Ten-hour day for skilled workers
1836	Texans proclaim independence from Mexico Martin Van Buren elected president
1837	Depression of 1837–1843 begins
1838	Trail of Tears
1840	William Henry Harrison elected president
1841	John Tyler succeeds to presidency Preemption Act

The Whigs and the Second Party System

A rich literature describes the emergence of the Whigs and the larger topic—the formation of the Second Party System. Books that deal broadly with the new party structure include Richard Hofstadter, *The Idea of a Party System* (1972); Daniel W. Howe, *The Political Culture of the American Whigs* (1979); Robert Kelley, *The Cultural Pattern in American Politics: The First Century* (1979); Lawrence F. Kohl, *The Politics of Individualism: Parties and the American Character in the Jacksonian Era* (1989); Richard P. McCormick, *The Second American Party System: Party Formation in the Jacksonian Era* (1966); and Joel H. Silbey, *The Partisan Imperative: The Dynamics of American Politics before the Civil War* (1985). Studies that are more specialized include Thomas Brown, *Politics and Statesmanship: Essays on the American Whig Party,* (1985); Ronald P. Formisano, *The Birth of Mass Political Parties: Michigan, 1827–1861* (1971), and *The Transformation of Political Culture: Massachusetts Parties, 1790s–1840s* (1983); William G. Shade, *Banks or No Banks: The Money Issue in Western Politics, 1832–1865* (1972); Harry L. Watson, *Jacksonian Politics and Community Conflict: The Emergence of the Second Party System in Cumberland County, North Carolina* (1981); and Chilton Williamson, *American Suffrage from Property to Democracy, 1760–1860* (1960).

The Shaker Community at Poland Hill, Maine (detail)

This Shaker community in Poland Hill, Maine, painted by Joshua H. Bussell around 1850, had typical Shaker architecture—unadorned buildings and a large central dwelling for communal living. (Collection of the United Society of Shakers)

CHAPTER 12 *Freedom's Crusaders,* 1820–1860

The Industrial Revolution and territorial expansion had contradictory effects on the way Americans thought about themselves as individuals and as a society. Growing economic opportunity seemed to liberate individuals, to make men and women believe that each person could become the master of his or her own fate.

But the changes also brought new restraints and obligations. The new economic order demanded social organization and an increasing degree of standardization. For one thing, men and women had to submit to common disciplines of work. And in order to solve a new array of social and economic problems, they had to accept a greater measure of discipline—working cooperatively, for example, within the Second Party System.

Alexis de Tocqueville observed the contest between the supremacy of the individual and the demands of social responsibility during his 1831–1832 tour of the United States. In *Democracy in America* he described the tendency of Americans to be moved in opposite ways, by self-interest but also by devotion to the interests of the community. Americans, he said, seemed at one time to be "animated by the most selfish cupidity; at another by the most lively patriotism." These opposing passions were so powerful, he thought, that Americans must have them "united and mingled in some part of their character."

It was on account of these conflicting passions that a wave of reform movements washed over America during the Industrial Revolution. The wave of reform movements was so strong that it spilled out of the conservative channels first carved by business-class reformers—those who had championed regular church attendance, abstinence from alcohol, and the embrace of evangelical religion—to challenge some basic premises of American society. The labor movement offered sweeping criticism of industrial society, but its appeal did not win wide support from middle-class Americans, and labor's power waned after the Panic of 1837. In contrast, the new reform movements won a growing middle-class following during the 1840s and 1850s, despite their radical edge. The radical movements also broke through the walls erected by national politicians to bring order to American public life and control debate over social issues. Radical reformers demanded action; they either sought change outside the political system or demanded that it respond immediately to their ideals.

The effort to abolish slavery was the most disruptive of the radical movements, and it confronted American politicians with their greatest challenge. Abolitionism's appeal was sectional. It won broad popular support in the North by condemning slavery for denying freedom to enslaved people and threatening the liberty of free people, but it provoked outrage throughout most of the South. Would the dominant parties address the issue of slavery? If so, could they still maintain their national support—and the unity of the republic? The answers to these questions would come during the 1840s and 1850s.

Transcendentalists and Utopians

Among the reformers who most vigorously championed individual freedom—the liberation of individuals to act freely on their own personal choices—were the transcendentalists. They were a group of intellectuals who emerged in the New England heartland of the Industrial Revolution. At first they sought primarily to loosen the constraints imposed by traditional Congregationalist faith, but some became so distressed over the difficulties of individual fulfillment that they rejected industrial society as well. Many of these radical transcendentalists, like other groups of Americans, withdrew into utopian experimental communities. These communities had diverse goals, ranging from the establishment of a separate, more rewarding society for like-minded people to the transformation of American society as a whole by setting an inspiring example.

Ralph Waldo Emerson

The first transcendentalists were young men—often young Unitarian ministers—and were generally members of wealthy and privileged New England families. They were American romantics; they focused on ideas they borrowed from philosopher Immanuel Kant and from German romanticism, as translated by Harvard professor Edward Everett, who had studied in Germany, and the English poet Samuel Taylor Coleridge. Like the German and English romantics, they believed that behind the concrete world of the senses was another, *ideal* order of reality. This reality "transcended," or went beyond, the usual ways by which people know the world. This ideal reality could be known only by mysterious intuitive powers through which, at moments of inspiration, people would travel past the limits of their ordinary experience and gain mystical knowledge of ultimate and eternal things. The intellectual leader of the transcendentalists—and the most popular of all of them—was a second-generation Unitarian minister, Ralph Waldo Emerson.

Emerson resigned his Boston pulpit in 1832, at the age of twenty-nine, after a crisis of conscience that led him to choose individual moral insight over organized religion. He moved to Concord, Massachusetts, and turned to writing essays and lecturing, supported in part by a legacy from his first wife. His message centered on the idea of the radically free individual. "Our age," Emerson's great complaint began, "is retrospective." People were trapped in their inherited institutions and societies. They wore the ideas of people from earlier times—the tenets of New England Calvinism, for example—as a kind of "faded masquerade." They needed to break free of the boundaries of tradition and custom. This could be done only if each individual discovered his or her own "original relation with Nature." Emerson celebrated individuality, self-reliance, dissent, and nonconformity as the only methods by which a person might become free to discover a private harmony with what he called, in almost mystical fashion, "currents of Universal Being." And for Emerson, the ideal setting for such a discovery was nature—solitude under an open sky, among nature's rocks and trees.

Emerson's message reached hundreds of thousands of people, primarily through his lectures. Public lectures had become a spectacularly successful new way of spreading information and fostering discussion across the boundaries of religious and political institutions. In 1826, an organization known as the American Lyceum formed to "promote the general diffusion of knowledge." The Lyceum organized lecture tours by speakers of all sort—poets, preachers, scientists, reformers—and soon it took firm hold, especially in the North. In 1839, 137 local Lyceum groups in Massachusetts invited slates of lecturers to their towns during the fall and winter "season" to speak to more than 33,000 subscribers. Of all the hundreds of lecturers on the Lyceum circuit, Emerson was the most popular. Between 1833 and 1860, he gave fifteen hundred lectures in more than three hundred different towns in twenty states.

Emerson's celebration of the liberated individual tapped currents of faith that already ran deep among his middle-class audiences. The publication of the autobiography of Benjamin Franklin in 1818 had earlier given Americans a down-to-earth model of an individual determined to reach "moral perfection" by the solitary cultivation of private virtues. Charles Grandison Finney's account of his own conversion experience in 1823 pointed in Emersonian directions, too. Finney pictured his conversion as a mystical union of an individual, alone in the woods, with God. In addition, Emerson's notion that a solitary individual could transcend the constraining boundaries of society, and discover a new self, was a familiar idea to the millions of Americans who read the fiction of Washington Irving and James Fenimore Cooper.

Emerson's romantic individualism, however, was more extreme. His pantheism stood outside Christian doctrine, and after he criticized organized religion in an address to the senior class of the Harvard Divinity School in 1838, Harvard refused to invite him back for thirty years. Moreover, Emerson criticized the new industrial society. He observed the life of New Englanders who had been forced to abandon their farms for factories, and sensed "the disproportion between their faculties and the work offered them." And he worried that a preoccupation with the consumption of factory-made goods would drain the moral energy of the more affluent. "Things are in the saddle," Emerson wrote, "and ride mankind."

Emerson's genius was his capacity to translate radical but vague ideas into examples that made sense—and were acceptable—to ordinary middle-class Americans. He soft-pedaled some of his more radical ideas in his lectures. Thus, he described his pantheism as the idea that all of nature was saturated with the presence of God. Emerson said that if God was everywhere, then he was present in even the most routine sights of everyday life, a bare pasture or a railroad. In the same way, Emerson took the edge off his hostility to materialism. He translated the celebration of the possibilities of human achievement into a celebration of common things that philosophers had traditionally ignored or scorned. At times he even celebrated money itself. It was not "the root of all evil." Instead, it "represents the prose of life. [It] is in its effects and laws, as beautiful as roses."

Emerson's Disciples

Emerson hoped to expand the influence of transcendentalism by revolutionizing literature—by creating a genuinely democratic American literature. In 1837 he had delivered an address at Harvard entitled "The American Scholar," intended as a literary declaration of independence from what he called the "courtly muse" of old Europe. He urged American writers to celebrate democracy and individual freedom, to find their inspiration in the "familiar, the low . . . the milk in the pan; the ballad in the street; the news of the boat; the glance of the eye; the form and gait of the body."

Henry David Thoreau. Henry David Thoreau heeded Emerson's call. Thoreau, who lived near Emerson in Concord, Massachusetts, decided to take Emerson's notion of solitude in nature quite literally. He built a cabin at the edge of Walden Pond, near Concord, and lived there from 1845 to 1847. In 1854, he published an account of his experiment in self-reliance, *Walden, Or Life in the Woods*. It was a story of a radical, nonconforming quest—his spiritual search for meanings that went beyond the traps and artificialities of life in a "civilized" society. On the practical side, Thoreau listed his accounts, a profit-and-loss statement that recorded his expenditures for a little sugar or a bit of string, and his income from the little surplus production he managed. He presented this accounting to lead readers to recall the pecuniary calculations of Benjamin Franklin in his *Autobiography*. Thoreau wanted to highlight his record of a "commerce" with the deeper, spiritual meaning of life. It was this kind of venture in self-discovery, rather than hermitlike subsistence farming, that he was really promoting:

> I went to the woods because I wished to live deliberately, confront only the essential facts of life, and see if I could not learn what it had to teach, and not, when I came to die, discover that I had not lived.

Although Thoreau's essay had little impact beyond transcendentalist circles during his lifetime, *Walden* has become an essential text of American literature and an inspiration to succeeding generations of utopian builders. And its most famous metaphor provides an enduring justification for independent thinking: "If a man does not keep pace with his companions, perhaps it is because he hears a different drummer."

Walt Whitman. Another writer who responded to Emerson's call was the poet Walt Whitman. He said that when he first encountered Emerson, he had been "simmering, simmering." Then Emerson "brought me to a boil." Whitman had been a journalist, an editor of the *Brooklyn Eagle* and other newspapers. But it was poetry that had been the "direction of his dreams." In *Leaves of Grass,* first published in 1855 and constantly revised and expanded for almost four decades thereafter, he recorded his attempt to pass a number of "invisible boundaries": between solitude and community; between body and spirit; between prose and poetry;

Walt Whitman

Whitman (1819–1892) took dangerous steps for an artist in the nineteenth century by condemning organized religion with its "creeds and priests" and treating sex explicitly. Emerson tried to persuade him to drop those sections from the *Leaves of Grass,* but Whitman explained that "if I had cut sex out," the poetry "would have been violated at its most sensitive spot."

even between the living and the dead. It was a wild, exuberant poem in both form and content. It self-consciously violated every poetic rule and every canon of respectable taste, daring readers either to shut the book in revulsion or to accept Whitman's idiosyncratic vision whole.

At the center of *Leaves of Grass* is the figure of the poet, "I, Walt." He begins alone: "I celebrate myself, and sing myself," loafing in nature, "observing a spear of summer grass." But because he has what Emerson calls an "original relation" with nature, the poet claims not solitude, finally, but perfect communion with others: "And what I assume you shall assume,/ For every atom belonging to me as good belongs to you." Whitman was celebrating democracy as well as himself. He argued militantly that a poet in a democracy could claim a profoundly intimate, mystical relationship with his mass audience. For both Emerson and Thoreau, the individual had a divine spark. For Whitman, however, the individual had expanded to *become* divine—infusing democracy with divinity and making organized religion irrelevant.

Whitman, Thoreau, and Emerson were not naively optimistic. Whitman wrote of human suffering with as much passion as he wrote of everything else. Emerson's accounts of the exhilaration that could come in nature were tinged with anxiety. "I am glad," he said, "to the brink of fear." Thoreau's gloomy judgment of everyday life is well known: "The mass of men lead lives of quiet desperation." Still, such dark murmurings were muted in their work, woven into their triumphant and expansive assertions that nothing was impossible for an individual able to break free from tradition, law, and other social restraints.

Nathaniel Hawthorne and Herman Melville. Emerson's influence also reached to two great novelists, Nathaniel Hawthorne and Herman Melville. Hawthorne, who for a time was a member of Emerson's circle, and Melville had more pessimistic visions. They dwelt on the vanities, corruption, and excesses of individualism—rather than on its positive potential. Both sounded powerful warnings that unfettered egoism could destroy individuals as well as their social arrangements. They embraced the ideal of individual freedom but at the same time urged the acceptance of an inner discipline.

Hawthorne's most brilliant exploration of this theme of excessive individualism was in his novel *The Scarlet Letter* (1850). The two main characters, Hester Prynne and Arthur Dimmesdale, challenge their seventeenth-century New England community in the most blatant way—by committing adultery, producing a child, and refusing to bend to the community's condemnation. The result of their assertion of individual freedom against communal discipline is not exaltation but tragedy. Wracked by guilt and unable to confess, Dimmesdale dies in anguish. Hester learns from the experience that the way to a truly virtuous life can be found only by a person who is willing to do good within the social order.

Melville, heavily influenced by Hawthorne, explored the same problem in even more extreme and tragic terms, and emerged a scathing critic of transcendentalism. His most powerful statement was in *Moby Dick* (1851). The novel begins as a whaling captain, Ahab, embarks on an obsessive hunt for a white whale, Moby Dick, that had severed Ahab's leg during an earlier expedition. Ahab is a version of Emerson's liberated individual, with an intuitive grasp of hidden meanings in nature. He believes that the whale is pure, demonic evil. Ahab's form of "self-reliance" is to hunt the whale down, no matter what the cost. The trouble, as Melville tells the story, is that Ahab can hunt the whale only in a social way. Ahab's ship, the *Pequod,* is an industrial community. In fact, the novel is perhaps the most detailed literary description of an actual industry, whaling,

Edgar Allan Poe, in 1848

Poe (1809–1849) was raised in Virginia, identified with the South, and defended slavery. But he rose above time and place in his poetry and fiction, never using southern subjects or problems. During his lifetime he was most famous as an editor and critic in Baltimore, Philadelphia, and New York. In these roles he advanced the ideas that art should strive for beauty, not truth, and that writers should calculate the effects on their readers with great precision.

ever written in the United States or in Britain. Ahab's transcendental adventure subverts the legitimate purposes of the whaling voyage. As a result, not only Ahab but the crew of workers die. Only one person, Ishmael, is left to tell the tale.

Moby Dick was a commercial failure. The middle-class audience that was the primary target of American publishers was unwilling to follow Melville into the dark, dangerous realms of individualism gone mad. They were also unenthusiastic about the visions of terror and evil that Edgar Allan Poe, a southern-born admirer of Hawthorne, created in "The Raven" (1845) and other poems and short stories. Poe won respect in New York literary circles but could not find a middle-class audience. Emily Dickinson, another poet whose work expressed doubts about individualism, did not even try to find readers. During the 1850s she kept private the poetry she had begun to write in isolation in Amherst, Massachusetts. At the same time, both *Walden* and *Leaves of Grass* also failed to find a large readership. The middle-class audience was unimpressed by Thoreau's extreme and demanding version of transcendentalism and by Whitman's boundless claims for the mystical union between the man of genius and the democratic mass. What they emphatically preferred was the more modest examinations of individualism offered by Emerson.

Emily Dickinson
Emily Dickinson (1830–1886), born into a well-to-do family in Amherst, was a rebellious student at South Hadley Female Seminary (now Mount Holyoke College), and may have had a brief love affair with a married Philadelphia minister. But after she was twenty-six she seldom left Amherst. Though she was a prolific writer—in 1862 alone she produced 356 poems—only seven poems were published during her lifetime.

Brook Farm

At one time or another, virtually all transcendentalists, including Emerson, felt that American society as it existed could not accommodate their aspirations for individual realization and achievement. Many of them acted on that perception and withdrew into insular communities. Their aim was to reform society by setting an example.

The most important communal experiment of the transcendentalists was Brook Farm, founded in 1841 by a Unitarian minister, George Ripley, in West Roxbury, Massachusetts. Free from the tension and degradation of a competitive society, community members hoped to create a harmonious environment for the full development of mind and soul. In the first few years the community's economy rested primarily on agriculture. The Brook Farmers did sell their milk, vegetables, and hay for cash. But they emphasized the way in which farming allowed them to remain relatively independent from the marketplace and to work close to nature. In addition, they acquired revenue by insisting that residents who did not work on the farm make cash payments—in effect, tuition for what was virtually a boarding school.

The intellectual life at Brook Farm was electric. Hawthorne lived there for a time and later used the setting for *The Blithedale Romance* (1852). All of the major transcendentalists, including Emerson and Margaret Fuller, the editor of the foremost transcendentalist journal, the *Dial,* were residents or at least frequent visitors. One former member recalled that the transcendentalists "inspired the young with a passion for study, and the middle-aged with deference and admiration, while we all breathed the intellectual grace that pervaded the atmosphere." Music, dancing, games, plays, parties, picnics, and dramatic readings filled leisure hours. Emerson wrote that Brook Farm meant "education" to most of its residents. It was, he said, "to many the most important period of their life . . . a French Revolution in small."

Brook Farm may have represented moral progress, but it faltered in providing economic self-sufficiency. Most of its members in the initial years were ministers, teachers, writers, and students. Relatively few families lived at Brook Farm; Ripley's message appealed mostly to young, single men and women who came from well-to-do Boston families, who were Unitarians, and who sought alternatives to careers devoted to the acquisition

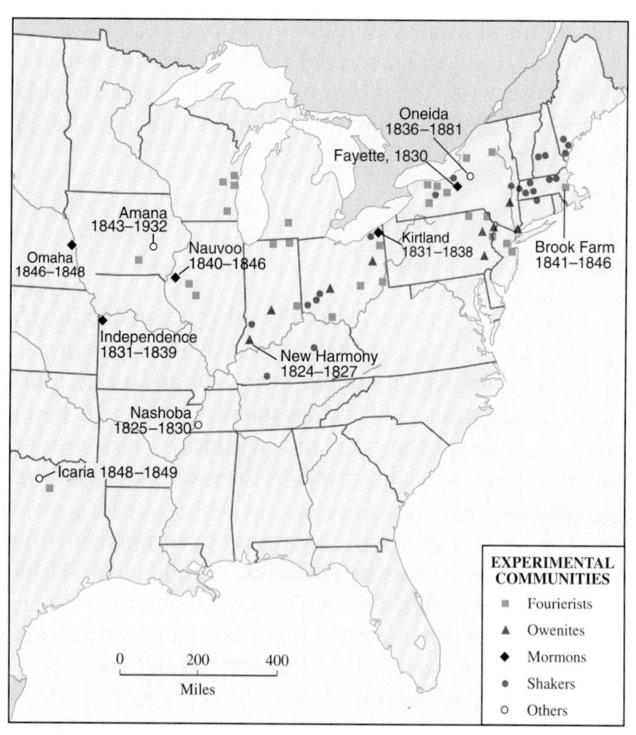

MAP 12.1

Communal Experiments Before 1860

Some experimental communities sought out frontier locations, but the vast majority simply looked for secluded areas in well-settled regions. The avoidance of the South by these groups is striking. For the trek of the Mormons, see Map 13.6, p. 404.

of wealth. Only a few farmers and artisans joined. And, for the first three years, Ripley and his individualistic followers paid little attention to the need to organize their farming and crafts efficiently.

In 1844, the residents began to run Brook Farm in a more disciplined fashion, particularly in arranging housekeeping chores to free women to produce handicrafts. Under their new plan, the Brook Farmers attracted some artisans and farmers. Still, the community made only marginal economic gains and did so at the cost of regimented routines that depressed many of the original members. One of the residents wrote that "the joyous spirit of youth was sobered." Finally, after a devastating fire in 1846, the organizers disbanded and sold the farm.

The Decline of Transcendentalism. After the failure of Brook Farm, the transcendentalists abandoned their attempts at comprehensive reform. Most became resigned to the structure of American industrial society; its material accomplishments seemed too great to resist. During the 1850s, the transcendentalists—as poets, historians, scientists, lawyers, and ministers—became thoroughly integrated into the cultural elite of New England. To the extent that they embraced reform of industrial communities, philanthropy, often focused on education for workers, was their program of choice. Some remained radicals on one issue, however—slavery. In the 1840s and 1850s, a few aging transcendentalists and a younger generation of their disciples applied their passion for individual freedom to liberate the slaves (see pages 366 and 369).

Communal Experiment at Bishop Hill

At Bishop Hill, a community founded by a sect of Swedish pietists in Illinois in 1848, women as well as men toiled in the fields and farm work was highly organized. But the younger members of Bishop Hill were unwilling to accept community discipline, and the community dissolved in 1862.

The Phalanxes

When the Brook Farmers reorganized their community in 1844, they adopted a constitution that embraced the ideas of Charles Fourier, a contemporary French utopian, as interpreted by his idealistic American disciple, Arthur Brisbane. Fourier and Brisbane envisioned cooperative work and living units—called "phalanxes"—in which those who labored would receive the largest portion of the community's earnings. The members of a phalanx would be its shareholders; they would own all property in common, including stores and a bank as well as a school and library. Fourier and Brisbane proposed a model for what they hoped would be a practical, more humane alternative to industrial society. "In society as it is now constituted," Brisbane wrote, "monotony, uniformity, intellectual inaction and torpor reign: distrust, isolation, separation, conflict and antagonism are almost universal: very little expansion of the generous affections and feelings obtain. . . . Society is spiritually a desert."

Brisbane skillfully promoted Fourier's ideas through an influential book, *The Social Destiny of Man* (1840), a regular column in Horace Greeley's New York *Tribune,* and hundreds of lectures, many of them in the towns along the Erie Canal. He inspired educated farmers and craftsmen to start close to 100 cooperative communities from Massachusetts to Michigan, most of them during the 1840s. However, almost all, like Brook Farm, were unable to support themselves and quickly died. Some contemporary observers, including the radical minister John Humphrey Noyes, believed that the Fourierists had failed because their communities lacked the strong religious ethic required for sustained altruism and cooperation.

The Shakers

When John Humphrey Noyes criticized the "Phalanxes," he had in mind, by way of contrast, the oldest and largest of the radical utopian experiments in America—the Shaker communities. Noyes described them as "the pioneers of modern Socialism."

The origins of the Shaker communities dated back to the era of the American Revolution. In 1770, Ann Lee (Mother Ann), a young cook in Manchester, England, had a vision that she was the second incarnation of Christ and thus the Second Coming. Four years later she led a tiny band of eight followers to America, where they established a new church near Albany, New York. Because of the ecstatic dances that became part of their religious worship, they became known as "Shaking Quakers," or, more simply, "Shakers."

After Mother Ann's death, the Shakers decided to withdraw from the evils of the world into strictly run communities of believers. Beginning in 1787, the Shakers founded twenty communities, mostly in New England, New York, and Ohio. During the 1820s they entered their most vigorous period of community formation, and during the 1830s they attracted more than three thousand converts.

Shakers embraced the common ownership of property, accepted the government of the church, pledged themselves to abstinence from alcohol, tobacco, politics, and war, and made a commitment to celibacy. Men and women lived apart in gender-segregated dormitories. Applicants had to declare themselves "sick of sin" and undertake a program of systematic confession that could last for years. To the Shakers, sin was wholly the product of a society that impeded a chaste and self-denying life.

The Shakers' beliefs that God was "a dual person, male and female" and that Mother Ann represented God's female element provided the underpinning for their attempt to give up marriage and banish distinctions between the sexes. In practice, they maintained a traditional division of labor between men and women, but the Shakers vested the authority for governing each community—in both its religious and economic spheres—in women and men alike, the Elders and the Eldresses.

New members flowed steadily into the Shaker communities, with women outnumbering men more than two to one. The communities welcomed blacks as well as whites. To Rebecca Cox Jackson, an African-American seamstress from Philadelphia, the Shakers seemed to be "loving to live forever." New members were drawn in by the highly structured nature of the community, by an opportunity to escape from the stresses of American life, by the chance offered to women to assume leadership roles, and by the economic success of the communities. Shaker agriculture and crafts, especially furniture making, acquired a reputation for quality that enabled most of the communities to become self-sustaining, even comfortable. However, during the 1840s and 1850s the communities stopped growing, and some began to decline. Because Shakers had no children of their own, they relied on converts to replenish their numbers. During the last part of the nineteenth century most of the communities disappeared, with only a few surviving into the twentieth century.

The celibate Shaker communities could never provide a model for society as a whole; they could serve only as a refuge from industrial society. But their marriage-less society highlighted the potent role of marriage and gender roles in defining social relationships in America as a whole.

AMERICAN VOICES

The Shakers *Rebecca Cox Jackson*

Rebecca Cox Jackson (1795–1871) was a free African-American woman who renounced a relatively secure life with her husband in Philadelphia to become an itinerant Methodist preacher. During the 1830s she traveled throughout the countryside, accompanied by a younger disciple, Rebecca Perot. In 1843 the "two Rebeccas" became committed Shakers, eventually settling in the community of Watervliet, near Albany, New York. They remained ambiguous about Shaker isolation, however, and in 1851 they resumed their ministry within the free black community. In 1858 Jackson founded her own Shaker family in Philadelphia. In the 1840s, Jackson began to write a memoir of her religious experiences, including powerful dreams and visions.

Monday evening, February 18, 1850. I was instructed concerning the atmosphere and its bounds. I saw its form—it is like the sea, which has her bounds. . . . It covered land and sea, so far above all moving things, and yet so far beneath the starry heavens. Its face is like the face of the sea, smooth and gentle when undisturbed by the wind. So is the atmosphere, when undisturbed by the power of the sun and moon. When agitated by these, it rages like the sea and sends forth its storms upon the earth. Nothing can live above it. A bird could no more live or fly above its face, than a fish can live or swim out of the water. It is always calm and serene between its face and the starry heaven. The sight, to me, was beautiful.

March 1, 1950. . . . Prayer given to me by Mother Ann Lee: "Oh God, my Everlasting Father, to Thee do I lift up my soul in prayer and thanksgiving for the gift of Thy dear Son, our Blessed Savior, who has begotten to us a living hope. And to Thee, Holy Mother Wisdom, do I lift up my soul in prayer and thanksgiving, for the gift of Thy Holy Daughter, whose blessed Spirit has led me and instructed me in this, the holy way of God, lo! these many years, and has borne with my infirmities and many shortcomings. And lo! Thou hast comforted me in all my sorrows and Thy blessed Spirit comforts me today."

Then I saw our Heavenly Parents look on me and smile, and Mother Ann gave me sweet counsel. And I was greatly strengthened in the way of God.

March 15, 1850. After I came to Watervliet . . . and saw how the Believers seemed to be gathered to themselves, in praying for themselves and not for the world, which lay in midnight darkness, I wondered how the world was to be saved, if Shakers were the only people of God on earth, and they seemed to be busy in their own concerns, which were mostly temporal. . . .

Then seeing these at ease in Zion, I cried in the name of Christ and Mother that He in mercy would do something for the helpless world. At that time, it seemed as if the whole world rested upon me. I cried to the Lord both day and night, for many months, that God would make a way that the world might hear the Gospel—that God would send spirits and angels to administer to their understanding, that they might be saved in the present tense, for I knew by revelation, that it was God's will that they should be.

Source: Jean McMahon Humez, *Gifts of Power: The Writings of Rebecca Jackson, Black Visionary, Shaker Eldress* (Amherst: University of Massachusetts Press, 1981), 220–21.

The Oneida Community

John Humphrey Noyes established a utopian experiment, the Oneida Community, after studying closely its Fourierist, Shaker, and other predecessors. He visited many of them, including Brook Farm. He intended that his community would offer a model for recasting all of industrial society on the basis of cooperation and Christian ethics.

Noyes and "Perfectionism." Noyes was a well-to-do Dartmouth College graduate who had left the study of law for the ministry after hearing Charles Finney preach in 1831. Noyes's divinity studies led him in radical directions, however, and the Congregationalist Church expelled him from the ministry for his unorthodox teachings. His doctrines, promoted through the religious magazines he edited, made him the leader of "perfectionism"—an evangelical cult that gathered thousands of followers during the 1830s, primarily among the New Englanders who had settled in New York. Perfectionists believed that the Second Coming of Christ had already occurred. Because the Kingdom of Heaven on earth was a reality, people could aspire to perfection—to freedom from sin. To Noyes, the major barrier to achieving this ideal state was marriage, which did not exist in heaven. "Exclusiveness, jealousy, quarreling have no place at the marriage supper of the Lamb," Noyes wrote. He sought to reform marriage to liberate individuals from sin, as had the Shakers. But his solution was dramatically different: Noyes and his followers embraced the doctrine of "complex marriage"—all the members of his community were married to one another.

"Complex Marriage." Like the Shakers, Noyes was attempting to gain community control over sexuality. His solution was love, usually expressed in sex without male orgasm, between successive partners, with childbearing strictly regulated by the community. Closely related objectives were to free women from being regarded as the property of husbands and to free children, who were raised in community nurseries, from being regarded as the property of their parents. Of all the founders of communities organized along socialist lines—with community ownership of property, Noyes presented the most radical alternative to traditional marriage and family life.

In the 1830s, Noyes began to collect like-minded followers in his hometown of Putney, Vermont. In 1848 the scandalousness of the doctrine of complex marriage forced Noyes to move his community to Oneida, New York. By the mid-1850s, more than two hundred people lived in the community, but it remained financially insecure. Their fortunes improved when the inventor of what proved to be a highly successful steel animal-trap joined the community. With the profits from the production of traps, Oneida diversified into the production of other products, notably silverware with the brand-name Community Plate. Its quality provided the basis for an economic success that continued long after 1879, when Noyes fled to Canada to avoid prosecution for adultery and the community abandoned complex marriage. In 1881 its members founded a joint-stock company, the Oneida Community, Ltd., which survived into the twentieth century.

In the case of both the Shakers and the Oneida Community, radical efforts to free individuals from sin, and from the constraints of industrial society, had extended to recasting the meaning of marriage and the family. Thus, in this period, when all kinds of changes seemed possible, some of the communitarians were willing to tinker with even the most deeply-rooted institutions in American society. Neither the Shakers nor the Oneidians aroused the kind of fierce hostility that would drive the Mormons into exile in the Great American Desert (see Chapter 13). But this was so only because to most outsiders the Shakers seemed pathetic eccentrics, and the followers of Noyes too few to be worrisome. Business-class evangelism had powerfully reinforced the institution of marriage, limiting the scope and appeal of communal experiments, and restricting the ability of women to develop a full-fledged feminist ideology.

Women and Reform

Women played instrumental roles in the radical reform movements of the Industrial Revolution. They had participated in the religious revivals and had joined the conservative temperance, moral reform, and educational reform movements. During the 1830s, some women went beyond these to movements aimed at removing limitations on individual freedom. Slavery was among their targets, and it was abolitionism that radicalized many of them. Abolitionism encouraged women to develop an ideology which argued that women had social and political rights equal to those of men.

Origins of the Women's Movement

The Industrial Revolution shaped in complex ways the movement to widen opportunities for women. On the surface, it seemed to limit economic opportunities for them and reinforce their confinement to a "separate sphere." The Industrial Revolution sharpened the lines of demarcation between the home and the workplace while accentuating the division of labor within the home. Middle-class women were now less involved in the production of goods (such as in household workshops) and more concerned with providing personal services in the home. Partly because of the influence of revivals, mothers increasingly became the keepers of religion and morality. They were preoccupied with setting a superior moral example and providing solace and support for the members who worked outside the home.

On a psychological level, however, these changes in the role of women within the family created a basis for greater independence and power. Middle-class women drew on the enhanced esteem attached to their family roles, reinforced each other through intensified community and kinship ties, and found sanctification for their roles in religion. With all this mutual reinforcement, middle-class women built a common identity in "womanhood." They used it to enlarge their influence over decisions in all areas of family life, including the bearing of children—the timing of pregnancies—and even their husbands' choice of work. For most middle-class women, greater influence over family life was enough. But some women seized on the logic implicit in the emphasis on the moral role of women to increase their involvement outside the home.

Young middle-class women in New York and New England entered the public arena through the religious revivals of the 1820s and 1830s. The evangelical revivals emphasized the power of individual free will—even for dependents such as wives and daughters—and provided a central role for women in the conversion process. The revivals also involved them more deeply in community life, enhanced their sense of self-esteem, and led them into other reform movements.

Moral reform was the first of their efforts in the public arena. Women reformers attempted to end prostitution, to punish those whose sexual behavior violated the Ten Commandments, to redeem fallen women, and to protect single women from moral corruption. The movement began in 1834, when a group of middle-class women founded the New York Female Moral Reform Society and elected Lydia Finney, the wife of the evangelical minister Charles Finney, as its president. By 1837 the New York society had 15,000 members and 250 chapters.

The American Female Moral Reform Society. In 1840 the New York society organized a national association, the American Female Moral Reform Society, with 555 chapters located throughout the North. Employing only women as its agents, bookkeepers, and staff, this society concentrated on the problems of young women who worked and lived away from their families. They focused on the need to provide moral "government" for factory girls, seamstresses, clerks, and servants who lived beyond the direct control of families and churches. The women reformers even visited brothels, where they sang hymns, offered prayers, searched for runaway daughters, and noted the names of clients. They founded homes of refuge for prostitutes, homeless girls, and migrant women. They petitioned for state laws regulating sexual behavior—including making seduction a crime—and succeeded in arranging the passage of such laws in Massachusetts in 1846 and New York in 1848.

Women with backgrounds in evangelical reform also turned their energies to the reform of social institutions. Almshouses, asylums, hospitals, and jails became targets for improvement in a movement that involved both men and women reformers. Women visited these places, which were growing in number during the 1830s and 1840s, with the aim of easing the condition of the residents. But what they saw inspired efforts toward more drastic action.

Dorothea Dix

Dorothea Dix (1802–1887) visited 18 state penitentiaries, 300 county jails and houses of correction, and more than 500 almshouses, in addition to innumerable hospitals and houses of refuge. At the outbreak of the Civil War, she was appointed superintendent of women nurses. This put her in charge of hospital nursing for the Union forces and made her the highest-ranking woman in the federal government.

Dorothea Dix. The most accomplished reformer of institutions for society's most dependent individuals was Dorothea Dix. In 1841 she visited a jail in Cambridge, Massachusetts, as a Sunday school teacher for the incarcerated women. Outraged that insane women were being put in jail with criminals, Dix conducted a two-year investigation of the treatment of the indigent insane in Massachusetts. Her report prompted Massachusetts to enlarge the state hospital in Worcester. And her success in Massachusetts led to a nationwide crusade to establish separate state hospitals for the insane. Between 1843 and 1854, supported by legacies from her grandparents, she traveled more than thirty thousand miles, visited hundreds of institutions, and prepared dozens of reports and memorials to state legislatures. Her success in arousing public opinion forced many states to create or significantly expand their state hospitals. Dix, however, despaired of state governments ever providing adequate support for such mental hospitals, and she dreamed of a national hospital system funded by the federal government. She came close to having her way. She persuaded Congress to pass a bill in 1854 that provided federal land grants for national hospitals, but President Franklin Pierce vetoed the bill, claiming it was both too expensive and unconstitutional, encroaching on a function of state government. Despite her defeats, Dix continued her work overseas. She enlisted the support of Queen Victoria, lectured the pope on conditions in Rome's asylum for the insane, and founded an international movement to improve treatment of the insane.

Abolitionism and Women

Under the influence of ideas and politics drawn from the movement to abolish slavery, a few women began to question whether they should continue to accept a restricted role in society. They faced severe opposition but in contrast with Frances Wright, who had denounced business-class evangelism, they advanced their ideas within a religious context and thus avoided the extreme forms of public outrage she had encountered in championing women's rights a decade earlier.

The Grimké Sisters. Shaping the ideas of the radical women were the abolitionist sisters Angelina and Sarah Grimké. They had left their father's South Carolina plantation, converted to Quakerism and abolitionism in Philadelphia, and become antislavery lecturers. In 1837, responding to the demand of some Congregationalist clergymen that she cease speaking to mixed male and female audiences, Sarah Grimké responded: "The Lord Jesus defines the duties of his followers in his Sermon on the Mount. . . without any reference to sex or condition. . . . Men and women are CREATED EQUAL! They are both moral and accountable beings and whatever is right for man to do is right for woman." The next year, Angelina Grimké declared that gender should not affect the manner in which people shape society:

> It is a woman's right to have a voice in all the laws and regulations by which she is governed, whether in Church or State. . . . The present arrangements of society, on these points are a *violation of human rights, a rank usurpation of power,* a violent seizure and confiscation of what is sacredly and inalienably hers.

By 1840, the Grimké sisters were asserting that traditional roles within the family amounted to the "domestic slavery" of women.

Not all abolitionist women shared these views. But they all gained experience and confidence outside the home and learned much about the organizational requirements for successful reform. And as their participation in the movement grew, many women demanded equality with men within the abolitionist movement. Equality to these women meant representation in antislavery societies equal to their numbers. At the same time, however, their activities, especially the vigorous antislavery lecturing by the Grimkés, aroused opposition from abolitionist clergymen who believed that the women's behavior was immoral. They also drew criticism from male abolitionists who feared that such visible departures from tradition would damage the political chances of the antislavery movement.

However, one leading abolitionist, William Lloyd Garrison argued that "our object is *universal* emancipation, to redeem women as well as men from a servile to an equal condition." At the convention of the American Anti-Slavery Society in 1840, he insisted on the right of women to participate equally in the organization. The

The Grimké Sisters

Sarah Moore Grimké (1792–1873) and Angelina Emily Grimké (1805–1879) joined the Philadelphia Female Anti-Slavery Society and began abolitionist lecturing in 1836. They drew crowds of thousands—and scathing criticism for having lost, as some Massachusetts clergymen put it, "that modesty and delicacy . . . which constitutes the true influence of women in society." The Grimké sisters responded with powerful statements protesting male domination of women.

votes of several hundred New England women elected Abby Kelley to the organization's business committee. This event precipitated the split between the supporters of Garrison and those who left the organization to found the American and Foreign Anti-Slavery Society.

A group of women abolitionists—led by Abby Kelley, Lucretia Mott, and Elizabeth Cady Stanton—remained with Garrison. They recruited new women agents, including Lucy Stone, to address hostile audiences on the common interests of slaves and free women. Stanton admired Frances Wright and kept her works on her library table, but she had learned from Wright's defeats. During the 1840s the women abolitionists focused on a pragmatic course of action for expanding the influence of women.

The Program of Seneca Falls

By the 1840s celebration of self—of individual identity and liberation—had become important to women in public life. Nonetheless, during the 1840s and 1850s, most critics of "domestic slavery," stopped short of challenging the institution of marriage or even the conventional division of labor within the family. They focused instead on using the American political system to strengthen the position of women under the law, within the existing social order. They wished women to come more into the mainstream of American life rather than to separate themselves from it.

Margaret Fuller. The new program had a radical dimension in that it emphasized the rights of women as free, rather than dependent, individuals. One of the key influences in this direction was transcendentalism, largely through the writings of Margaret Fuller. A transcendentalist who had never joined the abolitionists, Fuller had cogently asserted the rights of women in *Woman in the Nineteenth Century,* published in the *Dial* magazine in 1843 and as a book in 1845. Although she was well-read in the writings of Mary Wollstonecraft, her philosophy was based on a transcendental religious vision: that women had an independent relationship with God which gave them an identity having nothing to do with gender. She believed that every woman deserved psychological and social independence—the ability "to grow, as an intellect to discern, as a soul to live freely and unimpeded." She declared, "We would have every arbitrary barrier thrown down" and "every path laid open to Woman as freely as to Man." If societies placed men and women—"the two sides of the great radical dualism" of human nature—on an equal footing, they could end all injustice. After 1845, Fuller gained visibility as the New York *Tribune*'s literary critic and as a correspondent in Italy during that country's revolution of 1848. Her friends hoped that she would become a leader in the women's movement, but in 1850, returning to the United States at the age of forty, she drowned in a shipwreck.

Seneca Falls and After. In 1848 leaders of the nascent women's movement took a critical step. They called a convention in Seneca Falls, in upstate New York. Organized by Elizabeth Cady Stanton and Lucretia Mott, who had met at the World's Anti-Slavery Convention in 1840, and joined by a few sympathetic male abolitionists, the convention outlined, for the first time, a coherent program for women's equality. The delegates at Seneca Falls based their program on republican ideology, adopting resolutions patterned directly on the Declaration of Independence. Among their declared principles was "that all men and women are created equal; that they are endowed by the Creator with certain inalienable rights: that among these are life, liberty and the pursuit of happiness." They asserted, however, that "the history of mankind is a history of repeated injuries and usurpations on the part of man toward woman, having in direct object the establishment of an absolute tyranny over her." To educate the public as to

Margaret Fuller

Margaret Fuller (1810–1850) learned to read the classics of six languages when she was a child, educated her four siblings, and taught in a girls' school in Providence before she became interested in women's rights and transcendentalism. In 1839 she inaugurated a transcendental "conversation," or discussion group, for elite Boston women.

this reality, they resolved to "use every instrumentality within our power. . . . We shall employ agents, circulate tracts, petition the State and national legislatures, and endeavor to enlist the pulpit and the press on our behalf."

Throughout the 1850s, national women's rights conventions were held annually, as were numerous local and regional meetings. At these conventions, women promoted a diverse reform program: establishing the right of married women to control their own property and earnings; guaranteeing custody of children in the event of divorce; ensuring women's right to sue or testify in court; revising concepts of female inferiority found in established religious theology; and—above all else—winning the vote for women. The 1851 national convention of women resolved that the right of suffrage was "the corner-stone of this enterprise, since we do not seek to protect woman, but rather to place her in a position to protect herself."

The only legislative victories of the women's movement before the Civil War came in the area of women's property rights. Fourteen states followed New York's pioneering law of 1848 and adopted laws protecting the property of married women in the event of the death or incapacitation of their husbands. Joining the reformers in this effort were upper-class conservative males. Their principal motive was to protect propertied men in the event of bankruptcy (by preserving their spouses' assets intact) and to protect patriarchs with large estates who feared that dissolute or incompetent sons-in-law might lose or ruin their holdings; these men preferred to allow their daughters to hold assets independently.

Susan B. Anthony. Despite its dearth of victories before the Civil War, the suffrage effort did advance the organization of the women's movement. Meetings and publicity widened the participation of women in women's causes, and their leaders grew in number, and in their mastery of organization—as exemplified by Susan B. Anthony. While many women leaders of the 1830s and 1840s had been gifted lecturers, Anthony's foremost talents were organizational. Anthony, a member of a Massachusetts Quaker family that had moved to a farm near Rochester, New York, had participated in moral reform and in a female antislavery society. She had lectured on antislavery and religion, resigned a teaching position in bitter protest over discrimination against women, and joined the temperance movement as a paid

Elizabeth Cady Stanton

Elizabeth Cady Stanton (1815–1902) was born into the family of a judge in Johnstown, New York, and attended Emma Hart Willard's demanding Troy Female Seminary. In 1840 she married Henry B. Stanton, an abolitionist leader, and traveled to the World Anti-Slavery Convention in London, where she met Lucretia Mott and started down the intellectual path that led to Seneca Falls. (This photograph, with her grandson, was taken after the Civil War.)

Susan B. Anthony

As a child, Susan B. Anthony (1820–1906) worked on the Rochester, New York, farm of her father, who had failed in textile manufacturing. She served as "headmistress" of the Female Department at Canajoharie Academy before joining the temperance movement. As she passed "from town to town," she wrote, "I was made to feel the great evil of woman's utter dependence on man for the necessary means to aid reform movements."

AMERICAN VOICES

The Question of Women's Rights *Lucy Stone*

Lucy Stone (1818–1893) graduated from Oberlin College in 1847 and came to the issue of women's rights through abolitionist lecturing. This is an excerpt from a speech she delivered extemporaneously at a national women's rights convention in Cincinnati in 1855.

The last speaker alluded to this movement as being that of a few disappointed women. From the first years to which my memory stretches, I have been a disappointed woman. When, with my brothers, I reached forth after sources of knowledge, I was reproved with "It isn't fit for you; it doesn't belong to women." Then there was but one college in the world where women were admitted, and that was in Brazil. I would have found my way there, but by the time I was prepared to go, one was opened in the young state of Ohio—the first in the United States where women and negroes could enjoy opportunities with white men. I was disappointed when I came to seek a profession worthy of an immortal being—every employment was closed to me, except that of the teacher, the seamstress, and the housekeeper. In education, in marriage, in religion, in everything, disappointment is the lot of woman. It shall be the business of my life to deepen this disappointment in every woman's heart until she bows down to it no longer. I wish that women, instead of being walking showcases, instead of begging of their fathers and brothers the latest and gayest new bonnet, would ask of them their rights.

The question of Women's Rights is a practical one. . . . The flour merchant, the house-builder, and the postman charge us no less on account of our sex; but when we endeavor to earn money to pay all these, then, indeed, we find the difference. Man, if he have energy, may hew out for himself a path where no mortal has ever trod, held back by nothing but what is in himself; the world is all before him, where to choose; and we are glad for you, brothers, men, that it is so. But the same society that drives forth the young man, keeps woman at home—a dependent—working little cats on worsted, and little dogs on punctured paper; but if she goes heartily and bravely to give herself some worthy purpose, she is out of her sphere and she loses caste. . . . I know not what you believe of God, but I believe He gave yearnings and longings to be filled, and that He did not mean all our time should be devoted to feeding and clothing the body. The present condition of woman causes a horrible perversion of the marriage relation. It is asked of a lady, "Has she married well?" "Oh, yes, her husband is rich." Woman must marry for a home, and you men are the sufferers by this; for a woman who loathes you may marry you because you have the means to get money which she cannot have. But when woman can enter the lists with you and make money for herself, she will marry you only for deep and earnest affection.

Source: Elizabeth Cady Stanton, Susan B. Anthony, and Matilda Joslyn Gage, *History of Woman Suffrage* (New York, 1881), I,165–66.

fundraiser. In 1851, when she was thirty-one, Anthony joined the movement for women's rights and forged an enduring friendship with Elizabeth Cady Stanton. Her experience in the temperance movement proved valuable, especially because it had taught her "the great evil of woman's utter dependence on man for the necessary means to aid reform movements."

In promoting reforms during the 1850s, Anthony created a network of political "captains," all women. Because each of New York's counties had a captain, her group could collect thousands of signatures on petitions in just a few days. She lobbied the state legislature relentlessly. In 1860 her efforts culminated in New York giving women the legal right to collect their own wages (which fathers or husbands previously could insist on collecting), to bring suit in court, and to enjoy, if widowed, full control of their own property.

The organizational and legislative successes of the women's rights movement during the 1850s provided the basis for the more aggressive reform attempts that followed the Civil War. The political strategy of the more radical women had widened their support, winning the aid of moderate women abolitionists. During the 1850s, however, most Americans, even most abolitionists, did not regard the issues that the women's rights movement had raised to be of great concern. And most stressed a higher immediate priority: the abolition of slavery.

Harriet Beecher Stowe and Sojourner Truth. Women who had never joined an antislavery society could join with women's rights leaders in expressing evangelical outrage over slavery. The novelist Harriet Beecher Stowe, for example, did not participate in the organized movement against slavery but grew angry over slavery and, most importantly, moved other women to share her feelings. In her novel *Uncle Tom's Cabin,* she delivered an abolitionist message to more homes than any antislavery campaigner ever did. Beecher charged that among the greatest moral failings of slavery was its destruction of the slave family and the degradation of slave women. This charge was substantiated by a real-life former slave, Sojourner Truth, who was one of the numerous African-American women who lectured to both antislavery and women's rights conventions. Truth hammered home the point that women slaves were denied not only their basic human rights but also the protected, separate "sphere" enjoyed by free women. "I have ploughed and planted and gathered into barns, and no man could head me—and ain't I a woman?" she asked in 1851. "I have borne thirteen children, and seen most of 'em sold into slavery, and when I cried out with my mother's grief, none but Jesus heard me—and ain't I a woman?"

The Antislavery Movement

Sojourner Truth and other ex-slaves inspired what became the dominant movement to reform American society—the movement to abolish slavery. Beginning in the 1830s, white evangelists joined African-Americans in radical attacks on slavery.

By 1820, opposition to slavery—influenced by republican ideology and British antislavery advocates such as William Wilberforce—had already accomplished a good deal. Congress had outlawed the importation of slaves in 1808 (the earliest date permitted by the Constitution). Most northern states had already abolished slavery. And the Missouri Compromise had prohibited slavery in most of the Louisiana Purchase. But the most vocal opponents of slavery wanted to go much further. Three different approaches to ending slavery competed between 1820 and 1840: (1) gradual emancipation of the nation's slaves—1.5 million in 1820—and return of the freed slaves to Africa, with compensation paid to their former owners; (2) emancipation through slave flight or rebellion; and (3) emancipation through direct appeals to the conscience of slaveowners. Then, during the 1840s and 1850s, most opponents of slavery united as they turned to political tactics and developed a *fourth* approach to abolition: excluding slavery from the territories.

African Colonization

The American Colonization Society. Proponents of compensated emancipation and African colonization had founded the American Colonization Society in 1817. It was led by prominent representatives of the upper South who wanted to eradicate slavery in order to promote economic and social development along northern lines. However, Society members who were from New England and New York were interested primarily in removing free African-Americans from the North.

Northern colonizationists regarded the North's 250,000 free blacks as "notoriously ignorant, degraded and miserable, mentally diseased, brokenspirited, acted upon by no motive to honourable exertions, scarcely reached in their debasement by the heavenly light," in the words of the American Colonization Society's 1829 report. Colonizationists often played a key role in maintaining disfranchisement and segregation. By 1860, only five northern states (Maine, Massachusetts, New Hampshire, Rhode Island, and Vermont, which all together accounted for only 6 percent of the northern black population) had extended suffrage to all adult male African-Americans. New York imposed special property and residence requirements on black voters. Connecticut, New Jersey, and Pennsylvania denied African-Americans the right to vote, as did Ohio, Indiana, Illinois, and every southern state.

Southern supporters of colonization likewise believed that African-Americans lacked the capacity to succeed in American society. Colonization, they thought, was necessary to prevent a destructive race war, especially because slaves made up almost 40 percent of the southern population in 1820. Kentuckian Henry Clay, for example, wanted full emancipation but declared that emancipation without colonization "would be followed by instantaneous collisions between the two races, which would break out into a civil war that would end in the extermination or subjugation of the one race or the other." By 1830 the American Colonization Society, with money raised from individuals, state governments, and churches, had succeeded in transporting 1,400 African-Americans to a colony the society called Liberia, on the west coast of Africa. However, of the 1,400 colonists, only 200 had won freedom as a consequence of the society's efforts. In the last analysis, the society was far more interested in shoring up slavery by removing free African-Americans from the South than in a program of emancipation.

Liberia. The colonists declared Liberia an independent republic in 1847 and adopted a constitution modeled after that of the United States. The country did not receive American recognition until 1862, after the Confederate states had left the Union. The African-American colonists and their descendants, who remained Protestant and continued to speak English, formed a small ruling class—little more than 10 percent of the population by the mid-twentieth century—that dominated the indigenous tribes. Liberia's economic life remained closely tied to that of the United States, and in the twentieth century American rubber companies, working with the local elite, largely controlled the economy.

A Radical Solution

Most free blacks rejected colonization. In 1817, three thousand met in Philadelphia's Bethel Church and denounced it. They informed "the humane and benevolent inhabitants of the city" that "we have no wish to separate from our present homes for any purpose whatever." They explained that they were "contented with our present situation and condition" and wanted only "the use of those opportunities . . . which the Constitution and the laws allow to all." African-Americans throughout the North seconded these sentiments at conventions and in pamphlets and newspapers. They also called for an end to slavery—through rebellion, if necessary.

In 1827, John Russwurm and Samuel D. Cornish began the first African-American newspaper, *Freedom's Journal,* in New York. Their Boston agent for the newspaper was David Walker, a free African-American from North Carolina who made a living selling second-hand clothes. In 1829, Walker published a stirring pamphlet *Appeal . . . to the Colored Citizens,* which ridiculed the religious pretensions of slaveholders, justified slave rebellion, and warned America that the slaves would revolt if justice was delayed. To white Americans he said, "We must and shall be free . . . in spite of you. . . . And woe, woe, will be it to you if we have to obtain our freedom by fighting." He added: "I do declare that one good black man can put to death six white men." Within a year Walker's *Appeal* had gone through three printings and had begun to reach free blacks in the South.

In 1830, Walker and other African-American abolitionists called a national convention in Philadelphia. Walker died under mysterious circumstances later that year, but the convention became an annual event. The delegates never adopted a position as radical as Walker's, but they regularly condemned slavery, colonization, and northern discriminatory legislation. They also urged free blacks to use every legal means to improve the condition of their race and asked for divine assistance in breaking "the shackles of slavery."

Nat Turner's Rebellion. In 1831 the major violence that David Walker had contemplated took concrete form when Nat Turner, a slave in Southampton County, Virginia, staged a bloody revolt. Turner had taught himself how to read as a child and had hoped to be emancipated, but a new master forced him into field work and another master separated him from his wife. Turner became deeply spiritual, seeing visions and concluding that he might carry Christ's burden of suffering in a race war. Taking an eclipse of the sun as an omen, Turner plotted with a handful of relatives and close friends to meet the masters' terror with terror of their own. They killed almost sixty slaveowners and members of their families, in many cases dismembering and decapitating them. Turner had hoped that an army of slaves would join his liberation force, but he had mustered only sixty men by the time a white militia formed to protect two large plantations and dispersed Turner's poorly armed and exhausted followers. In retaliation, whites killed slaves at random all over the county. One company of cavalry killed forty in two days, putting the heads of fifteen on poles to warn "all those who should undertake a similar plot." Fifty slaves were tried formally, and twenty of these were hanged. After hiding for nearly two months, Turner too was captured and hanged, still identifying his mission with that of Christ.

Evangelical Abolitionism, to 1840

The threat of a bloody racial revolution, coupled with the inspiring example of free African-Americans who sought to eradicate slavery, had a profound effect on some young white opponents of slavery. Many were evangelical ministers and their supporters. They became evangelists against slavery, appealing to the Christian conscience of individual slaveowners for immediate emancipation. Gradual change or compromise had no place in their new campaign. The issue was absolute: slaveowners and their supporters were sinning by depriving slaves of their God-given status as free moral agents. If the slaveowners did not repent, the evangelical abolitionists believed, they inevitably faced the prospect of revolution in this world and damnation in the next.

William Lloyd Garrison. The two most influential leaders of the antislavery movement during the 1830s were William Lloyd Garrison and Theodore Dwight Weld. Garrison was an early antislavery advocate and was less influenced by the evangelical revivals than were Weld and other white abolitionists. A Massachusetts-born printer, Garrison had collaborated in Baltimore during the 1820s with a Quaker, Benjamin Lundy, who published the *Genius of Universal Emancipation,* the leading antislavery newspaper of the decade. In 1830, Garrison went to jail, convicted of libeling a New England merchant engaged in the domestic slave trade.

William Lloyd Garrison

The daguerreotype captures the moral intensity that Garrison displayed in 1854 when he publicly burned the Constitution and declared: "So perish all compromises with tyranny." His self-righteous defiance of proslavery laws was part of a passionate quest to destroy all institutions that prevented individuals from discovering their full potential. (The Metropolitan Museum of Art)

After seven weeks, he was released because, through Lundy's intervention, Arthur Tappan, a wealthy New York merchant, paid the fine. Garrison went on to found his own antislavery weekly, *The Liberator,* in Boston in 1831. In the following year he spearheaded the formation of the New England Anti-Slavery Society.

From the outset, *The Liberator* deplored gradual or compensated emancipation and demanded the immediate abolition of slavery, without any reimbursement for slaveholders. Garrison condemned the American Colonization Society, charging that its real aim was to strengthen slavery by removing troublesome African-Americans who were already free. He even attacked the Constitution for its recognition of slavery. It was, he pronounced, "a covenant with death, an agreement with Hell." Nothing was safe from Garrison's criticism. He denounced ministers and even the authenticity of Scripture itself whenever he felt slavery was sanctioned. Increasingly, he concluded that slavery was a sign of deep corruption infesting *all* institutions, and called for comprehensive reform of American society as a whole.

Garrison's radical position attracted many avid followers, and to them he became a cultural hero on the scale of Emerson or Finney. Like these men, he made thundering assertions of his own identity. In the first number of his weekly newspaper, *The Liberator,* he declared: "I will be harsh as truth and as uncompromising as justice. . . . I am in earnest—I will not equivocate—I will not excuse—I will not retreat a single inch—AND I WILL BE HEARD."

Theodore Dwight Weld. In contrast to Garrison, Theodore Dwight Weld came to abolitionism from the religious revivals of the 1830s. Weld was a more restrained abolitionist. The son of a Congregationalist minister, he made a commitment to reform after hearing Charles Finney preach in Utica, New York. Weld worked within the churches of New York and the Old Northwest and shifted his focus from temperance and educational reforms to abolitionism. In these churches, primarily Presbyterian and Congregational, he preached the moral responsibility of all Americans for the denial of liberty to the slaves. In 1834, Weld inspired a group of students at Lane Theological Seminary in Cincinnati to form an antislavery society. When Lane's president, Lyman Beecher, sought to repress the society, the "Lane rebels" left, enrolling at Oberlin College and joining Weld in his evangelism. Weld's crusade gathered force, buttressed by theological arguments he advanced in *The Bible Against Slavery* (1837). Collaborating closely with him were the two South Carolina abolitionists—Angelina Grimké, whom he married in 1838, and her sister, Sarah.

With the assistance of the Grimké sisters, Weld provided the antislavery movement with a new base of evidence in a massive book, *American Slavery as It Is: Testimony of a Thousand Witnesses* (1839). Weld addressed the reader "as a juror to try a plain case and bring in an honest verdict." The question he posed was: "What is the actual condition of the slaves in the United States?" In answering, Weld presented evidence from southerners themselves, some of it from the more than 20,000 editions of southern newspapers he had searched. Among the firsthand accounts he cited were those of Angelina Grimké, who recalled her childhood in Charleston. She told, for example, of a treadmill that Charleston slaveowners used for punishment and of a prominent white woman who sent slaves there regularly: "One poor girl, whom she sent there to be flogged, and who was accordingly stripped naked and whipped, showed me the deep gashes on her back—I might have laid my whole finger in them—*large pieces of flesh had actually been cut out by the torturing lash.*" Weld's book sold over 100,000 copies during its first year alone.

The American Anti-Slavery Society. In 1833 Weld, Garrison, Arthur and Lewis Tappan, and sixty other delegates, black and white, met in Philadelphia to establish the American Anti-Slavery Society. They received financial support from the Tappans, and with it aimed to reach the middle-class public. Led by this society, abolitionists developed two approaches—one to address the public, and the other aimed at politicians. First they sought to create a moral climate so intense that slave-owners would have to accept programs of abolition. They used the tactics of the religious revivalists: public meetings led by stirring speakers, small gatherings sponsored by local antislavery chapters, and home visits by agents of the movement. The abolitionists also used new techniques of mass communication. Garrison's radical individualism did not stand in the way of attempts to reach a mass market. Assisted by the new steam press, the American Anti-Slavery Society was able to distribute more than 100,000 pieces of literature in 1834 and more than a million in 1835. Most dramatic was the "great postal campaign," begun in 1835, which flooded the nation, including the South, with abolitionist pamphlets. In July 1835 alone, abolitionists mailed more than 175,000 items through the New York City post office.

The abolitionists' second broad strategy was to mobilize public pressure on legislative bodies—in particular, Congress. In 1835 the American Anti-Slavery Society encouraged local chapters and members to bombard Congress with petitions for specific action: the abolition of slavery in the District of Columbia, abolition of the domestic slave trade, removal of the "three-fifths compromise" from the Constitution, and the denial of admission of new slave states to the Union. By 1838, a total of nearly 500,000 signed petitions had arrived in Washington.

Anti-Slavery Almanac

The heart-wrenching break-up of families by the slave trade was a common theme in abolitionist literature.

These activities drew increasing numbers of middle-class men and women to abolitionism. During the 1830s local abolitionist societies grew swiftly, from about 200 in 1835 to more than 500 in 1836 and to nearly 2,000 by 1840. Almost 200,000 people joined them. Meanwhile, the leadership of the abolitionist movement broadened beyond the original core of free blacks, Quakers, and evangelical Christians. Some of the transcendentalists, for example, felt shattered by the stark contrast between their claims for individual potential and the reality of slavery. Thanks to their literary skills and in some instances their wealth, many became leaders of the movement in New England. Emerson was less interested in the condition of slaves than in the moral failure of a free society that tolerated slavery, but he spoke out frequently against the institution, and as the Civil War neared, condoned abolitionist violence.

Thoreau was eloquently transcendental in his condemnations of slavery and in his calls for civil disobedience. In 1846, Thoreau protested the Mexican War and slavery by refusing to pay his taxes and submitting to arrest. Two years later, he published anonymously an essay entitled "Civil Disobedience" that outlined how individuals, by resisting governments that sanctioned slavery and by loyalty to a higher moral law, could transcend their own complicity in slavery and even redeem the state from its crimes. Even if outnumbered, moral individuals could prevail if they were true to their beliefs. "A minority is powerless while it conforms to the majority," Thoreau explained. But it becomes "irresistible when it clogs by its whole weight."

The Role of Women. Women also contributed to the power of the abolitionist movement. African-American women were crucial, and one of them, Maria W. Stewart, was among the first abolitionists. Stewart spoke out in Boston during the early 1830s. Even earlier than the Grimké sisters, she made speeches to mixed audiences of men and women. As the movement grew, thousands of white women throughout the North followed her example. They condemned the immorality of slavery; they delivered lectures to audiences of men and women; they supplied more than half of the signatures on the petitions that the American Anti-Slavery Society sent to Congress; and they conducted home "visitations" to win converts among other women and their husbands.

Women abolitionists also established their own organizations, including the Philadelphia Female Anti-Slavery Society, founded by Lucretia Mott in 1833; the Boston Female Anti-Slavery Society, founded by Maria Weston Chapman and twelve other women; and the Anti-Slavery Conventions of American Women, formed by a network of local societies during the late 1830s. The women's societies raised money for *The Liberator* and the American Anti-Slavery Society, supported agents and speakers against slavery, distributed literature, and established schools for free blacks.

By the late 1830s the abolitionist movement had mobilized and merged the reform ideas and energies of both religious revivalism and transcendentalism. What remained uncertain was the ability of the movement to develop practical strategies that would actually succeed in eradicating slavery.

Hostility to Abolition

In the South the conjunction of Nat Turner's slave rebellion, the imminent abolition of slavery by the British in the West Indies, and the beginnings of Garrison's *Liberator* touched off an intense effort to defend slavery. The final effort to address the slavery problem peacefully came in 1831–1832, after Turner's rebellion, when the Virginia legislature considered a program of gradual emancipation and colonization. When the bill was rejected, by a vote of 73 to 58, the possibility that southern states would legislate an end to slavery faded forever. Instead, in the 1830s, the southern states toughened their slave codes, limiting the movement of slaves and prohibiting teaching them to read—to prevent them from absorbing abolitionist literature. Southern legislatures banned abolitionism and passed resolutions demanding that northern states follow suit. The Georgia legislature even offered a $5,000 reward to anyone who would kidnap Garrison and bring him to the South to be tried for inciting rebellion. Public meetings routinely offered rewards for the capture of anyone distributing abolitionist literature. In Nashville, vigilantes whipped a northern college student for distributing abolitionist pamphlets. In Charleston, in 1835, a mob attacked the post office and destroyed sacks of abolitionist mail from the North. After that, southern postmasters generally refused to deliver mail of suspected abolitionist origins.

The New Defense of Slavery. At the same time, southern leaders—politicians, newspaper editors, and clergy—developed a new intellectual defense of the institution. It was new in that they moved beyond the defense of slavery as a "necessary evil" and developed a "positive good" argument—linked to industrial conditions and buttressed with Christian doctrine. They argued that slavery provided the slave with protection against the evils of the industrial system; it promoted "harmony" in relations between the races; it provided for a more efficient, orderly labor supply than was available in the North; and it had a basis in Scripture. This last argument was particularly crucial to southerners who needed a rationalization for enslaving a population that was now overwhelmingly Christian. Defenders of slavery such as Thornton Stringfellow, a Baptist minister from Virginia, claimed that St. Paul had recognized Christian churches that contained both masters and servants. And Stringfellow cited Paul's injunction: "Servants, obey your masters."

According to this sharpening self-image of plantation society, only an exceptional person—the planter—deserved genuine freedom. He was seen as surrounded by people who were incompetent and incapable of freedom. His task was to achieve a "disinterested benevolence" so that he could lead and manage. Only his exceptional willpower, reason, and self-control made society and order possible. Indeed, southern leaders such as John C. Calhoun advised the northern business elite that it could hold northern society together only by asserting the power that flowed from its "natural superiority." Calhoun exhorted northern business leaders to think and act more like planters.

Northern Antiabolitionists. The southern arguments won considerable support in the North. Some wealthy northerners sympathized with the South's appeal for unity among social elites, and feared that the abolitionist attack on property held as slaves could turn into a more general assault on property rights. Traditional elites, as well as many members of the business class, were troubled by the tactics of the abolitionists, who seemed to threaten the stability of the family by encouraging the active participation of women in the movement. Economic self-interest of northerners also prompted hostility to abolitionism. For example, some New York merchants and New England textile producers found it profitable to support the arguments of their southern customers or suppliers. And some wage earners saw abolitionism as a threat to their jobs; they feared that freed slaves, willing to work for subsistence wages, would pour into northern communities. Finally, only a small minority of any class of northerners believed in African-American equality; the rest were sympathetic to the racism of the planters and abhorred the thought of racial mixing, which the abolitionists seemed to advocate indirectly through their attacks on racism and on the colonization movement. Within the North, the extreme tone of the abolitionists was particularly resented in the communities of the Ohio Valley, which southerners had founded and peopled, and where the fear of freed slaves was especially intense.

Northern opponents of abolition could be as violent as those in the South. Mobs, sometimes led by people whom the abolitionists described as "gentlemen of property and standing," intimidated free blacks and abolitionists. They disrupted abolitionist meetings and routinely destroyed abolitionist printing presses. In 1833, fifteen hundred New Yorkers, the first antiabolitionist mob, stormed a church in a search for William Lloyd Garrison and Arthur Tappan. The next year, prominent New Yorkers cheered a mob of casual laborers who vandalized and set fire to Lewis Tappan's house, and a white mob swept through Philadelphia's African-American neighborhoods, clubbing and stoning residents, destroying homes and churches, and forcing crowds of black women and children to flee the city. In 1835 in Utica, New York, a group of lawyers, local politicians, merchants, and bankers broke up an abolitionist convention and beat several delegates. In the same year a Boston mob dragged Garrison through the streets, threatening to hang him. And two years later in Alton, Illinois, a mob shot and killed an abolitionist editor, Elijah P. Lovejoy.

The "Gag-Rule." President Andrew Jackson, swayed by these demonstrations of northern hostility to abolition, privately approved of South Carolina's censorship of the United States mails. Publicly, in his 1835 annual message to Congress, Jackson called on northern states to suppress abolitionism, and he asked Congress to restrict the use of the mails by abolitionist groups. Congress did not respond, in part because Calhoun wanted an extreme measure—banning deliveries of abolitionist tracts in any state or territory that prohibited such material. In 1836, however, the House of Representatives did adopt the "gag rule." Under this rule, which remained in force until 1844, antislavery petitions were automatically tabled when they were received so the petitions could not become the subject of debate in the House. In the same year, Connecticut passed a "gag law" in an attempt to suppress abolitionist speakers, but no other northern state followed suit.

The violence and suppression stunned antislavery advocates and shocked many people who had not participated in abolitionism but had joined evangelical revivals. The disorder and violence seemed additional symptoms of a deeply troubled society. Evangelical Protestants redoubled their efforts to find the means to promote social harmony. Some of the abolitionists among them worked to build the Whig party. Others focused their efforts more specifically on slavery as a political question.

Antislavery after 1840: The Rise of the Free-Soil Movement

As assaults on the antislavery movement mounted, most abolitionists dissociated themselves from Garrison's broad attack on American institutions. Many evangelical Protestants, often following the Tappans, continued to work through their churches. Some of these, working with more secular abolitionists, drew on their experience in managing the postal and petition campaigns of the 1830s. They turned to practical politics. They wished to attract moderate Americans—people who neither supported nor opposed abolition—and to propose practical political solutions. They were no less radical than Garrison in terms of their commitment to abolition, but they were more willing to work within the existing political system. Most of these conservative abolitionists felt that American society, while seriously flawed by slavery, was at its core healthy.

Garrison and his supporters, however, became even more adamant that their American Anti-Slavery Society retain a broad platform, which included equal participation for women in the society, pacifism, abolition of prisons and asylums, and in 1843, expulsion of the slave states from the Union. The attacks on abolitionists had, in fact, made the Garrisonians even more radical. Then, in 1837, Garrison came under the influence of John Humphrey Noyes and the perfectionists. He began to emphasize emphatically his belief that institutions, rather than individuals, were the source of all sin and that virtually all American institutions were corrupt.

This growing rift in the abolitionist movement fractured Garrison's American Anti-Slavery Society in 1840. Some abolitionists left it to join the American and Foreign Anti-Slavery Society, with its leadership in New York and its major financial backing from Lewis Tappan. Others—such as Theodore Weld, who had left the organized movement along with the Grimkés in 1838—avoided both the Garrison and the Tappan camps, although he retained an evangelical approach to abolition. Weld sought to avoid factional disputes within the movement and, in any case, found both camps lacking. He disliked Garrison's dilution of abolitionism in a broad-based reform effort but found distasteful what he described as the "anti-woman" attitude of more conservative abolitionists.

The Liberty Party. In 1840 most of the abolitionist leaders who had split with Garrison began to emphasize electoral politics as a means to eliminate slavery. They established the Liberty party and nominated James G. Birney as its presidential candidate in 1840 and 1844. Birney was a former slaveowner who had lived in Alabama and Kentucky; after a Princeton education and conversion by Weld to abolitionism, he had founded an antislavery newspaper in Cincinnati. In contrast with Garrison and his demands for sweeping reform of the nation's institutions, Birney accepted working within the Constitution. He and the Liberty party took the position that the Constitution did not recognize slavery, regarding it as a state institution; that the Fifth Amendment, by barring any Congressional deprivation of "life, liberty, or property," prevented the federal government from sanctioning slavery; and that slaves became automatically free when they entered areas of federal authority, such as the District of Columbia or national territories. But even this more moderate stance failed to attract a substantial following; the Liberty party won less than 3 percent of northern votes for its presidential candidate in 1844.

After this defeat, the founders of the Liberty party relaxed even further the intensity of their moral demands and de-emphasized the moral and political rights of slaves. These political abolitionists cooperated with, and made major concessions to politicians in the major political parties. The leaders of the Liberty party agreed to recast abolitionism in terms of republican ideals, defining the problem of slavery not as an individual sin but as a threat to republican institutions. In 1848 the leaders of this new coalition redefined the antislavery position; they stressed that there was a tyrannical "Slave Power" conspiracy composed of southern planters and those northern business people who depended on them. The conspiracy was said to draw its strength from an absolute control over human beings that endangered the republic. House passage of the "gag rule" provided evidence of this conspiracy; the "Slave Power" imperiled the rights of free speech, free assembly, and the free press—in the North as well as in the South. In the new formulation, the key to defeating the "Slave Power" became prohibiting slavery in the national territories. This program became known as "free soil," and the reorganized antislavery party took on a new name: the Free Soil party. Under the new platform, the West, thought to be the key to the future of the republic, was to be kept pure of slavery and secure for freedom. The Free Soil party retained an enthusiasm for individual freedom, but it expressed a greater interest in the freedom of whites occupying new lands than in freedom for slaves. This shift of emphasis led Garrison to denounce the new Free Soil party as "whitemanism," a racist effort to make the territories white.

Despite Garrison's hostility, the new political approach won the support of many women and free black abolitionists, who themselves were denied the political rights that white men enjoyed. Women in the American and Foreign Anti-Slavery Society established dozens of new female societies throughout the Great Lakes states to work for free soil. In St. Cloud, Minnesota, Jane Swisshelm founded an antislavery newspaper, the *Visitor,* that commented on politics and won, she claimed, thousands of votes for free-soil candidates.

Free Soil Supporters. One supporter of free soil was Frederick Douglass, who emerged during the 1840s as a leading antislavery strategist, the most electrifying of all abolitionist orators, and the foremost African-American abolitionist. He and other African-American abolitionists established their independence from their white counterparts, including even the radical Garrisonians. In 1843 these African-American leaders called the convention of the Free People of Color, at which they advocated slave rebellions. Douglass, however, rejected Garrison's insistence on expulsion of the southern states, believing it would leave the slaves completely at the mercy of slaveowners. In 1848 Douglass and the other African-American abolitionists had decided that supporting the growing free-soil movement was their only sensible political choice.

The free-soil movement also attracted the remnants of the transcendentalists, who generally favored more radical approaches to abolition. Thomas Wentworth Higginson, a young Unitarian minister from Boston, ran unsuccessfully for Congress as a Free Soil candidate in 1850. During the Civil War, he would command a regiment of African-American soldiers. Another Unitarian minister, Theodore Parker, used his home as a station on the underground railroad for escaped slaves. In 1858, Parker, Higginson, and Franklin B. Sanborn, a young teacher who was a protégé of Emerson's, joined the "Secret Six," a group which financially backed the John Brown's scheme to invade the South and incite a slave rebellion.

The free-soil movement thus provided a convenient political umbrella for both antiblack opponents of slavery in the territories and at least some radical abolitionists. Many of the abolitionists who did support free soil believed that the terror used to maintain slavery would ultimately require a violent solution. They felt that the free-soil movement was the only way to provoke the necessary confrontation. Moreover, these abolitionists urged white free-soilers to pay greater attention to emancipation in the South and to civil rights for African-Americans in the North. They pointed out, for example, that no state admitted to the Union after Maine in 1820 had extended the suffrage to African-Americans.

During the 1840s and 1850s, the strategy of political abolitionism gained broader popular support. In 1848 the new Free Soil party received more than 290,000 votes cast in the presidential election—more than 10 percent of the total. During the 1850s, the Republican party would formulate a free-soil policy. Although many Americans did not believe that slaveowning was sinful or that African-Americans deserved equality, they could be convinced that slavery threatened liberty and economic opportunity for white people in the West.

By the 1850s, free-soil enthusiasm dominated popular support for the antislavery movement. Free soil had radical dimensions in that it threatened both slavery and the Second Party System. But it also had a conservative side. By preoccupying women reformers it delayed the development of a substantial critique of traditional roles within the family—a critique that was necessary for a fully developed feminist ideology. And the free-soil movement celebrated economic opportunity in the North, allowing conservative politicians to divert attention from the costs and limitations of the Industrial Revolution and, in particular, the dislocation and coercion of "free labor." Ironically, the vast reform energies of the era, which came to focus on the problem of slavery from the perspective of free soil, had the result of reinforcing the traditional family, industrialization, and the power of the business class.

AMERICAN LIVES

Frederick Douglass: Development of an Abolitionist

Frederick Douglass was born a slave in 1818, on the Eastern Shore of Maryland. He took his mother's family name of Bailey—derived perhaps from the Muslim *Belali.* He never knew who his father was, although talk in the slave-quarters pointed to a man Douglass later described as his "master."

For most of his time in slavery, Douglass's master was Thomas Auld, who acquired the young Frederick in 1827 as part of a property settlement and sent him to live with his brother Hugh in Baltimore. There were no other slaves in that home, and Frederick was treated much like the other children. He listened to Sophia Auld read the Bible, learned to read from a spelling book borrowed from the Auld children, figured out the meaning of "abolition" by reading newspapers, and heard about slaves running away to the North. At the age of twelve he purchased a copy of *The Columbian Orator,* a collection of practice speeches for young boys on the virtues of the republic—including its devotion to the "rights of man." Enthralled, Frederick memorized and recited the speeches to his friends, including the free blacks he sought out at Methodist and Baptist churches.

In 1833, Thomas Auld returned Frederick to the sleepy Eastern Shore town of St. Michaels, perhaps to prevent him from running away or becoming mixed up in antislavery agitation. Frederick hoped that Auld would get religion and free him. When he did not, Frederick became rebellious, organizing a Sabbath school and resisting the routines of work. In 1834 Auld hired Frederick out to Edward Covey, a farmer with a reputation for "breaking" unruly slaves. After six months of disciplined labor and regular beatings, Frederick had a brutal fight with Covey. Douglass recalled that the battle "was the turning point in my *'life as a slave.'* . . . I was nothing before; I WAS A MAN NOW." From that point he was determined "to be a FREEMAN."

The next year Auld hired Frederick out to a more lenient master. Frederick again organized a school and, with six other slaves, hatched a plan for escape up the Chesapeake. Betrayed by a fellow conspirator, he found himself in jail, facing sale into the Deep South. But Auld again intervened, returning Frederick to Baltimore with a promise that if he applied himself to a trade he would free him at the age of twenty-five.

Frederick Douglass

The daguerreotype was taken of Douglass when he was in his twenties. Describing Douglass, an admirer wrote: "He was more than six feet in height, and his majestic form . . . straight as an arrow, muscular, yet lithe and graceful, his flashing eye, and more than all, his voice, that rivaled Webster's in its richness, and in the depth and sonorousness of its cadences, made up such an ideal of an orator as the listeners never forgot."

Frederick did apply himself. He became a journeyman caulker in the shipyards and, in 1838, struck a deal with Hugh Auld that allowed him to control his living and working arrangements in return for a guaranteed weekly payment. Frederick plunged into Baltimore's free African-American community, almost 30,000 in number. He courted a free woman, Anna Murray, and joined a group of black caulkers—all free but him—called the East Baltimore Mental Improvement Society. But this life came to an abrupt end when he fell two days behind in his payment to Hugh Auld. Auld ordered him to give up his independent earnings, employment, and housing. Unwilling to surrender the small measure of independence he had gained, Frederick decided to run away. Less than a month later, in the fall of 1838, he stepped off a ferry in New York City; a few days later he married Anna Murray.

Frederick and Anna settled first in the seaport of New Bedford, Massachusetts, where he took a new name—Douglass—to avoid capture. He found work, made his first antislavery speech to a white audience, and heard William Lloyd Garrison lecture. At a meeting of the Massachusetts Anti-Slavery Society in 1841, he made a powerful address that won the admiration of Garrison and other leading abolitionists, who hired him as an agent of the American Anti-Slavery Society. His celebrated lecturing took him to hundreds of communities in the Northeast, where audiences were spellbound by his speeches. Elizabeth Cady Stanton described an 1842 address in Boston's Faneuil Hall:

> Around him sat the great antislavery orators of the day watching the effect of his eloquence on that immense audience, that laughed and wept by turns, completely carried away by the wondrous gifts of his pathos and humor. On this occasion, all the other speakers seemed tame after Frederick Douglass.

In his speeches Douglass denounced both slavery in the South and racial discrimination in the North. He was uncomfortable, however, with Garrison's perfectionism. Douglass did not take issue with Garrison's radicalism publicly, for he hoped it would motivate white America to take practical steps—such as abolishing slavery in the District of Columbia—toward the eradication of slavery. His differences with Garrison grew, however, and in 1847 he returned from a British tour determined to chart an independent course. (In an important way his independence was more secure because in 1841 admiring British abolitionists had financed the purchase of his freedom from Auld to ensure that Douglass would not be arrested as a fugitive.)

Douglass moved to Rochester, New York, where he founded an antislavery newspaper, the *North Star,* financed heavily by Gerrit Smith, a Liberty party leader. The next year Douglass attended the Buffalo convention that created the Free Soil party, and the *North Star* extended a cautious endorsement to the party. Also that year he attended the Seneca Falls convention, writing in the *North Star:* "We are free to say that in respect to political rights, we hold woman to be justly entitled to all we claim for men."

In 1851, Douglass publicly defied the American Anti-Slavery Society by defending the Constitution, and in 1852 he delivered what became known as his "Fifth of July" speech, probably the most moving and influential of his career. He denied that the Constitution was proslavery. "In *that* instrument, he declared, I hold there is no warrant, license, nor sanction of the hateful thing; but, interpreted as it *ought* to be interpreted, the Constitution is a GLORIOUS LIBERTY DOCUMENT."

Douglass's involvement in practical politics deepened during the 1850s. Although he believed that violence would be necessary to abolish slavery, he was cautious in encouraging slave insurrection, declining to join John Brown's raid on Harpers Ferry (see Chapter 14). Nonetheless, suspicion that he was a key conspirator led Douglass to flee to Canada and Britain. When he resumed speechmaking in America, during the summer of 1860, the victory of the Republican party and its free-soil program seemed imminent.

Douglass remained a key leader of former abolitionists and African-Americans for the rest of his life. During the Civil War, he pressed Abraham Lincoln and the Republicans to embrace abolition of slavery as a war aim and was delighted when Lincoln adopted his view of the Constitution. He helped the war department recruit black soldiers. Throughout Reconstruction he spoke and lobbied effectively for equal treatment—including the right to vote—for African-Americans. But his service to the Republican party went virtually unrewarded. Republican presidents appointed him to minor positions of marshal for the District of Columbia (1877) and recorder of deeds for the District (1881). It was not until the age of seventy that he finally received a significant appointment—as U.S. minister to Haiti. Nonetheless, he lost his optimism about the willingness of the republic to guarantee equality to all Americans only in the last few years before his death in 1895.

Summary

Industrialization challenged Americans to reconcile claims for the supremacy of the individual with society's need for cohesion. Americans' efforts to resolve this conflict produced an era of social reform.

The reform impulse embraced a widening variety of campaigns that expanded the social critique that the labor movement had initiated. Transcendentalists and other groups formed experimental communities that they hoped would reform society by setting an inspiring example. Women who had been involved in *moral* reform turned to the reform of *institutions*—including prisons, asylums, and hospitals. New religious sects like the Shakers sought to control sin by withdrawing into insular communities.

The most dramatic outlet for the reform enthusiasm was a new attack on slavery. In the 1830s, a group of abolitionists emerged who shared the moral intensity of the business-class evangelists but were far more radical. In attacking slavery, the abolitionists challenged traditional property rights, and some abolitionists condemned all institutions that seemed to limit human freedom. Participation in abolitionism led some women to begin the development of an ideology that challenged the traditional division of labor within the household.

In the late 1830s and early 1840s, conservative opposition in both the North and the South nearly halted the movement to abolish slavery, as well as all radical reform efforts. But later in the decade the abolitionists broadened their message. Increasingly, they described slavery as much more than the denial of freedom to individual slaves or an expression of the unbridled individualism of slaveholders. Slavery was, they said, a profound threat to the institution of "free labor" and to American family life. With this more conservative message, and with a new political tactic—calling for the exclusion of slavery from the territories—abolitionists won the support of a large middle-class audience in the North. By the 1850s, the issue of slavery completely dominated the way in which Americans thought about their future in an industrial society.

TOPIC FOR RESEARCH

Individualism and Reform: A Case Study

Powerful, dynamic individuals led the religious, social, and political reform movements that swept the United States before the Civil War. In a sense, the personal strength of these individuals demonstrated the potential of freedom in American society. But for all these reformers, for writers and philosophers, and for reflective politicians—in fact for everyone who thought seriously about the industrializing world—the main problem of the age was to reconcile the freedom of the individual with the legitimate demands of society. Consequently, many reformers who embraced the ideal of individual freedom at the same time urged others to accept an inner discipline—to make a religious commitment, for example, that would restrain excessive individualism.

Choose one of the leading reformers in the United States before the Civil War and read a biography of that reformer. (See the Bibliography for some possibilities.) You might look for a founder of a utopian community, an abolitionist, or a champion of women's rights. Also, consult the bibliography in the biography you have chosen for references to writings by the reformer that you might also read. As you read, think about how your reformer weighed the individual's need for freedom against society's for order. How did the goals and programs of your reformer reflect his or her assessment of what was the ideal balance between the two?

BIBLIOGRAPHY

Transcendentalists and Utopians

The leading study that connects transcendentalism with reform movements is Ann C. Rose, *Transcendentalism as a Social Movement, 1830–1850* (1981). See also Catherine L. Albanese, *Corresponding Motion: Transcendental Religion and the New American* (1977), and Lawrence Buell, *Literary Transcendentalism: Style and Vision in the American Renaissance* (1973). On communitarian experiments, see Arthur Bestor Jr., *Backwoods Utopias: The Sectarian and Owenite Phases of Communitarian Life in America* (1970); Lawrence Foster, *Religion and Sexuality: Three American Communal Experiments of the Nineteenth Century* (1981); Jean McMahon Humez, ed., *Gifts of Power: The Writings of Rebecca Jackson, Black Visionary, Shaker Eldress* (1981); Louis J. Kern, *An Ordered Love: Sex Roles and Sexuality in Victorian Utopias—The Shakers, the Mormons, and the Oneida Community* (1981); and Charles Nordhoff, *The Communistic Societies of the United States* (1875, reprinted 1960). Recent studies that link literary developments to reform themes include Harold Kaplan, *Democratic Humanism and American Literature* (1972); David S. Reynolds, *Beneath the American Renaissance: The Subversive Imagination in the Age of Emerson and Melville* (1988); and Larzar Ziff, *Literary Democracy, The Declaration of Cultural Independence in America*

(1981). On the linkages between religion and the utopians, see Whitney R. Cross, *The Burned-Over District, The Social and Intellectual History of Enthusiastic Religion in Western New York, 1800–1850* (1950); and Timothy L. Smith, *Revivalism and Social Reform: American Protestantism on the Eve of the Civil War* (1980).

Women and Reform

The most comprehensive history of women in the United States is Nancy Woloch, *Women and the American Experience* (1984). On the social history of women, see W. Elliot Brownlee and Mary M. Brownlee, *Women in the American Economy: A Documentary History, 1675–1929* (1976); Nancy F. Cott, *The Bonds of Womanhood: "Women's Sphere" in New England, 1780–1835* (1977); Carl N. Degler, *At Odds: Women and the Family in America from the Revolution to the Present* (1980); and Mary P. Ryan, *Cradle of the Middle Class, The Family in Oneida County, New York, 1790–1865* (1981). The most thorough description of the participation of women in benevolence and reform is Keith Melder, *Beginnings of Sisterhood: The American Women's Rights Movement, 1800–1850* (1977). For studies of more specific aspects of women's involvement in benevolence, see Barbara J. Berg, *The Remembered Gate: Origins of American Feminism, The Woman and the City, 1800–1860* (1978); and Estelle B. Freedman, *Their Sisters' Keepers: Women's Prison Reform in America, 1830–1860* (1981). The leading histories of feminists and the early women's rights movement include Kathleen Barry, *Susan B. Anthony—A Biography: A Singular Feminist* (1988); Paula Blanchard, *Margaret Fuller: From Transcendentalism to Revolution* (1978); Ellen Du Bois, *Feminism and Suffrage: The Emergence of an Independent Women's Movement, 1848–1869* (1978); and Eleanor Flexner, *Century of Struggle: The Woman's Rights Movement in the United States* (1959).

The Antislavery Movement

Surveys of reform that are useful in understanding the antislavery movement include works by C. S. Griffen, Alice F. Tyler, and Ronald G. Walters listed in the Bibliography for Chapter 13. Those that focus on antislavery include Robert H. Abzug, *Passionate Liberator, Theodore Dwight Weld and the Dilemma of Reform* (1980); Gilbert H. Barnes, *The Anti-Slavery Impulse, 1830–1844* (1933); David Brion Davis, *The Problems of Slavery in the Age of Revolution, 1770–1823* (1975); Louis Filler, *The Crusade Against Slavery, 1830–1860* (1960); Louis Gerteis, *Morality and Utility in American Antislavery Reform* (1987); Leon F. Litwack, *North of Slavery: The Negro in the Free States, 1790–1860*; Stephen B. Oates, *To Purge This Land with Blood: A Biography of John Brown* (1970); Lewis Perry, *Childhood, Marriage, and Reform: Henry Clarke Wright, 1797–1870* (1980); Benjamin Quarles, *Black Abolitionists* (1969); James B. Stewart, *Holy Warriors: The Abolitionists and American Slavery* (1976); John L. Thomas, *The Liberator: William Lloyd Garrison* (1963); and Bertram Wyatt-Brown, *Lewis Tappan and the Evangelical War Against Slavery* (1959). The leading studies of Frederick Douglass include Philip S. Foner, *Frederick Douglass: A Biography* (1964); Nathan I. Huggins, *Slave and Citizen: The Life of Frederick Douglass* (1980); Waldo E. Martin, *The Mind of Frederick Douglass* (1985); William S. McFeely, *Frederick Douglass* (1991); and Benjamin Quarles, *Frederick Douglass* (1948). Essential sources on Douglass are three versions of his autobiography: *The Narrative of the Life of Frederick Douglass, An American Slave* (1845), which he wrote as an antislavery tract; *My Bondage and My Freedom* (1855), which provides an elaborate, and highly personal analysis of slavery; *Life and Times of Frederick Douglass, Written by Himself* (1881), which added the Civil War and Reconstruction. For the role of women in the antislavery movement, consult Edmund Fuller, *Prudence Crandall: An Incident of Racism in Nineteenth-Century America* (1971); Blanche Hersh, *The Slavery of Sex: Female Abolitionists in Nineteenth-Century America* (1978); Gerda Lerner, *The Grimke Sisters from South Carolina: Pioneers for Women's Rights and Abolition* (1967); and Alma Lutz, *Crusade for Freedom: Women of the Antislavery Movement* (1968). On northern hostility to abolition, see Leonard L. Richards, *"Gentlemen of Property and Standing": Anti-Abolition Mobs in Jacksonian America* (1970).

TIMELINE

1817	American Colonization Society founded
1829	David Walker's *Appeal*
1831	William Lloyd Garrison begins publishing *The Liberator* Nat Turner's rebellion
1832	Ralph Waldo Emerson resigns his Boston pulpit New England Anti-Slavery Society founded
1834	New York Female Moral Reform Society established
1835	House of Representatives adopts "gag rule"
1837	Emerson's lecture "The American Scholar" Mob kills Elijah P. Lovejoy
1840	Liberty party launched
1841	Transcendentalists found Brook Farm Dorothea Dix begins her investigations
1844	Margaret Fuller's *Women in the Nineteenth Century*
1845	Thoreau withdraws to a cabin on Walden Pond
1847	Frederick Douglass founds the *North Star* Liberia declared an independent republic
1848	John Humphrey Noyes founds Oneida Community Free Soil party formed Seneca Falls convention
1851	Herman Melville's *Moby Dick* published
1852	Harriet Beecher Stowe's *Uncle Tom's Cabin*

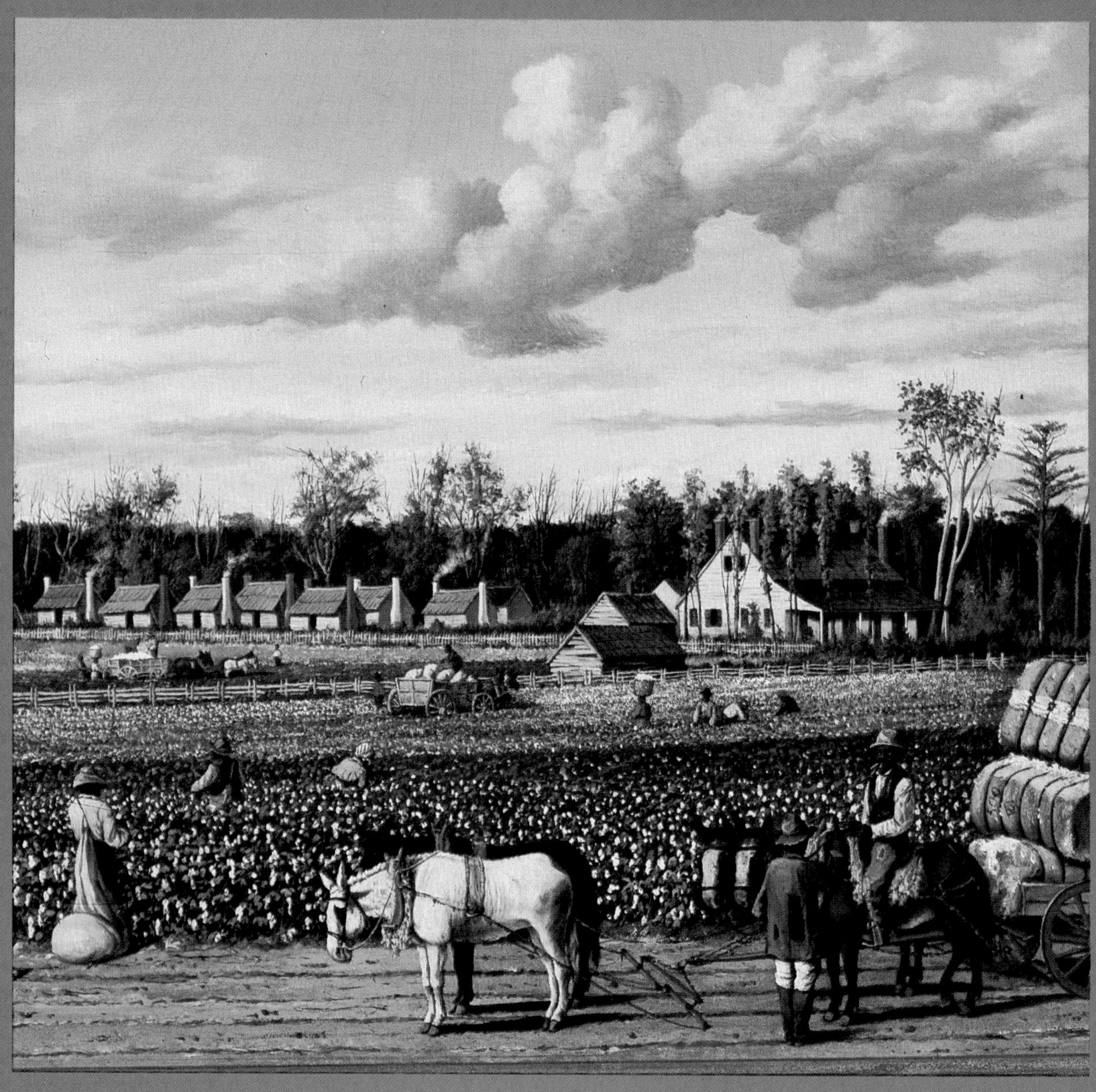

Plantation Economy in the Old South, c. 1876

Although this detail from a painting by William Aiken Walker idealizes life on the cotton plantation—much as the defenders of slavery did—it does suggest the importance of slavery and self-sufficiency to the largest plantations in the South. Small farms in the South outnumbered large plantations, but the plantations established economic and social styles that most white southerners tried to emulate. (The Warner Collection of Gulf States Paper Corp.)

CHAPTER 13 *Sections and Sectionalism,* 1840–1860

As the antislavery movement gathered force during the 1840s and 1850s, setting North against South, the accelerating Industrial Revolution accentuated the distinctiveness of the two sections. While the North grew increasingly industrial, the fortunes of the South became ever more tied to its "peculiar institution," as slavery was sometimes called. Two distinctly different economic and social systems were evolving, with two different ways of thinking about the relationship between the individual and society. And people in the two sections became acutely conscious of their differences. Indeed, they celebrated them—that is to say, *sectionalism* increased in the decades before the Civil War.

Westward expansion further intensified the sectionalism. Each society, southern and northern, believed that westward expansion was necessary in order to preserve its way of life. In the 1840s and 1850s, however, the acceleration of northern industrialization gave the North a major advantage. Northerners, motivated by the push of the Industrial Revolution and the pull of fresh land, came pouring into the West in vast numbers. The raw demographic advantage of northern society in the West, coupled with the popularity of the free-soil movement there and in the Northeast, led southerners to a condition of high anxiety about their ability to protect slavery within the Union.

The Slave South: A Distinctive Society

On a superficial level, southern planters were similar to northern capitalists. Both groups did what they considered necessary to protect their investments and maximize their profits. But the key investment for planters lay in human beings and land, rather than in factories and machines. That reality required a justification of slavery in which planters denied that they had significant economic motivations. As the profits from slaveowning mounted during the 1840s and 1850s, so did the efforts at rationalization. The planters increasingly described themselves as superior beings—natural aristocrats who altruistically protected their human property.

The Slave Economy

Between 1840 and 1860 the South's economy grew rapidly and generated high incomes for both slaveowners and other whites. Per capita income, even taking the meager incomes of slaves (food, clothing, and shelter) into account, increased more rapidly in the South than in the United States as a whole. In 1860, only the Northeast, Great Britain, and Australia had higher per capita incomes than the South. Southern prosperity was based on the export to Europe of tobacco, rice, sugar, and—above all—cotton. By the 1850s, after the Cotton Kingdom had swept across the Mississippi River into Texas, the South produced more than two-thirds of the world's cotton. In 1860 southern cotton accounted for almost two-thirds of the total value of exports from the United States.

Southern agriculture was highly productive, generating large revenues compared with the investment of labor, capital, and land. But unlike northern farmers, southern planters did not depend on domestic consumers or improvements in farm technology. Their high profits depended on three other factors—British markets, fresh land, and slavery.

The British connection was crucial. The buoyant demand of British textile mills drove up the export price of cotton, and British mercantile houses provided the major sources of capital for the southern planters. And because southern agriculture relied heavily on foreign markets, the region enjoyed a high degree of economic independence from the rest of the United States.

The availability of fresh land was equally significant because cotton ruined the soil more quickly than did most other crops. By 1860 nearly three-fourths of the South's cotton production came from the region's newer plantations—on lands stretching from western Georgia to eastern Texas. In the early 1850s one observer described Georgia's eastern plantation belt as "red old hills stripped of their native growth and virgin soil, and washed with deep gullies, with here and there patches of Bermuda grass, and stunted pine shrubs, struggling for a scanty subsistence on what was one of the richest soils in America." The ravaging of southern land moved westward and continued into the twentieth century.

Most important, southern planters became increasingly dependent on slave labor. Slavery allowed planters to organize labor into large-scale, specialized routines that resembled factory work but were far more demanding, intense, and brutal. While the northern business class relied heavily on the appeals of evangelical Christianity and the promise of economic rewards to discipline workers, southern planters emphasized coercion, terror, and suppression of open communication to keep their workers—the slaves—in line. Planters could use these tactics as long as they insulated their society from the rest of the nation.

Immigration offered little assistance to the South in building a labor force. Most migrants from the North and from Europe avoided the South, and the majority of those who did go there found jobs that did not force them to compete with cheap slave labor. Few immigrants settled there even during the 1850s, when there were growing opportunities for work in southern cities. The South actually *lost* free workers, because a significant portion of its white population, especially in the border states, migrated to the upper Ohio Valley and, during the 1850s, to Oregon and California. Few slaves arrived from Africa after 1808, when Congress banned their importation (and exportation). It was the high birthrate of the existing slave population that provided the necessary labor force for the Cotton Kingdom.

The Gang-labor System. Planters who grew cotton or sugar with more than twenty slaves forced their slaves into intensely specialized and disciplined work. In 1860 such planters were only about 10 percent of all slaveowners, but they owned about 50 percent of the slaves.

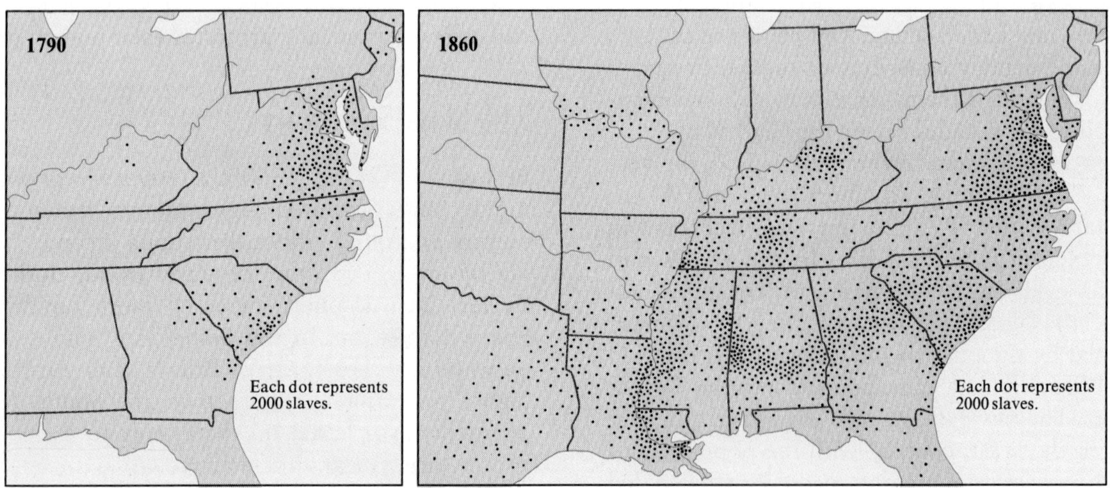

MAP 13.1

The Distribution of Slave Population, 1790–1860

The cotton boom was largely responsible for the westward shift of slave population. In 1790 slaves were concentrated most heavily on the tobacco plantations of the Chesapeake Bay and the rice and indigo areas of South Carolina. By 1860 slaves were most heavily concentrated on the cotton and sugar land of the lower Mississippi Valley, and along an arc of fertile cotton land—the "black belt"—sweeping from Mississippi through Georgia.

Harvesting Sugarcane
This watercolor by Franz Holzlhuber represents slaves harvesting sugarcane during the late 1850s in southern Louisiana, where American sugar production was concentrated. Sugar plantations, which had been the first to introduce gang labor, were even harder on slaves than cotton plantations because of the continuous ditching and draining of marsh lands, and the laborious processing of the cane. (*Sugarcane Harvest in Louisiana and Texas,* 1856–1860, Collection of Glenbow Museum)

These planters or their overseers assigned slaves specific tasks, which would vary by season, and organized the hands into disciplined "gangs," which worked in the fields at a feverish pace. Overseers, most of whom were white, and drivers, who were themselves slaves, used the threat of the whip to force their gangs into tight, coordinated units for plowing, hoeing, and picking. A traveler in Mississippi in 1854 watched an army of slaves return from the fields at the end of a summer day:

> First came, led by an old driver carrying a whip, forty of the largest and strongest women I ever saw together; they were all in a simple uniform dress of a bluish check stuff, the skirts reaching little below the knee; their legs and feet were bare; they carried themselves loftily, each having a hoe over the shoulder, and walking with a free, powerful swing.

Next marched the plowhands with their mules, "the cavalry, thirty strong, mostly men, but a few of them women." Finally, "a lean and vigilant white overseer, on a brisk pony, brought up the rear." As large-scale cotton and sugar production grew, gang labor became more common than the somewhat less demanding "task" system that prevailed in the cultivation of other crops and had been the most common organization of slave labor before 1820.

Plantation owners could not have organized *free* farm workers to labor under the discipline of slave gangs. On family farms, or on farms with only a few slaves, field workers insisted on a degree of independence and on work routines involving a variety of tasks. Throughout the country, whenever farm owners tried to organize free workers into gangs, the free laborers demanded wages that made their output unprofitable. Or they simply quit, preferring to find employment as sharecroppers, casual workers, or factory hands. There was a large difference between the high wages that free laborers would have demanded from cotton planters and the cost of rearing and maintaining slaves. This saving in labor costs was the economic gain that planters reaped from slavery.

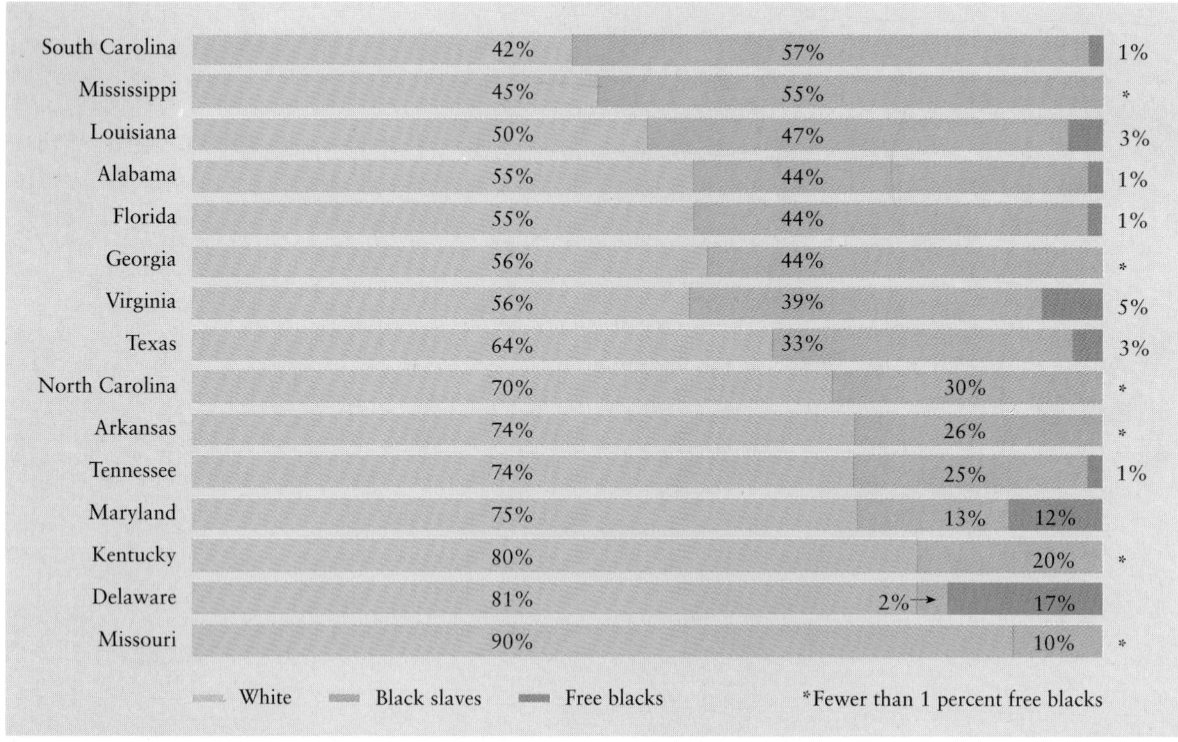

FIGURE 13.1

Proportion of Black and White Population in the South, 1860

The Economic Impact of Slavery. Because of the gang labor system, the availability of new land, and the enormous demand for cotton on world markets, the owning of slaves was extremely profitable. Planters—all except those farming the poorest land—made profits from their investments in slaves that averaged about 10 percent a year during the 1840s and 1850s. Even the most successful New England textile mills rarely produced a higher rate of return.

The high profits from cotton production and slavery created two long-term economic problems. First, southern investors concentrated their resources in cotton and slaves, rather than in manufacturing. Consequently, the percentage of people who lived in towns and cities and worked in manufacturing was twice as high in the North as in the South. The only major southern cities were the old seaports of Baltimore, Charleston, and New Orleans, and they remained predominantly commercial centers. A more tragic liability was slavery's discouragement of investment in human beings. Planters made little or no effort to educate or train their slaves or to provide schooling for poor whites. In fact, laws actually forbade education for slaves. Without large urban and industrial sectors, and without a large force of skilled, educated workers, the South faced severe difficulties in long-term economic development.

Realities and Ideals of the Planter Class

The planters made up a tiny minority of southern whites. In 1860, only about 46,000 individuals—little more than 0.5 percent of the white population of the South—owned twenty or more slaves. Only about 8,000 planters owned fifty or more slaves. Small as it was, this minority increased its influence during the 1840s and 1850s and came to dominate southern society more completely than the business elite controlled the North.

The planters were able to increase their power by holding out to the majority of whites the possibility of entering their elite class. Most planters lived in relatively unpretentious farmhouses. However, the enormous profits of the 1840s and 1850s enabled the wealthiest planters to build splendid plantations and indulge in displays of conspicuous consumption. In the new cotton lands of the Mississippi Valley, many large cotton planters had risen from modest circumstances. Their prosperity whetted the appetites of all slaveowners—more than 380,000 individuals, belonging to about a fourth of white southern families—and the small farmers who aspired to own slaves.

The "Cavaliers" and Their Wives. The elaborate defense of slavery that began to develop during the 1830s reinforced the message conveyed by the planters' wealth and conspicuous consumption. They promoted descriptions of themselves as superior, noble beings whom other whites should admire or at least treat with deference. Sermons, novels, and tracts defending slavery pictured the planter as a born leader who acted with grace and restraint. The planters were Christian patriarchs, it was said, who treated their dependents—slaves, wives, and children—with responsible generosity. They were described also as hospitable, courageous, loyal, and—in the spirit of Sir Walter Scott's novels, which were popular in the South—exceptionally chivalrous. In his novel *George Balcombe* (1836), Nathaniel Beverley Tucker described the planters as descendants of "the ancient cavaliers of Virginia." They were "men in whom the spirit of freedom was so blended with loyalty as to render them alike incapable of servility and selfishness."

Idealized along with the planter was his wife. Defenders of southern culture believed that the planter's wife had the exceptional qualities, such as generosity, graciousness, and charm, required to match those of her spouse. Especially prized was sexual purity—contrasted with what was described as the passionate sexuality of black women. Planters' wives became symbols of the moral superiority of whites over blacks.

The reality of plantation life was far more complex. Like northern women in their "separate sphere," most planters' wives educated their children and cared for the sick. In addition, they managed complicated households and often entire plantations when their husbands were away, fell ill, or died. Northern men disapproved of women giving orders to men, but southern white men did not object if white women directed the work of black men. However, southern white men drew a firm line that ruled out sexual intimacy between white women and black men. White men brutally punished any suspected black offenders and insisted that slavery was necessary to protect southern womanhood and prevent the mixing of the races.

This belief, and the strength of its appeal, in part reflected the guilt of planters who routinely had sex with their female slaves and fathered children by them. As one southern woman put it, "violations of the moral law made mulattoes as common as blackberries." Planters' wives generally kept quiet about this, perhaps doing nothing more than writing in their diaries.

A Racist Ideology. The planters increasingly relied on a racist ideology to maintain the loyalty of non-slaveholders. Central to this ideology was the claim that blacks were an inferior race permanently unsuited for freedom and requiring rigid social control. Supporters of slavery also argued that slavery had a highly positive result. It provided what South Carolina senator James H. Hammond described in 1858 as a "mud-sill" class—a class that provided the foundation on which whites, freed from the most degrading kinds of work, had built "progress, civilization, and refinement." During the 1850s, Hammond and other proslavery advocates increasingly saw slavery as guaranteeing equality, freedom, and democracy for whites and thereby protecting the highest values of the republic. As William Yancey of Alabama explained to a northern audience, "Your fathers and my fathers built this government on two ideas; the first is that the white race is the citizen and the master race, and the white man is the equal of every other white man. The second is that the Negro is the inferior race."

The planters faced no significant competition in maintaining the loyalty of the non-slaveholders, who constituted the majority of the white population. Manufacturers, merchants, lawyers, doctors, editors, and ministers comprised a far smaller proportion of the population in the South than they did in the North, and all were closely related to or dependent on wealthy planters. They might vote Whig because they supported government promotion of banking, transportation, and manufacturing, but defending slavery almost always had a higher priority.

Moreover, new ideas were slow to penetrate the South. Southern cities remained small and the sparse rural population was widely scattered. The vehicles for disseminating new ideas—schools, lecturers, magazines, newspapers—so common in the North, reached few southerners beyond the major cities. Before the Civil War, no southern state had a statewide public school system, and only Kentucky and North Carolina appropriated a significant share of public revenues for education. While wealthy southerners sent their children to private academies, poor whites typically taught their children at home. While less than half of one percent of the white population in New England was illiterate in 1850, nearly 20 percent of white southerners could not read or write. The cultural isolation meant that reform movements of nineteenth-century America were limited largely to the North and that the planters were able to exercise great influence over all aspects of life in the South.

Slave Life

The legal status of slaves remained unchanged in the antebellum South. They were regarded as *chattel*—personal property. They could be disciplined at will and bought and sold as though they were horses. As Thomas Ruffin, a justice of the North Carolina Supreme Court, said in 1829, "The power of the master must be absolute to render the submission of the slave perfect." The material lives of slaves did improve, however, reflecting the prosperity of the plantation system. Most slaves were somewhat better clothed and housed

AMERICAN VOICES

A Slaveholder's Diary *Mary Boykin Chesnut*

Mary Boykin Chesnut (1823–1886), the wife of South Carolina senator James Chesnut, lived most of her life on plantations near Camden, South Carolina. She made no secret of her hatred of slavery, but she believed that blacks were innately inferior. She revealed her views in the extensive diary she kept during the Civil War.

March 18, 1861 . . . I wonder if it be a sin to think slavery a curse to any land. [Massachusetts senator Charles] Sumner said not one word of this hated institution which is not true. Men and women are punished when their masters and mistresses are brutes and not when they do wrong—and then we live surrounded by prostitutes. An abandoned woman is sent out of any decent house elsewhere. Who thinks any worse of a negro or mulatto woman for being a thing we can't name? God forgive us, but ours is a *monstrous* system and wrong and iniquity. Perhaps the resent of the world is as bad—this *only* I see. Like the patriarchs of old our men live all in one house with their wives and their concubines, and the mulattoes one sees in every family exactly resemble the white children—and every lady tells you who is the father of all the mulatto children in everybody's household, but those in her own she seems to think drop from the clouds, or pretends so to think. Good women we have . . . the purest women God ever made. Thank God for my countrywomen—alas for the men! No worse than men everywhere, but the lower their mistresses, the more degraded they must be.

Mary Boykin Chesnut
(Portrait by Samuel Osgood, The National Portrait Gallery)

November 27, 1861 . . . Now what I have seen of my mother's life, my grandmother's, my mother-in-law's: These people were educated at Northern schools mostly—read the same books as their Northern contemners, the same daily newspapers, the same Bible—have the same ideas of right and wrong—are highbred, lovely, good, pious—doing their duty as they conceive it. They live in negro villages. They do not preach and teach hate as a gospel and the sacred duty of murder and insurrection, but they strive to ameliorate of the condition of these Africans in every particular. . . . These women are more troubled by their duty to negroes, have less chance to live their own lives in peace than if they were African missionaries. They have a swarm of blacks about them as children under their care—not as Mrs. Stowe's fancy paints them, but the hard, unpleasant, unromantic, undeveloped savage Africans. And they hate slavery worse than Mrs. Stowe. . . .

We are human beings of the nineteenth century—and slavery has to go, of course. All that has been gained by it goes to the North and to negroes. The slave-owners, when they are good men and women, are the martyrs. And as far as I have seen, the people here are quite as good as anywhere else. I hate slavery. I even hate the harsh authority I see parents think it their duty to exercise *toward their children.*

Source: C. Vann Woodward, *Mary Chesnut's Civil War* (New Haven: Yale University Press, 1981), 29–30, 245–246.

than the poorest whites of both the South and North. The slaves' food—particularly when supplemented by greens from their own garden plots and by game and fish that they caught—was probably better than that of unskilled workers in the North. On some large plantations, children, the sick, and the elderly received better care than northern society provided for these groups. But the slaves realized that planters gave them material favors primarily to protect their investment, rarely out of benevolent concern.

The working conditions of slaves varied widely. On small farms, slaves might work alongside their masters. And on every plantation some slaves were household servants, "drivers" who helped white overseers in the

Slaves on Auction in Richmond
The 1808 prohibition on the international slave trade meant that the new cotton planters in the deep South had to import most of their slaves from the older areas of the South, and that planters in those areas could reap huge profits from the slave trade. Upper South markets like this one in Richmond, Virginia, expedited that trade, and planters could use the threat of sale "down the River" to discipline their slaves. (Eyre Crowe, *Richmond Slave Market Auction*, The Collection of J.P. Altmayer)

fields, or skilled workers such as blacksmiths and carpenters. However, most slaves lived on farms or plantations that had more than twenty slaves, and they worked in the fields under the gang system.

The most oppressive conditions were to be found in the Old Southwest. The weather in Alabama, Mississippi, Louisiana, Arkansas, and Texas was hotter, the work routines more demanding, and the planters more brutal, than farther east. The slave population in those states increased from about 500,000 in 1840 to more than 1.5 million in 1860. These slaves accounted for about a fifth of the South's 2.4 million slaves in 1840 and more than a third of the 4 million slaves in 1860.

The Domestic Slave Trade. Many African-Americans came to the southwestern plantations through the growing domestic slave trade, which broke up families and communities. Masters in the coastal and border states sold slaves "down the river" (the Mississippi) both to increase their profits and to punish those whom they regarded as difficult to handle. During the 1840s and 1850s, profits in this trade became a major source of income to planters in the Chesapeake and the first-developed cotton areas of Georgia and South Carolina, which were suffering from soil depletion. By the 1850s slaveowners were shipping 25,000 slaves a year from the east to the west, and this trade helped to retain the grip of slavery on the older regions of the South.

The Slave Family. In response to intensified work loads and disrupted lives, slaves increased their resistance to bondage, using the same tactics of evasion and sabotage that they had employed for generations. Most important, slaves continued to nurture family relationships for protection and support and to foster personal identities independent from those of their masters. By mid-century slave families had become unusually resilient, despite the lack of legal protection. Because slaves could not make contracts, marriages between them could not be legally binding. The North Carolina Supreme Court brushed aside Christian tradition in 1853 when it ruled that:

A Slave Burial Around 1860
Burials, wakes, and memorials were rituals vital to African-American culture. Slave funerals often carried on West African traditions. They were major pageants bringing together friends and relatives who did not routinely see each other. By paying elaborate tribute to the dead, the funerals provided communal celebration of the living. (John Antrobus, *Plantation Burial*, c. 1860, The Historic New Orleans Collection)

> Our law requires no solemnity or form in regard to the marriage of slaves, and whether they "take up" with each other by express permission of their owners, or from a mere impulse of nature, in obedience to the command "multiply and replenish the earth" cannot, in the contemplation of the law, make any sort of difference.

Nevertheless, many slaves married outside the law and lived together throughout their lives. If not broken up by sale, couples usually maintained close nuclear families within plantation communities. Parents helped their children to be as independent as possible from the discipline of the master. Mothers not only worked alongside men, but also cooked, kept gardens, and raised children, often nursing babies in the field.

During this period, slaves also developed particularly elaborate kinship networks. These networks included distant relations and even individuals who had no blood or marital ties but who shared in the life of the family. Elderly slaves, for example, often played a special role as community patriarchs, conducting religious services and disciplining difficult children. Young slaves learned to address their elders by kin titles, such as "Aunt" or "Uncle," preparing them for the day when they might be separated from their parents. Even when parted by sale, members of both nuclear and extended families kept track of one another. Many runaway slaves returned to their home plantations and, after emancipation during the Civil War, thousands sought to reunite their families. If distances were too great to maintain marriages, many slaves started new families in their new location. When the Union army registered African-American marriages in Mississippi at the end of the Civil War, it was found that the slave trade had separated about a fourth of the men over forty years old from their previous wives.

AMERICAN VOICES

Slave Songs *Frederick Douglass*

In this selection from his autobiography, Frederick Douglass describes the singing during the days between Christmas and New Year's, typically allowed the slaves as holidays. He always took pains to urge his white audiences to find the hidden meanings in the words and rituals of slaves.

The fiddling, dancing, and "jubilee beating" was carried on in all directions. The latter performance was strictly southern. It supplied the place of violin, or of other musical instruments, and was played so easily that almost every farm had its "Juba" beater. The performer improvised as he beat the instrument, marking the words as he sang so as to have them fall pat with the movement of his hands. Among a mass of nonsense and wild frolic, once in a while a sharp hit was given to the meanness of slaveholders. Take the following example:

We raise de wheat,
Dey gib us de corn;
We bake de bread,
Dey gib us de crust;
We sif de meal,
Dey gib us de huss;
we peel de meat,
Dey gib us de skin;
And dat's de way
Dey take us in;
We skim de pot,
dey gib us de liquor,
And say dat's good enough
for nigger.
Walk over! Walk over!
Your butter and de fat;
Poor nigger you cant get over
dat...

This is not a bad summary of the palpable injustice and fraud of slavery, giving, as it does, to the lazy and the idle the comforts which God designed should be given solely to the honest laborer.

. . . I did not, when a slave, understand the deep meaning of those rude and apparently incoherent sounds [of the slaves' songs]. I was myself within the circle; so that I neither saw nor heard as those without might see and hear. They told a tale of woe which was then altogether beyond my feeble comprehension; they were tones loud, long, and deep; they breathed the prayer and complaint of souls boiling over with the bitterest anguish. Every tone was a testimony against slavery, and a prayer to God for deliverance from chains. The hearing of those wild notes always depressed my spirit, and filled me with ineffable sadness. I have frequently found myself in tears while hearing them. The mere recurrence to those songs, even now, afflicts me; and while I am writing these lines, an expression of feeling has already found its way down my cheek. To those songs I trace my first glimmering conception of the dehumanizing character of slavery, and quicken my sympathies for my brethren in bonds. . . .

I have often been utterly astonished, since I came to the north, to find persons who could speak of the singing, among slaves, as evidence of their contentment and happiness. It is impossible to conceive of a greater mistake. Slaves sing most when they are most unhappy. The songs of the slave represent the sorrows of the heart; and he is relieved by them, only as an aching heart by its tears.

Source: Frederick Douglass, *My Bondage and My Freedom* (New York, 1855), 253–54.

Slave Religion. In their quarters, slaves built a community life rich with mutual obligations. They shared insights regarding the world of their masters and news from the outside world. Religion was central to their culture. The Christianity of the slaves focused on the endurance of the Israelites in Egypt and on the caring of Christ for the oppressed. They sometimes had to conduct their services and prayers at night or in the woods, in "bush meetings" to keep them secret from the masters. Religion offered a message of hope—of eventual liberation from life's sorrows—and helped most slaves endure their bondage. Organized prayer enabled them to express love for one another and to share burdens with others. Confident of their special relationship with God, the slaves prepared themselves spiritually for emancipation, which they regarded as deliverance to the Promised Land.

Resistance and Rebellion

The Underground Railroad. Slave resistance sometimes took form in overt action. Tens of thousands of slaves ran away during the 1840s and 1850s, even though their chances of making it to the North or to Canada were slim. In the deep South white patrols with bloodhounds were constantly on the lookout for runaway slaves. All blacks on public roads or paths were presumed to be runaways unless they carried passes to prove otherwise. The odds for success were best for

Harriet Tubman
In 1849, Harriet Tubman (1823–1913, pictured far left with some of the slaves she helped to freedom) escaped from a Maryland plantation. During the next ten years she was a leader of the Underground Railroad and became a popular abolitionist speaker. She served as a spy for the Union Army during the Civil War and then set up schools for ex-slaves in North Carolina. In 1896 she played an active role in the founding of the National Association of Colored Women.

those who lived near a free state. They might receive aid from the "underground railroad," an informal network of white and, even more important, African-American abolitionists. Many escaped slaves, such as Harriet Tubman, who returned to the South nineteen times to free hundreds of slaves, risked reenslavement or death by working with the "railroad." Harriet Tubman knew the risks. She wrote:

> There was one of two things I had a *right* to, liberty, or death; if I could not have one, I would have the other; for no man should take me alive; I should fight for my liberty as long as my strength lasted, and when the time came for me to go, the Lord would let them take me.

Members of the small communities of free African-Americans in cities like Baltimore, Richmond, Charleston, and New Orleans were the most important source of help. In fact, they were virtually the only free people in the South who aided escapees. In doing so, they took enormous risks. In Baltimore, it was a free African-American sailor who lent his identification to Frederick Douglass. He disguised himself, used the papers to escape to New York, and then mailed the papers back to the sailor. Such acts were common, despite the consequences for the benefactor if the fugitive was unable to return the papers or was captured. Despite all the obstacles, thousands of slaves escaped to freedom.

Slave Rebellion. Discontented slaves might also resist by being deliberately careless with their master's property, losing or breaking tools, or setting fire to houses or barns. They could slow down the pace of work, perhaps playing roles in which they feigned illness or incompetence. In the instances of greatest desperation, they could make themselves useless by cutting off their fingers or even committing suicide. Or they might turn on the master and kill him.

The planters used the fear of violent slave rebellion to build support for slavery among poor whites. The fear of massacre became a binding, cohesive force among the whites, who recognized that their power over slaves depended on terror—and that slaves might want to repay the terror. Planters could point to many slave rebellions, including the bloody revolution on the island of Santo Domingo that overthrew the French and culminated in the creation of the republic of Haiti in 1803. Within the United States, revolts were local disturbances, such as that of Denmark Vesey in Charleston, South Carolina, in 1822. Although such revolts were small-scale, they were numerous. As many as two hundred of these small uprisings occurred during the first half of the nineteenth century, although some of the reported revolts undoubtedly took place mostly in the imaginations of slaveowners. The most dramatic example of the capacity of enslaved African-Americans to fight back was Nat Turner's rebellion of 1831 (see Chapter 12).

But slaves generally recognized, especially after Nat Turner's defeat, how heavily the odds were stacked against successful rebellion. The ratio of blacks to whites in the South was lower than in any other slave society in the Western Hemisphere. The South was not an island that could be captured and cut off from the outside world. Southern whites were well armed, unified, and militant; and the South had no impenetrable jungles, mountains, and swamps where a guerrilla army could hide out for a long period of time.

Still, few planters were entirely certain about their security, and their anxiety rose during the 1850s. In 1856, William Proctor Gould of Green County, Alabama, warned his slaves not to become involved in an alleged conspiracy. Although they pledged their loyalty, Gould was still uneasy enough to note, "What they might have done if there had been an actual outbreak must forever remain unknown to us."

Southern Imperialism

During the 1840s the South aggressively sought to establish and protect slavery in the region. Some planters wanted to make sure they did not run out of fertile land. Southern politicians also realized that every new free state in the West increased the threat of abolition by shifting power in Congress toward the North. Moreover, if the federal government did not protect slavery in the West, it would sanction what white southerners believed to be a denial of their rights as free Americans. They feared that if Congress failed to protect southern rights in the territories, it might not respect those rights in the South itself.

Anxiety about the future for slavery in the West was nothing new in the South. Southerners had pressed for the acquisition of Louisiana and Florida in order to gain new lands where slavery could expand. They had also cited the Monroe Doctrine to warn the British not to interfere with slavery anywhere in the Western Hemisphere. When Britain abolished slavery in the West Indies in 1833, southern planters feared that pressures for emancipation would release a wave of slave rebellions like Nat Turner's. The planters also feared the British would actively encourage abolition in the United States to undermine its plantation economy. In 1843, Calhoun proposed that the British wished to abolish slavery in the United States and Brazil to "transfer the production of cotton, rice, and sugar etc. to her colonial possessions, and . . . consummate the system of commercial monopoly, which she has been so long and systematically pursuing."

During the early 1840s the worries of the southern planters about the British intensified. They noted that in 1839 Britain, along with France, had intervened in Mexico to force it to pay its debts, and they heard rumors that Britain wanted California as payment. They saw evidence that Britain was encouraging Texas to remain independent, was expanding its involvement in Central America, and had designs on Cuba. It all seemed to add up to a grand scheme by the British to block American expansion by establishing an antislavery barrier from the West Indies through Mexican territory—a barrier sweeping from Texas all the way to California. The result, southerners feared, would be not only an end to economic opportunity but increasing pressure for emancipation in the South. Free-soil areas could serve as bases for abolitionist raids on plantations and provide havens for runaway slaves.

In the 1840s, to block the formation of a British antislavery barrier, southern politicians launched a program of establishing and protecting slavery on their southern boundary. This policy led the United States toward a war of conquest against Mexico. Ultimately, it put the South on a fateful collision course with the industrializing North.

The Northeast: The Industrial Revolution Accelerates

The business class of the Northeast drove industrialization forward at an accelerated pace during the 1840s and 1850s. The results were phenomenal. By 1860, the United States was second only to Great Britain and France in manufacturing. Northern industrial production already was more than two-thirds that of either of those two countries, and it was increasing even more rapidly. Sustaining that prosperity, however, required controlling western expansion.

Factories Triumphant

The accelerated pace of industrialization during the 1840s and 1850s resulted from the modernizing efforts of northern manufacturers. Hundreds of them built factories that relied on modern technology and large numbers of workers. Factory owners extended the use of power-driven machines and assembly lines from the processing of agricultural produce to the manufacture of guns, watches, sewing machines, and agricultural machinery. The manufacturers flourished not only in the first industrial towns, where falling water powered mills, but also in the older seaports and, with stunning swiftness, in the towns and cities of the Old Northwest. The industrialization of interior cities like Chicago and St. Louis meant that most of the Old Northwest became, in fact, a functional part of the Northeast.

Stationary Steam Engines. The most important technological innovation adopted by manufacturers during the 1840s was the stationary steam engine, which was used to power other machines. Steam engines freed manufacturers from their dependency on water power and enabled them to locate their factories in the nation's largest cities—the great Atlantic seaports and the booming ports on the Great Lakes. During the 1840s manufacturers for the first time took advantage of all the benefits offered by a big-city location: easy access to the cheapest immigrant labor, highly developed markets for capital, sophisticated trading services, and urban consumers. Manufacturers in the seaports and the largest western cities, particularly Chicago, broke the near-monopoly that the smaller inland cities had held on the most modern industries.

The manufacturers' growing demand for machinery stimulated the machine-tool industry, which became even more critical to the advance of industrialization. The same machines that made uniform parts for firearms were used to make parts for sewing machines. By the late 1850s five Connecticut clockmakers were using modern machine tools to make intricate works for

The McCormick Reaper, 1851
The McCormick reaper was a complex piece of machinery, but it was designed to be operated and repaired by average farmers. Company advertisements indicated that the various parts of the reaper were "numbered and marked with paint, showing the connection of the parts with one another so that they can readily be put together by the farmer."

half a million clocks a year. Some of the products of modern machine tools remained well known for generations—Colt revolvers, Remington rifles, Singer sewing machines, Waltham watches, Yale locks, and McCormick reapers.

Using the new sources of power and modern machine tools, some manufacturers began to introduce modern assembly lines during the 1850s. Cyrus McCormick of Chicago developed power-driven conveyor belts to assemble his reapers, and Samuel Colt built an assembly-line factory in Hartford, Connecticut, to produce his invention—the "six-shooter," as it was known in the Southwest. By the late 1850s, Colt's factory responded to the enormous demand for small arms by turning out 60,000 weapons annually.

Crystal Palace Exhibition. In 1851, at the Crystal Palace Exhibition in London, the first world's fair of the industrial era, Cyrus McCormick and Samuel Colt displayed their machine-tooled products. The amazement of British manufacturers quickly turned to anxiety when McCormick and Colt built factories in England using American machinery and production techniques. The British government dispatched two teams of technicians to investigate American factories. They reported that many different industries were organized "in large factories, with machinery applied to almost every process, the extreme subdivision of labor, and all reduced to an almost perfect system of manufacture."

The increasing scale and complexity of production, however, made it difficult for manufacturers to estimate the demand for their products. During the 1850s periods of overproduction followed by the layoff and dismissal of workers became more common. One such episode coincided with the Panic of 1857—a crisis produced by an overexpansion of railroad investment—and a long depression followed. Unemployment remained at about 10 percent until the outbreak of the Civil War in 1861.

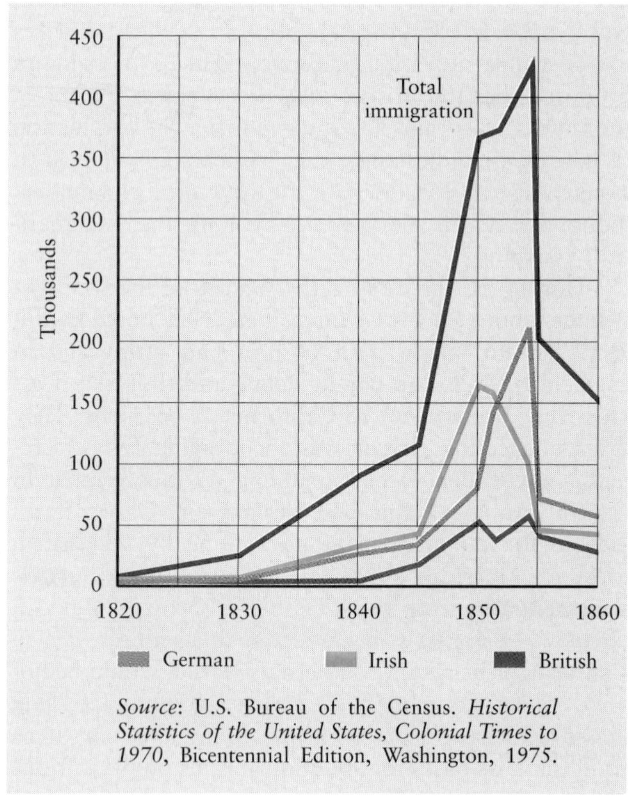

Source: U.S. Bureau of the Census. *Historical Statistics of the United States, Colonial Times to 1970*, Bicentennial Edition, Washington, 1975.

FIGURE 13.2

Immigration to the United States, 1820–1860
Immigration accelerated dramatically in the late 1840s. Fewer immigrants arrived in the mid- and late-1850s, as economic conditions improved in Ireland and the German states and the United States entered a depression in 1857.

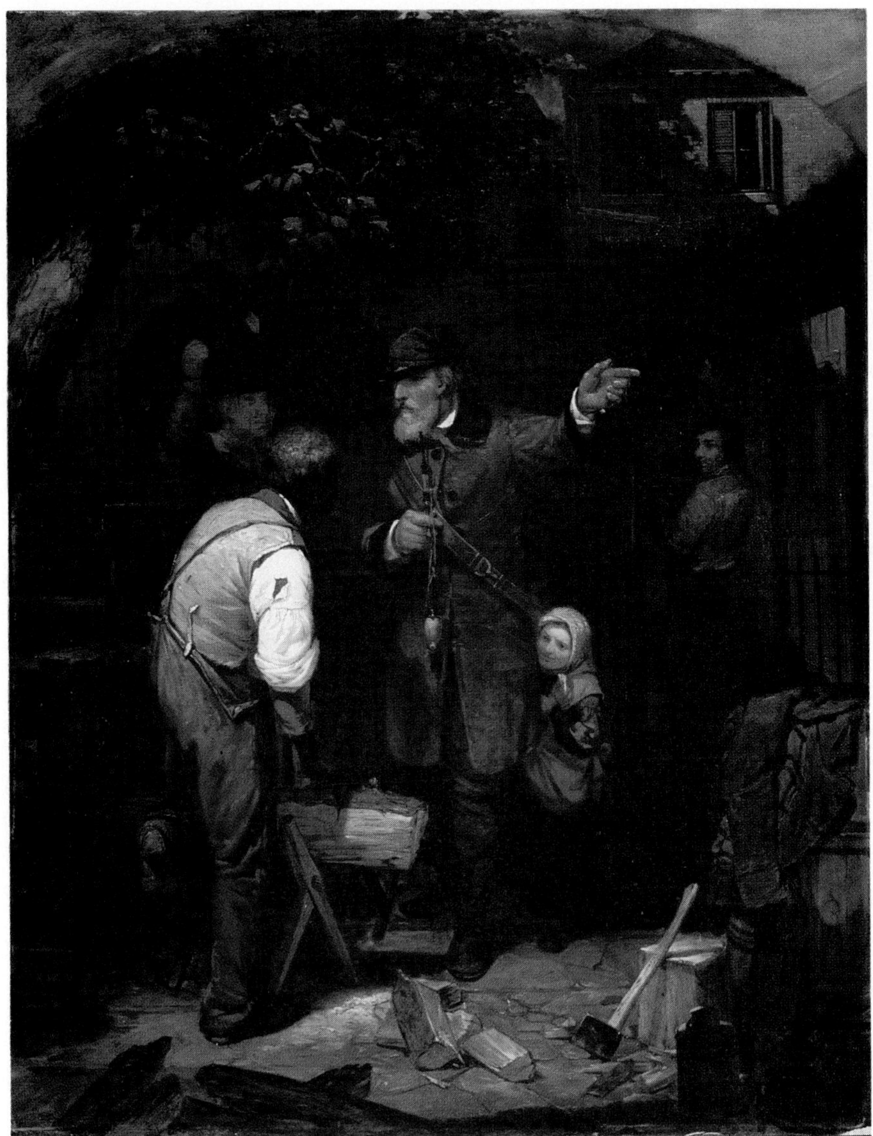

The Status of Immigrants, 1855
The painter Charles F. Blauvelt was one of the rare artists of the period who made immigrants his subject, and he treated them with realism and sympathy. Perhaps he meant to highlight the generosity of blacks by suggesting that they would help lost immigrants even though the new immigrants, simply by virtue of the color of their skin, enjoyed higher status. (*A German Immigrant Inquiring His Way,* North Carolina Museum of Art)

Immigration

Steam power and assembly lines further sharpened the class divisions that had begun to emerge during the 1820s and 1830s. To make the most of their large new investments, manufacturers increased the pace at which their workers toiled. Many workers resisted. For example, in 1845 a group of workers in Lowell, Massachusetts, under the leadership of Sarah G. Bagley, a weaver, formed the Lowell Female Labor Reform Association to protest such a speedup. As working conditions became more grueling, most of the young women who had poured into factory work chose to retire to the New England countryside and raised families.

Manufacturers now more and more turned to immigrants—men and women from Canada, Ireland, and the German states. Lacking the economic opportunities available to Americans, immigrants were willing to work for longer periods of time, at lower wages, and with greater intensity. As a result, in the 1840s immigrants began to fill the unskilled labor force.

By 1860 immigrants accounted for more than a fourth of the white adult men in the United States and more than a third of those in the North. Between 1820 and 1860, about 2 million Irish immigrants settled in the United States along with 1.5 million Germans and 750,000 Britons and Canadians. Some of these immigrants were skilled workers, but more than two-thirds were peasants, unskilled laborers, and farmers, dislocated by industrial and agricultural revolutions in Europe. Most of the newcomers took low-skilled jobs in factories, construction projects, docks, warehouses, and private homes. No federal legislation restricted immigration, and state immigration laws, which attempted to set minimum health standards and exclude paupers, were ineffective.

AMERICAN VOICES

A German Immigrant in Chicago *Nikolaus Schwenck*

Nikolaus Schwenck (1831–1869) emigrated to America from the German village of Langenau in 1854. His letters to his brother in Germany describe his efforts to achieve economic independence. He succeeded, opening his own shop in Chicago in the early 1860s.

Chicago, September 9, 1855. I am finally in a position to give you some news about me. . . . Now we have gathered a nice little *"convention" of people from Langenau* together, don't you see, dear brother! Oh well, you may feel like laughing, but I must say that so far they are quite well, everyone has work and therefore plenty to eat. . . .

I heard of a place where they were looking for a *coppersmith.* I went there right away and sure enough I got the job. And I will stay there for as long as it lasts. My masters are two Americans *in partnership*, a *coppersmith*, and a *tinsmith*. We have six coppersmiths in the workshop, among them two Englishmen, three Swedes, and one German, namely my humble self. The English language is still a problem, but soon it will surely work out better. I already went to school and tried to force it along. . . .

Chicago, November 15, 1856. As to my craft, dear brother—well . . . in America everything looks completely different. I have now decided to give up my craft for a while, and, if necessary, forever. Though it is a very good craft, you first have to find a job. But you have to hunt for these—I mean a job where I could function as a master, because to work for others as a journeyman, dear brother don't blame me, but that's not really what I want. . . . I would like . . . finally to take a step which, if luck would have it, could lead to independence.

[In] the 18 months which have elapsed since I started working in Chicago . . . I saved a respectable bit of capital and have bought good land with it, good farm land. By next spring I hope to settle there and, furthermore, to try to feed myself from it.

Chicago, March 20, 1857. I bought 160 acres of land in the state of *Iowa* for the sum of 450 *dollars*. In the meantime I heard of another, somewhat more *cultivated* farm in the state of *Indiana*. . . . I then sold my land. . . . I made quite a bit on it, as the value of land is constantly going up. . . . I don't have any other land except two large building sites in the state of *Michigan* and a lot, or building site, here in *Chicago*. . . . I'm still working for the same master. He was very much against my leaving, and for the first time raised my wages so that now, for 10 hours work, I earn a good 2 dollars. . . .

Chicago, November 17, 1857. Thousands of workers are unemployed and look with fearful hearts towards the approaching winter. . . . But I have no reason to complain. It is true that I am still not a master, and not a farmer either, but rather am still working at the same place as a coppersmith. Only just think, instead of 20 men we are now only three to four, which means that 16 workers have been laid off, which is a bit rough, don't you think?

. . . As you know, dear brother, I bought a lot last spring on a rather lively street here in Chicago, and in the course of this summer built a house on it, so I now live on my own land with a garden and house. . . .

Source: Hartmut Keil and John B. Jentz, *German Workers in Chicago: A Documentary History of Working-Class Culture from 1850 to World War I* (Urbana: University of Illinois Press, 1988), 24–33.

The economic situation of immigrants varied greatly by national group. The wealthiest were the British. Among them was a large number of professionals, former landowners, and skilled workers. Many German immigrants were also relatively prosperous. They were able to draw on their own savings in financing travel, and had sufficient resources to buy land in America. The poorest immigrants were the Irish.

The Irish. The immigration of the Irish had more to do with poverty in their homeland than economic opportunity in America. Although they arrived in increasing numbers during the 1830s, they began to come in force only in 1847, after a devastating potato famine in Ireland. They found new homes in the Northeast, especially in the cities of New England. By 1850 the Irish accounted for more than a third of the workers in Boston. Their labor enabled Boston industrialists to compete for the first time with manufacturers in the smaller mill towns of Massachusetts and Rhode Island. By 1860 each of the largest factories producing women's clothing in Boston employed about a hundred young Irishwomen. During the late 1840s and early 1850s, the Irish made only a modest contribution to the farm population. Although most of them had been farmers in Ireland, they were too poor to buy land in the United States.

Living conditions for many Irish immigrants, as for other unskilled immigrants and native-born day laborers, proved to be only marginally better than the grinding poverty and rampant disease that had filled their lives in the Old World. Per capita consumption of food increased during the Industrial Revolution, and most immigrants were much better nourished than they had been in Europe. Even so, many unskilled laborers could not afford to buy the food they needed to keep up the intense pace of factory work. In addition, the stress and insecurity of work drove many unskilled workers to spend an increasing portion of their income on the entertainment and alcoholic relief found in taverns. Malnutrition increased in the largest cities, resulting in higher rates of miscarriage and death from infectious diseases.

The crowding of immigrants in the old commercial cities of the Northeast threatened public health. Sanitation systems were primitive. Poorly sealed privies drained into drinking wells and open sewers ran through streets. Infectious diseases ravaged the weakened, malnourished poor. Epidemics of cholera, yellow fever, typhoid fever, smallpox, diphtheria, and tuberculosis struck the major cities with increasing frequency. In the summer of 1849, major cholera epidemics hit New York, St. Louis, and Cincinnati. More than five thousand people, mostly immigrants, died in New York. Many entire families succumbed. Wealthy families moved out of the cities during the epidemics, while, as one observer wrote, the immigrants remained crowded "into a few wretched hovels, amidst filth and bad air, suffering from personal neglect and poisoned by eating garbage [at] which a well-bred hog on a western farm would turn up his snout." In 1860 mortality rates in New York, Philadelphia, and Boston reached a level of more than thirty-four deaths per thousand population annually, compared with only about fifteen per thousand in rural areas.

Irish Identity and Anti-Catholicism

The Catholic Church. In the 1840s and 1850s the United States remained overwhelmingly Protestant in private allegiance and in public culture. But many of the new immigrants—the French-Canadians, many Germans, and particularly the Irish—relied on the Catholic Church not only to sustain their spiritual lives but also to reinforce their sense of class and ethnic identity. The church's expansion closely paralleled the growth of Irish immigration, increasing from sixteen dioceses and seven hundred churches in the 1840s to forty-five dioceses and three thousand churches by 1860. Throughout the areas settled by Irish immigrants, traveling priests were replaced by resident ones. The Irish purchased many church buildings from Protestant congregations that had moved to more spacious quarters. In towns and cities, using the church as a foundation, the Irish also built a network of charitable societies, orphanages, militia companies, parochial schools, newspapers, social clubs, and political organizations. These community institutions supported the Irish immigrants in their search for housing, jobs, education, and security.

The new institutions had no equivalent in Ireland. They developed in the United States in response to the desire of Irish immigrants to maintain their native culture, a culture to which existing American institutions were hostile or, at best, indifferent. The church network was important to immigrants who labored in large cities and especially to those who worked in big-city factories. It provided community services and a sense of group identity, much as a labor union might have done. The institutions that the Irish created had a great impact on later groups of Catholic immigrants. Because the Irish arrived early and because many spoke English, they built the church structure and the urban political machinery through which most European Catholic immigrants initially established a place for themselves in American life.

The relative autonomy of Catholic communities disturbed many American Protestants, who comprised the dominant majority in almost all of the United States. During the 1830s, when Irish immigration first started to increase, lurid anti-Catholic propaganda began to circulate. Its authors raised the specter of a sinister, highly organized menace. According to the propaganda, the pope, acting through Catholics over whom he exerted total authority, plotted to subvert republican institutions.

Samuel F. B. Morse. A leading anti-Catholic propagandist was Samuel F. B. Morse, who would later make the first commercial adaptation of the telegraph, based on a patent he and his partners obtained in 1841. In 1834 Morse published *Foreign Conspiracy Against the Liberties of the United States* anonymously. The book came out under his own name in 1835 and was endorsed by Protestant ministers of many denominations. Morse declared that the "past history" of Roman Catholics and "the fact that they everywhere act together, as if guided by one mind, admonish us to be jealous of their influence, and to watch with unremitted care all their movements in relation to our free institutions." He warned in particular of the political facility of Irish Catholics. They "in an especial manner clanned together, and kept alive their foreign feelings, associations, habits and manners." Morse advocated the formation of an "Anti-Popery Union" to resist the perceived Catholic threat.

Riot in Philadelphia
Philadelphia's anti-Irish rioting climaxed in Southwark on June 7, 1844. Pennsylvania's Governor John Cadwalader had called out the militia to protect Catholic churches, including one (pictured above) in which young Irish-Americans had stored muskets for self-defense. The Protestant rioters and the militia exchanged musket fire and the rioters even fired a cannon into the militia. Militia reinforcements ended the riots but Philadelphia's politics became focused on ethnic and racial issues.

Millions of young Americans read *Foreign Conspiracy* in Protestant Sunday schools and in public libraries and schools. It became a textbook for anti-Catholic crusaders. In 1838, the citizens of Sutton and Millbury, Massachusetts, asked Congress to investigate "whether there are not now those amongst us, who, by their oath of allegiance to a foreign despotic Prince or Power, are solemnly bound to support his interests and accelerate his designs."

Native-American Clubs. The anti-Catholic movement became exceptionally intense because of the dislocations associated with industrialization. It appealed especially to mechanics who had lost their jobs, or feared that they might lose them, as a consequence of the factory system. By attacking Catholics, they could blame cheap immigrant labor for their economic situation and, at the same time, persuade themselves that they at least had a superior culture and religion. Threatened workers took the lead in organizing Native American Clubs, which called for an extension of the waiting period before naturalization from five to twenty-one years, a restriction of public offices to native-born Americans, and exclusive use of the (Protestant) Authorized Version of the Bible in public schools.

Even workers who felt secure in their jobs feared that their children might face competition from immigrants. They strongly opposed the proposals from Catholic clergy and Democratic legislators in many northeastern states that Catholics' taxes be reserved for parochial (religious) schools—thus weakening the public schools. Another source of anti-Catholic sentiment was the temperance movement: a number of evangelical ministers denounced the abuse of alcohol among Irish immigrants. Such appeals won recruits to the business class among native-born Protestant workers, and it impeded the development of a labor movement across ethnic and religious lines. Many Protestant laborers became convinced that they had more in common with their employers and other members of the business class than with Catholic workers.

In almost every city with a large Catholic immigrant population, the anti-Catholic movement turned to violence. In 1834, in Charlestown, Massachusetts, a quarrel between Catholic laborers in an Ursuline convent and Protestant workers in a neighboring brickyard turned into a full-scale riot. The anti-Catholic mob, persuaded that a young Protestant woman was being held against her will, drove out the residents of the convent and burned it to the ground. Urban rioting escalated during the 1840s as the Irish began to acquire significant political power in eastern cities. In Philadelphia, the violence peaked in 1844 after the Catholic bishop persuaded public school officials to use both Protestant and Catholic versions of the Bible. Anti-Irish rioting, provoked by the city's Native American Clubs, lasted for two months and escalated into open warfare between the Protestants and the Pennsylvania militia, causing many casualties.

The Know-Nothings. In 1850 the secret anti-Catholic societies banded together in the Order of the Star-Spangled Banner; a year later they led in forming a new political party, the American party. Its members sometimes answered outsiders' questions by saying "I know nothing," which gave the party the name that stuck—"Know-Nothing." The program of the Know-Nothings, however, was not mysterious. They supported the program of the Native American Clubs and, in addition, advocated literary tests for voters, which they thought would disfranchise most recent immigrants. In the 1854 elections the Know-Nothings attempted to unite northern and southern voters behind a program of nativist opposition to Catholics—both Irish and German—and the "alien menace." They won a number of seats in Congress and temporarily gained control of the state governments of Massachusetts and Pennsylvania. Their conspiracy theory—suggesting a threat to republican institutions—paralleled the free-soilers' description of the "Slave Power" conspiracy and created the ideological basis for a new political coalition.

Business-Class Consumption

During the mid-1850s the annual increase in per capita income approached 2.5 percent, a remarkable rate that the United States has never since matched. The nation achieved this rate despite the fact that the great surges of immigration during the 1840s and 1850s tended to reduce per capita income.

The phenomenal income gains meant that native-born Americans with property or skills reaped an extraordinary material bonanza. During the 1840s and 1850s industrialization brought a sweeping wave of consumption to middle-class life in the North. New consumer goods served as badges of economic success and membership in the business class. The availability of inexpensive mass-produced goods, many of them new during the 1840s and 1850s, made the trappings of status widely accessible to the middle class. The new material culture reinforced a prideful sense of northern uniqueness—a sense that increasingly united affluent and upwardly mobile Americans from New England through the Great Lakes states.

Middle-Class Housing: The Balloon-Frame. When they could afford it, middle-class families built their homes of brick and stone. But wooden residences became much more numerous during the 1840s, and they were constructed very differently from log cabins or traditional frame buildings. In the 1830s, American carpenters had devised a faster method to construct housing: the *balloon frame*.

Constructing a Balloon-Frame House
The fragile-looking balloon frame shown on the left will provide a surprisingly strong skeleton for the substantial type of house on the right. Because people of modest means could build balloon-frame houses with the labor of family members, friends, or low-skilled carpenters, they could afford houses that had been available only to the very wealthy before the 1830s. (Engraving by W.W. Wilson, 1855, The Metropolitan Museum of Art)

Traditional wood construction had depended on the careful fitting together of heavy timbers; experienced housewrights fashioned a strong frame with mortise-and-tenon joints, while western farmers fitted trimmed logs together. The balloon frame, much lighter in weight (as its name implied) but almost as strong, formed a house with a vertical grid of thin wooden studs joined by nails to cross-pieces at top and bottom. Once the carpenter had thrown up the frame, he simply nailed wood sheathing to the studs as walls and then added a layer of clapboard siding. Even an inexperienced carpenter could erect a balloon frame. The process saved enough labor to reduce the cost of housing by 40 percent—and it was quick. The balloon frame made it possible for western cities like Chicago, where it was first introduced, to spring up almost overnight. The four-room balloon-frame house became the standard residence, replacing the one- or two-room house of preindustrial society.

Architects published self-help manuals with detailed plans of simple houses for carpenters and families building their own homes. In the 1840s and 1850s, the manuals featured larger houses with more numerous bedrooms to enhance the privacy of each member of the family. The leading architectural philosopher of the era was Andrew Jackson Downing, who lauded such designs in his most famous book, *The Architecture of Country Houses* (1850). Downing argued that his new houses would promote a "refinement of manners" and strengthen the life of the family, which was "the best social form." Within the single-family home, he proclaimed, "truthfulness, beauty, and order have the largest dominion." Ample homes, even if more standardized, would provide a medium for the success of republican ideals.

Household Goods. Prosperous urban families furnished their new homes with an array of new comforts, decorations, and devices. Furnaces heated both interiors and water. Europeans marveled at them and at the American desire for warmth. One visitor complained that it was impossible to escape hot air: "It meets you the moment the street-door is opened to let you in, rushes after you when you emerge again, half-stewed and parboiled into the wholesome air." In most homes, beds with springs of woven rope or iron wire replaced beds with wooden slats. Homemade featherbeds, mattresses, and down pillows spread rapidly after mass-produced ticking and sheeting became available in stores. Households acquired goods that made traditional chores more efficient. Beginning in the 1850s, some women purchased treadle-operated sewing machines. Most prosperous urban households now had stoves with ovens, including broilers and movable grates, instead of open hearths. Women used a wide variety of pots, pans, and kettles; some mechanical equipment, such as grinders and presses; and washboards. And these households had iceboxes that ice-company wagons filled daily. As early as 1825, the Underwood Company of Boston was marketing well-preserved Atlantic salmon in jars. With the introduction of the Mason jar in 1858, households vastly increased their ability to preserve other perishable foods.

The new household furnishings also included mass-produced clocks. Before 1820 townspeople and villagers relied on public clocks or bells; country folk told time by the sun. By the 1840s, inexpensive clocks and watches manufactured in Connecticut had become the main methods of keeping time. Clocks had revolutionary effects. People could organize themselves to meet the more intense pace of daily life produced by the Industrial Revolution.

The proliferation of low-cost textiles, furniture, lamps, glass, and ceramics enabled almost every home

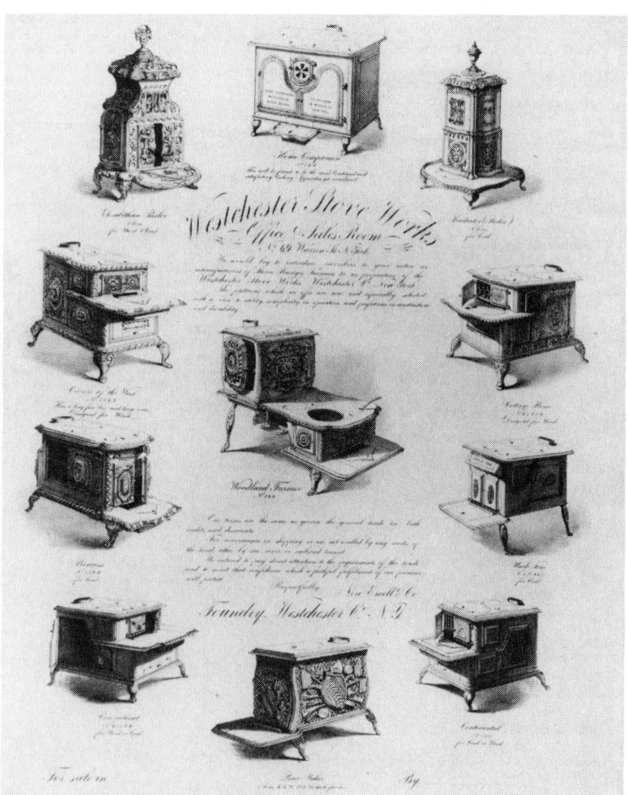

Advertisement for Stoves, 1856
The broadside advertisement was an early effort to use mass-produced media to sell expensive household goods. Westchester Stove Works gave romantic names to the various stove models to appeal to prosperous urban families. The manufacturer also offered terms "the same as govern the general trade in both credits and discounts."

Currier & Ives
By the 1850s, the most popular prints were those that showed idealized images of a prosperous rural life. This verdant scene, one of several entitled "Home, Sweet Home," dates from 1869. The apparently unscathed Union soldier returns to a perfect home, an orderly oasis in the woods. (Museum of the City of New York)

to have a unique appearance. Even families with very modest incomes added decorative touches to their homes—sheet glass (rather than blown glass) in large windows that brought full sunlight into the interior; tin and glassware that caught the light; colorful curtains; ruffles and flounces for chairs; tablecloths; floor coverings; and wall prints.

"Prints for the People." Many of these prints, or their reproductions from the clipped pages of illustrated magazines, were the "prints for the people" produced and distributed by Currier and Ives, the leading lithography firm of the nineteenth century. In contrast to the black and white prints available to earlier Americans, the mass-produced color prints were both more factual and more sensational. During the 1840s prints became an important means of disseminating national news, particularly in the North. They also brought drama, fashion, and social commentary to remote rural areas. Middle-class families bought prints depicting battles, fires, shipwrecks, notable personalities, new communities in the West, and the latest industrial technology. They also relied on prints to follow changing styles of architecture and to keep abreast of the latest fashions "out East." Women from New York to Cincinnati took pages from *Godey's Lady Book* to their seamstresses as patterns for new dresses. Businesses also used prints to advertise in new ways. Locomotive manufacturers, for example, commissioned prints not so much to reach the small market of locomotive buyers but to stimulate public interest in rail travel. Until moving pictures and home photography in the early twentieth century, the print was the most popular form of pictorial art in the United States.

Middle-Class Literature

During the 1840s and 1850s American democracy came to include a "democracy of print." Middle-class Americans provided a virtually insatiable market for books, magazines, and newspapers. By 1850, nine out of every ten adult white Americans could read, and millions bought books. Libraries were growing in both number and size. By 1860 there were over 50,000 public libraries, containing nearly 13 million volumes. The readers and the libraries were, however, concentrated in the North. The books were no doubt the most forceful component of the new material culture of the northern middle class; they fostered a powerful sense of community and reinforced values of individualism, self-control, and republican virtue.

The Industrial Revolution swept over American publishing, dramatically widening popular access to information. The Napier steam-driven press (1825) and the Hoe rotary press (1847) made it possible to mass-produce cheap books. Publishing houses in New York, Philadelphia, and Boston competed with each other, offering discounts to booksellers, advertising in magazines and newspapers, sending sales agents into the field, and recruiting authors the way manufacturers recruited gifted engineers and designers. Between 1820 and 1850, American book publishers, such as Harper Brothers and G. P. Putnam's Sons, increased their sales from about $2.5 million to $12.5 million. The religious press also contributed to the explosion. Dozens of Bible societies (led by the American Bible Society, founded in 1816) and tract societies published more than a million Bibles and six million books, pamphlets, and magazines each year.

A large part of the literary consumption of middle-class Americans was in the form of fiction. America's first successful writers of fiction were Washington Irving and James Fenimore Cooper. In *The Sketch Book*, Irving painted unforgettable portraits of two characters who became part of American folk culture, Ichabod Crane and Rip Van Winkle. An equally celebrated fictional character was the frontier scout Leatherstocking in the novels of Cooper. Beginning with *The Pioneers* (1823) and *The Last of the Mohicans* (1826) and ending with *The Deerslayer* (1841), Cooper built an enormously popular legend around his hero. The key personality trait about Leatherstocking—or "Hawkeye," "Natty Bumppo," or "Deerslayer," as he was also known—was his solitude in nature. His moral goodness grew directly out of his "original relation" with nature. He was a radically free individual, at odds with law and custom, comfortable only in the forest, a model of American self-reliance and nonconformity. Cooper fashioned his hero to represent the nobility, innocence, and strength of frontier Americans. Preoccupied with defending American democracy to Europeans, Cooper struck a responsive chord in his American readers. Corresponding in popularity to Irving and Cooper among poets was Henry Wadsworth Longfellow. Poems like *Hiawatha* (1855) and *The Courtship of Miles Standish* (1858) reused the American past and American settings in imaginative ballads infused with themes of God, nature, and moral improvement. For most nineteenth-century Americans, Longfellow defined what they meant by poetry.

Women Novelists. Even more popular was a group of women writers. They, at least as much as Irving, Cooper, and Longfellow, defined a new American literature—and new American themes. In their writing they reinforced the values promoted by business-class evangelism.

Women writers contributed to a redefinition of the role of women in middle-class life. Women formed growing majorities in most religious congregations. Middle-class women in northern communities played increasingly important roles in reform movements. They were marrying later—or not at all. They were having fewer children and employing more servants—two or three times as many servants by the 1860s as they had at the end of the Revolution. And they were prodigious readers, constituting a majority of the reading public. In the 1850s, according to the estimate of *Harper's Magazine*, four out of five readers of books or magazines were women. And women were writing many of those books, editing and filling the pages of magazines with stories and poems.

Novels by the leading women writers of the day often sold hundreds of thousands of copies in the North. Catharine Maria Sedgwick won wide popularity in the 1820s, as did Caroline Howard Gilman and Caroline Lee Hentz during the next decade. But the largest audiences were reached by Harriet Beecher Stowe in the 1840s and the 1850s, and by Sara Parton, Augusta Evans Wilson, and Susan Warner in the 1850s. Their sentimental melodramas, punctuated often by tearful domestic scenes, shared an assumption that had become increasingly popular in America since the 1790s: that women occupied a "separate sphere," with its own morality and its own possibilities.

The dominant message was that women could achieve their potential only within the sphere of marriage and family. For women, as Hentz wrote in *Ernest Linwood* (1856), "In the depth of the heart there is a lower deep, which is never sounded save by the hand that wears the *wedding-ring*." In her last novel, *Married or Single* (1857), Sedgwick concluded that "God has appointed marriage" for woman; marriage is "the great circumstance" of a woman's life.

For these writers, marriage did not imply a submissive or passive role; they were claiming a superior status for women within the sphere of family life. Women, they suggested, were ultimately responsible for forming the character of their husbands and sons. In *Means and Ends* (1839), Sedgwick wrote that "By an unobtrusive and unseen process, are the characters of men formed, at home, by the mother . . . where the moral basis is fixed."

The most successful woman novelist of the period was Harriet Beecher Stowe. Her *Uncle Tom's Cabin* (1852), which sold 350,000 copies in its first year, was not merely an antislavery novel but an extended discussion of the role of women and the family. Time after time, women and even little girls are shown to be morally more sensitive and superior to the men around them. In Stowe's portrayal of slave society, it is women who offer the best hope of eventual freedom for slaves and of salvation for both African-Americans and whites. Home and family held deeply religious meanings for Stowe. In *The Minister's Wooing* (1859), she wrote that home was the "appointed sphere for woman, more holy than cloister, more saintly and pure than church and altar."

The commercial success of women novelists put an ironic twist on their celebration of the private sphere of marriage and family. These writers were actually engaged in a very public—and commercial—enterprise. They often began their careers writing under assumed names—almost always female names—but they eventually dropped their anonymity. Bargaining with their publishers, often making their own livings and even supporting their families, they were, in fact, among the first successful professional women in the United States. Their success seemed to support Caroline Lee Hentz's judgment that "Mind, we verily believe, is of no sex."

The women writers offered a new justification for the independent woman—a justification used by the increasing numbers of women who participated in religious congregations and reform organizations in the North. If talented and energetic women could find a way to place their unusual abilities to a *moral* use, then the contradiction between "domestic" and "public" life could be softened. Given such a formula, women writers and their heroines could be seen as female versions of ministers. Stowe told her readers that she would make them feel "as if you had been hearing a sermon." Hentz could speak of her writing career as a legitimate calling, or "vocation . . . for which God has endowed me." These novelists, reaching a wide audience, influenced northern middle-class women to attempt to improve both family life and society at large.

Education

A hallmark of the northern business class was its investment in young people. Parents aspiring to higher status and income for their children tried to provide them with a healthier environment, better food, basic academic skills, and the personal and social qualities appropriate to urban life. They began to spend more money on educating their children, kept them in school longer, and devoted more attention to their upbringing.

Women Teachers. Improvement of schools attracted the support of women. From Maine through Wisconsin, women vigorously supported the movement led by Horace Mann to expand and standardize public elementary schools. During the 1840s and 1850s thousands of young middle-class women became teachers. Part of the reason was economic. Towns were predisposed to hire teachers at the lowest possible wages, and began, especially after the Panic of 1837 had restricted public credit, to fill teaching positions with young women, rather than men. In so doing, school boards recognized both the rise in the number of women with schooling and the degree to which the lack of jobs for them had depressed their wages.

Teaching drew young women into its ranks through its moral appeal as much as its economic reward. The message of Catharine Beecher, who became the intellectual leader of the thousands of young women who took teaching jobs, was most powerful. Beecher founded academies for young women in Hartford and Cincinnati in the 1820s and 1830s and argued that women should make a special commitment to education. Because "to enlighten the understanding and to gain the affections is a teacher's business," and because "the mind is to be guided chiefly by means of the affections," she asked: "is not *woman* best fitted to accomplish these important objects?" To Beecher, "moral and religious education must be the foundation of national instruction," and education must be carried out by "energetic and benevolent women."

Family Planning and Population Growth

Birth Control. Northern families found the time and money for better education for their children partly by limiting the size of their families. Families in cities and towns relied on primitive but moderately effective means of birth control—i.e., abstinence, coitus interruptus, condoms fashioned from animal skins and intestines, and abortions induced by potent herbs. The business-class families led the movement to restrict family size.

AMERICAN LIVES

The Beecher Family

The evangelical reform movements of the nineteenth century were led by powerful individuals, each of whom had a highly developed sense of self. Prominent among them were the members of an extraordinary family—the Beechers. No family had greater influence on business-class reform.

Born in New Haven, Connecticut, Lyman Beecher (1775–1863) studied theology at Yale University, and as the pastor of churches in New York and Boston, became a central figure of the Benevolent Empire. He published a best-selling book of sermons on temperance and helped found the American Bible Society. Married three times, Lyman had thirteen children, of which eleven survived into adulthood.

Lyman paid close attention to the spiritual development of each of his children. He believed in the presence of original sin, he expected each child to undergo a deep and intense conversion experience. Eventually each child found Lyman's spiritual code too strict. But Lyman moderated a harsh Calvinist determinism by preaching that individuals were responsible for their own salvation. This approach to personal salvation helped most of the children develop a sense of individuality and self-confidence in their own spiritual progress. They became convinced that they were making spiritual progress. And, in adulthoods inspired by Lyman's evangelical appeals to individual action, some of them turned from spiritual to worldly matters, embracing the belief that they were responsible for the moral welfare of others. Seven of Lyman's nine sons joined the ministry, while three of his four daughters became influential social reformers.

Lyman's most accomplished son was Henry Ward Beecher (1813–1887). He was a minister at the Congregationalist Plymouth Church in Brooklyn, where he held audiences spellbound with a message of hope and optimism. He became noted during the 1850s for sermons that dramatized the evils of slavery. However, his

The Beecher Family
Taken at the studio of photographer Mathew Brady around 1859, this Beecher family portrait includes Lyman (center, seated) and nine of his children: his sons, from the left, Thomas, William, Edward, Charles, and Henry Ward, and his daughters, from the left, Isabella, Catharine, Mary, and Harriet.

abolitionism was moderate. Although he believed that the system of slavery was sinful, he argued that individual slaveholders were not, and he worked, along with his father, to maintain church unity across sectional lines. Both he and his father embraced African colonization and the free-soil movement. Henry's flamboyancy and political influence, particularly within the new Republican party, increased in the 1850s.

None of the other six Beecher sons who became ministers became as influential or prosperous as Henry. They lived out their lives in the kind of genteel poverty that was typical for the Protestant ministry in the nineteenth century.

It was the Beecher daughters who became cultural innovators—even celebrities. While Lyman's sons found legitimate and familiar channels for fulfilling their father's expectations in the ministry, his daughters had to struggle to define their social roles. They had to innovate, working out their concern for the self-improvement of individuals within the family and, in turn, for the reform of society. In the process, they discovered ways of influencing the public beyond the limits imposed by women's separate sphere. But the Beecher daughters never agreed on a common agenda. The differences among them reflected the difficulties and ambiguities middle-class women generally experienced in working out their special mission.

Lyman's oldest daughter, Catharine Beecher (1800–1878), never married and never had a home of her own, and was often at odds with the rest of her family. Nonetheless, she became the nation's leading advocate on behalf of family life, and of a separate sphere in which women would draw on their superior moral authority. Her passion for educational reform extended beyond schools to the family. She led in the development of a popular self-help literature designed to inspire middle-class wives and mothers. In manuals and magazines Catharine Beecher instructed middle-class women on how to make their homes at once more efficient and more moral. To improve their homes, she argued, women had to first improve themselves—to adopt better health practices, physical activities, and diet. Catharine Beecher's *Treatise on Domestic Economy* (1841) was reprinted almost every year during the 1840s and the 1850s, becoming the standard text on housekeeping, child-rearing, and self-improvement for women.

Harriet Beecher Stowe (1811–1896), following the death of her mother in 1816, was placed under Catharine's care and attended one of her model schools, the Hartford Female Seminary. She found Catharine overbearing, chafing under her surrogate mothering. Harriet broke away from her sister's dominance in 1836 when she married a minister, Calvin Stowe. Despite having five children in the first seven years of marriage, she managed to publish her first article for money in 1838 and her first volume of fiction in 1843. (She had two other children later.) She gradually discovered that she could earn an income that helped relieve chronic financial problems that stemmed in part from Calvin's ill-health. Hiring others to care for their four children, she wrote *Uncle Tom's Cabin* in 1852. It launched her into worldwide fame and made her one of the wealthiest authors in the world. In 1853 she took over support of her family, including management of its money. As her income grew even larger during the 1860s and 1870s, she contributed to the support of her father and his third wife and sustained four of her adult children through a variety of financial difficulties.

In her novels Harriet popularized the same moral ideas that Catharine promoted. Her most successful novel, *Uncle Tom's Cabin,* carried the advancement of American family life into the realm of politics and the sectional crisis. She appealed to women as mothers to recognize how slavery destroyed family life and to use their moral authority to reform the nation.

Isabella Beecher Hooker (1822–1907), the youngest Beecher daughter, was the only one to challenge traditional assumptions of womanhood. Envying Harriet's fame, she became the leading advocate for women's rights in Connecticut, securing passage of a bill giving property rights to married women in 1877. She joined the more radical, New York branch of the suffrage movement and quickly assumed a leadership role. (The more moderate New England suffragists had named her half-brother Henry as its president.) But she was ostracized from her family only in 1875, when she defended the editor Victoria Woodhull, a free-love advocate who had published an article charging Henry Ward Beecher with adultery. During the sensational trial that followed, Isabella attacked the double standard that condemned Woodhull but exonerated Henry. Harriet and Catharine insisted on their brother's innocence and felt that Isabella was unfaithful to the family. Isabella was bitter that the family did not appreciate her work for suffrage and women's rights.

Mary Beecher Perkins (1805–1900) was the most traditional of the daughters, remaining aloof from the reform impulses that gripped her three sisters. She particularly disapproved of Isabella, but she supported all of them by offering her Hartford, Connecticut, home as a refuge. And ironically, it was Mary's granddaughter, Charlotte Perkins Gilman (1860–1935), who spun the family's reform history in a radical direction. During the 1890's, Charlotte left her husband and family to lead a liberated life and developed a powerful feminist argument for the economic independence of women.

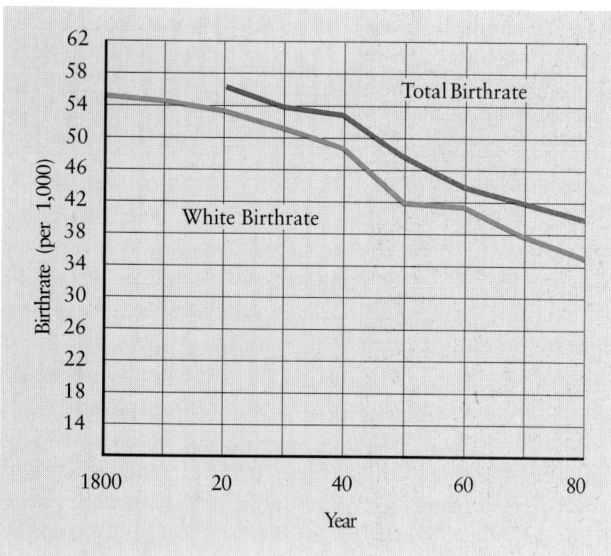

FIGURE 13.3

Birthrate by Race, 1800–1880

Although American birthrates fell steadily from 1800 to 1880, the sharpest decline took place during the 1840s.

They, more than families that owned little property, recognized the value of urban-based skills. More important, they did not feel a pressing need for their children to bring home wages or to support them in old age. Rather, they felt more pressure to buy new goods and, in order to purchase more goods, to restrict the number of children they had.

Some rural parents in long-settled agricultural areas of the Northeast also limited the size of their families. Farmers wanted to provide their children with ample land, which rising prices made more difficult to buy, or prepare them for skilled urban employment. In frontier areas fertility rates declined more slowly. There, only the most highly mobile, disrupted families restricted family size. On the frontier, where the price of land remained low, the labor of children retained greater relative value.

As a consequence of the birth control practiced by northern families, the average size of an American family declined from 5.8 to 5.3 members (including adults) between 1800 and 1860. The national birthrate, however, continued high—from forty-five to fifty live births per thousand people per year—compared with thirty per thousand in Europe. The vast majority of American parents, even in the Northeast, remained confident of their ability to provide for a large number of children.

The high birthrate and increasing immigration caused the American population to swell from 17 million in 1840 to over 31 million in 1860. By 1860 the American population exceeded the British in size and was about to overtake both the German and French. The North dominated this demographic surge; between 1840 and 1860, the northeastern and Great Lakes states accounted for nearly two-thirds of the growth in the nation's population.

The Dynamic West

Both South and North developed strategies of western expansion that were designed to protect their societies. The South established new plantations, selling slaves to the south and west, and tried to keep new territories open to such settlement. The North sent farmers and townspeople to occupy the land and to replicate the linkages among agriculture, community life, and industry that prevailed in the Northeast. Although the South did establish a dynamic society in Texas, overall the North was far more successful. By 1860 the westward movement had taken about half the nation's 31.4 million people west of the Appalachian Mountains, but the great majority of the westerners lived in the states of the Old Northwest, rather than Texas and the Old Southwest. As people moved westward, agriculture and industry developed in close conjunction, and the economies of the Northeast and the Old Northwest both converged in structure and became inextricably linked. All the peoples of two regions—even those of southern origin living in the Ohio Valley—became closely bound up in the economic and social life of the North.

The Old Northwest

Most settlers new to the West during the 1840s and 1850s migrated from New England and the Middle Atlantic states to the Old Northwest: Ohio, Indiana, Illinois, Michigan, and Wisconsin. Some pushed beyond the Mississippi into the fertile prairies of Iowa and Minnesota. These migrants established wheat farms, settled towns that serviced those farms, and built other, increasingly industrial towns. The demographic balance within the Old Northwest and the prairies beyond—which became known as the "Midwest"—shifted dramatically in favor of settlers of northeastern, rather than southern, origin.

Agriculture was buoyant in the Midwest, thanks to the products of industrial technology. The availability of low cost, labor-saving machinery quickened settlement, particularly on the fertile, grain-producing prairies bordering the Great Lakes. John Deere's steel plow, superior in strength to the cast iron plow, won widespread acceptance in the Midwest during the 1850s. In 1837, as a blacksmith in Grand Detour, Illi-

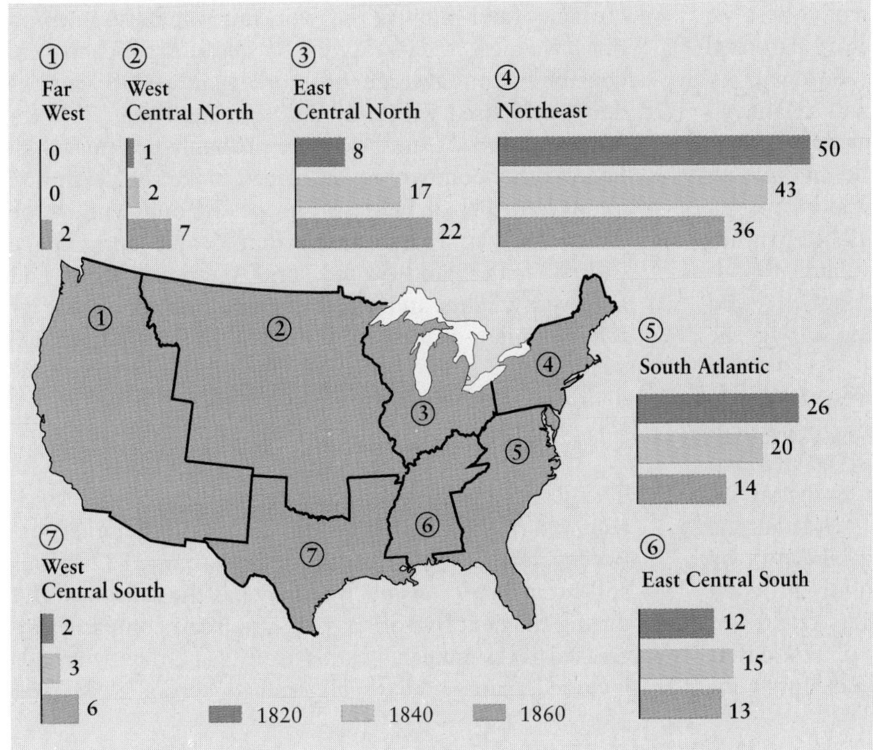

FIGURE 13.4

Population by Region, 1820–1860 (as percentages of U.S. total)

Between 1820 and 1860, the most dramatic population growth took place west of the Appalachians. The population of the Northeast and the South Atlantic regions declined from 76 percent of the national total in 1820 to 50 percent in 1860.

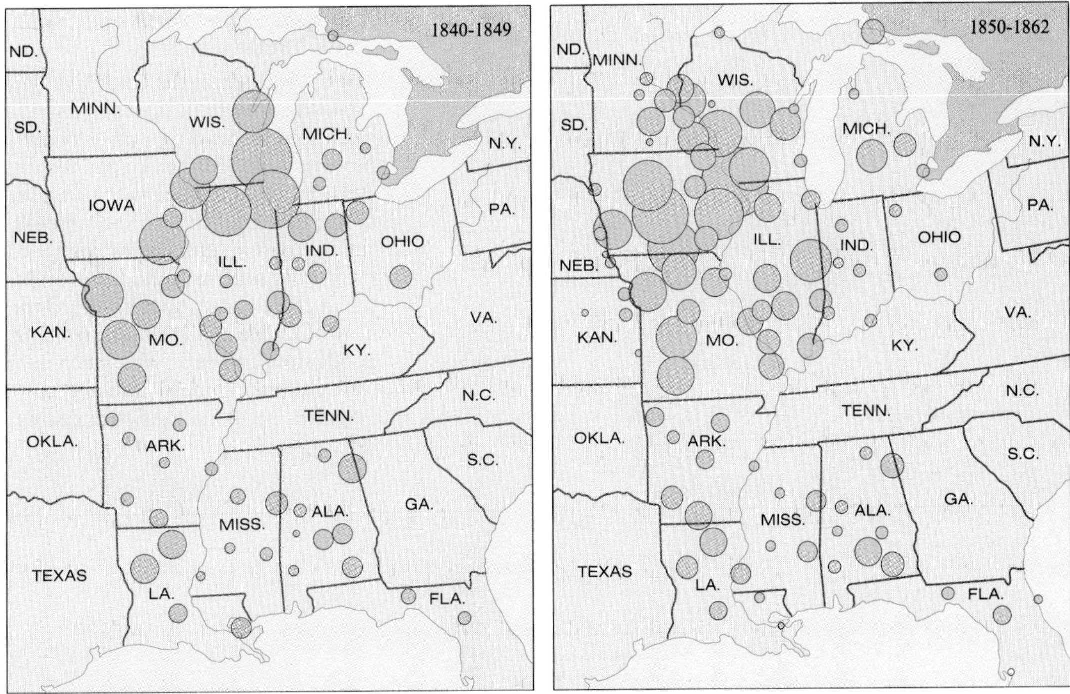

MAP 13.2

Western Land Sales, 1840–1862

Land offices continued to open up on the frontier to sell government land. Each of the circles centers on a land office and the size of each circle depends upon the relative amount of land sold at that office. During the 1840s and 1850s the tide of settlement shifted westerly and northwesterly into Indiana, Michigan, Iowa, Wisconsin, and Minnesota.

nois, Deere had made his first steel plow from old saws; ten years later, in Moline, he opened a factory that used mass-production techniques. In addition, various companies—McCormick, Hussey, Atkins, and Manny—made reapers that grain farmers found invaluable. Previously, one worker with a cradle scythe cut two to three acres a day. In the 1850s, with a self-raking reaper, that farmer cut twelve acres daily. Largely because midwestern farmers had begun to use the products of modern factories in their fields, their productivity and incomes increased more than 20 percent during the 1850s.

As agriculture flourished in the Midwest, its ties to the Northeast grew stronger. Wheat farmers, in particular, depended on northeastern urban markets reached by canal and rail, while the northeastern communities depended increasingly on wheat and flour from the Midwest. This imported wheat stimulated industry by lowering the cost of food. Without a rapidly growing food supply to augment their diet, workers could not have physically endured the long hours of work that factories required. And without a cheap and rapidly increasing food supply, the working population would not have increased as rapidly. By 1850, Americans were consuming an average of more than 4,000 calories daily, compared with only 2,000 or 2,500 in 1700. Infants and nursing mothers were probably healthier than in any other country, which helped make the death rate about half that of Western Europe. By mid-century the American diet was so ample that people born in the United States and raised on American diets had achieved heights and weights comparable to those of mid-twentieth-century Americans. The "breadbasket" of the Midwest had become vital to the health and productivity of the people of the Northeast.

The Railroads. It was another product of industrial technology—the railroad—that cemented the union between Northeast and Midwest. As late as 1852 canals still carried twice as much tonnage as the railroads. But during the next five or six years, railroad companies increased track mileage dramatically. The new railroads included trunk lines that stretched across New York

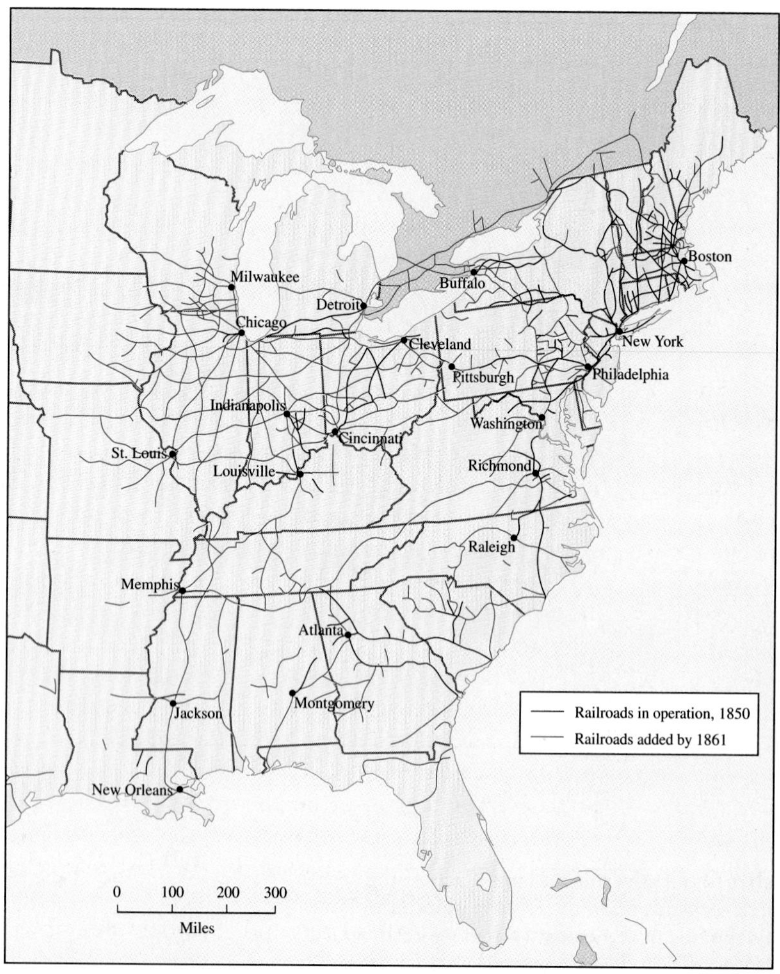

MAP 13.3

Railroads of the North and South, 1850–1860

The decade before the Civil War witnessed explosive growth in the nation's railroad network, but it was geographically uneven. The Northeast and Midwest acquired extensive, dense railroad systems that stimulated economic development. The South built a much simpler system. Numerous, highly competitive companies built railroad lines, often using different track gauges that hindered the efficient flow of traffic and made the transshipment of goods slow and expensive. Such problems were frustrating to the military, and proved especially severe in the South during the Civil War.

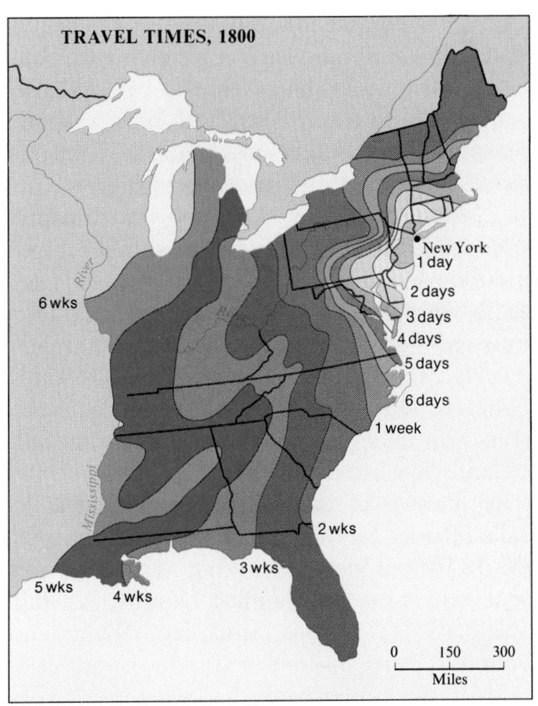

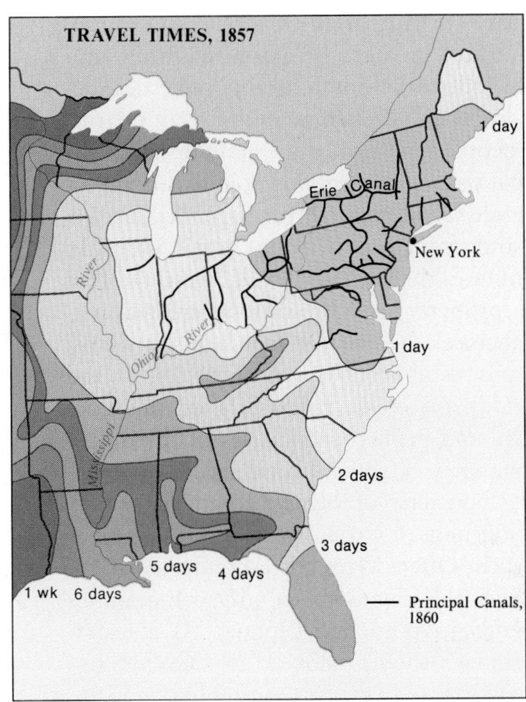

MAP 13.4

The New Mobility of Goods and People, 1800–1857

The transportation revolution dramatically decreased travel times by 1860. In 1800 a traveler from New York required an entire day to reach Philidelphia and a full week to reach Pittsburgh or western New York state. In 1860 a day on the railroad could take a New York traveler as far west as Cleveland. In a week the traveler could reach the Kansas Territory or the uppermost reaches of the Mississippi River.

and Pennsylvania to provide through traffic from New York City and Philadelphia to Cleveland and Chicago. More convenient and faster than canals, by 1859 the railroads had supplanted canals as the main carriers of freight.

Railroads promoted midwestern prosperity in a variety of ways. They hastened the advance of people onto fresh lands in remote areas that canal or river transport did not serve. They made western farming more profitable by lowering the costs of transporting farm goods. And they promoted commerce and manufacturing in the Midwest. Springing up at the points where trunk lines converged or rail routes met water transport were grain storehouses, warehouses, docks, flour mills, packing plants, and farm machinery factories, as well as mercantile and financial firms. In 1846, Cyrus McCormick moved his reaper production from western Virginia to Chicago to be closer to his customers. St. Louis and Chicago became boom towns largely because of the railroads. As early as 1860 they surpassed Boston and Baltimore in size and became the nation's third and fourth largest cities, respectively, behind New York and Philadelphia. Taking advantage of the stationary steam engine, St Louis and Chicago became major industrial centers with strong linkages to northeastern industrial centers and markets.

The trunk-line railroads undermined the economic base of other western cities, however, especially Cincinnati, Pittsburgh, Buffalo, and Rochester, which had been key regional centers along water routes. Thousands of dockworkers, teamsters, and warehouse workers in those cities lost their jobs when the railroads provided efficient through traffic. During the depression of the late 1850s, many of these workers roamed the country in search of casual employment or charity.

Railroads also became a force in modernizing the iron industry, a critical component of northeastern manufacturing. The industry responded to the demand of railroads for high-quality iron. By 1860 the railmills, located primarily in and around Philadelphia, were the largest and most technically advanced iron mills in the country. The engineering requirements for train engines had a similar effect on steam engine production. Moreover, to service complex locomotives, the railroads built a large network of machine shops that extended into the Midwest. The spread and expansion of these shops disseminated industrial skills and promoted the growth of a skilled labor force.

Links of Culture. The migration of people and capital insured that cultural linkages between Northeast and Midwest would follow the powerful economic ties, despite the high degree of geographic mobility. In migrating westward, people who owned property or had skills faced formidable risks. They knew that in new communities, as in the old, economic success depended heavily on the quality and strength of personal relationships. In the new communities throughout the Midwest, the first residents with property and aspirations created networks among themselves. The first merchants, artisans, and professionals established loyal clienteles, sound reputations, and good credit ratings. From this core came the leaders and prime beneficiaries of the Industrial Revolution. They celebrated their success, becoming the greatest "boosters" of the new communities.

Later-arriving migrants tried to seek out family or established friends. Often wives corresponded with sisters, cousins, and old friends to identify communities where their families would find support. As a result, westward migrants usually moved to communities founded by people of similar backgrounds. New Englanders, for example, largely avoided the towns of the Ohio Valley that southerners had established and settled instead in newer places in northern Ohio, northern Illinois, and Wisconsin. And in new communities, migrants immediately sought out familiar churches, fraternal lodges, crafts, and professions for their first friendships.

The first generations of community leaders became patrons of new migrants. They backed ambitious young men who had some education, skill, or family connections. They helped these young men acquire skills or loaned them money to start new businesses. Often they supported their daughters' decisions to marry one of these industrious migrants. Many of the young men, in turn, scouted western opportunities for relatives who still lived in the East. Conversely, success in the new communities usually required membership in the stable core of local property owners. Through this mechanism the business class of the Midwest established powerful linkages with its members in the older towns and cities of the Northeast.

Manifest Destiny

Even as Americans were settling the Midwest, American territorial ambitions soared, extending beyond the area of the Louisiana Purchase to encompass huge new chunks of the continent. Americans saw a continental vision—one captured by the term *Manifest Destiny*. It was coined in 1845 by John L. O'Sullivan, the editor of the *Democratic Review* and the *New York Morning News*. He wrote: "Our manifest destiny is to overspread the continent allotted by Providence for the free development of our yearly multiplying millions." O'Sullivan's vision was shared equally by southern imperialists seeking to export slavery to new territories and by the northern business class wanting to expand its dynamic mix of industry and agriculture.

Manifest Destiny expressed the romantic faith of Americans in their special mission to bind together nature, westward settlement, and political freedom. Virtually every aspect of mainstream American culture reinforced the imagery. Artists, for example, gave the message visual form. Thomas Cole (1801–1848) and Asher B. Durand (1796–1886), who started their careers as print engravers, established a national tradition of landscape art. They, their disciples, who were collectively known as the Hudson River School, and the so-called Rocky Mountain painters, who began working in the 1850s, all viewed painting as a patriotic art—a visual expression of Manifest Destiny. As Philip Hone, one of Cole's patrons, remarked, "Every American is bound to prove his love of country by admiring Cole."

Although other terms had been used to describe the nation's expansionist spirit, Manifest Destiny precisely captured the mood of the 1840s and 1850s and became a permanent part of the American vocabulary. O'Sullivan left the geographic scope of Manifest Destiny vague; America's continental mission might encompass only Oregon, where Britain and the United States had conflicting claims, or it could include parts of Canada and follow Texas as a model, reaching all of Mexico and even the islands of the Caribbean.

O'Sullivan meant to imply that the United States had a divinely inspired mission to bring its neighbors, including Mexico, within the American democratic experiment. For behind the rhetoric of Manifest Destiny was cultural arrogance—the assumption of the cultural, even racial, superiority of Americans. As "inferior" peoples were brought under American rule, they would be pushed to adopt American forms of government, convert to Protestantism, and learn from American teachers. This arrogance would long shape the nation's relationships with the rest of the world. Also behind the words of Manifest Destiny were economic motives that led Boston and New York merchants, southern planters, and small farmers throughout the nation to agree that the United States must expand at least to the shores of the Pacific.

Unlocking Japan. A few Americans may have looked even further and dreamed of bases in the Pacific. As the China trade declined in the 1840s, some northeastern merchants scouted new markets in the western Pacific. They persuaded the federal government to send its first mission to Japan in 1846. A subsequent naval expedition under Commodore Mathew C. Perry in 1853–1854 led Japan to sign, in 1858, a full commercial treaty with the United States, the first treaty Japan made with any industrial power.

The "Great American Desert" and "Oregon Fever"

By 1840, settlers had pushed westward into the Texas district of Mexico, but few other Americans had crossed the 95th meridian. Beyond this north-south line, which lay not far beyond the western boundary of Arkansas and Missouri, stretched what most Americans called the "Great American Desert." For fifty years map makers put that label on the Great Plains because they believed the 1820 report of an army explorer, Major Stephen H. Long, who claimed that the entire area between the Missouri River and the Rocky Mountains was "almost wholly unfit for cultivation." This assumption led the federal government to regard the 95th meridian as a permanent frontier between white settlement and the Indian reservations that Andrew Jackson had carved out to the west.

For the farmers who poured into the prairies of the Mississippi Valley from New England, New York, and Ohio in the 1840s and 1850s, the 95th meridian was not a meaningful barrier. They had plenty of room to settle in Wisconsin, Iowa, and Minnesota; they did not feel overcrowded on the land until after the Civil War. However, for the farmers who had filled in the best lands of Louisiana, Arkansas, Missouri, and the Ohio River Valley during the 1830s, the barrier was real. It forced those who sought new land to settle in Texas, which was still alien territory, to consider settling among the New Englanders, New Yorkers, and immigrants in the Midwest, or to cast their eyes beyond the Great Plains—to the forested valleys of Oregon.

Oregon under Joint Occupation. The United States and Britain both had claims to Oregon. In 1818 a British-American convention had failed to resolve the dispute, establishing the Canadian-American boundary only as far west as the Rocky Mountains. But the convention provided that both British and Americans could settle anywhere in the Oregon territory, which then stretched from the 42nd parallel in the south (the border with Mexico) to 54° 40' in the north (the border with Russian territory).

Settlement had proceeded without conflict under the joint occupation agreement. The Hudson's Bay Company carried on a lucrative fur trade while several hundred Americans, including a large group of Methodist missionaries, settled there during the 1830s.

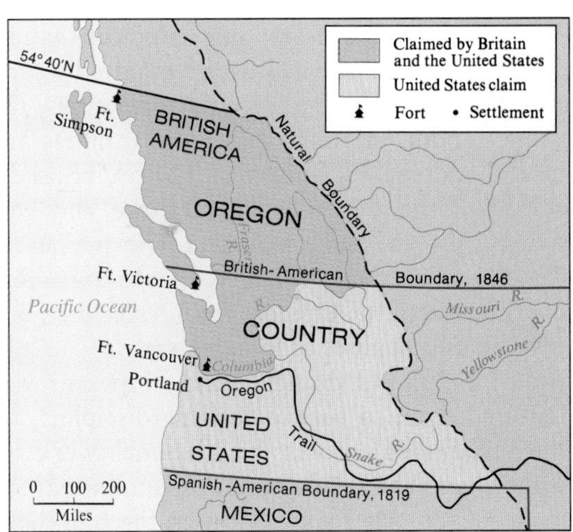

MAP 13.5

Territorial Conflict in Oregon

The American and British governments disputed whether the Oregon Territory should be divided along the Columbia River, to include Ft. Vancouver, or the more northerly boundary that eventually divided the two countries. An agreement granting the citizens of each country equal access to Oregon enabled thousands of Americans to pour into the area.

Most took up land south of the Columbia River, in the Willamette Valley, which was of little interest to the Hudson's Bay Company. Based on this settlement, the United States established a claim, unchallenged by the British, to the zone between the 42nd parallel and the Columbia River.

In 1842, American interest in Oregon increased dramatically. Navy lieutenant Charles Wilkes published widely circulated reports on his four years of Pacific explorations. He wrote glowingly of the potential harbors he had found in the Strait of Juan de Fuca, Admiralty Inlet, and Puget Sound—of great interest to the New England merchants plying the China trade. Also in 1842, the first large party, over one hundred people, crossed the Oregon Trail, blazed by fur traders and explorers through the Great Plains and the Rocky Mountains. Their reports told of a mild climate and fertile soil. The publicity and the beginnings of recovery in the rest of the nation from the depression that had followed the Panic of 1837 bred ambitious planning. "Oregon fever" suddenly raged.

The Oregon Trail. The following May a thousand men, women, and children gathered in Independence, Missouri, for the overland trek. They were farming and trading families from Missouri, Ohio, Indiana, Illinois,

Kentucky, and Tennessee; they had more than five thousand oxen and cattle and over a hundred wagons. With military-style organization and formations, they overcame flooding streams, dust storms, illness and death, insects and snakes, hunger and thirst, bruised feet and ruined clothes, overweight furniture and equipment, dying livestock, and encounters with Indians. (Most of these encounters, however, were ones of peaceful trade; over the life of the Oregon Trail, fewer than 400 travelers died as casualties of Indian attacks.) The trail was an ordeal for all, but women found it especially difficult. It required them to submit to male discipline, to add to their traditional chores the strenuous work of driving wagons and animals, and to give up domesticity and female friends. After six months on the trail they reached the Willamette Valley—more than 2,000 miles across the continent. During the next two seasons, another 5,000 people, still largely from the Ohio Valley, reached Oregon. By the Civil War, some 350,000 people had attempted the Oregon Trail, heading for California as well as Oregon; some 34,000 died in the effort—about 17 deaths per mile. The walking migrants wore 3-foot-deep paths, and their wagons carved 5-foot-deep ruts across sandstone formations; the tracks are still visible in southern Wyoming well over a century later.

For a time, Americans demanded all of Oregon, but in 1846 the United States reached an agreement with Britain to divide Oregon at the 49th parallel. Congress organized the Oregon Territory in 1848 and admitted the state of Oregon to the Union in 1859.

The Mormons and the Great Basin Frontier

As "Oregon Fever" raged, a group of utopians living in Nauvoo, Illinois, also dreamed of settling beyond the Rocky Mountains. These were the Mormons, the Church of Jesus Christ of Latter Day Saints. More interested in religious freedom than fat land, they founded the largest settlement in the truly arid portions of the "Great American Desert."

The Mormon migration resulted from the religious ferment that swirled along the route of the Erie Canal during the 1820s. In 1820, Joseph Smith, the founder of the Mormon Church, had a series of religious experiences that led him to believe that God had singled him out for a special, immediate, and private revelation of divine truth. In 1830, Smith published his revelations as *The Book of Mormon*, which he claimed he had translated from ancient hieroglyphics on gold plates shown

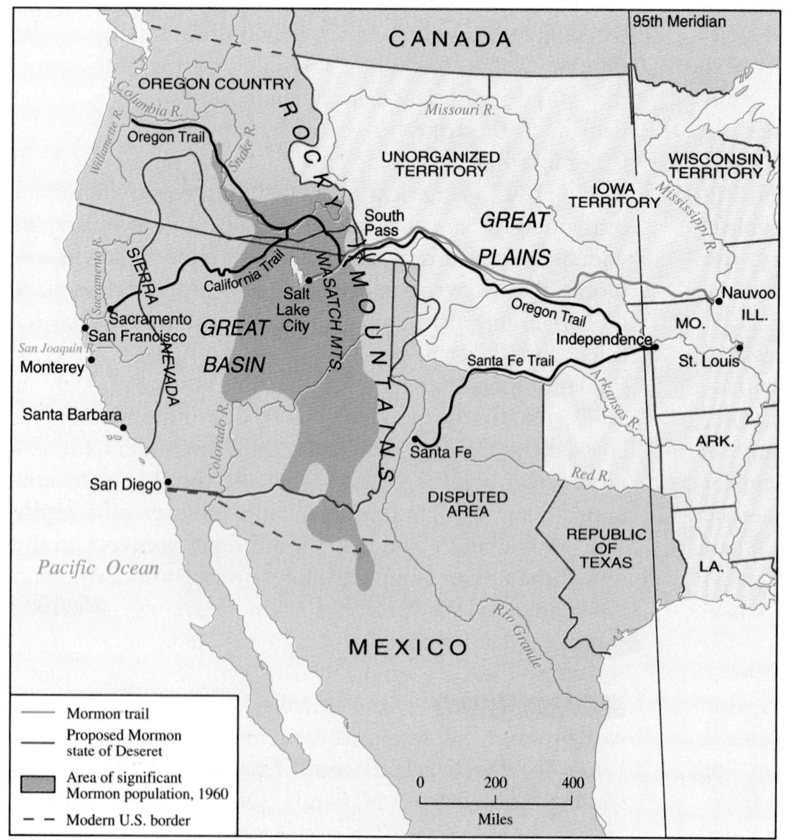

MAP 13.6

Settlement of the Trans–Missouri West, 1840s

The most successful communal experimenters were the Mormons, who ultimately sought extreme isolation and built an agrarian empire in Utah. Their proposed state of Deseret materialized in a way—in the form of a large area of the United States where Mormon culture became influential.

A Mormon Man and His Wives
Mormon families, such as this one pictured during the late 1840s, achieved a degree of prosperity that was unusual for pioneer farm families, partly because of the labor of multiple wives. This homesteader's cabin, although cramped for such a large family, is well built, with a brick chimney and—a luxury for any pioneer home—a glass window.

to him by an angel named Moroni. In the same year he organized a church in western New York. Smith encouraged his followers to adopt the patterns of behavior that were central to the Industrial Revolution—hard work, saving, and risk taking. At the same time, however, he imposed a communal framework that concentrated power in the church elders.

The success of Smith's message was phenomenal. By the early 1840s he had become perhaps the most successful of all the leaders of utopian communities, having attracted as many as 30,000 followers to Nauvoo. There, Smith had a new revelation, one that encouraged *polygamy*—taking more than one wife at the same time. But a large minority of the Mormon community rejected polygamy, producing internal dissension and violence, and the arrest of Smith. In 1844 an anti-Mormon mob led by members of the Illinois militia stormed the Carthage jail where Smith and his brother were being held and murdered them both.

Brigham Young and Utah. Now led by Brigham Young, an early convert of Smith's, the Mormon elders resolved that they could ensure their religious independence only by leaving the United States and seeking a home in the wilderness. In 1846, leaving the antipolygamy minority behind, Young began a phased migration of more than 10,000 people across the Great Plains. They reached Great Salt Lake, in what was still Mexican territory. Within a decade, Young and his theocracy transformed the alkaline desert landscape by building elaborate irrigation systems. The Mormons used communal labor and developed innovative principles of communal water rights that the federal government and all the states of the semiarid West later adopted. The Mormons quickly spread planned agricultural communities along the base of the Wasatch Range in present-day Utah.

But it was not long before the Mormons faced a challenge to their isolation from the United States government, which had acquired the area of Mormon settlement from Mexico. Congress rejected a Mormon petition to create a new state, Deseret, stretching all the way to Los Angeles and San Diego. Instead, it set up the much smaller Utah Territory in 1850, with Young as territorial governor. Thereafter, the federal government, under pressure from Protestant clergy, occasionally intervened in the territory's affairs, as in 1857 when President Buchanan removed Young from the governorship. But the nation's political leaders were too far from Utah and too absorbed in the sectional crisis to threaten Mormon society in a sustained way. Consequently, the Mormons were free to build their community, and Young was able to rule through figurehead governors until his death in 1877. The Mormons did not formally abolish polygamy until 1890, six years before Utah became a state. Protected by vast semiarid expanses, the Mormons had the security to make their communities the most successful utopian experiments of the nineteenth century.

Expansion into California

Long before the Mormons settled in northwestern Mexico, other Americans had discovered the economic opportunities of the region. In the late eighteenth century, Russia, Britain, and the United States all explored New Spain's northwestern coast. To secure its territory, Spain built a system of missions and presidios stretching from San Diego to San Francisco. Almost immediately, in the 1780s, New England merchants began trading with the Spanish settlements in California, largely for sea-otter pelts that they carried to China. Their commerce, and that of American traders throughout northern Mexico, increased after Mexico won its independence from Spain in 1822. Between Independence, Missouri, and Santa Fe, following the Sante Fe Trail, a few Americans ran a small but lucrative trade in gold, silver, furs, and mules. Literate mountain men like Jedediah Smith and James Ohio Pattie trapped and explored along the Sierra Nevada range and publicized California for eastern readers.

The Coastal Settlements. To promote economic development, the new Mexican government welcomed Yankee traders; secularized the missions, releasing the Indians, many of whom intermarried with the local *mestizos* ("mixed blood" Spanish-Indians); and promoted large-scale cattle ranching on former mission

The Monterey Colonial House
Thomas O. Larkin's house, completed in 1837, represented the fusing of American and Mexican building traditions and set architectural fashions during the early 1840s for the elite, both American and Mexican, in Monterey. The house combined eastern features, such as a symmetrical facade and a timber frame supporting an upper story, with adobe construction.

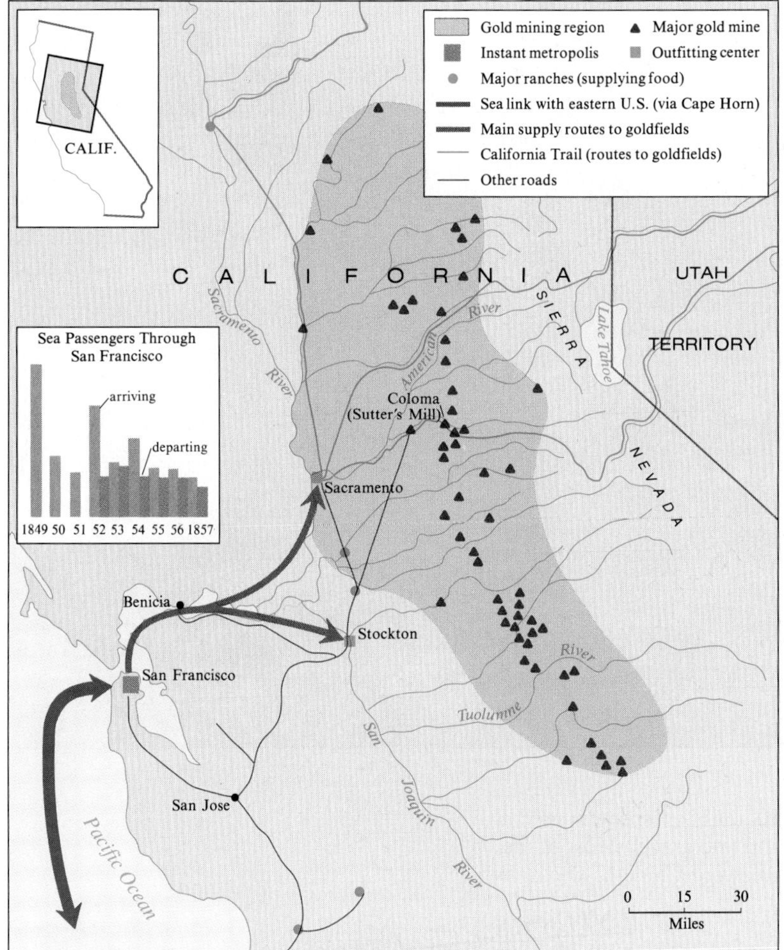

MAP 13.7

The California Gold Rush

Hundreds of thousands of fortune seekers converged on the California gold fields beginning in 1849. Miners traveling by sea landed at San Francisco, which became California's instant metropolis. They outfitted for their journey inland at Sacramento and Stockton, which were commercial outposts of San Francisco. The vast population influx placed great pressure on existing ranches for food and stimulated new farming enterprise in the Sacramento, American, and San Joaquin River valleys.

lands. All of this meant prosperity to the New England merchants who brought hides and tallow from California ranchos home to the boot and shoe industry. To handle the business, New Englanders dispatched dozens of resident agents to the coastal towns of California. More often than not, they fell in love with California, married into the families of the elite Mexicans—the *Californios*, became Catholics and Mexican citizens, and adopted the dress and manners of the *Californios*. A crucial exception was Thomas Oliver Larkin, the most successful merchant in Monterey. He established a close working relationship with Mexican authorities and often loaned them money, but he remained an American citizen and plotted for the peaceful annexation of Upper California. In 1843 he became U.S. consul in California.

The Sacramento Valley. The land-hungry farmers, mainly southerners from the Ohio River Valley, knew more about Oregon than California, and they felt more secure in settling where the United States had staked out a claim. However, about one in ten of the pioneers traveling the Oregon Trail turned left just past Fort Hall on the Snake River and struggled southward down the California Trail. Most of these settlers received dubious land grants or simply squatted without any title. By 1845 about a thousand Americans were living in California, mostly in the Sacramento Valley. Their number grew swiftly, while the coastal population of 7,000 Mexicans and roughly 300 Americans remained stable. The Americans in the interior did not wish to assimilate into Mexican society. They hoped, instead, to emulate the Americans in Texas: to colonize, to extinguish what they regarded as an inferior culture, and to make California another example of the beneficent workings of Manifest Destiny.

The Mexican War (1846–1847) gave the Americans the advantage in shaping California's development by winning Upper California for the United States (see Chapter 14). But their battle for control after the war would have been protracted and difficult had it not been for the gold rush.

Gold Prospectors
Working at the head of the Auburn Ravine in about 1850, these prospectors used a primitive technique—panning—to separate gold from sand and gravel. Most of the wage laborers in the early years of the gold rush were Indians or Chinese, who numbered over 25,000 in California by 1852.

The "Forty-Niners." In January 1848 workmen building a mill for John A. Sutter discovered flakes of gold in the Sierra Nevada foothills. Sutter was a German immigrant who had arrived in California in 1839, become a Mexican citizen, and established a kind of feudal barony in the Sacramento Valley, well removed from the Mexican authorities. He tried to keep the gold discovery a secret, but by May Americans from San Francisco were pouring into the foothills. In September the news reached the Northeast but newspaper readers remained skeptical until December, when President Polk confirmed the gold discoveries in his annual message to Congress. By January 1849, sixty-one crowded ships had departed from northeastern ports to sail around Cape Horn for San Francisco. By May, 12,000 wagons had crossed the Missouri River headed for the gold fields. In 1849 alone, more than 80,000 migrants—the "forty-niners"—arrived. In 1852 there were more than 200,000 Californians; by 1860 the state's population reached 380,000.

The demands of the "forty-niners" for effective government, and the national celebration of the California boom as a vindication of Manifest Destiny, brought California into the Union as a state in 1850. Using the instruments of both state government and vigilante tactics, the dominant Americans systematically restricted opportunities for the *Californios*. Violence and the state's Foreign Miners' Tax—which California applied to Mexicans in violation of the treaty that had ended the war—drove the *Californios* out of the gold fields. In agricultural districts American squatters invaded and engaged the *Californios* in costly legal battles over land titles. While a federal commission, created by the Land Act of 1851, ultimately upheld most Mexican titles that had been challenged, this usually came too late. Legal fees, heavy property taxes imposed by the California legislature, debts, and violence forced most *Californios* to sell their land. By the Civil War, the American migrants had completed the conquest of California and its people begun by the Mexican War.

The divergence between the South and the North was reflected in California society of the 1850s. California's two leading politicians reflected the dichotomy between South and North in the cultural origins of the migrants. Both had arrived in 1849, and both were Democrats, but both had very different constituencies. David C. Broderick, who had Irish parents and grew up in New York, appealed to the large number of Californians from northeastern cities, while William Gwin, who had a successful political career in his native Tennessee, was an old Jacksonian Democrat who represented people from the upper South and the Ohio River Valley.

The outcome of the rush to control California was not reassuring to the southern imperialists who hoped that the West might protect slavery. Despite their differences on many issues, both Broderick and Gwin, and their constituencies, were staunch opponents of the expansion of slavery. To be sure, their opposition to slavery was usually racist—an opposition couched as much in terms of hostility to African-Americans as to the institution of slavery. But that provided no comfort to southern slaveowners. The farmers from Tennessee and the Irish immigrants from New York shared a hatred of slavery and agreed that the future of California should resemble that of the free-soil Midwest.

While California voters disappointed southern imperialists, the state was a source of excitement for most Americans and represented the genuine culmination of Manifest Destiny. To the increasingly self-conscious North, California's success was a vindication of its social system. The excesses appalled only a few. Henry David Thoreau, for example, condemned the Gold Rush as an expression of the moral bankruptcy of industrial society. California, he said, was "three thousand miles nearer to hell." But for most Americans, the Gold Rush and the thrust to the Pacific Ocean dramatized the promise of American life. Even most of the old transcendentalists joined the celebration. While Emerson initially had his doubts about the "California dream," by 1851 he had come to believe that in California, as in America generally, "nature watches over all, and turns this malfeasance to good."

Summary

During the 1840s and 1850s southern society became increasingly dependent on slavery. Planters exploited the system of slavery more aggressively as a source of profits and developed an elaborate defense of it in order to control slaves and guarantee the loyalty of non-slaveholding whites. In response to the growing intensification of work and the disruption of their lives, slaves devised elaborate networks of family and community support. The South's commitment to a slave-labor system placed the region in direct competition with the North over the future of the West.

Meanwhile, industrialization accelerated and tightened its hold on northeastern society by stimulating spectacular gains in productivity, income, and middle-class consumption. In addition, it accelerated the settlement of the Old Northwest, helping to fill the land of the Great Lakes basin and the prairies of the Mississippi Valley with people from the Northeast, and to stimulate the flourishing of commerce and industry in new western towns and cities. In short, industrialization bound together the Northeast and the Old Northwest. Class distinctions further hardened, however, particularly because industrialization attracted immigrants, especially from Ireland, who were poor and Catholic.

Both northerners and southerners agreed on the need for continued westward expansion, and on the Manifest Destiny of continental expansion. Consequently, during the 1840s, they embarked on great migrations across the Great Plains to British-American Oregon, to the desolate terrain of the Great Basin, and to the vast territories of Mexican California. But southern planters faced disappointment when the future of California—the culmination of Manifest Destiny—proved to be one of free soil.

TOPIC FOR RESEARCH

Family Life and Religion Under Slavery

In recent years historians have explored the role of family life and religion in helping African-Americans cope with the oppression of slavery. The pioneering books were John W. Blassingame, *The Slave Community: Plantation Life in the Antebellum South* (1979); Eugene D. Genovese, *Roll, Jordan, Roll* (1974); Herbert G. Gutman, *The Black Family in Slavery and Freedom, 1750–1925* (1976); and Lawrence W. Levine, *Black Culture and Black Consciousness* (1977). More recent studies include Charles Joyner, *Down by the Riverside: A South Carolina Slave Community* (1984); Jacqueline Jones, *Labor of Love, Labor of Sorrow: Black Women, Work, and the Family from Slavery to the Present* (1986); Albert J. Raboteau, *Slave Religion: The "Invisible Institution" in the Antebellum South* (1978); Mechal Sobel, *Travelin' On: The Slave Journey to an*

Afro-Baptist Faith (1979); Sterling Stuckey, *Slave Culture* (1987); and Deborah G. White, *Ar'n't I a Woman? Female Slaves in the Plantation South* (1985). However, some planters may have attempted to shape slave family life and religion for a very different purpose: to strengthen slavery. For example, some planters may have promoted family life among slaves as a way of increasing their economic productivity, and promoted slave religion as a way of encouraging slaves to accept their bondage. In a research paper, focus on a small sample of slaves and analyze for yourself the role of family and religion in their lives. Base your analysis on the words of slaves themselves. A prime source is the massive collection of slave interviews conducted by the New Deal's Federal Writers' Project during the 1930s. These interviews can be found in Benjamin A. Botkin, *Lay My Burden Down: A Folk History of Slavery* (1945); Norman Yetman, ed., *Life Under the "Peculiar Institution": Selections from the Slave Narrative Collection* (1970); and George P. Rawick, *The American Slave: A Composite Autobiography* (19 volumes and supplements, beginning in 1972). The narratives have to be used with care, however, because the interviewers were mainly white, and most of the people interviewed were recalling events that had happened many decades earlier. For analysis of the interviews by historians, see Paul D. Escott, *Slavery Remembered: A Record of Twentieth-Century Slave Narratives* (1979), and John Blassingame's introduction to *Slave Testimony* (1977). You might also read one or more of the many diaries and first-hand accounts by slaves or freedmen. See, for example, Frederick Douglass, *My Bondage and My Freedom* (1855).

BIBLIOGRAPHY

The Slave South

Scholars have heatedly debated the issues of slavery's profitability and the productivity and welfare of slave labor. Most controversial is Robert W. Fogel and Stanley L. Engerman, *Time on the Cross: The Economics of American Negro Slavery* (1974), which should be read with Paul A. David et al., *Reckoning with Slavery* (1976).

The culture of the planter class and non-slaveholding whites can be explored in O. Vernon Burton, *In My Father's House Are Many Mansions: Family and Community in Edgefield, South Carolina* (1985); Jane T. Censer, *North Carolina Planters and Their Children, 1800–1860* (1984); J. William Harris, *Plain Folk and Gentry in a Slave Society: White Liberty and Black Slavery in Augusta's Hinterlands* (1985); John McCardell, *The Idea of a Southern Nation: Southern Nationalists and Southern Nationalism, 1830–1860* (1979); James Oakes, *The Ruling Race: A History of American Slaveholders* (1982); and Frank L. Owsley, *Plain Folk of the Old South* (1949). The best studies of women in southern slave society are Catherine Clinton, *The Plantation Mistress* (1983), and Elizabeth Fox-Genovese, *Within the Plantation Household: Black and White Women of the Old South* (1988). A pioneering effort to use literature to reflect on cultural themes remains William R. Taylor, *Cavalier and Yankee: The Old South and American National Character* (1961). Efforts to connect southern culture with southern politics include Clement Eaton, *The Freedom of Thought Struggle in the Old South* (1964); George M. Frederickson, *White Supremacy: A Comparative Study in American and South African History* (1981); and J. Mills Thornton III, *Politics and Power in a Slave Society: Alabama, 1800–1860* (1978). On the nature of violence in southern society, see John Hope Franklin, *The Militant South 1800–1861* (1956), and Bertram Wyatt-Brown, *Southern Honor: Ethics and Behavior in the Old South* (1982).

The first modern work to focus on slavery as repressive to African-Americans was Kenneth Stampp, *The Peculiar Institution* (1956). The first to emphasize the psychological costs of slavery was Stanley Elkins, *Slavery: A Problem in American Institutional and Intellectual Life* (3rd ed., 1976). For additional studies of the lives of slaves, see the works listed in the Topic for Research. On slave revolts, see Herbert Aptheker, *American Negro Slave Revolts* (1943); Stephen B. Oates, *The Fires of Jubilee: Nat Turner's Fierce Rebellion* (1975); and Eugene D. Genovese, *From Rebellion to Revolution: Afro-American Slave Revolts in the Making of the Modern World* (1979). On the ambiguous position of free blacks in slave society, see Ira Berlin, *Slaves Without Masters: The Free Negro in the Antebellum South* (1974), and Michael P. Johnson and James R. Roark, *Black Masters: A Free Family of Color in the Old South* (1984).

The Northeast

The economic changes in the North during the 1840s and 1850s can be studied in many of the economic history sources listed for Chapter 10. In addition, on railroads see Albert Fishlow, *American Railroads and the Transformation of the Ante-Bellum Economy* (1965); Peter Temin, *Iron and Steel in Nineteenth-Century America* (1964); Allan G. Bogue, *From Prairie to Corn Belt: Farming on the Illinois and Iowa Frontier* (1968); Lee Soltow, *Men and Wealth in the United States, 1850–1870* (1975); and Colin Forster and G. S. L. Tucker, *Economic Opportunity and White Fertility Ratios, 1800–1860* (1972).

On the sources and character of European immigration, consult Maldwyn Allen Jones, *American Immigration* (1960), and Philip Taylor, *The Distant Magnet: European Immigration to the U.S.A.* (1971). The most useful introduction to the nature of immigrant communities during the 1840s and 1850s is Oscar Handlin, *Boston's Immigrants: A Study in Acculturation* (1959). See also Jay P. Dolan, *The Immigrant Church: New York's Irish and German Catholics, 1815–1865* (1975); Kathleen Neils Conzen, *Immigrant Milwaukee, 1836–1860*

(1976); and Bruce Laurie, *Working People in Philadelphia, 1800–1850* (1980). For the nativist reaction, consult Michael Feldberg, *The Philadelphia Riots of 1844: A Study of Ethnic Conflict* (1975), and Robert F. Hueston, *The Catholic Press and Nativism, 1840–1860* (1976).

No scholarly book surveys the development of middle-class culture in the decades before the Civil War. Explorations of the relationship between women's roles and the development of popular literature include Ann Douglas, *The Feminization of American Culture* (1977), and Mary Kelley, *Private Woman, Public Stage: Literary Domesticity in Nineteenth-Century America* (1984). On birth control, see Linda Gordon, *Woman's Body, Woman's Rights: A Social History of Birth Control in America* (1976), and James Reed, *From Private Vice to Public Virtue: The Birth Control Movement and American Society since 1830* (1978). On educational reform, see Lawrence A. Cremin, *American Education: the National Experience, 1783–1876* (1980); Linda A. Pollock, *Forgotten Children: Parent-Child Relations from 1500–1900* (1983); and Stanley K. Schultz, *The Culture Factory: Boston Public Schools, 1789–1860* (1973). On the Beecher family, see Jeanne Boyston et al., eds., *The Limits of Sisterhood: The Beecher Sisters on Women's Rights and Woman's Sphere* (1988); Milton Rugoff, *The Beechers: An American Family in the Nineteenth Century* (1981); and Kathryn Kish Sklar, *Catharine Beecher: A Study in American Domesticity* (1973), which is a definitive biography.

The Dynamic West

Books treating Manifest Destiny include William Graebner, *Empire on the Pacific: A Study of American Continental Expansion* (1955); Reginald Horsman, *Race and Manifest Destiny: The Origins of American Racial Anglo-Saxonism* (1981); Frederick Merk, *Manifest Destiny and Mission in American History* (1963); and Albert K. Weinberg, *Manifest Destiny: A Study of Nationalist Expansionism in American History* (1935). On the Mormon experience, see Thomas F. O'Dea, *The Mormons* (1957) and Klaus J. Hansen, *Mormonism and the American Experience* (1981).

In recent years a number of books have opened up exciting new approaches to the history of western America. The leading examples of this scholarship include Patricia Nelson Limerick, *The Legacy of Conquest: The Unbroken Past of the Unbroken West* (1987); Ann Markeson, *Regions: The Economics and Politics of Territory* (1987); Kevin Starr, *Americans and the California Dream, 1850–1915* (1973); John Unruh, *The Plains Across: The Overland Emigrations and the Trans-Mississippi West, 1840–1860* (1979); and David J. Weber, *The Mexican Frontier, 1821–1846* (1982). This newer scholarship presents a more complete view of women in the West. See, for example, Susan Armitage and Elizabeth Jameson, eds., *The Women's West* (1987); John Mack Faragher, *Women and Men on the Overland Trail* (1979); Julie R. Jeffrey, *Frontier Women: The Trans-Mississippi West, 1840–1860* (1979); and Joanna L. Stratton, *Pioneer Women: Voices from the Kansas Frontier* (1981).

TIMELINE

1841	Catharine Beecher's *Treatise on Domestic Economy* appears Preemption Act
1842	Migration to Oregon begins
1843	Calhoun warns of a British conspiracy to block expansion
1844	Anti-Catholic rioting in Philadelphia
1845	Lowell Female Labor Reform Association formed Editor John L. O'Sullivan coins term Manifest Destiny Texas admitted to the Union as a slave state
1846	Mormons begin trek to Salt Lake Mexican War begins Cyrus McCormick opens Chicago factory
1847	Refugees from Irish potato famine arrive in large numbers Hoe rotary press introduced
1848	Gold discovered in California Oregon Territory organized
1849	Cholera epidemics in cities
1850	A. J. Downing's *The Architecture of Country Houses* appears
1851	Crystal Palace Exhibition American Party formed
1852	*Uncle Tom's Cabin* appears
1853	Perry expedition to Japan begins
1854	Know-Nothing movement peaks
1857	Economic panic begins depression
1859	Railroads carry more freight than do canals

John Brown (1800–1859)

Just before his hanging, John Brown wrote out a prophetic message: "I John Brown am now quite *certain* that the crimes of this *guilty land* : will never be purged *away;* but with Blood." (John Steuart Curry, *John Brown Mural*, 1941, Kansas State Capitol)

CHAPTER 14 *Disrupting the Union,* 1844–1860

For nearly a generation after the Missouri Compromise in 1820, the two major parties succeeded in preventing the slavery issue from polarizing the nation. This was so even after the democratization of politics under the Second Party System, and after a confrontation between evangelical abolitionism and proslavery movement. The two parties devised programs that were *national* in appeal and built coalitions of groups and interests that were national in scope. Both parties labored to avoid the slavery issue, recognizing its potential for fracturing the parties and the nation along sectional lines. During the early 1840s prospects for continuing to blunt the divisive potential of slavery seemed bright because abolitionism was stalled as a consequence of the antiabolitionist movement and the split between Garrisonians and anti-Garrisonians.

The sectional arrangement of 1820 had survived into the 1840s for another reason: both northern and southern societies had been able to expand into the West without appearing to threaten the other. But the Mexican War—and the acquisition of immense new territories in the West—changed everything.

After the Mexican War national politicians struggled to find a formula to resolve the status of slavery in the new lands. But their compromises became increasingly fragile, as Americans took matters into their own hands. Abolitionists fought off slave catchers in northern towns, and free-soilers and defenders of slavery attacked each other in "Bleeding Kansas." When the radical abolitionist John Brown attempted to incite a slave rebellion, many southerners became convinced that only secession would protect their "peculiar institution."

Sectional Conflict and Compromise, 1844–1850

In the 1830s southern leaders began to fear that the British, working with abolitionists, might ring the South with a free-soil belt that would block the expansion of slavery and bring about the institution's demise. To avoid containment, southerners had supported the annexation of Texas since it declared its independence in 1836. Both Andrew Jackson and Martin Van Buren had successfully deflected this push, in the interest of party and national unity. But in 1843 some southern leaders finally found a way to champion annexation that did not seem to threaten the unity of the Democratic party.

The Election of 1844

In 1843 "Oregon Fever" opened the door for southern leaders (see Chapter 13). Suddenly, northerners as well as southerners were calling for territorial expansion; Americans throughout the Ohio Valley and Great Lakes states called on the federal government to renounce joint occupation and oust the British from Oregon. Democrats and Whigs jointly organized "Oregon conventions" throughout the West. In July a bipartisan national convention demanded that the United States seize Oregon—all the way to 54° 40' north latitude, the southern limit of Russian-controlled Alaska.

Meanwhile, President John Tyler, disowned by the Whigs, had joined the Democratic party in hopes of becoming its nominee in 1844. In 1843, Tyler settled on a

TABLE 14.1

American Presidents and the Sectional Crisis, 1841–1861

	Term in Office	Party	Fate
William Henry Harrison	1841	Whig	Died in office
John Tyler	1841–1845	Whig	Broke with Whig party
James K. Polk	1845–1849	Democrat	Did not seek second term; died three months after leaving office
Zachary Taylor	1849–1850	Whig	Died in office
Millard Fillmore	1850–1853	Whig	1852 Whig nomination won by Winfield Scott
Franklin Pierce	1853–1857	Democrat	1856 Democratic nomination won by James Buchanan
James Buchanan	1857–1861	Democrat	Democratic party split, nominating Stephen Douglas and John Breckinridge

program designed to please expansionists among both southern and northern Democrats: the annexation of Texas and the seizure of Oregon to the 54° 40' line.

As a first step to annex Texas, Tyler appointed Senator John C. Calhoun of South Carolina as secretary of state in 1844. Calhoun had rejoined the Democratic party because he feared the national economic program and abolitionist tendencies of the Whigs. Convinced that it was necessary to prevent British domination of the West, Tyler and Calhoun submitted an annexation treaty to the Senate in April. In July Calhoun brushed aside an offer from the British, now fearful of American hostility, to settle the Oregon question.

The treaty encountered opposition from two leaders with presidential ambitions in 1844—Democrat Martin Van Buren and Whig Henry Clay. Each feared alienating northern voters by supporting the annexation of Texas. At their urging, Whigs and northern Democrats united to defeat the treaty.

The Candidacy of James K. Polk. The economic issues that had dominated the presidential campaign in 1840 gave way to the issues of Texas and Oregon in 1844. The Democrats had great success in unifying their party on Texas. They passed over both President Tyler, who had failed to win the trust of his adopted party, and Van Buren, whom southern Democrats despised for failing to support their position on Texas. Instead, they selected former Governor James K. Polk of Tennessee, a slaveowner who was Andrew Jackson's personal fa-

A Polk Political Banner, 1844

The "lone star" outside the group of twenty-six stars represented Texas. The banner was intended to leave no doubt about the importance of Texas annexation to Polk's presidental campaign.

Henry Clay
Clay (1777–1852) was the towering figure of Whig politics but he complained about his bad luck in seeking the presidency—"always run by my friends when sure to be defeated, and . . . betrayed for the nomination" when certain of election. He failed to win the Whig endorsement in 1840 but when he had it, in 1832 and 1844, he lost to Democrats. (J.W. Dodge, 1843, National Museum of American History, Smithsonian Institution)

vorite. Polk was unimpressive in appearance, but he was a man of iron will and boundless ambition for the nation. He and the Democrats called for the annexation of Texas and taking all of Oregon. "Fifty-four forty or fight!" became the war cry of his campaign.

The Whigs were less successful in uniting their party. They nominated Henry Clay, who once again championed his American System. Throughout his campaign Clay was defensive about his opposition to annexation of Texas. He finally suggested, but only hesitantly, that he might support annexation under certain circumstances. His position annoyed many southern Whigs. They were willing to bolt the party, sacrificing its economic program in return for the annexation of Texas. At the same time, Clay disappointed the thousands of northern Whigs who opposed any expansion of slavery. His waffling on Texas led them to support the Liberty party candidate, James G. Birney of Kentucky. Birney won less than 3 percent of the popular vote, but he may have taken away enough votes from Clay to deprive Clay of the electoral votes of New York and Michigan, with which he would have won. That was the conclusion of Clay's supporters, who blamed his defeat on the desertion of both proslavery and abolitionist Whigs.

Polk was elected by voters who had accepted the argument of Tyler and Calhoun that the British were determined to block the expansion of the republic into both Oregon and Mexico. Many Americans who might otherwise have opposed the extension of slavery had accepted Tyler and Calhoun's linkage of the Texas and Oregon issues and endorsed Polk's territorial ambitions. Thus, the strategy that Tyler and Calhoun devised, and Polk implemented, of uniting Democrats around expansion in both Texas and Oregon had succeeded.

The Agenda of the Polk Administration

Polk's victory led northern Democrats in Congress to reject Van Buren's leadership, close ranks with southern Democrats, and annex Texas even before Polk's inauguration. In February 1845 pro-annexation Democrats finessed the opposition of antislavery senators by approving annexation through a joint resolution, which required majority votes in both houses rather than the two-thirds Senate vote needed to ratify a treaty. Although Mexico challenged the legality of annexation—it had never recognized Texas's independence—and broke diplomatic relations with the United States, Texas was admitted as a slave state in December.

Polk and the Democrats, who won control of Congress in 1844, decided that they had a popular mandate not only to pursue territorial expansion but also to overturn Henry Clay's American System. So in 1846 they restored the Independent Treasury (see Chapter 11) and passed the Walker Tariff, which dramatically reduced tariffs and paid only lip service to the principle of protection. The Walker Tariff paralleled Britain's repeal of the Corn Laws (tariffs on imported bread grains) in the same year, and it seemed to herald the adoption of free trade throughout the Anglo-American world. Demoralized by this defeat, congressional Whigs never recaptured their enthusiasm for campaigning on their traditional economic program.

Polk's main goal remained territorial expansion. In December 1845 he delivered a bellicose message to Congress, claiming that British intentions in the Pacific Northwest violated the Monroe Doctrine. Polk intended to drive the British from Oregon and discourage them from taking California, which they wanted as compensation for debts owed them by Mexico. Polk was now resolved to go beyond his party's 1844 platform to acquire additional lands—New Mexico, Alta (upper) California, and perhaps even more of Mexico's territory.

The Mexican War, 1846–1848

The Polk administration had already hatched a plan to replicate the Texas experience in Alta California. Polk's secretary of state, James Buchanan, advised Thomas O. Larkin, his agent in the coastal town of Monterey, that the United States would welcome a declaration of independence and a petition for annexation by American settlers in California. Meanwhile, secret orders went to John Sloat, the commander of the U.S. naval squadron in the Pacific. He was to seize San Francisco and other California ports if Mexico declared war on the United States. In December 1845, shortly after Polk's message to Congress, Captain John C. Frémont led an "exploring" party of heavily armed soldiers to California. For two months he engaged in a show of force, even building fortifications near Monterey. But in March, when Mexican authorities threatened to fight, Frémont withdrew across the Oregon border. Later he described this as "the first step in the conquest of California."

The Slidell Mission. President Polk also sent a secret emissary, John Slidell, to Mexico City in December. Polk instructed Slidell not to discuss the right of the United States to annex Texas, including some territory—between the Nueces River and the Rio Grande to the south—that had never been part of Spanish or Mexican Texas and that Mexico claimed. Slidell was instructed, instead, to buy New Mexico and California for as much as $30 million. Mexico rejected the legality of America's annexing Texas and refused to see Slidell. It also insisted on the Nueces River as the southern boundary of the Texas Republic. The central objective of the Mexican government was simply to maintain national honor and protect valuable lands from an aggressive neighbor. To do anything else would have insured the fall of the government. The Mexican government hoped that the United States would become embroiled in a war with Britain and become diverted from its southwestern ambitions, but, if necessary, Mexico was prepared to fight.

Polk responded by creating an incident designed to insult the Mexicans. In January 1846 he sent General Zachary Taylor, an army veteran with almost forty years of service, to establish a fort near the Rio Grande, in the area south of the Nueces River. As Ulysses S.

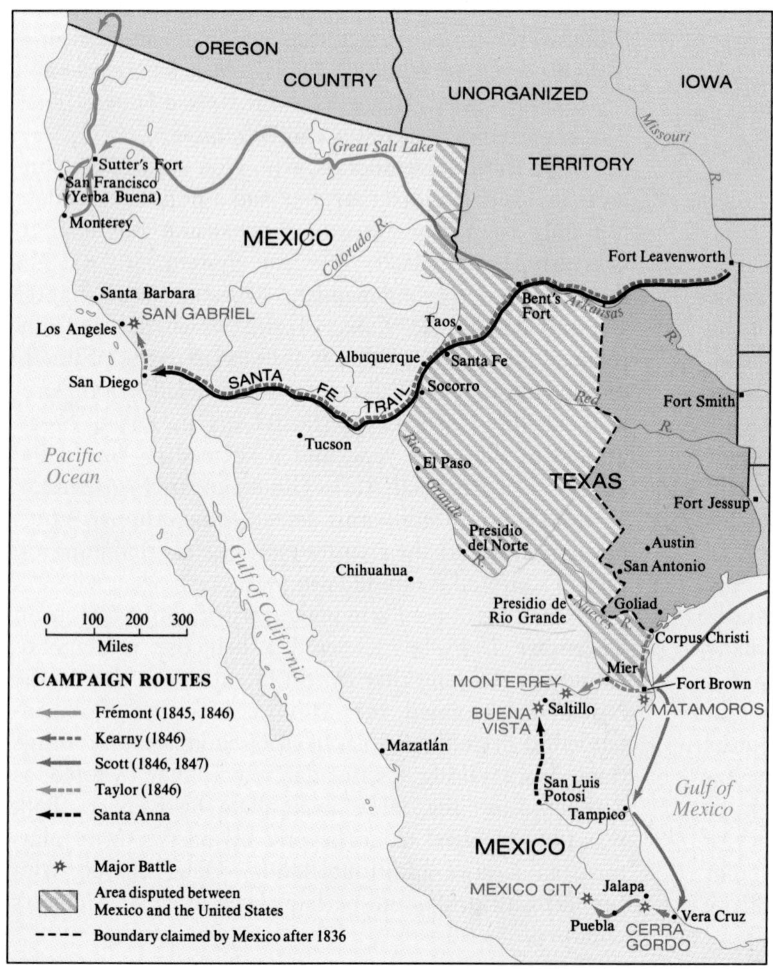

MAP 14.1

The Mexican War, 1846–1848

This map shows the major military expeditions which seized the northern frontier of Mexico and occupied Mexico City. In the last phase of the war, as Winfield Scott assembled his invasion army off the coast of Mexico, General Santa Anna tried to take advantage of the division of American forces by attacking the army of Zachary Taylor. At Buena Vista (February 1847), Taylor's smaller forces repulsed Santa Anna, who had to return to defend Mexico City. Scott's most significant victory in his march on Mexico City came in the mountains, at Cerro Gordo.

Grant, a young officer serving with Taylor, said much later, "We were sent to provoke a fight, but it was essential that Mexico should commence it." News of skirmishing between Mexican and American patrols reached Polk in early May. On May 9 he delivered the war message he had drafted long before: Mexico "has passed the boundary of the United States, has invaded our territory, and shed American blood on American soil." Congress declared war four days later, and its action was followed by large, almost hysterical demonstrations of support throughout the nation. The *New York Herald* editorialized that the war would "lay the foundation of a new age, a new destiny, affecting both this continent and the old continent of Europe."

Meanwhile, Polk worked to avoid a simultaneous war with Britain, even though this might mean betraying a promise to northern Democrats. He recommended that the Senate adopt the British proposal to divide the Oregon country at the 49th parallel. The Senate agreed, ratifying the Oregon treaty on June 15, 1846.

The War in California. Before delivering his war message, Polk sent secret orders to Frémont, who then marched back into California and established a base near Sacramento. In June 1846 the Americans in the interior, although unaware of the formal state of war between the United States and Mexico, staged a revolt and captured the Mexican town of Sonoma, all with the support of Frémont's forces. Frémont did not yet have formal authority to take California, so he prevented the rebelling Americans from flying the Stars and Stripes. The Americans designed a crude flag—one displaying the strongest animal in California—and proclaimed the Bear Flag Republic. In July, knowing that war with Mexico had been declared, Commander Sloat landed 250 marines and seamen in Monterey. He declared that California "henceforward will be a portion of the United States" and raised the United States flag.

American forces quickly moved to win control of New Mexico and all of California. A small army under General Stephen Kearney captured Santa Fe without opposition in August, occupied New Mexico, and marched toward California. By autumn, Frémont and Commodore Robert F. Stockton, who had assumed command of the United States forces in California, seemed to have subdued the province. But in the southern part of Alta California the Mexicans mounted stiff resistance, driving the Americans from Los Angeles and winning a victory at the Battle of San Pascual outside San Diego. Only the reinforcements of General Kearney turned the tide. By mid-January 1847 the combined American forces had captured the fortified towns of San Francisco, Monterey, Santa Barbara, Los Angeles, and San Diego. In his diary Polk wrote that he would accept no peace treaty with Mexico that did not yield New Mexico and California to the United States.

Across the Rio Grande. Meanwhile, Zachary Taylor's army, made up largely of untrained but enthusiastic volunteers, crossed the Rio Grande. On May 18, the American forces, outnumbered but with a great advantage in artillery, took Matamoros after two bloody battles. On

Mexican War Volunteers, 1846

This daguerreotype by an unknown photographer shows volunteers from Exeter, New Hampshire, preparing for war. When news of Zachary Taylor's victories reached most towns, men scrambled to volunteer before the war was over. In New York, Herman Melville wrote that "people here are all in a state of delirium . . . . Nothing is talked of but the 'Halls of the Montezumas.'" (Amon Carter Museum)

Street Fighting in Monterrey, 1846
The taking of Monterrey, which Spain's troops had been unable to capture during Mexico's war for independence, was a bloody affair of house-to-house fighting. Americans, however, immediately romanticized it. This is a typical lithograph of the day, picturing soldiers fighting in what seemed to be medieval settings.

May 24, 1846, after even heavier fighting, Taylor took the interior town of Monterrey. In November a naval squadron in the Gulf of Mexico seized Tampico as a base for an inland assault. Another force struck 900 miles southward from San Antonio and gained control of Chihuahua in December. By the end of 1846 the United States controlled a long line across northeastern Mexico.

Polk expected that the Mexicans, having lost large territories and with no chance of winning Britain as an ally, would sue for peace. But he had underrated Mexican national pride and strength. Mexico would not agree to a peace, let alone a cession of territory. So Polk and Winfield Scott, the commanding general of the army, decided to strike deep into the heart of Mexico. In November 1846 they decided to send Scott on a seaborne campaign to storm the port of Veracruz and advance 260 miles inland to Mexico City. As Scott gathered his forces, a large Mexican army under General Santa Anna attacked the depleted units of Zachary Taylor at Buena Vista on February 22, 1847. The outcome was uncertain, and the fighting fierce, but superiority in artillery enabled the American line in northeastern Mexico to hold.

AMERICAN VOICES

A Mexican War Diary *Henry S. Lane*

In June 1846, Henry S. Lane, a thirty-five-year-old lawyer from Montgomery County, Indiana, raised a company of volunteers for the Mexican War. His troops served without seeing battle throughout the war, and Lane rose from captain to lieutenant colonel. Before the war he served two terms as a Whig congressman. In 1860 Lane was elected as the first Republican governor of Indiana, and the next year the legislature sent him to the Senate, where he served until 1877. His war diary reflects the conflicts most Americans felt as they contemplated the extension of Manifest Destiny to Mexico.

July 5, 1846. Encamped on the ever memorable battle ground of New Orleans, & thought of Genl. [Andrew] Jackson until our hearts were filled with the mingled love of glory & love of country. . . .

August 21, 1846 [at the mouth of the Rio Grande]. The climate of this country is decidedly more pleasant than Indiana or indeed any place I have ever been in. It is one of the richest countries in the world. The necessaries & comforts of life are produced spontaneously. All the tropical fruits could be produced here in perfection, but the present inhabitants are altogether unworthy of such a country. It is an abuse of the bounty of providence to let such a race of drones & slaves [squander] so goodly a heritage, but they are do[o]med to be swallowed up in the all-engulfing vo[r]tex of Anglo-Saxon enterprise and ambition.

January 19, 1847 [in Matamoros]. A nation cannot be free with the popular mind enslaved. A man cannot be free with his soul in chains, whether spiritual or temporal. The only hope for Mexico is that she may be Americanised & religious toleration prevail. Then she may be free & never before.

February 14, 1847 [in Matamoros]. If all the money which has been expended in this war had been expended to give the Gospel to the poor & deluded Mexican, oh what a glorious conquest we should make. Not a conquest of barren territory which if it is ever annexed to our Republic will only introduce dissention & end in a dissolution of our glorious confederacy, but a conquest of souls, immortal souls, a conquest over ignorance, intolerance, & the mental thraldom of the Mother of Harlots.

April 12, 1847 [near Monterrey]. When will this war so fraught with misery to two nations have an end? . . . We began to fight about questions of abstract right, but mutual wrongs & aggressions have changed the character of the war & vengeance has largely mingled in the contest. Things are now done by each army that one year ago were not dreamed of & the bare mention of which would have sent the war blood freezing & curdling upon the heart.

April 30, 1847 [near Monterrey]. Creatures who for selfish ends embroil great nations in needless war should have the indignant thunders of outraged humanity sounding in their ear during this life, & during the life to come they should have the unending Hell of bitter remorse & deep despair.

May 4, 1847 [near Monterrey]. Why not bring an army here instead of a handful of men? Why not make a demonstration of power which will awe Mexico & show the world what Americans are? We should make this a short & glorious war for the moral effect it would have upon Europe. . . .

May 11, 1847 [near Monterrey]. Had something like sunstroke. Near fai[n]ting, become blind, succeeded by severe head ache. . . . Nearer dieing perhaps than ever before. Most anxious to leave this cursed country.

Source: Graham A. Barringer, ed., "The Mexican War Journal of Henry S. Lane," *Indiana Magazine of History* 53 (December 1957), 383–434.

In March 1847, Scott captured Veracruz with more than 14,000 troops and a talented group of West Point officers, most of them southerners. He then boldly moved his army inland. The well-read soldiers realized that they were following the route of Cortés's Spanish conquerors three centuries earlier, and they even looked for the locations of Cortés's battles. Scott's forces persistently outflanked the enemy during a 7,400-foot climb over rugged terrain. Scott never suffered a defeat, but both armies endured heavy casualties. On August 20, at the Battle of Churubusco, near Mexico City, General Santa Anna lost more than 4,000 of the 25,000 in his army while Scott lost 900 of his 10,000 men. Scott finally seized Mexico City on September 14, 1847, and a new Mexican government had no choice but to make peace.

National euphoria had accompanied the early phase of the war, peaking with Taylor's occupation of Matamoros. Many Americans initially viewed the war as a noble struggle to promote republican ideals, in the spirit of the American Revolution. An American victory, they believed, would secure American institutions in the West and free Mexico from a corrupt regime open to the influence of European monarchies. And at the end of the war, whatever they thought about its goals, even more Americans agreed with President Polk that it had demonstrated that a democratic republic could fight a foreign war "with the vigor" characteristic of "more arbitrary forms of government."

A few antislavery Whigs such as the "conscience Whigs" Charles Francis Adams of Massachusetts and Joshua Giddings of Ohio, had denounced the war from the start as part of a proslavery conspiracy. Most Whigs, however, had participated in or at least tolerated the national enthusiasm that accompanied the early phase of the war. But by the time news of Scott's victory in Mexico City reached Washington, the nation was badly divided over its war aims, and Whig opposition had become stronger and bolder. Northern Whigs drew confidence from the elections of 1846, which gave their party control of Congress, and increasing numbers of northern Whigs began to agree with the conscience Whigs. Additional slave states in the West might jeopardize the expansion of free agriculture and assure control of the federal government for the Democratic representatives of planters and immigrants. Also, northern Whigs grew anxious as they watched the casualties mount, particularly during the bloody march to Mexico City. Of the 92,000 Americans who served during the war, over 13,000 were killed or died of disease. After Taylor's victory at Buena Vista, the House passed a resolution thanking him—but not until the Whigs had amended it to declare that the war had been "unconstitutionally and unnecessarily begun by the President."

The Wilmot Proviso. It was a Democrat, however, who provided the most disruptive way of opposing the war. On a warm August evening in 1846, David Wilmot, a free-soil congressman from Pennsylvania, proposed a simple amendment to a military appropriation bill: slavery would be prohibited in any territory acquired from Mexico. This provision, known as the Wilmot Proviso, quickly became the rallying point for northerners who feared the expansion of slavery into the West. For the first time the antislavery movement had a well-defined proposal that could attract broad popular support. It was the Wilmot Proviso that enabled the free-soil movement to attract thousands of followers quickly.

Scott's costly invasion of Mexico enabled the Wilmot Proviso to gain bipartisan support—from northern Democrats as well as Whigs. In the House a minority of Democrats, including key supporters of Martin Van Buren, joined forces with most Whigs to pass it on several occasions, but the more heavily southern, more proslavery Senate killed it each time. The state legislatures of fourteen northern states passed resolutions urging their senators to vote for it.

Meanwhile, the most fervent expansionists among the Democrats became even more aggressive. They argued that the rising cost of the war meant that the nation should enlarge its war aims. The national Democratic party leaders—Polk, Secretary of State Buchanan, and senators Stephen A. Douglas of Illinois and Jefferson Davis of Mississippi—all wanted the United States to take at least a part of Mexico south of the Rio Grande.

This goal put the Democratic leadership at odds with the vocal free-soil minority of northeastern Democrats and many midwestern Democrats, who were already disappointed that Polk had failed to acquire more of Oregon. Moreover, a few southern Democratic leaders worried that the Mexican people would oppose slavery and that the United States could not absorb the Mexicans, whom they regarded as an "inferior" people. This group included John C. Calhoun, who supported the taking of only Alta California and New Mexico, the most sparsely populated areas of Mexico.

Once again, as during the administrations of Jackson and Van Buren, the president put the interests of party unity foremost. He and Buchanan backed away from their early support of "All Mexico" and threw their support to Calhoun's policy. Polk endorsed the Treaty of Guadalupe Hidalgo (February 2, 1848), in which the United States promised to pay Mexico $15 million in return for Texas north of the Rio Grande, New Mexico, and Alta California. The United States also agreed to assume all the damage claims of its citizens, totaling $3.2 million, against the Mexican government. The Senate quickly ratified the treaty in March 1848.

The Polk administration had gained northern Mexico, as well as Texas and Oregon, without sacrificing party unity. But now the nation faced an even more contentious issue: what would the future of slavery be in the newly acquired territory?

The Election of 1848

The sectional divisions among Democrats that had surfaced during the Mexican War continued into the election of 1848. Free-soil and midwestern Democrats unhappy with Polk's Oregon treaty would probably have forced their party to dump Polk in the 1848 election. But before that could happen, an exhausted Polk, who had worked from dawn late into the night throughout his presidency, declined to run; he would die only three months after leaving office. In search of a replacement who could unify the party, the Democrats nominated the dull, elderly Senator Lewis Cass of Michigan. Cass was an expansionist who had advocated the purchase of Cuba, the annexation of Mexico's Yucatan Peninsula, and the acquisition of all of Oregon. In an effort to hold both southerners and northerners in the party, the Democrats left their platform deliberately vague on the expansion of slavery. Cass promoted a new concept—*popular sovereignty*: each territorial government should have the right to determine the status of slavery in its territory.

The Cass nomination did not satisfy free-soil Democrats, who demanded unambiguous opposition to the expansion of slavery. Many of them threw their support to the newly formed Free Soil party. To win Democratic votes, the Free-Soilers nominated Martin Van Buren for president. Though still a Democrat, he ran out of a combination of idealism and vindictiveness. He had converted to free-soil beliefs and to support of the Wilmot Proviso, but he also wanted to punish southern Democrats for denying him the nomination in 1844. The Free-Soilers appealed to Whigs also, nominating Charles Francis Adams, the son of John Quincy Adams, for vice-president. He had inherited many of the conscience Whig supporters of his father, who died in 1848 after distinguished service as an antislavery congressman from Massachusetts.

The Candidacy of Zachary Taylor. The division among Democrats created an opportunity for the Whigs, and they did their best to suppress their own sectional disputes. Whig leaders avoided adopting a specific platform, even though northern Whigs generally supported the Wilmot Proviso. The Whigs nominated General Zachary Taylor. The fact that he came from Louisiana and owned a hundred slaves was less important to northern Whigs than his vagueness of the issue of slavery in the territories and his popularity throughout the nation. Known as "Old Rough and Ready," Taylor possessed a common touch that had won him the affection of his troops and made him the greatest hero of the Mexican War. Numerous biographers found him to be a "natural" American leader. "Our Commander on the Rio Grande," wrote Walt Whitman, "emulates the Great Commander of our revolution"—George Washington.

The tactic of running a military hero worked for the Whigs, just as it had when Harrison ran in 1840. Taylor won 51 percent of the popular vote and nearly two-thirds of the electoral votes of the South. In the North, the Free Soil party of Van Buren and Adams hurt the Democrats more than it did the Whigs. Van Buren received 10 percent of the popular vote nationally and about 14 percent of the northern vote. He may have pulled enough votes from Cass in New York to cost him the state and the election. Cass won 127 electoral votes to the 163 garnered by Taylor.

The swift growth of the Free Soil party and the popularity of the Wilmot Proviso left southerners—both Whigs and Democrats—stunned and fearful. Slaveowners became even more aggressive in seeking the expansion of slavery, demanding more explicit commitments from the two major parties. Consequently, in the future the two national parties would have difficulty maintaining ambiguity on the status of slavery in the territories.

Alternatives to the Wilmot Proviso

The election of 1848 persuaded virtually all southern politicians that they could not win support that was national in scope for their territorial ambitions. They also realized that they would have to secure a future for slavery in territory already acquired, rather than in new acquisitions from Mexico or Cuba. After the election they concentrated on meeting the challenge of the Wilmot Proviso. They tried to establish slavery firmly in the territories taken from Mexico. They developed three different approaches to achieve that objective.

Calhoun's "Common Property" Doctrine. John C. Calhoun advocated the most extreme position supporting the spread of slavery into federal territories. He held that Congress had no constitutional authority to regulate slavery in the territories and therefore could not exclude slavery from a territory prior to admission to statehood. According to Calhoun's "common property" doctrine, the citizens of any state had the same rights as the citizens of any other state to take their property into areas owned commonly by the states. His arguments won support from many Democrats and Whigs in the deep South, but they repelled too many northerners of both parties ever to gain much support in Congress.

Extending the Missouri Compromise Line. Most southern leaders of both parties advocated or were willing to accept a more moderate position: an extension of the Missouri Compromise line through the Mexican cession (the territory purchased from Mexico) to the Pacific coast. Their proposal would guarantee slaveowners access to at least some western territory, particularly southern California; it would remove the antislavery threat from the deep South's western boundary; and it would almost certainly add slave states to the Union. This approach appealed to Polk and even to some northern Democrats. Buchanan and Douglas, for example, hoped the offer of prohibiting slavery in northern territories would prevent free-soil Democrats from bolting the party. But free-soil advocates among the Democrats and Whigs were unequivocally opposed to *any* expansion of slavery as a matter of principle, and they rejected the scheme.

Popular Sovereignty. The third alternative was popular sovereignty, Lewis Cass's position in the 1848 election. It seemed to be an inherently fair, democratic approach. Moreover, because it relieved Congress of the responsibility of addressing the slavery issue by passing it on to territorial governments, popular sovereignty won support from many northern Democrats who otherwise might have converted to free soil.

Popular sovereignty, however, was a vague and slippery concept. It did not specify at what point the people of a territory could legalize or prohibit slavery; nor did it say how much authority territorial governments could exercise in regulating slavery. If Calhoun's doctrine were correct, the constitutional protection of slavery meant that territorial governments could decide the status of slavery only at the *end* of the territorial process, when they framed a constitution to apply for statehood. Southern Democrats preferred this interpretation, believing that it gave slavery a good chance to become established in the territories. Northern Democrats, on the other hand, believed that territorial legislatures had the power to exclude slavery and could do so as soon as a territory was organized.

As long as each side left this ambiguity unresolved, popular sovereignty held the greatest possibility of any of the approaches for maintaining the unity of the Democratic party—and national unity—on the slavery issue. However, the ability of popular sovereignty to unify was tested far sooner than anyone expected—in another major sectional confrontation.

The Compromise of 1850

Taylor and California Statehood. In California, as yet unorganized into a territory, American settlers—especially the "forty-niners," who lived in crowded, chaotic towns and mining camps—demanded effective government. Responding, President Zachary Taylor advised the Californians to apply for statehood immediately. Taylor's objectives were simple—to satisfy the forty-niners' demands, to avoid wrestling with the ambiguities of popular sovereignty, and to provide dramatic evidence that the Whigs could promote westward expansion without intensifying the slavery issue. Behind his approach was his desire to establish the Whigs as the dominant national party. On the one hand, he hoped to draw Free-Soilers and free-soil Democrats into the Whig party. On the other, he hoped to persuade southern Whigs that they could protect slavery in the South without insisting on slavery in the territories.

Taylor made his proposal when he took office in March 1849. By November, California voters had ratified a state constitution and applied for statehood. In the swift process of constitution-making, slavery advocates fared poorly. Few of the many southerners who flocked to the gold fields, San Francisco, or the farms of the Sacramento Valley owned slaves or wanted to own them. Only ranchers in sparsely populated southern California had a strong interest in promoting slavery. Consequently, the California constitutional convention, copying much of the new Iowa state constitution, prohibited slavery. When Congress convened in December 1849, President Taylor urged the admission of California and New Mexico as free states.

Southern defenders of slavery were startled and alarmed by the swift victory of the antislavery forces in California. Popular sovereignty now seemed to offer only empty promises of protection. Would not vast numbers of northerners overwhelm slavery anywhere they settled in the new territories, just as they had in California? The prospect of adding additional free states to the Union also disturbed the southerners. In 1845 the admission of Texas and Florida had given slavery a temporary edge of fifteen slave states against thirteen free states, but the admission of Iowa in 1846 and Wisconsin in 1848 reestablished the exact balance. California's admission would lend the free states a political advantage in shaping states carved from the Mexican cession and the unorganized areas of the Louisiana Purchase. Moreover, the new state of California would create a base for abolitionists within the territory acquired from Mexico.

Southern leaders were willing to accept California's admission as a free state only if the federal government adequately guaranteed the future of slavery. Southerners were not agreed on what they needed, but they knew it was more than popular sovereignty in the Mexican cession. And so, in passionate debates that lasted for eight months, southern leaders forced Congress to examine all the issues surrounding the present and future status of slavery.

The most extreme southern position was taken by Calhoun, who doubted that the North and South could arrive at a lasting compromise. In what would be his farewell address, read to Congress on his behalf shortly before he died, Calhoun said the nation could prevent the South's secession and eventual civil war only by guaranteeing slavery in all the territories and by adopting a constitutional amendment to establish a permanent balance of sectional power. He was thinking of an amendment that would turn the presidency into a dual office, providing executives from both South and North and giving each president the full power of veto.

Antislavery advocates in both parties lent credence to Calhoun's prediction of civil war. Senators Salmon P. Chase, an Ohio Free-Soiler who had been a Democrat,

Salmon P. Chase

Trained as a lawyer, Chase (1808–1873) was drawn to the antislavery movement by his defense of fugitive slaves. He served as U.S. senator (1849–1855), Republican governor of Ohio (1855–1860), secretary of the treasury (1861–64), and chief justice of the Supreme Court (1864–1873).

and William H. Seward, a New York Whig, urged the government to contain slavery within its existing limits. Their goal was its ultimate extinction. Seward declared that the government had a responsibility to "a higher law than the Constitution, which regulates our authority over the domain . . . the common heritage of mankind."

The issues were finally being clearly drawn, as were the risks to the future of the nation. The clash in Congress tore both national parties along sectional lines—and stirred fears that the Union might dissolve.

Forging a Compromise. Having moved to the brink of disaster, senior Whigs and Democrats did their best to back away and reach a compromise. Through a long, complex legislative process, the Whig leaders Henry Clay and Daniel Webster and Democrat Stephen A. Douglas organized a package that, when implemented, consisted of six distinct laws. These laws were known collectively as the Compromise of 1850. The Compromise, enacted in September, attempted to mollify the South by adopting the Fugitive Slave Act. This replaced a weak 1793 law with a strong one that put the federal government at the disposal of slaveowners chasing runaway slaves. The intent was to remove the free states as havens for runaway slaves and to reduce the ability of abolitionists to use free-soil bases to attack slavery. The Compromise tried to satisfy the North by establishing the principle of popular sovereignty in the Mexican cession. The Compromise of 1850 (1) admitted California as a free state, ending the equal balance of free and slave states; (2) organized (by two of the six laws) the rest of the Mexican cession into the territories of New Mexico and Utah on the implied basis of popular sovereignty; (3) resolved a boundary dispute between New Mexico and Texas in favor of New Mexico by the federal government assuming the $10 million in unpaid debts of the Republic of Texas; (4) abolished the slave trade, but not slavery itself, in the District of Columbia; and (5) passed the Fugitive Slave Act.

The Compromise averted a secession crisis in 1850—but only barely. In the end northern Democrats and southern Whigs accounted for most of the votes for the compromise. Northern Whigs like Seward and southern Democrats like Jefferson Davis all voted against it. Most southern Democrats objected to admitting California under any terms and regarded the Fugitive Slave Act as an inadequate protector of slavery. Robbed of their longtime leader by Calhoun's death prior to the vote, they would soon regroup to become an increasingly potent obstacle to sectional compromise. Northern Whigs opposed both the fugitive slave law and popular sovereignty. The northern Whigs held their ground even after Vice-President Millard Fillmore of New York—a northern Whig who supported popular sovereignty—succeeded to the presidency in July 1850. (Taylor had died suddenly of a violent stomach ailment and heat prostration suffered during a Fourth of July celebration.) In other words, most northern Whigs and southern Democrats in Congress were willing to defy the leadership of their parties, and to risk the Union, for the sake of their principles. The compromise did not augur well for the future.

Sectional Strife and the Third Party System, 1850–1858

The Compromise of 1850 was intended to prevent the slavery issue from disrupting politics and government. Both northern Democratic and southern Whig leaders hoped that the Compromise would be as effective as its predecessor in 1820 had been and that the new compromise—particularly its fugitive slave law and popular sovereignty elements—would enable each party to maintain national base of support. But any such hopes were quickly dashed, as northern hostility to slavery swelled and southern demands for slavery's protection grew more insistent.

Slave Catchers, 1838

Even though the fugitive slave law of 1793 was weak, the antislavery movement saw it as legitimizing slavery. The drawing, appearing in the *American Anti-Slavery Almanac,* pictured a free black in New York being "Kidnapped. . . under color of law" and "carried away from his wife and children into slavery."

The Fugitive Slave Act

The most controversial element of the Compromise proved to be the Fugitive Slave Act. Federal judges or special commissioners determined the status of blacks who denied they were runaways. The accused African-Americans were denied jury trials or the right to testify. A commissioner would receive a $10 fee if an alleged fugitive was found guilty but only $5 if the accused were found innocent—a tremendous incentive to render a guilty verdict. Federal marshals were instructed to support slave catchers, and could impose heavy penalties on anyone who helped a slave escape or obstructed the efforts of slaveholders to recover their slaves. Even slaves who had long ago fled to freedom could be subject to recapture. And African-Americans born free in the North ran the risk of kidnapping. The law was effectively enforced, and many fugitives were convicted and reenslaved.

Resistance in the North. The plight of the runaways and the appearance of slave catchers in northern communities personalized the message of abolitionism, and popular hostility to the Fugitive Slave Act grew. Abolitionists organized vigilante groups to defy the law and block its enforcement. Frederick Douglass abandoned pacifism, declaring that "the only way to make the Fugitive Slave Law a dead letter is to make half a dozen or more dead kidnappers." In October 1850, Theodore Parker and other Boston abolitionists defied the law by helping two slaves escape to freedom and driving a Georgia slave catcher out of town. In September 1851, in the Quaker village of Christiana, Pennsylvania, more than twenty African-American men, including two escaped slaves, exchanged gunfire with a group of slave catchers from Maryland; the slaveowner was killed and his son severely wounded. President Fillmore sent marines and federal marshals to arrest thirty-six blacks and four whites around Christiana and had them indicted for treason. But the jury acquitted one defendant, and a public uproar forced the government to drop charges against the rest. In Syracuse, New York, two thousand rioters broke into a courthouse and freed a fugitive slave in October 1851.

Some northern legislators and judges overtly resisted federal authority. Several state legislatures passed *personal liberty* laws to protect accused fugitive slaves from federal officers. In 1857 the Supreme Court of Wisconsin, in the case of *Ableman v. Booth,* held that a state court had the power to declare an act of Congress unconstitutional. The Fugitive Slave Act, the court ruled, violated the Constitution and could not be enforced in Wisconsin. In 1859 the case reached the Supreme Court, where Chief Justice Taney ruled against Wisconsin.

Uncle Tom's Cabin. It was in reaction to the Fugitive Slave Act that Harriet Beecher Stowe composed her abolitionist novel *Uncle Tom's Cabin*. Published first in 1851–1852 as a serial in a Washington Free Soil newspaper, the *National Era,* the novel tells of a compassionate but weak slavemaster in Kentucky who is forced by debts to sell two slaves, Tom and a five-year-old boy, to a slave trader. Beautiful Eliza Harris, the boy's mother, refuses to be separated from her son. With the child in her arms, she crosses the Ohio River on cakes of ice just ahead of the vicious slave trader. Eliza escapes to freedom and reaches the house of an Ohio politician who had voted for a fugitive slave law, having set aside his "private feeling." His wife persuades him to trust his heart, rather than his head, and to help Eliza and her child on their way to Canada. Meanwhile, Tom is eventually sold to Simon Legree, a brutal overseer on a southern plantation. Legree beats Tom to death but never conquers the slave's Christian soul.

Uncle Tom's Cabin further fueled the hostility to the Fugitive Slave Act in the North. When the novel first appeared in book form in 1852, more than three hundred thousand Americans bought copies. Countless families saw the stage version, produced by theater companies throughout the North. For most of these people Stowe's novel connected the abstract moral principles of abolitionism with heart-rending personal situations to which they could respond with anger or grief.

The Southern Response. To the South's political leaders the Fugitive Slave Act was important because it meant that the government recognized and protected their "property" everywhere. The fierce northern defiance of the act mobilized leading southern politicians who were already upset by the admission of California, the introduction of popular sovereignty, and the abolition of the slave trade in Washington, D.C. To protect what they called Southern Rights, they organized special conventions in South Carolina, Georgia, Mississippi, and Alabama in 1850 and 1851. The governor of South Carolina declared that there was not "the slightest doubt" but that his state would secede from the Union to protect slavery. Although all the conventions considered secession, moderates in Georgia, Mississippi, and Alabama defused the crisis by persuading the conventions to support the Compromise of 1850. In turn, the moderates agreed to support secession in the future if Congress abolished slavery anywhere, failed to recognize slavery in a new territory, or refused to admit a state into the Union because it permitted slavery. The victorious Georgia unionists declared in their Georgia Platform that the protection of Southern Rights, and the "preservation of our much beloved Union," depended most importantly on "a faithful execution of the Fugitive Slave Law." Moderate arguments carried less weight in South Carolina, however, where secession failed only because many secessionists doubted that they could go it alone, without the cooperation of other states.

The Election of 1852: A Shift in Party Balance

The northern Whigs, who dominated their party, carried their powerful hostility to the Fugitive Slave Act and popular sovereignty into the 1852 election. They passed over President Fillmore because he had vigorously enforced the act and supported popular sovereignty. Instead they nominated another general from the Mexican War, Winfield Scott, in the hope that a popular general, like Harrison in 1840 and Taylor in 1848, would attract national support. The southern Whigs were not satisfied by the Scott nomination and by the offhanded endorsement of the Compromise of 1850 that the northern Whigs and Scott offered to keep the southerners in the party. Many southern Whigs, particularly in the deep South, withheld support from their party; some went so far as to vote for the Democratic ticket.

The Whigs had problems in the North, too; while their economic program still had supporters, many northern Whigs wanted the party to address the slavery and immigration issues in a straightforward, compelling fashion. And the deaths of Henry Clay and Daniel Webster in 1852 had robbed the party of its most articulate leaders and its most effective voices for national unity.

Franklin Pierce. The Democrats displayed no more vision in 1852 than the Whigs, but they were more successful in avoiding a division along sectional lines. Some southern Democrats wanted to nominate a candidate who supported Calhoun's radical position that the federal government should protect slavery in all the territories. Most realized, however, that this would ensure defeat for the party in the North. The Democratic convention passed over all the advocates of popular sovereignty, including Lewis Cass, Stephen Douglas, and James Buchanan, none of whom could obtain the necessary two-thirds majority. On the forty-ninth ballot, it chose Franklin Pierce of New Hampshire. The public knew Pierce only as a handsome and congenial New Englander with no identifiable enemies, but southern Democrats were assured that he would be sympathetic to the South's interests.

Pierce and the Democrats crushed the Whigs in the 1852 election. The Democrats not only attracted southern Whigs but also won back some of the northern Democrats who had voted for the Free Soil party in 1848. Pleased by the outcome of popular sovereignty in California, these Free-Soilers were satisfied that the popular sovereignty provisions of the Compromise of 1850 would effectively prevent an expansion of slavery. Even Martin Van Buren, the former Free Soil candidate, supported Pierce. Votes for the Free Soil party and its candidate, John P. Hale of New Hampshire, declined to about 5 percent of the total—about half the share the party had won four years earlier. Although General Scott attracted more popular votes than Taylor had in 1848, Scott carried only four of the thirty-one states.

The Whigs never again waged a national campaign. The Compromise of 1850 had driven a wedge between northern and southern Whigs. The task of maintaining the political unity of the nation now fell to the Democrats.

Franklin Pierce
In this engraving (c. 1847), Franklin Pierce poses as a brigadier general of volunteers in the Mexican War.

In trying to maintain itself as a *national* party, the Democratic party had some powerful assets. Most Democratic leaders took the broadly appealing stance of supporting popular sovereignty. The Democrats also had a diverse base of voters, including the growing number of immigrant voters in northern cities and the many settlers of southern ancestry in the Ohio Valley. They also appealed to the many voters in all sections of the country who thought the Union was more important than the question of slavery or freedom for slaves.

But popular sovereignty was unacceptable both to many southerners—those who wanted slaves to be protected as property throughout the Union—and to the northerners who wanted the federal government to prohibit slavery in the western territories. The Democrats also lost those northern voters who resented the recruitment of immigrants, particularly Catholics, into the party, and those who wanted more vigorous federal programs to promote economic development.

Latin American Schemes

President Franklin Pierce set out to broaden his support and divert attention from sectional disputes with a familiar Democratic strategy—an expansionist foreign policy. An early success was a treaty with Japan. Pierce hoped that, like Polk in the early phases of the Mexican War, he could broaden support beyond slaveholders to Americans, both northern and southern, who were interested in the spread of republican institutions. Pierce cast his eyes toward Latin America, particularly Mexico, the Caribbean, and Central America.

The Gadsden Purchase. Pierce inherited an array of Mexican-American problems, including a dispute over New Mexico's southern boundary and American acquisition of transit routes across northwestern Mexico. Pierce and his secretary of war, Jefferson Davis, hoped to pressure the Mexican government of Santa Anna, who had just returned to the presidency, to sell land to America as part of a comprehensive settlement. Pierce sent James Gadsden, a South Carolina politician and railroad promoter, to Mexico to negotiate with Santa Anna. Gadsden threatened force if Mexico did not cede a major portion of northern Mexico and Baja (lower) California. Santa Anna refused but did agree to a settlement that included sale of about 30,000 square miles south of the Gila River, territory Gadsden wanted for a southern railroad to the Pacific Ocean. The Gadsden Purchase, as it became known, was the last territory acquired from Mexico, but it served to rub salt in Mexico's wounds, reminding it of the power of its northern neighbor.

Cuba. The early expansionist plans of the Polk administration had included purchasing Cuba from Spain. But the schemes had accomplished little, despite the vigorous efforts of some southerners and their northern supporters like the New York editor John Louis O'Sullivan. They tried to stir up a revolution in Cuba with hope that widespread republican hostility to the Spanish monarchy would then lead to the admission of Cuba, which would turn out, they hoped, to be a slave state. The expansionists funded three expeditions to the island by a Cuban exile, General Narciso López. President Pierce resumed these efforts in 1853 by covertly supporting another expedition to Cuba—one led by John A. Quitman, a former governor of Mississippi. By early 1854, Quitman had mobilized several thousand volunteers. Pierce instructed Pierre Soulé, U.S. minister to Spain, to attempt "to detach that island from the Spanish dominion." After failing to purchase Cuba, Soulé sent Pierce a message that became known as the Ostend Manifesto. In it, Soulé declared that the United States would be justified "by every law, human and Divine," in "wresting" Cuba from Spain "if we possess the power." By November, when the document arrived in Washington, Pierce realized that northern politicians would refuse to go to war for the purpose of adding a new slave state. Not wanting to lose support among northern Democrats, he persuaded Quitman to abandon his expedition. In 1855 the manifesto was leaked to the public and triggered a new wave of northern resentment against the South.

Nicaragua. In 1855 another American, William Walker, led an invasion of Nicaragua. Born and raised in Tennessee, Walker had acquired a taste for Latin American adventures in California, where he won popularity for his schemes for annexing Sonora and Baja California. In 1854 he had led forty-eight followers to La Paz to participate in a rebellion against Mexican rule. After the rebellion failed, he landed in Nicaragua with sixty men and succeeded in making himself dictator of that country. He announced a grand scheme to create a new nation that would include Central America and Cuba. Most of his followers had the simpler mission of bringing Nicaragua into the Union as a slave state. In 1856, Walker announced the reestablishment of slavery in Nicaragua. His government was recognized by the Pierce administration and won an endorsement in the Democratic party platform. But Walker alienated his Central American neighbors, was driven out of power in 1857, and died before a Honduran firing squad in 1860. The resistance of Latin American nations, coupled with the growing force of Free-Soil sentiment in the North, meant that foreign policy and plots for taking manifest destiny to Latin America could not be the Democrats' key to national cohesion.

Kansas-Nebraska and the Republicans

The Democrats' main hopes for sustaining their party as a national institution now depended on the success of popular sovereignty. The doctrine was put to its first test since California in the northern—and the largest—portion of the Louisiana Purchase.

The Kansas-Nebraska Act. Because the Missouri Compromise guaranteed free soil in the Louisiana Purchase north of 36° 30', southerners had blocked the political organization of this area, except for the admission of Iowa to the Union in 1846 and the formation of the Minnesota Territory. Even though most of the unorganized area was in the "Great American Desert," the appetite of people in the Ohio River Valley and the upper South for new land made them impatient. The same sense of confinement that had sent thousands of them to Oregon led them to demand that the government organize the vast northern region of the Louisiana Purchase into territories and open it for settlement. Democratic senator Stephen A. Douglas of Illinois became their foremost spokesman. He championed development of the West and wanted Chicago to become the eastern terminus of a transcontinental railroad. He also yearned to be president. In 1854, he introduced a bill to extinguish Indian rights and organize a large territory in what he called Nebraska.

Douglas's plan conflicted with the plans of southern senators, who wanted to guarantee slavery in the territories and hoped that New Orleans, Memphis, or St. Louis would be chosen as the eastern railroad terminus. To win southern support, Douglas made two major concessions. First, he agreed with southerners that the

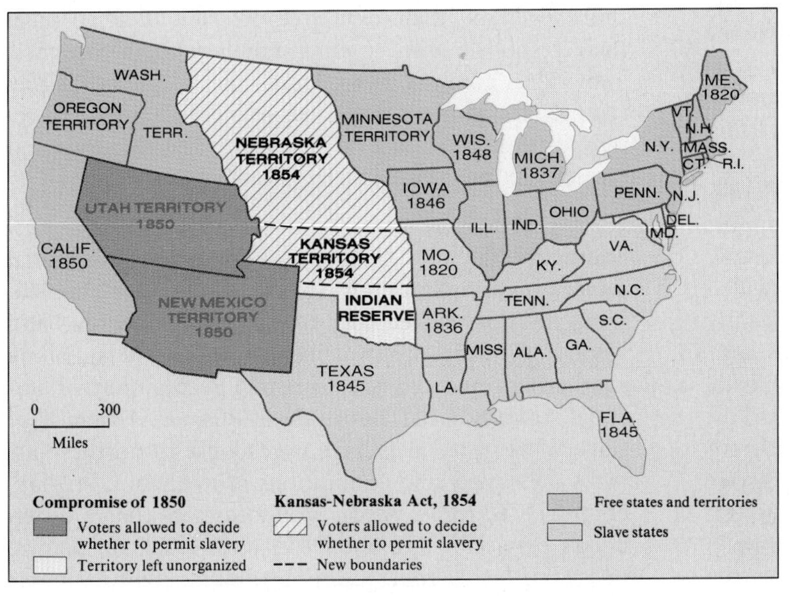

MAP 14.2

The Compromise of 1850 and the Kansas-Nebraska Act, 1854

Vast territories were at stake in the contest over the extension of slavery. The Compromise of 1850 and the Kansas-Nebraska Act provided that the future of slavery in most of the West—in the Kansas, Nebraska, Utah, and New Mexico territories—would be decided by popular sovereignty.

popular sovereignty principle embraced by the Compromise of 1850 had voided the Missouri Compromise's prohibition of slavery in the northern part of the Louisiana Purchase. Second, he advocated the formation of two new territories, Nebraska and Kansas, rather than one, giving slaveholders a chance to dominate the settlement of Kansas, the more southern territory. Douglas believed that the demographic advantage of non-slaveholders, coupled with geography that he thought would be hostile to plantation agriculture, would ensure that Kansas, like California earlier, would remain free. These concessions attracted the support of almost all southerners in Congress, and the Kansas-Nebraska Act passed in May 1854, despite the opposition of northern Whigs and half of Douglas's own northern Democrats, who were less sanguine about the future of free labor in the West.

Throughout the North, abolitionists and free-soilers denounced the Kansas-Nebraska Act; Douglas had seriously misread northern opinion. The repeal of the Missouri Compromise seemed to attack freedom in an area that had been secure for more than a generation. Suddenly, the idea caught fire that a "Slave Power" conspiracy had undertaken a dangerous program of aggression. Many free-soilers became convinced that the federal government had been captured by slaveholders and had abandoned sectional neutrality.

The Republican Party. Many northern Whigs, adrift without a national party, seized the opening Douglas had created. They began to cooperate with "Anti-Nebraska" Democrats. The two groups then joined with members of the Free-Soil party. In 1854 they began to organize a new party, reviving the Jeffersonian term *Republican* for themselves. The Republicans emphasized absolute opposition to the expansion of slavery into any new territories—generalizing the principle of the Wilmot Proviso—and ran their first candidates in the congressional elections of that year.

In these elections, they cooperated with the northern Know-Nothings, most of whom were also former Whigs. While the Republicans stressed free soil, the Know-Nothings emphasized anti-Catholic nativism—the other major program which had lacked support from a national party. The Republicans and Know-Nothings were wary of each other, uncertain which party might have the better formula for success. Many Republicans were uncomfortable with fervent anti-Catholicism, but they appreciated the fact that outside the South Know-Nothings applauded free-soil policy, regarding its potential antiblack thrust as consistent with the Know-Nothing program of excluding everyone but white Protestants from America. Together, the Republicans and Know-Nothings won a majority of seats in the House of Representatives in 1854. Suddenly the Republican/Know-Nothing coalition seemed a potent alternative to the Democrats and popular sovereignty.

Republican Ideology Versus the Defense of Slavery

Like most American political parties, the Republican party was a coalition, and its platform contained proposals designed to appeal to each of the groups that made up this alliance. But the party's ideas and political language were not just the sum of these proposals. Republican ideology was strongly shaped by a perception of the different kinds of human personalities and societies that would develop under slavery and freedom.

In the Republican view, slavery produced only two classes of people, masters and slaves. The master class was corrupted by wielding power that knew no limits. In their dealings with slaves—and with their poorer white neighbors—the slave masters would inevitably claim limitless privilege and inflict limitless injustice. This kind of excess could only produce habits of subservience, ignorance, and sloth among slaves and poor whites.

In the Republicans' description of free society, no person had unlimited power over another. The ancient divisions of society into permanent classes were eradicated by freedom and mobility. As Abraham Lincoln, a Whig who became a Republican after the passage of the Kansas-Nebraska Act, put it, in northern society "there is no permanent class of hired laborers among us." Every man had a chance to become an owner and an employer. And "if any continue through life in the condition of the hired laborers, it is not the fault of the system, but because of either a dependent nature which prefers it, or improvidence, folly, or singular misfortune." In the faith of Lincoln and his fellow Republicans, the typical men and women of such a society would be proudly independent, creative, ambitious, and energetic. Such people would be disciplined not by authority but by their own free determination to meet their responsibilities to their families, their churches, and their communities. Thus, the Republicans attempted to maintain the values of individualism and republicanism in the face of increasing class divisions and tensions in the industrializing North.

Southern Ideology. Southerners had long defended slavery on racist grounds—black people, they claimed, were inferior, lacked any capacity for freedom, and were dependent on their benevolent masters. Many southerners invoked the Christian recognition of unequal stations in life. But in the 1850s a new defense of slavery began to take shape in response to northern attacks on slavery and celebrations of free labor. Proslavery novelists, for example, produced more than a dozen books between 1852 and 1854 to counter the searing images of *Uncle Tom's Cabin* by making a positive case for slavery.

In a free-labor system, the new argument ran, labor

is simply a commodity whose price is determined by the ruthless laws of the market. In the market, greed is the only morality, supply and demand the only law, and money the only goal. Every member of such a society, rich or poor, becomes grasping and selfish. Anyone who is too old, too weak, or too young to sell labor in the market is "free" only to be hungry and homeless. In such a world, self-interest dominates; no one has a sense of community, civic values, or responsibility for others.

While slavery requires some people to work to enrich others, the argument continued, it produces a master class that differs greatly from the ruling class of a capitalist society. Masters assume lifelong responsibility for their slaves, including the old and the sick. The slaveowner, unlike the capitalist employer, is committed to community and civic responsibility. The master class in a slave society—whether in ancient Greece or Rome or the American South—cultivates the graces and virtues that can thrive only in a frankly aristocratic culture.

And so, in each section ideologies were being shaped that defined the differences between North and South in ways that utterly precluded political compromise. Each ideology suited the interests and the world view of the dominant groups—the planters in the South and the business class in the North. Northerners and southerners argued that slavery and free labor were not simply different labor systems but expressed different social orders and produced irreconcilably different kinds of men and women. Every passing year made it more likely that a majority of the voters in each section would be ready to decide that societies as different as the North and South could no longer be joined in a constitutional union.

"Bleeding Kansas"

The Kansas-Nebraska Act channeled the clash of rival ideologies into the settlement of the newly organized territory. In 1854 thousands of settlers began a rush into Kansas. Many believed they had a mission to defend the fundamental principles of their society, whether northern or southern; they were putting popular sovereignty to the test. On the side of slavery, Senator David R. Atchison of Missouri organized residents of his state to cross into Kansas and intervene in crucial elections. Opposing him were the agents of the New England Emigrant Aid Society, organized by abolitionists in 1854 to colonize Kansas with Free-Soilers. The preference of the Pierce administration was clear. In March 1855 the administration recognized a Kansas territorial legislature that had been elected largely by Missourians who crossed the border simply to cast ballots. The territorial legislature declared that questioning the legitimacy of slavery was a felony and that aiding a fugitive slave was a capital offense. Pierce assisted the legislature with federal troops and proslavery judicial appointees.

Violence peaked in the summer of 1856. A proslavery gang, seven hundred strong, sacked the free-soil town of Lawrence, destroying two newspaper offices, burning down buildings, and looting stores. While Lawrence burned, an abolitionist from New York and Ohio named John Brown, together with his four sons and two helpers, was on his way to Lawrence with a free-state volunteer militia to defend the town. Brown, born in 1800, had started more than twenty business ventures in six states, had gone through bankruptcy, and often had to defend himself against lawsuits.

Free-State Battery, 1856

For these free-soil settlers in Topeka, Kansas, there was a very real sense that the Civil War began in 1856, rather than 1861. Their cannon had seen service in the Mexican War.

AMERICAN VOICES

Six Months in "Bleeding Kansas" *Hannah Anderson Ropes*

In September 1855 Hannah Anderson Ropes moved with her two children from Brookline, Massachusetts, to join her husband in Lawrence, Kansas. But in March 1856, terrified by the violence, she abandoned Kansas and returned to Brookline, two months before the sack of Lawrence. During her six months in Kansas she wrote long letters to her mother and kept a diary.

November 21, 1855. Last week . . . a man living about six miles from here upon a claim . . . was shot down by a pack of Missourians, without any provocation. The border Missourians are a horseback people; always off somewhere; drink a great deal of whiskey, and are quite reckless of human life. There is no necessity for hard work to those who have long lived in this country, the earth yields so abundantly. They ride fine horses, and are strong, vigorous-looking animals themselves. To shoot a man is not much more than to shoot a buck. After killing this poor Yankee, they stood around him till they saw a man approach, and then rode deliberately away.

My dear mother, this is Saturday evening. . . . How strange it will seem to you to hear that I have loaded pistols and a bowie-knife upon my table at night, three of Sharp's rifles, loaded, standing in the room. . . . All the week every preparation has been made for our defence; and everybody is worn with want of sleep. . . .

The Missourians have taken awful oaths to destroy this Yankee town, and a price is set upon the heads of some of our most honored citizens. Already they have assembled to the number of two hundred at Franklin, a little town south of us, and many more at Douglas, a village farther up the river. They are moving with great secretiveness; but when was a Yankee 'caught napping,' in the faintest prospect of danger?

To-night everybody is at the hall. My orders are, if fire-arms sound like battle, to place Alice [her daughter] and myself as near the floor as possible, and be well covered with blankets. We already have one bullet in the wall, and, since that, one struck the 'shakes' close by the bed's head and glanced off. Now, for the first time, I begin to take an interest in Lawrence, as a city; and, prospectively, her destiny is almost as my own. How well her men bear themselves . . . [is] now so important as a matter of national history. . . .

December 5, 1855. Mother of mine . . . we now have an armed force of five hundred men, who are under the command of Dr. Robinson, now commander-in-chief, and Col. Lane, both of whom have had experience in actual battle, in Mexico and California. Out of my south window I can see them drilling. . . . Boys there are in the ranks; but the soberness of manhood is upon them, and the determination of "Seventy-six" [1776] in their step. The blood warms in my veins as I look. . . .

undated, December 1855. How we, at the North, have always believed implicitly in the chivalry of the South, and the wide-hearted generosity of the West. It is not till we arrive in Kansas, away from everything dear and familiar . . . that the truth really dawns upon us. Mother, there is no indignity to be mentioned which has not been heaped upon us. By it I feel myself robbed of a large estate—my faith in human nature.

undated, March 1856. I am not only proud, but thankful, very thankful, that New England is the land of my birth. Her laws and institutions are dearer to us than ever before; and Kansas, without a similar elevating basis of social and moral restraint, would not be worth travelling two thousand miles to secure. . . .

Source: Hannah Anderson Ropes, *Six Months in Kansas by a Lady* (Boston: John P. Jewett, 1856), *passim.*

Nonetheless, he had an intelligence and a moral intensity that won the trust of influential people, including leading abolitionists, whom he sought out beginning in the early 1830s. Brown believed, according to a free-soil minister who sheltered him, "that God had raised him up on purpose to break the jaws of the wicked." The day after Brown heard about the sack of Lawrence, he acted with vengeance. He and his followers, with broadswords honed like razors, murdered and mutilated five proslavery settlers in Kansas. We must "fight fire with fire" and "strike terror in the hearts of the proslavery people," Brown declared. The "Pottawatomie massacre," as the killings became known, provoked reprisals and initiated a guerrilla war that cost about two hundred lives.

The violence even reached the civilized halls of Congress. In an inflammatory speech, "The Crime against Kansas," Senator Charles Sumner of Massachusetts denounced the Pierce administration, the South, and Senator Andrew P. Butler of South Carolina, who Sumner said had taken "the harlot slavery" as his mistress. Butler's nephew and protégé, Preston Brooks, a member of the House, took personal offense at Sumner's attack and decided to punish him according to the southern code of chivalry. Brooks accosted Sumner at his desk while the Senate was not in session and began beating him on the head with a walking cane. Sumner struggled to his feet, wrenched his desk loose from the screws that held it to the floor, and finally fell, unconscious and bleeding. Sumner did not return to the Senate for two and a half years; Massachusetts kept his seat open for him to honor him, and create a symbol of his martyrdom. The House censured Brooks but the South Carolina voters returned him to Congress with an almost unanimous show of support. Many of them sent him new canes to replace the one he had broken in the attack.

The Election of 1856

The violence in Kansas and in the halls of Congress dominated the presidential election of 1856. The Democrats stayed with their policy of popular sovereignty, but with their party's center of gravity now resting in the South, they had to go beyond generalities and explicitly reaffirm the Kansas-Nebraska Act. To strengthen the party in the North in the face of Pierce's close association with "Bleeding Kansas," the Democrats turned away from him and nominated James Buchanan of Pennsylvania. A tall, dignified, white-haired figure of sixty-four years, Buchanan had more than forty years of experience in politics, but he was an unimaginative, uninspiring, and timid leader. Fortunately for his candidacy, he had been minister to Great Britain during the controversy over the Kansas-Nebraska Act and had no record on that volatile issue.

The Republicans counted on a northern backlash against Democrats over "Bleeding Kansas," despite the success of Pierce's third territorial governor, John W. Geary of Pennsylvania, in establishing peace in Kansas in September. The Republican platform denounced the Kansas-Nebraska Act and insisted that the federal government prohibit slavery in all the territories. The platform also called for federal subsidies to transcontinental railroads, reviving the element of the Whig economic program that was most popular among midwestern Democrats. The Republicans nominated John C. Frémont, a celebrated army explorer with a meager political record. He was a genuine free-soiler and famous throughout the nation for his role in the conquest of California.

The Know-Nothings had appeared to be strong early in 1856, but they proved to be only a minor factor in the election. They had quickly split into warring factions—North and South—over Kansas-Nebraska. The Republicans cleverly maneuvered the northern party—called the North American party—into endorsing Frémont. Meanwhile, the southern fragment of the American party nominated Millard Fillmore. He ran strongly in many southern states, but in the North most Know-

A Free-Soil Cartoon, 1856

This Republican cartoon, published during the presidential campaign of 1856, proposes that the Democrats and their platform would compel free soilers in Kansas to accept slavery. Using a black man to symbolize slavery, and presenting him in a derogatory fashion, suggests the racist aspect of the free-soil message.

Nothings disappeared into the ranks of the Republican party. By incorporating nativism but emphasizing free soil, the Republican message resonated more closely with the deepest concerns of northern voters.

For the Republicans the great issue of the election was the expansion of slavery. They grabbed the offensive—and the "Slave Power" conspiracy theory—charging that the South, through the Democratic party, was seeking to extend slavery throughout the nation. The sense of destiny, of impending doom, the election created was captured by the poet Walt Whitman, a former Democrat who campaigned for Republicans in 1856. "No man knows what will happen next," Whitman wrote, "but all know some such things are to happen as mark the greatest moral convulsions of the earth."

Many southern Democrats threatened to press for secession if Frémont won. Fearful of such a cataclysm—and still believing that popular sovereignty could solve the crisis—enough northern Democrats remained loyal to give the election to Buchanan. He drew 1.8 million votes to 1.3 million for Frémont. But the Republican party stunned the nation by running up impressive victories in the free states. Frémont attracted former Whigs, Know-Nothings, and free-soil Democrats to carry eleven free states. Buchanan took only five, and the race was very close in two of them—Illinois and Pennsylvania. A small shift of the popular vote in those two states to Frémont would have won him the presidency, even though he received no support in the South. In the slave states the race was simply a contest between Buchanan and Fillmore, who won only Maryland.

The Third Party System. A dramatic restructuring of parties had suddenly taken place: the Third Party System—Democrats and Republicans replacing Democrats and Whigs—had become a reality. The implications for the sectional crisis were ominous. The Republican party was within striking distance of the presidency after only one campaign despite the fact that it was a sectional party, with no support in the South. And the Democratic party had succeeded in bridging sectional conflicts only by the slenderest of margins. Many Americans, North and South, sensed that they stood on the brink of a revolution. The future of the Union would depend on the ability of President Buchanan to persuade the North that slavery would not threaten free labor in the West, and to convince the South that the federal government would protect slavery.

The Democratic Blunders of 1857–1858

The *Dred Scott* Decision. However attractive to northern voters, the free-soil program of the Republicans had never been subjected to a clear test of constitutionality. The Supreme Court had never reviewed the free-soil doctrine or the contrary proposition of John C. Calhoun, that the Constitution protected slavery in the territories, and that the people of a territory could prohibit slavery *only* at the moment of admission to statehood, not before. Many on both sides of the issue hoped the Court would resolve the question—in their favor. In 1857 the Court made an effort.

In 1856 the case of Dred Scott, a slave suing for his freedom, reached the Supreme Court. Scott had lived for a time with his master, an army surgeon, in the free state of Illinois and the Wisconsin Territory, where the Northwest Ordinance (1787) and the Missouri Compromise (1820) prohibited slavery. In his suit, which began in 1846 in the courts of Missouri, Scott claimed that his residence in a free state and a free territory had made him a free man. In March 1857, only two days after Buchanan's inauguration, the Court reached a decision, in *Dred Scott v. Sandford.*

There was little consensus among the justices on the issues raised by the case, but seven members of the court agreed on one critical matter—Scott remained a slave. There was no majority opinion; every justice wrote his own opinion. But Chief Justice Roger B. Taney's was the most influential. Taney ruled that blacks, free *or* slave, could not be citizens of the United States. Scott therefore had no right to sue in a federal court. Taney could have stopped there. Instead, he insisted on going further and making two broad points. First, he ruled that the Fifth Amendment's prohibition on taking property without due process of law meant that Congress could not pass a law depriving persons of their slave "property" in the territories. So the Missouri Compromise, voided three years earlier by the Kansas-Nebraska Act, had *always* been unconstitutional, and Scott's residence in the Wisconsin Territory had not freed him. Second, Congress could not extend to territorial governments any powers that Congress itself did not possess. Since Congress had no power to prohibit slavery in a territory, neither did the government of that territory. Thus Taney endorsed Calhoun's interpretation of the constitutional protection of slavery and his definition of popular sovereignty.

Five of the seven justices, including the chief justice, who was from Maryland, were southern Democrats. They and President Buchanan—who privately twisted the arm of fellow Pennsylvanian Justice Robert C. Grier to join the five—had a specific political purpose in mind when they arranged the decision. They prayed that it would be accepted by Democrats and Republicans alike, out of respect for the Court and for law and order, and thus ease the sectional crisis. Buchanan also hoped that the decision would strip Republicans of the basis of their support.

Dred Scott
Dred Scott's odyssey began in St. Louis in 1834, when he was sold to John Emerson and taken to Illinois, then to Fort Snelling in Wisconsin Territory, and finally back to Missouri. After Emerson died, Scott sued Emerson's wife for his freedom. Two months after the Supreme Court decision, the former Mrs. Emerson, who had married an antislavery politician from Massachusetts, freed Scott

But the decision did just the opposite of calming the sectional waters. After all, in a single stroke the Democratic Supreme Court had declared the Republicans' antislavery platform unconstitutional. It was a decision the Republicans could not tolerate. Led by Senator William H. Seward of New York, they accused the Supreme Court and President Buchanan of participating in the "Slave Power" conspiracy. Even many northern Democrats were outraged, including Stephen Douglas, who had labored so hard to protect his party's strength in the North with the popular sovereignty doctrine.

The Lecompton Constitution. President Buchanan then made an even more serious blunder—he decided to support the proslavery forces in Kansas. In early 1858 he recommended the admission of Kansas as a slave state under the so-called Lecompton constitution. Most observers—including Stephen Douglas—believed that the constitution had been obtained by fraud particularly because the antislavery majority in Kansas had rejected the constitution in a referendum. Douglas thought that admitting Kansas under the Lecompton constitution would be a travesty of democracy, a parody of popular sovereignty, and an embarrassment to the party in most of the North. Angered, Douglas broke with Buchanan and the southern Democrats and mobilized western Democrats and Republicans in the House of Representatives to defeat the Lecompton constitution. Kansas finally entered the Union as a free state in 1861, after secession was well under way and many southern representatives had left Congress.

Buchanan's support for Lecompton meant that he had decided to worry more about the anxieties of the South than those of the North. It was a catastrophic choice. He failed to organize Kansas on a proslavery basis; he fractured the Democratic party; and he provided the Republicans with more evidence that an insidious "Slave Power" was threatening the rights of free labor and, ultimately, the existence of the republic. Buchanan had made it virtually impossible for either the Democratic party or popular sovereignty to provide the basis for cementing national unity.

Abraham Lincoln and the Breaking of Union, 1858–1860

The disintegration of the national Democratic party that had begun over "Bleeding Kansas" accelerated after the elections of 1856 and the *Dred Scott* decision. Former Democrats and Whigs continued to switch into the new Republican party. During this crisis of Union, Abraham Lincoln (1809–1865) emerged as the pivotal figure in American politics. His rise to power illustrates how the issue of slavery came to dominate politics—and change the way Americans thought about the future of their society.

Lincoln's Early Career

Economic development and the rise of the business class in the small towns of the Ohio River Valley shaped Lincoln's early career. His restless farming family of modest means had moved from Kentucky to Indiana, and then to Illinois. In 1831, Lincoln set out on his own, settling in New Salem, a small town on the Sangamon River in central Illinois. He rejected the farming life and began working as a store clerk. He had already displayed signs of business entrepreneurship, having twice, in 1828 and 1831, taken flatboats laden with farm produce down the Mississippi River to New Orleans. The profits helped him to become a partner in a general store in New Salem.

In New Salem, Lincoln was equally at home with the rough, footloose young men of the town and its emerging business class. He excelled in the games, pranks, and combat of a gang of young men who hung out in a local saloon, and in 1831 they elected him captain of the company of New Salem men who volunteered for the Black Hawk War. He had little formal schooling but, studying with the local schoolmaster, he mastered English grammar and elementary mathematics. Another villager introduced him to Shakespeare. During Lincoln's very first winter in town he became a regular participant in the New Salem Debating Society.

Illinois State Legislator. Lincoln's ambition was, as a friend later described it, "a little engine that knew no rest." That ambition ran not to business but to politics. In 1832 Lincoln ran for the state legislature on a business-class program: increased state investment in internal improvements and education. Universal education, he said in his campaign, would provide "the advantages and satisfaction to be derived from all being able to read the scriptures and other works, both of a religious and moral nature, for themselves."

Lincoln lost the 1832 election, but he won almost all of the votes cast in New Salem and he rapidly extended his influence. He was appointed postmaster and deputy county surveyor and began the study of the law with a prominent attorney, who was also a state legislator and the foremost Whig in the county. In 1834 he ran again for the state legislature and won. Admitted to the bar in 1837, he moved to Springfield, the new state capital. There he met Mary Todd, the daughter of a successful Kentucky businessman and politician; they married in 1842. They were a picture in contrasts. Her tastes were aristocratic; his were humble. She was volatile; he was easygoing and deliberate. Bouts of depression, which plagued him throughout his life, tried her patience. Yet these episodes were bound up in the remarkable growth of his personality and mind.

During Lincoln's four terms in the lower house of the Illinois legislature he powerfully influenced the building of the Whig party. As Whig floorleader and chairman of the finance committee, Lincoln promoted state banking and extensive internal improvements—turnpikes, canals, and railroads—that the Whigs hoped would increase their appeal in the normally Democratic areas of southern and central Illinois. In 1840 he made two long campaign tours on behalf of William Henry Harrison in southern Illinois, and in 1844 he campaigned for his political hero, Henry Clay, in the southern Indiana towns of his boyhood. In 1846, Lincoln drew on his expanded network of Whig friends and supporters to win election to Congress.

Congressman. Until entering Congress in 1847, Lincoln had successfully avoided taking a stand on the contentious issue of slavery. But now the Mexican War and its implications for the future of slavery forced him to state his position.

Lincoln had concluded, perhaps as early as one of his youthful trips to New Orleans, that slavery was unjust. And, in 1837, he spoke out against the mob violence that was directed at abolitionists and had resulted in the killing of Elijah Lovejoy in nearby Alton. But Lincoln's roots in the Ohio River Valley towns settled largely by migrants from southern states, and his desire to build Whig support in those towns, worked against any sympathy for abolitionism, which emphasized the sinfulness of slaveholding. He knew, moreover, that abolitionism was a threat to the Whigs. This had come home to him in 1844 when he watched the Whig abolitionists in New York throw their votes to James G. Birney, the Liberty Party candidate, and seemingly deny Henry Clay the presidency. And he did not believe that the federal government had any authority to tamper with slavery where it existed.

Lincoln entered Congress in 1847 with a firm conviction that the Whigs had to abstain from abolitionism yet find a way to hold the allegiance of the growing number of people opposed to slavery. Consequently, he supported the appropriation bills necessary to sustain American forces in Mexico but, at the same time, condemned the Polk administration for its war of aggression, introduced resolutions pressing Polk on the constitutionality of the war, and, most important, voted for the Wilmot Proviso in various forms. In addition, Lincoln introduced a bill for the gradual abolition of slavery in the District of Columbia. His bill would have provided for compensation to slaveowners and required approval by a referendum of the "free white citizens" of the District. It was this kind of moderate program of opposition to slavery's expansion and encouragement of gradual emancipation, coupled with the colonization of freed slaves in Africa and elsewhere, that Lincoln argued was the only practical way to solve the problem of slavery. It was on the basis of this program that he argued, in 1848, while campaigning for Zachary Taylor in Massachusetts, Chicago, and even his own district, that antislavery Whigs should remain with the party because Whigs and Free-Soilers had similar views on the spread of slavery.

Corporate Lawyer. The abolitionists denounced Lincoln's approach. In response to his gradualist proposal for emancipation in the District of Columbia, abolitionist Wendell Phillips called Lincoln "the slave hound of Illinois." But Lincoln's position, particularly his condemnation of the Mexican War, put him too far out of step with the voters of his district. He went into a prudent retirement from politics that lasted from 1849 until 1854. While he engaged in an increasingly lucrative legal practice, one in which some of the leading rail-

Abraham Lincoln

Abraham Lincoln became the most photographed man of his time, yet none of the photographs suggests how striking and sparkling people found him. The photography of Lincoln's day required subjects to stand absolutely still, their heads against a rack, for long periods, and this caused Lincoln to lapse into a sad, abstracted mood.

roads and manufacturers of Illinois became his clients, Lincoln agonized over the disintegration of the Whig party and the apparent failure of moderate approaches to resolve the sectional crisis. In a speech eulogizing Henry Clay after his death in 1852, Lincoln condemned both the proslavery fanatics who denied the tenet of the Declaration of Independence that "all men are created equal" and the abolitionists, who would "shiver into fragments the Union of these States; tear to tatters its now venerated constitution; and even burn the last copy of Bible, rather than slavery should continue a single hour."

The Campaign of 1854. Lincoln's dual quest for the moral high ground on slavery and for a way to preserve the Union brought him back into politics in 1854, following the passage of the Kansas-Nebraska Act. The act "aroused" him "as he had never been before." The opening of Kansas to popular sovereignty placed freedom and slavery on the same ethical level and, at the same time, threatened the Union. Moreover, the act created an opportunity for the Whigs to win the allegiance of Democrats who feared that Douglas was betraying them by opening the West to slavery, and to blacks. Lincoln made a last, desperate effort to save the Whig party in Illinois. He plunged into the campaigns with an attack on Douglas, support for Whig candidates, and his own campaign for U.S. Senator.

Lincoln stated his position in what became known as his Peoria address. He did not want to threaten slavery where it existed. White southerners were, he said, "just what we would be in their situation." He believed that "some system of gradual emancipation might be adopted," but "for their tardiness in this, I will not undertake to judge our brethren of the south." But the Kansas-Nebraska Act repealed the Missouri Compromise and threatened to expand slavery. Politicians had to face the ethical issue that slavery was founded, he said, "in the selfishness of man's nature," while opposition to it was based "in his love of justice." However, the risks to the Union were obvious. These principles were in "eternal antagonism," and "when brought into collision so fiercely as slavery extension brings them, shocks, and throes, and convulsions must ceaselessly follow."

Lincoln concluded his Peoria address by appealing to Free-Soilers and abolitionists to join the Whigs in restoring the Missouri Compromise. Joining forces, they could both block slavery's extension and uphold the Union. In short, Lincoln expressed what would become key tenets of the Republican party: moral opposition to slavery, assertion of the right of the national government to exclude slavery from the territories, and the conviction that the nation must eventually cut out slavery like a "cancer."

Republican Party Leader. After a handful of "Anti-Nebraska" Democrats in the state legislature blocked Lincoln's election to the Senate, he decided, finally, to abandon the Whig party. That way, he might win the support of "Anti-Nebraska" Democrats who could not bring themselves to endorse a Whig. As the violence escalated in Kansas and the Whig party splintered, he worked to unite all the "Anti-Nebraska" forces—conservative Whigs, Free-Soilers, abolitionists, Know-Nothings, and bolting Democrats—in opposition to the Democratic party, and to Stephen Douglas and his doctrine of popular sovereignty. In May 1856, in a state convention of all the dissident groups, Lincoln emerged as the most powerful leader in the coalition that formed the Republican party in Illinois, and Illinois Republicans put him forward as their favorite-son candidate for vice-president.

The *Dred Scott* decision in 1857 gave Lincoln new ammunition in his campaign to win over Democrats. He warned that the Supreme Court, in its "next Dred Scott decision," would simply "decide that no State under the Constitution can exclude" slavery. If the followers of Buchanan had their way, "we shall *awake* to the *reality* . . . that the *Supreme* Court has made *Illinois* a *slave* State." The Court now seemed to be a partner in the "Slave-Power" conspiracy. Although Republicans would abide by the Court's decision, they would devote themselves to reversing it.

By 1858, Lincoln's position in the Illinois Republican party was even stronger, and he again received the party's nomination as the challenger to Stephen Douglas for U.S. senator. In accepting the nomination, he delivered the most radical statement of his career. Quoting from the Bible, "A house divided against itself cannot stand," he warned that the nation could not resolve the slavery issue without a crisis. There were only two possible outcomes:

> I believe this government cannot endure permanently half *slave* and half *free*. I do not expect the Union to be dissolved—I do not expect the house to *fall*—but I do expect it will cease to be divided. It will become *all* one thing, or *all* the other.

Thus Lincoln dismissed as insignificant the differences between Douglas and Buchanan on the issue of slavery. Americans had to choose, according to Lincoln, between opposition and advocacy.

Stephen Douglas

This photograph, taken in Matthew Brady's New York studio in 1860, suggests why Stephen Douglas (1813–1861) became known as the "Little Giant."

Lincoln Versus Douglas

Abraham Lincoln's eloquent challenge to Douglas's bid for reelection as a senator from Illinois proved to be the highlight of the elections in 1858. The political duel attracted national interest because of Douglas's prominence and his break with the Buchanan administration. Adding to the excitement was Lincoln's own reputation as a formidable attorney, politician, and stump speaker. To increase his national exposure, Lincoln challenged Douglas to a series of seven debates.

During those debates, Lincoln attacked slavery as an institution that subverted equality of opportunity. He did express doubts about the innate abilities of African-Americans, and he explicitly rejected formulas  that would give them social and political equality. But he declared that blacks were entitled to "all the natural rights enumerated in the Declaration of Independence." This meant, Lincoln explained, that "in the right to eat the bread, without leave of anybody else, which his own hand earns," the black was "the equal of every living man."

Lincoln described the master conspiracy he saw at work. The Kansas-Nebraska Act (which Douglas had introduced), the *Dred Scott* decision, and Buchanan's cynical endorsement of the fraudulent Lecompton constitution were part of a master plan to extend slavery throughout the territories. If the South succeeded, it would eventually insist that slavery be legalized throughout the United States. Lincoln then pressed Douglas to explain how he could accept the *Dred Scott* decision and at the same time advocate popular sovereignty.

In a debate in Freeport, Illinois, Douglas responded by elaborating on a reformulation of popular sovereignty that he had been working on since mid-1857. In what became known as the Freeport doctrine, Douglas asserted that settlers could exclude slavery from a territory in practice simply by not adopting local legislation to protect it. In other words, he claimed that even if territorial governments followed Taney and did not prohibit slavery, municipalities could still do so by failing to support the "peculiar institution." In effect, this was a legalistic formulation of his view that demography and geography made the victory of slavery in the territories almost impossible. To southerners, the Freeport doctrine meant that they could be denied the victory won in the *Dred Scott* decision.

The Republicans made great gains in 1858, including control of the House. Lincoln, however, was not among the victors. Douglas was reelected to the Senate by a narrow margin in the state legislature. But Lincoln had virtually buried popular sovereignty in Illinois. Douglas's victory resulted from the overrepresentation in the legislature of the staunchly Democratic counties in southern Illinois rather than any popularity of the Freeport doctrine—a doctrine that was too flimsy for rebuilding the Democratic party.

John Brown Pledging Allegiance to the Flag

This is the earliest known photograph of John Brown, probably taken in 1846. In 1847, Frederick Douglass had dinner with Brown and learned that he had a plan to establish abolitionist bases in the Appalachian mountains and induce slaves to escape to freedom.

The Election of 1860

The congressional elections of 1858 made southern Democrats intensely nervous. They knew that the Republicans might win in 1860, so they increased their demands. The more moderate Southern Rights Democrats insisted that the Democratic party and the federal government make specific commitments to protect slavery, such as the enactment of a territorial slave code that would counter the Freeport doctrine. One of their leading spokesmen was Senator Jefferson Davis, a Mississippi planter and Mexican War hero. More radical southern Democrats, like Robert Barnwell Rhett of South Carolina and William Lowndes Yancey of Alabama, demanded that Douglas and his followers support relegalizing the international slave trade. Called *the fire-eaters*, these radicals were secessionists who hoped to drive a wedge between North and South. In response, Douglas made it plain that if the Democratic party platform included such proposals in 1860, he would not support it. He had no choice in drawing a hard line. If he did not, he would sacrifice his home base of support.

John Brown's Raid. In the meantime a shocking event further deepened the anxiety of southerners. One night in October 1859, John Brown, leader of the Pottawatomie massacre, led eighteen heavily armed followers, both black and white, in a raid that seized the federal arsenal at Harpers Ferry, Virginia. Brown's explicit purpose was to arm a slave rebellion and create an African-American state within the South. The local militia and U.S. marines, under the command of Colonel Robert E. Lee, quickly reclaimed the arsenal; they captured Brown and killed ten of his party.

Republican leaders dismissed Brown as a criminal, but Democrats, North and South, called Brown's plot, in the words of Stephen Douglas, "a natural, logical, inevitable result of the doctrines and teachings of the Republican party." Fueling the Democratic charges were letters, discovered near Harpers Ferry and widely published in the press, that incriminated six leading abolitionists, known as the Secret Six, for financing Brown's raid. One of the six, the Unitarian minister Thomas Wentworth Higginson, admitted his involvement and declared that Brown's "acquittal or rescue would do half as much good as being executed; so strong is the personal sympathy with him."

Virginia gave the abolitionists the Christian martyr they wanted. The governor charged Brown with treason; a state court sentenced him to death; and Brown was hanged. At a church meeting in Concord, Massachusetts, Henry David Thoreau described Brown as "an angel of light," "the bravest and humanest man in all the country." Emerson proclaimed that Brown would "make the gallows as glorious as the cross." Slaveholders were horrified, assuming that these widely publicized utterances revealed the sentiments of the entire North and that abolitionists were organizing new slave rebellions. More than ever, slaveholders were convinced that a Republican victory would lead to the destruction of slavery.

Harpers Ferry from Jefferson Rock, 1893

The town of Harpers Ferry was situated at the confluence of the Shenandoah (flowing from the right) and Potomac rivers in the Blue Ridge Mountains of northern Virginia. The Baltimore and Ohio Railroad crossed the Potomac (on the left). Adding to the town's strategic importance were the shops of the federal armory, the federal arsenal (arms storehouse), and, on a nearby island in the Shenandoah, Hall's Rifle Works, where sixty gunsmiths produced firearms for the U.S. Army.

The Democrats Divide. When the Democratic party convened in Charleston, South Carolina, in April 1860, the southern wing was determined to force the party to embrace the program of Jefferson Davis and his followers—positive protection of slavery in the territories in line with the *Dred Scott* decision. Northern Democrats refused. They wanted only a vague endorsement of popular sovereignty and the suggestion that disputed issues be left to the Supreme Court. When the convention adopted the northern platform, the delegates from eight southern states left the hall. Because Buchanan had lost the confidence of northern Democrats, Douglas led the subsequent balloting for a presidential candidate. However, his determined foes denied him the two-thirds majority that the party rules required for nomination. The party adjourned and reconvened in Baltimore in June. Most of the southerners reappeared but soon walked out again. The Baltimore convention then nominated Stephen Douglas. The bolting southerners convened separately in Baltimore and nominated Buchanan's vice-president, John C. Breckinridge of Kentucky. The Democratic party had finally broken into two sectional pieces.

The Republicans Choose Lincoln. The Republicans sensed victory and acted cautiously. They settled on Abraham Lincoln, who had a more moderate position on slavery than the best-known Republicans, Senator William H. Seward of New York and Governor Salmon P. Chase of Ohio. Lincoln also conveyed a compelling egalitarian image that could appeal to small farmers and workers. And Lincoln's home territory—the Ohio River Valley of Illinois and Indiana—was a crucial "swing" area in the competition between Democrats and Republicans.

The Republican platform also attempted to strike a moderate tone. It adhered to free-soil doctrine but ruled out direct interference with slavery in the South. It denied the right of states to secede. It also endorsed the programs of economic development that had remained at the heart of Whig politics and that had gained increasing support among Democrats in the Midwest, especially since the onset of depression conditions in 1857.

Douglas campaigned nationally against three competitors, each of whom was, for all practical purposes, a regional candidate. However, in September and October he concentrated his efforts in the South, having concluded that Lincoln would win in the North. Douglas underscored the seriousness of the sectional crisis by shattering tradition and campaigning personally. He warned southerners about secession. He told them that the North and northern Democrats would not allow them to destroy the Union and argued that *his* Democratic party provided the only feasible instrument for compromise. Competing with Douglas in the South and also offering a Unionist message was John Bell, a former Tennessee senator who became the nominee of the Constitutional Union party, a residue of southern Whiggery. The forces of moderation were ebbing in the South. Since the shock of John Brown's raid on Harpers Ferry, waves of hysteria over slave rebellion had swept through the region. Southern panic intensified during the presidential campaign. Fires of unknown origin and the deaths of whites under peculiar circumstances initiated reports of arson and poisoning.

Lincoln's Victory. Lincoln won only a plurality of the popular vote—about 40 percent of the total—but received a majority of the electoral vote. His victory in the North was overwhelming: he won every state except New Jersey. Of crucial importance to Lincoln's election were Pennsylvania, Indiana, and his home state of Illinois, all of which had cast their electoral votes for Buchanan in 1856. In ten of the slave states, Lincoln was excluded from the ballot; in the other five slave states he won no electoral votes. Breckinridge won every state in the deep South as well as Delaware, Maryland, and North Carolina. Bell carried the upper southern states where the Whigs had been strongest—Kentucky, Tennessee, and Virginia. Douglas won three of New Jersey's seven electoral votes and carried only one state, Missouri, despite winning 21 percent of the popular vote. His broad support was wasted in a winner-take-all system.

The Republicans had united the Northeast, the Midwest, and the Far West behind free soil. They had been able to absorb abolitionism and still unify enough businessmen, workers, and farmers to achieve their victory. A political party with support in only one section of the country and a clear mission had finally come to power. To many southerners, it now seemed time to think carefully about the meaning of Lincoln's 1858 words, that the Union must "become all one thing, or all the other."

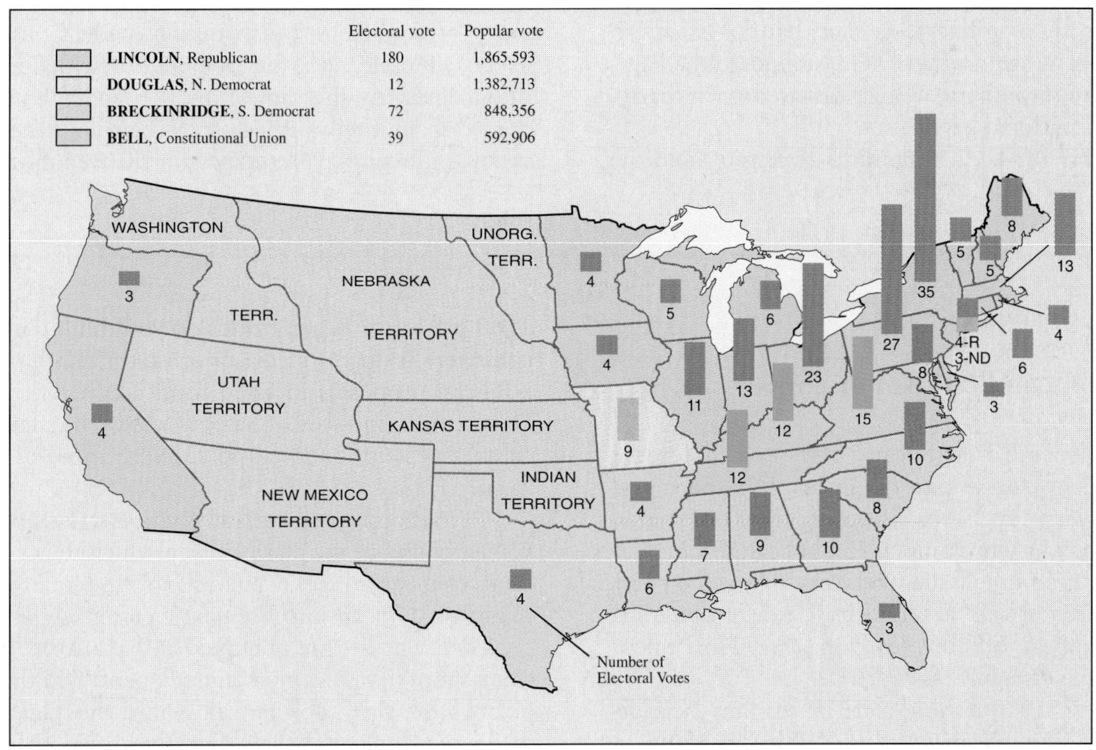

MAP 14.3

The Election of 1860

Four presidential candidates vied for election in 1860. Douglas's few electoral votes are striking when compared with his showing in the popular vote. In most states, Douglas ran second to Lincoln or Breckinridge, who took all of the electoral votes of the states they won.

Summary

The American experience, so full of material and spiritual promise, took a tragic turn during the two decades before the Civil War. That turn began when southern planters saw a possible solution to their anxiety over British and abolitionist threats to slavery: the seizure of northern Mexico. The South's ambitions led the United States into a war of conquest against Mexico. However, the Mexican War and continued western expansion doomed the Missouri Compromise as a means of reconciling the interests of the South and the North in the West. The sectional threat to the unity of the two major political parties, and to the Union itself, became so great that in 1850 leaders of both parties joined in framing a major settlement, known as the Compromise of 1850. The Compromise temporarily preserved the Second Party System, but most southern Democrats and most northern Whigs did not support the Compromise. They stood ready to risk the Union if they could not dominate the West.

The Compromise of 1850 and the Second Party System died in the violence of the 1850s, casualties of the first armed struggles over slavery. Antislavery northerners defied the Fugitive Slave Act, battling southern slave catchers. When northern Whigs opposed the Fugitive Slave Act, southern Whigs deserted their party, killing it as a national party.

The ability of the U.S. political system to hold the Union together then rested exclusively on the national appeal of the Democratic party and its doctrine of popular sovereignty. But the doctrine brought only more violence—"Bleeding Kansas"—as opponents and supporters of slavery fought a bitter guerrilla war over the meaning of popular sovereignty. "Bleeding Kansas" pushed North and South further apart and weakened the Democratic party.

Whigs and abolitionists joined with dissident Democrats and Know-Nothings to establish the Republican party, which firmly supported free-soil principles. By 1856 the Second Party System of Democrats and Whigs had given way to the Third Party System of Democrats and Republicans. The Republican party united a majority of voters in the Northeast and Northwest around free-soilism.

The national Democratic party finally fractured over the *Dred Scott* decision and President Buchanan's support for the Lecompton constitution. Former Democrats and Whigs continued to switch to the Republican party. In 1859, John Brown, an abolitionist veteran of the Kansas struggle, captured a federal arsenal in Virginia and tried to start a private war against slavery. Southerners then demanded more protection for slavery than northern Democrats would provide. Consequently, in the 1860 election, the Democrats divided along sectional lines. At the same time, Abraham Lincoln succeeded in uniting northern society around the free-soil vision and won the presidency for the Republican party.

TOPIC FOR RESEARCH

The Republican Platform in 1860

In 1856, when the Republicans first reached for the presidency, they seemed preoccupied with the moral issue of slavery. In 1860, however, they nominated Abraham Lincoln who, among Republicans, was relatively moderate on the issue of slavery. Thus, the party may have been trying to mute its idealism and thus broaden its appeal. Was this really the case? How calculating were the Republicans in 1860?

To answer this question, start by reading the platforms of the Republican party in 1856 and 1860. In what ways do the platforms suggest that the Republicans moderated their opposition to slavery in 1860? What exactly was their position on slavery in 1860, as represented by the Republican platform? Was their 1860 position on slavery internally consistent? What other programs did the Republicans endorse in the 1860 platform? What groups do you think the Republicans were trying to please or attract? Did all of the Republican proposals in 1860 form a coherent package? How consistent were Lincoln's views on slavery, and other aspects of national policy, with those of the platform?

Parties and presidents who win elections often conveniently ignore the platforms on which they ran. As a final element in your analysis of the platform, you might read ahead into the next chapter of the text and consider whether or not the 1860 platform was anything more than a campaign document. Did the Republicans, after they took power, regard this platform as a serious statement of their objectives? Which planks in the platform did they implement into law, and which planks did they ignore? In the last analysis, how important to the actual programs of the Republicans was the idealistic message they had fashioned during the 1850s?

Additional information on the development of the Republican party will be found in Michael Les Benedict,

A Compromise of Principle: Congressional Republicans and Reconstruction, 1863–1869 (1974); Eric Foner, *Free Soil, Free Labor, Free Men: The Ideology of the Republican Party Before the Civil War* (1970); William E. Gienapp, *The Origins of the Republican Party, 1852–1856* (1987); and Michael Holt, *The Political Crisis of the 1850s* (1978). You might also want to consult one of the biographies of Lincoln listed in the Suggestions for Further Reading.

BIBLIOGRAPHY

Sectional Conflict and Compromise

Study of 1840s expansionism should begin with Frederick Merk, *The Monroe Doctrine and American Expansion, 1843–1849,* (1972). On the coming of the Mexican War consult David Pletcher, *The Diplomacy of Annexation: Texas, Oregon, and the Mexican War* (1973), and Charles G. Sellers, *James K. Polk: Continentalist, 1843–1846* (1966). For an analysis of the relationship between the war experience and American culture, see Robert W. Johannsen, *To the Halls of the Montezumas: The Mexican War in the American Imagination* (1985). For the Mexican viewpoint, see Gene M. Brack, *Mexico Views Manifest Destiny, 1821–1846: An Essay on the Origins of the Mexican War* (1975). On congressional politics during the 1840s, see Chaplain Morrison, *Democratic Politics and Sectionalism: The Wilmot Proviso Controversy* (1967); Merrill Peterson, *The Great Triumverate: Webster, Clay, and Calhoun* (1987); and Joel H. Silbey, *The Shrine of Party: Congressional Voting Behavior, 1841–1852* (1967). On the Compromise of 1850 see Holman Hamilton, *Prologue to Conflict: The Crisis and Compromise of 1850* (1964). For an interpretation stressing the contingency of the South's commitment to the Union, consult William W. Freehling, *The Road to Disunion: Secessionists at Bay, 1776–1854* (1991).

Sectional Strife and the Third Party System

General studies of sectional conflict in the 1850s include Avery O. Craven, *The Growth of Southern Nationalism, 1848–1861* (1953); Roy F. Nichols, *The Disruption of American Democracy* (1948); and David M. Potter, *The Impending Crisis, 1848–1861* (1976). On the Fugitive Slave Act, consult Stanley W. Campbell, *The Slave Catchers* (1970). The best study of the politics of southern expansionism is Robert E. May, *The Southern Dream of a Caribbean Empire, 1854–1861* (1973). The crisis over Kansas is discussed in James A. Rawley, *Race and Politics: Bleeding Kansas and the Coming of the Civil War* (1969), and Gerald W. Wolff, *The Kansas-Nebraska Bill: Party, Section, and the Coming of the Civil War* (1977). For the Buchanan administration, see Kenneth M. Stampp, *America in 1857: A Nation on the Brink* (1990). On *Dred Scott,* see Don E. Fehrenbacher, *The Dred Scott Case: Its Significance in American Law and Politics* (1978). For a biography of Stephen A. Douglas, see Robert W. Johannsen, *Stephen A. Douglas* (1973). The best biography of John Brown is Stephen Oates, *To Purge This Land with Blood: A Biography of John Brown* (1970). On the early years of the Republican party, see the books cited in the Topic for Research.

Abraham Lincoln

Abraham Lincoln has inspired a host of biographies. Classic studies include James G. Randall, *Mr. Lincoln* (1957, distilled by Richard N. Current from Randall's four volume *Lincoln the President* with vol. 4 completed by Current); Carl Sandburg, *Abraham Lincoln: The Prairie Years* (1929); and Benjamin Thomas, *Abraham Lincoln: A Biography* (1952). For a stimulating set of essays, see Richard N. Current, *The Lincoln Nobody Knows* (1958). The most valuable book on Lincoln's formative political years is Don E. Fehrenbacher, *Prelude to Greatness: Lincoln in the 1850s* (1962). For more recent interpretations, see George B. Forgie, *Patricide and the House Divided* (1979), and Stephen Oates, *With Malice Toward None: A Life of Abraham Lincoln* (1977).

TIMELINE

1844	James Polk elected president
1845	Texas admitted to the Union as a slave state Slidell mission
1846	United States declares war on Mexico "Bear Flag Republic" proclaimed Zachary Taylor's victory at Monterrey Oregon treaty ratified Wilmot Proviso introduced in Congress
1847	Taylor's victory at Buena Vista Scott captures Mexico City
1848	Treaty of Guadalupe Hidalgo Taylor elected
1849	Taylor proposes immediate admission of California
1850	Compromise of 1850
1851	Christiana riot
1852	*Uncle Tom's Cabin* appears in book form Franklin Pierce elected president
1854	Kansas-Nebraska Act Republican party formed
1856	"Pottawatomie massacre" James Buchanan elected president
1857	*Dred Scott v. Sandford* overturns Missouri Compromise of 1820
1858	Buchanan backs Lecompton constitution Lincoln-Douglas debates
1859	John Brown's raid on Harpers Ferry
1860	Abraham Lincoln elected president

The Seventh Regiment Departing for the War, April 19, 1861 (detail)

Stunned by the massive demonstrations of support for the Union after Lincoln's call to arms, a New York woman wrote that "It seems as if we never were alive till now; never had a country till now." Thomas Nast evoked this spirit in this painting done in 1869.

CHAPTER 15 *Two Societies at War, 1861–1865*

For the political leaders of the South, the victory of Abraham Lincoln and the Republicans in the fateful election of 1860 presented a clear and immediate danger to the institution of slavery. They knew that Lincoln regarded slavery as morally wrong and that he had united northern society in opposition to the "Slave Power" and the extension of slavery into the territories. Moreover, unlike any preceding president, he owed the South not a single electoral vote. Soon, southern leaders were certain, he would appoint abolitionists and free blacks to federal jobs in the South and reopen the flow of abolitionist literature. The result would be disastrous, bloody waves of slave revolts. White southerners believed that no loyal American should have to fear such a cataclysm. They were convinced that the Constitution protected slavery. Moreover, in their view slavery was a bulwark of democracy: by guaranteeing equality and freedom for whites, it protected the highest values of the republic.

Many southerners swiftly concluded that they could protect slavery from the Republican threat only through secession. Southern states would leave the Union and establish their own nation, in accordance with John C. Calhoun's constitutional theory that sovereignty lay not with the American people as a whole but with collections of people acting through their state governments. If Lincoln would not recognize states' rights, the South would fight.

And so came the Civil War. Called the "War Between the States" by Confederates and the "War of the Rebellion" by Unionists, it tested the founding principles of the republic. It resolved once and for all the great dividing issue of slavery. And it cost as many lives as all of the nation's subsequent wars put together.

Choosing Sides, 1861

The two societies, South and North, were poised for confrontation in 1861. On the one hand, many southerners were convinced that in defending states' rights and slavery they were more true in their Americanism and stalwart in their support of republican ideals than the Republicans in the North. On the other hand, Lincoln and his party regarded secession as despicable and treasonous. There was only the slimmest chance that during the early months of 1861 the nation's politicians could emulate the architects of the great compromises of 1820, 1833, and 1850 and once again postpone the sectional confrontation.

The Secession Crisis

The movement toward secession was most rapid in South Carolina—the home of Calhoun and the state with the greatest concentration of slaves. The fire-eaters took the lead in organizing a convention to consider secession, which most of them had been calling for since 1850. On December 20, only six weeks after Lincoln's election, the convention unanimously enacted an ordinance dissolving "the union now subsisting between South Carolina and other States."

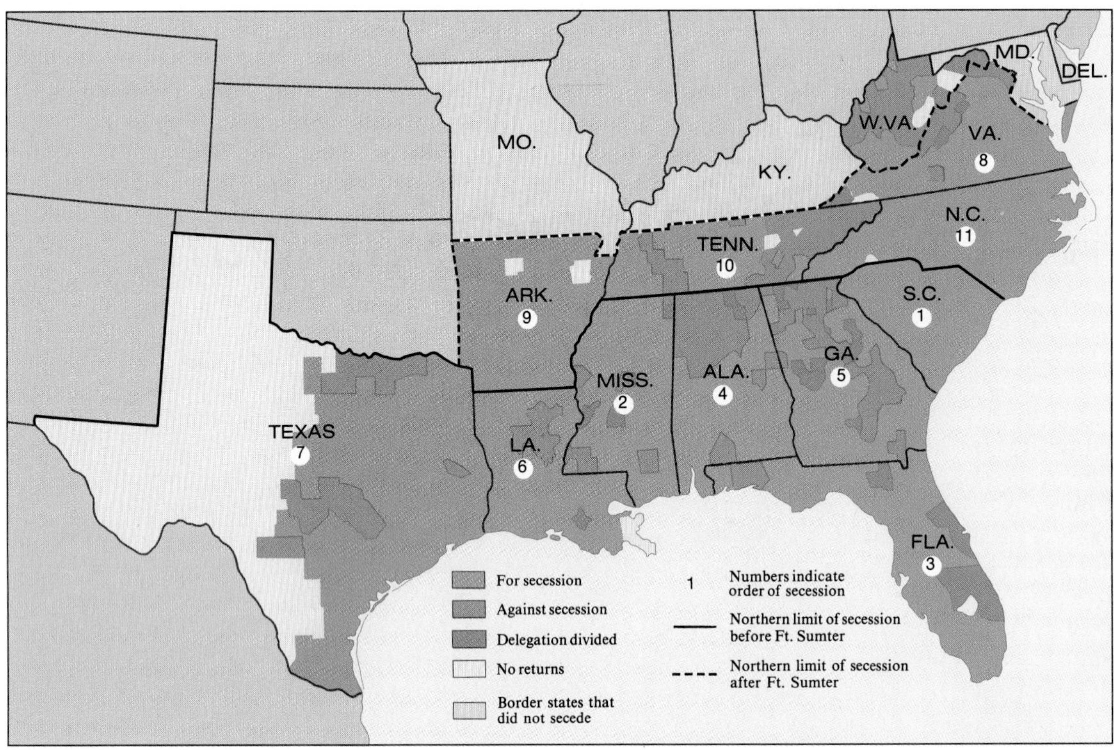

MAP 15.1

The Process of Secession

Comparing the order of secession with distribution of slaves on Map 13.1 (page 376), it is clear that states with the highest concentration of slaves led the movement to secede. The secession of the upper South followed the Confederate firing on Ft. Sumter. The map also shows how delegates to the secession conventions or special sessions of legislatures voted. Significant minorities in most states opposed secession.

During the next six weeks, fire-eaters in six other cotton states called conventions. They moved quickly, before southern unionists could mount an effective opposition. Meanwhile, vigilante groups and military companies organized, sometimes engaging in strong-arm intimidation of unionists, who usually preferred to wait and let Lincoln show his hand before seceding. In early January, in an atmosphere of public celebration, Mississippi enacted a secession ordinance. In less than a month, Florida, Alabama, Georgia, Louisiana, and Texas also left the Union. The jubilant secessionists proclaimed a new nation—the Confederate States of America. In early February commissioners from these states, meeting in Montgomery, Alabama, adopted a provisional constitution and named Jefferson Davis provisional president. Secession proceeded so briskly that all this had been done before James Buchanan left the White House.

Panic was less severe in the upper South, where concentrations of slaves were not as large. Nevertheless, secessionist fervor had been gathering momentum there from the time of Lincoln's election, and many political leaders in the eight upper South states (Arkansas, Delaware, Kentucky, Maryland, Missouri, North Carolina, Tennessee, and Virginia) defended the right of any state to secede. In January 1861 the Virginia and Tennessee legislatures pledged to resist any federal invasion of the seceded states. But they went no further. Upper South leaders proposed to seek federal guarantees for slavery in the states where it existed, hoping to relieve the anxieties of the seceding states and bring them back into the Union.

While the seceding states acted decisively, the Union government, still under control of the Democrats, floundered. President Buchanan did not support secession, but the southerners in his cabinet persuaded him that if he confronted the seceding states, he would only alienate southern Unionists and accelerate the secession drive. In his last message to Congress in December 1860, he declared secession illegal but said that the federal government lacked the authority to force a state to return to the Union. South Carolina responded quickly. It claimed that Buchanan's message implied recognition of its independence and demanded the surrender of Fort Sumter, a federal garrison in Charleston harbor. But even Buchanan was reluctant to turn over federal property; he decided to test cautiously the secessionists' resolve. In January 1861 he ordered an unarmed merchant ship to reinforce Fort Sumter. When South Carolinians fired on the ship as it entered the harbor, Buchanan backed off, declining to send the navy to escort the ship into the harbor.

The Crittenden Plan. As the South Carolina crisis worsened, Buchanan urged Congress to find a compromise. The proposal that received the most support was submitted by Senator John J. Crittenden of Kentucky, an aging follower of Henry Clay. Crittenden proposed amending the Constitution with a set of provisions that could never be changed. Congress would be prohibited from abolishing slavery in the states, and the Missouri Compromise line would be extended westward across the territories as far as the California border. While slavery would be barred north of the line, it would be recognized and protected south of the line, including in any territories "hereafter acquired."

After consulting with President-elect Lincoln, congressional Republicans rejected Crittenden's plan. Lincoln feared that extending the Missouri Compromise line would encourage the South to embark on an imperialist expansion of slavery into Mexico, the Caribbean, and Latin America. If adopted, Lincoln charged, Crittenden's plan would be "a perpetual covenant of war against every people, tribe, and State owning a foot of land between here and Tierra del Fuego." Lincoln was determined not to repudiate the Republicans' chief plank—free soil in the territories.

Lincoln Takes Command. In his inaugural address on March 4, 1861, Lincoln carefully balanced the possibility of reconciliation with his firm commitment to protect the Union. He promised to welcome back the seceded states after time had allowed passions to cool, and he repeated his support for the guarantee of slavery in states where it existed. But he continued to stand by free soil, offering no compromises on the future of slavery in the territories. Most important, he stated that secession was illegal and that acts of violence in support of secession constituted insurrection. He announced, equally clearly, that he intended to enforce federal law throughout the Union and—of particular relevance to Fort Sumter—to hold federal property in the seceded states. If force were necessary to preserve the Union, he promised to use it. The choice would be the South's—return to the Union or face war.

Lincoln had hoped to wait out the Fort Sumter crisis, but the fort urgently needed supplies. He was reluctant to appear aggressive, but he was unwilling to abandon the fort, fearing that his efforts to maintain the Union would lose credibility. Consequently, only a month after his inaugural, Lincoln dispatched an armed relief expedition and informed South Carolina of his intentions.

Jefferson Davis and his government received word of Lincoln's action on April 8. The next day they resolved to take the fort before Union reinforcements arrived. Believing that Lincoln's show of force would set the wavering southern states against the North and win foreign support for the Confederate cause, they welcomed Lincoln's move. Jefferson Davis ordered General P. G. T. Beauregard, the Confederate commander in Charleston, to take the fort—by force if necessary. When Major Robert Anderson refused to surrender, the Confederates opened fire. On April 14, after two days of bombardment that destroyed large portions of the fort but killed no one, Anderson surrendered. The next day, Lincoln called 75,000 state militiamen into federal service for ninety days. As he put it, they were needed to put down an insurrection "too powerful to be suppressed by the ordinary course of judicial proceedings." War had come.

In the North, Fort Sumter became a symbol of national unity and Major Anderson became a hero. Northern states responded enthusiastically to Lincoln's call to arms. Governor William Dennison of Ohio, when asked to provide thirteen regiments of volunteers, sent twenty. "The lion in us is thoroughly roused," he explained. Many northern Democrats were equally fervent. As Stephen Douglas explained just six weeks before his death: "There are only two sides to the question. Every man must be for the United States or against it. There can be no neutrals in this war, *only patriots—or traitors.*"

The Contest for the Upper South

After the fall of Fort Sumter, Lincoln hoped to hold as many of the eight states of the upper South as possible. If he could keep them from seceding, he might swiftly restore the Union. In the event of war, the upper South would be of great strategic value. The eight states accounted for two-thirds of the South's white population, more than three-fourths of its industrial production, and well over half of its food and fuel. They were home to many of the nation's best military leaders, including Colonel Robert E. Lee of Virginia, a career officer whom General-in-Chief Winfield Scott recommended to Lincoln as field commander of the new Union army. And they offered key geographic advantages. Kentucky, with its 500-mile border on the Ohio River, was essential to the movement of troops and supplies. Maryland was vital to national security because it surrounded the nation's capital on the north. It also contained the major port of Baltimore and adjoined the industrial state of Pennsylvania. Virginia was psychologically strategic as the home of Washington and Jefferson.

Virginia. Lincoln never had a chance to hold Virginia. His inaugural address, with its implied threat of invasion, had silenced Unionists in eastern Virginia. His call to arms prompted them to embrace secession. After the fall of Fort Sumter, William Poague, a former Unionist lawyer who quickly enlisted in a Virginia artillery unit, explained that "the North was the aggressor. The South resisted her invaders."

On April 17, Virginia's secession convention passed an ordinance of secession by a vote of 88 to 55—an almost direct reversal of the first vote taken earlier in April. The dissenting votes came mainly from the mountainous northwestern counties, where whites resented the power of the Tidewater planters and often looked more to Ohio and Pennsylvania for trade and leadership. On April 18, General Scott offered Robert E. Lee field command of the Union troops. Despite his description of himself as "one of those dull creatures that cannot see the good of secession," Lee not only declined the offer but resigned from the army. "Save in defense of my native state," Lee told Scott, "I never desire again to draw my sword." At the same time, Virginia's militia seized the federal armory and arsenal at Harpers Ferry and the Gosport navy yard at Newport. The upper South states of North Carolina, Tennessee, and Arkansas promptly joined Virginia in the Confederacy and sent their militias to that state's defense.

Western Virginia, Maryland, Kentucky, and Missouri. Lincoln moved aggressively to hold the rest of the upper South in the Union. In May he ordered General George B. McClellan, who had assembled a Union force in Ohio, to cross the Ohio River into Virginia. By June, McClellan's army had secured the route of the Baltimore and Ohio Railroad, which linked Washington with the Ohio River Valley. In July he established control of northwestern Virginia. In October the voters in fifty western Virginia counties overwhelmingly approved the creation of a new state. In 1863, West Virginia was admitted to the Union.

In Maryland southern sympathizers were quite militant, but Lincoln made it clear he would use force to keep the state in the Union. Less than a week after Fort Sumter fell, a pro-Confederate mob attacked Massachusetts troops marching between railroad stations in Baltimore and caused the war's first combat deaths—four soldiers and twelve civilians. A few days later Maryland secessionists destroyed railroad bridges and telegraph lines. Without delay Lincoln stationed Union troops along the state's railroad lines and imprisoned many suspected secessionists, including Baltimore's police chief and members of the state legislature. He released them only in November 1861, after the Union party had won a decisive victory in state elections.

In Kentucky secessionist and Unionist sentiments were evenly balanced, and Lincoln at first moved cautiously, trying to avoid pushing it into the Confederacy. He asserted his right to send troops into the state, but he took no immediate military action. In August, after Unionists had won control of the state legislature, he took steps to shut off Kentucky's thriving export of horses, mules, whiskey, and foodstuffs to the lower South and to the Confederate troops on its borders. Then the Confederacy played into Lincoln's hands by moving troops into Kentucky, seizing Columbus and Bowling Green. Outraged by this aggression, the Kentucky legislature called on the federal government to protect it from invasion. In September, Union troops—Illinois volunteers under the command of the relatively unknown brigadier general Ulysses S. Grant—crossed the Ohio River to drive out the Confederates. Thus the Confederates inadvertently helped keep Kentucky in the Union. Over the course of the war, most—about three-fifths—of the white Kentuckians who took up arms did so for the Union.

In Missouri, Lincoln moved promptly to control communications and trade on the upper Mississippi and Missouri rivers. By July a small Union force stationed in St. Louis, composed largely of regiments organized by the city's German-American community, had defeated Confederate sympathizers commanded by Governor Claiborne Jackson. Confederate guerrilla bands led by William Quantrill and Jesse and Frank James—dubbed "bushwhackers" (ambushers) by Unionists—waged campaigns throughout the war. But the Union maintained control of the state, and most Missouri men who fought joined the Union armies—80,000 whites and 8,000 blacks. Of the eight states of the upper South Lincoln had held four (including Delaware) and a portion of a fifth (western Virginia) in the Union.

War Aims and Resources, North and South

Setting Out War Aims. On July 4, 1861, Lincoln made his first major statement of war aims to a special session of Congress: the war was a noble crusade in which the future of democracy throughout the world would be determined. The issue of the war was "whether a constitutional republic, or a democracy—a government of the people, by the same people—can or cannot maintain its territorial integrity against its domestic foes." The war would test "whether discontented individuals, few in number, can arbitrarily break up their government and thus practically put an end to free government upon the face of the earth." Only by crushing the rebellion would the nation survive.

Lincoln did not foresee in 1861 how difficult it would be to defeat the rebellion. The Union had to break the will of the southern people, not just smash Confederate armies. To win, the Union had to fight a *total war*—a war against an entire society, not just its armies. But Lincoln's conception of the war aims, well-developed even at the war's outset, advanced the great task. His lofty statements of what was at stake helped rally the people of the Union to make deep and sustained commitments to the war. Like Lincoln, they came to perceive the war as a democratic crusade against southern society.

Confederate leaders also called on their people to fight for democracy. At his inauguration in February 1861, Jefferson Davis identified the Confederate cause with the principles of the American Revolution. He claimed that southerners were fighting, just as their grandfathers had done, against tyranny and on behalf of the "sacred right of self-government." A month later, shortly after his election as vice-president of the Confederacy, Alexander Stephens of Georgia defined more explicitly what Confederate democracy meant. The Confederacy's "cornerstone rests upon the great truth that the Negro is not equal to the white man, that slavery—subordination to the superior race—is his natural or normal condition." Slavery made democracy for whites possible, he argued, and the alternative to slavery for blacks was serfdom—dependence on economic elites—for whites.

Davis and other Confederate leaders stressed that their strategy for protecting democracy was defensive: to defend the independence of the Confederacy. As Davis put it in his inaugural, the Confederacy sought "no conquest, no aggrandizement, no concession of any kind from the states with which we were lately confederated; all we ask is to be let alone." This strategy gave Confederate leaders a major advantage. Although they might dream about a battlefield victory that would force formal recognition, they were willing to settle simply for the Union's abandoning the fight and implicitly accepting Confederate independence. If they could make the cost of the war high enough to induce the North to quit, their cause would be victorious. A draw on the battlefield would be good enough.

Resources, Human and Material. The Union entered the war with some obvious advantages. Lincoln's success in securing the border slave states gave the Union nearly total control over the Ohio River. With more than two-thirds of the American people, about two-thirds of the nation's railroad mileage, and very nearly 90 percent of American industrial output, the North's economy was far superior to the South's (see Figure

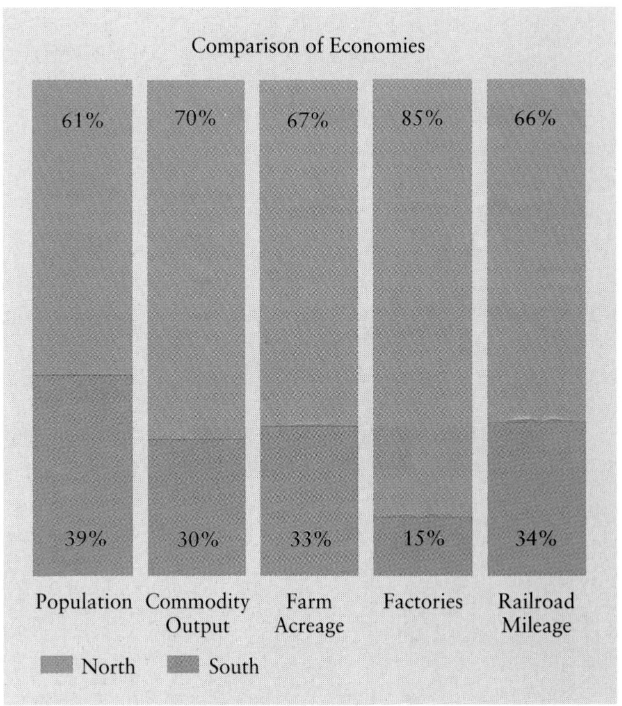

FIGURE 15.1

Economies, North and South, 1860

The economic advantages of the North were even greater than this chart suggests because the population figures included slaves, commodity output was dominated by farm goods, farm acreage included unimproved acres (greater in the South), and southern factories were, on the average, much smaller than northern factories.

Source: Stanley Engerman, "The Economic Impact of the Civil War," in Robert W. Fogel and Stanley L. Engerman, The Reinterpretation of American Economic History (New York: Harper & Row, 1971), 371; U.S. Census data.

15.1). The North produced all goods in larger quantities and had an especially great advantage in the manufacture of cannon and rifles because of earlier advances in mass-production technology.

But the Confederate's position was not as weak as these figures might suggest. Virginia, North Carolina, and Tennessee had substantial industrial capacity. Richmond, with its Tredegar Iron Works, was already an important industrial center, and in 1861 the Confederacy transported to Richmond the gun-making machinery captured at the U.S. armory at Harpers Ferry. With nine million people, the Confederacy could mobilize enormous armies. And, while one-third of the number were slaves, their masters expected to keep them in the fields, producing food for the armies and cotton for export. Indeed, this agricultural capacity of the South was crucial. The Confederacy was self-sufficient in food production and dominated world production of cotton—by far America's most lucrative export commodity. "King Cotton" could provide revenue to purchase the clothes, boots,

Industrial Richmond

Located at the falls of the James River, Richmond had flour mills, tobacco factories, railroad and port facilities, and, most important, a profitable and substantial iron industry. In 1861, the Tredegar Iron Works, employing nearly 1,000 workers, was the only facility in the South that could produce large machinery and heavy weaponry.

blankets, and weapons that the Confederacy needed but could not produce. Used as a weapon of diplomacy, cotton might induce the British, who depended on imports of southern cotton to supply their textile and clothing factories, to recognize the independence of the Confederacy and supply it with military and economic aid.

The Confederacy thus had sufficient resources to wage an extended and punishing war. It had other assets as well, notably a strong military tradition and a healthy supply of trained military officers. Moreover, it enjoyed important tactical advantages. It would be fighting largely on familiar terrain among local supporters. And even though its railroad system was inferior to the North's, it could move troops and supplies rapidly by interior lines within a defensive perimeter extending from Virginia to Texas. Its long, irregular coastline made it difficult to blockade. Finally, with a defensive stance the South could take full advantage of a new weapon—the rifle-musket. For the first time in military history, well-entrenched riflemen could repulse cavalry. Britain's Enfield rifles, together with 100,000 captured Union rifles and the production of the Richmond armory, enabled the Confederacy to provide each of its infantrymen with a modern weapon by 1863.

Thus the odds did not necessarily favor the Union, despite its superior resources. The citizens of the Union would have to decide to fight a total war and then learn how to fight such a war, both on the battlefield and the homefront. The decision and learning was painful and slow in coming. As late as November of 1864 the outcome could have gone either way.

War Machines, North and South

In mobilizing their peoples for war, Abraham Lincoln and Jefferson Davis faced similar challenges: to establish their powers as commander-in-chief, to recruit troops for their great armies, to suppress dissent, and to pay the enormous costs of the conflict. Lincoln, aided by a strong party and a talented cabinet, quickly consolidated his power and organized a strong central government. Davis was less successful, but his task was more formidable. He had to fight a war while leading eleven states that were deeply suspicious of centralized government.

NEW TECHNOLOGY *The Rifle-Musket*

In 1855, U.S. Secretary of War Jefferson Davis ordered an end to the production of the smooth-bore musket and began equipping American soldiers with rifle-muskets. Most Union infantrymen used the Springfield rifle, a rifle-musket first manufactured by the U.S. armory at Springfield, Massachusetts. Confederate soldiers often used the Enfield rifle, a similar weapon manufactured in England. These new weapons accounted for most of the casualties of the war.

Hunting rifles dating back to the eighteenth century had tapered barrels that were *rifled*—lined with spiral grooves—to give the bullet greater speed and accuracy. Unlike the smooth barrels of muskets, however, the grooved rifle barrel quickly accumulated gunpowder and required frequent cleaning, which was inconvenient and dangerous in combat.

In the early 1850s, James S. Burton, an American mechanic working at the Harpers Ferry Armory, developed a new form of bullet based on the innovations of Captain Claude E. Minie of the French army. Burton's cylindro-conoidal bullet, radically different from the round bullets of the day, was cast with a cavity at its base. When the rifle hammer exploded powder at the base of the barrel, hot gas expanded this cavity and forced the bullet to engage the grooves of the rifling as it sped through the barrel. The bullet thus cleaned the grooves with each shot.

For the first time infantrymen could be efficient, effective riflemen. Rifle-muskets built to fire the new bullets could hit targets half a mile away, whereas the maximum range of a musket was barely 250 yards. Firing two shots a minute, a veteran with a rifle-musket killed reliably at 300 yards; his aim with a musket was assured only at 100 yards or less.

The new gun was called a rifle-musket, rather than a rifle, because it retained certain musket characteristics. It fired a single shot, was loaded through the muzzle, and had a long barrel, usually 40 inches. Like the musket, the rifle-musket was still cumbersome to load. Before aiming and firing, a soldier had to take out a paper-wrapped cartridge of gunpowder, rip open the cartridge with his teeth, pour the powder down the barrel, insert the bullet into the barrel, jam the bullet and powder down with a ramrod, half-cock the hammer, insert a percussion cap, and finally, cock the hammer. Some soldiers could do all this lying on their backs, but most, in order to fire two or three times a minute, had to load from a kneeling or standing position, often exposing themselves to enemy fire. Clearly, soldiers could not reload and fire on the run.

The rifle-musket was not a modern rifle; it was not breech-loading and it did not fire multiple rounds. Although modern rifles were refined during the war and adopted in limited quantities, both sides preferred to stay with the familiar and proven rifle-musket.

The rifle-musket revolutionized warfare and military strategy. The greater range and accuracy and relatively quick reloading of the rifle-musket enormously strengthened defensive forces. Defenders could fire on attackers almost continually and, if the defenders were ensconced in well-protected positions with a broad field of vision—like the Union forces on Cemetery Hill—they could usually keep attackers from getting close enough for hand-to-hand combat. (Bayonets accounted for less than 1 percent of all wounds in the Civil War.) If attacking forces did manage to break through defensive lines, they were usually so weakened that they had to retreat or surrender in the face of counterattacks. Elaborate entrenchments strengthened defensive positions even more. Used by both sides in almost every battle by 1863, these trenches, together with the rifle-musket, enabled infantrymen to turn back assaults by forces three to four times their size.

Infantry commanders, however, were slow to change the tactics of assault they had inherited from the days of the musket and bayonet. They tried flanking maneuvers where possible; relied more heavily on "skirmishers," whose traditional role had been to explore the enemy's position; and experimented with deceptive rushing tactics. But to use these tactics extensively required more than the voice and visual communication to which the Civil War armies were limited. Consequently, commanders still attacked in dense, close-order formations, with thousands of infantrymen, assaulting enemy positions in successive waves. Officers tried to keep their men perfectly parallel to concentrate their fire and hit the enemy line with maximum shock.

In battle after battle, charging infantrymen went down like harvested wheat. Many units in both armies suffered losses of 40 to 80 percent in a single engagement. By 1863 the extraordinary number of casualties had become psychologically and politically intolerable. The terrible losses at Gettysburg finally forced a reform of military tactics. Commanders on both sides began to try to avoid situations that required frontal assaults and to force or induce enemy troops to leave defensive positions. The trench warfare that developed around Petersburg, Virginia, in the last weeks of the Civil War presaged the trenches of World War I and the further strengthening of defensive positions by true rifles, automatic rifles, and machine guns.

Union Soldiers Camped Near Cumberland Landing, 1862
The Civil War armies required encampments that were huge and intricate. The logistical demands on the Union armies were great because they generally fought in enemy territory and maintained long supply lines. The rule of thumb was that a Union army of 100,000 men consumed 600 tons of supplies each day and required 2,500 supply wagons and at least 35,000 animals.

Mobilizing Armies

At first both Abraham Lincoln and Jefferson Davis mobilized troops by calling for volunteers. But the initial surge of enlistments fell off in 1862, as Americans saw the realities of war—heavy losses to disease and dreadful battle carnage. Thus both presidents faced the necessity of a draft.

The Confederacy, with its relative shortage of military manpower, was the first to act. In April 1862, after the defeat at Shiloh (see page 458), the Confederate Congress imposed the first draft in American history. One law extended all enlistments for the duration of the war; another made all able-bodied men between eighteen and thirty-five liable to serve in the Confederate army for three years. In September a defeat at Antietam prompted the Congress to raise the upper age limit to forty-five. The same law exempted one white man—planter or overseer—for each twenty slaves. Drafted men could hire substitutes, and by 1863 the price for a substitute was $300 in gold—about three times the annual wage of a skilled worker in Richmond. (The substitute law was repealed in 1864.) Impoverished young farmers in the South angrily complained that it was "a rich man's war and a poor man's fight." Conscription proved unenforceable in some parts of the South, and nearly half the eligible non-volunteers never served.

By midsummer of 1862, the Union undertook a kind of quasi-draft. The Militia Act of 1862 used the draft as a threat. When Abraham Lincoln's secretary of state, Edwin M. Stanton, announced that any state that failed to meet its quota of volunteers would be subject to the draft, enough volunteers came forward to satisfy Union needs for a year. In 1863, as the scale of hostilities intensified, Congress passed the Enrollment Act, which subjected to the draft all able-bodied male citizens and aliens applying for naturalization, aged twenty to forty-five. Once again, the law was designed to encourage volunteers. Each congressional district was assigned a quota, based on its population, which it could meet with either conscripts or volunteers. Districts used cash bounties to compete for volunteers—sometimes bidding against one another to entice recruits. The federal government also offered bounties for enlistment, and it permitted men to avoid the draft by providing a substitute or paying a $300 commutation, or exemption, fee. The 46,000 draftees and 118,000 substitutes who enlisted under the act amounted to only about 10 percent of the Union soldiers. However, the bounties stimulated the voluntary enlistment or reenlistment of almost a million men.

Meanwhile, the Lincoln administration took steps to suppress any dissent that might impede mobilization. In September 1862, Lincoln proclaimed that during the "insurrection" all persons who discouraged enlistment, resisted the draft, or were guilty of any disloyal practice were subject to martial law. He did this so they would be tried by military courts rather than local juries. He suspended normal constitutional guarantees, such as the writ of *habeas corpus* (designed to protect people from arbitrary arrest and detention). By war's end his administration had imprisoned nearly 15,000 individuals, mostly in the border states, where pro-Confederate political movements were strongest.

The Draft Riots. Lincoln faced his most violent internal challenge of the war after the passage of the Enrollment Act of 1863. Conscription and the high commutation fee—at least half of a worker's annual income—generated resentment among men who were unenthusiastic about the war but could not afford to buy their way out. Democratic opponents of Lincoln exploited this resentment in urban working-class districts by making racist appeals to recent immigrants and wage earners. These Democrats argued that Lincoln was drafting poor whites in order to free the slaves and flood the cities with black workers. Thus the draft became a focal point for preexisting hostility to Republicans and African-Americans.

In July 1863 hostility to the draft spilled on to the streets. After draftees' names were announced in New York City, ferocious antidraft rioting broke out among immigrant Irish workers. Youths burned the draft office, sacked the homes of some important Republicans, assaulted police, and lynched at least a dozen African-Americans. Lincoln reacted with an iron fist. He rushed in Union troops. The police and soldiers of the Army of the Potomac, who had faced the Confederates at Gettysburg two weeks earlier, killed more than a hundred rioters and suppressed the urban insurrection.

President Davis was never able to match this degree of coercion. Most Confederate leaders, such as Governors Joseph Brown of Georgia and Zebulon Vance of North Carolina, had powerful states' rights convictions and wanted to avoid creating a federal government as

Draft Riots in New York City

The rioters went so far as to burn down a black orphanage, the Colored Orphan Asylum, on Fifth Avenue. The riots—perhaps the worst in all of U.S. history—demonstrated that powerful issues of class and race were not far from the surface of American politics. (But business-class denunciation of the riots and of Peace Democrats strengthened Lincoln's hand.)

centralized and powerful as the one they had left. Because the Confederate constitution vested sovereignty in the individual states, state governors could thwart the president's will. Brown and Vance simply ignored Davis's first draft call in early 1862. In parts of the South state judges issued writs of habeas corpus ordering the Confederate government to release draftees. The Confederate Congress was reluctant to impose its authority on the state courts; it granted Davis the authority to suspend the writ of habeas corpus, and thereby enforce conscription, for only two brief periods totaling sixteen months.

Nevertheless, Davis's failure to organize an effective draft did not cripple the Confederacy. About four-fifths of the Confederate men eligible for the draft actually served; by contrast, only one-half of the eligible Union men served. Moreover, the Davis government was able to keep armies in the field by requiring volunteers to extend their enlistments. But as the scale of the fighting grew, as the casualties mounted, and as the Union gained control of more Confederate territory, the manpower crisis became severe. By 1864, Confederate generals could not rotate their soldiers to rest areas for relief.

Mobilizing Money

The financial requirements of fighting a total war were enormous. In the Union war costs drove up government spending from less than 2 percent of the gross national product to an average of 15 percent, close to the 20 percent level reached in the early 1990s. To finance these expenditures, the Republicans had to go beyond their 1860 economic platform; they had to build the kind of revenue system necessary to establish a powerful modern state. The financial demands on the Confederacy were even greater, but it abstained from employing any revenue machinery that required centralized government coercion.

Taxes, almost all of them new, financed about 20 percent of Union war costs. For the first time the government levied an income tax—a graduated tax reaching a maximum rate of 10 percent. The Union placed excise taxes on virtually all consumer goods, license taxes on a wide variety of activities (including every profession except the ministry), special taxes on corporations, stamp taxes on legal documents, and taxes on inheritances. Each wartime Congress also raised the tariffs on foreign goods, doubling the average tariff rate by the end of the war.

The Union government financed most—about two-thirds—of the war by running deficits and borrowing money through the sale of bonds by the U.S. Treasury. Secretary of the Treasury Salmon P. Chase had no prior financial experience, but he learned quickly from Jay Cooke, a Philadelphia banker. Chase and Cooke adopted four key policies. First, they made interest on the bonds payable in gold, making them financially attractive. Second, they kept income tax rates low, thereby winning support among the wealthy for the bond program. Third, they pioneered in techniques for marketing bonds. Although banks and wealthy people in America and Britain bought most of the bonds, Cooke's newspaper advertisements and his 2,500 subagents persuaded nearly a million northerners—a fourth of all ordinary families—to buy them too. Working through a private financier, the Lincoln administration innovated in developing the propaganda techniques that would become essential to funding all the major wars in the twentieth century.

Fourth, Chase led in creating a national banking system—an important element of every modern centralized government. The National Banking acts of 1863 and 1864 established this system to induce bankers to purchase bonds. The federal government offered state-chartered banks national charters, allowing them to issue national banknotes. The national banks could acquire the notes only with U.S. bonds, which the national banks were required to buy with at least one-third of their capital. But because the national banks were more heavily regulated, state banks failed to rush into the new system. Consequently, in 1865 the federal government placed a crippling tax on the notes of state banks. By the end of 1865 the number of national banks had tripled, and their purchases of U.S. bonds had increased nearly four times.

The Union also financed the war by issuing paper money backed by faith in the government rather than by specie. In February 1862, Congress passed the Legal Tender Act, authorizing the issue of $150 million of Treasury notes, which became known as *greenbacks*. Congress required the public to accept these notes as legal tender. Only tariff duties and interest on the national debt still had to be paid in gold or silver coins. This paper money, nearly $500 million by the end of the war, funded only 13 percent of the war's cost. If the Union government had been weaker—less able to tax or induce Americans and Europeans to loan it money—it would have had to rely more heavily on the creation of money.

In short, the Union government built the financial foundations of a modern industrial nation-state. Imposing broad-based taxes, borrowing from the middle class as well as the wealthy, and creating a functional money supply mobilized huge sums for the Union cause. In the process, the Union's program of public finance created ties of mutual dependency between the war effort and the millions of Americans who had paid taxes, loaned their savings, and accepted paper money.

In sharp contrast with the Union, the Confederacy covered less than 5 percent of its expenditures through taxation. The Confederate Congress fiercely opposed taxes on cotton exports or on the property of planters. It did pass a modest property tax in 1861 but exempted slaves and left its collection to the states. Only one state, South Carolina, imposed the tax; the other states generally borrowed the money or paid the Confederacy with state-issued IOU's. In 1863 the Congress passed a more comprehensive tax law, but it still exempted property in slaves. As a result, the tax burden fell primarily on middle-class citizens and non-slaveholding small farmers, who commonly refused to pay, especially when Confederate armies were far away. An 1864 revision that included a 5 percent property tax on slaves came too late to raise much revenue or restore popular faith in the fairness of the Confederate tax system.

The Confederacy was able to borrow enough money for only 35 percent of its war effort. Although wealthy planters had enough capital to fund a relatively large part of the war, most rebuffed pleas that they buy Confederate bonds by pledging cotton revenues. At first they were unwilling to accept low interest rates; later they began to doubt that the Confederacy would prevail. Europeans came to share those doubts, and the only major loan to the Confederacy came from a French banking house in 1863.

And so the Confederacy was forced to finance about 60 percent of its expenses with unbacked paper money. This created a new problem—soaring inflation, compounded by a flood of counterfeit copies of the poorly designed and badly printed Confederate notes. The great battles and sieges created growing numbers of refugees, and this added to inflationary pressures by reducing the food supply and further escalating food prices. In the early spring of 1863 a wave of riots broke out in southern cities. In more than a dozen towns, women ransacked shops and supply depots for food. In Richmond several hundred women broke into bakeries, crying: "Our children are starving while the rich roll in wealth."

The inflation worsened in 1863, as an inflationary psychology—a panic—took hold. Southerners became convinced that inflation would accelerate, and they rushed to spend their depreciating paper money before it became even less valuable, producing run-away inflation—the only such episode since the Revolutionary War. By the spring of 1865 prices had risen to ninety-two times their 1861 level. A South Carolina judge wrote that "You take your money to the market in the market basket, and bring home what you buy in your pocketbook."

The run-away inflation severely hampered Confederate mobilization. The orderly supply of armies became impossible when farmers refused to accept Confederate money. Confederate supply officers then tried to confiscate what they needed, leaving behind worthless IOU's. Some cavalry units simply took what they needed without even pretending to pay. Ironically, partly because it was so fearful of taxation, the Confederacy was forced to resort to great violations of property rights in order to sustain the war effort.

The Union and Confederate Economic Programs

Lincoln mobilized men by introducing conscription, used force to suppress war resistance, and taxed the people of the North at unprecedented rates. But economic reforms were also needed, both to increase the effectiveness of wartime organization and to win the support of those who voted, paid taxes, and fought. Consequently, Lincoln and the Republican leadership enacted virtually the entire economic program they had inherited from Henry Clay and the Whigs.

The many Republicans who had begun their political careers as Whigs had been waiting more than twenty years for this opportunity. They faced the continued opposition of northern Democrats, but the war had eliminated almost all the southern Democrats from Congress while northern Democrats, who had become Republicans, relaxed their resistance to national banking and protective tariffs. Most fundamentally, the Republicans won new support from workers and small farmers, arguing that the Republican economic program would help prevent a return to the depression conditions of the late 1850s. And, by celebrating economic opportunity in the North and focusing on the threat that slavery posed to opportunity, the Republicans diverted attention from the failures and limitations of American industrialization. Finally, the southern challenge to northern society helped convince many farmers and workers to set aside their doubts about the Whig platform and support the nationalizing economic program of the Republican party and the business class in order to win the war.

Each element of the Republican economic program won a substantial following. The tariff received support from manufacturers and from those laborers and farmers who feared cheap foreign labor. Capitalists, large and small, applauded the national banking system. Republican land policy, designed to accelerate free-soil settlement, won the enthusiastic support of almost all farmers. In 1862, Congress passed the Homestead Act, giving heads of families or individuals twenty-one or older the right to 160 acres of public land after five years of residence and improvement. Although the act contained many loopholes, allowing speculators to put together large blocks of land, numerous small farmers also acquired land. In 1862, Lincoln followed through on the Republican promise to build transcontinental railroads. Congress chartered the Union Pacific and Central Pacific railways and subsidized them lavishly. It gave the railroads twenty sections (20 square miles) of federal land in alternate plots for every mile of track the railroads put down. Congress provided a similar charter and subsidy to the Northern Pacific in 1864.

The Confederate government, however, undertook almost no restructuring of national economic life. True to their states' rights philosophy, the Confederacy left much governmental intervention in the economy in the hands of the state governments operating under their police powers. When the Davis administration did intervene, it did so out of desperation over the inadequacy of the economy for fighting a total war. Consequently, the Confederacy adopted programs that were extremely coercive. With an economy that was less developed than that of the North, the Confederacy took extraordinary measures: it built and operated its own shipyards, armories, foundries, and textile mills; it commandeered food and scarce raw materials such as coal, iron, copper, nitre, and lead; it requisitioned slaves; and it exercised direct control over foreign trade. The unprecedented nature of these encroachments was all the more resented as the war wore on, because the Confederate government failed to explain its wartime needs or cope with misery on the homefront.

Rather than undertaking reforms designed to maintain loyalty and support through economic self-interest, the Confederate leadership simply relied on a defense of slavery and racial solidarity. Jefferson Davis told whites that they were fighting to be able to expand westward into new territories. Without expansion, he said, "an overgrown black population" would "crowd upon our soil . . . until there will not be room in the country for whites and blacks to subsist in." Containment would destroy slavery "and reduce the whites to the degraded position of the African race."

The Home Front: Civilian Support for the War

In both the Confederacy and the Union, civilians made enormous contributions to the war effort. No civilian effort was more important than relieving the suffering on the battlefield.

The Sanitary Commission. In the North the most important voluntary agency was the United States Sanitary Commission, established in April 1861 by prominent New Yorkers and endorsed by Lincoln two months later. Its task was to provide medical services and prevent a repeat of the debacle of the Crimean War (1854–1856), in which disease accounted for over three-fourths of the British dead. Through its network

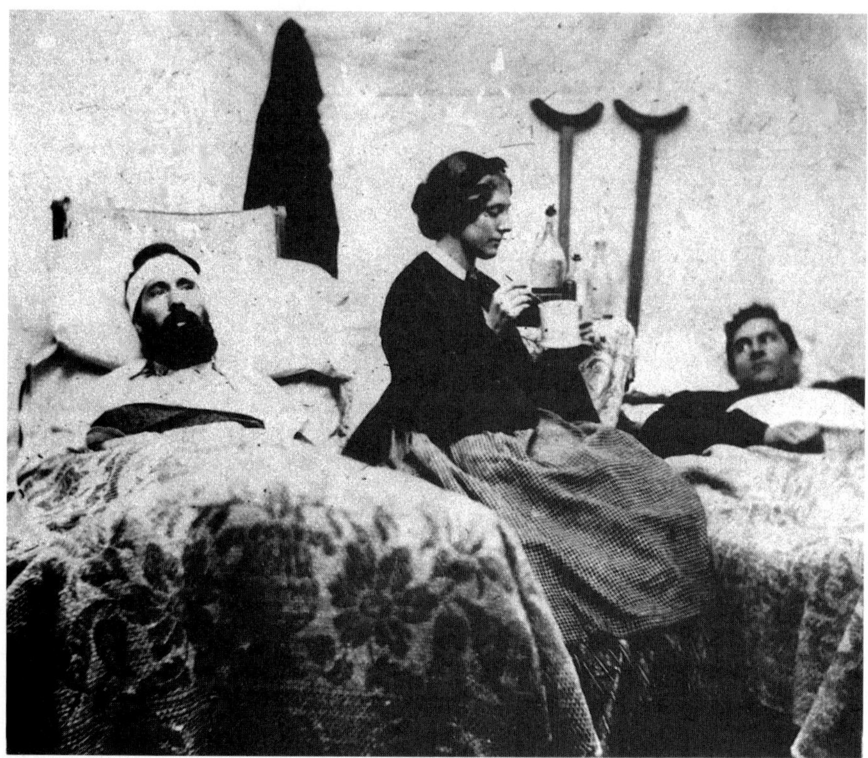

Hospital Nursing

Most Civil War nurses served as unpaid volunteers and spent most of their time cooking and cleaning for their patients. A sense of calm prevailed in this Union hospital in Nashville, well removed from the battle field. In contrast, conditions at field hospitals were chaotic under the pressure of heavy casualties and shifting battle sites.

of 7,000 local auxiliaries, the Sanitary Commission gathered supplies; distributed clothing, food, and medicine to the army; improved the sanitary standards of camp life; recruited battlefield nurses; and recruited doctors for the Union Army Medical Bureau, which came to be led by an innovative surgeon general, William A. Hammond. He professionalized the bureau, increasing the number of surgeons, building more hospitals, organizing a trained ambulance corps, and integrating the services of the Sanitary Commission into the war effort.

The results of all this organized medical effort were not readily visible. Diseases—primarily dysentery, typhoid, and malaria, but also childhood diseases like mumps and measles, to which many rural men had developed no immunity—killed twice as many Union soldiers (about 250,000) as combat did. Surgeons inadvertently took more lives by spreading infection than they saved. Nurses could do little more for the wounded than dress their wounds and comfort them with reminders of home. Still, the incidence of mortality from disease and wounds was substantially lower than in other major nineteenth-century wars, partly because of the attention given to sanitation and the quality of food.

The health care available to Union troops surpassed that in the Confederacy. Great numbers of southern women volunteered as nurses, but the Confederate health care and hospital system remained disorganized. Thousands of Confederate soldiers suffered from scurvy because of the lack of Vitamin C in their diets, and they died from camp diseases at even higher rates than did Union soldiers.

Women in the War Effort. Most of the Sanitary Commission nurses and workers were women. Organized by Dorothea Dix, the first woman to receive a major federal appointment—as Superintendent of Female Nurses—the nurses overcame prejudice against women treating men and opened a new occupation to women. Nurse Clara Barton, who later founded the American Red Cross, recalled that "At the war's end, woman was at least fifty years in advance of the normal position which continued peace would have assigned her." Barton may have been overoptimistic. But the war effort did open the way for middle-class women to participate not only in nursing but also in government, as women either replaced male clerks who went to war or took up new jobs in the expanding bureaucracies. This was true not only in the North but also in the South, where women staffed the efficient Confederate postal service.

While some women assumed new kinds of jobs, far more women, in both the North and the South, dramatically increased their responsibilities in their own  households, on their farms, in schools, and in textile, clothing, and shoe factories. They made possible mobilization in both the Union and the Confederacy, substituting their labor for that of men. On plantations, some women took over the management of slaves and production. On small farms in both the South and North, women worked with far greater intensity and effort than they had before the war, taking on chores that men had done. Some farm women, like Sarah Beaulieu, not only performed demanding chores but assumed jobs outside the home to make ends meet.

Military Deadlock, 1861–1863

Between 1861 and 1863 the Lincoln administration created a complex war machine and a powerful structure of command and production. Northern government, industry, and finance capital worked in an integrated manner, making the North's advantages of population and material resources available to the Union army. But the Union had not yet fully resolved to fight a total war against southern society. The Confederacy, successfully prosecuting its limited, defensive war, forced the Union into a deadlock on the battlefield.

Early Stalemate, 1861–1862

The First Battle of Bull Run. At the war's beginning, Lincoln rejected the military strategy proposed by his general-in-chief, Winfield Scott, who was a Virginia Unionist. This strategy, dubbed the "anaconda" (a large, constricting snake) plan by its opponents, involved blockading the South on all sides from the sea and the Mississippi River, and then gradually squeezing the Confederacy into submission through psychological pressure and economic sanctions. Instead, Lincoln chose a more aggressive beginning—a swift assault on P. G. T. Beauregard's Confederate force of over 20,000 based at Manassas, a major rail junction in Virginia only 30 miles southwest of Washington. Lincoln, along with many Union commanders with Mexican War experience, believed in vigorous offensives; he recognized that northern public opinion called for a strike toward Richmond, the Confederate capital; and he hoped an early Union victory would help discredit the secessionists. Consequently, in mid-July 1861, Lincoln sent Union General Irvin McDowell with an army of more than 30,000 to attack Beauregard's army.

Northern newspapers and southern spies advertised the advance of McDowell's army, so Beauregard had plenty of time to establish his army south of Bull Run, a small stream north of Manassas. He also brought reinforcements by rail from the Shenandoah Valley, thus seizing the advantage provided by having interior lines.

AMERICAN VOICES

The Union Home Front, 1865 *Sarah Beaulieu*

These selections are from a diary that was begun in the bleak Wisconsin winter of 1865 by a farm woman, Sarah Beaulieu (1843–1921). With the adult men of the family at war, Sarah, her sister-in-law Emma, and her mother were left to run a marginal farm in Morrison. Her favorite brother had been killed in July outside Atlanta, her father had been captured in the same battle and would die of starvation in a Confederate prison, and her brother "Bony" would be severely wounded and become addicted to cocaine as a consequence of his wounds.

January 14

Cleaned as usual. Ma went to the P.O. to get a letter from Brother Bony [Napoleon Bonaparte Beaulieu] which was very welcome, he being in the army, and we being very anxious about him.

February 10

Passed this day rather dilatory little caring whether I moved or not. I have almost come to the conclusion that this war is never coming to an end.

February 13

Arose very early. About ten A.M. Bony took his departure, left Emma [Bony's wife] and I very lonely. He having to join his regt. at Cairo, Ill. having been home on a thirty day furlough.

March 27

Did our usual work. In the afternoon yoked up the oxen and drawed logs for firewood then went to sugar bush with Mother and brought down some sap on the little sleigh and had a queer time driving oxen.

March 28

Did the washing and in the afternoon had a sugaring off. Ate all the warm sugar I wanted for once this year.

Sarah Beaulieu

In August 1865 Sarah Beaulieu married a returning Union veteran and the next year they had their first child, also pictured here. They named their son after her brother who had been killed in the war.

March 30

Ironed the clothes and gathered sap in the evening. . . .

March 31

Moved about twenty bushels of potatoes with Ma's help and put them in the cellar. . . .

April 3

Emma and myself carried in fifty bushels of turnips out of the pit. We did not think it was so hard a job until after we got at it. . . .

April 5

Passed this day in the bush boiling sap. Did not do anything of importance. In the afternoon I went home and felt very bad. Went to bed early.

April 13

Prepared to go to the Bay and pass examinations. If there is anything I dislike it is to have a man ask questions and be obliged to answer them in order to get that little paper licensing one to teach school.

April 14

Feel very tired having walked fourteen miles and at last arrived at my place of destination [Green Bay]. . . .

April 16

Went to the Methodist Church in the forenoon. Every article was draped in mourning. The assassination of our president has cast a gloom over everyone. Went to the Presbyterian Church in the evening.

April 25

Commenced school, had only eight scholars. Passed the day in teaching those little minds in the right direction of their books.

April 26

Taught school, one half day, cleaned the school house. . . . Went down to Mrs. Wagner's in the evening. Stayed all night, dressed that sick girl's hand which was so badly burned trying to save her mother.

April 29

Taught school, went home in the evening very lonesome and weary. I think I am getting very much like the old maid that sat down on Monday morning and cried because Saturday did not come twice a week. . . .

Source: W. Elliot Brownlee and Mary M. Brownlee, *Women in the American Economy, A Documentary History*, 1675 to 1929 (New Haven: Yale University Press, 1976) 126–130.

Farragut's Fleet
On April 24, 1862, Flag Officer David G. Farragut's fleet made a run past the forts guarding the southern approach to New Orleans, in the most spectacular naval battle of the war. New Orleans was forced to surrender the next day. (J. Joffray, *Farragut's Fleet Passing Fort Jackson and Fort Philip*)

McDowell attacked strongly on July 21, but panic swept through his troops during a Confederate counterattack. For the first time the Union troops, who had fought almost fourteen hours with little water to relieve the Virginia heat, heard the startling scream of the rebel yell. "The peculiar corkscrew sensation that it sends down your backbone under these circumstances can never be told," one Union veteran wrote. "You have to feel it."

McDowell's troops retreated to Washington, scrambling along with the many civilians who had come down from the capital with their Sunday picnic baskets and binoculars to observe the battle. The Confederate troops also dispersed. They were as confused as the beaten Unionists, and they lacked wagons and supplies to pursue McDowell's army. While Confederate leaders rejoiced in their victory, Lincoln replaced McDowell with young General George B. McClellan of Ohio. He also signed bills for enlistment of 100,000 additional men, who would serve for three years in what would soon be named the Army of the Potomac. In November 1861, when Scott retired, Lincoln made McClellan general-in-chief. Although neither Lincoln nor Davis fully anticipated total war as yet, it was now clear that the war would not be quick or easy.

The War in the West. While eastern armies were fighting to capture the opposing capital or demoralize the enemy's army, Union and Confederate troops in the West struggled to dominate territory—the great interior river valleys. Union control of communications and transportation along these strategic rivers would divide the Confederacy into isolated pieces and reduce its ability to supply and move armies. The Confederacy had already lost the Ohio Valley when Kentucky remained in the Union. Retaining the Tennessee and Mississippi valleys was vital to the South's communications with its vast western territory.

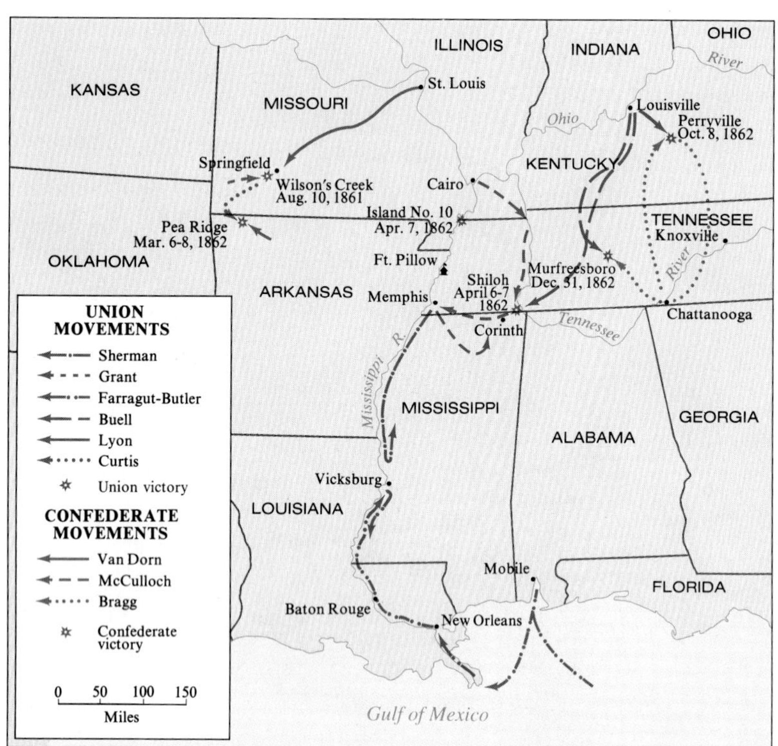

MAP 15.2

The Western Campaigns, 1861–1862

Control of the great valleys of the Ohio, Tennessee, and Mississippi rivers were at stake during the early part of the Civil War. By the end of 1862, Union armies had kept Missouri in the Union and driven the Confederate armies out of Kentucky and half of Tennessee. They also controlled New Orleans and almost all of the Mississippi River, and at Shiloh they had proven that they could not be driven out of the lower South.

In 1862 the Union launched a series of highly innovative land-and-water operations designed to seize control of the Tennessee and Mississippi rivers. In February, in a brilliant tactical maneuver, Ulysses S. Grant, still a relatively unknown Union commander, used river boats clad with iron plates to take Fort Henry on the Tennessee River and Fort Donelson on the Cumberland. Grant then moved south along the Tennessee to take control of critical railroad lines. Meanwhile, as the southern part of a giant pincer movement, Admiral David G. Farragut struck from the sea. In April 1862 he led a Union squadron up the Mississippi from the Gulf of Mexico and took New Orleans. In one naval offensive, the Union captured the South's financial center and largest city, acquired a major base for future operations, and denied the Confederacy an important port.

Shiloh. Confederates under Albert Sidney Johnston and P. G. T. Beauregard slowed Grant's advance by catching him by surprise a few miles from the Tennessee River near a small log church named Shiloh. In the ensuing battle on April 6–7, 1862, Grant relentlessly threw troops into the battle and forced a Confederate withdrawal. About 20,000 men were killed or wounded at Shiloh, making it the bloodiest battle thus far. Grant described a large field "so covered with dead that it would have been possible to walk over the clearing in any direction, stepping on dead bodies, without a foot touching the ground."

Grant's victory at Shiloh was a major turning point. It marked the beginning of the end of Confederate power in the Mississippi Valley; by June the Union controlled the Mississippi as far south as Memphis, Tennessee. Also, the ghastly triumph at Shiloh began to transform the Union's strategic thinking, persuading Lincoln and the most foresighted generals that a long, protracted war would be necessary, even in the West. Later, Grant wrote that after Shiloh he "gave up all idea of saving the Union except by complete conquest."

The Eastern Theater, 1862. After Bull Run both the Union and the Confederacy continued to seek a victory in the east that would end the war. Confederate and Union commanders jockeyed for position around Washington and Richmond. Each tried to outflank the other, place his army between the capital and its defenders, and, if possible, punish the opposing army. As they maneuvered, these commanders used virtually identical battlefield tactics, since almost all had been taught by the same instructors and read the same textbooks at West Point.

After meticulously training 150,000 men during the winter of 1861–1862, McClellan moved his troops up the peninsula between the York and James rivers toward Richmond. In a maneuver that required skillful logistics, he transported about 100,000 troops by boat down the Potomac River and Chesapeake Bay and then up the peninsula. But he failed to anticipate some major problems. In May, a Confederate army under Thomas J. ("Stonewall") Jackson marched rapidly north up the Shenandoah Valley, threatening the army of Nathaniel P. Banks that was protecting Washington. To head off Jackson, Lincoln diverted 30,000 troops from McClellan's army. Jackson proved a brilliant general; he defeated three Union armies in five battles in the valley. Then in June, as McClellan finally moved toward Richmond, Robert E. Lee, the new commander of the Army of Northern Virginia, with a force of 85,000, attacked McClellan ferociously in the Seven Days' battles (June 25–July 1). McClellan's troops inflicted heavy casualties (20,000 to the Union's 10,000), but he was unwilling to renew the offensive unless he received 50,000 fresh troops. Lincoln believed that McClellan would only find another excuse not to attack Lee, and he withdrew the Army of the Potomac from the peninsula. Richmond remained secure.

Lee's First Invasion of the North. Lee now went on the offensive, hoping for victories that would humiliate Lincoln's government. Lee sent Jackson to destroy a Union army under John Pope in northern Virginia before McClellan returned. On August 29–30, only 20 miles from Washington, Jackson's troops, joined by the forces of Lee and General James P. Longstreet, routed Pope's army in the Second Battle of Bull Run. Lee struck north through western Maryland, while Lincoln ordered McClellan to confront Lee's army. Lee almost met with disaster when he divided his force—sending Stonewall Jackson to capture Harpers Ferry—and a copy of his orders to Jackson fell into McClellan's hands. Once again, however, McClellan hesitated, and Lee had time to occupy a strong defensive position behind Antietam Creek, near Sharpsburg, Maryland. Although outnumbered 87,000 to 50,000, Lee repelled McClellan's attacks until Jackson's troops arrived, just as Union regiments were about to overwhelm Lee's right flank.

The fighting at Antietam was some of the most savage of the war. A Wisconsin officer described his men as "loading and firing with demoniacal fury and shouting and laughing hysterically." At a critical point in the battle, a sunken road, Bloody Lane, filled with Confederate bodies two and three deep, and the attacking Union troops knelt on "this ghastly flooring" to shoot at the retreating Confederates.

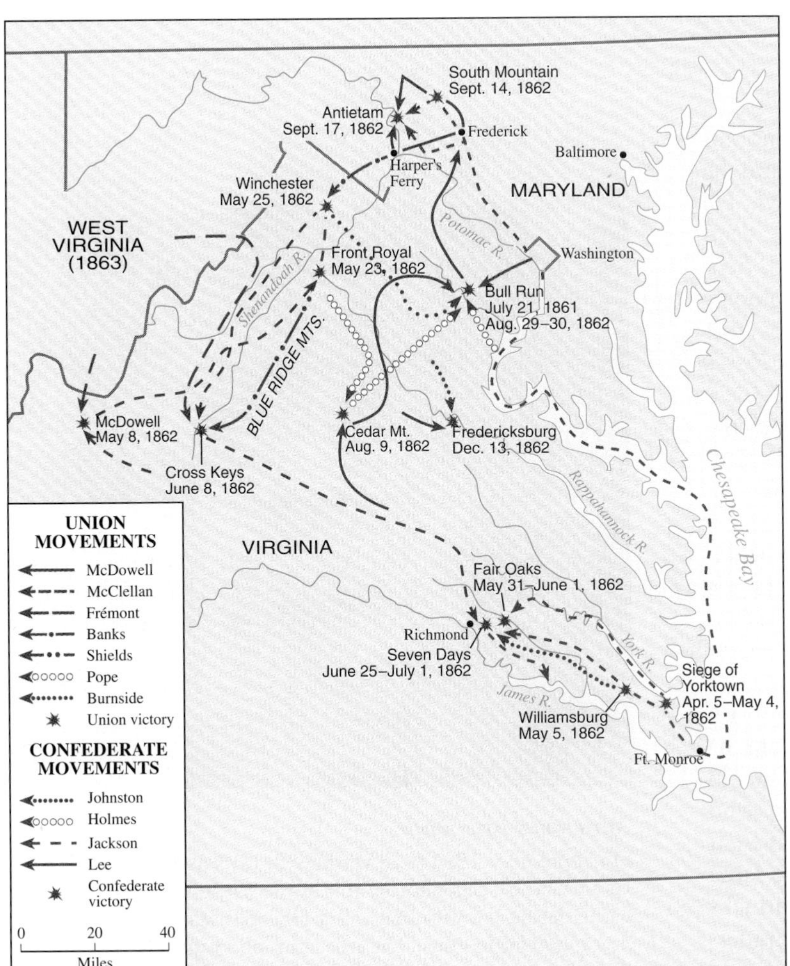

MAP 15.3

The Eastern Campaigns, 1861–1862

The greatest concentration of major Civil War battlefields was in the corridor between Washington and Richmond. There, during the eastern campaigns of 1861 and 1862, the audacity and imagination of Confederate generals Thomas J. "Stonewall" Jackson and Robert E. Lee almost produced decisive Confederate victories. But, as often in the Civil War, the victors were usually too exhausted to exploit their triumphs.

Antietam

This painting, *The Battle of Antietam: The Fight for Burnside's Bridge,* is the work of Captain James Hope of the 2nd Vermont Volunteers, who was a survivor of Antietam. The Rohrbach Bridge, nicknamed "Burnside's Bridge," was the scene of some of the heaviest fighting.

McClellan might have defeated Lee with another major effort, but the casualties appalled him and he feared that enemy troops might outnumber his own. He let Lee fall back to Virginia while he buried the dead and set up field hospitals to nurse the wounded. September 17, 1862, at Antietam proved to be the bloodiest single day in American military history. Lee lost somewhat fewer men than McClellan, but Lee's losses represented one-fourth of his army. Together, the Confederate and Union dead numbered 4,800 and the wounded 18,500, of whom 3,000 soon died. (In comparison, 6,000 Americans were wounded or killed on D-Day in World War II.)

The military setbacks prior to Antietam had begun to erode popular support for the war. To rally public opinion, Lincoln declared Antietam a victory. Privately, he believed that McClellan should have fought Lee to the finish. McClellan had been a masterful organizer of men and supplies, but had never been willing to risk major commitment of his forces, perhaps because he could not face the carnage that would follow. Lincoln replaced McClellan with Ambrose E. Burnside, who proved to be more daring but an even less competent battlefield tactician than McClellan. After losing large parts of the Army of the Potomac in futile attacks against well-entrenched Confederate forces at Fredericksburg, Virginia, on December 13, Burnside relieved

Antietam's Aftermath

On September 19, 1862, Mathew Brady's assistant Alexander Gardner took this photograph of the battlefield. These are Confederate infantrymen along Hagerstown Pike, raked down by Union guns. The Antietam photographs were the first ones Americans had ever seen of wartime carnage.

Lincoln With the Army of the Potomac
This formal photograph records Lincoln's visit to McClellan's headquarters near the Antietam battlefield on October 3, 1862. On this visit, Lincoln vigorously urged McClellan to advance on Richmond. McClellan (facing the president) did not respond and Lincoln removed him from command a month later.

himself of command. Lincoln replaced him with Joseph ("Fighting Joe") Hooker. As 1862 ended, the war was still a stalemate.

Emancipation

As the Union war dragged on during 1861 and 1862, Lincoln, some of his generals, and some Republican leaders began to redefine the war as a struggle not only against Confederate armies, but also against southern society. In particular, Lincoln and his administration decided they had to attack the very cornerstone of southern society—the institution of slavery.

At the beginning of the war, a few abolitionist leaders had hoped that the South would be allowed to secede, so as to rid the Union of the stain of slavery. But other abolitionists tried to persuade the Republican party to make abolition a goal of the war. They argued on grounds not just of morality but of "military necessity": it was the labor of the slaves that enabled the Confederacy to feed and supply its armies. Frederick Douglass wrote that "the very stomach of this rebellion is the Negro in the form of a slave. Arrest that hoe in the hands of the Negro, and you smite the rebellion in the very seat of its life."

"Contrabands." It was the slaves themselves who forced the issue of emancipation. From the very outset of the war, slaves exploited the disorder of wartime to seize their freedom. Over the course of the war, tens of thousands escaped from plantations and ran to Union lines.

The first Union officials who dealt with the status of escaped slaves were the commanders in the field. In May 1861, General Benjamin Butler, who had taken military control of Annapolis and Baltimore, was commanding a fort on the Virginia coast. When three slaves escaped to his lines, he refused to return them to their master. He did not declare them to be free but labeled them "contraband of war." His term stuck, and for the rest of the war slaves found within the Union lines were known as *contrabands*. By August 1861 a thousand contrabands were camping with Butler's army.

The increasingly large number of runaway slaves behind Union lines forced the government to establish a policy regularizing their status. In August 1861, Lincoln signed the First Confiscation Act, authorizing the seizure of all property—defined to include slaves—used to support the rebellion. This law applied only to slaves within reach of Union armies, and it did not actually emancipate them. The act was designed only to undermine the Confederate war effort, but it did begin the process that ended in abolition.

As early as the summer of 1861, almost all Republicans opposed slavery and were ready for some kind of emancipation. But they divided into three groups over the timing and method. The conservatives, the smallest of the three, wanted an end to slavery but believed that it should occur slowly, as the federal government blocked the extension of slavery into the territories; emancipation in existing states, they believed, should be left to state governments. More numerous were the radicals, who wanted the government to abolish slavery straightaway, wherever it existed. The moderates, most numerous of all and led by Lincoln, wanted emancipation to proceed more expeditiously than did the conservatives but feared that immediate abolition would cause a dramatic loss of Union support in the border states and stimulate a racist backlash in northern cities.

But as battlefield casualties mounted in 1861 and 1862, so did popular support for punishing slaveowners by taking away their slaves; so did support for emancipation as a means of mobilizing slaves against their masters; so did moral enthusiasm for freeing the slaves and thus ennobling the carnage on the battlefield; and so did the influence of the radical Republicans. Their leaders included Secretary of the Treasury Salmon P. Chase, Charles Sumner, chairman of the Senate Committee on Foreign Relations, and Thaddeus Stevens, chairman of the House Ways and Means Committee. Both Sumner and Stevens held stern and uncompromising views on slavery, but Stevens was the more masterful in manipulating Congress, where he served as a representative from Pennsylvania from 1849 to 1853 and from 1859 until his death in 1868. Of all the Republicans in Congress, Stevens was probably the one most completely committed to racial equality.

In the spring of 1862, Lincoln and moderate Republicans in Congress began to move slowly toward abolition. In April 1862, Congress enacted legislation abolishing slavery in the District of Columbia while promising compensation to the former slaveowners in the hopes of winning their loyalty to the Union. In June, Congress took its second step, abolishing slavery in the federal territories. This law affected only a few slaves, but it represented the fulfillment of the free-soil platform. Congress took a more radical step in July when it passed the Second Confiscation Act. It went beyond the first one by declaring "forever free" all captured and fugitive slaves of rebels. Although it affected only those slaves under the direct control of the Union army, it did for the first time embrace emancipation as an instrument of war. Also in July, Lincoln read a draft of a proclamation to his cabinet, testing out an even more radical conception of emancipation, one that would transform the Union armies into agents of liberation.

The Emancipation Proclamation. Lincoln was pondering how he could use his power to emancipate the slaves not affected by previous actions. Some lived in areas loyal to the Union but most were in areas controlled by the Confederacy. He was certain that he must leave the former alone because the Constitution protected slavery within the Union. But he believed he could free the latter under his wartime power to take enemy resources. He worried, however, that if he did that while the war was going badly, he would be seen as cynically trying to divert attention from military defeats. And abolishing slavery while the Union was losing the war would, in fact, be an empty gesture; if the tide of battle did not go Lincoln's way, he could free no additional slaves. After Antietam, Lincoln decided that the time had come. He declared Antietam a victory, and told his cabinet that he took it as "an indication of the Divine Will" that he should "move forward in the cause of emancipation." On September 22, 1862, he issued a preliminary Emancipation Proclamation. He declared that on January 1, 1863, slaves in all states wholly or partly in rebellion would be free. Thus Lincoln gave the rebellious states a hundred days to return to the Union and keep slavery intact. None chose to do so.

The proclamation was politically astute as well as constitutionally correct. Lincoln wanted to keep the loyalty of the border states, where racism was most severe, so he left slavery intact there. He also wanted to win the allegiance of the areas occupied by Union armies—western and middle-Tennessee, western Virginia, and southern Louisiana, including New Orleans—so he left slavery untouched there. Thus, the Emancipation Proclamation had no immediate, practical effect on the life of a single slave. Abolitionists were disappointed, but they were confident that emancipation would have to go further. Wendell Phillips believed Lincoln was "only stopping on the edge of Niagara." Jefferson Davis called the proclamation the "most execrable measure recorded in the history of guilty man." Lincoln himself predicted that the proclamation would change the nature of the war; it would now become a war of "subjugation" in which "the old South is to be destroyed and replaced by new propositions and ideas."

Many Union officers doubted whether they wanted to fight for emancipation and worried that the proclamation would incite slave rebellions. General McClellan, who had aspirations for a political career as a Democrat, privately admitted that he "could not make my mind to fight for such an accursed doctrine as that of a servile insurrection." But McClellan reminded his officers that the "remedy for political errors . . . is to be found only in the action of people at the polls."

The Elections of 1862. The Democrats, in fact, made emancipation the primary issue in the elections of 1862. Leading Democrats used emancipation to focus popular frustration over the seeming futility of the bloody war. They denounced emancipation as unconstitutional;

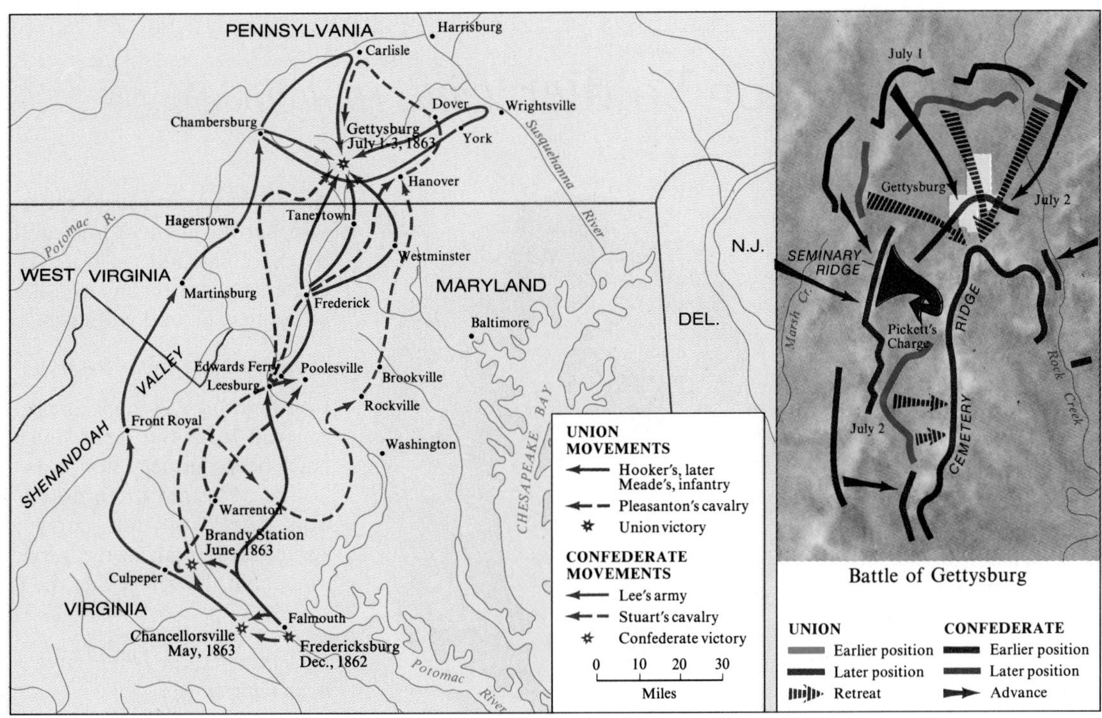

MAP 15.4

The Battle of Gettysburg

Lee's invasion of the North, following Confederate victories at Fredericksburg and Chancellorsville, was designed to threaten northern cities, persuade Europeans that the Confederacy would win the war, and strengthen the hand of the Peace Democrats. Lee's strategy might have ended the war if he had won at Gettysburg.

thousand of Pickett's men were killed, wounded, or captured, and the few Confederate soldiers who managed to charge over the Union fortifications were shot or forced to surrender. When ordered to rally his troops to repel a possible counterattack, Pickett answered, "General Lee, I *have* no division, now."

Gettysburg took more lives than any other Civil War battle. Meade lost 23,000 killed or wounded; Lee lost 28,000, one-third of the Army of Northern Virginia. Lee could never again invade the North. But he still had a substantial force, thanks largely to Meade, who was so pleased with his victory and wary of Lee that he allowed the remaining Confederate soldiers to escape. Lincoln believed that Meade could have ended the war at Gettysburg. "As it is," Lincoln brooded, "the war will be prolonged indefinitely." Lincoln's pessimism was justified; the two sides were still deadlocked.

The victory at Gettysburg did, however, increase popular support for the war in the North. During the fall of 1863, in state and local elections in Pennsylvania, Ohio, and New York, Democrats once again tested support for the war by challenging Republicans on the issue of emancipation, accusing them of favoring social equality for blacks. For Governor of Ohio, Democrats nominated Clement L. Vallandigham after Lincoln had banished him from the Union for treasonously denouncing the war as one fought "for the freedom of the blacks and the enslavement of the whites." Republicans, however, benefited from the patriotic pride in the victory at Gettysburg, from the heroics of African-American soldiers, and from white embarrassment over the New York draft riots that summer. Lincoln intervened in the election, declaring that when the war was won, "there will be some black men who can remember that, with silent tongue, and clenched teeth, and steady eye, and well-poised bayonet, they have helped mankind on to this great consummation; while, I fear, there will be some white ones, unable to forget that, with malignant heart, and deceitful speech, they have strove to hinder it." Lincoln made stick the charge that to oppose emancipation was to oppose northern victory, and Republicans swept to decisive victories across the three key states, including Ohio, where Vallandigham's opponent won a record share of the vote.

AMERICAN VOICES

The Diary of a Union Soldier *Elisha Hunt Rhodes*

In June 1861, nineteen-year-old Elisha Hunt Rhodes left his widowed mother and enlisted in the Second Rhode Island Volunteers. Over the next four years he participated in every campaign of the Army of the Potomac. Surviving twenty major battles, he rose from private to lieutenant colonel and commander of the regiment.

April, 1861 [Pawtuxet]

Sunday night after I had retired, my mother came to my room and with a spirit worthy of a Spartan mother of old said, "My son, other mothers must make sacrifices and why should not I? If you feel that it is your duty to enlist, I will give my consent." She showed a patriotic spirit that much inspired my young heart.

July 21, 1861 [Bull Run]

On reaching a clearing, . . . we were saluted with a volley of musketry, which, however, was fired so high that all the bullets went over our heads. I remember that my first sensation was one of astonishment at the peculiar whir of the bullets, and that the Regiment immediately laid down without waiting for orders.

As I emerged from the woods I saw a bomb shell strike a man in the breast and literally tear him to pieces. I passed the farm house which had been appropriated for a hospital and the groans of the wounded and dying were horrible. I then descended the hill to the woods which had been occupied by the rebels . . . . The bodies of the dead and dying were actually three and four deep . . . while the trees were spattered with blood.

September 23, 1862 [Antietam]

Sunday morning we found that the enemy had recrossed the river. O, why did we not attack them and drive them into the river? I do not understand these things. But then I am only a boy.

Elisha Rhodes (1842–1917)

After mustering out of the army Rhodes married and established a business supplying Rhode Island mills with cotton and wool. He traveled extensively in the South and West, establishing contact with other veterans. He was especially active in the Grand Army of the Republic, the primary organization of Union veterans.

July 3, 1863 [Gettysburg]

Soon the Rebel yell was heard, and . . . the Rebel General Pickett made a charge with his Division and was repulsed after reaching some of our batteries. Our lines of Infantry in front of us rose up and poured in a terrible fire. As we were only a few yards in rear of our lines we saw all the fight. The firing gradually died away, and but for an occasional shot all was still. But what a scene it was. Oh the dead and dying on this bloody field.

June 3, 1864 [Cold Harbor]

We have had a terrible battle today, and the killed and wounded number in thousands. . . . Nothing seems to have been gained by the attack today, except it may be that it settles the question of whether the enemy's line can be carried by direct assault or not. At any rate General Grant means to hold on, and I know that he will win in the end.

June 20, 1864 [near Petersburg]

Last night at 9 o'clock our Brigade was relieved from the front line where we had been under fire for thirty-six hours. . . . I am often asked the question "Are you not sorry that you agreed to remain in the service?" I answer "*No*, I want to see the end of the war."

December 22, 1864 [entrenchments near Petersburg]

We do not fear the result of an assault by the enemy on our works. . . . The forts and batteries . . . are within range of each other and are connected by curtains or rifle pits. In front of our works are deep ditches now filled with water and in front of this an abatis [barrier] made of limbs and trees driven slanting into the ground and with the points sharpened. Then we have wires stretched about in every direction about six inches or a foot above the ground. And still in front of all this the trees are slashed and are piled up in great confusion. I wish the Rebels would try to take our lines. It would be fun for us.

July 9, 1865 [Hall's Hill, Virginia]

Although I want to go home, yet as I think of the separation from comrades some of whom I have known for more than four years, I cannot help feeling sad . . . . I have been successful in my Army life simply because I have always been ready and willing to do my duty. I thank God that I have had an opportunity of serving my country freeing the slaves and restoring the Union.

Source: Robert Hunt Rhodes, ed., *All for the Union, The Civil War Diary and Letters of Elisha Hunt Rhodes* (New York: Orion, 1991), passim.

Wartime Diplomacy

Gettysburg also advanced the Union cause by neutralizing the European powers as factors in the outcome of the war. Great Britain, in particular, had been a key participant, as arms supplier to both the North and South and as a potential source of economic and additional military aid to the Confederacy.

At the beginning of the war, the Confederacy had begun diplomatic efforts to gain foreign recognition of its independence. Because Great Britain depended on the South for four-fifths of its raw cotton, southern leaders hoped that it would offer the Confederacy enough support to cause the Union to give up the fight. Moreover, France's emperor Napoleon III might be of assistance. He dreamed of an empire in Mexico and by the summer of 1862 had sent thousands of troops to overthrow a republican regime there. The French army, which grew to 35,000, succeeded in June 1863, and in 1864 Napoleon installed as Emperor of Mexico Archduke Ferdinand Maximilian, the brother of the emperor of Austria. France was bound by a diplomatic agreement to defer to the British in American affairs, but if Britain recognized the independence of the Confederacy, France was virtually certain to follow and might even challenge Union power west of the Mississippi.

Shortly after the onset of hostilities, Great Britain proclaimed its neutrality. This action meant that Britain recognized the Confederacy as a belligerent power and therefore regarded it as having the right, under international law, to borrow money and purchase weapons in neutral nations. A concerned Lincoln administration protested that the conflict was fighting a domestic insurrection and not a war and that Britain's declaration of neutrality might be taken to imply recognition of the Confederacy as a sovereign state. Lincoln feared that the British might next help break the ever-tightening naval blockade of the southern coast that he had established in April 1861.

The dispute with Britain came to a head over two issues. First, in November 1861 a Union sloop seized a British steamer, the *Trent,* on the high seas and arrested two Confederate commissioners, James Mason and John Slidell, who were on their way to Britain. In response, the British demanded release of the diplomats and ordered troops to Canada. Then, in spring 1862 British shipbuilders agreed to supply cruisers to the Confederacy. That summer a British firm also contracted to build the "Laird rams," two well-armed ironclads designed to break the blockade. The cruisers included the *Alabama,* which sailed from Liverpool in the summer of 1862 and sank or captured more than one hundred Union merchant ships.

Lincoln, Secretary of State William H. Seward, and the minister to Great Britain, Charles Francis Adams, released Mason and Slidell in December 1861, and adroitly avoided provoking Britain into siding with the Confederacy. In the summer of 1863 they even persuaded the British to impound the Laird rams.

"King Cotton" was less powerful than Lincoln had feared. Before the war British manufacturers had stockpiled textile products, and the blockade enabled them to reap extremely high profits from their sale. During the war they were able to buy raw cotton from Egypt and India. British munitions suppliers, who sold to both sides, and British shipowners, who profited from the South's attacks on the North's merchant marine, also had no interest in hastening the end of the war by choosing sides. British consumers had no wish to raise food prices by disrupting imports of grain from the North. In addition, British workers and reformers were enthusiastic champions of abolition, which the Emancipation Proclamation seemed to establish as a Union war aim.

The most important influence on the British, however, was Lee's defeat at Gettysburg. It convinced the British of the military might of the Union. The British did not want to risk their Canadian colonies or the British merchant marine by provoking the United States. Consequently, they decided not to recognize the Confederacy and to remain neutral. Napoleon still favored recognition but had no enthusiasm for facing Union forces alone, particularly after Lincoln, to warn France and Mexico, sent General Banks on a successful mission to capture Brownsville, Texas, just north of the Mexican border, in late 1863.

The Union Victorious, 1864–1865

Despite Gettysburg, the outcome of the war remained very much in doubt well into 1864. Even though the Confederacy could no longer mount an invasion of the North, the failure to crush Lee's army at Gettysburg meant that the Confederacy had new chances to erode northern support for the Union cause. If the war went poorly for the Union, the election of 1864 might enable the Democrats to challenge Lincoln's definition of war aims and persuade northern voters that the Union should end the war on terms favorable to the Confederacy. Two major developments, however, strengthened the ability of the Union to prosecute a total war: the enlistment of African-American soldiers, and the discovery of generals capable of fighting a modern war.

African-American Soldiers

From the beginning of the war, both free blacks and fugitive slaves had sought to enlist in the Union army to advance the cause of freedom. Abolitionists and a few Union generals had tried to help. Frederick Douglass embraced the liberating power of military service in the cause of Union. "Once let the black man get upon his person the brass letters, 'U.S.,' let him get an eagle on his buttons and a musket on his shoulder and bullets in his pockets, and there is no power on earth which can deny that he has earned the right to citizenship in the United States." But this is exactly what northern whites feared; enlistment of African-Americans could threaten traditional race relations in the North. And most Union generals doubted that they would fight. Consequently, until the Emancipation Proclamation the Lincoln administration gave little encouragement to black aspirations for military service. Nonetheless, in 1862 several regiments of free and "contraband" blacks formed in South Carolina, Louisiana, and Kansas.

The logic of tying abolition of slavery to the war effort, combined with the carnage of battle, helped produce a change in popular attitudes and government policy. Increasingly after the proclamation, northern whites concluded that if blacks were to benefit from a Union victory, then they, too, should share in the fighting and dying. In early 1863, the War Department began to authorize the enlistment of free blacks in the North and slaves in the areas of the South occupied by Union armies. During the summer of 1863, when the army's demand for soldiers increased and white resistance to the draft grew as well, the Lincoln administration began to recruit as many African-Americans as it could.

The performance of the first African-American regiments also helped shift policy. One of these was the First South Carolina Volunteers, under the command of Thomas Wentworth Higginson, a white abolitionist. In January 1863, he wrote a glowing newspaper account of the fighting of his troops: "No officer in this regiment now doubts that the key to the successful prosecution of the war lies in the unlimited employment of black troops." In July northerners read of the heroic and tragic attack on Fort Wagner, South Carolina, by another black regiment, the 54th Massachusetts Infantry, which was led by Robert Gould Shaw, son of a prominent abolitionist. These accounts convinced many white northerners, including Union officers, of the value of African-American soldiers.

Black Soldiers in the Union Army

These were the proud soldiers of a guard detail of the 107th Colored Infantry at Fort Corcoran, near Washington, D.C. In January 1865, their regiment participated in the daring capture of Fort Fisher, which protected Wilmington, North Carolina, the last of the Confederate ports open to blockade runners. Their chaplain declared that in nine battles the regiment "never faltered, gave way, or retreated, unless ordered by the General commanding."

By spring of 1865, there were nearly 200,000 African-Americans, primarily former slaves, serving as soldiers and sailors, constituting about 10 percent of those who served in the Union forces. Their regiments contributed to the Union cause in a number of major battles during 1864–1865, especially in Grant's grinding siege of Petersburg. During the election of 1864 Lincoln claimed that if the Union renounced emancipation and the recruiting of black soldiers, "we would be compelled to abandon the war in three weeks."

Black soldiers knew that they were fighting for freedom and that they were shifting the military odds in favor of the Union. Moreover, they hoped that victory would not only end slavery but also help them achieve full equality in American society. Nonetheless, the racial attitudes of northern whites underwent no fundamental change during the war, and the Union army, while developing more confidence in African-Americans as fighting soldiers, still held them in a second-class status. The army kept them in segregated regiments; used them primarily for menial labor or for garrisoning forts and guarding supply lines in occupied southern territory; routinely denied them commissions; and paid them less than white soldiers ($7 as against $13 per month) until June 1864, when the protests of black soldiers finally led Congress to equalize pay. In addition, the Lincoln administration did not protect captured African-Americans against Confederate violations of their rights as prisoners of war. The War Department ended exchanges of prisoners of war in 1863 when the Confederacy threatened to execute or enslave black prisoners of war. On the occasions when Confederates acted on these threats, however, Lincoln was unwilling to take sterner measures. In July 1863 he threatened retaliation—execution of rebel soldiers or their employment at hard labor on public works—but never followed through.

Despite second-class citizenship, black soldiers persisted and endured, understanding what was at stake. One soldier found himself facing his former master, who had been taken as a prisoner of war. "Hello, Massa," he said, "bottom rail on top dis time." The worst fears of the secessionists had come true; in a real sense, the great slave rebellion had materialized, though not as a slave revolt.

The New Military Strategy

Lincoln and Grant. The successful Vicksburg and Chattanooga campaigns convinced Lincoln that in Ulysses S. Grant he had finally found a military leader who produced results. He realized that Grant understood how to fight a modern war—a war relying on industrial technology and directed at an entire society.

During his cadet days at West Point, Grant had been bored with studying conventional tactics—ones that stressed, for example, the advantages of interior lines of supply. Now, new tactics offered a chance to win the war. During what was the first major war fought with railroads, the telegraph, and ironclad ships, Grant emphasized taking advantage of the ability to move troops and supplies rapidly and overcoming the Confederate advantage of interior lines.

Unlike McClellan and Meade, Grant was willing to accept heavy casualties in assaults on strongly defended positions. Grant was convinced that only by going on the offensive, even when it meant great loss of life, could the Union end the war swiftly. "To conserve life, in war," Grant wrote, "is to fight unceasingly." Grant's tactics earned him a reputation as a butcher—a reputation enhanced by his persistent efforts to destroy armies in retreat. Grant was certain that the only way to victory was to crush the southern people's will to resist.

Lincoln, frustrated with the stalemate on the battlefield and worried about re-election in 1864, finally implemented his approach to modern war. In March 1864 he placed Grant in charge of all the Union armies and created a command structure appropriate to the large, complex organization that the Union army had become. From now on the president would determine general strategy and Grant would decide how best to implement it. Aiding the process was General Henry W. Halleck, the consummate office soldier. He served as chief of staff, channeling communications and lifting administrative burdens from both Lincoln and Grant. Along with the Prussian General Staff, the Union's military command structure was the most efficient in the world.

Lincoln, advised by Grant, drew up a new strategy to defeat the Confederacy's will to resist. Instead of launching campaigns to take specific places, cities, and territory, he planned a simultaneous crushing advance of all Union armies, mustering the maximum manpower and resources in their support. Grant would seek victories with a will and power that, Lincoln hoped, would overcome any obstacle.

In early May 1864, Grant ordered the 115,000-man Army of the Potomac to destroy Lee's remaining 75,000 troops, regardless of the cost in Union lives. He ordered General William Tecumseh Sherman, who shared Grant's views on the nature of warfare, to move simultaneously against the Confederate army in Tennessee, invade Georgia, and take Atlanta. As Sherman prepared, he wrote that "all that has gone before is mere skirmish. The war now begins."

The Wilderness Campaign. In Virginia, General Grant advanced toward Richmond, hoping to force Lee's

75,000 troops to fight in open fields where the Union's superior manpower and artillery could prevail. Lee, remembering Gettysburg, maintained strong defensive positions, attacking only when he held a superior position. He twice seized such opportunities, making the Union take 32,000 casualties in return for 18,000 of his men in the battles of the Wilderness on May 5–7 and Spotsylvania Court House on May 8–12. Grant drove toward the railroad junction at Cold Harbor to outflank General Lee, who countered and met Grant there, 10 miles from Richmond. Disregarding his earlier losses, Grant attacked Lee on June 1–3, but broke off after losing 7,000 more men in a frontal assault that lasted less than sixty minutes.

During this month-long Wilderness campaign, Grant eroded Lee's forces, which suffered 31,000 casualties, but paid with 55,000 of his own men. A Union captain, Oliver Wendell Holmes, Jr., wrote that "Many a man has gone crazy since this campaign began from the terrible pressure on mind and body." Another Union officer described his men as feeling "a great horror and dread of attacking earthworks again." During

Grant Planning an Attack

On June 2, 1864, the day this photograph was taken, Grant moved his headquarters to Bethesda Church, carried the pews out under the shade of the surrounding trees, and planned the costly attack he would make at Cold Harbor the next day. While Grant leaned over the pew, gesturing at a map, other officers read reports of the war in newspapers that had just arrived from New York City.

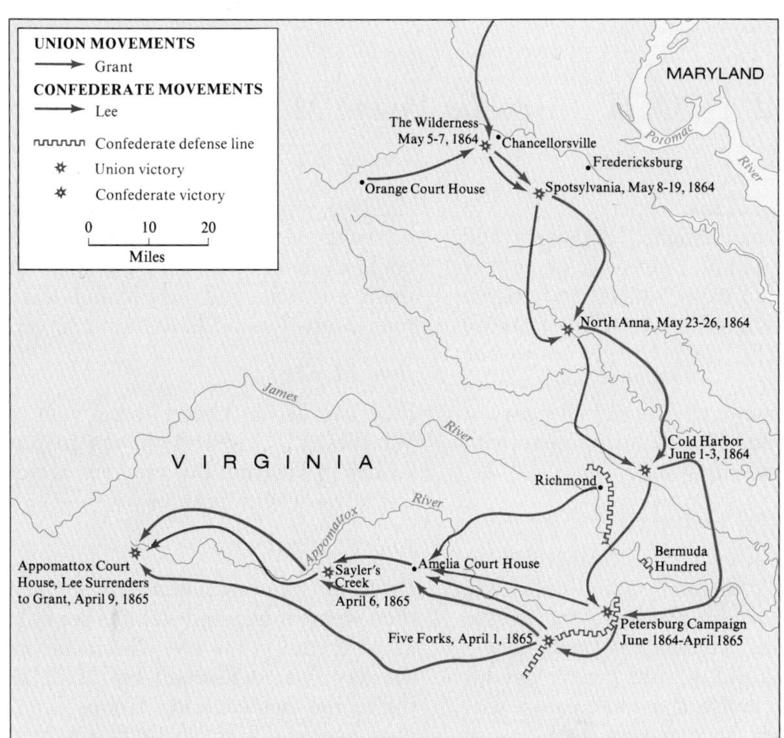

MAP 15.5

The Closing Virginia Campaigns

In 1865 the armies of Grant and Lee were locked in a deadly dance across the Virginia countryside. By threatening Lee's lines of communication, Grant attempted to force Lee into open battles. Until April 1865, Lee resisted, taking strong defensive positions that forced Grant to accept protracted sieges and steady casualties, which threatened to undermine northern support for the war.

1861–1863, battles had been relatively brief, typically lasting one to three days with intervals between the blood-lettings. But with the Wilderness campaign the fighting took on a sustained quality. In Virginia, General Grant's relentless offensive tactics and Lee's successful defensive tactics had turned the war into one of grueling attrition.

The Siege of Petersburg. On June 12, in a surprise maneuver, Grant pulled away from Lee and Richmond, now heavily fortified, and swung south toward Petersburg, a major railroad center. By occupying this, he hoped to force Lee into the final battle of the war. Lee, however, alertly entrenched his troops at Petersburg and denied Grant the advantage of position. In June 1864, Grant laid siege to Petersburg.

Protracted trench warfare, which foreshadowed that of World War I, ensued. The spade had become more important than the sword as soldiers on both sides, including many who had been engineers in civilian life, built complex networks of trenches, tunnels, artillery emplacements, barriers of debris, and clearings designed to be killing zones. The two armies extended the trenches for almost 50 miles around Richmond and Petersburg, as Grant inched toward control of Richmond's railroads. One officer described the continual artillery firing and sniping as "living night and day within the 'valley of the shadow of death.'" The stress was especially great for the Confederate troops because of the Confederacy's manpower crisis. Some of the Confederate regiments had to spend six months in the muddy, sickening trenches without rotation to the rear.

Lincoln and Grant were confident that their siege would eventually prevail, but time was not on their side. They feared that the enormous casualties and military stalemate might lead to Lincoln's defeat in the November election and, as a consequence, to the abandonment of the Union war effort.

The Shenandoah Campaign. Making matters worse were the daring raids of 15,000 Confederate cavalry under Jubal Early. Based in the Shenandoah Valley, Early's troops crossed the Potomac in early July, passed Union defenses in Maryland only 5 miles north of the White House, and caused Grant to send some of his best troops from Petersburg to chase Early back to the Shenandoah. Before returning, two of Early's brigades invaded Pennsylvania and burned the town of Chambersburg when the city council refused to pay a ransom of $500,000.

The Union struck back with a vengeance. To punish and control the valley, which served as both a refuge for Confederate cavalry and a breadbasket for the Army of Northern Virginia, Grant created a new army, the Army of the Shenandoah under his favorite cavalry officer, Philip H. Sheridan. Grant ordered Sheridan not only to destroy Early's forces but also to turn the Shenandoah Valley into "a barren waste . . . so that crows flying over

AMERICAN VOICES

The Confederate Home Front *Cornelia Peake McDonald*

Cornelia Peak McDonald (1822–1909) spent the first years of the war at her home in Winchester, Virginia, a major road-hub in the Shenandoah Valley. She began her diary to keep a record of events for her husband, a well-to-do lawyer and Confederate officer. In July 1863, when Confederate troops evacuated Winchester, she and her eight children were forced to flee to Lexington, Virginia.

November 1, 1862

Our army is still falling back, there are a very few here now. Northern papers say General [Ambrose E.] Burnside expects to occupy Winchester during the coming week. I scarcely have time now to think of them, or of anything but caring for my household which is more difficult to do every day as servants are not to be had, supplies are scarce, and Confederate money of little value.

December 24, 1862

. . . I beheld two [Union] cavalry men on their way through the yard stop and take the Christmas turkey that had been dressed and hung on a low branch of a tree for cooking on the morrow. . . . I flew after him, and in a commanding tone demanded the restoration of my property.

The man laughed derisively and told me I had no right to it, being "secesh" as he expressed it, and that it was confiscated to the United States. "Very well," said I, "go on to the camp with it, and I will go with you to the commanding officer." He gave it up then and I returned triumphantly to the kitchen with it. . . .

February 19, 1863

Daily, hourly there is something to annoy. Soldiers stalk in and out of the house, at their pleasure, for in the front room that was my husband's, a meek eyed old quarter master has his abode; an inoffensive old creature that I permitted to come in the hope of keeping away the offensive ones. . . .

March 17, 1863

I have to be constantly on the watch for fear of my boys doing something to provoke the persecution of the Yankees.

May 22, 1863

To day I received another intimation that my house would be wanted for a regimental hospital. I feel a sickening despair when I think of what will be my condition if they do take it. Where can I go, what can I do without home or shelter, and no means to buy it if it could be had? The children, some of them are sick, and how can I leave poor Aunt Winnie? [a domestic slave]

June 14, 1863

[Lee has driven Union forces out of Winchester.] Victory! thanks to our Father in Heaven; our enemies are at last powerless to harm us.

June 15, 1863

I did not lock my chamber door and then went to bed and slept as soundly as I ever did in my life. The scenes of the day floated through my brain all night, the maneuvering troops scudding over the hills, shells flying, men rushing back and forth, artillery, infantry and ambulances confusedly hurrying by, and amidst it all my little ones playing in the yard in the bright summer sunshine, as happy and unconcerned as if all was peace around them. Poor little things, they have long been used to scenes of strife and confusion, and I suppose it now seems to them the natural course of things.

Source: Minrose C. Gwin, ed., *A Woman's Civil War: A Diary, with Reminiscences of the War from March 1862* (Madison: University of Wisconsin Press, 1992), passim.

it for the balance of this season will have to carry their provender with them." During the fall, Sheridan's troops conducted a "scorched earth" campaign in the valley, destroying grain supplies, barns, farming implements, and grist mills, and burning the homes of people suspected of sheltering "bushwhackers" who had murdered three of Sheridan's officers. The goal was to destroy the valley's economy and break the will of its people to resist the Union. For the first time in the Civil War, a major army terrorized civilians.

Guerrillas had conducted terrorist activities against civilians in "Bleeding" Kansas during the 1850s, and in the upper South, particularly in the Shenandoah Valley and Missouri, since the outset of the war. Early's attack on Chambersburg was part of a gradual escalation of such warfare. And soldiers on both sides, frustrated and angered by the indecisiveness of the war, were increasingly tempted to turn to acts of vengeance against hostile civilians. But with Sheridan's campaign, terror directed at civilians took on a far more organized form.

The new terrorism was limited for the most part to destruction of property rather than life, but it nonetheless went beyond the traditional military norms of the day. Conventional generals like McClellan regarded civilians as innocents whom the military should protect, and they feared terrorism for the way it could disrupt military discipline. The decision of Lincoln, Grant, and the other Union generals in 1864 to carry the war to Confederate civilians in an organized fashion changed the definition of conventional warfare. The direction of organized terror against civilians was another way in which the Civil War approached the total warfare of the twentieth century.

Sherman, Atlanta, and the Election of 1864

As the siege at Petersburg dragged on, Lincoln and Grant knew that their hopes of proving to voters that the war could be won rested with Sherman in Georgia. At the beginning of the siege in Virginia, Sherman had penetrated to within about thirty miles of Atlanta, a great railway hub that controlled the heart of the Confederacy. Although his army outnumbered that of General Joseph E. Johnston, 90,000 to 60,000, he declined to attack Johnston directly. Sherman feared that his supply line, extending by rail all the way to Louisville, was overexposed to Confederate cavalry and guerrilla attacks, and he recognized the advantage to its defenders of the rugged terrain of northern Georgia. Johnston, for his part, was unwilling to risk his smaller army, and he gradually fell back southward toward Atlanta. Finally, on June 27, at Kennesaw Mountain, Sherman engaged Johnston in a set battle but took 3,000 casualties while inflicting only about 600. Sherman seemed to be stalled in his effort to destroy Johnston's army; Confederate morale soared.

In July, Jefferson Davis, tired of Johnston's defensive tactics, replaced him with General John B. Hood. Sherman, however, welcomed the change, which one of Sherman's generals remarked, was "to have our enemy grasp the hot end of the poker." What followed, as one Union soldier described it, was "a common slaughter of the enemy," out in the open and unprotected by fortifications. By late July, Sherman was laying siege to Atlanta. But the next month brought little gain; both Sherman and Grant seemed to be bogged down in hopeless campaigns.

As Union and Confederate audiences focused on the fate of Atlanta, the 1864 presidential campaign began. In June, the Republican party convention endorsed all of Lincoln's war measures, demanded unconditional surrender of the Confederacy, and called for a constitutional amendment to abolish slavery. In order to emphasize the need for restoration of the Union and attract Democratic support, the party temporarily renamed itself the National Union party and had nominated for vice-president Andrew Johnson, a Tennessee Democrat who had remained loyal and stayed in the Senate until 1862 when Lincoln named him military governor of Tennessee.

By August many Republican leaders thought Lincoln would lose the presidency to General George B. McClellan, the likely Democratic nominee. With the armies of both Grant and Sherman stalled, the expanded war effort seemed to promise little hope of success. Some Republicans talked about calling a new convention and dropping Lincoln from the ticket. The Republican National Committee urged Lincoln to abandon emancipation as a war aim and to offer Jefferson Davis peace in return only for "acknowledging the supremacy of the constitution." Lincoln was tempted, but he refused to abandon emancipation even though he had decided he would be beaten "and unless some great change takes place *badly* beaten." Meanwhile, Republicans rushed through the admission of Nevada to the Union, believing that its electoral votes might tip a close election in their favor.

The Democratic national convention met in late August, nominated McClellan, and declared their opposition to emancipation—and to Lincoln's harsh treatment of internal dissent. A slight majority—the War Democrats—wanted to continue the war, despite their criticisms of the Lincoln administration. But the rest—the Peace Democrats—wanted to end the war. By threatening to bolt the convention, they obtained nearly unanimous agreement on a platform calling for "a cessation of hostilities, with a view to an ultimate convention of the states, or other peaceable means, to the end that, at the earliest practicable moment, peace may be restored on the basis of the Federal Union." McClellan himself was a War Democrat but he gave private assurances to the Peace Democrats that he would recommend an immediate armistice and a peace convention. Alexander Stephens, the vice president of the Confederacy, declared that the platform offered "the first ray of real light I have seen since the war began." If Confederate forces could hold on to Atlanta and Richmond through the election of 1864, Lincoln—and the Union war effort—might well go down to defeat.

The Fall of Atlanta. Stephens wrote these remarks before he learned the fateful news: on September 2, Atlanta fell to Sherman. In a stunning move, he had pulled his troops back from the trenches and had swept around the city to destroy its roads and rail linkages to the rest of the Confederacy. After failing to stop Sherman, Hood abandoned Atlanta, fearing that Sherman would be able to trap and destroy his army. Sherman wired Lincoln: "Atlanta is ours, and fairly won." In her diary Mary Chesnut recorded that she "felt as if all were dead within me, forever." For the first time, she despaired of Confederate victory. "We are going to be wiped off the earth."

Amid the 100-gun salutes in northern cities that greeted news of Sherman's victory, McClellan repudiated the Democratic peace platform, and Republicans abandoned all efforts to dump Lincoln. They campaigned hard, pinning the peace platform to McClellan's campaign and charging, with some accuracy, that groups of Peace Democrats—or "Copperheads" (poisonous snakes), as the Republican press called them—had hatched or were hatching treasonous plots in the border states and in the southern part of the Old Northwest.

Lincoln's Election. Lincoln's victory in November was not a landslide, but it was clear-cut. He won 212 of 233 electoral votes, carrying every state except Delaware, Kentucky, and New Jersey. He increased his percentage of the popular vote in the free and border states from the 48 percent he had received in 1860 to 55 percent. His opposition was concentrated in border districts and the immigrant wards of large cities. Republicans also won 145 of the 185 seats in the House of Representatives and increased their Senate majority to 42 of 52 seats. The margin of victory in many places came from Union soldiers. The soldiers cast absentee ballots or returned home, briefly furloughed by commanders to cast ballots where the Democrats had blocked absentee balloting. More than three-fourths of the Union troops voted for Lincoln. They wanted the war to continue until the Confederacy met every Union demand, including emancipation. As in 1863, the elections of 1864 lent democratic sanction to the Union war effort. Grant wrote a friend that "the overwhelming majority received by Mr. Lincoln and the quiet with which the election went off . . . will be worth more than a victory in the field both in its effect on the Rebels and in its influence abroad."

Sherman's "March to the Sea"

After abandoning Atlanta, Hood marched north to Tennessee, convinced that his only chance to wear down Sherman was to lure him into giving chase. But Sherman declined to follow. He decided that rather than wear out his troops or spread them dangerously thin by protecting captured territory, he would simply "cut a swath through to the sea." Lincoln and Grant were dubious, but Sherman prevailed, arguing that if he marched through Georgia, "smashing things" all the way to the Atlantic coast, he would divide the Confederacy and win a major psychological victory. It would be "a demonstration to the world, foreign and domestic, that we have a power Davis cannot resist."

As he marched, Sherman implemented the concept of total war that Sheridan had pioneered in the Shenandoah Valley—destruction of the enemy's economic and psychological resources. "We are not only fighting hostile armies," Sherman wrote, "but a hostile people, and must make old and young, rich and poor, feel the hard hand of war." Union armies "cannot change the hearts of those people of the South but we can make war so terrible . . . that generations would pass away before they would again appeal to it." He promised to "make Georgia howl!"

Sherman left Atlanta in flames and he destroyed Confederate railroads, property, and supplies, terrorizing the civilian population in a 300-mile march to the sea. A Union veteran wrote that "[we] destroyed all we could not eat, stole their niggers, burned their cotton & gins, spilled their sorghum, burned & twisted their R.Roads and raised Hell generally." One Union officer described the march as "probably the most gigantic pleasure excursion ever planned." Letters from Georgia describing the havoc so demoralized Confederate soldiers on the front that many deserted and fled home to their loved ones. When Sherman reached Savannah, Georgia, in mid-December, the 10,000 Confederate troops defending the city evaporated almost at once. Sherman presented the city to President Lincoln as a Christmas gift.

In February 1865, Sherman turned his forces to sweep through South Carolina. He planned to link up with Grant at Petersburg and, along the way, punish the state where secession began. "The truth is, Sherman wrote, "the whole army is burning with an insatiable desire to wreak vengeance upon South Carolina." His troops cut a comparatively narrow swath across the state, but they ravaged the countryside even more thoroughly than they had in Georgia. On February 17, the business district, most churches, and the wealthiest residential neighborhoods of South Carolina's capital, Columbia, burned to the ground. "*This* disappointment," Jefferson Davis moaned, "to me is extremely bitter." By March Sherman had reached North Carolina and was on the verge of linking up with Grant and crushing Lee's army.

Confederate Morale. Sherman's march, taken with Lincoln's victory in 1864, proved that the Union had both the armies and the willpower to prevail in total war. Moreover, the military setbacks that culminated with

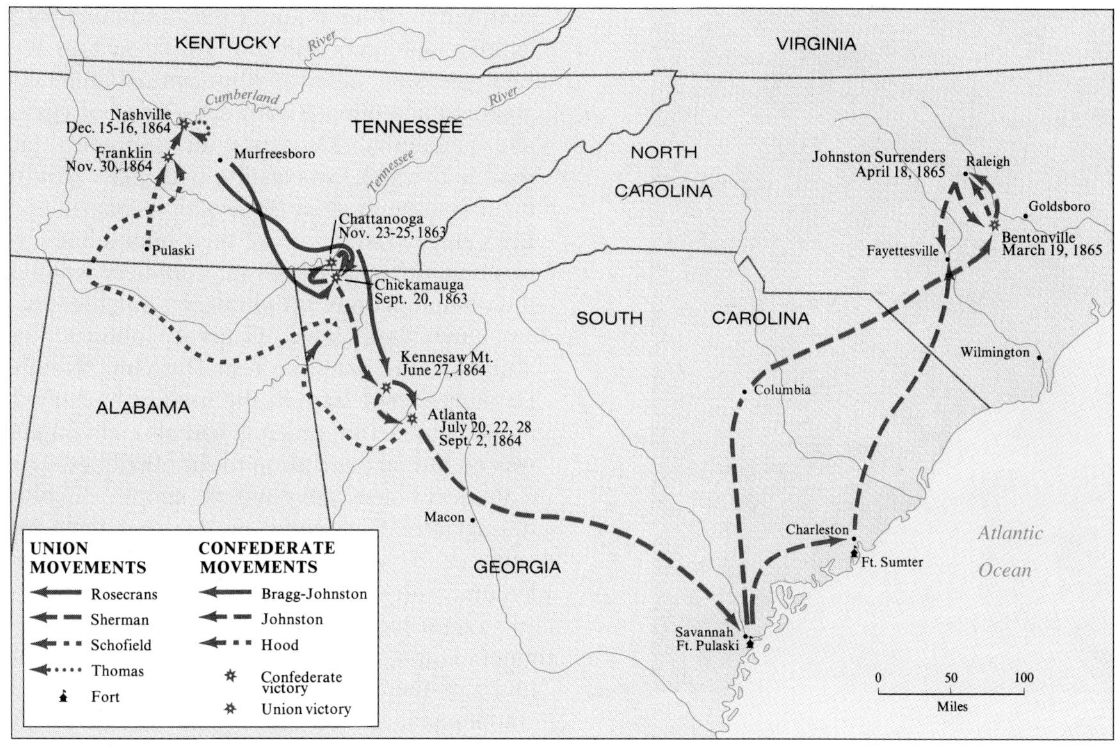

MAP 15.6

Sherman's March Through the Confederacy

The Union victory at Chattanooga in November 1863 was almost as critical as those at Gettysburg and Vicksburg. Having already split the Confederacy along the Mississippi, the Union was now in position to split the Confederacy again with a line running from Kentucky through Tennessee and Georgia to the sea. Sherman captured Atlanta and then, largely ignoring John B. Hood's failed invasion of Tennessee, swept to the Atlantic.

Sherman's march to the sea, coupled with the early "20-Negro Exemption," exposed an internal Confederate weakness: rising class resentment on the part of poor whites. Southern men resisted conscription at rates that increased dramatically and in 1865 desertion became epidemic. In all, over 100,000 Confederates deserted. Many deserters linked up with draft-evaders to form guerrilla forces that ruled many backcountry areas. To add to the South's troubles, secret societies of Unionists operated openly in the Appalachian Mountains, in the hill country of Alabama, in the Ozarks of Arkansas, in parts of Texas, and in all other areas where slavery barely existed. These Unionists aided northern troops and sometimes even enlisted in the Union army when it marched nearby.

By 1865 the Confederacy was experiencing a profound manpower crisis. In March its leaders decided on an extreme measure: to arm its own slaves. Howell Cobb, a powerful Georgia politician, had pointed out that "if slaves will make good soldiers our whole theory of slavery is wrong." Nonetheless, urged on by Lee, the Confederate Congress voted to enlist black soldiers. Davis added an executive order granting freedom to all blacks who served in the Confederate army. The war ended too soon, however, to reveal whether any slaves would seek freedom by joining their masters in defense of the Confederacy.

The End of the War

Appomattox. While Sherman marched, Grant continued his siege of the entrenched Army of Northern Virginia. In April 1865 he finally forced Lee into a showdown by gaining control of a crucial railroad junction near Richmond and cutting off Lee's supplies. Lee abandoned the defense of the city and turned west, hoping to meet Johnston in North Carolina. While Lincoln visited the ruins of Richmond, mobbed by joyful former slaves, Grant pursued Lee and his small army of 25,000. Grant

Lee's Surrender
Lee arrived in full-dress uniform to surrender his army at the village of Appomattox Courthouse. Mathew Brady photographed Lee with his son, left, and an aide. Lee's solemn expression suggests the terrible burden of his memories.

swiftly cut off his escape route, and on April 9, almost exactly four years after the attack on Fort Sumter, Lee surrendered to Grant at Appomattox Court House, Virginia. In accepting, Grant set a tone of egalitarianism and generosity. He wore an unpressed jacket and muddy trousers, contrasting with Lee's handsome uniform and sword in its gold-inlay scabbard, and allowed Lee's enlisted men to take their horses home for spring planting. Afterwards, Grant's soldiers willingly shared their ample rations with hungry Confederates.

Nine days later, General Johnston signed an armistice with Sherman near Durham, North Carolina. He surrendered later in the month; by May 26 all the other Confederate generals had also surrendered. There was no formal conclusion to the hostilities. The Confederate army and government simply dissolved. After fleeing from Richmond, hoping that the South would continue to resist, Jefferson Davis was captured by Union cavalry in Georgia.

The armies of the Union had destroyed the Confederacy. During four years of war, they had destroyed much of the South's productive capacity. Its factories, warehouses, and railroads were in ruins, as were many of its farms and cities. Nearly 260,000 Confederate soldiers—nearly one in three—had paid for secession with their lives. And most significant, the Union armies had destroyed slavery.

The Ruins of Fredericksburg
Many southern towns suffered terrible damage to property, business activity, and people's way of life during the Civil War. In December 1863, Union artillery levelled the town of Fredericksburg, Virginia. Then Union soldiers fought house by house, street by street to clean out Confederate sharpshooters. The method of combat, and the totality of the destruction it produced, presaged World Wars I and II.

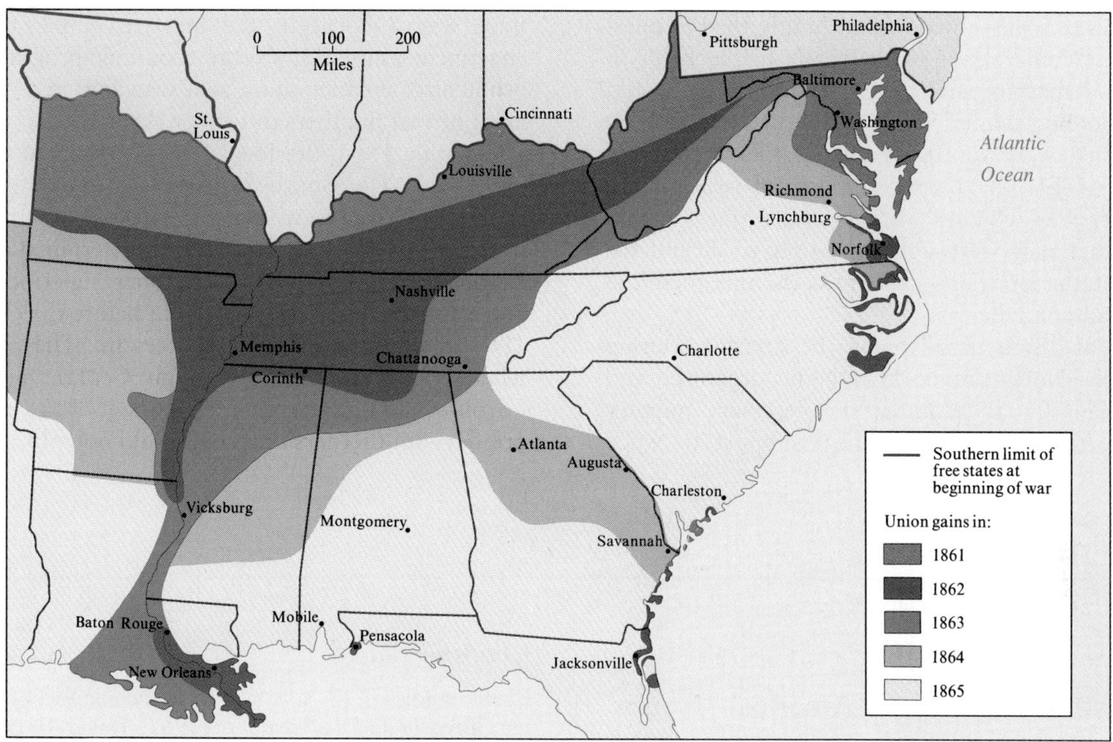

MAP 15.7

The Conquest of the South, 1861–1865

This map reveals how the Union slowly took control of Confederate territory. Nearly half of the territory of the Confederacy held fast until the last year of the war. The Union's victory depended primarily on its ability to control strategic lines of communication and destroy the armies of the Confederacy.

The Union's victory had been tragically costly. From Fort Sumter to Appomattox, more than 360,000 Union soldiers had died and hundreds of thousands of others had been maimed and crippled. But the hard and bitter war was won. Americans from the North and South, both blacks and whites, had to turn to the tasks of peace. Lincoln had spoken at Gettysburg of "finishing the work," and it was time to decide exactly what that "work" was. Freed slaves faced the questions of what freedom would bring. Their former masters began to try to salvage what they could from defeat. People in all parts of the North pondered the meaning of a victory so costly and so complete. They wondered whether the "terrible, swift sword" of the Battle Hymn of the Republic should be put away in reconciliation or loosed again in a hard and bitter peace.

Summary

The Democrats had divided along sectional lines in the 1860 elections because southerners sought more protection for slavery than northern Democrats would provide. When the Republicans took control of the federal government, the South concluded that it could no longer both preserve slavery and remain in the Union. The South seceded and used force to discourage the North from trying to maintain the Union.

The conflict became a total war, one of unsurpassed cost in American lives and resources, because of the great strength of the two regions and because of their conflict over fundamental political and social values. In 1861–1863 the Confederacy several times came close to a decisive victory—at Bull Run, Antietam, and Gettysburg. Meanwhile the Union learned that to win the war it had to smash southern society.

As the Civil War became a war between two peoples, the South and the North each had to address major issues of social unity. For the South, the key questions were: Would slaves work loyally in the fields to sustain their masters, and the war effort? And would non-slaveholding whites fight and die in a war if they believed they were simply defending the interests of slaveowners? For the North, the central issue of national unity was whether workers and farmers would conclude that they were fighting simply to defend the interests of the northern business-class and therefore refuse to fight and die.

The year 1864 turned out to be decisive. During that year the North proved to be better organized and more unified. It had acquired the necessary military leadership, resources, and political support to wage total war. Critical to the massive mobilization was enactment of the Republican economic program, establishment of emancipation as a war aim, and the enlistment of vast numbers of former slaves.

During 1864, President Lincoln mounted two great offensives. The South resisted vigorously, and once again came close to wearing down the will of the North to fight. But the equally stubborn determination of the Union armies, combined with their superior strength and a fortunate victory at Atlanta before the election of 1864, made both offensives successful. The war ended when Sherman's march through Georgia and South Carolina and Grant's relentless pursuit of Lee convinced ordinary southerners that they could not win the war.

TOPIC FOR RESEARCH

The Enlistment of African-American Troops

By the end of the Civil War, both Abraham Lincoln and Jefferson Davis had dropped their objections to arming slaves; in the course of fighting the war, each leader decided to enlist slaves in his armed forces. These decisions raise many questions. How did each leader arrive at his decision? What did the development of the thinking of Lincoln and Davis on arming slaves reveal about their attitudes toward slavery, and toward African-Americans? Did they change these attitudes during the course of the war? What other factors, such as shifting war aims and fortunes of war, accounted for their decisions to use African-American troops? And, finally, what impact did these troops have on the outcome of the war? Books that help in studying these questions include Ira Berlin et al., *Freedom, A Documentary History of Emancipation, 1861–1867, Series II, The Black Military Experience* (1982); Dudley Cornish, *The Sable Arm: Negro Troops in the Union Army, 1861–1865* (1956); Robert F. Durden, *The Gray and the Black: The Confederate Debate on Emancipation* (1972); and James M. McPherson, *The Negro's Civil War: How American Negroes Felt and Acted During the War for the Union* (1967).

BIBLIOGRAPHY

The most up-to-date, comprehensive one-volume survey of the Civil War is James M. McPherson, *Battle Cry of Freedom: The Civil War Era* (1988). Compelling older surveys include Shelby Foote, *The Civil War: A Narrative,* 3 vols. (1958–1974), and Allan Nevins, *War for the Union,* 4 vols. (1959–1971).

Choosing Sides

Classic studies of the secession crisis include Richard N. Current, *Lincoln and the First Shot* (1963); David M. Potter, *Lincoln and His Party in the Secession Crisis, 1860–61* (1950); and Kenneth M. Stampp, *And the War Came: The North and the Secession Crisis, 1860–61* (1950). Histories of the secession of the deep South include William L. Barney, *The Secessionist Impulse: Alabama and Mississippi in 1860* (1974), and Michael P. Johnson, *Toward a Patriarchal Republic: The Secession of Georgia* (1977). On the upper South, see Daniel W. Crofts, *Reluctant Confederates: Upper South Unionists in the Secession Crisis* (1989). For politics in a border state, consult William E. Parrish, *Turbulent Partnership: Missouri and the Union, 1861–1865* (1963).

War Machines

To study northern society and politics during the war, consult Adrian Cook, *The Armies of the Streets: The New York City Draft Riots of 1863* (1974); Emerson D. Fite, *Social and Economic Conditions in the North During the Civil War* (1910); George M. Fredrickson, *The Inner Civil War: Northern Intellectuals and the Crisis of Union* (1965); David Gilchrist and W. David Lewis, eds., *Economic Change in the Civil War Era* (1965); Frank L. Klement, *The Copperheads in the Middle West* (1960); Mary E. Massey, *Bonnet Brigades: American Women and the Civil War* (1966); William Q. Maxwell, *Lincoln's Fifth Wheel: The Political History of the United States Sanitary Commission* (1956); Joel Silbey, *A Respectable Minority: The Democratic Party in the Civil War Era* (1977); and Hans Trefousse, *The Radical Republicans* (1969). Important biographies on Union leaders include Frederick J. Blue, *Salmon P. Chase: A Life in Politics* (1987); Richard N. Current, *Old Thad Stevens* (1942); David Donald, *Charles Summer and the Rights of Man* (1970); William McFeely, *Grant: A Biography* (1981); Stephen B. Oates, *With Malice Towards None: The Life of Abraham Lincoln* (1977); Stephen W. Sears, *George B. McClellan: The Young Napoleon* (1988);

Benjamin F. Thomas, *Abraham Lincoln* (1952); and James G. Randall, *Mr. Lincoln* (1957).

The best summary histories of the Confederacy are Clement Eaton, *A History of the Southern Confederacy* (1954); Charles P. Roland, *The Confederacy* (1960); and Emory M. Thomas, *The Confederate Nation: 1861–1865* (1979). A classic study of the Confederate homefront is Charles W. Ramsdell, *Behind the Lines in the Southern Confederacy* (1944). Important biographies on leading Confederates include William C. Davis, *Jefferson Davis, The Man and His Hour: A Biography* (1991); Eli N. Evans, *Judah P. Benjamin, The Jewish Confederate* (1988); Douglas S. Freeman, *R. E. Lee: A Biography,* 4 vols. (1934–1935); and Thomas E. Schott, *Alexander H. Stephens of Georgia: A Biography* (1988).

Studies of non-slaveholders in the Confederacy include Paul Escott, *After Secession: Jefferson Davis and the Failure of Southern Nationalism* (1978); Drew Gilpin Faust, *The Creation of Confederate Nationalism: Ideology and Identity in the Civil War* (1988); Philip S. Paludan, Victims: *A True History of the Civil War* (1981); and Bell I. Wiley, *The Plain People of the Confederacy* (1943). Useful on the slaveowners is James L. Roark, *Masters Without Slaves* (1977), and the most revealing diary from the Confederacy: C. Vann Woodward, ed., *Mary Chesnut's Civil War* (1982).

Studies of wartime emancipation include Herman Belz, *A New Birth of Freedom: The Republican Party and Freedmen's Rights, 1861–1866* (1976); John Hope Franklin, *The Emancipation Proclamation* (1963); Louis S. Gerteis, *From Contraband to Freedom: Federal Policy Toward Southern Blacks, 1861–1865* (1973); William B. Hesseltine, *Lincoln's Plan of Reconstruction* (1960); James M. McPherson, *The Struggle for Equality: Abolitionists and the Negro in the Civil War and Reconstruction* (1964); and Benjamin Quarles, *The Negro in the Civil War* (1953). The best scholarship on the lives of slaves during the war is found in Ira Berlin et al., eds., *Freedom, A Documentary History of Emancipation, 1861–1867, Series I, Volume I: The Destruction of Slavery* (1985), and *Series I, Volume III: The Wartime Genesis of Free Labor: The Lower South* (1990). See, also, the works cited in the Topic for Research.

Fighting the Civil War

The most useful introductions to the military aspects of the war are T. Harry Williams, *The History of American Wars* (1981) and *Lincoln and His Generals* (1952). The classic studies of the experience of Civil War soldiers are Bell I. Wiley, *The Life of Johnny Reb* (1943) and *The Life of Billy Yank* (1952). For more modern scholarship, see Gerald F. Linderman, *Embattled Courage: The Experience of Combat in the American Civil War* (1987); Reid Mitchell, *Civil War Soldiers* (1988); and Joseph T. Glatthaar, *The March to the Sea and Beyond: Sherman's Troops in the Savannah and Carolinas Campaign* (1985). On Confederate military tactics, see Grady McWhiney and Perry D. Jamieson, *Attack and Die: Civil War Military Tactics and the Southern Heritage* (1982). An innovative exploration of the dynamics of violence is found in Charles Royster, *The Destructive War: William Tecumseh Sherman, Stonewall Jackson, and the Americans* (1991). The most graphic account of a single battle is Stephen W. Sears, *Landscape Turned Red: The Battle of Antietam* (1983). On the Civil War in the West consult Alvin M. Josephy, Jr., *The Civil War in the American West* (1991). The only comprehensive study of Civil War prisons is William B. Hesseltine, *Civil War Prisons: A Study in War Psychology* (1930). For insightful analysis of the war's outcome see Richard E. Beringer et al., *Why the South Lost the Civil War* (1986), and Herman Hattaway and Archer Jones, *How the North Won: A Military History of the Civil War* (1983).

TIMELINE

1861	Confederate States of America formed (February 4) Abraham Lincoln inaugurated (March 4) Confederates fire on Fort Sumter (April 12) First Battle of Bull Run (July 21)
1862	Battle of Shiloh (April 6–7) Confederacy introduces the first draft Homestead Act Battle of Antietam (September 17) Preliminary Emancipation Proclamation (September 22)
1863	Enrollment Act establishes draft in the North Battle of Gettysburg (July 1–3) Fall of Vicksburg (July 4) New York City draft riots
1864	Ulysses S. Grant takes command of all Union armies (March 9) Siege of Petersburg begins (June 15) The fall of Atlanta to William T. Sherman (September 2) The elections of 1864 Sherman's march through Georgia
1865	Robert E. Lee surrenders at Appomattox Court House (April 9)

Robert B. Elliott

Robert B. Elliott (1842–1884) was an African-American born in Boston and educated there, and in Jamaica and England. After studying law and serving in the U.S. Navy during the Civil War, he moved to Charleston. He won election to the South Carolina legislature (1868–1870), to two terms in Congress (1871–1874), and to Speaker of the House in South Carolina (1874–1876). He is pictured in this 1874 lithograph entitled, *The Shackle Broken by the Genius of Freedom,* addressing his fellow state legislators on civil rights. With the end of Reconstruction he left politics and moved to New Orleans where he practiced law.

CHAPTER 16 *The Union Reconstructed,* 1865–1877

When the Confederacy collapsed in the spring of 1865, President Lincoln hoped that he could achieve a swift reconciliation between the triumphant North and the shattered South. In his second inaugural address Abraham Lincoln had spoken of the need to "bind up the nation's wounds." But many questions remained unanswered. Who would control the rebuilding of the Union—the president or Congress? How long should the rebuilding last? How far should it go—should it exclude former Confederates from politics and reward freedmen with land confiscated from their former masters?

At the end of the war, most Republican leaders defined the task of rebuilding simply as *restoration.* These moderates wanted to establish loyal, pro-Union state governments and restore the southern states' representation in Congress. But the freedmen, former abolitionists, and some Republican politicians favored a more radical plan—one requiring a degree of *reconstruction* of the South. In their view, steps should be taken to ensure a measure of political and even economic equality for the freed slaves and to prevent the return to power of unrepentant planters. For radicals, the key to reconstructing the South was to make the Republican party dominant there.

When northern Republicans adopted a policy of radical reconstruction in 1867, ex-Confederates and their Democratic sympathizers in the North maintained that their goal should be the *redemption* of the South. They claimed that the Union's victory had defeated democracy in the South, depriving southerners of control over their economic, social, and political systems. The Union would be rebuilt, the redeemers claimed, only when white southerners had regained power over their own affairs.

The Reconstruction Era—the years from 1865 to 1877—was shaped by continuous struggles among the groups holding these differing views. It was a time of unparalleled peacetime turmoil and violence. In the struggles, every kind of tactic was brought to bear—the assassination of one president and the impeachment of another; the adoption of three amendments to the Constitution and a welter of new legislation; the use of violence, including nighttime terrorism by robed whites in the South; the creation of new institutions by African-Americans; and the conventional compromises and deals by politicians on all sides.

Presidential Restoration

Lincoln and his successor, Andrew Johnson, took the initiative for rebuilding the Union. Both presidents believed that the southern states had never legally left the Union; that rebuilding the nation was simply a process of restoring state governments loyal to the Union; and that this political process could take place quickly, largely under presidential direction. This moderate approach put the presidents on a collision course with those Republicans in Congress who sought a reconstruction of southern society.

Restoration Under Lincoln

The process of rebuilding had actually begun during the war as President Lincoln tried to subvert the southern war effort. Lincoln thought that a policy of moderation and reconciliation in those portions of the South occupied by federal troops would induce the Confederates to abandon the rebellion. In implementing his restoration plan, Lincoln relied on his power as military commander-in-chief. Lincoln assumed that states could not legally secede and that reorganizing the Union was purely an administrative matter. (In 1869, in *Texas v. White*, the Supreme Court accepted Lincoln's constitutional interpretation, ruling that secession was impossible under the Constitution.)

Lincoln's Plan. In December 1863, Lincoln announced his restoration plan. He offered a general amnesty to all Confederate citizens except high-ranking civil and military officials. Citizens of states seeking to reconstitute their governments would have to take an oath pledging their *future* loyalty to the Union and accepting the Union's wartime acts and proclamations concerning slavery. When 10 percent of the number of voters in 1860 had taken the loyalty oath, those individuals could organize a new state government.

President Lincoln aimed his plan at former southern Whigs, many of whom he had known well as former political allies. Under his plan, they would step forward, declare allegiance to the Union, and take charge of southern state governments. This is what happened in three states under military occupation—Louisiana, Arkansas, and Tennessee. The former Whigs who organized loyal governments under Lincoln's supervision often retained their economic power. In Louisiana, for example, Whig sugar planters who declared their loyalty to the Union received help from Generals Benjamin F. Butler and Nathaniel P. Banks, who used their troops to enforce labor discipline, transforming slaves into wage laborers and enabling the former Whigs to save their plantations.

Radical and Moderate Republicans. Many members of his own party, including some of his fellow moderates, disapproved of Lincoln's plan. Their opposition was based, in part, on a different constitutional interpretation. They argued that the southern states *had* left the Union and were now the equivalent of conquered provinces with territorial status. As such, they were subject to congressional rule rather than the president's executive authority.

The most strenuous criticism came from a group of radical Republicans, some of whom had abolitionist backgrounds. Led by Senator Charles Sumner of Massachusetts and Representative Thaddeus Stevens of Pennsylvania, the radicals wanted a harder, slower peace. In Stevens's words, the federal government should "revolutionize Southern institutions, habits, and manners." He declared that "the foundations of their institutions . . . must be broken up and relaid, or all our blood and treasure will have been spent in vain."

Stevens, Indiana congressman George W. Julian, and African-American leaders, including Frederick Douglass, staked out the most radical definition of what reconstruction should mean. The core of their program was an economic one—confiscation and redistribution of southern plantations to the freed slaves and white farmers who had been loyal to the Union. The program was meant to answer the dreams of the former slaves, whose expectations had been raised by emancipations,

Radical Republicans
Lincoln's readmission plan was harshly criticized by radical Republicans. One of their leaders was Thaddeus Stevens (front row, second from left) pictured here with fellow members of Congress in a photograph taken by Mathew Brady. Stevens outlined a radical economic plan that called for a redistribution of land in the South. He believed that the former slaves needed more than the vote to control their fate—they needed land. He was unable to muster support for this radical plan.

and even of the poor white farmers of the South. To the former slaves, emancipation and freedom meant control over their lives. But to control their fate in an agricultural economy, they knew they needed more than the vote—they needed to own land. But Stevens and Julian were unable to recruit other members of Congress to support a large-scale redistribution of land in the South. The majority of radical Republicans regarded such a plan as a violation of the Constitution's protection of property rights and a threat to the capitalist order.

The radical Republicans did agree on three key points: (1) The leaders of the Confederacy should not be allowed to return to power in the South; (2) Steps should be taken to establish the Republican party as a major, even dominant, force in southern political life; (3) The federal government should ensure that African-Americans participated in southern society with full *civil* equality by guaranteeing their voting rights. The last point was especially important. As Frederick Douglass declared in May 1865, "Slavery is not abolished until the black man has the ballot."

Moderate Republicans in Congress shared the radicals' view that Lincoln's program was too lenient, and they endorsed the first two points of the radical program. But as a group they hesitated in going further to support black suffrage and civil equality. Like virtually all conservative Republicans and Democrats, some moderates were profoundly racist and believed that African-Americans could never become responsible citizens. Other moderates, like Lincoln, had confidence in blacks' abilities. But they wanted to avoid the violent resistance that southern whites might offer to drastic changes in the relationship between the races.

The Wade-Davis Bill. In 1864 the radical and moderate Republicans in Congress devised an alternative to Lincoln's program, based on the two reconstruction principles on which they could agree. In the Wade-Davis bill, passed by Congress on July 2, 1864, they prescribed harsher conditions for former Confederate states to rejoin the Union. A *majority* of the state's adult white men would have to swear an oath of allegiance to the Union. The state could then hold a constitutional convention—but no one could vote in the election for delegates or serve as a delegate unless he could swear that he had never carried arms against the Union or aided the Confederacy in any way. Requiring this pledge, which became known as the *ironclad oath*, would exclude most southern whites, therefore leaving the task of constitution-making to those white men who had overtly opposed the Confederacy. Finally, the bill required slavery to be prohibited and Confederate civil and military leaders to be permanently disfranchised.

The Wade-Davis bill proposed going further than Lincoln's plan in punishing ex-Confederates, especially those who had led the South in rebellion. Despite this difference, Lincoln seemed ready to compromise with the congressional Republicans. Rather than openly challenging Congress by vetoing the Wade-Davis bill, he executed a "pocket" veto by not signing it before Congress adjourned. At the same time he initiated informal talks with members of Congress aimed at producing a compromise solution when the war ended. He even suggested that he might support the radical program of establishing federal control over race relations in the South and guaranteeing the vote to African-Americans there. In the last speech he ever delivered, on April 11, 1865, Lincoln demonstrated that he was moving pragmatically to endorse freedmen's suffrage, beginning with those who had served in the Union army.

The Assassination of Lincoln. Whether Lincoln and his party could have forged a unified approach to reconstruction is one of the great unanswered questions of American history. On April 14, 1865—Good Friday—Lincoln was shot in the head at Ford's Theater in Washington by an unstable actor named John Wilkes Booth. Ironically, Lincoln might have been spared if the war had dragged on longer, for Booth and his Confederate associates had originally plotted to kidnap the president to force a negotiated settlement. After Lee's surrender, Booth became desperate for revenge. In the middle of the play, he entered Lincoln's box, shot him at close range, stabbed a member of the president's party, and fled. Booth was hunted down and killed by Union troops. Eight people were eventually convicted as accomplices by military courts, and four of them were hanged.

Lincoln never regained consciousness and died on April 15. The Union—and the hundreds of thousands of African-Americans for whom his name had become synonymous with freedom—went into profound mourning. Even Lincoln's critics suddenly conceded his greatness. Millions of Americans honored his memory by waiting in silence to watch the train bearing his body back to Illinois for burial.

Lincoln's death dramatically changed the prospects for a moderate reconstruction. At one stroke, John Wilkes Booth had sent Lincoln to martyrdom, convinced many northerners that harsher measures against the South were necessary, and forced the presidency into the hands of Vice-President Andrew Johnson.

Restoration Under Johnson

Andrew Johnson was a self-made man and former slaveholder from the hills of eastern Tennessee. A Jacksonian Democrat, he saw himself as the champion of ordinary people. He hated what he called the "bloated, corrupt aristocracy" of the Northeast, and he blamed

Andrew Johnson

The president was not an easy man. This photograph of Andrew Johnson (1808–1875) conveys some of the personal qualities that contributed so centrally to his failure to reach agreement with Republicans on a program of moderate Reconstruction.

southern planters for the Civil War. His political career had led from the Tennessee legislature to the U.S. Senate, where he remained, loyal to the Union, after Tennessee seceded. He served as military governor of his home state after federal forces captured Nashville. In 1864 the Republicans gave him the vice-presidency in an effort to promote wartime political unity and to court the support of southern Unionists.

Like Lincoln, Johnson believed that the southern states had retained their constitutional status and that reunification was exclusively an executive matter. During the summer of 1865, when Congress was not in session, Johnson unilaterally executed his own plan of restoration. He insisted only that the states revoke their ordinances of secession and ratify the Thirteenth Amendment, which abolished slavery. He offered amnesty and a return of all property except slaves to almost all southerners if they took an oath of allegiance to the Union. Those southerners who were excluded from amnesty—high-ranking Confederate military officers and civil officials, and persons with taxable property of more than $20,000—could petition Johnson personally. By December 1865 all of the former Confederate states had functioning governments and had met Johnson's requirements to rejoin the Union.

Johnson's plan would not become complete until Congress accepted the senators and representatives from the former Confederacy. Under the Constitution, Congress is "the judge of the elections, returns and qualifications of its own members" (Article I, Section 5), and it would not convene again until December 1865. This step need not have been a problem for Johnson. While most moderate Republicans in Congress hoped to make changes in Johnson's program to bring it closer to the Wade-Davis bill, they supported the basic outline of his program. Perhaps most important, they agreed with Johnson that the federal government ought not to protect African-American suffrage or civil equality. Even most radicals were optimistic. They liked the stern treatment of Confederate leaders, and they hoped that the new southern governments would respond positively to Johnson's conciliatory attitude and offer the vote at least to those African-Americans who were literate and owned property—probably no more than 10 percent of adult African-American men.

During the summer and fall, however, Johnson lost any support from radical Republicans. They first became angered over a telegram that Johnson had sent in August to the provisional governor of Mississippi, who was presiding over the state's constitutional convention. Johnson urged that the vote be given to literate African-Americans—on the grounds that "the radicals, who are wild upon negro franchise, will be completely foiled." The telegram also embarrassed Republican moderates, who had hoped to win the support of the radicals as well as Johnson for a compromise program.

During the fall of 1865, news reports of conditions in the South alarmed the moderates and further outraged the radicals. They learned that ex-Confederates were frequently attacking freedmen and white Union supporters; that the new provisional governments were making no effort to enfranchise African-Americans; and that ex-Confederates had taken control of southern governments. Southern voters elected to Congress nine men who had served in the Confederate Congress, seven former officials of Confederate state governments, four generals and four colonels from the Confederate army, and even the vice-president of the Confederacy, Alexander Stephens. It turned out that Johnson had been exceedingly liberal in pardoning ex-Confederate leaders. He seemed less interested in punishing them than in humbling them by making them submit to his personal power.

As radical Republicans increased their attacks on Johnson, he shifted away from his strongly bipartisan stance. He began to believe he could build a coalition of white southerners, northern Democrats, and conservative Republicans to support the creation of a democracy for white southerners. To avoid embarrassing potentially supportive Republicans or ex-Whigs in the South, his banner would be "National Union." Democrats in both the North and South praised Johnson as the leader they needed to restore their party on a national basis. As the president warmed to Democratic applause, he granted more and more pardons to wealthy southerners—an average of a hundred a day in September.

The president's movement toward the Democrats further agitated radical Republicans and dismayed the moderates. By December 1865, when Congress convened, the moderates had become convinced that they had to join with the radicals in order to protect the Republican party. It would be necessary, they concluded, to take action to guarantee the civil rights of former slaves and to establish the Republican party in the South.

The Republican party acted quickly to reject the newly elected southern representatives and propose that Johnson work with Congress on a new program for reconstructing the South. A House-Senate committee—the Joint Committee on Reconstruction—was formed to develop that program in cooperation with the president.

The Joint Committee conducted public hearings on conditions in the former Confederacy and publicized alarming reports from army officers, federal officials, and white and black southerners. The testimony augmented the newspaper reports by revealing an astonishing level of violence, and by providing disturbing details on how southern planters and southern legislatures were attempting to resubjugate the freed slaves. Although most moderates were still not ready to impose black suffrage on the South, almost all were shocked by what they regarded as a movement to circumvent the Thirteenth Amendment.

Acting on Freedom

While congressmen discussed conditions in the South, African-Americans were already far advanced in acting on their idea of freedom. Exultant and hopeful, their main concern was economic independence, which they assumed was necessary to be truly free. During the Civil War they had acted on this assumption throughout the South, whenever Union armies drew near. But many officers actively sympathized with the planters, allowing planters who expressed loyalty to the Union to retain control of their plantations and their former slaves. Other officers wished to destroy the power of the planters but preserve a class system in the South. General Lorenzo Thomas, for example, devised a plan in 1863 to lease plantations in the Mississippi Valley to loyal northern men who would hire African-American laborers under conditions set by the army.

During the final months of the war, when the Union directed its military operations against civilians, the freedmen found greater opportunities to win control of land. Most visibly, General William T. Sherman reserved vast tracts of coastal lands in Georgia and South Carolina—the Sea Islands and the abandoned plantations within 30 miles of the coast—for African-American settlers and gave them "possessory titles" to 40-acre tracts. Sherman had little use for radicals or freedmen; he only wanted to relieve the pressure that African-American refugees placed on his army as it marched across the lower South. But the freedmen assumed that Sherman's order meant that the land would be theirs—a reasonable expectation after one of Sherman's generals told a large group of freedmen "that they were to be put in possession of lands, upon which they might locate their families and work out for themselves a living and respectability."

The resettlement of freedmen was organized by the Bureau of Refugees, Freedmen, and Abandoned Lands, which Congress created in March 1865. Known as the Freedmen's Bureau, it was charged with feeding and clothing war refugees of both races, renting confiscated land to "loyal refugees and freedmen," and drafting and enforcing labor contracts between freedmen and planters. The Freedmen's Bureau also worked with the large number of northern voluntary associations that sent missionaries and teachers to the South to establish schools for former slaves.

Schoolhouse, Port Hudson, Louisiana

This was probably the first schoolhouse built for freedmen by Union forces. In front, African-American soldiers from the Port Hudson "Corps d'Afrique" pose with their textbooks. In 1865 and 1866, most new schools in the South were established by blacks forming societies and raising money among themselves.

AMERICAN VOICES

Report on the Freedmen's Bureau *Eliphalet Whittlesey*

In October 1865, Colonel Eliphalet Whittlesey, an assistant commissioner for the Freedmen's Bureau in North Carolina, wrote the following report on the activities of the Bureau. He was later promoted to general and served as a trustee of the national Freedman's Savings Bank in Washington, D.C. He was typical of many Freedmen's Bureau officials in that he saw his role as one of mediating between two worthy groups—former slaves and former masters.

On the 22d of June I arrived at Raleigh with instructions . . . to take the control of all subjects relating to "refugees, freedmen, and the abandoned lands" within this State. I found these subjects in much confusion. Hundreds of white refugees and thousands of blacks were collected about this and other towns, occupying every hovel and shanty, living upon government rations, without employment and without comfort, many dying for want of proper food and medical supplies. A much larger number, both white and black, were crowding into the towns, and literally swarming about every depot of supplies to receive their rations. My first effort was to reduce this class of suffering and idle humanity to order, and to discover how large a proportion of these applicants were really deserving of help. . . .

It was evident at the outset that large numbers were drawing rations who might support themselves. . . . orders were issued that no able-bodied man or woman should receive supplies, except such as were known to be industrious, and to be entirely destitute. . . . The homeless and helpless were gathered in camps, where shelter and food could be furnished, and the sick collected in hospitals, where they could receive proper care. . . .

Suddenly set free [the freedmen] were at first exhilarated by the air of liberty, and committed some excesses. To be sure of their freedom, many thought they must leave the old scenes of oppression and seek new homes. Others regarded the property accumulated by their labor as in part their own, and demanded a share of it. On the other hand, the former masters, suddenly stripped of their wealth, at first looked upon the freedmen with a mixture of hate and fear. In these circumstances some collisions were inevitable. . . .

. . . [M]any freedmen need the presence of some authority to enforce upon them their new duties. . . . The efforts of the bureau to protect the freedmen have done much to restrain violence and injustice. Such efforts must be continued until civil government is fully restored, just laws enacted, or great suffering and serious disturbance will be the result.

Contrary to the fears and predictions of many, the great mass of colored people have remained quietly at work upon the plantations of their former masters during the entire summer. . . . In truth, a much larger amount of vagrancy exists among the whites than among the blacks. . . .

The report is confirmed by the fact that out of a colored population of nearly 350,000 in the State, only about 5,000 are now receiving support from the government. . . . Our officers . . . have visited plantations, explained the difference between slave and free labor, the nature and the solemn obligation of contracts. The chief difficulty met with has been a want of confidence between the two parties.

. . . Rev. F. A. Fiske, a Massachusetts teacher, has been appointed superintendent of education, and has devoted himself with energy to his duties. . . . the whole number of schools . . . is 63, the number of teachers 85, and the number of scholars 5,624. A few of the schools are self-supporting, and taught by colored teachers, but the majority are sustained by northern societies and northern teachers. The officers of the bureau have, as far as practicable, assigned buildings for their use, and assisted in making them suitable; but time is nearly past when such facilities can be given. The societies will be obliged hereafter to pay rent for school-rooms and for teachers homes. The teachers are engaged in a noble and self-denying work. They report a surprising thirst for knowledge among the colored people—children giving earnest attention and learning rapidly, and adults, after the day's work is done, devoting the evening to study. . . .

Source: Report of the Joint Committee on Reconstruction, 39th Cong., 1st sess. (Washington, D.C.: Government Printing Office, 1866), II: 186–92.

By the end of the war, the army and the Freedmen's Bureau had resettled about ten thousand families on half a million acres of "Sherman" land in Georgia and South Carolina. Reports of such actions inspired many African-American families to stay on their old plantations in the hope that they would own some of the land after the war. When South Carolina planter Thomas Pinckney returned home, his freed slaves told him, "We ain't going nowhere. We are going to work right here on the land where we were born and what belongs to us."

One Georgia freedman offered to sell to his former master the share of the plantation he expected to receive after the federal redistribution.

Andrew Johnson's amnesty plan allowed pardoned Confederates to recover their land if Union troops had confiscated or occupied it. In October, Johnson ordered General Oliver O. Howard, head of the Freedmen's Bureau, to tell Sea Island blacks that they did not hold legal title to the land and that they would have to come to terms with the white landowners. When Howard reluctantly obeyed, the dispossessed farmers protested: "Why do you take away our lands? You take them from us who have always been true, always true to the Government! You give them to our all-time enemies! That is not right!" When some of the Sea Islanders refused to deal with the restored white owners, Union soldiers forced them to leave or work for their old masters.

The former slaves resisted efforts to remove them. Often led by African-American veterans of the Union army, they fought pitched battles with plantation owners and bands of ex-Confederate soldiers. Whenever possible, landowners attempted to disarm and intimidate the returning soldiers. One of them wrote from Maryland: "The returned colard Solgers are in Many cases beten, and their guns taken from them, we darcent walk out of an evening. . . . they beat us badly and Sumtime Shoot us." In this warfare, federal troops often backed the local whites, who generally prevailed in recapturing their former holdings.

A New Labor System. Throughout the South, high postwar prices for cotton prompted returning planters not only to reclaim land but also to establish a labor system that was as close to slavery as they could make it. On paper, emancipation had cost the slaveowners about $3 billion—the value of their capital investment in former slaves—a sum that equaled nearly three-fourths of the nation's economic production in 1860. The *real* losses of planters, however, depended on whether they lost control of their former slaves. Planters attempted to reestablish that control and to substitute low wages for the food, clothing, and shelter that their slaves had previously received. They also refused to sell or rent land to blacks, hoping to force them to work for low wages.

The freedmen resisted the new wage system, as well as the loss of land. During the growing seasons of 1865 and 1866, thousands of former slaves abandoned their old plantations and farms. Many freedmen sought better lives in the towns and cities of the South. Those who remained in the countryside either refused to work in the cotton fields or tried to reduce the amount of time they worked there. When they could, freedmen developed their own garden plots, therefore, guaranteeing themselves a subsistence level of rations during the postwar disruptions. The freedmen who did return to work in the white-owned cotton fields refused to submit to the grueling gang system that had been the major tool of economic exploitation under slavery. Now they wanted a pace of work and independence that reflected their new status. What was freedom all about if not to have a bit more leisure time, to work less intensely than they had as slaves, and to work for themselves and their families?

Wage Labor of Ex-Slaves

This photograph, taken in South Carolina shortly after the Civil War, shows former slaves being led from the cotton fields. Although they now worked for wages, they were probably organized into a gang not far removed from the earlier slave gangs. Their plug-hatted crew leader is dressed much as his slave-driving predecessor would have been.

The Black Codes. The efforts of former slaves to control their own lives ran counter to deeply entrenched white attitudes. Emancipation had not destroyed the racist assumptions and fears that the planters had fostered in order to maintain and defend slavery. The former slaveowners and many of the poorer whites who looked to them for leadership attempted to maintain the South's caste system. Beginning in 1865, southern legislatures enacted sets of laws—known as Black Codes—that were designed to keep African-Americans in a condition close to slavery.

The codes varied from state to state, but virtually all required the arrest of blacks for vagrancy if they were found without employment. In most cases they could not pay the fine, and the county court would then hire them to an employer, who could hold them in slavery-like conditions. Several state codes established specific hours of labor, spelled out the duties expected of laborers, and declared that any laborer who did not meet these standards was a vagrant. The codes usually restricted black employment opportunities outside agriculture by requiring licenses for those who wished to pursue skilled work or even "irregular job work."

The state legislatures went even further, sanctioning the efforts of local governments to circumscribe narrowly the lives of blacks. Localities set curfews, required black agricultural workers to obtain passes from their employers, insisted that blacks who wished to live in town obtain white sponsors, and, in an effort to prevent political gatherings, sharply regulated meetings of blacks, including those held in churches. Fines and forced labor were the penalties for violators.

Congressional Initiatives

Reports of southern repression aroused moderate Republicans in Congress. They decided they must provide for some guarantees of the civil rights of freedmen. The moderates first drafted a bill to extend the life of the Freedmen's Bureau and enlarge its powers, including the authority to establish courts to protect the rights of freedmen.

The news from the South had not, however, convinced Republicans that they should confiscate land and give it to the freedmen. A large majority of Republicans voted down an amendment to the Freedmen's Bureau bill proposed by Thaddeus Stevens that would have made "forfeited estates of the enemy" available to freedmen. Still, Republicans were now willing to go further in creating opportunities for land ownership. Thus the Freedmen's Bureau bill countermanded Johnson's order to Howard to evict the freedmen from the confiscated lands on the Sea Islands. Also, two days after the bill's passage, the House passed another bill, sponsored by George Julian, that became the Southern Homestead Act of 1866. It designated about 45 million acres of public land in Alabama, Arkansas, Florida, Louisiana, and Mississippi for 80-acre grants to settlers who cultivated the land for five years. Congress prohibited anyone who had supported the Confederacy from filing a claim until 1867. Although Republicans were unwilling to violate planters' property rights, they offered freedmen the same chance to acquire land that northerners had enjoyed since the passage of the Homestead Act of 1862.

Republicans approved the Freedmen's Bureau bill almost unanimously, but in February 1866 Johnson vetoed it. The bill was unconstitutional, he argued, because the Constitution did not authorize a "system for the support of indigent persons" and because the states most directly affected by its provisions were not yet represented in Congress. His veto, implying that *any* Reconstruction legislation passed without southern representation was unconstitutional, enraged moderate Republicans. They tried to override the veto but failed, just barely, to hold the votes of enough conservative Republicans to collect the necessary two-thirds majority.

Democrats applauded Johnson's firmness. To celebrate the veto, and Washington's Birthday, a group of Democrats went to the White House to serenade him. The president emerged to deliver an impromptu, impassioned speech that suggested to many listeners that he was drunk. Accusing the radical Republicans of being traitors, he likened Stevens and Sumner to Confederate leaders because they all were "opposed to the fundamental principles of this Government." He mentioned himself two hundred times in the speech and suggested that the radicals were plotting to assassinate him.

The First Civil Rights Bill. Johnson's veto and his Washington's Birthday speech pushed the moderate Republicans close to a complete break with him. But they still expected his cooperation on their second major piece of legislation, a civil rights bill. Passed in March 1866, it defined the citizenship rights of the freedmen—for example, the rights to own and rent property, to make contracts, and to have access to the courts. And, it authorized federal authorities to bring suit against those who violated these rights and guaranteed that appeals in such cases could be heard in federal courts. The moderate Republicans were prepared to expand federal protection of civil rights, though they were still not ready to guarantee black suffrage.

Against the advice of his cabinet, Johnson vetoed the civil rights bill. He restated his constitutional point about absent southern representation and added a new objection, with the votes of Democratic wards in the large cities in mind. The bill, he argued, discriminated against whites by providing immediate citizenship for newly freed slaves. Under federal law, he pointed out, immigrants had to wait five years.

Johnson's veto was the last straw for almost all moderate Republicans. They now agreed with the radicals that Congress must take charge of Reconstruction. In April moderates engineered an override of Johnson's veto, and in July—after watering down the Freedmen's Bureau bill by requiring freedmen to buy the confiscated land on the Sea Islands—they won the votes of enough conservative Republicans to pass the Freedmen's Bureau bill over a second veto.

The Fourteenth Amendment. The central part of the independent plan that moderates and radicals now undertook was to provide freedmen with constitutional as well as legislative protection. In April the Joint Committee on Reconstruction drafted and submitted to Congress a proposal for a fourteenth amendment to the Constitution. It did not provide what the radicals wanted—a guarantee of black suffrage—but it went beyond the Civil Rights Act of 1866.

Section 1 declared that "all persons born or naturalized in the United States" were citizens. No state could abridge "the privileges or immunities of citizens of the United States" or deprive "any person of life, liberty, or property, without due process of law" or deny anyone "the equal protection of the laws." The drafters intended these phrases to be vague, but they hoped that their force would increase over time, especially since Section 5 gave Congress the power to enforce the amendment.

Section 2 penalized any state that denied suffrage to any adult male citizens. A state's representation in the House of Representatives would be reduced by the percentage of adult male citizens who were denied the vote.

Rising violence against African-Americans throughout the South clinched the support of moderates for the amendment. Most dramatic were three days of race rioting in Memphis in May. Forty-six blacks and two whites were left dead, and hundreds of black houses, churches, and schools were looted and burned. In June 1866, Congress forwarded the Fourteenth Amendment to the states for ratification.

President Johnson attacked the Fourteenth Amendment. Even its moderate provisions went too far in protecting African-Americans for his taste, and he wanted to create an issue for the 1866 elections. At his urging, ten ex-Confederate states, joined by Delaware and Kentucky, all turned it down, denying the amendment the necessary approval of three-fourths of the states. Among the former states of the Confederacy, only Tennessee approved the amendment, and it was formally readmitted to the Union in July 1866.

Resistance in the South

The engraving, subtitled "Verdict, 'Hang the D--- Yankee and Nigger,'" appeared in *Harper's Weekly* in March 1867. It may have led readers to recall the killing of the Republicans who attended the black suffrage convention in New Orleans the previous summer. We have no reliable estimates of the total number of Republicans, white and black, killed by ex-Confederates during Reconstruction.

The Congressional Elections of 1866. Johnson planned to attack the Fourteenth Amendment and advance his National Union movement during the congressional elections of 1866. In July a National Union Convention met for the purpose of uniting his supporters from around the nation. But the Republican and Democratic politicians in attendance were unwilling to share power across party lines, and the convention did not attempt to create a new national party. Another problem for Johnson's movement was a major race riot in the South, just two weeks before the convention assembled. A white mob in New Orleans attacked the delegates to a black suffrage convention and, aided by the local police, killed forty people, including thirty-seven blacks. Popular support in the North for radical Reconstruction seemed to grow instantly.

In August and September, Johnson tried to win back support in a disastrous "swing around the circle"—a railroad tour from Washington to Chicago and St. Louis and back. It was unprecedented for a president to campaign personally, and Johnson made matters worse by engaging in shouting matches with hecklers and insulting members of the hostile crowds. His message was consistent: Congress had acted illegally by approving the Fourteenth Amendment without the participation all of the southern states, southerners were now loyal to the Union, and the real traitors were the radical Republicans who were delaying restoration of the Union.

Moderate and radical Republicans responded by escalating their attacks on Democrats. They charged that ex-Confederates wanted to resume the Civil War, and, in a practice that became known as "waving the bloody shirt," they charged that the Democratic party had caused the Civil War and then sided with the traitors. Indiana's Republican governor, Oliver Morton, described the Democratic party as "a common sewer and loathsome receptacle, into which is emptied every element of treason North and South, every element of inhumanity and barbarism which has dishonored the age."

The 1866 congressional elections brought a humiliating defeat for the president, who still had two years left to serve. The Republicans won a three-to-one majority in Congress (margins of 42 to 11 in the Senate, and 143 to 49 in the House) and gained control of the governorship and legislature in every northern state, as well as West Virginia, Missouri, and Tennessee. The moderate Republicans interpreted the election results as a clear call for radical Reconstruction, rather than mere restoration, of the South. The most important policy shift was the moderates' acceptance of the radicals' proposition that the federal government must guarantee the vote for black men.

Radical Reconstruction

In the months following the 1866 elections, moderates and radicals in Congress joined together to take control of Reconstruction. They agreed on a more radical program than even the one proposed in the Wade-Davis bill.

The Congressional Program

In March, Congress passed the Reconstruction Act of 1867, which was designed to implement the radical plan. It organized the South as a conquered land, dividing it (with the exception of Tennessee) into five military districts, each under the command of a Union general. Each commander was ordered to register all adult black men in his district but was given considerable discretion in registering former Confederates. After the registration, the commander was to supervise the election of a convention to write a state constitution and to make certain that the constitution include guarantees for black suffrage. Congress would readmit the state to the Union if its voters ratified the new constitution, if that document proved acceptable to Congress, if the new state legislature approved the Fourteenth Amendment, and if enough states had already ratified the Fourteenth Amendment to make it part of the Constitution. Johnson vetoed the act, but Congress overrode the veto. During 1868, six states—North Carolina, South Carolina, Florida, Alabama, Louisiana, and Arkansas—met the requirements and were readmitted to the Union.

These measures were radical, but a few radical Republicans argued that even more dramatic measures were needed to guarantee racial equality. They pressed for the distribution of land to former slaves, federal support for black schools, and disfranchisement of ex-Confederates. Congressman George Julian warned that "the power of the great landed aristocracy in these regions, if unrestrained by power from without, would inevitably assert itself." But even the most extreme of the radicals accepted the new Reconstruction policies as all they could get in 1867.

The Tenure of Office Act. Republicans also acted to check the power of President Johnson to undermine their Reconstruction plan. At the same time the Reconstruction Act of 1867 became law, Congress passed the Tenure of Office Act, which required congressional consent for the removal of any official whose appointment had required Senate confirmation. Congress chiefly wanted to protect Secretary of War Edwin M. Stanton, a Lincoln appointee and the only member of Johnson's cabinet who favored radical Reconstruction. In his position Stanton could do much to prevent Johnson from frustrating the goals of Reconstruction. Congress also required the president to issue all orders to the army through its commanding general, Ulysses S. Grant, also a supporter of radical Reconstruction. In effect, Congress was attempting to reconstruct the presidency as well as the South.

Johnson appeared to cooperate with Congress at first, appointing generals recommended by Stanton and Grant to command the five military districts in the South. But he was just biding his time. In August 1867, after Congress had adjourned, he "suspended" Stanton until Congress reconvened and replaced him with Grant on a temporary basis, believing that Grant would act like a good soldier and follow orders. Next Johnson replaced four Republican generals who commanded southern districts, including Philip H. Sheridan, Grant's favorite cavalry general.

Johnson, however, had misjudged Grant, who wrote a letter protesting the president's thwarting of Congress and then deliberately leaked it to the press. When the Senate reconvened in the fall, it intensified the political drama by overruling Stanton's suspension. Grant increased the pressure on Johnson by resigning so

Stanton could resume his office. Johnson overreacted, publicly protesting Grant's resignation. Grant responded by becoming an open enemy of the president.

The Impeachment of Johnson. Johnson decided to challenge the constitutionality of the Tenure of Office Act. In February 1868 he formally dismissed Stanton. This time Stanton barricaded the door of his office, refusing to admit the replacement Johnson had appointed. Three days later, on February 24, the House of Representatives struck out against Johnson using the power granted by the Constitution to impeach—to charge federal officials with "Treason, Bribery, or other high Crimes and Misdemeanors." The House overwhelmingly (128–47) brought eleven counts of criminal misconduct, nine of which dealt with violations of the Tenure of Office Act, against the president.

The trial in the Senate, which the Constitution empowers to act as a court in impeachment cases, lasted eleven weeks and was presided over by Chief Justice Salmon P. Chase. On May 16 thirty-five senators voted for conviction—one vote short of the two-thirds majority required. Seven moderate Republicans had broken ranks, voting for acquittal along with twelve Democrats. The reluctant moderates were overwhelmed by the drastic nature of impeachment and conviction; Congress had removed federal judges from office, but never before had it seriously considered removing a president. While these moderates agreed that Johnson had broken the law, they felt the real issue was a disagreement between Congress and the president over a matter of policy. They feared that a conviction based on a policy dispute would establish a dangerous precedent and undermine the presidency. The Civil War had demonstrated to them the need for a strong federal government administered by a powerful executive. These moderates doubted that the nation could preserve internal unity, advance the Republican economic program, and defend itself against foreign enemies without a strong presidency.

The radical Republicans had failed to convict Johnson, but they had defeated him politically. For the remaining ten months of his term, Johnson was forced to allow Reconstruction to proceed under congressional direction.

The Elections of 1868. The impeachment controversy made Grant, already the North's most popular war hero, a hero of Reconstruction as well. He easily won the Republican presidential nomination. In the fall campaign he supported radical Reconstruction and "waved the bloody shirt," but he also urged reconciliation between the sections. His Democratic opponent was Horatio Seymour, a former governor of New York and Peace Democrat who almost declined the nomination, certain that Grant would win. In the face of rising violence in the South, Seymour and the Democrats received little support for their claim that the government should let southern state governments reorganize on their own. Grant won about the same share of the northern vote (55 percent) that Lincoln had in 1864, collected a majority of the national popular vote, and received 214 out of 294 electoral votes, including those of six of the eight reconstructed states. The Republicans also retained two-thirds majorities in both houses of Congress. The Republicans were convinced they had a strong popular mandate for their program of radical Reconstruction.

The Fifteenth Amendment. The Republicans quickly produced the last major piece of Reconstruction legislation—the Fifteenth Amendment. Intended to guarantee black manhood suffrage, the amendment forbade states to deny their citizens the right to vote on the grounds of race, color, or "previous condition of servitude."

Some radical Republicans would have preferred more aggressive protections of black citizenship, such as prohibiting state governments from using property ownership or literacy tests to disqualify blacks as voters. But Republican moderates did not want to ban tactics that northern and western states might want to employ to deny immigrants the vote. Massachusetts and Connecticut used literacy as a requirement for voting, as did California, which sought to deny the vote to Chinese immigrants. Even though it failed to prohibit such tactics, the Fifteenth Amendment was much more effective than the Fourteenth in promoting African-American suffrage. The amendment was passed in February 1869, and Congress required the unreconstructed states of Virginia, Mississippi, Texas, and Georgia to ratify it before they were readmitted to the Union.

The Issue of Suffrage for Women

Radical Reconstruction could have changed the legal status of women. Instead, by referring to adult "male citizens," the Fourteenth Amendment wrote the term "male" into the Constitution for the first time and, in effect, sanctioned the denial of the suffrage for women. Under the Fourteenth Amendment, suffrage limitations based on gender—alone among all the possible restrictions on suffrage—would not reduce a state's representation in Congress.

Former abolitionists such as Elizabeth Cady Stanton and Susan B. Anthony were deeply disappointed. They had organized a massive petition drive that collected almost 400,000 signatures in support for the Thirteenth Amendment; they believed that their male collaborators would reciprocate by supporting universal suffrage. In fact, many did, but most assumed that the public was not ready for the idea. As Wendell Phillips told women leaders, "One question at a time. This hour belongs to the Negro."

The leaders of the women's movement did not oppose ratification of the Fourteenth Amendment. They accepted defeat at the federal level and focused on the reform of state constitutions. Through a new organization, the American Equal Rights Association—which they formed in 1866, at their first women's rights convention since the Civil War—they launched a campaign to win *universal* suffrage at the state level.

The Fifteenth Amendment wounded those who sought the vote for women even more deeply; it made no reference to gender and thus permitted states to deny suffrage to women. In response, Stanton and Anthony concluded that feminists should develop a program independent of any political party. They broke with Republican abolitionists and refused to support the Fifteenth Amendment unless it was accompanied by a new amendment enfranchising women. Stanton argued that ratification of the Fifteenth Amendment alone would create an "aristocracy of sex." She declared, "All manhood will vote not because of intelligence, patriotism, property or white skin, but because it is male, not female." In promoting a new amendment, she made a special appeal to women of the business class:

> American women of wealth, education, virtue and refinement, if you do not wish the lower orders of Chinese, Africans, Germans and Irish, with the low ideas of womanhood to make laws for you and your daughters . . . to dictate not only the civil, but moral codes by which you shall be governed, awake to the danger of your present position and demand that woman, too, shall be represented in the government!

Other advocates of woman suffrage—including Lucy Stone and Frederick Douglass—saw the politics of suffrage differently. The Fifteenth Amendment had opened up a schism in the ranks of the women's movement. In 1868, Stone and Douglass broke with the American Equal Rights Association of Stanton and Anthony and formed a new group, the New England Woman Suffrage Association. Their goal was to maintain an alliance with Republicans and to support the Fifteenth Amendment. They believed that this was the best way to enlist Republican support for women's suffrage after Reconstruction issues had been settled.

The differences between the two groups increased in the postwar years. In 1869 the American Equal Rights Association renamed itself the National Woman Suffrage Association and elected Stanton as its first president. It concentrated on mobilizing local suffrage societies in communities around the country. Meanwhile, the New England Woman Suffrage Association reorganized itself as the American Woman Suffrage Association. Its members elected Henry Ward Beecher, a prominent Brooklyn minister, as president and cultivated strong ties with Republicans and men who had been abolitionists.

For twenty-one years, the two national organizations competed for the leadership of the women's movement. The "American" association tended to focus on suffrage, while the "National" association developed a more comprehensive reform posture. While the split weakened the movement in the short run, the formation of the "National" association meant that a major part of the women's movement had broken away from abolitionism and Republicanism and was free to develop independent political strategies.

A Woman Suffrage Quilt, Made Around 1875
Home-made quilts provided funds and a means of persuasion for the temperance and antislavery movements. But woman suffrage quilts, such as this detail from "The Suffragette Quilt" (c. 1860–1880), picturing a women's rights lecturer, were rare. The leaders of the woman suffrage movement usually regarded quilts and needlework as representing the domestic subjugation of women.

The First Vote

The lithograph appeared in *Harper's Weekly* in November 1867. The voters represent elements of African-American political leadership: an artisan with tools, a well-dressed member of the middle class, and a Union soldier.

The South During Radical Reconstruction

Between 1868 and 1871 all the southern states met the stipulations of Congress and rejoined the Union. The Reconstruction governments under Republican control remained in power for periods ranging from a few months for Virginia to nine years for South Carolina, Louisiana, and Florida. African-Americans were at the center of forming and maintaining these Republican governments. In Alabama, Florida, South Carolina, Mississippi, and Louisiana, they constituted an outright majority of all the registered voters. They provided the votes for Republican victories there and in Georgia, Virginia, and North Carolina as well where they accounted for nearly half the registered voters. But the Republican governments were more than African-American regimes; they also drew support from whites who had not owned slaves and from white northerners who moved south after the war.

Democratic ex-Confederates satirized and stereotyped the Republicans who dominated the reconstructed state governments. They mocked and scorned black Republicans as ignorant field hands who could only play at politics, and they ridiculed whites who became Republicans as *scalawags*—an ancient Scots-Irish term for underfed, runty, worthless animals. White settlers who had come from the North they denounced as *carpetbaggers*—transient exploiters who carried all their property in cheap suitcases called carpetbags. Carpetbaggers held more than half the Republican governorships in the South and almost half of its seats in Congress.

Actually, few southern Republicans conformed to these stereotypes. Some of the carpetbaggers did come south to seek personal profit, but they also brought capital and skills to invest in the region's future. Most were former officers of the Union army who had fallen in love with the South—its climate, people, and economic

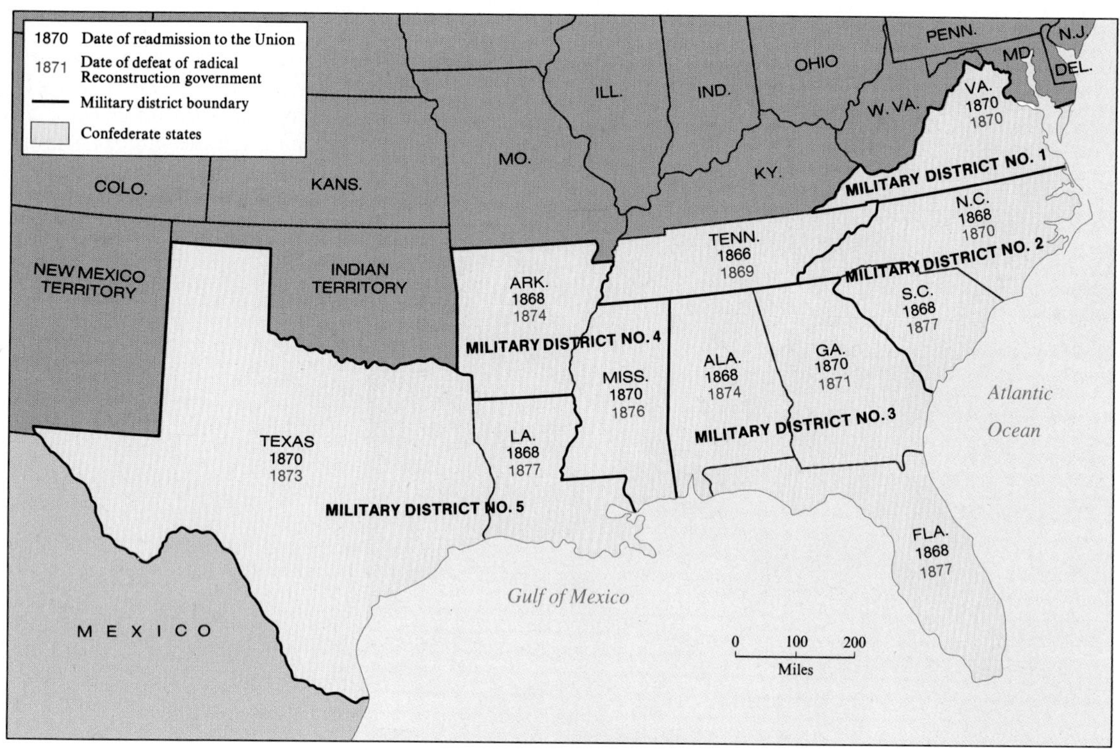

MAP 16.1

Reconstruction

The federal government organized the Confederate states into five military districts during radical Reconstruction. For each state the first date indicates when the state was readmitted to the Union; the second date is when radical Republicans lost control of the state government. All the ex-Confederate states rejoined the Union from 1868 to 1870, but the periods of radical rule varied widely. Radicals lasted only a few months in Virginia; they held on until the end of Reconstruction in Louisiana, Florida, and South Carolina.

opportunities. Many carpetbaggers were professionals and college graduates. The scalawags were even more diverse. Some were wealthy ex-Whigs and even former slaveowners. Some of these groups saw Republicanism as the best way to attract northern capital to southern railroads, mines, and factories. Immigrant workingmen and farmers were often found among the Republicans. The largest such group were the Germans in southwest Texas. They sent to Congress Edward Degener, an immigrant and San Antonio grocer, whom Confederate authorities had imprisoned and whose sons had been executed for treason. But most numerous among the scalawags were yeoman farmers from the backcountry districts. They wanted to rid the South of its slaveowning aristocracy, and scalawags had generally fought against, or at least refused to support, the Confederacy. They believed that slavery had victimized whites as well as blacks. "Now is the time," a Georgia scalawag wrote, "for every man to come out and speak his principles publickly and vote for liberty as we have been in bondage long enough."

African-American Political Leadership. The Democrats' stereotypes of black political leaders were just as false. Until 1867 most African-American leaders in the South, attracted to the movement for black suffrage, came from the elite that had been free before the Civil War. When Congress began to organize Republican governments in 1867, this diverse group of ministers, artisans, shopkeepers, and former soldiers reached out to the freedmen. African-American speakers, some financed by the Republican Congressional Committee, fanned out into the old plantation districts and drew ex-slaves into political leadership. Still, few of the new leaders were field hands; most had been preachers or artisans. The literacy of one ex-slave, Thomas Allen, who was a Baptist minister and shoemaker, helped him win election to the Georgia legislature. "In my county," he recalled, "the colored people came to me for instructions, and I gave them the best instructions I could. I took the *New York Tribune* and other papers, and in that way I found out a great deal, and I told them whatever I thought was right."

Many of the African-American leaders who emerged in 1867 had been born in the North or spent many years there. They moved south when congressional Reconstruction began to offer the prospect of meaningful freedom. Like white migrants, many were veterans of the Union army; some had fought in the antislavery crusade; some were employed by the Freedmen's Bureau or northern missionary societies; a few were from free families and had gone north for an education. Others had escaped from slavery and were now returning home, such as Blanche K. Bruce, who became one of two black U.S. senators from Mississippi. He had received tutoring on the Virginia plantation of his white father. During the war Bruce escaped to Kansas from Missouri, where his father had moved, and then returned to Missouri, establishing a school for African-Americans in Hannibal. He arrived in Mississippi in 1869 and entered politics; in 1874 he became the second African-American elected to the Senate and the first elected to a full term until 1966.

Hiram R. Revels

In 1870 Hiram R. Revels (1822–1901) was elected to the U.S. Senate from Mississippi to fill Jefferson Davis's former seat. Revels was a free black from North Carolina who had migrated North and attended Knox College in Illinois. He recruited blacks for the Union army and, as an ordained Methodist minister, served as chaplain of a black regiment in Mississippi, where he settled after the war.

Although the number of African-Americans who held office during Reconstruction never reflected their share of the electorate, they held positions of importance throughout the South, and their significance increased in every state under Republican rule. Sixteen African-Americans served in the U.S. House of Representatives in the Reconstruction Era. In 1870, Mississippi sent Hiram Revels, a minister born in North Carolina, to the Senate as its first African-American member. In 1868, African-Americans won a majority in one house of the South Carolina legislature; subsequently they won half of the state's eight executive offices, elected three members of Congress, and won a seat on the state supreme court. Over the entire course of Reconstruction, twenty African-Americans served as governor, lieutenant governor, secretary of state, treasurer, or superintendent of education, and more than six hundred served as state legislators. Almost all the African-Americans who became state executives had been freemen before the Civil War, while most of the legislators had been slaves. Because these African-Americans represented the districts that large planters had dominated before the Civil War, they embodied the potential of Reconstruction for revolutionizing class relationships in the South.

The Radical Program. Southern Republicans believed that the South needed to be fundamentally reconstructed. They wanted to end the South's dependence on cotton agriculture and unskilled labor and create an economy based on manufacturing, capital investment, and skilled labor. Southern Republicans fell far short of making this vision a reality. But they accomplished much more of it than their critics gave them credit for.

Southern Republicans made their societies more democratic. They repealed Black Codes and rejected new proposals for enforcing labor discipline. They modernized state constitutions, extended the right to vote, and made more offices elective. They established hospitals, penitentiaries, and asylums for orphans and the insane. South Carolina purchased medical care for the poor, while Alabama provided them with free legal counsel. Republican governments built roads in areas where roads had never existed. They supervised the rebuilding of the region's railroad network and subsidized investment in manufacturing and transportation. They undertook major public works programs. And they did all this without federal financing. To pay for their ambitious programs they introduced the taxes that northern states had relied on since the Jacksonian era. These were general property taxes that taxed not only real estate but the trappings of wealth—personal property such as furnishings, machinery, tools, and even cash. The goal was to force planters to pay their fair share of taxes and to force uncultivated land onto the market. In many plantation counties, especially in South Carolina, Louisiana, and Mississippi, former slaves served as tax assessors and collectors, administering the taxation of their onetime owners.

A Freedmen's School

An 1866 sketch from *Harper's Weekly* of a Vicksburg, Mississippi, school run by the Freedmen's Bureau illustrates the desire for education by ex-slaves of all ages. Because most southern blacks were farmers, schools commonly offered night classes that left students free for field work during the day.

The most important accomplishments of the southern Republicans came in education. The Republican state governments viewed schooling as the foundation for a democratic order in the South. Led by both black and white superintendents of education, many of whom had served in the Freedmen's Bureau, the Reconstruction governments built public schools that served more people, black and white, than had ever been reached by free education in the South. African-Americans of all ages rushed to attend the newly established schools, even when they had to pay tuition. One elderly man in Mississippi explained his desire to go to school: "Ole missus used to read the good book [the Bible] to us . . . on Sunday evenin's, but she mostly read dem places where it says, 'Servants obey your masters.' . . . Now we is free, there's heaps of tings in that old book we is just suffering to learn." By 1875 about half of all the children in Florida, Mississippi, and South Carolina were enrolled in school.

Virtually all the new schools were segregated by race; only Louisiana attempted to establish an integrated system. But most African-Americans seemed to agree that segregation was an issue for a later day; most shared Frederick Douglass's judgment that what was most important was the fact that separate schools were "infinitely superior" to no schools at all.

Social Institutions in Freedom. The building of schools was part of a larger effort by African-Americans to fortify the institutions that had sustained their spirit during the days of slavery. Most important, they strengthened their family life as the cornerstone of new communities. Families moved away from the slave quarters, usually building homes scattered around or near their old plantations and farms. Sometimes they established entirely new all-black villages. Husbands, wives, and children who had been separated by the slave trade often reunited, sometimes after journeys of hundreds of miles. Couples stepped forward to record marriages that had been unrecognized under slavery. As slavery crumbled, mothers rescued their children from the control of planters and overseers. Many women refused to work in the fields. Instead, they insisted on tending gardens, managing households, and bringing education and religion to their children. Many wives asserted their independence, opening individual bank accounts, refusing responsibility for their husbands' debts at country stores, and bringing complaints of abuse and lack of child support to the Freedmen's Bureau.

Christianity had played a central role in nineteenth-century slave society, and freed slaves buttressed their new communities by founding their own churches. Rather than participate in biracial congregations in which they had only second-class status, requiring them to worship in segregated balcony pews and denying them rights in church ownership or governance, they purchased land and built their own churches. These churches joined together to form African-American versions of the Southern Methodist and Southern Baptist denominations. The largest new denominations were the National Baptist Convention and the Colored Methodist Episcopal Church. The vigorous new churches served not only as places of worship but as schools, social centers, and political meeting halls. The ministers were community leaders and often held political offices during Reconstruction. Charles H. Pearce, a

Methodist minister in Florida, declared that "A man in this State cannot do his whole duty as a minister except he looks out for the political interests of his people." The religious message of black ministers, who called for a recognition of the brotherhood of man and a special destiny like that of the "Children of Israel," provided a powerful religious bulwark for the Republican politics of their congregations.

The Counterrevolution of the Planters

Even if radical Reconstruction had been adopted right at the end of the Civil War, it would have sparked southern resistance to federal power. But coming after Johnson's lenient policy of restoration, which had enabled ex-Confederates to resume control of the South, their reaction was especially intense. Former slaveowners were the most bitter opponents of the Republican program, especially the effort to expand political and economic opportunities for African-Americans, because it threatened their vested interest in traditional agriculture and their power and status in southern society. Led by former slaveowners, the ex-Confederates staged a massive counterrevolution—one designed to "redeem" the South by regaining control of southern state governments.

The former slaveowners united under the Democratic banner to oppose the Republicans. In the eight southern states where whites formed a majority of the population—all except Louisiana, Mississippi, and South Carolina—planters sought to return ex-Confederates to the rolls of registered voters. They appealed to racial solidarity and southern patriotism; they attacked black suffrage as a threat to the social status of whites. Relying primarily on conventional, albeit unsavory, means of political competition, Democrats recovered power in Tennessee in 1869 and Virginia in 1870.

But the Democrats were prepared to go far beyond conventional techniques. Throughout the deep South, and almost everywhere that Republicans and Democrats were nearly equal in number, planters and their supporters engaged in terrorism against people and property. They organized secret societies to frighten blacks and Republican whites from voting or taking other political action.

Klan Portrait, 1868
Two armed Klansmen from Alabama posed proudly in their disguises. Northern audiences saw a lithograph based on this photograph in *Harper's Weekly* in December 1868.

The Ku Klux Klan. The most widespread of these groups, the Ku Klux Klan, was organized in Tennessee in 1865 and quickly spread throughout the South. The Klan's first leader was Nathan Bedford Forrest, a former Confederate general. A skilled and ferocious leader, Forrest was notorious in the North for an incident at Fort Pillow, Tennessee, in 1864, when his troops killed African-American soldiers holding the fort after they had surrendered. Forrest based the initial organization of the Klan on Confederate army units and openly threatened to kill Republicans if they tried to suppress the Klan.

By 1870 the Klan was operating almost everywhere in the South as a military force serving the Democratic party. The Klan murdered and whipped Republican politicians, burned black schools and churches, and attacked party gatherings. In October 1870, a group of Klansmen assaulted a Republican rally in Eutaw, Alabama, killing four African-Americans and wounding fifty-four. For three weeks in 1873, Klansmen laid siege to the small town of Colfax, Louisiana, defended by black veterans of the Union army who were holding the county seat after a contested election. On Easter Sunday, armed with a small cannon, the whites overpowered the defenders and slaughtered fifty blacks and two whites after they had surrendered under a white flag. Such terrorist tactics enabled the Democrats to seize power in Georgia and North Carolina in 1870 and make substantial gains elsewhere. An African-American politician in North Carolina wrote that "Our former masters are fast taking the reins of government."

AMERICAN VOICES

The Intimidation of Black Voters *Harriet Hernandes*

The following testimony was given in 1871 by Harriet Hernandes, a black resident of Spartanburg, South Carolina, to the Joint Congressional Select Committee investigating conditions in the South. The terrorizing of black women through rape and other forms of physical violence were among the means of oppression used by the Ku Klux Klan.

Question: How old are you?

Answer: Going on thirty-four years. . . .

Q: Are you married or single?

A: Married.

Q: Did the Ku-Klux come to your house at any time?

A: Yes, sir; twice. . . .

Q: Go on to the second time. . . .

A: They came in; I was lying in bed. Says he, "Come out here, sir; come out here, sir!" They took me out of bed; they would not let me get out, but they took me up in their arms and toted me out—me and my daughter Lucy. He struck me on the forehead with a pistol, and here is the scar above my eye now. Says he, "Damn you, fall." I fell. Says he, "Damn you, get up." I got up. Says he," Damn you, get over this fence!" and he kicked me over when I went to get over; and then he went on to a brush pile, and they laid us right down there, both together. They laid us down twenty yards apart, I reckon. They had dragged and beat us along. They struck me right on top of my head, and I though they had killed me; and I said, "Lord o' mercy, don't, don't kill my child!" He gave me a lick on the head, and it liked to have killed me; I saw stars. He threw my arm over my head so I could not do anything with it for three weeks, and there are great knots on my wrist now.

Q: What did they say this was for?

A: They said, "You can tell your husband that when we see him we are going to kill him. . . ."

Q: Did they say why they wanted to kill him?

A: They said, "He voted the radical ticket [slate of candidates], didn't he?" I said, "Yes," that very way. . . .

Q: When did [your husband] get back home after this whipping? He was not at home, was he?

A: He was lying out; he couldn't stay at home, bless your soul!. . .

Q: Has he been afraid for any length of time?

A: He has been afraid ever since last October. He has been lying out. He has not laid in the house ten nights since October.

Q: Is that the situation of the colored people down there to any extent?

A: That is the way they all have to do—men and women both.

Q: What are they afraid of?

A: Of being killed or whipped to death.

Q: What has made them afraid?

A: Because men that voted radical tickets they took the spite out on the women when they could get at them.

Q: How many colored people have been whipped in that neighborhood?

A: It is all of them, mighty near.

Source: *Report of the Joint Select Committee to Inquire into the Condition of Affairs in the Late Insurrectionary States, House Reports*, 42d Cong., 2d sess. (Washington, D.C.: Government Printing Office, 1972), Vol. 5, South Carolina, December 19, 1871.

Congress responded to the Klan-led counterrevolution by passing the Force Acts in 1870 and 1871, which included the Ku Klux Klan Act (1871). The acts authorized the president to use federal prosecutions, military force, and martial law to suppress conspiracies to deprive citizens of the right to vote, hold office, serve on juries, and enjoy the equal protection of the laws. For the first time, the government had made private criminal acts violations of federal law.

Federal agents penetrated the Klan and gathered evidence that provided the basis for thousands of arrests. Federal grand juries indicted more than three thousand Klansmen. In South Carolina, where the Klan was most deeply entrenched, federal troops occupied nine counties, made hundreds of arrests, and drove as many as two thousand Klansmen from the state. The U.S. attorney general brought several dozen notorious Klansmen to trial and sent most to jail. Elsewhere, victories were only temporary. Justice Department attorneys usually faced all-white juries, and the department lacked the resources to prosecute effectively. Only about six hundred Klansmen were convicted under the Force Acts, and only a small fraction of them served significant prison terms.

The Grant administration's war against the Klan raised the spirits of southern Republicans, but if they were going to prevail, they required what one carpetbagger described as *"steady, unswerving power from without."* In particular, to defeat the well-armed paramilitary forces of the ex-Confederates, they needed sustained federal military aid. However, after seeming to defeat the Klan, northern Republicans increasingly lost enthusiasm for fighting—let alone enlarging—what amounted to a guerrilla war. Republican leaders continued to "wave the bloody shirt," but with each election it had less appeal for voters. Northerners grew weary of the financial costs of Reconstruction and the continuing bloodshed it seemed to produce. Moreover, they became preoccupied with the severe depression that began in 1873. Racism played a role as well; many moderate Republicans in the North began to conclude that Republican defeats in the South reflected the incompetence of black politicians. Because of the diminishing federal help, Republican governments in the South eventually found themselves overwhelmed by ex-Confederate politicians during the day and by terrorists at night. Democrats overthrew Republicans in Texas in 1873, in Alabama and Arkansas in 1874, and in Mississippi in 1875.

The defeat in Mississippi demonstrated the crucial role of federal aid. As elections neared in 1875, paramilitary groups such as the Rifle Clubs and Red Shirts operated openly. Often local Democratic clubs paraded armed, as if they were militia companies. They identified African-American leaders in assassination lists called "dead-books"; broke up Republican meetings; provoked rioting that left hundreds of African-Americans dead; and threatened voters, who still lacked the protection of the secret ballot. Mississippi's Republican governor, Adelbert Ames, a Congressional Medal of Honor winner from Maine, appealed to President Grant for federal troops, but he refused, fearing damage to Republicans in northern elections and lacking the heart for more bloodshed. Ames then contemplated organizing a state militia but decided against it, believing that only African-Americans would join. Rather than escalate the fighting and turn it into a racial war, he conceded victory to the terrorists.

By 1877, Republican governments, along with token U.S. military units, remained in only three states—Louisiana, South Carolina, and Florida. Southern Republicans had done their best to reconstruct southern society, but the ex-Confederates had exhausted the northern Republicans, who finally abandoned the southern members of their party.

The Economic Fate of the Former Slaves

The greatest failure of radical Reconstruction was in not redistributing land, along with the resources required to cultivate it, from the planters to the former slaves. The only major federal program enabling freedmen to obtain land, the Southern Homestead Act, turned out to provide little assistance. Although the land was free, very few freedmen had the capital to move their families and buy the necessary seed, tools, and draft animals to get in their first crop. Fewer than seven thousand ex-slaves claimed land, and only about a thousand eventually qualified for ownership, most of them in sparsely populated areas of Florida. Compounding the problem, state governments rarely had the resources to help freedmen buy and settle land. Alone among all the Republican state governments, South Carolina purchased land from planters and resold it to former slaves on long-term credit. Between 1872 and 1876, the South Carolina land commission enabled more than 14,000 African-American families (accounting for about one-seventh of the state's black population) to purchase homesteads.

Sharecropping

This sharecropping family seems proud of their new cabin and their crop of cotton, which they planted in every available bit of ground. But the presence of their white landlord in the background suggests the forces that led families like this one into debt peonage.

AMERICAN LIVES

Nathan Bedford Forrest

Nathan Bedford Forrest (1821–1877) became a hero by defending the honor of his family at the age of twenty-four. Armed with only a pistol and a bowie knife, he fought off four men who had a grudge against his uncle, a merchant in the hamlet of Hernando, Mississippi. The uncle died from a bullet meant for his nephew, but young Forrest had shown that he could meet violence with violence. He soon used his pistol again, facing down a well-armed planter who had just killed a friend of Forrest's. The local citizens rewarded Forrest's courage by making him town constable and county coroner, and a respectable young woman from Hernando agreed to marry him.

Forrest's father had been a yeoman farmer and blacksmith who followed the frontier from North Carolina to Tennessee, where Bedford, the eldest child of eleven, was born. His family moved to northern Mississippi in 1834, but three years later, when he was only sixteen, his father died, leaving Bedford the primary breadwinner. He had no more than six months of schooling in his life, but he supported the family, working on their small farm and then joining an uncle's horse-trading business. At the age of twenty-one, when his mother remarried, he left home for Hernando.

Recognized and respected in Hernando, the hard-driving young Forrest was able to scratch his way up the social ladder in the booming cotton economy. He took over his uncle's store, ran a stagecoach service between Hernando and Memphis, opened a brickyard, again traded horses and cattle, and then turned to buying and selling slaves. By 1850 he owned three of his own. In 1851, Forrest's ambition took him and his family to nearby Memphis, Tennessee. In this Mississippi river town he became one of the largest interstate slave traders and entered the ranks of the planter class. He purchased large land holdings, including a Mississippi plantation of more than 3,000 acres worked by dozens of slaves. He even entered politics, winning election to the Memphis Board of Aldermen in 1857.

The Civil War created new opportunities for Forrest. His reputation for boldness and shrewdness, as well as his riding and shooting skills, won him an appointment from the governor of Tennessee as a lieutenant colonel. He organized a cavalry regiment and, after distinguishing himself at Shiloh, was promoted to brigadier general in July 1862. In the course of the war he became the premier cavalry officer of the Confederacy—perhaps the best on either side. The Confederate government failed to make the best use of Forrest and his troops, but he almost always carried out his missions with dramatic success, protecting Confederate

Nathan Bedford Forrest

In his often violent career Forrest was a farmer, slave trader, planter, politician, cavalry general, Grand Wizard of the Ku Klux Klan, and railroad entrepreneur. This portrait was done by Nicola Marshall c. 1866. (Collection Tennessee State Museum)

armies in retreat, raiding Union lines of communications, and attacking Union posts, often deep within enemy lines.

Forrest's intimate knowledge of the countryside and the people of the Mississippi, Tennessee, and Cumberland river valleys, his superb organizational skills, his powerful tactical sense of when to use bluff and deception, his sobriety, and his ability to inspire his troops served him well. He had a ferocious temper, and he used it to good advantage in combat—turning a zest for fighting into enraged fury whenever his honor, or the honor of his troops, seemed at stake. He counted thirty Union soldiers that he had killed personally—one more than the number of horses shot out from under him. And he was wounded by saber cut or gunfire several times, including once by a junior Confederate officer whom Forrest quickly stabbed to death.

Forrest's code of honor, his readiness for violence, his racism, and his commitment to slavery, all honed and hardened by war, have suggested to many that Forrest played a role in the slaughter of black troops at Fort Pillow, Tennessee, on April 12, 1864. Forrest approached the assault on Fort Pillow with a combination of anger and contempt for the garrison there—largely white pro-Union Tennesseans and former slaves. The war in western Tennessee had taken a bitter turn in 1864, involving civilians more directly in combat, and Forrest was outraged at rumors that the garrison had been harassing local whites loyal to the Confederacy. Although Forrest's direct role in the slaughter remains uncertain, it is clear that his troops believed they were acting as he wished, that they experienced the same fury he usually displayed in battle, and that he accepted the outcome with equanimity.

The war left Forrest exhausted but determined to recreate as much of his old life as possible. This meant adapting to the new economic system and, when necessary, to the reality of Union victory. In 1866, to restore his plantation labor force, he rented his Mississippi land to seven former Union officers and worked closely with the Freedmen's Bureau, writing some of the highest-wage contracts. He drew on some of his old slave-trading skills to bring in workers from as far away as Georgia. At the same time he moved into new enterprises—provisioning the reorganized plantations, selling fire and life insurance, and contracting for paving the streets of Memphis and for laying railroad track. In building the Memphis and Little Rock Railroad, Forrest used labor supplied by the Freedmen's Bureau. Meanwhile, he sought a pardon from President Johnson, which was granted in 1868.

But Forrest was unprepared to accept a radical Reconstruction. As conflicts between ex-Confederates and coalitions of former Unionists and freedmen intensified, Forrest's ambition and loyalty to his comrades—a sense of honor defined by shared wartime experiences—led him to support the effort to restore the social world of 1860. In 1867 he joined secret organizations in Memphis and Nashville that became chapters of the Ku Klux Klan. He soon became the Klan's Grand Wizard and turned the organization into a major force throughout most of the South. Under cover of his insurance business, Forrest corresponded with perhaps thousands of Confederate veterans and traveled to neighboring states to confer with other ex-generals.

In 1868 the Republican governor of Tennessee, "Parson" William G. Brownlow, threatened to organize a militia of eastern Tennessee Unionists to root out the Klan. Forrest told his former troops to prepare for civil war, warning a reporter from the Cincinnati *Commercial* that he could "raise 40,000 men in five days, ready for the field." Forrest's intimidation worked, as it had so often in the past. Brownlow resigned in early 1869 to take up a seat in the U.S. Senate, and his replacement sought to appease the Democrats and the Klan. Victorious in Tennessee and hoping to reduce pressure from Washington on the Klan, Forrest ordered its members to destroy their regalia and moderate their excesses, such as whippings and jail breaks. Forrest knew full well that he had no power to implement such an order.

Forrest may have continued a secret life within the Klan, but after his political victory he appeared to devote his full attention to his businesses. He tried to combine northern capital with new sources of cheap labor. Marketing bonds in New York, he established the Selma, Marion, and Memphis Railroad. He promoted Chinese immigration to the South and made extensive use of convict labor on his railroad and plantation crews. But he achieved only modest success in the depression of the 1870s. In 1877 he died of a debilitating intestinal illness, perhaps related to his wartime wounds. Shortly before, he ended his litigation, which had grown massive in the years since the Civil War. He told his lawyer: "My life has been a battle from the start. . . . I have seen too much of violence, and I want to close my days at peace with all the world. . . ."

Without guaranteed economic independence, the content of freedom depended largely on thousands of conflicts between freedmen, acting individually and collectively, and the planter class. Here too the federal government failed to assist the freedmen in a significant way. The vast majority of army officers and federal marshals held the racist assumption that had been behind the Black Codes—that former slaves were suited only for agricultural labor. If these agents of the federal government had different ideas at first, they usually came to support the economic interests of the planters. One Louisiana freedman described the process as follows: "Whenever a new Provost Marshall comes he gives us justice for a fortnight or so; then he becomes acquainted with planters, takes dinners with them, receives presents; and then we no longer have any rights, or very little." In disputes between employers and laborers, federal marshals generally sided with the planters and sustained their authority. Army commanders complied with the requests of planters for help in forcing African-Americans to work. They expelled former plantation workers from towns and cities and punished them for disobedience, theft, vagrancy, and erratic labor.

Even agents of the Freedmen's Bureau often supported the planters. Many Bureau officials interpreted their mandate to promote a transition to free labor as meaning that they should teach former slaves to be industrious, reliable agricultural workers. They preached the gospel of work to African-Americans. To discourage labor violence, they warned that it was better "to suffer wrong than to do wrong." They urged former slaves to vindicate the cause of abolition by staying at home and working even harder than they had under slavery. One Bureau official told some freedmen that their former master "is not able to do without you, and you will . . . find him as kind, honest, and liberal as other men" and that "you can be as free and as happy in your old home, for the present, as anywhere else in the world." The agents of the Freedmen's Bureau who did side with African-Americans were stymied by northern racism, lack of funds, understaffing, poor coordination within the Bureau, and uncooperative military authorities.

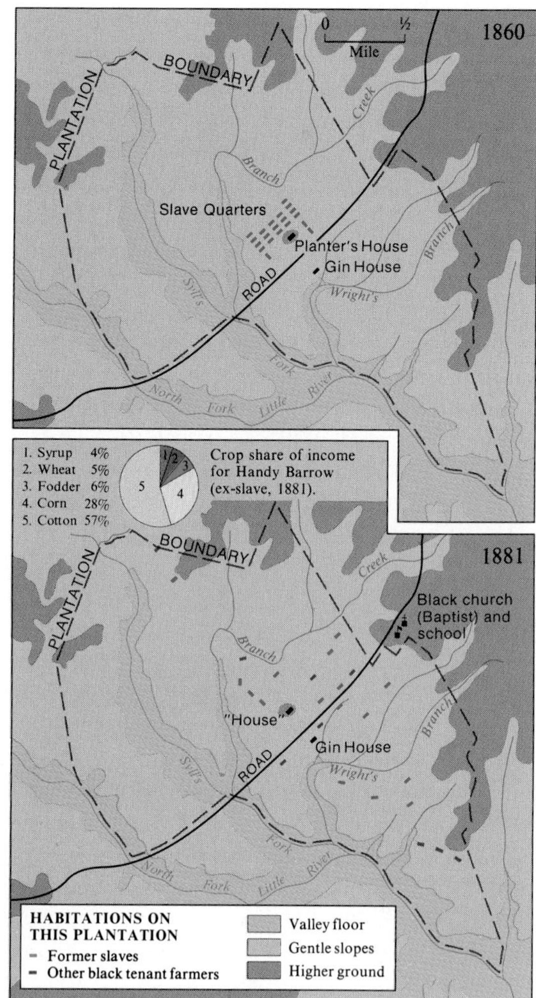

MAP 16.2

The Barrow Plantation

Comparing the map of this central Georgia plantation with the 1881 map reveals the changing patterns of black residence and farming. In 1860 the slave quarters clustered near the planter's house, which sat above them on a small hilltop. The free sharecroppers of 1881 built their cabins along the spurs or ridges of land between the streams, scattering their community over the plantation. A black church and school were built by this date. A typical sharecropper on the plantation earned most of his income from growing cotton.

Sharecropping. The Freedmen's Bureau helped change, however, the way planters controlled the labor of their former slaves. It encouraged, even compelled, planters and freedmen to agree on written contracts through a formal bargaining process. The labor contract system was a poor substitute for land ownership, but it assisted the freedmen in attaining something else they greatly desired: the elimination of gang labor.

As early as 1865, written contracts between freedmen and planters provided that the former slaves would work for wages. But, the contracts also provided for less supervision, a slower pace of work, and more free time than had been typical under slavery, as well as the elimination of drivers and overseers. By 1866 the process of bargaining between planters and freedmen had become more difficult, partly because a shrinking money supply reduced the amount of cash available to pay wages. To resolve the growing number of conflicts over labor contracts, Freedmen's Bureau agents introduced a form of compensation that was common, though not typical, in northern agriculture—payment of agricultural workers in shares of the crop rather than in wages. This system was known as *sharecropping.* While it came to involve many poor whites in the South, it was far more important for blacks. For them, sharecropping was the dominant mode of agricultural labor.

At first, freedmen were enthusiastic about sharecropping. It increased their control over working conditions and allowed them to improve their standard of living. Under typical sharecropping contracts, sharecroppers turned over between half and two-thirds of their harvested crops to their landlord. The owner's share was not necessarily excessive, because the landlord commonly provided land, seed, fertilizer, tools, and assistance in marketing.

The sharecropping system joined laborers and owners of land and capital in a common sharing of risks and returns. But it produced little upward mobility. By the end of Reconstruction, only a fraction of sharecroppers, no more than one-quarter of the total, had managed to save enough to rent land with cash payments, as most landless whites did. Even though these so-called "tenant farmers" could now sell their crops directly to market, they remained impoverished.

Land Ownership. Virtually all African-American farmers struggled long and hard to buy the land they tilled, and some of the cash renters gradually succeeded. They were willing to pay exorbitant prices for land just for the sake of being independent. But the system was stacked against them. African-American renters had far less access to land ownership than did their white counterparts. Planters made agreements among themselves to drive up the price of land to blacks or even refuse to sell to them. Some planters used the Ku Klux Klan to intimidate blacks who tried to buy land. Despite the adversity, by 1910 black farmers owned nearly a third of the land they cultivated. But black farm-owners usually occupied marginal land—in the coastal swamps of Georgia and South Carolina, for example—and the land had usually cost far more than its productivity warranted.

Debt Peonage. The financial condition of all African-American farmers was extremely difficult. Sharecropping, cash-renting of land, and land ownership enabled former slaves to raise their incomes but also increased their financial needs. They wanted more food and better clothing than they had received under slavery; they often needed more farm supplies than their landlords were willing to provide; and renters and owners had to purchase all their seed, fertilizer, and equipment. The purchase of major farm supplies almost always required borrowing. But southern banks were reluctant to lend money to black farmers, whom they saw as bad risks, and cash was generally in short supply.

The owners of country stores stepped in. Eager to lend money, they furnished everything the black farmers needed and extended credit for the purchases. The country merchants took advantage of the weak bargaining power of the former slaves, especially the sharecroppers, by charging unusually high prices and interest rates. In effect, these storekeepers became rural loan sharks.

Once African-American sharecroppers accepted credit from the country merchants, high interest rates made it difficult for them to settle their accounts. At best, after paying their debts they broke even. Most sharecroppers fell deeper and deeper into debt.

Throughout the South, when Democrats regained control of state governments, they passed laws that gave force to this economic system by providing merchants with the right to take liens on crops. Merchants could take crops to settle sharecroppers' debts and seek criminal prosecution of sharecroppers who could not pay the full amount of the interest they owed. Indebted African-American farmers faced imprisonment and forced labor unless they toiled on the land according to the instructions of the merchant-creditor. Increasingly, merchants and landlords cooperated to maintain this lucrative system, and many landlords themselves became merchants. The former slaves had become trapped in the vicious circle of *debt peonage,* which tied them to the land and robbed them of their earnings.

In sum, despite the odds against them, the freedmen won some modest economic gains. But their gains came only within the restrictions of the system of debt peonage that replaced slavery. Thus, most African-Americans and many whites remained mired in an agricultural poverty created by racism and economic forces.

The North During Reconstruction

Although the Republicans in Congress failed to break the hold of the planter elite on the South, they did reconstruct the economy of the North. They enacted nearly all of their nationalizing economic program—national banking, tariff protection, and subsidies for internal improvements—despite resistance from the Democrats. The Republican program promoted unprecedented economic growth and industrial development.

A Dynamic Economy

The Civil War disrupted the nation's economic life, yet by the 1870s Americans had become more productive than ever before. Northeastern industry led the way. Production of iron more than doubled between the end of the Civil War and 1870; it doubled again by 1880. Steel production grew even more rapidly, increasing fivefold between 1865 and 1870 and then nearly twenty times by 1880. The era began an *age of capital*—a period that lasted until World War I and was marked by great increases in investment in factories and railroads. It also began the era of big business, which was characterized by the rise of giant corporations.

The Republican Economic Program. During Reconstruction, Republicans expanded the ambitious economic program they had enacted during the war. The broad support that middle-class northerners gave to the program indicated that they now largely shared business-class values.

The scope of the Republican economic program was vast. Republicans strengthened government regulation of the banking system, winning praise from investors who appreciated a more predictable economic environment. Republican Congresses expanded subsidies to national rail systems and chartered new railroads; they expanded the national postal system; and they financed major river and harbor development throughout the North. They also funded the cavalry forces who fought the nation's wars against the Indians in the Great Plains (see Chapter 17). In fact, military spending accounted for 60 percent of the federal budget by 1880. Republicans used the Homestead Act of 1862 to subsidize the settling of the Great Plains.

Revenues raised from the Civil War tax system paid for these programs. Postwar Congresses kept the high tariffs, which had proven lucrative and appealed to average Republicans because they seemed to protect against foreign workers. Congress also retained the "emergency" wartime taxes on alcohol and tobacco, which were popular among many Republicans because they taxed "sin."

The tariffs and "sin" taxes not only funded programs but also provided money to pay back the Americans who had bought Union bonds during the war. Because the taxes increased the cost of everyday items, average Americans were paying a far higher share of their income for debt repayment than were the wealthy. Moreover, the repayment was going largely to the wealthy, who owned a disproportionate share of Civil War bonds. Republicans were self-consciously redistributing wealth from the poor to the rich, who were more likely to save and invest, as a way of increasing the supply of capital and accelerating the rate of economic growth.

The most popular Republican economic program was the Civil War pension program, which the government extended and broadened virtually every year. It provided disabled veterans and the widows and children of Union veterans with generous benefits, which were particularly welcome during the severe depressions of the 1870s and 1890s. At the same time, the pensions solidified the Republican loyalties of the families of the men who had served in the Union army.

An ideological shift also contributed to the Republicans' success in enacting their economic program. The Civil War had led many Americans to relax their traditional suspicion of concentrations of power—in both business and government. This was particularly true of the men and women who had served in the Union army and the Sanitary Commission. The war had given them their first direct experience of living and working within modern bureaucracies—elaborate hierarchies imposing a high degree of job specialization and rigorous discipline. Wartime service also had taken them, usually for the first time, far from home and placed them in intimate contact with people who came from distant places and yet served in the same cause. And the Union had won the war. This disciplined, collective, national—and successful—experience predisposed northerners to accept American business, the Republican party, and the federal government as the central agencies of national economic development.

Republican Foreign Policy

Some Republican leaders were alert to new possibilities for expansion abroad. The most important advocate of expansion was William H. Seward, Lincoln and Johnson's secretary of state. Believing in the importance of foreign commerce to the long-term health of the republic, Seward promoted the acquisition of colonies that could be used as trading bases in the Caribbean and the Pacific. But Seward was ahead of his time. During the Reconstruction Era, most Americans wanted to concentrate on the development of their own territory.

Seward inherited his most pressing foreign policy issues from the Civil War. In Mexico, Napoleon III's puppet government under Archduke Maximilian was still in power; the threat this European regime posed to American interests in the Southwest was especially great since it might draw die-hard Confederate soldiers to its support. "On to Mexico," Grant only half-jokingly told an aide just a day after he accepted Lee's surrender at Appomattox. It was a good guess as to where the next war might take place. Within a year, president Johnson and Seward sent General Philip Sheridan with 50,000 battle-hardened Union veterans to the Mexican border, while Seward negotiated the withdrawal of French troops. The threat of force worked. The French left in 1867, abandoning Maximilian to a Mexican firing squad.

The American government was also troubled over another Civil War issue: Great Britain's allowing the *Alabama* and other Confederate cruisers to sail from British shipyards to raid Union commerce. Seward claimed that Britain had violated international laws of neutrality and owed compensation for damages. Britain, fearing that Americans might build ships for British enemies in some future war, accepted Seward's legal point and agreed to submit the *Alabama* claims to arbitration. However, Charles Sumner, chairman of the Senate Foreign Relations Committee, insisted that the compensation cover "indirect" damages. Including lost shipping revenue and the costs of Britain's prolonging the war, his cost estimates reached more than $2 billion. Sumner was angry over English aid to the Confederacy during the war, and he wanted to acquire Canada as part of the financial deal with Britain. In 1866, Congress restricted Canadian trade and fishing privileges in an attempt to force Canadians to support annexation. However, with the stakes so high, the British refused to agree to a settlement during Johnson's presidency.

Meanwhile, American expansionist ambitions in the Caribbean and the Pacific met with only mixed success. Supporting the U.S. Navy's demands for a base in the Caribbean, Seward negotiated a treaty with Denmark to purchase the Virgin Islands, but Congress rejected the $7.5 million price. Congress also turned down his proposal to annex Santo Domingo (now the Dominican Republic), which had won independence from Spain in 1865. Seward did persuade Congress to annex the small Midway Islands west of Hawaii, after his effort to acquire the Hawaiian Islands had failed. Most important, Seward convinced the Senate, in 1867, to ratify a treaty to buy Alaska from Russia and to appropriate the $7.2 million for the purchase. Critics referred to Alaska as "Johnson's Polar Bear Garden" and "Seward's Folly," but its acquisition promised to obstruct any British ambitions in North America. Also, the price was reasonable when weighed against even the low estimates that Congress made of Alaska's fish, fur, lumber, and mineral resources.

When Ulysses S. Grant became president in 1869, he took up the cause of expansion in the Caribbean. He was influenced by American investors and adventurers in Santo Domingo, including Orville E. Babcock, his former military aide, who became his personal secretary in the White House. Grant proposed a treaty to annex the country as a colony for freed slaves dissatisfied with Reconstruction. The Senate defeated Grant's imperial ambition in 1870. Leading the attack was Charles Sumner, who feared that annexation would threaten the independence of the neighboring black republic of Haiti. "These islands by climate, occupation, and destiny . . . belong to the colored people," he declared.

Grant's secretary of state was genteel Hamilton Fish, a former Whig who had been governor of New York and a U.S. senator. Fish had less interest than Seward in acquiring new territory and concentrated on settling differences with Britain. Part of his goal was to strengthen the ties of capital and commerce between the two nations. Interest in annexing Canada still remained high, but Fish finally persuaded Grant that the British North America Act of 1867, uniting Canada in a confederation (the Dominion of Canada) and providing for greater self-government, had removed any serious Canadian interest in annexation. Fish then quickly negotiated the Treaty of Washington in 1871, which submitted for arbitration all the outstanding issues between the two countries, including the *Alabama* claims. In 1873, the British government obeyed the ruling of an international tribunal established under the treaty and presented a $15.5 million check to the United States government. A period of unprecedented good will between America and Britain followed.

The Politics of Corruption and the Grant Administration

During the Grant administration, the Democratic party, seeking to reestablish its national base of power, made the Republican economic program its primary target. Since the key elements of Republican policy had wide support, the Democrats avoided attacking specific programs. Instead, they renewed their traditional assault on "special privilege."

Democrats warned that Republican programs were creating islands of privilege, enabling wealthy individuals to buy favors from the federal government and the Republicans to buy support from the people their programs served. The result, Democrats charged, was increasing concentration of wealth and power in the hands of the wealthy and corruption of the republic. By stressing corruption, the Democrats tried to appeal to Americans who valued honesty and still cherished the Jeffersonian ideal—a society composed of independent and virtuous farmers, artisans, and small entrepreneurs. The Democrats claimed that they would restore a competitive economy, one that they said had been lost during the Industrial Revolution and the Civil War.

Dissident Republicans. Some Republicans joined the Democratic chorus condemning Grant's policies. These dissidents included radicals on Reconstruction like Charles Sumner but most numerous and influential were men like Charles Francis Adams—wealthy, well-educated members of established northeastern families—who resented the critical role professional politicians had come to play in the party. They attacked Grant for turning the Republican party into a self-serving bureaucracy, with too many professional politicians in executive positions, especially cabinet posts. And they faulted their party for requiring government workers to pay a portion of their salaries into the party's treasury.

The dissidents coined the term *Grantism* to describe this new system of party patronage. To counter it they endorsed a program of civil service reform, beginning with a *merit system* to replace the spoils system established under Jackson. A civil service commission would administer competitive examinations as the basis for appointments.

"Grantism"

Grant was lampooned on both sides of the Atlantic for the scandalous behavior of his administration. The British magazine *Puck* showed Grant only barely defying gravity in protecting corrupt members of his administration. Despite the scandals, the British public welcomed Grant with admiration on his triumphal foreign tour in 1877.

The Liberal Republicans and the Election of 1872. When the dissident Republicans failed to replace Grant as the party's nominee in 1872, they called themselves the Liberal Republicans and formed a new party. The name reflected their commitment to liberty, competition, and limited government. Their platform emphasized civil service reform and—in an appeal for Democratic support—amnesty for all former Confederates and removal of troops from the South. For president they nominated Horace Greeley, the influential editor and publisher of the *New York Tribune*. In an attempt to steal the Liberals' thunder, the Democrats nominated Greeley too, but with little enthusiasm. Although Greeley now supported reconciliation with ex-Confederates, he had earlier favored a radical approach to Reconstruction, and he supported high tariffs, which conflicted with the views of the Democrats.

In the election of 1872, Grant won an even larger percentage of the popular vote—56 percent—than in 1868. In fact, this was a higher percentage of the popular vote than any candidate had won since Andrew Jackson in 1828. Grant carried every northern state and, because of support for him among African-American voters and the distaste of ex-Confederates for Greeley, he carried all of the states of the former Confederacy except Tennessee, Georgia, and Texas.

Crédit Mobilier and the Whiskey Ring. During Grant's second term, the issue of corruption in the Republican party erupted again. In 1873 a congressional committee confirmed newspaper reports of a complicated deal in which high-ranking Republicans appeared to have cheated the taxpayers. The scandal centered on Crédit Mobilier, a construction company that contracted for work on the Union Pacific Railroad. It turned out that Crédit Mobilier was a dummy corporation. Union Pacific stockholders had formed it and made enormous purchases from it, sometimes for services that were never delivered, to be paid to the corporate conspirators in Union Pacific stock and federal subsidies. In an attempt to prevent a congressional investigation, the insiders had sold Crédit Mobilier stock at a discount to several members of Congress.

An even more dramatic scandal, which reached into the White House itself, involved the Whiskey Ring, a network of large whiskey distillers and Treasury agents who defrauded the Treasury of millions of dollars of excise taxes on liquor. The ring was organized by a Union general, John A. McDonald, whom Grant had appointed to the post of supervisor of internal revenue in St. Louis. Grant's private secretary, Orville Babcock, kept a protective eye on McDonald's activities and funnelled some of the spoils into the campaign chests of the Republican party. The game was up in 1875 when Benjamin Bristow, an upright and ambitious secretary of the Treasury, exposed the ring and brought indictments against more than 350 distillers and government officials. Babcock was later acquitted, but more than a hundred men, including McDonald, went to prison.

The Whiskey Ring scandal ruined Grant's second term in office and crushed whatever prospects Grant might have had for a third term. Grant had ordered Bristow to "Let no guilty man escape," but Grant protected his good friend Babcock with extraordinary measures, possibly even perjuring himself in a deposition he gave in the presence of Chief Justice Morrison Waite.

The Depression of 1873–1877. These scandals occurred in the midst of the worst depression the nation had ever endured. By 1876 nearly 15 percent of the labor force was unemployed, and thousands of farmers had gone bankrupt. The precipitating event was the Panic of 1873, which involved the bankruptcy of the Northern Pacific Railroad and its major investor, Jay Cooke. Both Cooke's privileged role as a financier of the Civil War and the extensive Republican subsidies to railroads suggested to many suffering Americans that Republican financial manipulations had caused the depression.

To Americans who had suffered economic loss or even ruin, the Grant administration seemed unresponsive. Especially troublesome was an important money issue: how much paper money should be in circulation. Rapidly decreasing prices hurt small farmers and all others who were heavily in debt. Forced to repay debts with dollars that were swiftly increasing in value, they called on the federal government to increase the nation's money supply—action that they hoped would stop prices from falling. The Grant administration ignored the debtors' pleas for relief and further angered them by insisting that Civil War bondholders be fully repaid in gold, even though they had bought their bonds with greenbacks and had received only the guarantee that the interest on the bonds would be paid in gold. In 1874, the Democrats gained sufficient support from Republicans to push through Congress a bill that would have increased the number of greenbacks in circulation, and eased the money pinch. But President Grant vetoed it, fueling Democratic charges that Republicans served only the special interests of capitalists. In the election of 1874, the Democrats rode their criticism of Grant's leadership to gains in both houses of Congress and a majority in the House of Representatives—for the first time since secession.

Before the new Congress met, however, the lame-duck Republicans passed the Specie Resumption Act of 1875. This law provided that the federal government would exchange gold for greenbacks, thus making federal paper money as "good as gold." It put the nation's money supply squarely on the gold standard, which increased the confidence of investors in the economy and helped foreign trade. But, by increasing the value of greenbacks, the act induced wealthy Americans to hoard them, reducing the amount of money in circulation, pushing prices up more sharply, and increasing still more the burden of debts. The severe financial pain felt by many Americans worsened even further the political prospects of the Grant administration.

The Political Crisis of 1877

Republican leaders approached the 1876 presidential campaign with a sense of foreboding. If they were to thwart the Democrats, they had to shake themselves free of the atmosphere of scandal and special privilege that had come to surround President Grant. They turned to the electoral-vote-rich state of Ohio for a candidate—Governor Rutherford B. Hayes, who had won three closely contested races. His scandal-free terms had won him a reputation for honesty; he had a good Civil War record; and he was a supporter of civil service reform. He was a moderate on Reconstruction and a former Whig, whose election strategy included an appeal to southern conservatives—especially former southern Whigs.

The Democrats concentrated on the Grant scandals. They nominated Governor Samuel J. Tilden of New York, a well-known fighter of corruption who had helped break the control of the infamous Tweed Ring over New York City politics. Their platform emphasized reform, especially of the civil service, promising to save the nation from "a corrupt centralism which has honeycombed the offices of the Federal government itself with incapacity, waste, and fraud."

The Election of 1876. On election night, the outcome seemed clear; headlines announced that Tilden had won. The Democrats celebrated, and the Republicans plunged into gloom. In Ohio, Hayes went to bed convinced that he had been defeated. Tilden had won a bare majority of the popular vote—51 percent. The Democrats had made deep inroads in the North, carrying New York, New Jersey, Connecticut, and Indiana, and they had apparently swept the southern states.

But by dawn two or three sleepless politicians at Republican headquarters in New York City had woven together a daring strategy. Republicans still controlled election procedures in three southern states—Louisiana, South Carolina, and Florida. If they could argue that Democratic fraud and intimidation had affected the election results in those states, they could certify Republican victories and report Republican electoral votes. Of course, newly elected Democratic officials in the three states would send in electoral votes for Tilden. As a result, there would be two sets of electoral votes from those states when Congress counted them early in 1877. If Congress accepted all the Republican votes, Hayes would have a one-vote electoral majority. The auda-

BALLOTS FOR REPUBLICANS!
BULLETS FOR DEMOCRATS!!
VOTE FOR HAYES!
LATEST FROM CHARLESTON.
DEATH TO COLORED DEMOCRATS!
ADMINISTRATION REFORM.
SOUTHERN LIBERTY.
WASHINGTON, July, 1876.
GENERAL SHERMAN:
You will not send any of the following troops, now in the South, to assist Gen. Crook in suppressing the Sioux, until after the Presidential election:
Texas—45 companies of infantry and 26 companies of cavalry.
Louisiana—12 companies of infantry.
Mississippi—10 companies of infantry.
South Carolina—8 companies of infantry and 2 companies of
WASHINGTON, Sept. 4, 1876.
To all U. S. Marshals:
You are hereby placed in command of all the Military Forces in the United States—militia, soldiers and marines—for use at the November elections.
You may also appoint all (Republican) citizens your deputies for the same occasion.
These instructions have been submitted to the President, and have his approval.
ALPHONSO TAFT.

Anti-Republican Sentiment, 1876

This Democratic cartoon portrays Union soldiers, with bayonets fixed, coercing African-Americans to vote Republican. The carpetbag in the foreground identifies the politics of the civilian at the voting table. To the far left, the individual casting a watchful eye on the proceedings is probably an ex-planter, supposedly powerless in the new politics of the South.

cious announcement came: Hayes had carried the three southern states and won the election.

The Compromise of 1877. The Constitution had established no method to resolve this unprecedented dispute over the validity of electoral votes, and the long period of uncertainty between the election in November and the inauguration the following March were filled with rumors: There might be a violent coup by Democrats if the Republicans tried to steal the election; President Grant might use the military to prevent Tilden from taking office; there might be a new election, or even a new civil war. While the rumors flew, various interests tried to gain some advantage from the situation. Railroad promoters jockeyed for new federal subsidies, promising to deliver blocs of support in Congress to the party that made the best promises. Politicians on all sides flirted with the opposition, hoping for rewards.

In the end, political compromise and accident won out. Congress decided to appoint an electoral commission to settle the question. The commission would include seven Republicans and seven Democrats. The fifteenth and deciding vote would go to Justice David Davis of the Supreme Court, a man with a reputation for being free of party loyalty. But Justice Davis resigned from the Court at the crucial moment to accept election to the Senate from Illinois and the deciding vote fell to Joseph P. Bradley, a lifelong Republican. When the commission completed its careful investigation of the election results in Florida, Louisiana, and South Carolina, the decision on each state was made by a straight party vote of eight to seven.

It remained to be seen whether Congress would accept the result. The Senate was controlled by the Republicans, the House by the Democrats. Southern Democrats held the balance of power, and Hayes's representatives sought their support. Some of these southerners were convinced that Hayes had made various promises to the "negotiators"—to confine federal troops to their barracks throughout the South, to appoint Democrats to major offices, and to support the construction of a railroad across Texas to the Pacific. Whether or not such promises were actually made, enough southerners in the House accepted the commission's findings to make Hayes president.

This sequence of events is often referred to as the Compromise of 1877, but historians remain uncertain as to whether any kind of deal was really struck. During

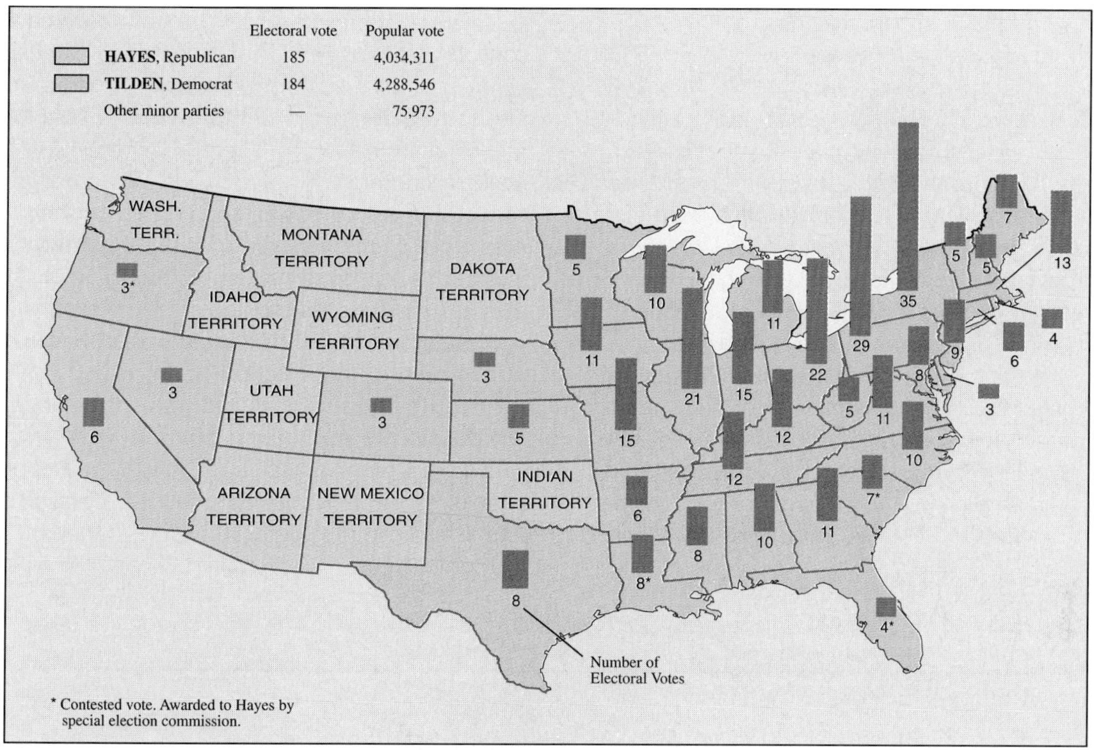

MAP 16.3

The Election of 1876

Tilden made such inroads in northern states that Hayes could not win without the contested votes of three states in the deep South.

his campaign Hayes had promised to end the military occupation of the South. He had also planned to appoint a few Democrats to his cabinet. And his faction of the Republican party did not support the Texas railroad scheme. The alleged compromise may have been a fiction created by southern Democrats to justify their votes for Hayes.

The End of Reconstruction. The only certainty was that Reconstruction had ended. The outcome was mixed and unclear; no single position emerged triumphant. In 1877 political leaders on all sides were ready to say that what Lincoln had called "the work" was complete. But for many Americans, especially the freed slaves, the work had clearly not been completed. To be sure, they had won three amendments to the Constitution, established public schools for African-American children, and gained some access to land for former slaves. But any work toward further improvement in the condition of African-Americans had been abandoned and left to the slow, frustrating, and imperfect processes of history.

Summary

In 1865, after the Civil War ended, the Thirteenth Amendment made slavery unconstitutional. President Abraham Lincoln's plan for quickly restoring the Union encountered opposition from radical Republicans in Congress, who believed that freedmen must vote, and moderate Republicans, who wished to punish the South and establish their party in southern states. Lincoln was assassinated before he could negotiate a unified Republican position.

Possibilities for a swift sectional reconciliation continued into the administration of Andrew Johnson, but he could not satisfy both moderate Republicans and the defeated Confederacy. His difficulties in working with Congress deepened the contest for the control of Reconstruction and resulted in an erratic policy that intensified the South's resistance to federal power.

Congressional Reconstruction extended the civil rights of former slaves through the Fourteenth Amendment, protected their suffrage through the Fifteenth Amendment, and encouraged the formation of southern state governments in which freedmen played crucial roles. Northern Republicans, however, failed to equip these governments to defeat the old planter elite, which managed to regain control through political appeals to racial solidarity and by means of terror and intimidation. By 1877 all the Reconstruction state governments had been overturned. The freedmen also won some modest economic gains during Reconstruction, but without access to land ownership they became ensnared in a system of debt peonage and once again found themselves dependent on the planters, who were now their landlords.

The Republicans proved to be more successful in consolidating the power of industrial capitalism than in reconstructing the South. Democrats attacked the Republican economic program with a Jeffersonian and Jacksonian critique of "special privilege," but most northerners came out of the Civil War more receptive to concentrations of power and to the values of the business class. Many believed that the Republican program was necessary for sustained prosperity and a strong nation. Although scandals during the Grant administration inflamed opposition to the Republicans, the Republicans took the election of 1876 by capitalizing on the South's hunger for an end to Reconstruction and for some influence in national politics. What is sometimes called the Compromise of 1877 kept the Republicans in control of the federal government by cementing an alliance between the northern business class and southern economic elites.

TOPIC FOR RESEARCH

The Overthrow of Radical Reconstruction

One by one, the Reconstruction state governments fell to counterrevolutions. This text has surveyed the general reasons for the victories of the Democratic "redeemers" over the Republicans, but the timing and particular circumstances differed from state to state. Choose one of the states of the former Confederacy and investigate how and why Reconstruction came to an end there. You should explore the methods of the redeemers, examining the extent to which they relied on conventional methods of political persuasion and organization as opposed to terrorism and guerrilla warfare. You should also consider the role of divisions among the various groups of Republicans—African-Americans, carpetbaggers, and scalawags—in the party's defeat. And, finally, examine the role of the federal government and the Union army. Could greater effort and commitment in Washington have saved the Republicans? General books on Reconstruction, such as Eric Foner, *Reconstruction: America's Unfinished Revolution, 1863–1877* (1988), have bibliographies listing books, articles, and other sources on the individual states. Be alert to the possibility of consulting the documents compiled by Congress as it struggled to understand the problems of Reconstruction. Especially fascinating, for example, are the hearings on the Ku Klux Klan: *Testimony Taken by the Joint Committee to Enquire into the Condition of Affairs in the Late Insurrectionary States,* indexed as 42d Cong., 2d sess., H. Rept. 22.

BIBLIOGRAPHY

Among the best general studies are three older works: W. E. B. Du Bois, *Black Reconstruction* (1935), the first to challenge traditional racist interpretations of Reconstruction; John Hope Franklin, *Reconstruction: After the Civil War* (1965); and Kenneth M. Stampp, *The Era of Reconstruction* (1965). More modern studies are Eric Foner, *Reconstruction: America's Unfinished Revolution* (1988), currently the best survey of Reconstruction, and James M. McPherson, *Ordeal by Fire: The Civil War and Reconstruction* (1982).

Presidential Restoration

For important studies of presidential efforts to rebuild the Union see the books on Abraham Lincoln listed in Chapter 15 and the following works on Andrew Johnson: Albert Castel, *The Presidency of Andrew Johnson* (1979); Eric L. McKitrick, *Andrew Johnson and Reconstruction* (1960), which initiated scholarly criticism of Johnson; and James Sefton, *Andrew Johnson and the Uses of Constitutional Power* (1979). Books that focus more closely on Congress include LaWanda Cox and John H. Cox, *Politics, Principle, and Prejudice, 1865–1867* (1963); David Donald, *The Politics of Reconstruction, 1863–1867* (1965); and William B. Brock, *An American Crisis: Congress and Reconstruction, 1865–1867* (1963). For insight into developments in the South, see Dan T. Carter, *When the War Was Over: The Failure of Self-Reconstruction in the South, 1865–1867* (1985). Michael Perman, *Reunion Without Compromise: The South and Reconstruction, 1865–1868* (1973), analyzes how the South manipulated Johnson.

Radical Reconstruction

For studies of Congress's role in radical Reconstruction, see Michael Les Benedict, *A Compromise of Principle: Congressional Republicans and Reconstruction* (1974); William Gillette, *Retreat from Reconstruction, 1863–1879* (1979); and Hans L. Trefousse, *Impeachment of a President: Andrew Johnson, the Blacks, and Reconstruction* (1975). William S. McFeely, *Grant: A Biography* (1981), deftly explains the politics of Reconstruction. Study of the South during radical Reconstruction should begin with the wealth of literature on the experience of blacks. Among the most useful works are Ira Berlin et al., *Freedom: A Documentary History of Emancipation, 1861–1867, The Wartime Genesis of Free Labor: The Lower South* (1990); Robert Cruden, *The Negro in Reconstruction* (1969); Jacqueline Jones, *Labor of Love, Labor of Sorrow: Black Women, Work, and the Family from Slavery to the Present* (1985); and Leon F. Litwack, *Been in the Storm So Long: The Aftermath of Slavery* (1979). The economic condition of the freedmen and the postwar South is the focus of Robert Higgs, *Competition and Coercion: Blacks in the American Economy, 1865–1914* (1977); Jay Mandle, *The Roots of Black Poverty: The Southern Plantation Economy After the Civil War* (1978); Roger L. Ransom and Richard Sutch, *One Kind of Freedom: The Economic Consequences of Emancipation* (1977); Jonathan M. Wiener, *Social Origins of the New South: Alabama, 1860–1885* (1975); and Gavin Wright, *The Political Economy of the Cotton South* (1978). Specialized studies of African-Americans and race relations, often focused on particular states, include John Blassingame, *Black New Orleans, 1860–1880* (1973); Barbara Fields, *Slavery and Freedom on the Middle Ground: Maryland During the Nineteenth Century* (1985); Thomas Holt, *Black over White: Negro Political Leadership in South Carolina During Reconstruction* (1977); Peter Kolchin, *First Freedom: The Responses of Alabama's Blacks to Emancipation and Reconstruction* (1972); Howard N. Rabinowitz, *Race Relations in the Urban South, 1865–1890* (1977); Willie Lee Rose, *Rehearsal for Reconstruction: The Port Royal Experiment* (1964); and Joel Williamson, *After Slavery: The Negro in South Carolina During Reconstruction, 1861–1877* (1965). Other instructive state studies of Reconstruction politics appear in Otto Olsen, ed., *Reconstruction and Redemption in the South* (1980). The best study of carpetbaggers is Richard N. Current, *Those Terrible Carpetbaggers: A Reinterpretation* (1988). On yeoman farmers, consult Steven Hahn, *The Roots of Southern Populism: Yeoman Farmers and the Transformation of the Georgia Upcountry, 1850–1890* (1983). The most thorough study of the Ku Klux Klan is Allen W. Trelease, *White Terror: The Ku Klux Klan Conspiracy and Southern Reconstruction* (1972). Biographies of Nathan Forrest include: Brian S. Wills, *A Battle from the Start: The Life of Nathan Bedford Forrest* (1992), and John A. Wyeth, *That Devil Forrest: A Life of General Nathan Bedford Forrest* (1989). To survey Reconstruction politics in the South consult Michael Perman, *The Road to Redemption: Southern Politics, 1869–1879* (1984).

TIMELINE

1864	Wade-Davis Bill
1865	Freedmen's Bureau established Lincoln assassinated; Andrew Johnson succeeds as president Joint Committee on Reconstruction formed
1866	Civil Rights Act passed over Johnson's veto Memphis and New Orleans riots American Equal Rights Association founded Johnson defeated in congressional elections
1867	Reconstruction Acts Tenure of Office Act Purchase of Alaska
1868	Impeachment crisis Fourteenth Amendment ratified Ulysses S. Grant elected president
1870	Ku Klux Klan at peak of power Fifteenth Amendment ratified
1873	Panic of 1873 ushers in depression of 1873–1877
1875	Whiskey Ring scandal undermines Grant administration
1877	Compromise of 1877; Rutherford B. Hayes becomes president Reconstruction ends

The North During Reconstruction

On state politics in the North, see Eugene H. Berwanger, *The West and Reconstruction* (1981), and James Mohr, ed., *The Radical Republicans in the North: State Politics During Reconstruction* (1976). Studies on national politics that extend beyond Reconstruction include Paul H. Buck, *The Road to Reunion, 1865–1900* (1937), and Morton Keller, *Affairs of State: Public Life in Late Nineteenth-Century America* (1977). The best studies of classic liberalism and liberals during the Reconstruction Era are John G. Sproat, *"The Best Men": Liberal Reformers in the Gilded Age* (1968), and Robert Kelley, *The Transatlantic Persuasion: The Liberal-Democratic Mind in the Age of Gladstone* (1968). On the monetary difficulties of the 1870s, see Walter T. K. Nugent, *The Money Question During Reconstruction* (1967). On the Compromise of 1877, see K. I. Polakoff, *The Politics of Inertia: The Election of 1876 and the End of Reconstruction* (1973), and C. Vann Woodward, *Reunion and Reaction* (1956).

PART 4

A Maturing Industrial Society, 1877–1914

THEMATIC TIMELINE

	Economy	Politics	Society	Culture	Diplomacy
	The triumph of industrialization	**From inaction to progressive reform**	**Racial, ethnic, and gender divisions**	**The rise of the city**	**An emerging world power**
1877	Andrew Carnegie launches modern steel industry Knights of Labor becomes national movement (1878)	Election of Rutherford B. Hayes ends Reconstruction	Defeat of the struggle for black equality End of nomadic Indian life High tide of women's "separate sphere"	Commercialization of leisure: National League founded (1876) Dwight L. Moody pioneers urban revivalism	U.S. becomes a net exporter
1880	Gustavus Swift pioneers vertically integrated firm American Federation of Labor founded (1886)	Ethnocultural issues dominate state and local politics Civil service reform (1883)	Chinese Exclusion Act (1882) Dawes Severalty Act divides tribal lands (1887)	Electrification transforms city life First *Social Register* defines high society (1888)	Diplomacy of inaction Naval build-up begins
1890	U.S. surpasses Britain in iron and steel output Economic depression (1893–97) Great merger movement	Populist party founded (1891) William McKinley wins presidency; defeats Bryan's free silver crusade (1896)	Black disfranchisement and racial segregation in the South Immigration from southeastern Europe rises sharply	Settlement houses spread progressive ideas to cities Hearst's *New York Journal* pioneers yellow journalism	Social Darwinism and Anglo-Saxonism promote expansionism Spanish-American War (1898–99); conquest of the Philippines
1900	Industry recruits immigrants for factory work Industrial Workers of the World founded (1905) Ford builds first automobile assembly line	Progressivism in national politics Theodore Roosevelt attacks the trusts Hepburn Act establishes government's regulatory power over railroads (1906)	Women take leading roles in social reform Revival of the struggle for civil rights Immigration restriction movement launched	Muckraking journalism Movies begin to overtake vaudeville	Panama cedes Canal Zone to United States (1903) Roosevelt Corollary of Monroe Doctrine (1904) Root-Takahira agreement (1908)
1910	U.S. business seeks foreign markets	Election of Woodrow Wilson (1912) New Freedom legislation creates Federal Reserve, FTC	NAACP founded (1910) Women win the right to vote in western states World War I ends the great European migration	Urban liberalism	Taft's Dollar Diplomacy promotes American business Woodrow Wilson proclaims U.S. neutrality in World War I

While the nation's attention had been riveted on the political dramas of Reconstruction, few people noticed an equally momentous watershed in American economic life. For the first time, as the decade of the 1870s passed, farmers no longer constituted a majority of working Americans. Henceforth, the nation's future would be linked irrevocably to its development as an industrial society.

The effects of accelerating industrialization were felt, first of all, in the manufacturing sector itself. As heavy industry emerged and the railroad system was completed, the modern techniques of industrial management took shape. Enterprise came increasingly to be carried on by big, nationwide firms. The trade union movement became firmly established, and, as immigration surged, the foreign-born and their children came to make up America's industrial workforce. What had been partial and limited became general and widespread as America turned into a land of factories, of great corporate enterprise, and of restless workers.

Second, the demands of industrialism largely drove the final surge of settlement across the Great Plains. Industry needed the West's mineral resources, while cities called for new sources of food. In the struggle for their way of life, the Plains Indians were ultimately defeated not so much by the rifles of army troopers as by events taking place far off in the nation's industries and cities. Rural America was likewise locked into the advancing Industrial Revolution. The distress American farmers experienced in this period resulted from their imperfect integration into the modern industrial order. They remained small-scale operators in an economic world increasingly dominated by far-flung railroads and giant corporations.

Third, industrialization transformed the physical and human make-up of the nation's cities. By 1900, one in five Americans lived in cities. That was where the jobs were—as workers in factories, as clerks and salespeople in offices and department stores, as members of a new salaried middle class of managers, engineers, and professionals, and, at the apex, as a wealthy elite of property owners and entrepreneurs. But the city was more than just a place to make a living. It provided a setting for an urban way of life unlike anything seen before in the United States.

Fourth, politics too marched in step with the industrial order. In the years of unprecedented economic expansion between 1877 and 1893, there seemed little need for government intervention. The major parties were robust and active, but their vitality stemmed from a political culture of popular participation, from ethnocultural conflicts linked to party loyalties, and from the informal functions the parties performed as highly organized political machines. Economic crisis during the 1890s triggered a major challenge to the political status quo, first, through the formation by the nation's distressed farmers of the Populist party, and then, as economic troubles spread across the land, over the explosive issue of free silver. The election of 1896 turned back that challenge. Still unresolved, however, was another economic concern—the enormous concentration of business power that had accompanied the nation's corporate development. This issue dominated the national politics of the Progressive Era years. Moreover, the nation belatedly began to address its social ills. From their bases in the settlement houses, women progressives took the lead in the struggle to make life better for America's urban masses. African-Americans, oppressed by disfranchisement and segregation, found allies among white progressives, and launched a new drive for racial equality.

Fifth and finally, the dynamism of America's economic development forced a decisive shift in the country's world relations. In the decades after the Civil War, America remained inward-looking, its indifference to global affairs reflected in an inactive diplomacy and a neglected navy. The economic crisis of the 1890s, however, brought home to American leaders the urgent need for secure access to overseas markets for the nation's surplus products. In short order, the United States fought a brief war with Spain, acquired an overseas empire, and forcefully asserted its national interests in Latin America and Asia. There was now no mistaking America's standing as a Great Power, nor, as World War I approached, any way to evade the responsibilities and entanglements that came with that exalted status.

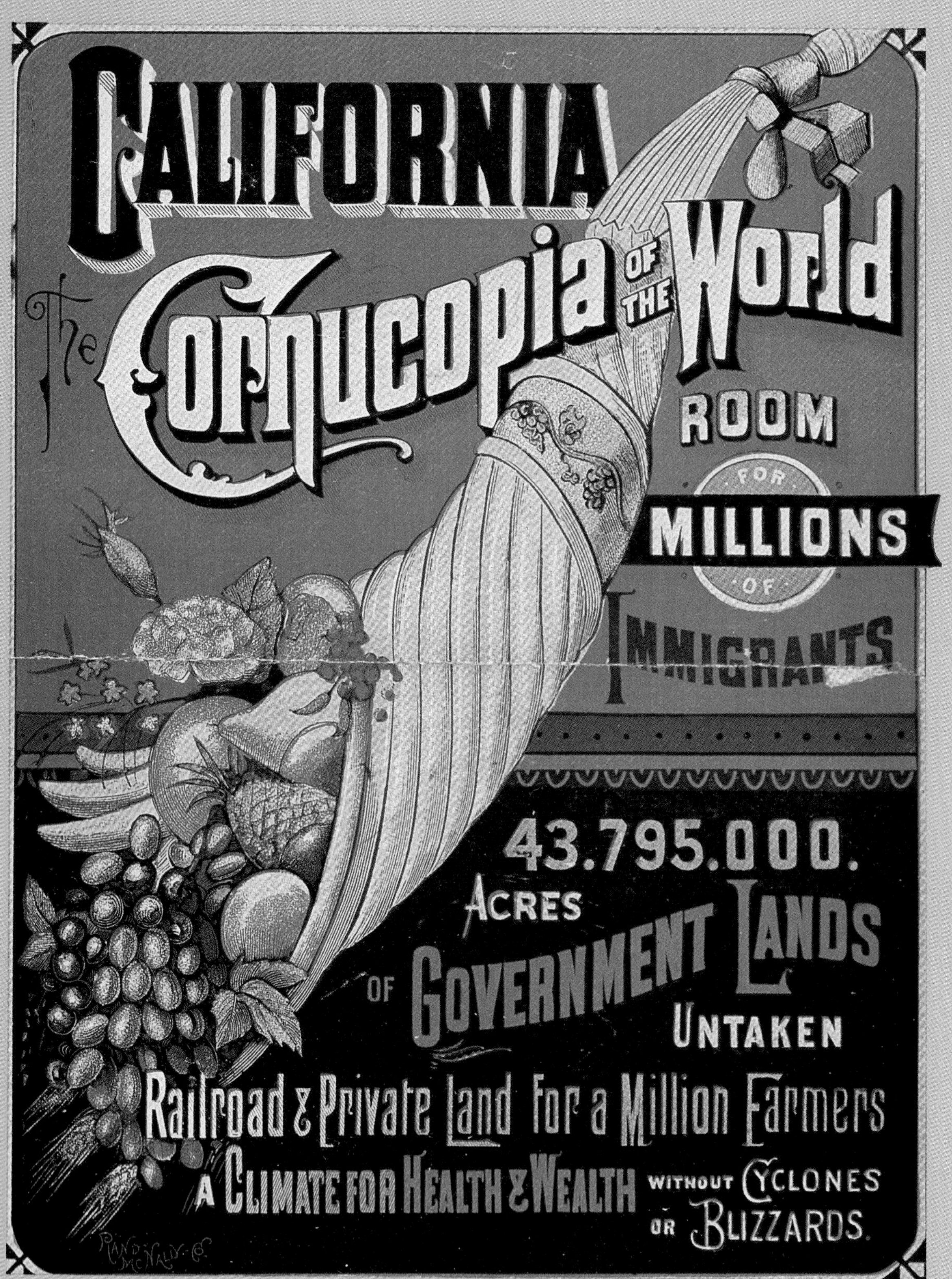

California Cornucopia of the World

In the 1880s there was a burst of publicity about the charms of Southern California. Eager for business, the Southern Pacific Railroad was responsible for this promotion.

CHAPTER 17 *The American West, 1865–1890*

During the last third of the nineteenth century, American society seemed to be at odds with itself. From one angle the nation looked like an advanced industrial society, with great factories and mills and enormous, crowded cities. But from another angle America still seemed to be a frontier country, with settlers streaming westward on to the Great Plains, repeating the old dramas of "settlement" they had been performing over and over ever since Europeans had first set foot on the continent. Not until the 1890 census would the federal government declare that the frontier no longer existed: the country's "unsettled area has been so broken into . . . that there can hardly be said to be a frontier line."

That same year, 1890, the country surpassed Great Britain in the production of iron and steel. Newspapers told about Indian wars and labor strikes in the same editions. The army's massacre of Indians at Wounded Knee, South Dakota, the final tragedy in the suppression of the Plains tribes, occurred only eighteen months before the great Homestead steel strike of July 1892.

This combination of events from the distant worlds of factory and frontier did not occur by accident. The final surge of westward settlement across the Great Plains was powered primarily by the dynamism of American industrialization. The Industrial Revolution likewise shaped the history of agricultural America in these years. Farmers had one foot in the Jeffersonian past and the other in the industrial age. They remained small-scale operators in an economic world increasingly dominated by far-flung railroads and giant corporations. They were producing for international markets but thinking as family farmers. The distress they experienced during this period resulted basically from their imperfect integration into the modern industrial order. Rural America could no longer be understood on its own terms. Its history had become linked ever more tightly to the larger industrial society.

The Great West

Before the Civil War, the vast lands west of the Mississippi seemed of little importance. Accustomed to woodlands and ample rainfall, farmers hung back from the dry country of the Great West. They saw it much as did Horace Greeley on his way to California in 1859: "a land of starvation," "a treeless desert," with a "terrible" climate of baking heat in the daytime and "chill and piercing" cold at night.

The Great West began at the edge of the prairie country several hundred miles west of the Mississippi River. Farther west, at roughly the ninety-eighth meridian running down from what are now North and South Dakota through central Texas, the tall grass of the prairies gave way to the short buffalo grass of the semi-arid country. The land of buffalo grass, the Great Plains, extended to the Rocky Mountains. Beyond the mountains lay a high, arid plateau that spread to the Sierra and Cascade ranges. Schoolbooks referred to the Great Plains as the Great American Desert. Major Stephen H. Long, after exploring the region west of the ninety-eighth meridian in 1820, had declared it "almost wholly unfit for cultivation, and of course uninhabitable by a people depending upon agriculture for their subsistence."

Indians of the Great Plains

Whites generally considered the Great Plains best left to the native American inhabitants—the Apache and Comanche in the Southwest; Arapaho and Pawnee on the central plains; and, to the north, Crow, Cheyenne, and the great Sioux nation. The Sioux, who had been spared the epidemics of smallpox and measles that had ravaged many of the rival tribes, became the dominant power on the northern Great Plains.

Originally, the Sioux had been eastern prairie people occupying semipermanent settlements in the lake country of northern Minnesota. Under pressure from the better-armed Ojibwa, and with dwindling sources of fish and game, some Sioux tribes began to drift westward during the early eighteenth century. Around 1760, they began to cross the Missouri River into the vast short-grass country. From tribes to the south and west, the Sioux acquired horses. Now mounted, they became hunters of the buffalo herds that ranged the Great Plains. The Sioux became a seminomadic people, living in portable skin tepees and claiming the entire Great Plains north of the Arkansas River as their hunting grounds. By the early nineteenth century, they had built an essentially new and robust Indian culture based on the horse, the buffalo, and the open land.

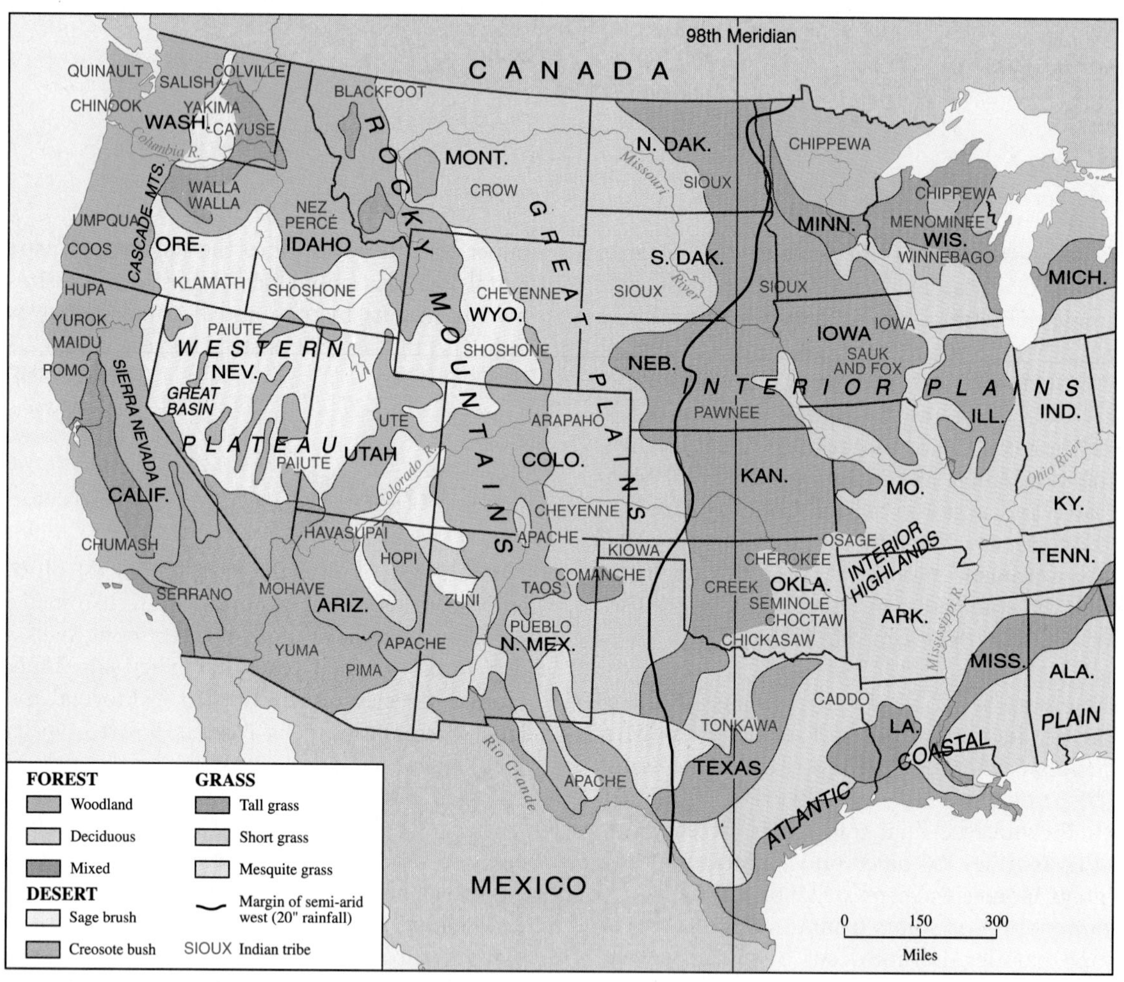

MAP 17.1

The Natural Environment and Peoples of the West

As settlers pushed into the Great Plains beyond the line of semiaridity, they sensed the overwhelming power of the natural environment. In a landscape without trees for fences and barns, without adequate rainfall, farmers had to relearn their business. The native Americans peopling the plains and mountains were also part of the western "environment," but ultimately they were easier to overcome than natural barriers. Pioneering whites never doubted that their country had the power to crush Indian resistance to the invasion of their ancestral lands.

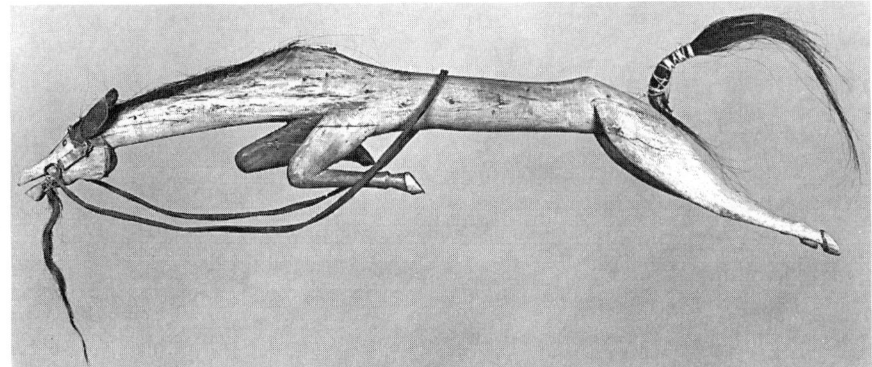

Sioux Horse Effigy

This Sioux horse effigy conveys powerfully the central place that the horse occupied in the life of the Plains Indians. (South Dakota State Historical Society)

The Teton Sioux. The westernmost Sioux—they called themselves the Teton people—made up a loose confederation of seven tribes: Oglala, Brulé, Hunkpapa, Minneconjou, Sans Arc, Two Kettle, and Blackfoot. In the winter months these tribes broke up into small bands, but each spring they would assemble and prepare for the summer hunt. Survival through the winter depended on the success of the buffalo hunt. This was conducted with much ritual, and required a high degree of organization. Summer was also the season for making war. Mostly, raiding parties of thirty or forty warriors went forth intent on capturing ponies and taking scalps, but larger, well-organized territorial campaigns were sometimes also mounted against rival tribes. The Sioux, it must be remembered, were an invading people. Warfare was the means by which they drove out or subjugated longer-settled tribes and made the Teton Sioux the dominant power on the Great Plains.

A society that celebrates the heroic virtues is likely to define gender roles sharply. Before the Sioux mastered the use of the horse, chasing down buffalo and antelope had been a group enterprise. The entire community—women as well as men—worked collectively to construct a "pound" and channel the herds in the right direction. Once on horseback, the male buffalo hunters were on their own, and gender roles became more distinct. The men did the fighting, hunting, and trading, while the women prepared the skins, made the clothing, and moved the camp. White observers frequently described Sioux women as "beasts of burden." Fanny Kelly, who had been a Sioux captive, considered "their life a servitude"; but she noticed also that Sioux women were "very rebellious, often displaying ungovernable and violent temper." Subordination to the men was not how Indian women understood their unrelenting labor; this was their allotted share in a partnership on which the proud, nomadic life of the Teton Sioux depended.

Living so close to nature, depending on its bounty for survival, the Sioux saw sacred meaning in every manifestation of the natural world. Unlike the white man, they conceived of God not as a supreme being, but (in the words of the ethnologist Clark Wissler) as "a controlling power or series of powers pervading the universe." The most sacred of these powers were the *wakan tanka.* First came the sun, Wi; then came Skan, the sky; Maka, the earth; Inyan, the rock. Below these came the moon, wind, buffalo, down through a hierarchy embodying the perceived natural order. The central experience of Sioux religion was to establish a bond with those mysterious powers through visions induced by prayer and fasting in some isolated place. Medicine men provided instruction, but the religious experience was essentially an individual matter, open both to women and men. The vision, when a supplicant achieved it, attached itself to some object—a feather, the skin of an animal, or a shell—which was tied up into a sacred bundle and became the Indian's lifelong talisman. For the tribe as a whole, Sacred Pipe bundles served as the symbolic and ceremonial core of Sioux religion. In the Sun Dance, the entire tribe engaged in the rites of coming of age, of fertility, of the hunt and combat, followed by four days of fasting and dancing in supplication to Wi, the sun.

The world of the Teton Sioux was not self-contained. From the very start of their westward trek, they had been traders, exchanging beaver and buffalo skins for the agricultural products of the sedentary eastern plains Indians, such as the Mandan. They soon extended these exchanges to the white traders who had appeared on the upper Missouri River during the eighteenth century and a substantial commerce in furs developed. Although the buffalo provided most of the essentials of life—not only food but clothing, shelter, fuel, carrying bags, and a variety of bone implements—the Sioux came to rely as well on the traders' pots, kettles, blankets, knives, and firearms. Sophisticated as this trade economy became, it was integrated into the Sioux way of life and indeed depended on the survival of the Great Plains as the Sioux had found it, wild grassland on which the antelope and buffalo ranged free.

Intruders

In 1834, Congress had formally created a permanent Indian country in the Great West. The army built border forts from Lake Superior to Fort Worth, Texas, to keep the Indians in and white settlers out. In 1838 the commanding general of the area, Edmund Gaines, recommended that the forts be constructed of stone because they would be there forever. The creation of an Indian country supported the contemporary belief that the Great American Desert could serve only as home, in the words of the explorer Zebulon M. Pike, "to the wandering and uncivilized aborigines of the country."

Though solemnly committed to the Indians, the Great West was put to new, more profitable uses almost immediately. The first encroachment came with the migration of settlers to Oregon and California during the 1840s. Instead of serving as a buffer against the British and the Mexicans, the Indian country became a bridge to the Pacific. The first wagon train headed west for Oregon from Missouri in 1842. Thousands of emigrants then traveled the Oregon Trail to the Willamette Valley or, cutting south beyond Fort Hall, down into California. Approaching that juncture in 1859, it seemed to Horace Greeley as if "the white coverings of the many emigrant and transport wagons dott[ing] the landscape" gave "the trail the appearance of a river running through great meadows, with many ships sailing on its bosom." Only these "ships" left behind not a trailing wake of foam, but a rutted landscape, devoid of grass and game, and littered with the debris of abandoned wagons and rotting garbage.

The migrants had no interest in the land they crossed; they considered it barren ground. But their journey marked the intrusion of the modernizing world on the habitat of the western Indians. And where the wagons came, the railroads were sure to follow.

As early as 1853, the federal government began surveying railway routes to the Pacific. A sectional stalemate over the proposed transcontinental route delayed railroad construction for a decade. Wagon freight lines, stagecoaches, and the horseback riders of the Pony Express furnished the first regular links between East and West. A telegraph line reached San Francisco in 1861. The tracks of the Union Pacific and Central Pacific railroads finally converged at Promontory Point, Utah, in 1869, uniting the continent by rail. A burst of western railway building followed. By 1883, two more continental routes had reached California—the Southern Pacific line from New Orleans and the Santa Fe from Kansas City—while the Northern Pacific linked Portland, Oregon, to St. Paul, Minnesota.

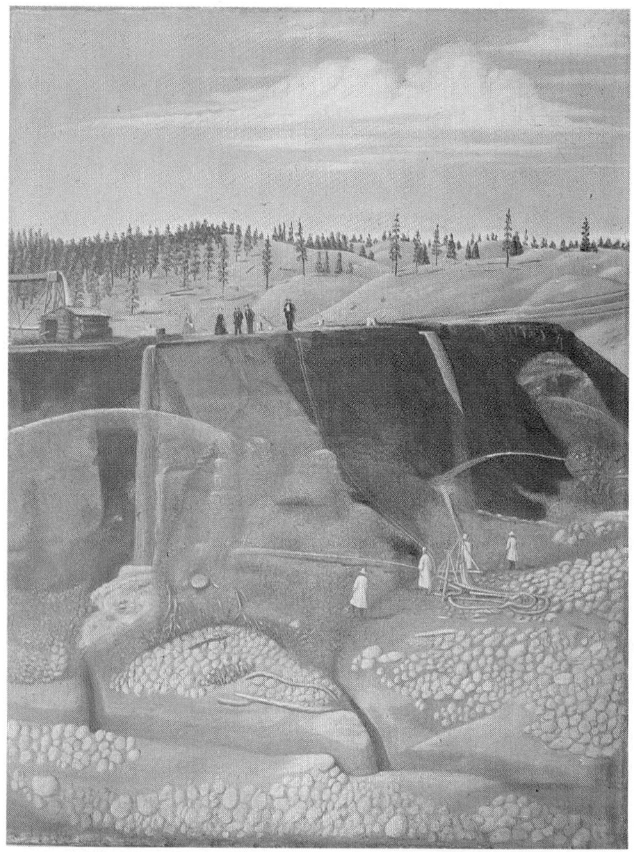

Hydraulic Mining in the Boise Basin, Idaho
Hydraulic mining, invented in the California gold fields in 1853, was a highly efficient method that yielded profits even with low-grade concentrations of gold. The technology was simple—it used high-pressure water jets to wash away hillsides of gold-bearing soil. Although building the necessary reservoirs, piping systems, and sluices required heavy investment, the profits from the hydraulic process helped transform western mining into big business. But, as Mary Brown's painting of 1875 suggests, hydraulic mining was environmentally disastrous.

The Mining Frontier. On the heels of the wagon traffic across the plains and mountains came the exploitation of the mineral wealth of the Great West. The rush to California had been triggered in 1848 by the discovery of gold in the foothills of the Sierras. By the mid-1850s, as easy pickings in the California gold country diminished, disappointed prospectors began to pull out and spread across the Great West in hopes of striking it rich elsewhere. Gold was discovered on the Nevada side of the Sierras, in the Colorado Rockies, and along the Fraser River in British Columbia. New strikes occurred

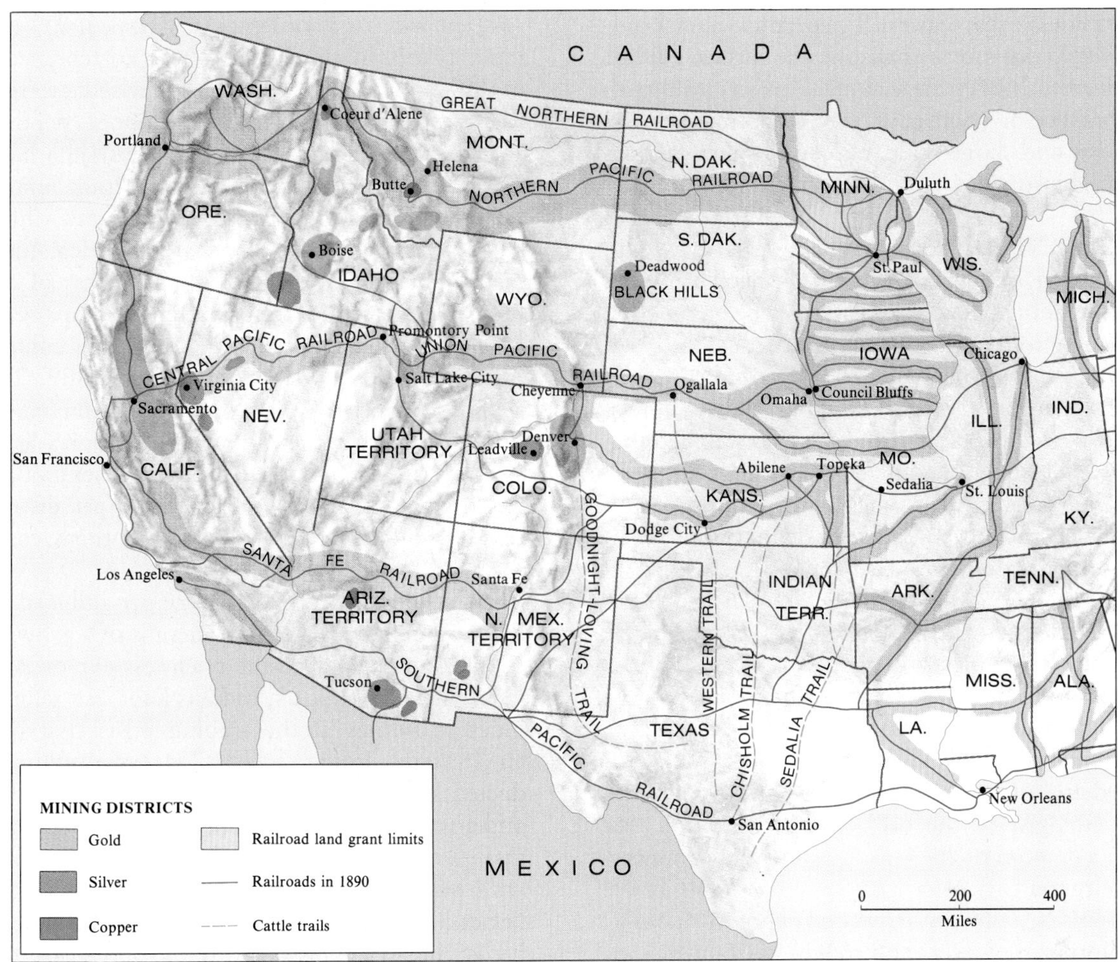

MAP 17.2

The Development of the West, 1860–1890

The first organized settlements—Mormons around Salt Lake, farmers in Oregon, ranchers and miners in California—were far from other populated areas. Mining sprang up in scattered places wherever gold and silver was discovered. The transportation routes of wagon trains, cattle trails, and railroads crossed wide expanses of open land. The final phase of western settlement thus broke from the earlier pattern of a frontier line moving westward and instead resembled a series of incursions that gradually enveloped an entire region.

in Montana and Wyoming during the 1860s, in the Black Hills of South Dakota in the 1870s, and in the Coeur d'Alene region of Idaho during the 1880s.

As the news of each gold strike spread, a wild, remote area turned almost overnight into a mob scene of prospectors, traders, gamblers, prostitutes, and saloon keepers. At least a hundred thousand fortune seekers flocked to the Pikes Peak area of Colorado in the spring of 1859. Always trespassers on government or Indian land, the prospectors made their own law. The mining codes, devised at community meetings, limited the size of a mining claim to what a person could reasonably work. This kind of informal law-making also became an instrument for excluding or discriminating against Mexicans, Chinese, and African-Americans in the gold fields. And it turned into hangman's justice for the many outlaws who infested the mining camps.

The heyday of the prospectors was always very brief. They were equipped only to skim gold from the surface of the earth and from streambeds. To extract the metal locked in the underground lodes required mine shafts and crushing mills, which took capital, technology, and business organization. The original claim holders quickly sold out after exhausting the surface gold or when a generous bidder came along. At every gold-rush site, the prospector soon gave way to entrepreneurial development and large-scale mining. Rough mining camps turned into cities.

Virginia City. Nevada's Virginia City was a case in point. It started out as a bawdy, ramshackle mining camp. But within a few years of the opening of the Comstock lode in 1859, Virginia City boasted a stock exchange, five newspapers and, in short order, ostentatious mansions for the mining kings, fancy hotels, opera, even Shakespearean theater. The underlying characteristics of a boom town persisted, however. In 1870, the ratio of men to women was two to one, and children made up only 10 percent of the population. There were a hundred saloons, and brothels lined D Street. Virginia City was a magnet for desperate job seekers of both sexes: the men who became miners and gambled their lives below ground for $4 a day, the working-class women who became dance-hall entertainers and prostitutes because that was the best chance offered many of them by Virginia City's bonanza economy. Nowhere among today's major cities, notes the leading sociologist of the subject, is prostitution "so central to community life" as it was in the miners' world of Virginia City.

When James Galloway arrived on February 4, 1875, from California, however, he brought his family with him, and so did many other miners. By 1880 there were as many women and children as men in Virginia City. Galloway's diary indicates a family life not out of the ordinary in its recording of church going, picnics, the purchase of a lot for a small house. But Galloway was infected by Virginia City's pervasive gambling fever: he speculated regularly in mining stock and always lost money. In the end, he fell victim of the extraordinary hazards of hard-rock mining. He was killed when his sleeve got caught in the gears of a mine machine. He might have survived had he agreed to having his arm hacked off, but he took a long chance on being cut loose and coming out whole, and lost.

Industrialization of Western Mining. In its final stage, the mining frontier passed into the industrial world. At some sites, gold and silver proved less important than the commoner metals with which they were intermixed. Beginning in the mid-1870s, copper mining thrived in the Butte district of Montana, especially after the opening of the fabulous Anaconda mine. It also flourished in the Globe and Copper Queen fields of New Mexico and Arizona. In the 1890s, following earlier finds at Leadville, Colorado, the Coeur d'Alene silver district became the nation's main source of lead and zinc.

The industrial order swiftly took hold of these remote places in the Great West. Entrepreneurs raised capital, built rail connections, devised the technology for treating the lower-grade copper deposits, constructed smelting facilities, and recruited a labor force. As elsewhere in American industry, trade union organization appeared among the miners (see Chapter 18). And, as elsewhere in corporate America, the western metal industries went through a process of consolidation. The Anaconda Copper Mining Company and other Montana mining firms came under the control of the Amalgamated Copper Company in 1899. That same year, the American Smelting and Refining Company brought together the bulk of the nation's lead-mining and copper-refining properties. Still Blackfoot and Crow country in the 1860s, the Butte copper district was a center of industrial capitalism barely thirty years later.

The Cattle Frontier. As with copper and lead mining in the mountain country, the demands of a growing industrial economy spurred the relentless exploitation of the Great Plains. For years, Indians had been selling buffalo hides to whites at the trading posts that dotted the Great Plains. In the early 1870s, eastern tanneries conducted successful experiments in curing buffalo hides, and a ready market developed among shoe and harness manufacturers. Parties of professional hunters, armed with high-powered rifles, swept across the plains and began a systematic slaughter of the buffalo. The great herds, already diminished by the spread of horses and cattle, almost vanished within ten years. Many people spoke out against this mass killing, but no method existed to curb people bent on making a quick dollar. Besides, as General Philip H. Sheridan assured the Texas legislature, the extermination of the buffalo brought benefits: the Indians would be starved into submission and feeding grounds would open up for a more valuable commodity, the Texas longhorn.

Since the eighteenth century, these tough Spanish cattle had spread westward across Texas from the grasslands between the Rio Grande and the Nueces River. About 5 million longhorns roamed the region in 1865, largely untended and unclaimed, and hardly worth bothering about because they could not be profitably marketed. That year, however, the Missouri Pacific Railroad reached Sedalia, Missouri. At that terminal, connecting as it did to hungry eastern markets, the $3 longhorn might command $40. This realization by Texas ranchers set off the famous Long Drive. Cowboys began to herd Texas cattle a thousand miles or more north to the railroads that were pushing west across Kansas.

At Abilene, Ellsworth, and, beginning in 1875, Dodge City, the stockmen sold the cattle and the trail-weary cowboys went on a binge. Like the mining

The Cowboy at Work
Open-range ranching, where cattle from different ranches grazed together, gave rise to distinctive traditions. At the roundup, cowboys separated the cattle by owner and branded the calves. The cowboy, traditionally a colorful figure, was really a kind of farmhand on horseback, with the skills to work on the range. He earned twenty-five dollars a month, plus his food and a bed in the bunkhouse, for long hours of grueling, lonesome work.

camps, the wide-open cattle towns captured the nation's imagination as symbols of the Wild West. The reality was much more ordinary. The cowboys, perhaps a third of them African-Americans and Hispanics, were in fact farm hands on horseback, working long hours under harsh conditions for small pay. Colorful though it seemed, the Long Drive was actually a makeshift method of bridging a gap in the developing transportation system. As soon as railroads reached the Texas range country during the 1870s, stockmen abandoned the hazardous and wasteful Long Drive for a more settled kind of ranching.

Others, meanwhile, introduced longhorns to the northern ranges and found that the cattle could survive the harsh winter climate. In hardly a decade, starting in the late 1860s, the Great Plains changed into ranching country. The land itself was treated as a free commodity, available to anyone who seized it and put it to use. Hopeful ranchers would spot a likely area along a creek and claim as much land as they could qualify for as settlers under federal homesteading laws, plus what might be added by the fraudulent claims taken out by one or two ranch hands. By a common usage that quickly became established, the rancher had a "range right" to all the adjacent land rising up to the divide—the point where the land sloped down to the next creek. As they improved the scrawny longhorns through crossbreeding with Hereford and Angus cattle, and as the herds multiplied, ranchers quickly became substantial operators. But they remained very much pioneers in relying on themselves and, through stock-raisers' associations, on each other to protect their rights as ranchers.

A cattle boom during the early 1880s hastened the end of open-range ranching. Eastern and British investors rushed in to benefit from the high profits. Overgrazing depleted the grasslands. Cattle prices had begun to slump at the Chicago stockyards in 1882, and they collapsed as stockmen dumped stricken cattle on the market during the cold weather and drought of 1885–1886. The following winter, the most terrible in memory, wiped out vast herds. Open-range ranching came to an end. Cattle ranchers built fences around their land and laid in hay crops for winter feed. No longer would cattle be left to fend for themselves on the open range. The Great Plains turned into ordinary ranch country. Sheep raising, previously scorned as unmanly work and resisted as a threat to the grass, now became respectable. Some ranchers even sold out to the despised "nesters"—those who wanted to try farming the Great Plains.

AMERICAN LIVES

Buffalo Bill and the Wild West

Scott County, Iowa, was still frontier country when William F. Cody was born there on February 26, 1846. Kansas, where his family moved in 1854, was even wilder, for it was not only frontier country but racked by bloody conflict between proslavery and free-soil settlers. Bill's father, Isaac Cody, was active on the free-soil side, serving in the Topeka legislature and frequently in harm's way from neighboring southern sympathizers and marauding Border Ruffians. One of Bill's first exploits was a wild gallop, with proslavery men in hot pursuit, to warn his father of a trap set for him near the family farm. Isaac Cody was less an idealist, however, than a typical enterprising westerner on the lookout for the main chance. He had been an Indian trader, a farm manager, a stagecoach operator, and, in Kansas, a land speculator around Grasshopper Falls. When he died suddenly in 1857, Cody left the family with a lot of land titles but little money.

Bill, never much for schooling anyway, had to find work. Only eleven, he was taken on by Majors and Waddell, the firm that freighted goods from Fort Leavenworth to army posts west of the Missouri River. Bill worked as a messenger boy, livestock herder, and teamster helper on the freight wagons going west. When his employers (now Russell, Majors, and Waddell) organized the short-lived Pony Express in 1860, Cody became a stocktender and occasional rider in the Colorado-Nebraska division. Most of this was hard and tedious labor, but there were flashes of excitement—scrapes with Indians and bandits (at fifteen, Bill killed one), buffalo stampedes, and brief encounters with Wild Bill Hickock and other tough western characters on which to model himself. In the early part of the Civil War, Cody was somewhat at loose ends. Among other things he engaged in some horse-thieving disguised as guerrilla activity in Missouri, and he became a heavy drinker. After a stint in the Seventh Kansas Cavalry and a half-hearted effort to settle down after the war (and an unhappy marriage), Cody got his lucky break in 1867.

Buffalo Bill's Wild West Show
(Buffalo Bill Historical Center)

The Kansas Pacific Railroad was building a line through Indian country to Sheridan, Kansas. To provision the work crews, the contractors hired Cody at $500 a month—excellent pay—to bring in twelve buffalo a day for the cooks. Cody was a crack shot, an excellent horseman, and he knew buffalo hunting. This assignment was duck soup for him, and the aplomb with which he carried it off soon gave him the name "Buffalo Bill."

The next summer, 1868, Indian war broke out in Kansas, and Cody got his second claim to fame. He was hired as chief scout for the U.S. Fifth Calvary. Cody knew the Kansas landscape intimately, he seemed to have a remarkable instinct for following a trail, and he was absolutely intrepid in the face of danger. At the height of the fighting in 1868-1869, Cody saw repeated action. In the climactic Battle of Summit Springs, his scouting played a decisive role and he himself shot the Cheyenne chief Tall Bull. Although the legends later built up around Buffalo Bill (and the claims of others) have inclined scholars to be skeptical, Buffalo Bill was in fact an authentic hero. Perhaps the best testimony was the extra $100 awarded him by the normally tight-fisted army "for extraordinarily good services as a trailer and fighter in the pursuit of hostile Indians."

Out of these promising materials there began to emerge a mythic figure. In July 1869, the dime novelist Ned Buntline (Edward Zane Carroll Judson) came through Kansas, met Cody, and, after returning to New York, wrote *Buffalo Bill, the King of the Border Men*—the first of some 1,700 potboilers to feature Cody's name and exploits. Then there were the buffalo hunting parties of the rich and famous that Cody periodically led, including a royal hunt in 1872 with the Grand Duke Alexis of Russia that had the entire country agog. With his white horse, buckskin suit, crimson shirt, and broad sombrero, Buffalo Bill began to play his part to the hilt. "He realized to perfection the bold hunter and gallant sportsman of the plains," wrote one appreciative participant. In 1872 Cody was persuaded to appear as himself in a play Ned Buntline proposed to put on in New York. Buntline was said to have dashed off *The Scouts of the Prairie* in four hours, and as a play critics pronounced it "execrable." But Buffalo Bill, who mostly ad-libbed, was a great hit, and so was the production. Cody was launched on his career as a showman.

From then on, the lines between reality and make-believe began to blur. Not only did Buffalo Bill draw on his past exploits when he went on stage, but he had the stage in mind when he returned to the real world. During the Sioux wars of 1875-1876, Cody was again out in the field as an army scout. (Fortunately, the fighting took place during the theatrical off-seasons in the East.) Shortly after the annihilation of Custer's troops at Little Big Horn, Cody gained a measure of vengeance in a famous skirmish in which he killed and scalped a Sioux chief named Yellow Hand. Cody rode into that engagement wearing his stage *vaquero* outfit—black velvet and scarlet with lace—so that when he reenacted the mayhem on stage, he could say he was wearing the very clothes in which he had seen action. Over time, with some help from Cody, the fight with Yellow Hand assumed legendary proportions, becoming a formal duel, with a challenge laid down by the Indian chief, and troopers and Indian warriors lined up on opposing sides watching Buffalo Bill and Yellow Hand fight it out.

Buffalo Bill Cody

The mythic West Cody was creating became full-blown in his Wild West Show. Modeled on the circus and rodeo, it was first staged in 1883. It was an open-air extravaganza, with displays of horsemanship, sharp-shooting by Little Annie Oakley, real Indians (in one season Chief Sitting Bull toured with the company), and reenactments of stagecoach robberies and great events like Custer's Last Stand. The Wild West toured the country every year—and was a smashing success in Europe as well.

Buffalo Bill had been keen enough to see the hunger of city people for a legendary West. He traded on his talents as a showman, but he relied as well on his grasp of the authentic world behind the make-believe. When Cody died in 1917, that world had long gone, but his Wild West Show kept it alive in legend, where it still remains in the mythic figures of cowboys and Indians that populate our movies and television screens.

The Impact on the Indians

And what of the Indians who had inhabited the Great West? Basically, their fate has been told in the foregoing account of western settlement. "The white children have surrounded me and have left me nothing but an island," lamented the great Sioux chief Red Cloud in 1870, the year after the completion of the transcontinental railroad. "When we first had all this land we were strong; now we are all melting like snow on a hillside, while you are grown like spring grass." Francis A. Walker, a knowledgeable government official, expressed that hard truth from the whites' point of view: "The freedom of territorial and industrial expansion, which is bringing industrial greatness to the nation, to the Indian brings wretchedness, destitution, beggary."

Every advance of the whites—the Oregon-bound wagon train, the railroad, the buffalo hunter, the miner, the cattle rancher, the farmer—intruded on the Indians' world. No historical equation could have been more precise: the progress of the settlers meant the end of the Indian's way of life.

The provision for a permanent Indian country, written into federal law and into treaties with various tribes, was swept away in the westward march of the settler. By 1860 all the resettled eastern tribes, treaties notwithstanding, had been forced to cede their lands and move farther west. The nomadic tribes presented a more formidable barrier. As miners and other pioneers thrust into Indian lands from the late 1850s on, they fought running battles with the Indians all along the frontier—from the Apache in the Southwest, to

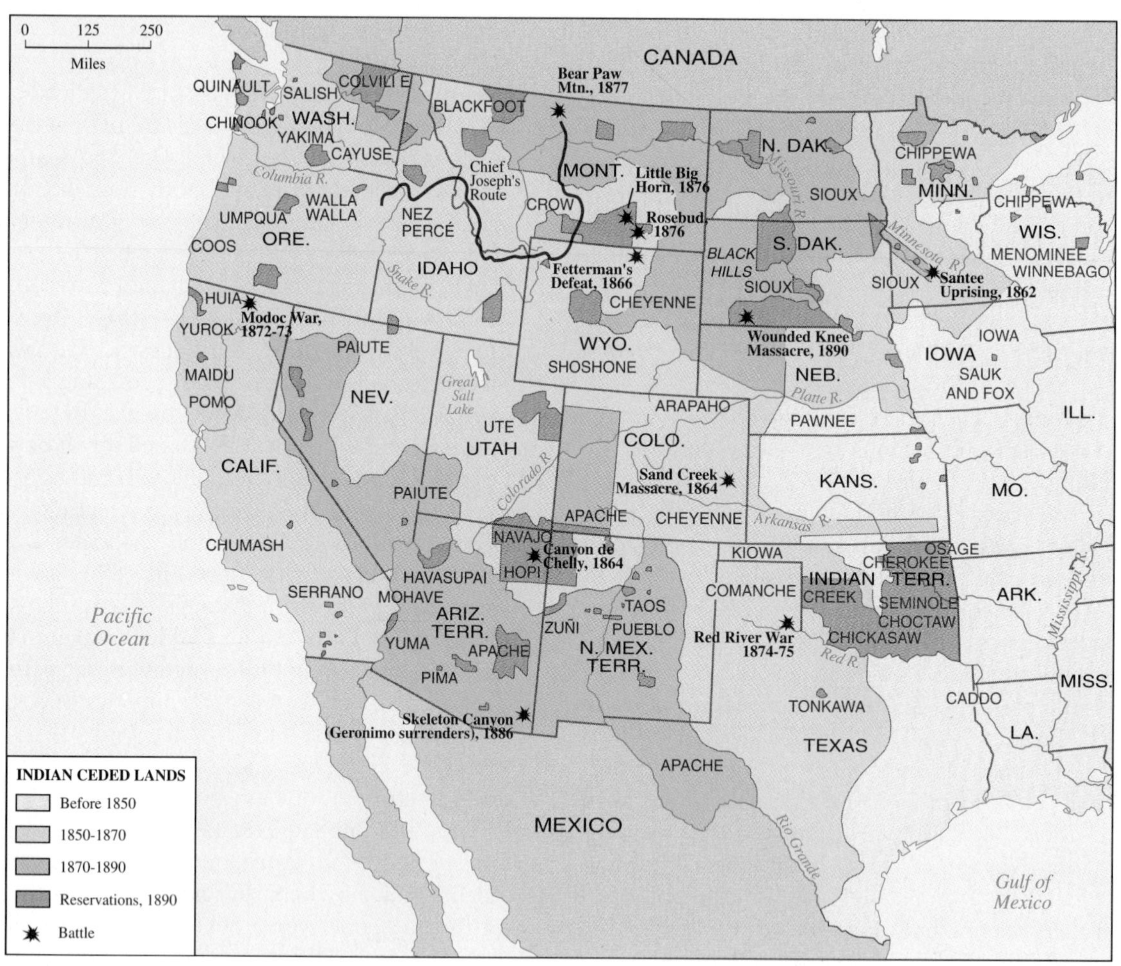

MAP 17.3

The Indian Frontier

As settlement pushed on to the Great Plains after the Civil War, the Indians put up bitter resistance, but ultimately to no avail. Over a period of decades, they ceded most of their lands to the federal government, and by 1890 they were confined to scattered reservations where most could expect an impoverished and alien way of life.

the Cheyenne and Arapaho in Colorado, to the Sioux in the Wyoming and Dakota territories. Fighting ferociously between 1865 and 1867, the Sioux prevented a wagon road from being built through their prized Powder River hunting grounds to the booming mining town of Bozeman in eastern Montana.

The Reservation Solution. This fierce resistance led to the formulation in 1867 of a new policy for dealing with the western Indians. Few whites questioned the necessity of moving the Indians out of the path of settlement, nor the idea that the Indians should be placed on reservations. This process had already begun intermittently. Now it would be pushed to a conclusion. And to it would be linked something new: a planned approach for weaning the Indians from their nomadic way of life. Under the guidance of the Office of Indian Affairs, they would be wards of the government until they learned "to walk on the white man's road."

The government set aside two extensive areas for the Indians. It allocated the southwestern quarter of the Dakota Territory—present-day South Dakota west of the Missouri River—to the Teton Sioux tribes. And it assigned what is now Oklahoma to the southern Plains Indians, as well as to the Five Civilized Tribes—the Choctaw, Cherokee, Chickasaw, Creek, and Seminole—and other eastern Indians already there. Scattered reservations went to the Apache, Navaho, and Ute in the Southwest and to the mountain Indians in the Rockies and beyond.

As in the past, the transfer of land went through the legal process of treaty making. And, as in the past, the whites bribed and tricked the Indian chiefs and in the end forced the chiefs to accept what they could not prevent. In 1868, the western Sioux tribes signed a treaty ceding all their land outside the Dakota reservation but explicitly retaining their hunting grounds in the Powder River country. "We have now selected and provided reservations for all, off the great road," concluded the western commanding general in September 1868. "All who cling to their old hunting-grounds are hostile and will remain so till killed off."

The Plains Indians, despite the treaties, inevitably tried to hold on to their way of life. Their subjugation was equally inevitable. The U.S. Army was thinly spread, having been cut back after the Civil War to a total of 27,000 for the entire country. But these were veteran troops, including 2,000 black cavalrymen of the Ninth and Tenth regiments, whom Indians called with grim respect "buffalo soldiers." Technology also favored the army. Telegraph communications and railroads enabled the troopers to be quickly concentrated; repeater rifles and Gatling guns increased their fire power against the Indians. As fighting in the mid-1870s intensified, a reluctant Congress made appropriations to augment the western troopers. Tribal rivalries prevented the Indians from ever concentrating their united power against a common enemy; on the contrary, the army generally counted on the help of friendly Indians in its campaigns. But the worst disadvantages facing the Indians derived less from a formidable U.S. Army or their own disunity than from the overwhelming impact of white settlement on their capacity to carry on the struggle.

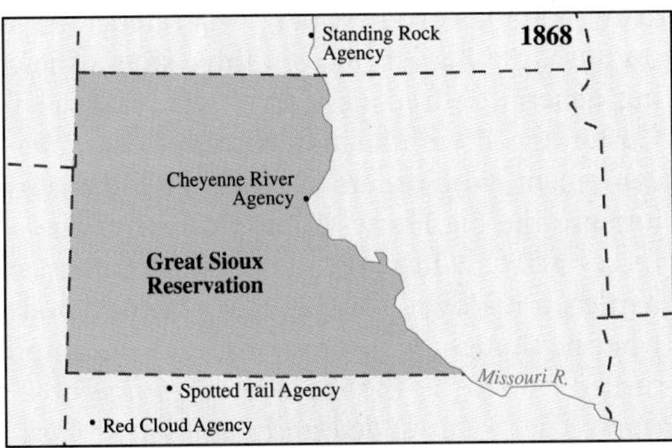

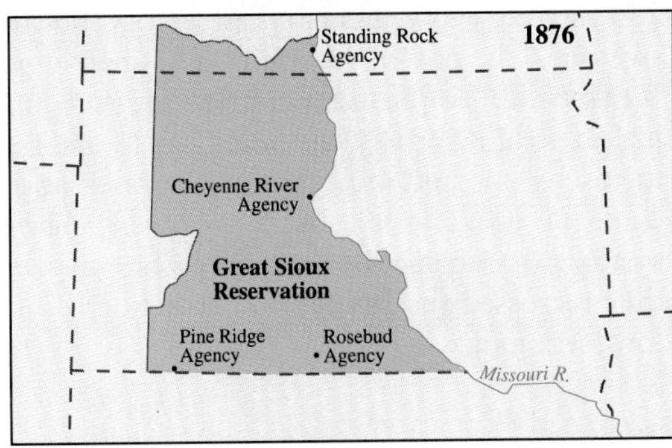

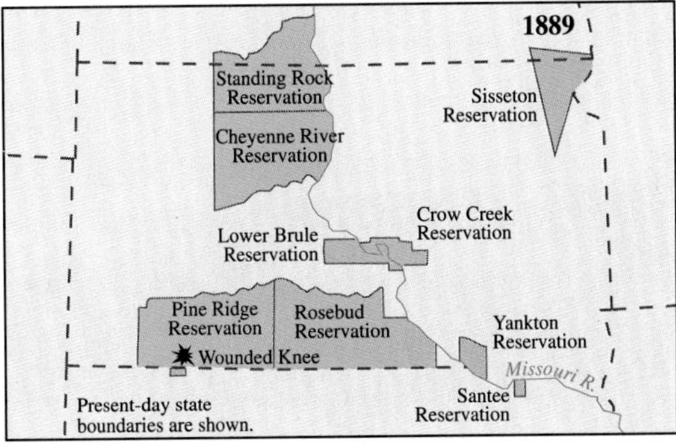

MAP 17.4

The Sioux Reservations in South Dakota, 1868–1890

When they bent to the demand in 1868 that they move on to the reservation, the Sioux thought they had gained secure rights to a substantial part of their ancestral hunting grounds. As they learned to their sorrow, however, fixed boundary lines only increased their vulnerability to the land hunger of the whites and sped up the process of expropriation.

Resisting the reservation solution, the Indians fought on for years—in Kansas in 1868–1869, in the Red River Valley of Texas in 1874, sporadically in New Mexico among the Apache until the capture of Geronimo in 1886. On the northern plains the crisis came in 1875, when the Indian Office—notwithstanding the treaty of 1868—ordered the Sioux to vacate their Powder River hunting grounds and withdraw to the reservation.

Led by Sitting Bull, Sioux warriors began to gather on the Little Big Horn River just to the east of the Powder River country. In a typical concentrating maneuver, army columns from widely separated forts converged on the Little Big Horn from three sides. The commanding general, Alfred H. Terry, sent Colonel George A. Custer ahead with a small force to locate the Sioux encampment, with orders to block the Indians from escaping into the Big Horn Mountains before the main army forces arrived. Instead, the reckless Custer sought out battle on his own. On June 25, 1876, he advanced on what he thought was a minor Indian encampment. This turned out to be the main Sioux force of 2,500 warriors. They surrounded and annihilated Custer and his 256 men. It was a great Indian victory, but not a decisive one. The day of reckoning was merely postponed. Weakened by unrelenting military pressure and increasing physical privation, the Sioux bands one by one gave themselves up and moved on to the reservation. Last to come in were Sitting Bull's followers. They had retreated to Canada, but in 1881 after five hard years they recrossed the border and surrendered at Fort Buford, Montana.

The Indians had no chance against the relentless white occupation of the land. Homesick bands of southern Cheyenne learned this bitter truth in 1878 when they escaped from their reservation in the Indian Territory of Oklahoma. Along the route to their native grounds in the Wyoming Territory lay three railroads, numerous telegraph lines, and ranchers and homesteaders eager to report the Cheyenne's movements. The Indians made their way through Kansas and Nebraska, but the army eventually caught up with and captured them. The surviving remnants declared that they preferred death to returning to the reservation. The government relented and permitted them to stay on their native land.

It was the whites, not the Indians, who wrecked the reservation policies of 1867. Prospectors began in 1873 to dig gold in the Black Hills, part of the Sioux reservation in Dakota. Unable to hold back the prospectors or to buy out the Indians, the government opened up the Black Hills to gold seekers at their own risk and then, when war with the Sioux broke out, forced the cession of the western third of the Sioux reservation.

The Indian Territory of Oklahoma met the same fate. Two million acres in the heart of the territory had not been assigned to any tribe, and white homesteaders coveted the fertile land of this area. The "Boomer" movement, stirred up initially by railroads running across the Indian Territory during the 1880s, agitated tirelessly to open this so-called Oklahoma District to settlers. In 1889, the government gave in and placed the Oklahoma District under the Homestead Act. On April 22, 1889, a horde of homesteaders rushed in and staked

The Cherokee Strip

This photograph captures the wild race into the Cherokee Strip in the northern part of Oklahoma Territory on September 16, 1893, the second such "run" that opened the region to white settlement. The winners staked out their claims under the Homestead Act, and looked forward to a prosperous future on some of the richest farmland in America. Those who lost out hoped for better luck as other parts of the territory opened up. The Indians who had lived on that land had nothing to hope for, because this process spelled the end of their way of life.

out the entire district within a few hours. Two tent cities—Guthrie with 15,000 people and Oklahoma City with 10,000—were in full swing by nightfall.

Severalty. The completion of the land-grabbing process was hastened, ironically, by the avowed friends of the native Americans. The Indians had never lacked sympathizers, especially in the East. After the Civil War, reformers created the Indian Rights Association. The movement got a big boost from Helen Hunt Jackson's powerful book *A Century of Dishonor* (1881), which told the story of the unjust treatment of the Indians. The reformers, however, had little sympathy for the tribal way of life. They could think of no other future for the Indian than assimilation into white society.

During the 1870s, the Indian Office had developed a program to train Indian children for farming and manual work and to prepare them for citizenship. Some attended reservation schools, while the less lucky were sent to boarding schools distant from family and home. The reformers approved of this educational program. They also favored the deliberate efforts by the Office of Indian Affairs to undercut tribal authority. In particular, they highly esteemed private property as a "civilizing" force.

The resulting policy was called *severalty:* the division of reservation lands into individually owned parcels. Notwithstanding that private ownership was a notion alien and repugnant to the Indians, or that earlier experiments with land allotments had failed dismally, the reformers remained unshaken in their faith that private property would transform the Indians into prudent, hard-working members of white society. With their blessing, the Dawes Severalty Act of 1887 authorized the president to divide tribal lands, giving 160 acres to each family head and smaller parcels to other individuals. The land would be held in trust by the government for twenty-five years, and the recipients would become U.S. citizens. Remaining reservation lands would be sold off, with the proceeds to be placed in an Indian education fund.

The Last Battle: Wounded Knee. The Sioux were among the first to feel the full effect of the Dawes act. According to the proposed allotments, roughly half their Dakota lands would become "surplus" and available for white settlement. The government drew up a plan breaking up the Sioux reservation into six smaller ones, and once again began the familiar process of negotiating assent from the unwilling Indians. This time the Sioux were determined not to be taken in: they would not bargain, they would simply say no. But once again they ultimately succumbed to coercion, golden promises, and division in their own ranks.

On February 10, 1890, the federal government announced that it had gained the required number of Sioux signatures (three quarters of the population) and threw the ceded land open to white settlement. But no surveys had yet been made for the reservation boundaries, nor any provision for land allotments for the Indians living in the ceded lands. On top of these signs of bad faith, there came drought that wiped out the Indians' crops. It seemed beyond endurance. They had lost their ancestral lands. They faced a future as sedentary farmers that was alien to all their traditions. And immediately confronting them was a hard winter of starvation.

But news of salvation had also come. An Indian Messiah, a holy man who called himself Wovoka, was preaching a new religion on a Paiute reservation in Nevada. In a vision, Wovoka had gone to heaven and received God's word that the world would be regenerated. The whites would disappear, all the Indians of past generations would return to earth, and life on the Great Plains would go back to the time of the roaming buffalo. All this would come to pass in the spring of 1891. Preparatory to that great day, the Indians should follow Wovoka's commandments and practice the Ghost Dance. This daylong submersion in dancing and praying brought participants into trancelike states during which their spirits rose to heaven. Wovoka's teachings were nonviolent and not specifically antiwhite, but among Wovoka's Sioux adherents the new religion took a belligerent and increasingly threatening turn toward white settlers. As the frenzy of the Ghost Dance swept through some of the Sioux encampments in the fall of 1890, resident whites became alarmed and called for army intervention.

Tragedy was almost inescapable. Confined as they were within their shrunken reservations, the Sioux had no hope of prevailing against the rapid military buildup. But neither did it seem possible to pacify them without letting loose a bloodbath. When Indian police backed by federal troops tried to arrest Sitting Bull on December 14, a gun battle broke out, killing the old chief and at least twelve others. Worse was to come. Among the Minneconjou, the medicine man Yellow Bird had stirred up a fervent Ghost Dance following. But, with their chief Big Foot desperately sick with pneumonia, they had given up and come in under military escort to an encampment at Wounded Knee Creek on December 28. The next morning, when the soldiers attempted to disarm the Indians, a battle exploded in the midst of the encampment. In the document on page 528, Black Elk describes what happened. Among the U.S. troopers, 25 died; among the Indians, 153 men, women, and children perished, plus probably 20 or more whose bodies were not found.

AMERICAN VOICES

Wounded Knee: "Something terrible happened. . . ."

Black Elk

Black Elk, an Oglala Sioux holy man, was at Wounded Knee when the killing happened. This is his account, as he recollected the event forty years later.

It was in the evening when we heard that the Big Foots were camped over there with the soldiers. . . . In the morning [December 29, 1890] I went out after my horses, and while I was out I heard shooting off toward the east, and I knew from the sound that it must be wagon guns [cannon] going off. The sounds went right through my body, and I felt that something terrible would happen. . . .

A little way ahead of us, just below the head of the dry gulch, there were some women and children who were huddled under a clay bank, and some cavalrymen were there pointing guns at them. . . .

I had no gun, and when we were charging, I just held the sacred bow out in front of me with my right hand. The bullets did not hit us at all. . . .

After the soldiers marched away, I heard from my friend, Dog Chief, how the trouble started, and he was right there by Yellow Bird when it happened. This is the way it was:

In the morning the soldiers began to take all the guns away from the Big Foots. Soldiers were on the little hill and all around, and there were soldiers across the dry gulch to the south and over east along Wounded Knee Creek too. The people were nearly surrounded, and the wagon-guns were pointing at them.

Some had not yet given up their guns, and so the soldiers were searching all the tepees, throwing things around and poking into everything. There was a man called Yellow Bird, and he and another man were standing in front of the tepee where Big Foot was lying sick. They had white sheets around and over them, with eyeholes to look through, and they had guns under these. An officer came to search them. He took the other man's gun, and then started to take Yellow Bird's. But Yellow Bird would not let go. He wrestled with the officer, and while they were wrestling, the gun went off and killed the officer. As soon as the gun went off, Dog Chief told me, an officer shot and killed Big Foot who was lying sick inside the tepee.

Then suddenly nobody knew what was happening, except that the soldiers were all shooting and the wagon-guns began going off right in among the people.

Many were shot down right there. The women and children ran into the gulch and up west, dropping all the time, for the soldiers shot them as they ran. There were only about a hundred warriors and there were nearly five hundred soldiers. The warriors rushed to where they had piled their guns and knives. They fought soldiers with only their hands until they got their guns. . . .

It was a good winter day when all this happened. The sun was shining. But after the soldiers marched away from their dirty work, a heavy snow began to fall. The wind came up in the night. There was a big blizzard, and it grew very cold. The snow drifted deep in the crooked gulch, and it was one long grave of butchered women and children and babies, who had never done any harm and were only trying to run away.

Source: John G. Neihardt, ed., *Black Elk Speaks: The Legendary 'Book of Visions' of an American Indian* (1932; New York: William Morrow and Co., 1971), pp. 216–23.

In December 1890, U.S. soldiers massacred about one hundred seventy-five Sioux men, women and children in the Battle of Wounded Knee in South Dakota. It was the last big fight on the northern plains between the Indians and the whites. Black Elk, a Sioux holy man, related that "after the soldiers marched away from their dirty work, a heavy snow began to fall . . . and it grew very cold." The body of Yellow Bird lay frozen where it had fallen.

Wounded Knee was the final episode in the long war of suppression of the Plains Indians, but not the end of their story. The process of severalty now proceeded without hindrance. On the Dakota lands, the Teton Sioux fared relatively well, and many of the younger generation settled down as small farmers and stock grazers. In general, however, the Indians gained little profit from the land to which they received title as individuals. Their vulnerability spawned an industry of land-leasing scams, followed by sale of their land once the twenty-five year trustee period forbidding the transfer of legal title expired. On the Indian reservations of the Oklahoma Territory, where this process went on with wild abandon, expropriation took scarcely two decades. When Oklahoma became a state in 1907, Indians made up a scattered minority of 70,000 among a million whites. As an Oklahoma editor put it in the year of statehood: "Sympathy and sentiment never stand in the way of the onward march of empire."

California and the Far West

In 1860, when the Great Plains was still Indian country, the booming state of California already had 300,000 residents, 57,000 of them in the bustling metropolis of San Francisco. California never conformed very closely to the prevailing conception of a "frontier" settlement. For one thing, California was not empty of "civilization" when the Americans began to arrive in significant numbers during the 1840s. Settled as an outpost of the Spanish empire in the late eighteenth century, California had roughly 8,000 Spanish-speaking inhabitants and a functioning ranching economy at the time that it was seized in 1848 by the United States from Mexico as part of the spoils of war. Moreover, although many Americans came overland, there was always sea access to California, and maritime commerce crucially shaped its growth from the outset. Finally, Indian resistance was nothing like what settlers had encountered farther east. Already subdued by half a century of Spanish rule, the California Indians lacked a tribal structure, a warrior tradition, or the farming skills of other sedentary Indians. These tribes were easy prey for the aggressive miners and settlers flooding into California, who, in short order, virtually exterminated them. Of the 100,000 Indians who had been living in California in the 1840s, scarcely 15,000 remained by 1900 in remote and barren reservations.

California was the anchor of two distinct far western regions. First, it joined with the present-day states of Oregon and Washington to form the Pacific slope. And second, by climate and Hispanic heritage, it was linked to the Southwest, which today includes Arizona and New Mexico.

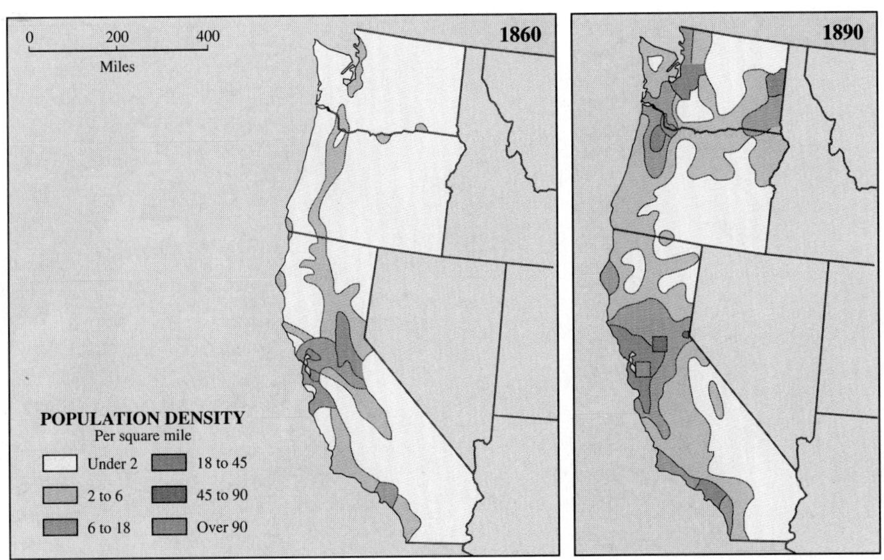

MAP 17.5

The Settlement of the Pacific Slope

In 1860 the settlement of the Pacific Slope was remarkably uneven—fully underway in northern California, scarcely begun anywhere else. By 1890, a new pattern had begun to emerge, with the swift growth of southern California already foreshadowed and the settlement of the Pacific Northwest well-launched.

Hispanics, Chinese, Anglos

The Hispanic Southwest. California was the westernmost end of a crescent of Spanish-speaking communities that extended across the American Southwest as far as San Antonio, Texas. The oldest and most stable settlements were along the upper Rio Grande Valley in New Mexico around Santa Fe, an adobe town that was over two hundred years old in 1860 and contained at that time 4,635 residents. The economy of this entire Hispanic crescent consisted primarily of cattle and sheep raising with some small-scale mining and trading. The social order was highly stratified and traditional. At the top was an aristocracy of large landowners; at the bottom, with little in between, was a Mexican peasantry that served as herders and farm hands on the big ranches or lived as subsistence farmers in small villages.

The survival of this Spanish-Mexican crescent after its incorporation into the United States depended very much on the rate of Anglo immigration. In New Mexico, which was off the beaten track before the arrival of railroads in the 1880s, the old culture more than held its own, incorporating through intermarriage and partnerships the Anglo newcomers into the Hispanic elite of Santa Fe. As the army broke the resistance of the warlike Navaho, Apache, and Ute tribes, moreover, New Mexican settlement expanded up into Colorado, and along the rivers and valleys into Texas and Arizona.

Most active in this Hispanic expansion were the New Mexico peasantry. The robustness of their subsistence culture stemmed from a division of labor that gave women a central productive role in the village economy. Women raised much of the family food in small gardens, engaged in village bartering trade, made the clothes, and plastered the adobe houses. When the Anglo economy pressed in during the 1880s, the men began to leave the villages seasonally to work on the railroads or in the Colorado mines and sugar-beet fields, thereby earning crucial dollars while leaving the village economy ever more firmly in their wives' hands.

Vaqueros in a Corral

On California cattle ranches, owners relied on Mexican cowhands—*vaqueros*—whose skills as riders and rope handlers were unexcelled. This striking painting was done in 1877 by the artist James Walker, who came from New York City but had a special enthusiasm for southwestern scenes. (The Thomas Gilcrease Institute)

When Texas cattle ranchers forced their way into an area known as the Las Vegas Grant, the Mexicans long settled there, *los pobres* (the poor ones), organized themselves into masked night-riding raiders and in 1889 and 1890 mounted an effective campaign of harassment against the Anglo interlopers. A vigorous Hispanic culture, with its hub around Santa Fe, thus stubbornly held its own within the American Southwest.

In California, on the other hand, the Spanish-speaking society was rapidly overwhelmed by the flood of Yankee migrants. The expropriation of the great ranchos was relentless, accomplished partly by legal challenges to the authenticity of the land grants, partly by the spendthrift ways of the *Californios* themselves. By the 1880s just a handful of the original families—the Dominguezes near Los Angeles, for example—managed to hold on to their Mexican land grants.

Only in the slow-growing southern part of the state did Hispanic communities retain a significant foothold. Overwhelmingly Spanish-speaking in the early decades, Los Angeles still counted 20 percent with Spanish surnames among its 11,000 inhabitants in 1880. Partly the remnants of the *Californio* working people, partly more recent migrants from Mexico, these Angelenos were mostly manual laborers and poor artisans, and they already formed what was identifiably a *barrio*—a distinct ethnic neighborhood—in the old downtown. At that point, an Anglo influx into southern California suddenly began, but so, more slowly, did the migration from old Mexico.

Mexican Immigrants. All along the Southwest borderlands, economic activity was picking up. Railroads were being built, copper mines were opening in Arizona, cotton and vegetable agriculture were developing in south Texas, and irrigated fruit growing was being introduced in southern California. There is no way of knowing precisely how many Mexicans migrated to the work thus created, since the borders were open until 1917 and few bothered to register when they entered the United States. But clearly their numbers were increasing from the 1880s onward; one estimate puts the number of immigrants arriving in 1900 at between 60,000 and 100,000. Some came as contract workers for railway track gangs and harvest labor; virtually all were relegated to the lowest-paying and most backbreaking work; and everywhere they were discriminated against and reviled by higher-status Anglo workers. Mostly the Mexicans came as short-term and casual workers, not as permanent settlers, but some remained and swelled the numbers and resources of the Mexican-American communities of the Southwest borderland cities from El Paso to Los Angeles.

What stimulated the Mexican immigration, of course, was the enormous need for labor by a region undergoing explosive economic development. Hence the exceptionally high numbers of immigrants generally in the California population of this era: between 1860 and 1890, roughly one-third were foreign-born, more than twice the level for the country as a whole. Many came from Europe; most numerous were the Irish, then the Germans and British. But there was also another group that was unique to the West—the Chinese.

The Chinese in California. Attracted first by the California gold rush of 1849, over 200,000 Chinese migrated to the United States over the next three decades. In those years they constituted a considerable minority of California's population—around 9 percent—and because virtually all were economically active, they represented a much larger proportion of the state's labor force—probably a quarter in 1870. The coming of the Chinese to California was not an isolated event, but part of a larger, world-wide pattern of Asian migration that began in the mid-nineteenth century. Driven by poverty from their overpopulated lands, Chinese went to Australia, Hawaii, and Latin America, Indians to Fiji and South Africa, and Javanese to Dutch colonies in the Caribbean. Most of these Asians migrated under the system of indentured or coerced servitude. That was not true of the Chinese who came to America. Contrary to the stubborn popular image of a "coolie trade," theirs was an essentially voluntary movement, mostly financed by a *credit-ticket system.* Under this system, migrants merely borrowed passage money from a broker; unlike indentured servants, they retained their personal freedom and the right to choose their employer.

Building the Central Pacific
Chinese laborers at work on the great trestle spanning the canyon at Secrettown in the Sierra Nevada.

Market Scene, Sansome Street
This exuberant painting by William Hahn captures downtown San Francisco as he saw it in 1872, a veritable boiling pot of races (note the black woman at left, the Chinese group at right) and classes (note, in the midst of the market bustle, the proper lady at far left, with her Lord-Fauntleroy son). It was its role as metropolis for the entire Far West that gave San Francisco the great vitality conveyed in this painting. (Crocker Art Museum)

Once they arrived, however, Chinese immigrants normally entered the orbit of the Six Companies—the powerful confederation of Chinese merchants in San Francisco's Chinatown. Most of the arrivals were unattached males eager to earn a stake and return to their native villages in Canton province. The Six Companies acted not only as an employment agency, but provided them with all the social and commercial services they needed to survive in an alien world. The small number of Chinese women—the male/female ratio was thirteen to one—worked mostly as prostitutes, sad victims drawn from the bottom of the world of poverty that drove the Chinese to America. Some were sold by impoverished parents; others had been enticed into fraudulent marriages or kidnapped by procurers and smuggled into American ports.

Until the early 1860s, when surface mining played out, Chinese men labored mainly in the gold fields—as prospectors where the white miners permitted it, as laborers and cooks where they did not. Then, when the transcontinental railroad was started in 1865, the Central Pacific began to recruit Chinese workers. Eventually they constituted four-fifths of the railroad's entire labor force. With as many as 11,000 working at any one time, the Chinese accomplished by their sheer physical labor the extraordinary feat of thrusting the railroad across the High Sierras. The Central Pacific perfected a system of contract labor for employing the Chinese. Many were recruited directly from around Canton by labor agents and worked as labor gangs under the control of "China bosses," who not only supervised but fed, housed, paid, and often cheated them.

When the transcontinental railroad was completed in 1869, the Chinese scattered. Some continued to work in construction gangs for the railroads, others labored on swamp-drainage and irrigation projects in the Central Valley and then became agricultural workers. Chinese settlements could be found across the Far West, but most Chinese remained in California. In San Francisco many of them became factory workers. The Chinese were excluded from higher-wage trades, but they soon dominated certain industries—such as cigar-making—that competed with eastern products and could survive only with cheap labor. "Wherever we put them, we found them good," remarked Charles Crocker, one of the Big Four of the Central Pacific. From the standpoint of employers, "their orderly and industrious habits make them a very desirable class of immigrants."

The Anti-Chinese Agitation. White workers, however, did not share this enthusiasm for Chinese labor. Why they should have taken so venomous a view of the Chinese has never been easy to explain. It involved, most certainly, a sense of unfair economic competition that pitted them against "Chinamen's wages" and "Chinamen's living conditions." But the hatred clearly went deeper. In other parts of the country, popular racism was directed against African-Americans; in California (where blacks were few in number) it found a target in the Chinese. They were "an infusible element" who could not be assimilated into American society, wrote the young journalist Henry George in a famous 1869 letter that made his reputation as a spokesman for California labor. "They practice all the unnameable vices of the East. [They are] utter heathens, treacherous, sensual, cowardly and cruel." Sadly, this vicious racism was intertwined with labor's republican ideals. The Chinese, argued George, would drive out free labor, "make nabobs and princes of our capitalists, and crush our working classes into the dust . . . substitut[ing] . . . a population of serfs and their masters for that population of intelligent freemen who are our glory and our strength."

The anti-Chinese agitation climaxed in San Francisco in the late 1870s when mobs ruled the streets, at one point threatening to burn the docks of the Pacific Mail Steamship Company from which the Chinese arrivals disembarked. The principal agitator, an Irish teamster named Denis Kearney, quickly became a dominant figure in the California labor movement. Under the slogan "The Chinese Must Go!" Kearney led a Workingmen's party which strongly challenged the state's major parties. Both of those parties, however, had already jumped on the anti-Chinese bandwagon—the Democrats enthusiastically, eager to recover their popularity after the Civil War, the Republicans more reluctantly, in the face of an issue too potent to resist. Finally, after renegotiating an end to the free-immigration provision of the Burlingame Treaty (1868) with China, Congress in 1882 adopted the Chinese Exclusion Act, which barred the further entry of Chinese laborers into the country.

Chinese immigration effectively came to an end, but not the demand for cheap labor that had drawn the Chinese to America in the first place. If anything, California's need intensified because its agriculture was shifting from wheat, the state's first great cash crop, to fruits and vegetables. These row crops needed lots of workers: stoop labor, meagerly paid, and mostly seasonal. This was not, as one San Francisco journalist put it, "white men's work."

That ugly phrase serves as a touchstone for California agricultural labor as it would thereafter develop—a kind of caste labor system, always drawing downtrodden, foot-loose whites into it, yet basically defined along color lines. But if not the Chinese, then who? First, Japanese immigrants, who came in increasing numbers and by the early twentieth century constituted half the state's agricultural labor force. Then, when rising anti-Japanese agitation closed off that population flow as well in 1908, Mexico became the next, essentially permanent, provider of migratory workers for California's booming commercial agriculture.

The irony of the state's social evolution is painful to behold. Here was California, the last, best hope of the American Dream, a land of limitless opportunity, boastful of its democratic egalitarianism. Yet simultaneously, and from its very birth, it was a racially torn society, at once exploiting and despising the Hispanic and Asian minorities whose hard labor helped make California the enviable land it was.

The Golden West

Had gold not been discovered at Sutter's mill in 1848, California's history would certainly have been very different. At that time it was a remote place, hard to get to, with a semiarid climate uninviting to American farmers. "The country is hilly and mountainous," noted a U.S. Navy officer in 1849. "Great dryness prevails during the summer, and occasionally excessive droughts parch up the soil." California, he concluded, would never be "susceptible of supporting a very large population." In fact, Oregon's Willamette Valley had been for the westward-bound settlers of the 1840s much the preferred place. And, but for gold rush, California's early development would likely have been very like that of the

Willamette Valley—an economic backwater, lacking markets for its products, slow to attract newcomers. In 1870, a decade after it had achieved statehood, Oregon still had scarcely 90,000 residents.

The hundreds of thousands of fortune seekers who descended on California changed everything. Mineral wealth poured in, first from the gold country, then from Nevada's Comstock Lode, and finally from mining sites up and down the Far West. Railroad building accelerated. Agriculture boomed. And so, as they found a market in California, did the timber industry, fisheries, and farms of Oregon and Washington. During the 1880s, both states grew prodigiously. By 1890, Oregon had 318,000 people, while Washington (which became a state in 1889) had a population of 357,000, and was by then finally linked to the east by the Northern Pacific and Great Northern railroads.

California counted over a million residents that year, fully a quarter of whom lived in San Francisco. Life in California offered all that the modern world of 1890 had to offer—a cosmopolitan city, comfortable travel, a high living standard, colleges and universities, even resident painters and writers.

And yet California was still remote from the rest of America, still a long journey away and, of course, differently and spectacularly endowed by nature. Location, environment, and history all conspired to set California somewhat apart from the American nation. And so, in certain ways, did the Californians.

California Culture. What Californians sought, first of all, was a cultural tradition of their own. Closest to hand was the bonanza era of the Forty-Niners. California had the great good fortune of attracting to its parts one Samuel Clemens. Clemens arrived in the Nevada Territory in 1861, did a bit of prospecting, became a reporter in Nevada City, adopted the pen name Mark Twain, and moved in 1864 to San Francisco, where he became a newspaper columnist writing about what he pronounced to be "the livest, heartiest community on our continent."

Exiled briefly in 1865 to Angel's Camp in the Sierra foothills because his sharp pen had made him some dangerous enemies, Twain listened to the tales of the old miners from the neighborhood. One he jotted in his notebook, as follows:

> Coleman with his jumping frog—bet stranger \$50—stranger had no frog, and C. got him one:—in the meantime stranger filled C's frog full of shot and he couldn't jump. The stranger's frog won.

In Twain's hands, this fragment was transformed into a marvelous tall tale that caught the imagination of the country and made his reputation as a humorist. What "The Celebrated Jumping Frog of Calaveras County" had somehow encapsulated was the entire world of make-or-break optimism in the mining camps.

In such short stories as "The Luck of Roaring Camp" and "The Outcasts of Poker Flat," Twain's fellow San Franciscan Bret Harte developed this theme in a more literary fashion and firmly implanted it in California's memory. Other writers—among them amateur historian Charles Howard Shinn in his *Mining Camps: A Study in American Frontier Government* (1885)—gave a more serious gloss to California's bonanza origins. Even so, this past was too raw, too suggestive of the tattered beginnings of so many of the state's leading citizens—in short, too disreputable—for an up-and-coming society.

Then, in 1884, Helen Hunt Jackson published her novel *Ramona.* In this story of a half-caste girl caught between two cultures, Jackson intended to advance the cause of the Indians, but she placed her tale in the evocative context of Old California, and that rang an immediate bell. By then, the Spanish missions—disestablished by the Mexican government back in 1833, long before the arrival of the Yankees—had fallen into total disrepair and the padres were wholly forgotten, their Indian acolytes scattered and in dire poverty. Now that lost world of "sun, silence and adobe" became all the rage. Sentimental novels and histories appeared in abundance. There was a movement to restore the missions (though not with aid to the Indians in mind). The Spanish-Mexican dons of the great ranchos became larger in death than they had ever been in life. Many communities began to stage Spanish fiestas, and the mission style of architecture enjoyed a great vogue among developers. In its Spanish past California found the cultural traditions it needed. Very much the same kind of discovery was taking place elsewhere in the Southwest, although, in the case of Santa Fe and Taos, with considerably more authenticity.

Land of Sunshine. All this enthusiasm was of course strongly tinged with commercialism. And this was even more true of a second distinctive feature of California's development. The southern part of the state was neglected, thinly populated and too dry for anything more than grazing and some chancy wheat growing. What it did have, however, was an abundance of sunshine. At the beginning of the 1880s there burst upon the country amazing publicity about the charms of southern California. "There is not any malaria, hay fever, loss of appetite, or languor in the air; nor any thunder, lightning, mad dogs . . . or cold snaps." This was mostly the work of the Southern Pacific Railroad, which had reached Los Angeles in 1876 and was anxious for business.

When the Santa Fe arrived in 1885, a furious rate war broke out, and it became possible to travel all the way from Chicago or St. Louis to Los Angeles for $25 or less. Thousands of people, mostly midwesterners, poured in; a dizzying real estate boom developed, along with the frantic building of such resort hotels as San Diego's opulent Hotel del Coronado. Los Angeles County had less than 3 percent of the state's population in 1870; it had 12 percent by 1900. Although the real estate bubble collapsed at the end of the 1880s, by then southern California had firmly established itself as the land of sunshine and orange groves. It had found a way to translate climate into riches.

The Great Outdoors. That California was specially favored by nature some Californians knew even as its great stands of redwoods and sugar pine were being hacked down, the soil depleted by the relentless cycle of wheat crops, the streams polluted, and the hills torn apart by reckless mining techniques. Back in 1864 influential Americans who had seen it prevailed on Congress to grant to the state of California "the Cleft, or Gorge in the granite peak of the Sierra Nevada Mountain, known as Yosemite Valley," which would thereafter be reserved "for public pleasuring, resort, and recreation." When the young naturalist John Muir arrived in California four years later, he made straight for Yosemite. Its "grandeur . . . comes as an endless revelation," he wrote. Muir, and others like him, became devoted to studying the High Sierras, and protecting them from "despoiling gain-seekers . . . eagerly trying to make everything immediately and selfishly commercial." One result was the creation of California's national parks in 1890—Yosemite, Sequoia, King's Canyon. Another was the formation in 1892 of the Sierra Club, which became a powerful voice for the defenders of California's wilderness.

They won some and lost some. In particular, there was an uphill battle against the advocates of water-resource development, who insisted that California's irrigated agriculture and thirsty cities could not grow without tapping the abundant snowpack of the Sierras. By the turn of the century, Los Angeles faced a water crisis that threatened its further growth. The answer was a 238-mile aqueduct to the Owens River in the southern Sierra. A bitter controversy blew up over this immense project, driven by objections by local residents and preservationists to the damming up of the beautiful Owens Valley. More painful yet was the defeat suffered by John Muir and his allies in their battle to save the Hetch-Hetchy gorge north of the Yosemite National Park. In 1913, after years of controversy, the federal government approved the damming of Hetch Hetchy to serve the water needs of San Francisco.

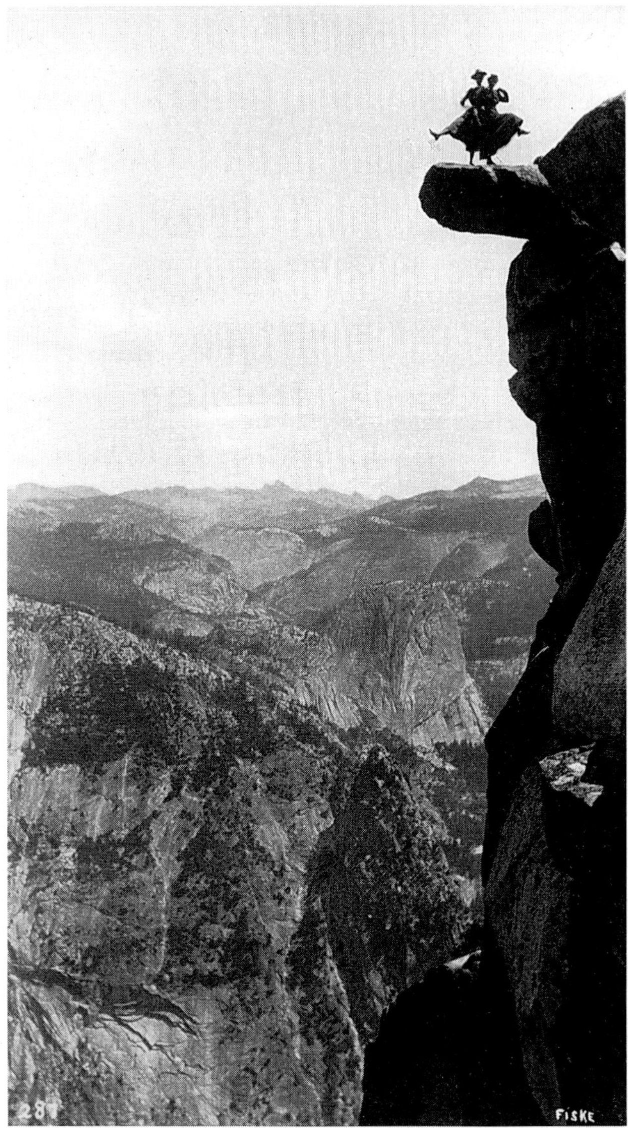

Kitty Tatch and Friend on Glacier Point, Yosemite

From the time the Yosemite Valley was first set aside in 1864 as a place for "public pleasuring, resort, and recreation," it attracted a stream of tourists eager to experience the grandeur of the American West. As is suggested by this photograph taken sometime in the 1890s, the magic of Yosemite was enough to set even staid young ladies a-dancing.

When the development stakes became high enough, nature lovers like John Muir generally came out on the short end. Even so, something original and distinctive had been added to California's heritage—the linking of a society's well-being with the preservation of its natural environment.

The Agricultural Interest

In certain grain-growing areas, as in California's Central Valley until the 1890s, farmers might be large-scale, even corporate, operators. In the South after Reconstruction, the typical farmer was a tenant or sharecropper. Elsewhere, and most generally, farmers were independent freeholders, operating their own family farms. The freeholder tradition was deeply rooted in the Jeffersonian ideal of a nation of virtuous yeomen farmers and was enshrined in the policy of free land for the settler. Generation after generation of farmers had joined the westward movement aspiring to this freeholder ideal. In the face of the treeless Great Plains, however, they had hesitated, permitting miners and ranchers to precede them. Then, in the 1870s, they overcame the mental barrier created by the notion of a Great American Desert.

The Farmers' Last Frontier

As the midwestern states filled up, farmers began to look hungrily farther west. Farmers in Europe, especially in Scandinavia, also were eager to find a place in America. Land speculators, steamship lines, and the western states and territories all encouraged settlement of the Great Plains. Railroads, anxious to sell their huge land holdings and develop traffic for their routes, became especially active sponsors of settlement programs.

Federal land policy also offered a strong attraction. Under the Homestead Act of 1862, settlers could obtain 160 acres of public land free, except for a filing fee, if they lived on it for five years. Aliens who had taken out their first naturalization papers were also eligible. Although married women could not file claims, widows and single women had the same rights as men. In fact, according to the land-office records for Colorado and Wyoming, 12 percent of the homestead filers were women. Beginning in 1873, with the passage of the Timber Culture Act, settlers could claim an additional 160 acres if they planted trees on at least a fourth of the land.

None of these forces, however, could have pushed the agricultural frontier far out on to the plains without the intervention of a highly inventive society. The notion of a Great American Desert, illusion though it was, did point to a plain truth: the grasslands could not be worked by the methods known to American farmers at the time.

Consider the absence of trees. Determined pioneers could manage the problem of shelter by cutting dugouts in the sides of hills. Then they built sod houses, using strips of turf cut from the ground. These crude homes served—often for years—until the settler had earned enough money to buy lumber for a proper house and barn. But what about fencing to protect the crops? A furious patent race developed to meet this crucial need. In 1874 Joseph F. Glidden, an Illinois farmer, invented barbed wire, which provided a cheap, effective barrier against roaming cattle.

The dry climate presented a tougher problem. The eastern, high-grass prairie received enough rain for grain crops. But west of the ninety-eighth meridian the annual rainfall averaged less than 20 inches. The Mormons living in the area near the Great Salt Lake had demonstrated how irrigation could turn a wasteland into a garden. But the Great Plains lacked the surface water needed for irrigation. The answer lay in dry-farming methods, which involved deep planting to bring subsoil moisture to the roots and quick harrowing after rainfalls to turn over a dry mulch that slowed evaporation.

Dry farming produced a low yield per acre. To be profitable, a semiarid farm had to operate on a scale much larger than an eastern farm. Therefore it had to rely much more on machinery. Western mechanized farming developed most fully on the corporate farms that covered up to 100,000 acres in the Red River Valley in the Dakota Territory. But even family farms, which remained the norm elsewhere, could not operate with less than 300 acres of cereal crops and so required machinery for plowing, planting, and harvesting. Such basic inventions as the McCormick reaper had

Homesteading on the Great Plains
This was what their homestead looked like when Peter Widvey, a Swedish Lutheran minister, and his family were starting out in 1891. At the upper lefthand corner is the dugout in which they lived before their house was built and a farm carved out of this bleak landscape north of Round Valley, Custer County, Nebraska.

AMERICAN VOICES

Swedish Emigrant in Frontier Kansas *Ida Lindgren*

Like many emigrants, Ida Lindgren did not find it easy to adjust to the harsh new life on the frontier. Her diary entries and letters home show that the adjustment for the first generation was never complete.

15 May 1870 [Lake Sibley, Nebraska]

What shall I say? Why has the lord brought us here? Oh, I feel so oppressed, so unhappy! Two whole days it took us to get here and they were not the least trying part of our travels. We sat on boards in the work-wagon packed in so tightly that we could not move a foot, and we drove across endless, endless prairies, on narrow roads; no, no, not roads, tracks like those in the fields at home when they harvested grain. No forest but only a few trees which grow along the rivers and creeks. And then here and there you see a homestead and pass a little settlement. The Indians are not so far away from here, I can understand, and all the men you see coming by, riding or driving wagons, are armed with revolvers and long carbines, and look like highway robbers.

No date [probably written July 1870]

Claus and his wife lost their youngest child at Lake Sibley and it was very sad in many ways. There was no real cemetery but out on the prairie stood a large, solitary tree, and around it they bury their dead, without tolling of bells, without a pastor, and sometimes without any coffin. A coffin was made here for their child, it was not painted black, but we lined it with flowers and one of the men read the funeral service, and then there was a hymn, and that was all.

August 25, 1874 [Manhattan, Kansas]

It has been a long time since I have written, hasn't it? . . . when one never has anything fun to write about, it is no fun to write . . . We have not had rain since the beginning of June, and then with this heat and often strong winds as well, you can imagine how everything has dried out. There has also been a general lamentation and fear for the coming year. We are glad we have the oats (for many don't have any and must feed wheat to the stock) and had hoped to have the corn leaves to add to the fodder. But then one fine day there came millions, trillions of grasshoppers in great clouds, hiding the sun, and coming down into the fields, eating up *everything* that was still there, the leaves on the trees, peaches, grapes, cucumbers, onions, cabbage, everything, everything. Only the peach stones still hung on the trees, showing what had once been there.

July 1, 1877 [Manhattan, Kansas]

. . . It seems so strange to me when I think that more than seven years have passed since I have seen you all . . . . I can see so clearly that last glimpse I had of Mamma, standing alone amid all the tracks of Eslov station. Oliva I last saw sitting on her sofa in her red and black dress, holding little Brita, one month old, on her lap. And Wilhelm I last saw in Lund at the station, as he rolled away with the train, waving his last farewell to me . . . .

Source: H. Arnold Barton, ed. *Letters from the Promised Land.* Minneapolis: University of Minnesota Press, 1975, 143–145, 150–156.

appeared before the Civil War; but only later did the farm-equipment industry pick up speed in response to the demand of western farmers.

Despite barbed wire, dry-farming methods, and harvesting machines, the push into the semiarid lands required a great deal of wish fulfillment. The Great Plains happened to experience a wet cycle between 1878 and 1886. "As the plains are settled up we hear less and less of drouth, hot winds, alkali and other bugbears that used to hold back the adventurous," remarked one Nebraska man. Some settlers attributed the increased rainfall to soil cultivation and tree planting, which somehow generated air moisture and caused more rain. Others credited God. As one settler on the southern plains remarked, "The Lord just knowed we needed more land an' He's gone and changed the climate." But no matter how they explained it—and no matter how much scientists warned otherwise—settlers moved westward convinced that the increased rainfall was permanent.

No amount of optimism, however, could take away the hardships of that migration, which seemed to fall disproportionately on the women. "That last separating word *Farewell!* sinks deeply into the heart," one pioneer woman recorded in her diary, thinking of family and friends left behind. Emigrants had always taken parting as a kind of death, with reunion unlikely "on this side of the dark river." But then came the treeless land, more alien and frightening than anything previously encountered in the westward settlement. "Endless, endless prairies," wrote the Swedish woman Ida Lindgren from her covered wagon in Kansas; or, from a

Nebraska-bound woman,"such an air of desolation"; and, from the Texas plains, "such a lonely country." There was a liberating side to frontier life as well, of course—the breakdown of gender roles as women shouldered men's work on new farms; for many, a heightened sense of self-reliance in the face of danger and hardship; and, as new communities sprang up, opportunities to teach school, run boardinghouses, participate in church and town affairs. Yet, one can surmise from Ida Lindgren's letters how hard life was for settlers, with the unrelenting round of toil, the harsh climate and primitive sod-house living, the crushed hopes when the rains failed or the grasshoppers swept in, and, of course, the loneliness.

Nothing, at any rate, seemed in the least to discourage the final frontier thrust across the continental United States. More land came under cultivation between 1870 and 1900 than in the previous 250 years. More than a million people went west from the settled Midwest during the 1880s. "Hardly anything else was talked about," recalled the short-story writer Hamlin Garland about his Iowa neighbors. "Every man who could sell out had gone west or was going. . . . Farmer after farmer joined the march to Kansas, Nebraska, and Dakota. . . . The movement . . . had . . . become an exodus, a stampede."

The Exodusters. For some southern blacks, Kansas briefly represented something even more precious—the modern land of Canaan. Blacks from Kentucky and Tennessee had been migrating to Kansas all through the 1870s. Then in the spring of 1879, with Reconstruction over and federal protection withdrawn, religious enthusiasm for Kansas swept through the terror-stricken black communities of Louisiana and Mississippi. Within a month or so, some 6,000 blacks arrived via St. Louis, most of them with nothing more than the clothes on their backs and faith in the Good Lord. How many of these Exodusters remained it is hard to say, but the 1880 Census reported 40,000 blacks in Kansas, by far the largest African-American concentration in the Great West aside from Texas, whose expanding cotton frontier attracted hundreds of thousands of black migrants during the 1870s and 1880s.

On the northern plains European immigration contributed a mighty share. At the peak of the "American fever" in 1882, over 105,000 Scandinavians emigrated to the United States. Swedish and Norwegian became the primary languages of entire areas of Minnesota and Dakota.

By 1880, Kansas was home to 850,000 people. Dakota, which had been very thinly settled when it became a territory in 1861, had 20,000 inhabitants in 1873. Its population jumped to 135,000 in 1880 and all the way to 550,000 in 1885. The dry years that followed reduced the population of North and South

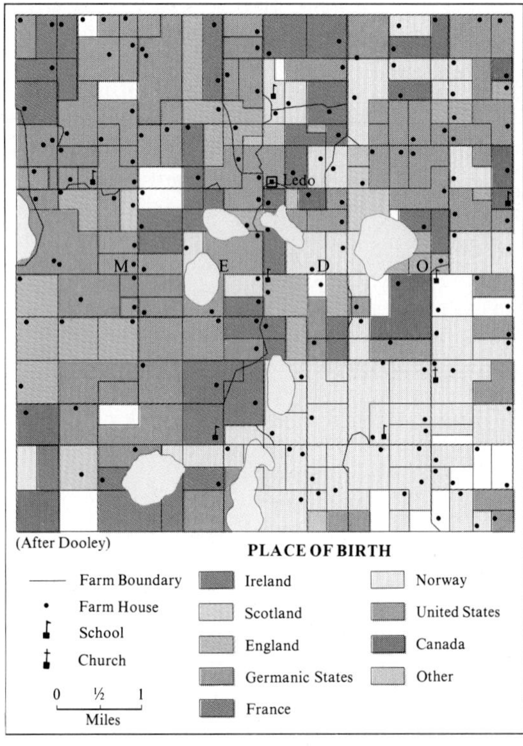

MAP 17.6

The Rural Ethnic Mosaic: Blue Earth County, Minnesota, 1880

What could have been more natural for emigrants like Ida Lindgren, in light of the isolation and hardship she describes (see document on page 537) than to settle next to others sharing common ties to a homeland? This map of Medo township reveals that in rural America, no less than in the cities, ethnicity determined where people lived.

Exodusters

Driven by terror raids from their homes, these southern blacks camped out on a Mississippi levee on the way to Kansas.

Dakota (they had become states in 1889) to 500,000 by 1890, and a comparable departure of drought-stricken farmers occurred up and down the Great Plains. But that vast region, where buffalo herds had thrived a few decades earlier, had been conquered. By 1900 about half the nation's cattle and sheep, a third of its cereal crops, and nearly three-fifths of its wheat came from the newly settled lands.

The Farming Business

With the settlement of the Great Plains, the regional patterns of American agriculture became well defined. The wheat belt lay on the western edge of the Midwest, from North Dakota down to Kansas and into northern Texas. Wheat had long been a virgin crop, the first to be planted when new land opened up. As the frontier moved on, wheat growing moved steadily westward. Wheat farming settled on the Great Plains, partly because of the suitability of the land and partly because of the arrival of hardy Russian varieties. Russian wheat prospered in the harsh plains climate and produced a bread flour superior to that from the soft wheat of milder regions. From Iowa eastward ran the corn belt, which devoted most of its product to feeding livestock. North of the corn belt, the dairy belt stretched from Minnesota as far east as New York and New England. It produced the nation's milk, butter, and cheese. In California, wheat raising gave way to orange groves and a wide variety of fruits and vegetables. In the South, cotton dominated, spreading steadily westward during the last third of the nineteenth century, from the old Cotton Kingdom into Texas to the semiarid line and northward up into Oklahoma and Arkansas.

American farmers stood at the center of a vast and

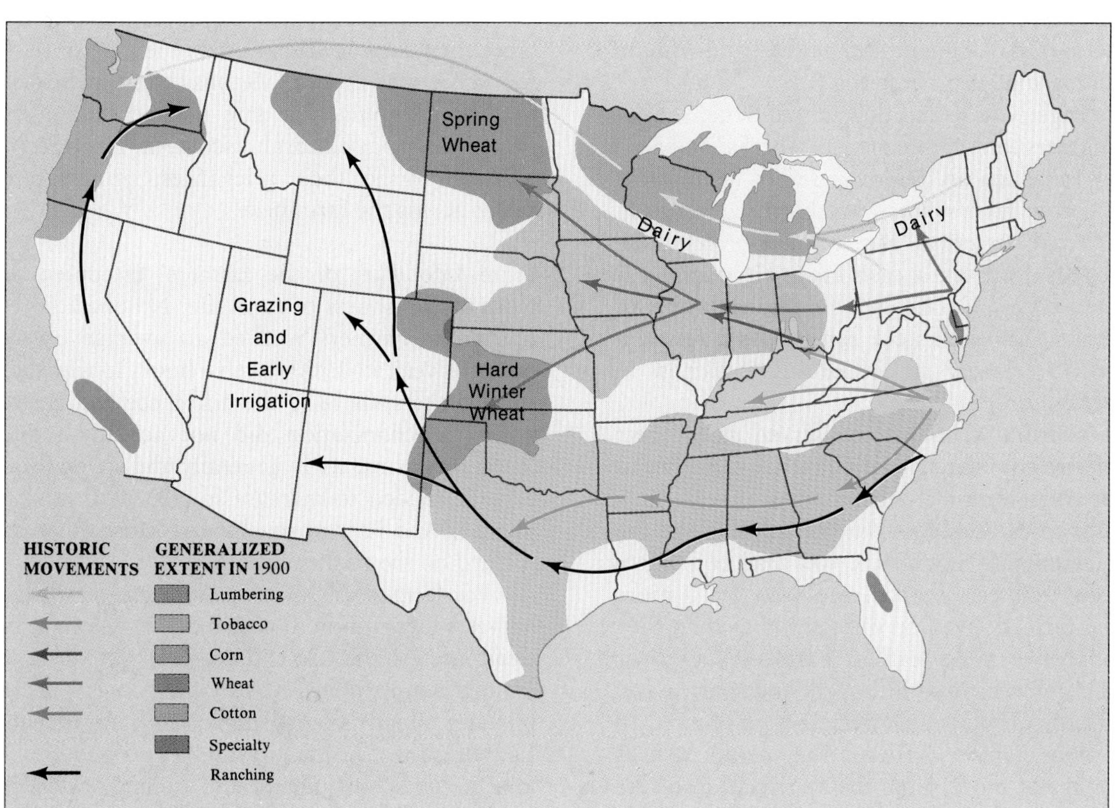

MAP 17.7

Agricultural Regions, 1900

The development of agricultural regions reflected the commercial bent of American agriculture—that is, farmers raised crops for market rather than for home consumption. Regional specialization matched climate and soil to the most suitable crops. The westward movement carried crops westward, of course. Wheat, generally a first crop choice in frontier areas, concentrated finally on the northern and central Plains and in the Northwest. By 1900, the basic pattern of crop specialization was well established in the United States.

complex system of trade. They depended on the railroads to carry their crops to market. A highly sophisticated network of commodity exchanges determined prices and found buyers throughout the country and beyond. Great processing industries turned wheat into flour, livestock into dressed meat, and fruit and vegetables into canned goods. Only through this modern commercial system could farmers gain access to the expanding urban markets in the United States and overseas. About 20 percent of American agricultural production went abroad during the late nineteenth century.

American farmers were likewise well supplied with modern goods and services. They met their credit needs through mortgage companies that drew on eastern and European capital. The McCormick Reaper Company, John Deere and Company, and other manufacturers sold them labor-saving farm machinery. Other industries supplied an increasing share of household and farming needs. "The old rule that a farmer should produce all he required is part of the past," noted a farm journal. "Agriculture, like all other business, is better for its subdivisions, each one growing that which is best suited for his soil, skill, climate and market, and with its proceeds purchasing his other needs."

Farmers eagerly followed this advice. True, subsistence farming persisted in infertile, hilly areas; and general farming, in which no crop represented as much as 40 percent of a farm's total production, went on throughout rural America. But farmers everywhere tended to concentrate on a cash crop, although—excepting in the cotton South—not to the exclusion of some gardening and small-stock raising. As a result, a high degree of regional specialization developed in American agriculture.

This agricultural specialization served as the best indicator of the commercial path taken by American farmers. But there were many other signs as well, such as the attitude toward land. Americans had little of the passionate identification with the soil that tied European peasants to their inherited plots. In 1910 more than half the farmers lived on different land than they had inhabited five years earlier. Farmers saw their acreage as a commodity—to be bought and sold, and to be valued for the price it could bring on the market. In developing areas, farmers believed they could earn as much profit, if not more, from the appreciation of the land's value as from the crops it produced. This attitude fostered the willingness to operate on borrowed capital. In boom times, farmers rushed into debt to extend their land holdings.

The commercial spirit also made farmers enthusiastic about the innovations of the industrial age. Between 1850 and 1900 farm machinery cut production costs for the leading crops by about half. The railroad, especially the prospect of local rail service, delighted the western pioneers. They happily supported whatever inducements might be necessary, such as the public purchase of railway bonds, to lure the line to their towns. And they developed an agricultural system of amazing abundance; farm output more than tripled between 1860 and 1900. To an Austrian observer, the surplus produced seemed "the greatest event of modern times."

Agrarian Distress

Family farms predominated throughout rural America in the late nineteenth century. The average farm comprised about 150 acres and employed an average of fewer than one hired hand. Farm ownership also was widespread. In 1880 owners occupied 75 percent of Iowa's farms. In an age of trusts and corporations, farmers succeeded as did no other group in retaining the *forms* of economic individualism. But their *functions* took them far from the self-sufficient yeoman farmer of Jeffersonian America. They had been fully inducted into the modern economic order.

Farmers participated eagerly in this market economy; they embraced its entrepreneurial spirit. Yet they found themselves more victims than beneficiaries of the modern economy. The late nineteenth century was a time of deep agricultural discontent. For thirty years, as farmers nursed their grievances, protest movements swept across the farm belt.

Farm Life. Part of the farmers' discontent stemmed from the harshness of rural life. No one labored longer or harder. Farmers worked an average of sixty-eight hours a week in 1900, twelve hours longer than industrial workers; in 1850 the difference had been only six hours. Mechanization did not actually reduce work loads on farms, as it generally did in factories. Crop acreage tended to increase in step with more efficient planting and harvest machinery. Most other chores remained on the farmer's shoulders.

For farm women too the burdens increased. Larger harvests meant more field hands for whom to cook and clean up. At the same time, work in the kitchen remained almost unaffected by the conveniences and appliances already commonplace in many urban homes. Laundry was "the most trying" of all household chores, long hours spent lugging and boiling water, bent over wash tubs and rubbing boards. Even on well-equipped farms, one Michigan woman observed, "the women must still do the work much as their mothers did before." "I have in mind a small, delicate woman," wrote another from Pennsylvania, "with a family of small children who does all her own housework, milks four or five cows, cooks for extra help, carries from the spring all the water—no time to read a paper or book. . . . Yet neither [her husband] nor she has any idea they could make her burden easier."

Laundry Day
Of all women's work on the farm, doing the wash was "the most trying . . . ."

On northern farms, women normally did not work in the fields after the pioneering days, although substantial numbers of widows and single women ran farms on their own—300,000 were recorded in the 1900 census. In the South, especially among tenant farmers, both black and white, wives did commonly go into the fields, making "a full hand at whatever the occasion demands—plowing, hoeing, chopping, putting down fertilizer, picking cotton."

Throughout rural America children, as soon as they were old enough, pitched in with the farm chores and field work. "Many a time a shudder has passed through the mother heart of me," said a Missouri woman, "at the sight of some little fellow struggling with the handles of a plow, jerking and stumbling over cloddy ground from daylight till dark. Boys 'making a full hand,' 'helping Pa.'" Farm children in 1900 attended school only two-thirds as many days as did city children, and they left school at an earlier age. In an era of rapidly advancing urban education, farm children still attended gloomy, ungraded one-room schools—hardly the little red schoolhouses of popular mythology.

Farm families may have accepted how hard they labored, how the men and women were worn out and the children sacrificed, for the living they wrested from the soil. It was harder to swallow the widening discrepancy in the quality of life between farm and city. Electricity, indoor plumbing, and paved roads had not yet come to the farm. The rural diet consisted of salt pork, bread, and potatoes for much of the year. Farm sanitation remained primitive. On two-thirds of all farms, according to a survey in 1918 by the U.S. Public Health Service, the water supply was threatened by "potentially dangerous contamination from privy contents."

Hardest to bear was the sense of isolation. On the Great Plains, with its cruel winters and the long, empty distances, loneliness was hard on everyone, but especially on the Scandinavian immigrants.

> Life in the fatherland was hard and toilsome [wrote one critic of dispersed American farming practices], but it was not lonesome. Think for a moment how great the change must be from the white-walled, red-roofed village on a Norway fiord . . . to an isolated cabin on a Dakota prairie, and say if it is any wonder that so many Scandinavians lose their mental balance.

Farm life everywhere, however, tended to be isolated and circumscribed. Rural neighborhoods, even in long-settled areas, totaled 3 or 4 square miles where perhaps a dozen families lived. As one writer remarked, "the end of the neighborhood was almost the end of the world." Hamlin Garland and other authors of the late nineteenth century wrote powerfully about the dullness of the countryside and the lure of the city. "I hate farm life," grumbled one of Garland's heroines. "It's nothing but fret, fret and work the whole time, never going any place, never seeing anybody but a lot of neighbors just as big fools as you are. I spend my time fighting flies and washing dishes and churning. I'm sick of it all."

Understandably, when farmers formed organizations they provided for social activity first of all. This was true of the National Grange of the Patrons of Husbandry, whose local granges spread by the thousands across rural America in the early 1870s. The Grange became the social center for farm families through its fraternal ceremonies and its dances, picnics, and lectures. Women and men joined on an equal footing. Oliver H. Kelley, the government clerk who founded the Grange in 1867, hoped that participation by "the young folks of both sexes . . . will have a tendency to instill in their

Granger Poster

This poster conveys all the longing for community and uplift that drove farmers to organize themselves in the late nineteenth century. It speaks as well of the underlying basis for the outrage they felt as victims of an exploitative economic order: that, as the farmer who produces the society's material wealth, "I pay for it all."

minds a fondness of rural life, and prevent in great measure so many of them flocking to the cities."

Economic Problems. The hunger for social activity cemented organizational ties, but the dynamism of agrarian movements came from economic grievances. The farmers' basic problem was their imperfect participation in the economic transformation of the late nineteenth century. They remained individual operators in a business world that was becoming ever more complex and highly organized. And they were, in certain ways, acutely aware of their predicament.

Farmers understood, for example, the disadvantages they faced as individuals dealing with the big businesses that supplied them with machinery, arranged their credit, and marketed their products. Cooperative activity, especially through stores and creameries, had started before the Civil War. The Grange took up the cooperative idea in a big way by organizing bulk purchasing from manufacturers, along with scattered cooperative banks, insurance companies, grain elevators, and processing plants. In Iowa, the state Grange started to manufacture farm implements in 1873.

Unfortunately, the cooperative record listed many more failures than successes. The opposition by private business was too unrelenting, cooperative managers too unskilled, and the pooled resources of the farmers too thin. Residual benefits did remain, among them an efficient mail-order business that emerged from farmers' hostility to middlemen. In 1872, Montgomery Ward and Company was founded specifically to "meet the wants" of Grange members for everything from clothes to toys and household goods by direct mail order. The early marketing cooperatives also led to more permanent institutions, especially for dairy farmers and fruit growers. Cooperative stores, grain elevators, and telephone exchanges became familiar parts of the countryside throughout rural America. As a solution to the organizational weakness of the late-nineteenth-century farmer in the marketplace, however, cooperative movements had to be accounted a failure.

Another solution was for farmers to enlist the power of government against economic monopoly. Western farmers, generally served by only one grain elevator or railroad, felt continually cheated on storage charges and wheat grading. They also complained about having to pay freight rates higher than those farther east. The Grange was itself strictly a social-educational organization, but it encouraged the formation of independent political parties during the early 1870s that ran on antimonopoly platforms. In a number of states, these parties won control of the legislatures and passed so-called Granger laws regulating grain elevators, fixing maximum railroad rates, and prohibiting discriminatory practices against small and short-haul shippers. In *Munn v. Illinois* (1877), the Supreme Court upheld these laws on the ground that such enterprises involved the public interest and were subject to the police powers of the states. But ten years later a more conservative Supreme Court drastically reduced the scope of state regulatory powers by invoking the interstate commerce clause of the U.S. Constitution. The Court declared that states exceeded their powers when they tried to regulate economic activity that was interstate in character. On that basis, *Wabash v. Illinois* (1886) voided an Illinois law prohibiting long- and short-haul rate discrimination. By then, however, a movement had started for federal regulation of the railroads. The Interstate Commerce Act (1887) created the Interstate Commerce Commission—the first federal regulatory agency—and made railroad regulation a permanent part of national public policy, although, for the next twenty years, not with very much practical effect.

Relief, at least in the short run, came mainly as the

TABLE 17.1

Freight Rates for Transporting Crops

Grand Island to Omaha (150 miles)				Grand Island to Chicago (650 miles)			
Date effective	Corn (In cents per hundredweight)	Wheat	Oats	Date effective	Corn (In cents per hundredweight)	Wheat	Oats
January 1, 1883	18	19½	18	January 7, 1880	32	45	32
April 16, 1883	15	16½	15	September 15, 1882	38	43	38
January 10, 1884	18	19½	18	April 5, 1887	34	39	34
March 1, 1884	17	19½	17	November 1, 1887	25	30	25
August 25, 1884	20	20	20	March 21, 1890	22½	30	25
April 5, 1887	10	16	10	October 22, 1890	22	26	22
November 1, 1887	10	12	10	January 15, 1891	23	28	25

Source: Sigmund Diamond, ed., *The Nation Transformed* (New York: George Braziller, 1963), 352. Reprinted by permission of George Braziller, Inc.

result of further economic development. After the 1870s, as improved technology reduced operating costs and the volume of western traffic increased, rail freight rates fell steadily and East-West differentials narrowed (see Chapter 18).

Farmers turned to cooperatives and government regulation out of a deep sense of organizational disadvantage. But this disadvantage, real as it was, did not really account for the unprofitability of farming in these years. Manufacturers and banks lacked the degree of market control ascribed to them by angry farmers. The much-maligned mortgage companies actually could not rig credit markets in the western states. Their interest rates matched those in the rest of the country. Nor, for the period from 1865 to 1890, could manufacturers establish a relative price advantage over agriculture. In fact, the wholesale price of all commodities fell at a slightly faster rate than did farm prices during those years.

The Wheat and Cotton Belts. The impact of this general fall in prices, or *deflation,* did have dire consequences for certain kinds of farmers, however. First, there were those whose crops were subject to wider, more unpredictable price swings. Of these crops two—both world-traded commodities—were especially prominent: cotton and wheat. The second category of farmers at risk in deflationary periods were those in debt, since falling prices meant they had to pay back more in real terms than they had borrowed. And who was most deeply in debt? The same two groups: cotton and wheat farmers.

The nature of their indebtedness was of course different. For the tenant farmers growing cotton, the debt was short-term, lasting only for a single season, but nevertheless painfully hard if they had to repay debt on earnings reduced by falling cotton prices. For the wheat farmer, indebtedness was a more deep-seated and entangling problem. This was because, in the nineteenth century, wheat was characteristically a virgin-land crop. Settling new land meant going into debt to start up—to pay for machinery, fencing, a new house, and so on. So wheat farmers were frequently debtors and hence under constant pressure when price levels dropped. And if, as commonly happened in frontier areas, a speculative spirit took hold and land prices were bid up, the debt levels of newly mortgaged farmers could become insupportable.

This happened for example in Harrison Township, Nebraska, which was first settled in 1872. Land that sold for $8 an acre in 1880 brought $25 and up a few years later. Given the price for wheat in the late 1880s, an investigator noted, no one taking out a mortgage to buy land at $25 an acre could hope to meet the payments, at 6 percent interest. "One is almost tempted to draw the moral that the would-be purchaser . . . had almost better throw his money away than invest it in farming operations in Nebraska."

In the 1870s the major wheat-growing states had been Illinois, Wisconsin, and Minnesota. These states had been at the center of the Granger agitation of that decade. By the 1880s wheat had moved on to the Great Plains. Among the indebted wheat farmers of Kansas, Nebraska, and the Dakotas, along with the tenant farmers of the cotton-growing South, the deflationary economy of the 1880s made for stubbornly hard times. All it would take was a sharp drop in world prices for wheat and cotton to bring on a real crisis.

Summary

In 1860 the Great Plains was still ancestral home to nomadic Indian tribes who had built a vibrant society based on the horse and the buffalo. By 1890 the Indians had been crowded onto reservations and forced to submit to the white man's notion that they should abandon their tribal way of life. The surge across the Great Plains and the Rockies, the final phase of America's westward movement, was strongly driven by the nation's economic development. Industry needed the West's mineral resources; the cities demanded agricultural products; and the railroad, barbed wire, and other symbols of an industrial age made the conquest of the West relatively easy. Doomed by the swift penetration of their lands, the western Indians were ultimately victims of events that occurred far off in the nation's industries and cities.

Anchor both to a crescent of Hispanic-Mexican settlement stretching into the Southwest and to the Pacific slope region reaching up into the Northwest, California never experienced in its American settlement the frontier process that characterized the rest of the country. The discovery of gold set off a huge migration that overwhelmed the thinly spread Hispanic inhabitants and swiftly transformed California into a populous state with a large urban sector. California developed a distinctive culture that capitalized on its rediscovered Hispanic heritage and on its climate and natural environment. The treatment of the Chinese, Japanese, and Mexicans who provided the state's cheap labor, however, infused a dark streak of racism into its society.

The settlement of the Great West completed the agricultural development characterized by regional crop specialization. American farming became integrated into the modern industrial order. However, that integration was imperfect—in particular because farming remained a family operation in an economy increasingly dominated by large-scale enterprise. Most aggrieved were the cotton farmers of the South and wheat farmers of the Great Plains.

TOPIC FOR RESEARCH

Women on the Frontier

Until recently historians paid little attention to the experience of women in the westward movement. When they did, they relied on a few well-worn stereotypes of the frontier woman as Victim, dragged down by a harsh and lonesome frontier life, or as Heroic Civilizer, uplifting by her example a raw frontier society. A number of recent books provide a more realistic and complex portrait of women on the frontier: Julie Roy Jeffrey, *Frontier Women: The Trans-Mississippi West, 1840–1880* (1979); Sandra L. Myres, *Westering Women and the Frontier Experience, 1800–1915* (1982); Glenda Riley, *Women and Indians on the Frontier, 1825–1915* (1984) and *The Female Frontier: A Comparative View of the Prairie and the Plains* (1988). Sarah Deutsch, *No Separate Refuge: Culture, Class, and Gender on an Anglo-Hispanic Frontier in the American Southwest, 1880–1940* (1987) focuses on Hispanic women. Another kind of frontierswoman—prostitutes—are discussed in Marion S. Goldman, *Gold Diggers and Silver Miners; Prostitution and Social Life on the Comstock Lode* (1981).

Choose one of these books to help you answer some of the questions posed by Sandra L. Myres:

> What preconceptions did women have about the frontier? How did they view the physical wilderness? What preconceptions did they have about Indians, Mexican-Americans, and other groups they would encounter in the West? How, if at all, were these ideas changed by life on the frontier? . . . Did women's ideas about their role in the family and the community change as a result of the westering experience? Did women take on new roles in the West . . . ? In what ways did women's reactions and adaptations to the frontier differ from those of men?

Since the books cited above seek to answer these questions through the voices of women themselves, they rely heavily on diaries and other contemporary writings, some of which have been published and may be available in college libraries. For a more ambitious paper, consult one or more of these primary sources in addition to a secondary work. The place to begin is with the notes and bibliographies of the books cited above.

BIBLIOGRAPHY

The Great West

A recent treatment of the West for this period is Rodman Paul, *The Far West and the Great Plains in Transition, 1859–1900* (1988). The liveliest general introduction is Robert V. Hine,

The American West (2nd ed., 1984). An important revisionist history, which emphasizes the hardships and costs of westward expansion, is Patricia N. Limerick, *The Legacy of Conquest: The Unbroken Past of the American West* (1987). The seminal 1893 statement on the significance of the frontier is in Frederick Jackson Turner, *The Frontier in American History* (1950). Another highly influential work is Walter P. Webb, *The Great Plains* (1931), which stresses the settlers' adaptation to the western climate and environment. The best book on western mining is Rodman Paul, *Mining Frontiers of the Far West: 1848–1880s* (1963). On railroad development, see Oscar O. Winther, *The Transportation Frontier: The Trans-Mississippi West, 1865–1890* (1964), and on the cattlemen, Lewis Atherton, *The Cattle Kings* (1961), and Robert R. Dykstra, *Cattle Towns* (1968). Cowboys receive full treatment in Joe B. Frantz and Julian Choate, *American Cowboy: Myth and Reality* (1955).

A useful introduction to native American history is William T. Hagan, *American Indians* (1961). More specific to the coverage of this chapter is Robert M. Utley, *The Indian Frontier of the American West, 1846–1890* (1984). Two valuable collections by deans of the subject are Wilfred E. Washburn, ed., *Indian and White Man* (1964), and Francis Paul Prucha, *Indian Policy in the United States: Historical Essays* (1981). Ralph K. Andrist, *Long Death: Last Days of the Plains Indians* (1964), and Francis Utley, *The Last Days of the Sioux Nation* (1963), eloquently retell that tragic story. On the religious life of the Plains Indians, see Howard L. Harrod, *Renewing the World: Plains Indians Religion and Morality* (1987). The best study of white attitudes is Richard Drinnon, *Facing West: The Metaphysics of Indian-Hating and Empire-Building* (1980).

California and the Far West

The best general history of California is Andrew F. Rolle, *California, A History* (2nd ed., 1969). Two valuable regional histories are Earl Pomeroy, *The Pacific Slope: A History of California, Oregon, Washington, Idaho, Utah, and Nevada* (1965), and Donald W. Meinig, *Southwest: Three Peoples in Geographical Change, 1600–1970* (1971). A very imaginative recent treatment of the New Mexican frontier is Sarah Deutsch, *No Separate Refuge* (1987). An important local study is Mario T. Garcia, *Desert Immigrants: The Mexicans of El Paso, 1880–1920* (1981). Leonard Pitt, *The Decline of the Californios: A Social History of the Spanish-Speaking Californians, 1846–1890* (1960) offers a narrative history of that subject, with an emphasis on the fate of the large ranchers. Two more recent studies focus on the Chicano peasantry: Albert Camarillo, *Chicanos in a Changing Society: From Mexican Pueblos to American Barrios in Santa Barbara and Southern California, 1848–1930* (1979), and Richard Griswold del Castillo, *The Los Angeles Barrio, 1850–1890* (1979). On the Chinese, the standard work is Gunther Barth, *Bitter Strength: A History of the Chinese in the United States, 1850–1870* (1964), which can be supplemented by a thorough recent study: Sucheng Chan, *This Bittersweet Soil: The Chinese in California Agriculture, 1860–1910* (1986). Labor's opposition to the Chinese is skillfully treated in Alexander Saxton, *The Indispensable Enemy: Labor and the Anti-Chinese Movement in California* (1971). On John Muir and the California wilderness, see Michael L. Smith, *Pacific Visions: California Scientists and the Environment, 1850–1915* (1987).

The Agricultural Interest

The standard works are Fred A. Shannon, *The Farmer's Last Frontier, 1860–1897* (1945), and Gilbert C. Fite, *The Farmer's Frontier, 1865–1900* (1966). For the farming pioneers, see Everett Dick, *Sod-House Frontier* (1954). On semiarid farming, see Mary W. M. Hargreaves, *Dry-farming in the Northern Great Plains, 1900–1925* (1957). A more far-ranging study of the impact of insufficient rainfall on the West is Donald Worster, *Rivers of Empire: Water Aridity and the Growth of the American West* (1985). On the black migration to Kansas, see the vivid treatment in Nell Irvin Painter, *Exodusters: Black Migration to Kansas after Reconstruction* (1976). The flavor of farm life can best be captured in fiction: Hamlin Garland, *Main-Travelled Roads* (1891), Willa Cather, *My Antonia* (1918), and O. E. Rölvaag, *Giants in the Earth* (1927). For women and the West, see the citations in the Topic for Research.

TIMELINE

1862	Homestead Act
1865	Long Drive of Texas longhorns begins
1867	Patrons of Husbandry (the Grange) founded
	U.S. government adopts Reservation policy for Plains Indians
1869	Union Pacific–Central Pacific transcontinental railroad completed
1874	Barbed wire invented
1876	Battle of Little Big Horn
1877	San Francisco anti-Chinese riots
	Munn v. Illinois
1879	Exoduster migration to Kansas
1882	Chinese Exclusion Act
1886	Dry cycle begins on the Great Plains
	Wabash v. Illinois
1887	Dawes Severalty Act
	Interstate Commerce Act
1889	Oklahoma opened to white settlement
1890	Indian massacre at Wounded Knee, South Dakota
	U.S. Census declares end of the frontier

Montgomery Ward & Co, Chicago

In 1872 Aaron Montgomery Ward began selling goods to rural customers through mail order catalogs. By the 1890s Montgomery Ward was one of the emerging retail and mail order giants along with Sears, Roebuck and Company.

CHAPTER 18 *Capital and Labor in the Age of Enterprise,* 1877–1900

The year 1877 marked the end of Reconstruction. That year also marked the conclusion of the first great crisis of the emerging system of industrial capitalism. Four years earlier, in 1873, the great banking house Jay Cooke & Co. had failed, triggering a financial panic. In the severe depression that followed, 47,000 firms went under. Wholesale prices fell about 30 percent. Railroad building ground almost to a halt. Orders for industrial goods disappeared. And with unemployment running as high as 25 percent, hundreds of thousands of workers lost their jobs. Suffering was widespread. Across the country workers demanded "bread for the needy, clothing for the naked, and houses for the homeless." Before long, the very foundations of the social order began to shake.

On July 16, 1877, railroad workers in West Virginia went on strike against the Baltimore and Ohio system to protest wage cuts. In railway towns along the B&O tracks, crowds cheered as the strikers attacked company property and prevented trains from running. The strike spread quickly to other lines. In Pittsburgh, the Pennsylvania Railroad roundhouse went up in flames on July 21, followed by the Union Depot the next day. Rioters and looters roamed freely. For nearly a week, riotous strikes swept other cities, including San Francisco, St. Louis, Omaha, and Chicago. President Rutherford B. Hayes called up the National Guard, which gradually restored order. On August 15, the president wrote in his diary: "The strikers have been put down *by force.*" The Great Strike of 1877 had been crushed. But never had the nation edged so close to social revolution.

And then recovery came. Within months the economy was booming again. The march toward industrial power resumed. The physical output of manufactured goods increased over 150 percent between 1877 and 1890. The vitality of industrial capitalism renewed America's confidence in the future. "Can there be any doubt that cheapening the cost of necessaries and conveniences of life is the most powerful agent of civilization and progress?" asked a railroad president in 1888. "History and experience demonstrate that . . . material progress must come first and . . . upon it is founded all other progress."

Industrial Capitalism Triumphant

Economic historians speak of the late nineteenth century as the age of the Great Deflation. Prices fell steadily worldwide, including in the United States. Following a brief upturn after 1877, wholesale prices declined by almost 30 percent between 1880 and 1892. Normally, falling prices are a sign of economic stagnation: there is not enough demand for the goods and services that are available. But that was not America's experience in these years. Because of increasing efficiencies in production and distribution, manufacturers were able both to cut prices *and* to earn profits and invest in better equipment. So that while in England the Great Deflation did indeed signal economic decline, in the United States it was associated with industrial expansion and technological progress.

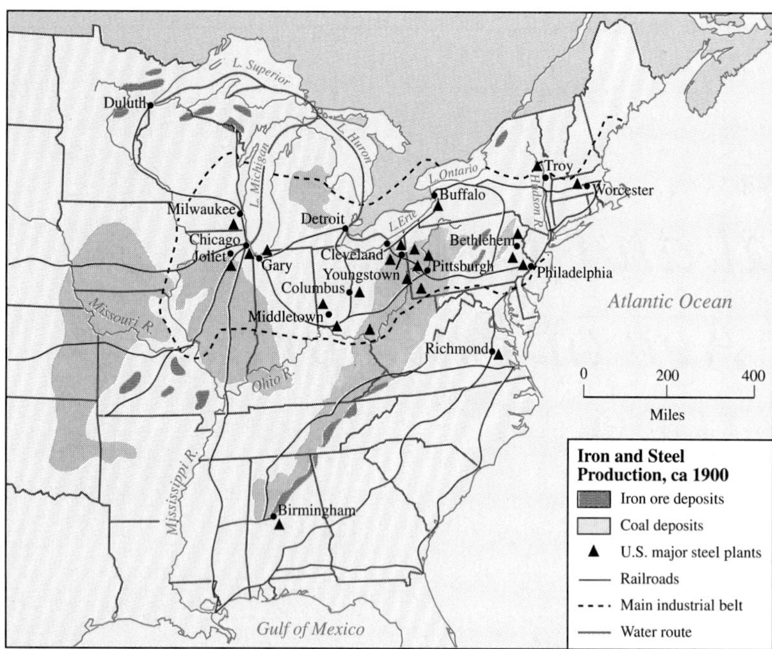

MAP 18.1

The Westward Movement of Iron and Steel Production

Before the Civil War, the iron industry was concentrated in eastern Pennsylvania and northern New Jersey. With the development of steel and the shift westward of population and industry, production moved first to western Pennsylvania, then to Ohio, Indiana, and Illinois, and also southward into Alabama. The specific locations—Pittsburgh, Youngstown, Chicago, Birmingham—were dictated by the rail network, new sources of coal and iron ore, and the markets for metal.

Basic Industry

By the 1870s, manufacturing already had a long history in America. But the early industries were an outgrowth of the larger agricultural economy. They processed farm and forest materials and relied on traditional sources of hand and water power. The goods they produced—textiles, boots and shoes, paper and furniture—were primarily consumer goods that could be substituted for existing home-made or artisan-made products. Gradually, however, a different kind of demand developed. This was the result of the surging economic growth of the country. Railroads needed locomotives, new factories called for machinery, and the expanding cities required vast quantities of building materials for trolley lines, sanitation systems, and commercial buildings. Locomotives, machinery, and construction materials were *capital goods*—that is, goods that themselves added to the productive capacity of the economy. And it was the manufacture of capital goods, as distinct from consumer products, that increasingly characterized America's industrial sector.

Central to this development was iron making. An extensive industry already existed, producing large quantities of wrought iron. This was a soft and malleable metal, ideally suited for use by country blacksmiths and farmers. But wrought iron was expensive—it was produced in small batches by skilled puddlers and rollers—and did not stand up well for heavy use as railway track. In 1856, the English inventor Sir Henry Bessemer perfected a new process for refining iron. Unlike the puddling furnaces that made wrought iron, Bessemer converters produced steel—a harder, more durable metal—and did so in large amounts with little labor. Others took up this invention, but it was Andrew Carnegie who demonstrated its revolutionary importance.

Andrew Carnegie and American Steel. Carnegie had arrived from Scotland in 1848 at the age of twelve with his poverty-stricken family. He became a telegraph operator, then went to work for the Pennsylvania Railroad and rapidly ascended the managerial ladder. Having become wealthy from a series of successful speculations, Carnegie resigned in 1865 to become an iron manufacturer. His main customers were his former associates in the railroad business.

Keenly aware of the possibilities of the Bessemer converter, Carnegie embarked in 1872 on a venture aimed at the fullest exploitation of the new refining process. He built a massive steel-rail mill outside Pittsburgh that utilized the most advanced equipment of the day. Equally important, the mill integrated all the stages of production—smelting, refining, and rolling—into a single operation that began with iron ore and ended with finished steel rails. Carnegie's mill, which he named the Edgar Thompson Works after his admired former boss at the Pennsylvania Railroad, fully repaid its investment in a few years and became a model for the modern steel industry.

Large, integrated steel plants swiftly replaced the older blast furnaces and puddling mills. At first, steel went mostly into railroad building. Steel rails made up nearly three-quarters of the total output in 1885. But thereafter, as railroad building slowed, the demand became more diversified. More and more steel went into bridges, skyscrapers, machinery, and a host of other industrial uses such as piping and tubing, sheet steel and wire, and armor for the nation's new navy.

TABLE 18.1

Increasing Output of Heavy Industry, 1870–1910

	Bituminous Coal (in thousands of tons)	Rolled iron and steel (in thousands of tons)	Copper (tons)	Industrial Machinery (in millions of dollars)
1870	20,471	850*	14,112	110.4†
1880	50,757	3,301	30,240	98.6‡
1890	111,302	6,746	129,882	185.6
1900	212,318	10,626	303,059	347.6
1910	417,111	24,216	544,119	512.4

*Approximate total.
†Data for 1869.
‡Data for 1874.

The Corliss Engine
The symbol of the Philadelphia Centennial in 1876 was the great Corliss engine, which towered over Machinery Hall and powered all the equipment on exhibit there. Yet the Corliss engine also signified the incomplete nature of American industrialism at that time; it soon became obsolete. Westinghouse turbines generating electricity would be the power source for the nation's next great World's Fair in Chicago in 1893.

The production of copper and other nonferrous metals went through a similar development. Before the Civil War, copper had been employed mainly in the manufacture of kettles, pots and pans, and other household products. Now it became a key ingredient in oil refining equipment, electric generators, and other new products such as telephone cable. Copper output grew at a phenomenal rate, increasing from 14,000 tons in 1870 to 130,000 tons in 1890.

The growth of the metal industries depended on the intensive exploitation of the country's mineral resources. Major discoveries of rich iron ore deposits occurred from the 1850s onward, first in upper Michigan and then in the huge Mesabi Range of Minnesota. These ores were readily shipped down the Great Lakes to the growing steel-making centers in Illinois, Ohio, and Pennsylvania.

Coal mining, a minor enterprise before 1850, grew rapidly thereafter, first in the anthracite region of eastern Pennsylvania and then in the soft-coal Appalachian fields of western Pennsylvania and Ohio. Coal production, scarcely half a million tons in 1860, reached 270 million tons in 1900.

It was the insatiable energy needs of American industrialism that spurred this remarkable expansion in coal mining. Carnegie's blast furnaces and Bessemer convertors burned prodigious amounts of coal. Coal-burning steam engines drove locomotives and ships, and increasingly became the power source for factories. Steam was as important as water power for running machinery by 1880, and six times as important twenty years later. At the Philadelphia Centennial Exhibition of 1876, visitors gazed in wonder at the enormous Corliss reciprocating engine, with a flywheel 30 feet in diameter and the capacity to drive all the other exhibits in Machinery Hall. Steam power became increasingly efficient, first through refinements in the reciprocating engine, then, in the 1880s, because of the steam turbine. The turbine was an inherently superior design because it utilized continuous rotation rather than the back-and-forth motion of the reciprocating engine. These advances in turn laid the basis for the next major innovation—the coupling of the steam turbine to the electric generator. After 1900 factories rapidly converted from steam to electric power.

Thus, in the decades following the Civil War, the modern metal-producing industries were established, the nation's mineral resources came under intensive exploitation, and energy was harnessed to the manufacturing system. All these basic elements of modern industrialism—steel, coal, and energy output—grew after 1870 at rates far exceeding that of manufacturing production itself.

NEW TECHNOLOGY *Iron and Steel*

Iron was not a product new to the nineteenth century in the sense that plastic was new to the twentieth century. Early Europeans made iron tools and weapons at least a thousand years before Christ. Nor did the underlying processes change, for they are dictated by the nature of iron metallurgy. Iron ore must be *smelted* into metal; the raw metal must be *refined* to acquire desired properties such as malleability or hardness; and the refined iron must be *shaped* into useable forms. What did begin to change, slowly at first, were the techniques for carrying out these processes. Only as iron became available in large quantities and at low cost could the Industrial Revolution proceed.

Metallurgical innovation took place in two great waves. The first began in smelting late in the Middle Ages, when blast furnaces appeared in Belgium around 1340. Ore was melted in a charcoal-burning furnace to which limestone had been added. A blast of air then set off a combustion process that combined carbon from the charcoal with the molten iron while its impurities combined with the limestone to form a slag. The slag was drawn off from the top of the furnace while the molten iron was tapped from the bottom into sand forms resembling piglets feeding from a sow—hence the term "pig iron."

By the eighteenth century, the shortage of wood for charcoal had become acute in England. The substitution of coke, made by superheating coal, broke this bottleneck in iron production. An improved refining furnace, with separate chambers for the fuel and iron, was also developing. In 1784, Henry Cort invented the puddling furnace. Molten iron collected in the hollowed-out bottom, where it worked with a long bar or paddle by hand from the outside. The resulting product was a malleable iron called *wrought iron.* Cort also made a crucial advance in the finishing stage at this time. For the laborious hammering process, he substituted the rolling mill, which shaped iron as it passed through grooved rolls.

This iron technology—blast furnace, puddling furnace, and rolling mill—formed the metallurgical basis for England's Industrial Revolution in the first half of the nineteenth century. Endowed with ample forests, the United States was slow to adopt the coke-using technology, but by 1860 it had caught up fairly well with England technologically and was producing nearly a million tons of iron annually. The iron industry, as it had developed to this point, met America's needs very well. Wrought iron was admirably suited for farm use because it was malleable and easily worked, and was also suitable for the localized machine- and engine-building characteristic of early industrialism. But wrought iron was too soft for the increasingly heavy service it received as railroad track. The search for a harder, more durable metal resulted in the invention in 1856 of an entirely different refining process by Henry Bessemer, an Englishman.

The Bessemer converter was a pear-shaped vessel open at the top, with a bottom perforated by many holes. Molten pig iron flowed into the top while the converter was tilted on its side. Air was blasted at great force through the perforated bottom, and the converter then swung back to its upright position. The resulting combustion set off a spectacular display of flame and smoke. Within fifteen minutes, the impurities in the molten iron had burned off and the flames died down. The converter was again tilted on its side and, after manganese and other chemicals had been added, the purified iron was emptied into ingot molds.

The refined metal, called steel, was harder than wrought iron and ideally suited for use as railroad track. The Bessemer process had one significant drawback: it operated successfully only with expensive, low-phosphorous iron. The open-hearth method, developed shortly after the Bessemer process, could handle low-quality iron and was more economical and flexible. By World War I, the open-hearth method was rapidly becoming the dominant refining process. But the Bessemer converter had given life to the modern steel industry.

The device that Bessemer had invented to produce a better metal also proved vastly more efficient than the hand-operated puddling furnace. The Bessemer converter turned out great quantities of steel with virtually

The Railroads

A transportation system capable of welding the nation into a vast, unified market had been developing since early in the nineteenth century. Until around 1850, the major advances had been in the improvement of water transportation. But while suitable for bulky raw materials, canal barges and riverboats could not provide the year-round, on-time service demanded by the growing industrial economy. Railroads performed this task far no labor. This forced changes up and down the line. To feed the converters' appetite for pig iron, blast furnaces grew even larger and, with the introduction of the hot blast, much more efficient. To handle the flow of steel from the converters, rolling mills became increasingly mechanized and automatic, so that the steel could move continuously through progressively narrower rolls set in tandem. By means of a variety of metal-handling devices, the stages of production became integrated, enabling the iron to proceed "with perfect regularity" from the blast furnace to the Bessemer converter to its emergence from the rolling mill as a finished rail or girder. The integrated steel plant of 1900, capable of producing 2,500 tons or more a day, was vastly more efficient than the small blast furnaces and iron mills of 1860.

The revolution in steelmaking changed the face of American industrialism. The geographic concentration of industrial activity intensified. The places best located in relation to raw materials, transportation, and markets—Pittsburgh, the steel towns along the Great Lakes, and Birmingham, Alabama—became the great centers of steel production.

A second result involved the scale of business enterprise. The principal steel companies evolved into vertically integrated firms that controlled their own raw materials, some of their transport facilities, and the marketing of their products. For the workers, the effects were no less sweeping. The skills of the puddler, heater, and hand roller became obsolete; gang labor was largely replaced by ore- and metal-handling equipment; and face-to-face relationships with employers disappeared. The typical steelworker of 1900 was a machine-tender in an impersonal, bureaucratic business organization.

Steel made possible dramatic changes in transportation and construction. With steel rails capable of withstanding heavy traffic, and steel locomotives capable of ever greater pulling power, the railroads became the primary carriers of the nation's enormous volume of goods. The efficiency of the railroads rose nearly 70 percent between 1870 and 1900, and freight charges per ton-mile fell by almost the same amount—thanks largely to the use of steel for rails and equipment. In the growth of America's cities, steel played a key role in the construction of skyscrapers, trolley lines, and subways, and the vast underground complexes of pipe that supplied the urban millions with water and gas and carried away their sewage. Steel battleships asserted the nation's new role as a world power. Without steel, the emerging automobile industry would not have grown, nor a host of other American industries. It is no wonder that historians have called the last decades of the nineteenth century America's Age of Steel.

The Bessemer Steel Furnace

better. They had started in the 1830s as feeders linking river and canal traffic to inland towns and cities but quickly grew into a system rivaling water transportation. By the 1860s, with a network of tracks covering the states east of the Mississippi, the dominance of the railroads was assured for both goods and passengers.

Between 1877 and 1893, in a remarkable burst of building activity, over 100,000 miles of new track were laid. The rail network doubled in size, mainly as a result of construction west of the Mississippi and in the South.

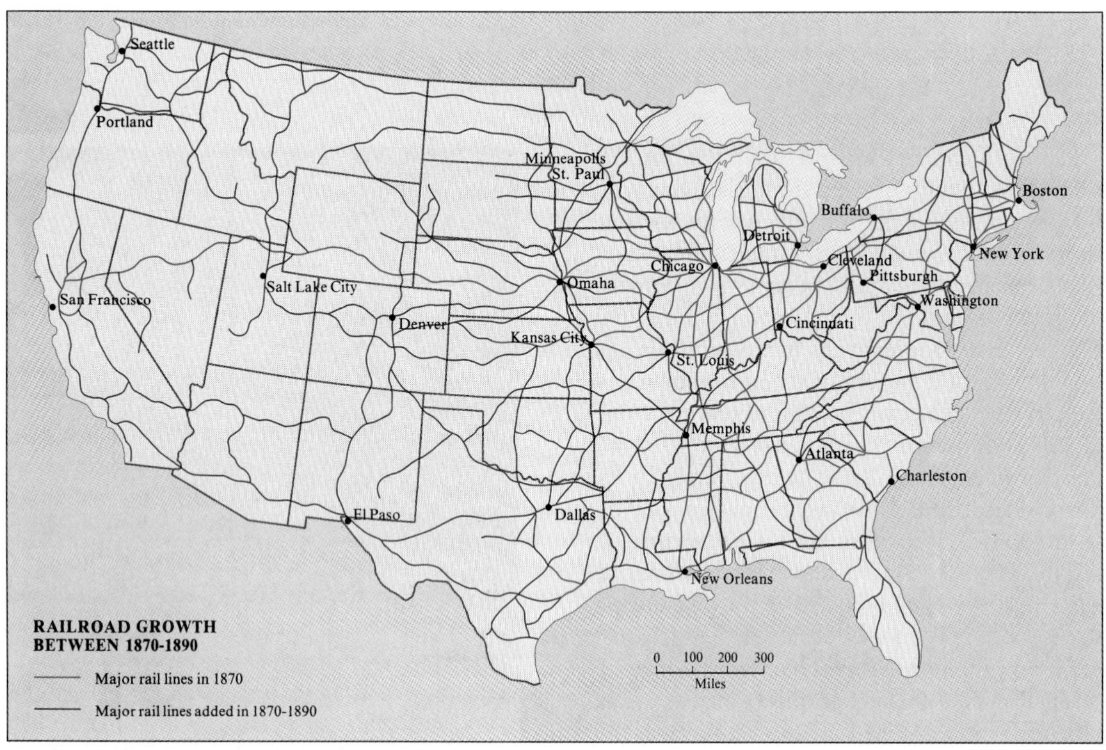

MAP 18.2

The Expansion of the Railroad System, 1870–1890

In 1870, the nation had 53,000 miles of rail track; in 1890, 167,000 miles. That burst of construction essentially completed the nation's rail network, although there would be additional expansion for the next two decades. The main areas of growth were in the South and west of the Mississippi. The Great Plains and Far West accounted for over 40 percent of all construction in this period.

By the early twentieth century, the American network, with more railway track than the rest of the world combined, brought virtually every populated area in the country within reach of railroad service.

Accompanying this physical growth was the rising efficiency of railway transportation. The early system, built by competing local companies, had been a jumble of discontinuous segments. Gauges of track—the width between the tracks—varied widely and at terminal points railroads were not physically connected. Many rivers lacked railroad bridges. Also, each railroad company reserved the use of its track exclusively for its own equipment. As late as 1880, a shipment of heavy textile machinery had to go through eight transfers en route from Massachusetts to South Carolina.

Beginning with the Civil War years, however, pressures increased for integration of the railroads. Track was hastily laid through Philadelphia, Richmond, and other cities to speed the huge shipments of troops and equipment. The postwar economy, as it grew more complex and interdependent, demanded a better-organized rail system. Much railroad integration took place through the expansion of such great trunk lines as the Pennsylvania, New York Central, and Illinois Central connecting different regions of the country. By the end of the 1880s, a standard track gauge (4 feet, 8½ inches) had been adopted across the country. Through the use of fast-freight firms and standard accounting procedures, the railroad network served shippers as if it were a single unit, moving their goods without breaks in transit, freight transfers between cars, or other delays that had once bedevilled smooth rail service.

At the same time, railroad technology was advancing. The key innovation was the shift to steel rails, which could bear much heavier loads than wrought-iron rails. Locomotives became heavier and more powerful, freight cars progressively larger, and freight trains longer. The Consolidation-type locomotive, with four sets of driving wheels, nearly tripled the pulling power of freight trains. To control the great mass and length of the new freight trains, the inventor George Westinghouse perfected the automatic coupler, the air brake, and the friction gear for starting and stopping a long line of cars.

Integrated service and advancing technology increased the efficiency of the railroads. Costs per ton-mile fell by 50 percent between 1870 and 1890, resulting in a steady drop in freight rates for shippers.

The railroads brilliantly met the transportation needs of the maturing industrial economy. However, this achievement did not stem from any orderly plan or design; it sprang from the competitive energy of a free-wheeling market economy. True, especially before the 1870s, federal, state, and city governments had provided financial assistance in the form of land grants, loans, and tax breaks. But the actual enterprise of building railroads remained, with a few early exceptions, entirely in private hands.

The Railroad Magnates. Railroad construction required, more than anything else, enormous amounts of capital. That was why, long before other businesses did so, the railroads organized themselves as corporations capable of raising funds from the public through the sale of stocks and bonds. Finance became the central entrepreneurial activity in railroading.

The key figures were those with access to capital—their own or that of others. For example, John Murray Forbes, a Bostonian who had made his fortune in the China trade, went on to develop the Chicago, Burlington and Quincy Railroad into the preeminent midwestern system. A more aggressive figure was Cornelius Vanderbilt, who left the steamboat business in 1863 to invest his fortune in the New York Central Railroad. Vanderbilt and his son William built the Central into an East-West trunk line rivaled only by the Pennsylvania Railroad. Forbes and the Vanderbilts aimed at creating well-constructed, well-financed railroad systems.

Jay Gould, a very different kind of entrepreneur, started out as a stock-market speculator. Gould earned early notoriety by his amazing attempt to corner the New York gold market. In 1869 he tried to acquire so much of the gold supply as to be able to force up gold prices almost at will. Many people at the time—and historians long after—considered Gould *a robber baron*, someone who loots commerce and gives nothing in return. But Gould did give something in return. His great talent lay in gaining control over weak properties—the Erie, the Union Pacific, the Wabash, and the Southwest lines during the 1880s—and making them turn a profit. Gould cared little for improving his properties, but he was a fierce competitor—for good reason. Gould's railroads generally were heavily in debt, and only a high volume of traffic enabled them to meet the interest charges. His wealthier rivals, such as Forbes and the Vanderbilts, bitterly resented his ruthless rate-cutting tactics, but shippers and consumers benefited from the lower transportation fees. In the free-market economy in which American railroads grew, even a buccaneer like Jay Gould made a positive contribution.

Railroad development in the United States was often sordid, fiercely competitive, and subject to boom and bust. When the Panic of 1893 hit, fully a third of the industry (by track mileage) went bankrupt. Yet vast sums of capital had been raised, an integrated, highly advanced rail system built, and the transportation needs of the nation amply met.

Mass Markets and Large-Scale Enterprise

The railway network, in turn, sparked a revolution in the distribution and marketing of goods. Until well into the industrial age, business firms were typically small. Most manufacturers produced goods in limited quantities, mainly for nearby markets. And they left the marketing to wholesale merchants and commission agents. Products normally passed through numerous hands on their way from the factory to final sale to the consumer.

Then after the Civil War the scale of economic activity began to grow dramatically. "Combinations of capital on a scale hitherto wholly unprecedented consti-

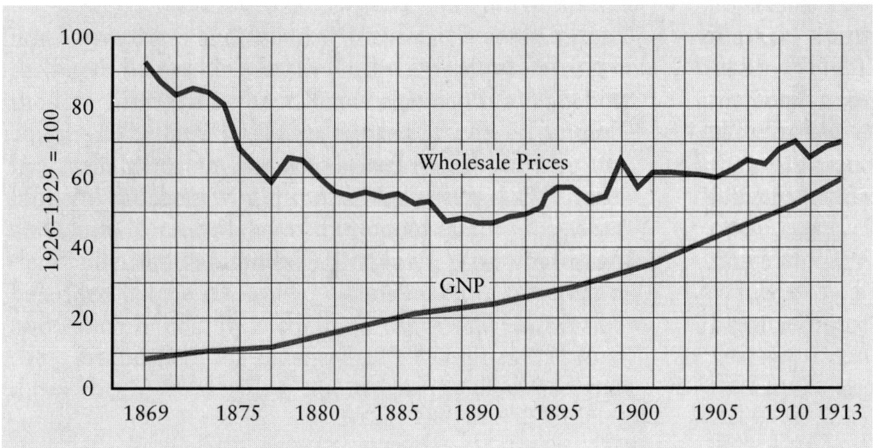

FIGURE 18.1

Business Activity and Wholesale Prices, 1865–1900

tute one of the remarkable features of modern business methods," the economist David A. Wells wrote in 1889. He already could see "no other way in which the work of production and distribution can be prosecuted." The increasing scale of enterprise seemed "not voluntary on the part of the possessors and controllers of capital, but necessary or even compulsory."

What was there about the nation's economic activity that led to Wells's sense of inevitability? The dynamic features of American growth—availability of capital, receptivity to technology, and the emergence of a heavy industrial base—certainly played a part. But the key to large-scale enterprise lay in the American market. Immigration and a very high birth rate swelled the population from 40 million in 1870 to over 60 million in 1890. People flocked to the cities, and the railroads brought these dense consuming markets within the reach of distant producers. The telegraph, in widespread use by the Civil War, eliminated communication barriers. Unlike Europe, America was not carved up into many national markets; no political frontiers impeded the flow of goods across the continent. Meanwhile, high tariffs protected American industry from foreign competition. Nowhere else did manufacturers have an internal market so vast and accessible for their products.

Gustavus Swift and Vertical Integration. The meat packing industry was a case in point. Before the Civil War, Cincinnati and Chicago had become great centers for the processing of preserved products like salt pork and smoked beef. But fresh meat remained the province of local butchers and slaughterhouses whose practices had scarcely changed since the preindustrial era. Fresh meat was a luxury item, and the diet of city dwellers, especially the poor, depended heavily on salt pork.

The coming of the railroads brought big changes to the fresh-meat business. Cattle raising shifted to the grazing ranges of the Great Plains and to the feed lots of the corn belt. Chicago, the rail terminal for the upper Midwest, became the hub of the American meat trade once the Union Stock Yards opened in 1865. Cattle were shipped by railroad from Chicago to eastern cities, where, as before, they were slaughtered in local

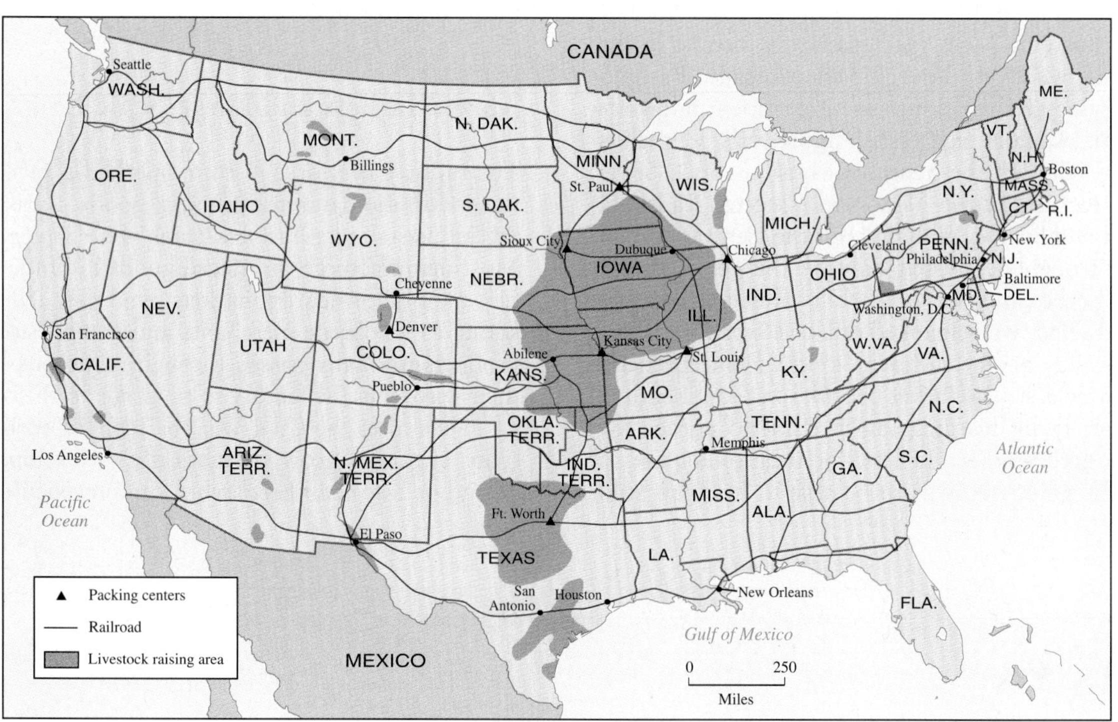

MAP 18.3

The Dressed Meat Industry

No industry better reveals than meat packing how transportation, supply, and demand combined to foster the growth of the American industrial economy. The main centers of beef production in 1900—Chicago, St. Paul, Kansas City, Fort Worth—were great rail hubs with connections westward to the cattle growing regions and eastward to the great cities hungry for cheap supplies of meat. Vertically integrated enterprise sprang from these elements, linked together by an efficient and comprehensive railroad network.

"butchertowns." By means of regional specialization and an efficient rail network, the meat trade serviced an exploding urban population and, without further development, might have done so indefinitely.

Gustavus F. Swift, a shrewd Massachusetts cattle dealer who settled in Chicago in 1875, saw the future differently. The system of marketing fresh meat seemed inefficient to him. Livestock in cattle cars deteriorated en route to the East, and local slaughterhouses were too small to utilize waste by-products and cut high labor costs. If a way could be found to keep the dressed beef fresh in transit, then processing operations could be concentrated in Chicago. Primitive refrigeration already enabled Chicago pork-packing plants to operate year-round. The problem was how to apply this technology to a railroad freight car. After Swift's engineers had figured out an effective system of air circulation, he built a fleet of refrigerator cars and constructed a central beef-processing plant at the Chicago stockyards.

This was only the beginning of Swift's activities. Since no refrigerated warehouses existed in the cities to which he shipped chilled beef, Swift had to build his own network of branch houses. Next, he established a fleet of wagons to distribute his products to retail butcher shops. Swift constructed additional facilities to process the fertilizer, chemicals, and other usable by-products from his slaughtering operations. He also added to his line of business other perishable commodities, including dairy products, so he could fully utilize his refrigerated cars and branch houses. As the demand grew, Swift built more packing houses in other stockyard centers, such as Kansas City, Fort Worth, and Omaha.

Step by step, Swift had created a new kind of enterprise, the *vertically integrated* firm—that is, a national company capable of handling within its own structure all the functions of an entire industry. In effect, Swift and Company replaced a large number of small specialized firms that had operated locally. Several other Chicago companies that had started as preserved pork packers—Armour and Company was the most prominent—followed Swift's lead. By the end of the 1890s five firms, all of them nationally organized and vertically integrated, produced nearly 90 percent of all the meat shipped in interstate commerce.

The Birth of Mass Marketing. The development of the refrigerator car had made all this possible in the fresh-meat trade. In most other fields, no such single event was so decisive. But other manufacturers did share Swift's insight that the essential step was to identify a mass market and then develop a national enterprise capable of serving it. In the petroleum industry, John D. Rockefeller built the Standard Oil Company partly by taking over rival firms; but he also developed a national distribution system to reach the enormous market for kerosene as a fuel for lighting and heating homes. The Singer Sewing Machine Company formed its own sales organization, using both retail stores and door-to-door salesmen. The McCormick Harvesting Machine Company set up a network of franchise dealers. Through such distribution systems, manufacturers provided technical information, credit, and repair facilities for their products. Like the meat packers, these companies became vertically integrated firms that served a national market.

To gain the benefits of mass distribution, retail business went through comparable changes. Montgomery Ward and Sears, Roebuck developed into national mail-order houses for rural consumers. From Vermont to California, farm families selected identical goods from mail-order catalogues, and became part of the nationwide consumer market. In the cities, mass distribution followed different strategies. Department stores, a form of retailing pioneered by John Wanamaker in Philadelphia, spread to every large city in the country. Sometimes this growth occurred through the efforts of a wholesale merchant, but more often—as with R. H. Macy of New York—it came through the

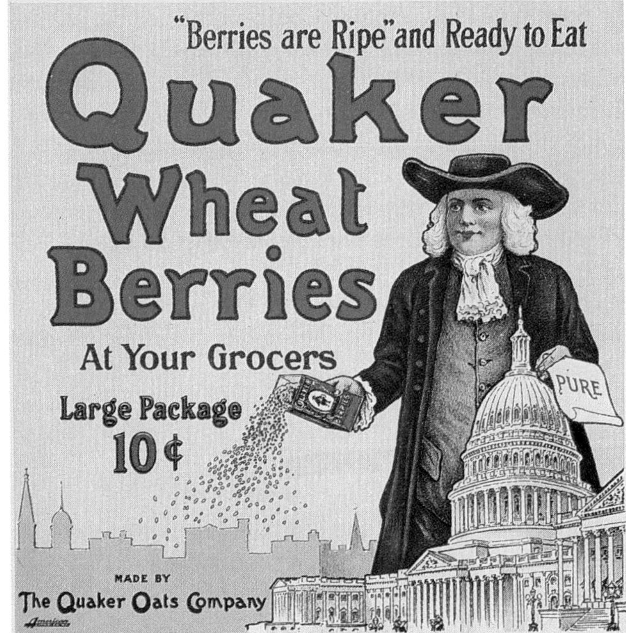

Quaker Oats

Like crackers, sugar, and other nonperishable foods, oatmeal had traditionally been marketed to consumers in bulk from barrels. In 1882, the grain merchant Henry P. Cowell completed the first continuous-process mill for oatmeal, cutting production costs and greatly increasing output. He also struck on the idea of selling oatmeal in boxes of standard size and weight to a national market. Broadsides showing the Quaker Oats man soon appeared in every American town, advertising a product of reliable quality and uniform price. (National Museum of American History, Smithsonian Institution) addition of departments to a dry goods store. The most important innovators in this field were such Jewish families as the Strauses of New York, the Lazaruses of Columbus, Ohio, and the Mays of Colorado, most of whose founders had started as peddlers or small dry good proprietors. An alternative route to urban distribution was the establishment of extensive chain store systems, which was the strategy of the Great Atlantic and Pacific Tea Company (A & P) and the F. W. Woolworth Company.

American society prepared citizens to be consumers of the standardized goods produced by national manufacturers and sold by mass marketers. The high rate of geographic mobility broke down loyalties to local custom and regional distinctiveness that were so strong in Europe. And social class in America, though by no means absent, was blurred at the edges. Equally important, it did not call for distinguishing ways of dressing. Foreign visitors often noted that ready-made clothing made it difficult to tell sales girls from debutantes on the city streets.

The American consumer's receptivity to standardized goods should not be exaggerated. Gustavus Swift, for example, encountered great resistance to his Chicago beef. How could it be wholesome weeks later in Boston or Philadelphia? Cheap prices helped, but advertising perhaps had a greater influence. Modern advertising was born during the late nineteenth century, bringing brand names and an urban landscape increasingly cluttered by billboards and signs. By 1900, advertisers were spending more than $90 million annually for space in newspapers and magazines. Advertisements urged readers to bathe with Pears' soap, to munch Uneeda biscuits, to sew on a Singer machine, and to snap pictures with a Kodak camera. The active molding of demand for brand names became a major function of American business.

The Managerial Revolution

At one time, observed the railroad expert Marshall M. Kirkman in 1896, it had been thought "practically impossible to manage a great railway effectively." On the early roads, "management had been personal and autocratic; the superintendent, a man gifted with energy and clearness of perception, moulded the property to his own will. But as the properties grew, he found himself unable to give his personal attention to everything. Undaunted, he sought to do everything and do it well. He ended by doing nothing."

It is not hard to understand the mistake of the early railroad superintendent. How could he know that methods which had worked brilliantly in the past would not work in the future? And where, in a world of small businesses, was there a model for running an enterprise other than by personal and direct control over its activities? How else could a business be run? No problem was harder to see clearly or, once discovered, more taxing on the business imagination. Nor was any industrial success, once achieved, fated to have more enduring consequences than the mastery of the techniques of modern management.

As trunk lines thrust westward from Baltimore, Philadelphia, and New York before the Civil War, they came up against a managerial crisis that had not troubled shorter roads. In 1856, in a classic statement of the problem, the Erie Railroad official Daniel C. McCallum compared a 50-mile road and a 500-mile road. On the short road, the superintendent could personally attend to every detail, "and any system, however imperfect, may prove comparatively successful." But not on long roads: "I am fully convinced that in the want of a system lies the true secret of their failure." McCallum's crucial insight was in realizing the need for a *system*—a formal administrative structure—for the successful operation of large-scale, complex enterprises. He knew he was working in the dark: "We have no precedent or experience upon which we can fully rely."

The railroads were the most complex form of nineteenth-century enterprise. They had to raise huge amounts of capital, and their properties stretched over ever greater distances. They employed armies of workers—nearly 50,000 on the Pennsylvania system by 1890. And, unlike the leisurely traffic on the canals, trains had to be precisely scheduled and closely coordinated. Even with telegraph communication, train accidents took a heavy toll.

Step by step, always under the prod of necessity, the early trunk lines pioneered in the main elements of modern business administration. They divided overall management from day-to-day operations and created separate departments along functional lines—maintenance of way, rolling stock, and traffic. Then they carefully defined the lines of communication from the operating divisions upward to the central office. When Albert Fink perfected his cost-accounting system for the Louisville and Nashville Railroad after the Civil War, managers at last had precise data on which to assess the performance of their roads. By the end of the 1870s, the managerial crisis on the railroads had been resolved.

As industrial enterprises became comparably complex, they confronted the same kind of managerial problems. However, manufacturers benefited from the experience of the railroads. Sometimes there was a direct link. Andrew Carnegie, for example, drew on his early career with the Pennsylvania Railroad. Whether by learning from the railroads or by trial and error, large companies everywhere moved toward a modern management structure and solved the problems of administering far-flung business empires.

By the beginning of the twentieth century, the main lines of managerial strategy had taken hold throughout large-scale American industry. With few exceptions, vertically integrated firms followed a centralized, functionally departmentalized plan (see Figure 18.2, below). The central office housed a number of departments, each charged with the overall responsibility for a specific area of activity—purchasing, auditing, production, transportation, or sales. These functionally defined departments provided "middle management," and they represented the heart of the managerial revolution in American industry. Middle managers were the key innovators; in matters of business practice they were equivalent to engineers who improved technology.

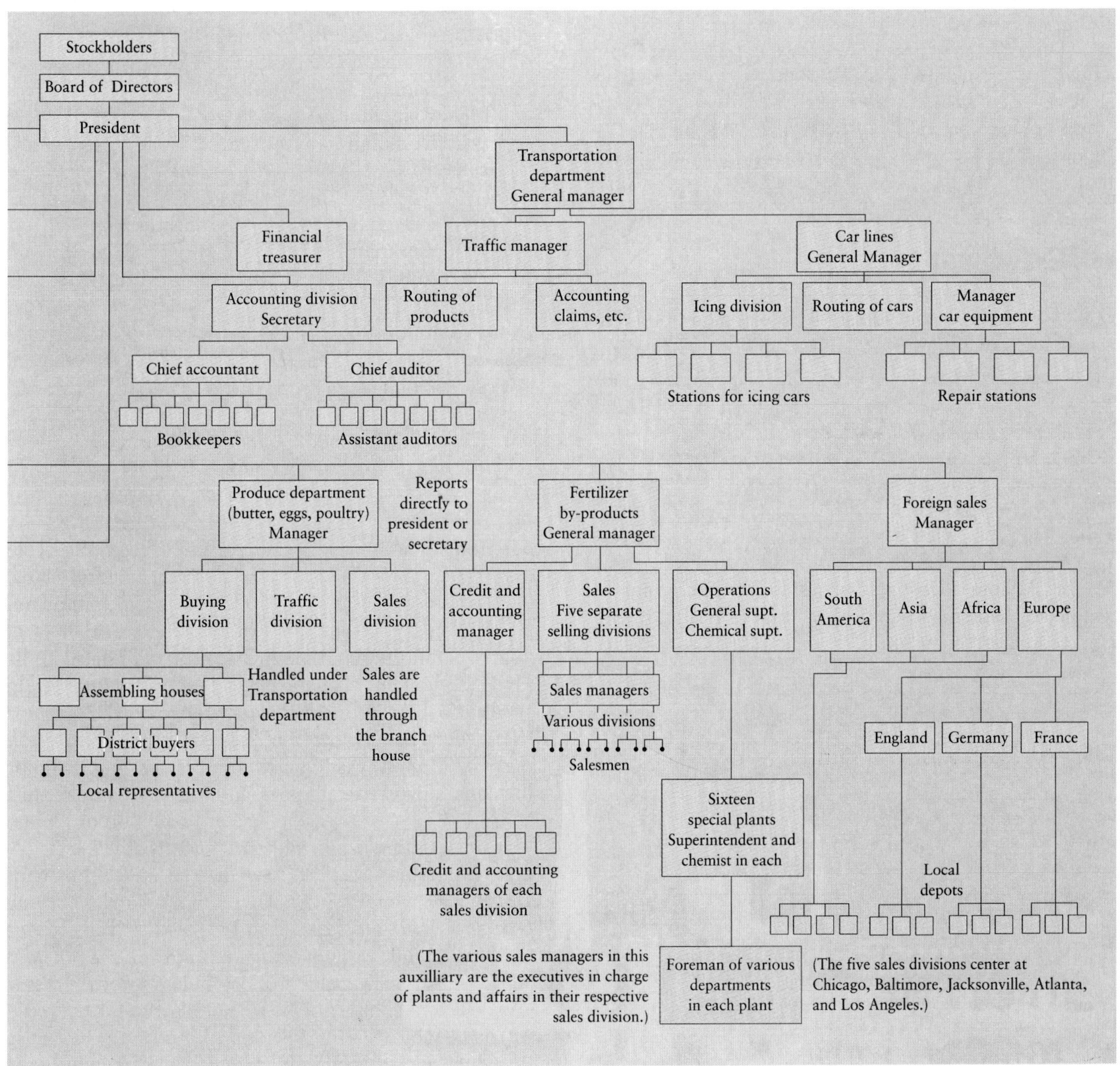

FIGURE 18.2

The Organization of Armour & Company in 1907

Their superiors, the top executives, could not claim such a complete achievement. The firms that developed through internal growth had been built by individual entrepreneurs—Gustavus Swift, Phillip D. Armour, and Cyrus McCormick. The successors, often their sons, were generally reluctant to surrender the tight supervision with which the founding fathers had developed their companies. In 1907, J. Ogden Armour spent his days reading operational reports and issuing orders to his buying, processing, and selling departments. All middle managers reported directly to him. Priding himself on his knowledge of the company and absorbed in the details of its operation, Armour had neither the time, the staff, nor the inclination to engage in long-term strategic planning or systematic evaluation of his firm's performance. Armour typified an entire generation of owner-managers. Brilliant in creating the subordinate administrative structure, they normally were slow to apply managerial principles to their own tasks.

The New South

"Shall we dethrone our idols?" This was a question that southerners had to ask themselves as they enviously observed the tremendous burst of economic activity in the North. For many, the answer was a resounding yes. Nostalgia for the glories of Old South became the chief target of the advocates of southern economic development. The South, they argued, had always given "the places of trust and honor" to "warriors and orators," forgetting that "what it would most need was the practical wisdom of businessmen." Led by Henry W. Grady of the Atlanta *Constitution,* an influential group of publicists made the "practical wisdom of businessmen" the credo of a "New South."

Catching up with the North was of course no easy task. The plantation economy of the Old South had strongly impeded industrial development. In 1860, railroad building lagged far behind, and there were few cities, a primitive distribution system, and not much manufacturing. After the devastation of the Civil War, this modest infrastructure was quickly restored. In 1879, with both Reconstruction and the economic depression ended, outside capital flowed in and a railroad boom developed. Track mileage doubled in the next decade and, at least by that measure, the South became nearly competitive with the rest of the country.

But the South remained overwhelmingly an agrarian society; two of every three persons wrested a livelihood from the soil. Farming and poverty are not necessarily linked. But in the South they were. Sharecropping, which required a cash crop (see Chapter 16), committed the South inflexibly to cotton, despite soil depletion and unprofitable prices. With leases on a year-to-year basis, neither tenant nor owner had an incentive to invest in long-term improvements. At a time of rapid advances in northern agriculture, cotton growing remained tied to the mule, the plow, and the hoe.

The result was a stagnant agricultural system. Low productivity and low cotton prices translated into low-wage agriculture. The price for southern farm labor fell steadily, until in South Carolina and Georgia it stood at scarcely half the national average by the 1890s—roughly 75 cents a day without board for a farm laborer.

Southern Industry. This low agricultural wage turned out to be the salvation of the South's hopes for industrialization. Consider, for example, how southern textile mills got started in the Piedmont upcountry of North Carolina, South Carolina, and Georgia in the mid-

The Industrial South
No development so buoyed the hopes of New South proponents as the success of the region's textile industry. After 1877, new mills sprung up in South Carolina, North Carolina, and Georgia. Investors received a high rate of return—average profits ran at 22 percent in 1882—and publicists boasted that new jobs were created for "the necessitous masses of poor whites." This 1887 engraving of a "model" mill at Augusta, Georgia, conveys the South's sense of pride in its new industrial prowess.

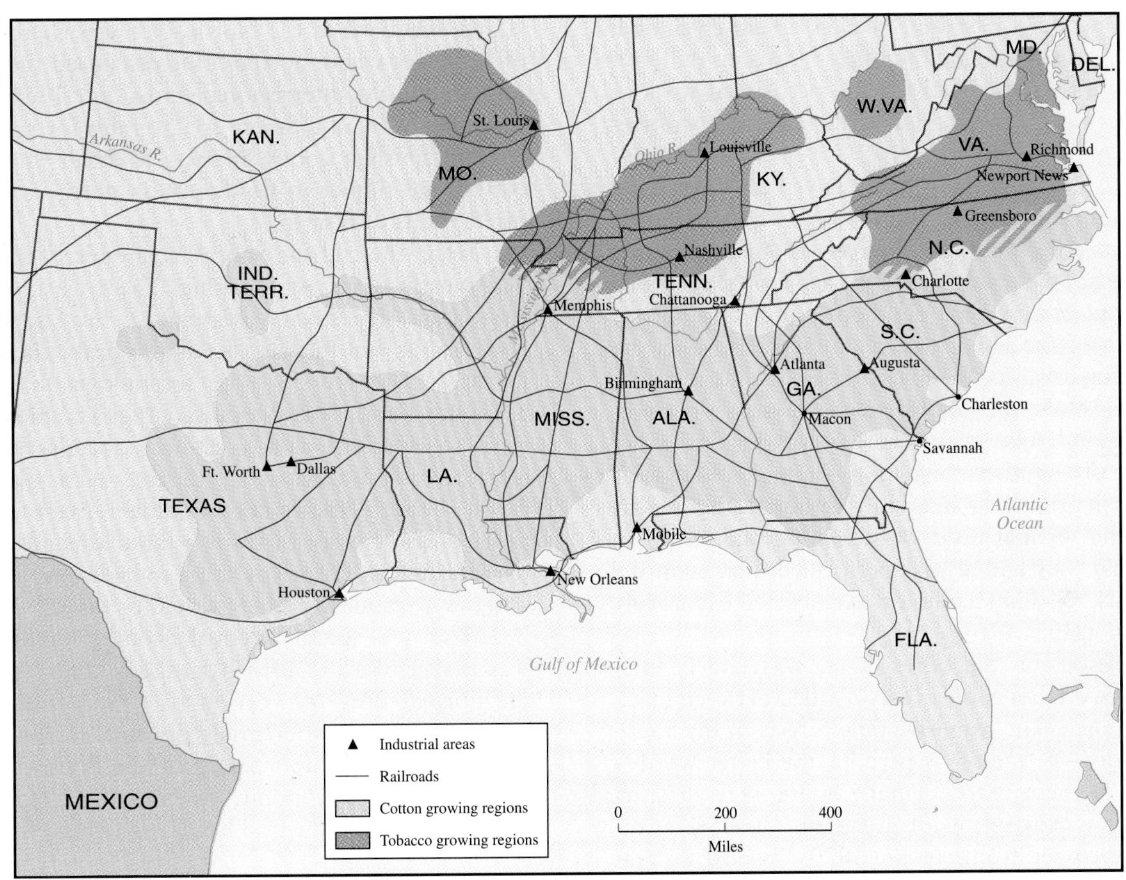

MAP 18.4

The New South, 1900

The economy of the Old South had concentrated heavily on the raising of staple crops—above all, cotton and tobacco. In the New South, staple agriculture continued to dominate, but there was marked industrial development as well. Industrial regions developed, producing textiles, coal and iron, and wood products. By 1900, the South's industrial pattern was well-defined.

1870s. Capital was raised locally, subscribed by investors large and small in an atmosphere of intense public boosterism. Workers were recruited mostly from the surrounding countryside, from the hardscrabble hill farms where people struggled to make ends meet. To attract them, mill wages had to be higher than their farm earnings, but wage-setting was pegged to that agricultural standard. And since the agricultural wage was so low in the South, the new mills had a great competitive advantage over the long-established New England industry. An 1897 report estimated the cost of cotton-mill labor as 40 percent lower in the South than in New England.

The labor system that evolved likewise reflected southern agrarian society. To begin with, it was a family system. "Papa decided he would come because he didn't have have nothing much but girls and they had to get out and work like men," recalled one woman. It was not Papa, in fact, but his girls whom the mills wanted, for work as spinners and loom tenders. Only they could not be recruited individually: no right-thinking parent would have permitted that. There was, on the other hand, no reason to object to hiring by families; after all, everyone had been expected to work on the farm. And so the family system of mill labor developed, in which half or more of the operatives were women, and in which, overall, the work force was very young. Fully a quarter of all southern textile workers in the 1880s were under fifteen years of age; three-quarters were twenty-four or younger.

The hours were long—twelve hours a day was the norm—but life in the mill villages was, in the words of one historian, "like a family." Employers tended to be highly paternalistic, providing company housing and a variety of services. The mill workers themselves built close-knit, supportive communities. However, mill jobs were for whites only. Blacks found occasional work as day laborers and janitors, but hardly ever as operatives inside the mills.

Cheap, abundant labor might have been termed the South's most valuable natural resource. But the South was rich in other natural resources. From its rich soil came tobacco, the region's second cash crop. Processing the leaf had always been southern work, and so had been much of the handicraft manufacture of chewing and smoking tobacco. When cigarettes became the fashion in the 1880s, the young North Carolina entrepreneur James B. Duke seized the new market by taking advantage of a southern invention—James A. Bonsack's machine for producing cigarettes automatically. Blacks retained the manual tasks of stemming and stripping the leaf that they had always performed, but, as in the textile mills, machine tending was restricted exclusively to white women.

Lumbering, on the other hand, was largely integrated, with a labor force evenly divided between black and white men. The extensive pine forests of the South were rapidly—*heedlessly* is perhaps the better word—exploited in these years. Finally, there were the rich coal and iron ore deposits of Alabama. These were vigorously developed from the late 1870s onward, so that by 1890 nearly a million tons of pig iron were being produced in the Birmingham district.

Contrary to the high hopes it raised for an emergent New South, this burst of industrial development did not lift the region out of poverty. Industrial output increased impressively, at a more rapid rate than in the North, but not enough to challenge the dominance of the agricultural sector. In 1900 two-thirds of all southerners made their living from the soil, just as they had in 1870. Moreover, the industries that did develop were usually extractive, such as forestry and mining. Nearly two-thirds of the South's labor force worked in the production of raw materials, compared with hardly one-eighth in the Middle Atlantic and New England states. Processing rarely went beyond coarse, semifinished goods, even in textiles. Industry by industry, the key statistic—the value added by manufacturing—showed the South consistently behind the North.

Southerners tended to blame the North. Theirs was a "colonial" economy controlled by New York and Chicago. There was something to this, certainly. Much of the capital—by no means all—did come from the North and from Britain. And the integrating processes of the economy did subordinate regional to national interests. When the railway network moved to a standard gauge, it was of course the southern railroads that had to conform to the national standard. In 1886, in one massive effort, the entire South converted to the 4 feet 8 ½ inch standard of the North. Nor was there any lack of instances where northern interests used their muscle to maintain the interregional status quo. Railroads, for example, charged different freight rates for raw materials and finished goods, making it cheap for southern cotton and timber to flow out and northern manufactured goods to flow in.

Yet in the end the South's economic backwardness was mostly of its own making. There was a crowning irony here. The great advantage of the South was its cheap labor. But this also acted as a brake on its capacity to develop into a more technologically advanced economy. First, low wages discouraged employers from replacing workers with machinery. Second, low wages attracted labor-intensive industry, such as textiles. Third, a cheap labor market inhibited investment in education. (In its way, this was a rational choice: the better educated workers would flee to higher-wage markets and the investment in them would be lost).

What was special about the southern labor market was that it was *insulated* from the rest of the country: the normal flow of workers back and forth did not occur and wage differentials did not narrow. And so long as this condition persisted, the South would remain a tributary economy, a supplier on unequal terms to the advanced industrial heartland of the North.

TABLE 18.2

Comparison of South and Non-South Value-Added per Worker, 1910

Type of Industry	South	Non-South
Lumber and timber products	820	1020
Cotton goods	544	764
Cars and general shop construction by steam railroad companies	657	746
Turpentine and resin	516	—
Tobacco manufactures	1615	1394
Foundry and machine shop products	1075	1307
Printing and publishing	1760	2100
Cotton seed oil and cake	1715	—
Hosiery and knit goods	461	724
Furniture and refrigerators	732	1052
Iron and steel	1182*	1433
Fertilizer	1833	1947

*Partially estimated
Source: Gavin Wright, *Old South, New South: Revolutions in the Southern Economy Since the Civil War* (New York: Basic Books), 1986, p. 163.

The World of Work

In a free enterprise system, profit drives the entrepreneur. But the industrial order is not populated only by profit makers. It includes—in vastly larger numbers—wage earners. What is done for profit always acts directly and powerfully on those working for wages. Never did those actions have more profound consequences than in the late nineteenth century. During that period, the modern factory system transformed the lives of American workers.

Autonomous Labor

No one supervised the nineteenth-century coal miner. He was a tonnage worker, paid for the amount of coal he produced. He provided his own tools, worked at his own pace, and knocked off early when he chose. Such autonomous craft workers—almost all of them men—flourished in many branches of nineteenth-century industry. They were mule spinners in cotton mills; puddlers and rollers in iron works; molders in stove making; and machinists, glass blowers, and skilled workers of many other types.

Within the shop, they abided by the *stint,* a limit placed by the workers themselves on the amount that they would produce each day. This informal system of limitation on output infuriated efficiency-minded engineers. But to the worker it signified personal dignity and "unselfish brotherhood" with his fellow employees. The male craft worker took pride in a "manly" bearing, both toward his fellows and toward the boss. One day a shop in Lowell, Massachusetts, posted regulations requiring all employees to be at their posts in work clothes at the opening bell and remain, with the shop door locked, until the dismissal bell. A machinist promptly packed his tools and quit, declaring that he had not "been brought up under such a system of slavery."

Underlying this ethical code was a keen sense of the craft group, each with its own history and customs. Hat finishers, masters of the art of applying fur felting to top hats and bowlers, had a language of their own. When a hatter was hired, he was "shopped"; if fired, he was "bagged"; when he quit work, he "cried off"; and when he took an apprentice, the boy was "under teach." The hatters, most of whom worked in Danbury, Connecticut, or Orange, New Jersey, formed a distinctive, self-contained community.

The craft worker's skills were crucial to nineteenth-century production. He was valued also for the responsibilities he assumed. He hired his own helpers, supervised their work, and paid them out of his earnings. In an era when the scale of production was expanding, autonomous craft workers relieved their employers of the mounting burdens of shop-floor management. Many factory managers tried to shift responsibility to employees. A system of inside contracting developed in metal-fabricating firms that did precise machining and complex assembling. Contractor-employees hired and paid their own men and supervised them completely.

The skilled worker was one central figure of nineteenth-century industry; the common laborer was another. Great numbers of laborers had been needed to dig canals, lay railroad tracks, and build cities. They were equally important in heavy industry. Until the last years of the century, virtually all hauling of materials was done by hand. In the steel mills, a third or more of the workers shoveled coal and iron ore from freight cars and pushed filled wheelbarrows to the furnaces. They also handled the tons of metal that passed through the mill daily at every stage of steel production. They worked in gangs, completely under the charge of the foreman or gang boss. He hired them, told them what to do, and disciplined and fired them.

Dispersal of authority was thus characteristic of nineteenth-century industry. The aristocracy of the workers—the craftsmen, the inside contractors, and the foremen—had a high degree of autonomy. However, their subordinates often paid dearly for that independence. The opportunities for abuse were endless. Any worker who paid his helpers from his own pocket might be tempted to exploit them. In the Pittsburgh area, foremen were known as "pushers," notorious for driving their gangs mercilessly. On the other hand, industrial labor in the nineteenth century was still on a human scale. People dealt with each other face-to-face and often developed cohesive ties within the shop. Striking craft workers commonly received the support of helpers and laborers, and labor gangs sometimes walked out on behalf of a popular foreman.

Labor Recruits

Wherever in the world industrialism took hold, it set people in motion. Artisans moved into factories. Farm folk migrated to manufacturing centers. An industrial labor force emerged. These events took place in all industrializing nations. But the United States built its work force in a distinctive way. Unlike European countries, it could not rely primarily on its own population.

For one thing, the demand for labor was enormous. American industry required nearly three times as many workers in 1900 as in 1870. No less important, people born in the United States after the 1850s could no

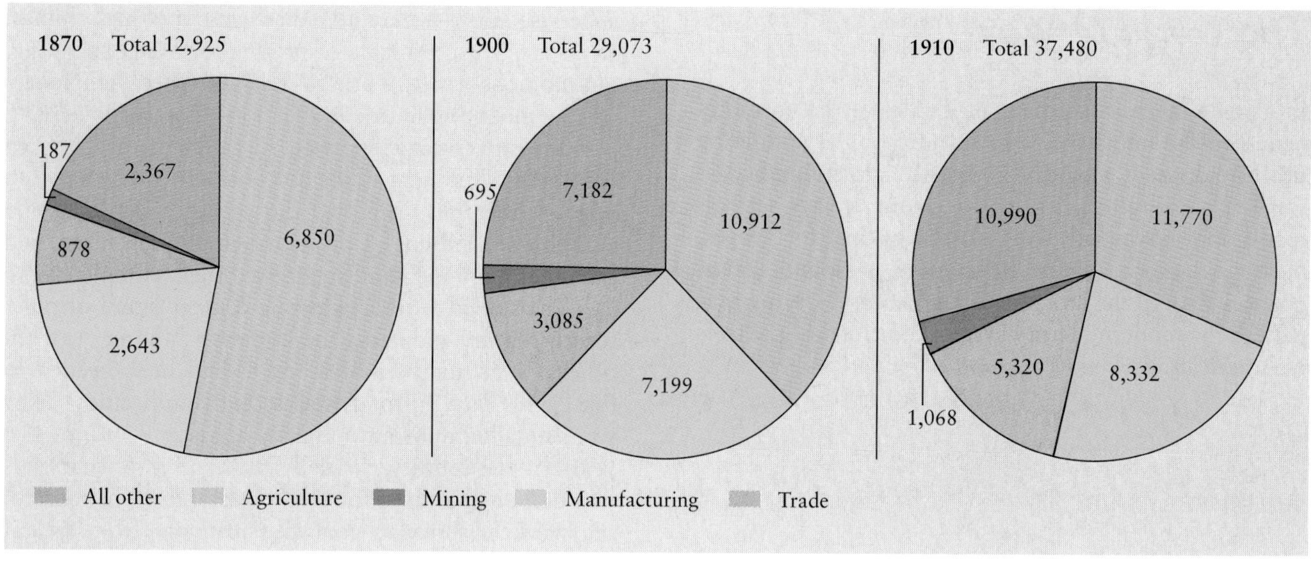

FIGURE 18.3

Changes in the Labor Force, 1870–1910

The numbers represent thousands of people (i.e., 12,925 = 12,925,000). They reveal both the enormous increase in the total labor force between 1870 and 1910 and the dramatic shift from agriculture to industry and other nonagricultural jobs.

longer be attracted into factories. It was not that rural people, who still made up about 75 percent of the population in 1870, refused to leave their land. Indeed, many went westward—but they remained farmers. About half of those leaving farms did move to cities, but they tended to avoid factory work. The desirable jobs—those of puddlers, rollers, molders, and machinists—required industrial skills not held by rural Americans. They did have a basic education. They could read and calculate, and they understood American institutions and ways of doing things. City-bound white Americans found their opportunities in the multiplying white-collar jobs in offices and retail stores rather than in the nation's factories.

As for rural blacks, even the lowest factory job probably seemed better than sharecropping or day labor on a farm. A trickle of blacks began to migrate northward and westward—roughly 80,000 between 1870 and 1890 and another 200,000 from 1890 to 1910. Most of them settled in cities, but they encountered in northern factories racial barriers just as impenetrable as those in the South. The great majority of the black men ended up as casual laborers and janitors, the women as maids and laundresses. Only 7 percent of all African-American men worked in industry in 1890. Industrial employers were able to exclude blacks because of an apparently limitless supply of foreign workers on which they could draw.

Immigrant Labor. The exodus from the Old World had started in the 1840s when the potato famine sent more than a million Irish peasants fleeing to America. During the following years, other traditional rural economies began to break down. As agriculture shifted to cash crops, peasant families lost their self-sufficiency. Increasing populations meant there was not enough land to go round. The erosion of peasant economies struck first in Germany and Scandinavia. Then later in the nineteenth century it spread east into Austria-Hungary and Russia, and south into Italy and the Balkans. In industrial districts of Europe, the forces of economic change also cut loose many workers in the declining artisan trades and obsolete occupations such as hand-loom weaving. A total of about 25 million European immigrants arrived in America between 1870 and 1914.

Ethnic origin largely determined the kind of work that the immigrants found in their new country. Many Western Europeans were seasoned artisans and industrial workers. They generally sought the same types of jobs they had held in the Old World. The nineteenth-century occupational structure took on an ethnic character: the Welsh worked as tin-plate workers, the English as miners, the Germans as machinists and traditional artisans, the Belgians as glass workers, and the Scandinavians as seamen on Great Lakes boats. For common labor, employers had long counted on the brawn of rural immigrants to dig canals, lay railroad

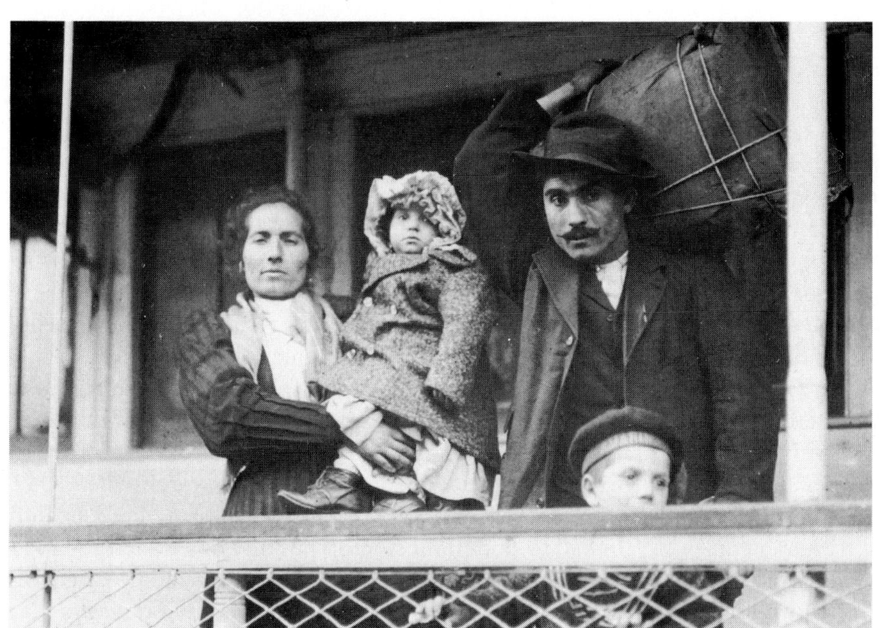

Immigrant Workers

Many native-born Americans resented the influx of peasant immigrants from eastern and southern Europe that began in the 1880s. In fact, however, the newcomers, more than any other group, manned the machines, laid the railroad tracks, and did the heavy construction labor that built the nation's cities. They were, in truth, Europe's gift—its most vigorous and hard-working people.

tracks, and provide unskilled labor in factory and construction gangs.

As industrialization advanced, the demand for unskilled workers increased and the nation's dependence on European craft skills moderated. These developments helped trigger the remarkable shift in immigration away from northern Europe that started in the 1880s. More than 9 million people migrated to America from eastern and southern Europe between 1900 and 1914. Italian and Slavic immigrants, almost wholly lacking in industrial skills, flooded into the lowest rungs of American industry. Heavy, low-paid factory labor became the domain of the recent immigrants. Blast-furnace jobs, a job-seeking investigator heard, were "Hunky work," not suitable for him or any other American.

Factors other than skills determined where immigrants ended up in American industry. Although most of the newcomers arrived alone, they moved within well-defined networks. The immigrants followed relatives or fellow villagers already in America, joined their households as family members or boarders, and relied on them to find a job. A high degree of ethnic clustering resulted, even within a single factory. At the Jones and Laughlin steel works in Pittsburgh, the carpentry shop was German, the hammer shop Polish, and the blooming mill Serbian. Distinctive ethnic characteristics also determined the jobs that immigrants found. For example, men from Italy preferred outdoor work to factory labor, and they were already accustomed to the form of gang labor under a *padrone* (boss) under which they performed construction and road work in America.

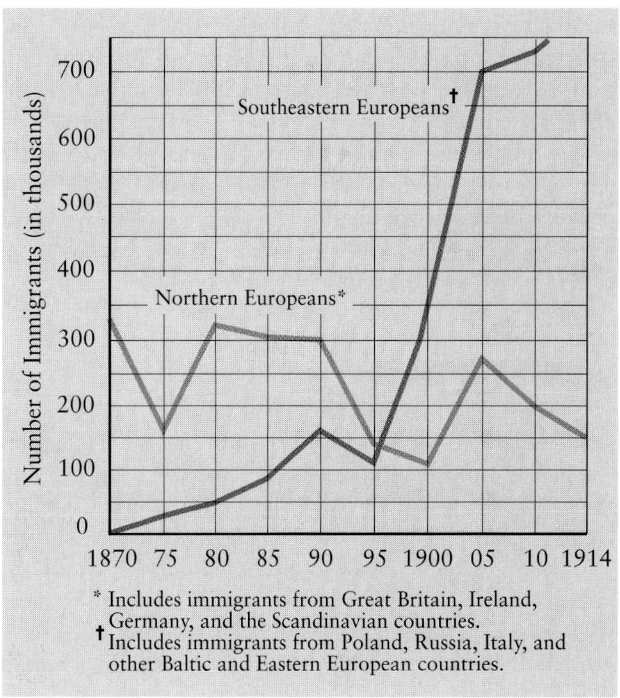

FIGURE 18.4

American Immigration, 1870–1914

The immigrants entered a modern industrial order, but they saw their surroundings through peasant eyes. With the disruption of the traditional rural economies of Eastern and southern Europe, many peasants had begun to lose their land. This meant an intolerable decline into the class of dependent, propertyless servants. Peasants could avoid such a bitter fate only if they had money to buy property. In Europe, job-seeking peasants commonly tried seasonal agricultural labor or temporary work in nearby cities. America represented merely a larger leap, made possible by cheap and speedy steamship transportation across the Atlantic. The peasant immigrants, most of them young and male, came with the purpose of earning enough money to buy land and then returning to their native villages.

As long as the work lasted, peasant workers were rarely inclined to protest against low wages, harsh conditions, or the hardships of their lives. When work ran out, as it almost always did, there was a safety valve. In depression years, they flooded back to Europe. As many as half of the new immigrants returned to their homelands. No one knows how many saved enough money to fulfill their peasant goals and how many left simply for lack of work. Clearly, however, the peasants' reasons for coming, and their tendency to leave in bad times, made them an ideal labor supply for the new industrial order.

A few fields, such as railroading, employed mostly native-born workers. Overall, however, immigrants manned American industry, constituting well over half the labor force of the nation's principal manufacturing and mining industries after the turn of the century.

Working Women

Between 1870 and 1900 the number of American women grew by half, but the number in wage-earning jobs jumped by almost two-thirds. Women became increasingly important to the industrial economy, and by 1900 they made up more than a fourth of the total nonfarm labor force. The role they found as wage earners was shaped by the fact that they were women. Contemporary beliefs about womanhood largely determined which women entered the work force and how they were treated once they became wage earners.

Wives were not supposed to hold jobs. In 1890 less than 5 percent of all married white women worked outside their homes. Black married women had a much higher labor participation rate, over 30 percent. Before marriage young women generally did go to work, at least those below the respectable middle class; indeed, in most working-class families they had no choice. The majority of all employed women in 1890 were from sixteen to twenty-four years old. When older women worked, remarked one observer, it "was usually a sign that something had gone wrong"—their husbands were gone, jobless, or incapacitated.

Since women were considered to be inherently different from men, it followed that they should not be permitted to do "men's work." And regardless of the value of their labor, they could not be paid at men's rates. The dominant view was that a woman did not require a "living wage" because, as one investigator reported, "it is expected that she has men to support her." Moreover, the occupation that served as the baseline for all women's jobs was domestic service, always very poorly paid, or, in a woman's own home, not paid at all. And because virtually all occupations employed either women or men exclusively, the job opportunities for women were always limited and overcrowded.

The sex-typing of occupations, although certainly linked to dominant stereotypes of women's lesser capacities, is not easy to explain. There were some originally male occupations, such as telephone operators and store clerks, that by the 1890s became female. In each case, as an occupation became feminized, it also became characterized as having female attributes, even though very similar or even identical work had been done by men. Once a job became identified with women, it became unsuitable for men. There were, literally, no male telephone operators by 1900.

At the turn of the century, women workers fell into three roughly equal categories. A third worked as maids or other types of domestic servants. Another third held "female" white-collar jobs in teaching, nursing, sales, and office work. Sex-typing affected the third of the women in industrial occupations as well. Few worked as supervisors, fewer in the crafts, nearly none as day laborers. Most female industrial workers were classified as *operatives*—machine tenders and hand workers. Women were heavily concentrated in the garment trades and textile mills but could be found throughout industry in "light" occupations—as packers, inspectors, assemblers, or as sausage stuffers in packing houses.

As with male workers, ethnicity and race played a big part in the distribution of women's jobs among particular groups. Exclusion from all but the most menial of jobs applied as rigidly to black women as to black men. White-collar jobs were reserved for the native-born, although in the cities these were often the second-generation daughters of immigrants. And, as with men, ethnicity created clustering patterns in the jobs held by wage-earning women, or, as in the case of Italian families, restricted them to subcontracting tasks like sewing that could be done at home.

But gender also mattered crucially. Women's identity give their work distinctive meaning. Department store clerks, for example, developed a work culture and language just as robust as that of the hard-drinking hatters of South Orange, New Jersey. Most important was the fact that wage-earning women were young and un-

Switchboard Operators
Telephone work offers a prime historical example of the process of sex-typing in American employment. When the first telephone exchange was set up in Boston in 1878, it was manned by teen-age boys, following the practice in the telegraph industry. During the 1880s, however, young women increasingly replaced the boys, and by 1900 switchboard operation was defined strictly as women's work. In this photograph of a telephone exchange in Columbus, Ohio, in 1907, the older woman at left has risen to be supervisor, but it is the two men in the picture who are clearly in charge. The other major occupations in this new industry—telephone installation and line maintenance—were just as strictly male as switchboard operation was female, but, of course, on a much higher pay scale.

married. For many, the first job was also the first escape from family discipline. It was an opportunity to gain some independence, to form friendships with other young women, and to experience, however briefly, a fun-loving time of nice clothes, dancing, and other "cheap amusements."

To some degree, these preoccupations made it easier to overlook or accept the miserable terms under which they worked. But working young women also developed a sense of group solidarity and self-respect. Fashionable clothes might appear frivolous to the casual observer, but they also conveyed the message that the working girl considered herself as good as anyone. And there were occasions, as with the Jewish garment workers of New York and the Irish-American telephone operators of Boston, when the rebellious youth culture united with feelings of job grievance to produce astonishing strike movements among working women.

Sex-typing of work was legitimized by the sentimental view of women as the weaker sex. But powerful interests also played a role. Craft workers protected their male domain, and employers profited from cut-rate work. Wherever they worked, women earned wages below those of the lowest male occupations. At the turn of the century, the weekly wage of women factory workers came to roughly $7—$3 less than unskilled males and $5 less than the average for all industrial employees.

The objection to working wives, also expressed in sentimental and moral terms, was likewise based on solid necessity. From the standpoint of the industrial economy, the basic economic unit consisted of the individual employee. For workers, however, the family was the economic unit. In this family economy, the wife contributed crucially. Cooking, cleaning, and tending the children were not income-producing or reckoned in terms of money. But everyone knew that the family household could not function without the wife's contribution. Therefore, her place was in the home.

Working-class families, however, found the going hard on a single income. Only among the highly skilled workers, wrote an investigator of the family budgets of coal and iron workers in the early 1890s, "was it possible for the husband unaided to support his family." For most working-class families, the hardest period came during the child-bearing years, when there were many mouths to feed and only the earnings of the father. Thereafter, the family income began to grow. Not only unmarried sons and daughters but the younger children as well contributed their share. In 1900, one of every five children below the age of sixteen worked, including probably a quarter of a million below the age of ten. "When the people own houses," remarked a printer from Fall River, "you will generally find that it is a large family all working together."

Obstacles to child labor, however, began to appear. By the 1890s, all the northern industrial states had passed laws prohibiting the employment of young children and regulating the work hours of teen-agers. Most of those states also required children from eight to four-

Breaker Boys

In the anthracite districts of eastern Pennsylvania, giant structures called breakers processed the coal as it came out of the mines, crushing it and sorting it by size for sale as domestic fuel. The boys shown in this photograph had the job of picking out the slate and refuse as the processed coal came down the shutes, working long hours in a constant cloud of coal dust for less than a dollar a day. Breaker boy was the the first job, often begun before the age of ten, in a lifetime in the mines. The photograph does not show any old men, but sick and disabled miners often ended their careers as breaker boys—hence the saying among coal diggers, "twice a boy and once a man is the poor miner's life."

teen years of age to go to school for a certain number of weeks each year. Working-class families continued to rely on second incomes, but this money was more and more likely to come from the wife than from the children. After 1890 the proportion of working married women crept steadily upward. For working-class women, entry into the labor market went forward especially rapidly. About a fifth of the wives of unskilled and semiskilled men in Chicago held jobs in 1920. Wage-earning wives, many with children, were on their way to becoming a primary part of America's labor force.

Systems of Control

As technology advanced and modern management emerged, controls over the work process increased. Workers might have preferred the older systems of autonomous work, but they had no choice. They increasingly lost the proud independence that had characterized nineteenth-century craft work.

When mine owners introduced undercutting machines in the 1880s, they deprived the coal miners of the pick work that was their most prized skill. "Anyone with a weak head and a strong back can load machine coal," grumbled one Kentucky miner. "But a man has to think and study every day like you was studying a book if he is going to get the best of the coal when he uses only a pick." Similar complaints came from many other craft workers as their skills fell victim to machinery—from hand-loom weavers early in the nineteenth century to glass-blowers a hundred years later.

What was primarily at work in this de-skilling process was a new system that we call *mass production.* This system applied to products that became standardized and found high-volume markets. Consider, for example, the great advances that accompanied the creation of a national market for dressed beef in the 1870s. The huge packing houses that sprang up in Chicago shifted from the traditional reliance on skilled butchers to a highly specialized division of labor. At the Armour plant, workers performed seventy-eight distinct jobs, working extremely efficiently and at high speed as the carcasses moved along, hooked to overhead conveyors. In a ten-hour day, a gang of 157 workers could handle 1,050 cattle, many more per employee than if one skilled butcher did everything. Machinery did not replace workers; rather, a minute division of labor vastly increased workers' output.

In most cases, however, the division of labor did lead to mechanization. This was because once jobs had been subdivided into simple, repetitive tasks, it was generally possible to design machines that could do those tasks. The greatest opportunity came in the manufacture of products assembled from standardized, interchangeable parts—such as agricultural implements, sewing machines, typewriters, bicycles, and, after 1900, the automobile. In all these cases, machine tools that cut, drilled, and ground the metal parts had originally been manned by skilled machinists. But as machine tools became more specialized, they became *dedicated* machines, that is, set up to do the same job over and over again, and the need for skilled operatives disappeared.

"A man never learns the machinist's trade now," a craft worker complained in 1883. In the manufacture of sewing machines, "the trade is so subdivided that a man is not considered a machinist at all. One man may make just a particular part of a machine and may not know anything whatever about another part of the same machine." Such a worker, noted an observer, "cannot be master of a craft, but only master of a fragment."

AMERICAN VOICES

The Impact of Mechanization *John Morison*

John Morison, a machinist, describes to a Senate investigating committee in 1883 what technological progress has meant to him and his fellow skilled workers.

Q. Is there any difference between the conditions under which machinery is made now and those which existed ten years ago?

A. A great deal of difference.

Q. State the differences as well as you can.

A. Well, the trade has been subdivided and those subdivisions have been again subdivided, so that a man never learns the machinist's trade now. Ten years ago he learned, not the whole of the trade, but a fair portion of it. Also, there is more machinery used in the business, which again makes machinery. In the case of making the sewing-machine, for instance, you find that the trade is so subdivided that a man is not considered a machinist at all. Hence it is merely laborers' work and it is laborers that work at that branch of our trade. Machinery is produced a great deal cheaper than it used to be formerly, and in fact, through this system of work, 100 men are able to do now what it took 300 or 400 men to do fifteen years ago.

Q. Have you noticed the effect upon the intellect of this plan of keeping a man at one particular branch?

A. Yes. It has a very demoralizing effect upon the mind throughout. The man thinks of nothing else but that particular branch; he knows that he cannot leave that particular branch and go to any other; he has got no chance whatever to learn anything else because he is kept steadily and constantly at that particular thing, and of course his intellect must be narrowed by it.

Q. And does he not finally acquire so much skill in the manipulation of his particular part of the business that he does it without any mental effort?

A. Almost. In fact he becomes almost a part of the machinery.

Q. What is the social condition of the machinists in New York and the surrounding towns and cities?

A. It is rather low compared to what their social condition was ten or fifteen years ago.

Q. Do you remember when it was better?

A. When I first went to learn the trade a machinist considered himself more than the average workingman; in fact he did not like to be called a workingman. He liked to be called a mechanic. Today he recognizes the fact that he is simply a laborer the same as the others. Ten years ago even, he considered himself a little above the average workingman; he thought himself a mechanic, and felt he belonged in the middle class; but today he recognizes the fact that he is simply the same as any other ordinary laborer, no more and no less.

Q. What is the social air about the ordinary machinist's house? Are there evidences of happiness, and joy, and hilarity, or is the general atmosphere solemn, and somber, and gloomy?

A. To explain that fully, I would state first of all, that machinists have got to work ten hours a day in New York, and that they are compelled to work very hard. In fact the machinists of America are compelled to do about one third more work than the machinists do in England in a day. . . . Of course when a man is dragged out in that way he is naturally cranky, and he makes all around him cranky; so, instead of a pleasant house it is every day expecting to lose his job by competition from his fellow workmen, there being so many out of employment, and no places for them, and his wages being pulled down through their competition, looking at all times to be thrown out of work in that way, and staring starvation in the face makes him feel sad, and the head of the house being sad, of course the whole family is the same, so the house looks like a dull prison instead of a home . . . .

Q. Where do you work?

A. I would rather not have it in print. Perhaps I would have to go Monday morning if I did. We are so situated in the machinist's trade that we daren't let them know much about us. If they know that we open our mouths on the labor question, and try to form organizations, we are quietly told that "business is slack," and we have got to go.

Source: U.S. Senate, Committee on Education and Labor, *Report on the Relations between Labor and Capital* (1885), I, 755–59.

The Killing Floor
To the modern eye, the labor process depicted in this 1882 engraving of a Chicago meat-packing plant seems primitive and inefficient, but in fact it contains the seeds of America's mass-production revolution. At the far left, the steer has already been stunned by one specialist, killed by a second, and attached to a chain that will lift it on to the overhead conveyor. The division of labor is already in place (each of the workers on the line does a single repetitive task) and the process is continuous. It would be only a small step from the killing floors of the Chicago packing plants to Henry Ford's assembly line.

Technology also took hold of the pace of operations. The machine, not the worker, determined how fast production would go. "If you need to turn out a little more," boasted a superintendent at Swift and Company, "you speed up the conveyor a little and the men speed up to keep pace." Complaints about speed-ups were a sure sign of workers' loss of control over their jobs.

Frederick W. Taylor and Scientific Management. The impact of machinery on workers was essentially unintentional, a by-product of decisions made for technological reasons. Employers doubtless recognized that mechanization would better enable them to discipline their workers. But this was only an incidental benefit added to the efficiencies that came from the machinery itself. Gradually, however, employers came to realize that managing workers might itself be a way of reducing the cost of production.

The pioneer in this field was Frederick W. Taylor. Taylor had made a name for himself as an expert on metal-cutting methods. In 1895 he published a landmark essay, "A Piece Rate System," that proposed a strategy for getting the maximum work from the individual worker. Taylor suggested two basic reforms. The first would eliminate the brain work from manual labor. Managers would assume "the burden of gathering together all of the traditional knowledge which in the past has been possessed by the workmen and then of classifying, tabulating, and reducing this knowledge to rules, laws, and formulae." The second reform, a logical consequence of the first, would deprive workers of the authority they had normally exercised on the shop floor. Workers would "do what they are told promptly and without asking questions or making suggestions . . . . The duty of enforcing . . . rests with the management alone."

Once they had the knowledge and power, according to Taylor, managers would put labor on a "scientific" basis. This meant subjecting each task to a *time-and-motion study,* by which an engineer with a stopwatch analyzed and timed each job. A personnel office would hire and train the right person for each job. Workers would be paid at a differential rate—that is, a certain amount if they met the stopwatch standard, a higher rate for any greater output. Taylor claimed that his techniques would guarantee the optimum level of worker efficiency. His simplistic assumption was that only money mattered to workers, and that they would be automatically responsive to the lure of higher earnings.

Taylor called his method *scientific management.* It was not, in practice, a roaring success. His reforms called for a total restructuring of factory administration. No company ever adopted Taylor's entire system, and the few that tried to do so paid dearly for the effort. The differential-rate method, which was widely used, met stubborn resistance. "It looks to me like slavery to have a man stand over you with a stopwatch," complained one iron molder. A union leader insisted that "this system is wrong, because we want our heads left on us."

Yet Taylor, a brilliant publicist, achieved something of fundamental importance. He and his disciples spread his scientific-management teachings throughout American industry. Taylor's successors moved beyond his simplistic economic psychology, creating the new professions of personnel administration and industrial psychology that purported to know how to extract more and better work from workers. A threshold had been crossed into the modern era of labor management.

So the circle closed on American workers. With each advance, the quest for efficiency cut deeper into their cherished autonomy. Mechanization, scientific management, and the growing scale of industrial activity diminished workers and cut them down to fit the production system. The process occurred unevenly. For textile workers, the loss had come early. Miners and iron workers felt it much more slowly. Others, such as craft workers in the building trades, escaped the process almost entirely. But increasing numbers of workers found themselves in an environment that crushed any sense of mastery or even understanding.

The Labor Movement

Wherever industrialization has taken hold, workers have organized and responded collectively. However, the movements they built have varied from one industrial society to another. In the United States, workers were especially uncertain about the path they wanted to take. Only in the 1880s did the American labor movement settle into a fixed course.

Reformers and Unionists

In 1883, a New York wagon driver named Thomas B. McGuire testified before a Senate committee. He had saved $300 from his wages, "so that I might become something of a capitalist eventually." But he soon failed. "A man in the express business today owning one or two horses and a wagon cannot even eke out an existence from the business," McGuire complained. "The competition is too great from the Adams Express Company and all those other monopolies." McGuire's prospects seemed no better in the hack (hired carriage) business:

> Corporations usually take that business themselves. They can manage to get men, at starvation wages, and put them on a hack, and put a livery on them with a gold band and brass buttons, to show that they are slaves—I beg pardon; I did not intend to use the word slaves; there are no slaves in this country now—to show that they are merely servants.

Slave or liveried servant, the symbolic meaning was the same to McGuire. He was speaking of the crushed aspirations of the independent American worker.

Labor Reform and the Knights of Labor. What would satisfy the Thomas McGuires of the nineteenth century? Only the restoration of a republican society in which all members were social and political equals and in which everyone might hope to become independent. To recapture the republican virtues did not require returning to the agrarian past but, rather, moving forward beyond the selfishness of the existing industrial order to a time when no distinction would exist between capitalists and workers. All would be "producers" laboring together in what was commonly called the "cooperative commonwealth." This ideal inspired wave after wave of labor-reform movements, going back to the workingmen's parties of the 1830s and culminating after the Civil War in the Noble and Holy Order of the Knights of Labor.

The Knights of Labor was founded in 1869 as a secret society of Philadelphia garment cutters. The organization gradually spread to other cities and by 1878 had become a national movement. Led by Grand Master Workman Terence V. Powderly, the Knights boasted an elaborate ritual and ceremony that appealed strongly to the fraternal spirit of the nineteenth-century worker. The Knights of Labor typified the American labor-reform tradition. The goal was to "give voice to that grand undercurrent of mighty thought, which is today [1880] crystallizing in the hearts of men, and urging them on to perfect organization through which to gain the power to make labor emancipation possible."

But how was "emancipation" to be achieved? The Knights tried a number of solutions, including cooperation. Funds would be raised to set up cooperative factories and shops that would be owned and run by the employees. As these cooperatives flourished and spread, American society would be transformed into a cooperative commonwealth. But little was actually done. In reality, the Knights concentrated mainly on "education." Powderly regarded the organization as a vast labor lyceum that almost anyone could join. The cooperative commonwealth would arrive in some mysterious way as more and more "producers" became members and learned the group's message from lectures, discussions, and publications. Social evil would not end in a day, but "must await the gradual development of educational enlightenment."

Trade Unionism. The labor-reform movement expressed the higher aspirations of American workers. Another kind of organization—the trade union—tended to their day-to-day needs. Unions had long been central to the lives of craft workers. Apprenticeship rules regulated entry into a trade, and the *closed shop*—by reserving all jobs for union members—kept out lower-wage and incompetent workers. Union rules specified the terms of work, sometimes in minute detail. Above all, trade unionism defended the craft worker's traditional skills and rights.

A Railroad Brotherhood

Locomotive firemen, who fed the boilers on nineteenth-century steam engines, ranked below the engineers, but still considered themselves a privileged occupation. This union certificate conveys the respectable values to which the locomotive firemen adhered and, as depicted in the scenes on the right-hand side—the need they felt to protect their families (through the affordable insurance provided by their union) in the event of accidents that were so much a part of the dangerous trade they followed.

The union also symbolized the social identity of a craft. Hatters took pride in their drinking prowess, an on-the-job privilege jealously guarded, and their unions sometimes resembled drinking clubs. More often, however, the craft union had an uplifting character. A Birmingham iron puddler claimed that his union's "main object was to educate mechanics up to a standard of morality and temperance, and good workmanship." Because operating trains was a high-risk occupation, the railroad brotherhoods stressed mutual aid, providing accident and death benefits and encouraging members to assist one another. On the job and off, the unions played a big part in the lives of craft workers.

The earliest unions were local groups of workers in the same trade. Many of them, especially among German workers, organized initially along ethnic lines. These local bodies grew into national unions. The first to survive, the International Typographical Union, was formed in 1852. By the 1870s, molders, iron workers, bricklayers, and about thirty other trades had formed national unions.

The protection of job interests might have seemed a far cry from the reform idealism of the Knights of Labor. But both kinds of motives arose from a single workers' culture. Seeing no conflict, many workers carried membership cards in both the Knights of Labor and a trade union. The careers of many labor leaders, including Powderly, likewise embraced both kinds of activity. For many years even the functional lines were indistinct. At the local level, little separated a trade assembly of the Knights from a local trade union; both engaged in fraternal and bargaining activities.

Trade unions generally barred women, and so had the Knights until, in 1881, women shoe workers in Philadelphia struck in support of their male co-workers and won the right to form their own local assembly. By 1886 probably 50,000 women belonged to the Knights of Labor. Their courage on the picket line prompted Powderly's rueful remark that women "are the best men in the Order." For a handful, like the hosiery worker Leonora M. Barry, the Knights provided a rare chance to take up leadership roles as organizers and officials. For many others, the liberation was more modest, but very real: "timid young girls—girls who have been overworked from their cradle—stand[ing] up bravely . . . swayed . . . by the wrongs heaped upon their comrades, talk[ing] nobly and beautifully of the hope of redress to be found in organization." Similarly, the Knights of Labor grudgingly expanded the opportunity for black workers to join up, recognizing the need for solidarity and, just as important, in deference to the Order's egalitarian principles. The Knights could rightly boast that their "great work has been to organize labor which was previously unorganized."

The American Federation of Labor

In the early 1880s the Knights began to act increasingly like a trade union. Boycott campaigns against the products of "unfair" employers achieved impressive results. With the economy booming and workers in short supply, the Knights began to win strikes, including a major victory against Jay Gould's Southwestern railway system in 1885. Workers flocked into the organization, and its membership jumped from 100,000 to perhaps 700,000 in less than a year. For a brief time, the Knights stood poised as a potential industrial-union movement capable of bringing all workers into its fold.

AMERICAN VOICES

On Strike *H. J. Thomas*

H. J. Thomas, a Welsh iron worker, writes home about a strike wave in the iron mills and coal mines of the Pittsburgh region. Note the mixture of labor dignity, craft pride, and ethnic identity that informs his account. Thomas is a Welshman, but in America he does not consider himself a "foreigner"—that term is reserved for the unskilled Swedish and Bohemian "rubbish" brought in to break the strike.

June 27, 1882 [Pittsburgh, Pennsylvania]

As yet there is no expectation that the strike wounds will be healed and there is little change in the situation. It is true that some mills are working, one in Cleveland, Ohio, one in Apollo, Armstrong County, Pennsylvania, and another near the city of Allegheny. These mills are worked by nonunion and unskilled labor, the sweepings of foreign countries, Swedes and Bohemians, who, it seems, were brought here to make good the shortage by the aristocratic elements for the purpose of bringing down the American workman to the low level in the European countries. No doubt much of this rubbish left their own lands for the good of those countries. Who knows but that the transporting of unskilled foreigners to this country, who undermine the rights of our workmen and help their oppressors to rob them of their just wages for their work and lower the dignity of the American workman, may provide the opportunity for someone in the federal government to put forward a law that will be second to the Chinese bill to prevent foreigners from emigrating to this country for ten or fifteen years.

Let the masters remember that the balance of power is in the hands of the sons of toil by the ballot box. It is a pity that someone does not whisper in the ears of the masters that there are breakers ahead. But this strike is not confined to the iron workers but also to a large number of the coal miners. Two thousand of them have been on strike since the 1st of last April. They are trying to get four cents a bushel for mining coal. . . .

Many of these miners are camping out in harmony like the Apostles long ago. They have two aims for adopting the gypsy life, thrift and to prepare tents if the masters throw them out of their cottages. Remember that the dignity of the workman in the United States is higher than on the Continent of Europe as the division between the rich John and the poor David is lower. . . .

On Saturday, 17th of this month, there was a majestic procession by different branches of industry. There were about thirty thousand in the procession but the rain fell in a flood and half of them fell out. Their banners were many and their mottoes showed their spirit. On one there was the outline of a male skeleton with the following words: "This is all of the man that works for nothing all day. All we ask is enough to make some stuffing." And another was "Competence obtained by honest labor is a blessing. Genius is gold in the mines. Talent is a miner who works and brings it out." Another was "Capital without labor like faith without works is dead."

P.S. Warn our nation from emigrating at this time for the strike is spreading rapidly. It would be too much to forecast what is in store for the sons of toil.

Source: Sigmund Diamond, ed., *The Nation Transformed* (New York: George Braziller, 1963), pp. 26–67.

The rapid growth of the Knights of Labor frightened the national trade unions. They tried to keep their local branches away from the Knights, but without success. The unions then began to insist on a clear separation of roles, with the Knights confined strictly to the field of labor reform. This was partly a battle over turf, but it reflected also a deepening divergence of labor philosophies.

This divergence is perhaps best seen in the debate over the shorter workday. For labor reformers, the need for more leisure arose from the duties workers had "to perform as American citizens and members of society." More leisure for workers was a precondition for a healthy republican society. Increasingly, however, the issue was seized by trade unionists, and they gave the demand for the eight-hour day a more practical bent: it was a way of spreading the available jobs among more workers, of protecting against overwork, and (like higher wages) of providing workers with a better life. "Eight hours for work, eight hours for rest, eight hours for what we will" was the slogan of the trade unions, not the Knights of Labor.

The Haymarket Square Riot. The trade unions set May 1, 1886, as the deadline for achieving the eight-hour day. As the time approached, a wave of strikes and demonstrations broke out. In Chicago, a battle on May 3 at the McCormick agricultural-implement works resulted in the deaths of four strikers. Chicago was a hotbed of American *anarchism*—the revolutionary advocacy of a stateless society—and local anarchists, most of them German immigrants, called a protest meeting the next evening at Haymarket Square. The meeting went off peacefully, but when police moved in at the end to break it up, someone threw a bomb and several policemen were killed or wounded. The anarchist organizers of the rally were charged wtih criminal conspiracy, a legal doctrine so broad as to require no proof of direct involvement in the bombing to justify a finding of guilt. There was, in fact, no evidence linking them to the bombing. Four men were executed, one committed suicide, and the others received long prison sentences. They were victims of one of the great miscarriages of American justice.

Seizing on the popular antiunion hysteria set off by the Haymarket affair, employers took the offensive against the campaign for an eight-hour day. They broke strikes violently, compiled blacklists of defeated strikers, and forced others to sign *yellow-dog contracts* (guarantees that, as a condition of employment, they would not join a union). If trade unionists needed any further confirmation of the tough world in which they lived, they found it in Haymarket and its aftermath.

Samuel Gompers and the AFL. In December 1886, having failed to prevail on the Knights of Labor to desist from union activity, the national trade unions formed the American Federation of Labor (AFL). The AFL embodied the belief of the national unions that they constituted a distinctive movement. The federation, in effect, locked into place the trade-union structure as it had evolved by the 1880s. Underlying this structure was the conviction that workers had to take the world as it was, not as they dreamed it might be.

The architect of the American Federation of Labor, and its president for nearly forty years, was Samuel Gompers. Gompers, a cigar maker from New York City, hammered out the philosophical position that would define American "pure and simple" unionism. First, there would be a steady focus on concrete, short-term gains. Second, unions would rely on economic power rather than politics. Third, they would limit their membership to workers, organized on strictly occupational lines. Finally, the unions strongly rejected the theories and grand schemes that had excited the labor reformers. "No matter how just a cause is," Gompers argued, "unless the cause is backed up with power to enforce it, it is going to be crushed and annihilated."

The steady growth of the trade unions after the formation of the AFL seemed to justify Gompers's confidence that he had hit on the correct formula for the American labor movement. The Knights of Labor faded away. The organization had been hard hit by the antilabor reaction to the Haymarket affair, and after a series of disastrous strikes, it retreated from the trade-union field. Grand Master Workman Powderly turned back to the rhetoric of labor reform. But the appeal to wage earners had disappeared. In its declining years, the Knights survived mainly in small-town America, no longer a workers' movement.

Industrial War

The Homestead Strike. Of America's workers, few had more reason to be satisfied with their lives than the skilled steelworkers of Homestead, Pennsylvania. They earned good wages, lived comfortably, and generally owned their own homes. The town was very much their community, with a municipal government run by officials elected from their own ranks. And in Andrew Carnegie the Homestead workers thought they had a truly sympathetic employer: for had not Good Old Andy said in a famous magazine article that the right of workers to combine was no less sacred than that of capitalists? Or that workers held a kind of moral claim on their jobs that forbade the use of strikebreakers by employers?

Carnegie, however, had other plans. In his view, the union had become too expensive. It deprived his steel company of the full benefits of the advanced machinery he was introducing; and with that machinery, the skills of his workers counted for less. Lacking the stomach for the hard battle ahead, Carnegie hid himself away in his remote castle in Scotland. But he left behind a second-in-command eminently qualified for the job at hand. This was Henry Clay Frick, a former coal baron with a deservedly fearsome reputation as an enemy of trade unionism.

After some perfunctory bargaining, Frick announced that, effective July 1, 1892, the company would no longer deal with the Amalgamated Association of Iron and Steel Workers. If the employees wanted to work, they would have to return on an individual basis. Frick's strategy was already clear. Preparations had been made to fortify the plant so that strikebreakers could be brought in to resume operations and defeat the union. At stake now was not just wage cuts but the defense of an entire way of life. To preserve their "workers' republic," Homesteaders thought they had the right to deny the company access to the plant, and town authorities turned away the county sheriff when he tried to take possession of the plant on behalf of the company. The entire community—women no less than men—mobilized in defense of the union.

At dawn on July 6, two bargeloads of Pinkerton guards were spied approaching Homestead up the Monongahela River. Behind hastily erected barricades, the strikers opened fire, and a bloody battle ensued. When the Pinkertons finally surrendered, they were mercilessly pummeled by the enraged women of Homestead as they retreated to the railway station. Frick appealed to the governor of Pennsylvania, who mobilized the state militia. Homestead was placed under martial law, strike leaders and town officials were arrested on charges of riot, murder, and treason, and the great steelworks was taken over and opened to strikebreakers.

The defeat at Homestead marked the beginning of

the end of trade unionism in the iron and steel industry. Ended too were any lingering illusions about the sanctity of workers' communities such as Homestead. "Men talk like anarchists or lunatics when they insist that the workmen of Homestead have done right," asserted one conservative journal. Nothing could be permitted to interfere with private property or threaten law and order. The Homestead strike ushered in an era of strife in which working people found arrayed against them not only the formidable power of corporate industry but the even more formidable power of their own government.

The Great Pullman Boycott. The fullest demonstration of that hard reality had its origins at a place that seemed an even less likely site for class warfare than Homestead. Pullman, Illinois, was a model factory town, famous for the amenities it offered to workers and the beauty of its landscaping and city plan. The town was named for its creator, George M. Pullman, who had made a great fortune as the inventor and manufacturer of the Pullman sleeping cars that brought comfort and luxury to railway travel. Still, when the Panic of 1893 struck, business fell off and the Pullman Company cut wages. But the rents for company housing, always higher than elsewhere, were not cut, and for many workers take-home pay shrank to pitiful levels.

When a committee finally called on him in May 1894 to present the workers' grievances, Pullman refused to budge. There was no connection between his role as employer and landlord, he insisted. In addition, he fired the committee members.

The strike that ensued might have become no more than a footnote in American labor history but for one thing—the Pullman workers belonged to the American Railway Union (ARU), a rapidly growing industrial union of railroad workers recently formed by the labor leader Eugene V. Debs. In response to the strikers' plea, the ARU directed its members not to handle Pullman sleeping cars, which were operated by the railroads but were owned and serviced by the Pullman Company. This was a classic example of a *labor boycott,* in which force is applied at a secondary point (the railroads) as a way to bring pressure on the primary target (Pullman). Railroad officials, already fearful of the growing power of the ARU, saw the Pullman boycott as their chance to break the union. The General Managers' Association, which represented the railroads serving Chicago, insisted on running the Pullman cars. Since ARU members refused to operate trains with Pullman cars, a far-flung rail strike soon spread across the country and threatened to disrupt the entire economy.

Quite deliberately, the railroad managers maneuvered to bring the federal government into the dispute. Their hook was the U.S. mail cars, which they took care to attach to every train hauling Pullman cars. When strikers tried to stop these trains, the General Managers' Association appealed to President Cleveland to send in troops to protect the U.S. mails and halt the growing violence. It so happened that in Attorney-General Richard Olney, a former railroad lawyer, the General Managers' Association had a direct link to the president. Overriding the protests of the liberal Illinois gov-

The Pullman Strike

Chicago was the hub of the midwestern railwork network, and the strategic center of the battle between the Pullman boycotters and the trunkline railroads. For the strikers, the crucial thing was to keep trains with Pullman cars attached from running, for the railroads, it was to get the trains through at any cost. The stage was thus set for violent confrontation, as is evident in this contemporary drawing of a standoff between armed railroad guards and angry strikers.

ernor, John P. Altgeld, Cleveland sent in federal troops. When this tactic failed to quell the popular resistance, Olney got court injunctions prohibiting the ARU leaders from conducting the strike. Debs and his subordinates refused to obey; they were held in contempt of court and jailed. Now leaderless and totally uncoordinated, the strike quickly disintegrated.

But no one could doubt what had defeated the great Pullman boycott of 1894: it had been crushed by the naked use of government power on behalf of the railroad companies.

American Radicalism in the Making

Oppression does not radicalize all its victims, but for some, it does. And when social injustice is most painfully felt, when the underlying power realities stand most openly revealed, the process of radicalization speeds up. Such was the case during the depression years of the 1890s. Out of the industrial strife of that decade emerged the main forces of twentieth-century American radicalism.

Eugene Debs and American Socialism. Very little in Eugene Debs's background suggested that he would one day become the nation's preeminent socialist. Born in 1855 of middle-class French-Alsatian parents, Debs grew up believing in the essential goodness of American society as he found it in his home town of Terre Haute, Indiana, a prosperous midwestern railroad center. Active in the Democratic party and very popular in the community, Debs might have made a career in politics or business. Instead, he returned to the railway yards where he had worked as a boy, became involved in the local labor movement, and in 1880, at the age of twenty-five, was elected national secretary-treasurer and journal editor of the Brotherhood of Locomotive Firemen.

This was one of the craft unions that had emerged to represent the skilled operating trades on the railroads. It was highly conservative, opposed to strikes, and indifferent to the well-being of the mass of low-paid track and yard laborers. This began to bother Debs, and in 1892 he unexpectedly resigned from his comfortable union post to devote himself to a new organization—the American Railway Union—that would organize all railroad workers irrespective of skill, that is, an *industrial union.*

The Pullman boycott, as it developed into a life-and-death struggle, visibly changed Debs. It had become "a contest between the producing classes and the money power of the country," Debs declared. Debs was sentenced to six months in the federal penitentiary—not for having violated any specific law, but for refusing to obey court orders he knew to be trumped-up and prejudicial. He came out of jail an avowed radical, committed to a lifelong struggle against a system that enabled employers to enlist the powers of government to enforce their arbitrary rule over working people. Initially Debs identified himself as a Populist, but he quickly gravitated toward the Socialist camp.

German refugees had brought the ideas of Karl Marx, the German radical philosopher, to America after the failed 1848 revolutions in Europe. Marx offered a powerful economic critique of capitalism. His prescription for revolution through class struggle inspired the most durable of radical movements throughout the industrial world. Although little noticed in most parts of American society, Marxist socialism struck deep roots in the growing German-American communities of Chicago and New York. In 1877 the Socialist Labor Party was formed, and from that time onward Marxist socialism maintained a continuing, if narrowly based, presence in American politics.

When Eugene Debs appeared in their midst in 1897, the Socialists were in a state of crisis. Their leader, Daniel De Leon, was a brilliant theorist but a poor political manager. He preferred an ideologically pure party to one that tried to appeal for the popular vote. De Leon's rigid beliefs prompted a revolt within the Socialist Labor Party, in which Debs joined. When the rival Socialist Party of America was formed in 1901, it was with the aim of building a broad-based political movement.

A spellbinding campaigner, Debs was a superb spokesman for his party. He had the common touch, and he attracted a devoted national following. Debs talked socialism in an American idiom, making Marxism understandable and persuasive to many ordinary Americans. Under him the new party began to break down ethnic barriers and attract American-born voters. Many trade unionists, disillusioned as Debs himself had been by the events of the 1890s, went through the same kind of radical evolution and joined up in large numbers. In Texas, Oklahoma, and Minnesota, socialism exerted a powerful appeal among cotton and wheat farmers. The party was also highly successful at attracting women activists. Inside of a decade, with a national network of branches and state organizations, the Socialist party had become a force to be reckoned with in American politics.

Western Radicalism. In the meantime, a different brand of American radicalism was taking shape in the West. After many years of mostly friendly labor relations, the situation in the western mining camps turned ugly during the 1890s. Powerful new corporations were taking over, and they wanted to be rid of the miners' union, the Western Federation of Miners (WFM). Moreover, silver and copper prices became increasingly unprofitable in the early 1890s, bringing pressure to cut the miners' wages. When strikes resulted, they took a particularly violent turn.

In 1892 at Coeur d'Alene, a silver-mining district in northern Idaho, striking miners engaged in gun battles with company guards, sent a car of explosive powder careening into the Frisco Mine, and threatened to blow up processing plants. Martial law was then declared, federal troops came in, the strikers were crowded into "bullpens" (enclosed stockades), and the strike was broken. Similarly violent strikes took place at Cripple Creek, Colorado, in 1894, at Leadville, Colorado, in 1896, and again in Coeur d'Alene in 1899.

In these western strikes, government intervention was particularly naked and unrestrained. This was partly a reaction to the level of violence, but it stemmed also from the character of politics in the lightly settled western states: either the miners would dominate state politics—as they did in coalition with the Populists during their successful strike at Cripple Creek in 1894—or, as was increasingly true, the mine owners would dominate, with disastrous consequences for the miners.

The union leaders—Ed Boyce, Charles Moyer, "Big Bill" Haywood—all served their time in the bullpens or on the barricades. And they drew the appropriately grim conclusions. Initially their radicalism led them, like Debs, into the Socialist party. But they also were strongly inclined toward direct action. In 1897, WFM President Boyce called on all union miners to arm themselves with rifles, and his rhetoric—that the wage system was "slavery in its worst form"—had a very hard edge. Any lingering faith in the political process died in the Colorado state elections of 1904, after the suppression of bitterly fought strikes across the state in the previous two years. The miners thought they had defeated their archenemy, the Republican governor James H. Peabody, only to have the Colorado Supreme Court overturn the election results and reinstall Peabody (who, by prearrangement, resigned in favor of his lieutenant governor).

In 1905 the Western Federation of Miners led the way in creating a new radical labor movement, the Industrial Workers of the World. Although the IWW initially had links to the Socialist party, it swiftly repudiated political action and settled on its own radical course. The Wobblies, as IWW members were called, fervently supported the Marxist class struggle—but strictly in the industrial field. By action at the point of production and by an unending struggle against employers—ultimately by a general strike—they believed that the workers themselves would bring about a revolution. A workers' society would emerge, run directly by the workers through their industrial unions. The term *syndicalism* describes this brand of workers' radicalism.

In both its major forms—the politically oriented Socialist party and the syndicalist IWW—American radicalism flourished after the crisis of the 1890s, but only on a limited basis. Socialists and Wobblies lived, in a sense, on the tolerance of society. They would later be crushed without ceremony. Nevertheless, they served a larger purpose. American radicalism, by its sheer vitality, bore witness to what was exploitative and unjust in the new industrial order.

Summary

American industrialism took its modern shape during the last decades of the nineteenth century. Heavy industry developed in these years, producing in vast quantities the capital goods and energy required by an expanding manufacturing economy. An efficient railway system provided access to national markets. The scale of enterprise grew very large, and the vertically integrated firm became the predominant form of business organization. A managerial revolution enabled entrepreneurs to gain mastery over the complex business organizations they were building. Only in the South did prevailing conditions—in particular, its insulated, low-wage labor market—retard the growth of an advanced industrial economy.

Workers felt these developments most strongly in the loss of control over the labor process. Mass production, the high-volume output of standardized products, had the effect of de-skilling workers and replacing them with machinery. Scientific management, the brainchild of Frederick W. Taylor, cut further into the traditional autonomy of American workers. The enormous demand for labor in the meantime led to a great influx of immigrants into the industrial economy, making ethnic diversity a distinctive feature of the American working class. Gender likewise defined occupational opportunity. Women joined the labor force in growing numbers, but almost universally they were subjected to a sex-typing process that relegated them to "women's work," always at wage rates below those of men.

The late nineteenth century gave rise to the American labor movement in its modern form. In the Knights of Labor, anticapitalist labor reform enjoyed one final surge during the mid 1880s, then succumbed to the "pure and simple" unionism of the American Federation of Labor. The bitter industrial warfare of the 1890s, however, stirred new radical impulses, leading on the one hand to the political socialism of Eugene Debs and on the other to the industrial radicalism of the IWW.

TOPIC FOR RESEARCH

The Making of the Modern Labor Movement

For much of the nineteenth century, American workers debated a defining question: What should be the goal of the labor movement? By the 1880s two answers had emerged: *labor reform,* the demand of the Knights of Labor for fundamental change in the economic system, and *pure-and-simple unionism,* the efforts of the American Federation of Labor to extract the best possible terms for workers from the existing system. Choose either the Knights or the AFL as the subject of your investigation. What were the organization's main goals, and why did it adopt those positions? What were some of the steps it took to achieve its goals, and how successful was it? For a more ambitious paper, compare and contrast both organizations, and explain why the "pure-and-simple" strategy of the AFL eventually prevailed.

The standard book on the struggle between labor reform and trade unionism is Gerald N. Grob, *Workers and Utopia, 1865–1900* (1961). For the Knights of Labor, it should be supplemented by Leon Fink, *Workingmen's Democracy: The Knights of Labor and American Politics* (1983), which captures the cultural dimensions of labor reform not seen by earlier historians. The pioneering work on the American labor movement is John R. Commons et al., *History of Labor in the United States* (4 vols., 1918–1935); volumes 2 and 4 cover the period of this chapter. The most recent survey, incorporating much of the latest scholarship, is Bruce Laurie, *Artisans Into Workers: Labor in Nineteenth Century America* (1989). The clash of ideas, however, is best understood through the words of the two leading exponents, Terence V. Powderly of the Knights, and Samuel Gompers of the AFL. Both have left autobiographies—Powderly, *The Path I Trod* (1940), and Gompers, *Seventy Years of Life and Labor* (2 vols., 1925). Moreover, the letters and papers of Gompers are being published in an authoritative multivolume edition by Stuart B. Kaufman. The volumes through the 1890s have appeared, and they contain a rich documentary record of the dispute. In Melvyn Dubofsky and Warren Van Tine, eds., *Labor Leaders in America* (1986), there are excellent brief biographies of Powderly and Gompers, with up-to-date bibliographical guides for further reading.

You may prefer to examine the views of the Knights and the AFL on another issue: the place of women and blacks in the labor movement. The starting points are two books by Philip S. Foner, *Women and the American Labor Movement From Colonial Times to the Eve of World War I* (1979), and *Organized Labor and the Black Worker* (1974).

BIBLIOGRAPHY

A Maturing Industrial Economy

The most useful introduction to the economic history of this period is Edward C. Kirkland, *Industry Comes of Age, 1860–1897* (1961). A more sophisticated analysis can be found in W. Elliot Brownlee, *Dynamics of Ascent* (rev. ed., 1979). For essays on many of the topics covered by this chapter, consult Glenn Porter, ed., *Encyclopedia of American Economic History* (3 vols., 1980).

On railroads, a convenient introduction is John F. Stover, *American Railroads* (1970). The growth of the railroads as an integrated system has been treated in George R. Taylor and Irene D. Neu, *The American Railway Network, 1861–1890* (1956). Thomas Cochran, *Railroad Leaders, 1845–1890* (1953), is a pioneering study of the industry's entrepreneurs. Julius Grodinsky, *Jay Gould: His Business Career, 1867–1892* (1957), is a complex study demonstrating the contributions this railroad buccaneer made to the transportation system. Books like Cochran's and Grodinsky's have gone a long way to resurrect Gilded Age businessmen from the debunking tradition first set forth with great power in Matthew Josephson, *Robber Barons: Great American Fortunes* (1934). Peter Temin, *Iron and Steel in the Nineteenth Century* (1964), is the best treatment of that industry. Joseph F. Wall, *Andrew Carnegie* (1970), is the definitive biography of the great steelmaster. Equally definitive on the oil king is Allan Nevins, *A Study in Power: John D. Rockefeller* (2 vols., 1953). Harold C. Passer, *The Electrical Manufacturers, 1875–1900* (1953), treats both the entrepreneurial and technological aspects of this emergent industry. On the development of mass production, the key book is David A. Hounsell, *From the American System to Mass Production, 1800–1932* (1984).

On the emergence of modern management, the magisterial work is Alfred D. Chandler, *The Visible Hand: The Managerial Revolution in American Business* (1977), not an easy book but one that will amply repay the labors of the interested student. Also worth reading is Chandler's earlier *Strategy and Structure: Chapters in the History of Industrial Enterprise* (1962). On the monetary system, the definitive book is Milton Friedman and Anna J. Schwartz, *Monetary History of the United States, 1867–1960* (1963).

On the New South, the standard work has long been C. Vann Woodward, *Origins of the New South, 1877–1913* (1951). A brilliant reinterpretation of the causes of the South's economic retardation is Gavin Wright, *Old South, New South: Revolutions in the Southern Economy Since the Civil War* (1986).

The World of Work

To understand the impact of industrialism on American workers, three collections of essays make the best starting points: Herbert G. Gutman, *Work, Culture and Society in Industrializing America* (1976); David Montgomery, *Workers' Control in America* (1979); and Michael S. Frisch and Daniel J. Walkowitz, eds., *Working-Class America: Essays on Labor, Community and American Society* (1983). On the introduction of Taylorism, the most useful book is Daniel Nelson, *Managers and Workers: Origins of the New Factory System* (1975). The impact of Taylorism on American workers is treated with great insight in David Montgomery, *The Fall of the House of Labor: The Workplace, the State, and American Labor Activism, 1865–1925* (1987). For a sweeping analysis of long-term change in American labor relations, see David M. Gordon et al., *Segmented Work, Divided Workers: The Historical Transformation of Labor in the United States* (1982). There are two valuable recent collections of essays on immigrant workers: Richard Ehrlich, ed., *Immigrants in Industrial America* (1977), and Dirk Hoerder, ed., *American Labor and Immigration History, 1877–1920: Recent European Research* (1983). David Brody, *Steelworkers in America: The Nonunion Era* (1960), examines workers in a single industry. John Bodnar, *Immigration and Industrialization: Ethnicity in an American Mill Town* (1977), is an important case study of a single community. On women workers, the best introduction is Alice Kessler-Harris, *Out to Work* (1982). Leslie Woodcock Tentler, *Wage-Earning Women: Industrial Work and Family Life, 1900–1930* (1979), and Mary H. Blewett, *Men, Women, and Work: Class, Gender, and Protest in the New England Shoe Industry, 1780–1910* (1988), are thoughtful treatments of the impact of industrial work on female identity. On black workers, the best introduction is William H. Harris, *The Harder We Run: Black Workers Since the Civil War* (1982).

The Labor Movement

The history of the Knights of Labor and the AFL can be studied in the books cited in the Topic for Research. The founder of the AFL is the subject of a lively brief biography by Harold Livesay, *Samuel Gompers and Organized Labor in America* (1978). Among the many books on individual unions, Robert Christie, *Empire in Wood* (1956), best reveals the way pure-and-simple unionism worked out in practice. On industrial conflict, the most vivid book is Robert V. Bruce, *1877: Year of Violence* (1959). Stanley Buder, *Pullman: An Experiment in Industrial Order and Community Planning, 1880–1930* (1967), provides an informed account of the great Pullman strike and places it in its local context. The best book on the IWW is Melvyn Dubofsky, *We Shall Be All* (1969). On socialism, David Shannon, *The Socialist Party of America* (1955), remains the standard account. There is, however, a fine biography of that party's leader that supersedes previous studies: Nick Salvatore, *Eugene V. Debs: Citizen and Socialist* (1982). A dimension of American radicalism long neglected has recently received sensitive attention in Mari Jo Buhle, *Women and American Socialism, 1870–1920* (1982).

TIMELINE

1869	Knights of Labor founded in Philadelphia
1872	Montgomery Ward, first mail-order house, founded
	Andrew Carnegie starts construction of Edgar Thompson steel works near Pittsburgh
1873	Panic of 1873 ushers in economic depression
1875	John Wanamaker establishes first department store in Philadelphia
1878	Gustavus Swift introduces refrigerator car
1886	Haymarket Square bombing in Chicago American Federation of Labor (AFL) founded
1890	U.S. passes Britain in producing iron and steel
1892	Homestead strike crushed
1893	Panic of 1893 starts depression of the 1890s
1894	President Cleveland sends troops to break Pullman boycott
1895	Frederick A. Taylor explains scientific management in "A Piece Rate System" essay
	Southeastern European immigration exceeds northern European immigration for the first time
1901	Eugene V. Debs helps found Socialist party
1905	Industrial Workers of the World (IWW) founded

Bandanna, 1888 Election Memorabilia

During the late nineteenth century, politics became a vibrant part of America's culture. Party paraphernalia, like the bandanna above, flooded the country. (Museum of American Political Life)

CHAPTER 19 *The Politics of Late Nineteenth-Century America*

In times of national ferment, as a rule, public life becomes magnified. Leaders emerge. Electoral campaigns debate great issues. The powers of government expand. That had certainly been true of the Civil War era. During the crises of Union and Reconstruction, the nation's public institutions had been tested to the utmost. The final challenge had occurred over the contested presidential election of 1876. In 1877, with the Republican Rutherford B. Hayes safely settled in the White House and the last federal troops withdrawn from the South, the era of sectional crisis finally ended. Political life went on, but was drained of its earlier drama. In the 1880s there were no Lincolns, no great national debates, and little exercise of governmental power. Public life was vigorous in other ways—highly organized and rife with cultural conflict—but not through the formal, public processes by which a nation confronts its central concerns. The politics of the status quo had arrived.

The Politics of the Status Quo (1877–1893)

The National Scene

There were five presidents from 1877 to 1893: Rutherford B. Hayes (Republican, 1877–1881), James A. Garfield (Republican, 1881), Chester A. Arthur (Republican, 1881–1885), Grover Cleveland (Democrat, 1885–1889), and Benjamin Harrison (Republican, 1889–1893). All were estimable men. Hayes, Garfield, and Harrison boasted distinguished war records. Hayes had served well as governor of Ohio for three terms, and Garfield had been a congressional leader for many years. Arthur, despite his cloudy reputation as a machine politician, had demonstrated fine administrative skills as head of the New York Customs House. Cleveland had made his mark as reform mayor of Buffalo and governor of New York. None was a charismatic leader, and only Cleveland, the lone Democrat of the lot, was an assertive public figure. But circumstances more than personal qualities explain why these presidents did not make a larger mark on history.

Their biggest job was to dispense political patronage. Under the spoils system, government appointments were treated as rewards for those who had served the victorious party. Reform of this system became a national issue after Charles Guiteau, a disappointed office seeker, assassinated President Garfield in 1881. The Pendleton Act of 1883 created a list of civil-service jobs to be filled on the basis of examinations administered by the new Civil Service Commission. The list originally included only 10 percent of all federal jobs. But each president added to it—generally at the close of his term in order to safeguard some of his appointees. But handling patronage remained a preoccupation in the White House. When the Democrats regained the presidency in 1884 for the first time in nearly thirty years, the pent-up hunger for jobs by the party faithful nearly overwhelmed Grover Cleveland. He was known to complain bitterly about the "damned, everlasting clatter for

Grover Cleveland

In the years after Reconstruction, Americans did not look for charismatic personalities or dramatic leadership in their presidents. They preferred men who accepted the limits of executive power, men of "sound conservatism." Grover Cleveland fitted this bill to perfection. For political reformers, Cleveland had the additional virtues of independence and personal integrity. He best represented the late nineteenth-century ideal of the American president.

office." The standards of public administration did rise measurably, but there was no American counterpart to the elite professional civil services taking shape in England and Germany in these years.

Other than dispensing patronage, presidents did not have a lot to do. As late as 1897, White House staff consisted of half a dozen assistants, plus a few clerks, doorkeepers, and messengers. The president exerted little control over the federal bureaucracy. Budgetary matters were not his province, but Congress's, and federal agencies accordingly paid much more heed to Capitol Hill and the key money-dispensing committees than to the White House.

The functions of the executive branch were, in any event, very limited in these years. Of the 100,000 federal employees in 1880, fully 56 percent worked for the Post Office. The largest item of expenditure—over a third of the 1890 federal budget—went for veterans' pensions. During the 1880s, the important government departments—Treasury, State, War, Navy, Interior—were sleepy places carrying on largely routine duties. Virtually all federal income came from customs duties and the excise tax on liquor and tobacco. These sources produced more money than the government spent. The problem of how to reduce the federal surplus ranked as one of the most troublesome issues of the 1880s.

As for setting a national agenda, this was—unlike in Lincoln's day, or our own—not to be looked for from the White House. "The office of President is essentially executive in nature," Cleveland insisted, not policy making. In fact, as a Democratic president facing a hostile Republican Senate, Cleveland did begin to assert himself on policy matters, but in an entirely negative way: in his first term, he vetoed three times as many bills as did all the previous presidents combined.

Congressional Government. On matters of national policy, the presidents took a back seat to Congress. But Congress was not well set up to do its work. In the House of Representatives, the rules had grown so complicated and numerous that they frequently brought business to a standstill. Party leaders were unable to exert discipline over the members of either house, and neither party ever stayed in power long enough to push through a coherent legislative program. From 1877 to 1893, neither Democrats nor Republicans controlled both houses for more than a single two-year term. Most of the time, the Democrats controlled the House, and the Republicans the Senate. Consequently, the ability of Congress to take forceful action was extremely limited.

Neither party, moreover, had much stomach for taking strong positions. Historically, they represented somewhat different traditions—the Democrats favoring states' rights and limited government, the Republicans supporting government encouragement of economic development. But after Reconstruction neither party was eager to translate these differences into well-defined positions. On most leading issues of the day—civil-service reform, the currency, and regulation of the railroads—the divisions occurred within the parties, not between them. The laws Congress passed could not be clearly identified as either Democratic or Republican.

The tariff was something of an exception. From Lincoln's day onward, high duties protected American industry against imported goods. It was an article of Republican faith, as President Harrison said in 1892, that "the protective system . . . has been a mighty instrument for the development of the national wealth."

The Democrats, free traders by tradition, regularly attacked Republican protectionism.

Actually, however, the parties disagreed only about the degree of protection. Congressmen voted according to their constituents' interests on tariffs, regardless of party rhetoric. As a result, every tariff bill was a patchwork of bargains among special interests. In 1887, President Cleveland made a mighty effort to sharpen the battle. He devoted his entire annual message to Congress to the need for tariff reform and campaigned for reelection on that issue. His narrow defeat seemed to confirm the political wisdom of evading big issues. "They told me it would hurt the party," he later wrote. "Perhaps I made a mistake from the party standpoint; but damn it, it was right. I had at least that satisfaction."

The Plumed Knight

In the fierce party politics of the Gilded Age, the political cartoon became a polished art form, and its high priest was Thomas Nast. In this cartoon, Nast pillories James G. Blaine, celebrated as the "Plumed Knight" among his Republican supporters, but fatally damaged in his ambitions to become president by reports that as Speaker of the House of Representatives he had taken bribes from an Arkansas railroad. Nast depicts the "knight" Blaine jousting in a tournament, with this ironic comment: "The 'Great American' Game of Public Office for Private Gain."

Electoral Politics. The major parties treated issues gingerly partly because they feared each other. The Democrats, in retreat immediately after the Civil War, quickly regrouped and, by the end of Reconstruction, stood on virtually equal terms with the Republicans. Every presidential election from 1876 to 1892 was decided by a thin margin, and neither party gained commanding control over Congress. Political caution seemed wise; any false move on national issues might tip the balance to the other side.

The Englishman James Bryce, accustomed to the philosophical divisions between Tories and Liberals, grumbled about the indistinctness of American politics. "Neither party has any principles, any distinctive tenets," he wrote in *The American Commonwealth* (1888). Perhaps Lord Bryce exaggerated when he added, "All has been lost, except office or the hope of it." But electoral success had unquestionably taken precedence over party principle.

This was evident particularly in the way the Republican party treated its Civil War legacy. The major unfinished business after 1877 involved the needs of the former slaves in the South. The Blair Education bill, which would have appropriated federal funds to combat illiteracy, was on the Republican agenda at the end of the 1880s, but did not pass into law. More threatening to the South was the Lodge Election bill, which would have provided federal protection for black voters in southern congressional elections. This last gasp of Reconstruction politics died in 1890. The Republican administrations, more interested in building white support in the South, back-pedaled on the race issue and gradually abandoned the blacks to their fate.

The Republicans were not so willing to abandon their identification with the Civil War itself, however. In every election campaign Republican orators "waved the bloody shirt" against the "treasonous" Democrats. Service in the Union army gave candidates a strong claim to public office. One-third of the Republican congressmen of the 1880s had a war record, and veterans' benefits always stood high on the Republican agenda. The Democrats played the same game in the South as the defenders of the Lost Cause. Bryce criticized American politicians for "clinging too long to outworn issues and neglecting . . . the problems which now perplex the country."

Alternatively, campaigns could descend into sideshows. In the hard-fought election of 1884, the personal reputations of the candidates overshadowed everything else. Was it more important that Grover Cleveland, a man of impeccable public honor, had years earlier fathered an illegitimate child? Or that James G. Blaine, perhaps the most gifted Republican of his generation, had taken favors from the railroads? In the midst of all the mudslinging, the issues got lost.

The characteristics of public life in the 1880s—the inactivity of the federal government, the evasiveness of both political parties, and the absorption in politics for its own sake—derived ultimately from the conviction that little was at stake in public affairs. In 1887, President Cleveland vetoed a small appropriation for drought-stricken Texas farmers with the remark that "though the people support the Government, the Government should not support the people." Government activity was in itself considered a bad thing. All that the state can do, said Republican Senator Roscoe Conkling, "is to clear the way of impediments and dangers, and leave every class and every individual free and safe in the exertions and pursuits of life." Conkling was expressing the political corollary to the doctrine of *laissez faire*—the mainstream belief of the late nineteenth century that that government was best which governed least.

The Ideology of Individualism

In 1885 at the height of the Knights of Labor, the cotton manufacturer Edward Atkinson gave a talk to the textile workers of Providence, Rhode Island. They had, he told them, no cause for discontent. "There is always plenty of room on the front seats in every profession, every trade, every art, every industry . . . There are men in this audience who will fill some of those seats, but they won't be boosted into them from behind." (There were certainly women as well in the audience—at least half of the Rhode Island labor force was female—but, as was characteristic of his times, Atkinson assumed economic opportunity to be of interest only to men.) Every man, Atkinson continued, gets what he deserves. For example, Cornelius Vanderbilt had amassed a fortune of $200 million by building the New York Central Railroad. Atkinson went through some rapid calculations. Every person in the audience consumed about a barrel of flour a year. In 1865, it had cost $3.45 to ship that barrel from Chicago to Providence. In 1885, the New York Central carried it for 68 cents, taking 14 cents as profit, while the workingman saved nearly $3. "Wasn't Vanderbilt a cheap man for you to employ as a teamster?" Atkinson asked. "Do you grudge him the fourteen cents?"

Atkinson's homely talk went to the roots of conservative American thought—that any man, however humble, could rise as far as his talents would carry him; that every person received his just reward, great or small; and that the success of the individual, so encouraged, contributed to the progress of the whole. How persuasive the workers listening to Atkinson found his message we have no way of knowing. But the confidence with which Atkinson presented his case is evidence of the continuing appeal of the ideology of individualism in the age of industrial expansion.

Facing the World

The cover of this Horatio Alger novel (1893) captures to perfection the myth of opportunity that Edward Atkinson extolled to his audience of textile workers. Our hero "Harry Vane" is a poor but earnest lad, valise packed, ready to make his way in the world and, despite the many obstacles thrown in his path, sure to succeed. In some 135 books, Horatio Alger repeated this story, with minor variations, for an eager reading public in the millions.

A wide variety of popular writings trumpeted the individualist creed, from the rags-to-riches tales of Horatio Alger to the stream of success manuals with such titles as *Thoughts for the Young Men of America, or a Few Practical Words of Advice to those Born in Poverty and Destined to be Reared in Orphanages* (1871). It was a lesson celebrated in the lives of such self-made men as Andrew Carnegie, whose book *Triumphant Democracy* (1886) paid homage to a nation in which a penniless Scottish child could rise from bobbin boy to steel magnate.

From the pulpit came the assurances of the Episcopal bishop William Lawrence of Massachusetts that "Godliness is in league with riches." In American Protestantism, there was a venerable tradition going back to the Puritans that linked success in one's earthly calling to the promise of eternal salvation. This link enabled a conservative ministry to make morally reassuring the furious acquisitiveness of industrial America. "To secure wealth is an honorable ambition," intoned the Baptist minister Russell H. Conwell in his lecture "Acres of Diamonds." "Money is power. Every good man and woman ought to strive for power, to do good with it when obtained." This notion of *stewardship*—that wealth carried with it a social obligation—Andrew Carnegie elevated into a formal doctrine that he called "the gospel of wealth." Carnegie argued that it was the responsibility of the rich to put their money to good use. This should be done not by coddling the less privileged, Carnegie said, but by providing the libraries, education, and cultural and scientific institutions by which they might prepare themselves for life's challenges.

Social Darwinism. American individualism drew strong intellectual support from the most important scientific theory of the age. In his great book *On the Origin of Species* (1859), the English naturalist Charles Darwin had presented a bold hypothesis to explain the evolution of plants and animals. In nature, Darwin wrote, all living things struggle and compete. Particular members of a species are born with characteristics that better enable them to survive. Future generations inherit these characteristics, and the species evolves. This process of evolution, which Darwin called *natural selection,* created a revolution in biological science.

Although not intended by Darwin, his theory also had an enormous impact on the study of human society. Drawing on Darwin, the British philosopher Herbert Spencer developed an elaborate analysis of how society evolved through constant competition and "the survival of the fittest." Social Darwinism, as Spencer's ideas became known, was championed in America by William Graham Sumner, a Yale sociology professor. Competition, said Sumner, is a law of nature that "can no more be done away with than gravitation." Furthermore, "if we do not like the survival of the fittest, we have only one possible alternative, and that is the survival of the unfittest. The former is the law of civilization; the latter is the law of anti-civilization." And who are the fittest? "The millionaires . . . They may fairly be regarded as the naturally selected agents of society. They get high wages and live in luxury, but the bargain is a good one for society."

Social Darwinists also argued that social processes must be permitted to take their course. "The great stream of time and earthly things will sweep on just the same in spite of us," Sumner wrote in his famous essay "The Absurd Attempt to Make the World Over" (1894). "That is why it is the greatest folly of which a man can be capable to sit down with a slate and pencil to plan out a new social world." As for the government, it had "at bottom . . . two chief things . . . with which to deal. They are the property of men and the honor of women. These it has to defend against crime." The political meaning of Social Darwinism was clear. As Sumner put it: "Minimize to the utmost the relations of the state and industry."

The Supremacy of the Courts. This antigovernment appeal not only paralyzed political initiative. It also shifted power away from the executive and legislative branches. "The task of constitutional government," declared Sumner, "is to devise institutions which shall come into play at critical periods to prevent the abusive control of the powers of a state by the controlling classes in it." Sumner meant the judiciary. From the 1870s onward, the courts increasingly took the role that he assigned to them.

During this period the states, rather than the federal government, took primary responsibility under their police powers for regulating the economy. So it was against the states that the courts began a concerted attack. The number of decisions striking down state social welfare and regulatory laws rose markedly in the 1880s.

The Supreme Court's crucial weapon in this campaign was the Fourteenth Amendment (1868), which prohibited the states from depriving "any person of life, liberty, or property, without due process of law." The due-process clause had been intended to protect the civil rights of the former slaves. But due process protected the property rights and contractual liberty of "any person," and the Supreme Court expanded the meaning of "person" to include corporations. So understood, the Fourteenth Amendment became an effective means of preventing the states from regulating business activity.

The Supreme Court erected similar barriers against the federal government through narrow interpretations of the Constitution. It ruled in 1895 that the federal power to regulate interstate commerce did not cover manufacturing and that the federal power to tax did not extend to personal incomes. And where federal power was undeniable—as in the regulation of railroads—the Supreme Court narrowly limited the exercise of that power. It reserved for itself the oversight of decisions that invaded property interests, such as how much railroads could charge their customers. With increasing aggressiveness, the courts took over the shaping of public policy on economic affairs.

Power conferred status. The legal profession and the courts, not politics, attracted the ablest people and held the public's esteem. A Wisconsin judge boasted: "The bench symbolizes on earth the throne of divine justice . . . . Law in its highest sense is the will of God." Judicial supremacy reflected the degree to which the ideology of individualism had become dominant in industrial America; it testified also to the low esteem to which American politics sank after Reconstruction.

Cultural Politics

Yet, for all the criticism leveled against it, politics still figured centrally in the nation's life. Proportionately more voters turned out in presidential elections from 1876 to 1892 than at any other time in American history. Party loyalty ran high, with little change from one election to the next. This loyalty manifested itself in high rates of party membership. Among Republican voters in New York City, a fourth were dues-paying party members. National conventions attracted huge crowds. "The excitement, the mental and physical strains," remarked an Indiana Republican after the 1888 convention, "are surpassed only by prolonged battle in actual warfare, as I have been told by officers of the Civil War who later engaged in convention struggles." The convention he described had nominated the colorless Benjamin Harrison on a routine platform. What was all the excitement about? Why did politics mean so much to late nineteenth-century Americans?

For one thing, politics had become a vibrant part of the nation's culture. The journalist George M. Towle told an English audience that America "is a land of conventions and assemblies, where it is the most natural thing in the world for people to get together in meetings, where almost every event is the occasion for speechmaking." Spellbinding orators like Herbert G. Ingersoll drew enormous crowds at Republican rallies. During the election season, the party faithful marched in impressive torchlight parades. Party paraphernalia flooded the country—handkerchiefs, mugs, posters, and buttons emblazoned with the Democratic donkey or the Republican elephant, symbols that had been adopted in the 1870s. In 1888, pictures of the presidential hopefuls appeared on cards, like baseball players, packed into Honest Long Cut tobacco. The campaigns had the suspense of baseball pennant races plus the excitement of the circus coming to town. In an age before movies and radio, politics ranked as one of the great American forms of mass entertainment.

Party loyalty was a deadly serious matter, however. Civil War emotions lasted a long time in both North and South. The Ohio Republican party, recalled the urban reformer Brand Whitlock, was "a synonym for patriotism, another name for the nation. It was inconceivable that any self-respecting person should be a Democrat." The two parties did, in fact, represent different sorts of people. Republicans tended to have higher incomes, and they prided themselves on being the respectable elements of northern society. Senator George F. Hoar of Massachusetts described them as the people "who do the work of piety and charity in our churches . . . administer the school systems, own and till their own farms . . . perform the skilled labor in the shops."

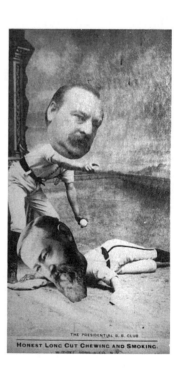

The Presidential B.B. Club (1888)

On the left, Grover Cleveland is the baseman; at center Benjamin Harrison is at bat; and, on the right, Cleveland tags Harrison out—not, alas, the right prediction, since Harrison won the 1888 election.

Ethnocultural Politics. More important than class, however, were religion and ethnic background. The two parties drew on different ethnic and cultural segments of society. Statistically, Democrats outside the South tended to be foreign-born and Catholic, while Republicans tended to be native-born and Protestant. Among Protestants, the more pietistic the theology—that is, the more personal and direct the person's relationship to God—the more likely he or she was to be a Republican. In political terms, this translated into a party policy favorable to using the powers of the state to legislate public morality and regulate individual behavior. The Democrats, on the other hand, favored "the largest individual liberty consistent with public order."

During the 1880s ethnic tensions began to build up in many cities. Education became an arena of bitter conflict. One issue was the place of foreign languages in schools. Immigrant groups, especially the Germans, wanted their children taught in their own language. However, native-born Americans pushed through laws making English the language of instruction. In St. Louis, a heavily German city, the long-standing policy of teaching German to all students was overturned after an acrimonious campaign.

Religion was an even more divisive school issue. The use of the King James Version of the Bible in school angered Catholics. They also fought a losing battle over public aid for parochial schools. By 1900 such aid had been prohibited by twenty-three states. In Boston a furious controversy broke out in 1888 over the use of an anti-Catholic history text. When the school board withdrew the offending book, angry Protestants mounted a campaign to throw the moderates off the board and put the text back into the curriculum.

Similar tensions developed over the regulation of public morals. Evangelical Protestants renewed their efforts to enforce the so-called blue laws, which restricted activity on Sundays. When Nebraska banned Sunday baseball, the state supreme court approved the law as a blow struck in "the contest between Christianity and wrong." But German and Irish Catholics, who saw nothing evil in a bit of fun on Sunday, considered blue laws a violation of their personal freedom.

The same kind of ethnocultural conflict flared over the liquor question. In a speech introducing the first constitutional amendment for national prohibition in 1876, Senator Henry W. Blair of New Hampshire laid down a challenge to his ethnic opponent: "Upon discussion of this issue Irishman and German will in due time demonstrate that they are Americans." Although the Blair amendment languished, the antiliquor movement intensified. Many states adopted strict licensing and local-option laws governing the sale and consumption of alcoholic beverages. Indiana permitted drinking, but only joylessly in rooms containing "no devices for amusement or music . . . of any kind."

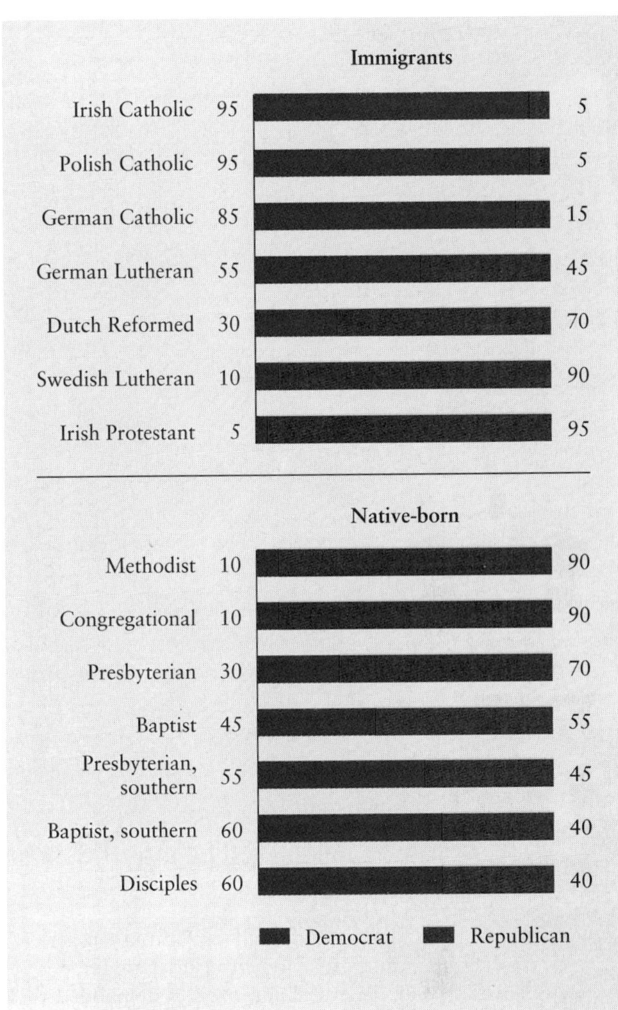

FIGURE 19.1

Ethnocultural Voting Patterns in the Midwest, 1870–1892

The hottest issues of the day—education, the liquor question, and observance of the Sabbath—were contested along ethnic and religious lines. Because they were also party issues—more so than tariffs, currency, or civil-service reform—they gave deep significance to party affiliation. Crusading Methodists thought of Republicans as the party of morality. For embattled Irish or German Catholics, the Democratic party was the defender of their freedoms. These cleavages occasionally surfaced in national elections. For example, when a Republican clergyman accused the Democrats in 1884 of being the party of "Rum, Romanism, and Rebellion," he undermined Republican efforts to woo the Irish-American vote and may have cost James G. Blaine the presidency. But the battles over public education and the liquor question were fought mostly at the state and local levels, mostly in the North. (In the South, which recieved few immigrants, politics lacked this ethnocul-

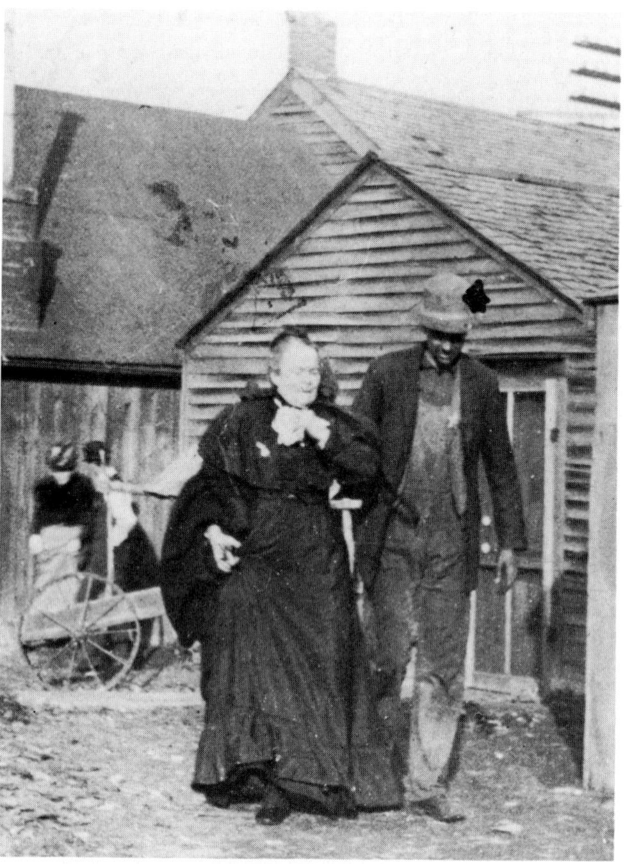

Carry Nation Under Arrest

Opponents of alcohol had traditionally advocated temperance; that is, self restraint. The Women's Christian Temperance Union took a more coercive approach. It demanded legal prohibition of alcohol. Some prohibitionists turned to direct action. Carry Nation became famous for her ax-wielding attacks on saloons. She meant to draw attention to the struggle, and so gladly went to jail—where she is headed in this photograph, taken in Enterprise, Kansas, in 1901.

tural dimension.) In the North ethnocultural issues gave a significance to party politics that would scarcely have been apparent to anyone looking only at the national scene.

Organizational Politics

Political life was also important because of the remarkable organizational activity that it generated. By the 1870s, both of the major parties had evolved a formal, well-organized structure. At the base lay the precinct or ward, whose meetings could be attended by all party members. County, state, and national committees ran the ongoing business of the parties. Conventions determined party rules, adopted platforms, and selected the party's candidates for public office.

At election time the party's main job was to get out the vote. In the South, where the Democratic nomination was equivalent to election, little organized effort went into election day. As a result, fewer people voted in southern states than anywhere else in the country. In states or communities with hard-fought elections, however, the parties mounted intensive efforts organized down to the individual voter. In Indiana, for example, the Republicans appointed 10,000 "district men" in 1884, each responsible for turning out a designated group of voters. The Pennsylvania Republican party maintained a list of 800,000 voters, classified according to degree of voting reliability.

Only professionals could manage such a highly organized political system. The German sociologist Max Weber remarked that Americans regarded "politics as a vocation." This factor, above all else, gave American politics its special character. The distinguishing trait of American politicians, James Bryce observed, was "that their whole time is more frequently given to political work, that most of them draw an income from politics . . . that they . . . are proficient in the arts of popular oratory, of electioneering, and of party management." The party system required professionals, and professionalism created careers. Politics, like professional sports and trade unionism, served as an avenue of upward mobility for many who, because of ethnic or class background, lacked the more conventional opportunities open to other Americans.

Machine Politics. Party administration was, on the face of it, highly democratic. In theory, all power derived from the party members in the precinct and ward organizations. In practice, however, the professionals ran the parties. They did this through unofficial, internal organizations called *machines*, which consisted of insiders willing to accept discipline and do work in exchange for getting on the public payroll or pocketing bribes and other profitable forms of "graft." The machines tended toward one-man rule, though this was based more on consensus than on dictatorship. Each state party had a "boss," such as, in New York, the Republican Thomas C. Platt and the Democrat David B. Hill. Sometimes the state leader held public office, generally as a U.S. senator, because it was the party-dominated state legislatures that chose senators until the adoption of the Seventeenth Amendment in 1913. But public office was not necessary for the boss to do his job.

Machine control affected the tone of party politics. Absorbed in the tasks of power brokerage, the machine boss tended to see public issues as somewhat irrelevant. The Republicans fought bitterly among themselves after President Grant left the White House in 1877. For the next six years, the party was divided into two warring factions—the Stalwarts, who followed Senator Roscoe Conkling of New York, and the Halfbreeds, led by James G. Blaine. The split resulted from a personal feud

The Levi P. Morton Association
The top-hatted gentlemen depicted in this photograph constituted the local Republican party organization of Newport, Rhode Island, named in honor of Levi P. Morton, Republican leader and vice president during the Benjamin Harrison administration (1889-1893). The maleness of party politics veritably leaps from the photograph and asserts more clearly than a thousand words why the suffragist demand for the right to vote was met with ridicule and disbelief.

between Conkling and Blaine, and it lasted because of a furious struggle over patronage. The Halfbreeds represented a newer Republican generation, more inclined to pay lip service to political reform and less committed to the old Civil War issues. But issues had little to do with the war between Stalwarts and Halfbreeds. They were really fighting over the spoils of the machine system.

And yet the record was by no means wholly negative. Machine politics raised the standards of government in certain ways. As seasoned machine politicians rose to higher office, their professionalism and party discipline measurably improved the performance of state legislatures and Congress. More important, the party machines filled a void in the nation's public life. They did informally much of what the governmental system left undone, especially in the cities (see Chapter 20).

The Mugwumps. For all its effectiveness, machine politics never managed to win public legitimacy. The social elite—professionals, intellectuals, well-to-do businessmen, and old-line families—deeply resented a politics that left little room for public service by people like themselves—the "best men." There was, too, a genuine clash of values. Political reformers called for "disinterestedness" and "independence"—the opposite of the self-serving careerism and party regularity fostered by the machine system. Many of them had earned their spurs as Liberal Republicans fighting the reelection of President Grant back in 1872.

In 1884, Carl Schurz, Edwin L. Godkin, and Charles Francis Adams, Jr., split from the Republican party again because they could not stomach its presidential candidate, James G. Blaine, whom they associated with corrupt party politics. Mainly from New York and Massachusetts, these Republicans became known as Mugwumps—a derisive bit of contemporary slang, supposedly of Indian origin, referring to pompous or self-important persons. The Mugwumps threw their support to the Democrat Grover Cleveland. After the 1884 election, something of a national reform movement sprang up, spawning good-government campaigns across the country. Although they won some municipal elections, the Mugwumps achieved greater importance as the nation's opinion molders. They controlled the respectable newspapers and journals and occupied a strategic place in the urban world.

Most of all, the Mugwumps defined the terms of political debate. They denounced the machine system for its violation of American political values. The potency of their attack was most evident in their campaign for the secret ballot, which had been used for the first time in Australia in 1857. Under this reform citizens would, in the privacy of a voting booth, mark an official ballot listing the candidates of all the parties instead of submitting in public view a party-supplied ticket at the polling place. The Australian ballot, adopted throughout the United States in the early 1890s, freed the voters from party surveillance as they exercised their right to vote.

The Mugwumps were reformers, but not on behalf of social justice. They had little sympathy for the problems of working people, nor any enthusiasm for using the powers of the state to alleviate the suffering of the poor and needy. As far as they were concerned, that government was best which governed least. Theirs was the brand of "reform" perfectly in keeping with a politics of the status quo.

Women's Political Culture

The young Theodore Roosevelt, an up-and-coming Republican state politician in 1884, referred to the Mugwump reformers contemptuously as "man-milliners." The sexual slur was not accidental. In attacking organizational politics, the Mugwumps were challenging one of the great bastions of male society of the late nineteenth century. Party meetings and conventions were occasions not only for carrying on the business of politics but also for performing the satisfying rituals of male sociability amidst cigar smoke and whiskey. Moreover, politics was identified with manliness. It was brutally competitive. It dealt in the commerce of power. It was frankly self-aggrandizing. Party politics, in short, was no place for a woman.

So it was no wonder that the woman suffrage movement met with serious opposition in these years. Susan B. Anthony succeeded in getting a constitutional amendment introduced in 1878, but the cause of woman suffrage made little headway through Congress. Suffragists mounted campaigns at the state level, but before 1900 women gained the right to vote in only four western states—Wyoming, Idaho, Colorado, and Utah. In other states, the most that women could win was the right to vote for school boards or on tax issues.

"Men are ordained to govern in all forceful and material things, *because they are men*," asserted one antisuffrage resolution, "while women, by the same decree of God and nature, are equally fitted to bear rule in a higher and more spiritual realm, where the strong frame and the weighty brain count for less"—that is to say, not in politics. Yet this same invocation of the doctrine of "separate spheres"—that men and women had different natures, and that women's nature fitted them for "a higher and more spiritual realm"—did open a channel for women to enter public life. "Women's place is Home," acknowledged the journalist Retha Childe Dorr. "But Home is not contained within the four walls of an individual house. Home is the community. The city full of people is the Family . . . . And badly do the Home and Family need their mother." So believing, socially conscious women had from the early nineteenth century onward engaged in charitable and reform activities. Women's organizations fought prostitution, assisted the poor, agitated for the reform of women's prisons, and tried to improve educational and job opportunities for women. Since many of these goals required state intervention, women's organizations of necessity became politically active, but not, they stressed, with any desire to participate in partisan politics or gain the ballot. Quite the contrary: women were bent on creating their own political sphere.

Thus in 1869, Sorosis, a women's professional club in New York City, convened a Women's Parliament in the hope of launching a parallel government responsible for public matters especially of concern to women. Nothing came of the Women's Parliament, but it did indicate the degree to which women's sphere had taken on a political dimension. If not a parallel government, the social activism of women certainly did give rise to a female political culture that made itself powerfully felt in the public life of late nineteenth-century America.

The Women's Christian Temperance Union. No issue joined home and politics more poignantly than the liquor question. Just before Christmas in 1873, the women of Hillsboro, Ohio, began to hold vigils and prayer meetings in front of the town's saloons, pleading with the owners to close down and end the suffering of families of hard-drinking fathers. Thus began a spontaneous uprising of women that spread across the country and, it was estimated, closed 3,000 saloons. The temperance movement had been inactive for twenty years. Now, from this groundswell of public agitation, came the Women's Christian Temperance Union, which after its formation in 1874, rapidly blossomed into the largest organization of women in the country. The WCTU put the liquor question back on the public agenda.

The WCTU quickly came to exemplify the vitality of women's political culture. It had a powerful consciousness-raising effect on its members and, because it was limited to women, created a whole generation of new leaders. Under the skilled guidance of Frances Willard, who became president in 1879, the WCTU broadened its concerns and adopted a "Do-Everything" policy. For one thing, women recognized that alcoholism was not so much a cause as a symptom of more deep-seated social problems. But just as important, Willard's "Do-Everything" strategy would attract members who had no particular interest in temperance. Local bodies were encouraged to undertake causes important for their own communities. By 1889, the WCTU had thirty-nine departments concerned with labor, social purity, health, international peace, as well as temperance.

Most important, the WCTU was drawn to woman suffrage. This was necessary, Willard argued, "because the liquor traffic is entrenched in law, and law grows out of the will of majorities, and majorities of women are against the liquor traffic." Women needed the vote, said Willard, in order to fulfill their social responsibilities *as women*. This was very different from the claim made by the suffragists—that the ballot was an inherent right of all citizens *as individuals*—and much less threatening to masculine culture. Not much changed in the short run. The WCTU was in fact internally divided on the suffrage issue and did not become a major participant in the later struggles for women's right to vote. But by linking women's social concerns and women's political participation, the WCTU helped lay the groundwork for a fresh, much broader attack on the bastion of male electoral politics in the early twentieth century.

AMERICAN VOICES

The Case for Women's Political Rights *Helen Potter*

In 1883, Helen Potter came to testify before the Senate Committee on Education and Labor about the sanitary conditions of the poor in New York City. But in the course of her testimony she was swept into a powerful indictment of the unequal treatment of women that speaks volumes about the evolving women's political culture of the late nineteenth century.

The Witness. It is really an important question—this of the condition of women in our community. When I was a young girl I had some ambition, and when I heard a good speaker, or when I read something written by a good writer, I had an ambition to do something of that kind myself. I was exceedingly anxious to preach, but the churches would not have me; why, they said that a woman must not be heard. . . .

Q. I suppose you have an idea that women might abolish some of the tricks of the politician's trade?

A. Well, sir, it would take them a long time to learn to dare to do those things that men do in the way of politics—to sell and buy votes. . . .

Q. What would be the effect of conferring suffrage upon women? Would not the effect be injurious to the moral character and high influence of woman, if she should devote herself to the tricks of the politician's trade, which you very properly criticize so severely?

A. . . . I certainly think it would clean our streets, and I think it would purify politics, at least for the next two hundred years. It would take about that time to get women to understand the tricks of politicians as at present practiced. I do not think that women would be injured by it. Men and women are raised in the same family, they go to school together, they marry together, they go to church together, and why they should separate just at that point I do not quite see. . . . This Government is based upon the will of the people—women are "people," yet we have not a word to say about the laws. You will hear women in the course of your acquaintance say they wish they were men; I never heard a man say he wished he was a woman.

Q. Do you think the only reason for that is that they want the suffrage?

A. Yes, sir. They want the power, and I do not blame them.

Q. Why do you think that the suffrage is not extended to women by men—what is the true reason, the radical reason, why men do not give up one half their political power to women?

A. Well, it may arise from a false notion of gallantry. I think most men feel like taking care of, and protecting the ladies. They do not stop to think that there are in New England alone 150,000 unmarried women, who can have no help, as things are. It would be all very well, perhaps, if all women had representatives, and if all had a generous, straightforward honorable man to represent them. But take the case of a good woman who has a drunken husband; how can he represent her? He votes for liquor and for everything he may happen to want, even though it may ruin her and turn her out of doors, and even though it may ruin her children. If the husband is a bad man would it not be better for that woman to represent herself?

Q. If she could vote, wherein would anything be changed?

A. I think the children raised would be better in every way. The mother could have something to say as to whether she should have a liquor saloon on each side of her home, so that her children would not have this terrible temptation constantly before them from the time they are brought into the world until they are grown up. If she had a vote she would have nine out of ten of these places put out of the way. . . .

Q. What effect do you think the extension of the suffrage to women would have upon their material condition, their wage-earning power and the like?

A. They would get equal pay for equal work of equal value. I do not think a woman ought to be paid the price of an expert, when she is not herself an expert, but I believe there would be a stimulus for a woman to fit herself for the very best work. What stimulus is there for woman to fit herself properly, if she never can attain the highest pay, no matter what sort of work she does? If women had a vote I think larger avenues of livelihood would be opened for them and they would be more respected by the governmental powers.

Source: U.S. Senate, Committee on Education and Labor, *Report upon Relations Between Labor and Capital* II, (1885), 627, 629–32.

The Crisis of American Politics: The 1890s

For a decade and more after the end of Reconstruction in 1877, the overriding characteristic of national politics had been the stalemate between two evenly balanced national parties. Such an equilibrium was, however, bound to break down sooner or later. In fact this began to happen at the end of the 1880s. The immediate cause was the intensification of debate over the tariff. The Republicans, in power after Benjamin Harrison defeated the incumbent Grover Cleveland in the 1888 presidential election, pushed through the highly protectionist McKinley Tariff of 1890. The unpopularity of this measure gave a strong edge to the Democrats in the 1890 elections. They gained 76 seats in the House of Representatives and won state offices in Pennsylvania, Massachusetts, and other normally Republican states. Two years later, Cleveland regained the presidency; in command of both the Congress and the White House, the Democrats seemed to have established a firm lock on national politics.

Had everything else remained equal, the events of 1890 and 1892 might have inaugurated a long period of Democratic supremacy. But everything else did not remain equal. On May 3, 1893, the stock market crashed. Even before the crash, there had been signs of economic trouble in the increasing number of railroad bankruptcies and reports of economic distress among farmers. Now the Panic of 1893 struck, followed by a deepening depression. Before the end of the year, 16,000 firms and hundreds of banks had failed. In Chicago, 100,000 jobless workers walked the streets; nationwide, the unemployment rate soared to over 20 percent; as always in hard times, suffering and unrest mounted alarmingly.

As the economic crisis of the 1890s set in, which party would prevail, and on what platform, became very much an open question. The first challenge swept up from the West and South in the form of the Populist party.

The Populist Revolt

Farmers were, of necessity, joiners. They needed organization to overcome their social isolation and to provide them with crucial economic services based on the cooperative principle. By the end of the 1880s, two great regional concentrations had emerged—the Southern Farmers' Alliance along with the Colored Farmers' Alliance and the Farmers' Alliance of the Northwest. The first was strongest among the cotton farmers of the Deep South, the second among the wheat growers of Kansas, Nebraska, and the Dakotas. The alliances were originally nonpolitical, but as economic conditions worsened, they were drawn into politics.

The Populist Program. How that happened is perhaps best seen in Texas, where the Southern Alliance had originated. Its great achievement had been the establishment of the Texas Exchange, a massive cooperative that marketed the crops of cotton farmers and provided them with cheap credit. When cotton prices fell sharply in 1891, the Texas Exchange failed. The Texas Alliance then proposed a new scheme—a *subtreasury system* that would enable farmers to store their crops in public warehouses. Farmers would be able to borrow against those crops from a federally supplied fund at low interest rates until prices rose enough so their cotton could be profitably marketed. The subtreasury plan would provide the same credit and marketing functions as had the defunct Texas Exchange, but with this crucial difference: now it was the federal government that would play the key role. The subtreasury plan was thus a *political* proposal, and when it was rejected by the Democratic party as being too radical, the Texas Alliance saw no choice but to strike out in politics independently.

A similar process—first economic failure, then a proposal political solution, and finally rejection by the established parties—turned Alliancemen across the South and West to political action. In 1890, third parties won control of the Nebraska and Kansas legisla-

Mary Elizabeth Lease

As a political movement, the Populists were short on cash and organization, but long on rank-and-file zeal and tub-thumping oratory. No one was more rousing on the stump than Mary Elizabeth Lease, who came from a Kansas homestead and pulled no punches. "What you farmers need to do," she proclaimed in her speeches, "is to raise less corn and more *Hell!*"

tures, and in the South they captured several governorships as well as eight state legislatures. These successes led to the formation of the national People's (Populist) party. In the 1892 election, with the veteran antimonopoly campaigner James B. Weaver as their presidential candidate, the Populists captured a million votes and carried four western states. For the first time agrarian protest had truly challenged the national two-party system.

The challenge went, however, beyond the contest for political office. Populism contained a strong radical bent. The problems afflicting farmers, Populists felt, could stem only from some basic evil. They identified this evil as the control of the "money power" over the levers of the economic system. "There are but two sides," proclaimed a Populist manifesto. "On the one side are the allied hosts of monopolies, the money power, great trusts and railroad corporations . . . . On the other are the farmers, laborers, merchants and all the people who produce wealth . . . . Between these two there is no middle ground."

This reasoning identified farmers and workers as a single producer class. Populists made a strong effort to ally themselves with the labor movement. Their best successes came in Colorado, among the metal miners, and in Illinois, where the union leadership favored independent labor politics. In its explicit class appeal—in recognizing that "the irrepressible conflict between capital and labor is upon us"—populism differed fundamentally from the two mainstream parties.

Equally distinguishing was the prominent role that women played in the Populist movement. The organizational basis of the established parties, the local political clubs, were for men only. Populism, on the other hand, had its roots in a network of suballiances that had formed for largely social purposes and that welcomed women without discrimination. Only a handful of women achieved high office either in the Alliances or in the Populist party structure. But they did participate actively and served prominently as speakers and lecturers. Most indefatigable was the fiery Mary Elizabeth Lease, who became famous for calling on farmers "to raise less corn and more hell." Populism brought women into politics to a degree unprecedented at that time. "No other movement in history—not even the antislavery cause," commented the writer Hamlin Garland, "appealed to the women like this movement here in Kansas."

In an age dominated by laissez-faire doctrine, what most distinguished Populism from the major parties was its positive attitude toward the state. The Populist platform declared: "We believe that the powers of government—in other words, of the people—should be expanded as rapidly and as far as the good sense of an intelligent people and the teachings of experience shall justify, to the end that oppression, injustice and

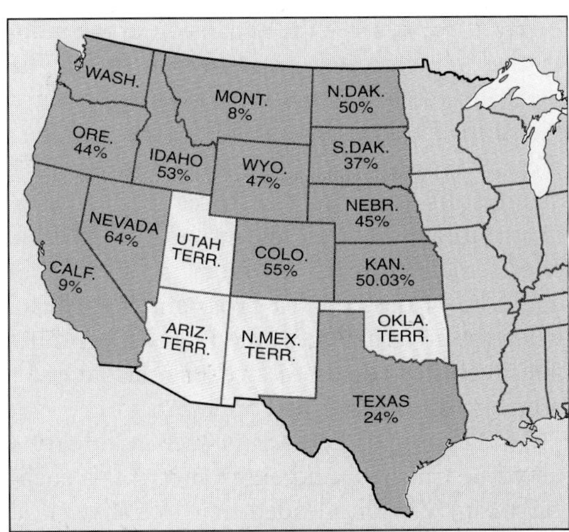

MAP 19.1

The Heyday of Western Populism, 1892

This map shows the percentage of the popular vote won by James B. Weaver, the People's party candidate, in the presidential election of 1892. Except for California and Montana, the Populists won broad support across the West and genuinely threatened the established parties in that region.

poverty should eventually cease in the land." The Populist program called for nationalization of the railroads and communications; protection of the land, including natural resources, from monopoly and foreign ownership; a graduated income tax; the creation of postal savings banks; and the Southern Alliance's subtreasury plan. In addition, the Populists adopted resolutions supporting organized labor, veterans' pensions, and such political reforms as the secret ballot and the direct election of senators. Finally, the Populists called for the free and unlimited coinage of silver. From a comprehensive program, the silver question quickly emerged as the overriding issue of the Populist party.

Free Silver. Cotton and grain farmers were especially vulnerable to falling commodity prices (see Chapter 17, page 543). In the early 1890s the bottom fell out of the market for cotton, wheat, and corn, wreaking havoc among those growers and making them the strongest supporters of Populism. They were strongly attracted to inflationary solutions to their problems. Increasing the money supply would raise farm prices and, since farmers would be paying back their loans in cheaper dollars, also lighten the burden of farm debt. But how to increase the money supply? One way was to get the government to issue paper dollars. This was one feature of the subtreasury plan: the funds lent to farmers on the collateral of their stored crops would be new money issued by the federal government.

But free silver—the expansion of the money supply by the unlimited coinage of silver—quickly became the more attractive alternative. For one thing, it was much the simpler course and, given the far-reaching nature of the subtreasury plan, much more likely to be implemented. In addition, free silver would bring in hefty contributions to the Populist party by silver-mining interests. These mine operators, scornful though they might be of the Populist program, yearned for the day when the government would buy at a premium price all the silver they could produce, and to that end they were prepared to support the Populists.

Urban social democrats such as Henry Demarest Lloyd of Chicago, and agrarian radicals such as Georgia's Tom Watson pleaded that free silver not be made the leading Populist issue. It would undercut the broader Populist program, they argued, and alienate wage earners, who had no particular enthusiasm for inflationary measures. Any chance of a farmer-labor alliance that might transform Populism into an American version of a social-democratic party would be doomed. As Lloyd complained, free silver was "the cowbird of reform," stealing in and taking over the nest that others had built.

Although fiercely debated within the party, the outcome was never in doubt. The practical appeal of free silver was simply too great. But once Populism made that choice, its capacity to maintain an independent existence was fatally compromised. For free silver was not an issue over which the Populists held any monopoly. It was, on the contrary, a question at the very center of mainstream politics in the 1890s.

Money and Politics

In a rapidly developing economy such as nineteenth-century America's, the money supply is bound to be a big political issue. The money supply has to increase rapidly enough to meet the economy's needs, or growth will be stifled. How fast the money supply should grow, however, is a question that creates sharp divisions. Borrowers and those suffering from low prices for their products want a larger money supply: more money in circulation inflates prices and reduces the real cost of borrowing. The "sound money" people—creditors, people on fixed incomes or in the slower-growing sectors of the economy—have an opposite interest. Touching people in the pocketbook as it does, the clash of interests can be very explosive.

Although the federal government always issued its own coins, the main source of the nation's money supply before the Civil War was the bank notes issued by several thousand state banks. Although more or less subject to state regulation, these banks issued their notes entirely in their private role as providers of credit to their customers. The notes given to borrowers circulated as money until presented for redemption at the originating bank. Economists tell us the burgeoning economy's need for money was amply met by the state banks, although the goodness of the bank notes—the ability of the issuing banks to stand behind their notes and redeem them at par—was always uncertain. During the Civil War, this freewheeling system came to an end. Bank notes still existed, but (under the National Banking Act of 1863) only to the extent that they were backed by U.S. government bonds.

The effects of the act were threefold. First, the money supply became inadequate for the country's needs. Second, the ensuing economic troubles—the deflation of prices and the scarcity of credit—magnified public debate over the money question. Finally, since solutions now depended so exclusively on the currency role of the federal government, the money question became much more politicized.

The constitutional power of the federal government to issue money was in theory unlimited. The Lincoln administration had not hesitated to pay for the Civil War largely by printing paper money—greenbacks, so-called—backed by nothing more than the government's declaration that the greenbacks were legal tender. The prevailing policy, however, going back to the founding years of the Republic, was to base the federal currency on the amount of *specie*—i.e., gold and silver—held by the U.S. Treasury.

Under the bimetallic standard, silver and gold were fixed in value at a ratio of sixteen to one: sixteen ounces of silver equaled one ounce of gold. Silver, however, had become scarce relative to the supply of gold after mid-century. As silver rose in market price, it became more valuable as metal than as money and disappeared from currency circulation. In 1873 silver was officially dropped as a medium of exchange. Soon thereafter, great silver discoveries occurred in Nevada, Arizona, and elsewhere in the West. With this new supply, silver prices dropped swiftly. If the government resumed the coinage of silver at the ratio of sixteen to one, silver would flow into the Treasury and greatly expand the volume of currency. It would also, of course, greatly enrich the silver-mining interests.

With so much at stake for so many people, the currency question became one of the staple issues of post-Reconstruction politics. Twice the prosilver coalition in Congress won modest victories. First, under the Bland-Allison Act of 1878, the U.S. Treasury was required to purchase and coin between $2 and $4 million worth of silver each month. Then, in the more sweeping Sherman Silver Purchase Act of 1890, 4.5 million ounces of silver bullion were to be purchased monthly to serve as the basis for new issues of U.S. Treasury notes. These legislative battles over silver coinage, although hard-fought, cut across party lines in a way that was wholly characteristic of the cautious party politics of the 1880s.

But in the early 1890s this situation changed. Silver now became a defining issue between the parties; in particular, it had a radicalizing effect on the Democratic party.

The Cleveland Administration and the Silver Question. When the Panic of 1893 hit, the Democrats were in power in Washington. The party in office usually gets blamed if the economy falters, but President Cleveland made things worse for the Democrats. When jobless marchers arrived in Washington in 1894 to agitate for federal relief, Cleveland's response was to disperse them forcibly and arrest their leader, Jacob S. Coxey. Cleveland's brutal handling of the Pullman strike further alienated the labor vote. Nor was he able to deliver on his campaign promise to reverse the protectionist McKinley Tariff of 1890. In a signal failure of presidential leadership, Cleveland lost control of the congressional battle for tariff reform. The resulting Wilson-Gorman Tariff of 1894, which he allowed to pass into law without his signature, caved in to special interests and cut average tariff rates only slightly.

Cleveland's worst failure, however, was his stand on the silver question. Cleveland was a committed sound-money man who had repeatedly denounced "the dangerous and reckless experiment of free, unlimited, and independent silver coinage." Nothing that happened after the depression set in—not collapsing prices, not the suffering of farmers, not the groundswell of support for free silver within his own party—budged Cleveland from that position.

Economic pressures, in fact, soon pushed him in the opposite direction. The problem was a persistent drain on U.S. gold reserves. This was caused partly by transfers of gold overseas to make up an unfavorable balance of international payments and partly by heavy redemptions of gold by holders of U.S. Treasury notes. To help stem the gold outflow, Cleveland persuaded Congress in 1893 to repeal the Sherman Silver Purchase Act, effectively sacrificing the country's painfully crafted effort at maintaining a partial bimetallic standard.

As his administration's difficulties deepened, Cleveland turned in 1895 to a syndicate of private bankers led by J. P. Morgan to finance the gold purchases needed to replenish the Treasury's depleted gold reserves. The administration's secret negotiations with Wall Street, once discovered, raised a furor among Democrats, and completed Cleveland's isolation from his own party.

William Jennings Bryan and the Election of 1896. In 1896, at their national convention in Chicago, the Democrats repudiated Cleveland and turned left. The leader of the triumphant silver Democrats was William Jennings Bryan of Nebraska. Bryan was truly a political phenomenon. Only thirty-six years old, he had already served two terms in Congress and become a passionate advocate of free silver. He was a consummate politician and, no less important, an inspiring public speaker. Bryan, remarked the journalist Frederic Howe, was "pre-eminently an evangelist . . . . He was a missionary . . . the *vox ex cathedra* of the Western self-righteous missionary mind." Bryan spoke with a Christian fervor that swept up his audiences, and he did so again when he joined the debate on free silver at the Democratic convention. He had been quietly building up delegate support while keeping a distance between himself and convention politicking. Bryan locked up the presidential nomination when he electrified the convention with his stirring attack on the gold standard: "You shall not press down upon the brow of labor this crown of thorns, you shall not crucify mankind on a cross of gold."

Bryan's nomination meant that the Democrats had identified themselves as the party of free silver; his "cross of gold" speech meant he would turn the money question into a national crusade.

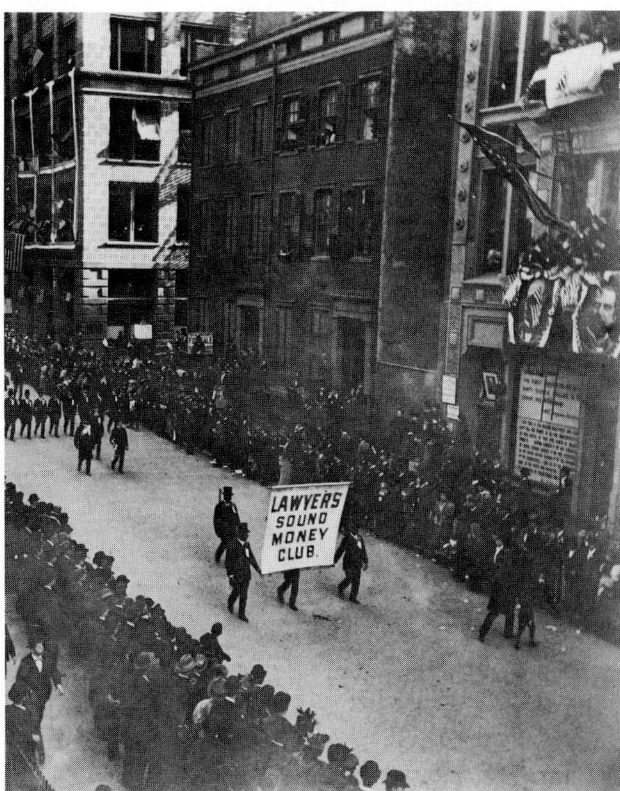

Lawyers March for the Gold Standard

Presidential campaigns of the late nineteenth century were always hard-fought, and none more so than the 1896 election. Big issues were at stake. Would the country stay on the gold standard, or drastically expand the money supply through the free coinage of silver? Lawyers paraded in the streets of New York City to demonstrate their conviction that the nation's fate hung on *sound money* and on the election of the Republican William McKinley.

AMERICAN VOICES

The Nomination of William Jennings Bryan *Edgar Howard*

Edgar Howard, a member of the Nebraska delegation, provides an eyewitness account of the heady idealism that swept the Democratic convention and launched William Jennings Bryan on his Free Silver crusade.

I have been asked by many friends to tell the convention story. I cannot do it. In common with countless thousands I was so overjoyed by the triumph of the people over the cohorts of Wall Street and monopoly that for once in my life I am unable to find words which will fittingly portray the scenes incident to this greatest convention in our country's history. I say it was the greatest convention of modern times because it was the only great political gathering in recent years which was not controlled by the representatives of the monied interests in our land, and to me there is no grander day than that in which the people rise in their majesty and break the cords which bind them to the enemy of mankind—the power of gold.

I frankly confess that we of the Nebraska delegation did not go to Chicago with strong hopes for success. We were ready to plead, pray or fight for Bryan, and yet we scarce dared hope that our pleas, prayers or our fights would avail. It has been said that Bryan could never have secured a nomination had he not made a speech. I am frank to admit that his speech went far to push him on to victory, but I also know that several states had resolved to support him before he made his speech, and I firmly believe he would have been nominated if he had never opened his mouth. He was not a candidate in an active sense. He refused to permit his friends to urge his name, begged the Nebraska delegates not to wear Bryan badges, and persistently refused to let us place his name before the convention, or before the delegates in hotel headquarters. He argued that if the People wanted him as their candidate they would call him to the leadership. . . . In short he was in Chicago the same, noble, clean, Christian gentleman that he has ever been in Nebraska, spurning all proffers of place and power, the receiving of which would be repugnant to his high sense of honor.

But about Bryan's great speech. There are no words in our language to picture the effect it produced upon the vast multitude which heard it. . . . At Bryan's first utterance all was still. The silence was broken at the close of his first beautiful paragraph by a powerful wave of approval which made the great iron building quiver. It was the polished effort of the day, and yet so plain and clear that the most untutored hearer could understand. Again and again the convention broke forth into the wildest demonstrations of approval, ceasing only when the speaker begged for opportunity to proceed. Then the thousands would be silent, every ear being bent to hear the wonderful flow of words, every eye straining to see the majestic man who was hurling defiance in the teeth of the money power. . . . At the conclusion of his speech—well, there's no use of a country editor like me trying to tell you about it. For ten seconds a deathlike silence prevailed. Then like a great cloud that monster assemblage rose to its feet. The cheers were deafening. . . . The demonstration continued nearly half an hour, only ceasing when the participants became exhausted. . . .

As this ironic portrait of him suggests, Bryan's special genius as a politician was to place himself above politics and to identify his cause with moral values deep in the American psyche.

When we went out upon the streets that night the air was full of Bryan enthusiasm, and especially among the laboring classes, who had already memorized his immortal words in his closing sentence: "You shall not press down this crown of thorns on labor's brow; you shall not crucify mankind upon a cross of gold." At our hotels we had hundreds of callers who begged us to get out a band and make a Bryan demonstration on the streets. . . .

At last the balloting began. . . . Bryan gained steadily from the start, reaching the necessary two-thirds on the fifth ballot, and was later declared the unanimous choice of the convention. Throughout the balloting there were wild demonstrations of approval at every mention of Bryan's name. And when victory came at last the scenes following the great speech were enacted over again. . . . It was not a stampede. Bryan was in the hearts of all the delegates who were not controlled by Wall street.

Source: William E. Christensen, ed., "The Cross of Gold Reburnished: A Contemporary Account of the 1896 Democratic Convention," *Nebraska History* 46 (September 1965), 225–33.

No campaign since Reconstruction evoked such a sharp division over issues. The silver Republicans bolted from their party; the gold Democrats went for a splinter Democratic ticket or supported the Republican party; even the Prohibition party split into gold and silver wings. The Populists, meeting after the Democratic convention, accepted Bryan as their candidate. The free silver issue had become so vital that they could not do otherwise. Despite their best efforts, the Populists found themselves, for all practical purposes, absorbed into the Democratic silver crusade.

The Republicans took up the challenge. Their key party leader was Mark Hanna, a wealthy Cleveland ironmaker, who was a brilliant political manager and an exponent of the new industrial capitalism. Hanna's candidate, William McKinley of Ohio, personified the virtues of Republicanism, standing solidly for prosperity, high tariffs, and honest money. While Bryan broke with tradition and criss-crossed the country in a furious whistle-stop campaign, the dignified McKinley received delegations at his home in Canton, Ohio. As Bryan orated with passionate moral fervor, McKinley talked of industrial progress and a full dinner pail.

Not since 1860 had the United States witnessed such a hard-fought election, and over stakes that loomed so high. The nation's currency had exceptional social significance in American life. For the middle class, sound money meant the soundness of the social order. With jobless workers tramping the streets and bankrupt farmers up in arms, Bryan's fervent assault on the gold standard struck fear in many hearts. Republicans denounced the Democratic platform as "revolutionary and anarchistic." They called Bryan's supporters "social misfits who have almost nothing in common but opposition to the existing order and institutions." The formidable party machinery was pumped up to the

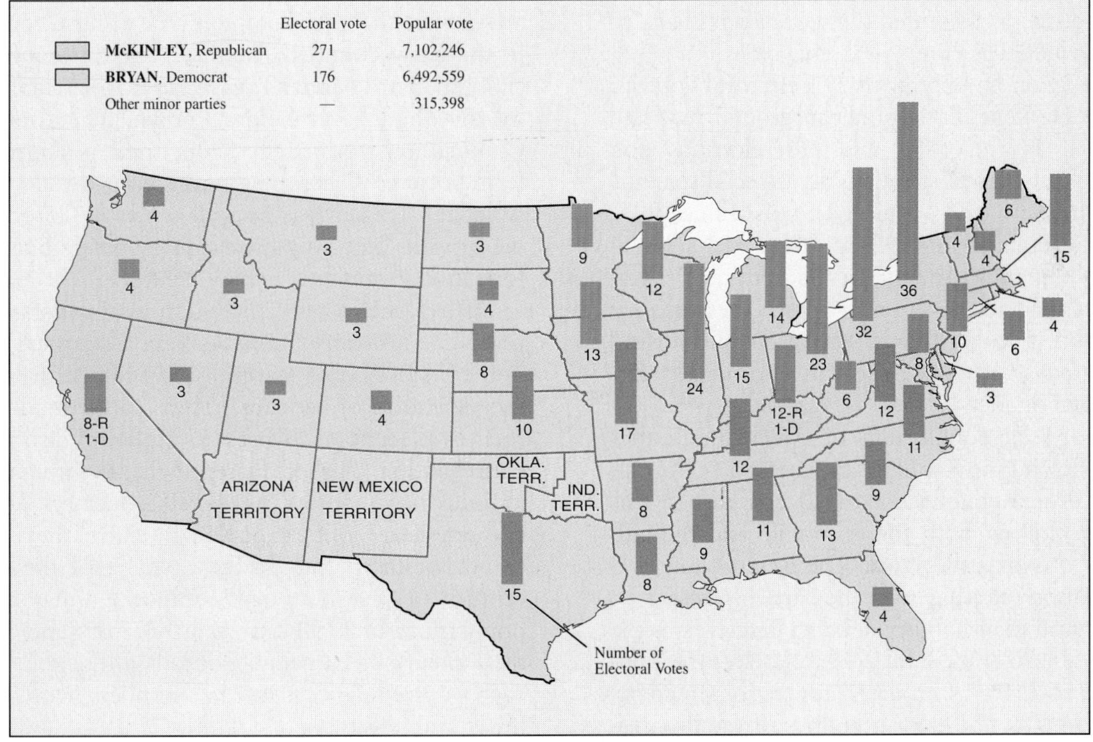

MAP 19.2

The Election of 1896

The 1896 election was one of the truly decisive elections in American history. The Republican party won by its largest margin since 1872. More important, the Republicans established a firm grip on the key midwestern and Middle Atlantic states—especially New York, Indiana, Ohio, and Illinois—that had been the decisive states in every national election since Reconstruction. The 1896 election broke a party stalemate of twenty years' duration and began a period of Republican domination that would last until 1932.

limit. Contributions flowed in from businessmen in record amounts. Hanna's network kept close tabs on the race in every state; and about 1,400 Republican speakers went out on the hustings. The political debate reached a level of intensity and significance unequaled since the days of the Lincoln-Douglas debates.

Although little noticed at the time, ethnocultural issues also figured strongly in the campaign. The Republicans, it will be recalled, had in the 1880s been the party of morality, appealing to native-born and evangelical Protestants on such issues as temperance and Sunday laws, but as a consequence alienating the foreign-born and Catholic vote. The Democrats had capitalized on these tensions in making their bid for electoral dominance in 1890 and 1892. Now, in 1896, the Republicans beat a strategic retreat from the politics of morality. McKinley himself had represented a mixed district of northeastern Ohio in Congress. In appealing to his immigrant and working-class constituents, he had learned the art of easy tolerance, as expressed in his phrase "live and let live." Of the two candidates, the prairie orator Bryan, with his biblical rhetoric and moral righteousness, presented the more alien image to traditional Democratic voters in the big cities.

McKinley won handily, with 271 electoral votes to Bryan's 176. He kept the Republican ground that had been regained in the 1894 mid-term elections and pushed into Democratic strongholds, especially in the cities. Boston, New York, Chicago, and Minneapolis, all taken by Cleveland in 1892, went for McKinley in 1896. Bryan ran strongly only in the South, in silver-mining states, and in the Populist West. The gains his evangelical style brought him in some Republican rural areas fell far short of what he lost in traditionally Democratic urban districts.

The paralyzing equilibrium of American politics ended in 1896, and the Republicans emerged as the majority party. The Republican party accomplished this victory by exploiting both the economic and the cultural aspects of party allegiance. The Republicans persuaded the nation that they were the party of prosperity, and they reduced their liability of being perceived as the party of moral intolerance. In 1896, too, electoral politics regained its place as an arena for national debate, setting the stage for the reform politics of the Progressive Era after 1900.

The Decline of Agrarian Radicalism. As for Populism, it simply faded away. Fusion with the Democrats in 1896 deprived the party of its identity and undermined its organizational structure. After the election, the issue on which populism had staked its fate—free silver—likewise vanished. During the 1890s, gold was discovered in South Africa, Colorado, and the Yukon, while the new cyanide refining method greatly increased ore yields.

The newly abundant gold supply did for the embattled farmers just what they had hoped to accomplish through free silver, ending the long deflation and easing their debt burdens. Wheat went from 72 cents a bushel in 1896 to 98 cents in 1909, corn from 27 cents to 57 cents, and cotton from 6 cents to 14 cents a pound. The world market for these products also turned more favorable. Farm prices rose faster than prices of other products, and as a result, so did the real income of farmers. A new spirit of prosperity and optimism took hold in the "golden age" of American agriculture before World War I.

The farmers' sense of inferiority and deprivation—that they were "rubes" and "hicks" and that life was inherently better in the city—began to subside after 1900. The new prosperity meant that more farmers could afford labor-saving home appliances and farm machinery to lighten field work. New inventions helped ease the isolation and monotony of rural life. The telephone became commonplace, not so much because of the spread of commercial service but through the determined efforts of farmers themselves. Telephone cooperatives were the most common type of farm cooperatives in the early twentieth century. The automobile, especially the Ford Model T, gave rural Americans a mobility they had never before known. The Country Life Commission, formed in 1908, took a sunny view of farm society: "There has never been a time when the American farmer was as well off as he is today, when we consider not only his earning powers but the comforts and advantages he may secure."

The farmer's self-conception also underwent an irreversible transformation. As long as farmers remained in the majority, they naturally considered themselves as representative Americans. They could readily regard their own economic distress as a general disorder of the entire nation. Pushed far enough, they might seek to mobilize their fellow producers—farmers and workers—to seize political power. In short, they could become Populists. But by the opening of the twentieth century, farmers no longer composed a majority of the population. In 1900 only a little more than a third of the labor force earned a living from the soil, and with each succeeding census, the numbers would become fewer and fewer.

There would be times in the twentieth century when distressed farmers would turn again to insurgent politics, but never with the potency generated by the Populist party. It was as an organized interest group, not as a political movement, that farmers in the future would advance their cause.

Agriculture had long been at the heart of American life. In the twentieth century, agriculture became just one more economic interest—an important one, but now subordinate in the larger scheme of the modern industrial order.

Race and Politics in the South

When Reconstruction came to an end in 1877, so did the hopes of African-Americans that they would enjoy the equal rights of citizenship promised them by the Fourteenth and Fifteenth amendments. In education there was strict segregation. Access to jobs, to justice, and to social welfare, was racially determined and unequal. And in 1883 the Supreme Court struck down the Civil Rights Act of 1875, exempting the discriminatory practices of private citizens—owners of restaurants, theaters, hotels—from the strictures of the Fourteenth Amendment. However, southern state laws did not yet *require* the exclusion or segregation of black patrons. After Reconstruction, segregation in public accommodation was general but not absolute: streetcars, for example, seem to have been largely integrated.

In politics, the picture was even more mixed. Blacks were routinely subject to white intimidation—but with the aim of controlling black participation, not eliminating it. In all southern states, blacks continued to vote in large numbers. In the black belt areas, where African-Americans sometimes constituted a majority, they claimed a share of the local offices and sent representatives to the state legislatures and, in Mississippi and the Carolinas, to Congress as well.

Whatever glimmer of hope blacks entertained for better things, however, was soon exploded by a terrible burst of racist terrorism and repression. What made this outcome so peculiarly tragic was that it had started as a positive effort to overcome racial divisions in the South. Black disfranchisement and rigid segregation stemmed directly from the crisis of the 1890s and, in particular, from a political upheaval that briefly challenged the southern status quo.

The Failure of Biracial Politics

Under normal conditions American politics serves to balance, or at least to give voice to, contending economic and social interests. In the New South the party system lacked that integrating capability. For one thing, there was no genuine competition between the parties. With the Republicans wholly discredited in southern eyes by Radical Reconstruction, the South became a one-party region. Whoever controlled the Democratic party controlled southern politics. This dominating group turned out to be, overwhelmingly, a business elite of new entrepreneurs and older plantation owners committed to southern economic development.

Because the Reconstruction struggle had been about home rule, the Democrats could portray themselves as the party of southern patriotism. In seizing control of the Democratic party, the economic elite thus had enormous advantages. Not only was there no effective opposition party, but those who controlled the Democratic party could cloak themselves in the mantle of the Lost Cause and present themselves as the champions of southern "redemption" from black Republican rule. The conservative Democrats, in fact, are most readily identified as the Redeemers.

White Supremacy Versus Class Solidarity. The crucial success of the Redeemers was their ability to exclude competing interests from the public arena. Class antagonism, although often muted, was never absent from southern society. There had been long-smoldering differences between hill-country farmers and the planters. Fresh sources of conflict now arose from the tenant-farmer system—which increasingly included whites as well as blacks—and from an emerging industrial working class. The Redeemers were occasionally challenged—for example, by the Readjuster movement, which after 1877 resisted the full repayment of discounted bonds issued by the Reconstruction state governments. On the whole, however, the Redeemers skillfully utilized the white-supremacist order to keep dissent in check.

"The white laboring classes here," wrote an Alabamian in 1886, "are separated from the Negroes, working all day side by side with them, by an innate consciousness of race superiority. This . . . excites a sentiment of sympathy and equality on their part with the classes above them, and in this way becomes a healthy social leaven." White workers expressed this "innate consciousness of race superiority" by claiming privileged rights above the blacks. Blacks were systematically driven from the many skilled jobs they had held after the Civil War; and they were excluded, except as janitors, from textile work, from the new factory jobs in cigarette manufacture, and in general from the opportunity to rise up in the industrial ranks.

The segregation and deference imposed on blacks were the social marks of their inferiority, asserting that "the lowest white man counts for more than the highest Negro." The pressure for a rigid system of social segregation came primarily from poor whites. "The best people of the South do not demand this separate [railroad] car business," wrote a North Carolina black man. By accepting segregation, he declared, they were "pandering to the lower instincts of the worst class of whites in the South."

In times of economic distress, however, the logic of class solidarity strongly challenged the doctrine of white supremacy. Blacks and whites worked together in many places, such as coal mines and timber camps and on the waterfronts of southern seaports. There they sometimes organized together into trade unions and even went on strike side by side. During the mid-1880s, the Knights of Labor preached the message of interracial unionism with considerable effect.

More significant in the predominantly agricultural South, was the fact that distressed white farmers showed some willingness to work with black farmers to achieve their common goals. "They are in the ditch just like we are," asserted a white Texan. Beginning in 1886, white dirt farmers began to agitate for agrarian reform through the Southern Alliance. Black farmers formed a separate organization, the Colored Farmers' Alliance, but the two bodies worked together. Once the farmers' movement entered politics around 1890, this formal racial division began to be overcome.

Unable to capture the Democratic party, the Southern Alliance formed independent parties or, as in North Carolina, fused with the Republicans. The southern Populists needed the black vote. "The accident of color can make no difference in the interest of farmers, croppers, and laborers," stated the Populist leader Tom Watson of Georgia. "You are kept apart that you may be separately fleeced of your earnings." By organizing interracially as a third party representing southern dirt farmers, the Populists endangered the structure of conservative southern politics.

The Repudiation of Racial Equality. The Populist challenge was put down, but at a terrible cost to racial justice in the South. In the contest for the black vote, the conservative Democrats had the advantages of money, power, and paternalistic influence over many blacks. The Redeemers also attacked the Populists at their most vulnerable point—that they were courting "Negro domination." When all this did not suffice, fraud at the polls enabled the Democrats to defeat the Populist challenge. Thus the Mississippian Frank Burkitt's bitter attack on the conservatives: they were "a class of corrupt office-seekers" who had "hypocritically raised the howl of white supremacy while they debauched the ballot boxes . . . disregarded the rights of the blacks . . . and actually dominated the will of the white people through the instrumentality of the stolen negro vote."

What was Burkitt's solution? A state constitutional convention to eliminate black Mississippians from politics! Thus, out of Populist frustration came the first decisive move to deprive blacks of their right to vote. And where it was the Populists who benefited from the black vote, as in North Carolina, the conservatives took much the same view. Black disfranchisement came through the constitutional adoption, beginning with Mississippi in 1890, of literacy tests, property requirements, and poll taxes.

The race issue had been instrumental in bringing down the Populists; now it served to reconcile them to defeat. Embittered poor whites, deeply ambivalent all along about interracial cooperation, turned their fury on the blacks. And southern conservatives, chastened by the Populist show of strength, encouraged this anger.

The poor whites favored disfranchisement as an expression of militant white supremacy. Their own voting rights were partially protected from the literacy tests by lenient enforcement and constitutional loopholes—such as Louisiana's grandfather clause, which exempted those entitled to vote on January 1, 1867, together with their sons and grandsons. But poor whites were not at all protected from property and poll-tax requirements. They might have objected more had they not been given a voice within the Democratic party.

From the 1890s onward, a new brand of southern politician spoke for the poor whites. He appealed now not to their class interests but to their racial prejudices. Tom Watson, the fiery Georgia Populist, rebuilt his political career as a brilliant practitioner of race baiting. Starting in the early 1900s, he and other racial demagogues thrived throughout the Deep South.

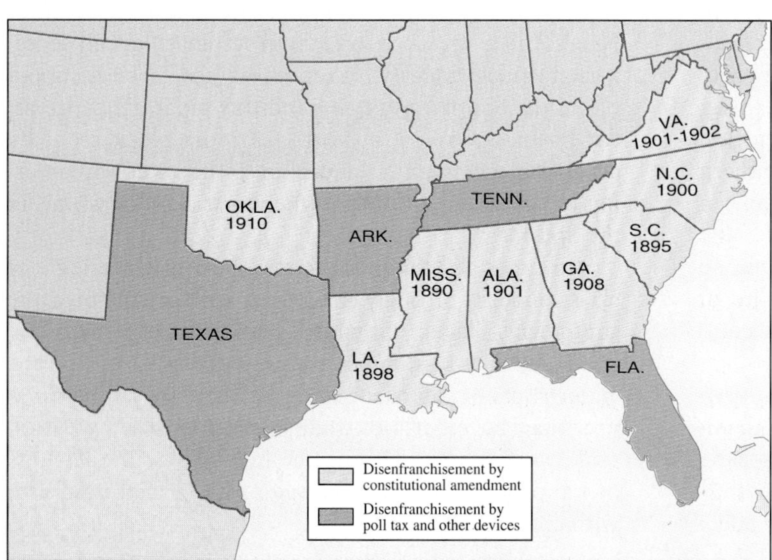

MAP 19.3

Disfranchisement in the South

In the midst of the Populist challenge to Democratic one-party rule in the South, a movement to deprive blacks of the right to vote spread from Mississippi across the South. By 1910 every state in the region except Tennessee, Arkansas, Texas, and Florida had made constitutional changes designed to prevent blacks from voting, and these four states accomplished much the same result through poll taxes and other exclusionary devices. For the next half-century, the political process in the South would be for whites only.

The Ascendancy of Jim Crow. The Populist struggle, tragically, produced a brand of white supremacy more virulent and impenetrable than anything the blacks had faced since Emancipation. The color line, hitherto incomplete, became rigid and comprehensive. Starting in Florida in 1887, state after state in the South passed laws requiring segregated seating in trains and other public accommodation. Such racial legislation, known as Jim Crow laws, soon applied to every type of public facility. In the 1890s, the South became for the first time a fully segregated society by law.

The Supreme Court of the United States soon ratified the South's decision. In the case of *Plessy v. Ferguson* (1896), the Court ruled that segregation was not discriminatory—that is, it did not violate black civil rights under the Fourteenth Amendment—provided that blacks had accommodations equal to those of whites. The "separate but equal" doctrine of course had little regard for the realities of southern life: segregated facilities were rarely if ever "equal" in any material sense, and segregation was itself intended to underscore the inferiority of blacks. With a similar disregard for the realities, the Supreme Court in *Williams v. Mississippi* (1898) validated the disfranchising devices of the southern states: so long as race was not a specified criterion for disfranchisement, the Fifteenth Amendment was not being violated—never mind that the practical effect was the virtually total exclusion of blacks from politics in the Deep South.

Race hatred became an accepted part of southern life, manifested in a wave of lynchings and race riots and in the public vilification of blacks. For example, Benjamin R. Tillman, governor of South Carolina and after 1895 a senator, excoriated blacks as "an ignorant and debased and debauched race." This ugly racism came from several sources, including intensified competition between whites and blacks during the depression of the 1890s and the reaction of whites against the less submissive black generation born after slavery. The nationwide spread of a pseudoscientific theory of racial inferiority played a part, as did American imperialism and its subjugation of Filipinos, Hawaiians, and Hispanics. Recent scholarship also suggests more deep-seated psychological causes for this unreasoning and often murderous racism, in which the rage against blacks served as a way of reasserting a traditional sense of southern "manhood" that was under siege in industrializing America.

But what had triggered the antiblack offensive was the crisis over Populism. From then on, white supremacy propped up the one-party system that had emerged from Reconstruction. If the southern elite had to share political power with demogagic poor white leaders like Tom Watson and James K. Vardaman, this sharing would be on terms agreeable to them—the exclusion from the political process of any serious challenge to the economic status quo.

The Black Response

Where did this leave blacks? In 1890, African-Americans comprised more than half the population of Grimes County, a cotton-growing area of east Texas. They had managed to keep the local Republican party going after Reconstruction and regularly sent black representatives to the Texas legislature during the 1870s and 1880s. More remarkable yet, the local Populist party that appeared in 1892 among white farmers proved immune to the Democrats' taunts of "black rule." A Populist-Republican coalition swept the county elections in 1896 and 1898, surviving well after the collapse of the national Populist movement.

In 1899 defeated Democratic office seekers and prominent citizens of Grimes County organized the secret White Man's Union. Armed men prevented blacks from voting in town elections that year. The two most important black county leaders were shot down in cold blood. Night riders terrorized both white Populists and black Republicans. When the Populist sheriff proved incapable of enforcing the law, the game was up. The White Man's Union, now out in the open, became the county Democratic party in a new guise. The Democrats won Grimes County by an overwhelming vote in 1900. The day after the election, members of the Union laid siege to the Populist sheriff's office. They killed his brother and a friend and drove the sheriff, badly wounded, out of the county forever.

The White Man's Union ruled Grimes County for the next fifty years. The whole episode was the handiwork of the county's "best citizens," suggesting how respectable the use of terror had become in the service of white supremacy. The Union intended, as one of its leaders said, to "force the African to keep his place." After 1900, blacks could survive in Grimes County only if they tended to their own business and stayed out of trouble with whites.

Like the blacks of Grimes County, southern blacks in many places resisted white oppression as best they could. When Georgia adopted the first Jim Crow law applying to streetcars in 1891, Atlanta blacks declared a boycott, and over the next fifteen years there were boycotts against segregated streetcars in at least twenty-five cities. "Do not trample on our pride by being 'jim crowed,'" the Savannah *Tribune* urged its readers: "Walk!" Ida Wells-Barnett emerged as the most outspoken crusader against lynching, so enraging the Memphis white community by the editorials in her newspaper *Free Speech* that she was forced in 1892 to leave the city. And there were individual blacks such as Robert Charles who, driven beyond endurance, struck back, at the inevitable sacrifice of their own lives.

Like Charles, some were drawn to the back-to-Africa movement. It was a sign of their despair that once again Africa was seen as the place of black salvation.

AMERICAN LIVES

Robert Charles: Black Militant

The trouble began in an ordinary way. The two black men were sitting quietly on the steps of a house on Dryades Street in New Orleans, between Washington and 6th Street. It was Monday evening, July 24, 1900. One of the two was nineteen-year-old Leonard Pierce, the other an older man named Robert Charles. They were waiting for a friend of Charles's, Virginia Banks, and her roommate to return from a day at Baton Rouge. Around 11 P.M., three policemen approached Pierce and Charles and began to question them roughly. When Charles stood up, Officer Mora grabbed him. A scuffle followed, and Mora began to beat Charles about the head with his billy club. Charles, a big man, broke away. There was an exchange of gunfire, wounding both in the thigh, Officer Mora more seriously. In a hail of bullets, Charles ran off.

"In any law-abiding community Charles would have been justified in delivering himself up immediately to the properly constituted authorities and asking for a trial by a jury of his peers," wrote the antilynching crusader Ida Wells-Barnett in her pamphlet on what followed. "Charles knew that his arrest in New Orleans, even for defending his life, meant nothing short of a long term in the penitentiary, and still more probable death by lynching at the hands of a cowardly mob." Those must have been Charles's thoughts. He made his way back to the room he shared with Pierce on 4th Street, took down his Winchester rifle, and got ready to fight.

In the meantime, Pierce had been brought to the police station, where Charles's name and address were soon "sweated" out of him. Captain John T. Day, a local hero who had rescued fourteen people from a hotel fire, led a squad to bring Charles in. The entrance to his room was along an alley. When the police arrived, Charles swung open the door, shot Day through the heart, then turned and fatally wounded a second officer. The other two policemen cowered along the wall and slipped into another house, where they hid in the dark. The officers on the street refused to enter the unlit alley. When reinforcements arrived at 5 A.M., Charles had slipped away, and the manhunt commenced.

MOB RULE

IN

NEW ORLEANS.

Robert Charles.

ROBERT CHARLES

AND

His Fight to the Death.

THE STORY OF HIS LIFE.
BURNING HUMAN BEINGS ALIVE.
OTHER LYNCHING STATISTICS.

IDA B. WELLS-BARNETT,

CHICAGO.

PRICE 25 CENTS.

Robert Charles

This is the only known picture of Charles, an engraving done for the cover of Ida Wells-Barnett's pamphlet on Charles' slaying.

The New Orleans newspapers labeled Charles a "fiend incarnate." No one who had known him would have said so. Robert Charles was one of thousands of rural blacks in this period who had sought to escape from grinding poverty by migrating to southern cities. Robert Charles was born just after the end of slavery, in 1865 or 1866, in Copiah County, Mississippi. His parents were sharecroppers, and he was one of ten children. He worked as a day laborer on the railroads and, after arriving in New Orleans around 1894, at a variety of odd jobs. In July 1900, he was unemployed. Charles was unmarried, rather stylish in his dress, favoring a brown derby hat. Acquaintances remembered him as quiet and intelligent. He had received little education, but in his room were the well-thumbed books and papers of a studious man. One other thing about Charles: he ardently believed that blacks should return to Africa.

The back-to-Africa movement, which enjoyed a revival in these hard years, reflected the despair that poor blacks like Robert Charles felt about life in America. Africa was their only salvation, preached Bishop Henry M. Turner, the combative leader of the movement. "I see no other shelter from the stormy blast, from the red tide of persecution, from the horrors of American prejudice." Charles was a reader of Bishop Turner's fiery paper *Voice of Missions,* and in 1899 he began to sell subscriptions. He also became a local agent for the International Migration Society, working on commission to sign up members who would secure transportation to Liberia if they contributed a dollar a month for forty months.

Recent events fortified Charles's conviction that blacks had no hope in America. He was said to have been infuriated by the most infamous lynching of the era, the burning and dismemberment of Sam Hose in Georgia in 1899. In Louisiana, moreover, blacks had been disfranchised in 1898, and a crisis was brewing in state politics. As 1900 elections approached, the Democrats vowed that on no account would they allow the Republicans and Populists to emerge as winners. In Charles's pocket was a newspaper clipping about an opposition leader calling upon his supporters to *"oil up their Winchesters* and prepare to fight" if Democrats tried to steal the election. In *Voice of Missions* there was a similarly desperate message: in one editorial Bishop Turner had urged that "Negroes Get Guns" in self-defense.

Charles, in fact, did habitually carry a Colt .38 revolver; it was in his belt when Officer Mora accosted him. There is no knowing what went through his mind when he chose not to submit to the policeman's abuse. But, having drawn his gun, Charles had stepped across the line. From then on, until his inevitable death, he was making a political statement.

That was how the whites of New Orleans saw Charles too: he was challenging the white power structure. As a leader of the mob that gathered in the streets on Wednesday put it:

> The only way you can teach these niggers a lesson and put them in their place is to go out and lynch a few of them as an object lesson. String up a few of them, and the others will trouble you no more. . . . On to the Parish Prison and lynch Pierce!

The mob couldn't get at Pierce, but they took their fury out on any other unfortunate black they encountered as they surged through the city. In the next two days, at least six people were killed, and dozens of others brutally beaten. Only late Thursday did the police and militia restore a semblance of law and order to New Orleans. But Charles remained at large. Then, on Friday afternoon, July 27, the police got a tip that he was hiding in a small house on Saratoga Street.

Springing from a back closet, Charles shot down the two police who came to investigate, then made his way up to the second story. A great crowd soon surrounded the house, peppering it with bullets. Dodging from window to window, Charles returned their fire for nearly two hours. In grudging admiration, one reporter wrote of his "diabolical coolness" and his "wonderful marksmanship [that] never failed him for a moment." More than twenty of his attackers were hit, three fatally. As dusk began to fall, the building was set ablaze, and Charles was forced out. Still defiant, he almost made it across the courtyard when he was felled by a bullet and went down. The crowd was at him in an instant, firing dozens of shots into him, stomping on his head. His body was carried off in a police wagon, his battered head hanging grotesquely from the back. Later that night, the mob broke loose again, burning buildings and murderously attacking six more blacks.

It would have meant certain death for any New Orleans black to say out loud that Robert Charles had done right. But Ida Wells-Barnett, writing from the safety of Chicago, insisted that he had. "The white people of this country may charge that he was a desperado, but to the people of his own race Robert Charles will always be regarded as the hero of New Orleans." Five weeks after Charles's burial in a potter's field, a neighbor of Fred Clark's on South Ramparts Street came up behind Clark, put a gun to his head and shot him dead. Fred Clark was the black man who had given away Charles's hiding place to the police.

But emigration was not a real choice, and, like the blacks of Grimes County, African-Americans everywhere had to bend to the raging forces of racism and find a way to survive.

The Atlanta Compromise. Booker T. Washington, the foremost black leader of the South of his day, responded to that grim reality in a famous speech in Atlanta in 1895. Washington marked out a line of retreat from the defiant stand of an older generation of black abolitionists exemplified by Frederick Douglass, who died the same year that the Atlanta speech launched Washington into national prominence. Washington was conciliatory toward the South; it was a society that blacks understood and loved. He considered "the agitation of the question of social equality the extremest folly." Washington accepted segregation, provided that blacks had equal facilities. He accepted educational and property qualifications for the vote, provided that they applied equally to blacks and whites.

Washington's doctrine came to be known as the Atlanta Compromise. His approach was "accommodationist," in the sense that it avoided any direct assault on white supremacy. Despite the humble face he put on before white audiences, however, Washington did not concede the struggle. Behind the scenes, Washington did his best to resist Jim Crow laws and disfranchisement. More important, his Atlanta Compromise, while abandoning the field of political protest, opened up a second front of economic struggle.

Washington sought to capitalize on a southern dilemma about the economic role of the black population. Racist dogma dictated that blacks be kept down and that they conform to their image as lazy, shiftless workers. But for the South to prosper, it needed an efficient labor force. Washington made this need the target of his efforts. As founder of the Tuskegee Institute in Alabama in 1881, Washington advocated *industrial education*—that is, manual and agricultural training. He preached the virtues of thrift, hard work, and property ownership. Washington's industrial education program won generous support from northern philanthropists and businessmen and, following his Atlanta speech, applause from progressive supporters of the New South.

Washington assumed that black economic progress would be the key to winning black political and civil rights. He regarded members of the white southern elite as his crucial allies, because ultimately only they had the power to act. More important, they could see "the close connection between labor, industry, education, and political institutions." When it was in their economic interest, and when they had grown dependent on black labor and black enterprise, white men of business and property would recognize the justice of black rights. As Washington put it, "There is little race prejudice in the American dollar."

Booker T. Washington

In an age of severe racial oppression, Washington emerged as the acknowledged leader of black people in the United States. He was remarkable both for his ability as spokesman to white Americans and his deep understanding of the aspirations of black Americans. Born a slave, Washington suffered the indignities experienced by all blacks after Emancipation. But, having been befriended by several whites as he grew to manhood, he also understood what it took to gain white support—and maneuver around white hostility—in the black struggle for equality.

Do the facts suggest that Washington was right? Or, to put the question as an economist might: was it the impersonal market or race prejudice that most determined the economic treatment of blacks? For southern industry, the answer seems mixed. Employers did not discriminate very much over wage rates—that is, they did not pay whites higher wages than blacks for the same work. But racial barriers certainly prevented blacks from moving up into better-paid and more highly skilled jobs. This hard truth is made graphically clear in the comparative wage distributions of whites and blacks shown in Figure 19.2. In agriculture, too, the picture is mixed. The opportunity for black farmers to advance themselves clearly did exist. The proportion who became landowners inched slowly upward to roughly 25 percent in 1900; and they were able to achieve this at a slightly younger age than earlier. But the racial gap remained very wide, with whites almost three times as likely to be landowners as blacks.

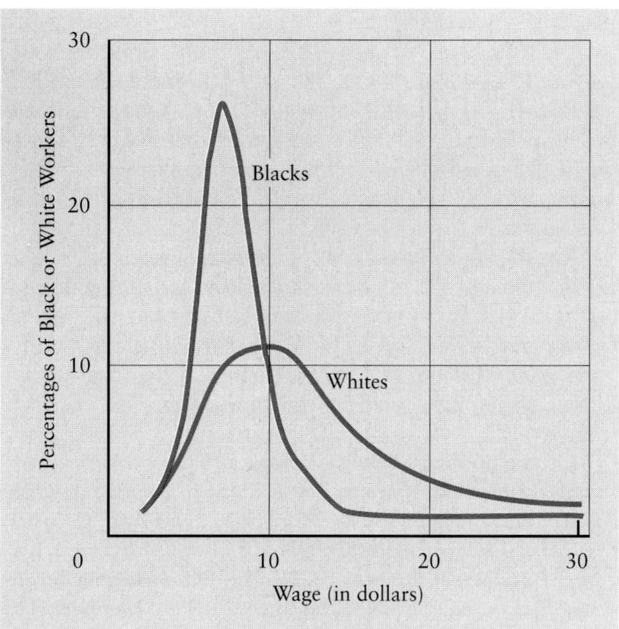

Source: Gavin Wright, *Old South, New South: Revolutions in the Southern Economy Since the Civil War* (New York: Basic Books, 1986), p. 184.

FIGURE 19.2

Wage Distributions of Black and White Workers in Virginia, 1907

To what extent black self-help—hard work, industrial education, the husbanding of small resources—might counterbalance the barriers thrown up by race prejudice was the nub of Booker T. Washington's problem. Where the almighty dollar reigned there was some hope of progress. Elsewhere, as Washington saw it, there was none.

For twenty years after his Atlanta address, Washington dominated organized black life in America. He was the authentic voice of black opinion in an age of severe racial oppression. No black dealt more skillfully with the leaders of white America or wielded more political influence. The black community knew him as a hard taskmaster. Intensely jealous of his authority, he did not regard opposition kindly. Black politicians, educators, and editors stood up to him at their peril.

Even so, a crack began to appear after 1900, especially among younger, educated blacks. They thought Washington was conceding too much. He instilled black pride, but of a narrowly middle-class and utilitarian kind. What about the special genius of blacks that W. E. B. DuBois celebrated in his collection of essays called *The Souls of Black Folk* (1903)? And what of the "talented tenth" of the black population whose promise could only be stifled by industrial education? Blacks also became increasingly impatient with Washington's silence over segregation and lynchings. By the time of his death in 1915, Washington's approach had been superseded by a strategy that relied on the courts and political leverage, not on black self-help and accommodation (see Chapter 21).

Summary

After Reconstruction ended in 1877, national politics became less issue-oriented and, as a formal process, less important in American life. This situation resulted from weaknesses in governmental institutions, from the prevailing philosophy of *laissez faire*, and from the paralysis of evenly matched political parties. Yet the politics of the years after 1877 had great vigor, evident in the high levels of popular participation. For one thing, politics was the arena in which the nation's ethnic and religious conflicts were largely fought out. Equally important, the party machines were very powerful and performed crucial functions that properly belonged to, but were still beyond the capacity of government institutions. Finally, despite the slow headway toward woman suffrage, women's organizations carved out for themselves a broadening public sphere of social reform activity.

During the 1890s, national politics again became an important arena. Threatened by the rise of Populism, the Democratic party committed itself to free silver and made the election of 1896 a contest over issues of real significance. The Republicans won decisively, ending the paralyzing party stalemate that had lasted for twenty years and assuring themselves of political dominance for the next thirty years. At the same time, the 1890s saw, in the failure of Populism, the last great challenge to the mainstream two-party system. And in the South the Populist failure turned into a grim reaction that disfranchised African-Americans, completed a rigid segregation system, and let loose a terrible cycle of racial hatred and violence. Blacks resisted, but had to bend to overwhelming white power. The accommodationist philosophy of Booker T. Washington seemed to be the best strategy for survival in an age of extreme racism.

TOPIC FOR RESEARCH

The Mugwump Critique of American Politics

In the years after the Civil War, the Mugwumps mounted a powerful critique of American party politics. What kind of people were the liberal reformers? What did they find objectionable in the machine system of politics? What was their attitude toward the immigrants who sustained the machine system? What was their attitude toward universal manhood suffrage? What kind of politics did they advocate, and what was their impact on the political process of the late nineteenth century? Among the many books that explore these questions, the most useful are Geoffrey T. Blodgett, *Gentle Reformers: Massachusetts Democrats in the Cleveland Era* (1966), John G. Sproat, *The "Best Men": Liberal Reformers in the Gilded Age* (1965), Gerald W. McFarland, *Mugwumps, Morals and Politics, 1884–1920* (1975), and Ari Hoogenboom, *Outlawing the Spoils: The Civil Service Reform Movement, 1865–1883* (1961). A good introduction to the subject, with ample notes on sources, is Chapter 3 in Michael E. McGerr, *The Decline of Popular Politics: The American North, 1865–1928* (1986). The Mugwumps were highly literate men, and they left an ample record of their views. You can find representative essays in 1880s issues of such journals as *The Nation, The North American Review,* and *Atlantic Monthly,* copies of which are available in many college libraries. Other accessible sources are the books or collected letters of many Mugwumps, such as Simon Sterne, Moorfield Storey, George William Curtis, and Henry Adams. (Citations to many of these published works can be found in McGerr's notes to Chapter 3 of his *Decline of Popular Politics.*) Adams's satirical novel *Democracy* (1880) conveys in lively fictional form the Mugwump critique of machine politics.

BIBLIOGRAPHY

The Politics of the Status Quo

The best introduction to American politics in the late nineteenth century is John A. Garraty, *The New Commonwealth, 1877–1890* (1968). Much more detailed is Morton Keller, *Affairs of State: Public Life in Late Nineteenth-Century America* (1977). Various aspects of national politics are discussed in Robert D. Marcus, *Grand Old Party: Political Structure in the Gilded Age* (1971), J. Rogers Hollingsworth, *The Whirligig of Politics: The Democracy of Cleveland and Bryan* (1963), H. Wayne Morgan, *From Hayes to McKinley: National Party Politics, 1877–1896* (1969), and David J. Rothman, *Politics and Power: The Senate, 1869–1901* (1966). On the development of public administration, see Leonard D. White, *The Republican Era, 1869–1901* (1958), and Stephen Skowronek, *Building a New American State: The Expansion of National Administrative Capacities* (1982).

The ideological basis for conservative national politics is fully treated in Robert L. Bannister, *Social Darwinism: Science and Myth* (1979), Sidney Fine, *Laissez Faire and the General Welfare State, 1865–1901* (1956), Richard Hofstadter, *Social Darwinism in American Thought* (rev. ed., 1955), and Robert G. McCloskey, *American Conservatism in the Age of Enterprise* (1951).

On the popular sources of political participation, see especially Michael E. McGerr, *The Decline of Popular Politics: The American North, 1865–1928* (1986), and Paul Kleppner, *The Third Electoral Party System, 1853–1892: Parties, Voters, and Political Cultures* (1979). The ethnocultural dimensions of party politics have been studied in Paul Kleppner, *The Cross of Culture: A Social Analysis of Midwestern Politics* (1970), and in Richard Jensen, *The Winning of the Midwest, 1888–1896* (1971). On the Mugwump reformers, see the citations in the Topic for Research. The existence of women's political culture in the late nineteenth century can be traced in Carl N. Degler, *At Odds: Women and the Family from the Revolution to the Present* (1979). A valuable book setting the stage is Ellen Carol DuBois, *Feminism and Suffrage: The Emergence of an Independent Women's Movement in America, 1848–1869* (1978).

The Crisis of the 1890s

The standard work on Populism is John D. Hicks, *The Populist Revolt* (1931). Richard D. Hofstadter, *The Age of Reform* (1955), stresses the darker side of Populism, in which intolerance and paranoia figure heavily. Hofstadter's thesis, which dominated debate among historians for some years, has now given way to a much more positive assessment. The key book here is Lawrence Goodwyn, *Democratic Promise: The Populist Moment in America* (1976), which argues that it was a broadly based, radical response to industrial capitalism. While Goodwyn stresses the southern roots of Populism, an earlier book makes a similar, but less complex, case for the radicalism of northwestern Populism: Norman Pollack, *The Populist Response to Industrial America* (1962). A highly stimulating book that traces the evolution of other strands of Populism into twentieth-century agrarian conservatism is Grant McConnell, *The Decline of Agrarian Democracy* (1953).

The money question is elucidated in Walter Nugent, *Money and American Society, 1865–1880* (1968), and Allan Weinstein, *Prelude to Populism: Origins of the Silver Issue* (1970). On the politics of the 1890s, see especially Peter H. Argesinger, *Populism and Politics: William A. Peffer and the People's Party* (1974), Robert F. Durden, *Climax of Populism: The Election of 1896* (1965), and Paul W. Glad, *McKinley, Bryan, and the People* (1964).

Race and Politics in the South

On southern politics, the seminal book for the post-Reconstruction period is C. Vann Woodward, *Origins of the New South, 1877–1913* (1951), which still defines the terms of discussion among historians. Two recent books stress the continuities between the Old South planters and the post–Civil War South: Dwight B. Billings, *Planters and the Making of "New South": North Carolina, 1865–1900* (1979), and Jonathan M. Wiener, *Social Origins of the New South: Alabama, 1860–1885* (1978). The standard book on New South thought is Paul M. Gaston, *The New South Creed: A Study of Southern Myth-Making* (1973). Gaston's book can profitably be read in conjunction with a much older study, Paul M. Buck, *The Road to Reunion, 1865–1900* (1937).

The classic book on segregation is C. Vann Woodward, *The Strange Career of Jim Crow* (2nd ed., 1968), but it should be supplemented by Howard N. Rabinowitz, *Race Relations in the Urban South, 1865–1890* (1978). A powerful analysis of southern racism, stressing its psychosocial roots, is Joel Williamson, *A Rage for Order: Black/White Relations in the American South Since Emancipation* (1986). Disfranchisement is treated with great analytic sophistication in J. Morgan Kousser, *The Shaping of Southern Politics: Suffrage Restriction and the Establishment of the One-Party South, 1880–1910,* (1974) and as an aspect of progressivism in Jack Temple Kirby, *Darkness at the Dawning: Race and Reform in the Progressive South* (1972). Rayford W. Logan, *The Betrayal of the Negro* (1965), is the standard history of blacks after Reconstruction. August Meier, *Negro Thought in America, 1880–1915* (1963), is a key analysis of black accommodation and protest. The preeminent exponent of accommodation is the subject of a superb two-volume biography by Louis B. Harlan, *Booker T. Washington: The Making of a Black Leader* (1973), and *Wizard of Tuskegee* (1983).

TIMELINE

1874	Women's Christian Temperance Union (WCTU) founded
1877	Rutherford B. Hayes inaugurated; end of Reconstruction
1881	President James A. Garfield assassinated
1883	Pendleton Civil Service Act
1884	Mugwump reformers bolt the Republican party to support Grover Cleveland, first Democrat elected president since 1856
1887	Interstate Commerce Act creates the Interstate Commerce Commission (ICC) to regulate railroads
1890	McKinley Tariff Mississippi becomes first state to adopt literacy test to disfranchise blacks
1892	People's (Populist) Party founded
1893	Panic of 1893 leads to national depression Repeal of Sherman Silver Purchase Act (1890)
1894	Coxey's Army
1895	Booker T. Washington sets out the Atlanta Compromise
1896	Election of William McKinley; free silver campaign crushed *Plessy v. Ferguson* upholds constitutionality of "separate-but-equal" facilities
1897	Economic depression ends

The Bowery at Night, 1895

This painting by W. Louis Sonntag, Jr., shows the Bowery crowded with shoppers and pleasure seekers. It was during this time that it gained its raffish reputation. (Museum of the City of New York)

CHAPTER 20 *The Rise of the City*

For the first two hundred years of its history, America remained a land of farmers. In 1820 barely 5 percent of the people lived in cities with a population of ten thousand or more. But after that, decade by decade, the urban population swelled, turning into a flood after mid-century. A comparable process was occurring in Europe, but at a slower pace. During the nineteenth century, the percentage of Europeans living in towns increased threefold, while in the United States the increase was sevenfold.

By 1900 one of every five Americans lived in an urban center of one hundred thousand or more residents. The greatest growth had taken place in the major metropolitan cities. Nearly a tenth of the nation—6.5 million persons—lived in cities of over a million. The late nineteenth century, an economist remarked in 1899, "was not only the age of cities, but the age of great cities."

The growth of the cities had enormous implications for American society. The city was the arena of the nation's vibrant economic life. Here the factories went up, and here the multitudes of working people settled. New immigrants swelled the ranks of the working class. At the turn of the century upwards of 30 percent of the residents of major cities in the United States were foreign-born. Here, too, lived the millionaires and a growing urban middle class of white-collar workers and businessmen. For all these people, the city was more than a place to make a living. It provided the setting for an urban culture unlike anything seen before in the United States. City people, although differing vastly among themselves, became distinctively and recognizably urban.

Urbanization

The march to the cities seemed inevitable to nineteenth-century Americans. "The greater part of our population must live in cities—cities much greater than the world has yet known," declared the Congregational minister and social critic Josiah Strong in 1898. "In due time we shall be a nation of cities." There was "no resisting the trend," said another writer. Urbanization became inevitable because of its link to another inevitability that gripped America—industrialization.

The Sources of City Growth

Until the Civil War, cities had been centers primarily of commerce, not industry. Located strategically along transportation routes, they were the places where merchants bought and sold goods for distribution into the interior or for shipment out to the world market. Early industrialism, on the other hand, was distinctly a rural phenomenon. Mills and factories needed water power from streams and rivers, ready access to sources of fuel and raw materials, and workers drawn from the surplus farm population. Of the nation's fifteen largest cities in 1860, only five reported as much as 10 percent of the labor force engaged in manufacturing activity.

After mid-century, industry began to abandon the countryside. With the arrival of steam power, mill operators no longer needed to locate along streams. In the iron industry, coal replaced charcoal as the primary fuel, so iron makers did not have to be near forests. Improved transportation, especially the railroads, gave entrepreneurs a greater choice in selecting the best sites in relation to supplies and markets. The result was the geographic concentration of industry. Iron makers gravitated to Pittsburgh because of its access not only to supplies of coal and iron ore but also to markets for iron and steel products. Chicago, ideally located between livestock suppliers and consuming markets, became a great meat-packing center in the 1870s.

Many smaller industrial cities depended on a high degree of economic specialization. Youngstown, Ohio, and Johnstown, Pennsylvania, specialized in iron and steel; Brockton and Haverhill, Massachusetts, in boots and shoes; Troy, New York, in collars and cuffs; East Liverpool, Ohio, in pottery. Other cities processed the raw materials of their regions. Sacramento canned fruits and vegetables, Richmond made cigarettes, Minneapolis milled grain, and Memphis handled lumber and produced cottonseed oil.

This geographic concentration of industry was one source of urban growth in the late nineteenth century. Another was the increasing scale of production that became characteristic of modern industry. A factory that employed thousands of workers instantly created a small city in its vicinity. The result was often a company town—Aliquippa, Pennsylvania, for example, became body and soul the property of the Jones and Laughlin Steel Company. Many firms set up their plants near a large city so they could draw on its labor supply and transportation facilities. George Pullman located his sleeping-car works and model town southwest of Chicago, and George Westinghouse built his electrical plant just east of Pittsburgh. Sometimes the nearby metropolis spread and absorbed the smaller city, as happened with Pullman, Illinois. Elsewhere, as in northern New Jersey or south of Chicago and across the state line into Indiana, smaller communities merged and formed an extended urban-industrial area. The same process could be seen in Europe, where industrial regions were emerging in northeastern France around Lille and in Germany's Ruhr Valley.

The established commercial cities also grew significantly in this era. They benefited from the tendency of a

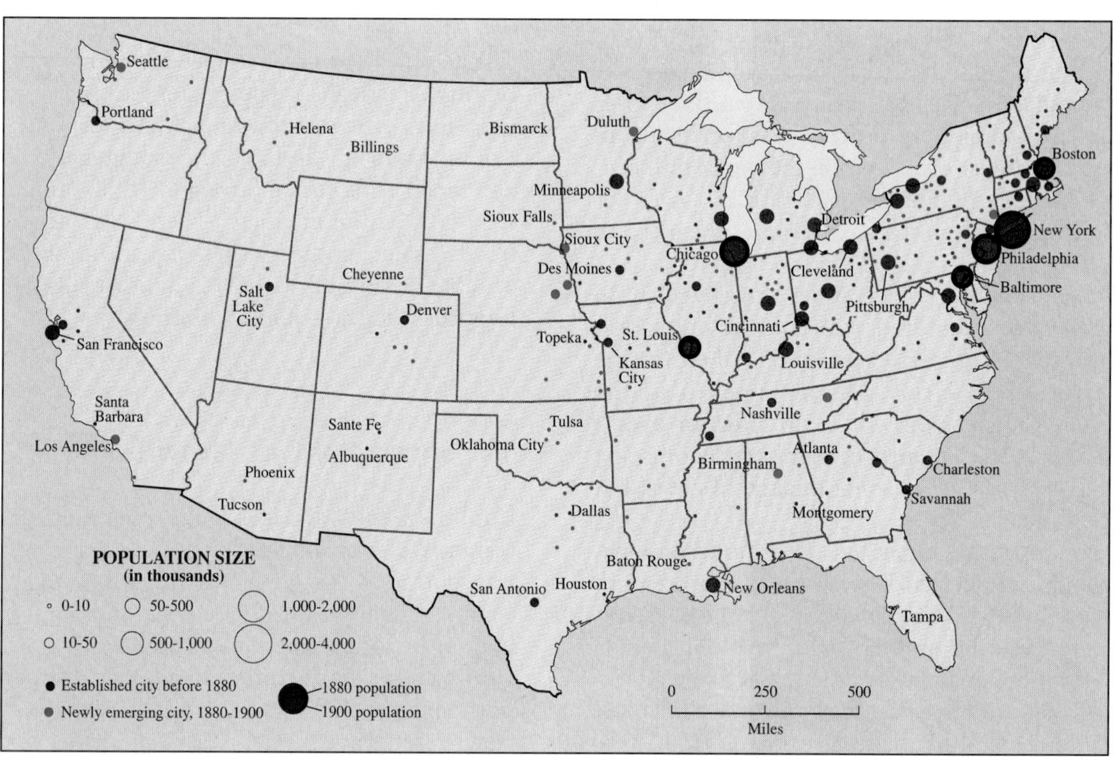

MAP 20.1

The Growth of America's Cities, 1880–1900

The number of Americans living in urban places more than doubled between 1880 and 1900. The most dramatic increases occurred in the largest metropolitan centers. New York went from 1.2 million to 3.4 million, Chicago from 0.5 million to 1.7 million. Notable among newly emerging cities—places that had been small towns or minor cities in 1880—were Los Angeles, Seattle, Birmingham, Omaha, and Atlanta.

maturing industrial economy to create complex marketing and administrative structures. The greatest centers—New York and Chicago—became headquarters for corporations operating across the country. Finance, publishing, distribution, advertising, and fashion were concentrated in the metropolitan centers.

These commercial centers also attracted certain kinds of industries. They had warehouse districts that could readily be converted to small-scale manufacturing, and they offered ample transportation and services. In addition, they could supply abundant cheap labor because they served as gateways for immigrants. Boston, Philadelphia, Baltimore, and San Francisco became hives of small-scale, labor-intensive industrial activity. New York's enormous pool of immigrant workers made it a magnet for the garment trades, cigar making, and diversified light industry. Preeminent as a city of trade and finance, New York also ranked as the nation's largest manufacturing center.

By 1870, a core industrial region had formed from New England down through the Middle Atlantic states to Maryland. In this region, the percentage of people living in urban places was twice the national average. Forty years later, in 1910, the original industrial core was nearly three-quarters urbanized. It had also thrust westward to include the Great Lakes states, which became America's industrial heartland. Important new centers for steel making, manufacturing, and food processing sprang up in this region. Pittsburgh, Cleveland, Detroit, Milwaukee, Minneapolis—all of them small cities or modest commercial centers in 1870—had by 1910 grown into major industrial cities ranging from 300,000 to well over half a million inhabitants.

TABLE 20.1

Ten Largest Cities by Population, 1870 and 1910

1870		1910	
City	Population	City	Population
1. New York	942,292	New York	4,766,883
2. Philadelphia	674,022	Chicago	2,185,283
3. Brooklyn*	419,921	Philadelphia	1,549,008
4. St. Louis	310,864	St. Louis	687,029
5. Chicago	298,977	Boston	670,585
6. Baltimore	267,354	Cleveland	560,663
7. Boston	250,526	Baltimore	558,485
8. Cincinnati	216,239	Pittsburgh	533,905
9. New Orleans	191,418	Detroit	465,766
10. San Francisco	149,473	Buffalo	423,715

*Brooklyn was consolidated with New York in 1898.
Source: U.S. Census data.

City Building

How would so many people move around, communicate, and satisfy their physical needs? "The only trouble about this town," wrote Mark Twain on arriving in New York in 1867, "is that it is too large. You cannot accomplish anything in the way of business, you cannot even pay a friendly call, without devoting a whole day to it. . . . The distances are too great." Finding ways of moving nearly a million New Yorkers around was not as hopeless an undertaking as it might have seemed to Twain, but it did pose daunting challenges to city builders. The city demanded innovation no less than did industry itself and, in the end, compiled an equally impressive record of technological achievement.

The preindustrial city had been a compact place, densely settled around a harbor or along a river. As late as 1850, when it had 565,000 people, greater Philadelphia covered only 10 square miles. From the foot of Chestnut Street on the Delaware River, a person could walk to almost anywhere in the city within forty-five minutes. Thereafter, however, Philadelphia—and, indeed, all American cities—tended to spread out and become less compact as they developed.

A downtown area emerged, usually in what had been the original commercial city. Downtown, in turn, broke up into shopping, financial, warehousing, manufacturing, hotel and entertainment, and red-light districts. Although somewhat fluid at their edges, all these districts were well-defined areas of specialized activity. Moving out from the center, industrial development tended to follow the arteries of transportation—railroads, canals, and rivers—and, at the city's outskirts, to spread out into complexes of heavy industry. At the same time the middle class moved in large numbers to new suburban areas.

The contrast with continental Europe was very marked. There, even rapidly growing cities remained physically compact, with boundaries that broke sharply at the surrounding countryside. In America, cities constantly expanded, spilling beyond the formal city boundaries and forming what the federal census began to designate in 1910 as *metropolitan areas.* While there was much congestion at the center, the population density of American cities was actually much below that of European cities—22 persons per acre for fifteen American cities in the 1890s, for example; 157.6 for a comparable group of German cities. It followed, of course, that the development of efficient urban transportation had a much higher priority in the United States than in Europe.

Mass Transit. The first step toward mass transit, dating back to the 1820s, was the omnibus, an elongated version of the horse-drawn coach. The omnibus was a con-

Traffic Jam in Downtown Chicago, 1905
The purpose of urban transit systems was to move masses of people rapidly and efficiently through the city. However, better transportation brought more congestion as well, like this scene of temporary gridlock at Randolph and Dearborn streets in Chicago.

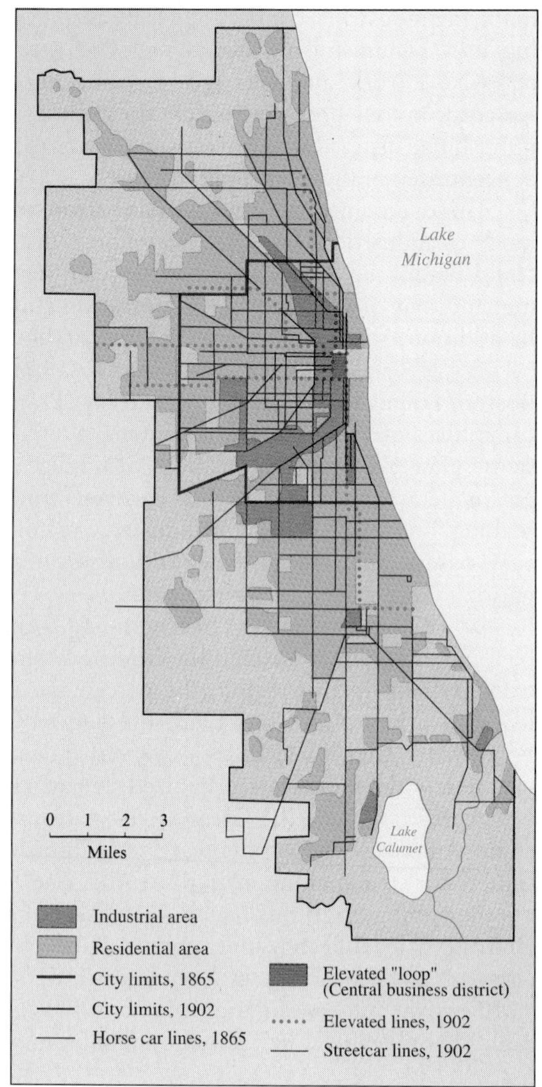

MAP 20.2

The Expansion of Chicago
In 1865 Chicagoans depended on slow horsecar transport to get around town. By 1900 the city limits had expanded enormously, accompanied by equally dramatic extension of streetcar service, by then all electrified. Elevated trains also now helped ease congestion in the urban core. New streetcar lines, some beyond the city limits, were important to suburban development in coming years.

venience, but it did not do much to relieve congestion; downtown, people could walk just as fast. Much more effective was the horsecar. The key thing was that it ran on iron tracks, so that it could carry more passengers, move them at a faster clip through congested city streets, and reach out into the residential areas. But it took a refinement of the railroad track—the invention in 1852 of a grooved rail that was flush with the pavement—to make the horsecar practical. For the next forty years, horsecars became the mainstay of urban transit across America, accounting for 70 percent of the traffic in 1890.

The horse was not, of course, an ideal source of locomotion. It moved slowly, had limited pulling power, and left piles of manure behind. Among various early improvements was the cable car, which was pulled by an underground cable set in below the tracks. The first cable cars ran in San Francisco in 1873, and more than twenty other cities used them during the 1880s. But the cable car could run only at a slow, unvarying speed; systemwide breakdowns occurred frequently.

Then came the electric trolley car. Its development was the work primarily of Frank J. Sprague, an electrical engineer once employed by the great inventor Thomas A. Edison. In 1887, Sprague designed an electric-driven system for Richmond, Virginia: a "trolley" carriage running along an overhead power line was attached by cable to streetcars equipped with an electric motor—hence the name trolley car. After Sprague's success, the electric trolley swiftly displaced the horsecar and became by 1900 the primary means of public transportation in most American cities.

In the great metropolitan centers, however, mounting congestion led to demands that public transit be moved off the streets. The railroad had long been used by well-to-do suburbanites to commute to the city. The problem was how to harness railway technology to serve the needs of ordinary city dwellers. In 1879, the first elevated lines went into operation on Sixth and

Ninth avenues in New York City. Powered at first by steam engines, the "els" converted to electricity following Sprague's success with the trolley. Chicago developed elevated transit most fully. New York, on the other hand, turned to the subway. Although Boston opened a short underground line in 1897, the completion in 1904 of a subway running the length of Manhattan demonstrated the full potential of underground rapid transit. Thinly settled areas of northern Manhattan and the Bronx, predicted the *New York Times*, would soon boast "a population of ten million . . . housed comfortably, healthfully and relatively cheaply." The subway would especially delight "all who travel with the sole purpose of 'getting there' in the least time possible." Mass transit had become *rapid* transit.

Nowhere else in the world was the demand for mass urban transit so acute. In 1890 the number of passengers carried on American street railways was more than 2 billion per year, over twice that of the rest of the world combined. Berlin, which boasted the best system in Europe, had a per capita usage that was exceeded by twenty-one American cities. In England, the horsecar remained dominant long after it had disappeared from American streets. In Tokyo, the biggest Asian city, the horsecar was not even introduced until 1882, while the first electric streetcar appeared only in 1903.

Manhattan's First Skyscraper
The Tower Building at 50 Broadway was completed in 1889. To the modern eye, this first New York skyscraper seems modest and old-fashioned. Compared with its squat neighbors, however, it was a revolutionary building based on new principles of slender, soaring architecture. (Museum of the City of New York)

The Skyscraper. If urban transit evolved in response to the geographic expansiveness of the American city, advances in construction techniques answered the need to create more space in the downtown business districts. New building materials made it possible to construct commercial buildings of greater height, interior space, and fire resistance. With the availability by the 1880s of steel girders, mass-produced durable plate glass, and the passenger elevator, a wholly new way of construction opened up. A steel skeleton would support the building, and the walls, hitherto weight-bearing, would serve as curtains enclosing the structure. The sky, so to speak, became the limit.

The first "skyscraper" to be built on this principle was the ten-story Home Insurance Building (1885) in Chicago. Although this pioneering effort was conventional in appearance—it looked just like the other commercial buildings in the downtown district—the steel-girdered structure swiftly liberated the aesthetic perceptions of American architects. A Chicago school sprung up, dedicated to the design of buildings whose form expressed, rather than masked, their structure and function. The masterpiece of the Chicago school was Louis Sullivan's Carson, Pirie, Scott and Company department store (1904). Chicago pioneered in skyscraper construction, but New York, with its unrelenting need for prime downtown space, took the lead after the mid-1890s. The climax of New York's construction surge came with the completion in 1913 of the fifty-five story Woolworth Building. Aptly called the "Cathedral of Commerce," the Woolworth Building towered over its neighbors and marked the beginning of the modern Manhattan skyline.

Bridges. Rivers, in earlier times the lifeline of trade, now became barriers that interrupted rail traffic and hindered city expansion. The second half of the nineteenth century became the great age of bridge construction. Hundreds of iron and steel bridges went up during this period. Some—including the Eads Bridge (1873) spanning the Mississippi River at St. Louis and the Brooklyn Bridge (1883) over New York's East River—are still in use. The Brooklyn Bridge, linking Brooklyn and Manhattan, took fifteen years to build. A giant suspension structure, the Brooklyn Bridge was not only an engineering marvel but the symbol of a new kind of functional architecture—"the first product of the age of coal and iron to achieve completeness of expression," wrote the architectural critic Lewis Mumford.

The Electric City. If the railroad was the economic lifeline of the industrial city, electricity was the source of its quickening tempo. Charles F. Brush's electric arc lamps, first installed in the windows of the Wanamaker department store in Philadelphia in 1878, soon replaced gaslight in stores and hotel lobbies and on city streets throughout the country. The following year, Thomas Edison created the first commercially practical incandescent lamp, which brought electric lighting into American homes. Before electricity had any significant effect on industry, it lifted and lowered elevators and powered streetcars and subway trains. No other invention so transformed America's urban life. Meanwhile the telephone, patented by Alexander Graham Bell in 1876, speeded up communication beyond anything imagined previously. Twain's complaint of 1867 that it was impossible to carry on business in New York had been answered: all he needed to do now was pick up the phone. By 1900, 1.5 million telephones were in use, linking urban activity into a network of instant communication.

The Private City

City building was very much an exercise in private enterprise. The great innovations—the trolley car, the skyscraper, the elevator, electric lighting, and the telephone—had been spurred by the lure of profit. So was urban real-estate development. The investment opportunities looked so tempting that new cities sprang up almost overnight from the ruins of the Chicago fire of 1871 and the San Francisco earthquake of 1906. Likewise, real-estate interests, anxious to develop subdivisions, were often partly instrumental in pushing streetcar lines outward from the central districts of cities.

Mass transit became big business. In the early 1880s, Peter A. B. Widener and William L. Elkins teamed up to unite much of Philadelphia's streetcar system within the Philadelphia Traction Company. They did the same in alliance with Charles T. Yerkes in Chicago and with William C. Whitney and Thomas Fortune Ryan in New York. By 1900 their syndicate controlled streetcar systems in more than a hundred cities and had expanded to include utilities supplying gas and electricity to urban customers. The city, like industry, became an arena for enterprise and profit.

This was a matter of choice, however. Under the law, cities had extensive powers of self-development. In a key decision in 1897, the New York state courts authorized New York City to build a municipally owned subway. There could be "no complete definition of 'a city purpose.'" Cities had to determine their needs and then carry out those responsibilities as they saw fit. If a city chose to have services provided by others, it did so by, in effect, turning a private corporation into a municipal instrumentality. Even the use of privately owned land was subject to whatever regulations the city might choose to impose.

But in sharp distinction from Europe, American cities generally hesitated to use the broad municipal powers granted them by the courts. America produced what the urban historian Sam Bass Warner has called "the private city"—one shaped primarily by the actions of many private individuals. All these persons pursued their own goals and tried to maximize their own profit. The prevailing belief was that the sum of such private activity would far exceed what the community could accomplish through public effort. This meant that the city itself handled only functions that could not be undertaken efficiently or profitably by private enterprise.

In that public realm, American cities actually compiled an impressive record of achievement in the late nineteenth century. Nowhere in the world were there more massive public projects: water aqueducts, sewage systems, street paving, bridge building, extensive park systems. Though by no means free of the corruption and wastefulness of earlier days, city governments became markedly more centralized in these years, better administered and more professional, and, above all, more expansive in the functions they undertook. How else could they have gathered the resources and built the infrastructure on which the modern industrial city depended? Massive though it was, however, this public contribution did not undercut the prevailing conception of the city as an arena for private enterprise.

The nation paid an enormous price for such unrestricted development. A century later, we are still adding up the costs in terms of the quality of American urban life.

The Urban Environment. Some of those costs could be seen right away. In 1879 an English visitor observed the blight that spread along streets on which elevated trains operated:

> The nineteen hours and more of incessant rumbling day and night from the passing trains; the blocking out of a sufficiency of light; the full, close view passengers on the cars can have into rooms on the second and third floors.

Skyscrapers also shut out the light, and added to downtown congestion. People regarded such conditions as sad but inevitable costs of progress.

Other consequences were more clearly the result of deliberate choice. Priority went to projects considered vital to a city's economic development. Thus bridge construction flourished. Grand public buildings, symbols of a city's eminence, enjoyed great popularity. Philadelphia's City Hall, said one critic, had been "projected on a scale of magnificence better suited for the capitol of an empire than the municipal building of a debt-burdened city." On the other hand, the condition of the streets, mainly a matter of convenience for the people, often remained scandalously bad. "Three or four days of warm spring weather," remarked a New York journalist, would turn Manhattan's garbage-strewn, snow-clogged streets into "veritable mud rivers."

A visitor to Pittsburgh noted "the heavy pall of smoke which constantly overhangs her . . . until the very sun looks coppery through the sooty haze." As for the lovely hills rising from the rivers, "they have been leveled down, cut into, sliced off, and ruthlessly marred and mutilated, until not a trace of their original outlines remain." Pittsburgh presented "all that is unsightly and forbidding in appearance, the original beauties of nature having been ruthlessly sacrificed to utility."

These failings resulted not only from the low value placed on the quality of urban life. The city's dynamism confounded efforts to provide adequate services. New York's Croton aqueduct, when completed in 1842, was hailed as "more akin in magnificence to the ancient and Roman aqueducts [than anything] achieved in our times." Yet less than a decade later, water consumption was outstripping the capacity of the aqueduct. In 1885, New York started to build a second, larger aqueduct. When that one also failed to meet the city's needs, New York built still another aqueduct a hundred miles away in the Catskill Mountains. Each new facility and innovation seemed to fall short, not merely outstripped by the rising demand, but also contributing further to that demand. This occurred with urban transportation, high-rise building, and modern sanitation systems. They attracted more users, created new necessities, and caused additional crowding and shortages.

It was not that America lacked an urban vision. On the contrary, an abiding rural ideal had exerted a powerful influence on American cities for many years. Frederick Law Olmsted, who designed New York's Central Park before the Civil War and many other city parks in later years, wanted cities that exposed people to the beauties of nature. One of Olmsted's projects, the Chicago World's Fair of 1893, gave rise to the influential "City Beautiful" movement. The results included larger park systems, broad boulevards and parkways, and after the turn of the century, zoning laws and planned suburbs.

Cities usually heeded urban planners too little and far too late. "Fifteen or twenty years ago a plan might have been adopted that would have made this one of the most beautiful cities in the world," the Kansas City Park Commissioners reported in 1893. At that time, "such a policy could not be fully appreciated." Nor, even if Kansas City had foreseen its future, would it have shouldered the "heavy burden" of trying to shape its development. The American city had placed its faith in the dynamics of the marketplace, not the restraints of a planned future.

Housing. The most disastrous impact of dynamic urban growth was on the living conditions of the poor. In the preindustrial city, low-income people had lived on a makeshift basis. They occupied small wooden structures in the alleys and back streets and, increasingly, in the subdivided homes of more prosperous families who had fled to other neighborhoods. When rising

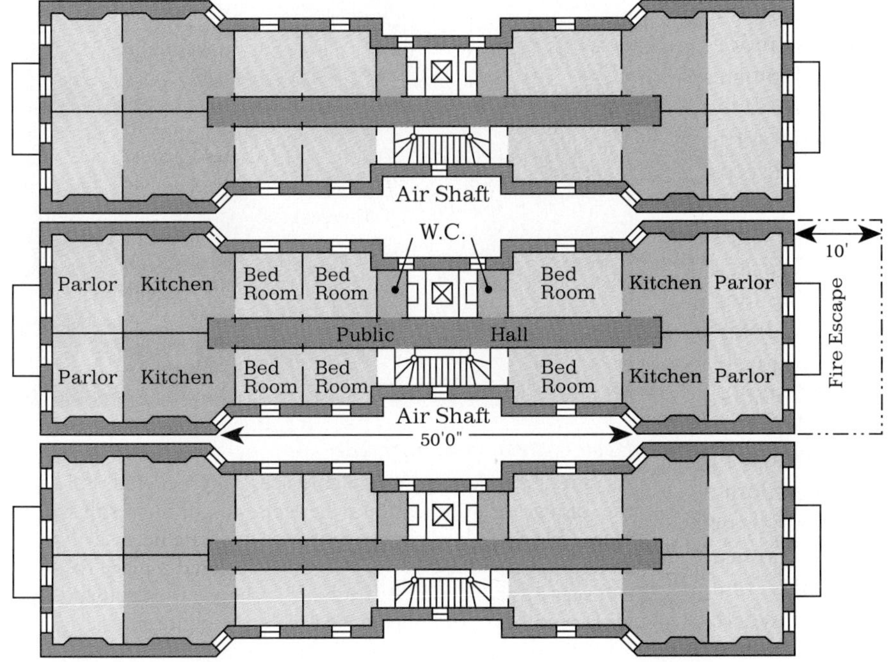

FIGURE 20.1

Floor Plan of a Dumbbell Tenement

land values after the Civil War made this practice uneconomical, speculators began to build housing specifically designed for the urban masses. In New York City, the dreadful result was the "dumbbell" tenement, so shaped as to utilize nearly all the standard 25 by 100–foot lot. A five-story building of this type could house twenty families in cramped, airless apartments (see Figure 20.1). In New York's Eleventh Ward, an average of 986 persons occupied each acre, a density matched only in Bombay, India. In other cities, the pressure for space was not quite as severe. Chicago, Boston, and St. Louis relied on two- and three-story buildings for low-income housing, while Philadelphia and Baltimore made do with dingy row houses.

But people everywhere considered these districts to be blights on the city. Here is how one investigator described Chicago's Halsted Street in 1896:

> The filthy and rotten tenements, the dingy courts and tumble-down sheds, the foul stables and dilapidated outhouses, the broken sewer pipes, the piles of garbage fairly alive with diseased odors, and . . . children filling every nook, working and playing in every room, eating and sleeping in every windowsill, pouring in and out of every door, and seeming literally to pave every scrap of "yard."

Reformers recognized the problem but seemed unable to solve it. Some favored model tenements financed by public-spirited citizens willing to accept limited dividends on their investments. When such private philanthropy failed to make much of a dent on the problem, cities tried to impose basic housing codes. The most advanced of these was New York's Tenement House Law of 1901, which applied stringent requirements for open courts, indoor toilets, and stronger fire safeguards on new housing, but did little to improve existing housing stock. Enforcement of housing standards was, moreover, always problematic. Commercial development had pushed up land values in downtown areas. Only high-density, cheaply built housing could earn a sufficient profit for the landlords of the poor. This basic economic fact defied nineteenth-century solutions.

A Balance Sheet: Chicago and Berlin. In 1902 Chicago and Berlin had virtually equal populations—1.8 million each. Their histories were, however, profoundly different. Seventy years earlier, when Chicago was just a muddy frontier outpost, Berlin already housed 250,000 people and had been for centuries the seat of the Hohenzollerns of Prussia. With German unification in 1871, the imperial authorities set about rebuilding Berlin on a grander scale. "A capital city is essential for the state, to act as a pivot for its culture," proclaimed the Prussian historian Heinrich von Treitschke, and Berlin served that national purpose—"a center where [Germany's] political, intellectual, and material life is concentrated, and its people can feel united." Chicago had no such pretensions. It was strictly a place of business, made great by virtue of its strategic grip on the commerce of America's industrial heartland. Nothing in Chicago evoked the grandeur of Berlin's boulevards or its monumental palaces and public buildings, nor were Chicagoans ever witness to the pomp and ceremony of the imperial parades through the Brandenburg Gate and up broad, tree-lined Unter den Linden to the national cathedral.

Yet as a functioning city Chicago was in many ways clearly superior to Berlin. For instance, Chicago's waterworks pumped 500 million gallons of water a day, providing 139 gallons of water per person, while a Berliner had to make do with 18 gallons. Flush toilets, a rarity in Berlin in 1900, could be found in 60 percent of Chicago's homes. Its streets were lit by electricity while Berlin was still relying mostly on gas lamps. Chicago had a much more extensive streetcar system, twice as much acreage devoted to parks, and a public library containing many more volumes than Berlin's. And Chicago had just completed an amazing sanitation project to protect its water supply in Lake Michigan. By

Hester Street, New York City

As cities grew, land values in core areas skyrocketed. For the immigrant poor, with nowhere else to go, the result was incredible crowding in tenement housing. Life necessarily spilled out into the streets. The streets offered a place to transact business, a bit of fresh air, a chance to socialize with neighbors, and playing space for the children.

means of the new Sanitary and Ship Canal, the course of the Chicago River had been reversed so that its waters—and the city's sewage—would flow away from the lake and southward down into the Illinois and Mississippi rivers. To create the giant canal, over 30 million cubic yards of dirt had had to be excavated. This was the greatest earth-moving project in municipal history up to that time.

Giant sanitation projects were one thing, an inspiring urban environment something else. "We are enormously rich," admitted the journalist Edwin L. Godkin, "but . . . what have we got to show? Almost nothing. Ugliness from an artistic point of view is the mark of all our cities." This, then, was the urban balance sheet: a utilitarian infrastructure superb by nineteenth century standards, but "no municipal splendors of any description, nothing but population and hotels."

City People

The city symbolized energy and enterprise, with its soaring skyscrapers, rushing subways and jostling traffic, and hum of business activity. When the budding writer Hamlin Garland and his brother arrived in Chicago from rural Iowa in 1881, they knew immediately that they had entered a new world: "Everything interested us. . . . Nothing was commonplace, nothing was ugly to us." In one way or another, every city-bound migrant, whether from the American countryside or a foreign land, experienced something of this exhilaration and wonder.

But with the opportunity and boundless variety came profound disorder and uncertainty. The urban world was utterly unlike the rural communities that the newcomers had left. In the countryside every person had been known to his or her neighbors. Mark Twain found New York "a splendid desert, where a stranger is lonely in the midst of a million of his race. A man walks his tedious miles through the same interminable streets every day, yet never seeing a familiar face, and never seeing a strange one the second time. . . . Every man rushes, rushes, rushes, and never has time to be companionable—never has any time at his disposal to fool away on matters which do not involve dollars and duty and business." If rural roles and obligations had been well understood, in the city the only predictable relationships were those dictated by the marketplace.

The newcomers could never recreate in the city the worlds they had left behind. But new ways developed to meet the social needs of urban dwellers—to give them a sense of their place in the community; to teach them how to function in an impersonal, heterogeneous environment; and to make the complex, dynamic city understandable. An urban culture emerged, and through it there developed a new breed of American entirely at home in the modern city.

Immigrants

At the turn of the century upwards of 30 percent of the residents of New York, Chicago, Boston, Cleveland, Minneapolis, and San Francisco were foreign-born. Except in the South, America's cities had attracted large numbers of immigrants for many years. In 1900 the dominant groups still represented mainly the older migration from northern Europe. The biggest ethnic group in Boston was Irish; in Minneapolis, Swedish; in most other northern cities, German. But by 1914 the influx from southern and Eastern Europe had changed the ethnic complexion of many of these cities. In Chicago, Poles and Russians (mostly Jewish) took the lead; in New York, Italians were second to Russians; in San Francisco, Italians became the largest foreign-born group.

For all of these immigrants—old and new—ethnic identity played a crucial role in forming an urban community. All of them carried experiences and customs from the homeland that shaped their lives in the new world. But for the later arrivals from southern and Eastern Europe, there was less intermingling with the older populations than had been possible in the earlier "walking cities." Beginning in the 1880s, observers invariably reported that only foreign-born people lived in the poorer downtown areas of the great eastern and midwestern cities. "One may find for the asking an Italian, a German, a French, African, Spanish, Bohemian,

TABLE 20.2

Foreign-Born Population of Philadelphia, 1870 and 1910

	1870	1910
Irish	96,698	83,196
German	50,746	61,480
Austrian	519	19,860
Italian	516	45,308
Russian	94	90,697
Hungarian	52	12,495
Foreign-born population	183,624	384,707
Total population	674,022	1,549,008

Source: Allen F. Davis and Mark Haller, *The Peoples of Philadelphia* (Philadelphia: Temple University Press, 1973). Reprinted by permission of Temple University Press.

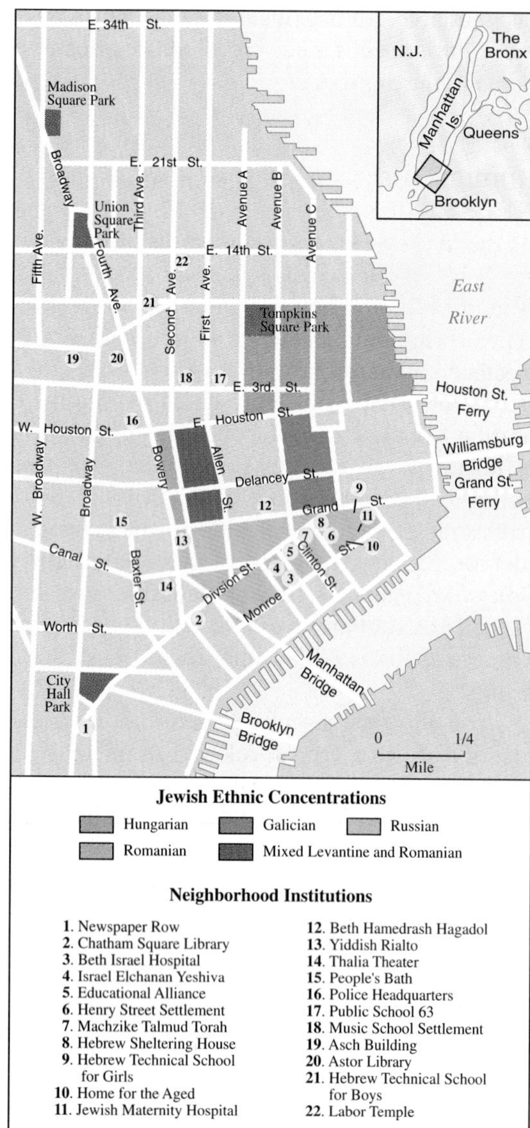

MAP 20.3

The Lower East Side, New York City

Jews from Eastern Europe concentrated in Manhattan's Lower East Side and, within that area, settled among others from their home regions. The feeling of group identity led to a remarkable flowering of institutions built by Jewish immigrants to meet their educational, cultural, and social needs.

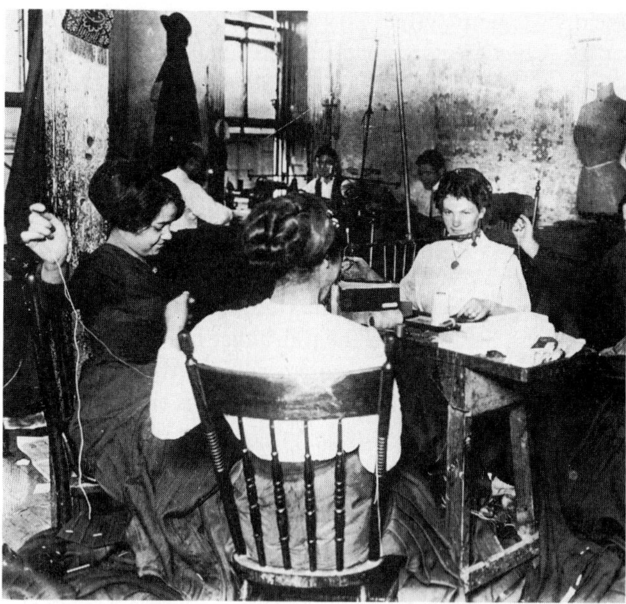

The Economy of the Ghetto

Downtown immigrant neighborhoods would not have struck the casual observer as industrial districts. But tucked away in the tenements were commercial lofts and small workshops. An entire ready-made clothing industry flourished within the ghettoes of large cities, drawing especially on the young women of the neighborhoods to do the low-paid sewing tasks.

Russian, Scandinavian, Jewish, and Chinese colony," remarked the Danish-American journalist Jacob Riis in his study of lower New York in 1890. "The one thing you shall vainly ask for in the chief city of America is a distinctively American community."

The foreign-born had little choice about where they lived: they needed to be near their jobs and could not afford better housing. Some gravitated to the factory districts; others settled in the congested downtown ghettoes. The immigrants did not arrive randomly in these districts, however. Even where this seemed to happen, as in Philadelphia, closer study revealed that ethnic groups clustered in certain houses and portions of blocks. More commonly, as Riis discovered, an ethnic group took over an entire neighborhood. In New York, Italians crowded into the Irish neighborhoods west of Broadway, and Russian and Polish Jews pushed the Germans out of the Lower East Side. A dense colony of Hungarians lived around Houston Street, and Bohemians occupied the Upper East Side between Fiftieth and Seventy-sixth streets.

Within ethnic groups, one could also spot clusterings of people from the same province or even the same village. Among New York Italians, for example, Neapolitans and Calabrians populated the Mulberry Bend district, while Genoese lived on Baxter Street. Other northern Italians occupied the Eighth and Fifteenth wards west of Broadway, while southern Italians moved into "little Italy" far up in Harlem. In 1903, along a short stretch of Elizabeth Street, lived several hundred families from a single Sicilian fishing town, Sciacca.

Capitalizing on the feeling of companionship that drew ethnic groups together, a variety of institutions

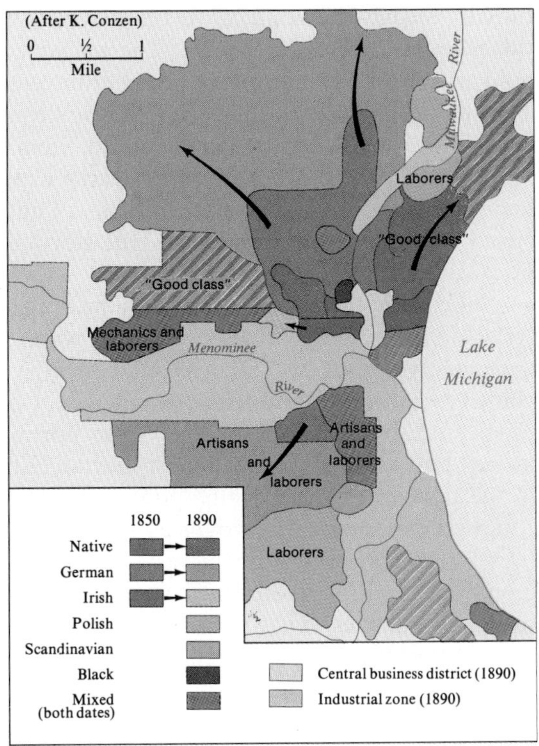

MAP 20.4

The Urban Ethnic Mosaic: Milwaukee, 1850–1890

Neighborhoods in American cities developed strong class and ethnic identities in the second half of the nineteenth century. Core areas near downtown Milwaukee expanded outward as immigrant populations increased and new residents arrived. Artisans and laborers tended to settle near their places of work in and near the industrial zone. The "good class" (upper and middle classes) and German residents have remained dominant in certain areas throughout Milwaukee's history.

sprang up to meet their needs. Wherever substantial numbers of immigrants lived, newspapers appeared. In 1911 the twenty thousand Poles in Buffalo, New York, supported two Polish-language daily papers. Immigrants throughout the country avidly read *Il Progresso Italo-Americano* and the Yiddish-language *Jewish Daily Forward*, both published in New York City. Convivality could always be found on street corners, in barbershops and club rooms, and in saloons. A 1905 survey showed that Chicago had as many saloons as grocery stores, meat markets, and dry-goods stores together. Italians marched in saint's day parades, Bohemians gathered in singing societies, and New York Jews patronized a vibrant Yiddish theater. To provide help in times of sickness and death, the immigrants organized mutual-aid societies. The Italians of Chicago had sixty-six of these organizations in 1903, composed mainly of people from particular provinces and towns. Immigrants built a rich and functional institutional life in urban America, to an extent unimagined in their native villages.

Urban Blacks. The vast majority of African Americans—85 percent in 1880—lived in the rural South. In the ensuing years some of them migrated to the modestly growing southern cities. By 1900 blacks constituted roughly a third of the South's total urban population, ranging from 20 percent in Louisville and Dallas to absolute majorities in Memphis and Charleston.

The great African-American migration to northern cities was just beginning. The black population of New York increased by 30,000 between 1900 and 1910, making it second only to Washington, D.C., as a black urban center. Still, the 91,000 blacks in New York in 1910 represented fewer than 2 percent of the population, as did Chicago's 45,000 black residents, and Cleveland's 6,000.

Despite their relatively small numbers, urban blacks could not escape becoming targets of the fierce racism of the age. In northern cities generally, residential segregation was intensifying, and the scattered black neighborhoods were giving way to concentrated ghettoes—Chicago's Black Belt on the south side, for example, or the early outlines of New York's Harlem. Job opportunities were likewise narrowing. While 26 percent of Cleveland's blacks had been skilled workers in 1870, only 12 percent were by 1890, and entire occupations like barbering (at least for a white clientele) disappeared. Two-thirds of all Cleveland's blacks in 1910 worked as domestic and day laborers, with little hope of pushing their way up the job ladder.

In the face of segregation and economic discrimination, urban blacks built their communities. They created a flourishing press, fraternal orders, a vast array of women's organizations, and a middle class of doctors, lawyers, and small entrepreneurs who catered to their needs. Above all, there were the black churches—twenty-five in Chicago in 1905, mainly Methodist and Baptist. More than any other institution, remarked one scholar in 1913, it was the church "which the Negro may call his own. . . . A new church may be built . . . and . . . all the machinery set in motion without ever consulting any white person. . . . [It] more than anything else represents the real life of the race." As in the southern countryside, the church was the central institution for city blacks, and the preacher—"a leader, a politician, an orator, a 'boss,' an intriguer, an idealist," as W. E. B. Du Bois described him—the most important local citizen. Manhattan's Union Baptist Church, housed like many others in a storefront, attracted the "very recent residents of this new, disturbing city" and, ringing with spirituals and fervent prayer, made Christianity come "alive Sunday mornings."

Ward Politics

Race and ethnicity tended to divide newcomers to the city and turn them inward. Politics acted in the opposite direction, serving as a powerful instrument for integrating immigrants and blacks into the larger urban society. The basic unit of city governance was the *ward*, each one entitled to its representative on the city council or board of aldermen. Whether realizing it or not, every migrant to an American city automatically belonged to a ward, and by virtue of residence on a particular street immediately acquired a spokesman at city hall. In earlier days, the aldermen had been the dominant figures in urban politics, but that was no longer the case in the late nineteenth century. Power had largely passed to the mayor's office and the various citywide administrative agencies. But the city council still represented the parochial interests of the wards, and immigrants learned very quickly that if they needed anything from city hall, the alderman was the person for them. That was how streets got paved, or water mains extended, or a variance granted—so that, for example, in 1888, Vito Fortounescere could "place and keep a stand for the sale of fruit, inside the stoop-line, in front of the northeast corner of Twenty-eighth Street and Fourth Avenue" in Manhattan, or that the parishioners of Saint Maria of Mount Carmel could set off fireworks at their Fourth of July picnic.

Interlinked with this formal representation was the pervasive presence of the party machines in the immigrant and black neighborhoods. Machine control of political parties existed at every level of American politics (see Chapter 19). The system flourished most luxuriantly, however, in the big cities. Most famous was Tammany Hall, the political machine that dominated Manhattan's Democratic party; but the major parties of most large cities—Democratic or Republican—had their versions of Tammany. The power of the urban machines depended on a loyal party constituency. This meant organization down to the grass roots. The wards were divided into election districts of a few blocks, each with a district captain who reported to the ward boss (who might or might not also be the alderman). It was the main job of these functionaries to be accessible and, as best they could, to serve the needs of the party's constituents.

The machine performed a similar function for the business community. Entrepreneurs of many kinds wanted something from the city. Contractors sought city business; gas companies and streetcar lines wanted licenses and privileges; manufacturers needed services and not-too-nosy inspectors; and the liquor trade and numbers racket relied on a tolerant police force. All of them turned to the machine boss and his lieutenants. In addition to these everyday functions, the machine continually mediated among conflicting interests and oiled the wheels of city government. The machines filled a void in the public life of the nineteenth-century city. They did informally much of what the municipal system left undone. "Nowhere else in the world," remarked the journalist Henry Jones Ford, "has party organization had to cope with such enormous tasks . . . and its efficiency in dealing with them is the true glory of our political system."

Of course, the machine exacted a price for all these services. The tenement dweller gave his vote. The businessman wrote a check. Those who became the machine's beneficiaries enabled it to function. Corruption permeated this informal system. Some portion of the money that changed hands almost inevitably ended up in the pockets of the machine politicians. This boodle could take the form of outright corruption—kickbacks by contractors, protection money from gamblers, saloonkeepers, and prostitutes, payoffs from gas and trolley companies. The Tammany ward boss George Washington Plunkitt, however, insisted that he had no need for kickbacks and bribes. He favored what he called "honest graft," the easy profits that came to political insiders from sure-fire investment—for example, by purchasing a vacant lot he knew would soon be needed for a city project—and the inside track on city contracts. Plunkitt himself made most of his money building wharves on Manhattan's waterfront. One way or another, legally or otherwise, machine politics rewarded its supporters.

For the young and ambitious, this was reason enough to favor the machine system. American society celebrated personal achievement but denied economic opportunity to poor immigrants. Not only did they lack the means to get started in business, remarked Robert A. Woods about the inhabitants of Boston's South End, "but they have to meet strong prejudices of race and religion. Politics, therefore, is for them apparently the easiest way to success in life." In the mid-1870s, over half of Chicago's forty aldermen were foreign-born, sixteen of them Irish immigrants. In 1885 the first Italian was elected to the board, and in 1888, the first Pole, followed in the 1890s by Czechs and Scandinavians. Blacks did not manage to get on to Chicago's board of aldermen until after 1900; but in Baltimore an African-American represented the Eleventh Ward from 1890 onward, and Philadelphia had three black aldermen by 1899. As a ladder for social mobility, machine politics (like professional sports, entertainment, and organized crime) was the most democratic of American institutions.

For most tenement dwellers, however, the machine had a more modest value. It acted as a rough-and-ready social service agency, providing jobs for the jobless, a helping hand for a bereaved family, and intercession against an unfeeling city bureaucracy. As a Boston ward boss remarked, "There's got to be in every ward somebody that any bloke can come to—no matter what he's done—and get help. *Help, you understand; none of your law and justice, but help.*" Tammany ward boss Plunkitt had a "regular system" when fires broke out in his district. "Any hour of the day or night, I'm usually there . . . as soon as the fire engines. If a family is burned out I don't ask whether they are Republicans or Democrats, and I don't refer them to the Charity Organization Society. . . . I just get quarters for them . . . and fix them up till they get things runnin' again. It's philanthropy, but it's politics, too—mighty good politics. . . . The poor look up to George W. Plunkitt as a father, come to him when they are in trouble—and don't forget him on election day."

Plunkitt was an Irishman, and so, indeed, were most of the ward politicians controlling Tammany Hall. But by the 1890s, Plunkitt's Fifteenth District was filling up with Italians and Eastern European Jews. In general, the New York Irish had no love for these newer immigrants. But Plunkitt played no favorites. On any given day (as recorded in a diary) he might be attending an Italian funeral in the afternoon and a Jewish wedding in the evening, and at each probably conveyed his respects with a few choice Italian words or a bit of Yiddish.

"Think what New York is and what the people of New York are," remarked Richard Croker, the powerful head of Tammany during the 1890s, and Plunkitt's boss.

> One half, more than half, are of foreign birth. . . . They do not speak our language, they do not know our laws, they are the raw material from which we have to build up the state. . . . [Tammany] looks after them for the sake of their vote, grafts them upon the Republic, makes citizens of them, in short. . . . Who else would do it if we did not? . . . There is not a mugwump in the city who would shake hands with the [immigrant voter].

The Mugwump reformer (see pp. 587) would doubtless have retorted that the nation could do without citizens whose notion of politics was only what was in it for themselves. But Croker spoke a powerful truth. In an era when so many forces acted to isolate the ghetto communities, politics served an *integrating* function, cutting across ethnic lines and giving immigrants and blacks a stake in the larger urban order.

Religion and Ethnic Identity

Among immigrant groups, religion was an abiding concern and so intertwined with ethnic identity as to be inseparable from the story of how the newcomers adapted to the American city.

Eastern European Jews. When Jews from Eastern Europe began their mass migration in the 1880s, about 250,000 Jews, mostly of German origin, were already living in America. The German Jews, well established and increasingly prosperous, had long since begun to embrace Reform Judaism. Reform Jews abandoned religious practices "not adapted to the views and habits of modern civilization." They practiced a form of Judaism very remote from the orthodoxy of Yiddish-speaking Jews. The Eastern Europeans founded their own Orthodox synagogues, often in vacant stores and ramshackle buildings. The number of synagogues in the United States jumped from 270 in 1880 to 1,901 in 1916.

Many Jews found it difficult to adhere to the traditional forms of their religion. In the isolated villages of Eastern Europe, Judaism comprised not only worship and belief but an entire way of life. Not even the closely confined urban American ghetto could re-create the communal environment essential for strict religious observance. "The very clothes I wore and the very food I ate had a fatal effect on my religious habits," confessed the hero of Abraham Cahan's novel *The Rise of David Levinsky* (1917). "If you . . . attempt to bend your religion to the spirit of your surroundings, it breaks. It falls to pieces." Levinsky shaved off his beard and plunged into the Manhattan clothing business. Orthodox Judaism survived this shattering of faith, but only by sharply reducing its claims on the lives of the faithful.

Catholic Immigrants. Catholics faced much the same problem. The issue, explicitly defined within the Roman Catholic Church as "Americanism," turned on how far Catholicism should respond to American society. Catholics fought out the question on many fronts. Should Catholic children attend parochial or public schools? Should they intermarry with non-Catholics? Should the traditional education for the clergy be changed? Bishop John Ireland of St. Paul, Minnesota, felt that "the principles of the Church are in harmony with the interests of the Republic." But traditionalists, led by Archbishop Michael A. Corrigan of New York, denied the possibility of such harmony. They argued, in effect, for insulating the church from a hostile environment.

In 1895, Pope Leo XIII announced his support of the traditionalists. In America, with its tradition of religious pluralism and sharp separation of church and state, was not "to be sought the type of the most desirable status of the Church." The pope regretted the absence of the benefits that came from state support and urged Catholics "to prefer to associate with Catholics, a course which will be very conducive to the safeguarding of their faith." Catholicism, because of its hierarchical structure, had a better chance than Judaism to resist American influences.

AMERICAN LIVES

Big Tim Sullivan: Tammany Politician

Timothy D. Sullivan was born on July 23, 1863, near the Hudson River docks in Lower Manhattan. His parents were Irish immigrants, part of the mass migration of potato famine victims that flooded into New York in the 1840s. Four years later Tim's father died, leaving the young widow Catherine Connelly Sullivan with four small children. Soon thereafter Catherine married Lawrence Mulligan, an Irish laborer, and the family moved to the notorious Five Points district on the Lower East Side. There the 1870 census found them, a household of ten (including three boarders), living in an overcrowded tenement at 25 Baxter Street (see Map 20.3, which can be consulted to trace the urban geography of Sullivan's career).

Tim had a harsh childhood. His stepfather drank heavily and regularly beat his wife and children. To make ends meet, Catherine took in washing, and Tim went to work at age seven bundling paper for $1.50 a week on Newspaper Row across from City Hall. Tim got through grammar school, but his family needed his earnings too much for him to go on to high school. "Free as it was," he later remarked, "it was not free enough for me to go there." Instead—Horatio Alger-style—he pushed his way up in the newspaper business and by age eighteen was well established as a wholesale newspaper dealer. He soon became the proprietor of two saloons and, in his early twenties, was ready for politics. Sullivan was a big fellow, over six feet tall, handsome, and quick with his fists. He gained a local reputation by thrashing a tough he had encountered on the street beating up a woman. True or not, the story helped him win the Democratic nomination at age twenty-three for the New York State Assembly from the Second District.

In 1889, Sullivan opposed a bill granting Manhattan's police virtually unlimited powers to detain people with jail records. The champion of the bill was Thomas F. Byrnes, chief inspector of the New York Police Department and the most celebrated detective in the country. Byrnes did not take kindly to opposition from small-time politicians. He raided Sullivan's saloons, arrested two barkeepers for excise tax violations, and denounced Sullivan as a consorter with criminals. Against the advice of friends, Sullivan took the Assembly floor to answer the charge. In tearful tones, Sullivan cast himself as an "honest Bowery boy," describing his impoverished childhood, his saintly mother, his struggle to rise in the world. "When, at the conclusion [so a reporter recorded], he asked if he had any time or money to spend with thieves, there was a 'No' on nearly every member's lips." It was the making of the obscure assemblyman. Although he gained a notoriety with uptown New Yorkers that would dog him throughout his career, he won the hearts of his own constituents, who revelled in the success story of one of their own. They thought "Big Tim" a fine fellow, and so did the Tammany leaders.

When the Tammany machine swept into power in the 1892 elections, Boss Richard Croker tapped Sullivan to run the new Third Assembly District centering around the Bowery. Sullivan swiftly consolidated his power. His inner circle was all Irish, but for election district captains he appointed Jews, Italians, and Germans who were well-connected in the immigrant communities that populated his fiefdom. Sullivan became famous for his summer "chowders," when he transported his constituents by riverboat to the country for a rowdy day of picnicking. At Christmas there was a fine dinner for all who were in need. And in February Sullivan handed out wool socks and shoes—always with the sentimental tale of how a teacher had given him free shoes one cold winter. Big Tim also attended assiduously to the nitty-gritty business of running a political machine. He got jobs for his supporters, visited the jails regularly to offer bail and other aid to the inmates, and, on election day, made sure his strong-arm crews patrolled the polling places. Sullivan's district became the best organized in the city, and Tammany hailed him as "the most popular man on the East Side."

In the meantime, Sullivan was making his fortune. His particular form of "honest graft" was commercial entertainment. In his bones Big Tim knew how important a good time was to city people. Besides, the main street of his district, the Bowery, was the gaudy center of low-life entertainment for the entire city, lined with burlesque houses, concert saloons, restaurants, and cheap hotels. In the mid-1890s he formed a partnership with two theatrical producers and began to invest in vaudeville houses. He contributed not only money and a shrewd head but the political contacts that assured lax enforcement of building codes and easy access to liquor licenses. Sullivan also became involved in professional boxing, horse racing, and, more illicitly, the gambling dens that dotted his district.

Big Tim Sullivan

Sullivan was accused of trafficking in East Side prostitution, but this he indignantly denied. "Nobody who knows me well will believe I would take a penny from any woman, much less from the poor creatures who are more to be pitied than any other human beings on earth. I'd be afraid to take a cent from a poor woman of the streets for fear my old mother would see me. I'd a good deal rather break into a bank and rob the safe. That would be a more manly and decent way of getting money."

When Boss Croker resigned in 1902, Sullivan might have succeeded him, but Big Tim preferred his own district and threw his support to Charles F. Murphy, who ruled Tammany for the next twenty-two years. Sullivan served briefly in Congress, made a lot more money investing in the early movie industry and in vaudeville syndicates across the country, and, in the final phase of his career, became a champion of progressive social legislation in the New York State Senate. In 1912, Sullivan suffered a severe mental breakdown, possibly caused by tertiary syphilis. A year later he died under the wheels of a freight train while trying to escape from his brother's house outside New York. His funeral procession down the Bowery was one of the largest in memory and brought out an immense crowd from every stratum of New York society, from statesmen to prizefighters and scrubwomen.

Immaculate Heart of Mary Church, 1908

In the crowded immigrant neighborhoods, only the church rose from the undistinguished mass to assert the centrality of religious belief in the life of the community. The photograph is a view of Immaculate Heart of Mary Church from Polish Hill in Pittsburgh taken in 1908.

The Church's traditional wing had the support of immigrant Catholics, who wanted to preserve their religion as they had known it in Europe. But the needs of the immigrants extended beyond purely religious matters. They wanted the Church also to be an expression of their ethnic identities. Newly arrived Catholics wanted their own parishes, where they could celebrate their own customs and holidays, speak their own languages, and educate their children in their own parochial schools. When they became numerous enough, they also demanded their own bishops. German Catholics had pressed these ethnic claims for years, and so did the southern and Eastern Europeans who flocked to America from the 1890s onward.

The Church had difficulty responding. The demands of its immigrant congregations seemed to challenge the Catholic hierarchy, which was dominated by Irish Catholics, and, more important, to challenge the integrity of the Church itself. The desire for ethnic parishes did more than divide Catholics; it also led to demands for local control of Church property. In addition, if the Church appointed bishops with jurisdiction over specific ethnic groups, this would mean disrupting the diocesan structure that unified the Church.

The severity of the conflict depended partly on the religious traditions of each ethnic group. Italians, for example, had a strong anticlerical feeling, much strengthened by the papacy's opposition to the unification of Italy. Italian men also had a tradition of religious apathy. On the other hand, the Church played such an important part in the lives of Polish immigrants that they sometimes tolerated no interference from the Catholic hierarchy. In 1907, fifty parishes formed the Polish National Catholic Church of America, which adhered to Catholic ritual without recognizing the pope's authority.

On the whole, however, the Church reconciled its authority with the ethnic needs of the immigrant faithful. It met the demand for representation in the hierarchy by appointing Polish and other immigrant priests as auxiliary bishops within existing dioceses. Before World War I, American Catholics worshiped in more than two thousand foreign-language churches and in many others that were bilingual. The Catholic Church thus became a central institution for the expression of ethnic identity in urban America.

Urban Protestantism. For the Protestant churches, the city posed different, but not easier, challenges than those faced by the largely immigrant Jewish and Catholic faiths. With the surge of immigration from southern and Eastern Europe, urban populations were becoming increasingly non-Protestant. At the same time, Protestant congregations were abandoning the older residential neighborhoods. Many formerly prosperous churches found themselves stranded in bleak working-class districts. During the twenty years after 1868, seventeen Protestant churches moved out of Lower Manhattan, as the area below Fourteenth Street filled up with immigrants.

Nearly every major city retained great downtown churches where wealthy Protestants worshiped. Some of these churches, richly endowed, took pride in nationally prominent pastors, including Henry Ward Beecher of Plymouth Congregational Church in Brooklyn and Phillips Brooks of Trinity Episcopal Church in Boston.

AMERICAN VOICES

The Salvation Army at Work

Maud Ballington Booth, daughter-in-law of the founder of the Salvation Army, describes the efforts of the Army's Slum Brigade in 1894.

When the Salvation Army launched out upon its work of raising and helping the outcast, it . . . reached, and is now reaching the poor, otherwise untouched by religious influence. Street loungers, drunkards, wife-beaters, wild, reckless youths, and fallen women, were attracted to its halls, by the hundreds of thousands, by the open-air procession, and through the lively and enthusiastic character of its services. . . .

It is now five years since we began the Slum Brigade work in New York City. . . . Perhaps the duty which absorbs the greatest part of their time is . . . the systematic house-to-house and room-to-room visitation of all the worst homes in their neighborhood. The visits paid in saloons and dives are naturally of a different character. There it has to be personal, dealing face to face with the people upon the danger of their wild lives, and the sorrow and misery that is coming to them. Sometimes it has to be very straight and earnest talk to some drunken man. At others gentle, affectionate pleading with some poor outcast girl, down whose painted cheeks the tears of bitter remorse fall. . . . Our women work entirely without escort, and this very fact appeals to the spark of gallantry in the hearts of those rough, hardened men, and if anyone dared to lay a finger upon the "Slum Sisters," or say an insulting word to them, champions would arise on every hand to defend them. . . . These visits are often lengthened into prayer-meetings, which include singing and speaking, to a more interested audience, and certainly a more needy one, than can be found within the walls of many a church. . . .

Street work is another phase of their mission. . . . In this they deal with the people whom they have not found within the saloons . . . many of them being sailors and members of the floating population. . . . They are talked to in a friendly and yet very practical way during the evening hours, when there is a great deal of street lounging. . . .

Yet another means of reaching these people is the gathering of them into our halls or meeting places. . . . The audiences are chiefly composed of men, very often young men such as from the toughest gangs in down-town sections of the city. . . . The bright, lively songs of the Salvation Army, the ever changing phases of the meetings, and the thorough bond of sympathy between the speakers on the platform and the roughs in the hall make these meetings a source of great power and interest. Of course, there are occasionally fights among the audience, chairs are upset every now and then, windows are broken . . . and yet through it all a deep, powerful wave of influence carries into the hearts of the people the sincerity and truth of things spiritual.

Source: Maud Ballington Booth, "Salvation Army Work in the Slums," *Scribner's Magazine* 17 (January 1895), pp. 103, 110–112, reprinted in Bayrd Still, *Urban America: A History with Documents* (Boston: Little, Brown, 1974), pp. 299–300.

The eminence of these churches, with their fashionable congregations and imposing edifices, emphasized the growing remoteness of Protestantism from much of its urban constituency. "Where is the city in which the Sabbath day is not losing ground?" lamented a minister in 1887. The families of businessmen, lawyers, and doctors could be seen in any church on Sunday morning, he noted, "but the workingmen and their families are not there."

To counter this decline, the Protestant churches responded in two ways. They evangelized among the unchurched and indifferent, for example, through the Sunday-school movement that blossomed in these years. Protestants also made their churches instruments of social uplift. Starting in the 1880s, many city churches provided reading rooms, day nurseries, clubhouses, and vocational classes. Sometimes the churches linked evangelism and social uplift. The Salvation Army, which arrived from England in 1879, spread the gospel of repentance among the urban poor and built up an assistance program that ranged from soup kitchens to homes for former prostitutes. When all else failed, the down-and-outers of American cities knew they could count on the Salvation Army.

The Young Men's and Women's Christian Associations attracted large numbers of the young single people flocking into the cities. Originating in England, the two organizations had arrived in the United States before the Civil War, and both grew prodigiously in the late nineteenth century. By the mid-1880s, virtually every large city had a YMCA equipped with gymnasiums, auditoriums, and dormitories. Housing for single women was an especially important mission of the YWCAs. No other organizations better met the needs of young adults for physical recreation, education, or companionship, or so effectively combine these services with an evangelizing appeal in the form of Bible classes, nondenominational worship, and a religious atmosphere.

The need of many people to unite religion with social uplift could be seen in the enormous popularity of a book called *In His Steps* (1896). The author, the Congregational minister Charles M. Sheldon, told the story of a congregation that resolved to live by Christ's precepts for one year. "If the church members were all doing as Jesus would do," Sheldon asked, "could it remain true that armies of men would walk the streets for jobs, and hundreds of them curse the church, and thousands of them find in the saloon their best friend?"

Urban Revivalism. The most potent form of urban evangelism—revivalism—said little about social uplift. From its beginnings in the eighteenth century, revivalism had steadfastly focused on the individual and had stressed personal redemption. The solution of earthly problems would follow the conversion of the people to Christ. Beginning in the mid-1870s, revival meetings swept the cities.

The pioneering figure was Dwight L. Moody, a former Chicago shoe salesman and YMCA official. After preaching in England for two years, Moody returned to America in 1875. With his talented chorister and hymn writer, Ira D. Sankey, Moody staged revival meetings that drew thousands of people. He preached an optimistic, uncomplicated, nondenominational message. Eternal life could be had for the asking, Moody shouted as he held up his Bible. His listeners needed only "to come forward and take, TAKE!"

Many other preachers followed in Moody's path. The most notable was Billy (William Ashley) Sunday, a hard-drinking outfielder for the Chicago White Stockings who mended his ways and found religion. Like Moody and other city revivalists, Sunday was a farm boy. His rip-snorting cries against "Charlotte-russe Christians" and the "booze traffic" carried the ring of rustic America. By realizing that many people remained villagers at heart, revivalists had found a key for bringing city dwellers back into the church fold.

In a larger sense, however, revivalism was expressive of a more general Fundamentalist movement seeking to preserve old-time religion against the increasing complacency and the doctrinal liberalism of mainstream Protestantism. Just as Methodism had arisen to challenge the Church of England in the eighteenth century, so now in the late nineteenth century new churches arose against Methodism. The Holiness evangelical movement was at first nondenominational, but then it began to spawn such new denominations as the Church of the Nazarene (1908). Out of the Holiness Revival came the still more radical Pentecostal movement, which by 1914 had brought together many local bodies into the Assemblies of God.

Luna Park, Coney Island

Luna Park was the Disneyland of the Industrial Age, but more unbuttoned and casual, intended to lift city dwellers out of their work-a-day lives for a few hours. The view is down the main thoroughfare looking toward the entrance.

Leisure in the City

City people divided life's activities into separate units, setting workplace apart from home, and working time apart from free time. Leisure became a defined function, marked by the clock and enjoyed in distinctive ways and at designated places. In the impersonal, anonymous world they inhabited, urban dwellers increasingly found themselves the paying customers of commercial entertainment. A new class of entrepreneurs emerged whose business it was to give the public what it wanted.

Amusement parks—Boston's Paragon Park, Philadelphia's Willow Grove, Atlanta's Ponce de Leon Park, Cleveland's Euclid Beach, San Francisco's The Chutes—went up at the end of trolley lines in cities across the country. Most remarkable perhaps was Luna Park at New York's Coney Island—"an enchanted, storybook land of trellises, columns, domes, minarets, lagoons, and lofty aerial flights. . . . It was a world removed—shut away from the sordid clatter and turmoil of the streets." In fact, that escape from everyday urban life was the lure of the amusement parks. The creators of Luna Park intended it to be "a different world—a dream world, perhaps a nightmare world—where all is bizarre and fantastic—crazier than the craziest parts of Paris—gayer and more different from the every-day world."

Theatrical entertainment likewise attracted huge audiences. Chicago had six vaudeville houses in 1896, and twenty-two in 1910. Evolving from cheap variety and minstrel shows, vaudeville moved from boisterous beer halls into grand theaters. It cleaned up its routines, making them suitable for the entire family, and turned into thoroughly professional entertainment handled by national booking agencies. With its standard program of nine acts of singing, dancing, and comedy, vaudeville attained enormous popularity just as the movies began to appear. The first primitive films, a minute or so of humor or glimpses of famous people, appeared in 1896 in penny arcades and as filler in vaudeville shows. Within a decade, millions of city people were watching story films of increasing length and artistry at nickelodeons (after the five-cent admission charge) across the country.

For young unmarried workers, the cheap amusements of the city created a new social space. "I want a good time," one New York clothing operator told an investigator. "And there is no . . . way a girl can get it on $8 a week. I guess if anyone wants to take me to a dance he won't have to ask me twice." Hence the widespread ritual in the urban working class of "treating." The girls spent what they had looking stylishly pretty; their beaus were expected to pay for the fun. Parental control over courtship broke down, and amid the bright lights and lively music of the dance hall and amusement park, working-class youth forged a more easy-going culture of sexual interaction and pleasure seeking.

Baseball. Of all forms of male diversion, none was more specific to the city, nor so spectacularly successful, as professional baseball. The game's promoters decreed that baseball had been created in 1839 by Abner Doubleday in the village of Cooperstown, New York. Actually, baseball was neither of American origin—it developed from the English game of rounders—nor a product of rural life.

Organized play began in the early 1840s in New York City, where a group of gentlemen enthusiasts competed among themselves on an empty lot. During the next twenty years, the aristocratic tone of baseball disappeared. Clubs sprang up across the country, and intercity competition developed on a scheduled basis. In 1868 baseball became openly professional, following the example of the Cincinnati Red Stockings in signing players to contracts at a negotiated salary for the season.

Big-time commercial baseball came into its own with the launching of the National League in 1876. The team owners were profit-minded businessmen who carefully shaped the sport to please the fans. Wooden grandstands gave way to the concrete and steel stadiums of the early twentieth century, such as Fenway Park in Boston, Forbes Field in Pittsburgh, and Shibe Park in Philadelphia.

For the urban multitudes, baseball grew into something more than an occasional afternoon at the ball park. By rooting for the home team, fans found a way of identifying themselves with the city they lived in. Amid the diversity and anonymity of urban life, the common experience and language of baseball acted as a bridge among city people.

Students of the game have suggested that baseball was peculiarly attuned to city life. It followed strict, precise rules, which suggested an underlying order to the chaotic city. Far from respecting the rules, however, the players tried to get away with whatever they could in order to win. Did this not match the competitive scramble of urban life? The blue-coated umpire, the symbol of authority, was scorned by players and derided by fans. What better substitute for the resentment against the powers-that-be who ruled the lives of city

The National Pastime

This lithograph celebrates the opening game of the 1889 season, with the Boston Base-Ball Club taking on the New York Base-Ball Club. The National League was then scarcely twelve years old. The fielders played barehanded, but otherwise the game remains today much as the artist pictured it a century ago, even down to the umpire's characteristic stance.

people? Baseball, like many other emerging urban institutions, served as a mechanism for inducting people into the life of the modern city.

Newspapers. The press undertook this task in a clear-eyed, calculated way. Ever since Benjamin H. Day had established the *New York Sun* in 1833, American newspapers had aimed for a broad audience. James Gordon Bennett, founder of the *New York Herald*, wanted to "record the facts . . . for the great masses of the community." Journalism defined the news to be whatever interested city readers. The *Herald* covered crime, scandal, and sensational events. After the Civil War, *Sun* editor Charles A. Dana added the human-interest story, which made news of ordinary, insignificant happenings. Newspapers also targeted specific audiences. A women's page offered recipes and fashion news, separate sections covered sports and high society, and the Sunday supplement helped fill the spare weekend hours.

Newspaper wars erupted periodically, as when Joseph Pulitzer, the owner of the *St. Louis Post-Dispatch*, invaded New York in 1883 by buying the *World*. In 1895, William Randolph Hearst, who owned the *San Francisco Examiner*, bought the *New York Journal* and challenged the *World*. Hearst developed a sensational style of newspaper reporting and writing that became known as *yellow journalism*. The term derived from the first comic strip to appear in color, "The Yellow Kid" (1895). In his combative zeal, Hearst often abandoned the journalistic canon of telling the truth. The *Journal*'s sensational reporting of the civil war in Cuba enabled Hearst's paper to win its circulation battle with the *World*; it also helped bring on the Spanish-American War of 1898 (see Chapter 22).

"He who is without a newspaper," said the great showman P. T. Barnum, "is cut off from his species." Barnum was speaking of city people and their hunger for information. By meeting this need, newspapers revealed their sensitivity to the public they served.

Joseph Pulitzer
Pulitzer (1847–1911) left Hungary at seventeen because he wanted to be a soldier and his best chance was with the Union Army in America. He ended up the greatest newpaper publisher of the century, extraordinary for his instincts as to what an urban reading public wanted from a newspaper, and extraordinary also because he came to this task as a foreigner, without English as his mother tongue and without native roots in the society.

Upper Class/Middle Class

Wealth, more than anything else, has determined social class in the United States. By that measure, American society was highly stratified during the nineteenth century. The top 1 percent of Americans held about a quarter of all wealth, and the upper 5 percent owned fully a half. The middle class, who made up the next 30 percent, owned most of the rest of the nation's wealth. The bottom half of the population owned virtually nothing. This sharply unequal division of wealth emerged early in America's Industrial Revolution and continued well into the twentieth century with little change. Income levels were likewise sharply unequal. In 1890 wage earners in manufacturing averaged $439 a year, clerical workers in manufacturing made twice that—$848 a year—while solidly middle-class people like doctors, lawyers, editors, and managers earned between $3,000 and $5,000. In the topmost ranks, of course, were those whose incomes came largely from investments rather than from salaries and wages. Given the great concentration of wealth at the top, America's wealthy necessarily enjoyed magnificent incomes.

In the compact preindustrial city, people had not defined their social position by where they lived. Class distinctions had been expressed by the way men and women dressed, how they behaved, and the deference they demanded from or granted to others. As the industrial city grew, these interpersonal marks of class began to lose their force. In the anonymity of a large city, recognition and deference no longer served very well as mechanisms for conferring status. Instead, people began to rely on external signs. These included conspicuous display of wealth, exclusive association in clubs and similar social organizations, and above all, choice of neighborhood.

People's place of residence had previously depended primarily on the location of their work. For the poor, that continued to be true. But for higher-income urbanites, where to live became much more a matter of personal means and social preference.

The Urban Elite

As early as the 1840s, Boston merchants took advantage of the new railway service to move out of the congested central city. Fine rural estates appeared in Milton, West Roxbury, Newton, and other outlying towns. By 1848 roughly 20 percent of Boston's businessmen were making the long trip from the countryside to their downtown offices. They traveled on 118 scheduled trains that served stations within 15 miles of the center of Boston. Ferries that plied the harbor between Manhattan and Brooklyn or New Jersey served the same purpose for New Yorkers.

As commercial development engulfed downtown residential areas and as transportation services improved, the exodus from cities by the well-to-do spread across America. In Cincinnati, wealthy families settled on the scenic hills rimming the crowded, humid tableland that ran down to the Ohio River. On those hillsides, a traveler noted in 1883, "the homes of Cincinnati's merchant princes and millionaires are found . . . elegant cottages, tasteful villas, and substantial mansions, surrounded by a paradise of grass, gardens, lawns, and tree-shaded roads." Residents of the area, called Hilltop, founded several country clubs, the Cincinnati Riding Club, the New England Society, five downtown gentlemen's clubs, and many other institutions that assured an exclusive social life for Cincinnati's elite.

Despite the temptations of country life, many of the very richest people preferred the heart of the city. Chicago had its Gold Coast; San Francisco, Nob Hill; Denver, Quality Hill; and Manhattan, Fifth Avenue. The New York novelist Edith Wharton recalled how the comfortable mid-century brownstones—"all so much alike that one could understand how easy it would be for a dinner guest to go to the wrong house"—gave way to the "'new' millionaire houses," which then spread northward beyond Fifty-ninth Street and up Fifth Avenue along Central Park. Great mansions, reminiscent of European aristocratic houses and filled with Old World artifacts, lined Fifth Avenue at the turn of the century.

By carving out fashionable areas in the heart of a city, the rich visibly demonstrated the power of money in American society. But great fortunes did not automatically mean high social standing. An established elite stood astride the social heights even in such relatively raw cities as San Francisco and Denver. It had taken only a generation—and sometimes less—for money made in commerce or real estate to shed its tarnish and become "old" and genteel. In more venerable cities, such as Boston, wealth passed intact through several generations. A high degree of intermarriage occurred there among the so-called Brahmin families. By withdrawing from trade, and by asserting a high cultural and moral code, the proper Bostonians kept moneyed newcomers at bay. Elsewhere, urban elites tended to be

The Breakers

The favorite summering place of the New York elite was the historic colonial port of Newport, Rhode Island. The opulent mansions there were known as "cottages." The Breakers was built in 1892 at a cost of $5 million for Cornelius Vanderbilt II. Designed in the style of an Italian palace, the Breakers had seventy-three rooms, thirty-three of them to house the small army of servants. The ornate dining room is shown in this photograph.

more open, but only to the socially ambitious who were prepared to make visible and energetic use of their money.

New York's Metropolitan Opera was one of the products of this ongoing struggle among the wealthy. The Academy of Music, home to the city's opera since 1854, was controlled by the Livingstons, the Bayards, the Beekmans, and other old New York families. Frustrated in their efforts to purchase boxes at the Academy, the Vanderbilts and their allies determined to sponsor a rival opera house. In 1883, with its glittering opening to the strains of Gounod's *Faust*, the Metropolitan proclaimed its ascendancy in the opera world and, in due course, won the patronage of even the Beekmans and Bayards. During this battle of the opera houses, the Vanderbilt circle achieved social recognition.

"High Society." New York became the home of a national elite. The most successful people gravitated from everywhere to this preeminent center of American economic and cultural life. Manhattan's extraordinary vitality, in turn, kept the city's high society fluid and relatively open. The tycoon Frank Cowperwood, in Theodore Dreiser's novel *The Titan* (1914), reassured his unhappy wife that if Chicago society would not accept them, "there are other cities. Money will arrange matters in New York—that I know. We can build a real place there, and go in on equal terms, if we have money enough." New York thus came to be a magnet for millionaires. The city attracted them not only by its importance as a financial center, but also by the opportunities it offered for display and social recognition.

From Manhattan an extravagant life of leisure radiated outward to such resort centers as Saratoga Springs, New York; Palm Beach, Florida; and Newport, Rhode Island. Newport featured a grand array of summer "cottages," crowned by the Vanderbilts' Marble House and The Breakers. To these resorts, and elsewhere, the affluent traveled in great comfort by private railway car. A style of living emerged that was incredible for its lavish excess, ranging from yachting and horseracing to huge feasts at such luxurious restaurants as Sherry's and Delmonico's. "Our forefathers would have been staggered at the cost of hospitality these days," remarked one New Yorker.

This infusion of wealth shattered the older elite society of New York. Seeking to be assimilated into the upper class, the flood of moneyed newcomers simply overwhelmed it. There followed a curious process of reconstruction, a deliberate effort to define the rules of conduct and identify those who properly "belonged" in New York society.

The key figure in this process was Ward McAllister, a southern-born lawyer who had made a quick fortune in gold rush San Francisco and then devoted himself to a second career as arbiter to New York society. McAllister compiled the first *Social Register* in 1888, to serve as a "record of society, comprising an accurate and careful list" of all those deemed acceptable to participate in New York society. McAllister instructed the socially ambitious on how to select guests, set a proper table, arrange a ball, and launch a young lady into society. McAllister fostered an ordered social round of assemblies, balls, and dinners that defined the boundaries of an elite society. The key lay in the creation of associations sponsored by established social leaders, "organized social powers, capable of giving a passport of society to all worthy of it." To top things off, McAllister came up with the idea of "the Four Hundred"—the true cream of New York society. His list corresponded to those invited to Mrs. William Astor's great ball of February 1, 1892.

Social registers, coming-out balls for debutantes, and lesser versions of Ward McAllister soon popped up in cities throughout the country. In this fashion, the socially ambitious struggled to master the fluidity at the height of the social order.

Americans were adept at making money, noted the journalist Edwin L. Godkin in 1896, but they lacked the European traditions for spending it. "Great wealth has not yet entered our manners," Godkin remarked. "No rules have yet been drawn to guide wealthy Americans in their manner of life." In their struggle to find the rules and establish the manners, the moneyed elite made an indelible mark on urban life. If there was magnificence in the American city, it was mainly their handiwork. And if there was conspicuous waste and vulgarity, it was likewise their doing. In a democratic society, wealth finds no easier outlet than through public display.

The Middle Class

The middle class left a smaller imprint on the public and cultural faces of urban society. Its members, unlike the rich, preferred privacy and retreated into the domesticity of suburban comfort and family life.

The emerging corporate economy spawned a new middle class. Bureaucratic organizations required managers, accountants, and clerks. Advancing technologies needed engineers, chemists, and designers. The distribution system sought salesmen, advertising executives, and buyers. These salaried ranks increased sevenfold between 1870 and 1910, much faster than any other occupational group. The traditional business class that had emerged in the first stages of industrialization before the Civil War—independent businessmen and professionals—also grew, but only at a third of the rate of salaried personnel. Nearly 9 million people held white-collar jobs in 1910, more than a fourth of all employed Americans.

The middle class, particularly its salaried portions,

AMERICAN VOICES

Throwing a Great Party During Hard Times

Frederick Townshend Martin

Gilded Age society was known for the magnificence of its parties. Here Frederick Townshend Martin describes the lavish affair his brother and sister-in-law put on for the cream of New York society in 1897 during a severe national depression.

Every year my brother Bradley and his wife spent their winters in New York, when they entertained largely. One morning at breakfast my brother remarked—

"I think it would be a good thing if we got up something; there seems to be a great deal of depression in trade; suppose we send out invitations for a concert."

"And pray, what good will that do?" asked my sister-in-law, "the money will only benefit foreigners. No, I've a far better idea; let us give a costume ball at so short notice that our guests won't have time to get their dresses from Paris. That will give an impetus to trade that nothing else will."

Directly Mrs. Martin's plan became known, there was a regular storm of comment. . . .

We were besieged by reporters, but my brother and his wife invariably refused to discuss the matter. Threatening letters arrived by every post, debating societies discussed our extravagance, and last, but not least, we were burlesqued unmercifully on the stage. . . .

I think every one anticipated a disturbance, but nothing of the kind took place, and the evening passed without any untoward incident.

The best way I can describe what is always known as the "Bradley Martin Ball," is to say that it reproduced the splendour of Versailles in New York, and I doubt if even the Roi Soleil himself ever witnessed a more dazzling sight. The interior of the Waldorf-Astoria Hotel was transformed into a replica of Versailles, and rare tapestries, beautiful flowers and countless lights made an effective background for the wonderful gowns and their wearers. I do not think there has ever been a greater display of jewels before or since; in many cases the diamond buttons worn by the men represented thousands of dollars, and the value of the historic gems worn by the ladies baffles description.

My sister-in-law personated Mary Stuart, and her gold embroidered gown was trimmed with pearls and precious stones. Bradley, as Louis XV, wore a Court suit of brocade, and I represented a gentleman of the period. The whole thing appealed most strongly to my imagination. . . .

The power of wealth with its refinement and vulgarity was everywhere. It gleamed from countless jewels, and it was proclaimed by the thousands of orchids and roses, whose fragrance that night was like incense burnt on the altar of the Golden Calf.

I cannot conceive why this entertainment should have been condemned. We Americans are so accustomed to display that I should have thought the ball would not have been regarded as anything very unusual. Every one said it was the most brilliant function of the kind ever seen in America, and it certainly was the most talked about.

After the ball the authorities promptly raised my brother's taxes quite out of proportion to those paid by any one else, and the matter was only settled after a very acrimonious dispute. Bradley and his wife resented intensely the annoyance to which they had been subjected, and they decided to sell their house in New York and buy a residence in London.

Source: Bulkley S. Griffin, ed., *Offbeat America* (Cleveland: World Publishing, 1967) pp. 221–24.

was an urban population. Some lived within the city, in the row houses of Baltimore or Boston, or in the comfortable apartment houses of New York or other metropolitan centers. But far more preferred to escape from the clamor and congestion of the city. They were attracted by a persisting rural ideal. They agreed with the landscape architect Andrew Jackson Downing, who thought that "nature and domestic life are better than the society and manners of town." With the extension of rapid transit service from the city center, middle-class Americans followed the wealthy into the countryside. All sought what a Chicago developer promised of his North Shore subdivision in 1875: "qualities of which the city is in a large degree bereft, namely, its pure air, peacefulness, quietude, and natural scenery." And advanced building techniques—mass-produced materials and balloon-frame construction—made suburban housing broadly affordable by the American middle class.

Cincinnati Suburb
The lives of the people inhabiting these neat homes were woven into the dynamic capitalism of a major industrial metropolis, including the children lounging on the corner. They were most certainly being educated for service in the new economic order. Looking at the bucolic setting of this Cincinnati street, no one would have thought so, and that was just the illusion which the suburb was intended to create: that Americans still partook of a rural ideal and could hold at bay the modern industrial order of which they were now a part. (The Cincinnati Historical Society)

No major American city escaped rapid suburbanization during the last third of the nineteenth century. City limits everywhere expanded rapidly. By 1900, more than half of Boston's people lived in "streetcar suburbs" outside the original city. The U.S. Census of 1910 reported that nationwide about 25 percent of the urban population lived in suburbs outside the city limits.

On the European continent, by contrast, cities remained highly concentrated and it was the poor, not the well-to-do, who inhabited the margins. Unlike their American counterparts, the European middle class was not attracted (except in England) to the rural ideal and valued urban life for its own sake. In Europe, mass transit developed much more slowly; more efficient balloon-frame construction techniques were not adopted; and there was little of the free-wheeling real-estate development that so powerfully encouraged American suburbanization. Nor, finally, did the culturally homogeneous European cities give rise to the impulse felt by middle-class Americans to escape the racially and ethnically diverse urban masses who occupied the city centers.

American suburbs were middle-class territory. But the middle class was not monolithic. It ranged from prosperous business proprietors and lawyers to clerks and traveling salesmen who earned no more than foremen and craft workers. Close in to the city, indeed, the suburbs increasingly took on a working-class character.

The geography of the suburbs was truly a map of class structure in America, because where a family lived told where it ranked. The farther the distance from the center of the city, the finer the houses and the larger the lots. This arrangement reflected the ability to pay and the work situations that went with varying income levels. The well-to-do had the leisure and flexible schedules to travel the long distance into town. People closer in wanted a direct transit line convenient to home and office. Lower-income suburbanites were likely to have more than one wage earner in the family, less security of employment, and jobs requiring movement around the city. They needed easy access to crosstown transit lines, which ran closer in to the city center.

Divisions within suburbs, although always a precise measure of economic ranking, never became rigidly fixed. People in the city center who wanted to better their lives moved to the cheapest suburbs. Fleeing from these newcomers, those already settled pushed the next higher group farther out in search of space and greenery.

Suburbanization was the sum of countless individual decisions. Each move represented an advance in living standards—not only more light, air, and quiet but also better housing than the city afforded. Suburban housing had more space and better design, as well as indoor toilets, hot water, central heating, and, by the turn of the century, electricity. Even people living in the inner suburbs came to regard these amenities as standard comforts. The suburbs also restored a basic opportunity that had seemed sacrificed by rural Americans when they moved to the city. In the suburbs, home ownership again became a norm. "A man is not really a true man until he owns his home," propounded the Reverend Russell H. Conwell in his famous sermon on the virtues of making money, "Acres of Diamonds."

The small town of the rural past had fostered community life. Not so the suburbs. The grid street pattern, while efficient for laying out lots and providing utilities, offered no natural focus for group life. Nor did stores and services that lay scattered along the trolley-car streets. Not even schools and churches were located to make them the centers of community life. Suburban development conformed to the economics of real estate and transportation, and so did the thinking of middle-class home seekers entering the suburbs. They wanted a house that gave them good value and convenience to the trolley line.

The need for community had lost some of its force

for middle-class Americans. Two other attachments assumed greater importance. One was work; the other was family.

Families

The family had been the primary productive unit in the preindustrial economy. Farmers, merchants, and artisans had carried on their work within a family setting, and the value of family members could be reckoned by their economic contribution. The family circle included not only blood relatives but all others living and working within the household. As industrialism progressed, the family gradually lost its function as a productive unit. For the middle class in particular, the family became disassociated from economic activity. The father left the home to earn his living; clothing was bought ready-made; food came increasingly in cans and packages; and the children spent more years in school. Families became smaller and excluded all but nuclear members. The typical middle-class family of 1900 consisted of husband, wife, and three children.

Within this small circle, relationships became intense and affectionate. "Home was the most expressive experience in life," recalled the literary critic Henry Seidel Canby of his growing up in the 1890s. "Though the family might quarrel and nag, the home held them all, protecting them against the outside world." In a sense, the family served as a refuge from the competitive, impersonal business world. The suburbs provided a fit setting for such middle-class families. The quiet, tree-lined streets created a domestic world insulated from the hurly-burly of commerce and enterprise.

The Wife's Role. The burdens of this domesticity fell heavily on the wife. It was nearly unheard of for her to seek an outside career; that was her husband's role. She had the job of managing the household. "The woman who could not make a home, like the man who could not support one, was condemned," Canby remembered. But with better household technology, greater reliance on purchased goods, and fewer children, the wife's workload declined. Moreover, servants still played an important part in middle-class households. In 1910 there were about two million domestic servants, the largest job category for women.

As the physical burdens of household work eased, higher-quality homemaking became the new ideal. This was the message of Catharine Beecher's best-selling book *The American Woman's Home* (1869) and of such magazines as the *Ladies' Home Journal* and *Good Housekeeping*, which first appeared during the 1880s. The wife did more than make sure that food was on the table, that clothes were washed and mended, and that the house was kept clean. She had the higher calling of bringing sensibility, beauty, and love to the household. "We owe to women the charm and beauty of life," wrote one educator. "For the love that rests, strengthens and inspires, we look to women." In this idealized view, the wife made the home a refuge for her husband and a place of nurture for their children.

Womanly virtue, even if a happy marriage depended on it, by no means put the wife on equal terms with her husband. Although the legal status of married women—the right to own property, to control separate earnings, to make contracts and bring suit, to get a divorce—improved markedly during the nineteenth cen-

Middle-Class Domesticity
For middle-class Americans, the home was a place of nurture, a refuge from the world of competitive commerce. Perhaps that explained why their residences were so heavily draped and cluttered with bric-a-brac, every space filled with overstuffed furniture. All of it emphasized privacy, and pride of possession. The young woman shown playing the piano symbolizes another theme of American domesticity—wives and daughters as ornaments, and as bearers of culture and refinement. (Mrs. Leoni's Parlor, 1894, Museum of the City of New York)

tury, sufficient legal discrimination remained to establish their subordinate role within the family. More important, custom dictated the wife's submission to her husband. She relied on his ability as the family breadwinner and, despite her superior virtues and graces, ranked as his inferior in vigor and intellect. Her mind could be employed "but little and in trivial matters," wrote one prominent physician, and her proper place was as "the companion or ornamental appendage to man."

Bright, independent-minded women understandably rebelled against marriage. The marriage rate in the United States fell to its lowest point during the last forty years of the nineteenth century. More than 10 percent of all women of marriageable age remained single, and the rate was much higher among college graduates and professionals. Only half of the Mount Holyoke College class of 1902 married. "I know that something perhaps, humanly speaking, supremely precious has passed me by," remarked the writer Vida Scudder. "But . . . how much it would have excluded!" Married life "looks to me often as I watch it terribly impoverished, for women."

The strains of marriage were manifest in the substantial number of middle-class families that broke apart. Most of these domestic failures remained unrecorded because of the stigma attached to divorce. In a Chicago suburb in the 1880s, at a time when divorce was virtually unknown there, about 10 percent of the households had an absent spouse. The national divorce rate increased from 1.2 per thousand marriages in 1860 to 7.7 in 1900. It was more difficult to document the other ways women responded to marriages that denied their autonomy and downplayed their sexuality. Middle-class women became the principal victims of neurasthenia, a disorder whose symptoms included depression and general disability. Some unhappy housewives found "silent friends" in opium and alcohol, both often dispensed in well-laced patent medicines.

A happier release came through the companionship of other women. In an age that defined separate spheres for men and women, close ties commonly formed between schoolmates, cousins, and mothers and daughters. The intimacy and intensity of such attachments can be sensed in surviving letters of separated friends. Such enduring female ties yielded emotional gratification not often found in marriage. Husbands, absorbed in business, frequently played a secondary and remote role in the lives of their wives. Women's own sphere often filled that emotional vacuum.

Changing Views of Sexuality. The middle-class family had long faced a difficult dilemma. Many couples wished to limit the number of their children, but birth control was not an easy matter. Antipornography laws, pushed through by the social-purity campaigner Anthony Comstock during the 1870s, banned the distribution of birth control information through the mail. Many states classified such material as obscene literature and prohibited its sale. Abortion became illegal except to save the mother's life. Although the practice of abortion was probably widespread, it was expensive and dangerous, and considered shameful. Family planning could be best achieved by delaying marriage and then by practicing abstinence. The repressed sexuality within the family resulted from practical necessity. A fulfilling sexual relationship could not be squared with the desire to limit and space childbearing.

The New Woman

John Singer Sargent's painting, *Mr. and Mrs. Isaac Newton Phelps Stokes* (1897), captures on canvas the essence of the "new woman" of the 1890s. Nothing about Mrs. Stokes, neither how she is dressed nor how she presents herself, suggests physical weakness or demure passivity. She confidently occupies center stage, a fit partner for her husband, who, indeed, is relegated to the shadows of the picture. (The Metropolitan Museum of Art)

Somewhere around 1890, change set in. Although the birth rate continued to decline, more young people married, and at an earlier age. These developments reflected the beginnings of a sexual revolution within the American middle-class family. With the growing acceptability of contraception—the Comstock laws notwithstanding—people no longer tightly linked sex and procreation. Experts began to abandon the notion, put forth by one popular medical text, that "the majority of women (happily for society) are not very much troubled by sexual feeling of any kind." In succeeding editions of his book *Plain Home Talk on Love, Marriage and Parentage*, the physician Edward Bliss Foote began to favor a healthy sexuality that gave pleasure to both women and men.

During the 1890s, the artist Charles Dana Gibson created the image of the "new woman" in his drawings for *Life* magazine. The Gibson girl was tall, spirited, athletic, and chastely sexual. Constricting bustles, hoop skirts, and hourglass corsets gave way to shirtwaists and other natural styles that did not hide or disguise the female form. In the city, moreover, women's sphere began to take on a more public character. Of the new urban institutions catering to women, the most important was the department store, which became a temple for their emerging role as consumers.

And the Children. The children of the middle class went through their own revolution. In the past, American children everywhere had been regarded chiefly as an economic asset—added hands for the family farm, shop, or counting house. That no longer held true for the urban middle class. Parents stopped treating their children as working members of the family. In the old days, remarked Ralph Waldo Emerson in 1880, "children had been repressed and kept in the background; now they were considered, cosseted, and pampered." There was such a thing as "the juvenile mind," lectured Jacob Abbott in his book *Gentle Measures in the Management and Training of the Young* (1871). The family had the responsibility of providing a nurturing environment in which the young personality could grow and mature.

Preparation for adulthood became increasingly linked to formal education. School enrollment went up one and a half times between 1870 and 1900. High school attendance, while still encompassing only a small percentage of teenagers, increased at the fastest rate. The years between childhood and adulthood began to stretch out, and a new stage of life—adolescence—emerged. Rooted in an extended period of family dependency, adolescence at the same time shifted much of the socializing role from parents to peer group. A youth culture—one of the hallmarks of American life in the twentieth century—was starting to take shape.

The Higher Culture

America's metropolitan centers, repositories of the nation's wealth, became the site for new institutions of higher culture. A hunger for the cultivated life did not, of course, originate in cities. Before the Civil War, the lyceum movement had sent lecturers to the remotest towns bearing messages of culture and learning. The Chautauqua movement, founded in upstate New York in 1874, carried on this work of cultural dissemination in the last decades of the nineteenth century. However, large cultural institutions such as museums, public libraries, opera companies, and symphony orchestras could flourish only in metropolitan centers.

The first outstanding art museum, the Corcoran Gallery of Art, opened in Washington, D.C., in 1869. New York's Metropolitan Museum of Art started in rented quarters two years later. In 1880 the museum moved to its permanent site in Central Park and launched an ambitious program of art acquisition. J. P. Morgan became chairman of the board in 1905, ensuring the Metropolitan's preeminence. The Boston Museum of Fine Arts was founded in 1876, and Chicago's Art Institute in 1879. By 1914 virtually every major city, and about three-fifths of all cities with more than a hundred thousand people, had an art museum.

Top-flight orchestras also appeared—first in New York under the conductors Theodore Thomas and Leopold Damrosch in the 1870s. Symphonies started in Boston and Chicago during the next decade. National tours by these leading orchestras planted the seeds for orchestral societies in many other cities. Public libraries grew from modest collections (in 1870 only seven had as many as fifty thousand books) into major urban institutions. The greatest library benefactor was Andrew Carnegie, who announced in 1881 that he would build a library in any city that was prepared to maintain it. By 1907, Carnegie had spent more than $32.7 million to establish about a thousand libraries throughout the country.

If the late nineteenth century was the great age of money making, it was also the great age of money *giving*. Surplus private wealth flowed in many directions, particularly to universities. These schools included Vanderbilt, Tulane, and Johns Hopkins universities, all named for their chief benefactors, and the University of Chicago, founded by John D. Rockefeller. Urban cultural institutions also received their share, partly as a matter of civic pride. To some extent patronage of the arts also served the need of the newly rich to establish themselves in society, as in the founding of the Metropolitan Opera in New York. But the higher culture, beyond being merely a commodity of civic pride and social display, also received support out of a sense of cultural deprivation.

The Metropolitan Museum of Art, New York

Standing in front of Emmanuel Luetze's *Washington Crossing the Delaware,* these visitors to the Metropolitan Museum (ca. 1908) were experiencing one of great transformations (although they were most certainly not aware of it) of modern urban life. In great civic institutions like the Metropolitan Museum, the artifacts of high culture became accessible and familiar beyond the dreams of ordinary people of an earlier age. (The Metropolitan Museum of Art)

"In America there is no culture," pronounced the English critic G. Lowes Dickinson in 1909. Science and the practical arts, yes, "every possible application of life to purposes and ends," but "no life for life's sake." Such condescending remarks received a respectful hearing in the United States because of a deep sense of cultural inferiority to the Old World. In 1873, Mark Twain and Charles Dudley Warner had published a novel, *The Gilded Age,* satirizing America as a land of money grubbers and speculators. This enormously popular book touched a nerve in the American psyche. Its title has, in fact, been appropriated by historians to characterize the late nineteenth century—America's "Gilded Age"—as an age of materialism and cultural shallowness.

Some members of the upper class, including the novelist Henry James, despaired of their country and moved to Europe. Others spent their lives in the kind of perpetual alienation that Henry Adams described in his caustic memoir *The Education of Henry Adams* (1907).

The more common response was to try to raise the nation's cultural level. The newly rich had a hard time of it. They did not have much opportunity to cultivate a taste for art, and a great deal of what they collected was mediocre and garish. On the other hand, George W. Vanderbilt, grandson of the rough-hewn Cornelius Vanderbilt, became a patron of the Art Students League in New York and an early champion of French Impressionism. And the coal and steel baron, Henry Clay Frick, built a brilliant art collection that still remains housed as a public museum in his mansion in New York City. The enthusiasm of moneyed Americans—not always well directed—largely fueled the great cultural institutions that arose in many cities during the Gilded Age.

A deeply conservative idea of culture sustained this generous patronage. The aim was to embellish urban life, not to probe or reveal its meaning. "Art," says the hero of the Reverend Henry Ward Beecher's sentimental novel *Norwood* (1867), "attempts to work out its end solely by the use of the beautiful, and the artist is to select out only such things as are beautiful."

Culture had also become firmly linked to femininity. In America, remarked one observer, culture was "left entirely to women. . . . It is they, as a general rule, who have opinions about music, or drama, or literature, or philosophy. . . . Husbands or sons rarely share in those interests." Men represented the "force principle," said the clergyman Horace Bushnell, and women symbolized the "beauty principle."

Literature. The treatment of life, wrote one eminent editor, "must be tinged with sufficient idealism to make it all of a truly uplifting character. We cannot admit stories which deal with false or immoral relations. . . . The finer side of things—the idealistic—is the answer for us." The *genteel tradition,* as this literary school came to be called, dominated American cultural agencies, such as universities and publishing companies, from the 1860s on.

Rebellion against the genteel tradition sparked the main creative impulses of late nineteenth-century American literature. *Realism* became the rallying cry of a new generation of writers. Their champion, William Dean Howells, resigned in 1881 as editor of the *Atlantic Monthly*, a stronghold of the genteel tradition. He became editor of *Harper's Monthly* and called for literature that "wishes to know and to tell the truth" and seeks "to picture the daily life in the most exact terms possible." In a series of realistic novels—*A Modern Instance* (1882), *The Rise of Silas Lapham* (1885), and *A Hazard of New Fortunes* (1890)—Howells captured the world of the urban middle class.

Henry James, a far greater writer, also treated the novel as "a direct impression of life" and aimed above all at achieving "an air of reality." He wrote about the world of leisured Americans, and his central concern was the study of moral decay and regeneration. This concern, often set in motion by the confrontation of American innocence with European corruption, appears in *The American* (1877), *Portrait of a Lady* (1882), and *The Golden Bowl* (1904).

The nostalgia of urbanized Americans for their agrarian past helped sustain a vigorous literature of local color and regionalism. These writings included the mining camp stories of Bret Harte, the Uncle Remus tales of Joel Chandler Harris, the Indiana poetry of James Whitcomb Riley, and the New England fiction of Sarah Orne Jewett. Such literature fit comfortably within the genteel tradition, for it was generally sentimental, reassuring, and morally uplifting.

Mark Twain was an entirely different kind of regional writer. Starting as a western journalist and humorist, Twain avoided the influence of the eastern literary establishment. His greatest novel, *The Adventures of Huckleberry Finn* (1884), violated the custom of keeping "low" characters in their proper place for the amused inspection of the culturally superior reader. Huck, an outcast boy, seizes control of the story. The words are his, and so is the innocence with which he questions right and wrong in America. No other novel so fully engaged the themes of racism, injustice, and brutality in nineteenth-century America.

Although not graced with Twain's genius, other novelists did begin to come to grips with the hard realities of city life. Stephen Crane's *Maggie: A Girl of the Streets* (1893), privately printed because no publisher would touch it, told unflinchingly of the destruction of a slum girl. In another urban novel, Henry Blake Fuller's *The Cliff-Dwellers* (1893), the city itself occupied the author's imagination. This story traces the fortunes of the occupants—"cliff-dwellers"—of an immense Chicago office building. In *McTeague* (1899), Frank Norris captured the sights, sounds, and, most acutely, the smells of the city. One reviewer called the story "a study in stinks." Although the novel was set in San Francisco, Norris insisted that it "could have happened in any big city, anywhere."

These *naturalistic* novels stressed the insignificance of the individual, and his or her helplessness in the face of urban life and the inexorable logic of Darwin's survival of the fittest. Frank Norris's character McTeague, more animal than man, is the creature of his instincts and his environment, and he cannot escape coming to a bad end. In Norris's *The Octopus* (1901), the implacable force is the Southern Pacific Railroad; in *The Pit* (1903) it is the Chicago grain market. The city itself, however, was the most powerful influence on the naturalistic writers.

The best of these authors, Theodore Dreiser, surmounted the crude determinism of Frank Norris. But the city people in his great novels *Sister Carrie* (1900), *Jennie Gerhardt* (1911), *The Financier* (1912), and *The Titan* (1914) are no less hostage to an urban world they cannot understand or control. Dreiser sought to capture this world in all its detail, "to talk about life as it is, the facts as they exist, the game as it is played."

Visiting his fiancée's Missouri farm home in 1894, Dreiser had been struck by "the spirit of rural America, its idealism, its dreams." But this was an "American tradition in which I, alas!, could not share." Said Dreiser, "I had seen Pittsburgh. I had seen Lithuanians and Hungarians in their 'courts' and hovels. I had seen the girls of the city—walking the streets at night." The city had entered the American imagination. By the early 1900s, it had become a main theme of American art and literature, and also an overriding concern of the Progressive Era.

Summary

America, an agrarian society since its birth, became increasingly urbanized after the Civil War. By 1900 about 20 percent of the population was living in cities of a hundred thousand or more people. City growth stemmed primarily from industrialization—the concentration of industry at key points, the increasingly large scale of production, and the need for commercial and administrative services that were best located in urban centers. A burst of innovation, including mass transit systems, steel frame buildings, electric lighting, and the telephone solved the problems arising from the concentration of an extremely large population in a confined area. Although amply endowed with regulatory powers, American cities left decision-making as much as possible in the hands of private interests. The result was dramatic growth, but not much attention to the impact of growth on the urban environment.

Within the city, geography defined the social order of the population. The poor were found in the city centers and the factory districts, the middle class spread out into the suburbs, and the rich lived insulated either in exclusive central sections of the cities or beyond the suburbs. A distinctive urban culture emerged, drawing heavily on ethnic social institutions and new leisure activities, enabling city dwellers to accommodate themselves to the world of the city. For the wealthy, an elite society emerged, stressing an opulent life style and exclusive social organizations. The middle class, on the other hand, withdrew into the private world of the family. For the wives, the cult of domesticity reigned, but its more repressive features began to relax as a new conception of female sexuality took hold. The nurturance of children persisted, but as the years of dependent childhood lengthened, a new phase of adolescence began to emerge that would draw teenagers out of the family orbit.

The great cities of the United States became the sites of a higher culture, including art museums, opera companies, symphony orchestras, and libraries. A new literature emerged that took the urban world as its subject. From the late nineteenth century on, American life would increasingly be defined by what happened in the nation's cities.

TOPIC FOR RESEARCH

The City Boss

How did machine politics come to play the key role in governing the industrial cities of the late nineteenth century? There is a rich contemporary literature describing the boss system by critics looking in from the outside—for example, James Bryce, *The American Commonwealth* (1888); Josiah Strong, *Our Country* (1891); and (on Boston) Robert A. Woods, *The City Wilderness* (1898). Historical studies of the subject include Zane Miller, *Boss Cox's Cincinnati* (1968); Humbert S. Nelli, "John Powers and the Italians: Politics in a Chicago Ward, 1896–1921," *Journal of American History* (June 1970); David C. Hammack, *Power and Society: Greater New York at the Turn of the Century* (1982); and Bruce M. Stave, ed., *Urban Bosses, Machines, and Progressive Reformers* (1972). But how did the system look from the inside? How did the bosses themselves see their role? What values did they hold? How did they explain the loyalty they engendered in the immigrant wards? How did they justify the "graft" that rewarded them for their labors? One Tammany boss—George Washington Plunkitt—gave a series of interviews in which he candidly addressed these questions. See William L. Riordon, ed., *Plunkitt of Tammany Hall* (1948). You might want to compare Plunkitt's views with those of contemporary critics such as Bryce, Strong, or Woods, or try to place Plunkitt's views in a more analytical context by reading one or more historical accounts of city machine politics. Or Plunkitt might be compared to Big Tim Sullivan, whose biography appears on page 620 of this chapter. A full account of his life can be found in Daniel Czitrom, "Underworlds and Underdogs: Big Tim Sullivan and Metropolitan Politics in New York, 1889–1913," *Journal of American History* (September 1991), 536–58.

BIBLIOGRAPHY

Urbanization

Useful as introductions to urban history are Charles N. Glaab and A. Theodore Brown, *A History of Urban America* (1967); Arthur M. Schlesinger, *The Rise of the City* (1936), a pioneering study; and Blake McKelvey, *The Urbanization of America, 1860–1915* (1963). A sampling of the innovative scholarship that opened new historical paths can be found in Stephan Thernstrom and Richard Sennett, eds., *Nineteenth-Century Cities: Essays in the New Urban History* (1969).

Allan Pred, *Spatial Dynamics of U.S. Urban Growth, 1800–1914* (1971), traces the patterns by which cities grew. On the revolution in urban transit, see the pioneering book by Sam B. Warner, *Streetcar Suburbs: The Process of Growth in Boston, 1870–1900* (1962). In a subsequent work, *The Private City: Philadelphia in Three Periods* (1968), Warner broadened his analysis to show how private decision making shaped the character of the American city. Innovations in urban construction are treated in Carl Condit, *American Building Art: Nineteenth Century* (1969) and *Chicago School of Architecture* (1964); Robert C. Twombly, *Louis Sullivan* (1986); and Alan Trachtenberg, *The Brooklyn Bridge* (1965). The problems of meeting basic human needs are treated in Jon C. Teaford, *The Unheralded Triumph: City Government in America, 1870–1900* (1984); Eric H. Monkkonnen, *Police in Urban America, 1860–1920* (1981); and David B. Tyack, *The One Best System: A History of American Urban Education*

(1974). The struggle to reshape the chaotic nineteenth-century city can be explored in Laura Wood Roper, *FLO: A Biography of Frederick Law Olmsted* (1973); William H. Wilson, *The City Beautiful Movement in Kansas City* (1964); and David Schuyler, *The New Urban Landscape: The Redefinition of City Form in Nineteenth-Century America* (1986).

City People

Much has been written on immigrants and the city. Among the leading books are Moses Rischin, *The Promised City: New York's Jews, 1870–1914* (1962); Joseph Barton, *Peasants and Strangers: Italians, Rumanians, and Slovaks in an American City, 1890–1950* (1975); and Humbert S. Nelli, *The Italians in Chicago, 1860–1920* (1970). On blacks in the city, see Gilbert Osofsky, *Harlem: The Making of a Ghetto, 1890–1930* (1966); Allan H. Spear, *Black Chicago, 1860–1920* (1966); and Kenneth L. Kusmer, *A Ghetto Takes Shape: Black Cleveland, 1870–1930* (1976). The encounter of Protestantism with the city is treated in Henry F. May, *Protestant Churches and Urban America* (1949); Aaron I. Abell, *The Urban Impact on American Protestantism* (1943); and William G. McLoughlin, *Modern Revivalism* (1959). On the Catholic Church, see Robert D. Cross, *The Emergence of Liberal Catholicism in America* (1958), and Cross, ed., *Church and City, 1865–1910* (1967). Aspects of an emerging city culture are studied in Gunther Barth, *City People: The Rise of Modern City Culture in Nineteenth-Century America* (1982); Susan Porter Benson, *Counter Cultures: Saleswomen, Managers, and Customers in American Department Stores, 1890–1940* (1986); John F. Kasson, *Amusing the Million: Coney Island at the Turn of the Century* (1978); Roy Rosenzweig, *Eight Hours for What We Will: Workers and Leisure in an Industrial City, 1870–1920* (1983); and Kathy Peiss, *Cheap Amusements: Working Women and Leisure in Turn-of-the-Century New York* (1986).

Upper Class/Middle Class

Urban social mobility is the focus of Stephan Thernstrom, *The Other Bostonians: Poverty and Progress in an American City, 1880–1970* (1973), which contains also a useful summary of mobility research on other cities. On the social elite, see Frederic C. Jaher, *The Urban Establishment: Upper Strata in Boston, New York, Charleston, Chicago, and Los Angeles* (1982); Dixon Wecter, *The Saga of American Society* (1937); and, for a personal account, Ward McAllister, *Society as I Have Found It* (1890). Two recent books greatly advance our understanding of the urban middle class: Stuart S. Blumin, *The Emergence of the Middle Class: Social Experience in the American City, 1760–1900* (1989) and Olivier Zunz, *Making Corporate America, 1870–1920* (1990). Aspects of middle-class life are revealed in Richard Sennett, *Families Against the City: Middle Class Homes of Industrial Chicago, 1872–1890* (1970); Kathryn Kish Sklar, *Catharine Beecher: A Study of Domesticity* (1973); Margaret Marsh, *Suburban Lives* (1990); Gwendolyn Wright, *Moralism and the Model Home: Domestic Architecture and Cultural Conflict in Chicago, 1873–1913* (1980); Susan Strasser, *Never Done: A History of American Housework* (1983); and, on the entry of immigrants into the middle class, Andrew R. Heinze, *Adapting to Abundance: Jewish Immigrants, Mass Consumption, and the Search for American Identity* (1990). Contemporary notions of sexuality are skillfully captured in John S. Haller and Robin M. Haller, *The Physician and Sexuality in Victorian America* (1980). Whether those views actually applied to the private world of the middle class is strongly questioned in Karen Lystra, *The Searching Heart: Women, Men, and Romantic Love in Nineteenth-Century America* (1989). On the fostering of high culture in the American city, see Daniel M. Fox, *Engines of Culture: Philanthropy and Art Museums* (1963). The best introduction to intellectual currents in the emerging urban society is Alan Trachtenberg, *The Incorporation of America: Culture and Society, 1865–1893* (1983).

TIMELINE

1871	Chicago fire
1873	Mark Twain and Charles Dudley Warner publish *The Gilded Age*
1875	Dwight L. Moody launches urban revivalist movement
1876	Alexander Graham Bell patents the telephone National Baseball League founded
1878	Electric arc-light system installed in Philadelphia
1879	Thomas Edison's incandescent light bulb Salvation Army arrives from England
1883	New York City's Metropolitan Opera founded Brooklyn Bridge opens Joseph Pulitzer purchases the *New York World*
1885	William Jenney builds first steel-framed structure, Chicago's Home Insurance Building
1888	First electric trolley line constructed in Richmond, Virginia
1893	Chicago World's Fair
1895	The comic strip "The Yellow Kid" appears
1897	Boston's subway
1900	Theodore Dreiser publishes *Sister Carrie*
1901	New York Tenement House Reform Law
1906	San Francisco earthquake
1913	Woolworth Building, New York City

The Cliff Dwellers

The 1913 painting by George Bellows shows a poor tenement neighborhood in New York's Lower East Side. (Los Angeles County Museum of Art)

CHAPTER 21 *The Progressive Era, 1900–1914*

On the face of it, the political ferment of the 1890s ended after the 1896 election. The bitter struggle over free silver left the victorious Republicans with no stomach for political crusades. The McKinley administration devoted itself to maintaining business confidence: sound money and high tariffs were the order of the day. The main thing, as party chief Mark Hanna said, was to "stand pat and continue Republican prosperity."

Yet beneath the surface a deep uneasiness was taking hold of the country. The depression of the 1890s had unveiled harsh truths not acknowledged in better days. One such discovery was the power of vested economic interests. In Wisconsin, for example, utility and transit companies had raised prices, reduced services, and received special tax relief—all at the expense of the public. This discovery of corporate arrogance launched movements in Wisconsin for tax reform, for municipal ownership of utilities, and for an end to boss-run party politics.

The labor unrest of the 1890s produced a similar response. The Cleveland administration had broken the great Pullman railway strike of 1894 by plotting with the railroad operators, issuing injunctions against the strike leaders, and sending in troops to get the trains moving again. The architect of this policy, Attorney General Richard Olney, took little satisfaction from his success in suppressing the strike. He asked himself what might be done in the future to avoid the need for such one-sided intervention. Olney began to advocate labor legislation, first expressed in the Erdman Mediation Act of 1898, that would regulate labor relations on the railroads and prevent crippling rail strikes. In such ways did the crisis of the 1890s turn the nation's thinking to reform.

The problems themselves, however, were of much older origin. For more than half a century, Americans had been absorbed in the furious development of their nation. Now, at the beginning of the twentieth century, they paused, looked around, and began to add up the costs. Industrialization had led to a frightening concentration of economic power in corporate hands, and an equally troubling growth of a restless working class. The cities had spawned widespread misery and corrupt machine politics. The heritage of an earlier America seemed to be succumbing to the demands of the new industrial order.

These problems had troubled the reform-minded for many years, but the crisis of the 1890s had forestalled action. Only now, after the threat of Populism had subsided, did it seem safe to return to the nation's festering problems. Reform became a central and absorbing concern of Americans. It was as if social awareness had reached a critical mass around 1900 that set reform activity going as a major, self-sustaining phenomenon of early twentieth-century America. For this reason the years from 1900 to World War I have come to be known as the Progressive Era.

The Course of Reform

Historians have sometimes spoken of a progressive "movement." But progressivism was not a movement in any meaningful sense. There was no single progressive constituency, no agreed-upon agenda, and no unifying organization or leadership. At different times and places, different social groups became active. People who were reformers on one issue might be conservative on another. The term *progressivism* embraces a widespread, many-sided effort after 1900 to build a better society. Progressive reformers shared only this objective, plus an intellectual style that can be called "progressive."

The Intellectual Roots of Progressivism

Intellectual climates change. It is usually hard to explain why they change, but not so difficult to tell when new ideas take hold. Such a change of ideas clearly seemed to be in the wind as the twentieth century began.

A Sense of Mastery. The Progressive Era was an age of scientific investigation. The federal government launched massive statistical studies of immigration, women's and children's labor, and working conditions in many industries. Vice commissions studied prostitution, gambling, and other moral ills of American cities. Among private investigations, the classic was the multivolume *Pittsburgh Survey* (1911–1914). Financed by Margaret Olivia Sage and other New York City philanthropists, a team of investigators recorded in great detail living and working conditions of the steel district.

The facts were important because they formed the basis for corrective action. When the young journalist Walter Lippmann wrote *Drift and Mastery* (1914), he asserted the progressive's confidence in people's ability to act purposefully and constructively. This sense of mastery expressed itself in many ways. For example, people had great faith in academic experts. In Wisconsin, the state university became a key resource for Robert M. La Follette's progressive administration. "The close intimacy of the university with public affairs explains the democracy, the thoroughness, and the scientific accuracy of the state in its legislation," boasted one La Follette supporter.

Scientific management exerted a particularly strong attraction on progressives. The original aim of scientific management had been to reorganize and rationalize work in factories (see Chapter 19). But its founder, Frederick W. Taylor, argued that his basic approach—the "scientific" analysis of human activity—offered solutions to waste and inefficiency in municipal government, in schools and hospitals, and even in homes and churches. "The fundamental principles of scientific management are applicable to all kinds of human activities," Taylor stressed, and could solve all the social ills that arise "through such of our acts as are blundering, ill-directed, or inefficient."

Attacking Nineteenth-Century Formalism. The essential thing, in the progressive view, was to resist intellectual formulations that denied people this sense of mastery. One of the worst offenders was the English philosopher Herbert Spencer, whose doctrine of Social Darwinism had exerted enormous influence on conservative American thought. Spencer argued that society developed "automatically," according to fixed laws that could not be changed. Spencer's intellectual approach was *formalistic*—that is, he based his conclusions on abstract theory rather than factual investigation. Critics of Spencer denied that the evolution of society was guided by absolute and unvarying rules. "It is folly," protested the Harvard philosopher William James, "to speak of the 'laws of history,' as of something inevitable, which science only has to discover, and which any one can then foretell and observe, but do nothing to alter or avert." Man could "shape environmental forces to his own advantage," argued the sociologist Lester F. Ward. Society could advance through "rational planning" and "social engineering."

A comparable attack on formalism took place in many academic disciplines. In classical economics, for example, scholars assumed that markets were perfectly competitive, and hence perfectly responsive to the laws of supply and demand. Such a system left no room for reform, which would only disrupt what could not be improved. Critics of classical economics—they called themselves "institutional economists"—denied that the market ever operated so perfectly. They conducted field research to determine how institutions and power relationships influenced the operation of the marketplace. In his *The Theory of the Leisure Class* (1899) and *The Instinct of Workmanship* (1914), the economist Thorstein Veblen lampooned the classical economists' abstract image of the economic man. In the real world, Veblen contended, people acted not out of pure economic calculation, but from complex motives ranging from vanity to pride in their work.

In legal thought, likewise, formalism had dominated the field. The courts treated the rights of property and liberty of contract as if these were eternal principles outside the realm of social reality. Thus in the famous *Lochner v. New York* decision (1905), the Supreme Court invalidated a law that would have limited the notoriously long hours of bakers in New York State. Such regulation, the Court concluded, violated the contractual rights of *both* employers and workers. Justice Oliver Wendell Holmes, the leading dissenter on the Supreme Court, objected; in his view, the *Lochner* decision was based on a fictional equality. If the choice was between working and starving, could it really be said that workers freely accepted jobs requiring that they labor fourteen hours a day? Or that state regulation limiting excessive working hours violated their liberty of contract in any meaningful sense?

Holmes had earlier asserted the essence of the progressive legal critique: "The life of the law has not been logic; it has been experience. The felt necessities of the time, even the prejudices which judges share with their fellow-men, have had a good deal more to do than [logic] in determining the rules by which men shall be governed." "Sociological jurisprudence," as Dean Roscoe Pound of the Harvard Law School termed it, called for "the adjustment of principles and doctrines to the human conditions they are to govern rather than assumed first principles."

In philosophy, it was William James who led the assault on formalism as an intellectual system. James denied the existence of absolute truths. His philosophy of *pragmatism* judged ideas by their consequences; ideas served as guides to action that produced desired results. Philosophy should concern itself with solving problems, said James, not with contemplating ultimate ends.

James's most important disciple was John Dewey. Like James, Dewey had a great interest in psychology, and was a pioneer in applying psychological insights to education. In his Laboratory School at the University of Chicago, Dewey broke from the rigid curriculum of traditional education and instead stressed problem solving and practical activity as the keys to children's educational growth. Children were encouraged to explore and discover for themselves rather than learning lessons by rote. Nowhere could the intellectual bent of progressivism in action be better seen than in Dewey's experiments. Fittingly, they came to be known as progressive education.

Idealism. Progressive reformers prided themselves on being tough-minded. They had confidence in people's capacity to take purposeful action. But there was another side to the progressive mind. It was deeply infused with idealism. Progressives framed their intentions in terms of high principle. The progressive cause, pronounced Theodore Roosevelt, "is based on the eternal principles of righteousness."

Much progressive idealism came from the American past. No American hero loomed larger in the minds of progressives than Abraham Lincoln. For many, like Jane Addams, the Great Emancipator served as a lifelong guide. Lincoln's example, in particular, inspired the battle for political reform. "Go back to the first principles of democracy; go back to the people," Robert La Follette told his audience when he first launched his attack on Wisconsin machine politics. Political reformers typically described theirs as a work of political restoration. They frequently said they had converted to reform after discovering how far party politics had drifted from the ideals of representative government.

Progressive idealism also derived from American radical traditions. Many progressives traced their conversion to a reading of Henry George's *Progress and Poverty* (1879), which asked why, in the midst of fabulous wealth, so many Americans should be condemned to want. George's answer—that private control of land siphoned the community's wealth into the hands of nonproductive landlords—led to a Single Tax movement that served as a school for many budding progressives. Others traced their awakening to Edward Bellamy's novel *Looking Backward* (1888), with its utopian vision of an ordered, affluent American socialism; or to the Chicago social democrat Henry Demarest Lloyd's *Wealth Against Commonwealth* (1894), with its powerful indictment of the Standard Oil trust. In later years, this radical tradition came to be transmitted mainly through the Socialist party, which flourished after 1900 under the leadership of Eugene Debs. Walter Lippmann and many other young reformers passed through socialism on their way to progressivism, while other reformers, like Charlotte Perkins Gilman, never left the socialist camp.

The most important source of progressive idealism, especially among social reformers, was religion. Within the Protestant churches, a new doctrine—the Social Gospel—took hold. The Baptist cleric Walter Rauschenbusch, its most influential exponent, had been deeply affected by his ministry near the squalid Hell's Kitchen section of New York City. Shocked by the conditions he found there, Rauschenbusch fought for more playgrounds and better housing in slum neighborhoods. The churches had to reassert the "social aims of Jesus," Rauschenbusch argued. The "Kingdom of God on Earth" would be achieved, he said, not by striving only for personal salvation but by struggling for social justice. The Social Gospel, increasingly heard from urban Protestant pulpits after the turn of the century, led to the formation of the Federal Council of Churches in 1908. The council aimed at "promoting the application of the law of Christ in every relation to human life."

The Social Gospel expressed the concerns of the Protestant ministry, but the underlying religious sentiment extended far beyond formal church boundaries. Progressive leaders of the Protestant faith characteristically grew up in families imbued with evangelical piety. Many went through a religious crisis, having sought and failed to experience a conversion, and ultimately settled on a career in social work, education, journalism, or politics. There they could translate inherited religious belief into modern secular action. Jane Addams, for example, had taken up settlement-house work with this intent. She believed that, by uplifting the poor in tenement districts, settlement workers would themselves be uplifted: they would experience "the joy of finding Christ" by acting "in fellowship" with those in need.

As a result, progressive thought contained a pervading Christian undercurrent. The philosopher John Dewey called democracy "a spiritual fact" and the "means by which the revelation of truth is carried on." Theodore Roosevelt launched his Progressive party in 1912 with the battle cry, "We stand at Armageddon and we battle for the Lord." His supporters at the party's national convention marched around the hall singing "Onward Christian Soldiers."

The Muckrakers. The progressive mode of thought—idealistic in intent and tough-minded in approach—nurtured a new kind of reform journalism. A growing urban audience had already given rise during the 1890s to a rash of popular magazines, including *Munsey's*, *McClure's*, and *Collier's*. Unlike the highbrow *Atlantic Monthly* or *Harper's*, these journals sold for only 10 cents and catered to a broad audience. Almost by accident—Lincoln Steffens's article "Tweed Days in St. Louis" in the October 1902 issue of *McClure's* is credited with getting things started—magazine editors discovered that what most excited their readers was the exposure of evildoing.

In a series of powerful articles, Steffens wrote about "the shame of the cities"—the corrupt ties between business and political machines. Ida M. Tarbell attacked Standard Oil, and David Graham Phillips told how money controlled the Senate. William Hard exposed industrial accidents in "Making Steel and Killing Men" (1907) and child labor in "De Kid Wot Works at Night" (1908). Others described prostitution, Wall Street abuses, and adulterated food. Hardly a sordid corner of American life escaped the scrutiny of these brilliant and tireless reporters. They were moralists as well. They made their writing powerful not only by uncovering facts, but also by telling the facts with great indignation.

President Roosevelt, among many others, thought they went too far. In a 1906 speech, he compared them to the man with the muckrake in *The Pilgrim's Progress*, by the seventeenth-century English preacher John Bunyan. The man was too absorbed with raking the filth on the floor to look up and accept a celestial crown. Thus the term *muckrakers* became attached to journalists who exposed the underside of American life. Their efforts were, in fact, health-giving. More than any other group, the muckrakers called the people to arms.

Political Reformers

Progressives infused their efforts with a deep sense of idealism. They were confident of the human capacity to take purposeful action. This much progressives had in common. But once in action, different groups took up different reforms, and to a greater or lesser degree, they did so out of self-interest. Nowhere were these crosscurrents stronger than in the battles for political reform.

Ida Tarbell Takes on Rockefeller

A popular biographer of Napoleon and Lincoln in the 1890s, Ida Tarbell turned her formidable journalistic talents to muckraking. Her first installment of "The History of the Standard Oil Company" appeared in *McClure's Magazine* in November 1902. John D. Rockefeller, she wrote, "was willing to strain every nerve to obtain for himself special and illegal privileges from the railroads which were bound to ruin every man in the oil business not sharing them with him." As Tarbell built her case, a crescendo of criticism rained down on Rockefeller. A more sympathetic cartoon in the magazine *Judge* pleads with Rockefeller's critics: "Boys, don't you think you have bothered the old man just about enough?"

AMERICAN VOICES

The Shame of the Cities *Lincoln Steffens*

One of the best-known muckraking journalists, Steffens aimed his pen at many aspects of city machine politics. In this article, published in *McClure's* in 1903, he describes corruption and bribe-taking—"boodling"—in St. Louis.

The convicted boodlers have described the system to me. There was no politics in it—only business. The city of St. Louis is normally Republican. . . . The State of Missouri, however, is normally Democratic, and the legislature has taken political possession of the city by giving to the governor the appointment of the Police and Election Boards. With a defective election law, the Democratic boss in the city became its absolute ruler.

This boss is Edward R. Butler, better known as "Colonel Ed," or "Colonel Butler," or just "Boss." He is an Irishman by birth, a master horseshoer by trade, a good fellow—by nature, at first, then by profession. . . .

His method was to dictate enough of the candidates on both tickets to enable him, by selecting the worst from each, to elect the sort of men he required in his business. In other words, while honest Democrats and Republicans were "loyal to party" (a point of great pride with the idiots) and "voted straight," the Democratic boss and his Republican lieutenants decided what part of each ticket should be elected; then they sent around Butler's "Indians" (repeaters) by the vanload to scratch ballots and "repeat" their votes, till the worst had made sure of the government by the worst, and Butler was in a position to do business.

His business was boodling, which is a more refined and a more dangerous form of corruption than the police blackmail of Minneapolis. It involves, not thieves, gamblers, and common women, but influential citizens, capitalists, and great corporations. For the stock-in-trade of the boodler is the rights, privileges, franchises, and real property of the city, and his source of corruption is the top, not the bottom, of society. . . .

Butler organized and systematized and developed [boodling] into a regular financial institution, and made it an integral part of the business community. He had for clients, regular or occasional, bankers and promoters; and the statements of boodlers, not yet on record, allege that every transportation and public convenience company that touches St. Louis has dealings with Butler's combine. And my best information is that these interests were not victims. Blackmail came in time, but in the beginning they originated the schemes of loot and started Butler on his career. Some interests paid him a regular salary, others a fee, and again he was a partner in the enterprise, with a special "rake-off" for his influence. . . .

Boodling was safe, and boodling was fat. Butler became rich and greedy, and neglectful of politics. Outside capital came in, and finding Butler bought, went over his head to the boodle combines. These creatures learned thus the value of franchises, and that Butler had been giving them an unduly small share of the boodle.

Then began a struggle, enormous in its vile melodrama, for control of corruption—Butler to squeeze the municipal legislators and save his profits, they to wring from him their "fair share."

. . . Such then, is the boodling system as we see it in St. Louis. Everything the city owned was for sale by the officers elected by the people. The purchasers might be willing or unwilling takers; they might be citizens or outsiders; it was all one to the city government. So long as the members of the combines got the proceeds they would sell out the town. Would? They did and they will. If a city treasurer runs away with $50,000 there is a great haloo about it. In St. Louis the regularly organized thieves who rule have sold $50,000,000 worth of franchises and other valuable municipal assets. This is the estimate made for me by a banker, who said that the boodlers got not one-tenth of the value of the things they sold, but were content because they got it all themselves. . . .

Preposterous? It certainly would seem so; but watch the people of St. Louis as I have, and as the boodlers have—then judge.

Source: Lincoln Steffens, "The Shamelessness of St. Louis," *McClure's* 20 (March 1903), 546–53.

Municipal Reform. In many cities the demand for better government came from local businessmen. They complained that the economic burdens of old-fashioned party rule had become too heavy. Taxes went up while services fell short of business's growing needs. There had to be an end, as one manufacturer said, to "the inefficiency, the sloth, the carelessness, the injustice and the graft of city administrations." The solution, argued John Patterson of the National Cash Register Company, lay in putting "municipal affairs on a strict business basis." Cities should be run "not by partisans, either Republican or Democratic, but by men who are skilled in business management and social service."

In 1900 a hurricane devastated Galveston, Texas. Local businessmen took over and, in the course of rebuilding the city, replaced the mayor and board of aldermen with a five-member commission. The Galveston plan, although widely copied, had a serious flaw. It gave too much power to the individual commissioners. Dayton, Ohio, resolved this problem by assigning legislative duties to a nonpartisan commission and administrative functions to an appointed city manager. The commission-manager system aimed at running the American city "in exactly the same way as a private business corporation." Municipal political reform was chiefly the work of the business community, and overtly a matter of the balance sheet.

It was also a way of grabbing power. Municipal reformers favored citywide elections, nonpartisanship, and professional city administration. All these reforms attacked the ward politics that traditionally had given ethnic and working-class groups access to political power and influence. As a result, municipal control moved into the hands of the urban middle class. In fact, municipal reform contained a decidedly antidemocratic bias. "Ignorance should be excluded from control," said former Mayor Abram Hewitt of New York in 1901. "City business should be carried on by trained experts selected upon some other principle than popular suffrage."

A different kind of urban progressive opposed such elitist reform. Mayor Brand Whitlock of Toledo, Ohio, believed "that the cure for the ills of democracy was not less democracy, as so many people were always preaching, but more democracy." The prototype of this new breed of urban politician was shoe manufacturer Hazen S. Pingree, who led the Republicans to victory against the Democratic machine in Detroit in 1889. Although drafted by a business coalition, Pingree skillfully appealed for support from trade unions and ethnic groups. His administration not only attacked municipal corruption and inefficiency but also concerned itself with the needs of Detroit's working people. An increasing number of other cities came under the leadership of such progressive mayors, including Samuel M. "Golden Rule" Jones in Toledo, Tom Johnson in Cleveland, and Mark Fagan in Jersey City. By combining popular programs and campaign magic, they won over the urban masses and challenged the rule of the entrenched machines.

State Politics. The major battleground for democratic political reform, however, was at the state level. Preeminent among state progressives was Robert M. La Follette of Wisconsin. La Follette was a seasoned politician. Born in 1855, he had followed a conventional party career—as a lawyer, a district attorney, and then a congressman for three terms—before breaking with the Wisconsin Republican machine in 1891 allegedly because of an attempt by the top party boss to bribe him. La Follette became a tireless exponent of political reform. "I was merely expressing a common and widespread, though largely unconscious, spirit of revolt among the people," La Follette said of his fight to unseat the Wisconsin Republican machine. At first, it was an uphill battle. But after a decade of unremitting campaigning, La Follette finally gained the Republican nomination and won the governorship in 1900 on a platform that demanded higher taxes for corporations, stricter utility and railroad regulation, and political reform.

La Follette's key proposal was a direct primary law, by which party candidates would be chosen through popular election rather than in machine-run conven-

Robert M. La Follette

La Follette was transformed into a political reformer when a Wisconsin Republican boss attempted to bribe him in 1891 to influence a judge in a railway case. As he described it in his *Autobiography,* "Out of this awful ordeal came understanding; and out of understanding came resolution. I determined that the power of this corrupt influence . . . should be broken." This photo captures La Follette at the top of his form, taking his case in 1897 to the people of Cumberland, Wisconsin.

tions. Pushed through by La Follette in 1903, this democratic reform both expressed his political ideals and suited his particular political talents. The party regulars opposing him were insiders, more comfortable in the caucus room than out on the hustings. But that was where La Follette excelled. A brilliant campaigner, La Follette aimed at dramatizing the issues and generating grass-roots support. The direct primary gave La Follette the means to maintain his control over the Republican party in Wisconsin. Through good times and bad, he kept it until his death twenty-five years later.

What was true of La Follette was more or less true of all successful progressive politicians. Albert B. Cummins of Iowa, Harold U'Ren of Oregon, and Hiram Johnson of California all espoused democratic ideals and made skillful use of the direct primary to win political power and push through reform programs. If they were newcomers—as was Woodrow Wilson when he left academic life to enter New Jersey politics in 1910—they showed a quick aptitude for politics and gained a solid mastery of the trade. Once in office, they asserted control over their parties and beat the political bosses at their own game. They practiced a new kind of popular politics. In a reform age, it could be a more effective way to power than the back-room techniques of the old-fashioned machine politicians.

Not even the most radical of progressive reforms—the initiative, the referendum, and the recall—quite lived up to their billings. All three reforms were intended to shift political power back to the people. The *initiative* empowered the voters to place issues on the ballot, the *referendum* enabled them to vote on those issues, while the *recall* empowered citizens to remove from office politicians who had lost the public's confidence. It very soon became clear, however, that direct democracy did not supplant organized politics but only gave it a different form. For initiative, referendum, and recall campaigns put a premium on organization, money, and expertise, and these were attributes not of the people at large but of private, well-organized interests. As with the direct primary, the initiative, referendum, and recall had as much to do with power relations as with democratic idealism.

The Woman Progressive

Reform movements arise through a process of *recruitment.* Why do people enlist in a great cause? Each reform group—like the progressive politicians just described—has its own particular history, mobilized to action by linkages of varying kinds to the evil crying out for correction. For middle-class women of the Progressive Era, the linkage was between their identity within women's domestic sphere—as wives and mothers—and the special responsibility this gave them for the social well-being of their communities.

There was nothing new about this linkage. It had been the basis of women's social reform movements for many decades (see Chapter 19). By the late nineteenth century women's clubs and reform organizations already occupied a broad public sphere. But the tempo of women's reform activity now manifestly increased, and attention focused above all on the nation's urban problems.

Middle-class women had long borne the burden of humanitarian work in American cities. Characteristically, they did most of the leg work for the charity organization societies that since the 1870s had sprung up to coordinate citywide private relief. As voluntary investigators, women visited needy families, assessed their problems, and referred them to the appropriate relief agencies.

After many years of such dedicated charity work, Josephine Shaw Lowell of New York City concluded that it was not enough to give assistance to the poor. "If the working people had all they ought to have, we should not have the paupers and criminals," she declared. "It is better to save them before they go under, than to spend your life fishing them out afterward." Lowell founded the New York Consumers League in 1890. Her goal was to improve the wages and working conditions of the female clerks in the city's stores. To bring pressure on reluctant merchants, the league issued a "White List"—a very short one at first—of shops that met its standards for a living wage and decent working conditions for clerks.

The league then expanded its interest beyond retail stores and spread to other cities. Most important, these women reformers came to recognize that voluntary action was insufficient, that only state action could meet the most pressing problems of the urban poor. Accordingly, they founded the National Consumers League in 1899 to push this struggle. Under the crusading leadership of Florence Kelley, formerly a chief factory inspector in Illinois, the league became a powerful lobby for protective legislation for women and children.

Among its achievements, none was more important than the *Muller v. Oregon* decision (1908), which upheld an Oregon law limiting to ten hours the workday of women workers. The Consumers League had pushed that law through the state legislature and recruited the brilliant Boston lawyer Louis D. Brandeis to defend the law before the Supreme Court. In his brief, Brandeis devoted a scant two pages to legal citations on the narrow constitutional issue—whether, under its police powers, Oregon had the right to regulate women's working hours. Instead Brandeis rested his case on a vast amount of data gathered by the Consumers League showing how long hours damaged women's health and family roles. The *Muller* decision, which accepted Brandeis's reasoning, was a signal victory for the new "sociological jurisprudence" (see p. 663) and cleared the way for a wave of protective laws across the country.

AMERICAN LIVES

Frances Kellor: Woman Progressive

From the day its doors opened in 1892, the University of Chicago was a major center of American learning. Financed by John D. Rockefeller, the university modeled itself on the great German research universities and, unlike Yale or Harvard, concentrated on graduate education. At Chicago and other American universities, modern social science was taking shape, breaking from its nineteenth-century links to moral philosophy and seeking a scientific foundation for the study of society. The disciplines that were emerging—economics, political science, sociology—demanded a rigorous course of study certified by the granting of the Ph.D. But if the social sciences were becoming professional and research-oriented, the motive force was not yet knowledge for its own sake, but social reform. The city of Chicago was, in fact, seen as a great laboratory within which the university would do its work. The students who came were being prepared (whether they knew it or not) to be in service to the American progressivism of the next decade. The University of Chicago, moreover, was receptive to the admission of women; and for them, in particular, the university was a breeding ground for careers as social reformers. Among the women entering in 1898 was Frances Alice Kellor, a recent graduate of Cornell.

Kellor was born in Columbus, Ohio, in 1873. Her father abandoned the family before she was two, and her mother made a hard living as a domestic and laundress. This was not the kind of privileged background from which most woman progressives sprang, but Kellor's experience came closer to the norm than her personal circumstances might have suggested. In 1875 her family moved to Coldwater, Michigan, a former abolitionist center (and station on the Underground Railroad) and a stronghold of Yankee culture. From the Coldwater community, with its high moral standards and strong educational institutions, Kellor received the reformist values that other budding progressives learned from their families. Kellor, moreover, had a remarkable talent for finding patrons, gaining by her wits the financial means her fellow progressives were born to. Her first patrons were the well-to-do librarians of Coldwater, Mary and Frances Eddy, who befriended her and then took her into their home. Born Alice, Kellor began to call herself "Frances" as a sign that she considered herself adopted by the Eddy sisters. She graduated from high school, became a reporter for the *Coldwater Republican*, and then, with the backing of the Eddys, enrolled at Cornell in 1895. Highly athletic, she made her first mark as a fighter for equal rights on a sports issue: she led the campaign for a women's crew. She got a solid education in the social sciences at Cornell and decided to become a criminologist.

Sociology was still an infant discipline when Kellor arrived in Chicago in 1898, with little in the way of systematic theory, and much emphasis on high-minded investigations of social problems. Kellor's interest in crime was accordingly encouraged by the Chicago faculty. The prevailing theory of the time, advanced by the Italian Cesare Lombroso, was that criminality was an inherited trait. Criminals were born criminal, and this was manifest in their physical features. Skeptical, Kellor conducted a study of the female inmates of five midwestern prisons. Comparing them to a control group of college women, she could find no physical differences. Rather, it was social environment, economic disadvantage, and poverty that made for criminality. Kellor also rejected "the prevailing opinion that when women are criminal they are more degraded and more abandoned than men." People thought so only because of "the difference in the standards which we set for the two sexes." A second project on southern prisons drew Kel-

Frances Kellor
This photograph of Kellor was taken in her early twenties, when she was a student at Cornell University.

lor to similar, antiracist conclusions: she found no inherent criminal propensity among blacks, only dire poverty, the ravages of centuries of slavery, and an unfair judicial system that came down with extreme hardness on black offenders.

Kellor's landmark studies resulted in a series of major research articles and a book but did not launch her into an academic career. Despite her brilliant record she left the university in 1902 without a degree. The reasons are not altogether clear, but doubtless had something to do with a painful truth of which Kellor must have been aware: Chicago almost never placed its female graduate students in tenure-track teaching jobs. To be a professor, it seemed, was still a male prerogative. There was, however, also a positive side to Kellor's decision. Like many of her fellow students, she had fallen under the spell of Jane Addams. Kellor lived periodically at Hull House, joined the circle of social reformers that congregated there, and began to see her future out among the disadvantaged rather than in the university. When she left Chicago, it was to do social research for New York's College Settlement Association.

Unemployment had hitherto been seen primarily as a personal problem afflicting the shiftless and incompetent. In her pioneering investigation *Out of Work* (1904), Kellor treated it as a social and economic phenomenon. She was especially concerned with the plight of jobless women and their exploitation by employment agencies. Representing the Women's Municipal League of New York, Kellor lobbied successfully for state regulatory legislation for these agencies. The combination of professional social investigation and robust political advocacy became the hallmark of Kellor's progressivism. Her next study, on the problems of immigrants in New York, led to the establishment of the state Bureau of Industries and Immigration in 1910. Kellor was chosen to be its head, the first woman to hold so major a post in New York state government.

The high point of Kellor's career came two years later, when Theodore Roosevelt launched the Progressive party. Convinced that social reform required strong government, Kellor was drawn to the New Nationalism. She linked it with her own fervent advocacy of women's political rights. Always a fighter, she was entirely at ease in the rough and tumble of partisan politics. After Roosevelt's defeat in 1912, the Progressive party set up the National Progressive Service, a kind of think tank to study social problems and formulate legislative proposals. The idea was mainly Frances Kellor's, and she was tapped to chair the Service. This was truly a pinnacle for a woman in American politics, at a time when women in most states could not vote in national elections. Unfortunately, Kellor's emphasis on scientific investigation put her at odds with the practical politicians, and she was forced out in early 1914. Hers was a brief run in national politics, exhilarating while it lasted and unique for a woman in that era.

Kellor never married. Like many other woman progressives, including Jane Addams, she found personal fulfillment in an enduring relationship with another woman. This was Mary Dreier, one of two wealthy sisters who played leading roles in New York progressivism. From the time Kellor moved into the Dreier home in Brooklyn Heights in 1904 until her death almost fifty years later, she and Mary were constant companions. Kellor's later professional life was devoted to a distinguished career as vice president of the American Arbitration Association.

Women's organizations became a mighty force in state legislatures and in Congress on behalf of women and children. Their victories included the first law providing public assistance for mothers with dependent children, in Illinois in 1911; the first minimum wage law for women and children, in Massachusetts in 1912; and the creation of the Children's and Women's bureaus in the U.S. Labor Department, in 1912 and 1920, respectively.

The Settlement Houses. A second thrust of women's urban activism, just as strong as public advocacy, aimed at direct engagement with the underprivileged. The settlement-house movement began in London in 1884, when Oxford University students founded Toynbee Hall. Inspired by that example, two young American women, Jane Addams and Ellen Gates Starr, established Hull House on Chicago's West Side in 1889. During the next fifteen years, scores of settlement houses sprang up in the slum neighborhoods of the nation's cities. The settlement houses served as community centers run by their middle-class residents, who acted as amateur social workers for the surrounding immigrant communities. Hull House had meeting rooms, an art gallery, clubs for children and adults, and a kindergarten. Jane Addams herself led battles for garbage removal, playgrounds, better street lighting, and police protection. At the Henry Street Settlement in New York City, Lillian D. Wald made visiting nursing a major service. Mary McDowell, head of the University of Chicago Settlement, installed a bathhouse, a children's playground, and a citizenship school for immigrants.

Beyond the modest good they did in slum neighborhoods, the settlement houses served as a breeding ground for social reform. At least half the women residents went on to careers in some branch of social service. The settlement houses thus contributed significantly to the emerging profession of social work. To a remarkable degree, too, the leaders of social reform—both men and women—served apprenticeships in settlement houses.

For the middle-class residents, more deep-seated needs were also being satisfied. In a famous essay, Jane Addams spoke of the "subjective necessity" of the settlement house. She meant that it was as much a response to the desire of educated young women to serve as it was to the needs of slum dwellers. Addams herself was a case in point. She had grown up in a comfortable Illinois family and graduated from Rockford College. Then she faced an empty future, an ornamental wife if she married, a sheltered spinster if she did not. Hull House became her salvation. It gave her contact with what she thought was the real world plus a useful career and a sense of purpose and personal worth.

The Revival of the Struggle for Women's Rights. Almost imperceptibly, women activists like Jane Addams and Florence Kelley began to breathe new life into the suffrage movement. Why should a woman who was capable of running a settlement house or lobbying a bill

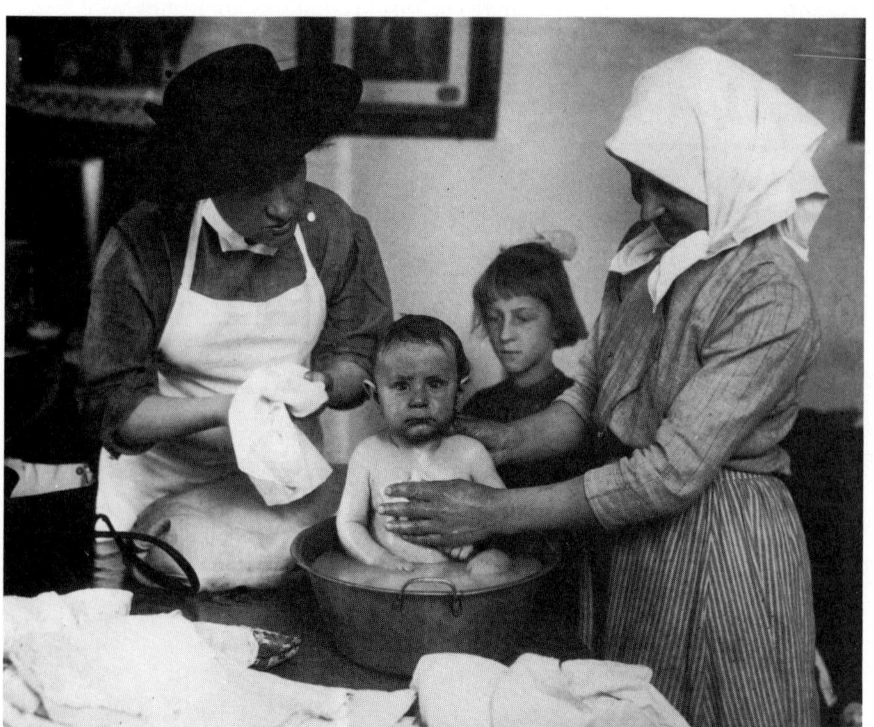

Saving the Children

In the early years at Hull House toddlers sometimes arrived for kindergarten tipsy from breakfasts of bread soaked in wine. To settlement-house workers, education in child care seemed the obvious answer to such ignorance, and so began the program to send visiting nurses into immigrant homes. They taught mothers the proper methods of caring for children—including, as this photograph shows, the daily infant bath, in a dishpan if necessary.

be denied the right to vote? Suffrage, moreover, became more firmly linked to social reform. If women had the right to vote, they and their male supporters argued, more enlightened legislation and better government would certainly result. Finally, by their activities among working-class women, the women progressives helped to broaden the social base of the suffrage movement.

Believing that working women should be encouraged to help themselves, social reformers founded the National Women's Trade Union League in 1903. Financed and led by wealthy supporters, the league organized women workers, played a considerable role in their strikes, and perhaps most important, developed working-class leaders. Rose Schneiderman, for example, became a union organizer among the garment workers in New York City; Agnes Nestor led the women glove workers in Illinois; and both were lobbyists for protective legislation. Such trade-union women identified their cause with the broader struggle for women's rights. When the state of New York held referenda on woman suffrage in 1915 and 1917, strong support came from the Jewish and Italian precincts inhabited by unionized garment workers.

Suffrage activity began to revive nationwide. Women won the right to vote in the state of Washington in 1910, in California in 1911, and in four more western states during the next three years. Women also altered their tactics. In England, suffragists had begun to picket Parliament, assault politicians, and go on hunger strikes in jail. This disruptive strategy, which infused the cause

Rose Schneiderman, 1913

In their battles for better conditions, women garment workers produced their own leaders, and none was more devoted to their cause, or more fiery on the platform, than Rose Schneiderman. The daughter of a widowed immigrant woman, Schneiderman went to work at thirteen, quickly became caught up in union activities, and fashioned for herself a lifetime career as a trade unionist, including becoming president of the National Women's Trade Union League.

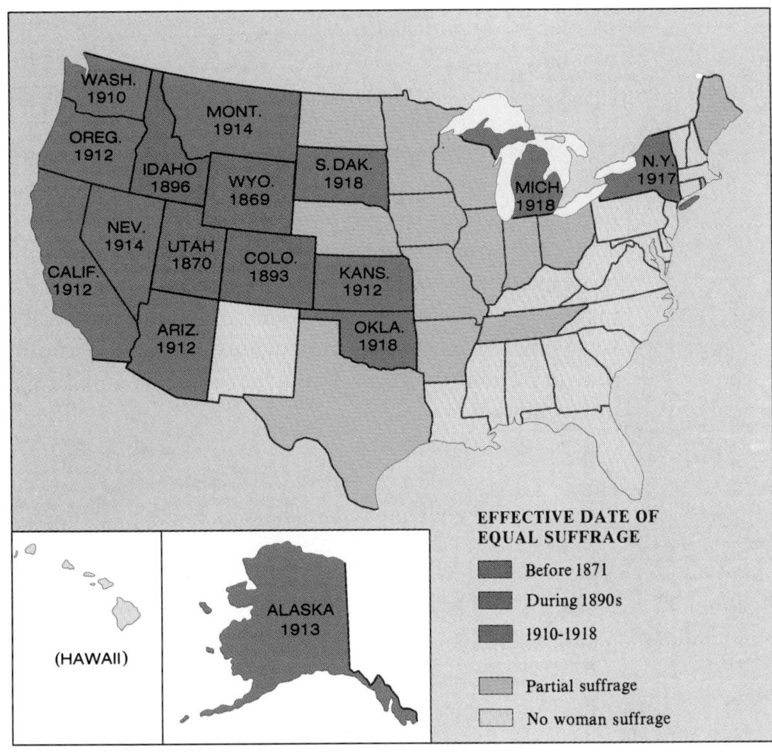

MAP 21.1

Woman Suffrage, 1869–1918

By 1909, after more than sixty years of agitation, only four lightly populated western states had granted women full voting rights. A number of other states granted partial suffrage, limited mostly to voting for school boards and such issues as taxes. Between 1910 and 1918, as the effort shifted to the struggle for a constitutional amendment, eleven states (and Alaska) joined the shortlist granting full suffrage. The most stubborn resistance was in the South.

Suffragists on Parade, 1912
After 1910 the suffrage movement went into high gear. Suffragist leaders decided to demand a constitutional amendment rather than relying solely on gaining the vote state by state. In 1912 they served notice on both parties that they meant business and, as in this suffragist parade in New York, made their demands a visible part of the presidential campaign.

of the English suffragists with new power, impressed their sisters in the United States.

Most important among the American converts was Alice Paul, a young Quaker who had lived in England and knew from firsthand experience how to apply the confrontational tactics of the English suffragists. Rejecting the slower route of enfranchisement by the states, Paul advocated a constitutional amendment that in one stroke would give women across the country the right to vote. In 1916, Paul organized the militant National Woman's party. The National American Woman Suffrage Association (NAWSA), from which Paul had split off, was also rejuvenated. Carrie Chapman Catt, a skilled political organizer from the New York movement, took over as national leader in 1915. Under her guidance, NAWSA brought a broad-based organization to the campaign for a federal amendment.

Feminism. In the midst of this suffrage struggle something new and more fundamental began to happen. A new generation of women activists was arising. They were college graduates or experienced trade unionists. Out in the world and self-supporting, these women were determined not to be hemmed in by the social constraints of women's "separate sphere." "Breaking into the Human Race" was the intention they proclaimed at a famous mass meeting in New York in 1914. "We intend simply to be ourselves," declared the chair Marie Jenny Howe, "not just our little female selves, but our whole big human selves."

The women at this meeting called themselves *feminists*, a term just then coming into use. In this, its first incarnation, feminism meant freedom for full personal development, which in its specifics covered many things—freedom to follow a career, freedom from the double standard in sexual morality, freedom from social convention—but in a larger sense meant above all freedom from the stifling stereotypes of woman's separate sphere. Thus did Charlotte Perkins Gilman, famous for her advocacy of communal kitchens as a means of liberating women from homemaking, imagine the new woman: "Here she comes, running, out of prison and off pedestal; chains off, crown off, halo off, just a live woman."

Feminists were militantly prosuffrage; but unlike their more traditional suffragist sisters, feminists did not stake their claim on any presumed uplifting effect of women's vote on American politics. Rather, they demanded the right to vote because they considered themselves full equals to men. At the point that the suffrage movement was about to triumph, it was being overtaken by a larger revolution that redefined the struggle for women's rights as a battle against all the constraints that prevented women from achieving their full potential as human beings.

Urban Liberalism

The social evolution of the suffrage movement—in particular, the recruitment of working-class women to what had been a middle-class struggle—was entirely characteristic of how progressivism evolved more generally.

When Hiram Johnson first ran for governor of California in 1910, he was the candidate of the middle class and the countryside. Launched into prominence by his successful prosecution of the corrupt San Francisco political boss Abe Ruef, Johnson pledged to purify California politics and to curb the Southern Pacific Railroad, the dominating power in the state's economic and political life. By his second term Johnson was championing social and labor legislation. His original base of middle-class support had eroded and been replaced by the immigrant, working-class vote that kept him in power for years. These events illustrated the most enduring achievement of progressivism: the activation of America's working people as a force in reform politics.

The cities served as the main arena for this development. Historians have called the result *urban liberalism*: that is, a reform movement by city people for social protection attained by state intervention. In New York, the activating event was a tragic fire.

Thirty minutes before quitting time on Saturday afternoon, March 25, 1911, fire broke out at the Triangle Shirtwaist Company in downtown New York City. The flames trapped the workers, mostly young immigrant women. Forty-seven leaped to their deaths; another ninety-nine never made it to the windows. The tragedy caused a national furor and led, two months later, to the creation of the New York State Factory Commission.

In the next four years, the commission developed a remarkable program of labor reform: fifty-six laws dealing with fire hazards, unsafe machines, home work, and wages and hours for women and children. The chairman of the commission was Robert F. Wagner; the vice-chairman, Alfred E. Smith. Both were Tammany Hall politicians and Democratic party leaders in the state legislature. Wagner and Smith sponsored the resolution establishing the commission, participated fully in its work, and marshaled the party regulars to pass the proposals into law. All this the two men did with the approval of the Tammany machine (see Chapter 20). The labor code that resulted was the most advanced in the United States.

Tammany's reform role reflected a trend in American cities. Urban political machines increasingly recognized their limits as social agencies in the modern industrial age. Only the state could prevent future Triangle fires or cope with the evils of factory work and city life. Also, a new generation had entered machine politics. Al Smith and Robert Wagner, men of social vision, absorbed the lessons of the Triangle investigation. They formed durable ties with such middle-class progressives as the social worker Frances Perkins, who sat on the commission as the representative of the New York Consumers League.

For all their organizational strength, moreover, the urban machines could not ignore the voters' sentiments. In the successes of such middle-class reform politicians as Toledo's Sam Jones and Cleveland's Tom Johnson, the urban machines saw the appeal of progressive pro-

The Triangle Shirtwaist Fire

The doors were the problem. Most were locked (to keep the working girls from leaving early); the few that were open became jammed by bodies as the flames spread. When the fire trucks finally came, the ladders were too short. Compared to those caught inside, the girls who leaped to their deaths were the lucky ones. "As I looked up I saw a love affair in the midst of all the horror," a reporter wrote. A young man was helping girls leap from a window. The fourth "put her arms about him and kiss[ed] him. Then he held her out into space and dropped her." He immediately followed. "Thud—dead, Thud—dead . . . I saw his face before they covered it . . . . he was a real man. He had done his best."

grams in working-class wards. There was a threat from the left as well. The Socialist party was making significant headway in the cities, electing Milwaukee's Victor Berger as the nation's first socialist congressman in 1910, and challenging the status quo by winning municipal elections in towns and cities across the country. The political universe of the urban machines had changed, and they had to pay more attention to opinion in the precincts.

The Labor Movement. Always highly pragmatic in their operations, the city machines adopted urban liberalism without much ideological struggle. The same could not be said of the trade unions, the other institution that represented American working people. During its early years the American Federation of Labor (AFL) had strongly opposed state interference in labor's affairs. Samuel Gompers preached that workers should not seek from government what they could accomplish through their own initiative and activities. Economic power and self-help, not the state, would be the worker's salvation. *Voluntarism*, as trade unionists called this antistate doctrine, did not die out, but it weakened substantially during the progressive years.

Organized labor enlisted in the cause of urban liberalism partly for defensive reasons. In the early twentieth century the labor movement came under severe attack by antiunion employers, who had at their disposal powerful legal weapons. For one thing, they could sue unions under the Sherman Antitrust Act. In the *Danbury Hatters* case (1908), the Supreme Court found a labor boycott—a call by the Hatters' Union for people not to patronize the antiunion D. E. Loewe & Company—to be a conspiracy in restraint of trade and awarded triple damages to the company. Hundreds of union members stood to lose their homes and life savings until the labor movement stepped in and raised the money to pay the fines. More harmful to the economic power of the unions was the employers' routine use of injunctions during labor disputes. (An *injunction* was a court order prohibiting a union from carrying on a strike or boycott.) The justification was to prevent "irreparable damage" to an employer while the legality of a union's acts was being adjudicated; but the effect of this "temporary" measure was to immobilize and defeat the union, as had happened, for example, to the American Railway Union in the great Pullman boycott of 1894 (see p. 573).

Only a political response might blunt these assaults on labor's economic weapons. In its "Bill of Grievances" of 1906, the AFL demanded that Congress grant unions immunity from court attack. Rebuffed, the labor movement decided to become more politically active, adopting as its strategy support on a nonpartisan basis for candidates who favored labor's program. Henceforth, the AFL intended to "reward our friends and punish our enemies." The practical effect of this "nonpartisan" strategy was to draw labor closer to the Democratic party, since it was more responsive than the Republicans to labor's pleas for a curb on the courts.

Having breached the political barriers for defensive reasons, the labor movement had difficulty denying the case for social legislation. The AFL, after all, claimed to speak for the entire working class. When muckrakers exposed exploitation of women and children and middle-class progressives came forward with solutions, how could the labor movement fail to respond? Gompers served on the Triangle factory commission, and if—according to Frances Perkins—he was a less eager student than the Tammanyite members, learn he did. In state after state, organized labor joined the battle for progressive legislation and increasingly became its strongest advocate. Conservative labor leaders found some consolation by making a careful distinction: protective laws were for women and children, who lacked the ability to defend themselves. In practice, however, the trade unions became more flexible about legislative protections for men as well, and on the issue of workmen's compensation, they lobbied vigorously for new legislation.

Accidents took an awful toll in American factories and mines. Two thousand coal miners were killed every year, dying from cave-ins and explosions at a rate, for example, 50 percent higher than in Germany's mines. Liability laws, still governed by common-law principles, were archaic and so heavily favored the employer that victims of industrial accidents rarely got compensated. Nothing cried out more for reform than the plight of maimed workers and penniless widows. In Germany and England, state-funded accident insurance guaranteed compensation regardless of fault. Efforts to provide comparable protections for American workers quickly received the backing of the trade unions. Between 1910 and 1917, workers' compensation for industrial accidents went into effect in all the industrial states.

In Defense of Cultural Pluralism. The economic needs of working people were not the only forces shaping urban liberal politics. It was also influenced by a sharpening attack on the cultural values and way of life of immigrants. Old-stock evangelical Protestants had long agitated for laws imposing their moral and cultural norms on American society. During the Progressive period, these activities gained a new lease on life. The Anti-Saloon League, which called itself "the Protestant church in action," became a formidable force for Prohibition in many states. Prohibiting the sale of liquor linked up with other reform objectives: the saloon made for dirty politics, poverty, and bad labor conditions.

AMERICAN VOICES

Working for the Triangle Shirtwaist Company

Pauline Newman

Pauline Newman was an organizer and educational director for the International Ladies Garment Workers Union until her death in 1986. As a child she worked at the notorious Triangle Shirtwaist factory in New York. This is her account of what life was like for women garment workers in the early twentieth century.

A cousin of mine worked for the Triangle Shirtwaist Company and she got me on there in October of 1901. It was probably the largest shirtwaist factory in the city of New York then. They had more than two hundred operators, cutters, examiners, finishers. Altogether more than four hundred people on two floors. The fire took place on one floor, the floor where we worked. You've probably heard about that. But that was years later.

We started work at seven-thirty in the morning, and during the busy season we worked until nine in the evening. They didn't pay you any overtime and they didn't give you anything for supper money. Sometimes they'd give you a little apple pie if you had to work very late. That was all. Very generous.

What I had to do was not really very difficult. It was just monotonous. When the shirtwaists were finished at the machine there were some threads that were left, and all the youngsters—we had a corner on the floor that resembled a kindergarten—we were given little scissors to cut the threads off. It wasn't heavy work, but it was monotonous, because you did the same thing from seven-thirty in the morning until nine at night.

Well, of course, there were [child labor] laws on the books, but no one bothered to enforce them. The employers were always tipped off if there was going to be an inspection. "Quick," they'd say, "into the boxes!" And we children would climb into the big boxes the finished shirts were stored in. Then some shirts were piled on top of us, and when the inspector came—no children. The factory always got an okay from the inspector, and I suppose someone at City Hall got a little something, too.

The employers didn't recognize anyone working for them as a human being. You were not allowed to sing. Operators would have liked to have sung, because they, too, had the same thing to do and weren't allowed to sing. We weren't allowed to talk to each other. Oh, no, they would sneak up behind if you were found talking to your next colleague. You were admonished: "If you keep on you'll be fired." If you went to the toilet and you were there longer than the floor lady thought you should be, you would be laid off for half a day and sent home. And, of course, that meant no pay. You were not allowed to have your lunch on the fire escape in the summertime. The door was locked to keep us in. That's why so many people were trapped when the fire broke out. . . .

I stopped working at the Triangle Factory during the strike in 1909 and I didn't go back. The union sent me out to raise money for the strikers. I apparently was able to articulate my feelings and opinions about the criminal conditions, and they didn't have anyone else who could do better so they assigned me. . . .

After the 1909 strike I worked with the union, organizing in Philadelphia and Cleveland and other places, so I wasn't at the Triangle Shirtwaist Factory when the fire broke out, but a lot of my friends were. I was in Philadelphia for the union and, of course, someone from here called me immediately and I came back. It's very difficult to describe the feeling because I knew the place and I knew so many of the girls. The thing that bothered me was the employers got a lawyer. How anyone could have *defended* them—because I'm quite sure that the fire was planned for insurance purposes. And no one is going to convince me otherwise. And when they testified that the door to the fire escape was open, it was a lie! It was never open. Locked all the time. One hundred and forty-six people were sacrificed, and the judge fined Blank and Harris seventy-five dollars!

Conditions were dreadful in those days. But there was something that is lacking today and I think it was the devotion and the belief. . . .

Even when things were terrible, I always had that faith. . . . Only now, I'm a little discouraged sometimes when I see the workers spending their free hours watching television—trash. We fought so hard for those hours and they waste them. We used to read Tolstoy, Dickens, Shelley, by candlelight, and they watch the "Hollywood Squares." Well, they're free to do what they want. That's what we fought for.

Source: Joan Morrison and Charlotte Fox Zabusky, eds., *American Mosaic: The Immigrant Experience in the Words of Those Who Lived It* (New York: E.P. Dutton, 1980), pp. 9–14.

The moral-reform agenda expanded to include a new goal: restricting the immigration of southern and Eastern Europeans into the United States. "The entrance . . . of such vast masses of peasantry, degraded below our utmost concepts, is a matter which no intelligent patriot can look upon without the gravest apprehension and alarm," warned Francis A. Walker, the president of the Massachusetts Institute of Technology. These concerns were shared by many progressive academics—for example, by La Follette's close adviser Edward A. Ross of the University of Wisconsin, who denounced the "pigsty mode of life" of the immigrants. The danger, respected social scientists argued, was that the nation's Anglo-Saxon population would be "mongrelized" and its American civilization swamped by "inferior" Mediterranean and Slavic cultures. Feeding on this fear, the Immigration Restriction League spearheaded a movement to end America's historic open-door policy. Like Prohibition, immigration restriction was considered by its proponents to be a progressive reform.

Urban liberals thought otherwise. They bitterly resented the demands for Prohibition and immigration restriction as unwarranted attacks on the personal liberty and worthiness of urban immigrants. Prohibition, protested one Catholic academic, was "despotic and hypocritical domination." The Tammany politician Martin McCue accused the Protestant ministry of "seeking to substitute the policeman's nightstick for the Bible."

Urban liberal leaders championed both the economic needs of city dwellers and their right to follow their religious and cultural preferences. In many ways, certainly until the Great Depression of the 1930s, ethnocultural issues provided the stronger basis for urban liberal politics. And because the Democrats were the party identified with tolerance and diversity, they became the beneficiaries of the rise of urban liberalism. The growing size of the city vote destined the Democrats to become the majority party. The shift from Republican domination, although not completed until the 1930s, began during the Progressive Era.

Racism in an Age of Reform

The direct primary was the flagship of progressive politics—the crucial reform, as La Follette said, for defeating the party bosses and returning politics to "the people." The primary electoral system of nominating party candidates originated not in Wisconsin, however, but in the South, and by the time La Follette got his primary law in 1903, it was already operating in seven southern states. As in the North, the southern primary was celebrated as a democratizing reform, and its adoption was frequently the opening victory that brought reform administrations into power.

In the South, however, it was a *white* primary; black voters were excluded, and since the Democratic nomination was tantamount to election, to be excluded from the primary meant in effect to be disfranchised. The direct primary was a reform *intended* among other things to drive blacks out of politics. How could democratic reform and white supremacy be thus wedded together?

The answer is to be found in the racist thinking of the age. "A black skin means membership in a race of men which has never of itself succeeded to reason," pronounced Professor John W. Burgess of Columbia University in a 1902 book on Reconstruction, and for Congress to have granted blacks the vote after the Civil War was a "monstrous thing." Burgess was a southern-born historian, but he was confident that his northern audience saw the "vast differences in political capacity" between blacks and whites and approved of black disfranchisement in the South. Even the Republican party, once it reconciled itself to relying on "lily white" organizations in the South midway through Roosevelt's administration, had no quarrel with this view. Indeed, as president-elect in 1908, William Howard Taft applauded the southern laws as necessary to "prevent entirely the possibility of domination by . . . an ignorant electorate" and reassured southerners that "the federal government has nothing to do with social equality."

In the North, the Progressive Era was marked by growing racial tensions. Over 200,000 blacks migrated from the South between 1900 and 1910. Their arrival in northern cities invariably sparked white resentment. Attacks on blacks became widespread. The worst episode was a bloody race riot in Springfield, Illinois, in 1908. Even more indicative of the popular racism infecting the North was the huge success of D. W. Griffith's epic film *Birth of a Nation* (1915), with its crude depiction of Reconstruction as a moral struggle between rampaging, childlike blacks and a chivalrous Ku Klux Klan. Woodrow Wilson found the film's history "all so terribly true." His Democratic administration marked a sad low point for the federal government as ultimate guarantor of the principle of equal rights: during Wilson's tenure, segregation of the U.S. civil service would have gone into effect but for the outcry it raised among black leaders and a handful of influential white progressives.

The Revival of the Civil Rights Struggle. In these bleak years, a core of young black professionals, mostly northern-born, began to fight back. The key figure was William Monroe Trotter, the pugnacious editor of the-

Boston *Guardian* and an outspoken critic of Booker T. Washington (see Chapter 19). "The policy of compromise has failed," argued Trotter. "The policy of resistance and aggression deserves a trial." In this endeavor, Trotter was joined in 1903 by W. E. B. Du Bois, a Harvard-trained sociologist and the preeminent black intellectual of his day. In 1906 the two of them, having broken with Washington, called a meeting of twenty-nine supporters at Niagara Falls—but in Canada, because no hotel on the U.S. side would admit blacks. The Niagara Movement, which resulted from that meeting, had an impact far beyond the scattering of members and local bodies it organized. The principles it affirmed would thereafter define the struggle for the rights of African-Americans: first, encouragement of black pride by all possible means; second, an uncompromising demand for full political and civil equality. Above all, "We refuse to allow the impression to remain that the Negro-American assents to inferiority, is submissive under oppression and apologetic before insults."

The revival of black protest found a small echo within white progressivism. Going against the grain, a handful of reformers were drawn to the plight of African-Americans. Among the most devoted was Mary White Ovington. By upper-class background and social outlook, she very much resembled Jane Addams, except that Ovington came from a family of abolitionists and thought of herself as a socialist. Like Addams, Ovington became a settlement-house worker, but among urban blacks rather than in an immigrant neighborhood. News of the bloody Springfield race riot of 1908 changed her life. Convinced that her duty lay in the struggle for equal rights, Ovington called a meeting of sympathetic white progressives that led to the formation of the National Association for the Advancement of Colored People in 1909.

The Niagara Movement, torn apart by internal disagreements, was breaking up, and most of the black activists joined the NAACP. Its national leadership was in the early years dominated by whites, however. The one exception proved to be of crucial importance. Du Bois became the editor of the NAACP's journal *The Crisis*. With a passion that only a black voice could provide, Du Bois used that platform to proclaim the demands for black equality.

In the social welfare field, the principal concern during the Progressive Era was over the needs of black migrants arriving in northern cities. In 1911 the National Urban League united the principal organizations that had sprung up to assist black migrants. Like the NAACP, the Urban League was interracial, including white reformers like Ovington and black welfare activists like William Lewis Bulkley, the New York school principal who played the single most important role in the founding of the Urban League.

Progressivism was a house of many chambers. Most were infected by the respectable racism of the age, but not all. There was a saving remnant of white progressives who allied themselves with black activists and created, in the NAACP and the Urban League, the national institutions that would dominate the black struggle for a better life over the next half-century.

Editorial Office, The Crisis

In its early years, no activity undertaken by the NAACP was more important than publication of its journal, *The Crisis*, which under the brilliant editorship of W. E. B. Du Bois became the strongest voice for equal rights and black pride in the country. In this photograph of the magazine's editorial office, Du Bois is the balding man at the right rear.

Progressivism and National Politics

The gathering forces of progressivism reached the national scene only slowly. Reformers had been activated by immediate concerns—by problems that affected them directly, and by evils visible and tangible to them. Washington seemed remote from the battles they were waging in their cities and states. But progressivism was bound to come to the capital. In 1906, Robert La Follette moved from the governor's office in Wisconsin to the U.S. Senate. Other seasoned progressives, also ambitious for a wider stage, made the same move. By 1910, a highly vocal progressive bloc was making itself heard in both houses of Congress.

The crucial entry point of progressivism into national politics was not Congress, however, but the presidency. This was partly because the presidential office was a "bully pulpit"—to use Theodore Roosevelt's words—for mobilizing opinion and defining national issues. But just as important was the twist of fate that brought Roosevelt—the epitome of the progressive politician—to the White House on September 14, 1901.

The Making of a Progressive President

Except for his rather aristocratic background, Theodore Roosevelt was cut from much the same cloth as other progressive politicians. Born in 1858, he came from a wealthy, old-line New York family, attended Harvard, and might well have chosen the life of a leisured, literary gentleman. Instead, scarcely out of college, he plunged into Republican politics and in 1882 entered the New York state legislature. His reasons matched the high-minded motives of other budding progressives. Like most of them, Roosevelt had received a moralistic, Christian upbringing. A political career would enable him to act constructively on those beliefs. Roosevelt always identified himself—loudly—with the side of righteousness. On the other hand, he did not scorn power and its uses. He showed contempt for the amateurism of the Mugwumps— "those political and literary hermaphrodites," he called them—and much preferred the professionalism of party politics. Roosevelt rose in the New York party because he skillfully translated his moral fervor into broad popular support and thus forced himself on reluctant state Republican bosses.

After returning from the Spanish-American War as the hero of San Juan Hill (see Chapter 22), Roosevelt won the New York governorship in 1898. During his single term he clearly indicated his inclinations toward reform. Roosevelt pushed through civil-service reform and a tax on corporate franchises. He discharged the corrupt superintendent of insurance over the Republican party's objections and asserted his confidence in the government's capacity to improve the life of the people.

In an attempt to neutralize him, the party bosses promoted Roosevelt in 1900 to what normally would have been a dead-end job as William McKinley's vice-president. Roosevelt accepted reluctantly. But on September 6, 1901, an anarchist named Leon F. Czolgosz shot the president. When McKinley died eight days later, Roosevelt became president. It was a sure bet, groaned Republican boss Mark Hanna, that "that damn cowboy" would make trouble in the White House.

Roosevelt in fact moved cautiously at the outset. In his first official statement, he reassured the nation that he would "continue absolutely unbroken" McKinley's policies. The conservative Republican bloc in Congress greatly limited his freedom of action. He treated the Senate leader, Nelson W. Aldrich of Rhode Island, with kid gloves. Much of Roosevelt's energy was devoted to consolidating his position. He skillfully used the patronage powers of his office to gain control of the Republican party. But Roosevelt was also restrained by uncertainty about what reform role the federal government ought to play. At first, the new president might have been described as a progressive without a cause.

Even so, Roosevelt gave early evidence of his activist bent. An ardent outdoorsman, he devoted part of his first annual message to conservation. A national movement had begun in the late nineteenth century to protect the country's natural resources and scenic wonders against reckless exploitation. With the establishment of Yellowstone National Park in 1872, the national park system had been launched, and the Forest Reserve Act of 1891 began the process of withdrawing timberlands from unregulated commercial use.

Unlike John Muir (see Chapter 17), Roosevelt was not a preservationist broadly opposed to the exploitation of the nation's wilderness. Rather, Roosevelt aimed at *conserving* the nation's public resources. He was not against commercial development, so long as it was regulated and mindful of the public interest. Roosevelt added more than 125 million acres to the national forest reserve and brought mineral lands and water power sites into the reserve system. In 1902 he backed the Newlands Reclamation Act, which designated the proceeds from public land sales for irrigation development in arid regions. His administration strongly upgraded the management of public lands and, to the chagrin of some Republicans, energetically prosecuted violators of federal land laws. In the cause of conservation, Roosevelt demonstrated his enthusiasm for exercising executive authority and his disdain for those who sought profit "by betraying the public."

The same inclinations influenced Roosevelt's handling of the anthracite coal strike of 1902. Hard coal was the main fuel for home heating in those days. As cold weather approached with no settlement in sight, the government faced a national emergency. The United Mine Workers, led by John Mitchell, were willing to submit to arbitration, but the coal operators adamantly opposed any recognition of the union. Roosevelt's advisers told him there was no legal basis for federal intervention. Nevertheless, the president called both sides to a conference at the White House on October 1, 1902. When the conference failed, Roosevelt threatened the operators with a government take-over of the mines. He also persuaded the financier J. P. Morgan to use his considerable influence with them. At this point the coal operators caved in. The strike ended with the appointment by Roosevelt of an arbitration commission to rule on the issues, another unprecedented step. Roosevelt did not especially support organized labor, but he became infuriated by what he labeled the "arrogant stupidity" of the mine employers.

"Of all the forms of tyranny the least attractive and the most vulgar is the tyranny of mere wealth," Roosevelt wrote in his autobiography. He was prepared to deploy all his presidential authority against the "tyranny" of irresponsible business.

The Trust Problem. The economic issue that most concerned Roosevelt was a disturbing assault on the competitive market by big business. The drift toward large-scale enterprise had been under way for many years, as entrepreneurs sought the efficiencies of nationwide, vertically integrated operations (see Chapter 18). But building larger business units was also a way of limiting competition and controlling markets. The depression of the 1890s, which had driven down prices and caused staggering business losses, led to an astonishing scramble to merge rival firms once economic recovery began in 1897. These mergers—*trusts*, as they were called—greatly increased the degree of business concentration in the economy. Of the 73 largest industrial companies in 1900, 53 had not existed three years earlier. By 1910, 1 percent of the nation's manufacturers accounted for 44 percent of the total industrial output.

The sheer economic power of the new combines was not their only disturbing feature. Most of them were heavily *watered*—that is, the stocks and bonds they issued much exceeded the real value of the properties they controlled. For their underwriting services in launching the new trusts, moreover, investment bankers such as J. P. Morgan charged huge fees. Worse yet, financiers did not relinquish control over the combines they had fathered, for they sat on the boards of directors of the new firms and behind the scenes exerted heavy influence on the operating executives. Almost overnight, a "money power"—a handful of Wall Street bankers—seemed to have gained a stranglehold on the American economy.

Roosevelt's sense of the nation's uneasiness became evident as early as his first annual message, in which he referred to the "real and grave evils" of economic concentration. But what weapons could the president use in response?

The basic legal principles upholding free competition were already firmly established. Under the common law—the body of court-made legal precedents that America had inherited from England—it was illegal for anyone to conspire to restrain or monopolize trade; persons economically injured by such actions could sue for damages. These common-law rights had been enacted into statute law in many states during the 1880s, and then, because the magnitude of the problem exceeded

Jack and the Wall Street Giants

In this vivid cartoon from the humor magazine *Puck*, Jack (Teddy Roosevelt) has come to slay the giants of Wall Street. To the country, trust busting took on the mythic qualities of the fairy tale—with about the same amount of awe for the fearsome Wall Street giants and hope in the prowess of the intrepid Roosevelt. J. Pierpont Morgan is the giant leering at front right.

state jurisdictions, had been incorporated into the Sherman Antitrust Act of 1890 and become part of federal law.

Neither the Cleveland nor the McKinley administrations had been much inclined to enforce the Sherman Act, except against organized labor. Of the eighteen federal suits brought before 1901, half were against trade unions. Nor were the courts any more enthusiastic about attacking business. In *U.S. v. E. C. Knight* (1895), the Supreme Court ruled that manufacturing was not covered by the Constitution's commerce clause and hence lay beyond the reach of federal antitrust regulation. This ruling crippled the Sherman Act but did not kill it. The potential of the act rested, above all, in the fact that it incorporated common-law principles of unimpeachable validity. In the right hands, the Sherman Act could be a strong weapon against the abuse of economic power.

Trust Busting. Roosevelt made his opening move when he strengthened the government's capacity to enforce the law. In 1903, despite considerable opposition, Congress accepted Roosevelt's proposal for a Bureau of Corporations within the newly created Department of Commerce and Labor. Empowered to investigate business practices, the bureau provided the factual record on which the Justice Department could mount antitrust suits. The first suit had already been filed in 1902 against the Northern Securities Company, a combination of the railroad systems of the Northwest. In a landmark 1904 decision, the Supreme Court ordered Northern Securities dissolved. The next year, the Court reversed the *Knight* doctrine: it ruled that manufacturing fell within the commerce clause and was therefore subject to federal antitrust law.

In 1904, Roosevelt handily defeated a weak conservative Democratic candidate, Judge Alton B. Parker. Now president in his own right, Roosevelt stepped up the attack on the trusts. He took on forty-five of the nation's giant firms, including Standard Oil, American Tobacco, and DuPont. The president accompanied these actions with a rising crescendo of rhetoric. He became the nation's trust buster, a crusader against "predatory wealth."

Despite his rhetoric, Roosevelt was not antibusiness; he regarded large-scale enterprise as a natural result of modern industrialism. Only firms that abused their power deserved punishment. But how would those companies be identified? Under the common law, and under the Sherman Act as originally intended, it had been up to the courts to decide whether a given act in restraint of trade was "unreasonable"—that is, actually harmed potential competitors or damaged the public interest. This was a highly flexible approach, enabling the courts to evaluate the actions of corporations on a case-by-case basis. In 1897, however, the Supreme Court had repudiated this "rule of reason" in the *Trans-Missouri* case. Now, even if the impact on the market was not harmful, actions that restrained or monopolized trade would automatically put a firm in violation of the Sherman law.

Little noticed when it was first decided, *Trans-Missouri* placed Roosevelt in an awkward position when he began to enforce the Sherman Act. Roosevelt had no desire to hamstring legitimate business activity. But he could not rely on the courts to distinguish between "good" and "bad" trusts. The only solution was for the executive to assume that responsibility. This the president could do because it was up to him—or his attorney general—to decide whether or not to initiate antitrust prosecutions in the first place.

That Roosevelt would use this discretionary power became clear in November 1904, shortly after the Bureau of Corporations began to investigate the United States Steel Corporation. The company chairman, Elbert H. Gary, asked for a meeting with Roosevelt. Gary proposed an arrangement: cooperation in exchange for preferential treatment. The company would open its books to the Bureau of Corporations. If the bureau found evidence of wrongdoing, the company would be

J. Pierpont Morgan

J. P. Morgan was the giant among American financiers. He had served an apprenticeship in investment banking under his father, a leading Anglo-American banker in London. A gruff man of few words, Morgan had a genius for instilling trust, and the strength of will to persuade others to follow his lead and do his bidding—qualities the great photographer Edward Steichen captured in this portrait. (The Museum of Modern Art, New York) advised privately and given a chance to set matters right. Roosevelt accepted this "gentlemen's agreement," which was followed by one with International Harvester the next year. J. P. Morgan controlled both firms. From the financier's standpoint, the arrangement seemed entirely sensible. Two great powers, one political and the other economic, would meet as equals and settle matters between them. For Roosevelt, the gentlemen's agreements eased a serious dilemma. He could accommodate the realities of the modern industrial order while maintaining his public image as the champion against the trusts.

Railroad Regulation. Abuse of economic power by the railroads posed a somewhat different kind of problem for Roosevelt. As quasi-public enterprises, the railroads had always been subject to public regulation. Initially, this had been the responsibility of the states, but with the passage of the Interstate Commerce Act of 1887, the federal government had entered the field, establishing in the Interstate Commerce Commission the nation's first federal regulatory agency. As with the Sherman Act, however, railroad regulation remained pretty much a dead letter in its early years. Restrained by a hostile Supreme Court, the ICC lapsed into a mere collector of statistics. Roosevelt was convinced, however, that the railroads needed firm regulation. The Elkins Act of 1903 empowered the ICC to act against discriminatory rebates—that is, reductions on published rates for preferred or powerful customers. Then, with the 1904 election behind him, Roosevelt made his push for a major expansion of railroad regulation.

The central issue was the setting of rates. Roosevelt considered it essential that the ICC have this power. Senator Nelson Aldrich and his conservative bloc opposed it just as firmly. In 1906, after nearly two years of wrangling, Congress passed the Hepburn Railway Act. This law empowered the ICC to set and put into effect maximum rates upon complaint of a shipper and gave it the authority to examine railroad books and prescribe uniform bookkeeping. But as a concession to the conservative bloc the courts retained broad powers to review ICC rate decisions.

The Hepburn Act stood as a testament to Roosevelt's skills as a political operator. He had maneuvered brilliantly against determined opposition and come away with the essentials of what he wanted. Despite grumbling by Senate progressives critical of any compromise, Roosevelt was satisfied. He had achieved a landmark expansion of the government's regulatory powers over business.

Consumer Protection. The regulation of consumer products, another hallmark of progressive reform, was very much the handiwork of muckraking journalists. In 1905 Samuel Hopkins Adams published a series of articles on the patent-medicine business in *Collier's*. The first paragraph opened with these riveting words:

> Gullible America will spend this year some seventy-five millions of dollars in the purchase of patent medicines. In consideration of this sum it will swallow huge quantities of alcohol, an appalling amount of opiates and narcotics, a wide assortment of varied drugs ranging from powerful and dangerous heart depressants to insidious liver stimulants; and, far in excess of all other ingredients, undiluted fraud. For fraud, exploited by the skillfullest of advertising bunco men, is the basis of the trade.

Numerous pure food and drug bills, introduced in Congress in 1905, had been stymied by industry lobbies. Then, in 1906, Upton Sinclair's novel *The Jungle* appeared. Sinclair had aimed at exposing labor exploitation in the Chicago meat-packing plants, but his graphic descriptions of rotten meat and filthy conditions excited—and sickened—the nation. President Roosevelt, hitherto not greatly concerned about consumer issues, now threw his weight into the legislative battle, initiating a federal investigation of conditions in the stockyards and threatening to make public its harsh findings unless Congress took swift action. The Pure

Campaigning for the Square Deal
When William McKinley ran for president in 1896, he sat on his front porch in Canton, Ohio, and received delegations of voters. That was not Theodore Roosevelt's way. He considered the presidency a "bully pulpit," and he used the office brilliantly to mobilize public opinion and to assert his leadership. The preeminence of the presidency in American public life begins with Roosevelt's administration. Here, at the height of his crusading powers, he stumps for the Square Deal in the 1904 election.

Food and Drug Act and the Meat Inspection Act passed within months. And another administrative agency was added to federal bureaucratic structure that Roosevelt was building—the Food and Drug Administration.

The Square Deal. During the 1904 presidential campaign, Roosevelt had taken to calling his program "the Square Deal." This kind of labeling was new to American politics. It introduced a political style that dramatized issues, mobilized public opinion, and asserted leadership. But the Square Deal meant something of substance as well. After many years of passivity and weakness, the federal government was reclaiming the large role it had abandoned after the Civil War. Now, however, the target had become the new economic order. When companies misused corporate power, the government had the responsibility for correcting matters and assuring ordinary Americans of a "square deal." Under Roosevelt's leadership, progressivism had come to national politics.

The Fracturing of Republican Progressivism

During his two terms as president, Theodore Roosevelt struggled to bring a modern corporate economy under control. He was well aware, however, that his Square Deal was built on nineteenth-century foundations; in particular, antitrust doctrine, which aimed at enforcing competition, seemed to Roosevelt inadequate to the demands of a large-scale industrial order. A better approach, he felt, would be to give the federal government the administrative powers to oversee and regulate big business. In his final presidential speeches, Roosevelt dwelt on the need for a reform agenda for the twentieth century. When he left office in 1909, he thought he had arranged matters so that there would be steady movement in that direction. He was mistaken. By the time Roosevelt returned from a year-long safari in Africa, turmoil reigned in Washington.

The Presidency of William Howard Taft. The agents of historical change sometimes take strange forms. A person out of tune with the times can, by the sheer friction he or she generates, serve as the catalyst for great events. Such became the fate of William Howard Taft, Roosevelt's hand-picked successor.

Taft's Democratic opponent in the 1908 campaign was William Jennings Bryan. This was Bryan's third—and last—try for the presidency, and he made the most of it. Eloquent as ever, Bryan showed again why he was known as the Commoner, the voice of the people. He attacked the Republicans as the party of the "plutocrats," and outdid them in urging stronger antitrust legislation, lower tariffs, stricter railway regulation, and labor legislation so favorable to the unions as to gain the support of the officially nonpartisan AFL. Bryan's campaign moved the Democratic party into the mainstream of national progressive politics, but this was not enough to offset Taft's advantages as President Roosevelt's candidate. Taft won comfortably, if by a smaller margin than Roosevelt's smashing 1904 victory, and he entered the White House with a mandate to pick up where TR had left off.

William Howard Taft was an estimable man in many ways. He had been an able jurist and a superb administrator. He had served Roosevelt loyally and well as governor general of the Philippines and as secretary of war. He was an avowed Square Dealer. But he was not by nature a progressive politician. Taft was incapable of dramatizing issues or of stirring the people. He disliked the give-and-take of politics, he distrusted power, and he generally deferred to Congress. In fundamental ways, moreover, Taft was deeply conservative. He sanctified property rights, he revered the processes of the law, and unlike Roosevelt, he found it hard to trim his means to fit his ends.

By 1909, the ferment of reform had unsettled the Republican party. On the right, the conservatives were girding themselves against further losses. Under Senator Aldrich, they were still a force to be reckoned with both on Capitol Hill and within the party. On the other hand, progressive Republicans were rebellious. They had broad popular support—especially in the Midwest—and, in Robert La Follette, a fiery leader. They felt that Roosevelt had made too many concessions to business interests. With the resourceful Roosevelt gone from the White House, the Congressional progressives were determined to have their way. Reconciling these conflicting forces within the Republican party would have been a daunting task for the most accomplished politician. For Taft, it spelled disaster.

First there was the tariff. Progressives generally considered high tariffs to be a major cause for the decline of competition and the rise of the trusts. Taft had campaigned for a "sizable reduction." During the lengthy drafting process, however, he was won over by the conservative Republican bloc and gave his approval for the protectionist Payne-Aldrich Tariff Act of 1909, which favored eastern industry.

Next came the battle over "Uncle Joe" Cannon, Speaker of the House of Representatives. A dyed-in-the-wool conservative, Cannon virtually controlled the flow of legislation in the House. Progressives were determined to depose him. Taft abandoned them in exchange for Cannon's help on administration legislation. When a House revolt finally broke the Speaker's power in 1910, Cannon's defeat was regarded as a defeat for the president as well.

Equally damaging to Taft was the Pinchot-Ballinger affair. U.S. Chief Forester Gifford Pinchot, an ardent conservationist and a chum of Roosevelt's, accused Secretary of the Interior Richard A. Ballinger of conspiring to transfer public coal lands in Alaska to a private syndicate. When Pinchot made the charges public in January 1910, Taft fired him for insubordination. The fact that Taft was actually a dedicated conservationist somehow did not matter. In the eyes of the progressives, the Pinchot-Ballinger affair marked Taft for life as a friend of the "interests" plundering the nation's resources.

Solemnly pledged to carry on in Roosevelt's tradition, Taft managed to work his way into the conservative Republican camp in less than two years. While doing so, he helped transform the reformers into a distinct faction of the Republican party. By 1910 they were calling themselves "Progressives" or, in more belligerent moments, "Insurgents." Taft responded by trying to purge them in the Republican primaries that year. This vendetta climaxed Taft's record of disastrous leadership.

The Progressive Insurgency. The Progressives emerged from the 1910 elections stronger and angrier than ever. In January 1911 they formed the National Progressive Republican League and began a drive to take control of the Republican party. La Follette was the Progressives' leader and their designated presidential candidate, but they knew that their best chance to win lay with Theodore Roosevelt.

Roosevelt, home from Africa, yearned to reenter the political fray. He was not easily reconciled to the absence of power and would have been troublesome for Taft under any circumstances. As it was, the president's handling of the Progressives fed Roosevelt's mounting sense of outrage. But Roosevelt was too loyal a party man to defy the Republican establishment, and too astute a politician not to recognize that a party split would benefit the Democrats. He could be spurred into rebellion only by the discovery of a true clash of principles. On the question of the trusts, such a clash materialized.

From the first, Roosevelt had been troubled by the Sherman Antitrust Act. To enforce competition seemed to him to fly in the face of the inevitable modern tendency toward economic concentration. By distinguishing between good and bad trusts, Roosevelt had managed to reconcile public policy and economic reality. But this was a makeshift solution, depending as it did on a president inclined to stretch his powers to the limit. Taft had no such inclination. His legalistic mind rebelled at the discretionary use of presidential authority over instituting antitrust suits. The Sherman Act was on the books. "We are going to enforce that law or die in the attempt," Taft promised grimly.

In its *Standard Oil* decision (1911), the Supreme Court eased Taft's dilemma by reasserting the common-law principle of the "rule of reason" on antitrust actions: once again, it would be up to the courts to distinguish between "good" and "bad" trusts. With that burden lifted from the executive branch, Attorney General George W. Wickersham stepped up the pace of antitrust actions.

The United States Steel Corporation immediately became a prime target. Among the charges against the Steel Trust was that it had violated the antimonopoly provision of the Sherman Act by acquiring the Tennessee Coal and Iron Company. The purchase had been made in 1907 from a banking house that had fallen into trouble and urgently needed to sell its TCI stock in order to raise capital. Roosevelt had personally approved the acquisition as a necessary step—so U.S. Steel representatives had explained it to him—to prevent a financial collapse on Wall Street. Taft's suit against U.S. Steel thus amounted to an attack on Roosevelt: he had as president entered into a private agreement with U.S. Steel to circumvent the Sherman Act. Nothing was better calculated to propel Roosevelt into action than an issue that was both an affair of personal honor and a question of broad principle.

The New Nationalism. The country did not have to choose between breaking up big business and submitting to corporate rule, Roosevelt argued. There was a third way. The federal government could be empowered to oversee big business to make sure it acted in the public interest. The tool would be a federal trade commission with powers comparable to those exerted by the Interstate Commerce Commission over the railroads. The nation's industrial corporations would be treated, in effect, as if they were natural monopolies or public utilities and placed under direct public oversight.

In a speech in Osawatomie, Kansas, in August 1910, Roosevelt made his case for what he called the New Nationalism. The central issue, he argued, was human welfare versus property rights. In modern society, property had to be controlled "to whatever degree the public welfare may require it." The government would become "the steward of the public welfare."

This formulation removed the restraints from Roosevelt's thinking. Ultimately, he did not stop short of advocating government price fixing for corporate industry. He took up the cause of social justice, adding to his program a federal child labor law, federal workmen's compensation, regulation of labor relations, and a national minimum wage for women. Most radical perhaps was Roosevelt's attack on the legal system. Insisting that the courts should not be making social policy, Roosevelt proposed sharp curbs on their powers, even raising the possibility of popular recall of court decisions.

Beyond these specifics, the New Nationalism presented a new political philosophy. The key source was a book by the journalist Herbert Croly, *The Promise of American Life* (1909), which called for a uniting of rival strains in the American political tradition. From Hamilton's federalism, Croly drew his emphasis on strong national government; from Jefferson's republicanism came Croly's enthusiasm for democracy and the primacy of the interests of the common citizen. The result, however, was a genuine break from America's political past. The New Nationalism offered a *statist* solution—an enormous expansion of the role of the federal government—to the problem of corporate power.

Early in 1912, Roosevelt announced his candidacy for the presidency and immediately swept the Progressive Republicans into his camp. A bitter and divisive party battle ensued. Taft proved to be a tenacious opponent. Roosevelt won the states that held primary elections, but Taft controlled the party organizations elsewhere. The party regulars dominated the national convention, and they threw the nomination to Taft.

Roosevelt, considering himself cheated out of the nomination, led his followers into a new Progressive party, soon nicknamed the "Bull Moose" party. In a crusading campaign, Roosevelt offered the New Nationalism to the people.

On to the White House

At the Democratic convention, Woodrow Wilson only narrowly defeated the front runner, Champ Clark of Missouri. *Harper's Weekly* triumphantly depicted Wilson immediately after his nomination—the scholar turned politician riding off on the Democratic donkey, his running mate, Thomas R. Marshall, hanging on behind. *Harper's* editor, George Harvey, had identified Wilson as of presidential timber as early as 1906, long before the Princeton president had thought of politics, and worked on his behalf ever since.

Woodrow Wilson and the New Freedom

While the Republicans battled among themselves, the Democrats were on the move. The scars caused by the free silver campaign of 1896 had faded, and in the 1908 campaign William Jennings Bryan had established the progressive credentials of the rejuvenated party. In the 1910 elections, the Democrats made dramatic gains, taking over the House of Representatives for the first time since 1892, winning ten Senate seats, and capturing a number of traditionally Republican governor ships. After fourteen years as party standard-bearer, Bryan now reluctantly made way for a new generation of leaders.

The ablest, by all odds, was Woodrow Wilson of New Jersey. Wilson was an academic, a noted political scientist who, as president of Princeton, had brought it to the front rank of American universities. In 1910, without ever before running for public office, he left Princeton to accept the Democratic nomination for governor of New Jersey. Wilson compiled a brilliant record as governor and went on, in a bruising battle, to win the Democratic presidential nomination in 1912. He could identify himself as a reformer by his achievements in New Jersey—defeat of the boss system and passage of a direct primary law, workmen's compensation, and the regulation of railroads and utilities.

Wilson possessed, to a fault, the moral certainty that characterized the progressive politician. A brilliant speaker, he almost instinctively assumed the mantle of righteousness and showed little tolerance for the views of his critics. Only gradually, however, did Wilson hammer out, in reaction to Roosevelt's New Nationalism, a coherent reform program, which he called the New Freedom.

It is important to recognize how much ground Wilson shared with Roosevelt. "*The old time of individual competition is probably gone by*," Wilson stressed. "We will do business henceforth, when we do it on a great and successful scale, by means of corporations." Like Roosevelt, Wilson opposed not bigness, but the abuse of economic power. Nor did Wilson think that the abuse of power could be prevented without a strong federal government. Where he parted company from Roosevelt was over *how* the authority of government should be used to restrain private power.

Direct control over corporations by the federal government as advocated by Roosevelt was an anathema to Wilson. As he warmed to the debate, Wilson cast the issue in the fundamental terms of slavery and freedom. "This is a struggle for emancipation," he proclaimed in October 1912. "If America is not to have free enterprise, then she can have freedom of no sort whatever." Wilson also scorned Roosevelt's social welfare program. It might be benevolent, he declared, but it also would be paternalistic and contrary to the traditions of a free people. The New Nationalism represented a future of collectivism, Wilson warned, whereas the New Freedom would conserve the political and economic liberties of the individual.

How, then, did Wilson propose to deal with the problem of corporate power? Court enforcement of the Sherman Act was Wilson's basic answer. His task was to figure out how to make that long-established antitrust approach work better. In this effort Wilson relied heavily on a new adviser, Louis D. Brandeis, famous as the "people's lawyer" for his public service in many progressive causes (including the landmark *Muller* case).

An expert on regulatory matters, Brandeis understood that an all-powerful trade commission was likely to end up not as the defender of the public interest but in a cozy relationship with the industries it was supposed to regulate. Nor did Brandeis believe that bigness meant efficiency. On the contrary, he argued that the trusts were inherently wasteful compared to firms vigorously competing in a free market. The main thing was to prevent the trusts from unfairly using their power to curb that free competition. The aim of public policy should be "so [to] restrict the wrong use of competition that the right use of competition will destroy monopoly."

The 1912 election fell far short of being a great referendum on the New Nationalism versus the New Freedom. The outcome turned on a more humdrum reality: Wilson was elected because he kept the traditional Democratic vote while the Republicans split between Roosevelt and Taft. Although he won by a landslide in the electoral college, Wilson received only 42 percent of the popular vote—115,000 fewer votes than Bryan had amassed against Taft in 1908.

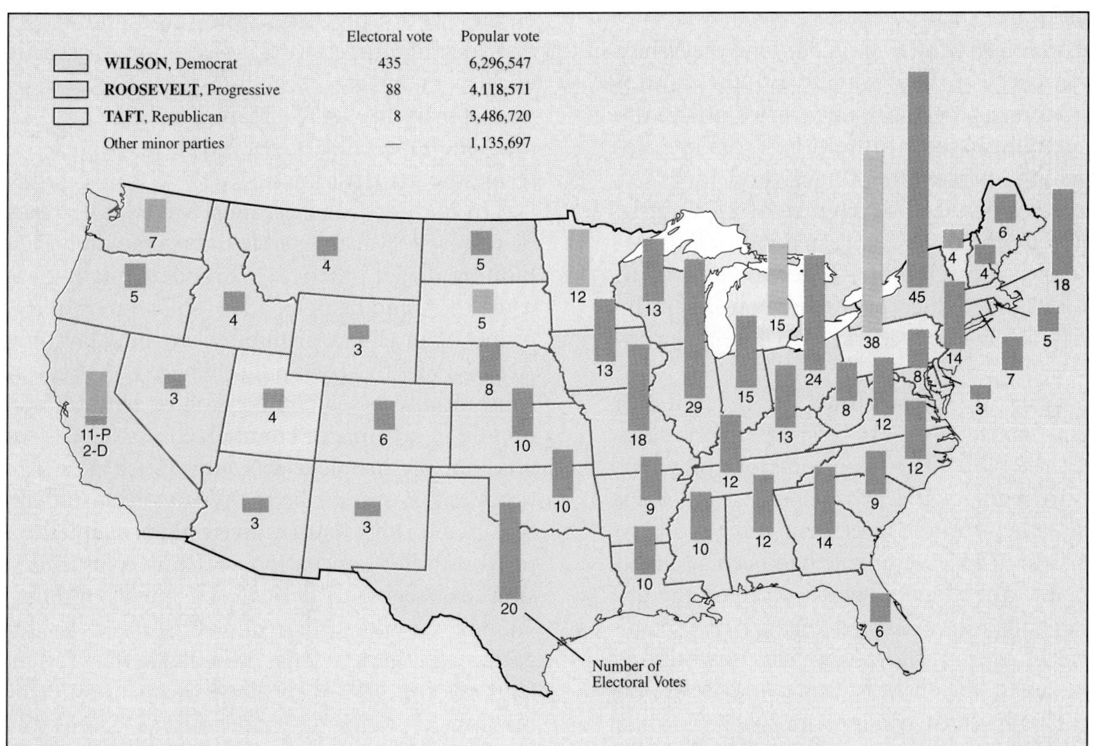

MAP 21.2

The Election of 1912

The 1912 election reveals why the two-party system has been so strongly rooted in American politics. The Democrats, although a minority party, won an electoral landslide because the Republicans divided their vote between Roosevelt and Taft. The disastrous result indicated the enormous incentive for major parties against splintering. The Socialists, despite a record vote of 900,000, got no electoral votes at all. To vote Socialist in 1912 meant, in effect, to throw away one's vote.

Moreover, voter turnout fell substantially, from 65.4 percent of eligible voters in 1908 to 58.8 in 1912. If there was a beneficiary of the reform ferment sparked by the presidential campaign, it was not Wilson, but the Socialist candidate, Eugene V. Debs, who captured a record 900,000 votes, 6 percent of the total. At best it could be said that the 1912 election signified that the American public was in the mood for reform: only 23 percent, after all, had voted for the one candidate who stood for the status quo, President Taft. Woodrow Wilson's own reform program, however, had received no particular mandate from the people.

As anticlimactic as the 1912 election might seem, it proved to be a decisive event in the history of national reform. Out of the searching campaign debate between Roosevelt and Wilson there emerged in the New Freedom a program capable of resolving the crisis over corporate power that had gripped the nation for the whole of the previous decade. And, just as important, the election created a rare opportunity for decisive legislative action in Washington. Wilson became president with the Democrats in firm control of both houses of Congress and united in their eagerness to get on with the New Freedom.

The New Freedom in Action. Upon entering the White House, Wilson chose a flank attack on the central problem of economic power. So long out of office, the Democrats were hungry for tariff reform. From the prevailing average of 40 percent, the Underwood Tariff Act of 1913 pared rates down to an average of 25 percent. Targeting especially the trust-dominated industries, Democrats confidently expected the Underwood Tariff to spur competition and reduce prices for consumers by opening protected American markets to foreign products.

The administration then turned to the nation's banking system, whose key weakness was the absence of a central reserve bank. The main functions of a central bank are to regulate the private banks and back them up in case they cannot meet their obligations to their depositors. In practice, this role had been assumed by the major New York banks, which accepted the deposits of lesser banks and assisted them if they came under pressure. However, if the New York institutions themselves weakened, the entire system could totter and even collapse. This had nearly happened in 1907, when the Knickerbocker Trust Company failed and panic swept through the nation's financial markets.

The need for a reserve system became widely accepted, but the form it should take was hotly debated. Wall Street wanted a centralized system, controlled by the bankers. Rural Democrats and their spokesman, Senator Carter Glass of Virginia, preferred a decentralized network of reserve banks. Progressives in both parties agreed that the essential feature should be public control over the reserve system. The bankers, already under severe criticism from a congressional investigation early in 1913, were on the defensive in this contest.

President Wilson, no expert to begin with, learned quickly and reconciled the reformers and bankers. The monumental Federal Reserve Act of 1913 gave the nation a banking system that was resistant to financial panic. The act delegated reserve functions to twelve district reserve banks, which would be controlled by the member banks. The Federal Reserve Board imposed public regulation on this regional structure. In one stroke, the act strengthened the banking system considerably and placed a measure of restraint on the "money trust."

The Clayton Act and the FTC. Having dealt with tariff and banking reform, Wilson turned at last to the central issue of corporate power: how to give full effect to the antitrust principles of the Sherman Act. Brandeis had already formulated two main approaches. One was to define with precision the prohibited practices—interlocking directorates, discriminatory pricing, and exclusive contracts that shut out competitors. The second approach was to create a new federal trade commission that would aid the executive branch in administering the antitrust laws.

In both approaches, there were knotty questions to be resolved. Was it feasible to be absolutely rigid in prohibiting illegal practices? Brandeis finally decided that it was not, and he persuaded Wilson to modify the definition of practices prohibited in the Clayton Antitrust Act of 1914 to apply only "where the effect may be to substantially lessen competition or tend to create a monopoly in any line of commerce." As for the trade commission, the problem was how much power and what functions it should have. Wilson was understandably sensitive on this matter, given his principled opposition to Roosevelt's conception of a powerful trade commission overseeing American business. Initially, Wilson wanted no more than an advisory and information-gathering agency. But ultimately the Federal Trade Commission (1914) received much broader powers to investigate companies and to issue "cease and desist" orders against unfair trade practices that violated antitrust law. FTC decisions, however, were subject to court review, so that Wilson's entire program was situated within the established judicial antitrust system based on the "rule of reason." As before, it would ultimately be up to the courts to decide which business practices were illegal.

Despite a good deal of commotion, an underlying consensus-building attended this arduous legislative process. Wilson himself had opened the debate in a conciliatory way. "The antagonism between business and government is over," he said, and the time was ripe for a program representing the "best business judgment in America." Afterward, Wilson felt he had brought the long controversy over corporate power to a successful conclusion. And, in fact, he had. Steering a course between Taft's conservatism and Roosevelt's radicalism, he had carved out a middle way—what the historian Martin J. Sklar has termed "corporate liberalism." This middle way brought to bear the powers of government without threatening the constitutional order; and it dealt in some measure with the abuses of corporate power without threatening the capitalist system.

Wilson's Social Program. On social policy, too, Wilson carved out a middle way. During the 1912 campaign he had denounced the social program of the New Nationalism as paternalistic. Compared to his dealings with big business, Wilson proved rather more resistant to special legislation for workers and farmers. He accepted cosmetic language in the Clayton Act stating that labor and farm organizations were not illegal combinations. But he rejected the exemptions they wanted from antitrust prosecution.

The labor vote had grown increasingly important to the Democratic party, however. As his second presidential campaign drew nearer, Wilson lost some of his scruples about prolabor legislation. In 1915 and 1916 he championed a host of bills beneficial to American workers. These included a model federal workmen's compensation law, a federal child labor law, the Adamson eight-hour law for railroad workers, and the landmark Seamen's Act, which eliminated age-old abuses of sailors aboard ship and granted them the individual rights held by all other workers. Likewise, after stubborn earlier resistance, Wilson approved in 1916 the Federal Farm Loan Act, providing the low-interest rural credit system long demanded by farmers.

Wilson encountered the same kind of dilemma that confronted all successful progressives—the claims of moral principle versus the unyielding realities of political and economic life. Progressives were high-minded but not radical. They saw evils in the system, but they did not consider the system itself evil. They also prided themselves on being realists as well as moralists. So it stood to reason that Wilson, like other progressives who achieved power, would find his place at the center.

Summary

A new chapter in American reform began at the start of the twentieth century. For decades, the problems resulting from industrialization and urban growth had been mounting. Now, after 1900, progressive activity sprang up and dominated the nation's public life until World War I. The unifying element in progressive reform was a common intellectual outlook, highly principled and idealistic as to goals, and confident of the human capacity to find the means.

Beyond this shared outlook, progressives broke up into diverse, often conflicting groups. Political reformers included business groups concerned chiefly with improving the efficiency of city government, while other progressives, such as Robert La Follette, opposed privilege and wanted to democratize the political process. Both groups worked to enhance their power at the expense of entrenched party machines.

Social welfare became very much the province of American women, and that effort in turn reinvigorated the struggle for women's rights. In the cities, working people and immigrants also became reform-minded and thereby set in motion a new political force, urban liberalism. While progressivism was sadly infected by the prevailing racism in American life, there was a reform wing that joined with black activists to forge the major institutions of black protest and uplift of the twentieth century, the National Association for the Advancement of Colored People and the Urban League.

At the national level, progressives focused primarily on controlling the economic power of corporate business. This overriding problem led to Theodore Roosevelt's Square Deal, then to his New Nationalism, and finally to Woodrow Wilson's New Freedom. The role of the federal government expanded dramatically, but in service to a cautious and pragmatic approach to the problems of the country.

TOPIC FOR RESEARCH

than the muckraking journalists. They investigated political corruption, child labor, adulterated food, business fraud, racial conflict, prostitution, and many other evils. Arthur and Lila Weinberg, eds., *The Muckrakers* (1961) is a representative collection of the most important muckraking articles, and contains an extensive bibliography of other such articles. Important muckraking books include Lincoln Steffens *The Shame of the Cities* (1904), Ida M. Tarbell's *The History of the Standard Oil Company* (1904). Most famous of the muckraking novels is Upton Sinclair, *The Jungle* (1906). Others are Frank Norris, *The Octopus* (1901) and *The Pit* (1903); David Graham Phillips, *The Great God Success* (1901), *The Plum Tree* (1905), and *Susan Lenox* (1917); and Robert Herrick, *The Memoirs of an American Citizen* (1905). Finally, the ideas and experiences of the muckrakers might be explored through their autobiographies, the best of which is *The Autobiography of Lincoln Steffens* (1931).

BIBLIOGRAPHY

The Course of Reform

The most recent survey of the Progressive Era is John Milton Cooper, *Pivotal Decades: The United States, 1900–1920* (1990). Two older but still serviceable narrative accounts are George E. Mowry, *The Era of Theodore Roosevelt, 1900–1912* (1958), and Arthur S. Link, *Woodrow Wilson and the Progressive Era, 1910–1917* (1954). Harold U. Faulkner, *The Quest for Social Justice, 1898–1914* (1931), is a useful portrait of the social setting in which progressivism developed. A highly influential interpretation of progressive re-

for progressivism, the key book is Morton White, *Social Thought in America: The Revolt Against Formalism* (1975). For leading figures in this antiformalist tradition, see Samuel Konefsky, *The Legacy of Holmes and Brandeis* (1956), and David Riesman, *Thorstein Veblen* (1963). Most useful on political thinkers is Charles Forcey, *The Crossroads of Liberalism: Croly, Weyl, Lippmann, and the Progressive Era* (1961). A provocative study set in an international context is James T. Kloppenberg, *Uncertain Victory: Social Democracy and Progressivism in European and American Thought, 1870–1920* (1986). Clarke A. Chambers, *Paul U. Kellog and the Survey* (1971), treats one of the key social investigators. For the muckrakers, see David M. Chalmers, *The Social and Political Ideas of the Muckrakers* (1964) and Harold S. Wilson, *McClure's Magazine and the Muckrakers* (1970).

Political reform has been the subject of a voluminous literature. Wisconsin progressivism can be studied in David P. Thelen, *The New Citizenship: Origins of Progressivism in Wisconsin, 1885–1900* (1972) and *Robert La Follette and the Insurgent Spirit* (1976), and Robert S. Maxwell, *La Follette and the Rise of Progressivism in Wisconsin* (1956). Other important progressives are treated in Spencer C. Olin, *California's Prodigal Son: Hiram Johnson and the Progressive Movement* (1968); Robert F. Wesser, *Charles Evans Hughes: Politics and Reform in New York State, 1905–1910* (1967); and Richard Lowitt, *George W. Norris: The Making of a Progressive* (1963). On city reform, see Bradley R. Rice, *Progressive Cities: The Commission Government Movement* (1972); Jack Tager, *The Intellectual as Urban Reformer: Brand Whitlock and the Progressive Movement* (1968); and Melvin G. Holli, *Reform in Detroit: Hazen S. Pingree and Urban Politics* (1969).

The best treatment of the settlement-house movement is Allen F. Davis, *Spearheads of Reform* (1967). Allen F. Davis, *American Heroine: Jane Addams* (1973), and George Martin, *Madame Secretary: Frances Perkins* (1976)

sippi Valley Historical Review (September 1962). Huthmacher's ideas have been fully developed in John D. Buenker, *Urban Liberalism and Progressive Reform* (1973). The relationship to organized labor can be followed in Irwin Yellowitz, *Labor and the Progressive Movement in New York State* (1965). The rise of anti-immigrant sentiment has received authoritative treatment in John Higham, *Strangers in the Land* (1955). James H. Timberlake, *Prohibition and the Progressive Crusade* (1963) covers another
of progressive moralism. On the South,
Kirby, *Darkness at the Dawning: Race a*
Progressive South (1972), and Dewey Gr
Progressivism (1983). The revival of blac
ously described in Stephen R. Fox, *The G*
William Monroe Trotter (1971).

Progressivism and National Politics

National progressivism is best approached
figures. John Milton Cooper, *The Warri*
(1983) is a provocative joint biography of
sevelt that emphasizes their shared world
biographies include William Harbau
Responsibility: The Life and Times of T
(1961); G. Wallace Chessman, *Theodore*
Politics of Power (1969); John Morton Blu
Roosevelt (1954); Donald E. Anderson, *Wi*
(1973); John Morton Blum, *Woodrow Wils*
of Morality (1956); and Melvin I. Urofsky,
and the Progressive Tradition (1981). Aspe
gressive politics can be followed in James
Politics and Conservation: The Balling
(1968); Robert Wiebe, *Businessmen and*
Gabriel Kolko, *The Triumph of Conservat*
Holt, *Congressional Insurgents and the Par*
and David Sarasohn, *The Party of Reform:*
the Progressive Era (1989). On the sociali
the books cited in Chapter 18, see Aileen
Radical Persuasion, 1890–1917 (1981), and
The Decline of American Socialism, 1912–1
mai Lamoreaux, *The Great Merger Mover*
Business, 1895–1904 (1985), offers a sop
analysis of trust activity, and Thomas K. M
lation in Perspective (1981), contains valu
essays on the problems of trust regulatio
Enterprise Denied: The Origins of the Decline of American Railroads, 1897–1917 (1971), assesses the impact of railway regulation. A comprehensive rethinking of the progressive struggle to fashion a regulatory policy for big business is offered in Martin J. Sklar, *The Corporate Reconstruction of American Capitalism, 1890–1916: The Market, the Law, and Politics* (1988).

inal sea
cased
eship.

CHAPTER 22 *An Emerging World Power,* 1877–1914

In 1881, England sent a new envoy to Washington. He was Sir Lionel Sackville-West, son of an earl, brother-in-law of the Tory leader Lord Denby, but otherwise distinguished only as the steadfast lover of a celebrated Spanish dancer. His well-connected friends wanted to park Sir Lionel somewhere comfortable, but out of harm's way. So they made him minister to the United States.

Twenty years later such an appointment would have been inconceivable. All the major European powers had by then elevated their missions in Washington to embassies and routinely staffed them with top-of-the-line ambassadors. And they treated the United States, without question, as a fellow Great Power.

When Sir Lionel arrived in Washington in 1881, the United States scarcely cast any shadow on world affairs. As a military power the United States was puny, even comical. Its army was smaller than Bulgaria's, and its navy ranked thirteenth in the world—and was a threat mainly to the crews who manned its unseaworthy ships. Twenty years later, however, the United States was flexing its muscles. It had just made short work of Spain in a brief but decisive war, and acquired for itself an empire that stretched from Puerto Rico to the Philippines. America's standing as a rising naval power was manifest, and so was its aggressive assertion of national interest in the Caribbean and in the Pacific.

In practice, the United States acted as a regional power in the early twentieth century, but Europeans had become keenly aware of its capacity to cut a larger swath whenever it chose to do so. "Are we to be confronted by an American peril . . . before which the Old World is to go down to irretrievable defeat?" wondered a former French foreign minister. The notion of an "American peril" became a lively topic after 1900 among Europeans surveying the industrial and military potential of the United States. No one could be quite sure what America's role would be, since the United States retained its traditional policy of nonalignment in European affairs. But in chanceries across the Continent, the importance of the United States was universally acknowledged and its likely response to every event carefully assessed.

How the United States emerged on to the world stage in the decades before World War I is the subject of this chapter.

The Roots of Expansionism

Diplomacy in the Gilded Age

In 1880 the United States had a population of 50 million and, by that measure, ranked easily with the great European powers. It was the world's leading producer of wheat and cotton. In industrial production, the United States was second only to Britain, and rapidly closing the gap. And if anyone doubted the military prowess of Americans, he or she only needed to recall the ferocity with which they had fought one another in the Civil War. The great campaigns of Lee, Sherman, and Grant entered the military textbooks and were closely studied by army strategists everywhere. In the encounter between the ironclads *Monitor* and *Merrimack* at Hampton Roads on March 9, 1862, the world had received its first example of modern naval warfare.

Nor, when its vital interests were at stake, had the United States shown itself to be lacking in diplomatic vigor. Both major crises with European powers arising from the Civil War had been settled to America's satisfaction. In 1867, France abandoned its imperial adventure in Mexico and withdrew its forces. And in 1871, Britain expressed its regrets for nonneutral acts against the Union during the war and agreed to the arbitration of the *Alabama* claims (see Chapter 16).

In the years that followed, the United States lapsed into diplomatic isolation, not out of inherent weakness, but for lack of any clear national purpose in world affairs. In this industrializing age, George Washington's warning against entangling alliances seemed as pertinent as it had when America was a thinly populated land of farmers. The business of building the nation's industrial economy absorbed Americans in these years and kept their attention inward-looking. And while the new international telegraphic cables provided the country with swift overseas communication after the 1860s, wide oceans still kept the world at a distance and gave Americans a sense of isolation and security. Nor did European power politics, which centered on Franco-German rivalry and on nationalistic conflict in the Balkans, seem to matter very much. As far as Cleveland's secretary of state Thomas F. Bayard was concerned, "we have not the slightest share or interest [in] the small politics and backstage intrigues of Europe . . . upon which we look with impatience and contempt."

As for the empire building in which the European powers were so avidly engaged, this expression of national prowess did not tempt the United States. Even so ardent an American nationalist as the young Theodore Roosevelt saw the folly of overseas expansion. "We want no unwilling citizens to enter our Union," he wrote in 1886. "European nations war for the possession of thickly settled districts which, if conquered, will for centuries remain alien and hostile to the conquerors; we, wiser in our generation, have seized the waste solitudes that lay near us."

In these circumstances, with no external threat to be seen, what was the point of maintaining a big navy? After making certain of the French departure from Mexico in 1867, the government began to dismantle the Civil War fleet. The ships that remained on duty gradually deteriorated. Of the 125 ships on the navy's active list, only about 25 were actually seaworthy at any one time. No effort was made to keep up with European advances in weaponry or battleship design. Indeed, the American fleet consisted mainly of sailing ships and obsolete ironclads.

During the administration of Chester A. Arthur (1881–1885), the navy began a modest upgrading program. New ships were put into service, standards for the officer corps were raised, and the Naval War College was founded. But the fleet remained small, and the squadrons lacked any unified naval command. The mission of the navy remained as before: to maintain coastal defenses and a modest cruising fleet capable of preying on enemy commerce at sea. An expenditure of 1 percent or less of the gross national product for the entire military establishment seemed entirely adequate in the 1880s.

The conduct of diplomacy was likewise small potatoes. Appointment to the foreign service was mostly through the spoils system. American ministers and consular officers were notoriously unskilled, and included an inordinate number of idlers and drunkards. Domestic politics, moreover, made it difficult to develop a coherent program. Although foreign relations was an executive responsibility, the U.S. Senate jealously guarded its right to give its "advice and consent" on treaties and diplomatic appointments. Partisan squabbling between Democrats and Republicans left the White House even less room for maneuver. For its part the State Department tended to be inactive, exerting little control either over policy making or over its missions abroad. It was remarkable how many actions (some of them subsequently repudiated or simply ignored by the State Department) were taken independently by ministers and naval officers out in the field. In the more remote parts of the world, the American presence was often primarily religious: the intrepid missionaries bent on Christianizing the native populations of Asia, Africa, and the Pacific islands.

Latin American Diplomacy. In the Caribbean, the United States remained the dominant power, but the expansionist enthusiasm of the Civil War era subsided. Nothing came of the grandiose dreams of William H. Seward, secretary of state under Presidents Lincoln and Johnson, for an American empire, perhaps with a capital in Mexico. President Grant's strongest efforts could not persuade the Senate to purchase Santo Domingo in 1870, and Congress likewise blocked later moves to acquire bases in Haiti, Cuba, and Venezuela. Nor did the United States pursue its long-expressed interest in an interoceanic canal in Central America. Despite its protests that no one else should build such a canal, the United States stood by when a French company headed by the builder of the Suez Canal, Ferdinand de Lesseps, started to dig across the Panama isthmus in 1880. That project failed after a decade—but the reason was bankruptcy, not American opposition.

On becoming secretary of state in 1881, James G. Blaine engaged in a flurry of diplomatic activity in Latin America. He got involved in a border dispute between Mexico and Guatemala, tried to settle a war Chile was waging against Peru and Bolivia, and called the first

Pan-American conference. Blaine's interventions in Latin American disputes proved disastrous, however, and the Pan-American conference seems mainly to have been a gesture to restore some lustre to his tarnished diplomatic reputation. Blaine had no particular strategic aims in mind. He was concerned mainly with his own political prospects at home, and, in any case, left office soon after sending out the invitations in late 1881. His successor canceled the conference. This was a characteristic instance of Gilded Age diplomacy, driven partly by partisan politics, and carried out without any clear sense of national purpose.

Pan-Americanism—the notion of a community of American states—took root, however, and in 1888 Congress requested President Cleveland to call a conference of American states to promote trade and peace in the Western Hemisphere. Blaine, returning in 1889 for a second stint at the State Department under the new Republican administration of Benjamin Harrison, took up the plans already laid for a new Pan-American conference. An impressive agenda called for a customs union, improved communications, and arbitration treaties. But the only result was the creation of an information agency in Washington, later renamed the Pan-American Union. Any Latin American goodwill garnered by Blaine's efforts was soon blasted by the humiliation he visited upon Chile because of a riot against American sailors in the port of Valparaiso in 1891. Threatened with war, Chile was forced to apologize to the United States and pay an indemnity of $75,000.

Pacific Episodes. In the Pacific, American interest centered on Hawaii. American missionaries had long been active among the Hawaiian islanders. With a climate ideal for raising sugar cane, Hawaii also attracted many American planters and investors. Nominally an independent nation with its own monarchy, Hawaii fell increasingly within the American orbit. In 1875 a treaty of commercial reciprocity opened the American market to Hawaiian sugar and declared that no Hawaiian territory could be ceded to a third power. A second treaty in 1887 granted the United States naval rights at Pearl Harbor.

Having encouraged the sugar economy in Hawaii, the United States abruptly withdrew Hawaii's trading advantages in the McKinley Tariff of 1890. All foreign sugar could now enter the United States duty free, while domestic producers received a special subsidy to compensate for the drop in sugar prices. Anxious to gain that benefit, American planters in Hawaii began to plot for annexation to the United States. Aided by the U.S. minister to Hawaii, and with American sailors conspicuously present, they revolted in January 1893 against Queen Liliuokalani. Within a month the provisional government they installed negotiated a treaty of annexation with the Harrison administration. Before annexation could be approved by the Senate, however, Grover Cleveland returned to the presidency, and, following an investigation of the Hawaiian episode, withdrew the treaty. To annex Hawaii, he declared, would violate both America's "honor and morality" and its "unbroken tradition" against acquiring territory far from the nation's shores.

In the meantime, the American presence elsewhere in the Pacific was growing. In 1867 the United States had purchased Alaska from imperial Russia. The deal was at the behest of the Russians, who were anxious to unload (to their everlasting subsequent regret) a possession they considered militarily indefensible and economically unprofitable. For $7.2 million the United States got not only the huge territory of Alaska with its vast natural resources but an unlooked-for presence stretching across the northern Pacific.

Far to the south, with even less forethought, the United States became involved in the remote Samoan islands. In 1878 the United States secured the right to a coaling station in Pago Pago harbor—a key link on the route to Australia—and in exchange promised local Polynesian leaders to use its good offices in Samoa's relations with other foreign powers. An informal protectorate resulted. In the mid-1880s, Germany began to press its claims to the islands, and the United States, stung by German arrogance, responded with equal fervor. In 1889 naval warfare might have broken out but for a fierce hurricane that wrecked both the German and the American fleets. At that point, agreement on a tripartite protectorate (the third European power was Britain) averted further strife and left the United States with its rights at Pago Pago.

American diplomacy in these years has been characterized as a series of incidents, not the pursuit of a foreign *policy*. Many things happened, but intermittently and without a plan, driven by individuals and pressure groups, not by any well-founded and coherent conception of national objectives. This was possible because, as the Englishman James Bryce remarked in 1888, America still sailed "upon a summer sea." In the stormier waters that lay ahead, a different kind of American diplomacy would be required.

Economic Sources of Expansionism

"A policy of isolation did well enough when we were an embryo nation," remarked Senator Orville Platt of Connecticut in 1893. "But today things are different. . . . We are 65 million people, the most advanced and powerful on earth, and regard to our future welfare demands an abandonment of the doctrines of isolation."

The Singer Sewing Machine

The sewing machine was an American invention, but it swiftly found markets abroad. The Singer Company, the dominant firm, not only exported large quantities, but was producing 200,000 machines annually at a Scottish plant that employed 6,000 workers. Singer's advertising rightly boasted of its prowess as an international company and of a product that was "The Universal Machine."

Why America's future welfare demanded an abandonment of isolation was first of all a matter of economics. In a sense the greatest danger to the country seemed to arise from its very success as a productive economy. The gross national product quadrupled between 1870 and 1900, and industrial output quintupled. But were there sufficient markets to absorb the staggering volume of goods flowing from America's farms and factories? It was true that America itself constituted an enormous market. Over 90 percent of American output in the late nineteenth century was consumed at home. Even so, foreign markets were important. Roughly a fifth of the nation's agricultural output was exported, and for the major staple crops—cotton, wheat, tobacco—the percentage ranged much higher, up to 80 percent, for example, in the case of cotton.

As the industrial economy expanded, so did factory exports. Between 1880 and 1900, the industrial share of total exports jumped from 15 percent to over 30 percent. Although only 9 percent of manufactured output went overseas in 1900, the export share for key industries loomed much larger: 57 percent for petroleum products, 50 percent for copper, 25 percent for sewing machines, 15 percent for iron and steel.

The importance of foreign trade was evident in the efforts of major firms to develop overseas production and marketing facilities. As early as 1868, the pioneering Singer Sewing Machine Company established its first foreign plant in Glasgow, Scotland. Most prominent among American firms doing business abroad was Standard Oil. Beginning with the Anglo-American Oil Company in 1888, Rockefeller's trust created affiliates across Europe to operate its tankers, establish bulk stations, and distribute its kerosene to foreign retailers. In Asia, Standard Oil's kerosene cans, made over into utensils and roofing tin, became an infallible index of American market penetration. Brand names such as Kodak (cameras), McCormick (agricultural equipment), and later Ford (the Model T) became household words around the world.

Foreign trade was important partly for reasons of international finance. As a developing economy, the United States attracted a lot of foreign capital, but sent relatively little abroad—scarcely 1 percent of all the money Americans were investing in the late nineteenth century. The result was a heavy outflow of dollars from the United States in the form of interest and dividend payments to foreign investors. To balance this account, the United States needed to ship overseas more goods than it imported. In fact, a favorable import-export balance was achieved in 1876 and was sustained almost every year thereafter. But because of its status as a net importer of capital, America would have to be constantly vigilant about the health of its export trade.

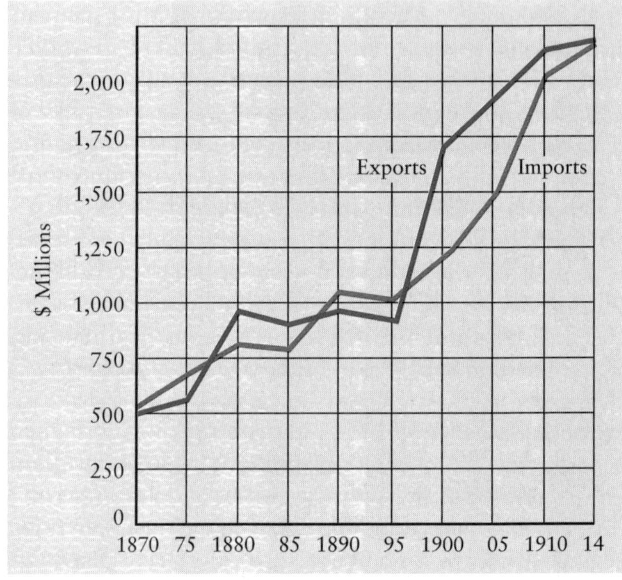

FIGURE 22.1

Balance of U.S. Imports and Exports, 1870–1914

Even more important, however, was the relationship that many Americans perceived between foreign markets and the nation's social stability. In hard times, as we have seen, farmers took up radical politics and workers became militant strikers. The problem, many thought, was that the nation's capacity to produce was outrunning its capacity to consume. And when the economy slowed and domestic demand fell, the impact on farmers and workers was devastating, driving down farm prices and wages, and cutting a swath of layoffs and farm foreclosures across the country. The answer was to make sure that there would always be enough buyers for America's surplus products, and this meant, more than anything else, access to foreign markets.

Overseas Trade and Foreign Policy. The nub of the question was how these concerns over foreign markets linked up to America's foreign policy. The bulk of American exports in the late nineteenth century—over 80 percent—went to Europe and Canada. In these countries, the normal instruments of diplomacy sufficed. In Europe, for example, a major issue for the United States during the 1880s was the restrictions placed by France and Germany on imports of American pork, allegedly on health grounds. The United States protested vigorously, threatened to embargo the imports of countries discriminating against American meat products, and in 1890–1891 negotiated a settlement of the dispute.

But there was a second category of foreign markets that seemed to demand a more vigorous kind of American intervention. These were the countries of Asia, Latin America, and other "backward" (by Western definition) parts of the world. Here the United States found itself in competition with other industrial powers. It was true that Asia and Latin America represented a rather modest part of America's export trade—roughly an eighth of the total in the late nineteenth century. Still, this trade was growing—it was worth $200 million in 1900—and parts of it mattered a great deal to specific industries, as, for example, the China market for American textiles.

Even more significant was the *potential* that these non-Western markets seemed to hold, because they, not Europe, constituted the future consumers of American goods. With its enormous population of potential customers, China exerted an especially powerful hold on the American mercantile imagination. Many felt that the China trade, although actually quite small, would one day be the key to American prosperity. Therefore, China and other beckoning markets must not be closed to the United States.

From the mid-1880s onward, with the surge of European imperialism, that feared prospect became more real. After the Berlin Conference of 1884, the African continent was rapidly carved up by the European powers. In the Far East, in a burst of modernizing energy, Japan transformed itself into a major power and began to challenge China's claims over Korea. In the Sino-Japanese war of 1894–1895, Japan won an easy victory and started a scramble among the great powers, including Russia, to carve China up into spheres of influence. In Latin America, U.S. interests began to be challenged more aggressively by Britain, France, and Germany. On the European continent, moreover, the free-trade liberalism of earlier years gave way after the 1870s to rising protectionism, threatening established European markets for American goods just at the point when empire building was closing off the likely new markets elsewhere. On top of all this came the Panic of 1893, setting in motion the movements of industrial and agrarian protest that many Americans, such as Cleveland's secretary of state Walter Q. Gresham, took to be "symptoms of revolution."

TABLE 22.1

Exports to Canada and Europe Compared with Exports to Asia and Latin America

Year	Exports to Canada and Europe	Percentage of Total	Exports to Asia and Latin America	Percentage of Total
1875	$ 494,000,000	86.1%	$ 72,000,000	12.5%
1885	637,000,000	85.8	87,000,000	11.7
1895	681,000,000	84.3	108,000,000	13.4
1900	1,135,000,000	81.4	200,000,000	14.3

Tables compiled from information in *Historical Statistics of the United States,* 1960; U.S. Department of Commerce, *Long Term Growth, 1860–1965,* 1966; National Bureau of Economic Research, *Trends in the American Economy in the Nineteenth Century,* 1960.

In these circumstances, with the nation's social stability seemingly at stake, securing the markets of Latin America and Asia became an urgent necessity, and from that urgent necessity sprang the expansionist diplomacy of the 1890s.

The Making of an Expansionist Foreign Policy

"Whether they will or not, Americans must now begin to look outward. The growing production of the country requires it." So wrote Captain Alfred T. Mahan, America's leading naval strategist, in his book *The Influence of Seapower upon History* (1890). An obscure naval officer posted to a rickety ship cruising Latin America in the mid-1880s, Mahan had spent his spare time reading history. In a library in Lima, Peru, he hit on the idea that great empires—first Rome and, in modern times, Great Britain—had depended for their power on the control of the seas. From this insight, Mahan developed a naval analysis that became the cornerstone of American strategic thinking.

The United States should no longer regard the oceans as barriers, Mahan argued, but as "a great highway . . . over which men pass in all directions." To traverse that highway required a robust merchant marine, which had fallen on hard times since its heyday in the 1850s, and a powerful navy to protect American commerce. "When a question arises of control over distant regions . . . it must ultimately be decided by naval power," Mahan advised. To sustain its navy and its commerce, the United States needed strategic overseas bases. Here technology played a part because, having converted to steam, navies required coaling stations far from home. Without such stations, Mahan warned, warships were "like land birds, unable to fly far from their own shores."

Alfred T. Mahan

Mahan's impressive theory of the influence of seapower on history, so he recalled, was sparked by reading he did on Roman history in a library in Lima, Peru, in 1885. His insight was personal as well as intellectual: embarrassed by the decrepit ships on which he served, Mahan thought the United States should have a modern fleet in which officers like himself could serve with pride (and with some hope of professional advancement).

Mahan called first of all for a canal across Central America to connect the Atlantic and Pacific oceans. Such a canal would enable the eastern United States to "compete with Europe, on equal terms as to distance, for the markets of East Asia." The canal's approaches would need to be guarded by bases in the Caribbean Sea. And Hawaii would have to be annexed to extend American power into the Pacific—a step that Mahan called "natural, necessary, irrepressible." Mahan was defining a distinctive and limited form of colonialism—not the rule over large territories and native populations to which European empire-builders aspired, but control over strategic bases from which American power could be asserted where Americans wanted to trade.

What Mahan offered was a *coherent* foreign policy for the United States: first, the securing of foreign markets for the nation's surplus products; second, of equal importance, the nation's development as a naval power; and, sustaining both these goals, an expansionist strategy anchored on an interoceanic canal and bases in the Caribbean and Pacific.

Mahan's reasoning was most eagerly taken up by other exponents of a powerful America, including publishers like Whitelaw Reid of the *New York Tribune*, and such young politicians as Theodore Roosevelt and Senator Henry Cabot Lodge of Massachusetts. The influence of these men, few in number but strategically placed, increased during the 1890s. They pushed steadily for what Lodge called a "large policy." But mainstream politicians also accepted Mahan's underlying logic, and from the inauguration of Benjamin Harrison's administration in 1889 onward, a surprising consistency began to emerge in the conduct of American foreign policy.

Rebuilding the Navy. This consensus was most evident in the rethinking of American naval strategy. The crucial thing, Mahan argued, was to drop the reliance on shore defense and lightly armed cruising ships and create instead a battleship fleet capable of roaming the far seas and of striking a decisive first blow against an enemy. This was precisely the line that Benjamin F. Tracy, Harrison's secretary of the navy, took in his first annual report. Battleships might be expensive, but they were "the premium paid by the United States for the in-

The Battleship Oregon
The battleship was the centerpiece of naval strategy in the industrial age, and the key marker in the naval arms race among the Great Powers. Building a battleship fleet was America's ticket of entry into that race.

surance of its acquired wealth and its growing industries." In 1890 Congress made appropriations for the first three battleships in the two-ocean fleet envisioned by Secretary Tracy, and by the time the Harrison administration left office in 1893, American naval power—thirteenth or worse in 1889—stood seventh in the world. "The sea will be the future seat of empire," predicted Tracy. "And we shall rule it as certain as the sun doth rise."

The incoming Cleveland administration was less spread-eagled and, by canceling Harrison's scheme for annexing Hawaii, established its antiexpansionist credentials. But after a brief period of hesitation, the Democrat Cleveland picked up the naval program of his Republican predecessor, pressing Congress just as forcefully for more battleships (five were authorized) and making the same basic argument. The nation's commercial vitality—"free access to all markets," in the words of Cleveland's second secretary of state, Richard Olney—depended on its naval power.

While rejecting the colonial aspects of Mahan's thinking, Cleveland absorbed the underlying strategic arguments about where America's vital interests lay. That this was so explains the remarkable crisis that suddenly blew up in 1895 with Great Britain over Venezuela.

The Venezuela Crisis. For years a border dispute had simmered between Venezuela and British Guiana. In the past the United States had urged arbitration, only to be told by the haughty British that they did not submit their interests to the judgments of third parties. Now that answer could no longer be accepted. For one thing, Britain's aggressive claims, if they prevailed, would strongly enhance its position in the Caribbean. Moreover, the Venezuela dispute seemed part of a larger pattern of European aggressiveness in Latin America, including ominous moves against Nicaragua, Brazil, Trinidad, and Santo Domingo. European empire building was carving up Africa and Asia in this period. How could the United States be sure that Europe did not have similar designs on Latin America? Indeed, prompted by President Cleveland, Secretary of State Olney made just that point in the bristling note he sent to London on July 25, 1895, demanding that Britain accept arbitration, or face the consequences.

Invoking the Monroe Doctrine, Olney warned that the United States could not tolerate any European attempt to intimidate or overthrow the nations of the Western Hemisphere. "Today the United States is practically sovereign upon this continent, and its fiat is law upon the subjects to which it confines its interposition," Olney asserted. Olney's words sound bombastic, but they were intended to convey a clear message to Britain and the European powers that the United States would brook no challenge to its perceived vital interests in the Caribbean. (Note that these were America's vital interests, not those of Venezuela, which was not consulted and was virtually ignored during the entire dispute.)

Because the Venezuela crisis blew up so suddenly, because it seemed so out of proportion to the boundary issue itself, and because it created war hysteria in the United States—for these reasons historians have found it difficult to recognize that the pugnacious stand of the Cleveland administration was not an aberration but a logical step in the new outward thrust of American foreign policy. Once the British realized that Cleveland meant business, they backed off and agreed to the arbitration of the boundary dispute. Afterward, Secretary of State Olney remarked with satisfaction that, as a great industrial nation, the United States needed "to accept [its] commanding position" and take its place "among the Powers of the earth." And these countries would have to accommodate to the American need for access to "more markets and larger markets for the consumption and products of the industry and inventive genius of the American people."

The Ideology of Expansionism. As policy makers hammered out a new foreign policy, a sustaining body of ideology took shape as well. One source of expansionist thinking was the Social Darwinist theory that so dominated the political thinking of this era (see Chapter 19). If animals and plants evolved through the survival of the fittest, so did nations. "Nothing under the sun is stationary," warned the American social theorist Brooks Adams in *The Law of Civilization and Decay* (1895). "Not to advance is to recede." By this criterion, the United States had no choice; if it wanted to survive, it had to expand.

Linked to Social Darwinism was a spreading belief in the inherent superiority of the Anglo-Saxon "race." On both sides of the Atlantic, Anglo-Saxonism had come into great vogue. John Fiske, an American philosopher and historian, popularized Social Darwinism and Anglo-Saxonism by lecturing the nation on its future responsibilities. "The work which the English race began when it colonized North America," Fiske declared, "is destined to go on until every land on the earth's surface that is not already the seat of an old civilization shall become English in its language, in its religion, in its political habits, and to a predominant extent in the blood of its people."

Fiske entitled his famous lecture "Manifest Destiny." This term had been used half a century earlier to convey the sense of national mission—America's "manifest destiny"—to sweep aside the native American peoples and occupy continental America. Now, in the 1890s, that process of westward expansion was declared by the U.S. Census to have come to an end: there was no longer a frontier line beyond which land remained to be conquered. The psychological impact of that news on Americans was profound, spawning among other things a new interpretation of America's past that stressed the shaping importance of the frontier on the nation's character. In his landmark essay first setting out this thesis—"The Significance of the Frontier in American History" (1893)—the young historian Frederick Jackson Turner suggested a linkage between the closing of the frontier and overseas expansion. "He would be a rash prophet who should assert that the expansive character of American life has now entirely ceased," Turner wrote. "Movement has been its dominant fact, and, unless this training has no effect upon a people, the American energy will continually demand a wider field for its exercise." As Turner predicted, Manifest Destiny did indeed now turn outward.

Thus a strong current of ideas, deep-rooted in American experience and ideology, justified the new diplomacy of expansionism. The United States was eager to step onto the world stage. All it needed was the right occasion.

An American Empire

The Cuban Crisis

Ever since Spain had lost hold of its vast empire in South America in the early nineteenth century, Cubans had yearned to join their mainland brothers and sisters in freedom. Cuban movements for independence had sprung up repeatedly, most recently in a rebellion that lasted from 1868 to 1875. In February 1895, Cuba rose up once more against Spanish rule. This time a bloody standoff developed; the Spaniards controlled the towns, the insurgents the countryside. In early 1896, the newly appointed Spanish captain general, Valeriano Weyler, adopted a brutal policy of *reconcentration*. The Spaniards forced entire populations into armed camps and treated any Cuban on the outside as a rebel. The strategy, while militarily effective, took a dreadful toll on the Cubans. Out of a population of 1,600,000 at least 200,000 died of starvation, exposure, or dysentery.

A wave of sympathy for the Cuban rebels swept across the United States. Cuban exiles skillfully played on public opinion. They got help from a yellow press eager to capitalize on the situation. Locked in a circulation war, William Randolph Hearst's *New York Journal* and Joseph Pulitzer's *New York World* elevated the atrocities and skirmishes into front-page news. Across the country powerful sentiments were stirred, mixing humanitarian concern for the Cubans, a superpatriotism that was tagged *jingoism*, and increasing demands that the Cubans be made free. Responding to public opinion, Congress passed resolutions in 1896 for Cuban autonomy, and early the next year, for complete independence.

The White House took a cooler view of the situation. Cleveland was still in office when the Cuban rebellion broke out. As with Venezuela, concern about America's vital interests—"by no means of a wholly sentimental or philanthropic character," he told the Congress—guided Cleveland's thinking. First, there were economic interests at stake. The rebellion was disrupting the sizable trade between the two countries and destroying profitable American investments, especially in Cuban sugar plantations. More important, the United States could no longer tolerate instability in the Caribbean. It became alarmed that Spain's troubles might draw other European powers into the situation. A chronically unstable Cuba was not compatible with America's increasing strategic interests in the region, especially its plans for an interoceanic canal whose approaches would have to be safeguarded. If Spain could put down the rebellion, that was fine from Cleveland's point of view. But as Spain's impotence became clearer, he began to urge the Spanish government to make reforms and to warn that the United States would have to intervene unless there was a speedy resolution of the Cuban crisis.

McKinley and the Road to War. On that central matter there was an essential continuity between Cleveland and the McKinley administration that took office in March 1897. Both were guided by the conception of the United States as the dominant Caribbean power, with vital interests that had to be defended. McKinley, however, was inclined to take a tougher line with the Spanish. For one thing, he was more appalled by Spain's "uncivilized and inhumane conduct" in Cuba and not so indifferent as Cleveland to the aspirations of the rebels. In addition, McKinley had to contend with the rising jingoism within the Republican party. At the 1896 national convention the Republicans had adopted a bristling platform calling for Cuban independence and proclaiming a new American imperialism. But the notion, long held by historians, that McKinley was swept along against his better judgment by popular opinion and by a Republican war faction led by Theodore Roosevelt, Henry Cabot Lodge, and other aggressive advocates of a "large policy" is not true. McKinley was very much his own man. He was a skilled politician and a canny, if undramatic, president. He would not proceed until he sensed a broad national consensus for war. In particular, he was sensitive to business interests fearful of any disruption to an economy just recovering from a depression.

On September 18, 1897, the American minister in Madrid asked the Spanish government "whether the time has not arrived when Spain . . . will put a stop to this destructive war." If Spain could not give assurances of an "early and certain peace," he warned, the United States would take whatever steps it "should deem necessary to procure this result." At first the Spanish response sparked some hope. The conservative regime fell, and a liberal government, upon taking office in October 1897, moderated its Cuban policy. Spain recalled Weyler, eased reconcentration, and adopted an autonomy plan that would grant Cuba a degree of self-rule, but not independence. Madrid's incapacity soon became clear, however. In January 1898, Spanish loyalists in Havana rioted against the offer of autonomy. The Cuban rebels, encouraged by the prospect of American intervention, demanded full independence.

Relations between the United States and Spain worsened. On February 9, 1898, the *New York Journal* published a private letter of Dupuy de Lôme, the Spanish minister to the United States. De Lôme called President McKinley "weak" and "a bidder for the admiration of the crowd." What was probably worse, De Lôme suggested that the Spanish government was not taking the American demands for reform seriously.

A week later, the U.S. battleship *Maine* blew up and sank in Havana harbor, with the loss of 260 seamen. "Whole Country Thrills with the War Fever," proclaimed Hearst's *New York Journal*. But McKinley kept his head. He assumed the sinking had been accidental: what motive could the Spanish have had for attacking the *Maine*? A naval board of inquiry, however, submitted a more damaging report. The explosion had been

"Remember the Maine!"

In late January 1898, the *Maine* entered Havana harbor on a courtesy call. On the evening of February 15, a mysterious blast sent the U.S. battleship to the bottom. This dramatic lithograph conveys something of the impact of that tragic event on American public opinion. Although no evidence ever linked the Spanish authorities to the explosion, the sinking of the *Maine* fed the emotional fires preparing the nation for war with Spain.

caused by a bomb, not, as experts had suspected, by a boiler rupture on the *Maine*. No evidence linked the Spanish to the explosion, but they had failed to meet their responsibility to protect the American vessel from attack.

This was damning evidence that Spanish control over Cuba had broken down, and it was reinforced by a memorable speech by Senator Redfield Proctor of Vermont after a visit to Cuba. The account by this anti-imperialist senior Republican of the devastation in the Cuban countryside made a deep impression and led even the skeptical to the conclusion that Spain had lost its claim to rule Cuba.

President McKinley had no stomach for the martial spirit engulfing the country. He was not swept along by the calls for blood to avenge the sinking of the *Maine*. But he did heed the advice of business leaders, earlier hesitant, but now impatient for the dispute with Spain to come to an end. War was preferable to the unresolved Cuban crisis. On March 27, McKinley cabled to Madrid what was in effect an ultimatum: an immediate armistice for six months, abandonment of the practice of reconcentration, and, with the United States as mediator, peace negotiations with the rebels. A telegram the next day added that only Cuban independence would be regarded as a satisfactory outcome to these negotiations.

In response, Spain made a series of desperate concessions, climaxed on April 9 by a unilateral declaration of an armistice whose duration would be at the discretion of the Spanish military. But it rejected American mediation, as well as the American demand for an independent Cuba. There had never been any chance that the proud Spanish would voluntarily accept that final humiliation.

On April 11, McKinley sent a message to Congress asking for authority to intervene to end the fighting in Cuba. His motives were as he described them: "In the name of humanity, in the name of civilization, in behalf of endangered American interests which give us the right and the duty to speak and to act, the war in Cuba must stop." The war hawks in Congress—a mixture of Republican jingoists and western Democrats who sympathized with the cause of Cuban independence—were impatient with McKinley's cautious progress. But the president did not lose control of things. On the one crucial difference he had with the war hawks, McKinley prevailed. He beat back their effort to grant recognition to the rebel republican government, which would have greatly reduced the administration's freedom of action in dealing with Spain.

The war hawks did push through the Teller amendment, by which the United States disclaimed any intention of taking Cuba. Senator Henry M. Teller wanted to make it impossible for European governments to say that "when we go out to make battle for the liberty and freedom of Cuban patriots, that we are doing it for the purpose of aggrandizement for ourselves or the increasing of our territorial holdings." This had to be made clear with regard to Cuba, "whatever," Senator Teller added, "we may do as to some other islands."

Did McKinley have in mind "some other islands"? Was this really a war of aggression, secretly motivated by a desire to seize strategic territory from Spain? In a strict sense, almost certainly not. It was not *because* of expansionist ambitions that McKinley pressed Spain into a corner. On the other hand, once war came he saw it as an opportunity to be exploited. As he wrote privately after hostilities began: "While we are conducting war and until its conclusion, we must keep all we get; when the war is over we must keep what we want." Precisely what would be forthcoming, of course, would depend on the fortunes of battle.

The Spoils of War

Hostilities formally began when Spain declared war on April 24, 1898. The day before, President McKinley had called for 125,000 volunteers. Across the country, regiments began to form up. Theodore Roosevelt immediately resigned as assistant secretary of the navy, ordered a fancy uniform, and was commissioned lieutenant colonel in a volunteer cavalry regiment that became famous as the Rough Riders. Raw recruits poured into the makeshift bases around Tampa, Florida. Confusion reigned. Tropical uniforms did not arrive; the food was bad, the sanitation worse; and rifles were in short supply. No provision had been made for getting the troops to Cuba; the government hastily began to collect a miscellaneous fleet of yachts, lake steamers, and commercial boats. Fortunately, the small regular army was a disciplined, highly professional force, and its seasoned 28,000 troops provided a nucleus for the 200,000 civilians who had to be turned into soldiers inside of a few weeks.

The navy was in better shape and, as it turned out, the real key to the outcome of the war. On April 23, acting on plans already drawn up, Commodore George Dewey's small Pacific fleet set sail from Hong Kong for the Philippines. Here, at this Spanish possession in the far Pacific, not in Cuba, the decisive engagement of the war was fought. On May 1, the American ships cornered the Spanish fleet in Manila harbor and destroyed it. The victory produced euphoria in the United States. Immediately, part of the army being trained for the Cuban campaign was diverted to the Philippines. Manila, the Philippine capital, fell on August 13, 1898.

With Dewey's naval victory, American strategic thinking suddenly clicked into place. "We hold the other side of the Pacific and the value to this country is almost beyond imagination," declared Senator Lodge.

"We must on no account let the [Philippine] Islands go." President McKinley agreed, and so did his key advisers. An anchor on the western Pacific had long been coveted by naval strategists. At this time, too, the great powers were carving up China into spheres of influence. If American commerce wanted a place in that glittering market, the power of the United States would have to be projected into Asia. "With a strong foothold in the Philippine Islands, we can and will take a large slice of the commerce of Asia," asserted Senator Mark Hanna. "That is what we want . . . and it is better to strike while the iron is hot."

Once the decision for a Philippine base had been made, other decisions followed almost automatically. For one, the question of Hawaii was quickly resolved. In 1897 McKinley had reintroduced an annexation proposal in the Congress, but it had stalled. In July 1898, Congress pushed Hawaiian annexation through by joint resolution. Hawaii had suddenly acquired a crucial strategic value: it was a halfway station on the way to the Philippines. The navy pressed for a coaling base in the central Pacific; that meant Guam, a Spanish island in the Marianas. There was need also for a strategically located base in the Caribbean; that meant Puerto Rico. By July, before the assault on Cuba, the full scope of McKinley's war aims had crystallized. Nor was there any question that he had the people behind him. In the wake of Dewey's victory, enthusiasm for colonial annexations swept the country and, so one close reader of the nation's press reported, was "getting so strong it will mean the political death of any man to oppose it pretty soon."

The campaign in Cuba, the main theater of operations, was something of an anticlimax. The Spanish fleet was bottled up in Santiago harbor, and the city itself became the strategic key to the military campaign. Half-trained and ill-equipped, the American forces moving on Santiago might have been checked by a determined opponent; but the Spaniards lacked the heart for battle. They would fight hard enough to maintain their honor, but they had no stomach for a real war against the Americans. There were two sharp engagements—the first at Las Guasimas on the road to Santiago, the second, on July 1, near the city on the heights

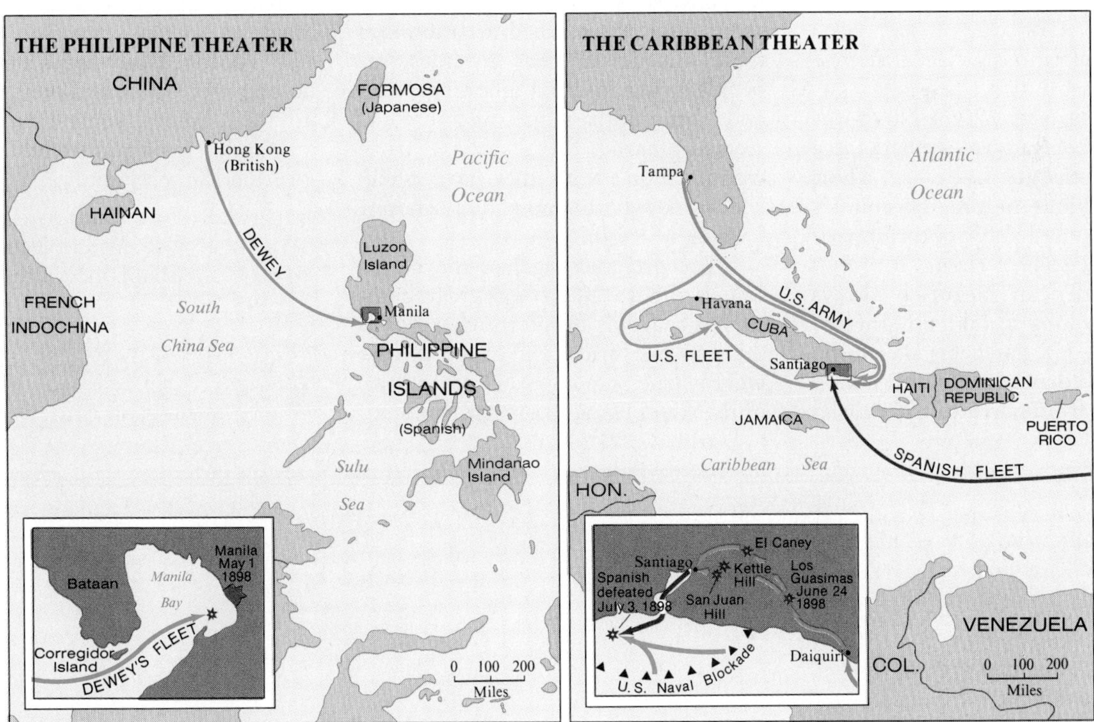

MAP 22.1

The Spanish-American War

The swift American victory in the Spanish-American War derived from overwhelming U.S. naval superiority. Dewey's destruction of the Spanish fleet in Manila harbor doomed the Spaniards in the Philippines. In Cuba, American ground forces won a hard victory on San Juan Hill, for they were ill-equipped and poorly supplied. With the United States in control of the seas, the Spaniards saw no choice but to give up the battle for Cuba.

AMERICAN VOICES

Black Soldiers in a White Man's War *George W. Prioleau*

The chaplain of the Ninth Cavalry regiment expresses his bitterness against the racism experienced by black troopers in the South on their way to battle in Cuba.

Hon. H. C. Smith
Editor, *Gazette*

Dear Sir:
The Ninth Cavalry left Chickamauga on the 30th of April for Tampa, Fla. We arrived here (nine miles from Tampa) on May 3. From this port the army will sail for Cuba. We have in this camp here and at Tampa between 7,000 and 8,000 soldiers, artillery, one regiment of cavalry (the famous fighting Ninth) and the Twenty-fourth and Twenty-fifth infantries. The Ninth Cavalry's bravery and their skillfulness with weapons of war . . . is well known by all who have read the history of the last Indian war. . . .

Yesterday, May 12, the Ninth was ordered to be ready to embark at a moment's notice for Cuba. . . . These men are anxious to go. The country will then hear and know of the bravery of these sable sons of Ham.

The American Negro is always ready and willing to take up arms, to fight and to lay down his life in defense of his country's flag and honor. All the way from northwest Nebraska this regiment was greeted with cheers and hurrahs. At places where we stopped the people assembled by the thousands. While the Ninth Cavalry band would play some national air the people would raise their hats, men, women and children would wave their handkerchiefs, and the heavens would resound with their hearty cheers. The white hand shaking the black hand. The hearty "goodbyes," "God bless you," and other expressions aroused the patriotism of our boys. . . . These demonstrations, so enthusiastically given, greeted us all the way until we reached Nashville. At this point we arrived about 12:30 A.M. There were about 6,000 colored people there to greet us (very few white people) but not a man was allowed by the railroad officials to approach the cars. From there until we reached Chattanooga there was not a cheer given us, the people living in gross ignorance, rags and dirt. Both white and colored seemed amazed; they looked at us in wonder. Don't think they have intelligence enough to know that Andrew Jackson is dead. . . .

The prejudice against the Negro soldier and the Negro was great, but it was of heavenly origin to what it is in this part of Florida, and I suppose that what is true here is true in other parts of the state. Here, the Negro is not allowed to purchase over the same counter in some stores that the white man purchases over. The southerners have made their laws and the Negroes know and obey them. They never stop to ask a white man a question. He (Negro) never thinks of disobeying. You talk about freedom, liberty, etc. Why sir, the Negro of this country is freeman and yet a slave. Talk about fighting and freeing poor Cuba and of Spain's brutality; of Cuba's murdered thousands, and starving reconcentrados. Is America any better than Spain? Has she not subjects in her very midst who are murdered daily without a trial of judge or jury? Has she not subjects in her own borders whose children are half-fed and half-clothed, because their father's skin is black. . . . Yet the Negro is loyal to his country's flag. . . .

The four Negro regiments are going to help free Cuba, and they will return to their homes, some then mustered out and begin again to fight the battle of American prejudice. . . .

Yours truly,
Geo. W. Prioleau
Chaplain, Ninth Cavalry

Source: Cleveland *Gazette* (May 13, 1898), reprinted in Willard B. Gatewood, *"Smoked Yankees" and the Struggle for Empire, 1898–1902* (Urbana: University of Illinois Press, 1971), pp. 27–29.

commanded by San Juan Hill. Roosevelt's dismounted Rough Riders (there had been no room for horses on the transports) and four black regiments took the brunt of the fighting. In the battle of San Juan, which was actually a close call for the Americans, white observers grudgingly credited much of the victory to the "superb gallantry" of the black soldiers. On July 3, in a last futile gesture, the Spanish fleet in Santiago harbor made a suicidal daylight attempt to run the American blockade—and was destroyed.

Three weeks later, Spain sued for peace. The two nations signed an armistice in which Spain agreed to give up Cuba and cede Puerto Rico and Guam to the United States. American forces would occupy Manila pending a peace treaty that would decide the fate of the Philippines.

The Battle of San Juan Hill

On July 1, 1898, the key battle for Cuba took place on heights overlooking Santiago. The brunt of the fighting was taken by African-American troops. Although generally overlooked, the black role in the San Juan battle is in fact done justice in this contemporary lithograph, and without the demeaning stereotypes by which blacks were normally depicted in an age of intensifying racism. Even so, the racial hierarchy is maintained. The blacks are the foot soldiers; their officers are white.

The Imperial Experiment

The big question was the Philippines. This was an archipelago of over 7,000 islands populated—as William R. Day, McKinley's secretary of state, put it with the characteristic racism of that era—by "eight or nine millions of absolutely ignorant and many degraded people." Not even the most avid of American expansionists had advocated colonial rule over such a population: that was European-style imperialism, not what Mahan and his followers had in mind. Both Mahan and Lodge initially advocated keeping only Manila as a western Pacific base. It gradually became clear, however, that Manila was not defensible without controlling the whole of Luzon, the large island on which the city is located.

McKinley and his advisers surveyed the options. One possibility would have been to return most of the islands to Spain, but the reputed evils of Spanish rule made that a "cowardly and dishonorable" solution. Another possibility would have been to partition the Philippines with one or more of the Great Powers. There would have been no dearth of takers, particularly Germany, whose ships were already prowling the nearby waters. But, as McKinley observed, to turn over valuable territory to "our commercial rivals in the Orient—that would have been bad business and discreditable."

Most plausible was the possibility of granting the Philippines independence. As in Cuba, Spanish rule had already stirred up a rebellion, led by the fiery patriot Emilio Aguinaldo. It would have been feasible to make an arrangement like the one being negotiated with the Cubans over Guantanamo Bay: the lease of a naval base to the Americans as a price for freedom. But after some hesitation McKinley was persuaded that "we could not leave [the Filipinos] to themselves—they were unfit for self-rule—and they would soon have anarchy and misrule over there worse than Spain's was."

The fact was that, having expended American lives and money on conquering the Philippines, the administration had no politically easy way of extricating itself. In October 1898, while the peace negotiations were in progress, McKinley made a two-week speaking tour of the Midwest to get a reading on public opinion. What he heard from the crowds confirmed his own belief that the United States would have to take the entire archipelago. On October 26 he cabled instructions to that effect to the American delegation in Paris. Afterward, to a visiting group of Methodist clergymen, McKinley provided a more sanctimonious explanation: after much prayer he had concluded "that there was nothing left for us to do but to take them all, and to educate the Filipinos, and uplift and civilize and Christianize them and by God's grace do the very best we could by them, as our fellow men, for whom Christ also died."

As for the Spaniards, they had little choice. In the Treaty of Paris, they ceded the Philippines to the United States for a payment of $20 million. The treaty encountered harder going at home. The seizure of the Philippines reawakened traditional antiexpansionist sentiment in the United States. An organized movement formed in many cities, starting with Boston, and grew into the formidable Anti-Imperialist League in October 1899. The Philippine issue delayed the treaty in the Senate for weeks. Senator George Hoar of Massachusetts protested that annexation violated the Constitution.

AMERICAN VOICES

Subduing the Filipinos — the Ideal

Major General Arthur MacArthur

In 1902 MacArthur, the commanding general of U.S. forces in the Philippines, appeared before a Senate committee investigating conditions there. In his presentation he expressed a widely held view of the necessity—and desirability—of American rule.

At the time I returned to Manila [May 1900] to assume the supreme command it seemed to me that we had been committed to a position by process of spontaneous evolution. . . . [o]ur permanent occupation of the islands was simply one of the necessary consequences in logical sequence of our great prosperity. . . . our conception of right, justice, freedom, and personal liberty was the precious fruit of centuries of strife; that we had inherited much in these respects from our ancestors, and in our own behalf have added much to the happiness of the world, and as beneficiaries of the past and as the instruments of future progressive social development we must regard ourselves simply as the custodians of imperishable ideas held in trust for the general benefit of mankind. In other words, I felt that we had attained a moral and intellectual height from which we were bound to proclaim to all as the occasion arose the true message of humanity as embodied in the principles of our own institutions. . . .

To my mind the archipelago is a fertile soil upon which to plant republicanism. . . . We are planting the best traditions, the best characteristics of Americanism in such a way that they never can be removed from that soil. That in itself seems to me a most inspiring thought. It encouraged me during all my efforts in those islands, even when conditions seemed most disappointing, when the people themselves, not appreciating precisely what the remote consequences of our efforts were going to be, mistrusted us; but that fact was always before me—that going down deep into that fertile soil were the imperishable ideas of Americanism.

AMERICAN VOICES

Subduing the Filipinos — the Realities

F. A. Blake and Richard T. O'Brien

MacArthur's voice was not the only one the Senate committee heard. News of battlefield atrocities reached them as well. This account by F. A. Blake, a Red Cross worker, for example, had appeared in the *San Francisco Call* on March 30, 1899.

I never saw such execution in my life and hope never to see such sights as met on all sides as our little corps passed over the field, dressing wounded legs and arms nearly demolished, total decapitation, horrible wounds in chest and abdomen, showing the determination of our soldiers to kill every native in sight.

Richard T. O'Brien, of M Company, 26th Infantry Volunteers, U.S. Army, told this story to the Senate Committee on the Philippines in 1902.

[H]ow the order started and who gave it I don't know, but the town was fired on. I saw an old fellow come to the door, and he looked out: he got a shot in the abdomen and fell to his knees and turned around and died. . . .

After that two old men came out, hand in hand. I should think they were over 50 years old, probably between 50 and 70 years old. They had a white flag. They were shot down. At the other end of the town we heard screams, and there was a woman there; she was burned up, and in her arms was a baby, and on the floor was another child. The baby was at her breast, the one in her arms, and this child on the floor was, I should judge, about 3 years of age. They were burned. Whether she was demoralized or driven insane I don't know. She stayed in the house.

"The power to conquer alien people and hold them in subjugation is nowhere expressly granted [and] nowhere implied," he protested. With only a vote to spare, the Senate approved the treaty on February 6, 1899.

War in the Philippines. Two days earlier, on February 4, fighting had broken out between American and Filipino patrols on the edge of Manila. Confronted by the prospect of American annexation, Aguinaldo asserted his nation's independence and turned his guns on the occupying American forces.

The ensuing conflict far exceeded in ferocity the war just concluded with Spain. Fighting tenacious guerrillas, the U.S. army resorted to the same tactics of reconcentration used by the Spaniards in Cuba, moving the people into the towns, carrying out indiscriminate attacks beyond the perimeters, and burning crops and villages.

Atrocities became commonplace on both sides. The American forces specialized in the "water cure"—forcing water into a person's stomach and then pounding it out—to force captured guerrillas to talk. In more than three years of warfare, forty-two hundred Americans and thousands of Filipinos died. The fighting ended in 1902, and Judge William Howard Taft, appointed governor in 1901, set up a civilian government. He intended to make the Philippines a model of American road building and sanitary engineering.

In the 1900 election, McKinley's convincing victory over William Jennings Bryan, an avid antiexpansionist, suggested popular satisfaction with America's overseas adventure. Yet a strong sense of misgivings was evident.

Emilio Aguinaldo

At the start of the war with Spain, U.S. military leaders brought the Filipino patriot Aguinaldo back from Singapore because they thought he would stir up a popular uprising that would help bring about the defeat of the Spaniards. Aguinaldo came because he thought the Americans favored an independent Philippines. These differing intentions—it has remained a matter of dispute as to what assurances Aguinaldo received—were the root cause of the tragic Filipino insurrection that proved far costlier in American and Filipino lives than the war with Spain that had preceded it.

Fighting the Filipinos

The United States went to war against Spain in 1898 partly out of sympathy with the Cuban struggle for independence. Yet the United States found it necessary to use very much the same brutal tactics to put down the Filipino struggle for independence as the Spaniards had used against the Cubans. Here the Twentieth Kansas Volunteers march through the burning village of Caloocan.

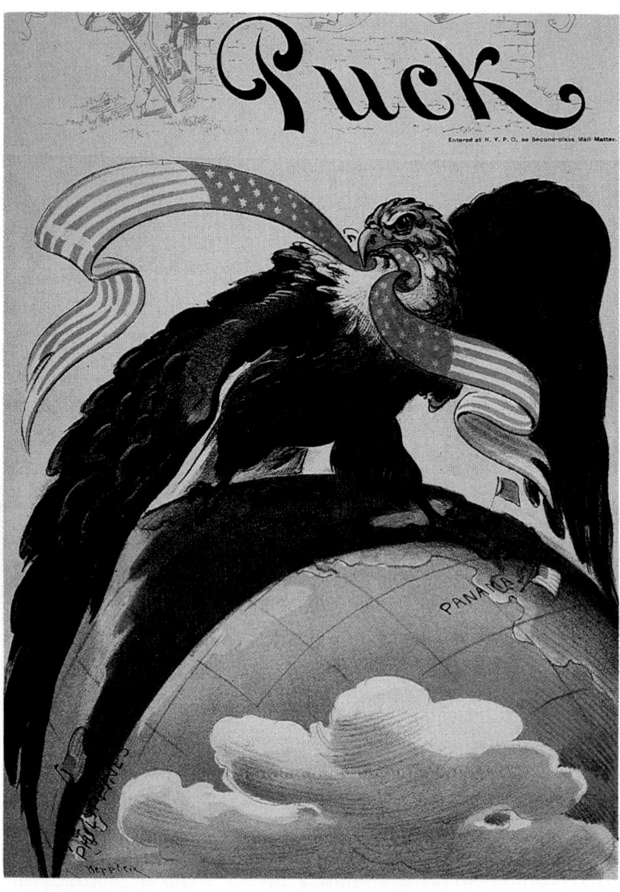

Second Thoughts About American Empire

After the shouting was over, and the United States had its empire, doubts began to creep in, as is evident in this *Puck* cover in celebration of July 4, 1904. There is the American eagle in all its glory, but with wings spreading far out to Philippines in one direction and Puerto Rico in the other, and grumbling: "Gee, but this is an awful stretch!"

Americans had not anticipated the brutal methods needed to subdue the Filipino guerrillas. "We are destroying these islanders by the thousands, their villages and cities," protested the philosopher William James. "No life shall you have, we say, except as a gift from our philanthropy after your unconditional surrender to our will. . . . Could there be any more damning indictment of that whole bloated ideal termed 'modern civilization'?"

There were, moreover, disturbing political issues to be resolved. Did the Constitution extend to the acquired territories? Did their inhabitants automatically become citizens? In 1901 the Supreme Court ruled negatively on both questions; these were matters for Congress to decide. In its report on administration for the Philippines, the special commission appointed by McKinley recommended ultimate independence after an indefinite period of U.S. rule, during which the Filipinos would be readied for self-government. In 1916, the passage of the Jones Act formally committed the United States to granting Philippine independence, but set no date.

The ugly business in the Philippines rubbed off some of the moralizing gloss but left undeflected the global aspirations driving the United States. In a few years the United States had acquired the makings of a strategic overseas empire—Hawaii, Puerto Rico, Guam, the Philippines, and finally, in 1900, several of the Samoan islands that had hitherto been jointly administered with Germany and Britain. The United States, remarked the legal scholar John Bassett Moore in 1899, had moved "from a position of comparative freedom from entanglements into a position of what is commonly called a world power."

Onto the World Stage

A Power Among Powers

In Europe the flexing of America's muscles against Spain caused a certain amount of consternation. The assault on an ancient, if decayed, European state seemed to many government leaders the work of a country that was (in the words of the French envoy to Washington) "ignorant, brutal, and quite capable of destroying the complicated European structure." At the instigation of Kaiser Wilhelm II of Germany, the major powers had tried before war broke out to intercede on Spain's behalf—but tentatively, because no one was looking for trouble with the Americans. President McKinley had listened politely to the representations of their envoys on April 6, 1898, and had then, dismissively, proceeded with his war.

The decisive outcome confirmed what the Europeans already suspected. After Dewey's naval victory, the semiofficial French paper *Le Temps* observed that "what passes before our eyes is the appearance of a new power of the first order." And, in a long editorial, the London *Times* concluded: "This war must . . . effect a profound change in the whole attitude and policy of the United States. In the future America will play a part in the general affairs of the world such as she has never played before."

Anglo-American Amity. Precisely what that part would be in the European balance of power remained uncertain. Germany toyed briefly with the notion of an American alliance, but only Great Britain had a clear view of what it wanted from the United States. In the late nineteenth century, Britain's position in Europe had steadily worsened. It was being challenged industrially and militarily by a unified Germany. Clashing expansionist ambitions in North Africa and across Asia soured Britain's relations with France and Russia. And there was general European hostility toward British imperial policy in South Africa, a policy that resulted in the Boer War against the independent-minded Dutch settlers at the end of the 1890s. In its growing isolation, Britain turned to the United States. This explained why Britain had meekly bowed to American demands in the Venezuela dispute of 1895. From that time onward, after a century of cool relations (or worse) with its former colonies, Britain strove consistently for a *rapprochement* (literally, a "coming together") with the United States.

In the Hay-Pauncefote Agreement (1901) Britain gave up its treaty rights to joint participation in any Central American canal project, thereby clearing the way for a canal exclusively under U.S. control. And two years later the last of the vexing U.S.–Canadian border disputes, this one involving British Columbia and Alaska, was settled—again, to American satisfaction. The lone British member of the U.S.–Canadian tribunal cast the deciding vote awarding to the United States the Pacific inlets and ports that provided the only convenient access to the Klondike gold fields of the Canadian Yukon. No formal alliance was forthcoming, but Anglo-American friendship had been placed on a firm basis, so much so that beginning in 1901 the British admiralty designed its war plans on the assumption of a friendly U.S. navy. The assumption was that America was "a kindred state with whom we shall never have a parricidal war."

The Caribbean—An American Lake

If America's role in Europe remained uncertain, that was certainly not the case closer to home. An exuberant exponent of the "large policy" of overseas expansionism, Theodore Roosevelt had been thrust into the presidency in 1901 just as the United States was concluding its brief burst of imperialism by subduing the Filipino independence movement. The next step was to consolidate the resulting strategic gains in the Caribbean and the Pacific. This was Roosevelt's main foreign policy task, and he welcomed it.

"All the great masterful races have been fighting races," Roosevelt declared. Nothing would be worse for the United States, already too commercial for his aristocratic taste, than "slothful and ignoble peace." But a nation's power had to be used only for good ends and, in particular, to keep the world from sliding into anarchy. The international forces for disorder were such, Roosevelt maintained, as to "render it incumbent on all civilized and orderly powers to insist on the proper policing of the world." This view licensed the United States to exert power as needed in the regions that, because of the country's overseas expansion, had fallen under its direct influence.

Roosevelt stated his foreign policy in the menacing phrase, "Speak softly and carry a big stick." By a "big stick" he meant above all naval power. Under Roosevelt, the battleship program went on apace. By 1904 the U.S. Navy stood fifth in the world, and by 1907, second. Roosevelt was a friend of Captain Mahan, and a close student of his geopolitical writings. Mahan's program called for a big navy and strategic bases—and, as a final step, a canal across Central America. Indeed, the Spanish-American War had demonstrated that strategic need in the most graphic way: the entire country had waited breathlessly as the battleship *Oregon* had sped for sixty days from the Pacific around the southern tip of Latin America to join in the final action against the Spanish fleet in Cuba.

The Panama Canal. A canal was at the top of Roosevelt's agenda. With Britain's treaty right to a joint canal enterprise surrendered in 1901, Roosevelt proceeded to more troublesome matters. For $40 million, the United States purchased from the New Panama Canal Company the assets of de Lesseps's earlier canal project. Panama was a province of Colombia, so the Roosevelt administration entered into negotiations with Colombia to lease the strip of land through which the canal would run. The Colombian legislature voted down the proposed treaty, partly because the company's rights would soon expire and the sale to the United States could then be renegotiated on terms more favorable to Colombia. Furious over what seemed to him a breach of faith, Roosevelt contemplated outright seizure of Panama but settled on a more devious solution.

The key intermediary in the sale of the de Lesseps assets, an engineer named Philippe Bunau-Varilla, let Roosevelt know that an independence movement was brewing in Panama. The United States in turn informed Bunau-Varilla that American ships were steaming toward Panama. The idea was that the Americans would provide cover for the expected uprising. There was a mix-up when the cruiser *Nashville* arrived at Colon, however, and the American commander failed to prevent 400 Colombian troops from disembarking at that small Atlantic port. Using their wits, the conspirators managed to keep these troops from proceeding to Panama City, and the bloodless revolution against Colombian rule went off on schedule. The next day, November 4, the United States recognized Panama. Less than two weeks later, with Bunau-Varilla serving as the representative of the new republic, Panama signed a treaty with the United States. The agreement granted the United States a perpetually renewable lease on a canal zone. These machinations were a dirty business, but they got Roosevelt what he wanted.

Roosevelt never regretted the victimization of Colombia, although the United States, as a kind of conscience money, paid Colombia $25 million in 1922. Building the canal was one of the heroic engineering feats of the century, involving a swamp-clearing project to rid the area of malaria and yellow fever, the construction of a series of great locks, and the excavation of 240 million cubic yards of earth. It took the U.S. Army Corps of Engineers eight years to finish the huge project. When it opened in 1914, the Panama Canal gave the United States a commanding commercial and strategic position in the Western Hemisphere.

Policeman of the Caribbean. Next came the task of making the Caribbean basin secure. The countries there, said Secretary of State Elihu Root, had been placed "in the front yard of the United States" by the Panama Canal. Therefore, as Roosevelt put it, they had to "behave themselves."

In the case of Cuba, this was readily managed in the settlement following the Spanish-American War. Before the United States withdrew from Cuba in 1902, it reorganized Cuban finances and concluded a swampclearing program that eliminated yellow fever, a disease that had ravaged Cuba for many years (and killed probably four thousand of the occupying U.S. troops). As a condition for gaining independence, Cuba was required to include in its constitution a proviso called the Platt amendment. The amendment gave the United States the right to intervene if Cuban independence was threatened or if Cuba failed to maintain internal order. Cuba also granted the United States a permanent lease on Guantanamo Bay, where the U.S. Navy built a large base.

Roosevelt believed that instability in the Caribbean invited the intervention of European powers. For example, Britain and Germany blockaded Venezuela in

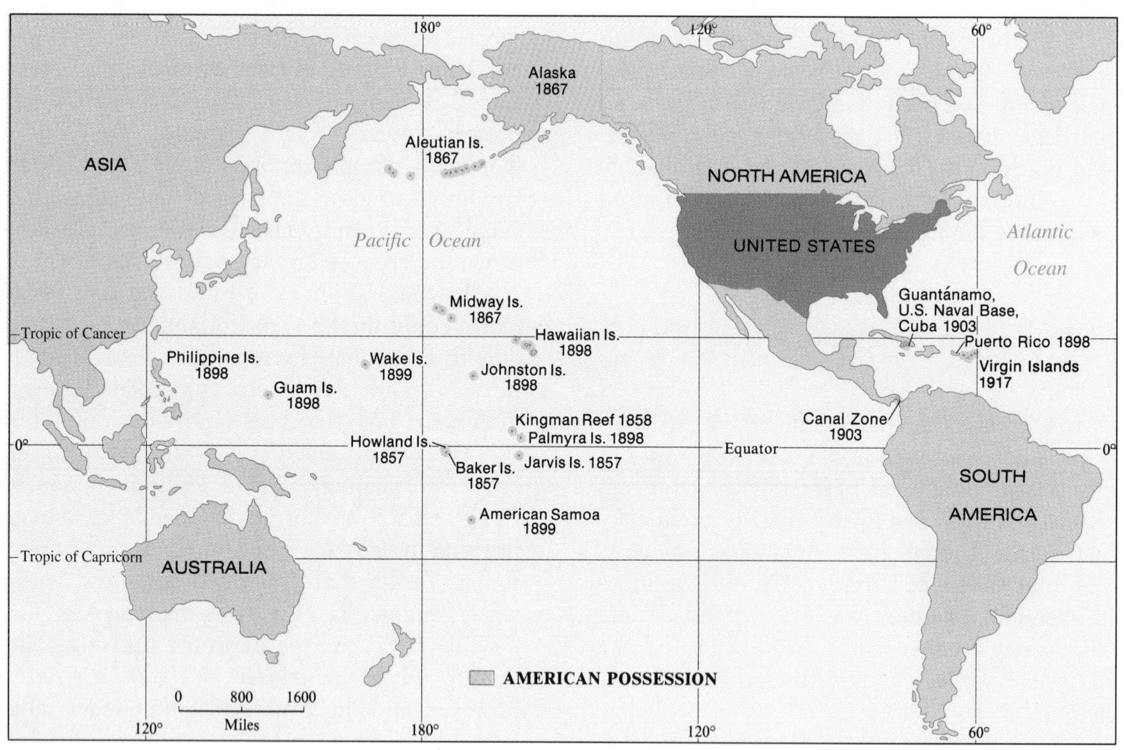

MAP 22.2

The American Empire

In 1890 Alfred T. Mahan wrote that the United States should regard the oceans as "a great highway" across which America would carry on world trade. That was precisely what resulted from the empire the United States acquired in the wake of the Spanish-American War. The Caribbean possessions, strategically located Pacific islands, and, in 1903, the Panama Canal Zone gave the United States commercial and naval access to a wider world.

The Panama Canal
The Canal Zone was acquired through devious means in which Americans could take little pride (and which led in 1978 to the Senate's decision to restore the property to Panama). But the building of the Panama Canal itself was a triumph of American ingenuity and drive. Dr. William C. Gorgas cleaned out the malarial mosquitoes that had earlier stymied the French. Under Col. George W. Goethels, the U.S. Army overcame formidable obstacles in a mighty feat of engineering. This photograph shows the massive effort under way in December 1904 to excavate the Culebra Cut so that ocean-going ships would be able to pass through.

1902–1903 for failing to meet its debt payments. In 1904, Roosevelt announced that the United States would act as "policeman" of the region, stepping in "however reluctantly, in flagrant cases . . . of wrong doing or impotence."

This policy became known as the Roosevelt Corollary to the Monroe Doctrine. It transformed what had been a broad principle of opposition against European expansionist ambitions in Latin America into an unrestricted American right to regulate Caribbean affairs. The Roosevelt Corollary was not a treaty with other states; it was a unilateral declaration sanctioned only by American power and national interest.

Under the Roosevelt Corollary the United States intervened regularly in the internal affairs of Caribbean states. In 1905, for example, American authorities took over the customs and debt management of the Dominican Republic. When similar financial intervention by the United States touched off a rebellion in Nicaragua in 1912, American marines landed and occupied the country.

Roosevelt's thinking was primarily strategic; his successor, William Howard Taft, took a more commercial view. American investments in the Caribbean region grew dramatically after 1900. The United Fruit Company owned about 160,000 acres in Central American countries by 1913, and U.S. investments in Cuban sugar plantations quadrupled in fifteen years. Taft quickly intervened when disorder threatened American property. But he also regarded business investment as a force for stability in underdeveloped areas. Taft spoke for *dollar diplomacy*—the aggressive coupling of American diplomatic and economic interests abroad.

The Open Door

In the Far East, commercial interests had always stood at the forefront of American policy—especially the huge China market. But by the late 1890s, Japan, Russia, Germany, France, and England had all moved into China, carved out spheres of influence, and instituted discriminatory trade practices in their zones. Fearful that the United States was being frozen out of China, Secretary of State John Hay in 1899 sent an "Open Door" note to the occupying powers: he wanted to establish the right of equal trade access—an Open Door—for all nations wanting to do business in China. Even with its control over the Philippines, the United States was in a weak position compared to the occupying powers on the scene. The best that Hay was able to achieve were responses that were ambiguous and highly conditional. But Hay chose to interpret them as accepting the American Open Door position.

When a secret society of Chinese nationalists launched the Boxer Rebellion in 1900, the United States sent 5,000 troops from the Philippines and joined the multinational campaign to raise the siege of the foreign legations in Beijing (Peking). America took the opportunity to assert a second principle to the Open Door: that China would be preserved as a "territorial and administrative entity." As long as the legal fiction of an independent China survived, so would American claims to equal access to the China market. The other powers gave their assent.

With a network of bases stretching across the Pacific, American power could now be projected into Asia. But here the United States faced formidable rivals.

The European powers had acceded to American claims to preeminence in the Caribbean, including the Roosevelt Corollary. In the Far East, however, Britain, Germany, France, and Russia were strongly entrenched, with no inclination to defer to American interests. The United States also confronted a strategically placed Asian nation—Japan—that had its own vital interests at stake.

The Japanese Challenge. Japan was a rising world power. It had unveiled its military strength in the Sino-Japanese War of 1894–1895, which had begun the dismemberment of China. With the signing of the Anglo-Japanese Alliance in 1902, the power balance in East Asia shifted in Japan's favor, giving Japan a freer hand in confronting Russia over their rival claims in Manchuria and Korea. In 1904, provoked by Russian demands for a military withdrawal from northern Korea, Japan suddenly attacked the tsar's fleet at Port Arthur, Russia's leased port in China. In a series of brilliant victories, the Japanese demolished the Russian military forces in Asia. Roosevelt, anxious to restore some semblance of a power balance, mediated a settlement of the Russo-Japanese War at Portsmouth, New Hampshire, in 1905. Japan emerged as the predominant power in East Asia.

Despite his robust rhetoric, Roosevelt took an accommodating stance toward Japanese expansionism. In exchange for Japanese acquiescence to American sovereignty over the Philippines, the United States approved of Japan's protectorate over Korea and raised no objection when this became full sovereignty in 1911. However, a surge of anti-Asian feeling in California complicated Roosevelt's efforts. In 1906 the San Francisco school board placed all Asian students in a segregated school, infuriating Japan. The "gentlemen's agreement" of 1907, in which Japan agreed to restrict immigration to the United States, smoothed matters over, but the periodic resurgence of racism in California led to continuing tensions with the proud Japanese.

Roosevelt meanwhile moved to balance Japan's military power by increasing American naval strength in the Pacific. American battleships visited Japan in 1908 and then made a global tour in an impressive display of sea power. Late that year, near the end of his administration, Roosevelt achieved his accommodation with Japan. The Root-Takahira Agreement confirmed the status quo in the Pacific, as well as the principles of free oceanic commerce and equal trade opportunity in China.

However, William Howard Taft entered the White House in 1909 convinced that the United States had been short-changed. An exponent of "dollar diplomacy," Taft pressed for a larger role for American bankers and investors in the Far East, especially in the railroad construction going on in China. Taft hoped that American capital could counterbalance Japanese power and pave the way for increased commercial opportunities. When the Chinese Revolution of 1911 toppled the ruling Manchu dynasty, Taft supported the Chinese Nationalists as a new counterforce to the Japanese. The United States thus entered a long-term conflict with Japan that would grow worse and end in war thirty years later.

The triumphant thrust across the Pacific lost some of its luster. The United States had become embroiled in a distant struggle that promised many future liabilities but little of the fabulous profits that had lured Americans to Asia. It was a chastening experience for an emerging world power.

The Japanese in California
The Japanese who flocked into California from 1890 onward made a mighty contribution to the state's agriculture, and by sheer hard work many of them became independent and highly productive farmers. But the prejudice against them was unrelenting, and when the San Francisco school board sought to segregate Japanese children in 1906, an international incident blew up. President Roosevelt got the segregation order rescinded, and Japan agreed to limit emigration to the United States voluntarily. Despite this so-called Gentlemen's Agreement, a festering wound had been opened in the relations between the two countries.

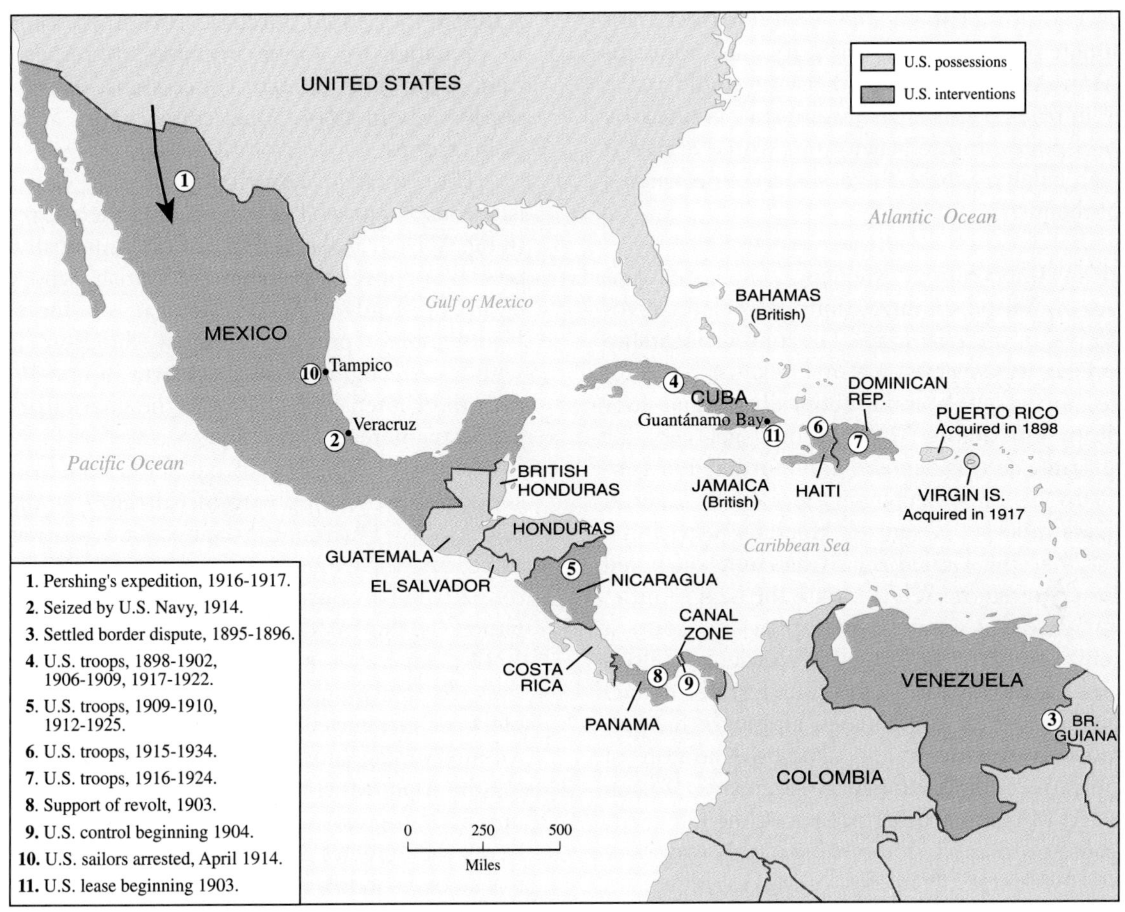

MAP 22.3

Policeman of the Caribbean, 1898–1917

After the Spanish-American War, the United States vigorously asserted its interest in the affairs of its neighbors to the south. As the record of interventions shows, the United States truly became the "policeman" of the Caribbean, and not only to maintain stability in the region. In the Mexican intervention, the United States was acting, at least in part, out of a sense that it had the right to impose its political values on its neighbors.

Woodrow Wilson and Mexico

When Woodrow Wilson became president in 1913, he was bent on reform in American foreign policy no less than in domestic politics. William Howard Taft's dollar diplomacy seemed to Wilson to be an extension abroad of the arrogant business practices that he and other progressives were trying to curb at home. On the importance of economic development overseas, Wilson did not really differ with his predecessors. He applauded the "tides of commerce" that would arise from the Panama Canal. But he was opposed to dollar diplomacy that bullied weaker countries into inequitable financial relationships and gave undue advantage to American business. It seemed to Wilson "a very perilous thing to determine the foreign policy of a nation in terms of material interest."

Within two weeks of taking office, Wilson demonstrated what he had in mind. American banks had joined an international consortium to provide a loan to China. When the investment banker J. P. Morgan sought his approval, Wilson refused, on the grounds that the terms of the loan threatened the independence of the Chinese government. The plan "was obnoxious to the principles upon which the government of our people rests."

The United States, Wilson insisted, should conduct its foreign policy in conformity with America's own democratic principles. He aimed to foster the "development of constitutional liberty in the world" and, above all, to extend it to the nation's neighbors in Latin America. In a major policy speech in October 1913, he promised those nations that the United States would "never again seek one additional foot of territory by conquest." The president said he would strive to advance "human rights, national integrity, and opportunity" in Latin America. To do otherwise would make "ourselves untrue to our own traditions." Guided by such a moral policy, future generations would arrive at "those great heights where there shines unobstructed the light of the justice of God."

The Mexican Intervention. Mexico became the primary object of Wilson's ministrations. A cycle of revolutions had begun there in 1911. The long dictatorship of Porfirio Diaz was overthrown by Francisco Madero, who spoke much as Wilson did about liberty and constitutionalism. But before Madero could get very far with his reforms, he was deposed and murdered in February 1913 by his chief lieutenant, Victoriano Huerta. Other powers quickly recognized Huerta's provisional government, but the United States had not yet acted when Wilson entered the White House the next month.

Wilson abhorred Huerta; he called his coup a "usurpation" and Huerta himself a murderer. Wilson pledged "to force him out." The United States denied recognition to Huerta's government, although this policy contradicted America's longstanding tradition of granting quick recognition to new governments. Wilson also subjected Mexico to other pressures, including the threatened use of force. By intervening in this way, Wilson insisted, "we act in the interest of Mexico alone. . . . We are seeking to counsel Mexico for its own good." Wilson meant that he intended to put the Mexican revolution back on the constitutional path started by Madero. Wilson was not deterred by the fact that American business interests, with enormous investments in Mexico, favored Huerta. On the contrary, that fact seemed to make Wilson all the more determined to get Huerta out.

The emergence of armed opposition to Huerta in northern Mexico under Venustiano Carranza strengthened Wilson's hand. Carranza's Constitutionalist movement, as it became known, gave Wilson some grounds for denying recognition to Huerta—his government did not fully control the country. More important, Carranza signified to Wilson the vitality of the reformist politics that he wanted to foster in Mexico.

But the Constitutionalists were ardent nationalists. They had no desire for American intervention in Mexican affairs. Carranza angrily rebuffed Wilson's efforts to bring about elections through a compromise between the rebels and the Mexican government. He also vowed to resist by force any intrusion of U.S. troops in his country. All he wanted from Wilson, Carranza asserted, was recognition of the Constitutionalists' belligerent status so they could purchase arms in the United States. In exchange for vague promises to respect property rights and "fair" foreign concessions, Carranza finally got his way in 1914. American weapons began to flow to his troops.

The American contribution to the Constitutionalists' cause went well beyond selling them arms. For one thing, Wilson isolated Huerta diplomatically. Huerta's crucial support came from the British, who wanted to ensure a steady flow of Mexican oil for their fleet. Under intense pressure from Washington, the British withdrew recognition from Huerta in late 1913. In return the United States became the guarantor of British property interests in Mexico.

When it became clear that neither the loss of British support nor the supplying of Carranza would turn the tide against Huerta, the United States threw its own forces into the game. Using the pretext of a minor insult to the U.S. Navy at Tampico, Wilson ordered the occupation of the major port of Vera Cruz on April 21, 1914. This action cost 19 American and 126 Mexican lives. At that point, the Huerta regime began to crumble. Carranza nevertheless condemned the United States for intervening, and his own forces came close to engaging the Americans. When he entered Mexico City in triumph in August 1914, Carranza had some cause to thank the Yankees. But if any sense of gratitude existed, it was overshadowed by the anti-Americanism inspired by Wilson's insensitivity to Mexican pride and revolutionary zeal.

This sad chapter in Mexican-American relations had a chastening effect on Wilson. It revealed to him the difficulties of acting on, or even of living up to, well-meant ideals amid the confusion of war, revolution, and clashing national interests. Indeed, there were even more egregious examples on which he might have drawn: despite his anti-imperialist pronouncements, Wilson acted no differently than had his predecessors in sending in the U.S. Marines when law and order broke down in Haiti in 1915 and in the Dominican Republic in 1916.

The Gathering Storm in Europe

In the meantime, Europe had begun to drift toward a great world war. There were two main sources of tension. One derived from the deadly rivalry between Germany, the new military and economic superpower of Europe, and the European states threatened by Germany's might—above all France, which had been humiliated in the Franco-Prussian War of 1870 and forced to cede the Alsace-Lorraine provinces to Germany. The second danger zone was the Balkans, where the Ottoman Empire was disintegrating and where, in the midst of explosive ethnic rivalries, Austria-Hungary and Russia were competing for dominance. On the basis of these conflicts an alliance system had emerged, with Germany, Austria-Hungary and Italy (the Triple Alliance) on one side and France and Russia (the Dual Alliance) on the other.

The tensions within Europe were to some degree released by European imperial adventures—most of all by France in Africa and by Russia in Asia. These activities placed France and Russia in opposition to imperial Britain, effectively excluding the latter from the European alliance system. Fearful of Germany, however, England in 1904 composed its differences with France, and the two countries reached a friendly understanding, or *entente*. When England came to a similar understanding with Russia in 1907, the basis was laid for the Triple Entente, and the potential was thereby much magnified for a deadly confrontation between two great European power blocs.

In these European quarrels the United States had no obvious stake, nor any inclination (in the words of a cautionary Senate resolution) "to depart from the traditional American foreign policy which forbids participation . . . [in] political questions which are entirely European in scope." But, on becoming president, Theodore Roosevelt had taken a lively interest in European affairs, and he was eager, as the head of a great power, to make a contribution to the cause of peace there. In 1905 he got his chance.

The Anglo-French entente of the previous year had been based partly on an agreement dividing up spheres of influence in North Africa: the Sudan was conceded to Britain, Morocco to France. Now Germany suddenly challenged France over Morocco. It was a disastrous move, contravening Germany's self-interest in keeping France's attention diverted away from Europe by its colonial involvements overseas. Instead, the Morocco issue brought France into conflict with Germany and produced a great European crisis. Kaiser Wilhelm turned to Roosevelt for help. Finding in an obscure commercial treaty with Morocco the basis for American involvement, Roosevelt persuaded France to participate in an international conference, which was held in January 1906 at Algeciras, Spain. With U.S. diplomats playing a key role, the crisis was defused: Germany got a few token concessions, but France's dominance over Morocco was sustained.

Algeciras marked, in actuality, an ominous turning point, in which the power blocs that would become locked in battle in 1914 first squared off against one another. But at the time it looked like a diplomatic triumph, and Roosevelt's secretary of state, Elihu Root, boasted of America's success in "preserv[ing] world peace because of the power of our detachment."

Root's words prefigured how the United States would define its role among the great powers: it would be the apostle of peace, distinguished by its "detachment," by its lack of selfish interests in European affairs. But cutting athwart this internationalist impulse was the tenacious grip of America's traditional isolationism.

The Peace Movement. Enthusiasm ran high in America for the international peace movement that had been launched by the Hague Peace Conference of 1899. The Permanent Court of Arbitration it created offered new hope for the peaceful settlement of international disputes. Both the Roosevelt and the Taft administrations negotiated arbitration treaties with other countries pledging to submit their disputes to the Hague Court, only to see the treaties emasculated by a Senate unwilling to permit the nation's sovereignty to be compromised in any significant way. Nor was there any sequel to Roosevelt's initiative at Algeciras. It had been coolly received in the Senate and by the nation's press. Roosevelt's successor, William Howard Taft, was not inclined to transgress the doctrine of nonentanglement.

When Woodrow Wilson became president, he chose William Jennings Bryan to be his secretary of state. Bryan was a great apostle of world peace, and he devoted himself to negotiating a series of "cooling off" treaties with other countries—so-called, because the parties agreed to wait for one year while issues in dispute were submitted to a conciliation process. These bilateral agreements were admirable, but they were of no relevance to the explosive power politics of Europe. As tensions there reached the breaking point in 1914, the United States remained effectively on the sidelines.

Yet at Algeciras Roosevelt had rightly seen what the future would demand of America. So did the French writer Andre Tardieu, who remarked in 1908:

> The United States is . . . a world power. . . . Its power creates for it . . . a duty—to pronounce upon all those questions that hitherto have been arranged by agreement only among European powers. These powers themselves, at critical times, turn toward the United States, anxious to know its opinion. . . . The United States intervenes thus in the affairs of the universe. . . . It is seated at the table where the great game is played, and it cannot leave it.

Summary

In 1877 the United States was, by any economic or population measure, already a great power. But America's orientation was inward-looking. The lax conduct of its foreign policy—and the neglect of its naval power—reflected the absence of significant overseas concerns. America's rapid economic development, however, began to force the country to look outward—in particular, because of the felt need for outlets for its surplus products. By the early 1890s a new strategic outlook had taken hold, best expressed in the writings of Alfred T. Mahan, that called for a battleship navy, an interoceanic canal, and overseas bases from which American naval power could be projected to ensure access to vital markets in Latin America and Asia. Accompanying this new expansionism were legitimating ideas drawn from Social Darwinism, Anglo-Saxon racism, and America's earlier tradition of Manifest Destiny.

With the Spanish-American War, the opportunity presented itself for acting on these imperialist impulses. On the one hand, America's traditional antiexpansionism was briefly silenced; on the other hand, swift victory enabled the United States to seize from Spain the key possessions it wanted. In taking the Philippines, however, the United States overstepped the bounds of the kind of colonialism palatable to the country—overseas bases, not the rule of alien populations. The result was a resurgence of anti-imperialist sentiment, deepened by Filipino resistance to annexation. Even so, the McKinley administration realized the strategic goals it had set for itself, and the United States entered the twentieth century poised to fulfill its destiny as a Great Power.

In Europe, the immediate consequences were few. Only in its *rapprochement* with England, and in Roosevelt's involvement in the Moroccan crisis, did the United States begin to depart from its traditional policy against European entanglements. Regarding its regional interests in the Caribbean and Asia, however, the United States moved much more decisively, building the Panama Canal, asserting its dominance over the nearby Latin states, and pressing for the Open Door in China. When Woodrow Wilson became president, he tried to bring the conduct of America's foreign policy into closer conformity with the nation's own political ideals, only to have the limitations of that new departure driven painfully home by his intervention in the Mexican revolution. That lesson was not so fundamental, however, as to stay Wilson's hand when a great world war engulfed Europe in 1914.

TOPIC FOR RESEARCH

The Anti-Imperialists (1898–1900)

During the 1890s, the attention grabbers were those advocating American expansionism. But America also had a long tradition of anti-imperialism—of opposition to the rule of other peoples by the United States—and this tradition was very much revived by the Spanish-American War and the sudden acquisition of an overseas empire. Although they had little political success, the anti-imperialists mounted a powerful critique of expansionism and, in particular, of the taking and subsequent bloody suppression of the Philippines. What were the ideas and arguments these anti-imperialists leveled against their nation's imperial adventure? The starting point for such an inquiry is Robert L. Beisner, *Twelve Against Empire: The Anti-Imperialists, 1898–1900* (1968), in particular the chapters on the philosopher William James, the industrialist Andrew Carnegie, the journalist E. L. Godkin (the editor of the *Nation*), and the Yankee businessman and historian Charles Francis Adams. A guide to the writings of these anti-imperialists is to be found in Beisner's "Note on Sources." Beisner links anti-imperialism to the Mugwump tradition. There were, however, many anti-imperialists outside that tradition. For labor, one might study the anti-imperialist Samuel Gompers; for a woman's perspective, Jane Addams; and, to see how humor was brought to bear on the pretensions of the expansionists, Mark Twain. As victims of American racism, African-Americans had particularly ambiguous feelings about the events of 1898–1900, and these might be explored in the writings of Booker T. Washington or in the contemporary black press. A useful source book is Philip S. Foner and Richard C. Winchester, eds., *The Anti-Imperialist Reader: A Documentary History of Anti-Imperialism in the U.S.* (1984).

BIBLIOGRAPHY

The Roots of Expansionism

Two useful surveys of late nineteenth-century diplomatic history are Foster R. Dulles, *Prelude to World Power, 1865–1900* (1965), and Charles S. Campbell, *The Transformation of American Foreign Relations, 1865–1900* (1976). Focusing more narrowly on the pre-expansionist era are

David M. Pletcher, *The Awkward Years: American Foreign Relations under Garfield and Arthur* (1963), and Milton Plesur, *America's Outward Thrust: Approaches to American Foreign Affairs, 1865–1890* (1971). Invaluable as an informed guide to recent scholarship is Robert L. Beisner, *From the Old Diplomacy to the New, 1865–1900* (2nd ed., 1986). Walter LaFeber's highly influential *The New Empire, 1860–1898* (1963) has placed economic interest—especially the need for overseas markets—at the center of scholarly debate over the sources of American expansionism. On American business overseas, the definitive work is Myra Wilkins, *The Emergence of the Multinational Enterprise: American Business Abroad from the Colonial Era to 1914* (1970). Other important books dealing with aspects of American expansionism are David Healy, *U.S. Expansionism: The Imperialist Urge in the 1890s* (1970); Robert Seager, *Alfred Thayer Mahan* (1977); Lester D. Langley, *Struggle for the American Mediterranean: United States–European Rivalry in the Gulf-Caribbean* (1976); and the early chapters of Akira Iriye, *Across the Pacific: An Inner History of American–East Asian Relations* (1967).

An American Empire

On the war with Spain and its settlement, see Lewis S. Gould, *The Spanish-American War and President McKinley* (1982); David S. Trask, *The War with Spain in 1898* (1981); Frank Freidel, *A Splendid Little War* (1958); and Julius W. Pratt, *The Expansionists of 1898: The Acquisition of Hawaii and the Spanish Islands* (1936). Lewis L. Gould, *The Presidency of William McKinley* (1980), emphasizes McKinley's strong leadership. Ernest R. May, *Imperial Democracy: The Emergence of America as a Great Power* (1961), exemplifies the earlier view—that McKinley was a weak figure, driven to war by jingoistic pressures—and is especially interesting because it shows the European view of America's emergence. On the Philippines, see Richard E. Welch, *Response to Imperialism: The United States and the Philippine-American War, 1898–1903* (1979), and, for the subsequent history, Peter Stanley, *A Nation in the Making: The Philippines and the United States, 1899–1921* (1974).

Onto the World Stage

On the European context, a useful introduction is to be found in the early chapters of Felix Gilbert, *The End of the European Era, 1890 to the Present* (4th ed., 1991), and, for a stimulating interpretation, L. C. B. Seaman, *From Vienna to Versailles* (1955). On American relations with Britain, the standard work is Bradford Perkins, *The Great Rapprochement: England and the United States, 1895–1914* (1968). On progressive diplomacy, the starting point remains Howard K. Beale, *Theodore Roosevelt and the Rise of America to World Power* (1956). There are keen insights into the diplomatic views of both Roosevelt and Wilson in John Milton Cooper, *The Warrior and the Priest* (1983). On the thrust into the Caribbean, see Walter LaFeber, *The Panama Canal* (1979); Dana G. Munro, *Intervention and Dollar Diplomacy in the Caribbean, 1900–1921* (1964); and David Healy, *The United States in Cuba, 1898–1902* (1963). America's Asian involvements are treated in Thomas J. McCormick, *China Market: America's Quest for Informal Empire, 1893–1901* (1967); Michael H. Hunt, *The Making of a Special Relationship: The United States and China to 1914* (1983); and Akira Iriye, *Pacific Estrangement: Japanese and American Expansion, 1897–1911* (1972). On the Mexican involvement, see P. Edward Haley, *Revolution and Intervention: The Diplomacy of Taft and Wilson with Mexico, 1910–1917* (1975). There is a lively and critical analysis of Wilson's misguided policies in Robert E. Quirk, *An Affair of Honor: Woodrow Wilson and the Occupation of Vera Cruz* (1962). The revolution as experienced by the Mexicans is brilliantly depicted in John Womack, *Zapata and the Mexican Revolution* (1968).

TIMELINE

1867	Purchase of Alaska
1871	Settlement of *Alabama* claims
1875	Reciprocity treaty with Hawaii
1876	United States achieves favorable balance of trade
1881	Secretary of State James G. Blaine inaugurates Pan-Americanism
1889	Conflict with Germany in Samoa President Harrison begins rebuilding U.S. Navy
1890	Alfred Thayer Mahan publishes *The Influence of Seapower on History*
1893	Annexation of Hawaii fails Frederick Jackson Turner's "The Significance of the Frontier in American History" Panic of 1893 ushers in economic depression (until 1897)
1894	Sino-Japanese war begins breakup of China into spheres of influence
1895	Venezuela crisis Cuban civil war
1898	Outbreak of Spanish-American War Hawaii annexed
1899	Treaty of Paris Guerrilla war in the Philippines "Open Door" policy in China
1901	Theodore Roosevelt becomes president; diplomacy of the "big stick"
1903	Panama Canal Treaty
1904	Roosevelt Corollary
1905	U.S. mediates Franco-German crisis over Morocco
1907	Gentlemen's Agreement with Japan
1908	Root-Takahira Treaty
1909	Taft becomes president; "dollar diplomacy"

PART 5

The Modern State and Society

1914–1945

THEMATIC TIMELINE

	Government	Diplomacy	Economy	Society	Culture
	The rise of the state	**From isolation to world leadership**	**Prosperity, depression, and war**	**Nativism, migration, and social change**	**The emergence of a mass national culture**
1914	Wartime agencies expand power of the federal government	U.S. enters World War I, 1917 Wilson's Fourteen Points, 1918	Agricultural glut	Southern blacks begin migration to northern cities	Silent screen; Hollywood becomes movie capital of the world
1920	Republican ascendancy Prohibition, 1920–33 Business-government partnership	Treaty of Versailles rejected by U.S. Senate, 1920 Washington Conference sets navy limits, 1922	Economic recession, 1920–21 Booming prosperity, 1922–29 Welfare capitalism	Rise of nativism National Origins Act (1924) Mexican-American immigration increases	The Jazz Age Advertising promotes consumer culture, supports radio and new magazines
1930	Franklin D. Roosevelt becomes president, 1933 The New Deal: unprecedented government intervention in economy, social welfare, arts	Roosevelt's Good Neighbor Policy toward Latin America, 1933 Abraham Lincoln Brigade fights in Spanish Civil War U.S. neutrality proclaimed, 1939	Great Depression, 1929–41 Rise of labor movement	Farming families migrate from Dust Bowl states to California and the West	Documentary impulse Federal patronage of the arts
1940	Government mobilizes industry for war production	U.S. enters World War II, 1941 Allies defeat Axis powers; bombing of Hiroshima, 1945	War moblization ends depression	Rural whites and blacks migrate to war jobs in cities Civil rights movement revitalized	Movies enlisted to aid war effort

No single event marked the birth of modern America in the twentieth century. But by 1914 industrialization, economic expansion abroad, and the growth of a vibrant urban culture had laid the foundations for a new, distinctly *modern* American society. The patterns of localism, autonomy, and isolation that had prevailed in industrializing America were being challenged by new forces of centralization and nationalism.

First, one of the strongest forces shaping modern American society was the rise of the state. The state came late to America, and it came haltingly, compared to Western European industrialized countries. Despite the trust-busting and worker protection laws of the Progressive Era, Americans remained uneasy about the idea of a strong national state. When the United States entered World War I, policymakers were wary of a permanent concentration of government power in Washington. State bureaucratic capacity expanded to fight the war, but the wartime agencies were quickly dismantled at the end of the conflict. During the 1920s the Republican administrations of Harding and Coolidge followed a philosophy of business-government partnership, which blurred the lines between public and private power but still relied heavily on private initiatives. Most Americans continued to believe that unrestricted corporate capitalism could provide adequately for the welfare of the American people. It took the Great Depression, with its uncounted business failures and unprecedented levels of unemployment and suffering, to overthrow that long-cherished idea. President Franklin D. Roosevelt's New Deal dramatically expanded federal responsibility for regulating the economy and guaranteeing the social welfare of ordinary citizens. While the New Deal resulted in a huge growth of federal power, an even greater expansion of the state came with the massive mobilization necessitated by World War II. Unlike the experience after World War I, the new state apparatus was not dismantled when the war ended.

Second, the United States was finally drawn, slowly and reluctantly, into the position of world leadership it still occupies today. In 1918, American troops provided the margin of victory for the Allies in World War I, and President Wilson helped shape the treaties that ended the war. But America was not prepared to embrace Wilson's internationalist vision and refused to join the League of Nations. America's self-imposed isolation from world events ended definitively in 1941, when the nation threw all its energies into defeating Germany and Japan. The United States became the leader of the alliance, and the dominant world power.

Third, by 1920 American society had been transformed by the great wave of European immigration and the migration from the farm to the cities. The growth of metropolitan areas gave the nation an increasingly urban tone, while geographic mobility broke down old regional differences. Many old-stock white Americans viewed these aspects of modern America with alarm; in 1924 nativists succeeded in all but eliminating immigration from the Eastern Hemisphere. But internal migration continued to change the human face of America, as African-Americans moved north to take up factory jobs and Dust Bowl farmers moved to the Far West in search of better land.

Fourth, a defining feature of modern America was the emergence of a mass national culture. Citizens were increasingly drawn into a web of interlocking cultural experiences. Advertising and the new entertainment media—the movies, radio, and magazines—disseminated the new values of consumerism. Not even the Great Depression could wean Americans from their desire for leisure, self-fulfillment, and consumer goods. The emphasis on consumption and a rising standard of living would define the American experience for the rest of the twentieth century.

Despite the many forces combining to centralize power and decisionmaking and nationalize American culture, modern America was still marked by great and deep-seated diversity. The lives of ordinary Americans were shaped by whether they lived in cities or rural areas, whether they were black or white, male or female, rich or poor, young or old. Describing the centralizing tendencies in modern American life while connecting them to the ongoing diversity of social experience offers clues to the complexity of America's history in the 1914–1945 period, and beyond.

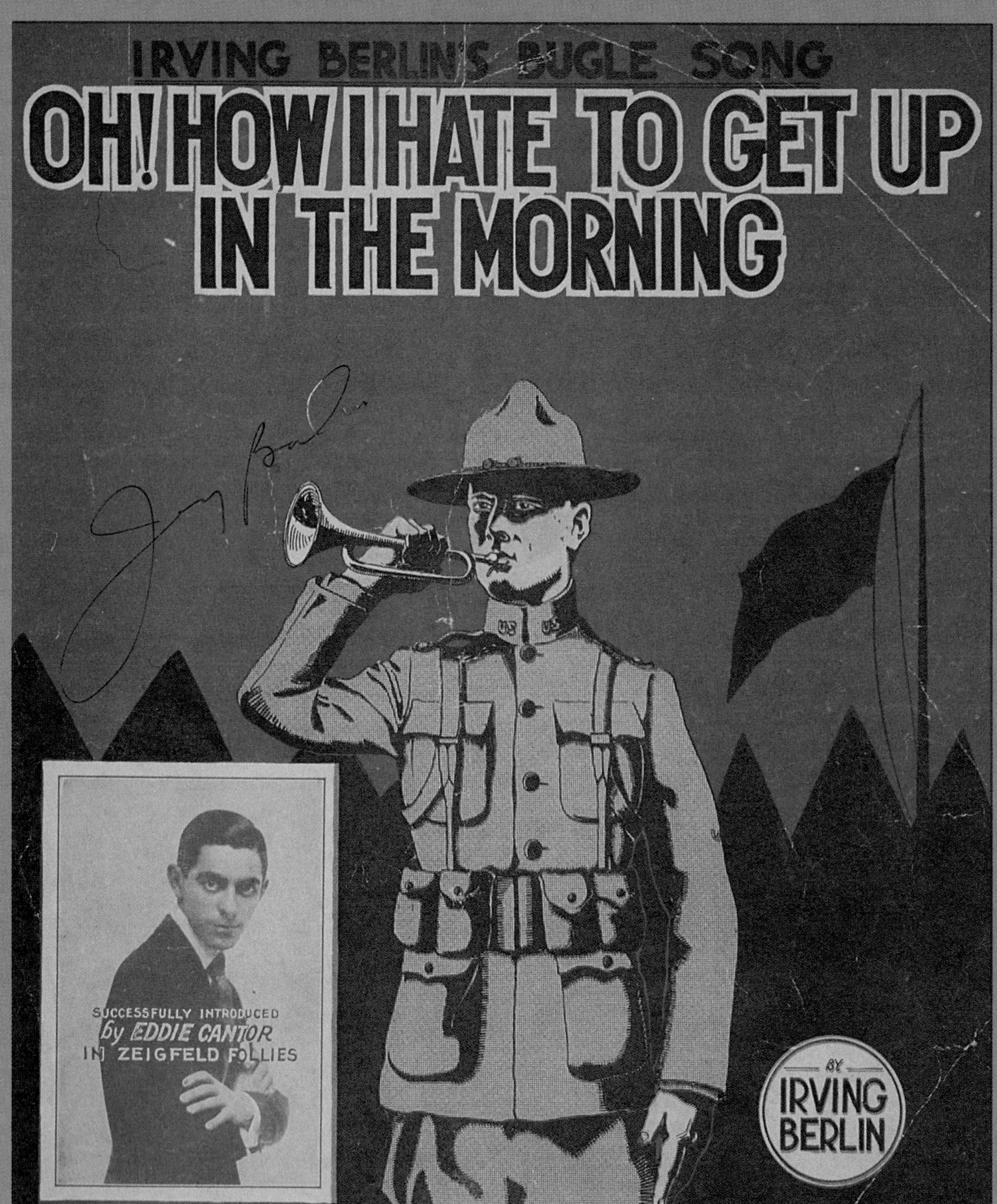

America and the War Effort

Irving Berlin's 1918 songsheet captured the ambivalence surrounding American participation in World War I: soldiers were proud to serve, but it was still hard to get up in the morning.

CHAPTER 23 *War and the American State,* 1914–1920

"It would be the irony of fate if my administration had to deal chiefly with foreign affairs," Woodrow Wilson confided to a friend early in his first term. But the United States was no longer just a regional power—it was seated at the table of the "great game" of international politics. When war broke out in Europe in August 1914 Wilson had to play his hand. For more than two years he tried to mediate as an honest broker between two sides. Only when Germany's resumption of unrestricted submarine attacks posed an unacceptable threat to American lives and shipping did he reluctantly ask for a declaration of war.

When the United States entered the conflict in 1917, President Wilson led the country with the same idealistic rhetoric he had brought to domestic concerns during the Progressive Era. American participation would make the world "safe for democracy," "end all wars," and "bring peace and safety to all nations." In the first major U.S. intervention in Great Power politics, Wilson aimed for no less than a new international order based on democratic American ideals.

Despite Woodrow Wilson's rhetoric, the United States was not ready to wage a modern war in 1917. Entirely new arms of the federal bureaucracy had to be created to coordinate the efforts of business, labor, and agriculture, a process that hastened the emergence of a national administrative state. War meant new opportunities—for women, for blacks, and for other ethnic minorities. It also meant new divisions among Americans and new hatreds, first of Germans and Austrians and then of "Bolshevik" Reds. When the war ended, the United States confronted the legacy of deep class, racial, and ethnic divisions that had surfaced during wartime mobilization.

The Great War, 1914–1918

When the Great War erupted in August 1914 (few anticipated a second world war just a generation later), most Americans saw no reason to get involved in a struggle among Europe's imperialistic powers. No vital American interests were at stake; indeed America had good relationships with both sides. But a combination of factors—economic interests, neutrality rights, cultural ties with Great Britain and France, and German miscalculations—would finally draw the United States into the war on the Allied side in 1917.

War in Europe

Almost from the moment that the Triple Entente was formed in 1907 to counter the Triple Alliance (see Chapter 22), European leaders prepared for what they saw as an inevitable conflict. The spark that ignited war came in Europe's perennial tinderbox, the Balkans. As the Ottoman Empire slowly disintegrated, Austria-Hungary and Russia competed for the remains of its Balkan possessions. Austria's seizure of the provinces of Bosnia and Herzegovina in 1908 enraged Russia and its client, the independent state of Serbia, who had wanted the provinces for itself. Serbian terrorists recruited Bosnians to agitate against Austrian rule and on

June 28, 1914, one of their number assassinated Franz Ferdinand, the heir to the Austro-Hungarian throne, and his wife in the Bosnian town of Sarajevo.

After the assassination, the complex European alliance system that had for years maintained a fragile peace now quickly pulled all the major powers into war. When Serbia failed to respond to a harsh Austrian ultimatum, Austria declared war on Serbia on July 28. Russia, which had a secret treaty with Serbia, began preparations for war. Germany in turn declared war on Russia and Russia's ally France, and invaded Belgium. On August 4, Great Britain declared war on Germany, and two days later Russia and Austria-Hungary formally entered the conflict.

The combatants were divided into two rival blocs. The Allied Powers were composed of Great Britain, France, Japan, Russia, and in 1915, Italy. They were pitted against the Central Powers, initially Germany, Austria-Hungary, Turkey, joined by Bulgaria in 1915. Because of the alliance system, the fighting spread to parts of the world beyond Europe. The Austrians and Germans faced the Russians on the Eastern Front; Turkey squared off against Russian and British troops (including units from Australia, New Zealand, and India) in the Middle East and Mesopotamia; and the British, French, and Japanese quickly seized German overseas territories in Africa, China, and the South Pacific. The resulting carnage, especially in battles such as Gallipoli in the Dardanelles, confirmed the conflict's designation as a world war. World War I was also the first modern war to involve extensive harm to civilian populations.

Since the Franco-Prussian War in 1870, massive industrialization and an escalating arms race among the Great Powers had completely transformed the technology of war. In the hands of every World War I soldier was a long-range, high-velocity rifle that could reach a target at 1000 yards, a vast improvement over the 300-yard range of the rifle-musket of the American Civil War. Significantly, the mass production of rifles in Europe was made possible by the adoption of technology first developed in Connecticut factories. Another innovation, the machine gun, also had American roots. Its Maine-born inventor, Hiram Maxim, had moved to England in the 1880s, heeding a friend's advice: "If you want to make your fortune, invent something which will allow those fool Europeans to kill each other more quickly." And make his fortune he did.

The concentrated fire of rifles and machine guns gave a tremendous advantage to defensive positions. For four bloody years between 1914 and 1918, the Allies and Central Powers faced each other on the Western Front, a small swath of territory in Belgium and northern France riddled with approximately 25,000 miles of heavily fortified trenches, enough to circle the globe. Trench warfare produced unprecedented casualties. If either side tried to break the stalemate by venturing into the "no man's land" between, soldiers were mowed down by artillery fire or poison gas, first used by the Germans at the battle of Ypres in April 1915. Between February and December 1916, the French suffered 550,000 casualties and the Germans 450,000 as Germany tried to break through the French lines at Verdun. The front did not move.

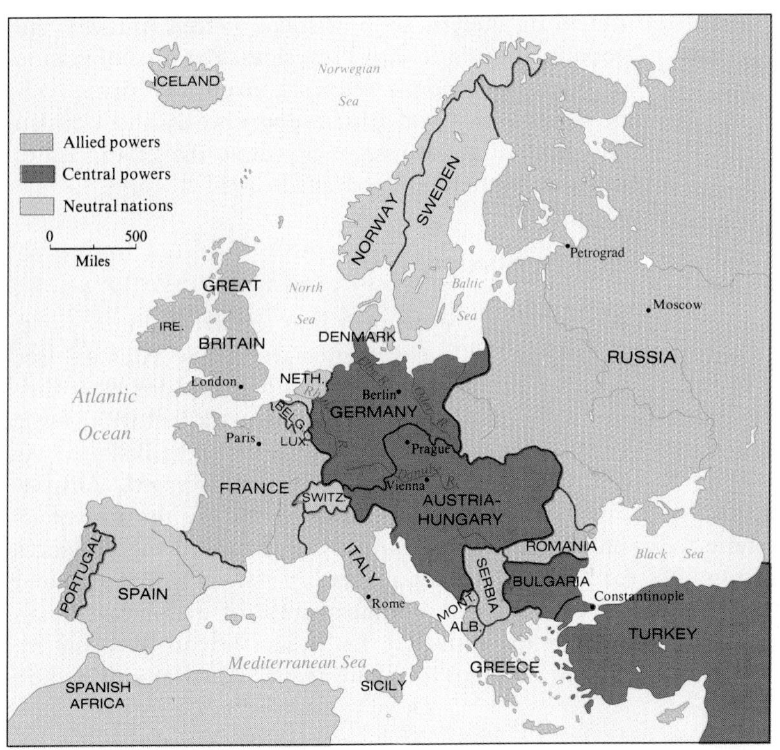

MAP 23.1

Europe at the Start of World War I

In early August 1914 a complex set of interlocking alliances drew the major European powers into war. At first the United States held aloof from the conflict. Not until April 1917 did the country enter the war on the Allied side.

The Landscape of War

World War I devastated the countryside: this was the battleground at Ypres in 1915. The carnage of trench warfare also scarred the soldiers who served in these surreal settings, causing the "burial-alive neurosis," "gas neurosis," and "soldiers' heart," all symptoms of shell-shock.

Military Technology. Military strategists struggled to find ways to break the stalemate on the Western Front. Tanks, first used in the battle of the Somme in the fall of 1916, proved effective against the machine gun and could crush through the barbed wire protecting enemy trenches, but they did not play the decisive military role they would in World War II. Nor did airplanes, despite the dramatic growth of aviation since the Wright brothers' 12-second, 120-foot flight at Kitty Hawk, North Carolina, in 1903. The technology of aerial bombardment was still primitive, so airplanes mainly flew photographic reconnaissance missions. An American Brigadier General marveled at the new perspective airplanes supplied on battle: a plane could cross the lines in a few minutes, survey enemy territory, and return quickly, "whereas the armies had been locked in the struggle, immovable, powerless to advance, for three years."

The Perils of Neutrality

Two weeks after the outbreak of war in Europe, President Wilson made the American position clear. In a widely publicized speech, the president called on Americans to be "neutral in fact as well as in name, impartial in thought as well as in action." Wilson wanted to keep out of war in order to play a larger, not a lesser, role in world affairs. The child of a Presbyterian minister, Woodrow Wilson approached foreign affairs with missionary zeal. He never doubted the superiority of the Christian values he had learned as a boy, nor did he question the chauvinistic belief that the United States was better than the rest of the world. Only if he kept America aloof from the European quarrel, Wilson reasoned, could he impartially arbitrate—and influence—its ultimate settlement.

The nation's divided loyalties also influenced President Wilson's neutrality policy. Many Americans, including Wilson himself, felt deep cultural ties to the Allies, especially Britain and France. And yet, most Catholic Irish-Americans fiercely resented the centuries-long British occupation of their home country and the cancellation of Irish Home Rule in 1914. On the other hand, 10 million immigrants had come from Germany or Austria-Hungary, and German-Americans made up the largest, best-established ethnic group in the United States. Many aspects of German culture, including classical music and Germany's university system, were widely admired. It would not have been easy for Wilson to rally the nation to the Allied side in 1914, had he chosen to try.

Many other Americans had no sympathy for either side. Pacifist sentiment was diffuse but broad. Progressive Republican senators, such as Robert La Follette of Wisconsin and George Norris of Nebraska, vehemently opposed American participation in the European conflict. Practically the entire political left, led principally by Eugene Debs and the Socialist party, condemned the war as imperialism. Pacifist groups, among them the American Union Against Militarism and the Women's Peace party founded in 1915, also mobilized popular opposition. Feminists Jane Addams and Crystal Eastman spoke out against war as an instrument of national policy. Prominent industrialists Andrew Carnegie and Henry Ford bankrolled antiwar activities. Ford spent almost half a million dollars in December 1915 to send more than a hundred men and women on a "peace ship" to Europe in the hope of negotiating an end to the war.

Conflict on the High Seas. With no stake in the territorial struggles among the European powers, the United States might well have remained neutral, had the conflict not spread to a new, undefined theater—the high seas. Here the United States initially had as many arguments with Britain as with Germany. The most troublesome issue concerned freedom of the seas and neutrality rights, that is, the freedom to trade with nations on both sides of a conflict.

By the end of August 1914, the British had succeeded in imposing a naval blockade on the Central Powers. The Allies were hoping to cut off military supplies and starve the German people into submission, but their action also effectively prevented neutral nations such as the United States from trading with Germany and its allies. American business was profiting handsomely from supplying food and arms to the combatants on both sides. The United States chafed at the British infringement of its neutrality rights, but chose to do little else, largely because the spectacular increase in trade with the Allies more than made up for the lost trade with the Central Powers. American trade with England and France grew from $824 million in 1914 to $3.2 billion in 1916, and by 1917, U.S. bankers had loaned the Allies $2.5 billion. In contrast, American trade with the Central Powers declined from $169 million in 1914 to $1 million in 1916.

To challenge British control of the seas, the German navy launched a devastating new weapon, the U-boat, short for *Unterseeboot* (undersea boat, or submarine). In February 1915, Germany announced its own naval blockade of Great Britain: German submarines would attack any ship transporting military supplies to the

Confrontation on the High Seas

These passengers and crew on a Spanish steamer have just been halted for inspection by a German submarine patrolling the North Sea in 1917. They are understandably nervous, since they know that the confrontation with the German sub could easily cost them their ship, and possibly their lives.

British Isles. Traditional rules of naval warfare required submarine commanders to warn and search a ship before it could be sunk. If a submarine surfaced to carry out this requirement, however, it lost its greatest advantage—surprise—and left itself vulnerable to attack. The Germans began sinking enemy ships, including passenger ships, without warning.

Although the Germans sank an American ship without warning on May 1, it was the sinking of a British luxury liner, the *Lusitania*, off the Irish coast on May 7, 1915, that brought the United States to the brink of war. When the *Lusitania* went down, 1,200 people died, including 128 Americans. The passenger ship, although unarmed, was carrying thousands of cases of ammunition, and passengers had been warned of the risk of attack. Yet many Americans shared the outrage of former president Theodore Roosevelt who characterized the attack as "an act of piracy." Newspapers called the loss of innocent civilian lives "mass murder." The National Security League intensified its calls for "preparedness," including a system of universal military training.

Woodrow Wilson sent a series of strongly worded notes to Germany protesting the assault on the freedom of nonbelligerents to travel on the high seas, although he did not take the additional precaution of banning Americans from traveling on the ships of Germany's enemies. The crisis continued until September when Germany announced that submarine commanders would not attack passenger ships without warning. (Eight months later the Germans halted, at least temporarily, attacks on merchant shipping.) For the Germans, the danger of drawing the United States into the war over neutrality rights and freedom of the seas far offset the benefits of attacking British ships. A temporary lull set into the naval war.

The *Lusitania* crisis divided Wilson's government into pro- and anti-British factions. Secretary of State William Jennings Bryan resigned in protest. Bryan could not support Wilson's harsh criticism of Germany's violation of neutrality rights, while the president remained silent about Britain's violation of American rights with its blockade. Throughout the stalemate years of 1915 and 1916, Wilson's attempt to mediate the European conflict came to naught.

The 1916 Election. The 1916 election failed to serve as a referendum on the American stance toward the European war. The Republicans passed over Theodore Roosevelt's prowar belligerence in favor of Justice Charles Evans Hughes of the Supreme Court, a former reform governor of New York. The Democrats renominated Woodrow Wilson. The foreign policies of the two candidates hardly differed, although the Democrats picked up votes with their widely circulated campaign slogan, "He kept us out of war." They won a narrow victory over a Republican party reunited after its 1912 split. Despite polling three million more votes than he had received in 1912, Wilson defeated Hughes by only about 600,000 popular votes and by 277 to 254 in the electoral college. This slender margin limited Wilson's options both in mobilizing the nation for war and planning the postwar peace.

Toward War. The events of early 1917 diminished whatever hopes Wilson had of staying out of the

The 1916 Campaign

This campaign van sponsored by the Women's Bureau of the Democratic National Committee linked Woodrow Wilson to the themes of prosperity and preparedness. Note the variation on the popular slogan, "Who keeps us out of war?"

conflict. On January 31, Germany announced the resumption of unrestricted submarine attacks, a decision dictated by the impasse of the ground war. Germany planned boldly to sever the trade links between America and the Allies. Although the Germans knew the renewal of attacks would almost certainly bring the United States into the war, the German General Staff assured the government that their submarines could paralyze Allied shipping before the Americans could join the fighting. In response, President Wilson broke off diplomatic relations with Germany on February 3, and though he still held off requesting a declaration of war from Congress, he ordered the War Department to prepare for hostilities.

The release of the "Zimmermann telegram" in late February 1917 also moved the country closer to war. Newspapers published an intercepted communication from Germany's foreign secretary, Arthur Zimmermann, to the German minister in Mexico City, which contained conclusive evidence of German interference in Mexican affairs. In a direct challenge to the Monroe Doctrine, Germany urged Mexico to join the war against the United States, and in return, Germany promised to help Mexico recover "the lost territory of Texas, New Mexico, and Arizona." When the telegram was decoded and made public on February 27, this threat to the territorial integrity of the United States jolted both Congressional and public opinion, especially in the West where support for the war had lagged. Combined with the resumption of unrestricted submarine warfare, this telegram further inflamed anti-German sentiments.

Although the likelihood of Mexico reconquering the border states was slim, American policymakers took this threat seriously because the situation there remained highly fluid. In the final stage of the Mexican revolution, the Constitutionalist movement led by Venustiano Carranza consolidated its power over challenger Pancho Villa. But Villa continued to stir up trouble along the border, killing sixteen U.S. citizens in January 1916 and razing the town of Columbus, New Mexico, in March. As the Mexican civil war threatened to spill over the Rio Grande into the United States, Wilson sent troops led by General John J. Pershing into Mexico after the elusive Villa; soon Pershing's force resembled an army of occupation rather than a punitive expedition. Mexican public opinion demanded that Pershing withdraw immediately. At the brink of war, the two governments backed off and U.S. troops began to leave in early 1917. The Carranza government received official recognition from Washington on March 13, 1917, less than a month before the United States entered World War I.

Declaring War. Throughout March, U-boats attacked American ships without warning, sinking three U.S. ships on March 18 alone. On April 2, 1917, after consulting the Cabinet and his own conscience, Wilson appeared before a special session of Congress to ask for a declaration of war. "The world must be made safe for democracy," he stated, in a memorable phrase intended to ennoble the conflict. America had no selfish aims: "We desire no conquest, no dominion. We seek no indemnities for ourselves, no material compensation for the sacrifices we shall freely make. We are but one of the champions of the rights of mankind."

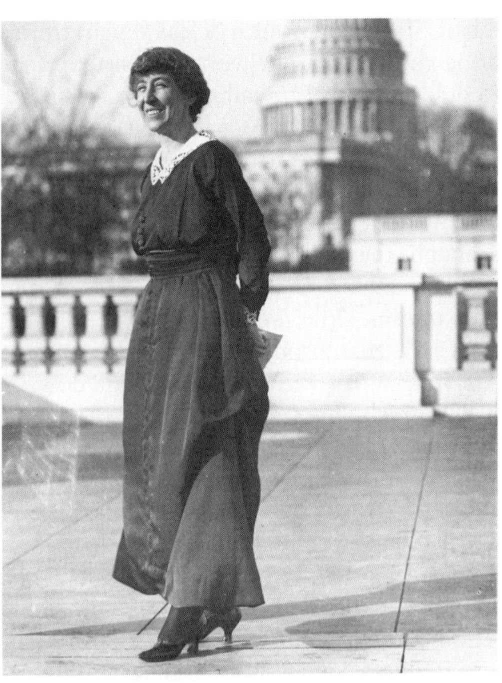

The First Woman in Congress
In 1916, Jeannette Rankin, a former suffrage organizer, became the first woman elected to Congress. Her vote against U.S. entry into World War I cost her the chance for election to the Senate in 1918. In 1940, Rankin once again won election to Congress from Montana. True to her lifelong pacifism, she cast the only vote against American entry into World War II.

Four days later, on April 6, 1917, the United States declared war on Germany. Six senators and fifty members of the House voted against the action, including Representative Jeannette Rankin of Montana, the first woman elected to Congress. "I want to stand by my country," she declared, "but I cannot vote for war."

Over There

To native-born Americans especially, Europe was a great distance away, literally "over there," as the lyrics of a popular World War I song described it. After the declaration of war, many citizens were surprised to learn that the United States planned to send troops to Europe—they had assumed that the nation's participation could be limited to military and economic aid.

In May 1917, General John J. Pershing, recently returned from pursuing Pancho Villa in Mexico, set sail for London and Paris to determine how the Americans could best support the war effort. The answer was clear: as the French Marshall Joseph Joffre put it, "Men, men, and more men." The problem was that the United States had always avoided having a large standing army in peacetime. There were only about 200,000 soldiers, mostly life-time volunteers, on active duty in early 1917. To field a credible fighting force, the government turned to conscription.

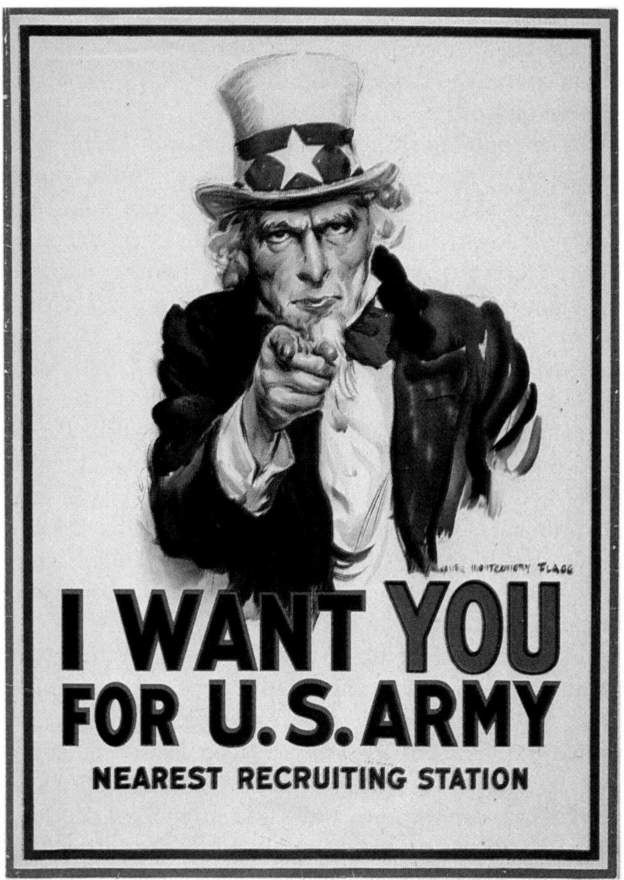

Call to Arms

To build popular support for the war effort, the government called on the services of such artists as Howard Chandler Christy, Charles Dana Gibson, and James Montgomery Flagg. This 1917 recruiting poster by Flagg was adapted from a June 1916 cover of *Leslie's Illustrated Weekly Newspaper*. The model was the artist.

Conscription. The passage of the Selective Service Act in May 1917 demonstrated the increasing impact of the state on ordinary Americans. Unlike the resistance to conscription during the Civil War, no major draft riots marred its implementation. The selective service system worked in part because it combined central direction from Washington with local administration and civilian control, and thus did not tread unnecessarily on traditions of individual freedom and local autonomy. On a single day, June 5, 1917, more than 9.5 million men between the ages of 21 and 30 were processed for military service at their local voting precincts. Draft registration demonstrated the potential bureaucratic capacity of the American state.

Although compliance was not universal, most male citizens went along with the draft's premise of service (a key Progressive word) as a responsibility of modern citizenship. By the end of the war, almost 4 million men, plus a few thousand female navy clerks and army nurses, were in uniform. Nearly 3 million men were inducted by a draft lottery; the rest volunteered. Over 300,000 men evaded the draft (they were called "slackers") and another 4,000 were classified as conscientious objectors.

President Wilson chose General Pershing to head the American Expeditionary Force (AEF), but the newly raised army did not have an immediate impact on the European fighting. The new recruits had to be trained and outfitted. Then they had to wait for one of the few available transport ships to take them thousands of miles across the submarine-infested Atlantic. By June 1917 only 15,000 AEF troops had arrived in France.

At first, the main contribution of the United States was to secure the safety of the seas. When the United States entered the war, German submarines were sinking Allied ships at the alarming rate of about 900,000 tons a month. The U-boats had seriously hampered the ability to send supplies and munitions to the Allies and threatened the transport of American troops to the European front. Adopting a plan that aimed for safety in numbers, the government began sending armed convoys across the Atlantic. The plan worked. No American soldiers were killed on their way to Europe. Allied shipping losses were cut to 400,000 tons a month by late 1917, to 200,000 tons by April 1918.

Meanwhile, trench warfare continued its deadly grind on the Western Front. Allied commanders pleaded for American reinforcements to be assigned to their units, but Pershing was reluctant to put his independent fighting unit under non-American commanders. Because the AEF was not ready as a fighting force until May 1918, the brunt of the fighting continued to fall on the French and British, and Britain's imperial troops, primarily from Canada and Australia.

The Russian Revolution and the Collapse of the Eastern Front. On the Eastern Front, the strain of fighting the Germans had exposed the weaknesses of the Russian government headed by Tsar Nicholas II, and a general mutiny of the troops led to the overthrow of the monarchy in March 1917. The new provisional government headed by Prince George Lvov and socialist Alexander Kerensky promised democratic reforms, but it also insisted on continuing the war. Russian workers and peasants were sick of war—sick of the seemingly endless food shortages at home, sick of the horrendous casualties at the front. Conditions were ripe for a second revolution.

The communist theorist Vladimir Ilych Lenin, who had been living in exile in Switzerland when the March revolution took place, saw his chance. Lenin was a follower of Karl Marx, and he anticipated that a period of the "dictatorship of the proletariat" [workers] would be necessary to root out capitalism before a classless society could emerge. The Germans, hoping to promote internal strife in Russia, cannily arranged Lenin's safe passage home on a sealed railroad car. Lenin and a group of Bolshevik revolutionaries arrived in Petrograd (later Leningrad, and now St. Petersburg) in April 1917 and began their agitation against the provisional government. On November 6, Lenin directed a Bolshevik-led coup against the government and quickly consolidated his control by promising "peace, land, and bread" to the long-suffering masses.

The new Bolshevik government kept the first part of its promise. Russia agreed to a cease-fire with Germany and Austria-Hungary on December 15, 1917, and signed the Treaty of Brest-Litovsk on March 3, 1918. The Bolsheviks surrendered massive territories—Russian Poland, the Ukraine, the Baltic provinces, and Finland—in return for an end to hostilities. Yet instead of peace, the Russian people got three more years of war, a vicious, devastating civil war.

Allied Victory in the West. The plight of the new Soviet state would command the Allies' attention after the armistice. When hostilities ended with Russia, Germany turned its full fighting force to break the stalemate on the Western Front. On March 21, 1918, the Germans launched a major offensive and by May the German army had advanced to the Marne River within 50 miles of Paris. Allied leaders intensified their calls for fresh American troops, and Pershing, who was under orders to keep the AEF a separate fighting unit, relented a bit to help the Allies bolster their defenses. About 60,000 American soldiers helped the French repel the Germans in the battles of Château-Thierry and Belleau Wood in May and June.

American reinforcements now began to arrive in force. Fresh troops flooded the ports of Liverpool in England and Brest and Saint Nazaire in France—245,000 in May 1918, 278,000 in June, and 306,000 in July. From there they worked their way slowly to the front along the clogged French transportation system. The Allied force, augmented by 85,000 American troops, brought the German offensive to a halt in mid-July. At that point, a million American troops were in France, and the counteroffensive began. On July 18, the Allies with 270,000 American troops began a drive to push the Germans back from their position on the Marne, which was successful. Approximately 100,000 American soldiers helped the British push the Germans back north of the Somme River.

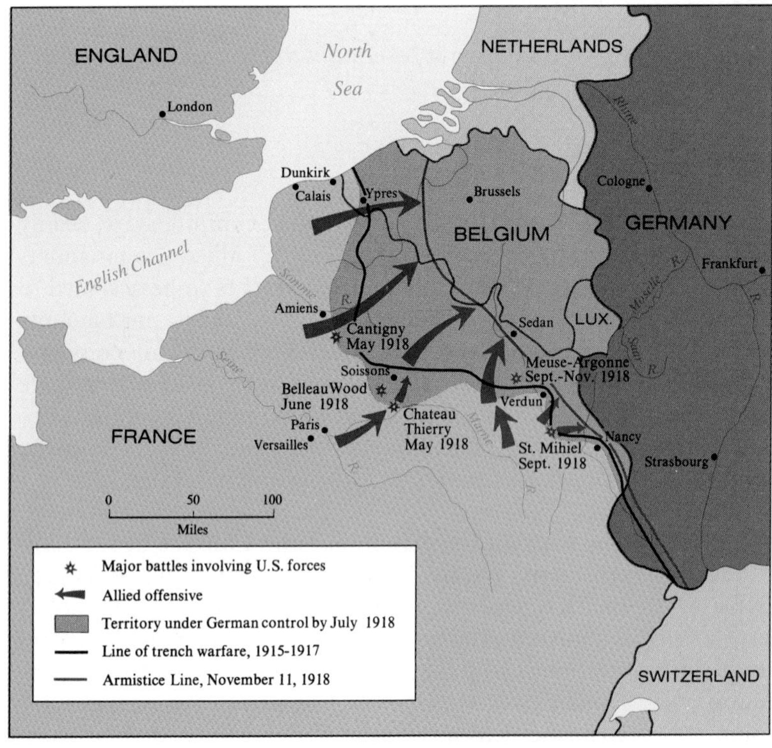

MAP 23.2

U.S. Participation on the Western Front, 1918

When American troops finally reached the European front in significant numbers in 1918, the Allied and Central powers had been grinding each other down in a war of attrition for almost four years. The influx of American troops and supplies broke the stalemate. Successful offensive maneuvers by the American Expeditionary Force included Belleau Wood, Château-Thierry, and the Meuse-Argonne campaign.

AMERICAN VOICES

Mustard Gas *Frederick Pottle*

Frederick Pottle volunteered for service as an enlisted man in the Medical Corps. He describes here the effects of mustard gas during the battles of Belleau Woods and Château-Thierry in June of 1918.

Indeed, those dreadful mustard-gas cases were probably the most painful we had to witness in all our service. As a matter of fact, the majority were in much less serious plight than the wounded men. Mustard gas (it has nothing to with mustard) is a heavy liquid, which, though fairly volatile, will remain for some time clinging to grass and undergrowth, and will burn any flesh with which it comes in contact. It is especially adapted for use by a retreating army. By soaking down with mustard gas the area through which the pursuing American troops had to advance, the Germans made sure that a large number of the advancing force would be incapacitated. The soldier's clothing soon becomes impregnated with the stuff as he brushes through the undergrowth, and the burns develop through the help of moisture. Those parts of the body subject to excessive perspiration are especially affected. The burns are extremely painful, but in general not fatal unless the gas has been inhaled, or (as with other surface burns) a third or more of the total skin area has been affected. A bad feature of mustard gas, however, is that it almost invariably produces temporary, but complete, blindness. Nothing demoralizes a man so much as the fear of losing his sight, and telling him that he will see again in a day or two generally fails to reassure him. The gas cases began to arrive at Juilly as early as June 12. Since most of them were immediately evacuable, we made temporary wards for them in the great cloisters which ran around two sides of the court in front of Wards F and G—the children's dormitories. By the sixteenth there were nearly seven hundred gassed men there, just out of the glare of the sunny court, lying fully dressed on blanket-covered cots, some of them badly gassed in the lungs and fighting horribly for breath, which could be a little prolonged by giving them oxygen; nearly all blinded, many delirious, all crying, moaning, tossing about. For most of the patients there was nothing to do but renew frequently the wet dressings which relieved somewhat the smart of the burns, and to try to restore their lost morale. For those who had been gassed worst, nothing effectual could be done. They were spared much by being in general delirious, but it required the constant attention of several orderlies to keep some of them in bed. Later on, the hospital service was so organized that the gas cases were handled by special gas hospitals. After we left Juilly we almost never received gas victims unless they were also wounded.

Source: Frederick A. Pottle, *Stretchers: The Story of a Hospital Unit on the Western Front* (New Haven: Yale University Press, 1929), 117–118.

In mid-September 1918, General Pershing, leading 500,000 Americans and 100,000 French soldiers, launched an offensive aimed at closing a hole in Allied lines at Saint-Mihiel. After four days of heavy artillery shelling of German positions, the Germans, who had been preparing to evacuate the area, retreated. On September 26, Pershing launched the last major assault of the war, which pushed the enemy back across the Selle River near Verdun and broke the German defenses. This forty-seven-day Meuse-Argonne campaign represented the main American military contribution to the fighting.

The flood of American troops and supplies during the last six months of fighting provided the Allied margin of victory. In many ways, this American contribution was emblematic of the shift in international power as European dominance declined and the United States emerged as a new world leader. World War I ended on November 11, 1918, when German representatives signed an armistice in the railway car of the French Marshall Foch.

The American Fighting Force

About two million American soldiers were in France when the war ended. Two-thirds of them had seen at least brief action on the western front, but most American "doughboys" escaped the horrors of sustained trench warfare that had sapped the morale of Allied and German troops. (The nickname may have derived from

AMERICAN LIVES

Edward Vernon Rickenbacker, Fighter Pilot

He was born Edward Rickenbacher in Columbus, Ohio, on October 8, 1890. Notice the slight but significant difference in the spelling: he adopted a less Germanic version of his last name, and added an English-sounding middle name, at the beginning of World War I. Even before his designation as the "American Ace of Aces" for shooting down more enemy craft than any other American pilot, Eddie Rickenbacker was front page news as a celebrity race car driver. He began racing at the age of sixteen, and in 1911 competed in the first Indianapolis 500 road race. The holder of the world speed record of 134 miles per hour, he earned the fabulous sum of $60,000 at the height of his racing career in 1916.

When the United States entered the war in 1917, Rickenbacker immediately enlisted. He was sent to France as a member of General John J. ("Black Jack") Pershing's motor car staff, although he was not Pershing's personal chauffeur, as legend sometimes has it. But his skills as a mechanic and a driver brought him to the attention of Colonel Billy Mitchell, one of Pershing's senior air staff, who helped arrange Rickenbacker's transfer to the Air Service. At that point, he had never flown a plane. He was originally told that at the age of twenty-eight he was too old to fly combat, but he proved the doubters wrong: his quick reflexes and competitive instincts from his racing career made him a superb pilot. Rickenbacker dutifully informed his mother about his change in assignment, telling her that flying was safer than race car driving because there was lots of room in the sky. She in turn cautioned him to be sure to fly slow and close to the ground.

In March 1918, Rickenbacker was posted to the 94th Aero Pursuit Squadron, the first all-American air squadron to go into action on the Western Front. The 94th was known as "hat-in-the ring," for the American custom of throwing a hat into the ring as an invitation to battle, and they adopted that representation as the insignia for their planes. But at first the American pilots did not have much of an impact on the fighting, hampered by antiquated French planes that did not even have machine guns. Only in August 1918 did the 94th get new planes, French-made SPADS, a single-seat pursuit fighter equipped with machine guns, which was fast and reliable.

When the war broke out, airplanes were used mainly for reconnaisance and artillery spotting, but the addition of machine guns transformed planes into offensive weapons. With guns mounted in front, combat pilots zoomed in on the tail of an enemy craft; to aim their machine gun, they simply aimed the plane at the intended target and poured bullets into both the plane and the pilot before beating a hasty retreat. French inventor Roland Garros made aerial combat possible by figuring out how to synchronize the firing of bullets with the rotation of the propeller.

Although German squadrons often hunted in packs (the so-called flying circus under the direction of Baron Manfred von Richthofen, the German ace known as the "Red Baron"), American pilots preferred to sneak up on their targets one at a time. These pilots had great respect for each other's skills, and would often joust in the air for position until one of them ran out of fuel and headed for home. Eddie Rickenbacker remembered no personal animosity against his German foes and was always delighted to learn that a downed pilot had escaped with his life. (This rarely happened since few aircraft were equipped with parachutes.) But once locked in a dogfight, Rickenbacker remembered, "I had no regrets over killing a fellow human being. I do not believe that at that moment I even considered the matter. Like nearly all air fighters, I was an automaton behind the gun barrels of my plane. I never thought of killing an individual but of shooting down an enemy plane." He fought in 134 air battles in all, and narrowly escaped death on several occasions.

Flying Aces
One of America's best known aces was former professional race car driver Eddie Rickenbacker (middle). Note the "hat-in-the ring" insigna on the plane.

In September 1918, Rickenbacker was named Commander of the 94th Squadron, and most of his victories came in the last two months of the war. In one encounter, for which he was later awarded the Congressional Medal of Honor, he singlehandedly took on seven German planes and downed two of them. He shot down fourteen enemy aircraft in the month of October alone, bringing his total to twenty-six confirmed victories and clinching his status as the American Ace of Aces. Under his leadership, the 94th "Hat in the Ring" Squadron became the most victorious American air unit of the war. Eddie Rickenbacker returned to the United-States a national hero, publishing a book about his war experiences, *Fighting the Flying Circus*, in 1919.

World War I dramatically accelerated the growth of aviation, both in its commercial and military applications. After the war, Eddie Rickenbacker dabbled in racing and automobile production before joining Eastern Airlines as its general manager in 1935; in1938 he became its president. As head of Eastern, then one of the flagships of modern aviation, Rickenbacker served as a spokesperson for commercial aviation until his retirement in 1963. Over the course of his lifetime (he died in 1973), this new industry grew up. Eddie Rickenbacker symbolized the fascination of early flight, even in the unlikely arena of war, and its possibilities for individual heroism. But just as significantly, he stood for the development of commercial aviation, which in the years after World War II would revolutionize world travel.

the buttons on the uniforms of American infantrymen, which resembled dumplings made of dough.) During the eighteen months that the United States fought in the war, 50,585 American servicemen were killed in action. Another 60,000 died from other causes, mainly the influenza epidemic that swept the world in 1918–1919. The nation suffered minimal casualties compared with the 8 million soldiers lost by the Allies and the Central Powers. The French lost far more soldiers in the siege of Verdun than the United States did in the entire war.

Although individual bravery grew increasingly anachronistic in the midst of modern warfare, the war generated its share of American heroes. Sergeant Alvin York singlehandedly killed twenty-five Germans and took 132 prisoners at the battle of Châtel-Chéhéry in the Meuse-Argonne campaign. Although air power played only a minor part in the actual conduct of the war, it captivated the popular imagination. One of America's best known aces was former professional race car driver Eddie Rickenbacker. The exploits of daredevil pilots, fighting it out in the skies like medieval knights in combat armor, provided a thrill that contrasted with the monotony of trench warfare. The popular fascination with Rickenbacker and York suggests a deep-seated need to annoint individual heroes in what had become an increasingly depersonalized and mechanized pursuit of war.

Fighting the Flu

The influenza epidemic of 1918–1919 strained the resources of a public health system already fully mobilized for the war effort. Here sanitation workers don protective masks to lessen their risk of contracting the often deadly disease.

Military Morality. High ideals set the tone for military service. Reformers urged the adoption of progressive solutions to the vices of alcohol and sex, and government and military officials agreed. Reflecting the anti-liquor fever taking hold in America, Secretary of the Navy Josephus Daniels declared navy ships dry. The army banned drinking by soldiers in uniform, and prohibited liquor on army bases and their surrounding localities.

The army also mounted an ambitious program of sex education. In an era when people rarely discussed sex in public, the army program brought the subject into the open. Concerned that venereal disease might sap the strength of the fighting men (antibiotics had not yet been developed), the army launched an anti-VD campaign. As soldiers ate dinner in their mess halls, they looked up at posters that proclaimed "A German Bullet is Cleaner than a Whore" or "How could you look the flag in the face if you were dirty with gonorrhea?" In France, the army continued its campaign against venereal disease, although it never totally stopped American soldiers from patronizing French prostitutes. Army-issue condoms and safety razors, a novelty that changed the shaving habits of an entire generation of men, were two of the souvenirs that American soldiers brought home from France.

Intelligence Testing. Intelligence testing joined the progressive belief in social science to wartime needs. To sort all the conscripts, the Army used the newly developed Stanford-Binet intelligence test. Army psychologists, who administered the test to all recruits, expressed shock at the level of illiteracy among draftees—as high as 25 percent. Racial and ethnic variations in the test scores reinforced stereotypes about the supposed intellectual inferiority of blacks and immigrants, who scored lower on the tests. But the lower scores stemmed from the cultural biases of the tests rather than innate differences in intelligence among ethnic groups. The army dropped the test in 1919, but revised versions of intelligence tests soon became a standard part of the American educational system.

Reformers expressed high hopes for the democratization and educational potential of military service. Theodore Roosevelt, whose offer to raise an independent regiment was politely but firmly refused by President Wilson, hoped that army duty would foster class unity. "The military tent where they all sleep side by side will rank next to the public school among the great agents of democratization," Roosevelt predicted. Yet the army reflected the same divisions found in American society. About a fifth of the American soldiers had been born in another country, leading some people to call the AEF the American Foreign Legion. Army censors had to be able to read forty-nine languages to check letters written home by American doughboys. The "Americanization" of even the American army remained imperfect at best.

Racism in the Armed Forces. African-American soldiers received the worst treatment. White Southerners became especially alarmed at training blacks to bear arms, and few whites from any part of the country would have consented to serve under a black officer. As a result, blacks were organized into rigidly segregated units, in all but a few cases under the control of white officers. In addition, blacks were always assigned to the most menial tasks, such as laborers, stevedores, and messboys. Although the policy of segregation minimized contact between black and white recruits, racial violence erupted at several camps. The worst incident occurred in Houston in August 1917, where black members of the Twenty-fourth Infantry's Third Battalion killed sixteen white soldiers and police officers after police beat up two black soldiers. The army immediately tried more than a hundred black soldiers in military courts, and disbanded the battalion. Thirteen black soldiers were executed within days, and six more were later hanged.

The black experience in World War I reflected the persistent gap between progressive rhetoric and reality. Over 400,000 black men served in the military, 13 percent of the armed forces; 92 percent were draftees, a far higher rate than for whites. In France, black soldiers found the French far more willing to socialize with them on an equal basis than many white American soldiers. Despite documented cases of extreme heroism, no black received the Congressional Medal of Honor, the nation's highest military award.

A Black Veteran Returns Home

Black soldiers received segregated and unequal treatment at every stage of their military service. When the war ended, black veterans faced hostility from many whites alarmed that blacks no longer "knew their place."

Demobilization. Just as it had taken months to get troops to Europe to join the fighting, similar delays, minus the U-boats, slowed demobilization at war's end. June 1919 was the peak month for returns, with 368,000 men—plus a few thousand women who had served in France as telephone operators, canteen workers, and nurses—arriving stateside to begin the process of readjusting to civilian life. When their ships sailed into New York harbor, many mouthed the old vaudeville saying, "If the Statue of Liberty wants to see my face again, she'll have to turn around" to emphasize that they had no desire to leave American shores again.

After the armistice, the war continued to live on in the minds of the men and women who had gone "over there" to serve. Spared the horror of sustained battle, many members of the AEF had experienced the war more as tourists than as soldiers. Before joining the army, recruits had barely traveled beyond their hometowns, and the journey across the ocean to Europe was a monumental, once-in-a-lifetime event. In 1919 a group of former AEF officers formed the American Legion "to preserve the memories and incidents of our association in the great war." The word "legion" perfectly captured the romantic, almost chivalric memories that many veterans chose to hold of their wartime service. Only later did disillusionment over the contested legacy of World War I set in.

Mobilizing the Home Front

Fighting World War I required extraordinary economic mobilization on the home front. Business, the work force, and the public all cooperated to win the war. At the height of mobilization, a fourth of the gross national product went for war production. Business and government proved especially congenial partners, a collaboration which typified the pattern of statebuilding in America. Similarly, the rapid dismantling of this apparatus when the war ended confirmed the ongoing unease that Americans felt with a strong bureaucratic state.

Financial and Economic Mobilization

Even before the formal declaration of war, the United States had geared up as the arsenal for Allied supplies and financing. As tons of American grain and military supplies crossed the Atlantic, America reversed its historic debtor position and become a leading creditor nation when Allies paid for their purchases in gold. In addition, U.S. financial institutions increasingly provided capital for foreign investment on the world market now that the British pound sterling was diverted to the Allied war effort. This shift from debtor to creditor status, which would last until the 1970s, guaranteed the nation a major role in international financial affairs after the war and confirmed the new role of the United States as a world power.

Paying for the War. The monetary cost to the United States of World War I reached $33 billion, a huge sum for a government unaccustomed to large expenditures. The disruption in international trade after the outbreak of war in 1914 had reduced the revenues raised by tariffs, ordinarily a major source of federal revenues. Wilson's Treasury Secretary William McAdoo had two options: impose a national sales tax or increase income taxes. (The Sixteenth Amendment to the Constitution which allowed a federal income tax had been approved in 1913.) Wilson and McAdoo, in conjunction with progressive Democratic leaders in Congress, chose the second option. The resulting Revenue Acts of 1916 and 1917 transformed the previously limited income tax into the foremost instrument of federal taxation, surely one of the most lasting legacies of World War I. The Wilson administration rejected a mass-based income tax falling on wages and salaries in favor of placing the burden on wealthier individuals and corporations. The corporate excess profits tax signaled a direct and unprecedented intrusion of the state into the workings of corporate capitalism. By 1918, U.S. corporations were paying over $2.5 billion in excess-profits taxes per year, more than half of all federal taxes.

In all, the United States raised about a third of the cost of the war from taxes; the rest came from loans, especially the popular Liberty Loans that encouraged public support for the war effort. The government also helped pay for the war by using the Federal Reserve System to expand the money supply, which made it easier to borrow money. Even so, the federal debt increased from $1 billion in 1915 to $20 billion in 1920. Federal expenditures never again dropped to their prewar levels, but by the 1920s the federal budget was posting a surplus.

Wartime Economic Regulation. In addition to financing the war, mobilization required coordination of economic production. The government never seriously considered exercising total control over the economy, but the war hastened the creation of a centralized national administrative structure to match the consolidated power of the business and banking communities. For economic expertise, the government turned primarily to those who knew the capacities of the economy best—the nation's business leaders. Executives flocked to Washington, regarding war work as both a duty and an opportunity for professional advancement.

A series of boards and agencies tried to rationalize and coordinate the economy. A network of industrial committees linked war agencies to organizations in private industry, and government leaders utilized a combination of public and private power to enforce their decisions. This semi-voluntarist approach was an attempt to find a middle ground between total state control of the economy and letting business operate without direction. Like most compromises, it had mixed results.

The Fuel Administration, directed by President Harry Garfield of Williams College, allocated the coal resources necessary for operation of the nation's railroads and factories. Its task became more difficult during the severe winter of 1917–1918, when coal shortages occurred in major northeastern cities and industries. At one point, Garfield ordered all factories east of the Mississippi River to shut down for four days. By raising the price of coal to artificially high levels, the Fuel Administration stimulated production of coal from previously unprofitable mines to meet the nation's energy needs.

The Railroad War Board, under Secretary of the Treasury William G. McAdoo, coordinated the nation's sprawling transportation system by taking over the railroads in December 1917. (The army needed the railroads to move its troops.) The board guaranteed railroad owners a "standard return" equal to average earnings between 1915 and 1917, and promised that the carriers would be returned to private control no later than twenty-one months after the war. The government quickly fulfilled that pledge after the armistice.

Perhaps the most successful government agency was the Food Administration, created in August 1917 and led by future president Herbert Hoover, a Stanford-trained engineer. Using the slogan "Food will win the war," Hoover encouraged the expansion of domestic production of wheat and other grains from 45 million acres in 1917 to 75 million in 1919. The increased output not only fed the large domestic market, but also allowed a threefold rise in food exports to war-torn Europe. At no time did the government contemplate domestic food rationing; most consumers patriotically followed government propaganda to "Serve Just Enough" and "Use All Left-Overs." "Wheatless" Mondays, "Meatless" Tuesdays, and "Porkless" Thursdays and Saturdays resulted in substantial conservation of food resources. Hoover emerged from the war as one of the nation's most admired public figures.

The War Industries Board. The central agency for mobilizing wartime industry was the War Industries Board (WIB), established in July 1917. After a fumbling start that showed the limits of voluntarism in a national emergency, the Wilson administration reorganized the board under the centralized control of Bernard Baruch, a Wall Street financier, in March 1918. Baruch's financial experience and his ability to cajole American business to cooperate with the government contributed significantly to the success of the WIB.

The WIB reflected the ambivalent attitude of Americans towards government intervention in the economy. When Wilson elevated Baruch to a position of "industrial czar," he recognized the need for central authority in wartime, but he always saw the WIB as a temporary expedient. Baruch proceeded to organize the WIB around specific commodities and industries, whose administrators then negotiated such issues as market allocation with their equivalents in private industry. This frequent consultation blurred the lines between the needs of business and government, and often left patterns of private power undisturbed.

The WIB produced an unparalleled expansion of the economic powers of the federal government. The board allocated scarce resources, gathered economic data and statistics, controlled the flow of raw materials, ordered conversion of factories to war production, set prices, imposed efficiency and standardization procedures, and coordinated purchasing. The board had the authority to compel compliance, but Baruch preferred to win voluntary acceptance from business. He saw himself as a partner of business, not its enemy. To a large degree, business supported this government expansion because federal growth coincided with its interests so well. Despite higher taxes, corporate profits soared, aided by the suspension of antitrust laws, competitive bidding during wartime, and guaranteed profits on war work. War profits produced an economic boom that continued without interruption until 1920.

With the signing of the armistice in November 1918, the United States scrambled to dismantle its wartime controls. Wilson disbanded the WIB effective January 1, 1919, resisting suggestions that keeping the board in place at least briefly would help stabilize the economy during the period of demobilization. Wilson was determined to take "the harness off." Like most Americans, he could tolerate planning power in the hands of the government during an emergency, but not as a permanent feature of the American economy.

Although U.S. participation in the war lasted only eighteen months, it left an important legacy for the modern bureaucratic state. Entire industries had been organized as never before, linked to a maze of government agencies and executive departments. The contours of the modern system of progressive income taxation took shape. The partnership between business and government had been mutually beneficial, a lesson that both partners would put to use in the statebuilding that occurred in the 1920s and beyond.

Mobilizing American Workers

Wars are never won solely by armies and business and government leaders. Farmers, factory workers, indeed the entire civilian population have crucial roles to play. However, World War I produced fewer rewards for workers than for owners and managers.

Organized Labor. Labor's position improved during the war, although it remained a junior partner to business and government. Samuel Gompers, leader of the American Federation of Labor (AFL), traded labor's support of the war for a voice in government policy. This bargain proved acceptable to government and business leaders concerned with averting crippling strikes. Gompers represented labor's interests on the National Defense Advisory Commission. Also, the War Labor Policies Board, headed by Felix Frankfurter, a Harvard law professor, coordinated labor and welfare programs in government and industry. The United States Employment Service placed four million workers in war jobs.

The National War Labor Board. Far more important to workers was the National War Labor Board, established in April 1918, which arbitrated labor disputes. Comprised of representatives of labor, management, and the public, the NWLB was chaired by former President William Howard Taft, representing management, and Frank P. Walsh, a labor lawyer. In some ways, the NWLB functioned more as a judicial than an administrative body; labor leaders often called it "labor's Supreme Court."

The board's decisions favored labor more often than management, giving important federal support to the goals of the labor movement. During the eighteen months of the NWLB's existence, it arbitrated about 1,250 cases. The board established an eight-hour day for war workers, with time-and-a-half pay for overtime; it also endorsed equal pay for women workers. Workers were not allowed to disrupt war production through strikes or other disturbances; in return, the NWLB supported the right of workers to organize unions and required employers to deal with shop committees. The NWLB had ample power to enforce its decisions and intervene in unresolved disputes. For example, when the Smith and Wesson arms plant in Springfield, Massachusetts, flouted NWLB rules by discriminating against union employees, the federal government took over the firm.

After years of federal hostility toward labor, the actions of the National War Labor Board improved labor's status and power. From 1916 to 1919, AFL membership grew by almost a million workers, reaching over three million by the end of the war. Few of these wartime gains lasted, however. Wartime inflation ate up most of the wage hikes, and a virulent postwar anti-union movement drove union membership into a rapid decline that lasted until the 1930s. The labor movement did not yet have enough power to bargain on an equal basis with business and government.

Black and Mexican-American Workers. When soldiers go to war, jobs open up for workers normally excluded from them. Black men, for example, found jobs in northern defense industries that never would have accepted them in peacetime. The magnet of industrial jobs and an escape from the southern agricultural system lured between 400,000 and 450,000 blacks to northern and midwestern cities such as St. Louis, Chicago, Cleveland, and Detroit during the war. Henry Ford sent agents to the South to recruit black workers for his automobile plants and even provided special trains to bring them north. In Detroit blacks shared in the unprecedented five-dollar daily wage that Ford had instituted in 1914. The migration of blacks from the South, which began in World War I and continued until the 1970s, represented one of the most fundamental population shifts of the twentieth century.

Mexican-Americans in California, Texas, New Mexico, and Arizona also found new opportunities during the war. The disruption of immigration from abroad opened up industrial opportunities, as did the conscription of U.S. citizens. Many left farm labor for new industrial opportunities, often settling in segregated neighborhoods (*barrios*) in urban areas. Other Mexican-Americans, however, feared they would be drafted into the army, and returned to Mexico. The exodus of so many workers increased the labor shortage in agriculture. The government quickly exempted agricultural workers from the draft, whereupon the migration resumed. At least a hundred thousand Mexican-Americans entered the United States between 1917 and 1920.

Wartime Opportunities

Women took on new jobs during the war, working as mail carriers, police officers, drill-press operators, and farm laborers attached to the Women's Land Army. These three women clearly enjoyed the camaraderie of working in a railroad yard in 1918. When the war ended, women usually lost such employment.

Women and the War Effort

Women made up the largest group that took advantage of new opportunities in wartime. White women and, to a lesser degree, black and Hispanic women, found jobs open to them in factories and war industries as never before. About one million women joined the labor force for the first time. In addition, many of the nation's eight million women who already held jobs switched from low-paying fields, such as domestic service, to higher-paying industrial work. Americans soon got used to the novel sight of woman streetcar conductors, train engineers, and defense workers. But everyone—including the women themselves—believed that these jobs would return to men after the war.

Professional women also found opportunities in government service. Mary Van Kleeck, an industrial sociologist and expert on the problems of woman workers, joined the Department of Labor to lobby for equal pay and better working conditions for woman workers. Pauline Goldmark, a social reformer from the National Consumers' League, acted as a women's rights advocate at the Railroad Administration. Mary Anderson, a trade unionist who had been Van Kleeck's assistant, became the first director of the Women's Bureau, established by the Labor Department in 1920. Women's groups failed, however, to get a woman named to the National War Labor Board.

World War I proved especially liberating for middle-class women outside the work force. Women's clubs and groups had grown steadily since the nineteenth century, and they turned much of their organizational energy to the war effort. Suffragist leaders such as Carrie Chapman Catt and Anna Howard Shaw mobilized women's support for the war through the Women's Committee of the Council of National Defense. Housewives played a crucial role in the success of Herbert Hoover's Food Administration. Other groups, including the American Red Cross and the Young Women's Christian Association (YWCA), sent volunteers to France, where they organized relief work and recreational activities in conjunction with the AEF.

Suffrage Victory. The war had an important impact on the battle for woman suffrage. The main suffrage organization, the National American Woman Suffrage Association (NAWSA), threw the support of its two million members solidly behind the Wilson administration. Carrie Chapman Catt, president of the organization, argued that women had to prove their patriotism in order not to jeopardize the suffrage movement. Only a small group of radical suffragists, led by Alice Paul and her Congressional Union, joined peace activists like Jane Addams in opposing the war.

Women's wartime contributions helped push their campaign for suffrage to its successful conclusion. Especially effective was a simple moral challenge: how could

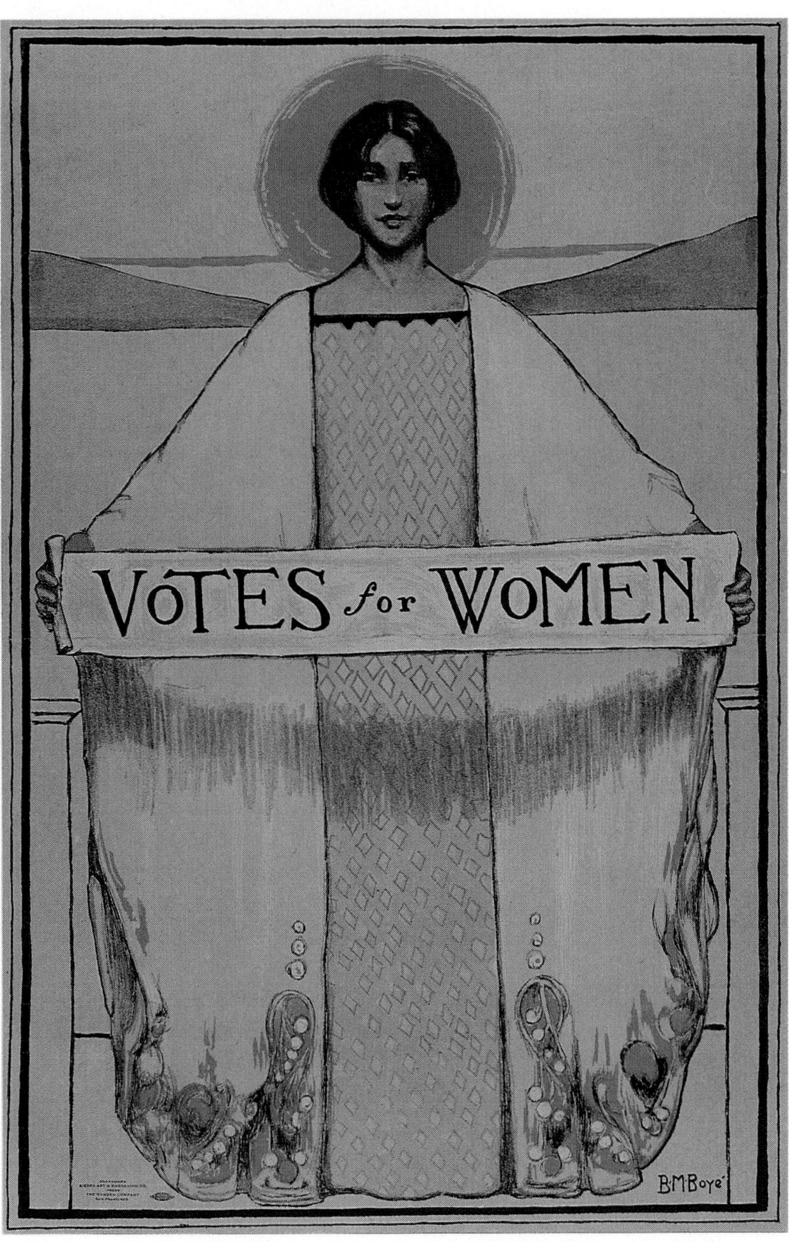

Votes for Women
Mass suffrage parades, introduced in the final stages of the campaign, provided an effective and eye-catching way to build popular support. Many of the banners and posters carried in the parades, such as this one by B. M. Boye, were in the suffrage colors of green, purple, or gold.

the United States fight to make the world safe for democracy while denying half its citizens their right to vote? Woodrow Wilson, who had accepted the Democratic platform's endorsement of woman suffrage in 1916 but preferred to leave the matter to the states, withdrew his opposition to a federal woman suffrage amendment in January 1918. The constitutional amendment quickly passed the House but took eighteen months to get through the Senate. Then came another year of hard work for ratification by the states. Finally, on August 26, 1920, Tennessee gave the Nineteenth Amendment the last vote it needed. The goal that had first been declared at the Seneca Falls convention in 1848 won approval seventy-two years later, partly because of women's contributions to the war effort.

A Human Statue of Liberty

Patriotic gestures knew no bounds, as demonstrated by the 18,000 soldiers at Camp Dodge in Iowa who formed a human replica of the Statue of Liberty. One wonders if the conscripts shared the photographer's enthusiasm for the project after what must have been a long, boring afternoon in the sun.

Promoting National Unity

The course of American participation in World War I was fundamentally shaped by the Progressive period that preceded it. Reformers eagerly embraced American involvement as an opportunity to put Progressive ideals into practice. Educator and philosopher John Dewey, a staunch supporter of the war, argued that wars represented a "plastic juncture" when societies became more open to reason and new ideas. In the collective effort of fighting and winning a war, society could be improved. Dewey's optimistic view matched the spirit of the times. Unfortunately, a dissenting observation by Randolph Bourne, an outspoken pacifist and intellectual who had once been a pupil of Dewey's, came closer to reality. "If the war is too strong for you to prevent," Bourne asked, "how is it going to be weak enough for you to control and mold to your liberal purposes?"

Although the enactment of woman suffrage confirmed Dewey's prediction that social progress could occur in a war context, the excesses committed in the name of building national unity corroborated Bourne's warnings about the passions that could get out of control during wartime. Wilson had shared Bourne's foreboding: "Once lead this people into war, and they'll forget there ever was such a thing as tolerance." But the president also realized the need to manufacture support for the war. "It is not an army we must shape and train for war, it is a nation."

Wartime Propaganda. In April 1917, Wilson designated the Committee on Public Information (CPI) to promote public backing for the war, which was never a foregone conclusion. This government propaganda agency, headed by journalist George Creel, acted as a magnet for Progressive reformers and muckraking journalists, such as Ida Tarbell and Ray Stannard Baker. The CPI professed high-sounding goals, such as educating citizens about democracy, promoting national unity, Americanizing immigrant groups, and breaking down the isolation of rural life. Indirectly, it acted as a nationalizing force by promoting the development of a common national ideology.

The Committee on Public Information touched the lives of practically every American during World War I. It distributed seventy-five million pieces of patriotic literature. At local movie theaters before the feature presentation (which might be a CPI-supported film, such as *The Prussian Cur* or *The Kaiser, Beast of Berlin*) a volunteer called a "four-minute man" made a short speech supporting the war. Such speeches reached an audience estimated at more than three hundred million, three times the population of the United States at the time. But the CPI sometimes went too far. By early 1918, for example, the CPI was encouraging speakers to use inflammatory stories of alleged German atrocities to build support for the war effort.

The Climate of Suspicion. As a spirit of conformity pervaded the home front, many Americans found themselves the targets of suspicion. Local businesses donated ads to newspapers and magazines that asked citizens to report to the Justice Department "the man who spreads pessimistic stories, cries for peace, or belittles our efforts to win the war." Posters encouraged Americans to be on the lookout for German spies. One of the most popular posters, called "Spies and Lies," began by warning that "German agents are everywhere." An unintended byproduct of this wartime propaganda was the stimulation of the advertising industry, which became a major force in shaping patterns of consumption in the 1920s.

The CPI also urged ethnic groups to give up their old-world customs and become "Unhyphenated Americans." German-Americans bore the brunt of the Americanization campaign. In an orgy of hostility generated by propaganda about German militarism and war atrocities, everything German became suspect. German music, especially opera, was banished from the concert repertoire. Publishers removed pro-German references from textbooks, and many communities banned the teaching of the German language. Sauerkraut was renamed "liberty cabbage," and hamburgers transformed into "liberty sandwiches" or Salisbury steaks. Even the German measles got a new name, "liberty measles." Anti-German hysteria dissipated quickly when the war ended, in large part because German-Americans were one of the best integrated immigrant groups in American society.

More aggressive than propaganda were quasi-vigilante groups, such as the American Protective League. This organization mobilized about 250,000 self-appointed "agents" to spy on their neighbors, fellow workers, and innocent bystanders. The American Protective League (whose members were furnished with badges issued by the Justice Department) and groups including the Sedition Slammers and the Boy Spies of America staged violent raids against draft evaders and other war opponents in 1918.

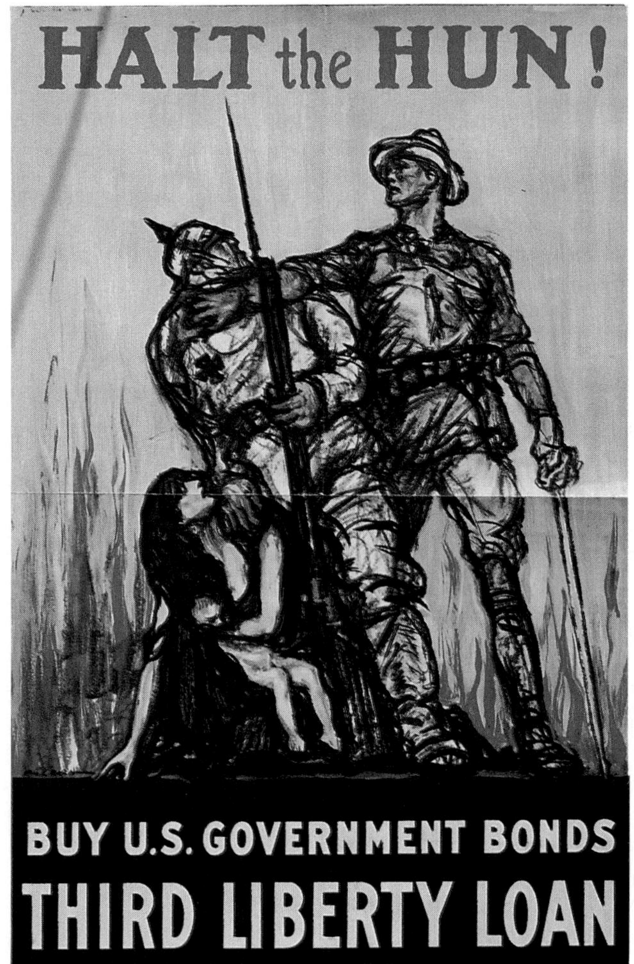

The Iconography of War

This poster made clear who the enemy was, and the proper patriotic American response. The iconography builds on traditional gender definitions, with the male American soldier pushing back the German Hun who is about to ravish a woman and her child, who stand for European civilization.

Curbing Dissent. Law enforcement officials tolerated little criticism of American values and institutions in wartime. For example, the Washington, D.C. police moved in quickly to arrest militant suffragists from the Congressional Union who chained themselves to the White House fence and burned copies of President Wilson's speeches on democracy to protest their lack of the vote. The suffragists, charged with obstructing traffic and blocking sidewalks, were sentenced to seven months in jail. In protest, Alice Paul and other women prisoners went on hunger strikes and were forcibly fed. Public shock at their treatment made them martyrs and ultimately aided the suffrage cause. But the suffragists' status as white middle-class women protected them from some of the harsher reprisals meted out to others who dared to criticize the government during wartime.

The main legal tools for curbing such dissent were the Espionage Act of 1917 and the Sedition Act of 1918. The espionage law set stiff penalties for antimilitary actions and empowered the federal government to ban treasonous material from the mails. The definition of treason was left to the discretion of the postmaster general. The sedition law went further, punishing anyone who might "utter, print, write or publish any disloyal, profane, scurrilous, or abusive language about the form of government in the United States, or the uniform of the Army or the Navy." More than a thousand people were convicted under these broad restrictions on freedom of speech in wartime.

AMERICAN VOICES

An Imprisoned Suffrage Militant *Rose Winslow*

Suffragist Rose Winslow smuggled out descriptions of the treatment she and Alice Paul, militant founder of the National Woman's Party, endured in Occuquan prison. The process of forcible feeding she mentions, which involved inserting a 20-inch-long tube through the nostril to the stomach while the patient was restrained, was excruciatingly painful as well as demeaning.

The women are all so magnificent, so beautiful. Alice Paul is as thin as ever, pale and large-eyed. We have been in solitary for five weeks. There is nothing to tell but that the days go by somehow. I have felt quite feeble the last few days—faint, so that I could hardly get my hair brushed, my arms ached so. But today I am well again. Alice Paul and I talk back and forth though we are at opposite ends of the building and a hall door also shuts us apart. But occasionally—thrills—we escape from behind our iron-barred doors and visit. Great laughter and rejoicing! . . .

Alice Paul is in the psychopathic ward. She dreaded forcible feeding frightfully, and I hate to think how she must be feeling. I had a nervous time of it, gasping a long time afterward, and my stomach rejecting during the process. I spent a bad, restless night, but otherwise I am all right. The poor soul who fed me got liberally besprinkled during the process. I heard myself making the most hideous sounds. . . . One feels so forsaken when one lies prone and people shove a pipe down one's stomach. . . .

We still get no mail; we are "insubordinate." It's strange, isn't it; if you ask for food fit to eat, as we did, you are "insubordinate"; and if you refuse food you are "insubordinate." Amusing. I am really all right. If this continues very long I perhaps won't be. I am interested to see how long our so-called "splendid American men" will stand for this form of discipline.

All news cheers one marvelously because it is hard to feel anything but a bit desolate and forgotten here in this place.

All the officers here know we are making this hunger strike that women fighting for liberty may be considered political prisoners; we have told them. God knows we don't want other women ever to have to do this over again.

Source: Doris Stevens, *Jailed For Freedom* (1920; rpt. New York: Schocken Books, 1976), 188–91.

The Justice Department also targeted the Industrial Workers of the World, or Wobblies (see Chapter 18). IWW organizers spoke out against militarism and threatened to disrupt war production in the western lumber and copper industries. In September 1917 the Justice Department arrested 113 top IWW leaders for interfering with the war effort. Vigilante groups contributed their own reprisals: a mob in Butte, Montana, dragged IWW organizer Frank Little through the streets and hanged him from a railroad trestle. By the end of the war, the Wobblies were decimated.

Socialists encountered similar attacks for criticizing the war and the draft. The postmaster general banned their publications from the mails. Party leader Eugene Debs drew ten years in jail for stating that the master classes caused wars while the subject classes fought them. Victor Berger, a Milwaukee Socialist, was twice prevented from taking his seat in the United States House of Representatives. Berger had served in the House from 1911 to 1913. He was reelected in 1918 and 1919, but the House refused to seat him because he had been jailed under the Espionage Act for his antiwar views. The Supreme Court reversed Victor Berger's sentence in 1921, and he served in the House again from 1923 to 1929.

The Supreme Court rarely overturned the wartime excesses. In *Schenck v. United States* (1919), Justice Oliver Wendell Holmes ruled in a unanimous decision that if an act of speech was uttered in circumstances that would "create a clear and present danger to the safety of the country," Congress could constitutionally restrict it. The defendant, the general secretary of the Socialist party, Charles T. Schenck, had been convicted for mailing pamphlets that urged draftees to resist induction. In *Abrams v. United States* (1919), the Court also upheld the sedition conviction of Jacob Abrams, a Russian anarchist and recent immigrant. Abrams had dumped Yiddish and English pamphlets from tenement windows in New York denouncing American military intervention in Russia. Holmes dissented in this case, seeing no clear threat to the conduct of the war. He and Justice Louis Brandeis made up the minority in the 7 to

2 decision. During a national war emergency, the Court upheld limits on freedom of speech that would not have been acceptable in peacetime.

An Unsettled Peace, 1919–1920

In January 1917, Woodrow Wilson had proposed a "peace without victory," since only "peace among equals" would be likely to last. His goal was "not a balance of power, but a community of power; not organized rivalries, but an organized common peace." With victory achieved, Wilson confronted the task of constructing the new moral international order he dreamed of. First he would have to win over a Senate openly hostile to the treaty he brought home. At the same time, ethnic and racial tensions that had smoldered during the war erupted in controversy and strife. And fears of domestic radicalism boiled over in the Red Scare.

The Treaty of Versailles

President Wilson scored an early victory when the Allies accepted his Fourteen Points as the basis for the peace negotiations that began in January 1919. First put forward in a speech to Congress in early 1918, the Fourteen Points represented Wilson's clearest articulation of his blueprint for the postwar world. The president called for open diplomacy, "absolute freedom of navigation upon the seas," removal of economic barriers to trade, an international commitment to territorial integrity, and arms reduction. The fifth point reaffirmed Wilson's long-standing commitment to national self-determination. He proposed redrawing national boundaries following the breakup of the Austro-Hungarian, Russian, and German empires, including the restoration of an independent Polish state. Essential to Wilson's vision was the creation of a multinational organization "for the purpose of affording mutual guarantees of political independence and territorial integrity to great and small States alike." This League of Nations became Wilson's obsession.

The Fourteen Points matched the spirit of Progressivism. Widely distributed as propaganda during the final months of the war, Wilson's declaration proposed to extend the benefits of the American way of life—democracy, freedom, and peaceful economic expansion—to the rest of the world. The League of Nations would serve as a mediator of international disputes so that future wars could be avoided and as a kind of Federal Trade Commission for the world. By pegging American involvement to such lofty goals, however, Wilson virtually guaranteed disappointment. When the Allies won the war, his ideals for world reformation were too far-reaching to be practical or attainable.

Many factors limited Wilson's ability to enforce his views of a just peace. Despite the president's plea to make the 1918 Congressional elections a referendum for his peace plan, American voters returned a Republican majority to Congress. Wilson shortsightedly failed to appoint even one Republican senator to the United States delegation to the peace conference, a political gaffe that later helped doom the treaty's chances for approval in the Senate.

Woodrow Wilson Triumphant
After the armistice, Woodrow Wilson toured Europe to tumultuous acclaim, such as here in Paris where citizens erected an electric sign saying "Vive [long live] Wilson." But his heady reception from the people contrasted sharply with the cool reception he received from the leaders of the major European powers.

The peace delegation sailed for Europe in December 1918. Wilson toured the major European capitals and received a tumultuous welcome. To European citizens the American president represented the hope for national self-determination that had become a major justification for the war. In Paris two million people lined the Champs-Élysées to pay tribute to "Wilson the Just." This reception encouraged Wilson to press ahead with his plans to dominate the peace conference.

Intervention in the U.S.S.R. The Allies deliberately excluded representatives of the new Bolshevik state from the peace conference. Wilson remained deeply disturbed by Lenin's calls for a proletarian revolution to liberate the world from capitalism and imperialism, a direct challenge to the Wilsonian international order. Not only did Wilson refuse to recognize Lenin's legitimacy, but he took steps to try to topple the Bolshevik regime. Under the ostensible excuse of helping 60,000 trapped Czechoslovakians who wanted to return to fight the Germans, Wilson deployed 5,000 American troops to Archangel in northern Russia in June 1918 and sent an additional 10,000 troops to Siberia in July. England and Japan also sent troops. The unstated purpose of this Allied military maneuver was to give support to anti-Bolshevik forces within Russia. American troops remained on Soviet soil until the spring of 1920, leaving a bitter legacy for American-Soviet relations.

Negotiating the Treaties. Twenty-seven countries sent representatives to the peace conference in Versailles, near Paris; like the Soviet Union, Germany was not invited. The Big Four—Wilson, Prime Minister David Lloyd George of Great Britain, Premier Georges Clemenceau of France, and Prime Minister Vittorio Orlando of Italy—did most of the negotiating. The three European leaders sought a peace that differed radically from Wilson's plan. They wanted to punish Germany through heavy reparations, and treat themselves to the spoils of war. In fact, Britain, France, and Italy had already made secret treaties to divide up territory of the defeated German empire before the conference began.

Territorial Settlements. It is a tribute to Woodrow Wilson that he managed to influence the peace agreement as much as he did. His presence at Versailles softened some of the harshest demands for reprisals against Germany. National self-determination, a fundamental American principle enunciated in Wilson's Fourteen Points, found fulfillment in the creation of the independent states of Austria, Hungary, Poland, Yugoslavia, and Czechoslovakia from the defeated empires of the Central Powers. The establishment of a *cordon sanitaire* (sanitary zone) of the new nations of Finland, Estonia, Lithuania, and Latvia further served Wilson's determination to isolate the Soviet Union from the rest of Europe. Even though Lenin did not attend the peace conference, Allied leaders realized that the new Soviet state was changing the complexion of power in Eastern Europe—and the world.

The president won only limited concessions regarding the colonial empires of the defeated powers. The old Central and Eastern European empires were dismantled, but the overseas empires of the victorious allies were actually enlarged by the addition of colonies taken from the defeated powers. The colonies were placed under a mandate system of protectorates, assigned to various powers for administration as trustees. France and England received parts of the old Turkish and German empires in the Middle East and Africa, and Japan assumed responsibility for the former German colonies in the Far East. Germany's loss of all its colonies, and their transfer to other imperialist powers like England and Japan, hardly constituted a blow for national self-determination.

Wilson had to back down on many other issues in the Fourteen Points as well. The secret negotiating sessions held by the Big Four at Versailles mocked Wilson's call for "open covenants of peace openly arrived at." Certain topics, such as freedom of the seas and free trade, never even made the agenda because of Allied resistance. Wilson yielded to French and British demands for a "war guilt" clause, which provided the justification for the heavy restitution demanded from Germany. France was especially adamant about reparations, since the war on the Western Front had been fought primarily on French soil. The final figure, set in 1921, was $33 billion. Although lower than France's original demands for $100 billion, it was still far more than the crippled German economy could bear.

In the face of his many disappointments, Wilson consoled himself with the peace conference's commitment to his proposed League of Nations. He acknowledged that the treaty had defects, but he expressed confidence that they could be resolved by a permanent international organization that brought nations together for the peaceful resolution of disputes.

The Fate of the Treaty

German leaders reacted with dismay at the severity of the treaty, but with the nation reduced almost to starvation by the Allied blockade they had no choice but to accept it. On June 28, 1919, representatives of the participating nations and Germany gathered in the Hall of Mirrors in the Palace of Versailles to sign the treaty. Wilson sailed home immediately after the ceremony and presented the treaty to the Senate on July 10. The treaty was already in trouble, however, with support in the Senate far short of the two-thirds vote necessary for ratification. Would Wilson compromise? "I shall consent to nothing," he told the French ambassador. "The Senate must take its medicine."

Congressional Opposition. Opposition to the Versailles treaty came from several sources. One group, called the "irreconcilables," consisted of such Western progressives as William E. Borah of Idaho, Hiram W. Johnson of California, and Robert M. La Follette of Wisconsin. They disagreed fundamentally with the premise of permanent U.S. participation in European affairs symbolized by the League of Nations. Moreover, they were horrified at the harsh terms of the treaty toward Germany.

Less dogmatic, but more influential, was a group of Republicans led by Senator Henry Cabot Lodge of Massachusetts. They too expressed strong reservations about the break with American isolationism represented by membership in the League of Nations. Lodge's Republicans proposed a list of amendments that, scholars now agree, would not have seriously weakened the peace treaty. Most of these changes centered around Article X, the section of the League of Nations covenant calling for collective security measures if a member nation were attacked. Lodge correctly argued that this provision restricted Congress's constitutional authority to declare war. More importantly, Lodge and many other senators felt that the treaty imposed unacceptable restrictions on the freedom of the United States to pursue a unilateral foreign policy.

Wilson still refused to budge, especially to placate Lodge, his hated political rival. Hoping to mobilize support for the treaty, the president launched an extensive speaking tour to take his case to the American people. He brought large audiences to tears with his impassioned defense of the treaty. But the strain proved too much for the ailing sixty-two-year-old president, and he collapsed in Pueblo, Colorado, in late September. One week later in Washington, Wilson suffered a severe stroke that left him paralyzed on one side of his body.

Defeat. We will never know whether a healthy Wilson could have mobilized public support for the League of Nations and gained Senate ratification. Perhaps if he had allowed the Democrats to compromise, the treaty might have been saved. From his sickbed, however, Wilson ordered the Democratic senators to vote against all Republican amendments. The treaty came up for a vote in November 1919 and failed to be ratified. Another attempt several months later fell seven votes short of approval, and the issue was dead.

While his wife, Edith Galt Wilson, and his physician oversaw the routine business of government, Wilson slowly recovered. But he was never the same again. He had delusions of making the 1920 election campaign "a great and solemn referendum" on the League of Nations, and even hoped to run for a third term as president. Neither dream was a serious possibility. Woodrow Wilson died in 1924, "as much a victim of the war," David Lloyd George noted, "as any soldier who died in the trenches."

The United States never signed the Versailles treaty or joined the League of Nations. Many wartime issues remained only partially resolved, notably the future of Germany, the fate of colonial empires, and rising nationalist demands for self-determination. These unsolved problems played a major role in the coming of World War II.

Racial Strife

Woodrow Wilson spent only ten days in the United States between December 1918 and June 1919. This striking circumstance illustrates his total preoccupation with the peacemaking process at Versailles. For more than six months, Wilson was practically an absentee president. Unfortunately, many urgent domestic problems demanded his attention.

The immediate postwar period brought a severe decline in race relations throughout the country. The volatile mix of black migration, American imperialism, intensified segregation in the South, and black service in World War I all combined to exacerbate white hostility to blacks. In the South, the number of lynchings rose from forty-eight in 1917 to seventy-eight in 1919. Several blacks were lynched while still wearing their military uniforms. Northern blacks also faced hostility. Serious racial violence broke out in more than twenty-five cities, and the resulting death toll for the summer of 1919 reached 120.

The riots resulted from the northward migration set in motion by World War I. Superficially at least, northern cities promised new freedoms. But southern blacks faced a difficult readjustment to the diverse urban environment after the South's traditional patterns of deference to whites. In turn, white northerners reacted hostilely to this perceived onslaught of unwelcome newcomers, especially when competition for jobs was added to racism. Violence between blacks and whites erupted as early as 1917 in Houston and Philadelphia. In East St. Louis, Illinois, nine whites and more than forty blacks died in a riot sparked by competition over jobs at a defense plant.

Racial Violence in Chicago
Much of the violence perpetrated against blacks during the 1919 race riot was perpetrated by young white men, many of Irish descent, who belonged to gangs such as the "Dirty Dozen" and "Our Flag." A city commission later concluded that without the gang activities, "it is doubtful if the riot would have gone beyond the first clash."

Riots in Chicago. One of the worst race riots took place in Chicago in July 1919. It began at a Lake Michigan beach when a black teenager named Eugene Williams swam into an area of the lake customarily reserved for whites. Someone threw a rock that hit him on the head, and he drowned. The incident touched off five days of rioting in which twenty-three blacks and fifteen whites died.

Chicago on the eve of the riot was a tinderbox waiting to ignite. The arrival of fifty thousand black newcomers during the war years had strained the city's social fabric. In politics black voters often provided the balance of power in close elections. Blacks and whites competed for jobs, and the more heavily unionized white population deeply resented the blacks who became strikebreakers—white stockyard workers considered the words "Negro" and "scab" synonymous. Blacks and whites competed for scarce housing as well, and blacks soon overflowed the racially segregated South Side into Chicago's intensely ethnic neighborhoods. Even before that sultry July afternoon at the beach, tensions had erupted in bombings of black homes and other forms of harassment.

Chicago blacks did not sit meekly by as whites destroyed their neighborhoods. They fought back, both in self-defense and for their rights as citizens. World War I had an indirect effect on their actions. Many blacks had served in the armed forces. The rhetoric about democracy and self-determination raised their expectations, too.

Labor Unrest

Workers had similar hopes as a result of the war. The war years had provided important breakthroughs for many industrial employees, including higher pay, shorter hours, and better working conditions. Soon after the armistice, however, many employers returned to older patterns of hostility toward union activity. Many consumers blamed workers for the rising cost of living, and many native-born Americans continued to identify unions with radicalism and foreigners. Nevertheless, workers hoped to expand their wartime gains. The worst problem was rapidly rising inflation, which threatened to wipe out their wage increases. By 1919 the cost of living had risen 77 percent over its prewar level.

1919—A Year of Strikes. More than four million workers—one out of every five—went on strike in 1919, a proportion never since equalled. The year began with a walkout by shipyard workers in Seattle. Their action spread into a general strike that crippled the city. In the fall, the Boston police force struck. The idea of public employees trying to unionize shocked many Americans. Governor Calvin Coolidge of Massachusetts propelled himself into the political spotlight by declaring, "There is no right to strike against the public safety by anybody, anywhere, any time." The strike failed, and the entire police force was fired by Coolidge. The public supported this harsh reprisal, and Coolidge was rewarded with the Republican vice-presidential nomination in 1920.

The most extensive labor disruption in 1919 was the great steel strike. More than 350,000 steelworkers across the country walked off the job in late September. The main issue was union recognition, but strikers were also protesting such conditions as twelve-hour shifts and seven-day weeks. Elbert H. Gary, chairman of the United States Steel Corporation, refused to meet with representatives of the steelworkers' union to discuss their demands. The company hired Mexicans and blacks to break the strike and maintained steel production at about 60 percent of the normal level.

The continued high production rate doomed the strike. Striker solidarity began to slacken as winter approached; by January, the strike had collapsed. The union charged that U.S. Steel's "arbitrary and ruthless misuse of power" had crushed the strike. Just as important to the union's defeat was the lack of public support for the goals of organized labor. Unions had made important gains during the war, but they were unable to hold on to them.

The Eighteenth Amendment

Another issue demanding national attention as the war ended was the century-old campaign for Prohibition. On the eve of World War I, nineteen states had passed Prohibition laws and many more provided that communities could regulate liquor if they desired. Generally only highly industrialized states with large immigrant populations, such as New York, Massachusetts, Rhode Island, Illinois, and California, had resisted the trend towards alcohol restriction.

In early twentieth-century America, Prohibition was viewed as a progressive reform, not as a repressive denial of individual freedom. Urban reformers, concerned about good government, urban poverty, and public morality, supported a nationwide ban on drinking. Among the Progressive-Era leaders who campaigned for Prohibition were Supreme Court Justice Louis Brandeis, former presidents William Howard Taft and Theodore Roosevelt, and settlement leader Jane Addams.

The drive for Prohibition also picked up substantial backing in rural communities. Many people equated liquor with all the sins of the city—prostitution, crime, machine politics, and public disorder. In addition, the churches with the greatest strength in rural areas such as the Methodists, Baptists, and Mormons strongly condemned drinking. Protestants from rural areas dominated the membership of the Anti-Saloon League, which by the 1910s had supplanted the Women's Christian Temperance Union as the leading proponent of Prohibition.

Support for the right to drink existed primarily in the nation's heavily urbanized areas, places where immigrants had settled. Alcoholic beverages, especially

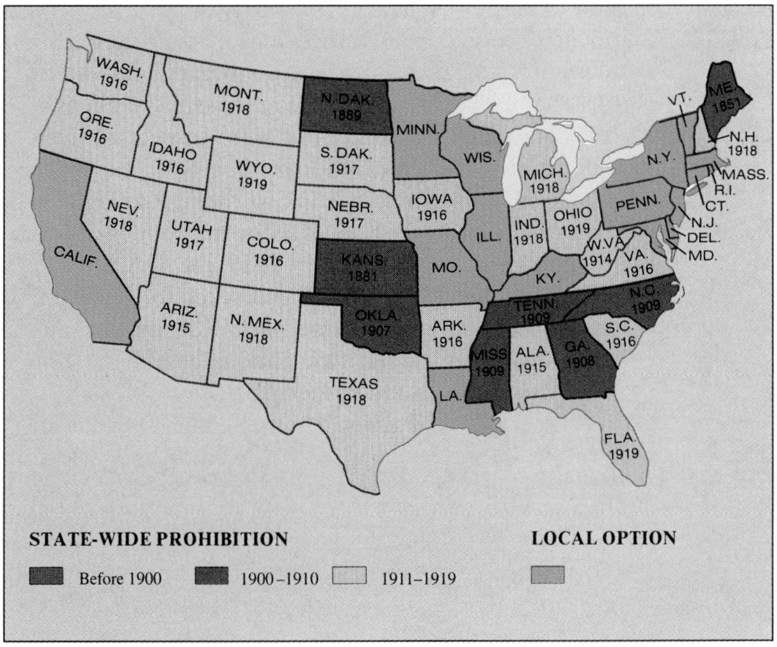

MAP 23.3

Prohibition on the Eve of the Eighteenth Amendment

Prohibition had already made strong headway in the states before the adoption of the Eighteenth Amendment in 1919. States such as Maine, North Dakota, and Kansas had been dry since the nineteenth century; by 1919, two-thirds of the states had already passed laws banning liquor. Most states that resisted the trend were industrial centers or had large immigrant populations.

beer and whiskey, played an important role in certain ethnic cultures, especially those of German- and Irish-Americans. Most saloons were in working-class neighborhoods and served as gathering places for workers at the end of the day. Machine politicians conducted much of their business in bars.

During World War I, those who supported a constitutional amendment to prohibit drinking had the political momentum. One spur to action was the intense anti-German hysteria of the war years. Because several major breweries (Pabst and Busch, for example) had German names, beer drinking became unpatriotic in many people's minds. As part of the drive to conserve food, Congress prohibited the use of food products to make distilled beverages. In December 1917 Congress passed the proposed Eighteenth Amendment prohibiting the manufacture, transport, or sale of intoxicating liquors. Every state with the exception of Connecticut and Rhode Island ratified it by 1919, and it went into effect on January 16, 1920. Among its few exemptions were alcohol prescribed for medicinal reasons and wine consumed for sacramental purposes.

The passage of the Eighteenth Amendent was another example of how "progressive" solutions to issues of purity, poverty, and public safety found success in the climate of war. It also amply demonstrated the widening influence of the state on matters of personal behavior. Yet the ethnic and urban-rural clashes over Prohibition also foreshadowed the ethnocultural debates after the war. Unlike woman suffrage, the other constitutional amendment that won wartime passage, Prohibition would never win general acceptance.

The Red Scare

Underlying and unifying many of the social tensions in the aftermath of World War I was fear of radicalism. Wartime hatred of the German Hun was quickly replaced by postwar hostility toward the Bolshevik Red. The Russian Revolution of 1917 set these fears in motion. The founding of the Third International (or Comintern) in 1919 to export revolution throughout the world threatened the Wilsonian vision of an international order based on democracy, capitalism, and harmony. As labor unrest increased, Americans suddenly began seeing radicals everywhere.

Ironically, as the public became increasingly concerned about domestic Bolshevism, American radicalism rapidly lost members and political power. No more than seventy thousand Americans belonged to the fledgling U.S. Communist party or the Communist Labor party in 1919. The IWW and the Socialist party had been weakened by wartime repression and internal dissension. Yet the public and the press continued to blame almost any disturbance, especially labor conflicts, on radicals. "REDS DIRECTING SEATTLE STRIKE—TO TEST CHANCE FOR REVOLUTION," warned a typical newspaper headline.

Then a series of bombings shocked the nation in early spring. "The word 'radical' in 1919," one historian observed, "automatically carried with it the implication of dynamite." Thirty-four mail bombs addressed to prominent government officials were discovered by alert postal workers before they exploded. Many people immediately suspected that the intended bombings had been timed to coincide with the communist celebration of International Labor Day on May 1. In June a bomb exploded outside the Washington townhouse of the recently appointed attorney general, A. Mitchell Palmer. His family escaped unharmed, but the bomber was blown to bits. Despite intensive efforts, law enforcement agencies never traced the origin of a single bomb.

As hysteria mounted in the fall of 1919, the federal government became involved. One aspect of the expansion of state power was increased surveillance of citizens and repression of dissent. President Wilson's debilitating stroke prevented him from providing decisive leadership, but Attorney General Palmer seized the moment. Angling for the presidential nomination, Palmer rode the crest of public hysteria about domestic radicalism into 1920.

The Palmer Raids. Palmer set up an antiradicalism division in the Justice Department and appointed a young government attorney named J. Edgar Hoover to direct it. Hoover's division shortly became the Federal Bureau of Intelligence. In November 1919, on the second anniversary of the Russian Revolution, the attorney general staged the first of what became known as "Palmer raids." Federal agents stormed the headquarters of radical organizations and captured such supposedly revolutionary booty as a set of drawings that turned out to be blueprints for an improved phonograph, not sketches for a bomb. The dragnet netted thousands of aliens who had committed no crime, but were suspect because of their anarchist or revolutionary beliefs or merely their immigrant backgrounds. Lacking the protection of U.S. citizenship, they faced deportation without formal trial or indictment. In December 1919 the U.S.S. *Buford*, nicknamed the "Soviet Ark," embarked for Finland and the Soviet state with a cargo of 294 deported radicals. Its passengers included two famous anarchists, Emma Goldman and Alexander Berkman.

The peak of Palmer's power came with his New Year's raids in January 1920. In one night, with the greatest possible newspaper publicity, Palmer rounded up six thousand radicals. Agents invaded private homes, union headquarters, and meeting halls. The government held both citizens and aliens without specific charges and denied them legal counsel, a violation of their civil liberties. Some prisoners were even forced to march through the streets handcuffed to one another. One of the few moments of comic relief came when "patriotic" prisoners in a Chicago jail rioted when ordered to share cells with arrested radicals. "There are some things at which even a Chicago crook draws the line," a local newspaper reported.

Palmer was riding high, and his ambitions for the presidency swelled. But then he overstepped himself. Palmer predicted that on May Day 1920 an unnamed conspiracy would attempt to overthrow the United States government. State militia units and police on twenty-four-hour alert guarded the nation against the threat of revolutionary violence. Not a single incident occurred. The hysteria of the Red Scare began to abate as the summer of 1920 passed without major labor strikes or renewed bombings.

The Sacco-Vanzetti Case. One dramatic episode kept the wartime legacy of antiradicalism alive well into the next decade. In May 1920, at the height of the Red Scare, Nicola Sacco, a shoemaker, and Bartolomeo Vanzetti, a fish peddler, were arrested for the robbery and murder of a shoe company paymaster in South Braintree, Massachusetts. Sacco and Vanzetti were self-proclaimed anarchists and Italian aliens who had evaded the draft; both were armed at the time of their arrest.

Sacco and Vanzetti were convicted in 1921 and sat on death row for six years while supporters tried unsuccessfully to appeal their verdicts. Regardless of their guilt or innocence, it is clear that they did not receive a fair trial from the American judicial system. Shortly before his execution in the electric chair on August 23, 1927, Vanzetti claimed triumph.

> If it had not been for these thing, I might have live out my life among scorning men. I might have die, unmarked, unknown, a failure. Now we are not a failure. This is our career and our triumph. Never in our full life can we hope to do such work for tolerance, for justice, for man's understanding of man, as now we do by an accident.
>
> Our words—our lives—our pains—nothing! The taking of our lives—lives of a good shoemaker and a poor fish-peddlar—all! That last moment belongs to us—that agony is our triumph.

This oft-quoted elegy captures the eloquence and tolerance of one victim caught in the last spasm of antiradicalism and fear that capped America's participation in World War I.

Summary

The outbreak of the Great War in 1914 posed the greatest challenge yet to American diplomacy. For more than two years, President Wilson kept the nation out of war, attempting to use American power and prestige to mediate between the two sides. The United States finally entered the war in 1917 because of violations of its neutrality rights at sea, but, more broadly, because the country's foreign policy reflected the same moral concerns that animated the domestic reform movement. On April 6, 1917, Congress declared war on Germany.

American participation in the war was brief but decisive. Two million freshly recruited "doughboys" turned the tide for the Allies on the Western Front in 1918. Flush with victory, Wilson sought a role in the peace commensurate with America's contribution. Yet the Versailles treaty only partially reflected the hopes of President Woodrow Wilson for such goals as freedom of the seas, peaceful economic expansion, and national self-determination. His postwar plans suffered a worse blow when the Senate refused to ratify the treaty, which included U.S. participation in the League of Nations.

As the Wilson administration put the nation on a war footing, Progressive reform energies were largely diverted to the war effort. An army had to be created almost from scratch, American agriculture and manufacturing had to be directed to produce for the Allies as well as the home market, and American workers had to be recruited for war work and kept on the job. All this absorbed the energies of a new group of professional experts turned government bureaucrats. World War I thus helped create the tools of the modern bureaucratic state which, laid aside temporarily at war's end, would be taken up again during the nation's greatest peacetime crisis, the Great Depression.

The government tried to mobilize the minds of the American people as well, but succeeded mainly in inflaming passions. Certain groups, such as woman suffragists, found success during the war. But others became targets of repression, including blacks who migrated to northern cities, labor activists who called widespread strikes, and Socialists and other radicals who criticized the government. Domestic tensions erupted in race riots in many northern cities, and in the Red Scare of 1919–1920.

TOPIC FOR RESEARCH

Free Speech in Wartime

How far does the First Amendment go in protecting the right of free speech? Does the state have a legitimate interest in imposing stringent regulations on public expression during wartime? Carefully analyze the reasoning of the Supreme Court in the 1919 cases of *Schenck v. United States* (249 U.S. 47) and *Abrams v. United States* (250 U.S. 616). What are the facts in each case? How is the doctrine of "clear and present danger" presented? Why did Justices Oliver Wendell Holmes and Louis Brandeis vote with the unanimous majority in *Schenck* but dissent in the *Abrams* case? Is there an absolute right to free speech? If not, then what are acceptable limits in a democratic society?

For background, Zechariah Chaffee, Jr.'s classic *Free Speech in the United States* (1941) can be supplemented by Richard Polenberg, *Fighting Faiths: The Abrams Case, the Supreme Court, and Free Speech* (1987). For further historical context, consult Harold C. Peterson and Gilbert Fite, *Opponents of War, 1917–1918* (1968); Donald Johnson, *The Challenge to American Freedoms: World War I and The Rise of the American Civil Liberties Union* (1963); William Preston, Jr., *Aliens and Dissenters: Federal Suppression of Radicals, 1903–1933* (1963); and Harry Schreiber, *The Wilson Administration and Civil Liberties, 1917–1921* (1960).

BIBLIOGRAPHY

David M. Kennedy, *Over Here: The First World War and American Society* (1980) provides a comprehensive overview. For the links between the Progressive Era and the war, see Neil A. Wynn, *From Progressivism to Prosperity: World War I and American Society* (1986); John A. Thompson, *Reformers and War* (1987); and Robert M. Crunden, *Ministers of Reform: The Progressives' Achievement in American Civilization, 1889–1920 (1982).* Ellis W. Hawley, *The Great War and the Search for a Modern Order, 1917–1933* (1979), stresses the continuities between the war years and the 1920s.

The Great War

On American entry into World War I, see John Coogan, *The End to Neutrality* (1981); Emily Rosenberg, *Spreading the American Dream* (1982); Ernest May, *The World War and American Isolationism* (1959); Ross Gregory, *The Origins of American Intervention in the First World War* (1971); Daniel Smith, *The Great Departure: The United States and World War I, 1914–1920* (1965); and Thomas A. Bailey and Paul Ryan, *The Lusitania Disaster* (1975). There is a large body of material on the policies and personality of Woodrow Wilson, beginning with Arthur Link's five-volume biography (1947–1965), as well as his *Wilson the Diplomatist* (1957). See also Alexander L. George and Juliette L. George, *Woodrow Wilson and Colonel House: A Personality Study* (1956), and John M. Blum, *Woodrow Wilson and the Politics of Morality* (1956). Later studies of Wilson include Robert Ferrell, *Woodrow Wilson and World War I* (1985); John Milton Cooper, Jr., *The Warrior and the Priest: Woodrow Wilson and Theodore Roosevelt* (1983); and Edwin Weinstein, *Woodrow Wilson: A Medical and Psychological Biography* (1981).

For American participation in the war, Russell Weigley, *The American Way of War* (1973); Edward M. Coffman, *The War to End All Wars* (1968); and Harvey deWeerd, *President Wilson Fights His War* (1968), provide useful introductions. They can be supplemented by Laurence Stallings, *The Doughboys: The Story of the AEF, 1917–1918* (1963), and A. E. Barbeau and Florette Henri, *The Unknown Soldiers: Black Troops in World War I* (1974). John Whiteclay Chambers II, *To Raise an Army* (1987), covers the draft. Allan Brandt, *No Magic Bullet* (1985), discusses the anti-venereal disease campaigns in the army and on the homefront. Paul Chapman, *Schools as Sorters* (1988), describes the intelligence testing movement. Material on Eddie Rickenbacker and other wartime aces can be found in his *Fighting the Flying Circus* (1919) and his autobiography, *Edward Rickenbacker* (1967). See also Robert Jackson, *Fighter Pilots in World War I* (1977) and Christopher Campbell, *Aces and Aircraft of World War I* (1981).

Mobilizing the Home Front

Robert D. Cuff, *The War Industries Board: Business-Government Relations During World War I* (1973), provides an excellent case study of war mobilization. See also Stephen Skowronek, *Building a New American State: The Expansion of National Administrative Capacities, 1877–1920* (1982); Charles Gilbert, *American Financing of World War I* (1970); and David F. Noble, *America By Design* (1977). Valerie Jean Conner, *The National War Labor Board* (1983), covers federal policies towards labor. Jordan Schwarz, *The Speculator* (1981), is a biography of Bernard Baruch.

Maurine Greenwald, *Women, War, and Work* (1980), and Barbara Steinson, *American Women's Activism in World War I* (1982), provide good overviews of women's wartime experiences. Anne F. Scott and Andrew Scott, *One Half the People* (1975), and Eleanor Flexner, *Century of Struggle* (1959), cover the final stages of the woman suffrage campaign. For the peace movement, see C. Roland Marchand, *The American Peace Movement and Social Reform, 1898–1918* (1973); Charles Chatfield, *for Peace and Justice: Pacifism in America, 1914–1941* (1971); and Charles DeBenedetti, *Origins of the Modern Peace Movement* (1978). Allen F. Davis, *American Heroine* (1974), is a biography of Jane Addams.

Efforts to promote national unity are covered in Stephen Vaughan, *Holding Fast the Inner Lines: Democracy, Nationalism, and the CPI* (1980); William J. Breen, *Uncle Sam at Home* (1984); Paul L. Murphy, *World War I and the Origins of Civil Liberties* (1979); George Blakey, *Historians on the Homefront* (1970); and Frederick Luebke, *Bonds of Loyalty: German-Americans and World War I* (1974). For the experiences of Mexican-Americans, see Rodolfo Acuna, *Occupied America* (1980), and Wayne Cornelius, *Building the Cactus Curtain: Mexican Migration and U.S. Responses From Wilson to Carter* (1980).

An Unsettled Peace

For Wilson's diplomacy, see Lloyd Ambrosius, *Woodrow Wilson and the American Diplomatic Tradition* (1987); Arthur Walworth, *Wilson and the Peacemakers* (1986); and N. Gordon Levin, Jr., *Woodrow Wilson and World Politics* (1968). For more on Versailles and the League of Nations, see Thomas Bailey, *Woodrow Wilson and The Great Betrayal* (1945); Ralph A. Stone, *The Irreconcilables: The Fight Against the League of Nations* (1970); and Arno J. Mayer, *Politics and Diplomacy of Peacemaking: Containment and Counter Revolution at Versailles* (1967). See also William Widenor, *Henry Cabot Lodge and the Search for an American Foreign Policy* (1980), and John A. Garraty, *Henry Cabot Lodge* (1953). Anglo-American responses to revolution between 1913 and 1923 are covered in Lloyd C. Gardner, *Safe for Democracy* (1984). On American intervention in Russia, see George F. Kennan, *The Decision to Intervene* (1958); John L. Gaddis, *Russia, the Soviet Union, and the United States* (1978); and Peter Filene, *Americans and the Soviet Experiment, 1917–1933* (1967). Ronald Steel's fine biography, *Walter Lippmann and the American Century* (1980), offers another view of the Versailles conference.

Robert K. Murray, *The Red Scare* (1955), summarizes the antiradicalism of the postwar period. See also James Weinstein, *The Decline of Socialism in America, 1912–1923* (1967); John Higham, *Strangers in the Land* (1955); and Burl Noggle, *Into the Twenties* (1974). David Brody, *Labor in Crisis* (1965), describes the steel strike of 1919; for a more general overview, see David Montgomery, *The Fall of the House of Labor: The Workplace, the State, and American Labor Activism, 1865–1925* (1987). For race relations, see James R. Grossman, *Land of Hope: Chicago, Black Southerners, and the Great Migration* (1989); William M. Tuttle, Jr., *Race Riot: Chicago in the Red Summer of 1919* (1970); Robert V. Haynes, *A Night of Violence: The Houston Riot of 1917* (1976); and Elliot M. Rudwick, *Race Riot at East St. Louis, July 2, 1917* (1964). For an introduction to the complicated Sacco and Vanzetti case, see Louis Joughin and Edmund Morgan, *The Legacy of Sacco and Vanzetti* (1948), and Roberta Strauss Feuerlicht, *Justice Crucified* (1977).

TIMELINE

1914	Outbreak of war in Europe United States declares neutrality (1914)
1915	German submarine sinks *Lusitania*
1916	Wilson reelected
1917	U.S. enters World War I War Industries Board established Revenue Act of 1917 passed Selective Service Act passed Suffrage militancy East St. Louis race riot Espionage Act Passed Bolshevik Revolution
1918	Wilson proposes Fourteen Points Armistice ends War Eugene Debs imprisoned under Sedition Act U.S. troops intervene in Soviet Union
1919	Treaty of Versailles Steel Strike Red Scare and Palmer Raids League of Nations defeated in Senate Eighteenth Amendment (Prohibition)
1920	Nineteenth Amendment (woman suffrage)

Advertising Modernity

Artist Maxfield Parrish's yearly calendars for General Electric, such as this 1920 "Prometheus" for Mazda lamps, brought him widespread visibility and suggest the power of modern advertising.

CHAPTER 24 *Modern Times: The 1920s*

In 1924 sociologists Robert Lynd and Helen Merrell Lynd arrived in Muncie, Indiana, to study the life of a small American city. They set about observing how citizens of Middletown (the fictional name they bestowed on the city, which had been chosen for its middle-of-the-road quality) went about their daily round of making a living, maintaining a home, educating the young, practicing religion, organizing community activities, and spending their leisure time. As the Lynds' field work proceeded, they were repeatedly struck by how much had changed over the past thirty-five years—the actual lifetime of a middle-aged Middletown resident. They decided to contrast the Muncie of the 1890s with the Muncie of the 1920s. When *Middletown* was published in 1929, this "study in modern American culture" became an unexpected bestseller.

Many characteristics of modern America were in place by the end of World War I. American participation in the war made the country a major player in the world economy; the foundations of the modern corporate economy were firmly established, as well as those of the modern state. The 1920s, rather than World War I, represented a watershed in the development of a mass national culture. The Protestant work ethic and the old values of self-denial and frugality gave way in the 1920s to a fascination with consumption, leisure, and self-realization, which is the essence of modern life. In economic organization, political outlook, and cultural values, the 1920s have more in common with the United States of today than with the industrializing America of the late nineteenth century.

The prosperity and economic innovation of the 1920s gave Americans the highest standard of living in the world, although not every American was lucky enough to benefit from this new way of life. Most farmers, urban blacks, and recent immigrants could not afford the new mass-produced consumer goods and sampled them only selectively, adapting them to their traditional lifestyles. Other Americans found that the new values conflicted with old religious and cultural ones. But despite ambivalence toward the changes under way, patterns of consumption that appeared during the "New Era" of the 1920s and ways of spending leisure time quickly became part of American life.

The Business-Government Partnership of the 1920s

The business-government partnership that accelerated during World War I expanded on an informal basis throughout the 1920s. The successful performance of the economy from 1922 to 1929 seemed to confirm its ability to regulate itself with minimal government intervention. The impulse toward reform that had animated the Progressive Era was gone, or had at least gone underground. Business leaders were no longer villains but respected public figures. President Warren Harding captured the prevailing political mood when he offered the American public "not heroics but healing, not nostrums but normalcy."

The Economy

America's transition from a wartime to a peacetime economy was not smooth. During the immediate postwar years, the worst problem was runaway inflation. Prices jumped by a third in 1919, accompanied by feverish economic activity. The postwar boom was less an indication of solid economic growth than a reflection of consumers' desire to buy before prices rose even higher. In an attempt to balance the budget, the Wilson administration sharply reduced federal expenditures and thus stopped the inflationary spiral. At the same time, in 1920, the Federal Reserve System tightened credit because its previous expansive money policies had encouraged people to borrow and spend, and thereby pushed prices even higher. The new policy resulted in a recession, demonstrating that the government had much to learn about how to achieve economic stability.

The recession of 1920–1921 was the sharpest short-term downturn the United States had ever faced. Unemployment reached 10 percent. Foreign trade dropped by almost half, from $13.5 billion in 1920 to less than $7 billion in 1921, as European nations returned to production after the disruptions of war. Prices fell so dramatically—more than 20 percent—that much of the inflation of World War I was wiped out. The recession lasted only a short time. By 1922 the economy had started to recover, and the recovery continued, broken only by brief, mild downturns, until 1929. Unemployment hovered around 3 or 4 percent and inflation was negligible. Between 1922 and 1929, the gross national product grew from $74.1 billion to $103.1 billion, approximately 40 percent. Per capita income rose proportionally from $641 in 1921 to $847 in 1929. Soon the federal government was recording a budget surplus. The boom of the 1920s provided the backdrop for the partnership between business and government which bloomed in that decade.

An abundance of new consumer products, particularly the automobile, stimulated the recovery and prosperity of the 1920s. Manufacturing output expanded 64 percent during the decade, with industries churning out automobiles, appliances, chemicals, electric power, radios, aircraft, and movies. Behind this growth lay new management and mass production techniques, which resulted in a 40 percent increase in worker productivity. The value of total new construction increased from $6 billion in 1921 to $12 billion in 1927. The demand for goods and services kept unemployment low throughout the 1920s, but the expanded demand was not so strong that it produced inflation.

One sector of the economy that never fully recovered from the 1920 recession was agriculture. During the inflationary period of 1914 to 1920, farmers had borrowed heavily to finance mortgages and buy farm equipment as they expanded production in response to government incentives, increased demand, and rising prices. When the war ended and European countries resumed agricultural production, the world market was glutted with agricultural products. The price of wheat dropped 40 percent as the government withdrew wartime price supports. Corn fell 32 percent, hogs 50 percent, and farm income plunged.

Since American farmers produced mainly for the world market, one key to agricultural recovery was to prevent worldwide surpluses from further depressing domestic prices. Farmers turned for help to the political system. The McNary-Haugen bill, a far-reaching attempt to create federal price supports for agricultural

The Assembly Line

The success of the automobile industry contributed significantly to the prosperity of the 1920s, and mass production made automobiles affordable to ordinary citizens, not just the well-to-do. By 1929 there were more than 23 million cars on the road.

products, used the idea of a "fair exchange value" to guarantee that farmers earned back at least their production costs, no matter what price prevailed on the world market. A 1924 bill restricting this principle to grain failed in Congress, where Eastern Republicans and President Coolidge opposed it as special interest legislation. When Midwestern supporters of the bill added cotton, rice, and tobacco to win southern farm support, the measure passed, only to be vetoed by President Coolidge in 1927 and again in 1928. By the end of the decade, the farmers' share of the national income had plummeted from 16 percent in 1919 to 8.8 percent.

Besides agriculture, certain "sick industries," like coal and textiles, also missed out on the prosperity of the 1920s. These industries had expanded in response to World War I demands only to face overcapacity or unprofitability, and grew sluggishly, if at all, in the 1920s. This underside of economic life foreshadowed the Depression of the 1930s.

The Republican Ascendancy

Except for two terms under Woodrow Wilson, the national government had been controlled by the Republican party since 1896. With Wilson's progressive coalition floundering in 1918, the Republicans were in a position to regain their edge in the upcoming election. In 1920 the Democrats passed over the ailing Wilson in favor of Governor James M. Cox of Ohio, with Assistant Secretary of the Navy Franklin D. Roosevelt as the vice-presidential candidate. The Democratic platform called for ratification of U.S. participation in the League of Nations and a continuation of Wilsonian progressivism, while the Republicans, represented by Warren G. Harding and Calvin Coolidge, promised a return to normalcy, which meant a strong pro-business stance and conservative cultural values. Harding and Coolidge won in a landslide, marking the beginning of a new Republican era that lasted until 1932.

Hardly a towering national figure, President Harding had built an uninspiring record in Ohio state politics before winning election to the United States Senate in 1914. With a Republican victory almost a certainty in 1920, party leaders wanted a candidate they could dominate. Genial, loyal, and mediocre, "Uncle Warren" fit the bill.

Harding knew his limitations and tried to assemble a strong cabinet to help him guide the government. Charles Evans Hughes, former presidential candidate and Supreme Court justice, headed the State Department. As Secretary of Agriculture, Henry C. Wallace set up conferences between farmers and government agencies, such as the Bureau of Agricultural Economics. Financier Andrew W. Mellon ran the Treasury Department, engineering a massive tax cut to reduce the federal surplus. Most of the benefits went to the wealthy, freeing up money for private investment, as Mellon intended.

By far the most active member of the Harding administration was Secretary of Commerce Herbert Hoover, who had successfully headed the food administration during the war. Hoover embodied the business-government cooperation of the 1920s, continuing the pattern of state-building begun during World War I. Unlike Secretary of the Treasury Mellon who sought to minimize government intervention, Hoover supported expansion of the federal government in what he called the spirit of "associationalism." Voluntary cooperation in the public interest, Hoover maintained, would stabilize prices and assure general economic stability in volatile sectors of the economy such as agriculture, construction, and mining. He used persuasion, educational conferences, and fact-finding commissions to accomplish his goals.

Hoover actively promoted trade associations as the key to "associated individualism." There were about two thousand of these instruments of voluntary cooperation, representing almost every major industry and commodity. Trade associations were supposed to lend stability to modern economic life through conferences, conventions, publicity, lobbying, and trade practice controls. Statistics gathered by the Commerce Department and by private groups, such as the National Bureau of Economic Research, were useful in corporate planning and in allocating investments and markets. Trade conferences organized by the Commerce Department provided a forum for the exchange of information. The Republican-dominated Federal Trade Commission conveniently ignored antitrust laws that forbade such restraints on trade, then approved the resulting agreements. Here it followed the lead of the Supreme Court, which in 1920 had dismissed the long-pending antitrust case against the United States Steel Corporation, ruling that the large size of a business was not in and of itself against the law as long as some competition remained.

Unfortunately, not all of Harding's appointees were as earnest as Hoover. Harding himself was an honest man, but some of his political associates lacked ethical standards. When Harding died suddenly in San Francisco in August 1923, evidence of widespread fraud and corruption in his administration had just started coming to light. The worst scandal concerned the government's leasing of oil reserves in Teapot Dome, Wyoming, and Elk Hills, California, to private companies. Secretary of the Interior Albert Fall was eventually convicted of taking $300,000 in bribes and became the first cabinet officer in American history to serve a prison sentence.

Following Harding's death, Vice-President Calvin

Coolidge moved to the White House. In contrast to Harding's political cronyism and outgoing style, Coolidge personified Vermont rectitude. As vice-president, "Silent Cal" often sat through official functions without uttering a word. His dinner partner once challenged him by saying, "Mr. Coolidge, I've made a rather sizable bet with my friends that I can get you to speak three words this evening." Coolidge replied, "You lose." Like Harding, Coolidge backed business and believed in limited government; he was said to have performed all his presidential duties in four hours a day. Coolidge's unimpeachable morality reassured voters in the wake of the Harding scandals, and he soon announced he would run for president in 1924.

The 1924 Election. The Democratic party found it difficult to mount an effective challenge to its more popular and better-financed rival, whose strength was drawn chiefly from the native-born Protestant middle class, augmented by small businesspeople, skilled workers, farmers, northern black voters, and wealthy industrialists. Democrats drew their support mainly from the South and from northern urban political machines, such as Tammany Hall in New York, but these were two constituencies whose interests often collided. Until the Democrats could build an effective national organization to rival the Republicans, they would remain a minority party.

When the Democrats gathered that year in the sweltering July heat of New York City, they were even more divided than usual. Their convention, the first to be broadcast live on national radio, lasted seventeen days, prompting the humorist Will Rogers to say, "This thing has got to come to an end. New York invited you people here as guests, not to live." The convention became hopelessly deadlocked between Governor Alfred E. Smith of New York, who had the support of northern urban politicians, and William G. McAdoo of California, Wilson's secretary of the treasury (and son-in-law), the western and southern choice. McAdoo had the backing both of former Progressives and a large faction of the Ku Klux Klan, causing opponents to jeer "Ku, Ku, McAdoo." After 103 ballots, the delegates compromised on candidate John W. Davis, a Wall Street lawyer who had served as a West Virginia congressman and ambassador to Great Britain. To attract rural voters, the Democrats chose as the vice-presidential candidate Governor Charles W. Bryan of Nebraska, brother of William Jennings Bryan.

The 1924 campaign also featured a third-party challenge by Senator Robert M. La Follette of Wisconsin, who ran on the Progressive ticket. His candidacy mobilized reformers and labor leaders, as well as disgruntled farmers. The Progressive party platform called for nationalization of the railroads, public ownership of utilities, and the right of Congress to overrule Supreme Court decisions. The platform also favored election of the president directly by the voters, rather than by the electoral college.

The Republicans won an impressive victory, with Coolidge receiving 15.7 million popular votes to 8.4 million for Davis and a decisive victory in the electoral college. Despite La Follette's vigorous campaign, he could not draw many midwestern farm leaders away from the Republican party; his labor support also proved soft. La Follette got almost 5 million popular votes but only Wisconsin supported him in the electoral college.

Perhaps the most significant fact about the 1924 election was voter apathy. Only 52 percent of the electorate bothered to vote, compared with more than 70 percent who voted in the presidential elections of the late nineteenth century. The nation's newly enfranchised women were not to blame, however: it was the drop in voting by men that was responsible for the decline.

Women in Politics. Instead of resting after the suffrage victory, women expanded their political activism throughout the 1920s. Partisan women tried to break into party politics, but the Democrats and Republicans granted them only token positions on party committees. For women, political officeholding remained a "widow's game": about two-thirds of the women in Congress were named to finish out their late husbands' terms.

Women were more influential as lobbyists. The Women's Joint Congressional Committee, a Washington-based coalition of ten major women's organizations including the newly formed League of Women Voters and the National Consumers' League, lobbied for reform legislation. Its major accomplishment was winning the passage in 1921 of the Sheppard-Towner Federal Maternity and Infancy Act, the nation's first federally funded health care program. In an attempt to reduce the high rates of death associated with childbirth, Congress appropriated $1.25 million for medical clinics, educational prenatal programs, and visiting-nurse projects. The Sheppard-Towner law passed because politicians feared that if it didn't, women would vote them out of office. As one supporter noted, "If the members could have voted in the cloak room, it would have been killed." However, in 1929, when politicians had realized that women did not vote as a bloc, they cut off appropriations for the program.

At mid-decade the Republicans were in an enviable position. The scandals of the Harding years were behind them and the economy continued to be strong, seeming to support their policy of vesting primary responsibility for the well-being of the country in the hands of corporate capitalism. The informal business-government partnership worked—or so it seemed, until the depression.

Corporate Capitalism

A revolution in management that had been reshaping American business since the late nineteenth century triumphed in the 1920s. Large-scale corporate organizations with bureaucratic structures of authority replaced family-run businesses. Ownership was divorced from control of daily operations; what the eighteenth-century economist Adam Smith had called the "invisible hand" of market forces gave way to the visible hand of management.

There were more mergers in the 1920s—368 in 1924 and 1,245 in 1929—than at any time since the heyday of combinations in the 1880s and 1890s. The largest number occurred in such rapidly growing industries as chemicals (Du Pont), electrical appliances and machinery (Westinghouse and General Electric), and automobiles (General Motors). By 1930 the two hundred largest corporations controlled almost half the nonbanking corporate wealth in the United States. It was rare for a corporation to monopolize an entire industry; rather, oligopolies, in which a few large producers controlled the market of an industry, became the norm.

By 1920 many industries, especially manufacturing industries, had modern organizational structures. The multi-unit enterprise coordinated production and distribution through divisions organized by functions, such as sales, operations, and investment. Alfred P. Sloan, Jr., an engineer and mid-level manager at General Motors, whose innovative structure set the pattern for large companies in the 1920s and 1930s, further refined this structure by relieving top management of all day-to-day control of production, freeing them to concentrate on long-range planning, while autonomous, integrated divisions met short-range production goals.

More important, corporations greatly increased their commitment to research and development, using current earnings to finance future profits. Corporate mergers were an important source of capital for this purpose. By 1927 more than a thousand corporations had set up independent research programs, among them Bell Laboratories, the research arm of the American Telephone and Telegraph Company, formally incorporated in 1925.

Running these huge modern corporate structures called for a new breed of man: the professional manager. (Women found few opportunities in the corporate hierarchy until the 1970s.) Increasingly, corporations relied on graduate schools of business, such as Wharton and Harvard, to produce managers, consultants, and executives, many of whom had engineering training. The chief executives at General Motors, General Electric, Singer, Du Pont, and Goodyear in the 1920s had been engineering classmates at the Massachusetts Institute of Technology several decades before.

River Rouge
Industrial photographers in the 1920s celebrated the power and raw beauty of industrial technology. Charles Sheeler's 1927 photograph shows Henry Ford's River Rouge plant outside Detroit. But where are the workers? (University Art Museum, University of New Mexico)

The nation's financial institutions expanded and consolidated along with its corporations. Total bank assets rose from almost $48 billion in 1919 to $72 billion in 1929, largely because of rising deposits in savings accounts and business and loan associations, along with life insurance policies and accounts. Mergers between Wall Street banks enhanced the role of New York as the financial center of the United States and, increasingly, the world. In 1929, almost half the nation's banking resources were controlled by 1 percent, or 250, of the nation's banks.

Business leaders enjoyed enormous popularity and respect in the 1920s, their reputations often surpassing those of the era's rather lackluster politicians, who often drew parallels between business leadership and religion. President Calvin Coolidge solemnly declared, "The man who builds a factory builds a temple. The man who works there worships there." The secularization of religion, or glorification of business, reached its height in a book called *The Man Nobody Knows* (1924), by advertising executive Bruce Barton. The man of the title was Jesus Christ, whom Barton portrayed as the founder of modern business, writing that Christ, "picked up twelve men from the bottom ranks of business and forged them into an organization that conquered the world." Barton's parable became an instant best seller.

The most respected businessman of the decade was Henry Ford, whose rise from a poor farm boy to corporate giant symbolized the values of rural society and American individualism in a rapidly changing world. Ford's factories, especially the River Rouge plant in suburban Detroit, represented the triumph of mass production. Ironically, this American capitalist hero achieved great popularity in the Soviet Union, selling the Russians twenty-five thousand tractors between 1920 and 1926, when the United States and the Soviet Union had no formal diplomatic relations.

Labor and Welfare Capitalism

Workers also shared in the prosperity of the 1920s, although labor lagged behind business in reaping the benefits of technology. Workers were given higher wages deliberately to increase their buying power. With a shorter work week (five days and a half day on Saturday), workers had more leisure time. Large firms like International Harvester offered employees two weeks annual paid vacation. But the scientific management techniques implemented in the 1920s reduced labor's control over the work environment. Decisions from the extremely pro-business Supreme Court, led by Chief Justice William Howard Taft, also adversely affected workers. For example, in *Colorado Coal Company v. United Mine Workers* the court ruled that a striking union could be prosecuted for illegal restraint of trade. It also struck down federal legislation regulating child labor and the minimum wage for women workers in the District of Columbia.

The 1920s were also the heyday of "welfare capitalism," a system of labor relations that stressed management's responsibility for the well-being of its employees. Though tinged with paternalism, such systems provided benefits to workers at a time when unemployment compensation and old age pensions did not exist. Employee security was not, however, the primary concern of such corporate programs, which existed mainly as a deterrent to the formation of unions.

Welfare capitalism took several forms. Workers could increase their stake in the company by buying the stock below the market price. Some firms subsidized mortgages or contributed to employee savings funds; others set up insurance and pension plans. Many adopted programs for consultation between management and elected representatives of the workers. These employee representation schemes, another device to avert unionization, were called the American Plan, so as to establish the idea that unions were un-American. Management's long-term goals included control over the workplace, an open (nonunion) shop, and worker loyalty.

However, the system had serious defects, the worst being the lack of protection against unemployment. Welfare capitalism appeared in the largest, most prosperous firms, such as General Electric and U.S. Steel, and reached only a minority of workers. Furthermore, corporate profits often dictated the nature of the programs. The Proctor & Gamble Company guaranteed forty-eight weeks of employment a year to its soap-manufacturing workers, because of the steady public demand for soap, but workers who processed vegetable oils, which were subject to wild sales fluctuations, received no such guarantee.

Welfare capitalism represented a form of labor relations squarely in keeping with the values of the 1920s. It placed the responsibility for economic welfare on the private rather than the public sector, avoiding the specter of government interference in the workplace. It also satisfied management's desire to reverse the tide of unionization: union membership dropped from 5.1 million in 1920 to 3.6 million in 1929, about 10 percent of the nonagricultural work force. The number of strikes also fell dramatically from the 1919 level. Welfare capitalism seemed to represent the wave of the future in industrial relations.

Economic Expansion Abroad

As the domestic economy expanded, so did the nation's position on the international scene. During the 1920s, the United States was the most productive country in the world, with an enormous capacity to compete in foreign markets. There was a growing demand from abroad for American products such as radios, telephones, automobiles, and sewing machines. Just as important was the demand for U.S. capital. America's emergence as the world's largest creditor nation, a reversal of its pre-World War I status as a debtor, represented a significant shift of power in the world capital markets. American investment abroad more than doubled between 1919 and 1930. By the end of the 1920s, American corporations had invested $15.2 billion in foreign countries.

Manufacturers led the way in foreign investment. Electric companies, including General Electric, built new plants in Latin America, China, Japan, and Australia. Ford had major facilities throughout the British Empire, and General Motors took over such established firms as Vauxhall in England and Opel in Germany. The International Telephone and Telegraph Corporation, founded in 1920, employed ninety-five thousand workers outside the country, more than any other U.S. company.

Other U.S. companies invested internationally during the 1920s to take advantage of lower production costs or to procure raw materials or supplies, concentrating mainly on Latin America. The three major American meat packers—Swift, Armour, and Wilson—built packing plants in Argentina to capitalize on lower livestock prices. Fruit growers, such as the United Fruit Company, developed plantations in Costa Rica, Honduras, and Guatemala. American capital also dominated sugar plantations in Cuba and rubber plantations in the Philippines, Sumatra, and Malaya.

American companies also invested heavily in mining and oil, especially in South America and Canada. The Anaconda Copper Corporation owned Chile's largest copper mine. Standard Oil of New Jersey led American oil companies in the acquisition of oil reserves in Mexico and Venezuela. American involvement in the oil-rich Persian Gulf became significant only after World War II.

American banks supported U.S. enterprises abroad, focusing much of their attention on Europe. European countries, especially Germany, desperately needed private American capital to finance economic recovery after World War I. Germany needed to rebuild its economy and pay reparations to the Allies; Britain and France had to repay wartime loans. As late as 1930, the Allies still owed the United States $4.3 billion. American political leaders, responding to the disenchantment with the nation's costly participation in the war, insisted on payment. "They hired the money, didn't they?" scoffed President Coolidge.

European countries had trouble repaying their debts because the United States maintained high protective tariffs to keep foreign-made goods out. The Fordney-McCumber Tariff of 1922 followed the long-standing Republican policy of protectionism, and the Hawley-Smoot Tariff of 1930 took economic nationalism even further. American manufacturers favored such tariffs because they feared that foreign competition would reduce their profits. But the difficulty European nations had in selling goods in the United States made it harder for them to use dollars to pay off their debts.

Concerned about debt repayment, the American banking community and many U.S. corporations with European investments opposed excessively high tariffs and urged modification of the debt structure. They recognized that a rapidly recovering Europe and a freer trade environment would help American business, while a weak European economy might undermine long-term loans and investments.

In 1924 at the prodding of the United States, France, Great Britain, and Germany joined with the United States in a plan to promote European financial stability. The Dawes plan, named for Charles G. Dawes, a Chicago banker who negotiated the agreement, offered substantial loans to Germany and a reduction in the amount of reparations owed the Allies. But the Dawes plan did not provide a permanent solution. The international economic system, dependent on the flow of American capital to Germany, reparations payments from Germany to the Allies, and the repayment of debts to the United States, was inherently unstable. If the flow of capital from the United States slowed or stopped, the whole international financial structure could collapse.

Foreign Policy in the 1920s

Foreign affairs in the period between the wars are often viewed through the lens of isolationism—that is, the view that the United States, disillusioned after World War I, willfully retreated from involvement in world affairs. But the term isolationism masks the active role that the United States was taking in world affairs, both before and after the Great War. Economic expansion into new markets was a major component of the 1920s prosperity, and the United States ardently sought a peaceful and stable world order to facilitate American investments in Latin American, European, and East Asian markets. This expansion abroad was abetted by the appropriate branches of the federal government, such as the State and Commerce departments.

In the 1920s the United States continued its quest for peaceful ways to dominate the Western Hemisphere, economically and diplomatically, but retreated slightly from its pattern of unchecked military intervention in Latin American affairs. The United States withdrew troops from the Dominican Republic in 1924, but maintained military forces in Nicaragua almost continuously from 1912 to 1933. American troops also occupied Haiti from 1915 to 1934. Relations with Mexico remained tense as a legacy of U.S. intervention during the Mexican Revolution.

There was little popular or political support, however, for entangling diplomatic commitments to allies, European or otherwise. The United States never joined the League of Nations or the Court of International Justice (the World Court). International cooperation had to come through other forums.

The Washington Conference and the Kellogg-Briand Pact. The 1921 Washington Naval Arms Conference represented a milestone in the history of disarmament. By placing limits on naval expansion, policymakers hoped to encourage stability in areas such as the Far East and protect the fragile postwar world economy from excessive arms spending. They also wished security to contain Japan, whose expansionist tendencies were already seen as threatening two decades before the outbreak of World War II.

Led by Secretary of State Charles Evan Hughes, the three leading naval powers—Britain, the United States, and Japan—joined other countries in agreeing to halt construction of large battleships for ten years and to maintain current tonnage among Britain, the United States, Japan, Italy, and France at a ratio of 5: 5: 3: 1.75: 1.75. (This maintained parity among the big three, since the Japanese fleet operated only in the Pacific.) The conferees even agreed to scrap some existing warships, leading one commentator to exclaim that in a thirty-five-minute speech the Secretary of State had sunk "more ships than all the admirals of the world have sunk in a cycle of centuries."

In a similar spirit of international cooperation, the 1928 Kellogg-Briand Peace Pact condemned militarism as a tool for advancing national interests. In 1927, French foreign minister Aristide Briand had asked the United States to sign an agreement guaranteeing France's territorial integrity and outlawing war between France and the United States. Instead, Coolidge's Secretary of State Frank Kellogg proposed a broader treaty, by which participating countries agreed to "condemn recourse to war for the solution of international controversies, and renounce it as an instrument of national policy." Fifteen nations signed the pact in Paris in 1928, with forty-eight additional nations approving it later. The Kellogg-Briand pact enjoyed the enthusiastic support of U.S. peace groups such as the Women's International League for Peace and Freedom and the Conference on the Cause and Cure of War, passing the U.S. Senate 85-1. Yet critics claimed that it was nothing more than an "international kiss": lacking enforcement machinery, it was only as effective as its signers made it. For many who abhorred war, however, the pact's broad moral statement was an important contribution to the maintenance of peace.

In the end, fervent hopes and pious declarations were no cure for the massive economic, political, and territorial problems that World War I left behind. The United States vacillated, as it would in the 1930s, between wanting to play a large role in world events and fearing that treaties or responsibilities would limit its ability to act unilaterally. Rather than criticize as naive or misguided the diplomatic efforts of the 1920s, it is perhaps best to see them as honest yet ultimately inadequate efforts to find a will to peace.

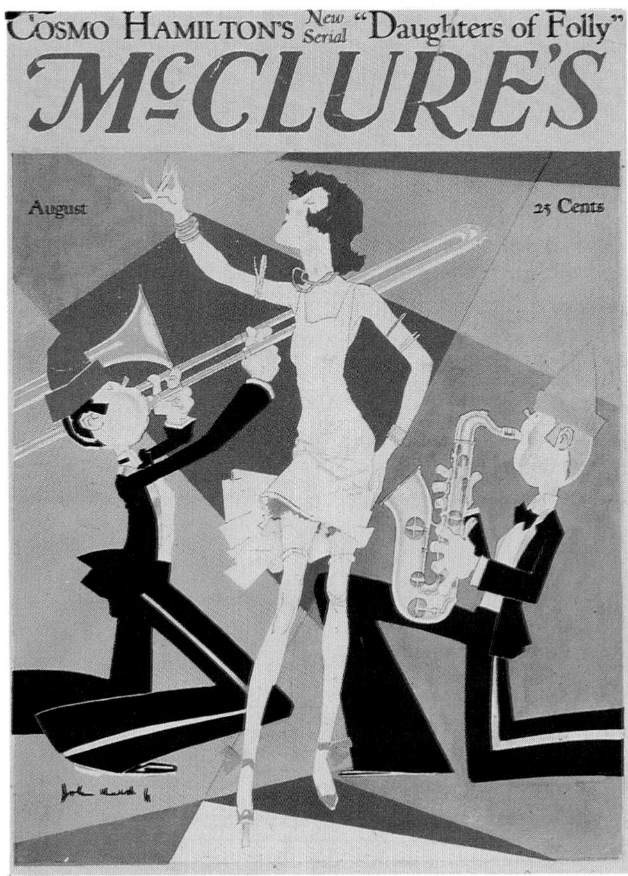

The Roaring Twenties

Rarely has a decade been defined so predominantly in cultural clichés as the 1920s—flappers, bathtub gin, speakeasies, the Charleston, and gangsters shooting it out on the streets of Chicago. John Held, Jr.'s cover for *McClure's* magazine suggests how the decade got its name of the "Roaring Twenties." But most Americans were too concerned with earning a living and raising a family to learn the latest dance craze.

A New National Culture

The 1920s represented an important watershed in the development of a mass national culture. Automobiles, paved roads, parcel post service, movies, radios, telephones, mass circulation magazines, brand names, and chain stores linked Americans—in the mill towns of the Southern Piedmont, to outposts on the Oklahoma plains, western mining settlements, and ethnic enclaves on the East and West coasts—in an ever-expanding web of national experience. A new emphasis on leisure, consumption, and amusement characterized the modern era, although its benefits were more accessible to the white middle class than to minorities and other disadvantaged groups.

Consumption and Advertising

In homes across the country during the 1920s, Americans sat down to a breakfast of Kellogg's corn flakes with toast prepared in a General Electric toaster. They got into the Ford Model T to go about their business—perhaps shopping at one of the new chain stores, such as Safeway or A. & P., which had sprung up across the country. In the evening, the family gathered to listen to radio programs, such as "Great Moments in History" and "True Story," read the latest issue of the *Saturday Evening Post*, *Reader's Digest*, or *Collier's*. On weekends they might hop into the car to take in the latest Charlie Chaplin film at the local movie theater. Millions of Americans now shared the same daily experiences.

The 1920s were a critical decade in the development of the American consumer society. Although not every family participated in this new lifestyle, consumption became a cultural ideal for most of the middle class, often providing the criterion for judging self-worth that was once supplied by character, religion, and social standing. Spending money became a form of self-fulfillment, a gratification of personal needs.

Yet participation in commercial mass culture did not necessarily mean a total sell-out to middle-class values. Buying a Victrola or a radio on credit and listening to the opera singer Enrico Caruso could be one way for Italian immigrants to keep their culture alive. Nor was owning a car simply a symbol of consumption. "I had bought a jalopy in 1924, and it didn't change me," remembered one Communist Party activist, "It just made it easier for me to function." One historian concluded, "Chicago's ethnic workers were not transformed into more Americanized, middle-class people by the objects they consumed. Buying an electric vacuum cleaner did not turn Josef Dobrowolski into 'True Story''s Jim Smith."

The unequal distribution of income limited some consumers' ability to buy the enticing new products. At the height of prosperity in the 1920s, about 65 percent of America's families had an income of less than $2,000 a year. The average family income for the bottom 40 percent of the population was $725. Of that amount, a family would spend about $290 a year for food, $190 for housing, and $110 for clothing, leaving only $135 for everything else.

Retailers and automobile manufacturers addressed this situation by selling on the installment plan. In those days "Buy now, pay later" was a revolutionary concept. Before World War I most urban families paid cash for everything except a house. Then, during the 1920s, the automobile was such an object of desire that consumers put aside their fears of buying on time. By 1927, two-thirds of the cars in the United States were being paid for on the installment plan. Once people saw how easy it was to finance a car, they bought radios, refrigerators, and sewing machines. "A dollar down and a dollar forever," a cynic remarked. By 1929 banks, finance companies, credit unions, and other institutions were extending consumers loans of over $7 billion a year, and consumer lending was the tenth largest business in the United States.

Consumers spent about $667 million for electric appliances in 1927. By 1930, 85 percent of the nation's nonfarm households had the electricity to run their favorite gadgets. Irons and vacuum cleaners were the most popular appliances, followed by phonographs, sewing machines, and washing machines. Radios,

Advertising on a National Scale

Refrigerators did not save as much time or labor as other appliances, such as electric irons and vacuum cleaners, but they did have advantages. For example, food stayed fresh longer, which reduced the need to shop every day and, as this ad from the *Saturday Evening Post* in August 1928 suggested, refrigerators made entertaining easier.

whose production increased twenty-five-fold in the 1920s, sold for around $75. One of the most expensive items was a refrigerator, which cost $900 at the beginning of the decade. Technology quickly brought the price down to $180, but many families still had to make do with an icebox.

Because much of the new technology was concentrated in the home, it had a dramatic impact on the lives of women. Domestic chores became less arduous. It was far easier to plug in an electric iron than it was to heat an iron on the stove, and quicker to use a vacuum cleaner than a broom and a rug beater. Paradoxically, however, all these conveniences made more work for women. Electric servants replaced human ones and more middle-class women began to do their own housework and laundry. Technology also raised standards of cleanliness so that a man could wear a clean shirt every day instead of just on Sunday, and a house could be vacuumed daily rather than weekly.

The Flapper
The flapper phenomenon was not limited to Anglos. This 1921 photograph of a young Mexican-American woman shows how American fads and fashions reached into Hispanic communities across the country.

Advertising became big business in the 1920s. By 1929 advertisers were spending an average of $15 annually for every man, woman, and child in the United States—a total of $2.6 billion—to entice them to buy automobiles, cigarettes, radios, and refrigerators. That year, the advertising industry, which one historian called the "town criers" of modernity, accounted for 3 percent of the gross national product, comparable to its share after World War II. Many of the major advertising firms relied on experts in the field of psychology. The prominent psychologist John B. Watson left Johns Hopkins University in 1920 to become vice-president of the J. Walter Thompson advertising agency, and the advertising pioneer Edward Bernays was the nephew of Sigmund Freud.

Few of the new consumer products could be considered necessities of life, so advertisements used psychology to stir desire in consumers. Advertisers often used a white-coated doctor to imply scientific approval of their products. They also appealed to people's social aspirations by projecting images of successful, elegant, sophisticated people, who smoked a certain brand of cigarettes or drove a recognizable make of car. Ad writers sold products by preying on people's insecurities. They came up with a variety of socially unacceptable diseases, including "sneaker smell," "paralyzed pores," "office hips," "ashtray breath," and the dreaded "B.O." (body odor). After the term *halitosis* was discovered in an obscure British medical journal, many consumers rushed out to buy Listerine mouth wash. Yet American consumers were hardly passive victims of advertisers—evil "captains of consciousness" manipulating their every whim. America gloried in its role as the world's first mass-consumption economy.

Many of these cultural images came together in the flapper, the emancipated woman of the 1920s. With her slim, boyish figure, bobbed hair, short skirt and rolled-down silk stockings, the flapper symbolized the personal freedom trumpeted by the movies, advertisements, and other elements of the emerging mass culture. The flapper wore makeup (previously associated with lower-class women out for sexual favors) and lit up her cigarettes in public, a shocking affront to ladylike decency, which suggested the new, looser morality of the times. Like so many cultural icons, the flapper represented only a tiny minority of women. Yet the image mass marketed the belief in women's postsuffrage emancipation.

The Automobile Culture

As the predominant symbol of the 1920s, the automobile typified the new consumer-based economy. "Why on earth do you need to study what's changing this country?" a Muncie, Indiana, resident asked sociologists Robert and Helen Lynd, who were studying American culture and values. "I can tell you what's happening in just four letters: A-U-T-O!" The showpiece of modern capitalism and the ultimate consumer toy, the automobile revolutionized the ways Americans spent their income and their leisure time. The isolation of rural life broke down in the wake of the automobile. New phrases, such as "filling station" (or, as they were known west of the Rockies, "service stations") entered the nation's vocabulary. The automobile even affected crime, providing gangsters with a "getaway car" and the possibility of "taking someone for a ride." Cars touched so many aspects of American life that the word *automobility* was coined to describe their revolutionary impact on production methods, the nation's landscape, and even American values.

The automobile stimulated the prosperity of the 1920s. Before the introduction of the moving assembly line in 1913, it took Ford workers twelve and a half

AMERICAN VOICES

The Automobile Culture *The Residents of "Middletown"*

In their study of community life in Muncie, Indiana, Robert and Helen Lynd found that the "horse culture" of the 1890s had been totally supplanted by the automobile culture of the 1920s. According to the sociologists, "ownership of an automobile has now reached the point of being an accepted essential of normal living," as these residents confirm.

"We'd rather do without clothes than give up the car. We used to go to his sister's to visit, but by the time we'd get the children shoed and dressed there wasn't any money left for carfare. Now no matter how they look, we just poke 'em in the car and take 'em along."

"We don't spend anything on recreation except for the car. We save every place we can and put the money into the car. It keeps the family together."

"No, sir, we've *not* got a car. *That's* why we've got a home."

"The Ford car has done an awful lot of harm to the unions here and everywhere else. As long as men have enough money to buy a second-hand Ford and tires and gasoline, they'll be out on the road and paying no attention to union meetings."

"We don't have no fancy clothes when we have the car to pay for. The car is the only pleasure we have."

"He don't like to go to church Sunday night. We've been away from church this summer more'n ever since we got our car."

"I'll go without food before I'll see us give up the car."

"An automobile is a luxury, and no one has a right to one if he can't afford it. I haven't the slightest sympathy for any one who is out of work if he owns a car."

Source: Robert S. Lynd and Helen Merrell Lynd, *Middletown: A Study In Modern American Culture*

hours to assemble an auto; it took ninety-three minutes on an assembly line. In 1927, Ford produced an auto every twenty-four seconds. Car sales climbed from 1.5 million in 1921 to 5 million in 1929, when Americans spent $2.58 billion on new and used cars. By the late 1920s, a new Ford Model T, which cost $1,000 in 1908, sold for only $295 (at a time when the average industrial worker earned about $5 a day). Lower cost and installment buying increased yearly car registrations from 8.5 million in 1920 to 23 million in 1929. By the end of the decade, Americans owned about 80 percent of the world's automobiles, with an average of one car for every five people.

The growth of the auto industry had a ripple effect on the American economy. In 1929, 3.7 million workers owed their jobs to the automobile, directly or indirectly. Auto production stimulated the steel, petroleum, chemical, rubber, and glass industries. Total U.S. demand for oil, mainly for gasoline, multiplied two and a half times in the United States between 1919 and 1929, and domestic oil production expanded to meet the need. (The United States was still the world's chief supplier of oil in the 1920s.) The advertising industry grew along with the automobile; cars and cigarettes were two of the most heavily marketed products of the decade. Highway construction became a billion-dollar-a-year enterprise financed by federal subsidies and state gasoline taxes. Car ownership also spurred the growth of suburbs and contributed to real estate speculation. It spawned the first shopping center, Country Club Plaza, in Kansas City in 1924. Not even the death of twenty-five thousand people a year in traffic accidents, 70 percent of them pedestrians, could cool America's passion for the automobile.

Nowhere was this more obvious than in the way Americans were spending their leisure time. They took to the roads, becoming a nation of tourists. The American Automobile Association, founded in 1902, reported that in 1929 about 45 million people—almost a third of the population—took vacations by automobile. Of the $10 billion spent on recreation in 1930, two-thirds went for cars and related expenses. People preferred the freedom of automobiles to the rigid timetables and predetermined routes of trains. With improved roads, mo-

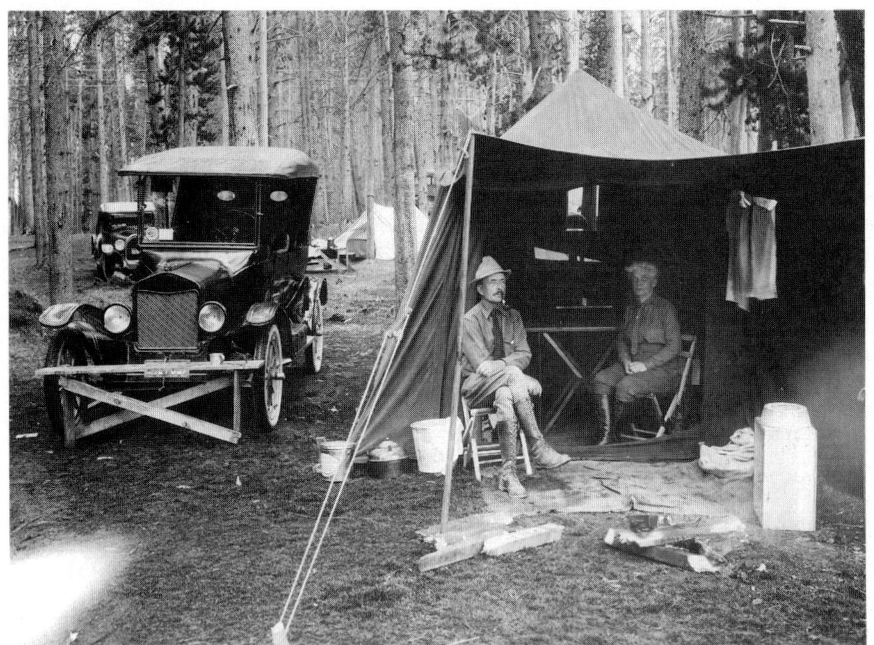

The Automobile Vacation
This contented couple was autocamping in Yellowstone Park in 1923. Autocamping was portrayed as a great liberation from seedy hotels and rigid railroad timetables. When farmers complained about auto tourists' tendency to camp right in their fields, towns instituted auto camps. When auto camps became associated with transients and hobos in the depression, tourist cabins (with a spot to park your car next to the cabin) became the vogue. By the 1940s, it was just a short step to the modern motel chain.

torists could average more than 45 miles per hour on their way to the "autocamps" and tourist cabins that were the forerunners of motels.

Young people embraced cars because they made it possible to escape parental supervision. Like movies and other products of the new mass culture, cars changed the dating patterns of young Americans. Contrary to many parents' views, sex was not invented in the back seat of a Ford, but a Model T offered more privacy and comfort than the family living room or front porch. City elders in Muncie, Indiana, overreacted by calling automobiles "prostitution on wheels."

The most popular car of the decade was the Model T. The Ford Motor Company manufactured over fifteen million Model T's between 1908 and 1927. "Tin Lizzies," as the dependable Model T's were called, required a driver who was mechanically inclined. The motorist had to handcrank the car to start it, and keep one hand on the accelerator and the other on the wheel while driving. There was no gas gauge—one had to remove the front seat and peer into the tank to see how much gas there was. As for color, Henry Ford said, "The customer can have a Ford any color he wants—so long as it's black." As late as 1919, only about 10 percent of the nation's cars had a roof.

Consumers eventually became discontented with the Model T and Ford faced stiff competition from General Motors. GM's five automobile divisions turned out cars for specialized markets: the luxury Cadillac cost the most and had the lowest volume of sales; the Chevrolet boasted the cheapest price tag and highest volume of sales; Oldsmobile, Pontiac, and Buick were geared to incomes in between. GM cars also featured self-starters and foot accelerators. Henry Ford finally bowed to consumer demands when he introduced the Model A in 1927. More than a million New Yorkers visited the Ford showroom during the five days after the new model was unveiled. At prices ranging from $495 to $570, the Model A lived up to consumers' demands for different styles, more colors, and greater comfort, and helped make the automobile a permanent part of American culture.

The Movies and Mass Culture

The movie industry probably did more than anything else to disseminate common values and attitudes throughout the United States. Its growth coincided with America's transformation into a predominantly urban, industrial society. In contrast to Europe, where cinema developed as an avant-garde, highbrow art form, American movies were part of popular culture almost from the start—a mass entertainment industry that was both democratic and highly profitable.

The Silent Era. Movies began around the turn of the century in nickelodeons, where for a nickel the mostly working-class audience could see a one-reel silent film such as *The Great Train Robbery* (1903). Because the films, mostly comedies and melodramas, were silent, they could be understood by immigrants who did not yet speak English. The new medium grew in popularity and profitability.

During the first years of the twentieth century, most films were made in New York City or Fort Lee, New Jersey. After 1910, moviemakers like D. W. Griffith and Cecil B. DeMille moved to southern California, drawn

The Tramp
Charlie Chaplin did not invent the tragicomic figure of the tramp, but it soon became his trademark screen persona. Chaplin grew up poor in the London slums, but the movies brought him wealth and fame. In 1919 he joined Douglas Fairbanks, Mary Pickford, and D. W. Griffith to form United Artists.

by cheap land, plenty of sunshine, and varied scenery—mountains, deserts, cities, and the Pacific Ocean all within easy reach—and by Los Angeles's reputation as an anti-union town. Actors also flocked to California, especially to Hollywood, a fast-growing suburb of Los Angeles. The new movie stars—comedians Buster Keaton, Charlie Chaplin, and Harold Lloyd, Mary Pickford ("America's Sweetheart"), the dashing Douglas Fairbanks, and Clara Bow (the "It" girl)—became national idols.

Movies quickly outgrew their working-class origins and reached middle-class audiences. D. W. Griffith's racist epic *Birth of a Nation* (1915) was a milestone in establishing the feature film as popular entertainment. The outbreak of World War I in Europe eliminated competition from Italian and French moviemakers (the same chemicals used to produce celluloid for film were crucial for the manufacture of gunpowder). By the war's end, the United States was making 90 percent of the world's films, and Hollywood reigned as the movie capital of the world for the next several decades. Foreign distribution of Hollywood films stimulated the market for the American material culture so lavishly displayed on the screen.

Movies fed the desires of a mass consumption economy, and set national trends in clothing and hairstyles. They also served as a form of sex education. Rudolph Valentino, best known as the romantic hero of *The Sheik* (1921), symbolized passion on the screen. The message was not wasted on the nation's youth. "It was directly through the movies that I learned to kiss a girl on her ears, neck, and cheeks, as well as on the mouth," confessed one boy. Many girls noticed that actresses kissed with their eyes closed, and so they too closed their eyes. A sociologist concluded that movies made young people more "sex-wise, sex-excited, and sex-absorbed" than any previous generation. The impact of the movies on sexual attitudes and morality has remained strong ever since.

The Coming of Sound. Movies were big business. Power in the industry was concentrated in large studios such as United Artists, Paramount, and Metro-Goldwyn-Mayer, which were controlled mainly by Eastern European Jewish immigrants, like Adolph Zukor and Samuel Goldfish (later Goldwyn). These studios were out for maximum profitability, not for artistic expression or creativity. In 1926 they grossed $1.5 billion a year. With distribution as well as production tightly controlled, the movie industry represented an example of a vertically integrated monopoly.

Though most of the movies were made in Hollywood, the studios were financed by eastern banks. Such financial connections were strained in the late 1920s because all the major studios borrowed huge sums of money to convert from silent production to "talkies." The total cost of conversion reached $300 million, but the overwhelming success of the new films quickly paid back the investment.

Warner Brothers' *The Jazz Singer* (1927), starring Al Jolson, was the first feature-length film to offer sound. By 1929 all the major studios had completed the changeover to talkies. While no one had thought of movies as silent until talkies took their place, silent films soon became obsolete. By the end of the 1920s, the nation had almost twenty-three thousand movie theaters, many of them elaborate movie palaces built by the studios in major cities. Movie attendance rose from 60 million in 1927 to 90 million in 1930. By then, movies were thoroughly entrenched as the most popular—and probably the most influential—form of the new urban-based mass media.

AMERICAN LIVES

Clara Bow
The "It" Girl

When Clara Bow, the "It" Girl of the 1920s, was asked to define what "it" meant, she replied, "I ain't real sure." To most fans, "it" was synonymous with sex appeal, but Elinor Glyn, the British writer who coined the phrase, had a more convoluted definition: "To have 'It' the fortunate possessor must have that strange magnetism which attracts both sexes. 'It' is purely virile quality belonging to a strong character. . . . There must be physical attraction, but beauty is unnecessary. Conceit or selfconsciousness destroys 'It' immediately." Whatever "it" was, when Paramount released a movie in 1927 based on the Elinor Glyn novella and starring Clara Bow, the film grossed $1 million. Soon Clara Bow was receiving almost 35,000 fan letters a month, many addressed simply to "The 'It' Girl, Hollywood U.S.A." In 1927 she was all of twenty-two years old.

The thin plot of the film hardly seems capable of launching a national obsession, but it did. Clara Bow plays a department store clerk named Betty Lou Spense, who is out to catch her rich, handsome boss. He too is smitten, and when he calls on her in her modest home, he finds her minding a friend's baby. However, he jumps to the mistaken conclusion that she is an unmarried mother, and propositions her. She is indignant at the insult, but after several twists of the plot they resolve their differences. In the final scene they kiss on the store owner's yacht, *Itola,* with the embrace obscuring all but the first two letters of the yacht's name. That's right—IT!

Clara Bow—the Twenties' Sex Symbol

"It" was typical of Hollywood's fascination with flapper themes in the 1920s. (The term *flapper* originated with women's fad of leaving galoshes unbuckled, which made them flap.) On screen and off the flapper was emancipated, urban, and young, befitting the worship of youth characteristic of the 1920s. She was a working girl with money to spend, time on her hands, and a wardrobe of mass-produced fashions, especially short skirts suitable for dancing and dating. On screen she was sensual, but not promiscuous, often marrying the male lead at the end. Hollywood stars Colleen Moore and Louise Brooks also played flapper roles.

Before Clara Bow became indelibly known as the "It" girl, her studio had tried to promote her as the "Brooklyn Bonfire." The name never stuck, but it revealed her background. Clara Bow was born on July 29, 1905, to an extremely poor family in Brooklyn, New York; her mother was mentally unstable and her father was often unemployed. She dropped out of school during the eighth grade. About the only place she found refuge from her grim family life was at the movies. Like so many other young girls, Clara Bow decided that she wanted to be an actress.

Her break came when she won a 1921 "Fame and Fortune" beauty contest sponsored by three movie magazines, which helped her land a bit part in *Beyond the Rainbow* (1922). Unfortunately, her scenes ended up on the cutting room floor, but they were restored after she became a hit. In 1923 she won a Hollywood contract, and by 1924 had made thirteen films, none memorable. Her roles improved when she signed with Paramount Studio in 1925; it was her performances in *Dancing Mothers* (1926) and *Mantrap* (1926), two movies with Jazz-Age themes, that led Elinor Glyn to pronounce that Clara Bow had "it" on the screen.

Clara Bow had an amazing screen presence. Studio executive B. P. Schulberg called her "the hottest jazz baby in films." Observed a young man who first saw her at age seventeen, "I've never taken dope, but it was like a shot of dope when you looked at this girl." Wrote the *New York Times* of her performance in *Mantrap*, "She could flirt with a grizzly bear." She had a boyish figure, and what one reviewer called "flirts eyes." She was especially known for her shock of red hair. (In the 1920s redheads were thought to be highly sexed. Just as the vamp of the 1910s had dark hair and the platinum blonde was the typical star of the 1930s, the 1920s was the decade of the redhead.) On screen, she never seemed to stay still.

Yet Clara Bow's career lasted less than five years after the success of *It*. Somewhat unstable emotionally, she had several nervous breakdowns. As she once said, "A sex symbol is a heavy load to carry when one is tired, hurt, and bewildered." She was also hurt by scandals in her personal life, including widely publicized affairs with Gary Cooper and director Victor Fleming and a legal dispute with a former secretary. Futhermore, like many silent stars she found the transition to talkies difficult. It was not simply a matter of her Brooklyn accent—voice lessons could smooth that out. But her whole style of acting, which was very emotional and involved constant movement around the set, was inimical to the early days of sound recording, where an actor had to stay close to a stationary microphone in order to speak dialogue.

In 1931, Clara Bow announced she was leaving Hollywood to live with Rex Bell, a Nevada rancher whom she married later that year. She returned briefly to make two films before declaring, "I've had enough" in 1933. She now devoted full time to her marriage, and her sons born in 1934 and 1938, but her emotional instability made it hard for her to find happiness and she and Bell eventually separated. She died in Los Angeles in 1965, long before her films had become cult classics. Said her son on seeing *It* for the first time in 1987, sixty years after its release, "If I ever saw Mother, I saw her in that movie. The tremendous facial expression. . . . It brought back so vividly what she was like." Or more likely, what she wished she was like.

Towards the end of her life, Clara Bow reflected on the differences between Hollywood in the 1920s and the 1960s in a way that makes clear where her sympathies lay. "We had individuality. We did as we pleased. We stayed up late. We dressed the way we wanted. Today, stars are sensible and end up with better health. But *we* had more fun."

"Rough-House Rosie"
A hand-painted poster was created for this 1927 film.

All That Jazz

George E. Lee's Singing Novelty Orchestra was a popular Kansas City act. Part of the novelty was his sister Julia Lee, who was both pianist and singer.

Jazz. It is perhaps no coincidence that the first talkie was *The Jazz Singer*. Jazz was such a popular part of the new mass culture that the 1920s are often called "the Jazz Age." This music remains one of the most distinctive American art forms. An improvisational form whose notes are rarely written down, jazz originated in the bordellos of New Orleans' Storyville quarter around the turn of the century. The origin of the word is obscure, but many link it to a vulgar term for the sex act. With its roots in urban culture, and drawing on earlier African-American music, such as ragtime and the blues, jazz gave African-Americans an outlet for expression of dissent and opposition to white values.

All the early jazz musicians were black. As they left the South, they took jazz rhythms to Chicago, New York, Kansas City, Los Angeles, and other cities. Some of the best known were composer-pianist Ferdinand ("Jelly Roll") Morton, who wrote "Dead Man Blues" and "Black Bottom Stomp"; trumpeter Louis Armstrong, who got his start with Joseph ("King") Oliver's Creole Jazz Band in Chicago in the early 1920s; and singer Bessie Smith, "the empress of the Blues." One of the most creative jazz innovators, Edward "Duke" Ellington, came to New York in 1927, and performed at the Cotton Club in Harlem. Phonograph records, especially those made by Louis Armstrong in the late 1920s, spread the appeal of jazz by capturing its spontaneity; in turn, jazz boosted the infant recording industry. Soon this uniquely American art form had caught on in Europe, especially in France.

Journalism and Radio. Other instruments of mass media helped establish national standards of taste and behavior. In 1922 ten magazines claimed a circulation of at least 2.5 million, and twelve others sold a million copies of each issue. The *Saturday Evening Post*, the *Ladies' Home Journal*, *Collier's Weekly*, and *Good Housekeeping* could be found in homes throughout the country. *Reader's Digest*, *Time*, and *The New Yorker* all started up in the 1920s. Thanks to syndicated columns and features in newspapers, people could read the same articles everywhere in the United States. They also bought the same books, partly because the Book of the Month Club was founded in 1926.

Tabloid newspapers—sometimes called jazz journalism—also became part of the national scene in this period. In 1919, just two days before the signing of the Versailles treaty, publisher Joseph Medill Patterson introduced *The New York Illustrated Daily News*. Half the size of a regular newspaper, with bold headlines, large photographs, and short, preferably sensational stories, tabloids were meant to be read quickly—for instance, while riding the subway to work. All the country's major cities had at least one tabloid competing with more sedate newspapers by 1932. As journalist Simon Bessie noted, the tabloid reflected the tenor of the times: "excitement, candid interest in sex and crime, hurry and an intense application to diversion."

The newest instrument of mass culture was truly a child of the 1920s. On November 2, 1920, professional radio broadcasting began when station KDKA in Pittsburgh carried the presidential election returns. By 1929 about 40 percent of the nation's households had a radio. There were more than eight hundred stations, most affiliated with either the Columbia Broadcasting Service (CBS), formed in 1928, or the National Broadcasting Company (NBC), started in 1926, which had two networks, Red and Blue. (These corporations would dominate the next leap forward in mass communication: television.) Unlike European networks, which were government monopolies, American radio stations operated for profit. The U.S. government licensed the stations, but their revenue came primarily from advertisers and corporate sponsors.

Americans loved radio. They listened to the World Series and other sports events, and to variety entertainment shows sponsored by advertisers of major brand-name products, which featured such composers as the Cliquot Club Eskimos, the Lucky Strike Orchestra, and the A. & P. Gypsies. One of the most popular radio shows of all time, "Amos 'n' Andy," which premiered on the NBC network in 1928, featured two white actors playing stereotypical black characters. Soon fractured phrases from "Amos 'n' Andy," like "Check and double check," became part of everyday speech. So many people "tuned in" (another new phrase of the 1920s) that the country almost seemed to come to a halt during favorite programs.

New Patterns of Leisure

One of the most significant developments in modern life has been the growing freedom of workers from constant physical toil. As the work week shrank and workers won the right to paid vacations, Americans had more time—and energy—to spend at leisure. Like so much else in the 1920s, leisure was increasingly tied to consumption and mass culture.

Sports and Recreation. Public recreation flourished during the 1920s. Cities and suburbs built baseball diamonds, tennis courts, swimming pools, and golf courses for their residents. In the New York metropolitan area, city planner Robert Moses masterminded a vast system of parks, playgrounds, and picnic areas. His greatest achievement was Jones Beach on Long Island. Moses not only created the state park but built limited-access highways to it. Any New Yorker with a car—an important limit on freedom of consumption—could escape to a public beach in less than forty minutes.

People not only played sports, but had time and money to watch them as well. Professional sports became increasingly commercialized. People could watch a game in a comfortable stadium, listen to it on the radio, or see highlights of it in a newsreel at the local movie theater. One of the most widely followed sports was boxing; Jack Dempsey was one of the decade's celebrity athletes. Baseball drew between nine and ten million fans a year. Tarnished in 1919 by the "Black Sox" scandal when gamblers bribed Chicago White Sox players to throw the World Series, baseball bounced back with the rise of such heroes as Babe Ruth of the Boston Red Sox and the New York Yankees. Nicknamed the "Sultan of Swat," Ruth electrified crowds by hitting more home runs—and hitting them farther—than any other player up to that time. Yankee Stadium became known as the "house that Ruth built." Reflecting the racism found in sports and in society as a whole, black athletes played in Negro Leagues, which were formed in the 1920s.

Boxing Heroes

Painter George Bellows (1882–1925) often painted boxing scenes. *Dempsey and Firpo* (1924) depicts a heavyweight fight between Jack Dempsey, the "Manassas Mauler," and challenger Luis Firpo, the "Wild Bull of the Pampas." Dempsey is the one being unceremoniously knocked out of the ring. Boxing was one of the most popular sports in the sports-crazy 1920s. (Whitney Museum of American Art)

Newspapers, especially the tabloids, capitalized on popular interest in sports. Sports coverage, especially the latest scores or fight results, sold papers. College football games, such as the annual Harvard-Yale game and the Rose Bowl, received national coverage. Football fans followed the fortunes of the Four Horsemen of Notre Dame, the most famous backfield in college football history. In 1924 Red Grange of the University of Illinois became nationally known for scoring five touchdowns against the University of Michigan the first five times he carried the ball.

Other sports gave the public more heroes. Bobby Jones ranked as the decade's best golfer. Bill Tilden dominated men's tennis, while Helen Wills and Suzanne Lenglen reigned in the women's game. The decade's best-known swimmer, male or female, was Gertrude Ederle, who shattered all records in 1926 by swimming the English Channel in just over fourteen hours. Thanks to the attention of the media, the popularity of sports figures rivalled that of movie stars.

Without a doubt, the decade's most popular hero was aviator Charles Lindbergh, a former stunt flyer and airmail pilot from Minnesota. On May 20, 1927, Lindbergh made the first successful solo nonstop flight between New York and Paris. For the 3,610 mile, 33½-hour flight, in *The Spirit of St. Louis*, Lindbergh took only five sandwiches and one day's worth of tinned rations, saying, "If I get to Paris, I won't need any more, and if I don't get to Paris, I won't need any more either." Lindbergh captivated America because he combined the mastery of new technology (the airplane) with the traditional American virtues of individualism, self-reliance, and hard work. His charm and boyish good looks didn't hurt, either. He was twenty-five years old at the time of his record-breaking flight, and in 1928 *Time* magazine chose him as its first Man of the Year.

Dissenting Values and Cultural Conflict

Many Americans were deeply disturbed by the secular values unleashed in the 1920s. To rural Americans, the new values were an affront to a more traditional way of life, rooted in small towns and farming communities of the nineteenth century. Cultural and political conflict broke out over such issues as immigration restriction, Prohibition, and race relations. Tension between city and country played a part in all these conflicts, but it was not the sole cause. Many city dwellers had been born and raised in the country and their memories were strong. Resistance to change and an ambivalence about modernity—feelings that transcended the urban-rural polarity—probably had a greater influence.

Urban Majority, Rural Minority

"The United States was born in the country and has moved to the city," the historian Richard Hofstadter observed. When the 1920 census revealed that for the first time city people outnumbered rural ones, Americans realized that a big change had taken place, rivalling the closing of the frontier in 1890. In 1920, 52 percent of the population lived in urban areas, compared with 28 percent in 1870, only fifty years earlier.

The 1920 census exaggerated the extent of urbanization by classifying as cities towns with only 2,500 people, but there was still no mistaking the trend. By 1929, ninety-three cities had a population of over 100,000. New York City exceeded 7 million in the 1920s, Chicago boasted close to 3 million, and the population of fast-growing Los Angeles doubled to more than 1.2 million. Outside the major cities, growth was even more impressive. Thanks to the availability of cheap land and better transportation—notably the automobile—metropolitan areas spread out and suburbs sprang up. This trend started long before the post-World War II suburban boom.

The conflict over values that had been building since the late nineteenth century took on special force in the 1920s. After the recession of 1920–1921, farmers continued to struggle, and rural communities lost people to the cities at an alarming rate. During the 1920s, about six million Americans left the farms for the cities, including many blacks who abandoned the South altogether for the seemingly greater freedom of the North. Political districts did not reflect this population shift, however, and rural areas still controlled most state legislatures. Battles over the equitable use of tax dollars, especially for city services, intensified the rural-urban political conflict.

Yet it would be wrong to describe this conflict as a last-ditch effort on the part of rural America to maintain political and cultural dominance. The lives of rural people, too, had been affected by the same forces that influenced urban life. Much of the new technology—especially electricity and automobiles—enhanced rural life. Rural people were tempted by the new materialistic values trumpeted by radio programs, magazines, and movies, and though they tried to resist, many found more to attract them than to repel them. The cultural conflicts in the 1920s may have been intensified by the realization, on the part of both rural and urban dwellers, of how far they had already strayed.

The Rise of Nativism

When native-born white Protestant Americans looked at their communities in 1920, they saw a different nation than the one they had been born into forty years earlier. During that time, more than 23 million immi-

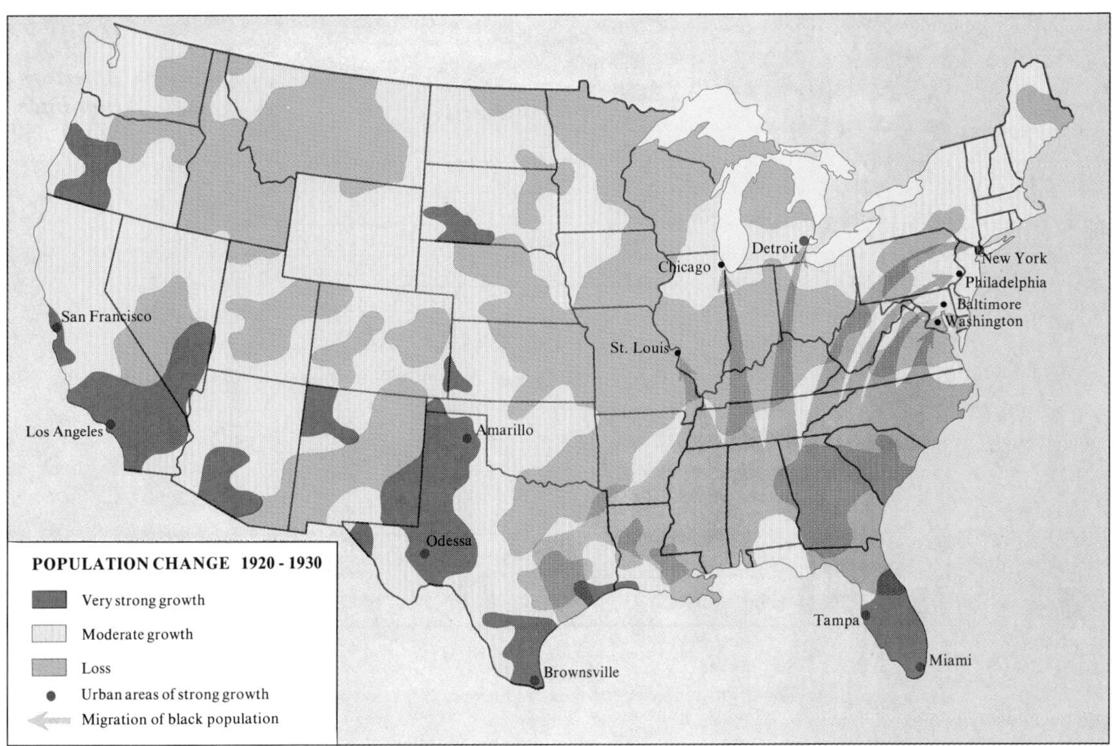

MAP 24.1

The Shift From Rural to Urban Population, 1920–1930

Despite the increasingly urban tone of modern America after 1920, regional patterns of population growth and decline were far from uniform. Cities in the South and West grew most dramatically, as southern farmers moved to more promising areas in familiar climates. One important component of the growth of northern cities, such as New York and Chicago, was the migration of southern blacks set in motion by World War I.

grants had come to America to seek a new life. Most of them came from peasant backgrounds, and many were Catholics or Jews. Senator William Bruce of Maryland called them "indigestible lumps" in the "national stomach," implying that the nation would be unable to absorb these immigrants from southeastern Europe and Russia. As President Coolidge said in 1924, "America must be kept American." Such sentiments, which were widely shared, came to be known as *nativism*.

These feelings were tapped in the 1920s to mount a successful drive against immigration. Originally, immigrants from Asia had been targets of restriction. In 1882 the Chinese were totally excluded, and Theodore Roosevelt negotiated a "gentleman's agreement" to limit Japanese immigrants in 1908. But now nativists demanded broader measures, aimed at European immigrants. In 1917 the United States required all immigrants to pass a literacy test, but it proved to be only a slight deterrent. If immigrants were determined to find a new life in America, they were willing to learn enough English to pass a simple test.

World War I and its aftermath had a direct impact on the immigration question. Nativists played up the immigrants' association with radicalism and labor unrest—a legacy of the Red Scare. The super-patriotism of the war years, especially the emphasis on Americanization, also fed into nativism. When the end of the war made it possible to cross the Atlantic in safety again, many feared that it would bring a new wave of immigrants to America, and they would take jobs away from Americans and cause social unrest. In 1921, Congress passed an emergency bill limiting the number of immigrants to 3 percent of each national group, as counted in the 1910 census. President Wilson refused to sign the legislation, but it was reintroduced and passed under Warren Harding. The new law produced immediate results. In the twelve-month period ending in June 1921, 805,228 immigrants had entered the United States; in the next twelve months, the number dropped to 309,556.

For many Americans, this quota system was still a sieve with too many holes. The National Origins Act of 1924 cut immigration back to 2 percent of each nationality, as reflected in the 1890 census, which included relatively small numbers of people from the "undesirable" areas of southeastern Europe and Russia. This cut the

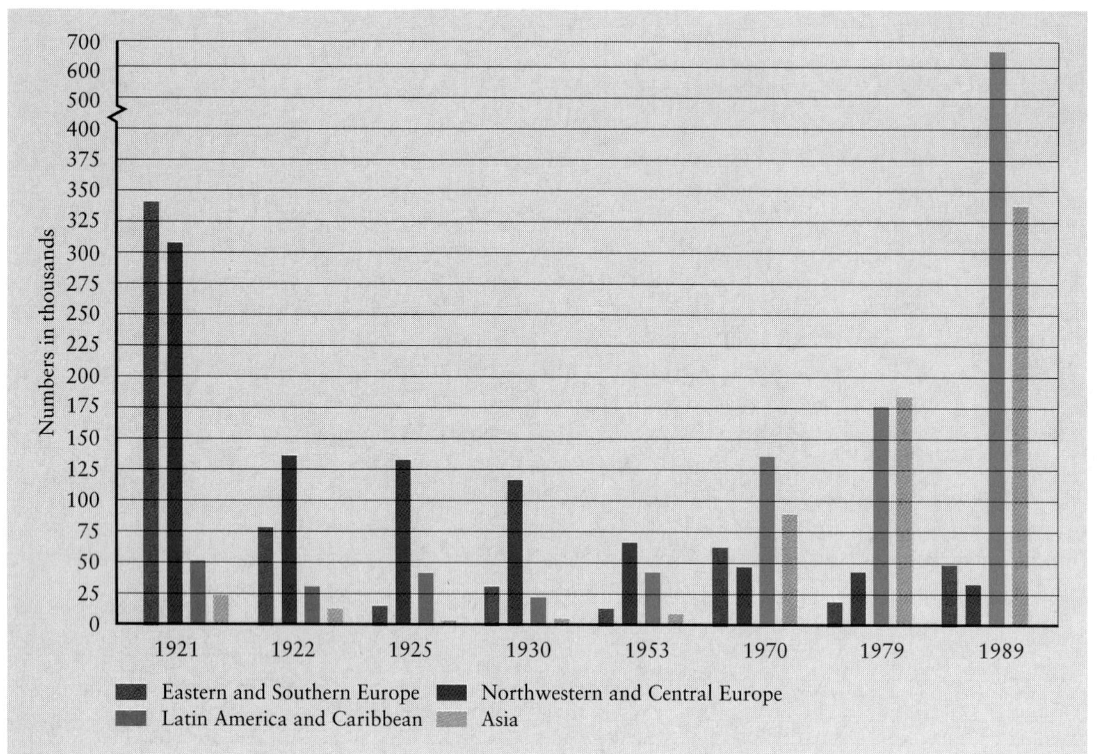

FIGURE 24.1

American Immigration since World War I

total immigration of 1924 to 164,000 persons, mostly from Great Britain, Ireland, and Germany. Japanese and Chinese immigrants continued to be excluded entirely.

In 1929 an even more restrictive quota went into effect, by which only 150,000 immigrants would be admitted each year, with national origins to be apportioned according to the 1920 census. President Herbert Hoover lowered the quota still further in 1931. The next year, during the depths of the Great Depression, more foreigners left the United States than entered. The last remaining loophole permitted unrestricted immigration from countries in the Western Hemisphere. This became increasingly significant over the years, as Central and Latin Americans crossed the border in increasing numbers, filling the places vacated by the cutoff of immigrants from Europe and the Pacific Rim.

Nativism took other forms as well during the 1920s. Many elite colleges instituted quotas to limit the enrollment of Jewish students, and many law firms refused to hire Jewish lawyers. Henry Ford spoke for many Americans when he warned of the menace of the "International Jew," referring to the supposed Jewish domination of international finance. Ford became so closely identified with anti-Semitism that some Jewish families could not bring themselves to buy one of his company's cars until decades later.

The New Klan. Another example of nativism in the 1920s was the revival of the Ku Klux Klan. Shortly after the premier in 1915 of *Birth of a Nation*, which glorified the Klan, a group of southerners gathered on Stone Mountain outside Atlanta, Georgia, to revive the KKK. Encouraged by the superpatriotism of the war years, Klan leaders chose as their motto "Native, white, Protestant supremacy." The modern Klan appealed to both urban and rural people, but it was mainly an urban phenomenon. Spreading out from its southern base, it found significant support in the far West, Southwest, and the Midwest, especially Indiana, Oklahoma, and Oregon. Unlike its earlier incarnation after the Civil War, the Klan of the 1920s did not limit its harassment to blacks. Its targets were just as likely to be Catholics and Jewish immigrants. Its tactics, however, were the same: nightriding, arson, tarring and feathering, and other forms of physical intimidation, as well as very effective economic boycotts directed at Klan targets. At the height of its power in 1925, the Klan had over three million members, including a strong contingent of women who pursued their own political agenda, combining racism, nativism, and a commitment to equal rights for white Protestant women.

After 1925, the Klan declined rapidly. Battles between rival factions and disclosures of rampant corruption hurt its image. Especially damaging was the revelation that Grand Dragon David Stephenson, the Klan's national leader, had kidnapped and sexually assaulted his former secretary, driving her to suicide. Nativism, which was a legacy of World War I, began to decline and that, along, with the passage of the 1924 immigration act, robbed the Klan of its most potent issue.

AMERICAN VOICES

The Klan Comes to Kokomo *Robert Coughlan*

Robert Coughlan grew up in Kokomo, Indiana, and as a young boy he witnessed a Ku Klux Klan Konklave, or gathering. As Catholics living in a strong pro-Klan neighborhood, Coughlan's family had reason to feel uncomfortable on the hot July day in 1923 when the Klan came to central Indiana.

Women of the Klan

The Ku Klux Klan was so well integrated into the daily life of white Protestants that one woman from rural Indiana remembered her time in the KKK in the 1920s as "just a celebration . . . a way of growing up." Perhaps as many as 500,000 women joined the Women of the Ku Klux Klan (WKKK) in the 1920s, including these Indiana Klanswomen in August 1924.

The Konklave was an important day in my life. I was nine years old, with a small boy's interest in masquerades and brass bands. But I was also a Catholic, the son of a Catholic who taught in the public schools and who consequently was the object of a good deal of Klan agitation. If anything worse was to come, the Konklave probably would bring it. Every week or so the papers had been reporting Klan atrocities in other parts of the country—whippings, lynchings, tar-and-feather parties—and my father and my family were logical game in our locality. . . .

As we sat on our front porch after watching the parade, we could see the Klansmen of our neighborhood trickling home. Some still wore their regalia, too tired to bother with taking it off before they came into sight. Others carried little bundles of white; they were the ones who still made some pretense of secrecy about being members. One of the last to come down the street was old Mrs. Crousore, who lived a few doors away. Her white robe clung damply, and her hood was pushed back. As she climbed her steps and sank solidly into a rocking chair on her porch, we could hear her groan, "Oh, my God, my feet hurt!"

Mrs. Crousore spoke with such feeling that her words seemed to summarize the whole day. My parents adopted her comment as a family joke. July 4, 1923, became for us the day when Mrs. Crousore's feet hurt. But it was clear to me when I grew a little older that my parents needed that joke as much as Mrs. Crousore needed her rocking chair. There were wild rumors in the town in the months that followed: Father Pratt, the pastor at St. Patrick's Church, was on the list for tar-and-feathering; the church was going to be burned; the Klan was going to "call" on the Jewish merchants; it was going to "get" my father and Miss Kinney, another Catholic who taught in the public schools. Considering all the violent acts committed by the Klan elsewhere in the country, it seemed quite possible that any or all of these notions might mature into action.

As it turned out none of them did. . . . Perhaps the answer lay in the dead level typicalness of the town; a population overwhelmingly white Protestant, with small, well-assimilated numbers of Catholics, Jews, foreigners, and Negroes, and an economy nicely balanced between farming and industry. There were few genuine tensions in Kokomo in 1923, and hence little occasion for misdirected hate to flame into personal violence.

It may be asked why, then, did the town take so wholeheartedly to the Klan, which made a program of misdirected hate? And the answer to that may be, paradoxically enough, that the Klan supplied artificial tensions. Though artificial, and perhaps never quite really believed in, they were satisfying. They filled a need—a need for Kokomo and all the big and little towns that resembled it during the early 1920s.

Source: Robert Coughlan, "Konklave in Kokomo," in Isabel Leighton, ed., *The Aspirin Age, 1919–1941*

Religious Fundamentalism

The religious debate between modernist and fundamentalist Protestants that had been simmering since the 1890s came to a boil in the 1920s. Modernists, or liberal Protestants, tried to reconcile religion with scientific discoveries, such as Darwin's theory of evolution, while fundamentalists clung to a literal interpretation of the Bible. Most major Protestant denominations struggled with conflicts in the 1920s, especially the Baptists and the Presbyterians, with the losers frequently splitting off to form their own churches. The most conspicuous evangelical figures were outside the established denominations, however. Popular preachers like Billy Sunday and Aimee Semple McPherson used revivals, storefront churches, and open-air preaching to reach their followers with their own brands of charismatic fundamentalism.

The modernist-fundamentalist controversy soon entered the political arena. The scientific theories in Charles Darwin's *On the Origins of the Species* (1859) conflicted with the account of creation in the book of Genesis, and legislation was designed to prevent teaching evolution in schools. In 1925 Tennessee passed a law providing that "it shall be unlawful . . . to teach any theory that denies the story of the Divine creation of man as taught in the Bible, and to teach instead that man has descended from a lower order of animals." The newly formed American Civil Liberties Union (ACLU) challenged the constitutionality of the Tennessee law in a test case involving John T. Scopes, a high school biology teacher in Dayton, Tennessee, who had taught evolution to his class. The famous criminal lawyer Clarence Darrow defended Scopes. The prosecuting attorney was William Jennings Bryan, three-time presidential candidate, a spellbinding orator and a fundamentalist.

The Scopes trial in July 1925 became known as the "monkey trial," referring both to Darwin's theory that human beings and other primates shared a common ancestor and to the circus atmosphere that prevailed at the trial. More than a hundred journalists crowded into the sweltering Dayton courthouse, and Chicago radio station WGN broadcast the proceedings live.

The trial quickly turned to volatile questions of faith and scientific theory. The judge rebuffed defense efforts to call expert scientific witnesses on evolution, dismissing such testimony as hearsay because the scientists had not been present when lower forms of life evolved. Darrow countered by calling Bryan to the stand as an expert on the Bible. Under oath, Bryan asserted his belief that Jonah had been swallowed by a "big fish," Eve created from Adam's rib, and the world created by God in six days. He hedged, however, about whether the days were literally twenty-four hours long, an inconsistency which Darrow ruthlessly exploited.

Even so, the jury took only eight minutes to find Scopes guilty. Although the Tennessee Supreme Court overturned Scopes's sentence on a technicality, the reversal prevented further appeal of the case and the controversial law remained technically in force for more than thirty years. As the 1920s ended, science and religion were locked in a standoff.

Intellectual Currents and Crosscurrents

The Lost Generation. The most articulate and embittered dissenters from American life in the 1920s were the writers and intellectuals who were profoundly disillusioned by the horrors of World War I and its uncertain legacy and by the crass materialism of the new American consumer culture. Some of the artists felt so at odds with what they saw as the complacent, anti-intellectual, moralistic tone of American life that they settled in Europe—some temporarily, like the novelists Ernest Hemingway and F. Scott Fitzgerald, others permanently. The poet T. S. Eliot, who left the United States before the war, became a British citizen. His despairing poem *The Waste Land* (1922), with its images of fragmented civilization in ruins after the war, influenced a generation of writers. Other writers also made powerful antiwar statements: John Dos Passos, whose first novel, *The Three Soldiers* (1921), was inspired by the war, the novelist Edith Wharton, and above all, Ernest Hemingway. Hemingway described the dehumanizing consequences and futility of the war in the novels *In Our Time* (1924), *The Sun Also Rises* (1926), and *A Farewell to Arms* (1929), which drew on his experience as an ambulance driver in Italy during the war.

But artists and writers who migrated to Europe, particularly to Paris, were not just a "lost generation" fleeing America; they were also drawn to Paris as the cultural and artistic capital of the world in the 1920s. Paris, as Gertrude Stein put it, was "where the twentieth century was happening." The *modernist* movement in literature, art, and music, which was marked by skepticism and technical experimentation, was in full swing, and its vitality invigorated American writing abroad and at home. Whether they settled in Paris, visited frequently, as Dos Passos did, or remained in their home country, as the poets Wallace Stevens and Marianne Moore and the novelists Willa Cather and William Faulkner did, American writers entered the modernist movement.

This movement began before the war as intellectuals began to react to the cultural and social changes that scientific advances, industrialization, and urbanization had brought to the American landscape. In the 1920s the new culture of business and the corruption of the Harding years caused intellectuals to cast a more critical eye on American society. One of the sharpest critics of American life and politics was H. L. Mencken, a Baltimore journalist and literary critic who founded the *American Mercury* in 1922. Mencken directed his mordant wit against small-town America and its guardians of public morals, American mass culture, and the "Booboisie," his contemptuous term for the middle class. In the *American Mercury* Mencken championed such writers as Sherwood Anderson, Sinclair Lewis, and Theodore Dreiser who satirized the provincialism of American society.

In *Main Street* (1920) Lewis scathingly depicted the narrow-mindedness of a midwestern farming town and in *Babbitt* (1922) he satirized the stifling conformity of a middle-class businessman. Dreiser wrote his naturalistic masterpiece *An American Tragedy* in 1925, an indictment of the American myth of success and materialism, as was John Dos Passos's *Manhattan Transfer*. In the same year Fitzgerald wrote *The Great Gatsby*, which showed the consequences of the mindless pursuit of wealth.

The literary outpouring of the 1920s was varied and rich as writers responded to the intellectual excitement of the decade and produced a large number of classics. Poetry enjoyed a renaissance, as Robert Frost, Wallace Stevens, Marianne Moore, and William Carlos Williams gave new strength to the genre. The novelist Edith Wharton, who had published many well-known novels in the first decades of the century, produced *The Age of Innocence* in 1920, which won a Pulitzer Prize. Warton's novels explored the human psyche and described the changing social relationships in a society where a new class of wealth was being created. Influenced by Freudian psychology, William Faulkner began his exploration of the mind of the South. Faulkner's first critical success, the novel *The Sound and the Fury* (1929), is set in the fictional Mississippi county of Yoknapatawpha with characters who cling to the old values of the agrarian South as they try to adjust to modern industrial capitalism.

The dramatist Eugene O'Neill also employed Freudian psychology in his experimental plays, which had the aspects of Greek tragedy. O'Neill was a brilliant and prolific playwright, producing thirteen plays between 1920 and 1933, including *The Hairy Ape* (1922) and *Desire Under the Elms* (1924).

Although William Faulkner and Eugene O'Neill went on to produce major works in the 1930s and American poets continued to write, the creative energy of the literary renaissance of the 1920s was not matched in the 1930s. The Great Depression, social and ideological unrest, and the rise of totalitarianism reshaped the intellectual landscape.

The Harlem Renaissance

Artist Aaron Douglas left his childhood home of Topeka, Kansas, in the mid-1920s for Harlem, "the Mecca of the New Negro." Douglas, whose paintings and murals often drew on African motifs, became the painter most closely associated with the New Negro Movement. This Douglas painting dates from around 1930. (The Howard University Gallery of Art)

Harlem Renaissance. A different kind of cultural affirmation took place in the black community of Harlem in the 1920s. In the words of Reverend Adam Clayton Powell, Sr., the pastor of the influential Abyssinian Baptist Church, Harlem loomed as "the symbol of liberty and the Promised Land to Negroes everywhere." In literature, its writers championed racial pride and cultural identity in the midst of white society. Poet Langston Hughes, who became a leading exponent of the Harlem Renaissance, captured its affirmative spirit when he asserted " I am a Negro—and beautiful."

The Harlem Renaissance was a creative group of young writers and artists who broke with the older genteel traditions of black literature to reclaim their cultural identity with its African roots. The intent of the movement was artistic, not political. The critic and teacher Alain Locke, editor of *The New Negro* (1926), an anthology that gave the writers of the Harlem Renaissance national exposure, summed up the character of the movement when he stated that through art, "Negro life is seizing its first chances for group expression and self-determination." Authors such as Claude McKay, Jean Toomer, Jessie Fauset, and Zora Neale Hurston explored the black experience and represented the "New Negro" in fiction. Countee Cullen and Langston Hughes turned to poetry, and Augusta Savage used sculpture to draw attention to black accomplishments. The outpouring of literary work showed the ongoing African-American struggle to find a way, as W. E. B. DuBois put it, "to be both a Negro and an American."

Jean Toomer, a writer passionately committed to African-American self-expression, wrote the influential novel *Cane* in 1923. With its poems, sketches, and stories about a northern black's discovery of the rural black South, it inspired other black artists and writers and was a stimulus to the movement. Langston Hughes drew on the black artistic forms of blues and jazz in *The Weary Blues* (1926), a groundbreaking collection of poems. Considered the most original of black poets and the most representative of African-American writers, Hughes also wrote novels, plays, and essays. Zora Neale Hurston, born in Florida to a family of poor tenant farmers, attended Howard University and won a scholarship to study anthropology at Barnard College. She spent a decade collecting folklore in the South and the Carribbean and incorporated this material into her short stories and novels. Her genius for storytelling and the tension between her rural folk education and her formal education, which she drew on in her writing, won her acclaim.

The vitality of the Harlem Renaissance was short-lived. Although the NAACP's magazine *The Crisis* was a forum for the Harlem Renaissance writers, the black middle class and intellectual elite in Harlem was relatively small and could not support the group's efforts. The movement was thus dependent on white patronage for support and access to publication. Many of the writers were ambivalent about this dependency as they struggled to attain an authentic black voice in their fiction. Langston Hughes became disillusioned with his white patron when she withdrew support for his work as he began to write about common black people in Kansas and New York rather than African themes. Claude McKay expressed the dilemma of black intellectuals in the novel *Home to Harlem*: how to be an intellectual and not lose the vitality and energy of the black heritage.

During the Jazz Age, when Harlem was very much in vogue in the public imagination, the publishing industry courted its writers, but the stock market crash of 1929 brought this interest to a sudden end. The movement waned in the 1930s as the depression continued. The writers of the Harlem Renaissance influenced a future generation of black writers when their works were rediscovered by black intellectuals during the civil rights movement of the 1960s.

Marcus Garvey and the UNIA. Although the cultural developments of the Harlem Renaissance had little impact on the African-American masses, other movements built racial pride and challenged white political and cultural hegemony. The most successful was the Universal Negro Improvement Association (UNIA), which championed black separatism under the leadership of Jamaican-born Marcus Garvey. Based in Harlem, the UNIA was the black working class's first mass movement. At its height it claimed four million followers, many of whom were recent migrants to northern cities. Like several nineteenth-century reformers, Marcus Garvey urged blacks to return to Africa because, he said, blacks would never be treated justly in countries ruled by whites. His wife, Amy Jacques Garvey, appealed to black women by combining her black nationalism with emphasis on women's contributions to culture and politics.

The UNIA grew rapidly in the early 1920s. It published a newspaper called *Negro World* and opened "liberty halls" in New York, Chicago, Detroit, Philadelphia, Pittsburgh, Cleveland, Cincinnati, and other northern cities. The UNIA also undertook extensive business ventures as part of its support for black capitalism. Its most ambitious project was the Black Star Line, a steamship company that would ferry cargo between the West Indies and the United States and take American blacks to Africa. The Black Star Line caused the downfall of the UNIA. Irregularities in fund raising led to Garvey's conviction on charges of mail fraud in 1925, and he was sentenced to five years in prison. President Calvin Coolidge paroled him in 1927, and Garvey was deported to Jamaica. Without his charismatic leadership, the movement soon collapsed.

Prohibition

The most notorious cultural debate of the 1920s was the battle over Prohibition. More than any other issue, Prohibition gave the decade its reputation as the Roaring Twenties. The Eighteenth Amendment, which took effect on January 20, 1920 (see Chapter 23), did make Americans drink less. Beer consumption declined the most, because beer was more difficult to manufacture and distribute illegally than hard liquor, but once people showed their willingness to flout the law, this effort to legislate private morality was doomed.

In major cities, support for Prohibition had always been limited. Before the law went into effect, the Yale Club of New York bought a fourteen-year supply of wine and hard liquor. Illegal saloons called speakeasies sprang up—more than 30,000 in New York City alone. People who preferred to drink at home and serve liquor to their guests emulated rural moonshiners and learned to distill their own "bathtub gin." Liquor smugglers op-

The Speakeasy
There aren't many photographs of speakeasies—after all, they were supposed to be private clubs tucked away beyond the reach of the law. Fancy hotels found themselves unable to compete with speakeasies once their bars were shut down, and many went out of business in the 1920s. But John Sloan's 1928 painting shows the rich enjoying themselves at New York's posh Lafayette Hotel. It is quite likely that these gentlemen and ladies had a flask concealed somewhere in the midst of their evening finery. (The Metropolitan Museum of Art)

erated with ease along borders and coastlines. Organized crime, already a factor in major cities, supplied a ready-made distribution network for bootleg liquor, and gangsters used "the noble experiment" to entrench themselves even more deeply in city politics. The decade's most notorious gangster, Al Capone, said "Everybody calls me a racketeer. I call myself a businessman. When I sell liquor, it's bootlegging. When my patrons serve it on a silver tray on Lake Shore Drive, it's hospitality."

By the middle of the decade, Prohibition was clearly failing. Government appropriations for the enforcement were woefully inadequate. The few highly publicized raids didn't make a dent in the liquor trade. In 1929, Attorney General William D. Mitchell conceded in 1929 that liquor could be bought "at almost any hour of the day or night, either in rural districts, the smaller towns, or the cities." Even a committee appointed by President Hoover in 1931 to study Prohibition only weakly urged that it be retained.

But Prohibition was in the Constitution, so the forces for repeal—the "wets," as opposed to the "drys," who continued to support the Eighteenth Amendment—undertook the long process of gaining the necessary majorities in Congress and state legislatures to amend the constitution once again. The Women's Organization for National Prohibition Repeal, headed by Pauline Sabin, a wealthy New York Republican, lobbied Congress and mobilized support from other national organizations.

The onset of the Great Depression hastened repeal. People argued that liquor production would provide jobs and prop up the faltering economy. On December 5, 1933, the Eighteenth Amendment was repealed. Ironically, drinking became more socially acceptable, although not necessarily more widespread, during Prohibition than it had been before.

The 1928 Election

Emotionally charged issues such as Prohibition, religious fundamentalism, and nativism eventually spilled over into national politics. The Democratic party, which drew on Protestant rural supporters in the South and West as well as ethnic voters from political machines in northern cities, was especially susceptible to the urban-rural conflicts of the 1920s. Four years earlier, the 1924 Democratic national convention had revealed a fissure between the party's urban forces and its rural wing.

Alfred E. Smith. The Democrats approached the 1928 campaign in somewhat better shape. The death of Senator Robert La Follette in 1925 ended the threat of another challenge by the Progressive party. William Jennings Bryan died the same year, just a week after his impassioned defense of fundamentalism in the Scopes trial, removing another potential spoiler from the field. Former contender William McAdoo was well into his sixties and considered too old for the nomination. As a result, Al Smith, who had just been elected to his fourth term as governor of New York, stood in a commanding position to win the Democratic nomination. In 1924 the Democrats had needed more than a hundred ballots to select a candidate, but in 1928 they nominated Smith on the first try.

Alfred E. Smith was the first presidential candidate to reflect the aspirations of the urban working classes. The grandson of Irish immigrants, and a Catholic, Smith had worked his way up in politics from Tammany Hall to the governor's mansion in Albany. He was proud of his urban background and adopted "The Sidewalks of New York" as his campaign song. Democrats hoped Smith would attract recent immigrants and workers who traditionally voted Republican. Belle Moskowitz, a New York social worker who served as Smith's political adviser, made Smith more attractive to women and liberal urban Jews.

But Smith had liabilities, too. He spoke in a heavy New York accent, sprinkling his speeches with "ain't" and "he don't," which did not play well on the radio. His early career in Tammany Hall troubled many voters, suggesting, unfairly, that he was little more than a cog in the political machine. Smith's stand on Prohibition alienated many voters. Although he promised, if elected, to enforce Prohibition, he made no secret of his support for repeal. Smith chose John J. Raskob, a wealthy entrepreneur and one of the nation's most ardent "wets," as head of the Democratic National Committee.

By far the most damaging handicap to Smith's campaign was his Catholicism. Protestant Americans were not ready for a Roman Catholic president in 1928. Although Smith insisted that his religion would not interfere with his duties as president, being Catholic cost him support from Democrats and Republicans alike. Protestant clergymen, who already opposed Smith because he had flouted Prohibition, led the drive against him. "No Governor can kiss the papal ring and get within gunshot of the White House," declared a Methodist bishop from Buffalo.

Herbert Hoover. Just as Smith marked a new kind of presidential candidate for the Democrats, so did Herbert Hoover as the Republican nominee. President Coolidge's unexpected decision not to run for reelection in 1928 opened the field, and Hoover led from the start. His popularity and power as secretary of commerce under Harding and Coolidge left no room for the other main contenders, Vice-President Charles G. Dawes and former Governor Frank O. Lowden of Illinois.

As a professional administrator and engineer, Hoover embodied the new managerial and technological elite. He had never been elected to any political office. During his campaign, in which he gave only seven speeches, Hoover promised that his vision of individualism and cooperative endeavor would banish poverty from the United States. Many voters considered him more progressive than Smith.

Hoover won a stunning victory. He received 58 percent of the popular vote to Smith's 41 percent, and 444 electoral votes to 87 for Smith. For the first time since Reconstruction, a Republican candidate carried Virginia, Texas, and North Carolina, largely because many Democratic voters refused to vote for a Catholic. The voter turnout rose from 52 percent in 1924 to 56.9 percent in 1928, partly due to extensive education campaigns undertaken by the League of Women Voters. The polling places were moved from their former location in saloons to schools and churches, which helped women feel more comfortable with their new role as citizens. Many Catholic and immigrant women voted for Smith, but even more native-born Republican women supported Herbert Hoover.

The 1928 election reflected important underlying

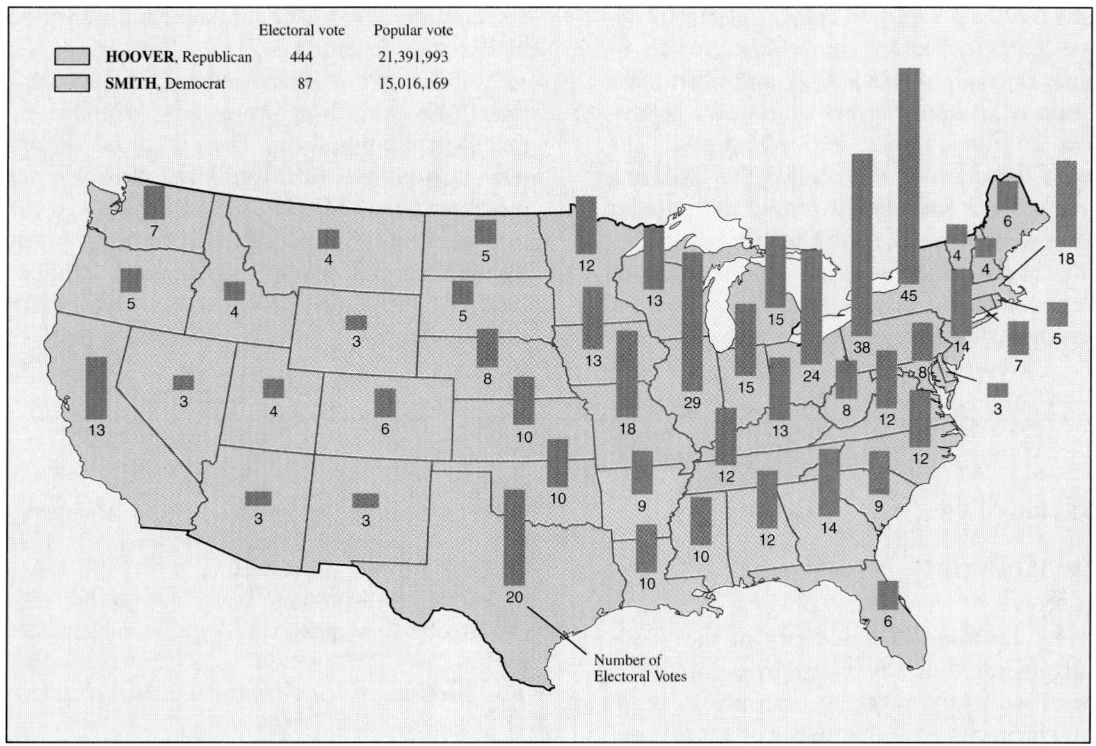

MAP 24.2

The Election of 1928

Historians still debate the extent to which 1928 was a critical election—that is, one that produced a significant realignment in voting behavior. Although Republican candidate Herbert Hoover swept the electoral college, Democrats were heartened that Alfred E. Smith won the heavily industrialized states of Rhode Island and Massachusetts. For the first time, the Democratic ticket carried the nation's twelve largest cities, garnering strong support from immigrants and urban dwellers.

political changes. The Democratic turnout, despite the party's overwhelming loss, increased substantially in urban areas. Smith won the heavily industrialized states of Massachusetts and Rhode Island, and carried the nation's twelve largest cities. The Democrats were on their way to a new identity as the party of the urban masses, including ethnic voters, a reorientation completed by the New Deal.

It is unlikely that any Democratic candidate, let alone a Catholic, could have won the presidency in 1928. With a seemingly prosperous economy, national consensus on foreign policy, and strong support from the business community, the Republicans were unbeatable. Herbert Hoover's victory put him in the unenviable position of leading the United States when the Great Depression struck in 1929. Having claimed credit for the prosperity of the 1920s, the Republicans found it difficult to escape blame for the depression. Twenty-four years passed before a Republican won the presidency again.

Summary

By the 1920s, modern America had arrived. The Republican party controlled the national government and cemented the partnership between business and government that had been accelerated by World War I. In foreign policy, the United States generally steered clear of European affairs, and concentrated on economic expansion abroad, especially in the Western Hemisphere. With the exception of the 1920–1921 recession, the economy performed well, although agriculture never recovered from the postwar slump and certain industries remained overextended following wartime expansion. The automobile industry typified the new mass production techniques that dominated economic life in the United States and revolutionized American society.

During the 1920s, a national culture began to develop. It was characterized by the wide diffusion of ideas and values through movies, radio, and other mass media, new ways of spending leisure time, and a heightened emphasis on consumption and advertising. The new lifestyles of the decade, often called the "Roaring Twenties" or the "Jazz Decade," captured the popular imagination but were limited to a minority of the population. Families had to enjoy at least a middle-class income to buy cars, radios, vacuum cleaners, and toasters. Those left outside the circle of prosperity included farmers, coal miners, textile workers, and minorities such as blacks and Hispanics.

Not everyone welcomed the new secular values of the 1920s. Conflicts arose over Prohibition, religion, race, and immigration. These cultural disputes spilled over into politics, disrupting the already fractured Democratic party. The 1928 election showed that the nation could not yet accept a Catholic as president. The Republican ascendancy continued under Herbert Hoover, who looked forward to a term filled with even greater prosperity and progress.

TOPIC FOR RESEARCH

Advertising Modernity

Nothing conveys the tone of modernity in the 1920s better than advertising, but ads (like movies) are not a simple mirror of society. Nonetheless, they are an excellent source for chronicling the emergence of a mass consumption economy. Pick a specific consumer good, such as the automobile, radio, an electrical appliance, cigarettes, or a hygiene product such as deodorant or mouthwash. Look for advertisements from the 1920s in a magazine like *The Saturday Evening Post, Ladies' Home Journal, Literary Digest, Fortune,* or *True Story.* How was the product marketed? Were any unusual stylistic or artistic devices used to sell the product? What was its audience? How representative of American society were the models or situations shown in the ads? What do the advertisements say about societal attitudes about race, class, and gender?

To place your own observations into a broader context, consult histories of advertising such as Roland Marchand, *Advertising the American Dream: Making Way for Modernity, 1920–1940* (1985), Daniel Pope, *The Making of Modern Advertising* (1983), and T. J. Jackson Lears, "From Salvation to Self-Realization: Advertising and the Therapeutic Roots of the Consumer Culture, 1880–1930," in Richard Wightman Fox and T. J. Jackson Lears, *The Culture of Consumption* (1983). Trade journals such as *Printers' Ink* and *Advertising Age* supply the industry perspective.

BIBLIOGRAPHY

General overviews of the 1920s are provided by Ellis Hawley, *The Great War and the Search for a Modern Order, 1917–1933* (1979); William Leuchtenburg, *The Perils of Prosperity* (1958); Frederick Lewis Allen, *Only Yesterday* (1931); and Geoffrey Perrett, *America in the Twenties* (1982). Robert S. Lynd and Helen Merrell Lynd, *Middletown: a Study in Modern American Culture* (1929), remains a superb study of American life and values in the 1920s. John Braeman, Robert H. Bremner, and David Brody, eds., *The Twenties* (1968), offers interpretations of the decade's major trends.

The Business-Government Partnership of the 1920s

Alfred Chandler provides a stimulating introduction to business life in *Strategy and Structure* (1962) and *The Visible Hand* (1977). Further discussion of corporate developments can be found in Louis Galambos, *Competition and Cooperation* (1966); Robert Himmelberg, *The Origins of the National Recovery Administration: Business, Government, and the Trade Association Ideal, 1921–1933* (1976); and James Gilbert, *Designing the Industrial State* (1972). Irving Bernstein, *The Lean Years* (1960), David Brody, *Steelworkers in America* (1960) and *Workers in Industrial America* (1980), and David Montgomery, *The Fall of the House of Labor* (1987), cover labor developments.

The domestic and international aspects of the economy are treated in Jim Potter, *The American Economy Between the Wars* (1974); Mira Wilkins, *The Maturing of Multinational Enterprise* (1974); Emily Rosenberg, *Spreading the American Dream* (1982); and Joan Hoff Wilson, *American Business and Foreign Policy, 1920–1933* (1968) and *Ideology and Economics: U.S. Relations with the Soviet Union, 1918–1933* (1974). Interpretations of foreign policy include Warren Cohen, *Empire Without Tears* (1987); William Appleman Williams, *The Tragedy of American Diplomacy* (1962); L. Ethan Ellis, *Republican Foreign Policy, 1921–1933* (1968); and Stephen Randall, *U.S. Foreign Oil Policy, 1919–1948* (1986). Walter LaFeber, *Inevitable Revolutions* (1983) covers the United States involvement in Central America.

General introductions to politics in the 1920s are found in John D. Hicks, *Republican Ascendancy* (1960), and Robert Murray, *The Politics of Normalcy* (1973). Biographies of the decade's major political figures include Donald McCoy, *Calvin Coolidge* (1967); David Burner, *Herbert Hoover* (1979); Joan Hoff Wilson, *Herbert Hoover: Forgotten Progressive* (1975); and Paula Elder, *Governor Alfred E. Smith: The Politician as Reformer* (1983). On women in politics, see J. Stanley Lemons, *The Woman Citizen* (1973); Clarke A.

Chambers, *Seedtime of Reform* (1963); Nancy Cott, *The Grounding of Modern Feminism* (1987); and Elisabeth Israels Perry, *Belle Moskowitz* (1987).

A New National Culture

Daniel Boorstin, *The Americans: The Democratic Experience* (1973) provides an excellent introduction to the emerging mass culture. On movies, see Robert Sklar, *Movie-Made America* (1975); Lary May, *Screening Out the Past* (1980); Lewis A. Erenberg, *Steppin' Out* (1981); and Neil Gabler, *An Empire of Their Own: How the Jews Invented Hollywood* (1988). Material on Clara Bow can be found in David Stenn, *Clara Bow, Runnin' Wild* (1988) and Sumiko Higashi, *Virgins, Vamps and Flappers: The American Silent Movie Heroine* (1978). Erik Barnouw, *A Tower in Babel: A History of American Broadcasting in the United States To 1933* (1966), Susan Douglas, *Inventing American Broadcasting* (1987), and Philip Rosen, *The Modern Stentors: Radio Broadcasting and the Federal Government,* 1920–1933 (1980), discuss radio. See also Melvin Patrick Ely, *The Adventures of Amos 'n' Andy: A Social History of an American Phenomenon* (1991). Stewart Ewen, *Captains of Consciousness* (1976), Daniel Pope, *The Making of Modern Advertising* (1983), Roland Marchand, *Advertising the American Dream* (1985), and Stephen Fox, *The Mirror Makers* (1984), cover advertising. Paula Fass, *The Damned and the Beautiful* (1977) and Beth L. Bailey, *From Front Porch to Back Seat* (1988), cover youth, while Susan Strasser, *Never Done* (1982), and Ruth Schwartz Cowan, *More Work For Mother* (1983), discuss white middle-class women's lives. Lizabeth Cohen, *Making A New Deal: Industrial Workers in Chicago,* 1919–1939 (1990), suggests how working-class communities adapted mass culture for their purposes.

The impact of the automobile on modern American life is amply documented by James Flink, *The Car Culture* (1975) and *The Automobile Age* (1988); John Rae, *The American Automobile* (1965); Ed Cray, *Chrome Colossus: General Motors and Its Times* (1980); Bernard A. Weisberger, *The Dream Maker* (1979); and Reynold Wik, *Henry Ford and Grass Roots America* (1972). For women and the automobile, see Virginia Scharff, *Taking The Wheel* (1991). For sports, see Allen Guttmann, *A Whole New Ball Game* (1988); Harvey Green, *Fit For America* (1986); and Larry Englemann, *The Goddess and the American Girl: The Story of Suzanne Lenglen and Helen Wills* (1988). Good sources for Charles Lindbergh are his two accounts, *"We"* (1927), and *The Spirit of St. Louis* (1953).

Dissenting Values and Cultural Conflict

Paul Carter, *Another Part of the Twenties* (1977), outlines the decade's deeply felt cultural controversies; many of the essays in Isabel Leighton, *The Aspirin Age, 1919–1941* (1949), also cover those themes. Background on rural and urban life is provided by Don Kirschner, *City and Country: Rural Responses to Urbanization in the 1920s* (1970); Zane Miller, *The Urbanization of America* (1973); and Jon Teaford, *The Twentieth-Century American City* (1986). John Higham, *Strangers in the Land* (1955), and Maldwyn A. Jones, *American Immigration* (1960), describe immigration restriction. Richard K. Tucker, *The Dragon and the Cross: the Rise and Fall of The Ku Klux Klan in Middle America* (1991), Kenneth Jackson, *The Ku Klux Klan in the City, 1915–1930* (1965), and David Chalmers, *Hooded Americanism* (1965), cover the KKK's rise and fall. Kathleen M. Blee, *Women of the Klan* (1991) offers a provocative discussion of racism and gender in the 1920s. Ray Ginger, *Six Days or Forever?* (1958), Norman F. Furniss, *The Fundamentalist Controversy, 1918–1933* (1954), George M. Marsden, *Fundamentalism and American Culture* (1980), and William G. McLoughlin, *Fundamentalism in American Culture* (1983), cover religion. Robert Crunden, *From Self to Society, 1919–1941* (1972), Roderick Nash, *The Nervous Generation: American Thought, 1917–1930* (1969), and Edmund Wilson, *The Twenties* (1975) cover intellectuals. For the Harlem Renaissance, see Jervis Anderson, *This Was Harlem, 1900–1950* (1982); Nathan Huggins, *Harlem Renaissance* (1971); and Gloria T. Hull, *Color, Sex, and Poetry: Three Women Writers of the Harlem Renaissance* (1987). David Cronin, *Black Moses* (1962), and Theodore Vincent, *Black Power and the Garvey Movement* (1970), describe Marcus Garvey. On prohibition, see Andrew Sinclair, *Prohibition: The Era of Excess* (1962); Joseph R. Gusfield, *Symbolic Crusade* (1963); and Norman Clark, *Deliver Us From Evil* (1976). The treatment of the 1928 election found in David Burner, *The Politics of Provincialism* (1967), and Oscar Handlin, *Al Smith and His America* (1958), should be supplemented by Kristi Andersen, *The Creation of a Democratic Majority, 1928–1936* (1979), and Allan J. Lichtman's quantitative study, *Prejudice and the Old Politics* (1979).

TIMELINE

1920–1921	Recession
1920	First commercial radio broadcast Warren G. Harding elected president
1921	Sheppard-Towner Act Immigration Act passed Washington Conference on naval disarmament
1923	Calvin Coolidge succeeds Harding as president *Time* magazine founded
1924	Dawes Plan reschedules German War reparations Teapot Dome scandal National Origins Act passed
1925	Scopes ("Monkey") trial
1927	First "talkies" Charles Lindbergh's solo flight Ford Model A Kellogg-Briand pact
1928	Herbert Hoover elected president

Employment Agency

Isaac Soyer's 1937 painting captures the resignation and despair of Americans searching for a job, any job, in the midst of the Great Depression. (Whitney Museum of American Art)

CHAPTER 25 *The Great Depression*

Flappers and movie stars in the 1920s, breadlines and hoboes in the 1930s: were the 1920s just "one long party" after which "everyone had a hangover—known as the depression—in the morning"? Did the country really go from unprecedented prosperity to the poorhouse practically overnight?

Obviously, the contrast between the flush times of the 1920s and the hard times of the 1930s is too starkly drawn. The vaunted prosperity of the 1920s was never as widespread or as firmly rooted as many believed at the time. Although America's mass-consumption economy was the envy of the world, many Americans lived on its margins. Nor was every American devastated by the depression of the 1930s. Those with secure jobs or fixed incomes survived the economic downturn in relatively sound shape—some people even managed to get rich in the decade. But few could escape contact with the wide-ranging social, political, and cultural developments of the depression.

Almost all of our impressions of the 1930s are black-and-white, in part because of the stark visual image of depression America etched on the popular consciousness through photographs taken by the Farm Security Administration. Although not every event of the 1930s should be viewed through the lens of the depression, more than any other factor, it provides the unifying theme for the decade.

The Coming of the Great Depression

Booms and busts are a permanent feature of the business cycle of capitalist economies. Since the beginning of the Industrial Revolution in the early nineteenth century, the United States had experienced recessions or panics at least every twenty years. The most recent downturn was the postwar recession of 1920–1921. But no slump was as severe and none lasted as long as the Great Depression.

The Causes of the Depression

The Great Depression began slowly and almost imperceptibly. After 1927, consumer spending declined, and housing construction slowed. Inventories piled up, and in 1928 and 1929 manufacturers began to cut back production and lay off workers. Reduced incomes and buying power reinforced the downturn. By the summer of 1929, the economy was clearly in a recession, although at that point not as severe as the one that had begun in 1920.

Stock Market Speculation and the Great Crash. Among the causes of the Great Depression, a flawed stock market played an important, but not dominant, role. By 1929 the market had become the symbol of the nation's prosperity and an icon in American business culture. Financier John J. Raskob captured this mentality in a *Ladies' Home Journal* article, "Everyone Ought to Be Rich." Invest $15 a month on sound common stocks, Raskob advised, and in twenty years the investment will grow to $80,000. Not everyone was playing the stock market, however. About four million Americans owned stock in 1929, representing about 10 percent of the nation's households. A mere 1.5 million had portfolios large enough to require the services of a stockbroker.

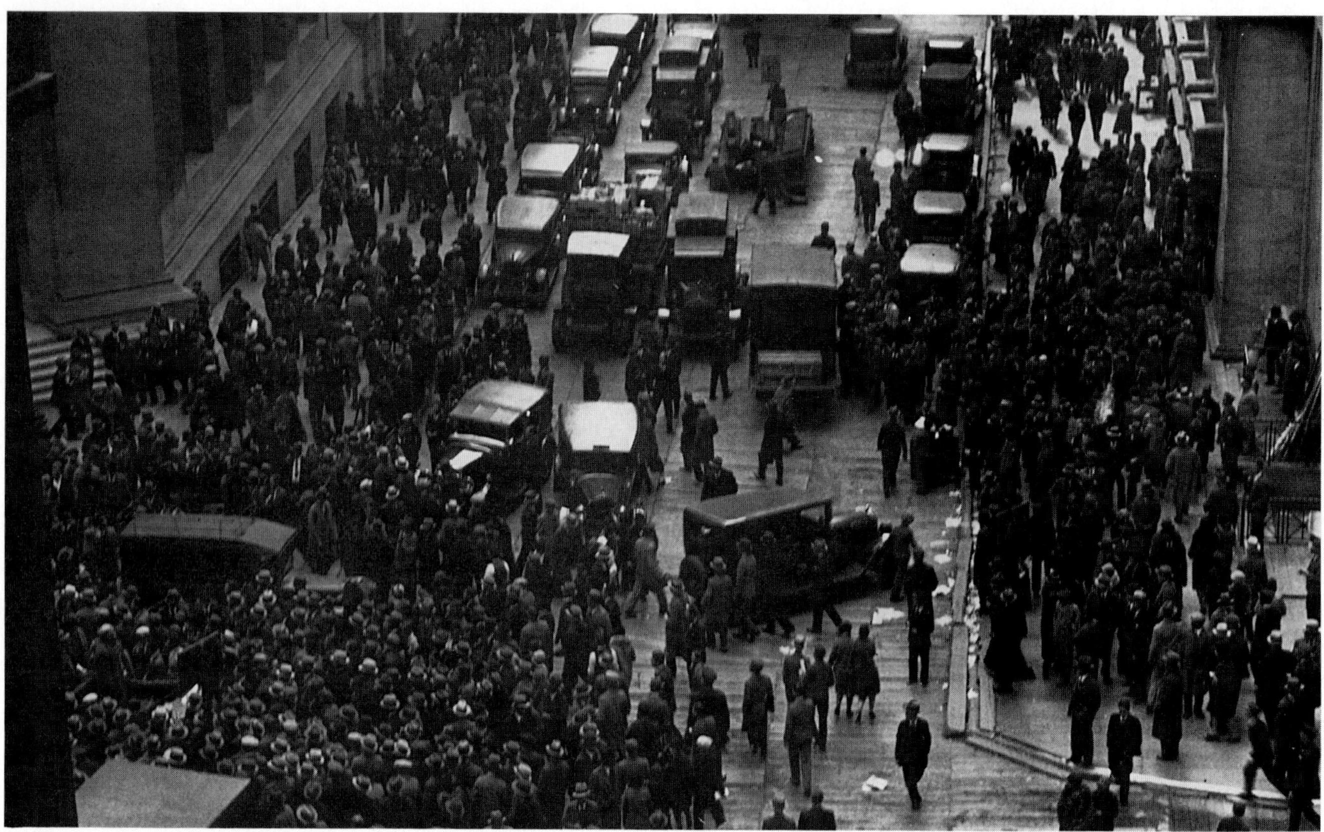

Wall Street, October 1929
When the stock market collapsed, Julius Rosenwald, the chairman of Sears, Roebuck and Company, offered to guarantee the accounts of Sears employees who had bought stocks on margin. Comedian Eddie Cantor jokingly asked for a job as a Sears office boy.

Stock market prices had been rising steadily since 1921, but in 1928 and 1929 they surged forward—the average price of stocks rising over 40 percent. All this economic activity was essentially unregulated. Margin buying, in particular, proceeded at a feverish pace: stockbrokers permitted many of their customers to borrow up to 75 percent of the purchase price of stocks. Such easy credit lured more speculators and less creditworthy investors into the market. The Federal Reserve Board warned member banks not to lend money for stock speculation—if prices dropped, many investors would not be able to pay their debts—but no one listened. As long as prices continued to soar, everyone felt like a winner. A noted economist proclaimed in mid-October 1929 that "stock prices have reached what looks like a permanently high plateau."

The stock market had been sliding since early September, but people ignored this warning. On "Black Tuesday"—October 29, 1929—the bubble burst. In frantic trading, more than 16 million stocks changed hands. Overextended investors, suddenly finding themselves heavily in debt, began to sell their stocks, inducing others to follow suit to protect their investments. This set off waves of panic selling, and many stocks found no buyers at all. Practically overnight, stock values fell from a peak of $87 billion (at least on paper) to $55 billion. The precipitous decline of stock prices became known as the Great Crash.

The impact of "Black Tuesday" was felt far beyond the trading floors of Wall Street. The stock market crash intensified the course of the Great Depression in several ways. It wiped out the savings of thousands of Americans and hurt commercial banks that had invested heavily in corporate stocks. Less tangibly, it destroyed the optimism of people who had regarded the stock market as the crowning symbol of America's economic prosperity, causing a crisis of confidence that prolonged the depression.

However, the stock market crash alone does not account for either the severity or the length of the Great Depression, especially the deep plunge between 1931 and 1933. The drag of "sick" industries, the growing inequality of wealth, the unstable international financial situation, and the monetary policies of the Federal Reserve System—all of these contributed to the prolonged decline.

Structural Weaknesses. The crash exposed long-standing weaknesses in the American economy. Agriculture was in the worst shape; farmers had never recovered from the recession of 1920–1921. They faced high fixed costs for equipment and mortgages incurred during the inflationary war years. At the same time, prices fell owing to overproduction and the resulting surpluses, forcing farmers to default on mortgage payments and risk foreclosure. In 1929 the yearly income of a farmer averaged only $273, compared to $750 for other occupations. Because farmers accounted for about a fourth of the nation's gainfully employed workers in 1929, their difficulties weakened the general economic structure.

Certain basic industries also had economic troubles during the otherwise prosperous 1920s, many of them dating back to World War I or the depression of 1920–1921. The textile industry, for example, had steadily declined after the war. Textile firms abandoned New England for cheaper labor markets in the South but continued to suffer from decreased demand and excess capacity. The railroad industry also suffered, hit by shrinking passenger revenues, stagnant freight levels, and inefficient management. In addition, the railroads faced stiff new competition from truck transportation on publicly subsidized roads.

Mining and lumbering, which had expanded in response to wartime demands, produced too much during peacetime. Coal mining, especially, was battered by overexpansion, technological obsolescence, and a legacy of bitter labor struggles. New sources, including hydroelectric power, fuel oil, and natural gas, now competed with coal. As secretary of commerce, Herbert Hoover had plans to help these ailing industries, but the trade associations he promoted were ineffectual.

Unequal Distribution of Wealth. The country's unequal distribution of wealth also contributed to the severity of the depression. During the 1920s, the share of national income going to families already in the upper- and middle-income brackets increased. The tax policies of Secretary of the Treasury Andrew Mellon contributed to this concentration of wealth by easing personal tax rates, eliminating the wartime excess-profits tax, and expanding deductions that favored wealthy individuals and corporations. In 1929, the lowest 40 percent of the population received only 12.5 percent of the aggregate family personal income, while the top 5 percent got 30 percent. Once the depression had begun, not enough people could afford to spend the money necessary to revive the economy.

The Worldwide Depression. The economic problems of the United States had an impact on the rest of the world, and vice versa. The international economic system had been out of kilter since World War I. It could function only as long as American banks exported enough capital for European countries to repay their debts and continue to buy American manufactured goods and agricultural products. By the late 1920s, European economies were staggering under the weight of large debts and trade imbalances with the United States, which undercut the recovery that looked possible earlier in the decade. By 1931, most European economies had collapsed.

In an interdependent world, the downturn of the American economy had enormous repercussions. In 1929 the United States had produced over 40 percent of the world's manufactured goods, twice as much as Great Britain and Germany combined. When American companies cut back production, they also cut back purchases of raw materials and supplies abroad, which had a devastating effect on many foreign economies. American financiers reduced foreign investments and consumers cut down on European goods, making debt repayment even more difficult. As economic conditions worsened on the continent, European demand for American exports fell drastically. When the Hawley-Smoot Tariff of 1930 raised rates to all-time highs, foreign governments retaliated with their own trade restrictions, further limiting the market for American goods, especially agricultural products, and deepening the worldwide depression.

The Deepening Economic Crisis

The Great Depression became self-perpetuating. The more the American economy contracted, the longer people expected the depression to last and the longer they expected it to last, the more afraid they were to spend or invest their money (if they had any), which was exactly what was necessary to stimulate economic recovery. Business investment plummeted 88 percent from 1931 to 1933. The economy showed some signs of recovery in the summer of 1931 as many inventories were eliminated and low prices encouraged renewed consumption, but plunged again in late fall.

At this point, the chronically depressed agricultural sector put pressure on the commercial banking system, worsening the economic contraction. The nation's banks had already been weakened by the stock market crash. When agricultural prices and incomes fell even more steeply than usual in 1930, many farmers went over the edge into bankruptcy. Rural banks failed in alarming numbers—particularly in the cotton belt—after the harvest of 1930. By November and December, so many rural banks had defaulted on their obligations that urban banks, too, began to fail. The wave of bank failures frightened depositors into withdrawing their savings, further deepening the banking crisis.

Flawed Monetary Policy. A change in the nation's monetary policy in 1931 added to the banking problems. During the first phase of the depression, the Federal Reserve System had reacted cautiously. In October 1931 the system's managers took several gravely incorrect steps. The New York Reserve Bank significantly increased the discount rate—that is, the interest rate it charged to loan money to member banks—and cut back the amount of money it placed in circulation through the purchase of government securities. These actions of the Federal Reserve hampered the ability of the banking system to meet domestic demands for currency and credit. By March 1933, when the economy reached its lowest point, the money supply had fallen from its August 1929 level by about a third.

The inadequate money supply forced prices down and deprived businesses of investment funds. In the face of such a money shortage, only by spending faster could the American people have pulled the country out of the depression. But because of falling prices, rising unemployment, and a banking system in disarray, Americans preferred to save their dollars, stashing them under the mattress rather than in the bank, thereby limiting even further the amount of money in circulation.

International Repercussions. Adherence to the gold standard had long been the most sacrosanct principle in the international business community, because gold provided a fixed standard against which the value of currencies throughout the world could be pegged. Great Britain unilaterally decided to abandon the gold standard in 1931, striking another blow to the already shaky international economic system. Currencies no longer had a definite value in relation to gold, and thus to each other, but now "floated" according to supply and demand, depriving the world market of a system for the orderly adjustment of values of international currencies. By 1932, forty-one countries had followed Britain's example and fear spread in Europe that, despite Herbert Hoover's unswerving support for the gold standard, the United States would follow suit. Consequently, holders of dollars abroad began to demand gold, and gold flowed out of the United States. The Federal Reserve's decision in October 1931 to drive up short-term interest rates successfully attracted gold holders to U.S. investments, thereby saving the gold standard, at least temporarily.

President Herbert Hoover later blamed the severity of the depression in the United States on the international economic situation. No other major trading nation was hit as hard as the United States. Although domestic factors far outweighed international ones in causing America's protracted decline, Hoover had a point. During the depression, no single country stepped forward to provide leadership and stability for the world market, as Britain had done prior to World War I. Instead, nations raised tariff barriers and imposed exchange controls to hoard precious gold, dollars, and pounds sterling, in a fit of economic nationalism that prolonged the depression. By 1933 the world economy finally showed signs of recovery, although progress remained uneven.

The Downward Spiral. Herbert Hoover personally chose the term *depression* to describe America's post-1929 economic downturn. He thought depression sounded less ominous than "panic" or "crisis." Whatever one calls the conditions of the American economy from 1929 to 1932, the statistics paint a stark picture.

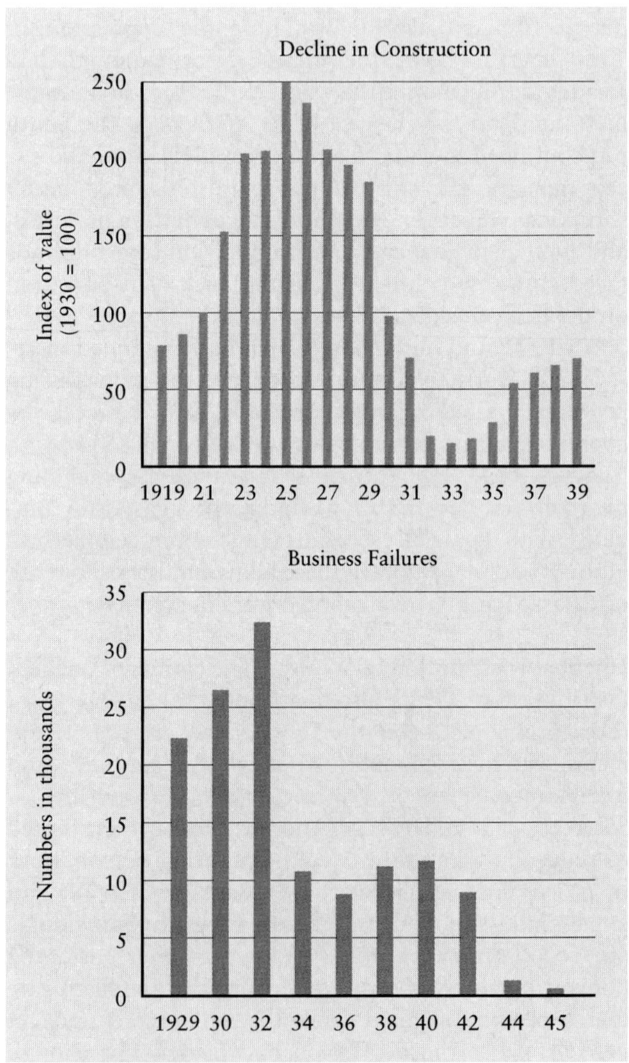

FIGURE 25.1

Statistics of the Depression

The top graph shows the decline in construction; bottom graph gives the numbers of business failures.

Source: Historical Statistics of the United States, Colonial Times to 1970, (Washington: Government Printing Office, 1975).

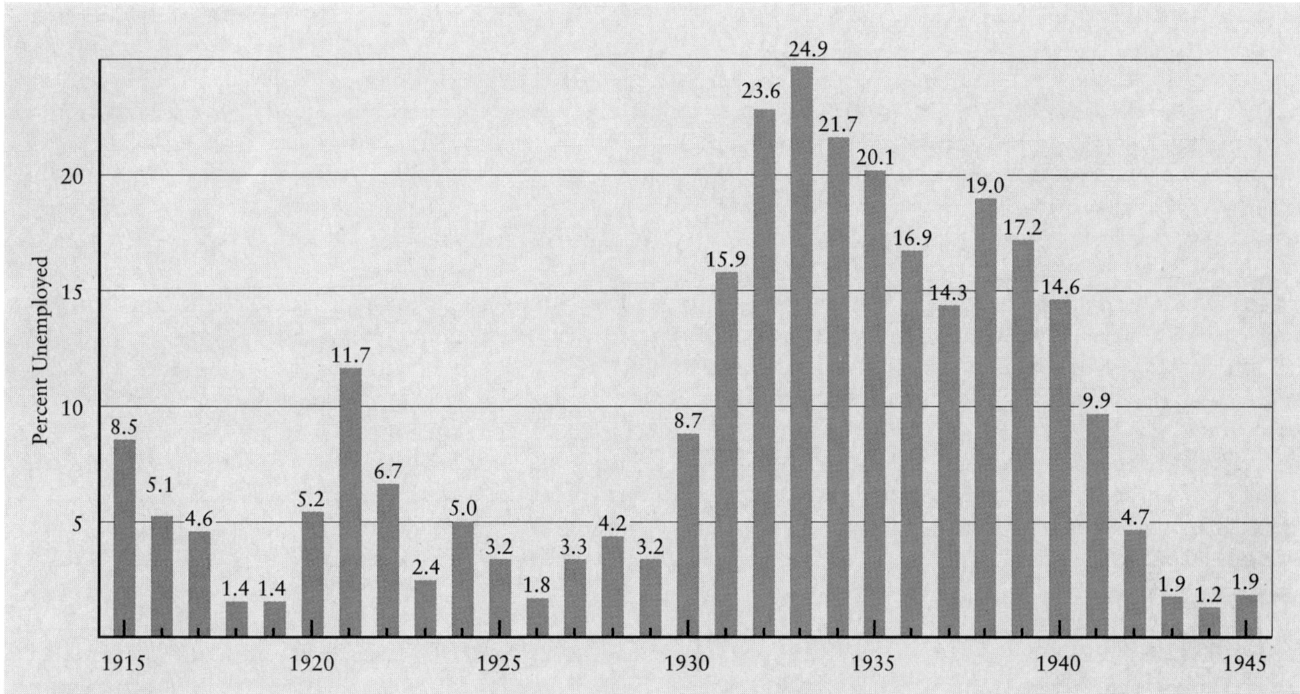

FIGURE 25.2

Unemployment, 1915–1945

From the height of the prosperity before the stock market crash in 1929 to the depths of the depression in 1932–1933, the gross national product dropped by almost half, declining from $103.1 billion to $58 billion in 1932; consumption expenditures dropped by 18 percent; construction fell by 78 percent; private investment plummeted by 88 percent; and farm income, already low, was more than cut in half. In this period, 9,000 banks either went bankrupt or closed their doors, and 100,000 businesses failed. The consumer price index declined by 25 percent, and corporate profits fell from $10 billion to $1 billion.

Most tellingly, unemployment rose from 3.2 percent to 24.9 percent, affecting approximately twelve million workers. The statistical measures at the time were fairly crude and unemployment was probably even higher. At least one of every four workers was out of a job. Even those who did have jobs faced wage cutbacks or the fear of being laid off. Their stories put a human face on the almost incomprehensible dimensions of this economic downturn.

Hard Times

"We didn't go hungry, but we lived lean." That sums up the experiences of many American families during the Great Depression. The vast majority were neither very rich nor very poor. For most, the depression did not mean losing thousands of dollars in the stock market or pulling children out of an expensive boarding school. Nor did it mean going on relief or living in shantytowns. In a typical family in the 1930s the husband had a job and the wife was a homemaker. Life was not easy, but it consisted of "making do" rather than stark deprivation.

The Invisible Scar

"You could feel the depression deepen," recalled the writer Caroline Bird, "but you could not look out the window and see it." Many people never saw a breadline or a man selling apples on the street corner. The depression caused a private kind of despair that often simmered behind closed doors. "I've lived in cities for many months broke, without help, too timid to get in breadlines," the writer Meridel LeSueur remembered. "I've known many women to live like this until they simply faint on the street from privations, without saying a word to anyone. A woman will shut herself up in a room until it is taken away from her, and eat a cracker a day and be as quiet as a mouse."

"Mass unemployment is both a statistic and an empty feeling in the stomach," observed a perceptive

Unemployment
The rate of unemployment was staggering during the depression. And, as Reginald Marsh's 1933 painting *The Park Bench,* illustrates, unemployment's effects on individuals were devasting. (Sheldon Memorial Art Gallery)

historian. "To fully comprehend it, you have to both see the figures and feel the emptiness." The victims of the depression were a varied group. The depression did not create poverty; it merely publicized the conditions of the poor. People who had always been poor were joined by the newly poor. These formerly solid working-class and middle-class families strongly believed in the Horatio Alger ethic of upward mobility through hard work but suddenly found themselves floundering in a society that no longer had a place for them. They were proud people who felt humiliated by their plight, and many of the down-and-out blamed themselves for their own misfortune. "What is going to become of us?" asked an Arizona man. "I've lost twelve and a half pounds this last month, just thinking. You can't sleep, you know. You wake up at 2 A.M. and you lie and think."

Hard times were distressing for old people, who faced total destitution in their final years. Some lost their savings in bank failures. In a cartoon from the 1930s, a squirrel asks a man on a park bench why he had not saved for a rainy day. "I did," the man replies listlessly. Children, on the other hand, often escaped the sense of bitterness and failure that gripped their elders. Some youngsters thought it was fun to stand in a soup line. Yet hard times made children grow up fast.

Downward mobility was especially hard for middle-class Americans. An unemployed Pittsburgh man told investigator Lorena Hickok, "Lady, you just can't know what it's like to have to move your family out of the nice house you had in the suburbs, part paid for, down into an apartment, down into another apartment, smaller and in a worse neighborhood, down, down, down, until finally you end up in the slums." Before a laid-off chauffeur started his relief construction job, he spent the day watching how the other men handled their picks and shovels so he could "get the hang of it and not feel so awkward." A wife broke into tears when her husband, formerly a white-collar worker, put on his first pair of overalls to go to work.

The key to surviving the depression was maintaining self-respect. One man spent two years painting his father's house (in fact, he painted it twice). Keeping up appearances, keeping life as close to normal as possible, was an essential strategy. Camaraderie and cooperation helped many families and communities survive, as people found that they were all in the same boat. When a truck driver "accidentally" dumped a load of oranges or coal off the back of his truck, he was probably contributing to the welfare of the neighborhood. Hoboes developed an elaborate system of sidewalk chalk marks to tell one another at which back doors they could get a meal, an old coat, or some spare change.

After savings and credit had been exhausted, many families faced the humiliation of going on relief. Seeking aid from the government hurt people's pride and disrupted the traditional pattern of turning to relatives, neighbors, churches, and mutual aid societies in time of need. A young caseworker tearfully remembered her embarrassment when investigating the homes of these proud people:

> The father was a railroad man who had lost his job. I was told by my supervisor that I really had to see the poverty. If the family needed clothing, I was to investigate how much clothing they had at hand. So I looked into this man's closet . . . he was a tall, gray-haired man, though not terribly old. He let me look into the closet—he was so insulted . . . He said, "Why are you doing this?" I remember his feeling of humiliation . . . this terrible humiliation. He said, "I really haven't anything to hide, but if you really must look into it . . ." I could see he was very proud. He was so deeply humiliated. And I was, too.

Even if families survived the demeaning process of being certified for state or local relief, the amount was a pittance: in New York State, for example, where benefits were among the highest in the nation, each family received only $2.39 per week.

Such hardships left deep wounds—the "invisible scar" described by author Caroline Bird. One elderly civil servant bought a plot of land outside Washington so that if the depression ever recurred, she would have the means to live. Labor organizer Larry Van Dusen described another common reaction: "The depression left a legacy of fear, but also a desire for acquisition—property, security. I now have twenty times more shirts than I need, because all during that time, shirts were something I never had." Virginia Durr, a white civil rights activist from Alabama, concurred: "The great majority reacted by thinking money is the most important thing in the world. Get yours. And get it for your children. Nothing else matters. Not having that stark terror come at you again." For many Americans, that was the Great Depression: "that stark terror" of losing control over their lives.

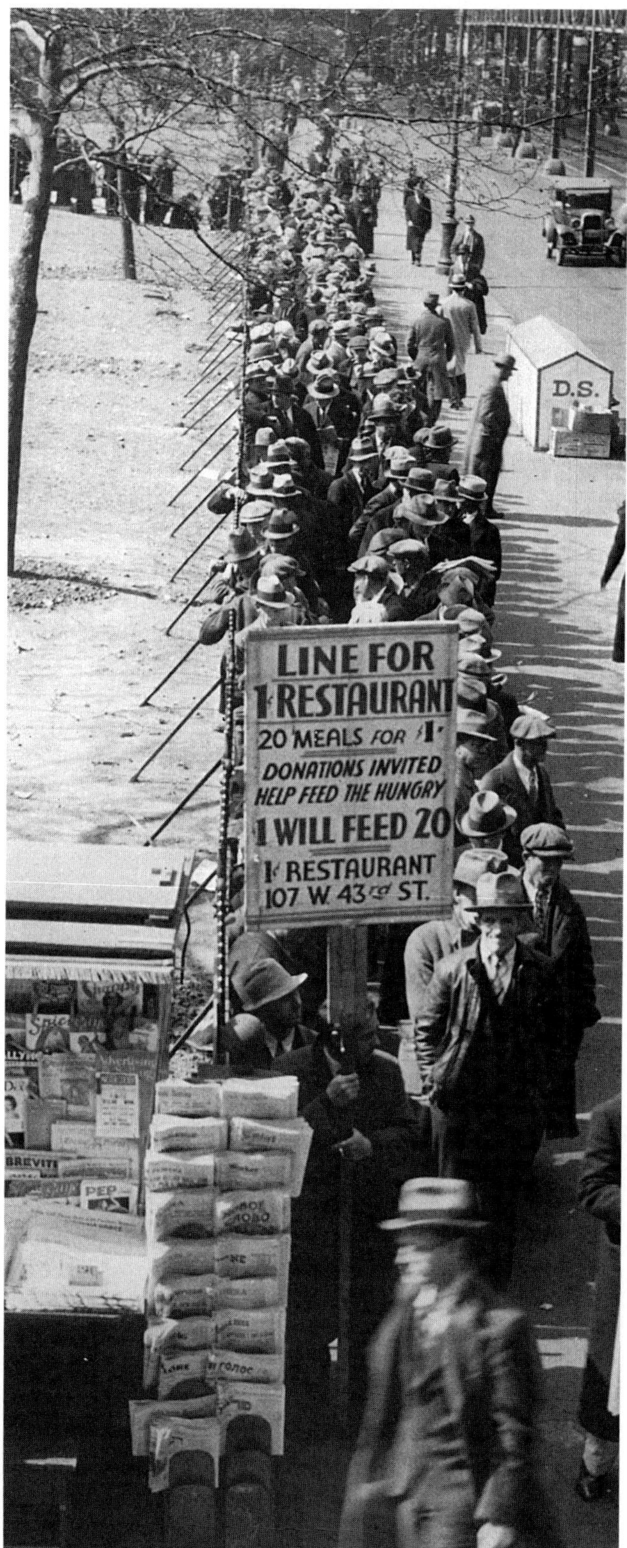

The Breadline

Some of the most vivid images from the depression were breadlines and men selling apples on street corners. Note that all the people in this breadline are men. Women rarely appeared in breadlines, often preferring to endure private deprivation rather than violate standards of respectable behavior for women.

The Family Faces the Great Depression

Sociologists who studied family life during the 1930s found that the depression usually intensified already existing behavior. For example, if a family had been stable and cohesive before the depression, it now pulled together to surmount the new obstacles. However, if a family had shown signs of disintegration, the depression made the situation worse. On the whole, researchers thought far more families hung together than broke apart.

In many ways, the depression disrupted women's lives less than men's. Millions of men lost their jobs, but few of the nation's 28 million homemakers lost their position in the home. In fact, women's domestic roles took on greater importance.

Men and women experienced the Great Depression differently, partly because of the traditional gender roles that governed male and female behavior in the 1930s. Men had been trained from childhood to be breadwinners for their families and they considered themselves failures if they could no longer support their families. Women, however, felt their self-importance increase as they struggled to keep their families afloat. The sociologists Robert and Helen Lynd noticed this phenomenon in their follow-up study of Middletown (Muncie, Indiana), published in 1937:

> The men, cut adrift from their usual routine, lost much of their sense of time and dawdled helplessly and dully about the streets; while in the homes the women's world remained largely intact and the round of cooking, housecleaning, and mending became if anything more absorbing.

Even if a wife took a job when her husband lost his, she still retained almost total responsibility for housework and childcare.

Women made many contributions to family survival during the depression years. With the national median annual income at $1,160, a typical woman had $20 to $25 a week to feed, clothe, and provide shelter for her family. Deflation had lowered the cost of living, so that milk sold for 10 cents a quart, bread 7 cents a loaf, and butter 23 cents a pound. Yet housewives still had to watch every penny. Two friends who often bought hamburger together split two pounds for 25 cents and took turns keeping the extra penny. Eleanor Roosevelt described the effect of the depression on these women's lives: "It means endless little economies and constant anxiety for fear of some catastrophe such as accident or illness which may completely swamp the family budget." The line between making do and doing without was often thin.

Despite the hard times, Americans managed to maintain a fairly high level of consumption. Continuing the pattern of the 1920s, households in the middle-income range, the 50.2 percent of American families with an income of $500 to $1,500 in 1935, did much of the buying. Several factors enabled these families more or less to keep up their former standard of living despite pay cuts or unemployment. Deflation lowered the cost of living almost 20 percent between 1929 and 1935. And families spent their reduced income differently. For example, telephone use and clothing sales dropped sharply during the depression, but people had a harder time giving up cigarettes, movies, radios, and newspapers, once considered luxuries but now regarded as necessities. An automobile proved to be one of the most depression-proof items in the family budget. Sales of new cars dropped, but gasoline sales stayed stable, suggesting that people bought used cars or kept their old models running longer.

Some families maintained their life-style in the 1930s through "deficit living"—that is, using installment payments and credit to stretch their income. This strategy added about 10 percent to a family income under $500, and 2 to 5 percent to a family in the $500 to $1,500 range. By 1936 consumer credit in the United States had increased by 20 percent over 1929 levels. A Middletown resident summed up the prevailing attitude toward installment buying: "Most of the families I know are after the same things today that they were after before the Depression, and they'll get them in the same way—on credit."

To maintain their families' life-style, housewives also substituted their own labor for goods and services they had formerly purchased. Women sewed their own clothes and canned fruits and vegetables. They practiced small economies such as buying day-old bread and heating several dishes in the oven at once to save fuel. Women who used to have servants now did their own housework. These economies helped pay for cars and movies, which could not be manufactured at home. Women generally accepted this new work stoically. "We had no choice," remembered one housewife. "We just did what had to be done one day at a time."

Demographic Trends

The depression directly affected demographic trends of the 1930s. The marriage rate fell from 10.14 per thousand persons in 1929 to 7.87 in 1932. The divorce rate dropped as well, because people could not afford the legal expense. Although marriage and divorce rates rebounded after 1933, postponement of marriage sometimes became no marriage at all. Elsa Ponselle, a Chicago schoolteacher who later became the principal of one of the city's largest elementary schools, recalled her experience:

> Do you realize how many people in my generation are not married? . . . It wasn't that we didn't have a chance. I was going with someone when the Depression hit. We probably would have gotten married. He was a commercial artist and had been doing very well . . . Suddenly he was laid off. It hit him like a ton of bricks. And he just disappeared.

The birthrate was the demographic factor most affected by the depression. Since 1800 the birthrate had fallen steadily, but in the years from 1930 to 1933 it dropped from 21.3 live births per thousand population to 18.4, a 13 percent decrease. The 1933 level, if maintained, would have led to a population decline. The overriding concern was whether a couple could afford to raise a child. The birthrate rose slightly after 1934 but by the end of the decade had reached only 18.8. In contrast, at the height of the baby boom following World War II, the birthrate was 25 per thousand population.

Birth Control. The extensive limitation of births during the Great Depression meant that people had access to effective contraception. The production of diaphragms and condoms was one business that thrived in the 1930s. Abortion remained illegal, but the number of women who had abortions increased. Because many abortionists operated under unsafe or unsanitary conditions, between eight and ten thousand women died each year from these illegal operations.

The 1930s marked a significant stage in the long history of the birth control movement in America. In 1936 a federal court decision in the case of *United States v. One Package of Japanese Pessaries* struck down all federal bans on the dissemination of contraceptive information. Doctors now had wide discretion in prescribing birth control for married couples, which became legal in all the states except Massachusetts and Connecticut. Public support for birth control also increased: a 1936 Gallup poll found that 63 percent of those interviewed favored the teaching and practice of contraception.

Margaret Sanger played a major part in encouraging popular acceptance of birth control in America. She had started her career as a public health nurse in the slums of New York in the 1910s. Anxious immigrant women continually asked Sanger to tell them the "secret" of how to avoid having more babies. When a patient who had been referred to her died from the effects of a botched abortion, Sanger dedicated her life to birth control. At first, she joined forces with socialist movements aimed at the working class. In the 1920s and 1930s, however, she appealed to the middle class for support, identifying this as the key to the movement's success. Sanger also courted the medical profession, pioneering the establishment of birth control clinics staffed by doctors and winning the American Medical Association's endorsement of contraception in 1937. Birth control became less a feminist demand and more a medical issue.

Birth control had long been a private decision between individuals. Its public acceptance increased greatly during the 1930s because of the widespread desire to limit family size for economic reasons. In 1942 the American Birth Control League, an organization Sanger had founded in 1921, became Planned Parenthood, an organization that remains active today.

Women on the Job

One way for families to make ends meet in the 1930s was to send an additional member of the household into the work force. At the turn of the century, this additional family worker probably would have been a child or a young unmarried adult. In the 1930s, it was increasingly a married woman. Instead of expelling women from the work force, the depression solidified their position in it: the 1940 census reported almost 11 million women in the work force, approximately a fourth of the nation's workers and a small increase over 1930. The number of married women employed outside the home rose by 50 percent.

Working women, especially married ones, encountered sharp resentment and outright discrimination when they entered the depression workplace. After calculating that the number of employed women roughly equaled the 1939 unemployment total, editor Norman Cousins suggested this tongue-in-cheek remedy: "Simply fire the women, who shouldn't be working anyway, and hire the men. Presto! No unemployment. No relief rolls. No depression." A 1936 Gallup poll asked whether wives should work when their husbands had a job, and a resounding 82 percent of the people interviewed said no. From 1932 to 1937 the federal government would not allow a husband and wife to hold government jobs at the same time. Many states adopted laws that prohibited married women from working; such laws were especially widespread in the field of education. Yet the proportion of married female school teachers rose from 17.9 percent in 1930 to 24.6 percent in 1940.

The attempt to make women scapegoats for the depression rested on shaky moral and economic grounds. Most women worked because they had to. A sizable minority were the sole support of their families, their husbands having either left home or lost their jobs. Single, divorced, or widowed women had no husbands to support them. Moreover, women rarely took jobs away from men. "Few of the people who oppose married women's employment," observed one feminist in 1940, "seem to realize that a coal miner or steel worker cannot very well fill the jobs of nursemaids, cleaning women, or the factory and clerical jobs now filled by women." Custom, rather than law or economics, made crossovers rare.

The division of the work force by gender gave women a small edge during the depression. Many fields with large numbers of female employees, including clerical work, sales, and service and trade occupations, suffered less from economic contraction than the steel industry, mining, and manufacturing, which employed men almost exclusively. As a result, unemployment rates for women, although extremely high, were somewhat lower than for men. This small bonus came at a heavy price, however. The jobs women held reinforced the traditional stereotypes of female work. When the depression ended, women found themselves even more concentrated in low-paying dead-end jobs than when it began.

This gender advantage benefited white women at the expense of minority women. To make ends meet, white women willingly took jobs usually held by blacks or minority workers—entering domestic service, for example—and employers were quick to act on their preference for a white work force. White men also took jobs previously held by minority males.

During the Great Depression, there were few feminist demands for equal rights either at home or on the job. On an individual basis, women's self-esteem probably rose because of their importance to family survival. Both men and women, however, continued to believe that the two sexes should have fundamentally different roles and responsibilities, and that a woman's life-style should be shaped by her marriage and her husband's career. The substantial contributions by women in the 1930s actually reinforced their overall identification with the home, laying the foundation for the so-called feminine mystique of the 1950s.

Hard Times for Youth

The depression hit the nation's 21 million young people especially hard. Although children only dimly glimpsed the sacrifices of life in the 1930s, adolescents knew that "making do" usually meant "doing without." The writer Maxine Davis, who traveled 10,000 miles in 1936 interviewing the nation's youth, described them as "runners, delayed at the gun." She added, "The depression years have left us with a generation robbed of time and opportunity just as the Great War left the world its heritage of a lost generation." Studies of social mobility confirm that the young men who entered their twenties during the depression era had less successful careers than those before or since. About 250,000 young people became so demoralized they simply took to the road as hoboes and "sisters of the road," as female tramps were called.

Because job prospects were so dim, some young people chose to stay in school longer. Public schools were free, and they were warm in winter. In 1930 less than half of the nation's youth attended high school, compared with three-fourths in 1940. This was partly due to increased attendance by boys, who had traditionally dropped out of school to work at an earlier age than girls.

College, on the other hand, remained the privilege of a distinct minority. About 1.2 million young people, or 7.5 percent of the population between eighteen and twenty-four, attended college in the 1930s, 40 percent of them women. After 1935 college became a little more affordable because of the National Youth Administration (NYA), which gave part-time employment to more than 2 million college and high school students. This government agency also provided work for 2.6 million out-of-school youths.

College students worked hard in the 1930s; financial sacrifices encouraged seriousness of purpose. The influence of fraternities and sororities declined on campus during the depression. Large numbers of students became involved in various political movements. Fueled by disillusionment with World War I, thousands took the "Oxford Pledge" never to support a war in which the United States might be involved. In 1936 the Student Strike Against War drew support from several hundred thousand students across the country.

Because young people spent more time in school, participating in organized athletics and extracurricular activities, adolescence became increasingly institutionalized in the 1930s, and teenagers developed their own values and patterns of behavior. Peers, rather than parents, influenced their values and tastes. Magazines and movies promoted a youth culture closely tied to an ethos of consumption. Teenagers throughout the country read the same comics, wore the same style clothes, and saw the same movies. They also experimented with necking, petting, and dating rituals that shocked their elders. The youth culture became a distinct feature of modern times.

Popular Culture

Popular culture played an important role in pulling the United States through the trauma of the Great Depression. As the novelist Josephine Herbst observed, there was "an almost universal liveliness that countervailed universal suffering." The mass culture that grew so dramatically in the 1920s flourished in the decade that followed.

Movie Palaces

In order to lure the more prosperous middle class to this new form of mass entertainment, movie theaters featured lavish interiors decorated to mimic European palaces. The recently restored Chicago Theatre shows the architectural grandeur of the picture palaces of the era.

Movies. The most popular form of entertainment during the 1930s was the movies. More than 60 percent of Americans saw at least one movie a week, with weekly attendance ranging from 60 to 75 million. In the 5,000 films made during the depression decade, moviegoers were transported to a world where hard times were practically unknown. Yet movies offered more than escapism. Hollywood in the 1930s, observed one film historian, "directed its enormous powers of persuasion to preserving the basic moral, social and economic tenets of traditional American culture."

Movies remained big business in the 1930s but the industry was not depression-proof. Although studios lowered admission prices from thirty cents to twenty, attendance dropped in the early 1930s, and by 1933 one-third of the nation's movie theaters were dark. Many of the major studios, dependent on Wall Street financing, were hurting. Not until 1934 did the industry begin to revive.

In many ways, films from the 1930s reflected the progress of the depression. In the grim early years gangster films were especially popular. Two of the most successful were *Little Caesar* (1930), starring Edward G. Robinson, and *The Public Enemy* (1931), in which James Cagney shoved a grapefruit in Mae Clark's face. These were replaced by extravagant Busby Berkeley musicals such as *Golddiggers of 1933,* suggesting an upswing in the public mood. The Marx brothers kept people laughing with such irreverent classics as *Animal Crackers* (1930) and *Duck Soup* (1933). Mae West titillated audiences with such lines as "It's not the men in my life, but the life in my men that counts" and "I used to be Snow White, but I drifted."

For some moviegoers, Mae West's sexual innuendoes went too far. To win back customers Hollywood made a highly publicized commitment to upholding ideals of decency and good taste. The Production Code Administration, headed by Joseph Breen, was Holly-

Dancing Cheek to Cheek
During the Great Depression, Americans turned to such inexpensive recreational activities as listening to the radio and going to the movies. One of the most popular attractions in Hollywood movies was the dance team of Fred Astaire and Ginger Rogers. Together Astaire and Rogers starred in ten movies.

wood's effort at self-censorship, an attempt to correct the perceived excesses of early talkies. Fearing a boycott from religious groups such as the Catholic Legion of Decency, studios in 1934 agreed to banish explicit sex, immorality, and violence from the screen. The standards promulgated were so narrow that censors barely permitted Rhett Butler to utter the famous last line of *Gone with the Wind:* "Frankly my dear, I don't give a damn." Critics charged that movies were cutting themselves off from reality, but the repressive standards held sway until the 1950s.

In part because of the Production Code, movies made after 1934 had a different feel than those made before. Sophisticated, fast-paced "screwball comedies" such as *It Happened One Night,* which swept the Oscars in 1934, epitomized Hollywood's new direction. Walt Disney emerged as a cultural mythmaker during the depression, producing 198 cartoons and such classics as *Snow White and the Seven Dwarfs* (1937), the first feature-length animated film. The 1940 Hollywood adaptation of John Steinbeck's novel *The Grapes of Wrath* was one of the few popular films to depict the depression. Otherwise, even the newsreels downplayed the depression in favor of heroes and heroines from the worlds of sport, entertainment, and popular culture.

At the height of the depression, movies continued to influence consumers. One of the decade's top box-office stars was a curly-headed little girl named Shirley Temple, who made twenty-one films by 1941. Shirley Temple dolls, books, and clothes flooded the market. Similarly, because of the popularity of such glamorous blondes as Jean Harlow, Carole Lombard, and Mae West, sales of peroxide hair rinse skyrocketed in the 1930s. Undershirt sales fell drastically after Clark Gable, a leading sex symbol of his day, took off his shirt in *It Happened One Night* and revealed his bare chest.

The Grapes of Wrath
John Steinbeck's bestselling 1939 novel became one of 1940's top movies, one of the few Hollywood films that tackled contemporary social problems. Ma Joad, played by Jane Darwell in the movie version, expressed the central message: "We're the people that live. They ain't gonna wipe us out. Why, we're the people—we go on."

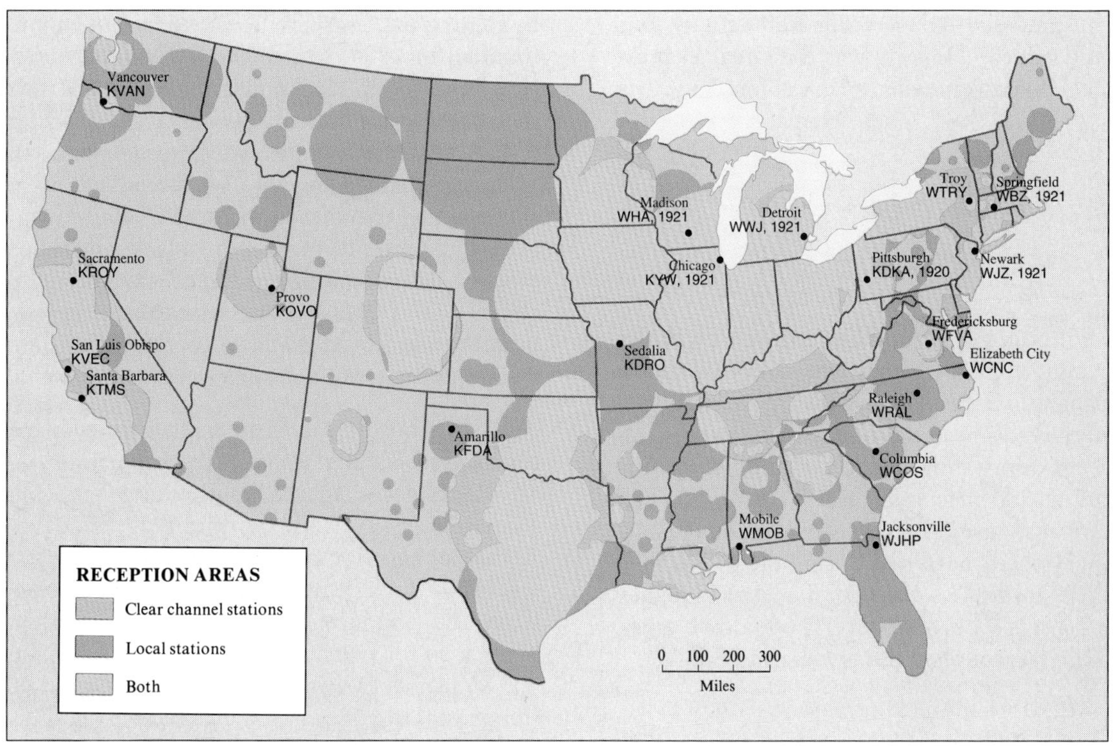

MAP 25.1

The Spread of Radio.

In 1938 more than 26 million American households, or about three-quarters of the population, had a radio. The date of first transmission is given for the earliest stations. By 1939 the period covered in this map, only a few sparsely populated areas were beyond radio's reach.

Headline History. Although movies had the greatest influence on popular culture, newspapers and newsreels provided quick coverage of world events. The kidnapping of the twenty-month-old son of Charles and Anne Morrow Lindbergh in 1932 instantly became a national news story. Seventy-five days later, the child's body was found in the woods near the Lindbergh home in New Jersey. "BABY DEAD" ran the headlines, and everyone knew what the two words meant. Other leading news events of the depression years included the birth of the Dionne quintuplets in Canada in 1934; the gunning down of John Dillinger, "Public Enemy Number One," by the FBI in 1934; the abdication in 1936 of King Edward VIII of Great Britain to marry "the woman I love," an American divorcee named Wallis Warfield Simpson; the disappearance of aviator Amelia Earhart on a round-the-world flight in 1937; and the fiery crash of the Hindenburg, a German dirigible, at Lakehurst, New Jersey, in 1937.

Radio Days. Radio occupied an increasingly large place in popular culture during the 1930s. At the beginning of the decade, about 13 million households had a radio set; by the end, 27.5 million owned one. Listeners tuned in to daytime serials such as "Ma Perkins" or picked up useful household hints on the "The Betty Crocker Hour." Variety shows featured Jack Benny, George Burns and Gracie Allen, and ventriloquist Edgar Bergen and his impudent dummy, Charlie McCarthy. Millions of listeners followed the adventures of the Lone Ranger ("Hi-Ho Silver"), Superman, the Shadow, and Dick Tracy.

Radio also brought music to depression-era audiences. Classical music devotees could listen to the Saturday afternoon broadcast of New York's Metropolitan Opera (premiered in 1931) or the NBC Symphony Orchestra under the baton of Arturo Toscanini. On the lighter side, people loved the new "swing" music of Benny Goodman, Duke Ellington, and Tommy Dorsey, which built on the jazz craze of the 1920s, and Cole Porter songs such as "Begin the Beguine" and "Night and Day" from Broadway hits. Radio increased the consumer market for 78 r.p.m. phonograph records of classical music, swing, and Broadway show tunes.

The depression also encouraged a return to traditional values. Church attendance rose slightly. The family again became a center of leisure activity, with an evening at home by the radio providing a cheap form of entertainment. Reading aloud from books borrowed from the public library was another affordable diversion. Columnist Russell Baker recalled an activity that everyone could afford: "Talking was the Great Depression pastime. Unlike the movies, talk was free."

The Social Fabric of Depression America

Much writing about the 1930s has focused on white working- or middle-class families who suddenly found themselves caught in a spiral of downward social mobility. For those already near the bottom, the depression had a much less devastating impact, both on their economic conditions and their self-esteem. For groups like African-Americans, farmers, and Mexican-Americans, times had always been hard and during the 1930s they just got a little harder. As the poet Langston Hughes noted, "The depression brought everybody down a peg or two. And the Negroes had but few pegs to fall."

Blacks and the Depression

Discrimination and limited opportunities had always been part of the lives of African-Americans, so they viewed the depression differently than most whites did. A black man didn't blame himself for his misfortune. "It didn't mean too much to him, the Great American Depression, as you call it," one remarked. "There was no such thing. The best he could be is a janitor or a porter or shoeshine boy. It only became official when it hit the white man." The novelist and poet Maya Angelou, who grew up in Stamps, Arkansas, recalled, "The country had been in the throes of the Depression for two years before the Negroes in Stamps knew it. I think that everyone thought the Depression, like everything else, was for the white folks."

Despite the pattern of black migration to northern cities begun in World War I, as late as 1940 more than 75 percent of all African-Americans were living in the South. Nearly all of the farmers who were black stayed in the South, their condition scarcely better than it was at the end of Reconstruction. Only 20 percent of black farmers owned their own land; the rest toiled on the bottom rung of the exploitative southern agricultural system, working as tenant farmers, farmhands, and sharecroppers. African-Americans rarely earned more than an average of $200 a year. The earnings of black women cotton pickers in one Louisiana parish averaged only $41.67 a year.

Throughout the 1920s southern agriculture had suffered from falling prices and overproduction. During the depression, an already desperate situation got worse. Some black farmers tried to protect themselves by joining the Southern Tenant Farmers Union (STFU), founded in 1934, one of the few southern groups that welcomed both blacks and whites. "The same chain that holds you holds my people, too," an elderly black farmer reminded whites on the organizing committee. "If we're chained together on the outside we ought to stay chained together in the union." Landowners, however, had a stake in keeping black and white sharecroppers from organizing, and they countered the STFU efforts with repression and harassment. In the end, the organization could do little to reform an agricultural system dependent on a single crop, cotton.

The Scottsboro Case. The Scottsboro case epitomized the harsh social and political discrimination that almost all blacks faced in the South during the 1930s. On March 25, 1931, a freight train pulled into Scottsboro, Alabama, carrying a number of hoboes and transients who had caught a free ride on the rails. Acting on a tip from the conductor, sheriff's deputies arrested nine black men for fighting with some of the white hoboes.

Suddenly, two white women wearing men's clothing stepped off the boxcar and claimed they had been raped by the nine blacks. The officers accepted without question the accusations of the women, Victoria Price and Ruby Bates, and barely restrained an angry white mob from lynching the men on the spot. Two weeks later, juries composed entirely of white men found the nine defendants guilty of rape and sentenced eight of them to death. (One defendant escaped the death penalty because he was a minor.) The U.S. Supreme Court overturned the sentences in 1932 and ordered new trials on the grounds that the defendants had been denied adequate legal counsel.

The youth of the Scottsboro defendants, their hasty trials, and especially their harsh sentences stirred public protest. The International Labor Defense (ILD), a labor organization closely tied to the Communist party, took over the defense of the so-called Scottsboro boys. The Communist party had targeted the struggle against racism as a priority in the early 1930s but was making little headway. "It's bad enough being black, why be red?" went a common retort. White southerners resented the interference of these radicals and also the fact that all those involved in the Scottsboro defense were northerners and Jews. In the words of a local solicitor, "Alabama justice cannot be bought and sold with Jew money from New York."

The case was complicated by the southern myth of the inviolate honor and chastity of white womanhood. The stories of the two women contained many inconsistencies, and Ruby Bates later recanted. However, in the South, when a white woman claimed to have been raped by a black man, she was taken at her word. As one court observer remarked, Victoria Price "might be a fallen woman, but by God she is a white woman."

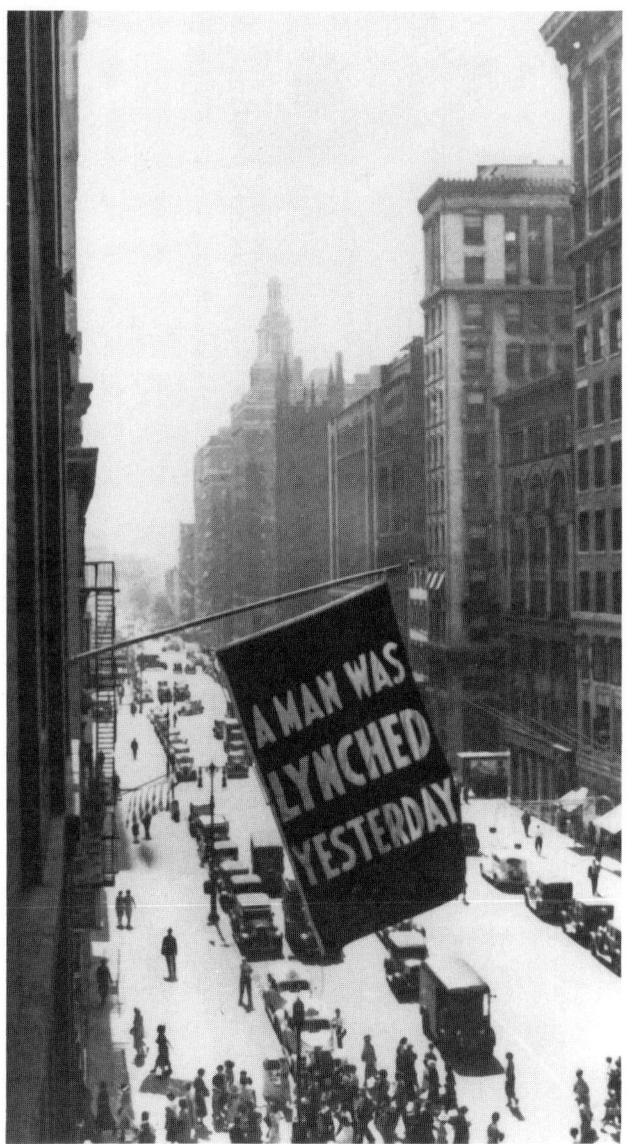

The Lynch Mob and Silent Witness
The threat of lynching remained a terrifying part of life for African-Americans in the 1930s, and not just in the South. The photograph on the left shows two young blacks who were lynched by an Indiana mob in 1930. Each day that a person was lynched, the NAACP hung a (right) banner outside the window of their New York office. NAACP appeals for federal anti-lynching legislation received little support from politicians, however.

The case dragged on through the courts for the next decade. In new trials held in 1936 and 1937, five of the defendants were convicted and sentenced to long prison terms. The charges against the other four were dropped in 1937. Four of the convicted men were paroled in 1944. The fifth escaped to Michigan, whose governor refused to return him to Alabama.

The Scottsboro case received wide coverage in black communities throughout the country. Along with the increase in lynching in the early 1930s (twenty blacks were lynched in 1930, twenty-four in 1933), it provided black Americans with a strong incentive to head for northern and midwestern cities. However, the lure of the North was offset by the lack of economic opportunities caused by the depression. About four hundred thousand black men and women left the South during the 1930s, only about half the number that left in the 1920s. By 1935 eleven cities had a black population of more than a hundred thousand. Two of the most popular destinations were the South Side of Chicago and Harlem in New York City.

Harlem in the 1930s. In the late nineteenth century, Harlem had been a neighborhood of wealthy white families—New York's first suburb. As late as 1900, blacks made up only a small minority of the Harlem population. Then World War I set in motion the great migration from the south. At the same time that blacks moved into Harlem, second-generation Italians and Jews began to move out.

Harlem reached the height of its fame in the 1920s, when it became a mecca for both whites and blacks. Adventurous New Yorkers associated Harlem with the Cotton Club and other glittering jazz palaces catering to white audiences. (Although the clubs featured African-American performers, they were white-only establishments, from which local blacks were excluded.) During the 1920s, the black population of New York City

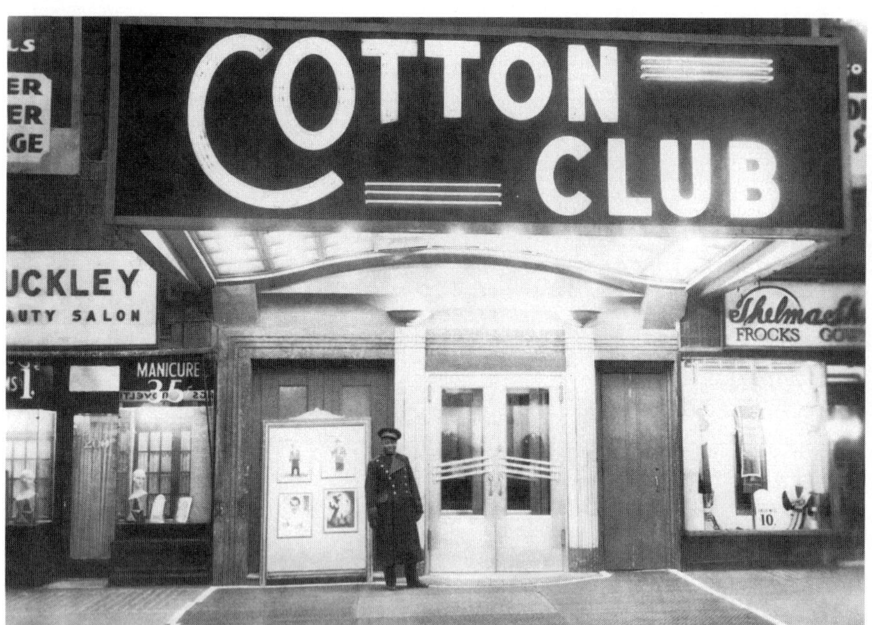

The Cotton Club

The Cotton Club, "the aristocrat of Harlem" at Lenox Avenue and 142nd Street, was home to such performers as Duke Ellington, Ethel Waters, and Cab Calloway. Even though blacks provided the entertainment and were hired as waiters and busboys at this swinging nightclub, they were not admitted as customers unless they were light-skinned enough to pass as white.

increased by about 115 percent, straining Harlem's housing facilities and community services. This once prosperous middle-class community was on its way to becoming a slum.

The depression aggravated the situation. Residential segregation kept blacks from moving elsewhere. African-Americans paid excessive rents to unscrupulous owners who allowed housing to deteriorate. Crowded living conditions caused disease and death rates to climb; tuberculosis became a leading cause of death in Harlem. At the height of the depression, shelters and soup kitchens staffed by the Divine Peace Mission, under the leadership of charismatic black religious leader Father Divine, provided 3,000 meals a day for Harlem's destitute. Unemployment rose to 50 percent, as whites now clamored for jobs traditionally held by blacks—waiters, domestic servants, elevator operators, and garbage collectors.

In March 1935 Harlem exploded in the nation's only major race riot of the decade. Its residents were angry about the lack of jobs, a slowdown in relief, and pervasive economic exploitation of the black community. Although entirely dependent on black trade, white-owned stores would not employ blacks. The arrest of a teenage black shoplifter, followed by rumors that he had been severely beaten by white police officers, triggered the riot. False reports of his death fueled the panic, and the city mobilized five hundred police officers. Four blacks were killed, and property damage totaled $2 million.

However, the picture was not totally bleak for blacks in the 1930s. The New Deal would channel significant amounts of relief money towards blacks outside the South, partly in response to the 1935 riot but mainly in return for growing black allegiance to the Democratic party (see Chapter 26). The National Association for the Advancement of Colored People continued to publicly challenge the status quo of race relations. Although calls for racial justice went largely unheeded during the depression, World War II and its aftermath would provide more fertile soil for the struggle for black equality.

Dust Bowl Migrations

Distressed conditions in agriculture had been one of the causes of the Great Depression. In the 1930s things only got worse, especially for farmers on the Great Plains. The decade became known as the "Dirty Thirties" because of the dust storms that blighted the land. The worst drought in the country's history began in 1930 and lasted until 1941. Throughout the decade the three words most often uttered by farmers were "if it rains."

Farmers who moved onto the semiarid Great Plains after the 1870s had always risked the ravages of drought (see Chapter 17). Even in wet years, the average rainfall was 20 inches or less—barely enough to raise grain crops. But low rainfall alone did not create the Dust Bowl. National and international market forces, such as the demand for wheat during World War I, caused farmers to push the farming frontier beyond its natural limits, expanding onto increasingly marginal land in order to capture a profit. After this land had been stripped of its natural vegetation, the delicate ecological balance of the plains was destroyed. Nothing remained to hold the soil when the rains dried up and the winds came.

AMERICAN VOICES

A Dust Bowl Diary *Ann Marie Low*

Born in 1912, Ann Marie Low kept diaries from 1927 to 1937 which describe the devastation wrecked by the drought and depression on her family's farm in the Badlands of southeastern North Dakota. They record both a young woman's coming of age and the harshness of life on the farm in the Dust Bowl.

April 25, 1934, Wednesday
Last weekend was the worst dust storm we ever had. We've been having quite a bit of blowing dirt every year since the drouth started, not only here, but all over the Great Plains. Many days this spring the air is just full of dirt coming, literally, for hundreds of miles. It sifts into everything. After we wash the dishes and put then away, so much dust sifts into the cupboards we must wash them again before the next meal. Clothes in the closet are covered with dust.

Last weekend no one was taking an automobile out for fear of ruining the motor. I rode Roany to Frank's place to return a gear. To find my way I had to ride right beside the fence, scarcely able to see from one fence post to the next.

Newspapers say the deaths of many babies and old people are attributed to breathing in so much dirt.

May 21, 1934, Monday
Ethel has been having stomach trouble. Dad has been taking her to doctors though suspecting her trouble is the fact that she often goes on a diet that may affect her health. The local doctor said he thought it might be chronic appendicitis, so Mama took Ethel by train to Valley City last week to have a surgeon there remove her appendix.

Saturday Dad, Bud, and I planted an acre of potatoes. There was so much dirt in the air I couldn't see Bud only a few feet in front of me. Even the air in the house was just a haze. In the evening the wind died down, and Cap came to take me to the movie. We joked about how hard it is to get cleaned up enough to go anywhere. . . .

May 30, 1934, Wednesday
Ethel got along fine, so Mama left her at the hospital and came to Jamestown by train Friday. Dad took us both home.

The mess was incredible! Dirt had blown into the house all week and lay inches deep on everything. Every towel and curtain was just black. There wasn't a clean dish or cooking utensil. . . It took until 10 o'clock to wash all the dirty dishes. That's not wiping them—just washing them. The cupboards had to be washed out to have a clean place to put them.

Saturday was a busy day. Before starting breakfast I had to sweep and wash all the dirt off the kitchen and dining room floors, wash the stove, pancake griddle, and dining room table and chairs. There was cooking, baking, and churning to be done for those hungry men. Dad is 6 feet 4 inches tall, with a big frame. Bud is 6 feet 3 inches and almost as big-boned as Dad. We say feeding them is like filling a silo.

Mama couldn't make bread until I carried water to wash the bread mixer. I couldn't churn until the churn was washed and scalded. We just couldn't do anything until something was washed first. Every room had to have dirt almost shoveled out of it before we could wash floors and furniture.

We had no time to wash clothes, but it was necessary. I had to wash out the boiler, wash tubs, and the washing machine before we could use them. Then every towel, curtain, piece of bedding, and garment had to be taken outdoors to have as much dust as possible shaken out before washing. The cistern is dry, so I had to carry all the water we needed from the well.

That evening Cap came to take me to the movie, as usual. Ixnay. I'm sorry I snapped at Cap. It isn't his fault, or anyone's fault, but I was tired and cross. Life in what the newspapers call "the Dust Bowl" is becoming a gritty nightmare.

Source: Ann Marie Low, *Dust Bowl Diary* (Lincoln, Nebraska: University of Nebraska Press, 1984), 95, 96–98.

Dust became a plague on everyday life throughout the Great Plains, but especially in Oklahoma, Texas, New Mexico, Colorado, Arkansas, and Kansas. When the clouds of dust rolled in, street lights blinked on as if night had fallen. Dust seeped into houses and "blackened the pillow around one's head, the dinner plates on the table, the bread dough on the back of the stove." The dust storms were not confined to the Plains. In May 1934, the wind took dust clouds to Chicago, where filth fell like snow, dumping on the city the equivalent of 4 pounds of debris per person. Several days later, the same clouds blackened the skies and dirtied the streets of Buffalo, Boston, New York, and Washington. That winter red snow fell on New England.

NEW TECHNOLOGY *Rural Electrification*

In 1935, less than one-tenth of the nation's 6.8 million farms had electricity. For millions of farm families, this stark fact meant a life of unremitting toil made even harsher by the lack of simple conveniences. Farm families used an average of 200 gallons of water a day. Any chore requiring water—and most did—meant pumping the water from a distant well and carrying it to the house or barn in a pair of buckets weighing as much as 60 pounds full. Hot water had to be heated on a wood stove that required constant tending. Meeting a family's yearly water needs took sixty-three eight-hour days and involved carrying water a distance of 1,750 miles.

Rural women suffered especially from the lack of electricity. Canning, a necessity before refrigeration, kept women standing over steaming vats of fruit or vegetables, often in the worst summer heat before the freshly harvested produce spoiled. Washday, traditionally Monday, called for three large zinc washtubs for washing, rinsing, and bleaching. A week's wash consisted of at least four to eight loads, each requiring three washtubs of clean water hauled from the well. Few rural households could afford commercial soap, so women used lye, which barely got ground-in dirt out of soiled clothes and was very harsh on their hands.

If farm women dreaded Monday, they hated Tuesday even more. Tuesday was ironing day, another all-day job. The iron, a six- or seven-pound wedge of metal, had to be heated on the stove, and because it did not retain heat for more than a few minutes, it took several irons to do a single shirt. The women in Texas's Hill Country called them "sad irons."

A day that began in darkness and was given over to twelve hours of backbreaking toil brought few comforts come evening. Reading by kerosene lamps strained the

Electrification

While a woman and her two children watch, workers install the power lines that will bring electricity to their nearby homestead. This sketch by C. David Stone Martin was done for a mural in Lenoir City, Tennessee.

This ecological disaster caused a mass exodus from the land. Their crops ruined, their lands barren and dry, their homes foreclosed for debts they could not pay, thousands of farm families loaded all their belongings into their beat-up Fords and headed west along Route 66 to the promised land of California. The migrants were called "Okies" whether or not they were from Oklahoma. John Steinbeck's classic novel *The Grapes of Wrath* (1939) immortalized their journey. The Joads abandoned their land not only because of drought, but also as a result of economic forces changing American agriculture. Large-scale commercialized farming had spread to the plains, where people like the Joads still farmed with animals. After the bank foreclosed on their

"Blue Monday"

Laundry was one of women's hardest household chores. Although this woman did not have to haul water from an outdoor well, she still had to pump it by hand in order to do the wash because her home lacked electricity. She also had to wring out the wet clothes manually, another arduous task.

eyes. Children's eyes might be strong enough to read in the semidarkness, but few older folks could read without squinting. The absence of electricity also meant no radios, which meant no contact with the outside world, no bit of amusement to brighten the darkness.

Studies showed that farmers would find many uses for electricity and would make good customers, but power companies balked at the prospect of electrifying the countryside. They claimed that it was economically unfeasible to run lines to individual farms. In 1935 the federal government made a commitment to bring power to rural America. The Rural Electrification Administration, an independent agency, promoted the formation of nonprofit farm cooperatives to bring electricity to their regions. For a $5 down payment, local farmers could join an association and become eligible for low-interest federal loans covering the cost of installing power lines. Each household was committed to a monthly minimum usage, usually about $3, but as usage increased, the rates came down. By 1940, 40 percent of the nation's farms had electricity; by 1950, the rate reached 90 percent.

Electricity brought relief from the drudgery and isolation of farm life. An electric milking machine saved hours of manual labor, most of it previously done, before dawn, by the faint glow of a kerosene lamp, so farmers could devote the daylight hours to outdoor chores. An electrically powered water pump lightened many chores, especially hauling water. Electric irons, vacuum cleaners, and washing machines eased the burden of women.

People's responses to rural electrification were poignant. A small child told his mother, "I didn't realize how dark our house was until we got electric lights." One farm woman remembered, "I just turned on the light and kept looking at Paw. It was the first time I'd ever really seen him after dark." Another family, caught unawares by the timing of the hookup, saw their house from a distance and thought it must be on fire. Schoolteachers noticed that children did better at school when they had light to do their homework by. Along with the automobile, electricity probably did more than any other technological innovation to break down the barriers between urban and rural life in twentieth-century America.

---

farm, a gasoline-engine tractor, the symbol of mechanized farming, plowed under their crops and demolished their house.

While powerful as fiction, the Joads' struggle does not convey the diversity of the westward migration, which was both a response to hard times and a part of the larger migration out of the nation's agricultural heartland that began around World War I and continued through the 1970s. Not all Okies were destitute dirt farmers; perhaps one in six was a professional, a business proprietor, or a white collar worker. Many were participating in chain migrations—that is, following family members or friends to a specific place. For most the drive west was fairly easy: Route 66 was a paved

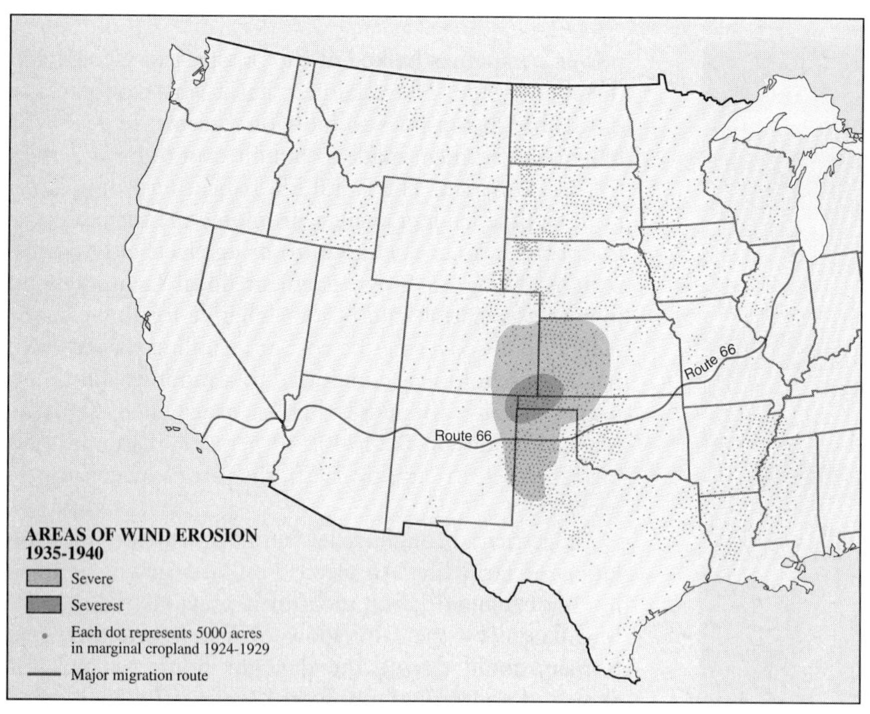

MAP 25.2

The Dust Bowl.

A U.S. Weather Bureau scientist called the drought of the 1930s "the worst in the climatological history of the country." Conditions were especially severe in the southern plains, where the dramatic increases in farming on marginal land had already strained production before the drought struck. Many farm families saw no choice but to follow Route 66, the highway that went straight west through Missouri, Oklahoma, and north Texas to California, the promised land.

Years of Dust

This 1936 Ben Shahn poster captured the despair and dislocation of the Dust Bowl years. Many farmers left their land to migrate to California.

two-lane road, and in a decent car, it took three to four days to make it from Oklahoma or Texas to California.

Before the 1930s California had already undergone changes that created a different type of agriculture from that practiced by southwestern and midwestern migrants. Farming in California was large-scale, intensive, and diversified. The state's wealth came from specialty crops whose staggered harvests required lots of transient labor for short picking seasons. The steady supply of cheap migrant labor provided by Chinese, Mexicans, Okies, and, briefly, even Hindustani made such farming economically feasible. Carey McWilliams, whose nonfiction *Factories in the Field* (1939) also focused national attention on migrant workers, noted that California agriculture was basically industrial in nature:

> Ownership is represented not by physical possession of the land, but by ownership of corporate stock; farm labor, no longer pastoral in character, punches a time clock, works at piece or hourly wage rates, and lives in a shack or company barracks, and lacks all contact with the real owners of the farm factory on which it is employed.

Encouraged by handbills promising good jobs in California, at least 350,000 southwesterners headed west during the 1930s. Some went to metropolitan areas, but about half settled in rural areas. White, native-born Americans had made up about 20 percent of the migratory farm labor force before the depression, but their proportion increased to more than 85 percent by the late 1930s. Since growers needed only 175,000 workers at the peak of the picking season, this surplus

Migrant Labor in California

By the 1930s, about 35,000 Filipinos were working as migrant laborers in California, including these lettuce workers in Salinas. At first, Filipinos were highly desired as migratory workers because they worked long hours for low wages. But they soon began to demand higher wages. In 1934, three thousand Filipino lettuce workers went on strike near Salinas. The strike was brutally broken, and many of the workers were driven from the community.

of labor assured them a cheap supply of labor, usually docile and willing to work at any price. That price was incredibly low in the 1930s. The average yearly family income for migrant farm workers in California ranged from $350 to $450, less than a third of the subsistence level. Yet what they earned in California was more than what they had left behind.

These migrants had a lasting impact on California culture. At first, they met outright hostility from old-time Californians, a demoralizing experience for these white, native-born Protestants, who were ashamed of the negative "Okie" stereotypes. But they stayed, filling important roles in the expanding California economy. Soon communities in the San Joaquin Valley—Bakersfield, Fresno, Merced, Modesto, Stockton—took on a distinctly Okie cast, identifiable by Southern-influenced evangelical religion and by the growing popularity of country music.

Mexican-American Communities

Mexican-Americans had a different experience in the west than Dust Bowl refugees did. In the depths of the depression, with fears about competition from foreign workers at their peak, perhaps a third of the Mexican-American population was deported or voluntarily relocated to Mexico. The 1930 census reported 617,000 Mexican-Americans; by 1940 the number had dropped to 377,000. A formal deportation policy instituted by the U.S. government was partly responsible for the decline, but many more Mexicans left voluntarily when work ran out, rather than be deported.

The deportation of Mexican-Americans was not in reaction to the arrival of migrants from the Dust Bowl. The largest number of Mexican-American deportations occurred under the Hoover administration, well before the Dust Bowl exodus reached its peak. Most deportations occurred in California and Texas, but Indiana, Illinois, and Colorado also repatriated unwanted workers. A one-way train ticket cost the equivalent of a week's relief allotment in 1932, and officials in many southwestern communities realized that it was cheaper to send migrant workers back to Mexico than to support them on relief during the winter, when there were no crops to pick. Pervasive racism and the proximity of Mexico made Mexicans the only immigrants targeted for deportation during the depression.

Mexican migration to the United States—legal and illegal—increased steadily throughout the twentieth century, except during the Great Depression and for short periods following the two world wars. The first *bracero* (day-laborer) program promoting Mexican immigration had been established during World War I to meet labor shortages. The importation of cheap Mexican labor continued throughout the 1920s. After being deported during the depression, Mexican workers found themselves being coaxed back again when World War II caused another labor shortage. The influx of Spanish-speaking migrants with their own distinct culture helped shape the patterns of life and work in the Southwest.

The experiences of his family as migrant workers during the 1930s influenced a Mexican-American named Cesar Chavez to become a farm union organizer. Chavez was a child of ten in 1934, when his father lost

Mexican-American Poverty in Texas
In 1937, Antonia and Pablo Martinez lived in a one-room house in San Antonio, Texas, with his parents and older brother. If either Pablo or Antonia was employed in 1937, it was probably in San Antonio's pecan-shelling industry, which depended heavily on the cheap labor of Mexican-Americans.

the family farm near Yuma, Arizona. The Chavez family joined the army of migrant workers that followed the crops in California. They experienced continual discrimination, even in restaurants where signs proclaimed "White Trade Only." Cesar's father became involved in several bitter labor struggles that hit the Imperial Valley in the mid-1930s. During 1933, thirty-seven major agricultural strikes occurred in California, including one in the San Joaquin Valley, which mobilized 18,000 cotton pickers. All these strikes failed, but they gave young Chavez a background in labor organizing, which he used to found a national farm workers' union in 1962.

Not all Mexican-Americans were migrant farm workers. A significant minority lived in cities and held industrial jobs. In 1930 Los Angeles was home to 150,000 Chicanos—people of Mexican birth or heritage—the largest concentration in the United States. By the 1930s, Mexican-Americans had spilled out of the downtown area known as "Sonoratown" into neighborhoods in East Los Angeles, where mutual aid societies, Spanish-language newspapers, and the Catholic Church fostered a sense of community.

In the cities, many Mexican-Americans found employment in fruit and vegetable processing plants, especially young single women who preferred cannery work to domestic service or farm labor. Corporate giants such as Del Monte (California Packing Corporation, or Cal Pak) and Libby, McNeill, and Libby dominated California's food processing industry. In these plants Mexican-American women earned around $2.50 a day, while their male counterparts earned $3.50 to $4.50. So pervasive was the "cannery culture" that workers could say, "We met in spinach, fell in love in peaches, and married in tomatoes," and their friends would know they were referring to the harvests of March, August, and October.

In 1939 labor unions came to the canneries in the form of the United Cannery, Agricultural, Packing, and Allied Workers of America (UCAPAWA), an unusually democratic union in which women, who formed a majority of the rank-and-file workers, played leading roles. This heritage of activism from the 1930s, in the fields and in the factories, foreshadowed later Chicano labor militancy.

Herbert Hoover and the Great Depression

During the presidential campaign of 1928, Herbert Hoover predicted that "the poorhouse is vanishing from among us" and that America was "nearer to the final triumph over poverty than ever before in the history of any land." Once elected, Hoover planned to preside over an era of Republican prosperity and governmental restraint. Even after the stock market crash in 1929, Hoover stubbornly insisted that the downturn was only temporary. He greeted a business delegation in June 1930 with these words: "Gentlemen, you have come sixty days too late. The Depression is over." In 1931 and 1932, as the country hit rock bottom, Hoover finally acted, but by then it was too little, too late.

The Republican Response

In 1932 the journalist William Allen White wrote an article about the outgoing president entitled "Herbert Hoover—The Last of the Old Presidents, or the First of the New?" White concluded that Hoover had been a little of both, as have historians ever since. Hoover's early efforts to fight the depression are now seen as predecessors of many New Deal programs, and his reputation among historians has risen steadily over the years. Hoover, who lived until 1964, offered a simple explanation for the improvement in his historical stature, telling Chief Justice Earl Warren of the Supreme Court that he had simply managed "to outlive the bastards."

Hoover's approach to the Great Depression was shaped by his priorities as secretary of commerce: he turned to the business community. Hoover asked business to maintain wages voluntarily, keep up production, and work with the government to build confidence in the system.

Fiscal Policy. Hoover did not rely solely on public pronouncements. He also used public budgets and federal action to encourage recovery. Soon after the stock market crash, he cut federal taxes and called on state and local governments to increase capital spending in the "energetic yet prudent pursuit" of public construction. The 1929 Agricultural Marketing Act gave the federal government its largest role to date in a program of agricultural stabilization and farm relief. In 1930 and the first half of 1931, Hoover raised the federal public works budget to $423 million, a dramatic increase in an area not traditionally seen as the federal government's responsibility. Hoover also eased the international crisis by bringing about, early in the summer of 1931, a moratorium on the payment of Allied debts and reparations. The federal government's efforts to stimulate business activity were moderately effective, but the depression continued.

By 1931 more drastic action was required. However, Hoover faced a cruel dilemma that had been created by the Federal Reserve's contraction of the money supply. If he embraced deficit financing and encouraged recovery through increased government spending, interest rates would remain high, since the federal government would be competing for capital with corporations and private investors. Hoover decided that significantly higher interest rates posed the greater danger to recovery, so in December 1931 he asked Congress for a 33 percent tax increase to balance the budget. The Revenue Act of 1932 represented the largest peacetime tax increase in the nation's history. Like monetary restriction, higher taxes choked both consumption and investment, and contributed significantly to the severity of the Great Depression.

Not all the steps taken by the Hoover administration were so ill-conceived. The president pushed Congress to create a system of government home loan banks in 1932. He also supported the Glass-Steagall Banking Act of 1932, which made government securities available to guarantee Federal Reserve notes and thereby counter credit contractions from gold withdrawals. This step temporarily propped up the ailing banking system. The federal government under Hoover spent $700 million—an unprecedented sum for the time—on public works.

However, Hoover remained adamant in his refusal to consider any plan for direct federal relief for unemployed Americans. Throughout his career, he had believed that private organized charities were sufficient to meet social welfare needs. During World War I, Hoover had headed the Commission for Relief of Belgium, a private group that distributed 5 million tons of food to relieve the suffering of Europe's civilian population. In 1927 he coordinated a rescue and cleanup operation after a devastating Mississippi River flood left 16.5 million acres of land under water in seven states. This effort involved private charities, including the Red Cross and the Rockefeller Foundation, as well as such government agencies as the U.S. Public Health Service and the National Guard. The success of these and other predominantly voluntary responses to public emergencies confirmed Hoover's belief that private charity, not federal aid, was the "American way." But charities and state and local relief agencies were unable to meet the growing needs of the unemployed.

The Reconstruction Finance Corporation. The centerpiece of Hoover's new initiative to combat the depression was the Reconstruction Finance Corporation (RFC), which Congress approved in January 1932. Modeled on the War Finance Corporation of World War I, and developed in collaboration with the business and banking communities, the RFC was the first federal institution that intervened directly in the economy during peacetime. It was designed to alleviate the credit crunch for business by providing federal loans to railroads, financial institutions, banks, and insurance companies, in a strategy that has been called *pump priming*. Money loaned at the top of the economic structure stimulates production, which in turn creates new jobs and increases consumer spending. Benefits thus "trickle down" to the rest of the economy.

Congress allocated $500 million for the RFC, but the agency's cautiousness in lending money limited its influence. In July 1932 Congress doubled this amount and authorized loans to the states for relief and public works. Once again the RFC acted far too cautiously, lending only $30 million by the end of 1932. It allocated and spent only 20 percent of the $1.5 billion appropriated for public works projects.

The Reconstruction Finance Corporation was a watershed in American political history and the rise of the state. When voluntary cooperation failed, the president turned to federal action to stimulate the economy. Yet Hoover's break with the past had clear limits. In many ways his support of the RFC was just another attempt to encourage business confidence. Compared with previous presidents, Hoover responded to the national emergency on an unprecedented scale. But the nation's needs during the Great Depression were also unprecedented, and federal programs failed to meet them.

Rising Discontent

As the depression deepened, many citizens came to hate Herbert Hoover. Once the symbol of business prosperity, Hoover became the scapegoat for the depression. His declarations that nobody was starving and that hoboes were better fed than ever before seemed cruel and insensitive. His apparent willingness to bail out business and banks while leaving individuals to fend

Hoovervilles

By 1930 shantytowns had sprung up in most of the nation's cities. In New York City, squatters camped out along the Hudson River railroad tracks, built makeshift homes in Central Park, or lived in the city dump. The two men in suits and hats are likely city inspectors or welfare officials.

for themselves added to his reputation for cold-heartedness. New terms entered the vocabulary: "Hoovervilles" (shanty towns where people lived in packing crates and other makeshift shelters), "Hoover flags" (empty pockets turned inside out), and "Hoover blankets" (newspapers). Columnist Russell Baker remembered his aunt's exaggerated recital of Hoover's faults:

> People were starving because of Herbert Hoover. My mother was out of work because of Herbert Hoover. Men were killing themselves because of Herbert Hoover, and their fatherless children were being packed away to orphanages . . . because of Herbert Hoover.

Signs of rising discontent and rebellion began to emerge as the country entered the fourth year of the depression. Farmers were among the most vocal groups, banding together to harass bank agents and government officers sent to enforce evictions and farm foreclosures, and protesting the low prices they received for their crops. Midwestern farmers had watched the price of wheat fall from three dollars a bushel in 1920 to barely thirty cents in 1932. Now they formed the Farm Holiday Association under the charismatic leadership of Milo Reno, the sixty-four-year-old former president of the Iowa Farmers' Union. Farmers barricaded local roads and dumped milk, vegetables, and other farm produce because the prices they would fetch on the market would not cover costs. Nothing better captured the cruel irony of underconsumption and maldistribution than farmers dumping food at a time when thousands of people were hungry.

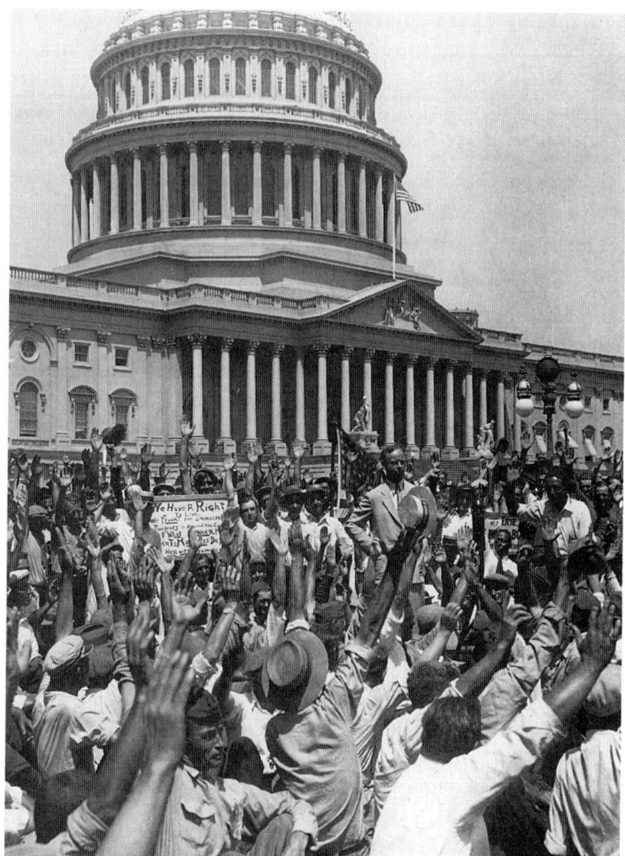

The Bonus Army

During this July 1932 rally on the Capitol grounds, Brigadier General Pelham D. Glassford, superintendent of the Washington, D.C., police, has just asked the assembled veterans whether they were 100 percent Americans. The raised hands provide the overwhelming answer.

AMERICAN VOICES

The Despair of the Unemployed

In 1931 an unemployed tool and die designer wrote to the director of the President's Organization for Unemployment Relief (POUR), but his letter drew only this penciled response: "no use answering."

Detroit, Mich.
September 29, 1931

Mr. Walter Gifford
Dear Sir:

You and Pres. Hoover shows at times about the same degree of intelligence as Andy [of the "Amos & Andy" radio show] does. The other night Andy was going to send a fellow a letter to find out his address.

You have told us to spend to end the slump, but you did not tell us what to use for money, after being out of work for two years you tell us this, Pres. Hoover on the other hand tells the working man to build homes, and in face of the fact nearly every working man has had his home taken off him, "some more intelligence." This is a radical letter but the time is here to be radical. when an average of two a day has to take their own life right in the City of Detroit because they can not see their way out. right in the city where one of the worlds riches men lives who made last year 259 000 000 dollars. where hundreds of peoples are starving to death . . . Mr. Gifford why not come clean. and stop bluffing us tell us the truth. remember you have the all seeing eye of God over you. Tell us the reason of the depression is the greed of Bankers and Industrialist who are taking too great of amount of profits . . . . The other day our Pres. Hoover came to Detroit and kidded the soldier boys out of their bonus. Pres Hoover a millionaire worth about 12 000 000 dollars drawing a salary of 75 000 per year from the government asking some boys to forgo their bonus some of them have not 12 dollars of their own "Some more nerve."

Am I right when I say you and he shows the same degree of intelligence as Andy.

J. B.

Source: Quoted in Robert S. McElvaine, *Down & Out in the Great Depression* (Chapel Hill: University of North Carolina Press, 1983), 46–47.

Protest was not confined to rural America. Bitter labor strikes occurred in the depths of the depression, despite the threat that strikers could lose their jobs. In Harlan County, Kentucky, miners struck in 1931 over a 10 percent wage cut, only to see their union crushed by the mine owners and the national guard. At the Ford River Rouge factory outside Detroit in 1932, a demonstration provoked violence from police and Ford security forces, with the result that three demonstrators were killed and fifty seriously injured. Some 40,000 people viewed the coffins under a banner that charged "Ford Gave Bullets for Bread."

In 1931 and 1932, violence broke out in the nation's cities. Groups of unemployed citizens battled local authorities over inadequate relief; people staged rent riots and hunger marches. Fearing the consequences of trying to stop this civil disorder, Mayor Anton J. Cermak of Chicago challenged a congressional committee to send relief or troops.

Many of these urban actions were organized by the Communist party as a challenge to the American capitalist system. For example, the Communist party helped to organize "unemployment councils" that agitated for jobs and food. Communists coordinated a hunger march on Washington, D.C., in 1931. The marches were well attended, and often got results from local and federal authorities, but they did not necessarily win converts to communism. In the early 1930s, the Communist party was still a tiny organization, with only 12,000 members.

It was not radicals, but veterans who staged the most publicized—and tragic—protest. In the summer of 1932 the "Bonus Army," a ragtag group of about fifteen thousand unemployed World War I veterans, hitchhiked to Washington to demand that their bonuses, originally scheduled for distribution in 1945, be paid immediately. While they unsuccessfully lobbied Congress, members of the "Bonus Expeditionary Force" (parodying the wartime American Expeditionary Force) camped out in the capital, a visible reminder of the plight of the unemployed. "We were heroes in 1917, but we're bums now," one veteran remarked bitterly. When the marchers refused to leave their Anacostia Flats camp, Hoover called out riot troops led by General Douglas MacArthur, assisted by Majors Dwight D. Eisenhower and George S. Patton, to clear the area. MacArthur's forces burned the encampment to the ground, and in the fight that followed, more than a hundred bonus marchers were injured. Newsreel footage captured the deeply disturbing spectacle of the U.S. Army firing on U.S. citizens, and Hoover's popularity plunged even further.

The 1932 Election

Despite evidence of discontent the nation was not in a revolutionary mood as it approached the 1932 election. Despair and apathy, more than anger, characterized the feelings of most citizens. The Republicans, who could find no credible way of dumping an incumbent president, unenthusiastically renominated Herbert Hoover. The Democrats turned to Governor Franklin Delano Roosevelt of New York, who capitalized on that state's innovative record of relief and unemployment programs to win the nomination.

Roosevelt's route to the presidential nomination began on a Hudson River estate north of New York City. Born into a wealthy family in 1882, he attended the Groton School, Harvard, and Columbia Law School. Roosevelt gave up his law career in 1910 for a seat in the New York legislature. He served as assistant secretary of the navy in the Wilson administration, which earned him the vice-presidential nomination on the losing Democratic ticket in 1920. Except for his allegiance to Democratic rather than Republican party ideology, he consciously modeled his career on that of his distant cousin Theodore Roosevelt, whose niece Eleanor he married in 1905.

Franklin Roosevelt was sidetracked in his path to the White House in 1921 by an attack of polio, which left him paralyzed in both legs for the rest of his life. Roosevelt fought back from his infirmity, emerging from the ordeal a stronger man. "If you had spent two years in bed trying to wiggle your toe, after that anything would seem easy," he said. Eleanor Roosevelt strongly supported her husband's return to public life, serving as his stand-in during the 1920s. She and Louis Howe, Roosevelt's devoted political aide, masterminded his reentry into Democratic politics. Roosevelt won the New York governorship in 1928 and the Democratic presidential nomination in 1932.

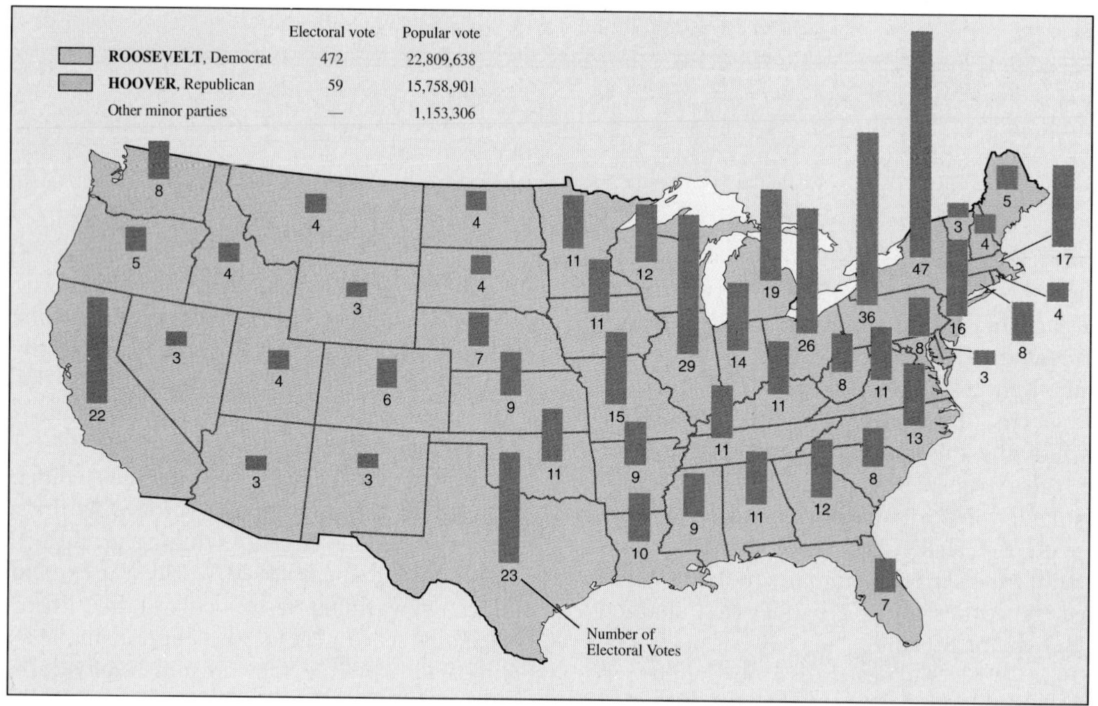

MAP 25.3

The Election of 1932.

Franklin Roosevelt's convincing electoral victory over Herbert Hoover in 1932 resulted from realignments in the Democratic party and dissatisfaction with the incumbent president. Even in the midst of the gravest crisis capitalism had ever faced, candidates of the Communist and Socialist parties received fewer than a million votes out of almost 40 million cast.

The 1932 campaign foreshadowed little of the New Deal. Roosevelt hinted at new approaches to the depression but stated his goals in vague terms. "The country needs and, unless I mistake its temper, the country demands bold, persistent experimentation," he said. Roosevelt won easily, receiving 22.8 million votes to Hoover's 15.7 million. Despite the economic collapse, Americans remained firmly committed to the two-party system. The Socialist party candidate, Norman Thomas, got fewer than a million votes. The Communist party drew only 100,000 votes for its candidate, party leader William Z. Foster.

The 1932 election marked a turning point in American politics: the emergence of a Democratic coalition that would dominate political life for the next four decades. In 1932 Roosevelt won with the support of the Solid South, which returned to the Democratic fold after defecting in 1928 because of Al Smith's religion and views on Prohibition. Roosevelt also drew substantial support in the West. An increasingly large urban vote continued the trend first noticed in the 1928 election, when the Democrats successfully appealed to recent immigrants and ethnic groups in the nation's cities. However, Roosevelt's election was hardly a mandate to reshape American political and economic institutions. Many people voted as much against Hoover as for Roosevelt.

The Interregnum. Having spoken, the voters had to wait until March 1933 before Roosevelt could put his ideas into action. (The interval between election and inauguration was shortened to the present January 20 by the Twentieth Amendment in 1933.) In the worst winter of the depression, Americans could do little but hope things would get better. According to the most conservative estimates, unemployment stood at 20 to 25 percent. The percentage was as high as 50 percent in Cleveland, 60 percent in Akron, and 80 percent in Toledo, all cities dependent on manufacturing jobs in industries that had basically shut down. The nation's banking system was so close to collapse that many state governors temporarily closed banks to avoid further panic.

By the winter of 1932–1933, the depression had totally overwhelmed public welfare institutions. Private charity and local public relief, whose expenditures had risen dramatically over earlier levels, still reached only a fraction of the needy. Hunger haunted cities and rural areas alike. When a teacher tried to send a coal miner's daughter home from school because she was weak from hunger, the girl replied, "It won't do any good . . . because this is sister's day to eat." In New York City, hospitals reported ninety-five deaths from starvation. This was the America that Roosevelt inherited when he took the oath of office on March 4, 1933.

Summary

The economic prosperity of the 1920s rested on shaky ground. After the stock market crash of 1929, the economy entered a downward spiral that did not bottom out until 1932–1933. In addition to the collapse of the stock market, the main causes of the depression were underconsumption, an unstable international situation, a legacy of "sick industries" and agricultural distress from the 1920s, and the flawed monetary policies of the Federal Reserve System. The Hoover administration authorized the first direct federal intervention in the economy during peacetime, the Reconstruction Finance Corporation, in an attempt to win business and public confidence. However, such measures did not end the Great Depression, and in 1932 the nation turned to Franklin D. Roosevelt and the Democrats.

The Great Depression left an "invisible scar" on many people who lived through the 1930s, especially on white middle-class Americans. Those who wanted to work blamed themselves if they could not find a job. The impact of the depression was less catastrophic for African-Americans and other minorities, for whom times had always been hard. But for farmers in the Midwest, things got even worse than they'd been in the 1920s. Drought and misguided agricultural practices created the Dust Bowl, forcing many farmers off their land.

Despite the devastating impact of the depression, many aspects of American life and culture continued to conform to traditional patterns. Families pulled together, with women taking on expanded roles—and often new jobs—to help support their households. Young people stayed in school longer. Families sought relief in popular culture, especially movies and radio programs. Only as the economy shifted towards war mobilization in the late 1930s did the depression finally ease.

TOPIC FOR RESEARCH

Remembering the Great Depression

One historian who studied the oral histories collected in the 1930s expressed surprise at how rarely people actually mentioned the Great Depression by name. "The Depression was not the singular event it appears in retrospect," she concluded. "It was one more hardship." On the other hand, the depression loomed larger in oral histories collected well after the event. As the years went by between hard times and the present, people's recollections of the depression's impact grew.

Test that hypothesis by comparing oral histories collected during the 1930s and those done later. Does the Great Depression take on an independent and different meaning as time goes by? How aware were people in the 1930s that they were living through "the Great Depression"? What does this tell us about the role historical memory plays in shaping our relation to the past? For an excellent introduction to Works Progress Administration (WPA) oral histories collected in the 1930s, see Ann Banks, ed., *First-Person America* (1980). Also of interest are the Federal Writers' Project, *These Are Our Lives* (1939), and Tom Terrill and Jerrold Hirsch, eds., *Such As Us: Southern Voices of the Thirties* (1978). The interviews Studs Terkel collected for *Hard Times: An Oral History of the Great Depression* (1970) provide an interesting counterpoint. See also Jeane Westin, *Making Do: How Women Survived the '30s* (1976). David Lowenthal's *The Past is a Foreign Country* (1985) discusses how the present influences our views of, and memories of, the past.

BIBLIOGRAPHY

Two useful overviews to begin the study of the Great Depression are John A. Garraty, *The Great Depression* (1987), and Robert S. McElvaine, *The Great Depression, 1929–1941* (1984).

The Coming of the Great Depression

Historians and economists continue to debate the causes of the Great Depression. See John Kenneth Galbraith, *The Great Crash* (1954); Milton Friedman and Anna Schwartz, *The Great Contraction, 1929–1933* (1965); Peter Temin, *Did Monetary Forces Cause the Great Depression?* (1976); and Michael Bernstein, *The Great Depression: Delayed Recovery and Economic Change in America, 1929–1939* (1988). For general overviews of economic developments, see Charles Kindelberger, *The World in Depression* (1974), and Jim Potter, *The American Economy Between the Wars* (1974). Irving Bernstein, *The Lean Years* (1960), offers a compelling portrait of hard times during the Hoover years.

Hard Times

A wealth of material brings the voices of the 1930s to life. The Federal Writers' Project, *These Are Our Lives* (1939); Tom Terrill and Jerrold Hirsch, eds., *Such As Us: Southern Voices of the Thirties* (1978); and Ann Banks, ed., *First-Person America* (1980), all draw on oral histories collected by the Works Progress Administration during the 1930s. See also Richard Lowitt and Maurine Beasley, eds., *One-Third of a Nation: Lorena Hickock Reports the Great Depression* (1981), and Robert S. McElvaine, ed., *Down & Out in the Great Depression* (1983), for first-hand accounts. Evocative secondary sources are Studs Terkel, *Hard Times: An Oral History of the Great Depression* (1970), and Caroline Bird, *The Invisible Scar* (1966).

Descriptions of family life in the 1930s include Robert and Helen Lynd, *Middletown in Transition* (1937); Mirra Komarovsky, *The Unemployed Man and His Family* (1940); and Roger Angell, *The Family Encounters the Depression* (1936). Russell Baker's autobiography, *Growing Up* (1982), provides an often humorous description of family life in the 1930s. Glen H. Elder, Jr., *Children of the Great Depression* (1974), looks at the long-term effects. For more on youth, see Maxine Davis, *The Lost Generation* (1936); Eileen Eagan, *Class, Culture, and the Classroom* (1981); Beth L. Bailey, *From Front Porch to Back Seat* (1988); and John Modell, *Into One's Own: From Youth to Adulthood, 1920–1975* (1989). Frederick Lewis Allen, *Since Yesterday* (1939), provides an impressionistic overview of the popular culture of the 1930s. Specific studies of movies and Hollywood include Robert Sklar, *Movie-Made America* (1975); Andrew Bergman, *We're in the Money* (1971); Molly Haskell, *From Reverence To Rape: The Treatment of Women in the Movies* (1974); Thomas Schatz, *The Genius of the System: Hollywood Film Making in the Studio Era* (1988); and Ed Sikov, *Screwball: Hollywood's Madcap Romantic Comedies* (1989).

Material on women in the 1930s is found in Susan Ware, *Holding Their Own* (1982); Winifred Wandersee, *Women's Work and Family Values, 1920–1940* (1981); Lois Scharf, *To Work and to Wed* (1981); and Alice Kessler-Harris, *Out to Work* (1982). For the special dimensions of white rural women's lives, see Margaret Hagood, *Mothers of the South* (1939). Jeane Westin, *Making Do: How Women Survived the '30s* (1976), is a lively account drawn from interviews. The birth control movement is surveyed in Linda Gordon, *Woman's Body, Woman's Right* (1976); James Reed, *From Private Vice to Public Virtue* (1978); and Estelle Freedman and John D'Emilio, *Intimate Matters: A History of Sexuality in America* (1988). See also *Margaret Sanger: An Autobiography* (1938).

The Social Fabric of Depression America

Developments in the black community during the 1930s are covered in Gilbert Osofsky, *Harlem: The Making of a Ghetto* (1966); Gunnar Myrdal, *An American Dilemma* (1944); David Lewis, *When Harlem Was in Vogue* (1981); Jervis Anderson, *This Was Harlem, 1900–1950* (1982); and Robert Weisbrot, *Father Divine and the Struggle for Racial Equality*

(1983). Dan T. Carter, *Scottsboro* (1969), remains the classic description of the case. Donald Grubbs, *Cry From Cotton* (1971), tells the story of the Southern Tenant Farmers Union. Robin D. G. Kelley, *Hammer and Hoe* (1990), is an excellent account of Alabama communists during the Great Depression.

For material on rural electrification, see D. Clayton Brown, *Electricity for Rural America* (1980), and Marquis Childs, *The Farmer Takes a Hand* (1952). The first volume of Robert Caro's biography of Lyndon Johnson, *The Path To Power* (1982), contains a moving portrait of the harshness of farm life before electricity.

Donald Worster, *Dust Bowl* (1979), evokes the plains during the "dirty thirties," as does Ann Marie Low's memoir, *Dust Bowl Diary* (1984). James N. Gregory, *American Exodus: The Dust Bowl Migration and Okie Culture in California* (1989), treats the experiences of the migrants in, and their impact on, California culture and the economy.

The experiences of Mexican-Americans during the 1930s are treated in Rodolfo Acuna, *Occupied America* (1981); Wayne Cornelius, *Building the Cactus Curtain* (1980); Mark Reisler, *By the Sweat of Their Brow* (1976); Abraham Hoffman, *Unwanted Mexican-Americans in the Great Depression: Repatriation Pressures, 1929–1939* (1974); and Francisco Balerman, *In Defense of La Raza: The Los Angeles Mexican Consulate and the Mexican Community, 1929–1936* (1982). For Mexican-American women's lives, see Vicki Ruiz, *Cannery Women, Cannery Lives: Mexican Women, Unionization, and the California Food Processing Industry, 1930–1950* (1987), and Patricia Zavella, *Women's Work and Chicano Families* (1987).

Herbert Hoover and the Great Depression

Hoover's response to the depression is chronicled in Alfred Romasco, *The Poverty of Abundance* (1965), and Jordan Schwartz, *The Interregnum of Despair* (1970). See also David Burner, *Herbert Hoover* (1978); Joan Hoff Wilson, *Herbert Hoover: Forgotten Progressive* (1975); and William Barber, *Herbert Hoover, the Economists, and American Economic Policy, 1921–1933* (1986). Eliot Rosen, *Hoover, Roosevelt, and the Brain Trust* (1977), treats the transition between the two administrations, as does Frank Freidel, *Launching the New Deal* (1973). For the 1932 election and the beginnings of the New Deal coalition, see David Burner, *The Politics of Provincialism* (1967); Samuel Lubell, *The Future of American Politics* (1952); and John Allswang, *The New Deal in American Politics* (1978).

TIMELINE

1929	Stock Market Crash
1930	Drought begins Hawley-Smoot Tariff
1931	Scottsboro case
1932	Reconstruction Finance Corporation Bonus Army
1933	Franklin Delano Roosevelt becomes President Birthrate drops to lowest level
1934	Southern Tenant Farmers Union *It Happened One Night* sweeps Oscars
1935	Rural Electrification Administration Harlem race riot
1936	Margaret Mitchell's *Gone with the Wind* Birth control legalized
1937	Amelia Earhart disappears
1939	John Steinbeck's *The Grapes of Wrath*

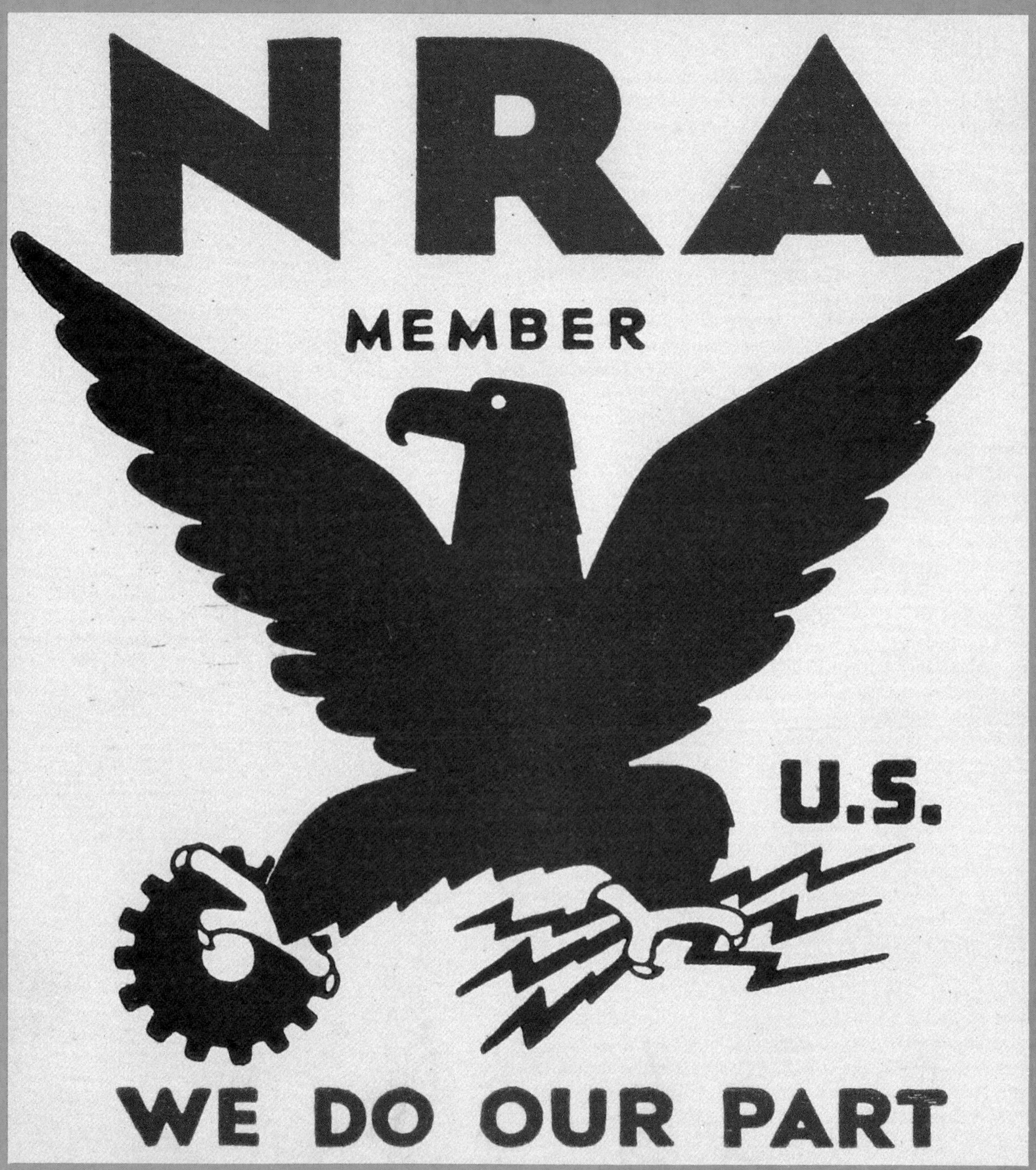

NRA Poster

Displaying the Blue Eagle and the slogan "We Do Our Part" symbolized compliance with the National Recovery Administration, one of the early programs of the New Deal.

CHAPTER 26 *The New Deal,* 1933–1939

In his bold inaugural address on March 4, 1933, President Franklin Delano Roosevelt declared, "The only thing we have to fear is fear itself." This memorable phrase rallied a nation that had already endured almost four years of the gravest economic contraction in its history, with no end in sight.

With his demeanor grim and purposeful, Franklin Roosevelt preached his first inaugural address like a sermon. He spoke of the economic and social problems the nation faced and their possible solutions only in the most general terms. Promising "a leadership of frankness and vigor," Roosevelt issued ringing declarations of his vision of governmental activism: "This Nation asks for action, and action now." Roosevelt repeatedly employed the analogy of fighting a war to combating the depression. The most explicit parallel was his willingness to ask Congress for "broad Executive power to wage a war against the emergency, as great as the power that would be given to me if we were in fact invaded by a foreign foe." Such a conception of presidential leadership was well suited to Roosevelt's self-confident personality and pragmatic political style.

In the end, however, Roosevelt intended not to scare the American people but to reassure them. The democratic system was basically sound, he told them, and hard times could be overcome, but only if a dispirited nation chose not to wallow in lethargy. On that cold March day in 1933, Roosevelt urged his fellow citizens to return to the values of hard work, cooperation, and sacrifice that had made the country great in the past. Roosevelt's restoration of hope and confidence was perhaps his greatest contribution to American life during the Great Depression of the 1930s.

The New Deal Takes Over, 1933–1935

When Franklin Roosevelt first used the term *New Deal* in his acceptance speech at the Democratic National Convention of 1932, he hardly realized that he had named his era. Plucked from deep in the speech by the newspaper cartoonist Rollin Kirby, the term came to stand for the Roosevelt administration's response to the depression. The federal government dominated political and economic life so thoroughly during the 1930s that the term *New Deal* is often used as a synonym for the decade itself.

The Roosevelt Style of Leadership

Every president since the 1930s has lived in the shadow of FDR. Few of his successors have matched his raw political talent; none had to face and surmount the twin crises of depression and war. "I have no expectation of making a hit every time I come to bat," he disarmingly told critics. "What I seek is the highest possible batting average." Roosevelt parlayed this experimental tone into a highly effective political and governmental style.

The New Deal represented many things to many people, but one unifying factor was the personality of its master architect, Franklin Roosevelt. The New Deal was "a very personal enterprise." Roosevelt, a superb and pragmatic politician, crafted his administration's program in response to shifting political and economic conditions, rather than by following a set ideology or plan. He experimented with one idea, and if it did not

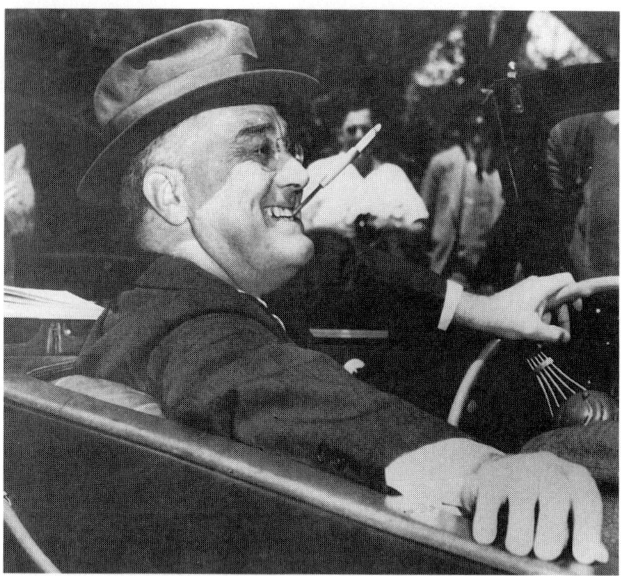

FDR
President Franklin Delano Roosevelt was a consummate politician who loved the adulation of a crowd. He consciously adopted a cheerful mien to keep people from feeling sorry for him because of his infirmity, knowing he could not be a successful politician if the public pitied him.

work, he tried another. Roosevelt juggled advice in the same way. Senator Huey Long of Louisiana complained, "When I talk to him, he says 'Fine! Fine! Fine!' But Joe Robinson [the Senate majority leader] goes to see him the next day and again he says 'Fine! Fine! Fine!' Maybe he says 'Fine!' to everybody."

President Roosevelt established an unusually close rapport with the American people. "Mr. Roosevelt is the only man we ever had in the White House who would understand that my boss is a son of a bitch," remarked one worker. Many ordinary citizens credited him with the positive changes in their lives, saying "He gave me a job" or "He saved my home." Roosevelt's masterful use of the new medium of radio, typified by the sixteen "fireside chats" he broadcast during his first two terms, fostered this personal identification. More than 450,000 letters poured into the White House in the week after the inauguration, and an average of 5,000 to 8,000 arrived weekly for the rest of the decade. One person had handled public correspondence during the Hoover administration, but it took a staff of fifty under Roosevelt. Understanding the importance of communicating with the public, Roosevelt became the first president to engage a press secretary.

Franklin Roosevelt continued the expansion of presidential power that dated to the administrations of Theodore Roosevelt and Woodrow Wilson. From the beginning, Roosevelt centralized decision making in the White House and dramatically expanded the role of the executive branch in initiating policy. For policy formulation, he turned to his talented cabinet, which included Interior Secretary Harold Ickes, Frances Perkins at Labor, Henry A. Wallace at Agriculture, and old friend Henry Morgenthau, Jr., who served as secretary of the Treasury. During the interregnum, he relied so heavily on the advice of Columbia University professors Raymond Moley, Rexford Tugwell, and Adolph A. Berle, Jr., that the press dubbed them the "Brains Trust."

When searching for new ideas and fresh faces, Roosevelt was just as likely to turn to advisers and administrators scattered throughout the New Deal bureaucracy. Eager young people flocked to Washington to join the New Deal—"men with long hair and women with short hair," wags quipped. Lawyers in their mid-20s fresh out of Harvard found themselves drafting legislation or being called to the White House for strategy sessions with the president. Paul Freund, a Harvard Law School professor who worked in the Reconstruction Finance Corporation and the Department of Justice, remembered, "It was a glorious time for obscure people." Many young New Dealers, who went on to distinguished careers in government or public service, later recalled that nothing matched the excitement of the early New Deal.

The Hundred Days

The first problem that the new president confronted was the banking crisis. Since the stock market crash, about 9 million people had lost their savings, a total of $2.5 billion. On the eve of his inauguration, thirty-eight states had closed their banks, and banks operated on a restricted basis in the rest. This collapse, far more than the stock market crash, brought the depression home to the middle class. Senator "Cotton Ed" Smith of South Carolina began carrying his cash in a money belt on the Senate floor rather than entrust it to a bank.

On March 5, the day after the inauguration, the president declared a national "bank holiday," a euphemism for closing all the banks and hurriedly called Congress into special session. On March 9, Congress passed Roosevelt's proposed banking bill, which permitted banks to reopen beginning on March 13, but only if a Treasury Department inspection showed they had sufficient cash reserves to operate on a sound basis. The House approved the plan after only thirty-eight minutes of debate.

Emergency Banking Act. The Emergency Banking Act, developed in consultation with banking leaders, was a conservative document. Herbert Hoover could have proposed it. The difference was the public's reaction. On the Sunday evening before the banks reopened, Roosevelt made his first "fireside chat" to a radio audience estimated at 60 million. In simple terms, he reassured the people that the banks were now safe—and they believed him. When the banks reopened on Monday morning, deposits exceeded withdrawals. "Capitalism was saved in eight days," observed Raymond Moley, who had served as Roosevelt's speechwriter in the 1932 campaign. The banking bill did its job: more than four thousand banks failed in 1933, but only sixty-one closed their doors in 1934.

The Banking Act was the first of fifteen pieces of major legislation enacted by Congress during the opening months of the Roosevelt administration. This legislative session, which came to be called the "Hundred Days," remains one of the most productive ever. Congress created the Home Owners Loan Corporation to refinance home mortgages threatened by foreclosure, and 20 percent of the nation's homeowners took advantage of it. A second banking law, the Glass-Steagall Act, curbed speculation by separating investment from commercial banking, and created the Federal Deposit Insurance Corporation (FDIC) which insured bank deposits up to $2,500. The Civilian Conservation Corps (CCC) sent 250,000 young men to live in camps where they performed reforestation and conservation work. The Tennessee Valley Authority (TVA) received legislative approval for its imaginative plan of government-sponsored regional development and public power. The price of electricity in the seven-state Tennessee Valley area soon dropped from ten cents a kilowatt hour to three cents. And in a move that lifted public spirits immeasurably, Roosevelt legalized beer in April. Full repeal of prohibition came eight months later, in December 1933.

The CCC
The Civilian Conservation Corps (CCC) was one of the most popular New Deal programs. Over ten years, it enrolled 2.75 million young Americans who worked for a dollar a day on such projects as soil conservation, disaster relief, reforestation, and flood control. The CCC was limited to men only, although a few camps benefited out-of-work young women.

The Agricultural Adjustment Act. The Roosevelt administration targeted three pressing problems: curbing agricultural overproduction, stimulating business recovery, and providing for the unemployed. Roosevelt considered a farm bill "the key to recovery." The Agricultural Adjustment Act (AAA) was developed by Secretary of Agriculture Henry A. Wallace, Assistant Secretary Rexford Tugwell, and agricultural economist M. L. Wilson, in close collaboration with leaders of major farm organizations. A domestic allotment system for seven major commodities (wheat, cotton, corn, hogs, rice, tobacco, and dairy products) gave cash subsidies to farmers in return for cutting production; these benefits were financed by a tax on processing (such as, milling of wheat), which was passed on to consumers. New Deal planners hoped prices would rise in response to the federally subsidized scarcity, and thus spur more general recovery.

The AAA stabilized the farm situation, but its benefits were distributed unevenly. The subsidies for reducing production went primarily to large and medium-sized farm owners, who in turn cut production by often reducing the acreage of their renters and sharecroppers but continued to farm their own land. In the South this strategy had a racial component, because many sharecroppers were black and the land owners and government administrators were white. As many as two hundred thousand black tenant farmers were displaced from their land by the AAA. Thus New Deal agricultural policies fostered the migration of marginal farmers in the South and Midwest to Northern cities and California and consolidated the economic and political clout of larger landholders.

TABLE 26.1

American Banks and Bank Failures, 1920–1940

Year	Total Number of Banks	Total Assets	Bank Failures
1920	30,909	$53.1 billion	168
1929	25,568	72.3	659
1931	22,242	70.1	2,294
1933	14,771	51.4	4,004
1934	15,913	55.9	61
1940	15,076	79.7	48

Source: Historical Statistics of the United States: Colonial Times to 1970, (Washington, D.C.: U.S. Government Printing Office, 1975), pp. 1019, 1038–1039.

NRA. The New Deal attacked the problem of economic recovery with the National Industrial Recovery Act, which created the National Recovery Administration (NRA). This agency drew on the World War I experience of Bernard Baruch's War Industries Board and extended the reliance on trade associations of the Coolidge and Hoover administrations. The NRA set up a system of industrial self-government to handle the problems of overproduction, cutthroat competition, and price instability. To achieve its objectives, the NRA established codes of fair competition, tailored to prevent the specific practices within each industry that had forced prices downward. In effect, these legally enforceable agreements suspended the antitrust laws. Each code also contained provisions covering working conditions. For example, the codes established minimum wages and maximum hours and outlawed child labor completely. One of the most far-reaching provisions, Section 7(a), guaranteed workers the right to organize and bargain collectively "through representatives of their own choosing," which dramatically spurred the growth of the labor movement.

General Hugh Johnson, a colorful if somewhat erratic administrator, headed the NRA. He oversaw negotiations for more than six hundred NRA codes, ranging from large industries such as coal, cotton, and steel, to dog food, costume jewelry, and even burlesque theaters. The code process theoretically included equal input from management, labor, and consumers, but business trade associations basically set the terms. Because large companies dominated the trade associations, the code-drafting process further solidified the power of large businesses at the expense of smaller enterprises. Labor had little input, consumer interests almost none. An extensive public relations campaign, complete with plugs in Hollywood films such as *Gold Diggers of 1933* and stickers with the NRA slogan, "We Do Our Part," attempted to sell this program to skeptical consumers and businesspeople.

Unemployment. The early New Deal also addressed the critical problem of unemployment. The total exhaustion of private and local sources of charity made some form of federal relief essential in this fourth year of the depression. Roosevelt moved reluctantly toward federal responsibility for the unemployed. The Federal Emergency Relief Administration (FERA), set up in May 1933 under the direction of Harry Hopkins, a New York social worker, offered federal money to the states for relief programs. It was designed to keep people from starving until other recovery measures had a chance to take hold. Hopkins distributed $5 million in his first two hours in office. When told that some of the projects he had just authorized might not be sound in the long run, Hopkins replied, "People don't eat in the long run—they eat every day." During its two-year existence, the FERA spent $1 billion.

Roosevelt always maintained a strong distaste for the dole. Wherever possible, his administration promoted work relief, no matter how makeshift, over cash subsidies; it also consistently favored relief jobs that did not directly compete with the private sector. The Public Works Administration (PWA), under Secretary of the Interior Harold L. Ickes, received a $3.3 billion appropriation in 1933 for a major public works program. However, Ickes's cautiousness in starting up projects limited the PWA's effectiveness in spurring recovery or providing jobs. In November 1933, Roosevelt assigned $400 million in PWA funds to a new agency, the Civil Works Administration (CWA), headed by Harry Hopkins. Within thirty days, the CWA put 2.6 million men and women to work; at its peak in January 1934, it employed 4 million. CWA workers received fifteen dollars a week for jobs such as repairing bridges, building highways, constructing public buildings, and setting up community projects. The CWA, regarded as a stopgap measure to get the country through the winter of 1933–1934, lapsed the next spring after spending all its funds.

Many of the emergency measures of the first hundred days were deliberately inflationary—that is, they were designed to trigger price rises thought necessary to stimulate recovery and halt the steep deflation. Another element of this strategy was Roosevelt's April 18 executive order to abandon the gold standard and let gold rise in value, just like any other commodity. As the price of gold rose, so too would agricultural prices, a key to general recovery. Budget director Lew Douglas warned that abandoning the gold standard would lead to "the end of Western civilization." That did not happen, but neither did it have much impact on the domestic economy. Its main significance lay in the adoption of a flexible currency system in which the value of the dollar could be manipulated by the Federal Reserve system according to economic conditions, rather than tied to a fixed standard. This action represented an important shift in control over the economy to the public sector.

When an exhausted Congress recessed in June 1933, much had been accomplished. Rarely had a president so dominated a legislative session. A mass of "alphabet agencies," as the New Deal programs came to be known, flowed from Washington. They gave the impression of action, but despite a slight economic upturn, they had not turned the economy around.

Nevertheless, Americans saw a ray of hope. In April 1933, at the height of the excitement over the Hundred Days, Walt Disney released a cartoon film called *Three Little Pigs*. Echoing FDR's assertion that they had nothing to fear but fear itself, many people hummed the cartoon's theme song, "Who's Afraid of the Big Bad Wolf?" as they started down the road toward renewed confidence.

Consolidating the Hundred Days

If the measures taken during Franklin Roosevelt's first hundred days had cured the Great Depression, the rest of the New Deal probably would not have occurred. When the Depression stubbornly persisted, FDR and Congress turned to more far-reaching structural reform rather than the emergency recovery measures of 1933.

Reforming Wall Street. One obvious target for reform was Wall Street, where insider trading, fraud, and other abuses had contributed to the 1929 crash. In 1934 Congress established the Securities and Exchange Commission (SEC) to regulate the stock market. The commission had the power to regulate buying stocks on credit, or margin buying, and to restrict speculation by those with inside information on corporate plans. The Public Utilities Holding Company Act of 1935 limited the widespread practice of pyramiding holding companies on top of utilities for the sole purpose of issuing stock and inflating profits.

The banking system came under scrutiny as well. The Banking Act of 1935 represented a significant consolidation of federal control over the nation's banks. The law authorized the president to appoint a new Board of Governors of the Federal Reserve System. This reorganization placed control of interest rates and other money market policies squarely at the federal level rather than with regional banks. By requiring all large state banks to join the Federal Reserve System by 1942 in order to use the federal deposit insurance system, the law further encouraged the centralization of the nation's banking system.

"Gulliver's Travels"
So many new agencies flooded out of Washington in the 1930s that you almost needed a scorecard to keep them straight. Here a July 1935 *Vanity Fair* cartoon by William Gropper substitutes Uncle Sam for Captain Lemuel Gulliver, tied to the ground by Lilliputians, in a parody of Jonathan Swift's satire *Gulliver's Travels*.

Roosevelt was not hostile toward business. He heartily accepted the capitalist system but realized that modern industrial life required more explicit federal control to limit some of capitalism's excesses. "To preserve we had to reform," Roosevelt commented succinctly. Even though he styled himself as the savior of capitalism, he provoked strong hostility from many well-to-do Americans. To the wealthy, Roosevelt became simply "That Man," a traitor to his class. Business leaders and conservative Democrats formed the Liberty League in 1934 to lobby against the New Deal and its "reckless spending" and "socialist" reforms.

The conservative majority on the Supreme Court also disagreed with the direction of the New Deal. On "Black Monday," May 27, 1935, the Supreme Court unanimously ruled that the National Industrial Recovery Act was an unconstitutional delegation of legislative power to an administrative agency in the case of *Schechter v. United States*. The so-called sick-chicken case concerned a Brooklyn, New York, firm convicted of violating NRA codes by selling diseased poultry. In the case, the court also held that the NRA was regulating commerce *within* an individual state and that the constitution limited federal regulation to *interstate* commerce. Roosevelt publicly protested that the Court's narrow interpretation would return the Constitution "to the horse-and-buggy definition of interstate commerce," but he could only watch helplessly as the court threatened to invalidate the entire New Deal.

Challenges from the Left

Other citizens thought the New Deal had not gone far enough. Francis Townsend, a Long Beach, California, doctor, spoke for the nation's elderly. Many Americans feared poverty in old age because few had pension plans. In 1933, Townsend proposed an Old Age Revolving Pension Plan, which would give $200 a month to citizens above the age of sixty. To receive payment, people would have to retire from their jobs, thereby opening the positions to others, and agree to spend the money within a month. Townsend Clubs soon sprang up throughout the country, with special strength in the Far West.

Father Charles Coughlin also challenged Roosevelt's leadership and attracted a large following, especially in the Midwest. Coughlin, a parish priest in the Detroit suburb of Royal Oak, had turned to the radio in the mid-1920s to enlarge his pastorate. In 1933 about 40 million Americans listened regularly to the "Radio

Priest." In many Roman Catholic neighborhoods during the summer, Coughlin's sermon could be heard blaring from open windows. At first he supported the New Deal but soon broke with Roosevelt over the president's refusal to support nationalization of the banking system and expansion of the money supply. Coughlin organized the National Union for Social Justice in 1935 to promote his views as an alternative to "Franklin Double-Crossing Roosevelt." As a Catholic priest who had been born in Canada, Coughlin could not run for president, but his rapidly growing constituency became a factor in the 1936 election.

The most direct political threat to Roosevelt came from Senator Huey Long. In a single term as governor of Louisiana, the flamboyant Long had achieved stunning popularity in his backward state. Voters applauded his attacks on big business, as he lowered their utility bills and increased the share of taxes paid by corporations. And Long's ambitious program of public works, which included the construction of new highways, bridges, hospitals, and schools, benefited all Louisianans and created many new jobs. But Long's accomplishments came at a price: to push through his reforms he seized almost dictatorial control of the state government. He maintained control over Louisiana's political machine even after his election to the U.S. Senate in 1930. Long supported Roosevelt in 1932 but made no secret of his own presidential ambitions.

In 1934, Senator Long broke with the New Deal, arguing that its programs did not go far enough. Like Father Coughlin, he established his own national movement, the Share Our Wealth Society which had over 4 million followers in 1935. Long argued that the unequal distribution of wealth in the United States was the fundamental cause of the depression. Long's solution was to tax 100 percent of all incomes over $1 million and all inheritances over $5 million, and distribute the money to the rest of the population. Every family would be guaranteed about $2,000 annually, he predicted. Huey Long's rapid rise in popularity suggested a potentially large volume of public dissatisfaction with the Roosevelt administration. The president's strategists feared that Long might join forces with Coughlin and Townsend to form a third party, enabling the Republicans to win the 1936 election.

The Kingfish
Huey Long, the Louisiana governor and senator, ranks as one of the most controversial figures in American political history. He took his nickname of the "Kingfish" from a character in the popular radio show "Amos 'n' Andy." Long inspired one of the most powerful political novels of all time, Robert Penn Warren's *All the King's Men*, which won a Pulitzer Prize in 1946.

The Second New Deal, 1935–1939

By 1935, Roosevelt had abandoned his hope of building a classless coalition of rich and poor, workers and farmers, and rural and urban dwellers. Pushed from the left to do more, and bitterly criticized by the right for what he had already done, the president had no choice but to abandon the middle ground. For both political and ideological reasons, and with an eye fixed firmly on the 1936 election, Roosevelt moved dramatically to the left. Historians use the term *Second New Deal* to describe the outpouring of legislation that followed.

Legislative Accomplishments

The first beneficiary of Roosevelt's change of direction was the labor movement. The rising number of strikes in 1934, about eighteen hundred involving a total of 1.5 million workers, reflected a growth of rank-and-file militancy. After the Supreme Court declared the NRA unconstitutional, labor demanded legislation that would protect its rights to organize and bargain collectively. That year, Senator Robert F. Wagner of New York, one of labor's staunchest supporters in Congress, introduced legislation to replace the ineffective (and now inoperative) Section 7(a) of the NRA. Only when Congress was on the verge of passing Wagner's bill did Roosevelt reluctantly support the legislation; he signed the National Labor Relations Act, also known as the Wagner Act, on July 5, 1935.

The Wagner Act placed the weight of the federal government on labor's side in the struggle to organize. Most importantly, it upheld the right of workers to join

General Strike, 1934
San Francisco's general strike began with the longshoremen and soon spread to almost every union member (and some middle-class supporters as well) in the city. Here the strikers are battling police. On July 19, union leaders voted to accept government arbitration, and the strike ended.

unions. The law also outlawed many unfair labor practices used by employers to squelch unions, such as spying on workers, requiring yellow-dog contracts (where workers had to agree not to join a union in order to be hired), and firing or blacklisting workers because of union activities. The act established the nonpartisan National Labor Relations Board (NLRB) to protect workers from employer coercion, to supervise representation elections, and to enforce the guarantee of collective bargaining. If a union won a majority of the votes in a secret election, usually conducted by the NLRB, it was entitled to recognition as the sole bargaining agent for all the employees in a factory or other appropriate bargaining unit. The NLRB had the authority to force employers to comply.

Social Security. The Social Security Act, signed by President Roosevelt on August 14, 1935, was the second major piece of legislation in this phase of the New Deal. The law was a response to the political mobilization of the nation's elderly through the Townsend and Long movements. It also reflected the prodding of social reformers such as Grace Abbott, head of the Children's Bureau, and Secretary of Labor Frances Perkins. The Social Security Act provided pensions for most workers in the private sector through a federal-state pension fund to which both employers and employees contributed. Roosevelt's advisers decided to fund this program with payroll deductions, rather than general tax revenues, in order to insulate it from political attack. The act also established a joint federal-state system of unemployment compensation, funded by an unemployment tax on employers and employees.

The Social Security Act represented a milestone in the creation of the modern welfare state. With this law, the United States joined such industrialized countries as Great Britain and Germany in providing old-age pensions and unemployment compensation benefits to its citizens. (The Roosevelt administration chose not to push for national health insurance, even though most other industrialized nations offered such protection.) The law also mandated categorical assistance, such as aid to the blind, deaf, and disabled, and to dependent children. These recipients were the so-called "deserving poor," people who could not support themselves through no fault of their own. The categorical assistance programs grew dramatically after the 1930s. Aid to Dependent Children covered only 700,000 youngsters in 1939; by 1974, its successor, Aid to Families with Dependent Children, enrolled 10.8 million Americans. Programs that had formed merely a small part of the New Deal gradually expanded through the years until they bore most of the burden of the American welfare system.

The WPA. Franklin Roosevelt was never enthusiastic about large expenditures for social welfare programs. As he said in January 1935, the government "must and shall quit this business of relief." But 10 million Americans were still out of work in the sixth year of the depression, a pressing political and moral issue for FDR and the Democrats. The Works Progress Administration (WPA), the main federal relief agency for the rest of the Depression, addressed the needs of the unemployed. Harry Hopkins, who had run the Federal Emergency Relief Administration from 1933 to 1935, took command of the new agency. Whereas the FERA had supplied grants to the states for relief programs, the WPA put relief workers on the federal payroll. Between 1935 and 1943 the WPA employed 8.5 million Americans and spent $10.5 billion. The agency constructed 651,087 miles of roads, 125,110 public buildings, 8,192 parks, 853 airports, and built or repaired 124,087 bridges.

The WPA, although an extravagant operation by the standards of the 1930s (it gave new meaning to the word "boondoggle" and inspired such nicknames as "We Putter Around"), never reached more than a third of the nation's unemployed. Its average wage of $55 a month, well below the government-defined subsistence

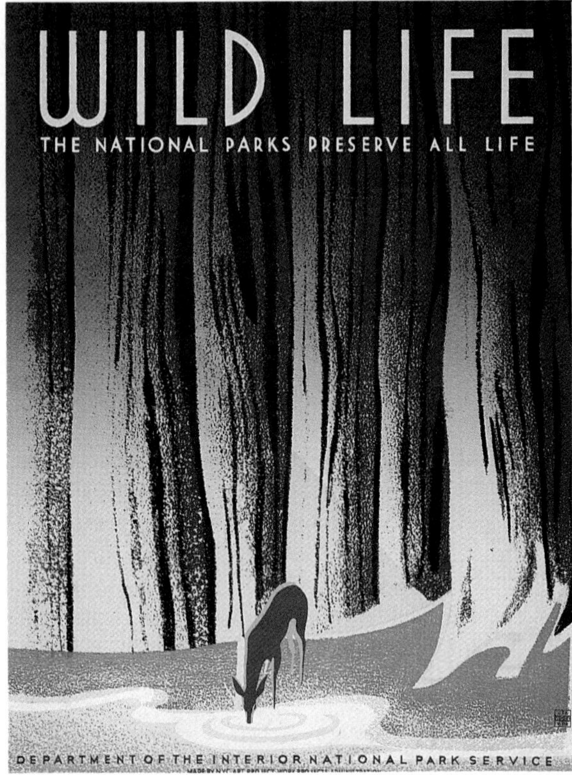

WILD LIFE
THE NATIONAL PARKS PRESERVE ALL LIFE
DEPARTMENT OF THE INTERIOR NATIONAL PARK SERVICE

Posters of the WPA
During its eight-year existence, the WPA produced two million posters from 35,000 designs. WPA posters such as this one designed for the National Park Service to support wildlife conservation show the vitality of American graphic design in the 1930s.

level of $100 a month, enabled workers to eke out only a bare living. The government cut back the program severely in 1941 and ended it in 1943, when the WPA was no longer needed in the full-employment economy resulting from World War II.

The Revenue Act of 1935 showed Roosevelt's willingness to push reforms considered too controversial earlier in his presidency. Much of the business community had already turned violently against Roosevelt in reaction to such measures as the NRA, the Social Security Act, the Wagner Act, and the Public Utilities Holding Companies Act. In 1935 he antagonized the wealthy further by proposing a tax reform bill that called for federal inheritance and gift taxes, higher personal income tax rates in the top brackets, and increased corporate taxes. Conservatives quickly labeled this legislation an attempt to "soak the rich." Roosevelt, seeking to defuse the popularity of Huey Long's Share Our Wealth plan, was just as interested in the political mileage of the tax bill as in its actual results. The final version of the bill increased revenues by only $250 million a year.

The 1936 Election

As the 1936 election approached, the broad range of New Deal programs brought many new voters into the Democratic coalition. Many had been personally helped by federal programs; others benefited because their interests had found new support in the expanded functions of the government. Roosevelt could now count on a potent urban-based coalition of workers, organized labor, northern blacks, white ethnic groups, Catholics, Jews, liberals, intellectuals, progressive Republicans, and middle-class families concerned about old-age dependence and unemployment. The Democrats also held on, though somewhat uneasily, to their traditional strength among white southerners.

The Republicans realized they could not compete directly with President Roosevelt's popularity and his potent New Deal coalition. To run against Roosevelt, they chose the progressive governor of Kansas, Alfred M. Landon, who accepted the general precepts of the New Deal. But Landon and the Republicans stridently criticized the inefficiency and expense of many New Deal programs, and even accused FDR of harboring dictatorial ambitions.

Roosevelt's victory in 1936 was one of the biggest landslides in United States history. The assassination of Huey Long in September 1935 had deflated the threat of a serious third party challenge; the candidate of the combined Long-Townsend-Coughlin camp, Congressman William Lemke of North Dakota, garnered fewer than 900,000 votes (1.9 percent) for the Union party ticket. Roosevelt received 60.8 percent of the popular vote and carried every state except Maine and Vermont; Landon received 36.5 percent. Landon fought such an uphill battle that columnist Dorothy Thompson quipped, "If Landon had given one more speech, Roosevelt would have carried Canada." The New Deal was at high tide.

Stalemate

"I see one-third of a nation ill-housed, ill-clad, ill-nourished," the president declared in his second inaugural address in January 1937. Roosevelt's frank appraisal suggested that he was considering the further expansion of the welfare state that had begun to form late in his first term. However, retrenchment, controversy, and stalemate, not further reform, marked the second term.

The Supreme Court Fight. Only two weeks after his inauguration, Roosevelt stunned Congress and the nation by asking for fundamental changes in the structure of the Supreme Court. He believed a grave constitutional crisis called for this drastic judicial reorganization.

After the Supreme Court found the NRA unconstitutional in the 1935 *Schechter* decision, it proceeded to strike down the Agricultural Adjustment Act, the Guffey-Snyder Coal Conservation Act, and New York's minimum wage law in the early months of 1936. With the Wagner Act, the TVA, and Social Security coming up on appeal, the whole future of New Deal reform legislation appeared in doubt.

In response, Roosevelt proposed adding one new justice to the Court for each one over the age of seventy. This scheme, which Roosevelt tried to pass off as concern for the workload of the elderly justices, would have increased the number of justices from nine to fifteen. Roosevelt's opponents quickly accused him of trying to "pack" the Court with justices favorable to the New Deal. The president's proposal was also regarded as an assault on the principle of separation of powers. The issue became moot when the Supreme Court, in what journalists called "a switch in time that saved nine," upheld several key pieces of New Deal legislation, including Washington state's minimum wage law and the Wagner Act.

Charitably, one could say that Roosevelt had lost a skirmish but won the war. In the spring of 1937 one conservative justice, Willis Van Devanter, resigned and other resignations soon followed. Within four years, Roosevelt reshaped the Supreme Court to suit his liberal philosophy with seven new appointments, including Hugo Black, Felix Frankfurter, Stanley F. Reed, and William O. Douglas. Yet his handling of the Court issue was a costly blunder at a time when he was vulnerable to the lameduck syndrome that often afflicts second-term administrations. No one yet suspected that FDR would break tradition to seek a third term.

Congressional conservatives had long opposed the direction of the New Deal, but the Court packing episode galvanized their opposition by demonstrating that Roosevelt was no longer politically invincible. Throughout Roosevelt's second term, a conservative coalition in Congress, composed mainly of southern Democrats and Republicans from rural areas, blocked or impeded further social legislation. Two pieces of reform legislation that did manage to win passage were the National Housing Act of 1937, which mandated the construction of low-cost public housing, and the Fair Labor Standards Act of 1938, which made permanent the minimum wage, maximum hours, and anti-child labor provisions first tried in the NRA codes.

Roosevelt's attempts to reorganize the executive branch met a different fate. In both 1937 and 1938 Congress refused to consider a Roosevelt plan that would have consolidated all independent agencies into cabinet-rank departments, extended the civil service system, and created the new position of auditor general. Conservatives effectively played on lawmakers' fears that centralized executive management would dramatically reduce congressional power. Opponents also linked Roosevelt's attempt to reorganize the executive branch with popular fears about fascism and dictatorship abroad. Roosevelt eventually settled for a weak bill in 1939, which allowed him to create the Executive Office of the President and name six administrative assistants to the White House staff. The White House also took control of the all-important budget process by moving the Bureau of the Budget to the Executive Office from its old home in the Treasury Department.

The Roosevelt Recession. The "Roosevelt recession" of 1937–1938 dealt the most devastating blow to the president's political standing in the second term. Until that point, the economy had made steady progress. From 1933 to 1937, the gross national product grew at a yearly rate of about 10 percent, and industrial output finally reached 1929 levels in 1937, as did real income. Unemployment declined from 25 percent to 14 percent, which meant that almost half the people without a job in 1933 had found one by 1937. Many Americans agreed with Senator James F. Byrnes of South Carolina that "the emergency has passed."

The steady improvement cheered Roosevelt. Reflecting his basic fiscal conservatism, he had never overcome his dislike of large deficits and huge federal expenditures for relief. Accordingly, Roosevelt slashed the federal budget in 1937. Congress cut the WPA's funding in half between January and August, which caused layoffs of about 1.5 million WPA workers. Moreover, the $2 billion withheld from workers' paychecks to initiate the new Social Security system further reduced purchasing power. Finally, the Federal Reserve, fearing inflation, tightened credit. The stock market promptly collapsed, and unemployment soared to 19 percent, which translated into more than 10 million workers without a job. Roosevelt found himself in the same situation that had confounded Hoover. Having taken credit for the recovery between 1933 and 1937, he now had to take the blame for the recession.

Roosevelt shifted gears and spent his way out of the downturn. Large WPA appropriations and a resumption of public works poured enough money into the economy to snap it out of the recession by early 1938. Roosevelt and his economic advisers were groping toward the general theories being advanced by John Maynard Keynes, a British economist. Keynes proposed that governments use deficit spending to stimulate the economy when private spending proved insufficient. But Keynes's theories would not be conclusively proved until the dramatic increase in federal defense spending for World War II finally ended the Great Depression.

As the 1938 election approached, Roosevelt decided to try to "purge" some of his most conservative opponents from the Democratic party. In the spring primaries, he campaigned against members of his own

TABLE 26.2

Major New Deal Legislation	
Agriculture	
1933	Agricultural Adjustment Act (AAA)
1935	Resettlement Administration (RA)
	Rural Electrification Administration
1937	Farm Security Administration (FSA)
1938	Second Agricultural Adjustment Act
Business and Industry	
1933	Emergency Banking Act Glass-Steagall (FDIC)
	National Industrial Recovery Administration (NIRA)
1934	Securities and Exchange Commission (SEC)
1935	Public Utilities Holding Company Act
	Banking Act of 1935
	Revenue Act (wealth tax)
Conservation and the Environment	
1933	Tennessee Valley Authority (TVA)
	Civilian Conservation Corps (CCC)
1963	Soil Conservation and Domestic Allotment Act
Labor and Social Welfare	
1933	Section 7(a) NIRA
1935	Wagner Act
	National Labor Relations Board (NLRB)
	Social Security Act
1937	National Housing Act
1938	Fair Labor Standards Act (FLSA)
Relief	
1933	Federal Emergency Relief Administration (FERA)
	Civil Works Administration (CWA)
	Public Works Administration (PWA)
1935	Works Progress Administration (WPA)
	National Youth Administration (NYA)

party who had blocked legislation in Congress and generally proven hostile or unsympathetic to New Deal initiatives. The purge failed abysmally (not one of his targets was unseated), and only served to widen the liberal-conservative rift in the Democratic party. In the general election, Republicans capitalized on the "Roosevelt recession" and the Court-packing backlash to pick up 8 seats in the Senate, 81 in the House, and gain 13 governorships.

By 1938 the New Deal had basically run out of steam. It had no climax; it simply withered away. For six years Franklin Roosevelt had inspired public confidence that hard times could be overcome. Roosevelt showed himself to be a superb politician, successfully balancing demands for more government programs with his own assessment of what was politically feasible. Throughout the New Deal, however, President Roosevelt always demonstrated clear limits on how far he was willing to go. His instincts were basically conservative, not revolutionary; he saved the capitalist economic system by reforming it. This new activism represented a major step beyond the informal (and one-sided) business-government partnership of the previous decade, but only because the emergency of the depression pushed Roosevelt in that direction. Under normal circumstances, he would have served out his second term and a new president would have been elected in 1940. Franklin Roosevelt won election to a third term (and eventually a fourth) primarily because the outbreak of World War II in Europe made Americans reluctant to risk a change in leadership during such perilous times.

The New Deal's Impact on Society

The New Deal was, as one historian put it, "somehow more than the sum of its parts." To understand its impact on society, we must look beyond the new federal programs coming out of Washington to consider broader changes in American political and social life. The New Deal set in motion dramatic growth in the federal bureaucracy. The Roosevelt administration opened unprecedented opportunities for women, African-Americans, and labor in public life. Its programs and priorities had an enormous impact on the public landscape, and it also laid the groundwork for the modern welfare system that shapes American life today.

Bureaucratic Growth

The New Deal accelerated the expansion of the federal bureaucracy that had been underway since the turn of the century. The number of civilian government employees increased 80 percent in just a decade, exceeding a million in 1940. The number of federal employees who worked in Washington grew at an even faster rate, doubling between 1929 and 1940. Power increasingly centered in the nation's capital, not in the states. In 1939 a British observer summed up this new orientation: "Just as in 1929 the whole country was 'Wall Street conscious,' now it is 'Washington conscious.'"

The new bureaucrats administered federal budgets

of unprecedented size. In 1930 the Hoover administration had spent $3.1 billion and had a surplus of almost $1 billion. With the increase in federal programs to fight the depression, federal expenditures grew steadily—$4.8 billion in 1932, $6.5 billion in 1934, and $7.6 billion in 1936. In 1939, the last year before war mobilization affected the federal budget, expenditures hit $9.4 billion. Government spending outstripped receipts throughout this period, producing yearly deficits of about $3 billion. Roosevelt had come close to balancing the budget in 1938, but he triggered a major recession. The deficit climbed toward $3 billion again the following year.

The beginnings of big government and bureaucracy have often been associated with the Roosevelt years, but many of the problems commonly ascribed to the New Deal belong to later eras. The real step toward big government spending came during World War II, not the depression. Federal outlays routinely surpassed $95 billion in the 1940s, and deficits grew to $50 billion. Although the deficit declined in the postwar era, government expenditures never returned to their pre–World War II levels.

Women and the New Deal

In the experimental climate of the New Deal, unprecedented numbers of women accepted positions in the Roosevelt administration, both as policy-makers and as middle-level bureaucrats. Frances Perkins served as Secretary of Labor throughout all four Roosevelt terms, the first woman in the cabinet. Molly Dewson, a social reformer-turned-politician, headed the Women's Division of the Democratic National Committee where she pushed an issue-oriented program that supported New Deal reforms. Roosevelt's appointments included the first woman director of the mint, head of a major WPA division, and judge of the Circuit Court of Appeals. Many of these women were close friends as well as professional colleagues, and they cooperated in an informal network to advance both feminist and reform causes.

Eleanor Roosevelt exemplified the growing prominence of women in public life. In the 1920s she worked closely with other reformers to increase women's power in political parties, labor unions, and education, an invaluable apprenticeship for the White House years. Franklin and Eleanor's marriage represented one of the most successful political partnerships of all time. He was a pragmatic politician, always aware of what could be done. She was an idealist, a gadfly, always pushing him—and the New Deal—to do more. Eleanor Roosevelt observed in her autobiography,

> He might have been happier with a wife who was completely uncritical. That I was never able to be, and he had to find it in other people. Nevertheless, I think I sometimes acted as a spur, even though the spurring was not always wanted or welcome. I was one of those who served his purposes.

Eleanor Roosevelt underestimated her influence. She served as the conscience of the New Deal.

Although Franklin Roosevelt's expansion of the personalized presidency had roots in the administrations of Theodore Roosevelt and Woodrow Wilson, the nation had never seen a First Lady like Eleanor Roosevelt. She held press conferences for woman journalists, wrote a popular syndicated news column called "My Day," and traveled extensively throughout the country. Some people wondered why the First Lady could not stay home at the White House like a good wife. But a Gallup poll in January 1939 showed that 67 percent approved of Eleanor Roosevelt's conduct, a higher approval rate than the president's at that time. In 1938 *Life* magazine hailed her as the greatest American woman alive.

Without the vocal support of prominent women such as Eleanor Roosevelt, Molly Dewson, and the rest of the female political network, women's needs during the depression might have been totally overlooked. Grave flaws still marred the treatment of women in New Deal programs. For example, a fourth of the NRA codes set a lower minimum wage for women than for men performing the same jobs. New Deal agencies such as the Civil Works Administration or Public Works Administration provided jobs almost exclusively to men, mainly because construction work was considered unsuitable for women; only 7 percent of the Civil Work Administration workers were female. The Social Security Act and Fair Labor Standards Act did not cover major areas of female employment, such as domestic service. The Civilian Conservation Corps excluded women entirely, leaving critics to ask, where is the "she-she-she"?

Women fared somewhat better under the Works Progress Administration. At the WPA's peak, 405,000 women were on its rolls. The Women's and Professional Projects Division of the WPA, headed by Ellen Sullivan Woodward, a Mississippi social worker, created hundreds of programs to put women to work. Still, at a time when women accounted for about 23 percent of the labor force, they comprised only between 14 percent and 19 percent of the WPA workers. For the most part, progress for women did not come from specific attempts to single them out as a group. It occurred as part of the broader effort to improve the economic security of all Americans.

AMERICAN LIVES

Frances Perkins, New Deal Reformer

How should the first woman to serve in the cabinet be addressed, the press wanted to know? "Miss Perkins," came her no-nonsense reply. But the press said "Mr. Secretary" to the Secretary of State—how were they to address a woman who was the Secretary of Labor? After consultation with Speaker of the House Henry Rainey and *Robert's Rules of Order*, the verdict came down: Frances Perkins was to be addressed as "Madam Secretary." As usual, the first woman in the cabinet took the attention to her sex in stride. She kept a deliberately low profile, dressing conservatively in black dresses and always wearing a distinctive tricorne hat. When asked later if being a woman had ever been a handicap, she replied matter-of-factly, "Only in climbing trees."

Frances Perkins's career shows the continuities between Progressive Era activism and New Deal reform. Born in 1880 in Massachusetts, Perkins took advantage of the new opportunities for higher education for women to graduate from Mount Holyoke College in 1902. She then worked in the settlement movement, in the woman suffrage campaign, and with reform groups trying to pass a fifty-four-hour work week bill for New York women and children. Her service on the commission set up to investigate New York factory conditions in the wake of the 1911 Triangle Shirtwaist Fire, which killed 146 female garment workers, confirmed her commitment to legislative solutions for social problems. "I'd much rather get a law passed than organize a union," she later said. That orientation shaped her priorities as Secretary of Labor.

In 1913, at the age of thirty-three, Frances Perkins married Paul C. Wilson, an economist and reformer. She kept her given name, and continued to work after her daughter Susanna was born in 1916. As she later recalled, "I suppose I had been somewhat touched by feminist ideas and that was one of the reasons I kept my maiden name. My whole generation was, I suppose, the first generation that openly and actively asserted—at least some of us did—the separateness of women and their personal independence in the family relationship." In 1918 her husband became seriously ill and spent the rest of his life in and out of mental institutions. Out of necessity, Perkins became the family breadwinner.

Perkins moved into government service in 1918 when newly-elected governor Alfred E. Smith, whom she had met during the Triangle investigation, appointed her a member of the New York State Industrial Commission. Smith appointed Perkins to the State Industrial Board in 1922, and made her its chairperson in 1926. In 1928, she became New York's industrial commissioner under Smith and then Franklin D. Roosevelt, who replaced Smith as governor that year. These positions made Perkins one of the highest-ranked women in state government in the immediate postsuffrage period.

When Franklin Roosevelt ran for president in 1932, talk began to circulate that Perkins might be offered a spot in the cabinet, a rumor which she dismissed as a "pipe dream." But to politicians like Molly Dewson, whose background in social welfare paralleled that of Perkins, Roosevelt's election offered an unprecedented opportunity for women to serve on the national level. Dewson set about convincing Roosevelt of the wisdom of choosing Perkins, and also overcoming Perkins's own doubts. Perkins was loathe to leave New York and a job she loved, she feared the effect of unwanted publicity on her husband and her teenage daughter, and the job would cause financial hardship. Molly Dewson blithely dismissed all these objections, emphasizing the importance of the appointment to the nation's women. "After all, you owe it to the women," Dewson argued repeatedly. "You probably will have this chance and you must step forward to do it." At other times, Dewson's pressure was less subtle. "Don't be such a baby. Frances, you do the right thing. I'll murder you if you don't!"

Duty to her sex finally carried the day. As Perkins later explained to suffrage leader Carrie Chapman Catt, "The overwhelming argument and thought which made me do it in the end in spite of personal difficulties was the realization that the door might not be opened to a woman again for a long, long time, and that I had a kind of duty to other women to walk in and sit down on the chair that was offered, and so establish the right of others long hence and far-distant in geography to sit in the high seats." Franklin Roosevelt announced Perkins's appointment on February 28, and she was sworn in five days later. Of Roosevelt's original cabinet, only Perkins and Secretary of the Interior Harold Ickes served for all four terms.

As secretary of labor, Frances Perkins took as her mandate the promotion of the general welfare of American workers rather than specific advocacy of the interests of organized labor. She built the Department of Labor into a smoothly functioning bureaucracy, and attracted many talented men and women to Washington. She played an important role in drafting the 1935 Social Security Act and the 1938 Fair Labor Standards Act. She did not ignore the labor movement, however, and after a period of initial doubt, labor leaders realized that Madam Secretary was an important ally in the turbulent era of union mobilization in the 1930s.

An important key to Perkins's success was her strong personal rapport with Franklin Roosevelt, who unlike many male politicians felt comfortable working with strong-minded women. (He, of course, was married to one, and he met many of the talented women he brought into the New Deal administration through Eleanor.) Perkins called Franklin Roosevelt the most complicated human being she had ever met, but she emphatically asserted that he had never let her down. In 1946 she published *The Roosevelt I Knew*, an autobiographical account of her participation in the New Deal which many believe offers the most perceptive account of the elusive Roosevelt personality.

After Roosevelt's death, Perkins served on the Civil Service Commission under President Harry Truman. When the Republicans regained power in 1952, she left government service for a fulfilling career as a lecturer, maintaining an affiliation with the Cornell School of Industrial and Labor Relations. Perkins died in 1965. Her role in laying the foundation for the modern welfare state was her greatest legacy, but just as important was her demonstration of the contributions that public-spirited women could make to politics and government.

Secretary of Labor
Frances Perkins being greeted by workers of the Carnegie Steel Company in Pittsburgh.

AMERICAN VOICES

The Great Depression in Harlem *Nora Mair*

Nora Mair and her husband Jack, both Jamaican immigrants, lived in Harlem throughout the 1930s. She worked in a linen shop on Madison Avenue, and he struggled to find employment of any kind. Like many other Americans, black and white, the WPA was their salvation.

We were poor. We didn't pretend. But our gas bill was always paid. Our rent bill was always paid. And we always knew where our next meal was coming from. We shopped on Eighth Avenue. We had everything there. We moved out of West Harlem to 100th Street and Madison Avenue in 1933 because the rent was less than half of what we were paying in West Harlem. We were paying thirty-two dollars a month for a five-room apartment. In Harlem, we would have paid sixty-five dollars, and we had a lovely landlord who painted our house every year. It was a lovely neighborhood—a potpourri of many nationalities. . . .

My husband worked in the day and went to school nights. He graduated from Mechanical Institute in 1928, and right after that the Depression came, and he couldn't get work in his profession. In the meantime he drove a cab. It was no living at all as a taxi driver. I've known him to work around the clock and only make a dollar and a half.

He would come in in the morning and eat his dinner for his breakfast and then go to bed. I've known him to be so cold, because in those days the cabs only had three doors, that he'd come in and all he would take off was his hat, his shoes, and his overcoat and then into the bed until he was warm. Those things I did resent, because he had more to offer. He met so many people on the cab line—people he knew from Jamaica. He met professors who were driving cabs and couldn't get a job. First it was color. Then it was color and Depression.

There was nothing my husband did not do to make a living. He did not want welfare, and he wanted to be independent. But he couldn't get work as a draftsman. Once, while he was driving a cab, he saw an ad in the paper for a draftsman. He went downtown to this office, and there was the receptionist. She didn't even look up. She waved him around the back, so he thought to himself, "She didn't ask what I wanted. She just motioned me to the back of the building. What kind of office could be back there?"

When he got back there, a white man with a pail and a mop said to him, "There is the pail and the mop."

"Pail and the mop for what?"

And said Mr. White Man, "Well, that's what you're here for, isn't it? A porter's job?"

Well, I won't tell you what my husband said when he came home, because he came home frothing at the mouth, and told me what he told him.

When the WPA came in, that was the first time he got to work in his profession. He worked on theaters, schools. They did everything, and it meant a lot that he was finally able to work in his field.

Source: Jeff Kisseloff, *You Must Remember This: An Oral History of Manhattan from the 1890s to World War II* (New York: Schocken, 1989), 326–327, 328.

Blacks and the New Deal

African-Americans had a similar experience. They benefited more from the general social and economic programs of the New Deal than from any concerted commitment to promote civil rights. There were striking parallels between the situation of blacks and women. (For black women, race proved more important than gender in determining treatment from the New Deal.) Mary McLeod Bethune, an educator who ran the Office of Minority Affairs of the National Youth Administration, headed the "black cabinet." This informal network worked for fairer treatment of blacks by New Deal agencies in the same way that the women's network advocated feminist causes. Both groups benefited greatly from the support of Eleanor Roosevelt. The First Lady's promotion of equal treatment for blacks in the New Deal ranks as one of her greatest legacies.

The vast majority of the American people did not regard civil rights as a legitimate object for federal intervention in the 1930s. The New Deal provided little specific aid for blacks, for whom hard times were a permanent feature, not just a product of the 1930s. Many New Deal programs reflected prevailing racist attitudes. CCC camps segregated blacks, and many NRA codes did not protect black workers. Most tellingly, Franklin Roosevelt repeatedly refused to support a federal antilynching bill, claiming it would antagonize southern members of Congress whose support he needed for passage of New Deal measures.

At the same time, blacks received enormous benefits from New Deal relief programs directed toward poor Americans regardless of race or ethnic background.

Eleanor Roosevelt and Civil Rights
One of Eleanor Roosevelt's greatest legacies was her commitment to civil rights. For example, she publicly resigned from the Daughters of the American Revolution (DAR) in 1939 when the group refused to let the black opera singer Marian Anderson perform at Constitution Hall. Eleanor Roosevelt developed an especially close working relationship with Mary McLeod Bethune of the National Youth Administration, shown here at a conference on black youth in 1939.

Public works projects channeled funds into black communities. Blacks made up about 18 percent of the WPA's recipients, although only 10 percent of the population. The Resettlement Administration, established in 1935 to help small farmers buy land and to aid in resettlement of sharecroppers and tenant farmers to more productive land, fought for the rights of black tenant farmers in the South, that is, until angry southerners in Congress cut its appropriations drastically. Still, many blacks reasoned that the tangible aid coming from Washington outweighed the discrimination that marred many federal programs.

Help from the WPA and other New Deal programs, and a belief that the White House—at least Eleanor Roosevelt—realized their plight, caused a dramatic change in blacks' voting behavior. Since the Civil War, blacks had voted Republican, a loyalty resulting from Abraham Lincoln's freeing of the slaves. As late as 1932, black voters in northern cities overwhelmingly supported Republican candidates.

Then, in fewer than four years, blacks turned Lincoln's portrait to the wall and substituted that of Franklin Roosevelt. Because of the harshness of the depression, national politics assumed a new relevance for black Americans outside the South. They gave Roosevelt 71 percent of their votes in 1936. In Harlem, where relief dollars increased dramatically in the wake of the 1935 riot (see Chapter 25), the support was an extraordinary 81.3 percent. Black voters have remained overwhelmingly Democratic ever since.

The Rise of Organized Labor

During the 1930s, labor relations became a legitimate arena for federal action and intervention, and organized labor claimed a place in national political life. Labor's dramatic growth in the 1930s represented one of the most important social and economic changes of the decade, an enormous contrast to its demoralized state at the end of the 1920s.

Several factors encouraged the growth of the labor movement: the inadequacy of welfare capitalism in the face of the Depression, New Deal legislation such as the Wagner Act, the rise of the Congress of Industrial Organizations (CIO), and the growing militancy of rank-and-file workers. By the end of the decade, the number of unionized workers had tripled to almost 9 million, covering 23 percent of the nonfarm work force. Union strength grew rapidly in manufacturing, transportation, and mining. Organized labor won not only the battle for union recognition, but also higher wages, seniority systems, and grievance procedures. Labor also greatly expanded its political involvement.

The CIO served as the cutting edge of the union movement. It did so by promoting industrial unionism—that is, it organized all the workers in an industry, both skilled and unskilled, into one union. John L. Lewis, leader of the United Mine Workers and a founder of the CIO, was the leading exponent of industrial unionism. His philosophy put him at odds with the American Federation of Labor, which favored organiz-

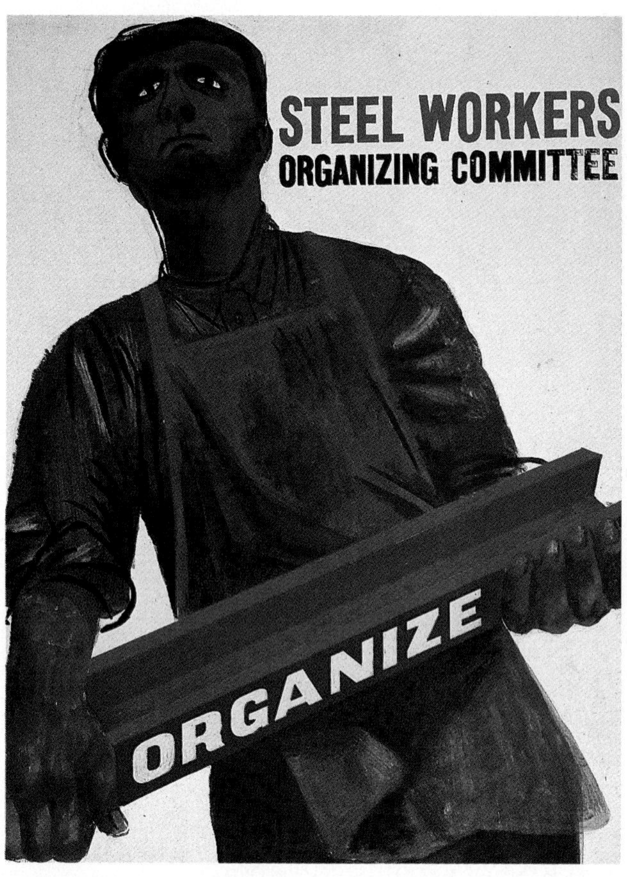

Organize
The Steelworkers' Organizing Committee was one of the most vital labor organizations contributing to the rise of the CIO. Note that artist Ben Shahn chose a male figure to represent the American labor movement in this poster designed in the late 1930s. Such iconography reinforced the notion that the typical worker was male, despite the large number of women who joined the CIO.

ing workers on a craft-by-craft basis. Lewis began to detach himself from the AFL in 1935, and the break became complete by 1938. Although the CIO generated much of the excitement on the labor front during the 1930s, the AFL gained more than a million new workers between 1935 and 1940.

The CIO scored its first major victory in the automobile industry. On December 31, 1936, General Motors workers in Flint, Michigan, staged a sit-down strike. They vowed to stay at their machines until management agreed to bargain collectively with them. The workers lived in the factories and machine shops for forty-four days before General Motors recognized the United Automobile Workers (UAW). The CIO soon won a second major victory, this time at the U.S. Steel Corporation. Despite a long history of bitter opposition to unionization (as demonstrated in the 1919 steel strike), "Big Steel" capitulated without a fight and recognized the Steel Workers Organizing Committee (SWOC) on March 2, 1937.

The victory in the steel industry was not complete, however. A group of companies known as "Little Steel" chose not to follow the lead of U.S. Steel in making peace with the CIO. Steelworkers struck the Republic Steel Corporation plant in South Chicago. On Memorial Day afternoon, May 31, 1937, strikers and their families gathered for a holiday picnic and rally outside the plant gates. Tension mounted, rocks were thrown, and the police fired on the crowd, killing ten protesters. All were shot in the back. A newsreel photographer recorded the scene, but Paramount Pictures considered the film of the "Memorial Day Massacre" too inflammatory for distribution. The road to recognition for labor, even with New Deal protections, was often still violent and protracted. Workers in Little Steel did not win union recognition until 1941.

The Sit-Down Strike
These members of the United Auto Workers helped to pioneer the sit-down tactic at a General Motors plant in Flint, Michigan in 1937. In their 44-day siege, workers made use of the car seats awaiting final assembly in GM cars while they passed the time. To avoid any taint of immorality, union leaders asked all women workers in the Flint plant to voluntarily leave once the sit-down strike began, and the women complied.

AMERICAN VOICES

Labor Militancy *Genora Johnson Dollinger*

During the Flint, Michigan, sit-down strike, Genora Johnson Dollinger, the wife of a General Motors striker and the mother of two small children, organized the Women's Emergency Brigade. Women like Dollinger played a major role in the Flint victory.

I was twenty-three years old on December 30, 1936, when the strike started. It lasted forty-four days, a very dramatic forty-four days, until February 11, 1937.

It was New Year's Eve when I realized women had to organize and join in the fight. I was on the picket lines when the men's wives came down. They didn't know why their husbands were sitting inside the plant. Living in a company town, you see, they got only company propaganda through the press and radio. So when they came down on New Year's Eve, many were threatening to divorce their striking husbands if they didn't quit and get back to work to bring home a paycheck.

I knew then that union women must organize on their own in order to talk with these wives. . . .

This was an independent move. It was not under the direction of the union or its administrators—I just talked it over with a few women—the active ones—and told them this is what we had to do.

Women might, after all, be called upon to give their lives. That was exactly the appeal I made while we were forming the brigade—I told the women, "Don't sign up for this unless you are prepared. If you are prone to hysteria or anything like that you'd only be in our way." I told them they'd be linking arms and withstanding the onslaughts of the police and if one of our sisters went down shot in cold blood there'd be no time for hysteria.

Around 500 women answered that call. We bought red berets and made arm bands with the white letters "EB" for Emergency Brigade. It was a kind of military uniform, yes, but it was mainly identification. We wore them all the time so we'd know who to call on to give help in an emergency. I had five lieutenants—three were factory women. I chose them because they could be called out of bed at any hour, if necessary, or sleep on a cot at the union hall. Mothers with children couldn't answer calls like that—although they did sign up for the brigade. Even a few grandmothers became brigadiers and, I remember, one young girl only sixteen.

We had no communication system to speak of. Very few people had telephones so we had to call one woman who was responsible for getting the messages through to many others.

We organized a first aid station and child care center—the women who had small children to tend and couldn't join the EB took care of these jobs.

Listen, I met some of the finest women I have ever come across in my life. When the occasion demands it of a woman and once she understands that she's standing in defense of her family—well, God, *don't fool around with that woman then. . . .*

It's a measure of the strength of those women of the Red Berets that they could perform so courageously in an atmosphere that was often hostile to them. We organized on our own without the benefit of professional leadership, and yet, we played a role, second to none, in the birth of a union and in changing working families' lives forever.

Source: Genora Johnson Dollinger, quoted in Jeane Westin, *Making Do* (Chicago: Follett Publishing, 1976), 223, 225–226, 229.

The 1930s were one of the most active periods of labor solidarity in American history. The sit-down tactic spread rapidly. In March 1937, 167,210 workers staged 170 sit-down strikes. Labor unions called nearly five thousand strikes that year and won favorable terms in 80 percent of them. Yet large numbers of middle-class Americans felt alienated by sit-down strikes, which they considered attacks on private property. The Supreme Court agreed, upholding a law that banned the practice in 1939.

The CIO attracted new groups to the union movement. Blacks, for example, found the CIO's commitment to racial justice a strong contrast to the AFL's long-established patterns of exclusion and segregation. About eight hundred thousand women workers also found a limited welcome in the CIO. Women participated in major CIO strikes and served as union organizers, especially in textile organizing drives in the South. Few blacks and women held union leadership positions, however.

Women found other ways beside joining a union to participate in the labor movement. During the Flint sit-down strike against General Motors in 1937, the Women's Emergency Brigade, a group of wives, sisters, and girlfriends of striking workers, supplied food and first aid. Wearing distinctive red berets and armbands, they picketed, demonstrated, and occasionally resorted to such tactics as breaking windows to dissipate the tear gas used against the strikers. After the strike, however, UAW leaders politely but firmly told the women to go back home where they belonged.

Labor's new vitality spilled over into political action. The AFL had always stood aloof from partisan politics, but the CIO quickly allied itself with the Democratic party. Through Labor's Nonpartisan League, the CIO gave $770,000 to Democratic campaigns in 1936. Labor also provided one of the few solid lobbies behind President Roosevelt's plan to reorganize the Supreme Court. In the 1940s the CIO's Political Action Committee became a major contributor to the Democratic war chest.

Despite the breakthroughs of the New Deal, the labor movement never developed into as dominant a force in American life as had seemed possible in the heyday of the late 1930s. Roosevelt never made the growth of the labor movement a high priority, and many workers remained indifferent or even hostile to calls for unionization. Although the Wagner Act guaranteed unions a permanent place in American industrial relations, it did not revolutionize actual working conditions. The important gain of collective bargaining did not redistribute power in American industry; it merely granted labor a measure of legitimacy. Management even found that unions could be a useful buffer against rank-and-file militancy. New Deal social welfare programs also diffused some of the pre-1937 radical spirit by channeling significant economic benefits to workers, whether they belonged to unions or not. In the 1940s, the labor movement entered a period of consolidation and then stagnation that continued for several decades.

Other New Deal Constituencies

The growth of the federal government in the 1930s increased the potential impact that its decisions (and its spending) had on various constituencies. The New Deal considered a broader cast of the population worthy of inclusion in the political process, especially if they were organized into pressure groups. Politicians realized the importance of satisfying the concerns of certain blocs of voters in order to cement their allegiance to the Democratic party. As a result, women, blacks, and labor received more attention from the federal government and had a higher visibility in public life than ever before.

But what about groups who were not politically mobilized or recognized as key components of the New Deal coalition? The New Deal's impact on their communities often came down to whether they had sympathetic government administrators in Washington to promote their interests.

Native Americans made up one of the nation's most disadvantaged and powerless minorities. Their annual average income in 1934 totaled only $48, and their unemployment rate was three times the national average. Concerned New Deal administrators, such as Secretary of the Interior Harold Ickes and Commissioner John Collier of the Bureau of Indian Affairs, tried to correct

New Deal Murals
Social realist painter William Gropper portrayed the contributions of labor to modern industry in the heroic, dynamic style that was typical of public art during the depression. His mural, *Construction of a Dam*, was commissioned in 1937 for the Department of the Interior Building in Washington, D.C. (National Museum of American Art)

some of these inequalities. The Indian Reorganization Act of 1934 reversed the Dawes Severalty Act of 1887 by promoting more extensive self-government through tribal councils and constitutions. The government also reversed the policy of forced integration into American society by pledging to help preserve Indian languages, arts, traditions, and other tribal heritages. The economic problems of native Americans were so severe, however, that these changes in federal policy produced only marginal results.

Hispanic Americans, scattered throughout the West in rural areas and urban barrios, had no such advocates within the New Deal bureaucracy. Too diverse to speak as an organized constituency, Hispanics found little help from the New Deal. Major legislation such as the Social Security Act and the Fair Labor Standards Act excluded agricultural workers, a major source of Hispanic employment. The Wagner Act did not cover farm workers' unions. And Mexican-Americans faced discrimination and prejudice, indeed the threat of deportation, when applying for relief (see Chapter 25). In part because Mexican-Americans were not mobilized politically in the 1930s, they did not know how to attract the attention—and federal dollars—of an increasingly activist state. Whatever benefits came their way were the result of generalized attacks on poverty and unemployment, rather than specific reforms addressed to the needs of Hispanic Americans.

The New Deal and the Land

Concern with the land was one of the dominant motifs of the New Deal, and the shaping of the public landscape was among its most visible and enduring legacies. Franklin Roosevelt brought to the presidency a love of forestry and a conservation ethic nurtured on his Hudson River estate. New Deal administrators like Interior Secretary Harold Ickes were avid conservationists. The expansion of federal responsibilities in the 1930s, especially the need to put the unemployed to work on public projects, created a climate conducive to action. So too did public concern heightened by the dramatic images of drought and devastation of the Dust Bowl. The resulting national resources policy stressed scientific management of the land, conservation over commercialism, and the often aggressive use of public authority to safeguard land that was either privately or publicly held.

The most extensive New Deal environmental undertaking was the Tennessee Valley Authority. The need for dams to control flooding and erosion in the Tennessee River Basin, a seven-state area with some of the country's heaviest rainfall, had been recognized as far back as World War I. During the 1920s progressives led by Senator George Norris of Nebraska pushed for the construction of a dam at Muscle Shoals on the Tennessee River, but utility companies successfully blocked the project. In the first hundred days of the Roosevelt administration in 1933, the Tennessee Valley Authority finally won approval to develop the region's resources under public control. The TVA was the ultimate watershed demonstration area, with its integrated plans for flood control, reforestation, and agricultural and industrial development, including a chemical fertilizer plant. Its hydroelectric grid provided cheap electrical power for the valley residents. The TVA was admired worldwide and became one of the most popular destinations for foreign visitors to the United States.

The Dust Bowl helped to focus attention on land use management and ecological balance. Agents from the Soil Conservation Service in the Department of Agriculture taught farmers the proper technique for tilling hillsides. (Quipped journalist Alistair Cooke, the New Deal's conception of the common man was someone who could "take up contour plowing late in life.") Government agronomists also worked to remove marginal land from cultivation and prevent soil erosion through better agricultural practices. One of their most widely publicized programs was the Shelterbelts, the planting of a line of some 220 million trees to run roughly along the ninety-ninth meridian from Abilene, Texas, north to the Canadian border. Planted as a wind break, these trees also prevented soil erosion. Shelterbelts were a personal favorite of Franklin Roosevelt's.

Sometimes political reality dictated specific legislation affecting the environment, such as the Soil Conservation and Domestic Allotment Act of 1936. This legislation filled the void created when the Supreme Court ruled the Agricultural Adjustment Act unconstitutional. Under the act, farmers received payments for cutting commercial production of crops like wheat and cotton, which depleted the soil, and planting instead soil-building grasses and legumes such as clover and soybeans. Not coincidentally, wheat and cotton were major surplus commodities, and the law provided a way to cut production as well as encourage soil conservation. The Agricultural Adjustment Act of 1938 continued the policy of price supports and payments to farmers to limit production and established soil conservation as a permanent program.

Another priority of the Roosevelt administration was helping rural Americans stay on the land. The Rural Electrification Administration established in 1935, which brought power to the nation's farms (see Chapter 25), was part of this attempt to improve the quality of rural life. The New Deal also encouraged urban dwellers to move back to rural areas. This "back to the land" motif animated many New Deal projects, especially those planned by the Resettlement Administration under the direction of Rexford Tugwell. Some of

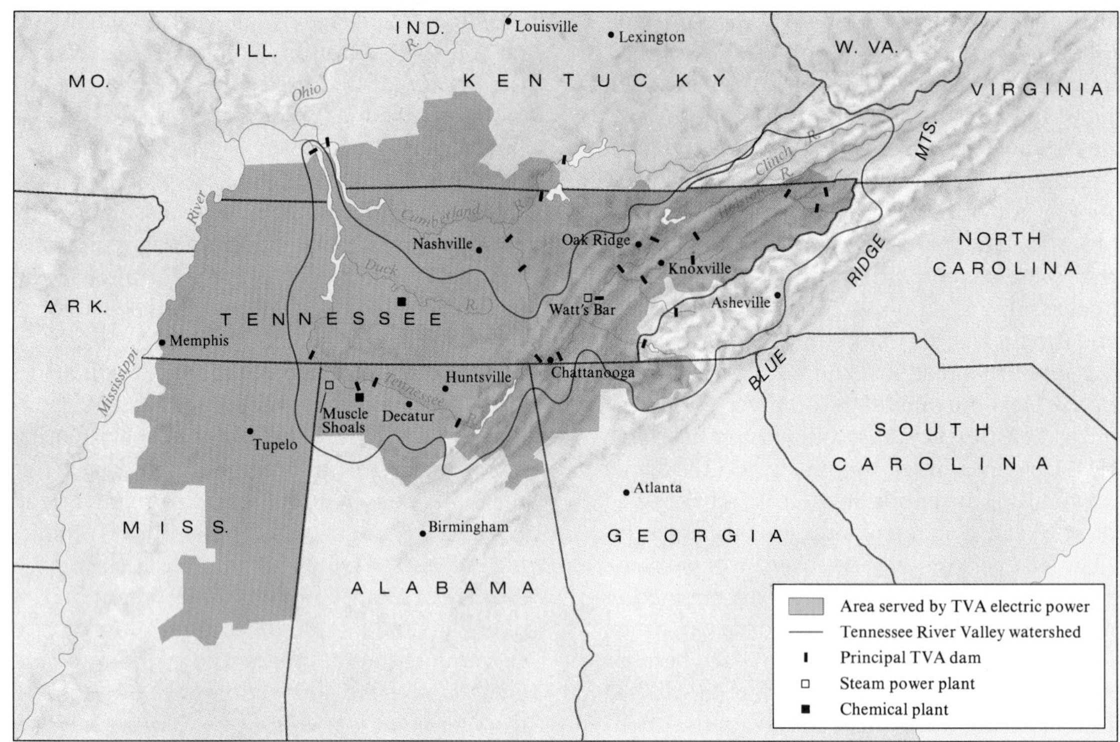

MAP 26.1

The Tennessee Valley Authority

The Tennessee Valley Authority was one of the New Deal's most far-reaching environmental projects. Between 1933 and 1952, the TVA built twenty dams and improved five others. The cheap hydroelectric power generated by the dams brought electricity to more local residents than ever before.

the best known examples were planned cooperative communities in rural areas, such as Arthurdale in West Virginia, or the "Greenbelt" residential towns outside Washington, D.C., Cincinnati, and Milwaukee.

Although the TVA, Shelterbelts, and Greenbelt towns were primarily environmental programs, they also put large numbers of the unemployed to work. The Civilian Conservation Corps, the so-called Tree Army, planted some 2 billion trees by 1941, a dozen for every American citizen at the time. Not only was this sound conservation, but it gave the 2.5 million CCC workers a job to do. Similarly, many WPA projects fulfilled conservation and recreational goals.

New Deal construction projects affecting the natural environment are all around us, artifacts from the depression era. CCC and WPA workers built the Blue Ridge highway, the consummate parkway of the 1930s, connecting the Shenandoah National Park in Virginia with the Great Smoky Mountain National Park in North Carolina. Government workers built the San Francisco Zoo, Berkeley's Tilden Park, and the canals of San Antonio; the CCC helped to complete the East Coast's Appalachian Trail and the West Coast's Pacific Crest Trail through the Sierras. In state parks throughout the country, cabins, shelters, picnic areas, lodges, and observation towers were built in a style that has been called "government rustic." All these projects shared the New Deal ethos of leisure and recreation co-existing with nature.

What was the long-term impact of the New Deal on land use and conservation? On the Great Plains, probably not very much. Without proper care, many of the shelterbelts deteriorated, and dust storms once again struck in the 1950s. When the Civilian Conservation Corps and the Works Progress Administration lost funding in the early 1940s, maintenance work lapsed. But many of these facilities still exist today, relics of the conservation ethic and the need to put citizens to work.

Although the New Deal was ahead of its time in its attention to conservation, its legacy to later environmental movements is more mixed. Many of the tactics of the New Deal projects—damming rivers, blasting fire roads, altering the natural landscape with buildings and shelters—would now be seen as too intrusive. The TVA especially came under attack in the 1970s for its overzealous application of technology, its longstanding

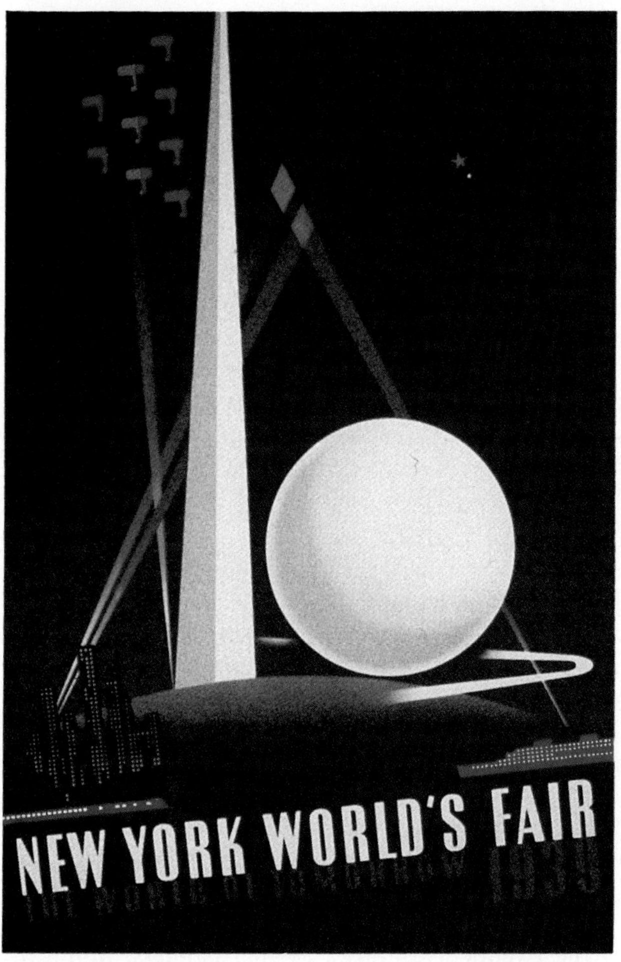

The New York World's Fair
The theme of the 1939 World's Fair was "Building the World of Tomorrow." After grimly struggling for a decade to overcome hard times, many Americans were more than ready to embrace a rosy future of social harmony, interdependence, and material progress. Joseph Binder's prize-winning poster featured the Trylon and Perisphere, the fair's instantly recognizable symbols. (The Queens Museum of Art)

practice of strip mining, and the pollution caused by its power plants and chemical factories. Because of environmental concerns, a project as massive as the TVA probably could never be built today, an ironic conclusion to what was hailed at the time as an enlightened use of government power for the public good.

The Legacies of the New Deal

The New Deal set in motion far-reaching changes, notably the growth of a modern state of significant size. For the first time, people experienced the federal government as a concrete part of everyday life. During the decade, more than a third of the population received direct government assistance from such new federal programs as Social Security, farm loans, relief, and mortgage guarantees. Furthermore, the government made a concrete commitment to intervene in the economy when private instruments of power proved insufficient to guarantee economic stability. New legislation regulated the stock market, reformed the Federal Reserve system by placing more power in the hands of Washington policy-makers, and brought many practices of modern corporate life under federal regulation. The New Deal thus continued the pattern begun during the progressive era of using federal regulation to bring order and regularity to modern economic life.

The New Deal also laid the foundations of America's welfare state, that is, the federal government's acceptance of primary responsibility for the individual and collective welfare of the people. Although the New Deal offered more benefits to American citizens than they had ever received before, its safety net had many holes, especially in comparison to the far more extensive welfare states found in Western Europe. The greatest defect of the emerging welfare system was its failure to reach a significant minority of American workers. For example, the Social Security program excluded domestic servants and farm workers entirely for many years. And since state governments administered the programs, benefits varied widely from state to state, with the South consistently providing the lowest amounts. Not until the Great Society programs of President Lyndon Johnson in the 1960s did social welfare programs reach significant numbers of America's poor.

To its credit, the New Deal recognized that poverty was a structural economic problem, not a matter of personal failure. New Deal reformers assumed that once the Depression was over, full employment and an active economy would take care of welfare needs, and poverty would simply wither away. It did not. When later administrations confronted the persistence of inequality and unemployment, they grafted welfare programs onto the modest jerrybuilt system left over from the New Deal. Thus the American welfare system would always be marked by its birth during the crisis atmosphere of the Great Depression.

New Deal Coalition. Even if the early welfare system set some ill-advised precedents, it was brilliant politics. The Democratic party courted the allegiance of citizens who benefited from New Deal programs. Organized labor aligned itself with the administration that had promoted it as a legitimate force in modern industrial life. Blacks voted Democratic in direct relation to the economic benefits that poured into their communities. The Women's Division mobilized eighty thousand women at the grassroots level who supported what the New Deal had done for their communities. The unemployed also looked kindly on the Roosevelt administration. According to one of the earliest Gallup polls, 84 percent of those on relief voted the Democratic ticket in 1936.

The Democratic party did not attract only the down and out. Franklin Roosevelt's magnetic personality and the dispersal of New Deal benefits to families throughout the social structure brought middle-class voters, many of them first- or second-generation immigrants, into the Democratic fold. The New Deal thus completed the transformation begun in the 1920s toward a Democratic party reflecting the interests of ethnic groups, city dwellers, organized labor, blacks, and a broad cross section of the middle class. These voters provided the backbone of the Democratic coalition for decades to come.

Yet even in the 1930s, the New Deal coalition contained lurking, potentially fatal, contradictions, mainly over the issue of race. Because Franklin Roosevelt depended on the support of southern white Democrats for passage of New Deal legislation, he was unwilling to challenge the economic and political marginalization of blacks in the South. At the same time, New Deal programs were themselves changing the face of southern agriculture by undermining the sharecropping tenant system and encouraging the migration of southern blacks to northern and western cities. Outside the South, blacks could vote, thus guaranteeing that civil rights would enter the national agenda. The resulting fissures would eventually weaken the coalition that had seemed so invincible at the height of Franklin Roosevelt's power.

Culture and Commitment

Many American artists redefined their relationship to society in response to the Depression. Never had there been a decade, noted critic Malcolm Cowley in 1939, "when literary events followed so closely on the flying coat-tails of social events." Political engagement replaced the personal alienation of the 1920s, as world events like the rise of fascism demanded intellectuals' energy. Although not all art in the decade was federally funded, the New Deal helped to foster creative expression in the 1930s with a wide-ranging, and controversial, experiment in federal patronage of the arts.

New Deal Culture

The depression had dried up traditional sources of private patronage and creative artists, like most Americans, had nowhere to turn except Washington. The WPA project known as "Federal One" put unemployed artists, actors, and writers to work. Federal One's spirit and purpose extended far beyond mere relief. New Deal administrators wanted to redefine the relationship between artists and the community, so that art no longer would be consumed only by the elite. "Art for the millions" became a popular New Deal slogan.

The Federal Art Project (FAP) gave work to many of the twentieth century's leading painters, muralists, and sculptors at a point in their careers when the lack of

Relief Blues

Between 1934 and 1939, an Italian immigrant O. Louis Guglielmi, found work on the Federal Art Project of the WPA, to which he submitted this painting in 1938. Entitled *Relief Blues,* it represents the social concern and urban realism prominent in American painting during the 1930s. The starkness of the room and its occupants is intensified by the bright red slippers, the pink rose on the floor, and the red lipstick and nail polish of the woman on the left. (National Museum of American Art)

AMERICAN VOICES

Artists on Relief *Anzia Yezierska*

Anzia Yezierska's powerful descriptions of immigrant life, particularly *Hungry Hearts* (1920) and *Bread Givers* (1925), brought her fame and a Hollywood movie contract in the 1920s, but she found herself penniless once the depression hit. The Federal Writers' Project was her salvation.

FOUR BILLION DOLLARS FOR JOBS . . . One after another picked up the newspaper, disbelieving. Perhaps because they had fought so hard for it they were stunned. It was too good to be true. And when they were finally convinced that their dream was about to be realized, the discussion became a joyous shouting celebration.

A new world was being born. A world where artists were no longer outcasts, hangers-on of the rich, but backed by the government, encouraged to produce their best work.

The President said so.

People who no longer hoped or believed in anything but the end of the world began to hope and believe again.

In the weeks that followed, radios boomed with it. Everywhere—at grocers, cigar stores, lunch counters, in the streets—people were discussing the President's plan to end unemployment. Every day we read announcements in the newspapers of the prominent men and women appointed by the President to direct the various departments of W.P.A.

One morning as I was in the kitchen of my rooming house fixing breakfast, the radio broadcast a special news item about W.P.A.: a headquarters had just been set up for the new Writers' Project. I hurried to the address, eager to work. Ever since I had marched with the unemployed I was full of ideas for stories. All I needed to begin writing again was the security of a W.P.A. wage to get my typewriter out of the pawnshop. . . .

Each morning I walked to the Project as lighthearted as if I were going to a party. The huge, barracks-like Writers' Hall roared with laughter and greetings of hundreds of voices. As we signed in, we stopped to smoke, make dates for lunch and exchange gossip. Our grapevine buzzed with budding love affairs, tales of salary raises, whispers of favoritism, the political maneuvers of the big shots, and the way Barnes told off Somervell over the phone. There was a hectic camaraderie among us, although we were as ill-assorted as a crowd on a subway express—spinster poetesses, pulp specialists, youngsters with school-magazine experience, veteran newspaper men, art-for-art's-sake literati, and the clerks and typists who worked with us—people of all ages, all nationalities, all degrees of education, tossed together in a strange fellowship of necessity. . . .

"Thank God for the depression!" a tall, gaunt man spouted. "The depression fathered W.P.A.!" His tattered coat hung loose on his shrunken body. A safety pin fastened the frayed collar of his shirt. Unaware of his rags, his ghastly appearance, he fixed his eyes on me. "Roosevelt will go down to posterity as the savior of art in America."

"The savior of art!" I laughed. "At the bargain price of $23.86 per artist."

Source: Anzia Yezierska, *Red Ribbon on a White Horse* (New York: Charles Scribner's Sons, 1950; reprint, Persea Books, 1981), 150, 156, 165.

private patronage might have prevented them from continuing their artistry. Jackson Pollack, Alice Neel, Willem de Kooning, and Louise Nevelson all received support. Under the direction of Holger Cahill, an expert on American folk art, the FAP commissioned murals for public buildings and post offices throughout the country. Huge WPA murals covered the walls and ceilings of terminals at the newly constructed La Guardia airport in New York. In the 1940s and 1950s as artistic tastes changed, most of La Guardia's murals were painted over, but those at its Marine Air Terminal have since been restored to their original splendor.

Under the direction of Nicholas Sokoloff, the conductor of the Cleveland Symphony Orchestra, the Federal Music Project employed fifteen thousand musicians. Government-sponsored orchestras toured the country, presenting free concerts of classical and popular music. Like many other New Deal programs, the Music Project emphasized American themes. Composer Aaron Copland wrote his *Billy the Kid* and *Rodeo* ballets for the WPA, compositions that specifically incorporated western folk melodies. Musicologist Charles Seeger, and his wife, composer Ruth Crawford Seeger, catalogued the American folk tradition.

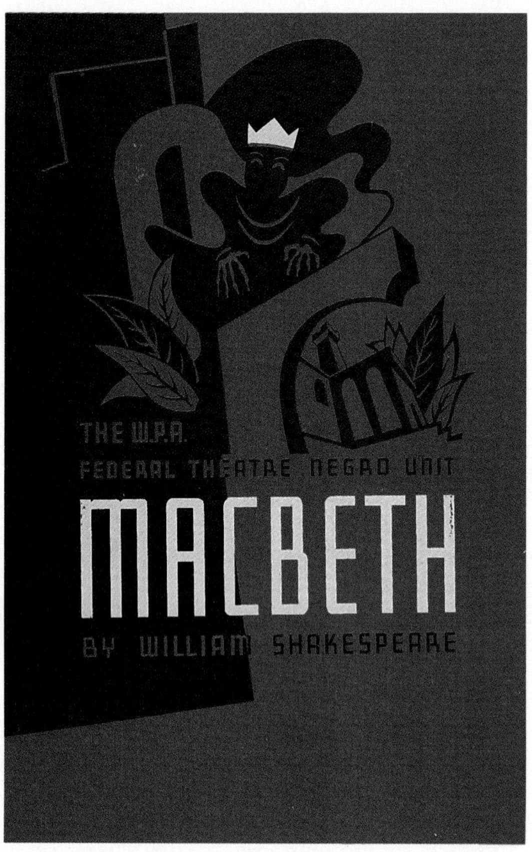

The Federal Theatre Project
The New Deal's Theatre Project promised "free, adult, uncensored theatre." One of the most popular plays was the version of Shakespeare's *Macbeth* produced by John Houseman and directed by Orson Welles. This 1936 production drew on the talents of Harlem's Federal Theatre Project, one of sixteen "Negro Units" across the country. (Poster by Anthony Velonis)

Former journalist Henry Alsberg headed the Federal Writers' Project (FWP), which employed about five thousand writers at its height. Young FWP writers who later achieved fame included Saul Bellow, Ralph Ellison, Tillie Olsen, and John Cheever. The black folklorist and novelist Zora Neale Hurston finished three novels while on the Florida FWP, among them *Their Eyes Were Watching God* (1937). Richard Wright won the 1938 *Story* magazine prize for the best tale by a WPA writer and used his spare time on the project to complete *Native Son* (1940).

The Federal Writers' Project produced more than a thousand publications. It collected oral histories of Americans in many walks of life, including a set of two thousand narratives of former slaves. Its most ambitious project was a set of state guidebooks. Fifty-one state and territorial guides, city guides, and twenty regional guides, including *U.S. One: Maine to Florida*, were published, mostly by commercial presses. Combining tourism, folklore, and history, they reflected the resurgence of interest in everything American. The guides became widely popular, but the choice of subjects occasionally annoyed politicians and state boosters. For example, the 675-page Massachusetts guide gave only fourteen lines to the Boston Tea Party and five to the Boston Massacre, while allotting thirty-one to the Sacco-Vanzetti case.

Of all the federal creative programs, the Federal Theatre Project (FTP) was the most ambitious. American drama thrived in the 1930s, the only time that the United States has had a federally supported national theater. Under the gifted direction of Hallie Flanagan, former head of Vassar College's Experimental Theater, the Theatre Project reached an audience of 25 to 30 million in the four years of its existence. Talented directors, playwrights, and actors, including Orson Welles, John Huston, and Arthur Miller, offered their services.

The Theatre Project's most successful productions included T. S. Eliot's *Murder in the Cathedral*, Mark Blitzstein's *The Cradle Will Rock*, William Shakespeare's *Macbeth* with an all-black cast in a Haitian voodoo setting, and the *Swing Mikado*, a jazz rendition of the Gilbert and Sullivan operetta. Sinclair Lewis's anti-fascist *It Can't Happen Here* opened simultaneously in eighteen cities across the country, including productions in Spanish and Yiddish. Also popular were mini-plays called "living newspapers," among them *Triple A Plowed Under*, about farm problems, and *Power*, concerning public ownership of utilities.

The theater was one of the most politically committed fields of American creative life in the 1930s. However, Congress proved unwilling to appropriate federal funds for its often controversial productions, and the Federal Theatre Project was terminated in 1939. Federal One limped on under federal-state sponsorship until 1943, when wartime priorities dealt it a final blow.

The Documentary Impulse

The WPA arts projects were influenced by a broad artistic trend called the *documentary impulse*. Combining social relevance with distinctively American themes, this approach characterized artistic expression in the 1930s. The documentary, probably the decade's most distinctive genre, influenced practically every aspect of American culture—literature, photography, art, music, film, dance, theater, and radio.

The documentary impulse was the communication of real life, the presentation of actual facts and events in a way that aroused the interest and emotions of its audience. Emphasizing observation and narration without relying on overembellished prose for impact, this technique exalted the ordinary, finding beauty and emotion in subjects not usually considered the province of art. It tried to make you, the audience, experience the subject as though you were actually on the scene.

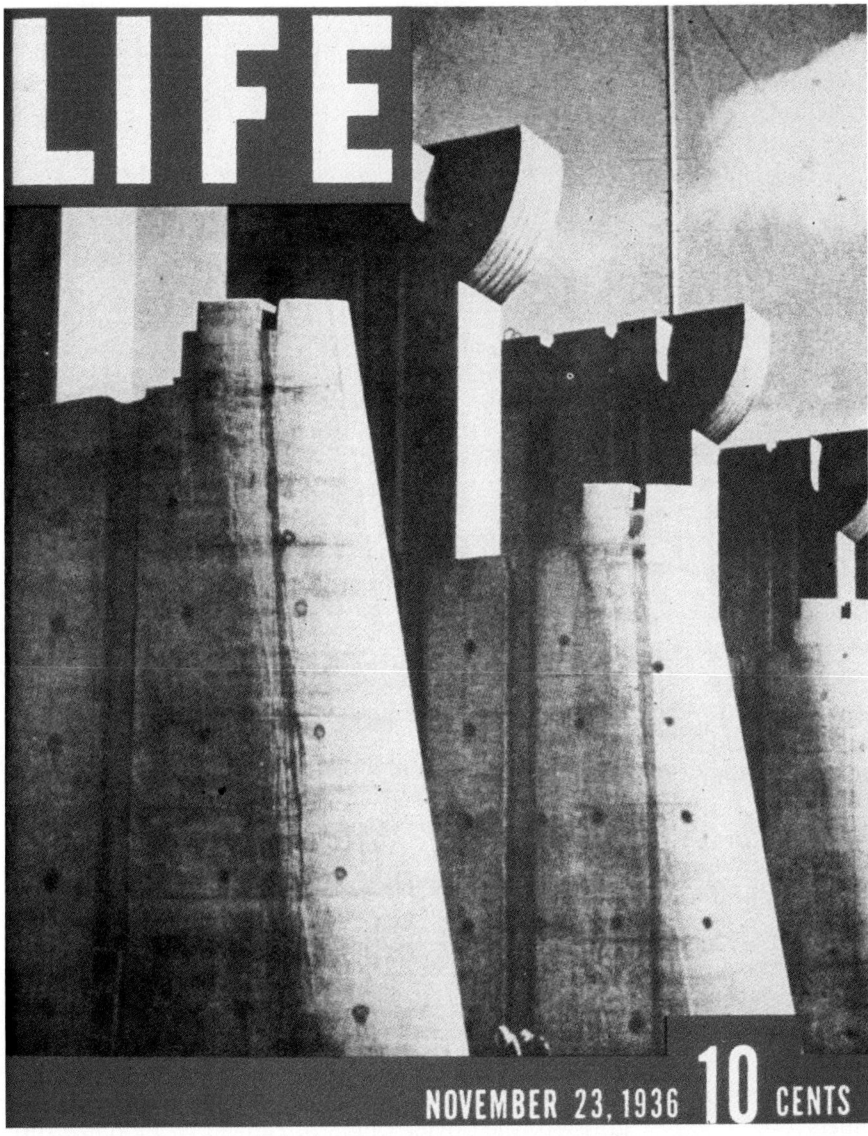

Life
Margaret Bourke-White's photograph of the Fort Peck Dam, with the two human figures in the foreground establishing its huge scale, graced the inaugural cover of *Life* magazine in 1936. Fort Peck was part of a series of dams the WPA was constructing in the Columbia River Basin for flood control. *Life*'s first issue also contained a photo essay about the town nearest to the Fort Peck Dam, which was named, appropriately, New Deal, Montana.

The documentary impulse is evident in John Steinbeck's fiction and in John Dos Passos's *U.S.A.* trilogy, which used actual newspaper clippings, dispatches, and headlines throughout its fictional story. The *March of Time* newsreels, which movie audiences saw before the feature film, presented images of the world for the pretelevision age. The standard opening of radio news broadcasts, "We now take you to . . . ," did the same thing. Filmmaker Pare Lorentz commissioned the composer Virgil Thompson to create music that set the mood for documentary movies such as *The Plow that Broke the Plains* (1936) and *The River* (1936). The new photojournalism magazines, including *Life* and *Look*, founded in 1936 and 1937, respectively, reflected this documentary approach. So did many creative works of the New Deal, from the living newspapers of the Federal Theatre Project to the American Guide series and oral history interviews prepared by the Federal Writers' Project. The New Deal actually institutionalized the documentary impulse. It sent investigators, such as journalist Lorena Hickok and writer Martha Gellhorn, into the field to report on conditions of people on relief.

The camera was the prime instrument of the documentary impulse. The use of cameras to document social conditions dated back to the probing photography of Jacob Riis and Lewis Hine at the turn of the century. When the nation entered another period of intense social and economic questioning in the 1930s, photographers revived and updated this technique. With their haunting images of sharecroppers, Dust Bowl migrants, and the urban homeless, photographers Dorothea Lange, Walker Evans, and Margaret Bourke-White permanently shaped the image of the Great Depression.

The federal government played a leading part in compiling the photographic record of the 1930s. In 1935 Roy Stryker, a Columbia economics instructor who had been a teaching assistant under brains trust member Rexford Tugwell, took charge of the Historical Section of the Resettlement Administration. He had a mandate to document and photograph the American scene for the government. Stryker gathered a talented group of photographers for this massive task, including Evans, Lange, Ben Shahn, Arthur Rothstein, and Marion Post Wolcott. The government hired these photographers solely for their professional skills, not to provide relief like Federal One's creative projects. The photographs collected by the Historical Section, which in 1937 became part of the newly created Farm Security Administration (FSA), rank as the best visual representation of life in the United States during the depression decade.

Intellectuals and the Popular Front

By the mid-1930s, the rise of fascism in Europe and the Far East called for new forms of political engagement by writers and other intellectuals. Many literary figures participated in a broad leftist movement dedicated to stopping the spread of fascism throughout the world. The Communist party played a leading role in rallying intellectuals against the fascist threat.

The period from 1935 to 1939 marked the Communist party's greatest appeal in American society. Marxism, having predicted the collapse of capitalism, provided an alternative vision of social and economic organization. Communists were scattered throughout all walks of life in the 1930s—working-class activists, intellectuals, housewives, union organizers, farmers, blacks, and even a few New Deal administrators. No longer a small sectarian group, party membership peaked at about a hundred thousand members.

The Communist party exerted an especially powerful influence on American writers in the 1930s. Although some intellectuals joined the Communist party, many others considered themselves "fellow travelers." They sympathized with the party's objectives, wrote for the *Daily Worker* and other party newspapers, and associated with organizations sponsored by the party. Author Mary McCarthy recalled the fascination that the party held for her and other intellectuals: "For me, the Communist Party was *the* party, and even though I did not join it, I prided myself on knowing that it was the pinnacle."

The Rise of Fascism in Europe. The courting of intellectuals was part of an important shift in Communist party tactics in response to the rise of fascism. Benito Mussolini had established the first fascist regime in Italy in 1922, but fascism did not become a worldwide threat until Adolf Hitler and the National Socialist party seized power in Germany in 1933 and began a program

The Abraham Lincoln Brigade
In the Spanish Civil War, most Americans sympathized with the Loyalists, who were fighting against Franco. This 1937 song by Lewis Allen shows how American volunteers associated their fight against fascism in Spain with the figure of Abraham Lincoln, symbol of American democracy and human rights.

of massive rearmament and expansion of the German state (see Chapter 27).

Fearful of a world war set in motion by fascist aggression, the Soviet Union attempted to mobilize support in democratic countries. In Europe and the United States, communist parties called for a "popular front" and welcomed cooperation with any group concerned about the threat of fascism to such areas as civil rights, organized labor, and world peace. As part of the popular front, the American Communist party adopted the slogan "Communism is 20th Century Americanism" and worked for President Roosevelt's reelection in 1936; Eleanor Roosevelt, once depicted as a slave of the ruling class, was lauded for her humanitarianism. This alliance with American liberal groups at mid-decade represented the height of the party's impact in the United States.

The Spanish Civil War. The popular-front strategy became even more urgent with the outbreak of the Spanish Civil War in 1936. Army forces led by Generalissimo Francisco Franco led a rebellion against the elected coalition government. Franco received strong support from the fascist regimes in Germany and Italy.

Only the Soviet Union and Mexico backed the Spanish government forces, called the Loyalists. The governments of the United States, Great Britain, and France sympathized with the Loyalists but stayed neutral. In the United States strict neutrality legislation in 1935, 1936, and 1937 forbade arms shipments to either side. Because Franco was receiving substantial military aid from Germany and Italy, the neutrality policy doomed the Loyalists.

Most American activists and intellectuals, overcoming their general distaste for war, expressed shock at the policy of nonintervention. The Spanish Civil War became the most vital issue of their generation. "People of my sort," observed writer Malcolm Cowley, "were more deeply stirred by the Spanish Civil War than by any other international event since the World War and the Russian Revolution." Ernest Hemingway immortalized the Spanish conflict in his novel *For Whom the Bell Tolls* (1940).

Approximately 3,200 American men and women volunteered to fight on the Loyalist side. Calling themselves the Abraham Lincoln Brigade, they formed part of an international force of soldiers, ambulance drivers, and support personnel. Years later, survivors recalled the struggle as the "good fight." Despite assistance from the Soviet Union, the Loyalists were outnumbered and inadequately supplied and in March 1939 the Spanish Republic fell to Franco's forces. More than half the American volunteers died in the carnage, which claimed over 700,000 lives altogether.

Although American intellectuals applauded the Soviet Union's active support of the Spanish Loyalists, many literary figures began to feel uncomfortable in leftist circles. The Communists remained suspicious of intellectuals, many of whom were too independent to submit to party discipline. A number of writers found it increasingly difficult to satisfy both their artistic urges and the party's demand for fiction that reflected working-class concerns. They were also deeply distressed by mounting evidence of Soviet leader Joseph Stalin's widespread political repression.

The Nazi-Soviet Pact. The final blow to the popular front came in August 1939, when the Soviet Union, eager to avoid war, signed a nonaggression pact with Nazi Germany. Stalin's willingness to deal with Hitler devastated many supporters of the popular front. Diehard party members loyally accepted Stalin's about-face, but others left the party in disgust. The heyday of American Communism ended abruptly.

With the signing of the Nazi-Soviet pact, the world again stood on the brink of war. Although many Americans considered themselves isolationists and hoped the United States could remain aloof from the coming European conflict, they began to realize that the nation faced a greater enemy than the economic problems that had gripped the country for the past decade. Barely twenty years after the war to end all wars, the United States prepared once again to enter a worldwide struggle for the survival of democracy.

Summary

The New Deal offered a broad-based program of political and economic reform, but its programs were hardly revolutionary. President Hoover had taken the first steps toward involving the federal government more actively in economic life, a trend Roosevelt continued. The New Deal never did cure the depression, but it restored confidence that hard times could be overcome. And it provided a measure of economic security against the worst depression in American history by greatly relieving many of the tragic effects of the depression.

The New Deal dramatically expanded the size and power of the federal government, continuing a trend which had begun in the late nineteenth and early twentieth centuries. Decisions made in Washington now touched millions of individual lives. The New Deal provided new opportunities and a larger role in public life for blacks, women, and the labor movement. In politics, the Democratic coalition of white Southerners and the urban working class that had begun to emerge in the 1920s reached its climax in the landslide victory of 1936. By 1938, however, the New Deal had run out of steam and hard times were far from over.

The collapse of the economy encouraged a reassertion of American values in literature and the arts. This artistic flowering was partly supported by a unique experiment in government patronage of the arts through the WPA. Many writers blended artistic concerns with intense political commitment. This activism culminated in the popular front, where liberals and Communists joined together to oppose the spread of fascism, especially in the Spanish Civil War. The brief alliance ended in 1939 when the Soviet Union signed an agreement with Nazi Germany, bringing the world to the brink of war again.

TOPIC FOR RESEARCH

The New Deal and Your Community

Historians say that the New Deal affected virtually every locality in the country—what did it mean to yours? Find examples of the impact of New Deal projects on your local area. Likely candidates include buildings, highways, or public works projects funded by the WPA; post office murals painted by the Federal Arts Project or Treasury Department; a nearby state park or recreation area, including playgrounds and golf courses; forestry or Shelterbelt projects, perhaps in connection with a CCC camp; and a traveling art project or theatrical performance funded by the WPA. As you play historical detective, consider these questions: What did it mean to the community to have the federal government enter its life? Did the federal presence mean different things to different segments of the community?

Several overviews suggest the kinds of places to start looking. Phoebe Cutler, *The Public Landscape of the New Deal* (1985), cites examples throughout the country. Marlene Park and Gerald Markowitz, *Democratic Vistas: Post Offices and Public Art in the New Deal* (1984), surveys New Deal murals and art. Carl Fleischhaeuer and Beverly Brannan, *Documenting America, 1935–1943* (1988) samples New Deal photography. For your community, visit the local historical society or library, check for town records and old newspaper clippings from the 1930s, and seek out senior citizens. If your town does not have enough material, investigate the New Deal's impact on a large urban area such as New York or San Francisco.

BIBLIOGRAPHY

Comprehensive introductions to the New Deal include Robert S. McElvaine, *The Great Depression* (1984); William E. Leuchtenburg, *Franklin D. Roosevelt and the New Deal* (1963); Barry Karl, *The Uneasy State* (1983); John A. Garraty, *The Great Depression* (1987); and Roger Biles, *A New Deal For the American People* (1991). Other useful surveys include Albert Romasco, *The Politics of Recovery* (1983); Paul Conkin, *The New Deal* (1967); and Harvard Sitkoff, ed., *Fifty Years Later: The New Deal Evaluated* (1985). Arthur M. Schlesinger, Jr., *The Age of Roosevelt* (3 vols., 1957–1960), and Frank Freidel, *Franklin D. Roosevelt: A Rendezvous With Destiny* (1990), examine the era and its leading protagonist in detail.

The New Deal Response

The New Deal has inspired a voluminous bibliography. Frank Freidel, *Launching the New Deal* (1973) covers the first hundred days in detail. Monographic studies include Bernard Bellush, *The Failure of the NRA* (1975); Thomas K. McCraw, *TVA and the Power Fight* (1970); John Salmond, *The Civilian Conservation Corps* (1967); Jerold Auerbach, *Labor and Liberty* (1966); Susan Kennedy, *The Banking Crisis of 1933* (1973); Michael Parrish, *Securities Regulation and the New Deal* (1970); Mark Leff, *The Limits of Symbolic Reform: The New Deal and Taxation, 1933–1939* (1984); James Olson, *Saving Capitalism: The Reconstruction Finance Corporation and the New Deal, 1933–1940* (1988); and Bonnie Fox Schwartz, *The Civilian Works Administration, 1933–1934* (1984). Ellis Hawley, *The New Deal and the Problem of Monopoly* (1966), provides a stimulating account of economic policy. Agricultural developments are covered in Theodore Saloutos, *The American Farmer and the New Deal* (1982); Richard S. Kirkendall, *Social Scientists and Farm Politics in the Age of Roosevelt* (1966); David Conrad, *The Forgotten Farmers* (1965); Paul Mertz, *The New Deal and Southern Rural Poverty* (1978); and Sidney Baldwin, *Poverty and Politics: The Rise and Decline of the Farm Security Administration* (1968). Alan Brinkley, *Voices of Protest* (1982), describes the Coughlin and Long movements; see also T. Harry Williams, *Huey Long* (1969), and Leo Ribuffo, *The Old Christian Right: The Protestant Far Right From the Great Depression to the Cold War* (1983). Roy Lubove, *The Struggle for Social Security*, and J. Joseph Huthmacher, *Senator Robert Wagner and the Rise of Urban Liberalism* (1968), cover major initiatives from the Second New Deal.

The second term has drawn far less attention than the 1933–1936 period. James MacGregor Burns, *Roosevelt: The Lion and the Fox* (1956), provides an overview, as does Barry Karl, *The Uneasy State.* For the Supreme Court fight, see Joseph Alsop and Turner Catledge, *168 Days* (1938), and Leonard Baker, *Back to Back* (1967). The growing opposition to the New Deal is treated in James T. Patterson, *Congressional Conservatism and the New Deal* (1967), and Frank Freidel, *FDR and the South* (1965). See also Richard Polenberg, *Reorganizing Roosevelt's Government* (1966), and Barry Karl, *Executive Reorganization and Reform in the New Deal* (1963). James T. Patterson, *The New Deal and the States* (1969), examines changing patterns of federalism, while Charles Trout, *Boston: The Great Depression* (1977), examines the impact of the New Deal on one city.

The New Deal's Impact on Society

Katie Louchheim, ed., *The Making of the New Deal: The Insiders Speak* (1983), provides an engaging introduction to some of the men and women who shaped the New Deal. See also Peter Irons, *New Deal Lawyers* (1982). On women in the New Deal, see Susan Ware, *Beyond Suffrage* (1981). Joseph

Lash, *Eleanor and Franklin* (1971), provides a comprehensive account of Eleanor Roosevelt's activities, which can be supplemented by her autobiographies, *This Is My Story* (1937), and *This I Remember* (1949). George Martin, *Madam Secretary* (1976), covers the career of Frances Perkins. Also of interest is Perkins's memoir, *The Roosevelt I Knew* (1946).

For minorities and the New Deal, see Harvard Sitkoff, *A New Deal For Blacks* (1978); Raymond Wolters, *Negroes and the Great Depression* (1970); John B. Kirby, *Black Americans in the Roosevelt Era: Liberalism and Race* (1980); Robert Zangrando, *The NAACP Crusade Against Lynching, 1909–1950* (1980); and Nancy J. Weiss, *Farewell to the Party of Lincoln* (1983).

Irving Bernstein, *The Turbulent Years* (1970) and *A Caring Society: The New Deal, the Worker, and the Great Depression* (1985), chronicle the story of the labor movement in compelling detail through 1941. Additional studies include Peter Friedlander, *The Emergence of a UAW Local* (1975); Melvin Dubofsky and Warren Van Tine, *John L. Lewis* (1977); Sidney Fine, *Sit-Down: The General Motors Strike of 1936–1937* (1969); David Brody, *Workers in Industrializing America* (1980); Ronald Schatz, *The Electrical Workers* (1983); David Milton, *The Politics of U.S. Labor: From the Great Depression to the New Deal* (1980); and Lizabeth Cohen, *Making A New Deal: Industrial Workers in Chicago, 1919–1939* (1990).

For Indian policy, see Donald Parman, *Navajoes and the New Deal* (1976); Laurence Hauptman, *The Iroquois and the New Deal* (1981); Laurence C. Kelly, *The Assault on Assimilation: John Collier and the Origins of Indian Policy Reform* (1983); and Kenneth Philp, *John Collier's Crusade for Indian Reform, 1920–1945* (1977).

The creation of the New Deal's welfare system is treated in James T. Patterson, *America's Struggle Against Poverty* (1981), which carries the story through 1980. See also Michael Katz, *In the Shadow of the Poorhouse: A Social History of Welfare in America* (1986); John Garraty, *Unemployment in History* (1978); and Otis Graham, *Towards a Planned Society: From Roosevelt to Nixon* (1976). Margaret Weir, Ann Shola Orloff, and Theda Skocpol, eds., *The Politics of Social Policy in the United States* (1988), and Amy Gutmann, ed., *Democracy and the Welfare State* (1988), provide perspectives from political science. For the enduring impact of Franklin Roosevelt on the political system, see William Leuchtenburg, *In the Shadow of FDR* (1983).

Culture and Commitment

The various New Deal programs have found their historians in Jerry Mangione, *The Dream and the Deal: The Federal Writers' Project, 1935–1943* (1972); Monty Penkower, *The Federal Writers' Project* (1977); Richard McKinzie, *The New Deal For Artists* (1973); and Jane DeHart Mathews, *The Federal Theater, 1935–1939* (1967). General studies of cultural expression include William Stott, *Documentary Expression and Thirties America* (1973); Richard Pells, *Radical Visions and American Dreams* (1973); and R. Alan Lawson, *The Failure of Independent Liberalism, 1933–1941* (1971). See also Karen Becker Ohrn, *Dorothea Lange and the Documentary Tradition* (1980) and F. Jack Hurley, *Portrait of a Decade: Roy Stryker and the Development of Documentary Photography in the Thirties* (1972).

Daniel Aaron, *Writers on the Left* (1961), provides an overview of literary currents in the decade. For selections from the 1930s, see Harvey Swados, ed., *The American Writer and the Great Depression* (1966), and Charlotte Nekola and Paula Rabinowitz, eds., *Writing Red: An Anthology of American Women Writers, 1930–1940* (1987). See also Paula Rabinowitz, *Labor and Desire: Women's Revolutionary Fiction in Depression America* (1991). Material on the relationship between intellectuals and the Communist party is in Harvey Klehr, *The Heyday of American Communism* (1984), and Irving Howe and Lewis Coser, *The American Communist Party* (1957). Warren Susman provides a provocative analysis of culture and commitment in the 1930s in *Culture as History* (1984). See also Alice Goldfarb Marquis, *Hopes and Ashes: The Birth of Modern Times, 1929–1939* (1986), and David P. Peeler, *Hope Among Us Yet: Social Criticism and Social Solace In Depression America* (1987).

TIMELINE

1933	Banking crisis Agricultural Adjustment Act National Industrial Recovery Act Roosevelt's first fireside chat Tennessee Valley Authority
1934	Securities and Exchange Commission Indian Reorganization Act
1935	National Labor Relations (Wagner) Act Social Security Act Works Progress Administration Huey Long assassinated CIO formed
1936	Roosevelt reelected Black Cabinet
1936–1939	Spanish Civil War
1937–1938	Recession
1937	Supreme Court reorganization fails Sitdown strikes
1938	Fair Labor Standards Act
1939	Nazi-Soviet Pact

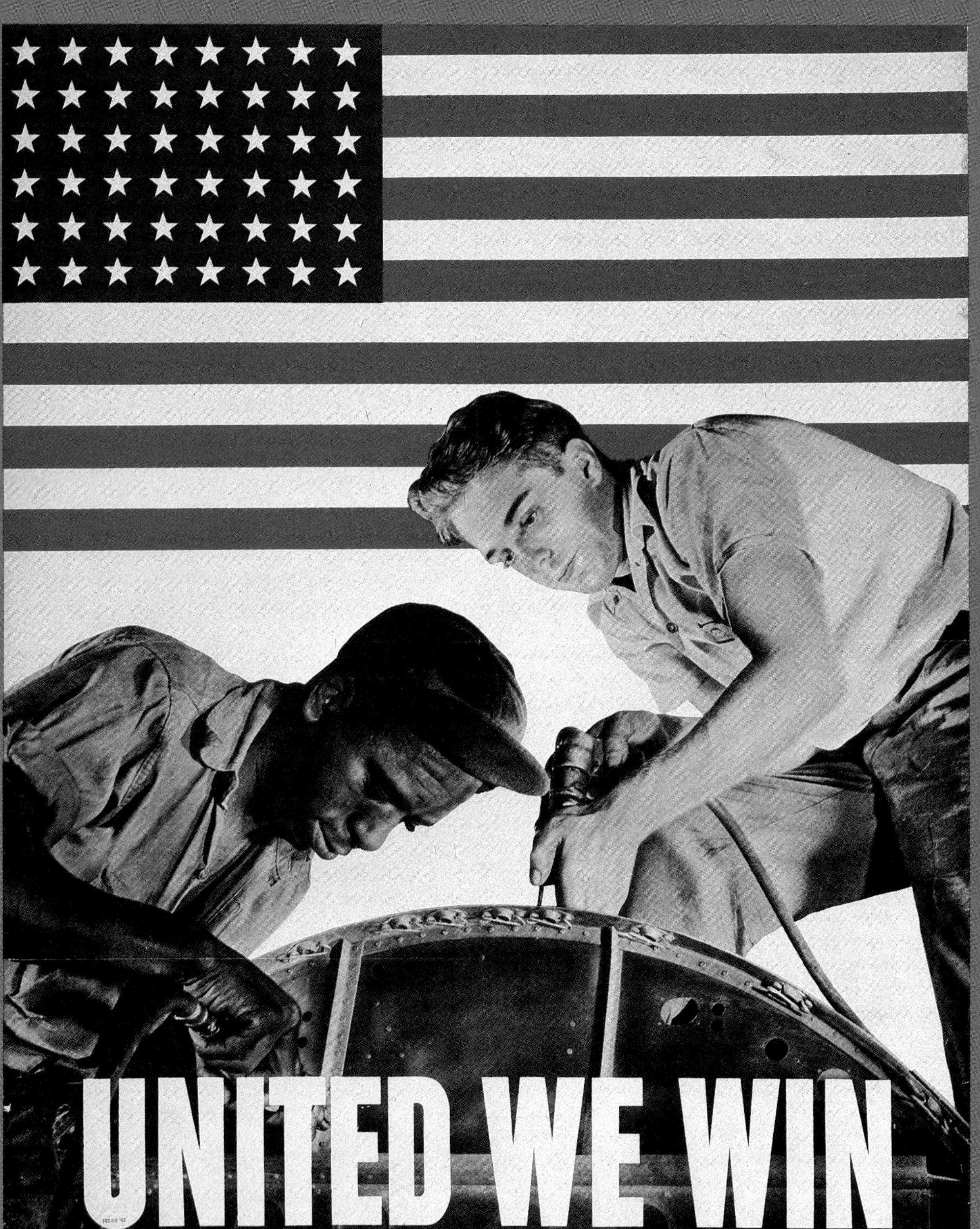

United We Win

This poster captured the spirit of unity and sacrifice needed to win World War II. At the same time it reminded Americans of the contributions blacks were making to the war effort, a spur to civil rights.

CHAPTER 27 *The World at War, 1939–1945*

On a Sunday night in October 1938, actor Orson Welles's "Mercury Theater of the Air" broadcast a modern version of *The War of the Worlds* (1898) by the English writer H. G. Wells. Using fictional news bulletins interspersed with simulated on-the-spot reports, Orson Welles convinced large numbers of people that Martians had landed near Princeton, New Jersey, and were invading the countryside. Even though the radio broadcast included four announcements that the attack was just a dramatization, many people fled from their homes. No one doubted the power of radio anymore.

One reason that so many people believed Orson Welles's fictional invasion may have been that during September 1938, radio programs had been repeatedly interrupted by ominous news bulletins about a possible European war. Even the news on September 30 of the Munich Agreement between England, France, and Germany, which prevented war for another year, did not ease public fears of imminent catastrophe.

By the late 1930s, popular culture, as represented by the "War of the Worlds" hoax, increasingly reflected America's involvement in international, if not cosmic, events. The coming of World War II would intensify this involvement. When radios announced on December 7, 1941, that the Japanese had attacked Pearl Harbor, Americans realized that this news flash was no hoax.

World War II ranks with the New Deal as a crucial period of political and economic change in America. Mobilization pumped money and confidence into the economy, ending the Great Depression. The task of fighting a global war increased government influence on American life and caused dramatic social changes on the home front. But the most far-reaching impact was the decision by the United States following the war to accept a leading, and continuing, role in world affairs.

The Road to War

The rise of fascism in Europe and Asia in the 1930s threatened the fragile world peace that had prevailed since the end of World War I. The League of Nations set up by the Versailles treaty, which the United States never joined, proved too weak to deal with threats to world peace. As early as 1936, Roosevelt foresaw the possibility of America's participation in another European war, but he bowed to the isolationist sentiment predominant in the country. By 1939, however, he was leading the nation toward war.

Depression Diplomacy

During the early years of the New Deal, America's involvement in international affairs remained limited. Roosevelt put national interests first, reasoning that only when the United States regained a stable economy at home could it be an effective international leader. His message to the 1933 London Economic Conference stating that the United States would not participate in plans to stabilize world currency killed any hope of common action. One of Roosevelt's few diplomatic initiatives was formal recognition of the Soviet Union in November 1933.

The Good Neighbor Policy. During his first term, Franklin Roosevelt followed the lead of the Republican administrations of the 1920s, working to consolidate American influence in the Western Hemisphere. His diplomatic strategy, which combined both political and economic goals, became known as the Good Neighbor Policy. Under the Reciprocal Trade Agreements Act of 1934, the president was empowered to raise or lower tariffs, without congressional approval, in return for reciprocal concessions from other nations. As a corollary to economic expansion, the United States also voluntarily renounced the use of military force and armed intervention in the Western Hemisphere. At the Pan-American Conference in Montevideo, Uruguay, in December 1933, Secretary of State Cordell Hull proclaimed that "no state has the right to intervene in the internal or external affairs of another." The U.S. Congress agreed in 1934 to repeal the Platt Amendment, a relic of the Spanish-American War, which had asserted the United States' right to intervene in the internal affairs of Cuba. The Navy still kept its major base at Cuba's Guantanamo Bay, a symbol of the American presence.

Isolationism. Although most Americans wished to steer clear of foreign entanglements during the early to mid-1930s, Roosevelt disagreed. An internationalist at heart, he wanted the United States to play a prominent role in an international economic and political system that would foster the long-term prosperity necessary for a lasting peace. But FDR was hampered in his wish for international action by the isolationism prevalent in Congress and the nation.

Isolationism had been building throughout the 1920s, as a product of disillusionment with American participation in World War I, and was fueled by the revelations of the Nye Committee in 1934 and 1935. Gerald P. Nye, a Republican senator from North Dakota, conducted a congressional investigation into the profits of munitions makers during World War I, and then widened the investigation to determine the influence of economic interests on America's decision to declare war. Nye's committee concluded that profiteers, whom it called "merchants of death," had maneuvered the United States into the war for financial gain.

Most of the Nye Committee's charges were dubious or simplistic, but they added momentum to the growing isolationist movement. In late 1934, President Roosevelt revived a proposal supported by the Republican administrations of the 1920s for the United States to join the World Court, a mild internationalist gesture of symbolic rather than real importance. In January 1935 the Senate rejected it.

The Neutrality Act of 1935 pushed the United States further along an isolationist course. The passage of this legislation showed the political power of such prominent isolationists as Nye, William Borah, Burton K. Wheeler, and Hiram Johnson in the senate, in addition to Joseph P. Kennedy, the Ambassador to Great Britain. Explicitly designed to prevent a recurrence of the events that had pulled the United States into World War I, the Neutrality Act imposed an embargo on arms trade with countries at war and declared that American citizens traveled on belligerent ships at their own risk.

In 1936, Congress expanded the Neutrality Act to ban loans to belligerents and, in 1937, it adopted a "cash and carry" provision. That is, if a country at war wanted to purchase nonmilitary goods from the United States, it had to pay for them in cash and pick them up in its own ships. The point of this restriction was to protect American commercial ships from attack. Roosevelt did not like it, because it gave him no discretion to decide whether some belligerents, such as the Spanish Loyalists, deserved American support. But he realized how strong the spirit of isolationism was and accepted the verdict of Congress. It would not be very long before the neutrality policy would be put to the test.

Aggression and Appeasement

World War II had its roots in the settlements of World War I. Germany deeply resented the international order laid down by the Treaty of Versailles, while other nations, notably Japan and Italy, revived their dreams of overseas empire after the war, in ways that fundamentally challenged the status quo. The League of Nations, the collective security system set up at Versailles, proved unable to stop aggression. After 1931, those who wanted to upset the status quo used force, but those who wanted to maintain it didn't.

The first challenge came from Japan. To develop as an industrial power, Japan needed raw materials and markets for its goods. By 1930 the country was under the leadership of an ultranationalist, militaristic regime, with designs on dominating the entire Pacific basin in a Greater East Asia Co-Prosperity Sphere. In 1931 the Japanese army occupied Manchuria, the northernmost province of China. China appealed to the League of Nations, which found Japan at fault, but imposed no sanctions and took no action. Japan simply resigned from the League of Nations.

Japan's defiance of the League encouraged a dictator half a world away, in Italy: Benito Mussolini. Mussolini had seized power in 1922, and introduced the system of *fascismo*. Fascism, in Italy and, later, in Germany, rested on an ideology of state control of economic affairs, the subordination of individual rights to the "collectivity," suppression of the labor movement and the Left, and in general a cult of the state, race, and war. Above all, fascism called for a strong, almost dictatorial leader. Parliamentary government and democratic guarantees were superseded by what Mussolini called, far too benevolently, a "dictatorship of the State over many classes cooperating."

Mussolini had long been unhappy with the provisions of the Versailles treaty, which did not give Italy any former German or Turkish colonies. Also, the Italians had never forgotten their stinging defeat by Abyssinia (modern Ethiopia) in 1896, the first time that Africans successfully defended themselves against white imperialists. In 1935, Italy invaded Ethiopia, one of the few independent countries left in Africa. The Ethiopian emperor Haile Selassie went before the League of Nations, which condemned the Italian action as aggression, and this time it imposed sanctions. However, member nations could not agree to include the vital sanction on oil, so the League's action had little effect. By 1936, Italian subjugation of Ethiopia was complete.

Not Italy but Germany presented the gravest threat to world order in the 1930s. The Weimar Republic of the 1920s was fundamentally unstable, saddled with huge reparations payments and a guilt clause for World War I that inflamed nationalist passions. Runaway inflation, fear of communism, labor unrest, and rising unemployment were conditions that Adolf Hitler and his National Socialist Party (Nazis) skillfully exploited. On January 20, 1933, Hitler became chancellor of Germany, and the *Reichstag* (legislature) soon gave him dictatorial powers. Hitler took the title of *Führer* (leader), proclaimed the Third Reich, and outlawed all other political parties. Hitler's goal was nothing short of world domination, which he made clear in his book *Mein Kampf*. He would seek to overturn the territorial settlements of the Versailles treaty, "restore" all the Germans of Central and Eastern Europe to a single greater German fatherland, and annex large areas of Eastern Europe to provide "living space" for Germans. "Inferior races," such as Jews and Slavs, would have to make way for the "master race."

Hitler's strategy was to provoke a series of crises which presented England and France with no alternative but to let him have his way. Hitler withdrew from the League of Nations in 1933; two years later he announced that he planned to rearm Germany in violation of the Versailles treaty. No one stopped him. In 1936, Germany reoccupied the Rhineland, which, under the treaty, had been declared a demilitarized zone, and once again France and Britain took no action. Later that year, Hitler and Mussolini joined forces in the Rome-Berlin Axis, a political and military alliance. After the Spanish Civil War broke out in 1936, Germany and Italy supplied the Spanish fascists.

To help him fulfill his global strategy, Hitler needed an Asian ally. The obvious choice was Japan. On November 26, 1936, Japan entered into the Anti-Comintern pact with Germany. The announced purpose was to oppose communism, but the pact was really a military alliance between Japan and the Axis, which was formalized in 1940. In 1937, Japan launched a full-scale invasion of China. Once again, the League of Nations was helpless to stop the aggression.

Hitler

Adolf Hitler seized power in Germany in 1933, and embarked on a plan for world domination. Here he addresses followers at a Nazi rally in Nuremberg in 1938. Note the swastika—the Nazi symbol—prominently displayed on the uniforms of the soldiers and on the *Führer* himself.

The Failure of Appeasement. Within Germany, persecution of the Jews escalated, and Hitler's ambitions grew. In 1938 he sent troops into Austria and annexed it, proclaiming an *Anschluss* (union) between Germany and Austria. France and Great Britain hoped he would go no further, as they had been hoping since he started on his road of conquest. But the German dictator was already scheming to seize part of Czechoslovakia, the keystone of Eastern Europe. Because Czechoslovakia had an alliance with France, war seemed imminent. At the Munich Conference in September 1938, Prime Minister Neville Chamberlain of Britain and Prime Minister Edward Daladier of France capitulated to Hitler, agreeing to let Germany annex the Sudetenland, the German-speaking border areas of Czechoslovakia, in return for Hitler's pledge that he would seek no more territory.

Within six months, Adolf Hitler overran the rest of Czechoslovakia and threatened to march into Poland, exposing the folly of Chamberlain's pronouncement that the Munich agreement guaranteed "peace with honor . . . peace for our time." Britain and France realized that their policy of appeasement wouldn't work and prepared to take a stand. In August 1939, Hitler signed a nonaggression pact with the Soviet Union, shocking Popular Front supporters but protecting Germany from having to wage war on two fronts. German troops attacked Poland on September 1, 1939, and two days later Britain and France declared war. World War II had begun.

American Neutrality, 1939–1941

Two days after the war started, the United States officially declared its neutrality. Roosevelt made no secret of his sympathies, however. He pointedly rephrased Woodrow Wilson's declaration in 1914, "This nation will remain a neutral nation, but I cannot ask that every American remain neutral in thought as well." The overwhelming majority of Americans supported the Allies over the Nazis—84 percent to 2 percent, with 14 percent neutral, according to a 1939 poll—but most Americans did not want to be drawn into another world war.

So began what *Time* magazine would later call America's "thousand-step road to war." After a bitter battle in Congress, Roosevelt won a modification of the neutrality laws in November 1939. The Allies could now buy weapons from the United States, but only on the same "cash and carry" basis established for nonmilitary goods by the 1937 Neutrality Act. To avoid a repetition of the conflicts that drew the United States into World War I, Congress authorized the president to restrict Americans and American ships from entering combat zones and to prevent merchant ships from carrying cargo to combatants' ports.

After the German conquest of Poland in September 1939, a false calm settled over Europe. This "phony war" lulled many Americans into the belief that supplying the Allies with arms would be enough to defeat Germany. Hitler soon shattered their complacency. In a few hours on April 9, 1940, Nazi tanks overran Denmark. Norway fell to the Nazi *blitzkrieg* (lightning war) next, and the Netherlands, Belgium, and Luxembourg soon followed. Then the Germans stormed into France, flanking the fixed defenses of the Maginot line and making short work of the combined English and French troops. On June 22, 1940, France fell. Only England stood between the United States and Hitler's plans for world domination.

Intervention Gains. During the summer and fall of 1940, German planes bombarded England mercilessly in the Battle of Britain, while in America the debate between interventionists and isolationists continued. Journalist William Allen White and the Committee to Defend America by Aiding the Allies led the interventionists. Isolationists, including aviator Charles

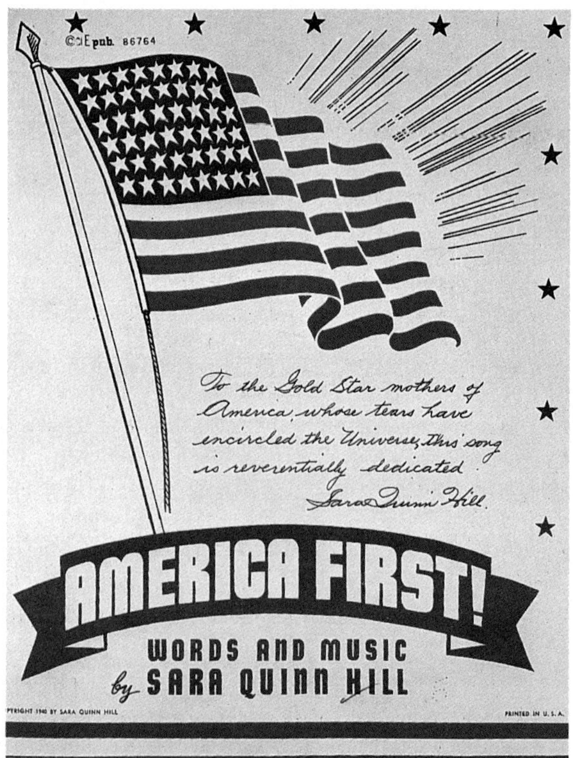

America First

In rallies, radio broadcasts, newspaper advertisements, and even in music (such as this 1940 songsheet by Sara Quinn Hill), the America First Committee expressed its opposition to U.S. entry into World War II. The movement was strongest in the Midwest, least successful in the South. After Pearl Harbor, however, the America First Committee pledged full support to the war effort.

Lindbergh, Senator Gerald Nye, and former NRA administrator Hugh Johnson, formed the America First Committee in 1940, to keep the nation out of the war. The *Chicago Tribune*, the Hearst newspapers, and other conservative publications, especially in the Midwest, gave full support to the isolationist cause.

Despite the efforts of America Firsters, in 1940 the United States moved closer to involvement. After the fall of France, the number of Americans who believed that a German victory would threaten national security increased from 43 percent (in March 1940) to 69 percent. Roosevelt began putting the economy and the government on a defense footing by creating the National Defense Advisory Commission and the Council of National Defense in May 1940. In June, he brought two prominent Republicans, Henry Stimson and Frank Knox, into his cabinet as the secretaries of war and navy, respectively, to give a bipartisan character to the war preparations. During the summer, the president traded fifty World War I destroyers to Great Britain for the right to build military bases on British possessions in the Atlantic, circumventing the 1939 neutrality legislation by an executive order. In October, a bipartisan majority in Congress approved a big increase in defense spending and instituted the first peacetime draft registration and conscription in American history. Another draft law, which came up in August 1941, lengthening draftees' service from one year to two and a half years, passed by a single vote.

The 1940 Election. In the midst of the deteriorating situation in Europe, the United States prepared for the 1940 election. Would Roosevelt seek an unprecedented third term? He had not designated a successor, and the Nazi *blitzkrieg* in the spring of 1940 convinced him that he should run again. He submitted to a "draft" at the Democratic National Convention. Although the delegates acclaimed Roosevelt's renomination, they balked at his choice for vice-president: liberal Secretary of Agriculture Henry A. Wallace, to replace John Nance Garner of Texas, a conservative who had long since broken with the New Deal. Wallace's nomination went through only after Eleanor Roosevelt flew to the convention in Chicago and asked the delegates to put politics aside in a national crisis.

The Republicans nominated a political newcomer, Wendell Willkie of Indiana, a lawyer and president of the Commonwealth and Southern Electric Utilities Company. Willkie, a former Democrat, supported many of the New Deal's domestic and international policies, including Roosevelt's destroyers for military bases deal with Britain. Trying to compete against the charismatic Roosevelt, Willkie portrayed himself as a man of the people, provoking crusty Secretary of the Interior Harold Ickes to call him "a simple barefoot Wall Street lawyer." The platforms of the two parties differed only slightly. Both pledged aid to the Allies but stopped short of calling for American participation in the war.

Initially Willkie conducted his campaign in a bipartisan spirit, but as the election approached, Republican leaders pressured him to go on the offensive. Charging that Roosevelt was leading the country into war, Willkie promised that he would not send "one American boy into the shambles of another war." Roosevelt's reply on October 28, 1940, probably clinched his victory: "I have said this before, but I shall say it again and again and again: Your boys are not going to be sent into foreign wars." Of course, if America was attacked, it would no longer be a foreign war. Willkie was a stronger contender than the Democrats had anticipated, and his spirited campaign resulted in a closer election than 1932 or 1936, but Roosevelt and the vital Democratic coalition won 55 percent of the popular vote and a lopsided victory in the electoral college.

Lend-Lease. The United States virtually entered the war when Congress passed the Lend-Lease Act in March 1941. This legislation enabled the nation to serve, in Roosevelt's words, as "the great arsenal of democracy." Great Britain, already at war for eighteen months and being bombed nightly by the German air force, could no longer afford to pay cash for arms. Roosevelt decided to "get away from the dollar sign." In a fireside chat to build support for Lend-Lease, Roosevelt used the analogy of lending a neighbor a garden hose to put out a fire: "I don't say to him, . . . 'Neighbor, my garden hose cost me fifteen dollars; you have to pay me fifteen dollars for it.' . . . . I don't want fifteen dollars—I want my garden hose back after the fire is over." Under the Lend-Lease Act, the president was empowered to "lease, lend, or otherwise dispose of" arms and other equipment to any country whose defense was considered vital to the security of the United States. In Roosevelt's view, the survival of Britain was the key to American security, so anything that helped Britain's defense was crucial to that of the United States. To administer the Lend-Lease program, Roosevelt turned to former relief administrator Harry Hopkins, who became one of his most trusted advisers during the war years.

Roosevelt's determination to aid Britain was reinforced by the personal rapport he was developing with British leader Winston Churchill. The two leaders communicated regularly. In January 1941, Roosevelt sent Harry Hopkins to meet with Churchill to lay the basis for the Anglo-American partnership. In August 1941, Roosevelt and Churchill, accompanied by the ever-present Hopkins, met secretly aboard a cruiser off the Newfoundland coast to discuss goals and military strategy. Defeating Germany was their top priority, especially since Germany had invaded the Soviet Union in June 1941, abandoning the Nazi-Soviet pact of two years earlier.

As in World War I, when Americans started supplying the Allies, the Germans attacked American and Allied ships. By September 1941, Nazi submarines and American vessels were fighting an undeclared naval war in the Atlantic, unbeknownst to the American public. In October, Congress authorized the arming of merchant vessels. However, without an actual enemy attack, Roosevelt still hesitated to ask for a declaration of war against Germany.

The Attack on Pearl Harbor

The final provocation came from Japan, not from Germany. Conflict between Japan and the United States had been building throughout the 1930s. Japanese military advances in China upset the balance of political and economic power in the Far East, where the United States had long enjoyed the economic benefits of the Open Door policy, especially control over the raw materials and large markets of China. After the Japanese invasion of China in 1937, Roosevelt denounced "the present reign of terror and international lawlessness," suggesting that aggressors like Japan be "quarantined" by peace-loving nations. But he deliberately left the meaning of "quarantine" vague, a political necessity when isolationism was so strong in the land.

Even when directly provoked, the United States avoided taking a stand. In 1937 the Japanese sank an American gunboat, the *Panay*, in the Yangtze River near Nanking. The United States allowed Japan to apologize and accepted more than $2 million in damages, and the incident was quickly forgotten.

Japanese intentions soon became more expansionist. In 1940, Japan signed the Tri-Partite Pact with Germany and Italy. By the fall of 1941, Japanese troops occupied the north part of French Indochina. The United States retaliated by effectively cutting off trade with Japan, including vital oil shipments. (At this time, the United States was producing two-thirds of the world's oil.) Before its supplies ran down, Japan had to decide whether to go forward into war or accept the demand of the American Secretary of State Cordell Hull that it cease its expansionist activities in Asia. In July 1941, Japanese troops occupied the rest of Indochina, and Roosevelt froze all Japanese assets in the United States.

In September 1941, the government of Prime Minister Hideki Tojo began secret preparations for war against the United States. By November, American military intelligence knew that Japan was planning an attack, but did not know where it would come. In fact, Japan had decided to mount simultaneous surprise attacks on all the principal British and U.S. naval bases in the Western Pacific. Early on Sunday morning, December 7, 1941, Japanese bombers attacked Pearl Harbor, killing more than 2,400 Americans. Eight battleships, three cruisers, three destroyers, and almost two hundred airplanes were destroyed or heavily damaged. There were no aircraft carriers in port at the time—vessels that were far more important in the war to come. The Japanese also failed to knock out Pearl Harbor's oil reserves, which would have stranded the navy in Hawaii until oil shipments arrived from the West Coast, thousands of miles away. From a military standpoint, the Japanese attack was actually something of a failure.

Pearl Harbor

The U.S. destroyer *Shaw* exploded into flames and smoke after receiving a direct hit during the surprise Japanese attack on Pearl Harbor on December 7, 1941. It was early Sunday morning and many of the servicemen were still asleep. More than 2,400 Americans were killed; the Japanese suffered only light losses.

But the psychological impact was devastating. Pearl Harbor Day is etched in the memories of millions of Americans, who remember precisely what they were doing when they heard about the Japanese attack. Many were relieved that the period of indecision was over. The next day, President Roosevelt went before Congress and, calling December 7 "a date which will live in infamy," asked for a declaration of war against Japan. The Senate unanimously voted for war, and the House concurred by a vote of 388 to 1. The lone dissenter was Jeannette Rankin of Montana, who had also opposed American entry into World War I. Three days later, Germany and Italy declared war on the United States, and the United States in turn declared war on Germany and Italy.

Mobilizing for Victory

The task of fighting a global war accelerated the growing influence of the state on all aspects of American life. Coordinating the changeover from civilian to war production, raising an army, and assembling the necessary work force taxed government agencies to their limits. Mobilization on such a scale demanded cooperation between business executives and political leaders in Washington, solidifying the partnership that had been growing since World War I. But the most dramatic expansion of power occurred at the presidential level, when Congress passed the War Powers Act of December 18, 1941, giving President Roosevelt unprecedented authority over the conduct of the war.

Defense Mobilization

Defense mobilization did more than end the Great Depression: it caused the economy to more than double. In 1940, the gross national product stood at $99.7 billion; it reached $211 billion by the end of the war, in 1945. After-tax profits of American business companies rose from $6.4 billion in 1940 to $10.8 billion in 1944. Agricultural output grew by a third.

During the war, the federal government spent $186 billion on war production, sometimes as much as $250 million a day. The peak of mobilization occurred in late 1943, when two-thirds of the economy was directly involved in the war effort, as opposed to only one quarter in World War I. By 1945, the United States had turned out 86,000 tanks, 296,000 airplanes, 15 million rifles and machine guns, 64,000 landing craft, and 6,500 ships. Mobilization on this gigantic scale gave a tremendous boost to the economy and, after years of depression, restored faith in the capitalist system.

The federal bureaucracy also grew far more than it had during the eight years of the New Deal. The number of civilians employed by the government increased almost fourfold, to 3.8 million. The government gave the civil service exam two or three times a day at the height of wartime hiring. The federal budget of $9.4 billion in 1939 was ten times that in 1945 at $95.2 billion. The national debt grew sixfold, topping out at $258.6 billion in 1945. Along with these astronomical federal budgets came greater acceptance of Keynesian economics—that is, the use of fiscal policy to spur economic growth.

Financing the War. Taxes paid about half the cost of the war, compared with 30 percent of the cost of World War I. The Revenue Act of 1942 continued the income tax reform begun during World War I by widening the system to reach beyond wealthy individuals and corporations to average citizens. The number of people paying income tax grew from 3.9 million in 1939 to 42.6 million in 1945; tax collections rose from $2.2 billion to $35.1 billion. This mass-based tax system, a revolutionary change in the financing of the modern state, was sold to the taxpayers as a way to express their patriotism. The system of payroll deductions and tax withholding was instituted in 1943 by the federal government to facilitate collection. Bond drives and war loans gave people the opportunity of putting their savings at the disposal of the government by buying long-term Treasury bonds, which financed the remaining cost of the war. War bonds had the side benefit of withdrawing money from circulation, which helped hold down inflation.

Roosevelt turned to business leaders to run the war economy, as had Woodrow Wilson during World War I. Defense preparations had been under way since 1940; 25 percent of the economy was already devoted to war production before Pearl Harbor. In January 1941, Roosevelt established the Office of Production Management under William Knudsen, the president of General Motors. After the Japanese attack, Roosevelt disbanded that agency and replaced it with the War Production Board (WPB), headed by Donald Nelson, a former Sears, Roebuck executive.

The War Production Board was a powerful, comprehensive agency that awarded defense contracts, evaluated military and civilian requests for scarce resources, and oversaw the conversion of industries to military production. Many business leaders, the depression still fresh in their minds, were reluctant to invest in plant expansion or new production, so as a spur, the government granted generous tax write-offs for plant construction. It also approved contracts with cost-plus provisions that guaranteed profits and promised that industries could keep the factories after the war.

In the interest of efficiency and maximum production, the WPB found it easier to deal with major corporations than with small businesses. The fifty-six largest corporations held three-fourths of the war contracts, with a full third going to the top ten. This system of allocating contracts, along with the suspension of antitrust prosecution during the war, hastened the trend toward large corporate structures. In 1940 the largest hundred companies manufactured 30 percent of the nation's industrial output; by 1945, their share had grown to 70 percent. These same corporations formed the core of the military-industrial complex of the postwar years (see Chapters 28 and 29).

The Office of Price Administration and Civilian Supply (OPA) oversaw the domestic economy, allocating resources and trying to keep inflation down. By February 1942 retail prices were rising rapidly at 2 percent a month. In April the OPA froze most prices and rents at their March 1942 level. When loopholes, especially regarding food prices, undermined the effort, Congress passed the Anti-inflation Act, which stabilized prices, wages, and salaries. The Consumer Price Index rose 28.3 percent between 1940 and 1945, but most of the inflation occurred before 1943.

Roosevelt remained unsatisfied with the mobilization effort; there were too many government agencies and they often overlapped. In October 1942 Roosevelt persuaded Justice James F. Byrnes to resign from the Supreme Court and head the Office of Economic Stabilization and, after 1943, the Office of War Mobilization. Byrnes soon became the second most powerful person in the administration and finally brought order to production goals for civilian and military needs. The results were remarkable.

Shipbuilding showed American productive capacity at full strength. By 1941, the German navy had crippled transatlantic transport, sinking about 12 million tons of Allied shipping—mainly U.S. built—in the North Atlantic. Producing replacement vessels became a high priority. By turning out easy-to-build but clunky Liberty ships, which Roosevelt, an experienced sailor, called "ugly ducklings," the United States produced 19 million tons of merchant shipping by 1943, up from a million tons just two years earlier.

Henry J. Kaiser, a West Coast shipbuilder, performed shipyard production miracles. Using the mass production techniques of the automobile industry, Kaiser cut the time needed to build a transport ship from three hundred days to seventeen. He motivated workers through high pay and fringe benefits, including one of the country's first prepaid medical programs.

Kaiser's name became synonymous with getting things done fast. Although not all industries could boast such relative freedom from snafus (an acronym coined during the war from the expression "*s*ituation *n*ormal, *a*ll *f*ouled *u*p"), business and government compiled an impressive record. As in World War I, industry played a significant role in the military victory.

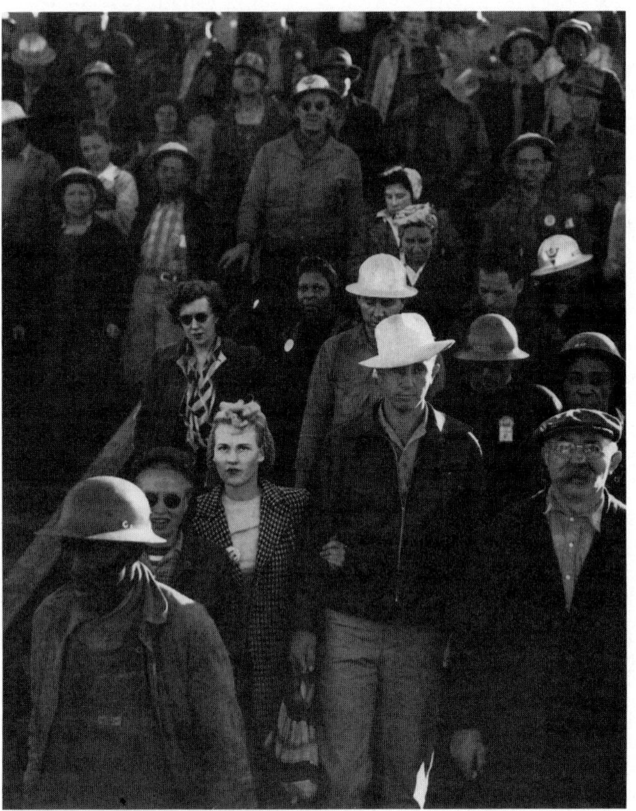

Wartime Workers

Photographer Dorothea Lange captured these shipyard construction workers coming off their shift at a factory in Richmond, California, in 1942. Note the large number of women workers, and also the presence of minority workers. Several of the workers are prominently wearing union buttons. (The Oakland Museum)

Mobilizing the American Fighting Force

Going to war meant mobilizing human resources, both for the battlefield and on the home front. During World War II, the armed forces of the United States numbered more than 15 million men and women. The army enlisted the most—about 10.5 million, including those who served in the Army Air Force—but almost 4 million served in the Navy, 600,000 in the Marines, and 240,000 in the Coast Guard.

Draft boards registered about 31 million men between the ages of eighteen and forty-four and ordered physical examinations for about a sixth of the male population. More than half the men failed to meet the physical standards: a height of 5 feet; weight of 105 pounds; correctable vision; at least half the number of natural teeth; no flat feet, hernia, or venereal disease. Defective teeth and eyes caused the greatest number of rejections. The military's attempts to screen out homosexuals were ineffectual. Once in the services, homosexuals found opportunities to participate in a gay subculture unavailable in civilian life.

Class distinctions and racial discrimination prevailed in the armed forces, mainly directed against the approximately seven hundred thousand blacks in uniform. Blacks served in all branches of the armed forces, but they were assigned the most menial duties; a great number served as messmen on navy ships, for example. The army segregated black and white blood banks, a practice without genetic or scientific merit. The NAACP and other civil rights groups chided the government with such reminders as "A Jim Crow army cannot fight for a free world," but the military remained rigidly segregated.

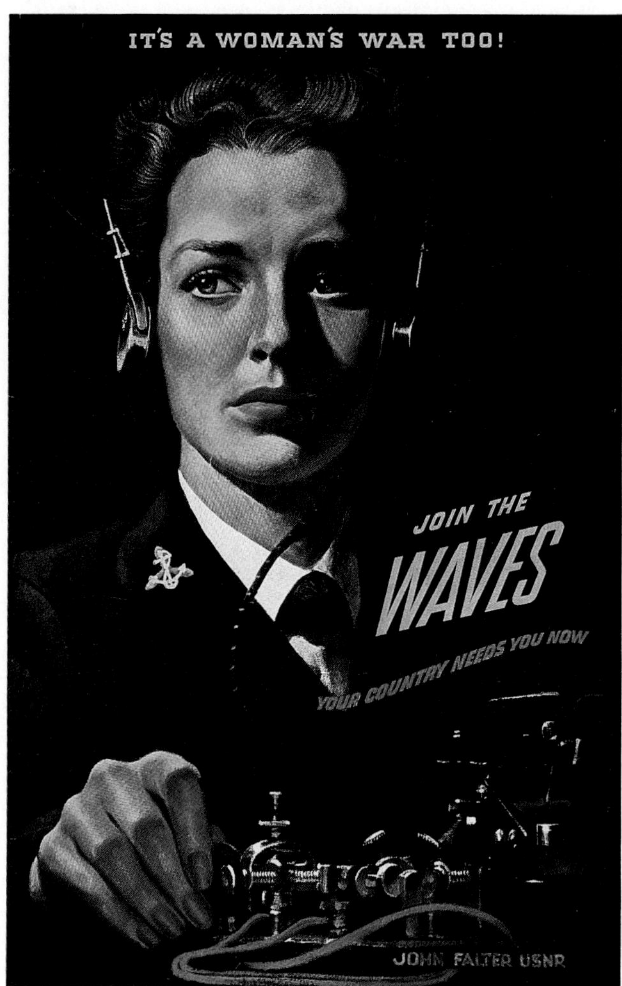

Join the Waves
Government ads pitched patriotic appeals to join the military, and women eagerly enlisted. As the poster said, "It's a Woman's War Too." Once in the navy, a WAVE would likely find herself stateside, working at jobs traditionally held by women, like clerical work. Not until 1944 were WAVES permitted to serve overseas.

Women in Military Service. About 350,000 American women, both black and white, enlisted in the armed services and achieved permanent status in the military establishment. There were about 140,000 WACS (Women's Army Corps), 100,000 WAVES (Women Appointed for Volunteer Emergency Service in the Navy), 23,000 members of the Marine Corps Women's Reserve, and 13,000 SPARs (for *S*emper *P*aratus, or *A*lways *R*eady, the Coast Guard motto) in the Coast Guard. In addition, about 1,000 WASPs (Women's Airforce Service Pilots) ferried planes and supplies in noncombat areas. A third of the nation's registered nurses volunteered for military duty: about 60,000 served in the army, and 14,000 in the navy.

The armed forces limited the types of duty assigned to women, as it did with blacks. Women were barred from combat, although nurses and medical personnel sometimes served close to the front lines, risking capture. Most jobs reflected stereotypes of women's roles in civilian life—clerical work, communications, and health care. The pin-ups of Betty Grable in a bathing suit, Rita Hayworth in a flimsy nightgown, and, for the black soldiers, the tempestuous singer Lena Horne, which were widely distributed to the troops, were probably closer to the average GI's view of women than a WAC or a WAVE was.

Women and the War Effort

When millions of citizens entered military service, a huge hole opened in the American work force. The backlog of Depression-era unemployment quickly disappeared, and the United States faced a critical labor shortage. The nation's defense industries provided jobs for about seven million new workers, including great numbers of women and blacks, who found employment opportunities for the first time.

Government planners "discovered" women while casting about for workers to fill the jobs vacated by departing servicemen. The recruiting campaign drew on patriotism. One poster urged, "Longing won't bring him back sooner . . . GET A WAR JOB!" Recruiters promised that women would take to riveting machines and drill presses "as easily as to electric cake-mixers and vacuum cleaners." The artist Norman Rockwell supported the campaign by creating his famous "Rosie the Riveter" cover for the *Saturday Evening Post*.

Although the government directed its propaganda at housewives, women who were already employed gladly abandoned low-paying "women's" jobs as domestic servants or file clerks for higher-paying jobs in defense factories. Suddenly the nation's factories were full of women, working as riveters, welders, blast furnace cleaners, and drill press operators. Women made up 36 percent of the labor force in 1945, compared with 24 percent at the beginning of the war. When the war ended, an overwhelming majority said they wanted to keep their jobs.

Women Aviators

WASPs piloted every type of military aircraft, from the huge B-29 bombers to sleeker fighter craft. Barred from combat duty, women pilots mainly ferried planes and supplies throughout the United States and Canada. As the smile on this aviator's face shows, the women were just glad to be able to fly at all. Because women pilots never achieved full military status, they were ineligible for military and veterans' benefits when the war ended.

However, government planners regarded women as just filling in while the men were away. Employers rarely offered such benefits as day care or flexible hours. Government child care programs set up by the 1940 Lanham Act reached only 10 percent of those who needed them. Because women were responsible for home care as well as for their jobs, they had a higher absentee rate than men did. Often, the only way to get shopping done or take a child to the doctor was to skip work. Women war workers also faced discrimination on the job. In shipyards, women with the most seniority and responsibility earned $6.95 a day, while the top men made as much as $22 a day.

When the men came home from war and the plants returned to peacetime operations, Rosie the Riveter was out of a job. However, many women refused to put on an apron and stay home. Women's participation in the labor force dropped temporarily when the war ended, but rebounded steadily for the rest of the 1940s.

Organized Labor

The labor movement also grabbed opportunities during the wartime mobilization effort. No dramatic changes occurred, but the war confirmed the industrial breakthroughs of the 1930s. By the end of the war, almost fifteen million workers—a third of the nonagricultural labor force, up from nine million at the end of the previous decade—belonged to unions.

Organized labor responded to the war with an initial burst of patriotic unity. On December 23, 1941, representatives of major unions made a "no strike" pledge—albeit nonbinding—for the duration of the war. To maintain industrial peace, in January 1942, President Roosevelt set up the National War Labor Board (NWLB), composed of representatives of labor, management, and the public. The board established wages, hours, and working conditions and had the authority to order government seizure of plants that did not comply. Forty plants were seized during the war.

During its tenure, the NWLB handled 17,650 disputes affecting 12 million workers. It faced two controversial issues: union membership and wage increases. Union organizers favored either the union shop or the closed shop, but management preferred the open shop. (In a union shop, the employees must belong to a certain union, or join it within a specified period. In a closed shop, the employer may hire only workers who are already members of a union. In an open shop, the employer usually uses only nonunion workers.) As a compromise, the NWLB imposed the principle of maintenance of membership. Workers did not have to join a union, but those already in a union had to maintain their membership during the life of the contract.

Agitation for wage increases caused a more serious disagreement. In contrast to the deflation of the depression, inflation pushed prices up throughout the war. Because management wanted to keep production (and profits) running smoothly, it was willing to pay the higher wages demanded by workers. However, such raises would conflict with the OPA policy of keeping inflation as low as possible. In 1942 the NWLB established the "Little Steel Formula," which granted a 15 percent wage increase to match the increase in the cost of living since January 1, 1941. Although the NWLB froze hourly wages in principle, it allowed them to rise another 24 percent by 1945. Actually, incomes rose as much as 70 percent because workers earned overtime pay, which was not covered by wage ceilings. The tremendous increase in output during World War II was largely because people worked overtime.

Although incomes were higher than anyone in the depression would have dreamed possible, many union members felt cheated as they watched corporate profits soar while their wages remained frozen. The high point

AMERICAN VOICES

"Rosie the Riveter" *Helen Studer*

Helen Studer was forty-four years old, and had a son in the armed forces, when she went to work at Douglas Aircraft in 1942. Overcoming blatant age discrimination, she eventually fought for a promotion to an inspection job before returning to full-time homemaking when the war ended.

We didn't train in the plant; we trained someplace else. You had classes and somebody'd be talking and get you familiar with what the process was going to be. We didn't get right down to basic working for, oh, probably three weeks or more. Then we went out to the plant.

I was awed, really awed. It is so huge. Well, you can imagine how big it would be to have that big airplane. And all these fluorescent lights. The place was just like daylight. Really, it takes you several hours almost to quit looking. I had never been inside anything like that. And the noise was absolutely terrible. There were times that the noise was just so bad, you'd have to really lay your tools down and walk outside. I wore earplugs a lot of times. . . .

I was going to work on the wing section; I was going to be a riveter or bucker. The one that drove the rivets had to have the drill and a whole set of different-sized bits, 'cause you never knew what size you were going to use. I didn't do a whole lot of bucking because I wasn't that strong. They furnished you with a rivet gun, but you had to have your own drill, your own hammer, your own flashlight. Small things.

They assigned you your job according to what they thought you could do. My husband's cousin's granddaughter, she went to work out there at the same time. She didn't rivet, either. She got a job with inspection right off the bat. Young and beautiful, see. An old lady didn't get anything like that. I was assigned to this wing section on the C-47. There were usually two of you paired together, and you stay with what you were doing, and then they'd have an inspector come along.

The men really resented the women very much, and in the beginning it was a little bit rough. You had to hold your head high and bat your eyes at 'em. You learned to swear like they did. However, I made myself stop because I don't think it's too ladylike. The men that you worked with, after a while, they realized that it was essential that the women worked there, 'cause there wasn't enough men and the women were doing a pretty good job. So the resentment eased. However, I always felt that they thought it wasn't your place to be there.

But some of the characters they had working there was just something else. We had a leadman and that was more or less a disaster. He was a young fellow, about the same age as my son who was overseas in the war—that was a primary reason to work, because I had a son that was in the service. Anyhow, this young fellow, they lived in Santa Ana and they were quite well-to-do people and his father bought him off. Got him a job in the defense plant so he was deferred. Boy, was he useless. He didn't know as much as we girls did. Time and time again, I've gone around the side of the plane, and he'd be sitting there playing mumblety-peg. And we women working our heads off! Just goes to show the politics.

Source: Sherna Berger Gluck, *Rosie the Riveter Revisited: Women, the War, and Social Change* (Boston: Twayne, 1987), 186–88.

of dissatisfaction came in 1943. First a nationwide railroad strike was narrowly averted. Then John L. Lewis led more than half a million United Mine Workers out on strike, demanding wages higher than the Little Steel Formula allowed. Lewis won concessions, but he alienated Congress, and by defying the government, he became one of the most disliked public figures of the 1940s.

Congress countered Lewis's action by overruling Roosevelt's veto of the Smith-Connally Labor Act of 1943, which required a thirty-day cooling-off period before a strike and prohibited strikes in defense industries entirely. Nevertheless, about fifteen thousand strikes occurred during the war. Less than one tenth of a percent of working hours were lost to strikes, but the public perceived the disruptions as far more costly. Labor unions won acceptance during the war years, but also provoked increased hostility.

Politics in Wartime

At a press conference late in 1943, President Roosevelt playfully announced that "Dr. Win the War" had replaced "Dr. New Deal." During the 1940s, Roosevelt rarely pressed for further social and economic change, thus placating conservative members of Congress whose support he needed to conduct the war in a bipartisan spirit. With little protest, he agreed to drop several popular New Deal programs. In 1942 the Civilian Conservation Corps was dismantled, followed in 1943 by the National Youth Administration and the Works Progress Administration. Severe budget cuts crippled the Farm Security Administration, which had represented the interests of poor farmers. The speed with which the government terminated these agencies suggested that they had been more a response to the crisis of the depression than a commitment to promoting the general welfare through federal programs. Such programs as Social Security remained untouched, however.

The war years brought a significant decline in the reform spirit that had flourished in Washington during the 1930s. Few public figures talked about using the war to bring about social change, as they did in World War I. One exception was the reform of the tax system. Business executives replaced the reformers and social activists who had staffed New Deal relief agencies in the 1930s. These executives became known as "dollar-a-year men" because they volunteered for government service while remaining on their corporate payrolls.

Roosevelt had hoped politics could be shelved for the duration of the war, but that expectation proved unreasonable. The Republicans picked up seats in both houses of Congress and increased their share of state governorships in the 1942 election. These gains reflected the general tendency of the party out of power to improve its position in off-year elections. The Republicans also benefited from a low voter turnout. Relocations, caused by enlistment, and residency requirements contributed to the low turnout.

Roosevelt himself did not give up politics for the duration. After concluding that continuation of the war made a fourth term necessary, Roosevelt went on a mild offensive to attract Democratic voters. In his state of the union address in 1944, the president called for a second Bill of Rights. As the basis of postwar prosperity, he pledged such rights as a job, adequate food and clothing, a decent home, proper medical care, and an education.

The president's sweeping commitment remained largely rhetorical. Congressional support for this vast extension of the welfare state did not exist in 1944. It was possible, however, to win some of these rights for a special group of American citizens: the veterans. The GI Bill of Rights, passed in 1944, provided education, job training, medical care, pensions, and mortgage loans for men and women who had served in the armed forces during the war.

The Election of 1944. "I am an old campaigner and I love a good fight," Franklin Roosevelt had said during the 1940 election. He approached the 1944 campaign with the same verve, but the years had taken their toll. Concern about Roosevelt's health and need for a succes-

Labor and Politics

The CIO Political Action Committee was formed to harness the political power of new recruits for labor's postwar agenda, especially full employment. Artist Ben Shahn's vivid 1944 poster reinforced the CIO's commitment to racial equality. (The Museum of Modern Art, New York) sor prompted the Democrats to drop Vice-President Henry Wallace, whose outspoken support for labor, civil rights, and domestic reform was too extreme for many party leaders. In Wallace's place, they chose Senator Harry S. Truman of Missouri.

Truman, a World War I veteran and Kansas City haberdasher whose business had failed in the 1920–1921 recession, found success in politics. Sponsored by Thomas Pendergast, the Democratic boss in Kansas City, he was elected to the Senate in 1934 and reelected in 1940. Truman became known for heading a Senate investigation of government waste and inefficiency in defense contracts during the war.

The Republicans nominated New York Governor Thomas E. Dewey. Only forty-two years old, Dewey had won fame fighting organized crime as a U.S. attorney. He accepted the broad outlines of the welfare state and belonged to the internationalist wing of the Republican party. The 1944 election was the closest since 1916. Roosevelt received 53.5 percent of the popular vote. The Democrats lost ground among farmers, but most ethnic groups remained solidly Democratic. Roosevelt got his customary support from the South, augmented by the overwhelming allegiance of members of the armed forces, who voted by absentee ballot. His margin of victory came from the cities. In urban areas with more than a hundred thousand people, the president drew 60 percent of the vote.

Roosevelt also received strong support from organized labor. Under the prodding of CIO leaders Sidney Hillman and Philip Murray, labor contributed more than $1.5 million, or about 30 percent of the Democratic party's election funds. The CIO's Political Action Committee canvassed door-to-door and conducted voter registration campaigns. Organized labor continued to play a significant role in the Democratic party after the war.

Life on the Home Front

In contrast to World War I, there was almost no domestic opposition to the nation's role in World War II. Americans fought for their way of life and for the preservation of democracy against the forces of Nazi and Japanese totalitarianism. Because the enemies seemed so evil, and America's will to fight was so strong, many remember it as the "good war." But those words have an ironic meaning for certain groups of Americans, notably Japanese-Americans.

"For the Duration"

Although the United States did not suffer the physical devastation that ravaged much of Europe and the Far East, the war affected the lives of those who stayed behind. Every time a family with a loved one overseas saw the Western Union boy on his bicycle, they were afraid it meant a telegram from the War Department telling them that their son or husband or father would not be coming home. Other Americans tolerated small deprivations daily. "Don't you know there's a war on?" be-

Wartime Prosperity

War mobilization brought prosperity to many American households. This photograph, taken in 1942, shows the Hall family of Sheffield, Alabama, in their comfortable home, part of a defense housing project connected with the TVA. The picture looks posed, but the new levels of consumption and affluence it represented were true for many Americans like the Halls.

came the standard reply to a request that could not be fulfilled. People accepted the fact that their lives would be different "for the duration."

Just like the soldiers in uniform, people on the home front had a job to do. They worked on civilian defense committees, performed volunteer work, donated blood, collected old newspapers and scrap material, and served on local rationing or draft boards. Advertising campaigns displaying the popular "V for Victory" slogan stressed patriotism. All seven war loan drives were oversubscribed. "Victory gardens" in about 20 million homes produced 40 percent of the vegetables grown in the United States.

However, many Americans remember the war years as much for the return of prosperity as for anything else. Unemployment disappeared and per capita income rose from $691 in 1939 to $1,515 in 1945. Despite geographical dislocations and shortages of various items, about 70 percent of the population admitted midway through the war that they had personally experienced "no real sacrifices." A Red Cross worker put it bluntly: "The war was fun for America. I'm not talking about the poor souls who lost sons and daughters. But for the rest of us, the war was a hell of a good time."

During the war years, demographic patterns rebounded from their depression-induced declines. Young people could afford to marry, and the imminent departure of men for military service induced many couples to take the step sooner rather than later. Not all these marriages survived the strain of separation or wartime relocation, and the divorce rate also rose. The birth rate went up, with many babies being conceived before their fathers went off to war. In effect, the wartime birth patterns marked the beginning of the pro-family "baby boom" that characterized American culture in the postwar period.

Entertaining the Troops

The original Stage Door Canteen opened in the basement of a Broadway theater in 1942. It served servicemen coffee, doughnuts, and big-time entertainment volunteered by Broadway and Hollywood stars. The canteen's popular weekly radio show was the inspiration for the 1943 movie *Stage Door Canteen.*

Popular Culture. Popular culture, especially the movies, reinforced the connections between the home front and the troops serving overseas. Hollywood escaped the restrictions and cutbacks that affected other industries, in part because studio heads argued that movies built morale. Many Hollywood directors leant their services to the military. Director Frank Capra's "Why We Fight" series, a documentary produced for the War Department, explained war aims to new soldiers and sailors. John Huston provided an intensely realistic portrayal of men in combat in *The Battle of San Pietro* (1944).

The average weekly movie attendance soared during the war, to over 100 million. Demand was so high that many theaters operated around the clock to accommodate defense workers on the swing and night shifts. Many movies had patriotic themes, and such films as *Wake Island* (1942) and *Thirty Seconds over Tokyo* (1945) portrayed life in the armed services. Dramas about struggles on the home front were also popular. In the box-office hit *Since You Went Away* (1943), Claudette Colbert took a war job after her husband went off to fight; Oscar-winning Greer Garson played a courageous British housewife in *Mrs. Miniver* (1942). Newsreels accompanied feature films and kept the public up-to-date on the war, as did on-the-spot radio broadcasts by commentators such as Edward R. Murrow. Thus popular culture reflected America's new international responsibilities at the same time as it built up home front morale.

Rationing. During the war, almost anything that Americans ate, wore, or used was subject to rationing or regulation. The first major scarcity was rubber. The Japanese conquest of Malaya and the Netherlands East Indies cut off 97 percent of America's imports of natural rubber, an essential raw material for war production. An entire new industry, synthetic rubber, was born, and by late 1944 the United States was producing 762,000 tons of it a year, mostly for the war effort.

Meanwhile, to conserve rubber, the government rationed tires, a hard sacrifice for the nation's 30 million car owners. Many people put their cars up on blocks for the duration. If people walked instead of drove, they wore out their shoes. In 1944 shoes were rationed to two pairs per person a year, barely half the average number people bought before the war.

The government also rationed gasoline and fuel oil. Shortages of fuel oil forced schools and restaurants to shorten their hours; home thermostats were lowered to 65 degrees. Gasoline rationing, introduced in December 1942, was both a response to depleted domestic gasoline supplies and an attempt to save wear on precious rubber tires. To further discourage gasoline consumption, Congress imposed a nationwide speed limit of 35 miles per hour, and highway death rates dropped dramatically.

People found it harder to cut back on eating. Among the many food items that were in short supply during the war, sugar disappeared quickly from grocery shelves. The government soon rationed it at the rate of 8 to 12 ounces per person a week. However, the manufacturers of such products as Coca-Cola and Wrigley's chewing gum received unlimited quantities of sugar by convincing the government that their products helped the morale of the men and women in the armed forces.

By 1943 the amount of meat, butter, and other foods Americans could buy was regulated by a complicated system of rationing points and coupons. Most people cooperated with the restrictions, but almost a fourth occasionally bought items on the black market.

Shortages of other consumer products also hit the home front. With the economy growing, people finally had enough money to buy refrigerators, cars, and radios, but the components of these items—such as rubber, copper, and steel—had been earmarked for war production. The last Ford rolled off the assembly line in 1942 and automobile plants converted to bomber production. To placate consumers, many companies ran advertisements promising delayed gratification. After the war, they told the public, you can buy that new house and fill it with all the appliances you dreamed of.

But some purchases just could not wait. One of the most sought-after items on the black market was women's stockings. In the 1930s, women had worn silk stockings, but when the war with Japan cut off imports of silk they switched to nylon stockings. Unfortunately for women, nylon was essential to war production: thirty-six pairs of nylons equaled one parachute. Many women began wearing slacks in public, a dramatic fashion change of the 1940s. The strict rationing of food and other items eased in the summer of 1944, when victory appeared on the horizon.

Migration and Family Life. The war caused people to move from one part of the country to another in unprecedented numbers. When men volunteered or were drafted into the armed services, their families often followed them to training bases or points of debarkation. The lure of high-paying defense jobs encouraged others to move. About 15 million Americans changed their residences during the war years, half of them moving to another state. The pace of urbanization increased, but this movement was not simply an exodus from rural to urban areas. About 5.4 million people left farms, but 2.5 million moved onto them. A million southerners, black and white, went north, but 600,000 migrants moved south. The greatest number of people went west.

As a center of defense production, California was affected by wartime migration more than any other state. During the war, one-tenth of all federal dollars went to California, and the state turned out one-sixth of the total war material. California welcomed nearly 3 million new residents during the war, a 53 percent population growth. They went where the defense jobs were—to Los Angeles, San Diego, and the San Francisco Bay Area. Some towns grew practically overnight. In just two years after the Kaiser Corporation opened a shipyard in Bay-area Richmond, the population quadrupled.

Migration and relocation often caused strains. Many towns with defense industries had scarce housing, inadequate public transportation, and tensions between old-timers and newcomers over public space and recreation. Of special concern were young people whom the war had set adrift from traditional community restraints. Newspapers were filled with stories of "latchkey" children, home alone while their mothers were at work in defense plants. Adolescents were even more of a problem. Teenage girls who hung around army bases looking for a good time were known as "victory girls."

In 1942 and 1943, juvenile delinquency seemed to be reaching epidemic proportions. In Los Angeles, male Hispanic teenagers organized *pachuco* (youth) gangs, dressing in broad felt hats, pegged trousers, and clunky shoes, wearing long slicked-down hair, and carrying pocket knives on gold chains. (This style was especially suitable for the jitterbug craze.) Such youths became known as "zoot suiters." Although this style was most popular among Hispanics, it was also taken up by blacks and by a few white working-class teenagers in Los Angeles, Detroit, New York, and Philadelphia. To adults, and many Anglos, the Zoot Suit came to symbolize wartime juvenile delinquency.

Zoot Suits
Zoot suit fashions gained wide popularity among young Americans during the war. In 1943, this well-dressed teenager greased his hair in a ducktail and wore a loosely cut coat with padded shoulders ("fingertips") that reached mid-thigh, baggy pleated pants cut tight ("pegged") around the ankles, and a long gold watch chain.

In Los Angeles, white hostility toward the Mexican-American community had been smoldering for some time, and zoot suiters became the targets. In July 1943 rumors that a Hispanic gang had beaten a white sailor set off a four-day riot, during which white servicemen entered Mexican-American neighborhoods and attacked zoot suiters, taking special pleasure in slashing the pegged pants of their victims. The attacks occurred within full view of white police officers, who did nothing to stop the violence.

Rising Winds of Change for African-Americans

"A wind is rising throughout the world of free men everywhere," Eleanor Roosevelt wrote during the war, "and they will not be kept in bondage." Unlike Mexican-Americans, for whom the war did little to bring about lasting change, African-Americans felt such a rising wind in the 1940s. The war disrupted a number of traditional patterns, and many barriers to racial equality tottered or fell.

Even before Pearl Harbor, there was evidence that the war might encourage greater black activism. In 1940 only 240 of the nation's 100,000 aircraft workers were black, and most of them were janitors. Black leaders demanded that the government require defense contractors to integrate their work forces. When the government took no action, A. Philip Randolph, head of the Brotherhood of Sleeping Car Porters, a black union, announced plans for a "March on Washington" in the summer of 1941. Roosevelt was not a strong supporter of civil rights, but he feared the embarrassment of such a massive public protest. Even more, he feared a disruption of war preparations. The president agreed to take action, and Randolph canceled the march.

In June 1941, Roosevelt issued an executive order declaring it to be the policy of the United States "that there shall be no discrimination in the employment of workers in defense industries or government because of race, creed, color, or national origin." To oversee the policy, the president established the Fair Employment Practices Committee (FEPC) in the Office of Production Management.

This federal commitment to black employment rights was unprecedented, but still limited in scope. For instance, it did not affect segregation in the armed forces. Moreover, the FEPC, which could not require compliance with its orders, often found that the needs of defense production took precedence over fair employment. The FEPC received more than eight thousand complaints, of which it resolved about a third. Blacks made up 8 percent of the defense workers in 1944, probably because of the labor shortage more than the FEPC prodding. Nevertheless, they got symbolic satisfaction from the federal action against discrimination in the work force.

Spurred by the new economic opportunities in defense and factory work, blacks migrated from the South in increasing numbers after the temporary slowdown of the depression. More than a million African-Americans moved to defense centers in California, Illinois, Michigan, Ohio, and Pennsylvania. Their need for jobs and housing led to racial conflict in several cities.

Some of the worst racial violence took place in Detroit, the new home of a large number of southern migrants, both black and white. Competition over scarce housing caused many of the disputes. Early in 1942, black families encountered resistance and intimidation when they tried to move into the Sojourner Truth housing project in the Polish community of Hamtramck. Similar tensions erupted into violence in June 1943, when a major race riot in Detroit left thirty-four people dead, including twenty-five blacks. Racial conflicts broke out in forty-seven cities throughout the country during 1943.

A new mood of militancy appeared among the nation's minorities during the war years. Black leaders pointed out parallels between anti-Semitism in Germany and racial discrimination in America. Civil rights leaders pledged themselves to a "Double V" campaign: victory over Nazism abroad and victory over racism and inequality at home.

Encouraged by the ideological climate of the war years, black organizations increased their membership. The NAACP grew ninefold, to 450,000 in 1945. In 1942, A. Philip Randolph helped found the Congress of Racial Equality (CORE). Unlike the NAACP, which favored lobbying and legal strategies, CORE was more aggressive; its tactics included demonstrations and sit-ins. In 1944, CORE forced several restaurants in Washington, D.C., to serve blacks after picketing them with signs that read "Are You for Hitler's Way or the American Way? Make Up Your Mind."

An awareness of civil rights was heightened in other ways as well. The Swedish sociologist Gunnar Myrdal wrote a monumental study of race relations, *An American Dilemma: The Negro Problem and Modern Democracy* (1944), focusing white Americans' attention on the issue for the first time. In 1944 the Supreme Court ruled in *Smith v. Allwright* that Texas's all-white primary election, a common device used to disfranchise blacks in southern states, was unconstitutional. Following the Court's decision, Congressman Wright Patman of Texas vowed that blacks in his district would vote "over my dead body." Soon, however, Patman was courting black voters at church picnics and other social events in his reelection campaigns. These wartime developments laid the groundwork for the civil rights revolution of the 1950s and 1960s.

Japanese Relocation

Although racial confrontations and Zoot Suit riots recalled the widespread racial tensions of World War I, the mood on the home front was generally calm in the 1940s. German culture and German-Americans did not come under suspicion, nor did Italian-Americans. Leftists and Communists were left alone mainly because after Pearl Harbor, the Soviet Union became an ally of the United States. There was one glaring exception to this record of tolerance: the internment of Japanese-Americans on the West Coast. The prejudice and hysteria directed at Japanese-Americans is a reminder of the fragility of civil liberties in wartime.

Immediately after Pearl Harbor, the West Coast remained calm. Then partly as a reflection of the region's vulnerability to attack, coastal residents began to demand protection against supposed Japanese spies. California had a long history of antagonism toward both Japanese and Chinese immigrants. The Japanese-Americans, who clustered together in highly visible communities, were a small, politically impotent minority. Unlike German- or Italian-Americans, the Japanese stood out. "A Jap's a Jap," an army general stated. "It makes no difference whether he is an American citizen or not."

Mounting fears on the West Coast brought a far-reaching decision from Washington in early 1942. President Roosevelt approved a War Department plan to intern Japanese-Americans in relocation camps for the duration of the war. In March 1942, Milton Eisenhower, a career civil servant and the brother of General Dwight D. Eisenhower, took over the War Relocation Authority, a civilian agency created to carry out the policy. Few public leaders opposed the plan. The Supreme Court upheld its constitutionality as a legitimate exercise of power during wartime in *Hirabayashi v. United States* (1943) and *Korematsu v. United States* (1944).

The relocation announcement shocked Japanese-Americans, more than two-thirds of whom were native-born American citizens. (They comprised the *Nisei* generation, the children of the foreign-born *Issei* generation.) The government gave families only a few

Japanese Internment

A Japanese-American family arrives at their new "home" in Heart Mountain, Wyoming, after being relocated from the West Coast military zone. The average internee spent 900 days—more than two and a half years—confined behind the barbed wire, which is not visible in this picture.

AMERICAN VOICES

The Insult and Injury of Internment *Peter Ota*

Peter Ota's father had come from Okinawa in 1904 and had built up a successful fruit and vegetable business in the Los Angeles area. Here the son, a member of the *Nisei* generation, remembers his family's internment during World War II. When Peter turned draft age, he was inducted into the army, even though his father and sister remained in the relocation camp for the duration of the war.

It was just my sister and myself. I was fifteen, she was twelve. In April, 1942, we were evacuated to Santa Anita. At the time we didn't know where we were going, how long we'd be gone. We didn't know what to take. A toothbrush, toilet supplies, some clothes. Only what you could carry. We left with a caravan.

Santa Anita is a race track. The horse stables were converted into living quarters. My sister and I were fortunate enough to stay in a barracks. The people in the stables had to live with the stench. Everything was communal. We had absolutely no privacy. When you went to the toilet, it was communal. It was very embarrassing for women, especially. . . .

We had orders to leave Santa Anita in September of 1942. We had no idea where we were going. Just before we left, my father joined us . . . . I can still picture it to this day; to come in like cattle or sheep being herded in the back of a pickup truck bed. We were near the gate and saw him come in. He saw us. It was a sad, happy moment, because we'd been separated for a year.

He never really expressed what his true inner feelings were. It just amazes me. He was never vindictive about it, never showed any anger. I can't understand that. A man who had worked so hard for what he had and lost it overnight. There is a very strong word in Japanese, *gaman*. It means to persevere. Old people instilled this into the second generation: you persevere. Take what's coming, don't react.

He had been a very outgoing person. Enthusiastic. I was very, very impressed with how he ran things and worked with people. When I saw him at Santa Anita, he was a different person.

We were out on a train, three of us and many trains of others. It was crowded. The shades were drawn. During the ride we were wondering, what are they going to do to us? We Niseis [first generation Japanese Americans] had enough confidence in our government that it wouldn't do anything drastic. My father had put all his faith in this country. This was his land.

Oh, it took days. We arrived in Amache, Colorado. That was an experience in itself. We were right near the Kansas border. It's a desolate, flat, barren area. The barracks was all there was. There were no trees, no kind of landscaping. It was like a prison camp. Coming from our environment, it was just devastating . . . .

When I think back to my mother and father, what they went through quietly, it's hard to explain. [Cries.] I think of my father without ever coming up with an angry word. After all those years, having worked his whole life to build a dream—an American dream, mind you—having it all taken away, and not one vindictive word. His business was worth more than a hundred thousand. He sold it for five. When he came out of camp, with what little money he had, he put a down payment on an apartment building. It was right in the middle of skid row, an old rooming house. . . . He died a very broken man.

Source: Studs Terkel, *"The Good War:" An Oral History of World War Two* (New York: Pantheon, 1984), 29–30, 32–33.

days to dispose of their belongings and prepare for relocation. Businesses that took a lifetime to build were liquidated overnight, and speculators snapped up Japanese real estate for a fraction of its value. A Japanese-American piano teacher got only $30 for her treasured piano. Another woman, rather than accept $17.50 from a secondhand dealer for her family's heirloom porcelain, broke every piece of it. The government later estimated that the total financial loss to Japanese-Americans was $400 million, but Congress appropriated only $38 million in compensation after the war. (Partial restitution came decades later, in 1988, when Congress voted to issue a public apology, and $20,000 in cash, to the 60,000 surviving internees.)

Relocation took place in two stages. First the government sent the Japanese-Americans to temporary assembly centers, such as the Santa Anita racetrack in Los Angeles, where they lived in stables that horses had occupied a few days earlier. Then they were moved to ten permanent camps away from the coast. These intern-

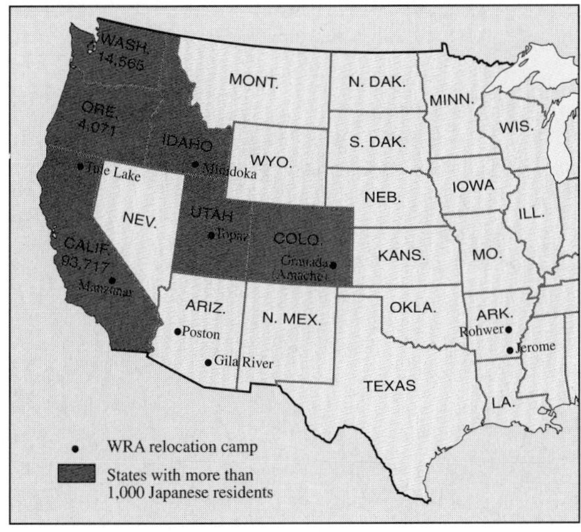

MAP 27.1

WRA Relocation Camps

In 1942 the government ordered 112,000 Japanese-Americans living on the West Coast into internment camps in the nation's interior because of their supposed threat to public safety. Some of the camps were as far away as Arkansas.

ment camps, located in California, Arizona, Utah, Colorado, Wyoming, Idaho, and Arkansas, "were in places where nobody had lived before and no one has lived since," one historian commented. Milton Eisenhower had hoped the relocation camps would resemble the CCC youth camps of the New Deal, but the barbed wire and enforced communal living mocked his hopes. Although sometimes compared to Nazi concentration camps, the relocation centers more closely resembled Indian reservations.

All ten camps were in hot, dusty places, and their communal bathroom and dining facilities made family life nearly impossible. Eight people often lived in a space measuring 25 by 20 feet. No one had any privacy and boredom was a major problem. Generational differences between the Issei, with an average age of fifty-five, and the Nisei, with an average age of seventeen, added to the tensions.

Almost every Japanese-American in California, Oregon, and Washington—a total of approximately 112,000 people—was involuntarily detained for some period during World War II. Ironically, the Japanese-Americans who made up one-third of the population of Hawaii, and presumably posed a greater threat because of their numbers and closer proximity to the Far East, were not affected. They were less vulnerable to detention, in part because of the island's multiracial heritage. More important, Japanese provided much of the unskilled labor on the island, and the Hawaiian economy could not function without them.

Cracks soon appeared in the relocation policy. Japanese-Americans had played an important role in California agriculture, and, even with stepped-up recruitment of Mexican-Americans through the *bracero* program, the labor shortage in farming led the government to furlough seasonal Japanese-American agricultural workers as early as 1942. In addition, about 4,300 young people who had been in college when the relocation order came through were allowed to stay in school—if they transferred out of the West Coast military zone. Another route out of the camps was enlistment in the armed services. The 442nd Infantry Combat Team, a segregated unit composed entirely of Nisei volunteers, became the most decorated unit in all the armed forces for its bravery in the European theater of operations.

Most Japanese-Americans accepted relocation stoically. They hoped that by proving their loyalty, they could reenter society after the war. Many Japanese-Americans of the third generation, called the *Sansei*, some of whom were born in the internment camps, and the fourth generation, the *Yonsei*, think their elders should have protested more strongly. With each generation, the memory of internment grows dimmer, but this shameful episode is burned into the national conscience.

Fighting and Winning the War

The Second World War was "the largest single event in human history, fought across six of the world's seven continents and all of its oceans," noted a military historian. "It killed fifty million human beings, left hundreds of millions of others wounded in mind or body and materially devastated much of the heartland of civilization." Dropping the atomic bomb on Hiroshima and Nagasaki in 1945 was the final stage in this most destructive and awesome of human conflicts.

Wartime Goals and Strategies

The Allied coalition was composed of Great Britain, the United States, the Soviet Union, and China. France, under German occupation until 1944, played a lesser role, although it was represented in Big Power discussions by Free French resistance leader General Charles De Gaulle. To America's dismay, Chinese leader Jiang Jieshi (Chiang Kai-shek) seemed more interested in fighting the communist revolution in his country (see Chapter 28) than in mobilizing the Chinese people to expel the Japanese invaders.

AMERICAN LIVES

The Quiet Diplomacy of Harry Hopkins

Winston Churchill called Harry Hopkins "Lord Root of the Matter" for his ability to dissect complex problems. President Franklin D. Roosevelt told Wendell Willkie that all presidents needed somebody like Hopkins "who asks for nothing except to serve you." Roosevelt put it more directly at the Teheran conference when he said simply, "Dear Harry, what would we do without you?"

In many ways, Hopkins's wartime service represented an unexpected career twist for this professional social worker. Born in Iowa in 1890, the son of a harness maker, he graduated from Grinnell College in 1912. Following in the footsteps of his older sister Adah, he became a social worker in New York, where he proved himself a competent and humane administrator. After the onset of the Great Depression, Hopkins became head of New York State's Temporary Emergency Relief Administration under Governor Franklin Roosevelt, whom he followed to Washington in 1933. During the New Deal, Hopkins headed emergency work relief programs such as the Civilian Works Administration (CWA), the Federal Emergency Relief Administration (FERA), and the Works Progress Administration (WPA), and served briefly as commerce secretary. He also made a run for the 1940 Democratic nomination, an unsuccessful foray into partisan politics that is universally regarded as the nadir of his career.

If Hopkins's government service had ended in 1940 (at the time he had severe health problems, which would continue until his death in 1946), he would be remembered as "the minister of relief." But Hopkins proved a remarkably quick learner when it came to diplomacy and international affairs, despite a total lack of background in these fields. In early 1941 Roosevelt sent him off as a special envoy to assess British morale and to offer assurance to Winston Churchill that American aid would be forthcoming. The two week trip stretched to six, and cemented Hopkins's relationship with Churchill. Hopkins modestly described his role as that of a "catalytic agent between two prima donnas," but from then on he proved indispensible to FDR. Later that year Hopkins undertook another mission of personal diplomacy: he went to the Soviet Union to reassure Russian leader Joseph Stalin that the United States would send military supplies to help the Soviets avoid defeat by Germany. In 1941, Hopkins also played a role in the administration of Lend-Lease aid to the Allies before the United States officially entered the war.

The kind of ad hoc arrangements that had characterized policy formulation during the New Deal continued after Pearl Harbor, and Hopkins found many opportunities to use his skills of crisis management. He always preferred troubleshooting and problem solving to being tied down in a bureaucratic chain of command; his only official position in the wartime bureaucracy was on the relatively minor Munitions Assignments Board. Instead, ensconced in a suite at the White House where he lived, he operated under the implied mantle of presidential authority. The key to Hopkins's unmatched working relationship with the president was his uncanny ability to anticipate FDR's views. But while Hopkins gave advice and counsel, Roosevelt always made up his own mind, especially on matters of military strategy.

The specter of illness haunted Hopkins's years of government service. Associates described him as a "bundle of energy," a chain-smoking workaholic, the worst possible lifestyle for a man plagued by stomach and digestive disorders. Because of his ongoing health problems, he often was forced to conduct government business from his White House suite dressed in his pajamas. The pajamas were usually silk—for a government bureaucrat, Hopkins had expensive tastes. He loved horse racing, fine dining, and first-class accomodations; he found it impossible to hold onto money and had trouble fulfilling his family obligations (he was married three times). But on the job Hopkins was scupulously honest and fair, and he inspired loyalty and high levels of performance from those who worked with him.

Hopkins's greatest contribution to the war effort came at the Teheran Conference in 1943, where he and Roosevelt tried to ensure Allied unity against competing Russian, British, and French demands. Functioning practically as the American secretary of state at Teheran since Roosevelt had not asked Cordell Hull to attend, Hopkins played an especially key role in convincing a reluctant Churchill to support the proposed invasion of France in 1944.

But at the height of Hopkins's power, illness once again struck. From January to July of 1944, Hopkins was out of Washington's (and FDR's) orbit entirely as he recuperated from surgery in Florida. Mounting one final comeback in late 1944, he regained his role as Roosevelt's chief adviser and confidante, in part by opposing Treasury Secretary Henry Morgenthau's postwar plans for German reorganization. In January 1945, Roosevelt tapped him for another major overseas assignment—meeting with French and English officials to review the plans for a postwar peace—before joining the American delegation at the Yalta conference in February.

By the time that Hopkins reached the Crimea, he was seriously weakened by the effects of wartime travel on his fragile system. His declining health prevented him from enjoying the personal triumphs he had experienced at Teheran: he attended only the major plenary sessions and instead used his dwindling energy to work with his staff in his quarters. He never doubted that Stalin's goal was to dominate Eastern Europe, but he still saw Yalta as the "dawn of a new day" for postwar cooperation. When he parted from FDR at the end of the conference (Hopkins was so ill he chose to fly home, rather than take the longer sea voyage with the president and his staff), it was the last time the two men saw each other. While Hopkins recuperated at the Mayo Clinic, he learned of Roosevelt's death. He performed one final act of government service by undertaking a personal mission to Moscow for Harry Truman before the Potsdam Conference, but ill health and his close identification with Franklin Roosevelt limited Hopkins's utility to the new president, and he declined Truman's invitation to join the official U.S. delegation.

In temporary retirement, Hopkins, who was only fifty-five, planned to rebuild his health and write his memoirs to provide financial stability for his family, but within eight months of Franklin Roosevelt, he too was dead. Appropriately for one who had contributed so much to the Anglo-American partnership during World War II, his last letter was to Winston Churchill.

Harry Hopkins and Joseph Stalin

While on his diplomatic mission to Moscow in 1941, Harry Hopkins took time-out from his discussions of the war situation to be photographed with Stalin at the Kremlin. The photo appeared in *Life* magazine.

The overall strategy for winning the war came out of give-and-take discussions among the dominant personalities of the Grand Alliance: Franklin Roosevelt, Prime Minister Winston Churchill of Great Britain, and Joseph Stalin, premier of the Soviet Union. Roosevelt's unswerving commitment to Britain's survival provided the basis for a strong, if not always smooth, relationship with Churchill. Stalin, however, was something of a mystery. He and Roosevelt did not even meet until late in 1943. Although the United States and Great Britain disagreed on such issues as the postwar fate of colonial empires, the potential for conflict with the Soviet Union was far greater. This uncertainty affected both the conduct of the war and the plans for the postwar peace.

The Atlantic Charter, drafted aboard ship during the Churchill-Roosevelt rendezvous off the Newfoundland coast in August 1941, provided the ideological foundation of the Allied cause and of the peace to follow, even before the Japanese attack on Pearl Harbor. It bore many similarities to Wilson's Fourteen Points of 1918. Calling for postwar economic collaboration and guarantees of political stability to ensure freedom from want, fear, and aggression, the Atlantic Charter supported free trade and condemned territorial gains achieved as the spoils of victory. It also supported the principle of collective security.

The Allied commitment to national self-determination was the most striking element of continuity with Wilson's Fourteen Points and presented the three leaders with their thorniest problem. Roosevelt's hope for self-determination in Eastern Europe conflicted with Stalin's desire for a band of Soviet-controlled satellite states to protect his western border. The fate of British colonies like India, where an independence movement had already begun, caused friction between Roosevelt and Churchill, though to a lesser degree. Despite such conflicts, Roosevelt hoped that the Allies could maintain friendly relationships, the basis of a constructive postwar system.

These long-term goals coexisted with the military necessities of fighting a global war. Defeating Germany always occupied top military priority, with the defeat of Japan in second place. One way to wear down the Germans was to open a second front on the European continent, preferably in France. The Russians strongly argued for this strategy, because it would draw German troops away from Russian soil. Roosevelt assured Stalin informally that such a front would be opened in 1942.

However, a combination of military priorities and British opposition caused a two-year delay in opening a second front. In 1942, the Allies did not have the necessary equipment, notably landing craft, to mount a successful invasion of the heavily defended French coast. Churchill adamantly opposed the invasion, fearing that the Allies would be trapped in a destructive ground war in France, as they had been in World War I.

The repeated delays in opening the second front proved damaging to harmony among the Allies. The issue came up so many times that Soviet Foreign Minister Vyacheslav Molotov was said to know only four English words: "yes," "no," and "second front." The delay meant that for most of the war, the Soviet Union bore the brunt of the land battle against Germany. Roosevelt and Churchill's unfulfilled pledges angered Soviet leaders, who were already suspicious about American and British intentions. This mistrust and bitterness carried over into the postwar world.

The War in Europe

During the first six months of 1942, the military news was so bad that it threatened to swamp the alliance completely. The Allies suffered severe defeats throughout Europe and on the Atlantic. German armies pushed deeper into Soviet territory, reaching the outskirts of Moscow and Leningrad, and simultaneously started an offensive in North Africa, aimed at seizing the Suez Canal. At sea, German submarines were crippling convoys of American supplies to Europe. Since the United States was the main supplier of oil for the Allies, these attacks went to the heart of the war effort, which was increasingly dependent on petroleum-based military technology such as tanks and airplanes.

The major turning point of World War II in Europe occurred in the winter of 1942–1943, when the Soviets halted the German advance in the Battle of Stalingrad. The Germans had taken most of the city in house-to-house fighting when the Soviets suddenly counterattacked. The Germans lost 330,000 soldiers and twenty-two divisions. Then came the task of pushing the Germans back through eastern Europe. By October 1943, Soviet armies stood on the east bank of the Dnieper River, ready to drive through the Ukraine into Romania. At the same time, the Allies launched a major offensive in North Africa, Churchill's substitute for a second front in France. Between November 1942 and May 1943, Allied troops under the leadership of Generals Dwight D. Eisenhower and George S. Patton defeated Germany's crack Afrika Korps led by General Erwin Rommel. From Africa the Allied command followed Churchill's strategy of attacking Europe through what he called its "soft underbelly": Sicily and the Italian mainland. In July 1943 the fascist regime of Benito Mussolini fell. The Allies invaded Italy the following fall, but encountered such heavy resistance from German troops that they did not enter Rome until June 1944.

D-Day. The long-awaited invasion of France came on D-Day, June 6, 1944. That morning, after an agonizing delay caused by bad weather, the largest armada ever

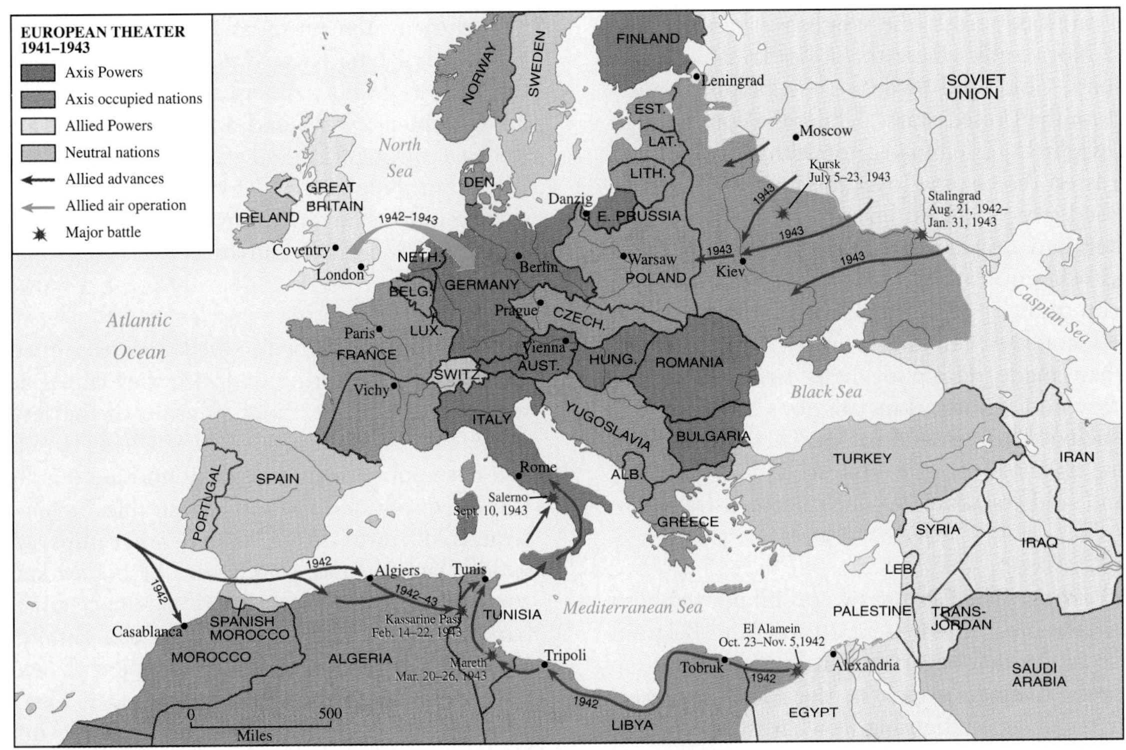

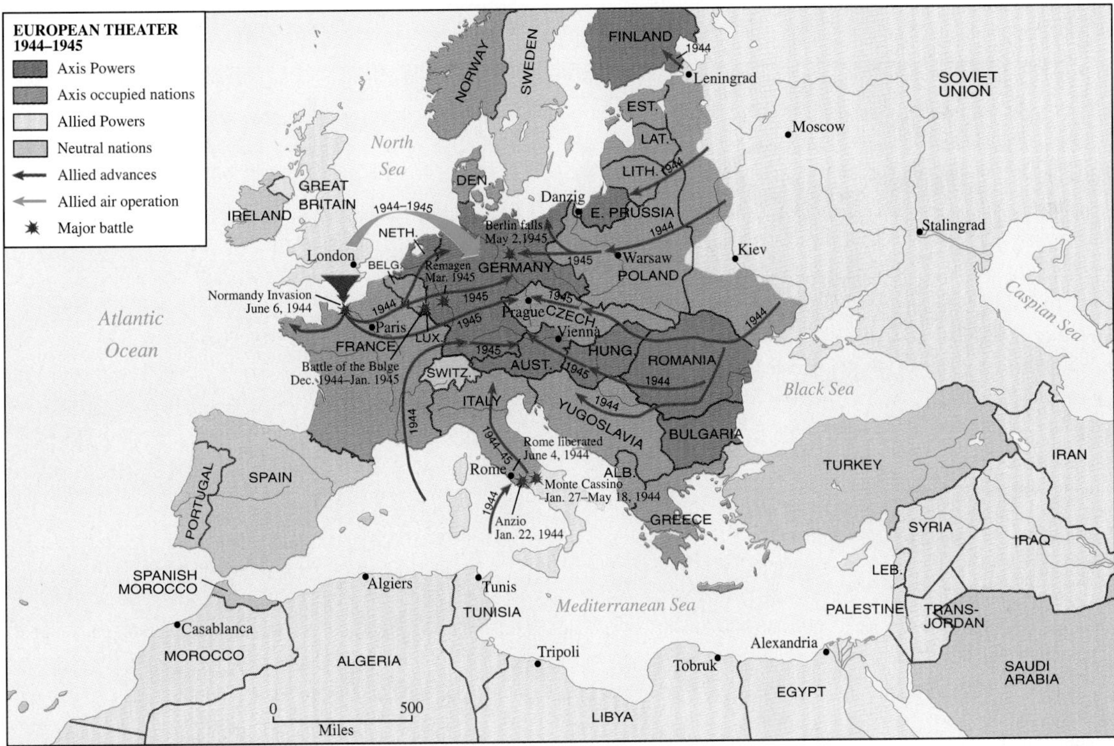

MAP 27.2

War in Europe

a. 1941–1943 Hitler's Germany reached its greatest extent in 1942, when Nazi forces finally stalled at Leningrad and Stalingrad. The tide of battle turned in the fall, when the Soviet army launched a massive counterattack at Stalingrad and Allied forces began to drive the Germans from North Africa. In 1943 the Allies invaded Sicily and the Italian mainland. ***b. 1944–1945*** On June 6, 1944 (D-Day), the Allies finally invaded France. It would take almost a year for the Allied forces to close in on Berlin—the Soviets from the east and the Americans, British, and French from the west. Germany surrendered on May 8, 1945.

assembled moved across the English Channel. The beaches of Normandy where the Allies landed—Utah, Omaha, Juno, Gold, and Sword—soon became household words in the United States. Under the command of General Dwight D. Eisenhower, more than 1.5 million soldiers crossed the channel over the next few days. In August, allied troops helped liberate Paris and by September, they had driven the Germans out of most of France and Belgium.

By the autumn of 1944, the German military situation looked hopeless. All that year, long-range Allied bombers had made daring daylight raids, damaging Nazi military and industrial installations and pulverizing cities such as Dresden and Berlin. The air campaign killed some 305,000 people and wounded 780,000, civilians and soldiers alike. No one remained free from attack.

Victory in Europe. The Germans were still not ready to give up. In December 1944, German forces in Belgium mounted an attack that began the Battle of the Bulge, so called because it made a dent in the Allied defenses. After ten days of heavy fighting in what turned out to be the final German offensive of the war, the Allies regained their momentum and pushed the Germans back across the Rhine River. Their goal was to take Berlin, the German capital. American and British troops led the drive from the west, and Soviet troops advanced from the east through Poland. On April 30, with much of Berlin in rubble from Allied bombing, Hitler committed suicide in his bunker. Germany surrendered on May 8, 1945, which became known as V-E (Victory in Europe) Day.

The Holocaust. When Allied troops advanced into Germany in the spring of 1945, they came face to face with Adolf Hitler's "final solution of the Jewish question": the extermination camps where 6 million Jews had been put to death as well as another 6 million Poles, Slavs, gypsies, and other "undesirables" such as homosexuals. Pictures from Nazi death camps at Buchenwald, Dachau, and Auschwitz, of bodies stacked like cords of wood, and survivors so emaciated they were barely alive, horrified the American public and the world. It is not as if no one knew about the existence of the camps before the German surrender. The Roosevelt administration, for example, had reliable information about the death camps as early as November 1942.

Hitting the Beach at Normandy

These American reinforcements landed on the Normandy beach two weeks after D-Day, June 6, 1944. More than a million Allied troops came ashore during the next month. The Allies liberated Paris in August and pushed the retreating Nazi forces back behind the German border by September.

The Living Dead
When Allied troops advanced into Germany in the spring of 1945, they came face to face with what had long been rumored—concentration camps, Adolf Hitler's "final solution of the Jewish question." Margaret Bourke-White was one of the first photographers on the scene. This haunting image from the Buchenwald death camp appeared in *Life* magazine soon after.

The lack of response by the U.S. government to the systematic annihilation of European Jewry ranks as one of the gravest failures of the Roosevelt administration. So few Jews got out because the United States, and the rest of the world, would not take them in. Strict State Department policies allowed only 21,000 refugees to enter this country during the war. The War Refugee Board, established in 1944 with little support from the Roosevelt administration, eventually helped save about 200,000 Jews. Several things combined to inhibit U.S. action: anti-Semitism; fears of economic competition from a flood of refugees in a country just recovering from the depression; the failure of the media to grasp the magnitude of the story and publicize it accordingly; and the failure of religious leaders, Jews and non-Jews alike, to speak out.

In justifying the American course of action, President Roosevelt claimed that winning the war would be the strongest contribution America could make to liberating the camps. But it is hard to escape the conclusion that the United States could have done more—much more—to lessen the Holocaust's terrible human toll.

The War in the Pacific

The United States still had to defeat Japan. At the beginning of 1942, the news from the Pacific was uniformly grim. In the wake of Pearl Harbor, Japan had scored quickly with seaborne invasions of Hong Kong, Wake Island, and Guam. Japanese forces conquered much of Burma, Malaya, and the Philippines, as well as the Solomon Islands, and threatened Australia and India. Japan managed this huge territorial expansion in only three months. One of the few boosts for American morale came on April 18, 1942, when Colonel James H. Doolittle led sixteen American bombers on the first air raid on Tokyo, but the attack had little military value.

The more significant battles were far to the south. On May 7–8, 1942, in the Battle of the Coral Sea near southern New Guinea, American naval forces halted the Japanese offensive against Australia. Then in June, at the Island of Midway, the Americans inflicted serious damage on the Japanese fleet. Dive bombers and fighters, launched from the aircraft carriers *Enterprise*, *Hornet*, and *Yorktown*, provided the margin of victory in both battles. For the first time, major sea battles were waged—and decided—primarily by planes launched from aircraft carriers that never even came in sight of each other. Submarines also played an important role in the naval battles, but the human cost was high: 22 percent of American submariners lost their lives during the war, the highest death rate of any branch of the armed services.

After the Battle of Midway, the American military command, under General Douglas MacArthur and Admiral Chester W. Nimitz, took the offensive in the Pacific. For the next eighteen months, American forces advanced arduously from one island to the next, winning major victories at Tulagi and Guadalcanal in the Solomon Islands and at Tarawa and Makin in the Gilberts. They reached the Marshall Islands in early 1944. In October 1944, MacArthur began the reconquest of the Philippines by winning the Battle of Leyte Gulf, a massive naval encounter, in which the Japanese lost practically their entire remaining fleet, and the Americans suffered only minimal losses.

AMERICAN VOICES

The War in the Pacific *Anton Bilek*

Anton Bilek was taken prisoner when the Japanese overran the Bataan penisula of the Philippines in April 1942. He describes here the infamous "Bataan Death March" and its aftermath.

The next morning, we got orders to get rid of all our arms and wait for the Japanese to come. General King had surrendered Bataan. They came in. First thing they did, they lined us up and started searchin' us. Anybody that had a ring or a wristwatch or a pair of gold-rimmed spectacles, they took 'em. Glasses they'd throw on the floor and break 'em and put the gold rims in their pockets. If you had a ring, you handed it over. If you couldn't get it off, the guy'd put the bayonet right up against your neck. Fortunately I never wore a ring. I couldn't afford one.

They moved us about on the road. Here was a big stream of Americans and Filipinos marchin' by. They told us to get in the back of this column. This was the start of the Death March. (A long, deep sigh.) That was a sixty-mile walk. Here we were, three, four months on half-rations, less. The men were already thin, in shock. Undernourished, full of malaria. Dysentery is beginning to spread. This is even before the surrender. We had two hospitals chuck-full of men. Bataan peninsula was the worst malaria-infected province of the Philippines.

The Japanese emptied out the hospitals. Anybody that could walk, they forced 'em into line. You found all kinda bodies along the road. Some of 'em bloated, some had just been killed. If you fell out to the side, you were either shot by the guards or you were bayoneted and left there. We lost somewhere between six hundred and seven hundred Americans in the four days of the march. The Filipinos lost close to ten thousand. At San Fernando, we were stuffed into boxcars and taken about thirty-five miles further north. The cars were closed, you couldn't get air. In the hot sun, the temperature got up there. You couldn't fall down because you were held up by the guys stacked around you. You had a lot of guys blow their top, start screamin'. From there, they marched us another seven, eight miles to Camp O'Donnell, which was built hurriedly for the Philippine army. It was built like the huts were built, of native bamboo and *nipa* and grass. There must've been about nine thousand of us and about fifty thousand Filipinos. Americans in one camp, Filipinos in the other. We had to leave after a month and a half. The monsoon season was starting. A hurricane blew down two of the barracks. Eighty men were killed. Just crushed.

I went blind, momentarily. It scared the hell out of me. I was at the hospital for about two weeks, and the doctor, an American, said, "There's nothing I can do with you. Rest is the only thing. Eat all the rice you can get. That's your only medicine." That's the one thing that pulled me through. He said, "You won't have to go on details." The Japanese were comin' in and they'd take two, three hundred and start 'em repairing a bridge that was blown up. We were losin' a lot of men there. They couldn't work any more. They were dyin'.

Every room at the hospital was full. They were built on stilts. It was cool underneath, where I was put. I started to swell. I got beriberi. Lack of vitamin B-1. Your kidneys stop functioning. The fluids just stay in your body. You blow up like a balloon. I was seein' guys die all around me. Americans, at 50 a day. Filipinos, around 350. We buried close to 2,000 Americans at Camp O'Donnell. They buried between 28,000 and 30,000 Filipinos.

They moved us to another camp at Cabanatuan, about fifty miles away. I rode on the back of a truck. . . . I was naked from the waist down. It was some ride. . . .

In camp, from the beginning to the end, you never talked of women. You never talked of sex. You never told stories. First thing you talked about is what you wanted in your stomach. Guys would tell stories about how their mother made this. Men would sit and listen very attentively. This was the big topic all the time.

I remember vividly this old Polack. One guy always wanted him to talk about how his mother made the cabbage rolls, the *golabki.* He had a knack of telling so you could almost smell 'em. He would say when he would be comin' home from school, he knew what he was gonna have to eat. When his mother made these *golabki,* he could smell 'em a block away. Oh, they'd get all excited. You'd see some of the fellas just lickin' their lips. Tasting it. You know?

I'm back home. It's all over with. I'd like to forget it. I had nothin' against the Japanese. But I don't drive a Toyota or own a Sony. . . . A lotta friends I lost. We had 185 men in our squadron when the war started. Three and a half years later, when we were liberated from a prison camp in Japan, we were 39 left. It's them I think about. Men I played ball with, men I worked with, men I associated with. I miss 'em.

Source: Studs Terkel, *"The Good War": An Oral History of World War Two* (New York: Pantheon, 1984), 85, 90–91, 95–96.

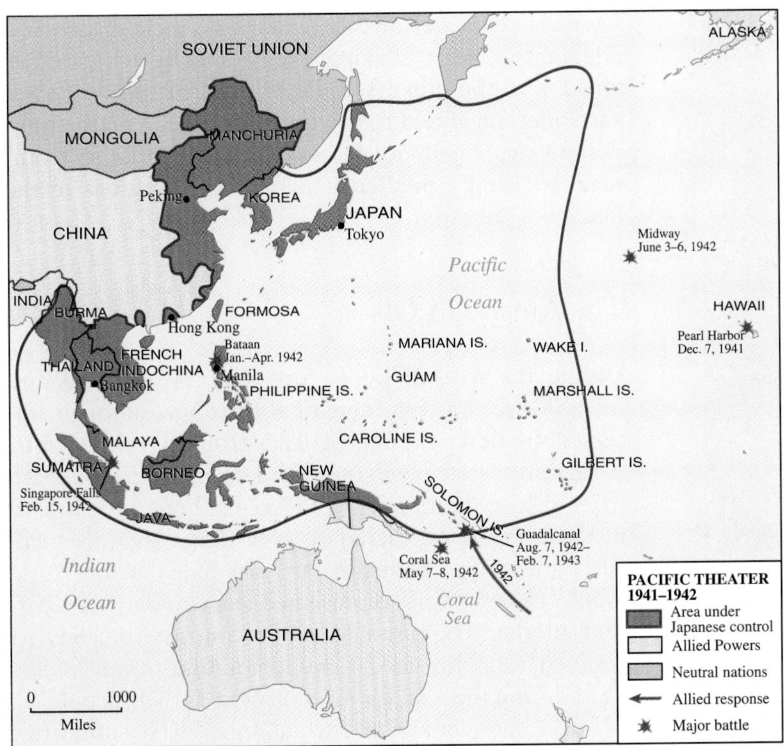

MAP 27.3

War in the Pacific

a. 1941–1942 After the attack on Pearl Harbor in December 1941, the Japanese rapidly extended their domination in the Pacific. The Japanese flag soon flew as far east as the Marshall and Gilbert Islands and as far south as the Solomon Islands and parts of New Guinea. Japan also controlled the Philippines, much of Southeast Asia, and parts of China, including Hong Kong. American naval victories at Coral Sea and Midway finally stopped further Japanese expansion.

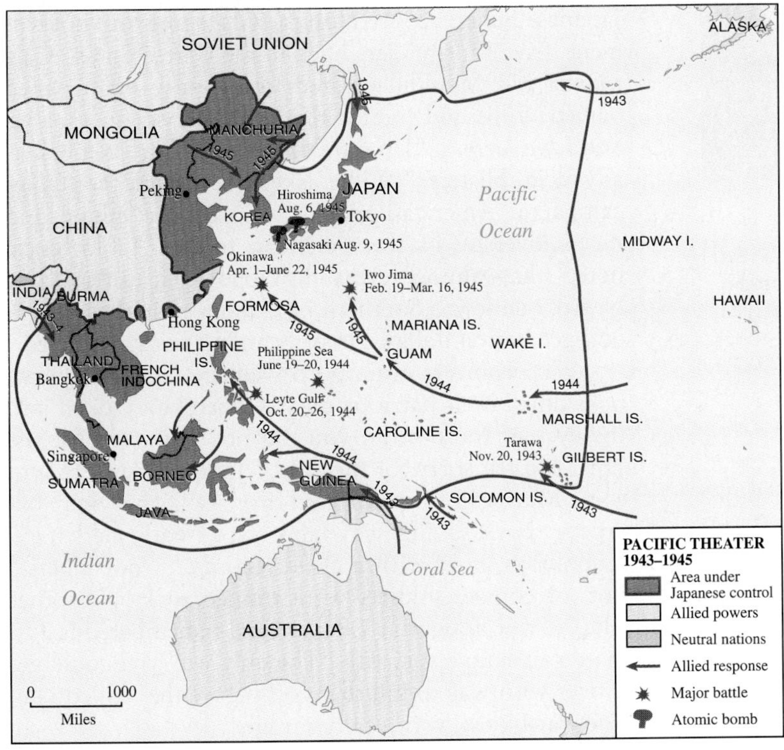

b. 1943–1945 Allied forces retook the islands in the Central Pacific in 1943 and 1944 and the Philippines in early 1945. The capture of Iwo Jima and Okinawa put U.S. bombers in position to attack Japan itself. The Japanese offered to surrender on August 10, after the United States dropped atomic bombs on Hiroshima and Nagasaki.

Throughout the war, the Japanese were far more hated than the Germans. While Americans often differentiated between evil Nazi leaders and ordinary "good Germans," forced to go along with Nazi excesses, they lumped all Japanese together. Racial epithets like "slant eyes" and "yellow monkeys" were widely used in conversation, and even respected magazines like *Time*, *Life*, and *Newsweek* routinely referred to the enemy as "Japs." Between American attitudes towards Japan, and Nazi atrocities against the Jews, racism was a constant undercurrent of World War II.

By early 1945, victory over Japan was in sight. The

A New Type of Naval Warfare
The battles of Coral Sea and Midway in 1942 marked a revolution in naval warfare. For the first time, major sea battles were waged—and decided—primarily by planes launched from aircraft carriers. This panorama shows the vastness of these naval encounters.

campaign in the Pacific moved slowly towards an anticipated massive and costly invasion of Japan. For a successful assault on the main Japanese island, the Americans needed to capture Iwo Jima and Okinawa. Airstrips there would put U.S. planes within striking distance of Tokyo. American Marines won the battles for Iwo Jima (February 1–March 20, 1945) and Okinawa (April 1–June 10) in some of the fiercest fighting of the war. At Iwo Jima, the Marines sustained more than 20,000 casualties, with 6,000 dead; at Okinawa, the toll reached 7,600 dead and 32,000 wounded.

By mid-1945, Japan's land troops, navy, and air force had suffered devastating losses. American bombing of the mainland had killed about 330,000 civilians and crippled the Japanese economy, which had difficulty functioning once oil imports were cut off. In a last-ditch effort to stem the tide, Japanese pilots began *kamikaze* (suicide) missions, crashing their planes and boats into American ships. This desperate action, combined with the Japanese military leadership's refusal to surrender, suggested that Japan would keep up the fight despite overwhelming losses. American military commanders grimly predicted millions of casualties in the upcoming invasion.

The American GIs

During the war, 292,000 Americans were killed and 671,000 wounded in the global fighting. Although stationed in deserts, jungles, and tropical rain forests, American service personnel faced no more risk of death from disease than they would have at home. Because of medical advances, including new drugs such as penicillin and sulfa, the death rate was half that of World War I. The casualties represented less than half of 1 percent of the U.S. population. In contrast, the Soviets counted as many as 20 million military and civilian dead during the war, about 8 percent of their people.

War correspondents such as John Hersey and Ernie Pyle (who was killed in a foxhole on Iwo Jima by a Japanese bullet) reported on the GIs (short for "government issue") for readers back in the United States. Cartoonist Bill Mauldin created two scruffy infantrymen named Willie and Joe for the armed service newspaper *Stars and Stripes*. "Do retreatin' blisters hurt as much as advancin' blisters?" Willie asked Joe during the Italian campaign. American movies stressed the ethnic and racial diversity of the American forces. A film critic noted that almost every war movie featured "one Negro, one Jew, a Southern boy, and a sprinkling of second-generation Italians, Irish, Scandinavians and Poles."

War reporters often portrayed the GIs as ordinary boys doing their patriotic duty. "When you looked into the eyes of those boys, you did not feel sorry for the Japs: you felt sorry for the boys," John Hersey wrote of some Marines in Guadalcanal in 1944. "They were ex-grocery boys, ex-highway laborers, ex-bank clerks, ex-schoolboys, boys with a clean record . . . not killers." But, of course, soldiers were trained to kill. Another Marine who fought at Guadalcanal remembered it as a matter of simple survival: "The only way you could get it over with was to kill them off before they killed you. The war I knew was totally savage."

By the spring of 1945, soldiers who had finished their military duty, which averaged sixteen months, were beginning to return home. Fighting had been a dirty, bloody job, a far cry from their visions of saving democracy or stopping fascism. Dreams of marriage, a house in the suburbs, and a new car sustained many soldiers through the horror and tedium of the war. In 1947, veterans and their families made up a fourth of the American population.

The Big Three at Yalta
With victory in Europe at hand, Roosevelt journeyed to Yalta, on the Black Sea, in February 1945, to meet one last time with Churchill and Stalin. It was here they discussed the problems of peace settlements. The Yalta agreements mirrored a new balance of power and set the stage for the Cold War.

Wartime Diplomacy

Throughout the war, the three leaders of the Grand Alliance continued to meet to discuss military strategy and plan the postwar peace. In January 1943 Roosevelt and Churchill met in Casablanca, Morocco; Stalin could not attend because the Soviet Union's battle against the Germans had reached a crucial point. The main outcome of the Casablanca conference was the Allied demand for unconditional surrender as a condition for victory. In November 1943, Roosevelt, Churchill, and Chiang Kai-shek of China met in Cairo to discuss military operations in the Pacific theater, a conference designed to keep China in the war as a major ally.

Traveling directly from Cairo to Teheran, Iran, Roosevelt finally met Stalin for the first time. As usual, Harry Hopkins was at Roosevelt's side. At the Teheran conference, Roosevelt and Churchill agreed to Stalin's demand for a second front within six months. In return, Stalin promised to join the fight against Japan after the war in Europe ended. Churchill and Roosevelt also agreed tacitly to Stalin's demand that Poland's borders be redrawn to give the Soviet Union more territory. The three men disagreed sharply, however, about who should control the rest of Poland and the other eastern European states. Roosevelt still expressed confidence that the personal rapport he developed with Stalin would aid postwar relations among the superpowers.

Yalta. The three leaders held their last conference in February 1945 at Yalta, a Black Sea resort. Victory in Europe was in sight, but no agreement had been reached on the shape of the peace to come. Roosevelt remained concerned about maintaining Allied unity after the war. Stalin had become increasingly inflexible on the issue of Eastern Europe, insisting that he needed governments there that were well disposed to the Soviet Union to provide a buffer for national security. Roosevelt acknowledged the legitimacy of this demand, but he also hoped for democratically elected regimes in Poland and the neighboring countries.

The compromise reached at Yalta was open to multiple interpretations. Admiral William D. Leahy, Roosevelt's chief military aide, described the agreement as "so elastic that the Russians can stretch it all the way from Yalta to Washington without technically breaking it." At Yalta, Roosevelt and Churchill agreed in principle to the idea of a Soviet sphere of influence in Eastern Europe, but they left its actual dimensions deliberately vague. In return, Stalin pledged to hold "free and unfettered elections" at an unspecified time. (These elections never took place.) Stalin also reaffirmed his commitment to enter the war against Japan.

The Yalta conference also proceeded with plans to divide Germany into four zones, to be controlled by the United States, Great Britain, France, and the Soviet Union. Berlin, which lay in the middle of the Soviet zone, would also be partitioned among the four powers. The issue of German reparations remained unsettled.

The Big Three made further progress towards a postwar international organization: the United Nations. Roosevelt, determined to avoid Woodrow Wilson's mistakes, had already cultivated congressional support; realizing that such an organization would be impotent without the Soviets' participation, he cultivated their support as well. British, American, and Soviet representatives had already met at Dumbarton Oaks, an estate in Washington, D.C., in September 1944 to begin planning the structure of the organization. At Yalta, the Big Three agreed that the Security Council of the United Nations should consist of the five major Allied powers—the United States, Britain, France, China, and the Soviet Union—plus six elected nations on a rotating basis. They also decided that the permanent members of the Security Council should have veto power over decisions of the United Nations General Assembly, in which all nations would be represented. Roosevelt, Churchill, and Stalin announced that the United Nations would convene in San Francisco on April 25, 1945.

Hiroshima

This was all that remained of Hiroshima's Museum of Science and Industry on August 6, 1945. The shell of the building later became the center of Hiroshima's memorial to those who had died in the atomic blast.

Roosevelt returned to the United States in February, visibly exhausted from his 14,000 mile trip. When he reported to Congress on the Yalta agreements, he made an unusual acknowledgment of his physical infirmity. Referring to the heavy steel braces he wore on his legs, he asked Congress to excuse him if he gave his speech sitting down. The sixty-three-year-old president was by now a very sick man, suffering from heart failure and hypertension. On April 12, 1945, during a short visit to his vacation home in Warm Springs, Georgia, the president suffered a cerebral hemorrhage and died. Many Americans could not imagine any leader other than Franklin Roosevelt in the White House. Those who reached adulthood in the 1930s and 1940s had never known another president.

V-E Day came less than a month after Roosevelt died and Harry Truman succeeded to the presidency. The war in the Pacific ended after Truman ordered the dropping of atomic bombs on two Japanese cities, Hiroshima on August 6, and Nagasaki on August 9. Many later questioned why the United States did not provide advance warning about the attack or choose a noncivilian target; the rationale for dropping the second bomb was even less clear. At the time, however, the belief that Japan's military leaders would never surrender unless their country was utterly devastated convinced policymakers that they had no choice but to deploy the new weapon. The atomic bombs killed a hundred thousand people at Hiroshima and sixty thousand at Nagasaki. Tens of thousands more Japanese died slowly of radiation poisoning. Japan offered to surrender on August 10 and signed a formal treaty of surrender on September 2, 1945. World War II had ended, but the atomic age of insecurity had just begun.

The Onset of the Atomic Age

The development of the atomic bomb was closely linked to wartime military strategy. In December 1938, German scientists had discovered that the nuclei of atoms could be split into yet smaller particles, a process called fission. With materials prepared from uranium, a chain reaction of nuclear fission would release tremendous amounts of energy. American scientists like Enrico Fermi and Leo Szilard, many of them refugees from Fascist Italy and Nazi Germany, produced the first controlled chain reaction on December 2, 1942, at the University of Chicago.

Scientists soon began working frantically to harness such nuclear reactions for military purposes. Their goal was the development of an atomic bomb for possible use against Germany or, later, Japan. The secret research, called the Manhattan Project, cost $2 billion, employed 120,000 people, and involved the construction of thirty-seven installations in nineteen states under the direction of General Leslie R. Groves of the U.S. Army Corps of Engineers. In the final stages, a team consisting of most of the country's top physicists assembled the bomb at an isolated desert site in Los Alamos, New Mexico. All of this was hidden from Congress, from the American people, even from Vice-President Truman. The secrecy and scope of this alliance between science and government is one of the most dramatic examples of how much the power of the state grew during wartime.

President Roosevelt followed the bomb's progress closely. He and his advisers planned to deploy the bomb to end the war without the dreadful number of American casualties that had been predicted for an invasion of

Japan. At the same time, policymakers hoped that merely possessing such a powerful weapon—the "master card," in the words of Secretary of War Henry Stimson—would enhance American power in the postwar world. Instead, the new weapon became the first step in a deadly arms race between the United States and the Soviet Union that characterized the postwar period.

Until the last moment, the scientists did not know if the atomic bomb would work. On July 16, 1945, near Alamogordo, New Mexico, they watched in wonder as the test bomb exploded into a huge mushroom cloud. President Truman received news of the successful detonation in Potsdam, near Berlin, where he was about to meet with Churchill and Stalin in the final wartime conference about the shape of postwar Europe. Truman, who had not even known about the bomb before he became president, was ecstatic about its potential. After the bombing of Hiroshima, he told aides, "This is the greatest thing in history." Others were not so sure. J. Robert Oppenheimer, one of the leading scientists on the Manhattan Project, watched the test on that early July morning in the New Mexico desert. Overwhelmed by its frightening power, he recalled the words from the *Bhagavad Gita*, the Hindu bible: "I am become Death, Destroyer of Worlds."

Summary

With the rise of fascism and totalitarianism in Germany, Italy, and Japan, the international situation deteriorated rapidly throughout the 1930s, and the world was again at war by 1939. Although most Americans opposed participation, clinging to strong isolationist sentiment, President Roosevelt began mobilizing public opinion for intervention. The Japanese attack on Pearl Harbor on December 7, 1941, brought the nation into World War II.

Defense mobilization ended the Great Depression. As had happened during World War I, mobilization led to a dramatic expansion of the state. On the home front, the war resulted in rationing and shortages of many items. Geographical mobility increased as labor shortages opened job opportunities for women, blacks, and Mexican-Americans. The ideological climate of fighting Nazism aided the cause of civil rights. However, Japanese-Americans on the West Coast suffered a devastating denial of civil liberties when the government moved them into internment camps.

World War II was a global war, consisting of massive military campaigns in both Europe and the Pacific. The war news was bleak at first, but by 1943 the Allies had started to move toward victory. At the same time, Roosevelt attempted to maintain harmony among the United States, Great Britain, and the Soviet Union. Many of the disagreements over wartime diplomacy turned into major problems in the postwar world. Of all the major powers that fought in World War II, only the United States emerged physically unharmed. And at the end of the war, only the United States had the powerful new weapon, the atomic bomb.

TOPIC FOR RESEARCH

Hollywood Goes to War

After Pearl Harbor, the Office of War Information asked Hollywood to concentrate on six subjects as part of the war effort: the enemy, the Allies, the armed forces, war production, the homefront, and the issues. Choose a film made during the war, either a popular film or a documentary, and analyze it as a document about American participation and attitudes about the war. How useful is it as a historical source? Is its historical accuracy, or lack thereof, less important than its role in boosting patriotism and morale? Films about the armed services include *Wake Island* (1942), *Guadalcanal Diary* (1943), *So Proudly We Hail* (1943), *Lifeboat* (1944), *Thirty Seconds Over Tokyo* (1945), and *Keep Your Powder Dry* (1945). Frank Capra's *Why We Fight* series and John Huston's *Battle of San Pietro* (1944) are powerful documentaries. The best homefront film is probably *Since You Went Away* (1943). A cult classic like *Casablanca* (1942) looks different when watched through the lens of wartime America.

John E. O'Connor, ed., *Image as Artifact: The His-*

torical Analysis of Film and Television (1990) is an excellent introduction to using films as historical sources. For Hollywood in the 1940s, see Clayton R. Koppes and Gregory D. Black, *Hollywood Goes to War: How Politics, Profits, and Propaganda Shaped World War II Movies* (1987). See also Douglas Gomery and Robert Allen, *Film History: Theory and Practice* (1985), and David Bordwell, Janet Staiger, and Kristin Thompson, *The Classical Hollywood Cinema: Film Style and Mode of Production to 1960* (1985).

BIBLIOGRAPHY

John Morton Blum, *V Was For Victory* (1976), offers a good introduction to American politics and culture during the war years. Also useful are Richard Polenberg, *War and Society* (1972); Geoffrey Perrett, *Days of Sadness, Years of Triumph* (1973); and Richard Lingeman, *Don't You Know There's a War On?* (1970). A powerful and provocative oral history of the war is Studs Terkel, "*The Good War*" (1984). John Keegan, *The Second World War* (1990) offers the best one-volume account of the battlefront aspects.

The Road to War

Depression and wartime diplomacy are effectively covered in Robert Dallek, *Franklin D. Roosevelt and American Foreign Policy, 1932–1945* (1979). For more on American policy between the wars, see Lloyd Gardner, *Economic Aspects of New Deal Diplomacy* (1964), and Selig Adler, *The Uncertain Giant* (1966). William L. Langer and S. Everett Gleason provide a detailed chronology of American entry in *The Challenge to Isolation, 1937–1940* (1952) and *The Undeclared War, 1940–1941* (1953); see also Robert Divine, *The Reluctant Belligerent* (1965). For American isolationism, see Wayne Cole, *Roosevelt and the Isolationists, 1932–1945* (1983) and *Charles S. Lindbergh and the Battle Against American Intervention in World War II* (1974); Selig Adler, *The Isolationist Impulse* (1957); and Manfred Jonas, *Isolationism in America* (1966). Warren T. Kimball, *The Most Unsordid Act* (1969), describes the Lend-Lease controversy of 1939–1941. Roberta Wohlstetter, *Pearl Harbor* (1962), Herbert Feis, *The Road to Pearl Harbor* (1950), and Gordon W. Prange, *At Dawn We Slept* (1981), describe the final chain of events that led to American entry. George McJimsey, *Harry Hopkins* (1987), covers both the New Deal and Hopkins's wartime contributions. See also the rich portrait supplied by former Roosevelt speechwriter Robert E. Sherwood in his *Roosevelt and Hopkins* (1948).

Mobilizing for Victory

George Flynn, *The Mess in Washington* (1979); Bruce Catton, *War Lords of Washington* (1964); Donald Nelson, *Arsenal of Democracy* (1946); Gerald T. White, *Billions for Defense* (1980); and Harold G. Vatter, *The U.S. Economy in World War II* (1985), discuss America's economic mobilization. David Brinkley, *Washington Goes to War* (1988), offers an engaging journalistic perspective. Alan Winkler, *The Politics of Propaganda* (1978), covers the Office of War Information. On labor's role during war, see Joel Seidman, *American Labor From Defense to Reconstruction* (1953); Nelson Lichtenstein, *Labor's War at Home: The CIO in World War II* (1982); Howell Harris, *The Right to Manage* (1982); and Paul Koistinen, *The Hammer and the Sword: Labor, the Military, and Industrial Mobilization, 1920–1945* (1979). James C. Foster, *The Union Politic* (1975), details the CIO's political involvement. For more on politics in wartime, see James McGregor Burns, *Roosevelt: The Soldier of Freedom* (1970).

Women's roles in wartime are covered by Susan Hartmann, *The Home Front and Beyond* (1982); Karen Anderson, *Wartime Women* (1980); Leila J. Rupp, *Mobilizing Women for War* (1978); William H. Chafe, *The American Woman* (1972); Ruth Milkman, *Gender at Work* (1987); and Sherna B. Gluck, *Rosie the Riveter Revisited: Women, the War, and Social Change* (1987).

Life on the Home Front

Additional material on America during the war can be gleaned from Richard Polenberg, ed., *The War at Home* (1968), and Lester Chandler, *Inflation in the United States, 1940–1948* (1951). Alan Clive, *State of War* (1979), provides a case study of Michigan during the war. See also Gerald D. Nash, *The American West Transformed: The Impact of the Second World War* (1985), and Marc Scott Miller, *The Irony of Victory: World War II and Lowell, Massachusetts* (1988). The experience of black Americans is treated by Albert Russell Buchanan, *Black Americans in World War II* (1977); Neil Wynn, *The Afro-American and the Second World War* (1975); and Louis Ruchames, *Race, Jobs, and Politics* (1953). For racial tensions, see Dominic Capeci, Jr., *Race Relations in Wartime Detroit* (1984), and Mauricio Mazan, *The Zoot Suit Riots* (1984). August Meier and Elliott Rudwick, *CORE* (1973), describes the founding of this important civil rights organization. Richard Dalfiume, *Desegregation of the U.S. Armed Forces* (1969), covers black soldiers in the military. Alan Berube, *Coming Out Under Fire* (1990), is an oral history of gay men and lesbians in the military; see also John D'Emilio, *Sexual Politics, Sexual Communities* (1983), for the impact of the war on gay Americans. Maurice Isserman,

Which Side Were You On? (1982), analyzes the American Communist party during the war. Two compelling accounts of Japanese relocation are Audre Girdner and Anne Loftus, *The Great Betrayal* (1969), and Roger Daniels, *Concentration Camps, U.S.A.* (1972). See also John Tateishi, ed., *And Justice for All: An Oral History of the Japanese-American Detention Camps* (1984), and Peter Irons, *Justice at War: The Story of the Japanese-American Internment Cases* (1983).

Fighting and Winning the War

Extensive material chronicles the American military experience during World War II. Albert Russell Buchanan, *The United States and World War II* (1962), and Russell F. Weigley, *The American Way of War* (1973), provide overviews; Ronald Schaffer, *Wings of Judgement: American Bombing in World War II* (1985), and Bradley F. Smith, *The Shadow Warriors: OSS and the Origins of the CIA* (1983) are more specialized. Cornelius Ryan, *The Last Battle* (1966), and John Toland, *The Last Hundred Days* (1966), describe the end of the fighting in Europe. David S. Wyman, *The Abandonment of the Jews* (1984), devastatingly describes the lack of American response to the Holocaust from 1941 to 1945. For the Far East, see John W. Dower, *War Without Mercy: Race and Power in the Pacific War* (1986); Ronald H. Spector, *Eagle Against the Sun: The American War With Japan* (1984); John Toland, *Rising Sun: The Decline and Fall of the Japanese Empire* (1970); William Manchester, *American Caesar* (1979) on General Douglas MacArthur; and Barbara Tuchman, *Stillwell and the American Experience in China* (1971).

American diplomacy and the strategy of the Grand Alliance are surveyed in Dallek, *Franklin D. Roosevelt and American Foreign Policy*; William McNeill, *America, Britain, and Russia, 1941–1946* (1953); and Gaddis Smith, *American Diplomacy During the Second World War* (1965). The relationship between the wartime conferences and the onset of the Cold War are treated by Walter LaFeber, *America, Russia, and the Cold War* (6th ed., 1990); Stephen Ambrose, *Rise to Globalism* (5th ed., 1988); John L. Gaddis, *The United States and the Origins of the Cold War* (1972); and Herbert Feis, *Between War and Peace* (1960). Richard Rhodes, *The Making of the Atomic Bomb* (1987); McGeorge Bundy, *Danger and Survival* (1988); and Martin Sherwin, *A World Destroyed* (1975), provide compelling accounts of the development of the bomb. See also Gar Alperowitz, *Atomic Diplomacy* (1965), and Gregg Herken, *The Winning Weapon* (1980). John Hersey, *Hiroshima* (2nd ed., 1985), on the aftermath of the bombing, retains its power forty years after its original publication.

TIMELINE

1935–1937	Neutrality Acts
1938	Munich agreement "War of the Worlds" broadcast
1939	World War II breaks out in Europe
1940	Conscription reinstated
1941	Lend-Lease Fair Employment Practices Commission Atlantic Charter Japanese attack Pearl Harbor
1942–1945	Rationing
1942	Women recruited for war industries Japanese relocation Revenue Act of 1942
1943	Race riots in Detroit and Los Angeles Fascism falls in Italy Teheran Conference
1944	D-Day (June 6) Reconquest of Philippines GI Bill
1945	Germany surrenders (May 8) Battles of Iwo Jima and Okinawa Yalta Conference Harry S. Truman becomes president upon Roosevelt's death United Nations Atomic bombs dropped on Hiroshima and Nagasaki Japan surrenders (September 2)

PART 6

America and the World

1945 to the Present

THEMATIC TIMELINE

	Diplomacy	Government	Economy	Society	Culture
	The Cold War Era—and after	**Redefining the role of the state**	**Rise and fall of *Pax Americana***	**Social movements and demographic diversity**	**A consumer society**
1945	Truman Doctrine (1947) Marshall Plan (1948) NATO founded (1949)	Truman's Fair Deal liberalism Employment Act	Bretton Woods system established: World Bank, IMF, GATT	Migration to cities accelerates Armed forces desegregated	End of wartime rationing Rise of television
1950	Permanent mobilization: NSC-68 (1950) Korean War (1950–53) McCarthyism	Eisenhower's modern Republicanism Interstate Highway Act (1956) Warren Court activism	Rise of military-industrial complex Labor movement at peak strength Service sector expands	*Brown v. Board of Education* (1954) Montgomery bus boycott SCLC founded	Growth of suburbia Baby boom Shopping malls spread
1960	Cuban missile crisis (1962) Nuclear Test-ban Treaty (1963) Gulf of Tonkin Resolution (1964); Vietnam War escalates	Kennedy and politics of expectation High tide of liberalism: the Great Society, War on Poverty Nixon ushers in conservative era	Kennedy-Johnson tax cut, military expenditures fuel economic growth	Student activism Civil Rights Act; Voting Rights Act Revival of feminism	Baby boomers swell college enrollments Youth counterculture
1970	Nixon visits China (1972) SALT initiates détente (1972) Paris Peace Accords (1973)	Watergate scandal; Nixon resigns (1974) Deregulation begins under Ford and Carter	Arab oil embargo (1973–74); inflation surges Deindustrialization begins	First Earth Day (1970) *Roe v. Wade* (1973) New Right urges conservative agenda	Gasoline shortages hit commuters, travel industry Apple introduces first personal computer (1977)
1980	Reagan arms buildup INF treaty Berlin Wall falls	Reagan Revolution Supreme Court conservatism	Reaganomics Budget and trade deficits soar Savings and loan bailout	Televangelists mobilize evangelical Protestants New Hispanic and Asian immigration	MTV debuts Wall Street greed AIDS epidemic
1990	War in the Persian Gulf U.S.S.R. disintegrates; end of the Cold War	Democratic party adopts "moderate" policies	Recession	Earth Summit (1992) Third wave of feminism	Health-care crisis Standard of living declines

Few years marked such a definitive turning point as 1945. In that year Americans celebrated the end of World War II and mourned the death of Franklin D. Roosevelt, who had led the country longer than any other president. The task of setting the goals for the United States in the postwar world fell to Harry S. Truman.

First, it was Truman and his advisers who shaped the diplomacy of the postwar world. With Germany and Japan prostrate in defeat and Britain and France severely weakened by six years of war, the normal balance of power was shattered. The United States, the most powerful country in the world, now played a hegemonic role in global affairs. The price of American hegemony was a permanent commitment to engagement in the international arena. When the Soviet Union challenged America's vision of postwar Europe, the Truman administration responded by crafting the policies and alliances that came to define the Cold War. American policymakers came to interpret almost every international event as a conflict between communism and the free world. The Cold War spawned two long "hot" wars, in Korea and Vietnam, and a terrifying direct confrontation between the two superpowers in the Cuban missile crisis. Although the policy of détente pursued by Richard Nixon and later presidents succeeded in easing tensions, the cold war mentality held sway until the final collapse and disintegration of the Soviet Union in 1991.

Second, thanks to the growth of a military-industrial complex of enormous size and the expansion of consumer culture, the quarter century after 1945 represented the heyday of American capitalism, an economic *Pax Americana*. Economic dominance abroad translated into years of unparalleled affluence at home. In the early 1970s competition from other countries began to challenge America's economic supremacy. And Americans learned that overseas commitments could have a severe and direct impact on their lives, as when the Arab nations cut off oil exports to the United States to retaliate for America's support for Israel.

Third, America's global commitments had dramatic consequences for American government and politics. Until the national consensus fractured over the Vietnam War, liberals and conservatives agreed on keeping the country in a state of permanent mobilization and maintaining a large and well-equipped military establishment. And all administrations, Republican or Democratic, were willing to intervene in the economy when private initiatives could not maintain steady economic growth. But liberals also pushed for a larger federal government role in the area of social welfare. Under Truman, John F. Kennedy, and especially Lyndon Johnson, the government went beyond the New Deal to erect an extensive federal and state apparatus to provide for the social well-being of the people. During Nixon's and, above all, Reagan's presidencies, conservatives cut back on many of the major programs but failed to eliminate any of them completely.

Fourth, the victory over fascism in World War II led to renewed calls for America to make good on its promise of liberty and equality for all. In great waves of protests in the 1950s and 1960s, African-Americans, then women, Hispanics, and other minorities challenged the political domination of elite white men. The resulting hard-won reforms dramatically expanded the democratic system, although the promise of full equality remains unfulfilled.

Today, half a century after the end of World War II, Americans are living in an increasingly interwoven mesh of national and international experience. Outside events shape ordinary lives in ways that would have been inconceivable a century earlier. As the Cold War Era fades into history, the outlines of a new world order are beginning to emerge. The United States remains the sole military superpower, but it shares economic leadership in the new interdependent global economy. Will international cooperation—to preserve the environment and alleviate hunger, to stop nuclear proliferation, civil strife, and regional conflicts—replace the old cold war patterns of confrontation? Or will the United States pull back from its global commitments to focus on domestic renewal? The next chapter of America's history remains to be written.

Danger and Survival

With its first successful test of a hydrogen bomb in 1952, America entered into the nuclear age.

CHAPTER 28 *Cold War America, 1945–1960*

When Harry Truman was summoned to the White House on April 12, 1945, after learning of Roosevelt's death, he asked the president's widow, "Is there anything I can do for you?" Eleanor Roosevelt responded with another question, "Is there anything we can do for you? For you are the one in trouble now."

Harry Truman inherited the presidency at one of the most important, and perilous, watersheds in modern American history. World War II ended two centuries of relative isolation from world diplomatic affairs and brought about a revolution in American foreign policy. The United States emerged from the war as the most powerful country in the world, and it deliberately set about to create conditions that maintained this global supremacy. Only the Soviet Union posed a real obstacle to American hegemony. Soon the two superpowers were locked in a Cold War that took economic, political, and military forms.

The dramatic shift in American foreign relations after 1945 had important domestic repercussions. In keeping with the centralization of American life and culture throughout the twentieth century, decisions made in Washington, and in other capitals across the world, now had an impact on ordinary lives. Reflecting the blurring of the lines between international and domestic events that characterized the postwar world, America's new global commitments fostered a climate of fear and suspicion about internal subversion at home. But the fruits of internationalism also fostered a period of unprecedented affluence and prosperity which gave the United States the highest standard of living in the world (see Chapter 29). America's global hegemony lasted through the early 1970s.

The Origins of the Cold War

The defeat of Germany and Japan did not bring stability to the world. Even before the end of World War II, the grand alliance among the United States, Britain, and the Soviet Union was disintegrating over differences in interpreting the Yalta and Potsdam agreements. Within two years the United States and the Soviet Union would be engaged in a global ideological and strategic struggle that historians call the Cold War. Cold war assumptions fundamentally shaped American and Soviet priorities for the next four decades.

Descent into Cold War, 1945–1946

Franklin Roosevelt had hoped that the establishment of the United Nations would provide a forum to help resolve postwar conflicts. When Roosevelt died in April 1945, American support for the United Nations became in part a memorial to the late president's hopes for the postwar peace. Avoiding the disagreements that had doomed American participation in the League of Nations after World War I, the Senate approved American participation in the United Nations by a margin of 80 to 2. One of the United Nations' most tireless supporters—and a member of the U.S. delegation from 1946 to 1953—was the president's widow, Eleanor Roosevelt.

Although Roosevelt heartily supported the United Nations, he also believed it was essential for the United States to continue good relations with the only other power whose strength realistically rivaled that of the

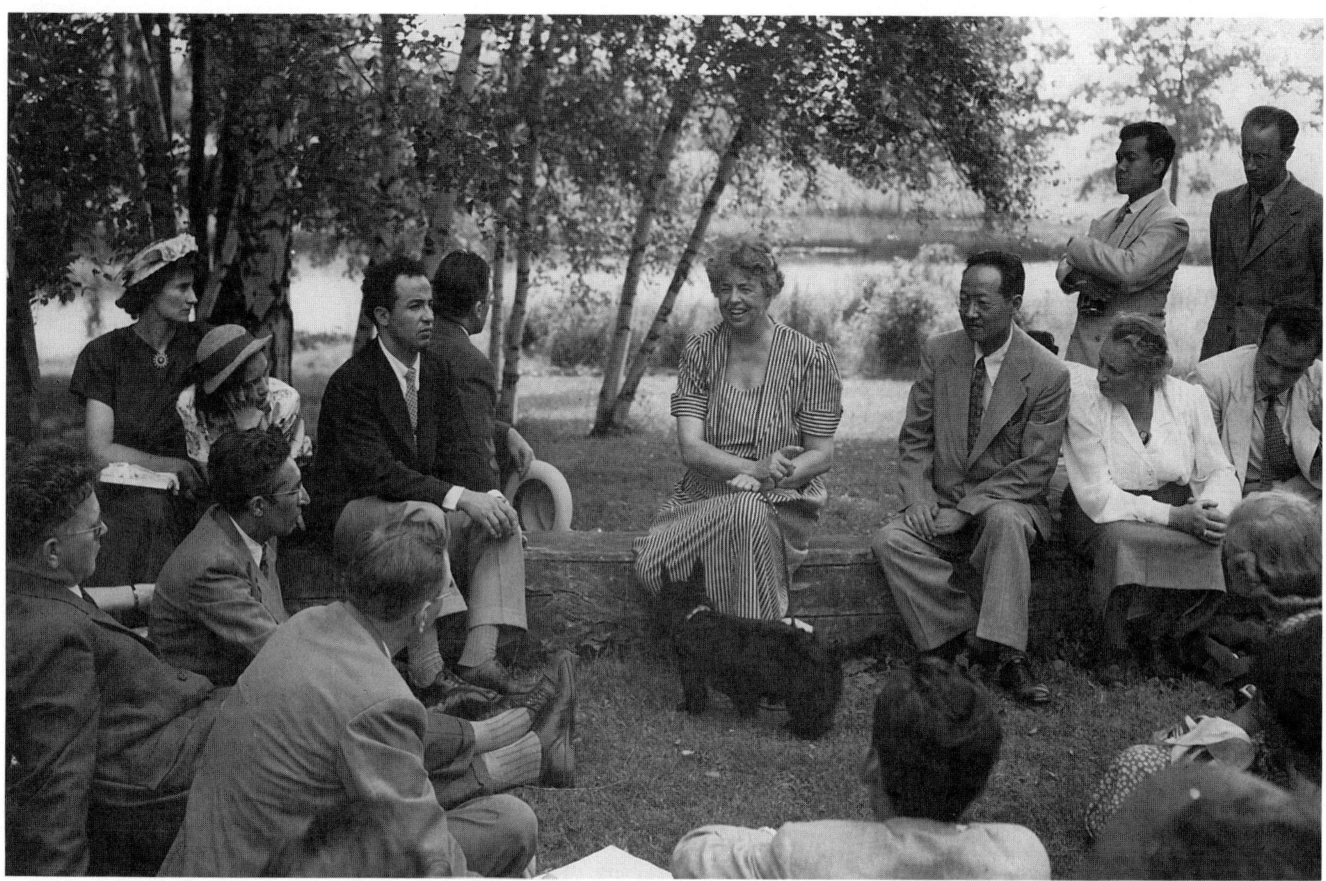

Eleanor Roosevelt, U.N. Representative

Eleanor Roosevelt won over her fellow members of the United Nations delegation by doing her homework and standing firm on her convictions. Republican John Foster Dulles admitted to her later, "I feel I must tell you that when you were appointed I thought it terrible and now I think your work here has been fine!" Eleanor Roosevelt was proudest of her role in drafting the 1948 Universal Declaration of Human Rights. Here she entertains delegates from UNESCO at her home in Hyde Park, New York, accompanied by the Roosevelt dog, Fala.

United States in 1945, the Soviet Union. Yet events in the immediate postwar period proved far too controversial to be settled amicably between the two great powers. Within twenty-four hours of taking over the presidency, Harry Truman questioned whether the United States could cooperate with its former wartime ally. "We must stand up to the Russians," he stated privately.

Why did the Grand Alliance fall into disarray so quickly in the immediate postwar period? Events in Eastern Europe caused the most bitter conflicts among the former allies. As the Soviet army drove the Germans out of Russia and back through Romania, Bulgaria, and Hungary, Soviet-sponsored, provisional governments were established in those countries. At the Yalta conference, both American and British diplomats, including President Roosevelt, had in effect agreed to recognize this Soviet "sphere of influence" in the region occupied by the Red Army along its borders. But as soon as the war ended, Truman backed away from the Yalta pledges. The new president berated Soviet Foreign Minister V. M. Molotov for imposing a Soviet-controlled government on Poland. Molotov had never "been talked to like that in my life," he told Truman. "Then keep your agreements!" Truman retorted. The Soviets had already gutted them anyway, by reneging on their pledge to allow free elections, suppressing democratic parties, and installing puppet governments.

No country so embodied the different visions that the United States and the Soviet Union had for the postwar world than Germany. At Yalta, the defeated German state had been divided into four occupation zones controlled by the United States, France, England, and the Soviet Union. By 1946, the United States was encouraging the gradual reindustrialization of the German industrial heartland within its zone as part of its general goal of reviving the European economy. For its part, the Soviet Union began to develop the industrial capacities of its zone. The economic base was thus laid for what eventually became the political division into East and West Germany.

A critical source of tension in 1946 was the question of atomic weapons. The United States enjoyed the sole possession of the atomic bomb, and while leaders were willing to consider international control of atomic energy in the long run, they were loathe to give up their immediate advantage. In a plan submitted to the United Nations, the United States proposed a system of international control that relied on mandatory inspection and control but preserved the American monopoly. The Soviets rejected the plan categorically. This climate of mutual suspicion and distrust undercut any hope for international cooperation to develop atomic energy for peaceful purposes.

Former British prime minister Winston Churchill articulated the deepening pessimism about the Soviet Union shared by American diplomats by 1946. Out of power and eager for a platform to put forward his views, Churchill accepted an invitation from President Truman to deliver a major policy address in March 1946 in Fulton, Missouri. Churchill had gone along with plans for a Soviet sphere of influence in Eastern Europe at Yalta, but now had second thoughts, warning ominously about the "expansive tendencies" of the Soviet Union: "From Stettin in the Baltic to Trieste in the Adriatic, an Iron Curtain has descended across the Continent." If the West hoped to preserve peace and freedom in the face of the Soviet challenge, Churchill declared, it must remember that "there is nothing they [the Soviets] admire so much as strength, and there is nothing for which they have less respect than for weakness, especially military weakness."

Churchill's widely publicized "Iron Curtain speech" helped convince many Americans that the Soviet Union posed a dangerous threat to national security. This shift represented a return to the American hostility towards Bolshevism first articulated by Woodrow Wilson after the 1917 revolution, a distrust that had delayed recognition of the Soviet Union until 1933. The wartime collaboration necessitated by the common fight against fascism receded quickly from memory. For the next forty years, the popular rhetoric adopted by American and Soviet leaders painted international relations in harsh ideological terms—democracy versus totalitarianism, the free world versus the Iron Curtain, capitalism versus communism.

The strident dichotomies of the Cold War mask a more complex global reality, however. As the dominant player in the world system after World War II, it was in the self-interest of the United States to make the world more unitary, more interdependent, more open to capitalist penetration. The domination of the Soviet Union over Eastern Europe violated this goal; so too did political instability or underdevelopment in third world countries. Behind American rhetoric about democracy, free trade, and anticommunism lay a commitment to fostering a world economy that provided the most conducive conditions for the major industrial countries like the United States to flourish. The integration of a reindustrialized Japan into the Asian economy, the creation of a revitalized common European market, and the Cold War isolation of the Soviet bloc were all goals designed to maintain American hegemony. This global context provides important background for understanding many of the key conflicts of the postwar world.

From the Truman Doctrine to NATO, 1947–1949

By 1947 a new American policy—called *containment*—was taking shape. Although its precepts were widely shared in Washington policymaking circles, containment is usually associated with George F. Kennan, an intense, scholarly diplomat who had devoted his entire career to the study of the Soviet Union. Kennan first articulated containment's basic premises in February 1946 in an eight-thousand-word cable from his post at the U.S. Embassy in Moscow to his superiors in Washington, where it was widely circulated. He expanded on these ideas in an influential article in the journal *Foreign Affairs* in July 1947. According to Kennan (who was identified only as "X"), the Soviets moved "inexorably along the prescribed path, like a persistent toy automobile wound up and headed in a given direction, stopping only when it meets unanswerable force." To stop this expansionism, it was necessary to pursue a policy of "firm containment, designed to confront the Russians with unalterable counterforce at every point where they show signs of encroaching upon the interests of a peaceful and stable world."

Kennan's initial formulation envisioned economic and diplomatic means as the way to enforce containment, but the policy soon took on a military cast. In one version or another, containment defined the foreign policy of every subsequent administration, both Democratic and Republican, well into the 1980s. It served at least three purposes. Identifying an evil, expansionist enemy, the containment doctrine called on Americans to unite behind the president in order to counter the threat; it justified the creation of a vast peacetime military machine; and it masked other objectives of American foreign policy in the economic arena and the Third World.

AMERICAN LIVES

The Wise Men

They were, as their biographers Walter Isaacson and Evan Thomas neatly tallied it up, two bankers (W. Averill Harriman, Robert Lovett), two lawyers (Dean Acheson, John McCloy), and two diplomats (Charles Bohlen, George Kennan). These six friends were among the main architects of the containment policy which dominated American foreign policy from the 1940s through at least the 1960s. Individually their names are not that well known—certainly not in comparison to the presidents and military leaders of the time—but collectively they had an enormous impact on postwar developments. They represent a cross section of what British journalist Henry Fairlie first called in 1955 "the establishment." In 1965, presidential aide McGeorge Bundy dubbed these senior statesmen "the wise men," and the name stuck.

At first glance, the social profile of the six men, all born between 1893 and 1904, suggests that the foreign policy elite was synonymous with the rich and the powerful in the United States. W. Averill Harriman was the son of the founder of the Union Pacific Railroad and Robert Lovett's father was the elder Harriman's second-in-command. Dean Acheson was the son of the Episcopal bishop of Connecticut, and Charles Bohlen was descended from the first American ambassador to France. But the establishment was more of a meritocracy than a closed club: John McCloy came from a poor family in Philadelphia and George Kennan was an outsider from Milwaukee. Access to education at the elite Eastern institutions that trained generations of leaders—prep schools like Groton and St. Paul, colleges such as Harvard, Yale, or Princeton—was crucial to membership. Averill Harriman taught Dean Acheson to row crew at Groton, they went off to Yale together, and their lives remained linked until they died.

After graduation from college, these privileged young men embarked on careers, mainly on Wall Street or in Washington. Charles Bohlen went into the foreign service, and became a specialist in Soviet affairs; he was assigned to the first United States mission to that country in 1934. George Kennan was also a foreign service officer in Moscow during the 1930s. Dean Acheson

President Truman (far left) confers with Secretary of State Robert Lovett and State Department aides George Kennan and Charles Bohlen (from left to right). In the photo on the right, Averill Harriman (left) and President Harry Truman (right) greet Secretary of State Dean Acheson on his return from a NATO conference in 1952. McCloy is not shown.

spent most of the 1920s and 1930s in private legal practice, as did John McCloy; W. Averill Harriman devoted his attention to business, and Robert Lovett worked with the banking firm of Brown Brothers, which merged with the Harriman empire in 1931.

One common thread among the six lives in the 1920s and 1930s was extensive contact with European affairs, including familiarity with the Soviet Union. The result was a collective internationalism which stood in stark contrast to the prevailing isolationism of the 1930s. Not surprisingly, all six ended up in Washington during World War II, a period when their personal and professional relationships coalesced. McCloy and Lovett served as assistant secretaries of war, where they were known as "the Heavenly Twins"; Harriman was ambassador to the Soviet Union, where one of his advisors was George Kennan; Acheson became assistant secretary of state for economic affairs; and Bohlen served as the State Department's chief translator and expert in Soviet affairs, accompanying Roosevelt to Teheran and Yalta.

When the war ended, the six men all joined the Truman administration and embarked on seven years of extraordinary power and influence at one of the most critical moments in modern American history: the onset of the Cold War, and the formulation of the policy of containment of the Soviet Union through diplomacy or force. Although containment is associated with George Kennan, its underlying assumptions were shared by all six. They fervently believed that the United States had a moral destiny to provide world leadership in the struggle against communism. The Truman Doctrine and the Marshall Plan epitomized the sweeping commitments they were willing to undertake to promote this world view.

The policy-making process in the Truman administration was fairly intimate and decentralized, and hence amenable to the kind of behind-the-scenes power these members of the establishment thrived on. Acheson was the most influential of the group, serving as undersecretary of state from 1945 to 1947 and then secretary of state from 1949 to 1953. Charles Bohlen was his special assistant, until Bohlen was named minister to France in 1949. George Kennan also served in various capacities in the State Department before being named ambassador to the Soviet Union in 1951. Averill Harriman joined the cabinet as secretary of commerce, and then became a special assistant to the president, where he played a key role in setting strategy for the conduct of the Korean war. John McCloy served as president of the World Bank and became a vigorous proponent of the Marshall Plan; in 1949 Truman named him U.S. high commissioner for Germany.

These six men wielded power individually, but their impact was enhanced by how they functioned as a group. They shared much in common, especially their belief in the Cold War ideology of containment. Just as important was their commitment to public service: remarkably free of personal ambition, they saw themselves as public servants above the fray of partisan politics. However, their pattern of moving in and out of government to lucrative positions on Wall Street suggests that they had no trouble reconciling public service with private gain.

Dwight Eisenhower's election sent most of the Wise Men into temporary retirement from public service, but the election of John Kennedy in 1960 called them in from what their biographers called "the wilderness years." Now generally in their fifties and sixties, this older generation served the young president in a variety of capacities—Bohlen and Kennan as ambassadors to France and Yugoslavia, respectively; Harriman as assistant secretary of state for Far Eastern affairs; McCloy, Lovett, and Acheson as advisers. Their service demonstrates the continuity of the postwar foreign policy elite from World War II through the 1960s.

After Kennedy's assassination, Lyndon Johnson continued to seek their counsel, especially as the Vietnam War escalated. But these six men, who had so forcefully supported standing up to communism in the 1940s and 1950s, now began to doubt the American commitment in Southeast Asia. One by one, they dropped their support for the war and some like Kennan, who was now a professor at Princeton's Institute for Advanced Study, criticized it publicly. At a March 1968 meeting of the Wise Men, even Dean Acheson, the epitome of the establishment, told Johnson that the United States had to get out of Vietnam. The defection of the foreign policy elite, those who had framed the Cold War, played a major role in Johnson's decision to begin negotiations to end the Vietnam War.

The Wise Men proved to be a hardy bunch, with Harriman, Lovett, and McCloy living into their nineties. They shared the experience of shaping America's Cold War policy and overseeing the dramatic expansion of American power and influence in the 1950s and 1960s. But of those who had been "present at the creation" (Acheson's modestly titled memoirs), only George Kennan was still alive to see the end of the Cold War and the dissolution of the Soviet Union. These events would no doubt have astounded, and pleased, the "wise men" who had so tirelessly served their country in the post war years.

The emerging policy of confronting the Soviets with counterforce crystallized in 1947 over the situation in Greece. Local Communist-inspired guerrillas, whom American advisers mistakenly believed were controlled by Moscow, had fought for control of Greece since the end of 1944. After postwar elections installed the royalist Popular Party in the spring of 1946, several thousand Communist guerrillas launched a full-scale civil war against the government and the British occupation authorities. In February 1947 the British informed Truman that they could no longer afford to assist the Greek anti-Communists. "If Greece was lost," Truman argued, Stalin "would then direct the Communist parties of Italy and France to grab for power" and thus threaten to bring the industrially developed regions of Western Europe into the Soviet sphere. Of more serious and immediate concern to the administration was the threat that potential Soviet domination posed to American and European influence in the eastern Mediterranean and the Middle East, especially in strategically located Turkey, and the oil-rich state of Iran.

To counter this perceived menace, the president announced what became known as the Truman Doctrine. In a speech to Congress on March 12, asking military and economic assistance to Greece and Turkey, President Truman called for all Americans to fight communism on a global level and "to support free peoples who are resisting attempted subjugation by armed minorities or by outside pressures." To win popular support for this unprecedented change in the U.S. stance toward the rest of the world, and to squeeze money out of a stingy Congress, the president followed the advice of Republican Senator Arthur Vandenberg "to scare the hell out of the country." Not just Greece, but freedom itself, was at issue, Truman declared: "If we falter in our leadership, we may endanger the peace of the world—and we shall surely endanger the welfare of our own Nation." Despite the open-endedness of this military and political commitment, Congress in a show of bipartisan support quickly approved Truman's request for $300 million in aid to Greece and $100 million for Turkey. This appropriation reversed the postwar policy of sharp cuts in foreign spending.

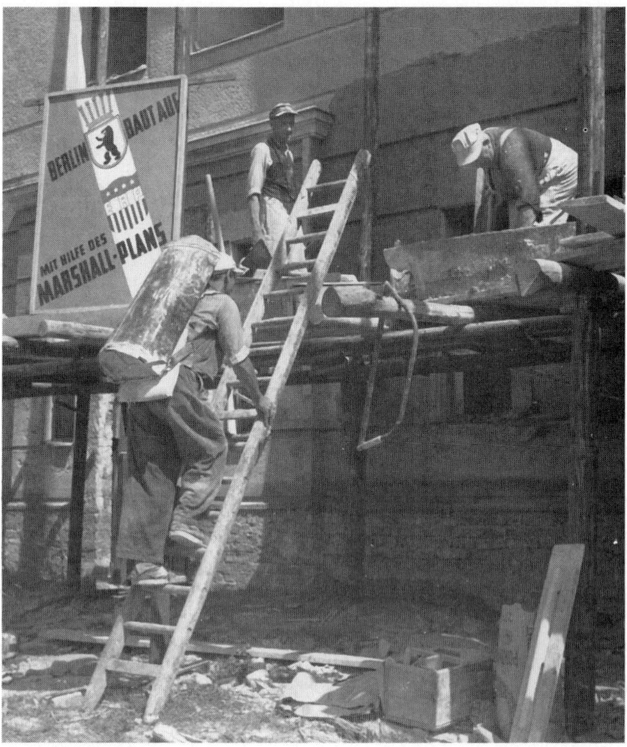

The Marshall Plan in Action

Between 1948 and 1951, the European Recovery Program, popularly known as the Marshall Plan for Secretary of State George C. Marshall, contributed over $13 billion toward its objective of "restoring the confidence of the European people in the economic future of their own countries and of Europe as a whole." Here a sign prominently announces that Berlin is being rebuilt with help from the Marshall Plan.

The Marshall Plan. Two weeks after Congress approved aid to Greece and Turkey, Secretary of State George Marshall proposed a plan to provide economic as well as military aid to Europe. European economies had been devastated by the war, and conditions worsened in the terrible winter of 1947. Only a massive influx of outside capital could begin the process of rebuilding and revitalization. Speaking at the Harvard University commencement in June 1947, George Marshall urged the nations of Europe to work out a comprehensive recovery program and then ask the United States for aid. "Any government that is willing to assist in the task of recovery," he promised, "will find full cooperation . . . on the part of the United States government." In Truman's words, the Marshall Plan was "the other half of the walnut." By bolstering European economies devastated by the war, Marshall and Truman believed, the United States could forestall the economic dislocation thought to give rise to communism. American economic self-interest was also a contributing factor—a revitalized Europe centered on a strong West German economy would provide a stronger market for U.S. goods and a European common market could serve as a model for economic multilateralism and interdependence.

Within the Congress, however, significant opposition remained to President Truman's pledge of economic aid to European economies. Republicans called the Marshall Plan a huge "international W.P.A.," a "European T.V.A.," and a "bold Socialist blue-print," none of which was meant as a compliment. In an election year, Republicans were loathe to give the Democratic president a major foreign policy triumph, but not all Republicans were opposed. Senator Vandenberg, the

Republican isolationist-turned-internationalist who chaired the Senate Foreign Relations Committee, supported the Marshall Plan, just as he had favored the appropriations for Greece and Turkey under the Truman Doctrine. In general, despite the continued influence of an isolationist wing of the Republican party, foreign policy in the 1940s and 1950s proceeded with bipartisan support.

In the midst of this stalemate came the communist coup in Czechoslovakia in March 1948, with its reminder of the menace of Soviet expansion in Eastern Europe. Czechoslovakia had been one of the few Eastern European countries to hold elections after the war ended. The Communists won 38 percent of the vote in the May 1946 elections, necessitating a coalition government; neither President Eduard Beneš nor Foreign Minister Jan Masaryk, who were both greatly admired in the West, were Communists. By early 1948 the fragile coalition had faltered, and the Communists took control in a coup on February 25, 1948. Two weeks later the Communist leadership assassinated Masaryk, an event which Truman said "sent a shock throughout the civilized world." To prevent similar situations in the rest of Europe, Truman argued, the Marshall Plan was imperative.

Congress agreed, overwhelmingly approving funds for the program in March of 1948. Historian Thomas J. McCormick calls the Marshall Plan "arguably the most innovative piece of foreign policy in American history." Over the next four years the United States contributed nearly $13 billion to a highly successful recovery effort. Western European economies revived and industrial production increased 64 percent, opening new areas for international trade. The Marshall Plan did not specifically exclude Eastern Europe or the Soviet Union, but it did require that all participating nations exchange economic information and work toward the mutual elimination of tariffs and other trade barriers. Soviet leaders denounced these conditions as attempts to draw Eastern Europe into the American orbit and forbade their satellites such as Czechoslovakia, Poland, and Hungary to participate.

The Berlin Airlift. Differing Soviet and American visions for postwar Germany continued to fuel the deepening Cold War. The United States wanted a unified, reindustrialized Germany that would be integrated into the European and world market. The Soviets feared the reemergence of a powerful German state, which had twice invaded the Soviet Union in the twentieth century. Especially troublesome was the fate of the city of Berlin, which lay deep within the Soviet zone of occupation and had been deemed so important that it was divided into four zones just like the country as a whole. The Soviet Union demanded control over the entire city, but the Allies refused. When Western nations took steps to revive the Berlin economy in the spring of 1948, the Soviet Union imposed a blockade on all highway, rail, and river traffic to West Berlin in June.

In this tense situation, Truman replied with an airlift. For nearly a year, American and British pilots, who had been dropping bombs on Berlin only four years earlier, flew in 2.5 million tons of food and fuel, nearly a ton for each Berlin citizen. On May 12, 1949, Stalin lifted the blockade, which by then had made West Berlin a symbol of resistance to communism.

The Berlin Airlift

For 321 days American planes like this DC-6 flew 272,000 missions to bring food and supplies to Berlin after the Soviet Union had blocked all surface routes into the city. The blockade was finally lifted on May 12, 1949.

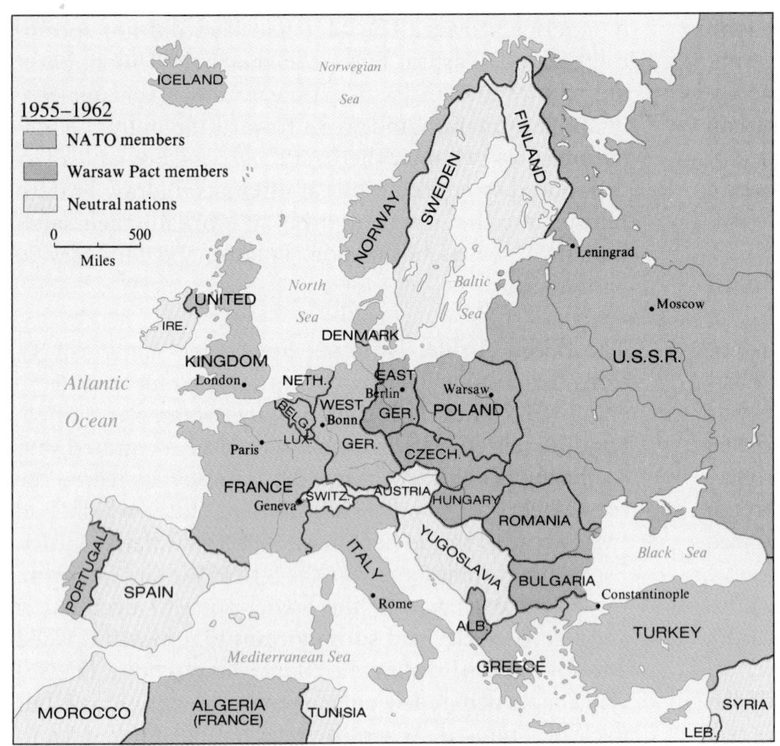

MAP 28.1

Cold War Europe, 1955

In 1949 the United States sponsored the creation of the North Atlantic Treaty Organization (NATO), an alliance of ten European nations, the United States, and Canada. West Germany was formally admitted to NATO membership in May 1955. A few days later the Soviet Union and seven other Communist nations established a rival alliance, the Warsaw Pact.

NATO. The Berlin airlift and the coup in Czechoslovakia led to another dramatic turning point in U.S. diplomatic history. In April 1949, for the first time since the American Revolution, the United States entered into a peacetime military alliance with Western Europe and Canada—the North Atlantic Treaty Organization (NATO). To back up America's new stance, Truman asked Congress for $1.3 billion in military assistance to NATO. Under the pact, the United States, Britain, France, Italy, Belgium, the Netherlands, Luxembourg, Denmark, Norway, Portugal, Iceland, and Canada agreed that "an armed attack against one or more of them in Europe or North America shall be considered an attack against them all." In May 1949 these nations also agreed to the creation of the Federal Republic of Germany (West Germany). All assumed that it would join NATO, which it did in 1955.

Distressed by the aggressive American effort to promote a new economic and political order in Western Europe and the presence of substantial numbers of American troops in Western Europe as part of the NATO commitment, the Soviet Union tightened its grip on Eastern Europe. It created a separate government for East Germany in October 1949, which became the German Democratic Republic. The Soviets also sponsored an economic association, the Council for Mutual Economic Assistance or COMECON (1949), and a military alliance for Eastern Europe, the Warsaw Pact (1955). The postwar division of Europe was nearly complete.

The "Fall" of China

Containment was developed primarily to prevent Soviet expansion beyond its sphere of influence in Eastern Europe. As the mutual suspicion between the United States and the Soviet Union deepened, cold war doctrines influenced the American stance toward Asia as well. Here China, rather than the Soviet Union, was the main counterweight to American influence. The developing American policy toward Asia was informed by the recognition of Asia's importance in the world economy as well as the desire to contain communism. For eighteen of the thirty years between 1945 and 1975, the United States was involved in Asian wars.

A civil war had been raging in China since the 1930s. Communist forces led by Mao Zedong (Mao Tse-tung) and Zhou Enlai (Chou En-lai) contended for power with conservative Nationalist forces under Jiang Jieshi (Chiang Kai-shek). Jiang had strong connections with the Chinese business community and with the western world. His wealthy wife had been educated at Wellesley College in Massachusetts. In contrast, Mao was the son of struggling peasants, a tough, uncompromising leader who inspired loyalty in his associates. Mao won the devotion of China's overtaxed, land-hungry peasants, whom Jiang had alienated with the widespread corruption of his regime and his suppression of agrarian reforms. The Communists also won support for their resistance against the Japanese forces occupying their country. By 1944 Mao's forces were gaining the upper hand.

The Truman administration stuck with its Nationalist allies almost until the bitter end. Between 1945 and 1949, the United States provided more than $2 billion to Jiang's forces, to no avail. In 1947, General Albert Wedemeyer, who had tried to work with Jiang, reported to President Truman that "until drastic political and economic reforms" were undertaken by the "corrupt, reactionary, and inefficient Chinese National government, United States aid cannot accomplish its purpose." When these reforms did not occur, the United States cut off aid to the Nationalists in August of 1949, sealing their fate. The People's Republic of China was formally established on October 1, 1949, and what was left of Jiang's government fled the Chinese mainland to the island of Formosa (Taiwan).

Many Americans viewed Mao's success as a defeat for the United States. The Republican statesman John Foster Dulles, who became Secretary of State under Eisenhower, called the communist victory in China "the worst defeat the United States has suffered in its history." A pro-nationalist "China lobby," supported by such Republicans as Senators Karl Mundt of South Dakota and William S. Knowland of California, protested that the State Department under Secretary of State Dean Acheson was responsible for the "loss of China." Publisher Henry R. Luce, born in China to missionary parents, spread these accusations through his magazines, including *Time* and *Life*. Bowing to pressure from the China lobby, most of the State Department's experts on the Far East were forced to resign for supposedly having been too sympathetic to the Chinese Communists. The United States refused to recognize the new communist state, instead giving diplomatic recognition to the Nationalists ensconced on Taiwan. The United States also used its influence to block China's admission to the United Nations. For almost twenty years afterward, U.S. administrations acted as if mainland China, the world's most populous country, did not exist.

Containment Militarized: NSC-68

September 1949 brought another shock to U.S. policymakers. American military intelligence detected a rise in radioactivity in the atmosphere, proof that the Soviet Union had set off an atomic bomb. The United States' atomic monopoly, which some military and political advisers had argued would last for decades, had ended in less than four years. In combination with the Communist takeover in China, the world looked even more threatening now that the Soviets had the bomb.

The end of the American atomic monopoly forced a major reassessment of the nation's foreign policy. To devise a new blueprint for diplomatic and military priorities, Truman turned to the National Security Council (NSC), an advisory body charged with assisting the president to set defense and military priorities. The NSC formed part of the unified military establishment set up by the National Security Act of 1947, which created a single Department of Defense to replace the previous Departments of War and the Navy. The recently established Joint Chiefs of Staff coordinated army, navy, and air force policy. And a new Central Intelligence Agency (CIA) gathered and analyzed military intelligence. These bureaucratic structures were a concrete reminder of the rise of the state.

In April 1950 the National Security Council delivered its report to President Truman. This document, known as NSC-68, reflected the bleak assumptions that American policymakers held about the Soviet Union: "It is quite clear from Soviet theory and practice that the Kremlin seeks to bring the free world under its dominion by the methods of the cold war." Because Moscow possessed tremendous military power that enabled the Soviet Union to "back up infiltration with intimidation," policymakers predicted an "indefinite period of tension and danger." In the immediate postwar period, the containment policy had relied primarily on economic and diplomatic means to counter Soviet expansionism and influence, but it became increasingly dependent on military force. The new stance thus pointed to far greater militarization of the Cold War.

NSC-68 made several specific recommendations. It favored development of a hydrogen bomb, an advanced weapon that was a thousand times more destructive than the atomic bombs that had destroyed Hiroshima and Nagasaki. (The United States exploded its first hydrogen bomb in November 1952, and the Soviet Union followed suit in 1953.) It supported increases in U.S. conventional forces and a strong system of alliances. Most importantly, it called for an increase in taxes to finance "a bold and massive program of rebuilding the West's defensive potential to surpass that of the Soviet world." NSC-68 envisioned defense budgets totaling up to 20 percent of the gross national product, four times their level at the time. The United States would function in a state approaching permanent mobilization, whether the country was officially at war or not.

The call for increased defense spending was linked directly to the end of atomic supremacy. The United States had been relying too heavily on atomic deterrence at the expense of its conventional military arsenal. Now that the nation's atomic monopoly had been broken, a general buildup of the American military arsenal was needed. The Korean War, which began just two months after NSC-68 was completed, provided the impetus to put this new policy into practice. Before 1950 the military budget stood at $13.5 billion. In just six months, Truman more than tripled it to nearly $50 billion.

The Korean War

Although Truman acknowledged that communist success in China raised urgent questions for American foreign policy, he recognized the limits of American power in Asia. In December 1949 Secretary of State Dean Acheson clarified American policy. The United States, he said, would help Asian nations realize their own aspirations but would consider itself bound to protect only a "defensive perimeter" that ran from the Aleutian Islands in Alaska to Japan, the Ryukyus (a chain of small islands that stretch from Japan to Taiwan), and the Philippines. If an attack occurred outside this perimeter—on Korea, Taiwan, or Southeast Asia, for example—"the initial reliance must be on the people attacked to resolve it and then upon . . . the United Nations."

A test of this new policy came quickly in Korea, a country whose artificial division after World War II contained seeds for later conflict. Both the United States and the Soviet Union had troops in Korea at the end of fighting in 1945, and neither side was willing to leave because of the peninsula's enormous strategic importance. As a compromise, the country was divided at the 38th parallel. Both occupying forces remained until 1948, when a Communist government led by Kim Il Sung took power in North Korea while Syngman Rhee, backed by the United States, took over in South Korea.

In 1950 the North Korean Communists decided to attempt to reunify the country. Whether the Soviet Union or the North Korean government initiated the action remains in dispute. Truman believed the attack to be Soviet-inspired, but in many ways the conflict was closer to a civil war. On June 25, North Korean troops launched a surprise attack across the 38th parallel. North Korean leaders may have expected Truman to ignore this armed challenge, but the president immediately asked the United Nations Security Council to authorize a "police action" against the invaders. Because the Soviet Union was temporarily boycotting the Security Council to protest the exclusion of the People's Republic of China from the U.N., it could not veto Truman's request, and the Security Council voted to send a peacekeeping force. Three days later Truman ordered General Douglas MacArthur, who was heading the American army of occupation that remained in Japan until 1951, to send American troops to help Rhee.

The outbreak of the Korean War further tipped the balance of foreign policy formulation from Congress to the president. When isolationist Republican Senator Robert A. Taft of Ohio objected that the president should have obtained congressional approval before committing American troops to Korea, Truman boldly insisted that he already had all the power he needed as commander-in-chief of the armed forces and as executor of the treaty binding the United States to the United Nations. The Truman administration enjoyed widespread popular support for this action: a July 1950 poll showed 77 percent approved of U.S. intervention in South Korea.

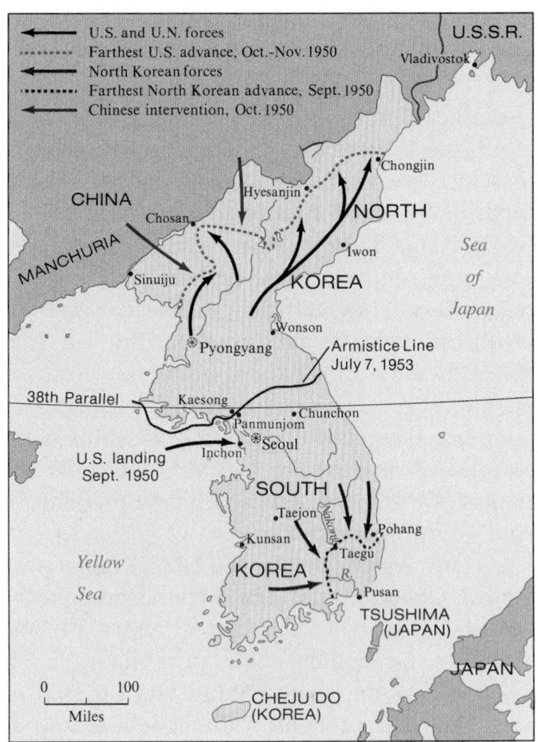

MAP 28.2

The Korean War, 1950–1953

The first months of the Korean War featured dramatic shifts in control up and down the 600-mile peninsula. From June to September 1950, North Korean troops overran most of the territory south of the 38th parallel. On September 15, U.N. forces under General Douglas MacArthur counterattacked behind enemy lines at Inchon and pushed north almost to the Chinese border. Massive Chinese intervention forced the U.N. troops to retreat to the 38th parallel in January 1951, and the war became a stalemate for the next two years.

Fighting the War. The rapidly assembled United Nations army in Korea remained overwhelmingly American, even though fourteen other non-Communist members sent troops, including Australia, Canada, and Great Britain. At the request of the Security Council, President Truman named General MacArthur to head the U.N. forces. At first, the North Koreans held an overwhelming advantage, controlling practically the entire peninsula except the Pusan beachhead. Then on September 15, 1950, MacArthur launched a brilliant amphibious attack at Inchon, far behind the lines of the North Korean invasion. Within two weeks, the U.N. forces controlled Seoul, the South Korean capital, and almost all the territory up to the 38th parallel.

Encouraged by this success, General MacArthur sought authority to lead his forces across the 38th parallel into North Korea itself. Truman's initial plan had been to restore the 1945 border; now he agreed to the broader goal of creating "a unified, independent and democratic Korea." The Chinese government in Beijing warned repeatedly that such a move would provoke its retaliation, but American officials failed to take these warnings seriously. MacArthur's troops drove rapidly northward, reaching the Chinese border at the Yalu River by the end of October. Just after Thanksgiving, however, a massive Chinese counterattack of almost 300,000 troops forced a retreat to the 38th parallel. On January 4, 1951, Communist troops reoccupied Seoul. "They really fooled us when it comes right down to it, didn't they?" a senator later asked Secretary of State Acheson. "Yes, sir," he replied.

Two months later, the American forces and their allies counterattacked, regained Seoul, and pushed back to the 38th parallel. Then a stalemate set in. Public support in the United States dropped after Chinese intervention increased the likelihood of a long war. By early January 1951, 66 percent thought the United States should withdraw, and 49 percent felt it was a mistake to have gone in in the first place.

Given those domestic and international constraints, Truman and his advisers in Washington decided to work for a negotiated peace. They did not wish to tie down large numbers of U.S. troops in a remote corner of Asia, far from what they considered more strategically important trouble spots in Europe and the Middle East. As Dean Acheson had said just before the Korean War broke out, "We cannot scatter our shots equally all over the world. We just haven't got enough shots to do that." If the Korean War had become a general war with China, reasoned General Omar N. Bradley, chairman of the Joint Chiefs of Staff, it would have been "the wrong war, at the wrong place, at the wrong time, and with the wrong enemy."

The Fate of MacArthur. MacArthur disagreed. Headstrong, arrogant, and brilliant, he fervently believed the nation's future opportunities lay in Asia, not in Europe. Disregarding Truman's instructions, General MacArthur traveled to Taiwan and urged the Nationalists to join in an attack on communist China. He pleaded for American use of the atomic bomb against targets in China. In an inflammatory letter to the House Minority Leader, Republican Joseph J. Martin of Massachusetts, he denounced the Korean stalemate. "We must win," MacArthur declared. "There is no substitute for victory."

Martin released MacArthur's letter on April 6, 1951, as part of a concerted Republican campaign to challenge President Truman's conduct of the war. The strategy backfired. On April 11, Truman relieved MacArthur of his command in Korea and Japan, accusing him of insubordination. "MacArthur left me no choice," Truman later insisted. "Even the Joint Chiefs of Staff came to the conclusion that civilian control of the military was at stake. . . . I didn't let it stay at stake very long."

The Korean War

The American GI's who fought in Korea were often the younger brothers of the men who had served in World War II. Unlike their older brothers, Korean War soldiers served in integrated units. Here members of a U.S. Combat Engineers battalion sweep a mountain trail for mines and booby traps.

MacArthur's Return From Korea

General Douglas MacArthur received a tumultuous welcome in San Francisco in 1951, the first time the popular general had set foot on the American mainland in fourteen years. The public outcry over President Truman's dismissal of MacArthur for insubordination reflected frustration with the stalemated Korean War.

Truman's decision was highly unpopular. According to a Gallup poll, 69 percent of the American people supported MacArthur rather than Truman. The allure of decisive victory under a charismatic military leader temporarily pushed aside doubts about the war. The general returned to tumultuous receptions in San Francisco, Chicago, and New York. In Washington, he delivered an impassioned address to a joint Congressional session that ended with a line from an old West Point ballad, "Old soldiers never die, they just fade away." But when the shouting died down, Truman had the last word. Failing to get the Republican presidential nomination in 1952, MacArthur did indeed fade from public view.

The war dragged on for more than two years after MacArthur's dismissal. Truce talks began in Korea in July 1951, but a final armistice was not signed until July 1953. Approximately 45 percent of American casualties were sustained in this period. The final settlement left Korea divided very near the 38th parallel in place when the war broke out, with a demilitarized zone dividing the two countries. North Korea remained firmly allied with the Soviet Union; South Korea signed a mutual defense treaty with the United States in 1954, allying itself to the American sphere of influence in the Pacific and playing host to large numbers of American troops stationed there. During the next thirty years, American and Japanese investments helped South Korea rapidly expand its economy.

The Impact of the Korean War. The Korean War had only a limited domestic impact on the United States. The government did not control the economy to the extent it had during World War II, although the military budget nearly quadrupled over the course of the war. Limited mobilization stimulated the economy and reduced unemployment, contributing to the general prosperity that characterized the 1950s.

Few soldiers felt the patriotic fervor that had characterized service during World War II. Struggling against heavy snow and subzero cold, the men grew to hate the endless fighting and "those damned hills of Korea." One griped, "You march up them but there's always the sinking feeling you are going to have to march right back down." A corporal from Chicago asserted, "I'll fight for my country, but I'm damned if I see why I'm fighting for this hell-hole." Showing the lack of engagement on the home front, when an Oregon newspaper prominently ran the same news dispatch from Korea two days in a row, not a single reader called the repetition to its attention.

Conditions did improve for black soldiers in Korea compared to the discrimination they faced in the service during World War II. President Truman had signed an executive order desegregating the armed forces in 1948, but little progress had been made before the war began. During the rapid mobilization, demands for quick processing of draftees outweighed such customary practices as keeping black and white draftees separate, thus speeding up integration. The generally successful experience of an integrated armed services during the Korean War hastened the emergence of the civil rights movement later in the 1950s.

The Korean War was costly for the United States: 54,200 American soldiers died, 103,000 were wounded, and military expenditures totaled $54 billion. It reminded Americans that global responsibilities required a heavy, ongoing commitment. In contrast to the triumphs on World War II battlefields, however, the protracted stalemate proved frustrating. "If we are so powerful," many asked, "why can't we win?" When the armistice was finally signed in 1953, there were few public celebrations. Similar frustration surfaced little more than a decade later over American intervention in Vietnam.

Harry Truman and the Fair Deal

Harry S. Truman brought a complex character to the presidency. Alternately humble and cocky, he had none of Roosevelt's patrician ease. Yet he handled affairs with an assurance and crisp dispatch that has endeared him to later generations. "If you can't stand the heat, stay out of the kitchen," he liked to say of presidential responsibility. The major domestic issues that he faced were reconversion to a peacetime economy and the fears of communist infiltration and internal subversion generated by the Cold War, fears which his own administration played a part in fanning. Truman kept the New Deal coalition alive by proposing new federal programs to advance the interests of its constituencies, and his "Fair Deal" shaped the Democratic party's agenda for the next twenty years.

The Challenge of Reconversion

Harry Truman never intended to be just a caretaker president for a Roosevelt fourth term. On September 16, 1945, just fourteen days after Japan surrendered and World War II ended, Truman staked his claim to domestic leadership with a plan for expanded federal responsibilities that he named the Fair Deal. Anticipating a period of affluence rather than the austerity that had shaped the New Deal, Truman phrased his proposals in terms of the rights of individual citizens—the right to a "useful and remunerative" job, protection from monopoly, good housing, "adequate medical care," "protection from the economic fears of old age," and a "good education." Later President Truman added support for civil rights as well.

When Truman took over the presidency, Americans welcomed him with an initial approval rate of 87 percent, according to Gallup polls. Within a year, his popularity had dropped to 32 percent, and new phrases such as "To err is Truman" had entered the political language. What had happened? New to the presidency, Truman had to oversee the complex conversion of a war economy to a peacetime one. In part because government planners had not known about the atomic bomb, they had assumed that reconversion could be phased in while the country went through the long process of winning a land war in Japan, which was expected to last through 1946. Instead the war ended before adequate reconversion plans were in place.

The main fear on the public's mind in 1945 was that the depression would return once war production ended. The specter of mass unemployment was very real to those who had lived through the grim sacrifices of the 1930s, as well as older Americans who remembered the recession that had followed World War I. To their relief, the economy managed to escape this fate. Despite a drop in government spending after the war, consumer spending increased, because workers had amassed substantial wartime savings that they were eager to spend. The Servicemen's Readjustment Act of 1944, popularly known as the GI Bill, also put money into the economy by providing a wide range of educational and economic assistance to returning veterans. Finally, despite some temporary dislocations as war production shifted back to civilian uses and veterans were reabsorbed into the workforce, unemployment did not soar. The most visible layoffs were the "Rosie the Riveters" who had taken on high-paying defense jobs during the war and were now forced to find jobs in traditional areas of women's employment at much lower pay.

But the transition was hardly trouble-free. One historian has called it the "morass of reconversion." The main domestic problem was inflation. Consumers wanted an end to wartime restrictions and price rationing, but Truman feared economic chaos if all controls were lifted immediately. In the summer of 1945, he eased industrial controls but retained the wartime Office of Price Administration. When the OPA was disbanded and almost all controls lifted in November 1946, prices soared. That year saw an annual inflation rate of 18.2 percent. The persistence of shortages of food and products also irritated consumers.

Helen Gahagan Douglas

Representative Helen Gahagan Douglas of California, a former Broadway and film star, illustrated a 1947 speech supporting the reestablishment of price controls by bringing a shopping basket of food to a press conference. Douglas served in Congress from 1944 until 1950, when she was defeated in a bid for the Senate by Representative Richard M. Nixon. In their bitterly fought campaign Nixon linked her with communism by calling her "pink."

With the Employment Act of 1946, the federal government began to develop mechanisms to pursue a coherent economic policy. The legislation formally integrated Keynesian ideas into American economic policy, proposing federal fiscal planning on a permanent basis, not just in times of crisis such as the Great Depression. Besides supporting the use of government spending to spur economic growth, the Employment Act envisioned the use of tax policy as a tool for managing the economy—cut taxes to spur economic growth, or raise taxes to slow inflation. Yet the legislation failed to establish clear economic priorities, such as the proper weight between the commitment to full employment and the need for a balanced budget. And the new three-member Council of Economic Advisers, appointed by the president and directly responsible to the White House, played only an advisory role. On balance, however, the Employment Act of 1946 marked an important turning point toward federal responsibility for the performance of the economy.

Postwar Strikes. The rapidly rising cost of living prompted demands for higher wages by the nation's workers. By 1945 the number of union members had swelled to more than 14 million—two-thirds of all workers in the mining, manufacturing, construction, and transportation industries. The labor movement had held the line on wages during the war but now was angered as corporate profits doubled while real wages declined due to the end of wartime overtime pay. Determined to make up for their war-induced sacrifices, workers mounted strikes in major sectors of the economy, crippling the automobile, steel, and coal industries. By the end of 1946, 5 million workers had idled factories and mines for a total of 107,476,000 work days.

Truman never doubted his proper course of action. Even if it meant alienating organized labor, an important component of the Democratic coalition, Truman felt it was the president's job to ensure economic stability. "If you think I'm going to sit here and let you tie up this whole country, you're crazy as hell," Truman told leaders of a nationwide railroad strike in the spring of 1946. Truman used his executive authority to place the nation's railroad system under federal control and asked Congress for power to draft striking workers into the army, a move that infuriated labor but pressured strikers back to work nonetheless. Three days later the president took a tough stand against labor leader John L. Lewis and the striking United Mine Workers by seizing control of the mines. Such actions won Truman support from Americans fed up with labor disruptions, but he incurred the enmity of organized labor.

The Election of 1946. These domestic upheavals did not bode well for the Democrats at the polls. In the 1946 elections Republicans capitalized on popular dissatisfaction with the myriad reconversion problems with the simple slogan, "Had enough?" (The original version was, "Have You Had Enough of the Alphabet?", a reference to the "alphabet soup" of New Deal agencies. Less was definitely more.) The Republicans gained control of both houses of Congress for the first time since 1928. Truman and the Democrats seemed thoroughly repudiated.

The Taft-Hartley Act. The Republican Congress elected in 1946 was determined to undo the New Deal's social welfare measures, and it singled out labor legislation as a special target. In 1947, Congress passed the Taft-Hartley Act, a direct challenge to several provisions of the 1935 National Labor Relations Act. This law outlawed the closed shop and restricted the political power of unions by prohibiting the use of union dues for political activity. It allowed the president to declare an 80-day cooling-off period in strikes with national impact. Unions especially disliked Section 14b of the act, which allowed states to pass "right to work" laws to prohibit the union shop. Truman issued a ringing veto of the Taft-Hartley bill in June 1947, calling it "bad for labor, bad for management, and bad for the country." Congress easily overrode Truman's veto, but his action brought labor back into the Democratic fold.

The 1948 Election

Most observers believed that Truman faced an impossible task in the presidential campaign of 1948. The Republicans were united and well led. They maintained the loyal support of most middle- and upper-income Protestants outside the South, and many farmers and skilled workers. Eager to attract votes from traditional Democratic constituencies, they nominated a moderate, Governor Thomas E. Dewey of New York. A well-known prosecuting attorney, Dewey had demonstrated his attractiveness as a national candidate in his 1944 campaign against Roosevelt. To increase their appeal in the West, the Republicans nominated Earl Warren, governor of California, for vice-president. Their brief platform promised to continue most New Deal reforms and supported a bipartisan foreign policy.

Truman, in contrast, led a party in severe disarray. Both the left and right wings of the Democratic party split off and nominated their own candidates. Henry A. Wallace, a former New Deal liberal whom Truman had fired as secretary of commerce in 1946 because he was

Taft-Hartley

No legislation angered organized labor more than the 1947 Labor-Management Relations Act, popularly known as Taft-Hartley, which rolled back many of the gains made by labor under the New Deal. The message to President Truman from these union members assembled at an American Federation of Labor rally at Madison Square Garden in 1947 is clear, even if they inverted the name of the bill to Hartley-Taft. Truman did veto the bill, but his veto was overridden by the Republican-controlled Congress.

perceived as too "soft" on communism, ran as the candidate of the new Progressive party. Wallace advocated increased government intervention in the economy, more power for labor unions, and greater cooperation with the Soviet Union.

Southern Democrats bolted the party over the issue of civil rights. At the Democratic national convention, leaders such as Mayor Hubert H. Humphrey of Minneapolis and gubernatorial candidate Adlai E. Stevenson of Illinois had pushed through a platform calling for the repeal of Taft-Hartley, the establishment of a permanent Fair Employment Practices Commission, and federal antilynching and anti-poll tax legislation. Many southerners would grudgingly support a greater role for the government in the economy, but they would not tolerate federal interference in race relations. Three days after the convention, southern Democrats met in Birmingham, Alabama, to set up the States' Rights, or Dixiecrat, party. They nominated Governor J. Strom Thurmond of South Carolina for president.

Truman responded to these challenges with one of the most effective presidential campaigns ever waged. He dramatically called Congress back into summer session to give the Republicans a chance to enact their platform into law. When, predictably, they failed to do so, he launched a strenuous cross-country speaking tour, hitting out at the "do-nothing Republican Congress." He also hammered away at the Republicans' support for the antilabor Taft-Hartley act and their

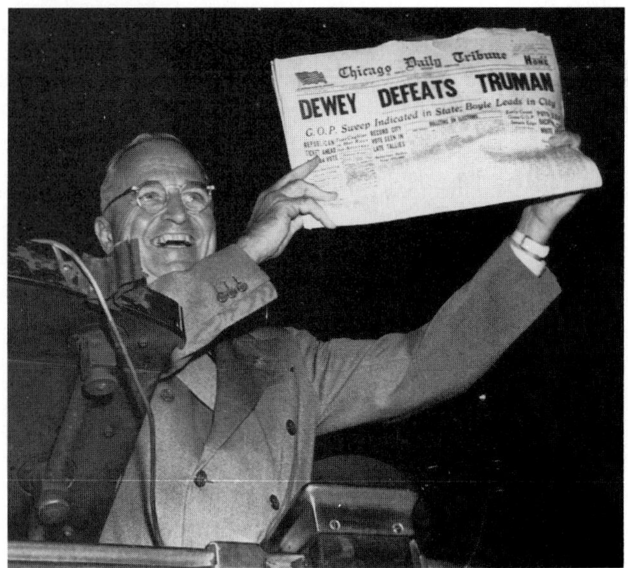

Truman Triumphant

In one of the most famous photographs in American political history, Harry S. Truman gloats over an inaccurate headline in the *Chicago Tribune*. Pollsters had predicted an overwhelming victory for Thomas E. Dewey. Their primitive polling techniques did not reflect the dramatic surge in support for Truman during the last days of the campaign.

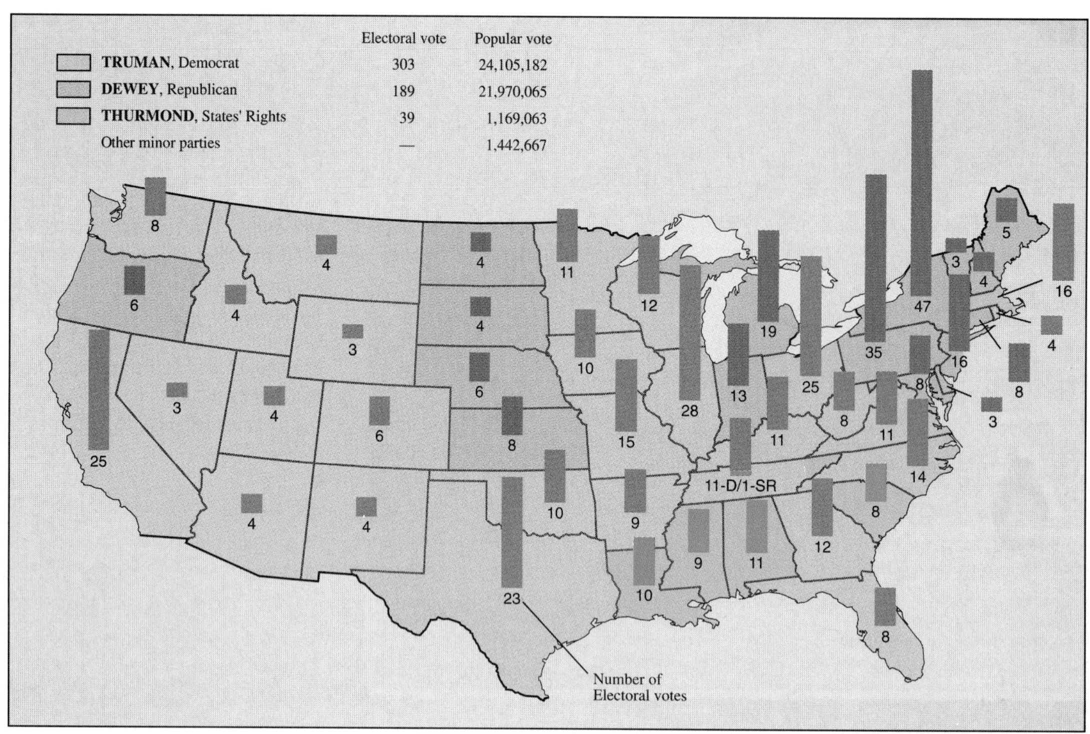

MAP 28.3

The Election of 1948

Political adviser Clark Clifford planned Truman's successful electoral strategy in 1948, arguing that the president should concentrate his campaign in urban areas where the Democrats had their greatest strength. In an election marked by low turnout, Truman held onto enough support from the Roosevelt coalition of blacks, union members, and farmers to defeat Dewey by more than 2 million votes.

opposition to full-parity price supports for farmers. Truman struck just the right chord. At his rallies enthusiastic listeners took up the cry, "Give 'em hell, Harry!"

Truman won a remarkable victory, receiving 49.6 percent of the vote to Dewey's 45.1 percent. Strom Thurmond and the Dixiecrats carried four southern states. Henry Wallace failed to win a single state. The Democrats also regained control of both houses of Congress. As a commentator in *The New Republic* observed, "Harry Truman won this election because Franklin Roosevelt had worked so well." Truman retained the support of organized labor and Jewish and Catholic voters in the big cities; the allegiance of northern black voters to the Democratic party offset the southern losses to the Dixiecrats. (The discovery that the Democrats could capture the presidency without the Solid South paved the way for later civil rights legislation.) Most importantly, Truman appealed effectively to people like himself who hailed from the farms, towns, and small cities in the nation's heartland. He had grasped something the pollsters had missed: "Everybody's against me but the people."

Fair Deal Liberalism

Truman's Fair Deal represented the essentials of postwar liberalism. Liberals' conception of the state was an expansive, Keynesian one, based on a willingness to use the fiscal powers of the federal government to stimulate economic growth, redress imbalances, and encourage social progress. With a rhetorical commitment to civil rights and economic abundance for all, liberalism committed the modern state to extending the benefits of capitalism to ever wider numbers of citizens. Postwar liberalism thus built on and surpassed the reforms begun during the New Deal.

Truman's ambitious agenda ran up against a generally hostile Congress. Despite its Democratic majority, the Senate and the House contained a fair number of conservatives of both parties. This same conservative coalition had blocked Roosevelt in his second term and dismantled or cut popular New Deal programs during wartime. With the exception of Taft-Hartley, the Truman administration forestalled any wholesale attacks on the New Deal. On the other hand, only parts of the

Fair Deal won adoption. The minimum wage was raised from forty cents an hour to seventy-five; the Social Security system was extended to cover 10 million new workers and its benefits raised by 75 percent. The National Housing Act of 1949 declared as public policy "the goal of a decent home and a suitable living environment for every American family" and called for the construction of 810,000 units of low-income housing.

Civil Rights. The Truman record on civil rights shows the combination of progress and stalemate that characterized most aspects of the Fair Deal. Civil rights became a national political issue in the 1940s. Black expectations had been raised by wartime opportunities as well as symbolic postwar victories, such as Jackie Robinson of the Brooklyn Dodgers breaking the color barrier in major league baseball in 1947. In addition, Truman realized that black voters played an increasingly large role in the Democratic party as they migrated from the South, where they were effectively disenfranchised, to northern cities. Finally, Truman was sensitive to the world's view of American treatment of blacks, especially since the Soviet Union often compared segregation of southern blacks with the Nazis' treatment of the Jews.

Lacking a popular mandate, Truman resorted to a variety of means to advance the cause of civil rights. In 1946 he appointed a National Civil Rights Commission; their 1947 recommendations called for an expanded federal role in civil rights that foreshadowed much of the legislation of the 1960s. He ordered the Justice Department to prepare *amicus curiae* (friend of the court) briefs in Supreme Court cases such as *Shelley v. Kraemer* (1948), which struck down as unconstitutional restrictive covenants designed to enforce residential segregation. By a 1948 executive order, he began the process of desegregating the armed forces which was hastened by the Korean War. And in 1949, safely after the election, the administration proposed a federal antilynching law, federal protection of voting rights (such as an end to poll taxes), and a permanent federal agency to guarantee equal employment opportunities. A filibuster by southern conservatives effectively blocked such legislation in Congress, however.

Interest groups successfully opposed other key items on the Fair Deal agenda. The American Medical Association squashed the movement for national health insurance by denouncing it as the first step toward "socialized medicine." Catholics successfully opposed any aid-to-education proposal that omitted subsidies for parochial schools. Farmers refused to join labor in supporting the outright repeal of Taft-Hartley. In general, the Truman administration failed to mobilize popular and congressional support for dramatically enlarged federal responsibilities in the economic and social spheres.

Two further factors limited the Fair Deal's chances for legislative success. One was the outbreak of the Korean War in 1950. The other was the nation's growing fear of internal subversion. The anticommunist crusade was just one manifestation of the increasing preoccupation with the cold war that was seeping into all facets of American life. Truman's own administration played a major role in fueling these domestic tensions.

The Great Fear

The deterioration of relations with the Soviet Union after 1945 underlay the fear of communism and the resulting domestic repression that gripped the country in the late 1940s and early 1950s. Americans often call this phenomenon "McCarthyism," after Senator Joseph R. McCarthy of Wisconsin, the decade's most vocal anticommunist. But this "great fear" was broader than the work of just one man. It built on the distrust of radicals and foreigners that had manifested itself in earlier periods such as the 1850s and the Red Scare after World War I. Worsening cold war tensions intersected with such deep-seated insecurities to spawn an obsessive concern over internal subversion, especially fears about how spies might pass the "secret" of the atomic bomb to the Soviet Union. Few spies or Communists were actually found in positions of power; far more Americans became innocent victims of the false accusations and innuendoes that flourished in the postwar climate of fear.

In the 1930s liberals and Communists had cooperated in a "popular front" against fascism. By the mid-1940s, however, Stalin's repressive dictatorship and fears of Russian expansionism into Eastern Europe and beyond made the Soviet Union seem as large a threat as fascism had been a decade earlier. Some postwar liberals, notably Henry Wallace and his followers in the Progressive party, continued to seek cooperation with the Soviet Union and were not disturbed by the presence of communist activists in their political movement. But many other liberal groups, particularly the Americans for Democratic Action, founded in 1947, broke from the popular front by including strident anticommunist planks in their political platforms.

Similarly, Communists had been active in the labor-organizing drives of the 1930s, and their contributions were welcomed, if not openly acknowledged. By the late 1940s, however, the labor movement reversed itself in the growing climate of fear and suspicion and suddenly purged Communists from its membership. CIO president Phillip Murray denounced communist sympathizers as "skulking cowards . . . apostles of hate." Unions that refused to oust their left-wing leaders, such as the United Electrical, Radio and Machine Workers of America, were expelled from the CIO.

The federal government also undertook its own an

AMERICAN VOICES

Testifying Before the House Committee on Un-American Activities *Pete Seeger*

Pete Seeger, a folk singer and songwriter, was one of many performers and artists called to testify before HUAC. This grilling by staff member Frank S. Tavenner, Jr., and Chairman Francis E. Walter was typical of the way investigators tried to force witnesses to divulge information against their will. After his 1955 appearance before the committee, Seeger and his group, the Weavers, were blacklisted.

Mr. Tavenner: When and where were you born, Mr. Seeger?

Mr. Seeger: I was born in New York in 1919.

Mr. Tavenner: What is your profession or occupation?

Mr. Seeger: Well, I have worked at many things, and my main profession is a student of American folklore, and I make my living as a banjo picker—sort of damning, in some people's opinion. . . .

Mr. Tavenner: You said that you would tell us about the songs. Did you participate in a program at Wingdale Lodge in the State of New York, which is a summer camp for adults and children, on the weekend of July Fourth of this year? [Witness consulted with counsel.]

Mr. Seeger: Again, I say I will be glad to tell what songs I have ever sung, because singing is my business.

Mr. Tavenner: I am going to ask you.

Mr. Seeger: But I decline to say who has ever listened to them, who has written them, or other people who have sung them.

Mr. Tavenner: Did you sing this song, to which we have referred, "Now Is the Time," at Wingdale Lodge on the weekend of July Fourth?

Mr. Seeger: I don't know any song by that name, and I know a song with a similar name. It is called "Wasn't That a Time." Is that the song?

Chairman Walter: Did you sing that song?

Mr. Seeger: I can sing it. I don't know how well I can do it without my banjo.

Chairman Walter: I said, Did you sing it on that occasion?

Mr. Seeger: I have sung that song. I am not going to go into where I have sung it. I have sung it many places. . . .

Chairman Walter: I direct you to answer the question. Did you sing this particular song on the Fourth of July at Wingdale Lodge in New York?

Mr. Seeger: I have already given you my answer to that question, and all questions such as that. I feel that is improper to ask about my associations and opinions. I have said that I would be voluntarily glad to tell you any song, or what I have done in my life.

Chairman Walter: I think it is my duty to inform you that we don't accept this answer and the others, and I give you an opportunity now to answer these questions, particularly the last one.

Mr. Seeger: Sir, my answer is always the same.

Source: Eric Bentley, ed., *Thirty Years of Treason: Excerpts From Hearings Before the House Committee on Un-American Activities, 1938–1968* (New York: Viking, 1971), 686, 690.

tisubversion campaign, which further inflamed the mounting hysteria. In March 1947, President Truman outraged many supporters by using an executive order to initiate a comprehensive investigation into the loyalty of all federal employees. More than 6 million individuals were subjected to security checks, and 14,000 underwent intensive FBI investigation. The case of Dorothy Bailey, a forty-one-year-old graduate of Bryn Mawr College and the University of Minnesota, was typical of the two thousand federal workers who were forced out of government service. A fourteen-year veteran of the U.S. Employment Service, Bailey lost her job because an unidentified informer claimed she was a Communist and associated with known Communists. Brought before the District of Columbia regional loyalty board, she denied the charge. No evidence against her was introduced and no witnesses testified to support the charges, but she lost her job anyway.

Following the lead from Washington, many state and local governments, colleges and universities, and private institutions and businesses undertook their own antisubversion campaigns. All 11,000 faculty members at the University of California were required to take a loyalty oath; UCLA alone fired 157 who refused to do so. In Hollywood, ex-FBI agents circulated a list of actors, directors, and writers whose names had been mentioned in congressional investigations or whose associations and friends had been described as dubious. Industry executives denied the existence of any such blacklist, but for ten years, hundreds of people were shut out of work in the entertainment industry. The Weavers, a popular group of folk singers, were blacklisted, and politically active actors such as Zero Mostel and John Garfield had difficulty finding work. One day actress Jean Muir headlined the popular radio show "The Aldrich Family"; the next she was out of a job—fired, the network said, not because she was a Communist but because gossip about her had made her too "controversial."

HUAC. The House Committee on Un-American Activities (HUAC) played an especially active role in fanning the anticommunist hysteria. HUAC had been ferreting out supposed Communists in government since its 1938 investigation into the Federal Theatre Project. In 1947, HUAC intensified its crusade by holding widely publicized hearings on communist infiltration in the film industry. A group of writers and directors, soon dubbed the "Hollywood Ten," went to jail for contempt of Congress when they cited the First Amendment rather than testify about their past associations.

HUAC next took up, with a vengeance, the case of Alger Hiss, a former New Deal State Department official who had accompanied Franklin Roosevelt to Yalta. The case against Hiss rested on the 1948 testimony of former Communist Whittaker Chambers, a senior editor at *Time*. Chambers claimed that Hiss had passed him classified documents in the 1930s as part of his duties as a member of a secret communist cell in the government, a charge that Hiss categorically denied. Congressman Richard M. Nixon of California orchestrated the HUAC investigation of Hiss, which culminated in the dramatic release of the so-called Pumpkin Papers, microfilm that Chambers had hidden in a pumpkin patch on his Maryland farm. (This supposedly incriminating cache, when declassified, contained only Navy Department documents on life rafts and fire extinguishers.) Because the statute of limitations on espionage had expired by 1949, Hiss was charged instead with perjury for denying Chambers's charges before HUAC. The first trial resulted in a hung jury; the second in early 1950 found Hiss guilty of perjury and sentenced him to five years in federal prison. The conviction of Hiss increased the paranoia about a communist conspiracy in the federal government.

The Rise and Fall of McCarthy. The hysteria soon intensified. Senator Joseph McCarthy, a Marine Air Corps veteran, had won election in the 1946 Republican landslide with the slogan, "Wisconsin Needs a Tail Gunner in the Senate." In late 1949, McCarthy discovered that a speech attacking a liberal Madison, Wisconsin, newspaper brought him favorable attention. In a February 1950 speech in Wheeling, West Virginia, he launched what one columnist later called his string of "multiple untruths" by declaring, "I have here in my hand a list of the names of 205 men that were known to the Secretary of State as being members of the Communist Party and who nevertheless are still working and shaping the policy of the State Department." McCarthy never revealed the names on his list, later changing the number to 81, then to 57. The public was so responsive to his charges that these inconsistencies failed to dent his momentum.

McCarthy's political genius was his ability to make his name synonymous with the cause of uncovering sub-

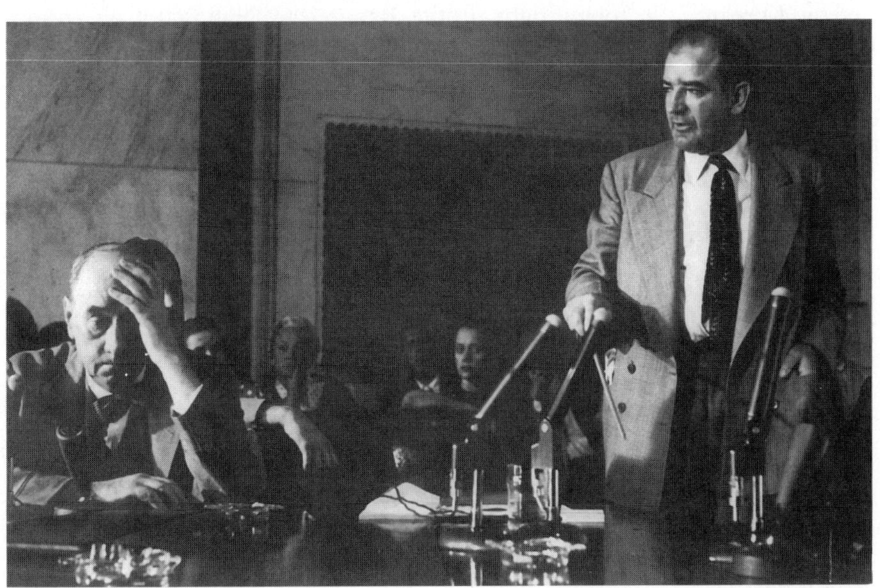

The Army-McCarthy Hearings

These 1954 hearings contributed to the downfall of Senator Joseph McCarthy by bringing his reckless accusations, bullying tactics, and snearing innuendoes to huge television audiences day after day. Some of the most heated exchanges took place between McCarthy (on right) and Joseph Welch (seated, on left), the lawyer representing the Army. When an exasperated Welch asked, "Have you no decency left, sir?", McCarthy merely shrugged. But the audience broke into applause because someone finally had the courage to stand up to the senator from Wisconsin.

versives in government. Politicians who attacked him exposed themselves to charges of being soft on communism, the kiss of death in the postwar political climate. At first McCarthy's supporters were more visible than his detractors; Democratic congressman John F. Kennedy of Massachusetts thought "McCarthy may have something." But President Truman called McCarthy's charges "slander, lies, character assassination," although he could do nothing to curb them. Even when Republican Dwight D. Eisenhower was elected president in 1952, he did not publicly challenge his party's most outspoken senator.

The momentum of international events allowed McCarthy to retain credibility, despite his failure to identify a single Communist in government. Alger Hiss was convicted in 1950. The Korean War broke out soon after, embroiling the United States in a frustrating fight against communism in a faraway land. And in a sensational but isolated case in 1951, Julius and Ethel Rosenberg were accused and convicted of passing atomic secrets to the Soviet Union. Despite conflicting evidence, they were executed in 1953.

In 1954, McCarthy finally overreached himself by launching an investigation into possible subversion in the U.S. Army. The lengthy televised hearings brought McCarthy's smear tactics and leering innuendoes into the nation's living rooms, and support for him declined. Later that year, the Senate voted 67 to 22 to censure McCarthy. He died three years later at the age of forty-eight, his name forever attached to a period of political repression of which he was only the most flagrant manifestation.

Modern Republicanism

The 1952 election occurred in the midst of the Korean stalemate and at the height of the Great Fear. The newly elected president, Dwight D. Eisenhower, worked quickly to end the Korean War; the grip of McCarthyism lasted longer. Eisenhower set the tone for the modern Republican party by emphasizing a slowdown, but not a dismantling, of federal responsibilities; his low-key style of governing was well suited to these seemingly prosperous and confident times. In foreign policy, the Republicans continued to see the world in Cold War polarities while expanding the defense buildup begun during the Korean War.

The Soldier Becomes President

The Republican party's greatest strength lay in the largely Protestant and rural states of the Midwest. Since only a third of the nation's registered voters were Republicans, however, the party had to find a candidate who could attract Democrats and independents. Republican leaders quickly realized that General Dwight D. Eisenhower would be just such a candidate.

Eisenhower's status as a war hero was his greatest political asset. Born in 1890 and raised in Abilene, Kansas, he graduated from the United States Military Academy at West Point in 1915. General Douglas MacArthur chose him as his aide in the early 1930s, and Eisenhower rose quickly through the ranks. After Pearl Harbor, he came to Washington under the sponsorship of a second mentor, General George C. Marshall. General Eisenhower oversaw the Allied invasion of North Africa in 1942, and in 1944 became Supreme Commander of Allied Forces in Europe, where he had the mammoth task of coordinating the D-Day invasion of France. To hundreds of thousands of soldiers, and to the millions who followed the war on newsreels, he was simply "Ike," the best known and best liked of the nation's military leaders.

Eisenhower had placed himself in a superb position for a presidential campaign. After serving as president of Columbia University from 1948 to 1950, he returned to active duty as the commander of NATO forces in Europe, serving at Truman's request. As a professional military man, he could insist that he stood "above politics." While in the army, in fact, he had never voted because he felt that such political activity would represent an intrusion of the military into civilian affairs. Many Democrats had hoped to make him their candidate for president in 1948, and again in 1952. Eisenhower did want the office, but as a Republican.

When conservative candidate Senator Robert A. Taft of Ohio did well in the early primaries of 1952, Eisenhower resigned his military position to campaign. He quickly proved an effective politician, winning several primaries and taking delegates away from Taft in a tough fight at the Republican National Convention. Eisenhower then asked Senator Richard M. Nixon of California to be his running mate. Young, tirelessly partisan, and with a strong anticommunist record from his crusade against Alger Hiss, Nixon brought an aggressive campaign style, as well as regional balance, to the ticket.

The Democrats never seriously considered renominating Harry Truman, who by 1952 was a thoroughly discredited leader. During the last two years of his presidency, his public approval rating had never risen above 32 percent and at one point had plunged to 23 percent. Lack of popular enthusiasm for the Korean War dealt the severest blow to Truman's support, but a series of widely publicized scandals involving federal officials in bribery, kickback, and influence-peddling schemes caused voters to complain about the "mess in Washington." With a certain relief, the Democrats turned to Governor Adlai E. Stevenson of Illinois, who enjoyed

They Liked Ike
In the 1952 election, Eisenhower's immense personal popularity, captured in the campaign slogan, "I Like Ike," propelled him to the largest popular vote of any candidate to that date. Here delegates show their enthusiasm at the Republican National Convention that year.

the support of respected liberals such as Eleanor Roosevelt and of organized labor. To appease southern voters who feared Stevenson's liberal agenda, the Democratic convention nominated Senator John A. Sparkman of Alabama for vice-president.

Throughout the 1952 campaign, Stevenson advocated New Deal–Fair Deal policies with an almost literary eloquence, but Eisenhower's artfully unpretentious speeches proved more effective with the voters. Eager to get maximum support from a broad electorate, Eisenhower played down specific questions of policy. Instead, he attacked the Democrats with the "K_1C_2" formula—"Korea, Communism, and Corruption." In a campaign pledge that clinched the election, he vowed to go to Korea to end the stalemated war if elected. Stevenson lamely quipped, "If elected, I shall go to the White House."

The only slip in the Republican campaign was the revelation that wealthy Californians had set up a secret "slush fund" for Richard Nixon. While Eisenhower contemplated dropping him from the ticket, Nixon adroitly used a televised speech to appeal directly for voters' sympathy, asserting that he had not misused campaign funds. Whereas Truman appointees had accepted mink coats from contractors—a reference to a widely reported case involving a loan examiner for the Reconstruction Finance Corporation—his wife wore only a "Republican cloth coat." Nixon did admit accepting one gift, a puppy his young daughters named Checkers. That gift he would not give back, he declared earnestly. Nixon's televised pathos turned an embarrassing incident into an advantage, as sympathetic viewers flooded Republican headquarters with telegrams and phone calls in his support. Outmaneuvered, Repub-

The "Checkers" Speech
Illustrating the power of the new medium of television, vice-presidential candidate Richard Nixon's "Checkers" speech kept him on the 1952 ticket despite allegations of an illegal campaign slush fund. Seen today, the half-hour speech seems stilted and amateurish, but viewers in 1952 were so impressed by Nixon's earnest delivery that they flooded Republican headquarters with telegrams demanding that he stay on the ticket.

lican leaders had no choice but to keep him on the ticket. The "Checkers speech" showed how the mass media—particularly television—were fundamentally changing the political process.

The Republican campaign paid off handsomely, with Eisenhower winning 55 percent of the popular vote. He carried all the northern and western states and won majorities in four southern states. Although Eisenhower won a great personal victory, Republican candidates for Congress ran far behind him. They won control of the House of Representatives by a slender margin of four seats and regained the Senate. In 1954 Democrats would regain control of both houses, an advantage they held even when the enormously popular Eisenhower won an easy reelection over Adlai Stevenson in 1956.

The Hidden-Hand Presidency

Seeking a middle ground between liberalism and conservatism, Eisenhower offered "modern Republicanism" as an alternative to the Democrats' liberal agenda. He did his best to set a quieter national mood, lessening the need for federal activism on social and economic issues. As columnist Richard L. Strout observed in *The New Republic*, "The less he does the more they love him. Here is a man who doesn't rock the boat." The nation's voters put it more simply in a popular slogan: "I Like Ike."

Yet Eisenhower was no stooge as president. Several historians have characterized his style of leadership as the "hidden-hand presidency." They point out that Eisenhower maneuvered deftly behind-the-scenes while maintaining a public demeanor of not concerning himself with partisan questions. They also cite the president's skillful handling of the press. When his press secretary, James Hagerty, asked what he would say at a press conference about a tricky foreign policy issue, Eisenhower replied, "Don't worry, Jim. If that question comes up, I'll just confuse them." He proved just as adept in personnel situations. In a characteristic move, Eisenhower recognized the outspoken anticommunism of Clare Booth Luce, an author, playwright, and former Republican member of Congress from Connecticut, by making her the nation's second woman ambassador. At the same time, by sending Luce to Italy, he removed her strident opinions from the Washington scene.

Eisenhower's presidential style deliberately avoided confrontation. He refused to speak out publicly against Senator Joseph McCarthy. Likewise, he displayed little leadership in the emerging area of civil rights. Inadvertently, though, he contributed to the advance of the black cause. In September 1953 he named Governor Earl Warren of California as chief justice of the Supreme Court. Warren's quiet persuasion convinced the Court to rule unanimously in *Brown v. Board of Education of Topeka* (1954) that racial segregation in the public schools was unconstitutional (see Chapter 31). Eisenhower remained disturbed by the decision, asserting, "I don't believe you can change the hearts of men with laws or decisions." Nonetheless, in 1957 he sent federal troops to enforce the integration of Central High School in Little Rock, Arkansas. He also signed the Civil Rights Act of 1957, a Democratic-inspired bill which though weak was the first national civil rights legislation passed since Reconstruction.

Eisenhower presided over other cautious increases in federal activity. When the Soviet Union launched the first satellite *Sputnik*—or "earth traveler"—in 1957, Eisenhower supported a U.S. space program to catch up with the Russians. Arguing that the Cold War required more scientists and experts on foreign affairs, he persuaded Congress to appropriate additional money for college and university scholarships and to increase support for research and development in universities and industry. He also yielded to demands of interest groups to increase federal outlays for veterans' benefits, unemployment compensation, housing, and Social Security. The minimum wage was raised from seventy-five cents an hour to a dollar. The creation of the new Department of Health, Education, and Welfare (HEW) confirmed the federal commitment to social welfare programs. When HEW head Oveta Culp Hobby, the second woman to hold a cabinet position, suggested that it would be "socialized medicine" for the government to

Sputnik
Given the size of the spacecraft that now take astronauts into space, we forget how tiny the original Soviet satellite was—a mere 184 pounds and 22 inches in diameter. Here a replica hangs in a Moscow exhibit hall—a symbol of pride for Soviet citizens, and in the Cold War atmosphere of 1957, an acute embarrassment for the United States government. When the American navy tried and failed to launch a satellite two months later (it only lifted six inches off the ground before exploding), newspaper headlines savagely pronounced, "Kaputnik!"

offer free distribution of the new Salk polio vaccine, she was forced from office by the adverse public reaction.

Under the Eisenhower administration, the government undertook new commitments on a more massive scale. It cosponsored with Canada the construction of the St. Lawrence Seaway to link the Great Lakes with the Atlantic Ocean, a project which had been under discussion since the 1930s. In a move that drastically altered the American landscape and favored the trend toward privately owned automobiles rather than mass transit, the Interstate Highway Act of 1956 authorized $26 billion over a ten-year period for the construction of a nationally integrated highway system. (This network of highways was also promoted to speed civilian evacuation in the event of nuclear attack.) Projects such as the St. Lawrence Seaway and interstate highways were the largest public works programs to date, surpassing anything the New Deal had undertaken. They confirmed the permanent role that federal spending now played in American life, even under Republican administrations.

President Eisenhower realized that the vast federal budget, which reached almost 23 percent of the gross national product by the late 1950s, gave the government a major responsibility for the overall health of the nation's economy. The president made the fight against inflation, not full employment, his top economic priority. Eisenhower and his advisers believed their policies would encourage business confidence and lead to prosperity, but the economy grew only at the modest rate of 2.9 percent per year between 1953 and 1960—too slowly to absorb all those who sought work. The unemployment rate fluctuated from a low of 2.9 percent in 1953 to a high of 6.8 percent in 1958. Furthermore, Eisenhower's drive for a balanced budget and stable prices contributed to the recessions of 1953–1954, 1957–1958, and 1960–1961.

Modern Republicanism, it turned out, resisted the unchecked expansion of the state but did not cut federal power back in any tangible fashion. The responsibilities now accepted by the federal government—social welfare programs inherited from the New Deal, Keynesian intervention in the economy, and increased defense expenditures necessitated by the United States' larger role abroad—foreclosed any return to the limited Republican government that had prevailed in the 1920s. When Eisenhower retired from public life in 1961, the federal government had become an even greater presence in everyday life than when he took office.

Alliances and Arms

Dwight Eisenhower had earned a reputation for excellent judgment in military and diplomatic affairs during his years in the armed forces. One of his first acts as president was to put that skill to use to negotiate an end to the Korean War. As he had pledged in the campaign, he visited Korea in December 1952. The final settlement was signed in July 1953 at Panmunjom after a compromise on the tricky issue of prisoner exchange was reached. Once the Korean matter had been settled, Eisenhower's attention turned back to Europe. Secretary of State John Foster Dulles played an important role in defining the administration's foreign policy. Dulles, an experienced international lawyer and diplomat, was an outspoken critic of "atheistic communism." Rather than just limiting further Soviet expansion, he argued, the United States ought to promote the "liberation" of the "captive nations" of Eastern Europe.

The Soviet Union Under Khrushchev. At the beginning of the Eisenhower administration, the Soviet Union briefly appeared more interested in better relations. Joseph Stalin died in March 1953, and Georgi Malenkov, who adopted a more conciliatory tone toward the West, assumed his duties. After an intraparty struggle that lasted until 1956, Nikita S. Khrushchev emerged as Stalin's successor. He soon startled Communists throughout the world by denouncing Stalin as "a distrustful man, sickly and suspicious," and detailing publicly for the first time Stalin's "crimes" and "tortures" of the 1930s and 1940s. Khrushchev likewise surprised Westerners by calling for "peaceful coexistence" between communist and capitalist societies. He also seemed more willing to tolerate different approaches to communism, such as that developed by Yugoslavia's Marshal Tito or Poland's Wladislaw Gomulka. When Gomulka, who had once been jailed in a Stalinist purge, insisted that his nation's Communists be allowed to work out Poland's problems in their own way, Khrushchev agreed.

On the other hand, Khrushchev made certain that Russia's Eastern European satellites did not deviate too far from the Soviet path. When a nationalist revolt erupted in Hungary in 1956, Soviet tanks rapidly moved into Budapest. Demonstrating their willingness to use massive force to retain control in Eastern Europe, the Soviets crushed the revolt and installed a puppet regime. Despite Dulles's rhetoric, there was little the United States could do beyond loosening immigration quotas for Hungarian refugees.

A Web of Alliances. The Soviet repression of the Hungarian revolt confirmed that American policymakers had few, if any, options to "roll back" Soviet power in Eastern Europe short of going to war with the U.S.S.R. An alternative strategy, already in force, sought to limit communism through a permanent alliance structure. Truman, Marshall, and Acheson had established key military alliances in Europe, such as NATO. In 1954, Dulles negotiated bilateral defense treaties with South Korea and the nationalist Chinese regime on Taiwan, and orchestrated the creation of the Southeast Asia Collective Defense and Treaty Organization (SEATO). In 1955 the United States sponsored, but did not join, the Baghdad Pact, a defensive alliance between Turkey and Iraq that was important to national security because of those countries' strategic location on the borders of the Soviet Union.

U.S. policymakers also displayed a tendency to support stable governments, no matter what their politics, as a bulwark against the supposed threat of communism. As a result, some of America's staunchest allies—the Philippines, Iran, Nicaragua, and the Dominican Republic—were military dictatorships or governments lacking broad-based popular support. The secretary of state regarded the establishment of these overtly anticommunist alliances as an imperative. "Neutrality," Dulles maintained, was not only "obsolete" but "immoral."

CIA Activities. Firm in the righteousness of his cause, Dulles did not shrink from covert interventions against governments that were, in his opinion, too closely aligned with communism. For such tasks, he used the Central Intelligence Agency, which was headed by his brother, Allen Dulles. During the Eisenhower administration, the CIA moved beyond its original mandate of intelligence gathering to active, if secret, involvement in the internal affairs of foreign countries where such covert action suited American objectives.

In the 1950s the CIA successfully directed the overthrow of several foreign governments. When Iran's nationalist premier, Mohammad Mossadegh, seized British oil properties in 1953, CIA agents helped the young shah, Mohammad Reza Pahlevi, depose him. Using both economic leverage and a repressive secret police, the shah soon solidified his power within Iran. In 1954 the CIA supported a coup in Guatemala against popularly elected Jacobo Arbenz Guzman, who had expropriated 250,000 acres held by the American-owned United Fruit Company and accepted arms from the communist government of East Germany. The CIA also tried, unsuccessfully, to overthrow Achmed Sukarno of Indonesia in 1958 and Fidel Castro of Cuba in 1961. Eisenhower specifically approved these efforts. "Our traditional ideas of international sportsmanship," he wrote privately in 1955, "are scarcely applicable in the morass in which the world now flounders."

The "New Look" in Foreign Policy. Although Eisenhower strongly opposed communism, he hoped to keep the cost of containment at a manageable level. His "New Look" in foreign policy tried to encourage the nation's allies to bear some of the responsibility for maintaining large armed forces, mainly through the extensive system of defense pacts. One byproduct was an increased role for the CIA, an agency that was relatively cheap as a foreign policy tool. (Another advantage was its ability to work covertly, removed from public scrutiny.) The administration also increased the flow of American military aid. Truman had emphasized economic assistance over military aid, but Eisenhower reversed the priorities.

As part of the "New Look," Eisenhower and Dulles also embraced the policy of "massive retaliation." They believed the United States could economize by developing an effective nuclear deterrent rather than relying solely on expensive conventional armed forces. Nuclear weapons delivered "more bang for the buck" in the words of Defense Secretary Charles E. Wilson. If the nation's major foreign enemy were a worldwide commu-

Testing An Atomic Bomb
Throughout the 1950s, the Atomic Energy Commission conducted above-ground tests of atomic and hydrogen bombs. Thousands of soldiers were exposed to fallout during the tests, such as this one at Yucca Flat, Nevada, in April 1952. The AEC, ignoring or suppressing medical evidence to the contrary, mounted an extensive public relations campaign to convince local residents that the tests did not endanger their health.

nist movement led by Moscow, they reasoned, the United States did not need to keep a large number of soldiers under arms, because atomic weapons could threaten the Soviet Union directly and force it to back down. To this end, the Eisenhower administration expanded its commitment to the hydrogen bomb, including extensive atmospheric testing in the South Pacific and Western states such as Nevada, Colorado, and Utah. To improve U.S. defenses against an air attack from the Soviet Union, the administration supported research to develop the long-range bombing capabilities of the Strategic Air Command and installed the Distant Early Warning (DEW) line of radar stations in Alaska and Canada in 1958.

These efforts did little to improve the nation's security, as the Soviets matched the United States weapon for weapon in an escalating arms race. The Soviet Union carried out its own atmospheric tests of hydrogen bombs between 1953 and 1958 and developed a fleet of long-range bombers. It briefly won the race to build an intercontinental ballistic missile (ICBM), but the United States launched its own ICBM in 1958. In 1960 an American nuclear submarine was the first to launch an atomic-tipped Polaris missile. Soviet leaders raced to produce equivalent weapons.

Although the Soviet Union viewed the Eisenhower and Dulles policies of anticommunist alliances and massive deterrence as inherently hostile, Eisenhower continued to work toward a negotiated arms limitation agreement. President Eisenhower was deeply disturbed by the implications of a nuclear policy that was based on the premise of annihilating your enemy, even if your own country was destroyed—the aptly named acronym MAD (Mutual Assured Destruction). Although preliminary discussions with Soviet leaders between 1955 and 1957 had not yielded the "open skies" mutual arms inspection treaty he had wanted, they did produce plans for a summit meeting with Khrushchev in May 1960. Then, on May 5, an American spy plane was shot down over Soviet territory. With Eisenhower's admission that he had authorized this and other secret flights by high-flying U-2 reconnaissance aircraft over the Soviet Union, his last chance to negotiate an arms agreement evaporated.

AMERICAN VOICES

An Atomic Bomb Veteran Remembers *George Mace*

George Mace's life was changed by his participation in atomic testing in the Pacific in the 1950s. He blames his ongoing health problems on the over thirty-five atomic and hydrogen bomb blasts he witnessed there. He became involved in the National Association of Atomic Veterans, founded in 1979, which has pressured the federal government to release the full story of what happened during the tests of the 1940s and 1950s.

I graduated from high school in 1953 and enlisted in the Air Force in 1955 to gain a trade. I originally went into communications as a teletype repairman, and by the last year of my enlistment I was a crypto and typographical equipment instructor at Lackland Air Force Base in San Antonio. In 1957, orders came down assigning me to Joint Task Force 7 on the Enewetak atoll in the Marshall Islands of the South Pacific. Initially it was for six months. So I took my wife and baby daughter back home to Hagerstown and left for Enewetak. I was twenty-two. . . .

Enewetak was so small that at first, I couldn't find it from the air; but then a single concrete airstrip came into view and it was as if we had landed on an aircraft carrier. Immediately we were briefed on the island's facilities and its very tight security. I remember being told that we couldn't write home about anything we saw or did and that our mail would be checked and edited. All of our standard uniforms were exchanged for khaki shorts, short sleeved shirts, and blue baseball caps. We wore that uniform all the time when we were on the island, for the next nine months. . . .

We were never told that a shot was going to occur until the day of the event. And every day there was a shot, they'd march us out to the beach and make us sit there with our backs to the lagoon. At the time, I always asked how far we were away from it, and I was always told about fifty miles. But in 1979, when I got the declassified documents, I found out that I was only five to fifteen miles from the bombs—never more than fifteen miles! So there was a clear deception on the part of the government.

Watching the shots got to be kind of pointless after a while; there was no follow-up study of us at all. They were just preparing the troops for the age of atomic war. We were never told about any effects of radiation, and being young and ignorant, I had no fear of it. But I *did* fear the tremendous strength of each blast. The enlisted men would sit on the sand with their heads on their knees, and the officers faced the bombs with dark goggles—welder's goggles really. We'd cover our eyes until the fireball passed. A few seconds after the explosion went off you would see this tremendous flash, and then a tremendous wave of heat you could feel like the sun coming up on your back. The biggest one I ever saw—code named Oak—got to the point of being uncomfortable.

The Oak explosion was nine megatons. I will never forget it; we sandbagged the island beforehand, because it was only seven feet above sea level. When it went off there was this wink of light that I sensed through my closed eyes and hands, just like a flashbulb behind me. And when I turned to see the column of water rising out of the lagoon, it was so tremendous that no one spoke. You could hear the sound waves bouncing off the island—Boom! Boom! And when the sound wave hit Enewetak, the whole island shook and a hot wind blew our baseball caps off.

The column was surrounded by ragged haloes of white shock waves which produced an electrical field. I actually experienced an electrical field passing through me; my hair stood up and there was a cracking sensation all through me that was as much felt as heard.

And that thing just continued to build and grow until it had risen about sixty or seventy thousand feet. The mushroom covered the entire island chain. Fifteen miles of islands were all shadowed by this terrifying, magnificent thing. I remember talk of an evacuation, but it never occurred.

After fifteen or twenty minutes, the water in the lagoon began to recede until the bottom was exposed for about two hundred yards. We could see sunken PT boats and equipment that was normally covered by fifteen or twenty feet of water. I really thought that they had cracked the earth and that the water was running into it! I mean, it had to go somewhere, right? But finally, the water stopped receding and it just stood there like a wall for a minute. Then it started coming back. I got a hell of a feeling then, because here we were on this dinky little island, not even half a mile wide, and here comes the whole ocean. It hit the island and sprayed up over the sandbags—all day long, the water kept seesawing back and forth like that. The column of water had just sucked it all up from fifteen miles away. I will never forget that.

After that shot the water was off limits for swimming for three days. But the ironic part of it was that the ocean was the source of our drinking water after it went through the desalinization plant. I didn't have any knowledge of radiation, so I wasn't afraid of it. They did give us dosimeters to wear sometimes to measure the gamma rays, but that was just another badge to take care of. I wasn't worried—I trusted my country. In 1958, I really did. To be truthful with you, I was proud to be there.

Source: Sam Totten and Martha Wescoat Totten, *Facing the Danger: Interviews with 20 Anti-Nuclear Activists* (Trumansburg, N.Y.: The Crossing Press, 1984), 52–56.

The Emerging Third World

Though preoccupied with the Soviet Union throughout the postwar period, American policymakers faced another challenge: developing a coherent policy toward the new nations that were rapidly emerging from the disintegrating European empires in Africa, Asia, and the Middle East. In the interests of global capitalism, it was imperative that such nations develop stable market economies which could be integrated into the world system. Also important was the commitment to national self-determination that had shaped American participation in both world wars. Third World political problems generally remained low priority, however, unless a short-term crisis demanded U.S. attention. And in certain areas, such as Latin America, traditional patterns of American penetration and dominance played a far larger role in determining United States policies than global politics.

Nationalism, socialism, and religion had already inspired powerful anticolonial movements before World War II; such forces intensified and spread, especially in the Middle East, Africa, and the Far East, during the 1940s and 1950s. Between 1947 and 1962, the British, French, Dutch, and Belgian empires all but disappeared. The British withdrawal from India in 1947, and the subsequent creation of the states of India (predominantly Hindu) and Pakistan (predominantly Muslim), was an especially important milestone.

The end to colonial empires fulfilled a goal the United States had sought in vain after World War I, and the nation in general welcomed the independence of the new states. At the same time, both the Truman and Eisenhower administrations were so caught up in the polarities of the Cold War that they often failed to recognize that indigenous nationalist or socialist movements in these emerging nations had their own goals and were not always under the strict control either of local communists or the Soviet Union. This failure to appreciate the complexity of local conditions limited the effectiveness of American policy toward the emerging Third World.

The Middle East, an oil-rich area that was playing an increasingly central role in strategic planning, presented one of the most complicated challenges. Zionism, the Jewish nationalist movement, had long encouraged Jews to return to their ancient homeland. After World War II, many of the Jews who had survived the Nazi extermination camps resettled in Palestine, still controlled by Britain under a World War I mandate. On November 29, 1947, the United Nations general assembly voted for the partition of Palestine into Jewish and Arab states. On May 14, 1948, the British mandate ended and Zionist leaders proclaimed the state of Israel. The Arab League states rejected the U.N. partition and invaded Israel. Israel survived, but the planned Palestinian state never came into existence, creating a large number of Palestinian refugees who now had no homeland. President Truman quickly recognized Israel, alienating the Arabs but winning crucial support from Jewish voters in the tight 1948 election.

Britain had been the dominant foreign power in the

The Birth of Israel, 1948
Prime Minister David Ben-Gurion reads Israel's Declaration of Independence to the new country's assembled officials.

Persian Gulf since the nineteenth century, and its withdrawal from Palestine in 1947 created a power vacuum in this already unstable area. When Gamal Abdel Nasser came to power in Egypt in 1954, two years after independence from Britain, he pledged to lead not just his country but the entire Middle East out of its dependent, colonial relationship through a form of pan-Arab socialism. Nasser obtained arms and promises of economic assistance from the Soviet Union in return for Egyptian cotton. When the Soviets offered to finance a dam on the Nile River at Aswan, Secretary of State Dulles countered with an offer of American assistance. Nasser refused to distance himself from the Russians, however, and in July 1956, Dulles abruptly withdrew the U.S. offer.

A week later Nasser retaliated against the withdrawal of Western financial aid by nationalizing the Suez Canal, over which Britain had retained administrative authority. Nasser said he would use the tolls from the canal to build the dam himself. After several months of fruitless negotiation, Britain and France, in alliance with Israel, attacked Egypt and retook the canal. When Eisenhower and the United Nations condemned this action, they reluctantly pulled back, although Israel retained the Gaza strip temporarily. In the end the Suez crisis increased Soviet influence in the Third World and produced dissension among the leading members of the NATO alliance.

In January 1957, showing concern that the Soviet Union might step into the vacuum created by the British withdrawal, the president persuaded Congress to approve the "Eisenhower Doctrine." This policy stated that American forces would assist any Middle Eastern nation "requiring such aid, against overt armed aggression from any nation controlled by International Communism." Invoking the doctrine, Eisenhower sent the U.S. Sixth Fleet to the Mediterranean Sea to aid King Hussein of Jordan in 1957. A year later, Eisenhower landed 8,000 troops to back up a pro-United States government in Lebanon.

The attention that the Eisenhower administration paid to developments in the Middle East in the 1950s demonstrated how the desire for access to steady supplies of oil increasingly affected strategic foreign policy considerations. (By 1955, two-thirds of the traffic through the Suez Canal was petroleum.) More broadly, attention to the Middle East confirmed that American policymakers no longer believed that containment of Soviet power in Eastern Europe was enough to guarantee American national security. Now the United States had to be concerned about communism and nationalism globally, especially in emerging Third World countries, for both economic and geopolitical reasons. The case of the small country of Vietnam, which won its independence from France in 1954, would show that localized wars for national liberation could be just as troubling for American foreign policy as the threat of worldwide Soviet domination.

Eisenhower's Farewell Address

When President Eisenhower left office in January 1961, he used his final address to warn the nation of a "military-industrial complex" that already employed 3.5 million Americans and whose "total influence—economic, political, even spiritual—is felt in every city, every statehouse, every office of the Federal Government." Even though his administration had fostered this growth in the defense establishment, Eisenhower was still gravely concerned about its implications for a democratic people:

> In the councils of government we must guard against the acquisition of unwarranted influence whether sought or unsought, by the military-industrial complex. . . . We must never let the weight of this combination endanger our liberties or democratic processes. We should take nothing for granted. Only an alert and knowledgeable citizenry can compel the proper meshing of the huge industrial and military machinery of defense with our peaceful methods and goals so that security and liberty may prosper together.

With those words, Dwight Eisenhower showed how well he understood the major transformations that the Cold War had brought to American life.

Summary

American foreign policy shifted dramatically at the end of World War II. The United States took the leading role in world affairs and tried to shape the structure of international relations and trade to further its own interests. A resurgent Soviet Union with its own agenda stood in the way of American goals, and the resulting clash between the two superpowers brought about the Cold War. Containment originally emerged in response to Soviet pressure on Eastern Europe, but that doctrine was expanded by succeeding administrations to include resistance to communism and left-wing revolution wherever they appeared. A cold war mentality shaped U.S. foreign policy well into the 1980s.

America's new international role had strong domestic repercussions. The new importance of foreign affairs enhanced the power of the president. Tension about communism abroad fostered a period of domestic repression and fear at home. Growing defense expenditures took up an ever-larger part of the gross national product. Besides paying for defense through taxes and growing deficits, American citizens now lived in a world where small foreign wars were a constant possibility and fear of nuclear attack became part of daily life.

The Democratic party set much of the legislative agenda for the postwar period, expanding the reforms first introduced by Franklin Roosevelt in the 1930s. Harry Truman's Fair Deal won only limited legislative victories but added civil rights to the national political agenda. The Republican administration of Dwight Eisenhower did not seek to roll back the New Deal and, in fact, presided over cautious increases in federal power.

TOPIC FOR RESEARCH

Truman and the Polls

The first Gallup polls appeared just before the 1936 election, and they have been a prominent aspect of political life ever since. For historians as well as politicians, polls offer a chance to sample a range of public opinion ("Americans believe . . .") on a wide variety of issues. Yet polls have proved imperfect sources, especially in their early days.

The Truman administration offers many cases to test the usefulness of public opinion polls as sources. The most obvious example is the 1948 election, where polls widely predicted a Dewey victory. Also of interest are the dramatic fluctuations in Truman's popularity and the seeming contradiction between popular dissatisfaction with the Korean War and public support for General Douglas MacArthur. What can polls tell us about political events? How useful are they for forming assessments of the Truman presidency? How closely can you correlate historical events with popular reaction? Conversely, can you show how public opinion shaped the course of political events and history?

Gallup polls from the 1940s have been collected in three volumes in George Gallup, *The Gallup Poll: Public Opinion,* 1935–1971 (New York: Random House, 1972). Alonzo Hamby, *Beyond the New Deal: Harry S. Truman and American Liberalism* (1973) is a good overview of the Truman administration. For the 1948 election, see Irwin Ross, *The Loneliest Campaign* (1968) and Jules Abels, *Out of the Jaws of Victory* (1959).

BIBLIOGRAPHY

The Origins of the Cold War

The two best overviews are Walter LaFeber, *America, Russia, and the Cold War, 1945–1990* (6th edition, 1990), and Stephen Ambrose, *Rise to Globalism* (5th ed., 1988). Thomas J. McCormick, *America's Half-Century* (1989) places the United States in the modern world-system. See also John Lewis Gaddis, *Strategies of Containment* (1982), plus his earlier *The United States and the Origins of the Cold War* (1972); Bernard Weisberger, *Cold War, Cold Peace* (1984); Thomas Paterson, *Meeting the Communist Threat* (1988); and Lloyd Gardner, *Architects of Illusion* (1970). Daniel Yergin, *Shattered Peace* (1977), focuses on the rise of the national security state. For perspectives critical of American aims, see Joyce and Gabriel Kolko, *The Limits of Power* (1970) and Robert J. Maddox, *The New Left and the Origins of the Cold War* (1977). Specialized studies include Laurence S. Kaplan, *The United States and NATO* (1984); Imanuel Wexler, *The Marshall Plan Revisited* (1983); Richard Freeland, *The Truman Doctrine and the Origins of McCarthyism* (1972); and Richard J. Barnet, *The Roots of War* (1972).

The descent into Cold War can also be viewed through individual policymakers. Indispensable are George F. Kennan, *American Diplomacy, 1900–1950* (1952) and *Memoirs, 1925–1950* (1967); and Dean Acheson's modestly titled *Present at the Creation* (1970). Walter Isaacson and Evan Thomas, *The Wise Men* (1986) traces the impact of John McCloy, Averill Harriman, Charles Bohlen, George Kennan, Dean Acheson, and Robert Lovett on postwar foreign policy. Walter Lippmann, *The Cold War* (1947) can be supplemented by Ronald Steel's fine biography, *Walter Lippmann and the American Century* (1980). Adam Ulam presents the Soviet point of view in *The Rivals: America and Russia Since World War II* (1971).

McGeorge Bundy, *Danger and Survival* (1989); Martin J. Sherwin, *A World Destroyed* (1975); and Gar Alperowitz, *Atomic Diplomacy* (1965) cover the impact of atomic weapons on policy formulation. For general discussion of America and nuclear weapons, see Paul Boyer, *By the Bomb's Early Light* (1985); Richard G. Hewlett and Jack Hall, *Atoms for Peace and War, 1953–1961* (1989); Gregg Herken, *Counsels of War* (1985); and Howard Ball, *Justice Downwind* (1986).

For developments in Asia, Akira Iriye, *The Cold War in Asia* (1974) is a good starting point. See also Warren I. Cohen, *America's Response to China* (2nd ed., 1980); Kenneth Shewmaker, *Americans and the Chinese Communists* (1971); and Michael Shaller, *The United States and China in the Twentieth*

Century (1979). E. J. Kahn, Jr., *The China Hands* (1975) and Ross Y. Kuen, *The China Lobby In American Politics* (1974) cover the domestic repercussions. On Japan, see Michael Schaller, *The American Occupation of Japan* (1985).

There has been a recent explosion of scholarship on the Korean War, including Clay Blair, *The Forgotten War* (1988); Max Hastings, *The Korean War* (1987); Callum McDonald, *Korea: The War Before Vietnam* (1987); Burton Kaufman, *The Korean War* (1986); and Rosemary Foot, *The Wrong War* (1985). Especially influential are the two volumes of *The Origins of the Korean War* by Bruce Cumings: *Liberation and the Emergence of Separate Regions, 1945–1947* (1981) and *The Roaring of the Cataract, 1947–1950* (1990). Earlier studies include Joseph C. Gouldens, *Korea* (1962); David Rees, *Korea: The Limited War* (1964); and Ronald J. Caridi, *The Korean War and American Politics* (1969). William Manchester, *American Caesar* (1979) and Michael Schaller, *Douglas MacArthur* (1989) offer stimulating biographies of a leading figure of the war.

Harry Truman and the Fair Deal

Two lively introductions to politics in the postwar period are William E. Leuchtenberg, *A Troubled Feast: American Society Since 1945* (1979) and John Patrick Diggins, *The Proud Decades: America in War and Peace, 1941–1960* (1988). Harry Truman's *Memoirs* (1952–1962) tell his story in characteristically pointed language; see also Merle Miller's oral history, *Plain Speaking* (1980). General accounts of the Truman presidency are found in Robert J. Donovan, *Tumultuous Years: The Presidency of Harry S Truman, 1949–1953* (1982), plus his earlier *Conflict and Crisis* (1977); Eric F. Goldman, *The Crucial Decade and After—America, 1945–1960* (1961); Donald R. McCoy, *The Presidency of Harry S Truman* (1984); William Pemberton, *Harry S Truman* (1989). Critical perspectives are presented in Barton J. Bernstein, ed., *Politics and Policies of The Truman Administration* (1970). Arthur M. Schlesinger, Jr., states the case for Fair Deal liberalism in *The Vital Center* (1949).

More specialized studies of the Truman years include Gary Reichard, *Politics as Usual* (1986); Andrew J. Dunar, *The Truman Scandals and the Politics of Morality* (1984); Jack Stokes Ballard, *The Shock of Peace: Military and Economic Demobilization After World War II* (1983); Stephen K. Bailey, *Congress Makes a Law* (1957) (the Employment Act of 1946); Allen J. Matusow, *Farm Policies and Politics in the Truman Years* (1967); Susan Hartmann, *Truman and the 80th Congress* (1971). The story of the Democratic coalition can be traced in Samuel Lubbell, *The Future of American Politics* (1965); V. O. Key, *Politics, Parties, and Pressure Groups* (1964); and Everett C. Ladd and Charles Hadley, *Transformations of the American Party System* (1978). On the Wallace challenge to Truman, see Norman D. Markowitz, *The Rise and Fall of the People's Century* (1973). Joseph P. Lash, *Eleanor: The Years Alone* (1972) describes the former First Lady's continuing work for liberal causes. James T. Patterson, *Mr. Republican: A Biography of Robert A. Taft* (1972), covers Truman's chief Republican critic.

The literature on McCarthyism is voluminous and intense. Two recent overviews are Richard Fried, *Nightmare in Red: The McCarthy Era in Perspective* (1990) and Stephen J. Whitfield, *The Culture of the Cold War* (1991). David Caute, *The Great Fear* (1978), provides another introduction, which can be supplemented by Victor Navasky, *Naming Names* (1980) and Athan Theoharis, *Spying on Americans* (1978). Two biographies are Thomas C. Reeves, *The Life and Times of Joe McCarthy* (1982), and David Oshinsky, *A Conspiracy So Immense* (1983); but Richard Rovere's *Senator Joseph McCarthy* (1959) still commands attention. Michael P. Rogin, *The Intellectuals and McCarthy* (1967), analyzes McCarthy's base of support, while Robert Griffith, *The Politics of Fear* (1970), and Richard Fried, *Men Against McCarthy* (1976), look at the politics involved. Ellen Schrecker, *No Ivory Tower* (1986) treats McCarthyism in academia, while Lary Ceplair and Steven Englund, *The Inquisition in Hollywood* (1983) looks at the impact on the film industry.

Allen Weinstein, *Perjury* (1978), covers the still-debated Hiss case. Walter and Miriam Schneir, *Invitation to an Inquest* (1965), and Ronald Radosh and Joyce Milton, *The Rosenberg File* (1983), cover the Rosenberg case. Lillian Hellman offers her biting, and not always reliable, memoir of the period in *Scoundrel Time* (1976). Eric Bentley, ed., *Thirty Years of Treason* (1971), collects excerpts from testimony before the House Committee on Un-American Activities. For the FBI and its controversial leader, see Richard Gid Powers, *Secrecy and Power: The Life of J. Edgar Hoover* (1987) and Athan Theoharis and John Stuart Case, *The Boss: J. Edgar Hoover and the Great American Inquisition* (1988).

Modern Republicanism

Two standard overviews of the Eisenhower administration, Herbert S. Parmet, *Eisenhower and the American Crusades* (1972), and Charles C. Alexander, *Holding the Line* (1975), can be supplemented by Fred I. Greenstein, *The Hidden-Hand Presidency* (1982) and Stephen Ambrose, *Eisenhower the President* (1984). Blanche Wiesen Cook, *The Declassified Eisenhower* (1984) contrasts the covert activities of the administration with its public image. Robert F. Burk, *The Eisenhower Administration and Black Civil Rights* (1984) looks at what the administration did, and did not, do. For scientific developments, consult James R. Killian, Jr., *Sputnik, Scientists, and Eisenhower* (1976). Richard M. Nixon, *Six Crisis* (1962) offers the perspective of the vice-president.

For the complex foreign policy of the 1950s, consult LaFeber, *America, Russia, and the Cold War,* Ambrose, *Rise to Globalism,* and McCormick, *America's Half Century.* Other overviews are Robert Divine, *Eisenhower and the Cold War* (1981), and Ronald Steel, *Pax Americana* (1967). An excellent book on the CIA is Victor Marchetti and John D. Marks, *The CIA and the Cult of Intelligence* (1974). For developments linking economics, corporations, and the defense industry, see Mira Wilkins, *The Maturing of Multinational Enterprise* (1974); Richard Barnet and Ronald Muller, *Global Reach* (1974); and Paul Hammond, *Organizing For Defense* (1971). Gabriel Kolko, *Confronting the Third World, 1945–1980* (1988), offers an opinionated overview; specific studies include Bruce Kuniholm, *The Origins of the Cold War in the Near East* (1980) and Michael Stoff, *Oil, War, and American Security* (1980).

On specific policy situations in the 1950s, see Robert Divine, *Blowing in the Wind: The Nuclear Test Ban Debate, 1954–1960* (1978); Robert Stookey, *America and the Arab States* (1975); John Snetsinger, *Truman, the Jewish Role and the Creation of Israel* (1974); Hugh Thomas, *Suez* (1967); and Melanie Billings-Yun, *Decision Against War: Eisenhower and Dien Bien Phu, 1954* (1988). Of interest for his later career are Henry Kissinger, *Nuclear Weapons and Foreign Policy* (1957) and *The Necessity of Choice* (1961).

TIMELINE

1945	Yalta and Potsdam conferences Harry S. Truman succeeds Roosevelt as president End of World War II
1946	Employment Act
1947	Taft-Hartley Act Truman Doctrine Marshall Plan
1948	Desegregation of armed forces State of Israel created Berlin airlift
1949	North Atlantic Treaty Organization (NATO) founded People's Republic of China established National Housing Act
1950–1953	Korean War
1950	Alger Hiss convicted of perjury NSC-68 (National Security Council report) calls for permanent mobilization
1952	Dwight D. Eisenhower elected president U.S. detonates hydrogen bomb
1954	Army-McCarthy hearings *Brown v. Board of Education of Topeka*
1956	Suez crisis Interstate Highway Act
1957	Eisenhower Doctrine U.S.S.R. launches *Sputnik*
1959	St. Lawrence Seaway completed

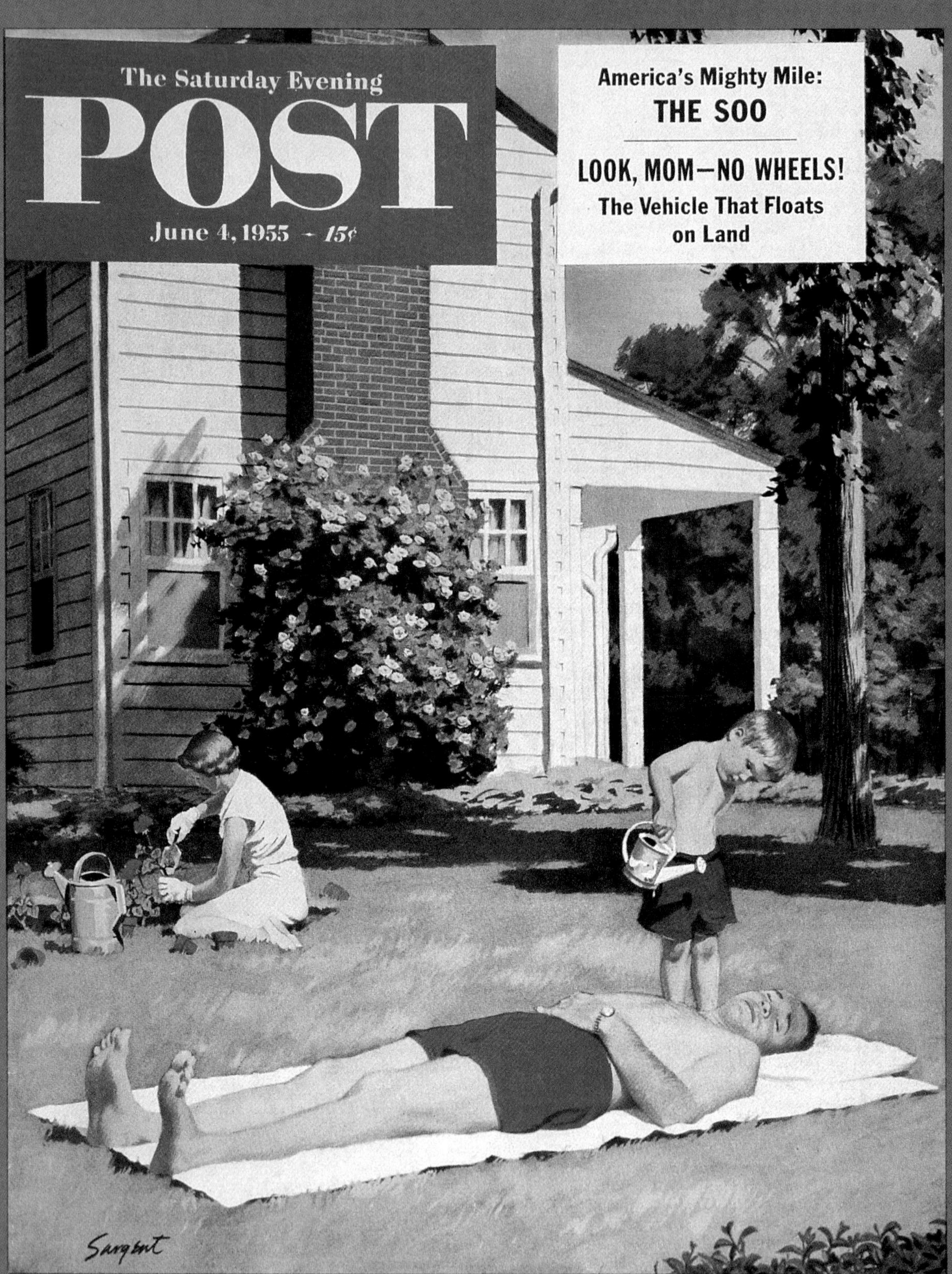
The Saturday Evening
POST
June 4, 1955 • 15¢
America's Mighty Mile:
THE SOO
LOOK, MOM—NO WHEELS!
The Vehicle That Floats
on Land
Sargent

Life in the Suburbs

During the 1950s the *Saturday Evening Post* celebrated the surburban ideal—family, leisure, and nurturing wife and mother.

CHAPTER 29 *Affluence and Its Contradictions, 1945–1965*

In 1959, Vice-President Richard M. Nixon traveled to Moscow to open the American National Exhibition. It was the height of both the Cold War and the postwar baby boom. After sipping from bottles of Pepsi-Cola, Nixon and Soviet Premier Nikita Khrushchev got into a heated debate about the relative merits of Soviet and American societies. But instead of debating rockets, submarines, and missiles, they talked dishwashers, toasters, and televisions. Both the subject of the animated conversation and its site (it took place in the kitchen of a model American home) led to its popular designation as the "kitchen debate."

The Moscow exhibition was designed to showcase American consumer and leisure goods. Its main attraction was a full scale model of a six-room, ranch-style house, filled with labor-saving appliances and devices that supposedly were typical of an American family back home. Over the next three weeks, more than 3 million Russians toured the exhibit, no doubt struck by, and the Americans hoped, jealous of all the gadgets and consumer appliances unavailable in Soviet society.

What was so striking about the kitchen debate was the way that affluence and mass consumption were enlisted in the service of American cold war politics. The suburban lifestyle trumpeted in the exhibit symbolized the superiority of capitalism over communism. The American way of life could win the Cold War.

After 1945, American citizens enjoyed the highest standard of living in the world, but this affluence was never as widespread as the Moscow exhibit implied. Moreover, the strong performance of the American economy was due in part to the relative weakness of all its competitors, who emerged from the war in far less secure economic shape than the United States. When the world economy returned to a more normal pattern in the 1960s and 1970s, the United States would face strong challenges to its postwar hegemony.

Technology and Economic Change

At the end of 1945, war-induced prosperity had made the American people the richest in the world. Over the next two decades, the gross national product more than tripled, and affluence reached a wider segment of society than anyone would have dreamed possible during the dark days of the depression. Industrial workers in the largest smokestack industries found their unions accepted at last, which translated into rising wages and expanding benefits. Employees of the successful large corporations—New York accountants, Georgia factory managers, Chicago engineers, San Francisco advertising executives, and Dallas office managers—were able to move their families into new homes in the suburbs. At the heart of this postwar prosperity lay the involvement of the federal government in national economic life. Federal outlays for defense and domestic programs, combined with galloping consumer spending, seemed to promise a continually rising standard of living.

The Economic Record

The impact of war mobilization laid the foundations for postwar economic success. The United States enjoyed overwhelming political and economic advantages at the end of World War II. Unlike the Soviet Union, which had lost more than 20 million citizens, or Western Europe and Japan, whose cities, factories, and population had been devastated by the fighting, the United States emerged physically unscathed from the war. Consumers had accumulated wartime savings of $140 billion, which created a strong market for the consumer goods that had been unavailable during the war. Business quickly applied the scientific and technological innovations developed for war production, such as plastics and synthetic fibers, to the production of consumer goods. The federal government eased conversion to a peacetime economy by allowing businesses to buy factories built for the war effort at a fraction of their cost.

The period from World War II through the late 1960s and early 1970s represented the heyday of modern American capitalism. U.S. corporations and banking institutions so dominated the world economy that the period has been called the *Pax Americana*. This American global supremacy rested on an institutional structure created at a United Nations economic conference held in Bretton Woods, New Hampshire, in July 1944. Its two key components were the International Bank for Reconstruction and Development (known commonly as the World Bank) and the International Monetary Fund (IMF), both founded in 1944. The World Bank provided private loans for the reconstruction of war-torn Europe as well as for developing Third World countries. The IMF was set up to stabilize currencies so that trade could function without fluctuations and devaluations. It did so by encouraging fixed exchange rates, which facilitated the free convertibility of currencies to gold or the currency of other trading nations; the strong U.S. dollar served as the benchmark. In 1947 multinational trade negotiations resulted in the General Agreement on Tariffs and Trade (GATT), which became the international body of rules and practices governing fair trade.

The World Bank, the IMF, and GATT were the cornerstones of the so-called Bretton Woods system that guided the world economy after the war. The United States in effect controlled the World Bank and the IMF, because it subscribed the most capital to them and because the dollar was designated as the principal reserve for world financial systems. Thus the independent international organizations worked along lines that favored American-style internationalism, rather than economic nationalism or autarky (self-sufficiency), adopting policies that encouraged stable prices, the liberalization of trade barriers and reduction of tariffs, flexible domestic markets, and free trade based on fixed exchange rates. As long as the dollar remained the strongest currency in the world, the Bretton Woods system effectively served America's global economic interests, paralleling many of the diplomatic goals the United States pursued in the Cold War.

This American hegemony abroad translated into affluence at home. The country's gross national product grew from $213 billion in 1945 to more than $500 billion in 1960; in 1970 the GNP approached $1 trillion. To working Americans, the steady economic growth meant a 25 percent rise in real income between 1946 and 1959. Most Americans rightly felt they had more money to spend than ever before. In 1940, 43 percent of American families owned their homes; by 1960, 62 percent did. But while the standard of living was rising, there was no redistribution of income—the top 10 percent still earned more than all the people in the bottom 50 percent put together.

One reason ordinary Americans felt better off was that inflation finally had been brought under control by the 1950s, a boon to both investors and individuals on fixed incomes. After the immediate postwar reconversion period, inflation slowed to 2 to 3 percent annually during the 1950s. It stayed low until 1965, when the increased military spending for the Vietnam War set off an inflationary spiral.

Despite high rates of economic growth, a rise in real income, and low inflation, there was an unevenness to the postwar economy that limited the rosy picture of economic success and affluence. Not all Americans shared in the general prosperity: the economy was plagued by periodic recessions accompanied by high unemployment. The permanently unemployed, the aged, female heads of households, and nonwhites all found themselves at a significant disadvantage. In *The Affluent Society* (1958), economist John Kenneth Galbraith

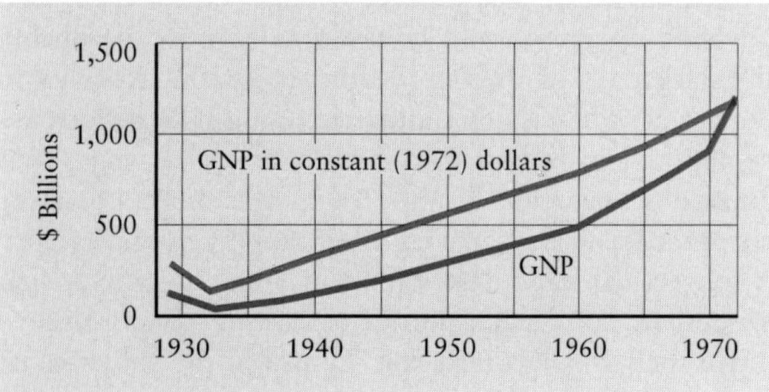

FIGURE 29.1

Gross National Product (GNP), 1929–1972

After a sharp dip during the Great Depression, the Gross National Product rose steadily in both real and constant dollars.

Consumer Culture
This 1962 painting by Tom Wesselmann mocks the consumer culture that it so lavishly illustrates with a table well stocked with brand-name goods. Realistic painting in the 1960s took on an air of cynicism, especially as practiced by artists such as Andy Warhol. Wesselman's *Still Life #24* treats the most ordinary objects of American life as icons, hinting at the new power of consumerism in popular culture. (The Nelson Atkins Museum of Art)

argued that the poor were only an "afterthought" in the minds of economists and politicians, who assumed that poverty was well on its way to extinction. Yet, as Galbraith noted, more than one family out of thirteen in the 1950s had a cash income of less than a thousand dollars.

The Military-Industrial Complex

An important linchpin of postwar prosperity was increased defense spending. The military-industrial complex that President Eisenhower identified in his 1961 farewell address had its immediate roots in the business-government partnerships of both world wars. But the massive commitment of government dollars to defense industries in the postwar era was unprecedented, a concrete reminder of how much the state had grown since the 1930s. Even though the country was technically at peace, the economy and government operated practically on a war footing—in a state of permanent mobilization.

In the late 1940s and 1950s, cold war mobilization and the Korean War led to a major expansion of the military establishment. Defense-related industries and the scientists and engineers they employed entered into a long-term relationship with the federal government in the name of national security. The Defense Department became practically a state within the state, with its headquarters at the sprawling Pentagon in Arlington, Virginia.

Certain companies did so much of their business with the government that they became almost exclusive vendors of the Defense Department. By the mid-1960s, Boeing and General Dynamics received 65 percent of their income from military contracts, Raytheon 60 percent, Lockheed 81 percent, and Republic Aviation 100 percent. The Pentagon reinforced the concentration of economic power at the top by awarding contracts to the largest firms. In 1967 the hundred largest corporations got 65 percent of the government contracts, while the top ten alone received more than 30 percent.

The impact of federal spending went deeper than just military contracts: science, corporate capitalism, and the federal government became increasingly intertwined in the postwar period. According to the National Science Foundation, federal money underwrote 90 percent of the cost of research on aviation and space, 65 percent on electricity and electronics, 42 percent on scientific instruments, and 24 percent on automobiles. With the government footing part of the bill, corporations transformed new ideas into useful products faster than ever before. After the Pentagon backed IBM's investment in integrated circuits in the 1960s, the new devices, crucial to the computer revolution, were in commercial production within three years.

The Pentagon

The Pentagon, so named because it has five sides, was the world's largest building when it was constructed in 1942. When the Department of Defense was established in 1947, the Pentagon became its sprawling headquarters, a symbol of America's postwar global responsibilities.

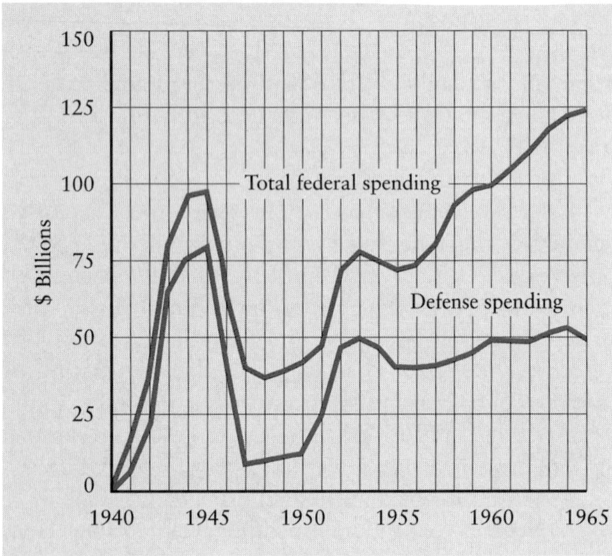

FIGURE 29.2

National Defense Spending, 1940–1965

In 1950 the defense budget was $13 billion, less than a third of the total federal outlays. In 1961 defense spending reached $47 billion—fully half of the federal budget and almost 10 percent of the nation's GNP.

The growth of this military-industrial establishment reflected a dramatic shift in national priorities. Military spending took up a greater percentage of national income as measured by the gross national product. Between 1900 and 1930, except for the two years that the United States fought in World War I, the country spent less than 1 percent of its GNP for military purposes. By 1960 the United States was regularly devoting close to 10 percent of its GNP to military spending.

The expansion of the military-industrial complex had a direct and ongoing impact on the American people. Channeling money into national security limited the resources available for domestic social needs. Critics of military spending added up the trade-offs—the cost of a subway system for Washington, D.C., equaled a nuclear aircraft carrier and support ships; sixty-six units of low-income housing matched the cost of one Huey helicopter.

The defense buildup also meant jobs, however, and lots of them. In 1966, 17 percent of California's workers were employed in jobs directly generated by defense contracts. Taking into account the multiplier effect, which measures the indirect benefits of such employment (the additional jobs created to serve and support the defense workers), perhaps as many as one worker in seven nationally owed his or her job to the military-industrial complex. This dependence of individual jobs on defense spending illustrates how the growth of a vast bureaucratic state, especially one committed to worldwide military responsibilities, affected daily life in the postwar period.

NEW TECHNOLOGY *The Computer Revolution*

The first modern computers—that is, information-processing machines capable of storing and manipulating data according to specified programs—appeared in the 1940s. During World War II, engineers and mathematicians at the University of Pennsylvania developed a general-purpose, programmable electronic calculator called ENIAC (Electronic Numerical Integrator and Computer), which could add 5,000 ten-digit decimal numbers in one second. It stood 8 feet tall, measured 80 feet long, and weighed 30 tons; it used 18,000 vacuum tubes for computations. When it performed complex mathematical computations, one scientist noted, ENIAC sounded "like a roomful of ladies knitting." Although ENIAC lacked a central memory and could not store a program, it was the bridge to the modern computer revolution.

Six computers were under construction by 1947, including UNIVAC (Universal Automatic Computer), the first commercial computer system. The word "UNIVAC" was synonymous with computer to the general public in the 1950s. UNIVAC was basically a data-processing system that could be tailored to individual customers' needs. In 1951 the U.S. Census Bureau bought the first UNIVAC. Soon CBS-TV signed on, using a UNIVAC to predict the outcome of the 1952 presidential election. At 9 P.M., only after the East Coast polls had closed and with only 7 percent of the votes counted, UNIVAC predicted that Dwight D. Eisenhower would sweep the election with 438 electoral votes. CBS programmers and network executives, who had expected a closer election, got jittery and altered the program to give Eisenhower a far narrower margin. When the final tally gave him 442 electoral votes, only four votes off the original projection, commentator Edward R. Murrow observed, "The trouble with machines is people."

Computers are essentially collections of switches, and programs tell the computer which switches to turn on and off. The puzzle that early computer scientists had to solve was how to increase the speed while lowering the cost of this basic operation. The first generation of computers need vacuum tubes for computation power and the use of punched cards for writing programs and analyzing data. Such computers were huge, room-sized machines, and programming them could take several days because programmers manually had to set thousands of switches in the On or Off position. The vacuum tubes were the weakest part of early computers; burnout of just a few tubes could shut down the entire system. Furthermore, vacuum tubes gave off enormous amounts of heat, necessitating noisy and cumbersome air-conditioning units wherever computers operated. After a critical signal relay stopped one early program, scientists finally located the problem—a dead moth trapped in the apparatus, the origin of the term "debugging."

The 1948 invention of the transistor, a development that revolutionized computers and also the whole field of electronics, made possible the second generation of computers. Transistors, like vacuum tubes, served as on-off switches, but they did not generate heat, burn out, or consume vast quantities of energy. They also were inexpensive to manufacture. The invention of integrated circuits (IC) in 1959 ushered in the third computer generation, (1965), characterized by greater sophistication in miniaturization, meant that the number of transistors that could be crammed on a silicon chip increased dramatically, with a corresponding increase in computational power. The fourth computer generation arrived in 1971 with development of the microprocessor, the entire central processing unit (CPU) of a computer on a single silicon chip about the size of the letter "O" on this page, soon followed. Miniaturization progressed so rapidly that by the mid-1970s, a $1 chip provided as much processing power as the ENIAC of 30 years earlier. Computers and computer technology have become so much a part of modern life that it is hard to remember how recent the origins of this technological revolution are.

This early computer-data processing center featured an IBM704 computer.

America's military responsibilities overseas had another effect on the lives of ordinary citizens: permanent mobilization meant a peacetime draft. In the past, the armed forces had shrunk dramatically to a skeleton volunteer force at the end of each war or foreign engagement. But when World War II ended, the draft was kept in place to meet the military commitments associated with the Cold War. Suddenly every neighborhood seemed to have a boy in the service; many made the military a career. By the late 1960s, more than 1.5 million military personnel were stationed in a hundred foreign countries.

Corporate Strategies

The Cold War and the growth of the state brought major changes to American life, hastening the concentration of power in ever larger economic and political structures. Successful corporate managers adopted flexible strategies to take advantage of the postwar economic climate. They tapped federal money for research and development, diversified their range of products, expanded their multinational operations, and sought to improve their ability to plan.

Diversification. Diversification was the most important corporate strategy of the postwar era. The classic corporation of the early twentieth century had produced a single line of products. After World War II, the most successful managers developed new product lines and moved into new markets. Because the largest corporations could afford research laboratories, they diversified more easily. CBS, for example, hired the Hungarian inventor Peter Goldmark, who perfected color television during the 1940s, long-playing records in the 1950s, and a video recording system in the 1960s. As head of CBS Laboratories, Goldmark patented more than a hundred new devices.

Postwar managers also diversified through mergers and acquisitions, creating larger firms to compete in the expanding world market. The nation's third great merger wave (the first two had taken place during the 1890s and the 1920s) reached its peak during the 1960s. International Telephone and Telegraph became a diversified conglomerate by acquiring Continental Baking, Sheraton Hotels, Avis Rent-a-Car, Levitt and Sons home builders, and Hartford Fire Insurance. Ling-Temco-Vought, another conglomerate, simultaneously produced steel, built ships, developed real estate, and brought cattle to market. In 1947 the largest two hundred corporations accounted for 30 percent of all value added by manufacturing, but by 1972 the largest two hundred, now heavily diversified, accounted for 43 percent of this sum.

Expansion into foreign markets also helped managers build giant corporations. At a time when "made in Japan" still meant shoddy workmanship, American products were the best made in the world. International strategies enabled American business to enter new areas when domestic markets became saturated or when American recessions cut into sales. By the 1970s, such corporations as Gillette, IBM, Mobil, and Coca-Cola earned more than half their profits from sales of their products abroad. ITT had a worldwide payroll of 425,000 workers in seventy countries.

In their effort to direct large organizations through the uncertainties of the postwar economy, managers placed more emphasis on planning. Top executives were increasingly recruited for their business-school training, their ability to manage information, and their skill in corporate planning, marketing, and investment. As a result, corporate managers found themselves working more closely with their counterparts in other corporations, large banks, investment firms, law firms, economic research organizations, the federal government, and such international agencies as the World Bank and the International Monetary Fund.

The New Oligopolies. The predominant thrust of modern corporate life after 1945 continued to be consolidation of economic and financial resources in oligopolies, where a few large producers controlled the national and, increasingly, the world market. In 1970 the top four U.S. firms produced 91 percent of all motor vehicles in the domestic market; the top four in tires produced 72 percent, in cigarettes 84 percent, and in detergents 70 percent. Despite laws restricting branch banking to a single state, in 1970 the four largest banks held 16 percent of the nation's banking assets; the top fifty banks held 48 percent.

A case study of the beer industry illustrates this growing concentration of economic power. Beer has always been a highly profitable, high-volume business. At the end of World War II, the United States had about 450 breweries. Each produced a distinctive-tasting brand of beer, due to variations in the local water and differences in brewing techniques. This pattern of competing products and regional diversity changed dramatically in the 1950s. Large corporations went after the national market that had been created in part by advertising on network television, especially for sports events. National companies such as Anheuser-Busch developed a beer that could be manufactured anywhere in the country, no matter what the local water was like. They then used modern marketing techniques to push this homogenized product.

Soon the national brands were driving out local competition. Whereas the seven leading breweries in 1946 had accounted for barely 20 percent of national

Cheers
The growth of national brands of beer such as Ballantine Ale went hand in hand with the popularity of television, especially sports, in the 1950s. These sports fans seem a bit overdressed, however, for an afternoon watching the game with their buddies.

sales, by 1970 the ten largest breweries had captured 70 percent of the beer market. American consumers could find the beer advertised on their favorite television programs at local supermarkets, but they were choosing among a much smaller selection of beers with much blander taste. Only in the economic climate of the 1980s did micro-breweries discover that small companies could compete in a national consumer market, at least in the beer industry.

The Changing World of Work

For most of the nineteenth century and the first half of the twentieth, the United States had been a nation of goods producers, but by 1956 a majority of Americans were white-collar workers. The shift of American workers from heavy industry and manufacturing into commerce, government, service industries, and the professions was as significant a watershed as the closing of the frontier in 1890. In 1940 two-thirds of all workers held industrial jobs that required them to use physical strength and skills to make products. From 1947 to 1957 the number of factory workers dropped 4 percent, while the ranks of clerical workers rose 23 percent and those of salaried middle-class workers jumped 61 percent. Instead of producing products, American workers increasingly provided services, the essence of a service economy.

The sociologist C. Wright Mills captured the new white-collar world in this riveting image: "What must be grasped is the picture of society as a great salesroom, an enormous file, an incorporated brain, a new universe of management and manipulation." Soon panelists on the popular quiz show "What's My Line?" learned to ask their mystery guests this question: "Do you deal in services?"

The new hierarchy of work altered old patterns of status and class. In the late nineteenth century, an office job as a secretary was a badge of upward social mobility and respectability for a working woman, as well as an opportunity for increased pay. By the 1950s the jobs of office workers were not too different from those of factory operatives—narrow, repetitive, and lacking in control and autonomy. Confounding the old formula that work with your brain counted for more than work with your hands, many unionized factory workers had higher incomes than those in such occupations as teaching and social work.

Many of these new workers in the service economy were women: twice as many women were at work in 1960 as in 1940. Because of the structural needs of the economy, there was a demand for workers in fields traditionally filled by women, such as clerical work, a predominantly female field that expanded as rapidly as any other white-collar sector in the economy. Teachers to staff the nation's burgeoning school systems were also in demand. Growing sectors of the economy such as restaurant and hotel work, hospitals, and beauty care offered low-paying jobs to women, jobs that have been called the "pink-collar ghetto." Nonwhite and working-class women predominated in such jobs.

Occupational segmentation remained a fundamental characteristic of women's work in the postwar period. More than 80 percent of all working women held jobs in stereotypical "women's work," as salespersons, health-care technicians, waitresses, flight attendants, domestic servants, receptionists, telephone operators, and secretaries. In 1960 women represented only 3.5 percent of all lawyers (many top law schools did not admit women at all) and 6.1 percent of all physicians, but 97 percent of the nurses, 85 percent of the librarians, and 57 percent of the social workers. Along with women's jobs went women's pay, which averaged 60 percent of men's in 1963.

The New Middle Class. America's transformation from a society of producers to one of white-collar workers created a new middle class. Corporate managers and salaried professionals, such as teachers, professors, and researchers, formed its core. They earned a salary, which distinguished them from self-employed entrepreneurs and from service and blue-collar workers who earned an hourly wage. The members of the new middle class had taken advantage of the great expansion of high school and college education after the 1920s, and the explosion of universities after 1945, to make themselves much better educated than their elders. Such skills enabled them to advance more quickly, and at a younger age, than previous generations.

As young managers and professionals advanced in their careers, they changed jobs frequently. Atlas Van Lines estimated in the 1950s that corporate managers moved an average of fourteen times—once every two and a half years—during their careers. Perpetually mobile IBM managers joked that the company's initials stood for "I've Been Moved." A building contractor and future multimillionaire summed up the fifties' mobility this way: "If you had a college diploma, a dark suit, and anything between the ears, it was like an escalator; you just stood there and moved up." (He was talking only about men—women were still generally excluded from these careers.) Such advancement usually led them through the giant corporate structures—big business, government agencies, universities, and other bureaucratic organizations—that came to dominate the latter half of the twentieth century.

Switching jobs, or even careers, necessitated personality traits such as adaptability and the ability to get along in a variety of situations. Corporate managers worked hard, sometimes with the assistance of the resident corporate psychologist, to be "well adjusted." Their philosophy was "Evade, don't confront." In *The Lonely Crowd* (1950), sociologist David Reisman contrasted the stern, formal small business and professional types of earlier years with the new managers of the postwar world. He concluded that members of the new middle class were "other-directed," more concerned about their relations with immediate associates than about adherence to fundamental principles. Sociologist William Whyte painted a more somber picture of "organization men" who left the home "spiritually as well as physically to take the vows of organization life."

Many commentators worried that the conformity demanded by marching off each day in gray flannel suits to work in huge corporations at interchangeable middle-management jobs was stifling men's creativity. Men were also weighted down by their responsibilities as breadwinners for the consumption-oriented family life-style that was the goal of many members of the new middle class. Such heightened expectations put enormous pressure on these men. In fact, it was in the 1950s that cardiologists first sounded the alarm about the role of stress in coronary heart disease. Fueled in part by death rates three times as high for men as for women from heart attacks and strokes, it looked like work was in fact dangerous for men's health.

Organization Men (and a Few Women)
What happened when the 5:57 discharged commuters in Park Forest, Illinois, a suburb of Chicago? This was the subject of William H. Whyte's *The Organization Man* (1956). Were these hordes of commuters thinking about their stressful day at the office, or the martini waiting for them when they walked in the door of their suburban home?

Challenges for the Labor Movement

The changing structural composition of the work force and the shifting nature of work itself posed challenges for the labor movement in the postwar world. Labor unions reached the peak of their strength immediately after World War II. The schisms of the 1930s had healed enough by 1955 that Walter P. Reuther of the United Auto Workers led the CIO back into an alliance with the AFL. This merger created a single organization, the AFL-CIO, that represented more than 90 percent of the nation's 17.5 million union members.

George Meany, a New York building-trade unionist, headed this organization from 1955 to 1979.

New priorities shaped labor-management relations after the war. Postwar inflation and changing patterns of consumption produced demands for higher incomes. Management agreed to contracts that brought many workers secure, predictable, and steadily rising incomes. In exchange, union leaders promised labor peace and stability—that is, fewer strikes. In 1950 General Motors and the United Automobile Workers signed a contract containing two novel provisions: an escalator clause providing that wages would be adjusted to reflect changes in the cost of living, and a productivity clause guaranteeing that wages would rise as productivity in the industry increased. Autoworkers won a guaranteed annual wage in 1955.

These contracts shared a common tendency to emphasize union members' status as consumers rather than workers. George Meany accepted the thrust of government-subsidized business prosperity; his goal was to ensure that labor got its share. Workers paid for these improved wages not only by limiting the number and duration of strikes, but also by putting aside their traditional claims for control over the pace of work. In return for higher wages and fringe benefits, workers allowed technologically minded managers to exert increasing control over their lives on the job.

But labor still had to fight for legitimacy in postwar society. The 1947 Taft-Hartley Act, which chipped away at some of the protections guaranteed by the 1935 National Labor Relations Act, represented the most virulent attack. Taft-Hartley showed that the New Deal labor reforms remained controversial a decade after their passage.

The Impact of Automation. Mechanization had long threatened skilled workers, but, in the 1950s, new technology affected the jobs of unskilled factory workers as well, many of them union members. In 1977, 400,000 workers in the steel industry produced twice as much steel as 600,000 had in 1947. Similar patterns held in coal mining and in the automobile industry, which had pioneered the assembly line. The Ford Motor Company introduced automatic drilling machines at a Cleveland engine plant in 1952, enabling 41 workers to do a job that formerly required 117.

When labor leader Walter Reuther inspected one of these automated engine plants, a Ford manager kidded him: "Well, you won't be able to collect dues from all these automated machines." "You know," Reuther replied, "that is not what is bothering me. What is bothering me is, how are you going to sell cars to all of these machines?" Reuther's reply was right on the mark. Without workers earning sufficient income to continue buying consumer goods, the American economy would falter.

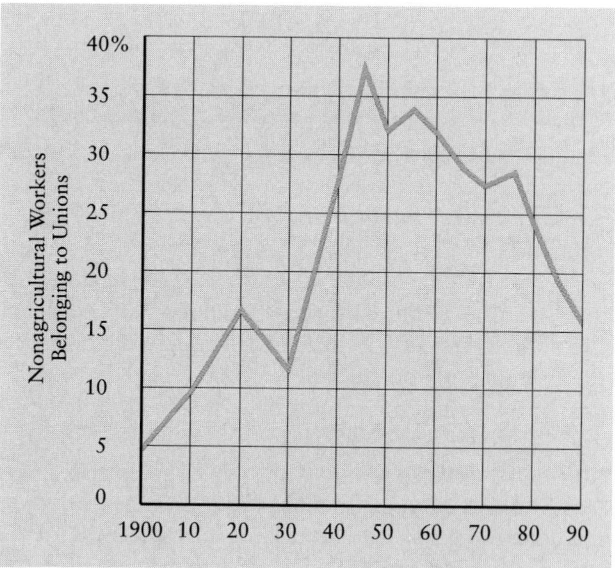

FIGURE 29.3

Labor Union Strength, 1900–1990

Labor unions reached their peak strength immediately after World War II. For thirty years they consistently represented more than a quarter of the nonfarm workforce. But labor union influence declined dramatically after 1975. (*Source:* AFL-CIO Information Bureau, Washington.)

New Recruits. These structural changes affected the labor movement in the postwar period. During the momentous 1930s and 1940s, unions had organized heavy industries such as mining, manufacturing, and transportation, but these sectors were no longer growing. The labor movement had to look elsewhere for new recruits, such as the less skilled, often black or Hispanic, workers in the lower-paying service and agricultural sectors or the millions of secretaries and file clerks in the nation's offices, who were predominantly women. The union movement needed to expand its industrial midwestern base into southern and western states, areas of rapid economic growth that were traditionally anti-union. Organized labor also had to woo younger workers who now saw unions as part of management, rather than as advocates of the rank and file. Finally, it had to branch out to organize white-collar employees in such previously untapped professions as teaching, nursing, and municipal services.

Organized labor met some, but not all, of these new challenges. By the mid-1950s, the labor movement had stalled. The unionized percentage of the nonagricultural work force peaked at 35.5 percent in 1946 and held level until 1954. Then union membership began a steady decline. This erosion of the labor movement stood in stark contrast to labor's vitality at the end of the New Deal.

The Agricultural Revolution

No sector of the economy changed more dramatically in the postwar period than agriculture. As late as 1945, a fourth of the American work force consisted of farmers. During the next twenty-five years, however, 25 million people left rural America; in 1969 only 5 percent of the population lived on farms. This farm-to-city migration was the result of two interrelated trends—a technological revolution in agriculture that reduced the need for labor, and the steady decline of the small family farm. A federal task force on rural development called this shift "one of the largest migrations of people in recorded history," rivaling European immigration to the New World and America's westward expansion.

The new technology that reduced the need for labor also contributed to an astonishing increase in agricultural productivity after 1945. Before the war, the typical American farm had been a small, modestly equipped family enterprise where horses and mules outnumbered tractors. In 1935 an hour of labor produced about 2 1/2 pounds of cotton, 2 bushels of wheat, just over 1 bushel of corn, 33 pounds of milk, or 3 chickens. During the postwar period, new machines and agricultural methods, including improved chemical fertilizers and pesticides, revolutionized farming. By 1978 a single hour's labor produced 50 pounds of cotton, 11 bushels of wheat, 25 bushels of corn, 250 pounds of milk, or 100 chickens. But mechanization required major capital investments. Between 1940 and 1955, the cost of fuel, fertilizer, and repairs for farm machines quadrupled, and total operating costs tripled. Family farms often lacked the capital to compete with the large, technologically advanced farm units in such areas as California and the Midwest, further disadvantaging the small farmer in an increasingly corporate economy.

TABLE 29.1

Trends in American Farming, 1935–1990

	Number of farms (thousands)	Farm population (thousands)	Percent of total population
1935	6,814	32,161	25.3%
1940	6,350	30,547	23.1
1945	5,967	24,420	17.5
1950	5,648	23,048	15.2
1956	4,514	18,712	11.1
1960	3,963	15,635	8.7
1965	3,356	12,363	6.4
1970	2,949	9,712	4.7
1975	2,521	8,864	4.2
1980	2,428	6,051	2.7
1985	2,293	5,355	2.4
1990*	2,143	4,801	2.1

*Data unavailable for 1989.

Source: Gilbert Fite, *American Farmers* (Bloomington: Indiana University Press, 1981), 101, used by permission; *U.S. Statistical Abstract* (1991).

The technological revolution transformed the lives of many of the farmers who remained on the land. They now managed specialized organizations—small factories that poured industrial materials into the land and extracted raw products for immediate sale. They relied on outside industrial sources for fertilizer, feed, seed, and pesticides and for the energy needed to run the expanding array of gasoline-powered equipment. Farm families purchased consumer goods from commercial sources, rather than producing them at home. These ties made farmers, like other businesspeople, increasingly dependent on national and international market conditions, on scientific and technological developments, and on the actions of the expanding federal bureaucracy.

Farmers' fortunes were especially tied to federal farm policies, further confirmation of the impact of the bureaucratic state on postwar American life. There was no such thing as a free market in agriculture: all farms operated under a complicated system of government price supports, subsidies, and loans, which were linked both to domestic needs and to exports for the world market. In 1956 the federal farm program cost $2.5 billion. As it had during the New Deal, this federal largesse tended to benefit larger farms. According to figures gathered in 1954 by Secretary of Agriculture Ezra Taft Benson, sixty-four large corn, wheat, and cotton operators received more than $100,000 each in government loans, including one $1.27 million loan on cotton bales to the Delta and Pine Land Corporation of Mississippi. In contrast, the average cotton grower in that state only received $372 in loan payments.

The fuller integration of farmers into the national economy, and the diminishing number of Americans who made farming their occupation, greatly reduced the differences between rural and urban life. Farmers, once a major force in political life, no longer wielded as much clout in electoral politics except in the United States Senate, where a bloc of farm states still affected national policy. Agribusiness took its place as part of corporate America. Measurable farm income, which ranged from only 40 to 60 percent of the national average between the 1930s and 1950s, rose above 80 percent—and briefly to 110 percent—in the 1970s. As farming came to resemble other occupations, those who remained on the farm increasingly shared the experiences, views, and aspirations of other Americans.

Cities and Suburbs

In the postwar years, Americans lived predominantly in metropolitan areas, largely because most jobs and housing were concentrated there. Economic activity in the twenty-five largest metropolitan areas picked up considerably after 1945. This growth did not occur in the central cities, which lost 300,000 jobs, but in the surrounding suburban areas, which gained an astounding 4 million jobs. By the late 1960s, suburbs surpassed cities in the number of jobs they offered. Only in white-collar office work did inner-city employment rise.

These patterns of employment and economic growth reinforced the growing gap between city dwellers and their suburban neighbors. Metropolitan areas developed a striking pattern of residential segregation that persists to this day. Poorer people, many of them nonwhites, clustered in the decaying inner cities, while the more prosperous middle class—whites and nonwhites—flocked to the suburbs.

Metropolitan Life

As early as 1880, demographers had noticed the appearance of sprawling metropolitan areas centered around one or more large cities and including scattered suburbs and satellite towns. That year, the U.S. Census identified twenty-five such regions, ranging in size from New York–Brooklyn–Newark, with 6,500,000 people, to Portland, Oregon, with 215,000. In 1920 the Census Bureau announced that urban population had surpassed rural for the first time, a major turning point in the modern era. At that time, a dozen metropolitan areas—located on the Atlantic Coast, near the Great Lakes or the Ohio River, or in California—had at least a million people each. Pilots flying along the East Coast

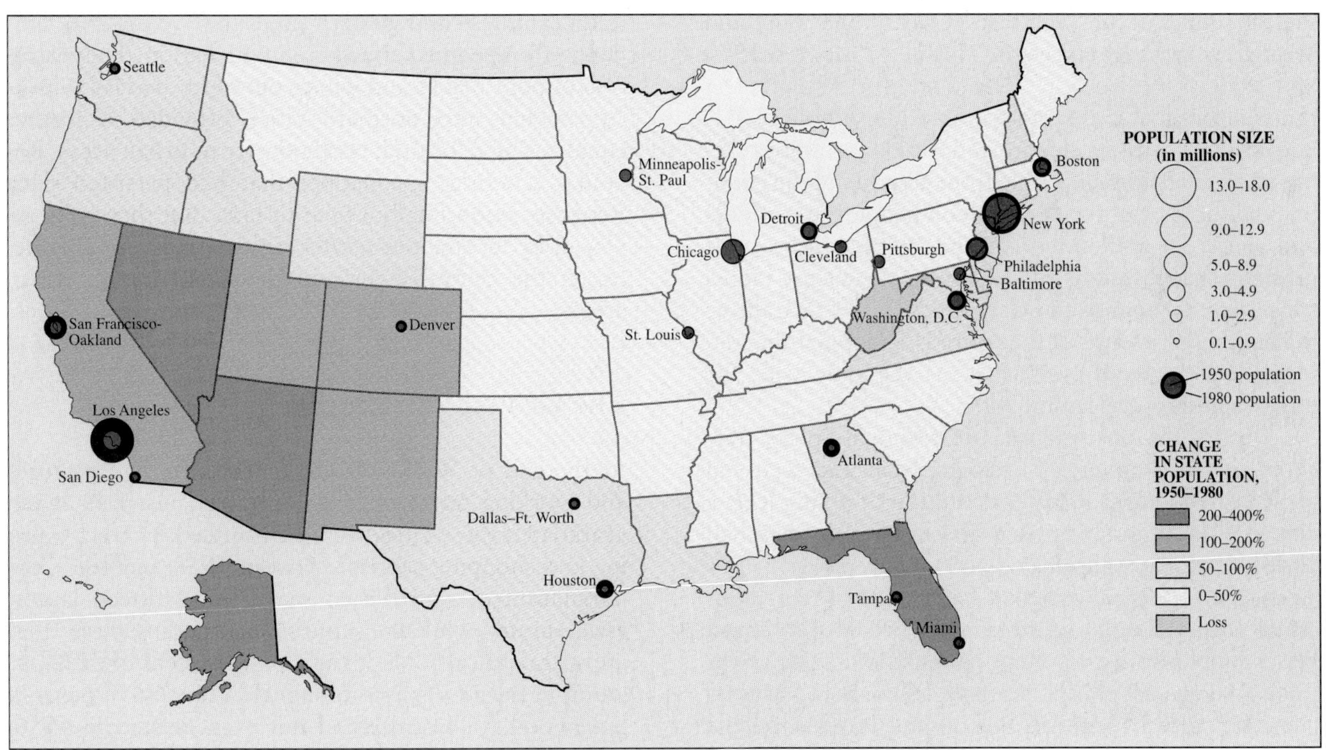

MAP 29.1

Metropolitan Growth, 1950–1980

A metropolitan area is generally defined as a central city which, in combination with its surrounding territory, forms an integrated economic and social unit. The U.S. Census Bureau introduced the "Standard Metropolitan Statistical Area" in 1950, but later changes in the definition of what comprises an SMSA make it difficult to generalize from the 1950 figures. This map compares the population of central cities in 1950 with population figures for the more broadly defined metropolitan areas in 1980 to illustrate the extent and geographic distribution of metropolitan growth in the postwar period.

at night began to notice that they could no longer distinguish one city from the next; a continuous strand of light stretched from Newport News, Virginia, past New York and up to Boston.

Urban migration, which had slowed to a trickle during the Great Depression, accelerated during the 1940s. In the years after World War II, metropolitan regions became the dominant form of settlement, providing a home for two-thirds of all Americans in 1960.

The Sun Belt. The growth of new metropolitan areas was most striking in the South and West, where large portions of the population had traditionally been rural and impoverished. Florida added 3.5 million people, many of them older or retired Americans, between 1940 and 1970. Texas cities grew as the petrochemical industry expanded rapidly after 1945; the oil and gas industries, together with the banks and law firms that served them, concentrated in Houston. Other expanding cities included Atlanta, Baton Rouge, Long Beach, Mobile, and Phoenix. Boosters heralded the booming metropolitan economies of the "Sun Belt." Overall, the South and West grew twice as fast as the Northeast between 1940 and 1970.

California was the most dramatic example of this new growth, with its climate and job opportunities acting as magnets to pull people from all parts of the country. California absorbed 2.6 million people in the 1940s and added 3.1 million more in the 1950s. Much of this growth was spurred by the expansion of defense industries, such as aircraft and electronics. In 1970, California had about a tenth of the entire U.S. population, and in 1972 it replaced New York as the state with the largest number of electoral votes.

During the postwar era, professional sports mirrored the new patterns of geographical and sectional growth, heralding a broader definition of a "big-league city." St. Louis had long been the westernmost baseball city. In 1958 baseball's Brooklyn Dodgers moved to Los Angeles and the New York Giants went to San Francisco. Teams in other professional sports also followed the sprawling metropolitan population. The New England Patriots played football in Foxboro, Massachusetts, halfway between Boston and Providence; the Detroit Lions moved to Pontiac, Michigan; and the Los Angeles Rams played in suburban Orange County.

The Northeast. While the older metropolitan areas in the Northeast grew less rapidly than the new Sunbelt centers, they experienced fundamental changes in their economies. Boston and nearby Lowell, Lawrence, and Salem, Massachusetts, lost most of their textile and manufacturing jobs, but high-technology industries that produced Polaroid instant cameras and Digital and Wang computers gave new life to the New England economy. So many companies built their corporate headquarters outside Boston along Route 128, one of the first peripheral highways to bypass downtown congestion, that it became known as the Technology Highway. New York City lost many of its garment-making and printing jobs, but outlying areas profited from the relocation of corporate headquarters to suburbs such as White Plains, New York, and Stamford, Connecticut. Reflecting the impact of military needs for defense production, Grumman and Northrop developed an important airplane and weapons-manufacturing industry on Long Island and the Electric Boat division of General Electric made submarines in Groton, Connecticut.

Blurring of Regional Differences. This redistribution of population, income, and economic activity gave metropolitan regions less sharply defined social and economic profiles than had prevailed in the late nineteenth and early twentieth centuries. The advent of metropolitan economies and the dramatic decline in small-scale farming caused by the agricultural revolution enabled people in the southern and western states to have incomes similar to those earned elsewhere in the nation. The migration of poor blacks and whites out of rural areas such as Appalachia into northern cities provided a further equalizer by relocating rural poverty to urban areas. Regional economic inequalities that had persisted since Reconstruction finally began to fade. But they were replaced by inequalities *within* regions, most notably between the central cities and their outlying suburban areas.

The Growth of Suburbia

At the end of World War II, many cities had pastures and working farms on their outskirts. Just five or ten years later, these cities were surrounded by tract housing and shopping centers. Between 1950 and 1960, the population of fourteen of the nation's fifteen largest cities shrank, while the suburbs surrounding these cities grew dramatically. New York lost 2 percent of its population in the 1950s, but its suburbs grew by 58 percent. Lakewood, California, had not even existed in 1950, but in 1960 this Los Angeles suburb counted more than 50,000 residents. Other areas that underwent rapid growth included San Mateo County, south of San Francisco; Cook and DuPage counties, north and west of Chicago; and Prince Georges County in Maryland, outside Washington, D.C. By 1960 more people lived in suburbs than in cities.

The Housing Boom. People flocked to the suburbs in part because they followed the available housing. Very little new housing had been built during the depression

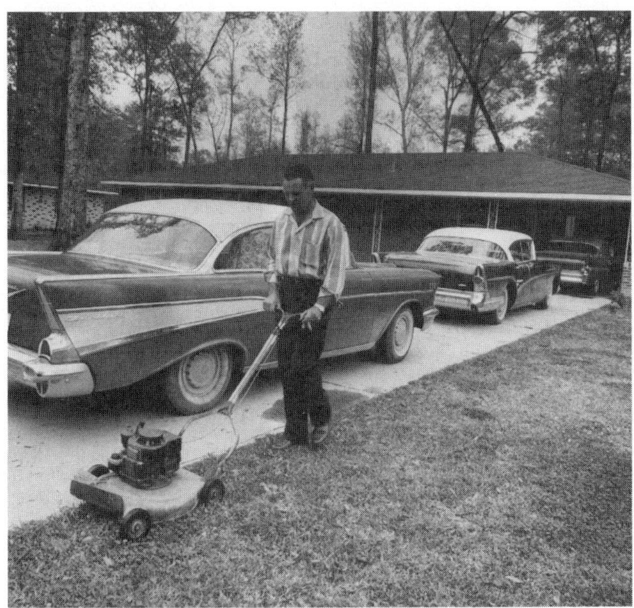

The Trappings of Suburbia
With a ranch house, three cars in the driveway, and a rotary lawn mower, this homeowner in Baton Rouge, Louisiana, embodied the middle-class suburban lifestyle.

or war years, and the returning World War II veterans and their families faced a critical housing shortage. The late 1940s and 1950s witnessed a dramatic surge in construction. A fourth of all housing in the country in 1960 had been built during the preceding decade. Most of it was single-family, owner-occupied homes.

The suburban housing market was revolutionized by a Long Island building contractor named Arthur Levitt, who applied mass-production techniques to home construction. His company could build as many as 150 homes a week, a rate of one every sixteen minutes. Levitt's basic four-room house, complete with kitchen appliances and an attic that could be finished on weekends by a handy homeowner into two additional bedrooms, was priced at less than ten thousand dollars in 1947. Levitt did not really need to advertise; word of mouth brought more customers than the firm could handle.

Levitt built planned communities in New York, New Jersey, and Pennsylvania (all named, not surprisingly, Levittown). The developments contained few old people and even fewer unmarried adults. Even the trees were young. Owners had to agree to cut their lawns once a week between April and November and not to hang out the laundry on weekends. (Reflecting cold war sentiments, Levitt asserted: "No man who owns his own house and lot can be a Communist. He has too much to do.") When residents complained that the streets and the houses were so similar that they could not find their way home, the developer added more variety in style and site placement. Soon other developers were snapping up cheap farmland surrounding urban areas, further hastening the exodus from both the farm and the central city.

Many families financed their homes with mortgages from the Federal Housing Administration and the Veterans' Administration. Before World War II, banks, primarily the savings and loan industry that served this fairly stable market, usually demanded a 50 percent down payment for homeowner's loans and granted no more than ten years to pay back the balance. After the war, the Federal Housing Administration required only a 5 to 10 percent down payment and gave homeowners up to thirty years to pay back mortgages at the modest rate of 2 to 3 percent. The Veterans' Administration was even more lenient, requiring only a token one-dollar down payment from qualified veterans. In 1955 these two agencies wrote 41 percent of all nonfarm mortgages. Such lending demonstrated the quiet, yet revolutionary, way in which the federal government was entering and influencing daily life.

These suburban developments—and much of the savings and loan and VA money—were almost exclusively for whites. Levittown homeowners had to sign a covenant with a restrictive clause prohibiting occupation "by members of other than the Caucasian Race." (*Shelley v. Kraemer* [1948] only made restrictive covenants unenforceable in court; the custom was still prevalent until the civil rights laws of the 1960s banned private discrimination.) Not until 1960 did Levitt sell houses directly to blacks. Even then, the company carefully screened black families and made sure that no two black families lived next door to each other. Restrictive covenants also applied in other communities to such groups as Jews and Asians.

While suburbia was often portrayed as a homogeneous, even bland, environment, there were strong cultural and class variations among the suburbs. Older, wealthy suburbs already occupied the most pleasant locations, including the hills north and west of Los Angeles, Chicago's North Shore, and the heights well to the east of Cleveland's industrial Cuyahoga Flats. When less affluent firefighters, plasterers, machine-tool makers, or sales clerks moved to the suburbs, they were far more likely to move to a modest Levittown than to an upper-middle-class suburb such as Winnetka, Illinois, or Shaker Heights, Ohio. Blacks shut out of white suburbs established their own communities, such as Lincoln Heights, outside Cincinnati; Robbins, on the edge of Chicago; and Kinloch, near St. Louis. In well-equipped living quarters at bargain prices, working-class and black families could share in the ultimate postwar suburban dream "to give every kid an opportunity to grow up with grass stains on his pants."

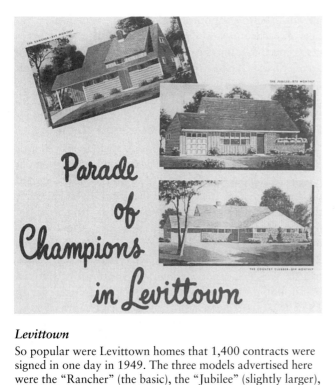

Levittown
So popular were Levittown homes that 1,400 contracts were signed in one day in 1949. The three models advertised here were the "Rancher" (the basic), the "Jubilee" (slightly larger), and the "Country Clubber" (the luxury edition). Homeowners especially enjoyed the privacy and space that such homes provided.

Cars and Highways. Automobiles and highways were essential to this dramatic suburban growth. Suburbanites needed cars to get to work or to take children to school and piano lessons. About 90 percent of suburban families owned cars, and 20 percent had more than one. Whereas 25 million cars had been registered in 1945, the number rose to 52 million in 1955 and increased to 75 million in 1965.

The car culture that had first emerged in the 1920s expanded dramatically during the 1950s, with cars becoming personal metaphors for status and success. With gas plentiful and cheap at fifteen cents a gallon, no one cared about fuel efficiency (8 miles to the gallon for the biggest gas guzzlers!). American cars became heavier and bigger, a disparity in size compared to Japanese or European models that remains to this day, even after American cars were downsized during the energy crisis of the 1970s.

More cars required more highways, which were funded largely by the federal government. In 1947, Congress authorized the construction of 37,000 miles of highway; the Interstate Highway Act of 1956 increased its commitment by another 42,500 miles. One of the largest civil engineering projects of world history, the new roads would be at least four lanes wide and would link the entire country in an integrated interstate system. Gas taxes and user fees for commercial vehicles provided the necessary funds.

The interstate system changed both the cities and the countryside. It rerouted traffic through rural areas, bypassing old main roads like Route 1 on the eastern seaboard and the cross-country Route 66, and creating new communities of gas stations, fast-food outlets, and motels at anonymous cloverleaf exchanges. In urban areas, new highways cut wide swaths through old neighborhoods. Cities were soon plagued by the problems that cars brought to modern life—air pollution and traffic jams. Critics now complained about "autosclerosis," a hardening of the urban arteries.

Highway construction had far-reaching effects on patterns of consumption and shopping. Instead of taking a train into the city or walking to a corner grocery store, people now hopped into their cars and drove to suburban shopping malls and supermarkets. Although the first mall had appeared in the 1920s, there were only eight in 1945; by 1960 the number mushroomed to almost four thousand. When a 110-store complex at Roosevelt Field on suburban Long Island opened in 1956, it was conveniently situated at an expressway exit and offered parking for eleven thousand cars. Downtown retail areas and department stores declined accordingly.

The federally constructed highways threatened the demise of mass transit. Los Angeles, a city now largely dependent on freeways, had a viable mass transit system as late as the 1940s. The Highway Trust Fund set up in 1956 specifically prohibited use of its collected fees to promote urban mass transit. By 1960, two-thirds of all Americans drove to work each day. The percentage was even higher—between 80 and 95 percent—in such places as Los Angeles, Albuquerque, and Phoenix.

State and Local Government

The task of governing cities and suburbs fell to state and local governments. The average citizen lived under multiple layers of government—local, county, state, and federal—but local governments often had the greatest impact on people's daily lives. They ran the schools, supplied fire and police protection, picked up the trash, and cleaned the streets. State governments licensed the services of workers ranging from beauticians to lawyers, enforced building and health codes, and protected workers through child-labor laws and workers' compensation.

Like the federal government, state and local governments experienced rapid growth in the postwar period. In fact, their expenditures and payrolls increased faster

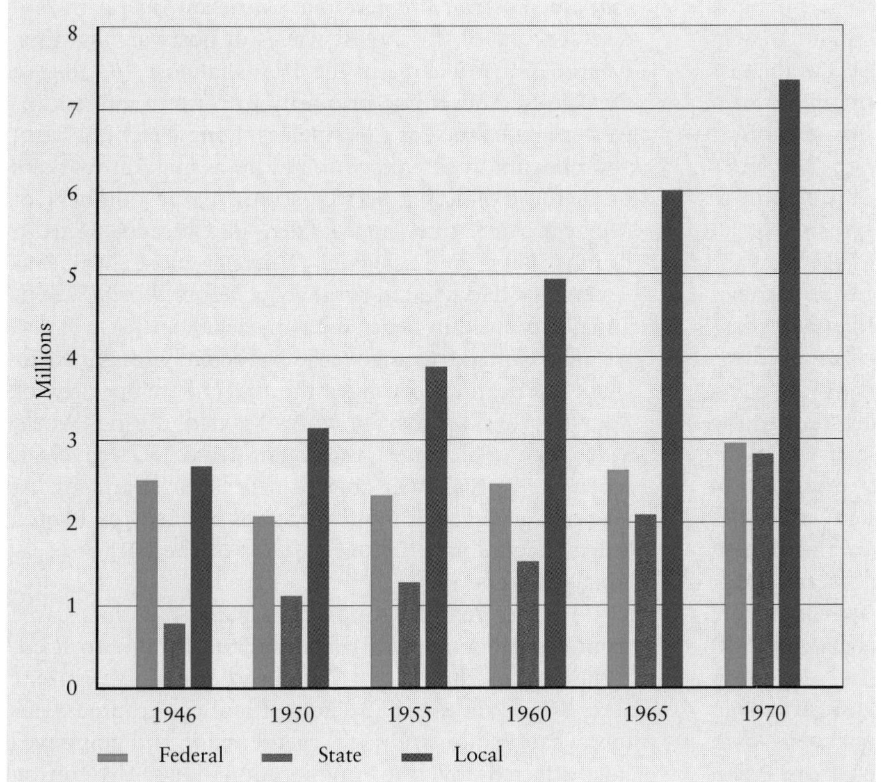

FIGURE 29.4

Federal, State, and Local Government Employees, 1946–1970

Although every level of government added employees in this period, the most dramatic growth took place in local government—counties, cities, and towns.

than the nondefense activities of the federal government during this time. State and local expenditures totaled $14 billion in 1946; in 1970 they had risen to almost $150 billion. Employment climbed correspondingly. In 1970, roughly one of seven Americans in the labor force worked for a government bureaucracy, yet another example of the rise of the state.

State and local revenues came from a variety of taxes. During the 1950s, state and local governments relied on property and sales taxes for almost half their revenues; state and city income taxes, and federal aid, were much less significant sources of revenue. State and local governments spent more money on education than on any other item, with expenditures for education in 1965 taking up approximately one-third of state and local budgets. The rest of the state and local budget went to welfare and social services (the second largest category), highways, health and hospitals, and other services.

Central cities and their surrounding suburban areas often had grossly unequal resources to meet local needs. Since the property tax provided a sizable part of local budgets, a wealthy community such as Grosse Pointe in suburban Detroit could far more easily provide funds for first-rate schools and adequate police departments than could Detroit, whose tax base shrank as businesses and middle-class residents relocated to the suburbs.

Although many of the problems of urban life—sewage, traffic, pollution, and police and fire protection—were shared by the cities and their surrounding areas, existing forms of government did not readily allow for cooperation. Political fragmentation was the rule. There were more than a thousand governmental units in the Chicago area, and fourteen hundred in the New York City region. Suburban communities remained reluctant to surrender their fiscal independence, to say nothing of the tradition of local self-rule, to the huge cities with their myriad social and economic problems.

City Dwellers and New Arrivals

Cities had always counted a heterogeneous population, one shaped by economic, religious, cultural, and racial diversity that changed neighborhood to neighborhood, sometimes from block to block. Migrants from other parts of the country and a new—if small—wave of immigration from abroad added to the postwar ethnic diversity of the nation's urban population.

Postwar Immigration. Until 1965 the United States immigration policy still followed the national origins quota system set up in 1924, whose purpose was generally to keep immigrants out, not let them in. Such restrictions, for example, had made it difficult to win entrance for Jews fleeing Hitler's Holocaust. But the dislocations caused by the war and its aftermath led to a slight loosening of the law. The Chinese Exclusion Act was repealed in 1943, a recognition of America's wartime alliance with China and a growing realization that the racism embodied in the total exclusion of all Asians was no longer tenable. The 1952 McCarran-Walter Act ended the former exclusion of certain racial and ethnic groups from immigration and naturalization. One impetus behind the change was a need inspired by the Cold War to strengthen the world's view of the United States as the symbol of democracy in the fight against communism.

Foreign policy shaped immigration priorities in other ways. In 1945 Congress passed the War Brides Act, which allowed the entrance and naturalization of the wives and children of Americans, mainly servicemen, abroad. As a result of the Korean War, approximately 17,000 Koreans entered the United States between 1950 and 1965, the vast majority war brides. In recognition of the independence of the Philippines from American control on July 4, 1946, this group received its own quota. The major increase in immigration from Asian countries would not occur until after 1965, however.

Changes in the immigration laws could have a large impact on the composition of immigrant communities. On the eve of World War II, the Chinatowns in the nation's major cities were populated primarily by Chinese men. Many of these men were married, but their wives had remained in China. The opening wedge of the 1943 legislation, coupled with the granting of the right of naturalization to Chinese already here, encouraged Chinese men to bring their wives to America. This increase of female immigrants led to a more balanced sex ratio, a pattern also seen in the Filipino-American and Japanese-American communities. There were approximately 135,000 men and 100,000 women of Chinese origin living in the United States in 1960, the majority in either New York State or California.

Proposals to admit displaced persons and refugees from Europe were more controversial. Many Americans feared being swamped with immigrants from devastated Europe, including displaced Jews who could or would not return to their former homelands. (In fact, most Jews headed to Israel once it became independent in 1948, one of the few alternatives open to them.) The 1948 Displaced Persons Act allowed approximately 415,000 Europeans to enter the United States before it expired in 1952. Among those who entered were a sizable number of Germans who had collaborated with the Nazis but whose expertise, in fields like rocketry, was deemed essential to national security.

Hispanic Postwar Immigration. Mexican-Americans represented one of the largest waves of postwar migrants. Nearly 275,000 came in the 1950s, almost 444,000 in the 1960s. They came primarily to western and southwestern cities such as Los Angeles, Long Beach, El Paso, and Phoenix, where they found jobs as migrant workers or in the expanding service sector. Large numbers of Mexican-Americans also settled in Chicago, Detroit, Kansas City, and Denver. Whereas most Mexican-Americans had lived in rural areas before World War II, a majority lived in urban areas by 1960.

The United States government actively sought Mexican-American labor under the *bracero* (temporary, or "day worker") program with Mexico during World War II labor shortages, then again from 1951 to 1964, when the Korean War created new labor shortages. At its peak in 1959, 450,000 braceros entered the United States, accounting for one-quarter of the nation's seasonal workers.

Another major group of Hispanic migrants came from the American-controlled territory of Puerto Rico. Residents of this island had been American citizens since 1917, and in 1952 Puerto Rico was granted commonwealth status. As such, their coming and going was not affected by the immigration laws. Migration increased dramatically after World War II, as Puerto Ricans were lured by the promise of better economic opportunities and social services. The inauguration of cheap, direct air service between San Juan and New York City (in the 1940s the fare was about $50, two weeks' wages) made Puerto Ricans this country's first group to immigrate by air, not by sea.

Most of the Puerto Rican migrants went to New York, where they settled first in East ("Spanish") Harlem and then in other areas throughout the city's five boroughs. This massive migration, which grew from 70,000 in 1940 to 613,000 just twenty years later, transformed the ethnic composition of the city. More Puerto Ricans now lived in New York City than in San Juan. They faced conditions common to all recent immigrants—crowded and deteriorating housing, segregation, unemployment or restriction to menial jobs, poor schools, and the problems of a bilingual existence.

Cuban refugees comprised the third large group of Hispanics. Nearly half a million people fled Cuba in the wake of Fidel Castro's seizure of power in 1959. The Cuban refugee community was so large and vigorous that it turned Miami into a cosmopolitan, bilingual city almost overnight. Unlike most new migrants to urban America, Miami's Cubans prospered, in large part because they had arrived with more resources. As the Castro regime consolidated its position, thus foreclosing prospects of returning home, Cuban-Americans increased their stakes in the United States. They differed

West Side Story

In 1961, United Artists released the movie version of Leonard Bernstein's 1957 Broadway hit, *West Side Story.* The plot recast Shakespeare's *Romeo and Juliet* to a Hispanic neighborhood on New York's West Side in the 1950s. Confrontations between members of youth gangs and adult figures of authority, such as pictured here in a still from the movie, were set to highly stylized song and dance routines.

from most other Hispanics as they were predominantly middle class and politically conservative.

Internal Migration. Internal migration also brought large numbers of people to the nation's cities, especially African-Americans, continuing a trend begun during World War I. Black migration was hastened by the transformation of southern agriculture. New Deal agricultural policies and the development of synthetic fibers such as rayon and Dacron after World War II caused cotton acreage in the South to decline from 43 million acres in 1929 to fewer than 15 million in 1959. In addition, the mechanization of farming drastically reduced the demand for farm labor. The mechanical cotton picker, introduced in 1944, fatally undermined the sharecropper system; it could pick 1,000 pounds an hour compared to 20 pounds by an experienced hand. As a result, the southern farm population fell from 16.2 million in 1930 to 5.9 million in 1960. Although both whites and blacks left the land, the starkest decline was among black farmers. By 1990 there were only 69,000 black farmers in the entire nation, just 1.5 percent of the country's farmers.

Where did they go? Some of the migrants settled in southern cities, where they obtained industrial jobs. White Southerners from Appalachia moved north to "hillbilly" ghettoes such as Cincinnati's Over the Rhine neighborhood or Chicago's Uptown. In the most dramatic population shift, as many as 3 million blacks headed to cities such as Chicago, New York, Washington, D.C., Detroit, and Los Angeles between 1940 and 1960. Certain sections of Chicago seemed like the Mississippi Delta transplanted, so pervasive were the migrants. The nation's cities saw their nonwhite populations swell at the same time that whites were flocking to the suburbs. From 1950 to 1960, the nation's twelve largest cities lost 3.6 million whites while gaining 4.5 million nonwhites. In 1960 about half of the African-American population was living outside the South.

Urban Neighborhoods, Urban Poverty

By the time that blacks, Mexican-Americans, and Puerto Ricans moved into the inner cities, urban America was in poor shape. Housing continued to be a crucial problem. One common response on the part of city planners, politicians, and real estate developers to the problem of deteriorating inner-city housing in the 1950s was *urban renewal*, razing blighted urban neighborhoods and replacing them with modern buildings. Local residents were rarely consulted about whether they wanted their neighborhoods "renewed." Urban renewal often produced grim high-rise housing projects that destroyed feelings of neighborhood pride and created combat zones for street crime. Between 1949 and 1961, urban renewal projects demolished almost 150,000 buildings and displaced 500,000 people. By 1967 the number of razed structures topped 400,000, and 1.4 million urban dwellers had been forced to relocate.

Urban renewal projects often benefited the wealthy at the expense of the poor. Many downtown "revitalization" projects supplanted established ethnic neighborhoods with expensive rental housing or shiny office

AMERICAN VOICES

Harlem: Dream and Reality *Claude Brown*

Claude Brown's *Manchild in the Promised Land* (1965) graphically described the conditions that awaited blacks when they journeyed to the promised land of Harlem in the postwar period. Brown dedicated the book to Eleanor Roosevelt, a benefactor of the Wiltwyck School for Boys, which helped troubled youth like Claude Brown break out of the ghetto.

Everybody I knew in Harlem seemed to have some kind of dream. I didn't have any dreams, not really. I didn't have any dreams for hitting the number. I didn't have any dreams for getting a big car or a fine wardrobe. I bought expensive clothes because it was a fad. It was the thing to do, just to show that you had money. I wanted to be a part of what was going on, and this was what was going on.

I didn't have any dreams of becoming anything. All I knew for certain was that I had my fears. I suppose just about everybody else knew the same thing. They had their dreams, though, and I guess that's what they had over me. As time went by, I was sorry for the people whose dreams were never realized.

When Butch was alive, sometimes I would go uptown to see him. He'd be sick. He'd be really messed up. I'd give him some drugs, and then he'd be more messed up than before. He wouldn't be sick, but I couldn't talk to him, I couldn't reach him. He'd be just sitting on a stoop nodding. Sometimes he'd be slobbering over himself.

I used to remember Butch's dream. Around 1950, he used to dream of becoming the best thief in Harlem. It wasn't a big dream. To him, it was a big dream, but I don't suppose too many people would have seen it as that. Still, I felt sorry for him because it was his dream. I suppose the first time he put the spike in his arm every dream he'd ever had was thrown out the window. Sometimes I wanted to shout at him or snatch him by the throat and say, "Butch, what about your dream?" But there were so many dreams that were lost for a little bit of duji. . . .

I used to feel that I belonged on the Harlem streets and that, regardless of what I did, nobody had any business to take me off the streets.

I remember when I ran away from shelters, places that they sent me to, here in the city. I never ran away with the thought in mind of coming home. I always ran away to get back to the streets. I always thought of Harlem as home, but I never thought of Harlem as being in the house. To me, home was the streets. I suppose there were many people who felt that. If home was so miserable, the street was the place to be. I wonder if mine was really so miserable, or if it was that there was so much happening out in the street that it made home seem such a dull and dismal place.

When I was very young—about five years old, maybe younger—I would always be sitting out on the stoop. I remember Mama telling me and Carole to sit on the stoop and not to move away from in front of the door. Even when it was time to go up and Carole would be pulling on me to come upstairs and eat, I never wanted to go, because there was so much out there in that street.

You might see somebody get cut or killed. I could go out in the street for an afternoon, and I would see so much that, when I came in the house, I'd be talking and talking for what seemed like hours. Dad would say, "Boy, why don't you stop that lyin'? You know you didn't see all that. You know you didn't see nobody do that." But I knew I had.

Source: Claude Brown, *Manchild in the Promised Land* (New York: Macmillan, 1965), 427–429.

buildings where suburban commuters worked. Boston's West End, a flourishing, if poor, Italian community, was razed by a private developer between 1958 and 1960 to build Charles River Park, an apartment complex whose rents were far too steep for the old-time residents. West Enders were forced into less desirable parts of the city, cut off from the vitality of their former neighborhood. The 575,000 units of public housing nationwide built by 1964 came nowhere near to filling the need for affordable housing in urban America.

Despite pockets of urban "gentrification," postwar cities were increasingly becoming a place of last resort for the nation's poor. Unlike earlier immigrants, for whom cities were gateways to social and economic betterment, inner-city residents in the postwar period faced diminishing hopes for improvement. Lured by the promise of plentiful jobs, migrants found that many of these supposed opportunities had relocated to the suburban fringe. Steady employment was out of reach for those who needed it most.

The Blight of Urban Renewal
The West End area of Boston is shown as it looked in 1960, after an urban renewal program had cleared the land. Of the thriving community where seven thousand people had lived just eighteen months earlier, only St. Joseph's Catholic Church still stood (far right). Within two years, the site was covered with 2,400 units of luxury housing, whose rents far exceeded what the former residents could afford.

That the poor were increasingly trapped in the cities was also due to racism. Migrants to the city, especially blacks, faced racial hostility and institutional barriers to mobility. Two separate Americas were emerging—a white society located in suburbs and peripheral areas and an inner city made up of blacks, Hispanics, and other disadvantaged groups. This widespread metropolitan segregation remains one of the most striking and disturbing aspects of modern urban life.

American Society During the Baby Boom

One of the most distinctive characteristics of the immediate postwar period was its family orientation. Couples, especially the white middle class, flocked to the new suburban developments, where they had children, lots of them. The effects of the postwar baby boom are still felt. In the 1950s children provided plenty of patients for doctors and dentists, and students for elementary teachers. In the 1960s the baby-boom generation swelled college enrollments, and not coincidentally, the ranks of student protesters. By the 1970s, when the baby-boom generation entered the workplace, it had to compete for a limited number of jobs in what had become a stagnant economy. In the 1980s the delayed marriages and later childbearing of the career-oriented baby-boomers temporarily caused the birthrate to rise again. In the 1990s baby boomers, now in their forties, took up positions of leadership in business, politics, and cultural life. The decisions made by many couples in the immediate postwar period to have large families will continue to ripple through American life well into the twenty-first century.

Consumer Culture

As we have seen, prosperity and affluence characterized much of postwar American life. In some respects, the consumer culture of the 1950s seemed like a return to the 1920s—an overabundance of new gadgets and appliances, the expansion of consumer credit and advertising, more leisure time, the growing importance of the automobile, and the development of new types of mass media. Yet there was a significant difference. The postwar economy was far better balanced than that of the 1920s; no depressed agricultural sector detracted from the prosperity and no Great Depression lurked on the horizon. By the 1950s consumption had become integral to middle-class culture. Due to rising incomes, even blue-collar families had discretionary income to spend on consumer goods.

As in the 1920s, though, the postwar prosperity was helped along by a dramatic increase in consumer credit, which enabled families to stretch their incomes. Between 1946 and 1958 short-term consumer credit rose from $8.4 billion to almost $45 billion. A hefty portion of this increase involved financing for the purchase of automobiles on the installment plan. The Diners Club credit card, introduced in 1950 and followed by the American Express card and Bank Americard in 1959, was initially geared toward the business traveler. But by the 1970s, the ubiquitous plastic credit cards had revolutionized personal and family finances. One casualty of the consumer credit phenomenon was the pawnshop, which no longer found much call for its services.

Advertising. Along with expanded consumer spending came a spurt in advertising, another example of the booming service sector. In 1951 businesses spent more on advertising ($6.5 billion) than taxpayers did on primary and secondary education ($5 billion); advertising expenditures topped $10 billion in 1960. The 1950s gave Americans the Marlboro Man; M & M's that melt in your mouth, not in your hand; the Hathaway eyepatch; Wonder Bread building strong bodies in twelve ways; and the "does she, or doesn't she?" Clairol woman. Motivational research delved into the subconscious to suggest how these messages should be pitched. The ads of the period reflected an uncritical view of American life that suggested, falsely, that all Americans were white and middle class, all women homemakers, and all families nuclear and intact.

Automobiles continued to be the most heavily advertised item in the 1950s, but advertising also promoted a variety of new consumer appliances to fill the suburban home. Production of some of these appliances had been halted during the war; others were new to the postwar market. In 1946 automatic washing machines replaced the old machines that required wringing out clothes by hand, and electric dryers came on the market that same year. In 1955, 1.2 million dryers were sold, twice the 1953 total, and commercial laundries across the country struggled to stay in business. Another new item on the market was the home freezer, which enabled families to eat seasonal foods, such as fruits and vegetables, all year and encouraged the dramatic growth of the frozen-food industry. Due in part to the purchases of electrical gadgets for the home, consumer use of electricity doubled during the 1950s.

Leisure Time. Consumers had more time to spend money than ever before. In 1960 the average worker put in a five-day week, with eight paid holidays each year (double the 1946 standard) plus a paid two-week vacation. The travel industry grew rapidly during the 1950s, with Americans devoting a seventh of the gross national product to spending on leisure and entertainment. Americans made use of the interstate highway system to travel domestically, encouraging the dramatic growth in motel chains, roadside restaurants, and fast-food eateries. (The first McDonald's restaurant opened in 1954 in San Bernardino, California; the Holiday Inn

Landmark for Hungry Americans

Conveniently located on major highways and in shopping centers, Howard Johnson's Motor Lodges and Restaurants (colloquially referred to as HoJo's) were instantly recognizable by their bright orange roofs. Like McDonald's Golden Arches, these roofs became familiar roadside beacons for travelers and suburbanites alike. (Henry Ford Museum & Greenfield Village)

motel chain started in Memphis in 1952.) Popular destinations were national and state parks, and Disneyland, the original theme park which opened in Anaheim, California, in 1955. Aided by the strong U.S. dollar and the introduction of jet air travel in 1958, families flooded Europe each summer, earning the unflattering epithet of "ugly Americans" for expecting things to be just like home.

Television

One of the most widespread leisure activities was watching television. TV's leap to cultural prominence was swift and overpowering. There were only ten broadcasting stations in the entire country in 1947, and a meager 7,000 sets in American homes. But in 1948 the CBS and NBC radio networks began offering regular programming on television. Just two years later, Americans had purchased 7.3 million TV sets. By 1955, 66 percent of American families had at least one television set; by 1960, 87 percent. More Americans owned a TV than a refrigerator.

In other countries, television developed as a government-controlled or subsidized service, but in the United States it emerged as private enterprise geared towards entertainment. Although stations were licensed by the Federal Communications Commission after 1941, television, like radio, depended entirely on advertising and corporate sponsorship for profits. Even though the radio networks, especially the corporate leaders NBC and CBS, played a large role in making TV happen, television soon supplanted radio as the chief diffuser of popular culture. Movies, too, lost the cultural predominance that they had enjoyed from the 1920s through the 1940s. Movie attendance shrank throughout the postwar period, and studios relied increasingly on overseas distribution of American films for their profits.

At first the novelty of television brought people together, at a neighbor's home or perhaps in a local tavern to watch the World Series or a political convention, but it soon had the opposite effect of isolating and atomizing leisure in the private home. Television fostered a mass national culture in a way similar to, but far more completely than, radio's effect in the 1920s. It promoted homogeneity and reduced regional and ethnic differences by its national network programming (the first live nationwide broadcast, the signing of the Japanese Peace Treaty ending the American military occupation, occurred in 1951). Viewers had only three or four channels to choose from; public television did not begin until 1967, and cable was a phenomenon of the 1980s.

Television encouraged the consumerism and advertising that has characterized mass culture since the 1920s. Like the golden era of radio in the 1920s and 1930s, corporations produced and sponsored major television shows, such as the "Texaco Star Theater" with Milton Berle, the "Camel News Caravan" with John Cameron Swayze, and the "General Electric Theater," hosted by Ronald Reagan. New items entered the home, such as frozen TV dinners of turkey, peas, and mashed potatoes, first introduced in 1954. Now a family could eat a meal in front of the television without having to talk. *TV Guide*, founded in television's breakthrough year of 1948, became the most successful new periodical of the 1950s. Television even affected city services. In 1954 the Toledo water commissioner wondered why water consumption rose dramatically during certain three-minute periods. The answer? All across Toledo, TV watchers flushed their toilets during commercials.

"The Honeymooners"

Sewer worker Ed Norton (left, played by Art Carney) and bus driver Ralph Kramden (Jackie Gleason) joust in an episode from the popular television series "The Honeymooners." Should Alice Kramden (played by Audrey Meadows) try to get a word in edgewise, Ralph's reply was likely to be, "One of these days, Alice, one of these days, pow! Right in the kisser!"

What Americans saw on television, besides the omnipresent commercials, was an overwhelmingly white, Anglo-Saxon world of nuclear families, suburban homes, and middle-class life. Shows like "The Honeymooners," starring Jackie Gleason as a Brooklyn bus driver, or "Life With Reilly" were rare in their treatment of working-class lives. Minorities appeared mainly as servants, such as Jack Benny's Rochester. Far more typical was "Father Knows Best," starring Robert Young and Jane Wyatt. We never knew what Father actually did for a living, except that he left home each morning wearing a suit and carrying a briefcase. Mother was a full-time housewife, always available and actively interested in her three children, but also prone to stereotypical female behavior such as bad driving and bursting into tears.

Probably the most popular situation comedy of the 1950s was "I Love Lucy," which revolved around the adventures of a wacky housewife and her Cuban-born bandleader husband, as portrayed by Lucille Ball and Desi Arnaz. Married in real life as well as on television, the show even incorporated Lucy's first pregnancy into the storyline. Twice as many Americans—44 million, the figure courtesy of the new sampling firm of A. C. Neilson—watched the 1956 show where Lucy had her baby as did the inauguration of President Dwight Eisenhower the next day.

The television genres developed in the 1950s still shape broadcasting today. Taking over a popular radio and movie category, television offered some thirty westerns on the air by 1959, including "Gunsmoke," "Have Gun, Will Travel," and "Bonanza," the first color show. National television coverage made professional sports big-time entertainment and big business. Programming geared to children, such as Walt Disney's Mickey Mouse Club, Howdy Doody, and Captain Kangaroo, meant that 1950s children were the first generation to grow up glued to the tube. The appeal of perennially popular quiz shows such as "Twenty-One" and "The $64,000 Question" was untarnished even when a scandal in 1959 revealed that contestants had been given the questions in advance. Although the new medium did offer some serious programming, notably live theater and documentaries, Federal Communications Commissioner Newton Minow concluded in 1963 that television was "a vast wasteland."

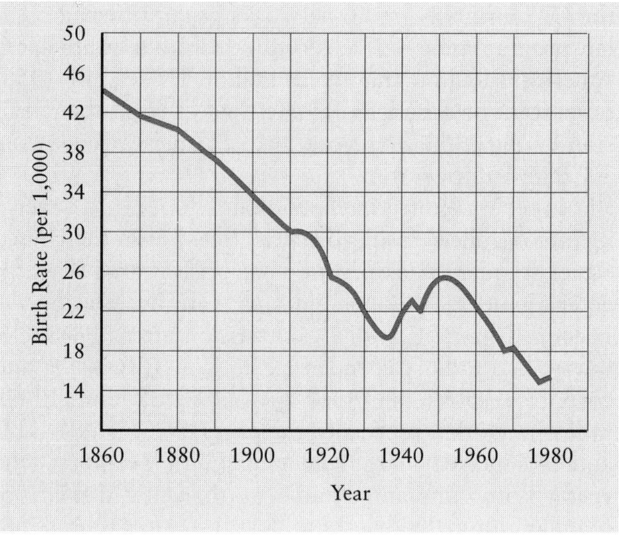

FIGURE 29.5

The Declining American Birthrate, 1860–1980

When viewed over more than a century, the postwar baby boom was clearly an aberration.

The Baby Boom

The dislocations of the depression and war years made both men and women yearn for a return to traditional family values. A popular 1945 song was "Gotta Make Up for Lost Time," and Americans did just that. The postwar generation approached life with an optimism and confidence notably absent from the depression cohort of the 1930s. The GI Bill and other federal programs aided their quest for unprecedented levels of material security, as did the general prosperity of the postwar era. As usual, these options were far more available to members of the white middle class than to minorities.

Such individual life choices were taking place against the backdrop of the Cold War. Just as the Marshall Plan and the Truman Doctrine were two halves of the same walnut, so too were cold war ideology and the 1950s emphasis on domesticity. One historian used the phrase "cold war, warm hearth" to capture how home and family seemed to offer a secure private retreat from the Cold War and the atomic age. (Note the semantic ironies of the *nuclear* family in the *nuclear* age.) As Richard Nixon argued in the "kitchen debate" with Nikita Khrushchev, stable suburban families (sexual "containment," no less) would provide the bulwark against the Soviet threat.

Two things were noteworthy about the men and women who formed families between 1940 and 1960. First, their marriages were remarkably stable. Not until the mid-1960s did the divorce rate begin to rise sharply. Second, they were strongly pronatal. Everyone expected to have at least several children—it was part of adulthood, almost a citizen's responsibility. "I'd like six kids," announced one young man. "It just seems like a minimum production goal." After a century and a half of declining family size, the birthrate shot up: more babies were born between 1948 and 1953 than in the previous thirty years. As a result, the American population rose dramatically, from 140 million in 1945 to 179 million in 1960, and 203 million in 1970.

There are several reasons for this twenty-year upsurge that demographers call the *baby boom*. Because a sustained rise in the birthrate did not occur in all the countries affected by World War II, it was not simply a response to the losses of war. Much more important was the drop in the marriage age, a trend that had begun during the war. The average age of marriage dropped to twenty-two for men, twenty for women; in 1951 a third of all women were married by the time they reached nineteen.

While younger couples were having babies earlier, they were not necessarily having huge numbers of children. Women who came of age in the 1930s had an average of 2.4 children; their counterparts in the 1950s averaged 3.2 children. What made the baby boom happen was that *everyone* was having children, and having them at the same time. This explosion in fertility peaked in 1957, and remained at a high level until the early 1960s. Since the 1960s the birthrate has generally declined, returning to more longstanding patterns. The postwar baby boom thus represents an aberration.

Increased Life Expectancy. In addition to the rising birthrate, the declining death rate contributed to the population growth. Life expectancy at birth had improved steadily over the first half of the twentieth century, from forty-seven years in 1900 to sixty-three years in 1940. Continued improvements in diet, public health, and surgical practices further lengthened the life span. So did "miracle drugs," such as penicillin, introduced in 1943, streptomycin (1945), and cortisone (1946). When Dr. Jonas Salk perfected a polio vaccine in 1954, he became a national hero. The free distribution of Salk's vaccine in the nation's schools, followed in 1961 by Dr. Albert Sabin's oral polio vaccine, demonstrated the potential of government-sponsored public health programs. The conquest of polio made the children of the 1950s one of the healthiest generations ever.

Scientific Child Rearing. For rearing all these baby boom children and keeping them healthy, middle-class parents increasingly relied on the advice of experts. Dr. Benjamin Spock's best-selling *Baby and Child Care* sold a million copies a year after its publication in 1946. Dr. Spock urged mothers to abandon the rigid feeding and baby-care schedules of an earlier generation. New mothers found Spock's common-sense approach liberating, but it did not totally soothe their insecurities. If mothers were too protective of their children, they might hamper their adjustment to a normal adult life. If they wanted to work outside the home, they felt guilty about neglecting their family. Dr. Spock could only recommend that mothers be constantly available to respond to their children's needs.

The baby boom had a broad and immediate impact on American society. The consumer needs of all those babies fueled the economy as families bought food, diapers, toys, and clothing for their expanding broods. Family spending on consumer goods joined federal expenditures on national security as the basis for the unparalleled prosperity and economic growth that characterized American society in the 1950s and 1960s.

The baby boom also encouraged a major expansion of the nation's educational system. The new middle class, America's first college-educated generation, placed a high value on education. To make schools into showplace community centers, suburbanites approved 90 percent of the proposed school bond issues during the 1950s. School expenditures accounted for 7.2 percent of the gross national product by 1970, double the 1950 level.

Polio Pioneers

These Provo, Utah, children each received a "Polio Pioneer" souvenir button for participating in the trial of the Salk vaccine in 1954. Dr. Jonas Salk's announcement the next year that the vaccine was safe and effective made him a national hero.

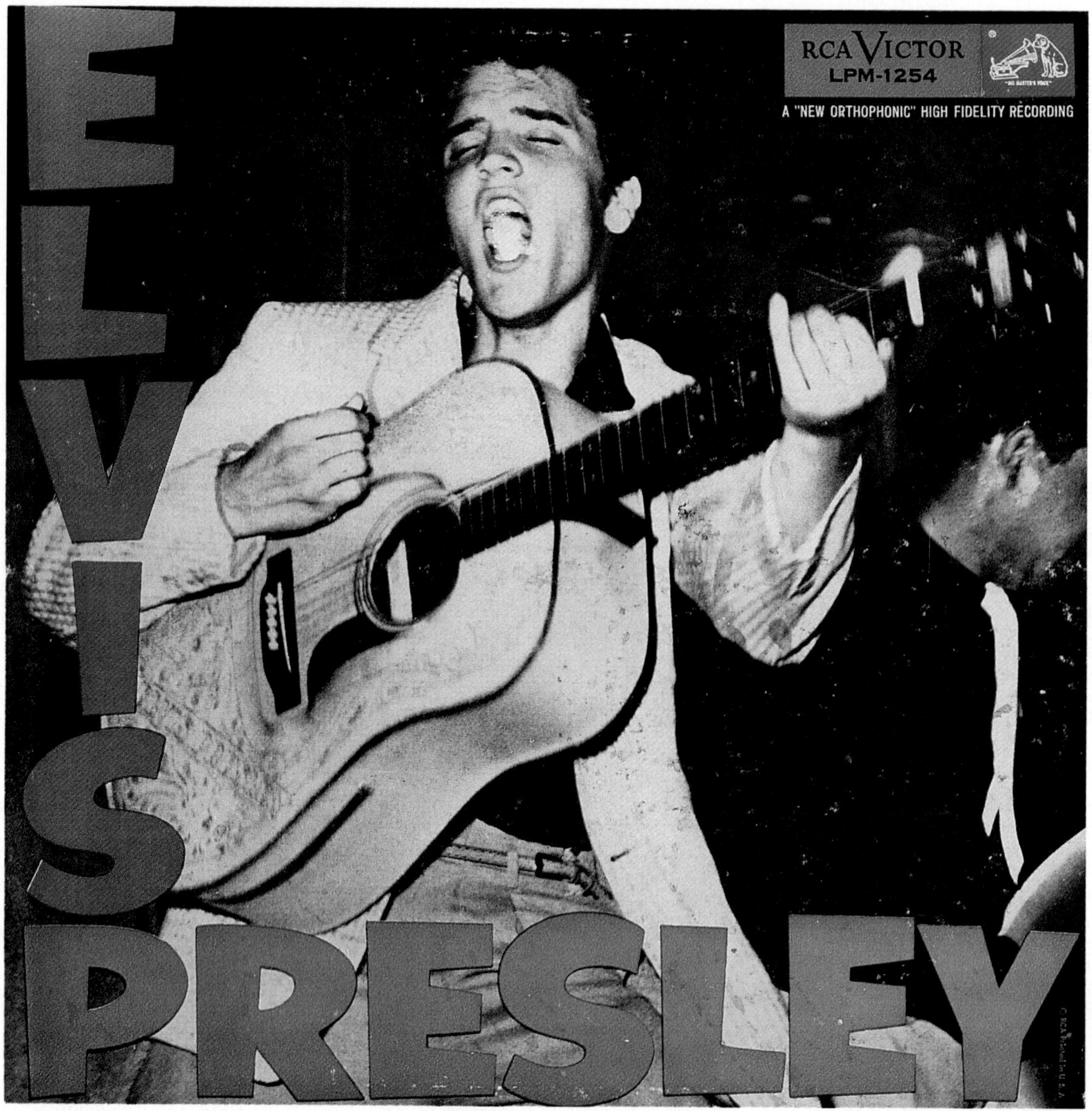

Elvis Presley

The young Elvis Presley (shown here on the cover of his first album in 1956) embodied cultural rebellion against the conservatism and triviality of adult life, but by the 1960s his music had lost its edge. He still remained enormously popular, however, especially after a 1968 comeback. After his death in 1977 from an accidental drug overdose, Elvis impersonators abounded and a major cult developed. Graceland, his home in Memphis, attracts more visitors each year than Mount Vernon.

Youth Culture

In 1956, only partly in jest, CBS radio commentator Eric Sevareid questioned "whether the teenagers will take over the United States lock, stock, living room, and garage." The centrality of youth culture to modern times, a trend first noticed in the 1920s and expanding ever since, had its roots in the democratization of education, the growth of peer culture, and what one historian has called the "burgeoning consumer independence" of teenagers in an age of affluence. Like so much else in the 1950s, the youth culture came down to money.

Market research convinced advertisers of the existence of a distinct teen market in the 1950s. A 1951 *Newsweek* story noted with awe that the $3 average weekly spending money of the typical teen was enough to buy 190 million candy bars, 130 million soft drinks, and 230 million sticks of gum. In 1956 advertisers projected an adolescent market of $9 billion for items such as transistor radios (first introduced in 1952), 45 rpm records, clothing, and fads such as silly putty (1950) and hula hoops (1958). Increasingly advertisers targeted their appeal to the young, both to capture their spending money and also for their influence on family spending patterns. Note the changing slogans for Pepsi-Cola: "Twice as much for a nickel" (1935); "Be Sociable—Have a Pepsi" (1948); "Now it's Pepsi for those who think young" (1960); and, finally, "The Pepsi Generation" (1965).

Hollywood movies played a large role in fostering, and legitimizing, this separate teenage culture. At a time when general movie attendance was declining because of competition from television, young people made up the largest audience for motion pictures. Soon Hollywood studios were catering to this youth orientation with such films as *The Wild One* (1951), starring Marlon Brando, and *Rebel Without A Cause* (1955), starring James Dean, Natalie Wood, and Sal Mineo. "What are you rebelling against?" a waitress asks Brando in *The Wild One*. "Whattaya got?" he replies.

What really defined this generation, however, was music. Just as wartime "bobby soxers" swooned over popular singers like Frank Sinatra, teenagers in the 1950s had rock and roll. Rock and roll developed from white country and western music and black-urban music known as rhythm and blues. Cleveland disk jockey Alan Freed played a large role in introducing white America to the new African-American sound by playing what were known as "race" records when he came to primetime radio in 1954. Soon the record companies realized the size of the market. Between 1953 and 1959 record sales increased from $213 million to $603 million, with rock and roll as the driving force. The market for stereos and transistor radios rose accordingly.

The breakthrough year for rock and roll was 1956, thanks largely to Elvis Presley. "If I could find a white man who had the Negro sound and the Negro feel, I could make a billion dollars," said the owner of a record company. Presley, born in 1935 in Tupelo, Mississippi, in a working-class family, proved an instant sensation with his hits "Hound Dog" and "Heartbreak Hotel." In 1956 his records sold 10 million copies, more than 10 percent of all popular records sold that year. Between 1956 and his induction into the army in 1958 (the long arm of the state reached even the most popular teen idol), Presley had fourteen consecutive million-copy selling hits.

Many adults were appalled. They saw in music, movies, and magazines like *Mad* (introduced in 1952) an invitation to rebellion, disorder, and juvenile delinquency. They found the new music especially troubling. A noted psychiatrist called rock and roll "a communicable disease" and "a cannibalistic and tribalistic kind of music." When Elvis Presley appeared on the "Ed Sullivan Show," television cameras showed the teen idol only from the waist up, censoring his skin-tight pants and gyrating pelvis. Young people got the message anyway.

Contradictions in Women's Lives

"The suburban housewife was the dream image of the young American woman," feminist Betty Friedan has said of the 1950s. "She was healthy, beautiful, educated, concerned only about her husband, her children, and her home." Friedan herself gave up a psychology fellowship and a career as a journalist to marry, move to the suburbs, and raise three children. "Determined that I find the feminine fulfillment that eluded my mother . . . I lived the life of a suburban housewife that was everyone's dream at the time," she said.

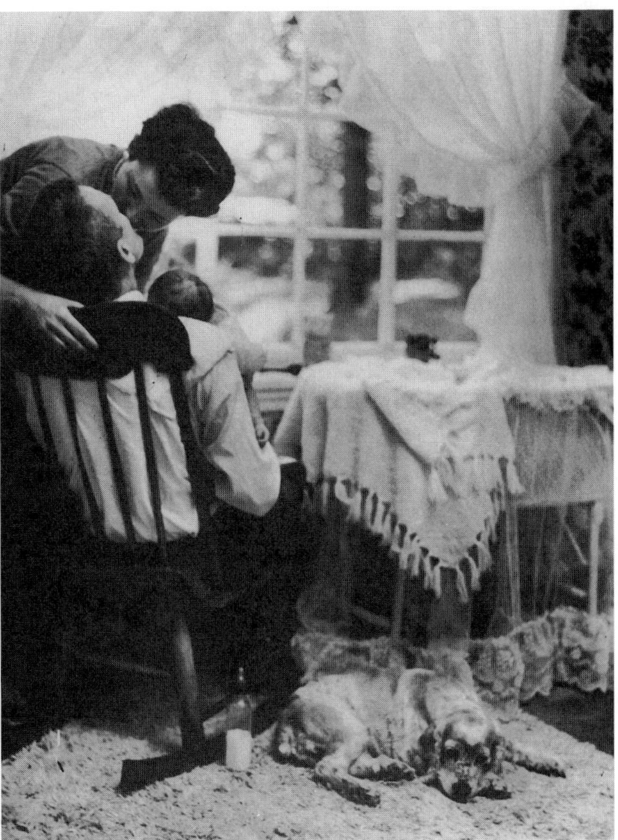

Home Life in the 1950s: The Ideal

This photograph reflects an idealized picture of family life in the 1950s. Taken in Long Island in 1958, it suggests the theme of "togetherness," a word coined by *McCall's* magazine in 1954. Many popular magazines promoted the notion of an idyllic home life for women who made a full-time career of homemaking, regardless of family size.

AMERICAN VOICES

The Feminine Mystique *Betty Friedan*

Betty Friedan drew on her own experiences as a suburban housewife to write her best-selling *The Feminine Mystique* (1963). This piece, published in 1974, describes her memories of "the way we were—1949."

I felt that I would never again, ever, be so happy as I was living in Queens. The floors were parquet, and the ceilings were molded white plaster, no pipes, and the plumbing worked. The rent was $118.50 a month, for four and one-half rooms, and we thought that was enormous. And now our friends were the other couples like us, with kids at the nursery school who squealed at each other from the baskets of the grocery carts we wheeled at the supermarket. It was fun at first, shopping in those new supermarkets. And we bought barbecue grills, and made dips out of sour cream and dried onion soup to serve with potato chips, while our husbands made the martinis as dry as in the city and cooked hamburgers on the charcoal, and we sat in canvas chairs on our terrace and thought how beautiful our children looked, playing in the twilight, and how lucky we all were, and that it would last forever.

There were six families in our group, and if your child smashed his finger in the manhole cover and you weren't home one of the others would take him to the doctor. We had Thanksgiving and Christmas and Passover Seders as a joint family, and in the summer rented houses together, on Lake George and Fire Island, that we couldn't afford separately. And the support we gave each other hid the cracks in our marriages—or maybe kept them from getting serious. As it is, of the six families, three couples are now divorced, one broken by suicide.

Having babies, the Care and Feeding of Children according to Doctor Spock, began to structure our lives. It took the place of politics. But the mystique was something else—that college graduates should make a *Career* of motherhood, not just one or two babies, but four, five, six. Why even go to college? . . .

Besides, the reality of the babies, the bottles, the cooking, the diapering, the burping, the carriage-wheeling, the pressure cooker, the barbecue, the playground, and doing-it-yourself was more comfortable, more safe, secure, and satisfying—that year and for a lot of years thereafter—than that supposedly glamorous "career" where you somehow didn't feel wanted, and where no matter what you did you knew you weren't going to get anywhere. There was a guilty feeling, too: it was somehow your fault, *pushy* of you, to want that good assignment for yourself, want the credit, the by-line, if the idea, even the writing, had been yours. *Pushy,* too, if you felt rejected when the men went out to lunch and talked shop in one of those bars where women were not allowed—even if one of those same men asked you out to lunch, alone, in the other kind of restaurant, and held your hand, or knee, under the tablecloth. It was uncomfortable, unreal in a way, working in that kind of office with "career" still driving you, but having no words to deal with, even *recognize,* that barrier that you could never somehow break through, that made you invisible as a person, that made them not take you seriously, that made you feel so basically unimportant, almost unnecessary, and—buried very deep—so angry.

At home, you *were* necessary, you were important, you were the boss, in fact—the mother—and the new mystique gave it the rationale of career. . . .

Shortly after 1949, I was fired from my job because I was pregnant again. They weren't about to put up with the inconvenience of another year's maternity leave, even though I was *entitled* to it under my union contract. It was unfair, *wrong* somehow to fire me just because I was pregnant, and to hire a man instead. I even tried calling a meeting of the people in the union where I worked. It was the first personal stirring of my own feminism, I guess. But the other women were just embarrassed, and the men uncomprehending. It was my own fault, getting pregnant again, a *personal* matter, not something you should take to the union. There was no word in 1949 for "sex discrimination."

Besides, it was almost a relief: I had begun to feel so guilty working, and I really wasn't getting anywhere in that job. I was more than ready to embrace the feminine mystique. I took a cooking course and started studying the suburban real-estate ads. And the next time the census taker came around, I was living in that old Charles Addams house we were fixing up, on the Hudson River in Rockland County. And the children numbered three. When the census taker asked my occupation, I said self-consciously, virtuously, with only the faintest stirrings of protest from that part of me I'd turned my back on—"housewife."

Source: Betty Friedan, *It Changed My Life* (New York: Dell, 1976), 33–37.

The 1950s were characterized by a pervasive, indeed pernicious, insistence that women's proper place was in the home. There was nothing new about this idea. What Betty Friedan tagged the *feminine mystique* of the 1950s—that "the highest value and the only commitment for women is the fulfillment of their own femininity"—bore remarkable similarities to the nineteenth-century's cult of true womanhood. But women's lives had changed dramatically since the nineteenth century, due to increased access to education and jobs, a declining birthrate, and the greater availability of consumer goods and services. It was much harder to convince women to stay in their homes in the 1950s than it had been in the 1850s. In fact, the shrillness with which the message of domesticity was trumpeted may have been in inverse relation to how far women had already strayed from total identification with the home.

The updated version of the cult of domesticity drew on new elements of twentieth-century science and culture, even Freudian psychology, to give it more force. Television, popular music, films, and advertising depicted career women as social and sexual misfits. As the postwar consumer culture took off, the media emphasized that women's primary role was to buy appliances and other consumer goods for home and family. "Love is said in many ways," ran an ad promoting a brand of toilet paper. Asked another, "Can a woman ever feel right cooking on a dirty range?"

While the feminine mystique held cultural sway in the postwar period, not all housewives were as unhappy or neurotic as Friedan later implied in her 1963 bestseller. Many women found constructive outlets for their energy in groups like the League of Women Voters, the PTA, the Junior League, and church women's groups. Blue-collar housewives proudly filled in census forms with "occupation: housewife"; unlike their mothers and unmarried sisters, they did not have to take routine employment outside the home. More fundamentally, not all American families could, or did, live by these norms. The ideals of suburban domesticity were out of reach, or totally irrelevant, to many minorities, inner-city residents, recent immigrants, rural Americans, and those on the margins of mainstream American culture, such as homosexuals. Once again, there was a large gap between popular culture and the reality of American lives.

Home Life: One Reality

This young mother in New Rochelle, a suburb of New York City, was photographed in 1955. Her frenzied situation hints at why 24,000 American women responded to a 1960 *Redbook* magazine article entitled "Why Young Mothers Feel Trapped."

Women at Work. Another way to widen our view beyond a domestic-bound 1950s is to confront the interesting and somewhat contradictory fact that at the height of the feminine mystique more than one-third of American women held jobs outside the home. As the service sector expanded, there was a steady demand for workers in fields traditionally filled by women. Economist Eli Ginzberg called the dramatic rise in the number and kind of women who worked for pay outside the home "the single most outstanding phenomenon of our century."

The increase in the number of working women was paralleled by another change of equally significant proportion—the dramatic rise in the number of older, married, middle-class women who took jobs. At the turn of the century, the average female worker was a young recent immigrant who worked only until she married. By mid-century, the average woman worker was in her forties, married, and had children in school. In 1940 only 15 percent of all wives worked. This percentage had doubled by 1960 and reached 40 percent by 1970.

Many women entered the paid labor force to supplement their family income. Changing consumption habits increasingly required two incomes to maintain a certain standard of living. The wages that many men earned even in the prosperous 1950s and 1960s could not pay for all the necessities of new middle-class life—cars, houses, vacations, and a college education for their children. For minority households, multiple wage earners were often necessary just to get by.

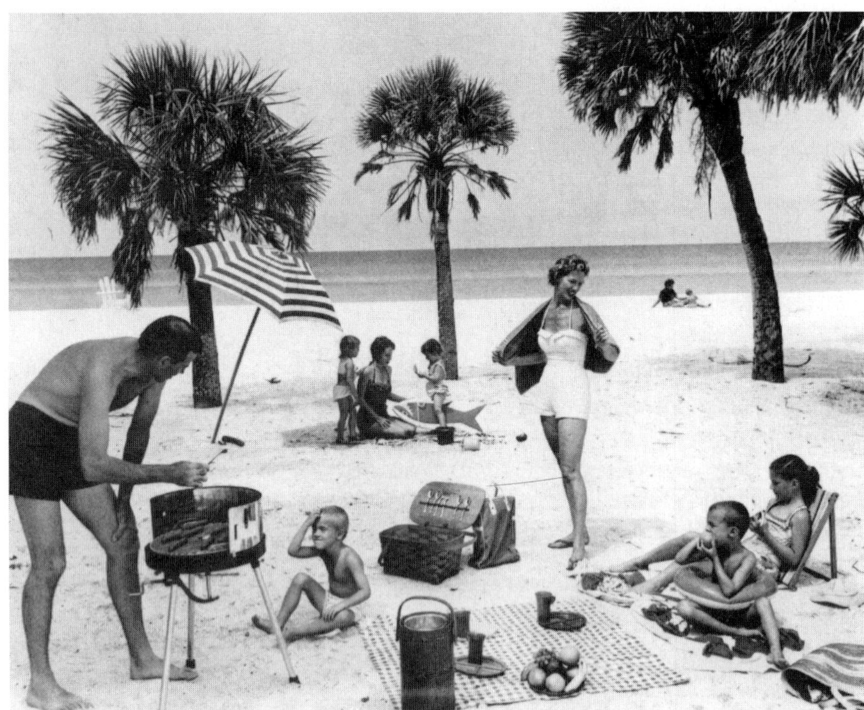

At the Beach

This 1958 photograph of Longboat Key, Florida, by Joe Steinmetz is packed with so many cultural clichés about family life in the 1950s that it is hard to know whether it is real or fake.

How could the society of the 1950s so steadfastly uphold the domestic ideal while an increasing number of wives and mothers took jobs? In many ways, the dramatic increase was kept invisible by the women themselves. Fearing public disapproval of their decisions, such women usually interpreted their work in very individual or family-oriented terms: "Of course I believe a woman's place is at home, but I took this job to save for college for our children." Moreover, when women took on jobs outside the home, they invariably maintained full responsibility for child care and household management, which allowed families and society to avoid the full implications of women's new roles. As one overburdened woman noted, she now had "two full-time jobs instead of just one—underpaid clerical worker and unpaid housekeeper." The absence of an active feminist movement in the 1940s and 1950s meant that few public figures or organizations paid attention to this major demographic and social shift. Similarly, few popular heroines from movies, television, or popular culture encouraged women's autonomy—quite the contrary. Women were left to cope on their own.

The Fifties: The Way We Were?

Like the 1920s, the 1950s are defined almost entirely in cultural terms. But once again, this emphasis on affluence, popular culture, and consumption is too superficial for understanding such a complex period of economic and social transformation. The popularized view of the "happy days" of the 1950s (a "decade" which really stretched from 1945 to the early 1960s) reflects only a tenuous rendering of reality.

In the popular mind the 1950s often represents the norm of American society. Families were close-knit and intact; children were happy; the economy was growing; and, despite the fear of nuclear annihilation, the United States was secure in its position as the strongest country, both economically and morally, in the world. Given all that has happened since the 1950s, changes in American family, political, and social life are often seen as declines from this ideal.

But perhaps the fifties were the aberration, not the norm—the result of a unique congruence of circumstances that would have been difficult to sustain on a permanent basis. The postwar baby boom was certainly an aberration in a two-hundred year trend toward smaller families. The stability of marriages in the 1940s and 1950s was also atypical in light of the liberalization of social mores in the 1920s and 1930s and the increasing divorce rates after the mid-1960s. Scarred by memories of war and depression-era dislocations, and scared by the ambiguities of living in the atomic age, this postwar generation embraced family life with a vengeance. When conditions changed, this profamily orientation slipped back more in line with the diversity and pluralism of the rest of the century.

Perhaps the greatest aberration, and the reason why

our view of the 1950s as the norm is so pernicious, is that the economic base on which this affluence rested was predicated on a set of international economic conditions that could not continue indefinitely. When the war-devastated economies of Japan and West Germany were rebuilt, they took advantage of new technology to compete, and eventually challenge, American economic supremacy in one industry after another: steel, rubber, automobiles, electronics, footwear, and textiles. So too did emerging industrial centers in the Pacific Rim, such as Korea, Hong Kong, and Singapore. Unfortunately, since the economic abundance and hegemony of the 1950s is taken as the norm, any decline is seen as a disturbing loss of American power and economic strength, rather than a return to a more normal state of economic affairs.

There are other ways that the stereotypes of the 1950s are misleading, if not downright false. The picture painted in popular culture of affluence unbounded hides, indeed makes invisible, those Americans who did not share equally in this postwar American dream. Many people—displaced factory workers, destitute old people, female heads of households, blacks and Hispanics—watched the affluent society from the outside and wondered why they were not permitted to share in its bounty. Not until the publication of Michael Harrington's *The Other America* in 1962 did Americans begin to realize that, in the richest country of the world, more than a quarter of the population was poor.

The contrasts between suburban affluence and the "other America," between the lure of the city for the poor and minorities and the grim reality of its segregated existence, between a heightened emphasis on domesticity and widening opportunities for women, would spawn protest and change in the turbulent 1960s. Amid the booming prosperity of the late 1940s and 1950s, however, these fundamental social and economic contradictions were barely noticed.

Summary

Postwar affluence rested on several foundations, especially the global hegemony enjoyed by the United States in the immediate postwar period. Federal intervention in the economy, especially in the form of defense spending, fueled prosperity, as did spending for consumer-goods. Consumer spending played an especially important role in the reconversion to a peacetime economy. Technological change stimulated productivity, notably in agriculture and industry.

Much of the economic activity in the postwar period concentrated in the growing metropolitan areas, especially in their expanding suburbs. Metropolitan areas exhibited a striking dichotomy, as poor migrants settled in the inner city while the more affluent took their families to the suburbs. For the new middle class, the postwar period brought a higher standard of living and access to an array of new consumer goods. Blacks, Puerto Ricans, and Mexican-Americans rarely shared in this affluence, however.

The structural changes transforming the American economy had a strong impact on individual Americans. White-collar workers now outnumbered blue-collar employees, and more women joined the work force. The labor movement could not maintain its momentum from the 1930s. Many of the smoldering contradictions of the postwar period—an unequally shared affluence, institutionalized racism that limited opportunities for nonwhite Americans, and tensions in women's lives—soon surfaced in the social protest movements of the 1960s.

TOPIC FOR RESEARCH

Poverty in the Age of Affluence

In 1962, Michael Harrington published *The Other America*, which described the persistence of poverty in postwar America. Assume you have been asked to review this book for a newspaper in 1962. You suspect that most of your readers will be surprised to learn that more than one-quarter of the population live in poverty and that the majority of the poor are white. Describe the findings of the book and analyze how successful it is in presenting its argument. How can you reconcile Harrington's picture with the general view of the 1950s as a period of unbounded affluence? Reflect on why the poor are so invisible and why modern capitalist societies, even those with welfare states, have been unable (or unwilling) to address the persistence of poverty.

For general background, sources on the history of poverty and social welfare include Michael B. Katz, *In the Shadow of the Poorhouse* (1986); Frances Fox Piven and Richard A. Cloward, *Poor People's Movements* (1977) and *Regulating the Poor* (1971); James Patterson, *America's Struggle Against Poverty, 1900–1980* (1981); and Oscar Lewis, *La Vida: A Puerto Rican Family in the Culture of Poverty* (1965). The classic text on the age of affluence in the 1950s remains John Kenneth Galbraith, *The Affluent Society* (1958).

BIBLIOGRAPHY

General introductions to postwar society include John Diggins, *The Proud Decades: America in War and Peace, 1941–1960* (1988); Elaine Tyler May, *Homeward Bound: American Families in the Cold War Era* (1988); William E. Leuchtenberg, *A Troubled Feast* (1979); James Gilbert, *Another Chance* (2nd ed., 1986); and William O'Neill, *American High* (1986).

Technology and Economic Change

For overviews on the economic changes of the postwar period, see W. Elliot Brownlee, *Dynamics of Ascent* (1979); David P. Calleo, *The Imperious Economy* (1982); and Harold G. Vatter, *The U.S. Economy in the 1950s* (1963). Robert Kuttner, *The End of Laissez-Faire* (1991) provides ample background on the Bretton Woods system. Herman P. Miller, *Rich Man, Poor Man* (1971) and Gabriel Kolko, *Wealth and Power in America* (1962), discuss inequality in income distribution. Michael Harrington, *The Other America* (1962), documents the persistence of poverty. John Kenneth Galbraith's lively books, *American Capitalism* (1952), *The Affluent Society* (1958), and *The New Industrial State* (1967), shaped much of the public discussion of the economy in the period. Robert L. Heilbroner, *The Limits of American Capitalism* (1965), is equally readable and more critical.

John L. Shover, *First Majority–Last Minority* (1976), analyzes the transformation of rural life in America. It can be supplemented by Willard W. Cochrane and Mary E. Ryan, *American Farm Policy, 1948–1973* (1976), and Gilbert C. Fite, *American Farmers: the New Minority* (1981). David Brody, *Workers in Industrial America* (1980); David Montgomery, *Workers' Control in America* (1979); and James R. Green, *The World of the Worker* (1980), provide overviews of labor in the twentieth century. On the impact of technology and automation, see Elting E. Morison, *From Know-how to Nowhere* (1974), and David F. Noble, *Forces of Production: A Social History of Industrial Automation* (1984). Harry Braverman, *Labor and Monopoly Capital* (1974) looks at the degradation of work from a Marxist perspective. In Studs Terkel's superb oral history, *Working* (1974), people from all walks of life talk about what they do and how they feel about it.

The most influential study of the new middle class remains David Reisman, with Nathan Glazer and Ruel Denney, *The Lonely Crowd* (1950). William H. Whyte, *The Organization Man* (1956), provides a similar perspective. See also the work of C. Wright Mills, especially *White Collar* (1951) and *The Power Elite* (1956). Samuel Lubbell describes middle-class voting patterns in *The Future of American Politics* (1956) and *Revolt of the Moderates* (1956).

Alfred D. Chandler, *The Visible Hand* (1977), is the definitive history of American corporate structure and strategy. Myra Wilkin, *The Maturing of Multinational Enterprise* (1974), and Richard J. Barnet and Ronald E. Muller, *Global Reach* (1974), describe American business abroad. See also Robert Sobel, *The Age of Giant Corporations* (1972), and the early sections of Barry Bluestein and Bennett Harrison, *The Deindustrialization of America* (1982).

Cities and Suburbs

Zane L. Miller, *The Urbanization of Modern America* (1973); Blake McKelvey, *The Emergence of Metropolitan America, 1915–1966* (1968); Jon C. Teaford, *The Twentieth Century American City* (1986); and Kenneth Fox, *Metropolitan America: Urban Life and Urban Policy in the United States, 1940–1980* (1985), are strong overviews of the growth of urban areas. See also Sam Bass Warner, Jr., *The Urban Wilderness* (1972), for a more interpretive view.

Kenneth Jackson, *Crabgrass Frontier* (1985), provides an overview of suburban development, which can be supplemented by Jon C. Teaford, *City and Suburb: The Political Fragmentation of Metropolitan America, 1850–1970* (1979) and Robert Fishman, *Bourgeois Utopias* (1987). Michael N. Danielson, *The Politics of Exclusion* (1976) describes how blacks were kept out of suburbia. Zane Miller, *Suburb* (1982), is a case study of Forest Park, Ohio. Herbert Gans, *The Levittowners* (1967), describes the two years he spent as a participant-observer in that New Jersey community. Bennett M. Berger, *Working-Class Suburb* (1960), and Scott Donaldson, *The Suburban Myth* (1969), question the homogeneity of the suburban experience. Mark H. Rose, *Interstate* (1979) describes the politics of building the highway system.

Nicholas Lemann offers an overview of postwar black migration in *The Promised Land* (1991). Herbert J. Gans, *The Urban Villagers* (1962), tells the story of an Italian community in Boston displaced by urban renewal. Jane Jacobs, *The Death and Life of Great American Cities* (1961), is an opinionated look at urban problems. Stephen Thernstrom, *The Other Bostonians* (1973), suggests why blacks in urban areas did not find upward social mobility. Robert A. Caro's biography of Robert Moses, *The Power Broker* (1974), provides a case study of the impact of highways on the landscape of metropolitan New York City through his career. Books that treatthe rise of the Sunbelt are Kirkpatrick Sale, *Power Shift* (1975), and Richard Bernard and Bradley Rice, eds., *Sunbelt Cities* (1983).

American Society During the Baby Boom

Books that highlight social and economic developments in the 1950s include Godfrey Hodgson, *America In Our Time* (1976); Carl Degler, *Affluence and Anxiety* (1968); and David Potter, *People of Plenty* (1954). See also Douglas T. Miller and Marion Nowak, *The Fifties: the Way We Really Were* (1977);

Jeffrey Hart, *When the Going Was Good! American Life in the Fifties* (1982); and Paul Carter, *Another Part of the Fifties* (1983).

For popular culture, George Lipsitz, *Time Passages: Collective Memory and American Popular Culture* (1991) surveys postwar television, music, film, and popular narrative. Eric Barnouw, *The Image Empire* (1970), chronicles the impact of television. Other treatments of the mass media include Marshall McLuhan, *Understanding Media* (1964); Todd Gitlin, *Inside Prime Time* (1983); Frank Mankiewicz and Joel Swerdlow, *Remote Control: Television and the Manipulation of American Life* (1978); and Edward J. Epstein, *News From Nowhere* (1973). Robert Sklar, *Movie-Made America* (1975), shows how movies reacted to the threat from television. See also Peter Biskind, *Seeing Is Believing: How Hollywood Taught Us to Stop Worrying and Love the Fifties* (1983). Vance Packard's influential unmasking of the advertising industry, *The Hidden Persuaders* (1957), can be supplemented by Stephen Fox, *The Mirror Makers* (1984).

Richard Easterlin, *American Baby Boom in Historical Perspective* (1962), and *Birth and Future: The Impact of Numbers on Personal Welfare* (1980), analyze the demographic changes, as does Landon Y. Jones, *Great Expectations: America and the Baby Boom Generation* (1980). See also Michael P. Nichols, *Turning Forty in the Eighties* (1986). Developments in medicine are treated in James Bordley and A. McGehee Harvey, *Two Centuries of American Medicine* (1967) and Jane S. Smith, *Patenting the Sun: Polio and the Salk Vaccine* (1990). Diane Ravitch describes education from 1945 to 1980 in *The Troubled Crusade* (1983). James Gilbert, *A Cycle of Outrage* (1986), looks at juvenile delinquency in the 1950s.

Elaine May's *Homeward Bound* is the best introduction to postwar family culture. See also Wini Breines, *Young, White, and Miserable: Growing Up Female in the Fifties* (1992). Betty Friedan, *The Feminine Mystique* (1963), provides a witty perspective on the lives of educated suburban women, which should be contrasted with Mirra Komarovsky, *Blue Collar Marriage* (1962). William H. Chafe, *The American Woman* (1972), and Carl Degler, *At Odds* (1982), survey women's public and private roles. Alice Kessler-Harris, *Out to Work* (1982), concentrates on women at work. Glenna Matthews, *Just A Housewife* (1987), and Susan Strasser, *Never Done* (1982), look at housewives and housework, respectively. Eugenia Kaledin surveys women in the 1950s in *Mothers and More* (1984), and Barbara Ehrenreich, *Hearts of Men* (1983), offers a provocative view of men's lives in the decade.

TIMELINE

1944	Bretton Woods economic conference World Bank and International Monetary Fund (IMF) founded
1946	Dr. Benjamin Spock publishes *Baby and Child Care*
1947	Levittown, New York, built General Agreement on Tariffs and Trade (GATT) UNIVAC computer developed
1948	Television's breakthrough year; CBS and NBC begin regular programming
1954	Polio vaccine developed by Dr. Jonas Salk First McDonald's opens
1955	AFL and CIO reunited Disneyland opens in Anaheim, California
1956	Interstate Highway Act Elvis Presley popularizes rock and roll
1957	Peak of postwar baby boom
1958	Brooklyn Dodgers move to Los Angeles Jet air travel introduced
1959	Nixon and Khrushchev's "Kitchen Debate"
1963	California passes New York as most populous state
1965	Immigration Act abolishes national quota system

Turbulent Sixties

Robert Rauschenberg's 1963 oil and silkscreen canvas *Kite*, prefigures the turmoil that rocked America during the 1960s, both on the domestic front and internationally with Vietnam. (©Robert Rauschenberg/VAGA New York)

CHAPTER 30 *Kennedy, Johnson, and the Liberal Consensus, 1960–1968*

As Franklin Roosevelt had reassured a nation that there was nothing to fear but fear itself in 1933, so did John Fitzgerald Kennedy seem to speak to a desire for national purpose in his 1961 inaugural address. "Let the word go forth from this time and place, to friend and foe alike, that the torch has been passed to a new generation of Americans, born in this century, tempered by war, disciplined by a hard and bitter peace, proud of our ancient heritage." He challenged his audience: "Ask not what your country can do for you, ask what you can do for your country." Without offering any radical or sweeping programs, John Kennedy fostered an atmosphere conducive to challenging the status quo, a climate that has been called the "politics of expectation." The social and political changes set in motion by this expansive national mood provide the focus for the next two chapters. This chapter examines the Kennedy and Johnson administrations and the American experience in Vietnam through 1968; Chapter 31 looks at the civil rights movement, the youth rebellion, and the revival of feminism.

The expansion of New Deal social welfare programs and the continuation of the Cold War were the twin pillars of postwar liberalism. The liberal conception of the state embraced government spending as a positive good. According to Keynesian economics, such spending served as a stimulus to economic growth. In addition, it also worked as a means toward social progress, spreading the abundance of a mass consumption economy to ever wider numbers of the citizenry. In essence, liberalism aimed to use the fiscal powers of the state to redress the imbalances of the private economy without directly challenging capitalism.

During the first half of the 1960s, the Democratic administrations of John Kennedy and Lyndon Johnson orchestrated the completion of much of the New Deal/Fair Deal agenda while also maintaining an activist stance abroad. A burst of legislation in 1964–1965 represented the high tide of postwar liberalism. Soon after, however, the growing American involvement in Vietnam began to crowd all other issues off the domestic and international stage. As the country tried simultaneously to wage, in historian Garry Wills's apt phrasing, a "welfare" and a "warfare" state, it found itself embroiled in domestic controversy that irrevocably shattered the liberal consensus.

John Kennedy and the Politics of Expectation

Franklin Roosevelt's enormously successful years in office had heightened expectations for presidential leadership, and by the 1960s citizens increasingly looked to Washington and the president for solutions to international, national, and local problems. Few presidents came to Washington more primed for action than John Fitzgerald Kennedy. Yet the accomplishments of what Kennedy speechwriter Theodore Sorenson first called the "New Frontier" were rather meager. Much of the Kennedy presidency was reactive and improvisational, far too often responding to events and crises rather than steering a clear ideological course.

The New Politics and the 1960 Campaign

The 1960 campaign marked the introduction to the national scene of political practices called the *new politics*. Charisma, style, and personality, rather than issues and platforms, were the hallmarks of the new politics. Although this new political style had roots in the nineteenth century, it took on new force when joined with the power of the modern media in the twentieth. Politicians paid special attention to the ability of television to reach individual voters. (By 1960, 88 percent of the nation's households owned at least one TV set.) Professional media consultants now advised candidates on their proper image, and professional pollsters not only told candidates whether they were leading their opponents, but also what issues to stress in order to get elected.

Originally developed in California in the late 1940s and early 1950s, this political style was well suited to a state that was growing so fast that it did not have entrenched political machines or active party organizations. The spread of the new politics contributed to a decline in the role of traditional political party organizations at the national level. Candidates now targeted their appeal to enthusiastic amateurs outside the traditional party organization, rather than to the ward bosses, state committee officials, and party machines that once delivered the votes on election day. By using the media, campaigns could bypass the party structures to touch, if only with a 30-second commercial, the ordinary citizen.

Running such campaigns took money, however, and the required funds often far exceeded those available through the traditional party coffers. Once candidates began to seek campaign funds from other sources, such as wealthy donors or mass mailings, the influence of political parties diminished even further. In addition, party loyalty declined as growing numbers of voters identified themselves as independents, a major shift from patterns of highly partisan political behavior in the nineteenth and early twentieth centuries. These factors set the context for the 1960 election.

The Republicans Choose Nixon. The crucial question for the Republicans in 1960 was whether they could hold on to the presidency without the popular Dwight D. Eisenhower. The Twenty-second Amendment now limited a president to two terms. A Republican-controlled Congress had passed the measure in 1951 to prevent another long-term presidency such as Franklin Roosevelt's. Ironically, it precluded another Eisenhower term.

The Republicans turned without opposition to Vice-President Richard M. Nixon, who, like a good 1950s junior executive, had patiently waited for his turn at the top. Nixon campaigned for an updated version of Eisenhower's policies, carefully staking out a position between the Republican conservative wing, now led by Senator Barry M. Goldwater of Arizona, and the liberal wing represented by New York Governor Nelson A. Rockefeller. Nixon was hampered, however, by the lukewarm support he received from Eisenhower. Asked whether Nixon had helped make any major policy decisions in his administration, Eisenhower replied, "If you give me a week I might think of one."

The Democrats Select Kennedy. After two unsuccessful tries with Adlai Stevenson as their candidate, the Democrats turned to Senator John Fitzgerald Kennedy of Massachusetts, who beat out Senators Hubert Humphrey of Minnesota and Lyndon Johnson of Texas

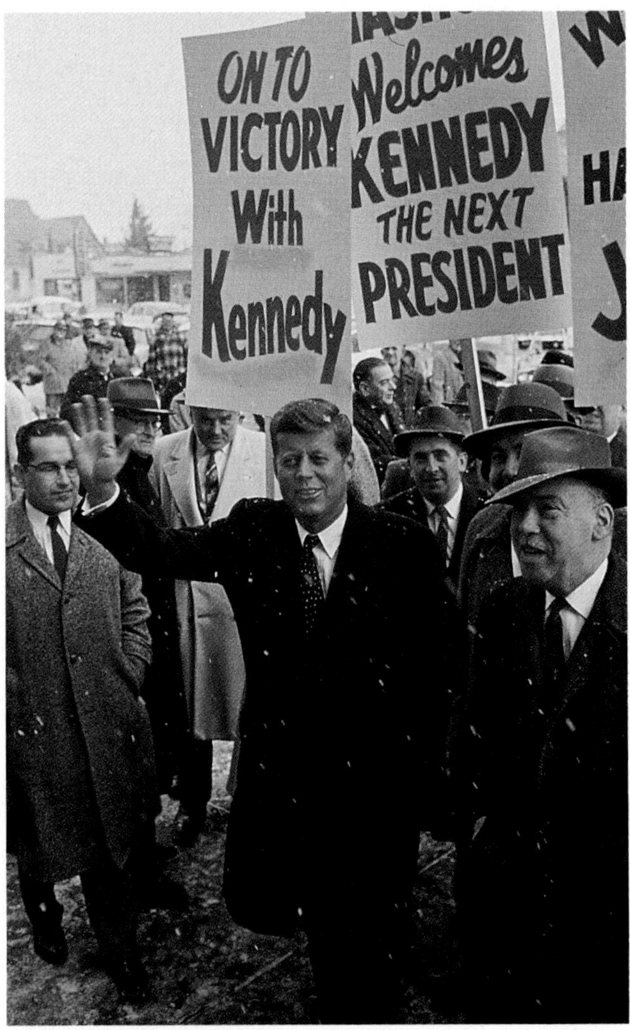

The New Politics Comes to New Hampshire
John Fitzgerald Kennedy, the first Catholic ever elected president, was also the first Democratic presidential nominee from New England in over one hundred years. Here the Massachusetts senator campaigned in neighboring New Hampshire, whose primary he won handily in February 1960.

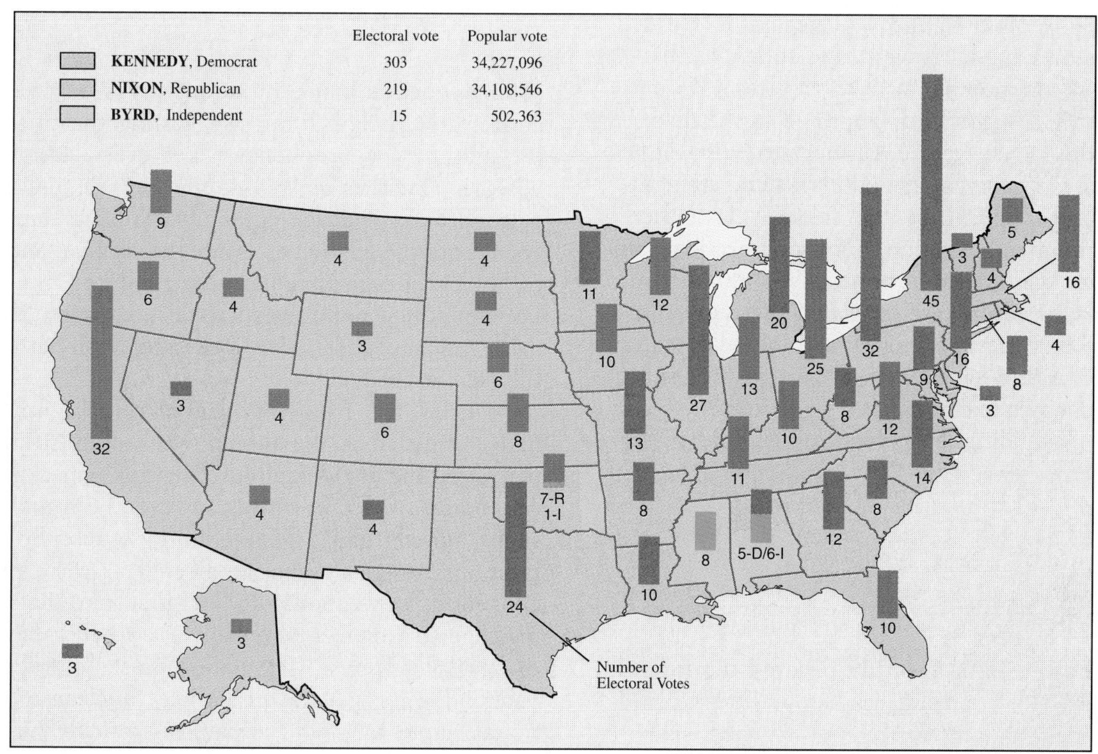

MAP 30.1

The Election of 1960

The Kennedy-Nixon contest produced the closest popular vote since 1884. Kennedy won 12 states, including Illinois, by less than 2 percent of the two-party vote tally; he lost 6 others, including California, by a similarly small margin. Fifteen electors cast their votes for the Independent Democrat, Harry F. Byrd. Despite his razor-thin margin of victory, Kennedy won 303 electoral votes, the same number as Truman in 1948, showing how the electoral college vote can be a misleading indicator of popular support.

for the nomination. Johnson joined the ticket as the vice-presidential nominee. Kennedy, an alumnus of Harvard and a World War II hero, had inherited his love of politics from his grandfathers, both of whom had been colorful Irish-Catholic politicians in Boston. His wealthy father, Joseph P. Kennedy, had headed the Securities and Exchange Commission and served as ambassador to Great Britain under Roosevelt. First elected to Congress in 1946, John Kennedy moved to the Senate in 1952. Ambitious, hard-driving and deeply aware of style, the forty-three-year-old candidate made full use of his many advantages to become, as novelist Norman Mailer put it, "our leading man." Besides his youth, Kennedy's main liability was his Catholicism: at that point, the United States had never elected a Catholic president.

Candidate Kennedy took the new politics to the national level in 1960, and his campaign altered the nature of American presidential contests. His family's wealth and the contributions he raised from sources outside traditional party donors paid for this expensive campaign. For example, his campaign bought its own airplane. Thanks to his media advisers and to his youthful and attractive personality, he projected a superb television image. His mastery of this method enabled him to appeal directly to voters, rather than just through the Democratic party.

A series of four televised debates between the two principal candidates, a major innovation of the 1960 campaign, reflected how important the media was becoming to political life. Nixon, a far less photogenic personality than Kennedy and at an added disadvantage because he was recovering from a minor illness, looked sallow and unshaven under the intense studio lights. Kennedy, in contrast, looked vigorous, cool, and self-confident on the TV screen, and he dispelled voters' doubts that he was not as well prepared for the presidency as the former vice-president. Public reaction demonstrated that appearances swayed political perceptions: voters who listened to the first debate on the radio concluded that Nixon had won, whereas TV viewers judged in Kennedy's favor.

Despite the ground Kennedy picked up in the debates, he won only the narrowest of victories, receiving 49.7 percent of the popular vote to Nixon's 49.5 percent. Kennedy had successfully appealed to the diverse elements of the Democratic coalition, attracting large proportions of Catholic voters and blacks and strengthening his party's appeal to the middle class; vice-presidential nominee Lyndon Johnson brought in southern white Democrats. Yet only 120,000 votes out of a total of 69 million cast separated the two candidates, and the shift of a few thousand votes in key states such as Illinois would have reversed the election results. Although Kennedy had campaigned on a promise to get America moving again, the electoral results hardly gave him a mandate for sweeping change.

The Kennedy Style

Unlike Eisenhower, John Kennedy believed the federal government should be strong, visible, and active, and that the president should set the tone for such leadership. Kennedy's activist bent attracted unusually talented and ambitious people to his administration. Robert S. McNamara, former president of the Ford Motor Company, introduced modern management techniques to the Department of Defense. Republican banker C. Douglas Dillon brought a corporate manager's desire for expanded markets and stable economic growth to the Department of the Treasury. The president's younger brother Robert took over the Department of Justice as attorney general, and his brother-in-law Sargent Shriver headed the popular Peace Corps. A host of "honorary Kennedys," trusted advisers and academics from leading universities, flocked to Washington to join the New Frontier. These advisers, dubbed "the best and the brightest" by journalist David Halberstam, also played a major role in plotting the Vietnam war.

The Kennedy administration, christened "Camelot" by the admiring media after the mythical realm of King Arthur in the popular musical of the same name, projected an aura of youth and energy. Secretary of State Dean Rusk recalled that Kennedy was "on fire, and he set people around him on fire." Vigor was one of Kennedy's favorite words, and he expected his appointees to move quickly. "The deadline for everything is the day before yesterday," exclaimed one cabinet member. House Speaker Sam Rayburn remained skeptical about this vigorous approach to government. Kennedy's people "might be every bit as intelligent as you say," he told his old friend Lyndon Johnson, "but I'd feel a whole lot better about them if just one of them had run for sheriff once."

Activism Abroad

John Kennedy's inaugural address was devoted almost entirely to foreign affairs, suggesting the priorities he brought to the presidency. "Let every nation know, whether it wishes us well or ill, that we shall pay any price, bear any burden, meet any hardship, support any friend, oppose any foe to assure the survival and success of liberty." Kennedy remained a resolute Cold Warrior. Foreign policy, not domestic affairs, captured the attention of most of those who flocked to Washington to join the New Frontier.

During the 1960 presidential campaign, Kennedy had charged that the Eisenhower administration had permitted the Soviet Union to develop superior nuclear capabilities. Once in office, however, he found that no such "missile gap" existed. In fact, Eisenhower had built up America's nuclear arsenal at the expense of conventional weapons. In his first national security message to Congress, Kennedy proposed a new policy of *flexible response*. The nation must be prepared "to deter all wars, general or limited, nuclear or conventional, large or small." Congress quickly acceded to Kennedy's military requests, boosting the number of combat-ready army divisions from eleven to sixteen and authorizing the construction of ten Polaris nuclear submarines and other warships. As Kennedy intended, the result was a major expansion of the military-industrial complex, as thousands of workers were recruited to build new weapons systems and military equipment.

These measures were designed to deter nuclear or conventional attacks by the Soviet Union. But what about the new kind of warfare, the wars of "national liberation" that had broken out in many Third World countries? Kennedy had a plan for these too: he adopted the new military doctrine of *counterinsurgency*. U.S. Army Special Forces, called the Green Berets for their distinctive headgear, received intensive training on how to repel the random and small-scale attacks typical of guerrilla warfare. The Vietnam war soon provided a testing ground for counterinsurgency techniques.

The Peace Corps. The New Frontier program that most captured the public imagination was the Peace Corps. The idea, Kennedy explained on March 1, 1961, was to create "a pool of trained American men and women" to be sent "overseas by the United States government or through private organizations and institutions to help foreign countries meet their urgent needs for skilled manpower." Thousands of idealistic Americans, many of them recent college graduates, responded to the call, agreeing to devote two or more years to teaching English to Philippine schoolchildren or helping African villagers obtain adequate supplies of water.

Kennedy also won congressional support for his ex-

AMERICAN VOICES

A Peace Corps Veteran Remembers *Thaine Allison*

The Peace Corps was the Kennedy program that most captured the nation's, and the world's, attention. Volunteers in parts of Africa were called *Wakina Kennedy* ("one who walks with Kennedy") and *los hijos de Kennedy* ("children of Kennedy") in Latin America. Thaine Allison and his wife spent from 1962 to 1964 in Borneo as Peace Corps volunteers.

When I was a kid, my parents took me to the YMCA to hear some missionaries speak about their experiences working and living in China. Their stories were fascinating. That's where I first started thinking that I might like to live in another country someday. When I went to college, I got involved with the Methodist Church youth movement and the option came up to work overseas as a missionary. But I didn't want to proselytize.

When the Peace Corps was announced, it just felt like the right thing to do after graduation. I had just gotten married and my wife wanted to get out of Iowa, where she'd lived all her life. At Chico State there were five graduates that year from the brand-new school of agriculture. Three of us went into the Peace Corps. The department chair was a bit upset that we were turning down real jobs.

When we found out we were going to Borneo, my dad said, "You guys quit running around. You sound like the wild man from Borneo."

My wife was assigned to teach English at a village school and I was an agricultural extension agent. I was told what the British colonial government was trying to do for agricultural development in my area and instructed to just go do it. "If you screw up," the Peace Corps said, "we'll see what we can do about it. Write us once a month and let us know how you're coming along." We were four hours by boat from the nearest volunteer.

I worked with Chinese and Muslim farmers. About a third of them were doing fairly well in that they had enough to eat: a lot of rice, some fresh fish, and sometimes dog or monkey. The rest grew just enough food to survive. I learned to speak Malay in training but it didn't help when I visited the Chinese farmers. They would say, "You Yankee Red dog, you come to talk to me and you don't even know my language." I took lessons in Mandarin Chinese from a school principal in the area and then went back to the Chinese farmers. They said, "You Yankee Red dog, since our language is obviously too difficult for you, why don't you just speak in English to us?"

I tried to tell the poorer farmers about ways to irrigate their crops, about the benefit of planting paddy rice instead of hill rice, and helped start some vegetable gardens. But much of the time, I never felt like I really knew what was happening. It seemed like it was more important that I show up in the villages for ceremonial purposes, rather than for anything I was able to do. These were people who wore loincloths and were barely able to grasp the notion that I had come from far away to help them, and there I was—asking them to plant their rows straight.

I took my wife with me to one village where they had never seen a white woman before. The women gathered around her and wanted to talk to her and touch her. I asked some of them to watch after her while I went to look at some crops and she had fifty women and kids following after her. She couldn't have gotten lost if she tried. In many of the villages, they'd never seen anyone with hairy arms before so they all liked to pet my arms.

Why my wife and I didn't have children was totally baffling to them. When we first got there, we used the excuse that we had just gotten married. But after we'd been there awhile and my wife obviously wasn't pregnant, they began asking questions. I knew I had gotten pretty good speaking Malay when I could tease them about Americans being like elephants, which take three years to gestate. When the time came for us to go on vacation, a group of women showed up at our door and gave my wife some money. They said, "We don't know what you have but we want some because we don't want any more babies."

Source: Karen Schwarz, *What You Can Do for Your Country: An Oral History of the Peace Corps* (New York: Morrow, 1991), 38, 44–45.

panded program of economic aid to foreign countries. The State Department's Agency for International Development coordinated foreign aid for the Third World, and its Food for Peace program distributed surplus agricultural products to developing nations. In March 1961 the president proposed "a ten-year plan for the Americas" called the Alliance for Progress, a $100 billion partnership between the United States and the republics of Latin America designed to reduce the appeal of communism in that region.

Reflecting his activist approach to presidential leadership, Kennedy often turned for foreign policy advice to a small circle of personal aides rather than relying on formal Pentagon and State Department channels. Taking the institutional changes of the 1947 National Security Act a step further, Kennedy enhanced the authority of the National Security Council by moving its chief directly into the White House. Such shifts further concentrated foreign policy initiation in the presidency.

The Bay of Pigs Invasion. The nation's strengthened military arsenal and streamlined defense establishment failed to bring Kennedy the universal diplomatic success he had anticipated. In April 1961, Kennedy confronted his first crisis. Its immediate roots lay in the January 1961 statement by Soviet Premier Nikita Khrushchev that conflicts in Vietnam, Cuba, and elsewhere were "wars of national liberation" worthy of Soviet support. Kennedy took Khrushchev's words as a challenge, especially as they applied to Cuba.

Ever since Cuba had won its independence in the Spanish-American War, it had been economically and politically dominated by its powerful neighbor to the north. In 1956, American companies owned 80 percent of Cuba's utilities, 90 percent of its mining operations, and 40 percent of its sugar plantations. On New Year's Day in 1959, Fidel Castro overthrew the unpopular dictatorship of Fulgencio Batista and called for a revolution to reshape Cuban society. He nationalized all its banks and industries, prompting the United States to embargo all exports to Cuba.

Concerned about Castro's growing friendliness with the Soviet Union, in early 1961 Kennedy used plans originally drawn up by the Eisenhower administration to dispatch Cuban exiles to foment an anti-Castro uprising. The invaders had been trained by the Central Intelligence Agency, but they were ill prepared for their task. After landing at Cuba's Bay of Pigs on April 17, the tiny force of 1,600 men was crushed by Castro's troops. Symptomatic of the inept CIA planning, pilots in Nicaragua who were supposed to provide air cover for the landing forces forgot to set their watches ahead to Cuban time and arrived at the beach an hour too soon. The anticipated rebellion never occurred.

The Bay of Pigs fiasco blighted the new administra-

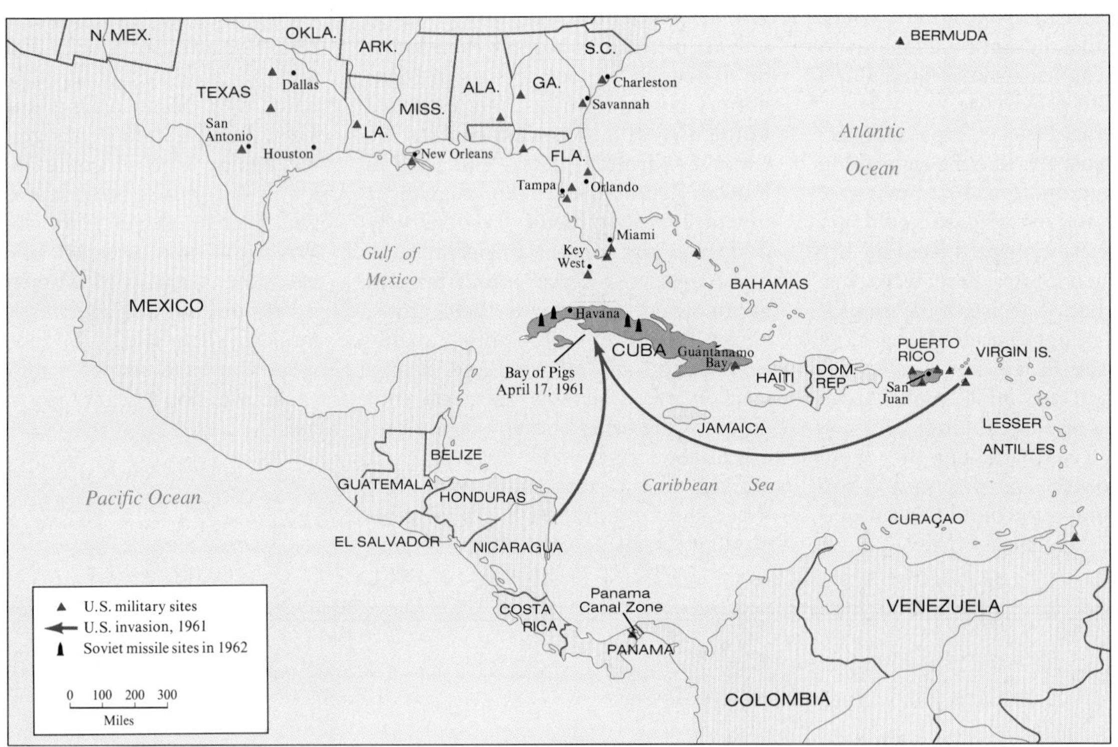

MAP 30.2

The United States and Cuba, 1961–1962

Fidel Castro's takeover in Cuba in 1959 soon brought cold war tensions to the Caribbean basin. In 1961 the United States tried unsuccessfully to overthrow Castro's regime by supporting an invasion of Cuban exiles launched from Nicaragua. In 1962 a major confrontation with the Soviet Union occurred over Soviet missile sites in Cuba. The Soviets removed the missiles after President Kennedy ordered a naval blockade of the island, which lies just 90 miles south of Florida.

tion with an embarrassing failure and cast doubts on Kennedy's activist approach to international affairs. It also affected U.S.-Soviet relations. Soviet leader Khrushchev interpreted the invasion as evidence of the United States's intent to launch a full-scale invasion of Cuba and stepped up military aid to Castro to protect against this contingency. A more subtle legacy was Khrushchev's view that he did not have to take the new American president seriously as an adversary.

The Berlin Wall. Kennedy's military response to the threat of a communist regime just 90 miles to the south confirmed how Cold War assumptions shaped foreign policy in the early 1960s, both in the Western Hemisphere and elsewhere. Kennedy never lost his preoccupation with the Soviet Union. In June 1961, weakened by the botched Cuban invasion, he met with Khrushchev in Vienna to discuss a test ban treaty, the civil war in Laos, and the status of Berlin. At the meeting, both men were truculent, especially about Berlin, which was part of a larger and longstanding disagreement about the status of Germany in postwar Europe. Khrushchev wanted it declared a "free city," which would mean the withdrawal of both Soviet and Western occupation forces, but he did not get his way.

Just days after this meeting, Khrushchev heightened international tensions by deploying soldiers to sever East Berlin from the western sector of the city. Determined to confront the Soviets publicly, Kennedy declared in a televised speech to the nation on July 25 that Berlin was the "great testing place of Western courage and will" and announced that he would ask Congress for large increases in military spending, a massive fallout shelter program, and the authority to mobilize the National Guard, call up reserves, and extend enlistments in response to this and future international crises. In mid-August, the East Germans under Soviet supervision erected the Berlin wall to stop the exodus of East Germans to the West and began policing the border with guards instructed to shoot to kill those trying to escape. Kennedy later visited the Berlin wall, where he invoked the solidarity of the free world by declaring "Ich bin ein Berliner" ("I am a Berliner"). The Berlin Wall stood as the supreme symbol of the Cold War until the fall of 1989 when it, and Soviet domination of Eastern Europe, crumbled.

The Berlin Wall

A West Berlin resident walks alongside a section of the Berlin Wall in 1962, a year after its construction. Note the two border guards on the East Berlin side, plus the numerous loud speakers, which East German communists used to broadcast propaganda over the barricade that divided the city.

The Cuban Missile Crisis. Tensions between the superpowers soon erupted again: for thirteen days in October 1962 the United States and the Soviet Union stood at the brink of war. The Soviets had stepped up their aid to the Castro regime after the Bay of Pigs invasion of the previous year, including sending 43,000 troops to join the 270,000 well-trained Cuban forces already assembled. In early October, American U-2 reconnaissance aircraft photographed Soviet bases under construction in Cuba, complete with missiles that, when assembled, would be able to reach U.S. targets as far as 2,200 miles away. It was later disclosed that the Soviets had supplied Havana with short-range nuclear weapons and that Soviet military commanders in Cuba were authorized to use them in the event of an American invasion.

Rather than work through State Department or diplomatic channels, Kennedy publicly confronted the Soviet Union over its actions in a somber televised address on Monday, October 22, 1962. The United States would use its newly enlarged navy to quarantine Soviet shipping to Cuba until the missiles were removed. Both the United States and the Soviet Union went on full military alert and the world held its breath—would this blockade lead to World War III? On the following Sunday, after one of the most harrowing weeks of the nuclear age, Kennedy and Khrushchev reached an agreement that the blockade would be lifted when the Soviets had removed their missiles from Cuba. "We're eyeball to eyeball," Secretary of State Dean Rusk observed, "and I think the other fellow just blinked." To allow Khrushchev to save face, the United States dismantled some outdated missiles in Turkey.

Although the risk of nuclear war was more grave during the Cuban missile crisis than at any other time in the postwar period, in retrospect it marked a turning point in U.S.-Soviet relations. In the words of presidential adviser McGeorge Bundy, "having come so close to the edge, the leaders of the two governments have since taken care to keep away from the cliff."

The Beginnings of Détente. Sobered by the Cuban missile crisis and the threat of nuclear annihilation, Kennedy began to seek ways to reduce international tensions. He turned away from the cold war rhetoric that had characterized his campaign and the first two years of his presidency and began to strive for world peace. In a notable speech at American University in June 1963, he stressed the need to "make the world safe for diversity." Russians and Americans alike, he observed, "inhabit this small planet. We all breathe the same air. We all cherish our children's future. And we are all mortal." Soviet leaders, also chastened by the confrontation over Cuba, were now willing to talk. In August 1963 the three nuclear powers—the United States, the Soviet Union, and Great Britain—agreed to ban the testing of nuclear weapons in the air or in the seas. Underground testing, however, was allowed to continue. The test-ban treaty was ratified by the Senate in the fall of 1963.

Kennedy's desire for peaceful coexistence with the Soviet Union resulted in a new foreign policy approach that came to be called *détente* (from the French word for a relaxation of tensions). Unlike containment, which called for confronting Soviet initiatives around the globe, détente accepted the Soviets as an adversary with whom the United States could negotiate and bargain. Mutual accommodation and coexistence was the ultimate goal. One concrete symbol was the establishment of a Washington-Moscow telephone "hotline" in 1963 so that leaders could quickly contact each other during potential crises.

But no matter how often American leaders talked about opening channels of communication with the Soviets, the obsession with the potential Soviet military threat to American national security remained a cornerstone of U.S. policy. Nor did Soviet leaders moderate their concern over the threat they believed the United States posed to the survival of the U.S.S.R. The two nations would maintain cold war tensions—and the escalating arms race that accompanied them—for another twenty-five years.

Kennedy's Thousand Days

The expansive vision of presidential leadership that Kennedy and his advisers brought to the White House worked less well at home than abroad. Kennedy, who was hampered by his lack of a popular mandate in the 1960 election, could not mobilize public support for the domestic agenda of the New Frontier. A conservative coalition of southern Democrats and western and midwestern Republicans effectively stalled most liberal initiatives.

One domestic program that did win both popular and congressional support was increased funding for space exploration. Seven astronauts had been chosen for America's Mercury space program in 1958. On May 5, 1961, just three months after Kennedy took office, Alan Shepard became the first American launched into space; on February 2, 1962, John Glenn became the first American to orbit the earth. (Soviet cosmonaut Yuri Gagarin held the distinction of being the first person in space with his 108-hour flight in April 1961.) At the height of American fascination with space, Kennedy proposed in 1961 that "this nation should commit itself to achieving the goal, before this decade is out, of landing a man on the moon and returning him safely to earth." To accomplish this mission, achieved in July 1969, he greatly increased the budget of the National Aeronautics and Space Administration (NASA), established in 1958.

Economic Policy. Kennedy's most striking domestic achievement was his use of modern economics to shape fiscal policy. Initially Kennedy had shared the belief of many business leaders that the federal government could best contribute to economic growth by reducing the national debt and balancing the budget. However, at the urging of Walter Heller, chairman of the Council of Economic Advisers, Kennedy decided on a different course. Rather than increase federal spending to stimulate the economy, he proposed a cut in the taxes paid by businesses and the public. A tax cut, he argued, would leave more money in the hands of taxpayers, enabling them to increase their investments and purchases, and thus bring about economic growth by creating more wealth and jobs. For a time, federal expenditures would exceed federal income, but after a year or two, the expanding economy would raise taxpayers' incomes, leading in turn to higher tax revenues.

Congress predictably balked at this unorthodox proposal. But Lyndon Johnson pressed for it after Kennedy's assassination and signed it into law in February 1964. The Kennedy-Johnson tax cut of 1964 marked a milestone in the purposeful use of the federal budget—fiscal policy—to encourage steady economic growth. Although economic expansion started before the effects of the tax cut could be felt, Kennedy and his economic advisers got credit for it anyway. The gross national product grew at a rate of 5 percent during the 1960s, nearly twice the rate of the Eisenhower years. Much of this growth, however, was fueled by massive defense expenditures linked to the growth of the military-industrial complex, as well as spending for the escalating Vietnam War.

A Limited Agenda. Kennedy's interest in stimulating economic growth did not include a corresponding commitment to spending for domestic social needs, although he did not entirely ignore the liberal legislative agenda Franklin Roosevelt and Harry Truman had set for the Democratic party. Kennedy proposed federal aid to elementary and secondary schools, civil rights legislation, federal investment in mass transportation, medical insurance for the elderly funded through Social Security, and wilderness preservation. But he failed to define any of these proposals in terms satisfactory to a majority in Congress and all were defeated.

Dissension within the Democratic coalition was particularly evident in the case of aid to education. Most northern Democrats favored such aid, but they disagreed about important details. Civil rights advocates insisted that federal school aid go only to desegregated schools, while Catholics insisted that federal assistance be extended to parochial systems. After great effort, Kennedy persuaded black leaders to accept a school aid plan that ignored existing segregation, but he told southern whites that federal aid would not be guaranteed to segregated schools in the future. Because Kennedy was himself a Catholic, however, he feared angering Protestants if he proposed a bill that permitted aid to parochial schools. In the absence of a bill acceptable to all these groups, the education proposal died in committee.

Kennedy failed to provide decisive leadership in other domestic fields. He appointed fewer women to federal positions than Eisenhower or Truman had, and made only a token attempt to address women's issues with the establishment of the Presidential Commission on the Status of Women in 1961. Most tellingly, he never made civil rights a top priority (see Chapter 31). He believed he would need the votes of southern whites to win reelection in 1964, and he sought to hold them in the Democratic coalition by delaying the civil rights reforms he had promised during the 1960 campaign. He doubted such measures would pass in any case. "There is no sense in raising hell," he insisted, "and then in not being successful."

The Warren Court. Some of the most controversial policies of the early 1960s came not from the Kennedy administration, but from the Supreme Court. Unlike the New Deal years, when the Supreme Court played an obstructionist role, during the postwar period it often acted as a catalyst for sweeping social change. So much of this judicial activism was linked to Earl Warren, the chief justice from 1953 to 1969, that the Supreme Court of these years is often referred to as the Warren Court.

The decisions of the Warren Court arguably had an equal or greater impact on American society than anything proposed by the president or the Congress. The most important decision of the Court, *Brown v. Board of Education*, requiring desegregation of public schools, had been handed down in 1954 during the Eisenhower administration (see Chapter 31). In the 1960s, the Court followed up with landmark decisions in the areas of defendants' rights and separation of church and state. In *Gideon v. Wainwright* (1963), *Escobedo v. Illinois* (1964), and *Miranda v. Arizona* (1966), the Supreme Court greatly expanded the rights of suspects accused of crimes. Tackling the issue of reapportionment of state legislatures in *Baker v. Carr* (1962) and *Reynolds v. Sims* (1964), the Court put forth the doctrine of "one person, one vote," which substantially increased the representation of both the suburbs and urban areas, with their concentration of black and Hispanic residents, at the expense of rural regions. Perhaps the most controversial decision was *Engel v. Vitale* (1962), which banned prayer in public schools as a violation of the First Amendment's injunction that "Congress shall make no law respecting an establishment of religion." President Kennedy, like President Eisenhower before him, pledged to uphold these decisions, even when he disagreed with the scope or content of this judicial activism.

The Kennedy Assassination

In the first two years of his presidency, Kennedy realized little of his promise. But in 1963 many political observers felt that he was maturing as a leader and was on the verge of even stronger presidential leadership. On November 22, 1963, Kennedy went to Texas, a state he needed to win for reelection in 1964, to heal divisions in the party organization there. As he rode in an open car past the Texas School Book Depository in Dallas, he was shot and killed. (Whether accused killer Lee Harvey Oswald, a twenty-four-year-old loner who had spent three years in the Soviet Union, was the sole gunman remains the source of considerable controversy.) Before Air Force One left Dallas to take the president's body back to Washington, a grim-faced Lyndon Johnson was sworn in as president. Kennedy's stunned widow, Jacqueline, still wearing a bloodstained pink suit, looked on.

By 1 P.M. Dallas time, just thirty minutes after the shooting, 68 percent of adults in the United States, about 75 million people, knew that Kennedy had been shot. By late afternoon, the proportion had risen to 99.8 percent, showing how within a few hours, the mass media could reach virtually every person in the nation. As on Pearl Harbor Day in 1941, people never forgot what they were doing when they first heard Kennedy had been shot. The shock that greeted the assassination reflected the personal identification that ordinary Americans now felt with the occupant of the White House, quite a change from the muted reaction to the last assassination of an American president, William McKinley, in 1901.

Americans suspended normal activities for four days as they sought reassurance in ceremonies of grief

Burying a President
A grief-stricken Jacqueline Kennedy walked behind her slain husband's casket at his 1963 funeral. To her left is brother-in-law Robert Kennedy, who himself would be assassinated five years later.

and continuity. The three television networks canceled their regular programs, and an estimated television audience of 100 million collectively mourned the slain president. Shared television images, such as the dignity of Jacqueline Kennedy as she and her two young children walked behind the casket, bound the American people together at a time of national grief.

Kennedy's buoyant youth, the trauma of his assassination, and the collective sense that Americans had been robbed of a promising leader contributed to a powerful Kennedy mystique. Only forty-six at the time of his death, he was the first president born in this century. The Kennedy mythologizing process had begun even before his tragic death. In June 1963 about 59 percent of the people surveyed claimed to have voted for Kennedy, a big jump over the 49.7 percent who actually had; after the assassination, this figure rose to 65 percent. A British journalist called it "a posthumous landslide."

The Kennedy assassination set off a national wave of self-examination. Americans debated whether the murder of the president had been an isolated act or the symbol of a tragic flaw in the democratic system. The argument that there was something wrong with the nation gained credence two days after the assassination, when Jack Ruby, a local nightclub owner, gunned down Lee Harvey Oswald in the basement of the Dallas police station. Since the television networks were covering Oswald as the police escorted him to another jail, his shooting by Ruby was shown live across the nation. Chief Justice Earl Warren warned ominously about "forces of hatred and malevolence" that made such acts possible, and newspapers and magazines asked, "What sort of nation are we?" Later in the 1960s, many Americans overwhelmed by the social conflict of the decade looked back on November 22, 1963, as the day when things began to come apart.

Lyndon Johnson and the Great Society

Lyndon Johnson, a seasoned politician who was best at negotiating in the backrooms of power, was no match for the Kennedy style, and he knew it. But less than a year after assuming office, Johnson won the 1964 presidential election in a landslide that far surpassed Kennedy's meager mandate in 1960. Johnson then used his astonishing energy and genius for compromise to bring to fruition many of Kennedy's stalled programs, and more than a few of his own. These legislative accomplishments are referred to as the Great Society, Johnson's own phrase to describe his commitment to end poverty and racial injustice. It was the Great Society, not the much less ambitious New Frontier, that fulfilled the New Deal liberal agenda of the 1930s.

The Great Coalition Builder

Lyndon Johnson brought to the presidency far more legislative experience than any modern president, and he used his talent to great effect. Born in the central Texas hill country in 1908, Johnson had served in Washington since 1932 as a congressional aide, New Deal administrator, congressman, senator, senate majority leader, and finally vice-president. A man of singular force, he often got his way by using what one journalist called the "Johnson treatment." Approaching unsuspecting colleagues, he moved "in close, his face a scant millimeter from his target, his eyes widening and narrowing, his eyebrows rising and falling. From his pockets poured clippings, memos, statistics. Mimicry, humor, and the genius of analogy made the Treatment an almost hypnotic experience." Johnson invariably left his targets overwhelmed and bruised—and willing to go along with his requests.

The "Johnson Treatment"
Lyndon B. Johnson, a shrewd and adroit politician, learned many of his legislative skills while serving as majority leader of the Senate from 1953 to 1960. Here he zeroed in on Senator Theodore Francis Green of Rhode Island. After assuming the presidency, Johnson remarked, "They say Jack Kennedy had style, but I'm the one who's got the bills passed."

The Civil Rights Act of 1964. With characteristic energy and determination, Johnson seized the initiative almost as soon as Kennedy's assassination thrust him into the presidency. As a memorial to the slain president, he called for rapid passage of New Frontier proposals, especially the tax cut and civil rights legislation. Dramatically reminding Congress that he himself, a white southerner, had supported civil rights in 1957 and 1960, he urged Congress "to enact a civil rights law so that we can move forward to eliminate from this nation every trace of discrimination and oppression that is based upon race or color."

By June, black pressure and Johnson's surehanded tactics had their impact. Breaking a southern filibuster, the Senate approved the most far-reaching civil rights legislation since Reconstruction. The 1964 Civil Rights Act guaranteed equal access to public accommodations and schools and prohibited discrimination by employers and unions. It granted new powers to the U.S. attorney general to enforce these guarantees and designated the Equal Employment Opportunity Commission to prevent job discrimination by race, religion, national origin, or sex.

The Election of 1964. If 1964 was a year of liberal triumph in Congress, it was a year of conservative retrenchment within the Republican party. The Republican nominee for president in 1964 was Senator Barry Goldwater of Arizona. Goldwater, who was determined to offer "a choice, not an echo," campaigned against the expansion of federal power in such areas as the economy and civil rights. Goldwater's crisp speeches rejected Republican efforts to build a moderate coalition. "Extremism in the defense of liberty is no vice," he stated. "Moderation in the pursuit of justice is no virtue."

President Johnson easily won his party's nomination. Reaffirming his commitment to the liberal Democratic agenda, but putting some distance between himself and the Kennedy clan, Johnson passed over Robert F. Kennedy for vice-president in favor of Senator Hubert H. Humphrey of Minnesota, who in 1948 had introduced the controversial civil rights plank that split the party. An attempt by an avowed segregationist, Governor George C. Wallace of Alabama, to exploit a white backlash against civil rights showed early strength but then fizzled. The Johnson-Humphrey ticket won by one of the largest margins in history, receiving 61.1 percent of the popular vote. It surpassed even the 1936 landslide of that great coalition builder, Franklin D. Roosevelt, Johnson's political idol and mentor. Johnson's sweeping victory brought with it Democratic gains in Congress and state legislatures.

The 1964 Campaign
Barry Goldwater's 1964 Republican campaign produced some very creative political memorabilia, such as bumper stickers that proclaimed "AuH_20" (the symbols for gold and water) and this gold elephant wearing glasses like the candidate's.

Enacting the Liberal Agenda

Like John Kennedy, Lyndon Johnson held an expansive view of presidential leadership. The 1964 election gave him the popular mandate, and more importantly, the filibuster-proof legislative majorities, to push forward legislation to achieve his "Great Society." "Hurry boys, hurry," he urged his staff. "Get that legislation up to the Hill and out. Eighteen months from now ol' Landslide Lyndon will be Lame-Duck Lyndon."

The Eighty-ninth Congress enacted more social-reform measures than any session since Roosevelt's first term, offering legislation for every important element of the Democratic coalition. Responding to growing black demands, Johnson increased federal support for civil rights. The Voting Rights Act of 1965 authorized the attorney general to send federal examiners to the South to register voters. In 1963 only a fourth of all southern blacks were registered to vote; when Johnson left office in 1969, their proportion had risen to two-thirds.

Johnson also found a way to break the congressional deadlock on aid to education. The Elementary and Secondary Education Act of 1965 authorized $1 billion in federal funds to benefit impoverished children, including Catholic children in parochial schools, rather than aiding the schools themselves. With his flair for the dramatic, he signed the education bill in the one-room Texas schoolhouse he had attended as a child.

The Eighty-ninth Congress also gave Johnson the votes to enact the federal health insurance legislation first proposed by Truman. Realizing that it could no longer block some form of federal health insurance, the American Medical Association now proposed that federal funds be used to pay doctors as well as hospitals. The result was two new programs: Medicare, a plan for the elderly funded from a surcharge on Social Security payroll taxes, and Medicaid, a health plan for poor recipients paid for by general tax revenues.

Administration programs did not just aid the poor—the middle class benefited too. Federal urban renewal and home mortgage assistance aided those who could afford to live in single-family homes or in modern apartments. Medicare assistance went to every elderly person covered by Social Security, regardless of need. Much of the federal aid to education benefited the children of the middle class. In addition, Johnson successfully pressed for expansion of the national park system, for legislation to improve the quality of the air and water, for increased land-use planning, and, at the insistence of his wife, Lady Bird Johnson, for the Highway Beautification Act of 1965. That year also saw the creation of the National Endowment for the Arts to support the performing and creative arts, and the National Endowment for the Humanities, which encouraged efforts to understand and interpret the nation's cultural and historical heritage.

The War on Poverty

Although Johnson's programs offered something for every constituency in the Democratic coalition, he always insisted that the top priority of his Great Society was "an end to poverty in our time." The problem of poverty was very real. Poor people made up about a fourth of the American population; three-fourths of the poor were white. The poor in the United States were isolated farmers and miners in Appalachia, blacks mired in urban ghettos, Hispanics in migrant labor camps and urban barrios, native Americans on reservations, women raising families on their own, and the abandoned and destitute elderly. As Michael Harrington had pointed out in *The Other America: Poverty in the United States* (1962), the poor were everywhere, but their poverty was curiously invisible in affluent America. Modern technology had "made a longer, healthier, better life possible," Harrington observed, yet it left the poor "on the margin": "They watch the movies and read the magazines of affluent America, and these teach them that they are internal exiles."

New Deal social welfare programs had failed to reach these people. Because unemployment insurance ran out after a few months, it did not protect against extended joblessness. Social Security and other social-insurance programs provided benefits to workers who paid for them through special taxes, but not all workers were covered. Social welfare programs such as Old Age Assistance, Aid to Dependent Children, and Aid to the Blind carried strict restrictions regarding eligibility.

One tactic tried by the Great Society to reduce poverty was expanding long-established social insurance and welfare programs. It broadened Social Security to include waiters and waitresses, domestic servants, farm workers, and hospital employees. Social welfare expenditures increased rapidly, especially for Aid to Families with Dependent Children (AFDC), as did public housing and rent subsidy programs. Food Stamps, begun in 1964 largely to stabilize farm prices, grew into a major program of assistance to low-income families. As in the New Deal, the social welfare system continued to develop in a piecemeal fashion, with no overall direction.

The Office of Economic Opportunity (OEO), established by the omnibus Economic Opportunity Act of 1964, became the Great Society's showcase in the "War on Poverty." Built around the twin strategies of equal opportunity and community action, OEO programs were so numerous and diverse that they recalled the alphabet agencies of the New Deal. Officials at the OEO quickly realized that identifying poverty was one thing; drafting and implementing programs to address it was quite another. Sargent Shriver, who left the Peace Corps to head the new agency, admitted, "It's like we went down to Cape Kennedy (the NASA space center in

Florida) and launched a half dozen rockets at once."

The War on Poverty produced some of the most significant measures of the Johnson administration. Head Start provided free nursery schools designed to prepare disadvantaged preschoolers for kindergarten. The Job Corps and the Neighborhood Youth Corps trained young people. Upward Bound gave low-income teenagers the skills and motivation to plan for college. The Appalachian Regional Development Act, the Metropolitan Area Redevelopment Act, and the Demonstration Cities Act were intended, like foreign aid, to spur development of impoverished areas. Volunteers in Service to America (VISTA), modeled on the Peace Corps, provided technical assistance to the rural and urban poor. The Community Action Program encouraged the poor to organize to demand "maximum feasible participation" in the decisions that affected them. Community Action organizers worked closely with the two thousand lawyers employed by the Legal Services Program to provide the poor with free access to the legal system.

The OEO quickly drew criticism, however. VISTA and Community Action Program agents encouraged poor people to mount militant demands for public services long withheld by unresponsive local governments. Community organizers on the government payroll in Syracuse, New York, for example, formed tenants' rights groups to protest conditions in public housing, conducted voter registration drives to unseat unpopular elected representatives, and even used public funds to bail out activists arrested for protesting at local welfare offices. Legal Services lawyers challenged welfare and housing administrations in class-action suits. Needless to say, such activism upset entrenched political elites. Such mayors as Sam Yorty of Los Angeles and Richard J. Daley of Chicago vociferously resisted OEO guidelines for including poor people in program planning and administration.

Lyndon Johnson's administration put issues of poverty, justice, and access at the center of national political life. But the mixed results suggest the difficulties of promoting fundamental political and economic change through federal initiatives. In the long-term, the War on Poverty did little to reduce poverty or redistribute wealth. Using a definition of poverty as half the median family income, the poverty line in 1963 was set at $3,000. That year, 20 percent of the population lived below the poverty line. In 1976 the median family income had risen to $15,000, but 20 percent of the nation still received less than half that amount. Technological change and economic growth had raised everyone's standard of living, so the poor were better off in an absolute sense. Relatively, however, they remained as far behind the middle class as ever. In effect, the War on Poverty and related social welfare efforts simply provided the nation's poor with about the same share of income they had always received.

Cracks in the New Deal Coalition

The Great Society represented the culmination of the liberal social agenda that had first been advanced during the crisis of the Great Depression. But the implementation of this liberal agenda revealed deep contradictions in the New Deal coalition. This coalition was inherently unstable, torn among its diverse constituencies and their conflicting priorities for the exercise of federal power. These contradictions had been lurking in political life since Franklin Roosevelt and Harry Truman began to expand the power of the federal government, but they surfaced forcefully in the climate fostered by the "politics of expectation."

During the 1960s, Kennedy's brilliant articulation of the aspirations of many Americans, and Johnson's genius at translating these unformed strivings for change into concrete legislative programs, set in motion a remarkable expansion of federal power. Kennedy and Johnson gathered an extraordinarily diverse set of groups into the New Deal coalition—middle-class and poor; white, black, and Hispanic; Protestant, Jewish, and Catholic; urban and rural. As the functions and responsibilities of the government grew, so did demands for further action from this widening cast of politically organized constituencies.

For a brief period between 1964 and 1966, the coalition held together. But inevitably the claims of certain groups—such as the demand of blacks for civil rights and of the urban poor for increased political power—conflicted with the interests of other Democratic supporters, such as white southerners and northern political bosses eager to maintain the status quo. In the end, the New Deal coalition, which had fostered a vast expansion of federal power, could not sustain a consensus over the purposes that such a government ought to serve.

The Great Society was not just a victim of the factionalism of the Democratic coalition. It was also, in the haunting phrase of civil rights leader Martin Luther King, Jr., "shot down on the battlefields of Vietnam." In 1966 the government spent $22 billion on the Vietnam War and only $1.2 billion on the War on Poverty. As Lyndon Johnson turned his full attention to the escalating war, the domestic programs of the Great Society fell by the wayside.

No one realized the trade-off more painfully than Johnson himself. In the crude language that characterized this tough-talking Texan, he posed the dilemma in this way: "If I left the woman I really loved—the Great Society—in order to get involved with that bitch of a war on the other side of the world, then I would lose everything at home. All my programs. All my hopes to feed the hungry and shelter the homeless. All my dreams to provide education and health care to the browns and the blacks and the lame and the poor. But if I left that

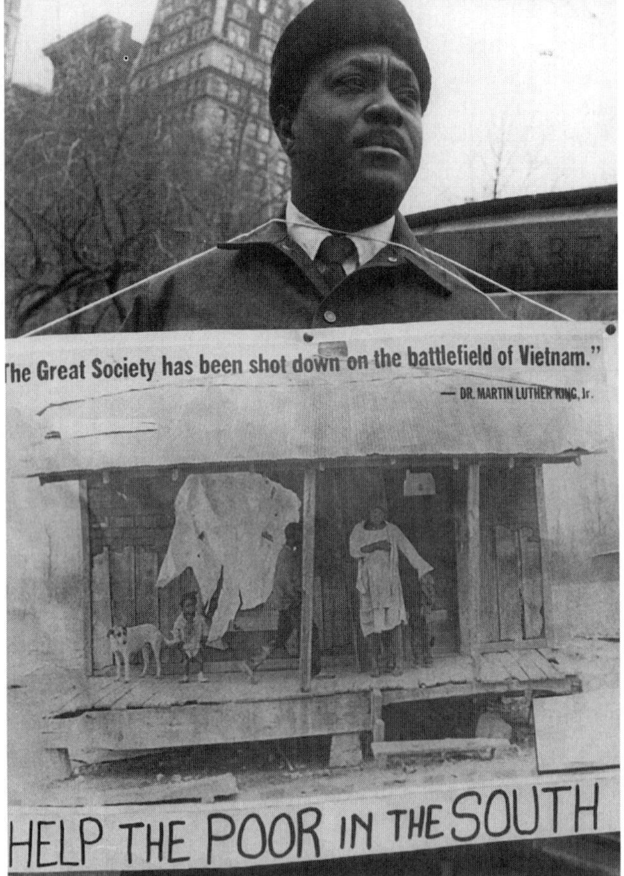

he Great Society has been shot down on the battlefield of Vietnam."
— DR. MARTIN LUTHER KING, Jr.
HELP THE POOR IN THE SOUTH

Butter, Not Guns

This placard graphically protested that the Vietnam War diverted money from government social and economic programs aimed at aiding the nation's poor. Many Americans shared this view, and antiwar demonstrations spread across the United States.

war and let the Communists take over South Vietnam, then I would be seen as a coward and my nation would be seen as an appeaser and we would both find it impossible to accomplish anything for anybody anywhere on the entire globe." In the end, his priorities were clear. "Losing the Great Society was a terrible thought, but not so terrible as the thought of being responsible for America's losing a war to the Communists. Nothing could possibly be worse than that."

America and the Vietnam Experience

Vietnam challenged American administrations from Harry Truman to Gerald Ford, and debates about the meanings and lessons of the war still resonate in American life today. American politicians tended to paint the conflict in the starkly ideological terms of the Cold War, but the story is more complicated than simplistic statements about supporting democracy and stopping communism. In postwar foreign relations, Third World concerns became increasingly central to the world order. The United States was in Vietnam not so much to stop the spread of communism as to protect its credibility as the leading noncommunist power in the postwar world order. Ironically, the course of the Vietnam War irrevocably damaged the very American credibility it was supposed to uphold.

The Roots of American Involvement

The roots of U.S. involvement in Vietnam lay in the instability produced by the decolonization of Southeast Asia after World War II. Vietnam had been part of the French colony of Indochina since the late nineteenth century, but was occupied by Japan during World War II. Native resistance to the Japanese was led by the French-educated communist Ho Chi Minh and the Vietnam Independence League, the Vietminh. After the Japanese surrender, Ho proclaimed an independent republic of Vietnam in September 1945. Seven months later the French recognized Vietnam as a "free state" within the French union. Ho and military strategist Vo Nguyen Giap responded by launching attacks to drive the French out completely, thus launching the first phase of the conflict that the Vietminh called the Anti-French War of Resistance.

President Truman came to support the French side in the Indochina war for several reasons. After the Chinese revolution of 1949, the United States was concerned about potential Chinese efforts to sponsor Asian wars of national liberation. Truman also wanted to maintain good relations with France, whose support was crucial to the success of the new NATO alliance. In addition, Indochina played a strategic role in U.S. plans for an integrated Pacific Rim regional economy centered around a reindustrialized Japan, both as a supplier of cheap raw materials and food and as a profitable market for Japanese goods and services.

When the Soviet Union and the new Chinese leaders recognized Ho's government as the legitimate ruler of Vietnam at the beginning of 1950, the United States and Great Britain in turn recognized the French-supported, noncommunist government of Bao Dai. Truman also decided to send supplies to French troops stationed in Vietnam, a policy continued by the Eisenhower administration. By 1954 the United States had sent more than $2 billion worth of military supplies to the French in Vietnam, plus another $703 million in technical and economic assistance, paying nearly 80 percent of the cost of continuing the war.

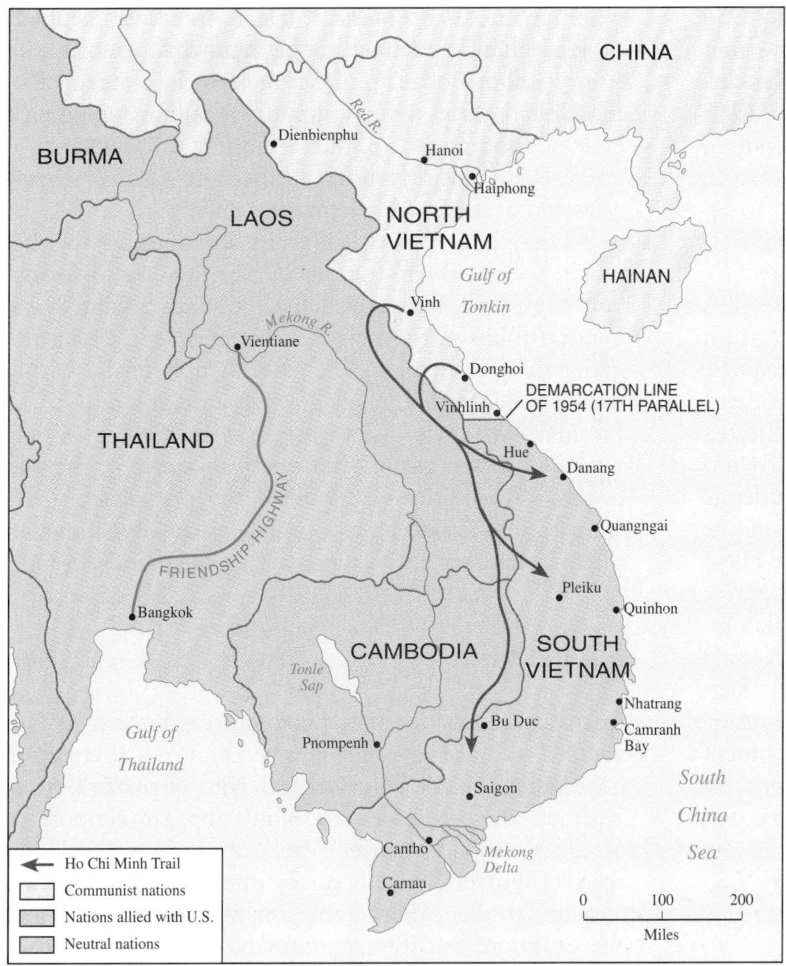

MAP 30.3

The Vietnam War, 1954–1975
The Vietnam War was a guerrilla war, fought in skirmishes and inconclusive encounters rather than decisive battles and major offensives. Supporters of the National Liberation Front filtered into South Vietnam along the Ho Chi Minh trail, which wound through Laos and Cambodia.

Despite these joint French-U.S. efforts, Vietminh forces gained strength in northern Vietnam. By the spring of 1954, they had trapped a large French force at the isolated administrative fortress of Dienbienphu. France asked the United States to launch direct air strikes from nearby carriers to break the siege. Despite the recommendation of several members of the Joint Chiefs of Staff to intervene, Eisenhower refused, and Dienbienphu fell in May 1954 after a fifty-six-day siege.

The dramatic turn of events at Dienbienphu enhanced the negotiating position of the Vietminh at a conference in Geneva just getting underway to discuss the fate of Vietnam. The resulting 1954 Geneva Accords temporarily partitioned Vietnam at the 17th parallel, committed France to withdraw its forces from north of that line within ten months, and forbade both North and South Vietnam from entering into any military alliance with an outside power. A final declaration provided that the two partitioned sectors would hold free elections within two years to choose a unified government for the entire nation. The United States was never an official party to the Geneva Accords, although it agreed to abide by them.

The Eisenhower administration made sure that a pro-American government headed by Ngo Dinh Diem took power in South Vietnam just before the accords were signed. Diem quickly consolidated his power and staged a rigged election in which his ballots were printed on red paper, a Vietnamese symbol of good luck, while his opponent's were green, which stood for misfortune. Diem refused to allow the national elections scheduled for 1956 to take place, mainly because he realized that the popular Ho Chi Minh would easily win in both the north and south. Diem's was just one in a long line of U.S.-backed governments which failed to win the allegiance of the Vietnamese population.

From the perspective of the Vietnamese, the Geneva Accords proved only an interlude between two wars, one to rid the country of French colonial control and a second to reunify Vietnam. (This second goal would not be accomplished until 1975, two years after the final U.S. withdrawal.) By January 1955 the United States had replaced France as the dominant power in South Vietnam. American policymakers now asserted that a noncommunist South Vietnam was vital to the security interests of the United States and they charted American policy accordingly. Said President Eisenhower: "You have a row of dominoes set up, you knock over the first one, and what will happen to the last one is the certainty that it will go over very quickly." Between 1955 and 1961 the Eisenhower administration sent Diem an average of $200 million a year in aid, mostly military. In addition, approximately 675 American military advisers were stationed in Saigon, the capital of South Vietnam.

Inheriting the Vietnam situation from the previous administration, President Kennedy saw Vietnam as an ideal laboratory to try out counterinsurgency tactics. But Kennedy, like all the other American presidents who guided policy, first had to prop up the faltering regime of Ngo Dinh Diem, who remained a highly unpopular leader because of his administration's endemic corruption and ruthless brutality, aloofness from the peasantry, and greedy land policy. Because the Diem regime was so weak, Kennedy increased the number of American military "advisers" (an elastic term which included helicopter units, special forces, minesweeping details, and air reconnaissance pilots) to more than 16,000 by November 1963. As part of the counterinsurgency strategy, he also sent in economic development specialists to win the "hearts and minds" of Vietnamese peasants away from the insurgents while also increasing agricultural production. Kennedy refused, however, to send American combat troops to assist the South Vietnamese. "In the final analysis," he told a journalist in November of 1963, "it is their war."

The American aid did little good. Diem's political inexperience and corruption, combined with his Catholicism in a predominantly Buddhist country, made it impossible for him to create a stable, popular government. He enjoyed much more support from his faraway American backers than he did in his native land. As the situation deteriorated, Diem consistently misled his American allies about South Vietnamese military and social progress. In December 1960 the North Vietnamese Communist party had organized its supporters in South Vietnam into a revolutionary front, the National Liberation Front (NLF). The front's guerrilla forces—called the Vietcong by Diem and his American advisers—made considerable headway against the Diem regime, using the revolutionary tactics of the Chinese leader Mao Zedong to blend into the South Vietnamese civilian population "like fish in the water." But opposition to Diem was far more widespread than just the communists. For example, large segments of the peasantry had been alienated by Diem's strategic hamlet program, which uprooted families and whole villages in a vain attempt to separate them from Ho Chi Minh's sympathizers.

Matters came to a head in late 1963. Militant Buddhists staged a dramatic series of demonstrations against Diem, including several self-immolations that were recorded by American television crews. Kennedy decided that Diem had to be removed. Ambassador Henry Cabot Lodge, Jr., let it be known in Saigon that the United States would support a military coup that had "a good chance of succeeding." On November 1, 1963, Diem was driven from office and assassinated by a faction of the South Vietnamese army.

Kennedy's advisers had given little thought to what would follow Diem's ouster. Before they could formulate any plans, Kennedy himself was assassinated and Lyndon Johnson took his place as president. "I am not going to lose Vietnam," he stated emphatically within weeks of becoming president. "I am not going to be the President who saw Southeast Asia go the way China went." A new phase in the Americanization of the war began. When Johnson assumed the presidency, there were 16,000 American troops in Vietnam. When he left office in January 1969, there were more than 500,000.

Escalation

In the period between Kennedy's assassination in November of 1963 and the summer of 1964, a coalition government headed by General Nguyen Khanh tried, without much success, to build popular support in South Vietnam. American policymakers realized that the Eisenhower-Kennedy policy of military advisers and supplies would probably no longer be enough to save the situation. But the commitment of U.S. forces in an offensive strategy would call for at least tacit congressional support, perhaps even a declaration of war. Originally, Johnson had wanted to wait until after the 1964 election to place this controversial request before Congress, but events gave him the opportunity to win authorization sooner.

The Gulf of Tonkin Resolution. During the summer of 1964, American naval forces had supported several South Vietnamese amphibious attacks on the North Vietnamese coast. The North Vietnamese resisted such attacks, and President Johnson told the nation that on two separate occasions North Vietnamese torpedo boats had fired on American destroyers in international waters in the Gulf of Tonkin. At Johnson's request, in early August Congress authorized him to "take all necessary measures to repel any armed attacks against the forces of the United States and to prevent further aggression." The Gulf of Tonkin resolution passed 88 to 2 in the Senate and 416 to 0 in the House. Only Senators Wayne Morse of Oregon and Ernest Gruening of Alaska opposed it as a "predated declaration of war" that further increased the president's ability to carry out foreign policy without consulting Congress.

Many questions were later raised about the resolution. A draft had been ready for several months awaiting just such an incident. The evidence of a North Vietnamese attack was sketchy at best. As the president admitted soon afterward, "For all I know, our navy was shooting at whales out there." But this trumped-up attack got Johnson what he wanted—the only formal approval of American intervention in Vietnam ever voted by Congress.

During the 1964 presidential campaign, Johnson declared, "We are not going to send American boys nine or ten thousand miles away from home to do what Asian boys ought to be doing for themselves." Yet plans were already under way for a major escalation of the United States effort, the only way, policymakers agreed, that the South Vietnamese government could prevent a Communist takeover. With Congressional support assured and the 1964 election safely over, the Johnson administration began the fateful moves toward the total Americanization of the war. The escalation, which was accomplished during the first several months of 1965, took two forms: the deployment of American ground troops and the initiation of direct U.S. bombing attacks against North Vietnam.

The Arrival of U.S. Ground Troops. The assignment of U.S. ground troops to combat duty in South Vietnam in March of 1965 marked a major turning point in the history of American involvement. Even with the help of numerous American advisers and millions of dollars of supplies, South Vietnamese troops were no longer able to resist the Vietcong. The first U.S. Marines waded ashore at Da Nang on March 8, 1965, ostensibly to protect the large American air base there. Soon they were patroling the countryside and skirmishing with the enemy. At the time the American people were not told that a major change in policy had occurred.

During the next three years, the number of U.S. troops in Vietnam grew dramatically. The war increasingly became an American struggle, fought for American aims. More than 75,000 soldiers were fighting there in June 1965, and 190,000 by the end of that year. In 1966, almost 400,000 American soldiers were stationed in Vietnam, 500,000 in 1967, and 540,000 in 1968. The escalating demands of General William Westmoreland, commander of the U.S. forces in Vietnam, confirmed a prediction made by presidential adviser George Ball in 1961. Ball had warned President Kennedy that if American ground troops were committed to Vietnam, there would be 300,000 there within five years. Kennedy had laughed and said, "George, you're crazier than hell." But as Kennedy observed before his death, requests for troops were like having a drink: "The effect wears off, and you have to take another."

The other major element of the escalation, which occurred simultaneously in March of 1965, concerned bombing attacks against North Vietnam. Retaliatory air strikes against North Vietnamese targets had already been selectively undertaken in February; what was significant about these new plans was that the bombing was not linked to a specific act of provocation, but was an open-ended policy. Such bombing raids, National Security Adviser McGeorge Bundy reasoned, would cripple the North Vietnamese economy and force the communists to the bargaining table. A special target was the Ho Chi Minh trail, an elaborate network of paths, bridges, and shelters that snaked from North Vietnam through Cambodia and Laos into South Vietnam. Some twenty thousand Vietnamese soldiers moved southward along this route each month by 1967, as well as the military hardware and other resources necessary to supply them.

Jungle Warfare in Vietnam

The horror of losing a buddy in war was plain in the faces of these marines as they tried to drag a comrade to safety under fire at the battle of Khe Sanh in 1968. Almost two-thirds of the American soldiers who died in action in Vietnam were twenty-one years old or younger.

Aerial Bombing in Vietnam
The bombs dropped by U.S. forces in an attempt to root out Vietcong sympathizers inflicted heavy damage on the countryside and led to civilian deaths. B-52 bombers dropped most of the bombs.

Between 1965 and 1968, Operation Rolling Thunder (named for a Protestant hymn) dropped a million tons of bombs on North Vietnam, 800 tons a day for three and a half years. Each of these B-52 bombing sorties cost $30,000, a measure of the escalating costs of the war; already by 1966 the direct costs of the air war exceeded $1.7 billion. From 1965 to 1973 the United States dropped three times as many bombs on North Vietnam, a country roughly the size of Texas, as had fallen on Europe, Asia, and Africa during World War II. The several hundred captured pilots downed in the raids then became pawns in negotiations with the North Vietnamese over the fate of prisoners of war.

Much to the amazement of American advisers, the bombing had little effect on the ability of the Vietnamese to wage war. Instead of destroying enemy morale and bringing the North Vietnamese to the bargaining table, the bombing rekindled Vietnamese nationalism and intensified its will to fight. The flow of troops and supplies to the south continued unabated. American leaders could have learned a lesson from World War II, when extensive bombing of Germany in 1944–1945 had failed to cripple Nazi industrial production. Because North Vietnam had little industry to destroy, the impact of similar bombing on an agricultural society would predictably be less. The bombing continued nevertheless.

The massive commitment of troops and airpower after 1965 threatened to destroy the fragile resources of this once beautiful country. Taking to the extreme Johnson's call "to leave the footprints of America in Vietnam," the campaign of extensive defoliation and military bombardment made it difficult for peasants to practice the agriculture that provided the economic and cultural base of Vietnamese society. After one devastating but not unusual engagement, the commanding U.S. officer claimed, using the logic of the times, "It became necessary to destroy the town in order to save it." Graffiti on a plane that dropped defoliants read, "Only you can prevent forests." (Only later did the devastating human effect of chemicals such as Agent Orange become clear.) Meanwhile, American soldiers and dollars flowed into Saigon and other cities, distorting the local economy, facilitating corruption and prostitution, and setting off wild, unmanageable inflation.

Why did the dramatically increased American presence in Vietnam after 1965 make so little difference to the outcome of the war? Certain advisers, like former Lieutenant Colonel John Paul Vann, argued that military intervention would do little unless accompanied by reform of the Saigon government and increased efforts at pacification in the countryside. Other critics claimed the war was lost because the United States never committed its full military might to total victory, although what total victory would have entailed remains in dispute. It is true, however, that no clear, overall military strategy guided American efforts. Instead, often for domestic reasons, policymakers searched for the illusive "middle ground" between all-out war and the politically unacceptable alternative of disengagement. This limited commitment was never enough to ensure victory, however defined.

The determination of the Vietnamese was also a major factor in the continuation of the war. In the 1940s, Ho Chi Minh had told his French imperialist foes, "You can kill ten of my men for every one I kill of yours, but even at those odds, you will lose and I will win." That same strategy held true twenty years later against the Americans. The Vietcong were prepared to accept limitless casualties and to fight for as many years as necessary. (Four million Vietnamese on both sides were either killed or wounded in the war, approximately 10 percent of the population.) North Vietnamese strategists astutely realized that the war did not have to be won on the battlefield. They accurately predicted that the United States would be unable to wage an extended war of attrition because American public opinion would eventually limit U.S. participation. Time was on the Vietcong side, although at an enormous cost to both sides.

Vietnam, From the Perspective of Americans Who Fought the War

The average age of the approximately 2.8 million Americans who served in Vietnam was nineteen. These kids were too young to vote or drink, but old enough to fight . . . and die. They served for a variety of reasons. Some responded to the kind of patriotic motives that had led their fathers to fight in World War II or Korea; others joined the army because they had no options at home and wanted to "see the world."

Many served because they were drafted. Until the country shifted to an all-volunteer force in 1973, the draft remained a concrete reminder of the impact of the state on individual lives. As the troop needs intensified, the draft reached deeper into the male population. The casualty figures reflected the increasing role of draftees in Vietnam. In 1965 draftees comprised 16 percent of total battle deaths; this had risen to 34 percent by 1967. By 1969, 62 percent of Army deaths were of draftees. Blacks were drafted, and died, in roughly the same proportion to their draft age population: about 12 to 13 percent.

Many draftees and enlistees initially shared cold war assumptions about the need to fight communism, and a corresponding belief in the superiority of American military strength. Arriving in Vietnam quickly disabused them of simple notions of patriotism or the inevitability of American victory. The first thing they noticed when they got off the plane was the stench—the smell of death, napalm, and human waste in this torrid jungle country. Sometimes they had to sprint from their plane to the safety of the base buildings because of incoming enemy mortar attacks, an augury of the boldness with which enemy forces operated throughout the country.

Unlike World War II soldiers, who served "for the duration," Vietnam soldiers had a tour of duty of exactly one year. For many, it was simply a matter of getting through three hundred and sixty-five days. For the first ninety days or so, they were a "cherry," sexual slang to designate youth and inexperience. Once they neared the end of their tour, soldiers might carry a "short-timer's stick" notched for the remaining days left; as each day passed, they would cut off another notch until left with a small stub. "Grunts" (the ordinary infantrymen) and "bloods" (what black draftees called themselves) were a suspicious lot, however, and they were always afraid of being "wasted" (killed) with only a few days to go. Some soldiers consciously tried not to make close friends, just in case their buddies caught a grenade or triggered a booby trap on a routine patrol.

In "Nam" (soldier's shorthand for Vietnam), days passed in boring menial work, punctuated by flashes of intense fighting. "Most of the time, nothing happened," a soldier recalled, "but when something did, it happened instantaneously and without warning." The pressure of waging war under these conditions drove many soldiers to seek escape with alcohol or cheap and readily available drugs.

The fighting had a certain surreal quality to it. Combat often intensified at night, with incoming and outgoing firepower lighting up the sky while soldiers huddled sleeplessly on watch. There were rarely large-scale battles, only skirmishes; no front lines or territory conquered, just operations during the day in areas that reverted to Vietcong control at night. Although whole units might sometimes be ambushed, casualties more typically came in twos and threes. A former Marine captain recalled:

> You never knew who was the enemy and who was the friend. They all looked alike. They all dressed alike. They were all Vietnamese. Some of them were Vietcong. Here's a woman of twenty-two or twenty-three. She is pregnant, and she tells an interrogator that her husband works in Danang and isn't a Vietcong. But she watches your men walk down a trail and get killed or wounded by a booby trap. She knows the booby trap is there, but she doesn't warn them. Maybe she planted it herself.

He concluded graphically, "It wasn't like the San Francisco Forty-Niners on one side of the field and the Cincinnati Bengals on the other. The enemy was all around you."

American success was measured not in territory gained, but in gruesome "body counts"—the number of enemy soldiers killed—and "kill ratios"—the ratio between enemy losses and American casualties. "If it's dead and Vietnamese, it's VC [Vietcong]" was the rule of thumb in the bush. Casualty figures were often deliberately inflated. As a twenty-four-year-old Special Forces captain recalled, "I went out and killed one VC and liberated a prisoner. Next day the major called me in and told me that I'd killed fourteen VC and liberated six prisoners. You want to see the medal?"

AMERICAN LIVES

John Paul Vann

The divisions over the Vietnam War haunted Arlington National Cemetery on June 16, 1972, when three hundred mourners assembled for the funeral of John Paul Vann. "The soldier of the war in Vietnam," Vann had been killed in a helicopter crash in the Central Highlands the week before. Politicians and military leaders closely associated with the war effort were very much in evidence—General William Westmoreland, CIA Director William Colby, conservative journalist Joseph Alsop, and Secretary of State William Rogers. But so were Daniel Ellsberg, a former Pentagon official who had publicly turned against the war, and Senator Edward Kennedy, another war opponent who had shared Vann's concern about the plight of its refugees. In a time of intense polarization over a war that was still going on, this assemblage of "hawks" and "doves" was highly unusual.

Vann's own family also showed the rifts over Vietnam that day. His wife of twenty-six years, Mary Jane, had requested two pieces of music: the upbeat "Colonel Bogie March" from the film *The Bridge on the River Kwai*, one of her husband's favorites, and the haunting antiwar ballad, "Where Have All the Flowers Gone?," her own expression of opposition to the war. One of Vann's sons, twenty-one-year-old Jesse, hated the war so profoundly that he tore his draft card in two at the funeral, placing half of it on his father's casket. He planned to give the other half to President Richard Nixon at the White House ceremony following the funeral, where his father would be presented posthumously with the Presidential Medal of Freedom. Only at the last moment was Jesse talked out of his act of defiance, agreeing that this was, after all, his father's day, and more than anything else, his father had believed in the war in Vietnam.

Also at the funeral was *New York Times* reporter Neil Sheehan, who decided at that moment to write a biography of Vann, which he finally published sixteen years later, *A Bright Shining Lie*. Sheehan, along with David Halberstam and other reporters, had fallen under

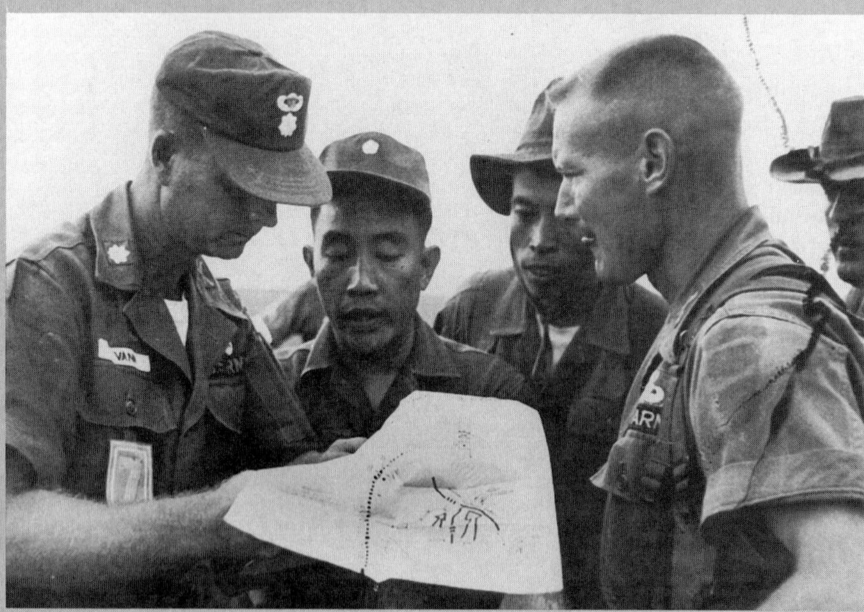

Planning Strategy
Lt. Col. John P. Vann (left) shown here during his tour of duty in Vietnam in 1963 discussing a tactical decision.

Vann's spell during his first tour of duty in Vietnam in 1963, when he seemed like the only American official who was willing to admit that the war was not going well. Sheehan had continued to rely on Vann's outspoken assessments for the rest of the war. "In this war without heroes, this man had been the one compelling figure," concluded Sheehan. "By an obsession, by an unyielding dedication to the war, he had come to personify the American endeavor in Vietnam."

John Paul Vann was an enormously complicated person—a born leader, a visionary, a man who knew no physical fear, but most of all, a true believer in America's mission to share democracy with countries "less fortunate" than ours. His early years were shaped by poverty and lack of opportunity. Born in 1924 to a working-class family in Norfolk, Virginia, he grew up dirt poor during the Great Depression. A colleague later recalled him as a "cocky little red-necked guy with a rural Virginia twang." World War II offered him his ticket out—when he turned eighteen in 1943, he enlisted and made the army his career. He served with distinction in the Korean War and then took assignments in West Germany and the United States. But in 1959 his service record was stained by accusations of the statutory rape of a fifteen-year-old girl. Even though the army eventually dropped the charges, the scandal effectively prevented him from moving up in the military bureaucracy. Neil Sheehan later concluded that Vann's "moral heroism" in speaking out against the conduct of the war to the seeming detriment of his career was rooted in his awareness that he had nothing to lose, although reporters did not know the full story at the time.

In 1963 the thirty-nine-year-old Lieutenant Colonel Vann was sent to Vietnam, where he served as a senior adviser to a South Vietnamese infantry division in the Mekong Delta. At the battle of Ap Bac, he watched his South Vietnamese counterpart purposely refuse to fight the battle the way it had been planned and let the enemy escape. In a moment of epiphany, Vann realized that the rosy reports being fed to Saigon and Washington were false, that Saigon suffered from "an institutionalized unwillingness to fight." After unsuccessful attempts to enlighten his superiors, he leaked his meticulously documented assessments to reporters like Halberstam and Sheehan. His candor won him few friends in the military, and at the end of his tour of duty he was reassigned to the Pentagon. He tried to alert the Joint Chiefs of Staff that the war was not being won, but at the last moment his scheduled briefing was canceled, in large part because the Joint Chiefs did not want to hear his version of the truth. He resigned from the army soon afterward.

Less than two years later, in 1965, Vann was back in Vietnam, just as the major escalation of the war was getting underway. Except for brief trips home, he stayed there until his death. His first position was as a civilian pacification representative for the Agency for International Development, where he worked to win over the peasants to the South Vietnamese side, rather than the National Liberation Front. His honesty and unmatched familiarity with conditions in the countryside led him to conclude that the communists were doing a far better job at appealing to the local population than the corrupt Saigon government: as he wrote to a friend in 1965, "If I were a lad of eighteen faced with the same choice—whether to support the GVN [Government of Vietnam] or the NLF—and a member of a rural community, I would surely choose the NLF." His concern for winning over the local peasantry made him an outspoken opponent of the heavy bombing inflicted on the Vietnamese countryside in an effort to rout out Vietcong sympathizers. He also strongly criticized General Westmoreland's strategy of sending in more American troops to wear down the Vietcong in a war of attrition, arguing that this would be useless without major reforms in the Saigon government.

Despite his role as a gadfly, and even though he was now a civilian, John Paul Vann assumed more and more responsibility in the day-to-day conduct of the war. In 1971 he was given authority over all the U.S. military forces in the Central Highlands, the equivalent of the position of major general. But by then, according to Sheehan, Vann had "lost his compass." He was no longer able to assess realistically the ability or the will of the South Vietnamese to fight without American aid. He continued to insist that the war could be won through pacification and reform in Saigon, despite evidence of growing Vietcong strength. When his helicopter went down at Kontum in 1972, he had almost singlehandedly saved the Central Highlands from a North Vietnamese offensive. Within six months, the United States formally ended its involvement. Two years later, Vietnam was reunited under Communist rule.

John Paul Vann never wavered in his belief that in Vietnam America's cause was just, its intentions good. He had no quarrel with the war itself, just the way it was fought. Vann thought he knew the answers, but Saigon and Washington chose not to listen. His life and death serve as a reminder of the complexities of the Vietnam experience—could it ever really have been "won" and what would "winning" have meant? Neil Sheehan is convinced that Vann "died believing he had won his war."

AMERICAN VOICES

A Vietnam Veteran Remembers *Ron Kovic*

Born on the Fourth of July in 1946, Ron Kovic wanted to be an American hero. He enlisted in the marines and was sent to Vietnam. He came home in a wheelchair and, after a long period of recovery, joined the antiwar movement.

Ron Kovic

I had been shot. The war had finally caught up with my body. I felt good inside. Finally the war was with me and I had been shot by the enemy. I was getting out of the war and I was going to be a hero. I kept firing my rifle into the tree line and boldly, with my new wound, moved closer to the village, daring them to hit me again. For a moment I felt like running back to the rear with my new million-dollar wound but I decided to keep fighting in the open. A great surge of strength went through me as I yelled for the other men to come out from the trees and join me. I was limping now and the foot was beginning to hurt so much, I finally lay down in almost a kneeling position, still firing into the village, still unable to see anyone. I seemed to be the only one left firing a rifle. Someone came up from behind me, took off my boot and began to bandage my foot. The whole thing was incredibly stupid, we were sitting ducks, but he bandaged my foot and then he took off back into the tree line.

For a few seconds it was silent. I lay down prone and waited for the next bullet to hit me. It was only a matter of time, I thought. I wasn't retreating, I wasn't going back, I was lying right there and blasting everything I had into the pagoda. The rifle was full of sand and it was jamming. I had to pull the bolt back now each time trying to get a round into the chamber. It was impossible and I started to get up and a loud crack went off next to my right ear as a thirty-caliber slug tore through my right shoulder, blasted through my lung, and smashed my spinal cord to pieces.

I felt that everything from my chest down was completely gone. I waited to die. I threw my hand back and felt my legs still there. I couldn't feel them but they were still there. I was still alive. And for some reason I started believing, I started believing I might not die, I might make it out of there and live and feel and go back home again. I could hardly breathe and was taking short little sucks with the one lung I had left. The blood was rolling off my flak jacket from the hole in my shoulder and I couldn't feel the pain in my foot anymore, I couldn't even feel my body. I was frightened to death. I didn't think about praying, all I could feel was cheated.

All I could feel was the worthlessness of dying right here in this place at this moment for nothing.

Source: Ron Kovic, *Born on the Fourth of July* (New York: McGraw-Hill, 1976), 221–22.

Racism was a fact of everyday life in Vietnam. It was difficult to differentiate between friendly South Vietnamese and Vietcong sympathizers, and many soldiers just lumped them all together as "gooks." A draftee noted of his indoctrination, "The only thing they told us about the Vietcong was they were gooks. They were to be killed. Nobody sits around and gives you their historical and cultural background. They're the enemy. Kill, kill, kill."

Fighting, and surviving, in such conditions took its toll. "War is not killing," recalled one soldier. "Killing is the easiest part of the whole thing. Sweating twenty-four hours a day, seeing guys drop all around you of heatstroke, not having food, not having water, sleeping only three hours a night for weeks at a time, that's what war is. Survival." Another vet echoed that sentiment: "The hardest thing to come to grips with was the fact that making it through Vietnam—surviving—is probably the only worthwhile part of the experience. It wasn't going over there and saving the world from communism or defending the country." Such cynicism and bitterness was common.

The 15,000 women who served in Vietnam shared many of these experiences. Half of these women were in the military, mainly with the WACS and as nurses; the rest were in civilian service, such as the USO. The nurses, like all medical personnel, had to deal with massive doses of death and mutilation, mainly inflicted on soldiers barely out of their teens. They tried not to get caught up in it emotionally, but as one navy nurse recalled, "it's pretty damn hard not getting involved when you see a nineteen- or twenty-year-old blond kid from the Midwest or California or the East Coast screaming and dying. A piece of my heart would go with each."

After the intensity, and the boredom, of the tour of duty, there remained one last hurdle. Unlike World War II or Korean veterans, who usually came back to this country in groups by a long boat ride, Vietnam veterans could literally be in Saigon one day and the American mainland the next. Soldiers from Vietnam returned home alone, with no deprogramming or counseling. Veterans found this transition enormously disorienting. Once home, they felt embarrassed when they dove under a table at the sound of firecrackers on the Fourth of July or froze when planes flew overhead. Mainly the Vietnam experience was just ignored. Recalled one vet, "Bringing up the Nam was like farting at the dinner table. Everybody looks away embarrassed and acts like nothing happened. Well, pardon me." The psychological tensions of serving in Vietnam, and the abrupt transition back to America, sowed the seeds of the post-traumatic stress disorder. Only in the 1980s did America begin to make its peace with those who had served in America's most unpopular war.

The Consensus Begins to Unravel

Throughout the Kennedy and early Johnson years, there was a broad consensus for the administration's conduct of foreign affairs, as there had been generally throughout the cold war period. Lyndon Johnson sought, and received, public support for the war by linking the fight to cold war principles:

> In the forties and fifties we took our stand in Europe to protect the freedom of those threatened by aggression. . . . Now, the center of attention has shifted to another part of the world where aggression is on the march and the enslavement of free men is its goal. . . . If we allow the Communists to win in Vietnam, it will become easier and more appetizing for them to take over other countries in other parts of the world. We will have to fight again some place else—at what cost no one knows. That is why it is vitally important to every American family that we stop the Communists in South Vietnam.

Note that the needs and desires of the Vietnamese people hardly entered into this formulation.

The Early Antiwar Movement. Although significant public opposition to the war did not surface until 1967, Vietnam became an issue for a small group of Americans well before then. The roots of the emerging antiwar movement date to the 1950s and the issue of atmospheric nuclear testing. Concern over fallout and traces of deadly strontium 90 in milk led to the founding of groups such as SANE (the National Committee for a Sane Nuclear Policy), Physicians for Social Responsibility, and Women's Strike for Peace. These activists opposed the escalating arms race in general and atmospheric testing in particular. Their mobilization played a role in the signing of the 1963 nuclear test-ban treaty between President Kennedy and Soviet Premier Nikita Khrushchev.

Between 1963 and 1965, as the American presence in Vietnam grew, the movement shifted from peace advocacy to opposition to the war. Again, no one organization unified this sentiment, although all were joined by a skepticism about the rationales for the growing American involvement. Critics of intervention argued that the war was morally wrong and antithetical to American ideals; that the goal of attaining an independent, anticommunist South Vietnam was futile; and that American military involvement would not necessarily help the Vietnamese people. At this point, dissenters included liberal activist groups like SANE, older peace or-

Women March for Peace, 1962
Members of the Women's Strike for Peace set up picket lines at the Capitol in December 1962 to urge an end to atmospheric testing of nuclear weapons by both the United States and the Soviet Union. Such protest groups were forerunners of the broader movement, which opposed the Vietnam War after 1965.

ganizations like the Women's International League for Peace and Freedom, newer ones like Women's Strike for Peace, radical pacifist groups such as the Fellowship for Reconciliation, student groups like Students for a Democratic Society and draft resisters' leagues, and antiwar religious groups. By the mid-1960s, a broad, diffuse movement against the war existed. "The antiwar movement is not a fixed group of people," observed one participant, "it is something that has been happening to America."

Norman Morrison is a symbol of how strongly some Americans felt about Vietnam. In November 1965, Morrison, a thirty-two-year-old Quaker activist, married and the father of an eighteen-month-old daughter, set himself on fire and burned to death near the gates of the Pentagon, barely 50 yards from Defense Secretary Robert McNamara's office. He undertook this protest against the immorality of the war after reading an account by a French priest who had despaired at seeing his Vietnamese parishioners burned by napalm during a bombing attack. Like the priest, Morrison was anguished about his inability to stop the carnage. To his wife of ten years, he left this note: "Know that I love thee but must act for the children of the priest's village."

The Johnson administration paid little heed to the emerging antiwar opposition, dismissing them as "nervous nellies," rebellious children, or communist dupes. Despite calls to "Support Our Boys—Bring Them Home," the president was increasingly adamant that the United States must not back down from its commitment to the South Vietnamese. Thus ensued a two-front offensive: a war for public opinion in America, to parallel the war in Vietnam itself.

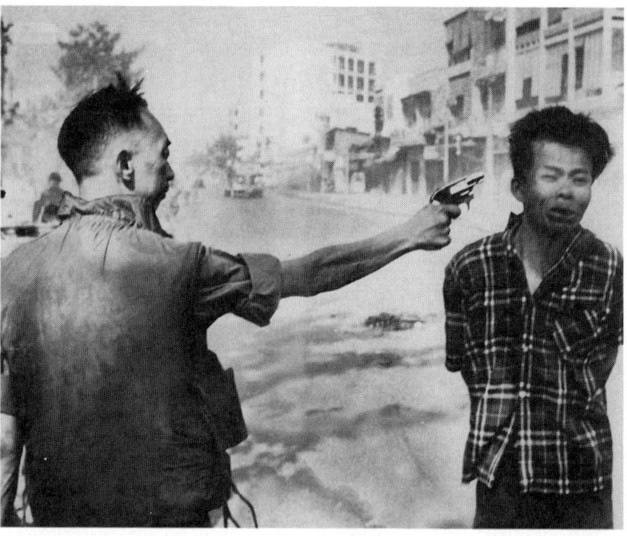

A Televised War
This harrowing scene from Saigon during the Tet offensive in 1968 was broadcast on U.S. network news. The NBC bureau chief described the film in a terse telex message: "A VC OFFICER WAS CAPTURED. THE TROOPS BEAT HIM. THEY BRING HIM TO [Brigadier General Nguyen Ngoc] LOAN WHO IS HEAD OF SOUTH VIETNAMESE NATIONAL POLICE. LOAN PULLS OUT HIS PISTOL, FIRES AT THE HEAD OF THE VC, THE VC FALLS, ZOOM ON HIS HEAD, BLOOD SPRAYING OUT. IF HE HAS IT ALL ITS STARTLING STUFF."

The Television War. Television had much to do with shaping American attitudes toward the war. Vietnam was television's first big war; it brought the fighting directly into the nation's living rooms. The escalation in Vietnam coincided with several trends in news broadcasting, notably the expansion of the nightly network newscast from fifteen minutes to half an hour in 1963. By 1967, CBS and NBC were spending $5 million a year to cover the war from their expanded Saigon bureaus. This investment guaranteed that Vietnam appeared on the news every night. Reporters soon learned that combat footage—what they called "shooting bloody"—had a better chance of airing than reports about pacification or political developments. Every night, the newscasts showed American soldiers steadily advancing in the countryside, while reported body counts suggested staggering Vietcong losses against minimal U.S. casualties.

Growing Doubts. Despite the glowing reports that were fed to the American public about the progress of the war, by 1967 many administration officials had privately reached more pessimistic conclusions. Pentagon analysts estimated that the Vietcong, with only minimal assistance from other Communist powers, could marshal 200,000 guerrillas a year indefinitely. Despite such a prognosis, President Johnson continued to insist that an American victory in Vietnam was vital to U.S. national security and prestige. Journalists, especially those who had spent time in Vietnam, soon commented that the Johnson administration suffered from a "credibility gap."

Economic events also forced Johnson and his advisers on the defensive. In 1966 the federal deficit stood at $9.8 billion. The deficit jumped to $23 billion in 1967, with the Vietnam War costing the taxpayers $27 billion that year. (The total cost of the war from 1965 to 1973 has been estimated at $120 billion.) Although the war was consuming only 3 percent of the gross national product, compared with 48 percent for World War II and 12 percent for the Korean War, Johnson could no longer hide the enormous expense of the war from the American people. But only in the summer of 1967 did he ask for a 10 percent surcharge on individual and corporate income, which Congress delayed approving until 1968. By then the inflationary spiral that plagued the American economy throughout the 1970s was already out of control.

The Tet Offensive

Then came Tet. On January 30, 1968, the Vietcong unleashed a massive, well-coordinated assault on major urban areas in the South. The offensive was timed to coincide with the festive Vietnamese holiday of Tet surrounding the lunar New Year, and perhaps also with the beginning of the 1968 presidential campaign in the United States. Vietcong forces struck thirty-six of the forty-four provincial capitals and five of the six major cities, including an assault on the supposedly impregnable U.S. embassy in Saigon. The United States and the South Vietnamese forces were caught off guard, once again having seriously underestimated the capabilities of their Vietcong foe who had been planning the attack since the previous fall. "Even had I known exactly what was to take place," explained an intelligence officer, "it was so preposterous that I probably would have been unable to sell it to anybody."

American forces recovered quickly and were able to counterattack. In strictly military terms, the Tet offensive was a defeat for the Vietcong—it failed to provoke the collapse of the South Vietnamese government headed since 1967 by Nguyen Van Thieu. But its long-term effect was quite different. As one historian observed, Tet was "probably unique in that the side that lost completely in the tactical sense came away with an overwhelming psychological and hence political victory." In the United States, Tet marked the beginning of a new phase of the war.

Television once again played a major role in shaping American attitudes. The success of the Vietcong made a mockery of official pronouncements that the United States was winning the war. Suddenly, television brought home more disturbing images—the American embassy in Saigon under siege, with a pistol-wielding staff member peering warily from a window; and the Saigon police chief placing a pistol to the head of a Vietcong suspect and executing him on the street. About 20 million viewers watched the latter scene, a symbol of the brutality of the war and the corruption and injustice that characterized the Thieu regime.

The Tet offensive set in motion a major shift in American public opinion about the war. Before Tet, a Gallup poll found that 56 percent of the people considered themselves "hawks" (supporters of the war), while only 28 percent identified themselves as "doves" (opponents); women and blacks consistently opposed the war more than white men did, younger people more than older. By April 1968, three months after the Tet offense, doves outnumbered hawks by 42 to 41 percent. This turnaround did not mean that a majority now supported the peace movement. Many who called themselves doves had simply concluded that the war was unwinnable and that America ought to cut its losses and get out. They opposed the war on pragmatic, rather than moral, grounds. As a housewife told a pollster, "I want to get out but I don't want to give up."

Tet also set in motion changes in the administration's conduct of the war. President Johnson turned down General Westmoreland's request for 206,000 additional troops, a request that would have required the politically explosive course of calling up the reserves. Congressional support was slipping, and even within the administration many advisers had concluded that the war was unwinnable, including the members of the foreign policy establishment dubbed "the Wise Men" (see Chapter 28). On March 31, 1968, Johnson announced a partial bombing halt and a willingness to search for a negotiated end to the war. Then, dramatically, he announced that he would not seek reelection and would devote himself to the search for peace (see Chapter 32). By late May 1968, preliminary peace talks between the United States and North Vietnam had begun in Paris. Johnson's decision to remove himself from the presidential race was a direct result of the lack of consensus at home. His attempts to lead the United States to victory in Vietnam and victory over poverty at home had both ended in stalemate and personal disappointment.

The first months of 1968 thus marked an important turning point in the long history of American involvement in Vietnam. The policy of incremental escalation in force since the 1950s came to an end when Westmoreland's request for more troops was turned down. Furthermore, the evaporating domestic consensus for the war meant that future leaders would have to find a way of disengaging, rather than escalating, the American commitment. But even though a corner had been turned in 1968, there was not yet Robert McNamara's proverbial "light at the end of the tunnel."

The struggle in Vietnam reflected problems characteristic of most new nations in the post-colonial world—nationalist ambitions, religious and cultural conflicts, economic needs, and political turmoil. In reality, Vietnam was too small to play a significant part in the international balance of power; its communism was intensely regional and nationalistic, not expansionist. Yet the Kennedy and Johnson administrations, their predecessors, and Nixon and Ford to follow, allowed their perception of a worldwide communist threat and the need to maintain American credibility to control their actions in Vietnam. By 1968 what Lyndon Johnson had once referred to as "a raggedy-ass little fourth-rate country" had brought the world's most powerful military giant to the bargaining table.

Lyndon Johnson never admitted to the American people the extent of the nation's growing involvement in Vietnam; nor did he confront the true cost of ending poverty through legislative activism. Johnson's attempt to pursue simultaneously the Vietnam War and the Great Society provoked by 1968 a profound crisis from which the Democratic coalition has yet to recover.

Summary

A liberal agenda, especially the commitment to expanding the responsibility of the state for social welfare and economic well-being first begun during the New Deal, shaped political life in the 1960s. The concentration of power in Washington led to a corresponding growth in the responsibilities of the president, whom citizens now invested with rising expectations of leadership. John F. Kennedy stimulated this "politics of expectation," but his expansive vision of presidential leadership was clipped by his limited popular mandate. Lyndon Johnson, building on the wave of public emotion after Kennedy's assassination, used his legislative skills to win enactment of a broad Democratic domestic agenda. By the late 1960s, however, the controversy over social programs at home and the escalating Vietnam war threatened the liberal consensus.

The same cold war mentality that characterized postwar foreign policy shaped American involvement in Vietnam. The American presence in Vietnam had been increasing gradually since the 1950s, but escalated dramatically after 1965 during the Johnson administration. Despite bombing attacks on North Vietnam and the deployment of half a million U.S. ground troops, the United States and its South Vietnamese allies found themselves no closer to victory. The 1968 Tet offensive and the beginning of peace talks in Paris signaled a major turning point in the war, although America did not officially end its involvement until 1973.

TOPIC FOR RESEARCH

The Vietnam War

In many ways Vietnam became an American war, fought for American aims. You have read about the war from the perspective of policymakers caught up in the Cold War and maintaining American credibility, and from the perspective of the American soldiers sent to "Nam." Yet those with the largest stake in the contest were the Vietnamese people themselves. How does the war look different from the Vietnamese perspective(s)? Who supported the insurgents, and who supported the American-backed governments? What role did religion and agriculture have in shaping loyalties? What is the relation between the kind of nationalistic communism practiced by Ho Chi Minh and Soviet (or Chinese) communism? What meaning would American democracy, however defined, have in a country such as Vietnam?

Several books concentrate on the Vietnamese themselves. An excellent introduction is Frances Fitzgerald, *Fire in the Lake: The Vietnamese and the Americans in Vietnam* (1972), especially Part I. The writings of French journalist Bernard Fall are also insightful, including *The Two Vietnams* (1963), *Vietnam Witness, 1953–1966* (1966), and *Last Reflections on a War* (1967). Marilyn Young, *The Vietnam Wars, 1945–1990* (1991), treats the Vietnamese and American sides with equal weight. Jeffrey P. Kimball, *To Reason Why: The Debate About the Causes of U.S. Involvement in the Vietnam War* (1990), is a collection of speeches and essays on the reasons for U.S. involvement.

BIBLIOGRAPHY

The best general introduction to the politics and social developments of the postwar world is William H. Chafe, *The Unfinished Journey: America Since World War II* (2nd ed., 1991). See also Godfrey Hodgson, *America in Our Time* (1976), and William E. Leuchtenberg, *A Troubled Feast* (1979). Standard overviews of American foreign policy are Stephen Ambrose, *Rise to Globalism* (5th ed., 1988); Walter LaFeber, *America, Russia, and the Cold War* (6th ed., 1990); and Thomas J. McCormick, *America's Half Century: United States Foreign Policy in the Cold War* (1989).

The Politics of Expectation

The best histories of politics of the 1960s are Allen J. Matusow, *The Unraveling of America: A History of Liberalism in the 1960s* (1984); Jim F. Heath, *Decade of Disillusionment: The Kennedy-Johnson Years* (1975); and James L. Sundquist, *Politics and Policy: The Eisenhower, Kennedy, and Johnson Years* (1968).

The indispensable account of the 1960 presidential campaign is Theodore H. White, *The Making of the President—1960* (1961). Arthur M. Schlesinger, Jr., *A Thousand Days* (1965), and Theodore Sorenson, *Kennedy* (1965), offer uncritical but highly readable accounts of the New Frontier. See also Roger Hilsman, another Kennedy aide, *To Move a Nation* (1967); David Burner, *JFK and A New Generation* (1988); and Thomas Brown, *John F. Kennedy: History of an Image* (1988). Critical views appear in David Halberstam, *The Best and the Brightest* (1972); Henry Fairlie, *The Kennedy Promise: The Politics of Expectation* (1973); and Garry Wills, *The Kennedy Imprisonment* (1980). The best account of President Kennedy's assassination is William Manchester's overwritten *The Death of the President* (1967); Anthony Summer, *Conspiracy* (1980), provides a careful review of the ongoing controversy.

For the Supreme Court, useful surveys include Bernard Schwartz, *Super Chief: Earl Warren and the Supreme Court* (1983); Archibald Cox, *The Warren Court* (1968); Alexander Bickel, *The Supreme Court and the Idea of Progress* (1970); and Philip B. Kurland, *Politics, the Constitution, and the Warren Court* (1970). Anthony Lewis, *Gideon's Trumpet* (1964), narrates one of the era's most famous cases, *Gideon v. Wainwright*.

For the foreign policy of the Kennedy years, see Richard Walton, *Cold War and Counterrevolution* (1972). Robert Kennedy, *Thirteen Days* (1969), provides a participant's account of the Cuban missile crisis, which can be supplemented by McGeorge Bundy, *Danger and Survival* (1989). For U.S. relations with the Third World, see Richard Barnet, *Intervention and Revolution* (1968); John L. S. Girling, *America and the Third World* (1980); Samuel Baily, *The United States and the Development of South America, 1945–1975* (1977); Richard Immerman, *The CIA in Guatemala* (1982); and Gabriel Kolko, *Confronting the Third World* (1988). Gerald T. Rice, *The Bold Experiment* (1985), and Karen Schwarz, *What You Can Do for Your Country* (1991), cover the Peace Corps.

Lyndon Johnson's own account of his presidency is *The Vantage Point* (1971). Doris Kearns, *Lyndon Johnson and the American Dream* (1976), and Merle Miller, *Lyndon: An Oral Biography* (1980), are based on extensive conversations with LBJ. Rowland Evans and Robert D. Novak offer a vigorous portrait in *Lyndon B. Johnson: The Exercise of Power* (1966). Robert A. Caro provides a critical interpretation of Johnson's early career in *The Path To Power* (1982) and *Means of Ascent* (1989). Eric F. Goldman, *The Tragedy of Lyndon Johnson* (1969), and George E. Reedy, *The Twilight of the Presidency* (1975), are sympathetic but critical views from former aides. For the 1964 election, see Theodore H. White, *The Making of the President—1964* (1965). Barry M. Goldwater presented his ideas in *The Conscience of a Conservative* (1960), which can be supplemented by Phyllis Schlafly, *A Choice Not an Echo* (1963).

Michael Harrington called attention to poverty in *The Other America* (1962). Charles Murray's conservative viewpoint in *Losing Ground: American Social Policy, 1950–1980* (1983), can be balanced by Michael Katz's liberal perspective in *The Undeserving Poor: From the War on Poverty to the War on Welfare* (1989). Other accounts of poverty include Harry M. Caudill, *Night Comes to the Cumberlands* (1963); J. Wayne Flynt, *Dixie's Forgotten People* (1979); and Susan Estabrook Kennedy, *If All We Did Was to Weep at Home* (1979). Sara A. Levitan describes the war on poverty in *The Great Society's Poor Law* (1969), and, with Robert Taggart, argues that it was quite effective in *The Promise of Greatness* (1976). Charles R. Morris, *A Time of Passion* (1984), offers thoughtful reflections from a former antipoverty administrator. Daniel P. Moynihan criticizes the community action program in *Maximum Feasible Misunderstanding* (1969). Other critical discussions of antipoverty programs include John Donovan, *The Politics of Poverty* (1973), and Richard Cloward and Frances Fox Piven, *Poor People's Movements* (1978). Marvin E. Gettleman and David Mermelstein, eds., *The Great Society Reader* (1965), criticize the prevailing assumptions behind many Johnson initiatives.

Vietnam and the American Experience

For insightful works on the Vietnam War, see the books listed in the Topic for Research. Two other books that provide an excellent introduction to the conflict and the American role in it are Stanley Karnow, *Vietnam: A History* (1983), and George Herring, *America's Longest War* (2nd ed., 1986). A fascinating source to digest is *The Pentagon Papers* (1971). David Halberstam, *The Best and the Brightest* (1972), gives a deft and biting portrait of the leaders who got the United States into Vietnam. Guenter Lewy offers a controversial defense of the commitment in *America in Vietnam* (1978). James C. Thompson, *Rolling Thunder* (1980), and John Galloway, *The Gulf of Tonkin Resolution* (1970), cover specific topics. The definitive book on the antiwar movement is Charles DeBenedetti, with Charles Chatfield, *An American Ordeal* (1990).

For a sense of what the war felt like to the soldiers who fought it, see Mark Baker, *Nam* (1982), and Ron Kovic, *Born on the Fourth of July* (1976). Wallace Terry, *Bloods* (1984), surveys the experiences of black veterans; Keith Walker, *A Piece of My Heart* (1985), introduces the often forgotten stories of women who served in Vietnam. See also Gloria Emerson, *Winners and Losers* (1976), and Michael Herr, *Dispatches* (1977). Neil Sheehan surveys the entire Vietnam experience through the life of career soldier John Paul Vann in *A Bright Shining Lie* (1988).

TIMELINE

1960	John F. Kennedy elected president
1961	Peace Corps established Bay of Pigs invasion (April 17) U.S. advisers in Vietnam Berlin Wall erected (August 15)
1962	John Glenn orbits earth Cuban missile crisis (October)
1963	Test-ban Treaty Coup ousts Ngo Dinh Diem in Vietnam Kennedy assassinated; Lyndon B. Johnson assumes presidency
1964	Tax cut Civil Rights Act War on Poverty Gulf of Tonkin Resolution (August 5) Johnson elected president
1965	Voting Rights Act Medicare and Medicaid Elementary and Secondary Education Act First U.S. combat troops arrive in Vietnam Beginnings of antiwar movement
1968	Tet offensive begins (January 30) Peace talks open in Paris (November)
1969	U.S. lands first person on the moon

La Huelga

Long live the cause, long live the strike, proclaimed Paul Davis's poster for a 1968 Carnegie Hall benefit for Cesar Chavez's farm workers' union, symptomatic of the challenges of protest movements in the 1960s. (Museum of American Political Life)

CHAPTER 31 *The Struggles For Equality and Diversity,* 1954–1975

The 1960s are often portrayed as a time of social protest and upheaval. Yet the era of questioning and confrontation was not confined to a single decade. From the early 1950s through the mid-1970s, new issues and movements crowded the national agenda. The struggle of African-Americans for their civil rights gained momentum in the 1950s with early victories against segregation in the South. The youth rebellion and resurgent feminism also had roots in the supposedly complacent 1950s, and the women's movement made its greatest impact on society in the 1970s.

Why did these demands for change occur when they did? Demographic shifts and earlier social changes were partly responsible. The black exodus from the South made civil rights a national, not a sectional, issue. The baby-boom generation swelled the enrollments of the nation's universities, providing recruits for student protest in the 1960s. Changes in women's lives, notably their increased access to education and greater participation in the work force, sparked the revival of feminism.

The civil rights movement was the first protest movement to develop in the postwar period. The tactics it pioneered—legislative and judicial challenges, nonviolent protests, and mobilization of public opinion—would later be adopted by other groups to press their demands. But even at the height of the protest movements, those who demanded change were always outnumbered by those who preferred the status quo. Although such resistance hindered the protestors' achievements, the movements for equality and diversity still had a large impact on American culture. By 1975 society had had its "consciousness raised" (a phrase from the women's movement) about a host of issues and problems that had not been topics of national concern in the two decades after World War II.

The Civil Rights Movement

The civil rights movement was enormously successful in its early days. The breakthroughs were especially dramatic in the South, where segregation, the legal separation of the races that had existed since before the turn of the century, was dismantled. The challenges posed by the civil rights movement to established customs and patterns of authority then rippled through the society in the climate of the "politics of expectation." Observed a northern white professor who participated in the movement, "What started as an identity crisis for Negroes turned out to be an identity crisis for the nation."

The Challenge to Segregation

Legal segregation of the races still governed the southern way of life in the early 1950s. In most states, it was illegal for whites and blacks to eat in the same rooms in restaurants or luncheonettes, use the same waiting rooms or toilet facilities at bus or train stations, or ride in the same taxis. All forms of public transportation were rigidly segregated, either by custom or law. On buses, for example, if whites had filled all the front

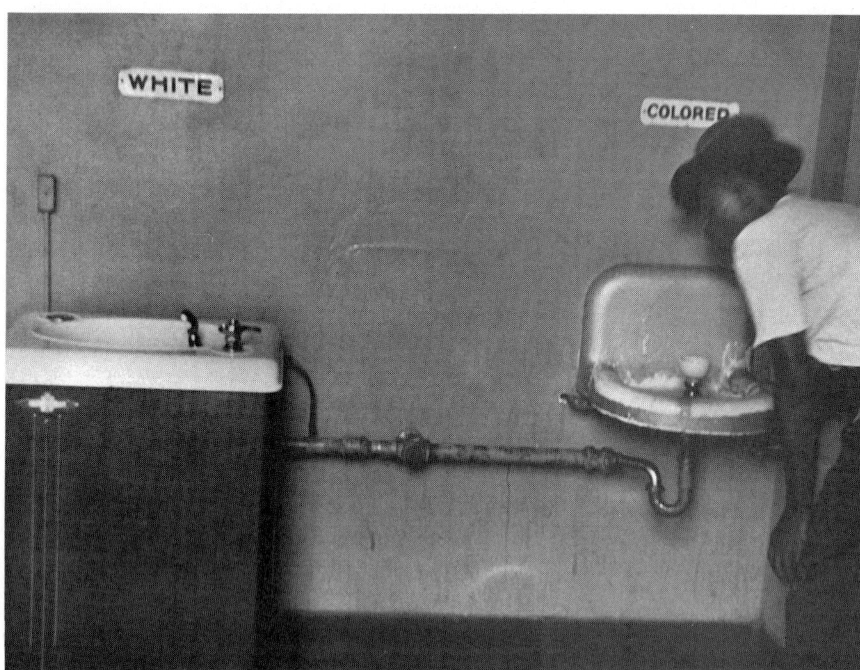

Racial Segregation, North Carolina, 1950

Some pictures are so powerful and shocking they hardly need captions. This is one of them.

seats, blacks were obliged to give up seats in the back until every white had a place. Even drinking fountains were labeled "White" and "Colored."

Usually blacks and whites observed local customs without comment. But there were exceptions. In August 1955, G. H. Mehta, India's ambassador to the United States, walked into a restaurant at the Houston airport. To his indignant surprise, Mehta was told he could not legally be served because he had taken a seat in the "Whites only" section. This incident exposed the southern system to the scrutiny of the world and embarrassed the U.S. government. Within less than a decade these laws would be totally gone.

Leadership in the battle against segregation and racial discrimination came not from the government but from national and community organizations, church groups, and ordinary citizens. Years of patient lobbying by the National Association for the Advancement of Colored People (NAACP) laid the groundwork for the challenge to segregation. Starting in the 1940s, NAACP lawyers such as Thurgood Marshall and William Hastie litigated a series of test cases challenging segregation. Their first victory came in 1944, when the Supreme Court declared that blacks could not be denied the right to vote in party primaries. In 1946 the Court ruled that states could not require segregated seating on interstate buses, and two years later it struck down restrictive residential covenants which prevented the sale of real estate to members of disfavored groups.

Brown v. Board of Education. In 1954, the Supreme Court handed down one of its most far-reaching decisions in a group of challenges to school segregation consolidated as *Brown v. Board of Education of Topeka, Kansas*. The NAACP had filed the Topeka case on behalf of Linda Brown, a black student who attended a segregated school several miles from her home rather than the white elementary school nearby. NAACP Chief Counsel Thurgood Marshall argued that the legal segregation mandated by the Topeka Board of Education was inherently unconstitutional because it stigmatized an entire race and thereby denied it the "equal protection of the laws" guaranteed by the Fourteenth Amendment. In a unanimous decision announced on May 17, 1954, the Supreme Court agreed, overturning the "separate but equal" doctrine of *Plessy v. Ferguson* (see Chapter 19). Speaking for the Court, Chief Justice Earl Warren ruled:

> To separate Negro children . . . solely because of their race generates a feeling of inferiority as to their status in the community that may affect their hearts and minds in a way unlikely ever to be undone. . . . We conclude that in the field of public education the doctrine of "separate but equal" has no place. Separate educational facilities are inherently unequal. . . . Any language in *Plessy v. Ferguson* contrary to these findings is rejected.

Blacks were especially proud that Marshall, a black lawyer, had won such a stunning judicial victory. White reaction was more mixed. White liberals were pleased, but President Eisenhower privately complained that his appointment of Chief Justice Earl Warren was "the biggest damn fool mistake I ever made."

In response to more NAACP suits over the next several years, the Supreme Court used the *Brown* precedent to overturn segregation in city parks, public beaches and golf courses, all forms of interstate and intrastate transportation, and public housing. Meanwhile progress in desegregating schools was frustratingly slow. In a 1955 decision implementing the Kansas decision, known as *Brown II*, the Court declared only that integration should proceed "with all deliberate speed." Many critics would later note that the deliberation was far more evident than the speed. By 1960 less than 1 percent of southern black children were attending desegregated schools. Significant levels of school integration would not be achieved until the 1970s.

Once it became clear that the Court was not going to back down on civil rights, white resistance solidified. In 1956, more than a hundred members of Congress signed a Southern Manifesto denouncing the *Brown* decision as "a clear abuse of judicial power" and encouraging their constituents to defy it. By the end of the year 500,000 southerners had joined White Citizens' Councils dedicated to blocking school integration and other civil rights measures. Some whites revived the old tactics of violence and intimidation, swelling the ranks of the Ku Klux Klan to levels not seen since the 1920s.

So far Eisenhower had accepted the *Brown* decision as the law of the land but had not committed federal power to enforcing it. A crisis in Little Rock, Arkansas, finally forced him to intervene, albeit reluctantly, on the side of desegregation. In September 1957, nine black students attempted to enroll at all-white Central High School after the local school board won a court order to implement a desegregation plan. Governor Orval Faubus called out the National Guard to bar them, despite the court order. Then the mob took over. Every day a white crowd taunted the poised but obviously terrified black students with such chants as "Go back to the jungle." As the vicious scenes were replayed on television night after night, Eisenhower reluctantly decided to act. He sent 1,000 federal troops to Little Rock and nationalized 10,000 members of the Arkansas National Guard, ordering them to protect the students. Eisenhower thus became the first president since Reconstruction to use federal troops to enforce the rights of blacks. This was the first of many times that white extremism provoked a far more sympathetic response from the federal government toward blacks than would otherwise have occurred.

Nonviolent Protest

The *Brown* decision had shown that the NAACP's strategy of judicial challenge could bring fundamental change. But the magnitude of white resistance to integration had also made it clear that winning in court was not enough. A new strategy was needed to challenge the pervasive racism and segregation that persisted in practice even if no longer in law. Sparked by one tiny but monumental act of defiance, southern black leaders embraced nonviolent protest.

The Montgomery Bus Boycott. On December 1, 1955, Rosa Parks, a seamstress and member of the NAACP in Montgomery, Alabama, refused to give up her seat on a city bus to a white man. She was promptly arrested and charged with violating a local segregation ordinance. "I felt it was just something I had to do," Parks stated simply. Black activist Eldridge Cleaver put her act of resistance in a broader context: "Somewhere in the universe a gear in the machinery had shifted."

Integration in Little Rock

Angry crowds taunted the nine black students who tried to register in 1957 at previously all-white Central High School in Little Rock, Arkansas, with chants such as "Two-four-six-eight, we ain't gonna integrate." The court ordered integration proceeded only after President Eisenhower reluctantly nationalized the Arkansas National Guard.

As the local black community met to discuss the proper response, it turned to the Reverend Martin Luther King, Jr., who had become pastor at Montgomery's Dexter Street Baptist Church the year before. The son of a prominent black minister in Atlanta, King had received a B.A. from Morehouse College and a Ph.D. in theology from Boston University. King embraced the teachings of Mahatma Gandhi, who had organized the brilliant campaigns of passive resistance that led to India's independence from Britain in 1947. Drawing on Gandhian principles, King suggested that blacks boycott Montgomery's bus system until it was integrated.

For the next 381 days, a united black community formed carpools or walked to work. "My feets is tired, but my soul is rested," said one woman. The bus company neared bankruptcy, and downtown stores complained about the loss of business. But not until the Supreme Court ruled in November 1956 that bus segregation was illegal did the city of Montgomery finally comply.

The Montgomery bus boycott catapulted King to national prominence. In 1957 with the Reverend Ralph Abernathy and other southern black clergy he founded the Southern Christian Leadership Conference (SCLC), based in Atlanta. The black church had long been the center of African-American social and cultural life. Now it lent its moral and organizational strength, as well as the voices of its most inspirational preachers, to the emerging civil rights movement. Black churchwomen supplied one of the strongest constituencies, transferring the skills they had honed through years of church work to fighting for racial change. The Southern Christian Leadership Conference joined the NAACP as one of the main spurs for racial justice.

Sit-Ins. The next phase of the nonviolent movement began in Greensboro, North Carolina, on February 1, 1960. Four black students from North Carolina Agricultural and Technical College—Ezell Blair, Jr., Franklin McCain, Joseph McNeill, and David Richmond—took seats at the "Whites only" lunch counter of a local Woolworth store, determined to "sit in" until they were served. When Blair ordered something to eat, "The waitress looked at me as if I were from outer space." The target of their protest demonstrated the capriciousness of southern segregation laws. Blacks could buy toothpaste, underwear, and magazines alongside whites at Woolworth's, but not a sandwich or a cup of coffee.

Although Blair and his fellow protestors were arrested, the sit-in tactic worked. White business owners quickly realized that they would lose business if the disruptions continued. By the end of the year, black activists and a number of white supporters had desegregated lunch counters in 126 cities throughout the South. About 50,000 people participated in sit-ins or other demonstrations, and 3,600 of them were jailed, usually for disturbing the peace. The Student Non-Violent Coordinating Committee (SNCC, pronounced "snick"), an offshoot of the SCLC, organized and coordinated the student sit-ins. Ella Baker, a SCLC administrator and lifelong activist, offered the students moral and tactical support.

Freedom Rides. The success of the upstart SNCC's unorthodox tactics encouraged the Congress of Racial Equality (CORE), an interracial group founded in 1942, to adopt a more confrontational strategy. In 1961, CORE's executive director James Farmer organized a series of "freedom rides" on interstate bus lines throughout the South. Farmer targeted buses, waiting rooms, toilets, and terminal restaurants throughout the deep South to call attention to the continuing illegal segregation of public transportation despite the Supreme Court rulings. Activists, mostly young, both black and white, signed on for the potentially dangerous trips. In Anniston, Alabama, club-wielding Ku Klux Klansmen attacked one of the buses with stones and set it on fire. The freedom riders escaped only moments before the bus exploded. Other riders were brutally beaten in Montgomery and Birmingham, but Alabama governor John Patterson refused to intervene, saying "I cannot guarantee protection for this bunch of rabble rousers."

As film of the beatings and bus burnings appeared on the nightly news, Attorney General Robert Kennedy intervened to protect the freedom riders. He also prodded the Interstate Commerce Commission to tighten regulations against segregation on interstate vehicles and terminal facilities. Faced with potential Justice Department intervention against those who defied the Interstate Commerce Commission rules, most southern communities quietly acceded to the changes. CORE meanwhile learned the lesson that nonviolent protest would succeed if it provoked vicious white resistance and generated lots of publicity. Only when forced to, it appeared, would federal authorities act.

JFK and Civil Rights

The accelerating momentum of the civil rights movement had profound implications for the federal government. The Civil Rights movement was arguably the most important force for change in postwar America, but President John Kennedy initially lacked any great empathy for the black cause. Instead, Kennedy seemed to view civil rights protests as irritating political embar-

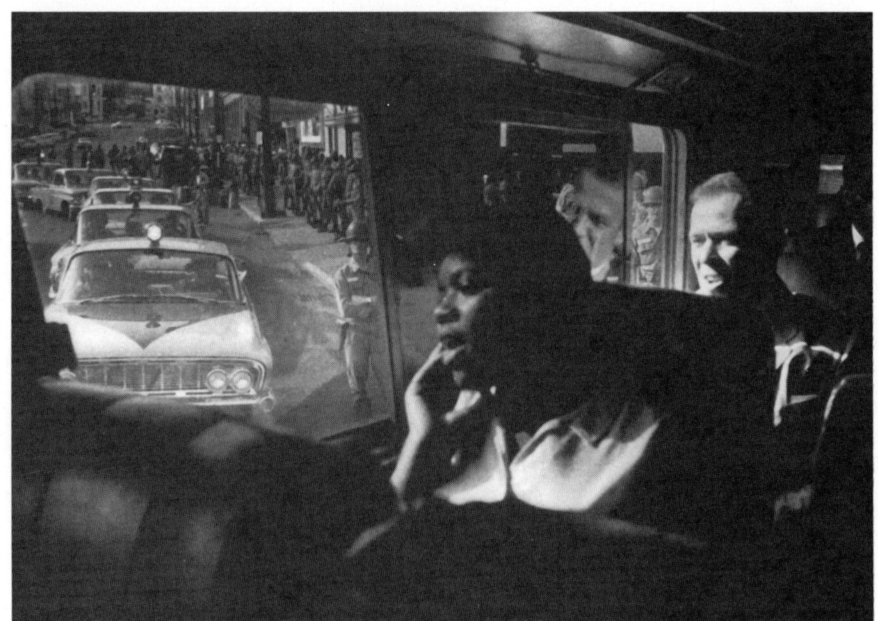

Freedom Riders

Black and white volunteers watch anxiously as they pull into the Montgomery, Alabama, bus station in 1961, while a hostile white crowd gathers outside. Civil rights leader James L. Farmer recalled their determination: "On the bus I noticed . . . boys writing notes and putting them in their pockets, and girls putting them in their brassieres. . . . They were writing names and addresses of next of kin. They really had not expected to live beyond that trip."

rassments that detracted from more important arenas for presidential leadership and action. The Kennedy administration's lack of a response to the emerging civil rights agenda was one of its greatest failures.

Political realities in part dictated Kennedy's reluctance to act, especially tensions within the Democratic coalition. On the one hand, Kennedy needed the votes of southern Democrats to get his programs through Congress, and he did not want to alienate them by embracing the civil rights cause. For the same reason, Kennedy appointed a number of white supremacist judges to the southern bench. On the other hand, blacks had given him strong support in the 1960 election, and Kennedy needed to keep them safely within the coalition. So he reached out to black constituencies with actions such as appointing Thurgood Marshall to the U.S. Circuit Court of Appeals.

But the darkest stain on Kennedy's civil rights record was his acquiescence in the FBI's clandestine surveillance of Martin Luther King, Jr., and the Southern Christian Leadership Conference. In the early 1960s, FBI director J. Edgar Hoover became convinced that the civil rights movement had ties to the Soviet Union. Fears of Communist infiltration found a receptive audience among the cold warriors in the Kennedy White House, and in 1962 Attorney General Robert Kennedy authorized wiretaps on King's Atlanta home and the SCLC headquarters. To its chagrin, the FBI found no evidence of Communist links, but it did uncover evidence of King's extramarital activity, which it then tried unsuccessfully to use to discredit him. Throughout the 1960s the FBI, with the tacit backing of the Kennedy administration and later Lyndon Johnson's as well, seemed to treat the civil rights movement, in Coretta Scott King's words, "as if it were an alien enemy attack on the United States."

Events in 1963 finally pushed the Kennedy administration to take a stronger stand. In Birmingham, Alabama, Martin Luther King, Jr., and the Reverend Fred Shuttlesworth called for a protest against conditions in what King called "the most segregated city in the United States." In April, thousands of black demonstrators marched downtown to picket Birmingham's department stores. They were met by Eugene ("Bull") Connor, the city's commissioner of public safety, who used snarling dogs, electric cattle prods, and high-pressure fire hoses to break up the crowd; the fire hoses were so strong that they ripped bark from trees and tore bricks from buildings. Television cameras captured the entire scene. "The civil rights movement should thank God for Bull Connor," President Kennedy noted. "He's helped it as much as Abraham Lincoln."

Realizing he could no longer straddle the issue, Kennedy determined to step up the federal role in civil rights. On June 11, 1963, he went on television to promise major civil rights legislation banning discrimination in public accommodations and empowering the Justice Department to seek desegregation on its own authority. Black leaders hailed the speech as a "Second Emancipation Proclamation." But for one person Kennedy's speech came too late. That same night, Medgar Evers, a prominent NAACP activist, was shot in the back and killed in Jackson, Mississippi. The martyred Evers became a spur to further action.

AMERICAN LIVES

Ella Baker

"Who the hell is this old lady here?" asked more than one impudent, and unknowing, newcomer to the offices of the Student Non-Violent Coordinating Committee (SNCC) in Atlanta. Regal, matronly, conservatively dressed in a business suit, and always referred to as "Miss Baker," fifty-seven-year-old Ella Baker did stand out from the black and white college students who flocked to SNCC in the early 1960s. But once activists watched her in action, few doubted that she belonged. Recalled veteran SNCC activist John Lewis, "She was much older in terms of age, but I think in terms of ideas and philosophy and commitment she was one of the youngest persons in the movement."

When Baker used her position as the executive secretary of the Southern Christian Leadership Conference (SCLC) to act as the midwife for the birth of SNCC in 1960, she already had years of experience as an organizer and facilitator of social change, almost all of it behind the scenes. As she recalled, "You didn't see me on television, you didn't see news stories about me. The kind of role that I tried to play was to pick up pieces or put together pieces out of which I hoped organization might come. My theory is, strong people don't need strong leaders." Ella Baker recognized the large, often unheralded roles that women played in the emergence of the civil rights movement: "the movement of the Fifties and the Sixties was carried largely by women, since it came out of church groups. . . . The number of women who carried the movement is much larger than that of the men." Her own life is a prime example.

Ella Baker was born in Norfolk, Virginia, in 1903, and grew up in rural North Carolina on land that her grandparents had originally farmed as slaves. She drew enormous strength from her family, with her mother's community and church work providing a model for her own later activism. Reflecting the importance placed on

Ella Baker

She was a woman of action whose lifelong commitment was dedicated to social change.

education by black families, especially for daughters who would need to work even if they married, Baker was sent to Shaw College in Raleigh, North Carolina. Soon after graduating in 1927, she headed north to Harlem, arriving just as the Great Depression dried up opportunities in the promised land of the North. Instead of going to graduate school in sociology as she had hoped, she worked as a journalist, did some political organizing, and was involved in WPA consumer projects. She also was married briefly, and unhappily, to a black minister. In the 1940s she traveled around the country as a field organizer for the National Association for the Advancement of Colored People (NAACP), but she quit that job when she took on the responsibility of raising a seven-year-old niece. Throughout her career, she rarely held regular jobs. "How did I make a living? I haven't. I have eked out existence."

When the SCLC was established in 1957 in the wake of the successful Montgomery bus boycott, Ella Baker was recruited "temporarily" to be its executive secretary. She ended up staying two and a half years. Her organizational skills were very important to the developing movement, but she found herself increasingly restive under King's cautious leadership. In addition, she realized, not for the first time, that her lack of deference to male leadership, her outspoken manner, and her willingness to talk back made black men uncomfortable. She had an especially hard time working with King, who held very traditional ideas about gender roles.

So when the student sit-ins erupted spontaneously in early 1960, Baker watched this development with interest and excitement. She convinced the SCLC to put up $800 toward a conference of student leaders to be held on the campus of her alma mater in Raleigh in April 1960. More than three hundred young people attended, a huge outpouring. At the convention Baker encouraged student leaders to chart an independent role, and not just to become the "youth wings" of established groups like SCLC, the NAACP, or CORE. She did not come right out and say, "Don't let Martin Luther King tell you what to do," recalled Julian Bond, but that was clearly what she meant. The students followed her advice, and SNCC remained independent from existing civil rights organizations. Baker's faith in the students was totally in keeping with her lifelong commitment to grassroots, "group-centered leadership." Probably her greatest dissatisfaction with the SCLC had been how it revolved so completely around Martin Luther King's leadership.

During the turbulent 1960s, Baker offered her organizational skills and material support to SNCC. She never intervened directly in the internal struggles and endless discussions that characterized the group, choosing instead to serve as a facilitator for group consensus and action. She provided not just a bridge across generations, but an incredibly powerful role model of political engagement and activism. This model was especially important to women, both black and white, who drew the lesson that women could be just as effective as organizers and participants as men. The non-hierarchical structure of SNCC, with its emphasis on local leadership and individual initiative, provided an egalitarian climate far more conducive to the utilization of female talent than the society at large. For some women, especially the white volunteers, their experience in SNCC laid the groundwork for the emergence of the women's movement later in the decade.

Voter registration had always been a top priority for SNCC, and in 1964 Ella Baker became involved in an attempt to wrest political power from the regular Democratic party, which remained rigidly all-white in the South. Denied access to the right to vote, SNCC organized an alternative political party—the Mississippi Freedom Democratic party (MFDP). Fannie Lou Hamer became the movement's most visible public orator, but Ella Baker played a crucial behind-the-scenes role. Testifying before the credentials committee at the Democratic convention in Atlantic City that summer, Hamer and Baker led the unsuccessful effort to unseat the all-white Mississippi delegation in favor of the MFDP. When President Johnson and the Democratic leadership offered the MFDP token representation in the delegation, the MFDP rejected this compromise as an insult. Baker was not bitter or discouraged by this outcome, or the many other setbacks she faced in her career. "I keep going because I don't see the productive value of being bitter. What else *do* you do?"

Ella Baker continued her lifelong commitment to participatory democracy and social change long after SNCC had lost its place as the cutting edge of the civil rights movement. She died in 1986 on her eighty-third birthday. At her memorial service, civil rights activist Bernice Johnson Reagon, the founder of the singing group Sweet Honey in the Rock, led the assembled friends in a favorite song that captured the determination and spirituality that shaped Ella Baker's lifelong activism: "Guide my feet while I run this race. . . . for I don't want to run this race in vain."

The March on Washington

To marshall support for Kennedy's bill—and to rouse the conscience of the country at large—civil rights leaders turned to a tactic that A. Phillip Randolph had suggested as early as 1941: a massive march on Washington. Martin Luther King of the SCLC, Roy Wilkins of the NAACP, Whitney Young of the National Urban League, and black socialist Bayard Rustin were the principal organizers. They drew support from a broad coalition, including the National Council of Churches, the National Conference of Catholics for Interracial Justice, the American Jewish Congress, and the AFL–CIO Industrial Union Department.

On August 28, 1963, about 250,000 black and white demonstrators—the largest protest assembled up to that time—gathered at the Lincoln Memorial. Speakers and performers alternately uplifted, challenged, and entertained the crowd. The March on Washington culminated in a memorable speech delivered, indeed preached, by Martin Luther King in the evangelical style of the black church:

> I have a dream that one day on the red hills of Georgia the sons of former slaves and the sons of former slaveowners will be able to sit down together at the table of brotherhood. I have a dream that one day even the state of Mississippi, a desert state sweltering with the heat of injustice and oppression, will be transformed into an oasis of freedom and justice. I have a dream that my four little children will one day live in a nation where they will not be judged by the color of their skin but by the content of their character.

He ended with an invocation from an old Negro spiritual, "Free at last! Free at last! Thank God almighty, we are free at last!"

King's eloquence, and the sight of blacks and whites marching solemnly together, did more than any other event to make black protest acceptable to white Americans. The March on Washington seemed to justify the liberal faith that blacks and whites could work together to promote racial harmony, and it marked the climax of the nonviolent phase of the civil rights movement. It also confirmed King's position, especially for the white liberal community, as the leading speaker for the black cause. His stature was further enhanced when he won the Nobel Peace Prize in 1964.

Despite the impact of the March on Washington on public opinion, even as ardent a civil rights supporter as Senator Hubert Humphrey realized that few congressional votes had been changed by the event. Southern senators continued to block Kennedy's legislation by threatening a filibuster. Even more troubling was a new outbreak of violence by white extremists, determined to oppose equality for blacks at all costs. In September a Baptist church in Birmingham was bombed, and four black girls attending Sunday school were killed. Only two months after the Birmingham bombing, President Kennedy was assassinated in Dallas.

Martin Luther King, Jr.
The Reverend Martin Luther King, Jr. (1929–1968) was one of the most eloquent advocates of the black cause in the 1950s and 1960s. For many, his speech at the 1963 March on Washington was the highpoint of the event.

Landmark Legislation

Lyndon Johnson promptly turned passage of civil rights legislation into a memorial to his slain predecessor, a slightly ironic twist given Kennedy's lukewarm support for the cause. The Civil Rights Act, finally passed in June 1964, was a landmark in the history of American race relations and one of the greatest achievements of the 1960s. Its keystone, a section known as Title VII,

AMERICAN VOICES

Registering to Vote in Mississippi *Fannie Lou Hamer*

Fannie Lou Hamer was the youngest of twenty children born into a sharecropping family in Montgomery county, Mississippi. When she attempted to register to vote in 1962, she lost her job as a timekeeper on a cotton plantation. In 1964 she led the challenge of the Mississippi Freedom Democratic party to the all-white party regulars in that state.

So then that was in 1962 when the civil rights workers came into this country. Now I didn't know anything about voter registration or nothin' like that, 'cause people had never been told that they could register to vote. . . . So they had a rally. I had gone to church that Sunday, and the minister announced that they were gon' have a mass meeting that Monday night. Well, I didn't know what a mass meeting was, and I was just curious to go to a mass meeting. So I did . . . and they was talkin' about how blacks had a right to register and how they had a right to *vote*. . . . Just listenin' at 'em, I could just see myself votin' people outa office that I know was wrong and didn't do nothin' to help the poor. I said, you know, that's sumpin' I really wanna be involved in, and finally at the end of that rally, I had made up my mind that I was gonna come out here when they said you could go down that Friday [August 31, 1962] to try to register. . . .

He [the registrar] brought a big old book out there, and he gave me the sixteenth section of the Constitution of Mississippi, and that was dealing with de facto laws, and I didn't know nothin' about no de facto laws, didn't know nothin' about any of 'em. I could copy it like it was in the book . . . but after I got through copying it, he told me to give a reasonable interpretation and tell the meaning of that section that I had copied. Well, I flunked out. . . .

Monday, the fourth of December, I went back to Indianola to the circuit clerk's office and I told him who I was and I was there to take that literacy test again.

I said, "Now, you cain't have me fired 'cause I'm already fired, and I won't have to move now, because I'm not livin' in no white man's house." I said, "I'll be here every thirty days until I become a registered voter."

I passed that second test, but it made us become like criminals. We would have to have our lights out before dark. It was cars passing that house all times of the night, driving real slow with guns, and pickups with white mens in it, and they'd pass that house just as slow as they could pass it . . . three guns lined up in the back. . . . Pap couldn't get nothin' to do. . . .

So I started teachin' citizenship class, and I became the supervisor of the citizenship class in this county. So I moved around the county to do citizenship education and later on I become a field secretary for SNCC.

Source: Howell Raines, *My Soul Is Rested* (New York: Putnam, 1977), 249–50, 252.

outlawed discrimination in employment based on race, religion, national origin, or sex. Another section barred discrimination in public accommodations. In addition, the law gave opponents of segregation two powerful new weapons. They could ask the attorney general to withhold federal funds from any state program that was not desegregated. And they could appeal discrimination in public accommodations and employment to the Equal Employment Opportunity Commission, which Kennedy had established soon after assuming office.

The Civil Rights Act had been passed over a southern filibuster, and many white southerners were determined to defy the new law. In particular, they continued to resist efforts to register blacks to vote. When SNCC and CORE had conducted voter registration drives in 1962–1963, blacks who tried to register faced pressure, economic intimidation, and outright violence. For example, when Fannie Lou Hamer participated in a SNCC voter registration campaign in 1962, she was evicted from the farm where she had sharecropped for eighteen years. The FBI agents sent to the South, supposedly to protect the voting rights activists, sided more often with white authorities, and occasionally the Ku Klux Klan, or did nothing at all.

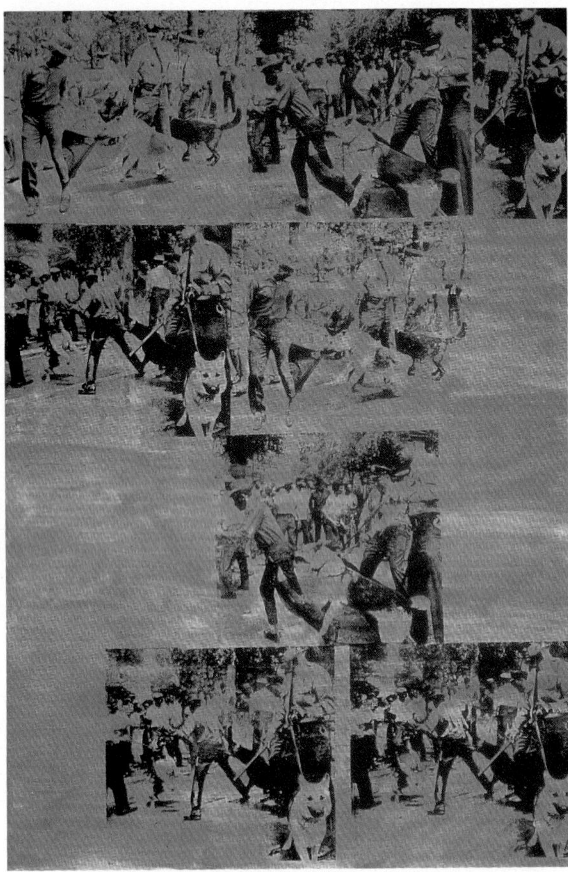

Andy Warhol on Race Relations
Artist Andy Warhol (1928–1987) is forever associated with his pop-art spoofs of consumer culture, such as paintings of Campbell soup cans or Brillo pads, along with his magnetic images of popular icons such as Marilyn Monroe and Elizabeth Taylor. Yet the artist also treated political subjects, such as this provocative (1963) painting *Red Race Riot* depicting violence at a civil rights demonstration. (The Andy Warhol Foundation for the Visual Arts, Inc.)

Freedom Summer. In 1964, with the Civil Rights Act on the brink of passage, black organizations and churches mounted a major registration drive. In that Freedom Summer they recruited several thousand volunteers from across the country, including many idealistic white college students. Violence struck quickly. In June, James Chaney, a CORE volunteer from Mississippi, Andrew Goodman, a student from New York, and Michael Schwerner, a New York social worker, disappeared from Philadelphia, Mississippi, and were presumed murdered. Like many white activists, Goodman and Schwerner were Jewish, a reflection of the large contributions that Jewish groups made to the civil rights movement. As public demand grew for an accounting of their disappearance, Rita Schwerner, Michael's wife, noted, "We all know that this search . . . is because Andrew Goodman and my husband are white. If only Chaney was involved, nothing would have been done." The three bodies were found several weeks later. Goodman and Schwerner had been killed by a single bullet each, while Chaney had been brutally beaten with a chain and shot several times. An investigation later determined that members of the Ku Klux Klan committed the crime. During Freedom Summer, fifteen civil rights workers were murdered; only 1,600 black voters were registered.

Voting Rights Act of 1965. The need for federal action to support voting rights became even clearer in 1965. In February sheriff's deputies in Marion, Alabama, killed Jimmy Lee Jackson, a black voting-rights advocate, during a voter registration march. In protest, Martin Luther King and other black leaders called for a massive march on Sunday, March 7, from nearby Selma to the state capital, Montgomery, 54 miles away. Governor George Wallace banned the march, disingenuously citing concern for public safety. As soon as the marchers left Selma, mounted state troopers attacked them in broad daylight with tear gas and clubs. The scene was shown on national television later that night; ironically, ABC broke into *Judgment at Nuremberg*, a film about Nazi war crimes, to show the Alabama police attacking American citizens on the Pettus Bridge.

Lyndon Johnson called Bloody Sunday "an American tragedy," and he redoubled his efforts to get Congress to pass his pending voting rights legislation. In a televised speech to a joint session of Congress on March 15, Johnson asserted, "It is wrong—deadly wrong, to deny any of your fellow Americans the right to vote in this country." Then, dramatically and repeatedly, Johnson invoked the best-known slogan of the civil rights movement, "We shall overcome." Watching the speech on television, Martin Luther King was moved to tears.

The Voting Rights Act of 1965, the second legislative landmark of the civil rights movement, marked the high tide of Johnson's Great Society. Passed and signed into law in August, it suspended the literacy tests that most southern states had used to prevent blacks from registering to vote. It also authorized the attorney general to send federal examiners to register voters in any county where less than 50 percent of the voting age population was on the voting lists, thus placing the entire registration and voting process under federal control. Together with the adoption in 1964 of the Twenty-fourth Amendment to the Constitution, which outlawed the federal poll tax, and successful legal challenges to state and local poll taxes, the Voting Rights Act made it possible for millions of blacks to register and vote for the first time. Congress extended the Voting Rights Act in 1970, 1975, and 1982. The results were stunning: in 1960 only 20 percent of eligible blacks were registered. In 1964 the figure had risen to 39 percent, and in 1971 to 62 percent.

Hartman Turnbow, a Mississippi farmer who had risked his life to register to vote in a SNCC-sponsored

Registering to Vote
Once black citizens could register to vote, they changed the nature of Southern politics, opening new channels of political participation and electoral success. In 1989, there were over 4,440 elected black officials in the South, including 578 in Mississippi alone, a dramatic change in the twenty-five years after the passage of the Voting Rights Act of 1965.

drive during the Freedom Summer of 1964, summed up the momentous changes that had occurred:

> Anybody had a jus told me 'fore it happened that conditions would make this much change between the white and the black in Holmes County here where I live, why I'da just said, "You're lyin'. It won't happen." But it got to workin' just like the citizenship class teacher told us—that if we redish to vote and just stick with it. . . . He said we gon' have difficults, gon' have troubles, folks gon' lose their homes, folks gon' lose their lives, people gon' lose all their money, and just like he said, all of that happened. . . . He hit it kadap on the head, and it's workin' now. It won't never go back where it was.

Rising Militance

Now that the system of legal (*de jure*) segregation had fallen, the civil rights movement turned to a more difficult task: eliminating the *de facto* segregation, enforced by custom, that made blacks second-class citizens throughout the nation. Racial discrimination was less flagrant outside the South, but it was real and pervasive, especially in education, housing, and employment opportunities. While the *Brown* decision outlawed separate but equal schools, it did nothing to change conditions in educational systems where schools were all-black or all-white because of patterns of residential segregation. In the 1960s, 90 percent of Chicago's black students attended predominantly all-black schools. Not until 1973 did federal judges begin to order the desegregation of schools in the rest of the country that had begun in the South two decades earlier.

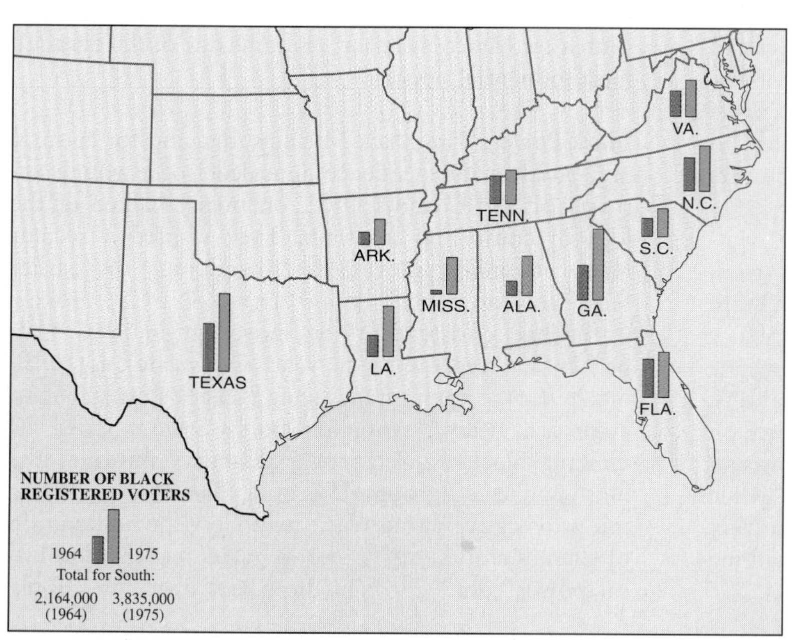

MAP 31.1

Black Voter Registration in the South
After passage of the Voting Rights Act of 1965, black registration in the South increased dramatically. The bars show the number of blacks registered in 1964, before the act was passed, and in 1975, after it had been in effect for ten years. States in the deep South, such as Mississippi, Alabama, and Georgia, had the biggest rises.

As civil rights leaders took on the new target of northern racism, the movement fractured along generational lines. Students who had risked assault to sit in at lunch counters or to register to vote grew impatient with the gradualism of their elders. Many of the freedom riders who had spent months in harsh southern jails found little relevance in Martin Luther King's commitment to nonviolence. Between 1963 and 1965 these activists repudiated the legalistic, nonviolent approach epitomized by the March on Washington and advocated immediate action of a more far-reaching nature. Symbolic of the new militance was their demand to be called blacks or Afro-Americans rather than Negroes, a term they found demeaning because of its historic association with slavery and racism.

Black Separatism. Some younger black activists, eager for confrontation and faster change, even questioned the goal of integration into white society. Black separatism dated back to the nineteenth century, but had been espoused by the Marcus Garvey movement in the 1920s (see Chapter 24). In the 1960s, black separatism was revived by the Nation of Islam, popularly known as the Black Muslims. The Nation of Islam had begun as a small sect in the 1930s, but by the 1960s it had more than 10,000 members, and many more sympathizers. The Black Muslims proselytized very effectively in prisons, urging black inmates to take charge of their lives by adopting a strict code of personal behavior, including the Islamic ban on the use of drugs, alcohol, and tobacco. The Black Muslim ideology was extremely hostile to whites, whom its leader Elijah Muhammad called "blue-eyed devils." Forcefully embracing black nationalism, the Nation of Islam stressed black pride, unity, and self-help. A prominent adherent was the boxer Cassius Clay, who changed his name to Muhammad Ali after his conversion in 1964.

The Black Muslims' most charismatic figure was Malcolm X. Born Malcolm Little in 1925, he converted to the Nation of Islam while serving time in prison for attempted burglary. Taking the name Malcolm X, he portrayed his transformation from petty criminal to minister of Islam as evidence of the redemptive powers of the Black Muslim faith.

A brilliant debater and spellbinding speaker, Malcolm X preached a philosophy quite different from Martin Luther King's. Malcolm advocated militant protest and separatism, although he condoned the use of violence only for self-defense and self-assertion. He was hostile to the traditional civil rights organizations, caustically referring to the 1963 march as the "farce on Washington" and mocking the "angry revolutionists all harmonizing 'We Shall Overcome . . . Suum Day' while tripping and swinging along arm-in-arm with the very people they were supposed to be angrily revolting against."

Malcolm X (1925–1965)

Charismatic, controversial, and caustic, Malcolm X rarely minced words. "Yes, I'm an extremist," he told writer Alex Haley. "The black race here in North America is in extremely bad condition. You show me a black man who isn't an extremist and I'll show you one who needs psychiatric attention!" Director Spike Lee's 1992 film, *Malcolm X,* reignited old controversies, and started some of its own.

In 1963, Malcolm X broke with Elijah Muhammad and the Nation of Islam. The next year he made a pilgrimage to Mecca, the holiest site of traditional Islam, and toured Africa, where he embraced the liberation struggles of all colonial peoples. On February 21, 1965, Malcolm X was assassinated while giving a speech at the Audubon Ballroom in Harlem. Although three Black Muslims were convicted of the murder, so many people opposed Malcolm X that there is a continuing debate over who was responsible for the killing. His autobiography, ghostwritten by Alex Haley and published soon after Malcolm's death, became one of the decade's most influential books.

Black Power. The Black Muslims' demand for cultural and political independence appealed to the young activists of SNCC and CORE, but many balked at the idea of converting to Islam. They wanted a secular black nationalist movement. Abandoning the earlier faith in interracial cooperation, SNCC's Stokely Carmichael christened a new movement in 1966: "We been saying freedom for six years and we ain't got nothing. What we gonna start saying is Black Power!" Soon afterward, Huey Newton and Bobby Seale founded the militant Black Panthers in Oakland, California, the most publicized group advocating Black Power. Newton provocatively told blacks to follow the admonition of China's communist leader Mao Zedong that "political power comes through the barrel of a gun." Only three years after Martin Luther King's "I have a dream" speech, radical black power activists proposed a new agenda: not nonviolence but armed self-defense, not integration but separatism, not working within the system but preparing for revolution.

As a result of this growing militancy, most black organizations went through major identity crises in 1965. By the next year, for all intents and purposes, whites had been kicked out of the civil rights movement. Whites were told they could not understand what it meant to be black; many whites themselves felt guilty about their own complicity in America's institutionalized racism. CORE's decision to bar whites from leadership positions symbolized this shift.

Blacks' new assertiveness alarmed many white Americans. They had been willing to go along with the moderate reforms of the 1950s and early 1960s, but they were wary when blacks started demanding immediate access to higher-paying jobs, better housing in previously white neighborhoods, integrated schools, and increased political power. In 1966, 84 percent of all whites thought blacks were demanding too much change, up from 34 percent just five years earlier.

Summer in the City

A major reason for the eroding white support were the riots that exploded in the nation's cities each summer from 1964 to 1968. The rapid growth of de facto segregation in metropolitan areas provided the backdrop for the riots. Without the education and skills needed for most city jobs, successive generations of blacks moving out of the rural South were unable to find employment that paid an adequate wage. Many were unemployed. Moreover, they were angry at white landlords who owned the substandard housing they were forced to live in; at white shopkeepers who earned money from black trade but would not hire black clerks or salespeople; and at all-white unions—especially in the construction industry—that controlled access to skilled jobs. Young adults especially were painfully aware of their exclusion from the dominant consumer culture. Stimulated by television coverage of southern blacks who had challenged whites and gotten results, young urban blacks expressed their grievances with their own brand of "direct action." Their parents and adult neighbors often supported them in spirit.

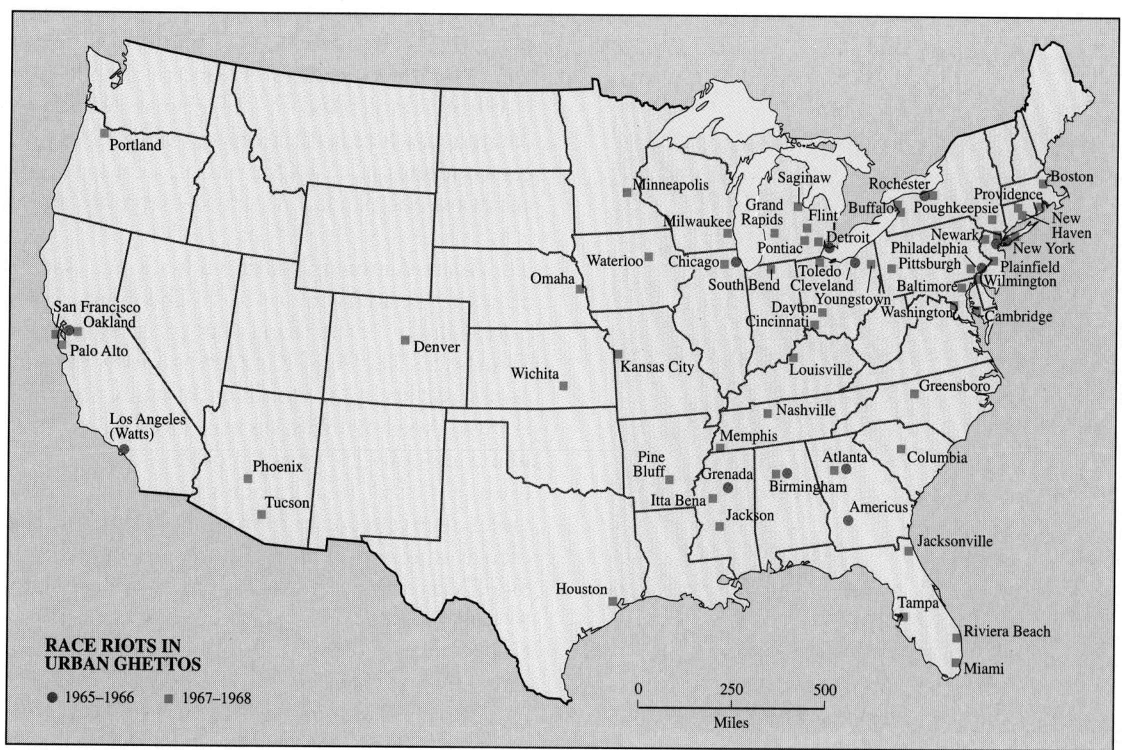

MAP 31.2

Racial Unrest in America's Cities, 1965–1968

American cities suffered four "long hot summers" of rioting in the mid-1960s. In 1967, the worst year, riots broke out in cities throughout the United States, including the South and West. Major riots usually did not occur in the same city two years in a row.

The first "long hot summer" began in July 1964 in New York City, when police shot a black criminal suspect in Harlem. Angry youths looted and rioted for a week. The volatile issue of police brutality would set off riots in a number of cities later that year, and in the years to come. In August rioting spread to several cities in New Jersey, as well as Philadelphia and Chicago.

Racial turmoil worsened the following summer. Thirty-four blacks died in a riot in the Watts section of Los Angeles, where 60 percent of the adult population was on relief. Ironically, Watts erupted only five days after President Johnson hailed passage of the Voting Rights Act of 1965 as the next great step toward racial equality. For many young urban blacks, however, the legal gains of the civil rights movement and the deferred promises of underfunded Great Society programs were irrelevant to their daily experiences of poverty and economic exploitation. Instead of "We shall overcome," Watts rioters shouted the frightening refrain, "Burn, baby, burn." "We won!" shouted a twenty-year-old unemployed rioter to onlooker Martin Luther King. How can we have won, King countered, when the community lay in ruins? "We won because we made the whole world pay attention to us," the rioter replied. "We made them come."

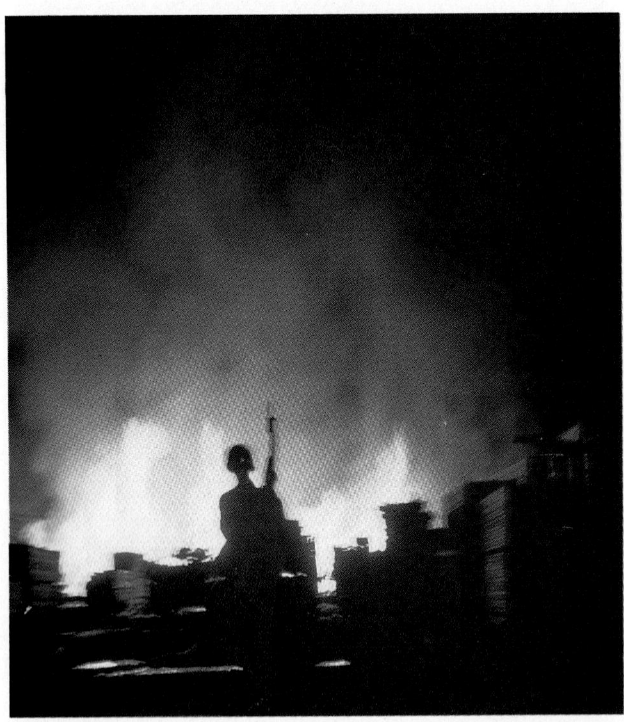

Watts in Flames

The nation's worst racial disturbance since the Detroit race riot of 1943 began in the Watts section of Los Angeles on August 11, 1965. An altercation broke out when white police officers stopped two blacks for a minor traffic violation. Thirty-four persons died in the Watts riot.

The riots of 1967 were the most serious of all. Rioting began in the spring in several southern cities, increased in number in June, and engulfed twenty-two cities in July and August. Large-scale disturbances hit Toledo, Ohio; Grand Rapids, Michigan; Plainfield, New Jersey; and Milwaukee, Wisconsin. Violent riots in Newark and Detroit produced widespread destruction and loss of life. Forty-three people were killed in Detroit alone, nearly all of them black, and at least a fourth of the city was burned, with $50 million worth of property destroyed. Federal paratroopers, some just back from service in Vietnam, were sent in to restore order, and Mayor Jerome Cavanaugh compared devastated Detroit to war-ravaged Berlin in 1945. As with most of the riots, the arson and looting were directed at white-owned stores and property, but there was little physical violence against white people. Almost all the reported sniping turned out to involve wild shooting by the police.

The riots finally provoked a response from the federal government. On July 29, 1967, President Lyndon Johnson appointed a special commission under Governor Otto Kerner of Illinois to investigate the reasons for the rioting. The final report of the National Advisory Commission on Civil Disorders, released in March 1968, detailed the patterns of inequality and racism embedded in urban life. It also issued a warning: "What white Americans have never fully understood—but what the Negro can never forget—is that white society is deeply implicated in the ghetto. White institutions created it, white institutions maintain it, and white society condones it. . . . Our nation is moving toward two societies, one black, one white—separate and unequal."

The Assassination of Martin Luther King. Barely a month after the Commission on Civil Disorders released its report, Martin Luther King was assassinated in Memphis, Tennessee. Reverend King had gone to that city to support a strike by predominantly black sanitation workers. On April 4, 1968, he was shot by James Earl Ray, a white ex-convict whose motive was unknown. King's death set off a final cataclysm of urban rioting. Major violence broke out in more than a hundred cities. As violence and looting engulfed most of Chicago's West Side, Mayor Richard J. Daley ordered police to "shoot to kill" suspected snipers. In Washington, National Guard troops with machine guns protected the Capitol; on television, it appeared framed by the fires from neighboring ghettoes.

With King's assassination, the civil rights movement lost the black leader most able to stir the conscience of white America. At the time of his death, he was only thirty-nine years old. During the last years of his life, King had moved toward a more comprehensive view of the structural problems of poverty and racism faced by blacks in contemporary America. In 1966 he had confronted the issue of residential segregation in a losing campaign for open housing in Chicago. He spoke out eloquently against the Vietnam War. In 1968 he was planning a poor people's campaign to raise issues of economic injustice and inequality.

King's death robbed the country of the one leader who could mediate between an increasingly fragmented black community and an ever more resistant white world. By the 1970s black Americans were too diverse economically and too divided politically to constitute a unified civil rights movement any longer. And the political climate had become too conservative to support further change.

The Legacy of the Civil Rights Movement. The 1950s and 1960s brought permanent, indeed revolutionary, changes in American race relations. Jim Crow segregation was overturned in less than a decade, and federal legislation granted black Americans their basic civil rights. The enfranchisement of African-Americans in southern states ended the political control there by a lily-white Democratic party, and candidates who had once been ardent segregationists now courted the black vote. In time Martin Luther King's greatness was recognized even in the South; in 1986 his birthday became a national holiday.

The Spreading Demand for Equal Rights

The civil rights movement inspired other groups, such as Hispanics and native Americans, to organize to press their claims. Until 1960 few Hispanic-Americans had participated in politics. Poverty, uncertain legal status, and language barriers kept them politically silent. This situation began to change when the Mexican-American Political Association (MAPA) mobilized support for John F. Kennedy in 1960, probably providing a margin of the victory in the closely contested states of Texas, New Mexico, and Illinois. In return, Kennedy appointed several Hispanic-American leaders to posts in Washington, and his administration paid increased attention to Hispanic issues.

Chicano activism. Younger Hispanics quickly grew impatient with MAPA, however. More radical and more inclined to celebrate cultural achievements and traditions, the younger leaders pursued increasingly diverse goals. The *barrios* of Los Angeles and other western cities produced the militant Brown Berets, who modeled themselves on the Black Panthers. In 1969, a new term, *Chicano*, was coined to replace Mexican-American. This revolution in consciousness also produced a political party, *La Raza Unida* (the united race), to promote Hispanic interests and candidates in public life.

Chicano strategists also pursued economic objectives. Working in the fields around Delano, California, labor leader Cesar Chavez organized the United Farm Workers, the first successful union to represent migrant workers. A 1965 grape pickers' strike and a nationwide boycott of table grapes brought Chavez and his union national publicity. Quietly advocating their cause, they won the support of the AFL–CIO and Senator Robert F. Kennedy of New York, and Chavez was soon receiving almost as much media attention as Martin Luther King, Jr. In 1968, Chavez undertook a twenty-five-day fast to protest the increasing strife and violence in the fields. Victory came in 1970, when California grape growers signed contracts recognizing the United Farm Workers.

Cesar Chavez

Mexican-American labor leader Cesar Chavez addresses a rally in Guadalupe, California. Chavez won national attention in 1965 during a strike of migrant farm workers, most of them Mexican-Americans, against California grape growers. Drawing on tactics from the civil rights movement, Chavez called for nonviolent action and effectively mobilized support from white liberals who boycotted non-union table grapes.

Asserting Rights for Native Americans. American Indians also found a model in the civil rights movement. Native Americans, who numbered nearly 800,000 in the 1960s, were an exceedingly diverse group, divided by language and tribal history, region, personal experience, and degree of integration into mainstream American life. But they shared certain things, such as an unemployment rate ten times the national average. Native Americans suffered the worst poverty, the most inadequate housing, the highest disease rates, and the least access to education of any group in the United States.

As early as World War II, the National Council of American Indians had lobbied for improvement. But now some Indian groups became more assertive. In 1961 representatives of sixty-seven tribes issued a Declaration of Indian Purpose that foreshadowed much of the later civil rights activism. During the War on Poverty, Indian groups successfully lobbied the Johnson administration to channel antipoverty funds into Indian communities. Paralleling the progression from liberal reform to more radical change seen in the civil rights movement, younger native Americans challenged the accommodationist approach of their elders. Like blacks and Hispanics, they proposed a new name for themselves—native Americans—and organized protests and demonstrations to build support for their cause. In 1968 several Chipewyan from Minnesota organized the militant American Indian Movement (AIM), which drew its strength from the third of the Indian population who lived in "red ghettoes" in cities throughout the West.

AIM consciously modeled itself on the black power movement, and for a few years its tactics attracted considerable public attention. In November 1969, AIM seized the deserted federal penitentiary on Alcatraz Island in San Francisco Bay, offering the government $24 worth of trinkets to pay for it. (This was supposedly what the Dutch had paid the local inhabitants for Manhattan Island in 1626.) The Indian occupation of Alcatraz lasted until the summer of 1971. In November 1972, a thousand protesters occupied the headquarters of the Federal Bureau of Indian Affairs in Washington, D.C., to many Indians a hated symbol of the inconsistent federal policy on behalf of tribal welfare. In February 1973, two hundred Sioux organized by AIM leaders began a seventy-one-day occupation of the tiny village of Wounded Knee, South Dakota, the site of the army

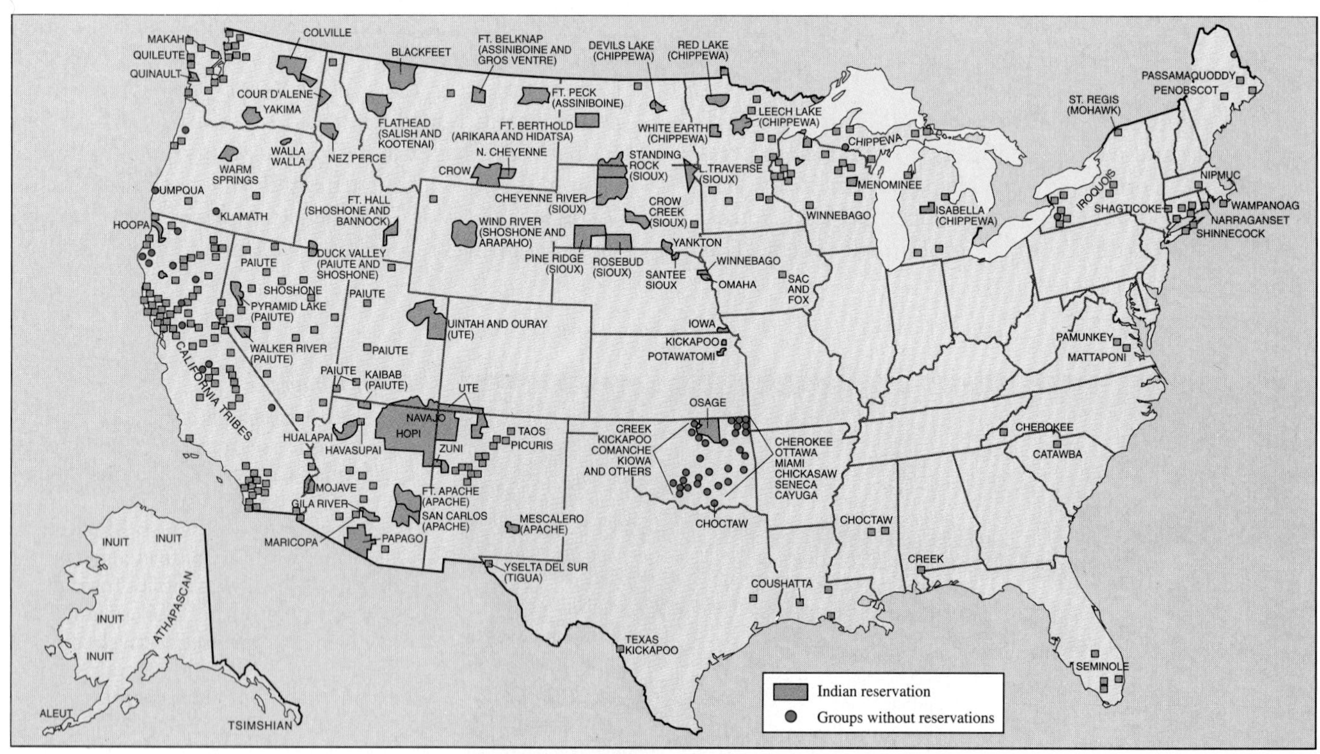

MAP 31.3

American Indian Reservations

Although native Americans have been able to preserve small enclaves in the northeastern states, most Indian reservations are in the West. In the 1990s various Indian tribes continue to press land claims against the federal and state governments.

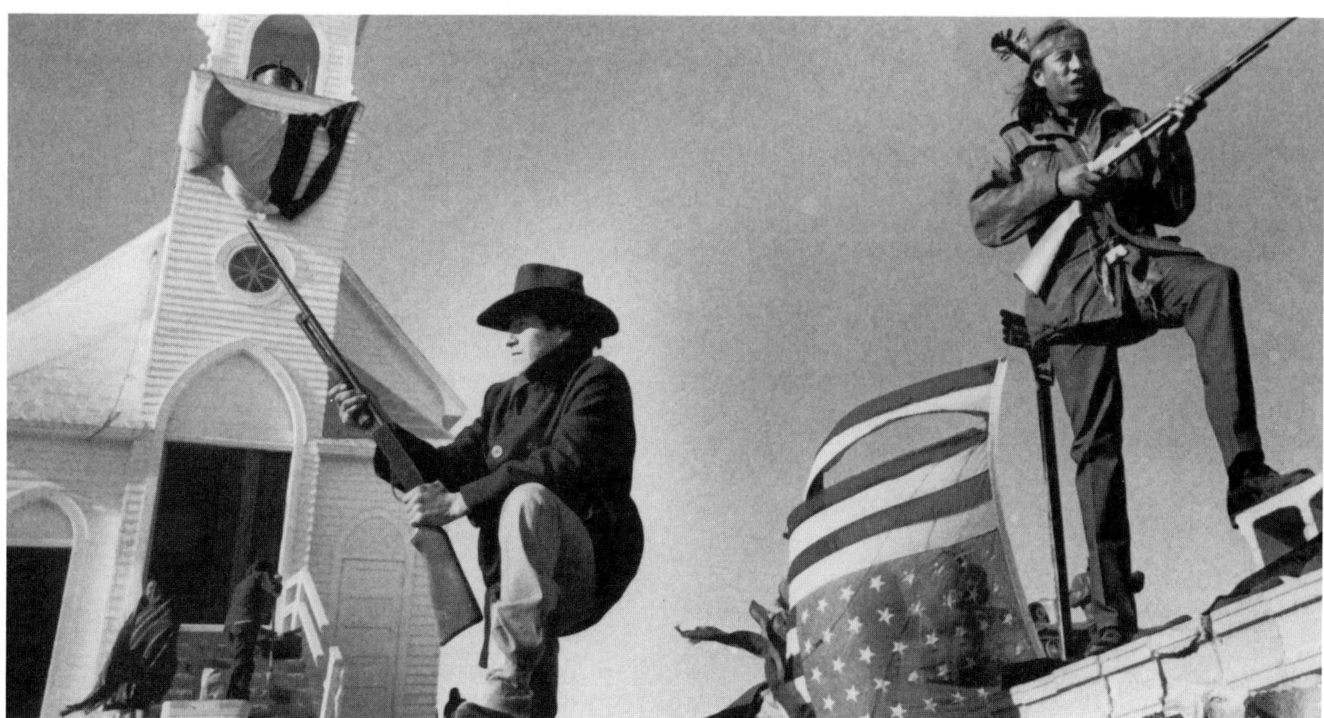

Wounded Knee Revisited

In 1973 members of the American Indian Movement staged a 71-day protest at Wounded Knee, South Dakota, the site of the 1890 massacre of two hundred Sioux by U.S. soldiers. The takeover was sparked by the murder of a local Sioux by a group of whites, but quickly expanded to include demands for basic reforms in federal Indian policy and tribal governance.

massacre of Sioux in 1890 (see Chapter 17). They were protesting the light sentences given a group of white men convicted of killing a Sioux in 1972. The protesters took eleven hostages and occupied several buildings to dramatize their cause. But when a gun battle with the FBI left one protester dead and another wounded, the siege collapsed.

These militant confrontations captured media attention, but often alienated public opinion. More effective in rousing white sympathy were a number of books published by a new generation of native American writers. *Custer Died for Your Sins* (1969), by Vine Deloria, Jr., a Sioux, N. Scott Momaday's Pulitzer Prize-winning novel *House Made of Dawn* (1968), and Dee Brown's best-selling *Bury My Heart at Wounded Knee* (1971) gave whites a better understanding of Indian history and concerns. As the nation marked the quincentenary of Columbus's arrival in 1492, historians continued to reconsider the meaning of that first encounter between native Americans and Europeans.

Other Voices. Civil rights, which began as a demand for the rights of black people, also spurred some predominantly white groups to claim justice, equality, and new identities. Americans of Polish, Italian, Greek, and Slavic descent, most of them working-class and Catholic, proudly embraced a new ethnic awareness modeled on black pride. George Wiley organized poor people, mostly women on welfare, into the National Welfare Rights Organization. Calling welfare a right, not a privilege, activists staged sit-ins at government offices to demand better treatment and higher benefits.

Homosexual men and women also banded together to protest legal and social discrimination based on sexual preference. The gay liberation movement was born in 1969 with the "Stonewall Riot" in New York City, when patrons of a gay bar in Greenwich Village fought back against police harassment. The assertion of gay pride that followed the Stonewall incident would probably not have occurred without the example of the civil rights movement. Adapting the model of the earlier movement, activists took the new name of gay rather than homosexual, founded advocacy groups, newspapers, and political organizations to challenge discrimination and prejudice, and provided emotional support for those who "came out" and publicly affirmed their homosexual identity. Models for increased political activism and heightened group identity represented one of the most important legacies of the African-American struggle to the rest of American society.

The Challenge of Youth

"There is everywhere protest, revaluation, attack on the Establishment," asserted social critic Paul Goodman at the end of the 1960s. Novelist Norman Mailer agreed. "We're in a time that's divorced from the past. . . . There's utterly no tradition anymore." The African-American drive for equality had ignited the challenge to established institutions. American youth joined in. New concerns roused young people, especially those from the white middle class, to mount colorful and sometimes shocking challenges to authority and traditional values. Vietnam would be the defining political issue of their generation.

Student Activism

The 1960s witnessed the first active student movement since the 1930s. The idealism of Kennedy's New Frontier raised students' expectations of what they and their society could accomplish. Then the civil rights movement exposed white youths to the brutality of race relations in the South and taught college students new protest tactics such as marches, sit-ins, and mass confrontations. In addition, the escalation of the Vietnam War in 1965 offered a compelling political cause to rally around, especially as the draft affected more college-age males.

The depression-scarred generation who came of age in the 1930s had been unable to afford higher education, but its children—the baby boomers—flocked to colleges and universities in the postwar period. In addition, many soldiers who had served during World War II and Korea used the benefits of the GI Bill to finance higher education that probably would have been out of their reach otherwise. In 1940, when only 15 percent of all college-age youth attended college, graduating was a major sign of upward social mobility for most minority and ethnic groups. In 1960, the year of John Kennedy's election, 40 percent of the college-age population was in college. In 1963, the year of his assassination, the proportion had reached almost 50 percent.

During the 1950s most students reflected the practical career-oriented values of their society. Engineering and business administration (for men) and home economics and teaching (for women) were the most popular courses of study, and students took little part in politics. Some critics suggested that students, responding to the repressive atmosphere of McCarthyism, had become a "silent generation." Even so, many young people felt dissatisfied in the 1950s. A vague awareness of the existence of poverty and the looming threat of nuclear war caused many to question the materialism of American society. J. D. Salinger's novel *Catcher in the Rye* (1951), which chronicled Holden Caulfield's quiet revulsion at the hypocrisy of his family, neighbors, and schoolmates, became a bestseller.

Early Stirrings. Student dissatisfaction began to coalesce in the early 1960s. In June 1962, forty students from Big Ten and Ivy League universities met at a United Auto Workers conference center in Port Huron, Michigan, to found the Students for a Democratic Society (SDS). Their manifesto, written by Tom Hayden, a University of Michigan student, drew heavily on the writing of radical Columbia sociologist C. Wright Mills. It expressed hostility toward bureaucracy, rejected cold war ideology, emphasized community participatory politics, and designated students as the major force for change in society. SDSers referred to their movement as the "New Left," to distinguish themselves from the "Old Left" Communists of the 1930s. SDS consciously adopted the activist tactics pioneered by SNCC and devoted much of its early attention to grass-roots organizing in the nation's cities and on campus.

The first student protests broke out at the University of California at Berkeley. In the fall of 1964 the university administration banned political activity near the Telegraph Avenue entrance to the campus, where student groups had traditionally distributed leaflets and recruited volunteers. In response, all the major student organizations, ranging from SNCC and SDS to the conservative Youth for Goldwater, formed a coalition to protest what they considered an abridgment of free speech. The Free Speech Movement organized a sit-in at the main administration building and persuaded the university to drop the ban.

The Free Speech Movement owed a strong debt to the civil rights movement. Berkeley had sent more volunteers to Freedom Summer in Mississippi in 1964 than any other campus, and the students had been radicalized by the experience. Free Speech leader Mario Savio spoke for many of them:

> Last summer I went to Mississippi to join the struggle there for civil rights. This fall I am engaged in another phase of the same struggle, this time in Berkeley. The two battlefields may seem quite different to some observers, but this is not the case. The same rights are at stake in both places—the right to participate as citizens in a democratic society and to struggle against the same enemy. In Mississippi an autocratic and powerful minority rules, through organized violence, to suppress the vast, virtually powerless majority. In California, the privileged minority manipulates the university bureaucracy to suppress the students' political expression.

On a deeper level, Berkeley students were challenging the university because it had grown too big, too impersonal, and too insulated from the major social issues of the day. The largest universities, like the largest cor-

Free Speech at Berkeley, 1964

These student activists at the University of California's Berkeley campus mounted an effective protest against the administration over the issue of free speech using tactics learned from the civil rights movement. In fact, some of these students may have just returned from Freedom Summer in Mississippi—Berkeley sent more volunteers than any other campus.

porations, had grown the fastest in the postwar era. In 1940, only two campuses had as many as 20,000 students. By 1969, thirty-nine were at least that large. Many students objected that they were treated as impersonally as a computer punch card in these "multiversities." "I am a student," one slogan ran, "Please do not fold, spindle, or mutilate." Emboldened by the Berkeley experience, students at institutions across the country were soon protesting everything from dress codes to course requirements, tenure decisions, and academic grading systems.

Students also protested the universities' complicity in the problems of the ghettoes that surrounded many urban campuses. Columbia, for example, was a major property owner in Harlem, which bordered on its campus. In 1968, Columbia announced plans to build a new gymnasium, displacing local stores and housing. Chanting "Gym Crow Must Go," students tore down the fence at the construction site and took over several Columbia buildings, including the office of President Grayson Kirk. (Photographs of protesters sampling Kirk's cigars and sherry did little to build public support.) At Berkeley, students and administrators clashed in 1969 over a parcel of vacant land near campus that a coalition of students and residents had turned into a "People's Park." When the university asserted its rights to the land, a violent confrontation broke out and an onlooker was killed. At both Columbia and Berkeley, the administration decided to use city police officers to break up the demonstrations; the brutality of the police radicalized far more students than had originally supported the protests. As campus disturbances spread, and more and more university buildings were blocked, occupied, or picketed, classes had to be canceled and academic life temporarily came to a halt.

Although black students participated in many of the protests, student movements increasingly split along racial lines, reflecting the separatism that affected the civil rights movement by the mid-1960s. Strongly inspired by the black power movement, black students at predominantly black institutions like Howard University and at mainly white universities demanded more courses in African-American history and culture. University administrators were open to such demands as a way to ease campus unrest, and many universities established separate Afro-American or Black Studies departments in the late 1960s and early 1970s. Black protestors also won university support for separate dormitories and cultural centers, a protest against the racism black students claimed pervaded university life on predominantly white campuses.

The Antiwar Movement. But no issue provoked more impassioned and sustained protest than the Vietnam War. In March 1965, several months after the Free Speech confrontation at Berkeley, President Johnson dramatically escalated the Vietnam War by committing American ground troops and bombing North Vietnam.

In response, faculty members and student activists at the University of Michigan organized a *teach-in* against the war. In marathon sessions they debated the political, diplomatic, and moral facets of U.S. involvement in Vietnam. Teach-ins quickly spread to other universities, as students turned their full attention to protesting the Vietnam war.

A strong spur to activism was a change in the Selective Service System. In the past, students could use deferments for college, graduate school, teaching, and parenthood to avoid the draft until they reached the cut-off age of twenty-six. But in response to criticisms about the unfairness of this system, the Selective Service System gradually phased out deferments. In January 1966 automatic student deferments were abolished altogether.

Young men's options were limited. Some enlisted in the National Guard or reserves to avoid being sent to Vietnam. Some reluctant draftees sought out sympathetic doctors to give them medical or psychiatric excuses or help them flunk the induction physical. Some filed for conscientious objector status, fulfilling their military commitment through alternative service in the United States or noncombatant duty in Vietnam. Several thousand ignored the induction notice entirely, risking prosecution for draft evasion. The Resistance, started at Berkeley and Stanford and widely recognized by its Omega symbol, provided support to draft resisters, but thousands left the country altogether (Canada and Sweden were the most popular destinations). Opponents of the war burned their draft cards in public acts of civil disobedience, closed down induction centers with mass protests, and on a few occasions broke into Selective Service offices to destroy or mutilate files.

As antiwar and draft protests increased after 1965, students realized that their own universities were deeply implicated in the war effort. In some cases as much as 60 percent of a university's research budget came from government contracts, especially from the Defense Department. Protesters blocked campus recruitment by the Dow Chemical Company because it produced the napalm used to burn Vietnamese villages and Agent Orange, which defoliated South Vietnam's forests. Arguing that universities should not train students for war, protesters demanded that the Reserve Officer Training Corps (ROTC) be removed from campus. ROTC was one of the main targets of the student protests at Columbia in 1968 and Harvard in 1969.

Mass Protests. Mass demonstrations against the war consumed much of the energy of the student movement in the late 1960s. Students became part of the much larger antiwar movement of peace activists, housewives, religious leaders, and a few elected officials. On October 15, 1969, millions joined a one-day "moratorium" on business as usual to demonstrate against the war. On November 15, 1969, hundreds of thousands of people mobilized in Washington to call for an end to the fighting in Vietnam.

The most extensive outbreak of student unrest came in the spring of 1970, after President Richard M. Nixon ordered American troops to invade Cambodia. Student leaders organized a national student strike in protest. At Kent State University outside Cleveland, panicky National Guardsmen fired into a crowd of students at a noontime antiwar rally on May 4. Four people were killed and eleven wounded. Only two of those killed, Jeffrey Miller and Alison Krause, had been at the demonstration; William Shroeder and Sandra Scheur were passing by on their way to class. Soon after, two black students were killed at Jackson State College in Mississippi. More than 450 colleges closed down on strike, and 80 percent of all American college campuses experienced some kind of protest.

In June 1970, immediately after the Kent State slayings, a Gallup poll reported that campus unrest was the main issue troubling Americans. But after 1970 the universities basically stayed calm. Student strikes in the spring of 1971 and 1972 never approached the intensity of the earlier demonstrations. Students had effectively challenged many aspects of university control over their lives, but their broader attack on American society had

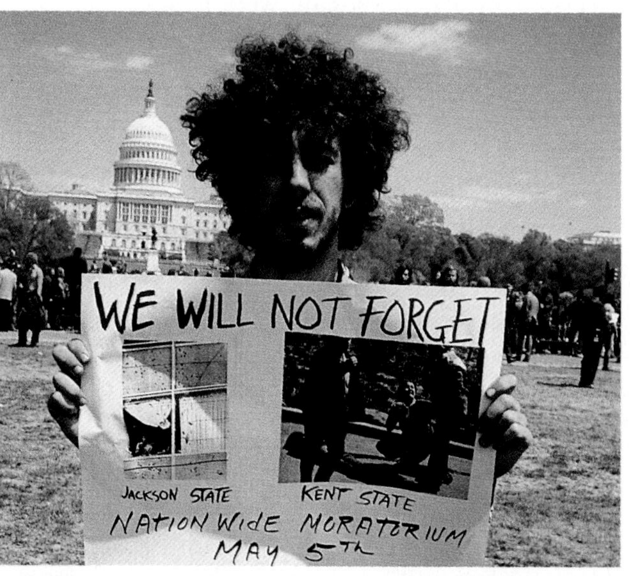

Kent State

The shootings by National Guardsmen of four students at Kent State University in Ohio on May 4, 1970, set off campus demonstrations and protests throughout the country. The protestor shown here holds a placard memorializing the slain students, as well as the two black students killed soon after at Jackson State College in Mississippi. The president of Columbia University called May 1970 "the most disastrous month . . . in the history of American higher education."

been less successful. They returned to the classroom, somewhat cynical, burned out, and no longer confident they could change the world.

The Rise of the Counterculture

Alongside student activism and protest, new forms of cultural expression emerged among the nation's young. In an amazingly short period of time, youth's clothing and hair styles changed radically. At Berkeley's Free Speech demonstrations in 1964, young men wore coats and ties, women skirts and sweaters. At the antiwar protests just three or four years later, youth defiantly dressed in a unisex fashion that featured ragged blue jeans, tie-dyed T-shirts, beads, and other adornments. Unorthodox clothes and long, unkempt hair identified a new phenomenon of American youth culture, the *hippie*. The uncomprehending older generation often had a simple response: "Get a haircut."

The Beats. The forerunners of the hippies were members of the Beat Generation of the 1950s. In the post-McCarthy climate of conformity, rebellion in the 1950s was more likely to take artistic than political forms. "Beats" such as poet Allen Ginsberg and writer Jack Kerouac were among the first to articulate the personal alienation that was at the heart of much of the rebelliousness of the 1960s. Kerouac's *On the Road* (1957), the tale of a group of drifters hitchhiking across the country, became the bible of the Beat Generation. Beats popularized beards for men, black tights for women, and sandals for both sexes. They experimented with sex and drugs and helped revive interest in folk music.

Popular Music. Throughout the 1960s, as one journalist noted, "popular music coincided uncannily with changing political moods." Folk singer Pete Seeger, free at last from the McCarthy-era blacklist, set the tone for the era's political idealism with such songs as the antiwar ballad "Where Have All the Flowers Gone?" In 1963, the year of the Birmingham demonstrations and President Kennedy's assassination, Bob Dylan's "Blowin' in the Wind" reflected the impatience of people whose liberalism was turning sour.

Early in 1964, the Beatles, four working-class youths from Liverpool, England, burst onto the American scene. Like Elvis Presley eight years earlier, they thrust their way into the national consciousness by a series of television appearances on the "Ed Sullivan Show." The Beatles's music, by turns lyrical and driving, was phenomenally successful, spawning a commercial and cultural phenomenon called Beatlemania. The more rebellious, angrier music of other British groups, notably the Rolling Stones, found a broad audience shortly afterward.

Sgt. Pepper's Lonely Hearts Club Band
The colorful collage on the cover of this 1967 Beatles's album allowed fans to debate (occasionally under the influence of marijuana or LSD) the symbolism of those chosen. Can you identify Mae West, Karl Marx, Bob Dylan, Albert Einstein, Lenny Bruce, Marilyn Monroe, as well as the "Fab Four" in their various disguises? (©Apple Corps Ltd.)

Drug Culture. Drugs were almost as important as rock music in the youth culture of the 1960s. Drugs were hardly new to the American scene: many jazz musicians from the 1920s on had used heroin and cocaine, and the Beats had experimented with mind-altering drugs in San Francisco. Now widespread recreational use of drugs extended beyond artistic and jazz circles.

Marijuana was the preferred drug among college students, but stronger drugs also gained popularity. The hallucinogen lysergic acid diethylamide, popularly known as LSD or "acid," was one of the most potent. It was popularized in California by writer Ken Kesey and his Merry Pranksters, who conducted "acid tests" (public "happenings" where tabs of LSD were distributed) in 1965 and 1966. San Francisco bands such as the Grateful Dead and the Jefferson Airplane, guitarist Jimi Hendrix, and Britain's Pink Floyd developed a style of music known as "acid rock." Even the Beatles, whose early songs had simply stated "I Want to Hold Your Hand" and "Please Please Me," now recorded tunes like "Lucy in the Sky with Diamonds," whose "tangerine trees and marmalade skies" celebrated the new drug-induced consciousness.

For a brief time, adherents of the *counterculture*—so named because it challenged so many established values—believed a new age was dawning. "The closest Western Civilization has come to uniting since the Congress of Vienna in 1815 was the week the *Sgt. Pepper* album was released," gushed a rock critic in 1968 about the newest Beatles's release. Others pointed to the "age of Aquarius" trumpeted in the 1968 Broadway rock musical *Hair.* In 1967, the "world's first Human Be-In" drew 20,000 people to Golden Gate Park in San Francisco. Allen Ginsberg "purified" the site with a Buddhist ritual, political activists embraced "drug freaks," and LSD advocate Timothy Leary, a former Harvard psychology instructor, urged the gathering to "turn on to the scene, tune in to what is happening, and drop out."

Hippies. "Tune in, turn on, drop out" and "Make love, not war" became catchwords for youthful alienation. By the summer of 1967, San Francisco's Haight-Ashbury, New York's East Village, Chicago's Uptown, and similar hippie neighborhoods in other large cities were crowded with young people, as well as swarms of reporters and busloads of tourists who gawked at the so-called flower children. The faith in instant love and peace quickly began to turn sour, however, as dropouts, drifters, and teenage runaways tried to cope with bad drug trips, venereal disease, loneliness, and violence. In 1967, seventeen murders and more than a hundred rapes were reported in Haight-Ashbury alone.

Another way to drop out was to join a commune. Many communes were located in isolated areas such as the mountains between Santa Cruz and San Francisco, the wide open spaces of New Mexico, or the rural solitude of Vermont, out of the watchful eye of mainstream America (and local drug enforcement agents). Communes, following in the utopian tradition, provided an economic and sexual alternative to nuclear families. They also promised a return to the land, as members banded together to grow their own food, bake their own bread, and reject the materialism and commercialism of American life. But the communes of the 1960s did not just look backward. Their advocacy of organic farming—growing food without chemicals or pesticides—anticipated the environmental concerns that would emerge in the 1970s and 1980s (see Chapter 32).

Meanwhile, the appeal of rock music and drugs continued to spread. In August 1969, four hundred thousand young people journeyed to Bethel, New York, to attend the Woodstock Music Festival. Despite torrential rain, people "got high" on music, drugs, and sex. The successful festival gave its name to the "Woodstock generation" of the late 1960s.

By 1970 the youth culture had revolutionized lifestyles and cultural expression. Even as political activism and rebellion waned, their spirit was absorbed and marketed by the consumer culture. The crowds at Woodstock and other rock festivals revealed the size of the youth market, and corporate entrepreneurs rushed to cash in on it.

The alternative values of the 1960s soon filtered into the dominant culture. *The Village Voice* and *Rolling Stone* outgrew their beginnings as underground publications and became respected voices of American journalism. Symbols of cultural defiance were coopted and homogenized by the mass culture. The ragged "bell bottoms" of the 1960s became the expensive designer jeans of the 1970s. The unkempt hair and beards of male hippies emboldened some middle-aged executives to sport a moustache or allow their hair to cover their ears. The "Afro" hairstyle, once worn only by radical black activists, was now favored by blacks and whites of both sexes who let their hair go natural. Women's fashion picked up the theme of personal liberation with the miniskirt, an innovation that had arrived from England in the mid-1960s. Women also found greater acceptance for wearing pants in public, even on the job. Many of these cultural changes continue to influence American life today.

Flower Children

Yale law professor Charles A. Reich celebrated the new freedom of youth in his best-selling book, *The Greening of America* (1970). Reich described a new consciousness that had "emerged out of the wasteland of the Corporate State, like flowers pushing up through the concrete pavement." Counterculture hippies were also called flower children.

The Revival of Feminism

In 1960, feminism was a dead issue. The words *sexism* and *Ms.* had not been coined. There were no rape crisis centers, women's health collectives, or battered women's shelters. Not a single university offered a course in women's studies, and women's sports programs were small and underfunded. At least ten thousand women a year lost their lives in illegal back-alley abortions.

All that changed during the next fifteen years. The women's movement rivaled the civil rights movement in the success it achieved in a short period of time. By the mid-1970s, however, feminism had provoked a backlash, and its progress too had stalled.

Women's Changing Lives

Social movements do not just spring up when leaders announce a set of demands. Leaders arise only when there is a constituency ready to be mobilized. Preconditions for feminism lay in the changing social and demographic bases of women's lives, especially increased labor force participation, greater access to higher education, the declining birthrate, and changing patterns of marriage.

The most important factor was the dramatic rise in women's participation in the work force during the postwar years. In 1950 almost one-third of women were employed, and one-quarter of them were married. By 1970, 42.6 percent of women were working, and four out of ten working women were married. Especially significant was the growth in the number of working women with preschool children—up from 12 percent in 1950 to 30 percent in 1970. Working mothers had become both socially accepted and economically necessary.

Women also benefited from increased access to education. Immediately after World War II the percentage of women college students had declined: the GI Bill gave men a temporary advantage in access to higher education, and many college women dropped out of school to marry and raise families at the height of the baby boom. By 1960, however, the percentage of women students had climbed to 35 percent, and by 1970 to 41 percent.

The meaning of marriage was changing too. The baby boom only temporarily interrupted the century-long decline in the birthrate. The introduction of the birth control pill, first marketed in 1960, and the intrauterine device (IUD) helped women control their fertility, as did the legalization of abortion in the 1970s. Women had fewer children and, because of increased life expectancy (75 years in 1970, up from 54 years in 1920), spent fewer years of their lives involved primarily in childcare. At the same time, the divorce rate, which had risen slowly through the twentieth century, shot up. It doubled from 15 per thousand marriages in 1960 to 32 per thousand in 1975. Women could no longer assume that their marriages would last until "death do us part."

As a result of these changes, traditional gender expectations were dramatically undercut. To be female in America now usually included work and marriage, often childrearing and a career, and possibly bringing up children as a single parent after a divorce. These changing social realities created a major constituency for the revival of feminism in the 1960s.

Paths to Feminism

During the 1960s, two distinct movements renewed the national interest in women's concerns. The *women's rights* branch of the new feminism, led by the National Organization for Women (NOW), consisted of older,

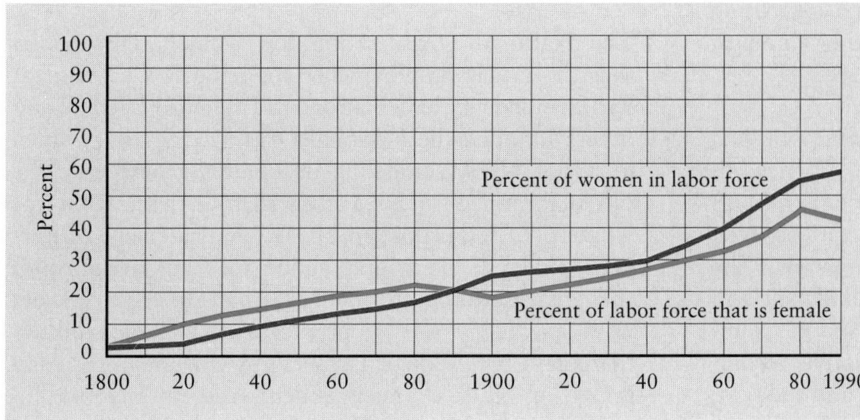

FIGURE 31.1

Women in the Labor Force, 1800–1990

Over the past two centuries, women have steadily increased their participation in the labor force. Paid employment outside the home is now part of the life cycle for most women.

Joanie Caucus, Modern Woman

The character of Joanie Caucus in Garry Trudeau's popular comic strip, *Doonesbury,* provided a running commentary on women's changing lives in the 1960s and 1970s. Caucus, a former housewife, ran away from her husband and family to a commune and then tried to raise the consciousness of the children at the day care center where she worked. Here she applies to law school. After graduation, she became a legislative aide to a female member of Congress, remarried, and had a child in her forties. (Doonesbury, By Garry Trudeau. Copyright, 1974, G. B. Trudeau. Reprinted with permission of Universal Press Syndicate. All rights reserved.)

politically active professional women who sought political change by working through the system. The *women's liberation* branch, on the other hand, attracted primarily younger women—especially recent college graduates who had been active in civil rights, the New Left, and the antiwar movement. Their vision of feminism was more radical and confrontational: mirroring the separatism of black power advocates, they were initially quite hostile to men.

Women's Rights. In 1961, President Kennedy established a Presidential Commission on the Status of Women, an attempt to counter criticism about his administration's poor record on women's issues. Eleanor Roosevelt served as honorary head of the commission. The group's 1963 report documented the employment and educational discrimination faced by women, but its impact extended beyond its rather conservative recommendations. The presidential commission, and the state commissions that were its offshoots, set up a rudimentary nationwide network of women in public life who were concerned about feminist issues.

One spark that ignited the revival of feminism was Betty Friedan's bestselling book, *The Feminine Mystique,* published in 1963. This book, a pointed indictment of the trap of women's suburban domesticity, grew out of her own experiences as a housewife in the 1950s. Friedan called it "the problem that has no name":

> As she made the beds, shopped for groceries, matched slipcover material, ate peanut butter sandwiches with her children, chauffeured Cub Scouts and Brownies, lay beside her husband at night—she was afraid to ask even of herself the silent question—"Is this all?"

Women responded enthusiastically to Friedan's story, especially the white, college-educated, middle-class women whose backgrounds resembled the author's. Friedan's book sold three million copies, and many more women read excerpts in major women's magazines. *The Feminine Mystique* gave women a vocabulary for their dissatisfaction and introduced many women to the powerful ideas of modern feminism.

Legislative Change. Like so many constituencies in postwar America, women's rights activists looked to the federal government for action. In 1963, as recommended by the Presidential Commission on the Status of Women, Congress passed the Equal Pay Act, which directed that men and women be paid the same wages for doing the same job.

Even more important was the Civil Rights Act of 1964, which had as great an impact on women as it did on blacks and other minorities. The key provision, Title VII, barred discrimination in employment on the basis of race, color, religion, national origin, or sex. The category of sex was added by a conservative representative, Howard Smith of Virginia. He did this not out of concern for women's equality—he called it "my little amendment"—but to make the civil rights bill so controversial as to kill it completely. His strategy backfired. Title VII eventually became a powerful legal tool in the fight against sex discrimination.

The National Organization for Women. Dissatisfied that the Equal Employment Opportunity Commission had avoided implementation of Title VII, Friedan and others founded the National Organization for Women in 1966. NOW, modeling itself after groups like the NAACP, aimed to be a civil rights organization for women. "The purpose of NOW," its statement of purpose declared, "is to take action to bring women into full participation in the mainstream of American society now, exercising all the privileges and responsibilities thereof in truly equal partnership with men." Friedan served as NOW's first president, and its membership grew from 1,000 in 1967 to 15,000 in 1971. Men made up a fourth of NOW's early membership. It is still the largest feminist organization in the United States.

Women's Liberation. Women's liberationists came to feminism by a different path. White women had made up about half the students who went South with SNCC in the 1964 Freedom Summer voter-registration project. While in Mississippi, they received conflicting messages. College women developed self-confidence and organizational skills and found role models in the black women and older southern white women who were prominent in the civil rights movement, such as Ella Baker, Anne Braden, and Virginia Foster Durr. Yet women volunteers also found that they were expected to do all the cleaning and cooking at the Freedom Houses where SNCC volunteers lived. "We didn't come down here to work as a maid this summer," one complained.

Intensely committed to civil rights, and lacking a feminist vocabulary to express their concerns, Freedom Summer volunteers raised their objections only tentatively. When they did, they compared women's position with that of blacks. "Assumptions of male superiority are as widespread and deeply rooted and every much as crippling to the woman as the assumptions of white superiority are to the Negro," they argued. Both black and white men in the movement laughed off these attempts to raise feminist issues. Stokely Carmichael made one of the most notorious retorts: "The only position for women in SNCC is prone."

Black power militancy made white women unwelcome in the civil rights movement after 1965. But when they transferred their energies to student and antiwar groups, they found the New Left equally male-dominated and unsupportive. Once again, women were expected to take notes or serve coffee, while men monopolized the leadership roles. As the New Left focused increasingly on draft resistance as a strategy to oppose the war, women found themselves treated primarily as sex objects. "Girls say yes to guys who say no," went a popular slogan. Women who tried to raise feminist issues at conventions were shouted off the platform with such jeers as "Move on, little girl, we have more important issues to talk about here than women's liberation." The "little girl" who received this taunt was Shulamith Firestone, whose *The Dialectic of Sex* (1971) was an early text of the women's movement.

Around 1967 groups of radical women realized that they needed their own movement. The contradictions between the New Left's commitment to egalitarianism and women's actual treatment by male leaders became so striking that women felt they had no other choice. This process occurred independently in five or six cities, including Chicago, San Francisco, and New York. In contrast to women's rights groups like NOW, which had traditional organizational structures and dues-paying members, radical women participated in loose collectives with shifting memberships that often lacked any coordinating structure at all.

The women's liberation movement (or "women's lib," as it was dubbed by the somewhat hostile media) went public when it staged a protest at the 1968 Miss America pageant. The demonstration included a "freedom trash can," into which women were encouraged to throw false eyelashes, hair curlers, brassieres, and girdles—all considered symbols of female oppression. The media quickly labeled the radical feminists "bra burners." The derisive name stuck, although no brassieres were actually burned.

A technique of more lasting impact was *consciousness raising*, group sessions in which women shared common experiences about being female. Swapping stories about being passed over for promotion, needing a husband's signature on a credit card application, or enduring the humiliation of whistles and leers while simply walking down the street helped participants to realize that their individual problems were part of wider patterns of oppression. (The women's movement called this moment of epiphany "click.") The slogan "The personal is political" became a watchword of the early radical feminists.

The High Tide of Feminism

Before 1969 most women learned about the feminist movement through word of mouth. After that, media attention brought women's issues to a much broader audience than could ever have been reached by NOW or the women's liberation collectives. A flood of new converts broke down the barriers between the two branches of the movement. Feminism's potential as a mass movement was demonstrated on August 26, 1970, when thousands of women throughout the country marched to celebrate the fiftieth anniversary of the Nineteenth Amendment.

The distinction between women's rights and women's liberation also began to blur because of the growing convergence of interests. Radical women learned that key feminist goals—child care, equal pay, abortion rights—could best be achieved in the political arena. At the same time, more traditional political activists developed a broader view of women's oppression, including tentative support for divisive issues like lesbianism and abortion. Feminists were beginning to think of themselves as part of a broad, growing, and increasingly influential social movement. "It's not a movement," said journalist Sally Kempton, "it's a state of mind." Robin Morgan's best-selling book, *Sisterhood is Powerful* (1970), similarly reflected feminist optimism. Only later did the movement grapple with the fact that perhaps as many issues divided women—race, class, age, sexual preference—as unified them.

AMERICAN VOICES

The Politics of Housework *Pat Mainardi*

The slogan "the personal is political" brought feminism into many aspects of daily life. Nowhere were disputes more heated than over housework, traditionally considered women's work. Painter Pat Mainardi, a member of the radical feminist group Redstockings, describes the ongoing debate with her husband over who would do what, a dialogue repeated in many households.

"I don't mind sharing the housework, but I don't do it very well. We should each do the things we're best at."

Meaning: Unfortunately I'm no good at things like washing dishes or cooking. What I do best is a little light carpentry, changing light bulbs, moving furniture *(how often do you move furniture?)*

Also Meaning: Historically the lower classes (black men and us) have had hundreds of years experience doing menial jobs. It would be a waste of manpower to train someone else to do them now.

Also Meaning: I don't like the dull stupid boring jobs, so you should do them.

"I don't mind sharing the work, but you'll have to show me how to do it."

Meaning: I ask a lot of questions and you'll have to show me everything everytime I do it because I don't remember so good. Also don't try to sit down and read while I'm doing my jobs because I'm going to annoy the hell out of you until it's easier to do them yourself.

"We used to be so happy!" (Said whenever it was his turn to do something.)

Meaning: I used to be so happy.

Meaning: Life without housework is bliss. *(No quarrel here. Perfect agreement.)*

"We have different standards, and why should I have to work to your standards. That's unfair."

Meaning: If I begin to get bugged by the dirt and crap I will say "This place sure is a sty" or "How can anyone live like this?" and wait for your reaction. I know that all women have a sore called "Guilt over a messy house" or "Household work is ultimately my responsibility." I know that men have caused that sore—if anyone visits and the place *is* a sty, they're not going to leave and say, "He sure is a lousy housekeeper." You'll take the rap in any case. I can outwait you.

Also Meaning: I can provoke innumerable scenes over the housework issue. Eventually doing all the housework yourself will be less painful to you than trying to get me to do half. Or I'll suggest we get a maid. She will do my share of the work. You will do yours. It's women's work.

"I've got nothing against sharing the housework, but you can't make me do it on your schedule."

Meaning: Passive resistance. I'll do it when I damned well please, if at all. If my job is doing dishes, it's easier to do them once a week. If taking out laundry, once a month. If washing the floors, once a year. If you don't like it, do it yourself oftener, and then I won't do it at all.

"I *hate* it more than you. You don't mind it so much."

Meaning: Housework is garbage work. It's the worst crap I've ever done. It's degrading and humiliating for someone of *my* intelligence to do it. But for someone of *your* intelligence . . .

"Housework is too trivial to even talk about."

Meaning: It's even more trivial to do. Housework is beneath my status. My purpose in life is to deal with matters of significance. Yours is to deal with matters of insignificance. You should do the housework.

"This problem of housework is not a man-woman problem! In any relationship between two people one is going to have a stronger personality and dominate."

Meaning: That stronger personality had better be *me*.

"In animal societies, wolves, for example, the top animal is usually a male even where he is not chosen for brute strength but on the basis of cunning and intelligence. Isn't that interesting?"

Meaning: I have historical, psychological, anthropological, and biological justification for keeping you down. How can you ask the top wolf to be equal?

"Women's liberation isn't really a political movement."

Meaning: The Revolution is coming too close to home.

Also Meaning: I am only interested in how *I* am oppressed, not how I oppress others. Therefore the [Vietnam] war, the draft, and the university are political. Women's liberation is not.

"Man's accomplishments have always depended on getting help from other people, mostly women. What great man would have accomplished what he did if he had to do his own housework?"

Meaning: Oppression is built into the System and I, as the white American male receive the benefits of this System. I don't want to give them up.

Postscript

Participatory democracy begins at home.

Source: Pat Mainardi, "The Politics of Housework," in Robin Morgan, ed., *Sisterhood is Powerful: An Anthology of Writings from the Women's Liberation Movement* (New York: Random House, 1970), 503–6.

Significant progress in the battle for women's equality occurred in the early 1970s. The media made new terms such as "sexism" and "male chauvinism" part of the national vocabulary. Many colleges across the country started women's studies programs. Former all-male bastions, including Yale, Princeton, and the U.S. Military Academy, admitted women undergraduates for the first time; women's colleges like Vassar and Sarah Lawrence admitted men. Gloria Steinem and other journalists founded *Ms.* magazine in 1972. The proportion of women in graduate and professional schools rose.

Women were increasingly visible in politics and public life. The National Women's Political Caucus, founded in 1971, actively promoted the election of women to public office. Bella Abzug, Elizabeth Holtzman, Shirley Chisholm, Patricia Schroeder, and Geraldine Ferraro served in Congress; Ella Grasso won election as Connecticut's governor in 1974, and Dixie Lee Ray as Washington's in 1976. Twenty thousand women came to Houston in November 1977 for the first National Women's Conference, part of the observance of the United Nations' International Women's Year. Their "National Plan of Action" represented a hard-won consensus on topics ranging from violence against women to homemakers' rights, the needs of older women, health, and, most controversially, reproductive freedom.

The women's movement achieved passage of significant federal legislation. The Equal Credit Opportunity Act of 1974 made it possible for women to get credit, including charge cards and mortgages, in their own names and based on their (not their husband's) incomes. Congress authorized child-care deductions for working parents and employment benefits for married female federal employees. In many cases, federal policies on civil rights were simply extended to include women as well as men. Title IX of the Educational Amendments Act of 1972 broadened the coverage of the 1964 Civil Rights Act to educational institutions; it prohibited colleges and universities that received federal funds from discriminating on the basis of sex. By requiring schools to fund sports programs for women at a comparable level to men, Title IX increased women's access to sports dramatically.

Supreme Court Victories. The Supreme Court also advanced the cause of women's rights, although not always as a result of pressure from the women's movement. In several rulings, the Court read a right of privacy into the Ninth and Fourteenth amendments' concept of personal liberty to give women more control over their reproductive lives. In 1965, the case of *Griswold v. Connecticut* overturned state laws against the sale of contraceptive devices to married adults; in 1972, *Baird v. Eisenstadt* extended this protection to single persons. In 1973, *Roe v. Wade* struck down Texas and Georgia statutes that allowed abortions only if the mother's life was in danger. According to this 7–2 decision, states could no longer outlaw abortions during the first trimester, or three months, of pregnancy. Rather than addressing the issue in feminist terms, such as women's right to control their bodies, the justices interpreted abortion as a medical issue, basing their decision on the confidentiality of the doctor-patient relationship as well as the right of privacy. *Roe v. Wade* nationalized the liberalization of state abortion laws that had begun in New York in 1970.

Running for Women's Rights

Feminists including Bella Abzug (in hat) and Betty Friedan (far right), join runners who carried a torch from Seneca Falls, New York, site of the first women's rights convention in 1848, to Houston for the 1977 National Women's Conference. Funded by Congress in honor of International Women's Year, the conference brought together two thousand delegates and twenty thousand observers who adopted a National Plan of Action for women's rights.

The Equal Rights Amendment. In the 1970s the women's movement increasingly united around the proposed Equal Rights Amendment to the Constitution (ERA), which stated in its entirety, "Equality of Rights under the law shall not be denied or abridged by the United States or any State on the basis of sex." The ERA, first introduced in Congress in 1923 by the National Woman's party, was dusted off by modern feminists. In 1970 the measure passed the House but died in the Senate. In the 1971–1972 session, it passed both houses and was submitted to the states for ratification. Thirty-four states quickly passed the ERA between 1972 and 1974. Then the momentum stopped, confirming the pattern that once a constitutional amendment becomes controversial, its chances for success plummet. Only Indiana ratified after that point, leaving the amendment three states short of the necessary three-fourths majority. Most of the non-ratifying states were in the South; Illinois also held out, despite spirited campaigns there by ERA supporters. Congress extended the deadline for ratification until June 30, 1982, but the Equal Rights Amendment still fell short.

Stalemate

The fate of the ERA suggested that, by the mid-1970s, the momentum of the women's movement was beginning to slow or even stop. Although 63 percent of women told the Harris poll in 1975 that they favored "efforts to strengthen and change women's status in society," a growing minority of men and women expressed concern over what seemed to be revolutionary changes in women's roles. A new conservatism was influencing political and social life by the mid-1970s, spearheaded by the Moral Majority and other organizations whose members belonged largely to evangelical Protestant groups (see Chapter 32). Especially disturbing to these conservatives were changes in attitudes that seemed to denigrate women who chose to stay home as full-time housewives.

Phyllis Schlafly, long active in conservative causes—she had written *A Choice, Not an Echo*, a best-seller extolling Barry Goldwater in 1963—led the antifeminist backlash. Despite her law degree and active career while raising five children, Schlafly advocated traditional

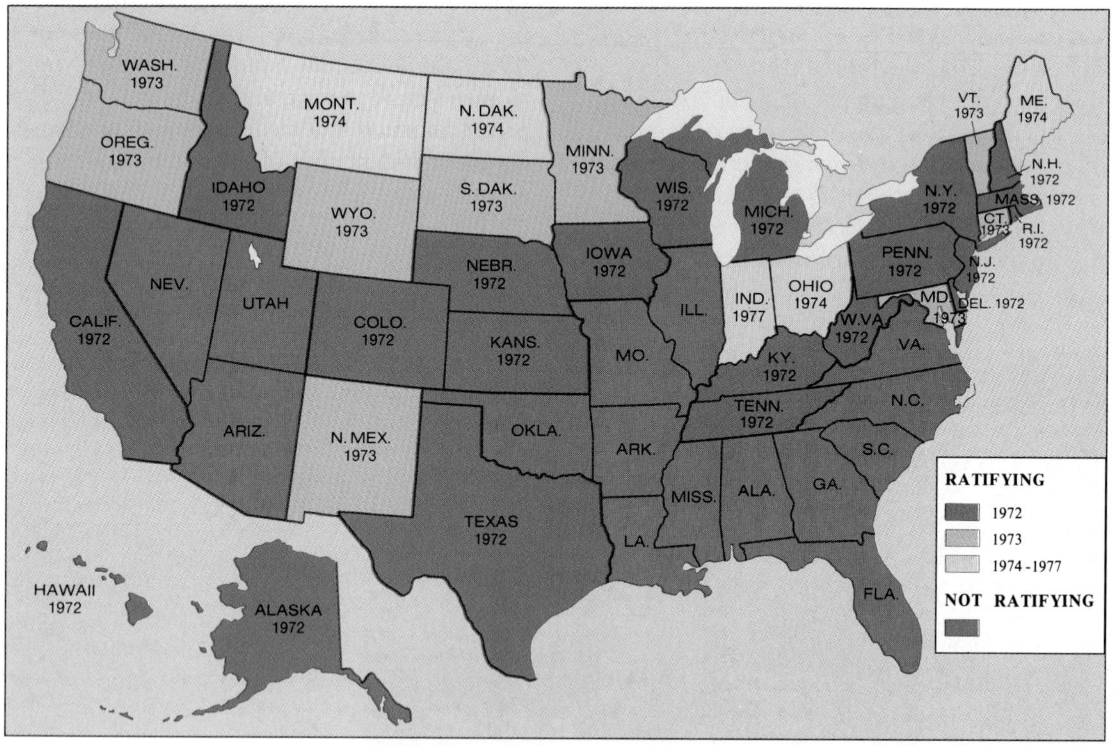

MAP 31.4

States Ratifying the Equal Rights Amendment

The Equal Rights Amendment quickly won state support in 1972 and 1973, but then it stalled. ERAmerica, a coalition of women's groups formed in 1976, lobbied extensively, particularly in Florida, North Carolina, and Illinois, but it failed to sway the conservative legislatures in those states. Efforts to revive the ERA in the 1980s were also unsuccessful.

roles for women. As she told audiences, "A man's first significant purchase is a diamond for his bride, and the major financial investment of his life is a home for her to live in." She baited feminists by opening her speeches, "I'd like to thank my husband for letting me be here tonight."

Schlafly's STOP ERA organization claimed the amendment would create an unnatural "unisex society," cause women to be drafted, legalize homosexual marriages, and prohibit separate toilets for men and women. (These charges have no basis in the language of the amendment.) Grass roots evangelical networks mobilized conservative women, who then showed up at state houses with home-baked bread and apple pies, symbols of their traditional domestic roles. The message that women would lose more than they would gain if the ERA passed found favor among many men and women, especially those deeply troubled by the rapid pace of social change.

Like the civil rights movement before it, the women's movement also found that choices were harder, and causes less clear-cut, as the 1970s progressed. Affirmative action guidelines, instituted by the Labor Department in 1968 to ensure nondiscriminatory hiring through quotas and preferential treatment to blacks and women, proved more politically unpopular than Title VII (see Chapter 32). Similarly, *comparable worth*, the doctrine that people with jobs involving similar levels of skill or responsibility, such as secretaries and maintenance workers, should be paid the same wages, was far more problematic than equal pay for equal work.

Abortion Controversy. But no issue could match the controversy that raged over abortion. The legalization of abortion in 1973 sparked a powerful Right to Life movement. Foes of abortion believed that the rights of a fetus took precedence over the right of the mother to choose whether to terminate her pregnancy. Therefore, they attempted to circumvent and overturn the *Roe v. Wade* decision. In 1976, Representative Henry Hyde of Illinois sponsored an amendment to deny Medicaid funds for abortions for poor women. Passed over a presidential veto, the amendment was upheld by the Supreme Court in 1980.

Although feminists had been forced on the defensive by the mid-1970s, women's lives showed no signs of returning to the patterns of 1950 or even of 1970. Pervasive changes were here to stay. So, too, were the victories won by blacks, Hispanics, native Americans, and gay people, incomplete though they may have been. American society had been permanently altered by the twenty-year struggle for equality.

Summary

Between 1954 and 1975, a series of social movements challenged the American status quo. The civil rights movement triggered the process, and its attacks on legalized segregation in the South expanded into challenges to institutionalized racism throughout the country. The tactics and ideology developed in the civil rights movement encouraged other groups, including Hispanics, native Americans, poor people, homosexuals, and women, to demand equality as well. Many were college students, who also challenged the policies of their universities and American participation in the Vietnam War.

All the protest movements had their roots in structural and demographic changes and shifting cultural values. Black migration from the South because of the transformation of agriculture made civil rights a national, not just a regional, problem. The postwar baby boom led to a rapid expansion of higher education. More women took jobs outside the home, faced rising divorce rates, and acquired better access to education.

The protest movements followed a similar progression. At first, efforts centered on the political or judicial front. These early successes led to heightened expectations, but the next stage—changing people's attitudes and gaining social and economic justice—proved more difficult. By the mid-1970s, the civil rights and women's movements each produced a backlash from those who thought change had gone far enough, but not before lasting alterations had been made in American society.

TOPIC FOR RESEARCH

The Life and Legacy of Malcolm X

Malcolm X (1925–1965) remains a controversial figures more than twenty-five years after his death. Was he a symbol of black pride and self-reliance, or was he a hatemonger? Which was more relevant to the 1960s—Malcolm X's message of self-defense and defiance or Martin Luther King's calls for integration and nonviolence?

Since advocates and detractors have variously distorted Malcolm's views over the years, the best way to understand his philosophy is to read his own speeches and writings. The place to begin this investigation of Malcolm X is through Alex Haley, *The Autobiography of Malcolm X* (1965). For his collected writings and speeches, see George Breitman, ed., *Malcolm X Speaks* (1965) and *Malcolm X: By Any Means Necessary* (1970). See also Bruce Perry, ed., *Malcolm X: The Last Speeches* (1989). What were the main tenets of Malcolm's philosophy? Did they change over time? Was his message better suited to northern urban residents than southern blacks?

In addition, you may wish to examine some broader questions: What was his impact on the civil rights movement, and what is his legacy today? Studies of Malcolm X's life include Peter Louis Goldman, *The Death and Life of Malcolm X* (1973), George Breitman, *The Last Year of Malcolm X: The Evolution of a Revolutionary* (1967), and John Henrik Clarke, ed., *Malcolm X: The Man and His Times* (1965). A full listing of secondary sources on Malcolm X's life is Timothy V. Johnson, *Malcolm X: A Comprehensive Annotated Bibliography* (1986).

BIBLIOGRAPHY

William H. Chafe, *The Unfinished Journey* (2nd ed., 1991), provides the best overview of the entire postwar period. Four strong surveys of the 1960s are Todd Gitlin, *The Sixties: Years of Hope, Days of Rage* (1987); Allen J. Matusow, *The Unraveling of America* (1984); William L. O'Neill, *Coming Apart* (1971); and Milton Viorst, *Fire in the Streets* (1979). For additional general material on the period, see Godfrey Hodgson, *America in Our Time* (1976), and Todd Gitlin, *The Whole World is Watching* (1980).

The Civil Rights Movement

Robert Weisbrot, *Freedom Bound* (1990), and Harvard Sitkoff, *The Struggle for Black Equality* (1981), offer comprehensive overviews. Richard Kluger, *Simple Justice* (1975), and Mark Tushnet, *The NAACP's Legal Strategy Against Segregated Education* (1987), analyze the *Brown* decision and its context, while Anthony Lewis, *Portrait of a Decade* (1964), covers southern reaction to the decision. J. Harvey Wilkinson III continues the story of the Supreme Court and integration through the 1970s in *From Brown to Bakke* (1979). Jules Tygiel, *Baseball's Great Experiment: Jackie Robinson and His Legacy* (1983), surveys integration on the field.

Histories of the major civil rights organizations include Clayborne Carson's study of SNCC, *In Struggle* (1981), and August Meier and Elliot Rudwick, *CORE* (1973). Mary Aickin Rothschild, *A Case of Black and White* (1982), describes northern volunteers during the Freedom Summer; Mary King, *Freedom Song* (1987), is a compelling personal memoir about SNCC. Victor Navasky, *Kennedy Justice* (1971), is extremely critical of President Kennedy's civil rights record; Carl Brauer, *John F. Kennedy and the Second Reconstruction* (1977), is more sympathetic. William H. Chafe, *Civilities and Civil Rights* (1980), is a superb case study of the impact of civil rights on Greensboro, North Carolina, from the 1950s through the 1970s.

Major texts of the civil rights movement include Stokely Carmichael and Charles Hamilton, *Black Power* (1967); James Baldwin, *The Fire Next Time* (1963); and Eldridge Cleaver, *Soul on Ice* (1968). Anne Moody, *Coming of Age in Mississippi* (1968), is a moving autobiography; Howell Raines, *My Soul is Rested* (1977), and Henry Hampton and Steve Fayer, *Voices of Freedom* (1990), are fine oral histories. Joanne Grant, *Black Protest* (1968), and August Meier and Elliot Rudwick, *Black Protest in the Sixties* (1970), are good anthologies of basic texts.

The material on Martin Luther King, Jr., is extensive and continues to grow. King tells his own story in *Stride Toward Freedom* (1958) and *Why We Can't Wait* (1964). Biographies of King include David Garrow, *Bearing the Cross* (1986); Taylor Branch, *Parting the Waters: America in the King Years, 1954–1963* (1988); Stephen Oates, *Let the Trumpet Sound* (1982); and David Lewis, *King* (1970). David Garrow, *The FBI and Martin Luther King, Jr.* (1981), chronicles the FBI surveillance of the civil rights movement.

Record of the National Advisory Commission on Civil Disorders (1968) analyzes the decade's major race riots. See also Joe R. Feagin and Harlan Hahn, *Ghetto Revolts* (1973), and Robert Fogelson, *Violence as Protest* (1971). Robert Conot, *Rivers of Blood, Years of Darkness* (1968), studies the Watts riot.

Stan Steiner, *La Raza* (1970), and Matt Meier and Feliciano Rivera, *The Chicanos* (1972), document early Hispanic political activity. Vine DeLoria, Jr., *Behind the Trail of Broken Treaties* (1974) and *Custer Died for Your Sins* (1969), convey the new Indian assertiveness. See also Stan Steiner, *The New Indians* (1968); Helen Hertzberg, *The Search for an American Indian Movement* (1971); and Wilcomb Washburn, *Red Man's Land, White Man's Law* (1971). John D'Emilio, *Sexual Politics, Sexual Communities* (1983), describes the emergence of gay identity between 1940 and 1970.

The Challenge of Youth

The student activism of the 1960s drew its share of scholarly chroniclers. See Kenneth Keniston, *The Uncommitted* (1965) and *Young Radicals* (1969); Daniel Bell and Irving Kristol, *Confrontation* (1969); Nathan Glazer, *Remembering the Answers* (1970); and Philip Slater, *The Pursuit of Loneliness* (1970). On student revolt, see W. J. Rorabaugh, *Berkeley at War* (1968); Seymour Lipset and Sheldon Wolin, eds., *The Berkeley Student Revolt* (1965); and Jerry Avorn, *Up Against the Ivy Wall* (1968). John P. Diggins, *The American Left in the Twentieth Century* (1973), and Irwin Unger, *The Movement: A History of the American New Left* (1974), provide general background. Kirkpatrick Sale, *SDS* (1973), can be supplemented by James Miller, *Democracy is in the Streets* (1987), which covers the years from the Port Huron Statement to the siege of Chicago in 1968. Lawrence Baskir and William A. Straus, *The Draft, the War, and the Vietnam Generation* (1978), explain who was drafted and why. For the antiwar movement, see Charles DeBenedetti, with Charles Chatfield, *An American Ordeal* (1990), and Nancy Zaroulis and Gerald

Sullivan, *Who Spoke Up? American Protest Against the War in Vietnam, 1963–1975* (1984).

Morris Dickstein, *Gates of Eden* (1977), is an excellent account of cultural developments in the 1960s. Todd Gitlin, *The Sixties*, also treats the counterculture extensively. Other sources include Theodore Roszak, *The Making of a Counter-Culture* (1969), and Charles Reich, *The Greening of America* (1970). Joyce Maynard, *Looking Back* (1973), provides a "chronicle of growing up old" in the 1960s. Todd Gitlin, *The Whole World is Watching* (1980), discusses the impact of the mass media on the New Left. Gerald Howard, ed., *The Sixties* (1982), is a good anthology of the decade's art, politics, and culture. Philip Norman, *Shout! The Beatles in Their Generation* (1981), and Jon Weiner, *Come Together: John Lennon in His Times* (1984), cover developments in popular music. Joan Didion, *Slouching Toward Bethlehem* (1968) and *The White Album* (1979), explore some of the darker sides of the hippie phenomenon.

For background on the Beat Generation of the 1950s, start with Ann Charters, *Kerouac* (1973); Dennis McNally, *Desolate Angel* (1979); and Jane Kramer, *Allen Ginsberg in America* (1969). John Tytell, *Naked Angels* (1976), covers the lives and literature of the Beat Generation. Tom Wolfe's *Electric Kool-Aid Acid Test* (1965) describes the antics of Beat survivors Ken Kesey and his Merry Pranksters in the 1960s.

The Revival of Feminism

Jo Freeman, *The Politics of Women's Liberation* (1975); Barbara Deckard, *The Women's Movement* (1975); and Judith Hole and Ellen Levine, *The Rebirth of Feminism* (1971), chronicle the revival of feminism in the 1960s and 1970s. Alice Echols, *Daring to Be Bad* (1989) traces radical feminism from 1967 to 1975. Gayle Graham Yates, *What Women Want* (1975), concentrates on feminist ideology, while William H. Chafe, *Women and Equality* (1977), draws comparisons between feminism and civil rights. Sara Evans, *Personal Politics* (1979), traces the roots of feminism in the civil rights movement and the New Left. General histories of women's postwar activism include Cynthia Harrison, *On Account of Sex: The Politics of Women's Issues, 1945–1968* (1988); Leila J. Rupp and Verta Taylor, *Survival in the Doldrums: The American Women's Rights Movement, 1945 to the 1960s* (1987); and Susan M. Hartmann, *From Margin to Mainstream* (1989).

Material on women's changing lives is found in Alice Kessler-Harris, *Out to Work* (1982); Carl Degler, *At Odds: Women and the Family in America from the Revolution to the Present* (1980); and Valerie Kincaid Oppenheimer, *The Female Labor Force in the United States* (1970). Ethel Klein, *Gender Politics* (1984), links demographic change with the revival of feminism. Phyllis Schlafly, *The Power of the Positive Woman* (1978); Andrea Dworkin, *Right Wing Women* (1983); and Rebecca E. Klatch, *Women of the New Right* (1987), present the ideas of antifeminist women that gained force in the 1970s. Mary Berry, *Why ERA Failed* (1986), and Jane J. Mansbridge, *Why We Lost the ERA* (1986), offer two perspectives on the demise of the Equal Rights Amendment. For the controversy over abortion, see Marion Faux, *Roe v. Wade* (1988), and Kristin Luker, *Abortion and the Politics of Motherhood* (1984).

TIMELINE

1954	*Brown v. Board of Education of Topeka, Kansas*
1955–1956	Montgomery bus boycott
1957	Southern Christian Leadership Conference (SCLC) founded
1960	Greensboro, North Carolina, sit-ins Birth control pill becomes available
1961	Presidential Commission on the Status of Women Freedom Rides
1962	Students for a Democratic Society (SDS) founded
1963	Betty Friedan's *The Feminine Mystique* March on Washington
1964	Civil Rights Act Free Speech Movement at Berkeley
1965	Voting Rights Act
1966	National Organization for Women (NOW) founded Stokely Carmichael proclaims Black Power
1967	Height of race riots in northern cities Hippie counterculture
1968	Martin Luther King, Jr., assassinated Robert F. Kennedy assassinated Women's liberation movement
1969	Vietnam moratorium Woodstock festival American Indian Movement (AIM) seizes Alcatraz Stonewall riot leads to gay liberation movement
1970	Kent State killings
1972	Congress passes Equal Rights Amendment
1973	*Roe v. Wade* legalizes abortion

In addition to the works of Betty Friedan, Robin Morgan, and Shulamith Firestone mentioned in the chapter, see Kate Millett, *Sexual Politics* (1970); Germaine Greer, *The Female Eunuch* (1972); and Susan Brownmiller, *Against Our Will: Men, Women, and Rape* (1975). Sara Ruddick and Pamela Daniels, eds., *Working It Out* (1977), chronicle the struggles of twenty-three women to find personal and professional fulfillment during a period of rapid change in women's lives.

Our Fragile Environment

NASA photographs from space captured both the beauty and the fragility of the planet Earth.

CHAPTER 32 *A More Conservative Era,* 1968–1980

In many ways, the years between 1963 and 1968 were distinct. The civil rights movement spurred the nation to debate the political issues of the day in terms of morality, justice, fairness, and equality. In the tumultuous year of 1968, the political system and social fabric seemed to unravel at an alarming pace. The events of 1968 ushered in an era of political, social, and cultural conservatism, which would dominate American life through the 1970s and 1980s. Richard Nixon won election as president in 1968 and again in 1972 by capitalizing on this shifting mood. But in 1974 the Watergate scandal forced Nixon from office, adding to the crisis of confidence that had been set in motion by the Vietnam War and the upheavals of the 1960s.

In the years after Nixon's resignation, the United States faced new challenges in national life. Economically, Americans found themselves in a period of limited growth, declining productivity, and runaway inflation, exacerbated by a dramatic rise in the price of imported oil after 1973. Internationally, the prolonged American withdrawal from Vietnam and increasing instability in the Middle East shared attention with continuing tense relations with the Soviet Union, as both superpowers engaged in an escalating nuclear arms race that threatened the fragile international peace.

Even after the election of Richard Nixon in 1968, activism continued, although civil rights was no longer the driving force. The women's movement made important gains in the early 1970s, and the birth of a new environmental movement was celebrated on Earth Day, April 22, 1970. Ironically, this was just two weeks before the killings of four students at Kent State in the last gasp of antiwar demonstrations. The ghost of Vietnam would hover over much of the 1970s.

The Watershed Year: 1968

Many historians point to 1968 as a watershed for America, "the pivotal dividing line of the postwar years." In the first half of the year, the pace of change seemed out of control, with events taking on special significance because it was a presidential election year. Yet by the time of the election in November, the tide had shifted decisively away from the previous period of protest and challenge.

A Year of Shocks

The first traumatic event of 1968 was the Tet offensive of January 30, a surprise Vietcong attack on major installations throughout South Vietnam, including the U.S. embassy in Saigon. Although U.S. forces repulsed the attack, the Vietcong's demonstrated strength mocked American claims that the enemy was being defeated. President Johnson's political stock fell accordingly. The war had "come home," affecting domestic politics, and especially the Democratic party, in a way that none of Johnson's advisers had anticipated.

At the urging of liberal antiwar activist Allard Lowenstein, Senator Eugene J. McCarthy of Minnesota had already entered the Democratic primaries as an alternative to Lyndon Johnson. (Lowenstein had first approached New York senator Robert Kennedy, whose instincts told him to run but whose advisers said he should wait until 1972.) A core of student activists "came clean for Gene," that is, they cut their hair and put away their blue jeans to avoid alienating voters. When the Tet offensive revealed how badly things were going in Vietnam, support for the war eroded further. Although President Johnson won the New Hampshire primary in early March, McCarthy received a stunning 42.2 percent of the vote. McCarthy's vote reflected profound dissatisfaction with the course of the war, including, ironically, those who believed Johnson was not hawkish enough. Sensing the president's vulnerability, Robert Kennedy changed his mind and entered the race. Johnson realized his political support was evaporating, and, in the midst of an otherwise mundane televised address on March 31, he stunned the nation by announcing he would not seek reelection. Johnson vowed to devote his remaining months in office to the search for peace in Vietnam. Johnson's vague pledge had little effect on the fighting, however, and protesters redoubled their efforts to stop the war.

Just five days after Johnson's withdrawal, Martin Luther King, Jr., was assassinated in Memphis, provoking urban riots across the country that left forty-three people dead. Soon after, a major student confrontation erupted at Columbia University, ending only when police violently removed protesters from the administration buildings they had occupied. Student unrest seemed likely to become a worldwide phenomenon in May, when a massive strike by students and labor unions toppled the French government.

Then came the final, and for many, the most painful tragedy of the year. As Robert Kennedy celebrated his California primary victory over Eugene McCarthy on June 5, 1968, he was assassinated by Sirhan Sirhan, a young Palestinian thought to oppose Kennedy's pro-Israel stand. Once again, the nation went through the ritual of burying a Kennedy. In two strokes—the assassinations of Martin Luther King and Robert Kennedy—liberalism had been, in the words of student leader Tom Hayden, "decapitated."

Robert Kennedy's assassination shattered the dreams of many who hoped that social change could be achieved through the political system. Kennedy's death also had major implications for the Democratic party, because only he had seemed able to mobilize a constituency broader than just the antiwar movement. In his brief but dramatic campaign, Robert Kennedy had excited, indeed energized, the traditional components of the New Deal coalition, including blue-collar workers and black voters, in a way that the more cerebral Eugene McCarthy never did. So widespread was Kennedy's appeal that election-day exit polls in Indiana found that many voters who had supported him in the primary actually voted for conservative candidate George Wallace in November.

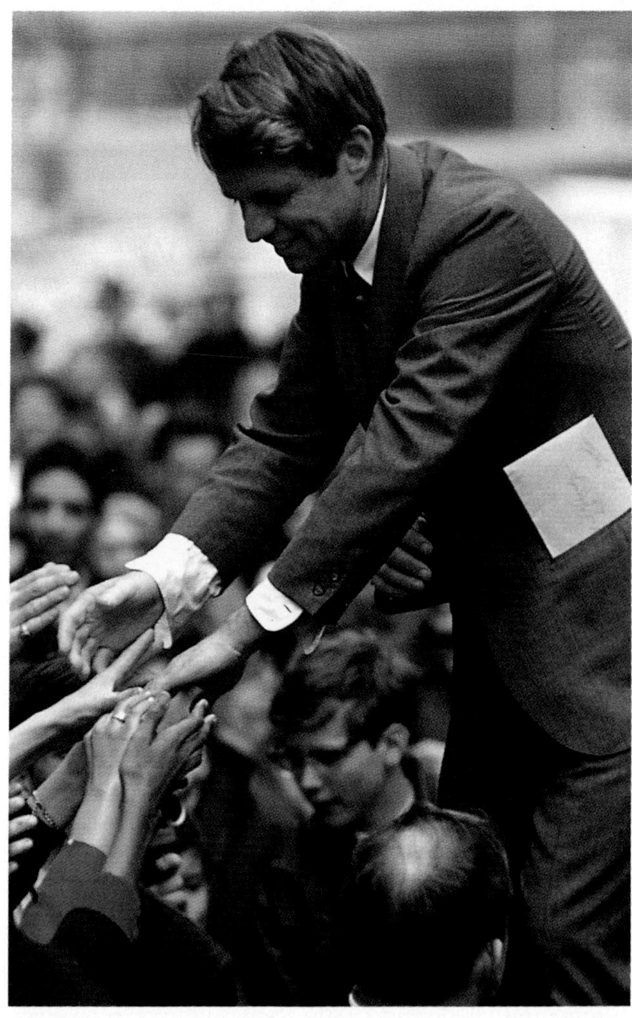

RFK

Bobby Kennedy inspired strong passions during his 1968 campaign. Followers often tore off his cufflinks as they tried to touch him or shake his hand.

The Democratic party, which was still reeling from Johnson's withdrawal when Kennedy was assassinated, never fully recovered. McCarthy proceeded listlessly through the rest of his campaign. Senator George S. McGovern of South Dakota entered the Democratic race in an effort to keep the Kennedy forces together. Meanwhile, Vice-President Hubert H. Humphrey lined up pledges from the traditional Democratic constituencies—unions, city machines, and state political organizations. The Democrats thus found themselves on the verge of nominating, not an antiwar candidate, but a public figure closely associated with Johnson's war policies. The stage was set for the Democratic National Convention in Chicago in August.

Chicago, 1968
Protesters gather in Chicago's Grant Park during the 1968 Democratic convention. The large structure in the background is the Conrad Hilton Hotel, where most of the delegates were staying.

Turmoil and Political Backlash

The Democrats had experienced disastrous conventions in the past, as in the 103-ballot meeting in 1924, but the 1968 convention hit a new low. Most of the drama occurred not in the convention hall but outside, on the streets of Chicago. Protesters led by Jerry Rubin and Abbie Hoffman, who the year before had tried to "levitate" the Pentagon as a way of ending the war, descended on Chicago, calling themselves the Youth International Party, or Yippies. With theatrics geared for maximum media exposure, they announced a platform that included an end to the war, the legalization of marijuana, and the abolition of money. To mock the "pigs" who ruled America, they nominated a live pig for president, which was promptly confiscated by the Chicago humane society. Their stunts diverted attention from the more serious, and far more numerous, antiwar activists who had come to Chicago as convention delegates or volunteers to take a stand against the Democrats' war policy.

Old-line Democratic mayor Richard J. Daley grew increasingly angry at the way the protesters were mocking *his* city and disrupting *his* convention. He called out the police and gave them broad discretion to break up the demonstrations. Several nights of skirmishes between protesters and police culminated on the evening that the names of candidates were put in nomination. In what an official report later described as a "police riot," the police dispersed protesters, who never numbered more than ten thousand, with mace, tear gas, and clubs. The tear gas was so strong that it wafted into the air conditioning ducts of the Conrad Hilton hotel, where most delegates were staying.

While protesters chanted, "The whole world is watching!" the television networks ran film of the riot in the midst of the nominating speeches. In one memorable exchange, Senator Abraham Ribicoff of Connecticut interrupted his nominating speech for Senator McGovern to interject, "With George McGovern we wouldn't have Gestapo tactics on the streets of Chicago." The cameras panned to Mayor Daley, livid with rage and clearly mouthing obscenities.

Television coverage of the riots was hardly excessive—about 32 minutes on CBS and less than 14 minutes on NBC—but it cemented an impression of the Democrats as the party of disorder. The Democrats dispiritedly gave the nomination to Hubert H. Humphrey, who chose Senator Edmund S. Muskie of Maine as his running mate. The convention approved a middle-of-the-road, pro-administration platform that endorsed the policy of continuing the fighting in Vietnam while exploring diplomatic means to end the conflict.

One result of the Democratic convention was the beginning of a backlash against protest. The general public did not differentiate between the antics of the small group of Yippies who wanted to shut the system down and the actions of a far greater number of antiwar activists who were still trying to work within the system. Polls showed overwhelming support for Mayor Daley and the police over the demonstrators. After 1968 the New Left splintered into factions, its energy

AMERICAN VOICES

The Siege of Chicago *Steve Lerner*

Steve Lerner published his account in *The Village Voice* of the altercation between protesters and the Chicago police during the Democratic convention in August 1968. The scene: Lincoln Park on Chicago's North Side, where many of the protesters hung out. The time: around midnight.

Around midnight on Tuesday some four hundred clergy, concerned local citizens, and other respectable gentry joined the Yippies, members of Students for a Democratic Society, and the National Mobilization Committee to fight for the privilege of remaining in the park. Sporting armbands decorated with a black cross and chanting pacifist hymns, the men of God exhorted their radical congregation to lay down their bricks and join in a nonviolent vigil.

Having foreseen that they could only wage a symbolic war with "little caesar Daley," several enterprising clergymen brought with them an enormous wooden cross which they erected in the midst of the demonstrators under a street lamp. Three of them assumed heroic poses around the cross, more reminiscent of the Marines raising the flag over Iwo Jima than any Christ-like tableau they may have had in mind.

During the half-hour interlude between the arrival of the clergy and the police attack, a fascinating debate over the relative merits of strict nonviolence versus armed self-defense raged between the clergy and the militants. While the clergy was reminded that their members were "over thirty, the opiate of the people, and totally irrelevant," the younger generation was warned that "by calling the police pigs and fighting with them you become as bad as they are." Although the conflict was never resolved, everyone more or less decided to do his own thing. By then the demonstrators, some eight hundred strong, began to feel the phalanx of police which encircled the park moving in; even the most militant forgot his quibbles with "the liberal-religious sellout" and began to huddle together around the cross.

When the police announced that the demonstrators had five minutes to move out before the park was cleared, everyone went into his individual kind of panic. One boy sitting near me unwrapped a cheese sandwich and began to stuff it into his face without bothering to chew. A girl standing at the periphery of the circle who had been alone all evening walked up to a helmented boy with a mustache and ground herself into him. People all over the park were shyly introducing themselves to each other as if they didn't want to die alone. "My name is Mike Stevenson from Detroit; what got you into this?" I heard someone asking behind me. Others became increasingly involved in the details of survival: rubbing Vaseline on their face to keep the Mace from burning their skin, buttoning their jackets, wetting their handkerchief and tying it over their nose and mouth. "If it's gas, remember, breathe through your mouth, don't run, don't pant, and . . . don't rub your eyes," someone thoughtfully announced over the speaker. A boy in the center of the circle got up, stepped over his seated friends, and made his way toward the woods. "Don't leave now," several voices called in panic. The boy explained that he was just going to take a leak.

It happened all in an instant. The night which had been filled with darkness and whispers exploded in a fiery scream. Huge tear-gas canisters came crashing through the branches, snapping them, and bursting in the center of the gathering. From where I lay, groveling in the grass, I could see ministers retreating with the cross, carrying it like a fallen comrade. Another volley shook me to my feet. Gas was everywhere. People were running, screaming, tearing through the trees. Something hit the tree next to me, I was on the ground again, someone was pulling me to my feet, two boys were lifting a big branch off a girl who lay squirming hysterically. I couldn't see. Someone grabbed onto me and asked me to lead them out of the park. We walked along, hands outstretched, bumping into people and trees, tears streaming from our eyes and mucus smeared across our faces. I flashed First World War doughboys caught in no-man's-land during a mustard gas attack. I felt sure I was going to die. I heard others choking around me. And then everything cleared.

Source: Steve Lerner account from *The Village Voice*, excerpted in Norman Mailer, *Miami and the Siege of Chicago: An Informal History of the Republican and Democratic Conventions of 1968* (New American Library, 1968), 151–52.

Hard Hats

Many construction workers (and the unions they belonged to) were vocal supporters of the Vietnam War. Sometimes hard hats clashed with long-haired protesters during antiwar marches and sidewalk demonstrations.

spent. One radical faction broke off from SDS to form the Weathermen (taking their name from a Bob Dylan song). A tiny band of self-styled revolutionaries, who embraced violence and bombings as tactics to bring about change, most were soon forced underground to avoid arrest. Broad-based antiwar protests continued, however, until at least 1970.

Conservative Backlash. Events in Chicago in August 1968 also strengthened support for proponents of "law and order," which became the catch phrase of the next several years. Many Americans were fed up with protest and dissent. Governor George C. Wallace of Alabama, a third-party candidate, skillfully exploited the public's growing hostility by making student protests and urban riots his chief campaign issues. He also spoke out against school desegregation and forced busing. Early polls showed that Wallace would receive as much as 20 percent of the vote, possibly enough to deadlock the electoral college and send the election to the House of Representatives.

Richard Nixon, even more than George Wallace, tapped the growing conservative mood of the electorate. After his unsuccessful presidential campaign in 1960 and his failure in the California gubernatorial race in 1962, Nixon engineered an amazing political comeback. In 1968 the "new" Nixon easily beat back primary challenges from three governors—Ronald Reagan of California, George Romney of Michigan, and Nelson Rockefeller of New York—to win the Republican nomination. He chose Maryland governor Spiro Agnew as his running mate to attract southern voters who opposed Democratic civil rights legislation, especially potential Wallace supporters. (One of Agnew's more memorable quotes was, "If you've seen one city slum, you've seen them all.") In the campaign, Nixon pledged to represent the "quiet voice" of the "great majority of Americans, the forgotten Americans, the non-shouters, the nondemonstrators." He declared, "The first civil right of every American is to be free from domestic violence."

Despite the Democratic debacle in Chicago, the election was close. Humphrey rallied in the last weeks of the campaign by gingerly disassociating himself from Johnson's war policies. Nixon countered by declaring that he had a "secret plan" to end the war. Nixon received 43.4 percent of the vote to Humphrey's 42.7 percent, defeating him by a scant 510,000 votes out of the 73 million cast. Wallace finished with 13.5 percent of the popular vote, becoming the most successful third-party candidate since Progressive Robert M. La Follette in 1924. Nixon's "southern strategy," his carefully crafted inroad into the once solidly Democratic South, certainly contributed to his victory. Yet Nixon owed his election more to the split in the Democratic coalition than to the emergence of a new Republican majority.

A Changing Mood. The closeness of the 1968 election suggested how polarized American society had become over the events of the 1960s. Nixon appealed to what came to be known as the *silent majority.* According to social scientists Ben J. Wattenberg and Richard Scammon in their influential book *The Real Majority* (1970), the typical American was a forty-seven-year-old machinist's wife from Dayton, Ohio, and this was what she was concerned about:

> To know that the lady in Dayton is afraid to walk the streets alone at night, to know that she has a mixed

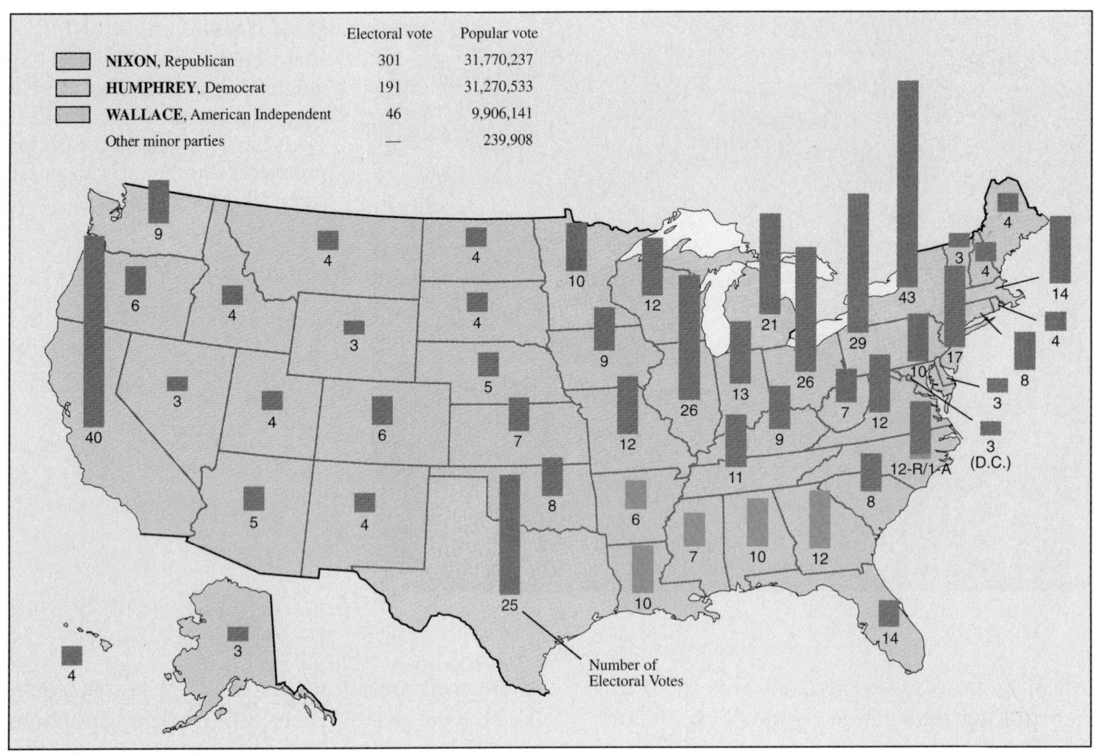

MAP 32.1

The Election of 1968

As late as mid-September, third-party candidate George C. Wallace of Alabama had the support of 21 percent of the voters. But in November he received only 13.5 percent of the vote, winning five states and showing that the South was no longer solidly Democratic. Republican Richard M. Nixon defeated Hubert H. Humphrey with only 43.4 percent of the popular vote.

> view about blacks and civil rights because before moving to the suburbs she lived in a neighborhood that became all black, to know that her brother-in-law is a policeman, to know that she does not have the money to move if her new neighborhood deteriorates, to know that she is deeply distressed that her son is going to a community junior college where LSD was found on campus—to know all this is the beginning of contemporary political wisdom.

But while political appeals after 1968 were targeted more to voters who were (in the words of Wattenberg and Scammon) "unblack, unpoor, and unyoung," protest and controversy would remain part of the political process until the divisive issue of the Vietnam War was resolved.

The Nixon Years

The figure and personality of Richard Nixon dominated, indeed haunted, the landscape of postwar American political history. Columnist Meg Greenfield defined the "Nixon Generation" in 1972:

> At regular intervals now, ever since the first vote in 1952, our generation has either been supporting or opposing Richard Nixon. The psychological implications of this fact are staggering. . . . What distinguishes us as a group from those who came before and those who have come after is that we are too young to remember a time when Richard Nixon was not on the political scene, and too old reasonably to expect that we shall live to see one.

What Greenfield could not have predicted when she wrote those words was that less than two years later, Nixon would be forced from office in order to avoid impeachment. But then too, who would have predicted Nixon's remarkable political resiliency, as he resurfaced in the 1980s as an influential author, television pundit, elder statesman, and unofficial adviser to Democratic and Republican presidents alike?

Domestic Agendas

Richard Nixon had waited eight years for his chance at the presidency, and he wanted to leave his mark on history. He anticipated ending his two terms in 1976 with a triumphant celebration of the nation's bicentennial.

Before the Watergate scandal brought his administration to an untimely end, Nixon had served his entire first term and part of the second. In that time, he counted both accomplishments and setbacks.

Richard Nixon proclaimed an ideological commitment to a *new federalism,* pledging to "reverse the flow of power and resources from the states and communities to Washington and start power and resources flowing back . . . to the people." One important innovation was the 1972 program of *revenue sharing,* whereby a portion of federal monies were turned back to the states to be spent as states saw fit. At the same time, however, the Nixon administration expanded the regulatory apparatus of the modern state. The Environmental Protection Agency (EPA) was set up in 1970 to coordinate the growing federal responsibilities for environmental action. The Occupational Safety and Health Administration (OSHA) and the Consumer Product Safety Commission were established in 1972 out of growing concern for the health and safety of workers and consumers.

Social Programs. In other areas Nixon worked to scale down government programs that had grown dramatically during the two previous Democratic administrations. Most Great Society programs received reduced funding and the Office of Economic Opportunity was totally dismantled in 1971. The administration claimed to support civil rights, but was embarrassed by a leaked 1970 memo by presidential adviser Daniel Patrick Moynihan, a Democrat who had joined the Nixon White House, which suggested that "the issue of race could benefit from a period of benign neglect." Nixon also vetoed a 1971 bill to establish a comprehensive national child care system because it would commit "the vast moral authority of the national government to communal approaches to child rearing, over against the family centered approach."

Despite these attacks on Democratic social programs, the administration put forward its own poverty program in an ambitious attempt to overhaul the jerry-built social welfare system dating from the New Deal. Following the advice of urban expert Moynihan, Nixon in 1969 proposed a Family Assistance Plan, which would guarantee a family of four an income of $1,600 a year, plus $860 in food stamps. One attraction of a guaranteed annual income was simplicity: it would eliminate the multiple layers of bureaucrats (caseworkers, local and state officials, and federal employees) who administered the burgeoning Aid to Families with Dependent Children program (AFDC), the largest welfare program by the 1960s. But the bill floundered in the Senate: conservatives attacked it for putting the federal government too deeply into the welfare business, while liberals and social welfare activists opposed it for not going far enough. No serious attempt at welfare reform has come as close to passage since.

The Supreme Court. The Nixon administration showed its commitment to conservative social values in its appointments to the Supreme Court. One of Nixon's first acts was to nominate hard-line conservative Warren Burger to replace retired Chief Justice Earl Warren in the spring of 1969. When another vacancy occurred later that year, Nixon attempted to appoint a conservative southern judge as a way of cementing his political support in that region. But two nominees in succession, Clement F. Haynsworth and G. Harrold Carswell, failed to win Senate confirmation. Haynsworth, a federal Circuit Court judge from South Carolina, was turned down after revelations that he had sat on cases in which he had a financial interest. Carswell failed, in part, because he had participated in a white segregationists' scheme in Tallahassee, Florida, to buy a public golf course to prevent its integration. Eventually, Nixon would name three more Supreme Court justices: Harry Blackmun, Lewis F. Powell, Jr., and William Rehnquist.

Conservative judges did not always give Nixon the conservative decisions he wanted. Despite attempts by the Justice Department to halt further desegregation, the Court ruled in *Swann v. Charlotte-Mecklenburg Board of Education* (1971) in favor of forced busing to achieve racial balance. The *Furman v. Georgia* decision (1972) contained strict guidelines restricting the implementation of capital punishment, although it did not rule the death penalty unconstitutional. And, in the controversial 1973 case of *Roe v. Wade,* the Court struck down Texas and Georgia laws that had prohibited abortion.

Foreign Policy

Some of Richard Nixon's most stunning first-term initiatives came in the realm of foreign policy. Paradoxes abound here. At the same time that he was prosecuting the war in Vietnam, ostensibly to halt the spread of communism, he was laying the groundwork for détente with the Soviet Union and China. As a lifelong anti-Communist crusader, Nixon had greater political maneuverability to reach out to these two Communist superpowers than a Democratic president. After all, no one could accuse Richard Nixon of being soft on communism. National Security Adviser Henry Kissinger, a former Harvard government professor, influenced the president's thinking in this direction. Like Nixon, Kissinger had a huge ego, and both wanted to leave their mark on history. Foreign policy gave them that chance.

Since the Chinese revolution of 1949, the United States had refused to recognize the government of the People's Republic of China, instead giving unconditional support to the Nationalist Chinese government that had set itself up in Taiwan. Nixon moved away from that policy, reasoning that the United States could profitably exploit the growing rift between the People's Republic of China and the Soviet Union. He sent Kissinger on a secret mission to Beijing in the summer of 1971 and in July told a startled world that he would visit the People's Republic in the near future. He did so in February 1972, walking along the Great Wall and toasting Chinese leaders in Beijing. Nixon's visit set the stage for the formal establishment of diplomatic relations, which took place in 1979.

In a similar spirit of détente, Nixon journeyed to Moscow in May of 1972 to sign SALT I, a treaty resulting from Strategic Arms Limitations Talks between the United States and the Soviet Union. (Both trips were timed to give him maximum television publicity in an election year.) Although President Nixon boasted that the SALT agreement was a dramatic step toward stopping the arms race, what the accords really did was limit production and deployment of intercontinental ballistic missiles (ICBMs) and antiballistic missile systems (ABMs), leaving untouched other equally destructive systems of nuclear warfare. Yet the treaty was also a recognition that the United States could no longer afford the massive military spending that would have been necessary to regain the nuclear and military superiority of the immediate postwar years. By the early 1970s, factors such as inflation, the decline in American hegemony over the world system, and domestic dissent were all limiting and reshaping American options in international relations.

Nixon's War

Vietnam, long Lyndon Johnson's war, also became Richard Nixon's. Fifteen thousand Americans would lose their lives in Vietnam during Nixon's presidency. Yet Nixon operated within political parameters that differed fundamentally from Johnson's. Realizing that the public would not support major sacrifices to win the war, Nixon and Kissinger searched for a way out. A new plan to reduce American troop involvement, called "Vietnamization," delegated most of the ground fighting to South Vietnamese troops. When Nixon took office, more than 543,000 American soldiers were serving in Vietnam; by the end of 1970, there were 334,000, and two years later 24,200. American casualties, and the political liabilities they generated, fell correspondingly. But the slaughter in Vietnam continued. As Ambassador to Vietnam Ellsworth Bunker noted cynically, it was just a matter of changing "the color of the bodies."

The companion policy to troop withdrawal was a dramatic increase in American bombing raids over North Vietnam. Expanded air support was an attempt to strengthen Nguyen Van Thieu's faltering South Vietnamese government while the gradual process of Vietnamization went into effect. The escalation of the air war was virtually concealed from the American public, who believed that the war was winding down, based on the much-publicized troop withdrawals.

Hanoi Devastated
The North Vietnamese capital of Hanoi sustained heavy damage from bombing raids by American B-52s. The most devastating raids occurred during the "Christmas bombing" in December 1972, just weeks before the Paris Peace Accords were signed.

In March 1969, Nixon went further and ordered secret bombing raids on neutral Cambodia, through which the Vietnamese transported supplies and reinforcements. To keep Congress ignorant about these sorties, accurate information about the raids was fed into one Defense Department computer, while data omitting the Cambodia targets were fed into another. The faulty projections from the second computer were the ones given to Congress. The secret war culminated in an April 30, 1970, "incursion" by American ground forces into Cambodia to destroy enemy troop havens there. The invasion of Cambodia triggered widespread protests and led to the Kent State killings on May 4 (see Chapter 31). No matter how much the United States escalated its activity, however, the Vietnamese fought on.

The War at Home. Like Lyndon Johnson, who by 1968 had become so unpopular that his appearance caused protests everywhere except on military bases, Richard Nixon seemed to inspire domestic conflict. To discredit critics, he denounced student demonstrators as "bums" and stated that "North Vietnam cannot defeat or humiliate the United States. Only Americans can do that." Vice-President Spiro Agnew added emphasis, attacking dissidents as "ideological eunuchs" and "nattering nabobs of negativism." Nixon staunchly insisted he would not be swayed by the mounting protests against the war. When close to half a million protesters marched on Washington in November 1969, the president barricaded himself in the White House and watched football games on television.

By 1970 dissatisfaction with the war had spread widely throughout society. Even American troops in Vietnam showed mounting opposition to their mission. They fought on, but many sewed peace symbols on their uniforms. A number of overbearing junior officers were "fragged"—that is, killed or wounded by a fragmentation grenade thrown by their own soldiers. A group called Vietnam Veterans Against the War turned in their combat medals at mass demonstrations at the U.S. Capitol.

My Lai. The Vietnam War was brought home forcefully to the American people in 1971, when Lieutenant William L. Calley was court-martialed for atrocities committed in the Vietnamese village of My Lai in March 1968. Calley had commanded a platoon on a routine search and destroy mission. Retaliating for casualties sustained by their buddies on an earlier engagement, the soldiers apparently murdered 350 Vietnamese villagers. The incident came to light because one member of the platoon refused to go along with a military cover-up; investigative reporter Seymour Hersh of the *New York Times* broke the story. In the court martial proceedings, a jury of six soldiers who had served in Vietnam sentenced Calley to life imprisonment for his part in the massacre. Yet conservatives called Calley a hero rather than a villain, and after President Nixon's intervention, his sentence was reduced to three years' house arrest.

The 1972 Election

The Democratic party, still divided over Vietnam and civil rights, would have had a difficult time countering Nixon at the end of his first term under any circumstances. Disarray within the party in 1972 made their task even harder. Following the 1968 national convention, the party had changed its way of selecting delegates and candidates, pledging to include "minority groups, young people and women in reasonable relationship to their presence in the population." The ratification of the Twenty-sixth Amendment in 1971, lowering the national voting age to eighteen, increased the impact of this procedural change.

The McGovern Campaign. South Dakota senator George McGovern reaped the greatest benefit from the new Democratic guidelines. By 1972 he was supported by an army of antiwar activists, who blitzed the precinct-level caucuses and won delegate commitments far beyond his voter support. In the past, an alliance of party bosses and union leaders would almost certainly have rejected an upstart candidate like McGovern. But few old-line party leaders qualified as delegates to the nominating convention under the changed rules. Typical of the new Democratic look, black leader Jesse Jackson replaced Mayor Richard Daley of Chicago as the head of the Illinois delegation.

McGovern's campaign against Nixon was an unrelieved disaster. Surprised to learn that his running mate, Senator Thomas F. Eagleton of Missouri, had undergone electroshock therapy for depression some years earlier, McGovern first supported him "1,000 percent," then abruptly insisted that he leave the ticket. Sargent Shriver, a brother-in-law of John and Robert Kennedy, was prevailed upon to join the ticket at the last minute. George McGovern was far too liberal for many traditional Democrats, who rejected his ill-defined proposals for welfare reform, did not rally around his calls for unilateral withdrawal from Vietnam, and ignored his charges that the Nixon administration had corruptly abused its power.

Nixon's campaign took full advantage of McGovern's weaknesses. Although the president had failed to end the war, his Vietnamization policy had reduced weekly American combat deaths from three hundred in 1968 to almost none in 1972. Just a few days before the election, Henry Kissinger returned from negotiations with the North Vietnamese in Paris and announced, somewhat disingenuously, that "peace is at hand." These initiatives robbed the Democrats of their greatest appeal—their antiwar stance. In addition, the improving economy helped the Republicans.

Nixon won handily, receiving nearly 61 percent of the popular vote and carrying every state except Massachusetts and the District of Columbia. (After the Watergate scandal gathered momentum, Bay State bumper stickers would proclaim, "Don't Blame Me—I'm from Massachusetts.") The threat of a conservative third-party challenge had ended abruptly the previous May, when George Wallace was shot and paralyzed from the waist down by an assailant in a suburban Maryland shopping mall. McGovern's vote demonstrated large cracks in the traditional Democratic coalition: he received only 18 percent of the southern white Protestant vote and 38 percent of the big-city Catholic vote. Only African-Americans, Jews, and low-income voters remained loyal to the Democratic cause. Yet Nixon failed to kindle strong Republican loyalties in the electorate. Only 55.7 percent of eligible voters bothered to go to the polls, and Democrats maintained their control of both houses of Congress.

American Withdrawal From Vietnam

Following his second election victory, Nixon moved to end American involvement in Vietnam. In a final destructive demonstration of American military strength for the benefit of South Vietnamese president Thieu, homefront hawks, and the Third World in general, he initiated the "Christmas bombings." From December 17 to December 30, 1972, American planes subjected North Vietnamese civilian and military targets to the most devastating bombing of the entire war. Then, on January 27, 1973, a ceasefire was signed in Paris by representatives of the United States, North and South Vietnam, and the Vietcong; it differed little from the proposal of the previous October. The Paris Peace Accords failed to deliver Nixon's often-repeated promise of peace with honor. Basically, they mandated the unilateral withdrawal of American troops in exchange for the return of American prisoners of war held in North Vietnam. For most Americans, that amount of face saving was enough.

The public outpouring of emotion that greeted the six hundred returning prisoners contrasted sharply with public indifference to ordinary Vietnam veterans. Advocates for Vietnam veterans would later charge that they experienced higher than average rates of divorce, suicide, and unemployment, as well as recurring physical and psychological problems that came to be associated with post-Vietnam trauma syndrome. For many Vietnam veterans, the war never ended.

The 1973 Peace Accords did not resolve the civil war that had raged in Vietnam for almost three decades. Without massive U.S. military and economic aid, and with Vietcong guerrillas operating freely throughout the countryside, it was only a matter of time before the South Vietnamese government of General Nguyen Van Thieu fell to the more disciplined and popular Communist forces. In April 1975 a North Vietnamese offensive reunited the country. On television, horrified American viewers watched South Vietnamese officials and soldiers struggle with American embassy personnel for space on the last helicopters that flew out of Saigon before the Vietcong entered the city. (As a testimonial to its founding leader, who had died in 1969, the Vietnamese government renamed it Ho Chi Minh City.) Strife still engulfs Vietnam and its neighbors Laos, Cambodia, and Thailand. The epitaph that journalist David Halberstam coined for American participation in the war applies to Southeast Asia itself: "No light at the end of the tunnel, only greater darkness."

Watergate

Watergate, the great constitutional crisis of the early 1970s, was a direct result of Richard Nixon's secretive style of governing and his obsession with opposition to the Vietnam War at home. Many Americans saw Watergate as only the evil deeds of one person (Richard Nixon) and one unlawful act (the obstruction of justice following a break-in). But Watergate was not just an isolated incident; it was part of a broad pattern of illegality and misuse of power that grew out of the era—and the war—that preceded it.

The new administration had begun to stretch the boundaries of the law under the guise of national security just four months into Nixon's first term. In the spring of 1969, after the *New York Times* reported the secret bombing of Cambodia, the White House arranged for the FBI to investigate the source of the story. Without seeking any judicial warrants, the FBI secretly (and illegally) taped phone conversations of several low-level staffers on the National Security Council, as well as five newspeople. The source was never found.

Over the next several years, the Nixon administration would repeatedly invoke supposed domestic threats to national security to conceal its actions. In 1970 the White House asked Tom Huston, a former army intelligence officer, to draw up an extensive plan for secret domestic counterintelligence—such as opening mail, tapping phones, and arranging break-ins—by the FBI, CIA, and Justice Department. President Nixon approved the scheme, only to have it blocked by FBI Director J. Edgar Hoover, who refused to cooperate with other government agencies in activities he interpreted as being exclusively within the scope of the FBI.

The Pentagon Papers. White House paranoia was next aroused in June 1971, when Daniel Ellsberg, a former Defense Department analyst who had grown disillusioned with the war, leaked the so-called Pentagon Papers to the *New York Times*. The Pentagon Papers were classified Defense Department documents commissioned by Secretary of Defense Robert McNamara in 1967 and completed eighteen months later. The report detailed so many American blunders and misjudgments that McNamara had commented on first reading it, "You know, they could hang people for what is in there." The Nixon administration unsuccessfully attempted to block publication of the Pentagon Papers, increasing Ellsberg's stature as a hero to the antiwar movement. In an effort to discredit Ellsberg, White House underlings burglarized his psychiatrist's office to look for damaging information.

In preparation for the 1972 campaign, the White House had established a clandestine intelligence group of its own, led by former CIA agents G. Gordon Liddy and Howard Hunt. Known as the "plumbers" because they were supposed to plug leaks of government information, they relied on such tactics as using the Internal Revenue Service and other agencies to harass opponents of the administration named on an "enemies list" drawn up by presidential counsel John Dean. A major target of the "plumbers" was the Democrats, whose primary frontrunner Edmund Muskie in 1972 was the beneficiary of several "dirty tricks." For example, New Hampshire primary voters were awakened in the middle of the night by callers from the "Harlem for Muskie" committee; posters appeared in Florida saying "Help Muskie in Busing More Children Now."

The Break-in. These secret and questionable activities led to the break-in that triggered the Watergate scandal. In the early morning of June 17, 1972, an alert security guard noticed something amiss at the door to the headquarters of the Democratic National Committee at the Watergate apartment complex in Washington. Five men carrying cameras and wiretapping equipment were arrested; two accomplices were apprehended soon after. Two of the accused men had worked as security consultants in the White House; a third had held a responsible position on the Committee to Re-Elect the President (aptly known as CREEP); the remaining four, all from Miami, had been involved in CIA-linked anti-Castro activities. Nixon's press secretary, Ronald Ziegler, archly dismissed the break-in as a "third-rate burglary attempt." Nixon himself stated categorically that "no one in the White House staff, no one in this administration, presently employed, was involved in this bizarre incident." The cover-up had begun.

It would later be revealed that six days after the break-in, the president ordered his chief of staff, H. R. Haldeman, to instruct the CIA to tell the FBI not to probe too deeply into connections between the White House and the burglars. This action constituted an obstruction of justice. Nixon apparently feared that the Watergate burglary would lead to an investigation of the dubious fundraising methods and political sabotage used by his re-election committee.

Trial and Investigations. The Watergate burglars were convicted and sent to jail in January 1973. White House counsel John Dean tried to buy their continued silence with $400,000 in hush money and hints of presidential pardons. But, prodded by the presiding judge, John Sirica, several of the convicted burglars began to talk. Two tenacious investigative reporters at the *Washington Post,* Carl Bernstein and Bob Woodward, kept the story alive. In February the Senate voted 70–0 to establish a select committee to investigate the scandal. Dean started to get nervous, and in March 1973 he warned Nixon, referring to the cover-up, that "there is a cancer within, close to the presidency, that is growing." On April 30, Nixon accepted the resignations of Haldeman and chief domestic adviser John Ehrlichman. He also fired Dean. As evidence mounted linking the scandal directly to the White House, press secretary Ziegler declared that all previous statements on Watergate were "inoperative."

Watergate Hearings
Some of the most damaging testimony against President Richard Nixon came from the former White House counsel, John Dean, shown here testifying before the Senate Watergate Committee in June 1973. Revelations from a secret taping system in the Oval Office later confirmed Dean's nearly total recall of conversations he had had with the president.

AMERICAN LIVES

Woodward and Bernstein, Investigative Reporters

"Woodstein"—that is how they were referred to around the newsroom of the *Washington Post.* Bob Woodward and Carl Bernstein, the two young reporters who broke the Watergate story, were definitely an odd couple. Woodward was a neatly dressed, Yale man who liked classical music and voted Republican; Bernstein was a rumpled Jewish college dropout who liked rock music and was definitely left-of-center in his political views. At times, the "kids" (as they were also called in the newsroom) seemed like a case of the Establishment versus the Counterculture, and not a likely combination for a Pulitzer Prize-winning series that eventually brought down the Nixon presidency.

In June 1972, when the Watergate break-in occurred, Bob Woodward had been at the *Washington Post* for only nine months, assigned to the not-so-prestigious metropolitan desk, where his most recent stories had been about restaurant health violations and police corruption. Born in 1943 in an affluent Chicago suburb, he had graduated from Yale in 1965 and then spent five years in the navy. He worked for a local Maryland paper for a year before wangling a position at the *Post.* His first day on the job he made over a hundred phone calls looking for a story. Ideologically, Woodward was no muckraker—he was always more interested in finding out the facts than changing the status quo.

Carl Bernstein was the shaggy-haired free spirit to Woodward's buttoned-down patrician. Born in 1944 in Washington, D.C., he began working for the *Washington Star* at age sixteen, rising from copy boy to reporter by 1965, and along the way dropping out of the University of Maryland after three years. Bernstein joined the staff of the *Washington Post* in 1966, where he covered Virginia politics. Permanently rumpled and with more than a trace of arrogance (a trait he shared with Woodward), Bernstein was notorious for his irregular hours and his barely concealed contempt for routine stories. He was also infamous for his penchant for high living, even when he did not have the money to pay for it. At the time Watergate broke, he was twenty-eight years old, a year younger than (and light years away from) his new partner in investigative journalism.

"Woodstein"
When Carl Bernstein (left) and Bob Woodward (right) began their investigation of the Watergate break-in, they were referred to as "Woodstein" around the newsroom. Their story won them a Pulitzer Prize for investigative reporting in March 1973.

When a tip came into the metropolitan desk of the *Post* on the morning of June 17, 1972, about a break-in at the Watergate headquarters of the Democratic National Committee, the story was assigned to city reporter Woodward rather than to one of the the more seasoned regulars who covered national politics for the capital's most influential paper. After all, the break-in was just local news. But this local story had some intriguing aspects, like the links of one of the burglars to the Central Intelligence Agency, and soon Carl Bernstein was snooping around too. Without really knowing where this was going, both Woodward and Bernstein found themselves working on the story fulltime; in six weeks, they were sharing a byline.

What followed was months of tough, boring, frustrating investigative journalism. Recalled Bernstein, "We knocked on doors, we talked to people at the bottom, which is to say secretaries and file clerks rather than starting at the top . . . and there was nothing glamorous about it." Slowly the case inched forward. Most of their sources pointed to the White House, especially to Nixon's re-election campaign. Eventually, of course, the tracks would lead directly to the Oval Office.

The *Washington Post* was the only major newspaper to devote significant resources to the story at first, and it made sure that the stories were airtight. Any significant facts had to be verified by at least two independent sources, and a senior editor had to approve each story before it appeared. As a result, only once did the *Post* have to back down from a story. Throughout, Bernstein and Woodward had the complete support of the newspaper brass, all the way up to executive editor Ben Bradlee and publisher Katherine Graham.

The two reporters might have been stymied more than once were it were not for the help of a highly placed confidential source nicknamed Deep Throat (from a pornographic movie popular at the time). This source rarely provided new information but was willing to corroborate things that Bernstein and Woodward had uncovered. In the cloak and dagger style that shaped much of the investigation, if Woodward wanted to meet with Deep Throat, he would move a flower pot with a red flag to the rear of his apartment balcony, a signal to meet at 2 A.M. in an underground garage. If Deep Throat wanted to meet Woodward, he would send a message via the copy of the *New York Times* delivered to Woodward's apartment, where, on the lower corner of page 20, clock hands would show the time of the designated rendezvous. To this day, the identity of Deep Throat remains a mystery.

The Watergate story entered a new phase in March 1973, when convicted burglar James McCord sent a letter to Judge John Sirica confirming what Woodward and Bernstein had patiently been proving over the last nine months—that the White House had been involved in the original break-in. Now all the major newspapers began covering the story more aggressively, and the *Post* lost its prime role in pursuing the scandal.

Watergate changed the lives of the two "cub" reporters. In March 1973 the *Washington Post* won a Pulitzer Prize for their investigative reporting on the Watergate story. Bernstein and Woodward received a $55,000 advance to write a book about their investigation (at the time, their combined salaries totalled only $30,000) and actor Robert Redford acquired the movie rights. *All the President's Men* was published in June 1974, and instantly made the bestseller list. The book, which was written in the third person like a fast-paced detective story ("Bernstein and Woodward called the White House. . . ."), came out just as the nation was moving into the final stage of the Watergate saga—the impeachment hearings. Bernstein and Woodward later took a leave of absence to write a second book, *The Final Days,* which covered the last summer of the Nixon presidency. That book was published in 1976, about the time that the movie of *All the President's Men* premiered, starring Robert Redford as Bob Woodward and Dustin Hoffman as Carl Bernstein. So convincing was the movie version that in many people's minds, Redford and Hoffman *are* Woodward and Bernstein.

Woodward and Bernstein?
Robert Redford and Dustin Hoffman starred in the screen version of Woodward and Bernstein's book *All the President's Men.* In fact, their performances were so believable that many people mistook the actors for the reporters.

Watergate set off, in Carl Bernstein's words, "an orgy of self-congratulation" about the power and importance of an independent press. Yet Watergate was less a victory for freedom of the press than a testament to the tenacity of two investigative journalists, who stuck with a story the rest of the media dismissed as a "caper." Bernstein and Woodward, now approaching fifty, are senior and respected journalists. Bob Woodward is the author of bestselling books on the Supreme Court and the CIA and has been the assistant managing editor of the *Washington Post* since 1981. Carl Bernstein is a correspondent for *Time* magazine, having formerly worked for ABC News. Neither reporter ever dreamed that when they set out to investigate a seemingly innocuous break-in they would help to topple a presidency. But that is precisely what Bob Woodward and Carl Bernstein did.

In May the Senate Watergate committee, chaired by Senator Sam Ervin of North Carolina, began a summer of nationally televised hearings. In five days of riveting testimony in late June, John Dean implicated President Nixon in the cover-up. Even more startling testimony from aide Alexander Butterfield revealed that Nixon had a secret taping system in the Oval Office. "I was hoping you fellows wouldn't ask me about that," Butterfield sheepishly told the committee. Until the existence of the tapes was disclosed, it had been Dean's word against Nixon's; now it appeared possible to find out what had actually been said. The president steadfastly "stonewalled," citing executive privilege and national security as he refused to release the tapes. When a lower federal court held in October that he had to give selected tapes to a special prosecutor, Nixon released heavily edited transcripts whose most frequent phrase seemed to be "expletive deleted," a phrase necessitated by the repeated profanity picked up on the tapes. Senate Republican leader Hugh Scott called these edited transcripts "deplorable, disgusting, shabby, immoral." Most suspicious was an eighteen-minute gap in the tape of a crucial meeting between Nixon, Haldeman, and Ehrlichman on June 20, 1972, three days after the break-in.

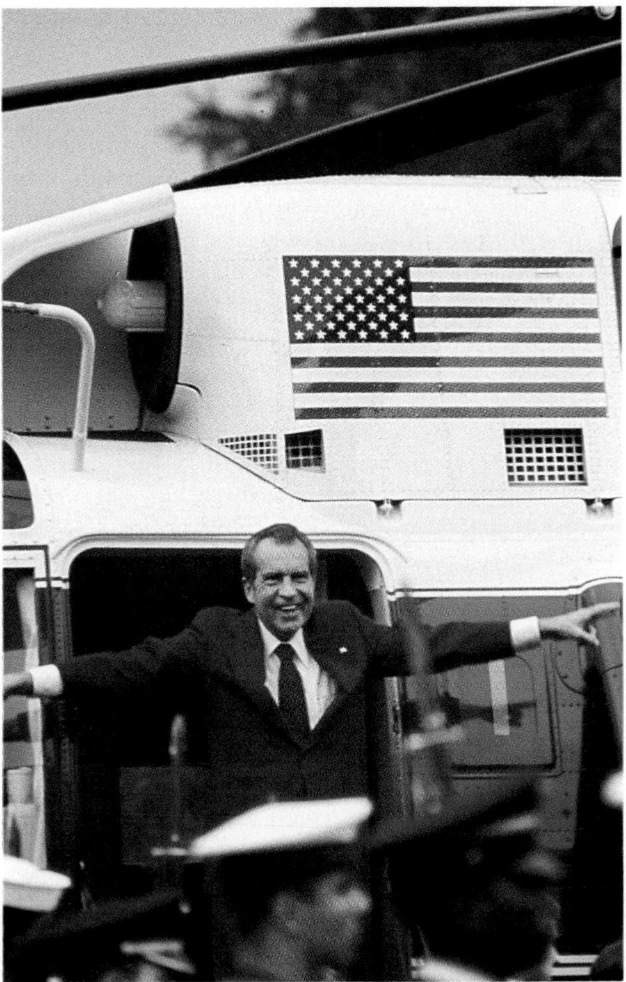

Nixon Resigns
On August 9, 1974, Richard M. Nixon became the first American president to resign. He is shown here minutes after turning over the presidency to Gerald R. Ford. He retired to his home in San Clemente, California, refusing to admit guilt for what had happened.

The Final Days. The Watergate affair moved into its final phase in the summer of 1974, when a committee of the House of Representatives convened impeachment hearings. On July 30, seven Republicans joined the Democratic majority to vote three articles of impeachment against Richard Nixon: obstruction of justice, abuse of power, and acting in a way subversive to the Constitution. Two days later the Supreme Court ruled unanimously that Nixon had no right to claim executive privilege as justification for refusing to turn over additional tapes requested by the special prosecutor. Under duress, Nixon released the unexpurgated tapes on August 5, which contained shocking evidence (the so-called "smoking gun") that he had indeed ordered the cover-up as early as six days after the break-in. In effect, the president had been lying to the American people ever since. Senator Barry Goldwater gravely informed the president that no more than fifteen senators still supported him. Facing certain conviction in a Senate trial, on August 9, 1974, Nixon became the first U.S. president to resign.

The transfer of power to Vice-President Gerald Ford went remarkably smoothly. In 1973 Ford had replaced Spiro Agnew, who had been forced to resign after being indicted for allegedly accepting kickbacks on construction contracts while governor of Maryland and vice-president. In the wake of the assassinations of John Kennedy, Robert Kennedy, and Martin Luther King, Jr., as well as the first resignation of an incumbent vice-president, the idea of substituting leaders was no novelty. The public had greater difficulty a month later in accepting President Ford's "full, free, and absolute" pardon of Nixon, on the grounds of sparing the country the agony of rehashing Watergate.

The Aftermath. In response to the abuses of the Nixon administration and the Vietnam era, Congress adopted several reforms to contain the power of what historian Arthur M. Schlesinger, Jr., named "the imperial presidency." The War Powers Act of 1973 required the president to report any use of military force—such as had occurred in Korea, Vietnam, and Cambodia—to Congress within forty-eight hours and directed that hostilities must cease within sixty days unless Congress declared war. The 1974 Congressional Budget and Impoundment Control Act restricted the president's authority to impound federal funds (that is, refuse to spend money appropriated by Congress for programs opposed by the White House.) The Fair Campaign Practices Act of 1974 limited campaign contributions and demanded stricter accounting of campaign expenditures. A strengthened Freedom of Information Act in 1974 gave citizens greater access to files that federal government agencies had amassed on them.

In the aftermath of Watergate, twenty-five members of the Nixon administration went to prison, including Nixon's closest advisers, H. R. Haldeman, John Ehrlichman, and Attorney General John Mitchell. Richard Nixon retired to his estate in San Clemente, California. He refused to admit guilt for what had happened, conceding only that Watergate represented an error of judgment.

Lowered Expectations and New Challenges

In 1973 the European economist E. F. Schumacher published *Small Is Beautiful*, a book whose message was well-timed for the 1970s. Schumacher challenged the "bigger is better" philosophy that had fueled the West's industrial growth and was posing a growing threat to the Third World. He was especially outspoken about the dangers of the dramatic world thirst for oil. "Less is more" became the watchword of the developing environmental movement, as the United States began to grapple with living in a world where resources were limited and American economic domination was no longer as secure as in the immediate postwar period.

The Hydrocarbon Age

"Without oil," Interior Secretary Harold Ickes had noted back in 1933, "American Civilization as we know it could not exist." That continues to be true to this day, when not only the United States but the entire modern world lives in a *hydrocarbon age,* totally dependent on petroleum and its byproducts. Oil supplanted coal as the main energy source for the industrial world, because it was cheaper, cleaner, and more abundant. Between 1949 and 1972, world energy consumption more than tripled, and the demand for oil increased by more than five and a half times. Access to oil, especially at the low prices that prevailed in the 1950s and 1960s, fostered rapid economic growth and rising standards of living throughout most of the world, and especially in the United States. Imported oil literally fueled the dramatic growth of the Japanese and Western European economies to positions of world dominance.

Until well into the twentieth century, the United States was both the world's leading producer and consumer of oil. During World War II, America still produced two-thirds of the world's oil, but its share of world production fell to only 22 percent in 1972, even though domestic production continued to rise. By the late 1960s the United States was buying more and more oil on the world market to keep up with shrinking domestic reserves and growing demand. Daily imports rose from 3.2 million barrels in 1970 to 6.2 million by the summer of 1973.

America imported oil primarily from the Middle East, where production increased a stupendous *1,500* percent in the twenty-five years after World War II. Oil had first been discovered in the region in 1908, when a vast "elephant" (oil industry jargon for a giant field) was uncovered in Persia (later Iran). Initially all Persian Gulf oil was extracted under a *concession* system—a foreign oil company or consortium would contract with a sovereign to explore for, own, and produce oil in a given territory, paying a rental fee in return. These arrangements proved enormously profitable to European and, after World War II, American oil companies.

With the postwar rise of nationalism and end of colonialism, Persian Gulf nations found the concession system demeaning. But rather than nationalizing their oil fields—and losing access to Western technology and equipment—most oil-rich countries renegotiated their agreements. The foreign companies still extracted the oil, but they recognized that it belonged to the exporting countries and split the profits accordingly. For example, a consortium of Western companies, including Jersey, Socony, Texaco, Standard of California, Gulf, and Shell, negotiated for access to Iran's oil on a 50–50 profit-sharing basis in 1947.

In 1960 oil-exporting countries in the Third World formed OPEC (Organization of Petroleum Exporting Countries) in an attempt to exercise more control over the world oil market. Five of the founding countries, the Middle Eastern states of Saudi Arabia, Kuwait, Iran, and Iraq, plus Venezuela, were the source of more than 80 percent of the world's crude oil exports. In 1960 the oil industry was in the middle of a twenty-year period of surplus capacity, and prices stayed low. In the early 1970s, however, the balance shifted. Several trends—a sharp increase in worldwide demand, the end of excess capacity, political instability in the Middle East, the shift of the United States from a net exporter to net importer of oil—came together to set up what would soon be OPEC's "golden age."

The year 1973 was the turning point. Between 1973 and 1975, OPEC deliberately raised the price of a barrel of oil from $3 to $12. At the end of the decade it peaked at $34 a barrel. Because the United States now depended heavily on Middle Eastern oil, the price rise set off furious inflation.

Also in 1973, OPEC instituted an oil embargo, showing that oil could be used as a weapon in global politics. On October 6, 1973, Egyptian and Syrian forces had coordinated a surprise invasion of Israel on Yom Kippur, the holiest day in Judaism. At first, American policymakers held back their support of Israel for fear of jeopardizing relations with the oil-producing countries, which supported the invaders. But the initial attack was so devastating that the United States reversed its stand and quickly sent enough supplies and military equipment to enable the Israelis to regain most of their lost territory in a few weeks. A ceasefire soon ended the fighting, but the international repercussions were just beginning. In retaliation against the United States, Western Europe, and Japan, which had all aided Israel in the Yom Kippur War, OPEC halted all exports to those countries. The embargo lasted until 1974.

The United States scrambled to meet its domestic energy needs. Americans were forced to curtail their driving or spend long hours in line at the pumps; gas prices climbed 40 percent in a matter of months. A national speed limit of 55 mph was instituted to conserve fuel. Drivers wanted to buy more fuel-efficient cars, but the U.S. automobile industry had nothing to offer except the "gas guzzlers" that had been built to run on cheap gasoline. Soon the domestic auto industry was in a recession, as Americans bought cheaper, more fuel-efficient foreign cars, primarily those manufactured in Japan and West Germany. Since the United States owed much of its twentieth-century prosperity to the automobile (one in six jobs was tied directly or indirectly to the industry in the 1970s), this downturn had profound implications for the American economy.

The energy crisis of the mid-1970s was an enormous shock to the American psyche. Suddenly Americans felt like hostages to economic forces beyond their control. As OPEC's oil ministers set even higher oil prices at their annual meetings, they seemed to be able to determine whether Western economies grew or stagnated. Despite extensive public education about energy conservation and a second gas shortage in 1979, it was impossible to wean the nation from foreign oil. In 1970 the United States imported $4 billion of foreign oil; the figure would grow to $90 billion by 1980. Inflation caused only part of the rise. Americans were using even more foreign oil after the energy crisis than before, testimony to the enormous thirst of modern industrial and consumer societies for petroleum.

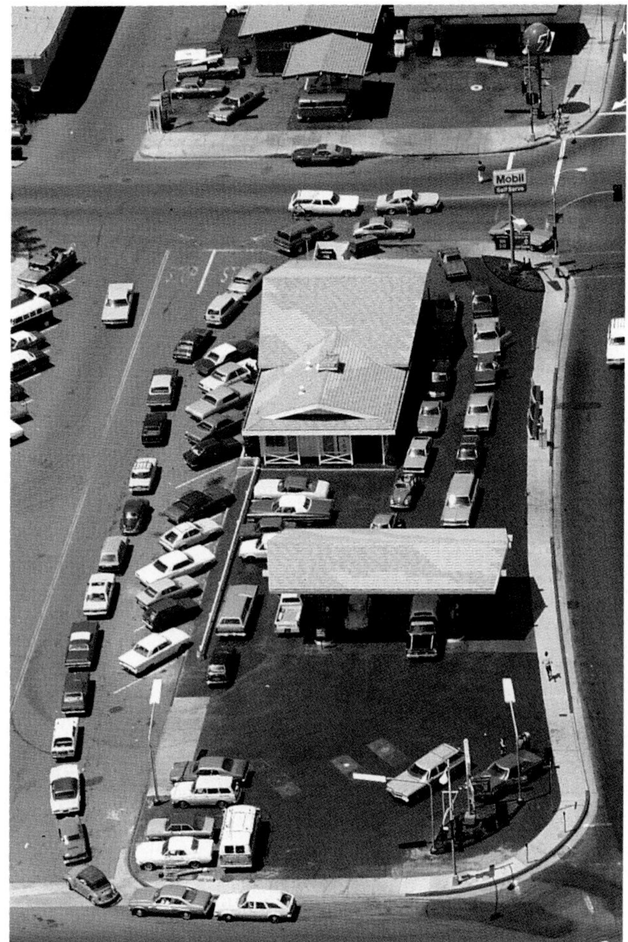

No Gas

During the energy crisis of 1973–1974, American motorists faced widespread gasoline shortages for the first time since World War II. Although gas was not rationed, gas stations were closed on Sundays, air travel was cut by 10 percent, and a national speed limit of 55 miles per hour was imposed.

The Environmental Movement

The energy crisis of the 1970s interacted with a growing awareness of environmental issues, which had been building since the 1960s. Along with the women's movement, the environmental movement had its greatest impact after 1970.

Emphasis on the environment and ecology did not originate in the postwar period, of course. John Muir and the Sierra Club had led the fight for the creation of the national park system in the late nineteenth century (see Chapter 17). This earlier conservation movement had advocated resource management and balancing open space and recreational needs against development. The post-1945 environmental movement operated in a different social and political context. Protecting nature in its pristine state became an inherent goal: activists talked about the "rights of nature," just as they did about the rights of women or blacks. Furthermore, there was a new awareness of the possible exhaustion of the earth's resources. Since America had always consumed vast quantities of natural resources, accepting the idea that there were "limits to growth" was revolutionary and troubling.

In some ways the environmental movement built on the activism of the 1960s. Protest tactics developed in the civil rights and antiwar movements were used to mobilize mass support for specific issues or legislation. Many 1960s radicals evolved into 1970s environmental activists. For example, the search for alternative technologies (especially solar power) could be a political statement against a corporate structure that seemed increasingly inhospitable to human-scale technology, and humans as well. Above all, the environmental movement was characterized by its grass-roots nature.

In other ways environmental activism represented something new—the mobilization of a broad mainstream constituency of people concerned about the air they breathed, the food they ate, and their desire to find recreation in undeveloped wilderness. Concern for environmental quality and ecological values can be seen as an offshoot of the advanced consumer economy that defined the postwar period. Now that most Americans had bought the basic necessities, and then some, they wanted an even higher standard of living, one that included a healthy environment and corresponding lifestyles. This desire led to new demands on the state—citizens expected the federal government to take responsibility for environmental issues. Governmental activism on consumer issues and the environment joined the welfare and warfare states of the post-1945 years.

The birth of the modern environmental movement is often dated to the 1962 publication of Rachel Carson's *Silent Spring,* a powerful analysis of the impact of pesticides, especially DDT, on the food chain. Citizen awareness of the fragility of the environment spurred both federal action and grass-roots involvement. Federal legislation in 1965, 1967, and 1970 covered water and air pollution; the 1970 Clean Air Act set standards for auto emissions to reduce smog and air pollution that still have not been met.

Environmental activists were also concerned about protecting wildlife, and they lobbied successfully for the Endangered Animals Act of 1964, widened to the Endangered Species Act of 1973. These acts gave species like snail darters, moths, and owls certain rights, which had to be balanced against human plans for development or recreation. Also important after 1970 were interagency provisions for an Environmental Impact Statement (EIS), an assessment of the consequences of changing use patterns on a particular ecological area. The EIS soon became a useful tool for citizens' groups trying to block unwanted development by private industry or government.

Early issues that galvanized public opinion included a huge oil spill in January 1969 off the coast of Santa Barbara, California; the environmental impact of such projects as the Alaska pipeline and a proposed airport in the Florida Everglades; and the harmful effects to the earth's atmosphere (ozone layer) caused by supersonic air transport. Environmentalism became a mass movement on the first Earth Day, April 22, 1970, when 20 million citizens gathered across the country to show their support for their endangered planet.

The environmental movement raised public awareness of the dangers inherent in the chemicals and petrochemical byproducts in American consumer goods, especially in foods and their packaging materials. Another concern was the careless dumping of toxic and radioactive wastes. The ironically named Love Canal housing development, near Niagara Falls, New York, had been built over an underground chemical waste disposal site. Residents noticed that trees turned black and sparks escaped from the pavement; even graver was the abnormally high rate of illness, miscarriages, and birth defects experienced by Love Canal families. In 1980 a state of emergency was declared, and the New York State government paid homeowners to relocate. Soon horror stories appeared about other poorly maintained waste-disposal sites across the country. "We just don't know how many potential Love Canals there are," admitted one federal official. "There are ticking time bombs all over."

One of the worst offenders was the federal government itself. In the cold war rush to produce bombs and weapons for national security, nuclear weapons plants carelessly released or dumped billions of gallons of radioactive waste into the environment. For example, the uranium processing plant built in 1954 at Fernald, Ohio, dumped liquid wastes into open-air waste-storage pits, which then leaked into regional waterways. At the Hanford Nuclear Reservation near Richland, Washington, plutonium waste and toxic chemicals contaminated the soil and seeped into the Columbia River. Outside of Denver, the Rocky Flats Plant and the Rocky Mountain Arsenal stored dangerous concentrations of plutonium, pesticide, and nerve gas wastes. Cleaning up the environmental morass resulting from forty years of reckless production will require one of the largest engineering projects ever undertaken.

Nuclear Energy. Nuclear energy also became a cause for citizen action in the 1970s, pitting environmental concerns against the need for alternative energy sources. In response to the energy crisis, some politicians and utility companies promoted the expansion of nuclear power to reduce American reliance on foreign oil. Forty-two nuclear power plants were in operation by January 1974 and more than a hundred others were planned. Construction of nuclear power plants and reactors, which generally went unchallenged in the 1950s and 1960s, now drew protests from community activists concerned about such issues as inadequate disaster evacuation plans and disposal of radioactive waste. At a reactor construction site in Seabrook, New Hampshire, the Clamshell Alliance staged protests reminiscent of the antiwar demonstrations of the previous decade.

Longstanding public fears about nuclear safety seemed to be confirmed in March 1979. At Three Mile Island, near Harrisburg, Pennsylvania, a nuclear plant came critically close to a meltdown of its central core reactor. (Fears were exacerbated by eerie similarities to *The China Syndrome,* a recently released movie starring Jane Fonda.) A hundred thousand residents were evacuated as a precaution. A prompt shutdown brought the problem under control before any radioactive material was released into the environment. As a member of the panel investigating the accident admitted, "We were damn lucky."

Three Mile Island made Americans reassess the future of nuclear power. Cost overruns, faulty construction, and waste disposal problems raised doubts that nuclear power was a viable solution to energy needs. Trying to think and act ecologically, Americans faced a difficult balancing act if they wanted to maintain the high level of consumer affluence they had grown accustomed to.

Three Mile Island

On March 30, 1979, the Three Mile Island nuclear power plant near Harrisburg, Pennsylvania, came close to suffering a dangerous meltdown of its central core reactor. The accident, caused in part by the failure of safety systems and by human error, helped undermine American faith in nuclear technology.

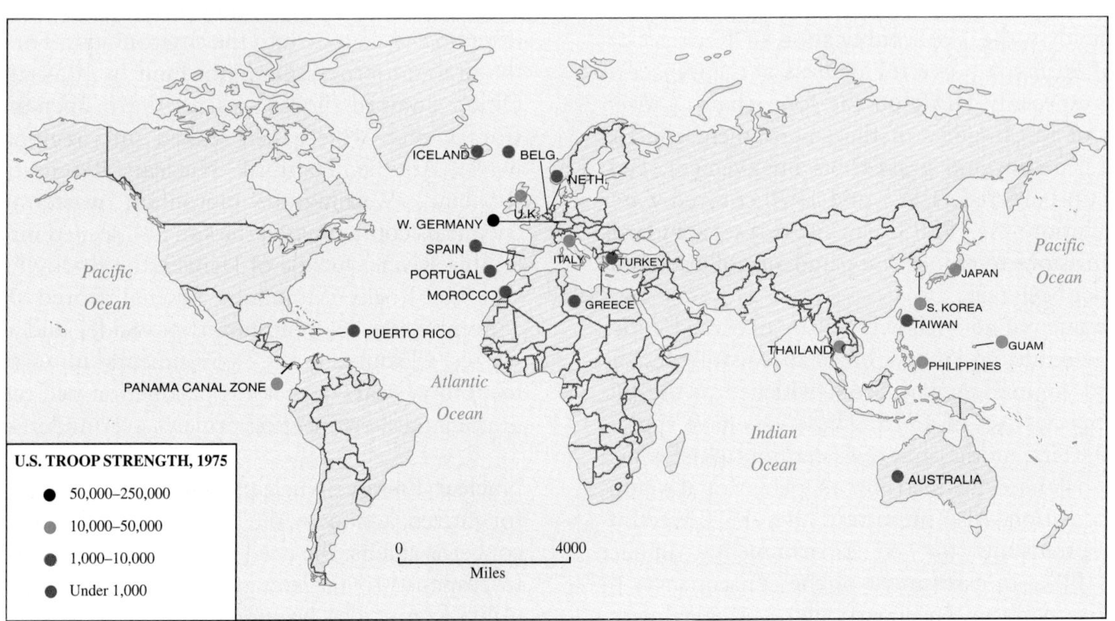

MAP 32.2

U.S. Troops Around the World, 1975

After its withdrawal from Vietnam, the United States maintained a substantial military presence around the world, especially in cold war troublespots in Europe and Asia. While the large military establishment provided millions of jobs for Americans, it also posed a continuing drain on the U.S. treasury.

Economic Trends

In retrospect, the 1970s marked the end of the *Pax Americana,* the overwhelming superiority the United States enjoyed in the world economy during the postwar era. The oil embargo of 1973–1974 and the energy crisis demonstrated that the domestic economy was vulnerable to world developments. The dollar was no longer the world's strongest currency. In 1971 the Bretton Woods system, set up at the United Nations monetary conference in 1944 (see Chapter 29), collapsed. The dollar now fluctuated in relation to the price of an ounce of gold, which increased from its former set price of $35 to as much as $800 on the international money market during the 1970s. Also in 1971, the United States posted its first balance of trade deficit in almost a century. Competition from the reviving economies of West Germany and Japan reduced demand for American goods worldwide. The U.S. share of world trade, which had declined by 16 percent between 1960 and 1970, dropped another 25 percent during the 1970s.

The more generalized prosperity of the postwar period also ended in the 1970s. The energy crisis merely speeded up a shift that was already underway. Overall economic growth as measured by the gross national product of the United States averaged 4.1 percent per year in the 1960s, but only 2.9 percent per year in the 1970s. Tellingly, all the real growth occurred before 1973. From 1973 to 1979 workers saw virtually no real income gain—instead of experiencing a rising standard of living, they found themselves worse off. By the early 1980s discretionary income per worker had declined 18 percent since 1973. Furthermore, the average price of a single-family house more than doubled during the 1970s, making home ownership inaccessible to wider segments of the working and middle class, including the baby boom generation that had now entered adulthood. By 1980, nine Western European countries had surpassed the United States in per capita GNP.

Deindustrialization. By the 1970s the industrial base of the United States had entered what would become a prolonged period of decline. Economists Barry Bluestone and Bennett Harrison estimate that the United States lost between 32 and 38 million jobs in the 1970s as a direct result of *deindustrialization*, "the widespread, systematic disinvestment in the nation's productive capacity." Instead of capital being invested in basic industries, it began to be diverted to speculation, to mergers and acquisitions, and to foreign investment. This was encouraged by policies that reduced taxes for corporations that could offset foreign expenses against their domestic profits. By the end of the 1970s, the hundred largest multinational corporations and banks earned more than a third of their overall profits abroad. For some corporations the proportion was much higher: in 1979, 94 percent of Ford's profits came from overseas operations, as did 83 percent of banking giant Citicorp's profits in 1977.

The most dramatic consequences of deindustrialization were found in the older industrial regions referred to as the Rust Belt. Nightly newscasts were full of stories of the closings of unprofitable plants. Corporations relocated overseas to take advantage of cheaper labor and production costs, or they dispersed their manufacturing functions into geographically disparate locations. The dominant images of mid-twentieth century American industry—huge factories such as Ford's River Rouge outside Detroit, the General Electric plant in Lynn, Massachusetts, or the U.S. Steel compound in Gary, Indiana—were becoming relics of a past stage of industrial development.

When a community's major employer closed up shop and left town, the effect was devastating. In 1977 the Lykes Corporation shut down the Campbell Works of the Youngstown Sheet and Tube Company, laying off 4,100 Ohio steelworkers. Two years later the community was still reeling. A third of the displaced workers, too old to retrain for new positions, had been forced to take early retirement, at half their previous salary. Ten percent had moved, and another 15 percent were still looking for work, their unemployment compensation long since exhausted. Of the 40 percent who were the "success stories" (those that found other jobs), many took huge wage cuts. A former rigger was selling women's shoes for $2.37 an hour. *Fortune* magazine tried to make Youngstown's story upbeat, titling it "Youngstown Bounces Back," but its cheerful conclusions belied the economic reality. The caption of a photograph of an unemployed steelworker sitting at a piano read, "Crane operator Ozie Williams, thirty-two, has a lot of time to practice his music." The impact of such plant closings rippled through communities across the heartland of America.

Challenges for Labor. The changed economic conditions that fostered foreign investment and plant closings posed enormous challenges for the labor movement. In labor's heyday during the 1940s and 1950s, American managers had learned grudgingly to cooperate with unions. With profits high, there was room for accommodation. But in the profit squeeze of the 1970s, industry was less willing to treat labor as a partner in making economic decisions. Union leaders might learn about a plant closing on the news at the same time as ordinary workers and the general public. Priorities of union leaders shifted to holding on to gains already won. But labor's bargaining position was increasingly vulnerable, given the resources and international mobility of multinational conglomerates. As employers turned to a cheaper workforce abroad, labor's prospects for regaining its earlier strength at home were dim.

Lifestyles and Social Trends

The Seventies as a decade defies easy generalization. Journalist Tom Wolfe labeled it the "Me Decade" for its widespread obsession with lifestyles and personal well-being. Historian Christopher Lasch referred derisively to its "culture of narcissism." Yet those labels hardly do justice to a decade in which the women's movement had its greatest impact, nor do they explain the broad-based activism of the environmental movement. Furthermore, such characterizations do not suggest the growing conservatism in social and political life. In fact, all these trends coexisted in a decade where, in the words of a popular history of the 1970s, "it seemed like nothing happened."

Turning Inward. In part due to the continuing influence of the counterculture, the 1970s featured a growing emphasis on personal fulfillment. One manifestation was the fitness craze. Millions of Americans, with the health-conscious baby boomers leading the way, began jogging, riding ten-speed bicycles, or working out on Nautilus machines. Jim Fixx's *Complete Book of Running* (1977) spurred the running boom—and the success of such athletic shoe companies as Nike and Adidas. (Reebok would be the success story of the 1980s.) The

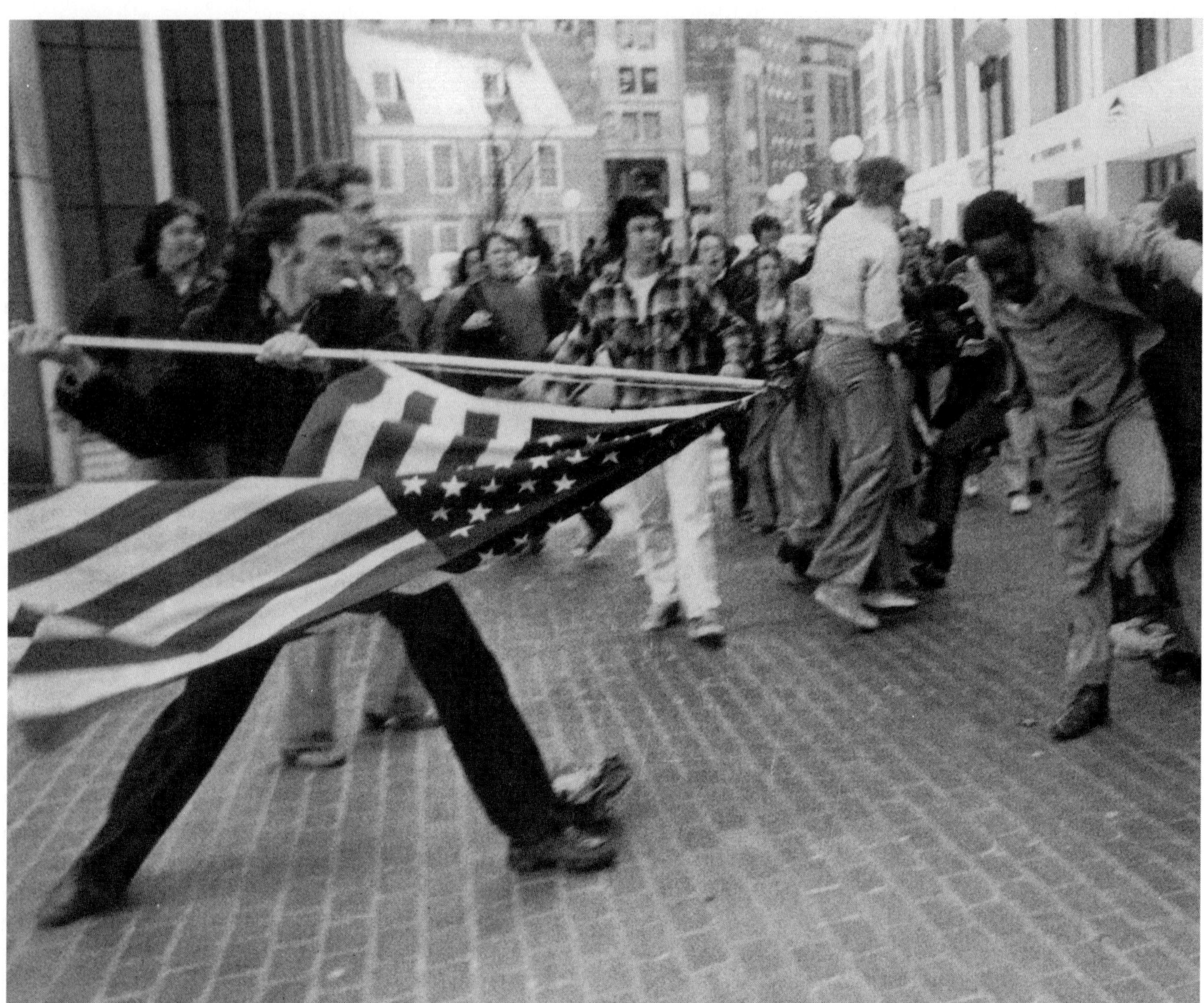

An Antibusing Confrontation in Boston

Tensions over court-ordered busing still ran high in Boston in 1976. When a black lawyer tried to cross the city hall plaza during an antibusing demonstration, he became another victim of Boston's climate of racial hate and violence. This photograph by Stanley Forman for the *Boston Herald American,* showing protesters trying to impale the man with a flagstaff, won a Pulitzer Prize.

nation's emphasis on health and fitness interacted with the heightened environmental awareness to spur demands for pesticide-free foods. Health foods soon became a multimillion-dollar business.

Another legacy of the counterculture was the *human potential* movement, which took the form of a variety of self-help and spiritual approaches. Some people joined encounter sessions—nicknamed "T-groups" for "sensitivity training"—in order to "get in touch with their feelings." Many couples attended marriage-renewal conferences. Other people turned to yoga, Zen Buddhism, Transcendental Meditation (TM), est (Erhard Seminars Training), and Gestalt movements in a quest for self. Numerous young adults joined religious cults, such as Hare Krishna, the Church of Scientology, or the Unification Church of the Reverend Sun Myung Moon (his followers were called "Moonies"); their parents often claimed that their children had been brainwashed to adopt a rigidly communal life and hired "deprogrammers" to rescue them. When hundreds of the predominantly African-American followers of the Reverend Jim Jones, a messianic cult leader, ritualistically committed suicide by drinking fruit punch laced with cyanide at the People's Temple in Guyana in 1978, the potential for excess in such cults was exposed.

The interest in religious cults and paths to inner awareness paralleled a major revival in mainstream religious denominations, which had been building since the 1950s. Much of this religious fervor occurred in evangelical Christian denominations, led by such charismatic preachers as Billy Graham, who learned to use the media, especially television, to spread the gospel. Soon evangelical groups set up their own school systems, newspapers, and broadcasting networks.

By the 1970s, 70 million Americans, almost a third of the population, were affiliated with Christian churches that fostered a "born-again" experience. President Jimmy Carter proudly proclaimed his direct personal relationship with Jesus Christ, as did singers Pat Boone and Johnny Cash, former Watergate convicts Jeb Magruder and Charles Colson, and black power activist Eldridge Cleaver. Religion entered public life when leaders like the Reverend Jerry Falwell, the founder of the Moral Majority, tried to inject their opinions on sensitive issues such as abortion, busing, school prayer, and censorship into politics.

Busing. The most disruptive social issue of the 1970s was the forced busing of children to achieve school integration. Following its 1954 ruling in *Brown v. Board of Education of Topeka,* the Supreme Court had called for desegregation "with all deliberate speed," but progress was limited before 1970. In the 1970s, however, the courts and the Justice Department pushed for more action, beginning in the South, which grudgingly complied, and then in the rest of the country. In 1971 the Supreme Court upheld a federal judge's order requiring the Charlotte-Mecklenberg, North Carolina, school system to transport students from neighborhood to more distant schools in order to integrate the citywide school system. In 1974 the Supreme Court rejected combining the schools of a city and its suburbs to achieve racial balance, but specified that cities with their deeply ingrained patterns of residential segregation must use busing within city boundaries to integrate their classrooms.

These court decisions provoked controversy and violence, with some of the worst occurring in Boston in 1974–1975. The strongly Irish Catholic working-class neighborhood of South Boston responded to the arrival of black students from the Roxbury section with mob scenes reminiscent of Little Rock in 1957. Only armed riot police kept South Boston High School open. Many white parents in Boston, and in other cities threatened by court-ordered busing, transferred their children to private schools; the resulting "white flight" increased the racial imbalance that busing was intended to solve. By the late 1970s the federal courts were backing away from their earlier insistence on busing to achieve racial balance.

Affirmative Action. Almost as divisive as busing was the implementation of *affirmative action* procedures and targets to achieve racial and sexual balance. First put forward by the Department of Labor in 1968, affirmative action was refined by a series of Supreme Court and lower court rulings that identified acceptable procedures for expanding the access of minority-group members to education and jobs. But whites, especially white men, soon raised the cry of "reverse discrimination," claiming they had been passed over in favor of less qualified minorities or women. In 1978 a white man named Allan Bakke sued the University of California Medical School at Davis for rejecting him while admitting minority candidates with lesser qualifications. The Supreme Court ruling in *Bakke v. University of California* was inconclusive: by a 5 to 4 margin, the Court proclaimed that the medical school's absolute quota was illegal and ordered Bakke admitted. At the same time, also by a 5 to 4 margin, it ruled that racial factors could properly be considered in making hiring or admission decisions, thus upholding the principle of affirmative action.

On balance the *Bakke* decision was a setback to the struggle for economic and racial equality that had concerned the nation throughout the 1960s. The often vociferous public opposition to busing, affirmative action, and the Equal Rights Amendment, along with the rapidly growing antiabortion "right to life" movement, constituted a broad backlash against the social changes of the previous decade. Signaling a new conservatism in the social order, many citizens said no to the use of federal power to encourage further change.

AMERICAN VOICES

Busing in Boston *Phyllis Ellison*

Nowhere in the North was busing a more divisive issue than in Boston in 1974–1975. Phyllis Ellison was one of fifty-six black students from the predominantly black neighborhoods of Columbia Point and Roxbury assigned to South Boston High School. Here she describes incidents from her sophomore year, including the day that a white student was stabbed by a black student during a melee at the school. The student's wound was not fatal, but the incident led to heightened resistance and recrimination.

I remember my first day going on the bus to South Boston High School. I wasn't afraid because I felt important. I didn't know what to expect, what was waiting for me up the hill. We had police escorts. I think there was three motorcycle cops and then two police cruisers in front of the bus, and so I felt really important at that time, not knowing what was on the other side of the hill.

Well, when we started up the hill you could hear people saying, "Niggers go home." There were signs, they had made a sign saying, "Black people stay out. We don't want any niggers in our school." And there were people on the corners holding bananas like we were apes, monkeys. "Monkeys get out, get them out of our neighborhood. We don't want you in our schools." So at that time it did frighten me somewhat, but I was more determined then to get inside South Boston High School, because of the people that were outside.

When I got off the bus, first of all I felt important, because of the news media that was there. [Television reporter] Natalie Jacobson out in front of your school getting the story on your school. So I felt really important going through the metal detectors and making sure that no one could come into the school armed. I felt like this was a big deal to me, to attend South Boston High School.

I felt like I was making history, because that was the first year of desegregation and all the controversies and conflicts at that time. I felt that the black students there were making history. . . .

On a normal day there would be anywhere between ten and fifteen fights. You could walk down the corridor and a black person would bump into a white person or vice versa. That would be one fight. And they'd try to separate us, because at that time there was so much tension in the school that one fight could just have the school dismissed for the entire day because it would just lead to another and another and another.

You can't imagine how tense it was inside the classroom. A teacher was almost afraid to say the wrong thing, because they knew that that would excite the whole class, a disturbance in the classroom. The black students sat on one side of the classes. The white students sat on the other side of the classes. The teachers didn't want to assign seating because there may be some problems in the classrooms. So the teachers basically let the students sit where they wanted to sit. In the lunchrooms, the black students sat on one side. The white students sat on the other side. And the ladies' room. It was the same thing. The black

Post-Watergate Politics: Failed Leadership

In the wake of Watergate, many citizens had become cynical about the federal government and politicians in general. "Don't vote. It only encourages them," read one bumper sticker during the 1976 presidential campaign. "The lesser of two evils is still evil," proclaimed another. Political leaders proved unable to deal with the rising inflation, stagnant growth, and declining productivity that plagued the U.S. economy in the 1970s. The fall of Saigon in 1975 reminded Americans of the failure of the Vietnam policy. The world was changing, and Americans had to grapple with the unsettling idea that perhaps the United States was no longer the all-powerful country it had been for much of the postwar era. As Americans approached the 1980 election, this growing sense of impotence erupted in fury over the Iranian hostage crisis.

Ford's Caretaker Presidency

Gerald Ford, the former congressman from Michigan who had become vice-president after Spiro Agnew's resignation, was unable to establish his legitimacy as president during the two years he held the office. His pardon students went to the right of the ladies' room; the white students went to the left of the ladies' room. So really, it was separate, I mean, we attended the same school, but we really never did anything together. Gym classes. If the blacks wanted to play basketball, the whites wanted to play volleyball. So we never played together. They would play volleyball. We would play basketball. . . .

I remember the day Michael Faith got stabbed vividly, because I was in the principal's office and all of a sudden you heard a lot of commotion and you heard kids screaming and yelling and saying, "He's dead, he's dead. That black nigger killed him. He's dead, he's dead." And then the principal running out of the office. There was a lot of commotion and screaming, yelling, hollering, "Get the niggers at Southie." I was really afraid. And the principal came back into the office and said, Call the ambulance and tell all the black students that were in the office to stay there. A police officer was in there and they were trying to get the white students out of the building, because they had just gone on a rampage and they were just going to hurt the first black student that they saw. Anyone that was caught in the corridor that day would be hurt. Once that happened, it probably took about fifteen, twenty minutes for the police officers to get all the white students out. The black students were locked in their rooms and all the white students were let go out of their classrooms. I remember us going into a room, and outside you just saw a crowd of people, I mean, just so many people, I can't even count. They just looked like little bumblebees or something, there was that many. And that Louise Day Hicks was on top of the stairs saying, Let the niggers go back to Roxbury. Send them back to Roxbury. And the crowd booing her. I remember the police cars coming up the street, attempting to, and people turning over the police cars, and I was just amazed that they could do something like that. The police tried to get horses up. They wouldn't let the horses get up. They stoned the horses. They stoned the cars. And I thought that day that we would never get out of South Boston High School. . . .

If I had it to do all over again, for the civil rights part of it, I would do it over, because I felt like my rights were being violated by the white people of South Boston telling me that I could not go to South Boston High School. As for as my education, I think I could have gotten a better education if I didn't spend so much time out of school with the fighting and the violence and being dismissed from school at least once or twice a week. We were allowed to go home early because there was just so much tension inside of the school that if we didn't, someone may be killed or really seriously injured. I think that I could have gotten a better education if I'd spent more time in school than out of school at that time.

Source: Henry Hampton and Steve Fayer, *Voices of Freedom: An Oral History of the Civil Rights Movement from the 1950s Through the 1980s* (New York: Bantam, 1990), 600–1, 610, 612–13, 618.

of Nixon a month after becoming president hurt his credibility as a political leader. Distrust toward politicians spilled onto his choice for vice-president, Nelson A. Rockefeller, the former governor of New York, whose extensive family financial holdings were subjected to acrimonious Senate hearings before he finally won confirmation. Rockefeller's moderate brand of Republicanism also put him out of step with the more hard-line conservatives in the party.

Ford's biggest problem as president was the economy, reeling with inflation set in motion by the Vietnam War and worsened by the OPEC price rises and the growing trade deficit. The 1974 inflation rate soared to almost 12 percent. In an attempt to curtail prices, the Federal Reserve tightened the money supply and drove up interest rates. In 1975 the economy entered its deepest downturn since the Great Depression, but the government refused to increase spending or cut taxes, generally acknowledged by economists as spurs to recovery. Production declined more than 10 percent, and nearly 9 percent of the work force was unemployed. The 1975 recession temporarily reduced the inflation rate to less than 5 percent, but it soon rose again. Ford's call to "Whip Inflation Now," complete with much-mocked "WIN" buttons, only served to draw attention to his inability to influence broader economic trends.

In foreign policy, Ford was equally lacking in presidential leadership. He maintained Nixon's initiatives to-

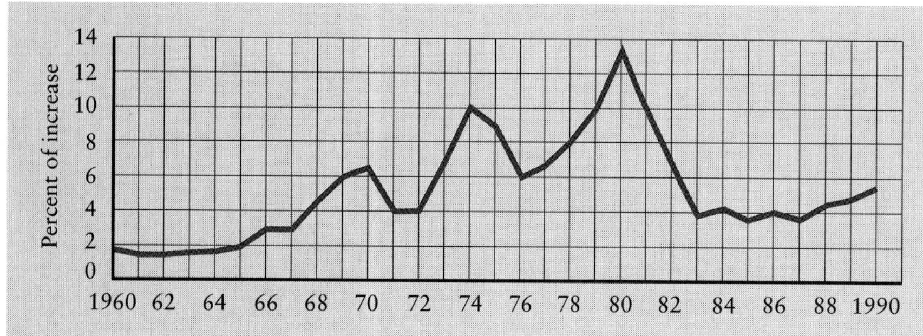

FIGURE 32.1

The Consumer Price Index, 1960–1990

The annual inflation rate peaked in 1980, the last year of Carter's presidency. *Source: U.S. Statistical Abstract, 1991.*

ward détente by asking Henry Kissinger to stay on as secretary of state, a position he had held since 1973. Ford met with Soviet leaders at Vladivostok to begin hammering out details of a hoped-for SALT II (Strategic Arms Limitation Talks) agreement, but there was little concrete progress on arms control. Ford and Kissinger also continued Nixon's policy of increasing American support for the Shah of Iran, failing to notice that the Shah's policy of rapid modernization was provoking bitter opposition and anti-Western sentiment among Iran's growing Muslim fundamentalist population.

After the paranoia and abuses of the Nixon era, Ford's personal style and candor were refreshing. But he failed to demonstrate the assurance and competence needed in a time of mounting economic and international problems. "Gerald Ford is an awfully nice man who isn't up to the presidency," the *New Republic* concluded, and the voters agreed.

The Outsider as President

Only in the skewed political atmosphere of post-Watergate America could the Democrats have chosen their 1976 nominee, James E. Carter, Jr. "Jimmy Who?" the media scoffed at first about this engineer and former entrepreneur in agricultural commodities from Plains, Georgia, popularly portrayed as a peanut farmer. But they soon changed their tune as Carter won key primaries, giving his candidacy momentum and credibility. Carter played up his role as a Washington outsider (his previous political experience had been as governor of Georgia, and before that as state senator), and pledged to restore morality to government. "I will never lie to you," he piously told voters.

The 1976 presidential campaign was one of the blandest in years. On the Republican side, President Ford staved off a conservative challenge from Governor Ronald Reagan of California; then he dumped Vice-President Nelson Rockefeller in favor of hard-line conservative Senator Robert J. Dole of Kansas. Carter chose as his running-mate Senator Walter F. Mondale of Minnesota, who had ties to the traditional Democratic constituencies of labor, liberals, blacks, and big-city machines. Avoiding issues and controversy, Carter won the election with 50 percent of the popular vote to Ford's 48 percent.

Jimmy Carter immediately tried to set a different tone for his administration. On Inauguration Day he renounced formal wear in favor of a business suit; instead of riding in a limousine, he and his wife, Rosalynn, walked from the Capitol to the White House. Throughout his term he relied heavily on symbolic gestures—dressing in an informal cardigan sweater for fireside chats to the nation, carrying his own luggage on and off planes, holding town meetings, and staying in the homes of ordinary citizens. Carter's homespun approach soon wore thin as people looked for substance behind the symbols. "If the Carter administration were a television show," quipped columnist Russell Baker, "it would have been canceled months ago."

Domestic Leadership. Part technocrat, part preacher, Carter failed to develop an effective style of domestic leadership, a task made even more difficult by the post-Watergate climate of cynicism and apathy. His campaign as an outsider had distanced him from traditional sources of power in Washington, and he did little to heal the breach. Well into the term, Carter's chief domestic aide, Hamilton Jordan, had never introduced himself to Thomas ("Tip") O'Neill, the Speaker of the House of Representatives and the most powerful Democrat on Capitol Hill. Shying away from established Democratic leaders, Carter turned to advisers and friends who had worked with him in Georgia, none of whom had national experience. When his budget director Bert Lance was questioned about financial irregularities at his Atlanta bank, the case undercut Carter's pledges to restore integrity and morality in government.

The nemesis of inflation was Carter's major domestic challenge. When he took office the nation was just coming out of the severe 1975 recession. To speed recovery, Carter called for increased government spending and lower taxes. When these actions provoked renewed inflation, he reversed himself, calling for spending cuts and a delay in the tax reductions. This zigzag fiscal policy eroded both business and consumer confidence. Unemployment hovered between 6 and 7 percent, and inflation rose from 6.5 percent in 1977 to the "double-digit" level of 12.4 percent in 1980. As the Federal Reserve Board raised rates to counter inflation, interest rates briefly topped 20 percent in 1980, a historic high. A deep recession finally broke the inflationary spiral in 1982, two years after Carter left office.

Among its domestic initiatives, the Carter presidency reformed the civil service system and created the separate cabinet-level departments of Energy and Education. It also oversaw the deregulation of the airline, trucking, and railroad industries. Carter supported gradual decontrol of oil and natural gas prices as a spur to domestic production and conservation. But his attempt to provide leadership during the energy crisis failed. He called efforts for energy conservation "the moral equivalent of war" (borrowing a phrase from the nineteenth-century philosopher William James). A hostile media, unable to find the specifics, wickedly reduced the phrase to "MEOW." By the summer of 1979, when gas lines once again reminded Americans of their dependence on foreign oil, Carter's approval rating was only 26 percent, lower even than Richard Nixon's at the height of the Watergate scandal.

A Framework for Peace
President Jimmy Carter's greatest foreign policy achievement was the personal diplomacy he exerted to persuade President Anwar Sadat of Egypt (left) and Prime Minister Menachem Begin of Israel (right) to sign a peace treaty in 1978.

Foreign Policy and Diplomacy. Jimmy Carter's commitment to human rights was the centerpiece of his new direction in foreign affairs. He criticized the suppression of dissent in the Soviet Union—especially as it affected the right of Jewish citizens to emigrate—and he withdrew economic and military aid from Argentina, Uruguay, Ethiopia, and other non-Communist countries that violated human rights. He also established an Office of Human Rights within the State Department. But he could not change the internal policies of longtime U.S. allies and serious human rights violators, such as the Philippines, South Korea, and South Africa.

President Carter did achieve a stunning success in the Middle East, a complex arena of international instability. Relations between Egypt and Israel had remained tense since the 1973 Yom Kippur War. In November 1975, Israel's prime minister, Menachem Begin, moved to break the ice by inviting the Egyptian president Anwar Sadat to Israel to discuss the possibility of peace. Sadat came in 1977, but the talks stalled. President Carter broke the stalemate in 1978 by inviting Begin and Sadat to Camp David, the presidential retreat in the Maryland mountains. Two weeks of discussions and Carter's promise of significant additional foreign aid for Egypt persuaded Sadat and Begin to agree on a "framework for peace." The framework included Israel's return of the Sinai peninsula, which it had occupied since 1967; the transfer of Sinai territory took place from 1979 to 1982.

In Latin America, Carter's most important contribution was resolution of the lingering dispute over control of the Panama Canal. In a treaty signed on September 7, 1977, the United States agreed to turn over control of the canal to Panama on December 31, 1999. In return, the United States retained the right to send its ships through the canal in case of war, even though the canal itself was declared neutral territory. Despite conservatives' outcry that the United States was giving away more than it got, the Senate narrowly approved the treaty.

Carter had campaigned to free the United States from its "inordinate fear of Communism," but relationships with the Soviet Union soon became tense. Recriminations surrounding the SALT II arms limitation talks were a major cause. By the time that Carter met Soviet leader Leonid Brezhnev in Vienna in July 1979 to sign the accords, the president had ordered the construction of a new category of ballistic missiles (Pershing II) and the Soviets had forged ahead with new SS-20 missiles. The SALT II treaty of 1979 was therefore already seriously behind the current technology and did little to stop the escalating arms race.

Ratification of the SALT II treaty was soon tabled

indefinitely, as part of the Carter administration's response to the Soviet Union's invasion of Afghanistan in December 1979. Carter called this the most serious threat to world peace since World War II, largely because he feared that the Soviet move was a stepping stone toward the rich Middle Eastern oil supplies. In retaliation, the United States curtailed grain sales to the U.S.S.R. and boycotted the 1980 summer Olympic games in Moscow. (The Soviets returned the gesture, boycotting the 1984 summer games in Los Angeles.) When Carter left office in 1980, relations with the Soviet Union were worse than when he came in.

The Iranian Hostage Crisis

The most serious foreign policy problem of the Carter administration occurred in Iran. Ever since the CIA had helped install Muhammad Riza Pahlavi on the throne in 1953, the United States had counted on his regime as a steady pillar (or more accurately, a heavy-handed police officer) in the troubled Middle East. The Shah was a major customer for American arms, using "petrodollars" from the sale of oil to the United States to purchase close to $20 billion worth of weapons between 1972 and 1979. (These arms sales were large enough to have a positive impact on the U.S. balance of payments deficit.) President Carter had visited Iran in late 1977 and declared it "an island of stability in one of the more troubled areas of the world." With this personal endorsement, the human rights advocate Carter overlooked the repressive tactics of Iran's CIA-trained secret police, SAVAK. For American policymakers, access to oil reserves and support for the Shah's consistently anti-Communist stance outweighed all other considerations.

Early in 1979, a revolution led by a fundamentalist Muslim leader, the Ayatollah Ruhollah Khomeini, overturned the Shah's government and drove him into exile. The United States had ignored warning signals that the Shah's efforts to westernize Iran had offended fundamentalist Islamic leaders; the CIA had also downplayed the extent to which hatred of the United States had helped to coalesce opposition to the Shah. Once the mullahs (religious leaders) were in power, the United States seemed unsure how to deal with the new Iranian officials, who denounced the Soviet Union and the United States with equal ferocity.

In late October 1979, the Carter administration made a controversial decision to admit the deposed Shah, who was suffering from incurable cancer, into the United States for medical treatment. Iran's new leaders had warned that such an action would provoke retaliation, but foreign policy leaders like Henry Kissinger and David Rockefeller argued that the United States owed this gesture to the Shah both for humanitarian reasons and in return for his years of support for American policy. In response, on November 4, 1979, fundamentalist Muslim students under Khomeini's direction seized the U.S. embassy in Teheran, taking American hostages in a flagrant violation of the principle of diplomatic immunity. After the release of nineteen hostages, primarily women, black marines, and those suffering from serious illness, fifty-two remained in captivity. The hostage-takers demanded that the Shah be returned to Iran for trial and punishment. The United States refused. President Carter suspended arms sales to Iran, froze Iranian assets in American banks, and threatened to deport Iranian students studying in the country, but no more hostages were released.

For the next fourteen months, the Iranian hostage

American Hostages in Iran
Images of blindfolded, handcuffed, American hostages seized by Iranian militants at the American Embassy in Teheran in November 1979 shocked Americans and created a foreign policy crisis that eventually cost Jimmy Carter the presidency.

crisis paralyzed the presidency of Jimmy Carter. Each night humiliating pictures of blindfolded hostages appeared on television newscasts. (Media-conscious Iranian students conveniently printed their anti-American placards in English.) The late night television news program, *Nightline,* featuring journalist Ted Koppel, originated as "America Held Hostage," a nightly update on the news from Iran which provided an unexpected way for ABC to compete with Johnny Carson's *Tonight Show.*

In many ways, Carter's insistence that the safe return of the hostages was his top priority actually enhanced their value to their captors. But amid mounting calls for strong American action, Carter could do little to win their release until a stable Iranian government was willing to negotiate. An attempt to mount a military rescue of the hostages failed miserably in April 1980, six months into the crisis, when helicopter equipment failures in the desert meant the rescue literally never got off the ground. Secretary of State Cyrus Vance resigned in protest over the attempt, claiming it would have endangered the lives of the hostages further. The abortive rescue mission reinforced the view of Carter as bumbling and ineffective.

The White House took on an embattled tone. President Carter decided not to enter the presidential primary elections underway in 1980, claiming that he wanted to devote all his energy to the safe return of the hostages. This "above politics" stance did help Carter beat back a challenge from Massachusetts senator Edward Kennedy for the Democratic nomination, but it worked to his detriment during the general presidential campaign against Republican challenger Ronald Reagan. In a scenario reminiscent of the 1932 election, Carter played the part of the embattled, defensive Hoover, while Reagan took the upbeat, decisive Roosevelt role. Candidate Reagan continually harped on the hostage stalemate, calling the Iranians "barbarians" and "common criminals" and hinting that he would take strong action to wrest their return. This rhetorical stance played a definite role in Reagan's decisive electoral victory in November 1980.

In all, the hostages spent 444 days in captivity. They were released at precisely the moment when Jimmy Carter turned over the presidency to Ronald Reagan on January 20, 1981. The hostages returned home to an ecstatic patriotic welcome, a reflection of American frustration over their long ordeal.

While most Americans continued to maintain that "We're Number One," the hostage crisis in Iran came to symbolize the loss of America's power to control world affairs. Its psychological impact was magnified because it came at the end of the decade that had witnessed Watergate, the American defeat in Vietnam, and the OPEC embargo. To a large extent, this decline in influence was magnified by the unusual predominance the United States had enjoyed after World War II, a dominance that could not realistically have been expected to last forever. The return to economic and political power of Japan and Western Europe, the control of vital oil resources by Middle Eastern countries, and the industrialization of some Third World nations had widened the cast of international actors. Still, many Americans were unable to accept anything less than the economic and political supremacy of the postwar years. Ronald Reagan rode their frustrations to victory in 1980.

Summary

The year 1968 saw an unprecedented level of domestic unrest, including the assassinations of Martin Luther King, Jr., and Robert F. Kennedy and major protests at the Democratic convention in Chicago. Richard Nixon was elected president by promising to restore quieter times. However, the nation continued to debate the value of American involvement in Vietnam, which did not end until the signing of the Paris Peace Accords in January 1973. Meanwhile, the Nixon administration took part in a series of illegal and questionable acts in connection with the president's campaign for reelection in 1972. The resulting Watergate scandal led to Nixon's resignation in 1974. Vice-President Gerald Ford became president, but he lost the 1976 election to Jimmy Carter of Georgia, who campaigned as an outsider.

During the rest of the decade, the United States struggled with economic problems including high inflation, skyrocketing energy costs, and a diminished position in world trade. Many citizens became cynical about national leadership in the wake of Watergate. The environmental movement promoted the vision that "small is beautiful," and many citizens sought federal action to promote clean air and water. A new, more conservative social mood limited further progress of the civil rights and women's movements; this mood injected values drawn from evangelical religion into political life. The end of the decade was dominated by the Iranian hostage crisis, as Islamic fundamentalists held fifty-two hostages at the U.S. embassy in Teheran for 444 days. The hostage crisis virtually paralyzed Carter's presidency, helping Ronald Reagan win election in 1980.

TOPIC FOR RESEARCH

The Alaska Pipeline and the Environment

In 1968 an "elephant" was found near Prudhoe Bay, Alaska, on the Arctic coast, that was twice as large as any oil field in North America. In 1977 completion of the 800-mile Trans-Alaska pipeline linked Prudhoe Bay to the port of Valdez at a cost of $7.7 billion. The delay in construction of the pipeline was due to extensive litigation that pitted oil companies against environmentalists. Environmental concerns included the impact of the pipeline on Alaskan wildlife and the risk of oil tanker accidents at Valdez in Prince William Sound.

Research the pros and cons of building the pipeline. What were the arguments on both sides? What strategies were pursued? What finally tipped the balance? In light of the *Exxon Valdez* accident in 1989 (which, as environmentalists had feared, saturated Prince William Sound with oil), were the earlier predictions of environmentalists accurate? Why had they failed to get their message across?

The best introduction to oil issues is Daniel Yergin, *The Prize* (1991). The public debate can be traced through newspapers and magazines in the 1970s, as well as the government hearings on the issue. Other sources include Potter Wickware, *Crazy Money: Nine Months on the Trans-Alaska Pipeline* (1979); Ed McGarth, *Inside the Alaska Pipeline* (1977); Robert Douglas Mead, *Journeys Down the Line: Building the Trans-Alaska Pipeline* (1978); and Mim Dixon, *What Happened to Fairbanks? The Effects of the Trans-Alaska Pipeline on the Community of Fairbanks* (1978).

BIBLIOGRAPHY

The Watershed Year

Material on 1968 as a turning point in postwar America can be found in various sources. See David Caute, *The Year of the Barricades* (1968); David Farber, *Chicago '68* (1988); and Lewis Chester, Godfrey Hodgson, and Bruce Page, *An American Melodrama* (1970). Norman Mailer provides his contemporary view on the conventions in *Miami and the Siege of Chicago* (1968). William H. Chafe's overview of the postwar period, *An Unfinished Journey* (2nd edition, 1991), gives a central role to developments in that year.

Kevin Phillips, *The Emerging Republican Majority* (1969), and Richard Scammon and Ben J. Wattenberg, *The Real Majority* (1970), describe the voters whom Richard Nixon tried to reach. Theodore H. White, *The Making of the President—1968* (1969) and *The Making of the President—1972* (1973), cover the election campaigns.

The Nixon Years

Jonathan Schell, *The Time of Illusion* (1976), offers an insightful discussion of the Nixon administration. Herbert Parmet, *Richard Nixon and His America* (1990), and Stephen Ambrose, *Nixon* (1987), are two of many biographies of this complicated political character. Kim McQuaid, *The Anxious Years: America in the Vietnam-Watergate Era* (1989), is an overview of the period. See also William Safire, *Before the Fall* (1975); Leonard Silk, *Nixonomics* (1972); and Garry Wills, *Nixon Agonistes* (1971).

Robert S. Litwak, *Détente and the Nixon Doctrine* (1984), and Tad Szulc, *The Illusion of Peace* (1978), are overviews of Nixon's foreign policy. Stanley Karnow, *Vietnam: A History* (1983), describes events through the fall of Saigon in 1975; Marilyn Young continues the story in *The Vietnam Wars, 1945–1990* (1991). William Shawcross, *Sideshow: Kissinger, Nixon, and the Destruction of Cambodia* (1979), is strongly critical of U.S. policy. Robert Jay Lifton, *Home from the War* (1973); Paul Starr, *The Discarded Army* (1973); and Lawrence Baskir and William A. Strauss, *Chance and Circumstance* (1978), discuss the problems of returning Vietnam veterans. Ron Kovic, *Born on the Fourth of July* (1976), is a moving personal memoir.

Stanley Kutler, *The Wars of Watergate* (1990); Anthony Lukas, *Nightmare: The Underside of the Nixon Years* (1976); and Theodore H. White, *Breach of Faith* (1975), are comprehensive accounts of the Watergate scandal. Also of interest are the books by the *Washington Post* journalists who broke the story, Carl Bernstein and Bob Woodward, *All the President's Men* (1974) and *The Final Days* (1976). John Dean, *Blind Ambition* (1976), is the best account by a participant; see also H. R. Haldeman, *The Ends of Power* (1978), and Richard M. Nixon, *RN: The Memoirs of Richard Nixon* (1978). Richard M. Cohen and Jules Witcover, *A Heartbeat Away* (1974), describes Spiro Agnew's fall from power. Arthur M. Schlesinger, Jr., *The Imperial Presidency* (1973), analyzes changes in the institution that provided a backdrop for the Watergate affair.

Lowered Expectations and New Challenges

Peter Carroll, *It Seemed Like Nothing Happened* (1982), provides a historian's view of the 1970s. General introductions to economic developments of the decade are in Barry Bluestone and Bennett Harrison, *The Deindustrialization of America* (1982); Richard J. Barnet and Ronald E. Muller, *Global Reach* (1974); Richard J. Barnet, *The Lean Years* (1980); John P. Hoerr, *And the Wolf Finally Came: The Decline of the Steel Industry* (1988); Robert Calleo, *The Imperious Economy* (1982); and Gardner Means et al., *The Roots of Inflation* (1975). John M. Blair, *The Control of Oil* (1976), and J. C. Hurewitz, ed., *Oil, the Arab-Israeli Dispute, and the Industrial World* (1976), treat OPEC developments.

Barry Commoner, *The Closing Circle* (1971) and *The Poverty of Power* (1976), and Robert Heilbroner, *An Inquiry into the Human Prospect* (1974), cogently assess the origins of the energy crisis and the prospects for the future. See also Lester C. Thurow, *The Zero-Sum Society* (1980), and Robert Stobaugh and Daniel Yergin, *Energy Future* (1980). For a general overview of the environmental movement, see Samuel P. Hays, *Beauty, Health, and Permanence: Environmental Politics in the United States, 1955–1985* (1987). Roderick Nash provides a history of environmental ethics in *The Rights of Nature* (1989). Influential books in shaping public awareness of ecological issues included Paul R. Ehrlich, *The Population Bomb* (1968); Frances Moore Lappe, *Diet for a Small Planet* (1971); and Philip Slater, *Earthwalk* (1974).

Much of the material on post-Watergate politics has been provided by journalists rather than historians. Richard Reeves, *A Ford, Not a Lincoln* (1975); J. F. ter Horst, *Gerald Ford and the Future of the Presidency* (1974); and John Osborne, *White House Watch: The Ford Years* (1977), cover the Ford presidency. See also A. James Reichley, *Conservatives in an Age of Change: The Nixon and Ford Administrations* (1981). Jules Witcover, *Marathon* (1977), describes the pursuit of the presidency in 1976, while Theodore H. White, *America in Search of Itself* (1982), looks more broadly at public life between 1954 and 1980.

Portraits of the Carter presidency, generally unfavorable, are found in Robert Shogan, *Promises to Keep* (1977); Haynes Johnson, *In the Absence of Power* (1980); and Clark Mollenhoff, *The President Who Failed* (1980). See also Erwin Hargrove, *Jimmy Carter as President* (1989), and Charles Jones, *The Trusteeship Presidency* (1988). James Wooten, *Dasher* (1978), and Betty Glad, *Jimmy Carter: From Plains to the White House* (1980), are competent biographies. See also Jimmy Carter's own campaign manifesto, *Why Not the Best?* (1975), and his presidential memoirs, *Keeping Faith* (1982). Rosalynn Carter contributes her perspective in *First Lady from Plains* (1984). James Fallows, *National Defense* (1981), is an incisive overview of defense developments. See also A. Glenn Mower, Jr., *Human Rights and American Foreign Policy: The Carter and Reagan Experiences* (1987). Stephen Ambrose, *The Rise to Globalism* (5th ed., 1988), includes a summary of the Iranian hostage crisis.

Stanley Aronowitz, *False Promises* (1973); Richard Krickus, *Pursuing the American Dream* (1976); and Michael Novak, *The Rise of the Unmeltable Ethnics* (1977), describe the concerns of the white ethnic middleclass. J. Anthony Lukas, *Common Ground* (1985), tells the story of the Boston busing crisis through the lives of three families in a compelling narrative. Nathan Glazer, *Affirmative Discrimination* (1975); Thomas Sowell, *Race and Economics* (1975); and Allan P. Sindler, *Bakke, Defunis, and Minority Admissions* (1978), treat the controversial topic of affirmative action.

Tom Wolfe gave the decade its name in "The Me Decade and the Third Great Awakening," *New York Magazine* (August 23, 1976). Influential books included Christopher Lasch, *The Culture of Narcissism: American Life in an Age of Diminishing Expectations* (1978), and Gail Sheehy, *Passages* (1976). Alan Crawford, *Thunder on the Right* (1980), surveys the new conservatism, as does Peter Steinfels, *The Neo-Conservatives* (1979). John Woodridge, *The Evangelicals* (1975), and Marshall Frady, *Billy Graham* (1979), analyze the rise of evangelical religion; James Reston, Jr., *Our Father Who Art in Hell* (1981), tells the story of Reverend Jim Jones and the Guyana tragedy. Carol Felsenthal's biography of Phyllis Schlafly, *The Sweetheart of the Silent Majority* (1981), shows how the Moral Majority identified feminism as a target.

TIMELINE

1968	Tet offensive Robert Kennedy assassinated Democratic convention marred by street violence in Chicago Nixon elected president
1970	U.S. troops invade Cambodia; renewed antiwar demonstrations Earth Day first observed Environmental Protection Agency established
1971	Pentagon Papers published Collapse of Bretton Woods system
1972	SALT initiates détente Watergate break-in Nixon reelected
1973–1974	Arab oil embargo
1973	Paris Peace Accords Spiro Agnew resigns; Gerald R. Ford appointed vice-president War Powers Act
1974	Nixon resigns; Ford becomes president
1974–1975	Busing controversy in Boston
1975	Recession Fall of Saigon
1976	Jimmy Carter elected president
1978	Camp David accords between Israel and Egypt *Bakke v. University of California* limits affirmative action
1979	Hostages seized at American embassy in Teheran, Iran Three Mile Island nuclear accident Formal recognition of People's Republic of China U.S.S.R. invades Afghanistan
1980	Ronald W. Reagan elected president

The Wall Comes Tumbling Down

The destruction of the Berlin Wall in November 1989 symbolized the end of the Cold War.

CHAPTER 33 *Toward a New World Order, 1980 to the Present*

In the 1920s, Americans were drawn into a national web of shared experience. In the 1980s, an international web linked Americans with the rest of the world. Political choices made in Washington, such as incurring huge budget deficits to maintain American defense and domestic spending while cutting taxes, had international economic implications. Similarly, decisions made in Tokyo, Hong Kong, Bonn, or Brussels affected what kind of consumer products Americans could buy, what the prime rate would be, and even whether American workers kept their jobs. More than ever, events in the United States and the rest of the world were inextricably intertwined.

A Coca-Cola executive captured why American corporations increasingly had to think in global terms. "Willie Sutton used to say he robbed banks because that's where the money is. Well, we are increasingly global because 95 percent of the world's consumers are outside this country. It's that simple." But not all American companies found it easy to adapt and compete in these new conditions. Lee Iaccoca, head of the Chrysler Corporation, which struggled throughout the 1980s to stay ahead of foreign competitors, often complained that international trade was an uneven football field on which United States industries had to play uphill. But the fact of the matter was that for the first time since the end of World War II, the field no longer tilted in America's favor.

The United States now shares dominance with other nations in an interconnected global economy that is constantly affected by changing international political realities. Most dramatically, the collapse of communism in Eastern Europe and the Soviet Union ended the Cold War, which had shaped American foreign and domestic policy for four decades. But the "new world order" that will replace the old economic and political relationships among nations is still emerging.

The Reagan Presidency

After 1968 the New Deal Democratic coalition that had dominated national politics since Franklin Roosevelt slowly but steadily declined. At the same time, the Republican party underwent a conservative rebirth that translated into electoral success. In 1989, when Vice-President George Bush succeeded Ronald Reagan, the Republicans had won five out of the last six presidential contests. The Democrats, on the other hand, continued to find more electoral success in Congress and in state government.

Ronald Reagan and the Conservative Agenda

Ronald Reagan's path to the presidency holds clues both to the resurgence of the Republican party and its core values. Born in 1911 in Tampico, Illinois, Reagan won a modest reputation as a Hollywood actor, then served as a corporate spokesperson on television for General Electric. During this time his political philosophy shifted from New Deal Democrat to conservative

Republican. After endorsing Barry Goldwater in 1964, Reagan decided to enter politics. He was twice elected governor of California, serving from 1966 to 1974. This positioned him well to try for the presidency in 1976, although he lost the nomination to Gerald Ford. During the 1980 primary season, he handily dispatched his opponents, including former U.N. ambassador and CIA director George Bush, whom he then chose as his running mate. In the general election, Reagan and Bush roundly defeated incumbent president Jimmy Carter as well as an independent candidate, Representative John B. Anderson of Illinois. The Republican landslide also gave the party control of the Senate for the first time since 1954, although the Democrats maintained their hold on the House.

One key to the Republican resurgence of the 1970s and 1980s was money. As the party of the well-to-do and the business community, Republicans were supported by financial resources that far exceeded those available to the Democrats, whose main support came from organized labor. Political action committees, or PACs, collected large sums for conservative candidates. The Republicans' financial superiority enabled them to make sophisticated and highly effective use of television to address voters directly.

Another key was a realignment of the electorate. The core of the Republican party that elected Ronald Reagan remained the upper-middle-class white Protestant voters who supported balanced budgets, disliked government activism, feared crime and communism, and believed in a strong national defense. These values were the essence of postwar conservatism. Now new groups gravitated toward the Republican vision, often for reasons of economic self-interest: southern whites disaffected by big government and blacks' civil rights gains; formerly urban ethnic group members who had moved to the suburbs; blue-collar workers, especially Catholics; young voters who identified as conservatives; and voters in the Sunbelt, a region traditionally more conservative than the Midwest or East. When California's Proposition 13, calling for sharp cuts in property taxes, was approved in a 1978 referendum, it suggested that voters were more concerned about their bank balances than with supporting public education or government services.

Perhaps the most significant constituency energizing the Republican party was the New Right, whose emphasis on traditional values and fundamentalist Christian morality dovetailed well with conservative Republican ideology. The New Right was particularly

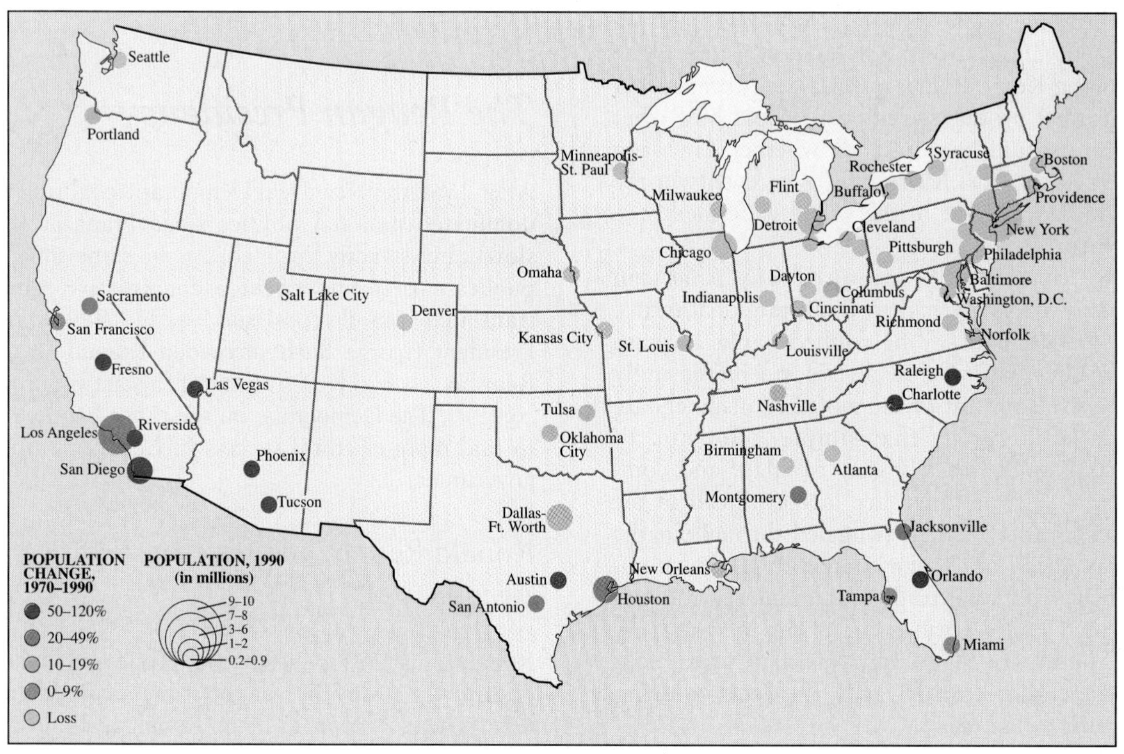

MAP 33.1

The Growth of the Sunbelt, 1970–1990

The Sunbelt states of the South and West were the key to the Republican resurgence in the 1980s. While older industrial cities like New York, Chicago, Philadelphia, and Detroit lost population, newer metropolises—Phoenix, Houston, and San Diego—grew spectacularly.

upset by the rapid social changes underway since the 1960s, especially those viewed as undermining traditional family and gender roles. Jimmy Carter, a southerner and a devout evangelical Protestant, had captured much of this vote in 1976, but four years later New Right voters were more comfortable in the Republican party. Their concerns formed the basis for the party's platform, which called for a constitutional ban on abortion, voluntary prayer in the public schools, and a mandatory death penalty for certain crimes; it also demanded an end to forced busing and, for the first time in forty years, opposed the Equal Rights Amendment, reflecting the New Right's strongly felt belief that women belonged at home with their families.

Back Home on the Ranch
Like many members of the Hollywood community, Nancy and Ronald Reagan preferred the southern California lifestyle to the frenetic rhythms of Washington and New York. Here they ride horseback at their California ranch.

The Reagan Style

When sixty-nine-year-old Ronald Wilson Reagan took office in January 1981, he became the oldest man ever to serve as president. (He was actually six years older than John F. Kennedy would have been, had he lived.) He showed his remarkable physical stamina just months into office when he survived an assassination attempt outside a Washington, D.C., hotel. Just as robust was his personal popularity, which remained high throughout his two terms. He became known as the "Great Communicator" for his ability to establish rapport with the American people through the medium of television.

During his long acting career and his stint in state government, Reagan developed a somewhat removed leadership style. Once, when asked what kind of governor he would be, he replied, "I don't know, I've never played a governor." Many observers found him better at general platitudes and encouragement than details: "We have a great task ahead of us," Reagan would say, but never state what that task was.

To maintain his hands-off style of governance, he depended on the support and advice of his appointees. Among his closest personal advisers were Chief of Staff James Baker, presidential counselor Edwin Meese, and Secretary of the Treasury Donald Regan, who became chief of staff in 1985 when Baker switched to the Treasury post. Reagan also relied heavily on his wife Nancy, who was fiercely protective of both his image and his schedule, even to the point of consulting an astrologer before planning major White House events.

Reaganomics

Buoyed by his electoral mandate and the conservative resurgence, Ronald Reagan seized the chance to redefine the nation's priorities. Ever since the New Deal, the public had generally assumed that the nation's social and economic problems could best be solved by expanding federal action. The election of Ronald Reagan ended almost half a century of activism. "Government is not the solution to our problem," he declared. "Government is the problem."

Reagan first moved to reshape the nation's fiscal and tax policies. The term *Reaganomics* came to stand for the tax cuts and domestic budget reductions enacted in 1981 and 1982 and the supply-side economic theory behind them. According to this theory, excessive taxation siphoned off capital that should be invested to stimulate economic growth. Tax cuts would give businesses and individuals more money to invest, investments would cause the economy to expand, and total tax revenues would be greater—despite the lower rates. Government expenditures would be trimmed by shrinking government benefits, especially entitlement programs begun during the New Deal. And the federal budget deficit would go down. That, at least, was the theory. Critics charged that conservatives deliberately cut taxes to mandate reductions in federal funding for social programs they abhorred.

The first part of this economic policy—tax cuts—was enacted in the Economic Recovery Tax Act of 1981, arguably the most significant legislation of the Reagan years. Building on a proposal originally developed by Senator William Roth of Delaware and Representative Jack Kemp of New York, this across-the-board tax cut reduced basic personal income tax rates 25 percent over three years. It also introduced the indexing of tax brackets, which kept tax rates constant when incomes rose solely because of inflation. According to budget director David Stockman, the tax cut was to be linked with large cutbacks in expenditures, especially in human services. Congressional resistance kept programs such as Social Security and Medicare intact, but more than half of Reagan's proposed cuts were enacted. If all had gone according to Stockman's plan, the budget should have been balanced by 1984. This did not happen. Despite what seemed like wrenching cuts in federal programs, the drop in revenues from the tax cuts was far steeper than the amount pruned from the budget. Deficits began to balloon alarmingly.

Another contribution to the deficit was the $1.7 trillion, five-year defense buildup advocated by the president and his Defense secretary, Caspar Weinberger. This huge increase fulfilled Republican campaign pledges to "make America Number One again" militarily. Especially favored was development of such equipment as the B-1 bomber, which Carter had canceled, and the MX mobile missile. Reagan's most ambitious, and controversial, weapons plan was the 1983 Strategic Defense Initiative (SDI), popularly known as "Star Wars" from the movie of the same name. SDI would be a satellite and laser shield to detect and intercept incoming missiles before they could strike. Reagan supporters claimed SDI would render nuclear war obsolete, but scientists doubted its feasibility.

Limiting Government. The Reagan administration also moved to abolish or reduce government regulations affecting the workplace, health care, consumer protection, and the environment. Reaganomics claimed such regulations were not only inefficient but also impeded productivity because of the high cost of compliance. (Much of the slack, and the cost, was transferred to the states.) Reagan's appointees to such formerly activist regulatory agencies as the National Labor Relations Board and the Environmental Protection Agency lessened the impact of existing regulations by scaling back budget requests, not spending allocated funds, or delaying action on pending cases.

Meanwhile, the Federal Reserve Board used monetary policy to combat the still troubling problem of inflation, which had been high since the mid-1970s. By raising the interest rate for corporate borrowers, the Federal Reserve did reduce inflation from 12.4 percent in 1980 to 4 percent in 1982. But tightening the money supply in this way also reduced business investment, contributing to a severe recession in 1981–1982. Slack industrial growth raised the unemployment rate to 10.7 percent, the highest since the Great Depression; thousands of workers were laid off, especially in the Midwest. The automobile and steel industries, already facing challenges from foreign competitors using newer and more efficient technologies as well as lower-paid workers, were particularly hard hit. Due to the severe cutbacks in entitlement programs under Reagan, only 45 percent of those who lost their jobs received unemployment compensation, compared with 75 percent at the height of the harsh 1975 recession.

It was a relatively brief recession: the economy began growing again in early 1983. For the rest of the decade inflation stayed low, aided by a worldwide drop in energy costs, and the Reagan administration presided over the longest peacetime economic expansion in American history. But in many ways this sense of economic well-being was an illusion, "an illusion based on borrowed time and borrowed money," as the federal budget deficit continued to mount.

Foreign Relations

In foreign relations, Ronald Reagan's first-term break with postwar traditions was less dramatic than in domestic social policy. Détente had collapsed late in the Carter administration over the Soviet Union's invasion of Afghanistan, and Reagan entered the presidency with a confrontational approach to the Soviet Union, including a strong commitment to stopping Communist expansion in developing nations. Giving voice to the beliefs of Republican hardliners, Reagan articulated some of the harshest anti-Soviet rhetoric heard in the United States since the 1950s. In March 1983 he called the Soviet Union an "evil empire" that was "the focus of evil in the modern world."

The Middle East continued to challenge policymakers, always mindful of America's dependence on the region for oil. Reagan's hopes for peace in the Middle East were thwarted when Israeli troops invaded southern Lebanon in 1982, intending to dislodge the Palestine Liberation Organization from its bases there. The Israelis overran much of Lebanon, and the Lebanese government disintegrated into warring factions. Reagan ordered a contingent of marines to Lebanon to help keep the peace, but instead they became a highly vulnerable target in the turmoil of Lebanon's civil war. The tragic result was the death of 241 American soldiers when an explosive-laden car rammed into their Beirut barracks in October 1983. The marines were soon withdrawn, although a number of American hostages remained in captivity in Beirut. (The last American hostages would not be released until 1991, after the Persian Gulf War.)

The Reagan administration devoted its most concerted attention to Central America. Halting what was seen as the spread of communism in the region became practically an obsession. In El Salvador, the United States supported a repressive right-wing regime that was fighting against leftists. In 1983 Reagan ordered

U.S. Marines to invade the tiny Caribbean island of Grenada, claiming that its Cuban-supported Communist regime was a threat to other states in the region. Reporters were kept uninformed about the military operation until it was over. The Grenada invasion, which featured the rescue of several dozen American medical students trapped on the island, occurred just days after the Lebanon bombing and helped shift public attention to a foreign policy "victory" rather than the Middle East policy failures.

Nicaragua's Sandinista government proved the most troubling to Reagan's foreign policy advisers. The Sandinistas, guerrillas who had overthrown the right-wing President Anastasio Somoza in 1979, were leftists but not Communists, although they were friendly with Marxist leaders such as Cuba's Fidel Castro. In 1981 the United States suspended aid to Nicaragua, charging that the Sandinista government, along with Cuba and the Soviet Union, was supplying arms to the rebels in El Salvador, a charge denied by the Sandinistas. At the same time, the CIA began to provide extensive support to Nicaragua's opposition forces, known as the "Contras" or counterrevolutionaries. Reagan called the Contras "freedom fighters," but Congress was not convinced. In 1984 it added the Boland Amendment banning military support to the Contras to a defense appropriations bill.

Reagan's Second Term

The 1984 Election. In 1984 the Democrats nominated Walter Mondale, Carter's vice-president and a former Minnesota senator, to run against Ronald Reagan. Mondale symbolized the New Deal coalition. He had been a protégé of Hubert Humphrey, with strong ties to labor unions, minority groups, and party leaders. He appealed to many women voters by selecting Representative Geraldine Ferraro of New York as his running mate, the first woman on a major party ticket. But the 1984 election was not even close. Reagan campaigned on the theme of "It's Morning in America," suggesting that a new day of prosperity was dawning. Voters gave him another landslide victory—59 percent of the popular vote. Reagan carried the entire country except Minnesota and the District of Columbia. He did especially well among young (eighteen- to twenty-one-year-old) voters, receiving 62 percent of their support.

After a string of administrations that had ended in discord (Johnson and Vietnam), disgrace (Nixon and Watergate), or frustration (Carter and Iran), many people responded warmly to Reagan's strong and confident leadership. Reagan was a convincing performer, and voters believed him when he said he could solve America's problems. Reagan's enormous personal popularity recalled Dwight Eisenhower's appeal in the 1950s. Also like Eisenhower, his coattails were short: Democrats maintained control of the House and picked up two seats in the Senate; they would regain control of the Senate in 1986.

Tax Reform. In its second term the Reagan administration continued to pursue its conservative agenda. The 1986 Tax Reform Act was the most sweeping overhaul of the tax code in history, but it was not designed to reduce the deficits accumulated since the 1981 tax cut. The 1986 act was *revenue-neutral* (that is, it did not change the amount of taxes raised, just how they were raised). It resulted from an unlikely alliance: liberal Democrats who wanted to close loopholes that allowed some wealthy individuals and corporations to avoid paying taxes altogether, joined supply-side Republicans who wanted so much to lower rates that they went along with the reforms, such as removing low-income taxpayers from the rolls. The act closed loopholes worth $300 billion over five years, balancing them with lower tax rates. It also raised corporate taxes by $120 billion over five years, the largest increase ever.

The Iran-Contra Affair. Reagan's second term was marred by a major scandal in 1986. Foreign newspapers broke the story that the administration had negotiated an arms-for-hostages deal with the revolutionary government of Iran, the same government Reagan had denounced at the height of the 1980 hostage crisis. Despite objections from Secretary of State George Shultz and Defense secretary Weinberger, but at the instigation of CIA director William Casey and National Security Advisor Robert McFarlane, the United States

A First for the Nation

Geraldine Ferraro, Walter Mondale's running mate in 1984, was the first woman nominated by a major party to its national ticket. Despite her presence, a majority of women voted for Reagan in the 1984 Republican landslide.

secretly sold arms to Iran, which was locked in a costly and lengthy war with neighboring Iraq. The intent was to gain Iran's help in freeing American hostages believed held by pro-Iranian forces in Lebanon. (Only one hostage was released.) These arm sales generated large profits, some of which, in the most controversial aspect of what became known as the Iran-Contra affair, were diverted as military aid for the Contras in Nicaragua. This diversion was both illegal (contravening the Boland Amendment) and unconstitutional (bypassing the sole right of Congress to appropriate funds).

The arms-for-hostages deal had been discussed at the highest levels of government, but the diversion of funds to the Contras seems to have been the brainstorm of Marine Lieutenant Colonel Oliver North, who was on assignment to the National Security Council. After the press picked up the story, North destroyed many incriminating documents, but he missed a key memo that linked the White House to the plan. Congress investigated the mounting scandal in 1986 and 1987; in their testimony, John Poindexter, the new National Security Advisor, North, and others provided details of the covert actions, but all insisted that the president knew nothing of the diversion. (William Casey, who died of a brain tumor in 1987, never testified.) Ronald Reagan's defense remained simple and consistent: "I don't remember."

The full story of the illegal arms operation may never be known. The scandal bore many similarities to Watergate, including the possibility that the president acted illegally, but there were no significant calls for Reagan's impeachment. The Democratic Congress was not keen to attack a president whose popularity remained remarkably high, nor were investigators able to shake the stonewalling by key presidential aides. Reagan's ability to weather "Iran-Contragate" further testified to what Representative Patricia Schroeder of Colorado, a leading Democratic critic in Congress, dubbed his "Teflon presidency"—bad news didn't stick; it just rolled off.

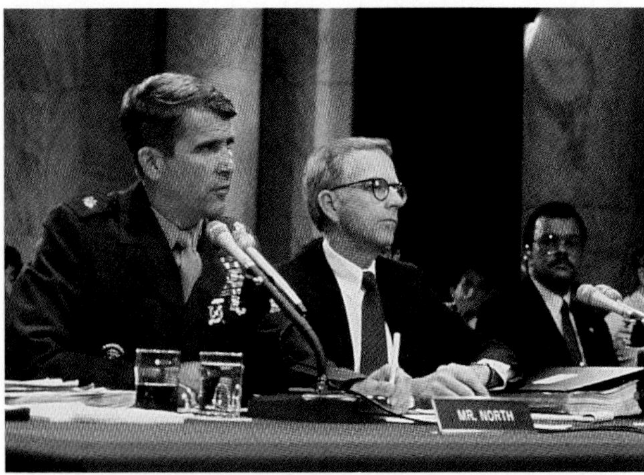

Oliver North
North's uncompromising stance before the congressional committee investigating the Iran-Contra affair made him a popular speaker before conservative audiences, especially those that shared his deep anti-Communist convictions. Indicted and tried for perjury and obstruction of justice, his conviction was overturned in 1990.

The Return of Détente. The most significant foreign policy development in Reagan's second term was a reduction in tensions with the Soviet Union. This process was set in motion by the ascent to power in 1985 of Soviet leader Mikhail Gorbachev. That same year, Gorbachev and Reagan met in Geneva, the first superpower summit meeting since 1979. They met again the following year in Reykjavik, Iceland. In 1987 the United States and the Soviet Union agreed to eliminate their short-range missiles based in Europe, the first time an existing category of weapons had been scrapped and the most significant postwar disarmament decision since the 1972 SALT I agreement. Although a fourth Reagan-Gorbachev summit in Moscow in mid-1988 produced no further nuclear arms cuts, it did demonstrate cordial relations between the two superpowers. When the Soviets announced soon after that they were withdrawing from Afghanistan, prospects for cooperation appeared even brighter.

Reagan Legacies

Ronald Reagan came into the presidency promising to dismantle an intrusive federal bureaucracy, reduce federal entitlements programs, give free-market forces more scope in the modern economy, and stand up to the Soviet menace. The so-called Reagan Revolution proved to be more a "Reagan revision." Although he changed the priorities of the national government and attempted to curb its expansion, he failed to reduce its size or scope. When he left office, government functions remained much as he found them. Defense spending had increased considerably; Social Security and most poverty programs were still in operation, although the latter at reduced levels. And events had brought the Soviet Union and the United States closer together.

One of Reagan's most enduring legacies was his conservative judicial appointments, the area where the New Right had its greatest impact on his administration. In 1981, Reagan nominated Sandra Day O'Connor to the Supreme Court, the first woman ever to serve; he later appointed two other conservatives, Antonin Scalia and Anthony Kennedy. Justice William Rehnquist, a noted conservative who had been appointed by Nixon, was elevated to chief justice in 1986. But when the Reagan administration tried to nominate federal judge Robert Bork in 1987, the Senate refused to confirm him because of Bork's outspoken opposition to judicial activism, with its potential threat to the protection of individual liberties.

Ironically, for a president who promised to balance the budget by 1984, Reagan's greatest legacy was the federal debt, which tripled during his two terms from the combined effect of vastly increased military spending, substantial tax reductions for high-income taxpayers, and Congress's refusal to approve the deep cuts in domestic programs requested by Reagan. There had been federal deficits before, but never on this scale. In 1989 the national debt stood at $2.8 trillion, more than $11,000 for every American citizen. Interest payments on the borrowed money, $216 billion by 1988, were the fastest growing item in the federal budget; by the year 2000, the accumulating interest was expected to consume one-quarter of the entire federal budget.

Trade with other nations was also running at a deficit, which peaked at $171 billion in 1987. Exports had been falling since the 1970s, as American products encountered increasing competition in world markets. The high exchange rate for dollars in the early 1980s made U.S. goods more expensive for buyers with other currencies, while foreign-made goods became more affordable in the United States. The decline in the value of the dollar in the late 1980s helped reduce the trade deficit to $95 billion in 1990.

The budget and trade deficits contributed to a major shift in 1985: for the first time since 1915, the United States was a debtor, not a creditor, nation. Since then, with phenomenal speed, the United States has accumulated the world's largest foreign debt.

These twin deficits have major economic and political ramifications. With so great a chronic budget deficit, money is channeled to servicing the debt rather than being invested to increase productivity; interest rates soar as the government competes with private-sector borrowers for the limited amount of investment capital. With less money to develop new products or purchase efficient modern equipment, American producers lose sales to those offering newer and better products at lower prices. An influx of foreign funds, especially after 1985, filled part of the investment gap and helped to keep interest rates low. But the growing debt to foreign lenders and trading partners meant that more dollars left the country as returns on foreign investment.

The political system was unable to address this mounting economic crisis. On the one hand, members of Congress were unwilling to cut programs their constituents depended on for services or jobs. Fearing unemployment in the military-industrial complex and lobbied by military leaders and defense contractors, they also hesitated to reduce the military budget, although it grew less dramatically after mid-decade. On the other hand, few politicians could buck the popular

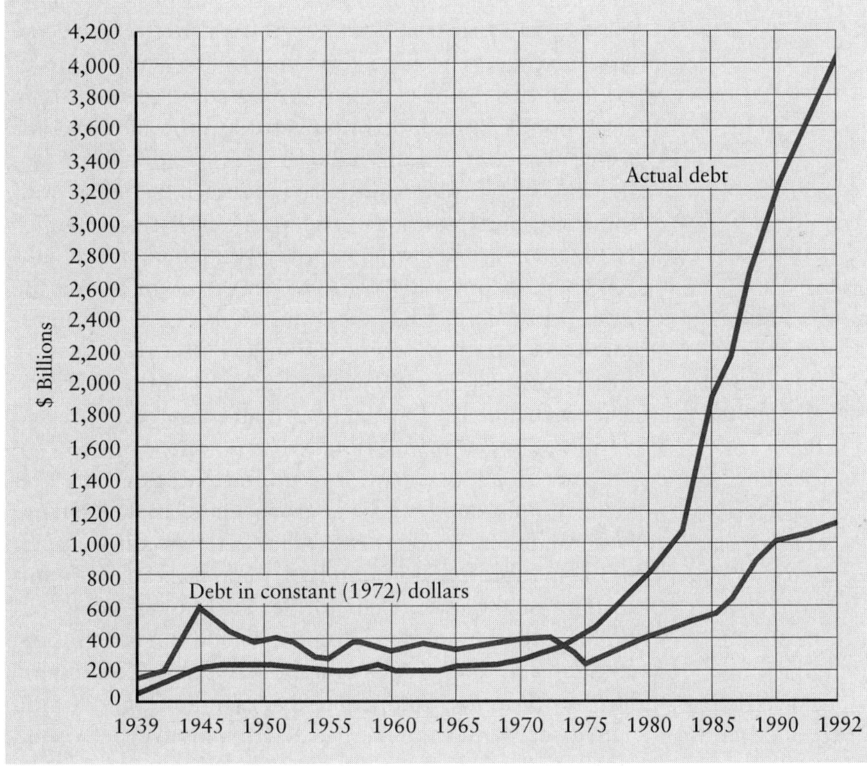

FIGURE 33.1

The Escalating Federal Debt, 1939-1992

The federal debt, which soared during World War II, remained relatively stable until the huge deficits of the 1980s.

Source: *U.S. Statistical Abstract, 1991; Economic Report of the President* (Feb. 1992).

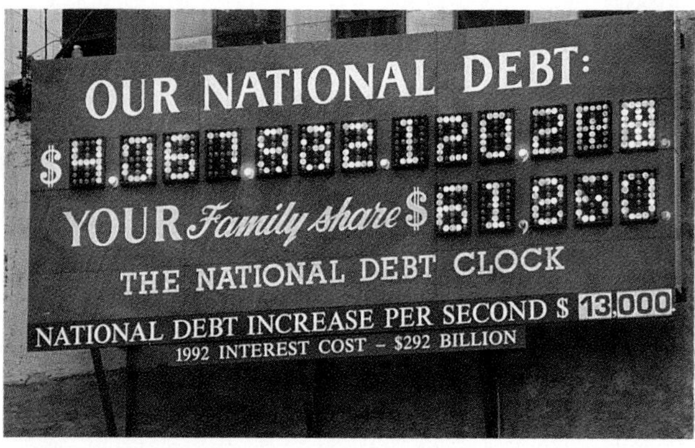

The National Debt
A "clock" in Times Square in New York City kept track of the mounting national debt. A 1990 tax hike slowed the rate of increase in the debt but did nothing to reduce the debt itself.

resistance to new taxes. In 1985, Congress passed the Gramm-Rudman Balanced Budget and Emergency Deficit Reduction Control Act, which tried to achieve a balanced budget by 1991 by mandating specific cuts that would automatically be instituted if deficit reduction targets were not met.

The budget deficit peaked at $221 billion in 1986, and then dropped slightly before leveling off, but the damage had been done. Ever since, both political parties have found it difficult to reverse the consequences of Reaganomics. A huge deficit remains, which, along with the interest needed to service it, will affect all political, economic, and social initiatives throughout the 1990s, and probably into the twenty-first century.

The Best of Times, The Worst of Times

The 1980s was a decade of stark contrasts: the billionaire Donald Trump (a tower, an airline, a casino, a best-selling book, even a board game) and a homeless person, living on the street and begging for change. In the 1980s the gap between poor and rich widened, largely because Reagan's policies reduced spending on social programs for poor people while putting tax-cut money in the pockets of the wealthy. Wage earners were on a treadmill, often working harder just to stay even financially. The population became even more diverse, as more immigrants entered the United States than at any time since the 1920s. Popular culture and technology increasingly reflected global trends, and AIDS touched off a medical crisis that transcended national boundaries.

The Second Gilded Age

Wealth, ostentation, and an unabashed glorification of material success set the tone for much of the 1980s. Corporate leaders such as Chrysler's Lee Iacocca or real estate developer Donald Trump, whose best-selling autobiographies detailed "the art of the deal," became popular icons.

Much of the action took place on Wall Street, which promoted unlimited riches and opportunities reminiscent of the bull market of the 1920s. Instead of investing venture capital to start new companies or increase the productivity of existing ones, investment bankers devised ways to make money through *paper entrepreneurship*. In these innovative and intricate financial arrangements—especially leveraged buyouts and managerial buybacks—existing corporations assumed heavy debt loads to acquire other companies or buy back their own stock. (These debt loads, manageable in the still-expanding economy of the 1980s, led to downsizing and bankruptcy as profits began to shrink in 1990 and beyond.) Most of these deals were initiated by the investment banking departments of established brokerage firms such as Shearson Lehman or Drexel Burnham Lambert, which made extraordinary profits. So did many corporate executives. Middle-level managers and assembly-line workers, however, might find themselves out of a job as the companies they worked for were taken over or restructured.

Much of this activity was fueled by *junk bonds*. Corporations and governments routinely sell bonds to investors to raise capital for various purposes, promising to pay interest and repay principal over a fixed period of time. The likelihood that the seller will make good on this promise depends on its stability and assets. Junk bonds were issued by relatively unstable corporations. To compensate bond buyers (lenders) for the higher risk, the sellers promised to return higher rates of interest than traditional—and safer—investments. Until the 1980s, few investors would buy such volatile, high-risk bonds, but they became central to many of the mergers, leveraged buyouts, and buybacks that restructured corporate America. So much in demand were these new paper investments that "junk bond king" Michael Milken of Drexel Burnham Lambert received $550 million compensation in 1987 alone.

As the 1980s went on, corporate deal-making and acquisition frenzy reached new heights. In 1985 there were eighteen separate deals for $1 billion or more, most financed by junk bonds. Capital Cities Communication bought ABC, General Electric bought RCA, and Philip Morris acquired General Foods. The tobacco company R. J. Reynolds bought Nabisco, becoming the largest consumer product company in the United States. Three years later the merged RJR Nabisco itself would be acquired for $25 billion, in a Wall Street deal that

Lifestyles of the Rich and Famous
Trump Tower in midtown Manhattan (named for its flamboyant developer, Donald Trump, a.k.a. "the Donald") catered to the super rich, the just plain wealthy, and the rest of us, who gawked at its ostentatious displays of conspicuous consumption.

came to symbolize the rapaciousness and greed of such corporate takeovers.

In 1986 financier Ivan Boesky told graduates of the University of California's business school at Berkeley, "I think greed is healthy. You can be greedy and still feel good about yourself." But there was something disturbing about young Wall Street traders making $200,000 or more a year, or executives voting themselves million-dollar *golden parachutes* (severance pay deals negotiated just before corporate restructuring or takeovers cost them their jobs). It turned out that some of the financial activities of the 1980s were illegal as well as unseemly: soon Boesky was jailed for *insider trading* (making advantageous trades based on information not yet made public) and Michael Milken for securities fraud. By decade's end the most excessive aspects of the "casino society" had run their course, although the long-term impact was just beginning to emerge.

That the rich had indeed been getting richer in the Reagan years was confirmed by Congressional Budget Office statistics, which showed that the richest *1 percent* of American families reaped most of the gains of the decade's prosperity. The country's wealthiest 666,000 families accounted for 60 percent of the growth in average after-tax income of all American families between 1977 and 1989—and 77 percent of the rise in average pre-tax income. The top quintile (fifth) saw a 29 percent increase in pre-tax income over that period. Economists debate the causes for the shift, with some stressing reduced tax rates for the wealthy and others pointing to factors like higher returns on capital gains and the explosion of executive pay. But the trend was clear—increasing concentration of riches at the top and growing inequality, the first significant widening of the gap since the 1920s.

The Struggling Middle Class

The Michelob beer slogan, "You can have it all," summed up the lifestyles of the fast-track, young, definitely upwardly mobile segment of society that the media dubbed "Yuppies" (young urban professionals). The Yuppies, with their BMWs, Perrier water, expense account lunches, and aggressive networking, captured the attention of advertisers and marketing directors because of their high disposable incomes and propensity to spend conspicuously. Yuppies were sometimes confused with the whole baby-boom generation, but this affluent set constituted only 5 percent of their age group. Far more baby boomers were confronting the realization that they would not necessarily do better than their parents, a startling slap to a generation raised in the affluence and optimism of the 1950s and 1960s.

Despite the apparent economic booms in the mid-1970s and throughout the 1980s, real income has stagnated since the early 1970s. The typical family saw only a 4 percent rise in pretax income between 1977 and 1989, while households in the bottom 40 percent saw their incomes decline in constant dollars. The federal tax cuts of the Reagan years did less to help middle-income taxpayers, who often saw their overall tax liability rise, as state and local taxes and payroll deductions for Social Security and other benefits increased steadily. (The surplus revenue accumulated for Social Security, which collects more than it currently pays out, was used in part to finance the deficit.) Soon many lower-income wage earners were paying more into Social Security than for federal income taxes.

In part, the stagnation in personal income was linked to broad trends, such as deindustrialization and the shift to a service economy (see Chapter 32), which decreased the number of blue-collar and white-collar jobs. Between 1954 and 1982, half of the 10,000 factories in Chicago shut down, a loss of 400,000 jobs. In their place were service jobs in supermarkets, fast-food outlets, check-cashing establishments, and the like, most at the low end of the pay scale. A hamburger flipper at Burger King or a security guard at a downtown office building did not earn enough to support a family. As a result, many households became dependent on two incomes. Some 70 percent of female baby boomers were in the workforce, compared to 30 percent of their mothers at that age. Some households became "three-income families," with one worker holding down a second job. Many also relied heavily on high levels of consumer debt (borrowing and buying on credit).

For certain occupations, a two-tiered compensation system appeared. To cut costs, and undercut the power of labor unions, companies hired new workers at lower wages than senior workers performing similar jobs. This strategy, along with overly stressful working conditions and other issues, led to the 1981 walkout of three-quarters of the nation's air controllers, who supervise takeoffs and landings at airports. In response, President Reagan fired all the strikers and destroyed their union, the Professional Air Traffic Controllers Organization (PATCO). Reagan's get-tough stance signaled the business community that it was okay to be anti-union. The labor movement, also facing dwindling membership due to the loss of blue-collar jobs, struggled to maintain its influence in the unfavorable economic climate of the 1980s.

Poverty in the 1980s

Here is a snapshot of poverty in America at the end of the 1980s: in 1989 about 31.5 million Americans, or 12.8 percent of the population, were classified by federal standards as poor, that is, their income was below $12,675 for a family of four. Many of the poor were employed, but at low wages. American poverty had racial variations: 10 percent of whites were poor, compared to 26 percent of Hispanics and 30 percent of blacks. Poverty was most common among families headed by women, who were often disadvantaged in the job market by their lack of skills, need for part-time jobs, or the scarcity of affordable child care. Nearly 40 percent of America's poor were children under eighteen, half of whom lived in female-headed households; one child in five, and two-thirds of all black children, would receive Aid to Families with Dependent Children (AFDC) payments at some point. By contrast, the elderly, who used to be among the poorer segments of the population, were relatively better off, thanks in part to Social Security and Medicare.

In many cities, Americans who did not have a roof over their heads at night became increasingly visible on the streets. Of course, there had been homeless people before. Called tramps or bums, they were usually white, middle-aged alcoholics. The 1980s homeless were far more diverse. Some were former mental patients who had been released as part of the 1960s movement toward deinstitutionalization. Some were drug addicts. Others ended up on the streets when loss of a job or cutbacks in social service and disability benefits reduced their ability to pay rent or a mortgage installment. Some were employed but earned too little for both food and rent. Men predominated, but there were growing numbers of homeless women and children, their shifting locations and disrupted lives a challenge to urban school systems.

The Homeless

The majority of homeless people on the nation's streets and sidewalks were men, but the number of homeless women and children has increased. Their needs for health care, housing, and education put demands on already stretched city budgets.

This problem was exacerbated by the lack of low-cost housing in the nation's cities. Urban renewal projects often demolished dilapidated but still liveable housing, replacing it with civic complexes and shiny office projects. SRO (single-room occupancy) rooming houses, which had provided cheap temporary or long-term housing for the poor, were often demolished as well. Construction of subsidized public housing failed to keep pace with the growing need for affordable apartments in urban America.

The Two Worlds of Black America

Until the 1960s, African-American neighborhoods had a mix of middle-class professionals, working-class members, and the poor. The civil rights revolution and affirmative action programs opened many doors for blacks to leave inner-city neighborhoods: armed with an improved education, a number of African-Americans secured business and professional jobs and were able to afford to move to suburban neighborhoods no longer closed by segregation. As upwardly mobile blacks moved out, so did black-owned businesses and the extensive family networks that had given stability to the community. Inner-city ghettoes deteriorated so badly after the 1960s in part because so many of their inhabitants found better lives elsewhere. They also deteriorated because of federal inaction. The peak of federal attention to urban areas occurred between 1964 and 1972; since then, but especially under Reaganomics, inner-city problems have been a low priority.

By the 1980s joblessness was a way of life, two-parent households scarce, and social contacts outside of the neighborhood rare for ghetto inhabitants. At the heart of the problem was the inability to find productive work. Unemployment rates rose as high as 60 percent, in part for demographic reasons: inner cities had a far larger proportion of young people than the general population, due to a higher birthrate and overall younger age of childbearing. Cities had too few entry-level jobs, and most of the inner cities' unemployed lacked the training to qualify for better-paying jobs.

Social scientists use the term *underclass* to describe people in the inner cities, often minorities, who lack resources to escape poverty and are cut off from mainstream society. Noted one social scientist, "venturing outside the neighborhood is like going to Mars." In the 1980s, conditions for young black men in urban areas became so bad that one sociologist called them "an endangered species." Black men were much more likely to be high school dropouts, unemployed, addicted to alcohol or drugs, or in prison than any other group. Especially disturbing was the homicide rate for black men, six times that for white men, and so high that the life expectancy of African-American men and women has been declining since 1986.

The struggles of black teenage mothers run on a parallel track. With so many black men unemployed or absent from the community, many black women do not marry, instead bearing and raising children on their own. In 1965, 26 percent of all black children were born out of wedlock. In 1989 this figure reached 66 percent. Most unmarried first-time mothers were teenagers, and virtually all dropped out of school while pregnant, leaving them unskilled and therefore unemployable, which contributed to the ongoing poverty of female-headed households.

By the 1980s the historical tide of black migration from the South that had begun in World War I was receding. Southern blacks who learned of the poor job prospects were less likely to seek new lives in urban areas; quite the contrary, anyone who could was leaving the inner cities, usually for a more stable neighborhood or to the suburbs. Some blacks were even making a reverse migration back to the South. Compared to living in a crime-ridden and dilapidated northern housing project, conditions in the post-civil rights South seemed attractive. From the Mississippi Delta to Chicago and back to Mississippi, all in one lifetime—what could say more about how the "promised land" of migration had failed?

In April 1992 the frustration and anger of impoverished black Americans erupted in five days of riots in Los Angeles, the worst civil disorders since the 1960s. The rioting was set off by the acquittal on all but one charge of four white Los Angeles police officers accused of using excessive force when arresting a black motorist, Rodney King, on March 3, 1991. The predominantly white jury was not swayed by a graphic 81-second amateur video of the arrest, which showed the officers kicking, clubbing, and beating King. The video, which was shown repeatedly on television, brought renewed attention to the issue of police brutality and the harassment of minorities. Three months later, the officers were indicted on federal charges of violating King's civil rights.

The violence in South-Central Los Angeles took sixty lives and caused $850 million in damage. A shaken Rodney King went on television to plead, "Can we all get along?" But when the fires were finally extinguished and order restored, the conditions in the central cities, as well as the racism that contributed to and perpetuated them, remained.

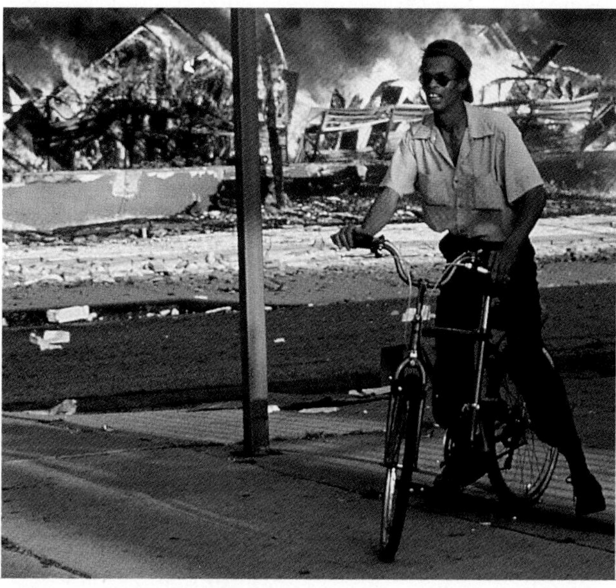

To Live and Die in L.A.

The images from South-Central Los Angeles in the wake of the 1992 riots looked eerily similar to those from Watts in 1965. The underlying causes were similar as well—police brutality, racism, and frustration about lack of jobs and opportunity.

Toward a Pluralistic Society

The 1990 census counted 246.9 million Americans. By far the most dramatic shift since the 1980 census was the changing racial composition of the United States. In 1990 one in four Americans had African, Asian, Hispanic, or American Indian ancestry, up from one in five just ten years earlier. In retrospect, the 1980s may emerge as a watershed decade in the emergence of the United States as a fully pluralistic society.

In the 1980s over 7 million immigrants entered the country, accounting for more than a third of the population growth in that decade. LAX and JFK, the Los Angeles and New York airports, were the main points of entry, not Ellis Island, which, after decades of abandonment and decay, was turned into a museum and tourist attraction. In the first major immigration legislation since 1965, the 1986 Immigration Reform and Control Act (Simpson-Mazzoli) attempted to establish a fair entry process. It also granted legal status to some illegal aliens, primarily Mexicans and other Latinos, who had entered the United States before 1982. Revisions to the law in 1990 expanded the number of immigrants allowed to enter, and gave priority to skilled workers and reunifying families.

Hispanic Immigration. A major component of the new immigration was from Latin America and the Caribbean. The terms *Hispanic* or *Latino*, which cover various Spanish-speaking groups from Mexico, Cuba, Puerto Rico, El Salvador, and other Latin American countries, represent a variety of distinctive heritages. Hispanics are the second largest minority group after blacks, and the second fastest growing, after Asians. Western states like California, Texas, and New Mexico, which border on Mexico, originally contained the most Hispanic immigrants, but in the postwar period Latinos from Puerto Rico, and Central and South America increasingly settled on the East Coast. Hispanics now live in urban areas throughout the country, making up one-tenth of the populations of Florida and New York, for example.

Asian-Americans. Asia was the other major source of immigration. The major components of this migration, which increased almost 108 percent from 1980 to 1990, were Chinese, Filipino, Vietnamese, Laotian, Cambodian, Korean, Pakistani, and Asian Indian. California had more Asian-Americans, almost 10 percent of the population, than any other state. Chinese-Americans are still the dominant Asian group in the United States, followed by Filipinos.

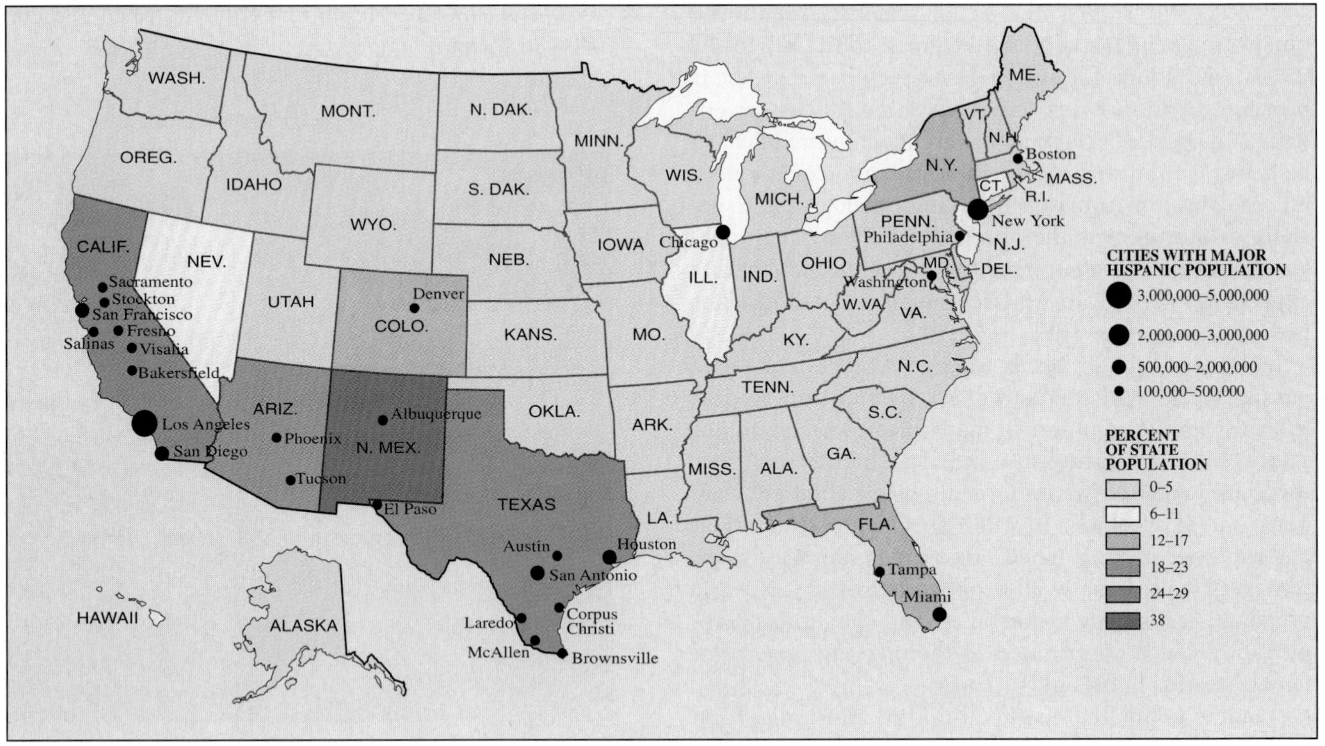

MAP 33.2

American Hispanic Population, 1990

The Hispanic population of the United States is concentrated in California, New York, Texas, Florida, and Illinois, mainly in urban areas. Hispanic Americans are the second largest minority group, after African-Americans.

AMERICAN VOICES

L.A. Journal *Rubén Martínez*

Rubén Martínez, born and raised in Los Angeles to Mexican and Salvadoran parents, describes himself as a member of the generation "that arrived too late for Che Guevara and too early for the fall of the Berlin Wall." Here he compares daily life in Los Angeles with San Salvador's state of siege.

June 1991
Was that a shotgun? In answer, a series of pops . . . a small automatic? I crouch by the window, look into the hazy balmy night. Mute buildings. Now, from afar, another sound begins, like the whine of a mosquito in the darkness of a stifling room in the tropics. The whine becomes a roar that rattles the windows. A shaft of light pours down from the sky. Sirens shriek in the distance. They come closer . . . closer: patrol cars race up the avenue.

I am not in San Salvador, I tell myself. Those are not soldiers down there, bursting through doors to ransack the apartments of high school kids who participated in a protest march . . . Y is okay, she works for a human rights organization in Los Angeles, she's not FMLN in San Salvador anymore, this is Los Angeles, not San Salvador, this is 1991, not 1979, this is gang strife, not civil war. I don't believe myself. Images past and present merge: It is 1979 and 1991 and San Salvador and Los Angeles and gang strife and civil war all at once.

When the helicopters thud-thud-thud-thud fades away, I light a cigarette. Did the bullets find their mark in a rival gangster, a three-year-old's skull? I wait for the ambulance's siren, but the neighborhood remains quiet. The bullets found nothing but the night, as though the night itself were both target and victim of the desperate rage that led the finger to pull on the trigger.

I return to my post next to the computer, in my Echo Park apartment (my latest stop in search of a home) whose living room holds my altar. Amidst votive candles and before a crucifix, I've gathered together objects from the living and the dead: a wallet-sized photo of Y, her stare questioning me across the distance of our latest—and final?—separation; on a cassette sleeve, a photo of Mexico City kids who look like a cross between Irish idealists U2 and the street toughs of *Los Olvidados;* a black-and-white snapshot of a graffiti artist cradling his brutally scarred arm, result of an evening when the bullets did find their mark; a brittle, yellowed leaf from Palm Sunday at La Placita, where Father Luis Olivares showered the thousands of Mexicanos and Centroamericanos surrounding him with holy water; the embossed card that says that one Fidel Castro Ruz, *Presidente del Consejo de Estado y del Gobierno de la República de Cuba,* requests my presence at a reception; a rather ugly postcard entitled "La Frontera, Tijuana, BC," that shows an antiseptic-clean highway on one side and a labyrinth of dusty paths on the other . . . shards of my identity . . . .

This jumble of objects is as close as I get to "home." As close as I get, because my home is L.A. and L.A. is an anti-home; that's why I've left it so many times, and returned just as many. Taking to the road, I've crossed and recrossed the border heading south and north—trying to put things back into place the way they were before . . . before what? The civil war? My grandfather's heart attacks? The gangland massacres? My father's alcoholism, the Latin American dictatorships, my first failed love, the treaty of Guadalupe Hidalgo?

I turn off the overhead light so that the candle flame transforms the shadow of the crucifix on the wall into a pair of wavering, reaching arms. I gaze upon the photos of my late grandparents. This is my history, I tell myself. "This is my home," I whisper, looking out through the window again at the avenues of Echo Park, which are now as deserted and tense as any in San Salvador during a state of siege. . . .

Source: Rubén Martínez, *The Other Side: Fault Lines, Guerilla Saints, and the True Heart of Rock 'n' Roll* (Verso: London and New York, 1992), 165–66.

Much of this immigration was traceable to the upheavals in Southeast Asia. More than 700,000 Indochinese refugees came in the decade after American involvement in Vietnam ended in 1975. The first of these refugees were highly educated, and after a few years they generally achieved economic success. Many of the later refugees, however, who came with less education and fewer skills, struggled for a foothold in new Indochinese neighborhoods that developed in places such as Arlington, Virginia, or Lowell, Massachusetts. When the Cambodian population in that former textile town increased from 3,500 in 1985 to 20,000 just three years later, local resources were strained, and the school system struggled to find bilingual teachers fluent in Khmer, the Cambodian language.

Asian-Americans are often referred to as a "model minority" for the educational and professional success achieved by many of their members. Yet this label masks their enormous diversity. They have also been subjected to racial slurs and blatant discrimination, often because people feared their success. Informal quotas, especially in college admissions, recall the similar expressions of anti-Semitism as late as the 1950s.

Ethnic Diversity. The new immigration has already affected the social, economic, and cultural landscape of the country. Thriving ethnic enclaves are one example: Little Saigon in Orange County, California; Little Havana in Miami; Koreatown in Los Angeles. Tens of thousands of Soviet Jews fleeing religious and political persecution created "Little Odessa" in Brooklyn, New York. At least 300 periodicals serve immigrant readers—*Nguoi Viet* in California, *La Voz de Houston* in Texas, and *Korea Times* in Queens, New York. Koreans have purchased and revitalized corner grocery stores in New York City, Los Angeles, and Washington, D.C. People from the Indian subcontinent manage small hotel chains in California, and Vietnamese now dominate the Gulf of Mexico shrimp fishing industry in Texas.

Occasionally, these newcomers have been the victims of racial altercations and conflicts. In 1982, Chinese-American Vincent Chin was beaten to death in a Detroit bar by two unemployed autoworkers, who apparently thought he was Japanese and thus a symbol of the foreign competition they believed had cost them their jobs. Several states have passed referendums to make English the official state language, a slap at the increasing use of bilingual documents, particularly to aid Spanish-speakers. Blacks have boycotted Korean-owned grocery stores, expressing the tensions between blacks still trapped in the nation's inner cities and more recent arrivals struggling to get ahead, and often succeeding. In the 1992 riots in Los Angeles, black protesters particularly targeted Korean-owned stores for arson and looting.

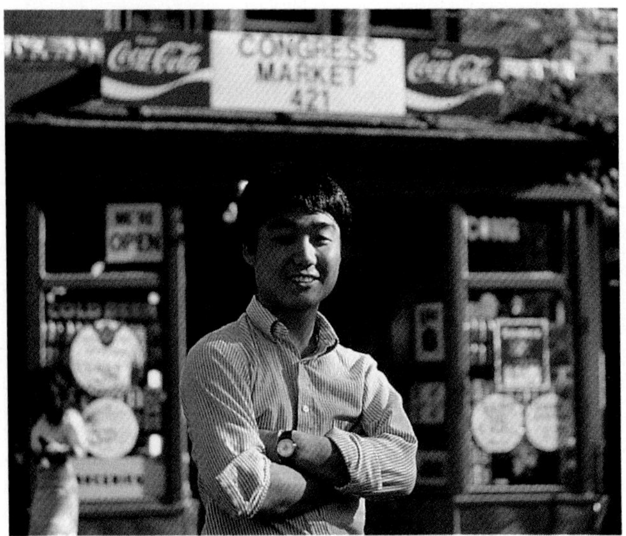

New Immigrants

In the 1980s many Korean immigrants got their start by opening small grocery stores in urban neighborhoods. Their success sometimes led to conflict with other racial groups, such as blacks and Hispanics, who were often their customers as well as competitors.

In contradiction to widespread fear that immigrants will strain resources and take jobs from American-born workers, economists generally believe that immigrants give more than they take. They provide a fresh source of predominantly youthful and highly motivated workers, who either take jobs that are not wanted by other people or move into new jobs in the growing service sector. They also create jobs to meet their own needs, such as *bodegas* in Hispanic neighborhoods, or travel agencies to facilitate family visits to and from the former homeland. To show good will toward the communities in which they set up small businesses, Koreans and other immigrant entrepreneurs may hire local workers and join neighborhood organizations.

Mainstream advertisers and producers are only now beginning to tap the huge consumer market represented by this increasingly multiracial society. For example, the major cosmetics companies have begun to sell cosmetics for darker complexions, a market previously monopolized by black-run companies. The process works the other way as well, as ethnic products, especially foods, enter the national market. New food treats such as stir-fry cooking, tacos, pita pockets, jalapeño peppers, and tofu have enriched the American palate, and the diversity of American life.

Health Care Costs and the Challenge of AIDS

The United States spends more on health care than any other country, and yet many citizens feel the health-care system is in crisis. By the late 1980s, nearly 12 percent of the gross national product went to health care, and the percentage was climbing, mainly due to what one journalist has called "the medical technology arms race." More and more, newspapers covered medical breakthroughs the way they did sports or local politics.

The United States is the only major industrialized country that does not provide national health insurance, in part because of the New Deal's decision not to push for a federal health care program in the 1930s. Instead, health care is financed primarily through group medical insurance provided by employers. This system has proven inadequate on several counts. With their employment-based benefits vulnerable to layoffs and corporate takeovers, workers avoided changing jobs because they or their families feared losing their medical coverage, a situation referred to by economists as "job lock." Spiraling medical costs (double the rate of inflation since 1970) and rising premiums stretched employers' ability to pay; a growing number of companies, often small businesses, fail to provide any health insurance to their workers. From the business perspective, health care was devouring profits just when those profits were shrinking in a competitive global economy.

About 35 million Americans, more than one-sixth of the population, had no health insurance in 1990, and many feared being bankrupted by a medical emergency or illness. Especially at risk were workers who had been unemployed for extended periods of time and individuals with preexisting medical conditions that made them ineligible for coverage. Rising costs put private health insurance out of the reach of many individuals. Only the very poorest Americans qualify for Medicaid, which despite vast expenditures fails to provide adequate medical services, especially for more cost-effective preventive care.

As medical costs escalated in the 1980s, health care became a political issue. Federal, state, and local governments now pay more than 40 percent of the nation's $600 billion yearly tab for health care. Economists fear that if costs are not brought under control, health spending will adversely affect national prosperity. Yet neither politicians nor medical administrators have found ways to reduce the costs of sophisticated, and ever more expensive, new medical equipments and procedures and a system that provides little incentive to control costs, since insurers and the government pay most of the bills. The goals are clear—universal access, reasonable cost, and top-quality care—but the means remain elusive.

AIDS. The AIDS epidemic, one of the most pressing medical and social issues of our times, and one with vast political implications as well, exemplifies the problems afflicting the American health-care system. Acquired Immune Deficiency Syndrome (AIDS) was first recognized in 1981. Its cause was soon identified as the human immunodeficiency virus (HIV), which weakens the immune system, causing infected persons to succumb to secondary infections such as pneumonia or the skin cancer known as Kaposi's Sarcoma. (HIV is transmitted through the exchange of infected body fluids, such as semen and blood.) Already about 18 million people worldwide are affected; most will experience lengthy debilitating illness and eventual death. By the year 2000, researchers project, more than 24 million people will have died from AIDS.

Initially, little organized action or government funding was directed to AIDS research or treatment, and critics charged that this reflected conservative antipathy toward homosexual men, who were the disease's earliest victims. AIDS began to gain public attention only when it became clear that heterosexuals, such as hemophiliacs who received the virus through blood transfusions, were affected as well. The October 1985 announcement of the death from AIDS of film star Rock Hudson, who had hidden his sexual orientation to maintain his Hollywood career, finally broke through the barriers of public apathy.

Many members of the gay community organized early on, but others were slow to respond to the implications of AIDS. Throughout the 1970s, the gay community's increased visibility and political clout, especially in New York and San Francisco, had been accompanied by a pattern of high-risk sexual practices that contributed to the spread of HIV infection. When it became clear that the disease was being transmitted through frequent casual sexual contacts, some were quick to advocate "safe-sex" practices, such as the use of condoms, which succeeded in slowing the spread of AIDS; others, however, balked at relinquishing their hard-won sexual freedoms.

After mid-decade, AIDS cases increased among heterosexuals, especially intravenous drug addicts and their sexual partners, as well as bisexuals. Especially tragic was the transmission of AIDS to infants by infected mothers. The marginal status of these new victims, often members of the urban underclass, did not command attention from the federal health establishment. The controversial advocacy group, ACT-UP (AIDS Coalition to Unleash Power), has found dramatic ways to confront drug manufacturers, politicians, and others in an effort to gain attention and funding. Caring for AIDS patients will put an even greater financial strain on the American health care system.

A few drugs such as AZT have been developed to delay the onset and reduce the severity of symptoms. There are blood tests to screen blood for transfusions and detect the HIV virus in infected individuals. But no cure or vaccine is in sight. The barriers are as much political and bureaucratic as medical. Many non-urban Americans see the AIDS epidemic as one more expres-

ACT UP

This poster *Untitled*, 1989 by artist Keith Haring for the group ACT UP (AIDS Coalition to Unleash Power) tries to mobilize public action against the deadly disease, which would later claim Haring's life. (© Estate of Keith Haring) sion of big-city decay. Federal red tape, and prohibitive expense, have limited the distribution of AZT and other medications. Already more Americans have died of AIDS than were killed in the Korean and Vietnam wars combined. The toll, in the United States and throughout the world, continues to rise.

Popular Culture and Popular Technology

Image was everything in the 1980s, or so commentators said, pointing to rock stars Michael Jackson and Madonna, and even to President Ronald Reagan. One strong influence on the images of the decade was MTV, which premiered in 1981. With its creative choreography, flashy colors, and rapid cuts, it seemed a perfect fit to the short attention spans of the TV generation raised on shows such as "Sesame Street." The MTV style soon showed up in mainstream advertising, network television shows like "Miami Vice," and even political campaigns. The national newspaper *USA Today*, which debuted in 1982, adapted the style, featuring flashy graphics, color photographs, and short, easy-to-read articles. Soon more staid newspapers followed suit.

New technology shaped television, especially with satellite transmission and live "mini-cam" broadcasting. Also new was the increased availability of cable channels. In the 1950s, Americans had only three networks to choose from; public television did not debut until 1967. By the end of the 1980s, such upstarts as Ted Turner's all-news CNN (Cable News Network), ESPN's all-sports channel, and the Fox network were challenging the major networks for viewers and profits.

Media, communications, and entertainment were big business, increasingly drawn into global financial networks and markets. Corporate mergers and takeovers reshaped these industries, as ownership of several entertainment conglomerates and major Hollywood studios passed into foreign, often Japanese, hands. In 1987, Sony acquired Columbia Pictures and CBS Records; in 1990 the consumer electronics firm Matsushita agreed to acquire MCA Inc., a large entertainment company, whose subsidiaries included theme parks, Universal Studios, recordings, and a talent agency. As manufacturers of "hardware" such as stereo components and VCRs, these investors saw a competitive advantage if they also produced "software" such as recordings and films to be used with that technology. This strategy reflected a widespread business belief, evident in the 1989 merger of Time Inc. and Warner Communications, that sheer size enhanced competitive ability in a global economy. Japanese companies acquired U.S. ones not from a desire to take over the American entertainment industry, but because certain American companies wanted to sell and others failed to bid. As Sony chairman Akio Morita put it, "If you don't want Japan to buy it, then don't sell it."

Technology also entered, and reshaped, the home. The 1980s saw the introduction of compact disc players, cellular phones, personal computers, and fax (facsimile) machines. By the end of the decade the vast majority of Americans had one or more of the new electronic toys. In 1990, for example, more than half of American households had a videocassette recorder (VCR). At first Hollywood feared decreasing box office admissions, but soon found that VCR's created a large new market for recent films, as well as for home videos. Video was everywhere—stores, elevators, airplanes, tennis courts, operating rooms. With the introduction of camcorders, the family photo album was supplanted by the video of the high school graduation, marriage, or birth. Personal computers, led by Apple's Macintosh and IBM's PC, enabled individual users to do everything from desktop publishing to tracking their investments, balancing checkbooks, and writing textbooks. Computers also made it possible to run a business from home or, with a fax machine and a telephone, to work at home and still be connected to an office.

The implications of this technology and communications revolution are staggering. When Federal Express and the U.S. Postal Service first introduced overnight deliveries, business practices changed, as people expected a response the next day instead of a week later. Then fax machines made possible instant communication with every corner of the world; now people expect a response the very same day. With cellular phones, business executives and sales representatives no longer fear being out of touch, whether driving on the freeway, flying across the country, or just walking down the street. Only a few voices questioned the stress and intensification that came with this new information technology. Most learned to live with it, and soon felt they could not live without it.

The End of the Eighties

The trends that characterize a decade are not always confined neatly to a ten-year period, and some of the images associated with the 1980s began to wane several years before the decade ended. The slipping popularity of television shows about the rich and fashionable, such as "Dallas" and "Dynasty," suggested a shift in values. Tom Wolfe's exposé of the moral bankruptcy of Wall Street, *The Bonfire of the Vanities* (1987), seemed remarkably prescient when the stock market fell 508 points on Black Monday, October 19, 1987. After the crash, some 15,000 Wall Street employees lost their jobs, and the investment firm Drexel Burnham Lambert declared bankruptcy. In the wake of the convictions of Ivan Boesky and Michael Milken, the world of investment banking suddenly seemed less appealing. Within a few years, Donald Trump's financial empire was on the verge of bankruptcy.

NEW TECHNOLOGY *The Electronic Office*

The 1980s witnessed an explosion in office and communications technology, as the early, bulky mainframe computers were replaced by more compact and efficient models.

The big breakthrough came from the upstart Apple Computer Company. Two young tinkerers and hobbyists, Steve Jobs and Steve Wozniak, operating from a bedroom and garage in Palo Alto, California, and using the $1,300 proceeds from the sale of an old Volkswagen, built the first easy-to-use, small, inexpensive computer. They achieved a runaway engineering and marketing success in 1977, when they offered the Apple II personal computer for only $1,195.

Belatedly, other companies scrambled to get into the market. IBM, already a leader in producing tabulating machines and mainframe computers for business and government, offered its first personal computer, the IBM PC, in the summer of 1981. Competition between IBM, Apple, and other low-cost models kept prices affordable, and by 1990 a quarter of American homes had at least one personal computer. But its greatest impact was on business. More than any other technological advance, the personal computer created the electronic office of today. Even the smallest business could keep all its records, do all its correspondence and billing, and run its own direct-mail advertising campaigns from a single desktop machine.

Personal computers' ability to store massive amounts of data increased every year. Small file boxes of floppy disks can now hold a decade's worth of business records, while optical disks can hold not only as many words as an encyclopedia but pictures and sounds as well. Optical disks are at the heart of CD-ROM (Compact Disk–Read Only Memory) multimedia systems, in which text, graphics, animation, video, music, and voice can be linked into one presentation. Many architects, engineers, and designers now use computer-aided design (CAD) software, which shows drawings in three dimensions on the screen, to design buildings, automobiles, clothing, and other products on their desktop computers.

Computers rely on *digital* technology, essentially a vast array of on-off switches. Today there are a host of other digital devices—modems, laser printers, cellular telephones, and fax machines—and all are able to be linked by wired and wireless communications. Fiber-optic cables, microwave relays, and satellites can transmit massive quantities of information to and from almost any place on earth, and even from space. Business people and scholars can readily study enormous databases of information, such as periodicals, specialized reference works, and government statistics, or they can get the latest financial information from the world's stock markets. The very structure of the office is changing, as people are able to work at home and "telecommute" via computer and fax machine. But there are perils in such easy exchanges of information, too. In particular, concerns have grown about protecting sensitive electronic files, such as credit and medical records and corporate financial data, from unauthorized users.

The electronic office of today has simplified arduous tasks. Here six people work on a car design using computer imaging in this "Capture Lab."

Computers have replaced much tedious work, as well as many unskilled workers who performed drudge jobs. They have created new jobs that require more education and new skills, and spawned entire new industries. Overall there has been a gain in number of jobs, productivity, and economic growth—despite the loss of low-skill, entry-level jobs. The electronic office of today and the workplace of the future belong to those who come prepared—prepared with current skills, and prepared to retrain as often as necessary during a career lifetime that is certain to see ever more technological change and challenge.

By the late 1980s, a new social mood was becoming evident. Jay McInerney's Yuppie classic, *Bright Lights, Big City* (1984), was transformed into a 1988 movie version only after "laser surgery" (as one studio executive put it) cut down the drug use in the plot. What caused the turnaround? Cocaine, the "drug of choice" for fast trackers, was not as harmless as many had believed. The appearance in mid-decade of crack, a highly addictive form of cocaine, took a deadly toll, especially in the inner cities where it led to an increase in drug-related violence.

The declining appeal of drugs ("Just say 'no,'" Nancy Reagan told the country) was part of adults' general rejection of chemicals and other stimulants, such as cigarettes and alcohol. (Drug use declined among teenagers as well, while smoking and drinking increased.) Widespread bans on smoking in public areas reduced cigarette smoking to an outdoor activity practiced furtively during breaks from work or classes. Fearing melanoma and clogged arteries, Americans also avoided excessive suntanning and high cholesterol. A "new prohibitionism" attacked alcohol consumption, causing wineries and distilleries to worry how to maintain consumption while allaying public fears. The "designated driver" was one solution; label warnings against alcohol consumption by pregnant women was another.

In sexual matters, Americans seemed to be saying "no" to the casual experimentation of the preceding decades. Here the AIDS crisis was central. Campaigns promoting safe sex and the fear of sexually transmitted diseases made many people more cautious about whom they slept with, and how often. Hedonism was out, monogamy—and even celibacy—was in.

Also at the end of the eighties came sexual scandals involving several New Right religious leaders who had been influential in the early Reagan years. First to fall from grace was the PTL (Praise the Lord) television empire of Jim and Tammy Bakker. Reverend Bakker lost his pulpit in March 1987 and ultimately went to jail after admitting he had paid a secretary $265,000 from PTL funds to keep quiet about a sexual relationship. The next year, Reverend Jimmy Swaggart of the Assemblies of God confessed his sin of patronizing prostitutes. While these scandals focused attention on the personal and financial excesses of some television preachers, evangelical religion continued strong.

Beyond the Cold War

"Jack, smile. We won." That's how General Colin Powell, head of the Joint Chiefs of Staff, greeted a glum U.S. NATO commander who remained preoccupied with the Soviet threat in Europe even as it receded and crumbled. The end of the Cold War removed the Soviet Union as America's main ideological enemy, but new post-Cold War challenges quickly appeared. During the Persian Gulf crisis in 1990, President George Bush called for a "new world order . . . in which nations recognize the shared responsibility for freedom and injustice." As events abroad progressed dramatically, especially the end of Soviet hegemony in Eastern Europe in 1989 and the collapse of communism within the Soviet Union itself in 1991, the United States grappled with the implications of this new world order.

The Bush Administration

George Herbert Walker Bush, the first sitting vice-president since Martin Van Buren in 1836 to be elected to the presidency, was no clone of Ronald Reagan. He lacked Reagan's abiding conservativism; in fact, many wondered if he had any ideological vision at all. In the 1988 campaign, Bush promised a "kinder, gentler administration," and announced his intention to go down in history as the education and environment president. Yet the deficit inherited from the Reagan years, along with Bush's own preference for foreign affairs, kept him from articulating a clear domestic agenda.

The 1988 Election. Bush won the Republican nomination by beating back challenges from Senate minority leader Robert Dole, television evangelist Pat Robertson, and tax-cutting representative Jack Kemp. In one of several controversial moves of his candidacy, Bush chose the young conservative Indiana senator Dan Quayle for vice-president. Even many Republicans questioned Quayle's qualifications to assume the duties of president, while Democrats, noting his hawkish views on defense, charged him with hypocrisy for having avoided service in Vietnam by joining the Indiana National Guard.

The early Democratic front runner, Colorado senator Gary Hart, was forced out of the race in early 1988 because of a sex scandal. Another senator, Al Gore of Tennessee, failed to inspire voters with his pro-environment message and withdrew after the New York and Pennsylvania primaries. The remaining primaries became a contest between Massachusetts governor Michael Dukakis and the charismatic civil rights leader Jesse Jackson. Audiences responded enthusiastically to Jackson's populist vision of a "Rainbow Coalition," but he was unable to convince enough Democrats that an African-American candidate could win. Dukakis, a somewhat bland figure known for a technocratic approach to state government, won the nomination. For his vice-president, Dukakis passed over Jackson in favor of Senator Lloyd Bentsen of Texas.

The 1988 campaign had a harsh cast to it, with negative commercials and brief televised *sound bites* replacing discussion of the issues. The sound bite, "Read My

Lips: No New Taxes," became the Republican campaign mantra. The Republicans portrayed the Democrats as liberals (the "L" word) who were unpatriotic, big spenders, soft on crime, and too generous to minorities. A television ad criticizing Massachusetts' prison furlough program pandered to racist fears by including a mug shot of Willie Horton, a black convicted murderer who had committed another murder while on parole. Forced on the defensive, Dukakis failed to mount an effective campaign. Bush carried thirty-eight states, winning the popular vote 54 to 46 percent. Only 50 percent of eligible voters went to the polls.

The Savings and Loan Crisis. The new Bush administration was almost immediately confronted by a major and embarrassing banking scandal. Its roots lay in decisions made during the Reagan administration and before, but its full impact hit only after Bush took office.

Savings and loan associations (S & L's), also called "thrifts," invest their depositors' savings in home mortgages. Since 1934 deposits in S & L's have been insured by the Federal Savings and Loan Insurance Corporation (FSLIC), which is distinct from the Federal Deposit Insurance Corporation (FDIC) established in 1933 to insure accounts in commercial banks. When S & L's complained in 1982 that high inflation and soaring interest rates were reducing their profits, Reagan's deregulation program permitted the thrifts to invest in commercial real estate and businesses. Such investments were more risky than home mortgages, and lack of supervision from Washington encouraged many speculative, and some fraudulent, deals.

For most of the 1980s the real estate market was booming, and so the loans and investments were profitable. But when construction and the Southwest oil boom slowed, and stock prices on Wall Street tumbled sharply in 1987, saving and loan associations losses mounted and the value of their assets plummeted. When the banks lost their depositors' funds, the government had to make good its guarantees to individual depositors. To recoup some of the massive losses, the federal government took over the insolvent banks, and, in 1989, set up a temporary agency to regulate the industry and sell the banks' remaining assets, primarily defaulted real estate. The total bill to American taxpayers is projected at $200 billion.

What was to blame? Reagan's commitment to diminished government regulation and a bullish business climate encouraged high-risk deals. Congress was lax in supervising the banking industry, on which lawmakers depended heavily for campaign contributions. The media had difficulty explaining this dry and technical issue to readers and viewers. Moreover, the public found it hard to grasp the size of the bailout. Only occasionally was there a live "villain" such as Charles Keating, whose failed Lincoln Savings and Loan in California alone added $2.5 billion to the bailout cost.

Economic Agendas. In his 1990 message to Congress, budget director Richard Darman compared the federal budget to Sesame Street's Cookie Monster for its "excessive tendencies towards consumption." The 1985 Gramm-Rudman Act mandated automatic cuts if budget targets were not met in 1991. Facing the prospect of a halt to non-essential government services and layoffs of thousands of government employees, the Congress struggled to produce a deficit-reduction plan. This compromise combined cuts with increased taxes and fees—recognition that the Reagan legacy of lower taxes and higher levels of spending was no longer tenable. Bush was forced, by inevitable circumstances, to break his "no new taxes" campaign promise.

The federal government can run up deficits, but state and local governments cannot. By the early 1990s, they were in bad fiscal shape. Reagan's new federalism had made states and localities responsible for formerly federal programs, but at the same time had cut back on grants to them for housing, education, transportation, public works, and social services. Social problems increased, but funding for services declined. Federal-state programs such as Medicaid, whose costs soared in the 1970s and 1980s due to inflation and higher demand, ate up increasingly large parts of state budgets, as did spending for welfare, education, and prisons. State and local governments could balance their budgets only by finding new sources of revenue (thus risking taxpayer revolts) or by reducing spending and services. Fiscal conditions were especially bad in the Northeast, but California and several other states also faced severe shortfalls.

Recession. A recession began in 1990, further eroding state and local tax revenues. In 1991 unemployment approached 7 percent nationwide; industrial and white-collar layoffs spread, and in many American families someone had either already lost a job or feared it might happen soon. Poverty increased sharply, and incomes declined: according to the Census Bureau, 2.1 million more Americans lived in poverty in 1990 than in 1989. Bankruptcies increased; so did defaults on mortgage payments. Unemployment grew as state and local governments laid off workers to save money, even as they faced greater demands for social services and unemployment compensation. The United States had had eight recessions since World War II, and in each case the economy rebounded within six to sixteen months. But in the early 1990s recovery was slowed by the massive federal debt, overburdened state and local governments, and decreasing consumer confidence.

Supreme Court Conservatism. During the Bush administration, the Supreme Court continued its transformation from liberal activism to a far more conservative stance. Former Supreme Court justice William Brennan used to tell his clerks, "Five votes can do anything

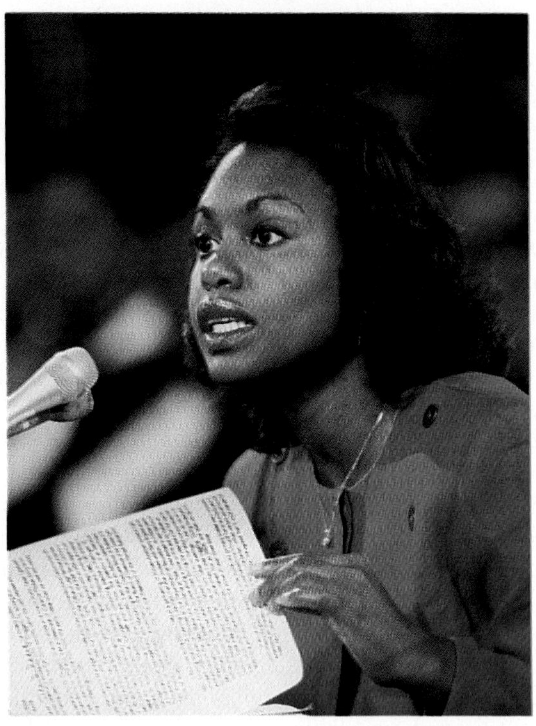

A Woman of Conscience
Accusations by University of Oklahoma professor Anita Hill that Supreme Court nominee Clarence Thomas had sexually harassed her sparked fierce political debate. Many felt that if there had been more women in the Senate, Professor Hill's charges would have been treated more seriously, and this played a role in many campaigns in the 1992 election.

around here," and under the leadership of Chief Justice William Rehnquist, the Court, often by 5–4 margins, chipped away at the Warren Court legacy in such areas as individual liberties and the rights of criminal defendants. The conservative shift was especially felt on the issue of abortion. The 1989 *Webster v. Reproductive Health Services* decision permitted states to restrict abortion, and the next year, in *Rust v. Sullivan*, the Court upheld a federal regulation which forbade personnel at federally funded health clinics from discussing abortion with their clients. In 1992, in *Planned Parenthood v. Casey*, another 5–4 decision upheld provisions of a Pennsylvania law mandating a 24-hour waiting period and informed-consent requirements. Yet the Court also reaffirmed what it called the "essential holding" of *Roe v. Wade*: that women have a constitutional right to abortion.

In Bush's rush to secure a conservative Court, presumed opposition to abortion became one of the "litmus tests" for potential nominees. David Souter, a little-known federal judge from New Hampshire, won confirmation easily in 1990. Clarence Thomas, a black conservative with little judicial experience who opposed affirmative action, had a much harder time in 1991, especially after former staff member Anita Hill accused him of sexually harassing her. After widely watched (and widely debated) televised testimony by both Thomas and Hill before the all-male Senate Judiciary Committee, the Senate confirmed Thomas by a narrow margin. In the wake of the hearings, national polls confirmed the pervasiveness of sexual harassment on the job: four out of ten women said they had been the object of unwanted sexual advances from men at work.

The Collapse of Communism

The image of young East and West Germans dancing on the Berlin Wall on November 9, 1989, symbolized the end of the Cold War. The breaching of this border between the two Germanies culminated in their reunification just one year later. During 1989, communism's grip on Eastern Europe loosened, then let go completely in a series of mostly nonviolent "velvet revolutions." For years, American policymakers had warned about the "domino" effect of countries falling to communism. Now the domino effect was unexpectedly working in the opposite way. Soon the Soviet Union also succumbed to the forces of change.

As modern technology and communications brought Soviet bloc states into contact with the rest of the world, the Iron Curtain became increasingly vulnerable. While the people of Eastern Europe experienced severe food, housing, and fuel shortages, as well as political repression, they saw televised scenes of prosperity and freedom from the outside world, images which state-controlled media could not counter. When Poland started to stir with workers' strikes led by the Solidarity union, its messages of freedom were spread to the rest of the Communist bloc by shortwave radios, television, and telephones. By the end of 1989, Poland had elected a non-Communist government headed by Solidarity founder and leader Lech Walesa, and hardline regimes in East Germany, Bulgaria, Czechoslovakia, and Romania had been toppled. The democratic movements in these countries quickly demanded and won guarantees of multiparty elections and more democratic governance. More than anything else, the swiftness of these changes and their generally peaceful course startled politicians and diplomats.

The background for the dramatic upheavals in Eastern Europe lay in the changes set in motion by Soviet president Mikhail Gorbachev, who came to power in 1985. His policies of *glasnost* (openness) and *perestroika* (economic restructuring) signaled a willingness to tolerate significant changes in the Soviet bloc and in Soviet relationships with the rest of the world. The new openness within the U.S.S.R. exposed severe problems. The economy was sluggish, the standard of living poor, and rates of growth had been declining since the 1960s; agricultural production was so low that the Soviet

AMERICAN VOICES

A Third-Wave Feminist *Laurie Ouellette*

Laurie Ouellette, born in 1966 and educated at the University of Minnesota, represents the generation of women who benefited from the changes set in motion by the revival of feminism but are confused about what feminism means. She considers herself a feminist, but calls on the movement to broaden its vision.

As a member of the first generation of women to benefit from the gains of the '70s women's movement without participating in its struggles, I grew up on the sidelines of feminism—too young to take part in those moments, debates, and events that would define the women's movement but old enough to experience firsthand the societal changes it had wrought.

Ironically, it is due to the modest success of feminism that many young women like myself were raised with an illusion of equality. Like most women my age, I never really thought much about feminism while I was growing up. Looking back, though, I believe it has always influenced me. Growing up with divorced parents, especially a father who was ambivalent about parental responsibilities, probably has much to do with this fact. I was only five when my parents separated in 1971, and I couldn't possibly have imagined or understood the ERA marches or the triumphal result of *Roe v. Wade* that would make history in just a few short years. Certainly I couldn't have defined the word *feminism*. Still, watching my mother struggle emotionally and financially as a single parent made the concept of gender injustice painfully clear, teaching me a lesson that would follow me always.

It was at the University of Minnesota that I first took an interest in feminist classics like *The Feminine Mystique, Sisterhood Is Powerful,* and *Sexual Politics.* They expressed the anger of an earlier generation that simultaneously captivated me and excluded me. Reading them so long after the excitement of their publication made my own consciousness-raising seem anticlimactic. Like many of my white middle-class friends, I believed that we wouldn't have to worry about issues like discrimination, oppression, and getting stuck in the housewife role. We wondered why we should join forces with a battle for women's equality that the media repeatedly declared was already "won."

My experiences after college made me think again about feminism. A public television internship where I was expected to perform menial secretarial tasks while my male (and, I might add, less experienced) co-interns worked on interesting and challenging projects shocked me into realizing the difficulties facing women in the workplace. Likewise, living in an inner-city neighborhood and being involved in community issues there showed me the dire need for feminism in the lives of the poor women, elderly women, and women of color who were my neighbors. Watching these women, many of them single mothers, struggle daily to find shelter, child care, and food made me realize that they had not been touched at all by the women's movement gains of the '70s. . . .

While the feminist movement of the '70s focused primarily on getting women into high-paying, powerful occupations and combating sexual discrimination on the job, these issues—while still critical—are not the only goals of feminism. My 24-year-old sister stands out as an example of other routes that feminism must move toward. Whereas I have focused my energies on attending graduate school and working toward a professional career, she has chosen to forfeit similar plans, for now, in favor of marrying young, moving to the country, and raising a family. Does she signify a regression into the homemaker role of the 1950s? On the contrary. For her, issues such as getting midwifery legalized and insured, providing information about breast-feeding to rural mothers, countering the male-dominated medical establishment by using and recommending natural and alternative healing methods, and raising her own daughter with positive gender esteem are central to a feminist agenda.

Only by recognizing and helping to provide choices—both lifestyle and reproductive—for women of all races, economic levels, and ages, as well as supporting all women in their struggles to make those choices, will the women of my generation, the first to be raised in the shadow of feminism and witness its successes and failures, be able to build a successful third wave of the feminist movement.

Source: Laurie Ouellette, "Our Turn Now: Reflections of a 26-Year-Old Feminist," *Utne Reader* (July-August, 1992), 118–20.

Union had to import grain. In addition, the costs of maintaining a vast military and political empire drained the resources of the state.

Gorbachev established strong personal rapport with both presidents Reagan and Bush, and raised enormous expectations worldwide about the possibilities of change within the U.S.S.R. But the Soviet leader soon found it was easier to call for the dismantling of the old system than to build something new. In addition, conflicts among the Soviet republics, some of which were

Gorbachev and Bush
The leaders of the two superpowers, shown here at a press conference during the Malta summit in December 1989 developed a warm personal relationship. Some later felt that Bush delayed reacting to changes in the Soviet Union out of loyalty to his friend.

eager to apply the lessons of Eastern Europe and gain their own independence, threatened the unity of the country. As Gorbachev moved to allow a rudimentary market economy and reduce price subsidies on some basic goods, he was attacked by hardliners who wanted to maintain the status quo and by reformers who wanted to move at once to a totally free market.

The dramatic, and generally peaceful, transfer of power in Eastern Europe, and the hesitant steps toward change within the Soviet Union, encouraged Chinese students in 1989 to undertake their own democratic movement. In June they staged a peaceful protest in central Beijing, only to be violently suppressed when Chinese leader Deng Xiaoping ordered a massive military attack. Troops killed dozens of protesting students who were camped out in Tiananmen Square and literally crushed the dissent. This harsh crackdown, broadcast live to the rest of the world, put China increasingly out of step with the political and economic loosening taking place everywhere else in the Communist world. George Bush and the rest of the world's leaders took no action against China, however.

In 1990, Soviet president Mikhail Gorbachev was awarded the Nobel Peace Prize for his efforts to restructure the Soviet Union, his introduction of quasi-democratic elections, the withdrawal of Soviet troops from Afghanistan, and his tacit support for the "velvet revolutions" that swept Communist regimes from power in Eastern Europe. But he was more popular outside the Soviet Union than at home. Symbolizing this discrepancy, Gorbachev did not travel to Stockholm to receive the Nobel Prize because events in his country were moving toward a crisis.

On August 19, 1991, while Gorbachev was vacationing at his summer home in the Crimea, officials in his own government attempted to oust him. The precipitating factor was the imminent signing of a Union Treaty that would have given limited autonomy to the fifteen Soviet republics and increased power to the republics' recently elected leaders. The plotters—officials of the Communist party, bureaucrats and overlords of the central economy, and leaders of the internal police force and KGB—stood to lose the most from decentralization. But by August 21, the coup had failed and the grip of the Communist party over the Soviet Union was broken. The Baltic republics of Latvia, Estonia, and Lithuania declared their independence, which was soon recognized by the United States and the rest of the world.

Why did the coup fail? The bland collective behind it had little appeal compared to the new generation of popularly elected leaders, and was unwilling or unable to use brutal force to consolidate its power. The coup's planning was also very disorganized, almost haphazard: "We knew the Communists couldn't do anything right," went one popular joke in Moscow. For example, the

A Defiant Boris Yeltsin
This image of Russian premier Boris Yeltsin defying Soviet authorities in August 1991 was broadcast worldwide and helped to turn the momentum against the coup. The impact of this gesture of individual defiance shows how telecommunications can affect political events.

MAP 33.3

The Collapse of Communism in Eastern Europe and the Soviet Union

The end of the Soviet empire in Eastern Europe and the collapse of communism in the Soviet Union itself dramatically changed the borders of Europe and Central Asia. West and East Germany reunited, while the nations of Czechoslovakia and Yugoslavia, created by the 1919 Versailles treaty, divided into smaller states. The old Soviet Union produced fifteen new countries, of which eleven remained loosely bound in the Confederation of Independent States (CIS).

plotters had ordered 250,000 pairs of handcuffs and preprinted blank arrest forms, but made no effort to detain the charismatic Boris N. Yeltsin, elected president of the Russian republic in 1989 and a leader of the movement for reform. When news of the coup attempt reached Moscow, Yeltsin defiantly mounted a Soviet tank to urge citizens to resist. Television coverage of this dramatic act, carried live throughout the U.S.S.R. and, indeed the world, solidified resistance. As in Eastern Europe two years earlier, instantaneous global communications fostered political and economic change.

The collapse of the coup left Gorbachev and Yeltsin uneasily co-leading what remained of the U.S.S.R., but its days were numbered. The twelve remaining Soviet republics struggled to find a way to cooperate in some kind of loose confederation, since none, not even the Russian republic, was strong enough to go it alone. In December 1991 the Union of Soviet Socialist Republics formally dissolved itself to make way for the Commonwealth of Independent States (CIS). Boris Yeltsin remained president of the largest and most populous Russian republic; Gorbachev was out of a job.

The breakup of the Soviet Union, which was hastened by the needs of long-suppressed ethnic and religious minorities within the republics, sharpened the focus on ethnic conflict as a threat to international stability. Events within the Soviet Union paralleled the struggle between Kurds and Shiite Muslims in Iran, the ethnic and religious disputes in India, the takeover of Ethiopia by secessionist rebels from Eritrea, and especially the deep internal divisions in former Soviet satellites such as Yugoslavia, which split into several states in 1991 and soon erupted into a violent civil war.

Economic issues were an even greater challenge. The end of Soviet domination over Eastern Europe and the dissolution of the union revealed that the Soviet economy was in more of a shambles than had been realized. Conversion from state-controlled production to a free-market economy would not be easy. Leaders of Russia and former Eastern bloc states turned eagerly to the West for economic aid, hoping for something similar to the Marshall Plan that had rebuilt Europe after World War II. Western leaders responded hesitantly, seeking signs of political stability from the CIS.

The dissolution of the Soviet Union left only one military superpower, the United States. With the end of the Cold War went much of the justification for maintaining permanent mobilization. Americans talked about how the country might spend the *peace dividend*, money that could be saved out of the military budget. Intellectuals, ordinary citizens, and politicians alike faced adjustment to a new climate where communism as a political and ideological force was dead. Nikita Khruschev had told the United States in 1956, "We will bury you." Now the tombstone read, "The Soviet Union, 1917–1991."

War in the Persian Gulf

Even as events in Eastern Europe and the Soviet Union were reshaping Cold War polarities, new challenges were arising in the Middle East. On August 2, 1990, Iraq invaded Kuwait. Saddam Hussein's brutal conquest of his oil-rich neighbor caught American policymakers by surprise, but within days President Bush articulated the position that eventually led to war: "This will not stand, this aggression against Kuwait." Bush orchestrated broad international support for a United Nations Security Council resolution condemning Iraq, calling for its withdrawal, and imposing an embargo and trade sanctions; for emphasis, the United Nations dispatched a multinational force of 150,000 troops to the area. The United Nations was finally working the way its Dumbarton Oaks planners had hoped in 1945, in large part because superpower tensions had abated with the end of the Cold War.

When Saddam Hussein showed no signs of complying with the U.N. resolution, Bush prodded the United Nations to create a legal framework for an international military offensive against the man he repeatedly called "the butcher of Baghdad." On November 29 the Security Council voted to use force if Iraq did not withdraw by January 15. A massive multinational build-up continued; eventually troops, supplies, and pledges of financial support came from thirty-seven countries, including several Arab states but not the Soviet Union. In early January, Congress debated whether to allow sanctions more time to work, then narrowly voted authorization for war. On January 16, President Bush announced to the nation, "the liberation of Kuwait has begun."

The United States commitment of 540,000 troops matched the height of the Vietnam mobilization in 1968. But this was a new, all-volunteer military, which included thousands of reservists called up from their civilian jobs. African-Americans and minorities, many of whom had been attracted to military service by benefits such as education and health care, made up a third of the force. Women, approximately 10 percent of the troops, were a far greater presence than in Vietnam. Although they served in support, not direct combat, positions, women would be among the relatively few casualties and POWs, raising questions about whether they should continue to be barred from combat when they were at risk anyway.

The 42-day war was a resounding success for the coalition forces, which, as in the Korean War, were predominantly American. The new post-Vietnam military was symbolized by General Colin Powell, head of the Chiefs of Staff, and General H. Norman Schwartzkopf, commander of first-stage Operation Desert Shield, renamed Desert Storm when the fighting began. Their air-land strategy involved a month of air strikes on Iraq designed to crush communications, destroy existing armaments, and pummel the morale of the Iraqi troops, followed by a ground offensive against Iraqi bases in Kuwait. As reported in daily Pentagon press briefings (about the only access to information the media was allowed), the laser-based technology and computerized weaponry seemed like a video game. Critics charged that such military jargon as "attriting" rather than killing enemy forces or "collateral damage" for destruction of civilian facilities sanitized the war's brutality. The ground phase of the war was finally launched on February 23; within days, thousands of Iraqi troops surrendered and the fighting quickly ended.

The rapid success of the ground war produced a euphoric reaction at home, a blizzard of yellow ribbons in support of the troops, and relief at the amazingly low U.S. casualties (145 Americans killed in action). The performance of American troops became for many a banishment of the ghost of Vietnam, the anti-military

Women at War

Women played key, and visible, roles in the Persian Gulf War, comprising approximately 10 percent of the American troops. Increasing numbers of women are choosing to make a career out of the military, despite widespread reports of sexual harassment and other forms of discrimination.

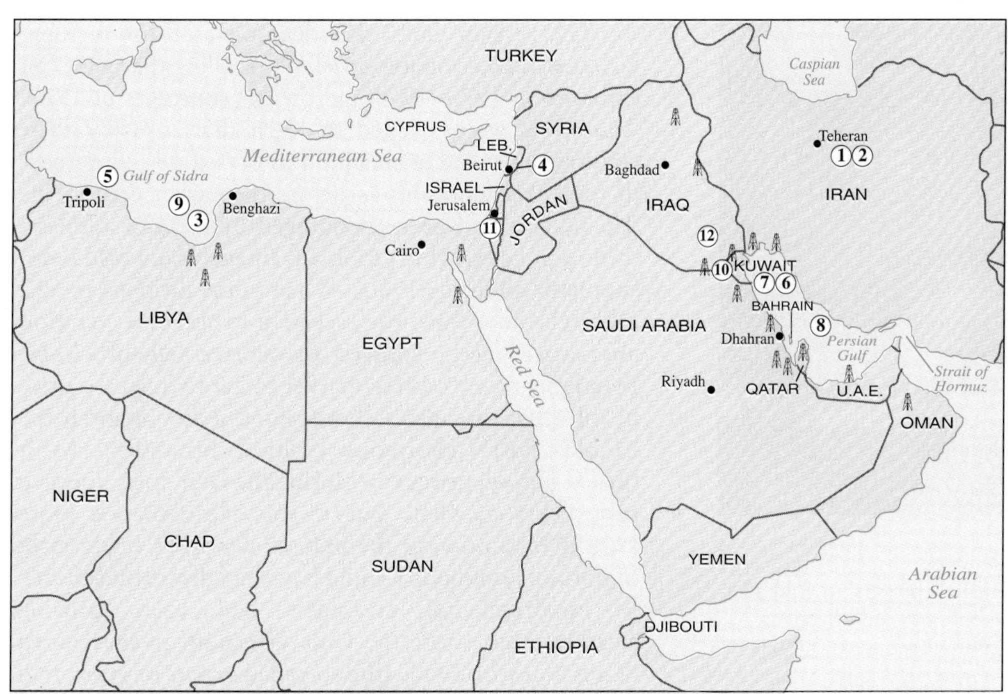

1. Teheran hostage taking, Nov.1979–Jan.1981
2. Hostage rescue attempt fails, Apr. 1980.
3. Libyan jets shot down, Aug. 1981.
4. 241 U.S. peacekeeping troops die in bombing, Oct. 1983.
5. U.S. air strikes, Mar.–Apr. 1986.
6. USS Stark hit by Iraqi missile, May 1987.
7. Kuwati tankers escorted by US Navy, July 1987.
8. U.S. Navy shoots down Iranian airliner, July 1988.
9. Libyan jets shot down, Jan. 1989.
10. Operation Desert Storm (Gulf War) Jan.-Feb. 1991.
11. U.S. Patriot missiles in Israel, Jan.–Feb.1991.
12. U.S. declares "no-fly zone" in southern Iraq, Sept. 1992.

Oil fields

MAP 33.4

U.S. Involvement in the Middle East, 1980–1992

The United States has long played an active role in the Middle East, pursuing the twin goals of protecting Israel's security and assuring a reliable supply of low-cost oil from the Persian Gulf states. By far the largest intervention came in 1991, when, under United Nations auspices, President Bush sent 540,000 American troops to liberate Kuwait from Iraq.

malaise resulting from the prolonged, inconclusive, and politically divisive war of two decades earlier. "By God, we've kicked the Vietnam Syndrome once and for all," gloated George Bush.

One of the biggest winners was the president himself, whose approval rating approached 90 percent. Appearing to act from strong, unequivocal beliefs, Bush made the brutality of the Iraqi aggression the main issue, rather than the need to maintain a steady supply of oil at reasonable prices. Bush profited from the support that often accompanies swift presidential action, such as Reagan's invasion of Grenada in 1983 or his own deployment of troops to Panama in December of 1989 to capture its president, suspected drug dealer Manuel Noriega.

Ironically, at war's end, very little had changed, except that Kuwait was liberated and Iraq no longer was an immediate military threat to its neighbors. Saddam Hussein was still in power. The war had been devastating for Iraqi civilians and as the fighting finished, Bush called on them to "take matters into their own hands" and force Saddam Hussein to "step aside." But when Iraq's minority Kurdish and Shiite rebels rose up against Saddam, only to be brutally repressed by Iraqi forces, the United States refused support. Perhaps as many as two million refugees fled over the border to Turkey or Iran, where, homeless and starving, they set up makeshift encampments. The United States offered only humanitarian aid.

Once the cheering stopped, doubts surfaced. Why wasn't George Bush providing the leadership on domestic issues that he had brought to the coalition against Saddam Hussein? If America could apply itself so purposefully to war, why couldn't it do the same for the problems of its inner cities, unemployment, the environment, or finding a cure for AIDS? Would the war help end the recession? Observed one consumer, "The country is feeling good about the war, I'm feeling good about it, but I still can't afford a new car."

The Spread of Environmentalism

The Persian Gulf War was the first conflict in modern history to stir public concern about environmental issues while it was being fought. In a deliberate act of sabotage before surrendering, the Iraqis opened Kuwait's oil storage tanks, letting a huge spill foul large

Kuwait Oil Fires
The fires in Kuwaiti oil fields set during the Persian Gulf War caused intense respiratory distress and heavy localized environmental damage, but their longterm effect on the global environment seem not to be as devastating as originally feared.

areas of the Persian Gulf. The spill, between four and ten times larger than that from the oil tanker *Exxon Valdez* off Alaska in 1989, damaged the gulf's delicate ecological balance and threatened to contaminate the desalination plants so essential to this arid region. The Iraqis also deliberately set fires in Kuwait's oil wells while retreating. The heavy acrid smoke from the fires blocked sunlight and caused pollution and respiratory distress over a wide area.

Be Kind to Your Mother (Earth)
The annual celebrations on Earth Day—April 22—began in 1970. Simple things that ordinary citizens can do to save the earth include stopping junk mail, recycling cans and bottles, carpooling, taking shorter showers, and recharging batteries rather than throwing them away.

The Persian Gulf crisis demonstrated the ongoing U.S. dependence on imported oil, recalling the OPEC oil embargo in 1973–1974 and the gas shortages of 1979. Americans were startled to learn that in 1990 their country depended as much on imported oil (42 percent of total consumption) as before the earlier crisis. This dependence had been encouraged by Reagan administration policies, which took advantage of a world oversupply of oil in the 1980s. When prices dropped to $12 a barrel, there was little incentive to conserve, develop alternative energy sources, or achieve self-sufficiency. By relying solely on free-market forces to keep the price of oil down, Reagan's shortsighted policy ignored the Middle East's enormous political instability. As it turned out, oil prices rose during the Gulf crisis but then subsided somewhat. But it was clear that a more lengthy disruption of the industrial world's single most important commodity could have had disastrous effects.

Environmental awareness had been growing steadily even before the Gulf War, both in the United States and worldwide (the so-called *greens* or *green politics*). A major impetus was the meltdown in a reactor at the Chernobyl nuclear energy plant in the Soviet Ukraine in 1986, the world's worst nuclear power accident to date. Chernobyl released a 50-ton cloud of radioactive dust into the air (ten times the fallout at Hiroshima), which soon spread throughout Europe. The accident raised grave questions about the safety of nuclear reactors worldwide.

Increasingly, environmental problems crossed national boundaries and demanded international action. Three pressing issues were the depletion of the ozone layer, acid rain, and global warming. Scientists have detected a gap in the ozone shield that protects the earth from the sun's ultraviolet rays, caused by the release of chlorofluorocarbons or CFCs (industrial chemicals used in refrigeration, air conditioning, and some aerosol products) into the atmosphere. Acid rain, which is caused by the release into the air of sulfur dioxide and oxides of nitrogen as byproducts of industrial processes, damages the water supply, plants, and stone structures. Global warming, or the "greenhouse effect," is believed to result from the widespread burning of fossil fuels or tropical rain forests, which releases carbon dioxide. This traps heat from the sun in the lower atmosphere (the equivalent of a "dirty window over the Earth"), which can gradually cause temperatures on earth to increase. A rise of between 2 and 5 degrees could produce such devastating effects as drought and the melting of polar and glacial ice, with a corresponding rise in sea level and flooding of low-lying coastal regions, including many of the world's most populated cities.

An important precedent for international action on environmental issues was the 1987 Montreal protocol, where thirty-four nations agreed to limit ozone-damaging chlorofluorocarbons over a period of time. In June 1992 a major environmental Earth Summit in Rio de Janeiro adopted a treaty on global warming. President Bush attended the conference and signed the treaty, but he refused to commit the United States to specific goals and timetables.

According to polls, more than three-quarters of Americans consider themselves environmentalists. The twentieth anniversary of Earth Day on April 22, 1990, drew millions worldwide to activities designed to encourage recycling, conservation, and more careful use of natural resources. Unfortunately, little progress had been made since the first Earth Day in 1970. Moving away from the convenience of a fuel-guzzling, "throw-away" society to one that conserves and recycles has been slow and halting.

The 1992 Election

With the end of the Cold War, domestic affairs returned to their more normal place at the center of American politics. As the election campaign of 1992 got underway, the economy, not the environment, was *the* overriding issue, as the recession that began in 1990 showed few signs of abating. As businesses failed and unemployment grew, the administration continued to respond with supply-side rhetoric and additional cuts in interest rates, hoping that this would lead to new investment and "trickle down" to create new jobs. Only it didn't.

It was a very disaffected nation that pondered a large field of Democratic contenders as the primary season began. Bill Clinton, long-time governor of Arkansas, one of the nation's poorest states, emerged as the front runner, surviving charges of marital infidelity and draft-dodging to win the Democratic nomination in July. For his running mate he chose Al Gore, a second-term senator from Tennessee who at age forty-four was a year and a half younger than Clinton, making them the first baby boom national ticket.

President Bush easily won renomination by facing down a primary challenge from conservative columnist Pat Buchanan to win renomination. But to solidify support with the New Right, Vice-President Dan Quayle spoke out strongly for family values and other conservative social agendas. Bush responded to criticism that he lacked a vision for domestic affairs by blaming the Democratic Congress for thwarting all his initiatives.

In the midst of the primary season, the television talk shows launched a third-party challenger, Texas billionaire H. Ross Perot, who more than any other candidate capitalized on voters' desire for change. On the last day of the Democratic convention, Perot dropped out almost as suddenly as he had entered. He then just as suddenly reentered the race less than five weeks before the election, adding a well-financed wildcard in this most unusual of election years.

Besides the state of the economy, the election focused attention on issues that had come to the fore in the preceding year. Women ran for office in unprecedented numbers, many galvanized by the insensitivity of the all-male, all-white Senate Judiciary Committee to Professor Anita Hill's charges of sexual harassment against Supreme Court nominee Clarence Thomas. "They just don't get it" became a rallying cry. Meanwhile, attacks on Hillary Rodham Clinton, a practicing lawyer and the wife of the Democratic candidate, suggested an uneasiness about women's roles in public life.

The Democrats, having learned something from the last three campaigns, mounted an aggressive, effective campaign that focused on Clinton's plans to solve domestic problems, especially education, health care, and revitalizing the economy, while Gore added expertise on defense and environmental issues. Opinion polls fluctuated through the fall, especially because it was hard to measure the impact of independent candidate Ross Perot. On election day, Clinton scored a decisive victory, winning 43 percent of the popular vote to Bush's

Clinton/Gore

Baby boomers Bill Clinton and Al Gore celebrated their 1992 victory to the strains of rock music. Billing themselves as representing a "new generation of leadership," they campaigned in dramatic new ways—appearing on MTV and the Arsenio Hall show, holding talk-show-style town meetings, and going on bus tours to out-of-the way locales all over the country.

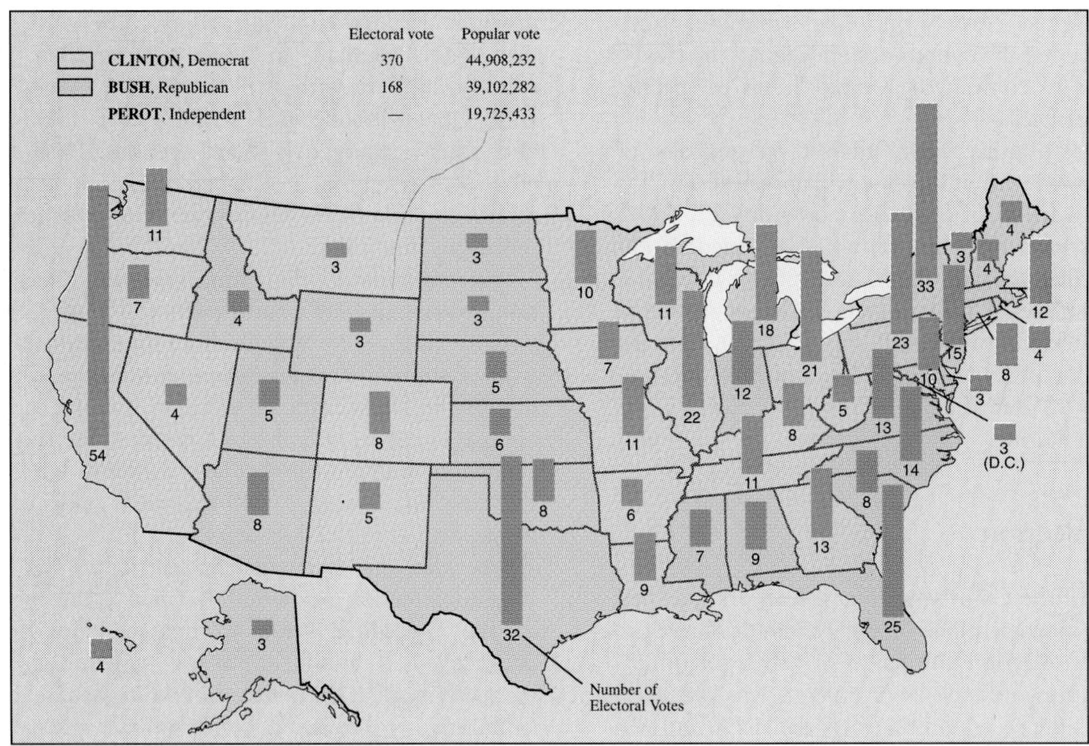

MAP 33.5

The Election of 1992

The first national election since the end of the Cold War was dominated by concern over the ailing economy. The first-ever all-southerner Democratic ticket of Bill Clinton and Al Gore won broad support across the country, cutting into the Republican strongholds of the South and West. Independent candidate H. Ross Perot won no electoral votes but polled an impressive 19 percent of the popular vote.

38 percent and Perot's 19 percent. The results in the electoral college were even more lopsided, with Clinton winning 370 votes to Bush's 168. Although Perot did not win a single state, his popular vote was the highest for an independent candidate since Theodore Roosevelt in 1912. The Democrats retained control of both houses of Congress, ending twelve years of divided government. And the number of women in Congress increased dramatically: forty-seven in the House of Representatives (up from twenty-eight) and an all-time high of six in the Senate, including Illinois Democrat Carol Moseley Braun, the first African-American woman elected to that body. Perhaps most important of all, voter turnout was up dramatically, suggesting a new engagement in the political process on the part of American citizens, as well as hope in Bill Clinton's promise of change.

The New World Order

In 1941, Henry Luce, the publisher of *Life* magazine, confidently predicted the beginning of an "American century" when World War II ended. As we approach the year 2000, it seems likely that the twenty-first century will be known not as an American century but as a "global century." Economically, power will be shared among multiple players, a sharp contrast to the immediate postwar period when the U.S. dominated the world economy. Militarily, superpower conflict will no longer be a threat, although smaller ethnic and religious conflicts will periodically rock international stability.

The new world order will be characterized by interdependent capitalist market economies organized around four major trading blocks. The first, North America, will be dominated by the United States and include Canada, Mexico, and the developing Central American countries. The second will be Russia and the other nations of the former Soviet Union and Eastern European bloc. The third, the Pacific Rim, will center on Japan, but also include China, South Korea, Hong Kong, Singapore, and Taiwan. The fourth will be the newly revitalized European Community (EC), with a strong Germany at its heart.

The early twenty-first century will likely be most favorable to the Pacific Rim and EC countries, already emerging as strong contenders in global markets as the United States no longer predominates and the CIS lags far behind. The strongest individual economies will likely continue to be those of Japan and Germany, who as the defeated enemies of World War II were kept out of the expensive arms race that absorbed the two superpowers from 1945 to 1991. Historians may later conclude that the United States and the former Soviet Union fell victim to "imperial overstretch," concentrating their resources on a vast military establishment while consumer-oriented production fell behind in the face of foreign competition. It would be a great irony if the United States "won" the Cold War only to have jeopardized its status as a world economic leader in the resulting peace.

The *Pax Americana* lasted from the end of World War II through the 1970s. That the United States no longer dominates the world does not mean that the country is on an inevitable decline toward obscurity and powerlessness. In the 1990s the world appears to be returning to a situation in which power, both economic and military, is dispersed among a number of key players, of which the United States still is one of the most important. This emerging new world order will shape the future of the United States and the globe in the twenty-first century and beyond.

Summary

Ronald Reagan's administration advocated a smaller role for the federal government in domestic programs and the restoration of American prestige abroad. Reagan remained enormously popular throughout his two terms, but left huge budget deficits to his successor, Vice-President George Bush. Reagan's economic policies, notably deregulation and tax cuts, added to the concentration of wealth in the 1980s. As Wall Street boomed, more Americans fell into poverty, and middle-income households struggled to stay afloat.

American society in the 1980s continued to be defined by diversity. Increased immigration, notably from Asia and Latin American countries, changed the demographic balance of many areas, especially the cities, and the postwar trend of population growth in the South, West, and metropolitan areas continued. The economy shifted toward the service sector, and traditional smokestack industries declined.

The most dramatic change of the decade was the end of the Cold War, which had been the guiding principle of American foreign policy since the end of World War II. The dramatic collapse of communism within the Soviet Union itself further complicated the old truisms. The post-Cold War future seemed to promise a fragile world peace, vulnerable to regional and ethnic conflicts, and an increasingly global economy, with the United States playing a leading role, but not dominating, as it did in the *Pax Americana* of the immediate postwar world.

TOPIC FOR RESEARCH

Feminism in the 1980s

In a widely read 1991 book, journalist Susan Faludi described a powerful backlash against the gains American women had won in the 1960s and 1970s. The media consistently held the women's movement responsible for every ill afflicting modern women—from infertility to eating disorders to rising divorce rates to the "man shortage." According to Faludi, the message that the women's movement was women's own worst enemy and that women were unhappy precisely because they had achieved equality was a myth. Instead, Faludi traced many of American women's problems to the fact that they do not have *enough* equality.

Use Faludi's thesis as a starting point for an assessment of the women's movement and women's lives in the 1980s and 1990s. Is there a backlash against women? How are women portrayed in the media and popular culture, especially in television, film, popular music, and advertising? Why is feminism often unappealing to younger women: have we moved into a postfeminist era? What do current debates about reproductive rights, sexual harassment, pay equity, the "glass ceiling," and the "mommy track" tell us about how much equality American women have actually achieved?

In addition to Susan Faludi, *Backlash: The Undeclared War Against American Women* (1991), see Naomi Wolf, *The Beauty Myth* (1991), and Marilyn French, *The War Against Women* (1992). Arlie Hochschild, *The Second Shift* (1989), challenges the notion that women can "do it all." Gloria Steinem's revealing memoir, *Revolution from Within* (1992), identifies self-esteem as the key to personal and political change.

BIBLIOGRAPHY

Few historians have turned their attention yet to the period since 1980, leaving the field to journalists, economists, and political scientists. For the stuff that history is made of, the Bureau of the Census offers an excellent introduction through the yearly *Statistical Abstract of the United States* (110th edition, 1990). Synthetic essays on important issues are also offered in the Congressional Quarterly's *Editorial Research Reports.* Indexes to newspapers and periodicals point toward coverage of major events.

The Reagan Presidency

Ronald Reagan has drawn his share of biographers. Historians who have tried their hand include Robert Dallek, *Ronald Reagan: The Politics of Symbolism* (1982), and Michael Rogin, *Ronald Reagan: The Movie* (1987). See also Ronnie Dugger, *On Reagan* (1983), and Lou Cannon, *Reagan* (1982). Nancy Reagan presented her interpretation of the Reagan years in her aptly named *My Turn* (1989), and speechwriter Peggy Noonan offered an insider's view in *What I Saw at the Revolution* (1990). Haynes Johnson, *Sleepwalking Through History* (1991), provides an excellent overview of America in the Reagan years.

On Reaganomics, George Gilder's *Wealth and Poverty* (1981) represents the views held by many in the Reagan administration. See also David Stockman's memoir, *The Triumph of Politics* (1986). John L. Palmer and Isabel Sawhill, eds., *The Reagan Record* (1984), offers a comprehensive assessment of the first term. See also Benjamin Friedman, *Day of Reckoning: The Consequences of American Economic Policy Under Reagan and After* (1988); William Greider, *The Education of David Stockman and Other Americans* (1982); and Robert Lekachman, *Greed Is Not Enough: Reaganomics* (1982). For the effects of deregulation and lax enforcement by government agencies, see Joan Claybrook, *Retreat from Safety: Reagan's Attack on American Health* (1984); Jonathan Lash, *A Season of Spoils: The Story of the Reagan Administration's Attack on the Environment* (1984); and Charles Noble, *Liberalism at Work: The Rise and Fall of OSHA* (1986).

For electoral politics, see Jack W. Germond and Jules Witcover, *Wake Us When It's Over: Presidential Politics of 1984* (1985); Thomas Ferguson and Joel Rogers, *Right Turn: The Decline of the Democrats and the Future of American Politics* (1986); Frances Fox Piven and Richard Cloward, *Why Americans Don't Vote* (1988); and Robert S. McElvaine, *The End of the Conservative Era: Liberalism after Reagan* (1987).

For foreign policy, Stephen Ambrose, *Rise to Globalism* (5th ed., 1988), provides a comprehensive overview of the Reagan years. The Iran-Contra scandal is covered in Jane Hunter et al., *The Iran-Contra Connection* (1987). Other surveys of covert Reagan initiatives are Bob Woodward, *Veil: The Secret Wars of the CIA* (1987), and Steven Emerson, *Secret Warriors: Inside the Covert Military Operations of the Reagan Era* (1988). For relations with the Soviet Union and the arms race, see Strobe Talbott, *Deadly Gambit: The Reagan Administration and the Stalemate in Nuclear Arms Control* (1984) and *The Master of the Game: Paul Nitze and the Nuclear Peace* (1988), and Seweryn Bialer and Michael Mandelbaum, eds., *Gorbachev's Russia and American Foreign Policy* (1988).

The material on the United States and Central and South America is extensive. Good introductions are Walter LaFeber, *Inevitable Revolutions* (1984); Abraham F. Lowenthal, *Partners in Conflict: The United States and Latin America* (1987); and Kenneth Coleman and George C. Herring, eds., *The Central America Crisis* (1985). On Nicaragua, see E. Bradford Burns, *At War in Nicaragua* (1987); Robert Pastor, *Condemned to Repetition* (1987); and Roy Gutman, *Banana Diplomacy, 1981–1987* (1988). On El Salvador, see Raymond Bonner, *Weakness and Deceit: U.S. Policy in El Salvador* (1984), and Tom Buckley, *Violent Neighbors: El Salvador, Central America and the United States* (1984). Other useful studies include Martin Diskin, ed., *Trouble in Our Backyard* (1984); J. Michael Hogan, *The Panama Canal in American Politics* (1986); and Hugh O'Shaughnessy, *Grenada* (1985).

The Best of Times, The Worst of Times

Kevin Phillips, *The Politics of Rich and Poor* (1989), provides a fairly unflattering view of the excesses of the 1980s. Journalists have chronicled the frenzied atmosphere of Wall Street in works that read like novels. Among the best are Connie Bruck, *The Predators' Ball: The Junk Bond Raiders and the Man Who Staked Them* (1988); Bryan Burroughs and John Helyar, *Barbarians at the Gate: The Fall of RJR Nabisco* (1990); Michael Lewis, *Liar's Poker* (1989); Donna Sammons Carpenter, *The Fall of the House of Hutton* (1989); Jeffrey Birnbaum and Allan S. Murray, *Showdown at Gucci Gulch: Lawmakers, Lobbyists, and the Unlikely Triumph of Tax Reform* (1987); and James B. Stewart, *Den of Thieves* (1991).

Books that address the growing inequality in the decade include Thomas Byrne Edsall, *The New Politics of Inequality* (1984); Leslie W. Dunbar, ed., *Minority Report: What Has Happened to Blacks, Hispanics, American Indians, and Other Minorities in the Eighties* (1984); Frances Fox Piven and Richard Cloward, *The New Class War* (1982); Michael Harrington, *The New American Poverty* (1984); Frank Levy, *Dollars and Dreams: The Changing American Income Distribution* (1987); and Michael Katz, *The Undeserving Poor: From the War on Poverty to the War on Welfare* (1989). For the poor and homeless in the inner cities, see Ken Auletta, *The Underclass* (1982); William J. Wilson, *The Truly Disadvantaged* (1987); Marian Wright Edelman, *Families in Peril* (1987); Jonathan Kozol, *Rachel and Her Children: Homeless Families in America* (1988); and Nicholas Lemann, *The Promised Land* (1989). For the problems of women and children, see Hilda Scott, *Working Your Way to the Bottom: The Feminization of Poverty* (1985); Ruth Sidel, *Women and Children Last* (1986); and Lenore Weitzman, *The Divorce Revolution* (1985). The struggles of contemporary American life are portrayed in Studs Terkel, *The Great Divide* (1988), and Bennett Harrison and Barry Bluestone, *The Great U-Turn: Corporate Restructuring and the Polarizing of America* (1988), which also offers an overview of economic developments in the 1980s.

David Reimers, *Still the Golden Door* (1986), covers immigration policy in the postwar period through the 1980s. See also Nathan Glazer, ed., *Clamor at the Gates: The New Amer-*

ican Immigration (1986); Thomas Muller and Thomas J. Espenshade, *The Fourth Wave: California's Newest Immigrants* (1985); and Al Santoli, *New Americans* (1988). On Hispanics, see Frank Bean and Marta Tienda, *The Hispanic Population of the United States* (1988), and James D. Cockcroft, *Outlaws in the Promised Land* (1986).

Barbara Ehrenreich's collection of essays, *The Worst Years of Our Lives* (1990), covers a variety of political and social topics from the perspective of the left. Randy Shilts, *And the Band Played On: Politics, People, and the AIDS Epidemic* (1987), is a devastating critique of the inaction in the early years of the AIDS epidemic. See also John Langone, *AIDS: The Facts* (1988). Steven Bach, *Final Cut: Dreams and Disaster in the Making of Heaven's Gate* (1985), provides an inside look at Hollywood and the modern studio system. Allan Bloom, *The Closing of the American Mind* (1987), and E. D. Hirsch, *Cultural Literacy* (1988) deal with issues of curriculum, learning, and literacy.

The New World Order

The emergence of a new world order has provoked commentary from economists, journalists, and historians. Paul Kennedy, *The Rise and Fall of the Great Powers* (1987), suggests that the United States, like other empires before it, fell victim to "imperial overstretch." This view has been questioned in such works as Joseph Nye, *Bound to Lead: The Changing Nature of American Power* (1990); Robert Kuttner, *The End of Laissez Faire: National Purpose and the Global Economy after the Cold War* (1991); and Henry R. Nau, *The Myth of America's Decline: Leading the World Economy into the 1990s* (1990). For developments in Eastern Europe, Bernard Gwertzman and Michael T. Kaufman, eds., *The Collapse of Communism* (1990), reviews the events of 1989 through articles published in the *New York Times*. Bob Woodward's treatment of military decision making in *The Commanders* (1991), also provides important background on Operation Desert Storm. H. Norman Schwartzkopf's entertaining autobiography, *It Doesn't Take a Hero* (1992), gives the commanding general's account of the Gulf War.

While there is no general overview of the environmental history in the 1980s and 1990s, many books survey the problems and call for action. The Earth Works Group, *50 Simple Things You Can Do to Save the Earth* (1989), offers a primer on what citizens can do. Barry Commoner, *Making Peace with the Planet* (1990), and the Conservation Foundation, *State of the Environment: An Assessment at Mid-Decade* (1984); and Al Gore, *Earth in the Balance* (1992), are report cards on how well, or poorly, the world is doing on environmental awareness. Daniel Yergin, *The Prize* (1991), chronicles how the commodity of oil dominates modern life, with both economic and environmental consequences. Among the books that try to look to the future are Robert B. Reich, *The Work of Nations: Preparing Ourselves for 2lst century Capitalism* (1991), and David Halberstam, *The Next Century* (1991). For discussions of American attitudes toward politics and leaders at the time of the 1992 election, see William Greider, *Who Will Tell the People?* (1992), and E. J. Dionne, *The War Against Public Life: Why Americans Hate Politics* (1991).

TIMELINE

1980	Ronald Reagan elected president
1981	Economic Recovery Tax Act Sandra Day O'Connor nominated to Supreme Court MTV premieres Beginning of AIDS epidemic
1982	Recession
1983	Star Wars proposed
1984	Geraldine Ferraro first woman on major party ticket
1985	Gramm-Rudman Balanced Budget Act United States becomes debtor nation Mikhail Gorbachev takes power in U.S.S.R.
1986	Iran-Contra affair Tax Reform Act Simpson-Mazzoli Immigration Act Chernobyl nuclear disaster
1987	Collapse of stock market
1988	George Bush elected president
1989	Savings and loan crisis *Exxon Valdez* oil spill Political revolutions in Eastern Europe Chinese crackdown at Tiananmen Square *Webster v. Reproductive Health Services*
1990	Recession begins Twentieth anniversary of Earth Day
1990–1991	Persian Gulf crisis
1991	Dissolution of Soviet Union; end of the Cold War
1992	Los Angeles riots Bill Clinton elected president

The Declaration of Independence

The Unanimous Declaration of the Thirteen United States of America

When in the Course of human events, it becomes necessary for one people to dissolve the political bands which have connected them with another, and to assume among the Powers of the earth, the separate and equal station to which the Laws of Nature and of Nature's God entitle them, a decent respect to the opinions of mankind requires that they should declare the causes which impel them to the separation.

We hold these truths to be self-evident, that all men are created equal, that they are endowed by their Creator with certain unalienable rights, that among these are Life, Liberty, and the pursuit of Happiness. That to secure these rights, Governments are instituted among Men, deriving their just powers from the consent of the governed. That whenever any Form of Government becomes destructive of these ends, it is the Right of the People to alter or to abolish it, and to institute new Government, laying its foundation on such principles and organizing its powers in such form, as to them shall seem most likely to effect their Safety and Happiness. Prudence, indeed, will dictate that Governments long established should not be changed for light and transient causes; and accordingly all experience hath shown, that mankind are more disposed to suffer, while evils are sufferable, than to right themselves by abolishing the forms to which they are accustomed. But when a long train of abuses and usurpations, pursuing invariably the same Object evinces a design to reduce them under absolute Despotism, it is their right, it is their duty, to throw off such Government, and to provide new Guards for their future security.—Such has been the patient sufferance of these Colonies; and such is now the necessity which constrains them to alter their former Systems of Government. The history of the present King of Great Britain is a history of repeated injuries and usurpations, all having in direct object the establishment of an absolute Tyranny over these States. To prove this, let Facts be submitted to a candid world.

He has refused his Assent to Laws, the most wholesome and necessary for the public good.

He has forbidden his Governors to pass Laws of immediate and pressing importance, unless suspended in their operation till his Assent should be obtained; and, when so suspended, he has utterly neglected to attend to them.

He has refused to pass other Laws for the accommodation of large districts of people, unless those people would relinquish the right of Representation in the Legislature, a right inestimable to them and formidable to tyrants only.

He has called together legislative bodies at places unusual, uncomfortable, and distant from the depository of their public Records, for the sole purpose of fatiguing them into compliance with his measures.

He has dissolved Representative Houses repeatedly, for opposing with manly firmness his invasions on the rights of the people.

He has refused for a long time, after such dissolutions, to cause others to be elected; whereby the Legislative powers, incapable of Annihilation, have returned to the People at large for their exercise; the State remaining in the mean time exposed to all the dangers of invasion from without and convulsions within.

He has endeavoured to prevent the population of these States; for that purpose obstructing the Laws of Naturalization of Foreigners; refusing to pass others to encourage their migrations hither, and raising the conditions of new Appropriations of Lands.

He has obstructed the Administration of Justice, by refusing his Assent to Laws for establishing Judiciary powers.

He has made Judges dependent on his Will alone, for the tenure of their offices, and the amount and payment of their salaries.

He has erected a multitude of New Offices, and sent hither swarms of Officers to harass our People, and eat out their substance.

He has kept among us, in times of peace, Standing Armies without the Consent of our legislature.

He has combined with others to subject us to a jurisdiction foreign to our constitution, and unacknowledged by our laws; giving his Assent to their Acts of pretended Legislation:

For quartering large bodies of armed troops among us:

For protecting them, by a mock Trial, from Punishment for any Murders which they should commit on the Inhabitants of these States:

For cutting off our Trade with all parts of the world:

For imposing taxes on us without our Consent:

For depriving us of many cases, of the benefits of Trial by jury:

For transporting us beyond Seas to be tried for pretended offences:

For abolishing the free System of English Laws in a neighbouring Province, establishing therein an Arbitrary government, and enlarging its Boundaries so as to render it at once an example and fit instrument for introducing the same absolute rule into these Colonies;

For taking away our Charters, abolishing our most valuable Laws, and altering fundamentally the Forms of our Governments:

For suspending our own Legislatures, and declaring themselves invested with Power to legislate for us in all cases whatsoever.

He has abdicated Government here, by declaring us out of his Protection and waging War against us.

He has plundered our seas, ravaged our Coasts, burnt our towns, and destroyed the lives of our people.

He is at this time transporting large armies of foreign mercenaries to compleat the works of death, desolation, and tyranny, already begun with circumstances of Cruelty & perfidy scarcely paralleled in the most barbarous ages, and totally unworthy the Head of a civilized nation.

He has constrained our fellow Citizens taken Captive on the high Seas to bear Arms against their Country, to become the executioners of their friends and Brethren, or to fall themselves by their Hands.

He has excited domestic insurrections amongst us, and has endeavoured to bring on the inhabitants of our frontiers, the merciless Indian Savages, whose known rule of warfare, is an undistinguished destruction of all ages, sexes, and conditions.

In every stage of these Oppressions We have Petitioned for Redress in the most humble terms: Our repeated Petitions have been answered only by repeated injury. A Prince, whose character is thus marked by every act which may define a Tyrant, is unfit to be the ruler of a free people.

Nor have We been wanting in attention to our British brethren. We have warned them from time to time of attempts by their legislature to extend an unwarrantable jurisdiction over us. We have reminded them of the circumstances of our emigration and settlement here. We have appealed to their native justice and magnanimity, and we have conjured them by the ties of our common kindred to disavow these usurpations, which, would inevitably interrupt our connections and correspondence. They too have been deaf to the voice of justice and of consanguinity. We must, therefore, acquiesce in the necessity, which denounces our Separation, and hold them, as we hold the rest of mankind, Enemies in War, in Peace Friends.

We, therefore, the Representatives of the United States of America, in General Congress, Assembled, appealing to the Supreme Judge of the world for the rectitude of our intentions, do, in the Name, and by Authority of the good People of these Colonies, solemnly publish and declare, That these United Colonies are, and of Right ought to be FREE AND INDEPENDENT STATES; that they are Absolved from all Allegiance to the British Crown, and that all political connection between them and the State of Great Britain, is and ought to be totally dissolved; and that as Free and Independent States, they have full Power to levy War, conclude Peace, contract Alliances, establish Commerce, and to do all other Acts and Things which Independent States may of right do. And for the support of this Declaration, with a firm reliance on the Protection of Divine Providence, we mutually pledge to each other our Lives, our Fortunes, and our sacred Honor.

John Hancock

Button Gwinnett
Lyman Hall
Geo. Walton
Wm. Hooper
Joseph Hewes
John Penn
Edward Rutledge
Thos. Heyward, Junr.
Thomas Lynch, Junr.
Arthur Middleton
Samuel Chase
Wm. Paca
Thos. Stone
Charles Carroll of Carrollton

George Wythe
Richard Henry Lee
Th. Jefferson
Benja. Harrison
Thos. Nelson, Jr.
Francis Lightfoot Lee
Carter Braxton
Robt. Morris
Benjamin Rush
Benja. Franklin
John Morton
Geo. Clymer
Jas. Smith
Geo. Taylor

James Wilson
Geo. Ross
Caesar Rodney
Geo. Read
Thos. M'Kean
Wm. Floyd
Phil. Livingston
Frans. Lewis
Lewis Morris
Richd. Stockton
Jno. Witherspoon
Fras. Hopkinson
John Hart
Abra. Clark

Josiah Bartlett
Wm. Whipple
Saml. Adams
John Adams
Robt. Treat Paine
Elbridge Gerry
Step. Hopkins
William Ellery
Roger Sherman
Sam'el Hunington
Wm. Williams
Oliver Wolcott
Matthew Thornton

The Constitution of the United States of America

We the People of the United States, in Order to form a more perfect Union, establish Justice, insure domestic Tranquility, provide for the common defence, promote the general Welfare, and secure the Blessings of Liberty to ourselves and our Posterity, do ordain and establish this Constitution for the United States of America.

Article I

Section 1 All legislative Powers herein granted shall be vested in a Congress of the United States, which shall consist of a Senate and a House of Representatives.

Section 2 The House of Representatives shall be composed of Members chosen every second Year by the People of the several States, and the Electors in each State shall have the Qualifications requisite for Electors of the most numerous Branch of the State Legislature.

No Person shall be a Representative who shall not have attained to the Age of twenty-five Years, and been seven Years a Citizen of the United States, and who shall not, when elected, be an Inhabitant of that State in which he shall be chosen.

Representatives and direct Taxes shall be apportioned among the several States which may be included within this Union, according to their respective Numbers, *which shall be determined by adding to the whole Number of free Persons, including those bound to Service for a Term of Years, and excluding Indians not taxed, three fifths of all other Persons.** The actual Enumeration shall be made within three Years after the first Meeting of the Congress of the United States, and within every subsequent Term of ten Years, in such Manner as they shall by Law direct. The Number of Representatives shall not exceed one for every thirty Thousand, but each State shall have at Least one Representative; and *until such enumeration shall be made, the State of New Hampshire shall be entitled to chuse three, Massachusetts eight, Rhode Island and Providence Plantations one, Connecticut five, New-York six, New Jersey four, Pennsylvania eight, Delaware one, Maryland six, Virginia ten, North Carolina five, South Carolina five, and Georgia three.*

When vacancies happen in the Representation from any State, the Executive Authority thereof shall issue Writs of Election to fill such Vacancies.

The House of Representatives shall chuse their Speaker and other Officers; and shall have the sole Power of Impeachment.

Section 3 The Senate of the United States shall be composed of two Senators from each State, *chosen by the Legislature thereof,*† for six Years; and each Senator shall have one Vote.

Immediately after they shall be assembled in Consequence of the first Election, they shall be divided as equally as may be into three Classes. The Seats of the Senators of the first Class shall be vacated at the Expiration of the second Year, of the second Class at the Expiration of the fourth Year, and of the third Class at the Expiration of the sixth Year, so that one-third may be chosen every second Year; *and if Vacancies happen by Resignation, or otherwise, during the Recess of the Legislature of any State, the Executive thereof may make temporary Appointments until the next Meeting of the Legislature, which shall then fill such Vacancies.*‡

No person shall be a Senator who shall not have attained to the Age of thirty Years, and been nine Years a Citizen of the United States, and who shall not, when elected, be an Inhabitant of that State for which he shall be chosen.

The Vice President of the United States shall be President of the Senate, but shall have no Vote, unless they be equally divided.

Note: The Constitution became effective March 4, 1789. Provisions in italics have been changed by constitutional amendment.

*Changed by Section 2 of the Fourteenth Amendment.

†Changed by Section 1 of the Seventeenth Amendment.

‡Changed by Clause 2 of the Seventeenth Amendment.

The Senate shall chuse their other Officers, and also a President pro tempore, in the absence of the Vice President, or when he shall exercise the Office of President of the United States.

The Senate shall have the sole Power to try all Impeachments. When sitting for that Purpose, they shall be on Oath or Affirmation. When the President of the United States is tried, the Chief Justice shall preside: And no Person shall be convicted without the Concurrence of two thirds of the Members present.

Judgment in Cases of Impeachment shall not extend further than to removal from Office, and disqualification to hold and enjoy any Office of honor, Trust or Profit under the United States: but the Party convicted shall nevertheless be liable and subject to Indictment, Trial, Judgment and Punishment, according to Law.

Section 4 The Times, Places and Manner of holding Elections for Senators and Representatives, shall be prescribed in each State by the Legislature thereof; but the Congress may at any time by Law make or alter such Regulations, except as to the Places of Chusing Senators.

The Congress shall assemble at least once in every Year, and such Meeting *shall be on the first Monday in December, unless they shall by Law appoint a different Day.**

Section 5 Each House shall be the Judge of the Elections, Returns and Qualifications of its own Members, and a Majority of each shall constitute a Quorum to do Business; but a smaller number may adjourn from day to day, and may be authorized to compel the Attendance of absent Members, in such Manner, and under such Penalties, as each House may provide.

Each House may determine the Rules of its Proceedings, punish its Members for disorderly Behavior, and, with the Concurrence of two thirds, expel a Member.

Each House shall keep a Journal of its Proceedings, and from time to time publish the same, excepting such Parts as may in their Judgment require Secrecy; and the Yeas and Nays of the Members of either House on any question shall, at the Desire of one-fifth of those Present, be entered on the Journal.

Neither House, during the Session of Congress, shall, without the Consent of the other, adjourn for more than three days, nor to any other Place than that in which the two Houses shall be sitting.

Section 6 The Senators and Representatives shall receive a Compensation for their Services, to be ascertained by Law, and paid out of the Treasury of the United States. They shall in all Cases, except Treason, Felony and Breach of the Peace, be privileged from Arrest during their Attendance at the Session of their respective Houses, and in going to and returning from the same; and for any Speech or Debate in either House, they shall not be questioned in any other Place.

No Senator or Representative shall, during the Time for which he was elected, be appointed to any civil Office under the Authority of the United States, which shall have been created, or the Emoluments whereof shall have been increased, during such time; and no Person holding any Office under the United States, shall be a Member of either House during his Continuance in Office.

Section 7 All Bills for raising Revenue shall originate in the House of Representatives; but the Senate may propose or concur with Amendments as on other Bills.

Every Bill which shall have passed the House of Representatives and the Senate, shall, before it becomes a Law, be presented to the President of the United States; If he approve he shall sign it, but if not he shall return it, with his Objections to that House in which it shall have originated, who shall enter the Objections at large on their Journal, and proceed to reconsider it. If after such Reconsideration two thirds of that House shall agree to pass the Bill, it shall be sent, together with the Objections, to the other House, by which it shall likewise be reconsidered, and if approved by two thirds of that House, it shall become a Law. But in all such Cases the Votes of both Houses shall be determined by Yeas and Nays, and the Names of the Persons voting for and against the Bill shall be entered on the Journal of each House respectively. If any Bill shall not be returned by the President within ten Days (Sundays excepted) after it shall have been presented to him, the Same shall be a Law, in like Manner as if he had signed it, unless the Congress by their Adjournment prevent its Return, in which Case it shall not be a Law.

Every Order, Resolution, or Vote to which the Concurrence of the Senate and the House of Representatives may be necessary (except on a question of Adjournment) shall be presented to the President of the United States; and before the Same shall take Effect, shall be approved by him, or being disapproved by him, shall be repassed by two thirds of the Senate and House of Representatives, according to the Rules and Limitations prescribed in the Case of a Bill.

Section 8 The Congress shall have Power To lay and collect Taxes, Duties, Imposts and Excises, to pay the Debts and provide for the common Defence and general Welfare of the United States; but all Duties, Imposts and Excises shall be uniform throughout the United States;

To borrow money on the credit of the United States;

To regulate Commerce with foreign Nations, and among the several States, and with the Indian Tribes;

To establish an uniform Rule of Naturalization, and uniform Laws on the subject of Bankruptcies throughout the United States;

To coin Money, regulate the Value thereof, and of foreign Coin, and fix the Standard of Weights and Measures;

To provide for the Punishment of counterfeiting the Securities and current Coin of the United States;

To establish Post Offices and post Roads;

To promote the Progress of Science and useful Arts, by securing for limited Times to Authors and Inventors the exclusive Right to their respective Writings and Discoveries;

To constitute Tribunals inferior to the supreme Court;

To define and punish Piracies and Felonies committed on the high Seas, and Offenses against the Law of Nations;

To declare War, grant Letters of Marque and Reprisal, and make Rules concerning Captures on Land and Water;

To raise and support Armies, but no Appropriation of Money to that Use shall be for a longer Term than two Years;

To provide and maintain a Navy;

*Changed by Section 2 of the Twentieth Amendment.

To make Rules for the Government and Regulation of the land and naval Forces;

To provide for calling forth the Militia to execute the Laws of the Union, suppress Insurrections and repel Invasions;

To provide for organizing, arming, and disciplining the Militia, and for governing such Part of them as may be employed in the Service of the United States, reserving to the States respectively, the Appointment of the Officers, and the Authority of training the Militia according to the discipline prescribed by Congress;

To exercise exclusive Legislation in all Cases whatsoever, over such District (not exceeding ten Miles square) as may, by Cession of particular States, and the acceptance of Congress, become the Seat of Government of the United States, and to exercise like Authority over all Places purchased by the Consent of the Legislature of the State in which the Same shall be, for the Erection of Forts, Magazines, Arsenals, dock-Yards, and other needful Buildings;—And

To make all Laws which shall be necessary and proper for carrying into Execution the foregoing Powers, and all other Powers vested by this Constitution in the Government of the United States, or in any Department or Officer thereof.

Section 9 *The Migration or Importation of such Persons as any of the States now existing shall think proper to admit, shall not be prohibited by the Congress prior to the Year one thousand eight hundred and eight but a tax or duty may be imposed on such Importation, not exceeding ten dollars for each Person.*

The privilege of the Writ of Habeas Corpus shall not be suspended, unless when in Cases of Rebellion or Invasion the public Safety may require it.

No Bill of Attainder or ex post facto Law shall be passed.

No capitation, or other direct, Tax shall be laid, unless in Proportion to the Census or Enumeration herein before directed to be taken.*

No Tax or Duty shall be laid on Articles exported from any State.

No Preference shall be given by any Regulation of Commerce or Revenue to the Ports of one State over those of another: nor shall Vessels bound to, or from, one State, be obliged to enter, clear, or pay Duties in another.

No Money shall be drawn from the Treasury, but in Consequence of Appropriations made by law; and a regular Statement and Account of the Receipts and Expenditures of all public Money shall be published from time to time.

No Title of Nobility shall be granted by the United States: And no Person holding any Office of Profit or Trust under them, shall, without the Consent of the Congress, accept of any present, Emolument, Office, or Title, of any kind whatever, from any King, Prince, or foreign State.

Section 10 No State shall enter into any Treaty, Alliance, or Confederation; grant Letters of Marque and Reprisal; coin Money; emit Bills of Credit; make any Thing but gold and silver Coin a Tender in Payment of Debts; pass any Bill of Attainder, ex post facto Law, or Law impairing the Obligation of Contracts, or grant any Title of Nobility.

*Changed by the Sixteenth Amendment.

No State shall, without the Consent of the Congress, lay any Imposts or Duties on Imports or Exports, except what may be absolutely necessary for executing its inspection Laws: and the net Produce of all Duties and Imposts, laid by any State on Imports or Exports, shall be for the Use of the Treasury of the United States; and all such Laws shall be subject to the Revision and Control of the Congress.

No State shall, without the Consent of the Congress, lay any duty of Tonnage, keep Troops, or Ships of War in time of Peace, enter into any Agreement or Compact with another State, or with a foreign Power, or engage in War, unless actually invaded, or in such imminent Danger as will not admit of delay.

Article II

Section 1 The executive Power shall be vested in a President of the United States of America. He shall hold his Office during the Term of four Years, and, together with the Vice President, chosen for the same Term, be elected, as follows:

Each State shall appoint, in such Manner as the Legislature thereof may direct, a Number of Electors, equal to the whole Number of Senators and Representatives to which the State may be entitled in the Congress; but no Senator or Representative, or Person holding an Office of Trust or Profit under the United States, shall be appointed an Elector.

*The Electors shall meet in their respective States, and vote by Ballot for two Persons, of whom one at least shall not be an Inhabitant of the same State with themselves. And they shall make a List of all the Persons voted for, and of the Number of Votes for each; which List they shall sign and certify, and transmit sealed to the Seat of the Government of the United States, directed to the President of the Senate. The President of the Senate shall, in the Presence of the Senate and House of Representatives, open all the Certificates, and the Votes shall then be counted. The Person having the greatest Number of Votes shall be the President, if such Number be a Majority of the whole Number of Electors appointed; and if there be more than one who have such Majority, and have an equal Number of Votes, then the House of Representatives shall immediately chuse by Ballot one of them for President; and if no Person have a Majority, then from the five highest on the List the said House shall in like Manner chuse the President. But in chusing the President, the Votes shall be taken by States, the Representation from each State having one Vote; a quorum for this Purpose shall consist of a Member or Members from two thirds of the States, and a Majority of all the States shall be necessary to a Choice. In every Case, after the Choice of the President, the Person having the greatest Number of Votes of the Electors shall be the Vice President. But if there should remain two or more who have equal Votes, the Senate shall chuse from them by Ballot the Vice President.**

The Congress may determine the Time of chusing the Electors, and the Day on which they shall give their Votes; which Day shall be the same throughout the United States.

No Person except a natural born Citizen, or a Citizen of the United States, at the time of the Adoption of this Constitution, shall be eligible to the Office of President; neither shall any Person be eligible to that Office who shall not have at-

*Superseded by the Twelfth Amendment.

tained to the Age of thirty five Years, and been fourteen Years a Resident within the United States.

In Case of the Removal of the President from Office, or of his Death, Resignation, or Inability to discharge the Powers and Duties of the said Office, the same shall devolve on the Vice President, *and the Congress may by Law provide for the Case of Removal, Death, Resignation, or Inability, both of the President and Vice President, declaring what Officer shall then act as President, and such Officer shall act accordingly, until the Disability be removed, or a President shall be elected.**

The President shall, at stated Times, receive for his Services a Compensation, which shall neither be increased nor diminished during the Period for which he shall have been elected, and he shall not receive within that Period any other Emolument from the United States, or any of them.

Before he enter on the Execution of his Office, he shall take the following Oath or Affirmation:—"I do solemnly swear (or affirm) that I will faithfully execute the Office of President of the United States, and will to the best of my Ability, preserve, protect and defend the Constitution of the United States."

Section 2 The President shall be Commander in Chief of the Army and Navy of the United States, and of the Militia of the several States, when called into the actual Service of the United States; he may require the Opinion, in writing, of the principal Officer in each of the executive Departments, upon any Subject relating to the Duties of their respective Offices, and he shall have Power to Grant Reprieves and Pardons for Offences against the United States, except in Cases of Impeachment.

He shall have Power, by and with the Advice and Consent of the Senate, to make Treaties, provided two thirds of the Senators present concur; and he shall nominate, and by and with the Advice and Consent of the Senate, shall appoint Ambassadors, other public Ministers and Consuls, Judges of the supreme Court, and all other Officers of the United States, whose Appointments are not herein otherwise provided for, and which shall be established by Law: but the Congress may by Law vest the Appointment of such inferior Officers, as they think proper, in the President alone, in the Courts of Law, or in the Heads of Departments.

The President shall have Power to fill up all Vacancies that may happen during the Recess of the Senate, by granting Commissions which shall expire at the End of their next Session.

Section 3 He shall from time to time give to the Congress Information of the State of the Union, and recommend to their Consideration such Measures as he shall judge necessary and expedient; he may, on extraordinary Occasions, convene both Houses, or either of them, and in Case of Disagreement between them, with Respect to the Time of Adjournment, he may adjourn them to such Time as he shall think proper; he shall receive Ambassadors and other public Ministers; he shall take Care that the Laws be faithfully executed, and shall Commission all the Officers of the United States.

*Modified by the Twenty-Fifth Amendment.

Section 4 The President, Vice President and all civil Officers of the United States, shall be removed from Office on Impeachment for, and Conviction of, Treason, Bribery, or other high Crimes and Misdemeanors.

Article III

Section 1 The judicial Power of the United States, shall be vested in one supreme Court, and in such inferior Courts as the Congress may from time to time ordain and establish. The Judges, both of the supreme and inferior Courts, shall hold their Offices during good Behaviour, and shall, at stated Times, receive for their Services a Compensation, which shall not be diminished during their Continuance in Office.

Section 2 The judicial Power shall extend to all Cases, in Law and Equity, arising under this Constitution, the Laws of the United States, and Treaties made, or which shall be made, under their Authority;—to all Cases affecting Ambassadors, other public Ministers and Consuls;—to all Cases of admiralty and maritime Jurisdiction;—to Controversies to which the United States shall be a Party;—to Controversies between two or more States;—*between a State and Citizens of another State;**—between Citizens of different States;—between Citizens of the same State claiming Lands under Grants of different States, and between a State, or the Citizens thereof, and foreign States, Citizens or Subjects.

In all Cases affecting Ambassadors, other public Ministers and Consuls, and those in which a State shall be Party, the supreme Court shall have original Jurisdiction. In all the other Cases before mentioned, the supreme Court shall have appellate Jurisdiction, both as to Law and Fact, with such Exceptions, and under such Regulations as the Congress shall make.

The trial of all Crimes, except in Cases of Impeachment, shall be by Jury; and such Trial shall be held in the State where said Crimes shall have been committed; but when not committed within any State, the Trial shall be at such Place or Places as the Congress may by Law have directed.

Section 3 Treason against the United States, shall consist only in levying War against them, or in adhering to their Enemies, giving them Aid and Comfort. No Person shall be convicted of Treason unless on the Testimony of two Witnesses to the same overt Act, or on Confession in open Court.

The Congress shall have Power to declare the Punishment of Treason, but no Attainder of Treason shall work Corruption of Blood, or Forefeiture except during the Life of the Person attainted.

Article IV

Section 1 Full Faith and Credit shall be given in each State to the public Acts, Records, and judicial Proceedings of every other State. And the Congress may by general Laws prescribe the Manner in which such Acts, Records, and Proceedings shall be proved, and the Effect thereof.

Section 2 The Citizens of each State shall be entitled to all Privileges and Immunities of Citizens in the several States.

*Restricted by the Eleventh Amendment.

A Person charged in any State with Treason, Felony, or other Crime, who shall flee from Justice, and be found in another State, shall on demand of the executive Authority of the State from which he fled, be delivered up, to be removed to the State having Jurisdiction of the Crime.

*No Person held to Service or Labour in one State, under the Laws thereof, escaping into another, shall, in Consequence of any Law or Regulation therein, be discharged from such Service or Labour, but shall be delivered up on Claim of the Party to whom such Service or Labour may be due.**

Section 3 New States may be admitted by the Congress into this Union; but no new State shall be formed or erected within the Jurisdiction of any other State; nor any State be formed by the Junction of two or more States, or parts of States, without the Consent of the Legislatures of the States concerned as well as of the Congress.

The Congress shall have Power to dispose of and make all needful Rules and Regulations respecting the Territory or other Property belonging to the United States; and nothing in this Constitution shall be so construed as to Prejudice any Claims of the United States, or of any particular State.

Section 4 The United States shall guarantee to every State in this Union a Republican Form of Government, and shall protect each of them against Invasion; and on Application of the Legislature, or of the Executive (when the Legislature cannot be convened) against domestic Violence.

Article V

The Congress, whenever two thirds of both Houses shall deem it necessary, shall propose Amendments to this Constitution, or, on the Application of the Legislatures of two thirds of the several States, shall call a Convention for proposing Amendments, which, in either Case, shall be valid to all Intents and Purposes, as Part of this Constitution, when ratified by the Legislatures of three fourths of the several States, or by Conventions in three fourths thereof, as the one or the other Mode of Ratification may be proposed by the Congress; Provided that no Amendment which may be made prior to the Year One thousand eight hundred and eight shall in any Manner affect the first and fourth Clauses in the Ninth Section of the first Article; and that no State, without its Consent, shall be deprived of its equal Suffrage in the Senate.

Article VI

All Debts contracted and Engagements entered into, before the Adoption of this Constitution, shall be as valid against the United States under this Constitution, as under the Confederation.

This Constitution, and the Laws of the United States which shall be made in Pursuance thereof; and all Treaties made, or which shall be made, under the Authority of the United States, shall be the supreme Law of the Land; and the Judges in every State shall be bound thereby, any Thing in the Constitution or Laws of any State to the Contrary notwithstanding.

The Senators and Representatives before mentioned, and the Members of the several State Legislatures, and all executive and judicial Officers, both of the United States and of the several States, shall be bound by Oath or Affirmation, to support this Constitution; but no religious Test shall ever be required as a Qualification to any Office or public Trust under the United States.

Article VII

The Ratification of the Conventions of nine States shall be sufficient for the Establishment of this Constitution between the States so ratifying the Same.

Done in Convention by the Unanimous Consent of the States present the Seventeenth Day of September in the Year of our Lord one thousand seven hundred and Eighty seven and of the Independence of the United States of America the Twelfth. In Witness whereof We have hereunto subscribed our Names.

*Superseded by the Twelfth Amendment.

Go. Washington
President and deputy from Virginia

New Hampshire
John Langdon
Nicholas Gilman

Massachusetts
Nathaniel Gorham
Rufus King

Connecticut
Wm. Saml. Johnson
Roger Sherman

New York
Alexander Hamilton

New Jersey
Wil. Livingston
David Brearley
Wm. Paterson
Jona. Dayton

Pennsylvania
B. Franklin
Thomas Mifflin
Robt. Morris
Geo. Clymer
Thos. FitzSimons
Jared Ingersoll
James Wilson
Gouv. Morris

Delaware
Geo. Read
Gunning Bedford jun
John Dickenson
Richard Bassett
Jaco. Broom

Maryland
James McHenry
Dan. of St. Thos. Jenifer
Danl. Carroll

Virginia
John Blair
James Madison, Jr.

North Carolina
Wm. Blount
Richd. Dobbs Spaight
Hu Williamson

South Carolina
J. Rutledge
Charles Cotesworth Pickney
Pierce Butler

Georgia
William Few
Abr. Baldwin

Amendments to the Constitution

Amendment I [1791]*

Congress shall make no law respecting an establishment of religion, or prohibiting the free exercise thereof; or abridging the freedom of speech, or of the press; or the right of the people peaceably to assemble, and to petition the Government for a redress of grievances.

Amendment II [1791]

A well regulated Militia, being necessary to the security of a free State, the right of the people to keep and bear Arms shall not be infringed.

Amendment III [1791]

No Soldier shall, in time of peace, be quartered in any house, without the consent of the Owner, nor in time of war, but in a manner to be prescribed by law.

Amendment IV [1791]

The right of the people to be secure in their persons, houses, papers, and effects, against unreasonable searches and seizures, shall not be violated, and no Warrants shall issue, but upon probable cause, supported by Oath or affirmation, and particularly describing the place to be searched, and the persons or things to be seized.

Amendment V [1791]

No person shall be held to answer for a capital or otherwise infamous crime, unless on a presentment or indictment of a Grand Jury, except in cases arising in the land or naval forces, or in the Militia, when in actual service in time of War or public danger; nor shall any person be subject for the same offence to be twice put in jeopardy of life or limb; nor shall be compelled in any criminal case to be a witness against himself, nor be deprived of life, liberty, or property, without due process of law; nor shall private property be taken for public use, without just compensation.

Amendment VI [1791]

In all criminal prosecutions, the accused shall enjoy the right to a speedy and public trial, by an impartial jury of the State and district wherein the crime shall have been committed, which district shall have been previously ascertained by law, and to be informed of the nature and cause of the accusation; to be confronted with the witnesses against him; to have compulsory process for obtaining witnesses in his favor, and to have the Assistance of Counsel for his defence.

Amendment VII [1791]

In suits at common law, where the value in controversy shall exceed twenty dollars, the right of trial by jury shall be preserved, and no fact tried by a jury, shall be otherwise reexamined in any Court of the United States, than according to the Rules of the common law.

Amendment VIII [1791]

Excessive bail shall not be required, nor excessive fines imposed, nor cruel and unusual punishments inflicted.

Amendment IX [1791]

The enumeration in the Constitution, of certain rights, shall not be construed to deny or disparage others retained by the people.

*The dates in brackets indicate when the amendments were ratified.

Amendment X [1791]

The powers not delegated to the United States by the Constitution, nor prohibited by it to the States, are reserved to the States respectively, or to the people.

Amendment XI [1798]

The Judicial power of the United States shall not be construed to extend to any suit in law or equity, commenced or prosecuted against one of the United States by Citizens of another State, or by Citizens or Subjects of any Foreign State.

Amendment XII [1804]

The Electors shall meet in their respective States and vote by ballot for President and Vice-President, one of whom, at least, shall not be an inhabitant of the same State with themselves; they shall name in their ballots the person voted for as President, and in distinct ballots the person voted for as Vice-President, and they shall make distinct lists of all persons voted for as President, and of all persons voted for as Vice-President, and of the number of votes for each, which lists they shall sign and certify, and transmit sealed to the seat of the government of the United States, directed to the President of the Senate;—The President of the Senate shall, in the presence of the Senate and House of Representatives, open all the certificates and the votes shall then be counted;—The person having the greatest number of votes for President, shall be the President, if such number be a majority of the whole number of Electors appointed; and if no person have such majority, then from the persons having the highest numbers not exceeding three on the list of those voted for as President, the House of Representatives shall choose immediately, by ballot, the President. But in choosing the President, the votes shall be taken by States, the representation from each State having one vote; a quorum for this purpose shall consist of a member or members from two-thirds of the States, and a majority of all the States shall be necessary to a choice. And if the House of Representatives shall not choose a President whenever the right of choice shall devolve upon them, before *the fourth day of March* next following, then the Vice-President shall act as President, as in the case of the death or other constitutional disability of the President.*—The person having the greatest number of votes as Vice-President, shall be the Vice-President, if such number be a majority of the whole number of Electors appointed, and if no person have a majority, then from the two highest numbers on the list, the Senate shall choose the Vice-President; a quorum for the purpose shall consist of two-thirds of the whole number of Senators, and a majority of the whole number shall be necessary to a choice. But no person constitutionally ineligible to the office of President shall be eligible to that of Vice-President of the United States.

Amendment XIII [1865]

Section 1 Neither slavery nor involuntary servitude, except as a punishment for crime whereof the party shall have been duly convicted, shall exist within the United States, or any place subject to their jurisdiction.

Section 2 Congress shall have power to enforce this article by appropriate legislation.

Amendment XIV [1868]

Section 1 All persons born or naturalized in the United States, and subject to the jurisdiction thereof, are citizens of the United States and of the State wherein they reside. No State shall make or enforce any law which shall abridge the privileges or immunities of citizens of the United States; nor shall any State deprive any person of life, liberty, or property, without due process of law; nor deny to any person within its jurisdiction the equal protection of the laws.

Section 2 Representatives shall be apportioned among the several States according to their respective numbers, counting the whole number of persons in each State, excluding Indians not taxed. But when the right to vote at any election for the choice of electors for President and Vice-President of the United States, Representatives in Congress, the Executive and Judicial officers of a State, or the members of the Legislature thereof, is denied to any of the male inhabitants of such State, being twenty-one years of age, and citizens of the United States, or in any way abridged, except for participation in rebellion, or other crime, the basis of representation therein shall be reduced in the proportion which the number of such male citizens shall bear to the whole number of male citizens twenty-one years of age in such State.

Section 3 No person shall be a Senator or Representative in Congress, or elector of President and Vice-President, or hold any office, civil or military, under the United States, or under any State, who, having previously taken an oath, as a member of Congress, or as an officer of the United States, or as a member of any State legislature, or as an executive or judicial officer of any State, to support the Constitution of the United States, shall have engaged in insurrection or rebellion against the same, or given aid or comfort to the enemies thereof. Congress may by a vote of two-thirds of each house, remove such disability.

Section 4 The validity of the public debt of the United States, authorized by law, including debts incurred for payment of pensions and bounties for services in suppressing insurrection or rebellion, shall not be questioned. But neither the United States nor any State shall assume or pay any debt or obligation incurred in aid of insurrection or rebellion against the United States, or any claim for the loss or emancipation of any slave; but all such debts, obligations and claims shall be held illegal and void.

Section 5 The Congress shall have power to enforce, by appropriate legislation, the provisions of this article.

Amendment XV [1870]

Section 1 The right of citizens of the United States to vote shall not be denied or abridged by the United States or by any State on account of race, color, or previous condition of servitude—

*Superseded by Section 3 of the Twentieth Amendment.

Section 2 The Congress shall have power to enforce this article by appropriate legislation.

Amendment XVI [1913]

The Congress shall have power to lay and collect taxes on incomes, from whatever source derived, without apportionment among the several States, and without regard to any census or enumeration.

Amendment XVII [1913]

The Senate of the United States shall be composed of two Senators from each State, elected by the people thereof, for six years; and each Senator shall have one vote. The electors in each State shall have the qualifications requisite for electors of the most numerous branch of the State legislatures.

When vacancies happen in the representation of any State in the Senate, the executive authority of such State shall issue writs of election to fill such vacancies: *Provided,* That the legislature of any State may empower the executive thereof to make temporary appointments until the people fill the vacancies by election as the legislature may direct.

This amendment shall not be so construed as to affect the election or term of any Senator chosen before it becomes valid as part of the Constitution.

Amendment XVIII [1919]

Section 1 After one year from the ratification of this article the manufacture, sale, or transportation of intoxicating liquors within, the importation thereof into, or the exportation thereof from the United States and all territory subject to the jurisdiction thereof for beverage purposes is hereby prohibited.

Section 2 The Congress and the several States shall have concurrent power to enforce this article by appropriate legislation.

Section 3 This article shall be inoperative unless it shall have been ratified as an amendment to the Constitution by the legislatures of the several States, as provided by the Constitution, within seven years from the date of submission hereof to the States by the Congress.*

Amendment XIX [1920]

The right of citizens of the United States to vote shall not be denied or abridged by the United States or by any State on account of sex.

Congress shall have power to enforce this article by appropriate legislation.

Amendment XX [1933]

Section 1 The terms of the President and Vice-President shall end at noon on the 20th day of January, and the terms of Senators and Representatives at noon on the 3d day of January, of the years in which such terms would have ended if this article had not been ratified; and the terms of their successors shall then begin.

Section 2 The Congress shall assemble at least once in every year, and such meeting shall begin at noon on the 3d day of January, unless they shall by law appoint a different day.

Section 3 If, at the time fixed for the beginning of the term of the President, the President elect shall have died, the Vice-President elect shall become President. If a President shall not have been chosen before the time fixed for the beginning of his term, or if the President elect shall have failed to qualify, then the Vice-President elect shall act as President until a President shall have qualified; and the Congress may by law provide for the case wherein neither a President elect nor a Vice-President elect shall have qualified, declaring who shall then act as President, or the manner in which one who is to act shall be selected, and such person shall act accordingly until a President or Vice-President shall have qualified.

Section 4 The Congress may by law provide for the case of the death of any of the persons from whom the House of Representatives may choose a President whenever the right of choice shall have devolved upon them, and for the case of the death of any of the persons from whom the Senate may choose a Vice-President whenever the right of choice shall have devolved upon them.

Section 5 Sections 1 and 2 shall take effect on the 15th day of October following the ratification of this article.

Section 6 This article shall be inoperative unless it shall have been ratified as an amendment to the Constitution by the legislavures of three-fourths of the several States within seven years from the date of its submission.

Amendment XXI [1933]

Section 1 The eighteenth article of amendment to the Constitution of the United States is hereby repealed.

Section 2 The transportation or importation into any State, Territory, or possession of the United States for delivery or use therein of intoxicating liquors, in violation of the laws thereof, is hereby prohibited.

Section 3 This article shall be inoperative unless it shall have been ratified as an amendment to the Constitution by conventions in the several States, as provided in the Constitution, within seven years from the date of submission hereof to the States by the Congress.

Amendment XXII [1951]

Section 1 No person shall be elected to the office of President more than twice, and no person who has held the office of President, or acted as President, for more than two years of a term to which some other person was elected President shall be elected to the office of the President more than once. But this Article shall not apply to any person holding the office of

*Repealed by Section 1 of the Twenty-First Amendment.

President when this Article was proposed by the Congress, and shall not prevent any person who may be holding the office of President, or acting as President, during the term within which this Article becomes operative from holding the office of President or acting as President during the remainder of such term.

Section 2 This article shall be inoperative unless it shall have been ratified as an amendment to the Constitution by the legislatures of three-fourths of the several States within seven years from the date of its submission to the States by the Congress.

Amendment XXIII [1961]

Section 1 The District constituting the seat of Government of the United States shall appoint in such manner as the Congress may direct:

A number of electors of President and Vice-President equal to the whole number of Senators and Representatives in Congress to which the District would be entitled if it were a State, but in no event more than the least populous State; they shall be in addition to those appointed by the States, but they shall be considered, for the purposes of the election of President and Vice-President, to be electors appointed by a State; and they shall meet in the District and perform such duties as provided by the twelfth article of amendment.

Section 2 The Congress shall have power to enforce this article by appropriate legislation.

Amendment XXIV [1964]

Section 1 The right of citizens of the United States to vote in any primary or other election for President or Vice-President, for electors for President or Vice-President, or for Senator or Representative in Congress, shall not be denied or abridged by the United States or any State by reason of failure to pay any poll tax or other tax.

Section 2 The Congress shall have power to enforce this article by appropriate legislation.

Amendment XXV [1967]

Section 1 In case of the removal of the President from office or of his death or resignation, the Vice-President shall become President.

Section 2 Whenever there is a vacancy in the office of the Vice-President, the President shall nominate a Vice-President who shall take office upon confirmation by a majority vote of both houses of Congress.

Section 3 Whenever the President transmits to the President pro tempore of the Senate and the Speaker of the House of Representatives his written declaration that he is unable to discharge the powers and duties of his office, and until he transmits to them a written declaration to the contrary, such powers and duties shall be discharged by the Vice-President as Acting President.

Section 4 Whenever the Vice-President and a majority of either the principal officers of the executive departments or of such other body as Congress may by law provide, transmit to the President pro tempore of the Senate and the Speaker of the House of Representatives their written declaration that the President is unable to discharge the powers and duties of his office, the Vice-President shall immediately assume the powers and duties of the office as Acting President.

Thereafter, when the President transmits to the President pro tempore of the Senate and the Speaker of the House of Representatives his written declaration that no inability exists, he shall resume the powers and duties of his office unless the Vice-President and a majority of either the principal officers of the executive department or of such other body as Congress may by law provide, transmit within four days to the President pro tempore of the Senate and the Speaker of the House of Representatives their written declaration that the President is unable to discharge the powers and duties of his office. Thereupon Congress shall decide the issue, assembling within forty-eight hours for that purpose if not in session. If the Congress, within twenty-one days after receipt of the latter written declaration, or, if Congress is not in session, within twenty-one days after Congress is required to assemble, determines by two-thirds vote of both Houses that the President is unable to discharge the powers and duties of his office, the Vice-President shall continue to discharge the same as Acting President; otherwise, the President shall resume the powers and duties of his office.

Amendment XXVI [1971]

Section 1 The right of citizens of the United States, who are eighteen years of age or older, to vote shall not be denied or abridged by the United States or by any state on account of age.

Section 2 The Congress shall have power to enforce this article by appropriate legislation.

Amendment XXVII [1992]

No law, varying the compensation for services of the Senators and Representatives, shall take effect, until an election of Representatives shall have intervened.

The American Nation

Admission of States into the Union

	State	Date of Admission		State	Date of Admission
1.	Delaware	December 7, 1787	26.	Michigan	January 26, 1837
2.	Pennsylvania	December 12, 1787	27.	Florida	March 3, 1845
3.	New Jersey	December 18, 1787	28.	Texas	December 29, 1845
4.	Georgia	January 2, 1788	29.	Iowa	December 28, 1846
5.	Connecticut	January 9, 1788	30.	Wisconsin	May 29, 1848
6.	Massachusetts	February 6, 1788	31.	California	September 9, 1850
7.	Maryland	April 28, 1788	32.	Minnesota	May 11, 1858
8.	South Carolina	May 23, 1788	33.	Oregon	February 14, 1859
9.	New Hampshire	June 21, 1788	34.	Kansas	January 29, 1861
10.	Virginia	June 25, 1788	35.	West Virginia	June 20, 1863
11.	New York	July 26, 1788	36.	Nevada	October 31, 1864
12.	North Carolina	November 21, 1789	37.	Nebraska	March 1, 1867
13.	Rhode Island	May 29, 1790	38.	Colorado	August 1, 1876
14.	Vermont	March 4, 1791	39.	North Dakota	November 2, 1889
15.	Kentucky	June 1, 1792	40.	South Dakota	November 2, 1889
16.	Tennessee	June 1, 1796	41.	Montana	November 8, 1889
17.	Ohio	March 1, 1803	42.	Washington	November 11, 1889
18.	Louisiana	April 30, 1812	43.	Idaho	July 3, 1890
19.	Indiana	December 11, 1816	44.	Wyoming	July 10, 1890
20.	Mississippi	December 10, 1817	45.	Utah	January 4, 1896
21.	Illinois	December 3, 1818	46.	Oklahoma	November 16, 1907
22.	Alabama	December 14, 1819	47.	New Mexico	January 6, 1912
23.	Maine	March 15, 1820	48.	Arizona	February 14, 1912
24.	Missouri	August 10, 1821	49.	Alaska	January 3, 1959
25.	Arkansas	June 15, 1836	50.	Hawaii	August 21, 1959

Territorial Expansion

Original states and territories	1783	Puerto Rico	1899
Louisiana Purchase	1803	Guam	1899
Florida	1819	Wake Island	1899
Texas	1845	The Philippines	1899–1946
Oregon	1846	American Samoa	1900
Mexican Cession	1848	Panama Canal Zone	1904–1978
Gadsden Purchase	1853	U.S. Virgin Islands	1917
Midway Islands	1867	Trust Territory of the Pacific Islands	1947
Alaska	1867	(North Mariana Islands, Micronesia, Marshall Islands, and Palau)	
Hawaii	1898		

Presidential Elections

Year	Candidates	Parties	Percent of Popular Vote	Electoral Vote	Percent Voter Participation
1789	**George Washington**	No party designations	*	69	
	John Adams†			34	
	Other candidates			35	
1792	**George Washington**	No party designations		132	
	John Adams			77	
	George Clinton			50	
	Other candidates			5	
1796	**John Adams**	Federalist		71	
	Thomas Jefferson	Democratic-Republican		68	
	Thomas Pinckney	Federalist		59	
	Aaron Burr	Democratic-Republican		30	
	Other candidates			48	
1800	**Thomas Jefferson**	Democratic-Republican		73	
	Aaron Burr	Democratic-Republican		73	
	John Adams	Federalist		65	
	Charles C. Pinckney	Federalist		64	
	John Jay	Federalist		1	
1804	**Thomas Jefferson**	Democratic-Republican		162	
	Charles C. Pinckney	Federalist		14	
1808	**James Madison**	Democratic-Republican		122	
	Charles C. Pinckney	Federalist		47	
	George Clinton	Democratic-Republican		6	
1812	**James Madison**	Democratic-Republican		128	
	DeWitt Clinton	Federalist		89	
1816	**James Monroe**	Democratic-Republican		183	
	Rufus King	Federalist		34	
1820	**James Monroe**	Democratic-Republican		231	
	John Quincy Adams	Independent Republican		1	
1824	**John Quincy Adams**	Democratic-Republican	30.5	84	26.9
	Andrew Jackson	Democratic-Republican	43.1	99	
	Henry Clay	Democratic-Republican	13.2	37	
	William H. Crawford	Democratic-Republican	13.1	41	
1828	**Andrew Jackson**	Democratic	56.0	178	57.6
	John Quincy Adams	National Republican	44.0	83	
1832	**Andrew Jackson**	Democratic	54.5	219	55.4
	Henry Clay	National Republican	37.5	49	
	William Wirt	Anti-Masonic	8.0	7	
	John Floyd	Democratic	‡	11	
1836	**Martin Van Buren**	Democratic	50.9	170	57.8
	William H. Harrison	Whig		73	
	Hugh L. White	Whig		26	
	Daniel Webster	Whig	49.1	14	
	W. P. Mangum	Whig		11	
1840	**William H. Harrison**	Whig	53.1	234	80.2
	Martin Van Buren	Democratic	46.9	60	

*Prior to 1824, most presidential electors were chosen by state legislators rather than by popular vote.

†Before the Twelfth Amendment was passed in 1804, the electoral college voted for two presidential candidates; the runner-up became vice-president.

‡Percentages below 2.5 percent have been omitted. Hence the percentage of popular vote may not total 100 percent.

Year	Candidates	Parties	Percent of Popular Vote	Electoral Vote	Percent Voter Participation
1844	**James K. Polk**	Democratic	49.6	170	78.9
	Henry Clay	Whig	48.1	105	
	James G. Birney	Liberty	2.3		
1848	**Zachary Taylor**	Whig	47.4	163	72.7
	Lewis Cass	Democratic	42.5	127	
	Martin Van Buren	Free Soil	10.1		
1852	**Franklin Pierce**	Democratic	50.9	254	69.6
	Winfield Scott	Whig	44.1	42	
	John P. Hale	Free Soil	5.0		
1856	**James Buchanan**	Democratic	45.3	174	78.9
	John C. Frémont	Republican	33.1	114	
	Millard Fillmore	American	21.6	8	
1860	**Abraham Lincoln**	Republican	39.8	180	81.2
	Stephen A. Douglas	Democratic	29.5	12	
	John C. Breckinridge	Democratic	18.1	72	
	John Bell	Constitutional Union	12.6	39	
1864	**Abraham Lincoln**	Republican	55.0	212	73.8
	George B. McClellan	Democratic	45.0	21	
1868	**Ulysses S. Grant**	Republican	52.7	214	78.1
	Horatio Seymour	Democratic	47.3	80	
1872	**Ulysses S. Grant**	Republican	55.6	286	71.3
	Horace Greeley	Democratic	43.9		
1876	**Rutherford B. Hayes**	Republican	48.0	185	81.8
	Samuel J. Tilden	Democratic	51.0	184	
1880	**James A. Garfield**	Republican	48.5	214	79.4
	Winfield S. Hancock	Democratic	48.1	155	
	James B. Weaver	Greenback-Labor	3.4		
1884	**Grover Cleveland**	Democratic	48.5	219	77.5
	James G. Blaine	Republican	48.2	182	
1888	**Benjamin Harrison**	Republican	47.9	233	79.3
	Grover Cleveland	Democratic	48.6	168	
1892	**Grover Cleveland**	Democratic	46.1	277	74.7
	Benjamin Harrison	Republican	43.0	145	
	James B. Weaver	People's	8.5	22	
1896	**William McKinley**	Republican	51.1	271	79.3
	William J. Bryan	Democratic	47.7	176	
1900	**William McKinley**	Republican	51.7	292	73.2
	William J. Bryan	Democratic; Populist	45.5	155	
1904	**Theodore Roosevelt**	Republican	57.4	336	65.2
	Alton B. Parker	Democratic	37.6	140	
	Eugene V. Debs	Socialist	3.0		
1908	**William H. Taft**	Republican	51.6	321	65.4
	William J. Bryan	Democratic	43.1	162	
	Eugene V. Debs	Socialist	2.8		
1912	**Woodrow Wilson**	Democratic	41.9	435	58.8
	Theodore Roosevelt	Progressive	27.4	88	
	William H. Taft	Republican	23.2	8	
	Eugene V. Debs	Socialist	6.0		

Year	Candidates	Parties	Percent of Popular Vote	Electoral Vote	Percent Voter Participation
1916	**Woodrow Wilson**	Democratic	49.4	277	61.6
	Charles E. Hughes	Republican	46.2	254	
	A. L. Benson	Socialist	3.2		
1920	**Warren G. Harding**	Republican	60.4	404	49.2
	James M. Cox	Democratic	34.2	127	
	Eugene V. Debs	Socialist	3.4		
1924	**Calvin Coolidge**	Republican	54.0	382	48.9
	John W. Davis	Democratic	28.8	136	
	Robert M. LaFollette	Progressive	16.6	13	
1928	**Herbert C. Hoover**	Republican	58.2	444	56.9
	Alfred E. Smith	Democratic	40.9	87	
1932	**Franklin D. Roosevelt**	Democratic	57.4	472	56.9
	Herbert C. Hoover	Republican	39.7	59	
1936	**Franklin D. Roosevelt**	Democratic	60.8	523	61.0
	Alfred M. Landon	Republican	36.5	8	
1940	**Franklin D. Roosevelt**	Democratic	54.8	449	62.5
	Wendell L. Willkie	Republican	44.8	82	
1944	**Franklin D. Roosevelt**	Democratic	53.5	432	55.9
	Thomas E. Dewey	Republican	46.0	99	
1948	**Harry S. Truman**	Democratic	49.6	303	53.0
	Thomas E. Dewey	Republican	45.1	189	
1952	**Dwight D. Eisenhower**	Republican	55.1	442	63.3
	Adlai E. Stevenson	Democratic	44.4	89	
1956	**Dwight D. Eisenhower**	Republican	57.6	457	60.6
	Adlai E. Stevenson	Democratic	42.1	73	
1960	**John F. Kennedy**	Democratic	49.7	303	64.0
	Richard M. Nixon	Republican	49.5	219	
1964	**Lyndon B. Johnson**	Democratic	61.1	486	61.7
	Barry M. Goldwater	Republican	38.5	52	
1968	**Richard M. Nixon**	Republican	43.4	301	60.6
	Hubert H. Humphrey	Democratic	42.7	191	
	George C. Wallace	American Independent	13.5	46	
1972	**Richard M. Nixon**	Republican	60.7	520	55.5
	George S. McGovern	Democratic	37.5	17	
1976	**Jimmy Carter**	Democratic	50.1	297	54.3
	Gerald R. Ford	Republican	48.0	240	
1980	**Ronald W. Reagan**	Republican	50.7	489	53.0
	Jimmy Carter	Democratic	41.0	49	
	John B. Anderson	Independent	6.6	0	
1984	**Ronald W. Reagan**	Republican	58.4	525	52.9
	Walter F. Mondale	Democratic	41.6	13	
1988	**George H. W. Bush**	Republican	53.4	426	50.1
	Michael Dukakis	Democratic	45.6	111*	
1992	**Bill Clinton**	Democratic	43.7	370	54.0
	George H. W. Bush	Republican	38.0	168	
	H. Ross Perot	Independent	19.0	0	

*One Dukakis elector cast a vote for Lloyd Bentsen.

Supreme Court Justices

Name	Terms of Service	Appointed by	Name	Terms of Service	Appointed by
John Jay*, N.Y.	1789–1795	Washington	Rufus W. Peckham, N.Y.	1896–1909	Cleveland
James Wilson, Pa.	1789–1798	Washington	Joseph McKenna, Cal.	1898–1925	McKinley
John Rutledge, S.C.	1790–1791	Washington	Oliver W. Holmes, Mass.	1902–1932	T. Roosevelt
William Cushing, Mass.	1790–1810	Washington	William R. Day, Ohio	1903–1922	T. Roosevelt
John Blair, Va.	1790–1796	Washington	William H. Moody, Mass.	1906–1910	T. Roosevelt
James Iredell, N.C.	1790–1799	Washington	Horace H. Lurton, Tenn.	1910–1914	Taft
Thomas Johnson, Md.	1792–1793	Washington	Charles E. Hughes, N.Y.	1910–1916	Taft
William Paterson, N.J.	1793–1806	Washington	**Edward D. White,** La.	1910–1921	Taft
John Rutledge, S.C.	1795	Washington	Willis Van Devanter, Wy.	1911–1937	Taft
Samuel Chase, Md.	1796–1811	Washington	Joseph R. Lamar, Ga.	1911–1916	Taft
Oliver Ellsworth, Conn.	1796–1800	Washington	Mahlon Pitney, N.J.	1912–1922	Taft
Bushrod Washington, Va.	1799–1829	J. Adams	James C. McReynolds, Tenn.	1914–1941	Wilson
Alfred Moore, N.C.	1800–1804	J. Adams	Louis D. Brandeis, Mass.	1916–1939	Wilson
John Marshall, Va.	1801–1835	J. Adams	John H. Clarke, Ohio	1916–1922	Wilson
William Johnson, S.C.	1804–1834	Jefferson	**William H. Taft,** Conn.	1921–1930	Harding
Brockholst Livingston, N.Y.	1807–1823	Jefferson	George Sutherland, Utah	1922–1938	Harding
Thomas Todd, Ky.	1807–1826	Jefferson	Pierce Butler, Minn.	1923–1939	Harding
Gabriel Duvall, Md.	1811–1835	Madison	Edward T. Sanford, Tenn.	1923–1930	Harding
Joseph Story, Mass.	1812–1845	Madison	Harlan F. Stone, N.Y.	1925–1941	Coolidge
Smith Thompson, N.Y.	1823–1843	Monroe	**Charles E. Hughes,** N.Y.	1930–1941	Hoover
Robert Trimble, Ky.	1826–1828	J. Q. Adams	Owen J. Roberts, Penn.	1930–1945	Hoover
John McLean, Ohio	1830–1861	Jackson	Benjamin N. Cardozo, N.Y.	1932–1938	Hoover
Henry Baldwin, Pa.	1830–1844	Jackson	Hugo L. Black, Ala.	1937–1971	F. Roosevelt
James M. Wayne, Ga.	1835–1867	Jackson	Stanley F. Reed, Ky.	1938–1957	F. Roosevelt
Roger B. Taney, Md.	1836–1864	Jackson	Felix Frankfurter, Mass.	1939–1962	F. Roosevelt
Philip P. Barbour, Va.	1836–1841	Jackson	William O. Douglas, Conn.	1939–1975	F. Roosevelt
John Cartron, Tenn.	1837–1865	Van Buren	Frank Murphy, Mich.	1940–1949	F. Roosevelt
John McKinley, Ala.	1838–1852	Van Buren	**Harlan F. Stone,** N.Y.	1941–1946	F. Roosevelt
Peter V. Daniel, Va.	1842–1860	Van Buren	James R. Byrnes, S.C.	1941–1942	F. Roosevelt
Samuel Nelson, N.Y.	1845–1872	Tyler	Robert H. Jackson, N.Y.	1941–1954	F. Roosevelt
Levi Woodbury, N.H.	1845–1851	Polk	Wiley B. Rutledge, Iowa	1943–1949	F. Roosevelt
Robert C. Grier, Pa.	1846–1870	Polk	Harold H. Burton, Ohio	1945–1958	Truman
Benjamin R. Curtis, Mass.	1851–1857	Fillmore	**Frederick M. Vinson,** Ky.	1946–1953	Truman
John A. Campbell, Ala.	1853–1861	Pierce	Tom C. Clark, Texas	1949–1967	Truman
Nathan Clifford, Me.	1858–1881	Buchanan	Sherman Minton, Ind.	1949–1956	Truman
Noah H. Swayne, Ohio	1862–1881	Lincoln	**Earl Warren,** Cal.	1953–1969	Eisenhower
Samuel F. Miller, Iowa	1862–1890	Lincoln	John Marshall Harlan, N.Y.	1955–1971	Eisenhower
David Davis, Ill.	1862–1877	Lincoln	William J. Brennan, Jr., N.J.	1956–1990	Eisenhower
Stephen J. Field, Cal.	1863–1897	Lincoln	Charles E. Whittaker, Mo.	1957–1962	Eisenhower
Salmon P. Chase, Ohio	1864–1873	Lincoln	Potter Stewart, Ohio	1958–1981	Eisenhower
William Strong, Pa.	1870–1880	Grant	Bryon R. White, Colo.	1962–1993	Kennedy
Joseph P. Bradley, N.J.	1870–1892	Grant	Arthur J. Goldberg, Ill.	1962–1965	Kennedy
Ward Hunt, N.Y.	1873–1882	Grant	Abe Fortas, Tenn.	1965–1969	Johnson
Morrison R. Waite, Ohio	1874–1888	Grant	Thurgood Marshall, Md.	1967–1991	Johnson
John M. Harlan, Ky.	1877–1911	Hayes	**Warren E. Burger,** Minn.	1969–1986	Nixon
William B. Woods, Ga.	1881–1887	Hayes	Harry A. Blackmun, Minn.	1970–	Nixon
Stanley Matthews, Ohio	1881–1889	Garfield	Lewis F. Powell, Jr., Va.	1971–1987	Nixon
Horace Gray, Mass.	1882–1902	Arthur	William H. Rehnquist, Ariz.	1971–1986	Nixon
Samuel Blatchford, N.Y.	1882–1893	Arthur	John Paul Stevens, Ill.	1975–	Ford
Lucius Q. C. Lamar, Miss.	1888–1893	Cleveland	Sandra Day O'Connor, Ariz.	1981–	Reagan
Melville W. Fuller, Ill.	1888–1910	Cleveland	**William H. Rehnquist,** Ariz.	1986–	Reagan
David J. Brewer, Kan.	1890–1910	B. Harrison	Antonin Scalia, Va.	1986–	Reagan
Henry B. Brown, Mich.	1891–1906	B. Harrison	Anthony M. Kennedy, Cal.	1988–	Reagan
George Shiras, Jr., Pa.	1892–1903	B. Harrison	David H. Souter, N.H.	1990–	Bush
Howell E. Jackson, Tenn.	1893–1895	B. Harrison	Clarence Thomas, Ga.	1991–	Bush
Edward D. White, La.	1894–1910	Cleveland	Ruth Bader Ginsburg, N.Y.	1993–	Clinton

*Chief Justices are printed in bold type.

The American People: A Demographic Survey

A Demographic Profile of the American People

Year	Life Expectancy from Birth		Average Age at First Marriage		Number of Children Under 5 (per 1,000 Women Aged 20–44)	Percent of Women in Paid Employment	Percent of Paid Workers Who Are Female
	White	Black	Male	Female			
1820					1,295	6.2%	7.3%
1830					1,145	6.4	7.4
1840					1,085	8.4	9.6
1850					923	10.1	10.8
1860					929	9.7	10.2
1870					839	13.7	14.8
1880					822	14.7	15.2
1890			26.1	22.0	716	18.2	17.0
1900	47.6	33.0	25.9	21.9	688	21.2	18.1
1910	50.3	35.6	25.1	21.6	643	24.8	20.0
1920	54.9	45.3	24.6	21.2	604	23.9	20.4
1930	61.4	48.1	24.3	21.3	511	24.4	21.9
1940	64.2	53.1	24.3	21.5	429	25.4	24.6
1950	69.1	60.8	22.8	20.3	589	29.1	27.8
1960	70.6	63.6	22.8	20.3	737	34.8	32.3
1970	71.7	65.3	22.5	20.6	530	43.3	38.0
1980	74.4	68.1	24.7	22.0	440	51.5	42.6
1990	76.2	71.4	26.1	23.9	377	57.4	45.2

Source: Historical Statistics of the United States, Colonial Times to 1970 (1975); *Statistical Abstract of the United States, 1991.*

American Population

Year	Population	Percent Increase	Year	Population	Percent Increase
1610	350	—	1810	7,239,881	36.4
1620	2,300	557.1	1820	9,638,453	33.1
1630	4,600	100.0	1830	12,866,020	33.5
1640	26,600	478.3	1840	17,069,453	32.7
1650	50,400	90.8	1850	23,191,876	35.9
1660	75,100	49.0	1860	31,443,321	35.6
1670	111,900	49.0	1870	39,818,449	26.6
1680	151,500	35.4	1880	50,155,783	26.0
1690	210,400	38.9	1890	62,947,714	25.5
1700	250,900	19.2	1900	75,994,575	20.7
1710	331,700	32.2	1910	91,972,266	21.0
1720	466,200	40.5	1920	105,710,620	14.9
1730	629,400	35.0	1930	122,775,046	16.1
1740	905,600	43.9	1940	131,669,275	7.2
1750	1,170,800	29.3	1950	150,697,361	14.5
1760	1,593,600	36.1	1960	179,323,175	19.0
1770	2,148,100	34.8	1970	203,235,298	13.3
1780	2,780,400	29.4	1980	226,545,805	11.5
1790	3,929,214	41.3	1990	248,709,873	9.8
1800	5,308,483	35.1			

Note: These figures largely ignore the native American population. Census takers never made any effort to count the native American population that lived outside their political jurisdictions and compiled only casual and incomplete enumerations of those living within their jurisdictions until 1890. In that year the federal government attempted a full count of the Indian population: the Census found 125,719 Indians in 1890, compared with only 12,543 in 1870 and 33,985 in 1880.

Source: Historical Statistics of the United States, Colonial Times to 1970 (1975); *Statistical Abstract of the United States, 1991.*

White/Nonwhite Population

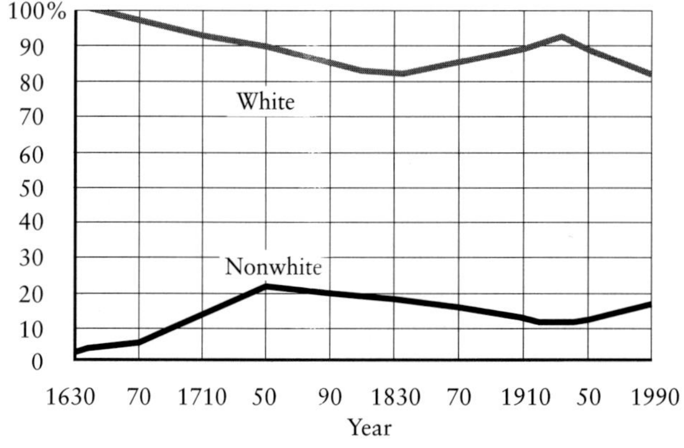

Urban/Rural Population

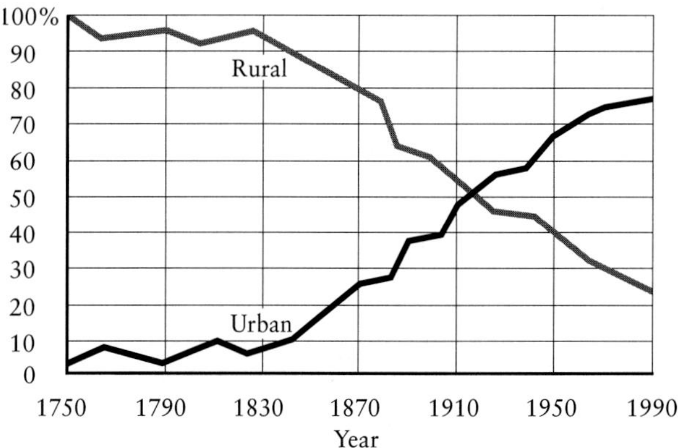

The Ten Largest Cities by Population, 1700–1990

Year	Rank	City	Population
1700	1.	Boston	6,700
	2.	New York	4,937*
	3.	Philadelphia	4,400†
1790	1.	Philadelphia	42,520
	2.	New York	33,131
	3.	Boston	18,038
	4.	Charleston, S.C.	16,359
	5.	Baltimore	13,503
	6.	Salem, Mass.	7,921
	7.	Newport, R.I.	6,716
	8.	Providence, R.I.	6,380
	9.	Marblehead, Mass.	5,661
	10.	Portsmouth, N.H.	4,720
1830	1.	New York	197,112
	2.	Philadelphia	161,410
	3.	Baltimore	80,620
	4.	Boston	61,392
	5.	Charleston, S.C.	30,289
	6.	New Orleans	29,737
	7.	Cincinnati	24,831
	8.	Albany, N.Y.	24,209
	9.	Brooklyn, N.Y.	20,535
	10.	Washington, D.C.	18,826
1850	1.	New York	515,547
	2.	Philadelphia	340,045
	3.	Baltimore	169,054
	4.	Boston	136,881
	5.	New Orleans	116,375
	6.	Cincinnati	115,435
	7.	Brooklyn, N.Y.	96,838
	8.	St. Louis	77,860
	9.	Albany, N.Y.	50,763
	10.	Pittsburgh	46,601
1870	1.	New York	942,292
	2.	Philadelphia	674,022
	3.	Brooklyn, N.Y.	419,921†
	4.	St. Louis	310,864
	5.	Chicago	298,977
	6.	Baltimore	267,354
	7.	Boston	250,526
	8.	Cincinnati	216,239
	9.	New Orleans	191,418
	10.	San Francisco	149,473
1910	1.	New York	4,766,883
	2.	Chicago	2,185,283
	3.	Philadelphia	1,549,008
	4.	St. Louis	687,029
	5.	Boston	670,585
	6.	Cleveland	560,663
	7.	Baltimore	558,485
	8.	Pittsburgh	533,905
	9.	Detroit	465,766
	10.	Buffalo	423,715
1930	1.	New York	6,930,446
	2.	Chicago	3,376,438
	3.	Philadelphia	1,950,961
	4.	Detroit	1,568,662
	5.	Los Angeles	1,238,048
	6.	Cleveland	900,429
	7.	St. Louis	821,960
	8.	Baltimore	804,874
	9.	Boston	781,188
	10.	Pittsburgh	669,817
1950	1.	New York	7,891,957
	2.	Chicago	3,620,962
	3.	Philadelphia	2,071,605
	4.	Los Angeles	1,970,358
	5.	Detroit	1,849,568
	6.	Baltimore	949,708
	7.	Cleveland	914,808
	8.	St. Louis	856,796
	9.	Washington, D.C.	802,178
	10.	Boston	801,444
1970	1.	New York	7,895,563
	2.	Chicago	3,369,357
	3.	Los Angeles	2,811,801
	4.	Philadelphia	1,949,996
	5.	Detroit	1,514,063
	6.	Houston	1,233,535
	7.	Baltimore	905,787
	8.	Dallas	844,401
	9.	Washington, D.C.	756,668
	10.	Cleveland	750,879
1990	1.	New York	7,322,564
	2.	Los Angeles	3,485,398
	3.	Chicago	2,783,726
	4.	Houston	1,630,553
	5.	Philadelphia	1,585,577
	6.	San Diego	1,110,549
	7.	Detroit	1,027,974
	8.	Dallas	1,006,877
	9.	Phoenix	983,403
	10.	San Antonio	935,933

*Figure from a census taken in 1698.
†Philadelphia figures include suburbs.
‡Annexed to New York in 1898.
Source: U.S. Census data.

Foreign Origins of the American People

Immigration by Decade

Year	Number	Percent of Total Population	Year	Number	Percent of Total Population
1821–1830	151,824	1.6	1921–1930	4,107,209	3.9
1831–1840	599,125	4.6	1931–1940	528,431	0.4
1841–1850	1,713,251	10.0	1941–1950	1,035,039	0.7
1851–1860	2,598,214	11.2	1951–1960	2,515,479	1.6
1861–1870	2,314,824	7.4	1961–1970	3,321,677	1.8
1871–1880	2,812,191	7.1	1971–1980	4,493,000	2.2
1881–1890	5,246,613	10.5	1981–1990	7,338,000	3.0
1891–1900	3,687,546	5.8	Total	23,338,835	
1901–1910	8,795,386	11.6			
1911–1920	5,735,811	6.2	1821–1990	56,993,620	
Total	33,654,785		Grand Total		

Source: U. S. Bureau of the Census, *Historical Statistics of the United States, Colonial Times to 1970* (1975), Part I, pp. 105–106; *Statistical Abstract of the United States, 1991.*

Regional Origins

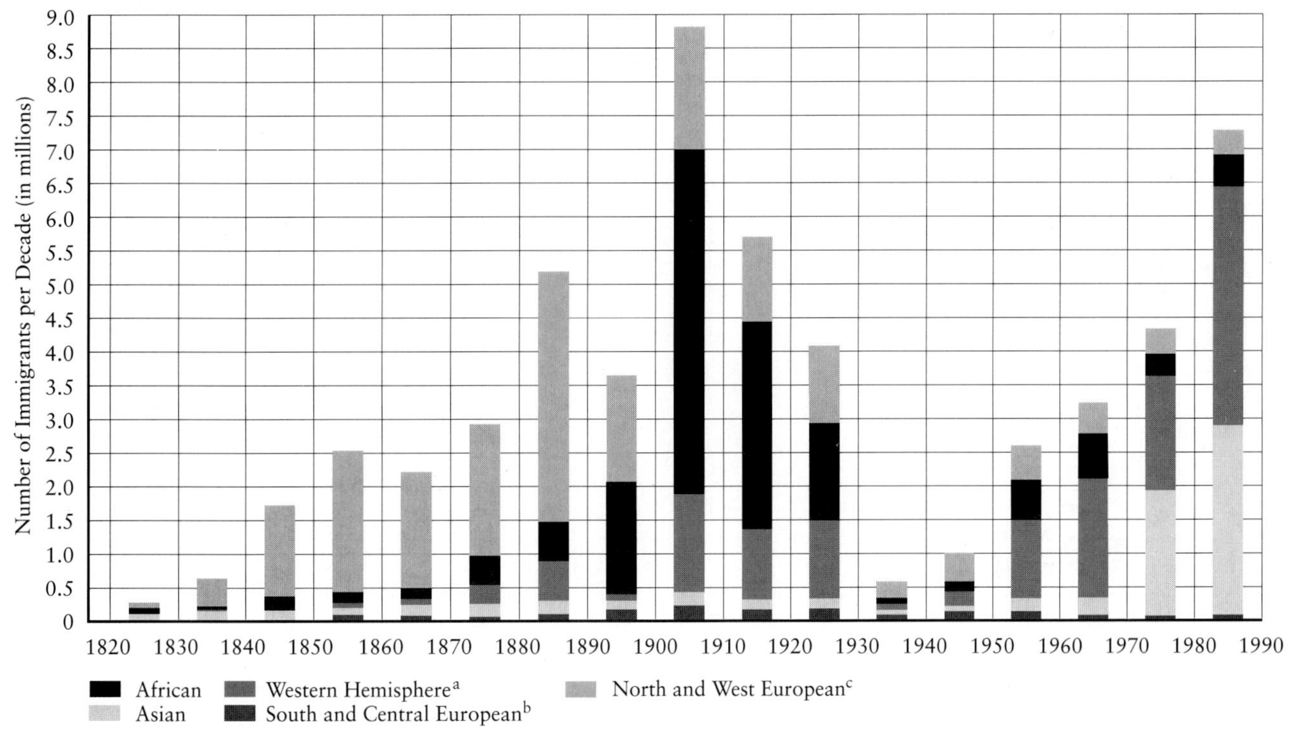

[a] Canada and all countries in South America and Central America.

[b] Italy, Spain, Portugal, Greece, Germany (Austria included, 1938–1945), Poland, Czechoslovakia (since 1920), Yogoslavia (since 1920), Hungary (since 1861), Austria (since 1861, except 1938–1945), former U.S.S.R. (excludes Asian U.S.S.R. between 1931 and 1963), Latvia, Estonia, Lithuania, Finland, Romania, Bulgaria, Turkey (in Europe), and other European countries not classified elsewhere.

[c] Great Britain, Ireland, Norway, Sweden, Denmark, Iceland, Netherlands, Belgium, Luxembourg, Switzerland, France.

Source: Stephan Thernstrom, ed., *Harvard Encyclopedia of American Ethnic Groups* (1980), p. 480; and U.S. Bureau of the Census, *Statistical Abstract of the United States, 1991.*

The Labor Force
(thousands of workers)

Year	Agriculture	Mining	Manufacturing	Construction	Trade	Other Services	Total
1810	1,956	11	75	—	—	288	2,330
1840	3,594	32	500	290	350	894	5,660
1850	4,520	102	1,200	410	530	1,488	8,250
1860	5,880	176	1,530	520	890	2,114	11,110
1870	6,790	180	2,470	780	1,310	1,400	12,930
1880	8,961	280	3,290	900	1,930	2,029	17,390
1890	9,960	440	4,390	1,510	2,960	4,060	23,320
1900	11,680	637	5,895	1,665	3,970	5,223	29,070
1910	11,770	1,068	8,332	1,949	5,320	9,041	37,480
1920	10,790	1,180	11,190	1,233	5,845	11,372	41,610
1930	10,633	1,009	9,884	1,988	8,122	17,194	48,830
1940	9,575	925	11,309	1,876	9,328	23,277	56,290
1950	7,870	901	15,648	3,029	12,152	25,870	65,470
1960	6,015	709	17,145	3,640	14,051	32,500	74,060
1970	3,463	623	19,367	3,588	15,040	36,597	78,678
1980	3,364	1,027	20,285	4,346	20,310	49,971	99,303
1990	3,186	711	19,111	5,136	25,888	63,882	117,914

Source: Stanley Lebergott, "Labor Force and Employment, 1800–1960," *Output, Employment, and Productivity in the United States After 1800* (New York: National Bureau of Economic Research, 1966); U.S. Bureau of Economic Analysis, *Long-Term Economic Growth, 1860–1970* (Washington, D.C., 1973), 260–263; U.S. Bureau of Labor Statistics, *Employment and Earnings* (October–December, 1991).

Changing Labor Patterns

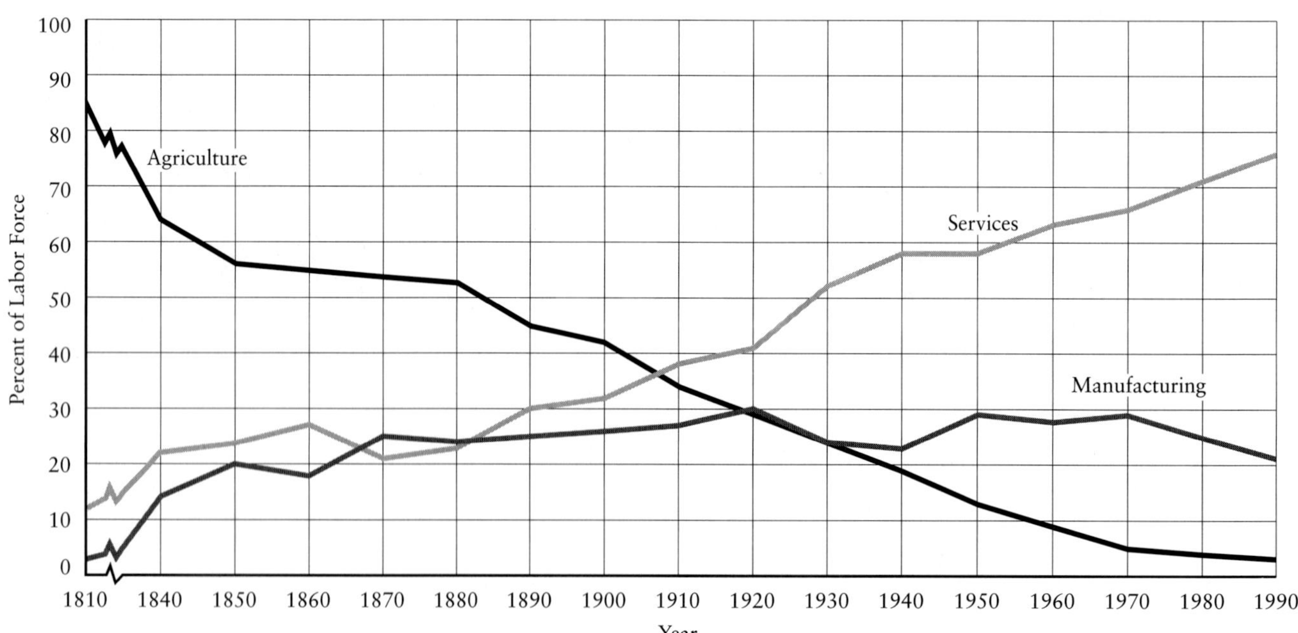

The Aging of the U. S. Population

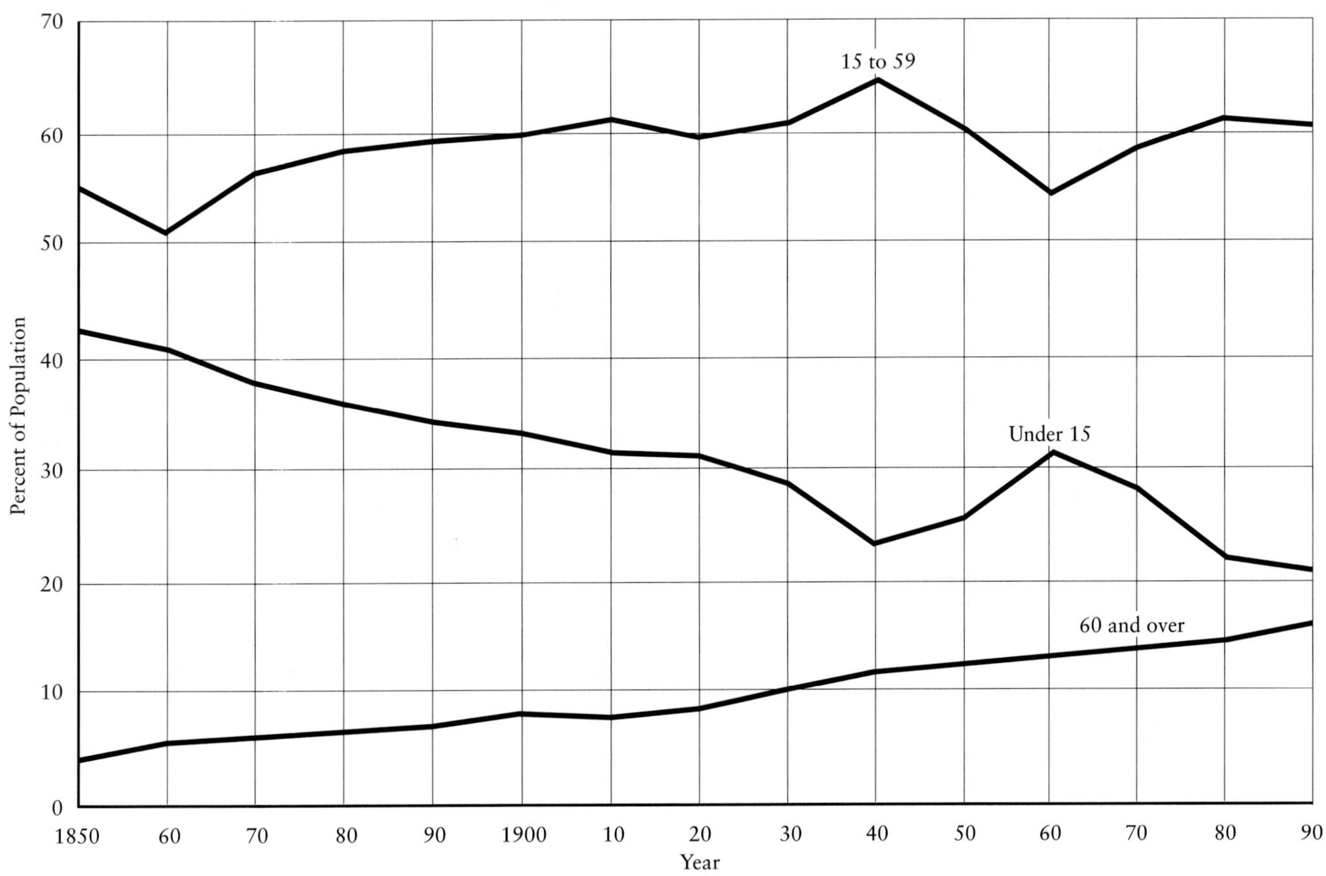

The American Government and Economy

The Growth of the Federal Government

The Federal Government, 1900–1980

Year	**Employees** (millions)		Year	**Receipts and Outlays** ($ millions)	
	Civilian	Military		Receipts	Outlays
1900	0.23	0.12	1900	567	521
1910	0.38	0.13	1910	676	694
1920	0.65	0.34	1920	6,649	6,358
1930	0.61	0.25	1930	4,058	3,320
1940	1.04	0.45	1940	6,900	9,600
1950	1.96	1.46	1950	40,900	43,100
1960	2.38	2.47	1960	92,500	92,200
1970	2.98	3.06	1970	193,700	196,600
1980	2.98	2.05	1980	517,112	590,920
1989	2.98	2.13	1990	1,031,462	1,251,850

Source: Statistical Profile of the United States, 1900–1980; Statistical Abstract of the United States, 1991.

Total Federal Debt, 1900–1990

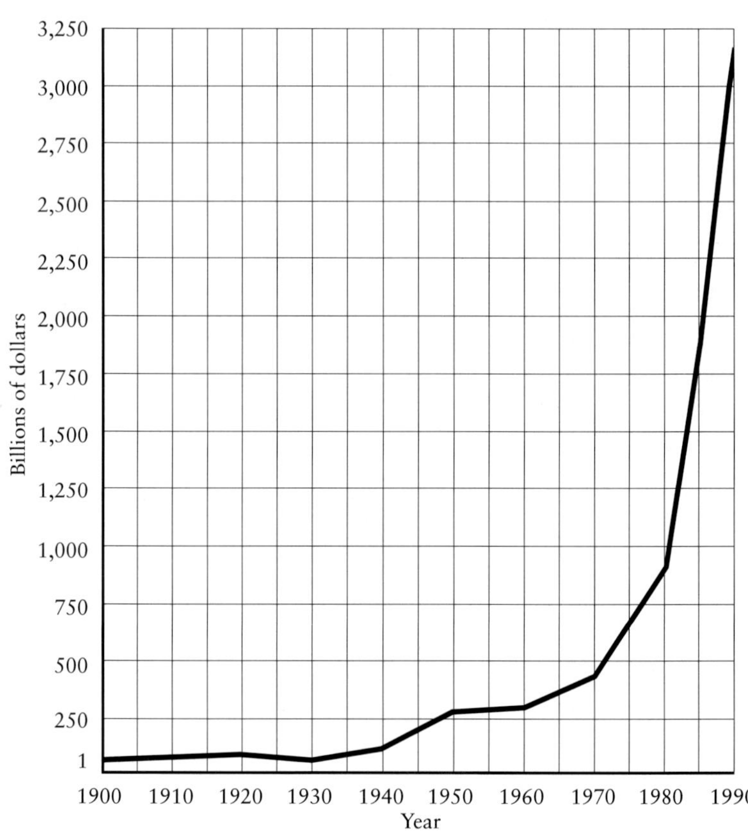

Gross National Product, 1840–1990

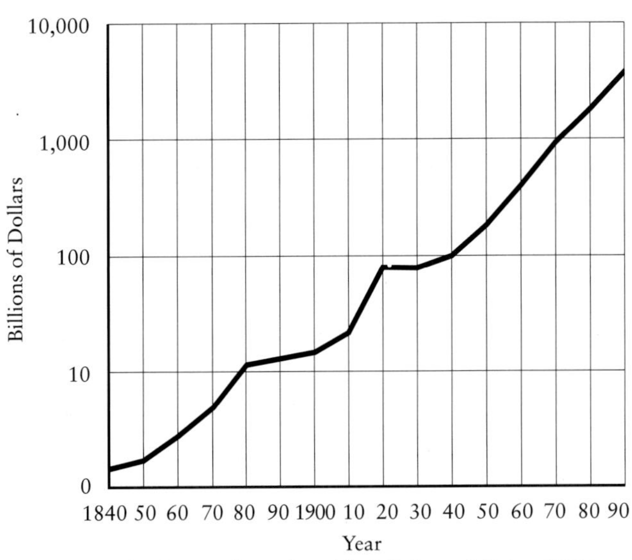

*Note: GNP values have not been adjusted for inflation or deflation. GNP is plotted here on a logarithmic scale.
Source: Statistical Abstract of the United States, 1991.

GNP per Capita, 1840–1990

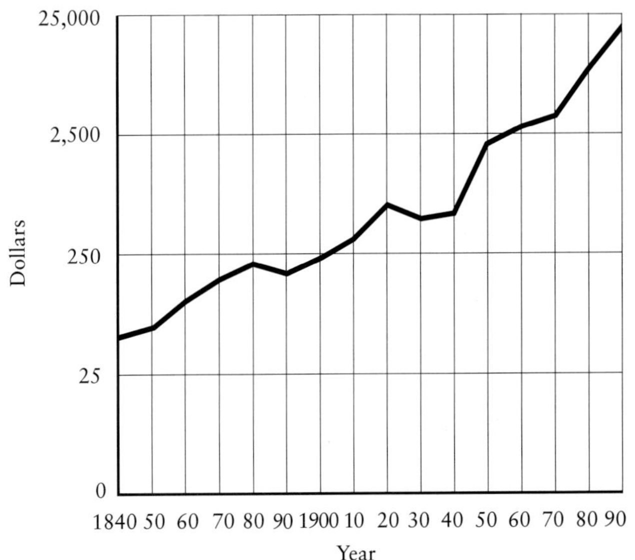

*Note: GNP values have not been adjusted for inflation or deflation. The GNP is plotted here on a logarithmic scale.

Consumer Price Index and Conversion Table

Year	Price Index* (1860 = 100)	Conversion Multiplier†	Year	Price Index	Conversion Multiplier	Year	Price Index	Conversion Multiplier
1700	130	53.3	1800	151	10.4	1900	101	15.5
1710	100	69.3	1810	148	10.6	1910	114	13.7
1720	76	91.3	1820	141	11.1	1920	240	6.5
1730	80	86.7	1830	111	14.1	1930	200	7.8
1740	66	105.1	1840	104	15.1	1940	168	9.3
1750	84	82.6	1850	94	16.6	1950	288	5.4
1760	96	72.3	1860	100	15.6	1960	354	4.4
1770	100	69.3	1870	157	9.9	1970	464	3.4
1780	165	9.5	1880	123	12.7	1980	985	1.6
1790	148	10.6	1890	109	14.3	1990	1563	1.0

* This index estimates how consumer prices changed on the average over ten-year intervals. Such estimates are highly uncertain, particularly when they are used to make comparisons over long periods of time. This is partly because it is extremely difficult to measure how the typical mix of goods (each with its own price) purchased by consumers changes over time.

† To convert £ (pounds Sterling, until 1770) or $ (U.S. dollars, beginning in 1780) from any date in the past to the equivalent in 1990 dollars, multiply the historical price by the appropriate number in this column. For example, £10 Sterling in 1730 would equal about $867 in 1990. (£10 × 86.7 = $867); or $10 in 1870 would equal about $99 in 1990 ($10 × 9.9 = $99).

Source: Adapted from John J. McCusker, "How Much Is That in Real Money? A Historical Price Index for Use as a Deflator of Money Value in the Economy of the United States," *Proceedings of the American Antiquarian Society,* Vol. 101, pt. 2, (1991), 297–390.

Illustration Credits

Chapter 1 **P. 2:** Flemish School, *The Cognoscenti* (detail), 17th century, reproduced by courtesy of the Trustees, The National Gallery, London. **P. 4:** Dumbarton Oaks Research Library and Collections, Washington, DC. **P. 5** (top): Hans Namuth/Photo Researchers. **P. 5** (bottom): George Holton/Photo Researchers. **P. 7:** Bailey/Howe Library, University of Vermont. **P. 8:** Peabody Museum, Harvard University. Photograph by Hillel Burger. **P. 10:** Musée Condé/Giraudon/Art Resource. **P. 12:** British Library, London. **P. 14:** Mathias Grünewald, *Isenheim Altarpiece* (central panel), early 16th century, Musée Unterlinden, Colmar/Giraudon/Art Resource. **P. 15:** Bibliothèque Nationale, Paris. **P. 17:** From *Sahinsahname,* Vol. I, Universite Kutuphanesi, Istanbul. Photograph by Ergun Cagutay. **P. 18:** Piero della Francesca, *The Ideal City,* 15th century, Scala/Art Resource. **P. 21:** Codex Florentino, courtesy of the Department of Library Services, American Museum of Natural History. **P. 22:** The Bettmann Archive. **P. 26:** Cornelius de Zeeuw, *Pierre de Moucheron and His Family,* n.d., Rijksmuseum, Amsterdam. **P. 29:** Unknown, *Sir Walter Raleigh and His Son,* c. 1602, courtesy of the National Portrait Gallery, London. **P. 30:** Marcus Gheeraerts, the Younger, *Elizabeth I,* c. 1592, courtesy of the National Portrait Gallery, London.

Chapter 2 **P. 34:** Ashmolean Museum, Oxford. **P. 37:** I. N. Phelps Stokes Collection, Miriam & Ira D. Wallach Division of Art, Prints and Photographs. The New York Public Library, Astor, Lenox and Tilden Foundations. **P. 41:** A. H. Robins Co. Photograph by Don Eiler. **P. 43:** Colonial Williamsburg Foundation. **Pp. 44 and 47:** Collection of the Maryland Historical Society, Baltimore. **P. 49:** George Ross. **P. 51:** Courtesy of the American Antiquarian Society. **P. 52:** Courtesy of the Pilgrim Society, Plymouth, MA. **P. 53:** Courtesy of the Essex Institute, Salem, MA. **P. 55:** Courtesy of the American Antiquarian Society. **P. 59:** Anon., *Mrs. Elizabeth Freake and Baby,* c.1671–74, Worcester Art Museum, Worcester, MA. Gift of Mr. and Mrs. Albert W. Rice. **P. 60:** Shelburne Museum, Shelburne, VT. Photograph by Ken Burris. **P. 62:** Service Hydrographique de la Marine, Paris.

Chapter 3 **P. 66:** English School, *Bristol Docks and Quay* (detail), early-18th century, City of Bristol Museum and Art Gallery/Bridgeman Art Library, London. **P. 68:** Mansell Collection. **P. 72:** Godfrey Kneller, *James II,* late-17th century, courtesy of the National Portrait Gallery, London. **P. 73:** New York State Historical Association, Cooperstown. **P. 76:** John Greenwood, *Sea Captains in Surinam,* 18th century, The Saint Louis Art Museum. Museum Purchase. **P. 77:** Benin Bronze Plaque: Mounted King and Attendants, c. 1550–1680, The Metropolitan Museum of Art, NY. The Michael C. Rockefeller Memorial Collection. **P. 79:** The Library Company of Philadelphia. **P. 80** (left): National Maritime Museum, London. **P. 80** (right): Library of Congress. **P. 82:** Courtesy of the Georgia Department of Archives and History, Atlanta. **P. 83:** Abby Aldrich Rockefeller Folk Art Center, Williamsburg, VA. **P. 84:** Augusta-Richmond County Museum, Augusta, GA. **P. 86:** Anon. (American), *The End of the Hunt,* c. 1800, National Gallery of Art, Washington, DC. Gift of Edgar William and Bernice Chrysler Garbisch. **P. 88:** Peter Cooper, *S. E. Prospect of the City of Philadelphia,* c. 1720, The Library Company of Philadelphia. **P. 91:** Joseph Steward, *George Wyllys,* c. 1770, The Connecticut Historical Society, Hartford.

Chapter 4 **P. 98:** Courtesy of the American Antiquarian Society. **P. 102:** Anon. (American), *The Cheney Family,* c. 1795, National Gallery of Art, Washington, DC. Gift of Edgar William and Bernice Chrysler Garbisch. **P. 103:** The Connecticut Historical Society, Hartford. **P. 105:** Attributed to Gerardus Duyckinck, *Lady Undressing for a Bath,* c. 1730–40, National Gallery of Art, Washington, DC. Gift of Edgar William and Bernice Chrysler Garbisch. **P. 106:** Courtesy of the Museum of Fine Arts, Boston. Bequest of Maxim Karolik. **P. 107:** Philadelphia Museum of Art, from the Clarence W. Brazer Collection. **P. 109:** Collection of the Maryland Historical Society, Baltimore. **P. 114:** John Steeper and Henry Dawkins, *A Southeast Prospect of the Pennsylvania Hospital,* c. 1761, The Library Company of Philadelphia. **P. 117:** Joseph Badger, *Rev. Jonathan Edwards,* 1720, Yale University Art Gallery. Bequest of Eugene Phelps Edwards, 1938. **P. 118:** John Wollaston, *George Whitefield,* c. 1742, courtesy of the National Portrait Gallery, London. **P. 123:** Anne S. K. Brown Military Collection, Brown University Library, Providence, RI. **P. 126:** Private Collection. **P. 128:** The Library Company of Philadelphia.

Chapter 5 **P. 132:** Ralph Earl, *Occupation of Concord by the British* (detail), n.d. Photograph courtesy of the Concord Antiquarian

Museum, Concord, MA. **P. 137:** Courtesy of the American Antiquarian Society. **P. 139:** Print Collection. Miriam and Ira D. Wallach Division of Art, Prints and Photographs. The New York Public Library, Astor, Lenox and Tilden Foundations. **P. 140:** Courtesy of the John Carter Brown Library at Brown University, Providence, RI. **P. 143:** John Singleton Copley, *Samuel Adams,* c. 1772. Courtesy of the Museum of Fine Arts, Boston. Deposited by the City of Boston. **P. 144:** Anon., *Patrick Henry,* n.d., Shelburne Museum, Shelburne, VT. Photograph by Ken Burris. **P. 145:** Courtesy of the Essex Institute, Salem, MA. **P. 149:** Print Collection. Miriam and Ira D. Wallach Division of Art, Prints and Photographs. The New York Public Library, Astor, Lenox and Tilden Foundations. **P. 153:** Courtesy of the John Carter Brown Library at Brown University, Providence, RI. **P. 154:** Joseph Cole, *George Hewes,* 1835. Courtesy of The Bostonian Society/Old State House. **Pp. 155 and 156:** Library of Congress. **P. 158:** Amos Doolittle, *The Battle of Lexington April 19, 1775,* late-18th century, the Carnegie Museum of Art, Pittsburgh. Howard N. Eavenson Americana Collection, 55-20-1.

Chapter 6 **P. 164:** Anon., *Attack on Bunker's Hill, with the Burning of Charles Town* (detail), c. 1783, National Gallery of Art, Washington, DC. Gift of Edgar William and Bernice Chrysler Garbisch. **P. 166:** John McRae, *Raising the Liberty Pole,* n.d., photograph courtesy of the Kennedy Galleries, Inc., NY. **P. 167:** John Zoffany, *Family of George III,* late-18th, early-19th century, Royal Collection, St. James's Palace. © H. M. Queen Elizabeth II. **P. 168:** Pine and Savage, *Declaration of Independence,* Library of Congress. **P. 169:** Thomas Sully, *George Washington at the Battle of Trenton,* 19th century, The Union League of Philadelphia. **P. 170:** William Mercer, *Battle of Princeton,* late-18th century, Historical Society of Pennsylvania, Philadelphia. **P. 171:** Library of Congress. **P. 173:** Charles Willson Peale, *Joseph Brant,* 1797, Independence National Historical Park Collection, Philadelphia, PA. **P. 174:** Library of Congress. **P. 178:** Virginia Historical Society, Richmond. **P. 179:** Anne S. K. Brown Military Collection, Brown University Library, Providence, RI. **P. 180** (top): Library of Congress. **P. 180** (bottom): Anne S. K. Brown Military Collection, Brown University Library, Providence, RI. **P. 182:** Benjamin West, *American Commission of the Preliminary Peace Negotiation with Great Britain* (detail), 1783, courtesy of the Winterthur Museum, Winterthur, DE. **P. 186:** Attributed to Copley, *Thomas Hutchinson,* Massachusetts Historical Society, Boston. **P. 187:** Massachusetts Historical Society, Boston.

Chapter 7 **P. 192:** Frederick Kemmelmeyer, *The American Star,* Metropolitan Museum of Art. Gift of Edgar William and Bernice Chrysler Garbisch, 1962. **P. 195** (left): Mather Brown, *John Adams,* late-18th century, Boston Atheneum. **P. 195** (right): Unknown, *Abigail Adams,* New York State Historical Association, Cooperstown. **P. 196:** Museum of Art, Rhode Island School of Design, Providence. Museum Appropriation. **P. 198:** Attributed to James Sharples, *Gouverneur Morris,* c. 1800, City of Bristol Museum and Art Gallery, England. **P. 200:** National Portrait Gallery, Washington, DC/Art Resource. **P. 202:** Gilbert Stuart, *Portrait of James Madison,* c. 1805–7, Bowdoin College Museum of Art, Brunswick, ME. Bequest of James Bowdoin III. **P. 207:** Courtesy of the New-York Historical Society, New York City. **P. 211** (left): Rembrandt Peale, *Thomas Jefferson,* c. 1800, © White House Historical Collection. Photograph by the National Geographic Society. **P. 211** (right): John Trumbull, *Alexander Hamilton,* n.d., Yale University Art Gallery, New Haven, CT. **P. 212:** Print Collection. Miriam and Ira D. Wallach Division of Art, Prints and Photographs. The New York Public Library, Astor, Lenox and Tilden Foundations. **P. 213:** Mansell Collection, London. **P. 214:** John Rubens Smith, *The Shop and Warehouse of Duncan Phyfe,* c. 1816–17. Watercolor, pen and brown ink on paper. The Metropolitan Museum of Art, Rogers Fund, 1922. **P. 215:** Ralph Earl, *Oliver Ellsworth and Abigail Wolcott Ellsworth,* c. 1792, Wadsworth Atheneum, Hartford, CT. Gift of the Ellsworth Heirs **P. 216:** Courtesy of the Winterthur Museum, Winterthur, DE. **P. 217:** By permission of the Huntington Library, San Marino, CA.

Chapter 8 **P. 222:** Thomas Birch, *Conestoga Wagon on the Pennsylvania Turnpike,* c. 1816, Shelburne Museum, Shelburne, VT. Photograph by Ken Burris. **P. 225:** Unknown, *Treaty of Greenville,* n.d., Chicago Historical Society. **P. 226:** Thomas Cole Ruckle, *Fairview Inn,* c. 1889, Collection of the Maryland Historical Society, Baltimore. **P. 227:** Courtesy of the Wethersfield Historical Society, CT. **P. 228:** Courtesy of the Cincinnati Historical Society. **P. 232:** Boqueto de Woieserie, *A View of New Orleans Taken from the Plantation of Marigny, Nov. 1803,* c. 1803, Chicago Historical Society. **P. 233:** Missouri Historical Society, St. Louis. **P. 235:** Library of Congress. **P. 236:** Library Company of Philadelphia. **P. 239:** Jean Hyacinthe de Laclotte, *Battle of New Orleans,* n.d., New Orleans Museum of Art. Gift of Edgar William and Bernice Chrysler Garbisch. **P. 240:** John Brewster, Jr., *Dr. and Mrs. Brewster,* Old Sturbridge Village, Sturbridge, MA. **P. 241:** Rare Book Department, Free Library of Philadelphia. Photograph by Joan Broderick. **P. 244:** Lewis Miller, *Slave Trader, Sold to Tennessee,* n.d., Abby Aldrich Rockefeller Folk Art Center, Williamsburg, VA. Gift of Dr. and Mrs. Richard M. Kain in memory of George Hay Kain. **P. 246:** Blue Ridge Heritage Archive. Ferrum College, Ferrum, VA. **P. 248:** Mount Bethel A.M.E. Church, Philadelphia. **P. 251:** *Se-Quo-Yah,* 19th century, Lithograph printed by Lehman & Duval after a painting by Charles Bird King, Philadelphia Museum of Art. Given by Miss William Adger.

Chapter 9 **P. 256:** Francis Guy, *Tontine Coffee House* (detail), c. 1747, courtesy of the New-York Historical Society, New York City. **P. 259:** Ralph Earl, *Elijah Boardman,* 1782, The Metropolitan Museum of Art, NY. Bequest of Susan W. Tyler, 1979. **P. 260:** Courtesy of the Lynn Historical Society, MA. **P. 263:** Chester Harding, *John Marshall,* c. 1830, Boston Atheneum. **P. 265:** John Lewis Krimmel, *Fourth of July at Center Square,* n.d., Historical Society of Pennsylvania, Philadelphia. **P. 267:** Frick Art Reference Library, New York City. **P. 269:** After William John Wilgus, *Ichabod Crane and the Headless Horseman,* c. 1855, National Gallery of Art, Washington, DC. Gift of Edgar William and Bernice Chrysler Garbisch. **P. 271:** Ambrose Andrews, *Schuyler Family,* c. 1824, Courtesy of the New-York Historical Society, New York City. **P. 272:** Unknown American, *The Sargent Family,* c. 1800, National Gallery of Art, Washington, DC. Gift of Edgar William and Bernice Chrysler Garbisch. **P. 274:** Courtesy Yates County Historical Society, Penn Yan, NY. **P. 275:** John L. D. Mathies, *Jemima Wilkinson,* c. 1816, collection of the Yates County Historical Society. Reproduced by courtesy of the Village Board, Penn Yan, NY. **P. 278:** Courtesy of the New-York Historical Society, New York City. Lithograph by Kennedy and Lucas after a painting by A. Rider. **P. 280:** George Lehman, *Dance in a Country Tavern,* n.d., Historical Society of Pennsylvania, Philadelphia.

Chapter 10 **P. 286:** Mary Keys, *Lockport on the Erie Canal* (detail), c. 1832. Watercolor, 19 $\frac{1}{2}$" x 24 $\frac{1}{2}$" Munson-Williams-Proctor Institute of Art, Utica, NY. **P. 288** (top): Courtesy of the New-York Historical Society, New York City. **P. 288** (bottom): The Cincinnati Historical Society. **P. 290:** Courtesy of the National Museum of History and Technology, Smithsonian Institution, Washington, DC. **P. 291:** J. W. Hill, *The Rotary or Circular Windmill,* c. 1833, The Edward W. C. Arnold Collection lent by The Metropolitan Museum of Art. Photograph courtesy of the Museum of the City of New York, #L1400.31. **P. 292:** Barfoot for Darton, *Progress of Cotton: No 6, Spinning,* n.d., Lithograph, Yale University Art Gallery. The Mabel Brady Garvan Collection. **P. 294:** Hagley Museum & Library, Wilmington, DE. **P. 296:** William Giles Munson, *The Eli Whitney Gun Factory,* c. 1826–28, Yale University Art Gallery. The Mabel

Brady Garvan Collection. **P. 297:** Unknown, *The Yankee Pedlar,* c. 1830, courtesy of the IBM Corporation, Armonk, NY. **P. 301** (top): George Tattersall, *Highways and Byeways of the Forest,* 19th century, Museum of Fine Arts, Boston. M. and M. Karolik Collection of American Watercolors and Drawings: 1800–75. **P. 301**(bottom): John William Hill, *Junction of the Erie and Champlain Canals,* c. 1832, courtesy of the New-York Historical Society, New York City. **P. 304:** Pavel Petrovich Svinin, *Deck Life on the Paragon.* Watercolor on paper. The Metropolitan Museum of Art, NY. Rogers Fund, 1942. **P. 307** (left): Nicolino Calyo, *George Cousin, The Patent Chimney Sweep Cleaner,* c. 1840–44, Museum of the City of New York. Gift of Mrs. Francis P. Garvan in memory of Francis P. Garvan. **P. 307** (right): Nicolino Calyo, *The Hot Corn Seller,* c. 1840–44, Museum of the City of New York. Gift of Mrs. Francis P. Garvan in memory of Francis P. Garvan. **P. 310:** Unknown, *York Pennsylvania Family with Negro Servant,* c. 1828, The Saint Louis Art Museum. Bequest of Edgar William and Bernice Chrysler Garbisch. **P. 312:** Oberlin College Archives. **P. 313** (top): J. Maze Burbank, *Religious Camp Meeting* (detail), c. 1839, New Bedford Whaling Museum. **P. 313** (bottom): Courtesy of the Newberry Library, Chicago.

Chapter 11 **P. 318:** Robert Cruikshank, *President's Levee or All Creation Going to the White House,* n.d., © by the White House Historical Association, Washington, DC. Photograph by the National Geographic Society. **P. 321:** Library of Congress. **P. 322:** Philip Haas, *John Quincy Adams* (daguerreotype), c. 1843, The Metropolitan Museum of Art, NY. Gift of I. N. Phelps Stokes, Edward S. Hawes, Alice Mary Hawes, Marion Augusta Hawes, 1937. **P. 323:** P. Desobry, *Opposition Blown Sky High, Sir . . .,* American Heritage Picture Collection. **P. 325:** Ralph E. W. Earl, *Tennessee Gentleman (Andrew Jackson),* c. 1830, courtesy of The Hermitage—Home of Andrew Jackson. **P. 327:** George Catlin, *Muk-a-tah-mish-o-kah-kaik, The Black Hawk,* mid-19th century, courtesy of The Thomas Gilcrease Institute of American History and Art, Tulsa, OK. Catalog #0226.1519. **P. 329:** Library of Congress. **P. 330:** S. Bernard, *View Along the East Battery, Charleston,* c. 1831, Yale University Art Gallery. The Mabel Brady Garvan Collection. **P. 331:** Unknown, *John C. Calhoun* (daguerreotype), The Gibbes Museum of Art, Carolina Art Association, Charleston, SC. **P. 334:** The Bettmann Archive. **P. 337:** General Research Division, The New York Public Library, Astor, Lenox and Tilden Foundations. **P. 339:** From *The Union,* 1835, courtesy of The New York Public Library. **Pp. 340, 342 and 345:** Courtesy of the New-York Historical Society, New York City.

Chapter 12 **P. 348:** Joshua H. Bussell, *The Shaker Community at Poland Hill, Maine* (detail), c. 1850, Collection of the United Society of Shakers, Sabbathday Lake, ME. **P. 351:** The Bettmann Archive. **P. 352:** The American Antiquarian Society. **P. 353:** The Bettmann Archive. **P. 354:** Olaf Krans, *Harvesting,* c. 1896, Bishop Hill State Historical Site, Illinois Historic Preservation Agency. **P. 358:** By permission of the Houghton Library, Harvard University, Cambridge, MA. **P. 359** (both): Library of Congress. **P. 360:** Culver Pictures. **P. 361** (left): Collection of Rhoda Jenkins and John Barney, Greenwich, CT. **P. 361** (right): The Bettmann Archive. **P. 365:** Unknown, *William Lloyd Garrison* (daguerreotype), 19th century, The Metropolitan Museum of Art, NY. Gift of I. N. Stokes, Edward S. Hawes, Alice Mary Hawes, Marion Augusta Hawes, 1937. **P. 371:** The Historical Society of Philadelphia, PA.

Chapter 13 **P. 374:** William Aiken Walker, *Plantation Economy in the Old South* (detail), c. 1876, The Warner Collection of Gulf States Paper Corporation, Tuscaloosa, AL. **P. 377:** Franz Holzlhuber, *Sugarcane Harvest in Louisiana and Texas,* c. 1856–60, Collection of Glenbow Museum, Calgary. **P. 380:** The National Portrait Gallery, The Smithsonian Institution, on loan from Serena Williams Miles Van Ronsselach. **P. 381:** Eyre Crowe, *Richmond Slave Market Auction,* n.d., The Collection of Jay P. Altmayer. **P. 382:** John Antrobus, *Plantation Burial,* c. 1860, The Historic New Orleans Collection. **P. 384:** Sophia Smith Collection, Smith College, MA. **P. 387:** Charles Blauvelt, *A German Immigrant Inquiring His Way,* c. 1855, North Carolina Museum of Art, Raleigh. Purchased with the funds from the State of North Carolina. **P. 390:** Library of Congress. **P. 391:** Engraving by W. W. Wilson, *Constructing a Balloon Frame House,* c. 1855, The Metropolitan Museum of Art, NY. Harris Brisbane Dick Fund, 1934. **P. 392:** Courtesy of the New-York Historical Society, New York City. **P. 393:** Currier & Ives, *Home Sweet Home,* c. 1869, Museum of the City of New York. The Harry T. Peters Collection. **P. 397:** Stowe-Day Foundation, Hartford, CT. **P. 405:** Culver Pictures. **P. 406:** The Pat Hathaway Collection of California Views. **P. 408:** California State Library, Sacramento. Daguerreotype Collection negative #912.

Chapter 14 **P. 412:** John Steuart Curry, *John Brown Mural* in the Kansas State Capitol, 1941, Kansas State Historical Society. Photograph as published in "The Story of America" © National Geographic Society, 1984. **P. 414:** From the Collection of the Dallas Historical Society. **P. 415:** National Museum of American History, The Smithsonian Institution, Department of Political History, Washington, DC. Photograph by Michael Freeman. **P. 417:** Courtesy of the Amon Carter Museum, Fort Worth, TX. **P. 418:** Samuel Chamberlain, *Street Fighting in the Calle de Iturbide,* 1855–61, The West Point Museum, United States Military Academy, West Point, NY. From *The Old West: The Mexican War.* Photograph by Paulus Leeser ©1978 Time/Life Books, Inc. **P. 423:** The Bettmann Archive. **P. 426:** The Bettmann Archive. **P. 429:** The Kansas Historical Society, Topeka, KS. **P. 431:** Library of Congress. **P. 433:** Missouri Historical Society, St. Louis. **P. 435:** The Lincoln Museum, Fort Wayne, IN, a part of the Lincoln National Corporation. **P. 436:** National Portrait Gallery, Washington, DC/Art Resource. **P. 437:** The Ohio Historical Society, Columbus. **P. 438:** Virginia State Library and Archives, Richmond.

Chapter 15 **P. 442:** The Seventh Regiment Fund, Inc. (detail), New York City. **P. 448:** Virginia State Library and Archives, Richmond. **P. 450:** Library of Congress. **P. 451:** From *Harper's Weekly,* August 1, 1863. Courtesy of the Newberry Library, Chicago. **P. 454:** Massachusetts Commandery Military Order of the Loyal Legion and the U.S. Army Military History Institute. **P. 456:** Elliot Brownlee. **P. 457:** Chicago Historical Society. **P. 460** (top): From *The Civil War: The Bloodiest Day.* Photograph by Larry Sherer ©1984 Time/Life Books, Inc. Courtesy of the Antietam National Battlefield, National Park Service, Sharpsberg, MD. **P. 460** (bottom): Library of Congress. **P. 461:** Library of Congress. **P. 463:** From *The Civil War: Twenty Million Yankees.* Photograph by Larry Sherer © 1985 Time/Life Books, Inc. Courtesy of the United States Senate Collection. **P. 466:** Courtesy of Robert Hunt Rhodes. **Pp. 468 and 470:** Library of Congress. **P. 476** (top): Culver Pictures. **P. 476** (bottom): Library of Congress.

Chapter 16 **P. 480:** Chicago Historical Society. **Pp. 482 and 484:** Library of Congress. **P. 485:** Chicago Historical Society. **P. 487:** Courtesy of the New-York Historical Society, New York City. **P. 489:** Library of Congress. **P. 492:** Collection of Mrs. Nancy W. Livingston and Mrs. Elizabeth Livingston Jaeger. Photograph courtesy of the Los Angeles County Museum of Art. **P. 493:** The Bettmann Archive. **P. 495:** Library of Congress. **P. 496:** *Harper's Weekly,* June 23, 1866. Courtesy of the Newberry Library, Chicago. **P. 497:** Rutherford B. Hayes Presidential Center, Spiegel Grove, Freemont, OH. **P. 499:** Brown Brothers. **P. 500:** Collection Tennessee State Museum. Photograph by Karina McDaniel. Courtesy of the Tennessee State Library & Archives, Nashville. **P. 506:** Historical Pictures/Stock Montage, Inc. **P. 508:** *Frank Leslie's Illustrated Newspaper,* September 23, 1876. Courtesy of the Newberry Library, Chicago.

Chapter 17 **P. 514:** Courtesy of the New-York Historical Society, New York City. Bella C. Landauer Collection. **P. 517:** South Dakota State Historical Society, Pierre. **P. 518:** Idaho State Historical Society, Boise. **P. 521:** Culver Pictures. **P. 522:** Buffalo Bill Historical Center, Cody, WY. Gift of the Coe Foundation. **P. 523:** Culver Pictures. **P. 526:** Archives & Manuscript Division of the Oklahoma Historical Society, Oklahoma City. **P. 528:** Smithsonian Institution Photo No. 3200–b–8. **P. 530:** The Thomas Gilcrease Institute of American History and Art, Tulsa, OK. **P. 531:** Bancroft Library, University of California, Berkeley. **P. 532:** William Hahn, *Market Scene, Sansome Street, San Francisco,* 1872. Oil on canvas, 60" x 96". © 1872 Crocker Collection, Crocker Art Museum, Sacramento, CA. **P. 535:** Yosemite National Park Research Library, Yosemite National Park, CA. **P. 536:** Solomon D. Butcher Collection, Nebraska State Historical Society, Lincoln. **P. 538:** Library of Congress. **P. 541:** Courtesy of the California Historical Society, San Francisco. FN 29120. **P. 542:** Library of Congress.

Chapter 18 **P. 546:** Chicago Historical Society. **P. 549:** Culver Pictures. **P. 551:** Historical Pictures/Stock Montage, Inc. **P. 555:** National Museum of American History, Smithsonian Institution Photo No. 89–5099. **P. 558:** *Harper's Weekly,* Vol. 31, 1887; pp. 158–159. Courtesy of the Newberry Library, Chicago. **P. 563:** International Museum of Photography at George Eastman House, Rochester, NY. **P. 565:** The Bettmann Archive. **P. 566:** Library of Congress. **P. 568:** The Bettmann Archive. **P. 570:** Library of Congress. **P. 573:** Historical Pictures/Stock Montage, Inc.

Chapter 19 **P. 578:** Museum of American Political Life, University of Hartford, West Hartford, CT. Photograph by Sally Andersen-Bruce. **P. 580:** Culver Pictures. **P. 582:** Brown Brothers. **P. 584:** Museum of American Political Life, University of Hartford, West Hartford, CT. Photograph by Sally Andersen-Bruce. **P. 586:** The Kansas State Historical Society, Topeka. **P. 587:** From the Collection of the Newport Historical Society, Newport, RI (P292). **P. 590:** Brown Brothers. **P. 593:** Courtesy of the New-York Historical Society, New York City. **P. 594:** Culver Pictures. **P. 600:** General Research Division, New York Public Library, Astor, Lenox, and Tilden Foundations. **P. 602:** Library of Congress.

Chapter 20 **P. 606:** W. Louis Sonntag, Jr., *The Bowery at Night,* 1895, Museum of the City of New York, Gift of Mrs. William B. Miles. **P. 610:** The Bettmann Archive. **P. 611:** Museum of the City of New York, Gift of Louis Stearns, 1889–1914. **P. 614:** Seaver Center for Western History Research, Natural History Museum of Los Angeles County. **P. 616:** New York Public Library, Astor, Lenox, and Tilden Foundations. **P. 621:** Culver Pictures. **P. 622:** Archives of Industrial Society, University Library System, University of Pittsburgh. **P. 624:** Culver Pictures. **P. 625:** Historical Pictures/Stock Montage, Inc. **P. 626:** Brown Brothers. **P. 627:** The Preservation Society of Newport County, Newport, RI. **P. 630:** Courtesy of the Cincinnati Historical Society. **P. 631:** Museum of the City of New York, Byron Collection. **P. 632:** John Singer Sargent, *Mr. and Mrs. Isaac Newton Phelps Stokes,* 1897. Oil on canvas, 84 $\frac{1}{4}$" x 39 $\frac{3}{4}$". The Metropolitan Museum of Art, New York. Bequest of Edith Minturn Phelps Stokes (Mrs. I.N.), 1938 (38.104). **P. 634:** The Metropolitan Museum of Art, New York.

Chapter 21 **P. 638:** George Wesley Bellows, *Cliff Dwellers,* 1913. Oil on canvas, 39 $\frac{1}{2}$" x 41 $\frac{1}{2}$". Los Angeles County Museum of Art, Los Angeles County Fund. **P. 642 (left):** Ida M. Tarbell Collection, Reis Library, Allegheny College, Meadville, PA. **P. 642 (right):** Culver Pic-tures. **P. 644:** State Historical Society of Wisconsin, Madison. **P. 647:** Schlesinger Library, Radcliffe College, Cambridge, MA. **P. 648:** Chicago Historical Society. **P. 649:** Brown Brothers. **P. 650:** The Bettmann Archive. **P. 651:** Brown Brothers. **P. 655:** Courtesy NAACP National Headquarters. **P. 657:** Library of Congress. **P. 658:** Edward Steichen, *J. Pierpont Morgan* (1903), Plate V from the boxed edition de Luxe of the Steichen Supplement to *Camera Work,* April 1906. Published simultaneously with No. XIV, April 1906. Gravure, 8 $\frac{1}{8}$" x 6 $\frac{1}{4}$". Collection, The Museum of Modern Art, New York. Gift of A. Conger Goodyear. **P. 659:** Library of Congress. **P. 662:** Woodrow Wilson—Democratic Nominee For President, *Harper's Weekly,* July 13, 1912. Courtesy of the Newberry Library, Chicago.

Chapter 22 **P. 668:** James G. Tyler, *Battle of Santiago de Cuba,* 1898. Courtesy of the Franklin D. Roosevelt Library, Hyde Park, NY. **P. 672:** Courtesy of the New-York Historical Society, New York City. Bella C. Landauer Collection. **P. 674:** Culver Pictures. **P. 675:** U.S. Naval Historical Center, Washington, DC. **P. 677:** Chicago Historical Society. **P. 681:** Library of Congress. **P. 683** (top): National Archives. **P. 683** (bottom): G. W. Peters, *Harper's Weekly,* April 22, 1899. Courtesy of the Newberry Library, Chicago. **P. 684:** Joseph Keppler, Jr., *His 126th Birthday—Gee, but this is an awful stretch!* From *Puck,* June 29, 1904. Courtesy of the Newberry Library, Chicago. **P. 687:** UPI/Bettmann. **P. 688:** The Pat Hathaway Collection of California Views.

Chapter 23 **P. 696:** The Lester Levy Collection of Sheet Music. Milton S. Eisenhower Library, The Johns Hopkins University, Baltimore, MD. *Oh, How I Hate to Get up in the Morning* © 1918 by Irving Berlin; © renewed 1945 by Irving Berlin; © assigned to Trustees of God Bless America Fund. **P. 699:** Imperial War Museum, London. **P. 700:** Culver Pictures. **Pp. 701 and 702:** UPI/Bettmann. **P. 703:** Library of Congress. **Pp. 706 and 708:** The Bettmann Archive. **P. 709:** UPI/Bettmann. **P. 712:** National Archives. Photograph by M. Rudolph Vetter. **P. 713:** Schlesinger Library, Radcliffe College, Cambridge, MA. **P. 714:** Library of Congress. **P. 715:** Historical Pictures/Stock Montage, Inc. **P. 717:** National Archives. Photograph by M. Rudolph Vetter **P. 720** (all): Chicago Historical Society. Photographs by Jun Fujita.

Chapter 24 **P. 726:** © Mazda, General Electric, courtesy of Baker Library, Dartmouth College, Hanover, NH. Photograph: © 1992 Jeffrey Nintzel. All rights reserved. **P. 728:** The Bettmann Archive. **P. 731:** Charles Sheeler, *Untitled (River Rouge Plant),* 1927, University Art Museum, University of New Mexico, Albuquerque. Gift of Eleanor and Van Deren Coke. **P. 734:** Culver Pictures. **P. 735:** Ruth Kravette, Jericho, NY. **P. 736:** *Portrait of Luisa Ronstadt Espinal,* c. 1921, Arizona Historical Society Library. Gift of Edward Ronstadt, Mexican Heritage Project. **P. 738:** Library of Congress. **P. 739:** Globe Photos. **P. 740:** Photofest. **P. 741:** Courtesy of Christopher Casler. **P. 742:** Kansas City Museum, Kansas City, MO. **P. 743:** George Bellows, *Dempsey and Firpo,* 1924. Oil on canvas, 51" x 63 $\frac{1}{4}$". Whitney Museum of American Art, New York. Purchased with funds from Gertrude Vanderbilt (Whitney. 31.95. Photograph by Geoffrey Clements). **P. 747:** W. A. Swift Collection, Archives and Special Collections, A. M. Bracken Library, Ball State University, Muncie, IN. **P. 749:** Aaron Douglas, *Rise, Shine for Thy Light Has Come,* c. 1930, The Howard University Gallery of Art, Permanent Collection, Washington, DC. **P. 751:** John Sloan, *The Lafayette,* 1928. Oil on canvas, 30 $\frac{1}{2}$" x 36 $\frac{1}{4}$". The Metropolitan Museum of Art, New York. Gift of Friends of John Sloan, 1928 (28.18).

Chapter 25 **P. 756:** Isaac Soyer, *Employment Agency,* 1937. Oil on canvas, 34 $\frac{1}{4}$" x 45". Whitney Museum of American Art, New York. Purchase 37.44. Photograph by Geoffrey Clements. **P. 758:** UPI/Bettmann. **P. 762:** Reginald Marsh, *The Park Bench,* 1933. Tempera on masonite. 24" x 36". Nebraska Art Association Collection, Sheldon Memorial Art Gallery, University of Nebraska, Lincoln. **P. 763:** Franklin D. Roosevelt Library, Hyde Park, NY. **P. 767:** Courtesy of William C. Kluver. **P. 768** (both): Courtesy of Steve

Schapiro. **P. 771** (left): UPI/Bettmann. **P. 771** (right): Schomburg Center for Research in Black Culture, The New York Public Library, Astor, Lenox, and Tilden Foundations. **P. 772:** The Bettmann Archive. **P. 774:** C. David Stone Martin, *Electrification.* Color sketch. Photograph courtesy of the Public Buildings Service, General Services Administration. **P. 775:** The Bettmann Archive. **P. 776:** Ben Shahn, *Years of Dust,* 1936, Library of Congress. **P. 777:** Library of Congress. **P. 778:** University of Texas, The Institute of Texan Cultures, *San Antonio Light* Collection. **P. 780 (top):** Brown Brothers. **P. 780 (bottom):** FPG International.

Chapter 26 **P. 786:** Library of Congress. **P. 788:** AP/Wide World Photos. **P. 789:** UPI/Bettmann. **P. 791:** Courtesy *Vanity Fair* © 1935 (renewed 1963) by The Condé Nast Publications, Inc. **P. 792:** UPI/Bettmann. **P. 793:** San Francisco Public Library. **P. 794:** Library of Congress. **P. 799:** Brown Brothers. **P. 801:** Franklin D. Roosevelt Library, Hyde Park, NY. **P. 802 (top):** Ben Shahn, *Steel Workers Organizing Committee* Poster, 1930s. Library of Congress. **P. 802 (bottom):** UPI/Bettmann. **P. 804:** William Gropper, *Construction of a Dam,* 1937. (Mural study, Department of the Interior), National Museum of American Art/Art Resource. **P. 807:** Joseph Binder, *World's Fair* Poster, Collection of The Queens Museum of Art, Queens, NY. Gift of Clara Binder. **P. 808:** O. Louis Guglielmi, *Relief Blues,* c. 1938, National Museum of American Art/Art Resource. **P. 810:**Anthony Velonis, WPA *Macbeth* Poster, Library of Congress.**P. 811:** Margaret Bourke-White, *Life Magazine* © 1936 Time Warner, Inc. **P. 812:** From *Champion,* November 1937. Library of Congress.

Chapter 27 **P. 816:** Library of Congress. **P. 819:** Hugo Jaeger, *Life Magazine* © Time Warner, Inc. **P. 820:** Library of Congress. **P. 822:** UPI/Bettmann. **P. 824:** Courtesy of the Dorothea Lange Collection. The City of Oakland, The Oakland Museum. 1982. **P. 825:** Library of Congress. **P. 826:** National Air and Space Museum, Smithsonian Institution, Washington, DC. **P. 828:** Ben Shahn, *For Full Employment After the War Register Vote,* 1944. Offset lithograph, printed in color, 30" x 39 $\frac{7}{8}$". Collection, The Museum of Modern Art, New York. Gift of the CIO Political Action Committee. **P. 829:** Library of Congress. **P. 830:** Lee Boltin Picture Library. **P. 832:** UPI/Bettmann. **P. 833:** Myron Davis, *Life Magazine* © Time Warner, Inc. **P. 837:** Margaret Bourke-White, *Life Magazine* © Time Warner, Inc. **P. 840:** UPI/Bettmann. **P. 841:** Margaret Bourke-White, *Life Magazine* © Time Warner, Inc. **P. 844:** Frank Scherschel, *Life Magazine* © 1942 Time Warner, Inc. **P. 845:** Franklin D. Roosevelt Library, Hyde Park, NY. (Photographed by U.S. Army Signal Corps.) **P. 846:** UPI/Bettmann.

Chapter 28 **P. 852:** Los Alamos National Laboratory. **P. 854:** FPG International. **P. 856** (left): UPI/Bettmann. **P. 856** (right): AP/Wide World Photos. **P. 858:** UPI/Bettmann. **P. 859:** Fenno Jacobs/Black Star. **P. 863:** UPI/Bettmann. **P. 864:** Wayne Miller/Magnum. **P. 865:** Western History Collections, University of Oklahoma Library, The Helen Gahagan Douglas Collection. **P. 867** (both): UPI/Bettmann. **P. 871:** Robert Phillips/Black Star. **Pp. 873, 874, and 875:** AP/World Wide Photos. **P. 877:** FPG International. **P. 879:** The Bettmann Archive.

Chapter 29 **P. 884:** © 1955 The Curtis Publishing Company. **P. 887:** Tom Wesselmann, *Still Life #24,* 1962, The Nelson-Atkins Museum of Art (Gift of the Guild of the Friends of Art), Kansas City, MO. **P. 888:** FPG International. **P. 889:** Charles Babbage Institute, University of Minnesota. **P. 891:** Ruth Kravette, Jericho, NY. **P. 892:** Photograph by Dan Weiner. Courtesy of Sarah Weiner. **P. 897:** Bern Keating/Black Star. **P. 898:** Levittown Public Library, Levittown, NY. **P. 901:** Globe Photos. **P. 903:** Photograph courtesy of Herbert Gans. Reprinted from Herbert Gans, *The Urban Villagers,* updated and expanded edition, Free Press/Macmillan (© 1962 Free Press; © 1982 Herbert J. Gans). **P. 904:** From the collections of Henry Ford Museum and Greenfield Village. Courtesy of Franchise Associates, Inc., South Weymouth, MA. **P. 905:** Photofest. **P. 907:** March of Dimes Birth Defects Foundation. **P. 908:** © 1956 BMG Music. **P. 909:** Eve Arnold/Magnum. **P. 911:** Elliott Erwitt/Magnum. **P. 912:** Joe Steinmetz, *Longboat Key, Florida,* 1958. Courtesy of the Carpenter Center for the Visual Arts, Harvard University, Cambridge, MA, and Mrs. Joe Steinmetz.

Chapter 30 **P. 916:** Robert Rauschenberg, *Kite,* 1963. Oil and silkscreen on canvas, 84" x 60". Courtesy of the Sonnabend Collection, NY. © Robert Rauschenberg/VAGA NY. **P. 918:** Hank Walker, *Life Magazine* © Time Warner, Inc. **P. 923:** UPI/Bettmann. **P. 926:** Charles Harbutt/Actuality, Inc. **P. 927:** Dewitt Collection, Museum of American Political Life, University of Hartford, West Hartford, CT. Photograph by Sally Andersen-Bruce. **P. 928:** George Tames/New York Times Pictures. **P. 930:** Michael Abramson/Gamma Liaison. **P. 933:** Robert Ellison, © 1968 *Empire News*/Black Star. **P. 934:** Larry Burrows, *Life Magazine* © Time Warner, Inc. **P. 936:** U.S. Army Photo. U.S. Department of Defense, Still Media Records Center, Washington, DC. **Pp. 938 and 939:** UPI/Bettmann. **P. 940:** AP/World Wide Photos.

Chapter 31 **P. 944:** Museum of American Political Life, University of Hartford, West Hartford, CT. Photograph by Sally Andersen-Bruce. **P. 946:** Elliott Erwitt/Magnum. **P. 947:** AP/Wide World Photos. **P. 949:** Bruce Davidson/Magnum. **P. 950:** Danny Lyon/Magnum. **P. 952:** AP/Wide World Photos. **P. 954:** Andy Warhol, *Red Race Riot,* 1963. Silkscreen ink on synthetic polymer paint on canvas. 137 $\frac{7}{8}$" x 82 $\frac{3}{4}$". The Andy Warhol Foundation for the Visual Arts. **Pp. 955 and 956:** Eve Arnold/Magnum. **P. 958:** Michael Alexander/Black Star. **P. 959:** FPG International. **P. 961:** UPI/ Bettmann. **P. 963:** Paul Fusco/Magnum. **P. 964:** Michael Abramson/Black Star. **P. 965:** © Apple Corps Ltd. **P. 966:** Paul Fusco/Magnum. **P. 971:** Steve Northup/*Time*.

Chapter 32 **P. 976:** NASA. **P. 978:** Steve Schapiro/Black Star. **P. 979:** Dennis Brack/Black Star. **P. 981:** Burt Glinn/Magnum. **P. 984:** Marc Riboud/Magnum. **P. 987:** UPI/Bettmann. **P. 988:** R. Mims/Sygma. **P. 989:** Photofest. **P. 990:** Dennis Brack/Black Star. **P. 992:** Tony Korody/Sygma. **P. 994:** Jim Anderson/Black Star. **P. 996:** © Stanley Forman. **P. 1001:** D. B. Owen/Black Star. **P. 1002:** Mingam/Gamma Liaison.

Chapter 33 **P. 1006:** R. Bossu/Sygma. **P. 1009:** Michael Evans/Sygma. **P. 1011:** Tannenbaum/Sygma. **P. 1012:** J. L. Atlan/Sygma. **P. 1014:** John Dolan, hand-coloring by Ann Rhoney. **P. 1015:** Naoki Okamoto/Black Star. **P. 1016:** Thomas Hoepker/Magnum. **P. 1017:** David Butow/Black Star. **P. 1020:** Kay Chernush/The Image Bank. **P. 1021:** © Estate of Keith Haring. **P. 1023:** W. Eastep/The Stock Market. **P. 1026:** Markel/Gamma Liaison. **P. 1028** (top): Reuters/Bettmann. **P. 1028** (bottom): East News/SIPA Press. **P. 1030:** Luc Delahaye/SIPA Press. **P. 1032** (top): S. Compoint/Sygma. **P. 1032** (bottom): Dagmar Fabricius/Gamma Liaison. **P. 1033:** Sobol/SIPA Press.

Copyright Notices

Chapter 2 **P. 51:** Reprinted by permission of the editor from *Letters from New England: The Massachusetts Bay Colony,* 1629–1638, ed. Everett H. Emerson (Amherst: University of Massachusetts Press, 1976).

Chapter 4 **P. 107:** Gottlieb Mittelberger, *Journey to Pennsylvania* (1756), ed. and trans. Oscar Handlin and John Clive (Cambridge, Mass.: Harvard University Press, 1960). Reprinted by permission of Harvard University Press.

Chapter 10 **P. 308:** Reprinted by permission of Dodd, Mead & Company, Inc. from *The Diary of Philip Hone,* 1828–1851, edited by Allan Nevins.

Chapter 11 **P. 326:** David Jackson, ed., *Black Hawk: An Autobiography.* Copyright 1955 University of Illinois. Reprinted by permission of University of Illinois Press.

Chapter 12 **P. 356:** Reprinted from *Gifts of Power: The Writings of Rebecca Jackson, Black Visionary, Shaker Eldress,* ed. Jean McMahon Humez (Amherst: University of Massachusetts Press, 1981), copyright © 1981 by The University of Massachusetts Press.

Chapter 13 **P. 388:** Hartmut Keil and John B. Jentz, *German Workers in Chicago: A Documentary History of Working-Class Culture from 1850 to World War I.* © 1988 by the Board of Trustees of the University of Illinois. Reprinted by permission of University of Illinois Press.

Chapter 15 **P. 466:** From *All for the Union* by Elisha Hunt Rhodes, edited by Robert Hunt Rhodes. Copyright © 1985 by Robert Hunt Rhodes. Reprinted by permission of Orion Books, a division of Crown Publishers, Inc. **P. 472:** Minrose C. Gwin, ed., *A Woman's Civil War: A Diary, with Reminiscences of the War from March 1862.* Reprinted by permission of the University of Wisconsin Press.

Chapter 17 **P. 528:** Reprinted from *Black Elk Speaks,* by John G. Neihardt, by permission of the University of Nebraska Press. Copyright 1932, 1959, 1972, by John G. Neihardt. Copyright © 1961 by the John G. Neihardt Trust. **P. 537:** H. Arnold Barton, ed., *Letters from the Promised Land* (Minneapolis: University of Minnesota Press, 1975). Copyright © 1975 by the University of Minnesota Press. Reprinted by permission of the University of Minnesota.

Chapter 18 **P. 571:** Sigmund Diamond, ed., *The Nation Transformed.* Copyright © 1963 by George Braziller, Inc. Reprinted by permission of George Braziller, Inc.

Chapter 19 **P. 594:** William E. Christensen, ed., "The Cross of Gold Reburnished: A Contemporary Account of the 1896 Democratic Convention," *Nebraska History* 46 (September 1965). Reprinted by permission of *Nebraska History.*

Chapter 21 **P. 653:** Joan Morrison and Charlotte Fox Zabusky, eds., *American Mosaic: The Immigrant Experience in the Words of Those Who Lived It* (New York: E. P. Dutton, 1980). Copyright © 1980, Joan Morrison and Charlotte Fox Zabusky. Currently available in a new edition published in 1992 by the University of Pittsburgh Press.

Chapter 23 **P. 705:** Frederick A. Pottle, *Stretchers: The Story of a Hospital Unit on the Western Front.* Copyright (1929) by Yale University Press. Reprinted by permission. **P. 716:** Reprinted from *Jailed for Freedom* by Doris Stevens, by permission of Liveright Publishing Corporation. Copyright 1920 by Boni & Liveright. Copyright renewed 1949 by Liveright Publishing Corporation.

Chapter 24 **P. 737:** Excerpts from *Middletown: A Study in American Culture* by Robert S. Lynd and Helen Merrell Lynd, copyright 1929 by Harcourt Brace Jovanovich, Inc. and renewed 1957 by Robert S. Lynd and Helen Merrell Lynd, reprinted by permission of the publisher.

Chapter 25 **P. 773:** Reprinted from *Dust Bowl Diary,* by Ann Marie Low, by permission of University of Nebraska Press. Copyright 1984 by the University of Nebraska Press. **P. 781:** Robert S. McElvaine, ed., *Down and Out on the Great Depression: Letters from the Forgotten Man.* Copyright © 1983 by The University of North Carolina Press. Reprinted by permission of the publisher.

Chapter 26 **P. 803:** Jeane Westin, *Making Do.* All rights reserved by Jeane Westin © 1976. Reprinted by permission. **P. 809:** Anzia Yezierska, *Red Ribbons on a White Horse.* Copyright © 1950 by Anzia Yezierska, Copyright renewed 1978 by Louise Levitas Henriksen. Reprinted by permission of Persea Books, Inc.

Chapter 27 **P. 827:** Excerpted with permission of Twayne Publishers, Inc., an imprint of Macmillan Publishing Company, from *Rosie the Riveter Revisited* by Sherna Berger Gluck. Copyright © 1987 by Sherna Berger Gluck. **P. 834:** From *The Good War: An Oral History of World War II* by Studs Terkel. Copyright © 1984 by Studs Terkel. Reprinted by permission of Pantheon Books, a division of Random House, Inc. **P. 842:** From *The Good War: An Oral History Of World War II* by Studs Terkel. Copyright © 1984 by Studs Terkel. Reprinted by permission of Pantheon Books, a division of Random House, Inc.

Chapter 28 **P. 870:** Eric Bentley, ed., *Thirty Years of Treason: Excerpts from Hearings Before the House Committee on Un-American Activities,* 1938–1968. Reprinted by permission of Eric Bently.

Chapter 29 **P. 902:** Reprinted with the permsission of Macmillan Publishing Company from *Manchild in the Promised Land* by Claude Brown. Copyright © 1965 by Claude Brown.

Chapter 31 **P. 953:** Reprinted by permission of The Putnam Publishing Group from *My Soul Is Rested* by Howell Raines. Copyright © 1977 by Howell Raines. **P. 970:** Pat Mainardi, "The Politics of Housework." From *Sisterhood Is Powerful: An Anthology of Writings from the Women's Liberation Movement,* edited by Robin Morgan. Copyright © 1970 by Robin Morgan. Reprinted with permission of Edite Kroll Literary Agency.

Chapter 32 **Pp. 998–999:** From *Voices of Freedom* by Henry Hampton and Steve Fayer. Copyright © 1990 by Blackside, Inc. Used by permission of Bantam Books, a division of Bantam Doubleday Dell Publishing Group, Inc.

Chapter 33 **P. 1027:** Laurie Ouellette, "Our Turn Now: Reflections of a 26-Year-Old Feminist." Excerpted by permission of the author from *On the Issues* (Fall 1992).

Index

Italic letters following pages refer to (*i*) illustrations, (*t*) tables, (*f*) figures, and (*m*) maps.

Abbott, Grace (1878–1939), 793
Abbott, Jacob, 633
Abbott, John, 272
Abelman v. Booth (1859), 414
Abenaki Indians, 8
  conversion to Catholicism, 37
Abernathy, Ralph (1926–1990), 948
Abilene, Texas, 520
abolitionism, 349, 363, 413
  African colonization and, 363–64
  American and Foreign Anti-Slavery Society, 368
  American Anti-Slavery Society and, 359, 365–66, 368
  Britain and, 385
  Civil War and, 461. *See also* Civil War
  Douglass and, 369, 370–71
  Emancipation Proclamation and, 464
  evangelical, 364–67
  free-soil movement and, 368–69
  Fugitive Slave Act and, 424
  Garrison and, 364–65
  growth of societies, 365–66
  hostility to, 367
  Liberty party and, 368–69
  New England Emigrant Aid Society, 429
  North and, 187–88, 261
  "slave power," 369, 428, 432
  transcendentalism and, 354
  underground railroad, 369, 383–84
  Weld and, 365
  Whig party and, 420
  Wilmot Proviso and, 420
  women involved in, 359–60
  World's Anti-Slavery Convention, 360
abortion, 632
  legalization of, 967
  rates during Great Depression, 765
  Right to Life movement and, 973, 996
  Roe v. Wade, 971, 973, 983, 1026, 1027
Abraham Lincoln Brigade, 812, 812*i*
Abrams v. United States (1919), 716
"Absurd Attempt to Make the World Over, The" (Sumner), 583
Abyssinia, 819. *See also* Ethiopia
Abzug, Bella (1920–), 971, 971*i*
Academy of Music (New York), 627
Acheson, Dean, Gooderham (1893–1971), 856, 857, 861, 862, 876
acid rain, 1032
acquired immunodeficiency syndrome. *See* AIDS
Act to Prevent Monopoly and Oppression (1777), 184
Act to Provide for the Payment of Debts, 186
Adams, Abigail (1744–1818), 187, 195*i*, 196, 273
Adams, Brooks (1848–1927), 676
Adams, Charles Francis (1807–1886), 421, 467
Adams, Charles Francis, Jr., 587
Adams, Henry (1838–1918), 634
Adams, John (1735–1826), 102*i*, 195*i*, 201, 205, 273, 320
  Boston Massacre of 1771 and, 149
  common law principle and, 142
  death of, 257
  family alliance in politics in New England colonies and, 91
  Federalist party nomination for president, 217
  foreign policy, 217–18
  Monroe Doctrine and, 253
  negotiations for peace during American Revolution, 182, 182*i*
  presidency, 217–18
  republicanism and, 194
  Thoughts on Government, 194
  vice-admiralty courts and, 138
  vice-presidential election, 207
Adams, John Quincy (1767–1848), 238, 253
  expansionist western policy, 253
  foreign policy, 253
  presidency, 1825–1829, 322–23
  presidential election of 1824, 320, 322
  presidential election of 1828, 323*i*, 324
  Rush-Bagot treaty of 1817 and, 253
  as secretary of state under Monroe, 253
  Whig party and, 341
Adams, Samuel (1722–1803)
  opposition to U.S. Constitution, 206–7
  Parliament's authority and, 150
  Shays's Rebellion and, 209
  Stamp Act crisis and, 143, 143*i*, 150
Addams, Jane (1860–1935), 648, 700, 713
adolescents. *See* youth
Adventures of Huckleberry Finn, The (Twain), 635
advertising industry, 905
  beer industry and, 890–91
  growth of, 556, 904
  1920s, 734–36, 737
  teen market, 908–9
affirmative action programs, 996, 1016
Affluent Society, The (Galbraith), 886–87
Afghanistan
  Soviet Union invasion of, 1002
  Soviet Union withdrawal from, 1012

Africa
  colonization of, 363–64
  impact of slavery on, 77–78
African-Americans. *See* blacks
Afro-American, use of term, 956
Afro hairstyle, 966
Agawam Indians, 7
aged, shelter for, 114
Agent Orange, 934, 964
age of capital, 504
Age of Exploration, 3
Age of Innocence, The (Wharton), 749
Agnew, Spiro Theodore (1918–), 981, 985, 998
  resignation as vice-president, 990
Agricultural Adjustment Act (AAA) (1933), 789–90
Agricultural Adjustment Act (1936), 795
Agricultural Adjustment Act (1938), 804
Agricultural Marketing Act (1929), 779
agricultural processing industry, 540
agricultural society, European, 3
agriculture. *See also* farmers; specific product
  advances in machinery, 227, 536, 537, 540, 894
  during American Revolution, women's role in, 184
  astrological chart and, 57
  Brook Farm, 353–54
  in California, 533, 539, 776
  cash crops, 540, 560
  Chesapeake colony, 42–43
  chinampas, 5
  commercialism of, 540
  cooperative, 10, 542, 543
  corn belt, 539
  cotton belt, 543
  dairy belt, 539
  decline, after American Revolution, 199
  dry-farming, 536
  economic problems (1870s–1880s), 542
  effect of gold supply on (1896–1909), 596
  English, 7
  European (1400s), 10–12
  exports. *See* under exports
  "fair exchange value," 729
  family farms, 540
  farm life (1850s–1900s), 540–42
  federal farm policies, 543, 894
  freehold society and, 99–102, 104. *See also* freehold society
  Great Depression and, 759, 761
  income from, 761, 894
  indigo, 126, 199
  Industrial Revolution effects on, 513, 515
  industries related to, 548
  Interstate Commerce Commission and, 542
  legislation related to, 542–43
  McCormick reaper, 386, 386*i*
  McNary-Haugen bill and, 728–29
  migrant labor in, 776–77, 778
  native American, 4, 5, 7, 7*i*, 9–10, 22, 250
  New Deal and, 805–7
  Northeast (1850s), 400
  organic farming, 966
  plantation. *See* plantation
  prices
    1896–1900, 596
    1920s, 728
  processing industry, 540
  production during World War I, 710
  rice industry, 81, 83
  rotation of crops, 227
  rural manufacturing effects on, 259–60
  Shaker, 355
  sharecropping, 502–3
  southern, 375–76, 558
    racial equality and, 598
  southwestern (1840s–1860s), 531
  Spanish missionaries and, 36
  specialization, 540
  substinence farming, 540
  subtreasury system, 590, 591
  technological developments, 227
    1820s–1830s, 300
    1850s, 398, 400
    Jefferson and, 212–13, 213–14
  tenant farmers, 46, 109–11
  tenant-farmer system, 597
  tobacco, 41, 42–43, 46
  transportation of crops (1790s), 227–28
  trends in (1935–1990), 894, 894*t*
  western expansion, 225–27, 299–300
    late nineteenth century, 536–43
  wheat belt, 539, 543
  yeomen tradition of, 156
Aguinaldo, Emilio (1869–1964), 681, 683, 683*i*
AIDS (acquired immunodeficiency syndrome), 1021–22, 1024
Aid to Families with Dependent Children (AFDC), 794, 928, 983, 1016
Aid to the Blind, 928
air traffic controllers strike, 1016
Aix-la-Chappelle, Treaty of (1748), 94
Alabama, 299
  coal and iron deposits of, 560
  secession of, 444
Alabama (claims), 505
Alaska, 661
  purchase of, 505
Albany, N.Y., 37, 39, 355
  British attack of, 172
Albemarle, George Monck, duke of (1608–1670), 70
Alcatraz Island penitentiary, seizing of, by American Indian Movement members, 960
alcohol
  antiliquor movement, 585
  Blair amendment and, 585
  customs duties and excise tax on, 580
  distilleries, 87
  Eighteenth Amendment and, 721
  ethnocultural conflict over (1876), 585
  excise tax on, 216
alcohol consumption
  among Irish immigrants, 390
  ethnocultural differences in, 585
  military policy during World War I, 708
  Prohibition and, 750–52. *See also* Prohibition
  temperance movement, 314
  Women's Christian Temperance Union and, 588
  by working class (1820s), 309
Aldrich, Nelson Wilmarth (1841–1915), 656, 659, 660
Aleutian Islands, 862
Alexis of Russia (Grand Duke), 523
Algeciras, Spain, 691
Alger, Horatio (1834–1899), 582, 582*i*, 762
Algiers, 231
Algonquin Indians, 38
  language of, 8
  northern, 8
Alien Act of 1798, 218
  expiration of, 231
Aliquippa, Penn., 608
All the President's Men (Woodward and Bernstein), 989
Allen, Ethan (1738–1789), 189
Allen, Gracie, 769
Allen, Richard (1760–1831), 248–49
Allen, Thomas, 494
Alliance for Progress, 921
Allison, Thaine, 921
almshouses, women's movement and, 358
Alsace-Lorraine, 690
Alsberg, Henry, 810
Alsop, Joseph, 936
Alta California, 416
Altgeld, John Peter (1847–1902), 574
Amalgamated Association of Iron and Steel Workers, 572
Amalgamated Copper Company, 520
amendments to the Constitution. *See* U.S. Constitution, specific amendments
Amenia, N.Y., 225
America First Committee, 820, 820*i*
America, Spain's discovery of, 19
American, The (James), 635
American and Foreign Anti-Slavery Society, 368
American Anti-Slavery Society, 365–66, 368
  convention of 1840, 359
American Automobile Association (AAA), 737
American Birth Control League, 765
American Civil Liberties Union (ACLU), 748
American Colonization Society, 363
American Commonwealth, The (Bryce), 581
American Dilemma: The Negro Problem and Modern Democracy, The (Myrdal), 833
American Education Society, 278
American Equal Rights Association, 492
American Expeditionary Force, 781
American Federation of Labor (AFL), 570–72, 652, 711, 801, 802, 804
  Bill of Grievances, 652
  Samuel Gompers and, 572

American Federation of Labor–Congress of Industrial Organizations (AFL–CIO), 892–93, 952
American Female Moral Reform Society, 358
American Foreign Legion, 708
American Geography (Morse), 241
American Home Missionary Society, 278
American Indian Movement, 960, 961, 961*i*
Americanism, 619
American Jewish Congress, 952
American Medical Association (AMA), 869, 927
American Mercury, 749
American National Exhibition of 1959, 885
American party
  Know-Nothings, 391, 428
  nomination of Fillmore, 431, 432
American Philosophical Society, 114
American Protective League, 715
American Railway Union (ARU), Pullman boycott of 1948, 573–74, 652
American Red Cross, 455, 712
American Renaissance of the 1840s and 1850s, 269
American Revolution, 165–83
  armies and strategies, 170–72
  Coercive Acts and, 152–53
  Continental Army in. *See* Continental Army
  Continental Congress and, 153, 156. *See also* Continental Congress
  events leading to, 150, 158–59, 165–69
  financial crisis during, 173, 174, 174*f*, 184, 185
  French alliance and, 175–76
  labor unions and, 338
  Loyalists' rights and, 186–87
  path to victory, 175–83
  Patriots and, 179–82
  peace talks related to, 182–83
  religion and, 188–89
  republicanism following, 183–89
  in rural communities, 156–58
  slavery issue and, 176, 187–88
  Tea Act of 1773 and, 150–53
  Treaty of Paris (1783), 183
  Valley Forge and, 174, 175
  victory at Saratoga, 172–73
  virtue v. self-interest and, 184
  war in the North, 169–70, 172*i*
  war in the South, 176–79
  women's roles in, 184
American Slavery as It Is: Testimony of a Thousand Witnesses (Weld), 365
American Smelting and Refining Company, 520
American Society for the Promotion of Temperance, 311, 314
American Sunday School Union, 278
American System, Clay's, 322
American Telephone and Telegraph Company, 731
American Tract Society, 278
American Tragedy, An (Dreiser), 749
American Union Against Militarism, 700
American Woman's Home, The (Beecher), 631
Americans for Democratic Action, 869
Ames, Fisher (1758–1808), 200
"Amos 'n' Andy," 743
amusement parks, 624, 624*i*
Anabaptists, 24, 120
Anaconda Copper Mining Company, 520, 733
Anderson, John Bayard (1922–), 1008
Anderson, Mary (1872–1964), 712
Anderson, Robert (1805–1871), 445
Anderson, Sherwood (1876–1941), 749
Andros, Sir Edmund (1637–1714), 71, 72, 73
Angelenos, 531
Angelou, Maya (1928–), 770
Anglican Church. *See* Church of England
Anglo-American Oil Company, 672
Anglo-Dutch wars, 38
Anglo-French entente (1904), 691
Anglo-Japanese Alliance (1902), 688
Anheuser-Busch, 890
Animal Crackers (1930), 767
Annapolis, Md., commercial convention of 1786 in, 201
Anniston, Ala., 948
Anson County, N.C., 129
Anthony, Susan Brownell (1820–1906), 361–62, 491, 492, 588
antiballistic missile systems (ABMs), 984
antibiotics, introduction of, 907
Antietam, battle of (1862), 459–60, 460*i*, 462, 466
Antifederalists, 204–5
  election of 1788 and, 207
Anti-inflation Act of 1942, 823
antinomianism, 54
Anti-Saloon League, 652, 721
anti-Semitism, 746, 841
Anti-Slavery Conventions of American Women, 366
antislavery. *See* abolitionism
antiwar movements, during Vietnam War, 939–40, 963–64, 977
Apache Indians, 516, 524, 525
Appalachian Regional Development Act, 929
Appeal . . . to the Colored Citizens (Walker), 364
Apple Computer Company, 1023
Appleton, Nathan, 291
appliances. *See* electric appliances
Appomattox Courthouse, Lee's surrender at, 475–76
Arabs
  civilization of, 14, 16
  as leaders in world trade, 3
  slave trade, 18
Arapaho Indians, 525
Arawak Indians, 20
Arbella (ship), 52
Architecture of Country Houses (Downing), 392
architecture, Spanish, in California, 534
Argus (newspaper), 320
aristocracy
  Chesapeake, 85–6
  English, price revolution and, 27
  European, 279
  Federalists and, 265
  legal profession and, 266
Arkansas, 403
  freedom of slaves, 464
Arkansas National Guard, 947
Arkwright, Sir Richard (1732–1792), 289, 290
Arlington, Va., 887
armed forces. *See also* army; draft; military; navy
  desegregation by Truman, 864
  Eisenhower's sending to Little Rock, 947
  expansion of (1880s), 670
  Reserve Officer Training Corp (ROTC), 964
  segregation in, during World War II, 832
  veterans pensions, 589
  volunteer, 935
  women in
    during Persian Gulf War, 1030, 1031
    during Vietnam War, 938
  world presence (1975), 994*m*
  during World War II, 844–45
Arminius, Jacob (1560–1609), 53
Armour, J. Ogden, 558
Armour, Philip Danforth (1832–1901), 558
Armour & Company, 555, 557*f*, 566
arms-for-hostages initiative, 1012
arms race
  escalation during Eisenhower administration, 877
  Kennedy and, 920
  MAD (Mutual Assured Destruction), 877
  Strategic Arms Limitations Talks and, 984, 1000, 1001–2
arms trade, Neutrality Act and, 818
Armstrong, (Daniel) Louis (1900–1971), 742
army. *See also* draft, military; Continental Army; Union Army
  Army-McCarthy Hearings, 871*i*, 872
  British
    deployments, 1763–1775, 147
    lodging for, Quartering Act of 1765 and, 139, 146, 156, 157*t*
  intelligence testing by, during World War I, 708–9
  military morality during World War I, 708
Army Air Force, 824
Arnaz, Desi, 905
Arnold, Benedict (1741–1801), 178, 180–81
art. *See also* literature; theater
  documentary impulse, 810
  Federal Art Project, 808, 809
  landscape, 402
  modernist movement, 748–49
  native American, 4, 5, 8, 9
  New Deal and, 808–10
  "prints for the people," 393
Art Institute (Chicago), 633
Art Students League (New York), 634
Arthur, Chester Alan (1830–1886), 579, 670

Articles of Confederation, 197–99, 201
  ratification of, 198
  revision of, 201
  U.S. Constitution and, 204
  Virginia Plan compared to, 202
artisans
  Committee on Prices, 184
  expansion of market, 258
  hostility toward Britain, 167
  labor unions and, 334
  in seaport cities (1700s), 89
Ashley, William (Billy), 624
Asia
  American policy toward (1940s–1970s), 866
  exports to (1875–1900), 673, 673*t*
Asian-Americans, 900
  immigration (1980s–1990s), 1018, 1019–1020
  migration to California (1840s–1870s), 531–32
Assemblies of God, 1024
assembly line, 736
assembly, rise of (1700s), 90–92
associationalism, 729
assumption plan, 209
Astor, John Jacob (1763–1848), 258
asylums, women's movement and, 358
Atchison, David Rice (1807–1886), 429
Atkinson, Edward, 582
Atlanta *Constitution,* 558
Atlanta, Ga., Sherman's capture of, 473–74
Atlantic Charter (1941), 838
Atlantic Monthly (magazine), 635, 642
Atlantic seaports, 298
atomic bomb
  dropping on Japan, 846
  Manhattan Project, 847
  radiation poisoning from, 846
  testing of, 877*i*, 878
atomic energy
  American monopoly on, 861
  international control of, 855
Audubon Ballroom, 956
Augsburg, Peace of (1555), 24
Augustine, Saint (354–430), 36
Auschwitz, 840
Austria, union with Germany, 820
Austria-Hungary, 698, 704
  declaration of war on Serbia (1914), 698
  Triple Alliance and, 691
Autobiography (Franklin), 310, 351
automation, impact on labor unions, 893
automobile industry, 596, 728
  assembly lines, 728*i*, 736
  buying on installment plan, 735
  effect of energy crisis of mid-1970s on, 992
  Great Depression effect on, 764
  growth of (1920s), 736–38
  guaranteed annual wage in, 893
  organized labor in, 802, 802*i*, 803
  during World War II, 831
Azores islands, 18
Aztecs, 5, 6*i*
  fall of, sixteenth century, 20–22
Babbitt (Lewis), 749
Babcock, Orville E., 505, 506
Baby and Child Care (Spock), 907
baby boom, 765, 830, 903, 906–7
  scientific child rearing, 907, 907*i*
baby boomers, 962, 996
Backus, Isaac (1724–1806), 119
Bacon, Nathaniel (1647–1676), rebellion, 47–48, 79
Bad Axe Massacre, 325–26
Bagley, Sarah G., 387
Bahamas, 19
Bailey, Dorothy, 870
Baird v. Eisenstadt (1972), 971
Baja California, Walker's attempt at annexation, 427
Baker v. Carr (1962), 925
Baker, Ella (1903–1986), 948, 950–52, 969
Baker, James, 1009
Baker, Ray Stannard (1870–1946), 714
Baker, Russell, 780
Bakke v. University of California (1978), 996
Bakker, Jim (1939–) and Tammy, 1024
Balboa, Vasco Núñez de (c. 1475–1519), 20
Balkans, World War I and, 697
Ball, George Wildman (1909–), 933
Ball, Lucille (1911–1989), 905
Ballinger, Richard Achilles (1858–1922), 661
ballistic missles (Pershing II), 1001
balloon frame house, 391–92
Baltimore and Ohio system, strikes against, 547
Baltimore, Benedict Calvert, Lord (1679–1715), 73
Baltimore, Cecilius Calvert, Lord (1605–1675), 42, 72
Baltimore, Charles Calvert, Lord (1637–1715), 72
Baltimore, Maryland, 298, 378, 618
  as major seaport (1700s), 88
Bancroft, George (1800–1891), 340
Bank of England, 72
  Panic of 1837 and, 342
Bank of the United States, 231
  charter of, 258
  Hamiltonian Program and, 210–11
  Second, 261, 263, 328–30
Banking Act of 1935, 791
banks, banking
  assets in 1920s, 731
  Banking Act of 1935, 791
  bank notes, 592
    lending of, 328
  Democratic party and, 344
  emergence of, 258
  Emergency Banking Act of 1933, 788–89
  failures (1930), 759
  Federal Deposit Insurance Corporation, 789
  Federal Reserve Act of 1913 and, 665
  Glass-Steagall Act, 789
  Great Depression and, 761
  land, 95, 111
  mergers in 1920s, 731
  National Banking Act of 1863 and 1864, 452
  oligopolies, 890–91
  pet banks, 330
  savings and loan crisis, 1025
  support for U.S. foreign investments, 733
Banks, Nathaniel Prentiss (1816–1894), 459, 482
Bannister, Thomas, 87
Baptists, Baptist Church, 23, 24, 121, 188
  attempts at suppression, 189
  baptism, 121
  childrearing practices, 272
  growth of, early nineteenth century, 276
  National Baptist Convention, 496
  republicanism and, 276
  revivals, 120–21
  Second Great Awakening and, 277
  separation of church and state and, 189
  slaves, 120–21, 250
Barbados, 76
Barbary States of North Africa, 231
barbed wire, 536
Barlow, Joel (1754–1812), 268
Barnum, Phineas Taylor (1810–1891), 626
Barron v. Baltimore (1833), 208
Barry, Leonora M., 570
barter prices, 11
Barton, Bruce, 731
Barton, Clara (1821–1912), 455
Baruch, Bernard Mannes (1870–1965), 711
baseball, 625, 625*i*, 743
  big-league cities, 896
Bataan peninsula, "Bataan Death March," 842
Bates, Ruby, 770
bathtub gin, 750
Battle of the Bulge (1944), 840
Battle of San Pietro, The, 830
Battle of the Thames (1813), 238, 344
Bayard, James Asheton (1767–1815), 219
Bayard, Nicholas, 73
Bayard, Thomas Francis (1828–1898), 670
Bay of Pigs, 922–23
beans, native American planting of, 7
Bear Flag Republic, 417
Beard, Charles Austin (1874–1948), 201
Beard, Ithamar, 310
Beat Generation, 965
Beatles, 965, 966
Beaulieu, Sarah (1843–1921), 456
Beauregard, Pierre Gustave Toutant (1818–1893), 445
  first Battle of Bull Run and, 455, 457
Becker, Carl Lotus (1873–1945), 193
Beckley, John, 235
Beecher, Catharine Esther (1800–1878), 395, 396, 631
Beecher, Harriet. *See* Stowe, Harriet Beecher
Beecher, Henry Ward (1813–1887), 343, 396, 622, 634
Beecher, Lyman (1775–1863), 279, 396, 311
beer industry, 890–91
Begin, Menachim (1913–1992), 1001, 1001*i*
Beijing (Peking), 687, 836

Belgium, 25
Belknap, Jeremy (1744–1798), 194
Bell, Alexander Graham (1847–1922), 612
Bell, Rex, 741
Bellamy, Edward (1850–1898), 641
Belleau Woods, battle of (1918), 705
Bell Laboratories, 731
Bellow, Saul (1915–), 810
Bellows, George Wesley (1882–1925), 638*i*, 743*i*
Beneš, Eduard (1884–1948), 859
Benevolent Empire, business class and, 311
Benezet, Anthony, 187
Ben-Gurion, David (1886–1973), 879*i*
Bennington, battle of (1777), 173
Benny, Jack (1894–1975), 769, 905
Benson, Ezra Taft (1899–), 894
Bentsen, Lloyd Millard, Jr. (1921–), 1024
Bergen, Edgar, 769
Berger, Victor Louis (1860–1929), 652, 716
Bering Strait, 4
Berkeley, Busby (1895–1976), 767
Berkeley, George (1685–1753), 68, 90
Berkeley, Sir William (1606–1677), 47, 48, 68
  Green Spring faction, 47
Berle, Adolph Augustus, Jr. (1895–1971), 788
Berle, Milton (1908–), 905
Berlin, compared to Chicago, early twentieth century, 614–15
Berlin decree, 234
Berlin, Irving (1888–1989), 696*i*
Berlin airlift, 859, 859*i*
Berlin Conference of 1884, 673
Berlin Wall
  destruction of, 1006*i*, 1026
  Kennedy and, 923, 923*i*
Bernard, Sir Francis (1712–1779), 138, 148
Bernard, Thomas, 273
Bernays, Edward, 736
Bernstein, Carl, 987, 988–89
Bernstein, Leonard (1918–1990), 901*i*
Bessemer, Sir Henry (1813–1898), 548
Bessemer converters, 548, 549
Bessemer steel furnace, 551*i*
Bethune, Joanna, 311
Bethune, Mary McLeod (1875–1955), 800
bettering house, 114
Beyond the Rainbow, 741
Bible, 23
bicameral legislature, 194, 205
Biddle, Nicholas (1786–1844), 328, 329, 329*i*
  recession of 1834 and, 330
Big Foot, 527, 528
Bilek, Anton, 842
Bill of Rights, 208
Billy the Kid (Copland), 809
Bingham, Caleb (1757–1817), 266
Bird, Caroline, 761, 763
Birmingham, Ala., Baptist church bombing in, 952
Birney, James Gillespie (1792–1857), 368, 434
  presidential campaign, 415
birth control, 271, 967
  business class and (1840s–1850s), 395, 398
  during Great Depression, 765
Birth of a Nation, The, 739, 746, 654
birthrate
  baby boom, 765, 830, 903, 906*f*, 906–7. *See also* baby boom
  decline in, early nineteenth century, 271
  demographic transition, 271
  during Great Depression, 765
  during World War II, 830
  during colonial period, 103, 104
  European peasantry (1400s), 11*f*
  late nineteenth century, 398*f*, 554, 633
Bishop Hill, Ill., communal living in, 354*i*
Black, Hugo Lafayette (1886–1971), 795
Black Ball Line, 299, 306
"black cabinet," 800
Black Codes, 488
  Reconstruction and, 502
Black Elk, 527, 528
Blackfoot tribe, 517
Black Hawk (Chief) (1767–1838), 325, 326, 327*i*
Black Hawk War, 325, 434
Black Hills, gold mining in, 526
black market, 831
Black Monday, 791
Blackmun, Harry Andrew (1908–), 983
Black Muslims, 956
Black Panthers, 956
black power movement, 963, 956–57
  white women in civil rights movement and, 969
Black Tuesday, 758
blacks. *See also* civil rights movement; slaves
  abolitionists, 369
  African colonization and, 363–64
  in American Revolution, 166, 176*t*
  in armed forces
    during Spanish-American War, 680
    during World War II, 825
  attitudes toward, early 1800s, 363
  "black rule," 599
  in Chesapeake colonies, status of, 78, 79
  civil rights of freedmen, 488
  in Civil War, 465
  Colored Farmers' Alliance, 598
  contracts between freedmen and planters, 502–3
  creation of African-American community, 81, 83–84
  debt peonage of former slaves, 503
  discrimination against, 519, 562, 770–71. *See also* racism
  drive for racial equality, 513. *See also* civil rights movement
  education of former slaves, 485, 485*i*, 496
  employment
    1870s–1890s, 562
    during World War I, 712, 832
    in tobacco industry, 560
  Ethiopian Regiment, 166
  Exodusters, 538, 538*i*
  Fifteenth Amendment and, 491
  first vote, 493*i*
  Fourteenth Amendment and, 489
  Great Depression's effects on, 770, 772
  Harlem population (1920s), 771–72
  Harlem Renaissance and, 749–50
  homicide rates for men, 1017
  in inner cities (1980s), 1017
  intimidation of voters during Reconstruction Era, 498
  jazz musicians, 742
  land ownership by former slaves, 499, 503
  Lodge Election bill and, 581
  lynching of, 719, 771, 771*i*
  manhood suffrage, 491
  married women, in labor force (1870s–1900s), 564
  migration
    to cities (1880–1913), 617
    to North, 654, 901
    to South (1980s), 1017
  New Deal and, 772, 800–801, 807
  newspapers, 364
  New York City population (1920s), 771–72
  participation in American Revolution, 187–88
  political leadership (1860s), 494–95
  population (1820s), 223
  Protestantism, 120–21, 277
  resettlement of freedmen, 485–87
  Scottsboro case and, 770–71
  Sea Island, 487
  segregation of. *See* segregation
  separatism, 956
  as servants in Chesapeake colonies, 40
  sharecropping, 502–3
  social institutions during Reconstruction Era, 496
  as soldiers in Union Army, 468
  southern population (1860s), 378*f*
  southern, resistance of suppression (1898–1900), 599–602
  status of, 79
  teenage mothers, 1017
  TV roles (1950s), 905
  Universal Negro Improvement Association, 750
  in urban politics, 618
  use of term, 956
  violence toward after World War I, 719–20
  voter registration drives, 953, 954
  voters, 581
    southern, protection of, 581
  voting rights, 320, 483
    in South (1897–1900), 598
    during World War II, 833
  Voting Rights Act of 1965 and, 927
  wage labor of former slaves, 487–88
  Washington, Booker T. and, 602–3
  women, 363
    abolitionist movement and, 366
    in politics, 1035
    as role models, 969

(blacks con't)
World War II effects on, 832–33
Blaine, James Gillespie (1830–1893), 581, 585, 586, 587
interventions in Latin America, 670–71
Blair, Exell, Jr., 948
Blair, Francis Preston (1821–1875), 325
Blair, Henry W., 585
Blair Education bill of 1880, 581
Blake, F. A., 682
Bland, Richard, 138
Bland-Allison Act of 1878, 592
blast furnaces, 550, 551
Bleeding Kansas, 413, 429–31
Blithedale Romance, The (Hawthorne), 353
Blitzstein, Mark, 810
blood banks, segregation of, 825
Bloody Lane, 459
blue laws, 585
Blue Ridge Highway, 806
Bluestone, Barry, 995
Board of Aldermen, 73
Board of Trade, 75, 95
appointment of judges and, 142
Boeing Corporation, military contracts to, 887
Boesky, Ivan, 1015, 1022
Bohlen, Charles Eustis (1904–1974), 856, 857
Boland amendment, 1011, 1012
Bolshevism, 704, 722
American hostility toward, 855
Bond, Julian, 951
bonds
Civil War, 452, 504, 507
Confederate, 453
junk, 1014
Bonfire of the Vanities, The (Wolfe), 1022
Bonsack, James A., 560
Bonus Army, 780*i*, 781
Bonus Bill (1817), 261, 322
Bonus Expeditionary Force, 781
bookbinders, journeymen, 338
Book of Mormon (Smith), 404
Boomer movement, 526
Boone, Pat, 996
Booth, John Wilkes (1838–1865), 483
Booth, Maud Ballington, 623
Booth, Nathaniel, 280
bootlegging, 751
Borah, William Edgar (1865–1940), 719, 818
Bork, Robert Heron (1927–), 1013
Bosnia and Herzegovina, 697, 1029*m*
Boston, 87, 298, 615
antibusing demonstrations (1975), 996, 997–98, 999
corporate headquarters in, 896
slaves and indentured servants in, 89
streetcar suburbs, 630
urban elite living in, 627
Boston Female Anti-Slavery Society, 366
Boston Guardian, 655
Boston Herald American, 996*i*
Boston Manufacturing Company, 297
Boston Massacre of 1770, 149
Boston Museum of Fine Arts, 633
Boston Tea Party, 151–53, 154*i*
Boston Transcript, 338
Boucher, Jonathan, 157
Bourne, Randolph Silliman (1886–1918), 714
Bow, Clara (1905–1965), 739, 740–41
Bowdoin, James, 149, 200
Bowie, James (c. 1796–1836), 333
Boxer Rebellion (1900), 687
boxing, 743, 743*i*
Boy Spies of America, 715
Boyce, Ed, 575
Boylston, Zabdiel (1679–1766), 113
bracero program, 777, 835, 900
Brackenridge, Hugh Henry (1748–1816), 215
Braddock, Edward (1695–1755), 123
Braden, Anne, 969
Bradford, William (1590–1657), 31
Bradley, Omar Nelson (1893–1981), 863
Bragg, Braxton (1817–1876), 464
Brahmin families, 627
Brandeis, Louis Dembitz (1856–1941)
Abrams v. United States (1919), 716
Muller v. Oregon (1908), 645, 663
Sherman Antitrust Act (1914) and, 663, 664
as Wilson's adviser, 663
Brando, Marlon, 909
Brandywine Creek, 172
Braun, Carol Mosely, 1034
Braxton, Carter (1736–1797), 198
Brazil, abolition of slavery, 385
Bread Givers (Yezierska), 809
breadline, 763*i*
breaker boys, 566*i*
Breckinridge, John Cabell (1821–1875), 438
Breed's Hill, British attack of, 165
Breen, Joseph, 767
Brennan, William Joseph, Jr. (1906–), 1025
Brent, Margaret (1600?–1671?), 44–45
Brest-Litovsk, Treaty of (1918), 704
Bretton Woods, N.H., U.N. conference in, 886, 995
bridges, construction of, late nineteenth century, 611
Brief Account of the Province of Pennsylvania (Penn), 69
Bright Lights, Big City (McInerney), 1024
Bright Shining Lie, A (Halberstam), 936
Brisbane, Arthur (1864–1936), 355
British Guiana, border dispute with Venezuela, 675–76
Broderick, David Colbreth (1820–1859), 408, 409
Brook Farm, 353–54*i*
Brooklyn Bridge, 611
Brooklyn, N.Y., 298*i*
Brooklyn Eagle (newspaper), 351
Brooks, Phillips (1835–1893), 622
Brotherhood of Sleeping Car Porters, 832
Brotherhood of Locomotive Firemen, 574
Brown, Charles Brockden (1771–1810), 268
Brown, Claude (1937–), 902
Brown, Dee, 961
Brown, John (1800–1859), 369, 412*i*, 413, 429, 430
raid at Harper's Ferry, 437, 439
Brown, Joseph Emerson (1821–1894), 451, 452
Brown, Mary, 518*i*
Brown, Moses (1738–1836), 289
Brown Berets, 959
Brown v. Board of Education of Topeka (1954), 874, 925, 946, 947, 955, 996
Bruce, Blanche Kelso (1841–1898), 495
Bruce, William, 745
Brulé Sioux tribe, 517
Brunelleschi, Filippo (1377–1446), 17
Brush, Charles F., 612
Bryan, Charles W., 730
Bryan, William Jennings (1860–1925), 683, 730, 752
cross of gold speech, 593
efforts for world peace, 691
free silver and, 593, 594–96
presidential campaigns, 660
presidential election of 1896, 593, 594
resignation as secretary of state, 701
as secretary of state under Wilson, 691
Scopes trial and, 748
Bryce, James Viscount (1838–1922), 581, 587, 671
Buchanan, James (1791–1868), 406, 414*t*, 425, 436
Dred Scott decision and, 432–33
Lecompton constitution and, 433
presidential election of 1856, 431–32
secession crisis and, 444–45
as secretary of state under Polk, 416, 420
Buchenwald, 840
"Buckskin" nickname for Virginians, 240
budget deficit, 1025
of 1980s, 1010, 1013*f*, 1013–14, 1014*i*
Buena Vista, battle of (1847), 418, 420
buffalo, 517
extermination of, 520
Buffalo Bill. *See* Cody, William Frederick
Buffalo Bill, the King of the Border Men (Buntline), 523
buffalo grass, land of. *See* Great Plains
"Buffalo soldiers," 525
Buffalo, N.Y., 297, 298*i*
Buford (ship), 722
building trade. *See also* construction workers
labor unions and, 334–35
Working Men's party, 335
Bulgaria, 698, 1026
Bulkley, William Lewis, 655
Bull, John, 241
Bull Run, battles of,
first (1861), 455, 457, 466
second (1862), 459
Bunau-Varilla, Philippe Jean (1859–1940), 685
Bundy, McGeorge, 856, 933
Bunker, Elsworth, 984
Bunker Hill, British attack on, 164*i*, 165
Buntline, Ned (Edward Zane Carroll Judson, 1823–1886), 523
bureaucracy, federal, 580

(bureaucracy, federal con't)
New Deal and, 796–97
during World War II, 823
Bureau of Agricultural Economics, 729
Bureau of Corporations, 658
Burger, Warren Earl (1907–), 983
Burgess, John W., 654
Burgoyne, John (1722–1792), 172, 173
Burke, Edmund (1729–1797), 93
Burkitt, Frank, 598
Burlingame Treaty (1868), 533
Burlington Railroad, 553
Burma, 841
Burns, George (1896–), 769
Burnside, Ambrose Everett (1824–81), 460
Burr, Aaron (1756–1836), 218
killing of Hamilton, 234
trial for treason, 234
Burrell & Burrell merchant house, 209
Bury My Heart at Wounded Knee (Brown), 961
Bush, George Herbert Walker (1924–)
economic agendas, 1025
Persian Gulf War and, 1024, 1030–31
presidential election of 1988, 1024–25
presidential election of 1992, 1033
savings and loan crisis and, 1025
Supreme Court and, 1025–26
Bush, Gerald, 1008
Bushwackers, 446
business. *See also* corporations
activity, from 1865–1900, *553f*
dollar-a-year men executives, 828
entrepreneurs, 258. *See also* entrepreneurs
immigrant-owned, 1020
machine politics in cities and, 618
mail-order houses, 555
mass markets and large-scale enterprises, 553–56
1980s–1990s, 1022
overseas production and marketing facilities (1880s), 672
partnership with government (1920s), 727–34
trusts, 657–59
vertically integrated firms, 555, 557
watered stocks and bonds, 657
business class, 309, 628. *See also* middle class
abolitionism and, 367
"Benevolent Empire" and, 311
education (1840s–1850s), 395
evangelism, 359
family planning and population growth (1840s–1860s), 395, 398
ideology of (1820s–1830s), 310
Industrial Revolution and, 385
origins of, 309
reformers, 349
revivalism and reform, 311–15
Bute, John Stuart, earl of (1713–1792), 135, 136, *144t*
Butler, Andrew P., 431
Butler, Benjamin Franklin (1818–1893), 482
Butler, Edward R., 643
Butler, Pierce, 203
Butte, Mont., copper mining in, 520
Butterfield, Alexander, 990
Byrnes, James Francis (1879–1972), 796, 824

Cabot, John (1450–1498), 28
Cahan, Abraham (1860–1951), 619
Cahill, Holger, 809
Cairo, 845
Calhoun, John Caldwell (1782–1850), 236, 261, *331i*, 415
abolitionism and, 367
annexation of Texas and, 414
common property doctrine, 421
Compromise of 1850 and, 422
death of, 423
joins Democratic party, 414
presidential election of 1824, 320, 322, 323, 324
presidential election of 1828, 323, 324
slavery and, 385
South Carolina's Ordinance of Nullification and, 331–32
view on states' rights argument, 331–32
Whig party and, 341
Wilmot Proviso and, 420
California, *514i*
admission as free state, 408, 422, 423
agriculture of, 533, 539, 776
application for statehood, 422
Bear Flag Republic, 417
Chinese in (1840s–1870s), 531–32
climate of, 534–35
coastal settlements, 406–7
culture of (1860s), 534
expansion into (1840s–1860s), 406–9
forty-niners, *408i*, 408–9, 534
Frémont expedition, 416
gold rush, 518–20
grape pickers joining of United Farm Workers Union, 959–60
Mexican population in (1860s–1890s), 531
Mexican War and, 417
migrant labor during Great Depression, 776–77, 778
migration to, during World War II, 831
movie industry in, 739
national parks, 535
Proposition 13, 1008
railroad expansion to, 518
Sacramento Valley, 407–8
settlement of (1840s–1860s), 529–35
society of (1850s), 408
Spanish settlement of, 406
Spanish-speaking culture in, 531
woman suffrage, 649
California Packing Corporation, 778
Californios, 407, 408, 531
Calley, William L., 985
Calvert, Benedict. *See* Baltimore, Benedict Calvert, Lord
Calvert, Cecilius. *See* Baltimore, Cecilius Calvert, Lord
Calvert, Leonard (1605–1675), 42
Calvin, John (1509–1564), 52
teaching of, 25
Calvinism, Calvinists, 25, 31, 278
Halfway Covenant and, 56
French, 108
Cambodia, 933, 986
immigrants from, 1019
U.S. bombing of, 985, 986
U.S. invasion of, 964
Cambridge Platform of 1648, 55
Camden, battle of (1780), 177
Canaan, 538
Canada, 505
American invasion of (1775), 169
British conquests in, 124
Dominion of, 505
exports to (1875–1900), *673t*
Loyalist migration to, 186
U.S. invasion of (1812), 237–38
canals, 228. *See also* specific canals
construction of, 301–3
freight rates, (1784–1900), *303f*
Canary Islands, 19
Canby, Henry Seidel (1878–1961), 631
Cane, (Toomer), 750
Cannon, Joseph Gurney (1836–1926), 660
Cape Kennedy, 928
capital goods, manufacture of, 548
capitalism
corporate, 731
industrial. *See* industrial capitalism
welfare, 732
capitalist(s)
agricultural, 109
feuds with laborers, 338, 340
capitalist individualism, 279–80
capitalist society
banking and credit, 258
market economy, 259–60, 276
merchants, 257–58
rural manufacturing, 258–59
state mercantilism, 261
Capitol Hill, 589
Capone, Alphonse (1899–1947), 751
Capra, Frank (1897–1991), 830
Carey, Mathew (1760–1839), 307
Caribbean Islands, 19
American expansionist ambitions in, 505, 670, 685–87, *689i*
European interference in, 686–87
Theodore Roosevelt's Corollary and, 687
Carib Indians, 20
Carlisle, Frederick Howard, earl of (1748–1825), 176
Carmichael, Stokely (1941–), 956, 969
Carnegie, Andrew (1835–1919), 548, 549, 556, 572, 582, 700
building of libraries by, 633
gospel of wealth and, 583
Carolina colonies, *69t*. *See also* North Carolina (colony); South Carolina (colony)
Charles II's grant of, 68
Cornwallis's relinquishment of, 182
demands for independence, 166
Fundamental Constitutions (1669), 68

(Carolina colonies con't)
proprietorship, 68, 75
Caroline County, Va., 121
carpetbaggers, 493, 494
Carranza, Venustiano (1859–1920), 690, 702
Carroll, Charles (1737–1832), 200
Carson, Johnny, 1003
Carson, Rachel Louise (1907–1964), 993
Carswell, G. Harrold, 983
Carter, Jimmy (James Earl, Jr., 1924–), 996, 1000, 1008, 1009
domestic leadership, 1000–1
foreign policy, 1001–2
Iranian hostage crisis and, 1002–3
Carter, John, 294
Carter, Rosalynn, 1000
Carteret, Sir George (c. 1610–1680), 68
Cartier, Jacques (1491–1557), 36
Casablanca, meeting of Roosevelt and Churchill in, 845
Casey, William, 1011, 1012
Cash, Johnny, 996
cash crop, 540, 560
Cass, Lewis (1782–1866), 421, 425
concept of popular sovereignty, 421, 422
caste system, 533
southern, 488
Castro, Fidel (1927–), 876, 900, 922*i*, 922
Catcher in the Rye (Salinger), 962
Cather, Willa (1873–1947), 748
Catherine of Aragon (1485–1536), 29
Catholic Church, Catholics, 13, 15
aid to parochial schools and, 869, 925, 927
anti-Catholicism (1840s–1850s), 389–91, 428
conversion of native Americans to, 36
Democratic party and, 585
Elementary and Secondary Education Act of 1965 and, 927
English, settlement in America and, 31
European (1600s), 24*i*
hierarchy of, 13–14
immigrants living in cities (1890s–1900s), 619, 622
Irish identity with (1840s–1850s), 389
New Spain colonization and, 36
pope, 13–14
priests, 14
Protestant Reformation and, 23–25
Quebec Act and, 153
republicanism and, 276
Smith's presidential campaign and, 752, 753
transsubstantiation, 14
Catholic Legion of Decency, 768
Cato's Letters (Gordon), 143
Catskill Mountains, 613
Catt, Carrie Chapman Lane (1859–1947), 712, 798
cattle industry
California, 530, 531*i*
cowboys, 521*i*
of Great Plains, 520–21
ranching, 521
Texas longhorns, 520–21
vaqueros, 531*i*
cavaliers, 378–79
cavalry forces, 504
Cavanaugh, Jerome, 958
Cayuga Indians, 223
"Celebrated Jumping Frog of Calaveras County, The" (Twain), 534
Census of Manufacturing of 1820, 260
Census, U.S.
of 1880, 895
of 1910, 630
of 1920, 744
of 1980, 1018
of 1990, 1018
Central America
canal project, Hay-Pauncefote Agreement and, 685
native Americans in, 3
Reagan and, 1010–11
Central Intelligence Agency (CIA), 986, 1002
under Eisenhower, 876
Central Pacific Railroad, 454, 518, 532, 533
Central Park (New York), 613
Century of Dishonor, A (Jackson), 527
Cermak, Anton J., 781
Ceuta, battle of (1415), 18
Chambers, Whittaker (1901–1961), 871
Champlain, Samuel de (1567–1635), 36
Chaney, James, 954
Channing, William Ellery (1780–1842), 278
Chaplin, Charlie (1889–1977), 739, 739*i*
Chapman, Maria Weston (1806–1885), 366
Charity Organization Society, 619
Charles I (1600–1649), 42, 50
dissolution of Parliament, 50
execution of, 56
Charles II (1630–1685), 55, 67–68, 128
Navigation Act of 1651 and, 70
new mercantilism, 69–70
Charles V (1500–1558), 23, 29
Charles, Robert, 599, 600–1
Charles River Park, 902
Charleston, S.C., 87, 378
British control of, 177, 178
as major seaport (1700s), 88
slave revolt in, 384
Charlotte-Mecklenberg, N.C., 996
Chase, Salmon Portland (1808–1873), 423, 423*i*, 438, 462, 491
Chase, Samuel (1741–1811), 231
Chastelleux, marquis de, 272
Château-Thierry, battle of (1918), 705, 708
Chattanooga, battle of (1863), 464
chattel slavery, 78, 379
Chauncy, Charles (1705–1787), 115
Chautauqua movement, 633–35
Chavez, Cesar Estrada (1927–1993), 777–78, 941*i*, 959–60
Cheever, John (1912–1982), 810
chemical warfare
Agent Orange, 934, 964
mustard gas, in World War I, 705
napalm, 939
nerve gas wastes, 993
in Vietnam War, 934
Chernobyl nuclear accident, 1032
Cherokee Indians, 326
attack on Patriot forces, 178
Cherokee Nation v. Georgia (1831), 327
cultural assimilation of, 251–52
divisions among, 251, 251*i*
Georgia's ceding of territory, 327
John Marshall and, 327
mixed-bloods, 251
national council, 251
patrilineal inheritance system, 251
Trail of Tears, 327
war with whites, 129
Cherokee Strip, 526
Chesapeake (ship), 234
Chesapeake colonies, 39
aristocracy, 85–86
Bacon's rebellion and, 48
emancipation of slaves in, 188
English invasion of, 39–43
founding of Maryland, 42
indentured servitude in, 43–46
Indian uprising of 1622 and, 41–42
life expectancy in, 49*i*
planter-merchants in, 47
political system, 91
royal government in, 42
slavery in, 48, 81–82, 83, 84
social order, 85–86
tenant farming in, 46
tobacco industry in, 42–43, 46–47
Chesnut, Mary Boykin (1823–1886), 380, 474
Chester County, Pa., 109, 110
Quakers in, 111
Cheyenne Indians, 525, 526
Chiang Kai-shek. *See* Jiang, Jieshi
Chicago, 297, 608
alderman, 618
black population (1880–1913), 617
compared to Berlin, early twentieth century, 614–15
Democratic convention of 1968 held in, 978–81
expansion of, late nineteenth century, 610*i*
fire of 1871, 612
Halsted Street, 614
Haymarket Square Riot of 1886, 570–72
as industrial center, 401
meat trade in, 554–55
racial violence after World War I in, 720
skyscraper construction, early twentieth century, 611
World's Fair (1893), 613
Chicago Railroad, 553
Chicago Tribune, 820
Chicano. *See* Mexican-Americans
Chickahominy Indians, 40
Chickamauga, battle of (1863), 464
Chickasaw Indians, 326
Chihuahua, Mexico, 418
child labor, 564
farm families in manufacturing, 260

(child labor con't)
federal laws related to, 564–65, 662
in southern mills, 559
in textile industry, (1830s), 292
childrearing
early nineteenth century, 271–73
scientific, 907
children. *See also* youth
effect of Great Depression on, 766
farm work performed by (1850s–1900s), 541
as indentured servants, 99–100
middle class (1870–1900), 633
parental control over, 271
status of, in European society, 1400s, 13
TV programs geared to (1950s), 906
Chile, riots against American sailors (1891), 671
Chin, Vincent, 1020
China. *See also* People's Republic of China; Taiwan
Boxer Rebellion (1900), 687
fall to communism, 860–61
Japanese invasion of (1937), 819
Open Door policy toward, 687–88
Sino-Japanese War (1894–1895), 688
U.S. loans to, 689
China bosses, 532
"China lobby," 861
China Syndrome, The, 994
chinampas cultivation system, 5
Chinatowns, 532, 900
Chinese-Americans
discrimination against, 519, 533
migration to California (1840s–1870s), 531–32
naturalization of, 900
Chinese Exclusion Act (1882), 533
repeal of, 900
Chippewyan Indians
American Indian Movement, 224, 960
Chisholm, Shirley Anita St. Hill (1924–), 971
chlorofluorocarbons (CFCs), 1032
Chocktaw Indians, 8, 9, 326
Choice, Not an Echo, A (Schlafly), 972
cholera epidemics, of 1849, 389
Chou En-lai. *See* Zhou Enlai
Christiana, Pa., 424
Christian Evangelist, The (magazine), 314
Christianity, 10, 255. *See also* religious reform; specific religions
African-American urban churches, 617
Benevolent Empire and, 311
"born again" experience, 996
church growth by denomination, 1700–1780, 119*f*
deists and, 113
Enlightenment and, 113
European (1400s), 13–15
evangelical denominations, 996
freed slave participation in, 496–97
Great Awakening, 115, 118–19, 140
interdenominational societies, 278
Maryland colony and, 42
native American conversion to, 36–37, 250, 251, 252
Old Lights v. New Lights, 115, 118–19, 175, 277
Pietism, 112, 114–15, 119
propagation of, 39
Protestant Reformation, 23–25, 30
redefining traditional moral injunctions, 310
republicanism and, 276–78
sabbath regulations, 311
Satan and, 14
scandals of religious leaders (1980s), 1024
Second Great Awakening, 276–78, 311
slave conversion to, 78, 79, 83, 120–21
slave marriage and, 381, 382
slavery and, 250, 367
television and, 1024
theological seminaries, 277–78
vestrymen, 120
women's activism in, 273–76, 277
Christy, Howard Chandler, 703*i*
Chumash people, 36
Churchill, Sir Winston Leonard Spencer (1874–1965), 821, 836, 837, 847, 855
at Casablanca Conference, 845
"Iron Curtain Speech," 855
"soft underbelly" strategy, 838
at Yalta Conference, 845*i*, 845–46
Church of England, 29–30, 67
after American Revolution, 188
in Maryland, 73
in Virginia, 42, 119, 120–21
Pilgrims and, 50
Puritans and, 52–53
separation from, 31
support of, 119, 120
Church of Jesus Christ of Latter Day Saints, 404. *See also* Mormons (1847)
Church of Scientology, 996
Church of the Nazarene, 624
Churumbusco, battle of, 419
Cibola, seven cities of, 35–36
Cincinnati, Ohio, 297, 627, 630*i*
pork packing industry in, 288–89*i*
cities. *See also* specific city
blacks living in (1880–1913), 617
bridges, 611
building of, 609–12
crowding of immigrants in (1840s–1860s), 389
culture, 633–35
disease in (1840s–1860s), 389
dumbbell tenements, 613*f*, 614
economy of the ghetto, 616*i*
electricity in, 612
environment, late nineteenth century, 612–13
ethnic diversity (1980s–1990s), 1022
ethnic tensions in (1880s), 585
family life in, 631–33
farm families move to (1870s), 562
ghettos, 616*i*, 1017
governing of (1946–1970), 898–99
growth of
(1820s–1840s), 297–99
(1950–1980), 895–96
housing, 613–14
immigrant population
early twentieth century, 615–17
after World War II, 900–1
industrial, 608–9
Industrial Revolution effects on, 513
leisure in, late nineteenth century, 624–26
major (1840s), 298*m*
mass transit, 609–11, 612
middle class living in, 628–31
migration to (1960s), 893
municipal powers granted to, 612
newspapers of (1800s), 241
Northeast, 896
northern (1700s), 87–88
population (1870–1910), 609*t*
progressive reform in, 643–44
racial unrest in (1965–1968), 957–59
religion and ethnic identity in, 619–21
sanitation systems (1840s–1860s), 389
seaboard, 87–88, 89, 378
settlement houses, 648
source of growth, 607–9
Sun Belt, 896
upper class in, 626–28
urban liberalism, 650–56
urban majority (1920s), 744, 745*f*
urban poor (1820s–1840s), 306–9
urban renewal projects, 901–2, 903*i*
ward politics, 618–19
western (1830s), 297–98
citizenship. *See* U.S. citizenship
City Beautiful movement, 613
civic humanism, 17
"Civil Disobedience" (Thoreau), 366
Civilian Conservation Corps (CCC), 789, 789*i*, 806, 828
Civilian Works Administration (CWA), 836
civil liberties, suspended during Civil War, 451
civil rights, Truman's efforts in, 865, 869
Civil Rights Act (1866), 488–89
Civil Rights Act (1875), defeat of, 597
Civil Rights Act (1957), 874
Civil Rights Act (1964), 927, 952, 953, 954
coverage of educational institutions, 971
impact on women, 968
civil rights laws, 897
civil rights movement, 945–61. *See also* women's movement
Black Muslims, 956
Black Power, 956–57
black separatism, 956
challenge to segregation, 945–48
ethnic groups joining, 959–61
freedom rides, 948, 949*i*
Freedom Summer (1964), 954, 969
Martin Luther King's assassination and, 958–59
legacy of, 959
legislation related to, 952, 953–55
Montgomery bus boycott, 947–48, 949*i*
National Civil Rights Commission, 869

(civil rights movement con't)
Niagara Movement, 655
during Progressive Era, 654–55
racial unrest in American cities (1965–1968), 957–59
sit-ins, 948
Voting Rights Act of 1965, 954–55, 955*m*
Civil Service Commission, 579
civil service jobs, Pendleton Act of 1883 and, 579
civil service reform, 506
Civil War, 443–77. *See also* Confederacy; Union; specific battles
African-American soldiers in, 468–69
aims and resources, 446–49
Atlanta, fall of (1864), 473–74
battlefields, 459*i*
bonds, 504, 507, 592
casualties, 460
civilian support for, 454–55, 456
contrabands of war, 461–62
Crittenden Plan and, 445
diplomacy during, 467
draft riots, 451–52
eastern theater, 458–59
economic programs, 453–54
emancipation and, 461–64
end of, 475–77
military deadlock, 455–67
mobilization of armies, 450–52
mobilization of money, 452–53
movement toward secession, 443–46
northern whites' racial attitudes during, 469
nursing during, 454*i*, 455
pension program 504
Petersburg, siege of (1864), 466, 471
Republican party and, 581
Shenandoah campaign, 471–73
tax system, revenues raised from, 504
Union gains in, 464–66
Union victory, 467–77
Vicksburg, fall of (1863), 464–65
western theater, 457–58
Civil Works Administration (CWA), 790, 797
Clamshell Alliance, 994
Clark, William (1770–1838), 233
class, social and economic. *See also* poor
aristocracy. *See* aristrocracy
barriers, 268
based on achievement, 279
blurring at edges, 556
business class 628. *See* business class
California society of 1850s, 408
caste system, southern 488
Chesapeake colonies, 85–86
childrearing practice and, 272
commercial society, 3
distinction in armed forces during World War II, 825
division in suburbs, 630
education and (1820s), 266–67
English
inflation during seventeenth century and, 27–28
price revolution and, 27
European hierarchy and authority, 12–13, 279
European peasantry, 10–12, 13, 14
Great Depression's effects on, 762
in Hispanic Southwest (1860s–1880s), 530, 531
of immigrants, 268, 388
Industrial Revolution and, 305–6
merchant. *See* merchants
middle class, 302–6. *See also* middle class
in middle colonies, 109
native American, 9
planter (1860s), 378–79
political power and (1700s), 91, 91*i*
property ownership and, 302
race and, 268
Renaissance and, 17
republicanism and, 265
in seaport cities (1700s), 88–96
sentimentalism and, 270
underclass, 1017
urban elite, 626–29, 631
urban poor, 302–6, 310
women in labor force and (1870s–1900s), 564, 565, 566
working class, 309
Clay, Henry (1777–1852), 261, 415*i*, 423, 434
American Revolution and, 236
American System 322, 345, 415
annexation of Texas and, 414
Bonus Bill (1817), 261, 322
Compromise of 1850, 423
Compromise Tariff (1833), 332
death of, 425
Harrison and, 344
Jackson's veto of Second Bank of the United States and, 329
Missouri Compromise and, 244
presidential election of 1824, 320, 322
presidential election of 1832, 329
presidential election of 1844, 415
Second Bank of the United States and, 261
as secretary of state under John Quincy Adams, 322
Whig party and, 340, 341, 342
Clayton Antitrust Act (1914), 664
Clean Air Act (1970), 993
Cleaver, Eldridge (1935–), 947
Clermont (steamship), 303
Clemenceau, Georges (1841–1929), 718
Clemens, Samuel. *See* Twain, Mark
Cleveland, (Stephen) Grover (1837–1908), 573, 574, 584*i*, 596, 579, 580*i*, 581, 587, 671
rebuilding of navy and, 675
presidential election of 1892, 590
silver and, 593
tariffs and, 581
vetoes, 580
Cleveland, Ohio, 297, 617
Cliff Dwellers, The (Bellows), 638*i*
Cliff-Dwellers, The (Fuller), 635
Clinton, De Witt (1769–1818), 237, 301
Clinton, George, 92–93
Clinton, George (1739–1812), 204, 224, 236
Clinton, Sir Henry (1738–1795), 172, 173, 176–77
Clinton, William Jefferson (1946–), 1033, 1033*i*
presidential election of 1992, 1033–34
clocks, mass-produced, 392
closed shops, 339, 569, 826
clothing industry. *See* textile industry
coal, allotment during World War I, 710
coal industry
anthracite coal strike of 1902, 657
breaker boys, 566*i*
coke-using technology, 550
conspiracy to transfer coal lands to private industry in Alaska, 661
Great Depression and, 759
growth of, 549
1920s, 729
output (1870–1910), 549*t*
Coast Guard, 824
Cobb, Howell (1815–1868), 475
Cody, Isaac, 522
Cody, William Frederick (Buffalo Bill, 1846–1917), 522, 523
coerced servitude, Asian migration and, 531
Coercive Acts, 152–53, 157, 171
Patriot response to, 157*t*, 157
Coeur d'Alene, Idaho, 519, 519*m*, 520, 575
Cohens v. Virginia (1821), 264
Colbert, Claudette, 830
Cold Harbor, Va., 466, 470
Colden, Calwallader (1688–1776), 141
Cold War, 887, 930
baby boom and, 906
Berlin airlift and, 859, 859*i*
Berlin Wall and, 923
containment policy and, 855–58, 861
election of 1948 and, 866–68
end of, 1006*i*, 1024, 1026
Fair Deal and, 865–66, 868–69
fall of China to Communists, 860–61
fear of communism and, 869–72
Kennedy and, 923
Korean War and, 862–64
militarization of, 861
origins of, 852–60
Cole, Nathan, 118
Cole, Thomas (1801–1848), 402
Coleridge, Samuel Taylor (1772–1834), 350
colleges and universities
colonial, 119, 120*t*
enrollment during Great Depression, 766
football, 744
quotas on Jewish students, 746
student unrest at (1960s), 962–63, 978
college students, protest against segregation, 948
Collier, John (1884–1968), 804
Colliers Magazine, 734
Collier's Weekly, 742
Collins, Samuel W., 295
Colombia, Panama Canal and, 685, 686
colonial governments, corporations and, 261

colonies, *38i*, *56t*, *69t*
  corporate, 39
  Dominion of New England, 71, 71*i*, 72, 73–74, 92
  Dutch, 37–39
  English, 35, 39–48, 67. *See also* specific colonies
  English troops in, 135
  French, 36–37, 121, 125. *See also* New France
  governors of, 75, 92
  growth of, 127
  imperial system 1763, 133–35
  legislatures, factions in, 217
  mercantilism and, 95
  natural and constitutional rights, 146
  Proclamation of 1763 and, 135
  proprietary, 42, 68–69
  Puritans in, 48–60
  Restoration, 67–68
  royal
    Maryland as, 73
    Massachusetts as, 72
    New Hampshire as, 71
    Virginia as, 42
  Spanish, 22–23, 36
  tobacco and disease and, 44–48
  voting rights in, 90–91
  waning of English authority in, 92
Colorado, 596
  gold mining in, 519
  Supreme Court, 575
Colorado Coal Company v. United Mine Workers, 732
Colored Farmers' Alliance, 590, 598
Colored Methodist Episcopal Church, 496
Colson, Charles, 997
Colt, Samuel (1814–1862), 386
Columbiad, The (Barlow), 268
Columbia Broadcasting Service (CBS), 742, 905
Columbia University, 266
  student protest at, 963–64, 978
Columbus, Christopher (1451–1506), 19–20
commerce. *See also* trade
  expansion of (1817–1819), 242
  foreign, 298
  new mercantilism, 70
  Portuguese (fifteenth century), 18
  state (1790s), 261
  sugar industry, 76–77
commercial society, European, 3
Commerce department, 729
Commission for Relief of Belgium, 779
Committee of Resistance, Philadelphia, 167
Committee of Safety, 186
Committee on Prices, 184
Committee on Public Information (CPI), 714, 715
Committee to Defend America by Aiding the Allies, 820
Committee to Re-Elect the President (CREEP), 987
Committees of Correspondence, 150
  Tea Act of 1773 and, 151, 152
commodity exchanges, 540
common (unskilled) laborers, wages (1825), 306
common law, 142, 262
  versus development, 262
common property doctrine, 421
Common Sense (Paine), 167–68
commonwealth systems, 261–62
Commonwealth of Independent States, 1029*m*
Commonwealth v. Hunt (1842), 344
Commonwealth v. Pullis (1805), 334
communal living, 354*m*
  Brook Farm, 353–54
  Mormons, 404–6
  Oneida Community, 356–57
  phalanxes, 355
  Shakers, 355–56
  1960s, 966
communications. *See also* newspapers; radio; television; telephone
  speed of business news, 303*m*
  telegraph, 554
  transportation revolution and, 302*m*
  westward expansion and, 518
communism, 876
  Anti-Cominterm pact, 819
  blacklists, 869, 870
  collapse of, 1026, 1027–30
  Eisenhower and, 877
  fear of 869–72
  House Committee on Un-American Activities and, 869, 870
  McCarthy and, 871–72
  North Korean, 862
  Truman Doctrine and, 858
Communist Labor party, 722
Communist party, 722
  election of 1932 and, 738
  fight against racism, 770
  1935–1939, 812
  unemployment councils, 781
  urban actions during Great Depression, 781
communities
  barrios, 531
  employer and wage earner separation, 309
  European (1400s), 13
  hippie, 966
  immigrant, 900
  mill villages, 559–60
  residential, 309
  rural (1850s–1900s), 541
  urban
    black, 617
    ethnic identity in, 615
Community Action Program, 929
Company of New France, 36
comparable worth, 973
Complete Book of Running (Fixx), 996
Compromise of 1850, 423, 425, 427*m*
Compromise of 1877, 508
Compromise Tariff (1833), 332
computers, 899, 1022
Concord, Mass.
  battle of (1775), 159, 165
  town meeting establishes "minutemen," 158
Conestoga tribe, massacre of, 128
Coney Island, 624, 624*i*
Confederacy
  aims of, 447
  British aid to, 505
  casualties, 445–46
  contest for upper South, 445–46
  destruction of, 476
  destruction of Fort Sumter, 445
  efforts in recognition of independence, 467
  first invasion of North, 459–61
  health care for troops, 455
  home front, 472
  mobilization of army, 450–52
  morale of army, 474–75
  resources of, 448
  secession crisis and, 443–45
  Wade-Davis bill (1864), 483
  war costs, 452, 453
Confederation Congress, 198–201
  Articles of Confederation, 197–98
  Land Ordinance (1785), 198
  Northwest Ordinance (1787), 198–99, 228, 432,
  Ordinance of 1784, 198, 214, 228
  settling of trans-Appalachian West, 198–99
  U.S. Constitution and, 204
Confederation notes, 209
Confiscation acts
  First (1861), 461
  Second (1862), 462
Congregational Church, 52, 56, 115, 189, 277
  Benevolent Empire and, 311
  non-Separatist, 31
  Republicanism, 276
  transfer to Ohio, 242
  westward migration of, 226–27
  women members, 273
Congress. *See* U.S. Congress
Congress of Industrial Organizations (CIO), 801, 802*i*, 802, 803, 804. *See also* American Federation of Labor–Congress of Industrial Organizations
  Anti-Communist sentiment, 869
  Political Action Committee, 818*i*, 819
Congress of Racial Equality (CORE), 832, 948, 951, 956
  voter registration drives, 953
Congressional Budget and Impoundment Control Act of 1974, 990
Congressional Union, 713
Conkling, Roscoe (1829–1988), 582, 596
Connecticut (colony), 55, 56*t*, 75
  Dominion of New England, 71
  Old Lights in, 118
  Puritans in, 53, 55
Connecticut (state), constitution, 193, 265
Connecticut River Valley, Puritan settlement in, 53, 55

Connor, Eugene ("Bull"), 949
conscientious objectors, 703, 964
consciousness raising, 969
conservation
  Endangered Animals Act of 1964 and, 993
  Theodore Roosevelt and, 656
Constitution. *See* U.S. Constitution
Constitutionalist movement, Mexican, 690
constitutions
  state, 193–96. *See also* specific states
    revision of (1818–1821), 265
  U.S. *See* U.S. Constitution
construction industry, steel and, 551
construction workers, labor unions and, 334–35
consumer credit. *See* credit, consumer
consumer culture (1950s), 903–6
consumer price index
  during Great Depression, 761, 764
  1960–1990, 999*f*
  during World War II, 823
Consumer Product Safety Commission, 983
consumer protection, Theodore Roosevelt and, 659–60
consumer revolution. *See* Industrial Revolution
consumerism, 884*i*, 885
  installment plan, 735
  of 1920s, 735
  television and advertising and, 905
consumption, 1920s, 734–36
containment policy, 855–58
  NSC-68 and, 861
Continental Army, 170, 198
  in Morristown, N.J., 183, 184
  strength of, 169, 171, 179
  support for, 171
Continental Congress, 168
  Articles of Confederation, 197–98
  currency issued by, 171, 185
  First, 153, 156
  Second, 165
Continental currency, 171, 185
Continental System, 234
contraception. *See* birth control
contract (s), obligation of, state legislature and, 204
contract clause, of U.S. Constitution, 264
Contras, 1011
Conwell, Russell Herman (1843–1925), 583, 630
Coode, John, 72
Cooke, Alistair, 804
Cooke, Jay (1821–1905), 452, 507, 547
Coolidge, John Calvin (1872–1933), 721, 729, 731, 733
  as president, 729–30
Cooper, Gary (1901–1961), 741
Cooper, James Fenimore (1789–1851), 269, 394
Cooper, Thomas (1759–1839), 189
cooperative farming, 10
cooperative movements, agricultural (1870s–1880s), 542, 543
coopers, 88
Cooperstown, N.Y., 625
Copland, Aaron (1900–1991), 809
copper industry, 520
  development of, 549
  output (1870–1910), 549*t*
Copperheads, 474
Coral Islands, 843*m*
Coral Sea, battle of (1942), 841, 844
Corcoran Gallery of Art, 633
cordwainers, 334. *See also* shoemakers
Corliss reciprocating engine, 549, 549*i*
corn, 7
corn belt, 539
Cornish, Samuel (1790–1859), 364
Corn Laws, 415
Cornwallis, Charles, marquess of (1738–1805), 178
  relinquishment of Carolinas, 182
  surrender at Yorktown, 178
Coronado, Francisco Vásquez de (c. 1510–1554), 35–36
corporate colonies, 39
corporate economy, middle class and, 628
corporate managers, 892
corporations
  commitment to research and development, 731
  deindustrialization effects on, 995
  diversification, 890
  excess profits tax, 710
  government charters for, 261, 305
  government contracts awarded to, 887
  junk bonds, 1014
  limited liability of, 261
  mergers of 1920s, 731
  monopoly privileges, 305
  oligopolies, 890–91
  paper entrepreneurs, 1014
  power of eminent domain, 261
  professional managers in, 731
  railroad organizations as, 552
Cort, Henry (1704–1800), 550
Cortés, Hernando (1485–1547), 20–21, 22, 415
cortisone, 907
"corrupt bargain," 322, 324
Cosby, William, 93
cotters, 27, 28
cotton, cotton industry
  acreage in South, after World War II, 901
  Civil War and, 467
  export of
    1780s–1790s, 214
    1820s, 297
  impact on slavery, 243–44
  prices, 342, 376, 596
  profits from, 378
  southern production of (1860s), 375–76
  westward expansion, 539
cotton belt, 543
Cotton Club, 742, 771
cotton gin, 214, 295–96
Cotton Kingdom, 375, 376
cotton-spinning machines, 290
Coughlan, Robert, 747
Coughlin, Charles Edward (1891–1979), 792
Council for Mutual Economic Assistance (COMECON), 860
Council of Economic Advisers, 866, 924
Council of National Defense, 821
counterculture, 965–66, 996, 997
counterinsurgency techniques, 920
counting houses, 22
Country Life Commission, 596
Country party, 93, 136
coureurs de bois, 36
Court of International Justice (the World Court), 733, 818
Court party, 93
courts, court system. *See also* U.S. Supreme Court
  colonial, appointment of judges, 142
  impeachment of judges, 231
  Judiciary Act of 1801 and, 231
  lower, establishment of, 208
  state, 208
  trial by jury, 142
  vice-admiralty courts, 137–38
Courtship of Miles Standish, The (Longfellow), 394
Cousins, Norman (1915–), 765
Cowell, Henry P., 555*i*
Cowley, Malcolm (1898–1989), 808, 812
Cox, James M., 729
Coxe, Tench (1755–1824), 211
Coxey, Jacob Sechler (1854–1951), 593
cradle, 109
Cradle Will Rock, The (Blitzstein), 810
craft guilds, 13
craft workers
  autonomous, 561
  ethical code of, 561
  sex discrimination in, 565
crafts, Shaker, 355
Craig, Sir James Henry (1748–1812), 236
Crane, Stephen (1871–1900), 635
Crawford, William Harris (1772–1834), presidential election of 1824, 320, 322
credit, banking and (1781–1811), 258
credit, consumer, 903–4
  Equal Credit Opportunity Act of 1974, 971
  installment buying, 735, 764
Crédit Mobilier, Grant's involvement in, 506
creditors
  public, 209
  rights of, after American Revolution, 200, 201
Creek nation, 8, 326
  John Quincy Adams and, 323
  battles against, 239
  migration legend, 9
  treaty with Georgia, 323
Creel, George, 714
Creswell, Nicholas, 84
Crèvecoeur, St. Jean de (1735–1813), 279
crime
  juvenile delinquency during World War II, 831–32

(crime con't)
organized, Prohibition and, 751
Cripple Creek, Colo., 575
Crisis, The (NAACP journal), 655, 655*i*, 750
Crittenden, John Jordan (1787–1863), 445
Crittenden Plan, 445
Crocker, Charles (1822–1888), 533
Crockett, David (1786–1836), 321, 333
Croker, Richard (1841–1922), 620, 621
Croly, Herbert, 662
Cromwell, Oliver (1599–1658), 56, 141
crop
rotation, 227
transportation of (1790s), 227–28
Croton aqueduct, 613
Crozer, John, 295
Crusades, 14–15
Crystal Palace Exhibition, 386
Cuba, 20, 876
Bay of Pigs invasion, 922–23
expansionist efforts in, 670
movements for independence from Spain (1868–1875), 676–78, 680
Ostend Manifesto, 426–27
Platt Amendment and, 686
Polk's attempt to purchase, 426–27
Soviet Union's relationship with (1960s), 922
Spanish–American War and, 679
U.S. involvement in (1930s), 818
U.S. withdrawal from, 686
Cuban missile crisis, 923
Cuban refugees, migration to Miami, 980–1
Cullen, Countee (1903–1946), 750
Culpepper, John, 68
cultural autonomy, 269
cultural conflict, 1920s, 744–50
cultural life, Renaissance and, 16–18
cultural movements, Enlightenment and Great Awakening, 112–21. *See also* Enlightenment; Great Awakening
cultural pluralism, in middle colonies, 112
culture. *See also* art; literature; music; theater
African-American, slave, 245–50
Californian (1860s), 534
counterculture, 965–66, 996, 997
ethnic, early 1900s, 616
Harlem Renaissance, 749–50
modernist movement, 748–49
native American dualism, 250
New Deal and, 810
1950s, 912–13
1980s, 1022
Old Northwest, 24–43
politics related to, 584–96
popular, during Great Depression, 766–70
Protestant, 257
regional diversity in (1800s), 241
support by private wealth, 633
television and, 904–6
transplantation to West, 240
urban (1870–1912), 633–35
during World War II, 830
youth (1950s), 908–9
"culture of narcissism," 996
Cumberland Gap, 226
Cummins, Albert Baird (1850–1926), 645
currency
Continental, 171, 185
floating, 760
gold, 592
Great Depression and, 760
greenbacks, 592
issuing of, state loss of power in, 204
paper money, 95, 111, 174, 175, 452, 453, 507, 591, 592
silver, 592
Currency Act of 1751, 70*t*, 95, 134
Currency Act of 1764, 135, 142
currency taxes, 185
Currier & Ives, 393, 393*i*
Custer, George Armstrong (1839–1876), 523, 526
Custer Died for Your Sins (Deloria), 961
customs duties. *See also* tariff(s)
Hamilton's program on, 212
Customs Service, Revenue Act of 1767 and, 146
Czechoslovakia, 1026
Communist control of, 859
German invasion of, 820
Czolgosz, Leon F. (1873–1901), 656

Da Nang, 933
Dachau, 840
Daily Worker (newspaper), 812
dairy belt, 539
Dakota. *See also* North Dakota; South Dakota
agricultural expansion in, 538
Scandinavian immigration to, 538
Daladier, Édouard (1884–1970), 820
Daley, Richard Joseph (1902–1976), 929, 958, 979, 981
Damrosch, Leopold (1832–1885), 633
dams, construction of, 262
Palmer v. Mulligan and, 262
Dana, Charles Anderson (1819–1897), 626
Danbury, Conn., 561
Danbury Hatters case (1908), 652
Dangers of an Unconverted Ministry (Gilbert), 119
Darman, Richard, 1025
Darrow, Clarence Seward (1857–1938), 748
Dartmouth, Lord, 156
Dartmouth (ship), 152, 154*i*
Dartmouth College v. Woodward (1819), 264
Daughters of Liberty, 147, 156
Darwin, Charles Robert (1809–1882), 583, 635, 748
Social Darwinism, 676
Davis, David (1815–1886), 508
Davis, Jefferson (1808–1889), 423, 426, 449, 454, 473
election of 1860 and, 437
mobilization of troops, 450–52
as president of Confederacy, 444, 447
Davis, John William (1873–1955), 730
Davis, Maxine, 766
Davis, Paul, 944*i*
Dawes, Charles Gates (1865–1951), 733, 752
Dawes Severalty Act (1887), 527, 804
Day, Benjamin Henry (1810–1889), 626
Day, John T., 600
Day, William Rufus (1849–1923), 681
Dayton, Ohio, progressive reform in, 644
Dayton, Tenn., 748
D-Day (June 6, 1944), 838, 839*i*, 840
DDT, 993
Dean, James (1931–1955), 909
Dean, John, 987, 987*i*, 990
Deane, Silas (1737–1789), 175
Dearborn, Henry (1751–1829), 230
death rate
in Chesapeake colonies, 43
England, sixteenth century, 26
European peasantry (1400s), 11, 11*f*, 12
of slaves, 80
Vietnam War-related, 935
Debs, Eugene Victor (1855–1926), 573, 574, 641, 700
American socialism and, 574
election of 1912 and, 664
imprisonment of, 716
debt, federal
private, sanctity of, after American Revolution, 201
World War I and, 710
1939–92, 1013*f*, 1013–14
debtor relief legislation, 200, 204
debt peonage, 503
Declaration of Independence, 165, 168–69
Jefferson and, 214
principle of popular sovereignty, 194. *See also* popular sovereignty
signing of, 168*i*
Declaration of Rights, 188
Declaration of Rights and Grievances, 153
Declaration of the Causes and Necessities of Taking Up Arms, 166
Declaratory Act of 1766, 145, 153
Deere, John (1804–1886), 398, 400
Deere, John and Company, 540
Deerfield, Mass., 74
Deerslayer, The (Cooper), 394
Defense, Department of
awarding of contracts by, 887
buildup after World War II, 888
mobilization during World War II, 823
Pentagon, 887, 888*i*
defense spending
1940–1965, 888*i*
NSC-68 and, 861
during Reagan administration, 1010
after World War II, 887, 888*f*, 888
deflation
effect on agriculture (1870s), 543
Great Deflation, 547
De Gaulle, Charles André Joseph Marie (1890–1970), 835

Degener, Edward, 494
deindustrialization, 995
deists, 113, 189
de Kooning, Willem (1904–), 809
Delano, Calif., 959
Delaware (colony), 69
Delaware (state), constitution of 1776, 193, 194, 206
Delaware Indians, 8, 224
Delaware River, 170
De Leon, Daniel (1852–1914), 574
Del Monte Corporation, 778
De Lôme, Dupuy, 677
Deloria, Vine, Jr., 961
De Mille, Cecil Blount (1881–1959), 739
Democracy in America (de Tocqueville), 279, 349
Democratic National Committee
  at Watergate apartments, break-ins at, 987–90
  Women's Division of, 797
Democratic party, Democrats, 339. *See also* elections, presidential elections
  antibanking party and, 344
  Calhoun's joining of, 414
  coalition of 1840s, 345–46
  Compromise of 1850 and, 423
  condemnation of Grant's policies, 505–7
  control of South (1877–1900), 597
  Copperheads, 474
  depression of 1837–1843 and, 344
  description of members, 584
  Dred Scott decision and, 432–33
  effect of Robert Kennedy's assassination on, 978
  election of 1852 and, 425–26
  election of 1856 and, 432
  election of 1860 and, 438
  election of 1862 and, 462–64
  electoral dominance in 1890 and 1892, 596
  Emancipation Proclamation and, 462–63
  emergence of, 323–24
  former slaveowners in, 497
  gains from New Deal, 807, 808
  Andrew Jackson and, 324, 325
  Lecompton constitution and, 433
  members, joining of Whig party, 341
  national convention in Chicago (1968), 978
  New Deal coalition and, 807–8
  nomination of Buchanan, 431
  nomination of John Kennedy, 918, 919
  nomination of Pierce, 425
  Peace Democrats, 474
  resurgence of (1840–1841), 345–46
  social programs, Nixon's attack on, 983
  stereotypes of black political leaders (1860s), 494
  Tammany Hall, 618, 619, 620–21, 651, 730
  Third Party System and, 432
  traditions, 580
  Tyler's joining of, 413
  unions and, 338, 804
  Wilmot Proviso and, 420
Democratic-Republicans, 217, 324
Democratic Review (magazine), 402
democratic tendencies, after American Revolution, 195–96
democratic values, of business class, 310
democratization, 1820–1829, 319–20
Demonstration Cities Act, 929
Dempsey, Jack (1895–1983), 743, 743*i*
Deng Xiaoping (1904–), 1028
Dennison, William, 445
Department of Defense. *See* Defense, Department of
Department of Health, Education and Welfare (HEW), 874
Department of Labor, 712, 996
department stores, growth of, 555, 556
deportation, Alien Act of 1798 and, 218
depressions. *See also* Great Depression
  of 1837–1843, 342–44
  of 1850s, 401
  of 1873–1877, 507, 547
  of 1890s, 574, 590, 658
  of 1920–1921, 759
  Panic of 1837, 342, 342*i*, 349, 386
  Panic of 1893, 553, 590, 593, 673
  Panic of 1907, 664
Desire Under the Elms (O'Neill), 749
DeSoto, Hernando (c. 1500–1542), 36
Destined to Be Reared in Orphanages (Alger), 582
détente, 924, 983, 984
  collapse of, 1010
  return under Reagan, 1012
Detroit, Mich., 225, 297, 732
  race riots in, 958
Dewey, George (1837–1917), 678
Dewey, John (1859–1952), 641, 714
  democracy and, 641–42
Dewey, Thomas Edmund (1903–1971), 866, 829
Dewson, Molly (1874–1962), 797
Dexter Street Baptist Church, 948
Dial (magazine), 353, 360
Dialectic of Sex (Firestone), 969
Diaz, Bartholomew, (c. 1450–1500), 18
Diaz, Porfirio (1830–1915), 690
Dickinson, Emily (1830–1886), 353, 353*i*
Dickinson, John (1732–1808), 143, 146, 166, 198
Dickinson, Goldsworthy Lowes (1862–1932), 634
Diedrich Knickerbocker's History of New York (Irving), 269
Diem, Ngo Dinh (1901–1963), 931 935
Dienbienphu, fall of, 931
diet, rural (1850s–1900s), 541
Dillinger, John (1903–1934), 769
Dinwiddie, Robert (1693–1770), 123
Dionne quintuplets, 769
diplomacy. *See* foreign policy
disabled, shelter for, 114
Discourses, The (Machiavelli), 17
discrimination. *See also* racism
  reverse, 996
disease
  AIDS epidemic, 1021–2, 1024
  antibiotics for, 907
  in Chesapeake colonies, 42–43
  cholera epidemics of 1849, 389
  during Civil War, 455
  in commercial cities (1840s–1860s), 389
  day laborers and (1830s), 307
  European peasantry (1400s), 11, 12
  European, spread to native Americans, 21
  influenza epidemic during World War I, 708, 708*i*
  in Harlem during Great Depression, 772
  measles epidemic of 1730s, 113
  polio vaccine, 907, 907*i*
  smallpox epidemics of 1633 and 1720s, 53, 113
  venereal, 708
Disney, Walter Elias (1901–1966), 906
Disneyland, 904
Displaced Persons Act of 1948, 900
dissent, during World War I, 715–16
Dissertation on the Canon and Feudal Law (Hancock), 142
Dissertation on the English Language (Webster), 269
distilleries, 87
District of Columbia. *See* Washington, D.C.
divorce, early nineteenth century, 270
divorce rate, Great Depression effect on, 632, 764, 967
Dix, Dorothea Lynde (1802–1887), 358*i*, 358–59, 455
Dixiecrat party, 867, 868
Dodge City, Texas, 520
Dodgers (baseball team), 896
Doeg Indians, 48
Dole, Robert Joseph (1923–), 1000, 1024
dollar-a-year men, 828
dollar diplomacy, 687, 688
Dollinger, Genora Johnson, 803
Dominican Republic, 505, 690. *See also* Haiti
  U.S. withdrawal of troops from (1920s), 733
Dominion of New England, 71, 71*m*, 92
  fall of, 72, 73–74
Doolittle, James Harold (1896–), 841
Doonesbury (Trudeau), 968*i*
Dorr, Retha Childe, 588
Dorsey, Tommy, 769
Dos Passos, John Rodrigo (1896–1970), 748, 749, 811
Doubleday, Abner (1819–1893), 625
doughboys, 705, 708
Douglas, Helen Gahagan, 865*i*
Douglas, Lew, 791
Douglas, Stephen Arnold (1813–1861), 420, 423, 425, 433, 435
  Freeport doctrine and, 436, 437
  Kansas-Nebraska Act and, 427
  Lincoln's challenge of, 436–37
  presidential election of 1860, 438–39
Douglas, William Orville (1898–1980), 795
Douglass, Frederick (1817–1895), 370–71, 371*i*, 483, 496, 602
  black soldiers in Union army and, 468

(Douglass, Frederick con't)
escape to New York, 384
free-soil movement and, 369
Fugitive Slave Act and, 424
Reconstruction and, 482
school segregation and, 496
slave songs and, 383
woman suffrage and, 492
Dover, N. H., women factory workers' strikes in, 338
dower rights, 12, 102
Downing, Andrew Jackson (1815–1852), 392, 629
draft, military
during Civil War, 450–52
conscientious objector status, 703, 964
resistance during Vietnam War, 964
riots, 451–52
Selective Service Act (1917), 703
substitute law, 450
during Vietnam War, 932–33, 935
during World War I, 703
during World War II, 824–25
Drake, Sir Francis (1540–1596), 28
Dred Scott v. Sanford, (1857), 263, 432
Lincoln and, 436, 437
Dreier, Mary, 647
Dreiser, Theodore Herman Albert (1871–1945), 627, 635, 749
Drexel Burnham Lambert, 1022
Drift and Mastery (Lippman), 640
drug culture, 965–66
dry-farming method, 536
Du Bois, William Edward Burghardt (1868–1963), 603, 617, 655, 750
Duck Soup (1933), 767
Duer, William (1747–99), 209
Dukakis, Michael Stanley (1035–), 1024, 1025
Duke, James B., 560
Dulles, Allen, 876
Dulles, John Foster, 854*i*, 861, 880
CIA and, 876
foreign policy under Eisenhower, 875–76
Dumbarton Oaks conference, 845
Dunmore, John Murray, earl of (1732–1809), 166
American slaves fighting for, 176
Durand, Asher Brown (1796–1886), 402
Durr, Virginia Foster, 763, 969
Dust Bowl, 804
migrations from, 772–77
Dutch East India Company, 25–26, 37
Dutch Reformed Church, factions of, 119
Dutch Republic. *See* Netherlands
Dutch West India Company, 38, 110
Dwight, Timothy (1752–1817), 103
Dylan, Bob, 965

Eads Bridge, 611
Earhart, Amelia (1898–1937), 769
Earth Day, 977, 1032*i*
Earth Summit, 1032–33
Eastern Woodlands, North America, native Americans of, 6–10
East Germany. *See* German Democratic Republic
East India Company, 28, 150
control of trade, 124
Tea Act of 1773 and, 151
Eastman, Crystal, 700
economic development, common law and, 262
Economic Interpretation of the Constitution of the United States (Beard), 201
economic policy. *See also* New Deal
Bush's, 1025
Hamiltonian, 208–13
Hoover's, 779
Kennedy's, 924
Populist party program, 591
Reaganomics, 1009–10
Republican party program during Reconstruction Era, 504, 505
during World War I, 710–11
during World War II, 823–24
following World War II, 866
economic power
concentration of, 890. *See also* Oligopolies
problem of, Wilson's attack on, 664
economic programs, during Civil War, 453–54
Economic Recovery Tax Act of 1981, 1009
economy. *See also* budget; capitalism; corporations; debt, financial crisis; inflation; money supply; recession; stock market
American Revolution and, 173–75, 184, 185, 199, 201
attack on formalism, 640
capitalist market economy, 276
capitalist society 257–61
common law v. development, 262
commonwealth system, 261–62
corporate, 628
deindustrialization, 995
development of corporations, 261. *See also* corporations
during Eisenhower's administration, 875
exchange system, 105
expansionism and, 671–74
foreign expansion of 1920s, 732–33
freeholder society and, 105
Great War for Empire effects on, 129, 135–36
greenbacks, 507
Hamiltonian program and, 209
household mode of production, 105
inequality in middle colonies, 109–11
integrating process of, 560
market economy, 259–60
during 1980s, 1014
1970s, 995
northern urban (1700s), 87–92
paper entrepreneurs, 1014, 1022
paper money, 95, 111, 452, 453, 507, 591, 592
price revolution of the sixteenth century, 26, 27
recession of 1834, 330
Republican party program, during Reconstruction Era, 504, 505
1780s–1790s, 214–217
slavery and, 80–81, 375–78
state regulation of (1870s), 583
after World War I, 865–66, 885–87
during World War II, 829*i*
Ederle, Gertrude Caroline (1907–), 744
Edgar Thompson Works, 548
Edison, Thomas Alva (1847–1931), 610, 612
education. *See also* colleges and universities
aid to parochial schools, 869, 925, 927
on African-American history and culture, 963
of baby boomers, 962
Blair Education bill, 581
building of schools in cities, early 1900s, 611
business class (1840s–1850s), 395
busing and, 997–98, 999
certification of teachers, 267
of Chesapeake aristocracy, 86
Civil Rights Act of 1964 and, 971
Elementary and Secondary Education Act of 1965, 927
elitist system, 267
ethnic tensions in (1880s), 585
of former slaves, 485, 485*i*
Great Depression effects on, 766
industrial, 602
integration of schools, 997
Kennedy and, 925
medical schools, colonial, 114
native American (1878), 527
nineteenth century, 243, 272
parochial schools, 390
prayer in schools, 925
private schools, 266
public funding for, 267, 268
public schools, 266, 267, 335
during Reconstruction Era, 496
reforms (1820s), 266–69
regional differences in (1800s), 240
religion and (1880s), 585
school enrollment (1870–1900), 633
segregation of schools, 496, 925, 955, 977
sex, 708
slavery and, 378
southern planter class (1860s), 379
state superintendents of education, 267
support by private wealth, 633
theological seminaries, 277–78
women's access to (1950–1970), 967
women teachers, nineteenth century, 276, 395
Educational Amendments Act of 1972, Title IX, 971
Education of Henry Adams, The (Adams), 634
Edwards, Jonathan (1703–1758), 115, 116–17, 117*i*, 119
Edward VIII (1894–1972), 769
Egypt, 879
invasion of Israel (1973), 991

(Egypt con't)
peace treaty with Israel, 1001*i*, 1001
Ehrlichman, John, 987, 990, 991
Eisenhower, Dwight David (1890–1969), 781, 857, 872, 889, 1011
on appointment of Earl Warren as Supreme Court justice, 946
command of army, 840, 841
Eisenhower Doctrine, 880
farewell address, 880
foreign policy, 876–77
Little Rock integration and, 947
military-industrial complex and, 887
Middle East and, 879
negotiations to end Korean War, 875
on Nixon, 918
presidency of, 874–75
presidential election of 1952, 872–74
Vietnam War and, 931, 935
Eisenhower, Milton Stover (1899–1985), 833, 835
elections. *See also* presidential elections
congressional
of 1818, 252
of 1866, 489–90
of 1890, 590
of 1946, 866
electoral college, 203
House of Representatives, 322
electric appliances
household (1920s), 735
production of, (1950s), 904
electricity, 612
effects on rural life, 774, 774*i*, 775
Electronic Numerical Integrator Computer (ENIAC), 889
Elementary and Secondary School Education Act of 1965, 927
Eliot, John N. (1604–1690), 54
Eliot, Thomas Stearns (1888–1965) 748, 810
Elizabeth I (1533–1603), 25, 29, 30*i*, 39
Elk Hills, Calif., 729
Elkins, William L., 612
Elkins Act of 1903, 659
Ellington, Duke (Edward Kennedy, 1899–1974), 742, 769
Elliott, Robert B., 480
Ellison, Phyllis, 998, 999
Ellison, Ralph (1914–), 810
Ellsberg, Daniel (1914–), 936, 987
Ellsworth, Abigail Wolcott, 215*i*
Ellsworth, Oliver (1745–1807), 215*i*
Ellsworth, Texas, 520
El Salvador, 1010, 1011
Ely, Ezra Stiles, 279
Emancipation Proclamation (1863), 462, 468
Embargo Act of 1807, 235, 261
Emergency Banking Act of 1933, 788–89
Emerson, Ralph Waldo (1803–1882), 350–51
at Brook Farm, 353
John Brown and, 437
Hawthorne and, 352–53
Melville and, 352–53
Thoreau and, 351
Whitman and, 351
eminent domain, power of, 261
employers
antiunion tactics (1830s), 339
separation from wage earners, 309
employment. *See also* labor; labor force; unemployment
of blacks in cities (1880–1913), 617
Civil Rights Act of 1964 and, 953
federal, tenure in, 325
1940s–1950s, 891
Employment Act of 1946, 866
Employment Agency, 756*i*
Enclosure acts, 27
Endangered Animals Act of 1964, 993
energy crisis of 1973–1974, 992, 992*i*, 995
Engel v. Vitale (1962), 925
England. *See also* specific acts; treaties; wars
abolitionism and, 385, 413
agriculture (1400s), 11
aid to Confederacy, 505
American loyalty to, 166–67. *See also* Patriots
Anglo-Dutch wars, 77, 177
Anglo-French entente, 691
antislavery barrier, 385
attack on American ships (1807), 234–35
authority, waning of (1742), 92
Battle of Britain (1940), 820
British North America Act (1867), 505
colonization of North America, 26–31. *See also* colonies; English
credit crisis of 1772, 150
declaration of war against Germany (1914), 698
economic and religious transformation, sixteenth century, 31
economic growth (1700s), 125–27
empire of 1713, 74–75
equality of sexes and, 197
expansionist ambitions (1890s), 685
Glorious Revolution of 1688, 71–73, 90
immigrants in U.S., 388
indentures from, 43–44
Industrial Revolution in, 287, 550
Lend-Lease (1941), 821
maritime policies (1809), 236
mechanics, 289
mercantilist expansion, 28–29, 69–70
ministerial instability in (1760–82), 144*t*
monarchy, 17–18
naval blockade, World War I and, 700–1
Navigation Acts, 70, 70*t*, 77
new mercantilism, 69–70
Panic of 1837 in, 342
Parliament. *See* Parliament
peasantry (1400s), 12
planting methods, 7
political parties (1700s), 93–94
politics of empire (1660–1713), 67–75
Puritans, migration to America, 48–60. *See also* Puritans
restrictions on neutral trade (1805), 234
restrictions on U.S. trade (1807), 234, 235
retaking of Suez Canal, 880
Rule of 1756 and, 216
Rush-Bagot treaty of 1817, 253
society, structure of (1688), 28*i*
sovereignty, debates on, 149–50
sugar industry, 76
textile industry, 291
trade with
Macon's Bill No. 2 and, 236
Non-intercourse Act and, 235
war with France, U.S. involvement in, 218
wars, 1650–1750, 74, 74*t*
withdrawal from India, 879
withdrawal from Palestine, 879
Enlightenment, 112
childrearing and, 272
European, 57, 113, 168
Franklin and, 113–14
impact on America, 113
reform movements and, 142
slavery and, 187
Enrollment Act of 1863, 451
entail, 100
Enterprise (aircraft carrier), 841
entrepreneurs, 258
in manufacturing and industry (1820s–1840s), 294, 295–96
view of property, 305
environment. *See also* conservation
air pollution, 1032
greenhouse effect, 1032
New Deal and, 806
urban, late nineteenth century, 612
Environmental Impact Statement (EIS), 993
environmental movements
Clean Air Act of 1970, 993
Earth Day, 977
Montreal protocol, 1032
of 1970s, 992–93
nuclear energy and, 993–94
spread of, 1031–33
Environmental Protection Agency (EPA), 983
epidemics. *See* under disease; specific diseases
Episcopal Church, 277
Equal Credit Opportunity Act (1974), 971
Equal Employment Opportunity Commission (EEOC), 953, 968
Equal Rights Amendment (ERA), 972–73, 996
states ratifying, 972*m*
Equiano, Olaudah, 79
Era of Good Feeling, 252
Erhard Seminars Training, 996
Erie Canal, 228, 300
construction of, 301
day laborers working on, 306
opening of, 298
Erie Railroad, 553
Eritrea, 1029
Ernest Linwood (Hentz), 394
Ervin, Samuel James, Jr. (1896–1985), 990
Escobedo v. Illinois (1964), 925
Escorial, 25

Espionage Act of 1917, 715
espionage, industrial, 289
Essay Concerning Human Understanding (Locke), 113
"Essay on the Trade of New England, An" (Bannister), 87
Essex, 234
Estonia, 1028
Ethiopia, 1029. *See also* Abyssinia
Ethiopian Regiment, 166
ethnic background, political party membership and, 585–86
ethnic groups, in middle Atlantic region, 106–8, 277*i*
Europe
  American artists living in (1920s), 748
  balance of power (1890–1901), 684
  collapse of Communism in, 1026, 1027–30
  economics, Marshall Plan and, 858–59
  erosion of peasant economies in, 562
  events leading to World War I in, 690–91, 697–99
  expansion and transformation of, 15–26
  exports to (1875–1900), 673*t*
  immigrants from (1870–1914), 562
  politics, late nineteenth century, 670
  powers, interference in Caribbean, 686–87
  religious diversity in (1600s), 24*i*
  Renaissance, 16–18
  rise of fascism in, 812, 817
  spheres of influence (1754), 122*m*
  transformation to commercial society, 3
  U.S. Civil War and, 467
  World War II fought in, 838–41
European Community (EC), 1034
European markets, American reliance on (1820s), 296
European middle class, 630
European peasantry
  employment in American industry, 562, 564
  erosion of, 562
European society
  hierarchy and authority, 12–13
  peasantry, 10–12
  religion, 13–15
Europeans
  impressions of U.S., late eighteenth century, 279
  as leaders in world trade, 3
  as settlers, 3
evangelical movement, 624, 996
evangelism
  abolitionism and, 364–67, 368
  business class, 359
  Second Great Awakening and, 277
Evans, Oliver (1755–1819), 288
Everett, Edward (1794–1865), 340–41, 350
Evers, Medgar Wiley (1926–1963), 949
Ewell, Richard Stoddert (1817–1872), 464
exchange rate, fixed, 886
excise taxes
  Hamilton's program on, 212
  Jefferson's abolition of, 231
  on liquor and tobacco, 580
  on spirits, 216
executive branch of government, 589
  antigovernment and, 583
Exodusters, 538, 538*i*
expansionism, continental, 413
  Anglo-American amity and, 684–85
  annexation of Texas, 413, 414
  Caribbean and, 685–87
  Cuban crisis of 1868–1875 and, 676–78
  economic sources of, 671–74
  foreign policy, 674–76
  ideology of, 676
  Manifest Destiny and, 402–3
  Mexico, Wilson and, 689–90
  Open Door policy, 687–89
  overseas trade and foreign policy and, 673–74
  Philippines and, 681–84
  Pierce and, 425–27
  Polk's goal in, 415
  roots of, 669–71
  slavery and, 385, 420
  Tyler and, 413, 414
  Venezuela crisis and, 675–76
exploration
  Christopher Columbus and, 19–20
  French, 36
  Portuguese, fifteenth century, 18–19
  Spanish, 35–36
exports, exportation
  agricultural, 109, 111
  American Revolution and, 184
  balance with imports (1870–1914), 672, 674*f*. *See also* trade deficit
  eighteenth-century, 126, 214
  Embargo Act of 1807 and, 235
  grain, 109
  from mid-Atlantic colonies, 109, 111
  1875–1900, 672, 673, 673*t*
  of native American crops, 7
  tobacco (1600s), 43
Exxon Valdez (oil tanker), 1032

factories
  assembly lines in, 386
  labor unions and, 338–39
  technological improvements in, 1820s–1830s, 288
Factories in the Field (McWilliams), 776
factory workers, unionized, 891
Fairbanks, Douglas (1883–1939), 739
Fair Campaign Practices Act of 1974, 991
Fair Deal, 865–66, 868–69
Fair Employment Practices Commission, 867
Fairfax, Thomas, baron (1693–1781), 128
Fair Labor Standards Act (1938), 795
Fairlie, Henry, 856
Fall, Albert Bacon (1861–1944), 729
Fallen Timber, battle of (1794), 224
fall-line towns, 289, 297
Fall River plan, 294
Falwell, Jerry (1933–), 996
families. *See also* children; farm families; marriage; parents
  African-American, 246–50, 381–82, 496
  in Chesapeake colonies, 43, 91
  during Great Depression, 764
  European (1400s), 12, 13
  farm. *See* farm families
  manufacturing, 306
  mercantile, 306
  nuclear, 906
  sharecropper, 499*i*
  size, early nineteenth century, 271–73
  southern, mills hiring, 559
  stem family system, 100–101, 102*i*
  women's movement and, 357
Family Assistance Plan, 983
family life
  1920s, 734–735
  1950s, 909, 909*i*, 912*i*
  urban (1870–1900), 631
  during World War II, 829–30, 831–32
family planning, 632. *See also* birth control
Farewell to Arms, A (Hemingway), 748
Farmer, James Leonard (1920–), 948, 949*i*
farmers. *See also* agriculture; farm families
  black, 602
  commercial paths taken by, 540
  debts, 540
    after American Revolution, 200
    1780s, 230
  expansion of holdings, 540
  "fair compensation," 262
  migration
    from Dust Bowl and, 772–77, 776*m*
    to West, 225–27
  New Deal and, 801
  Populist party and, 590–91
  protests during Great Depression, 780
  in Republican party, 494
  Resettlement Administration, 801
  social division among, in middle colonies, 109
  U.S. Constitution and, 206
  Whig party and, 341
Farmers' Alliance of the Northwest, 590
farm families, 229–30
  electrification and, effects on, 774, 774*i*, 775
  employment in cities (1870s), 562
  employment in textile industry (1820s), 292, 294
  freehold society and, 99–100
  Industrial Revolutions effect on, 299–300
  mail-order houses for, 555
  manufacturing by (1780s–1800s), 258–59
  standard of living (1800s), 242–43
  stem family system, 100–101, 102*i*
  westward expansion, 299–300
  yeoman, 60, 111
Farm Holiday Association, 780
farm life
  1850s–1900s, 540–42
  1896–1909, 596
  granges, 541–42
Farm Security Administration (FSA), 812, 828
Farragut, David Glasglow (1801–1870), 458

fascism, 869
  rise in Europe, 812, 817, 818–19
"Father Knows Best," 905
Faubus, Orval (1910–), 947
Faucett, Rachel (d. 1768), 208
Faulkner, William (1897–1962), 748, 749
Fauset, Jessie Redmon (1882–1961), 750
Fawkes, Guy (1570–1606), 140, 141
fax machines, 1022
Federal Art Project (FAP), 808
Federal Bureau of Investigation
(FBI), 986
  surveillance of Martin Luther King, Jr., and Southern Christian Leadership Conference, 949
  voter registration drives in South and, 953
  Watergate and, 986
Federal Communications Commission (FCC), 905
Federal Deposit Insurance Corporation (FDIC), 789
Federal Emergency Relief Administration (FERA), 790, 794
Federal Farm Loan Act of 1916, 665
federal government
  executive branch of, 583, 589
  expansion of, 729
  legislative branch, 583
  power to issue money, 592
federal land, price of (1820s–1830s), 300
Federal One project, 808
Federal Republic of Germany, 860, 860*m*
  reunification of, 1026
Federal Reserve System, 710, 728, 758, 791, 796, 1001
  contraction of money supply, 779
  Federal Reserve Act (1913), 664
  Great Depression and, 760
  reform of (1935), 791
Federal Savings and Loan Insurance Corporation (FSLIC), 1025
Federal Theatre Project (FTP), 810, 810*i*, 871
Federal Trade Commission (FTC), 729
  Wilson's broadening of power, 664
Federal Writers' Project, 811
Federalist, The, 205, 209
Federalist party, 204
  John Adams and, 217
  commonwealth ideology, 261–62
  in Congress (1794), 215, 216
  decline of, 238, 252, 320
  election of 1796 and, 217
  elections of 1788 and, 207
  Gazette of the United States, 218
  judges, 231
  Land Act of 1796, 230
  policies, Jefferson's modification of, 231
  property rights view, 262
  relinquishment of power, 219
  supporters of, 217
  U.S. Constitution and, 206, 207
  voting rights and, 265
  westward expansion and, 233
Federated Society of Journeymen Cordwainers, 334
fee simple title of land, 59, 69, 166
Fellowship for Reconciliation, 940
Female Charitable Society, 273, 313
Feminine Mystique, The (Friedan), 910
feminism, 650, 967
  consciousness raising, 969
  National Organization for Women, 967–68
  paths to, 967–69
  peak of, 969–71
  Redstockings, 970
  Supreme Court victories related to, 971–72
  "third wave," 1027
  women's liberation, 968–69
  women's rights, 967
Ferdinand, Franz, assassination of, 698
Fernald, Ohio, 993
Ferdinand II (1452–1516), 17, 19
Ferraro, Geraldine Anne (1935–), 971, 1011
feudal revival, 128
Few Practical Words of Advice to Those Born in Poverty (Alger), 582
Filipino-American communities, 900
Fillmore, Millard (1800–1874), 414*t*
  American party nominee in 1856, 431–32
  Fugitive Slave Act and, 424
  presidency, 423
  rejection by Whig party, 425
Filmer, Sir Robert (d. 1653), 90
Final Days, The (Woodward and Bernstein), 989
Finance Department. *See* U.S. Treasury Department
financial crisis. *See also* depressions
  American Revolution related, 173–75, 184, 185
  Panic of 1837, 306, 342, 342*i*, 349, 386
financial system, Hamilton's expansion of, 258
financiers, as public creditors, 209
Financier, The (Dreiser), 635
Fink, Albert, 556
Finney, Charles Grandison, (1792–1875), 311–14, 350, 356
Finney, Lydia, 312, 358
firearms
  Civil War rifle musket, 449
  Whitney's production of, 296
  World War I rifle, 698
Fire-eaters, 437, 443
  conventions, 444
Firestone, Shulamith, 969
First Confiscation Act of 1861, 461
First Rhode Island Company, 187
First South Carolina Volunteers, 468
fiscal crisis. *See* financial crisis
Fish, Hamilton (1808–1893), 505
Fish, Nathaniel, 60
fishing rights, 183
Fiske, John (1842–1901), 676
fitness craze of 1970s, 996
Fitzgerald, Francis Scott Key (1896–1940), 748, 749
Fixx, Jim, 996
Flagg, James Montgomery (1877–1960), 703*i*
Flanagan, Hallie, 810
Flapper, 736i
Fleming, Victor, 741
Florida, 36
  acquisition of, slavery and, 385
  American invasion of, 236
  East, annexation to U.S. (1819), 253
  growth of cities, 896
  secession of, 444
  Spanish control of, 183
flour, export trade in, 1700s, 126
Fonda, Jane (1937–), 994
Food Administration, 712
Food and Drug Administration, 660
food consumption, during Industrial Revolution, 389
  shortages, in 1768, 148
food rationing, during World War I, 710, 831
Foot, Samuel Augustus (1780–1846), 332
football, college, 744
Foote, Edward Bliss, 633
Force Acts of 1870 and 1871, 498
For Whom the Bell Tolls (Hemingway), 812
Forbes, John Murray, 553
Ford, Gerald Rudolph (1913–), 930, 941, 990, 1008
  presidency of, 998, 999–1000
Ford, Henry, 700, 738
  anti-Semitism, 746
Ford Motor Company, 732, 738
  automatic drilling machines, 893
  Model A, 738
  Model T, 596, 737, 738
  River Rouge plant, 731*i*, 995
Fordney-McCumber Tariff of 1922, 733
Foreign Affairs (journal), 855
Foreign Affairs Department. *See* State Department
foreign aid
  Marshall Plan and, 858–59
  Peace Corps, 920–21
foreign commerce, New York merchants seeking, 298
Foreign Conspiracy Against the Liberties of the United States (Morse), 389, 390
foreign policy. *See also* Cold War
  John Adams', 217, 218
  John Quincy Adams', 253
  Carter's, 1001–2
  Confederacy's, 467
  containment policy, 855–58
  détente, 924, 983, 984, 1010, 1012
  Dulles and, 875–76
  during Eisenhower administration, 874, 875–77
  expansionist, 674–76
  Grant's, 505
  immigration and, 900
  Andrew Johnson's, 504–5
  Kennedy's, 924
  Lincoln's, 467
  mission to Japan, 402–3

(foreign policy con't)
Monroe's, 253
during the 1920s, 733–34
Nixon's, 983–84
overseas trade and (1880s–1890s), 673–74
Pierce's, 426–27
Polk's, 415, 417, 420
Reagan's, 1010–11, 1012
Republican, during Reconstruction Era, 504–5
Franklin Roosevelt's, 817–18, 820–23, 838, 845–46
Washington's, 216
westward expansion, effects on, 236
Wilson's, 689–690
foreign relations, after World War II, 853
foreigners. *See also* immigrants
deportation of, Alien Act of 1798 and, 218
Forest Reserve Act of 1891, 656
formalism, nineteenth century, attack on, 640–41
Forman, Stanley, 996*i*
Forrest, Nathan Bedford (1821–1877), 497, 500–1
Fort Buford, Mont., Sioux surrender at, 526
Fort Donelson, Grant's taking of, 458
Fort Duquesne, 123, 124
Fort Henry, Grant's taking of, 458
Fort Pillow, Tenn., 497
Fort Pitt, 124
Fort Stanwix, Treaty of (1784), 223
Fort Sumter, Confederacy's destruction of, 445
Fort Wagner, 468
Fortune (magazine), 995
forty-niners, 408*i*, 408–9, 422, 534
Foster, William Z., 783
Fourier, Charles (1772–1837), 355
Fox, George (1624–1691), 105
France. *See also* French Revolution; French West Indies; specific treaties and wars
alliance with United States, during American Revolution, 175–76, 178, 198
Anglo-French entente, 691
challenge by Germany over Morocco, 691
Civil War and, 467
colonies, 36–37, 121, 125. *See also* New France
Continental System, 234
Franco-Prussian War (1870), 690, 698
French and Indian War, 121, 123–24
Germany's declaration of war on (1914), 698
Jacobin clubs, 215
monarchy, 17–18
Napoleonic wars, 234, 253
Paris, Treaty of, (1763) 124, 125
Paris, Treaty of, (1783) 183, 199, 223
purchase of Louisiana from, 231-34
recognition of Vietnam, 930
republican practices, 215
retaking of Suez Canal, 880
rule of Haiti, 231
trade with
Macon's Bill No. 2 and, 236
Non-intercourse Act and, 235
restrictions on (1805, 1807), 234, 235
U.S. support of troops in Vietnam, 930–31
war with Britain, U.S. involvment in, 218
war with Indochina, 930
withdrawal from Mexico, 505, 670
World War I casualties, 698
Franciscan monks, missions of, 36
Franco, Francisco (1892–1975), 812
Frankfurter, Felix (1882–1965), 711, 795
Franklin, Benjamin (1706–1790), 167, 201, 295
American Revolution and, 123, 182, 183
Autobiography, 350, 351
Enlightenment and, 113–14
Great Awakening and, 115
imperial system and, 148
Parliament's authority and, 149, 150
Paxton Boys and, 128
at Philadelphia Convention of 1787, 201
"Plan of Union" (1754), 123
scientific inventions, 114
Stamp Act and, 139, 146
Thoreau and, 351
treaty with France and, 175
U.S. Constitution and, 204
work ideal, 310
Franklin, Tenn.,199
Franklin Institute, 295
Fredericksburg, battle of (1862), 460, 476*i*
Free Speech (newspaper), 599
Free Speech Movement, 962
Freed, Alan, 909
freedmen, resettlement of, 485–87
Freedmen's Bureau, 486, 487, 488
support of planters, 502–3
Freedom and the Conference on the Cause and Cure of War, 734
Freedom of Information Act (1974), 991
freedom riders, freedom rides, 948, 949*i*,
Freedom's Journal (newspaper), 364
Freedom Summer (1964), 954, 969
freehold estates, stem family system, 101
freehold society
crisis of, 103–5
farm division, 100
Puritan, 57–60
voting rights, 203
women's place and, 101–3
freehold titles, 127, 203
Freeman, Elizabeth, 187*i*
freemen, in medieval towns, 13
Freeport doctrine, 436, 437
Free Presbyterian Church, 312–13
free society, Republicans' description of, 428
Free Soil party, 368–69
Dred Scott decision and, 423–33
election of 1848 and, 421
election of 1852 and, 425
Kansas-Nebraska Act and, 428
National Era (newspaper), 424
platform 462
freight rates, inland (1784–1900), 303*f*
Frelinghuysen, Theodore Jacob, 115
Frémont, John Charles (1813–1890), 417
Republican nomination of, 431, 432
French and Indian War, (1755–1763), 121, 123–24
French West Indies. *See also* Haiti; Martinique; Tobago
Sugar Act of 1764 and, 136
trade with, 95
French Revolution (1792–1801), 183, 208
American politics and, 215–16
economic effects on U.S., 214
Hamilton's economic program and, 216
Freneau, Philip (1752–1832), 189
Freund, Paul, 788
Frick, Henry Clay (1849–1919), 572, 634
Friedan, Betty Naomi (1921–), 909, 910, 911, 968, 971*i*
Frost, Robert (1874–1963), 749
frozen food industry, 904
Fuel Administration, 710
Fugitive Slave Act
of 1793, 244, 247, 423
of 1850, 423, 424–25
Fuller, Henry Blake, 635
Fuller, Margaret (1810–50), 360, 360*i*
Fulton, Robert (1765–1815), 303
Fundamental Constitutions of Carolina (1669), 68
Fundamentalist movement, 624, 748
Fundamental Orders, 55
Furman v. Georgia (1972), 983
fur trade, 35
Dutch, 39
French, sixteenth century, 36–37
native American dependence on, 62
New Netherland, 38

G. P. Putnam's Sons, 394
Gable, Clark (1901–1960), 768
Gadsden, Christopher (1724–1805), 148
Gadsden, James (1788–1858), 426
Gadsden Purchase, 426
Gage, Thomas (1721–1787), 128, 146, 169, 182
power in Boston, 158, 159
Quartering Act and, 139
gag rule (1836), 368, 369
Gaines, Edmund (1777–1849), 518
Galbraith, John Kenneth (1908–), 886–87
Gallatin, Albert (1761–1849), 231, 238, 259
Galloway, James, 520
Galloway, Joseph (c. 1731–1803), 153
Gallup Poll
1936, 765
on American attitudes toward Vietnam War, 941
on campus unrest (1960S), 964
Galveston, Texas, progressive reform in, 643–44
Gama, Vasco da (c. 1469–1524), 19
Gandhi, Mohandas (Mahatma, 1869–1948), 948
Garfield, Harry Augustus (1863–1942), 710

Garfield, James Abram (1831–1881), 579
Garfield, John, 871
Garland, Hamlin (1860–1940), 538, 540
Garner, John Nance (1863–1967), 821
Garrison, William Lloyd (1805–79), 359, 364–65, 365*i*, 366, 367, 368, 369
Garsed, Richard, 295
Garson, Greer, 830
Garvey, Marcus (1887–1940), 750, 956
Gary, Elbert Henry (1846–1927), 658, 721
gasoline. *See also* oil
  rationing during World War II, 831
Gaspé (ship), 150, 157*t*
Gates, Horatio (1727–1806), 173, 177
gay liberation movement, 961
Gazette (Boston), 258
Gazette (Maryland), 225, 266
Gazette of the United States, 218
Geddes, James, 301
General (magazine), 114
General Agreement on Tariffs and Trade (GATT, 1947), 886
General Dynamics Corporation, military contracts to, 887
General Electric Company, 731, 732
  Lynn, Mass. plant, 995
General Managers' Association, 573
General Motors Corporation, 732, 738, 803, 893
General Union for Promoting the Observance of the Christian Sabbath, 311
Genêt, Edmond Charles (1763–1834), 215
Geneva Accords (1964), 931
Geneva, Switzerland, John Calvin in, 25
Genius of Universal Emancipation (Lundy), 364
genteel tradition, 634–35
Gentle Measures in the Management and Training of the Young (Abbott), 633
gentry, English, price revolution and, 27
George I (1660–1727), 93
George II (1683–1760), 93
George III (1738–1820), 136, 264
  Proclamation of 1763, 135
George Balcombe (Tucker), 379
George, Henry (1839–1897), 533, 641
Georges, Sir Ferdinando (1566–1647), 29
Georgia (colony), founding of, 94
Georgia (state)
  abolitionism and, 367
  cotton plantations in, 376
  Creek nation, treaty with, 323
  Jim Crow law, 599
  secession of, 444
  seizure of native American land (1825, 1828), 327
  Sherman's capture of, 473–74
  textile industry, 558
Germain, George, viscount Sackville (1716–1785), 172
German-Americans
  Catholic, 622
  immigration to U.S., after World War II, 900
  World War I and, 700, 715
German Democratic Republic, 860, 860*m*, 1026
Germans
  immigrants, 388
  mercenaries in American Revolution, 173
  in New York colony, 110
  in Pennsylvania colony, 106–7, 107*i*, 112
Germany, 698, 704. *See also* Federal Republic of Germany; German Democratic Republic
  Anti-Comintern pact with Japan, 819
  Berlin airlift, 859, 859*i*
  challenge of France over Morocco, 691
  declaration of war on France (1914), 698
  declaration of war on U.S., 823
  erosion of peasant economy in, 562
  fascism in, 818–19
  Franco-Prussian War (1870), 690, 698
  invasion of Soviet Union, 839*i*
  joining with Italy (1936), 819
  naval blockade of Great Britain, World War I and, 700–1
  nonaggression pact with Soviet Union, 820
  occupational zones after World War II, 854
  outbreak of World War II (1939), 820
  persecution of Jews, 820. *See also* Holocaust
  Protestant Reformation and, 23–24
  reindustrialization after World War II, 854
  reparations payments after World War I, 733
  reunification of, 1026
  sinking of Allied ships during World War I, 703
  sinking of U.S. ships during World War II, 824
  surrender (1945), 840
  Third Reich, 818
  Tri-Partite Pact with Japan and Italy (1940), 822
  Triple Alliance and, 691
  U.S. declaration of war on (1917), 702, 823
  Weimar Republic of 1920s, 818
  withdrawal from League of Nations, 819
Geronimo (1829–1909), 525
Gestalt movements, 996
Gettysburg, battle of (1863), 464–65, 466
Ghent, Treaty of (1814), 238
Ghost Dance, 527
Giants (baseball team), 896
Giap, Vo Nguyen (1912–), 930
GI Bill. *See* Servicemen's Readjustment Act of 1944
Gibraltar, 75, 183
  Treaty of, 238
Gibbons v. Ogden (1824), 305
Gibson, Charles Dana (1867–1944), 633, 703*i*
Gibson girl, 633
Gideon v. Wainwright (1963), 925
Gila River, 426
Gilbert Islands, 841, 843*i*
Gilbert, Sir Humphrey (1539–1583), 29
Gilded Age, The (Twain and Warner), 634
Gilman, Caroline Howard, 394
Gilman, Charlotte Perkins (1860–1935), 397, 641, 650
Ginsberg, Allen (1926–), 965, 966
gins, cotton, 214
Ginzberg, Eli, 911
Glacier Point, 535*i*
glasnost, 1026
Glass, Carter (1858–1946), 665
Glassford, Pelham D., 780*i*
Glass-Steagall Banking Act (1932), 779, 789
Gleason, Jackie, 905, 905*i*
Glenn, John Herschel, Jr. (1921–), 924
Glidden, Joseph F., 536
Glorious Revolution of 1688, 71–73, 90, 93, 148, 168
Godey's Lady Book (magazine), 313*i*, 393
Godkin, Edwin Lawrence, 587, 628
gold, 19, 25, 592
  abundance of (1869–1909), 596
  bimetallic standard, 592
  drain of reserves, 593
  exchange for greenbacks, 507
Gold Diggers of 1933, 767, 790
Golden Bowl, The (James), 635
Golden Hill riots, 149
Goldmark, Pauline, 712
Goldmark, Peter, 890
gold rush, 407–9, 518–20
  in Black Hills, 526
  boom towns, 520
  effects on development of California, 533–34
  forty-niners, 408*i*, 408–9, 422, 534
gold standard
  Franklin Roosevelt's abandonment of, 791
  Great Depression and, 760
  lawyer's march for, 593*i*
Goldwater, Barry Morris, (1909–), 918, 927, 1008
  Youth for Goldwater, 962
Goldwyn, Samuel (1882–1974), 739
golf, 744
Gompers, Samuel (1850–1924), 652, 711
  AFL and, 572
Gomulka, Wladyslaw (1905–1982), 876
Gone With the Wind, 768
Gooch, Sir William, (1681–1751), 120
Good Hope Plantation, 246
Good Housekeeping, 631, 742
Goodman, Andrew, 954
Goodman, Benjamin David (Benny, 1909–1986), 769
Good Neighbor Policy, 818
goods, sharing of, in freehold society, 104
Gorbachev, Mikhail (1931–), 1012
  coup against, 1028–29
  glasnost and perestroika, 1026
  Nobel Peace Prize awarded to, 1028
  rapport with Reagan and Bush, 1027, 1028*i*
Gordon, Thomas, 143
Gore, Albert Arnold, Jr. (1948–) 1024, 1033, 1033*i*
Gosport navy yard, 446

Gould, Jay (1836–1892), 553, 570
Gould, William Proctor, 384
government. *See also* federal government; state government; local government
  mixed, English Whig theory of, 194
  partnership with business (1920s), 727–34
  Reagan's removal of regulations on, 1010
  spending, New Deal and, 797
  standards of, machine politics and, 587
  U.S., executive department, 208
governors, 194
  of colonies, 75, 92
Grable, Betty, 825
Grady, Henry Woodfin (1850–1889), 558
Graham, Isabella, 311
Graham, William Franklin (Billy, 1918–), 996
grain, grain industry
  in mid-Atlantic colonies, 109
  tariff on, 415
Gramm-Rudman Act of 1985, 1025
Grand Alliance, 838, 854
Grange, Harold Edward (Red, 1903–), 744
Granger, 542, 543
Granger, Gideon, 230
Granges, 541–42, 543
Grant, Ulysses Simpson (1822–1885), 446, 458, 490, 586, 587
  condemnation of policies, 505–7
  depression of 1873–1877 and, 507
  election of 1866, 491
  election of 1872, 506
  expansion in Caribbean and, 505
  as leader of Union Army, 469–73
  Mexican War and, 416, 417
  resignation as secretary of War, 490–91
  Tenure of Office Act and, 490
  victory at Shiloh, 458
  war against Ku Klux Klan, 498
Grantism, 506
Granville, County, 129
Granville John Carteret, earl of (1690–1763), 128
grape pickers, joining of United Farm Workers Union, 959–60
Grapes of Wrath (Steinbeck), 768, 774, 775
Grasse, François Joseph Paul, comte de (1722–1788), 178
Grasso, Ella Tambussi (1919–1981), 971
Grateful Dead, 965
Great American Desert, 403, 427. *See also* Great Plains
Great Atlantic and Pacific Tea Company (A & P), 556
Great Awakening. *See also* Second Great Awakening
  rebellion related to, 140
  social and intellectual significance of, 118–19
  George Whitefield and, 115
Great Britian. *See* England
Great Deflation, 547
Great Depression, 752, 757
  blacks and, 770–72
  Black Tuesday, 758
  Bonus Army, 780*i*, 781
  breadlines, 763*i*
  causes of, 757
  demographic trends, 764–65
  discontent and rebellion related to, 779–82
  Dust Bowl migration and, 772, 773–77
  effects on Harlem, 800
  election of 1932 and, 782–93
  family life during, 764
  Hoover and, 778–79
  international repercussions, 759, 760
  Mexican-American communities and, 777–78
  monetary policy and, 760, 779
  popular culture and, 766–70
  Reconstruction Finance Corporation and, 779
  self-perpetuation of, 759
  statistics of, 760–61
  victims of, 761–63
  women and, 765–66
  World War II and, 817–18
  young people and, 766
Great Gatsby, The (Fitzgerald), 749
Great Lakes, 225
Great Northern Railroad, 534
Great Plains, 515, 536. *See also* California; westward expansion
  cattle frontier, 520–21
  Dust Bowl, 772–77
  Indians of, 516–18
  settlement of farmers in, 515, 536–39, 536*i*
Great Salt Lake, 405
Great Salt Lake area, Mormons in, 536
Great Society, 807, 926–30
  New Deal coalition and, 929–30
  war on poverty, 928–29
Great Train Robbery, The, 738
Great War for Empire, (1756–1763) 124–25, 127, 137*i*
  economic conditions after, 129, 135–36
  imperial political system and, 133–35
  Paris, Treaty of, 137. *See also* Paris, Treaty of
  reform after, 136–38
Greece, civil war in, 858
Greeley, Horace (1811–1872), 355, 506, 515, 518
greenbacks, 452, 507, 592
Greenbelt residential towns, 806
Green Berets, 920
Greene, Nathaniel (1742–1786), 178
Greenfield, Meg, 982
greenhouse effect, 1032
green politics, 1032
Greensboro, N.C., sit-in, 948
Green Spring, 47, 90
Greenville, Treaty of (1795), 224
Grenada, U.S. invasion of, 1011
Grenville, George (1712–1770), 144*t*, 145
  Stamp Act and, 138–39
Gresham, Walter Quintin (1832–1895), 673
Grier, Robert Cooper (1794–1870), 432
Griffith, David Wark (1875–1948), 654, 739
Grimes County, Texas, 599
Grimké, Angelina Emily (1805–1879), 359–60, 365
Grimké, Sarah Moore (1792–1873), 359–60
Grimké, Thomas, 273
Griswold v. Connecticut (1965), 971
grog shops, 309
Gropper, William (1897–1977), 791, 791*i*
gross national product (GNP), A-24
  during Great Depression, 761
  1870–1900, 672
  1920–1921, 728
  1933–1937, 796
  1945–1960, 886
  1960s, 924
  Roosevelt recession of 1937–1938 and, 796
Gruening, Ernest Henry (1887–1974), 932
Guadalcanal, 841
Guadalupe Hidalgo, Treaty of (1848), 420
Guam, 679, 841
  U.S. acquisition of, 680
Guantanamo Bay, 818
Guatemala, 4, 876
Guerard, Peter Jacob, 82
Guffey-Snyder Coal Conservation Act of 1936, 795
Guinea Company, 28
Guiteau, Charles, 579
Gulf of Tonkin resolution (1964), 932–33
Guthrie, Okla., 527
Guzman, Jacobo Arbenz, 876
Gwin, William McKendree (1805–1885), 408–9

habeas corpus, writ of, 451
Hagerty, James, 874
Hague Peace Conference of 1899, 691
Haight-Ashbury, 966
Haile, Selassie (1891–1975), 818
Hair, 966
Hairy Ape, The (O'Neill), 749
Haiti, 20, 505, 690
  expansionist efforts in, 670, 689*m*
  French rule in, 231
  U.S. withdrawal of troops from (1920s), 733
Halberstam, David, 920, 936, 986
Haldeman, H. R., 987, 990, 991
Haldimand, James, 151
Halfbreeds, 586, 587
Halfway Convenant, 56
Halifax, Lord, 123
Halifax, Nova Scotia, Howe's headquarters in, 169
Hall, John H., 296
Halleck, Henry Wager (1815–1872), 469
Hall's Hill, Va., 466
Hamer, Fannie Lou, 953
Hamilton, Alexander (1755–1804)
  assumption plan, 209
  background of, 208, 209
  Bank of United States and, 210–11, 258

(Hamilton, Alexander con't)
Burr's killing of, 234
economic program, 209–13, 258, 261
expansion of financial system, 258
factions in Congress, 211
Federalist, The, 205, 209
fiscal structure and, 209*f*
national taxes, 212, 216
patronage of government, 211
at Philadelphia Convention of 1787, 201
"Report on Manufactures," 211
"Report on the Public Credit," 209–10
secretary of Treasury under Washington, 208
war debt and, 210
westward expansion and, 233–34
Hamilton, Elizabeth Schuyler, 208
Hammond, James Henry (1807–1864), 379
Hampton Roads, 669
Hancock, John (1737–1793), 136, 151
John Adams' defense of, 138, 142
opposition to U.S. Constitution, 206–7
trial of, 148
hand jenny, 290
Handsome Lake (1735–1815), 250
Hanford Nuclear Reservation, 993
Hanna, Marcus Alonzo (1837–1904), 595, 596, 656, 679
Hanoi, bombing of, 984*i*
Harding, Warren Gamaliel (1865–1923), 727, 729, 745
Hard, William, 642
Hare Krishna, 996
Hargreaves, James (1720–1778), 290
Harlan County, Ky., 781
Harlem, 617, 771–72, 902
cultural affirmation of 1920s in, 749–50
Great Depression and, 800
race riots in (1935), 772
Spanish Harlem, 900
Harlem Heights, battle of (1776), 170
Harlem Renaissance, 749–50
Harlow, Jean (1911–1937), 768
Harmar, Josiah, 224
Harper Brothers, 394
Harpers Ferry, Va., 446
John Brown's raid at, 437, 439
Jackson's capture of, 459
Harper's (magazine), 642
Harper's Monthly, 635
Harriman, William Averell (1891–1986), 856, 857
Harrington, Michael, 913, 928
Harris, Joel Chandler (1848–1908), 635
Harrison, Benjamin (1833–1901), 579, 584, 584*i*, 587*i*, 671, 675
presidential election of 1888, 590
view on tariffs, 580
Harrison, Bennett, 995
Harrison Township, Neb., 543
Harrison, William Henry (1773–1841), 414*t*
death of, 345
presidential election of 1836, 342
presidential election of 1840, 344–45, 434
purchase of native American land and, 225
War of 1812 and, 238
Harris poll, 972
Harte, (Francis) Brett (1836–1902), 534, 635
Hart, Gary Warren (1936–), 1024
Harvard University, 266, 731
Divinity School, 350
Hastie, William, 946
Hat Act of 1732, 70*t*, 95
hatters, 561
Hawaii
annexation of, 679
expansionist interest in (1880s), 671
Japanese-Americans living in, during World War II, 835
Hawkins, Sir John (1532–1595), 28
Hawley-Smoot Tariff of 1930, 733, 759
Hawthorne, Nathaniel (1804–1864), 302
transcendentalism and, 352, 353
Hayden, Tom, 962, 978
Hayes, Rutherford Birchard (1822–1893), 507
compromise of 1877 and, 508–9
presidential election of 1876, 507–8
Hay, John Milton (1838–1905), 687
Haymarket Square Riot, of 1886, 571–72
Hayne, Robert Young (1791–1839), Daniel Webster's debate with, 332
Haynsworth, Clement F., 983
Hay-Pauncefote Agreement (1901), 685
Haywood, William Dudley (Big Bill, 1869–1928) 575
Hayworth, Rita, 825
Hazard of New Fortunes, A (Howells), 635
headright system, 41, 46
Head Start, 929
health care. *See also* hospitals; nursing
during Civil War, 454i, 455
midwives, 103
healthcare costs, 1980s–1990s, 1020–22
health insurance, 1021
federal, Lyndon Johnson and, 927
Medicaid, 928, 1021
Medicare, 928
national, 794, 869
social programs, 928
Hearst, William Randolph (1863–1951), 626, 676
Heller, Walter (1915–1987), 924
Hemingway, Ernest Miller (1899–1961), 748, 812
Hendrix, Jimi, 965
Henry VII (1457–1509), 17
Henry VIII (1491–1547), 29
Henry, Patrick (1736–99), 143, 166, 188
Antifederalists and, 204
Hamiltonian program and, 209
Philadelphia Convention of 1787 and, 201
Henry Street Settlement, 648
Henry the Navigator, prince of Portugal (1394–1460), 18
Hentz, Caroline Lee, 394, 395
Hepburn Railway Act of 1906, 659
Herbst, Josephine, 766
Hernandes, Harriet, 498
Hersey, John Richard (1914–), 844
Hersh, Seymour, 985
Hessians, in American Revolution, 170
Hewitt, Abram Stevens (1822–1903), 644
Hiawatha (Longfellow), 394
Hickok, Lorena, 762
hierarchy, European, 1400s, 12–13
Higginson, Thomas Wentworth (1823–1911), 369, 437, 468
Highway Beautification Act of 1965, 928
Highway Trust Fund, 898
highways
construction of (1945–1965), 898
Interstate Highway Act (1956), 875, 898
New Deal and, 806
Hill, Anita, 1026, 1026*i*,
Hill, Jonathan (1646–1717), 101*i*
Hillman, Sidney (1887–1946), 829
Hillsboro, Ohio, Women's Christian Temperance Union and, 588
Hillsborough, Lord, 148
Hine, Lewis (1874–1940), 811
Hinman, David, 295
hippies, 965, 966
Hirabayashi v. United States (1943), 833
Hiroshima, dropping of atomic bomb on, 846, 847
Hispanics. *See also* Mexican-Americans
immigration
1980s–1990s, 1018, 1018*i*, 1019
after World War II, 900–1
New Deal and, 804
in Southwest (1860s–1880s), 530–31
Hiss, Alger (1904–), 871, 872
History of the American Revolution (Ramsay), 200
History of the Revolution (Warren), 268
Hitler, Adolf (1889–1945), 818, 819*i*
Hoar, George Frisbie (1826–1904) 584, 681
Hobbes, Thomas (1588–1679), 12, 43
Hobby, Oveta Culp (1905–), 874
Ho Chi Minh (1890–1969), 930, 931, 934
Ho Chi Minh City, 986
Ho Chi Minh trail, 933. *See also* Saigon
Hoe rotary press, 394
Hoffman, Abbie, 979
Hofstadter, Richard (1916–1970), 744
holidays, observance of, regional differences in, 240–41
Holland. *See* Netherlands
Holland Land Company, 230
Hollywood, Calif., 739
"Hollywood Ten," 871
Holmes, Isaac, 245
Holmes, Oliver Wendell (1841–1935), 470, 640–41
Abrams v. United States (1919), 716
Lochner v. New York (1905), 640
Schenck v. United States, 716
Holocaust, 840–41
Holtzman, Elizabeth, 971
homeless, of 1980s–1990s, 1016, 1016*i*
Home Owners Loan Corporation, 789
Homestead Act of 1862, 453–54, 536
Homestead Act of 1889, 526

homesteading, *536i*
Home to Harlem (McKay), 750
homicide rates, for black men, 1017
homosexuals
 AIDS epidemic and, 1021–22
 in armed forces during World War II, 824
 gay liberation movement, 961
Hone, Philip (1780–1851), 308, 402
Honeymooners, The, 905, *905i*
Hong Kong, 841, *843m*
Hood, John Bell (1831–1879) 473, 474
Hooker, Isabella Beecher (1822–1907), 397
Hooker, Joseph (1814–1879), 461, 464
Hooker, Thomas (1586–1647), 55
Hoover, Herbert Clark (1874–1964), 710, 751, 759, 760
 fiscal policy, 779
 Great Depression and, 760, 778–82
 immigration quota and, 746
 presidential election of 1928, 752–53
 presidential election of 1932, 782, *782m*
 Reconstruction Finance Corporation and, 779
 as secretary of commerce, 729
Hoover, John Edgar (1895–1972), 722, 949
 Watergate and, 986
Hoovervilles, 780, *780i*
Hopi Indians, 36
Hopkins, Harry Lloyd (1890–1946), 790, 794, 821, 836–37, 845
Hopkins, Samuel (1721–1803), 279
Horne, Lena (1917–), 825
Hornet (aircraft carrier), 841
Horseshoe Bend, battle of (1814), 239
Horton, Willie, 1025
hospitals
 colonial, 114
 women's movement and, 358
Hotel del Coronado, 535
household goods, purchase of, 1840s–1860s, 392–93
household mode of production, 105
House Committee on Un-American Activities, 869, 870
House Made of Dawn (Momaday), 961
House of Burgesses, 41, 47, 48
 property rights of Africans and, 79
 taxation on Virginia colony, 86
 Virginia, 148, 150
House of Commons, *56t*
House of Representatives. *See* U.S. Congress
Houseman, John, *810i*
House of Representatives. *See* U.S. House of Representatives
housing. *See also* communtities
 balloon frame, 391–92
 bettering house, 114
 among Chesapeake aristocracy, 86
 dumbbell tenements, *613f*, 614
 home mortgage assistance, 928
 low-cost, 614, 1016
 middle-class (1820s–1850s), 310, 391–92
 in middle colonies, 109
 mortgages in 1940s–1960s, 897
 National Housing Act of 1937, 795
 prices of 1970s, 995
 rooming houses, 1016
 subsidized public housing, 1016
 suburban (1940s–1960s), 896–99
 tenants' rights groups, 929
 tenements, 309
 urban (1890s–1901), 614
 of western settlers (1870s), *536*
Houston, Samuel (1793–1863), 333
Howard, Edgar, 594
Howard, Oliver Otis (1830–1909), 487
Howard University, 963
Howe, William, viscount (1729–1814), 169, 170, 171
 occupation of Philadelphia, 183
Howells, William Dean (1837–1920), 635
Hudson, Henry (d. 1611), 37
Hudson Bay, 75
Hudson River, 37
Hudson River School, 402
Hudson River Valley, 238
 manors, tenancy on, 109–11
Hudson's Bay Company, in Oregon territory, 403
Huerta, Victoriano (1854–1916), 690
Hughes, Charles Evans (1862–1948), 701, 729, 733
Hughes, James Langston (1902–1967), 749, 750
Huguenots (French Protestants), 36, 108
Huitzilopochtli, 5
Hull, Cordell (1871–1955), 818, 822, 837
Hull House, 648, *648i*
Hull, William (1753–1825), 237
humanism, Renaissance, 17
human potential movement, 996–97
Humphrey, Hubert Horatio (1911–1978), 867, 918, 927, 978
 presidential election of 1968, 979
Hungary. *See also* Austria-Hungary
 Soviet Union repression of revolt, 876
Hungry Hearts (Yezierska), 809
Hunkpapa tribe, 517
Hunt, Howard, 987
Huron Indians, conversion to Catholicism, 37
Hurston, Zora Neale (1901–1960), 750, 810
Husband, Herman, 129
Hussein, Saddam, 1030, 1031
Huston, John (1906–1987), 810, 830
Huston, Tom, 986
Hutchinson, Anne Marbury (1591–1643), 54–55
Hutchinson, Thomas (1711–1780), 140, 156, 157
 sovereignty and, 150
 Tea Act of 1773 and, 152
hydrocarbon age, 991
hydrogen bomb, *851i*, 861
 Eisenhower's commitment to, 877

Iacocca, Lee (1924–), 1014
Ice Age, 3
Ickes, Harold LeClaire (1874–1952), 788, 790, 804, 805, 821, 991
idealism, progressive, 641–42
illegal aliens, 1018
Illinois, 299
 constitution, 265
 migration to, 225
Illinois Central Railroad, 552
I Love Lucy, 905
immigrants. *See also* foreigners; specific nationalities
 Alien Act of 1798 and, 218
 European, social class of, 268
 German, 106–7, *387i*, 388
 Irish (1830s–1860s), 388–91
 in labor force (1840–1914), 562–64, 609
 living in cities (1880–1911), 615–17
 Naturalization Act of 1798 and, 218
 in Republican party, 494
immigration, 609
 advocates of restricting, 654, 744–47
 Chinese (1840s–1870s), 531–32
 1870–1914, *563f*
 1820–1860, *386f*
 European, to West (1880s), 538
 Hispanic (1860s–1880s), 531–33
 Industrial Revolution and, 287–91
 1980s, 1018–20
 1921–1979, *746f*
 quota system of 1920s, 745–46
 to West (1870s–1880s), 537, 538, *538m*
 after World War II, 899–901
Immigration Reform and Control Act of 1986 (Simpson-Mazzoli), 1018
Immigration Restriction League, 654
impeachment, of Andrew Johnson, 491
imperialism
 American. see expansionism
 in British colonies, 133–35
 weakening of, 94
imports, importation. *See also* tariff(s)
 American Revolution and, 184
 balance with exports (1870–1914), 672, *672f*
 boycott of (1768), 147–50
 British (1700s), *126f*
 duties on, 201, 291, 323. *See also* tariffs
  Articles of Confederation and, 198
  Hamilton's program on, 212
  protests against, 148–50, 156–58
  Townshend Act of 1767 and, 146–48
impressment, 234–35
Incas, 20
 Spanish conquest of, 21
income. *See also* Wage
 Industrial Revolution and, 306
 mid-1850s, 391
 1920s, 728, 735
 1945–1960, 886
 1973–1989, 995, 1015
 urban (1890s), 626
 wage labor of former slaves, 487–88
 during World War II, 830
income tax
 Economic Recovery Tax Act (1981), 1009, 1011
 financing of World War II by, 823

(income tax con't)
Kennedy-Johnson tax cut of 1964, 924
reform, Revenue Act of 1942, 823
Supreme Court rules unconstitutional, 583
Tax Reform Act, (1986), 1011
World War I and, 710
indentured servants, servitude, 46, 78
in Chesapeake colonies, 43–46
children as, 99–100
Chinese migration and, 531
northern urban, 89
India, 15*i*, 19
British withdrawal from, 879
ethnic and religious disputes in, 1029
Indiana, 299
constitution, 265
migration to, 225
Indian Removal Act (1830), 327
Indian Reorganization Act of 1934, 804
Indian Rights Association , 527
Indians, American. *See* native Americans
indigo industry, 126, 199
individualism, 279, 428. *See also* transcendentalists and utopians
associated, 729
competitive capitalistic, 279, 280
Emerson and, 350
ideology of, 582
Social Darwinism, 583
Indochina, French colony, 930
Indonesia, 876
industrial education, 602
industrial espionage, 289
industrialization
basic industry, 548–50
managerial revolution, 556–58
mass markets and large-scale enterprise, 553–56
new South and, 558–61
railroads and, 550–53
Industrial Revolution, 10, 169, 243, 287
Boston Manufacturing Company, 291–94
business class and, 391–93
democratization and, 319, 320
effects on farming families, 299–300
England in, 125
expansion of markets, 296–300
factories, 385–86
family planning and population growth and, 395–98
growth of cities and towns, 297–99
immigration, 1840–1860, and, 387–91
labor unions and, 334, 335
Northeast and, 385–98
reform movements arising during, 349
rise of northeastern manufacturing, 287–89
social structures related to, 305–15. *See also,* class, social and economic
technological innovations, 294–96
transportation revolution, 300–5
women's movement and, 357
industrial society, Emerson and, 350–51
Industrial Workers of the World (IWW, Wobblies), 575, 716
industry. *See also* factories; manufacturing; specific industries
African-Americans employed in (1890), 562
centralized, functionally departmentalized, plan, 557–58
cooperative factories and shops, 569
Crystal Palace Exhibition, 386
decline, after American Revolution, 199
deindustrialization, 995
electricity effects on, 612
geographic concentration, late nineteenth century, 608–9
Great Depression and, 759
impact of railroads on, 401
impact of slavery on, 81, 83
machine-tooled products, 295, 385, 386
in middle colonies, 109
middle management, 557
military-industrial complex, 887–96
move to cities, late nineteenth century, 607–8
National Industrial Recovery Act, 790
National Recovery Administration, 790
in Northeast (1840s–1860s), 385–86
northern urban (1700s), 87–92
output
1870–1900, 672
1933–1937, 796
sick industries, 729
stationary steam engines, 385–86
textile, 289–91. *See also* textile industry
vertically integrated firms, 557
War Industries Board, 711
workers employed in (1940–1950), 891
inflation
during American Revolution, 174, 185
during Carter administration, 1000–1
during Civil War, 453
lowering of, during 1950s, 886
of 1919, 728
of 1974, 999
during World War II, 826
following World War II, 865
Influence of Seapower upon History, The (Mahan), 674
influenza epidemic, after World War I, 708, 708*i*
Ingersoll, Herbert G., 584
Ingersoll, Jared (1749–1822), 140, 141
In His Steps (Sheldon), 624
injunctions, against labor unions, 652
In Our Time (Hemingway), 748
Inquisition, Spanish, 19
installment buying, 735
during Great Depression, 764
Instinct of Workmanship, The (Veblen), 640
Institutes of the Christian Religion (Calvin), 25
insurance, 928. *See also* health insurance
integrated circuits (IC*j*, 880
intelligence testing, by army, during World War I, 708–9
intercontinental ballistic missiles (ICBMs), 984
interest rates
in grain belt (1880s), 543
Great Depression and, 760
1974, 999
1977–1980, 1001
Internal Revenue Service (IRS), 987
internal taxes, Jefferson's abolition of, 231
International Bank for Reconstruction and Development. *See* World Bank
international economic system, impact of Great Depression on, 759
International Harvester, 658, 732
International Labor Defense (ILD), 770
international market, Great Depression and, 760
International Monetary Fund (IMF), 886
international money market, 995
International Telephone and Telegraph, 732, 890
International Typographical Union, 570
International Women's Year, 971, 971*i*
Interstate Commerce Act (1887), 542, 659
Interstate Commerce Commission (ICC), 659, 948
railroad regulation, 542
Interstate Highway Act (1956), 875, 897
Iowa, admission to Union, 427
Iowa Farmers' Union, 780
Iran
hostage crisis, 1002–3
import of oil from, 991
SAVAK, 1002
seizing of British oil properties (1953), 876
Iran-Contra affair, 1011–12
Iraq. *See also* Persian Gulf War
import of oil from, 991
invasion of Kuwait (1990), 1030–31
revolt of Kurds and Shiites (1991), 1031
Ireland, John (1838–1918), 619
Ireland
immigrants from
anti-Catholicism and, 389–91
1830s–1860s, 388–91
potato famine, 388
Irish Home Rule, cancellation of (1914), 700
Iron Act of 1750, 70*t*
ironclad oath, 483
ironclads, 669
iron industry, 515, 550, 608. *See also* steel industry
impact of railroads on, 401
output (1870–1910), 549*t*
puddling mills, 548, 550
westward movement of, 548*m*
Iroquois Indians, 7, 38, 74
alliance with British, 172
language of, 8
loss of land, 223
trade, 121
irrigation, 536
Irving, Washington (1783–1859), 269, 269*i*, 394
Isabella (1451–1504), 19
Ishki chito, 9
Isaacson, Walter, 856

isolationism, 818
abandonment of (1890s), 671
America First Committee (1940), 820–21
during 1930s, 818
Israel. *See also* Palestine
Gaza Strip, 880
invasion of Lebanon, 1010
peace treaty with Egypt, 1001, 1001*i*
Yom Kippur War, 992, 1001
It Can't Happen Here (Lewis), 810
It Happened One Night, 768
Italy, 3, 698
Allied invasion of (1943), 838
fascism in, 818–19
immigrants from, employment in American industry, 563
invasion of Ethiopia (1935), 818
Renaissance, 17
Tri-Partite Pact with Japan and Germany (1940), 822
Triple Alliance and, 691
U.S. declaration of war on, 823
Iwo Jima, U.S. capture of, 843*i*, 844

Jackson, Andrew (1767–1845), 253, 325i, 413, 414
attack on Second Bank of the United States, 328–30
Battle of New Orleans and, 238–39
Democratic party and, 324, 325
democratization movement and, 319
depression of 1837–1843 and, 344
inauguration, 318*i*
Kitchen Cabinet, 325
native American policy, 325–27
Nullification crisis and, 330–32
presidency of, 325–34
presidential election of 1824, 320, 322
presidential election of 1828, 323*i*, 323–24
presidential election of 1832, 329
restriction of abolitionists' use of mail and, 368
supporters of, attack on John Quincy Adams, 324
Texas Rebellion and, 333–34
Whig party and, 340, 341
Jackson, Helen Hunt (1830–1885), 527, 534
Jackson, Jesse (1941–), 1024
Jackson, Jimmy Lee, 954
Jackson, Michael, 1022
Jackson, Patrick Tracy, 291
Jackson, Rebecca Cox (1795–1871), 355, 356
Jackson, Richard, 138
Jackson, Thomas Jonathan ("Stonewall") (1824–1863), 459
capture of Harpers Ferry, 459
Jackson State College, killing of students at, 964, 964*i*
Jacobin clubs, 215
Jacobson, Natalie, 998
jails, women's movement and, 358
Jamaica, 76
James I (1566–1625), 30, 31, 42
James II (1633–1688), 68, 71, 73
overthrow of, 72
James, Frank, 446
James, Henry (1843–1916), 634, 635
James, Jesse (1847–1882), 446
James, William (1842–1910), 640, 641, 1001
James River, 40
Jamestown, Va., English settlement in, 25, 29, 40, 41*i*
Japan, 698
Anglo-Japanese Alliance (1902), 688
Anti-Comintern pact with Germany, 819
attack on Pearl Harbor, 822-23
commercial treaty with U.S. (1858), 402–3
dropping of atomic bomb on, 846
expansionism (early 1900s), 688–89, 733
invasions in Pacific, 841, 843*m*
kamikaze missions during World War II, 844
occupation of Vietnam, 930
protectorate over Korea, 688
resignation from League of Nations, 818
Russo-Japanese War (1904), 688
Sino-Japanese War (1894–1895), 673, 688
surrender of, 846
Tri-Partite Pact with Germany and Italy (1940), 822
U.S. declaration of war on, 823
U.S. victory over, 843
Japanese-Americans, 829
communities, 900
internment during World War II, 833–35
Issei generation, 833
Nisei generation, 833
Sansei generation, 835
Yonsei generation, 835
Japanese immigrants, 533
quotas on, 745
Jay, John (1745–1829), 182, 194, 201, 205, 225
Jay's Treaty (1795), 225
jazz, 742, 769
Jazz Age, 750
Jazz Singer, The, 739, 742
Jefferson, Thomas (1743–1826), 85, 262, 266, 296, 323
John Quincy Adams and, 322
Alien and Sedition Acts and, 218
Bill for Establishing Religious Freedom (1786), 188
cabinet, 230
Constitution and, 232
death of, 257
Declaration of Independence and, 168–69, 214
Embargo Act of 1807, 235
Louisiana Purchase and, 231–34
opposition to Hamilton's economic policy, 211, 211*i*
Ordinance of 1784 and, 214
peaceful coercion policy, 235
political parties and, 217, 218
politics and the court system and, 230–31
presidency, 230–31
presidential election of 1800, 218–19
as secretary of state under Washington, 208, 210
slavery and, 188
technology and, 212–13, 213–14
as vice-president, 217
westward expansion and, 223, 231–34
Jefferson Airplane, 965
Jenkinson, Charles, 137
Jenkins's Ear, War of (1739–1741), 94
Jennie Gerhardt (Dreiser), 635
Jesuits, (Society of Jesus), 36
Jewett, Sarah Orne (1849–1909), 635
Jews
anti-Semitism, 746, 841
in civil rights movement, 954
college quotas on, 746
displaced, immigration to U.S., 900
Eastern European, 619
Holocaust and, 840, 841
immigrants from Soviet Union, 1020
living in Manhattan's Lower East Side, 616*m*
in movie industry, 739
Orthodox Judaism, 619
persecution of
Crusades and, 15
Spanish Inquisition and, 19
Reform Judaism, 619
Zionism, 879
Jiang Jieshi (Chiang Kai-shek, 1887–1975), 835, 845, 860, 861
Jim Crow segregation, 599, 959
Job Corps, 929
Jobs, Steven Paul (1955–), 1023
Joffre, Joseph (Jacques Césaire, 1852–1931), 703
Johns Hopkins University, 736
Johnson, Andrew (1808–1875), 484*i*
amnesty plan, 487
congressional election of 1866 and, 489–90
Fourteenth Amendment and, 489
impeachment of, 491
National Union Movement and, 489
restoration under, 481, 483–85
Tenure of Office Act and, 490–91
veto of Civil Rights Act (1866), 488–89
Johnson, Edward, 59–60
Johnson, Gabriel, 94
Johnson, Hiram Warren (1866–1945), 645, 651
Johnson, Hugh Samuel (1882–1942), 790, 820
Johnson, Lady Bird (1912–), 928
Johnson, Lyndon Baines (1908–1973), 857, 917, 918, 925
Civil Rights Act of 1964 and, 927
civil rights movement and, 949
consensus on foreign affairs, 939
Great Society programs, 807, 926–30
investigation of race riots, 958
Kennedy-Johnson tax cut of 1964 and, 924

(Johnson, Lyndon Baines con't)
liberal agenda, 927–28
presidential election of 1964, 926, 927, 933
speech on voting rights, 954
as vice president, 919, 920
Vietnam War and, 932–33, 940, 941
War on Poverty, 928–29
Johnson, Tom Loftin (1854–1911) 644, 651
Johnson, Sir William (1715–1774), 121
Johnston, Albert Sidney (1803–1862), 458
Johnston, Joseph Eggleston (1807–1891), 473
surrender of, 476
Johnstown, Penn., 608
Joint Chiefs of Staff, 931
Joint Committee on Reconstruction, 485
joint-stock companies, 29
Joliet, Louis (1645–1700), 36
Jolson, Al (1888–1950), 739
Jones, Absalom (1746–1818), 248
Jones, Jim, 996
Jones, Robert Tyre, Jr. (Bobby, 1902–1971), 744
Jones, Samuel Milton ("Goldenrule," 1846–1904), 644, 651
Jones and Laughlin Steel Company, 608
Jones Beach, 743
Jordan, Hamilton, 1000
journalism. *See also* newspapers and magazines
muckrakers, 642, 643
1920s, 742
journeymen, 310, 335, 338
judges. *See also* U.S. Supreme Court justices
colonial, appointment of, 142
impeachment of, 231
judicial review, Supreme Court's power of, 263
judiciary, 194, 205
John Marshall and, 263. *See also* Marshall, John
Judiciary Act of 1789, 208
Judiciary Act of 1801, 231
Jefferson's repeal of, 231
Judson, Edward Zane Carroll. *See* Buntline, Ned
Julian, George Washington (1817–1899), 482, 483, 490
Jungle, The (Sinclair), 659
junk bonds, 1014
Justice, Department of, 986
justices. *See* Supreme Court justices
justices of the peace, 91
just price, 184

Kaiser, Henry John (1882–1967), 824
Kalm, Peter, 105, 106, 135
Kansas, 538
admission to Union, 433
Lecompton constitution, 433
Missourian voters in, 429
slavery and, violence related to, 429–31
Kansas City, Mo., 613
Kansas-Nebraska Act (1854), 432, 436
Lincoln and, 435
passage of, 428
Republican party and, 427–28
Kansas Pacific Railroad, 523
Kant, Immanuel (1724–1804), 350
Kearny, Stephen Watts (1794–1848), 417
Keating, Charles, 1025
Keaton, Buster (1895–1966), 739
Kelley, Abigail (1810–1887), 360
Kelley, Florence (1859–1932), 645
Kelley, Oliver Hudson (1826–1913), 541
Kellogg, Frank Billings (1856–1937), 734
Kellogg-Briand Pact (1928), 733, 734
Kellor, Frances (1873–1953), 646–47
Kelly, Fanny, 517
Kemp, Jack, 1009, 1024
Kempton, Sally, 969
Kendall, Amos (1789–1869), 325
Kennan, George Frost (1904–), 857
Kennedy, Anthony McLeod (1936–), 1012
Kennedy, Edward Moore (1932–), 936, 1003
Kennedy, Jacqueline, 925
Kennedy, John Fitzgerald (1917–1963), 857, 917, 918*i*, 941
assassination of, 925–26, 932
Bay of Pigs and, 922–23
Berlin Wall and, 923
cabinet of, 920
civil rights and, 948–49, 953
consensus on foreign affairs, 939
counterinsurgency doctrine, 920, 932
Cuban missile crisis and, 923
debates with Nixon, 919
détente and, 924
domestic programs, 924–25
economic policy, 924
expansion of military-industrial complex, 920
inaugural address, 920
New Frontier and, 917, 920. *See also* New Frontier
nuclear test-ban treaty with Khrushchev (1963), 939
Peace Corps and, 920–21
Presidential Commission on the Status of Women and, 968
presidential election of 1960, 918*i*, 919*m*, 918–20
Vietnam War and, 932, 933
Kennedy, Joseph Patrick (1888–1969), 818, 919
Kennedy, Robert Francis (1925–1968), 920, 927, 948, 959, 978, 978*i*
assassination of, 978
surveillance of Martin Luther King, Jr., 949
Kent, Conn., families, movement to Amenia, N.Y., 226
Kent, James (1763–1847), 189, 265
Kent State University, killing of students at, 964, 964*i*, 985
Kentucky, 299
entry into Union, 225
loyalty to Union, 446
secessionists, 446
Kerensky, Aleksandr Feodorovich (1881–1970), 703
Kerner, Otto, 958
kerosine, 555
Kerouac, Jack (1922–1969), 965
Kesey, Ken Elton (1935–), 965
Keynes, John Maynard, baron of Tilton (1883–1946), 796
Khanh, Nguyen, 932
Khomeini, Ayatollah Ruholla Mussavi (1900?–1989), 1002
Khrushchev, Nikita Sergeyevich (1894–1971), 876, 877, 885, 922, 923, 1030
Bay of Pigs invasion and, 923
Cuban missile crisis and, 923
kitchen debate, 885, 906
nuclear test-ban treaty with Kennedy (1963), 939
Kieft's War (1643–1646), 38
Kim Il Sung (1912–), 862
King, Coretta Scott, 949
King, Martin Luther, Jr. (1929–1968), 929, 948, 949, 952, 952*i*, 954
assassination of, 958, 978
birthday as national holiday, 959
FBI surveillance of, 949
"I have a dream" speech, 952, 957
Nobel Peace Prize, 952
opposition to violence, 956, 958
King, Rodney, 1017
King's Canyon, 535
kinship networks, 382
Kirby, Rollin, 787
Kirkman, Marshall M., 556
Kissinger, Henry Alfred (1923–), 983, 984, 1000, 1002
negotiations with North Vietnam, 985–86
Kitchen Cabinet, 325
kitchen debate, 885, 906
Kitty Hawk, N.C., 699
Klondike gold fields, U.S. access to, 685
Knickerbocker Trust Company, 664
Knights of Labor, 569–70, 571, 572, 582
interracial unionism and, 597
Know-Nothings, 391
Republicans and, 428
Knox, Henry (1750–1806), 208, 250
Knox, John (1514?–1572), 30
Knox, William Franklin (1874–1944), 821
Knudsen, William Signius (1879–1948), 823
Kokomo, Ind., Ku Klux Klan in, 747
Koppel, Edward James (Ted, 1940–), 1003
Korea, 688
immigrants from, population, 1950–1965, 900
Japan's protectorate over, 688
Korean War (1950–1953), 861, 862–64, 887
Communist reoccupation of Seoul, 863
domestic impact of, 864
Eisenhower's efforts to end, 875
Fair Deal and, 869
settlement of, 864
38th parallel, 862, 863, 864
U.S. regaining of Seoul, 863
U.S. troops in, 862–63

Korematsu v. United States (1944), 833
Kovic, Ron, 938, 938*i*
Krause, Alison, 964
Ku Klux Klan, 497*i*, 497–99, 654, 730, 947, 953
  attacks on freedom riders, 948
  murder of civil rights workers, 954
  of 1920s, 746–47
Ku Klux Klan Act of 1871, 498
Kurds in Iraq, 1031
Kuwait, 991, 1030–31

labor. *See also* child labor; employment; unemployment
  affirmative action, 996
  African-Americans (1870s–1890s), 562
  agricultural, 894
    southern (1800s), 558, 559
  aristocracy of workers, 561
  autonomous (1900s), 561
  blacklists, 339
  boycotts, 573
  bracero (day laborer) program, 777, 835, 900
  caste labor system, 533
  cheap labor of the South, 560
  Chinese immigrant (1860s–1880s), 532–33
  civil service jobs, 579
  comparable worth, 973
  cooperative factories and shops, 569
  demand for (1890s), 561
  depression of 1837–1843 and, 343–44
  differential-rate method, 568
  division of, 566, 568*i*
  division of work force by gender, 766
  English, sixteenth century, 28
  ethnic clustering in, 562, 563
  European society (1400s), 13
  Fair Labor Standards Act of 1938, 795
  in freehold society, 104
  gang-labor system, 376–77
  headright system, 46
  immigrant, 562, 609, 1020
  indentured servants, 43–44, 46, 78
  laborers, 561
  labor gangs, 561
  mechanization, effects on, 566
  in mid-Atlantic colonies, 110
  migrant workers, 553, 776–77, 778
  mill, family system of, 559
  National Labor Relations Act of 1935, 793
  National Labor Relations Board, 793
  National War Labor Board, 711–12
  1940s–1950s, 891–92
  1970s, 995
  organization of workers, 288
  outwork system, 28, 259, 260, 288
  "Piece Rate System, A" (Taylor), 568
  putting-out system, 28, 110, 259
  scientific management of, 568–69
  sex typing of occupations (1870s–1890s), 564, 565
  sharecropping, 503
  skilled workers, 561
  slave, 376
  slavery and, 429
  Smith-Connally Labor Act of 1943, 827
  in South
    1850s–1860s, 376
    following Civil War, 487–88
  stints, 561
  systems of control, 566–69
  Taft-Hartley Act and, 866
  time-and-motion studies, 568
  two and three income families, 1015–16
  United States Employment Service, 711
  unrest following World War I, 720–21
  unskilled workers, 291
  welfare capitalism, 732
  Whig party and, 341
  white collar workers (1940s–1950s), 891, 892
  during World War I, 711–12
  during World War II, 830
labor contracts, 502
  indentured servitude, 43–44
laborers
  anti-Catholicism, 391
  attitude toward banks 1820s, 328
  casual workers, 306, 307
  day, 306
  feuds with capitalists, 338, 340
  northern urban, 1700s, 89
  revivalism and, 313–15
  unskilled, 306–7
  wage, 306, 307, 308
labor force
  changes in (1870–1910), 562*t*
  women's participation in (1800–1980), 564–565, 911–912, 967, 967*f*
labor relations, 732, 893
labor theory of value, 335
labor unions, 513, 569, 570. *See also* strikes; specific union
  American Federation of Labor, Cesar Chavez and, 777–78
  artisans and, 334
  building trade workers and, 334–35
  closed shops, 339, 569, 826
  Commonwealth v. Hunt (1842) and, 344
  Congress of Industrial Organizations. *See* Congress of Industrial Organizations
  decline in memberships (1950s), 893
  depression of 1837–1843 and, 343–44
  employers and, 339
  factory workers, 338–39
  Haymarket Square Riot of 1886 and, 571–72
  impact of automation on, 893
  injunctions against, 652
  interracial, 597
  journey shoemakers, 335, 338
  mining, 520, 575, 657, 827, 866
  national, 570
  National Trades' Union, 338
  New Deal and, 801–4
  new recruits during 1950s, 893
  open shops, 826
  political activities of, 652
  radicalism, 574–75
  Franklin Roosevelt and, 793
  strength of (1900s), 892–93, 893*i*
  strikes. *See* strikes
  voluntarism, 652
  women's activism in, 649, 649*i*
  worker's compensation and, 652
  during World War I, 711
  during World War II, 826, 827, 828*i*
  yellow-dog contracts, 572
Labor's Nonpartisan League, 804
Ladies Home Journal, 631, 742, 757
Lady Day, 11
Lafayette, Marie Joseph, marquis de (1757–1834), 178
La Follette, Robert Marion (1855–1925), 654, 660, 661, 700, 730, 752, 981
  opposition to Treaty of Versailles, 719
  progressivism and, 640, 644*i*, 644–45
laissez faire, doctrine of, 582
Lake, Handsome, 250
Lake Champlain, battle of (1776), 238
Lake George, battle of (1755), 123*i*
Lake Texcoca, 5
Lancaster, Pa., 88, 298*i*
Lance, Bert, 1000
land. *See also* property
  colonial, conflicts, 127–28
  demands for (1800s), 225
  distribution, in New England colonies, 59
  fee simple titles, 59, 69, 166
  feudal revival and, 128
  freehold titles, 127
  headright system, 41
  ownership
    by former slaves, 503
    Homestead Act of 1862 and, 536
    in Massachusetts Bay colony, 59–60
    in middle colonies, 109–11
    Timber Culture Act of 1873 and, 536
  Preemption Act of 1841, 345
  prices
    1780s, 228
    1820s–1830s, 300
  purchase, by private corporations, 261
  redistribution, during Reconstruction Era, 499
  sales, western, 230, 299*m*, 399*m*
  tenancy, 109–11, 127
  tenure, open-field system of, 10
  Tory, redistribution of, 166–67
Land Act of 1796, 230
Land Act of 1820, 230
Land Act of 1851, 408
land banks, 95, 111
Landon, Alfred Mossman (1887–1987), 795
Land Ordinance (1785), 198
Lane, Henry S., 419
language
  diversity of (1800s), 241
  native American, 8, 9
Lanham Act (1940), 826
Laos, 933
La Raza Unida, 959

Larcom, Lucy (1824–1893), 293
Larkin, Thomas Oliver, 407, 416
La Salle, René Robert Cavelier, sieur de (1643–1687), 36
Las Casas, Bartolomé de (1474–1566), 22
Lasch, Christopher (1932–), 996
Las Guasimas, battle of (1898), 679
Last of the Mohicans, The (Cooper), 394
Las Vegas Grant, 531
Latin America
  exports to (1875–1900), 673, 673*t*
  Pierce's expanionist policy in, 426–27
  U.S. withdrawal of troops from (1920s), 733
Latinos. *See* Hispanics
Latvia, 1028
Laud, William, archbishop, (1573–1645), 51, 55
Laurens, Henry, (1724–1792), 183
law(s). *See also* specific laws
  common, 262
  equality in, 279
  formalism in, 640
  national, Supreme Court voiding of, 264
  Revealed Law of God, 262
  statute, 262
  supremacy of courts (1877–1900), 583
lawmaking, 204
  branch of government, 194
Law of Civilization and Decay, The (Adams), 676
Law of Nature, 262
Law of Reason, 262
Lawrence, William, 582
lawyers
  admission to bar, 266
  in Chesapeake colonies, 86
  march for gold standard, 593*i*
  as New Dealers, 788
  population of (1820s), 266
  professional aristocracy of, 266
  reform movement related to, 142, 266
  status of (1877–1893), 583
  untrained "pettifoggers," 266
Leadville, Colo., 575
League of Armed Neutrality (1780), 178
League of Nations, 717, 719, 729, 733, 818, 819
League of Women Voters, 752
Leahy, William Daniel (1875–1959), 845
Leary, Timothy, 966
Lease, Mary Elizabeth (1853–1933), 591
Leatherstocking Tales, The (Cooper), 269
Leaves of Grass (Whitman), 351, 352, 353
Lebanon, 1010, 1012, 1031*m*
Lecompton constitution, 433, 436
Lee, Ann (Mother Ann) (1736–1784), 273, 355
Lee, Arthur (1740–1792), 175
Lee, Charles (1731–1782), 201
Lee, Richard Henry (1732–1794), 168, 187
Lee, Robert Edward (1807–1870), 437, 445
  attack on McClellan's army, 459
  defeat at Gettysburg, 464–65, 467
  first invasion of North, 459–61
  refusal to command Union troops, 446
  surrender at Appomattox Court House, 475–76
  Wilderness campaign and, 470–71
leet men, 88
Leeward Islands, 76
legal profession. *See* lawyers
Legal Services Program, 929
Legal Tender Act (1882), 452
legislature
  after American Revolution, 195–96
  bicameral, 194, 205
  unicameral, 194
Leisler, Jacob, 73
leisure
  amusement parks, 624
  baseball, 626
  expenditures on (1920–1930), 737
  1920s, 743–44
  1950s, 904–06
  sports and recreation, 743–744
Lemke, William, 795
Lend-Lease Act (1941), 821
Lenglen, Suzanne, 744
Lenin, Vladimir Ilyich (1870–1924), 704, 718
Lenni mill, 294*i*
Leo X (Pope) (1475–1521), 23
Leo XIII (Pope), 619
Leonardo da Vinci (1452–1519), 17
Leopard (warship), 234
Lepanto, battle of (1571), 25
Lerner, Steve, 980
LeSueur, Meridel, 761
Letter on Manufactures (Gallatin), 259
Letters from a Farmer in Pennsylvania (Dickinson), 146
Letters from an American Farmer (Crèvecoeur), 279
Levant Company, 28
Leviathan (Hobbes), 12
Levi P. Morton Association, 587*i*
Levitt, Arthur, 897
  Levittown, 897
Lewis, Harry Sinclair (1885–1951), 749, 810
Lewis, John, 950
Lewis, John Llewellyn (1880–1969), 801–2, 827, 866
Lewis, Meriwether (1774–1809), 233
Lexington, battle of (1775), 157*t*, 158*i*, 165
Leyte, battle of (1944), 841
Libby, McNeill, and Libby Corporation, 778
liberalism
  Fair Deal and, 868–69
  Great Society, 928–29
  Kennedy administration, 917, 924–25
  urban, 650–56
Liberal Republican party, 506, 587
Liberator, The (newspaper), 365, 366, 367
Liberia, as independent republic, 363–64
liberty halls, 750
Liberty League, 791
Liberty Loans, 710
Liberty party, 415, 434
  establishment of, 368–89
Liberty ships, 824
libraries, 394
  public, 633
Liddy, G. Gordon, 987
Life (magazine), 633, 811, 843, 861
life expectancy. *See also* mortality rates
  in New England and Chesapeake colonies, 49*i*
  1900s–1950s, 907
Life of Washington (Weems), 269
Liliuokalani, Lydia Kamekeha (1838–1917), 671
limestone, 550
limited liability, 261
Lincoln, Abraham (1809–1865), 428, 433, 592
  appointment of Grant, 469
  assassination of, 483
  in Congress, 434
  as corporate lawyer, 434–35
  Crittenden Plan and, 445
  v. Douglas, 436–37
  education of, 434
  Emancipation Proclamation, 462
  first battle of Bull Run and, 455, 457
  Fort Sumter and, 445
  as Illinois state legislator, 434
  inaugural address, 445
  mobilization of troops, 450–52
  presidential campaign of 1854, 435
  presidential election of 1860, 438–39
  presidential election of 1864, 473–74
  progressive idealism of, 641
  as Republican party leader, 435–36
  restoration under, 481–83
  signing of First Confiscation Act, 461
  slavery and, 443
  statement of war aims, 446–47
  upper South, attempts to hold, 445–46
Lincoln, Levi, 230
Lincoln, Mary Todd (1818–1882), 434
Lincoln Memorial, 952
Lindbergh, Anne Morrow (1907–), 769
Lindbergh, Charles Augustus (1902–1974), 744, 769, 820–821
Lindgren, Ida, 537, 538
Lippmann, Walter (1889–1974), 640, 641
literacy tests, suspension of, in Voting Rights Act of 1965, 598, 954
literature. *See also* specific authors
  childrearing, 272, 907
  Communist party and, 812
  1880–1912, 634–35
  Federal Writers' Project, 810
  early American, 268–69
  feminism-related, 969
  fiction, 394
  genteel tradition, 634–35
  impact of Industrial Revolution on, 394–95
  on Indian history, 961
  of local color and regionalism, 635
  modernist movement, 748–49
  naturalistic, 635
  poetry (1920's), 749

(literature con't)
progressive, 641
realism, 635
religious, 278
transcendentalist, 350–53
women novelists (1840s–1850s), 394–95
Lithuania, 1028
Little, Malcolm. *See* Malcolm X
Little Big Horn River, Indian battles at, 523, 526
Little Caesar, 767
Little Rock, Ark., integration in (1957), 947, 947*i*
Little Steel Formula, 817
Little Turtle (c. 1752–1812), 224
living newspapers, 810
Livingston, Robert R. (1746–1813), 232
Livingston, William (1723–1790), 201
Lloyd, Harold (1893–1971), 739
Lloyd, Henry Demarest (1847–1903), 592, 641
Lloyd George, David, earl of Dwyfor (1863–1945), 718, 719
loans, federal, pump priming, 779
local government, growth of (1946–1970), 898–99
Lochner v. New York (1905), 640
Locke, Alain, 749
Locke, John (1632–1704), 68, 72, 113, 115, 142, 272
slavery and, 187
Lockheed Corporation, military contracts to, 887
Lodge, Henry Cabot (1850–1924), 674, 677
League of Nations and, 719
Lodge, Henry Cabot, Jr. (1902–1985), 932
Lodge Election bill of 1880, 581
Lombard, Carole, 768
London Economic Conference (1933), 817
Lonely Crowd, The (Reisman), 892
Long, Huey Pierce (1893–1935), 788, 792*i*
assassination of, 795
New Deal and, 792–93
Share Our Wealth plan, 794
Long, Stephen H., 515
Longfellow, Henry Wadsworth (1807–1882), 394
Long Island, 73
battle of (1776), 170
Longstreet, James P. (1821–1904), 459
Look (magazine), 811
Looking Backward (Bellamy), 641
López, Narciso, 426
Lords of Trade and Plantations, 70, 71, 73
Lorentz, Pare, 811
Los Angeles
barrios, 959
expansion of (1870s–1890s), 535
race riots
of 1992, 1017
in Watts section, 958
Louis XI (1423–1483), 17
Louis XIV (1638–1715), 36, 74
Louis XVI (1754–1793), 175
execution of, 215
Louisbourg, 121
Louisiana, 253
acquisition of, slavery and, 385
freedom of slaves, 464
Huey Long and, 792
secession of, 444
settlement of, 36
Louisiana Purchase, 223, 231–34
Missouri Compromise and, 428
threats to union, 233–34
Louisville, Ky., 297
Louisville Railroad, 556
Love Canal, 993
Lovett, Robert, 856, 857
Lovejoy, Elijah (1802–1837), 434
Low, Ann Marie, 773
Low, Thomas, 268
Lowden, Frank Orren (1861–1943), 752
Lowell, Francis Cabot (1775–1817), 291, 294, 306
Lowell, Josephine Shaw, 645
Lowell, Mass., 561
textile industry in (1820s), 292, 293
women factory workers' strikes in, 338
Lowell Female Labor Reform Association, 387
Lowenstein, Allard, 977, 978
Loyalists, 157, 176
exodus from America, 186–87
property, seizure of, 186
LSD (lysergic acid diethylamide), 965, 966
Luce, Claire Booth (1903–1987), 874
Luce, Henry Robinson (1898–1967), 861
"Luck of Roaring Camp, The" (Harte), 534
lugars, 82
lumber industry, 88
Great Depression and, 759
southern (1870s–1890s), 560
Lundy, Benjamin, 364, 365
Lusitania, sinking of, 701
Luther, Martin (1483–1546), 23
Lutheran Church, 241
Protestant Reformation and, 23
Lvov, Prince Georgi Yeugenievich (1861–1925), 703
Lyceum groups, 350
Lykes Corporation, 995
Lynd, Helen Merrell (1896–1982), and Robert Staughton (1892–1970), 727, 736, 737, 764
Lynn, Mass., journeymen shoemakers of, 338

MacArthur, Arthur (1845–1912), 682
MacArthur, Douglas (1880–1964), 781, 782, 841, 862, 872
in Korea, 862–63
Truman's firing of, 863, 864
Macbeth (Shakespeare), 810
Machiavelli, Niccolo (1469–1527), 17
machine building, innovators in, 295–96
machine industry, output (1870–1910), 549*t*
machine politics, 586–587
machine-tool industry, 295, 385, 386
machinist's trade, 566
Macon, Nathaniel (1758–1837), 236
Macon's Bill No. 2 (1810), 236
Mad (magazine), 909
Madeira islands, 18
Madero, Francisco Indalecio (1873–1913), 690
Madison, James (1751–1836), 166, 188, 201, 322
amendments to Constitution submitted by, 208
native Americans and, 250
Non-intercourse Act, 235
opposition to Hamilton's economic policy, 210, 211
political parties and, 217
presidency, 235–37
rechartering of Bank of the United States, 258
as secretary of state under Jefferson, 230
U.S. Constitution and, 205–6, 218
veto of Bonus Bill, 261
Virginia Plan, 202
Virginia resolution (1798), 218
War of 1812 and, 236, 237–38
magazines. *See also* newspapers and magazines
photojournalism, 811
women's, 631
Maggie: A Girl of the Streets (Crane), 635
Maginot Line, 820
Magna Charta (1215), 142
Magruder, Jeb Stuart, 996
Mahan, Alfred Thayer (1840–1914), 674, 674*i*, 686*m*
foreign policy, 674
Mailer, Norman (1923–), 962
mail-order houses, 555
Mainardi, Pat, 970
Main Street (Lewis), 749
Maine, 29
as free state, 244–245
slavery and, 244
Maine (battleship), sinking in Havana harbor, 677–78
majority, tyranny of, 262
malaria, in Chesapeake colonies, 43
Malaya, 841
Malcolm X (Malcolm Little, 1925–1965) 956, 956*i*
male(s)
involvement in property rights of women, 361
status in European society, 1400s, 12–13
suffrage. *See* suffrage
male chauvinism, 969, 971
Malenkov, Georgi Maximilianovich (1902–1988), 876
malnutrition, 389
Manchild in the Promised Land (Brown), 902
Manchuria, 688
Mandan Indians, 517
Manhattan Island, purchase of, 37
Manhattan Project, 847
Manifest Destiny, 402–3, 409
"Manifest Destiny" (Fiske), 676
Man Nobody Knows, The (Barton), 731

manorial lords, 13
Mansfield, James, 144
Mantrap, 741
manufacturing. *See also* factories; industry; machine-tool industry
assembly lines, 728*i*
of capital goods, 548
Census of 1820, 260
English, mercantilism, 28–29
entrepreneurs (1820s–1840s), 295–96
foreign investment, 732
Hamilton's report on, 211
Jefferson and, 212–13, 213–14
late eighteenth century, 214–15
managerial revolution, 556–58
mass production techniques, 728, 728*i*
national market, 259
northeastern, rise in, 287–89
organizational and technological innovations (1820s), 789
organizational structures, of 1920s, 731
output (1920s), 728
outwork system, 28, 259, 260, 288
putting-out system, 28, 110, 259
relative price advantage over agriculture, 543
rural, expansion of (1780s–1800s), 258–59
textile industry, 289–91. *See also* textile industry
wage earnings in (1890), 626
Manumission Act of 1782, 187
Mao Zedong (Mao Tse-tung, 1893–1976), 860, 861, 932, 956
Marbury v. Madison (1803), 263
March of Time newsreels, 811
Marcy, William L. (1786–1857), 325
margin buying, 758
Marianas Islands, 679
Marijuana, 965
Marine Corps Women's Reserve, 825
Marines, during World War II, 844
Marion, Francis (1732–1795), 178
Marion, Ala., 954
market economy (1790s–1800s), 259–60
markets, expansion of (1820s–1830s), 296–300
Marne River, 704
Marquette, Jacques (1637–1675), 36
marriage. *See also* divorce
arranged, 104
of blacks, after Civil War, 496
in Chesapeake colonies, 43
early nineteenth century, 269–71
in European society (1400s), 13
among farm families (1700s), 100
intermarriage among urban elite (1880s–1890s), 627
native American, 8
Oneida Community and, 357
parent-controlled, 270
politics and, 1700s, 91
polygamy, 405, 406
Quaker, 111–12
sentimentalism and, 270
among slaves, 246–50, 381, 382
women novelists and (1850s), 395
marriage contract, 271
marriage portion, 100
marriage rate
Great Depression's effect on, 764
late nineteenth century, 632
marriage-renewal conferences, 996
Married or Single (Sedgwick), 394
Marshall, George Catelett (1880–1959), 872, 876
Marshall Plan, 857
Marshall, John (1755–1835), 231
Burr's trial and, 234
Cherokee Nation v. Georgia (1831), 327
Cohens v. Virginia (1821), 264
corporate charters and, 305
Dartmouth College v. Woodward (1819), 264
death of, 264
Federalist principles, 262–64
Fletcher v. Peck (1810), 264
Gibbons v. Ogden (1824), 305
Indian policy, 327
Marbury v. Madison (1803), 263
McCulloch v. Maryland (1819), 263
property rights and, 264
Worcester v. Georgia (1832), 327
Marshall, Thurgood (1908–1993), 946, 949
Marshall Islands, 841, 843*m*
Martin, Frederick Townshend, 629
Martin, Joseph William, Jr. (1884–1968), 863
Martin, John, 166
Martin, William, 294, 294*i*
Martínez, Rubén, 1019
Martinique, 135
Marx Brothers, 767
Marx, Karl (1818–1883), 574, 704
Marxism, 575, 812
Mary II (1662–1694), 72
Maryland (colony), 56*t*
establishment of, 31, 42
slavery in, 81
uprisings of 1689, 72, 73
Maryland (state), 446
constitution, 193
freedom of slaves, 464
profarmer and prodebtor program of 1785 and 1786, 200
secessionists, 446
taxation, after American Revolution, 200
Masaryk, Jan (1886–1948), 859
Mason, George (1725–1792), 203
Mason, James (1798–1871), 467
Massachusetts (magazine), 114
Massachusetts (royal colony), 72
Massachusetts (state)
Confederacy attack on, 446
constitution, 186, 265
debtor-relief legislation, after American Revolution, 200
growth of cities, 896
Lyceum groups in, 350
Mill Dam Act (1795), 262
opposition to U.S. Constitution, 206–7
Riot Act, 200
Massachusetts Bay colony, 56*t*, 71
charter annulled, 71
Dominion of New England, 71
land ownership in, 59
separation of church and state in, 54
Puritan settlement of, 31, 51–52
Massachusetts "Bucks," 187
Massachusetts Institute of Technology, 731
mass marketing, mass markets, 553–56
mass media, 1920s, 742
mass production techniques, 728
mass transit, 612
Matamoros, 419
American capture of, 420
Mather, Cotton (1663–1728), 52, 54, 57, 113
Mather, Increase (1639–1723), 72
Mather, Richard (1596–1669), 55*i*
Mauldin, Bill, 844
Maxim, Sir Hiram Stevens (1840–1916), 698
Maximilian, emperor of Mexico (1832–1867), 504
"Maxims for the Republics," 273
Mayan civilization, 4, 6*i*, 20, 23
decline of 4–5
Mayflower Compact, 49
McAdoo, William Gibbs (1863–1941), 710, 730, 752
McAllister, Ward (1827–1895), 627
McCain, Franklin, 948
McCarran-Walter Act (1952), 900
McCarthy, Eugene Joseph (1916–), 977, 978
McCarthy, Joseph Raymond (1908–1957), 871–72
investigation of army, 871*i*, 872
"McCarthyism," 869, 962
McCarthy, Mary Therese (1912–1989), 812
McClellan, George Brinton (1826–1885), 446, 457, 458, 459, 460
battle of Antietam and, 459, 460
Emancipation Proclamation and, 462, 463
presidential election of 1864, 473, 474
McCloy, John Jay (1895–1989), 856, 857
McClure's (magazine), 642, 734
McCord, James, 989
McCormick, Cyrus Hall (1809–1884), 558
reaper, 386, 386*i*, 401, 536
McCormick, Thomas J., 859
McCormick Harvesting Machine Company, 540, 555
McCue, Martin, 654
McCulloch v. Maryland (1819), 263
McDonald, Cornelia Peake (1822–1909), 472
McDonald, John A. (1815–1891), 506
McDonald's restaurant, 904, 904*i*
McDowell, Irvin (1818–1885), first battle of Bull Run and, 455, 457
McFarlane, Robert, 1011
McGovern, George Stanley (1922–), 978, 979
presidential campaign of 1972, 985–86

McGready, James, 276
McGuire, Thomas B., 569
McInerney, Jay, 1024
McKay, Claude (1890–1948), 750
McKinley, William (1843–1901)
assassination of, 656, 925
conquest of Philippines and, 681, 683
presidential election of 1896, 596
presidential election of 1900, 683
Spanish-American War and, 677–78
McKinley Tariff of 1890, 590, 593, 671
McNamara, Robert Strange (1916–), 920, 941
Pentagon Papers and, 987
McNary-Haugen bill, 728–29
McNeill, Joseph, 948
McTeague (Norris), 635
McWilliams, Carey, 776
Meade, George Gordon (1825–1872), battle of Gettysburg, 464
Meany, George (1894–1980), 893
measles epidemic of 1730s, 113
meat industry, meat packing industry, 554, 733
foreign investments, 733
impact of mechanization on, 566, 568i
Meat Inspection Act (1906), 660
mechanics
British, 289
contribution to Industrial Revolution, 295
depression of 1837–43 and, 343
labor theory of value, 335
labor unions and, 334, 335–38
as manufacturing entrepreneurs, 294–96
Mechanics' Union of Trade Associations, 335
mechanization, impact on labor practices, 566–69
Medicaid, 928, 1021
state budget and, 1025
medical care. *See* health care
Medicare, 928
Meese, Edwin, 1009
Mein Kampf (Hitler), 818
Mellon, Andrew William (1855–1937), 729, 759
policies of, 759
Melville, Herman (1819–1891), 352–53
Mencken, Henry Louis (1880–1956), 748–49
Mennonites, 112
mercantilism
American
national, 261
state (1790s–1800s), 261, 262
English, 28–29, 95
mercenaries, German, in American Revolution, 173
merchant houses, 258
merchants, American (1780s–1800s), 257–58
New York, 298
northern, 88–90
Mercury space program, 924
Mesoamerica, 3. *See also* Central America; Mexico
native Americans in, 3, 5
mestizos, 23, 406
Metacom (King Philip, 1639?–1676), 60, 60*i*
metal industries, 520, 548–49
Methodism, Methodists, 121, 624
attempts at suppression, 189
childrearing practices, 272
growth of, early nineteenth century, 276
republicanism and, 276
Republican party and, 585
Second Great Awakening and, 277
slaves, 250
Metro-Goldwyn-Mayer, 739
Metropolitan Area Redevelopment Act, 929
metropolitan areas. *See* cities
Metropolitan Museum of Art (New York), 633, 634*i*
Metropolitan Opera (New York), 627, 633, 769
Meuse-Argonne campaign (1918), 705, 708
Mexican-American Political Association (MAPA), 959
Mexican-Americans, 777, 778. *See also* Hispanics
attacks on, during World War II, 832
bracero program, 777, 835, 900
Chicano activism, 959
deportation of, during Great Depression, 777–78
discrimination against, 519
employment during World War I, 712
immigration to Southwest (1840s–1900s), 531
immigration to U.S. after World War II, 900
New Deal and, 804
Mexican War (1846–48), 395, 407, 413, 416*m*, 416–20, 434
in California, 417
election of 1848 and, 420–21
in Mexico, 417–20
Slidell mission, 416, 417
volunteers in, 417*i*, 419
Wilmot Proviso, 420
Mexico
agriculture, native American, 4
civil war in, World War I and, 702
Constitutionalist movement, 690
expansionist ambitions in, 670, 689–90
French control of, 504–5
French withdrawal from, 505, 670
Gadsden Purchase and, 426
illegal aliens from, 1018
independence of, 333
Indian civilizations of, 3, 4, 8
migratory workers from, 533
Pierce's expansionist policy in, 426
revolution in, U.S. intervention in (1911), 690
Texas Rebellion of 1836 and, 333–34
U.S. relations with (1920s), 733
Mexico City, 5, 418
American capture of, 419
Miami, Cuban refugees living in, 900–1
Miami Indians, 224
Michelangelo Buonarroti (1475–1564), 17
Mickey Mouse Club, 906
Micmac Indians, 63
conversion to Catholicism, 37
mid-Atlantic colonies, 105
ethnic diversity in, 106–8
opportunity and equality in, 108–11
population of, 108–9
Quakers in, 105–6
Middle Atlantic states
culture of (1800s), 241
ethnic groups in (1780s–1830s), 177*i*
Middlebury Female Seminary, 276
middle class, 309. *See also* business class
employment rates (1940s–1950s), 891
family life (1870s–1900s), 631, 631*i*
Great Depression and, 762
housing (1840s–1850s), 391–92
literature, Industrial Revolution and, 394–95
1940s–1950s, 892
1980s, 1015
property owners, Industrial Revolution and, 306
urban (1870–1910), 628
Whig party and, 341
women's roles (1800–1830), 357–58
Middle East, 879–80. *See also* specific countries
Carter's successes in, 1001
Eisenhower Doctrine and, 880
import of oil from, 991
Persian Gulf War, 1024, 1030–31, 1032
Reagan and, 1010
U.S. involvement in (1980–1992), 1031*m*
Middlesex County Congress, 158
Middletown (Lynd and Lynd), 727, 737, 764
Midway, battle of (1942), 841, 844*i*
Midway Islands, annexation of, 505
Midwest
agriculture (1850s), 398, 400
cultural linkage to Northeast, 402
prosperity (1850s), 401
railroads (1850s), 401
wheat belt, 539
midwives, 103
migrant labor, 776
migration, during World War II, 831
Milan Decree (1807), 234
Milburne, Jacob, 73
military. *See also* army; draft; military spending
during Reconstruction Era, 504
military force, reporting to president, 990
military-industrial complex, 887–96
Kennedy's expansion of, 920
militia, 91, 183
Militia Act of 1862, 450
Puritan, 53
Milken, Michael, 1014, 1015, 1022
Mill Dam Act of 1795, 262
millennium, 55
Miller, Arthur Asher (1915–), 810
Miller, Jeffrey, 964

Mills, Charles Wright (1916–1962), 891
mill villages, 559–60
Milton, John (1608–1674), 30
Mineo, Sal, 909
mineral resources, metal industry growth and, 549
Mining Camps: A Study in American Frontier Government (Shinn), 534
mining industry
  foreign investment in 1920s, 733
  gold, 518*i*, 518–20, 534
  Great Depression and, 759
  Western Federation of Miners, 575
Minister's Wooing, The (Stowe), 395
Minneapolis, Minn., 615
Minneconjou tribe, 517, 527
Minnesota, Scandinavian immigration to, 538
Minnesota Territory, formation of, 427
minorities, TV roles, 905
Minuit, Peter (1580–1638), 37
Minutemen, 158
Miranda v. Arizona (1966), 925
missile gap, 920
missions, missionaries, 35, 278
  French, 37
  Spanish, 36, 534
Mississippi, 299
  black voting rights in (1962), 953
  Freedom Summer in, 962
  Union control of, 458, 464
Mississippian civilization, native Americans, 8, 9
Mississippi Freedom Democratic party (MFDP), 951
Mississippi River, 515
Mississippi Valley, Confederate power in, 458
Missouri, 299, 403
  commonwealth system and, 261
  loyalty to Union, 446
  secessionists, 446
  slavery and, 244, 245, 464
Missouri Compromise, 244–45, 334, 413, 427, 432
  extension of line, 421–22, 445
  Kansas-Missouri Act and, 435
  Louisiana Purchase and, 428
  repeal of, 428, 435
Missouri Pacific Railroad, 520
Mitchell, John, 657, 991
Mitchell, William D., 751
Mittelberger, Gottlieb, 106, 107, 111
Moby Dick (Melville), 352, 353
Moctezuma, 20, 21
Moderator movement, 129
Modern Instance, A (Howells), 635
modernist movement, 748–49
Mohawk Indians, 223
  customs, 39
Mohawk Valley, 121
molasses, 87, 95
Molasses Act (1733), 70*t*, 95, 135, 137
Moley, Raymond Charles (1886–1975), 788, 789
Molineaux, William, 152
Molotov, Vyacheslav Mikhailovich (1890–1986), 838, 854
Momaday, N. Scott, 961
Monacan Indians, 40
monarchs, 13. *See also* specific monarchs
  Renaissance, 17
  Spanish, 19, 25
Mondale, Walter Frederick (1928–)
  presidential campaign of 1984, 1011
  as vice-president under Carter, 1000
monetary policy, Great Depression and, 760
money supply. *See also* currency
  contraction of (1931–1933), 760
  land banks and, 95
  politics and, 592–93
  tightening of (1974), 999
  unlimited coinage of silver, 592
monopoly
  Act to prevent Monopoly and Oppression, 184
  privileges in corporate charters, 305
Monroe, James (1758–1831), 235, 320, 323
  Era of Good Feeling, 252
  foreign policy, 253
  presidency, 252
Monroe Doctrine (1823), 253, 415, 675, 702
  Roosevelt Corollary to, 687
Montana, gold mining in, 519
Montcalm, Louis Joseph, marquis de (1712–1759), 124
Monterey, Calif., 416
  American capture of, 417
Monterrey, Mexico, battle of (1846), 417–18, 418*i*, 419
Montesquieu, Charles Louis, baron de (1689–1755), 205, 206
Montgomery, Ala.
  bus boycott of 1955, 947–48, 949*i*
  march on, 954
Montgomery Ward and Company, 542, 546*i*, 555
Montreal, 124, 166
Moody, Dwight Lyman (1837–1899), 624
Moody, Paul, 291
Moore, Marianne Craig (1887–1972), 748
Moore's Creek Bridge, battle of (1776), 166
Moors, Spanish Inquisition and, 19
Moral Majority, 972, 996
Morgan, John Pierpont (1837–1913), 593, 633, 657, 658, 658*i*
  control of U.S. Steel and International Harvester, 658, 659
  Wilson's refusal to allow loans to China by, 689
Morgan, Robin, 969
Morgenthau, Henry, Jr. (1891–1967), 788, 837
Morison, John, 567
Morita, Akio, 1022
Mormons, 404–5
  in Great Salt Lake area, 536
  isolation from U.S. government, 405
  settlement in Utah, 405–6
Morocco, 231
  German challenge of France over, 691
Morris, Robert (1734–1806), 184, 198, 198*i*, 201, 230, 252, 258
Morris, Samuel, 120
Morrison, Norman, 940
Morristown, N.J., Continental army in, 183, 184
Morse, Jedidiah, 233, 241
Morse, Samuel F. B. (1791–1872)
  anti-Catholicism, 389–90
  Anti-popery Union, 389
Morse, Wayne Lyman (1900–1974), 932
mortality rates, 1860, 389
mortgage companies, 543
Morton, Jelly Roll (Ferdinand Joseph LaMenthe, 1885–1941), 742
Moscow
  American National Exhibition of 1959 in, 885
  U.S. boycott of summer Olympic games in, 1002
Moses, Robert (1888–1981), 743
Moskowitz, Belle, 752
Mossadegh, Muhammad, 876
Mostel, Zero, 871
motherhood, republican, 273
Mother's Magazine, 276
Mott, Lucretia Coffin (1793–1880), 360, 366
movie industry, 738
  blacklisting in, 869–71
  coming of sound, 739, 741–42
  during Great Depression, 767*i*, 767–69
  Production Code Administration, 767–68
  silent era, 738–39
  teen market, 909
  television's effects on, 905
  during World War II, 830
Moyer, Charles, 575
Mrs. Miniver, 830
Ms. (magazine), 971
MTV, 1022
muckrakers, 642, 643
Mugwumps, 587, 588, 619, 656
Muhammad, Elijah (1897–1975), 956
Muir, John (1838–1914), 535, 992
Muller v. Oregon (1908), 645, 663
Mumford, Lewis (1895–1990), 611
Muncie, Ind., 727, 737, 764
Mundt, Karl, 861
Munich Conference (1938), 820
Munn v. Illinois (1877), 542
Munsey's (magazine), 642
Murder in the Cathedral (Eliot), 810
Murray, Philip (1886–1952), 829, 869
Murray, Judith Sargent, 196
Murrow, Edward Roscoe (1908–1965), 830, 889
Muscovy Company, 28
museums, art, 633
music
  jazz, 742, 769
  modernist movement, 748–49
  New Deal and, 809
  popular (1960s), 965
  rock and roll, 909

(music con't)
- slave songs, 383
- symphony orchestras (1870s–1880s), 633

Muskhogean languages, 8, 9
Muskie, Edmund Sixtus (1914–), 987
Muslim faith
- Crusades against, 14–15
- spread of, 14

Muslims, 879
Mussolini, Benito (1883–1945), 812, 819
- fall of, 838

mustard gas, 705
Mutual Assured Destruction (MAD), 877
Mutual Benefit Society of Journeymen Cordwainers, 338
My Lai, 985
Myrdal, Karl Gunnar (1898–1987), 833

Nagasaki, Japan, dropping of atomic bomb on, 846
napalm, 939
Napier steam-driven press, 394
Napoleon I (1769–1821), 231
- Continental System, 234
- defeat of, 238
- Napoleonic wars (1802–15), 234, 253
- Sale of Louisiana, 232

Napoleon III (1808–1873), 467, 504
Napoleonic wars (1802–15), 234, 253
Narragansett Indians, 54
Nashville (ship), 685
Nashville Railroad, 556
Nasser, Gamal Abdel (1918–1970), 879, 880
- nationalization of Suez Canal, 880

Natchez people of Mississippi, 9
Nation, Carry Amelia Moore (1846–1911), 586*i*
National Advisory Commission on Civil Disorders, 958
National Aeronautics and Space Administration (NASA), 924
- space center, Cape Kennedy, 928

National American Woman Suffrage Association (NAWSA), 650, 712
National Association for the Advancement of Colored People (NAACP), 750, 825, 832, 948, 951
- *The Crisis*, 655, 655*i*, 772
- formation of, 655
- lawsuits protesting segregation, 946, 947

National Association of Atomic Veterans, 878
National Banking Act (1863), 592
National Banking Act (1864), 452
National Baptist Convention, 496
National Broadcasting Company (NBC), 742, 905
- Symphony Orchestra, 769

National Bureau of Economic Research, 729
National Civil Rights Commission, 869
National Committee for a Sane Nuclear Policy (SANE), 939
National Conference of Catholics for Interracial Justice, 952
National Consumers' League, 645, 712, 730
National Council of American Indians, 960
National Council of Churches, 952
National Defense Advisory Commission, 821
National Endowment for the Arts, 928
National Endowment for the Humanities, 928
National Era (newspaper), 424
national government, power of U.S. Constitution and, 204
National Grange of the Patrons of Husbandry, 540
National Guard, 779, 947, 964
National Housing Act (1937), 795
National Housing Act (1949), 868
national identity, 279
National Industrial Recovery Act of 1933, 790, 791
National Intelligencer (newspaper), 345
National Labor Relations Act of 1935 (Wagner Act), 793, 801, 804, 866
National Labor Relations Board (NLRB), 793
National Liberation Front (NLF), 932
National Mobilization Committee, 981
National Organization for Women (NOW), 967–68
National Origins Act (1924), 745–46
National Progressive Republican League, 661
National Recovery Administration (NRA), 787*i*, 790
- *Schechter v. United States* (1935) and, 791–92
- Supreme Court rulings on, 792, 793, 795

National Road, 301
National Science Foundation, 887
National Security Council (NSC), NSC–68, 861, 986
National Security League, 701
National Socialist party (Nazis), 818
National Trades' Union, 338
National Union Convention, 489
National Union for Social Justice, 792
National Union Movement, 489
National Urban League, 655
National War Labor Board (NWLB), 711–12, 826
National Welfare Rights Organization, 961
National Woman's Party, 650
National Woman Suffrage Association, 492
National Women's Conference, 971, 971*i*
National Women's Political Caucus, 971
National Women's Trade Union League, 649, 649*i*
National Youth Administration (NYA), 766, 828
- Office of Minority Affairs, 800

Nation of Islam. *See* Black Muslims
native Americans, 3–4, 6*i*, 7, 19. *See also* specific tribes
- Agawam, 7
- aggressive neutrality, 74
- agriculture, 7
- Algonquin, 8, 38
- American Indian Movement , 960, 961, 961*i*
- in American Revolution, 179
- assertion of rights (1960s), 960
- Aztecs, 5, 6*i*, 20–22
- Bureau of Indian Affairs, 804
- Californian, decline of, 529
- Cherokee. *See* Cherokee Indians
- Chickahominy, 40
- chinampas cultivation system, 5
- Choctaw, 8, 9, 326
- clubs, 390–91
- conversion to Christianity, 35, 36–37, 54, 250, 251, 252
- Creek. *See* Creek nation
- cultural and religious dualism, 250
- cultural assimilation of, 251–52
- Delaware tribe, 8, 224
- Doeg tribe, 48
- of eastern North America, 6–10
- education of (1878), 527
- English view of, 54
- English wars' effects on, 74
- European disease spread to, sixteenth century, 21
- five civilized tribes, 326–27
- French and Indian War, 121, 123–24
- of Great Plains, 516–18
- impact of fur trade on, 62–63
- Indian Removal Act (1830), 327
- Iroquois nations. *See* Iroquois Indians
- Andrew Jackson and, 325–27
- languages of, 8, 9
- loss of land, Treaty of Fort Stanwix and, 223
- maintenance of tribal identity, 250
- marriage customs, 8
- massacre of
  - Nathaniel Bacon and, 47–48
  - Bad Axe Massacre, 325–26
  - Paxton Boys and, 128
  - Wounded Knee, S.D., 515
- Mayan. *See* Mayan civilization
- medicine men, 517
- Metacom's war, 60
- Micmac tribe, 37, 63
- military alliances among, 236
- Mississippian culture, 8, 8*i*, 9
- Mohawk, 39, 223
- Monacan, 40
- New Deal and, 804–5
- Northwest Ordinance and, 199
- Onondaga, 223
- Pequot, 53–54
- placement under protection of U.S., 225
- Powhatan, 8, 40, 41
- pro-British, 223
- Proclamation Act of 1763 and, 135
- Pueblo, 36
- Puritans' relationship with, 53–54
- relinquishment of land, 223–25
- reservations, 525–27, 960*m*
- reserves, 152*i*
- rights
  - John Quincy Adams' support of, 323
  - Douglas and, 427

(native Americans con't)
Seneca, 7, 223
severalty, 527
Shawnee, 224, 236, 237
slaves, 53, 69
Spanish treatment of, 22
Sun Dance, 517
Susquehannock, 47
Teotihuac and Tula civilization, 4, 5
Toltecs, 5
trade with Britain, 236
Treaty of Greenville and, 224
tribal rivalries, 525
Tuscarora, 6
uprising of 1622, 41–42
voting rights (1840s), 320
Wampanoag, 60, 60*i*
warfare against, 35, 39
wars, 523, 525, 526
western confederacy, 224
western expansion's effects on, 524–29
Woodland, 6, 7, 8
Worcester v. Georgia, 327
nativism
Ku Klux Klan and, 746–47
rise of, 654, 744–47
Native Son (Wright), 810
Naturalization Act of 1798, 218
naturalization, Native-American clubs, 390–91
natural selection, Darwinian, 583
Naval War College, 570
naval warfare, during World War II, 844, 844*i*
Navigation Acts, 135, 150, 199
mercantilism and, 95
of 1651–1751, 70, 71*t*
of 1660 and 1663, 46
sugar industry and, 77
violation of, 138
navy, 824
anti-liquor policy during World War I, 708
Civil War fleet, dismantling of, 670
1881–1885, 670
rebuilding of (1880s–1890s), 674–75
Nazis. *See* National Socialist party
Nebraska, agricultural expansion in, 538. *See also* Kansas-Nebraska Act
Neel, Alice, 809
Negro World (newspaper), 750
Neighborhood Youth Corps, 929
Nelson, Donald, 823
Nelson, Horatio (1758–1805), 234
nerve gas wastes, 993
Nestor, Agnes, 649
Netherlands, 25
Anglo-Dutch wars, 77, 177
colonies of, 37–39
Holland Land Company, 230
inhabitants in New York colony, 73
Spanish, 25
trade, sixteenth century, 25–26
neutrality
World War I, 699–702
World War II, 820–22
Neutrality Act of 1794, 215, 216
Neutrality Act of 1935, 818
Neutrality Act of 1937, 820
Nevada, 534
gold discovered in, 518
New Amsterdam, 37
Newburgh, N.Y., 184
New Deal, 772, 778, 787–88, 883. *See also* Roosevelt, Franklin Delano
agriculture and, 790, 804–7
blacks and, 800–1
bureaucratic growth and, 796–97
coalitions, 807–8
cracks in, 929–30
constituencies, 804–5
culture, 808–10
demise of, 796
dismantling of programs during World War II, 828
documentary impulse, 810–12
impact on society, 796–804
legacies of, 807–8
lobbies against, 791
New Dealers, 788
rise of organized labor and, 801–4
Second, 793–94
social welfare programs, 928
unemployment and, 790–91
women and, 797
New England
Congregational churches in, 56
women in 273
Dominion of, 71, 92
educational levels in (1790s), 240
freehold society. *See* freehold society
regional identity in (1800s), 241
New England colonies
life expectancy in, 49*f*
migration from, 127–28
political system, 91
settlement patterns, 58*m*
New England Emigrant Aid Society, 429
New England Girlhood, A (Larcom), 293
new federalism, 983
Newfoundland, 75
fishing rights off, 183
New France
Anglo-American conquest of, 124, 124*i*
fur trade and religious conversion, 36–37
New Frontier, 917, 920
passage of proposals, 927
Peace Corps and, 920–21
New Hampshire (colony), 69*t*, 71
New Haven, Conn., 55
New Jersey (colony), 69*t*, 75, 105
James's grant of, 68
New Jersey (state)
constitution of 1776, 193, 196
ratification of U.S. Constitution, 206
New Jersey Plan, 203
Newlands Reclamation Act of 1902, 656
New Left, 969
New Light Presbyterians, 120, 175, 188, 277
ministers, 167
v. Old Lights, 115, 118–19, 277
Newman, Pauline, 652
New Mexico, 423, 529
American capture of, 417
copper mining in, 520
Hispanic settlement in, 530
New Nationalism, 661–62
New Negro, The (Locke), 749
New Netherland. *See* New York (colony)
New Orleans, La., 37, 297, 378
Battle of (1815), 238–39, 320
purchase of, 232
Newport, R.I., 54, 87
New Republic, The (magazine), 868, 874, 1000
New Right, 1008–9, 1012
New Salem, Ill., Lincoln in, 433–34
New Spain, 253, 406
colonization, 36
newspapers and magazines
African-American, 364
antislavery, 369
city, late nineteenth century, 626
colonial, 114
ethnic, 616, 1020
Free Soil party, 424
during Great Depression, 769
national identity and cultural values and (1800s), 241
native American, 251
sports coverage (1920s), 744
tabloid (1920s), 742–43
yellow journalism, 626
newsreels, 811
during Great Depression, 769
New Sweden, 38
Newsweek (magazine), 843, 908
Newton, Huey, 956
Newton, Sir Isaac (1642–1727), 113
New World Order, 1034–35
New York (colony), 37, 39, 68, 69*t*, 70, 75, 105
Leisler's rebellion in, 73–74
New York (city), 39, 87, 169, 256*t*, 609. *See also* Harlem
aqueducts, 613
black population
1880–1913, 617
1920s, 771–72
draft riots in (1863), 451*i*
East Village, 966
Eleventh Ward, 614
ethnic groups living in, 616, 616*i*
Hester Street, 614*i*
immigrants living in (1880–1911), 615–17
Lower East Side, 616*i*
organized baseball in, 625
Puerto Rican migrants to, after World War II, 900
racial unrest (1964), 958
rise of (1820s–1830s), 298–99
skyscraper construction, early twentieth century, 611
Tenement House Law of 1901, 614
threat to secede from state, 207
urban elite living in, 626, 627*i*, 628, 629

New York (magazine), 114
New York (state)
constitution of 1777, 189, 194, 265
Court of Appeals, 262
Emancipation Edict of 1799, 188
Palmer v. Mulligan (1805), 262
Republican party, Van Buren's changes in, 320
New York Central Railroad, 552, 553, 582
New York Consumers League, 645
New Yorker (magazine), 742
New York Female Moral Reform Society, 358
New York Herald, 417, 626
New York Illustrated Daily News, 742
New York Journal, 676, 677
New York Morning News, 402
New York Reserve Bank, 760
New York Stock Exchange, 298
New York Sun, 626
New York Supreme Court
closed shops and, 339
religious liberty and, 189
New York Times, 985, 986, 987, 989
New York Tribune, 506
New York World, 676
Niagara Movement, 655
Nicaragua
Sandinista government, 1011
U.S. support of Contras, 1011
U.S. withdrawal of troops from (1920s), 733
Walker's invasion of, 427
Nicholas II (1868–1918), 703
Nicholson, Francis, 73
Nielsen, A.C., 906
Nightline, 1003
Niles Weekly Register (newspaper), 241
Nimitz, Chester William (1885–1966), 841
Nixon, Richard Milhous (1913–), 872, 885, 941, 982
bombing of Cambodia (1969), 985
"Checkers" speech, 873, 874*i*
Christmas bombings of Vietnam (1972), 986
debates with Kennedy, 919
defeat of Douglas, 865*i*
domestic agendas, 982–83
foreign policy, 983–84
House Committee on Un-American Activities and, 871
invasion of Cambodia and, 964
kitchen debate, 906
new federalism and, 983
"Nixon Generation," 982
presidential election of 1960, 918–20, 919*m*
presidential election of 1968, 981
presidential election of 1972, 985–86
resignation of presidency, 990, 990*i*
silent majority and, 981
"slush fund," 873
Strategic Arms Limitations Talks and, 984
Watergate scandal and, 986–91
Vietnam War and, 984–85, 986
Nobel Peace Prize
awarded to Mikhail Gorbachev, 1028
awarded to Martin Luther King, Jr., 952
Non-intercourse Act (1809), 235
Normandy, landings (1944), 839*m,* 840, 840*i*
Norris, (Benjamin) Franklin (1870–1902), 635
Norris, George William (1861–1944), 700, 804
North, Frederick, Lord, (1732–1792), 144*t*, 149, 150, 156
North, Oliver Laurence (1943–), 1012*i*
North
abolition of slavery in, 187–88, 261
African colonization and, 363
American Revolution fought in, 169–70, 172*i*
antiabolitionists in, 367
antislavery sentiment in, 203
Fugitive Slave Act and, 424
Lee's first invasion of, 459–61
racial tensions in, during Progressive Era, 654
during Reconstruction Era, 503–9
urban economy (1700s), 87–92
North Africa
assault of American ships in, 231
expansionist ambitions (1890s), 685
North American party, 431
North American Review (newspaper), 241
North American trading block, 1034
North Atlantic Treaty Organization (NATO), 860, 860*m,* 930
North Carolina (colony), 69*t*, 75
North Carolina (state)
constitution, 193
Regulators, 129
segregation in (1950), 946*i*
Supreme Court, slave marriage and, 381, 382
textile industry, 558
North Carolina Agricultural and Technical College, 948
North Dakota, 515
emigration from (1880s), 538
Northeast
cultural linkage to Midwest, 402
growth of cities, 896
Industrial Revolution in, 385–88
migration to west from (1820s–1840s), 300
rise of manufacturing in, 287–89
Northern Confederacy plan, 233–34
Northern Pacific Railroad, 518, 534
bankruptcy of, 507
Northern Securities Company, 658
North Korea, 864
North Vietnam
attack of American destroyers, 933
bombing of, 934, 984*i*
Communist party, 932
Northwest Ordinance (1787), 198–99, 228, 432
Northwest Territory. *See also* Old Northwest
creation of, 228
government sale of land, 230
land divisions in, 229*m*
speculators, 229–30
townships, 228
Norwood (Beecher), 634
Notes on Virginia (Jefferson), 212, 214, 231
Nova Scotia, 69t, 75
fishing rights off, 183
novelists. *See also* specific novelists
proslavery, 428
women, 394–95
Noyes, John Humphrey (1811–1886), 355, 356, 368
nuclear family, 906
nuclear power plants, environmental hazards, 993–94
nuclear weapons. *See also* arms race
development during Eisenhower administration, 876–77
nuclear test ban treaty of 1963, 939
plants, radioactive waste from, 993
Nueces River, 416
nullification crisis (1832), 330–32
nursing, during Civil War, 454*i*, 455
nutrition. *See* malnutrition
Nye, Gerald Prentice (1892–1971), 818, 820
Nye Committee, 818

O'Brien, Richard T., 682
Occupational Safety and Health Administration (OSHA), 983
O'Connor, Sandra Day (1930–), 1012
Octopus, The (Norris), 635
office holding. *See also* specific offices
after American Revolution, 194
rotation in Andrew Jackson and, 325
Office of Economic Opportunity (OEO), 928, 929, 983
Office of Economic Stabilization, 823
Office of Human Rights, 1001
Office of Indian Affairs, 525, 527
Office of Price Administration and Civilian Supply (OPA), 823, 826, 865
Office of Production Management, Fair Employment Practices Committee (FEPC), 832
Office of War Mobilization, 823
Ogden, Aaron, 305
Oglala tribe, 517
Oglethorpe, James (1696–1785), 94
Ohio, 299
entry into union, 225
French presence in, 123
Republican party, 584
Ohio Land company, 230
Ohio River, Northwest Ordinance and, 199
oil, oil industry, 555
energy crisis of 1973–1974, 992, 992*i*, 995
foreign investment in 1920s, 733
fuel rationing during World War II, 831
refining equipment, 549
U.S. demand for (1920s), 737

(oil con't)
U.S. import of, 991
U.S. production of (1940s), 822, 991
Ojibwa Indians, 516
Okies, 774, 775
Okinawa, battle of (1945), 843*m*, 844
Oklahoma City, Okla., 527
Oklahoma, Indian territory of, 327, 526, 526*i*, 529
Old Age Assistance, 928
Old Age Revolving Pension Plan, 792
Old Light Presbyterians, 175
v. New Light, 115, 118–19, 277
Old Northwest
culture of (1800s), 241–43
expansion of, 225, 398–402
Old Southwest
slave life in, 243–50, 381
oligopolies, 890–91
Olive Branch petition, 166
Oliver, Andrew, 140
Oliver, King (Joseph, 1885–1938), 742
Oliver, Robert, 258
Olmec culture, 4
Olmsted, Frederick Law, (1822–1903), 613
Olney, Richard (1835–1917), 573, 675
Olsen, Tillie, 810
Olympics, in Moscow, U.S. boycott of, 1002
Omnibus Economic Opportunity Act of 1964, 928
Oneida Community, 356–57
O'Neill, Eugene Gladstone (1888–1953), 749
O'Neill, Thomas Philip, Jr. (1912–), 1000
Onondaga Indians, 223
"On the Equality of the Sexes" (Murray), 196
On the Origin of Species (Darwin), 583, 748
On the Road (Kerouac), 965
Opechancanough, 41
Open Door policy, toward China, 687–89
open shops, 826
Operation Rolling Thunder, 933
Oppenheimer, Julius Robert (1904–1967), 847
Orange County, N.C., 129
Orange, N.J., 561
Order of the Star-Spangled Banner, 391
Ordinance of Nullification (1832), 330–31, 332
Ordinance of 1784, 198, 214, 228
Oregon (battleship), 675
Oregon, 407, 529
admission to Union, 404
American acquisition of, 417, 420
development of (1880s), 534
joint occupation of, 403, 403*m*
migration to (1840s), 404
Oregon conventions, 413
Oregon Trail, 403–4, 407, 518
organic farming, 966
Organization of Petroleum Exporting Countries (OPEC), 991–92, 999
oil embargo (1973), 992
Organization Man, The (Whyte), 892*i*
Orphan Asylum Society, 311
Ostend Manifesto, 426–27
O'Sullivan, John Louis, 426
Manifest Destiny, 402–3
Oswald, Lee Harvey (1939–1963), 925, 926
Ota, Peter, 834
Other America: Poverty in the United States, The (Harrington), 913, 928
Otis, James (1725–1783), 142, 151
Ottawa Indians, 124, 224
Ottoman Empire, 690–91, 697
Ouellette, Laura, 1027
"Outcasts of Poker Flat, The" (Harte), 534
outwork system, 28, 259, 260
Ovington, Mary White, 655
Owens River, 535
Oxford Pledge, 766
ozone, 1032

Pacific, American expansionist ambitions in, 505, 671
Pacific Mail Steamship Company, 533
Pacific slope, settlement of (1860), 529, 529*m*
pacifist groups, during World War I, 700
packet service, transatlantic, 299
pagan traditions, 14
Pago Pago, 671
Pahlavi, Muhammad Riza (Shah of Iran), 876
American support of, 1000, 1002
Paine, Sarah Cobb, 184
Paine, Thomas (1737–1809), 167–68, 183, 189, 201
Pakistan, 879
Palestine. *See also* Israel
partition (1947), 879
Palestine Liberation Organization (PLO), 1010
Palmer, Alexander Mitchell (1872–1936), 722–23
Palmer v. Mulligan, (1805), 262
Panama Canal
construction of, 685–86, 687*i*
treaty (1978), 1001
Panama, U.S. recognition of, 685
Pan-American Conference, 818
Pan-American Union, 671
Panay (gunboat), 822
Panic of 1837, 306, 342, 342*i*, 346, 386
Panic of 1893, 553, 590, 593, 673
Panic of 1907, 664
paper dealers, 210
paper entrepreneurs, 1014
paper money, 95, 111, 452, 453, 507, 591, 592
American Revolution and, 174, 175
Paramount Studios, 739
parents
control over children, 271
marriage and, 270
Paris Peace Accords (1973), 986
Paris peace conference, 223
Paris, Treaty of (1763), 124, 125, 137, 199
Paris, Treaty of (1783), 183, 199, 216, 223
Paris, Treaty of (1899), 681
Parker, Alton Brooks (1852–1926), 658
Parker, Theodore (1810–1860), 369, 424
Parks, Rosa, 947
parks
city, 613
national, 535
Parliament, British
Board of Trade, 75
Charles I's dissolution of, 50
Stamp Act and, 139
supremacy over colonies, 153
parochial schools. *See* education; Catholicism
Patman, Wright, 833
patriotism, 268
Patriots, 157, 158, 167
Committee of Safety, 186
militia, 178
resistance movements, 1760–1775, 157*t*
rural, 156–58
state constitutions and, 194
support for, 158
patronage policies, Walpole's, 93, 94
patroon, 38
Patterson, John, Alabama governor, 948
Patterson, John, business executive, 643
Patterson, Joseph Medill, 742
Patterson, William, 203
Patton, George Smith, Jr. (1885–1945), 781, 838
Paul, Alice, 650, 713, 715, 716
Pawnee Indians, 516
Pax Americana, 886, 995, 1035
Paxton Boys, massacre of native Americans, 128
Payne-Aldrich Tariff Act of 1909, 660
Peabody, James H., 575
Peace Corps, 920–21
Peace Democrats, 474
peace movement, international, before World War I, 691
Pearce, Charles H., 496
Pearl Harbor, Japanese attack on, 822–23, 841
peasantry, 24. *See also* European peasantry
comparison with slaves, 84
English, inflation and, seventeenth century, 27
European, 10–12
Hispanic, 530, 531
peddler, Yankee, 297*i*
Peking. *See* Beijing
Pelham, Henry, 123, 124
Pendergrast, Thomas Joseph (1872–1945), 829
Pendleton, Edmund (1721–1803), 166
Pendleton Act (1883), 579
Penn, Richard, 166
Penn, William (1644–1718), 69, 90, 106, 127
Pennsylvania (colony), 69, 69*t*, 105
Germans in, 106–7
Quakers in, 105, 106, 111
trade and urban growth in, 89

Pennsylvania (state)
coal mining industry in, 549
constitution of 1776, 193, 194
Second Bank of the United States and, 330
Whiskey Rebellion and, 216
Pennsylvania assembly, 90
Pennsylvania *Gazette*, 115
Pennsylvania Manufacturing Society, 211
Pennsylvania Railroad, 552, 553, 556
strikes against, 547
Penobscot Indians, 8
pensioners, 136
pension programs
Civil War, 504
Social Security Act, 793
veterans, 580
Pentagon. *See* Defense, Department of
Pentagon Papers, 987
Pentecostal movement, 624
People's party. *See* Populist party
People's Republic of China, 861
exclusion from U.N., 862
intervention in Korean War, 863
Nixon's visit to, 984
student democratic protests in, 1028
U.S. refusal to recognize, 983
Pequot tribe
extermination of, 53
Puritan relationship with, 53–54
perestroika, 1026
perfectionism, perfectionists, 368
Noyes and, 356
Perkins, Frances (1882–1965), 651, 652, 788, 793, 797, 798–99, 799*i*
Perkins, Mary Beecher (1805–1900), 397
Permanent Court of Arbitration, 691
Perot, H. Ross, 1033
Perry, Matthew Colbraith (1794–1858), 403
Perry, Oliver Hazard (1785–1819), 238
Pershing, John Joseph (1860–1948), 702, 703, 704, 705
Persian Gulf, 733
import of oil from, 991
Persian Gulf War, 1024, 1030–31, 1032
personal liberty laws, 424
personal property laws, 244
Peru, 3, 4
pesticides, 993
pet banks, 330
Petersburg, siege of (1864), 466, 471
"pettifoggers," 266
Petty, William (1737–1805), 146
phalanxes, 355
Philadelphia, Miss., 954
Philadelphia, 69, 87, 88*i*, 298
British attack on, 172, 173, 175
Enlightenment in, 114
hostility toward Britain in, 167
Howe's occupation of, 183
Paxton Boys' march toward, 128*i*
ratification of Constitution, 206
religious denominations in, 105
streetcar system, 612
Philadelphia Centennial Exhibition of 1876, 549
Philadelphia Committee of Resistance, 167
Philadelphia Convention of 1787, 201–4, 243
Philadelphia Female Anti-Slavery Society, 366
Philadelphia Traction Company, 612
Philip II (1527–1598), 25
Philippines, 841, 843*m*
"Bataan Death March," 842
U.S. acquisition of, 680, 681–84
U.S. bases on, 679
U.S. capture of, 843*i*
Phillips, John, 294
Phillips, Wendell (1811–1884), 434, 462, 491
photography, 811, 812
Pickering, John, 231
Pickering, Timothy (1745–1829), 233
Pickett, George Edward (1825–1875), 464, 465
Pickford, Mary (1893–1979), 739
"Piece Rate System, A" (Taylor) 568
Pierce, Franklin (1804–1869), 359, 414*t*, 426*i*
Latin American expansionist policy and, 426–27
presidential election of 1852, 425–26
presidential election of 1856, 431
slavery and, 429
pietism, 119
in America, 114–15
revival, 120
pig iron, 550, 551
Pike, Zebulon Montgomery (1779–1813), 518
Pilgrims, 31
Church of England and, 50
Mayflower Compact, 49
at Plymouth, Mass., 49–50
as Separatists, 50, 54
Pinchot, Gifford (1865–1946), 661
Pinckney, Charles Cotesworth (1746–1825), 232
as presidential candidate, 235
Pinckney, Thomas (1750–1828), 217, 486
Pingree, Hazen S., 644
Pink Floyd, 965
Pioneers, The (Cooper), 394
Pit, The (Norris), 635
Pitt, William, earl of Chatham, (1708–1778), 123, 136, 137*i*, 144*t*, 156, 179
Great War for Empire and, 124–25
Stamp Act and, 139, 145
Pittsburgh, Penn., 297, 298*i*
environment, late nineteenth century, 613
iron industry in, 608
Pittsburgh Survey (Sage), 640
Pizarro, Francisco (c. 1470–1541), 21
placemen, 94, 136
Plain Home Talk on Love, Marriage and Parentage (Foote), 633
Planned Parenthood, 765
Planned Parenthood v. Casey (1992), 1026
plantation(s), 373*i*
confiscation and redistribution of, 482
society, 367, 378–79
of Virginia, 40*i*
plantation duty, 70
planter(s), 378–79
contracts with freedmen, 502
fear of slave rebellion, 384
opposition to radical Reconstruction, 497–99
racist ideology, 379
Platt, Orville Hitchcock (1827–1905), 671
Platt amendment, 686, 818
Platt, Thomas Collier (1833–1910), 586
Plessy v. Ferguson (1896), 599, 946
plow, cast iron, 227, 300
Plunkitt, George W., 619
pluralism, in religion, in mid-Atlantic colonies, 111–12
plutonium, 993
Plymouth (colony), 31, 35
Dominion of New England, 71
Pilgrims at, 49–50
Pocahontas (1595–1617), 41
Poe, Edgar Allan (1809–1849), 352*i*, 353
poetry. *See* literature
Poindexter, John, 1012
Poland
election of non-Communist government, 1026
German invasion of, 820
immigrants from, Catholic hierarchy, 622
Soviet control of, 854
polio vaccine, 907, 907*i*
political parties. *See also* specific parties
American, 391, 431–432
antimonopoly platforms, 542
city, machine control of (1880s–1890s), 618
congressional caucus of 1824 and, 322
Democratic. *See* Democratic party
Dixiecrat party, 867, 868
during 1820s, 320
English (1700s), 93–94, 136
Federalist. *See* Federalist party
Free Soil, 368–69. *See also* Free Soil party
La Raza Unida, 959
Liberal Republican, 506, 587
Liberty, 368–69
loyalty to (1876–1892), 584
membership in, ethnocultural differences in, 585–86
Mississippi Freedom Democratic party, 951
North American, 431
organizational activity, 586–87
Republican. *See* Republican party
rise of, 217–18
Second Party System, 319, 339–46, 413. *See also* Democratic party; Whig party (American)
States' Rights party, 867
Third Party System, 432
Working Men's, 335
Workingmen's party, 533

politics
following American Revolution, 200
control of, Jackson's changing of, 325
corruption during late nineteenth century, 618
crisis of the 1890s, 590–96
1876–1892, 581, 584–86
industrialization, effects on, 513
machine, 586–87, 618–19
new, 918–20
organizational, 586–87
progressivism and, 642–45, 656–60
reforms in, 587
representative system of, 90
rise of assembly, 1700s, 90–92
salutary neglect, 93–94
trade and (1763–1776), 148*i*
women in, 797, 971, 1034
during World War II, 828–29
Polk, James Knox (1795–1849), 408, 421
agenda of administration, 415
Mexican War and, 416–21
presidential election of 1844, 414–15
Pollock, Jackson (1912–1956), 809
poll tax, 200, 954
polygamy, Mormons and, 405, 406
Ponselle, Elsa, 764
Pontiac (d. 1769), 124, 135
Pony Express, 518, 522
poor. *See also* poverty
migration to cities, 902
urban, 310
Industrial Revolution and, 306–9
war on poverty, 928–29
Poor Law of 1601, 28
Poor Richard's Almanac (Franklin), 114
Pope, John (1822–1892), 459
popular rule, 194
popular sovereignty, doctrine of, 261, 262, 427
advocates of, 425
Cass's concept of, 421, 422
Compromise of 1850 and, 425, 426, 427–28
Douglas and, 427
election of 1852 and, 425, 426
principle of, 194
population. *See also* birthrate; disease; mortality
black (1820s), 223
city (1870–1910), 609*t*
1870–1890, 554
growth (1840s–1850s), 395, 398
by region (1820s–1860), 399*f*
in 1700s, 126*f*
1610–1910, A-18
slave (1775–1820), 243
white (1820s), 223
Populist (People's) party, 513, 590–91
decline of, 596
free silver issue, 591–92, 595
presidential election of 1892, 591*m*
southern, 598, 598*i*
pork packing industry, in Cincinnati, 289*i*
Porter, Cole, 769
Port Hudson, La., fall to Union forces, 464
Port Huron, Mich., 962
Portland, Ore., 518
Portrait of a Lady, The (James), 635
Portsmouth, R.I., 54
Portugal
maritime empire (fifteenth century), 18–19
slavery and, 77
Postal Service. *See* U.S. Postal Service
potato(es), growing of, in New England, 227
potato famine, 388
Potawatomi Indians, 224
Potomac River, 458, 469
Potsdam Conference (1945), 837, 847
Potter, Helen (1866–1943), 419, 589
Pottle, Frederick, 705
Pound, Roscoe (1890–1964), 641
poverty
Lyndon Johnson's program, 928–29
during 1980s, 1016, 1016*i*
Powderly, Terence Vincent (1849–1924), 569, 570, 572
Powder River, 525, 526
Powell, Colin, 1024, 1030
Powell, Lewis Franklin, Jr. (1907–), 983
Power, 810
power of eminent domain, 261
Powhatan Indians, 8, 40, 41
Preemption Act of 1841, 345
prejudice. *See* racism
Presbyterian Church, 30
Benevolent Empire and, 311
Free Presbyterian Church, 312–13
New Lights, 120
pietistic revival, 120
Scots-Irish, 183
Second Great Awakening and, 277
presbyters, 30
president, 205. *See also* specific presidents
election of, electoral college, 203
power of, 204
presidential campaigns. *See also* individual president
new styles to, 918–20
Presidential Commission on the Status of Women, 925, 968
presidential elections
1788, 207
1792, 211
1796, 217
1800, 218–19
1808, 235
1812, 237
1824, 320, 322
1828, 323–24, 323*i*
1832, 329
1836, 342
1840, 344–45, 345*i*
1844, 414–15
1848, 420–21
1852, 425
1856, 431–32
1860, 437–39, 439*m*
1864, 464
1868, 491
1872, 506
1876, 507–9, 509*m*
1876–1892, 581
1884, 581
1888, 578*i*, 590
1896, 593–96, 595*m*
1900, 683
1908, 660
1912, 663*m*, 663–64
1916, 701, 701*i*
1920, 729
1924, 730
1928, 752–53, 753*m*
1932, 782, 782*m*
1936, 794–95
1940, 821
1944, 828–29
1948, 966–68, 868*m*
1952, 872
1960, 918–20, 919*m*
1964, 926, 927
1968, 977, 981, 982*m*
1972, 985–6
1976, 1000
1980, 1008–9
1984, 1011
1988, 1024–25
1992, 1033–34, 1034*m*
President's Organization for Unemployment Relief (POUR), 781
presidios, 36
Presley, Elvis (1935–1977), 908*i*, 909, 965
press, Sedition Act of 1798 and, 218
Price, Victoria, 770
price(s). *See also* consumer price index; deflation; inflation
American Revolution and, 184
cattle (1880s), 521
commodity (1890s), 591
conversion table, A-25
decline (1880–1892), 547
Great Depression and, 760
housing prices of 1970s, 995
just price, 184
land (1820s–1830s), 300
Panic of 1837 and, 342, 343
wholesale, 1865–1900, 553*f*
price revolution of the sixteenth century, 26, 27
Priestly, Joseph (1733–1804), 114
Prince, The (Machiavelli), 17
Princeton, N.J., 170
American victories at, 171
battle of, 170*i*
Princeton University, 117, 120*t*
Principia Mathematica (Newton), 113
printers' unions, 338
"prints for the people," 393
Prioleau, George W., 680
Prison Discipline Society, 311
Privy Council, 70, 146
Proclamation for Suppressing Rebellion and Sedition, 166
Proclamation Line of 1763, 135, 152*m*, 157*t*
Proclamation of Neutrality, 214, 215

Proclamation of 1763, 135
Proctor, Redfield (1831–1908), 678
Proctor & Gamble Company, 732
Production Code Administration, 767–68
profarmer and predebtor program of 1785 and 1786, 200
Progress and Poverty (George), 641
Progressive Era, 513, 639–65
Progressive party, 752, 869
  1924 election and, 730
progressivism, 639
  attack on nineteenth-century formalism, 640–41
  course of, 639
  cultural pluralism and, 652–54
  idealism, 641–42
  intellectual roots of, 640–42
  labor movement, 652
  municipal reform, 643–44
  muckrakers, 642
  national politics and, 656–60
  political reformers, 642–45
  racism and, 654–55
  recruitment, 645
  republican, fracturing of, 660–62
  settlement houses, 648
  state politics and, 644–45
  urban liberalism, 650–56
  women and, 645–50
  Woodrow Wilson and New Freedom, 662–65
Prohibition, 652, 654, 721–22, 721*m*, 750–52
  repeal of, 752
Prohibitory Act of 1775, 166, 176
Promise of American Life, The (Croly), 662
Promontory Point, Utah, 518
propaganda, during World War I, 714
property. *See also* land
  entrepreneurial view of, 305
  intangible, 306
  ownership of
    day laborers and, 307
    Industrial Revolution and, 305–6
  slaves as, 379
  state legislature participation and, 194–95
  tangible, 305–6
  voting rights and, 265, 320
property owners, middle class, Industrial Revolution and, 306
property rights
  Federalist view, 262
  government's intrusion on, 262
  redistribution of Tory lands and goods and, 166–67
  republican view, 262
  social utility and, 262
  of women, 361
property taxes
  after American Revolution, 200
  labor unions and, 338
  during Reconstruction Era, 495
proprietary colonies, 42, 68–69
Prosser, Gabriel (1776–1800), 188, 247
Prosser, Martin, 250
Protestantism, 15
  black, 120–21, 277
  Huguenots, 36
  modernist-fundamentalist debate (1920s), 748
  progressive idealism and, 641
  republicanism and, 276
  revivalism, 311
  Second Great Awakening and, 277
  Social Gospel, 641
  urban (1870s–1890s), 622–24
Protestant Reformation, 23–25, 26, 31
  in England, 29–30
  Puritans and, 30
Providence, R. I., 54
PTL (Praise the Lord) television, 1024
publications. *See also* literature; newspapers and magazines
  African-American, 364
  revivalist, 314
Public Enemy, The, 767
public health, city crowding and (1840s–1860s), 389
Public Utilities Holding Companies Act (1935), 791, 794
Public Works Administration (PWA), 790, 797
Pueblo Indians, 36
Puerto Ricans, migration to U.S. after World War II, 900, 901
Puerto Rico, U.S. acquisition of, 680
Pulitzer, Joseph (1847–1911), 626*i*, 676
Pullman, George Mortimer (1831–1897), 573
Pullman boycott of 1894, 573–74, 652
pump priming, 779
Pure Food and Drug Act (1906), 659–60
Puritanism, Puritans, 30, 52
  Cambridge Platform of 1648, 55
  dissent in, 54–55
  as freeholding society, 57–60
  Fundamental Orders, 55
  Halfway Covenant, 55–57
  Anne Hutchinson and, 54
  in Massachusetts Bay colony, 51–52
  native American conversion to, 54
  pietistic movements in, 115
  relationship with native Americans, 53–54
  religious covenant, 52–53
  in Salem, Mass., 54
  settlement at Massachusetts Bay, 31, 51–52
  Roger Williams and, 54
  witch hunting, 57
  women's roles and, 103
putting-out system, 28, 110, 259
Pyle, Ernie (1900–1945), 844
Pynchon, John, 60
Pyramid of the Sun, 5

Quaker Oats, 555*i*
Quakers, 277
  abolitionism and, 366
  in Pennsylvania, 105–6
  permission to marry, 111–12
  republicanism and, 276
  separation of church and state, 189
  settlement in Pennsylvania, 69
  Shakers and, 355–56
  weekly meetings for worship, 105, 106, 111
  Welsh, 108
  women's roles and, 103
Quantrill, William Clarke (1837–1865), 446
Quartering Act (1765), 139, 146, 156
  Patriot response to, 157*t*
Quayle, James Danforth, 3rd (1947–), 1033
Quebec
  British capture of, 124
  French settlement in, 36
Quebec Act of 1774, 152*m*, 153
  Patriot response to, 157*t*
Queen Anne's War (1702–13), 74, 92
Queen's Own Loyal Virginians, 166
Quetzalcoatl, 5, 20
Quincy Railroad, 553
Quitman, John A., 426, 428

R. H. Macy, 556
race riots, 654
  in Harlem (1935), 772
  in Los Angeles (1992), 1017
  of 1960s, 957*m*, 958
  in Springfield (1908), 655
  following World War I, 719–20
race, social class and, 268
racial tension, 1980s, 1020
racism
  in armed forces, 709, 825
  against blacks, 533
  against Chinese (1860s), 533
  during Civil War, 469
  northern, 956
  of planters, 379
  during Progressive Era, 654–56
  during Reconstruction Era, 499
  in Vietnam, 938
  following World War I, 719
  during World War II, 825, 832, 833–35, 843
radicalism
  agrarian, decline of, 596
  American, 574–75
  fear of, following World War I, 722–23
  syndicalism, 575
  western, 574–75
radical movements. *See* reform movements
radio, 734
  during Great Depression, 769*m*, 769–70
  news broadcasts, 811
  1920s, 742
  during World War II, 830
radioactive waste, 993
Railroad Brotherhood Union, 570, 570*i*
railroad industry, 610
  Chinese immigrants employed by (1860s), 532–33

(railroad industrry con't)
coal-burning steam engines, 549
effect on westward expansion, 540
entrepreneurs, 553
freight rates (1784–1900), 303*f*
General Managers' Association, 573, 574
government control of, during World War I, 710
Great Depression and, 759
growth of (1860s–1890s), 550, 551–52
impact on meat industry, 554–55
ICC regulation of, 542
locomotives, 552
managerial problems (1850s–1890s), 556
metal industry and, 549
of North and South (1850–1860), 400–2
Pullman boycott of 1894, 573–74, 652
refrigerated cars, 555
Theodore Roosevelt's effort to regulate, 659
southern, 558, 560
steel industry and, 548, 551
strikes against (1877), 547
Truman's efforts for federal control of, 866
trunk lines, 556
Railroad War Board, 710
Rainbow Coalition, 1024
Rainey, Henry, 798
Raleigh, Sir Walter (1554–1618), 29
Ramona (Jackson), 534
Ramsay, David, 200
ranching. *See* cattle ranching
Randolph, Asa Philip (1889–1979), 832, 952
Randolph, Edward, 71
Rankin, Jeanette (1880–1973), 702*i*, 823
Raphael (1483–1520), 17
Raskob, John J., 752, 757
rationalists, childrearing and, 272
rationing, during World War II, 830–31
Rauschenberg, Robert (1925–), 916*i*
Rauschenbusch, Walter (1861–1918), 641
Ray, James Earl, 958
Rayburn, Samuel Taliaferro (1882–1961), 920
Reader's Digest, 734, 742
Readjuster movement, 597
Reagan, Nancy, 1024
Reagan, Ronald Wilson (1911–), 905, 981, 1000, 1003, 1009*i*
conservative agenda of, 1007–9
deregulation, 1010, 1025
firing of air traffic controllers, 1016
foreign relations, 1010–11
Iran-Contra Affair and, 1011–12
presidential election of 1980, 1008–9
Reaganomics, 1009–10
tax reform, 1011
reality, ideal order of , 350
Real Majority, The (Wattenberg and Scammon), 981
Real Whigs
American, 93–94, 136, 140
English, 93
reapers, 400, 401, 536, 540
Reason, The Only Oracle of Man (Paine), 189
Rebel Without a Cause, 909
recession(s)
following American Revolution, 199
of 1834, 330
of 1920–1921, 728, 744, 757, 759
of 1953–1954, 1957–1958, 1960–1961, 875
of 1975, 999, 1000
of 1982, 1001
"Roosevelt recession" of 1937–1938, 795–96
after World War II, 886
Reciprocal Trade Agreement Act of 1934, 818
Reconstruction, 538. *See also* Restoration
Black Codes and, 502
Civil Rights Act (1866), 488–89
congressional initiatives, 488–91
corruption and Grant administration, 505–7
counterrevolution of planters, 497–99
depression of 1873–1877, 507
economic fate of former slaves, 499–503
end of, 509
Fifteenth Amendment and, 491
first civil rights bill and, 488–89
Fourteenth Amendment and, 489
Joint Committee on Reconstruction, 485
labor system and, 487–88
North during, 503–9
political crisis of 1877, 507–9
politics related to, 581
radical, 490–503
Republican economic programs during, 504
Republican foreign policy during, 504–5
resettlement of freedmen, 485–87
South during, 493–97
Tenure of Office Act, 490–91
woman suffrage and, 491
Reconstruction Act of 1867, 490
Reconstruction Finance Corporation, 779
recreation. *See* leisure
Red Cloud (1822–1909), 524
Red Cross, 712, 779
Red Jacket (Sagoyewatha) (1758–1830), 250, 251
Red River Valley, 536
Redstockings, 970
Reed, Stanley Forman (1884–1980), 795
reformers, political, 587
reform movements, 349. *See also* abolitionism; civil rights movement; Progressivism; religious reform; women's movement
American
communal living, 353–54
education (1820s), 266–69
legal profession, 266
Oneida Community, 356–57
phalanxes, 355
transcendentalists and utopians, 350–57. *See also* transcendentalists and utopians
women and, 357–59
of British Imperial System
Currency Act of 1751 and, 134
Currency Act of 1764 and, 135
Great War for Empire and, 136–38
ideological roots of resistance to, 142–43
Molasses Act of 1733 and, 135
Navigation Acts and, 135. *See also* Navigation Acts
Revenue Act of 1762 and, 135
1763–1765, 133–37
Stamp Act and, 129–42, 143
Sugar Act of 1764 and, 137–38
Townshend Act of 1676 and, 146–48
refrigeration, meat industry and, 554
Regan, Donald T. (1918–), 1009
Regulators, 176
North Carolina, 129
South Carolina, 129
Rehnquist, William Hubbs (1924–), 983, 1012, 1026
Reid, Whitelaw (1837–1912), 674
Reisman, David, 892
religion. *See also* Christianity; specific religions
after American Revolution, 188–89
in cities (1890s–1900s), 619–24
deists, 189
education and (1880s), 585
English migration to America and, 29–31
European (1400s and 1600s), 11, 13–15, 24*i*
freedom of, 189
fundamentalism, 748
in mid-Atlantic colonies, 105, 111–12
native American, 4, 5, 8, 9, 250, 251
political party membership and, 585–86
progressive idealism and, 641
Puritan migration to America and, 50
reform movements. *See* reform movements; religious reform
republicanism and, 189
religious cults, 996
school prayer, 925
separation of church and state, 54, 55, 118, 188–89
of Sioux nation, 517
slave, 250, 383
women's involvement in, 273
religious reform, 349
Benevolent Empire and, 311
business class and, 311
urban revivalism, 624
religious test for office, 189
Renaissance, 16–18
American, 269
humanism and, 17
Italian, 17
princes of, 17–18
relocation, during World War II, 831
Reno, Milo, 780
"Report on Manufactures" (Hamilton), 211
"Report on the Public Credit" (Hamilton), 209–10
Rensselaer, Kiliaenvan, 38

Rensselaer family of New York, 73, 110, 111*m*
representation, slavery-related issues of, 203, 204
representative system of politics, 90
Republic Aviation Corporation, military contracts to, 887
republicanism, 183, 257, 428
doctrine of popular sovereignty, 261. *See also* popular sovereignty
education and, 266–69
ideal of, 183–84
Industrial Revolution and, 306
marriage and, 269–71
"Maxims for Republics," 273
political philosophy, 264–65
raising of children and, 271–73
religion and, 188, 278–79
Second Great Awakening and, 276–78
slavery and, 187
technology and, 212
de Tocqueville and, 279–81
women and, 196–97, 273–76
Republican party (1794–1828), 324, 339
commonwealth ideology, 261–62
election of 1796 and, 217
election of 1800 and, 218
election of 1824 and, 320
factions, 252
Federalists joining, 253
formation of, 217
national mercantilism and, 261
property rights view, 262
Sedition Act and, 218
Supreme Court justices appointed by, 264
supporters of, 217
Van Buren's changes in New York, 320
Republican party (founded 1854). *See also* presidential elections
carpetbaggers, 493, 494
condemnation of Grant's policies, 506
Crédit Mobilier and Whiskey Ring and, 506
economic program
during Civil War, 453–54
during Reconstruction Era, 504, 505
election of 1856 and, 431, 432
election of 1858 and, 436–37
election of 1860 and, 438–39
election of 1946 and, 866
Fifteenth Amendment and, 491
foreign policy during Reconstruction Era, 504–5
Great Depression and, 778–79
Halfbreeds, 586, 587
identification with Civil War, 581
ideology v. defense of slavery, 428–29
immigrant workingmen and farmers in, 494
Andrew Johnson's restoration plans and, 484–85
Kansas-Nebraska Act and, 427–28
Liberal Republican party, 506, 587
Lincoln as leader of, 435–36
Lincoln's restoration plan and, 482–83
loyalty of members (1877–1893), 584
Marshall Plan and, 858–59
Mugwumps, 587, 588, 619, 656
nomination of Frémont, 431
radical Reconstructon and, 493, 494, 495–96
resurgence during 1970s–1980s, 1008–9
scalawags, 493, 494
silver and, 595
Stalwarts, 586
Third Party System and, 432
traditions, 580
Wade-Davis Bill and, 483
during World War II, 828
republican society, 194
Republic Steel Corporation, 802
research and development
corporate involvement in (1920s), 731
federal support of, post World War II, 887
Reserve Officer Training Corps (ROTC), 964
Resettlement Administration, 801, 804
Historical Section of, 812
restoration. *See also* Reconstruction
under Andrew Johnson, 483–85
under Lincoln, 481–83
Restraining Act of 1767, 146
retail industry, 555–56
Reuther, Walter Philip (1907–1970), 892
Revels, Hiram (1822–1901), 495, 495*i*
Revenue Act of 1673, 70
Revenue Act of 1762, 135
Patriot response to, 157*t*
Revenue Act of 1767, 146
Revenue Acts of 1916 and 1917, 710
Revenue Act of 1932, 779
Revenue Act of 1935, 794
Revenue Act of 1942, 823
revenue, control of (1700s), 91
revenue, Federal (1880), 580
revenue sharing, new federalism and, 983
Revere, Paul (1735–1818), 152
revivalism, revivalists, 115, 118, 273, 276–78
urban, 624
Revolutionary War. *See* American Revolution
Reykjavik, Iceland, 1012
Reynolds v. Sims (1964), 925
Rhee, Syngman, 862
Rhett, Robert Brownwell, 437
Rhode Island (colony), 56*t*, 75
Dominion of New England, 71
Anne Hutchinson in, 55
paper currency, 95
separation of church and state in, 54
Rhode Island (state), constitution, 193
Rhodes, Elisha Hunt (1842–1917), 466
Ribicoff, Abraham Alexander (1910–), 979
rice industry, use of slaves in, 81,83
Richmond, David, 948
Rickenbacker, Edward Vernon (1890–1973), 706–7, 707*i*, 708
rifle-musket, 449
Right to Life movement, 973, 996
rights of citizens, Fair Deal and, 865
Riis, Jacob August (1849–1914), 811
Riley, James Whitcomb (1849–1916), 635
Rio de Janeiro, Earth Summit in, 1032–33
Rio Grande, 416, 417, 419
riots. *See also* race riots
at Democratic national convention in Chicago (1968), 978–81
draft, 451–52
food, 308
for gay rights, 961
Haymarket Square, 571–2
Ripley, George (1802–1880), 353, 354
Rise of David Levinsky, The (Cahan), 619
Rise of Silas Lapham, The (Howells), 635
Rittenhouse, David (1732–1796), 167
rivers
freight rates, (1784–1900), 303*f*
as source of energy, 289
steamboats on, 303–4
roads, building of (1830s), 301, 301*i*
Roaring Twenties, 734*i*
Robertson, Pat (1930–), 1024
Robinson, Edward G., 767
Robinson, Jackie (Jack Roosevelt, 1919–1972), 869
Robinson, Joseph Taylor (1872–1937), 788
Rochambeau, Jean Baptiste, comte de (1725–1807), 178
Rochester, N.Y., 297
revivalism in, 312
rock and roll, 909
Rockdale, Pa., industry in (1820s), 294–96
Rockefeller, David (1915–), 1002
Rockefeller, John Davidson (1839–1937), 555, 633, 646
Rockefeller, Nelson Aldrich (1908–1979), 918, 999, 1000
Rockefeller Foundation, 779
Rockingham, Charles Wentworth, marquis of (1730–1782), 144, 144*t*, 145
Rocky Mountain Arsenal, 993
Rocky Mountain painters, 402
Roe v. Wade (1973), 971, 973, 983, 1026, 1027
Rogers, William Penn Adair (1879–1935), 730
Rogers, William Pierce (1913–), 936
Rolfe, John (1585–1622), 40, 41
Rolling Stone (magazine), 966
Rolling Stones, 965
Roman Catholicism. *See* Catholicism
Romania, 838, 1026
Rome-Berlin Axis, 819
Rommel, Erwin (1891–1944), 838
Romney, George, 981
Roosevelt I Knew, The (Perkins), 799
Roosevelt, Eleanor (1884–1962), 782, 797, 801, 801*i*, 821, 832, 853, 902, 968
as U.N. representative, 854*i*
Roosevelt, Franklin Delano (1882–1945), 729, 782, 836. *See also* New Deal
Agricultural Adjustment Act and, 789–90
attack on Pearl Harbor and, 822
banking crisis and, 788–89
cabinet of, 788

(Roosevelt, Franklin Delano con't)
at Casablanca Conference, 845
death of, 837, 846
declaration of neutrality, 820
declaration of war against Japan, 823
expansion of presidential power, 788
financing of World War II and, 823
fireside chats, 788, 789
first hundred days of administration, 788–93
first inaugural address, 787
Good Neighbor Policy, 818
Holocaust and, 840, 841
Japanese-American internment and, 833
leadership style, 787–88
legislative accomplishments, 793–94
Lend-Lease Act, 821
meeting with Stalin in Teheran, 845
National War Labor Board and, 826
political activity during World War II, 828
political threats to, 792–93
presidential election of 1932, 782–83, 782*m*
presidential election of 1936, 794–95
presidential election of 1940, 821
presidential election of 1944, 828–29
recognition of Soviet Union, 821
"Roosevelt recession," 795–96
Social Security Act and, 793–94
Soviet sphere of influence and, 854
support for United Nations, 853
Supreme Court and, 795
unemployment and, 790–91
Wall Street reforms, 791–92
WPA and, 794
at Yalta Conference, 845*i*, 845–46
Roosevelt, Theodore (1858–1919), 641, 701, 708, 745, 782, 788
at Algeciras, Spain, 691
anthracite coal strike and, 656–57
conservation and, 656
consumer protection and, 659–60
Corollary to Monroe Doctrine, 687
expansionism and, 670, 674, 685, 686, 688
interest in European affairs, 691
as McKinley's vice president, 656
muckrakers and, 642
Mugwumps and, 588
New Nationalism and, 661–62
Panama Canal and, 685–86
political career of, 656
Progressive party and, 642, 647
railroad regulation, 659
Rough Riders, 678, 680
Sherman Antitrust Act and, 661
Square Deal and, 660
trusts and, 657–59
Wilson's view of, 662–63
Root, Elihu (1845–1937), 686, 691
Root-Takahira Agreement, 688
Root, Elisha K., 295
Ropes, Hannah Anderson, 430
Rosecrans, William Starke (1819–1898), 464
Rosenberg, Ethel (1916–1953) and Julius (1918–1953), 872
Rosenwald, Julius (1862–1932), 758*i*
"Rosie the Riveter," 865
Ross, Edward Alsworth (1866–1951), 654
Roth, William, 1009
Rothstein, Arthur, 812
rotten boroughs, 136
Rough Riders, 678, 680
Rowlandson, Mary, 61
royal colonies
Maryland as, 73
Massachusetts as, 72
New Hampshire as, 71
Virginia as, 42
"Royal Fifth," 25
rubber, scarcity during World War II, 830–32
Rubin, Jerry, 979
Ruby, Jack, 926
Ruef, Abraham (1864–1936), 651
Ruggles, Timothy, 189
Rule of 1756, 216
rum industry, 87, 95
rural Americans, Pietist revivals and, 119
rural communities
in Great West, 538, 538*m*, 541
loss of population (1920s), 744, 745*f*
Rural Electrification Administration, 804
Rush, Benjamin (1745–1813), 167, 183, 185, 266, 273
Rush-Bagot treaty of 1817, 253
Rusk, (David) Dean (1909–), 920
Russia, 1029*m*. *See also* Soviet Union
conflict with Austria-Hungary, 698
Revolution of 1917, 703–4, 722
Russo-Japanese War (1905), 688
Russwurm, John, 364
Rust Belt, 995
Rust v. Sullivan (1990), 1026
Rustin, Bayard, 952
Ruth, Babe (George Herman, 1895–1948), 743
Rutledge, John (1739–1800), 203
Ryan, Thomas Fortune, 612
Ryswick, Treaty of (1697), 74
Ryukyu Islands, 862

Sabbath observation
Benevolent Empire and, 311
blue laws, 585
Sabin, Albert Bruce (1906–), 907
Sabin, Pauline, 752
Sacco-Vanzetti case, 723
Sackville-West, Sir Lionel , 669
Sacramento, Ca., 417
Sacramento Valley, development of, 407–8
Sadat, Anwar as (1918–1981), 1001, 1001*i*
"Safety of the Plantation," 83
Saffin, John, 59
Sage, Margaret Olivia Slocum (1828–1918), 640
Saigon, South Vietnam, 935
fall of, 998
Vietcong invasion of, 986
St. Clair, Arthur (1734–1818), 224
Saint-Domingue. *See* Haiti
St. George Fields, Massacre of, 148
St. Lawrence Seaway, 874
St. Leger, Barry (1737–1789), 172
St. Louis, Mo., 297, 896
as industrial center, 401
St. Louis Post-Dispatch, 626
St. Paul, Minn., 518
St. Mary's City, 42
Salem, Mass.
Puritan Church in, 54
witchcraft trials of 1692, 57
Salinger, Jerome David (1919–), 962
Salk, Jonas, 907, 907i
Salmagundi (Irving), 269
salutary neglect, 93–94, 95
Great War for Empire and, 136
Salvation Army, 623
Samoan islands, expansionist efforts in, 671
Sanborn, Franklin Benjamin (1831–1917), 369
San Diego, 36, 417, 535
San Francisco, 36, 408, 529
anti-Chinese agitation in (1870s), 533
American capture of, 417
earthquake of 1906, 612
Haight-Ashbury, 966
San Francisco Examiner, 626
Sanger, Margaret Higgins (1883–1966), 765
sanitation, 613
farm (1850s–1900s), 541
sanitation systems, city crowding and (1840s–1860s), 389
San Jacinto, battle of (1836), 333
San Juan Hill, battle of (1898), 656, 680, 681*i*
Sankey, Ira D., 624
San Pascual, battle of (1846), 417
Sans Arc tribe, 517
Santa Anita, 834
Santa Anna, Antonio López de (1794–1876), 333, 418, 426
Santa Barbara, Ca., 36
American capture of, 417
Santa Fe, N.M.
American capture of, 417
Hispanic culture in, 531
Hispanic settlement in, 530
Santa Fe Trail, 406
Santiago de Cuba, battle of (1898), 668*i*
Santo Domingo. *See* Dominican Republic
Sarajevo, 698
Saratoga, battle of (1777), 172–73
Satan, 14
Saturday Evening Post, The, 734, 742
Saudi Arabia, import of oil from, 991
Savage, Augusta, 750
savings and loan crisis, 1025
Savio, Mario, 962
scalawags, 493, 494
Scalia, Antonin (1936–), 1012
Scammon, Richard, 981
Scandinavia
erosion of peasant economy in, 562
immigration to U.S. from, 538

Scarlet Letter, The (Hawthorne), 352
Schechter v. United States (1935), 716, 791–92, 795
Schenck v. United States (1919), 716
Schenectady, N.Y., destruction of (1690), 74
Scheur, Sandra, 964
Schlafly, Phyllis (1924–), 972, 973
Schlesinger, Arthur Meier, Jr. (1917–), 990
Schneiderman, Rose (1884–1972), 649, 649*i*
schools. *See* education
Schroeder, Patricia, 971, 1012
Schumacher, E. F., 991
Schurz, Carl, 587
Schuyler, Elizabeth. *See* Hamilton, Elizabeth Schuyler
Schuyler, Philip John (1733–1804), 171
Schwartzkopf, H. Norman (1934–), 1030
Schwenck, Nikolaus (1831–1869), 388
Schwerner, Michael, 954
science, Enlightenment and, 112, 113–14
scientific management, 568–69
Scopes trial, 748
Scioto land companies, 230
Scots-Irish
  in mid-Atlantic colonies, 108
  in New York colony, 110
  in Pennsylvania colony, 110
    Paxton Boys, 128
  Presbyterians, 183
Scott, Dred (c. 1795–1858), 432–33
Scott, Hugh Lenox (1853–1934), 990
Scott, Winfield (1786–1866), 327, 418, 445
  Whig nomination of, 425
Scottsboro case, 770–71
Scouts of the Prairie, The (Buntline), 523
Scudder, Vida, 632
Seabrook, N.H., 994
sea dogs, 28
Seale, Bobby, 956
Seamen's Act of 1915, 665
seaport cities
  Atlantic, 298
  growth of, 1700s, 87–88
  society in, 88–90
  southern, 378
Sears, Roebuck and Company, 555, 758*i*
Second Bank of the United States, 263
  recharter, Jackson's veto of, 328–29
  withdrawal of federal government deposits, 329–30
Second Confiscation Act of 1862, 462
Second Great Awakening, 311
Second Party System, 319, 339–46, 349, 369, 413. *See also* Democratic party; Whig party (American)
Secret Six, 369
sectionalism, 375
Securities and Exchange Commission (SEC), 791
Sedalia, Mo., 520
Sedgwick, Catharine Maria, 394
Sedition Act of 1798, 218
  expiration of, 231
Sedition Act of 1918, 715
Seeger, Charles, 809
Seeger, Pete (1919–), 965
  blacklisting of, 869, 870
Seeger, Ruth Crawford, 809
segregation
  of armed forces, during World War I, 709
  battle against, 945–48
  of blood banks, 825
  Brown v. Board of Education of Topeka, 874, 925, 946, 947, 955, 996
  de facto, 955
  1877–1900, 597–603
  Jim Crow, 959
  in North Carolina (1950), 946*i*
  residential, 997
  school, 496, 955
  Shelley v. Kraemer (1948), 897
  in suburban housing, 897
Selective Service Act (1917), 703
Selective Service System, phasing out of student deferments, 964
selectmen, 91
Sellars, John, 295
Sellars, Samuel, Jr., 295
Selma, Ala., march on, 954
Seminole Indians, 327
Senate. *See* U.S. Senate
Seneca Falls women's rights convention, 360–61, 714
Seneca Indians, 7, 223
sensitivity training, 996
sentimentalism, 270
Seoul, South Korea, Communist reoccupation of, 863
separate spheres, doctrine of, 588
Separatists, 31
  Pilgrims as, 50, 54
Sequoia National park, 535
Sequoyah, 251*i*
Serbia, 697
  Austria-Hungary declaration of war on (1914), 698
serfs, 10
Sgt. Pepper's Lonely Hearts Club Band, 965*i*, 966
Serra, Junipero (1713–1784), 36
Serrano people, 36
Servicemen's Readjustment Act of 1944 (GI Bill), 828, 865
Sevareid, Eric, 908
Seven Days' battle (1862), 459
Seven Years' War (1756–63), 124, 169
severalty, 527
Sewall, Samuel (1652–1730), 57
Seward, William H. (1801–1872), 433, 467, 670
  foreign policy, 504–5
  purchase of Alaska, 505
sex discrimination, occupational (1877–1900), 564–65
sex education, of army during World War I, 708
sexism, 971
sexuality
  changing views of (1870s–1890s), 632–33
  flapper, 736, 739, 740–41
  hippies, 966
  reproduction and, 971
  homosexuality. *See* homosexuals
  Oneida Community and, 357
  1750s–1800s, 276
  1980s, 1024
Seymour, Horatio (1810–1886), 491
Shah of Iran. *See* Pahlevi, Mohammad Reza
Shahn, Ben, 812, 828*i*
Shaker Heights, Ohio, 897
Shakers, 273, 276, 348*i*, 355–56
sharecropping, family, 499*i*, 502–3
Share Our Wealth plan, 794
Shattuck, Job, 200*i*
Shaw, Anna Howard (1847–1919), 712
Shaw, Lemuel, *Commonwealth v. Hunt* (1842), 344
Shaw (warship), 822*i*
Shawnee Indians, 224
  Tippecanoe, battle of (1811), 236, 237
Shays, Daniel (1747–1825), 200*i*, 202
Shays's Rebellion, 200, 201
Sheehan, Neil, 936, 937
Sheeler, Charles (1883–1965), 731*i*
sheep raising, 521, 530
Sheik, The, 739
Sheldon, Charles Monroe (1857–1946), 624
Shelley v. Kraemer (1948), 869, 897
shelters, 772
Shenandoah campaign, 471–73
Shenandoah Valley, 474
Sheppard-Towner Federal Maternity and Infancy Act of 1921, 730
Sheridan, Kansas, 523
Sheridan, Philip Henry (1831–1888), 472, 505, 520
Sherman, William Tecumseh (1820–1891), 469, 485
  capture of Atlanta, 473–74
  march to the sea, 474–75
Sherman Antitrust Act (1914), 652
  principles of, 664
  Theodore Roosevelt and, 658, 661
  Wilson and, 663
Sherman Silver Purchase Act (1890), 592
Shiite Muslims, in Iraq, 1031
Shiloh, battle of (1862), 458
Shinn, Charles Howard, 534
shipbuilding, 88
  industry, 822, 824
  steamboats, 303–4
shipping, shipping industry
  Black Ball Line, 299, 306
  Britain's restrictions on (1805), 234
  Embargo Act of 1807, 235
  impressment and, 234–35
  inland freight rates (1784–1900), 303*f*
  Napoleon's Continental System and, 234
  Rule of 1756, 216
  transatlantic packet service, 299
Shirley, William (1694–1771), 121
shoe and boot industry
  development of, 259–60
  putting-out system, 259

shoemakers
closed shops, 339
Commonwealth v. Pullis (1806), 334
Federated Society of Journeymen Cordwainers, 334
journeymen, 335, 338
Mutual Benefit Society of Journeymen Cordwainers, 338
ten footers, 335
Short Narrative of the Horrid Massacre in Boston, A (Bowdoin), 149
Shriver, Sargent, 920, 928
Shroeder, (Robert) William (1915–), 964
Shultz, George Pratt (1920–), 1011
Shuttlesworth, Fred, 949
Sierra Club, 535, 992
Sierra Nevada mountains, 535
Silent Generation, 962
Silent Majority, 981
Silent Spring, The (Carson), 993
Silliman, Benjamin, 212
silver, 25, 520
Bland-Allison Act (1878) and, 592
political issue of, 596
Sherman Silver Purchase Act (1890) and, 592
unlimited coinage of, Populist party and, 592
Sinai Peninsula, 1001
Sinatra, Frank, 909
Since You Went Away, 830
Sinclair, Upton Beall (1878–1968), 659
Singer Sewing Machine Company, 555
foreign plants, 672, 672*i*
Sino-Japanese War (1894–1895), 673, 688
Sioux nation, 525
battle at Wounded Knee, 527–29
Ghost Dance, 527
horse effigy, 517*i*
movement into Great Plains, 516–17
occupation of Wounded Knee (1973), 960, 961, 961*i*
reservations in South Dakota, 525, 525*m*
Teton people, 517, 525, 529
warfare, 517, 523
women's roles in, 517
Sirhan, Sirhan, 978
Sirica, John, 989
Sister Carrie (Dreiser), 635
Sisterhood is Powerful (Morgan), 969
sit-ins, 948
Sitting Bull (c. 1831–1890), 526, 527
Six Companies, 532
Sketch Book, The (Irving), 269
Sklar, Martin J., 665
skyscrapers, 611, 611*i*, 612
slackers, 703
Slater, Samuel (1768–1835), 289, 290, 291*i*
slaughterhouses, 260
slave(s), 187
African-American society and culture, 245–50
children of, freedom given to, 188
control over work lives, 247
death rate of, 80
emancipation of, 461–64
family, 246–47, 381–82
Gullah dialect, 83
Indian, 69
killing of, 364
kinship networks, 382
lives of, 379–83
northern urban, 89
oppression of, 84–85
as personal property, 379
planters' dependence on, 376
population, 243, 376*i*
punishment of, 247
religion of, 120–21, 250, 383
representation, 204
resistance and rebellion, 84–85, 247, 383–84
prevention of, 86
as soldiers during American Revolution, 176
as soldiers in Civil War, 469, 475
songs of, 383
women, planters' sexual activity with, 379
working conditions of, 380–81
slave catchers, 424
slave owners. *See* planters
"Slave Power" conspiracy, 369, 428, 432
slavery, 76
abolition in north, 187
abolitionism, 349, 359–62. *See also* abolitionism
American Revolution and, 176, 187–88
antislavery forces in California, 422–23
antislavery movements, 244–45
John Brown's raid and, 437–38
California and, 409
chattel, 78
in Chesapeake colonies, 48
common property doctrine and, 421
Compromise of 1850 and, 422–23
contrabands of war, 461–62
cotton industry and, 243–44
creation of an African-American society and, 81, 83–84
defense of, Republican party ideology v., 428–29
Dred Scott v. Sanford (1857) and, 432–33
economics of, 80–81, 375–78
election of 1852 and, 425–26
election of 1856 and, 431–32
election of 1860 and, 437–39
Enlightenment and, 187
extending Missouri Compromise line and, 421–22
first Confiscation Act (1861), 461
free states, 422
Freeport doctrine and, 437
Fugitive Slave Act
of 1793, 244, 247
of 1850, 423, 424–25
gang-labor system, 376–77
impact on Africa, 77–78
of Indians, 53
Jefferson and, 214
Kansas-Nebraska Act and, 429–30
Lecompton constitution and, 433
Lincoln and, 433–37, 443
"middle passage," 79, 80
Missouri Compromise and, 244–45, 334, 421–22
in Nicaragua, 427
northern defense of, 367–68
Northwest Ordinance and, 199
personal liberty laws, 244, 424
popular sovereignty and, 422
second Confiscation Act (1862), 462
"Slave Power" conspiracy, 369, 428, 432
slave states, 422
South Atlantic system and, 76–77
southern defense of, 367
southern imperialism and, 385
in Old Southwest, 243–50
Stono Rebellion and, 85
Texas rebellion and, 333, 334
underground railroad, 369, 383–84
U.S. Constitution and, 203–4
Virginia's decision for, 78–80
in West, 385
Whigs opposing, 420
slave trade
abolition of, in District of Columbia, 425
Arab, 18
Columbus's involvement in, 19
Dutch, 38
in 1400s, 18
internal, 243–44, 381
Portuguese, 18
transatlantic, 245
Slavic immigrants, American industry, 563
Slidell, John (1793–1871), 416, 417, 467
Sloan, Alfred Pitchard, Jr. (1875–1966), 731
Sloat, John Drake (1781–1867), 416
Sloughter, Henry, 73
Small Is Beautiful (Schumacher), 991
smallpox epidemics
of 1633, 53
of 1720s, 113
Smallwood, William, 171
Smith, Adam (1723–1790), 76, 211
Smith, Alfred Emanuel (1873–1944), 651, 730, 752, 798
Smith, "Cotton Ed," 788
Smith, John (1580–1631), 40
Smith, Jonathan, 206
Smith, Joseph (1805–1844), 404
Smith, Melancton, 204
Smith-Connally Labor Act of 1843, 827
Smith v. Allwright (1944), 833
smoking, bans in public areas, 1024
Snow White and the Seven Dwarfs, 768
social class. *See* class, social and economic
Social Darwinism, 583, 676
Social Destiny of Man, The (Brisbane), 355
Social Gospel, 641
social institutions, reform of, women's movement and, 358–59
social insurance, 928
Social Register, 627
Social Security Act (1935), 793
Social Security system, 796, 807, 928
National Housing Act of 1949 and, 868
payments by middle class (1980s), 1015

(Social Security system con't)
surcharge on payroll taxes, 928
socialism, Shakers and, 355–56
Socialist Labor party, 574
Socialist party, 574, 641, 651, 700, 722, 783
Society for Establishing Useful Manufacturers, 211
Society for the Promotion of Industry, 311
Society for the Relief of Poor Widows with Small Children, 311
Society of Friends. *See* Quakers
Society of Jesus (Jesuits), 36
sociological jurisprudence, 641
Soil Conservation and Domestic Allotment Act of 1936, 804
Soil Conservation Service, 804
Sokoloff, Nicholas, 809
Solemn League and Covenant (1638), 159
Solomon Islands, 841, 843*m*
Somme, battle of (1916), 699
Somoza Debayle, Anastasio (1925–), 1011
Sonoma, Ca., American capture of, 417
Sonora, Walker's attempt at annexation, 427
Sonoratown, 778
Sons of Liberty, 140, 141, 147, 157
Sorenson, Theodore, 917
Sorosis, 588
Soulé, Pierre (1801–1870), 426
Souls of Black Folks, The (Du Bois), 603
Sound and the Fury, The (Faulkner), 749
soup kitchens, 762, 772
Souter, David, 1026
South, 597. *See also* Confederacy
African colonization and, 363
American Revolution fought in, 176–77
attempts at slavery in Mexican Cession, 421–22
black and white population in (1860), 378*f*
black migration to (1980s), 1017
black population, during Great Depression, 770
blacks rioting in (1877–1900), 597
caste system, 488
commercial centers, 378
conquest of (1861–1865), 477*m*
culture (1800s), 241, 379
demands for independence, 166
economy, tie to Britain, 297
failure of biracial politics in, 597–98
farm labor, 558
hostility to abolitionism, 367
ideology, slavery and, 428
imperialism (1840s), 385
industrial development in (1877–1900), 558
lumber industry, 560
mill villages, 559–60
planter class, 378–79
racism during Progressive Era in, 654
during radical Reconstruction, 493–97
response to Fugitive Slave Act, 425
secession of, 443
segregation in, 945–48. *See also* segregation
1870s–1900s, 599, 597–603
social and religious conflict in, 119, 120–21
social order, 1700s, 85–86
Southern Rights Conventions (1850–1851), 425
States' Rights and Dixiecrat party, 867, 868
support for Whig party, 341
textile industry, 294
tobacco industry, 560
westward expansion (1820s–1840s), 299
South Africa, 596
South Atlantic system, 76–77
impact on northern economy, 88
South Boston High School, 997, 998
South Carolina (colony), 69*t*, 75
Regulator rule, 129
settlement of, 68–69
slavery in, 81, 82, 84, 85
South Carolina (state)
censorship of U.S. mails, 368
constitution of 1778, 194–95
"just rights of creditors," 200
land commission, 499
Nullification crisis, 330–32
secession, 425, 443, 445
Sherman's attack on, 474
textile industry, 558
South Carolina Exposition and Protest, The (Calhoun), 331, 332
South Dakota, 515
emigration from (1800s), 538
Sioux reservation in, 525, 525*m*
South Korea, mutual defense treaty with U.S., 864
South Vietnam, 984
bombing of, 934
National Liberation Front, 932
support of, 931–32
Vietcong invasion of, 986
Southeast Asia Collective Defense and Treaty Organization (SEATO), 876
Southern Christian Leadership Conference (SCLC), 948
FBI surveillance of, 949
Southern Farmers' Alliance, 590
Southern Pacific Railroad, 518, 534
Southern Tenant Farmers Union (STFU), 770
Southgate, Eliza, 270, 271
Southwest Railroad, 553
Soyer, Isaac, 756*i*
space exploration
Kennedy administration and, 924
NASA, 924, 928
Soviet Union launching of *Sputnik,* 874, 875*i*
Spain, 3
American Revolution and, 176
ceding of Philippines to U.S., 681
Civil War, 812*i*, 812–13
Columbus's discovery of America and, 19–20
conquests, sixteenth century, 20
Cuba's movement for independence from (1868–1875), 676–78, 680
Loyalists, 812, 818
monarchy, 17–19
rise and decline of, sixteenth century, 25–26
territory and missions, 35–36
Treaty of Paris and, 124
War of Jenkins' Ear (1739), 94
War of the Spanish Succession (1702–1714), 74
Spanish-American War (1898), 656, 678–80, 679*m,* 818
battle of San Juan Hill, 680, 681*i*
events leading to, 677–78
Spanish Armada, 25
Spanish-Indians, 406
Spanish Netherlands, 25
Spanish rule, revolt against, 253
Sparkman, John A., 873
SPARs, 825
speakeasies, 750, 751*i*
Specie Resumption Act (1875), 507
speculators, purchase of land in Northwest Territory, 229–30
Spencer, Herbert (1820–1903), 583, 640
spinning frame, 290, 290*i*
spinning jenny, 289
Spirit of the Laws, The (Montesquieu), 205
Spirit of St. Louis, The, 744
Spock, Benjamin, 907
spoils system, 325
sports. *See also* specific sport
beer advertising at events, 890–91
interest in (1920s), 743
urban involvement in, late nineteenth century, 625
Spotswood, Alexander, 86
Sprague, Frank Julian (1857–1934), 610
Sputnik, 874, 875*i*
Spy, The (Cooper), 269
Square Deal, 660
stagecoaches, 518
Stalin, Joseph Vissarionovich (1879–1953), 836, 837*i*, 847
death of, 876
meeting with Roosevelt in Teheran, 845
at Yalta Conference, 845*i*, 845–46
Stalingrad, battle of (1942–1943), 838
Stalwarts, 586
Stamford, Conn., 896
Stamp Act of 1765, 133, 138–39, 142, 143
Congress of, 144
crisis of, 142, 145
Patriot response to, 157*t*
protests against, 139–42, 143–45, 146
repeal of, 141, 144, 145
Resolves, 144, 150
standard of living
of business class (1820s–1830s), 309
1840s–1860s, 392–93
of farm families (1800s), 242–43
Great Depression's effects on, 764
Industrial Revolution and, 305
among Irish immigrants (1840s), 389
1920s, 727
1973–1979, 995
after World War II, 885

Standard Oil Company, 555, 661, 733
  foreign interests, 672
Stanford-Binet intelligence test, 708
Stanton, Edwin McMasters (1814–1869), 450, 490
  Johnson's dismissal of, 491
Stanton, Elizabeth Cady (1815–1902), 360 361*i*, 491, 492
Stanwix, John, 124
Staple Act of 1663, 70, 70*t*
Star Wars, 1010
Starr, Ellen Gates, 648
Stars and Stripes (newspaper), 844
state(s)
  European and American conceptions of, 17
  interference, protection against, 264
  mercantilism
    common law, 262
    1790s–1800s, 261
  power, division of, Adams's view, 194
  regulation of economy, 583
  regulatory powers, 542
state(s), U.S. *See also* specific states
  abortion laws, 971
  constitutions, 193–96
  debts
    following American Revolution, 199
    Hamiltonian program and, 210
  economies after American Revolution, 201
  funding of education, 268
  funding of programs, 1025
  governments
    charters to transportation corporations, 305
    growth of (1946–1970), 898–99
  mercantilism
    common law and, 262
    1790s–1800s, 261
  party bosses 586
  progressive reform in politics, 644–45
  revenue sharing, 983
  rights, Calhoun's view, 331–32
  superintendents of education, 267
state banks, notes issued by (1830s), 328
state courts, 208
State, Department of, 208
States' Rights party, 867
statute law, 262
steamboats, 303–4
steam engines, coal-burning, 549
steam engines, stationary, 385–86
steam power, 549
steel industry, 515, 550, 608
  Bessemer converters, 548
  Andrew Carnegie and, 548
  common laborers in, 561
  labor strikes against (1719), 721
  growth of, 548
  organized labor in, 802, 802*i*, 803
  revolution in, 551
steel rails, 552
steel workers, Homestead, Penn., strike, 572–73
Steel Workers Organizing Committee (SWOG), 803
Steffens, (Joseph) Lincoln (1866–1936), 642, 643
Stein, Gertrude (1874–1946), 748
Steinbeck, John (1902–1968), 768, 768*i*, 774, 775, 811
Steinem, Gloria (1936–), 971
stem family system, 100–101, 102*i*
Stephens, Alexander Hamilton (1812–1883), 447
Stephenson, David, 746
Steuben, Frederick William, Baron von (1730–1794), 175, 179
Stevens, Thaddeus (1792–1868), 462, 482, 482*i*, 483
Stevens, Wallace (1879–1955), 748, 749
Stevenson, Adlai Ewing (1900–1965), 872, 873, 918
stewardship, 583
Stewart, Maria W., 366
Stiles, Ezra, 129
Stimson, Henry Lewis (1867–1950), 821, 847
Stinkards, 9
stock market, 757
  collapse of 1893, 590
  crash of 1929, 758*i*, 758, 761
  crash of 1937, 796
  crash of 1987, 1022
  Great Depression and, 757–59
  insider trading, 1015
  margin buying, 758
  during 1980s, 1014–15
  reforms, New Deal and, 791–92
  Securities and Exchange Commission, 791
  speculation in, 757
Stockton, Robert Field (1795–1866), 417
Stone, Lucy (1818–1893), 360, 362, 492
Stone Mountain, Ga., 746
Stono Rebellion, 85
Stonewall Riot, 961
storekeeper-manufacturers, 294
Story, Joseph (1779–1845), 264
Story (magazine), 810
Stowe, Calvin E., 397
Stowe, Harriet Beecher (1811–1896), 363, 394, 395, 397, 397*i*
  reaction to Fugitive Slave Act, 424–25
Strategic Arms Limitation Talks (SALT)
  SALT I, 984, 1012
  SALT II, 1000, 1001–2
Strategic Defense Initiative (SDI), 1010
strikes, 571
  construction workers (1825), 335
  factory workers (1830s), 338–39
  during Great Depression, 781
  Homestead, Penn., strike, 572
  Knights of Labor and, 570
  mechanics and, 335–38
  Pullman, 573–74, 652
  railroad workers (1877), 547
  sit-down, 802*i*, 803
  for wages (1836–1837), 338
  after World War I, 721
  during World War II, 827
  following World War II, 866
Stringfellow, Thornton, 367
Strong, Josiah, 607
Strout, Richard L., 874
Strutt, Jedediah, 289
Stryker, Roy, 812
Student Non-Violent Coordinating Committee (SNCC), 948, 950, 951, 956, 962, 969
  voter registation drives, 953
student strike against war, 766
Students for a Democratic Society (SDS), 962
Studer, Helen, 827
Stuyvesant, Peter (c. 1610–1672), 38
substitute law, 450
subtreasury system, 590, 591
suburbs, 630*i*
  growth of, 630–31, 885, 896–98
  highway construction and, 898
  social divisions within, 630
Suez Canal, nationalization of, 880
suffrage
  black male, 491
  white male, 265, 320, 338
  woman, 196, 361, 491, 649–50, 649*m*, 713–14
Sugar Act of 1764, 137, 142, 143
  compromises on, 145
  Patriot response to, 157*t*
  protests against, 144
  vice-admiralty courts and, 137–38
Sugar Act of 1766, 149
sugar industry, 76. *See also* Sugar Act of 1764; Sugar Act of 1766
  harvesting of sugar, 377*i*
  Molasses Act of 1733 and, 95
  in New England (1700s), 87
  slavery and, 77–78, 80–81
  South Atlantic system, 76–77
sugar plantations, in Old Southwest, 243
sugar, rationing during World War II, 831
Sukarno (1901–1970), 876
Sullivan, Timothy D., 620–21, 621*i*
Summary View of the Rights of British America, A (Jefferson), 168
Summit Springs, battle of (1863), 523
Sumner, Charles (1811–1874), 380, 431, 462, 482, 505
Sumner, William Graham (1840–1910), 583
Sun Also Rises, The (Hemingway), 748
Sun Belt, 896
Sunday mail law, 311
Supreme Court. *See* U.S. Supreme Court
Surveyors of the Woods, 92
Susquehannock tribe, 47
Swaggart, Jimmy, 1024
Swann v. Charlotte Mecklenburg Board of Education (1971), 983
Swift, Gustavus, 554–55, 556, 558
Swing Mikado, 810
Swiss, in Pennsylvania colony, 107
Swisshelm, Jane, 369
syndicalism, 575
Syria, invasion of Israel (1973), 991

Taft, Robert Alphons (1889–1953), 872
Taft, William Howard (1857–1930), 654, 691, 711, 732
 Caribbean and, 687
 Colorado Coal Company v. United Mine Workers, 732
 dollar diplomacy, 687, 688
 presidency of, 660
Taft-Hartley Act (1947), 866, 867, 867*i*, 868, 869, 893
Taiwan, 983
Tall Bull, 523
Talleyrand-Périgord, Charles Maurice de (1754–1838), 217
Tallmadge, James, 244
Tammany Hall, 618, 619, 620–621, 651, 730, 752
 reform role, 651
Tampico, Mexico, 418
Taney, Roger Brooke (1777–1864), 325
 Charles River Bridge v. Warren Bridge (1837), 305
 Dred Scott v. Sanford (1857), 432–33
 Jackson's policies and, 330
Tappan, Arthur (1786–1865), 314, 365, 367
Tappan, Lewis (1788–1873), 314, 365
Tarbell, Ida Minerva (1857–1944), 642, 642*i*, 714
Tardieu, André (1876–1945), 691
tariff(s), 581
 after American Revolution, 201
 Compromise (1833), 332
 Corn Laws, 415
 of 1824, 291, 323
 of 1828 (Abominations), 331
 of 1846 (Walker), 415
 Fordney-McCumber Tariff of 1922, 733
 General Agreement on Tariffs and Trade, 886
 Harrison's view on, 580
 Hawley-Smoot Tariff of 1930, 733, 759
 McKinley Tariff of 1890, 590, 593, 671
 during Reconstruction Era, 504
 South Carolina Ordinance of Nullification and, 330–31
 Wilson and, 664
 Wilson-Gorman Tariff of 1894, 593
Tatch, Kitty, 535*i*
Tavenner, Frank S., Jr., 870
taxation, taxes. *See also* income taxes specific taxation acts
 American Revolution and, 174, 185, 199, 200, 201
 Articles of Confederation and, 198
 on banks in the Civil War, 452, 453, 504
 under Bush administration, 1025
 in Chesapeake colonies, 85–86
 Civil War system, revenues raised from, 504
 control of (1700s), 91
 currency, 185
 corporate excess profit tax, 710
 federal poll tax, 954
 Hamilton's program on, 212, 216
 on imports, 156–58, 291. *See also* tariff
 inheritance, 306
 on intangible property, 306
 internal and external, 146
 Jefferson and, 231
 Kennedy-Johnson tax cut of 1964, 924
 labor unions and, 338
 John Marshall's view, 263–64
 property, 338
 protests against, 1768, 146, 148–50
 Reagan's lowering of, 1009–10, 1011, 1015
 during Reconstruction Era, 495, 504
 reforms during World War II, 828
 Regulator rule and, 129
 religious, 188
 Revenue Act of 1767, 146
 Shays's Rebellion and, 200
 slavery-related issues of, 203
 Stamp Act, 138–39
 Tea Act of 1773, 150–53
 Townshend Act of 1767, 145–48
 unequal distribution of wealth and, 759
 Washington and, 198
Tax Reform Act of 1986, 1011
Taylor, Frederick Winslow (1856–1915), 568
Taylor, Zachary (1784–1850), 414*t*
 California statehood and, 422–23
 death of, 423
 in Mexican War, 416–18, 420
 presidential election of 1848, 421, 434
Tchikilli, Chief, 9
Tea Act of 1773, 150–53, 176
 Patriot response to, 157*t*
 resistance to, 151–53
teachers, 891. *See also* education
 certification of, 267
 women, early nineteenth century, 276
teach-ins, 964
Teapot Dome Scandal, 729
technology. *See also* manufacturing; industry
 agricultural, 894
  1850s, 398, 400
  1790s, 227
 computer revolution, 889, 1022, 1023
 effect on family life (1920s), 735
 effect on rural life (1920s), 744
 European, sixteenth century, 21
 innovations, 886
  (1820s–1840s), 294–96
 Jefferson and, 212–13, 213–14
 1980s, 1022
 republicanism and, 212
 rise in manufacturing and, 287–89
 stationary steam engines, 385–86
Technology Highway, 896
Tecumseh (1768?–1813), 236, 238
Teedyuscung, 74
Teheran, U.S. embassy in, seizure of, 1002
Teheran Conference of 1943, 837, 845
telegraph, 389, 518, 554
telephone, 596, 612
 cellular, 1022
 cooperatives, 596
television, 904–6
 American attitude toward Vietnam War and, 940, 940*i*, 941
 beer advertisements on, 891
 color, 906
 1980s–1990s, 1022, 1024
 presidential debates, 919
Teller, Henry Moore (1830–1914), 678
 Teller Ammendment, 678
temperance movement, 314
Temple, Shirley, 768
Temporary Emergency Relief Administration, 836
tenancy leaseholds, 127
tenant farmers, 109–11, 543, 597
 of Chesapeake colonies, 46
tenants rights goups, 929
tenement(s), 309
 dumbbell, 613*f*, 614
 workshops in, 616*i*
Tenement House Law (1901), 614
ten footers, 335
Tennent, Gilbert (1703–1764), 115, 119, 167
Tennent, William (1673–1746), 115
Tennessee
 Democrats recover power in, 497
 entry into union, 225
 freedom of slaves, 464
 political campaigning in, 321
 Union control of, 464
Tennessee Coal and Iron Company, 661
Tennessee Supreme Court, Scopes trial and, 748
Tennessee Valley Authority (TVA), 789, 804, 805*m*, 806
Tenochtitlán. *See* Mexico City
Tenskwatawa, 236
Tenure of Office Act (1867), 490–91
Teotihuacán civilization, 4, 5
terrorist actions, during Civil War, 472
Terry, Alfred Howe (1827–1890), 526
Test Act of 1704, 108
Tet offensive, 941, 977
Teton people. *See* Sioux nation
Texas, 423
 American settlement of, 333, 333*m*
 annexation of, 413, 414, 415, 416, 420
 black voting rights during World War II, 833
 cattle industry, 520–21
 growth of cities, 896
 rebellion against Mexico (1836), 333–34
 secession of, 444
 Spanish, 253
Texas Exchange, 591
Texas v. White (1869), 482
textile industry
 Boston Manufacturing Company, 291–94
 cotton-spinning machines, 290
 entrepreneurs in (1820s–1840s), 295
 failures in, 291
 Great Depression and, 759
 Industrial Revolution and, 289–91
 machine tools for, 295
 mill villages, 559–60
 1920s, 729

(textile industry con't)
ready-made clothing, 556
southern, 294, 558
unionization of, 649
Waltham and Fall River plans, 294
T-groups, 996
Thailand, 986
Thames, Battle of the (1813), 238, 344
Thanksgiving Day, 240
theater
Federal Theater Project, 810, 810*i*
1890s–1910, 624–25
Their Eyes Were Watching God (Hurston), 810
theological seminaries, 277–78
Theory of the Leisure Class, The (Veblen), 640
Thieu, Nguyen Van (1923–), 941, 984, 986
Third Party System, 432
Third World, development of, 879–80
Thirty-nine Articles (1563), 30
Thirty Seconds Over Tokyo, 830
Thomas, Clarence, 1026
Thomas, Evan, 856
Thomas, H. J., 571
Thomas, Norman Mattoon (1884–1968), 783
Thomas, Theodore, 633
Thomas Aquinas, Saint (1225–1274), 23
Thompson, Dorothy, 795
Thompson, J. Walter, advertising agency, 736
Thompson, Jeremiah, 306
Thomson, Charles, 167
Thoreau, Henry David (1817–1862), 409
abolitionism and, 366
John Brown and, 437
transcendentalism and, 351, 353
Thoughts for the Young Men of America (Alger), 582
Thoughts on Female Education (Rush), 273
Thoughts on Government (Adams), 194, 205
Three Little Pigs, 791
Three Mile Island, 994, 994*i*
Three Soldiers, The (Dos Passos), 748
Thurmond, Strom (James, 1902–), 868
Tiananmen Square, 1028
Tikal, 4
Tilden, Samuel Jones (1814–1886)
compromise of 1877 and, 508–9
presidential election of 1876, 507–8
Timber Culture Act (1873), 536
Time (magazine), 742, 744, 820, 861, 843
Times (London), 684
Tin Lizzies, 738
Tippecanoe, battle of (1811), 236, 237
tippling houses, 309
Titan, The (Dreiser), 627, 635
Tito, Josip Broz (1892–1980), 876
tobacco
duties on, 1600s, 46
excise tax on, 580
export of, 1700s, 126
native American planting of, 7
use and growth of, in Chesapeake colonies, 41, 42–43, 46
tobacco industry
crash of 1660 and, 46
decline, after American Revolution, 199
growth of, 560
in Maryland colony, 72
in Old Southwest, 243
use of slaves in, 81
Tobago, French control of, 183
Tocqueville, Alexis de (1805–1859), 279–81, 287
individualism and, 279
observations of Americans, 349
republicanism and, 279, 280–81
Tojo, Hideki (1885–1948), 822
Toledo, Ohio, 224, 644
Toleration Act of 1647, 42
Toltec Indians, 5
Toomer, Jean (1894–1957), 750
Topeka, Kans., free-soil settlers in, 429*i*
Tory party, Tories, 93, 179, 183, 185. *See also* Loyalists
exodus from America, 186
southern, 177
Toscanini, Arturo (1867–1957), 769
Toussaint L'Ouverture, François Dominique (1743–1803), 231
Towle, George M., 584
town(s)
fall-line, 297
growth of (1820s–1840s), 297–99
northern (1700s), 88
selectmen, 91
town councils, 13
town meetings, 59, 92
Townsend, Francis Everett (1867–1960), 792, 793
Townshend, Charles, viscount (1674–1738), 95, 144*t*, 145–46
Townshend Act of 1767, 146
Patriot response to, 157*t*
protests against, 146
repeal of, 149, 150
townships, 228
New England colonies, 59
Tracy, Benjamin Franklin (1830–1915), 674
trade. *See also* arms trade; commerce; exports; imports; world trade
after American Revolution, 199
Arab, 3, 16–17
Aztec, 5
Board of Trade, 75, 95, 142
deficit, American (1700s), 126*f*
deficit, American (1939–1992), 995, 1013*f*
disruption of, during World War I, 710
Dutch, sixteenth century, 25–26
1880s, 672
English, mercantilism, 28–29
European control of (1400s), 15, 16*m*
Europeans as leaders in, 3
exchange rates, 886
expansion into California, 406–7
foreign policy and (1880s–1890s), 673–74
fur. *See* fur trade
General Agreement on Tariffs and Trade, 886
International Monetary Fund and, 886
Macon's Bill No. 2 and, 236
naval blockade on (1775), 156
neutral, British restriction of (1805), 234
1920–1921, 728
Non-intercourse Act and, 235
northern seaboard cities and (1700s), 88
politics and (1763–76), 148*f*
Portuguese (fifteenth century), 18, 19
Proclamation of Neutrality and, 214
Prohibitory Act of 1775 and, 166
regional patterns (1820s–30s), 296–97
Sioux nation, 517
slave. *See* slave trade
surplus, 672, 672*f*
transportation revolution and, 303*i*
unfair, Federal Trade Commission and, 664
West Indian (1700s), 87
trade associations, 729
trade unions. *See* labor unions
Trafalgar, battle of (1805), 234
Tramp, The, 739*i*
trans-Appalachian West, 198–99, 223, 225–27
transatlantic packet service, 299
Transcendental Meditation, 996
transcendentalists and utopians, 350, 354*m*. *See also* Mormons, specific communities
Brook Farm and, 353–54
decline of, 354
Ralph Waldo Emerson and, 350–52
free-soil movement and, 369
Nathaniel Hawthorne and, 352–53
ideal reality, 350
Herman Melville and, 352–53
Walt Whitman and, 351–52
transcontinental railroad, 532
transistor, invention of, 880
Trans-Missouri case (1897), 658
transportation. *See also* railroad industry
Bonus Bill, 261
canals, 227, 228, 301–3
charters, power of eminent domain, 261
development of (1790s–1800s), 261
elevated trains, 612
government and business corporations and, 305
mass transit, 609–11, 612
protests against segregation of public transportation, 947–48, 949*i*
railroads (1850s), 400–2
revolution in (1820s–1840s), 300–5
roads, 301, 301*i*
state government charters to corporations, 305
steamboats, 303–4
steel and, 551
streetcar system, 612
turnpike companies, 227
westward expansion and, 227–28, 518, 519*m*
transsubstantiation, 14
travel industry, growth (1950s), 904

treason, 332
Burr's trial for, 234
Treasury department. *See* U.S. Treasury
Treasury notes, greenbacks, 452
treaties. *See* specific treaties
Treatise on Domestic Economy (Beecher), 396
Treaty of 1795, 225
Tree Army, 806
Treitschke, Heinrich von (1834–1896), 614
Trelawney, Edward, 51
Trelawney, Robert, 51
Trenchard, John, 143
trenchers, 109
trench warfare
during Civil War, 471
during World War I, 703
Trent (ship), 467
Trenton, N. J.
American victories at, 171
battle of, 169*i*
Washington's attack on, 170
Triangle Shirtwaist Company fire, 651, 651*i*, 653
Tribune (New York), 360
Triple A Plowed Under, 810
Triple Alliance, 691, 697
Triple Entente, 697
Tripoli, 231
Triumphant Democracy (Carnegie), 582
trolley car, 612
Trotter, William Monroe, 654–55
Troup, George M., 323
Trudeau, Garry, 968*i*
True Laws of Free Monarchy, The (James I), 31
Truman, Harry S. (1884–1972), 837, 847, 853, 876, 879, 930
atomic bombing of Japan and, 846
civil rights efforts, 869
Cold War and, 854
desegregation of armed forces by, 864
Fair Deal and, 865–66, 868–69
firing of MacArthur, 864, 864*i*
investigation of federal employees' loyalty and, 869
Korean War and, 862, 863
labor strikes and, 866
policymaking process, 857
presidency after Roosevelt's death, 853, 854
presidential election of 1948, 866–68
presidential election of 1952, 872
recognition of Israel, 879
support of France in war with Indochina, 930
Truman Doctrine, 858, 859
as U.S. senator, 829
Trump, Donald John (1946–), 1014, 1022
trusts
Brandeis and, 663
Clayton Antitrust Act (1914), 664
Theodore Roosevelt and, 657–59
Sherman Antitrust Act. *See* Sherman Antitrust Act (1914)
Truth, Sojourner (1797–1883), 363
Tryon, William, 129
Tubman, Harriet (c. 1820–1913), 384, 384*i*
Tucker, Nathaniel Beverley, 379
Tucker, St. George, 247
Tugwell, Rexford Guy (1891–1979), 788, 790, 804, 812
Tula civilization, 5
Tulagi, 841
Tunis, 231
turbine, steam-powered, 549
Turkey, 698
Turnbow, Hartman, 955
Turner, Frederick Jackson (1861–1932), 241–42, 676
Turner, Nat (1800–1831), 364, 384
Turner, Ted, 1022
turnpike companies, 227
Tuscarora Indians, 6
Tuskegee Institute, 602
TV Guide, 905
Twain, Mark (Samuel Clemens, 1835–1910), 534, 609, 612, 634, 635
Two Kettle tribe, 517
Two Treatises on Government (Locke), 72, 113
Tyler, John (1790–1862), 345, 414*t*, 415
joins Democratic party, 413
presidency of, 345, 413–14
Whig party and, 345

U-2 reconnaissance aircraft, 877
"Uncle Sam," 241
Uncle Tom's Cabin (Stowe), 363, 395, 397, 424–25, 428
underclass, 1017
underground railroad, 369, 383–84
Underwood Tariff Act of 1913, 664
unemployment
following American Revolution, 184
among blacks
during Great Depression, 772
1980s, 1017
in South (1886), 597
depression of 1837–1843 and, 343
1850s, 386
during Great Depression, 761–62, 781
New Deal and, 790–91
1915–1945, 728, 761*f*, 796
1970s, 995, 1001
1981–1982, 1010
1989–1990, 1025
panic of 1893, 593
during Roosevelt recession of 1937–1938, 796
welfare capitalism and, 732
during World War II, 830
unicameral assembly, 194
Unification Church of the Reverend Sun Myung Moon, 996
Union
home front, 456
resources, 447, 447*f*, 448
secret societies, 475
southern states loyal to, 446
war costs, 452–53
Union Army
African-American soldiers, 468–69
casualties, 460
gains in 1863, 464–66
health care for troops, 455
mobilization of, 450–52
new military strategy, 469–73
victory, 467–77
Union Army Medical Bureau, 455
Union Baptist Church, 617
Union Pacific Railroad, 454, 518, 553
Union of Soviet Socialist Republics (U.S.S.R.), 698, 1034
ally to U.S. during World War II, 833
arms race during Eisenhower administration, 877
battle of Stalingrad, 838
Berlin blockade, 859
Berlin Wall and, 923, 923*i*
Bolshevism, 722, 764, 855
Carter administration and, 1001, 1002
Churchill's view on, 855
collapse of Communism in, 1026, 1029–30
containment policy and, 855–58
coup of August 1991, 1028–29
Cuban missile crisis and, 923
détente and, 924
domination over Eastern Europe, 855
German invasion of (1942–1943), 838, 839*m*
Germany's nonaggression pact with, 820
invasion of Afghanistan, 1002
Jews emigrating from, 1020
launching of *Sputnik,* 874, 875*i*
Nixon's policy toward, 983
nuclear capacities, Kennedy's policy related to, 920
Reagan's relationship with, 1010, 1012
relations with Cuba (1960s), 922
repression of Hungarian revolt, 876
sphere of influence, 854, 855
Third International, 722
Treaty of Brest-Litovsk (1918), 704
Treaty of Versailles and, 718
Union Treaty, 1028
U.S. intervention in, following World War I, 718
withdrawal from Afghanistan, 1012
unions. *See* labor unions
Unitarianism, Unitarians, 278, 353
abolitionism and, 369
United Artists, 739
United Automobile Workers (UAW), 803, 892, 893
United Cannery, Agricultural, Packing, and Allied Workers of America (UCAPAWA), 778
United Farm Workers' Union, 959
grape pickers joining of, 959–60
United Fruit Company, 733, 876
United Mine Workers Union, 827, 866
anthracite coal strike of 1902, 657
United Nations, 845
American support for, 853–54

(United Nations con't)
Bretton Woods conference, 886
International Women's Year, 971, 971*i*
monetary conference, 995
partition of Palestine, 879
peacekeeping force in Korea, 862
vote to use force against Iraq (1991), 1030
U.S. Army Corps of Engineers, 686
U.S. bonds, purchase of, during Civil War, 452
U.S. Census. *See* Census
U.S. citizenship
Native-American clubs, 390–91
naturalization, 390
Naturalization Act of 1798 and, 218
right of naturalization to Chinese, 900
U.S. Congress. *See also* U.S. House of Representatives; U.S. Senate
American Anti-Slavery Society and, 366
approval of Marshall Plan, 859
caucus of 1824, 322
charter of Bank of the United States, 258
charter of national banks and, 263
charter of Second Bank of United States, 263, 328
Compromise Tariff (1833), 332
election of 1860 and, 437
election of 1866 and, 489–90
election of 1876 and, 508
establishment of executive departments, 208
extension of Voting Rights Act, 954
Force Acts of 1870 and 1871, 498
force bill (1833), 332
Homestead Act (1862), 453–54
immigration quotas and (1920s), 745
impeachment of Andrew Johnson, 491
implementation of Constitution, 208
Andrew Jackson and, 332
Andrew Johnson's restoration plans and, 484
Joint Committee on Reconstruction, 485
Ku Klux Klan Act (1871), 498
laws passed by, states' refusal to enforce, 218
Legal Tender Act of 1862, 452
Neutrality Act of 1794, 215, 216
opposition to Treaty of Versailles, 719
passage of social reform under Lyndon Johnson, 927–28
political parties controlling (1877–1893), 580
Reconstruction Act (1867) and, 490
reforms related to presidential powers, 990
reparation to Japanese-Americans, 834
savings and loan crisis and, 1025
Specie Resumption Act (1875), 507
Tenure of Office Act and, 490–91
Wade-Davis bill, 483, 484
women in, 971, 1034
U.S. Constitution, 201
Antifederalists and, 204–5
Article I, section 5, 484
Bill of Rights, 208
Calhoun's view, 331
compromise over slavery, 203, 243
contract clause, 264
Eighteenth Amendment, 721–22, 750–52
Equal Rights Amendment, 972–73. *See also* Equal Rights Amendment
The Federalist and, 205, 206–7
Fifteenth Amendment, 491, 492
Fourteenth Amendment, 208, 489, 491, 492, 583, 946
Hamilton's view, 211
implementation of, 207–8
interstate commerce clause, 542
Louisiana Purchase and, 232
Madison and, 218
Nationalist faction and, 201
national power and, 204
New Jersey Plan, 203
Nineteenth Amendment, 714, 969
Ordinance of Nullification and, 332
Philadelphia Convention and, 201–4
procedures for ratification, 204–6
Sedition Act of 1798 and, 218
Sixteenth Amendment, 710
slavery and, 432
Supreme Court interpretation of, 583
Thirteenth Amendment, 464, 491
Twelfth Amendment, 219
Twentieth Amendment, 783
Twenty-fourth Amendment, 954
Twenty-sixth Amendment, 985
Virginia Plan, 202–3
U.S. Employment Service, 711
U.S. government, division of power, 205
U.S. House of Representatives. *See also* U.S. Congress
African-Americans serving in, during Reconstruction Era, 495
antislavery sentiment in, 245
election of John Quincy Adams and, 322
Victor Berger and, 716
"gag rule," 368, 369
impeachment of judges, 231
selection of president
election of 1800 and, 218–19
election of 1824, 322
Virginia Plan and, 203
Whig coalition in, 341, 342
U.S. Postal Service
restriction of abolitionists' use of U.S. mails, 368, 369
Sunday mail law, 311
U.S. Public Health Service, 541, 779
U.S. Sanitary Commission, 454–55, 504
U.S. Senate. *See also* U.S. Congress
Foreign Relations Committee, 859
Gulf of Tonkin resolution, 932–33
Republican party control of (1970s–1980s), 1008
Virginia Plan and, 203
Watergate Committee, 990
U.S. Steel Corporation, 658, 721, 732
Gary, Ind., plant, 995
Sherman Antitrust Act and, 661
U.S. Supreme Court, 729. *See also* specific cases
conservatism during Bush administration, 1025–26
corporate charters and, 305
defeat of Civil Rights Act of 1875, 597
establishment of, 208
Fourteenth Amendment and, 583
NRA and, 793
power of judicial review, 263
Franklin Roosevelt's attempt to reorganize, 795
ruling on segregation, 599, 946, 947, 948
Scottsboro case and, 770
Standard Oil decision, 661
supremacy of, 583
women's rights and, 971–72
U.S. Supreme Court justices. *See also* specific justices
appointment by Republican party, 264
impeachment of, 231
Nixon's appointment of, 983
U.S. Treasury department, 208, 729
Bland-Allison Act of 1878 and, 592
Treasury bonds, 823
Treasury notes, 592, 593
United States v. E. C. Knight (1895), 658
United States v. One Package of Japanese Pessaries (1936), 765
Universal Automatic Computer (UNIVAC), 889
Universal Negro Improvement Association (UNIA), 750
Universalists, 276
universities. *See* colleges and universities
University of California, loyalty oath, 870
University of California at Berkeley, student protests, 962–63, 965
University of Chicago, 633, 646
University of Michigan, teach-in against Vietnam War, 964
University of Pennsylvania, 889
unskilled laborers. *See* common laborers
Unterseeboot (U-boat), 700
Upward Bound, 929
urban renewal projects, 901–2, 903*i*
federal, 928
urbanization, during World War II, 831
U'Ren, Harold, 645
USA Today, 1022
U.S.A. (Dos Passos), 811
USO, 939
Utah, 423
Mormon settlement in, 405–6
utopians. *See* transcendentalists and utopians; specific communities
Utrecht, Treaty of (1713), 94, 174

V-E (Victory in Europe) Day, 840, 846
Valentino, Rudolph (1895–1926), 739
Vallandigham, Clement Laird (1820–1871), 465
Valley Forge, 169
Continental Army at, 174, 175
Valley of the Shenandoah, The (Tucker), 247

values
business-class, 310
Great Depression's effects on, 769
1920s, 744–50
1980s, 1022
Van Buren, Martin (1782–1862), 327, 329, 413, 425
annexation of Texas and, 414
changes in New York Republican party and, 320
Depression of 1837–1840 and, 344
labor unions and, 344
presidential campaign of 1848, 421
presidential election of 1836, 342
as secretary of state under Jackson, 325
Vance, Cyrus, 1003
Vance, Zebulon Baird (1830–1894), 451, 452
Vandenberg, Arthur Hendrick (1884–1951), 858
Vanderbilt, Cornelius (1794–1877), 553, 582
Vanderbilt, George Washington (1862–1914), 634
Van Devanter, Willis, 795
Van Dusen, Larry, 763
Van Kleeck, Mary, 712
Vann, James, 252
Vann, John Paul (1924–1972), 934, 936*i*, 936–37
Vanzetti, Bartolomeo, 723
vaqueros, 531*i*
Vardaman, James Kimble (1861–1930), 599
Vasa, Gustavus, 79
VCR, 1022
Veblen, Thorstein, 640
venereal disease, army campaign against, during World War I, 708
Venezuela
border dispute with British Guiana, 675–76
British and German blockade of, 686–87
expansionist efforts in, 670
import of oil from, 991
Veracruz, 418
American capture of (1847), 419
American occupation of (1914), 690
Vergennes, Charles Gravier, comte de (1717–1787), 175
Versailles, Treaty of (1783), 183
Versailles, Treaty of (1919), 717–19, 817, 818
vertically integrated firms, 555, 557
Vesey, Denmark (1767?–1822), 247, 384
Vespucci, Amerigo (1451–1512), 19
vestrymen, 120
Veterans' Administration, mortgages and, 897
veto power, Jackson's use of, 332
vice-admiralty courts, 137–38
Vicksburg, Miss., fall to Union forces, 464
Victory gardens, 830
Vietcong, 933, 935
invasion of Saigon, 986
Tet offensive, 941, 977
Vietminh, 930
Vietnam. *See also* North Vietnam; South Vietnam; Vietnam War
immigrants from, 1019
Vietnam Independence League (Vietminh), 930
Vietnam War, 920, 930, 931*m*, 941
American casualty rate in, 935
American doubts related to, 940
American soldiers' perspective on, 935–39
American withdrawal from, 986
antiwar movement, and, 939–40, 963–64, 977–78, 985
Christmas bombings, 986
cost of, 929, 940
escalation of, 932–35, 963–64
Gulf of Tonkin Resolution and, 932–33
hawks and doves, 941
invasion of Saigon, 986
jungle warfare in, 933*i*
My Lai, 985
National Liberation Front, 932
Nixon and, 984–85
Operation Rolling Thunder, 934
Paris Peace Accords, 986
roots of American involvement in, 930–32
supporters of, 981
television coverage of, 940, 940*i*, 941
Tet offensive, 941, 977
U.S. ground troops in, 933–37
U.S. veterans of, 939
Vietcong, 935
"Vietnamization," 984
Villa, Pancho (Doroteo Arango, 1877–1923), 703
Village Voice, The (newspaper), 966
Vindication of the Rights of Woman, A (Wollstonecraft), 197
violence, politics-related, 1700s, 92. *See also* riots
Virginia (colony), 56*t*
Bacon's Rebellion in, 48
British attack on, 178
decision for slavery, 78
Franco-American unity at, 178
House of Burgesses, 148, 150
politics of, 91
religious conflict in, 119, 120–21
river plantations of, 40*m*
as royal colony, 42
Virginia (state), 299
abolitionism and, 367
cavaliers of, 379
Civil War battles in, 469–73
constitution, 193
Democrats recover power in, 497
literacy rate (1800s), 240
secession of, 446
Virginia City, Nev., 520
Virginia Company of London, 29, 39, 40
dissolution of, 42
Virginia Convention, Declaration of Rights, 188
Virginia Dynasty, 238
Virginia Plan, 202–3
Virgin Islands, 505
Visitor (newspaper), 369
Vladivostok, 1000
voluntarism, 652
Volunteers in Service to America (VISTA), 929
voodoo, 250
voting
after American Revolution, 194
apathy in 1924, 730
in Chesapeake colonies, 86
electoral college, 203
electoral votes and election of 1876 and, 507–8
ethnocultural patterns (1870–1892), 585*f*
federal poll tax, 955
lowering of voting age, 985
property-holding requirements for, 265
slaves and, 203–4
U.S. Constitution and, 207
Virginia Plan and, 202
voting rights. *See also* suffrage
blacks achieving in South (1960s), 953, 954, 955*m*
in English colonies, 90–91
Voting Rights Act of 1965, 927, 954–55, 955*m*, 958
extension of (1970–1982), 954

Wabash Railroad, 553
Wabash v. Illinois, 542
Wade-Davis bill, 483, 484
Wadsworth, Benjamin, 100
Wadsworth family, 230
wage(s). *See also* income
agricultural, southern (1800s), 558, 559
laborer's (1820s–1840s), 306–7
minimum, 795
raising of, 868, 874
1940s–1950s, 893
sex differences in (1977–1900), 564, 565
southern (1880s–1890s), 560, 560*t*
strikes for (1836–37), 338
urban (1890s), 626
during World War II, 826, 827
following World War II, 866
wage laborers, 306, 307
diseases among (1830s), 307
living conditions (1830s), 309
separation from employers, 309
Wagner, Robert Ferdinand (1877–1953), 651, 793
Wagner Act. *See* National Labor Relations Act of 1935
wagon freight lines, 518
Wake Island, 830, 841
Wald, Lillian D. (1867–1940), 648
Walden, Or Life in the Woods (Thoreau), 351, 353
Walesa, Lech, 1026
Walker, David, 364
Walker, Francis Amasa (1840–1897), 524, 654
Walker, William (1824–1860), 427
Walker Tariff, 415

Wallace, George Corley (1919–), 927, 954, 982*i*
  Democratic convention of 1968 and, 981
  shooting of, 986
Wallace, Henry Agard (1888–1965), 788, 790, 821, 829, 866, 868
  communism and, 869
Wallace, Henry Cantwell (1866–1924), 729
Wall Street. *See* stock market
Walpole, Robert, earl of Orford (1676–1745), 93, 94, 136
  patronage policies, 93, 94
Walsh, Frank P., 711
Walter, Francis E., 860
Waltham, Mass., Boston Manufacturing Company's textile plant in, 291, 292, 293, 294
Waltham plan, 294
Wampanoag Indians, 60, 60*i*
Wanamaker, John (1838–1922), 555
War Between the States. *See* Civil War
War Brides Act, 900
War department, 208
wards, 618–19
War Finance Corporation of World War I, 779
War Hawks, 236
Warhol, Andy (1928–1987), 954*i*
War Industries Board, 711
War Labor Policies Board, 711
Warner, Charles Dudley (1829–1900), 634
Warner, Sam Bass, 612
Warner Brothers, 739
War of 1812, 230, 237–38, 344
  causes of, 236, 237
War of Independence. *See* American Revolution
War of Jenkins' Ear (1739), 94
War of the League of Augsburg (1689–1697), 74
War of the Rebellion. *See* Civil War
War of the Spanish Succession (1702–1714), 74
War of the Worlds (Wells), 817
War on Poverty, 960
War Powers Act of 1941, 823
War Powers Act of 1973, 990
War Production Board (WPB), 823–24
War Refugee Board, 841
War Relocation Authority, 833
Warren, Earl (1891–1974), 778, 866
  Baker v. Carr, 925
  Brown v. Board of Education of Topeka, 874, 925
  Engel v. Vitale, 925
  Escobedo v. Illinois, 925
  Gideon v. Wainwright, 925
  Miranda v. Arizona, 925
  overrules *Plessy v. Ferguson,* 946
  Reynolds v. Sims, 925
Warren, Joseph (1741–1775), 143
Warren, Mercy Otis (1728–1814), 268
Warsaw Pact (1955), 860
Wasatch Range, 405
Washington, Booker Taliaferro (1856–1915), 602*i*, 602–3
Washington, George (1732–1799), 165, 169, 184, 188, 201, 670
  in American Revolution, 170–71
  at battle of Princeton, 170*i*
  at battle of Trenton, 169*i*
  cabinet of, 208
  as commander of Continental Army, 179, 182
  French and Indian War and, 123
  at Philadelphia Convention of 1787, 202
  presidency of, 207, 208
  presidential election of 1788, 207
  Proclamation of Neutrality, 214, 215
  refusal to seek third presidential term, 217
  taxation and, 198
  troops of, 169
  at Valley Forge, 175
  in Virginia, 178
Washington, D.C.
  abolition of slave trade in, 425
  British attack on, 238
  first inauguration held in, 230
  Lincoln's proposal for emancipation in, 434
  March on, 952
Washington (state), 529
  development of (1880s), 534
  women's right to vote in, 649
Washington Globe (newspaper), 325, 345
Washington Naval Arms Conference (1921), 733
Washington Post, 988, 989
Washington, Treaty of (1871), 505
Waste Land, The (Eliot), 748
water crisis, California (1890s–1913), 535
water frame, 290, 290*i*
Watergate scandal, 986
  break-ins, 987
  "plumbers," 987
  trial and investigations, 987–90
water power, manufacturing and, 288, 288*i*, 289, 297
water resource development, 535
Watson, John Broadus (1878–1958), 736
Watson, Thomas Edward (1856–1922) 592, 598, 599
Wattenberg, Ben, 981
Watts section of Los Angeles, race riots of 1964 in, 958
Wayne, Anthony (1745–1796), 224
wealth
  distribution, in northern cities, 1700s, 90*i*, 90
  state legislature membership and, 194–95
  unequal distribution of, 759, 1015
Wealth Against the Commonwealth (Lloyd), 641
Wealth of Nations, The (Smith), 76, 211
weaponry. *See* firearms
Weary Blues (Hughes), 750
Weaver, James Baird (1833–1912), 591
Weavers, 870, 871
Weber, Max (1864–1920), 587
Webster, Daniel (1782–1852), 238, 262, 263, 332, 344, 423
  Dartmouth College v. Woodward and, 264
  death of, 425
  debate with Hayne, 332
  Jackson's veto of Second Bank of the United States and, 329
  Whig party and, 340, 341
Webster, Noah (1758–1843), 269
Webster v. Reproductive Health Services, 1026
Wedemeyer, Albert Coady (1897–1989), 861
Weed, Thurlow (1797–1882), 265
Weems, Mason Locke (1759–1825), 269
Weimar Republic, 818
Weinberger, Caspar, 1010, 1011
Weld, Theodore Dwight (1803–1895), 364, 368
welfare
  Eisenhower's efforts in, 874–75
  LBJ, War on Poverty, 960
  National Welfare Rights Organization, 961
  New Deal and, 807
welfare capitalism, 732
Welles, (George) Orson (1915–1985), 810, 810*i*, 817
Well Ordered Family, The (Wadsworth), 100
Wells, David Ames (1828–1898), 554
Wells, H.G. (1866–1946), 817
Wells-Barnett, Ida, 599
Wentworth, Benning (1696–1770), 157
West. *See also* Old Northwest; Midwest; Old Southwest; trans-Appalachian West
  Civil War fought in, 457–58
  expansion of. *See* westward expansion
  farming expansion in (1820s–1840s), 299–300
  land sales
    1820–1839, 299*i*
    1840–1862, 399*i*
  migration to, 402
  Mormons in, 404–5
  Northwest Ordinance, 198–99
  slavery in, 385
  trans-Missouri, settlement of, 404*i*
  uprisings in (1700s), 128–9
West, Mae (1892–1980), 767, 768
West, Thomas, 40
Western Confederacy, revival of, 236
Western Federation of Miners (WFM), 575
West Indies
  Columbus's exploration of, 19
  economic systems (1700s), 87
  sugar islands of, 67
Westinghouse, George (1846–1914), 552, 608
Westinghouse Company, 731
Westmoreland, William Childs (1914–), 933, 936, 941
West Side Story, 901*i*
West Virginia, admission to the Union, 446

westward expansion, 223, 515
agricultural, 225–27, 536–44
into California, 406–9, 529–39. *See also* California
cattle frontier, 520–21
during 1860s, 398
foreign policy effects, 236
of Great Plains, 516–18
immigration, 518
impact on Indians, 524–25
Indians of Great Plains, 516–18
Jefferson and, 231–34
Louisiana Purchase, 231–34
mining frontier, 518–20
native American resistance to, 223–25
regional diversity and national identity, 240–53
slavery in Old Southwest, 243
speculators and settlers, 228–30
transportation and communication, 518
transportation related to, 227–28
Wharton, Edith Newbold Jones (1862–1937), 627, 748, 749
Wharton College, 731
Whatley, Thomas, 137
wheat
export trade in (1700s), 126
prices (1780s–1790s), 214
prices (1896–1900), 596
trade in middle colonies, 109, 109*f*
wheat belt, 539, 543
deflation effects on (1870s), 543
Wheeler, Burton Kendall (1882–1975), 818
Whig party (American), 319, 339, 368, 422
annexation of Texas and, 415
Calhoun and, 341
coalitions, 341–42, 346
Compromise of 1850 and, 423
conscience, 420
economic power, 482
election of 1848 and, 421
election of 1852 and, 425
emergence of, 340–42
Harrison and, 344–45
ideology of, 340–42
Know-Nothings and, 428
Lincoln and, 434, 435
Mexican War and, 420
opponents of slavery, 420
rejection of Fillmore, 425
Third Party System and, 432
Tyler and, 345
Whig party (English), 90, 93
Glorious Revolution and, 93
Real Whigs, 93–94, 136, 140
taxation and, 144
theory of mixed government, 194
Whiskey Rebellion of 1794, 231, 216*i*, 216
Whiskey Ring, Grant's involvement in, 506
White, Hugh Lawson (1773–1840), presidential campaign of 1836, 342
White, William Allen (1868–1944), 778, 820
White Citizen's Councils, 947
white collar workers (1940s–1950s), 891, 892
Whitefield, George (1714–1770), 115, 118, 120, 277
white male suffrage. *See* suffrage
White Man's Union, 599
White Plains, N.Y., 170, 896
whites
northern, racial attitudes, during Civil War, 469
population (1820s), 223
white supremacy, doctrine of, 597
Whitlock, Brand (1869–1934), 584, 644
Whitman, Walt (1819–1892), 351–52, 353, 421, 432
Whitney, Eli (1765–1825), 242, 295–96
Whitney, William C., 612
Whittlesey, Eliphalet, 486
Whyte, William, 892, 892*i*
Wickersham, George Woodward (1858–1936), 661
Widener, Peter A. B., 612
Wilberforce, William (1759–1833), 363
Wilderness, battle of the (1864), 469–71
wildlife, Endangered Animals Act of 1964, 993
Wild One, The, 909
Wiley, George, 961
Wilhelm II (1859–1941), 684, 691
Wilkes, John (1727–1797), 136
election to Parliament, 148–49
Wilkins, Roy (1901–1981), 952
Wilkinson, Eliza, 196
Wilkinson, James (1757–1825), 234
Wilkinson, Jemima (1752–1819), 273, 274–75, 275*i*
Willamette Valley, Oregon, 404, 518, 533
Willard, Emma (1787–1870), 276
Willard, Frances Elizabeth Caroline (1839–1898), 588
William III (1650–1702), 72
William and Mary, College of, 266
Williams, Roger (1603–1683), 54, 55
Williams, William Carlos (1883–1963), 749
Williams v. Mississippi (1898), 599
Willkie, Wendell (1892–1944), 821
Wills, Helen Newington (1906–), 744
Wilmot, David (1814–1868), 420
Wilmot Proviso, 420, 421, 428, 434
alternatives to, 421–22
Wilson, Charles Erwin (1890–1961), 876
Wilson, Edith Galt (1872–1961), 719
Wilson, Woodrow (1856–1924), 645, 697, 745, 788
attack on problem of economic power, 664
blacks and, 663
Committee on Public Information and, 714, 715
equal rights and, 654
Food Administration, 712
foreign policy, 689–90
Fourteen Points, 717, 838
income tax and, 710
intervention in Mexican Revolution, 690
League of Nations and, 717, 719
neutrality policy in World War I, 699–700, 820
political career, 662
presidential election of 1912, 663–65
presidential election of 1916, 701, 701*i*
progressive coalition, 729
Sherman Act and, 663
sinking of *Lusitania* and, 701
social program, 665
Treaty of Versailles and, 717
War Industries Board and, 711
Wilson-Gorman Tariff of 1890, 593
Windsor, Conn., 60
Winnetka, Ill., 897
Winslow, Rose, 716
Winthrop, John (1606–1676), 51, 51*i*, 52, 53, 54, 55, 59, 205, 206
Wise, John (1652–1725), 113
Wissler, Clark (1870–1947), 517
witchcraft trials, in Salem, Mass., of 1692, 57
Wolcott, Marion Post, 812
Wolfe, James (1727–1759), 124, 133, 137*i*
Wolfe, Tom, 996, 1022
Wollstonecraft, Mary (1759–1797), 197, 270, 273
women
abolitionists, 369
access to education (1950–1970), 967
activism in religion, 273–76, 277
African-American, 363
in armed forces
during Persian Gulf War, 1030, 1030*i*
during Vietnam War, 938
Benevolent Empire reform and, 311
Civil War efforts, 455
contributions during American Revolution, 184
dower rights, 102
education of, early nineteenth century, 276
employment in textile industry (1820s–1830s), 292, 292*i*, 293
employment in tobacco industry, 560
European peasantry, 10
factory workers, strikes by (1830s), 338
food riots during Civil War, 453
as head of household, 1016
help-mates, 334
impact of Civil Rights Act of 1964 on, 968
in labor force
black, married women (1870s–1900s), 564
during Great Depression, 765–66
1800s–1900s, 564–66, 967*f*
1940–1950, 891
1950s–1970s, 911–12, 967
during World War I, 712–13
during World War II, 825–26, 827
joining of unions, 803
of Ku Klux Klan, 747*i*
native American, 7, 7*i*, 8
New Deal and, 797, 807
novelists (1840s–1850s), 394–95
opportunities in corporate hierarchy, 731
planters' wives, 379

(women con't)
political activism, 1920s, 730
in politics, 797
in Populist party, 591
property ownership by, in Maryland colony, 44–45
property rights, during colonial period, 100, 102
reformers, 357–63
republicanism and, 195–97, 273
sexual harassment, 1026, 1033
slaves, 81, 82*i*, 379
social power of, 276
status in European society, 1400s, 12–13
suffrage, property ownership and, New Jersey constitution of 1776 and, 196
teachers, nineteenth century, 276, 395
technology effects on (1920s), 735
"Third-Wave Feminist, A" (Ouellette), 1027
uneasiness with role of, 1033
urban activism, 648
voting rights for, 713–14. *See also* suffrage
wages (1870s–1900s), 564–65, 891, 912, 968
white, southern myth of, 770
World War I contributions, 713–714
Women Appointed for Volunteer Emergency Services in the Navy (WAVES), 825, 825*i*
"Women in New England" (Dwight), 103
Women in the Nineteenth Century (Fuller), 360
Women's Airforce Service Pilots (WASPS), 825, 826*i*
Women's Army Corps (WACS), 825, 939
Women's Bureau, 712
Women's Christian Temperance Union (WCTU), 588
Women's Committee of the Council of National Defense, 712
Women's Emergency Brigade, 803
Women's International League for Peace and Freedom, 734, 940
Women's Joint Congressional Committee, 730
Women's Land Army, 712*i*
women's liberation, 968, 969
women's movement, 492*i*, 967, 996. *See also* feminism
abolitionism and, 359–60
American Equal Rights Association, 492
American Female Moral Reform Society, 358
Anthony and, 361, 362, 491, 492, 588
Dix and, 358–59
Frederick Douglass and, 492
Fifteenth Amendment and, 492
Fourteenth Amendment and, 492
Fuller and, 360
legislative victories of, 360
National American Woman Suffrage Association, 713
National Woman Suffrage Association, 492
New York Female Moral Reform Society, 358
origins of, 357–59
political rights and, 588–89
Potter and, 588
progressive reform, 645–50
property rights and, 361
during Reconstruction period, 491–92
Seneca Falls program and, 360–63
social institutions and, 358
Stanton and, 361, 362, 491, 492
Stone and, 362, 491
Stowe and, 363
Truth and, 363
Women's Rights Convention, 361
Women's Municipal League of New York, 647
Women's Organization for National Prohibition Repeal, 752
Women's Parliament, 588
Women's Peace Party, 700
women's rights. *See also* suffrage
distinguished from women's liberation, 969
eighteenth–nineteenth century, 271, 272, 273–76
to land ownership, 536
revival of struggle for (1910–1913), 648–50
women's roles
in abolitionism, 366–67
during American Revolution, 171
changes in (1950s–1970s), 967
colonial period, 102–3
early nineteenth century, 272
of farm women (1850s–1900s), 540–41
Great Depression and, 764
in Hispanic Southwest (1860s–1880s), 530
housework and, 970
native American, 250
1950s, 909–12
Puritans and, 54, 103
in Sioux nation, 517
in western frontier, 538
wife's role (1880s–1910), 631–32
women's work, 891
Women's Strike for Peace, 939, 939*i*, 940
Wonder-Working Providence of Zion's Saviour (Johnson), 60
Wood, Jethro, 300
Woodland Indians, 6, 7, 8
Woods, Robert Archey (1865–1925), 618
Woodward, Ellen Sullivan, 797
Woodward, Robert, 987, 988*i*, 988–89
Woolen Act of 1699, 70*t*, 95
wool trade, English, sixteenth century, 28
Woolworth Building, 611
Woolworth, F. W., Company, 556
Worcester v. Georgia (1832), 327
work ethic, revivalism and, 314–15
work force. *See* labor force
working class. *See also* laborers
alcohol consumption by (1820s), 309
Great Depression and, 762
women in, 565, 566
Workingmen's party, 533
workmen's compensation, 652
federal, 662
Works Progress Administration (WPA), 794, 794i, 796, 800, 828, 836
art and, 809
documentary impulse, 810
Federal One project, 808
music and, 809
Women's and Professional Projects Division, 797
World (newspaper), 626
World Bank (International Bank for Reconstruction and Development), 886
world capital markets, U.S. in, 732
World Court, 733, 818
World's Anti-Slavery Convention, 360
World's Fair of 1893, 613
World War I
Allied powers in, 698
Allied victory in the West, 704, 704*m*
American casualties in, 708
American declaration of war, 702
American fighting force, 705–9
American involvement in, 701–17
American neutrality in, 699–700
black and Mexican-American workers in, 712
Central Powers in, 698
conflict on the high seas, 700–1
demobilization after, 709
Eighteenth Amendment and, 721–22
election of 1916 and, 701
events leading to, 690–91, 697–99, 701–2
fear of radicalism after, 722–23
financial and economic mobilization, 710–11
intelligence testing and, 708–9
labor unrest following, 720–21
military morality during, 708
military technology in, 699
mobilization of American workers during, 711–14
mobilization of home front during, 709–14
mustard gas in, 705
National War Labor Board, 711–12
payments and debts by European countries following, 733
promoting national unity during, 714–17
racial strife following, 719–20
racism in armed forces, 709
settlements of, World War II and, 818
sinking of *Lusitania* and, 701
Treaty of Versailles, 717–19
trench warfare in, 703
women's involvement in, 712–14
World War II, 816, 816*i*
admission of displaced persons to U.S. after, 900
African-Americans and, 832–33
American GIs, 844–45
American isolationism in, 818
American neutrality in, 820–22
Atlantic Charter, 838

(World War II con't)
atomic bomb, 846–47
attack on Pearl Harbor, 822–23
Battle of Britain, 820
Battle of the Bulge, 840
black market during, 832
D-Day, 838, 839*m*, 840
defense mobilization, 823–25
events leading to, 817–23
financing of, 823–24
Grand Alliance, 838
Great Depression and, 817–18
Holocaust, 840, 841
home front during, 829–35
Lend-Lease Act and, 821–22
migration and family life during, 831–32
organized labor and, 826–27
politics during, 828–29
popular culture during, 830
rationing during, 830–31
V-E Day, 840, 846
war in Europe, 838–41
war in the Pacific, 841–44
wartime diplomacy, 845–46
wartime goals and strategies, 835–38
women and, 825–26
World War I settlements and, 818–20
Yalta Conference, 845–46
Wounded Knee, S.D.
battle at (1890), 515, 527–529
Sioux occupation of (1973), 960, 961, 961*i*
Wovoka, 527
Wozniak, Steve, 1023
Wright, Benjamin, 301
Wright, Frances (1795–1852), 336–37, 360
Wright, Henry, 336–37
Wright, Richard (1908–1960), 810
Wright, Wilbur (1867–1912) and Orville (1871–1948), 699
Writs of Assistance case, 142
Wyandot Indians, 224
Wyatt, Jane, 905
Wyoming, gold mining in, 519

XYZ affair, 217

Yalta, conference at, 845*i*, 845–46, 854
Yalu River, 863
Yancey, William Lowndes (1814–1863), 437
"Yankee," 240
Yeardley, Sir George (c. 1587–1627), 41
Yellow Bird, 527
yellow-dog contracts, 572
Yellow Hand, 523
yellow journalism, 626
Yellowstone National Park, 656
Yeltsin, Boris N., 1028*i*, 1029
yeomen, 46, 100, 310
English, price revolution and, 27
farm families, 60, 111
freeholding society, 99
independence, agricultural tradition of, 156
Yerkes, Charles Tyson (1837–1905), 612
Yezierska, Anzia, 809
Yippies (Youth International Party), 979
yoga, 996
Yom Kippur War, 992, 1001
York, Alvin, 708
Yorktown (aircraft carrier), 841
Yorktown, Va., 179*i*
Cornwallis's surrender at, 178
Franco-American victory at, 178
Yorty, Sam, 929
Yosemite National Park, 535, 535*i*
Young, Brigham (1801–1877), 405–6
Young, Robert, 905
Young, Thomas (1773–1829), 152
Young, Whitney, Jr. (1921–1971), 952
Young Men's Christian Association (YMCA), 623–24
Youngstown, Ohio, 608
Youngstown Sheet and Tube Company, Campbell Works of, 995
Young Women's Christian Association (YWCA), 623–24, 712
youth. *See also* children
counterculture, 965–66, 966, 967
Great Depression's effect on, 766
juvenile delinquency during World War II, 831–32
World War II effects on, 831
youth culture (1950s), 908–09
Youth for Goldwater, 962
Youth International Party (Yippies), 979
Ypres, battle of (1915), 698, 699*i*
Yugoslavia, 718, 1029, 1029*m*
Yukon, 596, 685
Yuppies (young urban professionals), 1015

Zen Buddhism, 996
Zhou Enlai (Chou En-lai, 1898–1976), 860
Ziegler, Ronald, 987
Zimmerman telegram, 702
Zionism, 879
Zoot suit, 831, 832*i*, 833
Zukor, Adolph, 739
Zuni Indians, 36

Political divisions as of January 1, 1993